THE
ANALYTICAL
LEXICON
TO THE
GREEK NEW
TESTAMENT

THE
ANALYTICAL
LEXICON
TO THE
GREEK NEW
TESTAMENT

WILLIAM D. MOUNCE

ZondervanPublishingHouse
Grand Rapids, Michigan

A Division of HarperCollinsPublishers

Analytical Lexicon to the Greek New Testament
Copyright © 1993 by William D. Mounce

Requests for information should be addressed to:
Zondervan Publishing House

Grand Rapids, Michigan 49530

Library of Congress Cataloging-in-Publication Data

Mounce, William D.
    Analytical lexicon to the Greek New Testament / by William D. Mounce.
       p.   cm.
    Includes index.
    ISBN 0-310-54210-3
    1. Greek language, Biblical--Dictionaries--English.   2. Bible. N.T.--Language, style.   I. Title.
PA881.M74   1992: aa15 11-24-92
476'.4--dc20   92-43226
                                                     CIP

Printed in the United States of America

00 01 02 / DH / 15 14 13 12 11 10 9

This edition is printed on acid-free paper and meets the American National Standards Institute Z39.48 standard.

Table of Contents

Preface vii

How to use the Analytical ix

Abbreviations xii

Explanation of the Morphological Tags and the Paradigms 1

Section One: Nouns and Adjectives
The Basic Rules Governing Case Endings 3
Case Endings 4
Article 5
Nouns 5
Adjectives 10

Section Two: Verb Formation
Augment (§31) 14
Reduplication (§32) 15
Verbal tense formation (§33) 16
Tense and mood formatives (§34) 17
Thematic and Athematic conjugations (§35) 17
Personal endings (§36) 18

Section Three: Tense Formation
Master Indicative Verb Chart 20
Overview of the thematic conjugation 21
Present indicative (§41) 24
Imperfect indicative (§42) 26
Future indicative (§43) 27
Aorist indicative (§44) 29
Perfect active indicative/Pluperfect (§45) 31
Perfect middle/passive indicative (§46) 32
Aorist/Future passive (§47) 34
Subjunctive (§50) 35
Optative (§60) 37
Imperative (§70) 39
Infinitive (§80) 41
Participle (§90) 42

Analytical Lexicon 47

Appendix

Quick reference chart 491

Methodology 492

Identical forms 493

Crasis 494

Goodrick/Kohlenberger's numbers compared to Strong's numbers 495

Strong's numbers compared to Goodrick/Kohlenberger's numbers 517

Principal parts of verbs occurring 50 times or more in the Greek New Testament 539

Preface

This volume is based on the latest version of the Greek text (UBS 3 edition, corrected). The database from which it was created has been checked against several databases, and many decisions as to the correct parsing were made by hand. The Index contains a listing of ambiguous passages, and reports other decisions that had to be made that might affect the frequency counts in the Analytical. We have tried to be as accurate as possible, but only arrogance would assume the text to be error free; any corrections are gladly appreciated. Just send them to Zondervan Publishing House, Academic books.

I would be remiss in not thanking those who have contributed so heavily to the completion of this work. My wife Robin has been a constant source of encouragement and help, from thinking through the philosophy behind the book as to its appearance on the page; Ian and Kathleen Lopez, who did so much of the manual typing for the dictionary; C. Jonathin Seraiah and Miles Van Pelt, two of the best students a teacher could ever hope for, who spent hours helping me proof dictionary entries, principal parts, etc.; Bryant Swenson and Aaron Sellers for their help; for the wonderful people at Zondervan, especially Ed van der Maas and Verlyn Verbrugge, who believe in what I am doing in Greek instructional methods, and who stood behind both this volume and the others that we are working on; and to my Greek teachers, who taught me both the love for the language and the necessity of knowing Greek for an accurate and persuasive proclamation of God's truth: Dr. E. Margaret Howe, Dr. Walter W. Wessel, Dr. Robert H. Mounce, Dr. William S. LaSor. Thank you.

Bill Mounce, 1992

Preface to Subsequent Printings

Zondervan has graciously allowed me to make corrections in subsequent printings of the *Analytical*, and many of you have notified me of errors you discovered. Thank you. In the second printing we have made corrections in the charts in the first forty-six pages. In subsequent printings, and when I am done with the *Morphology* grammar, other corrections may be made in the *Analytical* itself.

How to Use the Analytical

An Analytical can be both a person's friend and a person's enemy. For the pastor with limited time for sermon preparation, it can prevent spending 30 minutes on parsing. It can keep the translator from making a serious translation error. For the layperson, it can provide some access to the Greek Testament. However, it can also do great harm. If used as a crutch, the student will never develop a true facility with the language. And it may lull laypersons into a false sense of security, thinking that because they can parse a word, they therefore know what it means.

Who should not use this volume? (1) A first-year Greek student. The only way to learn the language is to struggle. If you use this volume instead of learning the basic paradigms, you are cheating yourself and most likely will never develop a true facility in the language. (2) Those who know a little Greek. This can be very dangerous, because a cursory exposure to Greek cannot convey the complexity and beauty of the language. For example, just because a verb is an aorist tells you nothing, necessarily, about its meaning. Only prolonged exposure with adequate guidance can do that.

When and who should use this volume?

- When you cannot discover the word's parsing or are not sure, and without the answer you cannot understand the text or the commentator. It is always preferable to struggle, and when you think you have the correct answer or just are unable to see it, then use this book.

- In second-year Greek it is helpful to read large portions of the biblical text. An analytical can help you from spending large portions of time on a very difficult word. However, if you find that you are consistently looking up forms you should know, go back to your beginning grammar and relearn the basic forms.

- Those who know a little Greek and are trying to do word studies. Because each form lists the dictionary form and the G/K number, it is possible to do elementary word studies once you discover what word is being used. If you do this kind of biblical study, please be sure you are aware of the limitations of word studies. For example, do not look at μετανοέω and assume the meaning of the word (*to repent*) on the basis of the fact it is comprised of two words, μετά and νοέω. Do not look at English cognates and define the Greek on the basis of the English. For example, δύναμις does not mean *dynamite*. And be aware of the fact that biblical Greek, or "koine," is different from classical Greek, and many of the nice and neat differences between words and grammatical functions that were present in classical times are ignored or minimized biblical times. A book like D.A. Carson's *Exegetical Fallacies* will send you well down the road in dealing with these types of problems.

Analytical

Instead of reproducing the old analytical, we have tried to include additional information that you will find helpful.

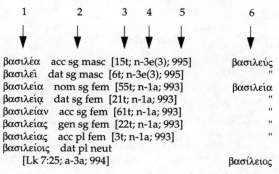

1. Inflected form

2. Parsing. See the list of abbreviations (below) if you are unsure.

3. Inside the square brackets the first information is either how many times that inflected form occurs or the verse reference if it occurs only once. If the entry is too long to fit on one line, the information in the square

brackets is indented on a second line, as is the case with βασιλείοις in the example.

4. The morphological tag. See below.

5. The G/K number for cross reference. This new numbering system replaces that of Strong. It includes all the Greek words used in our Greek Testament; the texts used by Strong were different in places from those used today. The Goodrick/Kohlenberger number ties the entry in with other reference works that use the systems. If you are still using the Strong numbering system, there is a cross reference between the two systems in the *Index*.

6. The lexical form of the word. If it is the same as the preceeding word, there are just ditto (") marks.

Lexicon

Inserted into the analytical listings is a dictionary. It has been greatly updated from the version in the earlier analytical. It is not designed to replace a full lexicon such as Bauer, Arndt, Gingrich, Danker (*BAGD*), but it is good for quick reference. The spellings of the words have been updated to match those used by *BAGD*, the old English has been removed from the definitions, and the definitions have been generally updated. For students, we have included very important information. The principal parts of verbs are listed, as well as the G/K number and the Mounce morphological tag. If a word occurs less than ten times we have usually listed all biblical passages of that word. The asterisk at the end of an entry confirms that all biblical references have been cited. We also discovered that the old lexicon was replete with errors; many of the biblical references were wrong. We have corrected these. And all dictionary entries are listed alphabetically and not grouped by root, as the older analytical did.

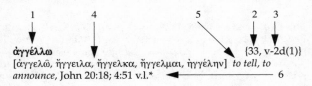

ἀγγέλλω   {33, v-2d(1)}
[ἀγγελῶ, ἤγγειλα, ἤγγελκα, ἤγγελμαι, ἠγγέλην] *to tell, to announce*, John 20:18; 4:51 v.l.*

ἁγνίζω   {49, v-2a(1)}
[-, ἥγνισα, ἥγνικα, ἥγνισμαι, ἡγνίσθην] *to purify; to purify morally, reform, to live like one under a vow of abstinence*, as the Nazarites

1. Lexical form

2. G/K number.

3. Morphological tag.

4. Principal parts if it is a verb.

5. Definitions and references.

6. If there is a final asterisk, then all biblical references have been cited.

Morphological tags

One of the unique features in this analytical is the fact that it is tied into the author's *Morphology of Biblical Greek* (*MBG*). This book categorizes all words in the biblical text on the basis of how they inflect. This way all words that behave similarly are grouped together. The morphological tag cited in the entry keys you in as to where you should look in *MBG* for more information about the word. The process works like this.

1. If you cannot parse a form, look it up in the analytical.

2. If you want more information about the form and why it is formed the way it is, see its tag and refer to the charts in the front of this volume. There we discuss the different classifications and the basic information for the class as a whole.

3. If you want to know more about the word, especially any irregularities experienced by the word that are

not common to the classification as a whole, turn to *MBG*.

Section numbers (§) refer to the sections in *MBG*. (Because *MBG* is still in its final stages, there may be some discrepancy between these section numbers and those actually used in *MBG*.) If your question is about the formation of verbs or tenses in general, look up the section number. If your question is about a specific word, look up the word using its morphological tag. The analytical is therefore much more than a mere lookup book.

Structure of the Analytical

The *Analytical* breaks down into three divisions.

1. A series of charts at the beginning show basic rules and inflectional patterns for every classification of Greek words in the New Testament.

    *   Section I: Nouns and Adjectives.
    *   Section II: Verb formation, where we discuss the verb from left to right (augment, reduplications, etc.).
    *   Section III: Tense formation, where we have a series of charts providing an overview of some basic verbal forms, and then break the discussion down by tense, voice, and mood with more detail.

    They spell out the rules for noun and verb formation, and then show the rules at work in the paradigms. These are an abridgment of the charts in *MBG*. We have limited our comments to those pertaining to the category of words as a whole; any comments necessary to explain the abnormalities of one specific word are to be found in *MBG*. We did not feel it helpful to discuss some of the difficult forms and omit others. The charts assume a basic knowledge of Greek, so discussion of fundamental concepts such as the nu-- movable are omitted.

2. The analytical itself with the lexicon interspersed throughout.

3. An *Index* of several important lists.

Principal parts

We followed the following rules when determining the principal parts listed in the lexicon.

1. We listed the tense stem if it occurs in the New Testament.

2. Other principal parts were included for the sake of completeness. If we do not list the principal part, there is a dash in its place [-, ἠγαλλίασα, -, -, ἠγαλλιάθην].

3. If the imperfect occurs, we have usually included it before the future tense form in parentheses [(ἠπείλουν), -, ἠπειλησάμην -, -, -].

4. If the word occurs in the optative or pluperfect, we have included it after the listing of the principal parts.

Analytical listings

We parsed the words in the analytical listings primary on the basis of form, not function. For example, when an accusative singular neuter of an adjective can function adverbially, we still list it as an adjective. If the accusative singular neuter form of the adjective is listed as its own word in *BAGD*, or if it is used widely adverbially, we mention the fact in the entry. See the Appendix for a further discussion.

Abbreviations

Symbols

* verbal root from which the other tense stems are formed

" this inflected form is from the same lexical form as the preceding entry

§ section numbers, in both the analytical and *MBG*.

‣ form on the left *develops into* the form on the right

Abbreviations

absol., absolutely, without case or adjunct

acc., accusative case

act., active voice

adj., adjective

al., *alibi*, in other texts

al. freq., *alibi frequenter*, in many other texts

Ant., *Antiquities* of Josephus

aor., aorist

Att., Attic dialect

compar., comparative

conj., conjunction

contr., contraction, contracted

dat., dative case

dep., deponent

dimin., diminutive

esp., especially

et., and

etc., *et cetera*

e.g., *exempli gratia*, for example

fem., feminine

freq., with al, *alibi frequenter*, in many other texts

fut., future

gen., genitive

genr., generally, in a general sense, not affected by

i.e., *id est*, that is, namely

id., *idem.*, the same

imperf., imperfect tense

impers., impersonal

impl., implication

indecl., indeclinable

ind., indicative mood

infin., infinitive

interj., interjection

interrog., interrogative, interrogation

intrans., intransitive

i.q., *idem quod*, the same as

Lat., Latin

lit., literally

LXX, Septuagint

masc., masculine gender

met., metaphorically

metath., metathesis, the transposition of letters

meton., by metonymy

mid., middle voice

n., noun

n/v, nominative and vocative case

neut., neuter gender

N.T., New Testament

nom., nominative case

obsol., obsolete

O.T., Old Testament

opt., optative mood

ptcp., participle

pass., passive voice

perf., perfect tense

pers., person

pl., plural

pluperf., pluperfect tense

pr., properly, proper

prep., preposition

pron., pronoun

q.v., *quod vide*, which see

rule refers to the noun rules

sc., *scilicet*, that is to say

seq., *sequente*, as seq. gen., *sequente genitivo*, with a genitive following

sg., singular

signif., significance

spc., specially, i.e., in a special and local meaning

subj., subjunctive mood

subscr., subscription

subst., substantive

superl., superlative

sync., syncope, contraction

synec., synecdoche

trans., transitively

trop., tropically, i.e., turned aside from its strict literal meaning

v(v)., verse(s)

v.r., a variant reading in the common text

viz., *videlicet*, that is, namely

voc., vocative case

2t., word occurs two times in the verse, 3(t) etc.

Books of the New Testament

Longer abbreviation is used in the lexicon; the shorter abbreviation is used in the analytical listing.

Matt	Mt
Mark	Mk
Luke	Lk
John	Jn
Acts	Ac
Rom	Rm
1 Cor	1C
2 Cor	2C
Gal	Ga
Eph	Ep
Phil	Pp
Col	Cl
1 Thess	1 Th
2 Thess	2 Th
1 Tim	1 Ti
2 Tim	2 Ti
Titus	Ti
Phlm	Pm
Heb	Hb
James	Jm
1 Peter	1P
2 Peter	2P
1 John	1J
2 John	2J
3 John	3J
Jude	Jd
Rev	Rv

Authors and works cited

BAGD, A Greek-English Lexicon of the New Testament and Other Early Christian Literature, W. Bauer, W.F. Arndt, F.W. Gingrich, F.W. Danker.

Funk, *A Beginning-Intermediate Grammar of Hellenistic Greek,* Robert W. Funk.

G/K, Goodrick Kohlenberger number.

LaSor, *Handbook of New Testament Greek,* William Sanford LaSor.

MBG, Morphology of Biblical Greek, William D. Mounce.

Smyth, *Greek Grammar,* Herbert Weir Smyth.

Explanation of
the Morphological Tags
and the Paradigms

We have developed a system for tagging inflected Greek forms so that words that inflect similarly can be grouped together and studied. Following a summary of that system.

Basic division

The first letter specifies the basic part of speech.

n- Noun
a- Adjective
v- Verb
cv- Compound verb

Other types of words do not use abbreviations (conjunction, preposition, interjection, adverb, particle).

Nouns

The second letter specifies the declension: "n-1" (first), "n-2" (second), "n-3" (third).

Adjectives

The second letter specifies how many different endings are used, and what declension those endings are.

a-1 (2-1-2) Uses three sets of case endings. The masculine uses second declension endings, the feminine uses first, and the neuter uses second.

a-2 (3-1-3) Uses three sets of case endings. The masculine uses third declension endings, the feminine uses first, and the neuter uses third.

a-3 (2-2) Uses two sets of case endings. The masculine and feminine use second declension endings, and the neuter uses second.

a-3 (3-3) Uses two sets of case endings. The masculine and feminine use third declension endings, and the neuter uses third.

Verbs

Verbs are categorized on the basis of how their verbal root is modified in order to form their present tense stem. A fuller discussion is given below in §33.

v-1 Present tense is the same as the verbal base (*αγαπα ‣ ἀγαπάω)

v-2 Present tense is formed by adding a consonantal iota to the verbal base (*βαπτιδ + ι ‣ βαπτίζω)

v-3 Present tense is formed by adding ν to the verbal base (*πι + ν ‣ πίνω)

v-4 Present tense is formed by adding τ to the verbal base (*κρυπ + τ ‣ κρύπτω)

v-5 Present tense is formed by adding (ι)σκ to the verbal base (*γνω ‣ γιγνω ‣ γινω + ισκ ‣ γινώσκω)

v-6 μι verbs

Many of the verbs within these categories also show other types of modifications. Verbs in almost all categories show ablaut in their stem vowel. Many of the verbs also use more than one verbal base in forming their different tense stems. Therefore, out of these 6 categories we have drawn all bases that undergo ablaut and use different verbal bases, and have repeated them in v-7 and v-8.

v-7　　Verbal bases that undergo ablaut (*καλε ‣ καλέω ‣ κέκληκα)

v-8　　Verbs that use more than one verbal base to form their different tense stems (*φερ ‣ φέρω; *οι ‣ οἴσω; *ενεκ ‣ ἤνεγκα)

Each of these categories can be broken down further, and they will done so in the charts that follow. For a fuller description of the categories and a discussion of individual forms, see *MBG*.

Paradigms

In order to preserve space and to allow the paradigms to be as readable as possible, we have omitted some of the labels on them. The cases are listed down the left side of the paradigm: *nom*, *n/v* (nominative and vocative), *gen*, *dat*, *acc*, *voc*. The left to right order in masculine, feminine, and neuter. In nouns and adjectives, the singular is on the top and the plural is below.

In verbs, the labels read *1 sg, 2 sg, 3 sg, 1 pl, 2 pl, 3 pl*. Usually the singular is on top and the plural on the bottom.

When a form is in parentheses such as "(γῆρας)," it means that no word in that classification occurs in the Greek Testament.

Section I

Nouns and Adjectives

The Basic Rules Governing Case Endings[1]

1. Stems ending in α or η are in the first declension, stems in ο are in the second, and consonantal stems are in the third.

2. Almost all neuter words are the same form in the nominative and accusative.

3. All neuter words, in the nominative and accusative plural, end in α.

   - In the second declension the α is the changed stem vowel; in the third it is the case ending.

4. In the dative singular, the ι subscripts if possible.

   - Because an ι can subscript only under a vowel (in which case the vowel lengthens), it subscripts only in the first and second declensions.

5. Vowels often change their length ("ablaut").

   - "Contraction" occurs when two vowels meet and form a different vowel or diphthong.

     λογο   +   ι   ‣   λόγῳ   (dative singular)
     λογο   +   ο   ‣   λόγου   (genitive singular)
     γραφη +   ων ‣   γραφῶν   (genitive plural)

   - "Compensatory lengthening" occur when a vowel is lengthened to compensate for the loss of another letter.

     λογο   +   νς ‣   λόγος ‣ λογους (accusative plural)

6. In the genitive and dative, the masculine and neuter will always be identical.

7. The Square of Stops.

Labials	π	β	φ
Velars	κ	γ	χ
Dentals	τ	δ	θ

   - Labials + σ form ψ; velars plus σ form ξ; dentals plus σ form σ.

   - The ντ combination drops out when followed by σ (παντ + ς ‣ πᾶς).

   - Whatever happens in the nominative singular third declension also happens in the dative plural. σαρκ + σ ‣ σαρξ. σαρκ + σι ‣ σάρξι.

8. A τ cannot stand at the end of a word and will drop off.

   - No case ending is used in stems ending in ματ. The τ then drops out.

     *ὀνοματ + - ‣ ὀνοματ ‣ ὄνομα

   - Sometimes the preceding vowel lengthens to compensate for the loss.

     *αρχοντ ‣ αρχον ‣ ἄρχων

---

[1] These rules come from the author's *The Basics of Biblical Greek.*

Case Endings

A dash means that no case ending is used. The underline means that the case ending has joined with the final stem vowel (cf. rule 5). The case endings for the masc/fem in the third declension are repeated for the sake of clarity, even though in several cases they are the same as in the first and second declensions.

Notice that the third declension case endings are not substantially different from those used for the first and second declensions. Because third declension stems end in a consonant, there are more changes than in the first and second declension words. Contrary to some, we do not list the final stem vowel of the first or second declension word as part of the case ending. For a fuller discussion of this method, see the author's *The Basics of Biblical Greek*.

	first/second declension			third declension		
	masc/fem	neut		masc/fem		neut
nom sg	ς	-	ν	ς	ς	- [2]
gen sg	υ [3]	ς	υ	ος	ος	ος
dat sg	ι [4]	ι	ι	ι [5]	ι	ι
acc sg	ν	ν	ν	α/ν [6]	α/ν	-
nom pl	ι	ι	α	ες	ες	α [7]
gen pl	ων	ων	ων	ων	ων	ων
dat pl	ις	ις	ις	σι(ν) [8]	σι(ν)	σι(ν)
acc pl	υς [9]	ς [10]	α	ας [11]	ας	α

---

[2] Be prepared for the final stem vowel to undergo changes (rule 8).

[3] The omicron contracts with the final stem vowel and forms ου (rule 5).

[4] The iota subscripts and the vowel lengthens (rule 5).

[5] Because third declension stems end in a consonant, the iota cannot subscript as it does in the first and second declensions; so it remains on the line.

[6] The case ending alternates between alpha and nu.

[7] As opposed to the first and second declensions, this alpha is an actual case ending and not a changed stem vowel.

[8] The nu is a nu-movable. Notice that the ending σι is a flipped version of ις found in the first and second declensions.

[9] The actual accusative plural case ending for the first and second declension is νς, but the nu drops out because of the following sigma.

In the first declension the alpha simply joins with the sigma (ὥρα + νς ‣ ὥρας).

In the second declension the omicron lengthens to ου (λογο + νς ‣ λογος ‣ λόγους; rule 5).

[10] See previous footnote.

[11] As opposed to the first declension, the alpha here is part of the case ending.

The Article

	masc	fem	neut		masc	fem	neut
nom sg	ὁ	ἡ	τό	nom pl	οἱ	αἱ	τά
gen sg	τοῦ	τῆς	τοῦ	gen pl	τῶν	τῶν	τῶν
dat sg	τῷ	τῇ	τῷ	dat pl	τοῖς	ταῖς	τοῖς
acc sg	τόν	τήν	τό	acc pl	τούς	τάς	τά

First Declension Noun Charts

Nouns that have stems ending in α or η follow the first declension pattern. Most are feminine.

n-1a   Feminine nouns with stems ending in εα, ια, or ρα, with a genitive in ας.
n-1b   Feminine nouns with stems ending in η and a genitive in ης.
n-1c   Feminine nouns with stems ending in α (where the preceding letter is not ε, ι, or ρ) and a genitive in ης.
n-1d   Masculine nouns with stems ending in ς and a genitive in ου.
n-1e   Masculine nouns with stems ending in α(ς) and a genitive in α.
n-1f   Masculine nouns with stems ending in η(ς) and a genitive in ου.
n-1g   Masculine nouns with stems ending in ης and a genitive in η.
n-1h   Contract nouns (which end in two consecutive vowels and have therefore contracted).

	n-1a	n-1b	n-1c	n-1d	n-1e	n-1f	n-1g	n-1h
nom sg	ὥρα	γραφή	δόξα	νεανίας	σατανᾶς	προφήτης	μανασσῆς	μνᾶ
gen sg	ὥρας	γραφῆς	δόξης	νεανίου	σατανᾶ	προφήτου	μανασσῆ	μνᾶς
dat sg	ὥρᾳ	γραφῇ	δόξῃ	νεανίᾳ	σατανᾷ	προφήτῃ		μνᾷ
acc sg	ὥραν	γραφήν	δόξαν	νεανίαν	σατανᾶν	προφήτην	μανασσῆ	μνᾶν
voc sg	ὥρα	γραφή	δόξα	νεανία	σατανᾶ	προφῆτα	–	μνᾶ
n/v pl	ὥραι	γραφαί	δόξαι	νεανίαι	–	προφῆται	–	μναῖ
gen pl	ὡρῶν	γραφῶν	δοξῶν	νεανιῶν	–	προφητῶν	–	μνῶν
dat pl	ὥραις	γραφαῖς	δόξαις	νεανίαις	–	προφήταις	–	μναῖς
acc pl	ὥρας	γραφάς	δόξας	νεανίας	–	προφήτας	–	μνᾶς

Second Declension Noun Charts

Nouns that have stems ending in ο follow the second declension pattern. Most are masculine or neuter.

n-2a   Masculine nouns with stems ending in ο(ς).
n-2b   Feminine nouns with stems ending in ο(ς).
n-2c   Neuter nouns with stems ending in ο(ν).
n-2d   Contract nouns. The stems actually end in two vowels, which contract when the case ending is added.
  n-2d(1)   Second declension masculine contract nouns with stems ending in εο.
  n-2d(2)   Second declension neuter contract nouns with stems ending in οο.
n-2e   Nouns with stems in εω (ἀπολλῶς, κώς).

	n-2a	n-2b	n-2c	n-2d(1)	n-2d(2)	n-2e
nom sg	λόγος	ὁδός	ἔργον	χειμάρρους	ὀστοῦν	κῶς
gen sg	λόγου	ὁδοῦ	ἔργου	χειμάρρου	ὀστοῦ	κῶ
dat sg	λόγῳ	ὁδῷ	ἔργῳ	χειμάρρῳ	ὀστῷ	κῷ
acc sg	λόγον	ὁδόν	ἔργον	χειμάρρουν	ὀστοῦν	–
voc sg	λόγε	ὁδέ	ἔργον	χειμάρρους	ὀστοῦν	κῶς
n/v pl	λόγοι	ὁδοί	ἔργα	χείμαρροι	ὀστᾶ	–
gen pl	λόγων	ὁδῶν	ἔργων	χειμάρρων	ὀστῶν	–
dat pl	λόγοις	ὁδοῖς	ἔργοις	χειμάρροις	ὀστοῖς	–
acc pl	λόγους	ὁδούς	ἔργα	χειμάρρους	ὀστᾶ	–

Third Declension Nouns

Stems that end in a consonant follow the third declension pattern. Because there is no intervening vowel, the case ending is added directly to the stem and there can be significant changes in the form of the word. But the changes are very predictable, if you know the rules (see *MBG*, §10 - §27). The most notable changes are in the nominative singular and dative plural where the case ending begins with a σ; sigmas are very volatile in that they can effect a significant amount of change depending on the preceding consonant.

The root of the noun is best seen by dropping the genitive singular case ending (*σαρκ ‹ σάρξ ‹ σαρκός)

n-3a-b   Stems ending in a labial or velar

When the σ of the case ending in the nominative singular and dative plural join with the final stem letter, the two letters are rewritten as a double consonant (rule #7).

n-3a   Stems ending in a labial
   n-3a(1)   Stems ending in π
   n-3a(2)   Stems ending in β
   n-3a(3)   Stems ending in φ (no examples in the NT)
n-3b   Stems ending in a velar
   n-3b(1)   Stems ending in κ
   n-3b(2)   Stems ending in γ
   n-3b(3)   Stems ending in χ

	n-3a(1)	n-3a(2)	n-3b(1)	n-3b(2)	n-3b(3)[12]
n/v sg	λαῖλαψ	ἄραψ	σάρξ	σάλπιγξ	θρίξ
gen sg	λαίλαπος	ἄραβος	σαρκός	σάλπιγγος	τριχός
dat sg	λαίλαπι	ἄραβι	σαρκί	σάλπιγγι	τριχί
acc sg	λαίλαπα	ἄραβα	σάρκα	σάλπιγγα	τρίχα
n/v pl	(λαίλαπες)	ἄραβες	σάρκες	σάλπιγγες	τρίχες
gen pl	(λαιλάπων)	ἀραβῶν	σαρκῶν	σαλπιγγῶν	τριχῶν
dat pl	(λαίλαψι(ν))	ἄραψι(ν)	σαρξί(ν)	σάλπιγξι(ν)	θριξί(ν)
acc pl	(λαίλαπας)	ἄραβας	σάρκας	σάλπιγγας	τρίχας

---

[12]   The changes between θ and τ in θρίξ are not indicative of this class of nouns. It is a peculiarity of this word. See *MBG* for discussion.

n-3c   Stems ending in a dental

The dental drops out of the nominative singular and dative plural because of the σ of the case ending (*χαριτ + ς ‣ χάρις; #22.3). The preceding vowel can lengthen to compensate for the loss (*οδοντ + ς ‣ οδος ‣ ὀδούς; #22).

n-3c(1)   Stems ending in τ. Use ν and not α in a accusative singular. The τ drops out before the ν.
n-3c(2)   Stems ending in δ
n-3c(3)   Stems ending in θ
n-3c(4)   Stems ending in ματ
n-3c(5)   Stems ending in ντ
  n-3c(5a)   Stems ending in ντ (with σ in the nominative singular). When the τ drops out in the nominative singular and dative plural due to the σ, the ν also drops out and the preceding vowels lengthen to compensate (e.g., ο ‣ ου; ο ‣ ω; rule 7).
  n-3c(5b)   Stems ending in ντ (with no ending in the nominative singular). A τ cannot stand at the end of a word so it drops off (rule 8). The preceding vowel can lengthen to compensate (*αρχοντ ‣ αρχον ‣ ἄρχων; rule 8).

	n-3c(1)	*n-3c(2)*	*n-3c(3)*	*n-3c(4)*	*n-3c(5a)*	*n-3c(5b)*
nom sg	χάρις	ἐλπίς	ὄρνις	ὄνομα	ὀδούς	ἄρχων
gen sg	χάριτος	ἐλπίδος	ὄρνιθος	ὀνόματος	ὀδόντος	ἄρχοντος
dat sg	χάριτι	ἐλπίδι	ὄνιθι	ὀνόματι	ὀδόντι	ἄρχοντι
acc sg	χάριν	ἐλπίδα	ὄρνιθα	ὄνομα	ὀδόντα	ἄρχοντα
n/v pl	χάριτες	ἔλπιδες	ὄρνιθες	ὀνόματα	ὀδόντες	ἄρχοντες
gen pl	χαρίτων	ἐλπίδων	ὀρνίθων	ὀνομάτων	ὀδόντων	ἀρχόντων
dat pl	χάρισι(ν)	ἔλπισι(ν)	ὄρνισι(ν)	ὀνόμασι(ν)	ὀδοῦσι(ν)	ἄρχουσι(ν)
acc pl	χάριτας	ἔλπιδας	ὄρνιθας	ὀνόματα	ὀδόντας	ἄρχοντας

n-3c(6)

Neuter nouns that do not end in a dental (except n-3c[6d]) but they decline as if they do.

n-3c(6a)   Stems ending in ας
n-3c(6b)   Stems ending in ρ
n-3c(6c)   Stems ending in ς
n-3c(6d)   Irregular stems

	n-3c(6a)	*n-3c(6b)*	*n-3c(6c)*	*n-3c(6d)*	*n-3c(6d)*	*n-3c(6d)*	*n-3c(6d)*
n/v sg	τέρας	ὕδωρ	φῶς	γάλα	γόνυ	μέλι	κρέας
gen sg	τέρατος	ὕδατος	φωτός	γάλακτος	γόνατος	(μέλιτος)	(κρέως)
dat sg	τέρατι	ὕδατι	φωτί				
acc sg	τέρας	ὕδωρ	φῶς				
n/v pl	τέρατα	ὕδατα	φῶτα				
gen pl	τεράτων	ὑδάτων	φώτων				
dat pl	τέρασι(ν)	ὕδασι(ν)			γόνασι		
acc pl	τέρατα	ὕδατα	φῶτα		γόνατα		κρέα

n-3d   Stems ending in ς

The nouns do not use any case ending for the nominative singular; the final ς is part of the stem. Most go undergo ablaut (rule 5). *γενες ‣ γένος; *σωσθενες ‣ σωσθένης.

n-3d(1)   Stems ending in ας
n-3d(2)   Stems ending in ες
  n-3d(2a)   Stems ending in ες that are masculine
  n-3d(2b)   Stems ending in ες that are neuter
n-3d(3)   Stems ending in ος

	n-3d(1)	*n-3d(2a)*	*n-3d(2b)*	*n-3d(3)*
nom sg	(γήρας)	σωσθένης	γένος	(αἰδώς)
gen sg	(γήρως)	(σωσθένους)	γένους	αἰδοῦς
dat sg	γήρει		γένει	
acc sg		σωσθένην	γένος	
voc sg			γένος	
n/v pl			γένη	
gen pl			γενῶν	
dat pl			γένεσι(ν)	
acc pl			γένη	

n-3e   Stems ending in a semi-vowel (digamma [Ϝ], consonantal iota [ι̯]).

The Ϝ and ι̯ were letters that used to be in the Greek alphabet, but had long since dropped out, centuries before the koine period. However, because they once had been part of the language, their presence has had a remarkable effect on the Greek language; when they dropped out, they usually changed the words with which they had been associated. For more discussion see *MBG*, §26(Ϝ) and §27 (ι̯; also §33.5 below). In most cases, the Ϝ became an υ or dropped out. The ι̯ either dropped out or became an ι or ε.

n-3e(1)   Stems ending in Ϝ
n-3e(2)   Stems ending in αϜ
n-3e(3)   Stems ending in εϜ
n-3e(4)   Stems ending in οϜ
n-3e(5)   Stems ending in ι̯
  n-3e(5a)   Stems ending in ι̯ (no ablaut)
  n-3e(5b)   Stems ending in ι̯ (ablaut, rule 5)
n-3e(6)   Stems ending in οι̯

	n-3e(1)	*n-3e(2)*	*n-3e(3)*	*n-3e(4)*	*n-3e(5a)*	*n-3e(5b)*	*n-3e(6)*
nom sg	ἰχθύς	(ναῦς)	βασιλεύς	νοῦς	(νῆστις)	πόλις	(πείθω)
gen sg	ἰχθύος	(νεώς)	βασιλέως	νοός		πόλεως	(πειθοῦς)
dat sg	ἰχθύϊ		βασιλεῖ	νοΐ		πόλει	πειθοῖ
acc sg	ἰχθύν	ναῦν	βασιλέα	νοῦν		πόλιν	
voc sg	ἰχθύ		βασιλεῦ	νοῦ		πόλι	
n/v pl	ἰχθύες		βασιλεῖς	νόες		πόλεις	
gen pl	ἰχθύων		βασιλέων	νοῶν		πόλεων	
dat pl	ἰχθύσι(ν)		βασιλεῦσι(ν)	νουσί(ν)		πόλεσι(ν)	
acc pl	ἰχθύας		βασιλεῖς	νόας	νήστεις	πόλεις	

n-3f   Stems in ν that show different degrees of ablaut

No case ending is used in the nominative singular. "Strong" ablaut means the vowel has shifted to a long vowel (ἡγεμόνος ‣ ἡγεμών). "Weak" ablaut means the vowel has shifted to a short vowel (ἀνηρ ‣ ἄνερ). "Zero" ablaut means the vowel has dropped out altogether (μητηρ ‣ μητρί). (Some prefer to speak of "strong," "middle," and "weak.")

For further discussion see rule 5 above, and §4 in *MBG*.

n-3f(1a)   Stems ending in ν
   n-3f(1a)   Stems ending in ν showing no ablaut
   n-3f(1b)   Stems ending in ν showing strong and weak ablaut
   n-3f(1c)   Stems ending in ν showing strong and zero ablaut
n-3f(2)   Stems ending in a liquid
   n-3f(2a)   Stems ending in a liquid showing no ablaut
   n-3f(2b)   Stems ending in a liquid showing strong and weak ablaut
   n-3f(2c)   Stems ending in a liquid showing strong, weak, and zero ablaut

	n-3f(1a)	*n-3f(1b)*	*n-3f(1c)*	*n-3f(2a)*	*n-3f(2b)*
nom sg	αἰών	ἡγεμών	κύων	σωτήρ	ῥήτωρ
gen sg	αἰῶνος	ἡγεμόνος	(κυνός)	σωτῆρος	ῥήτορος
dat sg	αἰῶνι	ἡγεμόνι		σωτῆρι	ῥήτορι
acc sg	αἰῶνα	ἡγεμόνα		σωτῆρα	ῥήτορα
voc sg	αἰών	ἡγεμών	κύων	σωτήρ	ῥῆτορ
n/v pl	αἰῶνες	ἡγεμόνες	κύνες	σωτῆρες	ῥήτορες
gen pl	αἰώνων	ἡγεμόνων		σωτήρων	ῥητόρων
dat pl	αἰῶσι(ν)	ἡγεμόσι(ν)	κυσίν	σωτῆρσι(ν)	ῥήτορσι(ν)
acc pl	αἰῶνας	ἡγεμόνας	κύνας	σωτῆρας	ῥήτορας

	n-3f(2c)	*n-3f(2c)*	*n-3f(2c)*	*n-3f(2c)*
nom sg	ἀνήρ	θυγάτηρ	μήτηρ	πατήρ
gen sg	ἀνδρός	θυγατρός	μητρός	πατρός
dat sg	ἀνδρί	θυγατρί	μητρί	πατρί
acc sg	ἄνδρα	θυγατέρα	μητέρα	πατέρα
voc sg	ἄνερ	θυγάτερ		πάτερ
n/v pl	ἄνδρες	θυγατέρες		πατέρες
gen pl	ἀνδρῶν	θυγατέρων		πατέρων
dat pl	ἀνδράσι(ν)			πατράσι(ν)
acc pl	ἄνδρας	θυγατέρας	μητέρας	πατέρας

n-3g   Irregular (n-3g[1], listed below) and indeclinable (n-3g[2]) stems

nom sg	Ζηνᾶς, ὁ	(Ζεύς), ὁ	Ἰησοῦς, ὁ	Λευίς, ὁ	Μωϋσῆς, ὁ	Λύδδα, ἡ
gen sg		Ζιός	Ἰησοῦ	Λευί	Μωϋσέως	Λύδδας
dat sg		Ζιί	Ἰησοῦ		Μωϋσεῖ	
acc sg	Ζηνᾶν	Ζία	Ἰησοῦν	Λευίν	Μωϋσῆν	Λύδδα
voc sg		Ζεῦ	Ἰησοῦ			

a-1 Adjectives

a-1a   Uncontracted stems (2-1-2)

Adjectives using three endings (2-1-2) that do not have contract stems. The masculine uses second declension case endings, the feminine uses first, and the neuter uses second.

a-1a(1)   Uncontracted stems (feminine in α).
a-1a(2a)   Uncontracted stems (feminine in η; neuter in ον)
a-1a(2b)   Uncontracted stems (feminine in η; neuter in ο). Included μέγας, πολύς, and the relative pronoun ὅς because they are either difficult to learn or important.

	a-1a(1)				*a-1a(2a)*		
nom sg	ἅγιος	ἁγία	ἅγιον		ἀγαθός	ἀγαθή	ἀγαθόν
gen sg	ἁγίου	ἁγίας	ἁγίου		ἀγαθοῦ	ἀγαθῆς	ἀγαθοῦ
dat sg	ἁγίῳ	ἁγίᾳ	ἁγίῳ		ἀγαθῷ	ἀγαθῇ	ἀγαθῷ
acc sg	ἅγιον	ἁγίαν	ἅγιον		ἀγαθόν	ἀγαθήν	ἀγαθόν
voc sg	ἅγιε	ἁγία	ἅγιον		ἀγαθέ	ἀγαθή	ἀγαθόν
n/v pl	ἅγιοι	ἅγιαι	ἅγια		ἀγαθοί	ἀγαθαί	ἀγαθά
gen pl	ἁγίων	ἁγίων	ἁγίων		ἀγαθῶν	ἀγαθῶν	ἀγαθῶν
dat pl	ἁγίοις	ἁγίαις	ἁγίοις		ἀγαθοῖς	ἀγαθαῖς	ἀγαθοῖς
acc pl	ἁγίους	ἁγίας	ἅγια		ἀγαθούς	ἀγαθάς	ἀγαθά

	a-1a(2b)				*a-1a(2b)*		
nom sg	οὗτος	αὕτη	τοῦτο		μέγας	μεγάλη	μέγα
gen sg	τούτου	ταύτης	τούτου		μεγάλου	μεγάλης	μεγάλου
dat sg	τούτῳ	ταύτῃ	τούτῳ		μεγάλῳ	μεγάλῃ	μεγάλῳ
acc sg	τοῦτον	ταύτην	τοῦτο		μέγαν	μεγάλην	μέγα
n/v pl	οὗτοι	αὗται	ταῦτα		μεγάλοι	μεγάλαι	μεγάλα
gen pl	τούτων	τούτων	τούτων		μεγάλων	μεγάλων	μεγάλων
dat pl	τούτοις	ταύταις	τούτοις		μεγάλοις	μεγάλαις	μεγάλοις
acc pl	τούτους	ταύτας	ταῦτα		μεγάλους	μεγάλας	μεγάλα

	a-1a(2b)				*a-1a(2b)*		
nom sg	πολύς	πολλή	πολύ		ὅς	ἥ	ὅ
gen sg	πολλοῦ	πολλῆς	πολλοῦ		οὗ	ἧς	οὗ
dat sg	πολλῷ	πολλῇ	πολλῷ		ᾧ	ᾗ	ᾧ
acc sg	πολύν	πολλήν	πολύ		ὅν	ἥν	ὅ
nom pl	πολλοί	πολλαί	πολλά		οἵ	αἵ	ἅ
gen pl	πολλῶν	πολλῶν	πολλῶν		ὧν	ὧν	ὧν
dat pl	πολλοῖς	πολλαῖς	πολλοῖς		οἷς	αἷς	οἷς
acc pl	πολλούς	πολλάς	πολλά		οὕς	ἅς	ἅ

a-1b   Contracted stems (2-1-2)

Adjectives using three endings (2-1-2) that have contract stems. This means that the stem actually ends in two vowels (εο), and those vowels have contracted according to the rules: ε + οσ ‣ ους (§2.6); ε + ον ‣ ους (§2.6)

nom sg	ἁπλοῦς	ἁπλῆ	ἁπλοῦν
gen sg	ἁπλοῦ	ἁπλῆς	ἁπλοῦ
dat sg	ἁπλῷ	ἁπλῇ	ἁπλῷ
acc sg	ἁπλοῦν	ἁπλῆν	ἁπλοῦν
nom pl	ἁπλοῖ	ἁπλαῖ	ἁπλᾶ
gen pl	ἁπλῶν	ἁπλῶν	ἁπλῶν
dat pl	ἁπλοῖς	ἁπλαῖς	ἁπλοῖς
acc pl	ἁπλοῦς	ἁπλᾶς	ἁπλᾶ

a-2 Adjectives

a-2 adjectives use three endings like a-1 adjectives, but a-2 use the third declension case endings for the masculine and neuter, and first declension case endings for the feminine (3-1-3).

a-2a   stems ending in ντ.
       The root of μέλας is *μελαν. A consonantal iota was added to the feminine, it switched places with the ν ("metathesis"), and the consonantal iota became an iota.

a-2b   stems ending in Ϝ.
       The digamma changes into an υ if the case ending begins with a consonant. Otherwise, it changes into an ε.

	a-2a				*a-2a*		
nom sg	πᾶς	πᾶσα	πᾶν		μέλας	μέλαινα	μέλαν
gen sg	παντός	πάσης	παντός		μέλανος	μελαίνης	μέλανος
dat sg	παντί	πάσῃ	παντί		μέλανι	μελαίνῃ	μέλανι
acc sg	πάντα	πᾶσαν	πᾶν		μέλανα	μέλαιναν	μέλαν
nom pl	πάντες	πᾶσαι	πάντα		μέλανες	μέλαιναι	μέλανα
gen pl	πάντων	πασῶν	πάντων		μελάνων	μελαινῶν	μελάνων
dat pl	πᾶσι	πάσαις	πᾶσι		μέλασι	μελαίναις	μέλασι
acc pl	πάντας	πάσας	πάντα		μέλανας	μελαίνας	μέλανα

	a-2a				a-2b		
nom sg	εἷς	μία	ἕν		ταχύς	ταχεῖα	ταχύ
gen sg	ἑνός	μιᾶς	ἑνός		ταχέως	ταχείας	ταχέως
dat sg	ἑνί	μιᾷ	ἑνί		ταχεῖ	ταχείᾳ	ταχεῖ
acc sg	ἕνα	μίαν	ἕν		ταχύν	ταχεῖαν	ταχύ
nom pl					ταχεῖς	ταχεῖαι	ταχέα
gen pl					ταχέων	ταχειῶν	ταχέων
dat pl					ταχέσι	ταχείαις	ταχέσι
acc pl					ταχεῖς	ταχείας	ταχέα

a-3 Adjectives

Adjectives using two endings, both second declension (2-2)

a-3a   Stems consistently using two endings
a-3b   Stems that alternate between using two endings and three endings.
           Sometimes they use a separate endings for the feminine. Normally, they are declined just like a-3a adjectives. When the feminine has a separate form, they are declined like ἅγιος (a-1a[1]), which has the α all the way through the singular. No example is listed below.
   a-3b(1)   Stems alternating between two (2-2) and three (2-1-2) endings (feminine in α)
   a-3b(2)   Stems alternating between two (2-2) and three (2-1-2) endings (feminine in η)

	masc/fem	neuter
nom sg	ἁμαρτωλός	ἁμαρτωλόν
gen sg	ἁμαρτωλοῦ	ἁμαρτωλοῦ
dat sg	ἁμαρτωλῷ	ἁμαρτωλῷ
acc sg	ἁμαρτωλόν	ἁμαρτωλόν
voc sg	ἁμαρτωλέ	ἁμαρτωλόν
nom pl	ἁμαρτωλοί	ἁμαρτωλά
gen pl	ἁμαρτωλῶν	ἁμαρτωλῶν
dat pl	ἁμαρτωλοῖς	ἁμαρτωλοῖς
acc pl	ἁμαρτωλούς	ἁμαρτωλά

a-4 Adjectives

Adjectives using two endings, both third declension (3-3). Most of the words undergo ablaut (rule 5).

a-4a   Stems ending in ες
a-4b(1)   Stems ending in ον
a-4b(2)   Stems ending in ν or ρ

| | *a-4a* | | *a-4b(1)* | | *a-4b(2)* | |
	masc/fem	*neuter*	*masc/fem*	*neuter*	*masc/fem*	*neuter*
nom sg	ἀληθής	ἀληθές	ἄφρων	ἄφρον	τίς	τί
gen sg	ἀληθοῦς	ἀληθοῦς	ἄφρονος	ἄφρονος	τίνος	τίνος
dat sg	ἀληθεῖ	ἀληθεῖ	ἄφρονι	ἄφρονι	τίνι	τίν
acc sg	ἀληθῆ	ἀληθές	ἄφρονα	ἄφρο͞ν	τίνα	τί
nom pl	ἀληθεῖς	ἀληθῆ	ἄφρονες	ἄφρονα	τίνες	τίνα
gen pl	ἀληθῶν	ἀληθῶν	ἀφρόνων	ἀφρόνων	τίνων	τίνων
dat pl	ἀληθέσι(ν)	ἀληθέσι(ν)	ἄφροσι(ν)	ἄφροσι(ν)	τίσι(ν)	τίσι(ν)
acc pl	ἀληθεῖς	ἀληθῆ	ἄφρονας	ἄφρονα	τίνας	τίνα

a-5 Adjectives

Irregular (a-5a) and indeclinable (a-5b) stems

nom sg	(δεῖνα)	ἵλεως	ἐγώ		σύ	
gen sg	(δεῖνος)	(ἵλεων)	ἐμοῦ	μου	σοῦ	σου
dat sg			ἐμοί	μοι	σοί	σοι
acc sg	δεῖνα		ἐμέ	με	σέ	σε
nom pl	δύο		ἡμεῖς		ὑμεῖς	
gen pl	δύο		ἡμῶν		ὑμῶν	
dat pl	δυσί		ἡμῖν		ὑμῖν	
acc pl	δύο		ἡμᾶς		ὑμᾶς	

Section II

Verb Formation

In this section we will look at how the Greek verb is formed, starting at the left side of the word with the augment and reduplication, and work through to the right and personal endings. The reference numbers (e.g., §31), refer to sections in *MBG*. We will skip over those discussions that are secondary in importance.

Augment (§31)

§31.2   **Syllabic Augment** If the word begins with a consonant, the syllabic augment ε is added before the initial consonant. λύω ‣ ἔλυον. It is called "syllabic" because it adds another "syllable" to the word.

§31.2a   Sometimes there is a η (temporal augment; §32.3) where we would expect to find an ε (syllabic augment; cf. §31.5). θέλω ‣ ἤθελον.

§31.2b   Verbs beginning with ρ sometime double the ρ before the augment. ῥαίνω ‣ ἔρρανα.

§31.2c   If the verb begins with a consonant cluster (except the combination of a stop and a liquid; §32.2), in the perfect the verb will augment instead of reduplicate. κτίζω ‣ ἔκτικα.

§31.2d   Sometimes words beginning with λ augment instead of reduplicate. *λαβ (λαμβάνω) ‣ εἴληφα.

§31.2e   Sometimes, words beginning with βλ or γλ augment instead of reduplicate.

§31.2f   Words beginning with γν always augment in the perfect instead of reduplicating. *γνω (γινώσκω) ‣ ἔγνωκα.

§31.3   **Temporal Augment**. Verbs with an initial vowel are augmented by lengthening that vowel. It is called a "temporal" augment because it lengthens the time required to say the word. Vowels lengthen according to the pattern in §2.4. ἀγαπάω ‣ ἠγάπησα.

§31.4   **Initial Diphthong**. Verbs with an initial diphthong lengthen the first vowel according to the pattern in §2.4. If the second vowel of the diphthong is an υ, it will remain. If the second vowel is an ι, it will subscript. αὐξάνω ‣ ηὔξανεν. οἰκοδομέω ‣ ᾠκοδόμησεν.

§31.4a   Initial diphthongs often are not augmented. ου is never augmented and ει only rarely. εὑρίσκω ‣ εὑρισκον. οὐδενέω ‣ οὐδενήθην.

§31.4b   Some words with an initial diphthong vary between augmenting and not augmenting. εὔχομαι ‣ εὐχόμην or ηὐχόμην.

§31.5   **Initial σ and Ϝ**. There are words that originally began with a σ or a digamma, but by the time of the koine these initial consonants had dropped out in the present tense. However, the words will augment as if the σ or Ϝ were still there.When the augment is added, the σ/Ϝ drops out and the vowels contract. *σεχ (ἔχω) ‣ εεχ ‣ εἶχον. *Ϝεπ ‣ εεπ ‣ εἶπον.

§31.6   **Compound verbs**. Compound verbs augment the verbal part of the compound (which is the second part of the compound). This makes sense since the augment indicates past time, and the non-verbal element of the compound cannot express time (Bl-D §67.2). καταβαίνω ‣ κατέβην.

§31.6a   Some compounds are treated as if they are not compounds, and therefore the augment will affect the first part of the word. ψευδομαρτυρέω ‣ ἐψευδομαρτύρησα.

§31.6b   Some compound verbs receive two augments, one for each element of the compound. For example, ἀνοίγω is actually a compound verb that can accent both parts (ἠνέῳξα) or just the preposition (ἤνοιγον) or just the verbal element (ἀνέῳξα).

§31.6c   If a compound is formed with a preposition ending in a vowel and a verb beginning with a consonant, the final vowel of the preposition will be dropped and the verb will receive the syllabic augment ("apocope"; §7.1). This is true for all prepositions except περί and πρό. ἐπικαλέω ‣ ἐπεκάλεσα.

§31.6d   If the verbal part of the compound begins with a vowel, the final vowel of the preposition will already have dropped out. In this case the initial vowel of the verbal part of the compound will receive the temporal augment. (As above, περί and πρό do not elide; §6.5d,e). ἐπί + αἴρω ‣ ἐπαίρω ‣ ἐπῆρα.

§31.6e When a preposition has undergone some morphological change in the formation of a compound verb such as elision or assimilation, when the augment is added the morphological change on the preposition is often reversed.

A good example is a compound using ἐκ. As discussed in §21.3, the preposition is properly ἐξ (i.e., "eks"). When the following word begins with a consonant, the σ in the ξ becomes interconsonantal and therefore drops out (§27.4). But when the verbal part of the compound is augmented, the σ is no longer interconsonantal and therefore remains εξ. ἐξ + βάλλω ‣ ἐκβάλλω ‣ ἐξέβαλον.

§31.7 **Lack of augment.** In certain circumstances it is not unusual to find a word in an augmented tense without an augment.

§31.7a Words beginning with diphthongs frequently do not augment. Verbs with initial ει rarely augment and verbs with ου never augment; cf. §31.3b. εὐλογέω ‣ εὐλόγησα.

§31.7b Compound verbs frequently lack augment.

§31.7c The pluperfect frequently has no augment (especially in compound verbs; Bl-D §66.1).

§31.8 **Double augment.** Some verbs receive double augments (see §32.6b). ὁράω ‣ εορων ‣ ἑώρων.

Reduplication (§32)

§32.1 Reduplication is primarily a characteristic of the perfect tense. Yet it is found in the present and even twice in the aorist.

In the present, v-6a verbs (and a few other isolated examples) alter their verbal base to form their present tense stem. A verb that is formed thus can also reduplicate in the perfect, but the vowel in between the reduplicated consonants will be different: ι in the present; ε in the perfect.

§32.2 **Single consonant.** If a word begins with a single consonant, that consonant is reduplicated and separated from the original with a vowel. If it is the perfect, the vowel is ε; if present it is an ι. λύω ‣ λέλυκα. *δω ‣ δίδωμι.

§32.2a If that consonant is an aspirate, when it reduplicates the reduplicated aspirate will deaspirate (§15.5). φανερόω ‣ φεφανεροω ‣ πεφανέρωκα. χαρίζομαι ‣ χεχαρισμαι ‣ κεχάρισμαι. θεραπεύω ‣ θεθεραπευμένον ‣ τεθεραπευμένον.

§32.3 **Consonant cluster.** In the perfect, if a verb begins with a consonant cluster composed of a stop + λ or ρ, the stop is usually reduplicated and the two stops are separated with an ε. γράφω ‣ γέγραφα.

§32.3a Words beginning with any other cluster will not reduplicate to form the perfect but will have a syllabic augment (§32.4).

§32.4 **Consonant cluster.** In the present, even if the word begins with a cluster, the first consonant of the cluster will reduplicate and be separated with an ι. *πτ ‣ πίπτω.

§32.5 **Compound verbs.** Compound verbs reduplicate the second element of the compound. ἐν + ἐργέω ‣ ἐνεργέω ‣ ἐνήργηκα.

§32.5a Some compounds became viewed as simple verbs, and therefore reduplicate the beginning of the first element. ἀνοίγω ‣ ἤνοιγον.

§32.6 **Attic reduplication.** This is a special form of reduplication. It applies only to certain words. If one of these verbs began with α, ε, or ο followed by a single consonant, the vowel and consonant were both reduplicated, and the second vowel was then lengthened. In other words, the word underwent both a reduplication and a lengthening. Cf. Funk §344. *ακο (ἀκούω) ‣ ακακο ‣ ἀκηκοα (second perfect).

§32.7 **Initial σ / F.** If a verb originally began with σ or F, the reduplicated σ or F may dissimilate to a rough breathing (§27.6b). *στα ‣ σιστημι ‣ ἵστημι. *Fορα ‣ FεF ωρακα ‣ ἐF ωρακα ‣ ἑώρακα.

Tense formation (§33)

§33.1 The "root" of a verb is its most basic form. For example, the root of ἀγαπάω is *αγαπα. We always preface the verbal root with an asterisk. This root shows itself in the verb ἀγαπάω as well as the noun ἀγάπη and the adjective ἀγαπητός.

§33.2 The "stem" of a verb is the basic form of that verb in a particular tense. The stem of the present tense λύω is λυ. The stem of the future tense λύσω is also λυ. (Usage differs with these terms, but this is how we will use them.)

§33.3 The present tense stem and the verbal root of some verbs are the same. For example, the root of ἀγαπάω is *αγαπα. The present tense stem is also αγαπα. In other words, the root and the present tense stem are identical.

In verbs where this is the case, the root is usually used without modification in all the tenses and is therefore quite recognizable. Most call these the "regular" verbs.

§33.4 Other verbs modify their verbal root when forming their different tense stems. This is especially true in the formation of the present tense. The present tense is by far the most "irregular" of all the tenses. If you assume that the present tense stem is the base form and all other tenses are derived from it, you will become very confused and potentially discouraged since this approach forces you to memorize hundreds of "irregular" forms. However, if you can learn that the different tense stems are formed from the verbal root and not the present tense stem, memorization and frustration can be kept to a minimum.

For example, the verbal root *βαλ is modified to form its present tense stem by doubling the lambda: βάλλω ("I throw"). However, when you arrive at the future, you will see that there is only one lambda: βαλῶ. The aorist tense also has one lambda: ἔβαλον. If you learn the present tense as the base form, both these forms will appear irregular. But if you learn the present form and its root, these two forms are perfectly regular.

Most grammars describe these changes by saying that the present tense stem has lost a lambda. Although this may be easier at first, it builds a significant error into your way of thinking and will come back to haunt you. The present tense stem is never altered to form another tense stem! The present tense stem is usually a modified form of the verbal root.

§33.5 **Consonantal iota**. One of the more important elements in this entire discussion is a letter in the Greek alphabet called the "consonantal iota," usually written in grammars as "ι". It fell out of use many centuries before the time of the koine, but the fact that it used to be present explains the formation of many words.

For example, the iota in the noun πόλις actually was a consonantal iota. Sometimes the consonantal iota stayed as an iota as it does here. But notice that in the genitive the form is πόλεως. The consonantal iota stayed as an epsilon.

Another example is the verb βάλλω, "I throw." In the future it is βαλῶ with the single lambda. Why the change? In the formation of the present tense stem, the consonantal iota was added to the root *βαλ, and a lambda and consonantal iota form two lambdas. *βαλ + ι ‣ βαλλ ‣ βάλλω.

§33.6 Verbs are properly classified by how the verbal base is modified in order to form the present tense stem.

v-1	Present tense = verbal base	*λυ ‣ λύω
v-2	Present tense = verbal base + ι	*βαπτιδ + ι ‣ βαπτίζω
v-3	Present tense = verbal base + ν	*πι + ν ‣ πίνω
v-4	Present tense = verbal base + τ	*θαπ + τ ‣ θάπτω
v-5	Present tense = verbal base + σκ	*αρε + σκ ‣ ἀρέσκω

§33.7 v-6. The sixth category is composed of μι verbs. These stems follow the athematic conjugation, use the alternate personal endings, and some of them reduplicate their verbal bases to form their present tense stems.

§33.8 These are the six basic categories. But many of the verbs within these categories also show other types of modifications. Verbs in almost all categories show ablaut in their stem vowel. Many of the verbs also use more than one verbal base in forming their different tense stems. Therefore, out of these 6 categories we have drawn all bases that undergo ablaut and use different verbal bases, and have repeated them in v-7 and v-8.

§33.9   v-7. Verbal bases that undergo ablaut (*καλε ‣ καλέω ‣ κέκληκα)

§33.10   v-8. Verbs that use more than one verbal base to form their different tense stems (*φερ ‣ φέρω; *οι ‣ οἴσω; *ενεκ ‣ ἤνεγκα)

Tense and Mood Formatives   (§34)

§34.1   Between the stem and the personal endings we find final stem consonants and vowels, tense formatives, connecting vowels, and mood formatives.

§34.2   **Final stem consonant**. If the word's stem ends in a consonant, and the next element in the inflectional form of the word begins with a consonant, the final stem consonant very frequently is modified. These types of changes are especially evident in the future and first aorist where the σ is added to the stem, and the perfect middle/passive where the endings are added directly to the stem without a connecting vowel. Our discussions in *MBG* (§21 - §29) cover all these types of changes that occur in the New Testament, especially §25 (σ) and §46.2 (stem changes in the perfect middle/passive). For illustrations see the discussion of the tenses below (§43–§46).

§34.3   **Final stem vowel**. If the stem of a word ends in a vowel, that vowel will be lengthened before all of the tense formatives, and before the personal endings in the perfect middle/passive, according to the pattern in §3.1.γεννάω ‣ γεννήσω, ποιέω ‣ ποιήσω, φανερόω ‣ φανερώσω.

§34.4   **Tense formatives**. The following suffixes are added in the formation of the different tenses.

future	σ	
1 aorist (act)	σα	(which becomes σε in the third person singular in order to distinguish it from the first person singular)
1 perfect (act)	κα	(which becomes κε in the third person singular in order to distinguish it from the first person singular)
2 perfect (act)	α	
1 pluperfect	κει	
2 pluperfect	ει	
1 aorist (pas)	θε	(which lengthens to θη)
2 aorist (pas)	ε	(which lengthens to η)
1 future (pas)	θησ	
2 future (pas)	ησ	

§34.5   **Mood formative**. The optative adds a mood formative between the stem and the personal ending.

         οι   All tenses (except the 1 aorist [act/mid])

         αι   1 aorist (act/mid)

         §34.5a   The subjunctive's use of lengthened connecting vowels (ω/η) function practically as if they were mood formatives.

Thematic and Athematic Conjugations   (§35)

§35.1   Certain verbs use a thematic vowel immediately before the personal endings ("thematic" conjugation). The "thematic" vowel is also called a "connecting" or "variable" vowel. Other verbs join the personal endings directly to the stem ("athematic" = α privative + "thematic").

         §35.1a   A verb that uses the athematic conjugation in a certain tense will use that conjugation consistently throughout that tense. But a verb can alternate between thematic and athematic conjugations from tense to tense.

§35.2   **Thematic**. In the indicative of some formations of the present, imperfect, second aorist (active/

middle), and all futures, a connecting vowel is inserted between the stem (or tense formative) and the personal ending.

§35.2a   In the indicative and optative, o is used with personal endings beginning with μ or ν and ε is used elsewhere. *λυ + ο + μεν ‣ λύομεν. *λυ + ε + τε ‣ λύετε.

§35.2b   In the subjunctive, the connecting vowels are lengthened so that ω is used with personal endings beginning with μ or ν. η is used elsewhere.

§35.2c   For the sake of simplicity, most beginning grammars teach that the connecting vowel is part of the personal ending. For example, the first person plural ending in the present middle indicative is ομεθα. But if you realize that the o is really not part of the personal ending, it makes it much easier to understand the similarity between the indicative (ομεθα) and subjunctive (ωμεθα), and between the present and the perfect middle/passive: μεθα.

§35.3   **Athematic conjugation.**   Some verbs add the personal endings directly to their stems (or tense formatives). These words will use the alternate personal endings (§39). διδω + μι ‣ δίδωμι.

§35.3a   Athematic conjugations are found in some present, imperfect, and second aorist constructions, and in all perfect (middle/passive), pluperfect (middle), and aorist (passive) constructions. It is also found in a few second perfect and pluperfect (active) constructions.

Personal Endings   (§36)

§36.1   Before studying the following discussion, be sure you understand connecting vowels (§35). In order to make the verb structure simple for beginners, most teach that the connecting vowel and the personal ending together form the personal ending. This may be necessary step at first, but one that must be refined. Following is a technically correct discussion of the personal endings (albeit with a few simplifications as any student of classical Greek will realize). If you wish even further discussion, see the major grammars: Smyth §463-464; F §318-319.

§36.2   The endings are broken down into primary and secondary, and for each there are regular and alternate endings.

§36.3   The primary endings are used on the unaugmented tenses. In the indicative these are the present, future, and perfect. In the subjunctive they are all tenses.

§36.4   The secondary endings are used on the augmented tenses (i.e., those that are past in time). In the indicative these are the imperfect, aorist, and pluperfect. In the optative they are all tenses.

§36.5   **Indicative**

	primary endings		*secondary endings*	
		active		
	regular	*alternate*	*regular*	*alternate*
1 sg	_ [13]	μι	ν [14]	
2 sg	σ [15]		ς	
3 sg	_ [16]	σι(ν)	-(ν) [17]	

---

[13]   No ending is used. The ω which stands at the end of the first person singular of verbs in the thematic conjugation is really the lengthened connecting vowel o.

[14]   The ending was originally μ. It assimilates to ν when preceded by a vowel. When it is preceded by a consonant it assimilates to an α (e.g., ἔλυσα; Smyth §464a).

[15]   The ending is actually σι. When added to the connecting vowel, the σ became intervocalic and dropped out. In the present this left, e.g., λυει which then added a final ς. The subjunctive also adds σ by analogy to the indicative. In the perfect σ (not σι) is the ending (Smyth §463b.2). There is an old alternate ending θα (derived from σθα) used only rarely.

1 pl	μεν		μεν	
2 pl	τε		τε	
3 pl	νσι(ν)[18]		ανσι(ν) [19]	ν

middle/passive

1 sg	μαι		μην	
2 sg	σαι [20]		σο [21]	
3 sg	ται		το	
1 pl	μεθα		μεθα	
2 pl	σθε		σθε	
3 pl	σαν		νται	ντο

§36.6　　**Subjunctive.** The subjunctive uses lengthened connecting vowels and primary endings. Exactly the same endings are found everywhere, regardless of tense. (In the first aorist passive, the η of the tense formative is absorbed.) See general discussion at §36.1,5, and especially Smyth §463.

1 sg	ω [22]				
2 sg	η	+	σι	▸	ης [23]
3 sg	η	+	ε	▸	η [24]
1 pl	ω	+	μεν	▸	ωμεν
2 pl	η	+	τε	▸	ητε
3 pl	ω	+	νσι	▸	ωσι [25]

---

[16]　The third singular ending is difficult. Smyth lists τι as the only ending (used for example by ἐστί) and adds that ει (e.g., λύει) cannot be derived from it (§463c). Many times no ending is used, and if the connecting vowel is ε, a movable ν may be added.

[17]　" - " indicates that no ending is used. If the connecting vowel is ε, then a movable ν may be added.

[18]　In every case the initial ν will drop out because of the σ (§24.4). What happens to the preceding stem vowel varies from case to case.

[19]　Funk says the ending was ανσι (short α) that, when ν dropped out (§24.4), was lengthened to ασι (long α).

[20]　The ending is properly σαι. When the connecting vowel ε precedes it, the σ becomes intervocalic (§27.4) and drops out (except in the athematic conjugation where there is no connecting vowel and the σ is not lost). Contraction differs from case to case.

[21]　The ending is properly σο. When the connecting vowel ε precedes it, the σ becomes intervocalic (§27.4) and drops out (except in the athematic conjugation where there is no connecting vowel and the σ is not lost). Contraction differs from case to case.

[22]　No ending is used. The connecting vowel stands alone.

[23]　Intervocalic σ drops out (§25.5), ι subscripts, and σ is added by analogy to the indicative.

[24]　ι is provided by analogy to the present indicative, and it subscripts.

[25]　ν drops out when immediately followed by σ (§24.4).

§36.7 **Imperative**. Following are the imperative endings.

	active	middle
2 sg	–	σο
3 sg	τω	σθω
2 pl	τε	σθε
3 pl	τωσαν	σθωσαν

§36.8 **Movable ν**. The basic rule is that a ν is added to a word ending in a vowel when the next word begins with a vowel. This is to prevent haitus (§6.3).

We often find movable ν when the following word begins with a consonant, thus deserving the name "irrational ν." On verbs it is found normally on the third person singular and plural primary endings (λύεν, λύουσιν) and on ἐστίν. In grammars, movable-ν is written in brackets; λυέ(ν).

Section III
Tense formation

In this section we will spell out the basic rules governing the formation of the different tenses. The reference numbers (e.g., §41) correspond to the reference numbers in *MBG*.

The paradigms are listed vertically first, second, and third person singular, first, second, and third person plural. When the active and middle/passive are both listed, they are usually listed to the right of the active. Following are a few master charts, and then the charts are broken down by tense.

Master Indicative Verb Chart

This chart summarizes the basic elements of the verb in each of the tenses in the indicative mood. If you can remember the parts, you can almost always determine the tense and voice of a verb.

Tense stem	Aug/ Redup	Tense stem	Tense form.	Conn. vowel	Personal endings	First sing paradigm
Present act		pres		o/ε	prim act	λύω
Present mid/pass		pres		o/ε	prim pass	λύομαι
Imperfect act	ε	pres		o/ε	sec act	ἔλυον
Imperfect mid/pass	ε	pres		o/ε	sec pass	ἐλυόμην
Future act		fut act	σ	o/ε	prim act	λύσω
Liquid fut act		fut act	εσ	o/ε	prim act	κρινῶ
Future mid		fut act	σ	o/ε	prim pass	ἐλεύσομαι
First future pass		aorist pass	θησ	o/ε	prim pass	λυθήσομαι
Second future pass		aorist pass	ησ	o/ε	prim pass	ἀποσταλήσομαι
First aorist act	ε	aorist act	σα		sec act	ἔλυσα
Liquid aorist act	ε	aorist act	α		sec act	ἔμεινα

Second aorist act	ε	aorist act		ο/ε	sec act	ἔλαβον
First aorist mid	ε	aorist act	σα		sec pass	ἐλυσάμην
Second aorist mid	ε	aorist act		ο/ε	sec pass	ἐλιπόμην
First aorist pass	ε	aorist pass	θη		sec act	ἐλύθην
Second aorist pass	ε	aorist pass	η		sec act	ἐγράφην
First perfect act	λε	perf act	κα		prim act	λέλυκα
Second perfect act	λε	perf act	α		prim act	γέγονα
Perfect mid/pass	λε	perf mid/pass			prim pass	λέλυμαι

Overview of the Thematic Conjugation

The following charts are meant to give you a quick overview of the main parts of the verbal system for thematic verbs. In the discussions that follow, you will find more specific information and additional charts, including contracted and athematic forms.

Overview of Indicative

	present	*imperfect*	*future*	*first aorist*	*second aorist*	*perfect*
Active indicative						
1 sg	λύω	ἔλυον	λύσω	ἔλυσα	ἔλιπον	λέλυκα
2 sg	λύεις	ἔλυες	λύσεις	ἔλυσας	ἔλιπες	λέλυκας
3 sg	λύει	ἔλυε(ν)	λύσει	ἔλυσε(ν)	ἔλιπε(ν)	λέλυκε(ν)
1 pl	λύομεν	ἐλύομεν	λύσομεν	ἐλύσαμεν	ἐλίπομεν	λελύκαμεν
2 pl	λύετε	ἐλύετε	λύσετε	ἐλύσατε	ἐλίπετε	λελύκατε
3 pl	λύουσι(ν)	ἔλυον	λύσουσι(ν)	ἔλυσαν	ἔλιπον	λελύκασι(ν)
Middle indicative						
1 sg	λύομαι	ἐλυόμην	λύσομαι	ἐλυσάμην	ἐλιπόμην	λέλυμαι
2 sg	λύῃ	ἐλύου	λύσῃ	ἐλύσω	ἐλίπου	λέλυσαι
3 sg	λύεται	ἐλύετο	λύσεται	ἐλύσατο	ἐλίπετο	λέλυται
1 pl	λυόμεθα	ἐλυόμεθα	λυσόμεθα	ἐλυσάμεθα	ἐλιπόμεθα	λελύμεθα
2 pl	λύεσθε	ἐλύεσθε	λύσεσθε	ἐλύσασθε	ἐλίπεσθε	λέλυσθε
3 pl	λύονται	ἐλύοντο	λύσονται	ἐλύσαντο	ἐλίποντο	λέλυνται
Passive indicative						
1 sg	λύομαι	ἐλυόμην	λυθήσομαι	ἐλύθην	ἐγράφην	λέλυμαι
2 sg	λύῃ	ἐλύου	λυθήσῃ	ἐλύθης	εγράφης	λέλυσαι
3 sg	λύεται	ἐλύετο	λυθήσεται	ἐλύθη	ἐγράφη	λέλυται
1 pl	λυόμεθα	ἐλυόμεθα	λυθησόμεθα	ἐλύθημεν	ἐγράφημεν	λελύμεθα
2 pl	λύεσθε	ἐλύεσθε	λυθήσεσθε	ἐλύθητε	ἐγράφητε	λέλυσθε
3 pl	λύονται	ἐλύοντο	λυθήσονται	ἐλύθησαν	ἐγράφησαν	λέλυνται

Overview of Subjunctive

	present	*first aorist*	*second aorist*

Active subjunctive

1 *sg*	λύω	λύσω	λίπω
2 *sg*	λύῃς	λύσῃς	λίπῃς
3 *sg*	λύῃ	λύσῃ	λίπῃ
1 *pl*	λύωμεν	λύσωμεν	λίπωμεν
2 *pl*	λύητε	λύσητε	λίπητε
3 *pl*	λύωσι (ν)	λύσωσι (ν)	λίπωσι (ν)

Middle subjunctive

1 *sg*	λύωμαι	λύσωμαι	λίπωμαι
2 *sg*	λύῃ	λύσῃ	λίπῃ
3 *sg*	λύηται	λύσηται	λίπηται
1 *pl*	λυώμεθα	λυσώμεθα	λιπώμεθα
2 *pl*	λύησθε	λύσησθε	λίπησθε
3 *pl*	λύωνται	λύσωνται	λίπωνται

Passive subjunctive

1 *sg*	λύωμαι	λυθῶ	λιπῶ
2 *sg*	λύῃ	λυθῇς	λιπῇς
3 *sg*	λύηται	λυθῇ	λιπῇ
1 *pl*	λυώμεθα	λυθῶμεν	λιπῶμεν
2 *pl*	λύησθε	λυθῆτε	λιπῆτε
3 *pl*	λύωνται	λυθῶσι (ν)	λιπῶσι (ν)

Overview of Imperative

	present	*first aorist*	*second aorist*

Active imperative

2 *sg*	λῦε	λῦσον	λίπε
3 *sg*	λυέτω	λυσάτω	λιπέτω
2 *pl*	λύετε	λύσατε	λίπετε
3 *pl*	λυέτωσαν	λυσάτωσαν	λιπέτωσαν

Middle imperative

2 *sg*	λύου	λῦσαι	λίπου
3 *sg*	λυέσθω	λυσάσθω	λιπέσθω
2 *pl*	λύεσθε	λύσασθε	λίπεσθε
3 *pl*	λυέσθωσαν	λυσάσθωσαν	λιπέσθωσαν

Passive imperative

2 sg	λύου	λύθητι	λίπηθι
3 sg	λυέσθω	λυθήτω	λιπήτω
2 pl	λύεσθε	λύθητε	λίπητε
3 pl	λυέσθωσαν	λυθήτωσαν	λιπήτωσαν

Overview of Infinitive

	present	*first aorist*	*second aorist*	*perfect*
Active infinitive	λύειν	λῦσαι	λιπεῖν	λελυκέναι
Middle infinitive	λύεσθαι	λύσασθαι	λίπεσθαι	λέλυσθαι
Passive infinitive	λύεσθαι	λυθῆναι	λιπῆναι	λέλυσθαι

Overview of Pluperfect Indicative

	active	*middle/passive*
1 sg	(ἐ)λελύκειν	(ἐ)λελύμην
2 sg	(ἐ)λελύκεις	(ἐ)λέλυσο
3 sg	(ἐ)λελύκει	(ἐ)λέλυτο
1 pl	(ἐ)λελύκειμεν	(ἐ)λελύμεθα
2 pl	(ε)λελύκειτε	(ἐ)λέλυσθε
3 pl	(ἐ)λελύκεισαν	(ἐ)λέλυντο

Overview of εἰμί

	present	*imperfect*	*future*

Indicative of εἰμί

1 sg	εἰμί	ἤμην	ἔσομαι
2 sg	εἶ	ἦς, ἦσθα	ἔσῃ
3 sg	ἐστί(ν)	ἦν	ἔσται
1 pl	ἐσμέν	ἦμεν, ἤμεθα	ἐσόμεθα
2 pl	ἐστέ	ἦτε	ἔσεσθε
3 pl	εἰσί(ν)	ἦσαν	ἔσονται

Non-indicative of εἰμί

	subjunctive	imperative	active infinitive
1 sg	ὦ		εἶναι
2 sg	ᾖς	ἴσθι	
3 sg	ᾖ	ἔστω	
1 pl	ὦμεν		
2 pl	ἦτε	ἔστε	
3 pl	ὦσι(ν)	ἔστωσαν	

Participle of εἰμί

	singular				plural		
	masc	fem	neut		masc	fem	neut
nom sg	ὤν	οὖσα	ὄν	nom pl	ὄντες	οὖσαι	ὄντα
gen sg	ὄντος	οὔσης	ὄντος	gen pl	ὄντων	οὐσῶν	ὄντων
dat sg	ὄντι	οὔσῃ	ὄντι	dat pl	οὖσι(ν)	οὔσαις	οὖσι(ν)
acc sg	ὄντα	οὖσαν	ὄν	acc pl	ὄντας	οὔσας	ὄντα

Formation of Tenses

Present Indicative (§41)

The present tense is subdivided between those words using a connecting vowel ("thematic" conjugation) and those not using a connecting vowel ("athematic" conjugation). "Thematic" is subdivided between stems ending in a consonant and those ending in a vowel. "Athematic" is subdivided among stems ending in different stem vowels.

Thematic: Uncontracted (§41.1a)

tense stem + connecting vowel + primary personal ending

	active	middle/passive
1 sg	λύω	λύομαι
2 sg	λύεις	λύῃ
3 sg	λύει	λύεται
1 sg	λύομεν	λυόμεθα
2 sg	λύετε	λύεσθε
3 sg	λύουσι(ν)	λύονται

Thematic: Contract verbs (§41.1b)

Tense stem (lengthened final vowel) + connecting vowel + primary personal endings

active

1 sg	γεννῶ	ποιῶ	φανερῶ
2 sg	γεννᾷς	ποιεῖς	φανεροῖς
3 sg	γεννᾷ	ποιεῖ	φανεροῖ
1 pl	γεννῶμεν	ποιοῦμεν	φανεροῦμεν
2 pl	γεννᾶτε	ποιεῖτε	φανεροῦτε
3 pl	γεννῶσι	ποιοῦσι	φανεροῦσι

middle/passive

1 sg	γεννῶμαι	ποιοῦμαι	φανεροῦμαι
2 sg	γεννᾷ	ποιῇ	φανεροῖ
3 sg	γεννᾶται	ποιεῖται	φανεροῦται
1 pl	γεννώμεθα	ποιούμεθα	φανερούμεθα
2 pl	γεννᾶσθε	ποιεῖσθε	φανεροῦσθε
3 pl	γεννῶνται	ποιοῦνται	φανεροῦνται

Athematic (§41.2)

The athematic conjugation (otherwise known as the μι verbs) is so named because these verbs do not use a thematic vowel between their stem and the personal ending. ("Athematic" being a compound of the alpha-privative and the word "thematic".) They have several peculiarities which if remembered, make recognition quite easy.

1. They use no connecting vowel.

2. They use the alternate personal endings μι, σι, and ασι.

3. They reduplicate their verbal base to form the present tense stem.

4. They lengthen the stem vowel in the singular active (ablaut: §4).

5. Most use a κα for their tense formative in the aorist active/middle.

All the μι verbs all collected in v-6. The only contraction in the paradigm below is with the third person plural as evidenced by the accent. As opposed to the thematic conjugation, the intervocalic σ of the σαι and σι endings does not drop out.

Reduplicated tense stem + primary personal endings (with alternate endings).

active

1 sg	ἵστημι (*στε)	τίθημι (*τε)	δίδωμι (*δο)	δείκνυμι (*δεικνυ)
2 sg	ἵστης	τίθης	δίδως	δείκνυς
3 sg	ἵστησι(ν)	τίθησι(ν)	δίδωσι(ν)	δείκνυσι(ν)
1 pl	ἵσταμεν	τίθεμεν	δίδομεν	δείκνυμεν
2 pl	ἵστατε	τίθετε	δίδοτε	δείκνυτε
3 pl	ἵστᾶσι	τιθέασι(ν)	διδόασι(ν)	δεικνύασι(ν)

middle/passive

1 sg	ἵσταμαι	τίθεμαι	δίδομαι	δείκνυμαι
2 sg	ἵστασαι	τίθεσαι	δίδοσαι	δείκνυσαι
3 sg	ἵσταται	τίθεται	δίδοται	δείκνυται
1 pl	ἱστάμεθα	τιθέμεθα	διδόμεθα	δεικνύμεθα
2 pl	ἵστασθε	τίθεσθε	δίδοσθε	δείκνυσθε
3 pl	ἵστανται	τίθενται	δίδονται	δείκνυνται

Imperfect Indicative   (§42)

Thematic: Uncontracted   §(§42.1)

augment + stem + connecting vowel + primary personal endings

	active	middle/passive
1 sg	ἔλυον	ἐλυόμην
2 sg	ἔλυες	ἐλύου
3 sg	ἔλυε	ἐλύετο
1 pl	ἐλύομεν	ἐλυόμεθα
2 pl	ἐλύετε	ἐλύεσθε
3 pl	ἔλυον	ἐλύοντο

Thematic: Contracted   (§42.2)

augment + stem (lengthened stem vowel) + connecting vowel + personal ending

active

1 sg	ἐγέννων	ἐποίουν	ἐφανέρουν
2 sg	ἐγέννας	ἐποίεις	ἐφανέρους
3 sg	ἐγέννα	ἐποίει	ἐφανέρου
1 pl	ἐγεννῶμεν	ἐποιοῦμεν	ἐφανεροῦμεν
2 pl	ἐγεννᾶτε	ἐποιεῖτε	ἐφανεροῦτε
3 pl	ἐγέννων	ἐποίουν	ἐφανέρουν

middle/passive

1 sg	ἐγεννώμην	ἐποιούμην	ἐφανερούμην
2 sg	ἐγεννῶ	ἐποιοῦ	ἐφανεροῦ
3 sg	ἐγεννᾶτο	ἐποιεῖτο	ἐφανεροῦτο
1 pl	ἐγεννώμεθα	ἐποιούμεθα	ἐφανερούμεθα
2 pl	ἐγεννᾶσθε	ἐποιεῖσθε	ἐφανεροῦσθε
3 pl	ἐγεννῶντο	ἐποιοῦντο	ἐφανεροῦντο

Athematic   (§42.3)

Since the imperfect is built off of the present tense stem, our comments there are appropriate here as well.
augment + present tense stem + secondary personal endings

active

1 sg	ἵστην	ἐτίθην	ἐδίδων	ἐδείκνυν
2 sg	ἵστης	ἐτίθης	ἐδίδως	ἐδείκνυς
3 sg	ἵστη	ἐτίθη	ἐδίδω	ἐδείκνυ
1 pl	ἵσταμεν	ἐτίθεμεν	ἐδίδομεν	ἐδείκνυμεν
2 pl	ἵστατε	ἐτίθετε	ἐδίδοτε	ἐδείκνυτε
3 pl	ἵστασαν	ἐτίθεσαν	ἐδίδοσαν	ἐδείκνυσαν

middle/passive

1 sg	ἱστάμην	ἐτιθέμην	ἐδιδόμην	ἐδεικνύμην
2 sg	ἵστασο	ἐτίθεσο	ἐδίδοσο	ἐδείκνυσο
3 sg	ἵστατο	ἐτίθετο	ἐδίδοτο	ἐδείκνυτο
1 pl	ἱστάμεθα	ἐτιθέμεθα	ἐδιδόμεθα	ἐδεικνύμεθα
2 pl	ἵστασθε	ἐτίθεσθε	ἐδίδοσθε	ἐδείκνυσθε
3 pl	ἵσταντο	ἐτίθεντο	ἐδίδοντο	ἐδείκνυντο

Future Indicative   (§43)

The only real variation in the future is how the tense formative affects the verbal stem.

Thematic: Uncontracted   (§43.1)

verbal stem + σ + thematic vowel + primary personal endings

	active	*middle*
1 sg	λύσω	λύσομαι
2 sg	λύσεις	λύσῃ
3 sg	λύσει	λύσεται
1 pl	λύσομεν	λυσόμεθα
2 pl	λύσετε	λύσεσθε
3 pl	λύσουσι(ν)	λύσονται

Contract Verbs   (§43.2)

Contract verbs lengthen their final stem vowel before the σ of the future. Other than this, they are identical to the uncontracted forms. ἀγαπάω ‣ ἀγαπήσω. ποιέω ‣ ποιήσω. πληρόω ‣ πληρώσω.

Athematic Conjugation (μι verbs) (§43.3)

μι verbs form their future with just their verbal base; there is no reduplication as there is in the present. The stem vowel is always long, and their conjugation is regular.

	active	middle
1 sg	δώσω	δώσομαι
2 sg	δώσεις	δώσῃ
3 sg	δώσει	δώσεται
1 pl	δώσομεν	δωσόμεθα
2 pl	δώσετε	δώσεσθε
3 pl	δώσουσι(ν)	δώσονται

Stems ending in a stop (§43.4)

labial   If a stem ends with a π, β, or φ, the final consonant and the σ will be written as a ψ (§22.1).

*βλεπ	+	σ	+ ω	‣	βλέψω
*θλιβ	+	σ	+ ω	‣	θλίψω
*γραφ	+	σ	+ ω	‣	γράψω

velar   If a stem ends with a κ, γ, or χ, the final consonant and the σ will be written as a ξ (§22.2).

*διωκ	+	σ	+ ω	‣	διώξω
*φευγ	+	σ	+ ομαι	‣	φεύξομαι
*ηκ	+	σ	+ ω	‣	ἥξω

dental   If a stem ends with a τ, δ, or θ, the final consonant becomes a σ, joins with the other σ, and then the double σ simplifies to one σ (§22.3).

*ερειδ	+	σ	+ ω	‣	ερεισσω ‣ ἐρείσω
*ψευδ	+	σ	+ ομαι	‣	ψευσσομαι ‣ ψεύσομαι
*πειθ	+	σ	+ ω	‣	πεισσω ‣ πείσω

Words ending in αζω or ιζω (§43.5)

§43.5a   The verbal stems in these categories really end in δ (v-2a(1)) or γ (v-2a(2)). In order to form the present stem, ι is added to the verbal stem. But δ or γ added to ι form ζ (§26.2), thus making it appear that the verb actually ends in ζ. Therefore, what we described in §43.3 above concerning dentals applies also to these words. (The original δ or γ reappear in the other tenses, only to be modified for other reasons.)

*βαπτιδ +	ι	+	ω	‣	βαπτίζω		(present)
*βαπτιδ +	σ	+	ω	‣	βαπτισσω	‣ βαπτίσω	(future)
*κραγ	ι	+	ω	‣	κράζω		(present)
*κραγ	σ	+	ω	‣	κρασσω	‣ κράσω	(future)

§43.5b   **Attic future.**   Certain verbs follow a different formula in the future. They are called "Attic futures" because this formation was used in the Attic dialect. In this formulation, if a verb ending in a dental had more than two syllables, it formed the future not by adding σ but by adding σε. Not only did the final dental of the stem drop out, but the σ of the tense formative was then intervocalic (because the stem would have had a vowel preceding the final dental), the σ dropped out (§24.4), and the two vowels contracted. Therefore, a verb with an Attic future will be conjugated just like a liquid verb (§43.6).*ελπιδ (ἐλπίζω) + σε ‣ ελπισε ‣ ελπιε ‣ ἐλπιῶ

Liquid stems (§43.6)

Verbs whose verbal stems end in a liquid (λ ρ) or a nasal (μ ν) are called "liquid verbs." They form their future by adding not σ but εσ and then the thematic vowel. The σ is therefore always between vowels ("intervocalic"), drops out (§25.5), and the ε of the tense formative and the connecting vowel contract. Liquid verbs are therefore conjugated in the future just as if they were ε contract verbs in the present. We included two other forms for comparison.

	future active liquid	*present contract*	*present liquid*	*future middle liquid*
1 sg	κρινῶ	ποιῶ	κρίνω	κρινοῦμαι
2 sg	κρινεῖς	ποιεῖς	κρίνεις	κρινεῖ
3 sg	κρινεῖ	ποιεῖ	κρίνει	κρινεῖται
1 pl	κρινοῦμεν	ποιοῦμων	κρίνομεν	κρινούμεθα
2 pl	κρινεῖτε	ποιεῖτε	κρίνετε	κρινεῖσθε
3 pl	κρινοῦσι(ν)	ποιοῦσι(ν)	κρίνουσι(ν)	κρινοῦνται

Aorist Active/Middle Indicative (§44)

The aorist is the most regular of the Greek tenses; the present is the most irregular (cf. §33 above). In fact, the second aorist tense stem is almost always exactly the same as the verbal root.

First Aorist (§44.1a)

augment + tense stem + tense suffix (σα) + secondary personal endings

	active	*middle*
1 sg	ἔλυσα	ἐλυσάμην
2 sg	ἔλυσας	ἐλύσω
3 sg	ἔλυσε	ἐλύσατο
1 pl	ἐλύσαμεν	ἐλυσάμεθα
2 pl	ἐλύσατε	ἐλύσασθε
3 pl	ἔλυσαν	ἐλύσαντο

Stems ending in a Stop (§44.1b)

As is the case in the future (§43.3), if a stem ends in a stop, the stop and the σ will be written as a different letter.

labial If a stem ends with a π, β, or φ, the final consonant and the σ will be written as a ψ (§22.1).

ε	+	*βλεπ	+ σα		▸ ἔβλεψα
ε	+	*τριβ	+ σα		▸ ἔτριψα
ε	+	*γραφ	+ σα		▸ ἔγραψα

velar If a stem ends with a κ, γ, or χ, the final consonant and the σ will be written as a ξ (§22.2).

ε	+	*διωκ	+ σα		▸ ἐδίωξα
ε	+	*πνιγ	+ σα		▸ ἔπνιξα
ε	+	*δεχ	+ σαμην		▸ ἐδεξάμην

dental If a stem ends with a τ, δ, or θ, the final consonant becomes a σ, joins with the other σ, and then the double σ simplifies to one σ (§22.3)

ε	+	*ψευδ	+ σα	+ μην	▸ εψευσσαμην	▸ ἐψευσάμην
ε	+	*πειθ	+ σα		▸ επεισσα	▸ ἔπεισα

Liquid Aorist (§44.1c)

Verbs whose verbal stems end in a liquid (λ ρ) or a nasal (μ ν) are called "liquid verbs." They form their aorist by adding only α (not σα) and by modifying their stem vowel.

augment + modified verbal base + σ + secondary personal endings

	active	middle
	active	*middle*
1 sg	ἔδειρα (*δερ)	ἠμυνάμην (*αμυν)
2 sg	ἔδειρας	ἠμύνω
3 sg	ἔδειρε	ἠμύνατο
1 pl	ἐδείραμεν	ἠμυνάμεθα
2 pl	ἐδείρατε	ἠμύνασθε
3 pl	ἔδειραν	ἠμύναντο

κ Aorists (§44.1d)

κ-aorists are formed just like regular first aorists, except that the tense formative is κα instead of σα. All examples in the New Testament are μι verbs; since this is the aorist there will not be reduplication of the verbal base. See the paradigms below (§44.2b).

τίθημι	ἔθηκα	(*θε)
δίδωμι	ἔδωκα	(*δο)
ἀφίημι	ἀφῆκα	(*σε)

Second Aorist: Thematic (§44.2a)

By and large, the stem of the second aorist is in fact that actual verbal base of the word.
augment + verbal base + connecting vowel + secondary personal ending

	active	*middle*
1 sg	ἔβαλον	ἐβαλόμην
2 sg	ἔβαλες	ἐβάλου
3 sg	ἔβαλε(ν)	ἐβάλετο
1 pl	ἐβάλομεν	ἐβαλόμεθα
2 pl	ἐβάλετε	ἐβάλεσθε
3 pl	ἔβαλον	ἐβάλοντο

Second Aorist: Athematic (§44.2b)

augment + verbal base (lengthened final stem vowel) + secondary personal endings

	ἵστημι	τίθημι	δίδωμι
active			
1 sg	ἔστην	ἔθην	ἔδων[26]
2 sg	ἔστης	ἔθης	ἔδως
3 sg	ἔστη	ἔθη	ἔδω

---

[26] First aorist, ἔδωκα.

1 pl	ἕστημεν	ἔθεμεν	ἔδομεν
2 pl	ἕστητε	ἔθετε	ἔδοτε
3 pl	ἕστησαν	ἔθεασαν	ἔδοσαν

middle

1 sg	ἐστάμην	ἐθέμην	ἐδόμην[27]
2 sg	ἔστω	ἔθου	ἔδου
3 sg	ἔστατο	ἔθετο	ἔδοτο
1 pl	ἐστάμεθα	ἐθέμεθα	ἐδόμεθα
2 pl	ἔστασθε	ἔθεσθε	ἔδοσθε
3 pl	ἔσταντο	ἔθεντο	ἔδοντο

Perfect Active Indicative (§45)

First Perfect (§45.1)

Two things of special note happen in the perfect active. Several times a final stem ν will drop out because of the following κ of the tense formative. Also, several times the final stem consonant, if it is a labial (π β) or a velar (κ γ), will aspirate to φ and χ respectively. There also is a substantial number of examples of ablaut (§4).

reduplication + verbal stem + tense formative (κα) + primary personal endings

1 sg	λέλυκα		*1 pl*	λελύκαμεν
2 sg	λέλυκας		*2 pl*	λελύκατε
3 sg	λέλυκε(ν)		*3 pl*	λελύκασι(ν)

Insertion of an η (§45.2)

Ten words in the New Testament insert an η between the verbal base and the perfect active tense formative. A similar insertion occurs in the other stems. *βαλ ‧ βάλλω ‧ βέβληκα.

Second Perfect Active Indicative (§45.3)

The second perfect is just like the first perfect except that it uses α and not κα as the tense formative.

reduplication + tense stem + α + primary personal endings

1 sg	γέγονα		*1 pl*	γεγόναμεν
2 sg	γέγονας		*2 pl*	γεγόνατε
3 sg	γέγονε(ν)		*3 pl*	γεγόνασι(ν)

Pluperfect Active (§45.4)

The pluperfect is formed from the fourth principal part. There are 22 verbs in the New Testament that appear as a pluperfect. As is the case with the perfect, a first pluperfect is formed with the tense formative (κ) where the second pluperfect has none. Following the tense formative are the connecting vowels ει. Preceding the reduplication can be an augment, although this is not necessary, so we have placed the augment in parentheses.

---

[27]   First aorist, ἐδωκάμην.

(augment +) reduplication + tense stem + (tense formative (κ) +) connecting vowels + secondary personal endings

	1 pluperfect	2 pluperfect
1 sg	(ἐ)λελύκειν	(ἐ)γεγράφειν
2 sg	(ἐ)λελύκεις	(ἐ)γεγράφεις
3 sg	(ἐ)λελύκει(ν)	(ἐ)γεγράφει(ν)
1 pl	(ἐ)λελύκειμεν	(ἐ)γεγράφειμεν
2 pl	(ἐ)λελύκειτε	(ἐ)γεγράφειτε
3 pl	(ἐ)λελύκεισαν	(ἐ)γεγράφεισαν

The first person singular forms of the μι verbs are ἑστήκειν, ἐτεθείκειν, and ἐδεδώκειν.

Perfect Middle/Passive Indicative   (§46)

The perfect middle/passive is built from the fifth principal part. The middle/passive does not use the tense formative and uses secondary endings. If the stem of the verb ends in a consonant, the third person plural is formed periphrastically.

Perfect middle/passive   (§46.1)

reduplication + stem + primary personal endings

1 sg	λέλυμαι	1 pl	λελύμεθα
2 sg	λέλυσαι	2 pl	λέλυσθε
3 sg	λέλυται	3 pl	λέλυνται

Stems ending in a Stop   (§46.2)

Because there is no connecting vowel or tense formative, the personal endings are added directly to the stem. When the stem ends in a consonant this will usually produce substantial consonantal change. Below is the basic paradigm.

μ	μαι/μεθα	labial	+ μ	›	μμ	(§21.1)
		velar	+ μ	›	γμ	(§21.2)
		dental	+ μ	›	σμ	(§21.3)
σ	σαι/σθε	labial	+ σ	›	ψ	(§22.1)
		velar	+ σ	›	ξ	(§22.2)
		dental	+ σ	›	σ	(§22.3)
τ	ται	labial	+ τ	›	ππ	(§20.1)
		velar	+ τ	›	κτ	(§20.2)
		dental	+ τ	›	σ	(§20.3)

If you take the rules above and apply them in paradigm form, this is how they will be put into effect.

	*labial (*γραφ)*	*velar (*διωκ)*	*dental (*πειθ)*
1 sg	γέγραμμαι	δεδίωγμαι	πέπεισμαι
2 sg	γέγραψαι	δεδίωξαι	πέπεισαι
3 sg	γέγραπται	δεδίωκται	πέπεισται

1 pl	γεγράμμεθα	δεδιώγμεθα	πεπείσμεθα
2 pl	γέγραφθε	δεδίωχθε	πέπεισθε
3 pl	εἰσὶ γεγραμμένοι	εἰσὶ δεδιωγμένοι	εἰσὶ πεπεισμένοι

Stems ending in ν   (§46.3)

The final stem consonant (ν) consonant will be changed if the personal ending begins with σ or μ. The σ is lost in the second plural, and the ν totally assimilates to a μ with endings beginning in μ (μαι; μεθα).

1 sg	κέκλιμμαι	1 pl	κεκλίμμεθα
2 sg	κέκλινσαι	2 pl	κέκλινθε
3 sg	κέκλινται	3 pl	κέκλινται

Insertion of a σ between the stem and personal ending   (§46.4)

A σ is inserted after the stem and before the personal ending. This same phenomena is found in the aorist passive (§47.3). κλείω › κέκλεισμαι.

Insertion of an η between the stem and the personal ending   (§46.5)

As in the other tenses, words may insert an η into this principal part between the tense stem and the personal endings. βάλλω › βέβλημαι.

Pluperfect middle/passive   (§46.6)

The middle passive of the pluperfect follows the same pattern as the active except that there is no tense formative and no connecting vowels.

(augment +) reduplication + tense stem + secondary personal endings

1 sg	(ἐ)λελύμην
2 sg	(ἐ)λέλυσο
3 sg	(ἐ)λέλυτο

1 pl	(ἐ)λελύμεθα
2 pl	(ἐ)λέλυσθε
3 pl	(ἐ)λέλυντο

The first person singular forms of the μι verbs are ἐστάμην, ἐτεθείμην, and ἐδεδόμην.

Aorist/Future Passive   (§47)

The aorist and future passive is built from the sixth principal part. The future passive does not augment.

First Aorist Passive   (§47.1)

augment + stem + tense formative (θη) + active secondary endings

1 sg	ἐλύθην	1 pl	ἐλύθημεν
2 sg	ἐλύθης	2 pl	ἐλύθητε
3 sg	ἐλύθη	3 pl	ἐλύθησαν

Stems ending in a stop (§47.2)

When a stem ends in a stop and is immediately followed by the θ of the tense formative, the stop will be altered.

A labial is aspirated (§20.1)

π	+	θ	*βλαπ	› βλαφθῆναι (› βλάπτω)	
β	+	θ › φθ	*συντρίβ	› συντετρίφθαι	
φ	+	θ	*ἐξαλείφ	› ἐξαλειφθῆναι	

A velar is aspirated (§20.2).

κ	+	θ			
γ	+	θ › χθ	*ανοιγ	› ἀνεῴχθη	
χ	+	θ			

A dental dissimilates to σ (§20.3).

τ	+	θ			
δ	+	θ › σθ	*θαυμαδ	› ἐθαυμάσθη (› θαυμάζω)	
θ	+	θ	*πείθ	› ἐπείσθησαν	

Insertion of a σ between the Stem and the Tense Formative (§47.3)

As is the case in the pefect middle/passive, some words insert a σ between the stem of the word and the θη of the aorist (and future) passive. ἀκούω › ἠκούσθην.

Insertion of an η between the stem and the tense formative (§47.4)

As is the case in other tenses, some stems insert an η between the tense stem and the θη tense formative. βάλλω › ἐβλήθην.

Second aorist passive (§47.5)

The second aorist passive is identical to the first aorist passive except that it uses only η and not θη as the tense formative.

augment + stem + tense formative (η) + active secondary endings

1 sg	ἐγράφην		*1 pl*	ἐγράφημεν
2 sg	ἐγράφης		*2 pl*	ἐγράφητε
3 sg	ἐγράφη		*3 pl*	ἐγράφησαν

First Future Passive (§47.6)

verb stem + tense formative (θη) + tense formative (σ) + thematic vowel + primary personal endings

1 sg	λυθήσομαι		*1 pl*	λυθησόμεθα
2 sg	λυθήσῃ		*2 pl*	λυθήσεσθε
3 sg	λυθησέται		*3 pl*	λυθήσονται

Second Future Passive Indicative (§47.7)

verbal base + tense formative (η) + tense formative σ + thematic vowel + primary middle/passive personal endings

1 sg	γραφήσομαι		*1 pl*	γραφησόμεθα
2 sg	γραφήσῃ		*2 pl*	γραφήσεσθε
3 sg	γραφήσεται		*3 pl*	γραφήσονται

Subjunctive (§50)

The subjunctive is easy to learn. It occurs only in the present, aorist, and the perfect tenses. The connecting vowel is lengthened to η or ω and behaves almost as a mood formative, and all tenses use the same primary personal endings.

In the aorist, there is no augment. Since only the indicative mood can indicate time, and since the augment indicates past time, there can be no augment in the aorist subjunctive. For the changes that will occur due to the connecting of the final stem consonant and the tense formative, see the aorist indicative (§44.1b).

The perfect is always formed periphrastically. It will use the perfect participle followed by the subjunctive of εἰμί.

Thematic: Uncontracted (§51)

The paradigms are ordered vertically active, middle, passive.

stem + (tense formative (σ) +) connecting vowel (η/ω) + primary personal endings

	present	aorist	perfect
active subjunctive			
1 sg	λύω	λύσω	λελύκω
2 sg	λύῃς	λύσῃς	λελύκῃς
3 sg	λύῃ	λύσῃ	λελύκῃ
1 pl	λύωμεν	λύσωμεν	λελύκωμεν
2 pl	λύητε	λύσητε	λελύκητε
3 pl	λύωσι(ν)	λύσωσι(ν)	λελύκωσι
middle subjunctive			
1 sg	λύωμαι	λύσωμαι	λελυμένος ὦ
2 sg	λύῃ	λύσῃ	λελυμένος ἦς
3 sg	λύηται	λύσηται	λελυμένος ἦ
1 pl	λυώμεθα	λυσώμεθα	λελυμένοι ὦμεν
2 pl	λύησθε	λύσησθε	λελυμένοι ἦτε
3 pl	λύωνται	λύσωνται	λελυμένοι ὦσι
passive subjunctive			
1 sg	λύωμαι	λυθῶ	λελυμένος ὦ
2 sg	λύῃ	λυθῇς	λελυμένος ἦς
3 sg	λύηται	λυθῇ	λελυμένος ἦ
1 pl	λυώμεθα	λυθῶμεν	λελυμένοι ὦμεν
2 pl	λύησθε	λυθῆτε	λελυμένοι ἦτε
3 pl	λύωνται	λυθῶσι(ν)	λελυμένοι ὦσι

Contract Verbs (§52)

Present active subjunctive

1 sg	γεννῶ	ποιῶ	φανερῶ
2 sg	γεννᾷς	ποιῇς	φανεροῖς
3 sg	γεννᾷ	ποιῇ	φανεροῖ
1 pl	γεννῶμεν	ποιῶμεν	φανερῶμεν
2 pl	γεννᾶτε	ποιῆτε	φανερῶτε
3 pl	γεννῶσι(ν)	ποιῶσι(ν)	φανερῶσι(ν)

Present middle/passive subjunctive

1 sg	γεννῶμαι	ποιῶμαι	φανερῶμαι
2 sg	γεννᾷ	ποιῇ	φανεροῖ
3 sg	γεννᾶται	ποιῆται	φανερῶται
1 pl	γεννώμεθα	ποιώμεθα	φανερώμεθα
2 pl	γεννᾶσθε	ποιῆσθε	φανερῶσθε
3 pl	γεννῶνται	ποιῶνται	φανερῶνται

μι Verbs (§53)

In the present, stems in α, ε, and υ are not altered. Stems in ο are altered due to contraction. The stem is reduplicated as in the indicative. In the aorist, the stem vowel contracts with the connecting vowel. The stem is not reduplicated, as in the indicative.

present active subjunctive

1 sg	ἱστῶ	τιθῶ	διδῶ
2 sg	ἱστῇς	τιθῇς	διδῷς
3 sg	ἱστῇ	τιθῇ	διδῷ
1 pl	ἱστῶμεν	τιθῶμεν	διδῶμεν
2 pl	ἱστῆτε	τιθῆτε	διδῶτε
3 pl	ἱστῶσι(ν)	τιθῶσι(ν)	διδῶσι(ν)

present middle/passive subjunctive

1 sg	ἱστῶμαι	τιθῶμαι	διδῶμαι
2 sg	ἱστῇ	τιθῇ	διδῷ
3 sg	ἱστῆται	τιθῆται	διδῶται
1 pl	ἱστώμεθα	τιθώμεθα	διδώμεθα
2 pl	ἱστῆσθε	τιθῆσθε	διδῶσθε
3 pl	ἱστῶνται	τιθῶνται	διδῶνται

second aorist active subjunctive

1 sg	στῶ[28]	θῶ	δῶ
2 sg	στῇς	θῇς	δῷς
3 sg	στῇ	θῇ	δῷ
1 pl	στῶμεν	θῶμεν	δῶμεν
2 pl	στῆτε	θῆτε	δῶτε
3 pl	στῶσι(ν)	θῶσι(ν)	δῶσι(ν)

second aorist middle subjunctive

1 sg	στῶμαι[29]	θῶμαι	δῶμαι
2 sg	στῇ	θῇ	δῷ
3 sg	στῆται	θῆται	δῶται
1 pl	στώμεθα	θώμεθα	δώμεθα
2 pl	στῆσθε	θῆσθε	δῶσθε
3 pl	στῶνται	θῶνται	δῶνται

Optative (§60)

There are only 67 examples of the optative in the New Testament, 15 of which are the Pauline phrase μὴ γένοιτο. It is found only in the present (linear aspect) and aorist (undefined aspect). The optative uses secondary personal endings except in the first person singular active, where it uses μι. Its mood formative in the thematic conjugation is ι and in the athematic conjugation it is ιη.

Thematic (§61)

Because the optative can have no real time significance, it can have no augment. The thematic vowel is o, and the mood formative is ι (except in the aorist passive where it is ιη). All forms of the present optative will have this οι. The tense formative for the aorist active/middle is σα which contracts with the mood formative so that all forms have σαι. The tense formative for the aorist passive in θε, and the mood formative in ιη, which result in θειη in all forms.

	present	*future*	*first aorist*	*second aorist*
active optative				
1 sg	λύοιμι	λύσοιμι	λύσαιμι	βάλοιμι
2 sg	λύοις	λύσοις	λύσαις	βάλοις
3 sg	λύοι	λύσοι	λύσαι	βάλοι
1 pl	λύοιμεν	λύσοιμεν	λύσαιμεν	βάλοιμεν
2 pl	λύοιτε	λύσοιτε	λύσαιτε	βάλοιτε
3 pl	λύοιεν	λύσοιεν	λύσαιεν	βάλοιεν

---

[28] First aorist, στήσω.

[29] First aorsit, στήσωμαι.

	present	*future*	*first aorist*	*first aorist*
middle optative				**passive optative**
1 sg	λυοίμην	λυσοίμην	λυσαίμην	λυθείην
2 sg	λύοιο	λύσοιο	λύσαιο	λυθείης
3 sg	λύοιτο	λύσοιτο	λύσαιτο	λυθείη
1 pl	λυοίμεθα	λυσοίμεθα	λυσαίμεθα	λυθείημεν
2 pl	λύοισθε	λύσοισθε	λύσαισθε	λυθείητε
3 pl	λύοιντο	λύσοιντο	λύσαιντο	λυθείησαν

Athematic μι Verbs   (§62)

In the aorist, ιη is added to the verbal base (with a short stem vowel).

present active optative

1 sg	ἱσταίην	τιθείην	διδοίην
2 sg	ἱσταίης	τιθείης	διδοίης
3 sg	ἱσταίη	τιθείη	διδοίη
1 pl	ἱσταίημεν	τιθείημεν	διδοίημεν
2 pl	ἱσταίητε	τιθείητε	διδοίητε
3 pl	ἱσταίνσαν	τιθείησαν	διδοίησαν

present middle optative

1 sg	ἱσταίμην	τιθείμην	διδοίμην
2 sg	ἵσταιο	τιθεῖο	διδοῖο
3 sg	ἵσταιτο	τιθεῖτο	διδοῖτο
1 pl	ἱσταίμεθα	τιθείμεθα	διδοίμεθα
2 pl	ἵσταισθε	τιθεῖσθε	διδοῖσθε
3 pl	ἵσταιντο	τιθεῖντο	διδοῖντο

second aorist active optative

1 sg	σταίην[30]	θείην	δοίην
2 sg	σταίης	θείης	δοίης
3 sg	σταίη	θείη	δοίη
1 pl	σταίημεν	θείημεν	δοίημεν
2 pl	σταίητε	θείητε	δοίητε
3 pl	σταίησαν	θείησαν	δοίησαν

---

[30] First aorist, στήσαιμι.

second aorist middle optative

1 sg	σταίμην[31]	θείμην	δοίμην
2 sg	σταῖο	θεῖο	δοῖο
3 sg	σταῖτο	θεῖτο	δοῖτο
1 pl	σταίμεθα	θείμεθα	δοίμεθα
2 pl	σταῖσθε	θεῖσθε	δοῖσθε
3 pl	σταῖντο	θεῖντο	δοῖντο

Imperative   (§70)

The imperative occurs in the New Testament only in the present and the aorist. In the present, the connecting vowel ε is used between the stem and the ending. In the aorist, the endings are added directly onto the tense formative. There will be no augment in the aorist, since the imperative cannot indicate time.

Thematic (Uncontracted)   (§71)

	present	*first aorist*	*second aorist*	*perfect*

active imperative

	present	*first aorist*	*second aorist*	*perfect*
2 sg	λῦε	λῦσον	βάλε	λέλυκε
3 sg	λυέτω	λυσάτω	βαλέτω	λελυκέτω
2 pl	λύετε	λύσατε	βάλετε	λελύκετε
3 pl	λυέτωσαν	λυσάτωσαν	βαλέτωσαν	λελυκέτωσαν

middle/passive imperative   **first aorist passive**

	present	*first aorist*	*second aorist*	*perfect*	first aorist passive
2 sg	λύου	λῦσαι	βαλοῦ	λέλυσο	λύθητι
3 sg	λύεσθω	λυσάσθω	βαλέσθω	λελύσθω	λυθήτω
2 pl	λύεσθε	λύσασθε	βάλεσθε	λέλυσθε	λύθητε
3 pl	λυέσθωσαν	λυσάσθωσαν	βαλέσθωσαν	λελύσθωσαν	λυθήτωσαν

Thematic (Contract Verbs)   (§72)

In the aorist, the final stem vowel will lengthen before the tense formative, and the endings will be like those in §71. In the present, the contractions are regular.

present active imperative

2 sg	γέννα	ποίει	φανέρου
3 sg	γεννάτω	ποιείτω	φανερούτω
2 pl	γεννᾶτε	ποιεῖτε	φανεροῦτε
3 pl	γεννάτωσαν	ποιείτωσαν	φανερούτωσαν

---

[31]   First aorist, στησαίμην.

present middle/passive imperative

2 sg	γεννῶ	ποιοῦ	φανεροῦ
3 sg	γεννάσθω	ποιείσθω	φανερούσθω
2 pl	γεννᾶσθε	ποιεῖσθε	φανεροῦσθε
3 pl	γεννάσθωσαν	ποιείσθωσαν	φανερούσθωσαν

Athematic (§73)

present active imperative

2 sg	ἵστη	τίθει	δίδου	δείκνυθι
3 sg	ἱστάτω	τιθέτω	διδότω	δεικνύτω
2 pl	ἵστατε	τίθετε	δίδοτε	δείκνυτε
3 pl	ἱστάτωσαν	τιθέτωσαν	διδότωσαν	δεικνύτωσαν

present middle/passive imperative

2 sg	ἵστασο	τίθεσο	δίδοσο	δείκνυσο
3 sg	ἱστάσθω	τιθέσθω	διδόσθω	δεικνύσθω
2 pl	ἵστασθε	τίθεσθε	δίδοσθε	δείκνυσθε
3 pl	ἱστάσθωσαν	τιθέσθωσαν	διδόσθωσαν	δεικνύσθωσαν

aorist active imperative

2 sg	στῆθι	θές	δός
3 sg	στήτω	θέτω	δότω
2 pl	στῆτε	θέτε	δότε
3 pl	στήτωσαν	θέτωσαν	δότωσαν

aorist middle imperative

2 sg	στάσο	θέσο	δόσο
3 sg	στάσθω	θέσθω	δόσθω
2 pl	στάσθε	θέσθε	δόσθε
3 pl	στάσθωσαν	θέσθωσαν	δόσθωσαν

Infinitive (§80)

There are three possible morphemes for active infinitives, and two for middle/passive infinitive. They are added to the tense stem (without augment); when used, the connecting vowel is always ε. The active morphemes are ειν, αι, and ναι. The middle passive morpheme is σθαι. The aorist passive uses ναι, the same morpheme that is used in the aorist active.

In the present, μι verbs will always have a short stem vowel. In the future, contract verbs lengthen their final stem vowel before the tense formative. In the aorist, contract verbs lengthen their final stem vowel before the tense formative. μι verbs lengthen their final stem vowel in various ways.

active infinitive

	present	future	first aorist	second aorist	first perfect	second perfect
thematic	λυείν	λύσειν	λῦσαι	βαλεῖν	λελυκέναι	γεγονέναι
contract (a)	γεννᾶν	γεννήσειν	γεννῆσαι		γεγεννηκέναι	
contract (e)	ποιεῖν	ποιήσειν	ποιῆσαι		πεποιηκέναι	
contract (o)	φανεροῦν	φανερώσειν	φανερῶσαι		πεφανερωκέναι	
μι	ἱστάναι	στήσειν	στῆσαι	στῆναι	ἑστηκέναι	
	τιθέναι	θήσειν		θεῖναι	τεθεικέναι	
	διδόναι	δώσειν		δοῦναι	δεδωκέναι	
	δεικνύναι					
	εἶναι					
liquid	μένειν	μενεῖν	μεῖναι			

middle/passive infinitive   **middle infinitive**

	present	future	perfect	first aorist	second aorist
thematic	λύεσθαι	λύσεσθαι	λελύσθαι	λύσασθαι	
contract (a)	γεννᾶσθαι	γεννήσεσθαι	γεννῆσθαι	γεννήσασθαι	
contract (e)	ποιεῖσθαι	ποιήσεσθαι	πεποιῆσθαι	ποιήσασθαι	
contract (o)	φανεροῦσθαι	φανερώσθαι	πεφανερῶσθαι	φανερώσασθαι	
μι	ἵστασθαι	στήσεσθαι		στήσασθαι	στάσθαι
	τίθεσθαι	θήσεσθαι			θέσθαι
	δίδοσθαι	δώσεσθαι			δόσθαι
	δείκνυσθαι				
	ἔσεσθαι				
liquid	μένεισθαι	μενεῖσθαι		μείνασθαι	

passive infinitive

thematic	future	first aorist	second aorist
thematic	λυθήσεσθαι	λυθῆναι	γραφῆναι
contract (a)	γεννηθήσεσθαι	γεννηθῆναι	
contract (e)	ποιηθήσεσθαι	ποιηθῆναι	
contract (o)	φανερωθήσεσθαι	φανερωθῆναι	

Participle (§90)

When we only list two forms for a participle and not the entire paradigm, the forms are the nominative and genitive singular. The order of the paradigms is from left to right, masculine, feminine, and neuter.

There are only four participle morphemes:

ντ	active (except perfect) and aorist passive
	(feminine formed by adding ι a to ντ to form ουσα)
μεν	middle/passive (future passive included)
τ	masculine/neuter perfect active (which uses the connecting vowel ο)
υσ	feminine in the perfect active (to which is added ι to form υια)

Thematic (Uncontracted)   (§91)

vτ is the morpheme for all active participles (except the perfect), and for the aorist passive participle. In the present, the participle is preceded by the connecting vowel o, making the participle appear to be οντ. In the aorist active it is preceded by the tense formative σα, forming σαντ. In the aorist passive it is preceded by θε, forming θεντ.

To form the feminine active, ϳα is added to vτ. τ + ϳ form σ (§26.4), ν drops out when followed immediately by σ, and o lengthens to ου in order to compensate for the loss (§24.4: οντ + ϳι + α ‣ ονσα ‣ οσα ‣ ουσα).

Present participle (§91.1)

The present active participle follows the pattern in a-2; the mid/pas follows the pattern from a-1a(2a).

stem + connecting vowel + tense formative + vτ (+ ϳα)

present active participle

nom sg	λύων	λύουσα	λῦον
gen sg	λύοντος	λυούσης	λύοντος
dat sg	λύοντι	λυούσῃ	λύοντι
acc sg	λύοντα	λύουσαν	λῦον
nom pl	λύοντες	λύουσαι	λύοντα
gen pl	λυόντων	λυουσῶν	λυόντων
dat pl	λύουσι	λυούσαις	λύουσι
acc pl	λύοντας	λυούσας	λύοντα

present middle/passive participle

nom sg	λυόμενος	λυομένη	λυόμενον
gen sg	λυομένου	λυομένης	λυομένου
dat sg	λυομένῳ	λυομένῃ	λυομένῳ
acc sg	λυόμενον	λυομένην	λυόμενον
nom pl	λυόμενοι	λυόμεναι	λυόμενα
gen pl	λυομένων	λυομένων	λυομένων
dat pl	λυομένοις	λυομέναις	λυομένοις
acc pl	λυομένους	λυομένας	λυόμενα

Future participle (§91.2)

Follows the same form as the present except that the tense formative is inserted between the tense stem and the participle. The passive is formed from the fifth principle part (aorist passive).

active	nom sg	λύσων	λύσουσα	λῦσον
	gen sg	λύσοντος	λυσούσης	λύσοντος
middle	nom sg	λυσόμενος	λυσόμενη	λυσόμενον
	gen sg	λυσομένου	λυσομένης	λυσομένου
first passive	nom sg	λυθησόμενος	λυθησομένη	λυθησόμενον
	gen sg	λυθησομένου	λυθησομένης	λυθησομένου
second passive	nom sg	γραψόμενος	γραψομένη	γραψόμενον
	gen sg	γραψομένου	γραψομένης	γραψομένου

First aorist participle (§91.3)

The aorist participle uses the same participle morpheme as does the present. There is no augment. The active and middle follow the third declension in the masculine and feminine, and the first declension in the feminine (3-1-3). The tense formative will affect the form (cf. aorist indicative).

The active inserts the tense formative σα between the stem and the participle and does not use a connecting vowel.

first aorist active participle

nom sg	λύσας	λύσασα	λῦσαν
gen sg	λύσαντος	λυσάσης	λύσαντος
dat sg	λύσαντι	λυσάσῃ	λύσαντι
acc sg	λύσαντα	λύσασαν	λῦσαν
nom pl	λύσαντες	λύσασαι	λύσαντα
gen pl	λυσάντων	λυσασῶν	λυσάντων
dat pl	λύσασι(ν)	λυσάσαις	λύσασι(ν)
acc pl	λύσαντας	λυσάσας	λύσαντα

first aorist middle participle

The middle uses the tense formative σα and no connecting vowel. It looks just like the present middle with σα replacing ο.

nom sg	λυσάμενος	λυσαμένη	λυσάμενον
gen sg	λυσομένου	λυσαμένης	λυσομένου

first aorist passive participle

The aorist passive uses the tense formative θε.

nom sg	λυθείς	λυθεῖσα	λυθέν
gen sg	λυθέντος	λυθείσης	λυθέντος
dat sg	λυθέντι	λυθείσῃ	λυθέντι
acc sg	λυθέντα	λυθεῖσαν	λυθέν
nom pl	λυθέντες	λυθεῖσαι	λυθέντα
gen pl	λυθέντων	λυθεισῶν	λυθέντων
dat pl	λυθεῖσι(ν)	λυθείσαις	λυθεῖσι(ν)
acc pl	λυθέντας	λυθείσας	λυθέντα

Second aorist participle (§91.4)

The second aorist participle is formed on the second aorist stem without the augment. The endings for the active and middle are exactly like those in the present of λύω. The second aorist passive uses the same forms as the aorist active.

active	*nom sg*	βαλών	βαλοῦσα	βαλόν
	gen sg	βαλόντος	βαλούσης	βαλόντος
middle	*nom sg*	βαλόμενος	βαλομένη	βαλόμενον
	gen sg	βαλόμενου	βαλομένης	βαλόμενου
passive	*nom sg*	γραφείς	γραφεῖσα	γραφέν
	gen sg	γραφέντος	γραφείσης	γραφέντος

Perfect (§91.5)

The perfect participle (masculine and neuter) is τ with a connecting vowel (o). It is otherwise very much like the aorist.

The feminine stem is totally different from the one used in the masculine and neuter. It is υσ to which is added ια. The σ becomes intervocalic and drops out (§25.5), and ι becomes vocalic ι resulting in υια. υσ + ια ‣ υια ‣ υια.

The middle/passive adds the participle directly onto the stem with no tense formative. The case endings are the same as λυόμενος, λυομένη, λυόμενον.

The only difference between first and second perfects is that first perfects include the tense formative κ while the second perfect does not (γεγονώς, γεγονυῖα, γεγονός).

perfect active participle

nom sg	λελυκώς	λελυκυῖα	λελυκός
gen sg	λελυκότος	λελυκυίας	λελυκότος
dat sg	λελυκότι	λελυκυίᾳ	λελυκότι
acc sg	λελυκότα	λελυκυῖαν	λελυκός
nom pl	λελυκότες	λελυκυῖαι	λελυκότα
gen pl	λελυκότων	λελυκυιῶν	λελυκότων
dat pl	λελυκόσι	λελυκυίαις	λελυκόσι
acc pl	λελυκότας	λελυκυίας	λελυκότα

perfect middle/passive participle

nom sg	λελυμένος	λελυμένη	λελυμένον
gen sg	λελυμένου	λελυμένης	λελυμένου

Thematic (contract verbs) (§92)

Contract verbs form their participles just like the uncontracted stems, except that if there is a tense formative it will lengthen (γεννάω ‣ γεννήσας). If there is no tense formative (as in the present), the final stem vowel will contract regularly with the connecting vowel (γεννα + οντ ‣ γενναον ‣ γεννῶν).

Athematic μι Verbs (§93)

μι verbs do not use a connecting vowel; they add the participle directly onto the stem. Their final stem vowel is always short. They are otherwise declined like a thematic stem. The genitive form is listed after the nominative.

present active participle

nom sg	ἱστάς	ἱστᾶσα	ἱστάν
gen sg	ἱστάντος	ἱστάσης	ἱστάντος
nom sg	τιθείς	τιθεῖσα	τιθέν
gen sg	τιθέντος	τιθεῖσα	τιθέντος
nom sg	διδούς	διδοῦσα	διδόν
gen sg	διδόντος	διδούσης	διδόντος
nom sg	δεικνύς	δεικνῦσα	δεικνύν
gen sg	δεικνύντος	δεικνύσης	δεικνύντος

present middle/passive participle

nom sg	ἱστάμενος	ἱσταμένη	ἱστάμενον
gen sg	ἱσταμένου	ἱσταμένης	ἱσταμένου
nom sg	τιθέμενος	τιθεμένη	τιθέμενον
gen sg	τιθεμένου	τιθεμένης	τιθεμένου
nom sg	διδόμενος	διδομένη	διδόμενον
gen sg	διδομένου	διδομένης	διδομένου
nom sg	δεικνύμενος	δεικνυμένη	δεικνύμενον
gen sg	δεικνυμένου	δεικνυμένης	δεικνυμένου

future active participle　　　　future middle participle

nom sg	στήσων	στησόμενος
gen sg	στήσοντος	στησομένου
nom sg	θήσων	θησόμενος
gen sg	θήσοντος	θησομένου
nom sg	δώσων	δωσόμενος
gen sg	δώσοντος	δωσομένου

first aorist active participle

nom sg	στήσας	θήκας
gen sg	στήσαντος	θηκάντος

second aorist active participle

nom sg	στάς	στᾶσα	στάν
gen sg	στάντος	στάσης	στάντος
nom sg	θείς	θεῖσα	θέν
gen sg	θέντος	θείσης	θέντος
nom sg	δούς	δοῦσα	δόν
gen sg	δόντος	δούσης	δόντος

first aorist middle participle

nom sg	στησάμενος	θηκάμενος
gen sg	στησαμένου	θηκομένου

second aorist middle participle

nom sg	στάμενος	σταμένη	στάμενον
gen sg	σταμένου	σταμένης	σταμένου
nom sg	θέμενος	θεμένη	θέμενον
gen sg	θεμένου	θεμένης	θεμένου

nom sg	δόμενος	δομένη	δόμενον
gen sg	δομένου	δομένης	δομένου

first aorist passive participle

nom sg	σταθείς	σταθεῖσα	σταθέν
gen sg	σταθέντος	σταθείσης	σταθέντος

nom sg	τεθείς	τεθεῖσα	τεθέν
gen sg	τεθέντος	τεθείσης	τεθέντος

nom sg	δοθείς	δοθεῖσα	δοθέν
gen sg	δοθέντος	δοθείσης	δοθέντος

perfect active participle

nom sg	ἑστηκώς	τεθεικώς	δεδωκώς
gen sg	ἑστκότος	τεθεικότος	δεδωκότος

Analytical Lexicon

Analytical Listings
and Lexicon

α

α   {1, n-3g(2)}
  alpha, first letter of the Greek alphabet; used as
  first in titles of N.T. writings

ἄ   nom pl neut [23t; a-1a(2b); 4005]   ὅς
ἄ   acc pl neut [95t; a-1a(2b); 4005]   "

Ἀαρών, ὁ   {2, n-3g(2)}
  Aaron, pr. name, indecl, the brother of Moses
  (Ex 4:14), Luke 1:15; Acts 7:40; Heb 5:4; 7:11;
  9:4*

Ἀαρών   indecl [5t; n-3g(2); 2]   Ἀαρών

Ἀβαδδών, ὁ   {3, n-3g(2)}
  Abaddon, pr. name, indecl, alternate spelling:
  Ἀββαδών, the angel who rules in hell, Rev 9:11*

Ἀβαδδών   indecl [Rv 9:11; n-3g(2); 3]   Ἀβαδδών
ἀβαρῆ   acc sg masc [2C 11:9; a-4a; 4]   ἀβαρής

ἀβαρής, ες, gen. οὓς   {4, a-4a}
  literally: *weightless*; figuratively: *not burdensome*,
  2 Cor 11:9*

ἀββά   {5, n-3g(2)}
  father, Mark 14:36; Rom 8:15; Gal 4:6*

ἀββα   indecl [3t; n-3g(2); 5]   ἀββά

Ἄβελ, ὁ   {6, n-3g(2)}
  Abel, pr. name, indecl, Matt 23:35; Luke 11:51;
  Heb 11:4; 12:24

Ἄβελ   indecl [4t; n-3g(2); 6]   Ἄβελ

Ἀβιά, ὁ   {7, n-3g(2)}
  Abiajah, pr. name, indecl. Hebrew is *Abijah*. (1)
  the son of Rehoboam (1 Chron 3:10) Matt 1:7;
  (2) the division of priests to which Zechariah
  belonged (1 Chron 24:10) Luke 1:5*

Ἀβιά   indecl [3t; n-3g(2); 7]   Ἀβιά

Ἀβιαθάρ, ὁ   {8, n-3g(2)}
  Abiathar, pr. name, indecl, Mark 2:26*

Ἀβιαθάρ   indecl [Mk 2:26; n-3g(2); 8]   Ἀβιαθάρ

Ἀβιληνή, ῆς, ἡ   {9, n-1b}
  Abilene, a district of the Syrian Decapolis; from
  Abila, the chief town, Luke 3:1*

Ἀβιληνῆς   gen sg fem [Lk 3:1; n-1b; 9]   Ἀβιληνή

Ἀβιούδ, ὁ   {10, n-3g(2)}
  Abihud, pr. name, indecl

Ἀβιούδ   indecl [2t; n-3g(2); 10]   Ἀβιούδ

Ἀβραάμ, ὁ   {11, n-3g(2)}
  Abraham, pr. name indecl

Ἀβραάμ   indecl [73t; n-3g(2); 11]   Ἀβραάμ

ἄβυσσον   acc sg fem [3t; n-2b; 12]   ἄβυσσος

ἄβυσσος, οῦ, ἡ   {12, n-2b}
  bottomless; place of the dead, Luke 8:31; Rom 10:7

ἀβύσσου   gen sg fem [6t; n-2b; 12]   "

Ἄγαβος, ου, ὁ   {13, n-2a}
  Agabus, pr. name, Acts 11:28; 21:10*

Ἄγαβος   nom sg masc [2t; n-2a; 13]   Ἄγαβος
ἀγαγεῖν   aor act inf [2t; v-1b(2); 72]   ἄγω
ἀγάγετε   aor act imperative 2 pl
  [3t; v-1b(2); 72]   "
ἀγάγῃ   aor act subj 3 sg [2t; v-1b(2); 72]   "
ἀγαγόντα   aor act ptcp acc sg masc
  [Hb 2:10; v-1b(2); 72]   "
ἀγαγόντες   aor act ptcp nom pl masc
  [Ac 5:27; v-1b(2); 72]   "
ἀγαθά   nom pl neut [Rm 3:8; a-1a(2a); 19]   ἀγαθός
ἀγαθά   acc pl neut [10t; a-1a(2a); 19]   "
ἀγαθάς   acc pl fem [2t; a-1a(2a); 19]   "
ἀγαθέ   voc sg masc [5t; a-1a(2a); 19]   "
ἀγαθή   nom sg fem [2t; a-1a(2a); 19]   "
ἀγαθῇ   dat sg fem [2t; a-1a(2a); 19]   "
ἀγαθήν   acc sg fem [8t; a-1a(2a); 19]   "
ἀγαθῆς   gen sg fem [2t; a-1a(2a); 19]   "
ἀγαθοεργεῖν   pres act inf
  [1Ti 6:18; cv-1d(2a); 14]   ἀγαθοεργέω

ἀγαθοεργέω   {14, cv-1d(2a)}
  [-, -, -, -, -] *to do good, confer benefits*, Acts 14:17;
  1 Tim 6:18*

ἀγαθοεργός, ον   {15, a-3a}
  doing good, used as a noun in Rom 13:3 v.l.*

ἀγαθοῖς   dat pl masc
  [1P 2:18; a-1a(2a); 19]   ἀγαθός
ἀγαθοῖς   dat pl neut [2t; a-1a(2a); 19]   "
ἀγαθόν   nom sg neut [7t; a-1a(2a); 19]   "
ἀγαθόν   acc sg masc [2t; a-1a(2a); 19]   "
ἀγαθοποιεῖτε   pres act imperative 2 pl
  [Lk 6:35; cv-1d(2a); 16]   ἀγαθοποιέω

ἀγαθοποιέω   {16, cv-1d(2a)}
  [-, ἠγαθοποίησα -, -, -] *to do good, do well; to do
  what is morally correct* (1 Pet 2:15, 20)

ἀγαθοποιῆσαι   aor act inf
  [Lk 6:9; cv-1d(2a); 16]   "
ἀγαθοποιῆτε   pres act subj 2 pl
  [Lk 6:33; cv-1d(2a); 16]   "

ἀγαθοποιΐα, ας, ἡ   {17, n-1a}
  well-doing, 1 Peter 4:19*

ἀγαθοποιΐα   dat sg fem
  [1P 4:19; n-1a; 17]   ἀγαθοποιΐα

ἀγαθοποιός, ον　　　　　　　　{18, a-3a}
doing good or *right; subst., a well-doer,* 1 Pet 2:14*

ἀγαθοποιοῦντας　pres act ptcp acc pl masc
　[3t; cv-1d(2a); 16]　　　　　　　ἀγαθοποιέω
ἀγαθοποιοῦντες　pres act ptcp nom pl masc
　[1P 2:20; cv-1d(2a); 16]　　　　　　　"
ἀγαθοποιοῦσαι　pres act ptcp nom pl fem
　[1P 3:6; cv-1d(2a); 16]　　　　　　　"
ἀγαθοποιῶν　gen pl masc
　[1P 2:14; a-3a; 18]　　　　　　ἀγαθοποιός
ἀγαθοποιῶν　pres act ptcp nom sg masc
　[3J 11; cv-1d(2a); 16]　　　　　　ἀγαθοποιέω

ἀγαθός, ή, όν　　　　　　　　{19, a-1a(2a)}
good, profitable, generous, upright, virtuous

ἀγαθός　nom sg masc [10t; a-1a(2a); 19]　　ἀγαθός
ἀγαθοῦ　gen sg masc [3t; a-1a(2a); 19]　　　"
ἀγαθοῦ　gen sg neut [5t; a-1a(2a); 19]　　　"
ἀγαθουργῶν　pres act ptcp nom sg masc
　[Ac 14:17; cv-1d(2a); 14]　　　　ἀγαθοεργέω
ἀγαθούς　acc pl masc [2t; a-1a(2a); 19]　　ἀγαθός
ἀγαθῷ　dat sg masc [2Th 2:17; a-1a(2a); 19]　　"
ἀγαθῷ　dat sg neut [6t; a-1a(2a); 19]　　　"
ἀγαθῶν　gen pl masc [Jm 3:17; a-1a(2a); 19]　　"
ἀγαθῶν　gen pl neut [5t; a-1a(2a); 19]　　　"

ἀγαθωσύνη, ῆς, ἡ　　　　　　{20, n-1b}
goodness, virtue, beneficence, Rom 5:14; Eph 5:9;
2 Thess 1:11; *generosity,* Gal 5:22*

ἀγαθωσύνη　nom sg fem
　[Ga 5:22; n-1b; 20]　　　　　　ἀγαθωσύνη
ἀγαθωσύνη　dat sg fem [Ep 5:9; n-1b; 20]　　"
ἀγαθωσύνης　gen sg fem [2t; n-1b; 20]　　　"
ἀγαλλιαθῆναι　aor pass inf
　[Jn 5:35; v-1d(1b); 22]　　　　　ἀγαλλιάω
ἀγαλλιάσει　dat sg fem
　[3t; n-3e(5b); 21]　　　　　　ἀγαλλίασις
ἀγαλλιάσεως　gen sg fem [Hb 1:9; n-3e(5b); 21]　"
ἀγαλλιᾶσθε　pres mid imperative 2 pl
　[Mt 5:12; v-1d(1b); 22]　　　　　ἀγαλλιάω
ἀγαλλιᾶσθε　pres mid ind 2 pl [2t; v-1d(1b); 22]　"

ἀγαλλίασις, εως, ἡ　　　　　　{21, n-3e(5b)}
exultation, extreme joy

ἀγαλλίασις　nom sg fem
　[Lk 1:14; n-3e(5b); 21]　　　　　ἀγαλλίασις

ἀγαλλιάω　　　　　　　　　　{22, v-1d(1b)}
[-, ἠγαλλίασα, -, -, ἠγαλλιάθην] *to celebrate,
praise;* usually in the middle in the N.T.
(ἀγαλλιάομαι) *to exult, rejoice exceedingly; to
desire ardently,* John 8:56

ἀγαλλιῶμεν　pres act subj 1 pl
　[Rv 19:7; v-1d(1b); 22]　　　　　ἀγαλλιάω
ἀγαλλιώμενοι　pres mid ptcp nom pl masc
　[1P 4:13; v-1d(1b); 22]　　　　　　"
ἀγάμοις　dat pl masc [1C 7:8; n-2a; 23]　　ἄγαμος

ἄγαμος, ου, ἡ or **ὁ**　　　　　{23, n-2b/n-2a}
unmarried (woman or man) 1 Cor 7:8, 11, 32, 34*

ἄγαμος　nom sg masc [1C 7:32; n-2a; 23]　　"
ἄγαμος　nom sg fem [2t; n-2a; 23]　　　　"

ἀγανακτεῖν　pres act inf
　[Mk 10:41; v-1d(2a); 24]　　　　ἀγανακτέω

ἀγανακτέω　　　　　　　　　{24, v-1d(2a)}
[-, ἠγανάκτησα, -, -, -] *to be pained; to be angry,
vexed, indignant; to manifest indignation,* Mark
14:4; Luke 13:14

ἀγανάκτησιν　acc sg fem
　[2C 7:11; n-3e(5b); 25]　　　　ἀγανάκτησις

ἀγανάκτησις, εως, ἡ　　　　　{25, n-3e(5b)}
indignation, 2 Cor 7:11*

ἀγανακτοῦντες　pres act ptcp nom pl masc
　[Mk 14:4; v-1d(2a); 24]　　　　ἀγανακτέω
ἀγανακτῶν　pres act ptcp nom sg masc
　[Lk 13:14; v-1d(2a); 24]　　　　　"
ἀγαπᾷ　pres act ind 3 sg
　[9t; v-1d(1a); 26]　　　　　　ἀγαπάω
ἀγαπᾷ　pres act subj 3 sg [3t; v-1d(1a); 26]　"
ἀγάπαις　dat pl fem [Jd 12; n-1b; 27]　　ἀγάπη
ἀγαπᾶν　pres act inf [8t; v-1d(1a); 26]　ἀγαπάω
ἀγαπᾷς　pres act ind 2 sg [2t; v-1d(1a); 26]　"
ἀγαπᾶτε　pres act imperative 2 pl
　[7t; v-1d(1a); 26]　　　　　　　"
ἀγαπᾶτε　pres act ind 2 pl [3t; v-1d(1a); 26]　"
ἀγαπᾶτε　pres act subj 2 pl [5t; v-1d(1a); 26]　"
ἀγαπάτω　pres act imperative 3 sg
　[Ep 5:33; v-1d(1a); 26]　　　　　"

ἀγαπάω　　　　　　　　　　{26, v-1d(1a)}
[ἀγαπήσω, ἠγάπησα, ἠγάπηκα, ἠγάπημαι
ἠγαπήθην] *to love, value, esteem, feel or manifest
generous concern for, be faithful towards; to delight
in, to set store upon,* Rev. 12:11

ἀγάπη, ῆς, ἡ　　　　　　　　{27, n-1b}
love, generosity, kindly concern, devotedness; pl.
love-feasts, Jude 12

ἀγάπη　nom sg fem [36t; n-1b; 27]　　　ἀγάπη
ἀγάπη　dat sg fem [28t; n-1b; 27]　　　"
ἀγαπηθήσεται　fut pass ind 3 sg
　[Jn 14:21; v-1d(1a); 26]　　　　ἀγαπάω
ἀγάπην　acc sg fem [33t; n-1b; 27]　　ἀγάπη
ἀγάπης　gen sg fem [18t; n-1b; 27]　　　"
ἀγαπήσαντος　aor act ptcp gen sg masc
　[2t; v-1d(1a); 26]　　　　　　ἀγαπάω
ἀγαπήσας　aor act ptcp nom sg masc
　[3t; v-1d(1a); 26]　　　　　　　"
ἀγαπήσατε　aor act imperative 2 pl
　[1P 1:22; v-1d(1a); 26]　　　　　　"
ἀγαπήσει　fut act ind 3 sg [4t; v-1d(1a); 26]　"
ἀγαπήσεις　fut act ind 2 sg [10t; v-1d(1a); 26]　"
ἀγαπήσητε　aor act subj 2 pl
　[Mt 5:46; v-1d(1a); 26]　　　　　"
ἀγαπήσω　fut act ind 1 sg
　[Jn 14:21; v-1d(1a); 26]　　　　　"
ἀγαπητά　nom pl neut
　[Ep 5:1; a-1a(2a); 28]　　　　　ἀγαπητός
ἀγαπητά　acc pl neut [1C 4:14; a-1a(2a); 28]　"
ἀγαπητέ　voc sg masc [3t; a-1a(2a); 28]　　"
ἀγαπητήν　acc sg fem [Rm 16:12; a-1a(2a); 28]　"
ἀγαπητοί　nom pl masc [3t; a-1a(2a); 28]　　"
ἀγαπητοί　voc pl masc [27t; a-1a(2a); 28]　　"
ἀγαπητοῖς　dat pl masc [2t; a-1a(2a); 28]　　"

ἀγαπητόν   nom sg neut   [1C 4:17; a-1a(2a); 28]   "
ἀγαπητόν   acc sg masc   [6t; a-1a(2a); 28]   "

ἀγαπητός   {28, a-1a(2a)}
  beloved, dear; worthy of love

ἀγαπητός   nom sg masc   [11t; a-1a(2a); 28]   "
ἀγαπητοῦ   gen sg masc   [Cl 1:7; a-1a(2a); 28]   "
ἀγαπητῷ   dat sg masc   [3t; a-1a(2a); 28]   "
ἀγαπητῷ   dat sg neut   [2Ti 1:2; a-1a(2a); 28]   "
ἀγαπῶ   pres act ind 1 sg
  [5t; v-1d(1a); 26]   ἀγαπάω
ἀγαπῶμαι   pres pass ind 1 sg
  [2C 12:15; v-1d(1a); 26]   "
ἀγαπῶμεν   pres act ind 1 pl   [3t; v-1d(1a); 26]   "
ἀγαπῶμεν   pres act subj 1 pl   [7t; v-1d(1a); 26]   "
ἀγαπῶν   pres act ptcp nom sg masc
  [14t; v-1d(1a); 26]   "
ἀγαπῶντας   pres act ptcp acc pl masc
  [3t; v-1d(1a); 26]   "
ἀγαπῶντι   pres act ptcp dat sg masc
  [Rv 1:5; v-1d(1a); 26]   "
ἀγαπῶντων   pres act ptcp gen pl masc
  [Ep 6:24; v-1d(1a); 26]   "
ἀγαπῶσιν   pres act ind 3 pl
  [Lk 6:32; v-1d(1a); 26]   "
ἀγαπῶσιν   pres act ptcp dat pl masc
  [4t; v-1d(1a); 26]   "

Ἁγάρ, ἡ   {29, n-3g(2)}
  pr. name, indecl, *Hagar* (Gen 16), Gal 4:24, 25*

Ἁγάρ   indecl   [2t; n-3g(2); 29]   Ἁγάρ
ἀγγαρεύουσιν   pres act ind 3 pl
  [Mk 15:21; v-1a(6); 30]   ἀγγαρεύω
ἀγγαρεύσει   fut act ind 3 sg
  [Mt 5:41; v-1a(6); 30]   "

ἀγγαρεύω   {30, v-1a(6)}
  [ἀγγαρεύσω, ἠγγάρευσα, -, -, -] *to press,* or
  compel another to go somewhere, or carry
  some burden, Matt 5:41; 27:32; Mark 15:21*

ἀγγείοις   dat pl neut
  [Mt 25:4; n-2c; 31]   ἀγγεῖον

ἀγγεῖον, ου, τό   {31, n-2c}
  a vessel, flask, Matt 25:4; 13:48 v.l.*

ἀγγελία, ας, ἡ   {32, n-1a}
  a messsage, doctrine, or *precept,* delivered in the
  name of any one; *command,* 1 John 1:5; 3:11*

ἀγγελία   nom sg fem   [2t; n-1a; 32]   ἀγγελία
ἀγγέλλουσα   pres act ptcp nom sg fem
  [Jn 20:18; v-2d(1); 33]   ἀγγέλλω

ἀγγέλλω   {33, v-2d(1)}
  [ἀγγελῶ, ἤγγειλα, ἤγγελκα, ἤγγελμαι, ἠγγέλην]
  to tell, to announce, John 20:18; 4:51 v.l.*

ἄγγελοι   nom pl masc   [23t; n-2a; 34]   ἄγγελος
ἀγγέλοις   dat pl masc   [9t; n-2a; 34]   "
ἄγγελον   acc sg masc   [22t; n-2a; 34]   "

ἄγγελος, ου, ὁ   {34, n-2a}
  one sent, a messenger, angel

ἄγγελος   nom sg masc   [47t; n-2a; 34]   "
ἀγγέλου   gen sg masc   [14t; n-2a; 34]   "

ἀγγέλους   acc pl masc   [20t; n-2a; 34]   "
ἀγγέλῳ   dat sg masc   [9t; n-2a; 34]   "
ἀγγέλων   gen pl masc   [31t; n-2a; 34]   "
ἄγγη   acc pl neut   [Mt 13:48; n-3d(2b); 35]   ἄγγος

ἄγγος, ους, τό   {35, n-3d(2b)}
  vessel, container, basket, Matt 13:48*

ἄγε   pres act imperative 2 sg
  [3t; v-1b(2); 72]   ἄγω
ἄγει   pres act ind 3 sg   [2t; v-1b(2); 72]   "
ἄγειν   pres act inf   [Ac 23:10; v-1b(2); 72]   "

ἀγέλη, ης, ἡ   {36, n-1b}
  flock, herd

ἀγέλη   nom sg fem   [6t; n-1b; 36]   ἀγέλη
ἀγέλην   acc sg fem   [Mt 8:31; n-1b; 36]   "

ἀγενεαλόγητος, ον   {37, a-3a}
  not included in a genealogy; independent of
  genealogy, Heb 7:3*

ἀγενεαλόγητος   nom sg masc
  [Hb 7:3; a-3a; 37]   ἀγενεαλόγητος
ἀγενῆ   acc pl neut   [1C 1:28; a-4a; 38]   ἀγενής

ἀγενής, ές, gen. οῦς   {38, a-4a}
  lit., *without kin;* fig., *base, low, insignificant,* 1 Cor
  1:28*

ἄγεσθαι   pres pass inf
  [Ac 21:34; v-1b(2); 72]   ἄγω
ἄγεσθε   pres pass ind 2 pl   [Ga 5:18; v-1b(2); 72]   "
ἁγία   nom sg fem   [6t; a-1a(1); 41]   ἅγιος
ἅγια   nom pl neut   [3t; a-1a(1); 41]   "
ἅγια   acc pl neut   [4t; a-1a(1); 41]   "
ἁγίᾳ   dat sg fem   [2Ti 1:9; a-1a(1); 41]   "
ἁγιάζει   pres act ind 3 sg
  [Hb 9:13; v-2a(1); 39]   ἁγιάζω
ἁγιάζεται   pres pass ind 3 sg
  [1Ti 4:5; v-2a(1); 39]   "
ἁγιαζόμενοι   pres pass ptcp nom pl masc
  [Hb 2:11; v-2a(1); 39]   "
ἁγιαζομένους   pres pass ptcp acc pl masc
  [Hb 10:14; v-2a(1); 39]   "
ἁγιάζον   pres act ptcp nom sg neut
  [Mt 23:19; v-2a(1); 39]   "

ἁγιάζω   {39, v-2a(1)}
  [-, ἡγίασα, -, ἡγίασμαι, ἡγιάσθην] *to separate,*
  consecrate; cleanse, purify, sanctify; regard or
  reverence as holy

ἁγιάζω   pres act ind 1 sg
  [Jn 17:19; v-2a(1); 39]   "
ἁγιάζων   pres act ptcp nom sg masc
  [Hb 2:11; v-2a(1); 39]   "
ἅγιαι   nom pl fem   [1P 3:5; a-1a(1); 41]   ἅγιος
ἁγίαις   dat pl fem   [3t; a-1a(1); 41]   "
ἁγίαν   acc sg fem   [6t; a-1a(1); 41]   "
ἁγίας   gen sg fem   [3t; a-1a(1); 41]   "
ἁγιάσαι   aor act opt 3 sg
  [1Th 5:23; v-2a(1); 39]   ἁγιάζω
ἁγιάσας   aor act ptcp nom sg masc
  [Mt 23:17; v-2a(1); 39]   "
ἁγιάσατε   aor act imperative 2 pl
  [1P 3:15; v-2a(1); 39]   "

ἁγιάση   aor act subj 3 sg [2t; v-2a(1); 39]   "
ἁγιασθήτω   aor pass imperative 3 sg
    [3t; v-2a(1); 39]   "
ἁγιασμόν   acc sg masc [3t; n-2a; 40]   ἁγιασμός

ἁγιασμός, οῦ, ὁ   {40, n-2a}
    sanctification, moral purity, sanctity

ἁγιασμός   nom sg masc [2t; n-2a; 40]   "
ἁγιασμῷ   dat sg masc [5t; n-2a; 40]   "
ἁγίασον   aor act imperative 2 sg
    [Jn 17:17; v-2a(1); 39]   ἁγιάζω
ἅγιε   voc sg masc [Jn 17:11; a-1a(1); 41]   ἅγιος
ἅγιοι   nom pl masc [6t; a-1a(1); 41]   "
ἅγιοι   voc pl masc [2t; a-1a(1); 41]   "
ἁγίοις   dat pl masc [19t; a-1a(1); 41]   "
ἅγιον   nom sg neut [22t; a-1a(1); 41]   "
ἅγιον   acc sg masc [7t; a-1a(1); 41]   ""
ἅγιον   acc sg neut [17t; a-1a(1); 41]   "

ἅγιος, ία, ον   {41, a-1a(1)}
    *separate from common condition and use;
    dedicated.* Luke 2:23; *hallowed;* used of things, τὰ
    ἅγια, *the sanctuary;* and of persons, *saints,* e.g.,
    members of the first Christian communities;
    pure, righteous, ceremonially or morally; *holy*

ἅγιος   nom sg masc [12t; a-1a(1); 41]   "
ἅγιος   voc sg masc [Rv 6:10; a-1a(1); 41]   "

ἁγιότης, ητος, ἡ   {42, n-3c(1)}
    holiness, sanctity, Heb 12:10; 2 Cor 1:12 v.l.*

ἁγιότητος   gen sg fem
    [Hb 12:10; n-3c(1); 42]   ἁγιότης
ἁγίου   gen sg masc [4t; a-1a(1); 41]   ἅγιος
ἁγίου   gen sg neut [38t; a-1a(1); 41]   "
ἁγίους   acc pl masc [12t; a-1a(1); 41]   "
ἁγίῳ   dat sg masc [Mt 24:15; a-1a(1); 41]   "
ἁγίῳ   dat sg neut [25t; a-1a(1); 41]   "
ἁγίων   gen pl masc [34t; a-1a(1); 41]   "
ἁγίων   gen pl neut [4t; a-1a(1); 41]   "

ἁγιωσύνη, ῆς, ἡ   {43, n-1b}
    sanctification, sanctity, holiness, Rom 1:4; 2 Cor
    7:1; 1 Thess 3:13*

ἁγιωσύνη   dat sg fem
    [1Th 3:13; n-1b; 43]   ἁγιωσύνη
ἁγιωσύνην   acc sg fem [2C 7:1; n-1b; 43]   "
ἁγιωσύνης   gen sg fem [Rm 1:4; n-1b; 43]   "
ἁγιωτάτῃ   dat sg fem superlative
    [Jd 20; a-1a(1); 41]   ἅγιος
ἀγκάλας   acc pl fem [Lk 2:28; n-1b; 44]   ἀγκάλη

ἀγκάλη, ῆς, ἡ   {44, n-1b}
    the arm, Luke 2:28*

ἄγκιστρον, ου, τό   {45, n-2c}
    a hook, fish-hook, Matt 17:27*

ἄγκιστρον   acc sg neut
    [Mt 17:27; n-2c; 45]   ἄγκιστρον

ἄγκυρα, ας, ἡ   {46, n-1a}
    an anchor, Acts 27:29, 30, 40; Heb 6:19*

ἄγκυραν   acc sg fem [Hb 6:19; n-1a; 46]   ἄγκυρα
ἀγκύρας   acc pl fem [3t; n-1a; 46]   "
ἀγνά   nom pl neut [Pp 4:8; a-1a(2a); 54]   ἁγνός

ἁγνάς   acc pl fem [Ti 2:5; a-1a(2a); 54]   "

ἄγναφος, ον   {47, a-3a}
    unshrunken; new, Matt 9:16; Mark 2:21*

ἀγνάφου   gen sg neut [2t; a-3a; 47]   ἄγναφος

ἁγνεία, ας, ἡ   {48, n-1a}
    purity, chastity, 1 Tim 4:12; 5:2*

ἁγνεία   dat sg fem [2t; n-1a; 48]   ἁγνεία
ἁγνή   nom sg fem [Jm 3:17; a-1a(2a); 54]   ἁγνός
ἁγνήν   acc sg fem [2t; a-1a(2a); 54]   "
ἁγνίζει   pres act ind 3 sg
    [1J 3:3; v-2a(1); 49]   ἁγνίζω

ἁγνίζω   {49, v-2a(1)}
    [-, ἥγνισα, ἥγνικα, ἥγνισμαι, ἡγνίσθην] *to purify;
    to purify morally, reform, to live like one under a
    vow of abstinence,* as the Nazarites

ἁγνίσατε   aor act imperative 2 pl
    [Jm 4:8; v-2a(1); 49]   "
ἁγνισθείς   aor pass ptcp nom sg masc
    [Ac 21:26; v-2a(1); 49]   "
ἁγνίσθητι   aor pass imperative 2 sg
    [Ac 21:24; v-2a(1); 49]   "

ἁγνισμός, οῦ, ὁ   {50, n-2a}
    purification, abstinence, Acts 21:26*

ἁγνισμοῦ   gen sg masc
    [Ac 21:26; n-2a; 50]   ἁγνισμός
ἁγνίσωσιν   aor act subj 3 pl
    [Jn 11:55; v-2a(1); 49]   ἁγνίζω
ἀγνοεῖ   pres act ind 3 sg
    [1C 14:38; v-1d(2a); 51]   ἀγνοέω
ἀγνοεῖν   pres act inf [6t; v-1d(2a); 51]   "
ἀγνοεῖται   pres mid ind 3 sg
    [1C 14:38; v-1d(2a); 51]   "
ἀγνοεῖτε   pres act ind 2 pl [2t; v-1d(2a); 51]   "

ἀγνοέω   {51, v-1d(2a)}
    [-, ἠγνόησα, -, -, -] *to be ignorant; not to
    understand; sin through ignorance*

ἀγνόημα, ατος, τό   {52, n-3c(4)}
    error, sin of ignorance, Heb 9:7*

ἀγνοημάτων   gen pl neut
    [Hb 9:7; n-3c(4); 52]   ἀγνόημα
ἀγνοήσαντες   aor act ptcp nom pl masc
    [Ac 13:27; v-1d(2a); 51]   ἀγνοέω

ἄγνοια, ας, ἡ   {53, n-1a}
    ignorance, willful, Acts 3:17; 17:30; Eph 4:18; 1
    Pet 1:14; 1 Pet 2:15 v.l.; 2 Pet 2:13 v.l.*

ἀγνοίᾳ   dat sg fem [1P 1:14; n-1a; 53]   ἄγνοια
ἄγνοιαν   acc sg fem [2t; n-1a; 53]   "
ἀγνοίας   gen sg fem [Ac 17:30; n-1a; 53]   "
ἁγνόν   acc sg masc
    [1Ti 5:22; a-1a(2a); 54]   ἁγνός
ἀγνοοῦμεν   pres act ind 1 pl
    [2C 2:11; v-1d(2a); 51]   ἀγνοέω
ἀγνοούμενοι   pres pass ptcp nom pl masc
    [2C 6:9; v-1d(2a); 51]   "
ἀγνοούμενος   pres pass ptcp nom sg masc
    [Ga 1:22; v-1d(2a); 51]   "
ἀγνοοῦντες   pres act ptcp nom pl masc
    [2t; v-1d(2a); 51]   "

ἀγνοοῦσιν   pres act ind 3 pl
  [2P 2:12; v-1d(2a); 51]   "
ἀγνοοῦσιν   pres act ptcp dat pl masc
  [Hb 5:2; v-1d(2a); 51]   "

ἀγνός, ή, όν   {54, a-1a(2a)}
  pure, chaste, modest, innocent, blameless

ἀγνός   nom sg masc [1J 3:3; a-1a(2a); 54]   ἀγνός

ἀγνότης, τητος, ἡ   {55, n-3c(1)}
  purity, life of purity, 2 Cor 6:6; 11:3*

ἀγνότητι   dat sg fem
  [2C 6:6; n-3c(1); 55]   ἀγνότης
ἀγνότητος   gen sg fem [2C 11:3; n-3c(1); 55]   "
ἀγνούς   acc pl masc
  [2C 7:11; a-1a(2a); 54]   ἀγνός
ἀγνοῶν   pres act ptcp nom sg masc
  [2t; v-1d(2a); 51]   ἀγνοέω

ἀγνῶς   {56, adverb}
  purely, with sincerity, Phil 1:17*

ἀγνῶς   adverb [Pp 1:17; adverb; 56]   ἀγνῶς

ἀγνωσία, ας, ἡ   {57, n-1a}
  ignorance, 1 Cor 15:34; 1 Peter 2:15*

ἀγνωσίαν   acc sg fem [2t; n-1a; 57]   ἀγνωσία

ἄγνωστος, ον   {58, a-3a}
  unknown, Acts 17:23*

ἀγνώστῳ   dat sg masc
  [Ac 17:23; a-3a; 58]   ἄγνωστος
ἀγόμενα   pres pass ptcp acc pl neut
  [2Ti 3:6; v-1b(2); 72]   ἄγω
ἄγονται   pres pass ind 3 pl [2t; v-1b(2); 72]   "
ἄγοντες   pres act ptcp nom pl masc
  [Ac 21:16; v-1b(2); 72]   "

ἀγορά, ᾶς, ἡ   {59, n-1a}
  a place of public concourse, forum, market-place;
  things said in the market, provision

ἀγορᾷ   dat sg fem [3t; n-1a; 59]   ἀγορά
ἀγοράζει   pres act ind 3 sg
  [2t; v-2a(1); 60]   ἀγοράζω
ἀγοράζοντας   pres act ptcp acc pl masc
  [2t; v-2a(1); 60]   "
ἀγοράζοντες   pres act ptcp nom pl masc
  [1C 7:30; v-2a(1); 60]   "

ἀγοράζω   {60, v-2a(1)}
  [-, ἠγόρασα, -, ἠγόρασμαι, ἠγοράσθην] *to buy;*
  redeem, acquire by a ransom or price paid

ἀγοραῖοι   nom pl fem
  [Ac 19:38; a-3a; 61]   ἀγοραῖος

ἀγοραῖος, ον   {61, a-3a}
  one who visits the forum; a lounger, one who idles
  away his time in public places, a low fellow, Acts
  17:5; *pertaining to the forum, judicial;* ἀγόραιοι,
  court days, Acts 19:38*

ἀγοραῖς   dat pl fem [6t; n-1a; 59]   ἀγορά
ἀγοραίων   gen pl masc
  [Ac 17:5; a-3a; 61]   ἀγοραῖος
ἀγοράν   acc sg fem [Ac 16:19; n-1a; 59]   ἀγορά
ἀγορᾶς   gen sg fem [Mk 7:4; n-1a; 59]   "
ἀγοράσαι   aor act inf [3t; v-2a(1); 60]   ἀγοράζω

ἀγοράσαντα   aor act ptcp acc sg masc
  [2P 2:1; v-2a(1); 60]   "
ἀγοράσας   aor act ptcp nom sg masc
  [Mk 15:46; v-2a(1); 60]   "
ἀγοράσατε   aor act imperative 2 pl
  [Mt 25:9; v-2a(1); 60]   "
ἀγορασάτω   aor act imperative 3 sg
  [Lk 22:36; v-2a(1); 60]   "
ἀγόρασον   aor act imperative 2 sg
  [Jn 13:29; v-2a(1); 60]   "
ἀγοράσωμεν   aor act subj 1 pl [3t; v-2a(1); 60]   "
ἀγοράσωσιν   aor act subj 3 pl [3t; v-2a(1); 60]   "
ἄγουσιν   pres act ind 3 pl [3t; v-1b(2); 72]   ἄγω

ἄγρα, ας, ἡ   {62, n-1a}
  a catching, thing taken, draught of fishes, Luke
  5:4, 9*

ἄγρᾳ   dat sg fem [Lk 5:9; n-1a; 62]   ἄγρα
ἀγράμματοι   nom pl masc
  [Ac 4:13; a-3a; 63]   ἀγράμματος

ἀγράμματος, ον   {63, a-3a}
  illiterate, unlearned, Acts 4:13*

ἄγραν   acc sg fem [Lk 5:4; n-1a; 62]   ἄγρα

ἀγραυλέω   {64, cv-1d(2)}
  [-, -, -, -, -] *to remain in the open air, to live outside,*
  especially *by night,* Luke 2:8*

ἀγραυλοῦντες   pres act ptcp nom pl masc
  [Lk 2:8; cv-1d(2); 64]   ἀγραυλέω
ἀγρεύσωσιν   aor act subj 3 pl
  [Mk 12:13; v-1a(6); 65]   ἀγρεύω

ἀγρεύω   {65, v-1a(6)}
  [-, ἤγρευσα, -, -, -] *to take in hunting, catch,* Mark
  12:13*

ἄγρια   nom pl neut [Jd 13; a-1a(1); 67]   ἄγριος

ἀγριέλαιος, ου, ἡ   {66, n-2b}
  a wild olive-tree, oleaster, Rom 11:17, 24*

ἀγριέλαιος   nom sg fem
  [Rm 11:17; n-2b; 66]   ἀγριέλαιος
ἀγριελαίου   gen sg fem [Rm 11:24; n-2b; 66]   "
ἄγριον   nom sg neut [Mt 3:4; a-1a(1); 67]   ἄγριος
ἄγριον   acc sg neut [Mk 1:6; a-1a(1); 67]   "

ἄγριος, ία, ιον   {67, a-1a(1)}
  belonging to the field, wild; fierce, raging, Matt 3:4;
  Mark 1:6; Jude 13*

Ἀγρίππα   voc sg masc [5t; n-1e; 68]   Ἀγρίππας
Ἀγρίππα   gen sg masc [Ac 25:23; n-1e; 68]   "

Ἀγρίππας, α, ὁ   {68, n-1e}
  Agrippa, pr. name

Ἀγρίππας   nom sg masc [5t; n-1e; 68]   "
ἀγρόν   acc sg masc [7t; n-2a; 69]   ἀγρός

ἀγρός, οῦ, ὁ   {69, n-2a}
  a field, especially *a cultivated field;* pl. *the country;*
  lands, farms, villages

ἀγρός   nom sg masc [3t; n-2a; 69]   "
ἀγροῦ   gen sg masc [7t; n-2a; 69]   "
ἀγρούς   acc pl masc [9t; n-2a; 69]   "

ἀγρυπνεῖτε pres act imperative 2 pl
[2t; cv-1d(2); 70] ἀγρυπνέω

ἀγρυπνέω {70, cv-1d(2)}
[-, -, -, -, -] *to be awake, watch; to be watchful,*
vigilant

ἀγρυπνία, ας, ἡ {71, n-1a}
want of sleep, watching, 2 Cor 6:5; 11:27*

ἀγρυπνίαις dat pl fem [2t; n-1a; 71] ἀγρυπνία
ἀγρυπνοῦντες pres act ptcp nom pl masc
[Ep 6:18; cv-1d(2); 70] ἀγρυπνέω
ἀγρυπνοῦσιν pres act ind 3 pl
[Hb 13:17; cv-1d(2); 70] "
ἀγρῷ dat sg masc [9t; n-2a; 69] ἀγρός
ἀγρῶν gen pl masc [Mk 11:8; n-2a; 69] "

ἄγω {72, v-1b(2)}
[ἄξω, ἤγαγον, -, ἦγμαι, ἤχθην] *to lead. bring; lead*
away, drive off, as a booty of cattle; *conduct,*
accompany; lead out, produce; conduct with force,
drag, hurry away; guide, incite, entice; convey ond's
self, go, go away; pass or *spend* as *time; celebrate*

ἄγω pres act ind 1 sg [Jn 19:4; v-1b(2); 72] ἄγω

ἀγωγή, ῆς, ἡ {73, n-1b}
guidance, mode of instruction, discipline, course of
life, 2 Tim 3:10*

ἀγωγῇ dat sg fem [2Ti 3:10; n-1b; 73] ἀγωγή
ἄγωμεν pres act subj 1 pl [7t; v-1b(2); 72] ἄγω

ἀγών, ῶνος, ὁ {74, n-3f(1a)}
place of contest, race-course, stadium; a contest,
strife, contention; peril, toil

ἀγῶνα acc sg masc [5t; n-3f(1a); 74] ἀγών
ἀγῶνι dat sg masc [1Th 2:2; n-3f(1a); 74] "

ἀγωνία, ας, ἡ {75, n-1a}
contest, violent struggle; agony, anguish, Luke
22:44*

ἀγωνίᾳ dat sg fem [Lk 22:44; n-1a; 75] ἀγωνία
ἀγωνίζεσθε pres mid imperative 2 pl
[Lk 13:24; v-2a(1); 76] ἀγωνίζομαι

ἀγωνίζομαι {76, v-2a(1)}
[-, ἠγωνισάμην, -, ἠγώνισμαι, -] *to be a combatant*
in the public games; to contend, fight, strive
earnestly

ἀγωνιζόμεθα pres mid ind 1 pl
[1Ti 4:10; v-2a(1); 76] "
ἀγωνιζόμενος pres mid ptcp nom sg masc
[3t; v-2a(1); 76] "
ἀγωνίζου pres mid imperative 2 sg
[1Ti 6:12; v-2a(1); 76] "
ἄγωσιν pres act subj 3 pl
[Mk 13:11; v-1b(2); 72] ἄγω

Ἀδάμ, ὁ {77, n-3g(2)}
Adam, pr. name, indecl

Ἀδάμ indecl [9t; n-3g(2); 77] Ἀδάμ
ἀδάπανον acc sg neut
[1C 9:18; a-3a; 78] ἀδάπανος

ἀδάπανος, ον {78, a-3a}
without expense, gratuitous, 1 Cor 9:18*

Ἀδδί, ὁ {79, n-3g(2)}
Addi, pr. name, indecl Luke 3:28*

Ἀδδί indecl [Lk 3:28; n-3g(2); 79] Ἀδδί
ἀδελφαί nom pl fem [4t; n-1b; 80] ἀδελφή
ἀδελφάς acc pl fem [5t; n-1b; 80] "
ἀδελφέ voc sg masc [6t; n-2a; 81] ἀδελφός

ἀδελφή, ῆς, ἡ {80, n-1b}
a sister; near kinswoman, or *female relative, a*
female member of the Christian community

ἀδελφή nom sg fem [8t; n-1b; 80] ἀδελφή
ἀδελφῇ dat sg fem [Pm 2; n-1b; 80] "
ἀδελφήν acc sg fem [5t; n-1b; 80] "
ἀδελφῆς gen sg fem [3t; n-1b; 80] "
ἀδελφοί nom pl masc [39t; n-2a; 81] ἀδελφός
ἀδελφοί voc pl masc [106t; n-2a; 81] "
ἀδελφοῖς dat pl masc [17t; n-2a; 81] "
ἀδελφόν acc sg masc [41t; n-2a; 81] "

ἀδελφός, οῦ, ὁ {81, n-2a}
a brother, near kinsman or *relative; one of the same*
nation or *nature; one of equal rank and dignity; an*
associate, a member of the Christian community

ἀδελφός nom sg masc [43t; n-2a; 81] "

ἀδελφότης, τητος, ἡ {82, n-3c(1)}
brotherhood, the body of the Christian brotherhood,
1 Peter 2:17; 5:9*

ἀδελφότητα acc sg fem
[1P 2:17; n-3c(1); 82] ἀδελφότης
ἀδελφότητι dat sg fem [1P 5:9; n-3c(1); 82] "
ἀδελφοῦ gen sg masc [17t; n-2a; 81] ἀδελφός
ἀδελφούς acc pl masc [39t; n-2a; 81] "
ἀδελφῷ dat sg masc [14t; n-2a; 81] "
ἀδελφῶν gen pl masc [21t; n-2a; 81] "
ᾅδη dat sg masc [Lk 16:23; n-1f; 87] ᾅδης
ἄδηλα nom pl neut [Lk 11:44; a-3a; 83] ἄδηλος
ἄδηλον acc sg fem [1C 14:8; a-3a; 83] "

ἄδηλος, ον {83, a-3a}
not apparent or *obvious; uncertain, not distinct,*
Luke 11:44; 1 Cor 14:8*

ἀδηλότης, τητος, ἡ {84, n-3c(1)}
uncertainty, 1 Tim 6:17*

ἀδηλότητι dat sg fem
[1Ti 6:17; n-3c(1); 84] ἀδηλότης

ἀδήλως {85, adverb}
not manifestly, uncertainly, dubiously, 1 Cor 9:26*

ἀδήλως adverb [1C 9:26; adverb; 85] ἀδήλως
ἀδημονεῖν pres act inf
[2t; cv-1d(2); 86] ἀδημονέω

ἀδημονέω {86, cv-1d(2)}
[-, -, -, -, -] *to be depressed* or *dejected, full of*
anguish or *sorrow,* Matt 26:37; Mark 14:33; Phil
2:26*

ἀδημονῶν pres act ptcp nom sg masc
[Pp 2:26; cv-1d(2); 86] "
ᾅδην acc sg masc [2t; n-1f; 87] ᾅδης

ᾅδης, ου, ὁ {87, n-1f}
the invisible abode or *mansion of the dead; the place*

of punishment, hell; the lowest place or *condition*,
Matt 11:23; Luke 10:15

ᾅδης　nom sg masc　[3t; n-1f; 87]　　　　　　"

ἀδιάκριτος, ον　　　　　　　　　{88, a-3a}
undistinguishing, impartial, James 3:17*

ἀδιάκριτος　nom sg fem
　[Jm 3:17; a-3a; 88]　　　　　ἀδιάκριτος
ἀδιάλειπτον　acc sg fem
　[2Ti 1:3; a-3a; 89]　　　　　ἀδιάλειπτος

ἀδιάλειπτος, ον　　　　　　　　{89, a-3a}
unceasing, constant, settled, Rom 9:2; 2 Tim 1:3*

ἀδιάλειπτος　nom sg fem　[Rm 9:2; a-3a; 89]　"

ἀδιαλείπτως　　　　　　　　　{90, adverb}
unceasingly, by an unvarying practice, Rom 1:9; 1
Thess 1:2; 2:13; 5:17*

ἀδιαλείπτως　adverb　[4t; adverb; 90]　ἀδιαλείπτως

ἀδιαφθορία, ας, ἡ　　　　　　　{91, n-1a}
incorruptness, genuineness, pureness, Titus 2:7
v.l.*

ἀδικεῖσθε　pres mid ind 2 pl
　[1C 6:7; v-1d(2a); 92]　　　　　ἀδικέω
ἀδικεῖτε　pres act ind 2 pl　[2t; v-1d(2a); 92]　"

ἀδικέω　　　　　　　　　　{92, v-1d(2a)}
[ἀδικήσω, ἠδίκησα, ἠδίκηκα, -, ἠδικήθην] *to act
unjustly; wrong; injure; violate a law*

ἀδικηθέντος　aor pass ptcp gen sg masc
　[2C 7:12; v-1d(2a); 92]　　　　　"
ἀδικηθῇ　aor pass subj 3 sg
　[Rv 2:11; v-1d(2a); 92]　　　　　"

ἀδίκημα, ατος, τό　　　　　　　{93, n-3c(4)}
an act of injustice, crime, Acts 18:14; 24:20; Rev
18:5*

ἀδίκημα　nom sg neut
　[Ac 18:14; n-3c(4); 93]　　　　ἀδίκημα
ἀδίκημα　acc sg neut　[Ac 24:20; n-3c(4); 93]　"
ἀδικήματα　acc pl neut　[Rv 18:5; n-3c(4); 93]　"
ἀδικῆσαι　aor act inf　[4t; v-1d(2a); 92]　ἀδικέω
ἀδικήσαντος　aor act ptcp gen sg masc
　[2C 7:12; v-1d(2a); 92]　　　　　"
ἀδικησάτω　aor act imperative 3 sg
　[Rv 22:11; v-1d(2a); 92]　　　　　"
ἀδικήσῃ　aor act subj 3 sg
　[Lk 10:19; v-1d(2a); 92]　　　　　"
ἀδικήσῃς　aor act subj 2 sg
　[Rv 6:6; v-1d(2a); 92]　　　　　"
ἀδικήσητε　aor act subj 2 pl
　[Rv 7:3; v-1d(2a); 92]　　　　　"
ἀδικήσουσιν　fut act ind 3 pl
　[Rv 9:4; v-1d(2a); 92]　　　　　"

ἀδικία, ας, ἡ　　　　　　　　{94, n-1a}
injustice, wrong; iniquity, falsehood, deceitfulness

ἀδικία　nom sg fem　[4t; n-1a; 94]　　ἀδικία
ἀδικίᾳ　dat sg fem　[5t; n-1a; 94]　　　"
ἀδικίαις　dat pl fem　[Hb 8:12; n-1a; 94]　"
ἀδικίαν　acc sg fem　[2t; n-1a; 94]　　　"
ἀδικίας　gen sg fem　[13t; n-1a; 94]　　"
ἄδικοι　nom pl masc　[2t; a-3a; 96]　ἄδικος

ἀδικοκρίτης, ου, ὁ　　　　　　　{95, n-1f}
unjust judge, Titus 1:9 v.l.*

ἄδικος, ον　　　　　　　　　{96, a-3a}
*unjust, unrighteous, iniquitous, vicious; deceitful,
fallacious*

ἄδικος　nom sg masc　[4t; a-3a; 96]　　　　"
ἀδικούμενοι　pres pass ptcp nom pl masc
　[2P 2:13; v-1d(2a); 92]　　　　　ἀδικέω
ἀδικούμενον　pres pass ptcp acc sg masc
　[Ac 7:24; v-1d(2a); 92]　　　　　"
ἀδίκους　acc pl masc　[2t; a-3a; 96]　　ἄδικος
ἀδικοῦσιν　pres act ind 3 pl
　[Rv 9:19; v-1d(2a); 92]　　　　　ἀδικέω
ἀδίκῳ　dat sg masc　[Lk 16:11; a-3a; 96]　ἄδικος
ἀδικῶ　pres act ind 1 sg
　[2t; v-1d(2a); 92]　　　　　ἀδικέω
ἀδίκων　gen pl masc　[3t; a-3a; 96]　ἄδικος
ἀδικῶν　pres act ptcp nom sg masc
　[3t; v-1d(2a); 92]　　　　　ἀδικέω

ἀδίκως　　　　　　　　　　{97, adverb}
unjustly, undeservedly, 1 Peter 2:19; 2:23 v.l.*

ἀδίκως　adverb　[1P 2:19; adverb; 97]　ἀδίκως

Ἀδμίν, ὁ　　　　　　　　　{98, n-3g(2)}
Admin, pr. name, indecl, Luke 3:33*

Ἀδμίν　indecl　[Lk 3:33; n-3g(2); 98]　　Ἀδμίν
ἀδόκιμοι　nom pl masc　[5t; a-3a; 99]　ἀδόκιμος
ἀδόκιμον　acc sg masc　[Rm 1:28; a-3a; 99]　"

ἀδόκιμος, ον　　　　　　　　{99, a-3a}
unable to stand test, rejected, refuse, worthless

ἀδόκιμος　nom sg masc　[1C 9:27; a-3a; 99]　"
ἀδόκιμος　nom sg fem　[Hb 6:8; a-3a; 99]　"
ἄδολον　acc sg neut　[1P 2:2; a-3a; 100]　ἄδολος

ἄδολος, ον　　　　　　　　　{100, a-3a}
without deceit, sincere, 1 Peter 2:2*

ᾄδοντες　pres act ptcp nom pl masc
　[2t; v-1b(3); 106]　　　　　ᾄδω
ᾅδου　gen sg masc　[4t; n-1f; 87]　　　ᾅδης
ᾄδουσιν　pres act ind 3 pl
　[3t; v-1b(3); 106]　　　　　ᾄδω

Ἀδραμυττηνός, ή, όν　　　　　{101, a-1a(2a)}
*of Adramyttium, a Greek city on the coast of
Aeolia, in Asia Minor,* Acts 27:2*

Ἀδραμυττηνῷ　dat sg neut
　[Ac 27:2; a-1a(2a); 101]　　　Ἀδραμυττηνός
Ἀδρίᾳ　dat sg masc　[Ac 27:27; n-1d; 102]　Ἀδρίας

Ἀδρίας, ου, ὁ　　　　　　　　{102, n-1d}
the Adriatic sea, Acts 27:27*

ἁδρότης, τητος, ἡ　　　　　　{103, n-3c(1)}
abundance, 2 Cor 8:20*

ἁδρότητι　dat sg fem
　[2C 8:20; n-3c(1); 103]　　　　　ἁδρότης
ἀδύνατα　nom pl neut
　[Lk 18:27; a-3a; 105]　　　　　ἀδύνατος

ἀδυνατέω　　　　　　　　　{104, cv-1d(2a)}
[ἀδυνατήσω, -, -, -, -] *not to be able; to be
impossible,* Matt 17:20; Luke 1:37*

ἀδυνατήσει   fut act ind 3 sg
   [2t; cv-1d(2a); 104]   ἀδυνατέω
ἀδύνατον   nom sg neut [6t; a-3a; 105]   ἀδύνατος
ἀδύνατον   acc sg neut [Rm 8:3; a-3a; 105]   "

ἀδύνατος, ον   {105, a-3a}
   impotent, weak; impossible

ἀδύνατος   nom sg masc [Ac 14:8; a-3a; 105]   "
ἀδυνάτων   gen pl masc [Rm 15:1; a-3a; 105]   "

ᾄδω   {106, v-1b(3)}
   [-, -, -, -, -] *to sing*, Eph 5:19; Col 3:16; Rev 5:9;
   14:3; 15:3*

ἀεί   {107, adverb}
   always, for ever, constantly

ἀεί   adverb [7t; adverb; 107]   ἀεί
ἀέρα   acc sg masc [5t; n-3f(2b); 113]   ἀήρ
ἀέρος   gen sg masc [Ep 2:2; n-3f(2b); 113]   "
ἀετοί   nom pl masc [2t; n-2a; 108]   ἀετός

ἀετός, οῦ, ὁ   {108, n-2a}
   an eagle, Rev 12:14; or *vulture*, Luke 17:37

ἀετοῦ   gen sg masc [2t; n-2a; 108]   "
ἀετῷ   dat sg masc [Rv 4:7; n-2a; 108]   "
ἄζυμα   nom pl neut [Mk 14:1; a-3a; 109]   ἄζυμος
ἄζυμοι   nom pl masc [1C 5:7; a-3a; 109]   "
ἀζύμοις   dat pl neut [1C 5:8; a-3a; 109]   "

ἄζυμος, ον   {109, a-3a}
   unleavened; τὰ ἄζυμα, *the feast of unleavened
   bread*; met. *pure from foreign matter,
   unadulterated, genuine*; τὸ ἄζυμον, *genuineness*, 1
   Cor 5:7, 8

ἀζύμων   gen pl neut [6t; a-3a; 109]   "

Ἀζώρ, ὁ   {110, n-3g(2)}
   Azor, pr. name, indecl, Matt 1:13f.; Luke 3:23-31
   v.l.*

Ἀζώρ   indecl [2t; n-3g(2); 110]   Ἀζώρ
Ἄζωτον   acc sg fem [Ac 8:40; n-2b; 111]   Ἄζωτος

Ἄζωτος, ου, ἡ   {111, n-2b}
   Azotus, Ashdod, a seaport in Palestine, Acts
   8:40*

ἀηδία, ας, ἡ   {112, n-1a}
   literally: *unpleasantness*; figuratively: *enmity*,
   Luke 23:12 v.l.*

ἀήρ, ἀέρος, ὁ   {113, n-3f(2b)}
   air, atmosphere

ἀήρ   nom sg masc [Rv 9:2; n-3f(2b); 113]   ἀήρ

ἀθανασία, ας, ἡ   {114, n-1a}
   immortality, 1 Cor 15:53, 54; 1 Tim 6:16*

ἀθανασίαν   acc sg fem [3t; n-1a; 114]   ἀθανασία
ἀθεμίτοις   dat pl fem
   [1P 4:3; a-3a; 116]   ἀθέμιτος
ἀθέμιτον   nom sg neut [Ac 10:28; a-3a; 116]   "

ἀθέμιτος, ον   {116, a-3a}
   unlawful, criminal, wicked, Acts 10:28; 1 Peter
   4:3*

ἄθεοι   nom pl masc [Ep 2:12; a-3a; 117]   ἄθεος

ἄθεος, ον   {117, a-3a}
   *an atheist; godless, estranged from the knowledge
   and worship of the true God*, Eph 2:12*

ἄθεσμος, ον   {118, a-3a}
   lawless, unrestrained, licentious, 2 Peter 2:7; 3:17*

ἀθέσμων   gen pl masc [2t; a-3a; 118]   ἄθεσμος
ἀθετεῖ   pres act ind 3 sg
   [4t; v-1d(2a); 119]   ἀθετέω
ἀθετεῖτε   pres act ind 2 pl
   [Mk 7:9; v-1d(2a); 119]   "

ἀθετέω   {119, v-1d(2a)}
   [ἀθετήσω, ἠθέτησα, -, -, -] pr. *to displace, set aside;
   to abrogate, annul, violate, swerve from; reject,
   condemn*

ἀθετῆσαι   aor act inf [Mk 6:26; v-1d(2a); 119] "
ἀθετήσας   aor act ptcp nom sg masc
   [Hb 10:28; v-1d(2a); 119]   "
ἀθέτησιν   acc sg fem
   [Hb 9:26; n-3e(5b); 120]   ἀθέτησις

ἀθέτησις, εως, ἡ   {120, n-3e(5b)}
   abrogation, annulling, Heb 7:18; 9:26*

ἀθέτησις   nom sg fem [Hb 7:18; n-3e(5b); 120] "
ἀθετήσω   fut act ind 1 sg
   [1C 1:19; v-1d(2a); 119]   ἀθετέω
ἀθετοῦσιν   pres act ind 3 pl
   [Jd 8; v-1d(2a); 119]   "
ἀθετῶ   pres act ind 1 sg
   [Ga 2:21; v-1d(2a); 119]   "
ἀθετῶν   pres act ptcp nom sg masc
   [4t; v-1d(2a); 119]   "

Ἀθηνᾶ, ᾶς, ἡ   {121, n-1h}
   Athens, one of the most important cities of
   Greece, called from Ἀθήνη, *Minerva*, to whom
   it was dedicated. Often listed as the plural
   Ἀθῆναι, ῶν, αἱ

Ἀθηναῖοι   nom pl masc
   [Ac 17:21; a-1a(1); 122]   Ἀθηναῖος
Ἀθηναῖοι   voc pl masc [Ac 17:22; a-1a(1); 122] "

Ἀθηναῖος, α, ον   {122, a-1a(1)}
   Athenian, inhabiting or *belonging to Athens*, Acts
   17:21, 22*

Ἀθήναις   dat pl fem [2t; n-1h; 121]   Ἀθῆναι
Ἀθηνῶν   gen pl fem [2t; n-1h; 121]   "

ἀθλέω   {123, v-1d(2a)}
   [-, ἤθλησα, ἤθληκα, -, -] *to strive, contend, be a
   champion in the public games*, 2 Tim 2:5*

ἀθλῇ   pres act subj 3 sg
   [2Ti 2:5; v-1d(2a); 123]   ἀθλέω
ἀθλήσῃ   aor act subj 3 sg
   [2Ti 2:5; v-1d(2a); 123]   "
ἄθλησιν   acc sg fem
   [Hb 10:32; n-3e(5b); 124]   ἄθλησις

ἄθλησις, εως, ἡ   {124, n-3e(5b)}
   contest, combat, struggle, conflict, Heb 10:32*

ἀθροίζω   {125, v-2a(1)}
   [-, ἤθροισα, -, ἤθροισμαι, ἠθροίσθην] *to collect,
   gather*, Luke 24:33*

ἀθυμέω   {126, cv-1d(2a)}
[-, -, -, -, -] *to be discouraged, lose heart*, Col 3:21*

ἀθυμῶσιν   pres act subj 3 pl
    [Cl 3:21; cv-1d(2a); 126]   ἀθυμέω
ἄθῷον   acc sg neut [Mt 27:4; a-3a; 127]   ἄθῷος

ἄθῷος, ον   {127, a-3a}
    unpunished; metaph. *innocent,* Matt 27:4, 24*

ἄθῷος   nom sg masc [Mt 27:24; a-3a; 127]   "
αἱ   nom pl fem [151t; a-1a(2b); 3836]   ὁ
αἱ   voc pl fem [3t; a-1a(2b); 3836]   "
αἰγείοις   dat pl neut
    [Hb 11:37; a-1a(1); 128]   αἴγειος

αἴγειος, εία, ειον   {128, a-1a(1)}
    belonging to a goat, Heb 11:37*

αἰγιαλόν   acc sg masc [6t; n-2a; 129]   αἰγιαλός

αἰγιαλός, οῦ, ὁ   {129, n-2a}
    seashore, beach, Matt 13:2, 48; John 21:4; Acts
    21:5; 27:39f.*

Αἰγύπτιοι   nom pl masc
    [Hb 11:29; a-1a(1); 130]   Αἰγύπτιος
Αἰγύπτιον   acc sg masc [2t; a-1a(1); 130]   "

Αἰγύπτιος, ια, ιον   {130, a-1a(1)}
    Egyptian

Αἰγύπτιος   nom sg masc [Ac 21:38; a-1a(1); 130]   "
Αἰγυπτίων   gen pl masc [Ac 7:22; a-1a(1); 130]   "
Αἴγυπτον   acc sg fem [12t; n-2b; 131]   Αἴγυπτος

Αἴγυπτος, οῦ, ἡ   {131, n-2b}
    Egypt

Αἴγυπτος   nom sg fem [Rv 11:8; n-2b; 131]   "
Αἰγύπτου   gen sg fem [8t; n-2b; 131]   "
Αἰγύπτῳ   dat sg fem [4t; n-2b; 131]   "
ἀϊδίοις   dat pl masc [Jd 6; a-3a; 132]   ἀΐδιος

ἀΐδιος, ον   {132, a-3a}
    always existing, eternal, Rom 1:20; Jude 6

ἀΐδιος   nom sg fem [Rm 1:20; a-3a; 132]   "
αἰδοῦς   gen sg fem [1Ti 2:9; n-3d(3); 133]   αἰδώς

αἰδώς, αἰδοῦς, ἡ   {133, n-3d(3)}
    modesty, reverence, 1 Tim 2:9; Heb 12:28 v.l.*

Αἰθιόπων   gen pl masc
    [Ac 8:27; n-3a(1); 134]   Αἰθίοψ

Αἰθίοψ, οπος, ὁ   {134, n-3a(1)}
    an Ethiopian, Acts 8:27*

Αἰθίοψ   nom sg masc [Ac 8:27; n-3a(1); 134]   "

αἷμα, ατος, τό   {135, n-3c(4)}
    blood; of the color of blood; bloodshed;
    blood-guiltiness; natural descent

αἷμα   nom sg neut [23t; n-3c(4); 135]   αἷμα
αἷμα   acc sg neut [20t; n-3c(4); 135]   "

αἱματεκχυσία, ας, ἡ   {136, n-1a}
    an effusion or *shedding of blood,* Heb 9:22*

αἱματεκχυσίας   gen sg fem
    [Hb 9:22; n-1a; 136]   αἱματεκχυσία
αἵματι   dat sg neut [20t; n-3c(4); 135]   αἷμα
αἵματος   gen sg neut [33t; n-3c(4); 135]   "

αἱμάτων   gen pl neut [Jn 1:13; n-3c(4); 135]   "

αἱμορροέω   {137, cv-1d(2}
    [-, -, -, -, -] *to have a flow of blood,* Matt 9:20*

αἱμορροοῦσα   pres act ptcp nom sg fem
    [Mt 9:20; cv-1d(2; 137]   αἱμορροέω
Αἰνέα   voc sg masc [Ac 9:34; n-1d; 138]   Αἰνέας
Αἰνέαν   acc sg masc [Ac 9:33; n-1d; 138]   "

Αἰνέας, ου, ὁ   {138, n-1d}
    Aeneas, pr. name, Acts 9:33f.*

αἰνεῖν   pres act inf
    [Lk 19:37; v-1d(2b); 140]   αἰνέω
αἰνεῖτε   pres act imperative 2 pl
    [2t; v-1d(2b); 140]   "
αἰνέσεως   gen sg fem
    [Hb 13:15; n-3e(5b); 139]   αἴνεσις

αἴνεσις, εως, ἡ   {139, n-3e(5b)}
    praise, Heb 13:15*

αἰνέω   {140, v-1d(2b)}
    [-, -, -, -, -] *to praise, celebrate*

αἴνιγμα, ατος, τό   {141, n-3c(4)}
    an enigma, riddle, any thing obscurely expressed or
    intimated, 1 Cor 13:12*

αἰνίγματι   dat sg neut
    [1C 13:12; n-3c(4); 141]   αἴνιγμα
αἶνον   acc sg masc [2t; n-2a; 142]   αἶνος

αἶνος, ου, ὁ   {142, n-2a}
    praise, Matt 21:16; Luke 18:43*

αἰνοῦντα   pres act ptcp acc sg masc
    [Ac 3:9; v-1d(2b); 140]   αἰνέω
αἰνοῦντες   pres act ptcp nom pl masc
    [2t; v-1d(2b); 140]   "
αἰνούντων   pres act ptcp gen pl masc
    [Lk 2:13; v-1d(2b); 140]   "

Αἰνών, ἡ   {143, n-3g(2)}
    Enon, pr. name, indecl, where John was
    baptizing, John 3:23*

Αἰνών   indecl [Jn 3:23; n-3g(2); 143]   Αἰνών
αἰνῶν   pres act ptcp nom sg masc
    [Ac 3:8; v-1d(2b); 140]   αἰνέω

αἴξ, αἰγός, ὁ or ἡ   {144, n-3b(2)}
    goat, Luke 15:29 v.l.*

αἶρε   pres act imperative 2 sg
    [3t; v-2d(2); 149]   αἴρω
αἴρει   pres act ind 3 sg [8t; v-2d(2); 149]   "
αἴρεις   pres act ind 2 sg [2t; v-2d(2); 149]   "
αἱρέσεις   nom pl fem
    [Ga 5:20; n-3e(5b); 146]   αἵρεσις
αἱρέσεις   acc pl fem [2t; n-3e(5b); 146]   "
αἱρέσεως   gen sg fem [3t; n-3e(5b); 146]   "
αἵρεσιν   acc sg fem [2t; n-3e(5b); 146]   "

αἵρεσις, εως, ἡ   {146, n-3e(5b)}
    strictly, *a choice* or *option;* hence, *a religious sect,*
    faction; by implication, *discord, contention*

αἵρεσις   nom sg fem [Ac 5:17; n-3e(5b); 146]   "
αἴρεται   pres pass ind 3 sg
    [Ac 8:33; v-2d(2); 149]   αἴρω

αἴρετε   pres act imperative 2 pl
   [Lk 9:3; v-2d(2); 149]   "

αἱρετίζω   {147, v-2a(1)}
   [-, ἡρέτισα, -, -, -] *to choose, choose with delight* or
   love, Matt 12:18*

αἱρετικόν   acc sg masc
   [Ti 3:10; a-1a(2a); 148]   αἱρετικός

αἱρετικός, ή, όν   {148, a-1a(2a)}
   one who creates or *fosters factions,* Titus 3:10*

αἱρέω   {145, v-1d(2a)}
   [αἱρήσω, εἷλα or εἷλον, -, ἥρημαι, ἡρέθην] some
   list as deponent αἱρέομαι, *to take;* mid. *to choose*

αἱρήσομαι   fut mid ind 1 sg
   [Pp 1:22; v-1d(2a); 145]   αἱρέω
αἱρόμενον   pres pass ptcp acc sg masc
   [Mk 2:3; v-2d(2); 149]   αἴρω
αἴροντος   pres act ptcp gen sg masc
   [2t; v-2d(2); 149]   "

αἴρω   {149, v-2d(2)}
   [ἀρῶ, ἦρα, ἦρκα, ἦρμαι, ἤρθην] *to take up, lift,*
   raise; bear, carry; take away, remove; destroy, kill

αἴρων   pres act ptcp nom sg masc
   [2t; v-2d(2); 149]   "
αἴρωσιν   pres act subj 3 pl
   [Mk 6:8; v-2d(2); 149]   "
αἷς   dat pl fem [14t; a-1a(2b); 4005]   ὅς

αἰσθάνομαι   {150, v-3a(2a)}
   [-, ἠσθόμην, -, -, -] *to perceive, understand,* Luke
   9:45*

αἰσθήσει   dat sg fem
   [Pp 1:9; n-3e(5b); 151]   αἴσθησις

αἴσθησις, εως, ἡ   {151, n-3e(5b)}
   perception, understanding, Phil 1:9*

αἰσθητήρια   acc pl neut
   [Hb 5:14; n-2c; 152]   αἰσθητήριον

αἰσθητήριον, ου, τό   {152, n-2c}
   an organ of perception; internal sense, Heb 5:14*

αἴσθωνται   aor mid subj 3 pl
   [Lk 9:45; v-3a(2a); 150]   αἰσθάνομαι
αἰσχροκερδεῖς   acc pl masc
   [1Ti 3:8; a-4a; 153]   αἰσχροκερδής
αἰσχροκερδῆ   acc sg masc [Ti 1:7; a-4a; 153]   "

αἰσχροκερδής, ές   {153, a-4a}
   eager for dishonorable gain, greedy, 1 Tim 3:3 v.l.,
   8; Titus 1:7*

αἰσχροκερδῶς   {154, adverb}
   for the sake of base gain, greedily, 1 Peter 5:2*

αἰσχροκερδῶς   adverb
   [1P 5:2; adverb; 154]   αἰσχροκερδῶς

αἰσχρολογία, ας, ἡ   {155, n-1a}
   vile or *obscene language, foul talk,* Col 3:8*

αἰσχρολογίαν   acc sg fem
   [Cl 3:8; n-1a; 155]   αἰσχρολογία
αἰσχρόν   nom sg neut [3t; a-1a(1); 156]   αἰσχρός

αἰσχρός, ά, όν   {156, a-1a(1)}
   strictly, *deformed,* opposed to καλός; metaph.

shameful, indecent, dishonorable, vile, 1 Cor 11:6;
   14:35; Eph 5:12; Titus 1:11*

αἰσχρότης, τητος, ἡ   {157, n-3c(1)}
   obscenity, indecency, Eph 5:4*

αἰσχρότης   nom sg fem
   [Ep 5:4; n-3c(1); 157]   αἰσχρότης
αἰσχροῦ   gen sg neut
   [Ti 1:11; a-1a(1); 156]   αἰσχρός
αἰσχύνας   acc pl fem
   [Jd 13; n-1b; 158]   αἰσχύνη
αἰσχυνέσθω   pres mid imperative 3 sg
   [1P 4:16; v-1c(2); 159]   αἰσχύνω

αἰσχύνη, ης, ἡ   {158, n-1b}
   shame, disgrace; cause of shame, dishonorable
   conduct

αἰσχύνη   nom sg fem [Rv 3:18; n-1b; 158]   αἰσχύνη
αἰσχύνη   dat sg fem [Pp 3:19; n-1b; 158]   "
αἰσχύνης   gen sg fem [3t; n-1b; 158]   "
αἰσχυνθήσομαι   fut pass ind 1 sg
   [2t; v-1c(2); 159]   αἰσχύνω
αἰσχυνθῶμεν   aor pass subj 1 pl
   [1J 2:28; v-1c(2); 159]   "

αἰσχύνομαι   {159, v-1c(2)}
   [-, -, -, ᾔσχυμμαι, ᾐσχύνθην] some list as an
   active αἰσχύνω, *to be ashamed, confounded*

αἰσχύνομαι   pres mid ind 1 sg
   [Lk 16:3; v-1c(2); 159]   "
αἰτεῖν   pres act inf
   [Ac 3:2; v-1d(2a); 160]   αἰτέω
αἰτεῖς   pres act ind 2 sg
   [Jn 4:9; v-1d(2a); 160]   "
αἰτεῖσθαι   pres mid inf [2t; v-1d(2a); 160]   "
αἰτεῖσθε   pres mid ind 2 pl [4t; v-1d(2a); 160]   "
αἰτεῖτε   pres act imperative 2 pl
   [3t; v-1d(2a); 160]   "
αἰτεῖτε   pres act ind 2 pl
   [Jm 4:3; v-1d(2a); 160]   "
αἰτείτω   pres act imperative 3 sg
   [2t; v-1d(2a); 160]   "

αἰτέω   {160, v-1d(2a)}
   [αἰτήσω, ᾔτησα, ᾔτηκα, ᾔτημαι, -] *to ask, request;*
   demand; desire, Acts 7:46

αἴτημα, ατος, τό   {161, n-3c(4)}
   a thing asked or *sought for; petition, request,* Luke
   23:24; Phil 4:6; 1 John 5:15*

αἴτημα   acc sg neut
   [Lk 23:24; n-3c(4); 161]   αἴτημα
αἰτήματα   nom pl neut [Pp 4:6; n-3c(4); 161]   "
αἰτήματα   acc pl neut [1J 5:15; n-3c(4); 161]   "
αἰτῆσαι   aor act inf
   [Mt 6:8; v-1d(2a); 160]   αἰτέω
αἰτήσας   aor act ptcp nom sg masc
   [2t; v-1d(2a); 160]   "
αἰτήσασθε   aor mid imperative 2 pl
   [Jn 15:7; v-1d(2a); 160]   "
αἰτήσει   fut act ind 3 sg [5t; v-1d(2a); 160]   "
αἰτήσεσθε   fut mid ind 2 pl
   [Jn 16:26; v-1d(2a); 160]   "

αἰτήσῃ   aor mid subj 2 sg
   [Jn 11:22; v-1d(2a); 160]   "
αἰτήσῃς   aor act subj 2 sg
   [Mk 6:23; v-1d(2a); 160]
αἰτήσηται   aor mid subj 3 sg
   [Mt 14:7; v-1d(2a); 160]   "
αἰτήσητε   aor act subj 2 pl   [5t; v-1d(2a); 160]   "
αἴτησον   aor act imperative 2 sg
   [Mk 6:22; v-1d(2a); 160]   "
αἰτήσουσιν   fut act ind 3 pl
   [Lk 12:48; v-1d(2a); 160]   "
αἰτήσωμαι   aor mid subj 1 sg
   [Mk 6:24; v-1d(2a); 160]   "
αἰτήσωμεν   aor act subj 1 pl
   [Mk 10:35; v-1d(2a); 160]   "
αἰτήσωνται   aor mid subj 3 pl
   [2t; v-1d(2a); 160]   "

αἰτία, ας, ἡ   {162, n-1a}
   cause, motive, incitement; accusation, crime, case

αἰτία   nom sg fem   [2t; n-1a; 162]   αἰτία

αἰτίαμα, τος, τό   {163, n-3c(4)}
   charge, accusation, Acts 25:7 v.l.*

αἰτίαν   acc sg fem   [16t; n-1a; 162]   "

αἰτιάομαι   {164, v-1d(1b)}
   [-, -, -, -, -] to charge, Rom 3:9 v.l.*

αἰτίας   gen sg fem   [Mk 15:26; n-1a; 162]   "
αἰτίας   acc pl fem   [Ac 25:27; n-1a; 162]   "
αἴτινες   nom pl fem   [10t; a-1a(2b); 4015]   ὅστις
αἴτιον   acc sg neut   [3t; a-1a(1); 165]   αἴτιος

αἴτιος, ια, ον   {165, a-1a(1)}
   causative; αἴτιος, an author or causer, Heb 5:9; τὸ
   αἴτιον, equivalent to αἰτία

αἴτιος   nom sg masc   [Hb 5:9; a-1a(1); 165] "
αἰτίου   gen sg neut   [Ac 19:40; a-1a(1); 165]   "

αἰτίωμα, ατος, τό   {166, n-3c(4)}
   charge, accusation, Acts 25:7*

αἰτιώματα   acc pl neut
   [Ac 25:7; n-3c(4); 166]   αἰτίωμα
αἰτοῦμαι   pres mid ind 1 sg
   [Ep 3:13; v-1d(2a); 160]   αἰτέω
αἰτούμεθα   pres mid ind 1 pl
   [Ep 3:20; v-1d(2a); 160]   "
αἰτούμενοι   pres mid ptcp nom pl masc
   [4t; v-1d(2a); 160]   "
αἰτοῦντι   pres act ptcp dat sg masc
   [3t; v-1d(2a); 160]   "
αἰτοῦσα   pres act ptcp nom sg fem
   [Mt 20:20; v-1d(2a); 160]   "
αἰτοῦσιν   pres act ind 3 pl
   [1C 1:22; v-1d(2a); 160]   "
αἰτοῦσιν   pres act ptcp dat pl masc
   [2t; v-1d(2a); 160]   "
αἰτώμεθα   pres mid subj 1 pl   [2t; v-1d(2a); 160]   "
αἰτῶμεν   pres act subj 1 pl
   [1J 3:22; v-1d(2a); 160]   "
αἰτῶν   pres act ptcp nom sg masc
   [2t; v-1d(2a); 160]   "

αἰφνίδιος, ον   {167, a-3a}
   unforeseen, unexpected, sudden, Luke 21:34; 1
   Thess 5:3*

αἰφνίδιος   nom sg masc
   [1Th 5:3; a-3a; 167]   αἰφνίδιος
αἰφνίδιος   nom sg fem   [Lk 21:34; a-3a; 167]   "

αἰχμαλωσία, ας, ἡ   {168, n-1a}
   captivity, state of captivity; captive multitude, Eph
   4:8; Rev 13:10; Heb 7:1 v.l.*

αἰχμαλωσίαν   acc sg fem
   [3t; n-1a; 168]   αἰχμαλωσία

αἰχμαλωτεύω   {169, v-1a(6)}
   [-, ἠχμαλώτευσα, -, -, -] to lead captive; met. to
   captivate, Eph 4:8; 2 Tim 3:6 v.l.*

αἰχμαλωτίζοντα   pres act ptcp acc sg masc
   [Rm 7:23; v-2a(1); 170]   αἰχμαλωτίζω
αἰχμαλωτίζοντες   pres act ptcp nom pl masc
   [2t; v-2a(1); 170]   "

αἰχμαλωτίζω   {170, v-2a(1)}
   [-, -, -, -, ἠχμαλωτίσθην] to lead captive; by impl.
   to subject, Luke 21:24; Rom 7:23; 2 Cor 10:5; 2
   Tim 3:6*

αἰχμαλωτισθήσονται   fut pass ind 3 pl
   [Lk 21:24; v-2a(1); 170]   "
αἰχμαλώτοις   dat pl masc
   [Lk 4:18; n-2a; 171]   αἰχμάλωτος

αἰχμάλωτος, ώτου, ὁ   {171, n-2a}
   a captive, Luke 4:18*

αἰών, ῶνος, ὁ   {172, n-3f(1a)}
   pr. a period of time of significant character; life; an
   era; an age: hence, a state of things marking an age
   or era; the present order of nature; the natural
   condition of man, the world; ὁ αἰών, illimitable
   duration, eternity; as also, οἱ αἰῶνες, ὁ αἰὼν τῶν
   αἰώνων, οἱ αἰῶνες τῶν αἰώνων; by an Aramaism
   οἱ αἰῶνες, the material universe, Heb 1:2

αἰῶνα   acc sg masc   [31t; n-3f(1a); 172]   αἰών
αἰῶνας   acc pl masc   [30t; n-3f(1a); 172]   "
αἰῶνι   dat sg masc   [8t; n-3f(1a); 172]   "
αἰώνια   nom pl neut
   [2C 4:18; a-3b(1); 173]   αἰώνιος
αἰωνίαν   acc sg fem   [2t; a-3b(1); 173]   "
αἰωνίοις   dat pl masc   [Rm 16:25; a-3b(1); 173]   "
αἰώνιον   nom sg neut   [1Ti 6:16; a-3b(1); 173]   "
αἰώνιον   acc sg masc   [2t; a-3b(1); 173]   "
αἰώνιον   acc sg fem   [38t; a-3b(1); 173]   "
αἰώνιον   acc sg neut   [4t; a-3b(1); 173]   "

αἰώνιος, ία, ον   {173, a-3b(1)}
   indeterminate as to duration, eternal, everlasting

αἰώνιος   nom sg fem   [4t; a-3b(1); 173]   "
αἰωνίου   gen sg masc   [Rm 16:26; a-3b(1); 173]   "
αἰωνίου   gen sg fem   [9t; a-3b(1); 173]   "
αἰωνίου   gen sg neut   [4t; a-3b(1); 173]   "
αἰωνίου   gen pl masc   [Ti 1:2; a-3b(1); 173]   "
αἰωνίους   acc pl fem   [Lk 16:9; a-3b(1); 173]   "
αἰωνίων   gen pl masc   [2t; a-3b(1); 173]   "
αἰῶνος   gen sg masc   [25t; n-3f(1a); 172]   αἰών
αἰώνων   gen pl masc   [27t; n-3f(1a); 172]   "

αἰῶσιν dat pl masc [Ep 2:7; n-3f(1a); 172] "

ἀκαθαρσία, ας, ἡ {174, n-1a}
uncleanness; lewdness; impurity of motive, 1 Thess 2:3

ἀκαθαρσία nom sg fem [2t; n-1a; 174] ἀκαθαρσία
ἀκαθαρσίᾳ dat sg fem [3t; n-1a; 174] "
ἀκαθαρσίαν acc sg fem [2t; n-1a; 174] "
ἀκαθαρσίας gen sg fem [3t; n-1a; 174] "
ἀκάθαρτα nom pl neut [3t; a-3a; 176] ἀκάθαρτος
ἀκάθαρτα acc pl neut [3t; a-3a; 176] "

ἀκαθάρτης, ητος, ἡ {175}
impurity, Rev 17:4 v.l.*

ἀκαθάρτοις dat pl neut [2t; a-3a; 176] "
ἀκάθαρτον nom sg neut [4t; a-3a; 176] "
ἀκάθαρτον voc sg neut [Mk 5:8; a-3a; 176] "
ἀκάθαρτον acc sg masc [Ac 10:28; a-3a; 176] "
ἀκάθαρτον acc sg neut [3t; a-3a; 176] "

ἀκάθαρτος, ον {176, a-3a}
impure, unclean; lewd; foul

ἀκάθαρτος nom sg masc [Ep 5:5; a-3a; 176] "
ἀκαθάρτου gen sg neut [5t; a-3a; 176] "
ἀκαθάρτῳ dat sg neut [5t; a-3a; 176] "
ἀκαθάρτων gen pl neut [4t; a-3a; 176] "

ἀκαιρέομαι {177, v-1d(2b)}
[-, -, -, -, ἠκαιρέθην] to be without opportunity or occasion, Phil 4:10*

ἀκαίρως {178, adverb}
unseasonably, 2 Tim 4:2*

ἀκαίρως adverb [2Ti 4:2; adverb; 178] ἀκαίρως

ἄκακος, ον {179, a-3a}
free from evil, innocent, blameless; simple, Rom 16:18; Heb 7:26*

ἄκακος nom sg masc [Hb 7:26; a-3a; 179] ἄκακος
ἀκάκων gen pl masc [Rm 16:18; a-3a; 179] "

ἄκανθα, ης, ἡ {180, n-1c}
a thorn, thornbush, Matt 7:16

ἄκανθαι nom pl fem [3t; n-1c; 180] ἄκανθα
ἀκάνθας acc pl fem [6t; n-1c; 180] "
ἀκάνθινον acc sg masc [2t; a-1a(2a); 181] ἀκάνθινος

ἀκάνθινος, η, ον {181, a-1a(2a)}
thorny, made of thorns, Mark 15:17; John 19:5*

ἀκανθῶν gen pl fem [5t; n-1c; 180] ἄκανθα
ἄκαρπα nom pl neut [Jd 12; a-3a; 182] ἄκαρπος
ἄκαρποι nom pl masc [Ti 3:14; a-3a; 182] "
ἀκάρποις dat pl neut [Ep 5:11; a-3a; 182] "

ἄκαρπος, ον {182, a-3a}
without fruit, unfruitful, barren; by impl. noxious

ἄκαρπος nom sg masc [3t; a-3a; 182] "
ἀκάρπους acc pl masc [2P 1:8; a-3a; 182] "
ἀκατάγνωστον acc sg masc [Ti 2:8; a-3a; 183] ἀκατάγνωστος

ἀκατάγνωστος, ον {183, a-3a}
pr. not worthy of condemnation by a judge; hence, irreprehensible, Tit 2:8*

ἀκατακάλυπτον acc sg fem [1C 11:13; a-3a; 184] ἀκατακάλυπτος

ἀκατακάλυπτος, ον {184, a-3a}
uncovered, unveiled, 1 Cor 11:5, 13*

ἀκατακαλύπτω dat sg fem [1C 11:5; a-3a; 184] "
ἀκατάκριτον acc sg masc [Ac 22:25; a-3a; 185] ἀκατάκριτος

ἀκατάκριτος, ον {185, a-3a}
uncondemned in a public trial, Acts 16:37; 22:25*

ἀκατακρίτους acc pl masc [Ac 16:37; a-3a; 185] "

ἀκατάλυτος, ον {186, a-3a}
incapable of dissolution, indissoluble; hence, enduring, everlasting, Heb 7:16*

ἀκαταλύτου gen sg fem [Hb 7:16; a-3a; 186] ἀκατάλυτος

ἀκατάπαστος, ον {187, a-3a}
unsatisfied, insatiable, 2 Pet 2:14 v.l. for ἀκατάπαυστος*

ἀκατάπαυστος, ον {188, a-3a}
also spelled ἀκατάπαστος, which cannot be restrained from a thing, unceasing, 2 Pet 2:14*

ἀκαταπαύστους acc pl masc [2P 2:14; a-3a; 188] ἀκατάπαυστος

ἀκαταστασία, ας, ἡ {189, n-1a}
pr. instability; hence, an unsettled state; disorder, commotion, tumult, sedition, Luke 21:9; 1 Cor 14:33; 2 Cor 6:5; 12:20; James 3:16*

ἀκαταστασία nom sg fem [Jm 3:16; n-1a; 189] ἀκαταστασία
ἀκαταστασίαι nom pl fem [2C 12:20; n-1a; 189] "
ἀκαταστασίαις dat pl fem [2C 6:5; n-1a; 189] "
ἀκαταστασίας gen sg fem [1C 14:33; n-1a; 189] "
ἀκαταστασίας acc pl fem [Lk 21:9; n-1a; 189] "
ἀκατάστατον nom sg neut [Jm 3:8; a-3a; 190] ἀκατάστατος

ἀκατάστατος, ον {190, a-3a}
unstable, inconstant; unquiet, turbulent, James 1:8; 3:8*

ἀκατάστατος nom sg masc [Jm 1:8; a-3a; 190] "

ἀκατάσχετος, ον {191, a-3a}
not coercible, irrestrainable, untamable, unruly, James 3:8 v.l.*

Ἀκελδαμάχ {192, n-3g(2)}
Akeldama, pr. name, indecl, Acts 1:19*

Ἀκελδαμάχ indecl [Ac 1:19; n-3g(2); 192] Ἀκελδαμάχ
ἀκέραιοι nom pl masc [2t; a-3a; 193] ἀκέραιος

ἀκέραιος, ον {193, a-3a}
pr. unmixed: hence, without mixture of vice or deceit, sincere, blameless, Matt 10:16; Rom 16:19; Phil 2:15*

ἀκεραίους acc pl masc [Rm 16:19; a-3a; 193] "

ἀκηδεμονέω, v.l. for ἀδημονέω at Mark 14:33* {195, v-1d(2a)}

ἀκηκόαμεν   perf act ind 1 pl
    [6t; v-1a(8); 201]   ἀκούω
ἀκηκόασιν   perf act ind 3 pl
    [Rm 15:21; v-1a(8); 201]   "
ἀκηκόατε   perf act ind 2 pl   [2t; v-1a(8); 201]   "
ἀκηκοότας   perf act ptcp acc pl masc
    [Jn 18:21; v-1a(8); 201]   "
ἀκλινῆ   acc sg fem   [Hb 10:23; a-4a; 195]   ἀκλινής

ἀκλινής, ες   {195, a-4a}
    not declining, unwavering, steady, Heb 10:23*

ἀκμάζω   {196, v-2a(1)}
    [-, ἤκμασα, -, -, -] *to flourish, ripen, be in one's
    prime,* Rev 14:18*

ἀκμήν   {197, adverb}
    pr. *the point of a weapon; point of time:* ἀκμήν, *for*
    κατὰκμήν, adv., *yet, still, even now,* Matt 15:16;
    Heb 5:13 v.l.*

ἀκμήν   adverb   [Mt 15:16; adverb; 197]   ἀκμήν
ἀκοαί   nom pl fem   [Mk 7:35; n-1b; 198]   ἀκοή
ἀκοαῖς   dat pl fem   [Hb 5:11; n-1b; 198]   "
ἀκοάς   acc pl fem   [4t; n-1b; 198]   "

ἀκοή, ῆς, ἡ   {198, n-1b}
    hearing; the act or *sense of hearing,* 1 Cor 12:17; 2
    Peter 2:8; *the instrument of hearing, the ear,* Mark
    7:35; *a thing heard;* announcement, *instruction,
    doctrine,* John 12:38; Rom 10:16; *report,* Matt
    4:24, et al

ἀκοή   nom sg fem   [5t; n-1b; 198]   "
ἀκοῇ   dat sg fem   [5t; n-1b; 198]   "
ἀκοήν   acc sg fem   [3t; n-1b; 198]   "
ἀκοῆς   gen sg fem   [5t; n-1b; 198]   "
ἀκολούθει   pres act imperative 2 sg
    [12t; v-1d(2a); 199]   ἀκολουθέω
ἀκολουθεῖ   pres act ind 3 sg   [4t; v-1d(2a); 199]   "
ἀκολουθεῖν   pres act inf
    [Mk 8:34; v-1d(2a); 199]   "
ἀκολουθείτω   pres act imperative 3 sg
    [4t; v-1d(2a); 199]   "

ἀκολουθέω   {199, v-1d(2a)}
    [ἀκολουθήσω, ἠκολούθησα, ἠκολούθηκα, -, -] *to
    follow; follow* as a disciple; *imitate*

ἀκολουθῆσαι   aor act inf   [2t; v-1d(2a); 199]   "
ἀκολουθήσαντες   aor act ptcp nom pl masc
    [Mt 19:28; v-1d(2a); 199]   "
ἀκολουθησάντων   aor act ptcp gen pl masc
    [Jn 1:40; v-1d(2a); 199]   "
ἀκολουθήσατε   aor act imperative 2 pl
    [2t; v-1d(2a); 199]   "
ἀκολουθήσεις   fut act ind 2 sg
    [Jn 13:36; v-1d(2a); 199]   "
ἀκολουθήσουσιν   fut act ind 3 pl
    [Jn 10:5; v-1d(2a); 199]   "
ἀκολουθήσω   fut act ind 1 sg   [3t; v-1d(2a); 199]   "
ἀκολουθοῦντα   pres act ptcp acc sg masc
    [Jn 21:20; v-1d(2a); 199]   "
ἀκολουθοῦντας   pres act ptcp acc pl masc
    [Jn 1:38; v-1d(2a); 199]   "
ἀκολουθοῦντες   pres act ptcp nom pl masc
    [4t; v-1d(2a); 199]   "

ἀκολουθοῦντι   pres act ptcp dat sg masc
    [Lk 7:9; v-1d(2a); 199]   "
ἀκολουθούσης   pres act ptcp gen sg fem
    [1C 10:4; v-1d(2a); 199]   "
ἀκολουθοῦσιν   pres act ind 3 pl
    [2t; v-1d(2a); 199]   "
ἀκολουθοῦσιν   pres act ptcp dat pl masc
    [Mt 8:10; v-1d(2a); 199]   "
ἀκολουθῶν   pres act ptcp nom sg masc
    [2t; v-1d(2a); 199]   "
ἄκουε   pres act imperative 2 sg
    [Mk 12:29; v-1a(8); 201]   ἀκούω
ἀκούει   pres act ind 3 sg   [14t; v-1a(8); 201]   "
ἀκούειν   pres act inf   [20t; v-1a(8); 201]   "
ἀκούεις   pres act ind 2 sg   [4t; v-1a(8); 201]   "
ἀκούεται   pres pass ind 3 sg
    [1C 5:1; v-1a(8); 201]   "
ἀκούετε   pres act imperative 2 pl
    [5t; v-1a(8); 201]   "
ἀκούετε   pres act ind 2 pl   [14t; v-1a(8); 201]   "
ἀκουέτω   pres act imperative 3 sg
    [7t; v-1a(8); 201]   "
ἀκούομεν   pres act ind 1 pl   [3t; v-1a(8); 201]   "
ἀκούοντα   pres act ptcp nom pl neut
    [Ac 13:48; v-1a(8); 201]   "
ἀκούοντα   pres act ptcp acc sg masc
    [Lk 2:46; v-1a(8); 201]   "
ἀκούοντας   pres act ptcp acc pl masc
    [6t; v-1a(8); 201]   "
ἀκούοντες   pres act ptcp nom pl masc
    [15t; v-1a(8); 201]   "
ἀκούοντι   pres act ptcp dat sg masc
    [Rv 22:18; v-1a(8); 201]   "
ἀκούοντος   pres act ptcp gen sg masc
    [2t; v-1a(8); 201]   "
ἀκουόντων   pres act ptcp gen pl masc
    [2t; v-1a(8); 201]   "
ἀκούουσιν   pres act ind 3 pl   [7t; v-1a(8); 201]   "
ἀκούουσιν   pres act ptcp dat pl masc
    [2t; v-1a(8); 201]   "
ἀκοῦσαι   aor act inf   [17t; v-1a(8); 201]   "
ἀκούσαντες   aor act ptcp nom pl masc
    [52t; v-1a(8); 201]   "
ἀκουσάντων   aor act ptcp gen pl masc
    [3t; v-1a(8); 201]   "
ἀκούσας   aor act ptcp nom sg masc
    [33t; v-1a(8); 201]   "
ἀκούσασα   aor act ptcp nom sg fem
    [2t; v-1a(8); 201]   "
ἀκούσασιν   aor act ptcp dat pl masc
    [Hb 4:2; v-1a(8); 201]   "
ἀκούσατε   aor act imperative 2 pl
    [10t; v-1a(8); 201]   "
ἀκουσάτω   aor act imperative 3 sg
    [8t; v-1a(8); 201]   "
ἀκουσάτωσαν   aor act imperative 3 pl
    [Lk 16:29; v-1a(8); 201]   "
ἀκούσει   fut act ind 3 sg   [2t; v-1a(8); 201]   "
ἀκούσεσθε   fut mid ind 2 pl
    [Ac 3:22; v-1a(8); 201]   "
ἀκούσετε   fut act ind 2 pl   [2t; v-1a(8); 201]   "
ἀκούσῃ   aor act subj 3 sg   [7t; v-1a(8); 201]   "

ἀκούσῃ　fut mid ind 2 sg
[Ac 25:22; v-1a(8); 201]　　　　"
ἀκούσητε　aor act subj 2 pl [5t; v-1a(8); 201]　　"
ἀκουσθεῖσιν　aor pass ptcp dat pl neut
[Hb 2:1; v-1a(8); 201]　　　　"
ἀκουσθῇ　aor pass subj 3 sg [4t; v-1a(8); 201]　"
ἀκουσθήσεται　fut pass ind 3 sg
[Lk 12:3; v-1a(8); 201]　　　　"
ἀκουσόμεθα　fut mid ind 1 pl
[Ac 17:32; v-1a(8); 201]　　　　"
ἀκούσονται　fut mid ind 3 pl [2t; v-1a(8); 201]　"
ἀκούσουσιν　fut act ind 3 pl [3t; v-1a(8); 201]　"
ἀκούσωσιν　aor act subj 3 pl [8t; v-1a(8); 201]　"

ἀκούω　　　　　　　{201, v-1a(8)}
[ἀκούσω, ἤκουσα, ἀκήκοα, -, ἠκούσθην] some
list the future active as a middle deponent,
ἀκούσομαι, *to hear; to hearken, listen to,* Mark 4:3;
Luke 19:48; *to heed, obey,* Matt 18:15; Acts 4:19;
to understand, 1 Cor 14:2; *to take in* or *admit to*
mental acceptance, Mark 4:33; John 8:43, 47

ἀκούω　pres act ind 1 sg [4t; v-1a(8); 201]　　"
ἀκούω　pres act subj 1 sg [2t; v-1a(8); 201]　　"
ἀκούων　pres act ptcp nom sg masc
[13t; v-1a(8); 201]　　　　"
ἀκούωσιν　pres act subj 3 pl
[Mk 4:12; v-1a(8); 201]　　　　"

ἀκρασία, ας, ἡ　　　　　{202, n-1a}
intemperance, self-indulgence, Matt 23:25; *unruly*
appetite, lustfulness, 1 Cor 7:5*

ἀκρασίαν　acc sg fem [1C 7:5; n-1a; 202]　　ἀκρασία
ἀκρασίας　gen sg fem [Mt 23:25; n-1a; 202]　"
ἀκρατεῖς　nom pl masc
[2Ti 3:3; a-4a; 203]　　　　ἀκρατής

ἀκρατής, ες　　　　　{203, a-4a}
without self-control, intemperate, 2 Tim 3:3

ἄκρατος, ον　　　　　{204, a-3a}
unmixed, unmingled wine, Rev 14:10*

ἀκράτου　gen sg masc
[Rv 14:10; a-3a; 204]　　　　ἄκρατος

ἀκρίβεια, ας, ἡ　　　　{205, n-1a}
accuracy, exactness; preciseness, or *rigor, severe*
discipline, Acts 22:3*

ἀκρίβειαν　acc sg fem
[Ac 22:3; n-1a; 205]　　　　ἀκρίβεια
ἀκριβεστάτην　acc sg fem superlative
[Ac 26:5; a-4a; 207]　　　　ἀκριβής

ἀκριβέστερον　　　　　{206, a-1a(2a)}
Comparative of ἀκριβῶς, *more exactly* or
accurately, Acts 18:26, Acts 24:22

ἀκριβέστερον　adverb-comparative
[4t; adverb; 209]　　　　ἀκριβῶς

ἀκριβής, ές　　　　　{207, a-4a}
exact, strict, Acts 26:5*

ἀκριβόω　　　　　　{208, v-1d(3)}
[-, ἠκρίβωσα, -, -, -] *to inquire accurately* or
diligently, Matt 2:7, 16 (see v. 8)*

ἀκριβῶς　　　　　　{209, adverb}
accurately, diligently, Matt 2:8; Luke 1:3; Acts
18:25; *circumspectly, strictly,* Eph 5:15; *precisely,*
distinctly, 1 Thess 5:2

ἀκριβῶς　adverb [5t; adverb; 209]　　"
ἀκρίδας　acc pl fem [Mk 1:6; n-3c(2); 210]　ἀκρίς
ἀκρίδες　nom pl fem [2t; n-3c(2); 210]　　"
ἀκρίδων　gen pl fem [Rv 9:7; n-3c(2); 210]　"

ἀκρίς, ίδος, ἡ　　　　　{210, n-3c(2)}
a locust, Matt 3:4; Mark 1:6; Rev 9:3, 7*

ἀκροαταί　nom pl masc [2t; n-1f; 212]　ἀκροατής

ἀκροατήριον, ου, τό　　　{211, n-2c}
a place of audience, Acts 25:23*

ἀκροατήριον　acc sg neut
[Ac 25:23; n-2c; 211]　　　　ἀκροατήριον

ἀκροατής, οῦ, ὁ　　　　{212, n-1f}
a hearer, Rom 2:13; James 1:22, 23, 25*

ἀκροατής　nom sg masc [2t; n-1f; 212]　ἀκροατής

ἀκροβυστία, ας, ἡ　　　{213, n-1a}
foreskin; uncircumcision, the state of being
uncircumcised, Rom 4:10; the abstract being put
for the concrete, *uncircumcised men,* i.e.,
Gentiles, Rom 4:9, et al

ἀκροβυστία　nom sg fem
[9t; n-1a; 213]　　　　ἀκροβυστία
ἀκροβυστίᾳ　dat sg fem [6t; n-1a; 213]　　"
ἀκροβυστίαν　acc sg fem [3t; n-1a; 213]　　"
ἀκροβυστίας　gen sg fem [2t; n-1a; 213]　　"
ἀκρογωνιαῖον　acc sg masc
[1P 2:6; a-1a(1); 214]　　　ἀκρογωνιαῖος

ἀκρογωνιαῖος, α, ον　　　{214, a-1a(1)}
literally: *lying at the extreme corner;* with λίθος,
corner or *foundation stone,* Eph 2:20; 1 Peter 2:6*

ἀκρογωνιαίου　gen sg masc
[Ep 2:20; a-1a(1); 214]　　　"

ἀκροθίνιον, ου, τό　　　{215, n-2c}
the first-fruits of the produce of the ground,
which were taken from the top of the heap and
offered to the gods; *the best and choicest of the*
spoils of war, usually collected in a heap, Heb
7:4*

ἀκροθινίων　gen pl neut
[Hb 7:4; n-2c; 215]　　　　ἀκροθίνιον

ἄκρον, ου, τό　　　　　{216, n-2c}
the top, tip, end, extremity, Mark 13:27; Luke
16:24; Heb 11:21

ἄκρον　acc sg neut [2t; n-2c; 216]　　　ἄκρον
ἄκρου　gen sg neut [2t; n-2c; 216]　　　"
ἄκρων　gen pl neut [2t; n-2c; 216]　　　"
Ἀκύλαν　acc sg masc [3t; n-3g(1); 217]　　Ἀκύλας

Ἀκύλας, ὁ　　　　　{217, n-3g(1)}
Aquila, pr. name, Paul's friend and Priscilla's
husband, Acts 18:2, 18, 21 v.l., 26; Rom 16:3; 1
Cor 16:19; 2 Tim 4:19*

Ἀκύλας　nom sg masc [3t; n-3g(1); 217]　　"

ἀκυροῖ   pres act ind 3 sg
  [Ga 3:17; v-1d(3); 218]   ἀκυρόω
ἀκυροῦντες   pres act ptcp nom pl masc
  [Mk 7:13; v-1d(3); 218]   "

ἀκυρόω   {218, v-1d(3)}
  [-, ἠκύρωσα, -, -, -] to deprive of authority, annul,
  cancel, Matt 15:6; Mark 7:13; Gal 3:17*

ἀκωλύτως   {219, adverb}
  without hindrance, freely, Acts 28:31*

ἀκωλύτως   adverb
  [Ac 28:31; adverb; 219]   ἀκωλύτως

ἄκων, ἄκουσα, ἄκον   {220, a-2a}
  unwilling, 1 Cor 9:17*

ἄκων   nom sg masc [1C 9:17; a-2a; 220]   ἄκων

ἄλα, see ἄλας   {221}

ἄλα   acc sg neut [Mk 9:50; n-3c(6a); 229]   ἄλας

ἀλάβαστρον, ου, τό   {222, n-2c}
  Can be used in all three genders ἀλάβαστρος,
  ου, ὁ (masc, n-2a), ἀλάβαστρος, ου, ἡ (fem, n-2b)
  and ἀλάβαστρον, ου, τό (neut, n-2c). The the
  N.T. it occurs twice as a fem. and twice as a
  neut. alabaster; a vase to hold perfumed ointment,
  properly made of alabaster, but also of other
  materials, Matt 26:7; Mark 14:3; Luke 7:37*

ἀλάβαστρον   acc sg fem
  [2t; n-2a; 223]   ἀλάβαστρος
ἀλάβαστρον   acc sg neut [2t; n-2a; 223]   "
ἀλαζόνας   acc pl masc
  [Rm 1:30; n-3f(1b); 225]   ἀλαζών

ἀλαζονεία, ας, ἡ   {224, n-1a}
  arrogance; presumptuous speech, James 4:16;
  haughtiness, 1 John 2:16*

ἀλαζονεία   nom sg fem
  [1J 2:16; n-1a; 224]   ἀλαζονεία
ἀλαζονείαις   dat pl fem [Jm 4:16; n-1a; 224]   "
ἀλαζόνες   nom pl masc
  [2Ti 3:2; n-3f(1b); 225]   ἀλαζών

ἀλαζών, όνος, ὁ   {225, n-3f(1b)}
  prideful, arrogant, boasting, Rom 1:30; 2 Tim 3:2*

ἀλαλάζον   pres act ptcp nom sg neut
  [1C 13:1; v-2a(1); 226]   ἀλαλάζω
ἀλαλάζοντας   pres act ptcp acc pl masc
  [Mk 5:38; v-2a(1); 226]   "

ἀλαλάζω   {226, v-2a(1)}
  [-, -, -, -, -] pr. to raise the war-cry, ἀλαλά: hence,
  to utter other loud sounds; to wail, Mark 5:38; to
  tinkle, ring, 1 Cor 13:1*

ἀλαλήτοις   dat pl masc
  [Rm 8:26; a-3a; 227]   ἀλάλητος

ἀλάλητος, ον   {227, a-3a}
  unutterable, or, unexpressed, Rom 8:26*

ἄλαλον   voc sg neut [Mk 9:25; a-3a; 228]   ἄλαλος
ἄλαλον   acc sg neut [Mk 9:17; a-3a; 228]   "

ἄλαλος, ον   {228, a-3a}
  unable to speak or artilculate, Mark 7:37; 9:17, 25*

ἀλάλους   acc pl masc [Mk 7:37; a-3a; 228]   "

ἅλας, ατος, τό   {229, n-3c(6a)}
  variant spellings of ἅλα and ἁλός, salt, Matt
  5:13; Mark 9:50; met. the salt of wisdom and
  prudence, Col 4:6

ἅλας   nom sg neut [6t; n-3c(6a); 229]   ἅλας
ἅλατι   dat sg neut [Cl 4:6; n-3c(6a); 229]   "
ἄλειψαι   aor mid imperative 2 sg
  [Mt 6:17; v-1b(1); 230]   ἀλείφω
ἀλείψαντες   aor act ptcp nom pl masc
  [Jm 5:14; v-1b(1); 230]   "
ἀλείψασα   aor act ptcp nom sg fem
  [Jn 11:2; v-1b(1); 230]   "
ἀλείψωσιν   aor act subj 3 pl
  [Mk 16:1; v-1b(1); 230]   "

ἀλείφω   {230, v-1b(1)}
  [-, ἤλειψα, -, -, ἠλείφθην] to anoint with oil or
  ointment

ἀλέκτορα   acc sg masc
  [5t; n-3f(2b); 232]   ἀλέκτωρ

ἀλεκτοροφωνία, ας, ἡ   {231, n-1a}
  the cock-crowing, the third watch of the night,
  intermediate to mid-night and daybreak, and
  termed cock-crow, Mark 13:35*

ἀλεκτοροφωνίας   gen sg fem
  [Mk 13:35; n-1a; 231]   ἀλεκτοροφωνία

ἀλέκτωρ, ορος, ὁ   {232, n-3f(2b)}
  a cock, rooster, Matt 26:34; Mark 14:30; Luke
  22:34; John 13:38

ἀλέκτωρ   nom sg masc [7t; n-3f(2b); 232]   ἀλέκτωρ

Ἀλεξανδρεύς, έως, ὁ   {233, n-3e(3)}
  a native of Alexandria, an Alexandrine, Acts 6:9;
  18:24

Ἀλεξανδρεύς   nom sg masc
  [Ac 18:24; n-3e(3); 233]   Ἀλεξανδρεύς
Ἀλεξανδρέων   gen pl masc [Ac 6:9; n-3e(3); 233]   "
Ἀλεξανδρῖνον   acc sg neut
  [Ac 27:6; a-1a(2a); 234]   Ἀλεξανδρῖνος

Ἀλεξανδρῖνος, η, ον   {234, a-1a(2a)}
  Alexandrian, Acts 27:6; 28:11; 6:9 v.l.*

Ἀλεξανδρίνῳ   dat sg neut
  [Ac 28:11; a-1a(2a); 234]   "
Ἀλέξανδρον   acc sg masc
  [Ac 19:33; n-2a; 235]   Ἀλέξανδρος

Ἀλέξανδρος, ου, ὁ   {235, n-2a}
  Alexander, pr. name. (1) The High Priest's
  kinsman, Acts 4:6. (2) A Jew of Ephesus, Acts
  19:33. (3) The coppersmith, 1 Tim 1:20; 2 Tim 4:14.
  (4) Son of Simon of Cyrene, Mark 15:21*

Ἀλέξανδρος   nom sg masc [4t; n-2a; 235]   "
Ἀλεξάνδρου   gen sg masc [Mk 15:21; n-2a; 235]   "

ἄλευρον, ου, τό   {236, n-2c}
  meal, flour, Matt 13:33; Luke 13:21*

ἀλεύρου   gen sg neut [2t; n-2c; 236]   ἄλευρον

ἀλήθεια, ας, ἡ   {237, n-1a}
  truth, Mark 5:33; love of truth, sincerity, 1 Cor
  5:8; divine truth revealed to man, John 1:17;

practice in accordance with Gospel *truth,* John 3:21; 2 John 4

ἀλήθεια   nom sg fem [14t; n-1a; 237]   ἀλήθεια
ἀληθείᾳ   dat sg fem [30t; n-1a; 237]   "
ἀλήθειαν   acc sg fem [22t; n-1a; 237]   "
ἀληθείας   gen sg fem [43t; n-1a; 237]   "
ἀληθεῖς   nom pl masc [2C 6:8; a-4a; 239]   ἀληθής
ἀληθές   nom sg neut [3t; a-4a; 239]   "
ἀληθές   acc sg neut [Jn 4:18; a-4a; 239]   "
ἀληθεύοντες   pres act ptcp nom pl masc
    [Ep 4:15; v-1a(6); 238]   ἀληθεύω

ἀληθεύω   {238, v-1a(6)}
   [-, -, -, -, -] *to speak* or *maintain the truth; to act truly* or *sincerely,* Gal 4:16; Eph 4:15*

ἀληθεύων   pres act ptcp nom sg masc
    [Ga 4:16; v-1a(6); 238]   "
ἀληθῆ   nom pl neut 2t; a-4a; 239]   ἀληθής
ἀληθῆ   acc sg fem [1P 5:12; a-4a; 239]   "
ἀληθῆ   acc pl neut [Jn 19:35; a-4a; 239]   "

ἀληθής, ες   {239, a-4a}
   true, John 4:18; *worthy of credit,* John 5:31; *truthful,* John 7:18

ἀληθής   nom sg masc [6t; a-4a; 239]   "
ἀληθής   nom sg fem [10t; a-4a; 239]   "
ἀληθιναί   nom pl fem
    [3t; a-1a(2a); 240]   ἀληθινός
ἀληθινή   nom sg fem [3t; a-1a(2a); 240]   "
ἀληθινῆς   gen sg fem [2t; a-1a(2a); 240]   "
ἀληθινοί   nom pl masc [4t; a-1a(2a); 240]   "
ἀληθινόν   nom sg neut [2t; a-1a(2a); 240]   "
ἀληθινόν   acc sg masc [3t; a-1a(2a); 240]   "
ἀληθινόν   acc sg neut [Lk 16:11; a-1a(2a); 240]   "

ἀληθινός, η, ον   {240, a-1a(2a)}
   sterling, Luke 16:11; *real,* John 6:32; 1 Thess 1:9; *unfeigned, trustworthy, true,* John 19:35

ἀληθινός   nom sg masc [6t; a-1a(2a); 240]   "
ἀληθινός   voc sg masc [Rv 6:10; a-1a(2a); 240]   "
ἀληθινῷ   dat sg masc [2t; a-1a(2a); 240]   "
ἀληθινῶν   gen pl neut [Hb 9:24; a-1a(2a); 240]   "
ἀληθοῦς   gen sg fem [2P 2:22; a-4a; 239]   ἀληθής
ἀλήθουσαι   pres act ptcp nom pl fem
    [2t; v-1b(3); 241]   ἀλήθω

ἀλήθω   {241, v-1b(3)}
   [-, -, -, -, -] *to grind,* Matt 24:41; Luke 17:35*

ἀληθῶς   {242, adverb}
   truly, really, Matt 14:33; *certainly, of a truth,* John 17:8; Acts 12:11: *truly, actually,* John 4:18

ἀληθῶς   adverb [18t; adverb; 242]   ἀληθῶς
ἁλιεῖς   nom pl masc [3t; n-3e(3); 243]   ἁλιεύς
ἁλιεῖς   acc pl masc [2t; n-3e(3); 243]   "
ἁλιεύειν   pres act inf
    [Jn 21:3; v-1a(6); 244]   ἁλιεύω

ἁλιεύς, έως, ὁ   {243, n-3e(3)}
   a fisherman, Matt 4:18, 19; Mark 1:16, 17; Luke 5:2

ἁλιεύω   {244, v-1a(6)}
   [-, -, -, -, -] *to fish,* John 21:3*

ἁλίζω   {245, v-2a(1)}
   [-, -, -, -, ἡλίσθην] *to salt, season with salt, preserve by salting,* Matt 5:13; Mark 9:49*

ἀλίσγημα, ατος, τό   {246, n-3c(4)}
   pollution, defilement, Acts 15:20*

ἀλισγημάτων   gen pl neut
    [Ac 15:20; n-3c(4); 246]   ἀλίσγημα
ἁλισθήσεται   fut pass ind 3 sg
    [2t; v-2a(1); 245]   ἁλίζω
ἀλλ᾽   particle [220t; particle; 247]   ἀλλά

ἀλλά   {247, particle}
   but; however; but still more; ἀλλάγε, *at all events;* ἀλλὴ, *unless, except.* Ἀλλά *also serves to introduce a sentence with keenness and emphasis,* Rom 6:5; 7:7; Phil 3:8; John 16:2

ἀλλά   particle [418t; particle; 247]   ἀλλά
ἄλλα   nom pl neut [8t; a-1a(2b); 257]   ἄλλος
ἄλλα   acc pl neut [8t; a-1a(2b); 257]   "
ἀλλαγησόμεθα   fut pass ind 1 pl
    [2t; v-2b; 248]   ἀλλάσσω
ἀλλαγήσονται   fut pass ind 3 pl
    [Hb 1:12; v-2b; 248]   "
ἄλλαι   nom pl fem [Mk 15:41; a-1a(2b); 257]   ἄλλος
ἀλλάξαι   aor act inf
    [Ga 4:20; v-2b; 248]   ἀλλάσσω
ἀλλάξει   fut act ind 3 sg [Ac 6:14; v-2b; 248]   "
ἄλλας   acc pl fem [2C 11:8; a-1a(2b); 257]   ἄλλος

ἀλλάσσω   {248, v-2b}
   [ἀλλάξω, ἤλλαξα, -, ἤλλαγμαι, ἠλλάγην] *to change, alter, transform,* Acts 6:14; Rom 1:23; 1 Cor 15:51, 52; Gal 4:20; Heb 1:12

ἀλλαχόθεν   {249, adverb}
   from another place or *elsewhere,* John 10:1*

ἀλλαχόθεν   adverb
    [Jn 10:1; adverb; 249]   ἀλλαχόθεν

ἀλλαχοῦ   {250, adverb}
   elsewhere, Mark 1:38*

ἀλλαχοῦ   adverb [Mk 1:38; adverb; 250]   ἀλλαχοῦ
ἄλλη   nom sg fem [12t; a-1a(2b); 257]   ἄλλος

ἀλληγορέω   {251, cv-1d(2)}
   [-, -, -, -, -] *to say what is either designed* or *fitted to convey a meaning other than the literal one, to allegorize;* ἀλληγορούμενος, *adapted to another meaning, otherwise significant,* Gal 4:24*

ἀλληγορούμενα   pres pass ptcp nom pl neut
    [Ga 4:24; cv-1d(2; 251]   ἀλληγορέω
ἀλλήλοις   dat pl masc
    [12t; a-1a(2b); 253]   ἀλλήλων
ἀλλήλοις   dat pl neut [Ga 5:17; a-1a(2b); 253]   "

ἀλληλουϊά   {252, n-3g(2)}
   (Hebrew) *hallelujah, praise Yahweh* or *the Lord,* Rev 19:1, 3, 4, 6*

ἀλληλουϊά   indecl [4t; n-3g(2); 252]   ἀλληλουϊά
ἀλλήλους   acc pl masc
    [67t; a-1a(2b); 253]   ἀλλήλων

ἀλλήλων   {253, a-1a(2b)}
   one another, each other

ἀλλήλων   gen pl masc   [19t; a-1a(2b); 253]   "

ἀλλήλων   gen pl neut   [1C 12:25; a-1a(2b); 253]   "

ἄλλην   acc sg fem   [9t; a-1a(2b); 257]   ἄλλος

ἄλλης   gen sg fem   [3t; a-1a(2b); 257]   "

ἄλλο   nom sg neut   [6t; a-1a(2b); 257]   "

ἄλλο   acc sg neut   [6t; a-1a(2b); 257]   "

ἀλλογενής, ες   {254, a-4a}
of another race or *nation*, i.e., not a Jew; *a stranger, foreigner,* Luke 17:18*

ἀλλογενής   nom sg masc
    [Lk 17:18; a-4a; 254]   ἀλλογενής

ἄλλοι   nom pl masc   [27t; a-1a(2b); 257]   ἄλλος

ἀλλοιόω   {255, v-1d(3)}
[-, ἠλλοίωσα -, -, ἠλλοιώθην] *to change,* Luke 9:29 v.l.*

ἄλλοις   dat pl masc   [6t; a-1a(2b); 257]   "

ἄλλομαι   {256, v-2d(1)}
[-, ἡλάμην, -, -, -] *to leap, jump, leap up,* Acts 3:8; 14:10; *to spring,* as water, John 4:14*

ἀλλόμενος   pres mid ptcp nom sg masc
    [Ac 3:8; v-2d(1); 256]   ἄλλομαι

ἀλλομένου   pres mid ptcp gen sg neut
    [Jn 4:14; v-2d(1); 256]   "

ἄλλον   acc sg masc   [17t; a-1a(2b); 257]   ἄλλος

ἄλλος, η, ο   {257, a-1a(2b)}
another, some other; ὁ ἄλλος, *the other;* οἱ ἄλλοι, *the others, the rest*

ἄλλος   nom sg masc   [25t; a-1a(2b); 257]   "

ἀλλοτρίᾳ   dat sg fem
    [Ac 7:6; a-1a(1); 259]   ἀλλότριος

ἀλλοτρίαις   dat pl fem   [1Ti 5:22; a-1a(1); 259]   "

ἀλλοτρίαν   acc sg fem   [Hb 11:9; a-1a(1); 259]   "

ἀλλοτριεπίσκοπος, ου, ὁ   {258, n-2a}
pr. *one who meddles with the affairs of others, a busybody in other men's matters; factious,* 1 Peter 4:15*

ἀλλοτριεπίσκοπος   nom sg masc
    [1P 4:15; n-2a; 258]   ἀλλοτριεπίσκοπος

ἀλλοτρίοις   dat pl masc
    [2C 10:15; a-1a(1); 259]   ἀλλότριος

ἀλλότριον   acc sg masc   [2t; a-1a(1); 259]   "

ἀλλότριος, ία, ιον   {259, a-1a(1)}
belonging to another, Luke 16:12; *foreign,* Acts 7:6; Heb 11:9; *a foreigner, alien,* Matt 17:25

ἀλλοτρίῳ   dat sg masc   [2t; a-1a(1); 259]   "

ἀλλοτρίῳ   dat sg neut   [2t; a-1a(1); 259]   "

ἀλλοτρίων   gen pl masc   [4t; a-1a(1); 259]   "

ἄλλου   gen sg masc   [Jn 19:32; a-1a(2b); 257]   ἄλλος

ἄλλους   acc pl masc   [12t; a-1a(2b); 257]   "

ἀλλόφυλος, ον   {260, a-3a}
of another race or *nation*, i.e., not a Jew, *a foreigner,* Acts 10:28; 13:19 v.l.*

ἀλλοφύλῳ   dat sg masc
    [Ac 10:28; a-3a; 260]   ἀλλόφυλος

ἄλλῳ   dat sg masc   [10t; a-1a(2b); 257]   ἄλλος

ἄλλων   gen pl masc   [3t; a-1a(2b); 257]   "

ἄλλως   {261, adverb}
otherwise, 1 Tim 5:25*

ἄλλως   adverb   [1Ti 5:25; adverb; 261]   ἄλλως

ἀλοάω   {262, v-1d(1a)}
[-, -, -, -, -] *to thresh; to tread,* 1 Cor 9:9, 10; 1 Tim 5:18*

ἄλογα   nom pl neut   [2t; a-3a; 263]   ἄλογος

ἄλογον   nom sg neut   [Ac 25:27; a-3a; 263]   "

ἄλογος, ον   {263, a-3a}
without speech or *reason, irrational, brute,* 2 Peter 2:12; Jude 10; *unreasonable, absurd,* Acts 25:27*

ἀλόη, ῆς, ἡ   {264, n-1b}
aloe, lign-aloe, a tree which grows in India and Cochin-China, the wood of which is soft and bitter, though highly aromatic. It is used by the Orientals as a perfume; and employed for the purposes of embalming, John 19:39*

ἀλόης   gen sg fem   [Jn 19:39; n-1b; 264]   ἀλόη

ἀλοῶν   pres act ptcp nom sg masc
    [1C 9:10; v-1d(1a); 262]   ἀλοάω

ἀλοῶντα   pres act ptcp acc sg masc
    [2t; v-1d(1a); 262]   "

ἅλς, ἁλός, ὁ, see ἅλς   {265}

ἁλυκόν   nom sg neut
    [Jm 3:12; a-1a(2a); 266]   ἁλυκός

ἁλυκός, ή, όν   {266, a-1a(2a)}
brackish, bitter, salt, James 3:12*

ἄλυπος, ον   {267, a-3a}
free from grief or *sorrow,* Phil 2:28*

ἀλυπότερος   nom sg masc comparative
    [Pp 2:28; a-3a; 267]   ἄλυπος

ἁλύσει   dat sg fem   [2t; n-3e(5b); 268]   ἅλυσις

ἁλύσεις   nom pl fem   [Ac 12:7; n-3e(5b); 268]   "

ἁλύσεις   acc pl fem   [Mk 5:4; n-3e(5b); 268]   "

ἁλύσεσι   dat pl fem   [Ac 21:33; n-3e(5b); 268]   "

ἁλύσεσιν   dat pl fem   [3t; n-3e(5b); 268]   "

ἅλυσιν   acc sg fem   [3t; n-3e(5b); 268]   "

ἅλυσις, εως, ἡ   {268, n-3e(5b)}
a chain, Mark 5:3, 4

ἀλυσιτελές   nom sg neut
    [Hb 13:17; a-4a; 269]   ἀλυσιτελής

ἀλυσιτελής, ες   {269, a-4a}
pr. *bringing in no revenue* or *profit;* hence, *unprofitable, useless; detrimental; ruinous, disastrous,* Heb 13:17*

ἄλφα, τό   {270, n-3g(2)}
first letter of Greek alphabet, *Alpha,* Rev 1:8, 11 v.l.; 21:6; 22:13*

ἄλφα   indecl   [3t; n-3g(2); 270]   ἄλφα

Ἀλφαῖος, ου, ὁ   {271, n-2a}
Alphaeus, pr. name   (1) *Father of James the less,* Matt 10:3; MArk 3:18; Luke 6:15; Acts 1:13.   (2) *Father of Levi,* (or Matthew) Mark 2:14, Luke 5:27 v.l.*

Ἀλφαίου   gen sg masc   [5t; n-2a; 271]   Ἀλφαῖος

ἄλων, ῶνος, ἡ   {272, n-3f(1a)}
a threshing-floor, a place where corn is trodden out;
meton. *the corn which is trodden out,* Matt 3:12;
Luke 3:17*

ἄλωνα   acc sg fem [2t; n-3f(1a); 272]   ἄλων
ἀλώπεκες   nom pl fem [2t; n-3b(1); 273]   ἀλώπηξ
ἀλώπεκι   dat sg fem [Lk 13:32; n-3b(1); 273]   "

ἀλώπηξ, εκος, ἡ   {273, n-3b(1)}
a fox, Matt 8:20; Luke 9:58; met. *a fox-like, crafty
man,* Luke 13:32*

ἄλωσιν   acc sg fem [2P 2:12; n-3e(5b); 274]   ἄλωσις

ἄλωσις, εως, ἡ   {274, n-3e(5b)}
a taking, catching, capture, 2 Peter 2:12*

ἅμα   {275, adverb}
also functions as an improper preposition with
the genmitive (2t), *with, together with; at the
same time*

ἅμα   adverb [10t; adverb; 275]   ἅμα
ἀμαθεῖς   nom pl masc [2P 3:16; a-4a; 276]   ἀμαθής

ἀμαθής, ές   {276, a-4a}
unlearned, uninstructed, rude, 2 Peter 3:16*

ἀμαράντινον   acc sg masc
   [1P 5:4; a-1a(2a); 277]   ἀμαράντινος

ἀμαράντινος, η, ον   {277, a-1a(2a)}
unfading; hence, *enduring,* 1 Peter 5:4*

ἀμάραντον   acc sg fem
   [1P 1:4; a-3a; 278]   ἀμάραντος

ἀμάραντος, ον   {278, a-3a}
unfading; hence, *enduring,* 1 Peter 1:4*

ἁμάρτανε   pres act imperative 2 sg
   [2t; v-3a(2a); 279]   ἁμαρτάνω
ἁμαρτάνει   pres act ind 3 sg [6t; v-3a(2a); 279]   "
ἁμαρτάνειν   pres act inf
   [1J 3:9; v-3a(2a); 279]   "
ἁμαρτάνετε   pres act imperative 2 pl
   [2t; v-3a(2a); 279]   "
ἁμαρτάνετε   pres act ind 2 pl
   [1C 8:12; v-3a(2a); 279]   "
ἁμαρτάνοντα   pres act ptcp acc sg masc
   [1J 5:16; v-3a(2a); 279]   "
ἁμαρτάνοντας   pres act ptcp acc pl masc
   [1Ti 5:20; v-3a(2a); 279]   "
ἁμαρτάνοντες   pres act ptcp nom pl masc
   [2t; v-3a(2a); 279]   "
ἁμαρτανόντων   pres act ptcp gen pl masc
   [Hb 10:26; v-3a(2a); 279]   "
ἁμαρτάνουσιν   pres act ptcp dat pl masc
   [1J 5:16; v-3a(2a); 279]   "

ἁμαρτάνω   {279, v-3a(2a)}
[ἁμαρτήσω, ἥμαρτον or ἡμάρτησα, ἡμάρτηκα, -, -]
pr. *to miss a mark; to be in error,* 1 Cor 15:34; Titus
3:11; *to sin,* John 5:14; *to be guilty of wrong,* Matt
18:15

ἁμαρτάνων   pres act ptcp nom sg masc
   [1J 3:6; v-3a(2a); 279]   "
ἁμάρτῃ   aor act subj 3 sg [2t; v-3a(2a); 279]   "

ἁμάρτημα, ατος, τό   {280, n-3c(4)}
an error; sin, offence, Mark 3:28; 4:12; Rom 3:25;
1 Cor 6:18

ἁμάρτημα   nom sg neut
   [1C 6:18; n-3c(4); 280]   ἁμάρτημα
ἁμαρτήματα   nom pl neut [Mk 3:28; n-3c(4); 280]   "
ἁμαρτήματος   gen sg neut [Mk 3:29; n-3c(4); 280]   "
ἁμαρτημάτων   gen pl neut [Rm 3:25; n-3c(4); 280]   "
ἁμαρτήσαντας   aor act ptcp acc pl masc
   [Rm 5:14; v-3a(2a); 279]   ἁμαρτάνω
ἁμαρτήσαντος   aor act ptcp gen sg masc
   [Rm 5:16; v-3a(2a); 279]   "
ἁμαρτησάντων   aor act ptcp gen pl masc
   [2P 2:4; v-3a(2a); 279]   "
ἁμαρτήσασιν   aor act ptcp dat pl masc
   [Hb 3:17; v-3a(2a); 279]   "
ἁμαρτήσει   fut act ind 3 sg
   [Mt 18:21; v-3a(2a); 279]   "
ἁμαρτήσῃ   aor act subj 3 sg [2t; v-3a(2a); 279]   "
ἁμαρτήσωμεν   aor act subj 1 pl
   [Rm 6:15; v-3a(2a); 279]   "
ἁμαρτήτε   aor act subj 2 pl
   [1J 2:1; v-3a(2a); 279]   "

ἁμαρτία, ας, ἡ   {281, n-1a}
error; offence, sin, Matt 1:21; *a principle* or *cause of
sin,* Rom 7:7; *proneness to sin, sinful propensity,*
Rom 7:17, 20; *guilt* or *imputation of sin,* John
9:41; Heb 9:26; *a guilty subject, sin-offering,
expiatory victim,* 2 Cor 5:21

ἁμαρτία   nom sg fem [28t; n-1a; 281]   ἁμαρτία
ἁμαρτίᾳ   dat sg fem [7t; n-1a; 281]   "
ἁμαρτίαι   nom pl fem [12t; n-1a; 281]   "
ἁμαρτίαις   dat pl fem [9t; n-1a; 281]   "
ἁμαρτίαν   acc sg fem [27t; n-1a; 281]   "
ἁμαρτίας   gen sg fem [34t; n-1a; 281]   "
ἁμαρτίας   acc pl fem [24t; n-1a; 281]   "
ἁμαρτιῶν   gen pl fem [32t; n-1a; 281]   "
ἁμάρτυρον   acc sg masc
   [Ac 14:17; a-3a; 282]   ἀμάρτυρος

ἀμάρτυρος, ον   {282, a-3a}
without testimony or *witness, without evidence,*
Acts 14:17*

ἁμαρτωλοί   nom pl masc
   [11t; a-3a; 283]   ἁμαρτωλός
ἁμαρτωλοί   voc pl masc [Jm 4:8; a-3a; 283]   "
ἁμαρτωλοῖς   dat pl masc [2t; a-3a; 283]   "
ἁμαρτωλόν   acc sg masc [Jm 5:20; a-3a; 283]   "

ἁμαρτωλός, ον   {283, a-3a}
one who deviates from the path of virtue, a sinner,
Mark 2:17; *depraved,* Mark 8:38; *sinful, detestable,*
Rom 7:13

ἁμαρτωλός   nom sg masc [6t; a-3a; 283]   "
ἁμαρτωλός   nom sg fem [3t; a-3a; 283]   "
ἁμαρτωλούς   acc pl masc [5t; a-3a; 283]   "
ἁμαρτωλῷ   dat sg masc [4t; a-3a; 283]   "
ἁμαρτωλῷ   dat sg fem [Mk 8:38; a-3a; 283]   "
ἁμαρτωλῶν   gen pl masc [13t; a-3a; 283]   "

Ἀμασίας, ου, ὁ   {284, n-1d}
(Hebrew) *Amaziah,* Matt 1:8 v.l.; Luke 3:23ff.
v.l.*

ἄμαχον   acc sg masc [1Ti 3:3; a-3a; 285]   ἄμαχος

ἄμαχος, ον   {285, a-3a}
not disposed to fight; not quarrelsome or
contentious, 1 Tim 3:3; Titus 3:2*

ἀμάχους   acc pl masc [Ti 3:2; a-3a; 285]   "

ἀμάω   {286, v-1d(1a)}
[-, ἤμησα, -, -, -] *to collect; to reap, mow* or *cut
down,* James 5:4*

ἀμέθυσος, ου, ἡ, v.l. for ἀμέθυστος   {n-1d}
an amethyst, Rev 21:20 v.l.*

ἀμέθυστος, οῦ, ἡ   {287, n-2b}
an amethyst, a gem of a deep purple or violet
color, so called from its supposed efficacy in
keeping off drunkenness, Rev 21:20*

ἀμέθυστος   nom sg fem
[Rv 21:20; n-2b; 287]   ἀμέθυστος
ἀμέλει   pres act imperative 2 sg
[1Ti 4:14; v-1d(2a); 288]   ἀμελέω

ἀμελέω   {288, v-1d(2a)}
[-, ἠμέλησα, -, -, -] *not to care for, to neglect,
disregard,* Matt 22:5; 1 Tim 4:14; Heb 2:3; 8:9; 2
Peter 1:12 v.l.

ἀμελήσαντες   aor act ptcp nom pl masc
[2t; v-1d(2a); 288]   "
ἄμεμπτοι   nom pl masc [2t; a-3a; 289]   ἄμεμπτος

ἄμεμπτος, ον   {289, a-3a}
blameless, irreprehensible, without defect, Luke
1:6; Phil 2:15; 3:6; 1 Thess 3:13; Heb 8:7*

ἄμεμπτος   nom sg masc [Pp 3:6; a-3a; 289]   "
ἄμεμπτος   nom sg fem [Hb 8:7; a-3a; 289]   "
ἀμέμπτους   acc pl fem [1Th 3:13; a-3a; 289]   "

ἀμέμπτως   {290, adverb}
blamelessly, unblamably, unexceptionably, 1 Thess
2:10; 5:23*

ἀμέμπτως   adverb [2t; adverb; 290]   ἀμέμπτως

ἀμέριμνος, ον   {291, a-3a}
free from care or *solicitude,* Matt 28:14; 1 Cor
7:32*

ἀμερίμνους   acc pl masc
[2t; a-3a; 291]   ἀμέριμνος
ἀμετάθετον   acc sg neut
[Hb 6:17; a-3a; 292]   ἀμετάθετος

ἀμετάθετος, ον   {292, a-3a}
unchangeable, Heb 6:17, 18*

ἀμεταθέτων   gen pl neut [Hb 6:18; a-3a; 292]   "
ἀμετακίνητοι   nom pl masc
[1C 15:58; a-3a; 293]   ἀμετακίνητος

ἀμετακίνητος, ον   {293, a-3a}
immovable, firm, 1 Cor 15:58*

ἀμεταμέλητα   nom pl neut
[Rm 11:29; a-3a; 294]   ἀμεταμέλητος
ἀμεταμέλητον   acc sg fem [2C 7:10; a-3a; 294]   "

ἀμεταμέλητος, ον   {294, a-3a}
not to be repented of ; by impl. *irrevocable,
enduring,* Rom 11:29; 2 Cor 7:10*

ἀμετανόητον   acc sg fem
[Rm 2:5; a-3a; 295]   ἀμετανόητος

ἀμετανόητος, ον   {295, a-3a}
impenitent, unrepentant, Rom 2:5*

ἄμετρα   acc pl neut [2t; a-3a; 296]   ἄμετρος

ἄμετρος, ον   {296, a-3a}
without or *beyond measure, regardless of measure,*
2 Cor 10:13, 15*

ἀμήν   {297, particle}
in truth, most certainly; so be it; ὁ ἀμήν, *the faithful
and true one,* Rev 3:14

ἀμήν   particle [129t; particle; 297]   ἀμήν
ἀμησάντων   aor act ptcp gen pl masc
[Jm 5:4; v-1d(1a); 286]   ἀμάω

ἀμήτωρ, τορος, τό   {298, n-3c(6b)}
pr. *without mother; independent of maternal
descent,* Heb 7:3*

ἀμήτωρ   nom sg masc
[Hb 7:3; n-3c(6b); 298]   ἀμήτωρ
ἀμίαντον   acc sg fem
[1P 1:4; a-3a; 299]   ἀμίαντος

ἀμίαντος, ον   {299, a-3a}
pr. *unstained, unsoiled;* met. *undefiled, chaste,*
Heb 7:26; 13:4; *pure, sincere,* James 1:27;
undefiled, unimpaired, 1 Peter 1:4*

ἀμίαντος   nom sg masc [Hb 7:26; a-3a; 299]   "
ἀμίαντος   nom sg fem [2t; a-3a; 299]   "

Ἀμιναδάβ, ὁ   {300, n-3g(2)}
Aminadab, pr. name, indecl, Matt 1:4; Luke
3:33*

Ἀμιναδάβ   indecl [3t; n-3g(2); 300]   Ἀμιναδάβ

ἄμμον, ου, τό   {301, n-2c}
sand, Rom 4:18 v.l.*

ἄμμον   acc sg fem [2t; n-2b; 302]   ἄμμος

ἄμμος, ου, ἡ   {302, n-2b}
sand, Matt 7:26; Rom 9:27; Heb 11:12; Rev 12:18,
20*

ἄμμος   nom sg fem [3t; n-2b; 302]   "

ἀμνός, οῦ, ὁ   {303, n-2a}
a lamb, John 1:29, 36; Acts 8:32; 1 Peter 1:19*

ἀμνός   nom sg masc [3t; n-2a; 303]   ἀμνός
ἀμνοῦ   gen sg masc [1P 1:19; n-2a; 303]   "
ἀμοιβάς   acc pl fem [1Ti 5:4; n-1b; 304]   ἀμοιβή

ἀμοιβή, ῆς, ἡ   {304, n-1b}
(adequate) *return, recompense,* 1 Tim 5:4*

ἄμμορφος, ον   {305, a-3a}
misshapen, ugly, 1 Cor 12:2 v.l.*

ἄμπελον   acc sg fem [Rv 14:19; n-2b; 306] ἄμπελος

ἄμπελος, ου, ἡ   {306, n-2b}
a vine, grape-vine

ἄμπελος   nom sg fem [3t; n-2b; 306]   "

ἀμπέλου   gen sg fem [4t; n-2b; 306]   "
ἀμπελουργόν   acc sg masc
  [Lk 13:7; n-2a; 307]   ἀμπελουργός

ἀμπελουργός, ου, ὁ   {307, n-2a}
  a vine-dresser, gardner, Luke 13:7*

ἀμπέλῳ   dat sg fem [Jn 15:4; n-2b; 306]   ἄμπελος

ἀμπελών, ῶνος, ὁ   {308, n-3f(1a)}
  a vineyard

ἀμπελῶνα   acc sg masc
  [11t; n-3f(1a); 308]   ἀμπελών
ἀμπελῶνι   dat sg masc [2t; n-3f(1a); 308]   "
ἀμπελῶνος   gen sg masc [10t; n-3f(1a); 308]   "
Ἀμπλιᾶτον   acc sg masc
  [Rm 16:8; n-2a; 309]   Ἀμπλιᾶτος

Ἀμπλιᾶτος, ου, ὁ   {309, n-2a}
  Ampliatus, pr. name, Rom 16:8*

ἀμύνομαι   {310, v-1c(2)}
  [-, ἠμυνάμην, -, -, -] to ward off; to help, assist; to
  repel from oneself, resist, make a defence; to assume
  the office of protector and avenger, Acts 7:24*

ἀμφιάζω, see ἀμφιέννυμι   {cv-2a(1)}

ἀμφιβάλλοντας   pres act ptcp acc pl masc
  [Mk 1:16; cv-2d(1); 311]   ἀμφιβάλλω

ἀμφιβάλλω   {311, cv-2d(1)}
  [-, -, -, -, -] to throw around; to cast a net, Mark
  1:16*

ἀμφίβληστρον, ου, τό   {312, n-2c}
  pr. what is thrown around, e.g., a garment; a large
  kind of fish-net, Matt 4:18; Mark 1:16 v.l.*

ἀμφίβληστρον   acc sg neut
  [Mt 4:18; n-2c; 312]   ἀμφίβληστρον
ἀμφιέζει   pres act ind 3 sg
  [Lk 12:28; cv-2a(1); 313]   ἀμφιέζω

ἀμφιέζω   {313, cv-2a(1)}
  [-, -, -, -, -] to clothe, see ἀμφιέννυμι. Our texts
  read ἀμφιέζει at Luke 12:28 and list ἀμφιέννυμι
  as a v.l.*

ἀμφιέννυμι   {314, v-3c(1)}
  [-, -, -, ἠμφίεσμαι, -] also spelled ἀμφιέζω and
  ἀμφιέννυμι, to clothe, invest, Matt 6:30; 11:8;
  Luke 7:25; 12:28 v.l. (where our text reads
  ἀμφιέζει, from ἀμφιέζω)*

ἀμφιέννυσιν   pres act ind 3 sg
  [Mt 6:30; cv-2a(1); 314]   ἀμφιάζω
Ἀμφίπολιν   acc sg fem
  [Ac 17:1; n-3e(5b); 315]   Ἀμφίπολις

Ἀμφίπολις, εως, ἡ   {315, n-3e(5b)}
  Amphipolis, a city of Thrace, on the river
  Strymon, Acts 17:1*

ἄμφοδον, ου, τό   {316, n-2c}
  pr. a road leading round a town or village; the street
  of a village, Mark 11:4; Acts 19:28 v.l.*

ἀμφόδου   gen sg neut [Mk 11:4; n-2c; 316]   ἄμφοδον
ἀμφότερα   acc pl neut
  [4t; a-1a(1); 317]   ἀμφότεροι

ἀμφότεροι, αι, α   {317, a-1a(1)}
  both. Only plural in the N.T.

ἀμφότεροι   nom pl masc [7t; a-1a(1); 317]   "
ἀμφοτέροις   dat pl masc [Lk 7:42; a-1a(1); 317]   "
ἀμφοτέρους   acc pl masc [Ep 2:16; a-1a(1); 317]   "
ἀμφοτέρων   gen pl masc [Ac 19:16; a-1a(1); 317]   "
ἄμωμα   nom pl neut [Pp 2:15; a-3a; 320]   ἄμωμος
ἀμώμητοι   nom pl masc
  [2P 3:14; a-3a; 318]   ἀμώμητος

ἀμώμητος, ον   {318, a-3a}
  blameless, unblemished, 2 Peter 3:14; Phil 2:15
  v.l.*

ἄμωμοι   nom pl masc [Rv 14:5; a-3a; 320]   ἄμωμος

ἄμωμον, ου, τό   {319, n-2c}
  amomum, an odoriferous shrub, from which a
  precious ointment was prepared, Rev 18:13*

ἄμωμον   acc sg masc [Hb 9:14; a-3a; 320]   "
ἄμωμον   acc sg neut [Rv 18:13; n-2c; 319]   ἄμωμον

ἄμωμος, ον   {320, a-3a}
  blameless, unblemished

ἄμωμος   nom sg fem [Ep 5:27; a-3a; 320]   ἄμωμος
ἀμώμου   gen sg masc [1P 1:19; a-3a; 320]   "
ἀμώμους   acc pl masc [3t; a-3a; 320]   "

Ἀμών, ὁ   {321, n-3g(2)}
  Amon, pr. name, indecl, v.l. for Ἀμώς at Matt
  1:10 *

Ἀμώς, ὁ   {322, n-3g(2)}
  Amos, pr. name, indecl, Matt 1:10; Luke 3:23ff.
  v.l.*

Ἀμώς   indecl [3t; n-3g(2); 322]   Ἀμώς

ἄν   {323, particle}
  For the various constructions of this particle,
  and their significance, consult a grammar. At
  the beginning of a clause, it is another form of
  ἐάν, if, John 20:23

ἄν   particle [166t; particle; 323]   ἄν

ἀνά   {324, prep}
  prep. used in the N.T. only in certain forms.
  ἀνὰ μέρος, in turn; ἀνὰ μέσον, through the midst,
  between; ἀνὰ δηνάριον, at the rate of a denarius;
  with numerals, ἀνὰ ἑκατόν, in parties of a
  hundred. In composition, step by step, up, back,
  again

ἀνά   prep-acc [13t; prep; 324]   ἀνά
ἀνάβα   aor act imperative 2 sg
  [Rv 4:1; cv-2d(6); 326]   ἀναβαίνω

ἀναβαθμός, οῦ, ὁ   {325, n-2a}
  the act of ascending; means of ascent, steps, stairs,
  Acts 21:35, 40*

ἀναβαθμούς   acc pl masc
  [Ac 21:35; n-2a; 325]   ἀναβαθμός
ἀναβαθμῶν   gen pl masc [Ac 21:40; n-2a; 325]   "
ἀναβαίνει   pres act ind 3 sg
  [4t; cv-2d(6); 326]   ἀναβαίνω
ἀναβαίνειν   pres act inf [3t; cv-2d(6); 326]   "
ἀναβαίνομεν   pres act ind 1 pl
  [3t; cv-2d(6); 326]   "

ἀναβαῖνον   pres act ptcp nom sg neut
   [Rv 11:7; cv-2d(6); 326]   "
ἀναβαῖνον   pres act ptcp acc sg neut
   [2t; cv-2d(6); 326]   "
ἀναβαίνοντα   pres act ptcp nom pl neut
   [Mk 4:8; cv-2d(6); 326]   "
ἀναβαίνοντα   pres act ptcp acc sg masc
   [2t; cv-2d(6); 326]   "
ἀναβαίνοντας   pres act ptcp acc pl masc
   [Jn 1:51; cv-2d(6); 326]   "
ἀναβαίνοντες   pres act ptcp nom pl masc
   [Mk 10:32; cv-2d(6); 326]   "
ἀναβαινόντων   pres act ptcp gen pl masc
   [2t; cv-2d(6); 326]   "
ἀναβαίνουσιν   pres act ind 3 pl
   [Lk 24:38; cv-2d(6); 326]   "

ἀναβαίνω   {326, cv-2d(6)}
  [ἀναβήσομαι, ἀνέβην, ἀναβέβηκα, -, -] *to go up,*
  ascend, Matt 5:1; *to climb,* Luke 19:4; *to go on*
  board, Mark 6:51; *to rise, mount upwards,* as
  smoke, Rev 8:4; *to grow* or *spring up,* as plants,
  Matt 13:7; *to spring up, arise,* as thoughts, Luke
  24:38

ἀναβαίνω   pres act ind 1 sg [2t; cv-2d(6); 326]   "
ἀναβαίνων   pres act ptcp nom sg masc
   [4t; cv-2d(6); 326]   "

ἀναβάλλω   {327, cv-2d(1)}
  [-, ἀνέβαλον, -, -, -] *to throw back;* mid. *to put off,*
  defer, adjourn, Acts 24:22*

ἀναβάντα   aor act ptcp acc sg masc
   [2t; cv-2d(6); 326]   "
ἀναβάντες   aor act ptcp nom pl masc
   [Lk 5:19; cv-2d(6); 326]   "
ἀναβάντων   aor act ptcp gen pl masc
   [Mt 14:32; cv-2d(6); 326]   "
ἀναβάς   aor act ptcp nom sg masc
   [7t; cv-2d(6); 326]   "
ἀνάβατε   aor act imperative 2 pl
   [Rv 11:12; cv-2d(6); 326]   "
ἀναβέβηκα   perf act ind 1 sg
   [Jn 20:17; cv-2d(6); 326]   "
ἀναβέβηκεν   perf act ind 3 sg
   [Jn 3:13; cv-2d(6); 326]   "
ἀναβήσεται   fut mid ind 3 sg
   [Rm 10:6; cv-2d(6); 326]   "
ἀνάβητε   aor act imperative 2 pl
   [Jn 7:8; cv-2d(6); 326]   "

ἀναβιβάζω   {328, cv-2a(1)}
  [-, ἀνεβίβασα, -, -, -] *to cause to come up* or *ascend,*
  draw or *bring up,* Matt 13:48*

ἀναβιβάσαντες   aor act ptcp nom pl masc
   [Mt 13:48; cv-2a(1); 328]   ἀναβιβάζω
ἀναβλέπουσιν   pres act ind 3 pl
   [2t; cv-1b(1); 329]   ἀναβλέπω

ἀναβλέπω   {329, cv-1b(1)}
  [-, ἀνέβλεψα -, -, -] *to look upwards,* Matt 14:19;
  to see again, recover sight, Matt 11:5

ἀναβλέψαντος   aor act ptcp gen sg masc
   [Jn 9:18; cv-1b(1); 329]   "

ἀναβλέψας   aor act ptcp nom sg masc
   [7t; cv-1b(1); 329]   "
ἀναβλέψασαι   aor act ptcp nom pl fem
   [Mk 16:4; cv-1b(1); 329]   "
ἀναβλέψῃ   aor act subj 3 sg
   [Ac 9:12; cv-1b(1); 329]   "
ἀναβλέψῃς   aor act subj 2 sg
   [Ac 9:17; cv-1b(1); 329]   "
ἀνάβλεψιν   acc sg fem
   [Lk 4:18; n-3e(5b); 330]   ἀνάβλεψις

ἀνάβλεψις, εως, ἡ   {330, n-3e(5b)}
  recovery of sight, Luke 4:18*

ἀνάβλεψον   aor act imperative 2 sg
   [2t; cv-1b(1); 329]   ἀναβλέπω
ἀναβλέψω   aor act subj 1 sg [2t; cv-1b(1); 329]   "

ἀναβοάω   {331, cv-1d(1a)}
  [-, ἀνεβόησα, -, -, -] *to cry out* or *aloud, exclaim,*
  Matt 27:46; Luke 1:42 v.l.; 9:38 v.l.; Mark 15:8
  v.l.*

ἀναβολή, ῆς, ἡ   {332, n-1b}
  delay, Acts 25:17*

ἀναβολήν   acc sg fem
   [Ac 25:17; n-1b; 332]   ἀναβολή
ἀναγαγεῖν   aor act inf
   [2t; cv-1b(2); 343]   ἀνάγω
ἀναγαγών   aor act ptcp nom sg masc
   [3t; cv-1b(2); 343]

ἀνάγαιον, ου, τό   {333, n-2c}
  an upper room, Mark 14:15; Luke 22:12*

ἀνάγαιον   acc sg neut [2t; n-2c; 333]   ἀνάγαιον
ἀναγγεῖλαι   aor act inf
   [2t; cv-2d(1); 334]   ἀναγγέλλω
ἀναγγελεῖ   fut act ind 3 sg [4t; cv-2d(1); 334]   "
ἀναγγέλλομεν   pres act ind 1 pl
   [1J 1:5; cv-2d(1); 334]   "
ἀναγγέλλοντες   pres act ptcp nom pl masc
   [Ac 19:18; cv-2d(1); 334]   "

ἀναγγέλλω   {334, cv-2d(1)}
  [ἀναγγελῶ, ἀνήγγειλα, -, -, ἀνηγγέλην] *to bring*
  back word, announce, report, Mark 5:14; *to declare,*
  set forth, teach, John 5:24

ἀναγγέλλων   pres act ptcp nom sg masc
   [2C 7:7; cv-2d(1); 334]   "
ἀναγεγεννημένοι   perf pass ptcp nom pl masc
   [1P 1:23; cv-1d(1a); 335]   ἀναγεννάω

ἀναγεννάω   {335, cv-1d(1a)}
  [-, ἀνεγέννησα, -, ἀναγεγέννημαι, -] *to beget* or
  bring forth again; to regenerate, 1 Peter 1:3, 23*

ἀναγεννήσας   aor act ptcp nom sg masc
   [1P 1:3; cv-1d(1a); 335]   "
ἀνάγεσθαι   pres mid inf
   [Ac 20:3; cv-1b(2); 343]   ἀνάγω
ἀνάγεσθαι   pres pass inf
   [Ac 27:21; cv-1b(2); 343]   "
ἀναγινώσκεις   pres act ind 2 sg
   [2t; cv-5a; 336]   ἀναγινώσκω
ἀναγινώσκετε   pres act ind 2 pl
   [2C 1:13; cv-5a; 336]   "

ἀναγινώσκηται   pres pass subj 3 sg
   [2C 3:15; cv-5a; 336]   "
ἀναγινωσκομένας   pres pass ptcp acc pl fem
   [Ac 13:27; cv-5a; 336]   "
ἀναγινωσκομένη   pres pass ptcp nom sg fem
   [2C 3:2; cv-5a; 336]   "
ἀναγινωσκόμενος   pres pass ptcp nom sg masc
   [Ac 15:21; cv-5a; 336]   "
ἀναγινώσκοντες   pres act ptcp nom pl masc
   [Ep 3:4; cv-5a; 336]   "
ἀναγινώσκοντος   pres act ptcp gen sg masc
   [Ac 8:30; cv-5a; 336]   "

ἀναγινώσκω   {336, cv-5a}
   [ἀναγνώσομαι, ἀνέγνων, -, -, ἀνεγνώσθην] *to*
   gather exact knowledge of, recognize, discern;
   especially, to read

ἀναγινώσκων   pres act ptcp nom sg masc
   [3t; cv-5a; 336]   "
ἀναγκάζεις   pres act ind 2 sg
   [Ga 2:14; v-2a(1); 337]   ἀναγκάζω
ἀναγκάζουσιν   pres act ind 3 pl
   [Ga 6:12; v-2a(1); 337]   "

ἀναγκάζω   {337, v-2a(1)}
   [-, ἠνάγκασα, -, -, ἠναγκάσθην] *to force, compel,*
   Acts 28:19; *to constrain, urge,* Luke 14:23

ἀναγκαῖα   nom pl neut
   [1C 12:22; a-1a(1); 338]   ἀναγκαῖος
ἀναγκαίας   acc pl fem [Ti 3:14; a-1a(1); 338] "
ἀναγκαῖον   nom sg neut [4t; a-1a(1); 338]   "

ἀναγκαῖος, α, ον   {338, a-1a(1)}
   necessary, indispensable, 1 Cor 12:22; *necessary,*
   needful, right, proper, Acts 13:46; 2 Cor 9:5; Phil
   1:24; 2:25; Heb 8:3; *near, intimate, closely*
   connected, as friends, Acts 10:24

ἀναγκαιότερον   nom sg neut comparative
   [Pp 1:24; a-1a(1); 338]   "
ἀναγκαίους   acc pl masc [Ac 10:24; a-1a(1); 338] "
ἀναγκαις   dat pl fem [2t; n-1b; 340]   ἀνάγκη
ἀναγκασον   aor act imperative 2 sg
   [Lk 14:23; v-2a(1); 337]   ἀναγκάζω

ἀναγκαστῶς   {339, adverb}
   by constraint or compulsion, unwillingly,
   opposite to ἑκουσίως, 1 Peter 5:2*

ἀναγκαστῶς   adverb
   [1P 5:2; adverb; 339]   ἀναγκαστῶς

ἀνάγκη, ῆς, ἡ   {340, n-1b}
   necessity, Matt 18:7; *constraint, compulsion,* 2 Cor
   9:7; *obligation of duty,* moral or spiritual
   necessity, Rom 13:5; *distress, trial, affliction,* Luke
   21:23; 1 Cor 7:26; 2 Cor 6:4; 12:10; 1 Thess 3:7

ἀνάγκη   nom sg fem [6t; n-1b; 340]   ἀνάγκη
ἀνάγκη   dat sg fem [1Th 3:7; n-1b; 340]   "
ἀνάγκην   acc sg fem [6t; n-1b; 340]   "
ἀνάγκης   gen sg fem [2t; n-1b; 340]   "
ἀναγόντες   aor act ptcp nom pl masc
   [Ac 15:31; cv-5a; 336]   ἀναγινώσκω
ἀναγνούς   aor act ptcp nom sg masc
   [Ac 23:34; cv-5a; 336]   "
ἀναγνῶναι   aor act inf [Lk 4:16; cv-5a; 336] "

ἀναγνωρίζω   {341, cv-2a(1)}
   [-, -, -, -, ἀνεγνωρίσθην] *to recognize;* pass. *to be*
   made known, or *to cause one's self to be recognized,*
   Acts 7:13*

ἀναγνώσει   dat sg fem
   [2t; n-3e(5b); 342]   ἀνάγνωσις
ἀναγνωσθῇ   aor pass subj 3 sg
   [2t; cv-5a; 336]   ἀναγινώσκω
ἀναγνωσθῆναι   aor pass inf
   [1Th 5:27; cv-5a; 336]   "
ἀνάγνωσιν   acc sg fem
   [Ac 13:15; n-3e(5b); 342]   ἀνάγνωσις

ἀνάγνωσις, εως, ἡ   {342, n-3e(5b)}
   reading, Acts 13:15; 2 Cor 3:14; 1 Tim 4:13*

ἀναγνῶτε   aor act subj 2 pl
   [Cl 4:16; cv-5a; 336]   ἀναγινώσκω
ἀναγομένοις   pres pass ptcp dat pl masc
   [Ac 28:10; cv-1b(2); 343]   ἀνάγω

ἀνάγω   {343, cv-1b(2)}
   [-, ἀνήγαγον -, -, ἀνήχθην] *to conduct; to lead* or
   convey up from a lower place to a higher, Luke
   4:5; *to offer up,* as a sacrifice, Acts 7:41; *to lead*
   out, produce, Acts 12:4; as a nautical term (in the
   middle or passive), *to set sail, put to sea,* Luke
   8:22

ἀναδείκνυμι   {344, cv-3c(2)}
   [-, ἀνέδειξα, -, -, -] pr. *to show anything by raising*
   it aloft, as a torch; *to display, manifest, show*
   plainly or *openly,* Acts 1:24; *to mark out,*
   constitute, appoint by some outward sign, Luke
   10:1*

ἀναδείξεως   gen sg fem
   [Lk 1:80; n-3e(5b); 345]   ἀνάδειξις

ἀνάδειξις, εως, ἡ   {345, n-3e(5b)}
   a showing forth, manifestation; public entrance
   upon the duty or *office to which one is consecrated,*
   Luke 1:80*

ἀνάδειξον   aor act imperative 2 sg
   [Ac 1:24; cv-3c(2); 344]   ἀναδείκνυμι
ἀναδεξάμενος   aor mid ptcp nom sg masc
   [2t; cv-1b(2); 346]   ἀναδέχομαι

ἀναδέχομαι   {346, cv-1b(2)}
   [-, ἀνεδεξάμην, -, -, -] *to receive,* as opposed to
   shunning or refusing; *to receive* with
   hospitality, Acts 28:7; *to embrace* a proffer or
   promise, Heb 11:17*

ἀναδίδωμι   {347, cv-6a}
   [-, ἀνέδωκα, -, -, -] *to give forth, up,* or *back; to*
   deliver, present, Acts 23:33*

ἀναδόντες   aor act ptcp nom pl masc
   [Ac 23:33; cv-6a; 347]   ἀναδίδωμι

ἀναζάω   {348, cv-1d(1a)}
   [-, ἀνέζησα, -, -, -] *to live again, recover life,* Rom
   14:9 v.l.; Rev 20:5 v.l.; *to revive, recover activity,*
   Rom 7:9; met. *to live a new and reformed life,*
   Luke 15:24, 32 v.l.*

ἀναζητέω   {349, cv-1d(2a)}
   [-, ἀνεζήτησα, -, -, -] *to track; to seek diligently,*
   inquire after, search for, Luke 2:44, 45; Acts 11:25*

ἀναζητῆσαι   aor act inf
   [Ac 11:25; cv-1d(2a); 349]   ἀναζητέω
ἀναζητοῦντες   pres act ptcp nom pl masc
   [Lk 2:45; cv-1d(2a); 349]   "

ἀναζώννυμι   {350, cv-3c(1)}
   [-, ἀνέζωσα, -, -, -] to gird with a belt or girdle;
   to gird one's self, 1 Peter 1:13*

ἀναζωπυρεῖν   pres act inf
   [2Ti 1:6; cv-1d(2a); 351]   ἀναζωπυρέω

ἀναζωπυρέω   {351, cv-1d(2a)}
   [-, ἀνεζωπύρησα, -, -, -] pr. to kindle up a dormant
   fire; met. to revive, excite; to stir up, quicken one's
   powers, 2 Tim 1:6*

ἀναζωσάμενοι   aor mid ptcp nom pl masc
   [1P 1:13; cv-3c(1); 350]   ἀναζώννυμι

ἀναθάλλω   {352, cv-2d(1)}
   [-, ἀνέθαλον, -, -, -] pr. to flourish again; met. to
   receive, to recover activity, Phil 4:10*

ἀνάθεμα, ατος, τό   {353, n-3c(4)}
   a devoted thing, Luke 21:5 v.l., but ordinarily in
   a bad sense, a person or thing accursed, Rom 9:3;
   1 Cor 12:3; 16:22; Gal 1:8, 9; a curse, execration,
   anathema, Acts 23:14*

ἀνάθεμα   nom sg neut [5t; n-3c(4); 353]   ἀνάθεμα
ἀναθέματι   dat sg neut [Ac 23:14; n-3c(4); 353]   "
ἀναθεματίζειν   pres act inf
   [Mk 14:71; cv-2a(1); 354]   ἀναθεματίζω

ἀναθεματίζω   {354, cv-2a(1)}
   [-, ἀνεθεμάτισα, -, -, -] to declare any one to be
   ἀνάθεμα;to curse, bind by a curse, Mark 14:71;
   Acts 23:12, 14, 21*

ἀναθεωρέω   {355, cv-1d(2a)}
   [-, -, -, -, -] to view, behold attentively, contemplate,
   Acts 17:23; Heb 13:7*

ἀναθεωροῦντες   pres act ptcp nom pl masc
   [Hb 13:7; cv-1d(2a); 355]   ἀναθεωρέω
ἀναθεωρῶν   pres act ptcp nom sg masc
   [Ac 17:23; cv-1d(2a); 355]   "

ἀνάθημα, ατος, τό   {356, n-3c(4)}
   a gift or offering consecrated to God, Luke 21:5*

ἀναθήμασιν   dat pl neut
   [Lk 21:5; n-3c(4); 356]   ἀνάθημα

ἀναίδεια, ας, ἡ   {357, n-1a}
   pr. shamelessness; hence, persistence, without
   regard to time, place, or person, Luke 11:8*

ἀναίδειαν   acc sg fem
   [Lk 11:8; n-1a; 357]   ἀναίδεια
ἀναιρεθῆναι   aor pass inf
   [2t; cv-1d(2a); 359]   ἀναιρέω
ἀναιρεῖ   pres act ind 3 sg
   [Hb 10:9; cv-1d(2a); 359]   "
ἀναιρεῖν   pres act inf
   [Ac 16:27; cv-1d(2a); 359]   "
ἀναιρεῖσθαι   pres pass inf
   [Ac 23:27; cv-1d(2a); 359]   "
ἀναιρέσει   dat sg fem
   [Ac 8:1; n-3e(5b); 358]   ἀναίρεσις

ἀναίρεσις, εως, ἡ   {358, n-3e(5b)}
   a taking up or away; a putting to death, murder,
   Acts 8:1; 13:28 v.l.; 22:20 v.l.*

ἀναιρέω   {359, cv-1d(2a)}
   [ἀνελῶ, ἀνεῖλα or ἀνεῖ˙λον, -, -, ἀνῃρέθην] pr. to
   take up, lift, as from the ground; to take off, put to
   death, kill, murder, Matt 2:16; to take away, abolish,
   abrogate, Heb 10:9; mid. to take up infants in
   order to bring them up, Acts 7:21

ἀναιρουμένων   pres pass ptcp gen pl masc
   [Ac 26:10; cv-1d(2a); 359]   ἀναιρέω
ἀναιρούντων   pres act ptcp gen pl masc
   [Ac 22:20; cv-1d(2a); 359]   "
ἀναίτιοι   nom pl masc
   [Mt 12:5; a-3a; 360]   ἀναίτιος

ἀναίτιος, ον   {360, a-3a}
   guiltless, innocent, Matt 12:5, 7; Acts 16:37 v.l.*

ἀναιτίους   acc pl masc [Mt 12:7; a-3a; 360]   "

ἀνακαθίζω   {361, cv-2a(1)}
   [-, ἀνεκάθισα, -, -, -] to set up; intrans. to sit up,
   Luke 7:15; Acts 9:40*

ἀνακαινίζειν   pres act inf
   [Hb 6:6; cv-2a(1); 362]   ἀνακαινίζω

ἀνακαινίζω   {362, cv-2a(1)}
   [-, -, -, -, -] to renovate, renew, Heb 6:6*

ἀνακαινούμενον   pres pass ptcp acc sg masc
   [Cl 3:10; cv-1d(3); 363]   ἀνακαινόω
ἀνακαινοῦται   pres pass ind 3 sg
   [2C 4:16; cv-1d(3); 363]   "

ἀνακαινόω   {363, cv-1d(3)}
   [-, -, -, -, -] to invigorate, renew, 2 Cor 4:16; Col
   3:10*

ἀνακαινώσει   dat sg fem
   [Rm 12:2; n-3e(5b); 364]   ἀνακαίνωσις
ἀνακαινώσεως   gen sg fem [Ti 3:5; n-3e(5b); 364]   "

ἀνακαίνωσις, εως, ἡ   {364, n-3e(5b)}
   renovation, renewal, Rom 12:2; Titus 3:5*

ἀνακαλυπτόμενον   pres pass ptcp nom sg neut
   [2C 3:14; cv-4; 365]   ἀνακαλύπτω

ἀνακαλύπτω   {365, cv-4}
   [-, -, -, ἀνακεκάλυμμαι, -] to unveil, uncover;
   pass. to be unveiled, 2 Cor 3:18; met. to be
   disclosed in true character and condition, 2 Cor
   3:14*

ἀνακάμπτω   {366, cv-4}
   [ἀνακάμψω, ἀνέκαμψα, -, -, -] pr. to reflect, bend
   back; hence, to bend back one's course, return,
   Matt 2:12; Luke 10:6; Acts 18:21; Heb 11:15; 2
   Pet 2:21 v.l.*

ἀνακάμψαι   aor act inf
   [2t; cv-4; 366]   ἀνακάμπτω
ἀνακάμψει   fut act ind 3 sg [Lk 10:6; cv-4; 366]   "
ἀνακάμψω   fut act ind 1 sg [Ac 18:21; cv-4; 366]   "

ἀνάκειμαι   {367, cv-6b}
   [-, -, -, -, -] to be laid up, as offerings; later, to lie,
   recline at table, Matt 9:10

ἀνακειμένοις   pres mid ptcp dat pl masc
[2t; cv-6b; 367]   ἀνάκειμαι

ἀνακείμενος   pres mid ptcp nom sg masc
[3t; cv-6b; 367]   "

ἀνακειμένου   pres mid ptcp gen sg masc
[2t; cv-6b; 367]   "

ἀνακειμένους   pres mid ptcp acc pl masc
[2t; cv-6b; 367]   "

ἀνακειμένων   pres mid ptcp gen pl masc
[4t; cv-6b; 367]   "

ἀνακεκαλυμμένῳ   perf pass ptcp dat sg neut
[2C 3:18; cv-4; 365]   ἀνακαλύπτω

ἀνακεφαλαιοῦται   pres pass ind 3 sg
[Rm 13:9; cv-1d(3); 368]   ἀνακεφαλαιόω

ἀνακεφαλαιόω   {368, cv-1d(3)}
[-, ἀνεκεφαλαίωσα, -, -, -] *to bring together several things under one, reduce under one head; to comprise,* Rom 13:9; Eph 1:10*

ἀνακεφαλαιώσασθαι   aor mid inf
[Ep 1:10; cv-1d(3); 368]   "

ἀνακλιθῆναι   aor pass inf
[Mt 14:19; cv-1c(2); 369]   ἀνακλίνω

ἀνακλιθήσονται   fut pass ind 3 pl
[2t; cv-1c(2); 369]   "

ἀνακλῖναι   aor act inf   [Mk 6:39; cv-1c(2); 369]   "

ἀνακλινεῖ   fut act ind 3 sg
[Lk 12:37; cv-1c(2); 369]   "

ἀνακλίνω   {369, cv-1c(2)}
[ἀνακλινῶ, ἀνέκλινα, -, -, ἀνεκλίθην] *to lay down,* Luke 2:7; *to cause to recline* at table, etc. Mark 6:39; Luke 9:15; 12:37; *to recline at table,* Matt 8:11

ἀνακόπτω   {370, cv-4}
[-, -, -, -, -] pr. *to beat back;* hence, *to check, impede, hinder, restrain,* Gal 5:7 v.l.*

ἀνακράζω   {371, cv-2a(2)}
[-, ἀνέκραξα or ἀνέκραγον, -, -, -] *to cry aloud, exclaim, shout,* Mark 1:23; 6:49; Luke 4:33; 8:28; 23:18*

ἀνακράξας   aor act ptcp nom sg masc
[Lk 8:28; cv-2a(2); 371]   ἀνακράζω

ἀνακραυγάζω   {372, cv-2a(1)}
[-, -, -, -, -] *to cry out,* Luke 4:35 v.l.*

ἀνακριθῶ   aor pass subj 1 sg
[1C 4:3; cv-1c(2); 373]   ἀνακρίνω

ἀνακρίναντες   aor act ptcp nom pl masc
[Ac 28:18; cv-1c(2); 373]   "

ἀνακρίνας   aor act ptcp nom sg masc
[3t; cv-1c(2); 373]   "

ἀνακρίνει   pres act ind 3 sg
[1C 2:15; cv-1c(2); 373]   "

ἀνακρίνεται   pres pass ind 3 sg
[3t; cv-1c(2); 373]   "

ἀνακρινόμεθα   pres pass ind 1 pl
[Ac 4:9; cv-1c(2); 373]   "

ἀνακρίνοντες   pres act ptcp nom pl masc
[3t; cv-1c(2); 373]   "

ἀνακρίνουσιν   pres act ptcp dat pl masc
[1C 9:3; cv-1c(2); 373]   "

ἀνακρίνω   {373, cv-1c(2)}
[-, ἀνέκρινα -, -, ἀνεκρίθην] *to sift; to examine closely,* Acts 17:11; *to scrutinize, scan,* 1 Cor 2:14, 15; 9:3; *to try* judicially, Luke 23:14; *to judge, give judgment upon,* 1 Cor 4:3, 4; *to put questions, be inquisitive,* 1 Cor 10:25, 27; Acts 11:12 v.l

ἀνακρίνω   pres act ind 1 sg
[1C 4:3; cv-1c(2); 373]   "

ἀνακρίνων   pres act ptcp nom sg masc
[1C 4:4; cv-1c(2); 373]   "

ἀνακρίσεως   gen sg fem
[Ac 25:26; n-3e(5b); 374]   ἀνάκρισις

ἀνάκρισις, εως, ἡ   {374, n-3e(5b)}
investigation, judicial examination, hearing of a cause, Acts 25:26*

ἀνακυλίω   {375, cv-4}
[-, -, -, -, -] *to roll back,* Mark 16:4 v.l.*

ἀνακύπτω   {376, cv-4}
[-, ἀνέκυψα, -, -, -] pr. *to raise up one's self, look up,* Luke 13:11; John 8:7, 10; met. *to look up* cheerily, *to be cheered,* Luke 21:28*

ἀνακύψαι   aor act inf
[Lk 13:11; cv-4; 376]   ἀνακύπτω

ἀνακύψας   aor act ptcp nom sg masc
[Jn 8:10; cv-4; 376]   "

ἀνακύψατε   aor act imperative 2 pl
[Lk 21:28; cv-4; 376]   "

ἀναλάβετε   aor act imperative 2 pl
[Ep 6:13; cv-3a(2b); 377]   ἀναλαμβάνω

ἀναλαβόντες   aor act ptcp nom pl masc
[3t; cv-3a(2b); 377]   "

ἀναλαβών   aor act ptcp nom sg masc
[2Ti 4:11; cv-3a(2b); 377]   "

ἀναλαμβάνειν   pres act inf
[Ac 20:13; cv-3a(2b); 377]   "

ἀναλαμβάνω   {377, cv-3a(2b)}
[-, ἀνέλαβον, ἀνείληφα, -, ἀνελήμφθην] *to take up, receive up,* Mark 16:19; *to take up, carry,* Acts 7:43; *to take on board,* Acts 20:13, 14; *to take* in company, Acts 23:31; 2 Tim 4:11

ἀναλημφθείς   aor pass ptcp nom sg masc
[Ac 1:11; cv-3a(2b); 377]   "

ἀναλήμψεως   gen sg fem
[Lk 9:51; n-3e(5b); 378]   ἀνάλημψις

ἀνάλημψις, εως, ἡ   {378, n-3e(5b)}
a taking up, receiving up, Luke 9:51*

ἀναλίσκω   {379, cv-5b}
[-, ἀνήλωσα, -, -, ἀνηλώθην] also spelled ἀναλόω, *to use up; to consume, destroy,* Luke 9:54; Gal 5:15; 2 Thess 2:8 v.l.*

ἀνάλλομαι   {380, v-2d(1)}
[-, -, -, -, -] *to jump up,* Acts 14:10 v.l.*

ἀναλογία, ας, ἡ   {381, n-1a}
analogy, ratio, proportion, Rom 12:6*

ἀναλογίαν   acc sg fem
[Rm 12:6; n-1a; 381]   ἀναλογία

ἀναλογίζομαι   {382, cv-2a(1)}
[-, ἀνελογισάμην, -, -, -] to consider attentively,
Heb 12:3*

ἀναλογίσασθε   aor mid imperative 2 pl
[Hb 12:3; cv-2a(1); 382]   ἀναλογίζομαι
ἄναλον   nom sg neut [Mk 9:50; a-3a; 383]   ἄναλος

ἄναλος, ον   {383, a-3a}
without saltness, without the taste and pungency of
salt, insipid, Mark 9:50

ἀναλόω, cf. ἀναλίσκω   {384}

ἀναλῦσαι   aor act inf
[Pp 1:23; cv-1a(4); 386]   ἀναλύω
ἀναλύσεως   gen sg fem
[2Ti 4:6; n-3e(5b); 385]   ἀνάλυσις
ἀναλύσῃ   aor act subj 3 sg
[Lk 12:36; cv-1a(4); 386]   ἀναλύω

ἀνάλυσις, εως, ἡ   {385, n-3e(5b)}
pr. dissolution; met. departure, death, 2 Tim 4:6*

ἀναλύω   {386, cv-1a(4)}
[-, ἀνέλυσα, -, -, -] pr. to loose, dissolve; intrans.
to loose in order to departure; to depart, Luke
12:36;to depart from life, Phil 1:23; Acts 16:26
v.l.*

ἀναλωθῆτε   aor pass subj 2 pl
[Ga 5:15; cf. ajnali; 384]   ἀναλόω
ἀναλῶσαι   aor act inf
[Lk 9:54; cf. ajnali; 384]   "

ἀναμάρτητος, ον   {387, a-3a}
without sin, guiltless, John 8:7*

ἀναμάρτητος   nom sg masc
[Jn 8:7; a-3a; 387]   ἀναμάρτητος
ἀναμένειν   pres act inf
[1Th 1:10; cv-1c(2); 388]   ἀναμένω

ἀναμένω   {388, cv-1c(2)}
[-, -, -, -, -] to await, wait for, expect, 1 Thess 1:10*

ἀναμιμνῄσκεσθε   pres pass imperative 2 pl
[Hb 10:32; v-5a; 389]   ἀναμιμνῄσκω
ἀναμιμνῃσκομένου   pres pass ptcp gen sg masc
[2C 7:15; v-5a; 389]   "

ἀναμιμνῄσκω   {389, v-5a}
[ἀναμνήσω, -, -, -, ἀνεμνήσθην] to remind, cause
to remember, 1 Cor 4:17; to exhort, 2 Tim 1:6; to
call to mind, recollect, remember, Mark 11:21;
14:72; 2 Cor 7:15; Heb 10:32; Acts 16:35 v.l.*

ἀναμιμνῄσκω   pres act ind 1 sg
[2Ti 1:6; v-5a; 389]   "
ἀναμνήσει   fut act ind 3 sg [1C 4:17; v-5a; 389]   "
ἀναμνησθείς   aor pass ptcp nom sg masc
[Mk 11:21; v-5a; 389]   "
ἀνάμνησιν   acc sg fem
[3t; n-3e(5b); 390]   ἀνάμνησις

ἀνάμνησις, εως, ἡ   {390, n-3e(5b)}
remembrance; a commemoration, memorial, Luke
22:19; 1 Cor 11:24, 25; Heb 10:3*

ἀνάμνησις   nom sg fem [Hb 10:3; n-3e(5b); 390]   "
ἀνανεοῦσθαι   pres pass inf
[Ep 4:23; cv-1d(3); 391]   ἀνανεόω

ἀνανεόω   {391, cv-1d(3)}
[-, -, -, -, -] also spelled ἀνανεόομαι, to renew;
pass. to be renewed, be renovated, by inward
reformation, Eph 4:23*

ἀνανήφω   {392, cv-1b(1)}
[-, ἀνένηψα -, -, -] to become sober; met. to recover
sobriety of mind, 2 Tim 2:26*

ἀνανήψωσιν   aor act subj 3 pl
[2Ti 2:26; cv-1b(1); 392]   ἀνανήφω
Ἁνανία   voc sg masc [2t; n-1d; 393]   Ἁνανίας
Ἁνανίαν   acc sg masc [Ac 9:12; n-1d; 393]   "

Ἁνανίας, ου, ὁ   {393, n-1d}
Ananias, pr. name I. A Christian of Jerusalem,
Acts 5:1, etc. II. A Christian of Damascus, Acts
9:12, etc. III. High Priest, Acts 23:2; 24:1

Ἁνανίας   nom sg masc [8t; n-1d; 393]   "

ἀναντίρρητος, ον   {394, a-3a}
not to be contradicted, indisputable, Acts 19:36*

ἀναντιρρήτων   gen pl neut
[Ac 19:36; a-3a; 394]   ἀναντίρρητος

ἀναντιρρήτως   {395, adverb}
pr. without contradiction or gainsaying; without
hesitation, promptly, Acts 10:29*

ἀναντιρρήτως   adverb
[Ac 10:29; adverb; 395]   ἀναντιρρήτως
ἀνάξιοι   nom pl masc [1C 6:2; a-3a; 396]   ἀνάξιος

ἀνάξιος, ον   {396, a-3a}
inadequate, unworthy, 1 Cor 6:2*

ἀναξίως   {397, adverb}
unworthily, in an improper manner, 1 Cor 11:27,
29 v.l.*

ἀναξίως   adverb [1C 11:27; adverb; 397]   ἀναξίως
ἀναπαήσονται   fut pass ind 3 pl
[Rv 14:13; cv-1a(5); 399]   ἀναπαύω
ἀναπαύεσθε   pres mid ind 2 pl
[2t; cv-1a(5); 399]   "
ἀναπαύεται   pres mid ind 3 sg
[1P 4:14; cv-1a(5); 399]   "
ἀναπαύου   pres mid imperative 2 sg
[Lk 12:19; cv-1a(5); 399]   "
ἀναπαύσασθε   aor mid imperative 2 pl
[Mk 6:31; cv-1a(5); 399]   "
ἀνάπαυσιν   acc sg fem
[5t; n-3e(5b); 398]   ἀνάπαυσις

ἀνάπαυσις, εως, ἡ   {398, n-3e(5b)}
rest, intermission, Matt 11:29; Rev 4:8; 14:11;
meton. place of rest, fixed habitation, Matt 12:43;
Luke 11:24*

ἀνάπαυσον   aor act imperative 2 sg
[Pm 20; cv-1a(5); 399]   ἀναπαύω
ἀναπαύσονται   fut mid ind 3 pl
[Rv 6:11; cv-1a(5); 399]   "
ἀναπαύσω   fut act ind 1 sg
[Mt 11:28; cv-1a(5); 399]   "

ἀναπαύω   {399, cv-1a(5)}
[ἀναπαύσω, ἀνέπαυσα, -, ἀναπέπαυμαι,
ἀνεπάην or ἀνεπαύθην] to cause to rest, to soothe,
refresh, Matt 11:28; mid. to take rest, repose,

refreshment, Matt 26:45; *to have a fixed place of rest, abide, dwell,* 1 Peter 4:14

ἀναπείθει   pres act ind 3 sg
  [Ac 18:13; cv-1b(3); 400]   ἀναπείθω

ἀναπείθω   {400, cv-1b(3)}
  [-, -, -, -, ἀνεπείσθην] *to persuade* to a different opinion, *to seduce,* Acts 18:13*

ἀνάπειρος, ον   {401, a-3a}
  also spelled ἀνάπηρος, *maimed, deprived of some member of the body,* or *at least of its use,* Luke 14:13, 21

ἀναπείρους   acc pl masc
  [2t; a-3a; 401]   ἀνάπειρος

ἀναπέμπω   {402, cv-1b(1)}
  [ἀναπέμψω, ἀνέπεμψα, -, -, -] *to send back,* Phil 12; *to send up, remit* to a tribunal, Luke 23:7, 11, 15; Acts 25:21; 27:1 v.l.*

ἀναπέμψω   aor act subj 1 sg
  [Ac 25:21; cv-1b(1); 402]   ἀναπέμπω
ἀναπέπαυται   perf pass ind 3 sg
  [2t; cv-1a(5); 399]   ἀναπαύω
ἀνάπεσε   aor act imperative 2 sg
  [2t; cv-1b(3); 404]   ἀναπίπτω
ἀναπεσεῖν   aor act inf   [3t; cv-1b(3); 404]   "
ἀναπεσών   aor act ptcp nom sg masc
  [Jn 13:25; cv-1b(3); 404]   "

ἀναπηδάω   {403, cv-1d(1a)}
  [-, ἀνεπήδησα, -, -, -] *to leap up, stand up,* MArk 10:50*

ἀναπηδήσας   aor act ptcp nom sg masc
  [Mk 10:50; cv-1d(1a); 403]   ἀναπηδάω

ἀνάπηρος, ον   {401, a-3a}
  maimed, deprived of some member of the body, or *at least of its use,* Luke 14:13 v.l., 21 v.l.*

ἀναπίπτω   {404, cv-1b(3)}
  [-, ἀνέπεσον or ἀνέπεσα, -, -, -] *to fall* or *recline backwards; to recline* at table, etc., Luke 11:37; *to throw one's self back,* John 21:20

ἀναπληροῦται   pres pass ind 3 sg
  [Mt 13:14; cv-1d(3); 405]   ἀναπληρόω

ἀναπληρόω   {405, cv-1d(3)}
  [ἀναπληρώσω, ἀνεπλήρωσα, -, -, -] *to fill up, complete,* 1 Thess 2:16; *to fulfil, confirm,* as a prophecy by the event, Matt 13:14; *to fill the place of any one,* 1 Cor 14:16; *to supply, make good,* 1 Cor 16:17; Phil 2:30;*to observe fully, keep the law,* Gal 6:2*

ἀναπληρῶν   pres act ptcp nom sg masc
  [1C 14:16; cv-1d(3); 405]   "
ἀναπληρῶσαι   aor act inf
  [1Th 2:16; cv-1d(3); 405]   "
ἀναπληρώσετε   fut act ind 2 pl
  [Ga 6:2; cv-1d(3); 405]   "
ἀναπληρώση   aor act subj 3 sg
  [Pp 2:30; cv-1d(3); 405]   "

ἀναπολόγητος, ον   {406, a-3a}
  inexcusable, Rom 1:20; 2:1*

ἀναπολόγητος   nom sg masc
  [Rm 2:1; a-3a; 406]   ἀναπολόγητος
ἀναπολογήτους   acc pl masc [Rm 1:20; a-3a; 406]   "
ἀνάπτει   pres act ind 3 sg
  [Jm 3:5; cv-4; 409]   ἀνάπτω
ἀναπτύξας   aor act ptcp nom sg masc
  [Lk 4:17; cv-2b; 408]   ἀναπτύσσω

ἀναπτύσσω   {408, cv-2b}
  [-, ἀνέπτυξα, -, -, -] *to roll back, unroll, unfold,* Luke 4:17*

ἀνάπτω   {409, cv-4}
  [-, -, -, -, ἀνήφθην] *to light, kindle, set on fire,* Luke 12:49; James 3:5; Acts 28:2 v.l.*

ἀναρίθμητος, ον   {410, a-3a}
  innumerable, Heb 11:12*

ἀναρίθμητος   nom sg fem
  [Hb 11:12; a-3a; 410]   ἀναρίθμητος
ἀνασείει   pres act ind 3 sg
  [Lk 23:5; cv-1a(3); 411]   ἀνασείω

ἀνασείω   {411, cv-1a(3)}
  [-, ἀνέσεισα, -, -, -] pr. *to shake up;* met. *to stir up, instigate,* Mark 15:11; Luke 23:5*

ἀνασκευάζοντες   pres act ptcp nom pl masc
  [Ac 15:24; cv-2a(1); 412]   ἀνασκευάζω

ἀνασκευάζω   {412, cv-2a(1)}
  [-, -, -, -, -] pr. *to collect one's effects* or *baggage* (σκεύη) in order to remove; *to lay waste by carrying off* or *destroying* every thing; met. *to unsettle, pervert, subvert,* Acts 15:24*

ἀνασπάσει   fut act ind 3 sg
  [Lk 14:5; cv-1d(1b); 413]   ἀνασπάω

ἀνασπάω   {413, cv-1d(1b)}
  [ἀνασπάσω, -, -, -, ἀνεσπάσθην] *to draw up, to draw out,* Luke 14:5; Acts 11:10*

ἀνάστα   aor act imperative 2 sg
  [2t; cv-6a; 482]   ἀνίστημι
ἀναστάν   aor act ptcp nom sg neut
  [Lk 23:1; cv-6a; 482]   "
ἀναστάντες   aor act ptcp nom pl masc
  [6t; cv-6a; 482]   "
ἀναστάς   aor act ptcp nom sg masc
  [36t; cv-6a; 482]   "
ἀναστᾶσα   aor act ptcp nom sg fem
  [2t; cv-6a; 482]   "
ἀναστάσει   dat sg fem
  [7t; n-3e(5b); 414]   ἀνάστασις
ἀναστάσεως   gen sg fem [17t; n-3e(5b); 414]   "
ἀνάστασιν   acc sg fem [12t; n-3e(5b); 414]   "

ἀνάστασις, εως, ἡ   {414, n-3e(5b)}
  a raising or *rising up; resurrection,* Matt 22:23; meton. *the author of resurrection,* John 11:25; met. *an uprising* into a state of higher advancement and blessedness, Luke 2:34

ἀνάστασις   nom sg fem [6t; n-3e(5b); 414]   "
ἀναστατοῦντες   pres act ptcp nom pl masc
  [Ga 5:12; cv-1d(3); 415]   ἀναστατόω

ἀναστατόω   {415, cv-1d(3)}
  [-, ἀνεστάτωσα, -, -, -] *to lay waste, destroy; to*

disturb, throw into commotion, Acts 17:6; *to excite to sedition and tumult,* Acts 21:38; *to disturb* the mind of any one by doubts, etc.; *to subvert, unsettle,* Gal 5:12*

ἀναστατώσαντες   aor act ptcp nom pl masc
 [Ac 17:6; cv-1d(3); 415]   "

ἀναστατώσας   aor act ptcp nom sg masc
 [Ac 21:38; cv-1d(3); 415]   "

ἀνασταυροῦντας   pres act ptcp acc pl masc
 [Hb 6:6; cv-1d(3); 416]   ἀνασταυρόω

ἀνασταυρόω   {416, cv-1d(3)}
 [-, -, -, -, -] *to crucify again,* Heb 6:6*

ἀναστενάξας   aor act ptcp nom sg masc
 [Mk 8:12; cv-2a(2); 417]   ἀναστενάζω

ἀναστενάζω   {417, cv-2a(2)}
 [-, ἀνεστέναξα, -, -, -] *to sigh, groan deeply,* Mark 8:12*

ἀναστῇ   aor act subj 3 sg
 [2t; cv-6a; 482]   ἀνίστημι

ἀνάστηθι   aor act imperative 2 sg
 [7t; cv-6a; 482]   "

ἀναστῆναι   aor act inf   [7t; cv-6a; 482]   "

ἀναστήσας   aor act ptcp nom sg masc
 [3t; cv-6a; 482]   "

ἀναστήσει   fut act ind 3 sg   [3t; cv-6a; 482]   "

ἀναστήσεται   fut mid ind 3 sg   [5t; cv-6a; 482]   "

ἀναστήσονται   fut mid ind 3 pl   [4t; cv-6a; 482]   "

ἀναστήσω   fut act ind 1 sg   [3t; cv-6a; 482]   "

ἀναστήσω   aor act subj 1 sg   [Jn 6:39; cv-6a; 482]   "

ἀναστράφητε   aor pass imperative 2 pl
 [1P 1:17; cv-1b(1); 418]   ἀναστρέφω

ἀναστρέφεσθαι   pres pass inf
 [2t; cv-1b(1); 418]   "

ἀναστρεφομένους   pres pass ptcp acc pl masc
 [2P 2:18; cv-1b(1); 418]   "

ἀναστρεφομένων   pres pass ptcp gen pl masc
 [Hb 10:33; cv-1b(1); 418]   "

ἀναστρέφω   {418, cv-1b(1)}
 [ἀναστρέψω, ἀνέστρεψα, -, -, ἀνεστράφην] *to overturn, throw down,* John 2:15 v.l.; *to turn back, return,* Acts 5:22; 15:16; *to abide, spend time,* Matt 17:22 v.l.; *to live, to conduct one's self,* 2 Cor 1:12; Eph 2:3; 1 Tim 3:15; Heb 13:18; 1 Peter 1:17; 2 Peter 2:18; *to gaze,* Heb 10:33

ἀναστρέψαντες   aor act ptcp nom pl masc
 [Ac 5:22; cv-1b(1); 418]   "

ἀναστρέψω   fut act ind 1 sg
 [Ac 15:16; cv-1b(1); 418]   "

ἀναστροφαῖς   dat pl fem
 [2P 3:11; n-1b; 419]   ἀναστροφή

ἀναστροφή, ῆς, ἡ   {419, n-1b}
 conversation, mode of life, conduct, deportment, Gal 1:13

ἀναστροφῇ   dat sg fem   [2t; n-1b; 419]   "
ἀναστροφήν   acc sg fem   [5t; n-1b; 419]   "
ἀναστροφῆς   gen sg fem   [5t; n-1b; 419]   "
ἀναστῶσιν   aor act subj 3 pl
 [2t; cv-6a; 482]   ἀνίστημι

ἀνασῴζω   {420, cv-2a(1)}
 [-, -, -, -, -] *to save,* Heb 10:14 v.l.*

ἀνατάξασθαι   aor mid inf
 [Lk 1:1; cv-2b; 421]   ἀνατάσσομαι

ἀνατάσσομαι   {421, cv-2b}
 [-, ἀνεταξάμην -, -, -] pr. *to arrange;* hence, *to compose,* Luke 1:1*

ἀνατεθραμμένος   perf pass ptcp nom sg masc
 [Ac 22:3; cv-1b(1); 427]   ἀνατρέφω

ἀνατείλαντος   aor act ptcp gen sg masc
 [2t; cv-2d(1); 422]   ἀνατέλλω

ἀνατείλῃ   aor act subj 3 sg
 [2P 1:19; cv-2d(1); 422]   "

ἀνατέλλει   pres act ind 3 sg
 [Mt 5:45; cv-2d(1); 422]   "

ἀνατέλλουσαν   pres act ptcp acc sg fem
 [Lk 12:54; cv-2d(1); 422]   "

ἀνατέλλω   {422, cv-2d(1)}
 [-, ἀνέτειλα, ἀνατέταλκα, -, -] *to cause to rise,* Matt 5:45; intrans. *to rise,* as the sun, stars, etc., Matt 4:16; *to spring* by birth, Heb 7:14

ἀνατέταλκεν   perf act ind 3 sg
 [Hb 7:14; cv-2d(1); 422]   "

ἀνατίθημι   {423, cv-6a}
 [-, ἀνέθηκα, -, -, -] in N.T. only mid., *to submit to* a person's *consideration, statement,* or *report* of matters, Acts 25:14; Gal 2:2*

ἀνατολή, ῆς, ἡ   {424, n-1b}
 pr. *a rising* of the sun, etc.; *the place of rising , the east,* as also pl. ἀνατολαί, Matt 2:1, 2; met. *the dawn* or *day-spring,* Luke 1:78

ἀνατολή   nom sg fem   [Lk 1:78; n-1b; 424]   ἀνατολή
ἀνατολῇ   dat sg fem   [2t; n-1b; 424]   "
ἀνατολῆς   gen sg fem   [4t; n-1b; 424]   "

ἀνατολικός, ή, όν   {425, a-1a(2a)}
 eastern, Acts 19:1 v.l.*

ἀνατολῶν   gen pl fem   [4t; n-1b; 424]   "
ἀνατρέπουσιν   pres act ind 3 pl
 [2t; cv-1b(1); 426]   ἀνατρέπω

ἀνατρέπω   {426, cv-1b(1)}
 [-, ἀνέτρεψα, -, -, -] pr. *to overturn, overthrow;* met. *to subvert, corrupt,* 2 Tim 2:18; Titus 1:11; James 2:15*

ἀνατρέφω   {427, cv-1b(1)}
 [-, ἀνέθρεψα, -, ἀνατέθραμμαι, ἀνετράφην] *to nurse,* as an infant, Acts 7:20; *to bring up, educate,* Acts 7:21; 22:3; Luke 4:16 v.l.*

ἀναφαίνεσθαι   pres pass inf
 [Lk 19:11; cv-2d(4); 428]   ἀναφαίνω

ἀναφαίνω   {428, cv-2d(4)}
 [-, ἀνέφανα, -, -, -] *to bring to light, display;* mid. and pass. *to appear,* Luke 19:11; a nautical term, *to come in sight of,* Acts 21:3*

ἀναφάναντες   aor act ptcp nom pl masc
 [Ac 21:3; cv-2d(4); 428]   "

ἀναφέρει   pres act ind 3 sg
 [2t; cv-1c(1); 429]   ἀναφέρω

ἀναφέρειν   pres act inf
[Hb 7:27; cv-1c(1); 429]   "

ἀναφέρω   {429, cv-1c(1)}
[-, ἀνήνεγκα or ἀνήνεγκον, -, -, -] *to bear* or *carry upwards, lead up*, Matt 17:1; *to offer* sacrifices, Heb 7:27; *to bear aloft* or *sustain* a burden, as sins, 1 Peter 2:24; Heb 9:28

ἀναφέρωμεν   pres act subj 1 pl
[Hb 13:15; cv-1c(1); 429]   "

ἀναφωνέω   {430, cv-1d(2a)}
[-, ἀνεφώνησα -, -, -] *to exclaim, cry out*, Luke 1:42*

ἀναχθέντες   aor pass ptcp nom pl masc
[3t; cv-1b(2); 343]   ἀνάγω
ἀναχθῆναι   aor pass inf   [2t; cv-1b(2); 343]   "
ἀνάχυσιν   acc sg fem
[1P 4:4; n-3e(5b); 431]   ἀνάχυσις

ἀνάχυσις, εως, ἡ   {431, n-3e(5b)}
a pouring out; met. *excess, stream, flood*, 1 Peter 4:4*

ἀναχωρεῖτε   pres act imperative 2 pl
[Mt 9:24; cv-1d(2a); 432]   ἀναχωρέω

ἀναχωρέω   {432, cv-1d(2a)}
[-, ἀνεχώρησα, -, -, -] *to go backward; to depart, go away*, Matt 2:12; *to withdraw, retire*, Matt 9:24; Acts 23:19; 26:31

ἀναχωρήσαντες   aor act ptcp nom pl masc
[Ac 26:31; cv-1d(2a); 432]   "
ἀναχωρησάντων   aor act ptcp gen pl masc
[Mt 2:13; cv-1d(2a); 432]   "
ἀναχωρήσας   aor act ptcp nom sg masc
[Ac 23:19; cv-1d(2a); 432]   "
ἀναψύξεως   gen sg fem
[Ac 3:20; n-3e(5b); 433]   ἀνάψυξις

ἀνάψυξις, εως, ἡ   {433, n-3e(5b)}
pr. *a refreshing coolness* after heat; met. *refreshing, recreation, rest*, Acts 3:20*

ἀναψύχω   {434, cv-1b(2)}
[-, ἀνέψυξα, -, -, -] *to recreate by fresh air; to refresh, cheer*, 2 Tim 1:16; Rom 15:32 v.l.*

ἄνδρα   acc sg masc [31t; n-3f(2c); 467]   ἀνήρ
ἀνδραποδισταῖς   dat pl masc
[1Ti 1:10; n-1f; 435]   ἀνδραποδιστής

ἀνδραποδιστής, οῦ, ὁ   {435, n-1f}
a man-stealer, kidnapper, 1 Tim 1:10*

ἄνδρας   acc pl masc [21t; n-3f(2c); 467]   ἀνήρ
ἀνδράσιν   dat pl masc [7t; n-3f(2c); 467]   "
Ἀνδρέᾳ   dat sg masc
[Jn 12:22; n-1d; 436]   Ἀνδρέας
Ἀνδρέαν   acc sg masc [4t; n-1d; 436]   "

Ἀνδρέας, ου, ὁ   {436, n-1d}
Andrew, pr. name

Ἀνδρέας   nom sg masc [6t; n-1d; 436]   "
Ἀνδρέου   gen sg masc [2t; n-1d; 436]   "
ἄνδρες   nom pl masc [31t; n-3f(2c); 467]   ἀνήρ
ἄνδρες   voc pl masc [32t; n-3f(2c); 467]   "
ἀνδρί   dat sg masc [19t; n-3f(2c); 467]   "

ἀνδρίζεσθε   pres mid imperative 2 pl
[1C 16:13; cv-; 437]   ἀνδρίζομαι

ἀνδρίζομαι   {437, cv2a(1)}
[-, -, -, -, -] *to render brave* or *manly;* mid. *to show* or *behave one's self like a man*, 1 Cor 16:13*

Ἀνδρόνικον   acc sg masc
[Rm 16:7; n-2a; 438]   Ἀνδρόνικος

Ἀνδρόνικος, ου, ὁ   {438, n-2a}
Andronicus, pr. name, Rom 16:7*

ἀνδρός   gen sg masc [16t; n-3f(2c); 467]   ἀνήρ
ἀνδροφόνοις   dat pl masc
[1Ti 1:9; n-2a; 439]   ἀνδροφόνος

ἀνδροφόνος, ου, ὁ   {439, n-2a}
a homicide, man-slayer, murderer, 1 Tim 1:9*

ἀνδρῶν   gen pl masc [7t; n-3f(2c); 467]   ἀνήρ
ἀνεβαίνομεν   imperf act ind 1 pl
[Ac 21:15; cv-2d(6); 326]   ἀναβαίνω
ἀνέβαινον   imperf act ind 3 pl
[Ac 3:1; cv-2d(6); 326]   "
ἀνεβάλετο   aor mid ind 3 sg
[Ac 24:22; cv-2d(1); 327]   ἀναβάλλω
ἀνέβη   aor act ind 3 sg
[22t; cv-2d(6); 326]   ἀναβαίνω
ἀνέβημεν   aor act ind 1 pl
[Ac 21:6; cv-2d(6); 326]   "
ἀνέβην   aor act ind 1 sg [3t; cv-2d(6); 326]   "
ἀνέβησαν   aor act ind 3 pl [10t; cv-2d(6); 326]   "
ἀνέβλεψα   aor act ind 1 sg
[2t; cv-1b(1); 329]   ἀναβλέπω
ἀνέβλεψαν   aor act ind 3 pl
[Mt 20:34; cv-1b(1); 329]   "
ἀνέβλεψεν   aor act ind 3 sg [5t; cv-1b(1); 329]   "
ἀνεβόησεν   aor act ind 3 sg
[Mt 27:46; cv-1d(1a); 331]   ἀναβοάω
ἀνεγίνωσκεν   imperf act ind 3 sg
[2t; cv-5a; 336]   ἀναγινώσκω

ἀνεγκλησία, ας, ἡ   {440, n -1a}
blameless, Phil 3:14 v.l.*

ἀνέγκλητοι   nom pl masc
[1Ti 3:10; a-3a; 441]   ἀνέγκλητος
ἀνέγκλητον   acc sg masc [Ti 1:7; a-3a; 441]   "

ἀνέγκλητος, ον   {441, a-3a}
unblamable, irreproachable, 1 Cor 1:8; Col 1:22; 1 Tim 3:10; Titus 1:6, 7*

ἀνέγκλητος   nom sg masc [Ti 1:6; a-3a; 441]   "
ἀνεγκλήτους   acc pl masc [2t; a-3a; 441]   "
ἀνεγνωρίσθη   aor pass ind 3 sg
[Ac 7:13; cv-2a(1); 341]   ἀναγνωρίζω
ἀνέγνωσαν   aor act ind 3 pl
[Jn 19:20; cv-5a; 336]   ἀναγινώσκω
ἀνέγνωτε   aor act ind 2 pl [10t; cv-5a; 336]   "
ἀνέδειξεν   aor act ind 3 sg
[Lk 10:1; cv-3c(2); 344]   ἀναδείκνυμι
ἀνέζησεν   aor act ind 3 sg
[2t; cv-1d(1a); 348]   ἀναζάω
ἀνεζήτουν   imperf act ind 3 pl
[Lk 2:44; cv-1d(2a); 349]   ἀναζητέω
ἀνεθάλετε   aor act ind 2 pl
[Pp 4:10; cv-2d(1); 352]   ἀναθάλλω

ἀνεθεματίσαμεν   aor act ind 1 pl
     [Ac 23:14; cv-2a(1); 354]   ἀναθεματίζω
ἀνεθεμάτισαν   aor act ind 3 pl
     [2t; cv-2a(1); 354]   "
ἀνεθέμην   aor mid ind 1 sg
     [Ga 2:2; cv-6a; 423]   ἀνατίθημι
ἀνέθετο   aor mid ind 3 sg [Ac 25:14; cv-6a; 423]   "
ἀνέθη   aor pass ind 3 sg
     [Ac 16:26; cv-6a; 479]   ἀνίημι
ἀνεθρέψατο   aor mid ind 3 sg
     [Ac 7:21; cv-1b(1); 427]   ἀνατρέφω
ἀνεῖλαν   aor act ind 3 pl
     [Ac 10:39; cv-1d(2a); 359]   ἀναιρέω
ἀνείλατε   aor act ind 2 pl
     [Ac 2:23; cv-1d(2a); 359]   "
ἀνείλατο   aor mid ind 3 sg
     [Ac 7:21; cv-1d(2a); 359]   "
ἀνεῖλεν   aor act ind 3 sg [2t; cv-1d(2a); 359]   "
ἀνεῖλες   aor act ind 2 sg
     [Ac 7:28; cv-1d(2a); 359]   "
ἀνείχεσθε   imperf mid ind 2 pl
     [2C 11:1; cv-1b(2); 462]   ἀνέχω
ἀνεκάθισεν   aor act ind 3 sg
     [2t; cv-2a(1); 361]   ἀνακαθίζω

ἀνεκδιήγητος, ον   {442, a-3a}
     which cannot be related, inexpressible, unutterable,
     indescribable, 2 Cor 9:15*

ἀνεκδιηγήτῳ   dat sg fem
     [2C 9:15; a-3a; 442]   ἀνεκδιήγητος
ἀνέκειτο   imperf mid ind 3 sg
     [Mt 26:20; cv-6b; 367]   ἀνάκειμαι

ἀνεκλάλητος, ον   {443, a-3a}
     unspeakable, ineffable, 1 Peter 1:8*

ἀνεκλαλήτῳ   dat sg fem
     [1P 1:8; a-3a; 443]   ἀνεκλάλητος
ἀνέκλειπτον   acc sg masc
     [Lk 12:33; a-3a; 444]   ἀνέκλειπτος

ἀνέκλειπτος, ον   {444, a-3a}
     unfailing, exhaustless, Luke 12:33*

ἀνέκλινεν   aor act ind 3 sg
     [Lk 2:7; cv-1c(2); 369]   ἀνακλίνω
ἀνέκραγον   aor act ind 3 pl
     [Lk 23:18; cv-2a(2); 371]   ἀνακράζω
ἀνέκραξαν   aor act ind 3 pl
     [Mk 6:49; cv-2a(2); 371]   "
ἀνέκραξεν   aor act ind 3 sg [2t; cv-2a(2); 371]   "

ἀνεκτός, ον   {445, a-3a}
     tolerable, supportable, Matt 10:15; 11:22, 24; Luke
     10:12, 14*

ἀνεκτότερον   nom sg neut comparative
     [Lk 10:14; a-3a; 445]   ἀνεκτός
ἀνεκτότερον   acc sg neut comparative, can
     function adverbially (3t)
     [Lk 10:12; a-3a; 445]   "
ἀνέκυψεν   aor act ind 3 sg
     [Jn 8:7; cv-4; 376]   ἀνακύπτω
ἀνελάβετε   aor act ind 2 pl
     [Ac 7:43; cv-3a(2b); 377]   ἀναλαμβάνω
ἀνελεήμονας   acc pl masc
     [Rm 1:31; a-4b(1); 446]   ἀνελεήμων

ἀνελεήμων   {446, a-4b(1)}
     unmerciful, uncompassionate, cruel, Rom 1:31;
     Titus 1:9 v.l.*

ἀνελεῖ   fut act ind 3 sg
     [2Th 2:8; cv-1d(2a); 359]   ἀναιρέω
ἀνελεῖν   aor act inf   [6t; cv-1d(2a); 359]   "

ἀνέλεος, ον   {447, a-3a}
     merciless, James 2:13*

ἀνέλεος   nom sg fem [Jm 2:13; a-3a; 447]   ἀνέλεος
ἀνελήμφθη   aor pass ind 3 sg
     [5t; cv-3a(2b); 377]   ἀναλαμβάνω
ἀνέλωσιν   aor act subj 3 pl
     [3t; cv-1d(2a); 359]   ἀναιρέω
ἀνεμιζομένῳ   pres pass ptcp dat sg masc
     [Jm 1:6; cv-2a(1); 448]   ἀνεμίζω

ἀνεμίζω   {448, cv-2a(1)}
     [-, -, -, -, -] *to agitate with the wind;* pass. *to be*
     agitated or *driven by the wind,* James 1:6*

ἀνεμνήσθη   aor pass ind 3 sg
     [Mk 14:72; v-5a; 389]   ἀναμιμνῄσκω
ἄνεμοι   nom pl masc [3t; n-2a; 449]   ἄνεμος
ἀνέμοις   dat pl masc [2t; n-2a; 449]   "
ἄνεμον   acc sg masc [Mt 14:30; n-2a; 449]   "

ἄνεμος, ου, ὁ   {449, n-2a}
     the wind; met. *a wind* of shifting doctrine, Eph
     4:14

ἄνεμος   nom sg masc [8t; n-2a; 449]   "
ἀνέμου   gen sg masc [7t; n-2a; 449]   "
ἀνέμους   acc pl masc [2t; n-2a; 449]   "
ἀνέμῳ   dat sg masc [4t; n-2a; 449]   "
ἀνέμων   gen pl masc [4t; n-2a; 449]   "
ἀνένδεκτον   nom sg neut
     [Lk 17:1; a-3a; 450]   ἀνένδεκτος

ἀνένδεκτος, ον   {450, a-3a}
     impossible, what cannot be, Luke 17:1*

ἀνενέγκαι   aor act inf
     [1P 2:5; cv-1c(1); 429]   ἀναφέρω
ἀνενέγκας   aor act ptcp nom sg masc
     [2t; cv-1c(1); 429]   "
ἀνενεγκεῖν   aor act inf
     [Hb 9:28; cv-1c(1); 429]   "
ἀνέντες   aor act ptcp nom pl masc
     [Ac 27:40; cv-6a; 479]   ἀνίημι
ἀνεξεραύνητα   nom pl neut
     [Rm 11:33; a-3a; 451]   ἀνεξεραύνητος

ἀνεξεραύνητος, ον   {451, a-3a}
     also spelled ἀνεξερεύνητος, *unfathomable,*
     incapable of human explanation, Rom 11:33*

ἀνεξερεύνητος, see ἀνεξεραύνητος.

ἀνεξίκακον   acc sg masc
     [2Ti 2:24; a-3a; 452]   ἀνεξίκακος

ἀνεξίκακος, ον   {452, a-3a}
     enduring or *patient under evils and injuries,* 2 Tim
     2:24*

ἀνεξιχνίαστοι   nom pl fem
     [Rm 11:33; a-3a; 453]   ἀνεξιχνίαστος
ἀνεξιχνίαστον   acc sg neut [Ep 3:8; a-3a; 453]   "

ἀνεξιχνίαστος, ον {453, a-3a}
to track out, ἴχνος, *a track which cannot be
explored, inscrutable, incomprehensible,* Rom
11:33; Eph 3:8*

ἀνέξομαι fut mid ind 1 sg
[3t; cv-1b(2); 462] ἀνέχω
ἀνέξονται fut mid ind 3 pl
[2Ti 4:3; cv-1b(2); 462] "
ἀνεπαίσχυντον acc sg masc
[2Ti 2:15; a-3a; 454] ἀνεπαίσχυντος

ἀνεπαίσχυντος, ον {454, a-3a}
without cause of shame, irreproachable, 2 Tim 2:15*

ἀνέπαυσαν aor act ind 3 pl
[1C 16:18; cv-1a(5); 399] ἀναπαύω
ἀνέπεμψα aor act ind 1 sg
[Pm 12; cv-1b(1); 402] ἀναπέμπω
ἀνέπεμψεν aor act ind 3 sg [3t; cv-1b(1); 402] "
ἀνέπεσαν aor act ind 3 pl
[2t; cv-1b(3); 404] ἀναπίπτω
ἀνέπεσεν aor act ind 3 sg [4t; cv-1b(3); 404] "
ἀνεπίλημπτοι nom pl masc
[1Ti 5:7; a-3a; 455] ἀνεπίλημπτος
ἀνεπίλημπτον acc sg masc [1Ti 3:2; a-3a; 455] "
ἀνεπίλημπτον acc sg fem [1Ti 6:14; a-3a; 455] "

ἀνεπίλημπτος, ον {455, a-3a}
also spelled ἀνεπίληπρος. pr. *not to be laid hold
of;* met. *beyond reproach, unblamable,* 1 Tim 3:2;
5:7; 6:14*

ἀνεπλήρωσαν aor act ind 3 pl
[1C 16:17; cv-1d(3); 405] ἀναπληρόω
ἄνερ voc sg masc [1C 7:16; n-3f(2c); 467] ἀνήρ

ἀνέρχομαι {456, cv-1b(2)}
[-, ἀνῆλθον, -, -, -] *to ascend, go up,* John 6:3; Gal
1:17, 18*

ἀνέσεισαν aor act ind 3 pl
[Mk 15:11; cv-1a(3); 411] ἀνασείω
ἄνεσιν acc sg fem [4t; n-3e(5b); 457] ἄνεσις

ἄνεσις, εως, ἡ {457, n-3e(5b)}
pr. *the relaxing* of a state of constraint; *relaxation*
of rigor of confinement, Acts 24:23; met. *ease,
rest, peace, tranquility,* 2 Cor 2:13; 7:5; 8:13; 2
Thess 1:7*

ἄνεσις nom sg fem [2C 8:13; n-3e(5b); 457] "
ἀνεσπάσθη aor pass ind 3 sg
[Ac 11:10; cv-1d(1b); 413] ἀνασπάω
ἀνέστη aor act ind 3 sg
[15t; cv-6a; 482] ἀνίστημι
ἀνέστησαν aor act ind 3 pl [2t; cv-6a; 482] "
ἀνέστησεν aor act ind 3 sg [4t; cv-6a; 482] "
ἀνεστράφημεν aor pass ind 1 pl
[2t; cv-1b(1); 418] ἀναστρέφω
ἀνεσχόμην aor mid ind 1 sg
[Ac 18:14; cv-1b(2); 462] ἀνέχω
ἀνετάζειν pres act inf
[Ac 22:29; cv-2a(1); 458] ἀνετάζω
ἀνετάζεσθαι pres pass inf
[Ac 22:24; cv-2a(1); 458] "

ἀνετάζω {458, cv-2a(1)}
[-, -, -, -, -] *to examine thoroughly; to examine* by
torture, Acts 22:24, 29*

ἀνέτειλεν aor act ind 3 sg
[3t; cv-2d(1); 422] ἀνατέλλω
ἀνετράφη aor pass ind 3 sg
[Ac 7:20; cv-1b(1); 427] ἀνατρέφω
ἀνέτρεψεν aor act ind 3 sg
[Jn 2:15; cv-1b(1); 427] "

ἄνευ {459, prep}
some classify as an improper preposition,
without, Matt 10:29; 1 Peter 3:1; 4:9; Mark 13:2
v.l.*

ἄνευ prep-gen [3t; prep; 459] ἄνευ

ἀνεύθετος, ον {460, a-3a}
unfavorable situated, inconvenient, Acts 27:12*

ἀνευθέτου gen sg masc
[Ac 27:12; a-3a; 460] ἀνεύθετος
ἀνεῦραν aor act ind 3 pl
[Lk 2:16; cv-5b; 461] ἀνευρίσκω

ἀνευρίσκω {461, cv-5b}
[-, ἀνεῦρα or ἀνεῦρον, -, -, -] *to find by diligent
search,* Luke 2:16; Acts 21:4*

ἀνευρόντες aor act ptcp nom pl masc
[Ac 21:4; cv-5b; 461] "
ἀνεφέρετο imperf pass ind 3 sg
[Lk 24:51; cv-1c(1); 429] ἀναφέρω
ἀνεφώνησεν aor act ind 3 sg
[Lk 1:42; cv-1d(2a); 430] ἀναφωνέω
ἀνέχεσθε pres mid imperative 2 pl
[Hb 13:22; cv-1b(2); 462] ἀνέχω
ἀνέχεσθε pres mid ind 2 pl [5t; cv-1b(2); 462] "
ἀνεχόμεθα pres mid ind 1 pl
[1C 4:12; cv-1b(2); 462] "
ἀνεχόμενοι pres mid ptcp nom pl masc
[2t; cv-1b(2); 462] "

ἀνέχω {462, cv-1b(2)}
[ἀνέξω, ἄνεσχον or ἠνεσχόμην, -, -, -] also
spelled ἀνέχομαι, *to endure patiently,* 1 Cor 4:12;
2 Cor 11:20; 2 Thess 1:4; *to bear with,* Matt 17:7;
to suffer, admit, permit, Acts 18:14; 2 Cor 11:4; 2
Tim 4:3; Heb 13:22

ἀνεχώρησαν aor act ind 3 pl
[Mt 2:12; cv-1d(2a); 432] ἀναχωρέω
ἀνεχώρησεν aor act ind 3 sg
[9t; cv-1d(2a); 432] "

ἀνεψιός, οῦ, ὁ {463, n-2a}
a nephew, cousin, Col 4:10*

ἀνεψιός nom sg masc
[Cl 4:10; n-2a; 463] ἀνεψιός
ἀνέψυξεν aor act ind 3 sg
[2Ti 1:16; cv-1b(2); 434] ἀναψύχω
ἀνέῳγεν perf act ind 3 sg
[2t; cv-1b(2); 487] ἀνοίγω
ἀνεῳγμένας perf pass ptcp acc pl fem
[Ac 16:27; cv-1b(2); 487] "
ἀνεῳγμένης perf pass ptcp gen sg fem
[2C 2:12; cv-1b(2); 487] "

ἀνεῳγμένον   perf pass ptcp acc sg masc
[Ac 10:11; cv-1b(2); 487]   "
ἀνεῳγμένος   perf pass ptcp nom sg masc
[Rm 3:13; cv-1b(2); 487]   "
ἀνεῳγμένων   perf pass ptcp gen pl masc
[Ac 9:8; cv-1b(2); 487]   "
ἀνεῳγότα   perf act ptcp acc sg masc
[Jn 1:51; cv-1b(2); 487]   "
ἀνέῳξεν   aor act ind 3 sg
[Jn 9:14; cv-1b(2); 487]   "
ἀνεῴχθη   aor pass ind 3 sg
[Lk 1:64; cv-1b(2); 487]   "
ἀνεῳχθῆναι   aor pass inf
[Lk 3:21; cv-1b(2); 487]   "
ἀνεῴχθησαν   aor pass ind 3 pl
[Mt 27:52; cv-1b(2); 487]   "
ἀνήγαγον   aor act ind 3 pl
[3t; cv-1b(2); 343]   ἀνάγω
ἀνήγγειλαν   aor act ind 3 pl
[Ac 15:4; cv-2d(1); 334]   ἀναγγέλλω
ἀνήγγειλεν   aor act ind 3 sg
[Jn 5:15; cv-2d(1); 334]   "
ἀνηγγέλη   aor pass ind 3 sg [2t; cv-2d(1); 334]   "
ἀνήγγελλον   imperf act ind 3 pl
[Ac 14:27; cv-2d(1); 334]   "

ἄνηθον, ου, τό   {464, n-2c}
dill, an aromatic plant, Matt 23:23; Luke 11:42
v.l.*

ἄνηθον   acc sg neut [Mt 23:23; n-2c; 464]   ἄνηθον
ἀνῆκεν   imperf act ind 3 sg
[2t; cv-1b(2); 465]   ἀνήκω
ἀνῆκον   pres act ptcp acc sg neut
[Pm 8; cv-1b(2); 465]   "

ἀνήκω   {465, cv-1b(2)}
[-, -, -, -, -] to come up to, to pertain to; ἀνήκει,
impers. it is fit, proper, becoming, Col 3:18; Eph
5:4; Phil 8*

ἀνῆλθεν   aor act ind 3 sg
[Jn 6:3; cv-1b(2); 456]   ἀνέρχομαι
ἀνῆλθον   aor act ind 1 sg [2t; cv-1b(2); 456]   "
ἀνήμεροι   nom pl masc
[2Ti 3:3; a-3a; 466]   ἀνήμερος

ἀνήμερος, ον   {466, a-3a}
savage, fierce, ferocious, 2 Tim 3:3*

ἀνήνεγκεν   aor act ind 3 sg
[1P 2:24; cv-1c(1); 429]   ἀναφέρω

ἀνήρ, ἀνδρός, ὁ   {467, n-3f(2c)}
a male person of full age and stature, as opposed
to a child or female, 1 Cor 13:11; a husband, Matt
1:16; a man, human being, individual, Luke 11:31;
used also pleonastically with other nouns and
adjectives, Luke 5:8; Acts 1:16

ἀνήρ   nom sg masc [51t; n-3f(2c); 467]   ἀνήρ
ἀνῃρέθη   aor pass ind 3 sg
[Ac 5:36; cv-1d(2a); 359]   ἀναιρέω
ἀνήφθη   aor pass ind 3 sg
[Lk 12:49; cv-4; 409]   ἀνάπτω
ἀνήχθη   aor pass ind 3 sg
[2t; cv-1b(2); 343]   ἀνάγω
ἀνήχθημεν   aor pass ind 1 pl [4t; cv-1b(2); 343] "

ἀνήχθησαν   aor pass ind 3 pl
[Lk 8:22; cv-1b(2); 343]   "
ἀνθ'   prep-gen [5t; prep; 505]   ἀντί
ἀνθέξεται   fut mid ind 3 sg
[2t; cv-1b(2); 504]   ἀντέχω
ἀνθέστηκεν   perf act ind 3 sg
[2t; cv-6a; 468]   ἀνθίστημι
ἀνθεστηκότες   perf act ptcp nom pl masc
[Rm 13:2; cv-6a; 468]   "
ἀνθίστανται   pres mid ind 3 pl
[2Ti 3:8; cv-6a; 468]   "
ἀνθίστατο   imperf mid ind 3 sg
[Ac 13:8; cv-6a; 468]   "

ἀνθίστημι   {468, cv-6a}
[-, ἀντέστην, ἀνθέστηκα, -, ἀντεστάθην] to
oppose, resist, stand out against

ἀνθομολογέομαι   {469, cv-1d(2a)}
[-, -, -, -, -] pr. to come to an agreement; hence, to
confess openly what is due; to confess, give thanks,
render praise, Luke 2:38*

ἄνθος, ους, τό   {470, n-3d(2b)}
a flower, James 1:10, 11; 1 Peter 1:24 (2t)*

ἄνθος   nom sg neut [4t; n-3d(2b); 470]   ἄνθος
ἄνθρακας   acc pl masc
[Rm 12:20; n-3b(1); 472]   ἄνθραξ

ἀνθρακιά, ᾶς, ἡ   {471, n-1a}
a mass or heap of live coals, John 18:18; 21:9

ἀνθρακιάν   acc sg fem [2t; n-1a; 471]   ἀνθρακιά

ἄνθραξ, ακος, ὁ   {472, n-3b(1)}
a coal, burning coal, Rom 12:20*

ἀνθρωπάρεσκοι   nom pl masc
[2t; a-3a; 473]   ἀνθρωπάρεσκος

ἀνθρωπάρεσκος, ον   {473, a-3a}
desirous of pleasing men, Eph 6:6; Col 3:22*

ἄνθρωπε   voc sg masc [9t; n-2a; 476]   ἄνθρωπος
ἀνθρωπίνη   dat sg fem
[2t; a-1a(2a); 474]   ἀνθρώπινος
ἀνθρωπίνης   gen sg fem [2t; a-1a(2a); 474]   "
ἀνθρώπινον   acc sg neut [Rm 6:19; a-1a(2a); 474] "

ἀνθρώπινος, η, ον   {474, a-1a(2a)}
human, belonging to man, 1 Cor 2:4, 13; 4:3; 10:13;
James 3:7; 1 Peter 2:13; suited to man, Rom 6:19;
1 Tim 1:15 v.l.; 3:1 v.l.*

ἀνθρώπινος   nom sg masc
[1C 10:13; a-1a(2a); 474]   "
ἀνθρωπίνων   gen pl fem [Ac 17:25; a-1a(2a); 474] "
ἄνθρωποι   nom pl masc [27t; n-2a; 476]   ἄνθρωπος
ἀνθρώποις   dat pl masc [44t; n-2a; 476]   "

ἀνθρωποκτόνος, ου, ὁ   {475, n-2a}
a homicide, murderer, John 8:44; 1 John 3:15*

ἀνθρωποκτόνος   nom sg masc
[3t; n-2a; 475]   ἀνθρωποκτόνος
ἄνθρωπον   acc sg masc [62t; n-2a; 476]   ἄνθρωπος

ἄνθρωπος, ου, ὁ   {476, n-2a}
a human being, John 16:21; Phil 2:7; an individual,
Rom 3:28, et al. freq.; used also pleonastically
with other words, Matt 11:19; et al.; met. the

spiritual frame of the inner *man*, Rom 7:22; Eph 3:16; 1 Peter 3:4

ἄνθρωπος   nom sg masc [123t; n-2a; 476]   "
ἀνθρώπου   gen sg masc [129t; n-2a; 476]   "
ἀνθρώπους   acc pl masc [31t; n-2a; 476]   "
ἀνθρώπῳ   dat sg masc [26t; n-2a; 476]   "
ἀνθρώπων   gen pl masc [99t; n-2a; 476]   "

ἀνθυπατεύω   {477, v-1a(6)}
[-, -, -, -, -] *to be proconsul*, Acts 18:12 v.l.*

ἀνθύπατοι   nom pl masc
   [Ac 19:38; n-2a; 478]   ἀνθύπατος
ἀνθύπατον   acc sg masc [Ac 13:8; n-2a; 478]   "

ἀνθύπατος, ου, ὁ   {478, n-2a}
a proconsul, Acts 13:7, 8, 12; 19:38

ἀνθύπατος   nom sg masc [Ac 13:12; n-2a; 478]   "
ἀνθυπάτου   gen sg masc [Ac 18:12; n-2a; 478]   "
ἀνθυπάτῳ   dat sg masc [Ac 13:7; n-2a; 478]   "
ἀνθωμολογεῖτο   imperf mid ind 3 sg
   [Lk 2:38; cv-1d(2a); 469]   ἀνθομολογέομαι
ἀνιέντες   pres act ptcp nom pl masc
   [Ep 6:9; cv-6a; 479]   ἀνίημι

ἀνίημι   {479, cv-6a}
[-, ἀνῆκα, -, -, ἀνέθην] (1) *to loose, slacken*, Acts 27:40; *to unbind, unfasten*, Acts 16:26; (2) *to omit, dispense with*, Eph 6:9; (3) *to leave* or *neglect*, Heb 13:5*

ἀνίλεως, ω   {480, n-2e}
see ἀνέλεος, *uncompassionate, merciless, stern*, James 2:13 v.l. for ἀνέλεος*

ἀνίπτοις   dat pl fem [2t; a-3a; 481]   ἄνιπτος

ἄνιπτος, ον   {481, a-3a}
literally: *unwashed*; figuratively: *ceremonially unclean* Matt 15:20; Mark 7:2, 5 v.l.*

ἀνιστάμενος   pres mid ptcp nom sg masc
   [Rm 15:12; cv-6a; 482]   ἀνίστημι
ἀνίστασθαι   pres mid inf [Hb 7:11; cv-6a; 482]   "
ἀνίσταται   pres mid ind 3 sg
   [Hb 7:15; cv-6a; 482]

ἀνίστημι   {482, cv-6a}
[ἀναστήσω, ἀνέστησα or ἀνέστην, -, -, -] trans. *to cause to stand up* or *rise*, Acts 9:41; *to raise up*, as the dead, John 6:39; *to raise up* into existence, Matt 22:24; intrans. and mid., *to rise up*, Matt 9:9; *to rise up* into existence, Acts 7:18; 20:30

Ἅννα, ας, ἡ   {483, n-1a}
Anna, pr. name, Luke 2:26*

Ἅννα   nom sg fem [Lk 2:36; n-1a; 483]   Ἅννα
Ἅννα   gen sg masc [Lk 3:2; n-1e; 484]   Ἅννας
Ἅνναν   acc sg masc [Jn 18:13; n-1e; 484]   "

Ἅννας, α, ὁ   {484, n-1e}
Annas, pr. name, short version of Ἅνανος, Luke 3:2; John 18:13, 24; Acts 4:6*

Ἅννας   nom sg masc [2t; n-1e; 484]   "
ἀνόητοι   nom pl masc [2t; a-3a; 485]   ἀνόητος
ἀνόητοι   voc pl masc [2t; a-3a; 485]   "
ἀνοήτοις   dat pl masc [Rm 1:14; a-3a; 485]   "

ἀνόητος, ον   {485, a-3a}
inconsiderate, unintelligent, unwise; Luke 24:25; Rom 1:14; Gal 3:1, 3; Titus 3:3; *brutish*, 1 Tim 6:9

ἀνοήτους   acc pl fem [1Ti 6:9; a-3a; 485]   "

ἄνοια, ας, ἡ   {486, n-1a}
want of understanding; folly, rashness, madness, Luke 6:11; 2 Tim 3:9*

ἄνοια   nom sg fem [2Ti 3:9; n-1a; 486]   ἄνοια
ἀνοίας   gen sg fem [Lk 6:11; n-1a; 486]   "
ἀνοίγει   pres act ind 3 sg
   [3t; cv-1b(2); 487]   ἀνοίγω
ἀνοίγειν   pres act inf
   [Ac 18:14; cv-1b(2); 487]   "
ἀνοιγήσεται   fut pass ind 3 sg
   [4t; cv-1b(2); 487]   "

ἀνοίγω   {487, cv-1b(2)}
[ἀνοίξω, ἀνέῳξα or ἠνέῳξα or ἤνοιξα, ἀνέῳγα, ἀνέῳγμαι, ἀνεῴχθην or ἠνοίχθην] trans. *to open*, Matt 2:11; intrans. *to be opened, to be open*, Matt 3:16; John 1:52

ἀνοίγων   pres act ptcp nom sg masc
   [Rv 3:7; cv-1b(2); 487]   "
ἀνοιγῶσιν   aor pass subj 3 pl
   [Mt 20:33; cv-1b(2); 487]   "

ἀνοικοδομέω   {488, cv-1d(2a)}
[ἀνοικοδομήσω, -, -, -, -] *to rebuild*, Acts 15:16 (2t); Jude 20 v.l.*

ἀνοικοδομήσω   fut act ind 1 sg
   [2t; cv-1d(2a); 488]   ἀνοικοδομέω
ἀνοῖξαι   aor act inf [7t; cv-1b(2); 487]   ἀνοίγω
ἀνοίξαντες   aor act ptcp nom pl masc
   [3t; cv-1b(2); 487]   "
ἀνοίξας   aor act ptcp nom sg masc
   [6t; cv-1b(2); 487]   "
ἀνοίξει   dat sg fem
   [Ep 6:19; n-3e(5b); 489]   ἄνοιξις
ἀνοίξῃ   aor act subj 3 sg
   [2t; cv-1b(2); 487]   ἀνοίγω

ἄνοιξις, εως, ἡ   {489, n-3e(5b)}
an opening, act of opening, Eph 6:19*

ἄνοιξον   aor act imperative 2 sg
   [2t; cv-1b(2); 487]   "
ἀνοίξω   fut act ind 1 sg
   [Mt 13:35; cv-1b(2); 487]   "
ἀνοίξωσιν   aor act subj 3 pl
   [Lk 12:36; cv-1b(2); 487]   "

ἀνομία, ας, ἡ   {490, n-1a}
lawlessness; violation of law, 1 John 3:4; *iniquity, sin*, Matt 7:23

ἀνομία   nom sg fem [1J 3:4; n-1a; 490]   ἀνομία
ἀνομίᾳ   dat sg fem [2t; n-1a; 490]   "
ἀνομίαι   nom pl fem [Rm 4:7; n-1a; 490]   "
ἀνομίαν   acc sg fem [6t; n-1a; 490]   "
ἀνομίας   gen sg fem [4t; n-1a; 490]   "
ἀνομιῶν   gen pl fem [Hb 10:17; n-1a; 490]   "
ἀνόμοις   dat pl masc [2t; a-3a; 491]   ἄνομος
ἀνόμοις   dat pl neut [2P 2:8; a-3a; 491]   "

ἄνομος, ον   {491, a-3a}
lawless, without law, not subject to law, 1 Cor 9:21;
lawless, violating law, wicked, impious, Acts 2:23;
a transgressor, Mark 15:28; Luke 22:37

ἄνομος   nom sg masc [3t; a-3a; 491]   "
ἀνόμους   acc pl masc [1C 9:21; a-3a; 491]   "
ἀνόμων   gen pl masc [2t; a-3a; 491]   "

ἀνόμως   {492, adverb}
without the intervention of *law*, Rom 2:12 (2t)

ἀνόμως   adverb [2t; adverb; 492]   ἀνόμως

ἀνόνητος, ον   {493, a-3a}
uselss, 1 Tim 6:9 v.l.*

ἀνορθόω   {494, cv-1d(3)}
[ἀνορθώσω, ἀνώρθωσα, -, -, ἀνωρθώθην] *to
restore to straightness* or *erectness*, Luke 13:13; *to
re-invigorate*, Heb 12:12; *to re-erect*, Acts 15:16*

ἀνορθώσατε   aor act imperative 2 pl
   [Hb 12:12; cv-1d(3); 494]   ἀνορθόω
ἀνορθώσω   fut act ind 1 sg
   [Ac 15:16; cv-1d(3); 494]   "
ἀνόσιοι   nom pl masc
   [2Ti 3:2; a-3a; 495]   ἀνόσιος
ἀνοσίοις   dat pl masc [1Ti 1:9; a-3a; 495]   "

ἀνόσιος, ον   {495, a-3a}
impious, unholy, 1 Tim 1:9; 2 Tim 3:2*

ἀνοχή, ῆς, ἡ   {496, n-1b}
forbearance, patience, Rom 2:4; 3:26*

ἀνοχῇ   dat sg fem [Rm 3:26; n-1b; 496]   ἀνοχή
ἀνοχῆς   gen sg fem [Rm 2:4; n-1b; 496]   "

ἀνταγωνίζομαι   {497, cv-2a(1)}
[-, -, -, -, -] *to contend, strive against*, Heb 12:4*

ἀνταγωνιζόμενοι   pres mid ptcp nom pl masc
   [Hb 12:4; cv-2a(1); 497]   ἀνταγωνίζομαι

ἀντάλλαγμα, ατος, τό   {498, n-3c(4)}
a price paid in exchange for a thing; *compensation,
equivalent ransom*, Matt 16:26; Mark 8:37*

ἀντάλλαγμα   acc sg neut
   [2t; n-3c(4); 498]   ἀντάλλαγμα

ἀνταναπληρόω   {499, cv-1d(3)}
[-, -, -, -, -] *to fill up, complete, supply*, Col 1:24*

ἀνταναπληρῶ   pres act ind 1 sg
   [Cl 1:24; cv-1d(3); 499]   ἀνταναπληρόω

ἀνταποδίδωμι   {500, cv-6a}
[ἀνταποδώσω, ἀνταπέδωκα, -, -, ἀνταπεδόθην] *to
repay, give back, return, recompense*, Luke 14:14
(2t); Rom 11:35; 12:19; 1 Thess 3:9; 2 Thess 1:6;
Heb 10:30

ἀνταποδοθήσεται   fut pass ind 3 sg
   [2t; cv-6a; 500]   ἀνταποδίδωμι

ἀνταπόδομα, ατος, τό   {501, n-3c(4)}
repayment, recompense, retribution, Luke 14:12;
Rom 11:9*

ἀνταπόδομα   nom sg neut
   [Lk 14:12; n-3c(4); 501]   ἀνταπόδομα
ἀνταπόδομα   acc sg neut [Rm 11:9; n-3c(4); 501]   "

ἀνταπόδοσιν   acc sg fem
   [Cl 3:24; n-3e(5b); 502]   ἀνταπόδοσις

ἀνταπόδοσις, εως, ἡ   {502, n-3e(5b)}
recompense, reward, Col 3:24*

ἀνταποδοῦναι   aor act inf
   [3t; cv-6a; 500]   ἀνταποδίδωμι
ἀνταποδώσω   fut act ind 1 sg [2t; cv-6a; 500]   "
ἀνταποκριθῆναι   aor pass inf
   [Lk 14:6; cv-1c(2); 503]   ἀνταποκρίνομαι

ἀνταποκρίνομαι   {503, cv-1c(2)}
[-, -, -, -, ἀνταπεκρίθην] occurs in the N.T. only
in the middle, *to answer, speak in answer*, Luke
14:6; *to reply against, contradict, dispute*, Rom
9:20*

ἀνταποκρινόμενος   pres mid ptcp nom sg masc
   [Rm 9:20; cv-1c(2); 503]   "
ἀντειπεῖν   aor act inf
   [2t; cv-1b(2); 515]   ἀντιλέγω
ἀντελάβετο   aor mid ind 3 sg
   [Lk 1:54; cv-3a(2b); 514]   ἀντιλαμβάνω
ἀντέλεγον   imperf act ind 3 pl
   [Ac 13:45; cv-1b(2); 515]   ἀντιλέγω
ἀντελοιδόρει   imperf act ind 3 sg
   [1P 2:23; cv-1d(2a); 518]   ἀντιλοιδορέω
ἀντέστη   aor act ind 3 sg
   [2Ti 4:15; cv-6a; 468]   ἀνθίστημι
ἀντέστην   aor act ind 1 sg [Ga 2:11; cv-6a; 468]   "
ἀντέστησαν   aor act ind 3 pl
   [2Ti 3:8; cv-6a; 468]   "
ἀντέχεσθε   pres mid imperative 2 pl
   [1Th 5:14; cv-1b(2); 504]   ἀντέχω
ἀντεχόμενον   pres mid ptcp acc sg masc
   [Ti 1:9; cv-1b(2); 504]   "

ἀντέχω   {504, cv-1b(2)}
[-, ἀνθέξω, -, -, -] *to hold firmly, cling* or *adhere to;
to be devoted to* any one, Luke 16:13; Titus 1:9; *to
exercise a zealous care for* any one, 1 Thess 5:14;
Mark 6:24*

ἀντί   {505, prep}
over against; hence, *in correspondence to,
answering to*, John 1:16; *in place of*, Matt 2:22; *in
retribution* or *return for*, Matt 5:38; *in
consideration of*, Heb 12:2, 16; *on account of*, Matt
17:27; ἀνθ᾽ ὧν, *because*, Luke 1:20

ἀντί   prep-gen [17t; prep; 505]   ἀντί
ἀντιβάλλετε   pres act ind 2 pl
   [Lk 24:17; cv-2d(1); 506]   ἀντιβάλλω

ἀντιβάλλω   {506, cv-2d(1)}
[-, -, -, -, -] pr. *to throw* or *toss from one to another;*
met. *to agitate, to converse* or *discourse about,*
Luke 24:17*

ἀντιδιατιθεμένους   pres mid ptcp acc pl masc
   [2Ti 2:25; cv-6a; 507]   ἀντιδιατίθημι

ἀντιδιατίθημι   {507, cv-6a}
[-, -, -, -, -] *to set opposite*; mid. (only in the N.T.)
to be of an opposite opinion, to be adverse; opponent,
2 Tim 2:25*

ἀντίδικος, ου, ὁ　　　　{508, n-2a}
　　an opponent in a lawsuit, Matt 5:25 (2t); Luke
　　12:58; 18:3; *an adversary,* 1 Peter 5:8*

ἀντίδικος　nom sg masc　[2t; n-2a; 508]　　ἀντίδικος
ἀντιδίκου　gen sg masc　[2t; n-2a; 508]　　"
ἀντιδίκῳ　dat sg masc　[Mt 5:25; n-2a; 508]　　"
ἀντιθέσεις　acc pl fem
　　[1Ti 6:20; n-3e(5b); 509]　　ἀντίθεσις

ἀντίθεσις, εως, ἡ　　　　{509, n-3e(5b)}
　　pr. *opposition;* hence, *a question proposed for
　　dispute, disputation,* 1 Tim 6:20*

ἀντικαθίστημι　　　　{510, cv-6a}
　　[-, ἀντικατέστην, -, -, -] trans. *to set in opposition;*
　　intrans. *to withstand, resist,* Heb 12:4*

ἀντικαλέσωσιν　aor act subj 3 pl
　　[Lk 14:12; cv-1d(2b); 511]　　ἀντικαλέω

ἀντικαλέω　　　　{511, cv-1d(2b)}
　　[-, ἀντεκάλεσα, -, -, -] *to invite in return,* Luke
　　14:12*

ἀντικατέστητε　aor act ind 2 pl
　　[Hb 12:4; cv-6a; 510]　　ἀντικαθίστημι

ἀντίκειμαι　　　　{512, cv-6b}
　　[-, -, -, -, -] pr. *occupy an opposite position;* met. *to
　　oppose, be adverse to,* Gal 5:17; 1 Tim 1:10;
　　opponent, hostile, Luke 13:7

ἀντικείμενοι　pres mid ptcp nom pl masc
　　[3t; cv-6b; 512]　　ἀντίκειμαι
ἀντικείμενος　pres mid ptcp nom sg masc
　　[2Th 2:4; cv-6b; 512]　　"
ἀντικειμένῳ　pres mid ptcp dat sg masc
　　[1Ti 5:14; cv-6b; 512]　　"
ἀντικειμένων　pres mid ptcp gen pl masc
　　[Pp 1:28; cv-6b; 512]　　"
ἀντίκειται　pres mid ind 3 sg　[2t; cv-6b; 512]　　"

ἀντικρύ, see ἄντικρυς.

ἄντικρυς　　　　{513, adverb}
　　can function as an improper preposition with
　　the gen., also spelled ἀντικρύ, *opposite to, over
　　against,* Acts 20:15*

ἄντικρυς　prep-gen
　　[Ac 20:15; adverb; 513]　　ἄντικρυς
ἀντιλαμβάνεσθαι　pres mid inf
　　[Ac 20:35; cv-3a(2b); 514]　　ἀντιλαμβάνω
ἀντιλαμβανόμενοι　pres mid ptcp nom pl masc
　　[1Ti 6:2; cv-3a(2b); 514]　　"

ἀντιλαμβάνω　　　　{514, cv-3a(2b)}
　　[-, ἀντέλαβον, -, -, -] *to aid, assist, help,* Luke 1:54;
　　Acts 20:35; *to be a recipient,* 1 Tim 6:2*

ἀντιλέγει　pres act ind 3 sg
　　[Jn 19:12; cv-1b(2); 515]　　ἀντιλέγω
ἀντιλέγεται　pres pass ind 3 sg
　　[Ac 28:22; cv-1b(2); 515]　　"
ἀντιλεγόμενον　pres pass ptcp acc sg neut
　　[Lk 2:34; cv-1b(2); 515]　　"
ἀντιλέγοντα　pres act ptcp acc sg masc
　　[Rm 10:21; cv-1b(2); 515]　　"
ἀντιλέγοντας　pres act ptcp acc pl masc
　　[2t; cv-1b(2); 515]　　"

ἀντιλέγοντες　pres act ptcp nom pl masc
　　[Lk 20:27; cv-1b(2); 515]　　"
ἀντιλεγόντων　pres act ptcp gen pl masc
　　[Ac 28:19; cv-1b(2); 515]　　"

ἀντιλέγω　　　　{515, cv-1b(2)}
　　[-, ἀντεῖπον, -, -, -] *to speak against, contradict; to
　　gainsay, deny,* Luke 20:27; *to oppose,* John 19:12;
　　Acts 13:45; 28:19; Rom 10:21; Titus 1:9; 2:9; pass.
　　to be spoken against, decried, Luke 2:34; Acts
　　28:22*

ἀντιλήμψεις　acc pl fem
　　[1C 12:28; n-3e(5b); 516]　　ἀντίλημψις

ἀντίλημψις, εως, ἡ　　　　{516, n-3e(5b)}
　　aid, assistance; meton, *one who aids* or *assists, a
　　help,* 1 Cor 12:28*

ἀντιλογία, ας, ἡ　　　　{517, n-1a}
　　contradiction, question, Heb 6:16; 7:7; *opposition,
　　rebellion,* Jude 11; *hostility,* Heb 12:3*

ἀντιλογίᾳ　dat sg fem
　　[Jd 11; n-1a; 517]　　ἀντιλογία
ἀντιλογίαν　acc sg fem [Hb 12:3; n-1a; 517]　　"
ἀντιλογίας　gen sg fem　[2t; n-1a; 517]　　"

ἀντιλοιδορέω　　　　{518, cv-1d(2a)}
　　[-, -, -, -, -] *to reproach* or *revile again* or *in return,*
　　1 Peter 2:23*

ἀντίλυτρον, ου, τό　　　　{519, n-2c}
　　a ransom, 1 Tim 2:6*

ἀντίλυτρον　acc sg neut
　　[1Ti 2:6; n-2c; 519]　　ἀντίλυτρον

ἀντιμετρέω　　　　{520, cv-1d(2a)}
　　[-, -, -, -, ἀντεμετρήθην] *to measure in return,*
　　Luke 6:38*

ἀντιμετρηθήσεται　fut pass ind 3 sg
　　[Lk 6:38; cv-1d(2a); 520]　　ἀντιμετρέω

ἀντιμισθία, ας, ἡ　　　　{521, n-1a}
　　a retribution, recompense, Rom 1:27; 2 Cor 6:13*

ἀντιμισθίαν　acc sg fem
　　[2t; n-1a; 521]　　ἀντιμισθία
Ἀντιοχέα　acc sg masc
　　[Ac 6:5; n-3e(3); 523]　　Ἀντιοχεύς

Ἀντιόχεια, ας, ἡ　　　　{522, n-1a}
　　Antioch, pr. name I. *Antioch,* the metropolis of
　　Syria, where the disciples first received the
　　name of Christians II. *Antioch,* a city of Pisidia,
　　Acts 13:14; 14:19; 2 Tim 3:11

Ἀντιοχείᾳ　dat sg fem [4t; n-1a; 522]　　Ἀντιόχεια
Ἀντιόχειαν　acc sg fem [11t; n-1a; 522]　　"
Ἀντιοχείας　gen sg fem [3t; n-1a; 522]　　"

Ἀντιοχεύς, έως, ὁ　　　　{523, n-3e(3)}
　　an inhabitant of Antioch, Acts 6:5*

ἀντιπαρέρχομαι　　　　{524, cv-1b(2)}
　　[-, ἀντιπαρῆλθον, -, -, -] *to pass over against, to
　　pass along* without noticing, Luke 10:31, 32*

ἀντιπαρῆλθεν　aor act ind 3 sg
　　[2t; cv-1b(2); 524]　　ἀντιπαρέρχομαι

Ἀντιπᾶς, ᾶ, ὁ   {525, n-1e}
  Antipas, pr. name, Rev 2:13*

Ἀντιπᾶς   nom sg masc
  [Rv 2:13; n-1e; 525]   Ἀντιπᾶς
Ἀντιπατρίδα   acc sg fem
  [Ac 23:31; n-3c(2); 526]   Ἀντιπατρίς

Ἀντιπατρίς, ίδος, ἡ   {526, n-3c(2)}
  Antipatris, pr. name, Acts 23:31*

ἀντιπέρα   {527, adverb}
  can function as an improper preposition with
  the gen., *opposite*, Luke 8:26*

ἀντιπέρα   adverb [Lk 8:26; adverb; 527]   ἀντιπέρα
ἀντιπίπτετε   pres act ind 2 pl
  [Ac 7:51; cv-1b(3); 528]   ἀντιπίπτω

ἀντιπίπτω   {528, cv-1b(3)}
  [-, -, -, -, -] pr. *to fall upon, rush upon* any one;
  hence, *to resist by force, oppose, strive against*,
  Acts 7:51*

ἀντιστῆναι   aor act inf
  [4t; cv-6a; 468]   ἀνθίστημι
ἀντίστητε   aor act imperative 2 pl
  [2t; cv-6a; 468]   "

ἀντιστρατεύομαι   {529, cv-1a(6)}
  [-, -, -, -, -] *to war against; to contravene, oppose*,
  Rom 7:23*

ἀντιστρατευόμενον   pres mid ptcp acc sg masc
  [Rm 7:23; cv-1a(6); 529]   ἀντιστρατεύομαι
ἀντιτάσσεται   pres mid ind 3 sg
  [3t; cv-2b; 530]   ἀντιτάσσω
ἀντιτασσόμενος   pres mid ptcp nom sg masc
  [Rm 13:2; cv-2b; 530]   "
ἀντιτασσομένων   pres mid ptcp gen pl masc
  [Ac 18:6; cv-2b; 530]   "

ἀντιτάσσω   {530, cv-2b}
  [-, -, -, -, -] *to post in adverse array*, as an army;
  mid. *to set oneself in opposition, resist*, Acts 18:6;
  Rom 13:2; James 5:6; *to be averse*, James 4:6; 1
  Peter 5:5*

ἀντίτυπα   acc pl neut
  [Hb 9:24; a-3a; 531]   ἀντίτυπος
ἀντίτυπον   nom sg neut [1P 3:21; a-3a; 531]   "

ἀντίτυπος, ον   {531, a-3a}
  of correspondent stamp or *form; corresponding, in
  correspondent fashion*, 1 Peter 3:21; τὸ ἀντίτυπον,
  a copy, representation, Heb 9:24*

ἀντίχριστοι   nom pl masc
  [1J 2:18; n-2a; 532]   ἀντίχριστος

ἀντίχριστος, ου, ὁ   {532, n-2a}
  antichrist, an opposer of Christ, 1 John 2:18, 22;
  4:3; 2 John 7; plural in 1 John 2:18*

ἀντίχριστος   nom sg masc [3t; n-2a; 532]   "
ἀντιχρίστου   gen sg masc [1J 4:3; n-2a; 532] "
ἀντλεῖν   pres act inf
  [Jn 4:15; v-1d(2a); 533]   ἀντλέω

ἀντλέω   {533, v-1d(2a)}
  [-, ἤντλησα, ἤντληκα, -, -] *to draw*, e.g., wine,
  water, etc.; John 2:8, 9; 4:7, 15*

ἄντλημα, ατος, τό   {534, n-3c(4)}
  pr. *that which is drawn; a bucket, vessel for
  drawing water*, John 4:11*

ἄντλημα   acc sg neut
  [Jn 4:11; n-3c(4); 534]   ἄντλημα
ἀντλῆσαι   aor act inf
  [Jn 4:7; v-1d(2a); 533]   ἀντλέω
ἀντλήσατε   aor act imperative 2 pl
  [Jn 2:8; v-1d(2a); 533]   "
ἀντοφθαλμεῖν   pres act inf
  [Ac 27:15; cv-1d(2); 535]   ἀντοφθαλμέω

ἀντοφθαλμέω   {535, cv-1d(2)}
  [-, -, -, -, -] pr. *to look in the face*, met. a nautical
  term, *to bear up against* the wind, Acts 27:15;
  6:10(11) v.l.*

ἄνυδροι   nom pl fem [2t; a-3a; 536]   ἄνυδρος

ἄνυδρος, ον   {536, a-3a}
  without water, dry, 2 Peter 2:17; Jude 12; τόποι
  ἄνυδροι, *dry places*, and therefore, in the East,
  barren, desert, Matt 12:43; Luke 11:24*

ἀνύδρων   gen pl masc [2t; a-3a; 536]   ἄνυδρος
ἀνυπόκριτον   acc sg fem
  [1P 1:22; a-3a; 537]   ἀνυπόκριτος

ἀνυπόκριτος, ον   {537, a-3a}
  unfeigned, real, sincere, Rom 12:9

ἀνυπόκριτος   nom sg fem [2t; a-3a; 537]   "
ἀνυποκρίτου   gen sg fem [2t; a-3a; 537]   "
ἀνυποκρίτῳ   dat sg fem [2C 6:6; a-3a; 537] "
ἀνυπότακτα   acc pl neut
  [Ti 1:6; a-3a; 538]   ἀνυπότακτος
ἀνυπότακτοι   nom pl masc [Ti 1:10; a-3a; 538] "
ἀνυποτάκτοις   dat pl masc [1Ti 1:9; a-3a; 538] "
ἀνυπότακτον   acc sg neut [Hb 2:8; a-3a; 538] "

ἀνυπότακτος, ον   {538, a-3a}
  not subjected, not made subordinate, Heb 2:8;
  *insubordinate, refractory, disorderly,
  contumacious, lawless*, 1 Tim 1:9; Titus 1:6, 10

ἄνω   {539, adverb}
  above, Acts 2:19; Gal 4:26; Col 3:1; *up, upwards*,
  John 11:41; ὁ, ἡ, τό, ἄνω, *that which is above*, John
  8:23; ἕως ἄνω, *to the top*

ἄνω   adverb [9t; adverb; 539]   ἄνω
ἀνῶ   aor act subj 1 sg
  [Hb 13:5; cv-6a; 479]   ἀνίημι

ἀνώγεον, see ἀνάγαιον

ἄνωθεν   {540, adverb}
  from above, from a higher place, John 3:31; of time,
  from the first or *beginning*, Acts 26:5; *from the
  source*, Luke 1:33; *again, anew*, John 3:3, 7; Gal
  4:9; with a prep., *the top* or *upper part*, Matt
  27:51

ἄνωθεν   adverb [13t; adverb; 540]   ἄνωθεν
ἀνωρθώθη   aor pass ind 3 sg
  [Lk 13:13; cv-1d(3); 494]   ἀνορθόω
ἀνωτερικά   acc pl neut
  [Ac 19:1; a-1a(2a); 541]   ἀνωτερικός

ἀνωτερικός, ή, ον   {541, a-1a(2a)}
  upper, higher, inland, Acts 19:1*

ἀνώτερον   {542, adverb}
is the acc sg neut of the adjective ἀνώτερος,
which occurs in our literature only as an
adverb, *higher, superior; to a higher place,* Luke
14:10; *above, before,* Heb 10:8*

ἀνώτερον   adverb-comparative
[2t; adverb; 542]   ἀνώτερον

ἀνωφελεῖς   nom pl fem
[Ti 3:9; a-4a; 543]   ἀνωφελής
ἀνωφελές   acc sg neut [Hb 7:18; a-4a; 543]   "

ἀνωφελής, ες   {543, a-4a}
useless, unprofitable, Titus 3:9; Heb 7:18*

ἄξει   fut act ind 3 sg [1Th 4:14; v-1b(2); 72]   ἄγω
ἀξία   nom sg fem [2t; a-1a(1); 545]   ἄξιος
ἄξια   nom pl neut [Rm 8:18; a-1a(1); 545]   "
ἄξια   acc pl neut [3t; a-1a(1); 545]   "

ἀξίνη, ης, ἡ   {544, n-1b}
an axe, Matt 3:10; Luke 3:9; 13:7 v.l.*

ἀξίνη   nom sg fem [2t; n-1b; 544]   ἀξίνη
ἄξιοι   nom pl masc [4t; a-1a(1); 545]   ἄξιος
ἄξια   nom sg neut [4t; a-1a(1); 545]   "
ἄξιον   acc sg masc [Mt 3:8; a-1a(1); 545]   "
ἄξιον   acc sg neut [4t; a-1a(1); 545]   "

ἄξιος, ια, ιον   {545, a-1a(1)}
pr. *of equal value; worthy, estimable,* Matt 10:11,
13; *worthy of, deserving,* either good or evil, Matt
10:10; *correspondent to,* Matt 3:8; Luke 3:8; Acts
26:20; *comparable, countervailing,* Rom 8:18;
suitable, due, Luke 23:41

ἄξιος   nom sg masc [19t; a-1a(1); 545]   "
ἀξιοῦμεν   pres act ind 1 pl
[Ac 28:22; v-1d(3); 546]   ἀξιόω
ἀξίους   acc pl masc [3t; a-1a(1); 545]   ἄξιος
ἀξιούσθωσαν   pres pass imperative 3 pl
[1Ti 5:17; v-1d(3); 546]   ἀξιόω

ἀξιόω   {546, v-1d(3)}
[ἀξιώσω, ἠξίωσα, -, ἠξίωμαι, ἠξιώθην] *to judge* or
esteem worthy or *deserving; to deem fitting, to
require,* Acts 15:38; 28:22

ἀξιωθήσεται   fut pass ind 3 sg
[Hb 10:29; v-1d(3); 546]   "

ἀξίως   {547, adverb}
worthily, Col 1:10; *suitably, in a manner becoming,*
Rom 16:2

ἀξίως   adverb [6t; adverb; 547]   ἀξίως
ἀξιώσῃ   aor act subj 3 sg
[2Th 1:11; v-1d(3); 546]   ἀξιόω
ἄξων   fut act ptcp nom sg masc
[Ac 22:5; v-1b(2); 72]   ἄγω
ἀόρατα   nom pl neut [2t; a-3a; 548]   ἀόρατος
ἀόρατον   acc sg masc [Hb 11:27; a-3a; 548]   "

ἀόρατος, ον   {548, a-3a}
invisible, Rom 1:20; Col 1:15, 16; 1 Tim 1:17; Heb
11:27

ἀοράτου   gen sg masc [Cl 1:15; a-3a; 548]   "
ἀοράτῳ   dat sg masc [1Ti 1:17; a-3a; 548]   "
ἀπ'   prep-gen [125t; prep; 608]   ἀπό

ἀπάγαγε   aor act imperative 2 sg
[Ac 23:17; cv-1b(2); 552]   ἀπάγω
ἀπαγαγών   aor act ptcp nom sg masc
[Lk 13:15; cv-1b(2); 552]   "
ἀπαγγεῖλαι   aor act inf
[3t; cv-2d(1); 550]   ἀπαγγέλλω
ἀπαγγείλατε   aor act imperative 2 pl
[5t; cv-2d(1); 550]   "
ἀπάγγειλον   aor act imperative 2 sg
[Mk 5:19; cv-2d(1); 550]   "
ἀπαγγελεῖ   fut act ind 3 sg
[Mt 12:18; cv-2d(1); 550]   "
ἀπαγγέλλομεν   pres act ind 1 pl
[2t; cv-2d(1); 550]   "
ἀπαγγέλλοντας   pres act ptcp acc pl masc
[Ac 15:27; cv-2d(1); 550]   "
ἀπαγγέλλοντες   pres act ptcp nom pl masc
[Lk 13:1; cv-2d(1); 550]   "
ἀπαγγέλλουσιν   pres act ind 3 pl
[1Th 1:9; cv-2d(1); 550]   "

ἀπαγγέλλω   {550, cv-2d(1)}
[ἀπαγγελῶ, ἀπήγγειλα, - ,- , ἀπηγγέλην] *to
announce that with which a person is charged,* or
*which is called for by circumstances; to carry back
word,* Matt 2:8; *to report,* Matt 8:33; *to declare
plainly,* Heb 2:12; *to announce* formally, 1 John
1:2, 3

ἀπαγγέλλων   pres act ptcp nom sg masc
[1C 14:25; cv-2d(1); 550]   "
ἀπαγγελῶ   fut act ind 1 sg [2t; cv-2d(1); 550]   "
ἀπάγετε   pres act imperative 2 pl
[Mk 14:44; cv-1b(2); 552]   ἀπάγω
ἀπαγόμενοι   pres pass ptcp nom pl masc
[1C 12:2; cv-1b(2); 552]   "
ἀπαγομένους   pres pass ptcp acc pl masc
[Lk 21:12; cv-1b(2); 552]   "
ἀπάγουσα   pres act ptcp nom sg fem
[2t; cv-1b(2); 552]   "

ἀπάγχω   {551, cv-1b(2)}
[-, ἀπῆγξα, -, -, -] *to strangle;* mid. *to choke* or
strangle one's self, hang one's self, Matt 27:5*

ἀπάγω   {552, cv-1b(2)}
[-, ἀπήγαγον, -, -, ἀπήχθην] *to lead away,* Matt
26:57; *to conduct,* Matt 7:13, 14; pass. *to be led off
to execution,* Acts 12:19; met. *to be led astray,
seduced,* 1 Cor 12:1

ἀπαίδευτος, ον   {553, a-3a}
uninstructed, ignorant; silly, unprofitable, 2 Tim
2:23*

ἀπαιδεύτους   acc pl fem
[2Ti 2:23; a-3a; 553]   ἀπαίδευτος

ἀπαίρω   {554, cv-2d(2)}
[-, -, -, -, ἀπήρθην] *to take away;* pass. *to be taken
away; to be withdrawn,* Matt 9:15; Mark 2:20;
Luke 5:35*

ἀπαίτει   pres act imperative 2 sg
[Lk 6:30; cv-1d(2a); 555]   ἀπαιτέω

ἀπαιτέω   {555, cv-1d(2a)}
[-, -, -, -, -] *to demand, require,* Luke 12:20; *to
demand back,* Luke 6:30*

ἀπαιτοῦσιν   pres act ind 3 pl
  [Lk 12:20; cv-1d(2a); 555]   "

ἀπαλγέω   {556, cv-1d(2a)}
  [-, -, ἀπήλγηκα, -, -] pr. *to desist from grief*; hence,
  to become insensible or *callous*, Eph 4:19*

ἀπαλλάξῃ   aor act subj 3 sg
  [Hb 2:15; cv-2b; 557]   ἀπαλλάσσω
ἀπαλλάσσεσθαι   pres pass inf
  [Ac 19:12; cv-2b; 557]   "

ἀπαλλάσσω   {557, cv-2b}
  [-, ἀπήλλαξα, -, ἀπήλλαγμαι, ἀπηλλάγην] *to set
free, deliver, set at liberty*, Heb 2:15; *to rid
judicially*, Luke 12:58; mid. *to depart, remove*,
Acts 19:12; 5:15 v.l.*

ἀπαλλοτριόω   {558, cv-1d(3)}
  [-, ἀπηλλοτρίωσα, -, ἀπηλλοτρίωμαι, -] pass. *to
be alienated from, be a stranger to; alien*, Eph 2:12;
4:18; Col 1:21*

ἀπαλός, ή, όν   {559, a-1a(2a)}
  soft, tender, Matt 24:32; Mark 13:28*

ἀπαλός   nom sg masc [2t; a-1a(2a); 559]   ἀπαλός
ἄπαν   nom sg neut [4t; a-2a; 570]   ἄπας
ἄπαντα   nom pl neut [2t; a-2a; 570]   "
ἄπαντα   acc sg masc [2t; a-2a; 570]   "
ἄπαντα   acc pl neut [6t; a-2a; 570]   "
ἄπαντας   acc pl masc [4t; a-2a; 570]   "

ἀπαντάω   {560, cv-1d(1a)}
  [ἀπαντήσω, ἀπήντησα, -, -, -] *to meet, encounter*,
Mark 14:13; Luke 17:12*

ἅπαντες   nom pl masc [11t; a-2a; 570]   "
ἀπαντήσει   fut act ind 3 sg
  [Mk 14:13; cv-1d(1a); 560]   ἀπαντάω
ἀπάντησιν   acc sg fem
  [3t; n-3e(5b); 561]   ἀπάντησις

ἀπάντησις, εως, ή   {561, n-3e(5b)}
  a meeting, encounter; εἰς ἀπάντησιν, *to meet*, Matt
25:6; 27:32 v.l.; Acts 28:15; 1 Thess 4:17*

ἁπάντων   gen pl neut [Mt 6:32; a-2a; 570]   ἅπας

ἅπαξ   {562, adverb}
  once, 2 Cor 11:25; *once for all*, Heb 6:4; 9:26, 28;
10:2; 1 Peter 3:18, 20; Jude 3; εἰδὼς ἅπαξ,
knowing once for ever, unfailingly, constantly,
Jude 5

ἅπαξ   adverb [14t; adverb; 562]   ἅπαξ
ἀπαράβατον   acc sg fem
  [Hb 7:24; a-3a; 563]   ἀπαράβατος

ἀπαράβατος, ον   {563, a-3a}
  not transient; not to be superseded, unchangeable,
Heb 7:24*

ἀπαρασκεύαστος, ον   {564, a-3a}
  unprepared, 2 Cor 9:4*

ἀπαρασκευάστους   acc pl masc
  [2C 9:4; a-3a; 564]   ἀπαρασκεύαστος
ἀπαρθῇ   aor pass subj 3 sg
  [3t; cv-2d(2); 554]   ἀπαίρω

ἀπαρνέομαι   {565, cv-1d(2a)}
  [ἀπαρνήσομαι, ἀπηρνησάμην, -, ἀπήρνημαι,

ἀπηρνήθην] *to deny, disown*, Matt 26:34; *to
renounce, disregard*, Matt 16:24

ἀπαρνηθήσεται   fut pass ind 3 sg
  [Lk 12:9; cv-1d(2a); 565]   ἀπαρνέομαι
ἀπαρνησάσθω   aor mid imperative 3 sg
  [2t; cv-1d(2a); 565]   "
ἀπαρνήσῃ   aor mid subj 2 sg
  [Lk 22:34; cv-1d(2a); 565]   "
ἀπαρνήσῃ   fut mid ind 2 sg [5t; cv-1d(2a); 565]   "
ἀπαρνήσομαι   fut mid ind 1 sg
  [2t; cv-1d(2a); 565]   "

ἀπαρτί   {566, adverb}
  This form occurs in our literature only as two
words, ἀπ' ἄρτι, *exactly, certainly, at once*, John
13:19; 14:7; *henceforward*, Matt 26:29; Rev 14:13;
hereafter, Matt 26:64; John 1:52

ἀπαρτισμόν   acc sg masc
  [Lk 14:28; n-2a; 568]   ἀπαρτισμός

ἀπαρτισμός, οῦ, ὁ   {568, n-2a}
  completion, perfection, Luke 14:28*

ἀπαρχή, ῆς, ή   {569, n-1b}
  pr. *the first act of a sacrifice*; hence, *the firstfruits,
first portion, firstling*, Rom 8:23

ἀπαρχή   nom sg fem [6t; n-1b; 569]   ἀπαρχή
ἀπαρχήν   acc sg fem [3t; n-1b; 569]   "

ἅπας, ασα, αν   {570, a-2a}
  all, the whole

ἅπας   nom sg masc [2t; a-2a; 570]   ἅπας
ἅπασαν   acc sg fem [2t; a-2a; 570]   "

ἀπασπάζομαι   {571, cv-2a(1)}
  [-, ἀπησπασάμην, -, -, -] *to take leave of, say farwell
to*, Acts 21:6; 20:1 v.l.*

ἀπάταις   dat pl fem [2P 2:13; n-1b; 573]   ἀπάτη
ἀπατάτω   pres act imperative 3 sg
  [Ep 5:6; v-1d(1a); 572]   ἀπατάω

ἀπατάω   {572, v-1d(1a)}
  [-, ἠπάτησα, -, -, ἠπατήθην] *to deceive, seduce into
error*, Eph 5:6; 1 Tim 2:14; James 1:26*

ἀπάτη, ῆς, ή   {573, n-1b}
  deceit, deception, delusion

ἀπάτη   nom sg fem [2t; n-1b; 573]   ἀπάτη
ἀπάτῃ   dat sg fem [2t; n-1b; 573]   "
ἀπάτης   gen sg fem [2t; n-1b; 573]   "
ἀπατῶν   pres act ptcp nom sg masc
  [Jm 1:26; v-1d(1a); 572]   ἀπατάω

ἀπάτωρ, τορος, τό   {574, n-3c(6b)}
  pr. *without a father, fatherless*; hence, *independent
of paternal descent*, Heb 7:3*

ἀπάτωρ   nom sg masc
  [Hb 7:3; n-3c(6b); 574]   ἀπάτωρ

ἀπαύγασμα, ατος, τό   {575, n-3c(4)}
  a radiance, Heb 1:3*

ἀπαύγασμα   nom sg neut
  [Hb 1:3; n-3c(4); 575]   ἀπαύγασμα

ἀπαφρίζω   {576, cv-2a(1)}
  [-, -, -, -, -] *to cast off like foam*, Jude 13 v.l.*

ἀπαχθῆναι aor pass inf
[Ac 12:19; cv-1b(2); 552] ἀπάγω
ἀπέβησαν aor act ind 3 pl
[Jn 21:9; cv-2d(6); 609] ἀποβαίνω
ἀπέβλεπεν imperf act ind 3 sg
[Hb 11:26; cv-1b(1); 611] ἀποβλέπω
ἀπέδειξεν aor act ind 3 sg
[1C 4:9; cv-3c(2); 617] ἀποδείκνυμι
ἀπεδέξαντο aor mid ind 3 pl
[Ac 21:17; cv-1b(2); 622] ἀποδέχομαι
ἀπεδέξατο aor mid ind 3 sg
[Lk 8:40; cv-1b(2); 622] "
ἀπέδετο aor mid ind 3 sg
[Hb 12:16; cv-6a; 625] ἀποδίδωμι
ἀπεδέχετο imperf mid ind 3 sg
[Ac 28:30; cv-1b(2); 622] ἀποδέχομαι
ἀπεδήμησεν aor act ind 3 sg
[5t; cv-1d(2a); 623] ἀποδημέω
ἀπεδίδουν imperf act ind 3 pl
[Ac 4:33; cv-6a; 625] ἀποδίδωμι
ἀπεδοκίμασαν aor act ind 3 pl
[4t; cv-2a(1); 627] ἀποδοκιμάζω
ἀπεδοκιμάσθη aor pass ind 3 sg
[Hb 12:17; cv-2a(1); 627] "
ἀπέδοντο aor mid ind 3 pl
[Ac 7:9; cv-6a; 625] ἀποδίδωμι
ἀπέδοσθε aor mid ind 2 pl [Ac 5:8; cv-6a; 625] "
ἀπέδωκεν aor act ind 3 sg [2t; cv-6a; 625] "
ἀπέθανεν aor act ind 3 sg
[32t; cv-5a; 633] ἀποθνήσκω
ἀπεθάνετε aor act ind 2 pl [2t; cv-5a; 633] "
ἀπεθάνομεν aor act ind 1 pl [2t; cv-5a; 633] "
ἀπέθανον aor act ind 1 sg [2t; cv-5a; 633] "
ἀπέθανον aor act ind 3 pl [10t; cv-5a; 633] "
ἀπέθεντο aor mid ind 3 pl
[Ac 7:58; cv-6a; 700] ἀποτίθημι
ἀπέθετο aor mid ind 3 sg [Mt 14:3; cv-6a; 700] "
ἀπέθνησκεν imperf act ind 3 sg
[Lk 8:42; cv-5a; 633] ἀποθνήσκω

ἀπεῖδον, see ἀφοράω

ἀπείθεια, ας, ἡ {577, n-1a}
an uncompliant disposition; obstinacy,
disobedience, unbelief, Rom 11:30, 32; Eph 2:2;
5:6; Heb 4:6, 11; Col 3:6 v.l.*

ἀπειθείᾳ dat sg fem
[Rm 11:30; n-1a; 577] ἀπείθεια
ἀπείθειαν acc sg fem [2t; n-1a; 577] "
ἀπειθείας gen sg fem [4t; n-1a; 577] "
ἀπειθεῖς nom pl masc [3t; a-4a; 579] ἀπειθής
ἀπειθεῖς acc pl masc [2t; a-4a; 579] "

ἀπειθέω {578, v-1d(2a)}
[-, ἠπείθησα, -, -, -] to be uncompliant; to refuse
belief, disbelieve, John 3:36; to refuse belief and
obedience, Rom 10:21; 1 Peter 3:20; to refuse
conformity, Rom 2:8

ἀπειθής {579, a-4a}
who will not be persuaded, uncompliant;
disobedient, Luke 1:17; Acts 26:19; Rom 1:30; 2
Tim 3:2; Titus 1:16; 3:3

ἀπειθής nom sg masc [Ac 26:19; a-4a; 579] "

ἀπειθήσαντες aor act ptcp nom pl masc
[Ac 14:2; v-1d(2a); 578] ἀπειθέω
ἀπειθήσασιν aor act ptcp dat pl masc
[3t; v-1d(2a); 578] "
ἀπειθοῦντα pres act ptcp acc sg masc
[Rm 10:21; v-1d(2a); 578] "
ἀπειθοῦντες pres act ptcp nom pl masc
[1P 2:8; v-1d(2a); 578] "
ἀπειθούντων pres act ptcp gen pl masc
[2t; v-1d(2a); 578] "
ἀπειθοῦσι pres act ptcp dat pl masc
[Rm 2:8; v-1d(2a); 578] "
ἀπειθοῦσιν pres act ind 3 pl
[1P 3:1; v-1d(2a); 578] "
ἀπειθῶν pres act ptcp nom sg masc
[Jn 3:36; v-1d(2a); 578] "
ἀπειλάς acc pl fem [Ac 4:29; n-1b; 581] ἀπειλή

ἀπειλέω {580, cv-1d(2a)}
[(ἠπείλουν), -, ἠπείλησα, -, -, -] to threaten,
menace, rebuke, Acts 4:17; 1 Peter 2:23*

ἀπειλή, ῆς, ἡ {581, n-1b}
threat, commination, Acts 4:29; 9:1; harshness of
language, Eph 6:9; Acts 4:17 v.l.*

ἀπειλήν acc sg fem [Ep 6:9; n-1b; 581] "
ἀπειλῆς gen sg fem [Ac 9:1; n-1b; 581] "
ἀπειλησώμεθα aor mid subj 1 pl
[Ac 4:17; cv-1d(2a); 580] ἀπειλέω

ἄπειμι {582, cv-6b}
[(ἀπήειν), -, -, -, -, -] to be absent, go away, depart,
Acts 17:10*

ἄπειμι pres act ind 1 sg
[Cl 2:5; cv-6b; 583] ἄπειμι
ἀπειπάμεθα aor mid ind 1 pl
[2C 4:2; cv-1b(2); 584] ἀπεῖπον

ἀπεῖπον {584, cv-1b(2)}
[-, ἀπειπάμην, -, -, -] to refuse, forbid, to renounce,
disclaim, 2 Cor 4:2*

ἀπείραστος, ον {585, a-3a}
inexperienced, untempted, incapable of being
tempted, James 1:13*

ἀπείραστος nom sg masc
[Jm 1:13; a-3a; 585] ἀπείραστος

ἄπειρος, ον {586, a-3a}
inexperienced, unskillful, ignorant, Heb 5:13*

ἄπειρος nom sg masc [Hb 5:13; a-3a; 586] ἄπειρος
ἀπεῖχεν imperf act ind 3 sg
[Mt 14:24; cv-1b(2); 600] ἀπέχω
ἀπεκαλύφθη aor pass ind 3 sg
[3t; cv-4; 636] ἀποκαλύπτω
ἀπεκάλυψας aor act ind 2 sg [2t; cv-4; 636] "
ἀπεκάλυψεν aor act ind 3 sg [2t; cv-4; 636] "
ἀπεκατεστάθη aor pass ind 3 sg
[3t; cv-6a; 635] ἀποκαθίστημι
ἀπεκατέστη aor act ind 3 sg
[Mk 8:25; cv-6a; 635] "
ἀπεκδέχεται pres mid ind 3 sg
[Rm 8:19; cv-1b(2); 587] ἀπεκδέχομαι

ἀπεκδέχομαι {587, cv-1b(2)}
[(ἀπεξεδεχόμην), -, -, -, -, -] to expect, wait or look

for, Rom 8:19, 23, 25; 1 Cor 1:7; Gal 5:5; Phil 3:20; Heb 9:28

ἀπεκδεχόμεθα   pres mid ind 1 pl
     [3t; cv-1b(2); 587]   "
ἀπεκδεχόμενοι   pres mid ptcp nom pl masc
     [Rm 8:23; cv-1b(2); 587]   "
ἀπεκδεχομένοις   pres mid ptcp dat pl masc
     [Hb 9:28; cv-1b(2); 587]   "
ἀπεκδεχομένους   pres mid ptcp acc pl masc
     [1C 1:7; cv-1b(2); 587]   "

ἀπεκδύομαι   {588, v-3a(1)}
     [-, ἀπεξεδυσάμην, -, -, -] *to put off, renounce,* Col
     3:9; *to despoil* a rival, Col 2:15*

ἀπεκδυσάμενοι   aor mid ptcp nom pl masc
     [Cl 3:9; v-3a(1); 588]   ἀπεκδύομαι
ἀπεκδυσάμενος   aor mid ptcp nom sg masc
     [Cl 2:15; v-3a(1); 588]   "
ἀπεκδύσει   dat sg fem
     [Cl 2:11; n-3e(5b); 589]   ἀπέκδυσις

ἀπέκδυσις, εως, ἡ   {589, n-3e(5b)}
     a putting or *stripping off, renunciation,* Col 2:11*

ἀπεκεφάλισα   aor act ind 1 sg
     [2t; cv-2a(1); 642]   ἀποκεφαλίζω
ἀπεκεφάλισεν   aor act ind 3 sg
     [2t; cv-2a(1); 642]   "
ἀπέκοψαν   aor act ind 3 pl
     [Ac 27:32; cv-4; 644]   ἀποκόπτω
ἀπέκοψεν   aor act ind 3 sg [2t; cv-4; 644]   "
ἀπεκρίθη   aor pass ind 3 sg
     [82t; cv-1c(2); 646]   ἀποκρίνομαι
ἀπεκρίθην   aor pass ind 1 sg [2t; cv-1c(2); 646]   "
ἀπεκρίθης   aor pass ind 2 sg
     [Lk 10:28; cv-1c(2); 646]   "
ἀπεκρίθησαν   aor pass ind 3 pl
     [19t; cv-1c(2); 646]   "
ἀπεκρίνατο   aor mid ind 3 sg [7t; cv-1c(2); 646]   "
ἀπέκρυψας   aor act ind 2 sg
     [Lk 10:21; cv-4; 648]   ἀποκρύπτω
ἀπεκτάνθη   aor pass ind 3 sg
     [Rv 2:13; cv-2d; 650]   ἀποκτείνω
ἀπεκτάνθησαν   aor pass ind 3 pl [4t; cv-2d; 650]   "
ἀπέκτειναν   aor act ind 3 pl [10t; cv-2d; 650]   "
ἀπεκτείνατε   aor act ind 2 pl
     [Ac 3:15; cv-2d; 650]   "
ἀπέκτεινεν   aor act ind 3 sg [2t; cv-2d; 650]   "
ἀπεκύησεν   aor act ind 3 sg
     [Jm 1:18; see ajpokt; 652]   ἀποκυέω
ἀπεκύλισεν   aor act ind 3 sg
     [Mt 28:2; cv-1d(2a); 653]   ἀποκυλίω
ἀπέλαβεν   aor act ind 3 sg
     [Lk 15:27; cv-3a(2b); 655]   ἀπολαμβάνω
ἀπέλαβες   aor act ind 2 sg
     [Lk 16:25; cv-3a(2b); 655]   "

ἀπελαύνω   {590, cv-3c(2)}
     [-, ἀπήλασα, -, -, -] *to drive away,* Acts 18:16*

ἀπελεγμόν   acc sg masc
     [Ac 19:27; n-2a; 591]   ἀπελεγμός

ἀπελεγμός, οῦ, ὁ   {591, n-2a}
     pr. *refutation;* by impl. *disrepute. contempt,* Acts
     19:27*

ἀπελεύθερος, ου, ὁ   {592, n-2a}
     a freed-man, 1 Cor 7:22*

ἀπελεύθερος   nom sg masc
     [1C 7:22; n-2a; 592]   ἀπελεύθερος
ἀπελεύσομαι   fut mid ind 1 sg
     [Rm 15:28; cv-1b(2); 599]   ἀπέρχομαι
ἀπελευσόμεθα   fut mid ind 1 pl
     [Jn 6:68; cv-1b(2); 599]   "
ἀπελεύσονται   fut mid ind 3 pl
     [Mt 25:46; cv-1b(2); 599]   "
ἀπεληλύθεισαν   pluperf act ind 3 pl
     [Jn 4:8; cv-1b(2); 599]   "
ἀπελήλυθεν   perf act ind 3 sg
     [Jm 1:24; cv-1b(2); 599]   "
ἀπελθεῖν   aor act inf   [11t; cv-1b(2); 599]   "
ἀπέλθῃ   aor act subj 3 sg
     [Mt 5:30; cv-1b(2); 599]   "
ἀπέλθητε   aor act subj 2 pl [2t; cv-1b(2); 599]   "
ἀπελθόντες   aor act ptcp nom pl masc
     [9t; cv-1b(2); 599]   "
ἀπελθόντι   aor act ptcp dat sg masc
     [Lk 9:59; cv-1b(2); 599]   "
ἀπελθόντων   aor act ptcp gen pl masc
     [Lk 7:24; cv-1b(2); 599]   "
ἀπελθοῦσα   aor act ptcp nom sg fem
     [Mk 7:30; cv-1b(2); 599]   "
ἀπελθοῦσαι   aor act ptcp nom pl fem
     [2t; cv-1b(2); 599]   "
ἀπέλθω   aor act subj 1 sg [2t; cv-1b(2); 599]   "
ἀπελθών   aor act ptcp nom sg masc
     [16t; cv-1b(2); 599]   "
ἀπέλθωσιν   aor act subj 3 pl
     [Mt 28:10; cv-1b(2); 599]   "
ἀπέλιπον   aor act ind 1 sg
     [3t; cv-1b(1); 657]   ἀπολείπω
Ἀπελλῆν   acc sg masc
     [Rm 16:10; n-1h; 593]   Ἀπελλῆς

Ἀπελλῆς, οῦ, ὁ   {593, n-1h}
     Apelles, proper name, Rom 16:10*

ἀπελογεῖτο   imperf mid ind 3 sg
     [Ac 26:1; cv-1d(2a); 664]   ἀπολογέομαι
ἀπελούσασθε   aor mid ind 2 pl
     [1C 6:11; cv-1a(8); 666]   ἀπολούω
ἀπελπίζοντες   pres act ptcp nom pl masc
     [Lk 6:35; cv-2a(1); 594]   ἀπελπίζω

ἀπελπίζω   {594, cv-2a(1)}
     [-, -, -, -, -] *to lay aside hope, despond, despair;* also,
     to hope for something *in return,* Luke 6:34, 35;
     Eph 4:19 v.l.*

ἀπέλυεν   imperf act ind 3 sg
     [Mk 15:6; cv-1a(4); 668]   ἀπολύω
ἀπελύθησαν   aor pass ind 3 pl
     [Ac 15:33; cv-1a(4); 668]   "
ἀπελύοντο   imperf mid ind 3 pl
     [Ac 28:25; cv-1a(4); 668]   "
ἀπέλυσαν   aor act ind 3 pl [4t; cv-1a(4); 668]   "
ἀπέλυσε   aor act ind 3 sg
     [Ac 23:22; cv-1a(4); 668]   "
ἀπέλυσεν   aor act ind 3 sg [8t; cv-1a(4); 668]   "

ἀπέναντι   {595, prep}
     some classify as an improper preposition,

opposite to, over against, Matt 21:2; 27:61;
contrary to, in oppositition to, against, Acts 17:7;
before, in the presence of, Matt 27:24; Rom 3:18;
Acts 3:16; Mark 12:41 v.l.*

ἀπέναντι prep-gen
    [5t; prep; 595]   ἀπέναντι

ἀπενεγκεῖν aor act inf
    [1C 16:3; cv-1c(1); 708]   ἀποφέρω

ἀπενεχθῆναι aor pass inf
    [Lk 16:22; cv-1c(1); 708]   "

ἀπενίψατο aor mid ind 3 sg
    [Mt 27:24; cv-4; 672]   ἀπονίπτω

ἀπεξεδέχετο imperf mid ind 3 sg
    [1P 3:20; cv-1b(2); 587]   ἀπεκδέχομαι

ἀπέπεσαν aor act ind 3 pl
    [Ac 9:18; cv-1b(3); 674]   ἀποπίπτω

ἀπεπλανήθησαν aor pass ind 3 pl
    [1Ti 6:10; cv-1d(1a); 675]   ἀποπλανάω

ἀπέπλευσαν aor act ind 3 pl
    [2t; cv-1a(7); 676]   ἀποπλέω

ἀπεπνίγη aor pass ind 3 sg
    [Lk 8:33; cv-1b(2); 678]   ἀποπνίγω

ἀπέπνιξαν aor act ind 3 pl
    [Lk 8:7; cv-1b(2); 678]   "

ἀπεράντοις dat pl fem
    [1Ti 1:4; a-3a; 596]   ἀπέραντος

ἀπέραντος, ον   {596, a-3a}
    unlimited, interminable, endless, 1 Tim 1:4*

ἀπερισπάστως   {597, adverb}
    without distraction, without care or *solicitude,* 1
    Cor 7:35*

ἀπερισπάστως adverb
    [1C 7:35; adverb; 597]   ἀπερισπάστως

ἀπερίτμητοι voc pl masc
    [Ac 7:51; a-3a; 598]   ἀπερίτμητος

ἀπερίτμητος, ον   {598, a-3a}
    pr. *uncircumcised;* met. *uncircumcised* in respect
    of untowardness and obduracy, Acts 7:51*

ἀπέρχεσθαι pres mid inf
    [Ac 23:32; cv-1b(2); 599]   ἀπέρχομαι

ἀπέρχῃ pres mid subj 2 sg [2t; cv-1b(2); 599] "

ἀπέρχομαι   {599, cv-1b(2)}
    [ἀπελύσομαι, ἀπῆλθον, ἀπελήλυθα, -, -]
    pluperfect, ἀπεληλύθειν v.l., *to go away, depart,*
    Matt 8:18; *to go forth, pervade,* as a rumor, Matt
    4:24; *to arrive at* a destination, Luke 23:33; *to
    pass away, disappear,* Rev 21:4; ἀπέρχομαι ὀπίσω,
    to follow, Mark 1:20

ἀπερχομένων pres mid ptcp gen pl fem
    [Mt 25:10; cv-1b(2); 599]   "

ἀπέσπασεν aor act ind 3 sg
    [Mt 26:51; cv-1d(1b); 685]   ἀποσπάω

ἀπεσπάσθη aor pass ind 3 sg
    [Lk 22:41; cv-1d(1b); 685]   "

ἀπεστάλη aor pass ind 3 sg
    [2t; cv-2d(1); 690]   ἀποστέλλω

ἀπεστάλην aor pass ind 1 sg [3t; cv-2d(1); 690] "

ἀπέσταλκα perf act ind 1 sg [2t; cv-2d(1); 690] "

ἀπεστάλκαμεν perf act ind 1 pl
    [Ac 15:27; cv-2d(1); 690]   "

ἀπέσταλκαν perf act ind 3 pl
    [Ac 16:36; cv-2d(1); 690]   "

ἀπεστάλκατε perf act ind 2 pl
    [Jn 5:33; cv-2d(1); 690]   "

ἀπέσταλκεν perf act ind 3 sg
    [7t; cv-2d(1); 690]   "

ἀπεσταλμένοι perf pass ptcp nom pl masc
    [5t; cv-2d(1); 690]   "

ἀπεσταλμένος perf pass ptcp nom sg masc
    [3t; cv-2d(1); 690]   "

ἀπεσταλμένους perf pass ptcp acc pl masc
    [2t; cv-2d(1); 690]   "

ἀπεστέγασαν aor act ind 3 pl
    [Mk 2:4; cv-2a(1); 689]   ἀποστεγάζω

ἀπέστειλα aor act ind 1 sg
    [4t; cv-2d(1); 690]   ἀποστέλλω

ἀπέστειλα aor act ind 3 pl
    [13t; cv-2d(1); 690]   "

ἀπέστειλας aor act ind 2 sg [7t; cv-2d(1); 690] "

ἀπέστειλεν aor act ind 3 sg
    [38t; cv-2d(1); 690]   "

ἀπεστερημένος perf pass ptcp nom sg masc
    [Jm 5:4; cv-1d(2a); 691]   ἀποστερέω

ἀπεστερημένων perf pass ptcp gen pl masc
    [1Ti 6:5; cv-1d(2a); 691]   "

ἀπέστη aor act ind 3 sg
    [2t; cv-6a; 923]   ἀφίστημι

ἀπέστησαν aor act ind 3 pl
    [Ac 22:29; cv-6a; 923]   "

ἀπέστησεν aor act ind 3 sg
    [Ac 5:37; cv-6a; 923]   "

ἀπεστράφησαν aor pass ind 3 pl
    [2Ti 1:15; cv-1b(1); 695]   ἀποστρέφω

ἀπεφθέγξατο aor mid ind 3 sg
    [Ac 2:14; cv-1b(2); 710]   ἀποφθέγγομαι

ἀπέχει pres act ind 3 sg
    [3t; cv-1b(2); 600]   ἀπέχω

ἀπέχεσθαι pres mid inf [5t; cv-1b(2); 600] "

ἀπέχεσθε pres mid imperative 2 pl
    [1Th 5:22; cv-1b(2); 600]   "

ἀπέχετε pres act ind 2 pl
    [Lk 6:24; cv-1b(2); 600]   "

ἀπέχῃς pres act subj 2 sg
    [Pm 15; cv-1b(2); 600]   "

ἀπέχοντος pres act ptcp gen sg masc
    [2t; cv-1b(2); 600]   "

ἀπέχουσαν pres act ptcp acc sg fem
    [Lk 24:13; cv-1b(2); 600]   "

ἀπέχουσιν pres act ind 3 pl [3t; cv-1b(2); 600] "

ἀπέχω   {600, cv-1b(2)}
    [-, -, -, -, -] trans. *to have in full* what is due or
    is sought, Matt 6:2, 5, 16; Luke 6:24; Phil 4:18; *to
    have altogether,* Phil 15; hence, *it is enough,* Mark
    14:41; intrans. *to be distant,* Luke 7:6; *to be
    estranged,* Matt 15:8; Mark 7:6, mid. *to abstain
    from,* Acts 14:20

ἀπέχω pres act ind 1 sg
    [Pp 4:18; cv-1b(2); 600]   "

ἀπεχωρίσθη aor pass ind 3 sg
    [Rv 6:14; cv-2a(1); 714]   ἀποχωρίζω

ἀπήγαγον aor act ind 3 pl
    [7t; cv-1b(2); 552]   ἀπάγω

ἀπήγγειλαν   aor act ind 3 pl
   [15t; cv-2d(1); 550]   ἀπαγγέλλω
ἀπήγγειλεν   aor act ind 3 sg
   [10t; cv-2d(1); 550]   "
ἀπηγγέλη   aor pass ind 3 sg
   [Lk 8:20; cv-2d(1); 550]   "
ἀπήγγελλον   imperf act ind 1 sg
   [Ac 26:20; cv-2d(1); 550]   "
ἀπήγξατο   aor mid ind 3 sg
   [Mt 27:5; cv-1b(2); 551]   ἀπάγχω
ἀπήεσαν   imperf act ind 3 pl
   [Ac 17:10; cv-6b; 583]   ἄπειμι
ἀπήλασεν   aor act ind 3 sg
   [Ac 18:16; cv-3c(2); 590]   ἀπελαύνω
ἀπηλγηκότες   perf act ptcp nom pl masc
   [Ep 4:19; cv-1d(2a); 556]   ἀπαλγέω
ἀπῆλθα   aor act ind 1 sg
   [Rv 10:9; cv-1b(2); 599]   ἀπέρχομαι
ἀπῆλθαν   aor act ind 3 pl [3t; cv-1b(2); 599]   "
ἀπῆλθεν   aor act ind 3 sg [40t; cv-1b(2); 599]   "
ἀπῆλθον   aor act ind 1 sg
   [Ga 1:17; cv-1b(2); 599]   "
ἀπῆλθον   aor act ind 3 pl [16t; cv-1b(2); 599]   "
ἀπηλλάχθαι   perf pass inf
   [Lk 12:58; cv-2b; 557]   ἀπαλλάσσω
ἀπηλλοτριωμένοι   perf pass ptcp nom pl masc
   [2t; cv-1d(3); 558]   ἀπαλλοτριόω
ἀπηλλοτριωμένους   perf pass ptcp acc pl masc
   [Cl 1:21; cv-1d(3); 558]   "
ἀπήνεγκαν   aor act ind 3 pl
   [Mk 15:1; cv-1c(1); 708]   ἀποφέρω
ἀπήνεγκεν   aor act ind 3 sg [2t; cv-1c(1); 708] "
ἀπήντησαν   aor act ind 3 pl
   [Lk 17:12; cv-1d(1a); 560]   ἀπαντάω
ἀπησπασάμεθα   aor mid ind 1 pl
   [Ac 21:6; cv-2a(1); 571]   ἀπασπάζομαι

ἀπιστέω   {601, v-1d(2a)}
   [(ἠπίστουν), -, ἠπίστησα, -, -, -] to refuse belief, be
   incredulous, disbelieve, Mark 16:11, 16; Luke
   24:11, 41; Acts 28:24; to prove false, violate one's
   faith, be unfaithful, 2 Tim 2:13; Rom 3:3
ἀπιστήσας   aor act ptcp nom sg masc
   [Mk 16:16; v-1d(2a); 601]   ἀπιστέω

ἀπιστία, ας, ἡ   {602, n-1a}
   unbelief, want of trust and confidence; a state of
   unbelief, 1 Tim 1:13; violation of faith,
   faithlessness, Rom 3:3; Heb 3:12, 19

ἀπιστία   nom sg fem [Rm 3:3; n-1a; 602]   ἀπιστία
ἀπιστίᾳ   dat sg fem [5t; n-1a; 602]   "
ἀπιστίαν   acc sg fem [4t; n-1a; 602]   "
ἀπιστίας   gen sg fem [Hb 3:12; n-1a; 602]   "
ἄπιστοι   nom pl masc [1C 14:23; a-3a; 603]   ἄπιστος
ἀπίστοις   dat pl masc [5t; a-3a; 603]   "
ἄπιστον   nom sg neut [Ac 26:8; a-3a; 603]   "
ἄπιστον   acc sg masc [1C 7:13; a-3a; 603]   "
ἄπιστον   acc sg fem [1C 7:12; a-3a; 603]   "

ἄπιστος, ον   {603, a-3a}
   unbelieving, without confidence in any one, Matt
   17:17; violating one's faith, unfaithful, false,
   treacherous, Luke 12:46; an unbeliever, infidel,
   pagan, 1 Cor 6:6; pass. incredible, Acts 26:8

ἄπιστος   nom sg masc [4t; a-3a; 603]   "
ἄπιστος   nom sg fem [1C 7:14; a-3a; 603]   "
ἄπιστος   voc sg fem [3t; a-3a; 603]   "
ἀπίστου   gen sg masc [2t; a-3a; 603]   "
ἀπιστοῦμεν   pres act ind 1 pl
   [2Ti 2:13; v-1d(2a); 601]   ἀπιστέω
ἀπιστούντων   pres act ptcp gen pl masc
   [Lk 24:41; v-1d(2a); 601]   "
ἀπιστοῦσιν   pres act ptcp dat pl masc
   [1P 2:7; v-1d(2a); 601]   "
ἀπίστων   gen pl masc [4t; a-3a; 603]   ἄπιστος

ἁπλότης, τητος, ἡ   {605, n-3c(1)}
   simplicity, sincerity, purity of mind, Rom 12:8;
   11:3; Eph 6:5; 2 Cor 1:12 v.l.; Col 3:22; liberality,
   as arising from simplicity and frankness of
   character, 2 Cor 8:2; 9:11, 13; 11:3*

ἁπλότητα   acc sg fem
   [2C 9:11; n-3c(1); 605]   ἁπλότης
ἁπλότητι   dat sg fem [5t; n-3c(1); 605]   "
ἁπλότητος   gen sg fem [2t; n-3c(1); 605]   "

ἁπλοῦς, ῆ, οῦν   {606, a-1b}
   pr. single; hence, simple, uncompounded; sound,
   perfect, Matt 6:22; Luke 11:34; Matt 10:16 v.l.*

ἁπλοῦς   nom sg masc [2t; a-1b; 606]   ἁπλοῦς

ἁπλῶς   {607, adverb}
   in simplicity; sincerely, really, or, liberally,
   bountifully, James 1:5*

ἁπλῶς   adverb [Jm 1:5; adverb; 607]   ἁπλῶς

ἀπό   {608, prep}
   pr. forth, from, away from; hence, it variously
   signifies departure; distance of time or place;
   avoidance; riddance; derivation from a quarter,
   source, or material; origination from agency or
   instrumentality

ἀπό   prep-gen [479t; prep; 608]   ἀπό

ἀποβαίνω   {609, cv-2d(6)}
   [ἀποβήσομαι, ἀπέβην, -, -, -] to step off; to
   disembark from a ship, Luke 5:2; John 21:9; to
   become, result, happen, Luke 21:13; Phil 1:19*

ἀποβάλητε   aor act subj 2 pl
   [Hb 10:35; cv-2d(1); 610]   ἀποβάλλω

ἀποβάλλω   {610, cv-2d(1)}
   [-, ἀπέβαλον, -, -, -] to cast or throw off, cast aside,
   Mark 10:50; Heb 10:35*

ἀποβαλών   aor act ptcp nom sg masc
   [Mk 10:50; cv-2d(1); 610]   "
ἀποβάντες   aor act ptcp nom pl masc
   [Lk 5:2; cv-2d(6); 609]   ἀποβαίνω
ἀποβήσεται   fut mid ind 3 sg [2t; cv-2d(6); 609] "

ἀποβλέπω   {611, cv-1b(1)}
   [(ἀπέβλεπον), -, -, -, -, -] pr. to look off from all
   other objects and at a single one; hence, to turn a
   steady gaze, to look with fixed and earnest
   attention, Heb 11:26*

ἀπόβλητον   nom sg neut
   [1Ti 4:4; a-3a; 612]   ἀπόβλητος

ἀπόβλητος, ον {612, a-3a}
pr. *to be cast away*; met. *to be condemned, regarded as vile*, 1 Tim 4:4*

ἀποβολή, ῆς, ἡ {613, n-1b}
a casting off; rejection, reprobation, Rom 11:15; *loss, deprivation*, of life, etc., Acts 27:22*

ἀποβολή   nom sg fem [2t; n-1b; 613]   ἀποβολή
ἀπογεγραμμένων   perf pass ptcp gen pl masc
  [Hb 12:23; cv-1b(1); 616]   ἀπογράφω
ἀπογενόμενοι   aor mid ptcp nom pl masc
  [1P 2:24; cv-1c(2); 614]   ἀπογίνομαι

ἀπογίνομαι {614, cv-1c(2)}
[-, ἀπεγενόμην, -, -, -] *to be away from, unconnected with; to die*; met. *to die to a thing by renouncing it*, 1 Peter 2:24*

ἀπογράφεσθαι   pres mid inf
  [Lk 2:3; cv-1b(1); 616]   ἀπογράφω
ἀπογράφεσθαι   pres pass inf
  [Lk 2:1; cv-1b(1); 616]   "

ἀπογραφή, ῆς, ἡ {615, n-1b}
a register, inventory; registration, enrollment, Luke 2:2; Acts 5:37*

ἀπογραφή   nom sg fem
  [Lk 2:2; n-1b; 615]   ἀπογραφή
ἀπογραφῆς   gen sg fem [Ac 5:37; n-1b; 615]   "

ἀπογράφω {616, cv-1b(1)}
[-, ἀπέγραψα, -, ἀπογέγραμμαι, -] pr. *to copy*; hence, *to register, enrol*, Luke 2:1; Heb 12:23; mid. *to procure the registration of one's name, to give in one's name for registration*, Luke 2:3, 5*

ἀπογράψασθαι   aor mid inf
  [Lk 2:5; cv-1b(1); 616]   ἀπογράφω
ἀποδεδειγμένον   perf pass ptcp acc sg masc
  [Ac 2:22; cv-3c(2); 617]   ἀποδείκνυμι
ἀποδεδοκιμασμένον   perf pass ptcp acc sg masc
  [1P 2:4; cv-2a(1); 627]   ἀποδοκιμάζω

ἀποδείκνυμι {617, cv-3c(2)}
[-, ἀπέδειξα, -, ἀποδέδειγμαι, -] *to point out, display; to prove, evince, demonstrate*, Acts 25:7; *to designate, proclaim, hold forth*, 2 Thess 2:4; *to constitute, appoint*, Acts 2:22; 1 Cor 4:9*

ἀποδεικνύντα   pres act ptcp acc sg masc
  [2Th 2:4; cv-3c(2); 617]   ἀποδείκνυμι
ἀποδεῖξαι   aor act inf [Ac 25:7; cv-3c(2); 617]   "
ἀποδείξει   dat sg fem
  [1C 2:4; n-3e(5b); 618]   ἀπόδειξις

ἀπόδειξις, εως, ἡ {618, n-3e(5b)}
manifestation, demonstration, indubitable proof, 1 Cor 2:4*

ἀποδεκατεύω {619, cv-1a(6)}
[-, -, -, -, -] *to tithe, give one tenth*, Luke 18:12*

ἀποδεκατοῦν   pres act inf
  [Hb 7:5; cv-1d(3); 620]   ἀποδεκατόω
ἀποδεκατοῦτε   pres act ind 2 pl
  [2t; cv-1d(3); 620]   "

ἀποδεκατόω {620, cv-1d(3)}
[-, -, -, -, -] *to pay* or *give tithes of*, Matt 23:23;

Luke 11:42; 18:12; *to tithe, levy tithes upon*, Heb 7:5*

ἀποδεκατῶ   pres act ind 1 sg
  [Lk 18:12; cv-1d(3); 620]   "
ἀπόδεκτον   nom sg neut [2t; a-3a; 621]   ἀπόδεκτος

ἀπόδεκτος, ον {621, a-3a}
acceptable, pleasant, 1 Tim 2:3; 5:4*

ἀποδεξάμενοι   aor mid ptcp nom pl masc
  [Ac 2:41; cv-1b(2); 622]   ἀποδέχομαι
ἀποδεξάμενος   aor mid ptcp nom sg masc
  [Lk 9:11; cv-1b(2); 622]   "
ἀποδέξασθαι   aor mid inf
  [Ac 18:27; cv-1b(2); 622]   "

ἀποδέχομαι {622, cv-1b(2)}
[-, ἀπεδεξάμην, -, -, ἀπεδέχθην] *to receive* kindly or heartily, *welcome*, Luke 8:40; 9:11; Acts 18:27; 28:30; *to receive* with hearty assent, *embrace*, Acts 2:41; *to accept* with satisfaction, Acts 24:3*

ἀποδεχόμεθα   pres mid ind 1 pl
  [Ac 24:3; cv-1b(2); 622]   "

ἀποδημέω {623, cv-1d(2a)}
[-, ἀπεδήμησα, -, -, -] *to be absent from one's home* or *country; to go on travel*, Matt 21:33; 25:14, 15; Mark 12:1; Luke 15:13; 20:9; 2 Cor 5:6 v.l.

ἀπόδημος, ον {624, a-3a}
absent in foreign countries, Mark 13:34*

ἀπόδημος   nom sg masc
  [Mk 13:34; a-3a; 624]   ἀπόδημος
ἀποδημῶν   pres act ptcp nom sg masc
  [Mt 25:14; cv-1d(2a); 623]   ἀποδημέω
ἀποδιδόναι   pres act inf
  [1Ti 5:4; cv-6a; 625]   ἀποδίδωμι
ἀποδιδόντες   pres act ptcp nom pl masc
  [2t; cv-6a; 625]   "
ἀποδιδότω   pres act imperative 3 sg
  [1C 7:3; cv-6a; 625]   "
ἀποδιδοῦν   pres act ptcp nom sg neut
  [Rv 22:2; cv-6a; 625]   "

ἀποδίδωμι {625, cv-6a}
[(ἀπεδέδουν), ἀποδώσω, ἀπέδωκα, -, -, ἀπεδόθην] *to give in answer to a claim* or *expectation; to render* a due, Matt 12:36; 16:27; 21:41; 22:21; *to recompense*, Matt 6:4, 6, 18; *to discharge* an obligation, Matt 5:33; *to pay* a debt, Matt 5:26; *to render back, requite*, Rom 12:17; *to give back, restore*, Luke 4:20; 9:42; *to refund*, Luke 10:35; 19:8; mid., *to sell*, Acts 5:8; 7:9; Heb 12:16; pass., *to be sold*, Matt 18:25; *to be given up* at a request, Matt 27:58

ἀποδίδωμι   pres act ind 1 sg
  [Lk 19:8; cv-6a; 625]   "
ἀποδίδωσιν   pres act ind 3 sg
  [Hb 12:11; cv-6a; 625]   "
ἀποδιορίζοντες   pres act ptcp nom pl masc
  [Jd 19; cv-2a(1); 626]   ἀποδιορίζω

ἀποδιορίζω {626, cv-2a(1)}
[-, -, -, -, -] pr. *to separate by intervening boundaries; to separate* or *divide*, Jude 19*

ἀποδοθῆναι   aor pass inf
   [2t; cv-6a; 625]   ἀποδίδωμι

ἀποδοκιμάζω   {627, cv-2a(1)}
   [-, ἀπεδοκίμασα, -, ἀποδεδοκίμασμαι,
   ἀπεδοκιμάσθην]   to reject upon trial; to reject,
   Matt 21:42; Mark 12:10; Luke 20:17; 1 Peter 2:4,
   7; pass., to be disallowed a claim, declared useless,
   Luke 9:22; 17:25; Heb 12:17

ἀποδοκιμασθῆναι   aor pass inf
   [3t; cv-2a(1); 627]   ἀποδοκιμάζω
ἀπόδος   aor act imperative 2 sg
   [3t; cv-6a; 625]   ἀποδίδωμι
ἀπόδοτε   aor act imperative 2 pl
   [5t; cv-6a; 625]   "
ἀποδοῦναι   aor act inf   [4t; cv-6a; 625]   "
ἀποδούς   aor act ptcp nom sg masc
   [Lk 4:20; cv-6a; 625]

ἀποδοχή, ῆς, ἡ   {628, n-1b}
   pr. reception, welcome; met. reception of hearty
   assent, 1 Tim 1:15; 4:9*

ἀποδοχῆς   gen sg fem   [2t; n-1b; 628]   ἀποδοχή
ἀποδῷ   aor act subj 3 sg
   [3t; cv-6a; 625]   ἀποδίδωμι
ἀποδῷς   aor act subj 2 sg   [2t; cv-6a; 625]   "
ἀποδώσει   fut act ind 3 sg   [7t; cv-6a; 625]   "
ἀποδώσεις   fut act ind 2 sg
   [Mt 5:33; cv-6a; 625]   "
ἀποδώσοντες   fut act ptcp nom pl masc
   [Hb 13:17; cv-6a; 625]   "
ἀποδώσουσιν   fut act ind 3 pl   [3t; cv-6a; 625] "
ἀποδώσω   fut act ind 1 sg   [3t; cv-6a; 625]   "
ἀποθανεῖν   aor act inf
   [16t; cv-5a; 633]   ἀποθνήσκω
ἀποθανεῖσθε   fut mid ind 2 pl   [3t; cv-5a; 633] "
ἀποθανεῖται   fut mid ind 3 sg
   [Rm 5:7; cv-5a; 633]   "
ἀποθάνῃ   aor act subj 3 sg   [13t; cv-5a; 633]   "
ἀποθανόντα   aor act ptcp nom pl neut
   [Jd 12; cv-5a; 633]   "
ἀποθανόντες   aor act ptcp nom pl masc
   [Rm 7:6; cv-5a; 633]   "
ἀποθανόντι   aor act ptcp dat sg masc
   [2C 5:15; cv-5a; 633]   "
ἀποθανόντος   aor act ptcp gen sg masc
   [1Th 5:10; cv-5a; 633]   "
ἀποθάνωμεν   aor act subj 1 pl
   [Jn 11:16; cv-5a; 633]   "
ἀποθανών   aor act ptcp nom sg masc
   [3t; cv-5a; 633]   "
ἀποθέμενοι   aor mid ptcp nom pl masc
   [4t; cv-6a; 700]   ἀποτίθημι
ἀποθέσθαι   aor mid inf   [Ep 4:22; cv-6a; 700]   "
ἀπόθεσθε   aor mid imperative 2 pl
   [Cl 3:8; cv-6a; 700]   "

ἀπόθεσις, εως, ἡ   {629, n-3e(5b)}
   a putting off or away, laying aside, a euphemism
   for death, 1 Peter 3:21; 2 Peter 1:14*

ἀπόθεσις   nom sg fem
   [2t; n-3e(5b); 629]   ἀπόθεσις
ἀποθήκας   acc pl fem   [2t; n-1b; 630]   ἀποθήκη

ἀποθήκη, ῆς, ἡ   {630, n-1b}
   a place where anything is laid up for preservation,
   repository, granary, storehouse, barn, Matt 3:12;
   6:26; 13:30; Luke 3:17; 12:18, 24

ἀποθήκη   nom sg fem   [Lk 12:24; n-1b; 630]   "
ἀποθήκην   acc sg fem   [3t; n-1b; 630]   "
ἀποθησαυρίζοντας   pres act ptcp acc pl masc
   [1Ti 6:19; cv-2a(1); 631]   ἀποθησαυρίζω

ἀποθησαυρίζω   {631, cv-2a(1)}
   [-, -, -, -, -]   pr. to lay up in store, hoard; met. to
   treasure up, secure, 1 Tim 6:19*

ἀποθλίβουσιν   pres act ind 3 pl
   [Lk 8:45; cv-1b(1); 632]   ἀποθλίβω

ἀποθλίβω   {632, cv-1b(1)}
   [-, -, -, -, -]   pr. to press out; to press close, press
   upon, crowd, Luke 8:45*

ἀποθνήσκει   pres act ind 3 sg
   [5t; cv-5a; 633]   ἀποθνήσκω
ἀποθνήσκειν   pres act inf   [5t; cv-5a; 633]   "
ἀποθνήσκομεν   pres act ind 1 pl
   [2t; cv-5a; 633]   "
ἀποθνήσκοντες   pres act ptcp nom pl masc
   [3t; cv-5a; 633]   "
ἀποθνήσκουσιν   pres act ind 3 pl
   [1C 15:22; cv-5a; 633]   "

ἀποθνήσκω   {633, cv-5a}
   [(ἀπέθνησκον), ἀποθανοῦμαι, ἀπέθανον, -, -, -]   to
   die, Matt 8:32; to decay, rot, as seeds, John 12:24;
   1 Cor 15:36; to wither, become dry, as a tree, Jude
   12; met. to die the death of final condemnation
   and misery, John 6:50; 8:21, 24; to die to a thing
   by renunciation or utter separation, Rom 6:2;
   Gal 2;19; Col 3:3; 1 Cor 15:31

ἀποθνήσκω   pres act ind 1 sg
   [1C 15:31; cv-5a; 633]   "
ἀποθνήσκωμεν   pres act subj 1 pl
   [2t; cv-5a; 633]   "
ἀποθνήσκων   pres act ptcp nom sg masc
   [2t; cv-5a; 633]   "
ἀποθώμεθα   aor mid subj 1 pl
   [Rm 13:12; cv-6a; 700]   ἀποτίθημι
ἀποκαθιστάνει   pres act ind 3 sg
   [Mk 9:12; cv-6a; 635]   ἀποκαθίστημι
ἀποκαθιστάνεις   pres act ind 2 sg
   [Ac 1:6; cv-6a; 635]   "

ἀποκαθιστάνω, alternate spelling for
   ἀποκαθίστημι   {634}

ἀποκαθίστημι   {635, cv-6a}
   [ἀποκαταστήσω, ἀπεκατέστην, -, -,
   ἀπεκατεστάθην] also spelled ἀποκαθιστάνω, to
   restore a thing to its former place or state, Matt
   12:13; 17:11; Mark 3:5; 8:25

ἀποκαλύπτεσθαι   pres pass inf
   [1P 5:1; cv-4; 636]   ἀποκαλύπτω
ἀποκαλύπτεται   pres pass ind 3 sg
   [4t; cv-4; 636]   "

ἀποκαλύπτω   {636, cv-4}
   [ἀποκαλύψω, ἀπεκάλυψα, -, -, ἀπεκαλύφθην] pr.
   uncover; to reveal, Matt 11:25; pass. to be

disclosed, Luke 2:35; Eph 3:5; *to be plainly signified, distinctly declared*, Rom 1:17, 18; *to be set forth, announced*, Gal 3:23; *to be discovered* in true character, 1 Cor 3:13; *to be manifested, appear*, John 12:38;Rom 8:18; 2 Thess 2:3, 6, 8; 1 Peter 1:5; 5:1

ἀποκαλυφθῇ   aor pass subj 3 sg [2t; cv-4; 636]   "
ἀποκαλυφθῆναι   aor pass inf [4t; cv-4; 636]   "
ἀποκαλυφθήσεται   fut pass ind 3 sg
   [3t; cv-4; 636]   "
ἀποκαλυφθῶσιν   aor pass subj 3 pl
   [Lk 2:35; cv-4; 636]   "
ἀποκαλύψαι   aor act inf [3t; cv-4; 636]   "
ἀποκαλύψει   dat sg fem
   [5t; n-3e(5b); 637]   ἀποκάλυψις
ἀποκαλύψει   fut act ind 3 sg
   [Pp 3:15; cv-4; 636]   ἀποκαλύπτω
ἀποκαλύψεις   acc pl fem
   [2C 12:1; n-3e(5b); 637]   ἀποκάλυψις
ἀποκαλύψεων   gen pl fem [2C 12:7; n-3e(5b); 637] "
ἀποκαλύψεως   gen sg fem [3t; n-3e(5b); 637]   "
ἀποκάλυψιν   acc sg fem [7t; n-3e(5b); 637]   "

ἀποκάλυψις, εως, ἡ   {637, n-3e(5b)}
a disclosure, revelation, Rom 2:5; *manifestation, appearance*, Rom 8:19; 1 Cor 1:7; 2 Thess 1:7; 1 Peter 1:7, 13; 4:13; met. spiritual *enlightenment*, Luke 2:32

ἀποκάλυψις   nom sg fem [Rv 1:1; n-3e(5b); 637] "

ἀποκαραδοκία, ας, ἡ   {638, n-1a}
earnest expectation, eager hope, Rom 8:19; Phil 1:20*

ἀποκαραδοκία   nom sg fem
   [Rm 8:19; n-1a; 638]   ἀποκαραδοκία
ἀποκαραδοκίαν   acc sg fem [Pp 1:20; n-1a; 638] "
ἀποκαταλλάξαι   aor act inf
   [Cl 1:20; cv-2b; 639]   ἀποκαταλλάσσω
ἀποκαταλλάξῃ   aor act subj 3 sg
   [Ep 2:16; cv-2b; 639]   "

ἀποκαταλλάσσω   {639, cv-2b}
[-, ἀποκατήλλαξα, -, -, -] *to transfer from a certain state to another which is quite different*; hence, *to reconcile, restore to favor*, Eph 2:16; Col 1:20, 22*

ἀποκατασταθῶ   aor pass subj 1 sg
   [Hb 13:19; cv-6a; 635]   ἀποκαθίστημι
ἀποκαταστάσεως   gen sg fem
   [Ac 3:21; n-3e(5b); 640]   ἀποκατάστασις

ἀποκατάστασις, εως, ἡ   {640, n-3e(5b)}
pr. *a restitution* or *restoration of* a thing to its former state; hence, *the renovation* of a new and better era, Acts 3:21*

ἀποκαταστήσει   fut act ind 3 sg
   [Mt 17:11; cv-6a; 635]   ἀποκαθίστημι
ἀποκατήλλαξεν   aor act ind 3 sg
   [Cl 1:22; cv-2b; 639]   ἀποκαταλλάσσω

ἀπόκειμαι   {641, cv-6b}
[-, -, -, -, -] *to be laid up, preserved*, Luke 19:20; *to be in store, be reserved, await* any one, Col 1:5; 2 Tim 4:8; Heb 9:27*

ἀποκειμένην   pres mid ptcp acc sg fem
   [2t; cv-6b; 641]   ἀπόκειμαι
ἀπόκειται   pres mid ind 3 sg [2t; cv-6b; 641] "
ἀποκεκρυμμένην   perf pass ptcp acc sg fem
   [1C 2:7; cv-4; 648]   ἀποκρύπτω
ἀποκεκρυμμένον   perf pass ptcp acc sg neut
   [Cl 1:26; cv-4; 648]   "
ἀποκεκρυμμένου   perf pass ptcp gen sg neut
   [Ep 3:9; cv-4; 648]   "
ἀποκεκυλισμένον   perf pass ptcp acc sg masc
   [Lk 24:2; cv-1d(2a); 653]   ἀποκυλίω
ἀποκεκύλισται   perf pass ind 3 sg
   [Mk 16:4; cv-1d(2a); 653]   "

ἀποκεφαλίζω   {642, cv-2a(1)}
[-, ἀπεκεφάλισα, -, -, -] *to behead*, Matt 14:10; Mark 6:16, 28; Luke 9:9

ἀποκλείσῃ   aor act subj 3 sg
   [Lk 13:25; cv-1a(3); 643]   ἀποκλείω

ἀποκλείω   {643, cv-1a(3)}
[-, ἀπέκλεισα, -, -, -] *to close, shut up*, Luke 13:25*

ἀποκόπτω   {644, cv-4}
[ἀποκόψω, ἀπέκοψα, -, -, -] *to cut off*, Mark 9:43, 45; John 18:10, 26; Acts 27:32; *to castrate, make a eunich*, Gal 5:12*

ἀπόκοψον   aor act imperative 2 sg
   [2t; cv-4; 644]   ἀποκόπτω
ἀποκόψονται   fut mid ind 3 pl
   [Ga 5:12; cv-4; 644]   "
ἀποκριθείς   aor pass ptcp nom sg masc
   [94t; cv-1c(2); 646]   ἀποκρίνομαι
ἀποκριθεῖσα   aor pass ptcp nom sg fem
   [Lk 1:60; cv-1c(2); 646]   "
ἀποκριθέν   aor pass ptcp nom sg neut
   [Ac 19:15; cv-1c(2); 646]   "
ἀποκριθέντες   aor pass ptcp nom pl masc
   [7t; cv-1c(2); 646]   "
ἀποκριθῇ   aor pass ind 3 sg
   [Mk 9:6; cv-1c(2); 646]   "
ἀποκριθῆναι   aor pass inf
   [Mt 22:46; cv-1c(2); 646]   "
ἀποκριθήσεται   fut pass ind 3 sg
   [Mt 25:45; cv-1c(2); 646]   "
ἀποκριθήσονται   fut pass ind 3 pl
   [2t; cv-1c(2); 646]   "
ἀποκρίθητε   aor pass imperative 2 pl
   [2t; cv-1c(2); 646]   "
ἀποκριθῆτε   aor pass subj 2 pl
   [Lk 22:68; cv-1c(2); 646]   "
ἀποκριθῶσιν   aor pass subj 3 pl
   [Mk 14:40; cv-1c(2); 646]   "

ἀπόκριμα, ατος, τό   {645, n-3c(4)}
a judicial sentence, 2 Cor 1:9*

ἀπόκριμα   acc sg neut
   [2C 1:9; n-3c(4); 645]   ἀπόκριμα
ἀποκρίνεσθαι   pres mid inf
   [Cl 4:6; cv-1c(2); 646]   ἀποκρίνομαι
ἀποκρίνεται   pres mid ind 3 sg
   [3t; cv-1c(2); 646]   "
ἀποκρίνῃ   pres mid ind 2 sg [3t; cv-1c(2); 646] "

ἀποκρίνη   pres pass ind 2 sg
  [Mk 15:4; cv-1c(2); 646]   "

ἀποκρίνομαι   {646, cv-1c(2)}
  [-, ἀπεκρινάμην, -, -, ἀπεκρίθην] *to answer*, Matt
  3:15; in N.T. *to respond* to certain present
  circumstances, *to avow*, Matt 11:25

ἀποκρίσει   dat sg fem
  [Lk 20:26; n-3e(5b); 647]   ἀπόκρισις
ἀποκρίσεσιν   dat pl fem [Lk 2:47; n-3e(5b); 647]   "
ἀπόκρισιν   acc sg fem [2t; n-3e(5b); 647]   "

ἀπόκρισις, εως, ἡ   {647, n-3e(5b)}
  an answer, reply, Luke 2:47; 20:26; John 1:22; 19:9

ἀποκρύπτω   {648, cv-4}
  [-, ἀπέκρυψα, -, ἀποκέκρυμμαι, -] *to hide away; to
  conceal, withhold from sight* or *knowledge*, Luke
  10:21; 1 Cor 2:7; Eph 3:9; Col 1:26; Matt 25:18
  v.l.*

ἀπόκρυφοι   nom pl masc
  [Cl 2:3; a-3a; 649]   ἀπόκρυφος
ἀπόκρυφον   nom sg neut [2t; a-3a; 649]   "

ἀπόκρυφος, ον   {649, a-3a}
  hidden away; concealed, Mark 4:22; Luke 8:17;
  stored up, Col 2:3*

ἀποκτανθείς   aor pass ptcp nom sg masc
  [Mk 9:31; cv-2d; 650]   ἀποκτείνω
ἀποκτανθῆναι   aor pass inf   [6t; cv-2d; 650]   "
ἀποκτανθῶσιν   aor pass subj 3 pl
  [Rv 13:15; cv-2d; 650]   "
ἀποκτεῖναι   aor act inf   [16t; cv-2d; 650]   "
ἀποκτεινάντων   aor act ptcp gen pl masc
  [1Th 2:15; cv-2d; 650]   "
ἀποκτείνας   aor act ptcp nom sg masc
  [2t; cv-2d; 650]   "
ἀποκτεινόντων   pres act ptcp gen pl masc
  [Lk 12:4; cv-2d; 650]   "
ἀποκτείνουσα   pres act ptcp voc sg fem
  [2t; cv-2d; 650]   "

ἀποκτείνω   {650, cv-2d}
  [ἀποκτενῶ, ἀπέκτεινα, -, -, ἀπεκτάνθην] also
  spelled ἀποκτέννω or ἀποκτένω, *to kill*, Matt
  14:5; *to destroy, annihilate*, Matt 10:28; *to destroy*
  a hostile principle, Eph 2:16; met. *to kill by*
  spiritual condemnation, Rom 7:11; 2 Cor 3:6

ἀποκτείνωμεν   aor act subj 1 pl [4t; cv-2d; 650]   "
ἀποκτείνωσιν   aor act subj 3 pl [7t; cv-2d; 650]   "
ἀποκτείνωσιν   pres act subj 3 pl
  [Mk 14:1; cv-2d; 650]   "
ἀποκτενεῖ   fut act ind 3 sg [2t; cv-2d; 650]   "
ἀποκτενεῖτε   fut act ind 2 pl
  [Mt 23:34; cv-2d; 650]   "
ἀποκτέννει   pres act ind 3 sg
  [2C 3:6; cv-2d; 650]   "
ἀποκτέννεσθαι   pres pass inf
  [Rv 6:11; cv-2d; 650]   "
ἀποκτέννοντες   pres act ptcp nom pl masc
  [Mk 12:5; cv-2d; 650]   "
ἀποκτεννόντων   pres act ptcp gen pl masc
  [Mt 10:28; cv-2d; 650]   "

ἀποκτέννω, see ἀποκτείνω   {651, cv-2d(5)}

ἀποκτενοῦσιν   fut act ind 3 pl   [6t; cv-2d; 650]   "

ἀποκτένω, see ἀποκτείνω

ἀποκτενῶ   fut act ind 1 sg   [Rv 2:23; cv-2d; 650]   "
ἀποκύει   pres act ind 3 sg
  [Jm 1:15; see ajpokt; 652]   ἀποκυέω

ἀποκυέω   {652, cv-1d(2a)}
  [-, ἀπεκύησα, -, -, -] pr. *to bring forth*, as women;
  met. *to generate, produce*, James 1:15; *to generate*
  by spiritual birth, James 1:18*

ἀποκυλίσει   fut act ind 3 sg
  [Mk 16:3; cv-1d(2a); 653]   ἀποκυλίω

ἀποκυλίω   {653, cv-1d(2a)}
  [ἀποκυλίσω, ἀπεκύλισα -, ἀποκεκύλισμαι, -] *to*
  roll away, Matt 28:2; Mark 16:3, 4; Luke 24:2*

ἀπολάβητε   aor act subj 2 pl
  [2J 8; cv-3a(2b); 655]   ἀπολαμβάνω
ἀπολαβόμενος   aor mid ptcp nom sg masc
  [Mk 7:33; cv-3a(2b); 655]   "
ἀπολάβωμεν   aor act subj 1 pl
  [Ga 4:5; cv-3a(2b); 655]   "
ἀπολάβωσιν   aor act subj 3 pl
  [Lk 6:34; cv-3a(2b); 655]   "
ἀπολαμβάνομεν   pres act ind 1 pl
  [Lk 23:41; cv-3a(2b); 655]   "
ἀπολαμβάνοντες   pres act ptcp nom pl masc
  [Rm 1:27; cv-3a(2b); 655]   "

ἀπολαμβάνω   {655, cv-3a(2b)}
  [ἀπολήμψομαι or ἀπολήμψομαι, ἀπέλαβον, -, -, -]
  to receive what is due, sought, or needed, Luke
  23:41; Rom 1:27; Gal 4:5; Col 3:24; 2 John 8; *to*
  receive in full, Luke 16:25; *to receive back, recover*,
  Luke 6:34; 15:27; 18:30; *to receive* in hospitality,
  welcome, 3 John 8 v.l.; mid. *to take aside, lead*
  away, Mark 7:33

ἀπόλαυσιν   acc sg fem
  [2t; n-3e(5b); 656]   ἀπόλαυσις

ἀπόλαυσις, εως, ἡ   {656, n-3e(5b)}
  beneficial participation, 1 Tim 6:17; *enjoyment*,
  pleasure, Heb 11:25*

ἀπολείπεται   pres pass ind 3 sg
  [3t; cv-1b(1); 657]   ἀπολείπω

ἀπολείπω   {657, cv-1b(1)}
  [-, ἀπέλιπον, -, -, -] *to leave, leave behind;* pass. *to*
  be left, remain, 2 Tim 4:13, 20; Heb 4:6, 9; 10:26;
  to relinquish, forsake, desert, Titus 1:5; Jude 6*

ἀπολεῖσθε   fut mid ind 2 pl
  [2t; cv-3c(2); 660]   ἀπόλλυμι
ἀπολεῖται   fut mid ind 3 sg
  [Ac 27:34; cv-3c(2); 660]   "

ἀπολείχω   {658, cv-1b(2)}
  [-, -, -, -, -] pr. *to lick off; to cleanse by licking, lick*
  clean, Luke 16:21*

ἀπολελυμένην   perf pass ptcp acc sg fem
  [2t; cv-1a(4); 668]   ἀπολύω
ἀπολελυμένον   perf pass ptcp acc sg masc
  [Hb 13:23; cv-1a(4); 668]   "
ἀπολέλυσαι   perf pass ind 2 sg
  [Lk 13:12; cv-1a(4); 668]   "

ἀπολελύσθαι   perf pass inf
　　[Ac 26:32; cv-1a(4); 668]   "
ἀπολέσαι   aor act inf
　　[7t; cv-3c(2); 660]   ἀπόλλυμι
ἀπολέσας   aor act ptcp nom sg masc
　　[3t; cv-3c(2); 660]   "
ἀπολέσει   fut act ind 3 sg   [9t; cv-3c(2); 660]   "
ἀπολέσῃ   aor act subj 3 sg   [8t; cv-3c(2); 660]   "
ἀπολέσητε   aor act subj 2 pl
　　[2J 8; cv-3c(2); 660]   "
ἀπολέσθαι   aor mid inf   [2t; cv-3c(2); 660]   "
ἀπολέσω   aor act subj 1 sg
　　[Jn 6:39; cv-3c(2); 660]
ἀπολέσωσιν   aor act subj 3 pl
　　[4t; cv-3c(2); 660]   "
ἀπολήμψεσθε   fut mid ind 2 pl
　　[Cl 3:24; cv-3a(2b); 655]   ἀπολαμβάνω
ἀπόληται   aor mid subj 3 sg
　　[7t; cv-3c(2); 660]   ἀπόλλυμι

ἀπολιμπάνω, v.l. of ὑπολιμπάνω at 1 Pet 2:21*   {659}

ἀπολιπόντας   aor act ptcp acc pl masc
　　[Jd 6; cv-1b(1); 657]   ἀπολείπω
ἀπόλλυε   pres act imperative 2 sg
　　[Rm 14:15; cv-3c(2); 660]   ἀπόλλυμι
ἀπολλύει   pres act ind 3 sg
　　[Jn 12:25; cv-3c(2); 660]
ἀπόλλυμαι   pres mid ind 1 sg
　　[Lk 15:17; cv-3c(2); 660]   "
ἀπολλύμεθα   pres mid ind 1 pl
　　[3t; cv-3c(2); 660]
ἀπολλυμένην   pres mid ptcp acc sg fem
　　[Jn 6:27; cv-3c(2); 660]
ἀπολλύμενοι   pres mid ptcp nom pl masc
　　[2C 4:9; cv-3c(2); 660]   "
ἀπολλυμένοις   pres mid ptcp dat pl masc
　　[4t; cv-3c(2); 660]   "
ἀπολλυμένου   pres mid ptcp gen sg neut
　　[1P 1:7; cv-3c(2); 660]   "

ἀπόλλυμι   {660, cv-3c(2)}
　　[ἀπολέσω or ἀπολῶ, ἀπώλεσα, ἀπολώλεκα or
　　ἀπόλωλα, -, -] to destroy utterly; to kill, Matt 2:13;
　　to bring to nought, make void, 1 Cor 1:19; to lose,
　　be deprived of, Matt 10:42; to be destroyed, perish,
　　Matt 9:17; to be put to death, to die, Matt 26:52; to
　　be lost, to stray, Matt 10:6

ἀπόλλυνται   pres pas ind 3 pl
　　[Mt 9:17; cv-3c(2); 660]   "
ἀπόλλυται   pres mid ind 3 sg
　　[Mk 2:2; cv-3c(2); 660]   "
ἀπόλλυται   pres pas ind 3 sg
　　[1C 8:11; cv-3c(2); 660]   "

Ἀπολλύων, ονος, ὁ   {661, n-3f(1b)}
　　Apollyon, Destroyer, i.q. Ἀβαδδών, Rev 9:11*

Ἀπολλύων   nom sg masc
　　[Rv 9:11; n-3f(1b); 661]   Ἀπολλύων
Ἀπολλῶ   acc sg masc   [4t; n-2e; 663]   Ἀπολλῶς
Ἀπολλῶ   gen sg masc   [3t; n-2e; 663]   Ἀπολλῶς
Ἀπολλῶ   acc sg masc   [Ac 19:1; n-2e; 663]   "

Ἀπολλωνία, ας, ἡ   {662, n-1a}
　　Apollonia, a city of Macedonia, Acts 17:1*

Ἀπολλωνίαν   acc sg fem
　　[Ac 17:1; n-1a; 662]   Ἀπολλωνία

Ἀπολλῶς, ῶ, ὁ   {663, n-2e}
　　Apollos, pr. name, Acts 18:24; 19:1; 1 Cor 1:12;
　　3:4-6, 22; 4:6; 16:12; Titus 3:13*

Ἀπολλῶς   nom sg masc   [4t; n-2e; 663]   Ἀπολλῶς
ἀπολογεῖσθαι   pres mid inf
　　[2t; cv-1d(2a); 664]   ἀπολογέομαι

ἀπολογέομαι   {664, cv-1d(2a)}
　　[(ἀπελογούμην), -, ἀπελογησάμην, -, -,
　　ἀπελογήθην] to defend one's self against a charge,
　　to make a defence, Luke 12:11; 21:14

ἀπολογηθῆναι   aor pass inf
　　[Lk 21:14; cv-1d(2a); 664]
ἀπολογήσησθε   aor mid subj 2 pl
　　[Lk 12:11; cv-1d(2a); 664]

ἀπολογία, ας, ἡ   {665, n-1a}
　　a verbal defence, Acts 22:1; 25:16

ἀπολογία   nom sg fem
　　[1C 9:3; n-1a; 665]   ἀπολογία
ἀπολογίᾳ   dat sg fem   [2t; n-1a; 665]   "
ἀπολογίαν   acc sg fem   [3t; n-1a; 665]   "
ἀπολογίας   gen sg fem   [2t; n-1a; 665]   "
ἀπολογοῦμαι   pres mid ind 1 sg
　　[Ac 24:10; cv-1d(2a); 664]   ἀπολογέομαι
ἀπολογούμεθα   pres mid ind 1 pl
　　[2C 12:19; cv-1d(2a); 664]   "
ἀπολογουμένου   pres mid ptcp gen sg masc
　　[2t; cv-1d(2a); 664]   "
ἀπολογουμένων   pres mid ptcp gen pl masc
　　[Rm 2:15; cv-1d(2a); 664]   "
ἀπολομένου   aor mid ptcp gen sg masc
　　[Lk 11:51; cv-3c(2); 660]   ἀπόλλυμι
ἀπολοῦνται   fut mid ind 3 pl   [4t; cv-3c(2); 660]   "
ἀπόλουσαι   aor mid imperative 2 sg
　　[Ac 22:16; cv-1a(8); 666]   ἀπολούω

ἀπολούω   {666, cv-1a(8)}
　　[-, ἀπέλουσα, -, -, -] to cleanse by bathing; mid. to
　　cleanse one's self; to procure one's self to be
　　cleansed; met., of sin, Acts 22:16; 1 Cor 6:11*

ἀπολύει   pres act ind 3 sg
　　[Mk 6:45; cv-1a(4); 668]   ἀπολύω
ἀπολύειν   pres act inf   [2t; cv-1a(4); 668]   "
ἀπολύεις   pres act ind 2 sg
　　[Lk 2:29; cv-1a(4); 668]   "
ἀπολύετε   pres act imperative 2 pl
　　[Lk 6:37; cv-1a(4); 668]   "
ἀπολυθέντες   aor pass ptcp nom pl masc
　　[2t; cv-1a(4); 668]   "
ἀπολυθήσεσθε   fut pass ind 2 pl
　　[Lk 6:37; cv-1a(4); 668]   "
ἀπολυθῆτε   aor pass subj 2 pl
　　[Ac 16:36; cv-1a(4); 668]   "
ἀπολῦσαι   aor act inf   [11t; cv-1a(4); 668]   "
ἀπολύσας   aor act ptcp nom sg masc
　　[2t; cv-1a(4); 668]   "
ἀπολύσασα   aor act ptcp nom sg fem
　　[Mk 10:12; cv-1a(4); 668]   "
ἀπολύσῃ   aor act subj 3 sg   [5t; cv-1a(4); 668]

ἀπολύσῃς   aor act subj 2 sg
[Jn 19:12; cv-1a(4); 668]   "
ἀπόλυσον   aor act imperative 2 sg
[6t; cv-1a(4); 668]   "
ἀπολύσω   aor act subj 1 sg   [6t; cv-1a(4); 668]   "
ἀπολύσω   fut act ind 1 sg   [2t; cv-1a(4); 668]   "
ἀπολυτρώσεως   gen sg fem
[2t; n-3e(5b); 667]   ἀπολύτρωσις
ἀπολύτρωσιν   acc sg fem   [6t; n-3e(5b); 667]   "

ἀπολύτρωσις, εως, ἡ   {667, n-3e(5b)}
*redemption, a deliverance, procured by the payment
of a ransom;* meton. the author of *redemption,* 1
Cor 1:30; *deliverance,* simply, the idea of a
ransom being excluded, Luke 21:28; Heb 11:35

ἀπολύτρωσις   nom sg fem   [2t; n-3e(5b); 667]   "

ἀπολύω   {668, cv-1a(4)}
[(ἀπέλυον), ἀπολύσω, ἀπέλυσα, -, ἀπολέλυμαι,
ἀπελύθην] pr. *to loose; to release* from a tie or
burden, Matt 18:27; *to divorce,* Matt 1:19; *to
remit, forgive,* Luke 6:37; *to liberate, discharge,*
Matt 27:15; *to dismiss,* Matt 15:23; Acts 19:40; *to
allow to depart, to send away,* Matt 14:15; *to
permit,* or, *signal departure* from life, Luke 2:29;
mid. *to depart,* Acts 28:25; pass. *to be rid,* Luke
13:12

ἀπολύων   pres act ptcp nom sg masc
[2t; cv-1a(4); 668]   ἀπολύω
ἀπολῶ   fut act ind 1 sg
[1C 1:19; cv-3c(2); 660]   ἀπόλλυμι
ἀπολωλός   perf act ptcp acc sg neut
[3t; cv-3c(2); 660]   "
ἀπολωλότα   perf act ptcp acc pl neut
[2t; cv-3c(2); 660]   "
ἀπολωλώς   perf act ptcp nom sg masc
[2t; cv-3c(2); 660]   "
ἀπόλωνται   aor mid subj 3 pl
[Jn 10:28; cv-3c(2); 660]   "
ἀπομασσόμεθα   pres mid ind 1 pl
[Lk 10:11; cv-2b; 669]   ἀπομάσσω

ἀπομάσσω   {669, cv-2b}
[-, -, -, -, -] *to wipe off;* mid. *to wipe off one's self,*
Luke 10:11*

ἀπονέμοντες   pres act ptcp nom pl masc
[1P 3:7; cv-1d(2c); 671]   ἀπονέμω

ἀπονέμω   {671, cv-1d(2c)}
[-, -, -, -, -] *to portion off; to assign, bestow,* 1 Peter
3:7*

ἀπονίπτω   {672, cv-4}
[-, ἀπένιψα, -, -, -] *to cleanse* a part of the body
by washing; mid., of one's self, Matt 27:24*

ἀπόντες   pres act ptcp nom pl masc
[2C 10:11; cv-6b; 583]   ἄπειμι

ἀποπέμπω   {673, cv-1b(1)}
[-, -, -, -, -] *to send out,* John 17:3 v.l.*

ἀποπίπτω   {674, cv-1b(3)}
[-, ἀπέπεσα, -, -, -] *to fall off* or *from,* Acts 9:18*

ἀποπλανᾶν   pres act inf
[Mk 13:22; cv-1d(1a); 675]   ἀποπλανάω

ἀποπλανάω   {675, cv-1d(1a)}
[-, -, -, -, ἀπεπλανήθην] *to cause to wander;* met.
to deceive, pervert, seduce, Mark 13:22; pass. *to
wander;* met. *to swerve from, apostatize,* 1 Tim
6:10*

ἀποπλεῖν   pres act inf
[Ac 27:1; cv-1a(7); 676]   ἀποπλέω
ἀποπλεύσαντες   aor act ptcp nom pl masc
[Ac 20:15; cv-1a(7); 676]   "

ἀποπλέω   {676, cv-1a(7)}
[-, ἀπέπλευσα, -, -, -] *to depart by ship, sail away,*
Acts 13:4; 14:26; 20:15; 27:1*

ἀποπλύνω   {677, cv-1c(2)}
[-, -, -, -, -] *to wash, rinse,* Luke 5:2 v.l.*

ἀποπνίγω   {678, cv-1b(2)}
[-, ἀπέπνιξα -, -, ἀπεπνίγην] *to choke, suffocate,*
Luke 8:7; *to drown,* Luke 8:33; Matt 13:7 v.l.*

ἀπορεῖσθαι   pres mid inf
[Lk 24:4; v-1d(2a); 679]   ἀπορέω

ἀπορέω   {679, v-1d(2a)}
[(ἠπόρουν), -, ἀπέριψα -, -, ἠπορήθην] also
spelled ἀπορρίπτω, pr. *to be without means;* met.
to hesitate, be at a stand, be in doubt and perplexity,
John 13:22; Acts 25:20; 2 Cor 4:8; Gal 4:20

ἀπορία, ας, ἡ   {680, n-1a}
doubt, uncertainty, perplexity, Luke 21:25*

ἀπορία   dat sg fem   [Lk 21:25; n-1a; 680]   ἀπορία

ἀπορίπτω   {681, cv-4}
[-, ἀπέριψα, -, -, -] *to throw off, throw down,* Acts
27:43*

ἀπορίψαντας   aor act ptcp acc pl masc
[Ac 27:43; cv-4; 681]   ἀπορίπτω
ἀποροῦμαι   pres mid ind 1 sg
[Ga 4:20; v-1d(2a); 679]   ἀπορέω
ἀπορούμενοι   pres mid ptcp nom pl masc
[2t; v-1d(2a); 679]   "
ἀπορούμενος   pres mid ptcp nom sg masc
[Ac 25:20; v-1d(2a); 679]   "

ἀπορφανίζω   {682, cv-2a(1)}
[-, -, -, -, ἀπωρφανίσθην] lit., *to make an orphan;*
fig., *to deprive, bereave,* 1 Thess 2:17*

ἀπορφανισθέντες   aor pass ptcp nom pl masc
[1Th 2:17; cv-2a(1); 682]   ἀπορφανίζω

ἀποσκευάζω   {683, cv-2a(1)}
[-, -, -, -, -] also listed as a middle/passive form
ἀποσκευάζομαι, *to prepare for a journey, take one's
departure,* Acts 21:15*

ἀποσκίασμα, ατος, τό   {684, n-3c(4)}
a shadow cast; met. *a shade, the slightest trace,*
James 1:17*

ἀποσκίασμα   nom sg neut
[Jm 1:17; n-3c(4); 684]   ἀποσκίασμα
ἀποσπᾶν   pres act inf
[Ac 20:30; cv-1d(1b); 685]   ἀποσπάω
ἀποσπασθέντας   aor pass ptcp acc pl masc
[Ac 21:1; cv-1d(1b); 685]   "

ἀποσπάω   {685, cv-1d(1b)}
[-, ἀπέσπασα, -, -, ἀπεσπάσθην] *to draw away
from; to draw out* or *forth,* Matt 26:51; *to draw
away, seduce,* Acts 20:30; *to separate one's self, to
part,* Luke 22:41; Acts 21:1*

ἀποσταλέντι   aor pass ptcp dat sg neut
   [1P 1:12; cv-2d(1); 690]   ἀποστέλλω
ἀποσταλῶσιν   aor pass subj 3 pl
   [Rm 10:15; cv-2d(1); 690]   "
ἀποστάντα   aor act ptcp acc sg masc
   [Ac 15:38; cv-6a; 923]   ἀφίστημι
ἀποστάς   aor act ptcp nom sg masc
   [Ac 19:9; cv-6a; 923]   "

ἀποστασία, ας, ἡ   {686, n-1a}
a falling away, a rebellion, apostasy, Acts 21:21; 2
Thess 2:3*

ἀποστασία   nom sg fem
   [2Th 2:3; n-1a; 686]   ἀποστασία
ἀποστασίαν   acc sg fem   [Ac 21:21; n-1a; 686]   "

ἀποστάσιον, ου, τό   {687, n-2c}
defection, desertion, as of a freedman from a
patron; in N.T. *the act of putting away a wife,
repudiation, divorce,* Matt 19:7; Mark 10:4;
meton. *a bill of repudiation, deed of divorce,* Matt
5:31*

ἀποστάσιον   acc sg neut
   [Mt 5:31; n-2c; 687]   ἀποστάσιον
ἀποστασίου   gen sg neut   [2t; n-2c; 687]   "

ἀποστάτης, ου, ὁ   {688, n-1f}
deserter. apostate, James 2:11 v.l.*

ἀποστεγάζω   {689, cv-2a(1)}
[-, ἀπεστέγασα -, -, -] *to remove* or *break through
a covering* or *roof* of a place, Mark 2:4*

ἀποστεῖλαι   aor act inf
   [Lk 4:18; cv-2d(1); 690]   ἀποστέλλω
ἀποστείλαντα   aor act ptcp acc sg masc
   [4t; cv-2d(1); 690]   "
ἀποστείλαντας   aor act ptcp acc pl masc
   [Ac 15:33; cv-2d(1); 690]   "
ἀποστείλαντες   aor act ptcp nom pl masc
   [Ac 11:30; cv-2d(1); 690]   "
ἀποστείλας   aor act ptcp nom sg masc
   [7t; cv-2d(1); 690]   "
ἀποστείλῃ   aor act subj 3 sg
   [2t; cv-2d(1); 690]   "
ἀπόστειλον   aor act imperative 2 sg
   [2t; cv-2d(1); 690]   "
ἀποστείλω   aor act subj 1 sg
   [Ac 7:34; cv-2d(1); 690]   "
ἀποστελεῖ   fut act ind 3 sg   [4t; cv-2d(1); 690] "
ἀποστέλλει   pres act ind 3 sg
   [4t; cv-2d(1); 690]   "
ἀποστέλλειν   pres act inf
   [Mk 6:7; cv-2d(1); 690]   "
ἀποστέλλῃ   pres act subj 3 sg
   [Mk 3:14; cv-2d(1); 690]   "
ἀποστελλόμενα   pres pass ptcp nom pl neut
   [Hb 1:14; cv-2d(1); 690]   "
ἀποστέλλουσιν   pres act ind 3 pl
   [2t; cv-2d(1); 690]   "

ἀποστέλλω   {690, cv-2d(1)}
[ἀποστελῶ, ἀπέστειλα or ἀποστείλω, ἀπέσταλκα,
ἀπέσταλμαι, ἀπεστάλην] *to send forth* a
messenger, agent, message, or command, Matt
2:16; 10:5; *to put forth into action,* Mark 4:29; *to
liberate, rid,* Luke 4:19; *to dismiss, send away,*
Mark 12:3

ἀποστέλλω   pres act ind 1 sg   [8t; cv-2d(1); 690] "
ἀποστελῶ   fut act ind 1 sg
   [Lk 11:49; cv-2d(1); 690]   "
ἀποστερεῖσθε   pres mid ind 2 pl
   [1C 6:7; cv-1d(2a); 691]   ἀποστερέω
ἀποστερεῖτε   pres act imperative 2 pl
   [1C 7:5; cv-1d(2a); 691]   "
ἀποστερεῖτε   pres act ind 2 pl
   [1C 6:8; cv-1d(2a); 691]   "

ἀποστερέω   {691, cv-1d(2a)}
[-, ἀπεστέρησα, -, ἀπεστέρημαι, -] *to deprive,
detach; to debar,* 1 Cor 7:5; *to deprive* in a bad
sense, *defraud,* Mark 10:19; 1 Cor 6:7; mid. *to
suffer one's self to be deprived* or *defrauded,* 1 Cor
6:8; pass. *to be destitute* or *devoid of,* 1 Tim 6:5; *to
be unjustly withheld,* James 5:4*

ἀποστερήσῃς   aor act subj 2 sg
   [Mk 10:19; cv-1d(2a); 691]   "
ἀποστῇ   aor act subj 3 sg
   [2C 12:8; cv-6a; 923]   ἀφίστημι
ἀποστῆναι   aor act inf   [Hb 3:12; cv-6a; 923]   "
ἀποστήσονται   fut mid ind 3 pl
   [1Ti 4:1; cv-6a; 923]   "
ἀπόστητε   aor act imperative 2 pl
   [2t; cv-6a; 923]   "
ἀποστήτω   aor act imperative 3 sg
   [2Ti 2:19; cv-6a; 923]   "

ἀποστολή, ῆς, ἡ   {692, n-1b}
a sending, expedition; office or *duty of one sent as a
messenger* or *agent; office of an apostle, apostleship,*
Acts 1:25; Rom 1:5; 1 Cor 9:2; Gal 2:8*

ἀποστολήν   acc sg fem   [2t; n-1b; 692]   ἀποστολή
ἀποστολῆς   gen sg fem   [2t; n-1b; 692]   "
ἀπόστολοι   nom pl masc
   [15t; n-2a; 693]   ἀπόστολος
ἀπόστολοι   voc pl masc   [Rv 18:20; n-2a; 693]   "
ἀποστόλοις   dat pl masc   [6t; n-2a; 693]   "
ἀπόστολον   acc sg masc   [2t; n-2a; 693]   "

ἀπόστολος, ου, ὁ   {693, n-2a}
one sent as a messenger or *agent, the bearer of a
commission, messenger,* John 13:16; *an apostle,*
Matt 10:2

ἀπόστολος   nom sg masc   [18t; n-2a; 693]   "
ἀποστόλου   gen sg masc   [2C 12:12; n-2a; 693]   "
ἀποστόλους   acc pl masc   [15t; n-2a; 693]   "
ἀποστόλων   gen pl masc   [22t; n-2a; 693]   "
ἀποστοματίζειν   pres act inf
   [Lk 11:53; cv-; 694]   ἀποστοματίζω

ἀποστοματίζω   {694, cv-2a(1)}
[-, -, -, -, -] pr. *to speak* or *repeat offhand;* also, *to
require* or *lead* others *to speak without
premeditation,* as by questions calculated to

elicit unpremeditated answers, *to endeavor to entrap into unguarded language*, Luke 11:53*

ἀποστραφῇς   aor pass subj 2 sg
[Mt 5:42; cv-1b(1); 695]   ἀποστρέφω

ἀποστρέφειν   pres act inf
[Ac 3:26; cv-1b(1); 695]   "

ἀποστρεφόμενοι   pres mid ptcp nom pl masc
[Hb 12:25; cv-1b(1); 695]   "

ἀποστρεφομένων   pres mid ptcp gen pl masc
[Ti 1:14; cv-1b(1); 695]   "

ἀποστρέφοντα   pres act ptcp acc sg masc
[Lk 23:14; cv-1b(1); 695]   "

ἀποστρέφω   {695, cv-1b(1)}
[ἀποστρέψω, ἀπέστρεψα, -, -, ἀπεστράφην] *to turn away; to remove*, Acts 3:26; Rom 11:26; 2 Tim 4:4; *to turn* a people from their allegiance, to their sovereign, *pervert, incite to revolt*, Luke 23:14; *to replace, restore*, Matt 26:52; *to turn away from* any one, *to slight, reject, repulse*, Matt 5:42; Titus 1:14; Heb 12:25; *to desert*, 2 Tim 1:15

ἀποστρέψει   fut act ind 3 sg
[Rm 11:26; cv-1b(1); 695]   "

ἀπόστρεψον   aor act imperative 2 sg
[Mt 26:52; cv-1b(1); 695]   "

ἀποστρέψουσιν   fut act ind 3 pl
[2Ti 4:4; cv-1b(1); 695]   "

ἀποστυγέω   {696, cv-1d(2a)}
[-, -, -, -, -] *to shrink from with abhorrence, detest*, Rom 12:9*

ἀποστυγοῦντες   pres act ptcp nom pl masc
[Rm 12:9; cv-; 696]   ἀποστυγέω

ἀποσυνάγωγοι   nom pl masc
[Jn 12:42; a-3a; 697]   ἀποσυνάγωγος

ἀποσυνάγωγος, ον   {697, a-3a}
expelled or *excluded from the synagogue, excommunicated, cut off from the rights and privileges of a Jew, excluded from society*, John 9:22; 12:42; 16:2*

ἀποσυνάγωγος   nom sg masc [Jn 9:22; a-3a; 697]   "

ἀποσυναγώγους   acc pl masc [Jn 16:2; a-3a; 697]   "

ἀποταξάμενος   aor mid ptcp nom sg masc
[4t; cv-2b; 698]   ἀποτάσσω

ἀποτάξασθαι   aor mid inf   [Lk 9:61; cv-2b; 698]   "

ἀποτάσσεται   pres mid ind 3 sg
[Lk 14:33; cv-2b; 698]   "

ἀποτάσσω   {698, cv-2b}
[-, ἀπέταξα, -, -, -] middle: *to take leave of, bid farewell to*, Luke 9:61; Acts 18:18, 21; 2 Cor 2:13; *to dismiss, send away*, Mark 6:46; fig: *to renounce, forsake*, Luke 14:33

ἀποτελεσθεῖσα   aor pass ptcp nom sg fem
[Jm 1:15; cv-1d(2b); 699]   ἀποτελέω

ἀποτελέω   {699, cv-1d(2b)}
[-, -, -, -, ἀπετελέσθην] *to complete;* pass. *to be perfected, to arrive at full stature* or *measure*, Luke 13:32; James 1:15*

ἀποτελῶ   pres act ind 1 sg
[Lk 13:32; cv-1d(2b); 699]   "

ἀποτίθημι   {700, cv-6a}
[-, ἀπέθηκα, -, -, -] mid: *to lay off, lay down* or *aside*, as garments, Acts 7:58; met. *to lay aside, put off, renounce*, Rom 13:12; Eph 4:22, 25; Col 3:8

ἀποτινάξας   aor act ptcp nom sg masc
[Ac 28:5; cv-2b; 701]   ἀποτινάσσω

ἀποτινάσσετε   pres act imperative 2 pl
[Lk 9:5; cv-2b; 701]   "

ἀποτινάσσω   {701, cv-2b}
[-, ἀπετίναξα, -, -, -] *to shake off*, Luke 9:5; Acts 28:5*

ἀποτίνω   {702, cv-3a(1)}
[ἀποτίσω, -, -, -, -] *to pay off* what is claimed or due; *to repay, refund, make good*, Phil 19*

ἀποτίσω   fut act ind 1 sg
[Pm 19; cv-3a(1); 702]   ἀποτίνω

ἀποτολμᾷ   pres act ind 3 sg
[Rm 10:20; cv-1d(1a); 703]   ἀποτολμάω

ἀποτολμάω   {703, cv-1d(1a)}
[-, -, -, -, -] *to dare* or *risk outright; to speak outright, without reserve* or *restraint*, Rom 10:20

ἀποτομία, ας, ἡ   {704, n-1a}
pr. *abruptness;* met. *severity, rigor*, Rom 11:22 (2t)*

ἀποτομία   nom sg fem
[Rm 11:22; n-1a; 704]   ἀποτομία

ἀποτομίαν   acc sg fem [Rm 11:22; n-1a; 704]   "

ἀποτόμως   {705, adverb}
sharply, severely, 2 Cor 13:10; Titus 1:13*

ἀποτόμως   adverb [2t; adverb; 705]   ἀποτόμως

ἀποτρέπου   pres mid imperative 2 sg
[2Ti 3:5; cv-1b(1); 706]   ἀποτρέπω

ἀποτρέπω   {706, cv-1b(1)}
[-, -, -, -, -] mid: *to turn* any one *away* from a thing; mid. *to turn one's self away* from any one; *to avoid, shun*, 2 Tim 3:5*

ἀπουσία, ας, ἡ   {707, n-1a}
absence, Phil 2:12*

ἀπουσία   dat sg fem
[Pp 2:12; n-1a; 707]   ἀπουσία

ἀποφέρεσθαι   pres pass inf
[Ac 19:12; cv-1c(1); 708]   ἀποφέρω

ἀποφέρω   {708, cv-1c(1)}
[-, ἀπήνεγκα, -, -, ἀπηνέχθην] *to bear* or *carry away, conduct away*, Mark 15:1; Luke 16:22; Acts 19:12; 1 Cor 16:3; Rev 17:3; 21:10*

ἀποφεύγοντας   pres act ptcp acc pl masc
[2P 2:18; cv-1b(2); 709]   ἀποφεύγω

ἀποφεύγω   {709, cv-1b(2)}
[-, ἀπέφυγον, -, -, -] *to flee from, escape;* met. *to be rid, be freed from*, 2 Peter 1:4; 2:18, 20*

ἀποφθέγγεσθαι   pres mid inf
[Ac 2:4; cv-1b(2); 710]   ἀποφθέγγομαι

ἀποφθέγγομαι   {710, cv-1b(2)}
[-, ἀπεφθεγξάμην, -, -, -] *to speak out, declare,*

particularly solemn, weighty, or pithy sayings, Acts 2:4, 14; 26:25*

ἀποφθέγγομαι pres mid ind 1 sg
[Ac 26:25; cv-1b(2); 710]   "

ἀποφορτίζομαι   {711, cv-2a(1)}
[-, -, -, -, -] *to unload*, Acts 21:3*

ἀποφορτιζόμενον pres mid ptcp nom sg neut
[Ac 21:3; cv-2a(1); 711]   ἀποφορτίζομαι

ἀποφυγόντες aor act ptcp nom pl masc
[2t; cv-1b(2); 709]   ἀποφεύγω

ἀποχρήσει dat sg fem
[Cl 2:22; n-3e(5b); 712]   ἀπόχρησις

ἀπόχρησις, εως, ἡ   {712, n-3e(5b)}
a using up, or, *a discharge of an intended use*, Col 2:22*

ἀποχωρεῖ pres act ind 3 sg
[Lk 9:39; cv-1d(2a); 713]   ἀποχωρέω

ἀποχωρεῖτε pres act imperative 2 pl
[Mt 7:23; cv-1d(2a); 713]   "

ἀποχωρέω   {713, cv-1d(2a)}
[-, ἀπεχώρησα, -, -, -] *to go from* or *away, depart*, Matt 7:23; Luke 9:39; Acts 13:13; Luke 20:20 v.l.*

ἀποχωρήσας aor act ptcp nom sg masc
[Ac 13:13; cv-1d(2a); 713]   "

ἀποχωρίζω   {714, cv-2a(1)}
[-, -, -, -, ἀπεχωρίσθην] *to separate*; pass. *to be swept aside*, Rev 6:14; mid. *to part*, Acts 15:39; Matt 19:6 v.l.*

ἀποχωρισθῆναι aor pass inf
[Ac 15:39; cv-2a(1); 714]   ἀποχωρίζω

ἀποψυχόντων pres act ptcp gen pl masc
[Lk 21:26; cv-1b(2); 715]   ἀποψύχω

ἀποψύχω   {715, cv-1b(2)}
[-, -, -, -, -] pr. *to breathe out, faint away, die*; met. *to faint at heart, be dismayed*, Luke 21:26*

Ἄππιος, ου, ὁ   {716, n-2a}
the forum or *marketplace, of Appius*; a village on the Appian road, near Rome, Acts 28:15*

Ἀππίου gen sg masc [Ac 28:15; n-2a; 716] Ἄππιος
ἀπρόσιτον acc sg neut
[1Ti 6:16; a-3a; 717]   ἀπρόσιτος

ἀπρόσιτος, ον   {717, a-3a}
unapproached, unapproachable, 1 Tim 6:16*

ἀπρόσκοποι nom pl masc
[2t; a-3a; 718]   ἀπρόσκοπος
ἀπρόσκοπον acc sg fem [Ac 24:16; a-3a; 718] "

ἀπρόσκοπος, ον   {718, a-3a}
not stumbling or *jarring*; met. *not stumbling* or *jarring against moral rule, unblamable, clear*, Acts 24:16; Phil 1:10; *free from offensiveness*, 1 Cor 10:32*

ἀπροσωπολήμπτως   {719, adverb}
without respect of persons, impartially, 1 Peter 1:17*

ἀπροσωπολήμπτως adverb
[1P 1:17; adverb; 719]   ἀπροσωπολήμπτως

ἄπταιστος, ον   {720, a-3a}
free from stumbling; met. *free from* moral *stumbling, offence; irreprehensible*, Jude 24*

ἀπταίστους acc pl masc
[Jd 24; a-3a; 720]   ἄπταιστος
ἅπτει pres act ind 3 sg [Lk 15:8; v-4; 721] ἅπτω
ἅπτεσθαι pres mid inf [2t; v-4; 721]   "
ἅπτεσθε pres mid imperative 2 pl
[2C 6:17; v-4; 721]   "
ἅπτεται pres mid ind 3 sg [2t; v-4; 721]   "
ἅπτηται pres mid subj 3 sg [Lk 18:15; v-4; 721] "
ἅπτου pres mid imperative 2 sg
[Jn 20:17; v-4; 721]   "

ἅπτω   {721, v-4}
[-, ἧψα, -, -, ἥφθην] pr. *to bring in contact, fit, fasten; to light, kindle*, Mark 4:21; Luke 8:16; *to touch*, Matt 8:3; *to meddle, venture to partake*, Col 2:21; *to have intercourse with, to know carnally*, 1 Cor 7:1; by impl. *to harm*, 1 John 5:18

Ἀπφία, ας, ἡ   {722, n-1a}
Apphia, pr. name, Phil 2 v.l., and in the inscr. and subscr*

Ἀπφίᾳ dat sg fem [Pm 2; n-1a; 722]   Ἀπφία
ἀπωθεῖσθε pres mid ind 2 pl
[Ac 13:46; cv-1b(4); 723]   ἀπωθέω

ἀπωθέω   {723, cv-1b(4)}
[-, ἀπῶσα, -, -, -] *to thrust away, repel from one's self, repulse*, Acts 7:27; *to refuse, reject, cast off*, Acts 7:39; 13:46; Rom 11:1, 2; 1 Tim 1:19*

ἀπώλεια, ας, ἡ   {724, n-1a}
consumption, destruction; waste, profusion, Matt 26:8; Mark 14:4; *destruction, state of being destroyed*, Acts 25:6; *eternal ruin, perdition*, Matt 7:13; Acts 8:20

ἀπώλεια nom sg fem [4t; n-1a; 724]   ἀπώλεια
ἀπώλειαν acc sg fem [9t; n-1a; 724]   "
ἀπωλείας gen sg fem [5t; n-1a; 724]   "
ἀπώλεσα aor act ind 1 sg
[2t; cv-3c(2); 660]   ἀπόλλυμι
ἀπώλεσεν aor act ind 3 sg [4t; cv-3c(2); 660] "
ἀπώλετο aor mid ind 3 sg [5t; cv-3c(2); 660] "
ἀπώλλυντο imperf pas ind 3 pl
[1C 10:9; cv-3c(2); 660]   "
ἀπώλοντο aor mid ind 3 pl [3t; cv-3c(2); 660] "
ἀπών pres act ptcp nom sg masc
[5t; cv-6b; 583]   ἄπειμι
ἀπωσάμενοι aor mid ptcp nom pl masc
[1Ti 1:19; cv-1b(4); 723]   ἀπωθέω
ἀπώσαντο aor mid ind 3 pl
[Ac 7:39; cv-1b(4); 723]   "
ἀπώσατο aor mid ind 3 sg [3t; cv-1b(4); 723] "

ἀρά, ᾶς, ἡ   {725, n-1a}
pr. *a prayer*; more commonly *a prayer for evil; curse, cursing, imprecation*, Rom 3:14*

ἄρα   {726, particle}
a particle which denotes, first, transition from one thing to another by natural sequence; secondly, logical inference; in which case the premises are either expressed, Matt 12:28, or to

be variously supplied, *therefore, then, consequently; as a result,* Acts 17:27

ἄρα   particle [49t; particle; 726]   ἄρα

ἆρα   {727, particle}
inferential particle, used mainly in interrogations, Luke 18:8; Acts 8:30; Gal 2:17*

ἆρα   particle [3t; particle; 727]   ἆρα

Ἄραβες   nom pl masc [Ac 2:11; n-3a(2); 732]   Ἄραψ

Ἀραβία, ας, ἡ   {728, n-1a}
Arabia, Gal 1:17; 4:25*

Ἀραβίᾳ   dat sg fem [Ga 4:25; n-1a; 728]   Ἀραβία
Ἀραβίαν   acc sg fem [Ga 1:17; n-1a; 728]   "

Ἄραβοι, v.l. in Acts 2:11, perhaps from the plural Ἀράβων, cf. *BAGD**   {729}

ἆραι   aor act inf [6t; v-2d(2); 149]   αἴρω

Ἀράμ, ὁ   {730, n-3g(2)}
Aram, pr. name, indecl, Matt 1:3-4; Luke 3:33 v.l.*

Ἀράμ   indecl [2t; n-3g(2); 730]   Ἀράμ
ἄραντες   aor act ptcp nom pl masc [2t; v-2d(2); 149]   αἴρω
ἄρας   gen sg fem [Rm 3:14; n-1a; 725]   ἀρά
ἄρας   aor act ptcp nom sg masc [5t; v-2d(2); 149]   αἴρω
ἄρατε   aor act imperative 2 pl [5t; v-2d(2); 149]   "
ἀράτω   aor act imperative 3 sg [4t; v-2d(2); 149]   "

ἄραφος, ον   {731, a-3a}
not sewed, seamless, John 19:23*

ἄραφος   nom sg masc [Jn 19:23; a-3a; 731]   ἄραφος

Ἄραψ, Ἄραβος, ὁ   {732, n-3a(2)}
an Arabian, Acts 2:11*

ἀργαί   nom pl fem [3t; a-1a(2a); 734]   ἀργός
ἀργεῖ   pres act ind 3 sg [2P 2:3; v-1d(2a); 733]   ἀργέω

ἀργέω   {733, v-1d(2a)}
[ἀργήσω, ἤργησα, ἤργηκα, ἤργημαι, ἠργήθην] pr. *to be unemployed; to be inoperative, to linger,* 2 Peter 2:3*

ἀργή   nom sg fem [Jm 2:20; a-1a(2a); 734]   ἀργός
ἀργοί   nom pl masc [Mt 20:6; a-1a(2a); 734]   "
ἀργόν   acc sg neut [Mt 12:36; a-1a(2a); 734]   "

ἀργός, ή, όν   {734, a-1a(2a)}
pr. *inactive, unemployed,* Matt 20:3, 6; *idle, averse from labor,* 1 Tim 5:13; Titus 1:12; met. 2 Peter 1:8; *unprofitable, hollow,* or by impl., *injurious,* Matt 12:36; James 2:20*

ἀργούς   acc pl masc [2t; a-1a(2a); 734]   "
ἀργυρᾶ   nom pl neut [2Ti 2:20; a-1b; 739]   ἀργυροῦς
ἀργυρᾶ   acc pl neut [Rv 9:20; a-1b; 739]   "

ἀργύρεος, see ἀργυροῦς   {735}
ἀργύρια   acc pl neut [8t; n-2c; 736]   ἀργύριον

ἀργύριον, ου, τό   {736, n-2c}
silver; meton. *money;* spc. *a piece of silver money, a shekel;* 1 Cor 3:12 v.l.

ἀργύριον   nom sg neut [2t; n-2c; 736]   "
ἀργύριον   acc sg neut [6t; n-2c; 736]   "
ἀργυρίου   gen sg neut [3t; n-2c; 736]   "
ἀργυρίῳ   dat sg neut [1P 1:18; n-2c; 736]   "

ἀργυροκόπος, ου, ὁ   {737, n-2a}
a forger of silver, silversmith, Acts 19:24*

ἀργυροκόπος   nom sg masc [Ac 19:24; n-2a; 737]   ἀργυροκόπος
ἄργυρον   acc sg masc [2t; n-2a; 738]   ἄργυρος

ἄργυρος, ου, ὁ   {738, n-2a}
silver; meton. *anything made of silver; money,* James 5:3

ἄργυρος   nom sg masc [Jm 5:3; n-2a; 738]   "
ἀργύρου   gen sg masc [Rv 18:12; n-2a; 738]   "

ἀργυροῦς, ᾶ, οῦν   {739, a-1b}
made of silver, Acts 19:24; 2 Tim 2:20; Rev 9:20*

ἀργυροῦς   acc pl masc [Ac 19:24; a-1b; 739]   ἀργυροῦς
ἀργύρῳ   dat sg masc [Ac 17:29; n-2a; 738]   ἄργυρος
Ἄρειον   acc sg masc [Ac 17:19; a-1a(1); 740]   ἄρειος

ἄρειος, α, ον   {740, a-1a(1)}
as an adj., *devoted to Ares, warlike,* in the N.T. used only as Ἄρειος πάγος, *the Areopagus* or *Hill of Mars* or *Ares,* in Athens, Acts 17:19, 22*

Ἀρείου   gen sg masc [Ac 17:22; a-1a(1); 740]   "

Ἀρεοπαγίτης, ου, ὁ   {741, n-1f}
a judge of the court of Areopagus, Acts 17:34*

Ἀρεοπαγίτης   nom sg masc [Ac 17:34; n-1f; 741]   Ἀρεοπαγίτης
ἀρέσαι   aor act inf [Rm 8:8; v-5a; 743]   ἀρέσκω
ἀρέσῃ   aor act subj 3 sg [4t; v-5a; 743]   "

ἀρεσκεία, ας, ἡ   {742, n-1a}
a pleasing, desire of pleasing, Col 1:10*

ἀρεσκείαν   acc sg fem [Cl 1:10; n-1a; 742]   ἀρεσκεία
ἀρέσκειν   pres act inf [3t; v-5a; 743]   ἀρέσκω
ἀρεσκέτω   pres act imperative 3 sg [Rm 15:2; v-5a; 743]   "
ἀρέσκοντες   pres act ptcp nom pl masc [1Th 2:4; v-5a; 743]   "
ἀρεσκόντων   pres act ptcp gen pl masc [1Th 2:15; v-5a; 743]   "

ἀρέσκω   {743, v-5a}
[(ἤρεσκον), ἀρέσω, ἤρεσα, -, -, -] *to please,* Matt 14:6; *to be pleasing, acceptable,* Acts 6:5; *to consult the pleasure of* any one, Rom 15:1, 2, 3; 1 Cor 10:33; *to seek favor with,* Gal 1:10; 1 Thess 2:4

ἀρέσκω   pres act ind 1 sg [1C 10:33; v-5a; 743]   "
ἀρεστά   acc pl neut [2t; a-1a(2a); 744]   ἀρεστός
ἀρεστόν   nom sg neut [2t; a-1a(2a); 744]   "

ἀρεστός   {744, a-1a(2a)}
    pleasing, acceptable, Acts 12:3; 1 John 3:22; 8:29,
    deemed proper, Acts 6:2

Ἀρέτα   gen sg masc [2C 11:32; n-1e; 745]   Ἀρέτας

Ἀρέτας, α, ὁ   {745, n-1e}
    Aretas, pr. name, 2 Cor 11:32*

ἀρετάς   acc pl fem [1P 2:9; n-1b; 746]   ἀρετή

ἀρετή, ῆς, ἡ   {746, n-1b}
    goodness, good quality of any kind; *a gracious act*
    of God, 1 Peter 2:9; 2 Peter 1:3; *virtue,*
    uprightness, Phil 4:8; 2 Peter 1:5*

ἀρετή   nom sg fem [Pp 4:8; n-1b; 746]   "
ἀρετῇ   dat sg fem [2t; n-1b; 746]   "
ἀρετήν   acc sg fem [2P 1:5; n-1b; 746]   "
ἄρῃ   aor act subj 3 sg [5t; v-2d(2); 149]   αἴρω

ἀρήν, ἀρνός, ὁ   {748, n-3f(1c)}
    a sheep, lamb, Luke 10:3*

ἄρῃς   aor act subj 2 sg [Jn 17:15; v-2d(2); 149] "
ἀρθῇ   aor pass subj 3 sg [1C 5:2; v-2d(2); 149]   "
ἀρθήσεται fut pass ind 3 sg [6t; v-2d(2); 149]   "
ἄρθητι   aor pass imperative 2 sg
           [2t; v-2d(2); 149]   "
ἀρθήτω   aor pass imperative 3 sg
           [Ep 4:31; v-2d(2); 149]   "
ἀρθῶσιν aor pass subj 3 pl
           [Jn 19:31; v-2d(2); 149]   "

ἀριθμέω   {749, v-1d(2a)}
    [-, ἠρίθμησα, -, ἠρίθμημαι, -] *to count,* Matt 10:30;
    Luke 12:7; Rev 7:9*

ἀριθμῆσαι aor act inf
           [Rv 7:9; v-1d(2a); 749]   ἀριθμέω
ἀριθμόν   acc sg masc [5t; n-2a; 750]   ἀριθμός

ἀριθμός, οῦ, ὁ   {750, n-2a}
    a number, Luke 22:3; John 6:10; Acts 4:4; Rev
    20:8; 13:18

ἀριθμός   nom sg masc [10t; n-2a; 750]   "
ἀριθμοῦ   gen sg masc [2t; n-2a; 750]   "
ἀριθμῷ   dat sg masc [Ac 16:5; n-2a; 750]   "

Ἀριμαθαία, ας, ἡ   {751, n-1a}
    Arimathea, a town of Palestine, Matt 27:57;
    Mark 15:43; Luke 23:51; John 19:38*

Ἀριμαθαίας gen sg fem [4t; n-1a; 751] Ἀριμαθαία
Ἀρίσταρχον acc sg masc
           [Ac 19:29; n-2a; 752]   Ἀρίσταρχος

Ἀρίσταρχος, ου, ὁ   {752, n-2a}
    Aristarchus, pr. name, Acts 19:29; 20:4; 27:2; Col
    4:10; Phlm 24*

Ἀρίσταρχος nom sg masc [3t; n-2a; 752]   "
Ἀριστάρχου gen sg masc [Ac 27:2; n-2a; 752]   "

ἀριστάω   {753, v-1d(1a)}
    [-, ἠρίστησα, -, -, -] *to take the first meal, breakfast,*
    John 21:12, 15; also, *to take a mid-day meal,* Luke
    11:37; 15:39 v.l.*

ἀριστερά nom sg fem
           [Mt 6:3; a-1a(1); 754]   ἀριστερός

ἀριστερός   {754, a-1a(1)}
    the left hand, Matt 6:3; so ἐξ ἀριστερῶν, sc. μερῶν,
    Luke 23:33; 2 Cor 6:7; Mark 10:37*

ἀριστερῶν gen pl fem [3t; a-1a(1); 754]   "
ἀριστήσατε aor act imperative 2 pl
           [Jn 21:12; v-1d(1a); 753]   ἀριστάω
ἀριστήσῃ aor act subj 3 sg
           [Lk 11:37; v-1d(1a); 753]   "

Ἀριστόβουλος, ου, ὁ   {755, n-2a}
    Aristobulus, pr. name, Rom 16:10*

Ἀριστοβούλου gen sg masc
           [Rm 16:10; n-2a; 755]   Ἀριστόβουλος

ἄριστον, ου, τό   {756, n-2c}
    pr. *the first meal, breakfast;* afterwards extended
    to signify also *a slight mid-day meal, luncheon,*
    Matt 22:4; Luke 11:38; 14:12; 14:15 v.l.*

ἄριστον   acc sg neut [2t; n-2c; 756]   ἄριστον
ἀρίστου   gen sg neut [Lk 11:38; n-2c; 756]   "
ἀρκεῖ   pres act ind 3 sg
           [2t; v-1d(2b); 758]   ἀρκέω
ἀρκεῖσθε pres pass imperative 2 pl
           [Lk 3:14; v-1d(2b); 758]   "
ἀρκέσῃ   aor act subj 3 sg
           [Mt 25:9; v-1d(2b); 758]   "
ἀρκεσθησόμεθα fut pass ind 1 pl
           [1Ti 6:8; v-1d(2b); 758]   "
ἀρκετόν   nom sg neut [2t; a-1a(2a); 757]   ἀρκετός

ἀρκετός, ή, όν   {757, a-1a(2a)}
    sufficient, enough, Matt 6:34; 10:25; 1 Peter 4:3*

ἀρκετός   nom sg masc [1P 4:3; a-1a(2a); 757] "

ἀρκέω   {758, v-1d(2b)}
    [-, ἤρκεσα, -, -, ἠρκέσθην] pr. *to ward off;* thence;
    to be of service, avail; to suffice, be enough, Matt
    25:9; pass. *to be contented, satisfied,* Luke 3:14; 1
    Tim 6:8; Heb 13:5; 3 John 10

ἄρκος, ου, ὁ or ἡ   {759, n-2b}
    also spelled ἄρκτος, *a bear,* Rev 13:2*

ἄρκου   gen sg masc [Rv 13:2; n-2b; 759]   ἄρκος
ἀρκούμενοι pres pass ptcp nom pl masc
           [Hb 13:5; v-1d(2b); 758]   ἀρκέω
ἀρκούμενος pres pass ptcp nom sg masc
           [3J 10; v-1d(2b); 758]   "
ἀρκοῦσιν pres act ind 3 pl
           [Jn 6:7; v-1d(2b); 758]   "

ἄρκτος, see ἄρκος   {760}

ἅρμα, ατος, τό   {761, n-3c(4)}
    a chariot, vehicle, Acts 8:28, 29, 38; Rev 9:9*

ἅρμα   acc sg neut [Ac 8:38; n-3c(4); 761]   ἅρμα

Ἀρμαγεδών   {762, n-3g(2)}
    Armageddon, Rev 16:16*

Ἀρμαγεδών indecl
           [Rv 16:16; n-3g(2); 762]   Ἀρμαγεδών
ἅρματι   dat sg neut [Ac 8:29; n-3c(4); 761]   ἅρμα
ἅρματος gen sg neut [Ac 8:28; n-3c(4); 761]   "
ἁρμάτων gen pl neut [Rv 9:9; n-3c(4); 761]   "

ἁρμόζω   {764, v-2a(1)}
[-, ἥρμοσα, -, ἥρμοσμαι, ἡρμόσθην] *to fit together;
to join, unite,* in marriage, *espouse, betroth,* 2 Cor
11:2*

ἁρμός, οῦ, ὁ   {765, n-2a}
a joint or *articulation* of the bones, Heb 4:12*

ἁρμῶν   gen pl masc [Hb 4:12; n-2a; 765]   ἁρμός
ἄρνας   acc pl masc [Lk 10:3; n-3f(1c); 748]   ἀρήν
ἀρνεῖσθαι   pres mid inf
    [Ac 4:16; v-1d(2a); 766]   ἀρνέομαι

ἀρνέομαι   {766, v-1d(2a)}
[ἀρνήσομαι, ἠρνησάμην, -, ἤρνημαι, ἠρνήθην] *to
deny, disclaim, disown,* Matt 10:33; *to renounce,*
Titus 2:12; *to decline, refuse,* Heb 11:24; absol. *to
deny, contradict,* Luke 8:15

ἀρνησάμενοι   aor mid ptcp nom pl masc
    [Ti 2:12; v-1d(2a); 766]   "
ἀρνησάμενος   aor mid ptcp nom sg masc
    [Lk 12:9; v-1d(2a); 766]   "
ἀρνήσασθαι   aor mid inf
    [2Ti 2:13; v-1d(2a); 766]   "
ἀρνησάσθω   aor mid imperative 3 sg
    [Lk 9:23; v-1d(2a); 766]   "
ἀρνήσεται   fut mid ind 3 sg
    [2Ti 2:12; v-1d(2a); 766]   "
ἀρνήσῃ   aor mid subj 2 sg
    [Jn 13:38; v-1d(2a); 766]   "
ἀρνήσηται   aor mid subj 3 sg
    [Mt 10:33; v-1d(2a); 766]   "
ἀρνήσομαι   fut mid ind 1 sg
    [Mt 10:33; v-1d(2a); 766]   "
ἀρνησόμεθα   fut mid ind 1 pl
    [2Ti 2:12; v-1d(2a); 766]   "

Ἀρνί, ὁ, τό   {767, n-3g(2)}
Arni, proper name, Luke 3:33*

Ἀρνί   indecl [Lk 3:33; n-3g(2); 747]   Ἀρνί
ἀρνία   acc pl neut [Jn 21:15; n-2c; 768]   ἀρνίον

ἀρνίον, ου, τό   {768, n-2c}
a young lamb, lamb, John 21:15; Rev 5:6, 8

ἀρνίον   nom sg neut [7t; n-2c; 768]   "
ἀρνίον   acc sg neut [Rv 5:6; n-2c; 768]   "
ἀρνίου   gen sg neut [16t; n-2c; 768]   "
ἀρνίῳ   dat sg neut [5t; n-2c; 768]   "
ἀρνούμενοι   pres mid ptcp nom pl masc
    [2t; v-1d(2a); 766]   ἀρνέομαι
ἀρνούμενος   pres mid ptcp nom sg masc
    [3t; v-1d(2a); 766]   "
ἀρνουμένων   pres mid ptcp gen pl masc
    [Lk 8:45; v-1d(2a); 766]   "
ἀρνοῦνται   pres mid ind 3 pl
    [Ti 1:16; v-1d(2a); 766]   "
ἀρξάμενοι   aor mid ptcp nom pl masc
    [2t; v-1b(2); 806]   ἄρχω
ἀρξάμενος   aor mid ptcp nom sg masc
    [8t; v-1b(2); 806]   "
ἀρξάμενου   aor mid ptcp gen sg masc
    [Mt 18:24; v-1b(2); 806]   "
ἄρξασθαι   aor mid inf   [2t; v-1b(2); 806]   "
ἄρξεσθε   fut mid ind 2 pl
    [Lk 13:26; v-1b(2); 806]   "

ἄρξῃ   fut mid ind 2 sg [Lk 14:9; v-1b(2); 806]   "
ἄρξησθε   aor mid subj 2 pl [2t; v-1b(2); 806]   "
ἄρξηται   aor mid subj 3 sg [2t; v-1b(2); 806]   "
ἄρξονται   fut mid ind 3 pl
    [Lk 23:30; v-1b(2); 806]   "
ἄρξωνται   aor mid subj 3 pl
    [Lk 14:29; v-1b(2); 806]   "
ἆρον   aor act imperative 2 sg
    [10t; v-2d(2); 149]   αἴρω
ἀροτριᾶν   pres act inf
    [1C 9:10; v-1d(3); 769]   ἀροτριάω

ἀροτριάω   {769, v-1d(3)}
[-, -, -, -, -] *to plow,* Luke 17:7; 1 Cor 9:10*

ἀροτριῶν   pres act ptcp nom sg masc
    [1C 9:10; v-1d(3); 769]   "
ἀροτριῶντα   pres act ptcp acc sg masc
    [Lk 17:7; v-1d(3); 769]   "

ἄροτρον, ου, τό   {770, n-2c}
a plow, Luke 9:62*

ἄροτρον   acc sg neut [Lk 9:62; n-2c; 770]   ἄροτρον
ἀροῦσιν   fut act ind 3 pl [4t; v-2d(2); 149]   αἴρω
ἁρπαγέντα   aor pass ptcp acc sg masc
    [2C 12:2; v-2a(1); 773]   ἁρπάζω
ἅρπαγες   nom pl masc [3t; n-3b(2); 774]   ἅρπαξ

ἁρπαγή, ῆς, ἡ   {771, n-1b}
plunder, pillage; the act of plundering, Heb 10:34;
prey, spoil, Matt 23:25; Luke 11:39*

ἁρπαγήν   acc sg fem [Hb 10:34; n-1b; 771]   ἁρπαγή
ἁρπαγῆς   gen sg fem [2t; n-1b; 771]   "
ἁρπαγησόμεθα   fut pass ind 1 pl
    [1Th 4:17; v-2a(1); 773]   ἁρπάζω
ἁρπαγμόν   acc sg masc
    [Pp 2:6; n-2a; 772]   ἁρπαγμός

ἁρπαγμός, οῦ, ὁ   {772, n-2a}
eager seizure; in N.T., *a thing retained with an
eager grasp,* or *eagerly claimed and conspicuously
exercised,* Phil 2:6*

ἁρπάζει   pres act ind 3 sg
    [2t; v-2a(1); 773]   ἁρπάζω
ἁρπάζειν   pres act inf [2t; v-2a(1); 773]   "
ἁρπάζοντες   pres act ptcp nom pl masc
    [Jd 23; v-2a(1); 773]   "
ἁρπάζουσιν   pres act ind 3 pl
    [Mt 11:12; v-2a(1); 773]   "

ἁρπάζω   {773, v-2a(1)}
[ἁρπάσω, ἥρπασα, -, ἥρπακμαι, ἡρπάσθην or
ἡρπάγην] *to seize,* as a wild beast, John 10:12;
take away by force, snatch away, Matt 13:19; John
10:28, 29; Acts 23:10; Jude 23; met. *to seize on
with avidity, eagerly, appropriate,* Matt 11:12; *to
convey away suddenly, transport hastily,* John 6:15

ἅρπαξ, αγος, ὁ   {774, n-3b(2)}
pr. *raveneous, ravening,* as a wild beast, Matt
7:15; met. *rapacious, given to extortion and
robbery, an extortioner,* Luke 18:11; 1 Cor 5:10, 11;
6:10; Titus 1:9 v.l.*

ἅρπαξ   nom sg masc [1C 5:11; n-3b(2); 774]   ἅρπαξ
ἅρπαξιν   dat pl masc [1C 5:10; n-3b(2); 774]   "
ἁρπάσαι   aor act inf   [2t; v-2a(1); 773]   ἁρπάζω

ἁρπάσει   fut act ind 3 sg
[Jn 10:28; v-2a(1); 773]   "

ἀρραβών, ῶνος, ὁ   {775, n-3f(1a)}
a pledge, earnest, 2 Cor 1:22; 5:5; Eph 1:14*

ἀρραβών   nom sg masc
[Ep 1:14; n-3f(1a); 775]   ἀρραβών
ἀρραβῶνα   acc sg masc [2t; n-3f(1a); 775]   "

ἄρραφος, see ἄραφος

ἄρρην, see ἄρσην   {776}

ἄρρητα   acc pl neut [2C 12:4; a-3a; 777]   ἄρρητος

ἄρρητος, ον   {777, a-3a}
pr. not spoken; what ought not to be spoken, secret;
which cannot be spoken or uttered, 2 Cor 12:4*

ἄρρωστοι   nom pl masc
[1C 11:30; a-3a; 779]   ἄρρωστος
ἀρρώστοις   dat pl masc [Mk 6:5; a-3a; 779]   "

ἄρρωστος, ον   {779, a-3a}
ill, sick, an invalid, Matt 14:14; Mark 6:5, 13;
16:18; 1 Cor 11:30

ἀρρώστους   acc pl masc [3t; a-3a; 779]   "
ἄρσεν   nom sg neut [2t; a-4b(1); 781]   ἄρσην
ἄρσεν   acc sg neut [3t; a-4b(1); 781]   "
ἄρσενα   acc sg masc [Rv 12:13; a-4b(1); 781]   "
ἄρσενες   nom pl masc [2t; a-4b(1); 781]   "
ἀρσενοκοῖται   nom pl masc
[1C 6:9; n-1f; 780]   ἀρσενοκοίτης
ἀρσενοκοίταις   dat pl masc [1Ti 1:10; n-1f; 780]   "

ἀρσενοκοίτης, ου, ὁ   {780, n-1f}
a male engaging in same-gender sexual activity, a
sodomite, pederast, 1 Cor 6:9; 1 Tim 1:10*

ἄρσεσιν   dat pl masc [Rm 1:27; a-4b(1); 781] ἄρσην

ἄρσην, ενος, εν   {781, a-4b(1)}
male, of the male sex, Matt 19:4; Mark 10:6; Luke
2:23; Rom 1:27; Gal 3:28; Rev 12:5, 13*

Ἀρτεμᾶν   acc sg masc
[Ti 3:12; n-1e; 782]   Ἀρτεμᾶς

Ἀρτεμᾶς, ᾶ, ὁ   {782, n-1e}
Artemas, pr. name, Titus 3:12*

Ἀρτέμιδος   gen sg fem [3t; n-3c(2); 783]   Ἄρτεμις

Ἄρτεμις, ιδος, ἡ   {783, n-3c(2)}
Artemis or Diana, Acts 19:24, 27, 28, 34, 35*

Ἄρτεμις   nom sg fem [2t; n-3c(2); 783]   "

ἀρτέμων, ῶνος, ὁ   {784, n-3f(1a)}
a topsail, foresail; or, according to others, the
dolon of Pliny and Pollux, a small sail near the
prow of the ship, which was hoisted when the
wind was too strong to use the larger sails, Acts
27:40*

ἀρτέμωνα   acc sg masc
[Ac 27:40; n-3f(1a); 784]   ἀρτέμων

ἄρτι   {785, adverb}
pr. at the present moment, close upon it either
before of after; now, at the present juncture, Matt
3:15; forthwith, presently; just now, recently, 1
Thess 3:6; ἕως ἄρτι, until now, hitherto, Matt

11:12; John 2:10; ἀπ' ἄρτι, or ἀπάρτι, from this
time, henceforth, Matt 23:39

ἄρτι   adverb [36t; adverb; 785]   ἄρτι
ἀρτιγέννητα   nom pl neut
[1P 2:2; a-3a; 786]   ἀρτιγέννητος

ἀρτιγέννητος, ον   {786, a-3a}
just born, new-born, 1 Peter 2:2*

ἄρτιος, ια, ον   {787, a-1a(1)}
entirely suited; complete in accomplishment,
ready, 2 Tim 3:17*

ἄρτιος   nom sg masc
[2Ti 3:17; a-1a(1); 787]   ἄρτιος
ἄρτοι   nom pl masc [4t; n-2a; 788]   ἄρτος
ἄρτοις   dat pl masc [Mk 6:52; n-2a; 788]   "
ἄρτον   acc sg masc [38t; n-2a; 788]   "

ἄρτος, ου, ὁ   {788, n-2a}
bread; a loaf or thin cake of bread, Matt 26:26; food,
Matt 15:2; Mark 3:20; bread, maintenance, living,
necessaries of life, Matt 6:11; Luke 11:3; 2 Thess
3:8

ἄρτος   nom sg masc [10t; n-2a; 788]   "
ἄρτου   gen sg masc [5t; n-2a; 788]   "
ἄρτους   acc pl masc [30t; n-2a; 788]   "
ἀρτυθήσεται   fut pass ind 3 sg
[Lk 14:34; v-1a(4); 789]   ἀρτύω
ἀρτύσετε   fut act ind 2 pl
[Mk 9:50; v-1a(4); 789]   "

ἀρτύω   {789, v-1a(4)}
[ἀρτύσω, -, -, ἤρτυμαι, ἠρτύθην] pr. to fit, prepare;
to season, make savoury, Mark 9:50; Luke 14:34;
Col 4:6*

ἄρτῳ   dat sg masc [2t; n-2a; 788]   ἄρτος
ἄρτων   gen pl masc [7t; n-2a; 788]   "

Ἀρφαξάδ, ὁ   {790, n-3g(2)}
Arphaxad, pr. name, indecl, Luke 3:36*

Ἀρφαξάδ   indecl [Lk 3:36; n-3g(2); 790]   Ἀρφαξάδ

ἀρχάγγελος, ου, ὁ   {791, n-2a}
an archangel, chief angel, 1 Thess 4:16; Jude 9*

ἀρχάγγελος   nom sg masc
[Jd 9; n-2a; 791]   ἀρχάγγελος
ἀρχαγγέλου   gen sg masc [1Th 4:16; n-2a; 791]   "
ἀρχαί   nom pl fem [2t; n-1b; 794]   ἀρχή
ἀρχαῖα   nom pl neut
[2C 5:17; a-1a(1); 792]   ἀρχαῖος
ἀρχαίοις   dat pl masc [2t; a-1a(1); 792]   "

ἀρχαῖος, αία, αιον   {792, a-1a(1)}
old, ancient, of former age, Matt 5:21, 27 v.l., 33; of
long standing, old, veteran, Acts 21:16; ἀφ'ἡμερῶν
ἀρχαίων, from early days, from an early period, of
the Gospel, Acts 15:7

ἀρχαῖος   nom sg masc [2t; a-1a(1); 792]   "
ἀρχαίου   gen sg masc [2P 2:5; a-1a(1); 792]   "
ἀρχαῖς   dat pl fem [4t; n-1b; 794]   ἀρχή
ἀρχαίῳ   dat sg masc
[Ac 21:16; a-1a(1); 792]   ἀρχαῖος
ἀρχαίων   gen pl masc [2t; a-1a(1); 792]   "
ἀρχαίων   gen pl fem [2t; a-1a(1); 792]   "

ἀρχάς   acc pl fem [4t; n-1b; 794]   ἀρχή
ἄρχειν   pres act inf [2t; v-1b(2); 806]   ἄρχω

Ἀρχέλαος, ου, ὁ   {793, n-2a}
Archelaus, pr. name, Matt 2:22*

Ἀρχέλαος   nom sg masc
[Mt 2:22; n-2a; 793]   Ἀρχέλαος

ἀρχή, ῆς, ἡ   {794, n-1b}
a beginning, Matt 24:8; *an extremity, corner*, or, *an attached cord*, Acts 10:11; 11:5; *first place, headship; high estate, eminence*, Jude 6; *authority*, Luke 20:20; *an authority, magistrate*, Luke 12:11; *a principality, prince*, of spiritual existence, Eph 3:10; 6:12; ἀπ᾽ ἀρχῆς, ἐξ ἀρχῆς, *from the first, originally*, Matt 19:4, 8; Luke 1:2; John 6:64; 2 Thess 2:13; 1 John 1:1; 2:7; ἐν ἀρχῇ, κατ᾽ ἀρχάς, *in the beginning* of things, John 1:1, 2; Heb 1:10; ἐν ἀρχῇ, *at the first*, Acts 11:15; τὴν ἀρχήν, used adverbially, *wholly, altogether*, John 8:25

ἀρχή   nom sg fem [7t; n-1b; 794]   ἀρχή
ἀρχῇ   dat sg fem [5t; n-1b; 794]   "
ἀρχηγόν   acc sg masc [4t; n-2a; 795]   ἀρχηγός

ἀρχηγός, οῦ, ὁ   {795, n-2a}
a chief, leader, prince, Acts 5:31; *a prime author*, Acts 3:15; Heb 2:10; 12:2*

ἀρχήν   acc sg fem [7t; n-1b; 794]   ἀρχή
ἀρχῆς   gen sg fem [26t; n-1b; 794]   "

ἀρχιερατικός, ον   {796, a-3a}
belonging to or *connected with the high-priest* or *his office*, Acts 4:6*

ἀρχιερατικοῦ   gen sg neut
[Ac 4:6; a-3a; 796]   ἀρχιερατικός
ἀρχιερέα   acc sg masc
[9t; n-3e(3); 797]   ἀρχιερεύς
ἀρχιερεῖ   dat sg masc [3t; n-3e(3); 797]   "
ἀρχιερεῖς   nom pl masc [40t; n-3e(3); 797]   "
ἀρχιερεῖς   acc pl masc [10t; n-3e(3); 797]   "

ἀρχιερεύς, έως, ὁ   {797, n-3e(3)}
a high-priest, chief-priest

ἀρχιερεύς   nom sg masc [28t; n-3e(3); 797]   "
ἀρχιερεῦσιν   dat pl masc [6t; n-3e(3); 797]   "
ἀρχιερέων   gen pl masc [10t; n-3e(3); 797]   "
ἀρχιερέως   gen sg masc [16t; n-3e(3); 797]   "

ἀρχιληστής, οῦ, ὁ   {798, n-1f}
robber, chieftain, John 18:40 v.l.*

ἀρχιποίμενος   gen sg masc
[1P 5:4; n-3f(1b); 799]   ἀρχιποίμην

ἀρχιποίμην, ενος, ὁ   {799, n-3f(1b)}
chief shepherd, 1 Peter 5:4*

Ἄρχιππος, ου, ὁ   {800, n-2a}
Archippus, pr. name, Col 4:17; Phlm 2, inscr. and subsc.*

Ἀρχίππῳ   dat sg masc [2t; n-2a; 800]   Ἄρχιππος
ἀρχισυνάγωγοι   nom pl masc
[Ac 13:15; n-2a; 801]   ἀρχισυνάγωγος
ἀρχισυνάγωγον   acc sg masc [Ac 18:17; n-2a; 801]   "

ἀρχισυνάγωγος, ου, ὁ   {801, n-2a}
a president or *moderating elder of a synagogue*, Mark 5:22, 35, 36, 38; Luke 8:49

ἀρχισυνάγωγος   nom sg masc [2t; n-2a; 801]   "
ἀρχισυναγώγου   gen sg masc [3t; n-2a; 801]   "
ἀρχισυναγώγῳ   dat sg masc [Mk 5:36; n-2a; 801]   "
ἀρχισυναγώγων   gen pl masc [Mk 5:22; n-2a; 801]   "

ἀρχιτέκτων, ονος, ὁ   {802, n-3f(1b)}
architect, head or *master-builder*, 1 Cor 3:10*

ἀρχιτέκτων   nom sg masc
[1C 3:10; n-3f(1b); 802]   ἀρχιτέκτων

ἀρχιτελώνης, ου, ὁ   {803, n-1f}
a chief publican, chief collector of the customs or *taxes*, Luke 19:2*

ἀρχιτελώνης   nom sg masc
[Lk 19:2; n-1f; 803]   ἀρχιτελώνης

ἀρχιτρίκλινος, ου, ὁ   {804, n-2a}
director of a feast, John 2:8, 9*

ἀρχιτρίκλινος   nom sg masc
[2t; n-2a; 804]   ἀρχιτρίκλινος
ἀρχιτρικλίνῳ   dat sg masc [Jn 2:8; n-2a; 804]   "
ἀρχόμεθα   pres mid ind 1 pl
[2C 3:1; v-1b(2); 806]   ἄρχω
ἀρχόμενος   pres mid ptcp nom sg masc
[Lk 3:23; v-1b(2); 806]   "
ἀρχομένων   pres mid ptcp gen pl neut
[Lk 21:28; v-1b(2); 806]   "
ἄρχοντα   acc sg masc [6t; n-3c(5b); 807]   ἄρχων
ἄρχοντας   acc pl masc [3t; n-3c(5b); 807]   "
ἄρχοντες   nom pl masc [8t; n-3c(5b); 807]   "
ἄρχοντες   voc pl masc [Ac 4:8; n-3c(5b); 807]   "
ἄρχοντι   dat sg masc [4t; n-3c(5b); 807]   "
ἄρχοντος   gen sg masc [Mt 9:23; n-3c(5b); 807]   "
ἀρχόντων   gen pl masc [5t; n-3c(5b); 807]   "
ἄρχουσιν   dat pl masc [Ac 14:5; n-3c(5b); 807]   "

ἄρχω   {806, v-1b(2)}
[ἄρξω, ἤρξα, -, -, -] (1) pr. (act.) *to be first; to rule*, Mark 10:42; Rom 15:12 (2) mid. *to begin*, Matt 4:17; *to take commencement*, Luke 24:27; 1 Peter 4:17

ἄρχων, οντος, ὁ   {807, n-3c(5b)}
one invested with power and dignity, chief, ruler, prince, magistrate, Matt 9:23; 20:25

ἄρχων   nom sg masc [8t; n-3c(5b); 807]   "
ἀρῶ   fut act ind 1 sg
[Jn 20:15; v-2d(2); 149]   αἴρω

ἄρωμα, ατος, τό   {808, n-3c(4)}
an aromatic substance, spice, etc., Mark 16:1; Luke 23:56; 24:1; John 19:40*

ἀρώματα   acc pl neut [3t; n-3c(4); 808]   ἄρωμα
ἀρωμάτων   gen pl neut [Jn 19:40; n-3c(4); 808]   "
ἅς   acc pl fem [2t; a-1a(2b); 4005]   ὅς

Ἀσά see Ἀσάφ   {809}

ἀσάλευτον   acc sg fem
[Hb 12:28; a-3a; 810]   ἀσάλευτος

ἀσάλευτος, ον   {810, a-3a}
    unshaken, immovable, Acts 27:41; met. *firm,
    stable, enduring,* Heb 12:28*

ἀσάλευτος   nom sg fem [Ac 27:41; a-3a; 810]   "

Ἀσάφ, ὁ   {811, n-3g(2)}
    Also spelled Ἀσά, *Asaph,* pr. name, indecl, Matt
    1:7, 8; Luke 3:23ff. v.l.*

Ἀσάφ   indecl [2t; n-3g(2); 811]   Ἀσάφ
ἄσβεστον   acc sg neut
    [Mk 9:43; a-3a; 812]   ἄσβεστος

ἄσβεστος, ον   {812, a-3a}
    unquenched; inextinguishable, unquenchable,
    Matt 3:12; Mark 9:43, 45 v.l.; Luke 3:17*

ἀσβέστῳ   dat sg neut [2t; a-3a; 812]   "

ἀσέβεια, ας, ἡ   {813, n-1a}
    impiety, ungodliness; dishonesty, wickedness, Rom
    1:18; 11:26; 2 Tim 2:16; Titus 2:12; Jude 15, 18*

ἀσέβειαν   acc sg fem [2t; n-1a; 813]   ἀσέβεια
ἀσεβείας   gen sg fem [2t; n-1a; 813]   "
ἀσεβείας   acc pl fem [Rm 11:26; n-1a; 813]   "
ἀσεβεῖς   nom pl masc [2t; a-4a; 815]   ἀσεβής
ἀσεβειῶν   gen pl fem
    [Jd 18; n-1a; 813]   ἀσέβεια
ἀσεβέσι   dat pl masc [1Ti 1:9; a-4a; 815]   ἀσεβής
ἀσεβέσιν   dat pl masc [2P 2:6; a-4a; 815]   "

ἀσεβέω   {814, v-1d(2a)}
    [-, ἠσέβησα, -, -, -] *to be impious, to act impiously
    or wickedly, live an impious life,* 2 Peter 2:6; Jude
    15*

ἀσεβῆ   acc sg masc [Rm 4:5; a-4a; 815]   "

ἀσεβής, ές   {815, a-4a}
    impious, ungodly; wicked, sinful, Rom 4:5; 5:6

ἀσεβής   nom sg masc [1P 4:18; a-4a; 815]   "
ἀσεβῶν   gen pl masc [3t; a-4a; 815]   "

ἀσέλγεια, ας, ἡ   {816, n-1a}
    intemperance; licentiousness, lasciviousness, Rom
    13:13; *insolence, outrageous behavior,* Mark 7:22

ἀσέλγεια   nom sg fem [2t; n-1a; 816]   ἀσέλγεια
ἀσελγείᾳ   dat sg fem [3t; n-1a; 816]   "
ἀσελγείαις   dat pl fem [4t; n-1a; 816]   "
ἀσέλγειαν   acc sg fem [Jd 4; n-1a; 816]   "

ἄσημος, ον   {817, a-3a}
    pr. *not marked;* met. *not noted, not remarkable,
    unknown to fame, ignoble, mean, inconsiderable,*
    Acts 21:39*

ἀσήμου   gen sg fem [Ac 21:39; a-3a; 817]   ἄσημος

Ἀσήρ, ὁ   {818, n-3g(2)}
    Asher, pr. name, indecl (Gen 30:13; 49:20; 2
    Chron 30:11) Luke 2:36; Rev 7:6*

Ἀσήρ   indecl [2t; n-3g(2); 818]   Ἀσήρ
ἀσθενεῖ   pres act ind 3 sg
    [5t; v-1d(2a); 820]   ἀσθενέω

ἀσθένεια, ας, ἡ   {819, n-1a}
    want of strength, weakness, feebleness, 1 Cor
    15:43; bodily *infirmity, state of ill health, sickness,*
    Matt 8:17; Luke 5:15; met. *infirmity, frailty,*

imperfection, intellectual and moral, Rom 6:19; 1
    Cor 2:3; Heb 5:2; 7:28; *suffering, affliction,
    distress, calamity,* Rom 8:26

ἀσθένεια   nom sg fem
    [Jn 11:4; n-1a; 819]   ἀσθένεια
ἀσθενείᾳ   dat sg fem [5t; n-1a; 819]   "
ἀσθενείαις   dat pl fem [4t; n-1a; 819]   "
ἀσθένειαν   acc sg fem [4t; n-1a; 819]   "
ἀσθενείας   gen sg fem [5t; n-1a; 819]   "
ἀσθενείας   acc pl fem [3t; n-1a; 819]   "
ἀσθενεῖς   nom pl masc [2t; a-4a; 822]   ἀσθενής
ἀσθενεῖς   acc pl masc [5t; a-4a; 822]   "
ἀσθενειῶν   gen pl fem [2t; n-1a; 819]   ἀσθένεια
ἀσθενές   nom sg neut
    [1C 1:25; a-4a; 822]   ἀσθενής
ἀσθενές   acc sg neut [Hb 7:18; a-4a; 822]   "
ἀσθενέσιν   dat pl masc [2t; a-4a; 822]   "
ἀσθενέστερα   nom pl neut comparative
    [1C 12:22; a-4a; 822]   "
ἀσθενεστέρῳ   dat sg neut comparative
    [1P 3:7; a-4a; 822]   "

ἀσθενέω   {820, v-1d(2a)}
    [ἀσθενήσω, ἠσθένησα, ἠσθένηκα, -, -] *to be weak,
    infirm, deficient in strength; to be inefficient,* Rom
    8:3; 2 Cor 13:3; *to be sick,* Matt 25:36; met. *to be
    weak* in faith, *to doubt, hesitate, be unsettled,
    timid,* Rom 14:1; 1 Cor 8:9, 11, 12; 2 Cor 11:29; *to
    be deficient in authority, dignity,* or *power, be
    contemptible,* 2 Cor 11:21; 13:3, 9; *to be afflicted,
    distressed, needy,* Acts 20:35; 2 Cor 12:10; 13:4, 9

ἀσθενῆ   acc sg masc [Mt 25:44; a-4a; 822]   "
ἀσθενῆ   acc pl neut [2t; a-4a; 822]   "

ἀσθένημα, ατος, τό   {821, n-3c(4)}
    pr. *weakness, infirmity,* met. *doubt, hesitation,*
    Rom 15:1*

ἀσθενήματα   acc pl neut
    [Rm 15:1; n-3c(4); 821]   ἀσθένημα

ἀσθενής, ες   {822, a-4a}
    without strength, weak, infirm, Matt 26:41; Mark
    14:38; 1 Peter 3:7; *helpless,* Rom 5:6; *imperfect,
    inefficient,* Gal 4:9; *feeble, without energy,* 2 Cor
    10:10; *infirm* in body, *sick, sickly,* Matt 25:39, 43,
    44; *weak,* mentally or spiritually, *dubious,
    hesitating,* 1 Cor 8:7, 10; 9:22; 1 Thess 5:14;
    afflicted, distressed, oppressed with calamities, 1
    Cor 4:10

ἀσθενής   nom sg masc [2t; a-4a; 822]   ἀσθενής
ἀσθενής   nom sg fem [4t; a-4a; 822]   "
ἀσθενήσας   aor act ptcp nom sg masc
    [Rm 4:19; v-1d(2a); 820]   ἀσθενέω
ἀσθενήσασαν   aor act ptcp acc sg fem
    [Ac 9:37; v-1d(2a); 820]   "
ἀσθενοῦμεν   pres act ind 1 pl
    [2C 13:4; v-1d(2a); 820]   "
ἀσθενοῦντα   pres act ptcp acc sg masc
    [3t; v-1d(2a); 820]   "
ἀσθενοῦντας   pres act ptcp acc pl masc
    [4t; v-1d(2a); 820]   "
ἀσθενούντων   pres act ptcp gen pl masc
    [3t; v-1d(2a); 820]   "

ἀσθενοῦς   gen sg masc [2t; a-4a; 822]   ἀσθενής
ἀσθενοῦσαν   pres act ptcp acc sg fem
   [1C 8:12; v-1d(2a); 820]   ἀσθενέω
ἀσθενῶ   pres act ind 1 sg
   [2C 11:29; v-1d(2a); 820]   "
ἀσθενῶ   pres act subj 1 sg
   [2C 12:10; v-1d(2a); 820]   "
ἀσθενῶμεν   pres act subj 1 pl
   [2C 13:9; v-1d(2a); 820]
ἀσθενῶν   gen pl masc [2t; a-4a; 822]   ἀσθενής
ἀσθενῶν   pres act ptcp nom sg masc
   [4t; v-1d(2a); 820]   ἀσθενέω

Ἀσία, ας, ἡ   {823, n-1a}
   Asia, the Roman province, Acts 19:27

Ἀσία   nom sg fem [Ac 19:27; n-1a; 823]   Ἀσία
Ἀσίᾳ   dat sg fem [5t; n-1a; 823]   "
Ἀσίαν   acc sg fem [5t; n-1a; 823]   "
Ἀσιανοί   nom pl masc
   [Ac 20:4; n-2a; 824]   Ἀσιανός

Ἀσιανός, οῦ, ὁ   {824, n-2a}
   belonging to the Roman province of Asia, Acts
   20:4*

Ἀσιάρχης, ου, ὁ   {825, n-1f}
   an Asiarch, an officer in the province of Asia, as
   in other eastern provinces of the Roman
   empire, selected, with others, from the more
   opulent citizens, to preside over the things
   pertaining to religious worship, and to exhibit
   annual public games at their own expense in
   honor of the gods, in the manner of the aediles
   at Rome, Acts 19:31*

Ἀσιαρχῶν   gen pl masc
   [Ac 19:31; n-1f; 825]   Ἀσιάρχης
Ἀσίας   gen sg fem [7t; n-1a; 823]   Ἀσία

ἀσιτία, ας, ἡ   {826, n-1a}
   abstinence from food, fasting, Acts 27:21*

ἀσιτίας   gen sg fem [Ac 27:21; n-1a; 826]   ἀσιτία
ἄσιτοι   nom pl masc [Ac 27:33; a-3a; 827]   ἄσιτος

ἄσιτος, ον   {827, a-3a}
   abstaining from food, fasting, Acts 27:33*

ἀσκέω   {828, v-1d(2a)}
   [(ἤσκουν), -, -, -, -, -] pr. to work materials; absol.
   to train or exert one's self, make endeavor, Acts
   24:16*

ἀσκοί   nom pl masc [4t; n-2a; 829]   ἀσκός

ἀσκός, οῦ, ὁ   {829, n-2a}
   a leathern bag or bottle, bottle of skin, Matt 9:17;
   Mark 2:22; Luke 5:37, 38

ἀσκούς   acc pl masc [8t; n-2a; 829]   "
ἀσκῶ   pres act ind 1 sg
   [Ac 24:16; v-1d(2a); 828]   ἀσκέω

ἀσμένως   {830, adverb}
   gladly, joyfully, Acts 21:17; 2:41 v.l.*

ἀσμένως   adverb [Ac 21:17; adverb; 830]   ἀσμένως
ἄσοφοι   nom pl masc [Ep 5:15; a-3a; 831]   ἄσοφος

ἄσοφος, ον   {831, a-3a}
   unwise; destitute of Christian wisdom, Eph 5:15*

ἀσπάζεσθαι   pres mid inf
   [Mk 15:18; v-2a(1); 832]   ἀσπάζομαι
ἀσπάζεται   pres mid ind 3 sg [11t; v-2a(1); 832]   "

ἀσπάζομαι   {832, v-2a(1)}
   [-, ἠσπασάμην, -, -, -] to salute, greet, welcome,
   express good wishes, pay respects, Matt 10:12;
   Mark 9:15, et al. freq.; to bid farewell, Acts 20:1;
   21:6; to treat with affection, Matt 5:47; met. to
   embrace mentally, welcome to the heart of
   understanding, Heb 11:13

ἀσπάζομαι   pres mid ind 1 sg
   [Rm 16:22; v-2a(1); 832]   "
ἀσπάζονται   pres mid ind 3 pl [9t; v-2a(1); 832]   "
ἀσπάζου   pres mid imperative 2 sg
   [3J 15; v-2a(1); 832]   "
ἄσπασαι   aor mid imperative 2 sg
   [2t; v-2a(1); 832]   "
ἀσπασάμενοι   aor mid ptcp nom pl masc
   [3t; v-2a(1); 832]   "
ἀσπασάμενος   aor mid ptcp nom sg masc
   [3t; v-2a(1); 832]   "
ἀσπάσασθε   aor mid imperative 2 pl
   [24t; v-2a(1); 832]   "
ἀσπάσησθε   aor mid subj 2 pl [2t; v-2a(1); 832]   "
ἀσπασμόν   acc sg masc
   [Lk 1:41; n-2a; 833]   ἀσπασμός

ἀσπασμός, οῦ, ὁ   {833, n-2a}
   salutation, greeting, Matt 23:7; Mark 12:38

ἀσπασμός   nom sg masc [4t; n-2a; 833]   "
ἀσπασμοῦ   gen sg masc [Lk 1:44; n-2a; 833]   "
ἀσπασμούς   acc pl masc [4t; n-2a; 833]   "
ἀσπίδων   gen pl fem
   [Rm 3:13; n-3c(2); 835]   ἀσπίς
ἄσπιλοι   nom pl masc [2P 3:14; a-3a; 834]   ἄσπιλος
ἄσπιλον   acc sg masc [Jm 1:27; a-3a; 834]   "
ἄσπιλον   acc sg fem [1Ti 6:14; a-3a; 834]   "

ἄσπιλος, ον   {834, a-3a}
   spotless, unblemished, pure, 1 Tim 6:14; James
   1:27; 1 Peter 1:19; 2 Peter 3:14*

ἀσπίλου   gen sg masc [1P 1:19; a-3a; 834]   "

ἀσπίς, ίδος, ἡ   {835, n-3c(2)}
   an asp, a species of serpent of the most deadly
   venom, Rom 3:13*

ἄσπονδοι   nom pl masc
   [2Ti 3:3; a-3a; 836]   ἄσπονδος

ἄσπονδος, ον   {836, a-3a}
   pr. unwilling to make a treaty; hence, implacable,
   irreconcilable, 2 Tim 3:3; Rom 1:31 v.l.*

ἀσσάριον, ου, τό   {837, n-2c}
   dimin. of the Latin, as, a Roman brass coin of
   the value of one-tenth of a denarius, or δραχμή,
   used to convey the idea of a trifle or very small
   sum, like the term a mil (equals one-tenth of a
   cent), Matt 10:29; Luke 12:6*

ἀσσαρίου   gen sg neut
   [Mt 10:29; n-2c; 837]   ἀσσάριον
ἀσσαρίων   gen pl neut [Lk 12:6; n-2c; 837]   "

Ἀσσάρων, ωνος, ὁ   {838, n-3f(1a)}
  Saron, a level tract of Palestine, between
  Caesarea and Joppa, see Σαρων, Acts 9:35 v.l.*

ἆσσον   {839, adverb}
  nearer; very nigh, close; used as the compar. of
  ἄγχι, Acts 27:13*

Ἆσσον   acc sg fem [2t; n-2b; 840]   Ἆσσος
ἆσσον   adverb-comparative
  [Ac 27:13; adverb; 839]   ἆσσον

Ἆσσος, ου, ἡ   {840, n-2b}
  Assos, a maritime city of Mysia, in Asia Minor,
  Acts 20:13-14*

ἀστατέω   {841, v-1d(2a)}
  [-, -, -, -, -] *to be unsettled, to be a wanderer, be
  homeless*, 1 Cor 4:11*

ἀστατοῦμεν   pres act ind 1 pl
  [1C 4:11; v-1d(2a); 841]   ἀστατέω
ἀστεῖον   acc sg neut
  [Hb 11:23; a-1a(1); 842]   ἀστεῖος

ἀστεῖος, α, ον   {842, a-1a(1)}
  pr. *belonging to a city; well bred, polite, polished;*
  hence, *elegant, fair, comely, beautiful*, Acts 7:20;
  Heb 11:23*

ἀστεῖος   nom sg masc [Ac 7:20; a-1a(1); 842]   "
ἀστέρα   acc sg masc [4t; n-3f(2b); 843]   ἀστήρ
ἀστέρας   acc pl masc [3t; n-3f(2b); 843]   "
ἀστέρες   nom pl masc [5t; n-3f(2b); 843]   "
ἀστέρος   gen sg masc [3t; n-3f(2b); 843]   "
ἀστέρων   gen pl masc [5t; n-3f(2b); 843]   "

ἀστήρ, έρος, ὁ   {843, n-3f(2b)}
  a star, luminous body like a star, luminary, Matt
  2:2, 7, 9, 10; Rev 1:16

ἀστήρ   nom sg masc [4t; n-3f(2b); 843]   "
ἀστήρικτοι   nom pl masc
  [2P 3:16; a-3a; 844]   ἀστήρικτος

ἀστήρικτος, ον   {844, a-3a}
  not made firm; unsettled, unstable, unsteady, 2
  Peter 2:14; 3:16*

ἀστηρίκτους   acc pl fem [2P 2:14; a-3a; 844]   "
ἄστοργοι   nom pl masc
  [2Ti 3:3; a-3a; 845]   ἄστοργος

ἄστοργος, ον   {845, a-3a}
  devoid of natural or *instinctive affection, without
  affection to kindred*, Rom 1:31; 2 Tim 3:3*

ἀστόργους   acc pl masc [Rm 1:31; a-3a; 845]   "

ἀστοχέω   {846, v-1d(2a)}
  [-, ἠστόχησα -, -, -] pr. *to miss the mark;* met. *to
  err, deviate, swerve from*, 1 Tim 1:6; 6:21; 2 Tim
  2:18*

ἀστοχήσαντες   aor act ptcp nom pl masc
  [1Ti 1:6; v-1d(2a); 846]   ἀστοχέω
ἄστρα   nom pl neut [Hb 11:12; n-2c; 849]   ἄστρον
ἀστραπαί   nom pl fem [4t; n-1b; 847]   ἀστραπή

ἀστραπή, ῆς, ἡ   {847, n-1b}
  lightning, Matt 24:27; *brightness, lustre*, Luke
  11:36

ἀστραπή   nom sg fem [3t; n-1b; 847]   "
ἀστραπῇ   dat sg fem [Lk 11:36; n-1b; 847]   "
ἀστραπήν   acc sg fem [Lk 10:18; n-1b; 847]   "
ἀστράπτουσα   pres act ptcp nom sg fem
  [Lk 17:24; v-4; 848]   ἀστράπτω
ἀστραπτούσῃ   pres act ptcp dat sg fem
  [Lk 24:4; v-4; 848]   "

ἀστράπτω   {848, v-4}
  [-, ἤστραψα, -, -, -] *to lighten, flash as lightning*,
  Luke 17:24; *to be bright, shining*, Luke 24:4*

ἄστροις   dat pl neut [Lk 21:25; n-2c; 849]   ἄστρον

ἄστρον, ου, τό   {849, n-2c}
  a constellation; a star, Luke 21:25; Acts 7:43;
  27:20; Heb 11:12*

ἄστρον   acc sg neut [Ac 7:43; n-2c; 849]   "
ἄστρων   gen pl neut [Ac 27:20; n-2c; 849]   "
Ἀσύγκριτον   acc sg masc
  [Rm 16:14; n-2a; 850]   Ἀσύγκριτος

Ἀσύγκριτος, ου, ὁ   {850, n-2a}
  Asyncritus, pr. name, Rom 16:14*

ἀσύμφωνοι   nom pl masc
  [Ac 28:25; a-3a; 851]   ἀσύμφωνος

ἀσύμφωνος, ον   {851, a-3a}
  discordant in sound; met. *discordant, at difference*,
  Acts 28:25*

ἀσύνετοι   nom pl masc [2t; a-3a; 852]   ἀσύνετος

ἀσύνετος, ον   {852, a-3a}
  unintelligent, dull, Matt 15:16; Mark 7:18;
  reckless, perverse, Rom 1:21, 31; *unenlightened,
  heathenish*, Rom 10:19

ἀσύνετος   nom sg fem [Rm 1:21; a-3a; 852]   "
ἀσυνέτους   acc pl masc [Rm 1:31; a-3a; 852]   "
ἀσυνέτῳ   dat sg neut [Rm 10:19; a-3a; 852]   "

ἀσύνθετος, ον   {853, a-3a}
  unable to be trusted, undutiful, Rom 1:31*

ἀσυνθέτους   acc pl masc
  [Rm 1:31; a-3a; 853]   ἀσύνθετος

ἀσφάλεια, ας, ἡ   {854, n-1a}
  pr. *state of security from falling, firmness; safety,
  security*, 1 Thess 5:3; *certainty, truth*, Luke 1:4;
  means of security, Acts 5:23*

ἀσφάλεια   nom sg fem
  [1Th 5:3; n-1a; 854]   ἀσφάλεια
ἀσφαλείᾳ   dat sg fem [Ac 5:23; n-1a; 854]   "
ἀσφάλειαν   acc sg fem [Lk 1:4; n-1a; 854]   "
ἀσφαλές   nom sg neut [Pp 3:1; a-4a; 855]   ἀσφαλής
ἀσφαλές   acc sg neut [3t; a-4a; 855]   "
ἀσφαλῆ   acc sg fem [Hb 6:19; a-4a; 855]   "

ἀσφαλής   {855, a-4}
  pr. *firm, secure from falling; firm, sure, steady,
  immovable*, Heb 6:19; met. *certain, sure*, Acts
  21:34; 22:30; 25:26; *safe, making secure*, Phil 3:1*

ἀσφαλίζω   {856, v-2a(1)}
  [-, ἠσφάλισα, -, -, ἠσφαλίσθην] mid: *to make fast,
  safe*, or *secure*, Matt 27:64, 65, 66; Acts 16:24, 30
  v.l.*

ἀσφαλίσασθε   aor mid imperative 2 pl
  [Mt 27:65; v-2a(1); 856]   ἀσφαλίζω
ἀσφαλισθῆναι   aor pass inf
  [Mt 27:64; v-2a(1); 856]   "

ἀσφαλῶς   {857, adverb}
  securely, safely; without fail, safely, Mark 14:44;
  Acts 16:23; *certainly, assuredly,* Acts 2:36*

ἀσφαλῶς   adverb [3t; adverb; 857]   ἀσφαλῶς
ἀσχήμονα   nom pl neut
  [1C 12:23; a-4b(1); 860]   ἀσχήμων
ἀσχημονεῖ   pres act ind 3 sg
  [1C 13:5; v-1d(2a); 858]   ἀσχημονέω
ἀσχημονεῖν   pres act inf
  [1C 7:36; v-1d(2a); 858]   "

ἀσχημονέω   {858, v-1d(2a)}
  [-, -, -, -, -] *to behave in an unbecoming manner or
  indecorously,* 1 Cor 13:5; *to behave in a manner
  open to censure,* 1 Cor 7:36*

ἀσχημοσύνη, ῆς, ἡ   {859, n-1b}
  pr. *external indecorum; nakedness, shame,
  pudenda,* Rev 16:15; *indecency, infamous lust or
  lewdness,* Rom 1:27*

ἀσχημοσύνην   acc sg fem
  [2t; n-1b; 859]   ἀσχημοσύνη
ἀσχήμων   {860, a-4b(1)}
  indecorous, uncomely, indecent, 1 Cor 12:23*

ἀσωτία, ας, ἡ   {861, n-1a}
  dissoluteness, debauchery, Eph 5:18; Titus 1:6; 1
  Peter 4:4*

ἀσωτία   nom sg fem [Ep 5:18; n-1a; 861]   ἀσωτία
ἀσωτίας   gen sg fem [2t; n-1a; 861]   "

ἀσώτως   {862, adverb}
  dissolutely, loosely, Luke 15:13*

ἀσώτως   adverb [Lk 15:13; adverb; 862]   ἀσώτως
ἀτακτέω   {863, v-1d(2a)}
  [-, ἡτάκτησα, -, -, -] pr. *to infringe* military *order;*
  met. *to be irregular, behave disorderly, to be lazy,* 2
  Thess 3:7*

ἄτακτος, ον   {864, a-3a}
  pr. used of soldiers, *disorderly;* met. *irregular* in
  conduct, *disorderly, lazy,* 1 Thess 5:14*

ἀτάκτους   acc pl masc
  [1Th 5:14; a-3a; 864]   ἄτακτος
ἀτάκτως   {865, adverb}
  disorderly, irresponsible, 2 Thess 3:6, 11*

ἀτάκτως   adverb [2t; adverb; 865]   ἀτάκτως
ἄτεκνος, ον   {866, a-3a}
  childless, Luke 20:28, 29*

ἄτεκνος   nom sg masc [2t; a-3a; 866]   ἄτεκνος
ἀτενίζετε   pres act ind 2 pl
  [Ac 3:12; v-2a(1); 867]   ἀτενίζω
ἀτενίζοντες   pres act ptcp nom pl masc
  [2t; v-2a(1); 867]   "

ἀτενίζω   {867, v-2a(1)}
  [-, ἡτένισα, -, -, -] *to fix one's eyes upon, look
  steadily, gaze intently,* Luke 4:20

ἀτενίσαι   aor act inf [2t; v-2a(1); 867]   "
ἀτενίσαντες   aor act ptcp nom pl masc
  [Ac 6:15; v-2a(1); 867]   "
ἀτενίσας   aor act ptcp nom sg masc
  [7t; v-2a(1); 867]   "
ἀτενίσασα   aor act ptcp nom sg fem
  [Lk 22:56; v-2a(1); 867]   "

ἄτερ   {868, prep}
  improper prep with the gen., *without,* Luke
  22:6, 35*

ἄτερ   prep-gen [2t; prep; 868]   ἄτερ
ἀτιμάζεις   pres act ind 2 sg
  [Rm 2:23; v-2a(1); 869]   ἀτιμάζω
ἀτιμάζεσθαι   pres pass inf
  [Rm 1:24; v-2a(1); 869]   "
ἀτιμάζετε   pres act ind 2 pl
  [Jn 8:49; v-2a(1); 869]   "

ἀτιμάζω   {869, v-2a(1)}
  [-, ἡτίμασα, -, -, ἡτιμάσθην] also spelled ἀτιμάω
  and ἀντιμόω, *to dishonor, slight,* John 8:49; Rom
  2:23; James 2:6; *to treat with indignity,* Mark
  12:4; Luke 20:11; Acts 5:41; *to abuse, debase,* Rom
  1:24*

ἀτιμάσαντες   aor act ptcp nom pl masc
  [Lk 20:11; v-2a(1); 869]   "
ἀτιμασθῆναι   aor pass inf
  [Ac 5:41; v-2a(1); 869]   "

ἀτιμάω   {870, cv-1d(1a)}
  [-, ἡτίμησα, -, -, -] see ἀτιμάζω, *to dishonor,
  outrage, treat shamefully,* Mark 12:4 v.l.*

ἀτιμία, ας, ἡ   {871, n-1a}
  dishonor, infamy, Rom 1:26; *shame,* 1 Cor 11:14;
  meanness, vileness, 1 Cor 15:43; 2 Cor 6:8; *a
  dishonorable use,* Rom 9:21; 2 Tim 2:20; κατὰ
  ἀτιμίαν, *slightingly, disparagingly,* 2 Cor 11:21

ἀτιμία   nom sg fem [1C 11:14; n-1a; 871]   ἀτιμία
ἀτιμία   dat sg fem [1C 15:43; n-1a; 871]   "
ἀτιμίαν   acc sg fem [3t; n-1a; 871]   "
ἀτιμίας   gen sg fem [2t; n-1a; 871]   "
ἄτιμοι   nom pl masc [1C 4:10; a-3a; 872]   ἄτιμος

ἄτιμος, ον   {872, a-3a}
  unhonored, without honor, Matt 13:57; Mark 6:4;
  despised, 1 Cor 4:10; 12:23*

ἄτιμος   nom sg masc [2t; a-3a; 872]   "
ἀτιμότερα   acc pl neut comparative
  [1C 12:23; a-3a; 872]   "

ἀτιμόω, see ἀτιμάω   {873}

ἄτινα   nom pl neut [5t; a-1a(2b); 4015]   ὅστις
ἀτιμίδα   acc sg fem [Ac 2:19; n-3c(2); 874]   ἀτμίς

ἀτμίς, ίδος, ἡ   {874, n-3c(2)}
  an exhalation, vapor, smoke, Acts 2:19; James
  4:14*

ἀτμίς   nom sg fem [Jm 4:14; n-3c(2); 874]   "

ἄτομος, ον   {875, a-3a}
  indivisible, and by impl. *exceedingly minute;* ἐν
  ἀτόμῳ, sc. χρόνῳ, *in an indivisible point of time, in
  an instant or moment,* 1 Cor 15:52*

ἀτόμῳ　dat sg neut [1C 15:52; a-3a; 875]　　ἄτομος
ἄτοπον　nom sg neut [Ac 25:5; a-3a; 876]　　ἄτοπος
ἄτοπον　acc sg neut [2t; a-3a; 876]　　"

ἄτοπος, ον　　　　　　　　{876, a-3a}
　　pr. *out of place; inopportune, unsuitable, absurd;*
　　new, unusual, strange; in N.T. *improper, amiss,*
　　wicked, Luke 23:41; Acts 25:5; 2 Thess 3:2;
　　noxious, harmful, Acts 28:6*

ἀτόπων　gen pl masc [2Th 3:2; a-3a; 876]　　"

Ἀττάλεια, ας, ἡ　　　　　　{877, n-1a}
　　Attalia, a city of Pamphylia, Acts 14:25*

Ἀττάλειαν　acc sg fem
　　[Ac 14:25; n-1a; 877]　　　　　Ἀττάλεια

αὐγάζω　　　　　　　　　{878, v-2a(1)}
　　[-, ηὔγασα, -, -, -] *to see distinctly, discern,* or
　　possibly *to shine, give light* at 2 Cor 4:4*

αὐγάσαι　aor act inf
　　[2C 4:4; v-2a(1); 878]　　　　　αὐγάζω

αὐγή, ῆς, ἡ　　　　　　　{879, n-1b}
　　radiance; daybreak, dawn, Acts 20:11*

αὐγῆς　gen sg fem [Ac 20:11; n-1b; 879]　　αὐγή

Αὔγουστος, ου, ὁ　　　　　{880, n-2a}
　　Caesar Augustus, Luke 2:1*

Αὐγούστου　gen sg masc
　　[Lk 2:1; n-2a; 880]　　　　　Αὔγουστος
αὐθάδεις　nom pl masc
　　[2P 2:10; a-4a; 881]　　　　　αὐθάδης
αὐθάδη　acc sg masc [Ti 1:7; a-4a; 881]　　"

αὐθάδης　　　　　　　　{881, a-4a}
　　one who pleases himself, willful, obstinate;
　　arrogant, stubborn, Titus 1:7; 2 Peter 2:10*

αὐθαίρετοι　nom pl masc
　　[2C 8:3; a-3a; 882]　　　　　αὐθαίρετος

αὐθαίρετος, ον　　　　　　{882, a-3a}
　　pr. *one who chooses his own course of action; acting*
　　spontaneously, of one's own accord, 2 Cor 8:3, 17*

αὐθαίρετος　nom sg masc [2C 8:17; a-3a; 882]　　"
αὐθεντεῖν　pres act inf
　　[1Ti 2:12; v-1d(2a); 883]　　　αὐθεντέω

αὐθεντέω　　　　　　　{883, v-1d(2a)}
　　[-, -, -, -, -] *to have authority over, domineer,* 1 Tim
　　2:12*

αὐλέω　　　　　　　　{884, v-1d(2a)}
　　[-, ηὔλησα, -, -, -] *to play on a pipe* or *flute, pipe,*
　　Matt 11:17; Luke 7:32; 1 Cor 14:7*

αὐλή, ῆς, ἡ　　　　　　　{885, n-1b}
　　pr. *an unroofed enclosure; court-yard; sheepfold,*
　　John 10:1, 16; *an exterior court,* i.q. προαύλιον, an
　　enclosed place between the door and the street,
　　Rev 11:2; *an interior court, quadrangle,* the open
　　court in the middle of Oriental houses, which
　　are commonly built in the form of a square
　　enclosing this court, Matt 26:58, 69; by synec. *a*
　　house, mansion, palace, Matt 26:3; Luke 11:21

αὐλῇ　dat sg fem [2t; n-1b; 885]　　　αὐλή
αὐλήν　acc sg fem [6t; n-1b; 885]　　　"

αὐλῆς　gen sg fem [4t; n-1b; 885]　　　"
αὐλητάς　acc pl masc
　　[Mt 9:23; n-1f; 886]　　　　　αὐλητής

αὐλητής, οῦ, ὁ　　　　　　{886, n-1f}
　　a player on a pipe or *flute,* Matt 9:23; Rev 18:22*

αὐλητῶν　gen pl masc [Rv 18:22; n-1f; 886]　　"

αὐλίζομαι　　　　　　　{887, v-2a(1)}
　　[(ηὐλιζόμην), -, -, -, -, ηὐλίσθην] pr. *to pass the*
　　time in a court-yard; to lodge; hence, *to pass the*
　　night in any place, *to lodge at night, pass* or
　　remain through the night, Matt 21:17; Luke 21:37*

αὐλός, οῦ, ὁ　　　　　　{888, n-2a}
　　a pipe or *flute,* 1 Cor 14:7*

αὐλός　nom sg masc [1C 14:7; n-2a; 888]　　αὐλός
αὐλούμενον　pres pass ptcp nom sg neut
　　[1C 14:7; v-1d(2a); 884]　　　αὐλέω
αὐξάνει　pres act ind 3 sg
　　[Lk 12:27; v-3a(1); 889]　　　αὐξάνω
αὐξάνειν　pres act inf [Jn 3:30; v-3a(1); 889]　　"
αὐξάνετε　pres act imperative 2 pl
　　[2P 3:18; v-3a(1); 889]
αὐξανόμενα　pres pass ptcp nom pl neut
　　[Mk 4:8; v-3a(1); 889]
αὐξανομένης　pres pass ptcp gen sg fem
　　[2C 10:15; v-3a(1); 889]
αὐξανόμενοι　pres pass ptcp nom pl masc
　　[Cl 1:10; v-3a(1); 889]
αὐξανόμενον　pres pass ptcp nom sg neut
　　[Cl 1:6; v-3a(1); 889]
αὐξάνουσιν　pres act ind 3 pl
　　[Mt 6:28; v-3a(1); 889]　　　　　"

αὐξάνω　　　　　　　　{889, v-3a(1)}
　　[(ηὔξανον), αὐξήσω, ηὔξησα, -, -, ηὐξήθην] also
　　spelled αὔξω, trans. *to cause to grow* or *increase;*
　　pass. *to be increased, enlarged,* Matt 13:32; 1 Cor
　　3:6, 7; intrans. *to increase, grow,* Matt 6:28; Mark
　　4:8

αὐξάνων　pres act ptcp nom sg masc
　　[1C 3:7; v-3a(1); 889]　　　　　"
αὔξει　pres act ind 3 sg [2t; v-3a(1); 889]　　"
αὐξηθῇ　aor pass subj 3 sg
　　[Mt 13:32; v-3a(1); 889]　　　　"
αὐξηθῆτε　aor pass subj 2 pl
　　[1P 2:2; v-3a(1); 889]　　　　　"
αὐξήσει　fut act ind 3 sg
　　[2C 9:10; v-3a(1); 889]　　　　"
αὔξησιν　acc sg fem [2t; n-3e(5b); 890]　　αὔξησις

αὔξησις, εως, ἡ　　　　　{890, n-3e(5b)}
　　increase, growth, Eph 4:16; Col 2:19*

αὐξήσωμεν　aor act subj 1 pl
　　[Ep 4:15; v-3a(1); 889]　　　　αὐξάνω

αὔξω, see αὐξάνω　　　　　{891}

αὔριον　　　　　　　　{892, adverb}
　　tomorrow, Matt 6:30; ἡ αὔριον, sc. ἡμέρα, *the next*
　　day, Matt 6:34

αὔριον　adverb [14t; adverb; 892]　　　αὔριον

αὐστηρός, ά, όν {893, a-1a(1)}
pr. *harsh, sour in flavor*; met. *harsh, rigid, ungenerous*, Luke 19:21, 22*

αὐστηρός nom sg masc
[2t; a-1a(1); 893] αὐστηρός
αὐτά nom pl neut [Jn 5:36; a-1a(2b); 899] αὐτός
αὐτά acc pl neut [56t; a-1a(2b); 899] "
αὗται nom pl fem [3t; a-1a(2b); 4047] οὗτος
αὐταῖς dat pl fem [20t; a-1a(2b); 899] αὐτός

αὐτάρκεια, ας, ἡ {894, n-1a}
a competence of the necessaries of life, 2 Cor 9:8; *a frame of mind viewing one's lot as sufficient, contentedness*, 1 Tim 6:6*

αὐτάρκειαν acc sg fem
[2C 9:8; n-1a; 894] αὐτάρκεια
αὐταρκείας gen sg fem [1Ti 6:6; n-1a; 894] "

αὐτάρκης {895, a-4a}
pr. *sufficient* or *adequate in one's self; contented with one's lot*, Phil 4:11*

αὐτάρκης nom sg masc
[Pp 4:11; a-4a; 895] αὐτάρκης
αὐτάς acc pl fem
[12t; a-1a(2b); 899] αὐτός
αὕτη nom sg fem [84t; a-1a(2b); 4047] οὗτος
αὐτῇ dat sg fem [107t; a-1a(2b); 899] "
αὐτήν acc sg fem [138t; a-1a(2b); 899] "
αὐτῆς gen sg fem [169t; a-1a(2b); 899] "
αὐτό nom sg neut [9t; a-1a(2b); 899] "
αὐτό acc sg neut [96t; a-1a(2b); 899] "
αὐτοί nom pl masc [86t; a-1a(2b); 899] "
αὐτοῖς dat pl masc [542t; a-1a(2b); 899] "
αὐτοῖς dat pl neut [16t; a-1a(2b); 899] "

αὐτοκατάκριτος, ον {896, a-3a}
self-condemned, Titus 3:11*

αὐτοκατάκριτος nom sg masc
[Ti 3:11; a-3a; 896] αὐτοκατάκριτος
αὐτομάτη nom sg fem
[2t; a-1a(2a); 897] αὐτόματος

αὐτόματος, η, ον {897, a-1a(2a)}
self-excited, acting spontaneously, spontaneous, of his own accord, Mark 4:8; Acts 12:10*

αὐτόν acc sg masc
[961t; a-1a(2b); 899] αὐτός
αὐτόπται nom pl masc
[Lk 1:2; n-1f; 898] αὐτόπτης

αὐτόπτης, ου, ὁ {898, n-1f}
an eye-witness, Luke 1:2*

αὐτός, αὐτή, αὐτό {899, a-1a(2b)}
self, very; alone, Mark 6:31; 2 Cor 12:13; *of one's self, of one's own motion*, John 16:27; used also in the oblique cases independently as a personal pron. of the third person; ὁ αὐτός, *the same; unchangeable*, Heb 1:12; κατὰ τὸ αὐτό, *at the same time, together*, Acts 14:1; ἐπὶ τὸ αὐτό, *in one and the same place*, Matt 22:34; *at the same time, together*, Acts 3:1

αὐτός nom sg masc [168t; a-1a(2b); 899] αὐτός

αὐτοῦ {899a, adverb}
pr. *in the very place; here, there, in this* or *that place*, Matt 26:36; Acts 15:34; 18:19; 21:4

αὐτοῦ adverb [4t; adverb; 899a] αὐτοῦ
αὐτοῦ gen sg masc [1372t; a-1a(2b); 899] αὐτός
αὐτοῦ gen sg neut [49t; a-1a(2b); 899] "
αὐτούς acc pl masc
[358t; a-1a(2b); 899] αὐτός

αὐτόφωρος, ον {900, a-3a}
pr. *caught in the act of theft*, John 8:4*

αὐτοφώρῳ dat sg neut
[Jn 8:4; a-3a; 900] αὐτόφωρος

αὐτόχειρ, ρος, ὁ {901, n-3f(2a)}
acting or *doing anything with one's own hands*, Acts 27:19*

αὐτόχειρες nom pl masc
[Ac 27:19; n-3f(2a); 901] αὐτόχειρ
αὐτῷ dat sg masc [838t; a-1a(2b); 899] "
αὐτῷ dat sg neut [20t; a-1a(2b); 899] "
αὐτῶν gen pl masc [513t; a-1a(2b); 899] "
αὐτῶν gen pl fem [20t; a-1a(2b); 899] "
αὐτῶν gen pl neut [34t; a-1a(2b); 899] "
αὐχεῖ pres act ind 3 sg
[Jm 3:5; v-1d(2a); 902] αὐχέω

αὐχέω {902, v-1d(2a)}
[-, -, -, -, -] *to boast*, James 3:5*

αὐχμηρός, ά, όν {903, a-1a(1)}
squalid, filthy; by impl. *dark, obscure, murky*, 2 Peter 1:19*

αὐχμηρῷ dat sg masc
[2P 1:19; a-1a(1); 903] αὐχμηρός
ἀφ' prep-gen [42t; prep; 608] ἀπό
ἀφαιρεθήσεται fut pass ind 3 sg
[Lk 10:42; cv-1d(2a); 904] ἀφαιρέω
ἀφαιρεῖν pres act inf
[Hb 10:4; cv-1d(2a); 904] "
ἀφαιρεῖται pres mid ind 3 sg
[Lk 16:3; cv-1d(2a); 904] "

ἀφαιρέω {904, cv-1d(2a)}
[ἀφελῶ, ἀφεῖλον, -, ἀφήρημαι, ἀφῃρέθην] *to take away, remove*, Luke 1:25; 10:42; *to take off, cut off, remove by cutting off*, Matt 26:15; Mark 14:47; Luke 22:50

ἀφανής, ες {905, a-4a}
out of sight; not manifest, hidden, concealed, Heb 4:13*

ἀφανής nom sg fem [Hb 4:13; a-4a; 905] ἀφανής
ἀφανίζει pres act ind 3 sg
[2t; v-2a(1); 906] ἀφανίζω
ἀφανιζομένη pres pass ptcp nom sg fem
[Jm 4:14; v-2a(1); 906] "
ἀφανίζουσιν pres act ind 3 pl
[Mt 6:16; v-2a(1); 906] "

ἀφανίζω {906, v-2a(1)}
[-, -, -, -, ἠφανίσθην] *to remove out of sight, cause to disappear*; pass. *to disappear, vanish*, James 4:14; by impl. *to destroy, consume*, so that nothing shall be left visible, Matt 6:19, 20; met.

to spoil, deform, disfigure, Matt 6:16; *to perish,*
Acts 13:41*

ἀφανίσθητε aor pass imperative 2 pl
[Ac 13:41; v-2a(1); 906] "

ἀφανισμός, οῦ, ὁ {907, n-2a}
a disappearing, vanishing away; met. *destruction,*
abolition, abrogation, Heb 8:13*

ἀφανισμοῦ gen sg masc
[Hb 8:13; n-2a; 907] ἀφανισμός

ἄφαντος, ον {908, a-3a}
not appearing, not seen, invisible; hence, ἄφαντος
γενέσθαι, *to disappear, vanish,* Luke 24:31*

ἄφαντος nom sg masc [Lk 24:31; a-3a; 908] ἄφαντος

ἀφεδρών, ῶνος, ὁ {909, n-3f(1a)}
a latrine, Matt 15:17; Mark 7:19*

ἀφεδρῶνα acc sg masc
[2t; n-3f(1a); 909] ἀφεδρών
ἀφεθῇ aor pass subj 3 sg
[3t; cv-6a; 918] ἀφίημι
ἀφέθησαν aor pass ind 3 pl [Rm 4:7; cv-6a; 918] "
ἀφεθήσεται fut pass ind 3 sg [12t; cv-6a; 918] "

ἀφειδία, ας, ἡ {910, n-1a}
pr. *the disposition of one who is* ἀφειδής,
unsparing; hence, in N.T. *unsparingness* in the
way of rigorous treatment, *non-indulgence,* Col
2:23*

ἀφειδίᾳ dat sg fem
[Cl 2:23; n-1a; 910] ἀφειδία
ἀφεῖλεν aor act ind 3 sg
[3t; cv-1d(2a); 904] ἀφαιρέω
ἀφεῖναι aor act inf
[Lk 5:21; cv-6a; 918] ἀφίημι
ἀφείς aor act ptcp nom sg masc
[5t; cv-6a; 918] "
ἀφεῖς pres act ind 2 sg [Rv 2:20; cv-6a; 918] "
ἀφελεῖ fut act ind 3 sg
[Rv 22:19; cv-1d(2a); 904] ἀφαιρέω
ἀφελεῖν aor act inf [Lk 1:25; cv-1d(2a); 904] "
ἀφέλῃ aor act subj 3 sg
[Rv 22:19; cv-1d(2a); 904] "

ἀφελότης, τητος, ἡ {911, n-3c(1)}
sincerity, simplicity, Acts 2:46

ἀφελότητι dat sg fem
[Ac 2:46; n-3c(1); 911] ἀφελότης
ἀφέλωμαι aor mid subj 1 sg
[Rm 11:27; cv-1d(2a); 904] ἀφαιρέω
ἀφέντες aor act ptcp nom pl masc
[15t; cv-6a; 918] ἀφίημι
ἄφες aor act imperative 2 sg
[15t; cv-6a; 918] "
ἀφέσει dat sg fem [2t; n-3e(5b); 912] ἄφεσις
ἄφεσιν acc sg fem [12t; n-3e(5b); 912] "

ἄφεσις, εως, ἡ {912, n-3e(5b)}
dismission, deliverance, from captivity, Luke 4:18
(2t); *remission, forgiveness, pardon,* Matt 26:28

ἄφεσις nom sg fem [3t; n-3e(5b); 912] "
ἄφετε aor act imperative 2 pl
[10t; cv-6a; 918] ἀφίημι

ἀφέωνται perf pass ind 3 pl [6t; cv-6a; 918] "

ἀφή, ῆς, ἡ {913, n-1b}
a fastening; a ligament, by which the different
members are connected, *commissure, joint,* Eph
4:16; Col 2:19*

ἀφῇ aor act subj 3 sg [3t; cv-6a; 918] "
ἀφῆκα aor act ind 1 sg [Mt 18:32; cv-6a; 918] "
ἀφήκαμεν aor act ind 1 pl [3t; cv-6a; 918] "
ἀφῆκαν aor act ind 3 pl [2t; cv-6a; 918] "
ἀφήκατε aor act ind 2 pl [Mt 23:23; cv-6a; 918] "
ἀφῆκεν aor act ind 3 sg [20t; cv-6a; 918] "
ἀφῆκες aor act ind 2 sg [Rv 2:4; cv-6a; 918] "
ἀφῆς gen sg fem [Ep 4:16; n-1b; 913] ἀφή
ἀφήσει fut act ind 3 sg [3t; cv-6a; 918] ἀφίημι
ἀφήσεις fut act ind 2 sg [Lk 17:4; cv-6a; 918] "
ἀφήσουσιν fut act ind 3 pl
[Lk 19:44; cv-6a; 918] "
ἀφήσω fut act ind 1 sg [2t; cv-6a; 918] "
ἀφῆτε aor act subj 2 pl [5t; cv-6a; 918] "

ἀφθαρσία, ας, ἡ {914, n-1a}
incorruptibility, 1 Cor 15:42, 53, 54; *immortality,*
Rom 2:7; 2 Tim 1:10; *soundness, purity;* ἐν
ἀφθαρσίᾳ, *purely, sincerely* or *constantly,*
unfailingly, Eph 6:24

ἀφθαρσίᾳ dat sg fem [2t; n-1a; 914] ἀφθαρσία
ἀφθαρσίαν acc sg fem [5t; n-1a; 914] "
ἄφθαρτοι nom pl masc
[1C 15:52; a-3a; 915] ἄφθαρτος
ἄφθαρτον acc sg masc [1C 9:25; a-3a; 915] "
ἄφθαρτον acc sg fem [1P 1:4; a-3a; 915] "
ἄφθαρτον acc sg neut [Mk 16:8; a-3a; 915] "

ἄφθαρτος, ον {915, a-3a}
incorruptible, immortal, imperishable, undying,
enduring, Rom 1:23; 1 Cor 9:25; 15:52

ἀφθάρτου gen sg masc [Rm 1:23; a-3a; 915] "
ἀφθάρτου gen sg fem [1P 1:23; a-3a; 915] "
ἀφθάρτῳ dat sg masc [1Ti 1:17; a-3a; 915] "
ἀφθάρτῳ dat sg neut [1P 3:4; a-3a; 915] "

ἀφθονία, ας, ἡ {916, n-1a}
willingness, Titus 2:7 v.l.*

ἀφθορία, ας, ἡ {917, n-1a}
pr. *incapability of decay;* met. *incorruptness,*
integrity, genuineness, purity, Titus 2:7*

ἀφθορίαν acc sg fem [Ti 2:7; n-1a; 917] ἀφθορία
ἀφίδω aor act subj 1 sg
[Pp 2:23; cv-1d(1a); 927] ἀφοράω
ἀφιέναι pres act inf [6t; cv-6a; 918] ἀφίημι
ἀφίενται pres pass ind 3 pl [4t; cv-6a; 918] "
ἀφίεται pres pass ind 3 sg [5t; cv-6a; 918] "
ἀφίετε pres act imperative 2 pl
[Mk 11:25; cv-6a; 918] "
ἀφίετε pres act ind 2 pl [2t; cv-6a; 918] "
ἀφιέτω pres act imperative 3 sg
[2t; cv-6a; 918] "

ἀφίημι {918, cv-6a}
[(ἤφιε (3rd sg), ἀφήσω, ἀφῆκα, -, ἀφέωμαι,
ἀφέθην] *to send away, dismiss, suffer to depart; to*
emit, send forth; τὴν φωνήν, *the voice, to cry out,*

utter an exclamation, Mark 15:37; τὸ πνεῦμα, *the spirit, to expire*, Matt 27:50; *to omit, pass over* or *by; to let alone, care not for*, Matt 15:14; 23:23; Heb 6:1; *to permit, suffer, let, forbid not; to give up, yield, resign*, Matt 5:40; *to remit, forgive, pardon; to relax, suffer to become less intense*, Rev 2:4; *to leave, depart from; to desert, forsake; to leave remaining* or *alone; to leave behind*, sc. at one's death, Mark 12:19, 20, 21, 22; John 14:27

ἀφίημι   pres act ind 1 sg   [2t; cv-6a; 918]   "

ἀφίησιν   pres act ind 3 sg   [4t; cv-6a; 918]   "

ἀφίκετο   aor mid ind 3 sg
    [Rm 16:19; cv-3b; 919]   ἀφικνέομαι

ἀφικνέομαι   {919, cv-3b}
    [-, ἀφικόμην -, -, -] *to come, arrive at; to reach* as a report, Rom 16:19*

ἀφιλάγαθοι   nom pl masc
    [2Ti 3:3; a-3a; 920]   ἀφιλάγαθος

ἀφιλάγαθος, ον   {920, a-3a}
    not a lover of good and *good men*, 2 Tim 3:3*

ἀφιλάργυρον   acc sg masc
    [1Ti 3:3; a-3a; 921]   ἀφιλάργυρος

ἀφιλάργυρος, ον   {921, a-3a}
    not fond of money, not covetous, generous, 1 Tim 3:3; Heb 13:5*

ἀφιλάργυρος   nom sg masc   [Hb 13:5; a-3a; 921]   "

ἄφιξιν   acc sg fem
    [Ac 20:29; n-3e(5b); 922]   ἄφιξις

ἄφιξις, εως, ἡ   {922, n-3e(5b)}
    arrival; departure, Acts 20:29*

ἀφίομεν   pres act ind 1 pl
    [Lk 11:4; cv-6a; 918]   ἀφίημι

ἀφίουσιν   pres act ind 3 pl
    [Rv 11:9; cv-6a; 918]   "

ἀφίστανται   pres mid ind 3 pl
    [Lk 8:13; cv-6a; 923]   ἀφίστημι

ἀφίστατο   imperf mid ind 3 sg
    [Lk 2:37; cv-6a; 923]   "

ἀφίστημι   {923, cv-6a}
    [ἀποστήσω, ἀπέστησα or ἀπέστην, -, -, -] trans. *to put away, separate; to draw off* or *away, withdraw, induce to revolt*, Acts 5:37; intrans., and mid., *to depart, go away from*, Luke 2:37; met. *to desist* or *refrain from, let alone*, Acts 5:38; 22:29; 2 Cor 12:8; *to make defection, fall away, apostatize*, Luke 8:13; 1 Tim 4:1; Heb 3:12; *to withdraw from, have no intercourse with*, 1 Tim 6:5; *to abstain from*, 2 Tim 2:19

ἄφνω   {924, adverb}
    suddenly, unexpectedly, Acts 2:2; 16:26; 28:6*

ἄφνω   adverb   [3t; adverb; 924]   ἄφνω

ἀφόβως   {925, adverb}
    fearlessly, boldly, intrepidly, Phil 1:14; *securely, peacefully, tranquilly*, Luke 1:74; 1 Cor 16:10; *boldly, shamelessly*, Jude 12*

ἀφόβως   adverb   [4t; adverb; 925]   ἀφόβως

ἀφομοιόω   {926, cv-1d(3)}
    [-, -, -, ἀφωμοίωμαι, -] *to assimilate, cause to resemble*, Heb 7:3*

ἀφοράω   {927, cv-1d(1a)}
    [-, ἀπεῖδον, -, -, -] *to view with undivided attention* by looking away from every other object; *to regard fixedly and earnestly*, Heb 12:2; *to see distinctly*, Phil 2:23*

ἀφορίζει   pres act ind 3 sg
    [Mt 25:32; cv-2a(1); 928]   ἀφορίζω

ἀφορίζω   {928, cv-2a(1)}
    [(ἀφώριζον), ἀφορίσω or ἀφοριῶ, ἀφώρισα, -, ἀφώρισμαι, ἀφωρίσθην] *to limit off; to separate, sever* from the rest, Matt 13:49; *to separate* from society, *cut off from all intercourse, excommunicate*, Luke 6:22; *to set apart, select*, Acts 13:2; Rom 1:1; Gal 1:15

ἀφοριοῦσιν   fut act ind 3 pl
    [Mt 13:49; cv-2a(1); 928]   "

ἀφορίσας   aor act ptcp nom sg masc
    [Ga 1:15; cv-2a(1); 928]   "

ἀφορίσατε   aor act imperative 2 pl
    [Ac 13:2; cv-2a(1); 928]   "

ἀφορίσει   fut act ind 3 sg
    [Mt 25:32; cv-2a(1); 928]   "

ἀφορίσθητε   aor pass imperative 2 pl
    [2C 6:17; cv-2a(1); 928]   "

ἀφορίσωσιν   aor act subj 3 pl
    [Lk 6:22; cv-2a(1); 928]   "

ἀφορμή, ῆς, ἡ   {929, n-1b}
    pr. *a starting point; means* to accomplish an object; *occasion, opportunity*, Rom 7:8, 11

ἀφορμήν   acc sg fem   [7t; n-1b; 929]   ἀφορμή

ἀφορῶντες   pres act ptcp nom pl masc
    [Hb 12:2; cv-1d(1a); 927]   ἀφοράω

ἀφρίζει   pres act ind 3 sg
    [Mk 9:18; cv-; 930]   ἀφρίζω

ἀφρίζω   {930, cv-2a(1)}
    [-, -, -, -, -] *to froth, foam*, Mark 9:18, 20*

ἀφρίζων   pres act ptcp nom sg masc
    [Mk 9:20; cv-; 930]   "

ἄφρονα   acc sg masc   [2t; a-4b(1); 933]   ἄφρων

ἄφρονες   nom pl masc   [Ep 5:17; a-4b(1); 933]   "

ἄφρονες   voc pl masc   [Lk 11:40; a-4b(1); 933]   "

ἀφρόνων   gen pl masc   [3t; a-4b(1); 933]   "

ἀφρός, οῦ, ὁ   {931, n-2a}
    froth, foam, Luke 9:39*

ἀφροσύνη, ῆς, ἡ   {932, n-1b}
    inconsiderateness, folly; boastful folly, 2 Cor 11:1, 17, 21; in N.T. *foolishness, levity, wickedness, impiety*, Mark 7:22*

ἀφροσύνη   nom sg fem
    [Mk 7:22; n-1b; 932]   ἀφροσύνη

ἀφροσύνῃ   dat sg fem   [2t; n-1b; 932]   "

ἀφροσύνης   gen sg fem   [2C 11:1; n-1b; 932]   "

ἀφροῦ   gen sg masc   [Lk 9:39; n-2a; 931]   ἀφρός

ἄφρων, ονος, ον   {933, a-4b(1)}
    unwise, inconsiderate, simple, foolish, Luke 11:40;

12:20; 1 Cor 15:36; *ignorant*, religiously
unenlightened, Rom 2:20; Eph 5:17; 1 Peter 2:15;
boastfully *foolish, vain*, 2 Cor 11:16, 19

ἄφρων nom sg masc [2t; a-4b(1); 933] ἄφρων
ἄφρων voc sg masc [2t; a-4b(1); 933] "

ἀφυπνόω {934, cv-1d(3)}
[-, ἀφύπνωσα, -, -, -] *to awake from sleep;* in N.T.
to go off into sleep, fall asleep, Luke 8:23*

ἀφύπνωσεν aor act ind 3 sg
[Lk 8:23; cv-1d(3); 934] ἀφυπνόω

ἀφυστερέω {935, cv-1d(2a)}
[-, -, -, -, -] *to withhold*, James 5:4 v.l.*

ἀφῶμεν aor act subj 1 pl
[Jn 11:48; cv-6a; 918] ἀφίημι
ἀφωμοιωμένος perf pass ptcp nom sg masc
[Hb 7:3; cv-1d(3); 926] ἀφομοιόω
ἀφῶν gen pl fem [Cl 2:19; n-1b; 913] ἀφή
ἄφωνα acc pl neut [1C 12:2; a-3a; 936] ἄφωνος
ἄφωνον nom sg neut [2t; a-3a; 936] "

ἄφωνος, ον {936, a-3a}
dumb, destitute of the power of speech, 1 Cor 12:2;
2 Peter 2:16; *silent, mute, uttering no voice*, Acts
8:32; *inarticulate, consisting of inarticulate
sounds, unmeaning*, 1 Cor 14:10*

ἄφωνος nom sg masc [Ac 8:32; a-3a; 936] "
ἀφώριζεν imperf act ind 3 sg
[Ga 2:12; cv-2a(1); 928] ἀφορίζω
ἀφώρισεν aor act ind 3 sg
[Ac 19:9; cv-2a(1); 928] "
ἀφωρισμένος perf pass ptcp nom sg masc
[Rm 1:1; cv-2a(1); 928] "

Ἀχάζ, ὁ {937, n-3g(2)}
Ahaz, pr. name, indecl, Matt 1:9*

Ἀχάζ indecl [2t; n-3g(2); 937] Ἀχάζ

Ἀχαΐα, ας, ἡ {938, n-1a}
Achaia, the Roman province, comprehending
all Greece to the south of Thessaly

Ἀχαΐα nom sg fem [2t; n-1a; 938] Ἀχαΐα
Ἀχαΐᾳ dat sg fem [3t; n-1a; 938] "
Ἀχαΐαν acc sg fem [2t; n-1a; 938] "
Ἀχαΐας gen sg fem [3t; n-1a; 938] "

Ἀχαϊκός, οῦ, ὁ {939, n-2a}
Achaicus, pr. name, 1 Cor 16:17, 15 v.l.*

Ἀχαϊκοῦ gen sg masc
[1C 16:17; n-2a; 939] Ἀχαϊκός
ἀχάριστοι nom pl masc
[2Ti 3:2; a-3a; 940] ἀχάριστος

ἀχάριστος, ον {940, a-3a}
unthankful, ungrateful, Luke 6:35; 2 Tim 3:2*

ἀχαρίστους acc pl masc [Lk 6:35; a-3a; 940] "

Ἄχας, see Ἀχάζ {941, n-3g(2)}

ἀχειροποίητον acc sg masc
[Mk 14:58; a-3a; 942] ἀχειροποίητος
ἀχειροποίητον acc sg fem [2C 5:1; a-3a; 942] "

ἀχειροποίητος, ον {942, a-3a}
not made with hands, Mark 14:58; 2 Cor 5:1; Col
2:11*

ἀχειροποιήτῳ dat sg fem [Cl 2:11; a-3a; 942] "
ἀχθῆναι aor pass inf [4t; v-1b(2); 72] ἄγω
ἀχθήσεσθε fut pass ind 2 pl
[Mt 10:18; v-1b(2); 72] "

Ἀχίμ, ὁ {943, n-3g(2)}
Achim, pr. name, indecl, Matt 1:14*

Ἀχίμ indecl [2t; n-3g(2); 943] Ἀχίμ

ἀχλύς, ύος, ἡ {944, n-3e(1)}
a mist; darkening, dimness, of the sight, Acts
13:11*

ἀχλύς nom sg fem [Ac 13:11; n-3e(1); 944] ἀχλύς
ἀχρεῖοι nom pl masc
[Lk 17:10; a-3a; 945] ἀχρεῖος
ἀχρεῖον acc sg masc [Mt 25:30; a-3a; 945] "

ἀχρεῖος, ον {945, a-3a}
useless, unprofitable, worthless, Matt 25:30;
unmeritorious, Luke 17:10*

ἀχρειόω {946, v-1d(3)}
[-, -, -, ἠχρείωμαι, ἠχρεώθην] also ἀχρεόω, pas.,
to render useless; met., *to become corrupt,
depraved*, Rom 3:12*

ἀχρηστον acc sg masc
[Pm 11; a-3a; 947] ἄχρηστος

ἄχρηστος, ον {947, a-3a}
unuseful, useless, unprofitable, and by impl.
detrimental, causing loss, Phil 11*

ἄχρι {948, prep}
improper prep with the gen., also functioning
as a conj., also spelled ἄχρις (Gal 3:19; Heb 3:13;
Rev 2:25), with respect to place, *as far as*; to
time, *until, during*; as a conj., *until*

ἄχρι prep-gen [46t; prep; 948] ἄχρι
ἄχρις prep-gen [3t; prep; 948] "

ἄχυρον, ου, τό {949, n-2c}
chaff, straw broken up by treading out the grain,
Matt 3:12; Luke 3:17*

ἄχυρον acc sg neut [2t; n-2c; 949] ἄχυρον
ἀψάμενος aor mid ptcp nom sg masc
[3t; v-4; 721] ἅπτω
ἅψαντες aor act ptcp nom pl masc
[Ac 28:2; v-4; 721] "
ἅψας aor act ptcp nom sg masc
[t; v-4; 721] "

ἀψευδής, ες {950, a-4a}
free from falsehood; incapable of falsehood, Titus
1:2*

ἀψευδής nom sg masc [Ti 1:2; a-4a; 950] ἀψευδής
ἅψῃ aor mid subj 2 sg [Cl 2:21; v-4; 721] ἅπτω
ἅψηται aor mid subj 3 sg [2t; v-4; 721] "

ἀψίνθιον, ου, τό {951, n-2c}
also spelled ἄψινθος, οῦ, η, *wormwood*, Rev 8:11;
where, as a proper name, it is masculine, Rev
8:11*

ἄψινθον   acc sg masc [Rv 8:11; n-2a; 952]   ἄψινθος

ἄψινθος, ου, ἡ, see ἀψίνθιον   {952, n-2b}

ἄψινθος   nom sg masc [Rv 8:11; n-2a; 952]   "
ἄψυχα   nom pl neut [1C 14:7; a-3a; 953]   ἄψυχος
ἄψυχος, ον   {953, a-3a}
    void of life or *sense, inanimate,* 1 Cor 14:7*

ἄψωμαι   aor mid subj 1 sg [2t; v-4; 721]   ἅπτω
ἄψωνται   aor act subj 3 pl [3t; v-4; 721]   "

β

β   {954, n-3g(2)}
    beta, second letter of Greek alphabet; used as
    second in titles of N.T. writings

Βάαλ, ὁ   {955, n-3g(2)}
    Baal, (Hebrew for *Master*) pr. name, indecl.,
    Rom 11:4*

Βάαλ   indecl [Rm 11:4; n-3g(2); 955]   Βάαλ

Βαβυλών, ῶνος, ἡ   {956, n-3f(1a)}
    Babylon, 1 Peter 5:13

Βαβυλών   nom sg fem [5t; n-3f(1a); 956]   Βαβυλών
Βαβυλών   voc sg fem [Rv 18:10; n-3f(1a); 956]   "
Βαβυλῶνι   dat sg fem [1P 5:13; n-3f(1a); 956]   "
Βαβυλῶνος   gen sg fem [5t; n-3f(1a); 956]   "
βαθέα   acc pl neut [Rv 2:24; a-2b; 960]   βαθύς
βαθεῖ   dat sg masc [Ac 20:9; a-2b; 960]   "
βαθέως   gen sg masc [Lk 24:1; a-2b; 960]   "
βάθη   acc pl neut [1C 2:10; n-3b(2b); 958]   βάθος
βαθμόν   acc sg masc [1Ti 3:13; n-2a; 957]   βαθμός

βαθμός, οῦ, ὁ   {957, n-2a}
    pr. *a step, stair;* met. *grade* of dignity, *degree,*
    rank, standing, 1 Tim 3:13*

βάθος, ους, τό   {958, n-3b(2b)}
    depth; τὸ βάθος, *deep water,* Luke 5:4; Matt 13:5;
    met. *fullness, abundance, immensity,* Rom 11:33;
    an extreme degree, 2 Cor 8:2; pl. *profundities,*
    deep-laid plans, 1 Cor 2:10; Rev 2:24

βάθος   nom sg neut [3t; n-3b(2b); 958]   βάθος
βάθος   acc sg neut [3t; n-3b(2b); 958]   "
βάθους   gen sg neut [2C 8:2; n-3b(2b); 958]   "
βαθύ   nom sg neut [Jn 4:11; a-2b; 960]   βαθύς

βαθύνω   {959, v-1c(2)}
    [-, -, -, -, -] *to deepen, excavate,* Luke 6:48*

βαθύς, εῖα, ύ   {960, a-2b}
    deep, John 4:11; met. *deep, profound,* Acts 20:9;
    Rev 2:24; ὄρθρου βαθέος, lit. *at deep morning*
    twilight, at the earliest dawn, Luke 24:1*

βαΐα   acc pl neut [Jn 12:13; n-2c; 961]   βάϊον

βάϊον, ου, τό   {961, n-2c}
    a palm branch, John 12:13*

Βαλαάμ, ὁ   {962, n-3g(2)}
    Balaam, pr. name, indecl.

Βαλαάμ   indecl [3t; n-3g(2); 962]   Βαλαάμ

Βαλάκ, ὁ   {963, n-3g(2)}
    Balak, pr. name, indecl., Jude 11 v.l.; Rev 2:14*

Βαλάκ   indecl [Rv 2:14; n-3g(2); 963]   Βαλάκ
βάλε   aor act imperative 2 sg
    [9t; v-2d(1); 965]   βάλλω
βαλεῖ   fut act ind 3 sg [Lk 12:58; v-2d(1); 965]   "
βαλεῖν   aor act inf [8t; v-2d(1); 965]   "
βάλετε   aor act imperative 2 pl
    [Jn 21:6; v-2d(1); 965]   "
βαλέτω   aor act imperative 3 sg
    [Jn 8:7; v-2d(1); 965]   "
βάλῃ   aor act subj 3 sg [2t; v-2d(1); 965]   "
βάλητε   aor act subj 2 pl [Mt 7:6; v-2d(1); 965]   "
βαλλάντια   acc pl neut
    [Lk 12:33; n-2c; 964]   βαλλάντιον

βαλλάντιον, ου, τό   {964, n-2c}
    also spelled βαλάντιον, *a bag, purse,* Luke 10:4;
    12:33; 22:35, 36*

βαλλάντιον   acc sg neut [2t; n-2c; 964]   "
βαλλαντίου   gen sg neut [Lk 22:35; n-2c; 964]   "
βάλλει   pres act ind 3 sg [6t; v-2d(1); 965]   βάλλω
βάλλειν   pres act inf [Rv 2:10; v-2d(1); 965]   "
βάλλεται   pres pass ind 3 sg [3t; v-2d(1); 965]   "
βάλλομεν   pres act ind 1 pl
    [Jm 3:3; v-2d(1); 965]   "
βαλλόμενα   pres pass ptcp acc pl neut
    [Jn 12:6; v-2d(1); 965]   "
βαλλόμενον   pres pass ptcp acc sg masc
    [2t; v-2d(1); 965]   "
βάλλοντας   pres act ptcp acc pl masc
    [2t; v-2d(1); 965]   "
βάλλοντες   pres act ptcp nom pl masc
    [2t; v-2d(1); 965]   "
βαλλόντων   pres act ptcp gen pl masc
    [2t; v-2d(1); 965]   "
βάλλουσαν   pres act ptcp acc sg fem
    [Lk 21:2; v-2d(1); 965]   "
βάλλουσιν   pres act ind 3 pl [4t; v-2d(1); 965]   "

βάλλω   {965, v-2d(1)}
    [βαλῶ, ἔβαλον or ἔβαλα, βέβληκα, βέβλημαι,
    ἐβλήθην] pluperfect, ἐβεβλήμην, *to throw, cast; to*
    lay, Rev 2:22; Matt 8:6, 14; *to put, place,* James
    3:3; *to place, deposit,* Matt 27:6; Mark 12:41-44;
    Luke 21:1-4; John 12:6; *to pour,* John 13:5; *to*
    thrust, John 18:11; 20:27; Mark 7:33; Rev 14:19;
    to send forth, Matt 10:34; *to assault, strike,* Mark
    14:65; met. *to suggest,* John 13:2; intrans. *to rush,*
    beat, as the wind, Acts 27:14

βάλλω   pres act ind 1 sg [2t; v-2d(1); 965]   "
βαλοῦσα   aor act ptcp nom sg fem
    [Mt 26:12; v-2d(1); 965]   "
βαλοῦσιν   fut act ind 3 pl [3t; v-2d(1); 965]   "
βάλω   aor act subj 1 sg [3t; v-2d(1); 965]   "
βάλωσιν   aor act subj 3 pl
    [Jn 8:59; v-2d(1); 965]   "
βαπτίζει   pres act ind 3 sg
    [2t; v-2a(1); 966]   βαπτίζω
βαπτίζειν   pres act inf [2t; v-2a(1); 966]   "
βαπτίζεις   pres act ind 2 sg
    [Jn 1:25; v-2a(1); 966]   "
βαπτίζομαι   prer pass ind 1 sg [2t; v-2a(1); 966]   "

βαπτιζόμενοι   pres pass ptcp nom pl masc
[1C 15:29; v-2a(1); 966]   "

βαπτίζονται   pres pass ind 3 pl
[1C 15:29; v-2a(1); 966]   "

βαπτίζοντες   pres act ptcp nom pl masc
[Mt 28:19; v-2a(1); 966]   "

βαπτίζοντος   pres act ptcp gen sg masc
[Mk 6:24; v-2a(1); 966]   "

βαπτίζω   {966, v-2a(1)}
[(ἐβαπτιζόμην), βαπτίσω, ἐβάπτισα, -,
βεβάπτισμαι, ἐβαπτίσθην] pr. *to dip, immerse; to
cleanse* or *purify by washing; to administer the rite
of baptism, to baptize*; met. *with various
reference to the ideas associated with Christian
baptism as an act of dedication, e.g.* marked
designation, devotion, trial, etc.; mid. *to procure
baptism for one's self, to undergo baptism*, Acts
22:16

βαπτίζω   pres act ind 1 sg [3t; v-2a(1); 966]   "

βαπτίζων   pres act ptcp nom sg masc
[7t; v-2a(1); 966]   "

βάπτισαι   aor mid imperative 2 sg
[Ac 22:16; v-2a(1); 966]   "

βαπτίσει   fut act ind 3 sg [3t; v-2a(1); 966]   "

βαπτισθείς   aor pass ptcp nom sg masc
[3t; v-2a(1); 966]   "

βαπτισθέντες   aor pass ptcp nom pl masc
[2t; v-2a(1); 966]   "

βαπτισθέντος   aor pass ptcp gen sg masc
[Lk 3:21; v-2a(1); 966]   "

βαπτισθῆναι   aor pass inf [10t; v-2a(1); 966]   "

βαπτισθήσεσθε   fut pass ind 2 pl
[3t; v-2a(1); 966]   "

βαπτισθήτω   aor pass imperative 3 sg
[Ac 2:38; v-2a(1); 966]   "

βάπτισμα, ατος, τό   {967, n-3c(4)}
pr. *immersion; baptism, ordinance of baptism*, Matt
3:7; Rom 6:4; met. *baptism in the trial of
suffering*, Matt 20:22, 23; Mark 10:38, 39

βάπτισμα   nom sg neut [5t; n-3c(4); 967]   βάπτισμα

βάπτισμα   acc sg neut [12t; n-3c(4); 967]   "

βαπτίσματος   gen sg neut [2t; n-3c(4); 967]   "

βαπτισμοῖς   dat pl masc
[Hb 9:10; n-2a; 968]   βαπτισμός

βαπτισμός, οῦ, ὁ   {968, n-2a}
pr. *an act of dipping* or *immersion: a baptism*, Col
2:12; Heb 6:2; *an ablution*, Mark 7:4, 8 v.l.; Heb
9:10*

βαπτισμούς   acc pl masc [Mk 7:4; n-2a; 968]   "

βαπτισμῷ   dat sg masc [Cl 2:12; n-2a; 968]   "

βαπτισμῶν   gen pl masc [Hb 6:2; n-2a; 968]   "

βαπτιστήν   acc sg masc [3t; n-1f; 969]   βαπτιστής

βαπτιστής, οῦ, ὁ   {969, n-1f}
one who baptizes, a baptist, Matt 3:1; 11:11, 12

βαπτιστής   nom sg masc [4t; n-1f; 969]   "

βαπτιστοῦ   gen sg masc [5t; n-1f; 969]   "

βαπτίσωνται   aor mid subj 3 pl
[Mk 7:4; v-2a(1); 966]   βαπτίζω

βάπτω   {970, v-4}
[βάψω, ἔβαψα, -, βέβαμμαι, -] *to dip*, John 13:26;
Luke 16:24; *to dye*, Rev 19:13*

βάρ   {97, n-3g(2)}
son, (Aramaic) Matt 16:17 v.l.*

Βαραββᾶν   acc sg masc [9t; n-1e; 972]   Βαραββᾶς

Βαραββᾶς, ᾶ, ὁ   {972, n-1e}
Barabbas, pr. name

Βαραββᾶς   nom sg masc [2t; n-1e; 972]   "

Βαράκ, ὁ   {973, n-3g(2)}
Barak, pr. name, indecl., Heb 11:32*

Βαράκ   indecl [Hb 11:32; n-3g(2); 973]   Βαράκ

Βαραχίας, ου, ὁ   {974, n-1d}
Barachias, pr. name, Matt 23:35

Βαραχίου   gen sg masc
[Mt 23:35; n-1d; 974]   Βαραχίας

βάρβαρος, ον   {975, a-3a}
pr. *one to whom a pure Greek dialect is not native;
one who is not a proper Greek, a barbarian*, Rom
1:14; Col 3:11; Acts 28:2, 4; *a foreigner speaking a
strange language*, 1 Cor 14:11*

βάρβαροι   nom pl masc [2t; a-3a; 975]   βάρβαρος

βαρβάροις   dat pl masc [Rm 1:14; a-3a; 975]   "

βάρβαρος   nom sg masc [3t; a-3a; 975]   "

βαρέα   acc pl neut [2t; a-2b; 987]   βαρύς

βάρει   dat sg neut [1Th 2:7; n-3d(2b); 983]   βάρος

βαρεῖαι   nom pl fem [2t; a-2b; 987]   βαρύς

βαρεῖς   nom pl masc [Ac 20:29; a-2b; 987]   "

βαρείσθω   pres pass imperative 3 sg
[1Ti 5:16; v-1d(2a); 976]   βαρέω

βαρέω   {976, v-1d(2a)}
[-, ἐβάρησα, -, βεβάρημαι, ἐβαρήθην] *to be heavy
upon, weigh down, burden, oppress*, as sleep, Matt
26:43; Mark 14:40; Luke 9:32; *surfeiting*, v.l.
Luke 21:34; *calamities*, 2 Cor 1:8; 5:4; or, *trouble,
care, expense*, etc. 1 Tim 5:16

βαρέως   {977, adverb}
heavily; met. *with difficulty, dully, stupidly*, Matt
13:15; Acts 28:27*

βαρέως   adverb [2t; adverb; 977]   βαρέως

βάρη   acc pl neut [Ga 6:2; n-3d(2b); 983]   βάρος

βαρηθῶσιν   aor pass subj 3 pl
[Lk 21:34; v-1d(2a); 976]   βαρέω

Βαρθολομαῖον   acc sg masc
[2t; n-2a; 978]   Βαρθολομαῖος

Βαρθολομαῖος, ου, ὁ   {978, n-2a}
Bartholomew, pr. name

Βαρθολομαῖος   nom sg masc [2t; n-2a; 978]   "

Βαριησοῦ   gen sg masc
[Ac 13:6; n-2d(1); 979]   Βαριησοῦς

Βαριησοῦς, οῦ, ὁ   {979, n-2d(1)}
Bar-jesus, pr. name, Acts 13:6*

Βαριωνᾶ, ὁ   {980, n-3g(2)}
also Βὰρ Ἰωνᾶ or Βαριωνᾶς, *Bar-jona*, pr. name,
Matt 16:17*

Βαριωνᾶ   indecl [Mt 16:17; n-3g(2); 980]   Βαριωνᾶ

Βαριωνᾶς, ᾶ, ὁ, see Βαριωνᾶ   {981, n-1e}

Βαρναβᾶ   gen sg masc [4t; n-1e; 982]   Βαρναβᾶς
Βαρναβᾶ   dat sg masc [6t; n-1e; 982]   "
Βαρναβᾶν   acc sg masc [8t; n-1e; 982]   "

Βαρναβᾶς, ᾶ, ὁ   {982, n-1e}
   Barnabas, pr. name, Acts 4:36; 13:1f.; 14:12;
   15:2f.; 1 Cor 9:6; Gal 2:1, 9, 13; Col 4:10

Βαρναβᾶς   nom sg masc [10t; n-1e; 982]   "

βάρος, ους, τό   {983, n-3d(2b)}
   weight, heaviness; a burden, anything grievous and
   hard to be borne, Matt 20:12; Acts 15:28; Gal 6:2;
   Rev 2:24; *burden, charge* or *weight, influence,*
   dignity, honor, 1 Thess 2:7; with another noun in
   government, *fulness, abundance, excellence,* 2
   Cor 4:17*

βάρος   acc sg neut [4t; n-3d(2b); 983]   βάρος
βαρούμενοι   pres pass ptcp nom pl masc
   [2C 5:4; v-1d(2a); 976]   βαρέω
Βαρσαββᾶν   acc sg masc [2t; n-1e; 984]   Βαρσαββᾶς

Βαρσαββᾶς, ᾶ, ὁ   {984, n-1e}
   Bar-sabas, pr. name (1) *Joseph, surnamed Justus,*
   Acts 1:23 (2) *Judas,* Acts 15:22*

Βαρτιμαῖος, ου, ὁ   {985, n-2a}
   Bartimaeus, pr. name, Mark 10:46*

Βαρτιμαῖος   nom sg masc
   [Mk 10:46; n-2a; 985]   Βαρτιμαῖος

βαρύς, εῖα, ύ   {987, a-2b}
   heavy; met. *burdensome, oppressive* or *difficult of*
   observance, as precepts, Matt 23:4; 1 John 5:3;
   weighty, important, momentous, Matt 23:23; Acts
   25:7; *grievous, oppressive, afflictive, violent,* Acts
   20:29; *authoritative, strict, stern, severe,* 2 Cor
   10:10*

βαρύτερα   acc pl neut comparative
   [Mt 23:23; a-2b; 987]   βαρύς

βαρύτιμος, ον   {988, a-3a}
   of great price, precious, Matt 26:7*

βαρυτίμου   gen sg neut
   [Mt 26:7; a-3a; 988]   βαρύτιμος
βασανιζομένη   pres pass ptcp nom sg fem
   [Rv 12:2; v-2a(1); 989]   βασανίζω
βασανιζόμενον   pres pass ptcp nom sg neut
   [Mt 14:24; v-2a(1); 989]   "
βασανιζόμενος   pres pass ptcp nom sg masc
   [Mt 8:6; v-2a(1); 989]   "
βασανιζομένους   pres pass ptcp acc pl masc
   [Mk 6:48; v-2a(1); 989]   "

βασανίζω   {989, v-2a(1)}
   [(ἐβασάνιζον), -, ἐβασάνισα, -, -, ἐβασανίσθην]
   pr. *to apply the lapis Lydius* or *touchstone;* met. *to*
   examine, scrutinize, try, either by words or
   torture; in N.T. *to afflict, torment;* pass. *to be*
   afflicted, tormented, pained, by diseases, Matt 8:6,
   29, 35; *to be tossed, agitated,* as by the waves,
   Matt 14:24

βασανίσαι   aor act inf [Mt 8:29; v-2a(1); 989]   "
βασανίσῃς   aor act subj 2 sg [2t; v-2a(1); 989]   "

βασανισθήσεται   fut pass ind 3 sg
   [Rv 14:10; v-2a(1); 989]   "
βασανισθήσονται   fut pass ind 3 pl
   [2t; v-2a(1); 989]   "
βασανισμόν   acc sg masc
   [Rv 18:7; n-2a; 990]   βασανισμός

βασανισμός, οῦ, ὁ   {990, n-2a}
   pr. *examination by torture; torment, torture,* Rev
   9:5; 14:11; 18:7, 10, 15*

βασανισμός   nom sg masc [2t; n-2a; 990]   "
βασανισμοῦ   gen sg masc [3t; n-2a; 990]   "
βασανισταῖς   dat pl masc
   [Mt 18:34; n-1f; 991]   βασανιστής

βασανιστής, οῦ, ὁ   {991, n-1f}
   pr. *an inquisitor, tormentor;* in N.T. *a keeper of a*
   prison, jailer, Matt 18:34*

βασάνοις   dat pl fem [2t; n-2b; 992]   βάσανος

βάσανος, ου, ἡ   {992, n-2b}
   pr. *lapis Lydius,* a species of stone from Lydia,
   which being applied to metals was thought to
   indicate any alloy which might be mixed with
   them, and therefore used in the trial of metals;
   hence, *examination* of a person, especially by
   torture; in N.T. *torture, torment, severe pain,* Matt
   4:24; Luke 16:23, 28*

βασάνου   gen sg fem [Lk 16:28; n-2b; 992]   "
βάσεις   nom pl fem [Ac 3:7; n-3e(5b); 1000]   βάσις
βασιλέα   acc sg masc [15t; n-3e(3); 995]   βασιλεύς
βασιλεῖ   dat sg masc [6t; n-3e(3); 995]   "

βασιλεία, ας, ἡ   {993, n-1a}
   a kingdom, realm, the region or country
   governed by a king; *kingly power, authority,*
   dominion, reign; royal dignity, the title and honor
   of king; ἡ βασιλεία, Matt 9:35, ἡ βασιλεία τοῦ
   θεοῦ· τοῦ Χριστοῦ· τοῦ οὐρανοῦ· τῶν οὐρανῶν,
   the reign or *kingdom of the Messiah,* both in a
   false and true conception of it; used also with
   various limitation, of its administration and
   coming history, as in the parables; its
   distinctive nature, Rom 14:17; its requirements,
   privileges, rewards, consummation

βασιλεία   nom sg fem [55t; n-1a; 993]   βασιλεία
βασιλείᾳ   dat sg fem [21t; n-1a; 993]   "
βασιλείαν   acc sg fem [61t; n-1a; 993]   "
βασιλείας   gen sg fem [22t; n-1a; 993]   "
βασιλείας   acc pl fem [3t; n-1a; 993]   "
βασιλείοις   dat pl neut
   [Lk 7:25; a-3a; 994]   βασίλειος
βασίλειον   nom sg neut [1P 2:9; a-3a; 994]   "

βασίλειος, ον   {994, a-3a}
   royal, regal; met. *possessed of high prerogatives and*
   distinction, 1 Peter 2:9; τὰ βαείλεια, sc. δώματα,
   regal mansion, palaces, Luke 7:25*

βασιλεῖς   nom pl masc [12t; n-3e(3); 995]   βασιλεύς
βασιλεῖς   acc pl masc [4t; n-3e(3); 995]   "
βασιλεῦ   voc sg masc [9t; n-3e(3); 995]   "
βασιλεύει   pres act ind 3 sg
   [Mt 2:22; v-1a(6); 996]   βασιλεύω

βασιλεύειν   pres act inf
  [1C 15:25; v-1a(6); 996]   "
βασιλευέτω   pres act imperative 3 sg
  [Rm 6:12; v-1a(6); 996]   "
βασιλευόντων   pres act ptcp gen pl masc
  [1Ti 6:15; v-1a(6); 996]   "

βασιλεύς, έως, ὁ   {995, n-3e(3)}
  a king, monarch, one possessing regal authority

βασιλεύς   nom sg masc   [48t; n-3e(3); 995]   βασιλεύς
βασιλεῦσαι   aor act inf
  [2t; v-1a(6); 996]   βασιλεύω
βασιλεύσει   fut act ind 3 sg   [2t; v-1a(6); 996]   "
βασιλεύσῃ   aor act subj 3 sg
  [Rm 5:21; v-1a(6); 996]   "
βασιλεῦσιν   dat pl masc
  [Rv 10:11; n-3e(3); 995]   βασιλεύς
βασιλεύσουσιν   fut act ind 3 pl
  [4t; v-1a(6); 996]   βασιλεύω

βασιλεύω   {996, v-1a(6)}
  [βασιλεύσω, ἐβασίλευσα, -, -, -] *to possess regal
  authority, be a king, reign; to rule, govern,* Matt
  2:22; met. *to be in force, predominate, prevail,* Rom
  5:14, 17, 21; met. *to be in kingly case, fare royally,*
  1 Cor 4:8

βασιλέων   gen pl masc   [11t; n-3e(3); 995]   βασιλεύς
βασιλέως   gen sg masc   [9t; n-3e(3); 995]   "
βασιλικήν   acc sg fem
  [Ac 12:21; a-1a(2a); 997]   βασιλικός
βασιλικῆς   gen sg fem   [Ac 12:20; a-1a(2a); 997]   "
βασιλικόν   acc sg masc   [Jm 2:8; a-1a(2a); 997]   "

βασιλικός, ή, όν   {997, a-1a(2a)}
  royal, regal, Acts 12:20, 21; βασιλικός, used as a
  subst. *a person attached to the king, courtier,* John
  4:46, 49; met. *royal, of the highest excellence,*
  James 2:8*

βασιλικός   nom sg masc   [2t; a-1a(2a); 997]   "

βασιλίκος, ου, ὁ   {998, n-2a}
  petty king, John 4:46 v.l., 49 v.l.*

βασίλισσα, ης, ἡ   {999, n-1c}
  a queen, Matt 12:42; Luke 11:31; Acts 8:27; Rev
  18:7*

βασίλισσα   nom sg fem   [3t; n-1c; 999]   βασίλισσα
βασιλίσσης   gen sg fem   [Ac 8:27; n-1c; 999]   "

βάσις, εως, ἡ   {1000, n-3e(5b)}
  pr. *a step; the foot,* Acts 3:7*

βασκαίνω   {1001, v-2d(4)}
  [-, ἐβάσκανα, -, -, -] pr. *to slander;* thence, *to
  bewitch* by spells, or by any other means; *to
  delude,* Gal 3:1*

βαστάζει   pres act ind 3 sg
  [Lk 14:27; v-2a(1); 1002]   βαστάζω
βαστάζειν   pres act inf   [2t; v-2a(1); 1002]   "
βαστάζεις   pres act ind 2 sg
  [Rm 11:18; v-2a(1); 1002]   "
βαστάζεσθαι   pres pass inf
  [Ac 21:35; v-2a(1); 1002]   "
βαστάζετε   pres act imperative 2 pl
  [2t; v-2a(1); 1002]   "

βαστάζοντες   pres act ptcp nom pl masc
  [Lk 7:14; v-2a(1); 1002]   "
βαστάζοντος   pres act ptcp gen sg neut
  [Rv 17:7; v-2a(1); 1002]   "

βαστάζω   {1002, v-2a(1)}
  [βαστάσω, ἐβάστασα, -, -, -] pr. *to lift, raise, bear
  aloft; to bear, carry* in the hands or about the
  person; *carry* as a message, Acts 9:15; *to take
  away, remove,* Matt 8:17; John 20:15; *to take up,*
  John 10:31; Luke 14:27; *to bear* as a burden
  endure, suffer; to sustain, Rom 11:18; *to bear with,
  tolerate; to sustain* mentally, *comprehend,* John
  16:12

βαστάζω   pres act ind 1 sg
  [Ga 6:17; v-2a(1); 1002]
βαστάζων   pres act ptcp nom sg masc
  [3t; v-2a(1); 1002]   "
βαστάσαι   aor act inf   [4t; v-2a(1); 1002]   "
βαστάσασα   aor act ptcp nom sg fem
  [Lk 11:27; v-2a(1); 1002]   "
βαστάσασι   aor act ptcp dat pl masc
  [Mt 20:12; v-2a(1); 1002]   "
βαστάσει   fut act ind 3 sg   [2t; v-2a(1); 1002]   "

βάτος, οῦ, ἡ and ὁ   {1003, n-2b}
  a bush, bramble, Mark 12:36

βάτος, ου, ὁ   {1004, n-2a}
  a bath, a measure for liquids, which is stated by
  Josephus (*Ant.* 8.57) to contain seventy-two
  sextarii, or about thirteen and one half gallons.
  Others estimate it to be nine gallons; and
  others, seven and one half gallons, Luke 16:6*

βάτου   gen sg masc   [2t; n-2b; 1004]   βάτος
βάτου   gen sg fem   [2t; n-2b; 1004]   "
βάτους   acc pl masc   [Lk 16:6; n-2b; 1003]   "
βάτραχοι   nom pl masc
  [Rv 16:13; n-2a; 1005]   βάτραχος

βάτραχος, ου, ὁ   {1005, n-2a}
  a frog, Rev 16:13

βατταλογέω   {1006, v-1d(2a)}
  [βατταλογήσω, ἐβατταλόγησα, -, -, -] also
  spelled βαττολογέω, pr. *to stammer;* hence, *to
  babble; to use vain repetitions,* Matt 6:7; Luke 11:2
  v.l.*

βατταλογήσητε   aor act subj 2 pl
  [Mt 6:7; v-1d(2a); 1006]   βατταλογέω
βάτῳ   dat sg fem   [Ac 7:35; n-2b; 1004]   βάτος
βάψας   aor act ptcp nom sg masc
  [Jn 13:26; v-4; 970]   βάπτω
βάψῃ   aor act subj 3 sg   [Lk 16:24; v-4; 970]   "
βάψω   fut act ind 1 sg   [Jn 13:26; v-4; 970]   "

βδέλυγμα, ατος, τό   {1007, n-3c(4)}
  an abomination, an abominable thing, Matt 24:15;
  Mark 13:14; *idolatry with all its pollution,* Luke
  16:15; Rev 17:4, 5; 21:27*

βδέλυγμα   nom sg neut
  [Lk 16:15; n-3c(4); 1007]   βδέλυγμα
βδέλυγμα   acc sg neut   [3t; n-3c(4); 1007]   "
βδελυγμάτων   gen pl neut   [2t; n-3c(4); 1007]   "

βδελυκτοί   nom pl masc
    [Ti 1:16; a-1a(2a); 1008]   βδελυκτός

βδελυκτός, ή, όν   {1008, a-1a(2a)}
    abominable, detestable, Titus 1:16*

βδελύσσομαι   {1009, v-2b}
    [-, -, -, ἐβδέλυγμαι, -] to abominate, loathe, detest,
    abhor, Rom 2:22; pass. to be abominable,
    detestable, Rev 21:8*

βδελυσσόμενος   pres mid ptcp voc sg masc
    [Rm 2:22; v-2b; 1009]   βδελύσσομαι
βεβαία   nom sg fem [2t; a-1a(1); 1010]   βέβαιος
βεβαίαν   acc sg fem [4t; a-1a(1); 1010]   "

βέβαιος, α, ον   {1010, a-1a(1)}
    firm, stable, steadfast, Heb 3:14; 6:19; sure, certain,
    established, Rom 4:16

βέβαιος   nom sg masc [Hb 2:2; a-1a(1); 1010]   "
βεβαιότερον   acc sg masc comparative
    [2P 1:19; a-1a(1); 1010]   "
βεβαιούμενοι   pres pass ptcp nom pl masc
    [Cl 2:7; v-1d(3); 1011]   βεβαιόω
βεβαιοῦντος   pres act ptcp gen sg masc
    [Mk 16:20; v-1d(3); 1011]   "
βεβαιοῦσθαι   pres pass inf
    [Hb 13:9; v-1d(3); 1011]   "

βεβαιόω   {1011, v-1d(3)}
    [βεβαιώσω, ἐβεβαίωσα, -, -, ἐβεβαιώθην] to
    confirm, establish; to render constant and
    unwavering, 1 Cor 1:8; to strengthen or establish
    by arguments or proofs, ratify, Mark 16:20; to
    verify, as promises, Rom 15:8

βεβαιῶν   pres act ptcp nom sg masc
    [2C 1:21; v-1d(3); 1011]   "
βεβαιῶσαι   aor act inf [Rm 15:8; v-1d(3); 1011]   "
βεβαιώσει   dat sg fem
    [Pp 1:7; n-3e(5b); 1012]   βεβαίωσις
βεβαιώσει   fut act ind 3 sg
    [1C 1:8; v-1d(3); 1011]   βεβαιόω
βεβαίωσιν   acc sg fem
    [Hb 6:16; n-3e(5b); 1012]   βεβαίωσις

βεβαίωσις, εως, ή   {1012, n-3e(5b)}
    confirmation, firm establishment, Phil 1:7; Heb
    6:16*

βεβαμμένον   perf pass ptcp acc sg neut
    [Rv 19:13; v-4; 970]   βάπτω
βεβαπτισμένοι   perf pass ptcp nom pl masc
    [Ac 8:16; v-2a(1); 966]   βαπτίζω
βεβαρημένοι   perf pass ptcp nom pl masc
    [2t; v-1d(2a); 976]   βαρέω
βεβήλοις   dat pl masc
    [1Ti 1:9; a-3a; 1013]   βέβηλος

βέβηλος, ον   {1013, a-3a}
    pr. what is open and accessible to all; hence,
    profane, not religious, not connected with religion;
    unholy; a despiser, scorner, 1 Tim 1:9; 4:7

βέβηλος   nom sg masc [Hb 12:16; a-3a; 1013]   "
βεβήλους   acc pl masc [1Ti 4:7; a-3a; 1013]   "
βεβήλους   acc pl fem [2t; a-3a; 1013]   "
βεβηλοῦσιν   pres act ind 3 pl
    [Mt 12:5; v-1d(3); 1014]   βεβηλόω

βεβηλόω   {1014, v-1d(3)}
    [-, ἐβεβήλωσα, -, -, -] to profane, pollute, violate,
    Matt 12:5; Acts 24:6*

βεβηλῶσαι   aor act inf [Ac 24:6; v-1d(3); 1014]   "
βεβληκότος   perf act ptcp gen sg masc
    [Jn 13:2; v-2d(1); 965]   βάλλω
βεβλημένην   perf pass ptcp acc sg fem
    [Mt 8:14; v-2d(1); 965]   "
βεβλημένον   perf pass ptcp acc sg masc
    [2t; v-2d(1); 965]   "
βεβλημένον   perf pass ptcp acc sg neut
    [Mk 7:30; v-2d(1); 965]   "
βεβλημένος   perf pass ptcp nom sg masc
    [Jn 3:24; v-2d(1); 965]   "
βέβληται   perf pass ind 3 sg [2t; v-2d(1); 965]   "
βεβρωκόσιν   perf act ptcp dat pl masc
    [Jn 6:13; v-5a; 1048]   βιβρώσκω

Βεελζεβούλ   {1015, n-3g(2)}
    variant spellings of Βεελζεβούβ and βεελζεβούλ,
    Beelzeboul, pr. name, indecl., Matt 10:25

Βεελζεβούλ   indecl [7t; n-3g(2); 1015]   Βεελζεβούλ
βέλη   acc pl neut [Ep 6:16; n-3d(2b); 1018]   βέλος

Βελιάρ, ὁ   {1016, n-3g(2)}
    Belial, pr. name, indecl., 2 Cor 6:15*

Βελιάρ   indecl [2C 6:15; n-3g(2); 1016]   Βελιάρ

βελόνη, ης, ή   {1017, n-1b}
    pr. the point of a spear; a needle, Luke 18:25*

βελόνης   gen sg fem [Lk 18:25; n-1b; 1017]   βελόνη

βέλος, ους, τό   {1018, n-3d(2b)}
    a missile weapon, dart, arrow, Eph 6:16*

βέλτιον   acc sg neut, can be used as a
    comparative adverb
    [2Ti 1:18; a-4b(1); 1019]   βελτίων

βελτίων, ον   {1019, a-4b(1)}
    better; βέλτιον, as an adv., very well, too well to
    need informing, Acts 10:28 v.l.; 2 Tim 1:18*

Βενιαμίν, ὁ   {1021, n-3g(2)}
    Benjamin, pr. name, indecl. Acts 13:21; Rom
    11:1; Phil 3:5; Rev 7:8*

Βενιαμίν   indecl [4t; n-3g(2); 1021]   Βενιαμίν

Βερνίκη, ης, ή   {1022, n-1b}
    Bernice, pr. name, Acts 25:13, 23; 26:30*

Βερνίκη   nom sg fem [2t; n-1b; 1022]   Βερνίκη
Βερνίκης   gen sg fem [Ac 25:23; n-1b; 1022]   "

Βέροια, ας, ή   {1023, n-1a}
    Berea, a town of Macedonia, Acts 17:10, 13*

Βεροία   dat sg fem [Ac 17:13; n-1a; 1023]   Βέροια

Βεροιαῖος, α, ον   {1024, a-1a(1)}
    belonging to Berea, Acts 20:4*

Βεροιαῖος   nom sg masc
    [Ac 20:4; a-1a(1); 1024]   Βεροιαῖος
Βέροιαν   acc sg fem [Ac 17:10; n-1a; 1023]   Βέροια

Βεώρ, ὁ, v.l. for Βοσόρ, Balaam's father, at 2 Peter
    2:15*   {1027, n-3g(2)}

Βηθαβαρά, ἡ   {1028}
Bethabara, a town of Palestine, v.l. for βηθανία at John 1:28*

Βηθανία, ας, ἡ   {1029, n-1a}
Bethany (1) A village near Jerusalem, at the Mount of Olives, Matt 21:17; Mark 11:1. (2) A village beyond the Jordan, John 1:28

Βηθανία   nom sg fem [Jn 11:18; n-1a; 1029] Βηθανία
Βηθανίᾳ   dat sg fem [3t; n-1a; 1029]   "
Βηθανίαν   acc sg fem [6t; n-1a; 1029]   "
Βηθανίας   gen sg fem [2t; n-1a; 1029]   "

Βηθεσδά, ἡ   {1031, n-3g(2)}
Bethesda, indecl., a pool in Jerusalem, John 5:2 v.l. for Βηθζαθά*

Βηθζαθά, ἡ   {1032, n-3g(2)}
Bethzatha, indecl., John 5:2 (which has a v.l. Βηθεσδά)*

Βηθζαθά   indecl [Jn 5:2; n-3g(2); 1032]   Βηθζαθά

Βηθλέεμ, ἡ   {1033, n-3g(2)}
Bethlehem, indecl., a town in Palestine

Βηθλέεμ   indecl [8t; n-3g(2); 1033]   Βηθλέεμ
Βηθσαϊδά   indecl [5t; n-3g(2); 1034]   Βηθσαϊδά

Βηθσαϊδα(ν), ἡ   {1034, n-3g(2)}
also spelled Βηθσαϊδα (1035) and Βηθσαϊδαν, *Bethsaida*, indecl. (1) A city of Galilee, Matt 11:21; Mark 6:45,. (2) A city of Lower Gaulanitis, near the Lake of Gennesareth, Luke 9:10

Βηθσαϊδάν indecl [2t; n-3g(2); 1034]

Βηθφαγή, ἡ   {1036, n-3g(2)}
Bethphage, indecl., a part of the Mount of Olives, Matt 21:1; Mark 11:1; Luke 19:29*

Βηθφαγή   indecl [3t; n-3g(2); 1036]   Βηθφαγή

βῆμα, ατος, τό   {1037, n-3c(4)}
a step, footstep, foot-breadth, space to set the foot on, Acts 7:5; *an elevated place ascended by steps, tribunal, throne*, Matt 27:19; Acts 12:21, 23 v.l.

βῆμα   acc sg neut [2t; n-3c(4); 1037]   βῆμα
βήματι   dat sg neut [Rm 14:10; n-3c(4); 1037]   "
βήματος gen sg neut [9t; n-3c(4); 1037]   "

βηρεύς, εως, ὁ   {1038, n-3e(3)}
Berens, Rom 16:15 v.l.*

βήρυλλος, ου, ὁ   {1039, n-2a}
a beryl, a precious stone of a sea-green color, found chiefly in India, Rev 21:20*

βήρυλλος   nom sg masc
           [Rv 21:20; n-2a; 1039]   βήρυλλος

βία, ας, ἡ   {1040, n-1a}
force, impetus, violence, Acts 5:26; 21:35; 24:7 v.l.; 27:41*

βιάζεται   pres mid ind 3 sg
           [Lk 16:16; v-2a(1); 1041]   βιάζω
βιάζεται   pres pass ind 3 sg
           [Mt 11:12; v-2a(1); 1041]   "

βιάζω   {1041, v-2a(1)}
[βιάσω, ἐβίασα, -, -, -] also written as a middle

deponent, βιάζομαι, *to urge, constrain, overpower by force; to press earnestly forward, to rush*, Luke 16:16; pass. *to be an object of a forceful movement*, Matt 11:12*

βιαίας   gen sg fem [Ac 2:2; a-1a(1); 1042]   βίαιος

βίαιος, α, ον   {1042, a-1a(1)}
violent, strong, Acts 2:2*

βίαν   acc sg fem [Ac 21:35; n-1a; 1040]   βία
βίας   gen sg fem [2t; n-1a; 1040]   "
βιασταί   nom pl masc
         [Mt 11:12; n-1f; 1043]   βιαστής

βιαστής, οῦ, ὁ   {1043, n-1f}
one who uses violence, or *is impetuous; one who is forceful* in eager pursuit, Matt 11:12*

βιβλαρίδιον, ου, τό   {1044, n-2c}
a small volume or *scroll, a little book*, Rev 10:2, 8 v.l., 9, 10*

βιβλαρίδιον acc sg neut
             [3t; n-2c; 1044]   βιβλαρίδιον
βιβλία   nom pl neut [Rv 20:12; n-2c; 1046] βιβλίον
βιβλία   acc pl neut [2t; n-2c; 1046]   "
βιβλίοις dat pl neut [Rv 20:12; n-2c; 1046]   "

βιβλίον, ου, τό   {1046, n-2c}
a written volule or *roll, book*, Luke 4:17, 20; *a scroll, bill, billet*, Matt 19:7; Mark 10:4

βιβλίον   nom sg neut [3t; n-2c; 1046]   "
βιβλίον   acc sg neut [15t; n-2c; 1046]   "
βιβλίου   gen sg neut [6t; n-2c; 1046]   "
βιβλίῳ   dat sg neut [6t; n-2c; 1046]   "

βίβλος, ου, ἡ   {1047, n-2b}
pr. *the inner bark* or *rind of the papyrus*, which was anciently used instead of paper; hence, *a written volume* or *roll, book, catalogue, account*, Matt 1:1; Mark 12:26

βίβλος   nom sg fem [Mt 1:1; n-2b; 1047]   βίβλος
βίβλου   gen sg fem [Rv 3:5; n-2b; 1047]   "
βίβλους   acc pl fem [Ac 19:19; n-2b; 1047]   "
βίβλῳ   dat sg fem [7t; n-2b; 1047]   "

βιβρώσκω   {1048, v-5a}
[-, -, βέβρωκα, βέβρωμαι, ἐβεβρώθην] *to eat*, John 6:13*

Βιθυνία, ας, ἡ   {1049, n-1a}
Bithynia, a province of Asia Minor, Acts 16:7; 1 Peter 1:1*

Βιθυνίαν   acc sg fem [Ac 16:7; n-1a; 1049] Βιθυνία
Βιθυνίας   gen sg fem [1P 1:1; n-1a; 1049]   "
βίον   acc sg masc [7t; n-2a; 1050]   βίος

βίος, ου, ὁ   {1050, n-2a}
life; means of living; sustenance, maintenance, substance, goods, Mark 12:44, Luke 8:14, 43; 15:12, 30; 21:4; 1 Tim 2:2; 2 Tim 2:4; 1 John 2:16; 3:17; 1 Peter 4:3 v.l.*

βίου   gen sg masc [3t; n-2a; 1050]   "

βιόω   {1051, v-1d(3)}
[-, ἐβίωσα, -, -, -] *to live*, 1 Peter 4:2*

βιῶσαι   aor act inf [1P 4:2; v-1d(3); 1051]   βιόω

βίωσιν acc sg fem
[Ac 26:4; n-3e(5b); 1052] βίωσις

βίωσις, εως, ἡ {1052, n-3e(5b)}
manner of life, Acts 26:4*

βιωτικά acc pl neut [2t; a-1a(2a); 1053] βιωτικός
βιωτικαῖς dat pl fem [Lk 21:34; a-1a(2a); 1053] "

βιωτικός, ή, όν {1053, a-1a(2a)}
pertaining to this life or *the things of this life,* Luke 21:34; 1 Cor 6:3, 4*

βλαβεράς acc pl fem
[1Ti 6:9; a-1a(1); 1054] βλαβερός

βλαβερός, ά, όν {1054, a-1a(1)}
hurtful, 1 Tim 6:9*

βλάπτω {1055, v-4}
[-, ἔβλαψα, -, -, ἐβλάφθην] pr. *to weaken, hinder, disable; to hurt, harm, injure,* Mark 16:18; Luke 4:35*

βλαστᾷ pres act subj 3 sg
[Mk 4:27; v-3a(2a); 1056] βλαστάνω

βλαστάνω {1056, v-3a(2a)}
[-, ἐβλάστησα, -, -, -] also spelled βλαστάω, intrans. *to germinate, bud, sprout, spring up,* Matt 13:26; Mark 4:27; Heb 9:4; trans. and causative, *to cause to shoot, to produce, yield,* James 5:18*

βλαστήσασα aor act ptcp nom sg fem
[Hb 9:4; v-3a(2a); 1056] "
Βλάστον acc sg masc
[Ac 12:20; n-2a; 1058] Βλάστος

Βλάστος, ου, ὁ {1058, n-2a}
Blastus, pr. name, Acts 12:20*

βλάσφημα acc pl neut
[Ac 6:11; a-3a; 1061] βλάσφημος
βλασφημεῖ pres act ind 3 sg
[2t; v-1d(2a); 1059] βλασφημέω
βλασφημεῖν pres act inf [3t; v-1d(2a); 1059] "
βλασφημεῖς pres act ind 2 sg
[Jn 10:36; v-1d(2a); 1059] "
βλασφημείσθω pres pass imperative 3 sg
[Rm 14:16; v-1d(2a); 1059] "
βλασφημεῖται pres pass ind 3 sg
[Rm 2:24; v-1d(2a); 1059] "

βλασφημέω {1059, v-1d(2a)}
[(ἐβλασφήμουν), -, ἐβλασφήμησα, -, -, ἐβλασφημήθην] *to defame, revile, slander,* Matt 27:39; *to speak of God* or *divine things in terms of impious irreverence, to blaspheme,* Matt 9:3; 26:65

βλασφημηθήσεται fut pass ind 3 sg
[2P 2:2; v-1d(2a); 1059] "
βλασφημῆσαι aor act inf
[Rv 13:6; v-1d(2a); 1059] "
βλασφημήσαντι aor act ptcp dat sg masc
[Lk 12:10; v-1d(2a); 1059] "
βλασφημήσῃ aor act subj 3 sg
[Mk 3:29; v-1d(2a); 1059] "
βλασφημήσωσιν aor act subj 3 pl
[Mk 3:28; v-1d(2a); 1059] "
βλασφημῆται pres pass subj 3 sg
[2t; v-1d(2a); 1059] "

βλασφημία, ας, ἡ {1060, n-1a}
slander, railing, reproach, Matt 15:19; Mark 7:22; *blasphemy,* Matt 12:31; 26:65

βλασφημία nom sg fem [4t; n-1a; 1060] βλασφημία
βλασφημίαι nom pl fem [3t; n-1a; 1060] "
βλασφημίαν acc sg fem [3t; n-1a; 1060] "
βλασφημίας gen sg fem [5t; n-1a; 1060] "
βλασφημίας acc pl fem [3t; n-1a; 1060] "
βλάσφημοι nom pl masc
[2Ti 3:2; a-3a; 1061] βλάσφημος
βλάσφημον acc sg masc [1Ti 1:13; a-3a; 1061] "
βλάσφημον acc sg fem [2P 2:11; a-3a; 1061] "

βλάσφημος, ον {1061, a-3a}
slanderous, railing, reproachful, 2 Tim 3:2; 2 Peter 2:11; *blasphemous,* Acts 6:11, 13; 1 Tim 1:13

βλασφημοῦμαι pres pass ind 1 sg
[1C 10:30; v-1d(2a); 1059] βλασφημέω
βλασφημούμεθα pres pass ind 1 pl
[Rm 3:8; v-1d(2a); 1059] "
βλασφημοῦντας pres act ptcp acc pl masc
[Ac 19:37; v-1d(2a); 1059] "
βλασφημοῦντες pres act ptcp nom pl masc
[5t; v-1d(2a); 1059] "
βλασφημούντων pres act ptcp gen pl masc
[Ac 18:6; v-1d(2a); 1059] "
βλασφημοῦσιν pres act ind 3 pl
[3t; v-1d(2a); 1059] "
βλάψαν aor act ptcp nom sg neut
[Lk 4:35; v-4; 1055] βλάπτω
βλάψῃ aor act subj 3 sg [Mk 16:18; v-4; 1055] "

βλέμμα, ατος, τό {1062, n-3c(4)}
a look; the act of seeing, sight, 2 Peter 2:8*

βλέμματι dat sg neut
[2P 2:8; n-3c(4); 1062] βλέμμα
βλέπε pres act imperative 2 sg
[Cl 4:17; v-1b(1); 1063] βλέπω
βλέπει pres act ind 3 sg [10t; v-1b(1); 1063] "
βλέπειν pres act inf [10t; v-1b(1); 1063] "
βλέπεις pres act ind 2 sg [10t; v-1b(1); 1063] "
βλέπετε pres act imperative 2 pl
[23t; v-1b(1); 1063] "
βλέπετε pres act ind 2 pl [10t; v-1b(1); 1063] "
βλεπέτω pres act imperative 3 sg
[2t; v-1b(1); 1063] "
βλέπῃ pres act subj 3 sg
[Jn 5:19; v-1b(1); 1063] "
βλέπῃς pres act subj 2 sg
[Rv 3:18; v-1b(1); 1063] "
βλέπομεν pres act ind 1 pl [5t; v-1b(1); 1063] "
βλεπόμενα pres pass ptcp nom pl neut
[2t; v-1b(1); 1063] "
βλεπόμενα pres pass ptcp acc pl neut
[2t; v-1b(1); 1063] "
βλεπομένη pres pass ptcp nom sg fem
[Rm 8:24; v-1b(1); 1063] "
βλεπόμενον pres pass ptcp acc sg neut
[Hb 11:3; v-1b(1); 1063] "
βλεπομένων pres pass ptcp gen pl neut
[2t; v-1b(1); 1063] "
βλέποντα pres act ptcp acc sg masc
[Ac 27:12; v-1b(1); 1063] "

βλέποντας pres act ptcp acc pl masc
  [2t; v-1b(1); 1063]   "
βλέποντες pres act ptcp nom pl masc
  [11t; v-1b(1); 1063]   "
βλεπόντων pres act ptcp gen pl masc
  [2t; v-1b(1); 1063]   "
βλέπουσι pres act ind 3 pl
  [Mt 18:10; v-1b(1); 1063]   "
βλέπουσιν pres act ind 3 pl [4t; v-1b(1); 1063]   "

βλέπω   {1063, v-1b(1)}
  [βλέψω, ἔβλεψα, -, -, -] *to have the faculty of sight,
  to see,* Matt 12:22; *to exercise sight, to see,* Matt
  6:4; *to look* towards or at, Matt 22:16; *to face,* Acts
  27:12; *to take heed,* Matt 24:4; in N.T., βλέπειν
  ἀπό, *to beware of, shun,* Mark 8:15; trans., *to cast
  a look on,* Matt 5:28; *to see, behold,* Matt 13:17; *to
  observe,* Matt 7:3; *to have an eye to, see to,* Mark
  13:9; Col 4:17; 2 John 8; *to discern* mentally,
  perceive, Rom 7:23; 2 Cor 7:8; James 2:22; *to
  guard against,* Phil 3:2; pass., *to be an object of
  sight, be visible,* Rom 8:24

βλέπω pres act ind 1 sg [5t; v-1b(1); 1063]   "
βλέπων pres act ptcp nom sg masc
  [12t; v-1b(1); 1063]   "
βλέπωσιν pres act subj 3 pl [7t; v-1b(1); 1063]   "
βλέψετε fut act ind 2 pl [2t; v-1b(1); 1063]   "
βλέψον aor act imperative 2 sg
  [Ac 3:4; v-1b(1); 1063]   "
βληθείς aor pass ptcp nom sg masc
  [Lk 23:19; v-2d(1); 965]   βάλλω
βληθείσῃ aor pass ptcp dat sg fem
  [Mt 13:47; v-2d(1); 965]   "
βληθέν aor pass ptcp nom sg neut
  [Mt 5:13; v-2d(1); 965]   "
βληθῇ aor pass subj 3 sg
  [Mt 5:29; v-2d(1); 965]   "
βληθῆναι aor pass inf [4t; v-2d(1); 965]   "
βληθήσεται fut pass ind 3 sg
  [Rv 18:21; v-2d(1); 965]   "
βληθήσῃ fut pass ind 2 sg
  [Mt 5:25; v-2d(1); 965]   "
βλήθητι aor pass imperative 2 sg
  [2t; v-2d(1); 965]   "
βλητέον nom sg neut
  [Lk 5:38; a-1a(1); 1064]   βλητέος

βλητέος, α, ον   {1064, a-1a(1)}
  requiring to be cast or *put,* Mark 2:22 v.l.; Luke
  5:38*

βοαί nom pl fem [Jm 5:4; n-1b; 1068]   βοή

Βοανηργές   {1065, n-3g(2)}
  Boanerges, pr. name, indecl., Mark 3:17*

βοανηργές indecl
  [Mk 3:17; n-3g(2); 1065]   Βοανηργές
βόας acc pl masc [2t; n-3e(4); 1091]   βοῦς

βοάω   {1066, v-1d(1a)}
  [(ἐβόων), βοήσω, ἐβόησα, -, -, -] *to cry out; to
  exclaim, proclaim,* Matt 3:3; 15:34; Acts 8:7; πρός
  τινα, *to invoke, implore the aid of any one,* Luke
  18:7

Βόες, ὁ   {1067, n-3g(2)}
  Boaz, pr. name, indecl., Matt 1:5*

Βόες indecl [2t; n-3g(2); 1067]   Βόες

βοή, ῆς, ἡ   {1068, n-1b}
  a cry, outcry, exclamation, James 5:4*

βοήθει pres act imperative 2 sg
  [2t; v-1d(2a); 1070]   βοηθέω

βοήθεια, ας, ἡ   {1069, n-1a}
  help, succor, Heb 4:16; meton. pl. *helps,
  contrivances for relief and safety,* Acts 27:17*

βοηθείαις dat pl fem
  [Ac 27:17; n-1a; 1069]   βοήθεια
βοήθειαν acc sg fem [Hb 4:16; n-1a; 1069]   "
βοηθεῖτε pres act imperative 2 pl
  [Ac 21:28; v-1d(2a); 1070]   βοηθέω

βοηθέω   {1070, v-1d(2a)}
  [-, ἐβοήθησα, -, -, -] *to run to the aid of those who
  cry for help; to advance to the assistance of any one,
  help, aid, succor,* Matt 15:25; Mark 9:22, 24

βοηθῆσαι aor act inf [Hb 2:18; v-1d(2a); 1070]   "
βοήθησον aor act imperative 2 sg
  [2t; v-1d(2a); 1070]   "

βοηθός, όν   {1071, a-3a}
  a helper, Heb 13:6*

βοηθός nom sg masc [Hb 13:6; a-3a; 1071]   βοηθός
βόησον aor act imperative 2 sg
  [Ga 4:27; v-1d(1a); 1066]   βοάω

βόθρος, ου, ὁ   {1072, n-2a}
  pit, cistern, Matt 15:14 v.l.*

βόθυνον acc sg masc [3t; n-2a; 1073]   βόθυνος

βόθυνος, ου, ὁ   {1073, n-2a}
  a pit, well or *cistern,* Matt 12:11; 15:14; Luke
  6:39*

βολή, ῆς, ἡ   {1074, n-1b}
  *a cast, a throw; the distance to which a thing can be
  thrown,* Luke 22:41*

βολήν acc sg fem [Lk 22:41; n-1b; 1074]   βολή

βολίζω   {1075, v-2a(1)}
  [-, ἐβόλισα, -, -, -] *to take soundings, sound* Acts
  27:28*

βολίς, ίδος, ἡ   {1076, n-3c(2)}
  a missile weapon, dart, javelin, Heb 12:20 v.l.;
  also, *a plummet, lead for sounding*

βολίσαντες aor act ptcp nom pl masc
  [2t; v-2a(1); 1075]   βολίζω

Βόος, ὁ   {1077, n-3g(2)}
  Boaz, pr. name, indecl., v.l. spelling for Βόος,
  Matt 1:5 v.l.; Luke 3:32 v.l.*

Βόος, ὁ   {1078, n-3g(2)}
  also spelled Βόοζ, *Boaz,* pr. name, indecl., Luke
  3:32*

Βόος indecl [Lk 3:32; n-3g(2); 1078]   Βόος

βόρβορος, ου, ὁ   {1079, n-2a}
  mud, mire, dung, filth, 2 Peter 2:22*

βορβόρου   gen sg masc
    [2P 2:22; n-2a; 1079]   βόρβορος
βορρᾶ   gen sg masc [2t; n-1e; 1080]   βορρᾶς

βορρᾶς, ᾶ, ὁ   {1080, n-1e}
    pr. *the north* or *N.N.E. wind*; meton. *the north*,
    Luke 13:29; Rev 21:13*

βόσκε   pres act imperative 2 sg
    [2t; v-5a; 1081]   βόσκω
βόσκειν   pres act inf [Lk 15:15; v-5a; 1081]   "
βοσκομένη   pres pass ptcp nom sg fem
    [3t; v-5a; 1081]   "
βόσκοντες   pres act ptcp nom pl masc
    [3t; v-5a; 1081]   "

βόσκω   {1081, v-5a}
    [-, -, -, -, -] *to feed, pasture, tend while grazing*;
    βόσκομαι, *to feed, be feeding*, Matt 8:30, 33; Luke
    8:32, 34

Βοσόρ, ὁ   {1082, n-3g(2)}
    Bosor, pr. name, indecl., 2 Peter 2:15*

Βοσόρ   indecl [2P 2:15; n-3g(2); 1082]   Βοσόρ

βοτάνη, ης, ἡ   {1083, n-1b}
    herb, herbage, produce of the earth, Heb 6:7*

βοτάνην   acc sg fem [Hb 6:7; n-1b; 1083]   βοτάνη
βότρυας   acc pl masc
    [Rv 14:18; n-3e(1); 1084]   βότρυς

βότρυς, υος, ὁ   {1084, n-3e(1)}
    a bunch or *cluster of grapes*, Rev 14:18*

βουλάς   acc pl fem [1C 4:5; n-1b; 1087]   βουλή
βούλει   pres mid ind 2 sg
    [Lk 22:42; v-1d(2c); 1089]   βούλομαι
βούλεσθε   pres mid ind 2 pl [2t; v-1d(2c); 1089]   "
βούλεται   pres mid ind 3 sg [2t; v-1d(2c); 1089]   "
βουλεύομαι   pres mid ind 1 sg
    [2t; v-1a(6); 1086]   βουλεύω
βουλεύσεται   fut mid ind 3 sg
    [Lk 14:31; v-1a(6); 1086]   "

βουλευτής, οῦ, ὁ   {1085, n-1f}
    a counsellor, senator; member of the Sanhedrin,
    Mark 15:43; Luke 23:50*

βουλευτής   nom sg masc [2t; n-1f; 1085]   βουλευτής

βουλεύω   {1086, v-1a(6)}
    [(ἐβουλευόμην), βουλεύσω, ἐβούλευσα, -,
    βεβούλευμαι, -] mid., *to give counsel; to
    deliberate*, Luke 14:31; John 12:10; 11:53; Acts
    5:33 v.l.; *to purpose, determine*, Acts 15:37 v.l.;
    27:39; 2 Cor 1:17*

βουλή, ῆς, ἡ   {1087, n-1b}
    counsel, purpose, design, determination, decree,
    Luke 7:30; 23:51, et al. freq.; by impl. *secret
    thoughts, cogitations of the mind*, 1 Cor 4:5

βουλή   nom sg fem [3t; n-1b; 1087]   βουλή
βουλῇ   dat sg fem [3t; n-1b; 1087]   "
βουληθείς   aor pass ptcp nom sg masc
    [Jm 1:18; v-1d(2c); 1089]   βούλομαι
βουληθῇ   aor pass subj 3 sg
    [Jm 4:4; v-1d(2c); 1089]   "

βούλημα, ατος, τό   {1088, n-3c(4)}
    purpose, will, determination, Acts 27:43; Rom
    9:19; 1 Peter 4:3*

βούλημα   acc sg neut
    [1P 4:3; n-3c(4); 1088]   βούλημα
βουλήματι   dat sg neut [Rm 9:19; n-3c(4); 1088]   "
βουλήματος   gen sg neut [Ac 27:43; n-3c(4); 1088] "
βουλήν   acc sg fem [4t; n-1b; 1087]   βουλή
βουλῆς   gen sg fem [Hb 6:17; n-1b; 1087]
βούληται   pres mid subj 3 sg
    [2t; v-1d(2c); 1089]   βούλομαι
βούλοιτο   pres mid opt 3 sg
    [Ac 25:20; v-1d(2c); 1089]

βούλομαι   {1089, v-1d(2c)}
    [(ἐβουλόμην), -, -, -, -, ἐβουλήθην] *to be willing,
    disposed*, Mark 15:15; Acts 25:20; 28:18; *to intend*,
    Matt 1:19; Acts 5:28; 12:4; 2 Cor 1:15; *to desire*, 1
    Tim 6:9; *to choose, be pleased*, John 18:39; Acts
    18:15; James 3:4; *to will, decree, appoint*, Luke
    22:42; James 1:18; 1 Cor 12:11; 1 Tim 2:8; 5:14;
    ἐβουλόμην, *I could wish*, Acts 25:22

βούλομαι   pres mid ind 1 sg [6t; v-1d(2c); 1089]   "
βουλόμεθα   pres mid ind 1 pl
    [Ac 17:20; v-1d(2c); 1089]   "
βουλόμενοι   pres mid ptcp nom pl masc
    [1Ti 6:9; v-1d(2c); 1089]   "
βουλόμενος   pres mid ptcp nom sg masc
    [7t; v-1d(2c); 1089]   "
βουλόμενος   pres pass ptcp nom sg masc
    [2P 3:9; v-1d(2c); 1089]   "
βουλομένου   pres mid ptcp gen sg masc
    [2t; v-1d(2c); 1089]   "
βουλομένους   pres mid ptcp acc pl masc
    [3J 10; v-1d(2c); 1089]   "
βοῦν   acc sg masc [3t; n-3e(4); 1091]   βοῦς
βουνοῖς   dat pl masc [Lk 23:30; n-2a; 1090]   βουνός

βουνός, οῦ, ὁ   {1090, n-2a}
    a hill, rising ground, Luke 3:5; 23:30*

βουνός   nom sg masc [Lk 3:5; n-2a; 1090]   "

βοῦς, ὀς, ὁ   {1091, n-3e(4)}
    an ox, a bull or *cow*, an animal of the ox kind,
    Luke 13:15

βοῦς   nom sg masc [Lk 14:5; n-3e(4); 1091]   βοῦς
βοῶν   gen pl masc [2t; n-3e(4); 1091]   "
βοῶντα   pres act ptcp acc pl neut
    [Ac 8:7; v-1d(1a); 1066]   βοάω
βοῶντες   pres act ptcp nom pl masc
    [2t; v-1d(1a); 1066]   "
βοῶντος   pres act ptcp gen sg masc
    [4t; v-1d(1a); 1066]   "
βοώντων   pres act ptcp gen pl masc
    [Lk 18:7; v-1d(1a); 1066]   "

βραβεῖον, ου, τό   {1092, n-2c}
    a prize bestowed on victors in the public games,
    such as a crown, wreath, chaplet, garland, etc.,
    1 Cor 9:24; Phil 3:14*

βραβεῖον   acc sg neut [2t; n-2c; 1092]   βραβεῖον
βραβευέτω   pres act imperative 3 sg
    [Cl 3:15; v-1a(6); 1093]   βραβεύω

βραδεῖς   voc pl masc [Lk 24:25; a-2b; 1096]   βραδύς

βραβεύω   {1093, v-1a(6)}
[-, -, -, -, -] pr. *to be a director* or *arbiter in the public games;* in N.T. *to preside, direct, rule, govern, be predominate,* Col 3:15*

βραδύνει   pres act ind 3 sg
[2P 3:9; cv-3a(1); 1094]   βραδύνω

βραδύνω   {1094, cv-3a(1)}
[-, -, -, -, -] *to be slow, to delay,* 1 Tim 3:15; 2 Peter 3:9*

βραδύνω   pres act subj 1 sg
[1Ti 3:15; cv-3a(1); 1094]   "

βραδυπλοέω   {1095, cv-1a(7)}
[-, -, -, -, -] *to sail slowly,* Acts 27:7*

βραδυπλοοῦντες   pres act ptcp nom pl masc
[Ac 27:7; cv-1a(7); 1095]   βραδυπλοέω

βραδύς, εῖα, ύ   {1096, a-2b}
slow, not hasty, James 1:19; *slow* of understanding, *heavy, stupid,* Luke 24:25*

βραδύς   nom sg masc [2t; a-2b; 1096]   βραδύς

βραδύτης, ητος, ἡ   {1097, n-3c(1)}
slowness, tardiness, delay, 2 Peter 3:9*

βραδύτητα   acc sg fem
[2P 3:9; n-3c(1); 1097]   βραδύτης
βραχέων   gen pl masc [Hb 13:22; a-2b; 1099] βραχύς
βραχίονι   dat sg masc
[Lk 1:51; n-3f(1b); 1098]   βραχίων
βραχίονος   gen sg masc [Ac 13:17; n-3f(1b); 1098] "

βραχίων, ονος, ὁ   {1098, n-3f(1b)}
the arm; the arm as a symbol of power, Luke 1:51; John 12:38; Acts 13:17*

βραχίων   nom sg masc [Jn 12:38; n-3f(1b); 1098] "
βραχύ   acc sg neut, can also function
adverbially (4t), [6t; a-2b; 1099]   βραχύς

βραχύς, εῖα, ύ   {1099, a-2b}
short, brief; few, small, Luke 22:58; John 6:7; Acts 5:34; 27:28; Heb 2:7, 9; 13:22; 1 Peter 5:12 v.l.*

βρέξαι   aor act inf
[Jm 5:17; v-1b(2); 1101]   βρέχω
βρέφη   nom pl neut [1P 2:2; n-3d(2b); 1100] βρέφος
βρέφη   acc pl neut [2t; n-3d(2b); 1100]   "

βρέφος, ους, τό   {1100, n-3d(2b)}
a child; whether unborn, *an embryo, fetus,* Luke 1:41, 44; or just born, *an infant,* Luke 2:12, 16; Acts 7:19; or partly grown, Luke 18:15; 2 Tim 3:15; met. *a babe* in simplicity of faith, 1 Peter 2:2*

βρέφος   nom sg neut [2t; n-3d(2b); 1100]   "
βρέφος   acc sg neut [2t; n-3d(2b); 1100]   "
βρέφους   gen sg neut [2Ti 3:15; n-3d(2b); 1100]   "
βρέχει   pres act ind 3 sg
[Mt 5:45; v-1b(2); 1101]   βρέχω
βρέχειν   pres act inf [Lk 7:38; v-1b(2); 1101]   "
βρέχῃ   pres act subj 3 sg
[Rv 11:6; v-1b(2); 1101]   "

βρέχω   {1101, v-1b(2)}
[-, ἔβρεξα, -, -, -] *to wet, moisten,* Luke 7:38; *to rain, cause* or *send rain,* Matt 5:45; Luke 17:29

βρονταί   nom pl fem [7t; n-1b; 1103]   βροντή

βροντή, ῆς, η   {1103, n-1b}
thunder, Mark 3:17; John 12:29

βροντήν   acc sg fem [Jn 12:29; n-1b; 1103]   "
βροντῆς   gen sg fem [3t; n-1b; 1103]   "
βροντῶν   gen pl fem [Rv 19:6; n-1b; 1103]   "

βροχή, ῆς, ἡ   {1104, n-1b}
rain, Matt 7:25, 27*

βροχή   nom sg fem [2t; n-1b; 1104]   βροχή
βρόχον   acc sg masc [1C 7:35; n-2a; 1105]   βρόχος

βρόχος, ου, ὁ   {1105, n-2a}
a cord, noose, 1 Cor 7:35*

βρυγμός, οῦ, ὁ   {1106, n-2a}
gnashing of teeth together, Matt 8:12, 13, 42, 50; 22:13; 24:51; 25:30; Luke 13:28*

βρυγμός   nom sg masc [7t; n-2a; 1106]   βρυγμός
βρύει   pres act ind 3 sg
[Jm 3:11; v-1a(4); 1108]   βρύω

βρύχω   {1107, v-1b(2)}
[(ἔβρυχον), -, -, -, -, -] *to grate* or *gnash* the teeth, Acts 7:54*

βρύω   {1108, v-1a(4)}
[-, -, -, -, -] pr. *to be full, to swell* with anything; *to emit, send forth,* James 3:11*

βρῶμα, ατος, τό   {1109, n-3c(4)}
food, Matt 14:15; Mark 7:19; *solid food,* 1 Cor 3:2

βρῶμα   nom sg neut [3t; n-3c(4); 1109]   βρῶμα
βρῶμα   acc sg neut [3t; n-3c(4); 1109]   "
βρώμασιν   dat pl neut [3t; n-3c(4); 1109]   "
βρώματα   nom pl neut [1C 6:13; n-3c(4); 1109]   "
βρώματα   acc pl neut [4t; n-3c(4); 1109]   "
βρώματι   dat sg neut [Rm 14:15; n-3c(4); 1109]   "
βρώματος   gen sg neut [Rm 14:20; n-3c(4); 1109]   "
βρωμάτων   gen pl neut [1Ti 4:3; n-3c(4); 1109]   "
βρώσει   dat sg fem
[Cl 2:16; n-3e(5b); 1111]   βρῶσις
βρώσεως   gen sg fem [2t; n-3e(5b); 1111]   "
βρώσιμον   acc sg neut
[Lk 24:41; a-3a; 1110]   βρώσιμος

βρώσιμος, ον   {1110, a-3a}
eatable, that may be eaten, Luke 24:41*

βρῶσιν   acc sg fem [4t; n-3e(5b); 1111]   βρῶσις

βρῶσις, εως, ἡ   {1111, n-3e(5b)}
eating, the act of eating, Rom 14:17; 1 Cor 8:4; *meat, food,* John 6:27; Heb 12:16; *a canker* or *rust,* Matt 6:19, 20

βρῶσις   nom sg fem [4t; n-3e(5b); 1111]   "
βυθίζεσθαι   pres pass inf
[Lk 5:7; v-2a(1); 1112]   βυθίζω
βυθίζουσιν   pres act ind 3 pl
[1Ti 6:9; v-2a(1); 1112]   "

βυθίζω   {1112, v-2a(1)}
[-, -, -, -, ἐβυθίσθην] *to immerse, submerge, cause*

to sink, Luke 5:7; *to plunge deep, drown*, 1 Tim 6:9*

βυθός, οῦ, ὁ   {1113, n-2a}
the bottom, lowest part; the deep, sea, 2 Cor 11:25*

βυθῷ   dat sg masc [2C 11:25; n-2a; 1113]   βυθός
βυρσεῖ   dat sg masc [2t; n-3e(3); 1114]   βυρσεύς

βυρσεύς, έως, ὁ   {1114, n-3e(3)}
a tanner, leather-dresser, Acts 9:43; 10:6, 32*

βυρσέως   gen sg masc [Ac 10:32; n-3e(3); 1114]   "
βύσσινον   nom sg neut
      [Rv 19:8; a-1a(2a); 1115]   βύσσινος
βύσσινον   acc sg neut [3t; a-1a(2a); 1115]   "

βύσσινος, η, ον   {1115, a-1a(2a)}
made of fine linen or *fine cotton*, Rev 18:16; 18:8 (2t), 14*

βυσσίνου   gen sg neut [Rv 18:12; a-1a(2a); 1115]   "
βύσσον   acc sg fem [Lk 16:19; n-2b; 1116]   βύσσος

βύσσος, ου, ἡ   {1116, n-2b}
byssus, a species of fine cotton highly prized by the ancients, Luke 16:19; Rev 18:12 v.l.*

βωμός, οῦ, ὁ   {1117, n-2a}
pr. *a slightly-elevated spot, base, pedestal*; hence, *an altar*, Acts 17:23*

βωμόν   acc sg masc
      [Ac 17:23; n-2a; 1117]   βωμός

γ

γ   {1118, n-3g(2)}
gamma, third letter of the Greek alphabet; *third* in titles of N.T. writings

Γαββαθᾶ   {1119, n-3g(2)}
Gabbatha, pr. name, indecl., John 19:13*

Γαββαθα   indecl [Jn 19:13; n-3g(2); 1119]   Γαββαθᾶ

Γαβριήλ, ὁ   {1120, n-3g(2)}
Gabriel, pr. name, indecl., Luke 1:19, 26*

Γαβριήλ   indecl [2t; n-3g(2); 1120]   Γαβριήλ

γάγγραινα, ης, ἡ   {1121, n-1c}
gangrene, mortification, 2 Tim 2:17*

γάγγραινα   nom sg fem
      [2Ti 2:17; n-1c; 1121]   γάγγραινα

Γάδ, ὁ   {1122, n-3g(2)}
Gad, pr. name, indecl., Rev 7:5*

Γάδ   indecl [Rv 7:5; n-3g(2); 1122]   Γάδ

Γαδαρηνός, ή, όν   {1123, a-1a(2a)}
an inhabitant of Gadara, the chief city of Perea, Matt 8:28; Mark 5:1 v.l.; Luke 8:26 v.l.; 8:37 v.l.*

Γαδαρηνῶν   gen pl masc
      [Mt 8:28; a-1a(2a); 1123]   Γαδαρηνός

Γάζα, ης, ἡ   {1124, n-1c}
Gaza, a strong city of Palestine, Acts 8:26*

γάζα, ης, ἡ   {1125, n-1c}
treasure, treasury, Acts 8:27*

Γάζαν   acc sg fem [Ac 8:26; n-1c; 1124]   Γάζα
γάζης   gen sg fem [Ac 8:27; n-1c; 1125]   γάζα

γαζοφυλάκιον, ου, τό   {1126, n-2c}
also spelled γαζοφυλακεῖον, *a treasury; the sacred treasure*, Mark 12:41, 43; Luke 21:1; John 8:20*

γαζοφυλάκιον   acc sg neut
      [3t; n-2c; 1126]   γαζοφυλάκιον
γαζοφυλακίου   gen sg neut [Mk 12:41; n-2c; 1126]   "
γαζοφυλακίῳ   dat sg neut [Jn 8:20; n-2c; 1126]   "
Γάϊον   acc sg masc [2t; n-2a; 1127]   Γάϊος

Γάϊος, ου, ὁ   {1127, n-2a}
Gaius, pr. name. (1) Of Macedonia, Acts 19:29. (2) Of Corinth, 1 Cor 1:14. (3) Of Derbe, Acts 20:4. (4) A Christian to whom John addressed his third Epistle, 3 John 1; Rom 16:23*

Γάϊος   nom sg masc [2t; n-2a; 1127]   "
Γαΐῳ   dat sg masc [3J 1; n-2a; 1127]   "

γάλα, ακτος, τό   {1128, n-3c(6d)}
milk, 1 Cor 9:7; met. spiritual *milk*, consisting in the elements of Christian instruction, 1 Cor 3:2; Heb 5:12, 13; spiritual *nutriment*, 1 Peter 2:2*

γάλα   acc sg neut [2t; n-3c(6d); 1128]   γάλα
γάλακτος   gen sg neut [3t; n-3c(6d); 1128]   "
Γαλάται   voc pl masc [Ga 3:1; n-1f; 1129]   Γαλάτης

Γαλάτης, ου, ὁ   {1129, n-1f}
a Galatian, inhabitant of Galatia, Gal 3:1*

Γαλατία, ας, ἡ   {1130, n-1a}
Galatia or *Gallo-Graecia*, a province of Asia Minor, 1 Cor 6:1; Gal 1:2; 2 Tim 4:10; 1 Peter 1:1*

Γαλατίαν   acc sg fem
      [2Ti 4:10; n-1a; 1130]   Γαλατία
Γαλατίας   gen sg fem [3t; n-1a; 1130]   "
Γαλατικήν   acc sg fem
      [2t; a-1a(2a); 1131]   Γαλατικός

Γαλατικός, ή, όν   {1131, a-1a(2a)}
Galatian, Acts 16:6; 18:23*

γαλήνη, ης, ἡ   {1132, n-1b}
tranquillity of the sea, a calm, Matt 8:26; Mark 4:39; Luke 8:24*

γαλήνη   nom sg fem [3t; n-1b; 1132]   γαλήνη

Γαλιλαία, ας, ἡ   {1133, n-1a}
Galilee, a district of Palestine north of Samaria, Matt 4:15

Γαλιλαία   nom sg fem
      [Mt 4:15; n-1a; 1133]   Γαλιλαία
Γαλιλαίᾳ   dat sg fem [6t; n-1a; 1133]   "
Γαλιλαίαν   acc sg fem [17t; n-1a; 1133]   "
Γαλιλαίας   gen sg fem [37t; n-1a; 1133]   "
Γαλιλαῖοι   nom pl masc
      [3t; a-1a(1); 1134]   Γαλιλαῖος
Γαλιλαῖοι   voc pl masc [Ac 1:11; a-1a(1); 1134]   "

Γαλιλαῖος, α, ον   {1134, a-1a(1)}
a native of Galilee, Matt 26:69; Mark 14:70; Luke 13:1; John 4:45; Acts 1:11

Γαλιλαῖος   nom sg masc [4t; a-1a(1); 1134]   "

Γαλιλαίου   gen sg masc [Mt 26:69; a-1a(1); 1134]   "
Γαλιλαίους   acc pl masc [Lk 13:2; a-1a(1); 1134]   "
Γαλιλαίων   gen pl masc [Lk 13:1; a-1a(1); 1134]   "

Γαλλία, ας, ἡ   {1135, n-1a}
Gaul, v.l. in 2 Tim 4:10 for Γαλατία *

Γαλλίων, ῶνος, ὁ   {1136, n-3f(1a)}
Gallio, pr. name, Acts 18:12, 14, 17*

Γαλλίων   nom sg masc
[Ac 18:14; n-3f(1a); 1136]   Γαλλίων
Γαλλίωνι   dat sg masc [Ac 18:17; n-3f(1a); 1136]   "
Γαλλίωνος   gen sg masc [Ac 18:12; n-3f(1a); 1136]   "

Γαμαλιήλ, ὁ   {1137, n-3g(2)}
Gamaliel, pr. name, indecl.

Γαμαλιήλ   indecl [2t; n-3g(2); 1137]   Γαμαλιήλ
γαμεῖν   pres act inf [3t; v-1d(2a); 1138]   γαμέω
γαμείτωσαν   pres act imperative 3 pl
[1C 7:36; v-1d(2a); 1138]   "

γαμέω   {1138, v-1d(2a)}
[(ἐγάμουν), -, ἔγημα or ἐγάμησα, γεγάμηκα, -,
ἐγαμήθην] *to marry*, Matt 5:32, et al.; absol. *to
marry, enter the marriage state*, Matt 19:10, et al.;
mid. *to marry, be married*, Mark 10:12; 1 Cor 7:39

γαμηθῆναι   aor pass inf
[1C 7:39; v-1d(2a); 1138]   "
γαμῆσαι   aor act inf [2t; v-1d(2a); 1138]   "
γαμήσας   aor act ptcp nom sg masc
[1C 7:33; v-1d(2a); 1138]   "
γαμήσασα   aor act ptcp nom sg fem
[1C 7:34; v-1d(2a); 1138]   "
γαμησάτωσαν   aor act imperative 3 pl
[1C 7:9; v-1d(2a); 1138]   "
γαμήσῃ   aor act subj 3 sg [4t; v-1d(2a); 1138]   "
γαμήσῃς   aor act subj 2 sg
[1C 7:28; v-1d(2a); 1138]   "
γαμίζονται   pres pass ind 3 pl
[3t; v-2a(1); 1139]   γαμίζω
γαμίζοντες   pres act ptcp nom pl masc
[Mt 24:38; v-2a(1); 1139]   "

γαμίζω   {1139, v-2a(1)}
[(ἐγάμιζον), -, -, -, -, -] also spelled γαμίσκω, *to
give in marriage, permit to marry*, 1 Cor 7:38

γαμίζων   pres act ptcp nom sg masc
[2t; v-2a(1); 1139]   "
γαμίσκονται   pres pass ind 3 pl
[Lk 20:34; v-5a; 1140]   γαμίσκω

γαμίσκω, see γαμίζω   {1140}

γάμον   acc sg masc [Jn 2:2; n-2a; 1141]   γάμος

γάμος, ου, ὁ   {1141, n-2a}
a wedding; nuptial festivities, a marriage festival,
Matt 22:2; 25:10; John 2:1, 2; Rev 19:7, 9; any
feast or *banquet*, Luke 12:36; 14:8; *the marriage
state*, Heb 13:4

γάμος   nom sg masc [5t; n-2a; 1141]   "
γάμου   gen sg masc [3t; n-2a; 1141]   "
γαμοῦντες   pres act ptcp nom pl masc
[Mt 24:38; v-1d(2a); 1138]   γαμέω
γάμους   acc pl masc [6t; n-2a; 1141]   γάμος

γαμοῦσιν   pres act ind 3 pl
[4t; v-1d(2a); 1138]   γαμέω
γάμων   gen pl masc [Lk 12:36; n-2a; 1141]   γάμος
γαμῶν   pres act ptcp nom sg masc
[2t; v-1d(2a); 1138]   γαμέω

γάρ   {1142, conj}
for; it is, however, frequently used with an
ellipsis of the clause to which it has reference,
and its force must then be variously expressed:
Matt 15:27; 27:23, et al.; it is also sometimes
epexegetic, or introductory of an intimated
detail of circumstances, *now, then, to wit*, Matt
1:18

γάρ   conj [1041t; conj; 1142]   γάρ
γαστέρες   nom pl fem
[Ti 1:12; n-3f(2c); 1143]   γαστήρ

γαστήρ, γαστρός, ἡ   {1143, n-3f(2c)}
the belly, stomach; the womb, Luke 1:31; ἐν γαστρὶ
ἔχειν, *to be with child*, Matt 1:18, 23; 24:19, et al.;
γαστέρες, *gluttons*, Titus 1:12

γαστρί   dat sg fem [8t; n-3f(2c); 1143]   "

γέ   {1145, particle}
an enclitic particle imparting emphasis;
indicating that a particular regard is to be had
to the term to which it is attached. Its force is
to be conveyed, when this is possible, by
various expression; *at least, indeed, even*

γε   particle [26t; particle; 1145]   γέ
γεγαμηκόσιν   perf act ptcp dat pl masc
[1C 7:10; v-1d(2a); 1138]   γαμέω
γεγενημένον   perf pass ptcp acc sg neut
[Jn 2:9; v-1c(2); 1181]   γίνομαι
γεγενῆσθαι   perf pass inf
[Rm 15:8; v-1c(2); 1181]   "
γεγέννηκα   perf act ind 1 sg
[3t; v-1d(1a); 1164]   γεννάω
γεγέννημαι   perf pass ind 1 sg
[2t; v-1d(1a); 1164]   "
γεγεννήμεθα   perf pass ind 1 pl
[Jn 8:41; v-1d(1a); 1164]   "
γεγεννημένα   perf pass ptcp nom pl neut
[2P 2:12; v-1d(1a); 1164]   "
γεγεννημένον   perf pass ptcp nom sg neut
[3t; v-1d(1a); 1164]   "
γεγεννημένον   perf pass ptcp acc sg masc
[1J 5:1; v-1d(1a); 1164]   "
γεγεννημένος   perf pass ptcp nom sg masc
[4t; v-1d(1a); 1164]   "
γεγεννημένου   perf pass ptcp gen sg masc
[Jn 9:32; v-1d(1a); 1164]   "
γεγέννηται   perf pass ind 3 sg
[5t; v-1d(1a); 1164]   "
γέγονα   perf act ind 1 sg
[5t; v-1c(2); 1181]   γίνομαι
γεγόναμεν   perf act ind 1 pl [2t; v-1c(2); 1181]   "
γέγοναν   perf act ind 3 pl [2t; v-1c(2); 1181]   "
γέγονας   perf act ind 2 sg [3t; v-1c(2); 1181]   "
γεγόνασιν   perf act ind 3 pl [2t; v-1c(2); 1181]   "
γεγόνατε   perf act ind 2 pl [2t; v-1c(2); 1181]   "
γεγόνει   pluperf act ind 3 sg
[Ac 4:22; v-1c(2); 1181]   "

γέγονεν　perf act ind 3 sg [31t; v-1c(2); 1181]　　"
γεγονέναι　perf act inf [4t; v-1c(2); 1181]　　"
γεγονός　perf act ptcp nom sg neut
　　[Mk 5:14; v-1c(2); 1181]　　"
γεγονός　perf act ptcp acc sg neut
　　[7t; v-1c(2); 1181]　　"
γεγονότας　perf act ptcp acc pl masc
　　[Jm 3:9; v-1c(2); 1181]　　"
γεγονότες　perf act ptcp nom pl masc
　　[2t; v-1c(2); 1181]　　"
γεγονότι　perf act ptcp dat sg neut
　　[Ac 4:21; v-1c(2); 1181]　　"
γεγονυῖα　perf act ptcp nom sg fem
　　[1Ti 5:9; v-1c(2); 1181]　　"
γεγονώς　perf act ptcp nom sg masc
　　[Ga 3:17; v-1c(2); 1181]　　"
γεγραμμένα　perf pass ptcp nom pl neut
　　[3t; v-1b(1); 1211]　　γράφω
γεγραμμένα　perf pass ptcp acc pl neut
　　[4t; v-1b(1); 1211]　　"
γεγραμμένας　perf pass ptcp acc pl fem
　　[Rv 22:18; v-1b(1); 1211]　　"
γεγραμμένην　perf pass ptcp acc sg fem
　　[Mt 27:37; v-1b(1); 1211]　　"
γεγραμμένοι　perf pass ptcp nom pl masc
　　[Rv 21:27; v-1b(1); 1211]　　"
γεγραμμένοις　perf pass ptcp dat pl neut
　　[2t; v-1b(1); 1211]　　"
γεγραμμένον　perf pass ptcp nom sg neut
　　[10t; v-1b(1); 1211]　　"
γεγραμμένον　perf pass ptcp acc sg neut
　　[7t; v-1b(1); 1211]　　"
γεγραμμένος　perf pass ptcp nom sg masc
　　[3t; v-1b(1); 1211]　　"
γεγραμμένων　perf pass ptcp gen pl masc
　　[Rv 22:19; v-1b(1); 1211]　　"
γεγραμμένων　perf pass ptcp gen pl neut
　　[Rv 20:12; v-1b(1); 1211]　　"
γέγραπται　perf pass ind 3 sg
　　[67t; v-1b(1); 1211]　　"
γέγραφα　perf act ind 1 sg [2t; v-1b(1); 1211]　　"
γεγυμνασμένα　perf pass ptcp acc pl neut
　　[Hb 5:14; v-2a(1); 1214]　　γυμνάζω
γεγυμνασμένην　perf pass ptcp acc sg fem
　　[2P 2:14; v-2a(1); 1214]　　"
γεγυμνασμένοις　perf pass ptcp dat pl masc
　　[Hb 12:11; v-2a(1); 1214]　　"

Γεδεών, ὁ　　　　　　　　{1146, n-3g(2)}
　　Gideon (Judges 6-8), pr. name, indecl., Heb
　　11:32*

Γεδεών　indecl [Hb 11:32; n-3g(2); 1146]　　Γεδεών

γέεννα, ης, ἡ　　　　　　　{1147, n-1c}
　　Gehenna, pr. the valley of Hinnom, south of
　　Jerusalem, once celebrated for the horrid
　　worship of Moloch, and afterwards polluted
　　with every species of filth, as well as the
　　carcasses of animals, and dead bodies of
　　malefactors; to consume which, in order to
　　avert the pestilence which such a mass of
　　corruption would occasion, constant fires were
　　kept burning; hence, hell, the fires of Tartarus, the

place of punishment in Hades, Matt 5:22, 29, 30;
　　10:28; 18:9, et al.

γέενναν　acc sg fem [8t; n-1c; 1147]　　γέεννα
γεέννῃ　dat sg fem [Mt 10:28; n-1c; 1147]　　"
γεέννης　gen sg fem [3t; n-1c; 1147]　　"

Γεθσημανί　　　　　　　　{1149, n-3g(2)}
　　Gethsemane, pr. name, indecl., Matt 26:36; Mark
　　14:32*

Γεθσημανί　indecl [2t; n-3g(2); 1149]　　Γεθσημανί
γείτονας　acc pl masc [2t; n-3f(1b); 1150]　　γείτων
γείτονας　acc pl fem [Lk 15:9; n-3f(1b); 1150]　　"
γείτονες　nom pl masc [Jn 9:8; n-3f(1b); 1150]　　"

γείτων, ονος, ὁ and ἡ　　　　{1150, n-3f(1b)}
　　a neighbor, Luke 14:12; 15:6, 9; John 9:8*

γελάσετε　fut act ind 2 pl
　　[Lk 6:21; v-1d(1b); 1151]　　γελάω

γελάω　　　　　　　　　{1151, v-1d(1b)}
　　[γελάσω, ἐγέλασα, -, -, -] to laugh, smile; by impl.
　　to be merry, happy, to rejoice, Luke 6:21, 25*

γελῶντες　pres act ptcp voc pl masc
　　[Lk 6:25; v-1d(1b); 1151]　　"

γέλως, ωτος, ὁ　　　　　　{1152, n-3c(1)}
　　laughter; by impl. mirth, joy, rejoicing, James 4:9*

γέλως　nom sg masc [Jm 4:9; n-3c(1); 1152]　　γέλως
γέμει　pres act ind 3 sg [2t; v-1c(2); 1154]　　γέμω
γεμίζεσθαι　pres pass inf
　　[Mk 4:37; v-2a(1); 1153]　　γεμίζω

γεμίζω　　　　　　　　　{1153, v-2a(1)}
　　[-, ἐγέμισα, -, -, ἐγεμίσθην] to fill, Matt 4:37;
　　15:36, et al.

γεμίσας　aor act ptcp nom sg masc
　　[Mk 15:36; v-2a(1); 1153]　　"
γεμίσατε　aor act imperative 2 pl
　　[Jn 2:7; v-2a(1); 1153]　　"
γεμισθῇ　aor pass subj 3 sg
　　[Lk 14:23; v-2a(1); 1153]　　"
γέμον　pres act ptcp acc sg neut
　　[Rv 17:4; v-1c(2); 1154]　　γέμω
γέμοντα　pres act ptcp nom pl neut
　　[Rv 4:6; v-1c(2); 1154]　　"
γέμοντα　pres act ptcp acc sg neut
　　[Rv 17:3; v-1c(2); 1154]　　"
γεμόντων　pres act ptcp gen pl masc
　　[Rv 21:9; v-1c(2); 1154]　　"
γεμούσας　pres act ptcp acc pl fem
　　[2t; v-1c(2); 1154]　　"
γέμουσιν　pres act ind 3 pl [3t; v-1c(2); 1154]　　"

γέμω　　　　　　　　　{1154, v-1c(2)}
　　[(ἔγεμον), -, -, -, -, -] to be full, Matt 23:27; Luke
　　11:39, et al.

γενεά, ᾶς, ἡ　　　　　　　{1155, n-1a}
　　pr. birth; hence, progeny; a generation of
　　mankind, Matt 11:16; 23:36, et al.; a generation,
　　a step in a genealogy, Matt 1:17; a generation, an
　　interval of time, an age; in N.T. course of life, in
　　respect of its events, interests, or character,
　　Luke 16:8; Acts 13:36

γενεά   nom sg fem [8t; n-1a; 1155]   γενεά
γενεά   voc sg fem [3t; n-1a; 1155]   "
γενεᾷ   dat sg fem [6t; n-1a; 1155]   "
γενεαί   nom pl fem [5t; n-1a; 1155]   "
γενεαῖς dat pl fem [2t; n-1a; 1155]   "

γενεαλογέω   {1156, cv-2a(1)}
[-, -, -, -, -] *to reckon one's descent, derive one's
origin,* Heb 7:6*

γενεαλογία, ας, ἡ   {1157, n-1a}
*genealogy, catalogue of ancestors, history of
descent,* 1 Tim 1:4; Titus 3:9*

γενεαλογίαις   dat pl fem
   [1Ti 1:4; n-1a; 1157]   γενεαλογία
γενεαλογίας   acc pl fem [Ti 3:9; n-1a; 1157]   "
γενεαλογούμενος   pres pass ptcp nom sg masc
   [Hb 7:6; cv-2a(1); 1156]   γενεαλογέω
γενεάν   acc sg fem [4t; n-1a; 1155]   γενεά
γενεᾶς   gen sg fem [10t; n-1a; 1155]   "
γενεάς   acc pl fem [3t; n-1a; 1155]   "

γενέθλιος, ον   {1159, a-3a}
relating to birth, Mark 6:21 v.l.*

γένει   dat sg neut [5t; n-3d(2b); 1169]   γένος
γενέσει   dat sg fem
   [Lk 1:14; n-3e(5b); 1161]   γένεσις
γενέσεως   gen sg fem [3t; n-3e(5b); 1161]   "
γενέσθαι   aor mid inf
   [37t; v-1c(2); 1181]   γίνομαι
γενέσθω   aor mid imperative 3 sg
   [1C 3:18; v-1c(2); 1181]   "

γενέσια, ίων, τά   {1160, n-2c}
pr. *a day observed in memory of the dead;* in N.T.
equivalent to γενέθλια, *celebration of one's
birthday, birthday-festival,* Matt 14:6; Mark 6:21*

γενεσίοις   dat pl neut [2t; n-2c; 1160]   γενέσια

γένεσις, εως, ἡ   {1161, n-3e(5b)}
birth, nativity, Matt 1:18; Luke 1:14; James 1:23;
successive generation, descent, lineage, Matt 1:1;
meton. *life,* James 3:6; Matt 1:18*

γένεσις   nom sg fem
   [Mt 1:18; n-3e(5b); 1161]   γένεσις

γενετή, ῆς, ἡ   {1162, n-1b}
birth, John 9:1*

γενετῆς   gen sg fem [Jn 9:1; n-1b; 1162]   γενετή
γενεῶν   gen pl fem [2t; n-1a; 1155]   γενεά
γένη   nom pl neut [2t; n-3d(2b); 1169]   γένος
γένη   acc pl neut [1C 12:28; n-3d(2b); 1169]   "
γενηθέντας   aor pass ptcp acc pl masc
   [Hb 6:4; v-1c(2); 1181]   γίνομαι
γενηθέντες   aor pass ptcp nom pl masc
   [2t; v-1c(2); 1181]   "
γενηθέντων   aor pass ptcp gen pl neut
   [Hb 4:3; v-1c(2); 1181]   "
γενηθῆναι   aor pass inf [Hb 5:5; v-1c(2); 1181] "
γενήθητε   aor pass imperative 2 pl
   [1P 1:15; v-1c(2); 1181]   "
γενηθήτω   aor pass imperative 3 sg
   [7t; v-1c(2); 1181]   "

γενηθῶμεν   aor pass subj 1 pl
   [Ti 3:7; v-1c(2); 1181]   "

γένημα, ατος, τό   {1163, n-3c(4)}
natural produce, fruit, increase, Matt 26:29; Mark
14:25; Luke 12:18; 22:18; 2 Cor 9:10*

γενήματα   acc pl neut
   [2C 9:10; n-3c(4); 1163]   γένημα
γενήματος   gen sg neut [3t; n-3c(4); 1163]   "
γενήσεσθε   fut mid ind 2 pl
   [Jn 8:33; v-1c(2); 1181]   γίνομαι
γενήσεται   fut mid ind 3 sg [9t; v-1c(2); 1181] "
γένησθε   aor mid subj 2 pl [8t; v-1c(2); 1181]   "
γενησόμενον   fut mid ptcp acc sg neut
   [1C 15:37; v-1c(2); 1181]   "
γενήσονται   fut mid ind 3 pl
   [Jn 10:16; v-1c(2); 1181]   "
γένηται   aor mid subj 3 sg [46t; v-1c(2); 1181] "
γεννᾶται   pres pass ind 3 sg
   [Mt 2:4; v-1d(1a); 1164]   γεννάω

γεννάω   {1164, v-1d(1a)}
[γεννήσω, ἐγέννησα, γεγέννηκα, γεγέννημαι,
ἐγεννήθην] *to beget, generate,* Matt 1:2-16, et al.;
of women, *to bring forth, bear, give birth to,* Luke
1:13, 57, et al.; pass. *to be born, produced,* Matt
2:1, 4, et al.; met. *to produce, excite, give occasion
to, effect,* 2 Tim 2:23; from the Hebrew, *to
constitute as son, to constitute as king,* or *as the
representative* or *viceregent of God,* Acts 13:33;
Heb 1:5; 5:5; by impl. *to be a parent to* any one;
pass. *to be a son* or *child to* any one, John 1:13; 1
Cor 4:15, et al.

γεννηθείς   aor pass ptcp nom sg masc
   [3t; v-1d(1a); 1164]   "
γεννηθέν   aor pass ptcp nom sg neut
   [Mt 1:20; v-1d(1a); 1164]   "
γεννηθέντος   aor pass ptcp gen sg masc
   [Mt 2:1; v-1d(1a); 1164]   "
γεννηθέντων   aor pass ptcp gen pl masc
   [Rm 9:11; v-1d(1a); 1164]   "
γεννηθῇ   aor pass subj 3 sg [3t; v-1d(1a); 1164] "
γεννηθῆναι   aor pass inf [3t; v-1d(1a); 1164]   "

γέννημα, ατος, τό   {1165, n-3c(4)}
what is born or *produced, offspring, progeny,
brood,* Matt 3:7; 12:34, et al.; *fruit, produce,* Matt
26:29; Mark 14:25, et al.; *fruit, increase,* Luke
12:18; 2 Cor 9:10

γεννήματα   voc pl neut [4t; n-3c(4); 1165]   γέννημα
γεννήσαντα   aor act ptcp acc sg masc
   [1J 5:1; v-1d(1a); 1164]   γεννάω

Γεννησαρέτ, ἡ   {1166, n-3g(2)}
Gennesaret, a lake of Palestine, called also the
Sea of Tiberias, Matt 14:34; Mark 6:53; Luke 5:1*

Γεννησαρέτ   indecl [3t; n-3g(2); 1166]   Γεννησαρέτ
γεννήσει   fut act ind 3 sg
   [Lk 1:13; v-1d(1a); 1164]   γεννάω
γεννήσῃ   aor act subj 3 sg
   [Jn 16:21; v-1d(1a); 1164]   "

γέννησις, εως, ἡ   {1167, n-3e(5b)}
birth, nativity, v.l. in Matt 1:18, Luke 1:14, and 1
John 5:18*

γεννητοῖς   dat pl masc
  [2t; a-1a(2a); 1168]   γεννητός
γεννητός, ή, όν   {1168, a-1a(2a)}
  born or *produced of,* Matt 11:11; Luke 7:28*

γεννώμενον   pres pass ptcp nom sg neut
  [Lk 1:35; v-1d(1a); 1164]   γεννάω
γεννῶσα   pres act ptcp nom sg fem
  [Ga 4:24; v-1d(1a); 1164]   "
γεννῶσιν   pres act ind 3 pl
  [2Ti 2:23; v-1d(1a); 1164]   "
γένοιτο   aor mid opt 3 sg
  [17t; v-1c(2); 1181]   γίνομαι
γενόμενα   aor mid ptcp acc pl neut
  [7t; v-1c(2); 1181]   "
γενόμεναι   aor mid ptcp nom pl fem
  [4t; v-1c(2); 1181]   "
γενομένην   aor mid ptcp acc sg fem
  [4t; v-1c(2); 1181]   "
γενομένης   aor mid ptcp gen sg fem
  [33t; v-1c(2); 1181]   "
γενόμενοι   aor mid ptcp nom pl masc
  [6t; v-1c(2); 1181]   "
γενομένοις   aor mid ptcp dat pl masc
  [2t; v-1c(2); 1181]   "
γενομένοις   aor mid ptcp dat pl neut
  [Mt 14:6; v-1c(2); 1181]   "
γενόμενον   aor mid ptcp acc sg masc
  [3t; v-1c(2); 1181]   "
γενόμενον   aor mid ptcp acc sg neut
  [2t; v-1c(2); 1181]   "
γενόμενος   aor mid ptcp nom sg masc
  [26t; v-1c(2); 1181]   "
γενομένου   aor mid ptcp gen sg masc
  [5t; v-1c(2); 1181]   "
γενομένου   aor mid ptcp gen sg neut
  [2t; v-1c(2); 1181]   "
γενομένων   aor mid ptcp gen pl masc
  [Ac 21:17; v-1c(2); 1181]   "
γενομένων   aor mid ptcp gen pl fem
  [Lk 24:5; v-1c(2); 1181]   "
γενομένων   aor mid ptcp gen pl neut
  [Hb 9:11; v-1c(2); 1181]   "

γένος, ους, τό   {1169, n-3d(2b)}
  offspring, progeny, Acts 17:28, 29; *family, kindred,
  lineage,* Acts 7:13, et al.; *race, nation, people,*
  Mark 7:26; Acts 4:36, et al.; *kind, sort, species,*
  Matt 13:47, et al.

γένος   nom sg neut [5t; n-3d(2b); 1169]   γένος
γένος   acc sg neut [2t; n-3d(2b); 1169]   "
γένους   gen sg neut [5t; n-3d(2b); 1169]   "
γένωμαι   aor mid subj 1 sg
  [2t; v-1c(2); 1181]   γίνομαι
γενώμεθα   aor mid subj 1 pl
  [2C 5:21; v-1c(2); 1181]   "
γένωνται   aor mid subj 3 pl [4t; v-1c(2); 1181]   "

Γερασηνός, ή, όν   {1170, a-1a(2a)}
  also spelled Γεργεσηνός, *from Gerasene,*
  belonging to the city of Gerasa, Mark 5:1; Luke
  8:26, 37; v.l. for Γαδαρηνός at Matt 8:28 v.l.

Γερασηνῶν   gen pl masc
  [3t; a-1a(2a); 1170]   Γερασηνός

Γεργεσηνός, η, ον   {1171, a-1a(2a)}
  see Γερασηνός, v.l. at Matt 8:28, Mark 5:1, and Luke
  8:26, 37*

γερουσία, ας, ή   {1172, n-1a}
  a senate, assembly of elders; the elders of Israel
  collectively, Acts 5:21*

γερουσίαν   acc sg fem
  [Ac 5:21; n-1a; 1172]   γερουσία

γέρων, οντος, ό   {1173, n-3c(5b)}
  an old man, John 3:4*

γέρων   nom sg masc [Jn 3:4; n-3c(5b); 1173]   γέρων

γεύομαι   {1174, v-1a(6)}
  [γεύσομαι, ἐγευσάμην, -, -, -] *to taste,* Matt 27:34;
  John 2:9; absol. *to take food,* Acts 10:10, et al.;
  met. *to have perception of, experience,* Heb 6:4, 5;
  1 Peter 2:3; θανάτου γεύεσθαι, *to experience
  death, to die,* Matt 16:28, et al.

γευσάμενος   aor mid ptcp nom sg masc
  [2t; v-1a(6); 1174]   γεύομαι
γευσαμένους   aor mid ptcp acc pl masc
  [2t; v-1a(6); 1174]   "
γεύσασθαι   aor mid inf [2t; v-1a(6); 1174]   "
γεύσεται   fut mid ind 3 sg
  [Lk 14:24; v-1a(6); 1174]   "
γεύσῃ   aor mid subj 2 sg
  [Cl 2:21; v-1a(6); 1174]   "
γεύσηται   aor mid subj 3 sg [2t; v-1a(6); 1174] "
γεύσωνται   aor mid subj 3 pl [3t; v-1a(6); 1174] "
γεωργεῖται   pres pass ind 3 sg
  [Hb 6:7; v-1d(2a); 1175]   γεωργέω

γεωργέω   {1175, v-1d(2a)}
  [-, -, -, -, -] *to cultivate, till the earth,* Heb 6:7*

γεώργιον, ου, τν   {1176, n-2c}
  cultivated field or *ground, a farm,* 1 Cor 3:9*

γεώργιον   nom sg neut
  [1C 3:9; n-2c; 1176]   γεώργιον
γεωργοί   nom pl masc [5t; n-2a; 1177]   γεωργός
γεωργοῖς   dat pl masc [5t; n-2a; 1177]   "
γεωργόν   acc sg masc [2Ti 2:6; n-2a; 1177]   "

γεωργός, ου, ό   {1177, n-2a}
  a farmer, one who tills the earth, 2 Tim 2:6; James
  5:7; in N.T. spc. *a vine-dresser, keeper of a
  vineyard,* i.q. ἀμπελουργός, Matt 21:33, 34, et al.

γεωργός   nom sg masc [2t; n-2a; 1177]   "
γεωργούς   acc pl masc [5t; n-2a; 1177]   "
γεωργῶν   gen pl masc [Mk 12:2; n-2a; 1177]   "

γῆ, ῆς, ή   {1178, n-1h}
  earth, soil, Matt 13:5; Mark 4:8, et al.; *the ground,
  surface of the earth,* Matt 10:29; Luke 6:49, et al.;
  the land, as opposed to the sea or a lake, Luke
  5:11; John 21:8, 9, 11; *the earth, world,* Matt 5:18,
  35, et al.; by synec. *the inhabitants of the earth,*
  Matt 5:13; 6:10; 10:34; *a land, region, tract,
  country, territory,* Matt 2:20; 14:34; by way of
  eminence, *the* chosen *land,* Matt 5:5; 24:30;
  27:45; Eph 6:3; *the inhabitants of a region* or
  country, Matt 10:15; 11:24, et al.

γῆ   nom sg fem [23t; n-1h; 1178]   γῆ

γῆ   voc sg fem [Mt 2:6; n-1h; 1178]   "
γῆ   dat sg fem [13t; n-1h; 1178]   "
γήμας   aor act ptcp nom sg masc
     [Mt 22:25; v-1d(2a); 1138]   γαμέω
γήμῃ   aor act subj 3 sg
     [1C 7:28; v-1d(2a); 1138]   "
γῆν   acc sg fem [78t; n-1h; 1178]   γῆ

γῆρας, ρως, τό   {1179, n-3d(1)}
     gen. also in ρους, *old age,* Luke 1:36*

γηράσῃς   aor act subj 2 sg
     [Jn 21:18; v-5a; 1180]   γηράσκω
γηράσκον   pres act ptcp nom sg neut
     [Hb 8:13; v-5a; 1180]

γηράσκω   {1180, v-5a}
     [-, ἐγήρασα, γεγήρακα, -, -] *to be* or *become old,*
     John 21:18; Heb 8:13*

γήρει   dat sg neut [Lk 1:36; n-3d(1); 1179]   γῆρας
γῆς   gen sg fem [135t; n-1h; 1178]   γῆ
γίνεσθαι   pres mid inf
     [9t; v-1c(2); 1181]   γίνομαι
γίνεσθε   pres mid imperative 2 pl
     [25t; v-1c(2); 1181]   "
γινέσθω   pres mid imperative 3 sg
     [7t; v-1c(2); 1181]   "
γίνεται   pres mid ind 3 sg [26t; v-1c(2); 1181]   "

γίνομαι   {1181, v-1c(2)}
     [(ἐγινόμην), γενήσομαι, ἐγενόμην, γέγονα,
     γεγένημαι, ἐγενήθην] pluperfect, ἐγενόει (3rd
     sg), *to come into existence; to be created, exist by
     creation,* John 1:3, 10; Heb 11:3; James 3:9; *to be
     born, produced, grow,* Matt 21:19; John 8:58, et
     al.; *to arise, come on, occur,* as the phenomena of
     nature, etc.; Matt 8:24, 26; 9:16, et al.; *to come,
     approach,* as morning or evening, Matt 8:16;
     14:15, 23; *to be appointed, constituted, established,*
     Mark 2:27; Gal 3:17, et al.; *to take place, come to
     pass, happen, occur,* Matt 1:22; 24:6, 20, 21, 34, et
     al. freq.; *to be done, performed, effected,* Matt
     21:42, et al.; *to be fulfilled, satisfied,* Matt 6:10;
     26:42, et al.; *to come into a particular state* or
     condition; to become, assume the character and
     appearance of anything, Matt 5:45; 02:45, et al.;
     to become or *be made anything, be changed* or
     converted, Matt 4:3; 21:42; Mark 1:17, et al.; *to be,*
     Matt 11:26; 19:8; γίνεσθαι ὑπό τινα, *to be subject
     to,* Gal 4:4; γίνεσθαι ἐν ἑαυτῷ, *to come to one's
     self, to recover from a trance* or *surprise,* Acts
     12:11; μὴ γένοιτο, *let it not be, far be it from, God
     forbid,* Luke 20:16; Rom 3:4, 31, et al.; *to be kept,
     celebrated, solemnized,* as festivals, Matt 26:2, et
     al.; *to be finished, completed,* Heb 4:3

γινόμενα   pres mid ptcp acc pl neut
     [4t; v-1c(2); 1181]   "
γινόμεναι   pres mid ptcp nom pl fem
     [Mk 6:2; v-1c(2); 1181]   "
γινομένας   pres mid ptcp acc pl fem
     [Ac 8:13; v-1c(2); 1181]   "
γινομένη   pres mid ptcp nom sg fem
     [Ac 12:5; v-1c(2); 1181]   "
γινομένῃ   pres mid ptcp dat sg fem
     [1P 4:12; v-1c(2); 1181]   "

γινομένης   pres mid ptcp gen sg fem
     [Ac 23:10; v-1c(2); 1181]   "
γινόμενοι   pres mid ptcp nom pl masc
     [2t; v-1c(2); 1181]   "
γινομένοις   pres mid ptcp dat pl neut
     [Lk 13:17; v-1c(2); 1181]   "
γινόμενον   pres mid ptcp nom sg neut
     [Ac 12:9; v-1c(2); 1181]   "
γινόμενον   pres mid ptcp acc sg masc
     [Jn 6:19; v-1c(2); 1181]   "
γινόμενον   pres mid ptcp acc sg neut
     [2t; v-1c(2); 1181]   "
γινομένου   pres mid ptcp gen sg neut
     [Jn 13:2; v-1c(2); 1181]   "
γινομένων   pres mid ptcp gen pl neut
     [Ac 24:2; v-1c(2); 1181]   "
γίνου   pres mid imperative 2 sg
     [5t; v-1c(2); 1181]   "
γινώμεθα   pres mid subj 1 pl [2t; v-1c(2); 1181]   "
γίνωνται   pres mid subj 3 pl
     [1C 16:2; v-1c(2); 1181]   "
γίνωσκε   pres act imperative 2 sg
     [2Ti 3:1; v-5a; 1182]   γινώσκω
γινώσκει   pres act ind 3 sg [12t; v-5a; 1182]   "
γινώσκειν   pres act inf [2t; v-5a; 1182]   "
γινώσκεις   pres act ind 2 sg [7t; v-5a; 1182]   "
γινώσκεται   pres pass ind 3 sg [2t; v-5a; 1182]   "
γινώσκετε   pres act imperative 2 pl
     [6t; v-5a; 1182]   "
γινώσκετε   pres act ind 2 pl [16t; v-5a; 1182]   "
γινωσκέτω   pres act imperative 3 sg
     [3t; v-5a; 1182]   "
γινώσκῃ   pres act subj 3 sg
     [Jn 17:23; v-5a; 1182]   "
γινώσκητε   pres act subj 2 pl
     [Jn 10:38; v-5a; 1182]   "
γινώσκομεν   pres act ind 1 pl [9t; v-5a; 1182]   "
γινωσκομένη   pres pass ptcp nom sg fem
     [2C 3:2; v-5a; 1182]   "
γινώσκοντες   pres act ptcp nom pl masc
     [6t; v-5a; 1182]   "
γινώσκουσι   pres act ind 3 pl
     [Jn 10:14; v-5a; 1182]   "
γινώσκουσιν   pres act ptcp dat pl masc
     [Rm 7:1; v-5a; 1182]   "

γινώσκω   {1182, v-5a}
     [γνώσομαι, ἔγνων, ἔγνωκα, ἔγνωσμαι, ἐγνώσθην]
     to know, whether the action be inceptive or
     complete and settled; *to perceive,* Matt 22:18;
     Mark 5:29; 8:17; 12:12; Luke 8:46; *to mark,
     discern,* Matt 25:24; Luke 19:44; *to ascertain by
     examination,* Mark 6:38; John 7:51; Acts 23:28; *to
     understand,* Mark 4:13; Luke 18:34; John 12:16;
     13:7; Acts 8:30; 1 Cor 14:7, 9; *to acknowledge,*
     Matt 7:23; 2 Cor 3:2; *to resolve, conclude,* Luke
     16:4; John 7:26; 17:8; *to be assured,* Luke 21:20;
     John 6:69; 8:52; 2 Peter 1:20; *to be skilled, to be
     master of* a thing, Matt 16:3; Acts 21:37; *to know
     carnally,* Matt 1:25; Luke 1:34; from the
     Hebrew, *to view with favor,* 1 Cor 8:3; Gal 4:9

γινώσκω   pres act ind 1 sg [7t; v-5a; 1182]   "

γινώσκωμεν   pres act subj 1 pl
    [1J 5:20; v-5a; 1182]   "
γινώσκων   pres act ptcp nom sg masc
    [2t; v-5a; 1182]   "
γινώσκωσιν   pres act subj 3 pl
    [Jn 17:3; v-5a; 1182]   "

γλεῦκος, ους, τό   {1183, n-3d(2b)}
    pr. *the unfermented juice of grapes;* hence, *sweet new wine,* Acts 2:13*

γλεύκους   gen sg neut
    [Ac 2:13; n-3d(2b); 1183]   γλεῦκος
γλυκύ   nom sg neut [2t; a-2b; 1184]   γλυκύς
γλυκύ   acc sg neut [2t; a-2b; 1184]   "

γλυκύς, εῖα, ύ   {1184, a-2b}
    sweet, James 3:11-12; Rev 10:9, 10*

γλῶσσα, ης, ἡ   {1185, n-1c}
    the tongue, Mark 7:33, 35, et al.; meton. *speech, talk,* 1 John 3:18; *a tongue, language,* Acts 2:11; 1 Cor 13:1, et al.; meton. *a language not proper to a speaker, a gift* or *faculty of such language,* Mark 16:17; 1 Cor 14:13, 14, 26, et al.; from Hebrew, *a nation,* as defined by its language, Rev 5:9, et al.; let. *a tongue-shaped flale,* Acts 2:3

γλῶσσα   nom sg fem [7t; n-1c; 1185]   γλῶσσα
γλῶσσαι   nom pl fem [4t; n-1c; 1185]   "
γλώσσαις   dat pl fem [15t; n-1c; 1185]   "
γλῶσσαν   acc sg fem [7t; n-1c; 1185]   "
γλώσσας   acc pl fem [Rv 16:10; n-1c; 1185]   "
γλώσσῃ   dat sg fem [7t; n-1c; 1185]   "
γλώσσης   gen sg fem [4t; n-1c; 1185]   "

γλωσσόκομον, ου, τό   {1186, n-2c}
    pr. *a box for keeping the tongues, mouth-pieces,* or *reeds* of musical instruments; hence, genr. *any box* or *receptacle;* in N.T. *a purse, money-bag,* John 12:6; 13:29*

γλωσσόκομον   acc sg neut
    [2t; n-2c; 1186]   γλωσσόκομον
γλωσσῶν   gen pl fem [5t; n-1c; 1185]   γλῶσσα

γναφεύς, έως, ὁ   {1187, n-3e(3)}
    a fuller, a bleacher, Mark 9:3*

γναφεύς   nom sg masc
    [Mk 9:3; n-3e(3); 1187]   γναφεύς
γνήσιε   voc sg masc
    [Pp 4:3; a-1a(1); 1188]   γνήσιος
γνήσιον   acc sg neut [2C 8:8; a-1a(1); 1188]   "

γνήσιος, α, ον   {1188, a-1a(1)}
    lawful, legitimate, as children; *genuine,* in faith, etc.; 1 Tim 1:2; Titus 1:4; *true, sincere,* 2 Cor 8:8; Phil 4:3*

γνησίῳ   dat sg neut [2t; a-1a(1); 1188]   "

γνησίως   {1189, adverb}
    genuinely, sincerely, Phil 2:20*

γνησίως   adverb [Pp 2:20; adverb; 1189]   γνησίως
γνοῖ   aor act subj 3 sg [3t; v-5a; 1182]   γινώσκω
γνόντα   aor act ptcp acc sg masc
    [2C 5:21; v-5a; 1182]   "
γνόντες   aor act ptcp nom pl masc
    [5t; v-5a; 1182]   "

γνούς   aor act ptcp nom sg masc
    [12t; v-5a; 1182]   "

γνόφος, ου, ὁ   {1190, n-2a}
    a thick cloud, darkness, Heb 12:18*

γνόφῳ   dat sg masc [Hb 12:18; n-2a; 1190]   γνόφος
γνῶ   aor act subj 1 sg
    [2C 2:9; v-5a; 1182]   γινώσκω
γνῷ   aor act subj 3 sg [3t; v-5a; 1182]   "
γνῶθι   aor act imperative 2 sg
    [Hb 8:11; v-5a; 1182]   "

γνώμη, ης, ἡ   {1191, n-1b}
    the mind, as the means of knowing and judging; *assent,* Phil 14; *purpose, resolution,* Acts 20:3; *opinion, judgment,* 1 Cor 1:10; 7:40; *suggestion, suggested advice,* as distinguished from positive injunction, 1 Cor 7:25; 2 Cor 8:10; Acts 4:18 v.l.; 20:3

γνώμη   dat sg fem [1C 1:10; n-1b; 1191]   γνώμη
γνώμην   acc sg fem [6t; n-1b; 1191]   "
γνώμης   gen sg fem [2t; n-1b; 1191]   "
γνῶναι   aor act inf [15t; v-5a; 1182]   γινώσκω
γνωριζέσθω   pres pass imperative 3 sg
    [Pp 4:6; v-2a(1); 1192]   γνωρίζω
γνωρίζομεν   pres act ind 1 pl
    [2C 8:1; v-2a(1); 1192]   "

γνωρίζω   {1192, v-2a(1)}
    [γνωρίσω, ἐγνώρισα, -, -, ἐγνωρίσθην] *to make known, reveal, declare,* John 15:15; 17:26, et al.; *to know,* Acts 7:13 v.l.; Phil 1:22

γνωρίζω   pres act ind 1 sg [4t; v-2a(1); 1192]   "

γνώριμος, ον   {1193, a-3a}
    acquainted with, known, John 18:16 v.l.*

γνωρίσαι   aor act inf [3t; v-2a(1); 1192]   "
γνωρίσας   aor act ptcp nom sg masc
    [Ep 1:9; v-2a(1); 1192]   "
γνωρίσει   fut act ind 3 sg [2t; v-2a(1); 1192]   "
γνωρίσῃ   aor act subj 3 sg
    [Rm 9:23; v-2a(1); 1192]   "
γνωρισθέντος   aor pass ptcp gen sg neut
    [Rm 16:26; v-2a(1); 1192]   "
γνωρισθῇ   aor pass subj 3 sg
    [Ep 3:10; v-2a(1); 1192]   "
γνωρίσουσιν   fut act ind 3 pl
    [Cl 4:9; v-2a(1); 1192]   "
γνωρίσω   fut act ind 1 sg
    [Jn 17:26; v-2a(1); 1192]   "
γνῷς   aor act subj 2 sg
    [Rv 3:3; v-5a; 1182]   γινώσκω
γνώσει   dat sg fem [8t; n-3e(5b); 1194]   γνῶσις
γνώσεσθε   fut mid ind 2 pl
    [6t; v-5a; 1182]   γινώσκω
γνώσεται   fut mid ind 3 sg [Jn 7:17; v-5a; 1182]   "
γνώσεως   gen sg fem [12t; n-3e(5b); 1194]   γνῶσις
γνώσῃ   fut mid ind 2 sg
    [Jn 13:7; v-5a; 1182]   γινώσκω
γνωσθέντες   aor pass ptcp nom pl masc
    [Ga 4:9; v-5a; 1182]   "
γνωσθῇ   aor pass subj 3 sg [Lk 8:17; v-5a; 1182]   "
γνωσθήσεται   fut pass ind 3 sg [4t; v-5a; 1182]   "

γνωσθήτω   aor pass imperative 3 sg
   [Pp 4:5; v-5a; 1182]   "
γνῶσιν   acc sg fem [6t; n-3e(5b); 1194]   γνῶσις
γνῶσιν   aor act subj 3 pl
   [Rv 3:9; v-5a; 1182]   γινώσκω

γνῶσις, εως, ἡ   {1194, n-3e(5b)}
   knowledge, Luke 1:77; knowledge of an especial
   kind and relatively high character, Luke 11:52;
   Rom 2:20; 1 Tim 6:20; more particularly in
   respect of Christian enlightenment, Rom 15:14;
   1 Cor 8:10; 12:8; 2 Cor 11:6, et al.

γνῶσις   nom sg fem [3t; n-3e(5b); 1194]   γνῶσις
γνώσομαι   fut mid ind 1 sg
   [2t; v-5a; 1182]   γινώσκω
γνωσόμεθα   fut mid ind 1 pl [1J 3:19; v-5a; 1182] "
γνώσονται   fut mid ind 3 pl [3t; v-5a; 1182]   "
γνωστά   acc pl neut
   [Ac 15:18; a-1a(2a); 1196]   γνωστός
γνώστην   acc sg masc [Ac 26:3; n-1f; 1195]   γνώστης

γνώστης, ου, ὁ   {1195, n-1f}
   one acquainted with a thing, knowing, skilful, Acts
   26:3*

γνωστοί   nom pl masc
   [Lk 23:49; a-1a(2a); 1196]   γνωστός
γνωστοῖς   dat pl masc [Lk 2:44; a-1a(2a); 1196]   "
γνωστόν   nom sg neut [10t; a-1a(2a); 1196]   "

γνωστός, ἡ, όν   {1196, a-1a(2a)}
   known, John 18:15, 16, et al.; certain,
   incontrovertible, Acts 4:16; τὸ γνωστόν, that which
   is known or is cognizable, the unquestionable
   attributes, Rom 1:19; subst. an acquaintance,
   Luke 2:44; 23:49

γνωστός   nom sg masc [2t; a-1a(2a); 1196]   "
γνῶτε   aor act imperative 2 pl
   [Lk 21:20; v-5a; 1182]   γινώσκω
γνῶτε   aor act subj 2 pl [5t; v-5a; 1182]   "
γνώτω   aor act imperative 3 sg
   [Mt 6:3; v-5a; 1182]   "
γογγύζετε   pres act imperative 2 pl
   [2t; v-2a(1); 1197]   γογγύζω
γογγύζοντος   pres act ptcp gen sg masc
   [Jn 7:32; v-2a(1); 1197]   "
γογγύζουσιν   pres act ind 3 pl
   [Jn 6:61; v-2a(1); 1197]   "

γογγύζω   {1197, v-2a(1)}
   [(ἐγόγγυζον), γογγύσω, ἐγόγγυσα, -, -, -] to speak
   privately and in a low voice, mutter, John 7:32; to
   utter secret and sullen discontent, express
   indignant complaint, murmur, grumble, Matt
   20:11; Luke 5:30; John 6:41, 43, 61; 1 Cor 10:10*

γογγυσμός, οῦ, ὁ   {1198, n-2a}
   a muttering, murmuring, low and suppressed
   discourse, John 7:12; the expression of secret and
   sullen discontent, murmuring, complaint, Acts
   6:1; Phil 2:14; 1 Peter 4:9*

γογγυσμός   nom sg masc [2t; n-2a; 1198] γογγυσμός
γογγυσμοῦ   gen sg masc [1P 4:9; n-2a; 1198]   "
γογγυσμῶν   gen pl masc [Pp 2:14; n-2a; 1198]   "
γογγυσταί   nom pl masc
   [Jd 16; n-1f; 1199]   γογγυστής

γογγυστής, οῦ, ὁ   {1199, n-1f}
   a murmurer, grumbler, Jude 16*

γόης, ητος, ὁ   {1200, n-3c(1)}
   a juggler, diviner; hence, by impl. an impostor,
   cheat, 2 Tim 3:13*

γόητες   nom pl masc [2Ti 3:13; n-3c(1); 1200]   γόης

Γολγοθᾶ, ἡ   {1201, n-3g(1)}
   Golgotha, pr. name, Matt 27:33; Mark 15:22;
   John 19:17*

Γολγοθᾶ   indecl [3t; n-3g(1); 1201]   Γολγοθᾶ
γόμον   acc sg masc [3t; n-2a; 1203]   γόμος

Γόμορρα, ων, τα or ας, ἡ   {1202, n-2c}
   Gomorrha (Genesis 19), pr. name, Matt 10:15;
   Mark 6:11 v.l.; Rom 9:29; 2 Peter 2:6; Jude 7*

Γόμορρα   nom sg fem [2t; n-2c; 1202]   Γόμορρα
Γομόρρας   gen sg fem [2P 2:6; n-2c; 1202]   "
Γομόρρων   gen pl neut [Mt 10:15; n-2c; 1202]   "

γόμος, ου, ὁ   {1203, n-2a}
   the cargo of a ship, Acts 21:3; by impl.
   merchandise, Rev 18:11, 12*

γόνασιν   dat pl neut [Lk 5:8; n-3c(6d); 1205]   γόνυ
γόνατα   acc pl neut [8t; n-3c(6d); 1205]   "
γονεῖς   nom pl masc [9t; n-3e(3); 1204]   γονεύς
γονεῖς   acc pl masc [5t; n-3e(3); 1204]   "

γονεύς, έως, ὁ   {1204, n-3e(3)}
   a father; pl. in N.T. parents, Matt 10:21; Luke
   2:27, 41; 2 Cor 12:14

γονεῦσιν   dat pl masc [5t; n-3e(3); 1204]   "
γονέων   gen pl masc [Lk 21:16; n-3e(3); 1204]   "

γόνυ, ατος, τό   {1205, n-3c(6d)}
   the knee, Luke 22:41; Heb 12:12, et al.

γόνυ   nom sg neut [2t; n-3c(6d); 1205]   γόνυ
γόνυ   acc sg neut [Rm 11:4; n-3c(6d); 1205]   "

γονυπετέω   {1206, v-1d(2a)}
   [-, ἐγονυπέτησα, -, -, -] to fall upon one's knees, to
   kneel before, Matt 17:14; 27:29; Mark 1:40; 10:17*

γονυπετήσαντες   aor act ptcp nom pl masc
   [Mt 27:29; v-1d(2a); 1206]   γονυπετέω
γονυπετήσας   aor act ptcp nom sg masc
   [Mk 10:17; v-1d(2a); 1206]   "
γονυπετῶν   pres act ptcp nom sg masc
   [2t; v-1d(2a); 1206]   "

γράμμα, ατος, τό   {1207, n-3c(4)}
   pr. that which is written or drawn; a letter,
   character of the alphabet, a writing, book, John
   5:47; an acknowledgment of debt, an account, a bill,
   note, Luke 16:6, 7; an epistle, letter, Acts 28:21;
   Gal 6:11; ἱερὰ γράμματα, Holy writ, the sacred
   books of the Old Testament, the Jewish Scriptures, 2
   Tim 3:15; spc. the letter of the law of Moses, the
   bare literal sense, Rom 2:27, 29; 7:6; 2 Cor 3:6, 7;
   pl. letters, learning, John 7:15; Acts 26:24*

γράμμα   nom sg neut [2C 3:6; n-3c(4); 1207] γράμμα
γράμμασιν   dat pl neut [3t; n-3c(4); 1207]   "
γράμματα   nom pl neut [Ac 26:24; n-3c(4); 1207] "
γράμματα   acc pl neut [5t; n-3c(4); 1207]   "

γραμματεῖς nom pl masc
[28t; n-3e(3); 1208] γραμματεύς
γραμματεῖς voc pl masc [6t; n-3e(3); 1208] "
γραμματεῖς acc pl masc [5t; n-3e(3); 1208] "

γραμματεύς, έως, ὁ {1208, n-3e(3)}
a scribe; a clerk, town-clerk, registrar, recorder,
Acts 19:35; *one skilled in the Jewish law, a teacher*
or *interpreter of the law,* Matt 2:4; 5:20, et al. freq.;
genr. *a religious teacher,* Matt 13:52; by synec.
any one distinguished for learning or *wisdom,* 1
Cor 1:20

γραμματεύς nom sg masc [5t; n-3e(3); 1208] "
γραμματεῦσιν dat pl masc [2t; n-3e(3); 1208] "
γραμματέων gen pl masc [17t; n-3e(3); 1208] "
γράμματι dat sg neut
[Rm 2:29; n-3c(4); 1207] γράμμα
γράμματος gen sg neut [3t; n-3c(4); 1207] "
γραπτόν acc sg neut
[Rm 2:15; a-1a(2a); 1209] γραπτός

γραπτός, ή, όν {1209, a-1a(2a)}
written, Rom 2:15*

γραφαί nom pl fem [3t; n-1b; 1210] γραφή
γραφαῖς dat pl fem [4t; n-1b; 1210] "
γραφάς acc pl fem [9t; n-1b; 1210] "
γράφε pres act imperative 2 sg
[Jn 19:21; v-1b(1); 1211] γράφω
γράφει pres act ind 3 sg
[Rm 10:5; v-1b(1); 1211] "
γράφειν pres act inf [7t; v-1b(1); 1211] "
γράφεσθαι pres pass inf
[1Th 5:1; v-1b(1); 1211] "

γραφή, ῆς, ἡ {1210, n-1b}
a writing; in N.T. *the Holy Scriptures, the Jewish
Scriptures,* or *Books of the Old Testament,* Matt
21:42; John 5:39, et al.; by synec. *doctrines,
declarations, oracles,* or *promises* contained in the
sacred books, Matt 22:29; Mark 12:24, et al.;
spc. *a prophecy,* Matt 26:54; Mark 14:49; Luke
4:21; 24:27, 32; with the addition of προφητική,
Rom 16:26; of τῶν προφητῶν, Matt 26:56

γραφή nom sg fem [21t; n-1b; 1210] γραφή
γραφῇ dat sg fem [2t; n-1b; 1210] "
γραφήν acc sg fem [4t; n-1b; 1210] "
γραφῆς gen sg fem [3t; n-1b; 1210] "
γράφηται pres pass subj 3 sg
[Jn 21:25; v-1b(1); 1211] γράφω
γράφομεν pres act ind 1 pl [2t; v-1b(1); 1211] "
γραφόμενα pres pass ptcp acc pl neut
[Jn 21:25; v-1b(1); 1211] "

γράφω {1211, v-1b(1)}
[(ἔγραφον), γράψω, ἔγραψα, γέγραφα, γέγραμμαι,
ἐγράφην] *to engrave, write,* according to the
ancient method of writing on plates of metal,
waxes tables, etc., John 8:6, 8; *to write* on
parchment, paper, etc., generally, Matt 27:37, et
al.; *to write letters to another,* Acts 23:25; 2 Cor
2:9; 13:10, et al.; *to describe in writing,* John 1:46;
Rom 10:5; *to inscribe* in a catalogue, etc., Luke
10:20; Rev 13:8; 17:8, et al.; *to write* a law,
command, or *enact in writing,* Mark 10:5; 12:19;
Luke 2:23, et al.

γράφω pres act ind 1 sg [13t; v-1b(1); 1211] "
γραφῶν gen pl fem [4t; n-1b; 1210] γραφή
γράφων pres act ptcp nom sg masc
[2J 5; v-1b(1); 1211] γράφω
γράψαι aor act inf [5t; v-1b(1); 1211] "
γράψαντες aor act ptcp nom pl masc
[Ac 15:23; v-1b(1); 1211] "
γράψας aor act ptcp nom sg masc
[3t; v-1b(1); 1211] "
γράψῃς aor act subj 2 sg
[Rv 10:4; v-1b(1); 1211] "
γράψον aor act imperative 2 sg
[14t; v-1b(1); 1211] "
γράψω aor act subj 1 sg
[Ac 25:26; v-1b(1); 1211] "
γράψω fut act ind 1 sg [Rv 3:12; v-1b(1); 1211] "
γραώδεις acc pl masc
[1Ti 4:7; a-4a; 1212] γραώδης

γραώδης, ες {1212, a-4a}
old-womanish; by impl. *silly, absurd,* 1 Tim 4:7*

γρηγορεῖτε pres act imperative 2 pl
[10t; v-1d(2a); 1213] γρηγορέω

γρηγορέω {1213, v-1d(2a)}
[-, ἐγρηγόρησα, -, -, -] *to be awake, to watch,* Matt
26:38, 40, 41; Mark 14:34; 37, 38; *to be alive,* 1
Thess 5:10; met. *to be watchful, attentive, vigilant,
circumspect,* Matt 25:13; Mark 13:35, et al.

γρηγορῇ pres act subj 3 sg
[Mk 13:34; v-1d(2a); 1213] "
γρηγορῆσαι aor act inf [2t; v-1d(2a); 1213] "
γρηγορήσατε aor act imperative 2 pl
[1P 5:8; v-1d(2a); 1213] "
γρηγορήσῃς aor act subj 2 sg
[Rv 3:3; v-1d(2a); 1213] "
γρηγοροῦντας pres act ptcp acc pl masc
[Lk 12:37; v-1d(2a); 1213] "
γρηγοροῦντες pres act ptcp nom pl masc
[Cl 4:2; v-1d(2a); 1213] "
γρηγορῶμεν pres act subj 1 pl
[2t; v-1d(2a); 1213] "
γρηγορῶν pres act ptcp nom sg masc
[2t; v-1d(2a); 1213] "
γυμνά nom pl neut
[Hb 4:13; a-1a(2a); 1218] γυμνός
γύμναζε pres act imperative 2 sg
[1Ti 4:7; v-2a(1); 1214] γυμνάζω

γυμνάζω {1214, v-2a(1)}
[-, -, -, γεγύμνασμαι, -] pr. *to train in gymnastic
discipline;* hence, *to exercise* in anything, *train to
use, discipline,* 1 Tim 4:7; Heb 5:14; 12:11; 2 Peter
2:14*

γυμνασία, ας, ἡ {1215, n-1a}
pr. *gymnastic exercise;* hence, *bodily discipline* of
any kind, 1 Tim 4:8*

γυμνασία nom sg fem
[1Ti 4:8; n-1a; 1215] γυμνασία
γυμνήν acc sg fem
[Rv 17:16; a-1a(2a); 1218] γυμνός
γυμνιτεύομεν pres act ind 1 pl
[1C 4:11; v-1a(6); 1217] γυμνιτεύω

γυμνητεύω, v.l. for γυμνιτεύω   {1216, v-1a(6)}

γυμνιτεύω   {1217, v-1a(6)}
[-, -, -, -, -] *to be poorly clad*, 1 Cor 4:11*

γυμνοί nom pl masc [2t; a-1a(2a); 1218] γυμνός
γυμνόν acc sg masc [3t; a-1a(2a); 1218]   "

γυμνός, ή, όν   {1218, a-1a(2a)}
naked, without clothing, Mark 14:51, 52; *without
the upper garment, and clad only with an inner
garment* or *tunic*, John 21:7; *poorly* or *meanly
clad, destitute of proper and sufficient clothing*,
Matt 25:36, 38, 43, 44; Acts 19:16; James 2:15;
met. *unclothed* with a body, 2 Cor 5:3; *not
covered, uncovered, open, manifest*, Heb 4:13; *bare,
mere*, 1 Cor 15:37; *naked of* spiritual *clothing*, Rev
3:17; 16:15; 17:16

γυμνός nom sg masc [6t; a-1a(2a); 1218]   "

γυμνότης, ητος, ή   {1219, n-3c(1)}
nakedness; want of proper and sufficient clothing,
Rom 8:35; 2 Cor 11:27; spiritual *nakedness, being
destitute of* spiritual *clothing*, Rev 3:18*

γυμνότης nom sg fem
   [Rm 8:35; n-3c(1); 1219]   γυμνότης
γυμνότητι dat sg fem [2C 11:27; n-3c(1); 1219]   "
γυμνότητος gen sg fem [Rv 3:18; n-3c(1); 1219]   "
γυμνοῦ gen sg neut
   [Mk 14:51; a-1a(2a); 1218]   γυμνός
γυμνούς acc pl masc [Ac 19:16; a-1a(2a); 1218]   "
γύναι voc sg fem [10t; n-3b(1); 1222]   γυνή
γυναῖκα acc sg fem [52t; n-3b(1); 1222]   "
γυναικάρια acc pl neut
   [2Ti 3:6; n-2c; 1220]   γυναικάριον

γυναικάριον, ου, τό   {1220, n-2c}
a little woman; a trifling, weak, silly woman, 2 Tim
3:6*

γυναῖκας acc pl fem [11t; n-3b(1); 1222]   γυνή

γυναικεῖος, α, ον   {1221, a-1a(1)}
pertaining to women, female, 1 Peter 3:7*

γυναικείῳ dat sg neut
   [1P 3:7; a-1a(1); 1221]   γυναικεῖος
γυναῖκες nom pl fem [12t; n-3b(1); 1222]   γυνή
γυναῖκες voc pl fem [3t; n-3b(1); 1222]   "
γυναικί dat sg fem [15t; n-3b(1); 1222]   "
γυναικός gen sg fem [22t; n-3b(1); 1222]   "
γυναικῶν gen pl fem [11t; n-3b(1); 1222]   "
γυναιξί dat pl fem [Ac 21:5; n-3b(1); 1222]   "
γυναιξίν dat pl fem [5t; n-3b(1); 1222]   "

γυνή, αικος, ή   {1222, n-3b(1)}
a woman, Matt 5:28, et al.; *a married woman,
wife*, Matt 5:31, 32; 14:3, et al.; in the voc. ὦ
γύναι, *O woman!* an ordinary mode of
addressing females under every circumstance;
met. used of the Church, as united to Christ,
Rev 19:7; 21:9

γυνή nom sg fem [73t; n-3b(1); 1222]   "

Γώγ, ὁ   {1223, n-3g(2)}
Gog, pr. name of a nation, indecl., Rev 20:8*

Γώγ indecl [Rv 20:8; n-3g(2); 1223]   Γώγ

γωνία, ας, ή   {1224, n-1a}
an exterior *angle, projecting corner*, Matt 6:5;
21:42; *an* interior *angle;* by impl. *a dark corner,
obscure place*, Acts 26:26; *corner, extremity*, or
quarter of the earth, Rev 7:1; 20:8

γωνίᾳ dat sg fem [Ac 26:26; n-1a; 1224]   γωνία
γωνίαις dat pl fem [2t; n-1a; 1224]   "
γωνίας gen sg fem [5t; n-1a; 1224]   γωνία
γωνίας acc pl fem [Rv 7:1; n-1a; 1224]   "

δ

δ' particle [24t; particle; 1254]   δέ

Δαβίδ, see Δαυίδαυίδ   {1226}

δαίμονες nom pl masc
   [Mt 8:31; n-3f(1b); 1230]   δαίμων
δαιμόνια nom pl neut [8t; n-2c; 1228]   δαιμόνιον
δαιμόνια acc pl neut [24t; n-2c; 1228]   "
δαιμονίζεται pres pass ind 3 sg
   [Mt 15:22; v-2a(1); 1227]   δαιμονίζομαι

δαιμονίζομαι   {1227, v-2a(1)}
[-, -, -, -, ἐδαιμονίσθην] in N.T. *to be possessed,
afflicted, vexed, by a demon* or *evil spirit*, i.q.
δαιμόνιον ἔχειν, Matt 4:24; 8:16, 28, 33

δαιμονιζόμενοι pres pass ptcp nom pl masc
   [Mt 8:28; v-2a(1); 1227]   "
δαιμονιζόμενον pres pass ptcp acc sg masc
   [2t; v-2a(1); 1227]   "
δαιμονιζόμενος pres mid ptcp nom sg masc
   [Mt 12:22; v-2a(1); 1227]   "
δαιμονιζομένου pres pass ptcp gen sg masc
   [Jn 10:21; v-2a(1); 1227]   "
δαιμονιζομένους pres pass ptcp acc pl masc
   [3t; v-2a(1); 1227]   "
δαιμονιζομένῳ pres pass ptcp dat sg masc
   [Mk 5:16; v-2a(1); 1227]   "
δαιμονιζομένων pres pass ptcp gen pl masc
   [Mt 8:33; v-2a(1); 1227]   "
δαιμονίοις dat pl neut
   [1C 10:20; n-2c; 1228]   δαιμόνιον

δαιμόνιον, ου, τό   {1228, n-2c}
a heathen god, deity, Acts 17:18; 1 Cor 10:20, 21;
Rev 9:20; in N.T., *a demon, evil spirit*, Matt 7:22;
9:33, 34; 10:8; 12:24

δαιμόνιον nom sg neut [5t; n-2c; 1228]   "
δαιμόνιον acc sg neut [10t; n-2c; 1228]   "
δαιμονίου gen sg neut [4t; n-2c; 1228]   "
δαιμονισθείς aor pass ptcp nom sg masc
   [2t; v-2a(1); 1227]   δαιμονίζομαι

δαιμονιώδης, ες   {1229, a-4a}
pertaining to or *proceeding from demons; demonic,
devilish*, James 3:15*

δαιμονιώδης nom sg fem
   [Jm 3:15; a-4a; 1229]   δαιμονιώδης
δαιμονίων gen pl neut [11t; n-2c; 1228]   δαιμόνιον

δαίμων, ονος, ὁ   {1230, n-3f(1b)}
a god, a superior power; in N.T. *a malignant*

demon, evil angel, Matt 8:31; Mark 5:12 v.l.; Luke 8:29; Rev 18:2 v.l.*

δάκνετε pres act ind 2 pl
[Ga 5:15; v-3a(1); 1231] δάκνω

δάκνω {1231, v-3a(1)}
[-, -, -, -, ἐδήχθην] *to bite, sting;* met. *to molest, vex, injure,* Gal 5:15*

δάκρυον, ου, τό {1232, n-2c}
also spelled δάκρυ, *a tear*

δάκρυον acc sg neut [2t; n-2c; 1232] δάκρυον
δάκρυσιν dat pl neut [2t; n-2c; 1232] "

δακρύω {1233, v-1a(4)}
[-, ἐδάκρυσα, -, -, -] *to shed tears, weep,* John 11:35*

δακρύων gen pl neut [6t; n-2c; 1232] "
δακτύλιον acc sg masc
[Lk 15:22; n-2a; 1234] δακτύλιος

δακτύλιος, ου, ὁ {1234, n-2a}
a ring for the finger, Luke 15:22*

δάκτυλον acc sg masc [2t; n-2a; 1235] δάκτυλος

δάκτυλος, ου, ὁ {1235, n-2a}
a finger, Matt 23:4; Mark 7:33; from Hebrew, *power,* Luke 11:20

δακτύλου gen sg masc [Lk 16:24; n-2a; 1235] "
δακτύλους acc pl masc [Mk 7:33; n-2a; 1235] "
δακτύλῳ dat sg masc [3t; n-2a; 1235] "
δακτύλων gen pl masc [Lk 11:46; n-2a; 1235] "

Δαλμανουθά, ἡ {1236, n-3g(2)}
Dalmanutha, indecl., a small town on the shore of the Sea of Tiberias, Mark 8:10*

Δαλμανουθά indecl
[Mk 8:10; n-3g(2); 1236] Δαλμανουθά

Δαλματία, ας, ἡ {1237, n-1a}
Dalmatia, 2 Tim 4:10*

Δαλματίαν acc sg fem
[2Ti 4:10; n-1a; 1237] Δαλματία
δαμάζεται pres pass ind 3 sg
[Jm 3:7; v-2a(1); 1238] δαμάζω

δαμάζω {1238, v-2a(1)}
[-, ἐδάμασα, -, δεδάμασμαι, -] also spelled δανείζω, *to subdue, tame,* Mark 5:4; James 3:7; met. *to restrain within proper limits,* James 3:8*

δαμάλεως gen sg fem
[Hb 9:13; n-3e(5b); 1239] δάμαλις

δάμαλις, εως, ἡ {1239, n-3e(5b)}
a heifer, young cow, Heb 9:13*

Δάμαρις, ιδος, ἡ {1240, n-3c(2)}
Damaris, pr. name, Acts 17:34*

Δάμαρις nom sg fem
[Ac 17:34; n-3c(2); 1240] Δάμαρις
δαμάσαι aor act inf [2t; v-2a(1); 1238] δαμάζω

Δαμασκηνός, ή, όν {1241, a-1a(2a)}
A Damascene, a native of Damascus, 2 Cor 11:32*

Δαμασκηνῶν gen pl masc
[2C 11:32; a-1a(2a); 1241] Δαμασκηνός

Δαμασκόν acc sg fem [7t; n-2b; 1242] Δαμασκός

Δαμασκός, οῦ, ἡ {1242, n-2b}
Damascus, the capital city of Syria

Δαμασκῷ dat sg fem [8t; n-2b; 1242] "

Δάν, ὁ {1243, n-3g(2)}
Dan (Genesis 30:6), pr. name, indecl., Rev 7:5 v.l.*

δανείζω, see δανίζω {1244, v-2a(1)}

δάνειον, ου, τό {1245, n-2c}
a loan, debt, Matt 18:27*

δάνειον acc sg neut
[Mt 18:27; n-2c; 1245] δάνειον

δανειστής, οῦ, ὁ, see δανιστής {1246, n-1f}

δανίζετε pres act imperative 2 pl
[Lk 6:35; v-2a(1); 1247] δανίζω
δανίζουσιν pres act ind 3 pl
[Lk 6:34; v-2a(1); 1247] "

δανίζω {1247, v-2a(1)}
[-, ἐδάνισα, -, -, -] *to lend money,* Luke 6:34 (2t), 35; mid. *to borrow money,* Matt 5:42*

Δανιήλ, ὁ {1248, n-3g(2)}
Daniel, pr. name, indecl., Matt 24:15; Mark 13:14 v.l.*

Δανιήλ indecl
[Mt 24:15; n-3g(2); 1248] Δανιήλ
δανίσασθαι aor mid inf
[Mt 5:42; v-2a(1); 1247] δανίζω
δανίσητε aor act subj 2 pl
[Lk 6:34; v-2a(1); 1247] "
δανιστῇ dat sg masc
[Lk 7:41; n-1f; 1250] δανιστής

δανιστής, ου, ὁ {1250, n-1f}
a money-lender, creditor, Luke 7:41*

δαπανάω {1251, v-1d(1a)}
[δαπανήσω, ἐδαπάνησα, -, -, ἐδαπανήθην] *to expend, be at expense,* Mark 5:26; Acts 21:24; 2 Cor 12:15; *to spend, waste, consume by extravagance,* Luke 15:14; James 4:3*

δαπάνη, ης, ἡ {1252, n-1b}
expense, cost, Luke 14:28*

δαπάνην acc sg fem [Lk 14:28; n-1b; 1252] δαπάνη
δαπανήσαντος aor act ptcp gen sg masc
[Lk 15:14; v-1d(1a); 1251] δαπανάω
δαπανήσασα aor act ptcp nom sg fem
[Mk 5:26; v-1d(1a); 1251] "
δαπανήσητε aor act subj 2 pl
[Jm 4:3; v-1d(1a); 1251] "
δαπάνησον aor act imperative 2 sg
[Ac 21:24; v-1d(1a); 1251] "
δαπανήσω fut act ind 1 sg
[2C 12:15; v-1d(1a); 1251] "
δαρήσεσθε fut pass ind 2 pl
[Mk 13:9; v-1c(1); 1296] δέρω
δαρήσεται fut pass ind 3 sg [2t; v-1c(1); 1296] "

Δαυίδ, ὁ {1253, n-3g(2)}
also spelled Δανείδ and Δαβίδ, *David,* pr. name,

indecl., Matt 1:6; Luke 1:27; Acts 2:29; Rom 1:3;
2 Tim 2:28

Δαυίδ   indecl [59t; n-3g(2); 1253]   Δαυίδ

δέ   {1254, particle}
a conjunctive particle, marking the
superaddition of a clause, whether in
opposition or in continuation, to what has
preceded, and it may be variously rendered
but, on the other hand, and, also, now, etc.; καὶ δέ,
when there is a special superaddition in
continuation, *too, yea,* etc. It sometimes is
found at the commencement of the apodosis of
a sentence, Acts 11:17. It serves also to mark
the resumption of an interrupted discourse, 2
Cor 2:10; Gal 2:6

δέ   particle [2768t; particle; 1254]   δέ
δεδάμασται   perf pass ind 3 sg
    [Jm 3:7; v-2a(1); 1238]   δαμάζω
δεδεκάτωκεν   perf act ind 3 sg
    [Hb 7:6; v-1d(3); 1282]   δεκατόω
δεδεκάτωται   perf pass ind 3 sg
    [Hb 7:9; v-1d(3); 1282]   "
δέδεκται   perf mid ind 3 sg
    [Ac 8:14; v-1b(2); 1312]   δέχομαι
δεδεκώς   perf act ptcp nom sg masc
    [Ac 22:29; v-1d(2b); 1313]   δέω
δέδεμαι   perf pass ind 1 sg
    [Cl 4:3; v-1d(2b); 1313]   "
δεδεμένα   perf pass ptcp nom pl neut
    [Mt 18:18; v-1d(2b); 1313]   "
δεδεμένην   perf pass ptcp acc sg fem
    [Mt 21:2; v-1d(2b); 1313]   "
δεδεμένον   perf pass ptcp nom sg neut
    [Mt 16:19; v-1d(2b); 1313]   "
δεδεμένον   perf pass ptcp acc sg masc
    [5t; v-1d(2b); 1313]   "
δεδεμένος   perf pass ptcp nom sg masc
    [4t; v-1d(2b); 1313]   "
δεδεμένους   perf pass ptcp acc pl masc
    [4t; v-1d(2b); 1313]   "
δέδεσαι   perf pass ind 2 sg
    [1C 7:27; v-1d(2b); 1313]   "
δεδέσθαι   perf pass inf [Mk 5:4; v-1d(2b); 1313] "
δέδεται   perf pass ind 3 sg [3t; v-1d(2b); 1313] "
δεδικαίωμαι   perf pass ind 1 sg
    [1C 4:4; v-1d(3); 1467]   δικαιόω
δεδικαιωμένος   perf pass ptcp nom sg masc
    [Lk 18:14; v-1d(3); 1467]   "
δεδικαίωται   perf pass ind 3 sg
    [Rm 6:7; v-1d(3); 1467]   "
δεδιωγμένοι   perf pass ptcp nom pl masc
    [Mt 5:10; v-1b(2); 1503]   διώκω
δεδοκιμάσμεθα   perf pass ind 1 pl
    [1Th 2:4; v-2a(1); 1507]   δοκιμάζω
δεδομένην   perf pass ptcp acc sg fem
    [2C 8:1; v-6a; 1443]   δίδωμι
δεδομένον   perf pass ptcp nom sg neut
    [4t; v-6a; 1443]   "
δεδόξασμαι   perf pass ind 1 sg
    [Jn 17:10; v-2a(1); 1519]   δοξάζω
δεδοξασμένη   perf pass ptcp dat sg fem
    [1P 1:8; v-2a(1); 1519]   "

δεδοξασμένον   perf pass ptcp nom sg neut
    [2C 3:10; v-2a(1); 1519]   "
δεδόξασται   perf pass ind 3 sg
    [2C 3:10; v-2a(1); 1519]   "
δέδοται   perf pass ind 3 sg
    [6t; v-6a; 1443]   δίδωμι
δεδουλεύκαμεν   perf act ind 1 pl
    [Jn 8:33; v-1a(6); 1526]   δουλεύω
δεδουλωμένας   perf pass ptcp acc pl fem
    [Ti 2:3; v-1d(3); 1530]   δουλόω
δεδουλωμένοι   perf pass ptcp nom pl masc
    [Ga 4:3; v-1d(3); 1530]   "
δεδούλωται   perf pass ind 3 sg
    [2t; v-1d(3); 1530]   "
δέδωκα   perf act ind 1 sg [5t; v-6a; 1443]   δίδωμι
δέδωκας   perf act ind 2 sg [11t; v-6a; 1443]   "
δεδώκει   pluperf act ind 3 sg [2t; v-6a; 1443]   "
δεδώκεισαν   pluperf act ind 3 pl
    [Jn 11:57; v-6a; 1443]   "
δέδωκεν   perf act ind 3 sg [13t; v-6a; 1443]   "
δεδωρημένης   perf mid ptcp gen sg fem
    [2P 1:3; v-1d(2a); 1563]   δωρέομαι
δεδώρηται   perf mid ind 3 sg
    [2P 1:4; v-1d(2a); 1563]   "
δέῃ   pres act subj 3 sg [2t; v-1d(2c); 1256]   δεῖ
δεηθέντων   aor pass ptcp gen pl masc
    [Ac 4:31; v-1d(2c); 1289]   δέομαι
δεήθητε   aor pass imperative 2 pl
    [3t; v-1d(2c); 1289]   "
δεήθητι   aor pass imperative 2 sg
    [Ac 8:22; v-1d(2c); 1289]   "
δεήσει   dat sg fem [5t; n-3e(5b); 1255]   δέησις
δεήσεις   acc pl fem [3t; n-3e(5b); 1255]   "
δεήσεσιν   dat pl fem [3t; n-3e(5b); 1255]   "
δεήσεως   gen sg fem [2t; n-3e(5b); 1255]   "
δέησιν   acc sg fem [2t; n-3e(5b); 1255]   "

δέησις, εως, ἡ   {1255, n-3e(5b)}
entreaty; prayer, supplication, Luke 1:13; 2:37;
5:33

δέησις   nom sg fem [3t; n-3e(5b); 1255]   "
δεθῆναι   aor pass inf [2t; v-1d(2b); 1313]   δέω

δεῖ   {1256, v-1d(2c)}
[(ἔδει), -, -, -, -, -] *it is binding, it is necessary, it is
proper; it is inevitable,* Acts 21:22

δεῖ   pres act ind 3 sg [77t; v-1d(2c); 1256]   δεῖ

δεῖγμα, ατος, τό   {1257, n-3c(4)}
pr. *that which is shown, a specimen, sample;* met.
an example by way of warning, Jude 7*

δεῖγμα   acc sg neut [Jd 7; n-3c(4); 1257]   δεῖγμα

δειγματίζω   {1258, v-2a(1)}
[-, ἐδειγμάτισα, -, -, -] *to make a public show* or
spectacle of, Matt 1:19; Col 2:15*

δειγματίσαι   aor act inf
    [Mt 1:19; v-2a(1); 1258]   δειγματίζω
δεικνύειν   pres act inf
    [Mt 16:21; v-3c(2); 1259]   δείκνυμι
δεικνύεις   pres act ind 2 sg
    [Jn 2:18; v-3c(2); 1259]   "

δείκνυμι   {1259, v-3c(2)}
[δείξω, ἔδειξα, δέδειχα, δέδειγμαι, ἐδείχθην] *to
show, point out, present to the sight,* Matt 4:8; 8:4;
to exhibit, permit to see, cause to be seen, John 2:18;
10:32; 1 Tim 6:15; *to demonstrate, prove,* James
2:18; 3:13; met. *to teach, make known, declare,
announce,* Matt 16:21; John 5:20; Acts 10:28

δείκνυμι   pres act ind 1 sg
   [1C 12:31; v-3c(2); 1259]   "
δεικνύοντος   pres act ptcp gen sg masc
   [Rv 22:8; v-3c(2); 1259]   "
δείκνυσιν   pres act ind 3 sg   [2t; v-3c(2); 1259]   "

δειλία, ας, ἡ   {1261, n-1a}
   timidity, 2 Tim 1:7*

δειλίας   gen sg fem   [2Ti 1:7; n-1a; 1261]   δειλία
δειλιάτω   pres act imperative 3 sg
   [Jn 14:27; v-1d(1b); 1262]   δειλιάω
δειλιάω   {1262, v-1d(1b)}
   [-, ἐδειλίασα, -, -, -] *to be timid, be in fear,* John
   14:27*

δειλοί   nom pl masc   [2t; a-1a(2a); 1264]   δειλός
δειλός, ή, όν   {1264, a-1a(2a)}
   timid, fearful, cowardly, Matt 8:26; Mark 4:40;
   Rev 21:8*

δειλοῖς   dat pl masc   [Rv 21:8; a-1a(2a); 1264]   "
δεῖν   pres act inf   [3t; v-1d(2c); 1256]   δεῖ
δεῖνα, ὁ   {1265, a-5a}
   such a one, a certain one, Matt 26:18*

δεῖνα   acc sg masc   [Mt 26:18; a-5a; 1265]   δεῖνα
δεινῶς   {1267, adverb}
   dreadfully, grievously, greatly, terribly, Matt 8:6;
   Luke 11:53*

δεινῶς   adverb   [2t; adverb; 1267]   δεινῶς
δεῖξαι   aor act inf   [2t; v-3c(2); 1259]   δείκνυμι
δείξατε   aor act imperative 2 pl
   [Lk 20:24; v-3c(2); 1259]   "
δειξάτω   aor act imperative 3 sg
   [Jm 3:13; v-3c(2); 1259]   "
δείξει   fut act ind 3 sg   [4t; v-3c(2); 1259]   "
δεῖξον   aor act imperative 2 sg
   [6t; v-3c(2); 1259]   "
δείξω   aor act subj 1 sg   [Ac 7:3; v-3c(2); 1259]   "
δείξω   fut act ind 1 sg   [4t; v-3c(2); 1259]   "

δειπνέω   {1268, v-1d(2a)}
   [δειπνήσω, ἐδείπνησα, -, -, -] *to eat* or *dine,* Matt
   20:28 v.l.; Luke 17:8; 22:20; 1 Cor 11:25; Rev 3:20

δειπνῆσαι   aor act inf
   [2t; v-1d(2a); 1268]   δειπνέω
δειπνήσω   aor act subj 1 sg
   [Lk 17:8; v-1d(2a); 1268]   "
δειπνήσω   fut act ind 1 sg
   [Rv 3:20; v-1d(2a); 1268]   "
δείπνοις   dat pl neut   [3t; n-2c; 1270]   δεῖπνον

δεῖπνον, ου, τό   {1270, n-2c}
   pr. *a meal; supper, the principal meal taken in the
   evening,* Luke 14:12; John 13:2, 4; meton. *food,* 1
   Cor 11:21; *a feast, banquet,* Matt 23:6; Mark 6:21;
   12:39

δεῖπνον   acc sg neut   [8t; n-2c; 1270]   "
δείπνου   gen sg neut   [4t; n-2c; 1270]   "
δείπνῳ   dat sg neut   [Jn 21:20; n-2c; 1270]   "
δείραντες   aor act ptcp nom pl masc
   [4t; v-1c(1); 1296]   δέρω
δεισιδαιμονεστέρους   acc pl masc comparative
   [Ac 17:22; a-4b(1); 1273]   δεισιδαίμων

δεισιδαιμονία, ας, ἡ   {1272, n-1a}
   fear of the gods; in a bad sense, *superstition; a
   form of religious belief,* Acts 25:19*

δεισιδαιμονίας   gen sg fem
   [Ac 25:19; n-1a; 1272]   δεισιδαιμονία

δεισιδαίμων, ον   {1273, a-4b(1)}
   reverencing the gods and divine things, religious;
   in a bad sense, *superstitious;* in N.T. *careful and
   precise in the discharge of religious services,* Acts
   17:22*

δειχθέντα   aor pass ptcp acc sg masc
   [Hb 8:5; v-3c(2); 1259]   δείκνυμι
δέκα   {1274, a-5b}
   ten, Matt 20:24; 25:1; ἡμερῶν δέκα, *ten days, a few
   days, a short time,* Rev 2:10

δέκα   indecl   [25t; a-5b; 1274]   δέκα
δεκαδύο, v.l. for δώδεκα   {1275}
δεκαοκτώ   {1277, a-5b}
   eighteen, Luke 13:4, 11*

δεκαοκτώ   indecl   [2t; a-5b; 1277]   δεκαοκτώ
δεκαπέντε   {1278, a-5b}
   fifteen, indecl., John 11:18; Acts 27:5 v.l., 28; Gal
   1:18*

δεκαπέντε   indecl   [3t; a-5b; 1278]   δεκαπέντε
Δεκαπόλει   dat sg fem
   [Mk 5:20; n-3e(5b); 1279]   Δεκάπολις
Δεκαπόλεως   gen sg fem   [2t; n-3e(5b); 1279]   "
Δεκάπολις, εως, ἡ   {1279, n-3e(5b)}
   Decapolis, a district of Palestine beyond Jordan,
   Mark 5:20; 7:31; Matt 4:25*

δεκάτας   acc pl fem   [2t; a-1a(2a); 1281]   δέκατος
δεκατέσσαρες, ων   {1280, a-5b}
   fourteen, Matt 1:17; 2 Cor 12:2; Gal 2:1*

δεκατέσσαρες   indecl
   [3t; a-5b; 1280]   δεκατέσσαρες
δεκατεσσάρων   indecl   [2t; a-5b; 1280]   "
δεκάτη   nom sg fem
   [Jn 1:39; a-1a(2a); 1281]   δέκατος
δεκάτην   acc sg fem   [2t; a-1a(2a); 1281]   "
δέκατον   nom sg neut   [Rv 11:13; a-1a(2a); 1281]   "
δέκατος, η, ον   {1281, a-1a(2a)}
   tenth, John 1:39; Rev 11:13; 21:20; δεκάτη, sc.
   μερίς, *a tenth part, tithe,* Heb 7:2, 4, 8, 9*

δέκατος   nom sg masc   [Rv 21:20; a-1a(2a); 1281]   "
δεκατόω   {1282, v-1d(3)}
   [-, -, δεδεκάτωκα, δεδεκάτωμαι, -] *to cause to pay
   tithes;* pass. *to be tithed, pay tithes,* Heb 7:6, 9*

δεκτήν   acc sg fem
[Pp 4:18; a-1a(2a); 1283]   δεκτός
δεκτόν   acc sg masc [Lk 4:19; a-1a(2a); 1283]   "

δεκτός, ή, όν   {1283, a-1a(2a)}
accepted, acceptable, agreeable, approved, Luke
4:24; Acts 10:35; Phil 4:18; by impl. when used
of a certain time, *marked by* divine *acceptance,
propitious,* Luke 4:19; 2 Cor 6:2*

δεκτός   nom sg masc [2t; a-1a(2a); 1283]   "
δεκτῷ   dat sg masc [2C 6:2; a-1a(2a); 1283]   "
δελεαζόμενος   pres pass ptcp nom sg masc
[Jm 1:14; v-2a(1); 1284]   δελεάζω
δελεάζοντες   pres act ptcp nom pl masc
[2P 2:14; v-2a(1); 1284]   "
δελεάζουσιν   pres act ind 3 pl
[2P 2:18; v-2a(1); 1284]   "

δελεάζω   {1284, v-2a(1)}
[-, -, -, -, -] pr. *to entrap, take* or *catch* with a bait;
met. *allure, entice,* James 1:14; 2 Peter 2:14, 18*

δένδρα   nom pl neut [Jd 12; n-2c; 1285]   δένδρον
δένδρα   acc pl neut [3t; n-2c; 1285]   "

δένδρον, ου, τό   {1285, n-2c}
a tree, Matt 3:10; 7:17; 13:32

δένδρον   nom sg neut [12t; n-2c; 1285]   "
δένδρον   acc sg neut [5t; n-2c; 1285]   "
δένδρων   gen pl neut [4t; n-2c; 1285]   "
δέξαι   aor mid imperative 2 sg
[3t; v-1b(2); 1312]   δέχομαι
δεξαμένη   aor mid ptcp nom sg fem
[Hb 11:31; v-1b(2); 1312]   "
δεξάμενοι   aor mid ptcp nom pl masc
[1Th 1:6; v-1b(2); 1312]   "
δεξάμενος   aor mid ptcp nom sg masc
[3t; v-1b(2); 1312]   "
δέξασθαι   aor mid inf [3t; v-1b(2); 1312]   "
δέξασθε   aor mid imperative 2 pl
[4t; v-1b(2); 1312]   "
δέξηται   aor mid subj 3 sg [8t; v-1b(2); 1312]   "
δεξιά   nom sg fem [3t; a-1a(1); 1288]   δεξιός
δεξιᾷ   dat sg fem [13t; a-1a(1); 1288]   "
δεξιά   acc pl neut [Jn 21:6; a-1a(1); 1288]   "
δεξιάν   acc sg fem [4t; a-1a(1); 1288]   "
δεξιᾶς   gen sg fem [4t; a-1a(1); 1288]   "
δεξιάς   acc pl fem [Ga 2:9; a-1a(1); 1288]   "
δεξιοῖς   dat pl neut [Mk 16:5; a-1a(1); 1288]   "

δεξιολάβος, ου, ὁ   {1287, n-2a}
*one posted on the right hand; a flank guard; a light
armed spearman,* Acts 23:23*

δεξιολάβους   acc pl masc
[Ac 23:23; n-2a; 1287]   δεξιολάβος
δεξιόν   acc sg masc
[Rv 10:2; a-1a(1); 1288]   δεξιός
δεξιόν   acc sg neut [2t; a-1a(1); 1288]   "

δεξιός, ά, όν   {1288, a-1a(1)}
right, as opposed to left, Matt 5:29, 30; Luke 6:6;
ἡ δεξιά, sc. χείρ, *the right hand,* Matt 6:3; 27:29;
τὰ δεξιά, sc. μέρη, *the parts towards the right hand,
the right hand side;* καθίζειν, or, καθῆσθαι, or,
ἑστάναι, ἐκ δεξιῶν (μερῶν) τινος, *to sit* or *stand at*

the right hand of any one, as a mark of the highest
honor and dignity which he can bestow, Matt
20:20; 26:64; εἶναι ἐκ δεξιῶν (μερῶν) τινος, *to be at
one's right hand,* as a helper, Acts 2:25; δεξιὰς
(χεῖρας) διδόναι, *to give the right hand* to any one,
as a pledge of sincerity in one's promises, Gal
2:9

δεξιός   nom sg masc [Mt 5:29; a-1a(1); 1288]   "
δεξιῶν   gen pl fem [3t; a-1a(1); 1288]   "
δεξιῶν   gen pl neut [20t; a-1a(1); 1288]   "
δέξωνται   aor mid subj 3 pl
[2t; v-1b(2); 1312]   δέχομαι

δέομαι   {1289, v-1d(2c)}
[(ἐδεῖτο, 3rd sg), -, -, -, -, ἐδεήθην] *to be in want,
to need; to ask, request,* Matt 9:38; Luke 5:12; 8:28,
38; in N.T. absol. *to pray, offer prayer, beseech,
supplicate,* Luke 21:36; 22:32; Acts 4:31; 8:22, 24

δέομαι   pres mid ind 1 sg
[4t; v-1d(2c); 1289]   δέομαι
δέομαι   pres pass ind 1 sg [3t; v-1d(2c); 1289]   "
δεόμεθα   pres mid ind 1 pl
[2C 5:20; v-1d(2c); 1289]   "
δεόμενοι   pres mid ptcp nom pl masc
[Lk 21:36; v-1d(2c); 1289]   "
δεόμενοι   pres pass ptcp nom pl masc
[2t; v-1d(2c); 1289]   "
δεόμενος   pres mid ptcp nom sg masc
[Rm 1:10; v-1d(2c); 1289]   "
δεόμενος   pres pass ptcp nom sg masc
[Ac 10:2; v-1d(2c); 1289]   "
δέον   pres act ptcp nom sg neut
[2t; v-1d(2c); 1256]   δεῖ
δέοντα   pres act ptcp acc pl neut
[1Ti 5:13; v-1d(2c); 1256]   "

δέος, ους, τό   {1290, n-3d(2b)}
fear, Heb 12:28*

δέους   gen sg neut [Hb 12:28; n-3d(2b); 1290]   δέος

Δερβαῖος, α, ον   {1291, a-1a(1)}
an inhabitant of Derbe, Acts 20:4*

Δερβαῖος   nom sg masc
[Ac 20:4; a-1a(1); 1291]   Δερβαῖος

Δέρβη, ης, ἡ   {1292, n-1b}
Derbe, a city of Lycaonia, Acts 14:6, 20; 16:0*

Δέρβην   acc sg fem [3t; n-1b; 1292]   Δέρβη
δέρει   pres act ind 3 sg
[2C 11:20; v-1c(1); 1296]   δέρω
δέρεις   pres act ind 2 sg
[Jn 18:23; v-1c(1); 1296]   "

δέρμα, ατος, τό   {1293, n-3c(4)}
the skin of an animal, Heb 11:37*

δέρμασιν   dat pl neut
[Hb 11:37; n-3c(4); 1293]   δέρμα
δερμάτινην   acc sg fem
[2t; a-1a(2a); 1294]   δερμάτινος

δερμάτινος, η, ον   {1294, a-1a(2a)}
made of skin, leathern, Matt 3:4; Mark 1:6*

δέροντες   pres act ptcp nom pl masc
[2t; v-1c(1); 1296]   δέρω

δέρρις, εως, ἡ {1295, n-3e(5b)}
skin, Mark 1:6 v.l.*

δέρω {1296, v-1c(1)}
[-, ἔδειρα, -, -, ἐδάρην] *to skin, flay;* hence, *to eat, scourge, beat,* Matt 21:35; Mark 12:3, 5; 13:9

δέρων pres act ptcp nom sg masc
[2t; v-1c(1); 1296]   "
δεσμά nom pl neut [2t; n-2a; 1301]   δεσμός
δεσμά acc pl neut [Lk 8:29; n-2a; 1301] "
δέσμας acc pl fem [Mt 13:30; n-1b; 1299]   δέσμη
δεσμεύουσιν pres act ind 3 pl
[Mt 23:4; v-1a(6); 1297]   δεσμεύω

δεσμεύω {1297, v-1a(6)}
[(ἐδέσμευον), -, -, -, -, -] *to bind, bind up,* as a bundle, Matt 23:4; *to bind, confine,* Luke 8:29; Acts 22:4*

δεσμεύων pres act ptcp nom sg masc
[Ac 22:4; v-1a(6); 1297]   "

δεσμέω {1298, v-1d(2a)}
to bind, confine, v.l. for δεσμεύω at Luke 8:29*

δέσμη, ης, ἡ {1299, n-1b}
a bundle, as of tares, Matt 13:30*

δέσμιοι nom pl masc
[Ac 16:25; n-2a; 1300]   δέσμιος
δεσμίοις dat pl masc [Hb 10:34; n-2a; 1300] "
δέσμιον acc sg masc [5t; n-2a; 1300] "

δέσμιος, ου, ὁ {1300, n-2a}
one bound, a prisoner, Matt 27:15, 16; Mark 15:6

δέσμιος nom sg masc [7t; n-2a; 1300] "
δεσμίους acc pl masc [Ac 16:27; n-2a; 1300] "
δεσμίων gen pl masc [Hb 13:3; n-2a; 1300] "
δεσμοῖς dat pl masc [6t; n-2a; 1301]   δεσμός

δεσμός, οῦ, ὁ {1301, n-2a}
a bond, anything by which one is bound, a cord, chain, fetters, etc.; and by meton. *imprisonment,* Luke 8:29; Acts 16:26; 20:23; *a string* or *ligament,* as of the tongue, Mark 7:35; met. *an impediment, infirmity,* Luke 13:16

δεσμός nom sg masc [Mk 7:35; n-2a; 1301] "
δεσμοῦ gen sg masc [Lk 13:16; n-2a; 1301] "
δεσμούς acc pl masc [Pp 1:13; n-2a; 1301] "
δεσμοφύλακι dat sg masc
[Ac 16:23; n-3b(1); 1302]   δεσμοφύλαξ

δεσμοφύλαξ, ακος, ὁ {1302, n-3b(1)}
a keeper of a prison, jailer, Acts 16:23, 27, 36*

δεσμοφύλαξ nom sg masc [2t; n-3b(1); 1302] "
δεσμῶν gen pl masc [6t; n-2a; 1301]   δεσμός
δεσμώτας acc pl masc [2t; n-1f; 1304]   δεσμώτης

δεσμωτήριον, ου, τό {1303, n-2c}
a prison, Matt 11:2; Acts 5:21, 23; 16:26*

δεσμωτήριον acc sg neut
[2t; n-2c; 1303]   δεσμωτήριον
δεσμωτηρίου gen sg neut [Ac 16:26; n-2c; 1303] "
δεσμωτηρίῳ dat sg neut [Mt 11:2; n-2c; 1303] "

δεσμώτης, ου, ὁ {1304, n-1f}
a prisoner, i.q. δέσμιος, Acts 27:1, 42*

δέσποτα voc sg masc [2t; n-1f; 1305]   δεσπότης
δεσπόταις dat pl masc [2t; n-1f; 1305] "
δεσπότας acc pl masc [2t; n-1f; 1305] "
δεσπότῃ dat sg masc [2Ti 2:21; n-1f; 1305] "
δεσπότην acc sg masc [2t; n-1f; 1305] "

δεσπότης, ου, ὁ {1305, n-1f}
a lord, master, especially of slaves, 1 Tim 6:1, 2; 2 Tim 2:21; Titus 2:9; 1 Pet 2:18; by impl. as denoting the possession of supreme authority, *Lord, sovereign,* used of God, Luke 2:29; Acts 4:24; Rev 6:10; and of Christ, 2 Peter 2:1; Jude 4

δεσπότης nom sg masc [Rv 6:10; n-1f; 1305] "

δεῦρο {1306, adverb}
here; used also as a sort of imperative, *come, Come here!* Matt 19:21; Mark 10:21; used of time, ἄχρι τοῦ δεῦρο, sc. χρόνου, *to the present time,* Rom 1:13

δεῦρο adverb [9t; adverb; 1306]   δεῦρο

δεῦτε {1307, adverb}
come, Matt 4:19; 01:28; as a particle of exhortation, incitement, etc., and followed by an imperative, *come now,* etc., Matt 21:38; 28:6

δεῦτε adverb [12t; adverb; 1307]   δεῦτε
δευτέρα nom sg fem [3t; a-1a(1); 1311]   δεύτερος
δευτέρᾳ dat sg fem [Lk 12:38; a-1a(1); 1311] "
δευτεραῖοι nom pl masc
[Ac 28:13; a-1a(1); 1308]   δευτεραῖος

δευτεραῖος, αία, ον {1308, a-1a(1)}
on the second day of a certain state or process, and used as an epithet of the subject or agent, Acts 28:13*

δευτέραν acc sg fem [6t; a-1a(1); 1311]   δεύτερος
δευτέρας gen sg fem [Hb 8:7; a-1a(1); 1311] "
δεύτερον nom sg neut [Rv 4:7; a-1a(1); 1311] "
δεύτερον acc sg neut, can function
adverbially (5t) [9t; a-1a(1); 1311] "

δευτερόπρωτος, ον {1310. a-3a}
second-first, an epithet of uncertain meaning, but probably appropriated of unleavened bread, Luke 6:1 v.l.*

δεύτερος, α, ον {1311, a-1a(1)}
second, Matt 22:26; τὸ δεύτερον, *again, the second time, another time,* Jude 5; so ἐκ δευτέρου, Matt 26:42; and ἐν τῷ δευτέρῳ, Acts 7:13

δεύτερος nom sg masc [12t; a-1a(1); 1311] "
δευτέρου gen sg masc [Rv 2:11; a-1a(1); 1311] "
δευτέρου gen sg neut [7t; a-1a(1); 1311] "
δευτέρῳ dat sg masc [Ac 13:33; a-1a(1); 1311] "
δευτέρῳ dat sg neut [Ac 7:13; a-1a(1); 1311] "
δέχεται pres mid ind 3 sg
[8t; v-1b(2); 1312]   δέχομαι
δέχηται pres mid subj 3 sg
[Mk 9:37; v-1b(2); 1312]   "

δέχομαι {1312, v-1b(2)}
[δέξομαι, ἐδεξάμην, -, δέδεγμαι, ἐδέχθην] *to take into one's hands,* etc., Luke 2:28; 16:6, 7; *to receive,* Acts 22:5; 28:21; Phil 4:18; *to receive into and retain, contain,* Acts 3:21; met. *to receive by*

the hearing, *learn, acquire a knowledge of,* 2 Cor 11:4; James 1:21; *to receive, admit, grant access to, receive kindly, welcome,* Matt 10:40, 41; 18:5; *to receive* in hospitality, *entertain,* Luke 9:53; Heb 11:31; *to bear with, bear patiently,* 2 Cor 11:16; met. *to receive, approve, assent to,* Matt 11:14; Luke 8:13; Acts 8:14; 11:1; *to admit,* and by impl. *to embrace, follow,* 1 Cor 2:14; 2 Cor 8:17

δεχόμενος   pres mid ptcp nom sg masc
   [4t; v-1b(2); 1312]   "
δέχονται   pres mid ind 3 pl
   [Lk 8:13; v-1b(2); 1312]   "
δέχωνται   pres mid subj 3 pl   [3t; v-1b(2); 1312]   "

δέω   {1313, v-1d(2b)}
[δήσω, ἔδησα, δέδεκα, δέδεμαι, ἐδέθην] *to bind, tie,* Matt 13:30; 21:2; *to bind, confine,* Matt 27:2; 14:3; *to impede, hinder,* 2 Tim 2:9; *to bind with* infirmity, Luke 13:16; *to bind* by a legal or moral tie, as marriage, Rom 7:2; 1 Cor 7:27, 39; by impl. *to impel, compel,* Acts 20:22; in N.T. *to pronounce* or *declare to be binding* or *obligatory,* or, *to declare to be prohibited and unlawful,* Matt 16:19; 18:18

δή   {1314, particle}
a particle that adds an intensity of expression to a term or clause. Its simplest and most ordinary uses are when it gives impressiveness to an affirmation, *indeed, really, doubtless,* Matt 13:23; or earnestness to a call, injunction, or entreaty, Luke 2:15; Acts 6:3 v.l.; 13:2; 15:36; 1 Cor 16:20*

δή   particle [5t; particle; 1314]   δή

δηλαυγῶς   {1315, adverb}
very clean, Mark 8:25 v.l.*

δηλοῖ   pres act ind 3 sg
   [Hb 12:27; v-1d(3); 1317]   δηλόω
δῆλον   nom sg neut [2t; a-1a(2a); 1316]   δῆλος
δῆλον   acc sg masc [Mt 26:73; a-1a(2a); 1316]   "

δῆλος, η, ον   {1316, a-1a(2a)}
pr. *clearly visible; plain, manifest, evident,* Matt 26:73; 1 Cor 15:27; Gal 3:11; 1 Tim 6:7 v.l.*

δηλοῦντος   pres act ptcp gen sg neut
   [Hb 9:8; v-1d(3); 1317]   δηλόω

δηλόω   {1317, v-1d(3)}
[δηλώσω, ἐδήλωσα, -, δεδήλωμαι, ἐδηλώθην] *to render manifest* or *evident; to make known, to tell, relate, declare,* 1 Cor 1:11; Col 1:8; *to show, point out, bring to light,* 1 Cor 3:13; *to indicate, signify,* Heb 8:9; 12:27; 1 Peter 1:11

δηλώσας   aor act ptcp nom sg masc
   [Cl 1:8; v-1d(3); 1317]   "
δηλώσει   fut act ind 3 sg
   [1C 3:13; v-1d(3); 1317]   "

Δημᾶς, ᾶ, ὁ   {1318, n-1e}
Demas, pr. name, Col 4:14; 2 Tim 4:10; Phlm 24*

Δημᾶς   nom sg masc [3t; n-1e; 1318]   Δημᾶς

δημηγορέω   {1319, v-1d(2a)}
[(ἐδημηγόρουν), -, -, -, -, -] *to address a public assembly, to deliver a public oration,* Acts 12:21*

Δημήτριος, ου, ὁ   {1320, n-2a}
Demetrius, pr. name (1) *The Ephesian silversmith,* Acts 19:24, 38 (2) *A certain Christian,* 3 John 12*

Δημήτριος   nom sg masc [2t; n-2a; 1320]   Δημήτριος
Δημητρίῳ   dat sg masc [3J 12; n-2a; 1320]   "

δημιουργός, οῦ, ὁ   {1321, n-2a}
pr. *one who labors for the public,* or, *exercises some public calling; an architect,* especially, the Divine *Architect* of the universe, Heb 11:10

δημιουργός   nom sg masc
   [Hb 11:10; n-2a; 1321]   δημιουργός
δῆμον   acc sg masc [2t; n-2a; 1322]   δῆμος

δῆμος, ου, ὁ   {1322, n-2a}
the people, Acts 12:22; 17:5; 19:30, 33*

δῆμος   nom sg masc [Ac 12:22; n-2a; 1322]   "
δημοσίᾳ   dat sg fem [4t; a-1a(1); 1323]   δημόσιος

δημόσιος, ία, ιον   {1323, a-1a(1)}
public, belonging to the public, Acts 5:18; δημοσίᾳ, *publicly,* Acts 16:37; 18:28; 20:20*

δήμῳ   dat sg masc [Ac 19:33; n-2a; 1322]   δῆμος
δηνάρια   acc pl neut [3t; n-2c; 1324]   δηνάριον

δηνάριον, ον, τό   {1324, n-2c}
Latin *denarius,* a Roman silver coin; the name originally meant *ten asses,* Matt 18:28; Mark 6:37; Rev 6:6

δηνάριον   acc sg neut [5t; n-2c; 1324]   "
δηναρίου   gen sg neut [4t; n-2c; 1324]   "
δηναρίων   gen pl neut [4t; n-2c; 1324]   "

δήποτε   {1325, adverb}
whenever, an intensive combination of the particle δή with ποτε as an intensive, John 5:4*

δήπου   {1327, adverb}
now in some way, surely, Heb 2:16*

δήπου   adverb [Hb 2:16; adverb; 1327]   δήπου
δῆσαι   aor act inf   [2t; v-1d(2b); 1313]   δέω
δήσαντες   aor act ptcp nom pl masc
   [3t; v-1d(2b); 1313]   "
δήσας   aor act ptcp nom sg masc
   [Ac 21:11; v-1d(2b); 1313]   "
δήσατε   aor act imperative 2 pl
   [Mt 13:30; v-1d(2b); 1313]   "
δήσῃ   aor act subj 3 sg   [2t; v-1d(2b); 1313]   "
δήσῃς   aor act subj 2 sg
   [Mt 16:19; v-1d(2b); 1313]   "
δήσητε   aor act subj 2 pl
   [Mt 18:18; v-1d(2b); 1313]   "
δήσουσιν   fut act ind 3 pl
   [Ac 21:11; v-1d(2b); 1313]   "
δι᾽   prep-gen [105t; prep; 1328]   διά
δι᾽   prep-acc [43t; prep; 1328]   "

διά   {1328, prep}
(1) gen., *through,* used of place or medium, Matt 7:13; Luke 6:1; 2 Cor 11:33; *through,* of time, *during, in the course of,* Heb 2:15; Acts 5:19; *through,* of immediate agency, causation, instrumentality, *by means of, by,* John 1:3; Acts 3:18; of means or manner, *through, by, with,*

Luke 8:4; 2 Cor 5:7; 8:8; of state or condition, *in a state of*, Rom 4:11; (2) acc., used of causation which is not direct and immediate in the production of a result, *on account of, because of, for the sake of, with a view to*, Mark 2:27; John 1:31; rarely, *through, while subject to* a state of untoward circumstances, Gal 4:13

διά   prep-acc [237t; prep; 1328]   διά
διά   prep-gen [282t; prep; 1328]   "
Δία   acc sg masc [Ac 14:12; n-3g(1); 2416]   Ζεύς

διαβαίνω   {1329, cv-2d(6)}
[-, διέβην, -, -, -] *to pass through* or *over*, Luke 16:26; Acts 16:9; Heb 11:29*

διαβάλλω   {1330, cv-2d(1)}
[-, -, -, -, διεβλήθην] *to throw* or *convey through* or *over; to thrust through; to defame, inform against*, Luke 16:1*

διαβάς   aor act ptcp nom sg masc
[Ac 16:9; cv-2d(6); 1329]   διαβαίνω

διαβεβαιόομαι   {1331, cv-1d(3)}
[-, -, -, -, -] *to assert strongly, insist*, 1 Tim 1:7; Titus 3:8*

διαβεβαιοῦνται   pres mid ind 3 pl
[1Ti 1:7; cv-1d(3); 1331]   διαβεβαιόομαι
διαβεβαιοῦσθαι   pres mid inf
[Ti 3:8; cv-1d(3); 1331]   "
διαβῆναι   aor act inf
[Lk 16:26; cv-2d(6); 1329]   διαβαίνω

διαβλέπω   {1332, cv-1b(1)}
[διαβλέψω, διέβλεψα, -, -, -] *to look through; to view steadily*, Mark 8:25; *to see clearly* or *steadily*, Matt 7:5; Luke 6:42*

διαβλέψεις   fut act ind 2 sg
[2t; cv-1b(1); 1332]   διαβλέπω
διάβολοι   nom pl masc
[2Ti 3:3; a-3a; 1333]   διάβολος
διάβολον   acc sg masc [Hb 2:14; a-3a; 1333]   "

διάβολος, ον   {1333, a-3a}
slanderer, 1 Tim 3:11; 2 Tim 3:3; Titus 2:3; *a treacherous informer, traitor*, John 6:70; ὁ διάβολος, *the devil*

διάβολος   nom sg masc [16t; a-3a; 1333]   "
διαβόλου   gen sg masc [13t; a-3a; 1333]   "
διαβόλους   acc pl fem [2t; a-3a; 1333]   "
διαβόλῳ   dat sg masc [4t; a-3a; 1333]   "
διαγγελῇ   aor pass subj 3 sg
[Rm 9:17; cv-2d(1); 1334]   διαγγέλλω
διάγγελλε   pres act imperative 2 sg
[Lk 9:60; cv-2d(1); 1334]   "

διαγγέλλω   {1334, cv-2d(1)}
[-, -, -, -, διηγγέλην] *to publish abroad*, Luke 9:60; Rom 9:17; *to certify* to the public, Acts 21:26; *to tell, announce, give notice of, divulge, publish abroad*, Acts 21:26; *to declare, promulgate, teach*, Mark 5:19 v.l.*

διαγγέλλων   pres act ptcp nom sg masc
[Ac 21:26; cv-2d(1); 1334]   "
διαγενομένου   aor mid ptcp gen sg masc
[Ac 27:9; cv-1c(2); 1335]   διαγίνομαι

διαγενομένου   aor mid ptcp gen sg neut
[Mk 16:1; cv-1c(2); 1335]   "
διαγενομένων   aor mid ptcp gen pl fem
[Ac 25:13; cv-1c(2); 1335]   "

διαγίνομαι   {1335, cv-1c(2)}
[-, διεγενόμην, -, -, -] pas., *to continue through; to intervene, elapse* of time, Mark 16:1; Acts 25:13; 27:9*

διαγινώσκειν   pres act inf
[Ac 23:15; cv-5a; 1336]   διαγινώσκω

διαγινώσκω   {1336, cv-5a}
[διαγνώσομαι, -, -, -, -] pr. *to distinguish; to resolve determinately; to examine, inquire into*, judicially, Acts 23:15; 24:22*

διαγνωρίζω   {1337, v-2a(1)}
[-, διεγνώρισα, -, -, -] *to tell abroad, publish*, Luke 2:17 v.l. for ἐγνώρισαν*

διάγνωσιν   acc sg fem
[Ac 25:21; n-3e(5b); 1338]   διάγνωσις

διάγνωσις, εως, ἡ   {1338, n-3e(5b)}
pr. *an act of distinguishing* or *discernment; a determination; examination* judicially, *hearing, trial*, Acts 25:21*

διαγνώσομαι   fut mid ind 1 sg
[Ac 24:22; cv-5a; 1336]   διαγινώσκω

διαγογγύζω   {1339, cv-2a(1)}
[(διεγόγγυζον), -, -, -, -, -] *to murmur, mutter*, Luke 15:2; 19:7*

διάγοντες   pres act ptcp nom pl masc
[Ti 3:3; cv-1b(2); 1341]   διάγω

διαγρηγορέω   {1340, cv-1d(2a)}
[-, διεγρηγόρησα, -, -, -] *to remain awake; to wake thoroughly*, Luke 9:32*

διαγρηγορήσαντες   aor act ptcp nom pl masc
[Lk 9:32; cv-1d(2a); 1340]   διαγρηγορέω

διάγω   {1341, cv-1b(2)}
[-, -, -, -, -] *to conduct* or *carry through* or *over; to pass* or *spend* time, *live*, Luke 7:25 v.l.; 1 Tim 2:2; Titus 3:3*

διάγωμεν   pres act subj 1 pl
[1Ti 2:2; cv-1b(2); 1341]   διάγω
διαδεξάμενοι   aor mid ptcp nom pl masc
[Ac 7:45; cv-1b(2); 1342]   διαδέχομαι

διαδέχομαι   {1342, cv-1b(2)}
[-, διεδεξάμην, -, -, -] *to receive by transmission; to receive in return*, Acts 7:45*

διάδημα, ατος, τό   {1343, n-3c(4)}
pr. *a band* or *fillet; a diadem*, the badge of a sovereign, Rev 12:3; 13:1; 19:12*

διαδήματα   nom pl neut
[Rv 19:12; n-3c(4); 1343]   διάδημα
διαδήματα   acc pl neut [2t; n-3c(4); 1343]   "

διαδίδωμι   {1344, cv-6a}
[(διεδίδων), -, διέδωκα, -, -, -] *to deliver from hand to hand; to distribute, divide*, Luke 11:22; 18:22; John 6:11; Acts 4:35; Rev 17:13 v.l.*

διαδίδωσιν pres act ind 3 sg
[Lk 11:22; cv-6a; 1344]   διαδίδωμι
διάδος aor act imperative 2 sg
[Lk 18:22; cv-6a; 1344]   "
διάδοχον acc sg masc
[Ac 24:27; n-2a; 1345]   διάδοχος

διάδοχος, ου, ὁ   {1345, n-2a}
 a successor, Acts 24:27*

διαζώννυμι   {1346, cv-3c(1)}
 [-, διέζωσα, -, διέζωσμαι, -] *to gird firmly round,*
 John 13:4, 5; mid. *to gird round one's self,* John
 21:7*

διαθέμενος aor mid ptcp nom sg masc
[Hb 9:17; cv-6a; 1416]   διατίθημι
διαθεμένου aor mid ptcp gen sg masc
[Hb 9:16; cv-6a; 1416]   "
διαθῆκαι nom pl fem [2t; n-1b; 1347]   διαθήκη

διαθήκη, ης, ἡ   {1347, n-1b}
 a testamentary disposition, will; a covenant, Heb
 9:16, 17; Gal 3:15; in N.T., *a covenant* of God
 with men, Gal 3:17; 4:24; Heb 9:4; Matt 26:28;
 the writings of the old covenant, 2 Cor 3:14

διαθήκη nom sg fem [7t; n-1b; 1347]   "
διαθήκῃ dat sg fem [2t; n-1b; 1347]   "
διαθήκην acc sg fem [5t; n-1b; 1347]   "
διαθήκης gen sg fem [16t; n-1b; 1347]   "
διαθηκῶν gen pl fem [Ep 2:12; n-1b; 1347]   "
διαθήσομαι fut mid ind 1 sg
[2t; cv-6a; 1416]   διατίθημι
διαιρέσεις nom pl fem
[3t; n-3e(5b); 1348]   διαίρεσις

διαίρεσις, εως, ἡ   {1348, n-3e(5b)}
 a division; a distinction, difference, diversity, 1 Cor
 12:4, 5, 6*

διαιρέω   {1349, cv-1d(2a)}
 [-, διεῖλον, -, -, -] *to divide, to divide out, distribute,*
 Luke 15:12; 1 Cor 12:11*

διαιροῦν pres act ptcp nom sg neut
[1C 12:11; cv-1d(2a); 1349]   διαιρέω

διακαθαίρω   {1350, cv-2d(2)}
 [-, ἐδιεκάθαρα, -, -, -] *to cleanse thoroughly,* Luke
 3:17*

διακαθᾶραι aor act inf
[Lk 3:17; cv-2d(2); 1350]   διακαθαίρω
διακαθαριεῖ fut act ind 3 sg
[Mt 3:12; cv-2a(1); 1351]   διακαθαρίζω

διακαθαρίζω   {1351, cv-2a(1)}
 [διακαθαριῶ, -, -, -, -] *to cleanse thoroughly,* Matt
 3:12; Luke 3:17 v.l.*

διακατελέγχομαι   {1352, cv-1b(2)}
 [(διακατηλεγχόμην), -, -, -, -, -] *to maintain
 discussion strenuously and thoroughly, to totally
 refute,* Acts 18:28*

διακατηλέγχετο imperf mid ind 3 sg
[Ac 18:28; cv-1b(2); 1352]   διακατελέγχομαι

διακελεύω   {1353, v-1a(6)}
 [-, -, -, -, -] dat., *to order,* John 8:5 v.l.*

διακόνει pres act imperative 2 sg
[Lk 17:8; v-1d(2a); 1354]   διακονέω
διακονεῖ pres act ind 3 sg
[1P 4:11; v-1d(2a); 1354]   "
διακονεῖν pres act inf [2t; v-1d(2a); 1354]   "
διακονείτωσαν pres act imperative 3 pl
[1Ti 3:10; v-1d(2a); 1354]   "

διακονέω   {1354, v-1d(2a)}
 [(διηκόνουν), διακονήσω, διηκόνησα, -, -,
 διηκονήθην] *to wait, attend upon, serve,* Matt
 8:15; Mark 1:31; Luke 4:39; *to be an attendant* or
 assistant, Acts 19:22; *to minister to, relieve, assist,*
 or *supply with the necessaries of life, provide the
 means of living,* Matt 4:11; 27:55; Mark 1:13;
 15:41; Luke 8:3; *to fill the office of* διάκονος,
 deacon, perform the duties of deacon, 1 Tim 3:10,
 13; 1 Peter 4:11; *to convey in charge, administer,* 2
 Cor 3:3; 8:19, 20; 1 Peter 1:12; 4:10; pass. *to
 receive service,* Matt 20:28; Mark 10:45

διακονῇ pres act subj 3 sg [3t; v-1d(2a); 1354]   "
διακονηθεῖσα aor pass ptcp nom sg fem
[2C 3:3; v-1d(2a); 1354]   "
διακονηθῆναι aor pass inf [2t; v-1d(2a); 1354]   "
διακονῆσαι aor act inf [2t; v-1d(2a); 1354]   "
διακονήσαντες aor act ptcp nom pl masc
[2t; v-1d(2a); 1354]   "
διακονήσει fut act ind 3 sg
[Lk 12:37; v-1d(2a); 1354]   "

διακονία, ας, ἡ   {1355, n-1a}
 *serving, service, waiting, attendance, the act of
 rendering friendly offices,* Luke 10:40; 2 Tim 4:11;
 Heb 1:14; *relief, aid,* Acts 6:1; 11:29; 2 Cor 8:4; 9:1,
 12, 13; *a commission,* Acts 12:25; Rom 15:31; *a
 commission* or *ministry* in the service of the
 Gospel, Acts 1:17, 25; 20:24; Rom 11:13; 2 Cor
 4:1; 5:18; 1 Tim 1:12; *service* in the Gospel, Acts
 6:4; 21:19; 1 Cor 16:15; 2 Cor 6:3; 11:8; Eph 4:12;
 Rev 2:19; *a function, ministry,* or *office* in the
 Church, Rom 12:7; 1 Cor 12:5; Col 4:17; 2 Tim
 4:5; *a ministering* in the conveyance of a
 revelation from God, 2 Cor 3:7, 8, 9

διακονία nom sg fem [6t; n-1a; 1355]   διακονία
διακονίᾳ dat sg fem [4t; n-1a; 1355]   "
διακονίαν acc sg fem [16t; n-1a; 1355]   "
διακονίας gen sg fem [7t; n-1a; 1355]   "
διακονιῶν gen pl fem [1C 12:5; n-1a; 1355]   "
διάκονοι nom pl masc [7t; n-2a; 1356] διάκονος
διακόνοις dat pl masc [3t; n-2a; 1356]   "
διάκονον acc sg masc [Rm 15:8; n-2a; 1356]   "
διάκονον acc sg fem [Rm 16:1; n-2a; 1356]   "

διάκονος, οῦ, ὁ or **ἡ**   {1356, n-2a}
 one who renders service to another; *an attendant,
 servant,* Matt 20:26; 22:13; John 2:5, 9; *one who
 executes a commission, a deputy,* Rom 13:4;
 Χριστοῦ, Θεοῦ, ἐν κυρίῳ, etc. *a commissioned
 minister* or *preacher* of the Gospel, 1 Cor 3:5; 2
 Cor 6:4; *a minister* charged with an
 announcement or sentence, 2 Cor 3:6; Gal 2:17;
 Col 1:23; *a minister* charged with a significant
 characteristic, Rom 15:8; *a servitor, devoted
 follower,* John 12:26; *a deacon* or *deaconess,* whose
 official duty was to superintend the alms of the

Church, with other kindred services, Rom 16:1; Phil 1:1; 1 Tim 3:8, 12

διάκονος nom sg masc [15t; n-2a; 1356] "

διακονουμένη pres pass ptcp dat sg fem
[2t; v-1d(2a); 1354] διακονέω

διακονοῦντες pres act ptcp nom pl masc
[2t; v-1d(2a); 1354] "

διακονούντων pres act ptcp gen pl masc
[Ac 19:22; v-1d(2a); 1354] "

διακόνους acc pl masc [2t; n-2a; 1356] διάκονος

διακονοῦσαι pres act ptcp nom pl fem
[Mt 27:55; v-1d(2a); 1354] διακονέω

διακονῶν pres act ptcp nom sg masc
[4t; v-1d(2a); 1354] "

διακόσιαι nom pl fem
[Ac 27:37; a-1a(1); 1357] διακόσιοι

διακοσίας acc pl fem [2t; a-1a(1); 1357] "

διακόσιοι, αι, ον {1357, a-1a(1)}
two hundred, Mark 6:37; John 6:7; 21:8; Acts 23:23f.*

διακοσίους acc pl masc [2t; a-1a(1); 1357] "
διακοσίων gen pl masc [Jn 21:8; a-1a(1); 1357] "
διακοσίων gen pl neut [2t; a-1a(1); 1357] "
διακούσομαι fut mid ind 1 sg
[Ac 23:35; cv-1a(8); 1358] διακούω

διακούω {1358, cv-1a(8)}
[διακούσομαι -, -, -, -] *to hear* a thing *through; to hear* judicially, Acts 23:35*

διακριθῇ aor pass subj 3 sg
[Mk 11:23; cv-1c(2); 1359] διακρίνω

διακριθῆτε aor pass subj 2 pl
[Mt 21:21; cv-1c(2); 1359] "

διακρῖναι aor act inf [1C 6:5; cv-1c(2); 1359] "

διακρίναντα aor act ptcp acc sg masc
[Ac 11:12; cv-1c(2); 1359] "

διακρίνει pres act ind 3 sg
[1C 4:7; cv-1c(2); 1359] "

διακρίνειν pres act inf
[Mt 16:3; cv-1c(2); 1359] "

διακρινέτωσαν pres act imperative 3 pl
[1C 14:29; cv-1c(2); 1359] "

διακρινόμενος pres mid ptcp nom sg masc
[5t; cv-1c(2); 1359] "

διακρινομένους pres mid ptcp acc pl masc
[Jd 22; cv-1c(2); 1359] "

διακρίνω {1359, cv-1c(2)}
[(διέκρινον), -, διέκρινα, -, -, διεκρίθην] *to separate, sever; to make a distinction* or *difference,* Acts 15:9; 1 Cor 11:29; *to make to differ, distinguish, prefer, confer a superiority,* 1 Cor 4:7; *to examine, scrutinize, estimate,* 1 Cor 11:31; 14:29; *to discern, discriminate,* Matt 16:3; *to judge, to decide a cause,* 1 Cor 6:5; *to dispute, contend,* Acts 11:2; Jude 9; *to make a distinction* mentally, James 2:4; Jude 22; in N.T. *to hesitate, be in doubt, doubt,* Matt 21:21; Mark 11:23

διακρίνων pres act ptcp nom sg masc
[1C 11:29; cv-1c(2); 1359] "

διακρίσεις nom pl fem
[1C 12:10; n-3e(5b); 1360] διάκρισις

διακρίσεις acc pl fem [Rm 14:1; n-3e(5b); 1360] "
διάκρισιν acc sg fem [Hb 5:14; n-3e(5b); 1360] "

διάκρισις, εως, ἡ {1360, n-3e(5b)}
a separation; a distinction, or, *doubt,* Rom 14:1; *a discerning, the act of discerning* or *distinguishing,* Heb 5:14; *the faculty of distinguishing and estimating,* 1 Cor 12:10*

διακωλύω {1361, cv-1a(4)}
[διεκώλυον], -, -, -, -, -] *to hinder, restrain, prohibit,* Matt 3:14*

διαλαλέω {1362, cv-1d(2a)}
[-, -, -, -, -] *to talk with;* by impl. *to consult, deliberate,* Luke 6:11; *to divulge, publish, spread by rumor,* Luke 1:65*

διαλέγεται pres mid ind 3 sg
[Hb 12:5; cv-1b(2); 1363] διαλέγομαι

διαλέγομαι {1363, cv-1b(2)}
[(διελεγόμην), -, διελεξάμην, -, -, διελέχθην] *to discourse, argue, reason,* Acts 17:2, 17; 24:12; *to address, speak to,* Heb 12:5; *to contend, dispute,* Mark 9:34; Jude 9

διαλεγόμενον pres mid ptcp acc sg masc
[Ac 24:12; cv-1b(2); 1363] "

διαλεγόμενος pres mid ptcp nom sg masc
[2t; cv-1b(2); 1363] "

διαλεγομένου pres mid ptcp gen sg masc
[2t; cv-1b(2); 1363] "

διαλείπω {1364, cv-1b(1)}
[-, διέλιπον, -, -, -] *to leave an interval; to intermit, cease,* Luke 7:45*

διάλεκτος, ου, ἡ {1365, n-2b}
speech; manner of speaking; peculiar language of a nation, *dialect, vernacular idiom,* Acts 1:19; 2:6, 8; 21:40; 22:2; 26:14

διαλέκτῳ dat sg fem [6t; n-2b; 1365] διάλεκτος

διαλιμπάνω {1366}
[(διελίμπανον), -, -, -, -, -] *stop, cease,* Acts 8:24 v.l.; 17:13 v.l.*

διαλλάγηθι aor pass imperative 2 sg
[Mt 5:24; cv-2b; 1367] διαλλάσσομαι

διαλλάσσομαι {1367, cv-2b}
[-, -, -, -, διηλλάγην] *to be reconciled* to another, Matt 5:24*

διαλογίζεσθαι pres mid inf
[Lk 5:21; cv-2a(1); 1368] διαλογίζομαι

διαλογίζεσθε pres mid ind 2 pl
[4t; cv-2a(1); 1368] "

διαλογίζομαι {1368, cv-2a(1)}
[(διελογιζόμην), -, -, -, -, -] pr. *to make a settlement of accounts; to reason, deliberate, ponder, consider,* Matt 16:7, 8; Mark 2:6, 8; John 11:50; *to dispute, contend,* Mark 9:33

διαλογιζόμενοι pres mid ptcp nom pl masc
[Mk 2:6; cv-2a(1); 1368] "

διαλογιζομένων pres mid ptcp gen pl masc
[Lk 3:15; cv-2a(1); 1368] "

διαλογίζονται pres mid ind 3 pl
[Mk 2:8; cv-2a(1); 1368] "

διαλογισμοί   nom pl masc
  [4t; n-2a; 1369]   διαλογισμός
διαλογισμοῖς   dat pl masc [Rm 1:21; n-2a; 1369]   "
διαλογισμόν   acc sg masc [Lk 9:47; n-2a; 1369]   "

διαλογισμός, οῦ, ὁ   {1369, n-2a}
  reasoning, thought, cogitation, purpose, Matt
  15:19; Mark 7:21; *discourse, dispute, disputation,*
  contention, Luke 9:46; *doubt, hesitation, scruple,*
  Luke 24:38

διαλογισμός   nom sg masc [Lk 9:46; n-2a; 1369]   "
διαλογισμοῦ   gen sg masc [1Ti 2:8; n-2a; 1369]   "
διαλογισμούς   acc pl masc [3t; n-2a; 1369]   "
διαλογισμῶν   gen pl masc [3t; n-2a; 1369]   "

διαλύω   {1370, cv-1a(4)}
  [-, -, -, -, διελύθην] *to dissolve, dissipate, disperse,*
  Acts 5:36; 27:41 v.l.*

διαμαρτυράμενοι   aor mid ptcp nom pl masc
  [Ac 8:25; cv-1c(1); 1371]   διαμαρτύρομαι
διαμαρτύρασθαι   aor mid inf   [2t; cv-1c(1); 1371]   "
διαμαρτύρεται   pres mid ind 3 sg
  [Ac 20:23; cv-1c(1); 1371]   "
διαμαρτύρηται   pres mid subj 3 sg
  [Lk 16:28; cv-1c(1); 1371]   "

διαμαρτύρομαι   {1371, cv-1c(1)}
  [-, διεμαρτυράμην, -, -, -] *to make solemn*
  affirmation, protest; to make a solemn and earnest
  charge, Luke 16:28; Acts 2:40; *to declare solemnly*
  and earnestly, Acts 8:25; 18:5

διαμαρτύρομαι   pres mid ind 1 sg
  [2t; cv-1c(1); 1371]   "
διαμαρτυρόμενος   pres mid ptcp nom sg masc
  [4t; cv-1c(1); 1371]   "

διαμάχομαι   {1372, cv-1b(2)}
  [(διεμαχόμην), -, -, -, -, -] *to fight out, to fight*
  resolutely; met. *to contend vehemently, insist,* Acts
  23:9*

διαμείνῃ   aor act subj 3 sg
  [Ga 2:5; cv-1c(2); 1373]   διαμένω
διαμεμενηκότες   perf act ptcp nom pl masc
  [Lk 22:28; cv-1c(2); 1373]   "
διαμεμερισμένοι   perf pass ptcp nom pl masc
  [Lk 12:52; cv-2a(1); 1374]   διαμερίζω
διαμένει   pres act ind 3 sg
  [2P 3:4; cv-1c(2); 1373]   διαμένω
διαμένεις   pres act ind 2 sg
  [Hb 1:11; cv-1c(2); 1373]   "

διαμένω   {1373, cv-1c(2)}
  [(διέμενον), -, διέμεινα, διαμεμένηκα, -, -] *to*
  continue throughout; to continue, be permanent or
  unchanged, Luke 1:22; Gal 2:5; Heb 1:11; 2 Peter
  3:4; *to continue, remain constant,* Luke 22:28

διαμεριζόμεναι   pres pass ptcp nom pl fem
  [Ac 2:3; cv-2a(1); 1374]   διαμερίζω
διαμεριζόμενοι   pres mid ptcp nom pl masc
  [Lk 23:34; cv-2a(1); 1374]   "
διαμερίζονται   pres mid ind 3 pl
  [Mk 15:24; cv-2a(1); 1374]   "

διαμερίζω   {1374, cv-2a(1)}
  [(διεμέριζον), -, διεμέρισα, -, διαμεμέρισμαι,

διεμερίσθην] *to divide into parts and distribute,*
  Matt 27:35; Mark 15:24; Acts 2:3; pass. in N.T. *to*
  be in a state of dissension, Luke 11:17, 18; 12:52, 53

διαμερίσατε   aor act imperative 2 pl
  [Lk 22:17; cv-2a(1); 1374]   "
διαμερισθεῖσα   aor pass ptcp nom sg fem
  [Lk 11:17; cv-2a(1); 1374]   "
διαμερισθήσονται   fut pass ind 3 pl
  [Lk 12:53; cv-2a(1); 1374]   "
διαμερισμόν   acc sg masc
  [Lk 12:51; n-2a; 1375]   διαμερισμός

διαμερισμός, οῦ, ὁ   {1375, n-2a}
  division; met. in N.T. *disunion, dissension,* Luke
  12:51*

διανεμηθῇ   aor pass subj 3 sg
  [Ac 4:17; cv-1d(2c); 1376]   διανέμω

διανέμω   {1376, cv-1d(2c)}
  [-, -, -, -, διενεμήθην] *to distribute; to divulge,*
  spread abroad, Acts 4:17*

διανεύω   {1377, cv-1a(6)}
  [-, -, -, -, -] *to signify by a nod, beckon, make signs,*
  Luke 1:22*

διανεύων   pres act ptcp nom sg masc
  [Lk 1:22; cv-1a(6); 1377]   διανεύω

διανόημα, ατος, τό   {1378, n-3c(4)}
  thought, Luke 11:17; 3:16 v.l.*

διανοήματα   acc pl neut
  [Lk 11:17; n-3c(4); 1378]   διανόημα

διάνοια, ας, ἡ   {1379, n-1a}
  pr. *thought, intention; the mind, intellect,*
  understanding, Matt 22:37; Mark 12:30; Luke
  10:27; *an operation of the understanding, thought,*
  imagination, Luke 1:51; *insight, comprehension,* 1
  John 5:20; *mode of thinking and feeling, disposition*
  of mind and heart, the affection, Eph 2:3; Col 1:21

διανοίᾳ   dat sg fem   [5t; n-1a; 1379]   διάνοια
διάνοιαν   acc sg fem   [4t; n-1a; 1379]   "
διανοίας   gen sg fem   [2t; n-1a; 1379]   "
διανοῖγον   pres act ptcp nom sg neut
  [Lk 2:23; cv-1b(2); 1380]   διανοίγω

διανοίγω   {1380, cv-1b(2)}
  [-, διήνοιξα, -, διήνοιγμαι, διηνοίχθην] *to open,*
  Mark 7:34, 35; Luke 2:23; 24:31; Acts 7:56; met.
  to open the sense of a thing, *explain, expound,*
  Luke 24:32; Acts 17:3; διανοίγειν τὸν νοῦν, τὴν
  καρδίαν, *to open the mind, the heart,* so as to
  understand and receive, Luke 24:45; Acts
  16:14*

διανοίγων   pres act ptcp nom sg masc
  [Ac 17:3; cv-1b(2); 1380]   "
διανοίχθητι   aor pass imperative 2 sg
  [Mk 7:34; cv-1b(2); 1380]   "
διανοιῶν   gen pl fem   [Ep 2:3; n-1a; 1379]   διάνοια

διανυκτερεύω   {1381, cv-1a(6)}
  [-, -, -, -, -] *to pass the night, spend the whole night,*
  Luke 6:12*

διανυκτερεύων   pres act ptcp nom sg masc
  [Lk 6:12; cv-; 1381]   διανυκτερεύω

διανύσαντες   aor act ptcp nom pl masc
 [Ac 21:7; cv-1a(4); 1382]   διανύω

διανύω   {1382, cv-1a(4)}
 [-, διήνυσα, -, -, -] *to complete, finish,* Acts 21:7*

διαπαντός   {1383}
 written in our texts as two words, διὰ παντός,
 through all time; throughout; always, Mark 5:5;
 continually by stated routine, Luke 24:53; Heb
 9:6

διαπαρατριβαί   nom pl fem
 [1Ti 6:5; n-1b; 1384]   διαπαρατριβή

διαπαρατριβή, ῆς, ἡ   {1384, n-1b}
 constant disputation, 1 Tim 6:5*

διαπεράσαντες   aor act ptcp nom pl masc
 [2t; cv-1d(1b); 1385]   διαπεράω
διαπεράσαντος   aor act ptcp gen sg masc
 [Mk 5:21; cv-1d(1b); 1385]   "

διαπεράω   {1385, cv-1d(1b)}
 [-, διεπέρασα, -, -, -] *to pass through* or *over,* Matt
 9:1; 14:34; Mark 5:21; 6:53; Luke 16:26; Acts
 21:2*

διαπερῶν   pres act ptcp acc sg neut
 [Ac 21:2; cv-1d(1b); 1385]   "
διαπερῶσιν   pres act subj 3 pl
 [Lk 16:26; cv-1d(1b); 1385]   "
διαπλεύσαντες   aor act ptcp nom pl masc
 [Ac 27:5; cv-1a(7); 1386]   διαπλέω

διαπλέω   {1386, cv-1a(7)}
 [-, διέπλευσα, -, -, -] *to sail through* or *over,* Acts
 27:5*

διαπονέομαι   {1387, cv-1d(2a)}
 [-, -, -, -, -] pr. *to be thoroughly exercised with
 labor; to be wearied; to be vexed,* Mark 14:4 v.l.;
 Acts 4:2; 16:18*

διαπονηθείς   aor pass ptcp nom sg masc
 [Ac 16:18; cv-1d(2a); 1387]   διαπονέομαι
διαπονούμενοι   pres mid ptcp nom pl masc
 [Ac 4:2; cv-1d(2a); 1387]   "
διαπορεύεσθαι   pres mid inf
 [Lk 6:1; cv-1a(6); 1388]   διαπορεύομαι

διαπορεύομαι   {1388, cv-1a(6)}
 [(διεπορευόμην), -, -, -, -, -] *to go* or *pass through,*
 Luke 6:1; 13:22; Acts 16:4; *to pass by,* Luke 18:36

διαπορευόμενος   pres mid ptcp nom sg masc
 [Rm 15:24; cv-1a(6); 1388]   "
διαπορευομένου   pres mid ptcp gen sg masc
 [Lk 18:36; cv-1a(6); 1388]   "

διαπορέω   {1389, cv-1d(2a)}
 [(διηπόρουν), -, -, -, -, -] *to be utterly at a loss; to be
 in doubt and perplexity,* Luke 9:7; Acts 2:12; 5:24;
 10:17

διαπραγματεύομαι   {1390, cv-1a(6)}
 [-, διεπραγματευσάμην, -, -, -] *to despatch a matter
 thoroughly; to make profit in business, gain in
 trade,* Luke 19:15*

διαπρίω   {1391, cv-2a(1)}
 [(διέπριον), -, -, -, -, -] *to divide with a saw, saw

asunder; to grate the teeth in a rage; pass. met. *to
 be cut* to the heart, *to be enraged,* Acts 5:33; 7:54*

διαρήσσω   {1393, cv-2b}
 [-, διέ(ρ)ρηξα, -, -, διε(ρ)ράγη] also spelled
 διαρρήγνυμι or διαρρήσσω, *to break,* Luke 8:29
 asunder, rend, tear, burst, Matt 26:65; Mark 14:63;
 Luke 5:6; Acts 14:14*

διαρθρόω   {1392, v-1d(3)}
 to make articulate speech possible, Luke 1:64 v.l.*

διαρπάζω   {1395, cv-2a(1)}
 [διαρπάσω, διήρπασα, -, -, -] *to plunder, spoil,
 pillage,* Matt 12:29, 30 v.l.; Mark 3:27 (2t)*

διαρπάσαι   aor act inf
 [Mk 3:27; cv-; 1395]   διαρπάζω
διαρπάσει   fut act ind 3 sg [2t; cv-; 1395]   "

διαρρήγνυμι, see διαρήσσω   {1396, cv-3c(2)}

διαρρήξαντες   aor act ptcp nom pl masc
 [Ac 14:14; cv-3c(2); 1396]   διαρρήγνυμι
διαρρήξας   aor act ptcp nom sg masc
 [Mk 14:63; cv-3c(2); 1396]   "

διαρρήσσω, see διαρήσσω

διαρρήσσων   pres act ptcp nom sg masc
 [Lk 8:29; cv-; 1393]   διαρήσσω

διασαφέω   {1397, cv-1d(2a)}
 [-, διεσάφησα -, -, -] *to make known, declare, tell
 plainly,* or *fully,* Matt 13:36; 18:31; Acts 10:25
 v.l.*

διασάφησον   aor act imperative 2 sg
 [Mt 13:36; cv-1d(2a); 1397]   διασαφέω
διασείσητε   aor act subj 2 pl
 [Lk 3:14; cv-1a(3); 1398]   διασείω

διασείω   {1398, cv-1a(3)}
 [-, διέσεισα, -, -, -] pr. *to shake thoroughly* or
 violently; to harass, intimidate, extort from, Luke
 3:14*

διασκορπίζω   {1399, cv-2a(1)}
 [-, διεσκόρπισα, -, διεσκόρπισμαι, διεσκορπίσθην]
 to disperse, scatter, Matt 26:31; Mark 14:27; *to
 dissipate, waste,* Luke 15:13; 16:1; *to winnow,* or,
 to strew, Matt 25:24, 26

διασκορπίζων   pres act ptcp nom sg masc
 [Lk 16:1; cv-2a(1); 1399]   διασκορπίζω
διασκορπισθήσονται   fut pass ind 3 pl
 [2t; cv-2a(1); 1399]   "
διασπαρέντες   aor pass ptcp nom pl masc
 [2t; cv-2d(3); 1401]   διασπείρω
διασπασθῇ   aor pass subj 3 sg
 [Ac 23:10; cv-1d(1b); 1400]   διασπάω

διασπάω   {1400, cv-1d(1b)}
 [-, -, -, διέσπασμαι, διεσπάσθην] *to pull* or *tear
 asunder* or *in pieces, burst,* Mark 5:4; Acts 23:10*

διασπείρω   {1401, cv-2d(3)}
 [-, -, -, -, διεσπάρην] *to scatter abroad* or *in every
 direction,* as seen; *to disperse,* Acts 8:1, 4; 11:19*

διασπορά, ᾶς, ἡ   {1402, n-1a}
 pr. *a scattering,* as of seed; *dispersion;* in N.T.
 meton. *the dispersed portion* of the Jews,

specially termed *the dispersion,* John 7:35; James
1:1; 1 Peter 1:1*

διασπορᾷ   dat sg fem
[Jm 1:1; n-1a; 1402]   διασπορά
διασποράν   acc sg fem [Jn 7:35; n-1a; 1402]   "
διασποράς   gen sg fem [1P 1:1; n-1a; 1402]   "
διαστάσης   aor act ptcp gen sg fem
[Lk 22:59; cv-6a; 1460]   διΐστημι
διαστελλόμενον   pres pass ptcp acc sg neut
[Hb 12:20; cv-2d(1); 1403]   διαστέλλω

διαστέλλω   {1403, cv-2d(1)}
[(διέστελλον), -, διέστειλα, -, -, -] *to determine,
issue a decision; to state* or *explain distinctly and
accurately;* hence, *to admonish, direct, charge,
command,* Acts 15:24; Heb 12:20; when
followed by a negative clause, *to interdict,
prohibit,* Matt 16:30; Mark 5:43

διάστημα, ατος, τό   {1404, n-3c(4)}
interval, space, distance, Acts 5:7

διάστημα   nom sg neut
[Ac 5:7; n-3c(4); 1404]   διάστημα
διαστήσαντες   aor act ptcp nom pl masc
[Ac 27:28; cv-6a; 1460]   διΐστημι

διαστολή, ῆς, ἡ   {1405, n-1b}
distinction, difference, Rom 3:22; 10:12; 1 Cor
14:7*

διαστολή   nom sg fem [2t; n-1b; 1405]   διαστολή
διαστολήν   acc sg fem [1C 14:7; n-1b; 1405]   "
διαστρέφοντα   pres act ptcp acc sg masc
[Lk 23:2; cv-1b(1); 1406]   διαστρέφω

διαστρέφω   {1406, cv-1b(1)}
[-, διέστρεψα -, διέστραμμαι, -] *to distort, turn
away;* met. *to pervert, corrupt,* Matt 17:17; Luke
9:41; *to turn out of the way, cause to make defection,*
Luke 23:2; Acts 13:8; διεστραμμένος, *perverse,
corrupt, erroneous*

διαστρέφων   pres act ptcp nom sg masc
[Ac 13:10; cv-1b(1); 1406]   "
διαστρέψαι   aor act inf
[Ac 13:8; cv-1b(1); 1406]   "

διασῴζω   {1407, cv-2a(1)}
[-, διέσωσα, -, -, διεσώθην] *to bring safely through;
to convey in safety,* Acts 23:24; pass. *to reach a
place* or *state of safety,* Acts 27:43, 44; 28:1, 4; 1
Peter 3:20; *to heal, to restore to health,* Matt 14:36;
Luke 7:3*

διασωθέντα   aor pass ptcp acc sg masc
[Ac 28:4; cv-2a(1); 1407]   διασῴζω
διασωθέντες   aor pass ptcp nom pl masc
[Ac 28:1; cv-2a(1); 1407]   "
διασωθῆναι   aor pass inf
[Ac 27:44; cv-2a(1); 1407]   "
διασῶσαι   aor act inf [Ac 27:43; cv-2a(1); 1407]   "
διασώσῃ   aor act subj 3 sg
[Lk 7:3; cv-2a(1); 1407]   "
διασώσωσι   aor act subj 3 pl
[Ac 23:24; cv-2a(1); 1407]   "
διαταγάς   acc pl fem [Ac 7:53; n-1b; 1408]   διαταγή

διαταγείς   aor pass ptcp nom sg masc
[Ga 3:19; cv-2b; 1411]   διατάσσω

διαταγή, ῆς, ἡ   {1408, n-1b}
an injunction, institute, ordinance, Rom 13:2;
Acts 7:53*

διαταγῇ   dat sg fem [Rm 13:2; n-1b; 1408]   διαταγή

διάταγμα, ατος, τό   {1409, n-3c(4)}
a mandate, commandment, ordinance, Heb 11:23*

διάταγμα   acc sg neut
[Hb 11:23; n-3c(4); 1409]   διάταγμα
διαταξάμενος   aor mid ptcp nom sg masc
[Ac 24:23; cv-2b; 1411]   διατάσσω
διατάξομαι   fut mid ind 1 sg
[1C 11:34; cv-2b; 1411]   "
διατάσσομαι   pres mid ind 1 sg
[1C 7:17; cv-2b; 1411]   "

διαταράσσω   {1410, cv-2b}
[-, -, -, -, διεταράχθην] *to throw into a state of
perturbation, to move* or *trouble greatly,* Luke
1:29*

διατάσσω   {1411, cv-2b}
[διατάξω, διέταξα, διατέταχα, διατέταγμαι,
διετάχθην or διετάγην] pr. *to arrange, make a
precise arrangement; to prescribe,* 1 Cor 11:34;
16:1; Titus 1:5; *to direct,* Luke 8:55; Acts 20:13; *to
charge,* Matt 11:1; *to command,* Acts 18:2; *to
ordain,* Gal 3:19

διατάσσων   pres act ptcp nom sg masc
[Mt 11:1; cv-2b; 1411]   "
διαταχθέντα   aor pass ptcp acc pl neut
[2t; cv-2b; 1411]   "
διατελεῖτε   pres act ind 2 pl
[Ac 27:33; cv-1d(2b); 1412]   διατελέω

διατελέω   {1412, cv-1d(2b)}
[-, -, -, -, -] *to complete, finish;* intrans. *to continue,
persevere,* in a certain state or course of action,
Acts 27:33*

διατεταγμένον   perf pass ptcp acc sg neut
[2t; cv-2b; 1411]   διατάσσω
διατεταγμένος   perf pass ptcp nom sg masc
[Ac 20:13; cv-2b; 1411]   "
διατεταχέναι   perf act inf
[Ac 18:2; cv-2b; 1411]   "

διατηρέω   {1413, cv-1d(2a)}
[(διετήρουν), -, -, -, -, -] *to watch carefully, guard
with vigilance; to treasure up,* Luke 2:51; ἑαυτὸν
ἐκ, *to keep one's self from, to abstain wholly from,*
Acts 15:29*

διατηροῦντες   pres act ptcp nom pl masc
[Ac 15:29; cv-1d(2a); 1413]   διατηρέω

διατί   {1414}
written in our texts as two words, διὰ τί, *For
what? Why? Wherefore?* Matt 9:14; 13:10; Luke
19:23, 31

διατίθεμαι   pres mid ind 1 sg
[Lk 22:29; cv-6a; 1416]   διατίθημι

διατίθημι   {1416, cv-6a}
[διαθήσω, διέθηκα, -, -, -] in N.T. only mid., so

some list as διατίθεμαι, *to arrange; to arrange according to one's own mind; to make a disposition, to make a will; to settle the terms of a covenant, to ratify,* Acts 3:25; Heb 8:10; 10:16; *to assign,* Luke 22:29

διατρίβοντες   pres act ptcp nom pl masc
   [Ac 16:12; cv-1b(1); 1417]   διατρίβω

διατρίβω   {1417, cv-1b(1)}
   [(διέτριβον), -, διέτριψα, -, -, -] pr. *to rub, wear away by friction;* met. *to pass* or *spend* time, *to remain, stay, tarry, continue,* John 3:22; 11:54; Acts 12:19; 14:3, 28

διατρίψας   aor act ptcp nom sg masc
   [Ac 25:6; cv-1b(1); 1417]   "

διατροφάς   acc pl fem
   [1Ti 6:8; n-1b; 1418]   διατροφή

διατροφή, ῆς, ἡ   {1418, n-1b}
   food, sustenance, 1 Tim 6:8*

διαυγάζω   {1419, cv-2a(1)}
   [διαυγάσω, διηύγασα, -, -, -] *to shine through, shine out, dawn,* 2 Cor 4:4 v.l.; 2 Pet 1:19*

διαυγάσῃ   aor act subj 3 sg
   [2P 1:19; cv-2a(1); 1419]   διαυγάζω

διαυγής, ές   {1420, a-4a}
   translucent, transparent, Rev 21:21*

διαυγής   nom sg fem [Rv 21:21; a-4a; 1420] διαυγής

διαφανής, ες   {1421, a-4a}
   transparent, Rev 21:21 v.l.*

διαφέρει   pres act ind 3 sg
   [4t; cv-1c(1); 1422]   διαφέρω

διαφέρετε   pres act ind 2 pl [4t; cv-1c(1); 1422]   "

διαφερομένων   pres pass ptcp gen pl masc
   [Ac 27:27; cv-1c(1); 1422]   "

διαφέροντα   pres act ptcp acc pl neut
   [2t; cv-1c(1); 1422]   "

διαφέρω   {1422, cv-1c(1)}
   [(διέφερον), -, διήνεγκα, -, -, -] *to convey through, across,* Mark 11:16; *to carry different ways* or *into different parts, separate;* pass. *to be borne, driven,* or *tossed hither and thither,* Acts 27:27; *to be proclaimed, published,* Acts 13:49; intrans. met. *to differ,* 1 Cor 15:41; *to excel, be better* or *of greater value, be superior,* Matt 6:26; 10:31; impers. διαφέρει, *it makes a difference, it is of consequence;* with οὐδέν, *it makes no difference, it is nothing,* Gal 2:6

διαφεύγω   {1423, cv-1b(2)}
   [-, διέφυγον, -, -, -] *to flee through, escape by flight,* Acts 27:42*

διαφημίζειν   pres act inf
   [Mk 1:45; cv-2a(1); 1424]   διαφημίζω

διαφημίζω   {1424, cv-2a(1)}
   [-, διεφήμισα, -, -, διεφημίσθην] *to report, proclaim, publish, spread abroad,* Matt 9:31; 28:15; Mark 1:45*

διαφθεῖραι   aor act inf
   [Rv 11:18; cv-2d(3); 1425]   διαφθείρω

διαφθείρει   pres act ind 3 sg
   [Lk 12:33; cv-2d(3); 1425]   "

διαφθείρεται   pres pass ind 3 sg
   [2C 4:16; cv-2d(3); 1425]   "

διαφθείροντας   pres act ptcp acc pl masc
   [Rv 11:18; cv-2d(3); 1425]   "

διαφθείρω   {1425, cv-2d(3)}
   [-, διέφθειρα, -, διέφθαρμαι, διεφθάρην] *to corrupt* or *destroy utterly; to waste, bring to decay,* Luke 12:33; 2 Cor 4:16; *to destroy,* Rev 8:9; 11:18; met. *to corrupt, pervert utterly,* 1 Tim 6:5; Rev 19:2 v.l.*

διαφθορά, ας, ἡ   {1426, n-1a}
   corruption, dissolution, Acts 2:27, 31; 13:34, 35, 36, 37*

διαφθοράν   acc sg fem [6t; n-1a; 1426]   διαφθορά
διάφορα   acc pl neut
   [Rm 12:6; a-3a; 1427]   διάφορος
διαφόροις   dat pl masc [Hb 9:10; a-3a; 1427]   "

διάφορος, ον   {1427, a-3a}
   different, diverse, of different kinds, Rom 12:6; Heb 9:10; *excellent, superior,* Heb 1:4; 8:6*

διαφορωτέρας   gen sg fem comparative
   [Hb 8:6; a-3a; 1427]   "
διαφορώτερον   acc sg neut comparative
   [Hb 1:4; a-3a; 1427]   "
διαφύγῃ   aor act subj 3 sg
   [Ac 27:42; cv-1b(2); 1423]   διαφεύγω
διαφυλάξαι   aor act inf
   [Lk 4:10; cv-2b; 1428]   διαφυλάσσω

διαφυλάσσω   {1428, cv-2b}
   [-, διεφύλαξα -, -, -] *to keep* or *guard carefully* or *with vigilance; to guard, protect,* Luke 4:10*

διαχειρίζω   {1429, cv-2a(1)}
   [-, διεχείρισα, -, -, -] pr. *to have in the hands, to manage;* mid. later, *to kill,* Acts 5:30; 26:21*

διαχειρίσασθαι   aor mid inf
   [Ac 26:21; cv-2a(1); 1429]   διαχειρίζω
διαχλευάζοντες   pres act ptcp nom pl masc
   [Ac 2:13; cv-2a(1); 1430]   διαχλευάζω

διαχλευάζω   {1430, cv-2a(1)}
   [-, -, -, -, -] *to jeer outright, deride,* Acts 2:13*

διαχωρίζεσθαι   pres mid inf
   [Lk 9:33; cv-2a(1); 1431]   διαχωρίζω

διαχωρίζω   {1431, cv-2a(1)}
   [-, -, -, -, -] *to depart, go away,* Luke 9:33*

διγαμιά, ας, ἡ   {1432, n-1a}
   second marriage, Titus 1:9 v.l.*

δίγαμος, ον   {1433, a-3a}
   married for the second time, Titus 1:9 v.l.*

διδακτικόν   acc sg masc
   [2t; a-1a(2a); 1434]   διδακτικός

διδακτικός, ή, όν   {1434, a-1a(2a)}
   apt or *qualified to teach,* 1 Tim 3:2; 2 Tim 2:24*

διδακτοί   nom pl masc
   [Jn 6:45; a-1a(2a); 1435]   διδακτός
διδακτοῖς   dat pl masc [2t; a-1a(2a); 1435]   "

διδακτός, ή, όν   {1435, a-1a(2a)}
pr. *taught, teachable,* of things; in N.T. *taught,* of person, John 6:45; 1 Cor 2:13*

διδάξαι   aor act inf [3t; v-5a; 1438]   διδάσκω
διδάξει   fut act ind 3 sg [2t; v-5a; 1438]   "
διδάξη   aor act subj 3 sg [2t; v-5a; 1438]   "
διδάξον   aor act imperative 2 sg
     [Lk 11:1; v-5a; 1438]   "
διδάξωσιν   aor act subj 3 pl
     [Hb 8:11; v-5a; 1438]   "
διδάσκαλε   voc sg masc
     [31t; n-2a; 1437]   διδάσκαλος

διδασκαλία, ας, ή   {1436, n-1a}
the act or *occupation of teaching,* Rom 12:7; 1 Tim 4:13; *information, instruction,* Rom 15:4; 2 Tim 3:16; *matter taught, precept, doctrine,* Matt 15:9; 1 Tim 1:10

διδασκαλία   nom sg fem
     [1Ti 6:1; n-1a; 1436]   διδασκαλία
διδασκαλία   dat sg fem [10t; n-1a; 1436]   "
διδασκαλίαις   dat pl fem [1Ti 4:1; n-1a; 1436]   "
διδασκαλίαν   acc sg fem [3t; n-1a; 1436]   "
διδασκαλίας   gen sg fem [3t; n-1a; 1436]   "
διδασκαλίας   acc pl fem [3t; n-1a; 1436]   "
διδάσκαλοι   nom pl masc
     [4t; n-2a; 1437]   διδάσκαλος
διδάσκαλον   acc sg masc [5t; n-2a; 1437]   "

διδάσκαλος, ου, ό   {1437, n-2a}
a teacher, master, Rom 2:20; in N.T. as an equivalent, to ῥαββί, John 1:39

διδάσκαλος   nom sg masc [15t; n-2a; 1437]   "
διδασκάλους   acc pl masc [3t; n-2a; 1437]   "
διδασκάλων   gen pl masc [Lk 2:46; n-2a; 1437]   "
δίδασκε   pres act imperative 2 sg
     [2t; v-5a; 1438]   διδάσκω
διδάσκει   pres act ind 3 sg [3t; v-5a; 1438]   "
διδάσκειν   pres act inf [13t; v-5a; 1438]   "
διδάσκεις   pres act ind 2 sg [7t; v-5a; 1438]   "
διδάσκη   pres act subj 3 sg
     [1J 2:27; v-5a; 1438]   "
διδάσκοντες   pres act ptcp nom pl masc
     [9t; v-5a; 1438]   "
διδάσκοντι   pres act ptcp dat sg masc
     [Mt 21:23; v-5a; 1438]   "
διδάσκοντος   pres act ptcp gen sg masc
     [Lk 20:1; v-5a; 1438]   "

διδάσκω   {1438, v-5a}
[(ἐδίδασκον), διδάξω, ἐδίδαξα, -, -, ἐδιδάχθην] *to teach,* Matt 4:23; 22:16; *to teach* or *speak in a public assembly,* 1 Tim 2:12; *to direct, admonish,* Matt 28:15; Rom 2:21

διδάσκω   pres act ind 1 sg [1C 4:17; v-5a; 1438]   "
διδάσκων   pres act ptcp nom sg masc
     [22t; v-5a; 1438]   "
διδάσκων   pres act ptcp voc sg masc
     [Rm 2:21; v-5a; 1438]   "
διδαχαῖς   dat pl fem [Hb 13:9; n-1b; 1439]   διδαχή

διδαχή, ῆς, ή   {1439, n-1b}
instruction, the giving of instruction, teaching, Mark 4:2; 12:38; *instruction, what is taught,*

doctrine, Matt 16:12; John 7:16, 17; meton. *mode of teaching and kind of doctrine taught,* Matt 7:28; Mark 1:27

διδαχή   nom sg fem [3t; n-1b; 1439]   "
διδαχῇ   dat sg fem [13t; n-1b; 1439]   "
διδαχήν   acc sg fem [7t; n-1b; 1439]   "
διδαχῆς   gen sg fem [6t; n-1b; 1439]   "
διδόασιν   pres act ind 3 pl
     [Rv 17:13; v-6a; 1443]   δίδωμι
διδόμενον   pres pass ptcp nom sg neut
     [Lk 22:19; v-6a; 1443]
διδόναι   pres act inf [6t; v-6a; 1443]   "
διδόντα   pres act ptcp nom pl neut
     [1C 14:7; v-6a; 1443]   "
διδόντα   pres act ptcp acc sg masc
     [1Th 4:8; v-6a; 1443]   "
διδόντες   pres act ptcp nom pl masc
     [2t; v-6a; 1443]   "
διδόντι   pres act ptcp dat sg masc
     [2t; v-6a; 1443]   "
διδόντος   pres act ptcp gen sg masc
     [2t; v-6a; 1443]   "
δίδοται   pres pass ind 3 sg [3t; v-6a; 1443]   "
δίδοτε   pres act imperative 2 pl
     [2t; v-6a; 1443]   "
δίδου   pres act imperative 2 sg
     [2t; v-6a; 1443]   "
διδούς   pres act ptcp nom sg masc
     [5t; v-6a; 1443]   "
δίδραχμα   acc pl neut [2t; n-2c; 1440]   δίδραχμον

δίδραχμον, ου, τό   {1440, n-2c}
a didrachmon or *double drachma,* a silver coin equal to the drachma of Alexandria, to two Attic drachmas, to two Roman denarii, and to the half-shekel of the Jews, Matt 17:24 (2t)*

Δίδυμος, ου, ό   {1441, n-2a}
a twin; Didymus, the Greek equivalent to the name Thomas, John 11:16; 20:24; 21:2*

Δίδυμος   nom sg masc [3t; n-2a; 1441]   Δίδυμος

διδῶ   {1442}
I give (by-form of δίδωμι), Rev 3:9 v.l.*

διδῶ   pres act ind 1 sg
     [Rv 3:9; v-6a; 1443]   δίδωμι

δίδωμι   {1443, v-6a}
[(ἐδίδων), δώσω, ἔδωκα, δέδωκα, δέδομαι, ἐδόθην] pluperfect, ἐδεδώκειν, *to give, bestow, present,* Matt 4:9; 6:11; John 3:16; 17:2, et al. freq.; *to give, cast, throw,* Matt 7:6; *to supply, suggest,* Matt 10:19; Mark 13:11; *to distribute* alms, Matt 19:21; Luke 11:41; *to pay* tribute, etc., Matt 22:17; Mark 12:14; Luke 20:22; *to be the author* or *source of* a thing, Luke 12:51; Rom 11:8; *to grant, permit, allow,* Acts 2:27; 13:35; Matt 13:11; 19:11; *to deliver to, entrust, commit to the charge* of anyone, Matt 25:15; Mark 12:9; *to give* or *deliver up,* Luke 22:19; John 6:51; *to reveal, teach,* Acts 7:38; *to appoint, constitute,* Eph 1:22; 4:11; *to consecrate, devote, offer in sacrifice,* 2 Cor 8:5; Gal 1:4; Rev 8:3; *to present, expose* one's self in a place, Acts 19:31; *to recompense,* Rev 2:23; *to attribute, ascribe,* John 9:24; Rev 11:13; from the Hebrew,

to place, put, fix, inscribe, Heb 8:10; 10:16; *to infix,
impress,* 2 Cor 12:7; Rev 13:16; *to inflict,* John
18:22; 19:3; 2 Thess 1:8; *to give in charge, assign,*
John 5:36; 17:4; Rev 9:5; *to exhibit, put forth,* Matt
24:24; Acts 2:19; *to yield, bear* fruit, Matt 13:8;
διδόναι ἐργασίαν, *to endeavor, strive,* Luke 12:58;
διδόναι ἀπόκρισιν, *to answer, reply,* John 1:22;
διδόναι τόπον, *to give place, yield,* Luke 14:9;
Rom 12:19

δίδωμι   pres act ind 1 sg   [9t; v-6a; 1443]   "
δίδωσιν   pres act ind 3 sg   [11t; v-6a; 1443]   "
διέβησαν   aor act ind 3 pl
   [Hb 11:29; cv-2d(6); 1329]   διαβαίνω
διέβλεψεν   aor act ind 3 sg
   [Mk 8:25; cv-1b(1); 1332]   διαβλέπω
διεβλήθη   aor pass ind 3 sg
   [Lk 16:1; cv-2d(1); 1330]   διαβάλλω
διεγείρειν   pres act inf
   [2P 1:13; cv-2d(3); 1444]   διεγείρω
διεγείρετο   imperf pass ind 3 sg
   [Jn 6:18; cv-2d(3); 1444]   "

διεγείρω   {1444, cv-2d(3)}
[(διήγειρον or διέγειρον), -, διήγειρα, -, -,
διηγέρθην] *to arouse* or *awake thoroughly,* Matt
1:24; Mark 4:38, 39; Luke 8:24; pass. *to be raised,
excited, agitated,* as a sea, John 6:18; met. *to stir
up, arouse, animate,* 2 Peter 1:13; 3:1

διεγείρω   pres act ind 1 sg
   [2P 3:1; cv-2d(3); 1444]   "
διεγερθείς   aor pass ptcp nom sg masc
   [2t; cv-2d(3); 1444]   "
διεγόγγυζον   imperf act ind 3 pl
   [2t; cv-2a(1); 1339]   διαγογγύζω
διεδίδετο   imperf pass ind 3 sg
   [Ac 4:35; cv-6a; 1344]   διαδίδωμι
διέδωκεν   aor act ind 3 sg   [Jn 6:11; cv-6a; 1344]   "
διεζώσατο   aor mid ind 3 sg
   [Jn 21:7; cv-3c(1); 1346]   διαζώννυμι
διέζωσεν   aor act ind 3 sg
   [Jn 13:4; cv-3c(1); 1346]   "
διεζωσμένος   perf pass ptcp nom sg masc
   [Jn 13:5; cv-3c(1); 1346]   "
διέθετο   aor mid ind 3 sg
   [2t; cv-6a; 1416]   διατίθημι
διεῖλεν   aor act ind 3 sg
   [Lk 15:12; cv-1d(2a); 1349]   διαιρέω
διεκρίθη   aor pass ind 3 sg
   [Rm 4:20; cv-1c(2); 1359]   διακρίνω
διεκρίθητε   aor pass ind 2 pl
   [Jm 2:4; cv-1c(2); 1359]   "
διέκρινεν   aor act ind 3 sg
   [Ac 15:9; cv-1c(2); 1359]   "
διεκρίνομεν   imperf act ind 1 pl
   [1C 11:31; cv-1c(2); 1359]   "
διεκρίνοντο   imperf mid ind 3 pl
   [Ac 11:2; cv-1c(2); 1359]   "
διεκώλυεν   imperf act ind 3 sg
   [Mt 3:14; cv-1a(4); 1361]   διακωλύω
διελαλεῖτο   imperf pass ind 3 sg
   [Lk 1:65; cv-1d(2a); 1362]   διαλαλέω
διελάλουν   imperf act ind 3 pl
   [Lk 6:11; cv-1d(2a); 1362]   "

διελέγετο   imperf mid ind 3 sg
   [4t; cv-1b(2); 1363]   διαλέγομαι
διελέξατο   aor mid ind 3 sg   [2t; cv-1b(2); 1363]   "
διελεύσεται   fut mid ind 3 sg
   [Lk 2:35; cv-1b(2); 1451]   διέρχομαι
διελέχθησαν   aor pass ind 3 pl
   [Mk 9:34; cv-1b(2); 1363]   διαλέγομαι
διεληλυθότα   perf act ptcp acc sg masc
   [Hb 4:14; cv-1b(2); 1451]   διέρχομαι
διελθεῖν   aor act inf   [6t; cv-1b(2); 1451]   "
διελθόντα   aor act ptcp acc sg masc
   [Ac 19:1; cv-1b(2); 1451]   "
διελθόντες   aor act ptcp nom pl masc
   [4t; cv-1b(2); 1451]   "
διέλθω   aor act subj 1 sg
   [1C 16:5; cv-1b(2); 1451]   "
διέλθωμεν   aor act subj 1 pl   [3t; cv-1b(2); 1451]   "
διελθών   aor act ptcp nom sg masc
   [3t; cv-1b(2); 1451]   "
διέλιπεν   aor act ind 3 sg
   [Lk 7:45; cv-1b(1); 1364]   διαλείπω
διελογίζεσθε   imperf mid ind 2 pl
   [Mk 9:33; cv-2a(1); 1368]   διαλογίζομαι
διελογίζετο   imperf mid ind 3 sg
   [2t; cv-2a(1); 1368]   "
διελογίζοντο   imperf mid ind 3 pl
   [5t; cv-2a(1); 1368]   "
διελύθησαν   aor pass ind 3 pl
   [Ac 5:36; cv-1a(4); 1370]   διαλύω
διεμαρτυράμεθα   aor mid ind 1 pl
   [1Th 4:6; cv-1c(1); 1371]   διαμαρτύρομαι
διεμαρτύρατο   aor mid ind 3 sg
   [2t; cv-1c(1); 1371]   "
διεμαρτύρω   aor mid ind 2 sg
   [Ac 23:11; cv-1c(1); 1371]   "
διεμάχοντο   imperf mid ind 3 pl
   [Ac 23:9; cv-1b(2); 1372]   διαμάχομαι
διέμενεν   imperf act ind 3 sg
   [Lk 1:22; cv-1c(2); 1373]   διαμένω
διεμέριζον   imperf act ind 3 pl
   [Ac 2:45; cv-2a(1); 1374]   διαμερίζω
διεμερίσαντο   aor mid ind 3 pl
   [2t; cv-2a(1); 1374]   "
διεμερίσθη   aor pass ind 3 sg
   [Lk 11:18; cv-2a(1); 1374]   "
διενέγκῃ   aor act subj 3 sg
   [Mk 11:16; cv-1c(1); 1422]   διαφέρω

διενθυμέομαι   {1445, cv-1b(2a)}
[-, -, -, -, -] *to revolve thoroughly in the mind,
consider carefully, ponder, reflect,* Acts 10:19*

διενθυμουμένου   pres mid ptcp gen sg masc
   [Ac 10:19; cv-1b(2a); 1445]   διενθυμέομαι

διεξέρχομαι   {1446, cv-1b(2)}
[διεξελεύσομαι, διεξῆλθον, διεξελήλυθα, -, -] *to
come out through* anything, *find one's way out,*
Acts 28:3*

διέξοδος, ου, ἡ   {1447, n-2b}
a passage throughout; a line of road, a thoroughfare,
Matt 22:9*

διεξόδους   acc pl fem
   [Mt 22:9; n-2b; 1447]   διέξοδος

διεπέρασεν   aor act ind 3 sg
  [Mt 9:1; cv-1d(1b); 1385]   διαπεράω
διεπορεύετο   imperf mid ind 3 sg
  [Lk 13:22; cv-1a(6); 1388]   διαπορεύομαι
διεπορεύοντο   imperf mid ind 3 pl
  [Ac 16:4; cv-1a(6); 1388]   "
διεπραγματεύσαντο   aor mid ind 3 pl
  [Lk 19:15; cv-1a(6); 1390]   διαπραγματεύομαι
διεπρίοντο   imperf pass ind 3 pl
  [2t; cv-2a(1); 1391]   διαπρίω

διερμηνεία, ας, ἡ   {1448, n-1a}
  explanation, interpretation, translation, 1 Cor
  12:10 v.l.*

διερμηνευέτω   pres act imperative 3 sg
  [1C 14:27; cv-1a(6); 1450]   διερμηνεύω
διερμηνεύῃ   pres act subj 3 sg
  [2t; cv-1a(6); 1450]   "
διερμηνευομένη   pres pass ptcp nom sg fem
  [Ac 9:36; cv-1a(6); 1450]   "
διερμηνεύουσιν   pres act ind 3 pl
  [1C 12:30; cv-1a(6); 1450]   "
διερμήνευσεν   aor act ind 3 sg
  [Lk 24:27; cv-1a(6); 1450]   "

διερμηνευτής, ου, ὁ   {1449, n-1f}
  an interpreter, 1 Cor 14:28*

διερμηνευτής   nom sg masc
  [1C 14:28; n-1f; 1449]   διερμηνευτής

διερμηνεύω   {1450, cv-1a(6)}
  [-, διερμήνευσα, -, -, -] *to explain, interpret,*
  translate, Luke 24:27; Acts 9:36; 18:6 v.l.; 1 Cor
  14:5, 13, 27; *to be able to interpret,* 1 Cor 12:30*

διέρρηξεν   aor act ind 3 sg
  [Mt 26:65; cv-3c(2); 1396]   διαρρήγνυμι
διερρήσσετο   imperf pass ind 3 sg
  [Lk 5:6; cv-; 1393]   διαρήσσω
διέρχεσθαι   pres mid inf
  [2t; cv-1b(2); 1451]   διέρχομαι
διέρχεται   pres mid ind 3 sg   [2t; cv-1b(2); 1451]   "

διέρχομαι   {1451, cv-1b(2)}
  [(διηρχόμην), διελεύσομαι, διῆλθον, διελήλυθα, -,
  -] *to pass through,* Mark 10:25; Luke 4:30; *to pass*
  over, cross, Mark 4:35; Luke 8:22; *to pass along,*
  Luke 19:4; *to proceed,* Luke 2:15; Acts 9:38; *to*
  travel through or *over* a country, *wander about,*
  Matt 12:43; Luke 9:6; *to transfix, pierce,* Luke
  2:35; *to spread abroad, be prevalent,* as a rumor,
  Luke 5:15; met. *to extend to,* Rom 5:12

διέρχομαι   pres mid ind 1 sg
  [1C 16:5; cv-1b(2); 1451]   "
διερχόμενον   pres mid ptcp acc sg masc
  [Ac 9:32; cv-1b(2); 1451]   "
διερχόμενος   pres mid ptcp nom sg masc
  [3t; cv-1b(2); 1451]   "
διέρχωμαι   pres mid subj 1 sg
  [Jn 4:15; cv-1b(2); 1451]   "

διερωτάω   {1452, cv-1d(1a)}
  [-, διηρώτησα, -, -, -] *to sift by questioning,* of
  persons; in N.T., of things, *to ascertain by*
  inquiry, Acts 10:17*

διερωτήσαντες   aor act ptcp nom pl masc
  [Ac 10:17; cv-1d(1a); 1452]   διερωτάω
διεσάφησαν   aor act ind 3 pl
  [Mt 18:31; cv-1d(2a); 1397]   διασαφέω
διεσκόρπισα   aor act ind 1 sg
  [Mt 25:26; cv-2a(1); 1399]   διασκορπίζω
διεσκόρπισας   aor act ind 2 sg
  [Mt 25:24; cv-2a(1); 1399]   "
διεσκόρπισεν   aor act ind 3 sg
  [2t; cv-2a(1); 1399]   "
διεσκορπίσθησαν   aor pass ind 3 pl
  [Ac 5:37; cv-2a(1); 1399]   "
διεσκορπισμένα   perf pass ptcp acc pl neut
  [Jn 11:52; cv-2a(1); 1399]   "
διεσπάρησαν   aor pass ind 3 pl
  [Ac 8:1; cv-2d(3); 1401]   διασπείρω
διεσπάσθαι   perf pass inf
  [Mk 5:4; cv-1d(1b); 1400]   διασπάω
διεστειλάμεθα   aor mid ind 1 pl
  [Ac 15:24; cv-2d(1); 1403]   διαστέλλω
διεστείλατο   aor mid ind 3 sg
  [4t; cv-2d(1); 1403]   "
διεστέλλετο   imperf mid ind 3 sg
  [2t; cv-2d(1); 1403]   "
διέστη   aor act ind 3 sg
  [Lk 24:51; cv-6a; 1460]   διΐστημι
διεστραμμένα   perf pass ptcp acc pl neut
  [Ac 20:30; cv-1b(1); 1406]   διαστρέφω
διεστραμμένη   perf pass ptcp voc sg fem
  [2t; cv-1b(1); 1406]   "
διεστραμμένης   perf pass ptcp gen sg fem
  [Pp 2:15; cv-1b(1); 1406]   "
διεσώθησαν   aor pass ind 3 pl
  [2t; cv-2a(1); 1407]   διασῴζω
διέταξα   aor act ind 1 sg
  [1C 16:1; cv-2b; 1411]   διατάσσω
διεταξάμην   aor mid ind 1 sg
  [Ti 1:5; cv-2b; 1411]   "
διετάξατο   aor mid ind 3 sg
  [Ac 7:44; cv-2b; 1411]   "
διέταξεν   aor act ind 3 sg   [2t; cv-2b; 1411]   "
διεταράχθη   aor pass ind 3 sg
  [Lk 1:29; cv-2b; 1410]   διαταράσσω
διετήρει   imperf act ind 3 sg
  [Lk 2:51; cv-1d(2a); 1413]   διατηρέω

διετής, ές   {1453, a-4a}
  of two years; of the age of two years, Matt 2:16*

διετία, ας, ἡ   {1454, n-1a}
  the space of two years, Matt 2:16 v.l.; Acts 24:27;
  28:30*

διετίαν   acc sg fem   [Ac 28:30; n-1a; 1454]   διετία
διετίας   gen sg fem   [Ac 24:27; n-1a; 1454]   "
διετοῦς   gen sg masc   [Mt 2:16; a-4a; 1453]   διετής
διέτριβεν   imperf act ind 3 sg
  [2t; cv-1b(1); 1417]   διατρίβω
διέτριβον   imperf act ind 3 pl
  [3t; cv-1b(1); 1417]   "
διετρίψαμεν   aor act ind 1 pl
  [Ac 20:6; cv-1b(1); 1417]   "
διέτριψαν   aor act ind 3 pl
  [Ac 14:3; cv-1b(1); 1417]   "

διεφέρετο   imperf pass ind 3 sg
  [Ac 13:49; cv-1c(1); 1422]   διαφέρω
διεφήμισαν   aor act ind 3 pl
  [Mt 9:31; cv-2a(1); 1424]   διαφημίζω
διεφημίσθη   aor pass ind 3 sg
  [Mt 28:15; cv-2a(1); 1424]   "
διεφθάρησαν   aor pass ind 3 pl
  [Rv 8:9; cv-2d(3); 1425]   διαφθείρω
διεφθαρμένων   perf pass ptcp gen pl masc
  [1Ti 6:5; cv-2d(3); 1425]   "
διεχειρίσασθε   aor mid ind 2 pl
  [Ac 5:30; cv-2a(1); 1429]   διαχειρίζω
διήγειραν   aor act ind 3 pl
  [Lk 8:24; cv-2d(3); 1444]   διεγείρω

διηγέομαι   {1455, cv-1d(2a)}
  [διηγήσομαι, διηγησάμην, -, -, -] pr. *to lead
  throughout; to declare thoroughly, detail, recount,
  relate, tell*, Mark 5:16; 9:9; Luke 8:39; Acts 8:33;
  Heb 11:32

διηγήσαντο   aor mid ind 3 pl
  [2t; cv-1d(2a); 1455]   διηγέομαι
διηγήσατο   aor mid ind 3 sg [2t; cv-1d(2a); 1455]   "
διηγήσεται   fut mid ind 3 sg
  [Ac 8:33; cv-1d(2a); 1455]   "
διήγησιν   acc sg fem
  [Lk 1:1; n-3e(5b); 1456]   διήγησις

διήγησις, εως, ἡ   {1456, n-3e(5b)}
  a narration, relation, history, Luke 1:1*

διηγήσωνται   aor mid subj 3 pl
  [Mk 9:9; cv-1d(2a); 1455]   διηγέομαι
διηγοῦ   pres mid imperative 2 sg
  [Lk 8:39; cv-1d(2a); 1455]   "
διηγούμενον   pres mid ptcp acc sg masc
  [Hb 11:32; cv-1d(2a); 1455]   "
διηκόνει   imperf act ind 3 sg
  [4t; v-1d(2a); 1354]   διακονέω
διηκονήσαμεν   aor act ind 1 pl
  [Mt 25:44; v-1d(2a); 1354]   "
διηκόνησεν   aor act ind 3 sg
  [2Ti 1:18; v-1d(2a); 1354]   "
διηκόνουν   imperf act ind 3 pl
  [5t; v-1d(2a); 1354]   "
διῆλθεν   aor act ind 3 sg
  [2t; cv-1b(2); 1451]   διέρχομαι
διῆλθον   aor act ind 1 sg
  [Ac 20:25; cv-1b(2); 1451]   "
διῆλθον   aor act ind 3 pl [4t; cv-1b(2); 1451]   "
διηνεκές   acc sg neut [4t; a-4a; 1457]   διηνεκής

διηνεκής, ές   {1457, a-4a}
  *continuous, uninterrupted; εἰς τὸ διηνεκές,
  perpetually*, Heb 7:3; 10:1, 12, 14*

διήνοιγεν   imperf act ind 3 sg
  [Lk 24:32; cv-1b(2); 1380]   διανοίγω
διηνοιγμένους   perf pass ptcp acc pl masc
  [Ac 7:56; cv-1b(2); 1380]   "
διήνοιξεν   aor act ind 3 sg [2t; cv-1b(2); 1380]   "
διηνοίχθησαν   aor pass ind 3 pl
  [Lk 24:31; cv-1b(2); 1380]   "
διηπόρει   imperf act ind 3 sg
  [2t; cv-; 1389]   διαπορέω
διηπόρουν   imperf act ind 3 pl [2t; cv-; 1389]   "

διήρχετο   imperf mid ind 3 sg
  [4t; cv-1b(2); 1451]   διέρχομαι
διήρχοντο   imperf mid ind 3 pl
  [2t; cv-1b(2); 1451]   "
διθάλασσον   acc sg masc
  [Ac 27:41; a-3a; 1458]   διθάλασσος

διθάλασσος, ον   {1458, a-3a}
  *surrounded on both sides by the sea; τόπος
  διθάλασσος, a shoal* or *sand-bank formed by the
  confluence of opposite currents*, Acts 27:41*

διϊκνέομαι   {1459, cv-3b}
  [-, -, -, -, -] *to go* or *pass through; to penetrate*, Heb
  4:12*

διϊκνούμενος   pres mid ptcp nom sg masc
  [Hb 4:12; cv-3b; 1459]   διϊκνέομαι

διΐστημι   {1460, cv-6a}
  [-, διέστησα or διέστην, -, -, -] *to set at an interval,
  apart; to station at an interval* from a former
  position, Acts 27:28; intrans. *to stand apart; to
  depart, be parted*, Luke 24:51; of time, *to
  intervene, be interposed*, Luke 22:59*

διϊσχυρίζετο   imperf mid ind 3 sg
  [2t; cv-; 1462]   διϊσχυρίζομαι

διϊσχυρίζομαι   {1462, cv-2a(1)}
  [(διϊσχυριζόμην), -, -, -, -, -] *to feel* or *express
  reliance; to affirm confidently, insist*, Luke 22:59;
  Acts 12:15: 15:2 v.l.

δικαία   nom sg fem [2t; a-1a(1); 1465]   δίκαιος
δίκαια   nom pl neut [2t; a-1a(1); 1465]   "
δίκαιαι   nom pl fem [3t; a-1a(1); 1465]   "
δικαίαν   acc sg fem [2t; a-1a(1); 1465]   "
δικαίας   gen sg fem [2Th 1:5; a-1a(1); 1465] "
δίκαιε   voc sg masc [Jn 17:25; a-1a(1); 1465] "
δίκαιοι   nom pl masc [9t; a-1a(1); 1465]   "
δικαιοῖ   pres act ind 3 sg
  [Ga 3:8; v-1d(3); 1467]   δικαιόω
δικαίοις   dat pl masc
  [Lk 15:7; a-1a(1); 1465]   δίκαιος

δικαιοκρισία, ας, ἡ   {1464, n-1a}
  just or *righteous judgment*, Rom 2:5, 2 Thess 1:5
  v.l.*

δικαιοκρισίας   gen sg fem
  [Rm 2:5; n-1a; 1464]   δικαιοκρισία
δίκαιον   nom sg neut [6t; a-1a(1); 1465]   δίκαιος
δίκαιον   acc sg masc [9t; a-1a(1); 1465]   "
δίκαιον   acc sg neut [3t; a-1a(1); 1465]   "

δίκαιος, ία, ιον   {1465, a-1a(1)}
  just, equitable, fair, Matt 20:4; Luke 12:57; John
  5:30; Col 4:1; of persons, *just, righteous,
  absolutely*, John 17:25; Rom 3:10, 26; 2 Tim 4:8;
  1 Pet 3:18; 1 John 1:9; 2:1, 29; Rev 16:5; *righteous
  by account and acceptance*, Rom 2:13; 5:19; in
  ordinary usage, *just, upright, innocent, pious*,
  Matt 5:45; 9:13, et al. freq.; ὁ δίκαιος, *the Just
  One*, one of the distinctive titles of the Messiah,
  Acts 3:14; 7:52; 22:14

δίκαιος   nom sg masc [20t; a-1a(1); 1465]   "

δικαιοσύνη, ης, ἡ   {1466, n-1b}
  fair and equitable dealing, justice, Acts 17:31; Heb

11:33; Rom 9:28; *integrity, virtue,* Luke 1:75; Eph
5:9; in N.T. *generosity, alms,* 2 Cor 9:10, v.r.; Matt
6:1; *piety, godliness,* Rom 6:13; *investiture with
the attribute of righteousness, acceptance as
righteous, justification,* Rom 4:11; 10:4, et al.
freq.; *a provision* or *mean for justification,* Rom
1:17; 2 Cor 3:9; *an instance of justification,* 2 Cor
5:21

δικαιοσύνη   nom sg fem
    [12t; n-1b; 1466]   δικαιοσύνη
δικαιοσύνη   dat sg fem   [14t; n-1b; 1466]   "
δικαιοσύνην   acc sg fem   [37t; n-1b; 1466]   "
δικαιοσύνης   gen sg fem   [29t; n-1b; 1466]   "
δικαίου   gen sg masc   [6t; a-1a(1); 1465]   δίκαιος
δικαιούμενοι   pres pass ptcp nom pl masc
    [Rm 3:24; v-1d(3); 1467]   δικαιόω
δικαιοῦντα   pres act ptcp acc sg masc
    [2t; v-1d(3); 1467]   "
δικαιοῦντες   pres act ptcp nom pl masc
    [Lk 16:15; v-1d(3); 1467]   "
δικαίους   acc pl masc   [6t; a-1a(1); 1465]   δίκαιος
δικαιοῦσθαι   pres pass inf
    [Rm 3:28; v-1d(3); 1467]   δικαιόω
δικαιοῦσθε   pres pass ind 2 pl
    [Ga 5:4; v-1d(3); 1467]   "
δικαιοῦται   pres pass ind 3 sg
    [4t; v-1d(3); 1467]   "

δικαιόω   {1467, v-1d(3)}
    [δικαιώσω, ἐδικαίωσα, -, δεδικαίωμαι,
    ἐδικαιώθην] pr. *to make* or *render right* or *just;*
    mid. *to act with justice,* Rev 22:11; *to avouch to be
    good and true, to vindicate,* Matt 11:19; Luke 7:29;
    to set forth as good and just, Luke 10:29; 16:15; in
    N.T. *to hold as guiltless, to accept as righteous, to
    justify,* Rom 3:26, 30; 4:5; 8:30, 33; pass. *to be held
    acquitted, to be cleared,* Acts 13:39; Rom 3:24; 6:7;
    *to be approved, to stand approved, to stand
    accepted,* Rom 2:13; 3:20, 28

δικαίῳ   dat sg masc   [2t; a-1a(1); 1465]   δίκαιος
δικαιωθέντες   aor pass ptcp nom pl masc
    [3t; v-1d(3); 1467]   δικαιόω
δικαιωθῆναι   aor pass inf   [2t; v-1d(3); 1467]   "
δικαιωθῇς   aor pass subj 2 sg
    [Rm 3:4; v-1d(3); 1467]
δικαιωθήσεται   fut pass ind 3 sg
    [2t; v-1d(3); 1467]   "
δικαιωθήσῃ   fut pass ind 2 sg
    [Mt 12:37; v-1d(3); 1467]   "
δικαιωθήσονται   fut pass ind 3 pl
    [Rm 2:13; v-1d(3); 1467]   "
δικαιωθῶμεν   aor pass subj 1 pl
    [2t; v-1d(3); 1467]   "

δικαίωμα, ατος, τό   {1468, n-3c(4)}
    pr. *a rightful act, act of justice, equity; a sentence,*
    of condemnation, Rev 15:4; in N.T., of
    acquittal, *justification,* Rom 5:16; *a decree, law,
    ordinance,* Luke 1:6; Rom 1:32; 2:26; 8:4; Heb 9:1,
    10; *a meritorious act, an instance of perfect
    righteousness,* Rom 5:18; Rev 19:8*

δικαίωμα   nom sg neut
    [Rm 8:4; n-3c(4); 1468]   δικαίωμα
δικαίωμα   acc sg neut   [2t; n-3c(4); 1468]   "

δικαιώμασιν   dat pl neut   [Lk 1:6; n-3c(4); 1468]   "
δικαιώματα   nom pl neut   [3t; n-3c(4); 1468]   "
δικαιώματα   acc pl neut   [2t; n-3c(4); 1468]   "
δικαιώματος   gen sg neut   [Rm 5:18; n-3c(4); 1468]   "
δικαίων   gen pl masc   [6t; a-1a(1); 1465]   δίκαιος
δικαιῶν   pres act ptcp nom sg masc
    [Rm 8:33; v-1d(3); 1467]   δικαιόω

δικαίως   {1469, adverb}
    justly, with strict justice, 1 Peter 2:23; *deservedly,*
    Luke 23:41; *as it is right, fit* or *proper,* 1 Cor 15:34;
    uprightly, honestly, piously, religiously, 1 Thess
    2:10; Titus 2:12*

δικαίως   adverb   [5t; adverb; 1469]   δικαίως
δικαιῶσαι   aor act inf
    [Lk 10:29; v-1d(3); 1467]   δικαιόω
δικαιώσει   fut act ind 3 sg
    [Rm 3:30; v-1d(3); 1467]   "
δικαίωσιν   acc sg fem
    [2t; n-3e(5b); 1470]   δικαίωσις

δικαίωσις, εως, ἡ   {1470, n-3e(5b)}
    pr. *a making right* or *just; a declaration of right* or
    justice; a judicial sentence; in N.T., *acquittal,
    acceptance, justification,* Rom 4:25; 5:18*

δικαστήν   acc sg masc   [2t; n-1f; 1471]   δικαστής

δικαστής, οῦ, ὁ   {1471, n-1f}
    a judge, Luke 12:14 v.l.; Acts 7:27, 35*

δίκη, ης, ἡ   {1472, n-1b}
    right, justice; in N.T. *judicial punishment,
    vengeance,* 2 Thess 1:9; Jude 7; *sentence of
    punishment, judgment,* Acts 25:15; personified,
    the goddess of justice or *vengeance, Nemesis,
    Paena,* Acts 28:4

δίκη   nom sg fem   [Ac 28:4; n-1b; 1472]   δίκη
δίκην   acc sg fem   [2t; n-1b; 1472]   "
δίκτυα   nom pl neut   [Lk 5:6; n-2c; 1473]   δίκτυον
δίκτυα   acc pl neut   [7t; n-2c; 1473]   "

δίκτυον, ου, τό   {1473, n-2c}
    a net, fishing-net, Matt 4:20, 21

δίκτυον   nom sg neut   [Jn 21:11; n-2c; 1473]   "
δίκτυον   acc sg neut   [3t; n-2c; 1473]   "

δίλογος, ον   {1474, a-3a}
    pr. *saying the same thing twice;* in N.T.
    *double-tongued, speaking one thing and meaning
    another, deceitful in words,* 1 Tim 3:8*

διλόγους   acc pl masc
    [1Ti 3:8; a-3a; 1474]   δίλογος

διό   {1475, conj}
    inferential conj., *on which account, wherefore,
    therefore,* Matt 27:8; 1 Cor 12:3

διό   conj   [53t; conj; 1475]   διό
διοδεύσαντες   aor act ptcp nom pl masc
    [Ac 17:1; cv-1a(6); 1476]   διοδεύω

διοδεύω   {1476, cv-1a(6)}
    [(διώδευον), -, διώδευσα, -, -, -] *to travel through*
    a place, *traverse,* Luke 8:1; Acts 17:1

Διονύσιος, ου, ὁ   {1477, n-2a}
    Dionysius, pr. name, Acts 17:34*

Διονύσιος   nom sg masc
   [Ac 17:34; n-2a; 1477]   Διονύσιος

διόπερ   {1478, conj}
   inferential conj., *on this very account, for this very
   reason, wherefore,* 1 Cor 8:13; 10:14; 14:13 v.l.*

διόπερ   conj [2t; conj; 1478]   διόπερ

διοπετής, ές   {1479, a-4a}
   which fell from Jupiter, or *heaven;* τοῦ Διοπετοῦς,
   sc. ἀγάλματος, Acts 19:35*

διοπετοῦς   gen sg neut
   [Ac 19:35; a-4a; 1479]   διοπετής

διόρθωμα, ατος, τό   {1480, n-3c(4)}
   correction, emendation, reformation, Acts 24:2*

διορθωμάτων   gen pl neut
   [Ac 24:2; n-3c(4); 1480]   διόρθωμα
διορθώσεως   gen sg fem
   [Hb 9:10; n-3e(5b); 1481]   διόρθωσις

διόρθωσις, εως, ή   {1481, n-3e(5b)}
   a complete rectification, reformation, Heb 9:10

διορύσσουσιν   pres act ind 3 pl
   [2t; cv-2b; 1482]   διορύσσω

διορύσσω   {1482, cv-2b}
   [-, -, -, -, διωρύχθην] *to dig* or *break through,* Matt
   6:19, 20; 24:43; Luke 12:39*

διορυχθῆναι   aor pass inf [2t; cv-2b; 1482]   "
Διός   gen sg masc [Ac 14:13; n-3g(1); 2416]   Ζεύς

Διόσκουροι, ων, οἱ   {1483, n-2a}
   the Dioscuri, Castor and Pollux, sons of Jupiter
   by Leda, and patrons of sailors, Acts 28:11*.

Διοσκούροις   dat pl masc
   [Ac 28:11; n-2a; 1483]   Διόσκουροι

διότι   {1484, conj}
   on the account that, because, Luke 2:7; 21:28; *in as
   much as,* Luke 1:13; Acts 18:10

διότι   conj [23t; conj; 1484]   διότι

Διοτρέφης, φους, ὁ   {1485, n-3d(2a)}
   Diotrephes, pr. name, 3 John 9*

Διοτρέφης   nom sg masc
   [3J 9; n-3d(2a); 1485]   Διοτρέφης
διπλᾶ   acc pl neut [Rv 18:6; a-1b; 1487]   διπλοῦς
διπλῆς   gen sg fem [1Ti 5:17; a-1b; 1487]   "

διπλόος, see διπλοῦς   {1486}

διπλότερον   acc sg neut from διπλοῦς,
   functioning as a comparative adverb
   [Mt 23:15; a-1b; 1487]   "
διπλοῦν   acc sg neut, functioning as an
   adverb [Rv 18:6; a-1b; 1487]   "

διπλοῦς, ῆ, οῦν   {1487, a-1b}
   double, Matt 23:15; 1 Tim 5:17; Rev 18:6

διπλόω   {1488, v-1d(3)}
   [-, ἐδίπλωσα, -, -, -] *to double; to render back
   double,* Rev 18:6*

διπλώσατε   aor act imperative 2 pl
   [Rv 18:6; v-1d(3); 1488]   διπλόω

δίς   {1489, adverb}
   twice, Mark 14:30, 72; in the sense of *entirely,
   utterly,* Jude 12; ἅπαξ καὶ δίς, *once and again,
   repeatedly,* Phil 4:16

δίς   adverb [6t; adverb; 1489]   δίς
δισμυριάδες   nom pl fem
   [Rv 9:16; n-3c(2); 1490]   δισμυριάς

δισμυριάς, άδος, ή   {1490, n-3c(2)}
   twice ten thousand, two myriads, Rev 9:16*

διστάζω   {1491, v-2a(1)}
   [διστάσω, ἐδίστασα, -, -, -] *to doubt, waver,
   hesitate,* Matt 14:31; 28:17*

δίστομον   acc sg fem [2t; a-3a; 1492]   δίστομος

δίστομος, ον   {1492, a-3a}
   pr. *having two mouths; two-edged,* Heb 4:12; Rev
   1:16; 2:12; 19:15 v.l.*

δίστομος   nom sg fem [Rv 1:16; a-3a; 1492]   "

δισχίλιοι, αι, α   {1493, a-1a(1)}
   two thousand, Mark 5:13*

δισχίλιοι   nom pl masc
   [Mk 5:13; a-1a(1); 1493]   δισχίλιοι
διϋλίζοντες   pres act ptcp voc pl masc
   [Mt 23:24; cv-; 1494]   διϋλίζω

διϋλίζω   {1494, cv-2a(1)}
   [-, -, -, -, -] *to strain, filter thoroughly; to strain out*
   or *off,* Matt 23:24*

διχάζω   {1495, v-2a(1)}
   [-, ἐδίχασα, -, -, -] *to cut asunder, disunite;* met. *to
   cause to disagree, set at variance,* Matt 10:35*

διχάσαι   aor act inf
   [Mt 10:35; v-2a(1); 1495]   διχάζω

διχοστασία, ας, ή   {1496, n-1a}
   a standing apart; a division, dissension, Rom
   16:17; 1 Cor 3:3 v.l.; Gal 5:20*

διχοστασίαι   nom pl fem
   [Ga 5:20; n-1a; 1496]   διχοστασία
διχοστασίας   acc pl fem [Rm 16:17; n-1a; 1496]   "

διχοτομέω   {1497, v-1d(2a)}
   [διχοτομήσω, -, -, -, -] pr. *to cut into two parts, cut
   asunder;* in N.T. *to inflict a punishment of extreme
   severity,* Matt 24:51; Luke 12:46*

διχοτομήσει   fut act ind 3 sg
   [2t; v-1d(2a); 1497]   διχοτομέω
διψᾷ   pres act subj 3 sg
   [2t; v-1d(1a); 1498]   διψάω

διψάω   {1498, v-1d(1a)}
   [διψήσω, ἐδίψησα, -, -, -] *to thirst, be thirsty,* Matt
   25:35, 37, 42, 44; met. *to thirst after* in spirit, *to
   desire* or *long for ardently,* Matt 5:6; John 4:14;
   6:35

δίψει   dat sg neut
   [2C 11:27; n-3d(2b); 1499]   δίψος
διψήσει   fut act ind 3 sg
   [3t; v-1d(1a); 1498]   διψάω
διψήσουσιν   fut act ind 3 pl
   [Rv 7:16; v-1d(1a); 1498]   "

δίψος, ους, τό   {1499, n-3d(2b)}
    thirst, 2 Cor 11:27*

δίψυχοι   voc pl masc [Jm 4:8; a-3a; 1500]   δίψυχος

δίψυχος, ον   {1500, a-3a}
    double-minded, inconstant, fickle, James 1:8; 4:8*

δίψυχος   nom sg masc [Jm 1:8; a-3a; 1500]   "
διψῶ   pres act ind 1 sg
    [Jn 19:28; v-1d(1a); 1498]   διψάω
διψῶ   pres act subj 1 sg
    [Jn 4:15; v-1d(1a); 1498]   "
διψῶμεν   pres act ind 1 pl
    [1C 4:11; v-1d(1a); 1498]   "
διψῶν   pres act ptcp nom sg masc
    [Rv 22:17; v-1d(1a); 1498]   "
διψῶντα   pres act ptcp acc sg masc
    [2t; v-1d(1a); 1498]   "
διψῶντες   pres act ptcp nom pl masc
    [Mt 5:6; v-1d(1a); 1498]   "
διψῶντι   pres act ptcp dat sg masc
    [Rv 21:6; v-1d(1a); 1498]   "
διωγμοῖς   dat pl masc [3t; n-2a; 1501]   διωγμός
διωγμόν   acc sg masc [Ac 13:50; n-2a; 1501]   "

διωγμός, οῦ, ὁ   {1501, n-2a}
    pr. *chase, pursuit*; *persecution* (specifically for
    religious reasons), Matt 13:21; Mark 4:17; 10:30

διωγμός   nom sg masc [2t; n-2a; 1501]   "
διωγμοῦ   gen sg masc [2t; n-2a; 1501]   "
διωγμούς   acc pl masc [2Ti 3:11; n-2a; 1501]   "
διωγμῶν   gen pl masc [Mk 10:30; n-2a; 1501]   "
διώδευεν   imperf act ind 3 sg
    [Lk 8:1; cv-1a(6); 1476]   διοδεύω
δίωκε   pres act imperative 2 sg
    [2t; v-1b(2); 1503]   διώκω
διώκεις   pres act ind 2 sg [6t; v-1b(2); 1503]   "
διώκετε   pres act imperative 2 pl
    [3t; v-1b(2); 1503]   "
διώκομαι   pres pass ind 1 sg
    [Ga 5:11; v-1b(2); 1503]   "
διωκόμενοι   pres pass ptcp nom pl masc
    [2t; v-1b(2); 1503]   "
διώκοντα   pres act ptcp nom pl neut
    [Rm 9:30; v-1b(2); 1503]   "
διώκοντας   pres act ptcp acc pl masc
    [Rm 12:14; v-1b(2); 1503]   "
διώκοντες   pres act ptcp nom pl masc
    [Rm 12:13; v-1b(2); 1503]   "
διωκόντων   pres act ptcp gen pl masc
    [Mt 5:44; v-1b(2); 1503]   "
διώκτην   acc sg masc
    [1Ti 1:13; n-1f; 1502]   διώκτης

διώκτης, ου, ὁ   {1502, n-1f}
    a persecutor, 1 Tim 1:13*

διώκω   {1503, v-1b(2)}
    [(ἐδίωκον), διώξω, ἐδίωξα, -, δεδίωγμαι,
    ἐδιώχθην] *to put in rapid motion; to pursue; to
    follow, pursue the direction of*, Luke 17:23; *to
    follow eagerly, endeavor earnestly to acquire*, Rom
    9:30, 31; 12:13; *to press forwards*, Phil 3:12, 14; *to
    pursue* with malignity, *persecute*, Matt 5:10, 11,
    12, 44

διώκω   pres act ind 1 sg [2t; v-1b(2); 1503]   διώκω
διώκωμεν   pres act subj 1 pl
    [Rm 14:19; v-1b(2); 1503]   "
διώκων   pres act ptcp nom sg masc
    [3t; v-1b(2); 1503]   "
διώκωνται   pres pass subj 3 pl
    [Ga 6:12; v-1b(2); 1503]   "
διώκωσιν   pres act subj 3 pl
    [Mt 10:23; v-1b(2); 1503]   "
διωξάτω   aor act imperative 3 sg
    [1P 3:11; v-1b(2); 1503]   "
διώξετε   fut act ind 2 pl
    [Mt 23:34; v-1b(2); 1503]   "
διώξητε   aor act subj 2 pl
    [Lk 17:23; v-1b(2); 1503]   "
διώξουσιν   fut act ind 3 pl [3t; v-1b(2); 1503]   "
διώξωσιν   aor act subj 3 pl
    [Mt 5:11; v-1b(2); 1503]   "
διωχθήσονται   fut pass ind 3 pl
    [2Ti 3:12; v-1b(2); 1503]   "

δόγμα, ατος, τό   {1504, n-3c(4)}
    a decree, statute, ordinance, Luke 2:1; Acts 16:4;
    17:7; Eph 2:15; Col 2:14*

δόγμα   nom sg neut [Lk 2:1; n-3c(4); 1504]   δόγμα
δόγμασιν   dat pl neut [2t; n-3c(4); 1504]   "
δόγματα   acc pl neut [Ac 16:4; n-3c(4); 1504]   "
δογματίζεσθε   pres pass ind 2 pl
    [Cl 2:20; v-2a(1); 1505]   δογματίζω

δογματίζω   {1505, v-2a(1)}
    [-, -, -, δεδογμάτισμαι, -] *to decree, prescribe an
    ordinance*; mid. *to suffer laws to be imposed on
    one's self, to submit to, bind one's self by,
    ordinances*, Col 2:20*

δογμάτων   gen pl neut
    [Ac 17:7; n-3c(4); 1504]   δόγμα
δοθεῖσα   aor pass ptcp nom sg fem
    [Mk 6:2; v-6a; 1443]   δίδωμι
δοθεῖσαν   aor pass ptcp acc sg fem
    [7t; v-6a; 1443]   "
δοθείσῃ   aor pass ptcp dat sg fem
    [1C 1:4; v-6a; 1443]   "
δοθείσης   aor pass ptcp gen sg fem
    [3t; v-6a; 1443]   "
δοθέντος   aor pass ptcp gen sg neut
    [Rm 5:5; v-6a; 1443]   "
δοθῇ   aor pass subj 3 sg [3t; v-6a; 1443]   "
δοθῆναι   aor pass inf [5t; v-6a; 1443]   "
δοθήσεται   fut pass ind 3 sg [16t; v-6a; 1443]   "
δοῖ   aor act subj 3 sg [Mk 8:37; v-6a; 1443]   "
δοκεῖ   pres act ind 3 sg
    [20t; v-1b(4); 1506]   δοκέω
δοκεῖν   pres act inf [Lk 19:11; v-1b(4); 1506]   "
δοκεῖς   pres act ind 2 sg
    [Mt 26:53; v-1b(4); 1506]   "
δοκεῖτε   pres act imperative 2 pl
    [Jn 5:45; v-1b(4); 1506]   "
δοκεῖτε   pres act ind 2 pl [9t; v-1b(4); 1506]   "

δοκέω   {1506, v-1b(4)}
    [(ἐδόκουν), δόξω, ἔδοξα, -, -, -] *to think, imagine,
    suppose, presume*, Matt 3:9; 6:7; *to seem, appear,*

Luke 10:36; Acts 17:18; *it seems; it seems good, best,* or *right, it pleases,* Luke 1:3; Acts 15:22, 25

δοκῇ   pres act subj 3 sg [Hb 4:1; v-1b(4); 1506]   "
δοκιμάζει   pres act ind 3 sg
  [Rm 14:22; v-2a(1); 1507]   δοκιμάζω
δοκιμάζειν   pres act inf [4t; v-2a(1); 1507]   "
δοκιμάζεις   pres act ind 2 sg
  [Rm 2:18; v-2a(1); 1507]   "
δοκιμαζέσθωσαν   pres pass imperative 3 pl
  [1Ti 3:10; v-2a(1); 1507]   "
δοκιμάζετε   pres act imperative 2 pl
  [3t; v-2a(1); 1507]   "
δοκιμαζέτω   pres act imperative 3 sg
  [2t; v-2a(1); 1507]   "
δοκιμαζομένου   pres pass ptcp gen sg neut
  [1P 1:7; v-2a(1); 1507]   "
δοκιμάζοντες   pres act ptcp nom pl masc
  [Ep 5:10; v-2a(1); 1507]   "
δοκιμάζοντι   pres act ptcp dat sg masc
  [1Th 2:4; v-2a(1); 1507]   "

δοκιμάζω   {1507, v-2a(1)}
  [δοκιμάσω, ἐδοκίμασα, -, δεδοκίμασμαι,
  ἐδοκιμάσθην] *to test, assay* metals, 1 Peter 1:7; *to prove, try, examine, scrutinize,* Luke 14:19; Rom 12:2; *to put to the proof, tempt,* Heb 3:9; *to approve* after trial, *judge worthy, choose,* Rom 14:22; 1 Cor 16:3; 2 Cor 8:22; *to decide upon* after examination, *judge of, distinguish, discern,* Luke 12:56; Rom 2:18; Phil 1:10

δοκιμάζων   pres act ptcp nom sg masc
  [2C 8:8; v-2a(1); 1507]   "
δοκιμάσαι   aor act inf [Lk 14:19; v-2a(1); 1507]   "
δοκιμάσει   fut act ind 3 sg
  [1C 3:13; v-2a(1); 1507]   "
δοκιμάσητε   aor act subj 2 pl
  [1C 16:3; v-2a(1); 1507]   "

δοκιμασία, ας, ἡ   {1508, n-1a}
  proof, probation, testing, examination, Heb 3:9*

δοκιμασίᾳ   dat sg fem
  [Hb 3:9; n-1a; 1508]   δοκιμασία

δοκιμή, ῆς, ἡ   {1509, n-1b}
  trial, proof by trial, 2 Cor 8:2; *the state or disposition of that which has been tried and approved, approved character* or *temper,* Rom 5:4; 2 Cor 2:9; Phil 2:22; *proof, document, evidence,* 2 Cor 8:2; 13:3*

δοκιμή   nom sg fem [Rm 5:4; n-1b; 1509]   δοκιμή
δοκιμῇ   dat sg fem [2C 8:2; n-1b; 1509]   "
δοκιμήν   acc sg fem [4t; n-1b; 1509]   "
δοκιμῆς   gen sg fem [2C 9:13; n-1b; 1509]   "

δοκίμιον, ου, τό   {1510, n-2c}
  that by means of which anything is tried, proof, criterion, test; trial, the act of trying or *putting to proof,* James 1:3; *approved character,* 1 Peter 1:7*

δοκίμιον   nom sg neut [2t; n-2c; 1510]   δοκίμιον
δόκιμοι   nom pl masc [2t; a-3a; 1511]   δόκιμος
δόκιμον   acc sg masc [2t; a-3a; 1511]   "

δόκιμος, ον   {1511, a-3a}
  proved, tried; approved after examination and

trial, Rom 16:10; James 1:12; by impl. *acceptable,* Rom 14:18

δόκιμος   nom sg masc [3t; a-3a; 1511]   "
δοκόν   acc sg fem [5t; n-2b; 1512]   δοκός

δοκός, οῦ, ἡ   {1512, n-2b}
  a beam or *spar* of timber, Matt 7:3, 4, 5; Luke 6:41, 42*

δοκός   nom sg fem [Mt 7:4; n-2b; 1512]
δοκοῦμεν   pres act ind 1 pl
  [1C 12:23; v-1b(4); 1506]   δοκέω
δοκοῦν   pres act ptcp acc sg neut
  [Hb 12:10; v-1b(4); 1506]   "
δοκοῦντα   pres act ptcp nom pl neut
  [1C 12:22; v-1b(4); 1506]   "
δοκοῦντες   pres act ptcp nom pl masc
  [3t; v-1b(4); 1506]   "
δοκούντων   pres act ptcp gen pl masc
  [Ga 2:6; v-1b(4); 1506]   "
δοκοῦσα   pres act ptcp nom sg fem
  [Jn 20:15; v-1b(4); 1506]   "
δοκοῦσιν   pres act ind 3 pl
  [Mt 6:7; v-1b(4); 1506]   "
δοκοῦσιν   pres act ptcp dat pl masc
  [Ga 2:2; v-1b(4); 1506]   "
δοκῶ   pres act ind 1 sg [2t; v-1b(4); 1506]   "
δοκῶν   pres act ptcp nom sg masc
  [1C 10:12; v-1b(4); 1506]   "
δόλιοι   nom pl masc
  [2C 11:13; a-1a(1); 1513]   δόλιος

δόλιος, ία, ιον   {1513, a-1a(1)}
  fraudulent, deceitful, 2 Cor 11:13*

δολιόω   {1514, v-1d(3)}
  [(ἐδολίουν), -, -, -, -, -] *to deceive, use fraud* or *deceit,* Rom 3:13*

δόλον   acc sg masc [2t; n-2a; 1515]   δόλος

δόλος, ου, ὁ   {1515, n-2a}
  pr. *a bait* or *contrivance for entrapping, fraud, deceit, cunning, guile,* Matt 26:4; Mark 7:22; 14:1

δόλος   nom sg masc [3t; n-2a; 1515]   "
δόλου   gen sg masc [2t; n-2a; 1515]   "
δολοῦντες   pres act ptcp nom pl masc
  [2C 4:2; v-1d(3); 1516]   δολόω

δολόω   {1516, v-1d(3)}
  [-, -, -, -, -] pr. *to entrap, beguile; to adulterate, corrupt, falsify,* 2 Cor 4:2; 1 Cor 5:6 v.l.*

δόλῳ   dat sg masc [4t; n-2a; 1515]   δόλος

δόμα, ατος, τό   {1517, n-3c(4)}
  a gift, present, Matt 7:11; Luke 11:13; Eph 4:8; Phil 4:17*

δόμα   acc sg neut [Pp 4:17; n-3c(4); 1517]   δόμα
δόματα   acc pl neut [3t; n-3c(4); 1517]   "
δόντα   aor act ptcp acc sg masc
  [2t; v-6a; 1443]   δίδωμι
δόντι   aor act ptcp dat sg masc
  [2C 8:16; v-6a; 1443]   "
δόντος   aor act ptcp gen sg masc
  [2t; v-6a; 1443]   "

δόξα, ης, ή   {1518, n-1c}
pr. *a seeming; appearance; a notion, imagination,*
opinion; the opinion which obtains respecting one;
reputation, credit, honor, glory; in N.T. *honorable*
consideration, Luke 14:10; *praise, glorification,*
honor, John 5:41, 44; Rom 4:20; 15:7; *dignity,*
majesty, Rom 1:23; 2 Cor 3:7; *a glorious*
manifestation, glorious working, John 11:40; 2
Peter 1:3; pl. *dignitaries,* 2 Peter 2:10; Jude 8;
glorification in a future state of bliss, 2 Cor 4:17; 2
Tim 2:10; *pride, ornament,* 1 Cor 11:15; 1 Thess
2:20; *splendid array, pomp, magnificence,* Matt
6:29; 19:28; *radiance, dazzling lustre,* Luke 2:9;
Acts 22:11

δόξα   nom sg fem [36t; n-1c; 1518]   δόξα
δοξάζειν   pres act inf
   [Mk 2:12; v-2a(1); 1519]   δοξάζω
δοξάζεται   pres pass ind 3 sg
   [1C 12:26; v-2a(1); 1519]   "
δοξαζέτω   pres act imperative 3 sg
   [1P 4:16; v-2a(1); 1519]   "
δοξάζηται   pres pass subj 3 sg
   [2t; v-2a(1); 1519]   "
δοξάζητε   pres act subj 2 pl
   [Rm 15:6; v-2a(1); 1519]   "
δοξαζόμενος   pres pass ptcp nom sg masc
   [Lk 4:15; v-2a(1); 1519]   "
δοξάζοντες   pres act ptcp nom pl masc
   [2t; v-2a(1); 1519]   "

δοξάζω   {1519, v-2a(1)}
[(ἐδόξαζον), δοξάσω, ἐδόξασα, -, δεδόξασμαι,
ἐδοξάσθην] *to think, suppose, judge; to extol,*
magnify, Matt 6:2; Luke 4:15; in N.T. *to adore,*
worship, Rom 1:21; *to invest with dignity or*
majesty, 2 Cor 3:10; Heb 5:5; *to signalize with a*
manifestation of dignity, excellence, or *majesty,*
John 12:28; 13:32; *to glorify* by admission to a
state of bliss, *to beatify,* Rom 8:30

δοξάζω   pres act ind 1 sg
   [Rm 11:13; v-2a(1); 1519]   "
δοξάζων   pres act ptcp nom sg masc
   [4t; v-2a(1); 1519]   "
δόξαν   acc sg fem [58t; n-1c; 1518]   δόξα
δόξαντες   aor act ptcp nom pl masc
   [2t; v-1b(4); 1506]   δοκέω
δόξας   acc pl fem [3t; n-1c; 1518]   δόξα
δοξάσαι   aor act inf
   [Rm 15:9; v-2a(1); 1519]   δοξάζω
δοξάσατε   aor act imperative 2 pl
   [1C 6:20; v-2a(1); 1519]   "
δοξάσει   fut act ind 3 sg [5t; v-2a(1); 1519]   "
δοξάσῃ   aor act subj 3 sg
   [Jn 17:1; v-2a(1); 1519]   "
δοξασθῇ   aor pass subj 3 sg [3t; v-2a(1); 1519]   "
δοξασθῶσιν   aor pass subj 3 pl
   [Mt 6:2; v-2a(1); 1519]   "
δόξασον   aor act imperative 2 sg
   [3t; v-2a(1); 1519]   "
δοξάσω   aor act subj 1 sg
   [Jn 8:54; v-2a(1); 1519]   "
δοξάσω   fut act ind 1 sg
   [Jn 12:28; v-2a(1); 1519]   "

δοξάσωσιν   aor act subj 3 pl [2t; v-2a(1); 1519]   "
δόξῃ   dat sg fem [21t; n-1c; 1518]   δόξα
δόξῃ   aor act subj 3 sg [2t; v-1b(4); 1506]   δοκέω
δόξης   gen sg fem [48t; n-1c; 1518]   δόξα
δόξητε   aor act subj 2 pl
   [Mt 3:9; v-1b(4); 1506]   δοκέω
δόξω   aor act subj 1 sg [2C 10:9; v-1b(4); 1506]   "

Δορκάς, άδος, ή   {1520, n-3c(2)}
Dorcas, pr. name, signifying a *gazelle* or *antelope,*
Acts 9:36, 39*

Δορκάς   nom sg fem [2t; n-3c(2); 1520]   Δορκάς
δός   aor act imperative 2 sg
   [16t; v-6a; 1443]   δίδωμι
δόσεως   gen sg fem [Pp 4:15; n-3e(5b); 1521]   δόσις

δόσις, εως, ή   {1521, n-3e(5b)}
pr. *giving, outlay;* Matt 6:1 v.l.; Phil 4:15; *a*
donation, gift, James 1:17*

δόσις   nom sg fem [Jm 1:17; n-3e(5b); 1521]   "
δότε   aor act imperative 2 pl
   [14t; v-6a; 1443]   δίδωμι
δότην   acc sg masc [2C 9:7; n-1f; 1522]   δότης

δότης, ου, ό   {1522, n-1f}
a giver, 2 Cor 9:7*

δότω   aor act imperative 3 sg
   [Mt 5:31; v-6a; 1443]   δίδωμι
δοῦλα   acc pl neut [2t; a-1a(2a); 1529]   δοῦλος

δουλαγωγέω   {1524, v-1d(2a)}
[-, -, -, -, -] pr. *to bring into slavery; to treat as a*
slave; to discipline into subjection, 1 Cor 9:27*

δουλαγωγῶ   pres act ind 1 sg
   [1C 9:27; v-1d(2a); 1524]   δουλαγωγέω
δούλας   acc pl fem [Ac 2:18; n-1b; 1527]   δούλη
δοῦλε   voc sg masc [6t; n-2a; 1528]   δοῦλος

δουλεία, ας, ή   {1525, n-1a}
slavery, bondage, servile condition; in N.T. met.
with reference to degradation and
unhappiness, Rom 8:15, 21; Gal 4:24; 5:1; Heb
2:15*

δουλείαν   acc sg fem [Ga 4:24; n-1a; 1525]   δουλεία
δουλείας   gen sg fem [4t; n-1a; 1525]   "
δουλεύει   pres act ind 3 sg
   [Ga 4:25; v-1a(6); 1526]   δουλεύω
δουλεύειν   pres act inf [8t; v-1a(6); 1526]   "
δουλεύετε   pres act imperative 2 pl
   [2t; v-1a(6); 1526]   "
δουλευέτωσαν   pres act imperative 3 pl
   [1Ti 6:2; v-1a(6); 1526]   "
δουλεύοντες   pres act ptcp nom pl masc
   [3t; v-1a(6); 1526]   "
δουλεύουσιν   pres act ind 3 pl
   [Rm 16:18; v-1a(6); 1526]   "
δουλεύσει   fut act ind 3 sg
   [Rm 9:12; v-1a(6); 1526]   "
δουλεύσουσιν   fut act ind 3 pl
   [Ac 7:7; v-1a(6); 1526]   "

δουλεύω   {1526, v-1a(6)}
[δουλεύσω, ἐδούλευσα, δεδούλευκα, -, -] *to be a*
slave or *servant; to be in slavery* or *subjection,*

John 8:33; Acts 7:7; Rom 9:12; *to discharge the
duties of a slave* or *servant*, Eph 6:7; 1 Tim 6:2; *to
serve, be occupied in the service of, be devoted,
subservient*, Matt 6:24; Luke 15:29; Acts 20:19;
Rom 14:18; 16:18; met. *to be enthralled, involved
in a slavish service*, spiritually or morally, Gal
4:9, 25; Titus 3:3

δουλεύω   pres act ind 1 sg [2t; v-1a(6); 1526]   "
δουλεύων   pres act ptcp nom sg masc
      [2t; v-1a(6); 1526]   "

δούλη, ης, ἡ   {1527, n-1b}
      female slave, bondmaid, Luke 1:38, 48; Acts 2:18*

δούλη   nom sg fem [Lk 1:38; n-1b; 1527]   δούλη
δούλης   gen sg fem [Lk 1:48; n-1b; 1527]   "
δοῦλοι   nom pl masc [19t; n-2a; 1528]   δοῦλος
δοῦλοι   voc pl masc [3t; n-2a; 1528]   "
δούλοις   dat pl masc [7t; n-2a; 1528]   "
δοῦλον   acc sg masc [18t; n-2a; 1528]   "

δοῦλος, ου, ὁ   {1528, n-2a}
      a male slave, or *servant*, of various degrees, Matt
      8:9, et al. freq.; *a servitor, person of mean
      condition*, Phil 2:7; fem. δούλη, *a female slave; a
      handmaiden*, Luke 1:38, 48; Acts 2:18; δοῦλος,
      used figuratively, in a bad sense, *one involved in*
      moral or spiritual *thraldom*, John 8:34; Rom
      6:17, 20; 1 Cor 7:23; 2 Peter 2:19; in a good
      sense, *a* devoted *servant* or *minister*, Acts 16:17;
      Rom 1:1; *one pledged* or *bound to serve*, 1 Cor
      7:22; 2 Cor 4:5

δοῦλος, η, ον   {1529, a-1a(2a)}
      enslaved, enthralled, subservient, Rom 6:19;

δοῦλος   nom sg masc [35t; n-2a; 1528]   "
δούλου   gen sg masc [6t; n-2a; 1528]   "
δούλους   acc pl masc [19t; n-2a; 1528]   "

δουλόω   {1530, v-1d(3)}
      [δουλώσω, ἐδούλωσα, -, δεδούλωμαι, ἐδουλώθην]
      *to reduce to servitude, enslave, oppress by retaining
      in servitude*, Acts 7:6; 2 Peter 2:19; met. *to render
      subservient*, 1 Cor 9:19; pass. *to be under restraint*,
      1 Cor 7:15; *to be in bondage*, spiritually or
      morally, Gal 4:3; Titus 2:3; *to become devoted to
      the service of*, Rom 6:18, 22*

δούλῳ   dat sg masc [6t; n-2a; 1528]   δοῦλος
δουλωθέντες   aor pass ptcp nom pl masc
      [Rm 6:22; v-1d(3); 1530]   δουλόω
δούλων   gen pl masc [5t; n-2a; 1528]   δοῦλος
δουλώσουσιν   fut act ind 3 pl
      [Ac 7:6; v-1d(3); 1530]   δουλόω
δοῦναι   aor act inf [33t; v-6a; 1443]   δίδωμι
δούς   aor act ptcp nom sg masc
      [11t; v-6a; 1443]   "

δοχή, ῆς, ἡ   {1531, n-1b}
      pr. *reception* of guests; in N.T. *a banquet, feast*,
      Luke 5:29; 14:13

δοχήν   acc sg fem [2t; n-1b; 1531]   δοχή
δράκοντα   acc sg masc
      [Rv 20:2; n-3c(5b); 1532]   δράκων
δράκοντι   dat sg masc [Rv 13:4; n-3c(5b); 1532]   "
δράκοντος   gen sg masc [2t; n-3c(5b); 1532]   "

δράκων, οντος, ὁ   {1532, n-3c(5b)}
      a dragon or *large serpent*; met. *the devil* or *Satan*,
      Rev 12:3, 4, 7, 9, 13, 16, 17; 13:2, 4, 11; 16:13; 20:2

δράκων   nom sg masc [9t; n-3c(5b); 1532]   "
δραμών   aor act ptcp nom sg masc
      [3t; v-1b(2); 5556]   τρέχω

δράσσομαι   {1533, v-2b}
      [-, -, -, -, -] pr. *to grasp with the hand, clutch; to lay
      hold of, seize, take, catch*, 1 Cor 3:19*

δρασσόμενος   pres mid ptcp nom sg masc
      [1C 3:19; v-2b; 1533]   δράσσομαι
δραχμάς   acc pl fem [Lk 15:8; n-1b; 1534]   δραχμή

δραχμή, ῆς, ἡ   {1534, n-1b}
      a drachma, an Attic silver coin of nearly the
      same value as the Roman *denarius*, Luke 15:8,
      9*

δραχμήν   acc sg fem [2t; n-1b; 1534]   "

δρέπανον, ου, τό   {1535, n-2c}
      an instrument with a curved blade, as *a sickle*,
      Mark 4:29; Rev 14:14, 15, 16, 17, 18, 19*

δρέπανον   acc sg neut [8t; n-2c; 1535]   δρέπανον
δρόμον   acc sg masc [3t; n-2a; 1536]   δρόμος

δρόμος, ου, ὁ   {1536, n-2a}
      a course, race, race-course; met. *course* of life or
      ministry, *career*, Acts 13:25; 20:24; 2 Tim 4:7*

Δρούσιλλα, ης, ἡ   {1537, n-1c}
      Drusilla, pr. name, Acts 24:24, 27 v.l.*

Δρουσίλλη   dat sg fem
      [Ac 24:24; n-1c; 1537]   Δρούσιλλα
δυναίμην   pres pass opt 1 sg
      [Ac 8:31; v-6b; 1538]   δύναμαι
δύναιντο   pres pass opt 3 pl [2t; v-6b; 1538]   "

δύναμαι   {1538, v-6b}
      [(ἠδυνάμην), δυνήσομαι, -, -, -, ἠδυνήθην or
      ἠδυνάσθην] *to be able*, either intrinsically and
      absolutely, which is the ordinary signification;
      or, for specific reasons, Matt 9:15; Luke 16:2

δύναμαι   pres pass ind 1 sg [7t; v-6b; 1538]   "
δυνάμεθα   pres pass ind 1 pl [9t; v-6b; 1538]   "
δυνάμει   dat sg fem [26t; n-3e(5b); 1539]   δύναμις
δυνάμεις   nom pl fem [13t; n-3e(5b); 1539]   "
δυνάμεις   acc pl fem [7t; n-3e(5b); 1539]   "
δυνάμενα   pres pass ptcp acc pl neut
      [2t; v-6b; 1538]   δύναμαι
δυνάμεναι   pres pass ptcp nom pl fem
      [Hb 9:9; v-6b; 1538]   "
δυναμένη   pres pass ptcp nom sg fem
      [Lk 13:11; v-6b; 1538]   "
δυνάμενοι   pres pass ptcp nom pl masc
      [3t; v-6b; 1538]   "
δυνάμενον   pres pass ptcp acc sg masc
      [4t; v-6b; 1538]   "
δυνάμενος   pres pass ptcp nom sg masc
      [5t; v-6b; 1538]   "
δυναμένου   pres pass ptcp gen sg masc
      [2t; v-6b; 1538]   "
δυναμένου   pres pass ptcp gen sg neut
      [Ac 27:15; v-6b; 1538]   "

δυναμένους   pres pass ptcp acc pl masc
  [Ac 27:43; v-6b; 1538]   "
δυναμένῳ   pres pass ptcp dat sg masc
  [4t; v-6b; 1538]   "
δυναμένων   pres pass ptcp gen pl masc
  [Mt 10:28; v-6b; 1538]   "
δυνάμεσι   dat pl fem
  [Ac 2:22; n-3e(5b); 1539]   δύναμις
δυνάμεσιν   dat pl fem   [2t; n-3e(5b); 1539]   "
δυνάμεων   gen pl fem   [3t; n-3e(5b); 1539]   "
δυνάμεως   gen sg fem   [21t; n-3e(5b); 1539]   "
δύναμιν   acc sg fem   [33t; n-3e(5b); 1539]   "

δύναμις, εως, ἡ   {1539, n-3e(5b)}
  power; strength, ability, Matt 25:15; Heb 11:11;
  efficacy, 1 Cor 4:19, 20; Phil 3:10; 1 Thess 1:5; 2
  Tim 3:5; *energy,* Col 1:29; 2 Tim 1:7; *meaning,*
  purport of language, 1 Cor 14:11; *authority,* Luke
  4:36; 9:1; *might, power, majesty,* Matt 22:29;
  24:30; Acts 3:12; Rom 9:17; 2 Thess 1:7; 2 Peter
  1:16; in N.T. *a manifestation* or *instance of power,*
  mighty means, Acts 8:10; Rom 1:16; 1 Cor 1:18,
  24; ἡ δύναμις, *omnipotence,* Matt 26:64; Luke
  22:69; Matt 14:62; pl. *authorities,* Rom 8:38; Eph
  1:21; 1 Peter 3:22; *miraculous power,* Mark 5:30;
  Luke 1:35; 5:17; 6:19; 8:46; 24:49; 1 Cor 2:4; *a*
  miracle, Matt 11:20, 21, et al. freq.; *a worker of*
  miracles, 1 Cor 12:28, 29; from the Hebrew αἱ
  δυνάμεις τῶν οὐρανῶν, *the heavenly luminaries,*
  Matt 24:29; Mark 13:25; Luke 21:26; αἱ δυνάμεις,
  the spiritual *powers,* Matt 14:2; Mark 6:14

δύναμις   nom sg fem   [13t; n-3e(5b); 1539]   "
δυναμούμενοι   pres pass ptcp nom pl masc
  [Cl 1:11; v-1d(3); 1540]   δυναμόω

δυναμόω   {1540, v-1d(3)}
  [-, ἐδυνάμωσα, -, δεδυνάμωμαι, ἐδυναμώθην] *to*
  strengthen, confirm, Col 1:11; Heb 11:34; Eph
  6:10 v.l.*

δύνανται   pres pass ind 3 pl
  [9t; v-6b; 1538]   δύναμαι
δύνασαι   pres pass ind 2 sg   [7t; v-6b; 1538]   "
δύνασθαι   pres pass inf   [8t; v-6b; 1538]   "
δύνασθε   pres pass ind 2 pl   [27t; v-6b; 1538]   "
δυνάστας   acc pl masc
  [Lk 1:52; n-1f; 1541]   δυνάστης

δυνάστης, ου, ὁ   {1541, n-1f}
  a potentate, sovereign; prince, Luke 1:52; 1 Tim
  6:15; *a person of rank and authority,* Acts 8:27*

δυνάστης   nom sg masc   [2t; n-1f; 1541]   "
δυνατά   nom pl neut   [6t; a-1a(2a); 1543]   δυνατός
δύναται   pres pass ind 3 sg
  [71t; v-6b; 1538]   δύναμαι
δυνατεῖ   pres act ind 3 sg
  [3t; v-1d(2a); 1542]   δυνατέω

δυνατέω   {1542, v-1d(2a)}
  [δυνατήσω, -, -, -, -] *to be powerful, mighty, to*
  show one's self powerful, 2 Cor 9:8; 13:3 v.l.; Rom
  14:4*

δυνατοί   nom pl masc   [4t; a-1a(2a); 1543]   δυνατός
δυνατόν   nom sg neut   [8t; a-1a(2a); 1543]   "
δυνατόν   acc sg neut   [Rm 9:22; a-1a(2a); 1543]   "

δυνατός, ή, όν   {1543, a-1a(2a)}
  able, having power, powerful, mighty; δυνατὸς
  εἶναι, *to be able,* i.q. δύνασθαι, Luke 14:31; Acts
  11:17; ὁ δυνατός, *the Mighty One, God,* Luke 1:49;
  τὸ δυνατόν, *power,* i.q. δύναμις, Rom 9:22; *valid,*
  powerful, efficacious, 2 Cor 10:4; *distinguished for*
  rank, authority, or *influence,* Acts 25:5; 1 Cor
  1:26; *distinguished for skill* or *excellence,* Luke
  24:19; Acts 7:22; Rom 15:1; δυνατόν and δυνατά,
  possible, capable of being done, Matt 19:26; 24:24

δυνατός   nom sg masc   [13t; a-1a(2a); 1543]   "
δύνῃ   pres pass ind 2 sg   [4t; v-6b; 1538]   δύναμαι
δυνηθῆτε   aor pass subj 2 pl
  [Ep 6:13; v-6b; 1538]   "
δυνήσεσθε   fut mid ind 2 pl   [2t; v-6b; 1538]   "
δυνήσεται   fut mid ind 3 sg   [Mk 9:39; v-6b; 1538]   "
δυνήσεται   fut pass ind 3 sg   [4t; v-6b; 1538]   "
δυνήσῃ   fut pass ind 2 sg   [Ac 24:8; v-6b; 1538]   "
δυνησόμεθα   fut mid ind 1 pl
  [Ac 19:40; v-6b; 1538]   "
δυνήσονται   fut pass ind 3 pl
  [Lk 21:15; v-6b; 1538]   "
δύνηται   pres pass subj 3 sg
  [Rv 13:17; v-6b; 1538]   "
δύνοντος   pres act ptcp gen sg masc
  [Lk 4:40; v-3a(1); 1544]   δύνω

δύνω   {1544, v-3a(1)}
  [-, ἔδυσα or ἔδυν, δέδυκα, δέδυμαι, ἐδύην] *to sink,*
  go down, set as the sun, Mark 1:32; Luke 4:40*

δύνωνται   pres pass subj 3 pl
  [Lk 16:26; v-6b; 1538]   δύναμαι

δύο   {1545, a-5a}
  two, Matt 6:24; 21:38, 31, et al. freq.; οἱ δύο, *both,*
  John 20:4; δύο ἢ τρεῖς, *two* or *three, some, a few,*
  Matt 18:20; from the Hebrew, δύο δύο, *two and*
  two, Mark 6:7, i.q. ἀνὰ δύο, Luke 10:1, and κατὰ
  δύο, 1 Cor 14:27

δύο   nom pl masc   [33t; a-5a; 1545]   δύο
δύο   nom pl fem   [8t; a-5; 1545]   "
δύο   nom pl neut   [Mt 10:29; a-5; 1545]   "
δύο   gen pl masc   [10t; a-5; 1545]   "
δύο   gen pl neut   [3t; a-5; 1545]   "
δύο   acc pl masc   [46t; a-5; 1545]   "
δύο   acc pl fem   [8t; a-5; 1545]   "
δύο   acc pl neut   [17t; a-5; 1545]   "
δυσβάστακτα   acc pl neut
  [2t; a-3a; 1546]   δυσβάστακτος

δυσβάστακτος, ον   {1546, a-3a}
  difficult or *grievous to be borne, oppressive,* Luke
  11:46; Matt 23:4 v.l.*

δυσεντέριον, ου, τό   {1547}
  a dysentery, Acts 28:8 v.l., G/K list as δυσεντερία

δυσεντέριον, ου, τό   {1548, n-2c}
  dysentery, Acts 28:8*

δυσεντερίῳ   dat sg neut
  [Ac 28:8; n-2c; 1548]   δυσεντέριον

δυσερμήνευτος, ον   {1549, a-3a}
  difficult to be explained, hard to be understood, Heb
  5:11*

δυσερμήνευτος   nom sg masc
   [Hb 5:11; a-3a; 1549]   δυσερμήνευτος
δύσεως   gen sg fem [Mk 16:8; n-3e(5b); 1550] δύσις
δυσί   dat pl masc [2t; a-5; 1545]   δύο
δυσί   dat pl fem [Ac 21:33; a-5; 1545]   "
δυσίν   dat pl masc [4t; a-5; 1545]   "
δυσίν   dat pl fem [2t; a-5; 1545]   "

δύσις, εως, ἡ   {1550, n-3e(5b)}
   west, Mark 16:8 (shorter ending)

δύσκολον   nom sg neut
   [Mk 10:24; a-3a; 1551]   δύσκολος

δύσκολος, ον   {1551, a-3a}
   pr. peevish about food; hard to please, disagreeable;
   in N.T., difficult, Mark 10:24*

δυσκόλως   {1552, adverb}
   with difficulty, hardly, Matt 19:23; Mark 10:23;
   Luke 18:24*

δυσκόλως   adverb [3t; adverb; 1552]   δυσκόλως

δυσμή, ῆς, ἡ   {1553, n-1b}
   a sinking or setting; pl. δυσμαί, the setting of the
   sun; hence, the west, Matt 8:11; 24:27

δυσμῶν   gen pl fem [5t; n-1b; 1553]   δυσμή
δυσνόητα   nom pl neut
   [2P 3:16; a-3a; 1554]   δυσνόητος

δυσνόητος, ον   {1554, a-3a}
   hard to be understood, 2 Peter 3:16*

δυσφημέω   {1555, cv-1d(2a)}
   [-, -, -, -, -] pr. to use ill words; to reproach, revile,
   1 Cor 4:13*

δυσφημία, ας, ἡ   {1556, n-1a}
   ill words; words of ill omen; reproach, contumely, 2
   Cor 6:8*

δυσφημίας   gen sg fem
   [2C 6:8; n-1a; 1556]   δυσφημία
δυσφημούμενοι   pres pass ptcp nom pl masc
   [1C 4:13; cv-; 1555]   δυσφημέω
δῷ   aor act subj 3 sg [6t; v-6a; 1443]   δίδωμι

δώδεκα   {1557, a-5b}
   twelve, Matt 9:20; 10:1; οἱ δώδεκα, the twelve
   apostles, Matt 26:14, 20

δώδεκα   indecl [75t; a-5b; 1557]   δώδεκα

δωδέκατος, η, ον   {1558, a-1a(2a)}
   the twelfth, Rev 21:20*

δωδέκατος   nom sg masc
   [Rv 21:20; a-1a(2a); 1558]   δωδέκατος

δωδεκάφυλον, ου, τό   {1559, n-2c}
   twelve tribes, Acts 26:7*

δωδεκάφυλον   nom sg neut
   [Ac 26:7; n-2c; 1559]   δωδεκάφυλον
δώῃ   aor act opt 3 sg [4t; v-6a; 1443]   δίδωμι
δώῃ   aor act subj 3 sg [2t; v-6a; 1443]   "

δῶμα, ατος, τό   {1560, n-3c(4)}
   pr. a house; synec. a roof, Matt 10:27; 24:17

δῶμα   acc sg neut [2t; n-3c(4); 1560]   δῶμα
δώματος   gen sg neut [3t; n-3c(4); 1560]   "

δωμάτων   gen pl neut [2t; n-3c(4); 1560]   "
δῶμεν   aor act subj 1 pl [5t; v-6a; 1443]   δίδωμι
δῶρα   nom pl neut [Hb 9:9; n-2c; 1565]   δῶρον
δῶρα   acc pl neut [7t; n-2c; 1565]   "

δωρεά, ᾶς, ἡ   {1561, n-1a}
   a gift, free gift, benefit, John 4:10; Acts 2:38

δωρεά   nom sg fem [2t; n-1a; 1561]   δωρεά
δωρεᾷ   dat sg fem [2C 9:15; n-1a; 1561]   "

δωρεάν   {1562, adverb}
   gratis, gratuitously, freely, Matt 10:8; Rom 3:24;
   in N.T. undeservedly, without cause, John 15:25;
   in vain, Gal 2:21

δωρεάν   acc sg fem [5t; n-1a; 1561]   "
δωρεάν   adverb [9t; adverb; 1562]   δωρεάν
δωρεᾶς   gen sg fem [3t; n-1a; 1561]   δωρεά

δωρέομαι   {1563, v-1d(2a)}
   [-, ἐδωρησάμην, -, δεδώρημαι, -] to give freely,
   grant, Mark 15:45; 2 Peter 1:3, 4*

δώρημα, ατος, τό   {1564, n-3c(4)}
   a gift, free gift, Rom 5:16; James 1:17*

δώρημα   nom sg neut [2t; n-3c(4); 1564]   δώρημα
δώροις   dat pl neut [Hb 11:4; n-2c; 1565]   δῶρον

δῶρον, ου, τό   {1565, n-2c}
   a gift, present, Matt 2:11; Eph 2:8; Rev 11:10; an
   offering, sacrifice, Matt 5:23, 24; 8:4; δῶρον, sc.
   ἐστι(ν), it is consecrated to God, Matt 15:5; Mark
   7:11; contribution to the temple, Luke 21:1, 4

δῶρον   nom sg neut [4t; n-2c; 1565]   "
δῶρον   acc sg neut [5t; n-2c; 1565]   "

δωροφορία, ᾶς, ἡ   {1567, n-1a}
   the bringing of a gift, Rom 15:31 v.l.*

δώρῳ   dat sg neut [Mt 23:18; n-2c; 1565]   "
δῷς   aor act subj 2 sg
   [Mk 6:25; v-6a; 1443]   δίδωμι
δώσει   fut act ind 3 sg [19t; v-6a; 1443]   "
δώσεις   fut act ind 2 sg [2t; v-6a; 1443]   "
δώσῃ   aor act subj 3 sg [Jn 17:2; v-6a; 1443] "
δῶσιν   aor act subj 3 pl [Rv 13:16; v-6a; 1443] "
δώσομεν   fut act ind 1 pl [Mk 6:37; v-6a; 1443] "
δώσουσιν   fut act ind 3 pl [5t; v-6a; 1443]   "
δώσω   fut act ind 1 sg [23t; v-6a; 1443]   "
δώσωμεν   aor act subj 1 pl [Rv 19:7; v-6a; 1443] "
δῶτε   aor act subj pl [3t; v-6a; 1443]   "

ε

ε   {1567, n-3g(2)}
   five, as a numeral, Acts 19:9 v.l.*

ἔα   {1568, interj}
   Ha! an expression of surprise or displeasure,
   Matt 1:24 v.l.; Luke 4:34*

ἔα   interjection [Lk 4:34; interj; 1568]   ἔα

ἐάν   {1569, conj}
   if, ἐὰν μή, except, unless; also equivalent to
   ἀλλά, Gal 2:16. Ἐάν, in N.T. as in the later

Greek, is substituted for ἄν after relative
words, Matt 5:19. Tends to be an indicator for
the subjunctive mood.

ἐάν   conj [333t; conj; 1569]   ἐάν

ἐάνπερ   {1570, conj}
  if it be that, if indeed, if at all events, Heb 3:6, 14;
  6:3

ἐάνπερ   conj [3t; conj; 1570]   ἐάνπερ
ἐάσαντες   aor act ptcp nom pl masc
  [Ac 23:32; v-1d(1b); 1572]   ἐάω
ἐάσει   fut act ind 3 sg
  [1C 10:13; v-1d(1b); 1572]   "
ἐᾶτε   pres act imperative 2 pl
  [Lk 22:51; v-1d(1b); 1572]   "
ἑαυτά   acc pl neut
  [1J 5:21; a-1a(2b); 1571]   ἑαυτοῦ
ἑαυταῖς   dat pl fem [Mt 25:9; a-1a(2b); 1571]   "
ἑαυτάς   acc pl fem [Lk 23:28; a-1a(2b); 1571]   "
ἑαυτάς   acc pl fem [3t; a-1a(2b); 1571]   "
ἑαυτῇ   dat sg fem [2t; a-1a(2b); 1571]   "
ἑαυτήν   acc sg fem [7t; a-1a(2b); 1571]   "
ἑαυτῆς   gen sg fem [6t; a-1a(2b); 1571]   "
ἑαυτοῖς   dat pl masc [50t; a-1a(2b); 1571]   "
ἑαυτόν   acc sg masc [68t; a-1a(2b); 1571]   "

ἑαυτοῦ, ῆς, οῦ   {1571, a-1a(2b)}
  himself, herself, itself, Matt 8:22; 12:26; 9:21; also
  used for the first and second persons, Rom
  8:23; Matt 23:31; John 18:34 v.l.; also equivalent
  to ἀλλήλων, Mark 10:26; John 12:19; ἀφ᾽ ἑαυτοῦ,
  ἀφ᾽ ἑαυτῶν, *of himself, themselves, voluntarily,
  spontaneously*, Luke 12:57; 21:30; *of one's own
  will merely*, John 5:19; δι᾽ ἑαυτοῦ, *of itself, in its
  own nature*, Rom 14:14; ἐξ ἑαυτῶν, *of one's own
  self* , 2 Cor 3:5; καθ᾽ ἑαυτόν, *by one's self, alone,*
  Acts 28:16; James 2:17; παρ᾽ ἑαυτῷ, *with one's
  self, at home*, 1 Cor 16:2; πρὸς ἑαυτόν, *to one's self,
  to one's home*, Luke 24:12; John 20:10; or, *with
  one's self*, Luke 18:11

ἑαυτοῦ   gen sg masc [41t; a-1a(2b); 1571]   "
ἑαυτοῦ   gen sg neut [6t; a-1a(2b); 1571]   "
ἑαυτούς   acc pl masc [64t; a-1a(2b); 1571]   "
ἑαυτῷ   dat sg masc [29t; a-1a(2b); 1571]   "
ἑαυτῶν   gen pl masc [34t; a-1a(2b); 1571]   "
ἑαυτῶν   gen pl fem [5t; a-1a(2b); 1571]   "
ἑαυτῶν   gen pl neut [Jd 13; a-1a(2b); 1571]   "

ἐάω   {1572, v-1d(1b)}
  [(εἴων), ἐάσω, εἴασα, -, -, -] *to let, allow, permit,
  suffer to be done*, Matt 24:43; Luke 4:41; *to let be,
  let alone, desist from, stop*, Luke 22:51; Acts 5:38
  v.l.; Rom 2:20 v.l.; *to commit* a ship to the sea, *let
  her drive*, Acts 27:40

ἐβάθυνεν   aor act ind 3 sg
  [Lk 6:48; v-1c(2); 959]   βαθύνω
ἔβαλαν   aor act ind 3 pl
  [Ac 16:37; v-2d(1); 965]   βάλλω
ἔβαλεν   aor act ind 3 sg [21t; v-2d(1); 965]   "
ἔβαλλον   imperf act ind 3 pl
  [Mk 12:41; v-2d(1); 965]   "
ἔβαλον   aor act ind 3 pl [8t; v-2d(1); 965]   "

ἐβάπτιζεν   imperf act ind 3 sg
  [2t; v-2a(1); 966]   βαπτίζω
ἐβαπτίζοντο   imperf pass ind 3 pl
  [5t; v-2a(1); 966]   "
ἐβάπτισα   aor act ind 1 sg [4t; v-2a(1); 966]   "
ἐβάπτισεν   aor act ind 3 sg [4t; v-2a(1); 966]   "
ἐβαπτίσθη   aor pass ind 3 sg [5t; v-2a(1); 966]   "
ἐβαπτίσθημεν   aor pass ind 1 pl
  [3t; v-2a(1); 966]   "
ἐβαπτίσθησαν   aor pass ind 3 pl
  [3t; v-2a(1); 966]   "
ἐβαπτίσθητε   aor pass ind 2 pl
  [4t; v-2a(1); 966]   "
ἐβαρήθημεν   aor pass ind 1 pl
  [2C 1:8; v-1d(2a); 976]   βαρέω
ἐβασάνιζεν   imperf act ind 3 sg
  [2P 2:8; v-2a(1); 989]   βασανίζω
ἐβασάνισαν   aor act ind 3 pl
  [Rv 11:10; v-2a(1); 989]   "
ἐβασίλευσαν   aor act ind 3 pl
  [Rv 20:4; v-1a(6); 996]   βασιλεύω
ἐβασίλευσας   aor act ind 2 sg
  [Rv 11:17; v-1a(6); 996]   "
ἐβασιλεύσατε   aor act ind 2 pl
  [2t; v-1a(6); 996]   "
ἐβασίλευσεν   aor act ind 3 sg [4t; v-1a(6); 996] "
ἐβάσκανεν   aor act ind 3 sg
  [Ga 3:1; v-2d(4); 1001]   βασκαίνω
ἐβάσταζεν   imperf act ind 3 sg
  [Jn 12:6; v-2a(1); 1002]   βαστάζω
ἐβαστάζετο   imperf pass ind 3 sg
  [Ac 3:2; v-2a(1); 1002]   "
ἐβάστασαν   aor act ind 3 pl
  [Jn 10:31; v-2a(1); 1002]   "
ἐβάστασας   aor act ind 2 sg [2t; v-2a(1); 1002]   "
ἐβάστασεν   aor act ind 3 sg
  [Mt 8:17; v-2a(1); 1002]   "
ἐβδελυγμένοις   perf pass ptcp dat pl masc
  [Rv 21:8; v-2b; 1009]   βδελύσσομαι
ἑβδόμη   dat sg fem
  [Hb 4:4; a-1a(2a); 1575]   ἕβδομος

ἑβδομήκοντα   {1573, a-5b}
  seventy, indecl., Acts 7:14; οἱ ἑβδομήκοντα, *the
  seventy* disciples, Luke 10:1, 17; Acts 23:23*

ἑβδομήκοντα   indecl
  [5t; a-5b; 1573]   ἑβδομήκοντα

ἑβδομηκοντάκις   {1574, a-5b}
  indecl, *seventy times*, Matt 18:22*

ἑβδομηκοντάκις   indecl
  [Mt 18:22; a-5b; 1574]   ἑβδομηκοντάκις
ἑβδόμην   acc sg fem [2t; a-1a(2a); 1575]   ἕβδομος
ἑβδόμης   gen sg fem [Hb 4:4; a-1a(2a); 1575]   "

ἕβδομος, η, ον   {1575, a-1a(2a)}
  seventh, John 4:52; Heb 4:4; Jude 14; Rev 8:1

ἕβδομος   nom sg masc [4t; a-1a(2a); 1575]   "
ἑβδόμου   gen sg masc [Rv 10:7; a-1a(2a); 1575]   "
ἐβεβαιώθη   aor pass ind 3 sg
  [2t; v-1d(3); 1011]   βεβαιόω
ἐβέβλητο   pluperf pass ind 3 sg
  [Lk 16:20; v-2d(1); 965]   βάλλω

Ἔβερ, ὁ {1576, n-3g(2)}
Heber, pr. name, indecl., Luke 3:35*

Ἔβερ indecl [Lk 3:35; n-3g(2); 1576] Ἔβερ
ἐβλάστησεν aor act ind 3 sg
[2t; v-3a(2a); 1056] βλαστάνω
ἐβλασφήμει imperf act ind 3 sg
[Lk 23:39; v-1d(2a); 1059] βλασφημέω
ἐβλασφήμησαν aor act ind 3 pl
[3t; v-1d(2a); 1059] "
ἐβλασφήμησεν aor act ind 3 sg
[Mt 26:65; v-1d(2a); 1059] "
ἐβλασφήμουν imperf act ind 3 pl
[2t; v-1d(2a); 1059] "
ἔβλεπεν imperf act ind 3 sg
[Ac 9:8; v-1b(1); 1063] βλέπω
ἔβλεπον imperf act ind 3 pl
[Jn 13:22; v-1b(1); 1063] "
ἔβλεψα aor act ind 1 sg [Rv 22:8; v-1b(1); 1063] "
ἐβλήθη aor pass ind 3 sg
[9t; v-2d(1); 965] βάλλω
ἐβλήθησαν aor pass ind 3 pl [3t; v-2d(1); 965] "
ἐβοήθησα aor act ind 1 sg
[2C 6:2; v-1d(2a); 1070] βοηθέω
ἐβοήθησεν aor act ind 3 sg
[Rv 12:16; v-1d(2a); 1070] "
ἐβόησεν aor act ind 3 sg
[3t; v-1d(1a); 1066] βοάω
ἐβούλετο imperf mid ind 3 sg
[Ac 15:37; v-1d(2c); 1089] βούλομαι
ἐβουλεύοντο imperf mid ind 3 pl
[Ac 27:39; v-1a(6); 1086] βουλεύω
ἐβουλεύσαντο aor mid ind 3 pl
[2t; v-1a(6); 1086] "
ἐβουλήθη aor pass ind 3 sg
[Mt 1:19; v-1d(2c); 1089] βούλομαι
ἐβουλήθην aor pass ind 1 sg
[2J 12; v-1d(2c); 1089] "
ἐβουλόμην imperf mid ind 1 sg
[3t; v-1d(2c); 1089] "
ἐβούλοντο imperf mid ind 3 pl
[2t; v-1d(2c); 1089] "
Ἑβραΐδι dat sg fem [3t; n-3c(2); 1579] Ἑβραΐς

Ἑβραϊκός, ή, όν {1577, a-1a(2a)}
Hebrew, Luke 23:38 v.l.*

Ἑβραῖοι nom pl masc
[2C 11:22; n-2a; 1578] Ἑβραῖος

Ἑβραῖος, ου, ὁ {1578, n-2a}
a Hebrew, one descended from Abraham the
Hebrew, 2 Cor 11:22; Phil 3:5; in N.T., a Jew of
Palestine, one speaking Aramaic, opp. to
Ἑλληνιστής, Acts 6:1*

Ἑβραῖος nom sg masc [Pp 3:5; n-2a; 1578] "
Ἑβραίους acc pl masc [Ac 6:1; n-2a; 1578] "

Ἑβραΐς, ΐδος, ἡ {1579, n-3c(2)}
the Hebrew dialect, i.e., the Hebrew-Aramaic
dialect of Palestine, Acts 21:40; 22:2; 26:14*

Ἑβραϊστί {1580, adverb}
in Hebrew or Aramaic, John 5:2; 19:13, 17, 20;
20:16; Rev 9:11; 16:16*

Ἑβραϊστί adverb [7t; adverb; 1580] Ἑβραϊστί

Ἑβραίων gen pl masc
[Pp 3:5; n-2a; 1578] Ἑβραῖος
ἔβρεξεν aor act ind 3 sg
[3t; v-1b(2); 1101] βρέχω
ἔβρυχον imperf act ind 3 pl
[Ac 7:54; v-1b(2); 1107] βρύχω
ἐγάμησεν aor act ind 3 sg
[Mk 6:17; v-1d(2a); 1138] γαμέω
ἐγαμίζοντο imperf pass ind 3 pl
[Lk 17:27; v-2a(1); 1139] γαμίζω
ἐγάμουν imperf act ind 3 pl
[Lk 17:27; v-1d(2a); 1138] γαμέω
ἐγγεγραμμένη perf pass ptcp nom sg fem
[2t; cv-1b(1); 1582] ἐγγράφω
ἐγγέγραπται perf pass ind 3 sg
[Lk 10:20; cv-1b(1); 1582] "
ἐγγιεῖ fut act ind 3 sg
[Jm 4:8; v-2a(1); 1581] ἐγγίζω
ἐγγίζει pres act ind 3 sg [2t; v-2a(1); 1581] "
ἐγγίζειν pres act inf [2t; v-2a(1); 1581] "
ἐγγίζομεν pres act ind 1 pl
[Hb 7:19; v-2a(1); 1581] "
ἐγγίζοντες pres act ptcp nom pl masc
[Lk 15:1; v-2a(1); 1581] "
ἐγγίζοντι pres act ptcp dat sg masc
[Ac 22:6; v-2a(1); 1581] "
ἐγγίζοντος pres act ptcp gen sg masc
[Lk 19:37; v-2a(1); 1581] "
ἐγγιζόντων pres act ptcp gen pl masc
[Ac 10:9; v-2a(1); 1581] "
ἐγγίζουσαν pres act ptcp acc sg fem
[Hb 10:25; v-2a(1); 1581] "
ἐγγίζουσιν pres act ind 3 pl
[Mk 11:1; v-2a(1); 1581] "

ἐγγίζω (Root) {1581, v-2a(1)}
[ἐγγιῶ, ἤγγισα, ἤγγικα, -, -] pr. to cause to
approach; in N.T. intrans. to approach, draw near,
Matt 21:1; Luke 18:35; met. to be at hand, Matt
3:2; 4:17; μέχρι θανάτου ἐγγίζειν, to be at the point
of death, Phil 2:30; from Hebrew to draw near to
God, to offer Him reverence and worship, Matt
15:8; Heb 7:19; James 4:8; used of God, to draw
near to men, assist them, bestow favors on them,
James 4:8

ἐγγίσαι aor act inf [Ac 23:15; v-2a(1); 1581] "
ἐγγίσαντος aor act ptcp gen sg masc
[Lk 18:40; v-2a(1); 1581] "
ἐγγίσας aor act ptcp nom sg masc
[2t; v-2a(1); 1581] "
ἐγγίσατε aor act imperative 2 pl
[Jm 4:8; v-2a(1); 1581] "

ἐγγράφω {1582, cv-1b(1)}
[-, -, -, ἐγγέγραμμαι, -] to engrave, inscribe, Luke
10:20; met. ἐγγεγραμμένος, imprinted, 2 Cor 3:2,
3*

ἔγγυος, ον {1583, a-3a}
a guarantee, sponsor, Heb 7:22*

ἔγγυος nom sg masc [Hb 7:22; n-2a; 1583] ἔγγυος

ἐγγύς {1584, adverb}
some view as an improper prep., followed by
gen. or dat., near, as to place, Luke 19:11; close at

hand, Rom 10:8; *near,* in respect of ready interposition, Phil 4:5; *near,* as to time, Matt 24:32, 33; *near* to God, as being in covenant with him, Eph 2:13; οἱ ἐγγύς, *the people near* to God, the Jews, Eph 2:17

ἐγγύς   adverb [30t; adverb; 1584]   ἐγγύς

ἐγγύτερον, comparative of ἐγγύς   {1585}

ἐγγύτερον   adverb-comparative
  [Rm 13:11; adverb; 1584]   "

ἐγεγόνει   pluperf act ind 3 sg
  [Jn 6:17; v-1c(2); 1181]   γίνομαι

ἐγεῖραι   aor act inf [2t; v-2d(3); 1586]   ἐγείρω

ἐγείραντα   aor act ptcp acc sg masc
  [2t; v-2d(3); 1586]   "

ἐγείραντος   aor act ptcp gen sg masc
  [3t; v-2d(3); 1586]   "

ἐγείρας   aor act ptcp nom sg masc
  [3t; v-2d(3); 1586]   "

ἔγειρε   pres act imperative 2 sg
  [14t; v-2d(3); 1586]   "

ἐγείρει   pres act ind 3 sg [2t; v-2d(3); 1586]   "

ἐγείρειν   pres act inf [2t; v-2d(3); 1586]   "

ἐγείρεσθε   pres pass imperative 2 pl
  [3t; v-2d(3); 1586]   "

ἐγείρεται   pres pass ind 3 sg
  [6t; v-2d(3); 1586]   "

ἐγείρετε   pres act imperative 2 pl
  [Mt 10:8; v-2d(3); 1586]   "

ἐγείρηται   pres pass subj 3 sg
  [Mk 4:27; v-2d(3); 1586]   "

ἐγείρομαι   pres pass ind 1 sg
  [Mt 27:63; v-2d(3); 1586]   "

ἐγείρονται   pres pass ind 3 pl
  [9t; v-2d(3); 1586]   "

ἐγείροντι   pres act ptcp dat sg masc
  [2C 1:9; v-2d(3); 1586]   "

ἐγείρουσιν   pres act ind 3 pl
  [Mk 4:38; v-2d(3); 1586]   "

ἐγείρω   {1586, v-2d(3)}
  [ἐγερῶ, ἤγειρα, -, ἐγήγερμαι, ἠγέρθην] *to excite, arouse, awaken,* Matt 8:25; mid. *to awake,* Matt 2:13, 20, 21; met. mid. *to rouse one's self* to a better course of conduct, Rom 13:11; Eph 5:14; *to raise* from the dead, John 12:1; and mid. *to rise* from the dead, Matt 27:52; John 5:21; met. *to raise* as it were from the dead, 2 Cor 4:14; *to raise up, cause to rise up* from a prone posture, Acts 3:7; and mid. *to rise up,* Matt 17:7; *to restore to health,* James 5:15; met. et seq. ἐπή, *to excite* to war; mid. *to rise up against,* Matt 24:7; *to raise up again, rebuild,* John 2:19, 20; *to raise up* from a lower place, *to draw up* or *out of* a ditch, Matt 12:10; from Hebrew, *to raise up, to cause to arise* or *exist,* Acts 13:22, 23; mid. *to arise, exist, appear,* Matt 3:9; 11:11

ἐγέμισαν   aor act ind 3 pl
  [2t; v-2a(1); 1153]   γεμίζω

ἐγέμισεν   aor act ind 3 sg
  [Rv 8:5; v-2a(1); 1153]   "

ἐγεμίσθη   aor pass ind 3 sg
  [Rv 15:8; v-2a(1); 1153]   "

ἐγένεσθε   aor mid ind 2 pl
  [4t; v-1c(2); 1181]   γίνομαι

ἐγένετο   aor mid ind 3 sg [202t; v-1c(2); 1181]   "

ἐγενήθη   aor pass ind 3 sg [12t; v-1c(2); 1181]   "

ἐγενήθημεν   aor pass ind 1 pl
  [7t; v-1c(2); 1181]   "

ἐγενήθην   aor pass ind 1 sg
  [Ep 3:7; v-1c(2); 1181]   "

ἐγενήθησαν   aor pass ind 3 pl
  [6t; v-1c(2); 1181]   "

ἐγενήθητε   aor pass ind 2 pl [5t; v-1c(2); 1181] "

ἐγεννήθη   aor pass ind 3 sg
  [7t; v-1d(1a); 1164]   γεννάω

ἐγεννήθημεν   aor pass ind 1 pl
  [Ac 2:8; v-1d(1a); 1164]   "

ἐγεννήθης   aor pass ind 2 sg
  [Jn 9:34; v-1d(1a); 1164]   "

ἐγεννήθησαν   aor pass ind 3 pl
  [3t; v-1d(1a); 1164]   "

ἐγέννησα   aor act ind 1 sg [2t; v-1d(1a); 1164]   "

ἐγέννησαν   aor act ind 3 pl
  [Lk 23:29; v-1d(1a); 1164]   "

ἐγέννησεν   aor act ind 3 sg
  [42t; v-1d(1a); 1164]   "

ἐγενόμην   aor mid ind 1 sg
  [12t; v-1c(2); 1181]   γίνομαι

ἐγένοντο   aor mid ind 3 pl [13t; v-1c(2); 1181]   "

ἐγένου   aor mid ind 2 sg [2t; v-1c(2); 1181]   "

ἐγερεῖ   fut act ind 3 sg
  [3t; v-2d(3); 1586]   ἐγείρω

ἐγερεῖς   fut act ind 2 sg
  [Jn 2:20; v-2d(3); 1586]   "

ἐγερθείς   aor pass ptcp nom sg masc
  [13t; v-2d(3); 1586]   "

ἐγερθέντι   aor pass ptcp dat sg masc
  [2t; v-2d(3); 1586]   "

ἐγερθῇ   aor pass subj 3 sg [2t; v-2d(3); 1586]   "

ἐγερθῆναι   aor pass inf [5t; v-2d(3); 1586]   "

ἐγερθήσεται   fut pass ind 3 sg
  [7t; v-2d(3); 1586]   "

ἐγερθήσονται   fut pass ind 3 pl
  [4t; v-2d(3); 1586]   "

ἐγέρθητε   aor pass imperative 2 pl
  [Mt 17:7; v-2d(3); 1586]   "

ἐγέρθητι   aor pass imperative 2 sg
  [Lk 7:14; v-2d(3); 1586]   "

ἔγερσιν   acc sg fem
  [Mt 27:53; n-3e(5b); 1587]   ἔγερσις

ἔγερσις, εως, ἡ   {1587, n-3e(5b)}
  pr. *the act of waking* or *rising up; resurrection resuscitation,* Matt 27:53*

ἐγερῶ   fut act ind 1 sg
  [Jn 2:19; v-2d(3); 1586]   ἐγείρω

ἐγεύσασθε   aor mid ind 2 pl
  [1P 2:3; v-1a(6); 1174]   γεύομαι

ἐγεύσατο   aor mid ind 3 sg
  [Jn 2:9; v-1a(6); 1174]   "

ἐγηγερμένον   perf pass ptcp acc sg masc
  [2t; v-2d(3); 1586]   ἐγείρω

ἐγήγερται   perf pass ind 3 sg
  [9t; v-2d(3); 1586]   "

ἔγημα   aor act ind 1 sg
  [Lk 14:20; v-1d(2a); 1138]   γαμέω
ἐγίνετο   imperf mid ind 3 sg
  [3t; v-1c(2); 1181]   γίνομαι
ἐγίνωσκεν   imperf act ind 3 sg
  [4t; v-5a; 1182]   γινώσκω
ἐγίνωσκον   imperf act ind 3 pl
  [Lk 18:34; v-5a; 1182]   "
ἐγκαθέτους   acc pl masc
  [Lk 20:20; a-3a; 1588]   ἐγκάθετος

ἐγκαίνια, ίων, τά   {1589, n-2c}
  initiation, consecration; in N.T. *the feast of
  rededication,* an annual festival of eight days in
  the month Kislev, John 10:22*

ἐγκαίνια   nom pl neut
  [Jn 10:22; n-2c; 1589]   ἐγκαίνια

ἐγκαινίζω   {1590, cv-2a(1)}
  [-, ἐνεκαίνισα, -, ἐγκεκαίνισμαι, -] *to initiate,
  consecrate, dedicate, renovate; to institute,* Heb
  9:18; 10:20*

ἐγκακεῖν   pres act inf
  [2t; cv-1d(2a); 1591]   ἐγκακέω
ἐγκακήσητε   aor act subj 2 pl
  [2Th 3:13; cv-1d(2a); 1591]   "
ἐγκακοῦμεν   pres act ind 1 pl
  [2t; cv-1d(2a); 1591]   "
ἐγκακῶμεν   pres act subj 1 pl
  [Ga 6:9; cv-1d(2a); 1591]   "
ἐγκαλεῖσθαι   pres pass inf
  [Ac 19:40; cv-1d(2b); 1592]   ἐγκαλέω
ἐγκαλείτωσαν   pres act imperative 3 pl
  [Ac 19:38; cv-1d(2b); 1592]   "
ἐγκαλέσει   fut act ind 3 sg
  [Rm 8:33; cv-1d(2b); 1592]   "

ἐγκαλέω   {1592, cv-1d(2b)}
  [(ἐνελάλουν), ἐγκαλέσω, -, -, -, -] can be
  followed by a dative, *to bring a charge against,
  accuse; to institute judicial proceedings,* Acts
  19:38, 40; 23:28, 29; 26:2, 7; Rom 8:33

ἐγκαλοῦμαι   pres pass ind 1 sg
  [2t; cv-1d(2b); 1592]   "
ἐγκαλούμενον   pres pass ptcp acc sg masc
  [Ac 23:29; cv-1d(2b); 1592]   "
ἐγκαταλειπόμενοι   pres pass ptcp nom pl masc
  [2C 4:9; cv-1b(1); 1593]   ἐγκαταλείπω
ἐγκαταλείποντες   pres act ptcp nom pl masc
  [Hb 10:25; cv-1b(1); 1593]   "

ἐγκαταλείπω   {1593, cv-1b(1)}
  [ἐγκαταλείψω, ἐγκατέλιπον, -, -, ἐγκατελείφθην]
  to leave, leave behind; to forsake, abandon, Matt
  27:46; Mark 15:34; Acts 2:27, 30; Rom 9:29; 2
  Cor 4:9; 2 Tim 4:00, 16; Heb 10:25; 13:5*

ἐγκαταλείψεις   fut act ind 2 sg
  [Ac 2:27; cv-1b(1); 1593]   "
ἐγκαταλίπω   aor act subj 1 sg
  [Hb 13:5; cv-1b(1); 1593]   "
ἐγκατελείφθη   aor pass ind 3 sg
  [Ac 2:31; cv-1b(1); 1593]   "
ἐγκατέλιπεν   aor act ind 3 sg
  [2t; cv-1b(1); 1593]   "

ἐγκατέλιπες   aor act ind 2 sg
  [2t; cv-1b(1); 1593]   "
ἐγκατέλιπον   aor act ind 3 pl
  [2Ti 4:16; cv-1b(1); 1593]   "

ἐγκατοικέω   {1594, cv-1d(2a)}
  [-, -, -, -, -] *to dwell in,* or *among,* 2 Peter 2:8*

ἐγκατοικῶν   pres act ptcp nom sg masc
  [2P 2:8; cv-1d(2a); 1594]   ἐγκατοικέω

ἐγκαυχάομαι   {1595, cv-1d(1a)}
  [-, -, -, -, -] *to boast in,* or *of,* 2 Thess 1:4*

ἐγκαυχᾶσθαι   pres mid inf
  [2Th 1:4; cv-1d(1a); 1595]   ἐγκαυχάομαι
ἐγκεκαίνισται   perf pass ind 3 sg
  [Hb 9:18; cv-2a(1); 1590]   ἐγκαινίζω

ἐγκεντρίζω   {1596, cv-2a(1)}
  [-, ἐνεκέντρισα, -, -, ἐγκεντρίσθην] *to ingraft;*
  met. Rom 11:17, 19, 23, 24*

ἐγκεντρίσαι   aor act inf
  [Rm 11:23; cv-2a(1); 1596]   ἐγκεντρίζω
ἐγκεντρισθήσονται   fut pass ind 3 pl
  [2t; cv-2a(1); 1596]   "
ἐγκεντρισθῶ   aor pass subj 1 sg
  [Rm 11:19; cv-2a(1); 1596]   "

ἐγκλείω   (1597, bv-1a(3))
  [-, -, -, ἐγκέκλεισμαι, -] *to lock up,* Luke 3:20 v.l.*

ἔγκλημα, ατος, τό   {1598, n-3c(4)}
  an accusation, charge, crimination, Acts 23:29;
  25:16; 23:24 v.l.*

ἔγκλημα   acc sg neut
  [Ac 23:29; n-3c(4); 1598]   ἔγκλημα
ἐγκλήματος   gen sg neut
  [Ac 25:16; n-3c(4); 1598]   "

ἐγκομβόομαι   {1599, cv-1d(3)}
  [-, ἐνεκομβωσάμην, -, -, -] pr. *to put on a garment
  which is to be tied;* in N.T. *to put on, clothe one's
  self with;* met. 1 Peter 5:5*

ἐγκομβώσασθε   aor mid imperative 2 pl
  [1P 5:5; cv-1d(3); 1599]   ἐγκομβόομαι

ἐγκοπή, ῆς, ἡ   {1600, n-1b}
  alsn spelled ἐκκοπή, pr. *an incision,* e.g. a trench,
  etc., cut in the way of an enemy; *an impediment,
  hindrance,* 1 Cor 9:12*

ἐγκοπήν   acc sg fem [1C 9:12; n-1b; 1600]   ἐγκοπή
ἐγκόπτεσθαι   pres pass inf
  [1P 3:7; cv-4; 1601]   ἐγκόπτω

ἐγκόπτω   {1601, cv-4}
  [(ἐνέκοπτον), -, ἐνέκοψα, -, -, -] pr. *to cut* or *strike
  in;* hence, *to impede, interrupt, hinder,* Rom 15:22;
  1 Thess 2:18; 1 Peter 3:7; Gal 5:7; Acts 24:4*

ἐγκόπτω   pres act subj 1 sg
  [Ac 24:4; cv-4; 1601]   "

ἐγκράτεια, ας, ἡ   {1602, n-1a}
  self-control, continence, temperance, Acts 24:25;
  Gal 4:23; 2 Peter 1:6*

ἐγκράτεια   nom sg fem
  [Ga 5:23; n-1a; 1602]   ἐγκράτεια
ἐγκρατείᾳ   dat sg fem [2P 1:6; n-1a; 1602]   "

ἐγκράτειαν acc sg fem [2P 1:6; n-1a; 1602]   "
ἐγκρατείας gen sg fem [Ac 24:25; n-1a; 1602]   "
ἐγκρατεύεται pres mid ind 3 sg
   [1C 9:25; cv-; 1603]   ἐγκρατεύομαι

ἐγκρατεύομαι   {1603, cv-1a(6)}
   [-, -, -, -, -] to possess the power of self-control or
   continence, 1 Cor 7:9; to practise abstinence, 1 Cor
   9:25*

ἐγκρατεύονται pres mid ind 3 pl
   [1C 7:9; cv-; 1603]   "
ἐγκρατῆ acc sg masc
   [Ti 1:8; a-4a; 1604]   ἐγκρατής

ἐγκρατής, ές   {1604, a-4a}
   strong, stout; possessed of mastery; master of self,
   Titus 1:8*

ἐγκρῖναι aor act inf
   [2C 10:12; cv-1c(2); 1605]   ἐγκρίνω

ἐγκρίνω   {1605, cv-1c(2)}
   [-, ἐνέκρινα, -, -, -] to judge or reckon among,
   consider as belonging to, adjudge to the number of;
   class with, place in the same rank, 2 Cor 10:12*

ἐγκρύπτω   {1606, cv-4}
   [-, ἐνέκρυψα, -, -, -] to conceal in anything; to
   mix, intermix, Matt 13:33; Luke 13:21 v.l.*

ἐγκύψ dat sg fem [Lk 2:5; a-3a; 1607]   ἔγκυος
ἔγνω aor act ind 3 sg [16t; v-5a; 1182]   γινώσκω
ἔγνωκα perf act ind 1 sg [2t; v-5a; 1182]   "
ἐγνώκαμεν perf act ind 1 pl [6t; v-5a; 1182]   "
ἔγνωκαν perf act ind 3 pl [Jn 17:7; v-5a; 1182]   "
ἔγνωκας perf act ind 2 sg [Jn 14:9; v-5a; 1182]   "
ἐγνώκατε perf act ind 2 pl [5t; v-5a; 1182]   "
ἐγνώκειτε pluperf act ind 2 pl
   [Mt 12:7; v-5a; 1182]   "
ἔγνωκεν perf act ind 3 sg [3t; v-5a; 1182]   "
ἐγνωκέναι perf act inf [1C 8:2; v-5a; 1182]   "
ἐγνωκότες perf act ptcp nom pl masc
   [2J 1; v-5a; 1182]   "
ἔγνων aor act ind 1 sg [6t; v-5a; 1182]   "
ἐγνώρισα aor act ind 1 sg
   [2t; v-2a(1); 1192]   γνωρίζω
ἐγνωρίσαμεν aor act ind 1 pl
   [2P 1:16; v-2a(1); 1192]   "
ἐγνώρισαν aor act ind 3 pl
   [Lk 2:17; v-2a(1); 1192]   "
ἐγνώρισας aor act ind 2 sg
   [Ac 2:28; v-2a(1); 1192]   "
ἐγνώρισεν aor act ind 3 sg
   [Lk 2:15; v-2a(1); 1192]   "
ἐγνωρίσθη aor pass ind 3 sg [2t; v-2a(1); 1192]   "
ἔγνως aor act ind 2 sg [3t; v-5a; 1182]   γινώσκω
ἔγνωσαν aor act ind 3 pl [17t; v-5a; 1182]   "
ἐγνώσθη aor pass ind 3 sg [2t; v-5a; 1182]   "
ἔγνωσται perf pass ind 3 sg [1C 8:3; v-5a; 1182]   "
ἐγόγγυζον imperf act ind 3 pl
   [3t; v-2a(1); 1197]   γογγύζω
ἐγόγγυσαν aor act ind 3 pl
   [1C 10:10; v-2a(1); 1197]   "
ἔγραφεν imperf act ind 3 sg
   [Jn 8:8; v-1b(1); 1211]   γράφω
ἐγράφη aor pass ind 3 sg [4t; v-1b(1); 1211]   "

ἔγραψα aor act ind 1 sg [19t; v-1b(1); 1211]   "
ἔγραψαν aor act ind 3 pl
   [Ac 18:27; v-1b(1); 1211]   "
ἐγράψατε aor act ind 2 pl
   [1C 7:1; v-1b(1); 1211]   "
ἔγραψεν aor act ind 3 sg [8t; v-1b(1); 1211]   "
ἐγρηγόρησεν aor act ind 3 sg
   [Mt 24:43; v-1d(2a); 1213]   γρηγορέω

ἔγκυος, ον   {1607, a-3a}
   with child, pregnant, Luke 2:5*

ἐγχρῖσαι aor act inf
   [Rv 3:18; cv-1a(1); 1608]   ἐγχρίω

ἐγχρίω   {1608, cv-1a(1)}
   [-, ἐνέχρισα, -, -, -] to rub in, anoint, Rev 3:18*

ἐγώ   {1609, a-5a}
   I, gen., ἐμοῦ (μου), dat., ἐμοί (μοι), acc., ἐμέ (με)

ἐγώ nom sg [347t; a-5a; 1609]   ἐγώ
ἐδάκρυσεν aor act ind 3 sg
   [Jn 11:35; v-1a(4); 1233]   δακρύω

ἐδαφίζω   {1610, v-2a(1)}
   [ἐδαφιῶ, -, -, -, -] pr. to form a level and firm
   surface; to level with the ground, overthrow, raze,
   destroy, Luke 19:44*

ἐδαφιοῦσιν fut act ind 3 pl
   [Lk 19:44; v-2a(1); 1610]   ἐδαφίζω

ἔδαφος, ους, τό   {1611, n-3d(2b)}
   pr. a bottom, base; hence, the ground, Acts 22:7*

ἔδαφος acc sg neut
   [Ac 22:7; n-3d(2b); 1611]   ἔδαφος
ἐδεήθη aor pass ind 3 sg
   [Lk 5:12; v-1d(2c); 1289]   δέομαι
ἐδεήθην aor pass ind 1 sg [2t; v-1d(2c); 1289]   "
ἔδει imperf act ind 3 sg
   [16t; v-1d(2c); 1256]   δεῖ
ἐδειγμάτισεν aor act ind 3 sg
   [Cl 2:15; v-2a(1); 1258]   δειγματίζω
ἔδειξα aor act ind 1 sg
   [Jn 10:32; v-3c(2); 1259]   δείκνυμι
ἔδειξεν aor act ind 3 sg [6t; v-3c(2); 1259]   "
ἔδειραν aor act ind 3 pl [2t; v-1c(1); 1296]   δέρω
ἐδεῖτο imperf mid ind 3 sg
   [Lk 8:38; v-1d(2c); 1289]   δέομαι
ἐδεξάμεθα aor mid ind 1 pl
   [Ac 28:21; v-1b(2); 1312]   δέχομαι
ἐδέξαντο aor mid ind 3 pl [5t; v-1b(2); 1312]   "
ἐδέξασθε aor mid ind 2 pl [4t; v-1b(2); 1312]   "
ἐδέξατο aor mid ind 3 sg [3t; v-1b(2); 1312]   "
ἐδεσμεύετο imperf pass ind 3 sg
   [Lk 8:29; v-1a(6); 1297]   δεσμεύω
ἐδήλου imperf act ind 3 sg
   [1P 1:11; v-1d(3); 1317]   δηλόω
ἐδηλώθη aor pass ind 3 sg
   [1C 1:11; v-1d(3); 1317]   "
ἐδήλωσεν aor act ind 3 sg
   [2P 1:14; v-1d(3); 1317]   "
ἐδημηγόρει imperf act ind 3 sg
   [Ac 12:21; v-1d(2a); 1319]   δημηγορέω
ἔδησαν aor act ind 3 pl [2t; v-1d(2b); 1313]   δέω
ἔδησεν aor act ind 3 sg [4t; v-1d(2b); 1313]   "

ἐδίδαξα   aor act ind 1 sg
  [Jn 18:20; v-5a; 1438]   διδάσκω
ἐδίδαξαν   aor act ind 3 pl   [Mk 6:30; v-5a; 1438]   "
ἐδίδαξας   aor act ind 2 sg
  [Lk 13:26; v-5a; 1438]   "
ἐδίδαξεν   aor act ind 3 sg   [3t; v-5a; 1438]   "
ἐδίδασκεν   imperf act ind 3 sg   [14t; v-5a; 1438]   "
ἐδίδασκον   imperf act ind 3 pl   [2t; v-5a; 1438]   "
ἐδιδάχθην   aor pass ind 1 sg
  [Ga 1:12; v-5a; 1438]   "
ἐδιδάχθησαν   aor pass ind 3 pl
  [Mt 28:15; v-5a; 1438]   "
ἐδιδάχθητε   aor pass ind 2 pl   [3t; v-5a; 1438]   "
ἐδίδοσαν   imperf act ind 3 pl
  [Jn 19:3; v-6a; 1443]   δίδωμι
ἐδίδου   imperf act ind 3 sg   [9t; v-6a; 1443]   "
ἐδίδουν   imperf act ind 3 pl   [2t; v-6a; 1443]   "
ἐδικαιώθη   aor pass ind 3 sg
  [6t; v-1d(3); 1467]   δικαιόω
ἐδικαιώθητε   aor pass ind 2 pl
  [1C 6:11; v-1d(3); 1467]   "
ἐδικαίωσαν   aor act ind 3 pl
  [Lk 7:29; v-1d(3); 1467]   "
ἐδικαίωσεν   aor act ind 3 sg   [2t; v-1d(3); 1467]   "
ἐδίστασαν   aor act ind 3 pl
  [Mt 28:17; v-2a(1); 1491]   διστάζω
ἐδίστασας   aor act ind 2 sg
  [Mt 14:31; v-2a(1); 1491]   "
ἐδίψησα   aor act ind 1 sg
  [2t; v-1d(1a); 1498]   διψάω
ἐδίωκεν   imperf act ind 3 sg
  [Ga 4:29; v-1b(2); 1503]   διώκω
ἐδίωκον   imperf act ind 1 sg   [2t; v-1b(2); 1503]   "
ἐδίωκον   imperf act ind 3 pl
  [Jn 5:16; v-1b(2); 1503]   "
ἐδίωξα   aor act ind 1 sg   [2t; v-1b(2); 1503]   "
ἐδίωξαν   aor act ind 3 pl   [3t; v-1b(2); 1503]   "
ἐδίωξεν   aor act ind 3 sg
  [Rv 12:13; v-1b(2); 1503]   "
ἐδόθη   aor pass ind 3 sg   [31t; v-6a; 1443]   δίδωμι
ἐδόθησαν   aor pass ind 3 pl   [2t; v-6a; 1443]   "
ἐδόκει   imperf act ind 3 sg
  [Ac 12:9; v-1b(4); 1506]   δοκέω
ἐδοκιμάσαμεν   aor act ind 1 pl
  [2C 8:22; v-2a(1); 1507]   δοκιμάζω
ἐδοκίμασαν   aor act ind 3 pl
  [Rm 1:28; v-2a(1); 1507]   "
ἐδόκουν   imperf act ind 3 pl
  [2t; v-1b(4); 1506]   δοκέω
ἐδολιοῦσαν   imperf act ind 3 pl
  [Rm 3:13; v-1d(3); 1514]   δολιόω
ἔδοξα   aor act ind 1 sg
  [Ac 26:9; v-1b(4); 1506]   δοκέω
ἐδόξαζεν   imperf act ind 3 sg
  [2t; v-2a(1); 1519]   δοξάζω
ἐδόξαζον   imperf act ind 3 pl
  [6t; v-2a(1); 1519]   "
ἔδοξαν   aor act ind 3 pl   [2t; v-1b(4); 1506]   δοκέω
ἐδόξασα   aor act ind 1 sg
  [2t; v-2a(1); 1519]   δοξάζω
ἐδόξασαν   aor act ind 3 pl   [4t; v-2a(1); 1519]   "
ἐδόξασεν   aor act ind 3 sg   [4t; v-2a(1); 1519]   "

ἐδοξάσθη   aor pass ind 3 sg   [6t; v-2a(1); 1519]   "
ἔδοξε   aor act ind 3 sg   [2t; v-1b(4); 1506]   δοκέω
ἔδοξεν   aor act ind 3 sg   [2t; v-1b(4); 1506]   "
ἐδουλεύσατε   aor act ind 2 pl
  [Ga 4:8; v-1a(6); 1526]   δουλεύω
ἐδούλευσεν   aor act ind 3 sg
  [Pp 2:22; v-1a(6); 1526]   "
ἐδουλώθητε   aor pass ind 2 pl
  [Rm 6:18; v-1d(3); 1530]   δουλόω
ἐδούλωσα   aor act ind 1 sg
  [1C 9:19; v-1d(3); 1530]   "
ἑδραῖοι   nom pl masc   [2t; a-3b(1); 1612]   ἑδραῖος

ἑδραῖος, (αία), αῖον   {1612, a-3b(1)}
  sedentary; met. *settled, steady, firm, steadfast,*
  constant, 1 Cor 7:37; 15:58; Col 1:23*

ἑδραῖος   nom sg masc   [1C 7:37; a-3b(1); 1612]   "

ἑδραίωμα, ατος, τό   {1613, n-3c(4)}
  a basis, foundation, 1 Tim 3:15*

ἑδραίωμα   nom sg neut
  [1Ti 3:15; n-3c(4); 1613]   ἑδραίωμα
ἔδραμεν   aor act ind 3 sg
  [2t; v-1b(2); 5556]   τρέχω
ἔδραμον   aor act ind 1 sg   [2t; v-1b(2); 5556]   "
ἔδραμον   aor act ind 3 pl
  [Mt 28:8; v-1b(2); 5556]   "
ἔδυ   aor act ind 3 sg
  [Mk 1:32; v-3a(1); 1544]   δύνω
ἐδυναμώθησαν   aor pass ind 3 pl
  [Hb 11:34; v-1d(3); 1540]   δυναμόω
ἐδύνασθε   imperf pass ind 2 pl
  [1C 3:2; v-6b; 1538]   δύναμαι
ἐδύνατο   imperf pass ind 3 sg   [11t; v-6b; 1538]   "
ἔδωκα   aor act ind 1 sg   [2t; v-6a; 1443]   δίδωμι
ἐδώκαμεν   aor act ind 1 pl   [1Th 4:2; v-6a; 1443]   "
ἔδωκαν   aor act ind 3 pl   [8t; v-6a; 1443]   "
ἔδωκας   aor act ind 2 sg   [8t; v-6a; 1443]   "
ἐδώκατε   aor act ind 2 pl   [3t; v-6a; 1443]   "
ἔδωκεν   aor act ind 3 sg   [64t; v-6a; 1443]   "
ἐδωρήσατο   aor mid ind 3 sg
  [Mk 15:45; v-1d(2a); 1563]   δωρέομαι
Ἐζεκίαν   acc sg masc
  [Mt 1:9; n-1d; 1614]   Ἐζεκίας

Ἐζεκίας, ου, ὁ   {1614, n-1d}
  Hezekiah, pr. name, Matt 1:9f.; Luke 3:23ff. v.l.*

Ἐζεκίας   nom sg masc   [Mt 1:10; n-1d; 1614]   "
ἐζημιώθην   aor pass ind 1 sg
  [Pp 3:8; v-1d(3); 2423]   ζημιόω
ἔζησα   aor act ind 1 sg
  [Ac 26:5; v-1d(1a); 2409]   ζάω
ἔζησαν   aor act ind 3 pl   [2t; v-1d(1a); 2409]   "
ἔζησεν   aor act ind 3 sg   [4t; v-1d(1a); 2409]   "
ἐζῆτε   imperf act ind 2 pl
  [Cl 3:7; v-1d(1a); 2409]   "
ἐζήτει   imperf act ind 3 sg
  [7t; v-1d(2a); 2426]   ζητέω
ἐζητεῖτε   imperf act ind 2 pl
  [Lk 2:49; v-1d(2a); 2426]   "
ἐζητεῖτο   imperf pass ind 3 sg
  [Hb 8:7; v-1d(2a); 2426]   "

ἐζητήσαμεν   aor act ind 1 pl
  [Ac 16:10; v-1d(2a); 2426]   "
ἐζήτησαν   aor act ind 3 pl
  [Lk 20:19; v-1d(2a); 2426]   "
ἐζήτησεν   aor act ind 3 sg
  [2Ti 1:17; v-1d(2a); 2426]   "
ἐζητοῦμεν   imperf act ind 1 pl
  [Lk 2:48; v-1d(2a); 2426]   "
ἐζήτουν   imperf act ind 3 pl
  [18t; v-1d(2a); 2426]   "
ἐζυμώθη   aor pass ind 3 sg
  [2t; v-1d(3); 2435]   ζυμόω
ἐζωγρημένοι   perf pass ptcp nom pl masc
  [2Ti 2:26; v-1d(2a); 2436]   ζωγρέω
ἔζων   imperf act ind 1 sg
  [Rm 7:9; v-1d(1a); 2409]   ζάω
ἐζώννυες   imperf act ind 2 sg
  [Jn 21:18; v-3c(1); 2439]   ζώννυμι
ἐθαμβήθησαν   aor pass ind 3 pl
  [Mk 1:27; v-1d(2a); 2501]   θαμβέω
ἐθαμβοῦντο   imperf pass ind 3 pl
  [2t; v-1d(2a); 2501]   "
ἐθανατώθητε   aor pass ind 2 pl
  [Rm 7:4; v-1d(3); 2506]   θανατόω
ἐθαύμαζεν   imperf act ind 3 sg
  [2t; v-2a(1); 2513]   θαυμάζω
ἐθαύμαζον   imperf act ind 3 pl
  [7t; v-2a(1); 2513]   "
ἐθαύμασα   aor act ind 1 sg
  [Rv 17:6; v-2a(1); 2513]   "
ἐθαύμασαν   aor act ind 3 pl   [8t; v-2a(1); 2513]   "
ἐθαύμασας   aor act ind 2 sg
  [Rv 17:7; v-2a(1); 2513]   "
ἐθαύμασεν   aor act ind 3 sg   [4t; v-2a(1); 2513]   "
ἐθαυμάσθη   aor pass ind 3 sg
  [Rv 13:3; v-2a(1); 2513]   "
ἔθαψαν   aor act ind 3 pl   [3t; v-4; 2507]   θάπτω
ἐθεάθη   aor pass ind 3 sg
  [Mk 16:11; v-1d(1b); 2517]   θεάομαι
ἐθεασάμεθα   aor mid ind 1 pl
  [2t; v-1d(1b); 2517]   "
ἐθεάσαντο   aor mid ind 3 pl   [2t; v-1d(1b); 2517]   "
ἐθεάσασθε   aor mid ind 2 pl
  [Ac 1:11; v-1d(1b); 2517]   "
ἐθεάσατο   aor mid ind 3 sg
  [Lk 5:27; v-1d(1b); 2517]   "
ἔθει   dat sg neut [Ac 15:1; n-3d(2b); 1621]   ἔθος

ἐθελοθρησκία, ας, ἡ   {1615, n-1a}
  also spelled ἐθελοθρησκεία, *self-made religion*,
  Col 2:23*

ἐθελοθρησκίᾳ   dat sg fem
  [Cl 2:23; n-1a; 1615]   ἐθελοθρησκία
ἐθεμελίωσας   aor act ind 2 sg
  [Hb 1:10; v-1d(3); 2530]   θεμελιόω
ἔθεντο   aor mid ind 3 pl   [4t; v-6a; 5502]   τίθημι
ἐθεράπευεν   imperf act ind 3 sg
  [Lk 4:40; v-1a(6); 2543]   θεραπεύω
ἐθεραπεύθη   aor pass ind 3 sg
  [3t; v-1a(6); 2543]   "
ἐθεραπεύθησαν   aor pass ind 3 pl
  [Ac 8:7; v-1a(6); 2543]   "

ἐθεράπευον   imperf act ind 3 pl
  [Mk 6:13; v-1a(6); 2543]   "
ἐθεραπεύοντο   imperf pass ind 3 pl
  [3t; v-1a(6); 2543]   "
ἐθεράπευσεν   aor act ind 3 sg
  [13t; v-1a(6); 2543]   "
ἐθερίσθη   aor pass ind 3 sg
  [Rv 14:16; v-2a(1); 2545]   θερίζω
ἐθερμαίνοντο   imperf mid ind 3 pl
  [Jn 18:18; v-2d(4); 2548]   θερμαίνω
ἔθεσθε   aor mid ind 2 pl
  [Ac 5:25; v-6a; 5502]   τίθημι
ἔθεσι   dat pl neut [Ac 28:17; n-3d(2b); 1621]   ἔθος
ἔθεσιν   dat pl neut [Ac 21:21; n-3d(2b); 1621]   "
ἔθετο   aor mid ind 3 sg [7t; v-6a; 5502]   τίθημι
ἐθεώρει   imperf act ind 3 sg
  [Mk 12:41; v-1d(2a); 2555]   θεωρέω
ἐθεώρησαν   aor act ind 3 pl
  [Rv 11:12; v-1d(2a); 2555]   "
ἐθεώρουν   imperf act ind 1 sg
  [Lk 10:18; v-1d(2a); 2555]   "
ἐθεώρουν   imperf act ind 3 pl
  [3t; v-1d(2a); 2555]   "
ἔθη   acc pl neut [2t; n-3d(2b); 1621]   ἔθος
ἔθηκα   aor act ind 1 sg [3t; v-6a; 5502]   τίθημι
ἔθηκαν   aor act ind 3 pl [7t; v-6a; 5502]   "
ἔθηκας   aor act ind 2 sg [2t; v-6a; 5502]   "
ἔθηκεν   aor act ind 3 sg [11t; v-6a; 5502]   "
ἐθήλασας   aor act ind 2 sg
  [Lk 11:27; v-2a(1); 2558]   θηλάζω
ἐθηριομάχησα   aor act ind 1 sg
  [1C 15:32; v-1d(2a); 2562]   θηριομαχέω
ἐθησαυρίσατε   aor act ind 2 pl
  [Jm 5:3; v-2a(1); 2564]   θησαυρίζω

ἐθίζω   {1616, v-2a(1)}
  [-, -, -, εἴθισμαι, -] *to accustom;* pass. *to be
  customary,* Luke 2:27*

ἐθνάρχης, ου, ὁ   {1617, n-1f}
  a governor, chief of any tribe or nation, 2 Cor
  11:32*

ἐθνάρχης   nom sg masc
  [2C 11:32; n-1f; 1617]   ἐθνάρχης
ἔθνει   dat sg neut [7t; n-3d(2b); 1620]   ἔθνος
ἔθνεσιν   dat pl neut [32t; n-3d(2b); 1620]   "
ἔθνη   nom pl neut [24t; n-3d(2b); 1620]   "
ἔθνη   voc pl neut [2t; n-3d(2b); 1620]   "
ἔθνη   acc pl neut [26t; n-3d(2b); 1620]   "
ἐθνικοί   nom pl masc
  [2t; a-1a(2a); 1618]   ἐθνικός

ἐθνικός, ή, όν   {1618, a-1a(2a)}
  national; in N.T. *Gentile, heathen, not Israelites,*
  Matt 5:47; 6:7; 18:17; 3 John 7*

ἐθνικός   nom sg masc [Mt 18:17; a-1a(2a); 1618]   "
ἐθνικῶν   gen pl masc [3J 7; a-1a(2a); 1618]   "

ἐθνικῶς   {1619, adverb}
  *after the manner of the Gentiles, heathenishly, like
  the rest of the world,* Gal 2:14*

ἐθνικῶς   adverb [Ga 2:14; adverb; 1619]   ἐθνικῶς

ἔθνος, ους, τό {1620, n-3d(2b)}
a multitude, company, Acts 17:26; 1 Peter 2:9; Rev
21:24; *a nation, people,* Matt 20:25; 21:43; pl. ἔθνη,
from the Hebrew, *nations* or *people* as
distinguished from the Jews, *the heathen,*
Gentiles, Matt 4:15; 10:5; Luke 2:32

ἔθος, ους, τό {1621, n-3d(2b)}
a custom, usage, habit, Luke 2:42; 22:39; *an*
institute, rite, Luke 1:9; Acts 6:14; 15:1

ἔθνος   nom sg neut [6t; n-3d(2b); 1620]   ἔθνος
ἔθνος   acc sg neut [12t; n-3d(2b); 1620]   "
ἔθνους   gen sg neut [7t; n-3d(2b); 1620]   "
Ἰθνῶν   gen pl neut [46t; n-3d(2b); 1620]   "
ἐθορύβουν   imperf act ind 3 pl
   [Ac 17:5; v-1d(2a); 2572]   θορυβέω
ἔθος   nom sg neut [3t; n-3d(2b); 1621]   ἔθος
ἔθος   acc sg neut [3t; n-3d(2b); 1621]   "
ἔθου   aor mid ind 2 sg [Ac 5:4; v-6a; 5502]   τίθημι
ἐθρέψαμεν   aor act ind 1 pl
   [Mt 25:37; v-1b(1); 5555]   τρέφω
ἔθρεψαν   aor act ind 3 pl
   [Lk 23:29; v-1b(1); 5555]   "
ἐθρέψατε   aor act ind 2 pl
   [Jm 5:5; v-1b(1); 5555]   "
ἐθρηνήσαμεν   aor act ind 1 pl
   [2t; v-1d(2a); 2577]   θρηνέω
ἐθρήνουν   imperf act ind 3 pl
   [Lk 23:27; v-1d(2a); 2577]   "
ἐθυμώθη   aor pass ind 3 sg
   [Mt 2:16; v-1d(3); 2597]   θυμόω
ἔθυον   imperf act ind 3 pl
   [Mk 14:12; v-1a(4); 2604]   θύω
ἔθυσας   aor act ind 2 sg
   [Lk 15:30; v-1a(4); 2604]   "
ἔθυσεν   aor act ind 3 sg
   [Lk 15:27; v-1a(4); 2604]   "
ἐθῶν   gen pl neut [Ac 26:3; n-3d(2b); 1621]   ἔθος

εἰ {1623, particle}
if, Matt 4:3, 6; 12:7; Acts 27:39, freq.; *since,* Acts
4:9; *whether,* Mark 9:23; Acts 17:11; *that,* in
certain expressions, Acts 26:8, 23; Heb 7:15; by
a suppression of the apodosis of a sentence, εἰ
serves to express a wish; *O if! O that!* Luke
19:42; 22:42; also a strong negation, Mark 8:12;
Heb 3:11; 4:3; εἰ καί, *if even, though, although,*
Luke 18:4; εἰ μή, *unless, except,* Matt 11:27; also
equivalent to ἀλλά, *but,* Matt 12:4; Mark 13:32;
Luke 4:26, 27; εἰ μήτι, *unless perhaps, unless it be,*
Luke 9:13; εἴ τις, εἴ τι, pr. *if any one; whosoever,*
whatsoever, Matt 18:28. The syntax of this
particle must be learned from the grammars.
As an interrogative particle, *whether,* Acts 17:11;
in N.T. as a mere note of interrogation, Luke
22:49

εἰ   particle [502t; particle; 1623]   εἰ
εἶ   pres act ind 2 sg [92t; v-6b; 1639]   εἰμί
εἴα   imperf act ind 3 sg
   [Lk 4:41; v-1d(1b); 1572]   ἐάω
εἴασαν   aor act ind 3 pl
   [Ac 27:32; v-1d(1b); 1572]   "
εἴασεν   aor act ind 3 sg [4t; v-1d(1b); 1572]   "

εἴδαμεν   aor act ind 1 pl
   [Ac 4:20; v-1d(1a); 3972]   ὁράω
εἴδαν   aor act ind 3 pl [5t; v-1d(1a); 3972]   "

εἰδέα, ας, ἡ {1624, n-1a}
appearance, face, Matt 28:3*

εἰδέα   nom sg fem [Mt 28:3; n-1a; 1624]   εἰδέα
εἴδει   dat sg neut [Lk 3:22; n-3d(2b); 1626]   εἶδος
εἶδεν   aor act ind 3 sg
   [42t; v-1d(1a); 3972]   ὁράω
εἰδέναι   perf act inf [11t; v-1b(3); 3857]   οἶδα
εἶδες   aor act ind 2 sg [8t; v-1d(1a); 3972]   ὁράω
εἴδετε   aor act ind 2 pl [5t; v-1d(1a); 3972]   "
εἰδῇς   perf act subj 2 sg
   [1Ti 3:15; v-1b(3); 3857]   οἶδα
εἰδήσουσιν   fut act ind 3 pl
   [Hb 8:11; v-1b(3); 3857]   "
εἰδῆτε   perf act subj 2 pl [6t; v-1b(3); 3857]   "
εἴδομεν   aor act ind 1 pl
   [9t; v-1d(1a); 3972]   ὁράω

εἶδον {1625, v-1d(1a)}
[-, εἶδον, -, -, -] *see, perceive,* used as second
aorist of ὁράω (3972)

εἶδον   aor act ind 1 sg [54t; v-1d(1a); 3972]   "
εἶδον   aor act ind 3 pl [22t; v-1d(1a); 3972]   "

εἶδος, ους, τό {1626, n-3d(2b)}
form, external appearance, Luke 3:22; 9:29; John
5:37; *kind, species,* 1 Thess 5:22; *sight, perception,*
2 Cor 5:7*

εἶδος   nom sg neut [Lk 9:29; n-3d(2b); 1626]   εἶδος
εἶδος   acc sg neut [Jn 5:37; n-3d(2b); 1626]   "
εἰδόσιν   perf act ptcp dat pl masc
   [2Th 1:8; v-1b(3); 3857]   οἶδα
εἰδότα   perf act ptcp nom pl neut
   [1Th 4:5; v-1b(3); 3857]   "
εἰδότας   perf act ptcp acc pl masc
   [2t; v-1b(3); 3857]   "
εἰδότες   perf act ptcp nom pl masc
   [23t; v-1b(3); 3857]   "
εἰδότι   perf act ptcp dat sg masc
   [Jm 4:17; v-1b(3); 3857]   "
εἴδους   gen sg neut [2t; n-3d(2b); 1626]   εἶδος
εἰδυῖα   perf act ptcp nom sg fem
   [2t; v-1b(3); 3857]   οἶδα
εἰδῶ   perf act subj 1 sg [2t; v-1b(3); 3857]   "
εἴδωλα   acc pl neut [3t; n-2c; 1631]   εἴδωλον

εἰδωλεᯮον, ου, τό {1627, n-2c}
a heathen temple, 1 Cor 8:10*

εἰδωλείῳ   dat sg neut
   [1C 8:10; n-2c; 1627]   εἰδωλεᯮον
εἰδωλόθυτα   acc pl neut
   [3t; a-3a; 1628]   εἰδωλόθυτος
εἰδωλόθυτον   nom sg neut [1C 10:19; a-3a; 1628]   "
εἰδωλόθυτον   acc sg neut [2t; a-3a; 1628]   "

εἰδωλόθυτος, ον {1628, a-3a}
idolatry, worship of idols, 1 Cor 10:14; Gal 5:23;
Gal 5:20; Col 3:5; as a noun *meat offered to an*
idol, Acts 15:29; 21:25; 1 Cor 8:1, 4, 7, 10; 10:19,
28 v.l.; Rev 2:14, 20*

εἰδωλοθύτων   gen pl neut [3t; a-3a; 1628]   "

εἰδωλολάτραι   nom pl masc
[3t; n-1f; 1629]   εἰδωλολάτρης
εἰδωλολάτραις   dat pl masc [2t; n-1f; 1629]   "

εἰδωλολάτρης, ου, ὁ   {1629, n-1f}
an idolater, worshipper of idols, 1 Cor 5:10, 11; 6:9;
10:7; Eph 5:5; Rev 21:8; 22:15*

εἰδωλολάτρης   nom sg masc [2t; n-1f; 1629]   "

εἰδωλολατρία, ας, ἡ   {1630, n-1a}
idolatry, worship of idols, 1 Cor 10:14; Gal 5:20;
Col 3:5; 1 Peter 4:3*

εἰδωλολατρία   nom sg fem
[2t; n-1a; 1630]   εἰδωλολατρία
εἰδωλολατρίαις   dat pl fem [1P 4:3; n-1a; 1630]   "
εἰδωλολατρίας   gen sg fem [1C 10:14; n-1a; 1630]   "

εἴδωλον, ου, τό   {1631, n-2c}
pr. *a form, shape, figure; image* or *statue;* hence, *an
idol, image of a god,* Acts 7:41; *a heathen god,* 1 Cor
8:4, 7; for εἰδωλόθυτον, *the flesh of victims
sacrificed to idols,* Acts 15:20; Rom 2:22; 1 Cor
10:19; 12:12; 2 Cor 6:16; 1 Thess 1:9; 1 John 5:21;
Rev 9:20*

εἴδωλον   nom sg neut [2t; n-2c; 1631]   εἴδωλον
εἰδώλου   gen sg neut [1C 8:7; n-2c; 1631]   "
εἰδώλῳ   dat sg neut [Ac 7:41; n-2c; 1631]   "
εἰδώλων   gen pl neut [4t; n-2c; 1631]   "
εἰδῶμεν   perf act subj 1 pl
[1C 2:12; v-1b(3); 3857]   οἶδα
εἰδώς   perf act ptcp nom sg masc
[21t; v-1b(3); 3857]   "
εἴη   pres act opt 3 sg [12t; v-6b; 1639]   εἰμί
εἰθισμένον   perf pass ptcp acc sg neut
[Lk 2:27; v-2a(1); 1616]   ἐθίζω

εἰκῇ   {1632, adverb}
without plan or *system; without cause, rashly,*
Matt 5:22 v.l.; Col 2:18; *to no purpose, in vain,*
Rom 13:4; 1 Cor 15:2; Gal 3:4; 4:11*

εἰκῇ   adverb [6t; adverb; 1632]   εἰκῇ
εἰκόνα   acc sg fem [10t; n-3f(1b); 1635]   εἰκών
εἰκόνι   dat sg fem [4t; n-3f(1b); 1635]   "
εἰκόνος   gen sg fem [3t; n-3f(1b); 1635]   "

εἴκοσι   {1633, a-5b}
twenty, Luke 14:31; Acts 27:28

εἴκοσι   indecl [11t; a-5b; 1633]   εἴκοσι

εἴκω   {1634, v-1b(2)}
[εἴξω, εἶξα, -, -, -] (1) *to yield, give place, submit,*
Gal 2:5. (2) the perfect form ἔοικα (2036) is
from this same root and functions as a present,
Jm 1:6, 23 (ἔοικεν, 3 sg). Some list it as a
separate word, but see the discussion in
Liddell and Scott*

εἰκών, όνος, ἡ   {1635, n-3f(1b)}
a material image, likeness, effigy, Matt 22:20;
Mark 12:16; *a representation, exact image,* 1 Cor
11:7; 15:49; Rev 13:14f.; *resemblance,* Rom 1:23;
8:29; Col 3:10; Heb 10:1

εἰκών   nom sg fem [6t; n-3f(1b); 1635]   εἰκών
εἵλατο   aor mid ind 3 sg
[2Th 2:13; v-1d(2a); 145]   αἱρέω

εἴληφα   perf act ind 1 sg
[Rv 2:28; v-3a(2b); 3284]   λαμβάνω
εἴληφας   perf act ind 2 sg [2t; v-3a(2b); 3284]   "
εἴληφεν   perf act ind 3 sg [3t; v-3a(2b); 3284]   "
εἰληφώς   perf act ptcp nom sg masc
[Mt 25:24; v-3a(2b); 3284]   "

εἰλικρίνεια, ας, ἡ   {1636, n-1a}
clearness, purity; met. *sincerity, integrity,
ingenuousness,* 1 Cor 5:8; 2 Cor 1:12; 2:17*

εἰλικρινείᾳ   dat sg fem
[2C 1:12; n-1a; 1636]   εἰλικρίνεια
εἰλικρινείας   gen sg fem [2t; n-1a; 1636]   "
εἰλικρινεῖς   nom pl masc
[Pp 1:10; a-4a; 1637]   εἰλικρινής
εἰλικρινῆ   acc sg fem [2P 3:1; a-4a; 1637]   "

εἰλικρινής, ές, gen. **οὖς**   {1637, a-4a}
pr. *that which being viewed in the sunshine is
found clear and pure;* met. *spotless, sincere,
ingenuous,* Phil 1:10; 2 Peter 3:1*

εἷλκον   imperf act ind 3 pl
[Ac 21:30; v-1a(4); 1816]   ἑλκύω
εἵλκυσαν   aor act ind 3 pl
[Ac 16:19; v-1a(4); 1816]   "
εἵλκυσεν   aor act ind 3 sg [2t; v-1a(4); 1816]   "
εἱλκωμένος   perf pass ptcp nom sg masc
[Lk 16:20; v-1d(3); 1815]   ἑλκόω

εἰμί   {1639, v-6b}
[(ἤμην, ἔσομαι, -, -, -, -] *to be, to exist,* John 1:1;
17:5; Matt 6:30; Luke 4:25, freq.; ἐστί(ν), *it is
possible, proper,* Heb 9:5; a simple linking verb
("copula") to the subject and predicate, and
therefore in itself affecting the force of the
sentence only by its tense, mood, etc., John 1:1;
15:1, freq.; it also forms a frequent
circumlocution with the participles of the
present and perfect of other verbs, Matt 19:22;
Mark 2:6

εἰμί   pres act ind 1 sg [140t; v-6b; 1639]   εἰμί

εἶμι   {1640, v-6b}
[-, -, -, -, -] In Attic used as future of ἔρχομαι, *I
shall go,* John 7:34 v.l.*

εἶναι   pres act inf [124t; v-6b; 1639]   εἰμί

εἵνεκεν   {1641, prep}
see ἕνεκα, *on account of,* Luke 4:18; Acts 28:20; 2
Cor 3:10*

εἵνεκεν   improper prep-gen
[2t; prep; 1641]   εἵνεκεν
εἴξαμεν   aor act ind 1 pl
[Ga 2:5; v-1b(2); 1634]   εἴκω
εἶπα   aor act ind 1 sg [3t; v-1b(2); 3306]   λέγω
εἶπαν   aor act ind 3 pl [95t; v-1b(2); 3306]   "
εἶπας   aor act ind 2 sg [4t; v-1b(2); 3306]   "
εἶπας   aor act ptcp nom sg masc
[4t; v-1b(2); 3306]   "
εἴπατε   aor act imperative 2 pl
[13t; v-1b(2); 3306]   "
εἴπατε   aor act ind 2 pl [Lk 12:3; v-1b(2); 3306] "
εἰπάτω   aor act imperative 3 sg
[Rv 22:17; v-1b(2); 3306]   "

εἰπάτωσαν   aor act imperative 3 pl
   [Ac 24:20; v-1b(2); 3306]   "
εἰπέ   aor act imperative 2 sg
   [15t; v-1b(2); 3306]   "
εἰπεῖν   aor act inf   [16t; v-1b(2); 3306]   "
εἶπεν   aor act ind 3 sg   [613t; v-1b(2); 3306]   "

εἴπερ   {1642, particle}
   if indeed, if it be so that, granted, Rom 8:9; 1 Cor
   15:15; *since indeed, since*, 2 Thess 1:6; 1 Peter 2:3;
   although indeed, 1 Cor 8:5

εἴπερ   particle [6t; particle; 1642]   εἴπερ
εἶπες   aor act ind 2 sg
   [Mk 12:32; v-1b(2); 3306]   λέγω
εἴπῃ   aor act subj 3 sg   [22t; v-1b(2); 3306]   "
εἴπῃς   aor act subj 2 sg   [4t; v-1b(2); 3306]   "
εἴπητε   aor act subj 2 pl   [8t; v-1b(2); 3306]   "
εἰπόν   aor act imperative 2 sg
   [4t; v-1b(2); 3306]   "
εἶπον   aor act ind 1 sg   [32t; v-1b(2); 3306]   "
εἶπον   aor act ind 3 pl   [26t; v-1b(2); 3306]   "
εἰπόντα   aor act ptcp acc sg masc
   [3t; v-1b(2); 3306]   "
εἰπόντες   aor act ptcp nom pl masc
   [3t; v-1b(2); 3306]   "
εἰπόντος   aor act ptcp gen sg masc
   [4t; v-1b(2); 3306]   "
εἰποῦσα   aor act ptcp nom sg fem
   [3t; v-1b(2); 3306]   "
εἴπω   aor act subj 1 sg   [7t; v-1b(2); 3306]   "
εἴπωμεν   aor act subj 1 pl   [10t; v-1b(2); 3306]   "
εἰπών   aor act ptcp nom sg masc
   [29t; v-1b(2); 3306]   "

εἴπως   {1643}
   cf. εἴ, *if by any means, if possibly*, Acts 27:12 v.l.

εἴπωσιν   aor act subj 3 pl   [6t; v-1b(2); 3306]   "
εἰργασάμεθα   aor mid ind 1 pl
   [2J 8; v-2a(1); 2237]   ἐργάζομαι
εἰργάσαντο   aor mid ind 3 pl
   [Hb 11:33; v-2a(1); 2237]   "
εἰργασμένα   perf pass ptcp nom pl neut
   [Jn 3:21; v-2a(1); 2237]   "
εἴρηκα   perf act ind 1 sg   [4t; v-1b(2); 3306]   λέγω
εἴρηκαν   perf act ind 3 pl
   [Rv 19:3; v-1b(2); 3306]   "
εἴρηκας   perf act ind 2 sg
   [Jn 4:18; v-1b(2); 3306]   "
εἰρήκασιν   perf act ind 3 pl
   [Ac 17:28; v-1b(2); 3306]   "
εἰρήκατε   perf act ind 2 pl
   [Ac 8:24; v-1b(2); 3306]   "
εἰρήκει   pluperf act ind 3 sg
   [3t; v-1b(2); 3306]   "
εἴρηκεν   perf act ind 3 sg   [8t; v-1b(2); 3306]   "
εἰρηκέναι   perf act inf
   [Hb 10:15; v-1b(2); 3306]   "
εἰρηκότος   perf act ptcp gen sg masc
   [Mt 26:75; v-1b(2); 3306]   "
εἰρημένον   perf pass ptcp nom sg neut
   [2t; v-1b(2); 3306]   "
εἰρημένον   perf pass ptcp acc sg neut
   [2t; v-1b(2); 3306]   "

εἰρηνεύετε   pres act imperative 2 pl
   [3t; v-1a(6); 1644]   εἰρηνεύω
εἰρηνεύοντες   pres act ptcp nom pl masc
   [Rm 12:18; v-1a(6); 1644]   "

εἰρηνεύω   {1644, v-1a(6)}
   [εἰρηνεύσω, εἰρήνευσα, -, -, -] *to be at peace; to*
   cultivate peace, concord, or *harmony*, Matt 9:50;
   Rom 12:18; 2 Cor 13:11; 1 Thess 5:13*

εἰρήνη, ης, ἡ   {1645, n-1b}
   peace, Luke 14:32; Acts 12:20; *tranquillity*, Luke
   11:21; John 16:33; 1 Thess 5:3; *concord, unity, love*
   of peace, Matt 10:34; Luke 12:51; meton. *the*
   author of peace, Eph 2:14; from the Hebrew *every*
   kind of blessing and good, Luke 1:79; 2:14, 29;
   meton. *a salutation expressive of good wishes, a*
   benediction, blessing, Matt 10:13

εἰρήνη   nom sg fem [40t; n-1b; 1645]   εἰρήνη
εἰρήνη   dat sg fem [8t; n-1b; 1645]   "
εἰρήνην   acc sg fem [25t; n-1b; 1645]   "
εἰρήνης   gen sg fem [19t; n-1b; 1645]   "
εἰρηνική   nom sg fem
   [Jm 3:17; a-1a(2a); 1646]   εἰρηνικός
εἰρηνικόν   acc sg masc
   [Hb 12:11; a-1a(2a); 1646]   "

εἰρηνικός, ή, όν   {1646, a-1a(2a)}
   pertaining to peace; peaceable, disposed to peace,
   James 3:17; from the Hebrew, *profitable, blissful*,
   Heb 12:11*

εἰρηνοποιέω   {1647, cv-1d(2a)}
   [-, εἰρηνοποίησα, -, -, -] *to make peace*, Col 1:20*

εἰρηνοποιήσας   aor act ptcp nom sg masc
   [Cl 1:20; cv-1d(2a); 1647]   εἰρηνοποιέω
εἰρηνοποιοί   nom pl masc
   [Mt 5:9; a-3a; 1648]   εἰρηνοποιός

εἰρηνοποιός, όν   {1648, a-3a}
   a peace-maker, one who cultivates peace and
   concord, Matt 5:9*

εἴρηται   perf pass ind 3 sg
   [Lk 4:12; v-1b(2); 3306]   λέγω

εἰς   {1650, prep}
   to, as far as, to the extent of, Matt 2:23; 4:24; *until*,
   John 13:1; *against*, Matt 18:15; Luke 12:10; *before*,
   in the presence of, Acts 22:30; *in order to, for, with*
   a view to, Mark 1:38; *for the use* or *service of*, John
   6:9; Luke 9:13; 1 Cor 16:1; *with reference to*, 2 Cor
   10:13, 16; *in accordance with*, Matt 12:41; Luke
   11:32; 2 Tim 2:26; also equivalent to ἐν, John
   1:18; *by*, in forms of swearing, Matt 5:35; from
   the Hebrew, εἶναι, γίνεσθαι εἰς, *to become, result*
   in, amount to, Matt 19:5; 1 Cor 4:3; εἰς τί, *why*,
   wherefore, Matt 26:8

εἰς   prep-acc [1767t; prep; 1650]   εἰς

εἷς, μία, ἕν   {1651, a-4b(2)}
   numeral *one*, Matt 10:29, freq.; *only*, Mark 12:6;
   one virtually by union, Matt 19:5, 6; John 10:30;
   one and the same, Luke 12:52; Rom 3:30; *one in*
   respect of office and standing, 1 Cor 3:8;
   equivalent to τις, *a certain one*, Matt 8:19; 16:14;
   a, an, Matt 21:19; James 4:13; εἷς ἕκαστος, *each*
   one, every one, Luke 4:40; Acts 2:3; εἷς τὸν ἕνα,

one another, 1 Thess 5:11; εἷς καὶ εἷς, the one- and the other, Matt 20:21; εἷς καθ᾽ εἷς and ὁδὲ καθ᾽ εἷς, one by one, one after another, in succession, Mark 14:19; John 8:9; as an ordinal, first, Matt 28:1

εἷς   nom sg masc [98t; a-4b(2); 1651]   εἷς
εἰσάγαγε   aor act imperative 2 sg
   [Lk 14:21; cv-1b(2); 1652]   εἰσάγω
εἰσαγαγεῖν   aor act inf
   [Lk 2:27; cv-1b(2); 1652]   "
εἰσαγάγῃ   aor act subj 3 sg
   [Hb 1:6; cv-1b(2); 1652]   "
εἰσάγεσθαι   pres pass inf   [2t; cv-1b(2); 1652]   "

εἰσάγω   {1652, cv-1b(2)}
   [-, εἰσήγαγον, -, -, -] to lead or bring in, introduce, conduct or usher in or to a place or person, Luke 2:27; 14:21; 22:54; John 18:16; Acts 9:8; 21:28f., 37; Heb 1:6

εἰσακουσθείς   aor pass ptcp nom sg masc
   [Hb 5:7; cv-1a(8); 1653]   εἰσακούω
εἰσακουσθήσονται   fut pass ind 3 pl
   [Mt 6:7; cv-1a(8); 1653]   "
εἰσακούσονται   fut mid ind 3 pl
   [1C 14:21; cv-1a(8); 1653]   "

εἰσακούω   {1653, cv-1a(8)}
   [εἰσακούσω, -, -, -, εἰσηκούσθην] to hear or hearken to, to heed, 1 Cor 14:21; to listen to the prayers of any one, accept one's petition, Matt 6:7; Luke 1:13; Acts 10:31; Heb 5:7*

εἰσδέξομαι   fut mid ind 1 sg
   [2C 6:17; cv-1b(2); 1654]   εἰσδέχομαι

εἰσδέχομαι   {1654, cv-1b(2)}
   [εἰσδέξομαι, -, -, -, -] to admit; to receive into favor, receive kindly, accept with favor, 2 Cor 6:17*

εἰσδραμοῦσα   aor act ptcp nom sg fem
   [Ac 12:14; cv-1b(2); 1661]   εἰστρέχω

εἴσειμι   {1655, cv-6b}
   [(εἴσῃειν, 3 sg), -, -, -, -, -] to go in, enter, Acts 3:3; 21:18, 26; Heb 9:6*

εἰσελεύσεσθαι   fut mid inf
   [Hb 3:18; cv-1b(2); 1656]   εἰσέρχομαι
εἰσελεύσεται   fut mid ind 3 sg
   [3t; cv-1b(2); 1656]   "
εἰσελεύσομαι   fut mid ind 1 sg
   [Rv 3:20; cv-1b(2); 1656]   "
εἰσελεύσονται   fut mid ind 3 pl
   [5t; cv-1b(2); 1656]   "
εἰσεληλύθασιν   perf act ind 3 pl
   [Jm 5:4; cv-1b(2); 1656]   "
εἰσεληλύθατε   perf act ind 2 pl
   [Jn 4:38; cv-1b(2); 1656]   "
εἰσέλθατε   aor act imperative 2 pl
   [Mt 7:13; cv-1b(2); 1656]   "
εἰσελθάτω   aor act imperative 3 sg
   [Mk 13:15; cv-1b(2); 1656]   "
εἴσελθε   aor act imperative 2 sg
   [4t; cv-1b(2); 1656]   "
εἰσελθεῖν   aor act inf   [36t; cv-1b(2); 1656]   "
εἰσέλθῃ   aor act subj 3 sg   [9t; cv-1b(2); 1656]   "
εἰσέλθῃς   aor act subj 2 sg
   [4t; cv-1b(2); 1656]   "

εἰσέλθητε   aor act subj 2 pl
   [10t; cv-1b(2); 1656]   "
εἰσελθόντα   aor act ptcp nom pl neut
   [2t; cv-1b(2); 1656]   "
εἰσελθόντα   aor act ptcp acc sg masc
   [2t; cv-1b(2); 1656]   "
εἰσελθόντες   aor act ptcp nom pl masc
   [5t; cv-1b(2); 1656]   "
εἰσελθόντι   aor act ptcp dat sg masc
   [Lk 17:7; cv-1b(2); 1656]   "
εἰσελθόντος   aor act ptcp gen sg masc
   [3t; cv-1b(2); 1656]   "
εἰσελθόντων   aor act ptcp gen pl masc
   [2t; cv-1b(2); 1656]   "
εἰσελθοῦσα   aor act ptcp nom sg fem
   [Mk 6:25; cv-1b(2); 1656]   "
εἰσελθοῦσαι   aor act ptcp nom pl fem
   [2t; cv-1b(2); 1656]   "
εἰσελθούσης   aor act ptcp gen sg fem
   [Mk 6:22; cv-1b(2); 1656]   "
εἰσέλθωμεν   aor act subj 1 pl
   [Mk 5:12; cv-1b(2); 1656]   "
εἰσελθών   aor act ptcp nom sg masc
   [20t; cv-1b(2); 1656]   "
εἰσέλθωσιν   aor act subj 3 pl
   [2t; cv-1b(2); 1656]   "
εἰσενεγκεῖν   aor act inf
   [Lk 5:18; cv-1c(1); 1662]   εἰσφέρω
εἰσενέγκῃς   aor act subj 2 sg
   [2t; cv-1c(1); 1662]   "
εἰσενέγκωσιν   aor act subj 3 pl
   [Lk 5:19; cv-1c(1); 1662]   "
εἰσεπήδησεν   aor act ind 3 sg
   [Ac 16:29; cv-1d(1a); 1659]   εἰσπηδάω
εἰσεπορεύετο   imperf mid ind 3 sg
   [Mk 6:56; cv-1a(6); 1660]   εἰσπορεύομαι
εἰσέρχεσθε   pres mid ind 2 pl
   [Mt 23:13; cv-1b(2); 1656]   εἰσέρχομαι
εἰσερχέσθωσαν   pres mid imperative 3 pl
   [Lk 21:21; cv-1b(2); 1656]   "
εἰσέρχεται   pres mid ind 3 sg
   [Hb 9:25; cv-1b(2); 1656]   "
εἰσέρχησθε   pres mid subj 2 pl
   [Lk 10:8; cv-1b(2); 1656]   "

εἰσέρχομαι   {1656, cv-1b(2)}
   [εἰσελεύσομαι, εἰσῆλθον, εἰσελήλυθα, -, -] to go or come in, enter, Matt 7:13; 8:5, 8; spc. to enter by force, break in, Mark 3:27; Acts 20:29; met. with εἰς κόσμον, to begin to exist, come into existence, Rom 5:12; 2 John 7; or, to make one's appearance on earth, Heb 10:5; to enter into or take possession of, Luke 22:3; John 13:27; to enter into, enjoy, partake of, Matt 19:23, 24; to enter into any one's labor, be his successor, John 4:38; to fall into, be placed in certain circumstances, Matt 26:41; to be put into, Matt 15:11; Acts 11:8; to present one's self before, Acts 19:30; met. to arise, spring up, Luke 9:46; from the Hebrew, εἰσέρχεσθαι καὶ ἐξέρχεσθαι, to go in and out, to live, discharge the ordinary functions of life, Acts 1:21

εἰσερχόμεθα   pres mid ind 1 pl
   [Hb 4:3; cv-1b(2); 1656]   "

εἰσερχομένην　pres mid ptcp acc sg fem
　　[Hb 6:19; cv-1b(2); 1656]　　　　　　　"
εἰσερχόμενοι　pres mid ptcp nom pl masc
　　[2t; cv-1b(2); 1656]　　　　　　　　　"
εἰσερχόμενον　pres mid ptcp nom sg neut
　　[Mt 15:11; cv-1b(2); 1656]　　　　　　"
εἰσερχόμενος　pres mid ptcp nom sg masc
　　[3t; cv-1b(2); 1656]　　　　　　　　　"
εἰσερχομένου　pres mid ptcp gen sg masc
　　[Lk 17:12; cv-1b(2); 1656]　　　　　　"
εἰσερχομένους　pres mid ptcp acc pl masc
　　[2t; cv-1b(2); 1656]　　　　　　　　　"
εἰσήγαγεν　aor act ind 3 sg
　　[3t; cv-1b(2); 1652]　　　　　　εἰσάγω
εἰσήγαγον　aor act ind 3 pl [3t; cv-1b(2); 1652]　"
εἰσῄει　imperf act ind 3 sg
　　[2t; cv-6b; 1655]　　　　　　　εἴσειμι
εἰσηκούσθη　aor pass ind 3 sg
　　[2t; cv-1a(8); 1653]　　　　　εἰσακούω
εἰσήλθατε　aor act ind 2 pl
　　[Lk 11:52; cv-1b(2); 1656]　　εἰσέρχομαι
εἰσῆλθεν　aor act ind 3 sg [43t; cv-1b(2); 1656]　"
εἰσῆλθες　aor act ind 2 sg [2t; cv-1b(2); 1656]　"
εἰσήλθομεν　aor act ind 1 pl
　　[2t; cv-1b(2); 1656]　　　　　　　　　"
εἰσῆλθον　aor act ind 1 sg [2t; cv-1b(2); 1656]　"
εἰσῆλθον　aor act ind 3 pl [10t; cv-1b(2); 1656]　"
εἰσηνέγκαμεν　aor act ind 1 pl
　　[1Ti 6:7; cv-1c(1); 1662]　　　　εἰσφέρω
εἰσίασιν　pres act ind 3 pl
　　[Hb 9:6; cv-6b; 1655]　　　　　εἴσειμι
εἰσιέναι　pres act inf　[Ac 3:3; cv-6b; 1655]　"
εἰσιν　pres act ind 3 pl [157t; v-6b; 1639]　εἰμί

εἰσκαλέομαι　　　　　　　{1657, cv-1d(2b)}
　　[-, εἰσεκαλεσάμην, -, -, -] to call in; to invite in,
　　Acts 10:23*

εἰσκαλεσάμενος　aor mid ptcp nom sg masc
　　[Ac 10:23; cv-1d(2b); 1657]　　εἰσκαλέομαι
εἴσοδον　acc sg fem [3t; n-2b; 1658]　εἴσοδος

εἴσοδος, ου, ἡ　　　　　　　{1658, n-2b}
　　a place of entrance; the act of entrance, Heb 10:19;
　　admission, reception, 1 Thess 1:9; 2 Peter 1:11; a
　　coming, approach, access, 1 Thess 2:1; entrance
　　upon office, commencement or beginning of
　　ministry, Acts 13:24*

εἴσοδος　nom sg fem [2P 1:11; n-2b; 1658]　"
εἰσόδου　gen sg fem [Ac 13:24; n-2b; 1658]　"

εἰσπηδάω　　　　　　　{1659, cv-1d(1a)}
　　[-, εἰσεπήδησα, -, -, -] to leap or spring in, rush in
　　eagerly, Acts 14:14 v.l.; 16:29*

εἰσπορεύεται　pres mid ind 3 sg
　　[3t; cv-1a(6); 1660]　　　　εἰσπορεύομαι

εἰσπορεύομαι　　　　　　　{1660, cv-1a(6)}
　　[(εἰσεπορευόμαι), -, -, -, -, -] to go or come in, enter,
　　Mark 1:21; 5:40; to come to, visit, Acts 28:30; to be
　　put in, Matt 15:17; Mark 7:15, 18, 19; to intervene,
　　Mark 4:19

εἰσπορευόμεναι　pres mid ptcp nom pl fem
　　[Mk 4:19; cv-1a(6); 1660]　　　　　　"

εἰσπορευόμενοι　pres mid ptcp nom pl masc
　　[4t; cv-1a(6); 1660]　　　　　　　　　"
εἰσπορευόμενον　pres mid ptcp nom sg neut
　　[3t; cv-1a(6); 1660]　　　　　　　　　"
εἰσπορευόμενος　pres mid ptcp nom sg masc
　　[2t; cv-1a(6); 1660]　　　　　　　　　"
εἰσπορευομένους　pres mid ptcp acc pl masc
　　[Ac 28:30; cv-1a(6); 1660]　　　　　　"
εἰσπορευομένων　pres mid ptcp gen pl masc
　　[Ac 3:2; cv-1a(6); 1660]　　　　　　　"
εἰσπορεύονται　pres mid ind 3 pl
　　[2t; cv-1a(6); 1660]　　　　　　　　　"
εἱστήκει　pluperf act ind 3 sg
　　[7t; v-6a; 2705]　　　　　　　　ἵστημι
εἱστήκεισαν　pluperf act ind 3 pl
　　[7t; v-6a; 2705]　　　　　　　　　　"

εἰστρέχω　　　　　　　{1661, cv-1b(2)}
　　[-, εἰσέδραμον -, -, -] to run in, Acts 12:14*

εἰσφέρεις　pres act ind 2 sg
　　[Ac 17:20; cv-1c(1); 1662]　　　　εἰσφέρω
εἰσφέρεται　pres pass ind 3 sg
　　[Hb 13:11; cv-1c(1); 1662]　　　　　　"

εἰσφέρω　　　　　　　{1662, cv-1c(1)}
　　[-, εἰσήνεγκα or εἰσήνεγκον, -, -, -] to bring in or
　　into, Luke 5:18, 19; 1 Tim 6:7; Heb 13:11; to bring
　　to the ears of any one, to announce, Acts 17:20; to
　　lead into, Matt 6:13; Luke 11:4; drag in, Luke
　　12:11*

εἰσφέρωσιν　pres act subj 3 pl
　　[Lk 12:11; cv-1c(1); 1662]　　　　　　"

εἶτα　　　　　　　{1663, adverb}
　　then, afterwards, Mark 4:17, 28; Luke 8:12; in the
　　next place, 1 Cor 12:28; besides, furthermore, Heb
　　12:9

εἶτα　adverb [15t; adverb; 1663]　　εἶτα

εἴτε　　　　　　　{1664, particle}
　　whether, Rom 12:6, 7, 8; 1 Cor 3:22; 2 Cor 1:6; 1
　　Thess 5:10

εἴτε　particle [65t; particle; 1664]　　εἴτε
εἶχε　imperf act ind 3 sg
　　[Hb 9:1; v-1b(2); 2400]　　　　　　ἔχω
εἶχεν　imperf act ind 3 sg [23t; v-1b(2); 2400]　"
εἶχες　imperf act ind 2 sg
　　[Jn 19:11; v-1b(2); 2400]　　　　　　"
εἴχετε　imperf act ind 2 pl [3t; v-1b(2); 2400]　"
εἴχομεν　imperf act ind 1 pl [2t; v-1b(2); 2400]　"
εἶχον　imperf act ind 1 sg [3t; v-1b(2); 2400]　"
εἶχον　imperf act ind 3 pl [16t; v-1b(2); 2400]　"
εἴχοσαν　imperf act ind 3 pl [2t; v-1b(2); 2400]　"

εἴωθα　　　　　　　{1665, v-1b(3)}
　　[-, -, εἴωθα, -, -] perfect of an obsolete present
　　ἔθω, pluperfect is εἰώθειν, to be accustomed, to be
　　usual, Matt 27:15; Mark 10:1; Luke 4:16; Acts
　　17:2*

εἰώθει　pluperf act ind 3 sg [2t; v-1b(3); 1665] εἴωθα
εἰωθός　perf act ptcp acc sg neut
　　[2t; v-1b(3); 1665]　　　　　　　　　"
εἴων　imperf act ind 3 pl
　　[2t; v-1d(1b); 1572]　　　　　　　ἐάω

ἐκ   {1666, prep}
ἐξ before vowels, with genitive, *from, out of,* a
place, Matt 2:15; 3:17; *of, from, out of,* denoting
origin or source, Matt 1:3; 21:19; *of, from* some
material, Matt 3:9; Rom 9:21; *of, from, among,*
partitively, Matt 6:27; 21:31; Mark 9:17; *from,*
denoting cause, Rev 8:11; 17:6; means or
instrument, Matt 12:33, 37; *by, through,*
denoting the author or efficient cause, Matt
1:18; John 10:32; *of,* denoting the distinguishing
mark of a class, Rom 2:8; Gal 3:7; of time, *after,*
2 Cor 4:6; Rev 17:11; *from, after, since,* Matt
19:12; Luke 8:27; *for, with,* denoting a rate of
payment, price, Matt 20:2; 27:7; *at,* denoting
position, Matt 20:21, 23; after passive verbs, *by,
of, from,* marking the agent, Matt 15:5; Mark
7:11; forming with certain words a periphrasis
for an adverb, Matt 26:42, 44; Mark 6:51; Luke
23:8; put after words of freeing, Rom 7:24; 2
Cor 1:10; used partitively after verbs of eating,
drinking, etc., John 6:26; 1 Cor 9:7

ἐκ   prep-gen [680t; prep; 1666]   ἐκ
ἐκαθάρισεν   aor act ind 3 sg
   [2t; v-2a(1); 2751]   καθαρίζω
ἐκαθαρίσθη   aor pass ind 3 sg
   [3t; v-2a(1); 2751]   "
ἐκαθαρίσθησαν   aor pass ind 3 pl
   [2t; v-2a(1); 2751]   "
ἐκαθέζετο   imperf mid ind 3 sg
   [2t; v-2a(1); 2757]   καθέζομαι
ἐκαθεζόμην   imperf mid ind 1 sg
   [Mt 26:55; v-2a(1); 2757]   "
ἐκάθευδεν   imperf act ind 3 sg
   [Mt 8:24; v-1b(3); 2761]   καθεύδω
ἐκάθευδον   imperf act ind 3 pl
   [Mt 25:5; v-1b(3); 2761]   "
ἐκάθητο   imperf mid ind 3 sg
   [11t; v-6b; 2764]   κάθημαι
ἐκάθισα   aor act ind 1 sg
   [Rv 3:21; v-2a(1); 2767]   καθίζω
ἐκάθισαν   aor act ind 3 pl [3t; v-2a(1); 2767]   "
ἐκάθισεν   aor act ind 3 sg [13t; v-2a(1); 2767]   "
ἐκάκωσαν   aor act ind 3 pl
   [Ac 14:2; v-1d(3); 2808]   κακόω
ἐκάκωσεν   aor act ind 3 sg
   [Ac 7:19; v-1d(3); 2808]   "
ἐκάλεσα   aor act ind 1 sg
   [Mt 2:15; v-1d(2b); 2813]   καλέω
ἐκάλεσεν   aor act ind 3 sg [10t; v-1d(2b); 2813]   "
ἐκάλουν   imperf act ind 3 pl
   [2t; v-1d(2b); 2813]   "
ἐκάμμυσαν   aor act ind 3 pl
   [2t; v-1a(4); 2826]   καμμύω
ἔκαμψαν   aor act ind 3 pl
   [Rm 11:4; v-4; 2828]   κάμπτω
ἐκαρτέρησεν   aor act ind 3 sg
   [Hb 11:27; v-1d(2a); 2846]   καρτερέω
ἑκάστη   nom sg fem
   [1C 7:2; a-1a(2a); 1667]   ἕκαστος
ἑκάστην   acc sg fem [Hb 3:13; a-1a(2a); 1667]   "
ἕκαστοι   nom pl masc [Pp 2:4; a-1a(2a); 1667]   "
ἕκαστον   nom sg neut [Lk 6:44; a-1a(2a); 1667]   "
ἕκαστον   acc sg masc [10t; a-1a(2a); 1667]   "

ἕκαστον   acc sg neut [2t; a-1a(2a); 1667]   "
ἕκαστος, η, ον   {1667, a-1a(2a)}
   each (one), every (one) separately, Matt 16:27;
   Luke 13:15

ἕκαστος   nom sg masc [40t; a-1a(2a); 1667]   "
ἑκάστοτε   {1668, adverb}
   always, 2 Peter 1:15*

ἑκάστοτε   adverb
   [2P 1:15; adverb; 1668]   ἑκάστοτε
ἑκάστου   gen sg masc [6t; a-1a(2a); 1667]   ἕκαστος
ἑκάστου   gen sg neut [Ep 4:16; a-1a(2a); 1667]   "
ἑκάστῳ   dat sg masc [18t; a-1a(2a); 1667]   "
ἑκάστῳ   dat sg neut [1C 15:38; a-1a(2a); 1667]   "
ἑκατόν   {1669, a-5b}
   one hundred, Matt 13:8; Mark 4:8

ἑκατόν   indecl [17t; a-5b; 1669]   ἑκατόν
ἑκατονταετής, ές   {1670, a-4a}
   a hundred years old, Rom 4:19*

ἑκατονταετής   nom sg masc
   [Rm 4:19; a-4a; 1670]   ἑκατονταετής
ἑκατονταπλασίονα   acc sg masc
   [Lk 8:8; a-4b(1); 1671]   ἑκατονταπλασίων
ἑκατονταπλασίονα   acc pl neut
   [2t; a-4b(1); 1671]   "
ἑκατονταπλασίων, ον   {1671, a-4b(1)}
   a hundredfold, Matt 19:29; Mark 10:30; Luke 8:8;
   18:30 v.l.*

ἑκατοντάρχας   acc pl masc
   [Ac 21:32; n-1f; 1672]   ἑκατοντάρχης
ἑκατοντάρχῃ   dat sg masc [4t; n-1f; 1672]   "
ἑκατοντάρχης, ου, ὁ   {1672, n-1f}
   the text varies between this form and
   ἑκατόνταρχος, *commander of a hundred men, a
   centurion,* Luke 23:47; Acts 10:1; 27:1ff.

ἑκατοντάρχης   nom sg masc [8t; n-1f; 1672]   "
ἑκατόνταρχον   acc sg masc [Ac 22:25; n-1f; 1672]   "
ἑκατόνταρχος, ου, ὁ   {1673, n-2a}
   the text varies between this form and
   ἑκατόνταρχης, *commander of a hundred men, a
   centurion,* Matt 8:5, 8; 27:54; Luke 7:2; Acts 22:25

ἑκατόνταρχος   nom sg masc [3t; n-1f; 1672]   "
ἑκατοντάρχου   gen sg masc [Lk 7:2; n-1f; 1672]   "
ἑκατονταρχῶν   gen pl masc [2t; n-1f; 1672]   "
ἐκαυματίσθη   aor pass ind 3 sg
   [2t; v-2a(1); 3009]   καυματίζω
ἐκαυματίσθησαν   aor pass ind 3 pl
   [Rv 16:9; v-2a(1); 3009]   "
ἐκβαίνω   {1674, cv-2d(6)}
   [-, ἐξέβην, -, -, -] *to go forth, go out of,* Heb 11:15*

ἔκβαλε   aor act imperative 2 sg
   [5t; cv-2d(1); 1675]   ἐκβάλλω
ἐκβαλεῖν   aor act inf [4t; cv-2d(1); 1675]   "
ἐκβάλετε   aor act imperative 2 pl
   [2t; cv-2d(1); 1675]   "
ἐκβάλῃ   aor act subj 3 sg [5t; cv-2d(1); 1675]   "

ἐκβάλλει   pres act ind 3 sg
   [10t; cv-2d(1); 1675]   "

ἐκβάλλειν   pres act inf   [6t; cv-2d(1); 1675]   "

ἐκβάλλεις   pres act ind 2 sg
   [Mt 8:31; cv-2d(1); 1675]   "

ἐκβάλλεται   pres pass ind 3 sg
   [Mt 15:17; cv-2d(1); 1675]   "

ἐκβάλλετε   pres act imperative 2 pl
   [Mt 10:8; cv-2d(1); 1675]   "

ἐκβαλλόμενοι   pres mid ptcp nom pl masc
   [Ac 27:38; cv-2d(1); 1675]   "

ἐκβαλλομένους   pres pass ptcp acc pl masc
   [Lk 13:28; cv-2d(1); 1675]   "

ἐκβάλλοντα   pres act ptcp acc sg masc
   [2t; cv-2d(1); 1675]   "

ἐκβάλλουσιν   pres act ind 3 pl
   [3t; cv-2d(1); 1675]   "

ἐκβάλλω   {1675, cv-2d(1)}
   [ἐκβαλῶ, ἐξέβαλον, ἐκβέβληκα, -, ἐξεβλήθην]
   pluperfect, ἐκβεβλήκειν, to cast out, eject by force,
   Matt 15:17; Acts 27:38; to expel, force away, Luke
   4:29; Acts 7:58; to refuse, John 6:37; to extract,
   Matt 7:4; to reject with contempt, despise, contemn,
   Luke 6:22; in N.T. to send forth, send out, Matt
   9:38; Luke 10:2; to send away, dismiss, Matt 9:25;
   Mark 1:12; met. to spread abroad, Matt 12:20; to
   bring out, produce, Matt 12:35; 13:52

ἐκβάλλω   pres act ind 1 sg   [5t; cv-2d(1); 1675]   "

ἐκβάλλων   pres act ptcp nom sg masc
   [2t; cv-2d(1); 1675]   "

ἐκβαλόντες   aor act ptcp nom pl masc
   [2t; cv-2d(1); 1675]   "

ἐκβαλοῦσα   aor act ptcp nom sg fem
   [Jm 2:25; cv-2d(1); 1675]   "

ἐκβαλοῦσιν   fut act ind 3 pl
   [Mk 16:17; cv-2d(1); 1675]   "

ἐκβάλω   aor act subj 1 sg   [3t; cv-2d(1); 1675]   "

ἐκβαλών   aor act ptcp nom sg masc
   [3t; cv-2d(1); 1675]   "

ἐκβάλωσιν   aor act subj 3 pl
   [3t; cv-2d(1); 1675]   "

ἔκβασιν   acc sg fem   [2t; n-3e(5b); 1676]   ἔκβασις

ἔκβασις, εως, ἡ   {1676, n-3e(5b)}
   a way out, egress; hence, result, issue, Heb 13:7;
   means of clearance or successful endurance, 1 Cor
   10:13*

ἐκβεβλήκει   pluperf act ind 3 sg
   [Mk 16:9; cv-2d(1); 1675]   ἐκβάλλω

ἐκβλαστάνω   {1677, v-3a(1)}
   [-, ἐκεβλάστησα, -, -, -] sprout up, Mark 4:5 v.l.*

ἐκβληθέντος   aor pass ptcp gen sg neut
   [Mt 9:33; cv-2d(1); 1675]   "

ἐκβληθήσεται   fut pass ind 3 sg
   [Jn 12:31; cv-2d(1); 1675]   "

ἐκβληθήσονται   fut pass ind 3 pl
   [Mt 8:12; cv-2d(1); 1675]   "

ἐκβολή, ῆς, ἡ   {1678, n-1b}
   a casting out; especially, a throwing overboard of
   a cargo, Acts 27:18*

ἐκβολήν   acc sg fem
   [Ac 27:18; n-1b; 1678]   ἐκβολή

ἐκγαμίζω   {1679, cv-2a(1)}
   to give in marriage, marry, Matt 22:30; 24:38 v.l.;
   Luke 17:27; 20:35; 1 Cor 7:38 v.l. (2t), see
   γαμίζω*

ἔκγονα   acc pl neut   [1Ti 5:4; a-3a; 1681]   ἔκγονος

ἔκγονος, ον   {1681, a-3a}
   born of, descended from; as a noun ἔκγονα,
   descendants, grandchildren, 1 Tim 5:4*

ἐκδαπανάω   {1682, cv-1d(1a)}
   [-, -, -, -, ἐξεδαπανήθην] to expend, consume,
   exhaust, 2 Cor 12:15*

ἐκδαπανηθήσομαι   fut pass ind 1 sg
   [2C 12:15; cv-1d(1a); 1682]   ἐκδαπανάω

ἐκδέχεσθε   pres mid imperative 2 pl
   [1C 11:33; cv-1b(2); 1683]   ἐκδέχομαι

ἐκδέχεται   pres mid ind 3 sg
   [Jm 5:7; cv-1b(2); 1683]   "

ἐκδέχομαι   {1683, cv-1b(2)}
   [(ἐξεδεχόμην), -, -, -, -, -] pr. to receive from
   another; to expect, look for, Acts 17:16; to wait for,
   to wait, John 5:3 v.l.; 1 Cor 11:33; 16:11; Heb
   11:10; 10:13; James 5:7*

ἐκδέχομαι   pres mid ind 1 sg
   [1C 16:11; cv-1b(2); 1683]   "

ἐκδεχόμενος   pres mid ptcp nom sg masc
   [Hb 10:13; cv-1b(2); 1683]   "

ἐκδεχομένου   pres mid ptcp gen sg masc
   [Ac 17:16; cv-1b(2); 1683]   "

ἔκδηλος, ον   {1684, a-3a}
   clearly manifest, evident, 2 Tim 3:9*

ἔκδηλος   nom sg fem   [2Ti 3:9; a-3a; 1684]   ἔκδηλος

ἐκδημέω   {1685, cv-1d(2a)}
   [-, ἐξεδήμησα, -, -, -] pr. to be absent from home, go
   abroad, travel; hence, to be absent from any place
   or person, 2 Cor 5:6, 8, 9*

ἐκδημῆσαι   aor act inf
   [2C 5:8; cv-1d(2a); 1685]   ἐκδημέω

ἐκδημοῦμεν   pres act ind 1 pl
   [2C 5:6; cv-1d(2a); 1685]   "

ἐκδημοῦντες   pres act ptcp nom pl masc
   [2C 5:9; cv-1d(2a); 1685]   "

ἐκδίδωμι   {1686, cv-6a}
   [ἐκδώσομαι, ἐξέδωκα, -, -, -] middle, to give out,
   to give up; to put out at interest; in N.T. to let out
   to tenants, Matt 21:33, 41; Lark 12:1; Luke 20:9*

ἐκδιηγέομαι   {1687, cv-1d(2a)}
   [-, -, -, -, -] to narrate fully, detail, Acts 13:14; 15:3*

ἐκδιηγῆται   pres mid subj 3 sg
   [Ac 13:41; cv-; 1687]   ἐκδιηγέομαι

ἐκδιηγούμενοι   pres mid ptcp nom pl masc
   [Ac 15:3; cv-; 1687]   "

ἐκδικεῖς   pres act ind 2 sg
   [Rv 6:10; cv-1d(2a); 1688]   ἐκδικέω

ἐκδικέω   {1688, cv-1d(2a)}
   [ἐκδικήσω, ἐξεδίκησα, -, -, -] pr. to execute right

and justice; to punish, 2 Cor 10:6; Rev 6:10; 19:2; in N.T. *to right, avenge* a person, Luke 18:3, 5; Rom 12:9*

ἐκδικῆσαι   aor act inf
  [2C 10:6; cv-1d(2a); 1688]   "

ἐκδικήσεως   gen sg fem
  [Lk 21:22; n-3e(5b); 1689]   ἐκδίκησις

ἐκδίκησιν   acc sg fem [6t; n-3e(5b); 1689]   "

ἐκδίκησις, εως, ἡ   {1689, n-3e(5b)}
  vengeance, punishment, retributive justice, Luke 21:22; Rom 12:19; 2 Cor 7:11; 1 Peter 2:14; ἐκδίκησιν ποιεῖν, *to vindicate, avenge,* Luke 18:7, 8; διδόναι ἐκδίκησιν, *to inflict vengeance,* Acts 7:24; 2 Thess 1:8; Heb 10:30*

ἐκδίκησις   nom sg fem [2t; n-3e(5b); 1689]   "

ἐκδίκησον   aor act imperative 2 sg
  [Lk 18:3; cv-1d(2a); 1688]   ἐκδικέω

ἐκδικήσω   fut act ind 1 sg
  [Lk 18:5; cv-1d(2a); 1688]   "

ἔκδικος, ον   {1690, a-3a}
  an avenger, one who inflicts punishment, Rom 13:4; 1 Thess 4:6*

ἔκδικος   nom sg masc [2t; a-3a; 1690]   ἔκδικος

ἐκδικοῦντες   pres act ptcp nom pl masc
  [Rm 12:19; cv-1d(2a); 1688]   ἐκδικέω

ἐκδιώκω   {1691, cv-1b(2)}
  [ἐκδιώξω, ἐξεδίωξα, -, -, -] pr. *to chase away, drive out;* in N.T. *to persecute, vex, harass,* Luke 11:49 v.l.; 1 Thess 2:15*

ἐκδιωξάντων   aor act ptcp gen pl masc
  [1Th 2:15; cv-1b(2); 1691]   ἐκδιώκω

ἔκδοτον   acc sg masc [Ac 2:23; a-3a; 1692]   ἔκδοτος

ἔκδοτος, ον   {1692, a-3a}
  delivered up, Acts 2:23*

ἐκδοχή, ῆς, ἡ   {1693, n-1b}
  a looking for, expectation, Heb 10:27*

ἐκδοχή   nom sg fem [Hb 10:27; n-1b; 1693]   ἐκδοχή

ἐκδυσάμενοι   aor mid ptcp nom pl masc
  [2C 5:3; cv-3a(1); 1694]   ἐκδύω

ἐκδύσαντες   aor act ptcp nom pl masc
  [2t; cv-3a(1); 1694]   "

ἐκδύσασθαι   aor mid inf
  [2C 5:4; cv-3a(1); 1694]   "

ἐκδύω   {1694, cv-3a(1)}
  [-, ἐξέδυσα, -, -, -] pr. *to go out from; to take off, strip, unclothe,* Matt 27:28, 31; mid. *to lay aside, to put off,* Mark 15:20; Luke 10:30; 2 Cor 5:3f.*

ἐκδώσεται   fut mid ind 3 sg
  [Mt 21:41; cv-6a; 1686]   ἐκδίδωμι

ἐκεῖ   {1695, adverb}
  there, in that place, Matt 2:13, 15; *to that place,* Matt 2:22; 17:20

ἐκεῖ   adverb [95t; adverb; 1695]   ἐκεῖ

ἐκεῖθεν   {1696, adverb}
  from there, Matt 4:21; 5:26

ἐκεῖθεν   adverb [27t; adverb; 1696]   ἐκεῖθεν

ἐκεῖνα   acc pl neut
  [Ac 20:2; a-1a(2b); 1697]   ἐκεῖνος

ἐκεῖναι   nom pl fem [5t; a-1a(2b); 1697]   "

ἐκείναις   dat pl fem [16t; a-1a(2b); 1697]   "

ἐκείνας   acc pl fem [2t; a-1a(2b); 1697]   "

ἐκείνη   nom sg fem [9t; a-1a(2b); 1697]   "

ἐκείνῃ   dat sg fem [38t; a-1a(2b); 1697]   "

ἐκείνην   acc sg fem [10t; a-1a(2b); 1697]   "

ἐκείνης   gen sg fem [19t; a-1a(2b); 1697]   "

ἐκεῖνο   nom sg neut [Mk 7:20; a-1a(2b); 1697]   "

ἐκεῖνο   acc sg neut [3t; a-1a(2b); 1697]   "

ἐκεῖνοι   nom pl masc [16t; a-1a(2b); 1697]   "

ἐκείνοις   dat pl masc [8t; a-1a(2b); 1697]   "

ἐκεῖνον   acc sg masc [12t; a-1a(2b); 1697]   "

ἐκεῖνος, -η, -ο   {1697, a-1a(2b)}
  demonstrative adjective or noun, *that, this, he,* etc., Matt 17:27; 10:14; 2 Tim 4:8; in contrast with οὗτος, referring to the former of two things previously mentioned, Luke 18:14

ἐκεῖνος   nom sg masc [58t; a-1a(2b); 1697]   "

ἐκείνου   gen sg masc [20t; a-1a(2b); 1697]   "

ἐκείνου   gen sg neut [2t; a-1a(2b); 1697]   "

ἐκείνους   acc pl masc [5t; a-1a(2b); 1697]   "

ἐκείνῳ   dat sg masc [9t; a-1a(2b); 1697]   "

ἐκείνων   gen pl masc [6t; a-1a(2b); 1697]   "

ἐκείνων   gen pl fem [Mt 24:29; a-1a(2b); 1697]   "

ἐκείνων   gen pl neut [2t; a-1a(2b); 1697]   "

ἐκεῖσε   {1698, adverb}
  there, at that place, Acts 21:3; 22:5*

ἐκεῖσε   adverb [2t; adverb; 1698]   ἐκεῖσε

ἔκειτο   imperf mid ind 3 sg
  [4t; v-6b; 3023]   κεῖμαι

ἐκέκραξα   aor act ind 1 sg
  [Ac 24:21; v-2a(2); 3189]   κράζω

ἐκέλευον   imperf act ind 3 pl
  [Ac 16:22; v-1a(6); 3027]   κελεύω

ἐκέλευσα   aor act ind 1 sg [2t; v-1a(6); 3027]   "

ἐκέλευσεν   aor act ind 3 sg [15t; v-1a(6); 3027]   "

ἐκένωσεν   aor act ind 3 sg
  [Pp 2:7; v-1d(3); 3033]   κενόω

ἐκέρασεν   aor act ind 3 sg
  [Rv 18:6; v-3c(1); 3042]   κεράννυμι

ἐκέρδησα   aor act ind 1 sg
  [2t; v-2d(6); 3045]   κερδαίνω

ἐκέρδησας   aor act ind 2 sg
  [Mt 18:15; v-2d(6); 3045]   "

ἐκέρδησεν   aor act ind 3 sg [2t; v-2d(6); 3045]   "

ἐκεφαλίωσαν   aor act ind 3 pl
  [Mk 12:4; v-1d(3); 3052]   κεφαλιόω

ἐκζητέω   {1699, cv-1d(2a)}
  [-, ἐξεζήτησα, -, -, ἐξεζητήθην] *to seek out, investigate diligently, scrutinize,* 1 Peter 1:10; *to ask for, beseech earnestly,* Heb 12:17; *to seek diligently* or *earnestly after,* Acts 15:17; Rom 3:11; Heb 10:6; from the Hebrew, *to require, exact, demand,* Luke 11:50, 51; Heb 12:07*

ἐκζητηθῇ   aor pass subj 3 sg
  [Lk 11:50; cv-1d(2a); 1699]   ἐκζητέω

ἐκζητηθήσεται   fut pass ind 3 sg
  [Lk 11:51; cv-1d(2a); 1699]   "

ἐκζητήσας   aor act ptcp nom sg masc
  [Hb 12:17; cv-1d(2a); 1699]   "
ἐκζητήσεις   acc pl fem
  [1Ti 1:4; n-3e(5b); 1700]   ἐκζήτησις

ἐκζήτησις, εως, ἡ   {1700, n-3e(5b)}
  useless speculation, 1 Tim 1:4*

ἐκζητήσωσιν   aor act subj 3 pl
  [Ac 15:17; cv-1d(2a); 1699]   ἐκζητέω
ἐκζητοῦσιν   pres act ptcp dat pl masc
  [Hb 11:6; cv-1d(2a); 1699]   "
ἐκζητῶν   pres act ptcp nom sg masc
  [Rm 3:11; cv-1d(2a); 1699]   "
ἐκηρύξαμεν   aor act ind 1 pl
  [2t; v-2b; 3062]   κηρύσσω
ἐκήρυξαν   aor act ind 3 pl [2t; v-2b; 3062]   "
ἐκήρυξεν   aor act ind 3 sg [2t; v-2b; 3062]   "
ἐκήρυσσεν   imperf act ind 3 sg [3t; v-2b; 3062] "
ἐκήρυσσον   imperf act ind 3 pl
  [Mk 7:36; v-2b; 3062]   "
ἐκηρύχθη   aor pass ind 3 sg
  [1Ti 3:16; v-2b; 3062]   "
ἐκθαμβεῖσθαι   pres pass inf
  [Mk 14:33; cv-1d(2a); 1701]   ἐκθαμβέω
ἐκθαμβεῖσθε   pres pass imperative 2 pl
  [Mk 16:6; cv-1d(2a); 1701]   "

ἐκθαμβέω   {1701, cv-1d(2a)}
  [-, -, -, -, ἐξεθαμβήθην] pas., to be amazed,
  astonished, awe-struck, Mark 9:15; 14:33; 16:5, 6*

ἔκθαμβοι   nom pl masc
  [Ac 3:11; a-3a; 1702]   ἔκθαμβος

ἔθαμβος, ον   {1702, a-3a}
  amazed, awe-struck, Acts 3:11*

ἐκθαυμάζω   {1702, cv-2a(1)}
  [-, -, -, -, -] to wonder at, wonder greatly, Mark
  12:17*

ἔκθετα   acc pl neut [Ac 7:19; a-3a; 1704]   ἔκθετος

ἔκθετος, ον   {1704, a-3a}
  exposed, cast out, abandoned, Acts 7:18*

ἐκινδύνευον   imperf act ind 3 pl
  [Lk 8:23; cv-1a(6); 3073]   κινδυνεύω
ἐκινήθη   aor pass ind 3 sg
  [Ac 21:30; v-1d(2a); 3075]   κινέω
ἐκινήθησαν   aor pass ind 3 pl
  [Rv 6:14; v-1d(2a); 3075]   "

ἐκκαθαίρω   {1705, cv-2d(2)}
  [-, ἐξεκάθαρα, -, -, -] to cleanse thoroughly, purify,
  2 Tim 2:21; to purge out, eliminate, 1 Cor 5:7*

ἐκκαθάρατε   aor act imperative 2 pl
  [1C 5:7; cv-2d(2); 1705]   ἐκκαθαίρω
ἐκκαθάρῃ   aor act subj 3 sg
  [2Ti 2:21; cv-2d(2); 1705]   "

ἐκκαίω   {1706, cv-2c}
  [-, ἐξέκαυσα, -, -, ἐξεκαύθην] pas., to blaze out, to
  be inflamed, Rom 1:27*

ἐκκακέω, see ἐγκακέω   {1707, cv-1d(2a)}

ἐκκεντέω   {1708, cv-1d(2a)}
  [-, ἐξεκέντησα, -, -, -] to stab, pierce deeply, John
  19:37; Rev 1:7*

ἐκκεχυμένον   perf pass ptcp nom sg neut
  [Lk 11:50; cv-1a(7); 1772]   ἐκχέω
ἐκκέχυται   perf pass ind 3 sg
  [2t; cv-1a(7); 1772]   "

ἐκκλάω   {1709, cv-1d(1b)}
  [-, -, -, -, ἐξεκλάσθην] to break off, pas., be broken,
  Rom 11:17, 19, 20*

ἐκκλεῖσαι   aor act inf
  [Ga 4:17; cv-1a(3); 1710]   ἐκκλείω

ἐκκλείω   {1710, cv-1a(3)}
  [-, ἐξέκλεισα, -, -, ἐξεκλείσθην] to shut out,
  exclude; to shut of, separate, insulate; Gal 4:17; to
  leave no place for, eliminate, Rom 3:27*

ἐκκλησία, ας, ἡ   {1711, n-1a}
  a popular assembly, Acts 19:32, 39, 41; in N.T. the
  congregation of the children of Israel, Acts 7:38;
  transferred to the Christian body, of which the
  congregation of Israel was a figure, the Church,
  1 Cor 12:28; Col 1:18; a local portion of the
  Church, a local church, Rom 16:1; a Christian
  congregation, 1 Cor 14:4

ἐκκλησία   nom sg fem [9t; n-1a; 1711]   ἐκκλησία
ἐκκλησίᾳ   dat sg fem [24t; n-1a; 1711]   "
ἐκκλησίαι   nom pl fem [7t; n-1a; 1711]   "
ἐκκλησίας   gen sg fem [26t; n-1a; 1711]   "
ἐκκλησίας   acc pl fem [3t; n-1a; 1711]   "
ἐκκλησίαν   acc sg fem [20t; n-1a; 1711]   "
ἐκκλησίας   acc pl fem [29t; n-1a; 1711]   "
ἐκκλησιῶν   gen pl fem [7t; n-1a; 1711]   "
ἐκκλινάτω   aor act imperative 3 sg
  [1P 3:11; cv-1c(2); 1712]   ἐκκλίνω
ἐκκλίνετε   pres act imperative 2 pl
  [Rm 16:17; cv-1c(2); 1712]   "

ἐκκλίνω   {1712, cv-1c(2)}
  [-, ἐξέκλινα -, -, -] to deflect, deviate, Rom 3:12; to
  decline or turn away from, avoid, Rom 16:17; 1
  Peter 3:11

ἐκκολυμβάω   {1713, cv-1d(1a)}
  [-, ἐξεκολύμβησα, -, -, -] to swim out to land, Acts
  27:42*

ἐκκολυμβήσας   aor act ptcp nom sg masc
  [Ac 27:42; cv-1d(1a); 1713]   ἐκκολυμβάω

ἐκκομίζω   {1714, cv-2a(1)}
  [(ἐξεκόμιζον), -, -, -, -, -] to carry out, bring out;
  especially, to carry out a corpse for burial, Luke
  7:12*

ἐκκοπή, ῆς, ἡ   {1715, n-1b}
  see ἐγκοπή, 1 Cor 9:02 v.l.*

ἐκκοπήσῃ   fut pass ind 2 sg
  [Rm 11:22; cv-4; 1716]   ἐκκόπτω
ἐκκόπτεται   pres pass ind 3 sg [3t; cv-4; 1716] "

ἐκκόπτω   {1716, cv-4}
  [ἐκκόψω, ἐξέκοψα, -, -, ἐξεκόπην] to cut out; to
  cut off, Matt 3:10; 5:30; met. to cut off an
  occasion, remove, prevent, 2 Cor 11:12; to render

ineffectual, Matt 7:19; 18:8; Luke 3:9; 12:7, 9; Rom 11:22, 24; 1 Peter 3:7*

ἐκκόψεις   fut act ind 2 sg [Lk 13:9; cv-4; 1716]   "

ἔκκοψον   aor act imperative 2 sg
[3t; cv-4; 1716]   "

ἐκκόψω   aor act subj 1 sg [2C 11:12; cv-4; 1716]   "

ἐκκρεμάννυμι   {1717, cv-3c(1)}
[(ἐξεκρεμάμην), -, -, -, -, -] mid., *to hang upon* a speaker, *fondly listen to, be earnestly attentive*, Luke 19:48*

ἔκλαιεν   imperf act ind 3 sg
[2t; v-2c; 3081]   κλαίω
ἔκλαιον   imperf act ind 1 sg [Rv 5:4; v-2c; 3081]   "
ἔκλαιον   imperf act ind 3 pl
[Lk 8:52; v-2c; 3081]   "

ἐκλαλέω   {1718, cv-1d(2a)}
[-, ἐξελάλησα, -, -, -] *to speak out; to tell, utter, divulge*, Acts 23:22*

ἐκλαλῆσαι   aor act inf
[Ac 23:22; cv-1d(2a); 1718]   ἐκλαλέω

ἐκλάμπω   {1719, cv-1b(1)}
[ἐκλάμψω, ἐξέλαμψα, -, -, -] *to shine out* or *forth*, Matt 13:43*

ἐκλάμψουσιν   fut act ind 3 pl
[Mt 13:43; cv-1b(1); 1719]   ἐκλάμπω

ἐκλανθάνομαι   {1720, cv-3a(2b)}
[-, -, -, ἐκλέλησμαι -] *to make to forget; to forget entirely*, Heb 12:5*

ἔκλασα   aor act ind 1 sg
[Mk 8:19; v-1d(1b); 3089]   κλάω
ἔκλασεν   aor act ind 3 sg [6t; v-1d(1b); 3089]   "
ἐκλαύσατε   aor act ind 2 pl
[Lk 7:32; v-2c; 3081]   κλαίω
ἔκλαυσεν   aor act ind 3 sg [3t; v-2c; 3081]   "

ἐκλέγομαι   {1721, cv-1b(2)}
[(ἐξελεγόμην), -, ἐξελεξάμην, -, ἐκλέλεγμαι, -] *to pick out;* in N.T. *to choose, select*, Luke 6:13; 10:42; in N.T. *to choose out* as the recipients of special favor and privilege, Luke 6:44, v.l. for συλλεγω; Acts 13:17; 1 Cor 1:27

ἐκλείπω   {1722, cv-1b(1)}
[ἐκλείψω, ἐξέλιπον, -, -, -] *to fail, die out*, Luke 22:32; *to come to an end*, Heb 1:12; *to be defunct*, Luke 16:9; 23:45*

ἔκλεισεν   aor act ind 3 sg
[Rv 20:3; v-1a(3); 3091]   κλείω
ἐκλείσθη   aor pass ind 3 sg [2t; v-1a(3); 3091]   "
ἐκλείσθησαν   aor pass ind 3 pl
[Ac 21:30; v-1a(3); 3091]   "
ἐκλείψουσιν   fut act ind 3 pl
[Hb 1:12; cv-1b(1); 1722]   ἐκλείπω
ἐκλεκτῇ   dat sg fem
[2J 1; a-1a(2a); 1723]   ἐκλεκτός
ἐκλεκτῆς   gen sg fem [2J 13; a-1a(2a); 1723]   "
ἐκλεκτοί   nom pl masc [3t; a-1a(2a); 1723]   "
ἐκλεκτοῖς   dat pl masc [1P 1:1; a-1a(2a); 1723]   "
ἐκλεκτόν   nom sg neut [1P 2:9; a-1a(2a); 1723]   "
ἐκλεκτόν   acc sg masc [3t; a-1a(2a); 1723]   "

ἐκλεκτός, ή, όν   {1723, a-1a(2a)}
chosen out, selected; in N.T. *chosen* as a recipient of special privilege, *elect*, Col 3:12; *specially beloved*, Luke 23:35; *possessed of prime excellence, exalted*, 1 Tim 5:21; *choice, precious*, 1 Peter 2:4, 6

ἐκλεκτός   nom sg masc [Lk 23:35; a-1a(2a); 1723]   "
ἐκλεκτούς   acc pl masc [7t; a-1a(2a); 1723]   "
ἐκλεκτῶν   gen pl masc [4t; a-1a(2a); 1723]   "
ἐκλελεγμένος   perf pass ptcp nom sg masc
[Lk 9:35; cv-1b(2); 1721]   ἐκλέγομαι
ἐκλέλησθε   perf mid ind 2 pl
[Hb 12:5; cv-3a(2b); 1720]   ἐκλανθάνομαι
ἐκλεξαμένοις   aor mid ptcp dat pl masc
[Ac 15:25; cv-1b(2); 1721]   ἐκλέγομαι
ἐκλεξάμενος   aor mid ptcp nom sg masc
[Lk 6:13; cv-1b(2); 1721]   "
ἐκλεξαμένους   aor mid ptcp acc pl masc
[Ac 15:22; cv-1b(2); 1721]   "
ἔκλεψαν   aor act ind 3 pl
[Mt 28:13; v-4; 3096]   κλέπτω
ἐκλήθη   aor pass ind 3 sg
[7t; v-1d(2b); 2813]   καλέω
ἐκλήθης   aor pass ind 2 sg [2t; v-1d(2b); 2813]   "
ἐκλήθητε   aor pass ind 2 pl [7t; v-1d(2b); 2813]   "
ἐκληρώθημεν   aor pass ind 1 pl
[Ep 1:11; v-1d(3); 3103]   κληρόω
ἔκλιναν   aor act ind 3 pl
[Hb 11:34; v-1c(2); 3111]   κλίνω
ἐκλίπῃ   aor act subj 3 sg
[2t; cv-1b(1); 1722]   ἐκλείπω
ἐκλιπόντος   aor act ptcp gen sg masc
[Lk 23:45; cv-1b(1); 1722]   "

ἐκλογή, ῆς, ἡ   {1724, n-1b}
the act of choosing out, election; in N.T. *election* to privilege by divine grace, Rom 9:11; 11:5, 28; 1 Thess 1:4; 2 Peter 1:10; ἡ ἐκλογή, *the elect*, Rom 11:7; ἐκλογῆς, equivalent to ἐκλεκτόν, by Hebraism, Acts 9:15*

ἐκλογή   nom sg fem [Rm 11:7; n-1b; 1724]   ἐκλογή
ἐκλογήν   acc sg fem [5t; n-1b; 1724]   "
ἐκλογῆς   gen sg fem [Ac 9:15; n-1b; 1724]   "
ἐκλυθήσονται   fut pass ind 3 pl
[Mk 8:3; cv-1a(4); 1725]   ἐκλύω
ἐκλυθῶσιν   aor pass subj 3 pl
[Mt 15:32; cv-1a(4); 1725]   "
ἐκλυόμενοι   pres pass ptcp nom pl masc
[2t; cv-1a(4); 1725]   "
ἐκλύου   pres pass imperative 2 sg
[Hb 12:5; cv-1a(4); 1725]   "

ἐκλύω   {1725, cv-1a(4)}
[-, -, -, -, ἐξελύθην] *to be weary, exhausted, faint*, Matt 15:32; Mark 8:3; Gal 6:9; *to lose courage, to faint*, Heb 12:3, 5*

ἐκμάξασα   aor act ptcp nom sg fem
[Jn 11:2; cv-2b; 1726]   ἐκμάσσω
ἐκμάσσειν   pres act inf [Jn 13:5; cv-2b; 1726]   "

ἐκμάσσω   {1726, cv-2b}
[(ἐξέμασσον), -, ἐξέμασα, -, -, -] *to wipe off; to wipe dry*, Luke 7:38, 44; John 11:2; 12:3; 13:5*

ἐκμυκτηρίζω   {1727, cv-2a(1)}
[(ἐξεμυκτήριζον), -, -, -, -, -] to mock, deride, scoff
at, Luke 16:14; 23:35*

ἐκνεύω   {1728, cv-1a(6)}
[-, ἐξένευσα, -, -, -] pr. to swim out, to escape by
swimming; hence, generally, to escape, get clear of
a place, John 5:13; though ἐκνεύσας, in this
place, may be referred to ἐκνεύω, to deviate,
withdraw*

ἐκνήφω   {1729, cv-1b(1)}
[-, ἐξένηψα -, -, -] pr. to awake sober after
intoxication; met. to shake off mental
bewilderment, to wake up from delusion and
folly, 1 Cor 15:34*

ἐκνήψατε   aor act imperative 2 pl
    [1C 15:34; cv-1b(1); 1729]   ἐκνήφω
ἐκοιμήθη   aor pass ind 3 sg
    [2t; v-1d(1a); 3121]   κοιμάω
ἐκοιμήθησαν   aor pass ind 3 pl
    [2t; v-1d(1a); 3121]   "
ἐκοινώνησαν   aor act ind 3 pl
    [Rm 15:27; v-1d(2a); 3125]   κοινωνέω
ἐκοινώνησεν   aor act ind 3 sg
    [Pp 4:15; v-1d(2a); 3125]   "
ἐκολάφισαν   aor act ind 3 pl
    [Mt 26:67; v-2a(1); 3139]   κολαφίζω
ἐκολλήθη   aor pass ind 3 sg
    [Lk 15:15; v-1d(1a); 3140]   κολλάω
ἐκολλήθησαν   aor pass ind 3 pl
    [Rv 18:5; v-1d(1a); 3140]   "
ἐκολοβώθησαν   aor pass ind 3 pl
    [Mt 24:22; v-1d(3); 3143]   κολοβόω
ἐκολόβωσεν   aor act ind 3 sg [2t; v-1d(3); 3143] "
ἐκομισάμην   aor mid ind 1 sg
    [Mt 25:27; v-2a(1); 3152]   κομίζω
ἐκομίσαντο   aor mid ind 3 pl
    [Hb 11:39; v-2a(1); 3152]   "
ἐκομίσατο   aor mid ind 3 sg
    [Hb 11:19; v-2a(1); 3152]   "
ἐκόπασεν   aor act ind 3 sg
    [3t; v-2a(1); 3156]   κοπάζω
ἐκοπίασα   aor act ind 1 sg
    [2t; v-1d(1b); 3159]   κοπιάω
ἐκοπίασεν   aor act ind 3 sg [2t; v-1d(1b); 3159] "
ἔκοπτον   imperf act ind 3 pl
    [Mt 21:8; v-4; 3164]   κόπτω
ἐκόπτοντο   imperf mid ind 3 pl [2t; v-4; 3164]   "
ἐκόσμησαν   aor act ind 3 pl
    [Mt 25:7; v-1d(2a); 3175]   κοσμέω
ἐκόσμουν   imperf act ind 3 pl
    [1P 3:5; v-1d(2a); 3175]   "
ἑκοῦσα   nom sg fem [Rm 8:20; a-2a; 1776]   ἑκών
ἑκούσιον   acc sg neut
    [Pm 14; a-1a(1); 1730]   ἑκούσιος

ἑκούσιος, ία, ιον   {1730, a-1a(1)}
voluntary, spontaneous, Phil 14*

ἑκουσίως   {1731, adverb}
voluntarily, spontaneously, Heb 10:26; 1 Peter
5:2*

ἑκουσίως   adverb [2t; adverb; 1731]   ἑκουσίως

ἐκούφιζον   imperf act ind 3 pl
    [Ac 27:38; v-2a(1); 3185]   κουφίζω
ἐκόψασθε   aor mid ind 2 pl
    [Mt 11:17; v-4; 3164]   κόπτω

ἔκπαλαι   {1732, adverb}
of old, long since, 2 Peter 2:3; 3:5*

ἔκπαλαι   adverb [2t; adverb; 1732]   ἔκπαλαι

ἐκπειράζω   {1733, cv-2a(1)}
[ἐκπειράσω, ἐξεπείρασα -, -, -] to tempt, put to the
test, Matt 4:7; Luke 4:12; 1 Cor 10:9; to try, sound,
Luke 10:25*

ἐκπειράζωμεν   pres act subj 1 pl
    [1C 10:9; cv-2a(1); 1733]   ἐκπειράζω
ἐκπειράζων   pres act ptcp nom sg masc
    [Lk 10:25; cv-2a(1); 1733]   "
ἐκπειράσεις   fut act ind 2 sg
    [2t; cv-2a(1); 1733]   "

ἐκπέμπω   {1734, cv-1b(1)}
[-, ἐξέπεμφα, -, -, ἐξεπέμφθην] to send out, or
away, Acts 13:4; 17:10*

ἐκπεμφθέντες   aor pass ptcp nom pl masc
    [Ac 13:4; cv-1b(1); 1734]   ἐκπέμπω
ἐκπεπλήρωκεν   perf act ind 3 sg
    [Ac 13:33; cv-1d(3); 1740]   ἐκπληρόω
ἐκπέπτωκεν   perf act ind 3 sg
    [Rm 9:6; cv-1b(3); 1738]   ἐκπίπτω

ἐκπερισσῶς   {1735, adverb}
exceedingly, vehemently, Mark 14:31*

ἐκπερισσῶς   adverb
    [Mk 14:31; adverb; 1735]   ἐκπερισσῶς
ἐκπεσεῖν   aor act inf
    [2t; cv-1b(3); 1738]   ἐκπίπτω
ἐκπέσητε   aor act subj 2 pl
    [2P 3:17; cv-1b(3); 1738]   "
ἐκπέσωμεν   aor act subj 1 pl
    [Ac 27:29; cv-1b(3); 1738]   "
ἐκπέσωσιν   aor act subj 3 pl
    [Ac 27:17; cv-1b(3); 1738]   "

ἐκπετάννυμι   {1736, cv-3c(1)}
[-, ἐξεπέτασα, -, -, -] pluperfect, ἐκπεπετάκειν, to
stretch forth, expand, extend, Rom 10:21*

ἐκπεφευγέναι   perf act inf
    [Ac 16:27; cv-1b(2); 1767]   ἐκφεύγω

ἐκπηδάω   {1737, cv-1d(1a)}
[-, ἐξεπήδησα or ἐξέπηδεσον, -, -, -] to leap forth,
rush out, Acts 14:14; get up quickly, Acts 10:25,
v.l.*

ἐκπίπτω   {1738, cv-1b(3)}
[-, ἐξέπεσον or ἐξέπεσα, ἐκπέπτωκα, -, -] to fall off
or from, Acts 12:7; 27:32; met. to fall from, forfeit,
lose, Gal 5:4; 2 Peter 3:17; to be cast ashore, Acts
27:17, 26, 29; to fall to the ground, be fruitless,
ineffectual, Rom 9:6; to cease, come to an end, 1
Cor 13:8, v.l.; James 1:11; 1 Peter 1:24*

ἐκπλεῦσαι   aor act inf
    [Ac 15:39; cv-1a(7); 1739]   ἐκπλέω

ἐκπλέω   {1739, cv-1a(7)}
[-, ἐξέπλευσα, -, -, -] *to sail out of* or *from a place*,
Acts 15:39; 18:18; 20:6*

ἐκπληρόω   {1740, cv-1d(3)}
[-, -, ἐκπεπλήρωκα, -, -] *to fill out, complete, fill up*;
met. *to fulfil, perform, accomplish*, Acts 13:33*

ἐκπλήρωσιν   acc sg fem
[Ac 21:26; n-3e(5b); 1741]   ἐκπλήρωσις

ἐκπλήρωσις, εως, ἡ   {1741, n-3e(5b)}
pr. *a filling up, completion*; hence, *a fulfilling,
accomplishment*, Acts 21:26*

ἐκπλήσσεσθαι   pres pass inf
[Mt 13:54; cv-2b; 1742]   ἐκπλήσσω
ἐκπλησσόμενος   pres pass ptcp nom sg masc
[Ac 13:12; cv-2b; 1742]   "

ἐκπλήσσω   {1742, cv-2b}
[(ἐξέπλησσον), -, ἐξέπληξα, -, -, ἐξεπλάγην] pr. *to
strike out of*; hence, *to strike out of* one's *wits*, *to
astound, amaze*; pass., *overwhelmed*, Matt 7:28;
13:54

ἐκπνέω   {1743, cv-1a(7)}
[-, ἐξέπνευσα, -, -, -] *to breathe out*; *to expire, die*,
Mark 15:37, 39; Luke 23:46*

ἐκπορεύεσθαι   pres mid inf
[2t; cv-1a(6); 1744]   ἐκπορεύομαι
ἐκπορευέσθω   pres mid imperative 3 sg
[Ep 4:29; cv-1a(6); 1744]   "
ἐκπορεύεται   pres mid ind 3 sg
[7t; cv-1a(6); 1744]   "

ἐκπορεύομαι   {1744, cv-1a(6)}
[(ἐξεπορευόμην), ἐκπορεύσομαι, -, -, -, -] *to go
from* or *out of* a place, *depart from*, Mark 11:19;
13:1; *to be voided*, Mark 7:19; *to be cast out*, Matt
17:21; *to proceed from, be spoken*, Matt 4:4; 15:11;
to burst forth, Rev 4:5; *to be spread abroad*, Luke
4:37; *to flow out*, Rev 22:1; from the Hebrew,
ἐκπορεύομαι καὶ εἰσπορεύομαι. See εἰσέρχομαι,
Acts 9:28

ἐκπορευόμενα   pres mid ptcp nom pl neut
[2t; cv-1a(6); 1744]   "
ἐκπορευομένη   pres mid ptcp nom sg fem
[Rv 1:16; cv-1a(6); 1744]   "
ἐκπορευόμενοι   pres mid ptcp nom pl masc
[Mk 6:11; cv-1a(6); 1744]   "
ἐκπορευομένοις   pres mid ptcp dat pl masc
[2t; cv-1a(6); 1744]   "
ἐκπορευόμενον   pres mid ptcp nom sg neut
[2t; cv-1a(6); 1744]   "
ἐκπορευόμενον   pres mid ptcp acc sg masc
[Rv 22:1; cv-1a(6); 1744]   "
ἐκπορευόμενος   pres mid ptcp nom sg masc
[Ac 9:28; cv-1a(6); 1744]   "
ἐκπορευομένου   pres mid ptcp gen sg masc
[3t; cv-1a(6); 1744]   "
ἐκπορευομένου   pres mid ptcp gen sg neut
[Rv 9:18; cv-1a(6); 1744]   "
ἐκπορευομένῳ   pres mid ptcp dat sg neut
[Mt 4:4; cv-1a(6); 1744]   "
ἐκπορευομένων   pres mid ptcp gen pl masc
[Mt 20:29; cv-1a(6); 1744]   "

ἐκπορεύονται   pres mid ind 3 pl
[2t; cv-1a(6); 1744]   "
ἐκπορεύσονται   fut mid ind 3 pl
[Jn 5:29; cv-1a(6); 1744]   "
ἐκπορνεύσασαι   aor act ptcp nom pl fem
[Jd 7; cv-1a(6); 1745]   ἐκπορνεύω

ἐκπορνεύω   {1745, cv-1a(6)}
[-, ἐξεπόρνευσα, -, -, -] *to be given to fornication,
indulge in immorality*, Jude 7*

ἐκπτύω   {1746, cv-1a(4)}
[-, ἐξέπτυσα, -, -, -] lit., *to spit out*; met. *to reject*,
Gal 4:14*

ἐκπυρόω   {1747, cv-1d(3)}
[-, -, -, -, ἐκπυρωθήσομαι] *to set on fire, destroy by
fire, to be burned up* or *destroyed by burning*, 2
Peter 3:10*

ἔκραζεν   imperf act ind 3 sg
[5t; v-2a(2); 3189]   κράζω
ἔκραζον   imperf act ind 3 pl [8t; v-2a(2); 3189]   "
ἔκραξαν   aor act ind 3 pl [7t; v-2a(2); 3189]   "
ἔκραξεν   aor act ind 3 sg [10t; v-2a(2); 3189]   "
ἐκραταιοῦτο   imperf pass ind 3 sg
[2t; v-1d(3); 3194]   κραταιόω
ἐκρατήσαμεν   aor act ind 1 pl
[Ac 24:6; v-1d(2a); 3195]   κρατέω
ἐκράτησαν   aor act ind 3 pl [4t; v-1d(2a); 3195]   "
ἐκρατήσατε   aor act ind 2 pl
[2t; v-1d(2a); 3195]   "
ἐκράτησεν   aor act ind 3 sg [3t; v-1d(2a); 3195]   "
ἐκρατοῦντο   imperf pass ind 3 pl
[Lk 24:16; v-1d(2a); 3195]   "
ἐκραύγαζον   imperf act ind 3 pl
[Jn 12:13; v-2a(1); 3198]   κραυγάζω
ἐκραύγασαν   aor act ind 3 pl [4t; v-2a(1); 3198]   "
ἐκραύγασεν   aor act ind 3 sg
[Jn 11:43; v-2a(1); 3198]   "

ἐκριζόω   {1748, cv-1d(3)}
[-, ἐξερίζωσα, -, -, ἐξεριζώθην] *to root up,
eradicate, pull out by the roots*, Matt 13:29; 15:13;
Luke 17:6; Jude 12*

ἐκριζωθέντα   aor pass ptcp nom pl neut
[Jd 12; cv-1d(3); 1748]   ἐκριζόω
ἐκριζωθήσεται   fut pass ind 3 sg
[Mt 15:13; cv-1d(3); 1748]   "
ἐκριζώθητι   aor pass imperative 2 sg
[Lk 17:6; cv-1d(3); 1748]   "
ἐκριζώσητε   aor act subj 2 pl
[Mt 13:29; cv-1d(3); 1748]   "
ἐκρίθη   aor pass ind 3 sg
[Ac 27:1; v-1c(2); 3212]   κρίνω
ἐκρίθησαν   aor pass ind 3 pl [2t; v-1c(2); 3212]   "
ἔκρινα   aor act ind 1 sg [3t; v-1c(2); 3212]   "
ἔκρινας   aor act ind 2 sg [2t; v-1c(2); 3212]   "
ἔκρινεν   aor act ind 3 sg [2t; v-1c(2); 3212]   "
ἐκρινόμεθα   imperf pass ind 1 pl
[1C 11:31; v-1c(2); 3212]   "
ἐκρύβη   aor pass ind 3 sg [4t; v-4; 3221]   κρύπτω
ἔκρυψα   aor act ind 1 sg [Mt 25:25; v-4; 3221]   "
ἔκρυψαν   aor act ind 3 pl [Rv 6:15; v-4; 3221]   "
ἔκρυψας   aor act ind 2 sg [Mt 11:25; v-4; 3221]   "

ἔκρυψεν   aor act ind 3 sg [2t; v-4; 3221]   "
ἐκστάσει   dat sg fem
   [3t; n-3e(5b); 1749]   ἔκστασις
ἐκστάσεως   gen sg fem [Ac 3:10; n-3e(5b); 1749]   "

ἔκστασις, εως, ἡ   {1749, n-3e(5b)}
   pr. *a displacement;* hence, *a displacement of the
   mind from its ordinary state and self-possession;
   amazement, astonishment,* Mark 5:42; *excess of
   fear; fear, terror,* Mark 16:8; Luke 5:26; Acts 3:10;
   in N.T. *an ecstasy, a trance,* Acts 10:10; 11:5;
   22:17*

ἔκστασις   nom sg fem [3t; n-3e(5b); 1749]   "

ἐκστρέφω   {1750, cv-1b(1)}
   [-, -, -, ἐξέστραμμαι, -] pr. *to turn out of, to turn
   inside out;* hence, *to change entirely;* in N.T. pass.
   to be perverted, Titus 3:11*

ἐκσῴζω   {1751, cv-2a(1)}
   [-, ἐξέσωσα, -, -, -] *to save from,* either to keep or
   to rescue from danger, v.l. for ἐξωθέω in Acts
   27:39*

ἐκταράσσουσιν   pres act ind 3 pl
   [Ac 16:20; cv-2b; 1752]   ἐκταράσσω

ἐκταράσσω   {1752, cv-2b}
   [-, -, -, -, -] *to disturb, disquiet, throw into
   confusion,* Acts 16:20; 15:24, v.l.*

ἐκτεθέντος   aor pass ptcp gen sg masc
   [Ac 7:21; cv-6a; 1758]   ἐκτίθημι
ἐκτείνας   aor act ptcp nom sg masc
   [7t; cv-2d(5); 1753]   ἐκτείνω
ἐκτείνειν   pres act inf [2t; cv-2d(5); 1753]   "
ἔκτεινον   aor act imperative 2 sg
   [3t; cv-2d(5); 1753]   "

ἐκτείνω   {1753, cv-2d(5)}
   [ἐκτενῶ, ἐξέτεινα, -, -, -] *to stretch out,* Matt 8:3;
   12:13; *to lay* hands on any one, Luke 22:53; *to
   exert* power and energy, Acts 4:30; *to cast out, let
   down* an anchor, Acts 27:30

ἐκτελέσαι   aor act inf
   [2t; cv-1d(2b); 1754]   ἐκτελέω

ἐκτελέω   {1754, cv-1d(2b)}
   [-, ἐξετέλεσα, -, -, -] *to bring to an end, to finish,
   complete,* Luke 14:29, 30*

ἐκτένεια, ας, ἡ   {1755, n-1a}
   pr. *extension;* in N.T. *intenseness, intentness;* ἐν
   ἐκτενείᾳ, *intently, perseverance, earnestness,* Acts
   12:5, v.l.; 26:7*

ἐκτενείᾳ   dat sg fem
   [Ac 26:7; n-1a; 1755]   ἐκτένεια
ἐκτενεῖς   fut act ind 2 sg
   [Jn 21:18; cv-2d(5); 1753]   ἐκτείνω
ἐκτενέστερον   adverb-comparative
   [Lk 22:44; adverb; 1757]   ἐκτενῶς
ἐκτενῆ   acc sg fem [1P 4:8; a-4a; 1756]   ἐκτενής

ἐκτενής, ές   {1756, a-4a}
   pr. *extended;* met. *intense, earnest, fervent, eager,*
   Acts 12:5, v.l.; 1 Peter 4:8*

ἐκτενῶς   {1757, adverb}
   intensely, fervently, earnestly, Luke 22:44; Acts
   12:5; 1 Peter 1:22*

ἐκτενῶς   adverb [2t; adverb; 1757]   ἐκτενῶς
ἔκτη   nom sg fem [3t; a-1a(2a); 1761]   ἕκτος
ἔκτην   acc sg fem [3t; a-1a(2a); 1761]   "
ἔκτης   gen sg fem [2t; a-1a(2a); 1761]   "
ἐκτησάμην   aor mid ind 1 sg
   [Ac 22:28; v-1d(1a); 3227]   κτάομαι
ἐκτήσατο   aor mid ind 3 sg
   [Ac 1:18; v-1d(1a); 3227]   "

ἐκτίθημι   {1758, cv-6a}
   [(ἐξετίθην), -, ἐξέθηκα, -, -, ἐξετέθην] pr. *to place
   outside, put forth; to expose* an infant, Acts 7:21;
   met. *to set forth, declare, explain,* Acts 11:4; 18:26;
   28:23*

ἐκτιναξάμενοι   aor mid ptcp nom pl masc
   [Ac 13:51; cv-2b; 1759]   ἐκτινάσσω
ἐκτιναξάμενος   aor mid ptcp nom sg masc
   [Ac 18:6; cv-2b; 1759]   "
ἐκτινάξατε   aor act imperative 2 pl
   [2t; cv-2b; 1759]   "

ἐκτινάσσω   {1759, cv-2b}
   [-, ἐξετίναξα, -, -, -] *to shake out, shake off,* Matt
   10:14; Mark 6:11; Luke 9:5, v.l.; Acts 13:51; 18:6*

ἔκτισας   aor act ind 2 sg
   [Rv 4:11; v-2a(1); 3231]   κτίζω
ἔκτισεν   aor act ind 3 sg [3t; v-2a(1); 3231]   "
ἐκτίσθη   aor pass ind 3 sg [2t; v-2a(1); 3231]   "
ἐκτίσθησαν   aor pass ind 3 pl
   [Rv 4:11; v-2a(1); 3231]   "
ἔκτισται   perf pass ind 3 sg
   [Cl 1:16; v-2a(1); 3231]   "

ἐκτός   {1760, adverb}
   also functions as an improper prep. (4t),
   without, on the outside; τὸ ἐκτός, *the exterior,
   outside,* Matt 23:26; met. *besides,* Acts 26:22; 1
   Cor 15:27; ἐκτὸς εἰ μή, *unless, except,* 1 Cor 14:5

ἐκτός   adverb [8t; adverb; 1760]   ἐκτός

ἕκτος, η, ον   {1761, a-1a(2a)}
   sixth, Matt 20:5; 27:45

ἕκτος   nom sg masc [4t; a-1a(2a); 1761]   ἕκτος
ἐκτραπῇ   aor pass subj 3 sg
   [Hb 12:13; cv-1b(1); 1762]   ἐκτρέπω
ἐκτραπήσονται   fut pass ind 3 pl
   [2Ti 4:4; cv-1b(1); 1762]   "
ἐκτρεπόμενος   pres mid ptcp nom sg masc
   [1Ti 6:20; cv-1b(1); 1762]   "

ἐκτρέπω   {1762, cv-1b(1)}
   [-, -, -, -, ἐξετράπην] mid. and pas., *to turn out* or
   aside, Heb 12:13; *to turn aside* or *away, swerve,* 1
   Tim 1:6; 5:15; 2 Tim 4:4; *to turn from, avoid,* 1 Tim
   6:20*

ἐκτρέφει   pres act ind 3 sg
   [Ep 5:29; cv-1b(1); 1763]   ἐκτρέφω
ἐκτρέφετε   pres act imperative 2 pl
   [Ep 6:4; cv-1b(1); 1763]   "

ἐκτρέφω   {1763, cv-1b(1)}
[-, ἐξέθρεψα, -, -, -] *to nourish, promote health and strength,* Eph 5:29; *to bring up, educate,* Eph 6:4*

ἔκτρομος, ον   {1764, a-3a}
trembling, Heb 12:21, v.l.*

ἔκτρωμα, ατος, τό   {1765, n-3c(4)}
an abortion, baby prematurely born, 1 Cor 15:8*

ἐκτρώματι   dat sg neut
    [1C 15:8; n-3c(4); 1765]   ἔκτρωμα
ἔκτῳ   dat sg masc [2t; a-1a(2a); 1761]   ἔκτος
ἐκύκλευσαν   aor act ind 3 pl
    [Rv 20:9; v-1a(6); 3238]   κυκλεύω
ἐκύκλωσαν   aor act ind 3 pl
    [Jn 10:24; v-1d(3); 3240]   κυκλόω
ἐκυλίετο   imperf mid ind 3 sg
    [Mk 9:20; v-1a(1); 3244]   κυλίω
ἐκφέρειν   pres act inf
    [Ac 5:15; cv-1c(1); 1766]   ἐκφέρω
ἐκφέρουσα   pres act ptcp nom sg fem
    [Hb 6:8; cv-1c(1); 1766]   "

ἐκφέρω   {1766, cv-1c(1)}
[ἐξοίσω, ἐξήνεγκα or ἐξήνεγκον, -, -, -] *to bring forth, carry out,* Luke 15:22; Acts 5:15; 1 Tim 6:7; *to carry out* for burial, Acts 5:6, 9, 10; *to produce, yield,* Mark 8:23; Heb 6:8*

ἐκφεύγω   {1767, cv-1b(2)}
[ἐκφεύξομαι, ἐξέφυγον, ἐκπέφευγα, -, -] intrans. *to flee out, to make an escape,* Acts 16:27; 19:16; trans. *to escape, avoid,* Luke 21:36; Rom 2:3

ἐκφεύξῃ   fut mid ind 2 sg
    [Rm 2:3; cv-1b(2); 1767]   ἐκφεύγω
ἐκφευξόμεθα   fut mid ind 1 pl
    [Hb 2:3; cv-1b(2); 1767]   "
ἐκφοβεῖν   pres act inf
    [2C 10:9; cv-1d(2a); 1768]   ἐκφοβέω

ἐκφοβέω   {1768, cv-1d(2a)}
[-, -, -, -, -] *to terrify,* 2 Cor 10:9*

ἔκφοβοι   nom pl masc [Mk 9:6; a-3a; 1769]   ἔκφοβος

ἔκφοβος, ον   {1769, a-3a}
frightened, horrified, Mark 9:6; Heb 12:21*

ἔκφοβος   nom sg masc [Hb 12:21; a-3a; 1769]   "
ἐκφυγεῖν   aor act inf
    [2t; cv-1b(2); 1767]   ἐκφεύγω
ἐκφύγωσιν   aor act subj 3 pl
    [1Th 5:3; cv-1b(2); 1767]   "
ἐκφύῃ   pres act subj 3 sg
    [2t; cv-1a(4); 1770]   ἐκφύω

ἐκφύω   {1770, cv-1a(4)}
[-, -, -, -, -] lit. *to cause to grow, to generate; to put forth, shoot,* Matt 24:32; Mark 13:28*

ἐκφωνέω   {1771, v-1d(2a)}
[-, -, -, -, -] *cry out,* Luke 16:24, v.l.*

ἐκχέαι   aor act inf
    [Rm 3:15; cv-1a(7); 1772]   ἐκχέω
ἐκχέετε   pres act imperative 2 pl
    [Rv 16:1; cv-1a(7); 1772]   "
ἐκχεῖται   pres pass ind 3 sg
    [Mt 9:17; cv-1a(7); 1772]   "

ἐκχέω   {1772, cv-1a(7)}
[ἐκχεῶ, ἐξέχεα, -, ἐκκέχυμαι, ἐξεχύθην] *to pour out,* Rev 16:1, 2, 3; *to shed* blood, Matt 26:28; Mark 14:24; pass. *to gush out,* Acts 1:18; *to spill, scatter,* Matt 9:17; John 2:15; met. *to give largely, bestow liberally,* Acts 2:17, 18, 33; 10:45; pass. *to rush headlong* into anything, *be abandoned to,* Jude 11

ἐκχεῶ   fut act ind 1 sg [2t; cv-1a(7); 1772]   "
ἐκχυθήσεται   fut pass ind 3 sg
    [Lk 5:37; cv-1a(7); 1772]   "
ἐκχυννόμενον   pres pass ptcp nom sg neut
    [4t; cv-1a(7); 1772]   "
ἐκχωρείτωσαν   pres act imperative 3 pl
    [Lk 21:21; cv-1d(2a); 1774]   ἐκχωρέω

ἐκχωρέω   {1774, cv-1d(2a)}
[-, ἐξεχώρησα, -, -, -] *to go out, depart from, flee,* Luke 21:21*

ἐκψύχω   {1775, cv-1b(2)}
[-, ἐξέψυξα, -, -, -] *to expire, give up one's spirit,* Acts 5:5, 10; 12:23*

ἐκωλύθην   aor pass ind 1 sg
    [Rm 1:13; v-1a(4); 3266]   κωλύω
ἐκωλύομεν   imperf act ind 1 pl
    [2t; v-1a(4); 3266]   "
ἐκωλύσατε   aor act ind 2 pl
    [Lk 11:52; v-1a(4); 3266]   "
ἐκώλυσεν   aor act ind 3 sg [2t; v-1a(4); 3266]   "

ἑκών, ἑκοῦσα, ἑκόν   {1776, a-2a}
willing, voluntary, Rom 8:20; 1 Cor 9:17*

ἑκών   nom sg masc [1C 9:17; a-2a; 1776]   ἑκών
ἔλαβε   aor act ind 3 sg
    [Ac 28:15; v-3a(2b); 3284]   λαμβάνω
ἔλαβεν   aor act ind 3 sg [20t; v-3a(2b); 3284]   "
ἔλαβες   aor act ind 2 sg [2t; v-3a(2b); 3284]   "
ἐλάβετε   aor act ind 2 pl [12t; v-3a(2b); 3284]   "
ἐλάβομεν   aor act ind 1 pl [7t; v-3a(2b); 3284]   "
ἔλαβον   aor act ind 1 sg [6t; v-3a(2b); 3284]   "
ἔλαβον   aor act ind 3 pl [20t; v-3a(2b); 3284]   "
ἔλαθεν   aor act ind 3 sg
    [Lk 8:47; v-3a(2b); 3291]   λανθάνω
ἔλαθον   aor act ind 3 pl
    [Hb 13:2; v-3a(2b); 3291]   "

ἐλαία, ας, ἡ   {1777, n-1a}
an olive tree, Matt 21:1; 24:3; *an olive, fruit of the olive tree,* James 3:12, ὄρος τῶν ἐλαιῶν, *the Mount of Olives,* Matt 21:1

ἐλαίᾳ   dat sg fem [Rm 11:24; n-1a; 1777]   ἐλαία
ἐλαῖαι   nom pl fem [Rv 11:4; n-1a; 1777]   "
ἐλαίας   gen sg fem [Rm 11:17; n-1a; 1777]   "
ἐλαίας   acc pl fem [Jm 3:12; n-1a; 1777]   "

ἔλαιον, ου, τό   {1778, n-2c}
olive oil, oil, Matt 25:3, 4, 8; Mark 6:13

ἔλαιον   acc sg neut [6t; n-2c; 1778]   ἔλαιον
ἐλαίου   gen sg neut [2t; n-2c; 1778]   "
ἐλαίῳ   dat sg neut [3t; n-2c; 1778]   "

ἐλαιών, ῶνος, ὁ   {1779, n-3f(1a)}
an olive garden; in N.T. the mount *Olivet,* Luke 19:29; 21:37; Acts 1:12*

ἐλαιῶν   gen pl fem [11t; n-1a; 1777]   ἐλαία
ἐλαιῶνος   gen sg masc
  [Ac 1:12; n-3f(1a); 1779]   ἐλαιών
ἐλάκησεν   aor act ind 3 sg
  [Ac 1:18; v-1d(1a); 3279]   λακάω
ἐλάλει   imperf act ind 3 sg
  [20t; v-1d(2a); 3281]   λαλέω
ἐλαλήθη   aor pass ind 3 sg [2t; v-1d(2a); 3281]   "
ἐλάλησα   aor act ind 1 sg [8t; v-1d(2a); 3281]   "
ἐλαλήσαμεν   aor act ind 1 pl
  [2C 7:14; v-1d(2a); 3281]   "
ἐλάλησαν   aor act ind 3 pl [11t; v-1d(2a); 3281]   "
ἐλαλήσατε   aor act ind 2 pl
  [Lk 12:3; v-1d(2a); 3281]   "
ἐλάλησεν   aor act ind 3 sg [31t; v-1d(2a); 3281]   "
ἐλαλοῦμεν   imperf act ind 1 pl
  [Ac 16:13; v-1d(2a); 3281]   "
ἐλάλουν   imperf act ind 1 sg
  [1C 13:11; v-1d(2a); 3281]   "
ἐλάλουν   imperf act ind 3 pl
  [5t; v-1d(2a); 3281]   "
ἐλάμβανον   imperf act ind 3 pl
  [Ac 8:17; v-3a(2b); 3284]   λαμβάνω
Ἐλαμῖται   nom pl masc
  [Ac 2:9; n-1f; 1780]   Ἐλαμίτης

Ἐλαμίτης, ου, ὁ   {1780, n-1f}
an Elamite; an inhabitant of Elam, a province of Persia, Acts 2:9*

ἔλαμψεν   aor act ind 3 sg
  [3t; v-1b(1); 3290]   λάμπω
ἐλάσσονι   dat sg masc comparative
  [Rm 9:12; a-4b(1); 1781]   ἐλάσσων
ἐλάσσω   acc sg masc comparative
  [Jn 2:10; a-4b(1); 1781]   "

ἐλάσσων, ον   {1781, a-4b(1)}
ἐλάττων (1784) is the Attic form of this word. Twice it is used with σσ (John 2:10; Rom 9:12) and twice with ττ (1 Tim 5:9; Heb 7:7, cf. Mt 20:28 v.l.). It is used as the comparative of μικρός, *less; less* in age, *younger,* Rom 9:12; *less* in dignity, *inferior,* Heb 7:7; *less* in quality, *inferior, worse,* John 2:10; 1 Tim 5:9; Matt 20:28 v.l.*

ἐλατόμησεν   aor act ind 3 sg
  [Mt 27:60; v-1d(2a); 3300]   λατομέω
ἐλάτρευσαν   aor act ind 3 pl
  [Rm 1:25; v-1a(6); 3302]   λατρεύω
ἔλαττον   nom sg neut comparative
  [Hb 7:7; a-4b(1); 1781]   ἐλάσσων
ἔλαττον   adverb-comparative
  [1Ti 5:9; a-4b(1); 1781]   "

ἐλαττονέω   {1782, v-1d(2a)}
[-, ἠλαττόνησα, -, -, -] trans. *to make less;* intrans. *to be less, inferior; to have too little, want, lack,* 2 Cor 8:15*

ἐλαττοῦσθαι   pres pass inf
  [Jn 3:30; v-1d(3); 1783]   ἐλαττόω

ἐλάττων, ον   {1784, a-4b(1)}
see ἐλάσσων (1781)

ἐλαττόω   {1783, v-1d(3)}
[-, ἠλάττωσα, -, ἠλάττωμαι, -] *to make less* or *inferior,* Heb 2:7; 2 Cor 12:13 v.l.; pass. *to be made less* or *inferior,* Heb 2:9; *to decline* in importance, John 3:30*

ἐλαύνειν   pres act inf
  [Mk 6:48; v-3c(2); 1785]   ἐλαύνω
ἐλαυνόμενα   pres pass ptcp nom pl neut
  [Jm 3:4; v-3c(2); 1785]   "
ἐλαυνόμεναι   pres pass ptcp nom pl fem
  [2P 2:17; v-3c(2); 1785]   "

ἐλαύνω   {1785, v-3c(2)}
[(ἤλαυνον), -, ἤλασα, ἐλήλακα, -, -] *to drive, urge forward, spur on,* Luke 8:29; James 3:4; 2 Peter 2:17; *to impel* a vessel by oars, *to row,* Mark 6:48; John 6:19*

ἐλαφρία, ας, ἡ   {1786, n-1a}
lightness in weight; hence, *lightness of mind, levity,* 2 Cor 1:17*

ἐλαφρίᾳ   dat sg fem
  [2C 1:17; n-1a; 1786]   ἐλαφρία
ἐλαφρόν   nom sg neut [2t; a-1a(1); 1787]   ἐλαφρός

ἐλαφρός, ά, όν   {1787, a-1a(1)}
light, not heavy, Matt 11:30; 2 Cor 4:17*

ἔλαχε   aor act ind 3 sg
  [Lk 1:9; v-3a(2b); 3275]   λαγχάνω
ἔλαχεν   aor act ind 3 sg
  [Ac 1:17; v-3a(2b); 3275]   "
ἐλαχίστη   nom sg fem superlative
  [Mt 2:6; a-1a(2a); 1788]   ἐλάχιστος
ἐλάχιστον   acc sg neut superlative
  [2t; a-1a(2a); 1788]   "

ἐλάχιστος, ίστη, ιστον   {1788, a-1a(2a)}
used as the superlative of μικρός, *smallest, least;* Matt 2:6; 5:19

ἐλάχιστος   nom sg masc superlative
  [2t; a-1a(2a); 1788]   "
ἐλαχιστοτέρῳ   dat sg masc comparative
  [Ep 3:8; a-1a(2a); 1788]   "
ἐλαχίστου   gen sg neut superlative
  [Jm 3:4; a-1a(2a); 1788]   "
ἐλαχίστῳ   dat sg neut superlative
  [3t; a-1a(2a); 1788]   "
ἐλαχίστων   gen pl masc superlative
  [2t; a-1a(2a); 1788]   "
ἐλαχίστων   gen pl fem superlative
  [Mt 5:19; a-1a(2a); 1788]   "
ἐλαχίστων   gen pl neut superlative
  [1C 6:2; a-1a(2a); 1788]   "

Ἐλεάζαρ, ὁ   {1789, n-3g(2)}
Eleazar, pr. name, indecl., Matt 1:15*

Ἐλεάζαρ   indecl [2t; n-3g(2); 1789]   Ἐλεάζαρ
ἐλεᾶτε   pres act imperative 2 pl
  [2t; v-1d(1a); 1790]   ἐλεάω

ἐλεάω   {1790, v-1d(1a)}
[-, -, -, -, -] see ἐλεέω, *have mercy on,* Rom 9:16; Jude 22, 23*

ἔλεγεν   imperf act ind 3 sg
[71t; v-1b(2); 3306]   λέγω

ἐλέγετε   imperf act ind 2 pl
[Lk 17:6; v-1b(2); 3306]   "

ἐλεγμόν   acc sg masc
[2Ti 3:16; n-2a; 1791]   ἐλεγμός

ἐλεγμός, οῦ, ὁ   {1791, n-2a}
   reproof, 2 Tim 3:16, a later equivalent to ἔλεγχος*

ἐλέγξαι   aor act inf
[Jd 15; v-1b(2); 1794]   ἐλέγχω

ἐλέγξει   fut act ind 3 sg
[Jn 16:8; v-1b(2); 1794]   "

ἔλεγξιν   acc sg fem
[2P 2:16; n-3e(5b); 1792]   ἔλεγξις

ἔλεγξις, εως, ἡ   {1792, n-3e(5b)}
   reproof, rebuke, 2 Peter 2:16*

ἔλεγξον   aor act imperative 2 sg
[2t; v-1b(2); 1794]   ἐλέγχω

ἔλεγον   imperf act ind 1 sg
[4t; v-1b(2); 3306]   λέγω

ἔλεγον   imperf act ind 3 pl [75t; v-1b(2); 3306]   "

ἔλεγχε   pres act imperative 2 sg
[3t; v-1b(2); 1794]   ἐλέγχω

ἐλέγχει   pres act ind 3 sg
[Jn 8:46; v-1b(2); 1794]   "

ἐλέγχειν   pres act inf   [Ti 1:9; v-1b(2); 1794]   "

ἐλέγχεται   pres pass ind 3 sg
[1C 14:24; v-1b(2); 1794]   "

ἐλέγχετε   pres act imperative 2 pl
[Ep 5:11; v-1b(2); 1794]   "

ἐλεγχθῇ   aor pass subj 3 sg
[Jn 3:20; v-1b(2); 1794]   "

ἐλεγχόμενα   pres pass ptcp nom pl neut
[Ep 5:13; v-1b(2); 1794]   "

ἐλεγχόμενοι   pres pass ptcp nom pl masc
[Jm 2:9; v-1b(2); 1794]   "

ἐλεγχόμενος   pres pass ptcp nom sg masc
[2t; v-1b(2); 1794]   "

ἔλεγχος, ου, ὁ   {1793, n-2a}
   pr. *a trial in order to proof, a proof;* meton. *a certain persuasion,* Heb 11:1; *reproof, refutation,* 2 Tim 3:16 v.l.*

ἔλεγχος   nom sg masc [Hb 11:1; n-2a; 1793] ἔλεγχος

ἐλέγχω   {1794, v-1b(2)}
   [ἐλέγξω, ἤλεγξα, -, -, ἠλέγχθην] *to put to proof, to test; to convict,* John 8:46; James 2:9; *to refute, confute,* 1 Cor 14:24; Titus 1:9; *to detect, lay bare, expose,* John 3:20; Eph 5:11, 13; *to reprove, rebuke,* Matt 18:15; Luke 3:19; 1 Tim 5:20; *to discipline, chastise,* Heb 12:5; Rev 3:19; pass. *to experience conviction,* John 8:9; 1 Cor 14:24

ἐλέγχω   pres act ind 1 sg
[Rv 3:19; v-1b(2); 1794]   ἐλέγχω

ἐλέει   dat sg neut [2t; n-3d(2b); 1799]   ἔλεος

ἐλεεῖ   pres act ind 3 sg
[Rm 9:18; v-1d(2a); 1796]   ἐλεέω

ἐλεεινός, ή, όν   {1795, a-1a(2a)}
   pitiable, wretched, miserable, 1 Cor 15:19; Rev 3:17*

ἐλεεινός   nom sg masc
[Rv 3:17; a-1a(2a); 1795]   ἐλεεινός

ἐλεεινότεροι   nom pl masc comparative
[1C 15:19; a-1a(2a); 1795]   "

ἐλεέω   {1796, v-1d(2a)}
   [ἐλεήσω, ἠλέησα, -, ἠλέημαι, ἠλεήθην] *to pity, have compassion on;* pass. *to receive pity, experience compassion,* Matt 5:7; 9:27; 15:22; *to be gracious to* any one, *show gracious favor and saving mercy towards;* pass. *to be an object of gracious favor and saving mercy,* Rom 9:15, 16, 18; 11:30, 31, 32; spc. *to obtain pardon and forgiveness,* 1 Tim 1:13, 16

ἐλεηθέντες   aor pass ptcp nom pl masc
[1P 2:10; v-1d(2a); 1796]   ἐλεέω

ἐλεηθήσονται   fut pass ind 3 pl
[Mt 5:7; v-1d(2a); 1796]   "

ἐλεηθῶσιν   aor pass subj 3 pl
[Rm 11:31; v-1d(2a); 1796]   "

ἐλεήμονες   nom pl masc
[Mt 5:7; a-4b(1); 1798]   ἐλεήμων

ἐλεημοσύναι   nom pl fem
[2t; n-1b; 1797]   ἐλεημοσύνη

ἐλεημοσύνας   acc pl fem [2t; n-1b; 1797]   "

ἐλεημοσύνη, ῆς, ἡ   {1797, n-1b}
   pity, compassion; in N.T. *an act of kindness, alms, almsgiving,* Matt 6:2, 3, 4; Luke 11:41

ἐλεημοσύνη   nom sg fem [Mt 6:4; n-1b; 1797]   "

ἐλεημοσύνην   acc sg fem [7t; n-1b; 1797]   "

ἐλεημοσυνῶν   gen pl fem [Ac 9:36; n-1b; 1797]   "

ἐλεήμων, ον   {1798, a-4b(1)}
   merciful, pitiful, compassionate, Matt 5:7; Heb 2:17*

ἐλεήμων   nom sg masc
[Hb 2:17; a-4b(1); 1798]   ἐλεήμων

ἐλεῆσαι   aor act inf
[Mt 18:33; v-1d(2a); 1796]   ἐλεέω

ἐλεήσῃ   aor act subj 3 sg
[Rm 11:32; v-1d(2a); 1796]   "

ἐλέησον   aor act imperative 2 sg
[11t; v-1d(2a); 1796]   "

ἐλεήσω   fut act ind 1 sg
[Rm 9:15; v-1d(2a); 1796]   "

ἔλεος, ους, τό   {1799, n-3d(2b)}
   pity, mercy, compassion, Matt 9:13; 12:7; Luke 1:50, 78; meton. *benefit* which results from compassion, *kindness, mercies, blessing,* Luke 1:54, 58, 72; 10:37; Rom 9:23

ἔλεος   nom sg neut [7t; n-3d(2b); 1799]   ἔλεος

ἔλεος   acc sg neut [13t; n-3d(2b); 1799]   "

ἐλέους   gen sg neut [5t; n-3d(2b); 1799]   "

ἐλευθέρα   nom sg fem
[3t; a-1a(1); 1801]   ἐλεύθερος

ἐλευθέρας   gen sg fem [4t; a-1a(1); 1801]   "

ἐλευθερία, ας, ἡ   {1800, n-1a}
   liberty, freedom, 1 Cor 10:29; Gal 2:4

ἐλευθερία   nom sg fem [2t; n-1a; 1800]   ἐλευθερία

ἐλευθερίᾳ   dat sg fem [2t; n-1a; 1800]   "

ἐλευθερίαν   acc sg fem [5t; n-1a; 1800]   "

ἐλευθερίας   gen sg fem [2t; n-1a; 1800]   "
ἐλεύθεροι   nom pl masc
    [6t; a-1a(1); 1801]   ἐλεύθερος

ἐλεύθερος, έρα, ερον   {1801, a-1a(1)}
    free, in a state of freedom as opposed to slavery, 1
    Cor 12:13; Gal 3:28; *free, exempt,* Matt 17:26; 1
    Cor 7:39; *unrestricted, unfettered,* 1 Cor 9:1; *free*
    from the dominion of sin, etc., John 8:36; Rom
    6:20; *free* in the possession of Gospel privileges,
    1 Peter 2:16

ἐλεύθερος   nom sg masc [8t; a-1a(1); 1801]   "
ἐλευθέρους   acc pl masc
    [Rv 13:16; a-1a(1); 1801]   "

ἐλευθερόω   {1802, v-1d(3)}
    [ἐλευθερώσω, ἠλευθέρωσα, -, -, ἠλευθερώθην] *to*
    free, set free, John 8:32, 36; Rom 6:18, 22; 8:2, 21;
    Gal 5:1*

ἐλευθερωθέντες   aor pass ptcp nom pl masc
    [2t; v-1d(3); 1802]   ἐλευθερόω
ἐλευθερωθήσεται   fut pass ind 3 sg
    [Rm 8:21; v-1d(3); 1802]   "
ἐλευθέρων   gen pl masc
    [Rv 19:18; a-1a(1); 1801]   ἐλεύθερος
ἐλευθερώσει   fut act ind 3 sg
    [Jn 8:32; v-1d(3); 1802]   ἐλευθερόω
ἐλευθερώσῃ   aor act subj 3 sg
    [Jn 8:36; v-1d(3); 1802]   "
ἐλεύκαναν   aor act ind 3 pl
    [Rv 7:14; v-2d(4); 3326]   λευκαίνω
ἐλεύσεται   fut mid ind 3 sg
    [5t; v-1b(2); 2262]   ἔρχομαι
ἐλεύσεως   gen sg fem
    [Ac 7:52; n-3e(5a); 1803]   ἔλευσις

ἔλευσις, εως, ἡ   {1803, n-3e(5a)}
    a coming, advent, Acts 7:52; Luke 21:7 v.l.; 23:42
    v.l.*

ἐλεύσομαι   fut mid ind 1 sg
    [6t; v-1b(2); 2262]   ἔρχομαι
ἐλευσόμεθα   fut mid ind 1 pl
    [Jn 14:23; v-1b(2); 2262]   "
ἐλεύσονται   fut mid ind 3 pl
    [10t; v-1b(2); 2262]   "
ἐλεφάντινον   acc sg neut
    [Rv 18:12; a-1a(2a); 1804]   ἐλεφάντινος

ἐλεφάντινος, η, ον   {1804, a-1a(2a)}
    ivory, made of ivory, Rev 18:12*

ἐλεῶ   pres act subj 1 sg
    [Rm 9:15; v-1d(2a); 1796]   ἐλεέω
ἐλεῶν   pres act ptcp nom sg masc
    [Rm 12:8; v-1d(2a); 1796]   "
ἐλεῶντος   pres act ptcp gen sg masc
    [Rm 9:16; v-1d(2a); 1796]   "
ἐληλακότες   perf act ptcp nom pl masc
    [Jn 6:19; v-3c(2); 1785]   ἐλαύνω
ἐλήλυθα   perf act ind 1 sg
    [7t; v-1b(2); 2262]   ἔρχομαι
ἐλήλυθας   perf act ind 2 sg [2t; v-1b(2); 2262]   "
ἐληλύθει   pluperf act ind 3 sg
    [6t; v-1b(2); 2262]   "

ἐληλύθεισαν   pluperf act ind 3 pl
    [Jn 11:19; v-1b(2); 2262]   "
ἐλήλυθεν   perf act ind 3 sg [8t; v-1b(2); 2262]   "
ἐληλυθότα   perf act ptcp acc sg masc
    [2t; v-1b(2); 2262]   "
ἐληλυθότες   perf act ptcp nom pl masc
    [Lk 5:17; v-1b(2); 2262]   "
ἐληλυθυῖαν   perf act ptcp acc sg fem
    [Mk 9:1; v-1b(2); 2262]   "
ἐλθάτω   aor act imperative 3 sg
    [Mt 10:13; v-1b(2); 2262]   "
ἐλθέ   aor act imperative 2 sg
    [2t; v-1b(2); 2262]   "
ἐλθεῖν   aor act inf [40t; v-1b(2); 2262]   "
ἐλθέτω   aor act imperative 3 sg
    [2t; v-1b(2); 2262]   "
ἔλθῃ   aor act subj 3 sg [32t; v-1b(2); 2262]   "
ἔλθῃς   aor act subj 2 sg
    [Lk 23:42; v-1b(2); 2262]   "
ἔλθητε   aor act subj 2 pl
    [Mk 14:38; v-1b(2); 2262]   "
ἐλθόν   aor act ptcp nom sg neut
    [2t; v-1b(2); 2262]   "
ἐλθόντα   aor act ptcp nom pl neut
    [Mt 13:4; v-1b(2); 2262]   "
ἐλθόντα   aor act ptcp acc sg masc
    [Mt 17:25; v-1b(2); 2262]   "
ἐλθόντας   aor act ptcp acc pl masc
    [Lk 5:7; v-1b(2); 2262]   "
ἐλθόντες   aor act ptcp nom pl masc
    [21t; v-1b(2); 2262]   "
ἐλθόντι   aor act ptcp dat sg masc
    [Mt 9:28; v-1b(2); 2262]   "
ἐλθόντος   aor act ptcp gen sg masc
    [6t; v-1b(2); 2262]   "
ἐλθόντων   aor act ptcp gen pl masc
    [3t; v-1b(2); 2262]   "
ἐλθοῦσα   aor act ptcp nom sg fem
    [5t; v-1b(2); 2262]   "
ἐλθοῦσαι   aor act ptcp nom pl fem
    [Mk 16:1; v-1b(2); 2262]   "
ἐλθούσης   aor act ptcp gen sg fem
    [2t; v-1b(2); 2262]   "
ἔλθω   aor act subj 1 sg [6t; v-1b(2); 2262]   "
ἐλθών   aor act ptcp nom sg masc
    [50t; v-1b(2); 2262]   "
ἔλθωσιν   aor act subj 3 pl [4t; v-1b(2); 2262]   "

Ἐλιακίμ, ὁ   {1806, n-3g(2)}
    also spelled Ἐλιακείμ, *Eliakim,* pr. name,
    indecl., Matt 1:13; Luke 3:30, 23 ff. v.l.*

Ἐλιακίμ   indecl [3t; n-3g(2); 1806]   Ἐλιακίμ

ἔλιγμα, ατος, τό   {1807, n-3c(4)}
    a roll, package, John 19:39 v.l.*

Ἐλιέζερ, ὁ   {1808, n-3g(2)}
    Eliezer, pr. name, indecl., Luke 3:29*

Ἐλιέζερ   indecl [Lk 3:29; n-3g(2); 1808]   Ἐλιέζερ
ἐλιθάσθην   aor pass ind 1 sg
    [2C 11:25; v-2a(1); 3342]   λιθάζω
ἐλιθάσθησαν   aor pass ind 3 pl
    [Hb 11:37; v-2a(1); 3342]   "

ἐλιθοβόλησαν   aor act ind 3 pl
   [Mt 21:35; v-1d(2a); 3344]   λιθοβολέω
ἐλιθοβόλουν   imperf act ind 3 pl
   [2t; v-1d(2a); 3344]   "
ἑλίξεις   fut act ind 2 sg
   [Hb 1:12; v-2b; 1813]   ἑλίσσω

Ἐλιούδ, ὁ   {1809, n-3g(2)}
   Eliud, pr. name, indecl., Matt 1:14f.; Luke 3:23ff.
   v.l.*

Ἐλιούδ   indecl [2t; n-3g(2); 1809]   Ἐλιούδ

Ἐλισάβετ, ἡ   {1810, n-3g(2)}
   Elisabeth, pr. name, indecl., Luke 1:5, 7, 13, 24,
   36, 40f., 46 v.l., 57*

Ἐλισάβετ   indecl [9t; n-3g(2); 1810]   Ἐλισάβετ

Ἐλισαῖος, ου, ὁ   {1811, n-2a}
   also spelled Ἐλισσαῖος, Elisha, pr. name, Luke
   4:27*

Ἐλισαίου   gen sg masc
   [Lk 4:27; n-2a; 1811]   Ἐλισαῖος
ἑλισσόμενον   pres pass ptcp nom sg neut
   [Rv 6:14; v-2b; 1813]   ἑλίσσω

ἑλίσσω   {1813, v-2b}
   [ἑλίξω, -, -, -, ἥλιχθην] to roll, fold up, as
   garments, Heb 1:12; Rev 6:14*

ἕλκη   acc pl neut [Lk 16:21; n-3d(2b); 1814]   ἕλκος

ἕλκος, ους, τό   {1814, n-3d(2b)}
   pr. a wound; hence, an ulcer, sore, Luke 16:21;
   Rev 16:2, 11*

ἕλκος   nom sg neut [Rv 16:2; n-3d(2b); 1814]   "
ἕλκουσιν   pres act ind 3 pl
   [Jm 2:6; v-1a(4); 1816]   ἕλκω

ἑλκόω   {1815, v-1d(3)}
   [-, -, -, εἵλκωμαι, -] pass. to be afflicted with ulcers,
   Luke 16:20*

ἑλκύσαι   aor act inf [Jn 21:6; v-1a(4); 1816]   "
ἑλκύσῃ   aor act subj 3 sg
   [Jn 6:44; v-1a(4); 1816]   "
ἑλκύσω   fut act ind 1 sg
   [Jn 12:32; v-1a(4); 1816]

ἕλκω   {1816, v-1a(4)}
   [(εἷλκον), ἑλκύσω, εἵλκυσα, -, -, -] also spelled
   ἕλκω, to draw, drag, John 21:6, 11; Acts 16:19;
   21:30; James 2:6; to draw a sword, unsheath, John
   18:10; met. to draw mentally and morally, John
   6:44; 12:32*

ἑλκῶν   gen pl neut
   [Rv 16:11; n-3d(2b); 1814]   ἕλκος
Ἑλλάδα   acc sg fem
   [Ac 20:2; n-3c(2); 1817]   Ἑλλάς

Ἑλλάς, άδος, ἡ   {1817, n-3c(2)}
   Hellas, Greece; in N.T. the southern portion of
   Greece as distinguished from Macedonia, Acts
   20:2*

Ἕλλην, ηνος, ὁ   {1818, n-3f(1a)}
   a Greek, Acts 18:17; Rom 1:14; one not a Jew, a
   Gentile, Acts 14:1; 16:1, 3

Ἕλλην   nom sg masc [4t; n-3f(1a); 1818]   Ἕλλην

Ἕλληνας   acc pl masc [5t; n-3f(1a); 1818]   "
Ἕλληνες   nom pl masc [3t; n-3f(1a); 1818]   "
Ἕλληνι   dat sg masc [2t; n-3f(1a); 1818]   "
Ἑλληνίδων   gen pl fem
   [Ac 17:12; n-3c(2); 1820]   Ἑλληνίς
Ἑλληνικῇ   dat sg fem
   [Rv 9:11; a-1a(2a); 1819]   Ἑλληνικός

Ἑλληνικός, ή, όν   {1819, a-1a(2a)}
   Greek, Grecian, Rev 9:11; Luke 23:38 v.l.*

Ἑλληνίς, ίδος, ἡ   {1820, n-3c(2)}
   a female Greek, Mark 7:26; Acts 17:12*

Ἑλληνίς   nom sg fem
   [Mk 7:26; n-3c(2); 1820]   Ἑλληνίς
Ἑλληνιστάς   acc pl masc
   [2t; n-1f; 1821]   Ἑλληνιστής

Ἑλληνιστής, οῦ, ὁ   {1821, n-1f}
   pr. one who uses the language and follows the
   customs of the Greeks; in N.T. a Jew by blood, but a
   native of a Greek-speaking country, Hellenist, Acts
   6:1; 9:29; 11:20*

Ἑλληνιστί   {1822, adverb}
   in the Greek language, John 19:20; Acts 21:37*

Ἑλληνιστί   adverb [2t; adverb; 1822]   Ἑλληνιστί
Ἑλληνιστῶν   gen pl masc
   [Ac 6:1; n-1f; 1821]   Ἑλληνιστής
Ἕλληνος   gen sg masc [3t; n-3f(1a); 1818]   Ἕλλην
Ἑλλήνων   gen pl masc [3t; n-3f(1a); 1818]   "
Ἕλλησιν   dat pl masc [5t; n-3f(1a); 1818]   "
ἐλλόγα   pres act imperative 2 sg
   [Pm 18; cv-1d(2a); 1824]   ἐλλογέω

ἐλλογάω, see ἐλλογέω

ἐλλογεῖται   pres pass ind 3 sg
   [Rm 5:13; cv-; 1824]

ἐλλογέω   {1824, cv-1d(2a)}
   [-, -, -, -, -] to enter in an account, to put or charge
   to one's account, Phil 18; in N.T. to impute, Rom
   5:13*

Ἐλμαδάμ, ὁ   {1825, n-3g(2)}
   also spelled Ἐλμωδάμ, Elmadam, pr. name,
   indecl., Luke 3:28*

Ἐλμαδάμ   indecl
   [Lk 3:28; n-3g(2); 1825]   Ἐλμαδάμ

Ἐλμωδάμ, see Ἐλμαδάμ

ἐλογιζόμην   imperf mid ind 1 sg
   [1C 13:11; v-2a(1); 3357]   λογίζομαι
ἐλογίσθη   aor pass ind 3 sg [8t; v-2a(1); 3357]   "
ἐλογίσθημεν   aor pass ind 1 pl
   [Rm 8:36; v-2a(1); 3357]   "
ἐλοιδόρησαν   aor act ind 3 pl
   [Jn 9:28; v-1d(2a); 3366]   λοιδορέω
ἑλόμενος   aor mid ptcp nom sg masc
   [Hb 11:25; v-1d(2a); 145]   αἱρέω
ἔλουσεν   aor act ind 3 sg
   [Ac 16:33; v-1a(8); 3374]   λούω
ἐλπίδα   acc sg fem [18t; n-3c(2); 1828]   ἐλπίς
ἐλπίδι   dat sg fem [12t; n-3c(2); 1828]   "
ἐλπίδος   gen sg fem [13t; n-3c(2); 1828]   "

ἐλπίζει   pres act ind 3 sg
    [3t; v-2a(1); 1827]   ἐλπίζω
ἐλπίζετε   pres act ind 2 pl
    [Lk 6:34; v-2a(1); 1827]   "
ἐλπίζομεν   pres act ind 1 pl
    [Rm 8:25; v-2a(1); 1827]   "
ἐλπιζομένων   pres pass ptcp gen pl neut
    [Hb 11:1; v-2a(1); 1827]   "
ἐλπίζουσαι   pres act ptcp nom pl fem
    [1P 3:5; v-2a(1); 1827]   "

ἐλπίζω   {1827, v-2a(1)}
    [ἐλπιῶ, ἤλπισα, ἤλπικα, -, -] *to hope, expect,* Luke
    23:8; 24:21; *to repose hope and confidence in, trust,*
    confide, Matt 12:21; John 5:45

ἐλπίζω   pres act ind 1 sg   [10t; v-2a(1); 1827]   "
ἐλπίζων   pres act ptcp nom sg masc
    [2t; v-2a(1); 1827]   "
ἐλπιοῦσιν   fut act ind 3 pl   [2t; v-2a(1); 1827]   "

ἐλπίς, ίδος, ἡ   {1828, n-3c(2)}
    pr. *expectation; hope,* Acts 24:15; Rom 5:4;
    meton. *the object of hope, thing hoped for,* Rom
    8:24; Gal 5:5; *the author* or *source of hope,* Col
    1:27; 1 Tim 1:1; *trust, confidence,* 1 Peter 1:21; ἐπ᾽
    ἐλπίδι, *in security, with a guarantee,* Acts 2:26;
    Rom 8:20

ἐλπίς   nom sg fem   [10t; n-3c(2); 1828]   ἐλπίς
ἐλπίσατε   aor act imperative 2 pl
    [1P 1:13; v-2a(1); 1827]   ἐλπίζω
ἔλυεν   imperf act ind 3 sg
    [Jn 5:18; v-1a(4); 3395]   λύω
ἐλύετο   imperf pass ind 3 sg
    [Ac 27:41; v-1a(4); 3395]   "
ἐλύθη   aor pass ind 3 sg
    [Mk 7:35; v-1a(4); 3395]   "
ἐλύθησαν   aor pass ind 3 pl
    [Rv 9:15; v-1a(4); 3395]   "
ἐλυμαίνετο   imperf mid ind 3 sg
    [Ac 8:3; v-2d(4); 3381]   λυμαίνω

Ἐλύμας, ᾶ, ὁ   {1829, n-1e}
    Elymas, pr. name, Acts 13:8*

Ἐλύμας   nom sg masc [Ac 13:8; n-1e; 1829]   Ἐλύμας
ἐλυπήθη   aor pass ind 3 sg
    [Jn 21:17; v-1d(2a); 3382]   λυπέω
ἐλυπήθησαν   aor pass ind 3 pl
    [2t; v-1d(2a); 3382]   "
ἐλυπήθητε   aor pass ind 2 pl
    [3t; v-1d(2a); 3382]   "
ἐλύπησα   aor act ind 1 sg
    [2C 7:8; v-1d(2a); 3382]   "
ἐλύπησεν   aor act ind 3 sg
    [2C 7:8; v-1d(2a); 3382]   "
ἔλυσεν   aor act ind 3 sg
    [Ac 22:30; v-1a(4); 3395]   λύω
ἐλυτρώθητε   aor pass ind 2 pl
    [1P 1:18; v-1d(3); 3390]   λυτρόω

ἐλωΐ   {1830, n-3g(2)}
    Aramaic for, *my God,* Mark 15:34; Matt 27:46
    v.l.*

ἐλωι   indecl [2t; n-3g(2); 1830]
ἐμά   nom pl neut [6t; a-1a(2a); 1847]

ἐμά   acc pl neut   [3t; a-1a(2a); 1847]   "
ἔμαθεν   aor act ind 3 sg
    [Hb 5:8; v-3a(2b); 3443]   μανθάνω
ἔμαθες   aor act ind 2 sg   [2t; v-3a(2b); 3443]   "
ἐμάθετε   aor act ind 2 pl   [4t; v-3a(2b); 3443]   "
ἐμαθητεύθη   aor pass ind 3 sg
    [Mt 27:57; v-1a(6); 3411]   μαθητεύω
ἔμαθον   aor act ind 1 sg
    [Pp 4:11; v-3a(2b); 3443]   μανθάνω
ἐμαρτύρει   imperf act ind 3 sg
    [Jn 12:17; v-1d(2a); 3455]   μαρτυρέω
ἐμαρτυρεῖτο   imperf pass ind 3 sg
    [Ac 16:2; v-1d(2a); 3455]   "
ἐμαρτυρήθη   aor pass ind 3 sg
    [Hb 11:4; v-1d(2a); 3455]   "
ἐμαρτυρήθησαν   aor pass ind 3 pl
    [Hb 11:2; v-1d(2a); 3455]   "
ἐμαρτυρήσαμεν   aor act ind 1 pl
    [1C 15:15; v-1d(2a); 3455]   "
ἐμαρτύρησαν   aor act ind 3 pl
    [3J 6; v-1d(2a); 3455]   "
ἐμαρτύρησεν   aor act ind 3 sg
    [5t; v-1d(2a); 3455]   "
ἐμαρτύρουν   imperf act ind 3 pl
    [Lk 4:22; v-1d(2a); 3455]   "
ἐμάς   acc pl fem
    [Jn 14:15; a-1a(2a); 1847]   ἐμός
ἐμαστίγωσεν   aor act ind 3 sg
    [Jn 19:1; v-1d(3); 3463]   μαστιγόω
ἐμασῶντο   imperf mid ind 3 pl
    [Rv 16:10; v-1d(1a); 3460]   μασάομαι
ἐματαιώθησαν   aor pass ind 3 pl
    [Rm 1:21; v-1d(3); 3471]   ματαιόω
ἐμαυτόν   acc sg masc
    [18t; a-1a(2a); 1831]   ἐμαυτοῦ

ἐμαυτοῦ, ῆς, οῦ   {1831, a-1a(2a)}
    myself, my own, Luke 7:7; John 5:31

ἐμαυτοῦ   gen sg masc [14t; a-1a(2a); 1831]   "
ἐμαυτῷ   dat sg masc [5t; a-1a(2a); 1831]   "
ἐμάχοντο   imperf mid ind 3 pl
    [Jn 6:52; v-1b(2); 3481]   μάχομαι
ἐμβαίνοντος   pres act ptcp gen sg masc
    [Mk 5:18; cv-2d(6); 1832]   ἐμβαίνω

ἐμβαίνω   {1832, cv-2d(6)}
    [-, ἐνέβην -, -, -] *to step in; to go on board* a ship,
    embark, Matt 8:23; 9:1; 13:2

ἐμβαλεῖν   aor act inf
    [Lk 12:5; cv-2d(1); 1833]   ἐμβάλλω

ἐμβάλλω   {1833, cv-2d(1)}
    [-, ἐνέβαλον -, -, -] *to cast into,* Luke 12:5*

ἐμβάντα   aor act ptcp acc sg masc
    [2t; cv-2d(6); 1832]   ἐμβαίνω
ἐμβάντες   aor act ptcp nom pl masc
    [Jn 6:17; cv-2d(6); 1832]   "
ἐμβάντι   aor act ptcp dat sg masc
    [Mt 8:23; cv-2d(6); 1832]   "

ἐ· ·ίζω   {1834, cv-2a(1)}
    -, -, -, -] *dip (in[to]),* Mark 14:20 v.l.*

· ·νος   pres mid ptcp nom sg masc
    [Mk 14:20; cv-4; 1835]   ἐμβάπτω

ἐμβάπτω {1835, cv-4}
[-, ἐνέβαψα, -, -, -] *to dip in*, Matt 26:23; *to dip* for
food in a dish, Mark 14:20*

ἐμβάς aor act ptcp nom sg masc
[5t; cv-2d(6); 1832] ἐμβαίνω

ἐμβατεύω {1836, cv-1a(6)}
[-, -, -, -, -] pr. *to step into* or *upon*; met. *to search
into, investigate; to pry into intrusively*, Col 2:18*

ἐμβατεύων pres act ptcp nom sg masc
[Cl 2:18; cv-; 1836] ἐμβατεύω

ἐμβάψας aor act ptcp nom sg masc
[Mt 26:23; cv-4; 1835] ἐμβάπτω

ἐμβῆναι aor act inf
[2t; cv-2d(6); 1832] ἐμβαίνω

ἐμβιβάζω {1837, cv-2a(1)}
[-, ἐνεβίβασα, -, -, -] *to cause to step into* or *upon;
to set in* or *upon*; especially, *to put on board*, Acts
27:6*

ἐμβλέποντες pres act ptcp nom pl masc
[Ac 1:11; cv-1b(1); 1838] ἐμβλέπω

ἐμβλέπω {1838, cv-1b(1)}
[-, ἐνέβλεψα, -, -, -] *to look attentively, gaze
earnestly*, at an object, followed by εἰς, Mark
6:26; Acts 1:11; *to direct a glance, to look
searchingly* or *significantly*, at a person, followed
by the dat., Mark 10:21; 14:67; Luke 22:61;
absol. *to see clearly*, Mark 8:25; Acts 22:11

ἐμβλέψας aor act ptcp nom sg masc
[6t; cv-1b(1); 1838] "

ἐμβλέψασα aor act ptcp nom sg fem
[Mk 14:67; cv-1b(1); 1838] "

ἐμβλέψατε aor act imperative 2 pl
[Mt 6:26; cv-1b(1); 1838] "

ἐμβριμάομαι {1839, cv-1d(1a)}
[-, ἐνεβριμησάμην, -, -, ἐνεβριμήθην] Attic
spelling, ἐμβριμόομαι, *to be greatly agitated*, John
11:33, 38; *to charge* or *forbid sternly* or *vehemently*,
Matt 9:30; Mark 1:43; *to express indignation, to
censure*, Mark 14:5*

ἐμβριμησάμενος aor mid ptcp nom sg masc
[Mk 1:43; cv-1d(1a); 1839] ἐμβριμάομαι

ἐμβριμώμενος pres mid ptcp nom sg masc
[Jn 11:38; cv-1d(1a); 1839] "

ἐμέ acc sg [90t; a-5a; 1609] ἐγώ

ἐμεγάλυνεν imperf act ind 3 sg
[2t; v-1c(2); 3486] μεγαλύνω

ἐμεγαλύνετο imperf pass ind 3 sg
[Ac 19:17; v-1c(2); 3486] "

ἐμεθύσθησαν aor pass ind 3 pl
[Rv 17:2; v-5a; 3499] μεθύσκω

ἐμείναμεν aor act ind 1 pl
[2t; v-1c(2); 3531] μένω

ἔμειναν aor act ind 3 pl [2t; v-1c(2); 3531] "

ἔμεινεν aor act ind 3 sg [10t; v-1c(2); 3531] "

ἔμελεν imperf act ind 3 sg
[2t; v-1d(2c); 3508] μέλει

ἐμελέτησαν aor act ind 3 pl
[Ac 4:25; v-1d(1a); 3509] μελετάω

ἔμελλεν imperf act ind 3 sg
[3t; v-1d(2c); 3516] μέλλω

ἔμελλον imperf act ind 3 pl [3t; v-1d(2c); 3516] "

ἔμενεν imperf act ind 3 sg
[3t; v-1c(2); 3531] μένω

ἔμενον imperf act ind 3 pl
[Ac 20:5; v-1c(2); 3531] "

ἐμέρισεν aor act ind 3 sg
[5t; v-2a(1); 3532] μερίζω

ἐμερίσθη aor pass ind 3 sg [2t; v-2a(1); 3532] "

ἐμέσαι aor act inf
[Rv 3:16; v-1d(2b); 1840] ἐμέω

ἐμεσίτευσεν aor act ind 3 sg
[Hb 6:17; v-1a(6); 3541] μεσιτεύω

ἐμέτρησεν aor act ind 3 sg
[2t; v-1d(2a); 3582] μετρέω

ἐμέω {1840, v-1d(2b)}
[-, ἤμεσα, -, -, -] *to vomit*, Rev 3:16*

ἐμῇ nom sg fem [12t; a-1a(2a); 1847] ἐμός

ἐμῇ dat sg fem [6t; a-1a(2a); 1847] "

ἐμήν acc sg fem [13t; a-1a(2a); 1847] "

ἐμήνυσεν aor act ind 3 sg
[Lk 20:37; v-1a(4); 3606] μηνύω

ἐμῆς gen sg fem [2t; a-1a(2a); 1847] ἐμός

ἔμιξεν aor act ind 3 sg
[Lk 13:1; v-3c(2); 3624] μίγνυμι

ἐμίσησα aor act ind 1 sg
[Rm 9:13; v-1d(2a); 3631] μισέω

ἐμίσησαν aor act ind 3 pl
[Jn 15:25; v-1d(2a); 3631] "

ἐμίσησας aor act ind 2 sg
[Hb 1:9; v-1d(2a); 3631] "

ἐμίσησεν aor act ind 3 sg [2t; v-1d(2a); 3631] "

ἐμισθώσατο aor mid ind 3 sg
[Mt 20:7; v-1d(3); 3636] μισθόω

ἐμίσουν imperf act ind 3 pl
[Lk 19:14; v-1d(2a); 3631] μισέω

ἐμμαίνομαι {1841, cv-2d(4)}
[-, -, -, -, -] *to be mad against, be furious toward*,
Acts 26:11*

ἐμμαινόμενος pres mid ptcp nom sg masc
[Ac 26:11; cv-2d(4); 1841] ἐμμαίνομαι

Ἐμμανουήλ, ὁ {1842, n-3g(2)}
Emmanuel, pr. name, indecl., Matt 1:23*

Ἐμμανουήλ indecl
[Mt 1:23; n-3g(2); 1842] Ἐμμανουήλ

Ἐμμαοῦς, οῦ, ἡ {1843, n-2d(1)}
Emmaus, pr. name, indecl., of a village near
Jerusalem, Luke 24:13*

Ἐμμαοῦς nom sg fem
[Lk 24:13; n-2d(1); 1843] Ἐμμαοῦς

ἐμμένει pres act ind 3 sg
[Ga 3:10; cv-1c(2); 1844] ἐμμένω

ἐμμένειν pres act inf
[Ac 14:22; cv-1c(2); 1844] "

ἐμμένω {1844, cv-1c(2)}
[-, ἐνέμεινα, -, -, -] pr. *to remain in* a place; met.
to abide by, to continue firm in, persevere in, Acts
14:22; 28:30; Gal 3:10; Heb 8:9*

Ἐμμώρ, ὁ {1846, n-3g(2)}
also spelled Ἐμμόρ, *Hamor*, pr. name, indecl.,
Acts 7:16

Ἐμμώρ indecl [Ac 7:16; n-3g(2); 1846] Ἐμμώρ
ἐμνημόνευον imperf act ind 3 pl
[Hb 11:15; v-1a(6); 3648] μνημονεύω
ἐμνημόνευσεν aor act ind 3 sg
[2t; v-1a(6); 3648] "
ἐμνήσθη aor pass ind 3 sg
[2t; v-5a; 3630] μιμνήσκομαι
ἐμνήσθημεν aor pass ind 1 pl
[Mt 27:63; v-5a; 3630] "
ἐμνήσθην aor pass ind 1 sg
[Ac 11:16; v-5a; 3630] "
ἐμνήσθησαν aor pass ind 3 pl [5t; v-5a; 3630] "
ἐμνηστευμένη perf pass ptcp dat sg fem
[Lk 2:5; v-1a(6); 3650] μνηστεύω
ἐμνηστευμένη perf pass ptcp acc sg fem
[Lk 1:27; v-1a(6); 3650] "
ἐμοί nom pl masc
[2t; a-1a(2a); 1847] ἐμός
ἐμοί dat sg [93t; a-5a; 1609] ἐγώ
ἐμοῖς dat pl neut [2t; a-1a(2a); 1847] ἐμός
ἐμοίχευσεν aor act ind 3 sg
[Mt 5:28; v-1a(6); 3658] μοιχεύω
ἐμόλυναν aor act ind 3 pl
[Rv 3:4; v-1c(2); 3662] μολύνω
ἐμολύνθησαν aor pass ind 3 pl
[Rv 14:4; v-1c(2); 3662] "
ἐμόν nom sg neut [3t; a-1a(2a); 1847] ἐμός
ἐμόν acc sg masc [2t; a-1a(2a); 1847] "
ἐμόν acc sg neut [6t; a-1a(2a); 1847] "

ἐμός, ή, όν {1847, a-1a(2a)}
my, mine, John 7:16; 8:37

ἐμός nom sg masc [6t; a-1a(2a); 1847] "
ἐμοσχοποίησαν aor act ind 3 pl
[Ac 7:41; cv-1d(2a); 3674] μοσχοποιέω
ἐμοῦ gen sg [108t; a-5a; 1609] ἐγώ
ἐμοῦ gen sg neut [5t; a-1a(2a); 1847] ἐμός
ἐμούς acc pl masc [3t; a-1a(2a); 1847] "

ἐμπαιγμονή, ῆς, ἡ {1848, n-1b}
mocking, scoffing, derision, 2 Peter 3:3*

ἐμπαιγμονῇ dat sg fem
[2P 3:3; n-1b; 1848] ἐμπαιγμονή

ἐμπαιγμός, οῦ, ὁ {1849, n-2a}
mocking, scoffing, scorn, Heb 11:36*

ἐμπαιγμῶν gen pl masc
[Hb 11:36; n-2a; 1849] ἐμπαιγμός
ἐμπαίζειν pres act inf
[Lk 14:29; cv-2a(2); 1850] ἐμπαίζω
ἐμπαίζοντες pres act ptcp nom pl masc
[2t; cv-2a(2); 1850] "

ἐμπαίζω {1850, cv-2a(2)}
[ἐμπαίξω, ἐνέπαιξα, -, -, ἐνεπαίχθην] *to play
upon, deride, mock, treat with scorn, ridicule,* Matt
20:19; 27:29; by impl. *to delude, deceive,* Matt
2:16

ἐμπαῖκται nom pl masc
[2t; n-1f; 1851] ἐμπαίκτης

ἐμπαίκτης, ου, ὁ {1851, n-1f}
a mocker, derider, scoffer, 2 Peter 3:3; Jude 18*

ἐμπαῖξαι aor act inf
[Mt 20:19; cv-2a(2); 1850] ἐμπαίζω
ἐμπαίξας aor act ptcp nom sg masc
[Lk 23:11; cv-2a(2); 1850] "
ἐμπαίξουσιν fut act ind 3 pl
[Mk 10:34; cv-2a(2); 1850] "
ἐμπαιχθήσεται fut pass ind 3 sg
[Lk 18:32; cv-2a(2); 1850] "

ἐμπέμπω {1852, cv-1b(1)}
[-, -, -, -, -] *send (in)*, Luke 19:14 v.l.*

ἐμπεπλησμένοι perf pass ptcp voc pl masc
[Lk 6:25; cv-6a; 1858] ἐμπίπλημι

ἐμπεριπατέω {1853, cv-1d(2a)}
[ἐμπεριπατήσω, -, -, -, -] pr. *to walk about in* a
place; met. in N.T. *to live among, be conversant
with,* 2 Cor 6:16*

ἐμπεριπατήσω fut act ind 1 sg
[2C 6:16; cv-1d(2a); 1853] ἐμπεριπατέω
ἐμπεσεῖν aor act inf
[Hb 10:31; cv-1b(3); 1860] ἐμπίπτω
ἐμπέσῃ aor act subj 3 sg [3t; cv-1b(3); 1860] "
ἐμπεσόντος aor act ptcp gen sg masc
[Lk 10:36; cv-1b(3); 1860] "
ἐμπεσοῦνται fut mid ind 3 pl
[Lk 6:39; cv-1b(3); 1860] "

ἐμπιμπλάω, see ἐμπίμπλημι {1854, cv-1d(1a)}

ἐμπίμπλημι {1855, cv-6a}
[(ἐνεπίμπλατο 3 sg pass), -, ἐνέπλησα, -,
ἐμπέπλησμαι, ἐνεπλήσθην] also spelled
ἐμπίπλημι and ἐμπιμπλάω, *to fill,* Acts 14:17;
pass. *to be satisfied, satiated, full,* Luke 1:53; 6:25;
John 6:12; met. *to have the full enjoyment of,* Rom
15:24*

ἐμπίμπρημι {1856, cv-6a}
[-, ἐνέπρησα, -, -, -] also spelled ἐμπίπρημι and
ἐμπρήθω, *to set on fire, burn down,* Matt 22:7; Acts
28:6 v.l.*

ἐμπιπλῶν pres act ptcp nom sg masc
[Ac 14:17; cv-6a; 1858] ἐμπίπλημι
ἐμπίπτουσιν pres act ind 3 pl
[1Ti 6:9; cv-1b(3); 1860] ἐμπίπτω

ἐμπίπτω {1860, cv-1b(3)}
[ἐμπεσοῦμαι, ἐνέπεσον, -, -, -] *to fall into,* Matt
12:11; Luke 14:5; *to encounter,* Luke 10:36; *to be
involved in,* 1 Tim 3:6, 7; 6:9; εἰς χεῖρας, *to fall
under the chastisement of,* Heb 10:31

ἐμπλακέντες aor pass ptcp nom pl masc
[2P 2:20; cv-1b(2); 1861] ἐμπλέκω
ἐμπλέκεται pres pass ind 3 sg
[2Ti 2:4; cv-1b(2); 1861] "

ἐμπλέκω {1861, cv-1b(2)}
[-, -, -, ἐμπέπλεγμαι, ἐνεπλάκην] pr. *to intertwine;*
met. *to implicate, entangle, involve;* pass. *to be
implicated, involved,* or *to entangle one's self in,* 2
Tim 2:4; 2 Peter 2:20*

ἐμπλησθῶ   aor pass subj 1 sg
[Rm 15:24; cv-6a; 1858]   ἐμπίπλημι

ἐμπλοκή, ῆς, ἡ   {1862, n-1b}
braiding or *plaiting* of hair, 1 Peter 3:3*

ἐμπλοκῆς   gen sg fem
[1P 3:3; n-1b; 1862]   ἐμπλοκή

ἐμπνέω   {1863, cv-1a(7)}
[-, -, -, -, -] gen., *to breathe into* or *upon; to respire,
breathe;* met. *to breathe of, be animated with the
spirit of,* Acts 9:1*

ἐμπνέων   pres act ptcp nom sg masc
[Ac 9:1; cv-1a(7); 1863]   ἐμπνέω

ἐμπορεύομαι   {1864, cv-1a(6)}
[ἐμπορεύσομαι, -, -, -, -] *to travel; to travel for
business' sake; to trade, traffic,* James 4:13; by
impl., trans., *to make a gain of, deceive for one's
own advantage,* 2 Peter 2:3*

ἐμπορευσόμεθα   fut mid ind 1 pl
[Jm 4:13; cv-1a(6); 1864]   ἐμπορεύομαι
ἐμπορεύσονται   fut mid ind 3 pl
[2P 2:3; cv-1a(6); 1864]   "

ἐμπορία, ας, ἡ   {1865, n-1a}
business, trade, Matt 22:5*

ἐμπορίαν   acc sg fem
[Mt 22:5; n-1a; 1865]   ἐμπορία

ἐμπόριον, ου, τό   {1866, n-2c}
a mart, marketplace, emporium; met. *traffic,* John
2:16*

ἐμπορίου   gen sg neut
[Jn 2:16; n-2c; 1866]   ἐμπόριον
ἔμποροι   nom pl masc [4t; n-2a; 1867]   ἔμπορος

ἔμπορος, ου, ὁ   {1867, n-2a}
pr. *a passenger by sea; a traveller; one who travels
about for traffic, a merchant,* Matt 13:45; Rev 18:3,
11, 15, 23*

ἐμπόρῳ   dat sg masc [Mt 13:45; n-2a; 1867]   "

ἐμπρήθω, see ἐμπίμπρημι   {1868, cv-1b(3)}

ἔμπροσθεν   {1869, adverb}
also an improper prep., *before, in front of,* Luke
19:4; Phil 3:14; *before, in the presence of, in the face
of,* Matt 5:24; 23:14; *before, previous to,* John 1:15,
27, 30; from the Hebrew, *in the sight* or
estimation of, Matt 11:26; 18:14

ἔμπροσθεν   adverb, [48t; adverb; 1869]   ἔμπροσθεν
ἐμπτύειν   pres act inf
[Mk 14:65; cv-1a(4); 1870]   ἐμπτύω
ἐμπτύσαντες   aor act ptcp nom pl masc
[Mt 27:30; cv-1a(4); 1870]   "
ἐμπτυσθήσεται   fut pass ind 3 sg
[Lk 18:32; cv-1a(4); 1870]   "
ἐμπτύσουσιν   fut act ind 3 pl
[Mk 10:34; cv-1a(4); 1870]   "

ἐμπτύω   {1870, cv-1a(4)}
[ἐμπτύσω, ἐνέπτυσα, -, -, ἐνεπτύσθην] followed
by the dat., or εἰς and the acc., *to spit upon,* Matt
26:67; 27:30

ἐμφανῆ   acc sg masc
[Ac 10:40; a-4a; 1871]   ἐμφανής

ἐμφανής, ές   {1871, a-4a}
apparent, conspicuous, obvious to the sight, Acts
10:40; met. *manifest, known, comprehended,* Rom
10:20*

ἐμφανής   nom sg masc [Rm 10:20; a-4a; 1871]   "
ἐμφανίζειν   pres act inf
[Jn 14:22; cv-2a(1); 1872]   ἐμφανίζω
ἐμφανίζουσιν   pres act ind 3 pl
[Hb 11:14; cv-2a(1); 1872]   "

ἐμφανίζω   {1872, cv-2a(1)}
[ἐμφανίσω, ἐνεφάνισα, -, -, ἐνεφανίσθην] *to cause
to appear clearly; to communicate, report,* Acts
23:15, 22; *to bring charges against,* Acts 24:1; 25:2,
15, *to manifest, intimate plainly,* Heb 11:14; *to
reveal, make known,* John 14:21, 22; pass. *to
appear, be visible,* Matt 27:53; *to present one's self,*
Heb 9:24*

ἐμφανίσατε   aor act imperative 2 pl
[Ac 23:15; cv-2a(1); 1872]   "
ἐμφανισθῆναι   aor pass inf
[Hb 9:24; cv-2a(1); 1872]   "
ἐμφανίσω   fut act ind 1 sg
[Jn 14:21; cv-2a(1); 1872]   "
ἔμφοβοι   nom pl masc [2t; a-3a; 1873]   ἔμφοβος

ἔμφοβος, ον   {1873, a-3a}
terrible; in N.T. *terrified,* Luke 24:5, 37; Acts 10:4;
24:25; Rev 11:13*

ἔμφοβος   nom sg masc [2t; a-3a; 1873]   "
ἐμφόβων   gen pl fem [Lk 24:5; a-3a; 1873]   "

ἐμφυσάω   {1874, cv-1d(1a)}
[-, ἐνεφύσησα, -, -, -] *to blow* or *breathe into,
inflate;* in N.T. *to breathe upon,* John 20:22*

ἔμφυτον   acc sg masc [Jm 1:21; a-3a; 1875]   ἔμφυτος

ἔμφυτος, ον   {1875, a-3a}
implanted, ingrafted, infixed, James 1:21*

ἐμῷ   dat sg masc
[Jn 8:31; a-1a(2a); 1847]   ἐμός
ἐμῷ   dat sg neut [2t; a-1a(2a); 1847]   "
ἐμῶν   gen pl neut [Jn 10:26; a-1a(2a); 1847]   "
ἐμώρανεν   aor act ind 3 sg
[1C 1:20; v-2d(4); 3701]   μωραίνω
ἐμωράνθησαν   aor pass ind 3 pl
[Rm 1:22; v-2d(4); 3701]   "

ἐν   {1877, prep}
followed by the dat., *in,* Matt 8:6; Mark 12:26;
Rev 6:6,; *upon,* Luke 8:32; *among,* Matt 11:11;
before, in the presence of, Mark 8:38; *in the sight,
estimation of,* 1 Cor 14:11; *before, judicially,* 1 Cor
6:2; *in,* of state, occupation, habit, Matt 21:22;
Luke 7:25; Rom 4:10; *in the case of,* Matt 17:12; *in
respect of,* Luke 1:7; 1 Cor 1:7; *on occasion of, on
the ground of,* Matt 6:7; Luke 1:21; used of the
thing by which an oath is made, Matt 5:34; *of
the instrument, means, efficient cause,* Rom
12:21; Acts 4:12; *equipped with, furnished with,* 1
Cor 4:21; Heb 9:25; *arrayed with, accompanied by,*
Luke 14:31; Jude 14; *of time, during, in the course*

of, Matt 2:1; in N.T. of demoniacal possession, *possessed by*, Mark 5:2

ἐν   prep-dat [2752t; prep; 1877]   ἐν
ἕν   nom sg neut [45t; a-4b(2); 1651]   εἷς
ἕν   acc sg neut [26t; a-4b(2); 1651]   "
ἕνα acc sg masc [42t; a-4b(2); 1651]   εἷς

ἐναγκαλίζομαι   {1878, cv-2a(1)}
   [-, ἐνηγκαλίμην, -, -, -] *to take into* or *embrace in one's arms*, Mark 9:36; 10:16*

ἐναγκαλισάμενος   aor mid ptcp nom sg masc
   [2t; cv-2a(1); 1878]   ἐναγκαλίζομαι

ἐνάλιος, ον   {1879, a-3a}
   marine, living in the sea, James 3:7*

ἐναλίων   gen pl neut
   [Jm 3:7; a-3a; 1879]   ἐνάλιος

ἐνάλλομαι   {1880, cv-2d(1)}
   [-, -, -, -, -] *leap upon*, Acts 19:16 v.l.*

ἐνανθρωπέω   {1881, cv-1d(2a)}
   [-, -, -, -, -] *take on human form*, 1 John 4:17 v.l.*

ἔναντι   {1882, prep}
   also an improper prep, *over against, in the presence of*, Luke 1:8; Acts 8:21; 7:10 v.l.*

ἔναντι   prep-gen [2t; prep; 1882]   ἔναντι
ἐναντία   acc pl neut
   [Ac 26:9; a-1a(1); 1885]   ἐναντίος
ἐναντίας   gen sg fem [2t; a-1a(1); 1885]   "

ἐναντίον   {1883, prep}
   acc sg neut of ἐναντίος used adverbially; the adj. does not appear in the N.T., improper prep., *before, in the presence of*, Mark 2:12 v.l.; Luke 1:6; 20:26; Acts 8:32; 2 Cor 2:7; Gal 2:7; 1 Peter 3:9; from the Hebrew, *in the sight* or *estimation of*, Acts 7:10; with τοῦ θεοῦ, an intensive expression, Luke 24:19*

ἐναντίον   prep-gen [6t; prep; 1883]   ἐναντίον

ἐναντιόομαι   {1884, cv-1d(3)}
   [-, -, -, -, -] dat., *oppose (oneself)*, Acts 13:45 v.l.*

ἐναντίος, α, ον   {1885, a-1a(1)}
   opposite to, over against, Mark 15:39; *contrary*, as the wind, Matt 14:24; Acts 26:9; 28:17; ὁ ἐξ ἐναντίας, *an adverse party, enemy*, Titus 2:8; *adverse, hostile, counter*, 1 Thess 2:15

ἐναντίος   nom sg masc
   [2t; a-1a(1); 1885]   ἐναντίος
ἐναντίους   acc pl masc [Ac 27:4; a-1a(1); 1885]   "
ἐναντίων   gen pl masc [1Th 2:15; a-1a(1); 1885]   "

ἐναργής, ές   {1886, a-4a}
   clear, evident, Heb 4:12 v.l.*

ἐναρξάμενοι   aor mid ptcp nom pl masc
   [Ga 3:3; cv-1b(2); 1887]   ἐνάρχομαι
ἐναρξάμενος   aor mid ptcp nom sg masc
   [Pp 1:6; cv-1b(2); 1887]   "

ἐνάρχομαι   {1887, cv-1b(2)}
   [-, ἐνηρξάμην, -, -, -] *to begin, commence*, Gal 3:3; Phil 1:6*

ἐνάτη   dat sg fem
   [Mk 15:34; a-1a(2a); 1888]   ἔνατος
ἐνάτην   acc sg fem [5t; a-1a(2a); 1888]   "
ἐνάτης   gen sg fem [3t; a-1a(2a); 1888]   "

ἔνατος, η, ον   {1888, a-1a(2a)}
   the ninth, Matt 20:5; 27:45f.; Mark 15:33f.; Luke 23:44; Acts 3:1; 10:3, 30; Rev 21:20*

ἔνατος   nom sg masc [Rv 21:20; a-1a(2a); 1888]   "
ἐναυάγησα   aor act ind 1 sg
   [2C 11:25; v-1d(2a); 3728]   ναυαγέω
ἐναυάγησαν   aor act ind 3 pl
   [1Ti 1:19; v-1d(2a); 3728]   "

ἐναφίημι   {1889, cv-6a}
   [-, -, -, -, -] *let, permit*, Mark 7:12 v.l.*

ἐνδεδυμένοι   perf pass ptcp nom pl masc
   [2t; cv-; 1907]   ἐνδύω
ἐνδεδυμένον   perf mid ptcp acc sg masc
   [Mt 22:11; cv-; 1907]   "
ἐνδεδυμένος   perf pass ptcp acc sg masc
   [Rv 1:13; cv-; 1907]   "
ἐνδεδυμένος   perf pass ptcp nom sg masc
   [Mk 1:6; cv-; 1907]   "

ἐνδεής, ές   {1890, a-4a}
   indigent, poor, needy, Acts 4:34*

ἐνδεής   nom sg masc [Ac 4:34; a-4a; 1890]   ἐνδεής

ἔνδειγμα, ατος, τό   {1891, n-3c(4)}
   a token, evidence, proof, 2 Thess 1:5*

ἔνδειγμα   nom sg neut
   [2Th 1:5; n-3c(4); 1891]   ἔνδειγμα
ἐνδεικνύμενοι   pres mid ptcp nom pl masc
   [2C 8:24; cv-3c(2); 1892]   ἐνδείκνυμι
ἐνδεικνυμένους   pres mid ptcp acc pl masc
   [2t; cv-3c(2); 1892]   "

ἐνδείκνυμι   {1892, cv-3c(2)}
   [-, ἐνέδειξα, -, -, -] *to manifest, display*, Rom 9:17, 22; Heb 6:10; *to give outward proof of*, Rom 2:15; *to display* a certain bearing towards a person; hence, *to perpetrate openly*, 2 Tim 4:14*

ἐνδείκνυνται   pres mid ind 3 pl
   [Rm 2:15; cv-3c(2); 1892]   "
ἐνδείκνυσθαι   pres mid inf
   [Hb 6:11; cv-3c(2); 1892]   "
ἐνδείξασθαι   aor mid inf
   [Rm 9:22; cv-3c(2); 1892]   "
ἐνδείξηται   aor mid subj 3 sg
   [2t; cv-3c(2); 1892]   "
ἔνδειξιν   acc sg fem [3t; n-3e(5b); 1893]   ἔνδειξις

ἔνδειξις, εως, ἡ   {1893, n-3e(5b)}
   a pointing out; met. *manifestation, public declaration*, Rom 3:25, 26; *a token, sign, proof*, i.q. ἔνδειγμα, 2 Cor 8:24; Phil 1:28*

ἔνδειξις   nom sg fem [Pp 1:28; n-3e(5b); 1893]   "
ἐνδείξωμαι   aor mid subj 1 sg
   [Rm 9:17; cv-3c(2); 1892]   ἐνδείκνυμι

ἔνδεκα   {1894, a-5b}
   eleven, indecl. numeral, Matt 28:16; Mark 16:14; Luke 24:9, 33; Acts 1:26; 2:14*

ἔνδεκα   indecl [6t; a-5b; 1894]   ἔνδεκα

ἐνδεκάτην   acc sg fem
   [2t; a-1a(2a); 1895]   ἐνδέκατος

ἐνδέκατος, η, ον   {1895, a-1a(2a)}
  eleventh, Matt 20:6, 9; Rev 21:20*

ἐνδέκατος   nom sg masc
   [Rv 21:20; a-1a(2a); 1895]   "

ἐνδέχεται   pres mid ind 3 sg
   [Lk 13:33; cv-1b(2); 1896]   ἐνδέχομαι

ἐνδέχομαι   {1896, cv-1b(2)}
  [-, -, -, -, -] *to admit, approve; to be possible,*
  impersonal, *it is possible,* Luke 13:33*

ἐνδημέω   {1897, cv-1d(2)}
  [-, ἐνεδήμησα, -, -, -] *to dwell in* a place, *be at
  home,* 2 Cor 5:6, 8, 9*

ἐνδημῆσαι   aor act inf
   [2C 5:8; cv-1d(2); 1897]   ἐνδημέω

ἐνδημοῦντες   pres act ptcp nom pl masc
   [2t; cv-1d(2); 1897]   "

ἐνδιδύσκουσιν   pres act ind 3 pl
   [Mk 15:17; cv-; 1898]   ἐνδιδύσκω

ἐνδιδύσκω   {1898}
  [(ἐνεδίδυσκον), -, -, -, -, -] a later form,
  equivalent to ἐνδύω, *to dress (oneself),* Mark
  15:17; Luke 8:27 v.l.; 16:19*

ἔνδικον   nom sg neut [Rm 3:8; a-3a; 1899]   ἔνδικος
ἔνδικον   acc sg fem [Hb 2:2; a-3a; 1899]   "

ἔνδικος, ον   {1899, a-3a}
  fair, just, Rom 3:8; Heb 2:2*

ἐνδόμησις, εως, ἡ   {1900, n-3e(5b)}
  pr. *a thing built in;* in N.T. *a building, structure,*
  Rev 21:18 v.l. for ἐνδώμησις*

ἐνδοξάζομαι   {1901, cv-2a(1)}
  [-, -, -, -, ἐνεδοξάσθην] *to invest with glory;* pass.
  to be glorified, to be made a subject of glorification,
  2 Thess 1:10, 12*

ἐνδοξασθῇ   aor pass subj 3 sg
   [2Th 1:12; cv-2a(1); 1901]   ἐνδοξάζομαι
ἐνδοξασθῆναι   aor pass inf
   [2Th 1:10; cv-2a(1); 1901]   "

ἔνδοξοι   nom pl masc [1C 4:10; a-3a; 1902]   ἔνδοξος
ἐνδόξοις   dat pl neut [Lk 13:17; a-3a; 1902]   "
ἔνδοξον   acc sg fem [Ep 5:27; a-3a; 1902]   "

ἔνδοξος, ον   {1902, a-3a}
  honored, 1 Cor 4:10; *notable, memorable,* Luke
  13:17; *splendid, gorgeous,* Luke 7:25; *in unsullied
  array,* Eph 5:27*

ἐνδόξῳ   dat sg masc [Lk 7:25; a-3a; 1902]   "

ἔνδυμα, ατος, τό   {1903, n-3c(4)}
  clothing, a garment, Matt 6:25, 28; 22:11, 12; in
  particular, *an outer garment, cloak, mantle,* Matt
  3:4; 7:15; 28:3; Luke 12:23*

ἔνδυμα   nom sg neut
   [Mt 28:3; n-3c(4); 1903]   ἔνδυμα
ἔνδυμα   acc sg neut [3t; n-3c(4); 1903]   "
ἐνδύμασιν   dat pl neut [Mt 7:15; n-3c(4); 1903]   "
ἐνδύματος   gen sg neut [3t; n-3c(4); 1903]   "

ἐνδυναμοῦ   pres pass imperative 2 sg
   [2Ti 2:1; cv-1d(3); 1904]   ἐνδυναμόω
ἐνδυναμοῦντι   pres act ptcp dat sg masc
   [Pp 4:13; cv-1d(3); 1904]
ἐνδυναμοῦσθε   pres pass imperative 2 pl
   [Ep 6:10; cv-1d(3); 1904]   "

ἐνδυναμόω   {1904, cv-1d(3)}
  [-, ἐνεδυνάμωσα, -, ἐνδεδυνάμωμαι,
  ἐνεδυναμώθην] *to empower, invigorate,* Phil 4:13;
  1 Tim 1:12; 2 Tim 4:17; mid. *to summon up vigor,
  put forth energy,* Eph 6:10; 2 Tim 2:1; pass. *to
  acquire strength, be invigorated, be strong,* Acts
  9:22; Rom 4:20*

ἐνδυναμώσαντι   aor act ptcp dat sg masc
   [1Ti 1:12; cv-1d(3); 1904]   "
ἐνδύνοντες   pres act ptcp nom pl masc
   [2Ti 3:6; cv-3a(1); 1905]   ἐνδύνω

ἐνδύνω   {1905, cv-3a(1)}
  [-, -, -, -, -] *enter, creep in,* 2 Tim 3:6*

ἐνδυσάμενοι   aor mid ptcp nom pl masc
   [3t; cv-; 1907]   ἐνδύω
ἐνδυσάμενος   aor mid ptcp nom sg masc
   [Ac 12:21; cv-; 1907]   "
ἐνδύσασθαι   aor mid inf   [3t; cv-; 1907]   "
ἐνδύσασθε   aor mid imperative 2 pl
   [3t; cv-; 1907]
ἐνδύσατε   aor act imperative 2 pl
   [Lk 15:22; cv-; 1907]   "
ἐνδύσεως   gen sg fem
   [1P 3:3; n-3e(5b); 1906]   ἔνδυσις
ἐνδύσησθε   aor mid subj 2 pl
   [4t; cv-; 1907]   ἐνδύω
ἐνδύσηται   aor mid subj 3 sg [2t; cv-; 1907]   "

ἔνδυσις, εως, ἡ   {1906, n-3e(5b)}
  a putting on, or *wearing* of clothes, 1 Peter 3:3*

ἐνδυσώμεθα   aor mid subj 1 pl
   [Rm 13:12; cv-; 1907]   "

ἐνδύω   {1907, cv-1a(4)}
  [-, ἐνέδυσα, -, ἐνδέδυμαι, -] *to enter,* 2 Tim 3:6; *to
  put on, clothe, invest, array,* Matt 27:31; Mark
  15:17, 20; mid. *clothe one's self, be clothed,* Matt
  22:11, 27, 31; trop. *to be clothed* with spiritual
  gifts, graces, or character, Luke 24:49; Rom
  13:14

ἐνδώμησις, εως, ἡ   {1908, n-3e(5b)}
  construction, material, Rev 21:18*

ἐνδώμησις   nom sg fem
   [Rv 21:18; n-3e(5b); 1908]   ἐνδώμησις
ἐνέβη   aor act ind 3 sg
   [2t; cv-2d(6); 1832]   ἐμβαίνω
ἐνέβησαν   aor act ind 3 pl [2t; cv-2d(6); 1832]   "
ἐνεβίβασεν   aor act ind 3 sg
   [Ac 27:6; cv-2a(1); 1837]   ἐμβιβάζω
ἐνέβλεπεν   imperf act ind 3 sg
   [Mk 8:25; cv-1b(1); 1838]   ἐμβλέπω
ἐνέβλεπον   imperf act ind 1 sg
   [Ac 22:11; cv-1b(1); 1838]   "
ἐνέβλεψεν   aor act ind 3 sg
   [Lk 22:61; cv-1b(1); 1838]   "

ἐνεβριμήθη   aor pass ind 3 sg
 [Mt 9:30; cv-1d(1a); 1839]   ἐμβριμάομαι
ἐνεβριμήσατο   aor mid ind 3 sg
 [Jn 11:33; cv-1d(1a); 1839]   "
ἐνεβριμῶντο   imperf mid ind 3 pl
 [Mk 14:5; cv-1d(1a); 1839]   "
ἐνέγκαι   aor act inf
 [Mk 6:27; v-1c(1); 5770]   φέρω
ἐνέγκας   aor act ptcp nom sg masc
 [2t; v-1c(1); 5770]   "
ἐνέγκατε   aor act imperative 2 pl
 [Jn 21:10; v-1c(1); 5770]   "
ἐνεδείξασθε   aor mid ind 2 pl
 [Hb 6:10; cv-3c(2); 1892]   ἐνδείκνυμι
ἐνεδείξατο   aor mid ind 3 sg
 [2Ti 4:14; cv-3c(2); 1892]   "
ἐνεδιδύσκετο   imperf mid ind 3 sg
 [Lk 16:19; cv-; 1898]   ἐνδιδύσκω

ἐνέδρα, ας, ἡ   {1909, n-1a}
  pr. *a sitting in* or *on a* spot; *an ambush,* or *lying in
  wait,* Acts 23:16; 25:3*

ἐνέδραν   acc sg fem [2t; n-1a; 1909]   ἐνέδρα
ἐνεδρεύοντες   pres act ptcp nom pl masc
 [Lk 11:54; cv-; 1910]   ἐνεδρεύω
ἐνεδρεύουσιν   pres act ind 3 pl
 [Ac 23:21; cv-; 1910]   "

ἐνεδρεύω   {1910, cv-1a(6)}
  [-, -, -, -, -] *to lie in wait* or *ambush for,* Acts 23:21;
  to endeavor to entrap, Luke 11:54*

ἔνεδρον, ου, τό   {1911, n-2c}
  ambush, v.l. for ἐνέδρα at Acts 23:16*

ἐνεδυναμοῦτο   imperf pass ind 3 sg
 [Ac 9:22; cv-1d(3); 1904]   ἐνδυναμόω
ἐνεδυναμώθη   aor pass ind 3 sg
 [Rm 4:20; cv-1d(3); 1904]   "
ἐνεδυνάμωσεν   aor act ind 3 sg
 [2Ti 4:17; cv-1d(3); 1904]   "
ἐνέδυσαν   aor act ind 3 pl [2t; cv-; 1907]   ἐνδύω
ἐνεδύσασθε   aor mid ind 2 pl
 [Ga 3:27; cv-; 1907]   "
ἐνεδύσατο   aor mid ind 3 sg [Lk 8:27; cv-; 1907]   "

ἐνειλέω   {1912, cv-1d(2a)}
  [-, ἐνείλησα, -, -, -] *to envelope,* Mark 15:46*

ἐνείλησεν   aor act ind 3 sg
 [Mk 15:46; cv-1d(2a); 1912]   ἐνειλέω

ἔνειμι   {1913, cv-6b}
  [-, -, -, -, -] *to be in* or *within;* τὰ ἐνόντα, *those
  things which are within,* Luke 11:41*

ἐνεῖχεν   imperf act ind 3 sg
 [Mk 6:19; cv-1b(2); 1923]   ἐνέχω

ἕνεκα   {1914, prep}
  some list ἕνεκα as an improper prep., although
  BAGD does not; also spelled ἕνεκεν, with the
  genitive, *on account of, for the sake of, by reason of,*
  Matt 5:10, 11; 10:18, 39

ἕνεκα   prep-gen [4t; prep; 1914]   ἕνεκα
ἐνεκαίνισεν   aor act ind 3 sg
 [Hb 10:20; cv-2a(1); 1590]   ἐγκαινίζω

ἐνεκάλουν   imperf act ind 3 pl
 [Ac 23:28; cv-1d(2b); 1592]   ἐγκαλέω
ἕνεκεν, see ἕνεκα   {1915}
ἕνεκεν   improper prep-gen [20t; prep; 1914]   ἕνεκα
ἐνεκεντρίσθης   aor pass ind 2 sg
 [2t; cv-2a(1); 1596]   ἐγκεντρίζω
ἐνεκοπτόμην   imperf pass ind 1 sg
 [Rm 15:22; cv-4; 1601]   ἐγκόπτω
ἐνέκοψεν   aor act ind 3 sg [2t; cv-4; 1601]   "
ἐνέκρυψεν   aor act ind 3 sg
 [2t; cv-4; 1606]   ἐγκρύπτω
ἐνέμειναν   aor act ind 3 pl
 [Hb 8:9; cv-1c(2); 1844]   ἐμμένω
ἐνέμεινεν   aor act ind 3 sg
 [Ac 28:30; cv-1c(2); 1844]   "
ἐνένευον   imperf act ind 3 pl
 [Lk 1:62; cv-1a(6); 1935]   ἐννεύω

ἐνενήκοντα   {1916, a-5b}
  indecl, *ninety,* Matt 18:12, 13; Luke 15:4, 7*

ἐνενήκοντα   indecl
 [Lk 15:7; a-5b; 1916]   ἐνενήκοντα
ἐνενήκοντα   indecl
 [Mt 18:13; n-3g(2); 1916]   "
ἐνενήκοντα   indecl [2t; n-3g(2); 1916]   "
ἐνεοί   nom pl masc [Ac 9:7; a-1a(1); 1917]   ἐνεός

ἐνεός, ά, όν   {1917, a-1a(1)}
  dumb, speechless, Acts 9:7*

ἐνέπαιζον   imperf act ind 3 pl
 [Lk 22:63; cv-2a(2); 1850]   ἐμπαίζω
ἐνέπαιξαν   aor act ind 3 pl [4t; cv-2a(2); 1850]   "
ἐνεπαίχθη   aor pass ind 3 sg
 [Mt 2:16; cv-2a(2); 1850]   "
ἐνέπλησεν   aor act ind 3 sg
 [Lk 1:53; cv-6a; 1858]   ἐμπίπλημι
ἐνεπλήσθησαν   aor pass ind 3 pl
 [Jn 6:12; cv-6a; 1858]   "
ἐνέπρησεν   aor act ind 3 sg
 [Mt 22:7; cv-6a; 1856]   ἐμπίμπρημι
ἐνέπτυον   imperf act ind 3 pl
 [Mk 15:19; cv-1a(4); 1870]   ἐμπτύω
ἐνέπτυσαν   aor act ind 3 pl
 [Mt 26:67; cv-1a(4); 1870]   "
ἐνεργεῖ   pres act ind 3 sg
 [1C 12:11; cv-1d(2a); 1919]   ἐνεργέω

ἐνέργεια, ας, ἡ   {1918, n-1a}
  energy, efficacy, power, Phil 3:21; Col 2:12; *active
  energy, operation,* Eph 1:19; 3:7; 4:16; Col 1:29; 2
  Thess 2:9, 11*

ἐνέργειαν   acc sg fem [7t; n-1a; 1918]   ἐνέργεια
ἐνεργείας   gen sg fem [Cl 2:12; n-1a; 1918]   "
ἐνεργεῖν   pres act inf
 [Pp 2:13; cv-1d(2a); 1919]   ἐνεργέω
ἐνεργεῖται   pres mid ind 3 sg
 [3t; cv-1d(2a); 1919]   "

ἐνεργέω   {1919, cv-1d(2a)}
  [-, ἐνήργησα, -, -, -] *to effect,* 1 Cor 12:6, 11; Gal
  3:5; Eph 1:11; Phil 2:13; *to put into operation,* Eph
  1:20; absol. *to be active,* Matt 14:2; Mark 6:14;
  Eph 2:2; in N.T. *to communicate energy and*

efficiency, Gal 2:8; pass. or mid. *to come into activity, be actively developed; to be active, be in operation*, towards a result, 2 Cor 4:12; 2 Thess 2:7; *to be an active power* or *principle*, Rom 7:5; 1 Thess 2:12; *instinct with activity; in action, operative*, 2 Cor 1:6; Gal 5:6; Eph 3:20; Col 1:29; *earnest*, James 5:16

ἐνέργημα, ατος, τό   {1920, n-3c(4)}
an effect, thing effected, activity, 1 Cor 12:6; *operation, working*, 1 Cor 12:10*

ἐνεργήματα   nom pl neut
   [1C 12:10; n-3c(4); 1920]   ἐνέργημα
ἐνεργημάτων   gen pl neut
   [1C 12:6; n-3c(4); 1920]   "

ἐνεργής, ές   {1921, a-4a}
active, Phil 6; *efficient, energetic*, Heb 4:12; *adapted to accomplish* a thing, *effectual*, 1 Cor 16:9*

ἐνεργής   nom sg masc
   [Hb 4:12; a-4a; 1921]   ἐνεργής
ἐνεργής   nom sg fem [2t; a-4a; 1921]   "
ἐνεργήσας   aor act ptcp nom sg masc
   [Ga 2:8; cv-1d(2a); 1919]   ἐνεργέω
ἐνεργουμένη   pres mid ptcp nom sg fem
   [2t; cv-1d(2a); 1919]   "
ἐνεργουμένην   pres mid ptcp acc sg fem
   [2t; cv-1d(2a); 1919]   "
ἐνεργουμένης   pres mid ptcp gen sg fem
   [2C 1:6; cv-1d(2a); 1919]   "
ἐνεργοῦντος   pres act ptcp gen sg masc
   [Ep 1:11; cv-1d(2a); 1919]   "
ἐνεργοῦντος   pres act ptcp gen sg neut
   [Ep 2:2; cv-1d(2a); 1919]   "
ἐνεργοῦσιν   pres act ind 3 pl
   [2t; cv-1d(2a); 1919]   "
ἐνεργῶν   pres act ptcp nom sg masc
   [3t; cv-1d(2a); 1919]   "
ἐνέστηκεν   perf act ind 3 sg
   [2Th 2:2; cv-6a; 1931]   ἐνίστημι
ἐνεστηκότα   perf act ptcp acc sg masc
   [Hb 9:9; cv-6a; 1931]   "
ἐνεστῶσαν   perf act ptcp acc sg fem
   [1C 7:26; cv-6a; 1931]   "
ἐνεστῶτα   perf act ptcp nom pl neut
   [2t; cv-6a; 1931]   "
ἐνεστῶτος   perf act ptcp gen sg masc
   [Ga 1:4; cv-6a; 1931]   "
ἐνετειλάμην   aor mid ind 1 sg
   [Mt 28:20; cv-2d(1); 1948]   ἐντέλλω
ἐνετείλατο   aor mid ind 3 sg
   [8t; cv-2d(1); 1948]   "
ἐνετρεπόμεθα   imperf pass ind 1 pl
   [Hb 12:9; cv-1b(1); 1956]   ἐντρέπω
ἐνετύλιξεν   aor act ind 3 sg
   [2t; cv-2b; 1962]   ἐντυλίσσω
ἐνέτυχον   aor act ind 3 pl
   [Ac 25:24; cv-3a(2b); 1961]   ἐντυγχάνω

ἐνευλογέω   {1922, cv-1d(2a)}
[-, -, -, -, ἐνευλογήθην] *to bless in respect of*, or *by means of*, Acts 3:25; Gal 3:8*

ἐνευλογηθήσονται   fut pass ind 3 pl
   [2t; cv-1d(2a); 1922]   ἐνευλογέω
ἐνεφάνισαν   aor act ind 3 pl
   [3t; cv-2a(1); 1872]   ἐμφανίζω
ἐνεφάνισας   aor act ind 2 sg
   [Ac 23:22; cv-2a(1); 1872]   "
ἐνεφανίσθησαν   aor pass ind 3 pl
   [Mt 27:53; cv-2a(1); 1872]   "
ἐνεφύσησεν   aor act ind 3 sg
   [Jn 20:22; cv-1d(1a); 1874]   ἐμφυσάω
ἐνέχειν   pres act inf
   [Lk 11:53; cv-1b(2); 1923]   ἐνέχω
ἐνέχεσθε   pres pass imperative 2 pl
   [Ga 5:1; cv-1b(2); 1923]   "
ἐνεχθεῖσαν   aor pass ptcp acc sg fem
   [2P 1:18; v-1c(1); 5770]   φέρω
ἐνεχθείσης   aor pass ptcp gen sg fem
   [2P 1:17; v-1c(1); 5770]   "

ἐνέχω   {1923, cv-1b(2)}
[(ἐνεῖχον), -, -, -, -, -] *to hold within; to fix upon;* in N.T. intrans. (sc. χόλον) *to entertain a grudge against*, Mark 6:19; *to be exasperated against*, Luke 11:53; pass. *to be entangled, held fast in*, Gal 5:1; 2 Thess 1:4 v.l.*

ἐνηργεῖτο   imperf mid ind 3 sg
   [Rm 7:5; cv-1d(2a); 1919]   ἐνεργέω
ἐνήργησεν   aor act ind 3 sg
   [2t; cv-1d(2a); 1919]   "

ἐνθάδε   {1924, adverb}
pr. *to this place*, John 4:15, 16; also, *here, in this place*, Luke 24:41; Acts 10:8; 16:28; 17:6; 25:17, 24*

ἐνθάδε   adverb [8t; adverb; 1924]   ἐνθάδε

ἔνθεν   {1925, adverb}
from this place, Matt 17:20; Luke 16:26*

ἔνθεν   adverb [2t; adverb; 1925]   ἔνθεν
ἐνθυμεῖσθε   pres mid ind 2 pl
   [Mt 9:4; cv-1b(2a); 1926]   ἐνθυμέομαι

ἐνθυμέομαι   {1926, cv-1b(2a)}
[-, -, -, -, -, ἐνεθυμήθην] *to ponder in one's mind, think of, meditate on*, Matt 1:20; 9:4; Acts 10:19 v.l.*

ἐνθυμηθέντος   aor pass ptcp gen sg masc
   [Mt 1:20; cv-1b(2a); 1926]   "
ἐνθυμήσεις   acc pl fem
   [2t; n-3e(5b); 1927]   ἐνθύμησις
ἐνθυμήσεων   gen pl fem [Hb 4:12; n-3e(5b); 1927] "
ἐνθυμήσεως   gen sg fem
   [Ac 17:29; n-3e(5b); 1927]   "

ἐνθύμησις, εως, ἡ   {1927, n-3e(5b)}
the act of thought, reflection, Matt 9:4; 12:25; Heb 4:12; *the result of thought, invention, device*, Acts 17:29*

ἔνι   {1928, cv-6b}
shortened form of ἔνεστιν, see ἔνειμι

ἐνί   dat sg masc [13t; a-4b(2); 1651]   εἷς
ἑνί   dat sg neut [9t; a-4b(2); 1651]   "
ἔνι   pres act ind 3 sg [6t; cv-6b; 1928] ἔνι
ἐνιαυτόν   acc sg masc [8t; n-2a; 1929]   ἐνιαυτός

ἐνιαυτός, ου, ὁ   {1929, n-2a}
a year, more particularly as being a cycle of
seasons, and in respect of its revolution, John
11:49, 51; 18:13; in N.T. an era, Luke 4:19

ἐνιαυτοῦ   gen sg masc [4t; n-2a; 1929]   "
ἐνιαυτούς   acc pl masc [2t; n-2a; 1929]   "
ἐνίκησα   aor act ind 1 sg
      [Rv 3:21; v-1d(1a); 3771]   νικάω
ἐνίκησαν   aor act ind 3 pl
      [Rv 12:11; v-1d(1a); 3771]   "
ἐνίκησεν   aor act ind 3 sg
      [Rv 5:5; v-1d(1a); 3771]   "

ἐνίοτε   {1930, adverb}
sometimes, Matt 17:15 v.l.*

ἐνίστημι   {1931, cv-6a}
[ἐνστήσω, ἐνέστην, ἐνέστηκα, -, -] to place in or
upon; intrans., to stand close upon; to be at hand,
impend, to be present, Rom 8:38; 2 Thess 2:2; Heb
9:9

ἐνίσχυσεν   aor act ind 3 sg
      [Ac 9:19; cv-1a(4); 1932]   ἐνισχύω

ἐνισχύω   {1932, cv-1a(4)}
[-, ἐνίσχυσα -, -, ἐνισχύθην] to strengthen, impart
strength and vigor, Luke 22:43; intrans. to gain,
acquire, or recover strength and vigor, be
strengthened, Acts 9:19; 19:20 v.l.*

ἐνισχύων   pres act ptcp nom sg masc
      [Lk 22:43; cv-1a(4); 1932]   "
ἔνιψα   aor act ind 1 sg
      [Jn 13:14; v-4; 3782]   νίπτω
ἐνιψάμην   aor mid ind 1 sg [Jn 9:15; v-4; 3782]   "
ἐνίψατο   aor mid ind 3 sg [Jn 9:7; v-4; 3782]   "
ἔνιψεν   aor act ind 3 sg [2t; v-4; 3782]   "

ἐννέα   {1933, a-5b}
indecl, nine, Matt 18:12f.; Luke 15:4, 7; 17:17*

ἐννέα   indecl [5t; a-5b; 1933]   ἐννέα

ἐννεός, see ἐνεός   {1934, a-1a(1)}
stupid; dumb; struck dumb with amazement,
bewildered, stupefied, Acts 9:7

ἐννεύω   {1935, cv-1a(6)}
[(ἐνένευον), -, -, -, -, -] to nod at, signify by a nod;
to make signs; to intimate by signs, Luke 1:62*

ἔννοια, ας, ἡ   {1936, n-1a}
notion, idea; thought, purpose, intention, Heb
4:12; 1 Peter 4:1*

ἔννοιαν   acc sg fem [1P 4:1; n-1a; 1936]   ἔννοια
ἐννοιῶν   gen pl fem [Hb 4:12; n-1a; 1936]   "

ἔννομος, ον   {1937, a-3a}
within law; lawful, legal, Acts 19:39; in N.T.
subject or under a law, obedient to a law, 1 Cor
9:21*

ἔννομος   nom sg masc [1C 9:21; a-3a; 1937] ἔννομος
ἐννόμῳ   dat sg fem [Ac 19:39; a-3a; 1937]   "

ἐννόμως   {1938, adverb}
with ἐν νόμῳ in Rom 2:12 v.l., subject to or
possession of the law*

ἔννυχα   acc pl neut used adverbially
      [Mk 1:35; a-3a; 1939]   ἔννυχος

ἔννυχος, ον   {1939, a-3a}
nocturnal, while still dark, Mark 1:35*

ἐνοικείτω   pres act imperative 3 sg
      [Cl 3:16; cv-1d(2a); 1940]   ἐνοικέω

ἐνοικέω   {1940, cv-1d(2a)}
[ἐνοικήσω, ἐνῴκησα, -, -, -] to dwell in inhabit; in
N.T. met. to be indwelling spiritually, Rom 8:11;
Col 3:16; 2 Tim 1:14; to be infixed mentally, 2 Tim
1:5; of the Deity, to indwell, by special presence,
2 Cor 6:16; Luke 13:4 v.l.; Rom 7:17 v.l.*

ἐνοικήσω   fut act ind 1 sg
      [2C 6:16; cv-1d(2a); 1940]   "
ἐνοικοῦντος   pres act ptcp gen sg neut
      [2t; cv-1d(2a); 1940]   "
ἐνόμιζεν   imperf act ind 3 sg
      [Ac 7:25; v-2a(1); 3787]   νομίζω
ἐνομίζετο   imperf pass ind 3 sg
      [Lk 3:23; v-2a(1); 3787]   "
ἐνομίζομεν   imperf act ind 1 pl
      [Ac 16:13; v-2a(1); 3787]   "
ἐνόμιζον   imperf act ind 3 pl
      [Ac 21:29; v-2a(1); 3787]   "
ἐνόμισαν   aor act ind 3 pl
      [Mt 20:10; v-2a(1); 3787]   "
ἐνόμισας   aor act ind 2 sg
      [Ac 8:20; v-2a(1); 3787]   "
ἐνόντα   pres act ptcp acc pl neut
      [Lk 11:41; cv-6b; 1913]   ἔνειμι

ἐνορκίζω   {1941, cv-2a(1)}
[-, -, -, -, -] to adjure, 1 Thess 5:27*

ἐνορκίζω   pres act ind 1 sg
      [1Th 5:27; cv-2a(1); 1941]   ἐνορκίζω
ἑνός   gen sg masc [26t; a-4b(2); 1651]   εἷς
ἑνός   gen sg neut [7t; a-4b(2); 1651]   "
ἐνοσφίσατο   aor mid ind 3 sg
      [Ac 5:2; v-2a(1); 3802]   νοσφίζω

ἑνότης, ητος, ἡ   {1942, n-3c(1)}
oneness, unity, Eph 4:3, 13*

ἑνότητα   acc sg fem [2t; n-3c(1); 1942]   ἑνότης

ἐνοχλέω   {1943, cv-1d(2a)}
[-, -, -, -, -] to trouble, annoy; to be a trouble, Luke
6:18; Heb 12:15*

ἐνοχλῇ   pres act subj 3 sg
      [Hb 12:15; cv-1d(2a); 1943]   ἐνοχλέω
ἐνοχλούμενοι   pres pass ptcp nom pl masc
      [Lk 6:18; cv-1d(2a); 1943]   "
ἔνοχοι   nom pl masc [Hb 2:15; a-3a; 1944]   ἔνοχος
ἔνοχον   acc sg masc [Mk 14:64; a-3a; 1944]   "

ἔνοχος, ον   {1944, a-3a}
held in or by; subjected to, Heb 2:15; subject to,
liable to, guilty, deserving, Matt 5:21, 22; 26:66;
Mark 3:29; 14:64; an offender against, 1 Cor 11:27;
James 2:10*

ἔνοχος   nom sg masc [8t; a-3a; 1944]   "
ἐνστήσονται   fut mid ind 3 pl
      [2Ti 3:1; cv-6a; 1931]   ἐνίστημι

ἔνταλμα, ατος, τό {1945, n-3c(4)}
a precept, commandment, ordinance, Matt 15:9;
Mark 7:7; Col 2:22*

ἐντάλματα acc pl neut
[3t; n-3c(4); 1945] ἔνταλμα
ἐνταφιάζειν pres act inf
[Jn 19:40; cv-2a(1); 1946] ἐνταφιάζω

ἐνταφιάζω {1946, cv-2a(1)}
[-, ἐνεταφίασα, -, -, -] *to prepare a body for burial,*
Matt 26:12; absol. *to make the ordinary
preparations for burial,* John 19:40*

ἐνταφιάσαι aor act inf
[Mt 26:12; cv-2a(1); 1946] "
ἐνταφιασμόν acc sg masc
[Mk 14:8; n-2a; 1947] ἐνταφιασμός

ἐνταφιασμός, οῦ, ὁ {1947, n-2a}
preparation of a corpse *for burial, burial* itself,
Mark 14:8; John 12:7*

ἐνταφιασμοῦ gen sg masc [Jn 12:7; n-2a; 1947] "
ἐντειλάμενος aor mid ptcp nom sg masc
[Ac 1:2; cv-2d(1); 1948] ἐντέλλω
ἐντελεῖται fut mid ind 3 sg
[2t; cv-2d(1); 1948] "
ἐντέλλομαι pres mid ind 1 sg
[2t; cv-2d(1); 1948] "

ἐντέλλω {1948, cv-2d(1)}
[ἐντελοῦμαι, ἐνετειλάμην, -, ἐντέλαμαι, -] some
list as ἐντέλλομαι, mid., *to enjoin, charge,
command,* Matt 4:6; 15:4; 17:9; *to direct,* Matt
19:7; Mark 10:3

ἐντέταλται perf mid ind 3 sg
[Ac 13:47; cv-2d(1); 1948] "
ἐντετυλιγμένον perf pass ptcp acc sg neut
[Jn 20:7; cv-2b; 1962] ἐντυλίσσω
ἐντετυπωμένη perf pass ptcp nom sg fem
[2C 3:7; cv-; 1963] ἐντυπόω

ἐντεῦθεν {1949, adverb}
hence, from this place, Matt 17:20; Luke 4:9;
ἐντεῦθεν καὶ ἐντεῦθεν, *on each side,* Rev 22:2;
hence, from this cause, James 4:1

ἐντεῦθεν adverb [10t; adverb; 1949] ἐντεῦθεν
ἐντεύξεις acc pl fem
[1Ti 2:1; n-3e(5b); 1950] ἔντευξις
ἐντεύξεως gen sg fem [1Ti 4:5; n-3e(5b); 1950] "

ἔντευξις, εως, ἡ {1950, n-3e(5b)}
pr. *a meeting with;* hence *address; prayer,
supplication, intercession,* 1 Tim 2:1; 4:5*

ἐντίθημι {1951, cv-6a}
[-, -, -, -, -] *put in, implant,* Acts 18:4 v.l.*

ἔντιμον acc sg masc [2t; a-3a; 1952] ἔντιμος

ἔντιμος, ον {1952, a-3a}
honored, estimable, dear, Luke 7:2; 14:8; Phil 2:29;
highly-valued, precious, costly, 1 Peter 2:4, 6*

ἔντιμος nom sg masc [Lk 7:2; a-3a; 1952]
ἐντιμότερος nom sg masc comparative
[Lk 14:8; a-3a; 1952] "
ἐντίμους acc pl masc [Pp 2:29; a-3a; 1952] "
ἐντολαί nom pl fem [1J 5:3; n-1b; 1953] ἐντολή

ἐντολαῖς dat pl fem [3t; n-1b; 1953] "
ἐντολάς acc pl fem [18t; n-1b; 1953] "

ἐντολή, ῆς, ἡ {1953, n-1b}
an injunction; a precept, commandment, law, Matt
5:19; 15:3, 6; *an order, direction,* Acts 17:15; *an
edict,* John 11:57; *a direction,* Mark 10:5; *a
commission,* John 10:18, *a charge* of matters to be
proclaimed or received, John 12:49, 50; 1 Tim
6:14; 2 Peter 2:21

ἐντολή nom sg fem [14t; n-1b; 1953] "
ἐντολήν acc sg fem [19t; n-1b; 1953] "
ἐντολῆς gen sg fem [9t; n-1b; 1953] "
ἐντολῶν gen pl fem [3t; n-1b; 1953] "
ἐντόπιοι nom pl masc
[Ac 21:12; a-1a(1); 1954] ἐντόπιος

ἐντόπιος, ία, ιον {1954, a-1a(1)}
in or *of a place; an inhabitant, citizen,* Acts 21:12*

ἐντός {1955, prep}
improper prep., gen., *inside, within,* Luke 17:21;
τὸ ἐντός, *the interior, inside,* Matt 23:26*

ἐντός prep-gen [2t; prep; 1955] ἐντός
ἐντραπῇ aor pass subj 3 sg
[2t; cv-1b(1); 1956] ἐντρέπω
ἐντραπήσονται fut pass ind 3 pl
[3t; cv-1b(1); 1956] "
ἐντρέπομαι pres pass ind 1 sg
[Lk 18:4; cv-1b(1); 1956] "
ἐντρεπόμενος pres pass ptcp nom sg masc
[Lk 18:2; cv-1b(1); 1956] "

ἐντρέπω {1956, cv-1b(1)}
[-, -, -, -, ἐνετράπην] mid., *to revere, reverence,
regard,* Matt 21:37; Mark 12:6; absol. *to feel
shame, be put to shame,* 2 Thess 3:14; Titus 2:8;
pas., *be put to shore,* 2 Thess 3:14; Titus 3:8

ἐντρέπων pres act ptcp nom sg masc
[1C 4:14; cv-1b(1); 1956] "
ἐντρεφόμενος pres pass ptcp nom sg masc
[1Ti 4:6; cv-1b(1); 1957] ἐντρέφω

ἐντρέφω {1957, cv-1b(1)}
[-, -, -, -, -] *to nourish in, bring up* or *educate in,* 1
Tim 4:6*

ἔντρομος, ον {1958, a-3a}
trembling, terrified, Acts 7:32; 16:29; Heb 12:21;
Luke 8:47 v.l.*

ἔντρομος nom sg masc [3t; a-3a; 1958] ἔντρομος

ἐντροπή, ῆς, ἡ {1959, n-1b}
humiliation; in N.T. *shame,* 1 Cor 6:5; 15:34*

ἐντροπήν acc sg fem [2t; n-1b; 1959] ἐντροπή

ἐντρυφάω {1960, cv-1d(1a)}
[-, -, -, -, -] *to live luxuriously, riot, revel,* 2 Peter
2:13*

ἐντρυφῶντες pres act ptcp nom pl masc
[2P 2:13; cv-1d(1a); 1960] ἐντρυφάω
ἐντυγχάνει pres act ind 3 sg
[3t; cv-3a(2b); 1961] ἐντυγχάνω
ἐντυγχάνειν pres act inf
[Hb 7:25; cv-3a(2b); 1961] "

ἐντυγχάνω   {1961, cv-3a(2b)}
[-, ἐνέτυχον, -, -, -] *to fill in with, meet; to have*
conversation with, address; to address or *apply to*
any one, Acts 25:24; ὑπέρ τινος, *to intercede for*
any one, plead the cause of, Rom 8:27, 34; Heb
7:25; κατά τινος, *to address a representation* or *suit*
against any one, to accuse, complain of, Rom 11:2*

ἐντυλίσσω   {1962, cv-2b}
[-, ἐνετύλιξα -, ἐντετύλιγμα, -] *to wrap up in,*
inwrap, envelope, Matt 27:59; Luke 23:53; *to wrap*
up, roll or *fold together,* John 20:7*

ἐντυπόω   {1963, cv-1d(3)}
[-, -, -, ἐντετύπωμαι, -] *to impress a figure,*
instamp, engrave, 2 Cor 3:7*

ἐνυβρίζω   {1964, cv-2a(1)}
[-, ἐνύβρισα, -, -, -] *to insult, outrage,* Heb 10:29*

ἐνυβρίσας   aor act ptcp nom sg masc
   [Hb 10:29; cv-2a(1); 1964]   ἐνυβρίζω
ἔνυξεν   aor act ind 3 sg [Jn 19:34; v-2b; 3817] νύσσω

ἐνυπνιάζομαι   {1965, v-2a(1)}
[-, -, -, -, ἐνυπνιάσθην] *to dream,* in N.T. *to dream*
under supernatural impression, Acts 2:17; *to*
dream delusion, have visions, Jude 8*

ἐνυπνιαζόμενοι   pres pass ptcp nom pl masc
   [Jd 8; v-2a(1); 1965]   ἐνυπνιάζομαι
ἐνυπνιασθήσονται   fut pass ind 3 pl
   [Ac 2:17; v-2a(1); 1965]   "
ἐνυπνίοις   dat pl neut
   [Ac 2:17; n-2c; 1966]   ἐνύπνιον

ἐνύπνιον, ου, τό   {1966, n-2c}
a dream; in N.T. *a supernatural suggestion* or
impression received during sleep, a sleep-vision,
Acts 2:17*

ἐνύσταξαν   aor act ind 3 pl
   [Mt 25:5; v-2a(2); 3818]   νυστάζω
ἐνῴκησεν   aor act ind 3 sg
   [2Ti 1:5; cv-1d(2a); 1940]   ἐνοικέω

ἐνώπιον   {1967, prep}
gen., *before, in the presence of,* Luke 5:25; 8:47; *in*
front of, Rev 4:5, 6; *immediately preceding* as a
forerunner, Luke 1:17; Rev 16:19; *from the*
Hebrew, in the presence of, metaphysically, *i.e.* in
the sphere of sensation or thought, Luke 12:9;
15:10; Acts 10:31; *in the eyes of, in the judgment of,*
Luke 16:15; 24:11; Acts 4:19

ἐνώπιον   prep-gen
   [94t; prep; 1967]   ἐνώπιον

Ἐνώς, ὁ   {1968, n-3g(2)}
Enos, pr. name, indecl., Luke 3:38*

Ἐνώς   indecl [Lk 3:38; n-3g(2); 1968]   Ἐνώς

ἐνωτίζομαι   {1969, cv-2a(1)}
[-, ἐνωτισάμην, -, -, -] *to give ear, listen, pay*
attention to, Acts 2:14*

ἐνωτίσασθε   aor mid imperative 2 pl
   [Ac 2:14; cv-2a(1); 1969]   ἐνωτίζομαι

Ἐνώχ, ὁ   {1970, n-3g(2)}
Enoch, pr. name, indecl., Luke 3:37; Heb 11:5; 1
Peter 3:19; Jude 14*

Ἐνώχ   indecl [3t; n-3g(2); 1970]   Ἐνώχ

ἔξ   {1971, a-5b}
   six, indecl., Matt 17:1; Mark 9:2

ἐξ   indecl [13t; a-5b; 1666]   "
ἐξ   prep-gen [234t; prep; 1666]   ἐκ
ἐξαγαγεῖν   aor act inf
   [Hb 8:9; cv-1b(2); 1974]   ἐξάγω
ἐξαγαγέτωσαν   aor act imperative 3 pl
   [Ac 16:37; cv-1b(2); 1974]   "
ἐξαγαγόντες   aor act ptcp nom pl masc
   [Ac 16:39; cv-1b(2); 1974]   "
ἐξαγαγών   aor act ptcp nom sg masc
   [2t; cv-1b(2); 1974]   "
ἐξαγγείλητε   aor act subj 2 pl
   [1P 2:9; cv-2d(1); 1972]   ἐξαγγέλλω

ἐξαγγέλλω   {1972, cv-2d(1)}
[-, ἐξήγγειλα, -, -, -] *to tell forth, divulge, publish;*
to declare abroad, celebrate, 1 Peter 2:9, shorter
ending of Mark*

ἐξάγει   pres act ind 3 sg
   [Jn 10:3; cv-1b(2); 1974]   ἐξάγω
ἐξαγοραζόμενοι   pres mid ptcp nom pl masc
   [2t; cv-2a(1); 1973]   ἐξαγοράζω

ἐξαγοράζω   {1973, cv-2a(1)}
[-, ἐξηγόρασα, -, -, -] *to buy out* of the hands of a
person; *to redeem, set free,* Gal 3:13; 4:5; mid. *to*
redeem, buy off, to secure for one's self or *one's own*
use; to rescue from loss or misapplication, Eph
5:16; Col 4:5*

ἐξαγοράσῃ   aor act subj 3 sg
   [Ga 4:5; cv-2a(1); 1973]   "
ἐξάγουσιν   pres act ind 3 pl
   [Mk 15:20; cv-1b(2); 1974]   ἐξάγω

ἐξάγω   {1974, cv-1b(2)}
[-, ἐξήγαγον, -, -, -] *to bring* or *lead out, conduct*
out of, Mark 8:23; 15:20; Luke 24:50

ἐξαιρέω   {1975, cv-1d(2a)}
[ἐξελῶ, ἐξεῖλον, -, -, -] *to take out of; to pluck out,*
tear out, Matt 5:29; 18:9; mid. *to take out of, select,*
choose, Acts 26:17; *to rescue, deliver,* Acts 7:10, 34;
12:11; 23:27; Gal 1:4*

ἐξαιρούμενος   pres mid ptcp nom sg masc
   [Ac 26:17; cv-1d(2a); 1975]   ἐξαιρέω

ἐξαίρω   {1976, cv-2d(2)}
[-, ἐξῆρα, -, -, -] pr. *to lift up out of;* in N.T. *to*
remove, eject, 1 Cor 5:2 v.l., 13*

ἐξαιτέω   {1977, cv-1d(2a)}
[-, ἐξῄτησα, -, -, -] *to ask for; to demand;* mid. *to*
demand for one's self, Luke 22:31; also, *to obtain*
by asking

ἐξαίφνης   {1978, adverb}
suddenly, unexpectedly, Mark 13:36; Luke 2:13;
9:39; Acts 9:3; 22:6*

ἐξαίφνης   adverb [5t; adverb; 1978]   ἐξαίφνης

ἐξακολουθέω   {1979, cv-1d(2a)}
[ἐξακολουθήσω, ἐξηκολούθησα, -, -, -] *to follow*
out; to imitate, 2 Peter 2:2, 15; *to observe as a*
guide, 2 Peter 1:16*

ἐξακολουθήσαντες   aor act ptcp nom pl masc
  [2t; cv-1d(2a); 1979]   ἐξακολουθέω
ἐξακολουθήσουσιν   fut act ind 3 pl
  [2P 2:2; cv-1d(2a); 1979]   "

ἐξακόσιοι, αι, ον   {1980, a-1a(1)}
  six hundred, Rev 13:18; 14:20*

ἐξακόσιοι   nom pl masc
  [Rv 13:18; a-1a(1); 1980]   ἐξακόσιοι
ἐξακοσίων   gen pl masc   [Rv 14:20; a-1a(1); 1980]   "
ἐξαλειφθῆναι   aor pass inf
  [Ac 3:19; cv-1b(1); 1981]   ἐξαλείφω

ἐξαλείφω   {1981, cv-1b(1)}
  [ἐξαλείψω, ἐξήλειψα -, -, ἐξηλείφθην] pr. *to*
  anoint or *smear over;* hence, *to wipe off* or *away,*
  Rev 7:17; 21:4; *to blot out, obliterate,* Col 2:14;
  Rev 3:5; met. *to wipe out* guilt, Acts 3:19*

ἐξαλείψας   aor act ptcp nom sg masc
  [Cl 2:14; cv-1b(1); 1981]   "
ἐξαλείψει   fut act ind 3 sg   [2t; cv-1b(1); 1981]   "
ἐξαλείψω   aor act subj 1 sg
  [Rv 3:5; cv-1b(1); 1981]   "

ἐξάλλομαι   {1982, cv-2d(1)}
  [-, -, -, -, -] *to leap* or *spring up* or *forth,* Acts 3:8;
  14:10 v.l.*

ἐξαλλόμενος   pres mid ptcp nom sg masc
  [Ac 3:8; cv-2d(1); 1982]   ἐξάλλομαι
ἐξανάστασιν   acc sg fem
  [Pp 3:11; n-3e(2b); 1983]   ἐξανάστασις

ἐξανάστασις, εως, ἡ   {1983, n-3e(2b)}
  a raising up; a dislodgment; a rising up; a
  resurrection from the dead, Phil 3:11*

ἐξαναστήση   aor act subj 3 sg
  [2t; cv-6(a); 1985]   ἐξανίστημι

ἐξανατέλλω   {1984, cv-2d(1)}
  [-, ἐξανέτειλα, -, -, -] *to raise up, make to spring*
  up; intrans. *to rise up, sprout, spring up* or *forth,*
  Matt 13:5; Mark 4:5*

ἐξανέστησαν   aor act ind 3 pl
  [Ac 15:5; cv-6(a); 1985]   "
ἐξανέτειλεν   aor act ind 3 sg
  [2t; cv-2d(1); 1984]   ἐξανατέλλω

ἐξανίστημι   {1985, cv-6a}
  [ἐξαναστήσω, ἐξανέστησα or ἐξανέστην, -, -, -] *to*
  cause to rise up, raise up; from the Hebrew, *to*
  raise up into existence, Mark 12:19; Luke 20:28;
  intrans. *to rise up from, stand forth,* Acts 15:5*

ἐξανοίγω   {1986, cv-1b(2)}
  to open (fully), Acts 12:16 v.l.*

ἐξαπατάτω   pres act imperative 3 sg
  [1C 3:18; cv-1d(1a); 1987]   ἐξαπατάω

ἐξαπατάω   {1987, cv-1d(1a)}
  [-, ἐξηπάτησα, -, -, -] pr. *to deceive thoroughly; to*
  deceive, delude, Rom 7:11; 16:18; 1 2 Cor 3:18;
  11:3; 2 Thess 2:3; 1 Tim 2:14*

ἐξαπατηθεῖσα   aor pass ptcp nom sg fem
  [1Ti 2:14; cv-1d(1a); 1987]   "
ἐξαπατήση   aor act subj 3 sg
  [2Th 2:3; cv-1d(1a); 1987]   "

ἐξαπατῶσιν   pres act ind 3 pl
  [Rm 16:18; cv-1d(1a); 1987]   "
ἐξαπεστάλη   aor pass ind 3 sg
  [Ac 13:26; cv-2d(1); 1990]   ἐξαποστέλλω
ἐξαπέστειλαν   aor act ind 3 pl
  [5t; cv-2d(1); 1990]   "
ἐξαπέστειλεν   aor act ind 3 sg
  [6t; cv-2d(1); 1990]   "

ἐξάπινα   {1988, adverb}
  suddenly, immediately, unexpectedly, Mark 9:8*

ἐξάπινα   adverb [Mk 9:8; adverb; 1988]   ἐξάπινα

ἐξαπορέω   {1989, cv-1d(2a)}
  [-, -, -, -, ἐξηπορήθην] some list as a deponent
  ἐξαπορέομαι, pas., *to be in the utmost perplexity*
  or *despair,* 2 Cor 1:8; 4:8*

ἐξαπορηθῆναι   aor pass inf
  [2C 1:8; cv-1d(2a); 1989]   ἐξαπορέω
ἐξαπορούμενοι   pres mid ptcp nom pl masc
  [2C 4:8; cv-1d(2a); 1989]   "

ἐξαποστέλλω   {1990, cv-2d(1)}
  [ἐξαποστελῶ, ἐξαπέστειλα, -, -, -] *to send out* or
  forth; to send away, dismiss, Luke 1:53; *to dispatch*
  on a service or agency, Acts 7:12; *to send forth* as
  a pervading influence, Gal 4:6

ἐξαποστελῶ   fut act ind 1 sg
  [Ac 22:21; cv-2d(1); 1990]   ἐξαποστέλλω
ἐξάρατε   aor act imperative 2 pl
  [1C 5:13; cv-2d(2); 1976]   ἐξαίρω

ἐξαρτάω   {1991, cv-1d(1a)}
  [-, -, -, -, -] *to be attached to, be an adherent of,*
  Mark 3:21 v.l.*

ἐξαρτίζω   {1992, cv-2a(1)}
  [-, ἐξήρτισα -, ἐξήρτισμαι, -] *to equip* or *furnish*
  completely, 2 Tim 3:17; *to complete* time, Acts
  21:5*

ἐξαρτίσαι   aor act inf
  [Ac 21:5; cv-2a(1); 1992]   ἐξαρτίζω

ἐξαστράπτω   {1993, cv-4}
  [-, -, -, -, -] pr. *to flash forth;* hence, *to glisten as*
  lightning, Luke 9:29*

ἐξαστράπτων   pres act ptcp nom sg masc
  [Lk 9:29; cv-4; 1993]   ἐξαστράπτω

ἐξαυτῆς   {1994, adverb}
  at the very time; presently, instantly, immediately,
  Mark 6:25; Acts 10:33; 11:11

ἐξαυτῆς   adverb [6t; adverb; 1994]   ἐξαυτῆς
ἐξέβαλεν   aor act ind 3 sg
  [5t; cv-2d(1); 1675]   ἐκβάλλω
ἐξέβαλλον   imperf act ind 3 pl
  [Mk 6:13; cv-2d(1); 1675]   "
ἐξεβάλομεν   aor act ind 1 pl
  [Mt 7:22; cv-2d(1); 1675]   "
ἐξέβαλον   aor act ind 3 pl [7t; cv-2d(1); 1675]   "
ἐξέβησαν   aor act ind 3 pl
  [Hb 11:15; cv-2d(6); 1674]   ἐκβαίνω
ἐξεβλήθη   aor pass ind 3 sg
  [Mt 9:25; cv-2d(1); 1675]   ἐκβάλλω

ἐξεγερεῖ   fut act ind 3 sg
  [1C 6:14; cv-2d(3); 1995]   ἐξεγείρω

ἐξεγείρω   {1995, cv-2d(3)}
  [ἐξεγερῶ, ἐξήγειρα, -, -, -] *to excite, arouse* from
  sleep, Luke 6:45 v.l.; *to raise up* from the dead, 1
  Cor 6:14; *to raise up* into existence, or into a
  certain condition, Rom 9:17*

ἐξέδετο   aor mid ind 3 sg
  [3t; cv-6a; 1686]   ἐκδίδωμι
ἐξεδέχετο   imperf mid ind 3 sg
  [Hb 11:10; cv-1b(2); 1683]   ἐκδέχομαι
ἐξεδίκησεν   aor act ind 3 sg
  [Rv 19:2; cv-1d(2a); 1688]   ἐκδικέω
ἐξέδυσαν   aor act ind 3 pl
  [2t; cv-3a(1); 1694]   ἐκδύω
ἐξεζήτησαν   aor act ind 3 pl
  [1P 1:10; cv-1d(2a); 1699]   ἐκζητέω
ἐξεθαμβήθησαν   aor pass ind 3 pl
  [2t; cv-1d(2a); 1701]   ἐκθαμβέω
ἐξεθαύμαζον   imperf act ind 3 pl
  [Mk 12:17; cv-2a(1); 1703]   ἐκθαυμάζω
ἐξέθεντο   aor mid ind 3 pl
  [Ac 18:26; cv-6a; 1758]   ἐκτίθημι
ἕξει   fut act ind 3 sg [6t; v-1b(2); 2400]   ἔχω
ἐξειλάμην   aor mid ind 1 sg
  [Ac 23:27; cv-1d(2a); 1975]   ἐξαιρέω
ἐξείλατο   aor mid ind 3 sg [2t; cv-1d(2a); 1975]   "

ἔξειμι   {1996, cv-6b}
  [(ἐξῄειν), -, -, -, -, -] *to go out* or *forth,* Acts 13:42;
  to depart, Acts 17:15; 20:7; ἐπὶ τὴν γῆν, *to get to*
  land, from the water, Acts 27:43

ἕξεις   fut act ind 2 sg [4t; v-1b(2); 2400]   ἔχω
ἐξεκαύθησαν   aor pass ind 3 pl
  [Rm 1:27; cv-2c; 1706]   ἐκκαίω
ἐξεκέντησαν   aor act ind 3 pl
  [2t; cv-1d(2a); 1708]   ἐκκεντέω
ἐξεκλάσθησαν   aor pass ind 3 pl
  [3t; cv-1d(1b); 1709]   ἐκκλάω
ἐξεκλείσθη   aor pass ind 3 sg
  [Rm 3:27; cv-1a(3); 1710]   ἐκκλείω
ἐξέκλιναν   aor act ind 3 pl
  [Rm 3:12; cv-1c(2); 1712]   ἐκκλίνω
ἐξεκομίζετο   imperf pass ind 3 sg
  [Lk 7:12; cv-2a(1); 1714]   ἐκκομίζω
ἐξεκόπης   aor pass ind 2 sg
  [Rm 11:24; cv-4; 1716]   ἐκκόπτω
ἐξεκρέματο   imperf mid ind 3 sg
  [Lk 19:48; cv-3c(1); 1717]   ἐκκρεμάννυμι
ἔξελε   aor act imperative 2 sg
  [2t; cv-1d(2a); 1975]   ἐξαιρέω
ἐξελέγοντο   imperf mid ind 3 pl
  [Lk 14:7; cv-1b(2); 1721]   ἐκλέγομαι

ἐξελέγχω   {1998, cv-1b(2)}
  [-, -, -, -, -] *to search thoroughly, to test; to convict,*
  condemn, Jude 15 v.l.*

ἐξελεξάμην   aor mid ind 1 sg
  [4t; cv-1b(2); 1721]   "
ἐξελέξαντο   aor mid ind 3 pl
  [Ac 6:5; cv-1b(2); 1721]   "
ἐξελέξασθε   aor mid ind 2 pl
  [Jn 15:16; cv-1b(2); 1721]   "

ἐξελέξατο   aor mid ind 3 sg
  [10t; cv-1b(2); 1721]   "
ἐξελέξω   aor mid ind 2 sg
  [Ac 1:24; cv-1b(2); 1721]   "
ἐξελέσθαι   aor mid inf
  [Ac 7:34; cv-1d(2a); 1975]   ἐξαιρέω
ἐξελεύσεται   fut mid ind 3 sg
  [3t; cv-1b(2); 2002]   ἐξέρχομαι
ἐξελεύσονται   fut mid ind 3 pl
  [2t; cv-1b(2); 2002]   "
ἐξεληλύθασιν   perf act ind 3 pl
  [1J 4:1; cv-1b(2); 2002]   "
ἐξεληλύθει   pluperf act ind 3 sg
  [2t; cv-1b(2); 2002]   "
ἐξελήλυθεν   perf act ind 3 sg
  [2t; cv-1b(2); 2002]   "
ἐξεληλυθός   perf act ptcp acc sg neut
  [Mk 7:30; cv-1b(2); 2002]   "
ἐξεληλυθότας   perf act ptcp acc pl masc
  [Hb 7:5; cv-1b(2); 2002]   "
ἐξεληλυθυῖαν   perf act ptcp acc sg fem
  [Lk 8:46; cv-1b(2); 2002]   "
ἐξέληται   aor mid subj 3 sg
  [Ga 1:4; cv-1d(2a); 1975]   ἐξαιρέω
ἐξέλθατε   aor act imperative 2 pl
  [2t; cv-1b(2); 2002]   ἐξέρχομαι
ἔξελθε   aor act imperative 2 sg
  [10t; cv-1b(2); 2002]   "
ἐξελθεῖν   aor act inf [9t; cv-1b(2); 2002]   "
ἐξέλθη   aor act subj 3 sg [3t; cv-1b(2); 2002]   "
ἐξέλθης   aor act subj 2 sg [2t; cv-1b(2); 2002]   "
ἐξέλθητε   aor act subj 2 pl [3t; cv-1b(2); 2002]   "
ἐξελθόντα   aor act ptcp nom pl neut
  [2t; cv-1b(2); 2002]   "
ἐξελθόντα   aor act ptcp acc sg masc
  [Mt 26:71; cv-1b(2); 2002]   "
ἐξελθόντες   aor act ptcp nom pl masc
  [18t; cv-1b(2); 2002]   "
ἐξελθόντι   aor act ptcp dat sg masc
  [Lk 8:27; cv-1b(2); 2002]   "
ἐξελθόντος   aor act ptcp gen sg masc
  [2t; cv-1b(2); 2002]   "
ἐξελθόντος   aor act ptcp gen sg neut
  [Lk 11:14; cv-1b(2); 2002]   "
ἐξελθόντων   aor act ptcp gen pl masc
  [2t; cv-1b(2); 2002]   "
ἐξελθοῦσα   aor act ptcp nom sg fem
  [3t; cv-1b(2); 2002]   "
ἐξελθοῦσαι   aor act ptcp nom pl fem
  [Mk 16:8; cv-1b(2); 2002]   "
ἐξελθοῦσαν   aor act ptcp acc sg fem
  [Mk 5:30; cv-1b(2); 2002]   "
ἐξελθούση   aor act ptcp dat sg fem
  [Rv 19:21; cv-1b(2); 2002]   "
ἐξελθών   aor act ptcp nom sg masc
  [21t; cv-1b(2); 2002]   "
ἐξελκόμενος   pres pass ptcp nom sg masc
  [Jm 1:14; cv-1a(4); 1999]   ἐξέλκω

ἐξέλκω   {1999, cv-1a(4)}
  [-, -, -, -, -] *to draw* or *drag out; met. to withdraw,*
  allure, hurry away, James 1:14*

ἐξέμαξεν   aor act ind 3 sg
   [2t; cv-2b; 1726]							ἐκμάσσω

ἐξέμασσεν   imperf act ind 3 sg
   [Lk 7:38; cv-2b; 1726]							"

ἐξεμυκτήριζον   imperf act ind 3 pl
   [2t; cv-2a(1); 1727]							ἐκμυκτηρίζω

ἐξενέγκαντες   aor act ptcp nom pl masc
   [2t; cv-1c(1); 1766]							ἐκφέρω

ἐξενέγκατε   aor act imperative 2 pl
   [Lk 15:22; cv-1c(1); 1766]							"

ἐξενεγκεῖν   aor act inf
   [1Ti 6:7; cv-1c(1); 1766]							"

ἐξένευσεν   aor act ind 3 sg
   [Jn 5:13; cv-1a(6); 1728]							ἐκνεύω

ἐξένισεν   aor act ind 3 sg
   [2t; v-2a(1); 3826]							ξενίζω

ἐξενοδόχησεν   aor act ind 3 sg
   [1Ti 5:10; v-1d(2a); 3827]							ξενοδοχέω

ἐξέπεμψαν   aor act ind 3 pl
   [Ac 17:10; cv-1b(1); 1734]							ἐκπέμπω

ἐξέπεσαν   aor act ind 3 pl
   [Ac 12:7; cv-1b(3); 1738]							ἐκπίπτω

ἐξεπέσατε   aor act ind 2 pl
   [Ga 5:4; cv-1b(3); 1738]							"

ἐξέπεσεν aor act ind 3 sg [2t; cv-1b(3); 1738]							"

ἐξεπέτασα   aor act ind 1 sg
   [Rm 10:21; cv-3c(1); 1736]							ἐκπετάννυμι

ἐξεπήδησαν   aor act ind 3 pl
   [Ac 14:14; cv-1d(1a); 1737]							ἐκπηδάω

ἐξεπλάγησαν   aor pass ind 3 pl
   [Lk 2:48; cv-2b; 1742]							ἐκπλήσσω

ἐξέπλει   imperf act ind 3 sg
   [Ac 18:18; cv-1a(7); 1739]							ἐκπλέω

ἐξεπλεύσαμεν   aor act ind 1 pl
   [Ac 20:6; cv-1a(7); 1739]							"

ἐξεπλήσσετο   imperf pass ind 3 sg
   [Mk 11:18; cv-2b; 1742]							ἐκπλήσσω

ἐξεπλήσσοντο   imperf pass ind 3 pl
   [9t; cv-2b; 1742]							"

ἐξέπνευσεν   aor act ind 3 sg
   [3t; cv-1a(7); 1743]							ἐκπνέω

ἐξεπορεύετο   imperf mid ind 3 sg
   [3t; cv-1a(6); 1744]							ἐκπορεύομαι

ἐξεπορεύοντο   imperf mid ind 3 pl
   [Mk 11:19; cv-1a(6); 1744]							"

ἐξεπτύσατε   aor act ind 2 pl
   [Ga 4:14; cv-1a(4); 1746]							ἐκπτύω

ἐξέραμα, ατος, τό							{2000, n-3c(4)}
   vomit, 2 Peter 2:22*

ἐξέραμα   acc sg neut
   [2P 2:22; n-3c(4); 2000]							ἐξέραμα

ἐξεραυνάω							{2001, cv-1d(1a)}
   [-, ἐξηραύνησα, -, -, -] *to search out, to examine closely,* 1 Peter 1:10*

ἐξέρχεσθε   pres mid imperative 2 pl
   [2t; cv-1b(2); 2002]							ἐξέρχομαι

ἐξέρχεται   pres mid ind 3 sg
   [3t; cv-1b(2); 2002]							"

ἐξέρχομαι							{2002, cv-1b(2)}
   [ἐξελεύσομαι, ἐξῆλθον, ἐξελήλυθα, -, -] *to go* or *come out of; to come out,* Matt 5:26; 8:34; *to*

proceed, emanate, take rise from, Matt 2:6; 15:18; 1 Cor 14:36; *to come abroad,* 1 John 4:1; *to go forth, go away, depart,* Matt 9:31; Luke 5:8; *to escape,* John 10:39; *to pass away, come to an end,* Acts 16:19

ἐξερχόμενοι   pres mid ptcp nom pl masc
   [5t; cv-1b(2); 2002]							"

ἐξερχόμενος   pres mid ptcp nom sg masc
   [Lk 21:37; cv-1b(2); 2002]							"

ἐξερχομένων   pres mid ptcp gen pl masc
   [Mt 9:32; cv-1b(2); 2002]							"

ἐξέρχονται   pres mid ind 3 pl
   [2t; cv-1b(2); 2002]							"

ἐξερχώμεθα   pres mid subj 1 pl
   [Hb 13:13; cv-1b(2); 2002]							"

ἐξεστακέναι   perf act inf
   [Ac 8:11; cv-6a; 2014]							ἐξίστημι

ἐξέστη aor act ind 3 sg [Mk 3:21; cv-6a; 2014]							"

ἐξέστημεν   aor act ind 1 sg
   [2C 5:13; cv-6a; 2014]							"

ἐξέστησαν aor act ind 3 pl [5t; cv-6a; 2014]							"

ἔξεστι							{2003, cv-6b}
   3rd person sing of the unused ἔξειμι used impersonally, *it is possible; it is permitted, it is lawful,* Matt 12:2, 4; Mark 3:4; Luke 6:9; Acts 22:25; 1 Cor 6:12

ἔξεστιν   pres act ind 3 sg
   [28t; cv-6b; 1997]							ἔξειμι

ἐξέστραπται   perf pass ind 3 sg
   [Ti 3:11; cv-1b(1); 1750]							ἐκστρέφω

ἐξετάζω							{2004, cv-2a(1)}
   [-, ἐξήτασα, -, -, -] *to search out; to inquire by interrogation, examine strictly,* Matt 2:8; 10:11; *to interrogate,* John 21:12*

ἐξετάσαι   aor act inf
   [Jn 21:12; cv-2a(1); 2004]							ἐξετάζω

ἐξετάσατε   aor act imperative 2 pl
   [2t; cv-2a(1); 2004]							"

ἔξετε   fut act ind 2 pl
   [Rv 2:10; v-1b(2); 2400]							ἔχω

ἐξετείνατε   aor act ind 2 pl
   [Lk 22:53; cv-2d(5); 1753]							ἐκτείνω

ἐξέτεινεν aor act ind 3 sg [2t; cv-2d(5); 1753]							"

ἐξετίθετο   imperf mid ind 3 sg
   [2t; cv-6a; 1758]							ἐκτίθημι

ἐξετράπησαν   aor pass ind 3 pl
   [2t; cv-1b(1); 1762]							ἐκτρέπω

ἐξέφυγον   aor act ind 1 sg
   [2C 11:33; cv-1b(2); 1767]							ἐκφεύγω

ἐξέφυγον   aor act ind 3 pl
   [Hb 12:25; cv-1b(2); 1767]							"

ἐξέχεαν   aor act ind 3 pl
   [Rv 16:6; cv-1a(7); 1772]							ἐκχέω

ἐξέχεεν aor act ind 3 sg [10t; cv-1a(7); 1772]							"

ἐξεχύθη   aor pass ind 3 sg
   [Ac 1:18; cv-1a(7); 1772]							"

ἐξεχύθησαν   aor pass ind 3 pl
   [Jd 11; cv-1a(7); 1772]							"

ἐξεχύννετο   imperf pass ind 3 sg
   [Ac 22:20; cv-1a(7); 1772]							"

ἐξέχω   {2006, cv-1b(2)}
[-, -, -, -, -] *to stand out, be prominent*, Matt 20:28
v.l.*

ἐξέψυξεν   aor act ind 3 sg
[3t; cv-1b(2); 1775]   ἐκψύχω
ἐξήγαγεν   aor act ind 3 sg
[5t; cv-1b(2); 1974]   ἐξάγω
ἐξήγγειλαν   aor act ind 3 pl
[Mk 16:8; cv-2d(1); 1972]   ἐξαγγέλλω
ἐξήγειρα   aor act ind 1 sg
[Rm 9:17; cv-2d(3); 1995]   ἐξεγείρω
ἐξηγεῖτο   imperf mid ind 3 sg
[Ac 21:19; cv-1d(2a); 2007]   ἐξηγέομαι

ἐξηγέομαι   {2007, cv-1d(2a)}
[-, ἐξηγησάμην, -, -, -] *to be a leader; to detail, to set
forth in language; to tell, narrate, recount*, Luke
24:35; Acts 10:8; *to make known, reveal*, John 1:18;
Acts 15:12, 14; 21:19*

ἐξηγησάμενος   aor mid ptcp nom sg masc
[Ac 10:8; cv-1d(2a); 2007]   "
ἐξηγήσατο   aor mid ind 3 sg
[2t; cv-1d(2a); 2007]   "
ἐξηγόρασεν   aor act ind 3 sg
[Ga 3:13; cv-2a(1); 1973]   ἐξαγοράζω
ἐξηγουμένων   pres mid ptcp gen pl masc
[Ac 15:12; cv-1d(2a); 2007]   ἐξηγέομαι
ἐξηγοῦντο   imperf mid ind 3 pl
[Lk 24:35; cv-1d(2a); 2007]   "
ἐξῄεσαν   imperf act ind 3 pl
[Ac 17:15; cv-6b; 1997]   ἔξειμι

ἐξήκοντα   {2008, a-5b}
indecl, *sixty*, Matt 13:8, 23

ἐξήκοντα   indecl [9t; a-5b; 2008]   ἐξήκοντα
ἐξῆλθαν   aor act ind 3 pl
[2t; cv-1b(2); 2002]   ἐξέρχομαι
ἐξήλθατε   aor act ind 2 pl [9t; cv-1b(2); 2002]   "
ἐξῆλθεν   aor act ind 3 sg [67t; cv-1b(2); 2002]   "
ἐξῆλθες   aor act ind 2 sg
[Jn 16:30; cv-1b(2); 2002]   "
ἐξήλθομεν   aor act ind 1 pl
[Ac 16:13; cv-1b(2); 2002]   "
ἐξῆλθον   aor act ind 1 sg [9t; cv-1b(2); 2002]   "
ἐξῆλθον   aor act ind 3 pl [14t; cv-1b(2); 2002]   "
ἐξήνεγκεν   aor act ind 3 sg
[Mk 8:23; cv-1c(1); 1766]   ἐκφέρω
ἐξηπάτησεν   aor act ind 3 sg
[2t; cv-1d(1a); 1987]   ἐξαπατάω
ἐξηραμμένη   perf pass ptcp acc sg fem
[2t; v-2d(4); 3830]   ξηραίνω
ἐξήρανεν   aor act ind 3 sg
[Jm 1:11; v-2d(4); 3830]   "
ἐξηράνθη   aor pass ind 3 sg [10t; v-2d(4); 3830] "
ἐξήρανται   perf pass ind 3 sg
[Mk 11:21; v-2d(4); 3830]   "
ἐξηραύνησαν   aor act ind 3 pl
[1P 1:10; cv-1d(1a); 2001]   ἐξεραυνάω
ἐξηρτισμένος   perf pass ptcp nom sg masc
[2Ti 3:17; cv-2a(1); 1992]   ἐξαρτίζω
ἐξήρχετο   imperf mid ind 3 sg
[2t; cv-1b(2); 2002]   ἐξέρχομαι

ἐξήρχοντο   imperf mid ind 3 pl
[2t; cv-1b(2); 2002]   "

ἑξῆς   {2009, adverb}
successively, in order; in N.T. with the article ὁ, ἡ,
τό, ἑξῆς, *next*, Luke 7:11; 9:37; Acts 21:1; 25:17;
27:18*

ἑξῆς   adverb [5t; adverb; 2009]   ἑξῆς
ἐξητήσατο   aor mid ind 3 sg
[Lk 22:31; cv-1d(2a); 1977]   ἐξαιτέω

ἐξηχέω   {2010, cv-1d(2a)}
[-, -, -, ἐξήχημαι -] act., *to make to sound forth;*
pas., *to sound forth*, 1 Thess 1:8*

ἐξήχηται   perf pass ind 3 sg
[1Th 1:8; cv-1d(2a); 2010]   ἐξηχέω
ἐξιέναι   pres act inf [2t; cv-6b; 1997]   ἔξειμι
ἕξιν   acc sg fem [Hb 5:14; n-3e(5b); 2011]   ἕξις
ἐξιόντων   pres act ptcp gen pl masc
[Ac 13:42; cv-6b; 1997]   ἔξειμι

ἕξις, εως, ἡ   {2011, n-3e(5b)}
a condition of body or *mind,* strictly, as resulting
from practice; *habit*, Heb 5:14*

ἐξίσταντο   imperf mid ind 3 pl
[6t; cv-6a; 2014]   ἐξίστημι
ἐξιστάνων   pres act ptcp nom sg masc
[Ac 8:9; cv-6a; 2014]   "
ἐξίστασθαι   pres mid inf [Mk 2:12; cv-6a; 2014] "
ἐξίστατο   imperf mid ind 3 sg
[Ac 8:13; cv-6a; 2014]   "

ἐξίστημι   {2014, cv-6a}
[(ἐξίστην), -, ἐξέστησα or ἐξέστην, ἐξέστακα -, -]
pr. *to put out of its place; to astonish, amaze,* Luke
24:22; Acts 8:9, 11; intrans. *to be astonished,* Matt
12:23; *to be beside one's self,* Mark 3:21; 2 Cor 5:13

ἐξισχύσητε   aor act subj 2 pl
[Ep 3:18; cv-1a(4); 2015]   ἐξισχύω

ἐξισχύω   {2015, cv-1a(4)}
[-, ἐξίσχυσα, -, -, -] *to be fully able, be strong,* Eph
3:18*

ἔξοδον   acc sg fem [2t; n-2b; 2016]   ἔξοδος

ἔξοδος, ου, ἡ   {2016, n-2b}
*a way out, a going out; a going out, departure, the
exodus,* Heb 11:22; met. *a departure* from life,
decease, death, Luke 9:31; 2 Peter 1:15*

ἐξόδου   gen sg fem [Hb 11:22; n-2b; 2016]   "
ἐξοίσουσιν   fut act ind 3 pl
[Ac 5:9; cv-1c(1); 1766]   ἐκφέρω
ἐξολεθρευθήσεται   fut pass ind 3 sg
[Ac 3:23; cv-1a(6); 2017]   ἐξολεθρεύω

ἐξολεθρεύω   {2017, cv-1a(6)}
[-, ἐξωλέθρευσα -, -, ἐξωλεθρεύθην] *to destroy
utterly, root out,* Acts 3:23*

ἐξομολογεῖσθε   pres mid imperative 2 pl
[Jm 5:16; cv-1d(2a); 2018]   ἐξομολογέω

ἐξομολογέω   {2018, cv-1d(2a)}
[ἐξομολογήσω, ἐξωμολόγησα, -, -, -] *to agree, bind
one's self, promise,* Luke 22:6; mid. *to confess,*
Matt 3:6; *to profess openly,* Phil 2:11; Rev 3:5; *to*

make open avowal of benefits; to praise, celebrate,
Matt 11:25; Luke 10:21

ἐξομολογήσεται   fut mid ind 3 sg
   [Rm 14:11; cv-1d(2a); 2018]   "

ἐξομολογήσηται   aor mid subj 3 sg
   [Pp 2:11; cv-1d(2a); 2018]   "

ἐξομολογήσομαι   fut mid ind 1 sg
   [Rm 15:9; cv-1d(2a); 2018]   "

ἐξομολογοῦμαι   pres mid ind 1 sg
   [2t; cv-1d(2a); 2018]   "

ἐξομολογούμενοι   pres mid ptcp nom pl masc
   [3t; cv-1d(2a); 2018]   "

ἐξόν   pres act ptcp nom sg neut
   [3t; cv-6b; 1997]   ἔξειμι

ἐξορκίζω   {2019, cv-2a(1)}
   [-, -, -, -, -] to put an oath to a person, to adjure,
   Matt 26:63; to exorcise, Acts 19:13 v.l., 14 v.l.*

ἐξορκίζω   pres act ind 1 sg
   [Mt 26:63; cv-2a(1); 2019]   ἐξορκίζω

ἐξορκιστής, οῦ, ὁ   {2020, n-1f}
   pr. one who puts an oath; in N.T. an exorcist, one
   who by various kinds of incantations, etc.,
   pretended to expel demons, Acts 19:13*

ἐξορκιστῶν   gen pl masc
   [Ac 19:13; n-1f; 2020]   ἐξορκιστής

ἐξορύξαντες   aor act ptcp nom pl masc
   [2t; cv-2b; 2021]   ἐξορύσσω

ἐξορύσσω   {2021, cv-2b}
   [-, ἐξώρυξα, -, -, -] to dig out or through, force up,
   Mark 2:4; to pluck out the eyes, Gal 4:15*

ἐξουδενέω   {2022, cv-1d(2a)}
   [-, -, -, -, ἐξουδενήθην] also spelled ἐξουδενόω, to
   treat with contempt, Mark 9:12*

ἐξουδενηθῇ   aor pass subj 3 sg
   [Mk 9:12; cv-1d(2a); 2022]   ἐξουδενέω

ἐξουθενεῖς   pres act ind 2 sg
   [Rm 14:10; cv-; 2024]   ἐξουθενέω

ἐξουθενεῖτε   pres act imperative 2 pl
   [1Th 5:20; cv-; 2024]   "

ἐξουθενείτω   pres act imperative 3 sg
   [Rm 14:3; cv-; 2024]   "

ἐξουδενόω, see ἐξουδενέω   {2023, cv-1d(3)}

ἐξουθενέω   {2024, cv-1d(2a)}
   [-, ἐξουθένησα, -, ἐξουθένημαι, ἐξουθενήθην] also
   spelled ἐξουθενόω, to make light of, set at naught,
   despise, treat with contempt and scorn, Luke 18:9;
   to neglect, disregard, 1 Thess 5:20; ἐξουθενημένος,
   contemptible, 2 Cor 10:10; of small account, 1 Cor
   1:28; 6:4; by impl. to reject with contempt, Acts
   4:11

ἐξουθενηθείς   aor pass ptcp nom sg masc
   [Ac 4:11; cv-; 2024]   "

ἐξουθενημένα   perf pass ptcp acc pl neut
   [1C 1:28; cv-; 2024]   "

ἐξουθενημένος   perf pass ptcp nom sg masc
   [2C 10:10; cv-; 2024]   "

ἐξουθενημένους   perf pass ptcp acc pl masc
   [1C 6:4; cv-; 2024]   "

ἐξουθενήσας   aor act ptcp nom sg masc
   [Lk 23:11; cv-; 2024]   "

ἐξουθενήσατε   aor act ind 2 pl
   [Ga 4:14; cv-; 2024]   "

ἐξουθενήσῃ   aor act subj 3 sg
   [1C 16:11; cv-; 2024]   "

ἐξουθενοῦντας   pres act ptcp acc pl masc
   [Lk 18:9; cv-; 2024]   "

ἐξουθενόω, see ἐξουθενέω   {2025, cv-1d(3)}

ἐξουσία, ας, ἡ   {2026, n-1a}
   power, ability, faculty, Matt 9:8; 10:1; efficiency,
   energy, Luke 4:32; liberty, licence, John 10:18;
   Acts 5:4; authority, rule, dominion, jurisdiction,
   Matt 8:9; 28:18; meton. pl. authorities, potentates,
   powers, Luke 12:11; 1 Cor 15:24; Eph 1:21; right,
   authority, full power, Matt 9:6; 21:23; privilege,
   prerogative, John 1:12; perhaps, a veil, 1 Cor
   11:10

ἐξουσία   nom sg fem [13t; n-1a; 2026]   ἐξουσία
ἐξουσίᾳ   dat sg fem [16t; n-1a; 2026]   "
ἐξουσιάζει   pres act ind 3 sg
   [2t; cv-2a(1); 2027]   ἐξουσιάζω
ἐξουσιάζοντες   pres act ptcp nom pl masc
   [Lk 22:25; cv-2a(1); 2027]   "

ἐξουσιάζω   {2027, cv-2a(1)}
   [-, -, -, -, ἐξουσιάσθην] to have or exercise power
   or authority over anyone, Luke 22:25; to possess
   independent control over, 1 Cor 7:4 (2t); pass. to be
   subject to, under the power or influence of, 1 Cor
   6:12*

ἐξουσίαι   nom pl fem
   [Cl 1:16; n-1a; 2026]   ἐξουσία
ἐξουσίαις   dat pl fem [3t; n-1a; 2026]   "
ἐξουσίαν   acc sg fem [56t; n-1a; 2026]   "
ἐξουσίας   gen sg fem [9t; n-1a; 2026]   "
ἐξουσίας   acc pl fem [3t; n-1a; 2026]   "
ἐξουσιασθήσομαι   fut pass ind 1 sg
   [1C 6:12; cv-2a(1); 2027]   ἐξουσιάζω

ἐξουσιαστικός, ή, όν   {2028, a-1a(2a)}
   authoritative, Mark 1:27 v.l.*

ἔξουσιν   fut act ind 3 pl [2t; v-1b(2); 2400]   ἔχω
ἐξουσιῶν   gen pl fem
   [1P 3:22; n-1a; 2026]   ἐξουσία

ἐξοχή, ῆς, ἡ   {2029, n-1b}
   pr. prominence, anything prominent; in N.T.
   eminence, distinction, Acts 25:23*

ἐξοχήν   acc sg fem [Ac 25:23; n-1b; 2029]   ἐξοχή

ἐξυπνίζω   {2030, cv-2a(1)}
   [ἐξυπνίσω, -, -, -, -] to awake, arouse from sleep,
   John 11:11*

ἐξυπνίσω   aor act subj 1 sg
   [Jn 11:11; cv-2a(1); 2030]   ἐξυπνίζω

ἔξυπνος, ον   {2031, a-3a}
   awake, aroused from sleep, Acts 16:27*

ἔξυπνος   nom sg masc
   [Ac 16:27; a-3a; 2031]   ἔξυπνος
ἐξυρημένη   perf pass ptcp dat sg fem
   [1C 11:5; v-1d(1a); 3834]   ξυράω

ἔξω   {2032, adverb}
can function as an improper prep., *without, out
of doors;* Matt 12:46, 47; ὁ, ἡ, τὸ ἔξω, *outer,
external, foreign,* Acts 26:11; 2 Cor 4:16; met. *not
belonging to one's community,* Mark 4:11; 1 Cor
5:12, 13; *out, away,* from a place or person, Matt
5:13; 13:48; as a prep., *out of,* Mark 5:10

ἔξω   adverb [63t; adverb; 2032]   ἔξω

ἔξωθεν   {2033, adverb}
can function as an improper prep., *outwardly,
externally,* Matt 23:27, 28; Mark 7:15; ὁ, ἡ, τὸ
ἔξωθεν, *outer, external,* Matt 23:25; Luke 11:39; τὸ
ἔξωθεν, *the exterior,* Luke 11:40; οἱ ἔξωθεν, *those
who are without* the Christian community, 1 Tim
3:7

ἔξωθεν   adverb, [13t; adverb; 2033]   ἔξωθεν

ἐξωθέω   {2034, cv-1b(4)}
[-, ἐξῶσα, -, -, -] *to expel, drive out,* Acts 7:45; *to
propel, urge forward,* Acts 27:39*

ἐξωμολόγησεν   aor act ind 3 sg
    [Lk 22:6; cv-1d(2a); 2018]   ἐξομολογέω
ἐξῶσαι   aor act inf
    [Ac 27:39; cv-1b(4); 2034]   ἐξωθέω
ἐξῶσεν   aor act ind 3 sg
    [Ac 7:45; cv-1b(4); 2034]   "
ἐξώτερον   acc sg neut comparative
    [3t; a-1a(1); 2035]   ἐξώτερος

ἐξώτερος, α, ον   {2035, a-1a(1)}
comparative in form but used as a superlative,
outer, exterior, external, Matt 8:12; 22:13; 25:30*

ἔοικα   {2036, a-1a(1)}
see εἴκω (1634a), dat., *to be like,* James 1:6, 23*

ἔοικεν   perf act ind 3 sg
    [2t; v-1b(2); 2036]   ἔοικα
ἑόρακα   perf act ind 1 sg
    [1C 9:1; v-1d(1a); 3972]   ὁράω
ἑόρακαν   perf act ind 3 pl
    [Cl 2:1; v-1d(1a); 3972]   "
ἑόρακεν   perf act ind 3 sg
    [Cl 2:18; v-1d(1a); 3972]   "

ἑορτάζω   {2037, v-2a(1)}
[-, -, -, -, -] *to keep a feast, celebrate a festival,* 1 Cor
5:8*

ἑορτάζωμεν   pres act subj 1 pl
    [1C 5:8; v-2a(1); 2037]   ἑορτάζω

ἑορτή, ῆς, ἡ   {2038, n-1b}
a solemn feast, public festival, Luke 2:41; 22:1;
John 13:1; spc. used of *the passover,* Matt 26:5;
27:15

ἑορτή   nom sg fem [4t; n-1b; 2038]   ἑορτή
ἑορτῇ   dat sg fem [7t; n-1b; 2038]   "
ἑορτήν   acc sg fem [9t; n-1b; 2038]   "
ἑορτῆς   gen sg fem [5t; n-1b; 2038]   "
ἐπ'   prep-gen [21t; prep; 2093]   ἐπί
ἐπ'   prep-dat [39t; prep; 2093]   "
ἐπ'   prep-acc [85t; prep; 2093]   "
ἐπαγαγεῖν   aor act inf
    [Ac 5:28; cv-1b(2); 2042]   ἐπάγω

ἐπαγγειλάμενον   aor mid ptcp acc sg masc
    [Hb 11:11; cv-2d(1); 2040]   ἐπαγγέλλομαι
ἐπαγγειλάμενος   aor mid ptcp nom sg masc
    [2t; cv-2d(1); 2040]   "

ἐπαγγελία, ας, ἡ   {2039, n-1a}
annunciation, 2 Tim 1:1; *a promise, act of
promising,* Acts 13:23, 32; 23:21; meton. *the thing
promised, promised favor and blessing,* Luke 24:49;
Acts 1:4

ἐπαγγελία   nom sg fem [6t; n-1a; 2039]   ἐπαγγελία
ἐπαγγελίᾳ   dat sg fem [Ep 6:2; n-1a; 2039]   "
ἐπαγγελίαι   nom pl fem [3t; n-1a; 2039]   "
ἐπαγγελίαις   dat pl fem [Hb 8:6; n-1a; 2039]   "
ἐπαγγελίαν   acc sg fem [16t; n-1a; 2039]   "
ἐπαγγελίας   gen sg fem [17t; n-1a; 2039]   "
ἐπαγγελίας   acc pl fem [6t; n-1a; 2039]   "
ἐπαγγελιῶν   gen pl fem [2t; n-1a; 2039]   "

ἐπαγγέλλομαι   {2040, cv-2d(1)}
[-, ἐπηγγειλάμην, -, ἐπήγγελμαι, -] *to declare, to
promise, undertake,* Mark 14:11; Rom 4:21; *to
profess,* 1 Tim 2:10

ἐπαγγελλομέναις   pres mid ptcp dat pl fem
    [1Ti 2:10; cv-2d(1); 2040]   ἐπαγγέλλομαι
ἐπαγγελλόμενοι   pres mid ptcp nom pl masc
    [2t; cv-2d(1); 2040]   "

ἐπάγγελμα, ατος, τό   {2041, n-3c(4)}
a promise, 2 Peter 3:13; meton. *promised favor* or
blessing, 2 Peter 1:4*

ἐπάγγελμα   acc sg neut
    [2P 3:13; n-3c(4); 2041]   ἐπάγγελμα
ἐπαγγέλματα   acc pl neut [2P 1:4; n-3c(4); 2041] "
ἐπάγοντες   pres act ptcp nom pl masc
    [2P 2:1; cv-1b(2); 2042]   ἐπάγω

ἐπάγω   {2042, cv-1b(2)}
[-, ἐπήγαγον or ἔπηξα, -, -, -] *to bring upon, cause
to come upon,* 2 Peter 2:1, 5; met. *to cause to be
imputed* or *attributed to, to bring* guilt *upon,* Acts
5:28; 14:2 v.l.*

ἐπαγωνίζεσθαι   pres mid inf
    [Jd 3; cv-2a(1); 2043]   ἐπαγωνίζομαι

ἐπαγωνίζομαι   {2043, cv-2a(1)}
[-, -, -, -, -] *to contend strenuously in defence of,*
Jude 3*

ἔπαθεν   aor act ind 3 sg [5t; v-5a; 4248]   πάσχω
ἐπάθετε   aor act ind 2 pl [2t; v-5a; 4248]   "
ἔπαθον   aor act ind 1 sg [Mt 27:19; v-5a; 4248] "
ἐπαθροιζομένων   pres pass ptcp gen pl masc
    [Lk 11:29; cv-2a(1); 2044]   ἐπαθροίζω

ἐπαθροίζω   {2044, cv-2a(1)}
[-, -, -, -, -] act., *to gather together, to collect close
upon,* or *beside;* pas., *to crowd upon,* Luke 11:29*

ἐπαιδεύθη   aor pass ind 3 sg
    [Ac 7:22; v-1a(6); 4084]   παιδεύω
ἐπαίδευον   imperf act ind 3 pl
    [Hb 12:10; v-1a(6); 4084]   "
ἐπαινεσάτωσαν   aor act imperative 3 pl
    [Rm 15:11; cv-1d(2b); 2046]   ἐπαινέω

ἐπαινέσω   aor act subj 1 sg
[1C 11:22; cv-1d(2b); 2046]   "

Ἐπαίνετον   acc sg masc
[Rm 16:5; n-2a; 2045]   Ἐπαίνετος

Ἐπαίνετος, ου, ὁ   {2045, n-2a}
Epaenetus, pr. name, Rom 16:5*

ἐπαινέω   {2046, cv-1d(2b)}
[ἐπαινέσω, ἐπήνεσα, -, -, -] to praise, commend,
applaud, Luke 16:8; Rom 15:11; 1 Cor 11:2, 17, 22
(2t)*

ἔπαινον   acc sg masc [7t; n-2a; 2047]   ἔπαινος

ἔπαινος, ου, ὁ   {2047, n-2a}
praise, applause, honor paid, Rom 2:29; 2 Cor 8:18;
meton. ground or reason of praise or
commendation, Phil 4:8; approval, Rom 13:3; 1
Peter 2:14; 1 Cor 4:5

ἔπαινος   nom sg masc [4t; n-2a; 2047]   "
ἐπαινῶ   pres act ind 1 sg
[3t; cv-1d(2b); 2046]   ἐπαινέω
ἐπαίρεται   pres mid ind 3 sg
[2C 11:20; cv-2d(2); 2048]   ἐπαίρω
ἐπαιρόμενον   pres pass ptcp acc sg neut
[2C 10:5; cv-2d(2); 2048]   "
ἐπαίροντας   pres act ptcp acc pl masc
[1Ti 2:8; cv-2d(2); 2048]   "

ἐπαίρω   {2048, cv-2d(2)}
[-, ἐπῆρα, ἐπῆρκα, -, ἐπήρθην] to lift up, raise,
elevate; to hoist, Acts 27:40; τὴν φωνήν, to lift up
the voice, to speak in a loud voice, Luke 11:27; τὰς
χεῖρας, to lift up the hands in prayer, Luke 24:50;
1 Tim 2:8; τοὺς ὀφθαλμούς, to lift up the eyes, to
look, Matt 17:8; τὴν κεφαλήν, to lift up the head, to
be encouraged, animated, Luke 21:28; τὴν
πτέρναν, to lift up the heel, to attack, assault; or, to
seek one's overthrow or destruction, John 13:18;
pass. to be borne upwards, Acts 1:9; met. mid. to
exalt one's self, assume consequence, be elated, 2
Cor 10:5

ἔπαισεν   aor act ind 3 sg [2t; v-1a(2); 4091]   παίω
ἐπαισχύνεσθε   pres pass ind 2 pl
[Rm 6:21; cv-1c(2); 2049]   ἐπαισχύνομαι
ἐπαισχύνεται   pres pass ind 3 sg
[2t; cv-1c(2); 2049]   "
ἐπαισχύνθη   aor pass ind 3 sg
[2Ti 1:16; cv-1c(2); 2049]   "
ἐπαισχυνθῇ   aor pass subj 3 sg
[2t; cv-1c(2); 2049]   "
ἐπαισχυνθῇς   aor pass subj 2 sg
[2Ti 1:8; cv-1c(2); 2049]   "
ἐπαισχυνθήσεται   fut pass ind 3 sg
[2t; cv-1c(2); 2049]   "

ἐπαισχύνομαι   {2049, cv-1c(2)}
[-, -, -, -, ἐπαισχύνθην] to be ashamed of, Mark
8:38; Luke 9:26; Rom 1:16; 6:21; 2 Tim 1:8, 12, 16;
Heb 2:11; 11:16*

ἐπαισχύνομαι   pres mid ind 1 sg
[Rm 1:16; cv-1c(2); 2049]   "
ἐπαισχύνομαι   pres pass ind 1 sg
[2Ti 1:12; cv-1c(2); 2049]   "

ἐπαιτεῖν   pres act inf
[Lk 16:3; cv-1d(2a); 2050]   ἐπαιτέω

ἐπαιτέω   {2050, cv-1d(2a)}
[-, -, -, -, -] to prefer a suit or request in respect of
certain circumstances; to ask alms, beg, Luke 16:3;
18:35; Mark 10:46 v.l.*

ἐπαιτῶν   pres act ptcp nom sg masc
[Lk 18:35; cv-1d(2a); 2050]   "

ἐπακολουθέω   {2051, cv-1d(2a)}
[-, ἐπηκολούθησα, -, -, -] to follow upon; to
accompany, be attendant, Mark 16:20; to appear
later, 1 Tim 5:24; met. to follow one's steps, to
imitate, 1 Peter 2:21; to follow a work, pursue,
prosecute, be studious of, devoted to, 1 Tim 5:10*

ἐπακολουθήσητε   aor act subj 2 pl
[1P 2:21; cv-1d(2a); 2051]   ἐπακολουθέω
ἐπακολουθούντων   pres act ptcp gen pl neut
[Mk 16:20; cv-1d(2a); 2051]   "
ἐπακολουθοῦσιν   pres act ind 3 pl
[1Ti 5:24; cv-1d(2a); 2051]   "

ἐπακούω   {2052, cv-1a(8)}
[ἐπακούσω, ἐπήκουσα, -, -, -] gen., to listen or
hearken to; to hear with favor, 2 Cor 6:2*

ἐπακροάομαι   {2053, cv-1d(1a)}
[(ἐπηκροώμην), -, -, -, -, -] gen., to hear, hearken,
listen to, Acts 16:25*

ἐπάν   {2054, conj}
with subj., whenever, as soon as, Matt 2:8; Luke
11:22, 34*

ἐπάν   conj [3t; conj; 2054]   ἐπάν
ἐπανάγαγε   aor act imperative 2 sg
[Lk 5:4; cv-1b(2); 2056]   ἐπανάγω
ἐπαναγαγεῖν   aor act inf
[Lk 5:3; cv-1b(2); 2056]   "

ἐπάναγκες   {2055, adverb}
of necessity, necessarily; τὰ ἐπάναγκες, necessary
things, Acts 15:28*

ἐπάναγκες   adverb
[Ac 15:28; adverb; 2055]   ἐπάναγκες
ἐπανάγω   {2056, cv-1b(2)}
[-, ἐπανήγαγον, -, -, -] to bring up or back; intrans.
to return, Matt 21:18; a nautical term, to put off
from shore, Luke 5:3, 4*

ἐπανάγων   pres act ptcp nom sg masc
[Mt 21:18; cv-1b(2); 2056]   ἐπανάγω

ἐπαναμιμνήσκω   {2057, cv-5a}
[-, -, -, -, ἐπανεμνήσθην] to remind, put in
remembrance, Rom 15:15*

ἐπαναμιμνήσκων   pres act ptcp nom sg masc
[Rm 15:15; cv-5a; 2057]   ἐπαναμιμνήσκω
ἐπαναπαήσεται   fut pass ind 3 sg
[Lk 10:6; cv-1a(5); 2058]   ἐπαναπαύομαι
ἐπαναπαύῃ   pres mid ind 2 sg
[Rm 2:17; cv-1a(5); 2058]   "

ἐπαναπαύομαι   {2058, cv-1a(5)}
[-, -, -, -, ἐπανεπάην] pr. to make to rest upon; mid.
to rest upon; to abide with, Luke 10:6; to rely on,

confide in, abide by confidingly, Rom 2:17; 1 Peter 4:14 v.l.*

ἐπαναστήσονται   fut mid ind 3 pl
[2t; cv-6a; 2060]   ἐπανίστημι
ἐπανελθεῖν   aor act inf
[Lk 19:15; cv-1b(2); 2059]   ἐπανέρχομαι
ἐπανέρχεσθαι   pres mid inf
[Lk 10:35; cv-1b(2); 2059]   "

ἐπανέρχομαι   {2059, cv-1b(2)}
[-, ἐπανῆλθον, -, -, -] to come back, return, Luke 10:35; 19:15*

ἐπανίστημι   {2060, cv-6a}
[ἐπαναστήσω, ἐπανέστην, -, -, -] to raise up against; mid. to rise up against in rebellion, Matt 10:21; Mark 13:12*

ἐπανόρθωσιν   acc sg fem
[2Ti 3:16; n-3e(5b); 2061]   ἐπανόρθωσις

ἐπανόρθωσις, εως, ἡ   {2061, n-3e(5b)}
correction, reformation, improvement, 2 Tim 3:16*

ἐπάνω   {2062, adverb}
can function as an improper prep., above, over, upon, of place, Matt 2:9; 5:14; over, of authority, Luke 19:17, 19; above, more than, Mark 14:5

ἐπάνω   adverb, [19t; adverb; 2062]   ἐπάνω
ἐπάξας   aor act ptcp nom sg masc
[2P 2:5; cv-1b(2); 2042]   ἐπάγω
ἐπᾶραι   aor act inf
[Lk 18:13; cv-2d(2); 2048]   ἐπαίρω
ἐπάραντες   aor act ptcp nom pl masc
[2t; cv-2d(2); 2048]   "
ἐπάρας   aor act ptcp nom sg masc
[5t; cv-2d(2); 2048]   "
ἐπάρασα   aor act ptcp nom sg fem
[Lk 11:27; cv-2d(2); 2048]   "
ἐπάρατε   aor act imperative 2 pl
[2t; cv-2d(2); 2048]   "
ἐπάρατοι   nom pl masc
[Jn 7:49; a-3a; 2063]   ἐπάρατος

ἐπάρατος, ον   {2063, a-3a}
accursed, John 7:49*

ἐπαρκείτω   pres act imperative 3 sg
[1Ti 5:16; cv-1d(2b); 2064]   ἐπαρκέω
ἐπαρκέσῃ   aor act subj 3 sg
[1Ti 5:16; cv-1d(2b); 2064]   "

ἐπαρκέω   {2064, cv-1d(2b)}
[-, ἐπήρκεσα, -, -, -] dat., pr. to ward off; to assist, relieve, succor; 1 Tim 5:10, 16 (2t)*

ἐπαρρησιάζετο   imperf mid ind 3 sg
[Ac 19:8; v-2a(1); 4245]   παρρησιάζομαι
ἐπαρρησιασάμεθα   aor mid ind 1 pl
[1Th 2:2; v-2a(1); 4245]   "
ἐπαρρησιάσατο   aor mid ind 3 sg
[Ac 9:27; v-2a(1); 4245]   "

ἐπαρχεία, ας, ἡ   {2065, n-1a}
province, Acts 23:34; 25:1*

ἐπαρχείᾳ   dat sg fem
[Ac 25:1; n-1a; 2065]   ἐπαρχεία
ἐπαρχείας   gen sg fem [Ac 23:34; n-1a; 2065]   "

ἐπάρχειος, ον   {2066, a-3a}
also spelled ἐπαρχία, a prefecture, province, Acts 25:1 v.l.*

ἐπαρχία, see ἐπάρχειος

ἐπάταξεν   aor act ind 3 sg
[2t; v-2b; 4250]   πατάσσω
ἐπατήθη   aor pass ind 3 sg
[Rv 14:20; v-1d(2a); 4251]   πατέω

ἔπαυλις, εως, ἡ   {2068, n-3e(5b)}
pr. a place to pass the night in; cottage, farm; in N.T. a dwelling, habitation, farm, Acts 1:20*

ἔπαυλις   nom sg fem
[Ac 1:20; n-3e(5b); 2068]   ἔπαυλις
ἐπαύοντο   imperf mid ind 3 pl
[Ac 5:42; v-1a(5); 4264]   παύω

ἐπαύριον   {2069, adverb}
tomorrow; ἡ ἐπαύριον, sc. ἡμέρα, the next or following day, Matt 27:62; Mark 11:12

ἐπαύριον   adverb [17t; adverb; 2069]   ἐπαύριον
ἐπαυσάμην   aor mid ind 1 sg
[Ac 20:31; v-1a(5); 4264]   παύω
ἐπαύσαντο   aor mid ind 3 pl [3t; v-1a(5); 4264]   "
ἐπαύσατο   aor mid ind 3 sg [2t; v-1a(5); 4264]   "

ἐπαυτοφώρῳ   {2070}
pr. in the very theft; in N.T. in the very act, v.l. for αὐτοφώρῳ (a-3a) at John 8:4*

Ἐπαφρᾶ   gen sg masc [Cl 1:7; n-1e; 2071]   Ἐπαφρᾶς

Ἐπαφρᾶς, ᾶ, ὁ   {2071, n-1e}
Epaphras, pr. name, Col 1:7; 4:12; Phlm 23*

Ἐπαφρᾶς   nom sg masc [2t; n-1e; 2071]   "
ἐπαφρίζοντα   pres act ptcp nom pl neut
[Jd 13; cv-; 2072]   ἐπαφρίζω

ἐπαφρίζω   {2072, cv-2a(1)}
[-, -, -, -, -] to foam out; to pour out like foam, vomit forth, Jude 13*

Ἐπαφρόδιτον   acc sg masc
[Pp 2:25; n-2a; 2073]   Ἐπαφρόδιτος

Ἐπαφρόδιτος, ου, ὁ   {2073, n-2a}
Epaphroditus, pr. name, Phil 2:25; 4:18*

Ἐπαφροδίτου   gen sg masc [Pp 4:18; n-2a; 2073]   "
ἐπαχύνθη   aor pass ind 3 sg
[2t; v-1c(2); 4266]   παχύνω
ἐπέβαλεν   aor act ind 3 sg
[3t; cv-2d(1); 2095]   ἐπιβάλλω
ἐπέβαλλεν   imperf act ind 3 sg
[Mk 4:37; cv-2d(1); 2095]   "
ἐπέβαλον   aor act ind 3 pl [5t; cv-2d(1); 2095]   "
ἐπέβην   aor act ind 1 sg
[Ac 20:18; cv-2d(6); 2094]   ἐπιβαίνω
ἐπεβίβασαν   aor act ind 3 pl
[Lk 19:35; cv-2a(1); 2097]   ἐπιβιβάζω
ἐπέβλεψεν   aor act ind 3 sg
[Lk 1:48; cv-1b(1); 2098]   ἐπιβλέπω
ἐπεγέγραπτο   pluperf pass ind 3 sg
[Ac 17:23; cv-1b(1); 2108]   ἐπιγράφω

ἐπεγείρω   {2074, cv-2d(3)}
[-, ἐπήγειρα, -, -, ἐπηγέρθην] to raise or stir up

against, excite or *instigate against,* Acts 13:50; 14:2*

ἐπεγίνωσκον   imperf act ind 3 pl
  [3t; cv-5a; 2105]   ἐπιγινώσκω
ἐπεγνωκέναι   perf act inf
  [2P 2:21; cv-5a; 2105]   "
ἐπεγνωκόσι   perf act ptcp dat pl masc
  [1Ti 4:3; cv-5a; 2105]   "
ἐπέγνωμεν   aor act ind 1 pl
  [Ac 28:1; cv-5a; 2105]   "
ἐπέγνωσαν   aor act ind 3 pl [4t; cv-5a; 2105]   "
ἐπεγνώσθην   aor pass ind 1 sg
  [1C 13:12; cv-5a; 2105]   "
ἐπέγνωτε   aor act ind 2 pl [2t; cv-5a; 2105]   "
ἐπεδίδου   imperf act ind 3 sg
  [Lk 24:30; cv-6a; 2113]   ἐπιδίδωμι
ἐπεδόθη   aor pass ind 3 sg
  [Lk 4:17; cv-6a; 2113]   "
ἐπέδωκαν   aor act ind 3 pl [2t; cv-6a; 2113]   "
ἐπεζήτησεν   aor act ind 3 sg
  [Ac 13:7; cv-1d(2a); 2118]   ἐπιζητέω
ἐπεζήτουν   imperf act ind 3 pl
  [Lk 4:42; cv-1d(2a); 2118]   "
ἐπέθεντο   aor mid ind 3 pl
  [Ac 28:10; cv-6a; 2202]   ἐπιτίθημι
ἐπέθηκαν   aor act ind 3 pl [6t; cv-6a; 2202]   "
ἐπέθηκεν   aor act ind 3 sg [5t; cv-6a; 2202]   "
ἐπεθύμει   imperf act ind 3 sg
  [Lk 15:16; cv-1d(2a); 2121]   ἐπιθυμέω
ἐπεθύμησα   aor act ind 1 sg
  [2t; cv-1d(2a); 2121]   "
ἐπεθύμησαν   aor act ind 3 pl
  [2t; cv-1d(2a); 2121]   "

ἐπεί   {2075, conj}
  when, after, as soon as, Luke 7:1 v.l.; *since, because, in as much as,* Matt 18:32; 27:6; *for, for then, for else, since in that case,* Rom 3:6; 11:6

ἐπεί   conj [26t; conj; 2075]   ἐπεί
ἐπεῖδεν   aor act ind 3 sg
  [Lk 1:25; cv-1d(1a); 2393]   ἐφοράω

ἐπειδή   {2076, conj}
  since, because, in as much as, Matt 21:46; Luke 11:6; Acts 13:46

ἐπειδή   conj [10t; conj; 2076]   ἐπειδή

ἐπειδήπερ   {2077, conj}
  since now, since indeed, considering that, Luke 1:1*

ἐπειδήπερ   conj [Lk 1:1; conj; 2077]   ἐπειδήπερ

ἐπεῖδον, see ἐφοράω   {2078}

ἔπειθεν   imperf act ind 3 sg
  [Ac 18:4; v-1b(3); 4275]   πείθω
ἐπείθετο   imperf pass ind 3 sg
  [Ac 27:11; v-1b(3); 4275]   "
ἔπειθον   imperf act ind 3 pl
  [Ac 13:43; v-1b(3); 4275]   "
ἐπείθοντο   imperf pass ind 3 pl
  [3t; v-1b(3); 4275]   "

ἔπειμι   {2079, cv-6b}
  [-, -, -, -, -] *to come upon; to come after; to succeed*

immediately, Acts 7:26; 16:11; 18:19 v.l.; 20:15; 21:18; 23:11*

ἐπείνασα   aor act ind 1 sg
  [2t; v-1d(1b); 4277]   πεινάω
ἐπείνασαν   aor act ind 3 pl
  [Mt 12:1; v-1d(1b); 4277]   "
ἐπείνασεν   aor act ind 3 sg [7t; v-1d(1b); 4277]   "

ἐπείπερ   {conj}
  since indeed, seeing that, Rom 3:30 v.l.*

ἐπείραζεν   imperf act ind 3 sg
  [Ac 9:26; v-2a(1); 4279]   πειράζω
ἐπείραζον   imperf act ind 3 pl
  [Ac 16:7; v-2a(1); 4279]   "
ἐπείρασαν   aor act ind 3 pl [2t; v-2a(1); 4279]   "
ἐπείρασας   aor act ind 2 sg
  [Rv 2:2; v-2a(1); 4279]   "
ἐπείρασεν   aor act ind 3 sg [2t; v-2a(1); 4279]   "
ἐπειρῶντο   imperf mid ind 3 pl
  [Ac 26:21; v-1d(1a); 4281]   πειράω

ἐπεισαγωγή, ῆς, ἡ   {2081, n-1b}
  a superinduction, a further introduction, whether by way of addition or substitution, Heb 7:19*

ἐπεισαγωγή   nom sg fem
  [Hb 7:19; n-1b; 2081]   ἐπεισαγωγή
ἔπεισαν   aor act ind 3 pl
  [Mt 27:20; v-1b(3); 4275]   πείθω
ἐπεισελεύσεται   fut mid ind 3 sg
  [Lk 21:35; cv-1b(2); 2082]   ἐπεισέρχομαι

ἐπεισέρχομαι   {2082, cv-1b(2)}
  [ἐπεισελεύσομαι, -, -, -, -] *to come in upon, invade, surprise,* Luke 21:35*

ἐπείσθησαν   aor pass ind 3 pl
  [2t; v-1b(3); 4275]   πείθω

ἔπειτα   {2083, adverb}
  thereupon, then, after that, in the next place, afterwards, Mark 7:5; Luke 16:7

ἔπειτα   adverb [16t; adverb; 2083]   ἔπειτα
ἐπεῖχεν   imperf act ind 3 sg
  [Ac 3:5; cv-1b(2); 2091]   ἐπέχω
ἐπεκάθισεν   aor act ind 3 sg
  [Mt 21:7; v-2a(1); 2125]   ἐπικαθίζω
ἐπεκάλεσαν   aor act ind 3 pl
  [Mt 10:25; cv-1d(2b); 2126]   ἐπικαλέω
ἐπεκαλύφθησαν   aor pass ind 3 pl
  [Rm 4:7; cv-4; 2128]   ἐπικαλύπτω
ἐπέκειλαν   aor act ind 3 pl
  [Ac 27:41; cv-2d(1); 2131]   ἐπικέλλω

ἐπέκεινα   {2084, adverb}
  BAGD say it is an adverb with the gen.; others classify it as an improper prep., gen., *on yonder side, beyond,* Acts 7:43*

ἐπέκεινα   adverb [Ac 7:43; adverb; 2084]   ἐπέκεινα
ἐπέκειντο   imperf mid ind 3 pl
  [Lk 23:23; cv-6b; 2130]   ἐπίκειμαι
ἐπέκειτο   imperf mid ind 3 sg
  [Jn 11:38; cv-6b; 2130]   "
ἐπεκέκλητο   pluperf mid ind 3 sg
  [Ac 26:32; cv-1d(2b); 2126]   ἐπικαλέω

ἐπεκλήθη   aor pass ind 3 sg
   [Ac 1:23; cv-1d(2b); 2126]   "
ἐπέκρινεν   aor act ind 3 sg
   [Lk 23:24; cv-1c(2); 2137]   ἐπικρίνω

ἐπεκτείνομαι   {2085, cv-2d(5)}
   [-, -, -, -, -] pr. *to stretch out farther*; in N.T. mid.
   to reach out towards, strain for, Phil 3:13*

ἐπεκτεινόμενος   pres mid ptcp nom sg masc
   [Pp 3:13; cv-2d(5); 2085]   ἐπεκτείνομαι
ἐπελάβετο   aor mid ind 3 sg
   [2t; cv-3a(2b); 2138]   ἐπιλαμβάνομαι
ἐπελάθετο   aor mid ind 3 sg
   [Jm 1:24; cv-3a(2b); 2140]   ἐπιλανθάνομαι
ἐπελάθοντο   aor mid ind 3 pl
   [2t; cv-3a(2b); 2140]   "
ἐπέλειχον   imperf act ind 3 pl
   [Lk 16:21; cv-; 2143]   ἐπιλείχω
ἐπελεύσεται   fut mid ind 3 sg
   [Lk 1:35; cv-1b(2); 2088]   ἐπέρχομαι
ἐπέλθῃ   aor act subj 3 sg [2t; cv-1b(2); 2088]   "
ἐπελθόντος   aor act ptcp gen sg neut
   [Ac 1:8; cv-1b(2); 2088]   "
ἐπελθών   aor act ptcp nom sg masc
   [Lk 11:22; cv-1b(2); 2088]   "
ἐπέλυεν   imperf act ind 3 sg
   [Mk 4:34; cv-1a(4); 2147]   ἐπιλύω
ἐπέμεινα   aor act ind 1 sg
   [Ga 1:18; cv-1c(2); 2152]   ἐπιμένω
ἐπεμείναμεν   aor act ind 1 pl
   [2t; cv-1c(2); 2152]   "
ἐπεμελήθη   aor pass ind 3 sg
   [Lk 10:34; cv-1d(2c); 2150]   ἐπιμελέομαι
ἐπέμενεν   imperf act ind 3 sg
   [Ac 12:16; cv-1c(2); 2152]   ἐπιμένω
ἐπέμενον   imperf act ind 3 pl
   [Jn 8:7; cv-1c(2); 2152]
ἐπέμφθη   aor pass ind 3 sg
   [Lk 4:26; v-1b(1); 4287]   πέμπω
ἔπεμψα   aor act ind 1 sg [9t; v-1b(1); 4287]   "
ἐπέμψαμεν   aor act ind 1 pl
   [1Th 3:2; v-1b(1); 4287]   "
ἐπέμψατε   aor act ind 2 pl
   [Pp 4:16; v-1b(1); 4287]   "
ἔπεμψεν   aor act ind 3 sg [3t; v-1b(1); 4287]   "

ἐπενδύομαι   {2086, cv-3a(1)}
   [-, ἐπενεδυσάμην, -, -, -] *to put on over* or *in
   addition to*; mid. *to put on one's self in addition; to
   be further invested*, 2 Cor 5:2, 4*

ἐπενδύσασθαι   aor mid inf
   [2t; cv-3a(1); 2086]   ἐπενδύομαι
ἐπενδύτην   acc sg masc
   [Jn 21:7; n-1f; 2087]   ἐπενδύτης

ἐπενδύτης, ου, ὁ   {2087, n-1f}
   the outer or *upper tunic*, worn between the inner
   tunic and the external garments, John 21:7*

ἐπενεγκεῖν   aor act inf
   [Jd 9; cv-1c(1); 2214]   ἐπιφέρω
ἐπένευσεν   aor act ind 3 sg
   [Ac 18:20; cv-1a(6); 2153]   ἐπινεύω
ἐπενθήσατε   aor act ind 2 pl
   [1C 5:2; v-1d(2a); 4291]   πενθέω

ἐπέπεσαν   aor act ind 3 pl
   [Rm 15:3; cv-1b(3); 2158]   ἐπιπίπτω
ἐπέπεσεν   aor act ind 3 sg [7t; cv-1b(3); 2158]   "
ἐπεποίθει   pluperf act ind 3 sg
   [Lk 11:22; v-1b(3); 4275]   πείθω
ἐπερίσσευον   imperf act ind 3 pl
   [Ac 16:5; v-1a(6); 4355]   περισσεύω
ἐπερίσσευσαν   aor act ind 3 pl
   [Jn 6:13; v-1a(6); 4355]   "
ἐπερίσσευσεν   aor act ind 3 sg
   [4t; v-1a(6); 4355]   "

ἐπέρχομαι   {2088, cv-1b(2)}
   [ἐπελεύσομαι, ἐπῆλθον, -, -, -] *to come to*, Acts
   14:19; *to come upon*, Luke 1:35; 21:26; Acts 1:8;
   James 5:1; *to come upon* unexpectedly, *overtake*,
   Luke 21:35 v.l.; *to be coming on, to succeed*, Eph
   2:7; *to occur, happen to*, Acts 8:24; 13:40; *to come
   against, attack*, Luke 11:22*

ἐπερχομέναις   pres mid ptcp dat pl fem
   [Jm 5:1; cv-1b(2); 2088]   ἐπέρχομαι
ἐπερχομένοις   pres mid ptcp dat pl masc
   [Ep 2:7; cv-1b(2); 2088]   "
ἐπερχομένων   pres mid ptcp gen pl neut
   [Lk 21:26; cv-1b(2); 2088]   "
ἐπερωτᾶν   pres act inf
   [Lk 20:40; cv-1d(1a); 2089]   ἐπερωτάω
ἐπερωτάτωσαν   pres act imperative 3 pl
   [1C 14:35; cv-1d(1a); 2089]   "

ἐπερωτάω   {2089, cv-1d(1a)}
   [(ἐπηρώτων), ἐπερωτήσω, ἐπηρώτησα, -, -,
   ἐπηρωτήθην] *to interrogate, question, ask*, Matt
   12:10; 17:10; in N.T. *to request, require*, Matt 16:1;
   from the Hebrew, ἐπερωτᾶν τὸν θεόν, *to seek
   after, desire an acquaintance with God*, Rom 10:20

ἐπερωτηθείς   aor pass ptcp nom sg masc
   [Lk 17:20; cv-1d(1a); 2089]   "

ἐπερώτημα, ατος, τό   {2090, n-3c(4)}
   pr. *an interrogation, question*; in N.T. *profession,
   pledge*, 1 Peter 3:21*

ἐπερώτημα   nom sg neut
   [1P 3:21; n-3c(4); 2090]   ἐπερώτημα
ἐπερωτῆσαι   aor act inf
   [3t; cv-1d(1a); 2089]   ἐπερωτάω
ἐπερωτήσας   aor act ptcp nom sg masc
   [Ac 23:34; cv-1d(1a); 2089]   "
ἐπερωτήσατε   aor act imperative 2 pl
   [Jn 9:23; cv-1d(1a); 2089]   "
ἐπερωτήσω   fut act ind 1 sg
   [Mk 11:29; cv-1d(1a); 2089]   "
ἐπερωτῶ   pres act ind 1 sg
   [Lk 6:9; cv-1d(1a); 2089]   "
ἐπερωτῶντα   pres act ptcp acc sg masc
   [Lk 2:46; cv-1d(1a); 2089]   "
ἐπερωτῶσιν   pres act ind 3 pl
   [Mk 7:5; cv-1d(1a); 2089]   "
ἐπερωτῶσιν   pres act ptcp dat pl masc
   [Rm 10:20; cv-1d(1a); 2089]   "
ἔπεσα   aor act ind 1 sg [4t; v-1b(3); 4406]   πίπτω
ἔπεσαν   aor act ind 3 pl [12t; v-1b(3); 4406]   "
ἔπεσεν   aor act ind 3 sg [29t; v-1b(3); 4406]   "

ἐπεσκέψασθε   aor mid ind 2 pl
   [2t; cv-4; 2170]   ἐπισκέπτομαι
ἐπεσκέψατο   aor mid ind 3 sg   [3t; cv-4; 2170]   "
ἐπεσκίαζεν   imperf act ind 3 sg
   [Lk 9:34; cv-2a(1); 2173]   ἐπισκιάζω
ἐπεσκίασεν   aor act ind 3 sg
   [Mt 17:5; cv-2a(1); 2173]   "
ἐπέσπειρεν   aor act ind 3 sg
   [Mt 13:25; cv-2d(3); 2178]   ἐπισπείρω
ἐπέστειλα   aor act ind 1 sg
   [Hb 13:22; cv-2d(1); 2182]   ἐπιστέλλω
ἐπεστείλαμεν   aor act ind 1 pl
   [Ac 21:25; cv-2d(1); 2182]   "
ἐπέστη   aor act ind 3 sg
   [2t; cv-6a; 2392]   ἐφίστημι
ἐπεστήριξαν   aor act ind 3 pl
   [Ac 15:32; cv-2a(2); 2185]   ἐπιστηρίζω
ἐπέστησαν   aor act ind 3 pl
   [5t; cv-6a; 2392]   ἐφίστημι
ἐπεστράφητε   aor pass ind 2 pl
   [1P 2:25; cv-1b(1); 2188]   ἐπιστρέφω
ἐπέστρεψα   aor act ind 1 sg
   [Rv 1:12; cv-1b(1); 2188]   "
ἐπέστρεψαν   aor act ind 3 pl
   [2t; cv-1b(1); 2188]   "
ἐπεστρέψατε   aor act ind 2 pl
   [1Th 1:9; cv-1b(1); 2188]   "
ἐπέστρεψεν   aor act ind 3 sg
   [2t; cv-1b(1); 2188]   "
ἐπέσχεν   aor act ind 3 sg
   [Ac 19:22; cv-1b(2); 2091]   ἐπέχω
ἐπέταξας   aor act ind 2 sg
   [Lk 14:22; cv-2b; 2199]   ἐπιτάσσω
ἐπέταξεν   aor act ind 3 sg   [3t; cv-2b; 2199]   "
ἐπετίθεσαν   imperf act ind 3 pl
   [Ac 8:17; cv-6a; 2202]   ἐπιτίθημι
ἐπετίμα   imperf act ind 3 sg
   [Mk 3:12; cv-1d(1a); 2203]   ἐπιτιμάω
ἐπετίμησαν   aor act ind 3 pl
   [2t; cv-1d(1a); 2203]   "
ἐπετίμησεν   aor act ind 3 sg
   [14t; cv-1d(1a); 2203]   "
ἐπετίμων   imperf act ind 3 pl
   [3t; cv-1d(1a); 2203]   "
ἐπετράπη   aor pass ind 3 sg
   [Ac 28:16; cv-1b(1); 2205]   ἐπιτρέπω
ἐπέτρεψεν   aor act ind 3 sg   [6t; cv-1b(1); 2205]   "
ἐπέτυχεν   aor act ind 3 sg
   [3t; cv-3a(2b); 2209]   ἐπιτυγχάνω
ἐπέτυχον   aor act ind 3 pl
   [Hb 11:33; cv-3a(2b); 2209]   "
ἐπεφάνη   aor pass ind 3 sg
   [2t; cv-2d(4); 2210]   ἐπιφαίνω
ἐπεφώνει   imperf act ind 3 sg
   [Ac 12:22; cv-1d(2a); 2215]   ἐπιφωνέω
ἐπεφώνουν   imperf act ind 3 pl
   [3t; cv-1d(2a); 2215]   "
ἐπέφωσκεν   imperf act ind 3 sg
   [Lk 23:54; cv-; 2216]   ἐπιφώσκω
ἔπεχε   pres act imperative 2 sg
   [1Ti 4:16; cv-1b(2); 2091]   ἐπέχω
ἐπεχείρησαν   aor act ind 3 pl
   [2t; cv-1d(2a); 2217]   ἐπιχειρέω

ἐπεχείρουν   imperf act ind 3 pl
   [Ac 9:29; cv-1d(2a); 2217]   "
ἐπέχοντες   pres act ptcp nom pl masc
   [Pp 2:16; cv-1b(2); 2091]   ἐπέχω
ἐπέχρισεν   aor act ind 3 sg
   [2t; cv-1a(1); 2222]   ἐπιχρίω

ἐπέχω   {2091, cv-1b(2)}
   [(ἐπεῖχον), -, ἐπέσχον, -, -, -] trans. *to hold out,*
   present, exhibit, display, Phil 2:16; Luke 4:42 v.l.;
   intrans. *to observe, take heed to, attend to,* Luke
   14:7; Acts 3:5; 1 Tim 4:16; *to stay, delay,* Acts
   19:22*

ἐπέχων   pres act ptcp nom sg masc
   [Lk 14:7; cv-1b(2); 2091]   ἐπέχω
ἐπηγγείλαντο   aor mid ind 3 pl
   [Mk 14:11; cv-2d(1); 2040]   ἐπαγγέλλομαι
ἐπηγγείλατο   aor mid ind 3 sg
   [5t; cv-2d(1); 2040]   "
ἐπήγγελται   perf mid ind 3 sg
   [Hb 12:26; cv-2d(1); 2040]   "
ἐπήγγελται   perf pass ind 3 sg
   [2t; cv-2d(1); 2040]   "
ἐπήγειραν   aor act ind 3 pl
   [2t; cv-2d(3); 2074]   ἐπεγείρω
ἐπηκολούθησεν   aor act ind 3 sg
   [1Ti 5:10; cv-1d(2a); 2051]   ἐπακολουθέω
ἐπήκουσα   aor act ind 1 sg
   [2C 6:2; cv-1a(8); 2052]   ἐπακούω
ἐπηκροῶντο   imperf mid ind 3 pl
   [Ac 16:25; cv-; 2053]   ἐπακροάομαι
ἐπῆλθαν   aor act ind 3 pl
   [Ac 14:19; cv-1b(2); 2088]   ἐπέρχομαι
ἐπήνεσεν   aor act ind 3 sg
   [Lk 16:8; cv-1d(2b); 2046]   ἐπαινέω
ἔπηξεν   aor act ind 3 sg
   [Hb 8:2; v-3c(2); 4381]   πήγνυμι
ἐπῆραν   aor act ind 3 pl
   [2t; cv-2d(2); 2048]   ἐπαίρω
ἐπηρεάζοντες   pres act ptcp nom pl masc
   [1P 3:16; cv-; 2092]   ἐπηρεάζω
ἐπηρεαζόντων   pres act ptcp gen pl masc
   [Lk 6:28; cv-; 2092]   "

ἐπηρεάζω   {2092, cv-2a(1)}
   [-, -, -, -, -] *to harass, insult,* Matt 5:44 v.l.; Luke
   6:28; *to mistreat, abuse,* 1 Peter 3:16*

ἐπῆρεν   aor act ind 3 sg
   [2t; cv-2d(2); 2048]   ἐπαίρω
ἐπήρθη   aor pass ind 3 sg
   [Ac 1:9; cv-2d(2); 2048]   "
ἐπήρκεσεν   aor act ind 3 sg
   [1Ti 5:10; cv-1d(2b); 2064]   ἐπαρκέω
ἐπηρώτα   imperf act ind 3 sg
   [10t; cv-1d(1a); 2089]   ἐπερωτάω
ἐπηρώτησαν   aor act ind 3 pl
   [7t; cv-1d(1a); 2089]   "
ἐπηρώτησεν   aor act ind 3 sg
   [16t; cv-1d(1a); 2089]   "
ἐπηρώτων   imperf act ind 3 pl
   [10t; cv-1d(1a); 2089]   "

ἐπί   {2093, prep}
   (1) with the gen., *upon, on,* Matt 4:6; 9:2; 27:19;

in, of locality, Mark 8:4; *near upon, by, at*, Matt
21:19; John 21:1; *upon, over*, of authority, Matt
2:22; Acts 8:27; *in the presence of*, especially in a
judicial sense, 2 Cor 7:14; Acts 25:9; *in the case
of, in respect of*, John 6:2; Gal 3:16; *in the time of,
at the time of*, Acts 11:28; Rom 1:10; ἐπ' ἀληθείας,
really, bona fide, Mark 12:32; (2) with the dat.,
upon, on, Matt 14:8; Mark 2:21; Luke 12:44; *close
upon, by*, Matt 24:33; John 4:6; *in the
neighborhood* or *society of*, Acts 28:14; *over*, of
authority, Matt 24:47; *to*, of addition, *besides*,
Matt 25:20; Eph 6:16; Col 3:14; supervening
upon, after, 2 Cor 1:4; 7:4; *immediately upon*, John
4:27; *upon*, of the object of an act, *towards, to*,
Mark 5:33; Luke 18:7; Acts 5:35; *against*, of
hostile posture or disposition, Luke 12:52; *in
dependence upon*, Matt 4:4; Luke 5:5; Acts 14:3;
upon the ground of, Matt 19:9; Luke 1:59; Phil 1:3;
Heb 7:11; 8:6; 9:17; *with a view to*, Gal 5:13; 1
Thess 4:7; (3) with the acc., *upon*, with the idea
of previous or present motion, Matt 4:5; 14:19,
26; *towards*, of place, *to*, Matt 3:13; 22:34;
towards, of the object of an action, Luke 6:35;
9:38; *against*, of hostile movement, Matt 10:21;
over, of authority, Luke 1:33; *to the extent of*, both
of place and time, Rev 21:16; Rom 7:1; *near, by*,
Matt 9:9; *about, at, of time*, Acts 3:1; *in order to,
with a view to, for the purpose of*, Matt 3:7; Luke
7:44

ἐπί   prep-gen [193t; prep; 2093]   ἐπί
ἐπί   prep-dat [132t; prep; 2093]   "
ἐπί   prep-acc [338t; prep; 2093]   "
ἐπίασαν   aor act ind 3 pl
    [Jn 21:3; v-2a(1); 4389]   πιάζω
ἐπιάσατε   aor act ind 2 pl
    [Jn 21:10; v-2a(1); 4389]   "
ἐπίασεν   aor act ind 3 sg
    [Jn 8:20; v-2a(1); 4389]   "
ἐπιάσθη   aor pass ind 3 sg
    [Rv 19:20; v-2a(1); 4389]   "
ἐπιβαίνειν   pres act inf
    [Ac 21:4; cv-2d(6); 2094]   ἐπιβαίνω

ἐπιβαίνω   {2094, cv-2d(6)}
[-, ἐπέβην, ἐπιβέβηκα, -, -] pr. *to step upon; to
mount*, Matt 21:5; *to go on board*, Acts 21:2; 27:2,
to enter, Acts 20:18; *to enter upon*, Acts 21:4; 25:1*

ἐπιβαλεῖν   aor act inf
    [Lk 20:19; cv-2d(1); 2095]   ἐπιβάλλω
ἐπιβάλλει   pres act ind 3 sg
    [2t; cv-2d(1); 2095]   "
ἐπιβάλλον   pres act ptcp acc sg neut
    [Lk 15:12; cv-2d(1); 2095]   "
ἐπιβάλλουσιν   pres act ind 3 pl
    [Mk 11:7; cv-2d(1); 2095]   "

ἐπιβάλλω   {2095, cv-2d(1)}
[ἐπιβαλῶ, ἐπέβαλον, -, -, -] *to cast* or *throw upon*,
Mark 11:7; 1 Cor 7:35; *to lay on, apply to*, Luke
9:62; *to put on, sew on*, Matt 9:16; Luke 5:36; τὰς
χεῖρας, *to lay hands on, offer violence to, seize*,
Matt 26:50; also, *to lay hand to, undertake,
commence*, Acts 12:1; intrans. *to rush, dash, beat
into*, Mark 4:37; *to ponder, reflect on*, Mark 14:72;
to fall to one's share, pertain to, Luke 15:12

ἐπιβαλοῦσιν   fut act ind 3 pl
    [Lk 21:12; cv-2d(1); 2095]   "
ἐπιβάλω   aor act subj 1 sg
    [1C 7:35; cv-2d(1); 2095]   "
ἐπιβαλών   aor act ptcp nom sg masc
    [2t; cv-2d(1); 2095]   "
ἐπιβάντες   aor act ptcp nom pl masc
    [2t; cv-2d(6); 2094]   ἐπιβαίνω

ἐπιβαρέω   {2096, cv-1d(2a)}
[-, ἐπεβάρησα, -, -, -] *to burden*; met. *to be
burdensome, chargeable to*, 1 Thess 2:9; 2 Thess
3:8; *to bear hard upon, overcharge*, 2 Cor 2:5*

ἐπιβαρῆσαι   aor act inf
    [2t; cv-1d(2a); 2096]   ἐπιβαρέω
ἐπιβαρῶ   pres act subj 1 sg
    [2C 2:5; cv-1d(2a); 2096]   "
ἐπιβάς   aor act ptcp nom sg masc
    [Ac 25:1; cv-2d(6); 2094]   ἐπιβαίνω
ἐπιβεβηκώς   perf act ptcp nom sg masc
    [Mt 21:5; cv-2d(6); 2094]   "

ἐπιβιβάζω   {2097, cv-2a(1)}
[-, ἐπεβίβασα, -, -, -] *to cause to ascend* or *mount,
to set upon*, Luke 10:34; 19:35; Acts 23:24*

ἐπιβιβάσαντες   aor act ptcp nom pl masc
    [Ac 23:24; cv-2a(1); 2097]   ἐπιβιβάζω
ἐπιβιβάσας   aor act ptcp nom sg masc
    [Lk 10:34; cv-2a(1); 2097]   "

ἐπιβλέπω   {2098, cv-1b(1)}
[-, ἐπέβλεψα, -, -, -] *to look upon; to regard* with
partiality, James 2:3; *to regard* with kindness
and favor, Luke 1:48; 9:38*

ἐπιβλέψαι   aor act inf
    [Lk 9:38; cv-1b(1); 2098]   ἐπιβλέπω
ἐπιβλέψητε   aor act subj 2 pl
    [Jm 2:3; cv-1b(1); 2098]   "

ἐπίβλημα, ατος, τό   {2099, n-3c(4)}
that which is put over or *upon*; in N.T. *a patch*,
Matt 9:16; Mark 2:21; Luke 5:36 (2t)*

ἐπίβλημα   nom sg neut
    [Lk 5:36; n-3c(4); 2099]   ἐπίβλημα
ἐπίβλημα   acc sg neut   [3t; n-3c(4); 2099]   "

ἐπιβοάω   {2100, cv-1d(1a)}
[-, -, -, -, -] *to cry out to* or *against*, Acts 25:24 v.l.*

ἐπιβουλαῖς   dat pl fem
    [Ac 20:19; n-1b; 2101]   ἐπιβουλή

ἐπιβουλή, ῆς, ἡ   {2101, n-1b}
a purpose or *design against* any one; *conspiracy,
plot*, Acts 9:24; 20:3, 19; 23:30*

ἐπιβουλή   nom sg fem   [Ac 9:24; n-1b; 2101]   "
ἐπιβουλῆς   gen sg fem   [2t; n-1b; 2101]   "
ἐπιγαμβρεύσει   fut act ind 3 sg
    [Mt 22:24; cv-; 2102]   ἐπιγαμβρεύω

ἐπιγαμβρεύω   {2102, cv-1a(6)}
[ἐπιγαμβρεύσω, -, -, -, -] *to marry* a wife *by the
law of affinity*, Matt 22:24*

ἐπιγεγραμμένα   perf pass ptcp acc pl neut
    [Rv 21:12; cv-1b(1); 2108]   ἐπιγράφω

ἐπιγεγραμμένη   perf pass ptcp nom sg fem
   [Mk 15:26; cv-1b(1); 2108]   "
ἐπίγεια   nom pl neut
   [1C 15:40; a-3a; 2103]   ἐπίγειος
ἐπίγεια   acc pl neut [2t; a-3a; 2103]   "

ἐπίγειος, ον   {2103, a-3a}
   pr. *on the earth*, Phil 2:10; *earthly, terrestrial*, John
   3:12; 1 Cor 15:40; 2 Cor 5:1; Phil 3:19; *earthly,
   low, grovelling*, James 3:15*

ἐπίγειος   nom sg fem [2t; a-3a; 2103]   "
ἐπιγείων   gen pl masc [Pp 2:10; a-3a; 2103]   "
ἐπιγείων   gen pl neut [1C 15:40; a-3a; 2103]   "
ἐπιγενομένου   aor mid ptcp gen sg masc
   [Ac 28:13; cv-1c(2); 2104]   ἐπιγίνομαι

ἐπιγίνομαι   {2104, cv-1c(2)}
   [-, ἐπεγενόμην, -, -, -] *to come on, spring up,* as the
   wind, Acts 28:13; 27:27 v.l.*

ἐπιγινώσκει   pres act ind 3 sg
   [2t; cv-5a; 2105]   ἐπιγινώσκω
ἐπιγινώσκεις   pres act ind 2 sg
   [Ac 25:10; cv-5a; 2105]   "
ἐπιγινώσκετε   pres act imperative 2 pl
   [1C 16:18; cv-5a; 2105]   "
ἐπιγινώσκετε   pres act ind 2 pl
   [2t; cv-5a; 2105]   "
ἐπιγινωσκέτω   pres act imperative 3 sg
   [1C 14:37; cv-5a; 2105]   "
ἐπιγινωσκόμενοι   pres pass ptcp nom pl masc
   [2C 6:9; cv-5a; 2105]   "

ἐπιγινώσκω   {2105, cv-5a}
   [ἐπιγνώσομαι, ἐπέγνων, ἐπέγνωκα, -,
   ἐπεγνώσθην] pr. *to make* a thing *a subject of
   observation*; hence, *to arrive at knowledge from
   preliminaries; to attain to a knowledge of,* Matt
   11:27; *to ascertain,* Luke 7:37; 23:7; *to perceive,*
   Mark 2:8; 5:30; *to discern, detect,* Matt 7:16, 20; *to
   recognize,* Mark 6:33; Luke 24:16, 31; Acts 3:10;
   to acknowledge, admit, 1 Cor 14:37; 1 Tim 4:3;
   pass. *to have one's character discerned and
   acknowledged,* 2 Cor 6:9; from the Hebrew, *to
   regard* with favor and kindness, 1 Cor 16:18

ἐπιγνόντες   aor act ptcp nom pl masc
   [5t; cv-5a; 2105]   "
ἐπιγνούς   aor act ptcp nom sg masc
   [5t; cv-5a; 2105]   "
ἐπιγνοῦσα   aor act ptcp nom sg fem
   [2t; cv-5a; 2105]   "
ἐπιγνοῦσιν   aor act ptcp dat pl masc
   [2P 2:21; cv-5a; 2105]   "
ἐπιγνῶ   aor act subj 3 sg
   [Ac 22:24; cv-5a; 2105]   "
ἐπιγνῶναι   aor act inf [4t; cv-5a; 2105]   "
ἐπιγνῷς   aor act subj 2 sg
   [Lk 1:4; cv-5a; 2105]   "
ἐπιγνώσει   dat sg fem
   [7t; n-3e(5b); 2106]   ἐπίγνωσις
ἐπιγνώσεσθε   fut mid ind 2 pl
   [3t; cv-5a; 2105]   ἐπιγινώσκω
ἐπιγνώσεως   gen sg fem
   [2t; n-3e(5b); 2106]   ἐπίγνωσις
ἐπίγνωσιν   acc sg fem [10t; n-3e(5b); 2106]   "

ἐπίγνωσις, εως, ἡ   {2106, n-3e(5b)}
   the coming at the knowledge of a thing,
   ascertainment, Rom 3:20; *a distance perception* or
   impression, acknowledgment, insight, Col 2:2

ἐπίγνωσις   nom sg fem [Rm 3:20; n-3e(5b); 2106]   "
ἐπιγνώσομαι   fut mid ind 1 sg
   [1C 13:12; cv-5a; 2105]   ἐπιγινώσκω

ἐπιγραφή, ῆς, ἡ   {2107, n-1b}
   an inscription; a legend of a coin, Matt 22:20;
   Mark 12:16; Luke 20:24; *a label* of a criminal's
   name and offence, Mark 15:26; Luke 23:38*

ἐπιγραφή   nom sg fem [4t; n-1b; 2107]   ἐπιγραφή
ἐπιγραφήν   acc sg fem [Lk 20:24; n-1b; 2107]   "

ἐπιγράφω   {2108, cv-1b(1)}
   [ἐπιγράψω, -, -, ἐπιγέγραμμαι, ἐπεγράφην]
   pluperfect pass., ἐπεγεγράμμην, *to imprint a
   mark on; to inscribe, engrave, write on,* Mark
   15:26; Acts 17:23; Rev 21:12; met. *to imprint,
   impress deeply on,* Heb 8:10; 10:16*

ἐπιγράψω   fut act ind 1 sg
   [2t; cv-1b(1); 2108]   ἐπιγράφω
ἔπιδε   aor act imperative 2 sg
   [Ac 4:29; cv-1d(1a); 2393]   ἐφοράω
ἐπιδεικνύμεναι   pres mid ptcp nom pl fem
   [Ac 9:39; cv-3c(2); 2109]   ἐπιδείκνυμι

ἐπιδείκνυμι   {2109, cv-3c(2)}
   [ἐπιδείξω, ἐπέδειξα, -, -, -] *to exhibit,* Matt 16:1;
   Acts 9:39; *to show,* Matt 22:19; Luke 17:14; *to
   point out,* Matt 24:1; *to demonstrate, prove,* Acts
   18:28; Heb 6:17*

ἐπιδεικνύς   pres act ptcp nom sg masc
   [Ac 18:28; cv-3c(2); 2109]   "
ἐπιδεῖξαι   aor act inf [3t; cv-3c(2); 2109]   "
ἐπιδείξατε   aor act imperative 2 pl
   [2t; cv-3c(2); 2109]   "
ἐπιδέχεται   pres mid ind 3 sg
   [2t; cv-1b(2); 2110]   ἐπιδέχομαι

ἐπιδέχομαι   {2110, cv-1b(2)}
   [-, -, -, -, -] *to admit; to receive kindly, welcome,
   entertain,* 3 John 10; met. *to admit, approve, assent
   to,* 3 John 9; Acts 15:40 v.l.*

ἐπιδημέω   {2111, cv-1d(2)}
   [-, -, -, -, -] *to dwell among a people; to be at home
   among one's own people;* and in N.T. *to sojourn as
   a stranger among another people,* Acts 2:10; 17:21;
   18:27 v.l.*

ἐπιδημοῦντες   pres act ptcp nom pl masc
   [2t; cv-1d(2); 2111]   ἐπιδημέω
ἐπιδιατάσσεται   pres mid ind 3 sg
   [Ga 3:15; cv-2b; 2112]   ἐπιδιατάσσομαι

ἐπιδιατάσσομαι   {2112, cv-2b}
   [-, -, -, -, -] *to enjoin* anything *additional, superadd*
   an injunction, Gal 3:15*

ἐπιδίδωμι   {2113, cv-6a}
   [(ἐπιδίδουν), ἐπιδώσω, ἐπέδωκα, ἐπιδέδωκα, -,
   ἐπιδόθην] *to give in addition;* also, *to give to,
   deliver to, give into one's hands,* Matt 7:9, 10; Luke
   4:17; 11:11f.; 24:30, 42; Acts 15:30; intrans.

probably a nautical term, *to commit a ship to the wind, let her drive,* Acts 27:15*

ἐπιδιορθόω   {2114, cv-1d(3)}
[-, ἐπεδιόρθωσα, -, -, -] *to set further to rights, to carry on an amendment, correct,* Titus 1:5*

ἐπιδιορθώσῃ   aor mid subj 2 sg
   [Ti 1:5; cv-1d(3); 2114]   ἐπιδιορθόω
ἐπιδόντες   aor act ptcp nom pl masc
   [Ac 27:15; cv-6a; 2113]   ἐπιδίδωμι
ἐπιδυέτω   pres act imperative 3 sg
   [Ep 4:26; cv-3a(1); 2115]   ἐπιδύω

ἐπιδύω   {2115, cv-3a(1)}
[-, -, -, -, -] *to set upon, to set during,* Eph 4:26*

ἐπιδώσει   fut act ind 3 sg
   [4t; cv-6a; 2113]   ἐπιδίδωμι

ἐπιείκεια, ας, ἡ   {2116, n-1a}
also spelled ἐπιεικία, *reasonableness, equity;* in N.T. *gentleness, mildness,* 2 Cor 10:1; *clemency,* Acts 24:4*

ἐπιεικείᾳ   dat sg fem
   [Ac 24:4; n-1a; 2116]   ἐπιείκεια
ἐπιεικείας   gen sg fem [2C 10:1; n-1a; 2116]   "
ἐπιεικεῖς   acc pl masc
   [Ti 3:2; a-4a; 2117]   ἐπιεικής
ἐπιεικές   nom sg neut [Pp 4:5; a-4a; 2117]   "
ἐπιεικέσιν   dat pl masc [1P 2:18; a-4a; 2117]   "
ἐπιεικῆ   acc sg masc [1Ti 3:3; a-4a; 2117]   "

ἐπιεικής, ές   {2117, a-4a}
pr. *suitable; fair, reasonable; gentle, mild, patient,* 1 Tim 3:3; Titus 3:2; James 3:17; 1 Peter 2:18; τὸ ἐπιεικές, *mildness, gentleness,* Phil 4:5*

ἐπιεικής   nom sg fem [Jm 3:17; a-4a; 2117]   "

ἐπιεικία, see ἐπιείκεια

ἔπιεν   aor act ind 3 sg [2t; v-3a(1); 4403]   πίνω
ἐπιζητεῖ   pres act ind 3 sg
   [3t; cv-1d(2a); 2118]   ἐπιζητέω
ἐπιζητεῖτε   pres act ind 2 pl
   [Ac 19:39; cv-1d(2a); 2118]   "

ἐπιζητέω   {2118, cv-1d(2a)}
[(ἐπεζήτουν), -, ἐπεζήτησα, -, -, -] *to seek for, make search for,* Acts 12:19; *to require, demand,* Matt 12:39; 16:4; Acts 19:39; *to desire, endeavor to obtain,* Rom 11:7; Heb 11:14; *to seek with care and anxiety,* Matt 6:32

ἐπιζητήσας   aor act ptcp nom sg masc
   [Ac 12:19; cv-1d(2a); 2118]   "
ἐπιζητοῦμεν   pres act ind 1 pl
   [Hb 13:14; cv-1d(2a); 2118]   "
ἐπιζητοῦσιν   pres act ind 3 pl
   [3t; cv-1d(2a); 2118]   "
ἐπιζητῶ   pres act ind 1 sg [2t; cv-1d(2a); 2118]   "

ἐπιθανάτιος, ον   {2119, a-3a}
condemned to death, under sentence of death, 1 Cor 4:9*

ἐπιθανατίους   acc pl masc
   [1C 4:9; a-3a; 2119]   ἐπιθανάτιος
ἐπιθεῖναι   aor act inf
   [Ac 15:10; cv-6a; 2202]   ἐπιτίθημι

ἐπιθείς   aor act ptcp nom sg masc
   [5t; cv-6a; 2202]   "
ἐπιθέντα   aor act ptcp acc sg masc
   [Ac 9:12; cv-6a; 2202]   "
ἐπιθέντες   aor act ptcp nom pl masc
   [3t; cv-6a; 2202]   "
ἐπιθέντος   aor act ptcp gen sg masc
   [2t; cv-6a; 2202]   "
ἐπίθες   aor act imperative 2 sg
   [Mt 9:18; cv-6a; 2202]   "
ἐπιθέσεως   gen sg fem
   [4t; n-3e(5b); 2120]   ἐπίθεσις

ἐπίθεσις, εως, ἡ   {2120, n-3e(5b)}
the act of placing upon, imposition of hands, Acts 8:18; 1 Tim 4:14; 2 Tim 1:6; Heb 6:2*

ἐπιθῇ   aor act subj 3 sg
   [3t; cv-6a; 2202]   ἐπιτίθημι
ἐπιθῇς   aor act subj 2 sg
   [Mk 5:23; cv-6a; 2202]   "
ἐπιθήσει   fut act ind 3 sg
   [Rv 22:18; cv-6a; 2202]   "
ἐπιθήσεται   fut mid ind 3 sg
   [Ac 18:10; cv-6a; 2202]   "
ἐπιθήσουσιν   fut act ind 3 pl
   [Mk 16:18; cv-6a; 2202]   "
ἐπιθυμεῖ   pres act ind 3 sg
   [2t; cv-1d(2a); 2121]   ἐπιθυμέω
ἐπιθυμεῖτε   pres act ind 2 pl
   [Jm 4:2; cv-1d(2a); 2121]   "

ἐπιθυμέω   {2121, cv-1d(2a)}
[(ἐπεθύμουν), ἐπιθυμήσω, ἐπεθύμησα, -, -, -] with the gen. or acc., *to set the heart upon; to desire, long for, have earnest desire,* Matt 13:17; Luke 15:16; *to lust after,* Matt 5:28; spc. *to covet,* Rom 13:9

ἐπιθυμῆσαι   aor act inf
   [Mt 5:28; cv-1d(2a); 2121]   "
ἐπιθυμήσεις   fut act ind 2 sg
   [2t; cv-1d(2a); 2121]   "
ἐπιθυμήσετε   fut act ind 2 pl
   [Lk 17:22; cv-1d(2a); 2121]   "
ἐπιθυμήσουσιν   fut act ind 3 pl
   [Rv 9:6; cv-1d(2a); 2121]   "
ἐπιθυμητάς   acc pl masc
   [1C 10:6; n-1f; 2122]   ἐπιθυμητής

ἐπιθυμητής, οῦ, ὁ   {2122, n-1f}
one who has an ardent desire for anything, 1 Cor 10:6*

ἐπιθυμία, ας, ἡ   {2123, n-1a}
earnest desire, Luke 22:15; *irregular* or *violent desire,* Mark 4:19; spc. impure *desire, lust,* Rom 1:24; met. *the object of desire, what enkindles desire,* 1 John 2:16, 17

ἐπιθυμία   nom sg fem [4t; n-1a; 2123]   ἐπιθυμία
ἐπιθυμίᾳ   dat sg fem [4t; n-1a; 2123]   "
ἐπιθυμίαι   nom pl fem [Mk 4:19; n-1a; 2123]   "
ἐπιθυμίαις   dat pl fem [10t; n-1a; 2123]   "
ἐπιθυμίαν   acc sg fem [5t; n-1a; 2123]   "
ἐπιθυμίας   gen sg fem [3t; n-1a; 2123]   "
ἐπιθυμίας   acc pl fem [10t; n-1a; 2123]   "

ἐπιθυμιῶν gen pl fem [1P 2:11; n-1a; 2123] "
ἐπιθυμοῦμεν pres act ind 1 pl
  [Hb 6:11; cv-1d(2a); 2121] ἐπιθυμέω
ἐπιθυμοῦσιν pres act ind 3 pl
  [1P 1:12; cv-1d(2a); 2121] "
ἐπιθυμῶν pres act ptcp nom sg masc
  [Lk 16:21; cv-1d(2a); 2121] "

ἐπιθύω {2124, cv-1a(4)}
  [-, -, -, -, -] offer as a sacrifice, Acts 14:13 v.l.*

ἐπιθῶ aor act subj 1 sg
  [Ac 8:19; cv-6a; 2202] ἐπιτίθημι

ἐπικαθίζω {2125, cv-2a(1)}
  [-, ἐπεκάθισα, -, -, -] to cause to sit upon, seat
  upon, Matt 21:7 (where some mss read
  ἐπεκάθισεν, intrans. to sit upon)*

ἐπικαλεῖσθαι pres pass inf
  [Hb 11:16; cv-1d(2b); 2126] ἐπικαλέω
ἐπικαλεῖσθε pres mid ind 2 pl
  [1P 1:17; cv-1d(2b); 2126] "
ἐπικαλεῖται pres pass ind 3 sg
  [2t; cv-1d(2b); 2126] "
ἐπικαλεσάμενος aor mid ptcp nom sg masc
  [Ac 22:16; cv-1d(2b); 2126] "
ἐπικαλεσαμένου aor mid ptcp gen sg masc
  [2t; cv-1d(2b); 2126] "
ἐπικαλέσασθαι aor mid inf
  [Ac 28:19; cv-1d(2b); 2126] "
ἐπικαλέσηται aor mid subj 3 sg
  [2t; cv-1d(2b); 2126] "
ἐπικαλέσωνται aor mid subj 3 pl
  [Rm 10:14; cv-1d(2b); 2126] "

ἐπικαλέω {2126, cv-1d(2b)}
  [ἐπικαλέσω, ἐπεκάλεσα, -, ἐπικέκλημαι,
  ἐπεκλήθην] pluperfect, ἐπεκέκλητο (3 sg), to call
  on; to attach or connect a name, Acts 15:17; James
  2:7; to attach an additional name, to surname, Matt
  10:3; pass. to receive an appellation or surname,
  Heb 11:16; mid. to call upon, invoke, 2 Cor 1:23;
  to appeal to, Acts 25:11, 12, 21

ἐπικαλοῦμαι pres mid ind 1 sg
  [2t; cv-1d(2b); 2126] "
ἐπικαλουμένοις pres mid ptcp dat pl masc
  [1C 1:2; cv-1d(2b); 2126] "
ἐπικαλούμενον pres mid ptcp acc sg masc
  [Ac 7:59; cv-1d(2b); 2126] "
ἐπικαλούμενον pres pass ptcp acc sg masc
  [Ac 11:13; cv-1d(2b); 2126] "
ἐπικαλούμενος pres pass ptcp nom sg masc
  [Ac 10:18; cv-1d(2b); 2126] "
ἐπικαλουμένου pres pass ptcp gen sg masc
  [Ac 12:12; cv-1d(2b); 2126] "
ἐπικαλουμένους pres mid ptcp acc pl masc
  [3t; cv-1d(2b); 2126] "
ἐπικαλουμένων pres mid ptcp gen pl masc
  [2Ti 2:22; cv-1d(2b); 2126] "

ἐπικάλυμμα, ατος, τό {2127, n-3c(4)}
  a covering, veil; met. a cloak, 1 Peter 2:16*

ἐπικάλυμμα acc sg neut
  [1P 2:16; n-3c(4); 2127] ἐπικάλυμμα

ἐπικαλύπτω {2128, cv-4}
  [-, -, -, -, ἐπεκαλύφθην] to cover over; met. to cover
  or veil by a pardon, Rom 4:7*

ἐπικατάρατος, ον {2129, a-3a}
  cursed, accursed; subject to the curse of
  condemnation, Gal 3:10; infamous, Gal 3:13;
  outcast, vile, Luke 6:5 v.l.*

ἐπικατάρατος nom sg masc
  [2t; a-3a; 2129] ἐπικατάρατος

ἐπίκειμαι {2130, cv-6b}
  [(ἐπεκείμην), -, -, -, -, -] to lie upon, be placed upon,
  John 11:38; 21:9; to press, urge upon, Luke 5:1;
  Acts 27:20; be urgent, importunate upon, Luke
  23:23; to be imposed upon, be imposed by law, Heb
  9:10; by necessity, 1 Cor 9:16

ἐπικείμενα pres mid ptcp nom pl neut
  [Hb 9:10; cv-6b; 2130] ἐπίκειμαι
ἐπικείμενον pres mid ptcp acc sg neut
  [Jn 21:9; cv-6b; 2130] "
ἐπικειμένου pres mid ptcp gen sg masc
  [Ac 27:20; cv-6b; 2130] "
ἐπικεῖσθαι pres mid inf [Lk 5:1; cv-6b; 2130] "
ἐπίκειται pres mid ind 3 sg
  [1C 9:16; cv-6b; 2130] "
ἐπικέκλησαι perf mid ind 2 sg
  [Ac 25:12; cv-1d(2b); 2126] ἐπικαλέω
ἐπικέκληται perf pass ind 3 sg
  [Ac 15:17; cv-1d(2b); 2126] "

ἐπικέλλω {2131, cv-2d(1)}
  [-, ἐπέκειλα, -, -, -] to push a ship to shore, Acts
  27:41*

ἐπικερδαίνω {2132, cv-2d(6)}
  [-, -, -, -, -] gain in addition, Matt 25:20 v.l., 22 v.l.*

ἐπικεφάλαιον, ου, τό {2133, n-2c}
  poll tax, Mark 12:14 v.l.*

ἐπικληθείς aor pass ptcp nom sg masc
  [Ac 4:36; cv-1d(2b); 2126] "
ἐπικληθέν aor pass ptcp acc sg neut
  [Jm 2:7; cv-1d(2b); 2126] "
ἐπικληθέντα aor pass ptcp acc sg masc
  [Ac 12:25; cv-1d(2b); 2126] "

Ἐπικούρειος, ου, ὁ {2134, n-2a}
  an Epicurean, follower of the philosophy of
  Epicurus, Acts 17:18*

Ἐπικουρείων gen pl masc
  [Ac 17:18; n-2a; 2134] Ἐπικούρειος

ἐπικουρία, ας, ἡ {2135, n-1a}
  help, assistance, Acts 26:22*

ἐπικουρίας gen sg fem
  [Ac 26:22; n-1a; 2135] ἐπικουρία

ἐπικράζω {2136, cv-2a(1)}
  [-, -, -, -, -] shout threats, Acts 16:39 v.l.*

ἐπικράνθη aor pass ind 3 sg
  [Rv 10:10; v-2d(4); 4393] πικραίνω
ἐπικράνθησαν aor pass ind 3 pl
  [Rv 8:11; v-2d(4); 4393] '

ἐπικρίνω   {2137, cv-1c(2)}
[-, ἐπέκρινα, -, -, -] *to decide; to decree,* Luke
23:24*

ἐπιλαβέσθαι   aor mid inf
[Lk 20:26; cv-3a(2b); 2138]   ἐπιλαμβάνομαι
ἐπιλαβόμενοι   aor mid ptcp nom pl masc
[5t; cv-3a(2b); 2138]   "
ἐπιλαβόμενος   aor mid ptcp nom sg masc
[5t; cv-3a(2b); 2138]   "
ἐπιλαβομένου   aor mid ptcp gen sg masc
[Hb 8:9; cv-3a(2b); 2138]   "
ἐπιλαβοῦ   aor mid imperative 2 sg
[1Ti 6:12; cv-3a(2b); 2138]   "
ἐπιλάβωνται   aor mid subj 3 pl
[2t; cv-3a(2b); 2138]   "
ἐπιλαθέσθαι   aor mid inf
[Hb 6:10; cv-3a(2b); 2140]   ἐπιλανθάνομαι
ἐπιλαμβάνεται   pres mid ind 3 sg
[2t; cv-3a(2b); 2138]   ἐπιλαμβάνομαι

ἐπιλαμβάνομαι   {2138, cv-3a(2b)}
[-, ἐπελαβόμην, -, -, -] *to take hold of,* Matt 14:31;
Mark 8:23; *to lay hold of, seize,* Luke 23:26; Acts
16:19; met. *to seize on* as a ground of accusation,
Luke 20:20, 26; *to grasp, obtain* as if by seizure, 1
Tim 6:12, 19; *to assume a portion of, to assume the
nature of,* or, *to attach* or *ally one's self to,* Heb 2:16

ἐπιλάμπω   {2139, cv-1b(1)}
[-, ἐπέλαμψα -, -, -] *shine out, forth,* Acts 12:7 v.l.*

ἐπιλανθάνεσθε   pres mid imperative 2 pl
[2t; cv-3a(2b); 2140]   ἐπιλανθάνομαι

ἐπιλανθάνομαι   {2140, cv-3a(2b)}
[-, ἐπελαθόμην, -, ἐπιλέλησμαι, -] *to forget,* Matt
16:5; *to be forgetful, neglectful of, to disregard,* Phil
3:14; Heb 6:10; in N.T. in a passive sense,
forgotten, Luke 12:6

ἐπιλανθανόμενος   pres mid ptcp nom sg masc
[Pp 3:13; cv-3a(2b); 2140]   "
ἐπιλεγομένη   pres pass ptcp nom sg fem
[Jn 5:2; cv-1b(2); 2141]   ἐπιλέγω

ἐπιλέγω   {2141, cv-1b(2)}
[-, ἐπέλεξα -, -, -] *to call,* John 5:2; mid. *to select
for one's self, choose,* Acts 15:40*

ἐπιλείπω   {2142, cv-1b(1)}
[ἐπιλείψω, -, -, -, -] *to be insufficient, to run short,
to fail,* Heb 11:32*

ἐπιλείχω   {2143, cv-1b(2)}
[(ἐπέλειχον), -, -, -, -, -] *to lick,* Luke 16:21*

ἐπιλείψει   fut act ind 3 sg
[Hb 11:32; cv-1b(1); 2142]   ἐπιλείπω
ἐπιλελησμένον   perf pass ptcp nom sg neut
[Lk 12:6; cv-3a(2b); 2140]   ἐπιλανθάνομαι
ἐπιλεξάμενος   aor mid ptcp nom sg masc
[Ac 15:40; cv-1b(2); 2141]   ἐπιλέγω

ἐπιλησμονή, ῆς, ἡ   {2144, n-1b}
forgetfulness, oblivion, James 1:25*

ἐπιλησμονῆς   gen sg fem
[Jm 1:25; n-1b; 2144]   ἐπιλησμονή
ἐπίλοιπον   acc sg masc
[1P 4:2; a-3a; 2145]   ἐπίλοιπος

ἐπίλοιπος, ον   {2145, a-3a}
remaining, still left, 1 Peter 4:2; Luke 24:43 v.l.*

ἐπιλυθήσεται   fut pass ind 3 sg
[Ac 19:39; cv-1a(4); 2147]   ἐπιλύω
ἐπιλύσεως   gen sg fem
[2P 1:20; n-3e(5b); 2146]   ἐπίλυσις

ἐπίλυσις, εως, ἡ   {2146, n-3e(5b)}
a loosing, liberation; met. *interpretation of* what is
enigmatical and obscure, 2 Peter 1:20*

ἐπιλύω   {2147, cv-1a(4)}
[(ἐπέλυον), -, -, -, -, ἐπελύθην] *to loose* what has
previously been fastened or entangled, as a
knot; met. *to solve, to explain,* what is
enigmatical, as a parable, Mark 4:34; *to settle,
put an end to* a matter of debate, Acts 19:39*

ἐπιμαρτυρέω   {2148, cv-1d(2a)}
[-, -, -, -, -] *to bear testimony to; to testify solemnly,*
1 Peter 5:12*

ἐπιμαρτυρῶν   pres act ptcp nom sg masc
[1P 5:12; cv-1d(2a); 2148]   ἐπιμαρτυρέω
ἐπιμεῖναι   aor act inf
[3t; cv-1c(2); 2152]   ἐπιμένω

ἐπιμέλεια, ας, ἡ   {2149, n-1a}
care, attention, Acts 27:3*

ἐπιμελείας   gen sg fem
[Ac 27:3; n-1a; 2149]   ἐπιμέλεια

ἐπιμελέομαι   {2150, cv-1d(2c)}
[ἐπιμελήσομαι, -, -, -, ἐπεμελήθην] gen., *to take
care of,* Luke 10:34f.; 1 Tim 3:5*

ἐπιμελήθητι   aor pass imperative 2 sg
[Lk 10:35; cv-1d(2c); 2150]   ἐπιμελέομαι
ἐπιμελήσεται   fut pass ind 3 sg
[1Ti 3:5; cv-1d(2c); 2150]   "

ἐπιμελῶς   {2151, adverb}
carefully, diligently, Luke 15:8*

ἐπιμελῶς   adverb
[Lk 15:8; adverb; 2151]   ἐπιμελῶς
ἐπίμενε   pres act imperative 2 sg
[1Ti 4:16; cv-1c(2); 2152]   ἐπιμένω
ἐπιμένειν   pres act inf
[Pp 1:24; cv-1c(2); 2152]   "
ἐπιμένετε   pres act ind 2 pl
[Cl 1:23; cv-1c(2); 2152]   "
ἐπιμένῃς   pres act subj 2 sg
[Rm 11:22; cv-1c(2); 2152]   "
ἐπιμενόντων   pres act ptcp gen pl masc
[Ac 21:10; cv-1c(2); 2152]   "

ἐπιμένω   {2152, cv-1c(2)}
[(ἐπέμενον), ἐπιμενῶ, ἐπέμεινα, -, -, -] *to stay
longer, prolong a stay, remain on,* Acts 10:48;
15:34; *to continue, persevere,* John 8:7; Acts 12:16;
to adhere to, continue to embrace, Acts 13:43; Rom
11:22; *to persist in,* Rom 6:1; 1 Cor 16:8

ἐπιμενῶ   fut act ind 1 sg
[1C 16:8; cv-1c(2); 2152]   "
ἐπιμένωμεν   pres act subj 1 pl
[Rm 6:1; cv-1c(2); 2152]   "

ἐπιμένωσιν   pres act subj 3 pl
[Rm 11:23; cv-1c(2); 2152]   "

ἐπινεύω   {2153, cv-1a(6)}
[-, ἐπένευσα, -, -, -] to nod to; met. to assent to,
consent, Acts 18:20*

ἐπίνοια, ας, ἡ   {2154, n-1a}
thought, purpose, device, intent, Acts 8:22*

ἐπίνοια   nom sg fem
[Ac 8:22; n-1a; 2154]   ἐπίνοια
ἔπινον   imperf act ind 3 pl
[3t; v-3a(1); 4403]   πίνω
ἐπίομεν   aor act ind 1 pl
[Lk 13:26; v-3a(1); 4403]   "
ἔπιον   aor act ind 3 pl   [2t; v-3a(1); 4403]   "

ἐπιορκέω   {2155, v-1d(2a)}
[ἐπιορκήσω, -, -, -, -] to forswear one's self, to fail
of observing one's oath, Matt 5:33*

ἐπιορκήσεις   fut act ind 2 sg
[Mt 5:33; v-1d(2a); 2155]   ἐπιορκέω
ἐπιόρκοις   dat pl masc
[1Ti 1:10; a-3a; 2156]   ἐπίορκος

ἐπίορκος, ον   {2156, a-3a}
one who violates his oath, perjured, 1 Tim 1:10*

ἐπιοῦσα, ης, ἡ, the next day, see ἔπειμι   {n-1c}

ἐπιούσῃ   dat sg fem   [3t; cv-6b; 2079]   ἔπειμι
ἐπιούσῃ   pres act ptcp dat sg fem
[2t; cv-6b; 2079]   "
ἐπιούσιον   acc sg masc
[2t; a-3a; 2157]   ἐπιούσιος

ἐπιούσιος, ον   {2157, a-3a}
This word occurs nowhere else in Greek
literature except in the context of the Lord's
prayer, Guesses include, necessary for today,
necessary for tomorrow, daily, sufficient, Matt 6:11;
Luke 11:3*

ἐπιπεπτωκός   perf act ptcp nom sg neut
[Ac 8:16; cv-1b(3); 2158]   ἐπιπίπτω
ἐπιπεσόντες   aor act ptcp nom pl masc
[Ac 20:37; cv-1b(3); 2158]   "
ἐπιπίπτειν   pres act inf
[Mk 3:10; cv-1b(3); 2158]   "

ἐπιπίπτω   {2158, cv-1b(3)}
[-, ἐπέπεσον, ἐπιπέπτωκα, -, -] to fall upon; to
throw one's self upon, Luke 15:20; John 13:25;
Acts 20:10, 37; to press, urge upon, Mark 3:10; to
light upon, Rom 15:3; to come over, Acts 13:11; to
come upon, fall upon mentally or spiritually,
Luke 1:12; Acts 8:16; 10:10, 44; 11:15; 19:17

ἐπιπλήξῃς   aor act subj 2 sg
[1Ti 5:1; cv-2b; 2159]   ἐπιπλήσσω

ἐπιπλήσσω   {2159, cv-2b}
[-, ἐπέπληξα, -, -, -] pr. to inflict blows upon; met.
to chide, reprove, 1 Tim 5:1*

ἐπιποθεῖ   pres act ind 3 sg
[Jm 4:5; cv-1da)(2; 2160]   Ͻθέω

ἐπιποθέω   da)(2}
[-, ἐπεπόθησα, -, -, -] to desire ʼ   ), to

desire earnestly, long for, 2 Cor 5:2; to have a strong
bent, James 4:5; by impl. to love, have affection for,
2 Cor 9:14

ἐπιποθήσατε   aor act imperative 2 pl
[1P 2:2; cv-1da)(2; 2160]   '
ἐπιπόθησιν   acc sg fem
[2t; n-3e(5b); 2161]   ἐπιπόθησις

ἐπιπόθησις, εως, ἡ   {2161, n-3e(5b)}
earnest desire, strong affection, 2 Cor 7:7, 11*

ἐπιπόθητοι   voc pl masc
[Pp 4:1; a-3a; 2162]   ἐπιπόθητος

ἐπιπόθητος, ον   {2162, a-3a}
earnestly desired, longed for, Phil 4:1*

ἐπιποθία, ας, ἡ   {2163, n-1a}
earnest desire, Rom 15:23*

ἐπιποθίαν   acc sg fem
[Rm 15:23; n-1a; 2163]   ἐπιποθία
ἐπιποθοῦντες   pres act ptcp nom pl masc
[2t; cv-1da)(2; 2160]   ἐπιποθέω
ἐπιποθούντων   pres act ptcp gen pl masc
[2C 9:14; cv-1da)(2; 2160]   '
ἐπιποθῶ   pres act ind 1 sg   [2t; cv-1da)(2; 2160]   '
ἐπιποθῶν   pres act ptcp nom sg masc
[2t; cv-1da)(2; 2160]   '

ἐπιπορεύομαι   {2164, cv-1a(6)}
[-, -, -, -, -] to travel to; to come to, Luke 8:4*

ἐπιπορευομένων   pres mid ptcp gen pl masc
[Lk 8:4; cv-1a(6); 2164]   ἐπιπορεύομαι
ἐπίπρασκον   imperf act ind 3 pl
[Ac 2:45; v-5a; 4405]   πιπράσκω
ἔπιπτεν   imperf act ind 3 sg
[Mk 14:35; v-1b(3); 4406]   πίπτω
ἐπιράπτει   pres act ind 3 sg
[Mk 2:21; cv-4; 2165]   ἐπιράπτω

ἐπιράπτω   {2165, cv-4}
[-, -, -, -, -] also ἐπιρράπτω, to sew on, Mark 2:21*

ἐπιρίπτω   {2166, cv-4}
[-, ἐπέριψα -, -, ἐπερρίφην] to throw upon, cast
upon, Luke 19:35; 1 Peter 5:7*

ἐπιρίψαντες   aor act ptcp nom pl masc
[2t; cv-4; 2166]   ἐπιρίπτω

ἐπισείω   {2167, cv-1a(3)}
[-, -, -, -, -] urge on, incite, Acts 14:19 v.l.*

ἐπίσημοι   nom pl masc
[Rm 16:7; a-3a; 2168]   ἐπίσημος
ἐπίσημον   acc sg masc   [Mt 27:16; a-3a; 2168]   "

ἐπίσημος, ον   {2168, a-3a}
pr. bearing a distinctive mark or device; noted,
eminent, Rom 16:7; notorious, Matt 27:16*

ἐπισιτισμόν   acc sg masc
[Lk 9:12; n-2a; 2169]   ἐπισιτισμός

ἐπισιτισμός, οῦ, ὁ   {2169, n-2a}
supply of food, provisions, Luke 9:12*

ἐπισκέπτεσθαι   pres mid inf
[Jm 1:27; cv-4; 2170]   ἐπισκέπτομαι

ἐπισκέπτη   pres mid ind 2 sg
[Hb 2:6; cv-4; 2170]   "

ἐπισκέπτομαι   {2170, cv-4}
[ἐπισκέψομαι, ἐπεσκεψάμην, -, -, -] *to look at
observantly, to inspect; to look out, select,* Acts 6:3;
to go see, visit, Acts 7:23; 15:36; *to visit* for the
purpose of comfort and relief, Matt 25:36, 43;
James 1:27; from the Hebrew, of God, *to visit,*
Luke 1:68, 78

ἐπισκευάζομαι   {2171, cv-2a(1)}
[-, ἐπεσκευασάμην, -, -, -] *to prepare for a journey,*
Acts 21:15*

ἐπισκευασάμενοι   aor mid ptcp nom pl masc
[Ac 21:15; cv-2a(1); 2171]   ἐπισκευάζομαι
ἐπισκέψασθαι   aor mid inf
[Ac 7:23; cv-4; 2170]   ἐπισκέπτομαι
ἐπισκέψασθε   aor mid imperative 2 pl
[Ac 6:3; cv-4; 2170]   "
ἐπισκέψεται   fut mid ind 3 sg
[Lk 1:78; cv-4; 2170]   "
ἐπισκεψώμεθα   aor mid subj 1 pl
[Ac 15:36; cv-4; 2170]   "

ἐπισκηνόω   {2172, cv-1d(3)}
[-, ἐπεσκήνωσα, -, -, -] *to quarter in* or *at;* met. *to
abide upon,* 2 Cor 12:9*

ἐπισκηνώσῃ   aor act subj 3 sg
[2C 12:9; cv-1d(3); 2172]   ἐπισκηνόω
ἐπισκιάζουσα   pres act ptcp nom sg fem
[Mk 9:7; cv-2a(1); 2173]   ἐπισκιάζω

ἐπισκιάζω   {2173, cv-2a(1)}
[ἐπισκιάσω, ἐπεσκίασα, -, -, -] *to overshadow,*
Matt 17:5; met. *to shed influence upon,* Luke 1:35

ἐπισκιάσει   fut act ind 3 sg
[Lk 1:35; cv-2a(1); 2173]   "
ἐπισκιάσῃ   aor act subj 3 sg
[Ac 5:15; cv-2a(1); 2173]   "

ἐπισκοπέω   {2174, cv-1d(2a)}
[ἐπισκοπήσω, ἐπεσκόπησα, -, ἐπεσκόπημαι, -] *to
look at, inspect;* met. *to be circumspect, heedful,*
Heb 12:15; *to oversee, to exercise the office of*
ἐπίσκοπος, 1 Peter 5:2*

ἐπισκοπή, ῆς, ἡ   {2175, n-1b}
inspection, oversight, visitation; of God,
visitation, interposition, whether in mercy or
judgment, Luke 19:44; 1 Peter 2:12; *the office of
an ecclesiastical overseer,* 1 Tim 3:1; from the
Hebrew, *charge, function,* Acts 1:20*

ἐπισκοπήν   acc sg fem
[Ac 1:20; n-1b; 2175]   ἐπισκοπή
ἐπισκοπῆς   gen sg fem   [3t; n-1b; 2175]   "
ἐπισκόποις   dat pl masc
[Pp 1:1; n-2a; 2176]   ἐπίσκοπος
ἐπίσκοπον   acc sg masc   [3t; n-2a; 2176]   "

ἐπίσκοπος, ου, ὁ   {2176, n-2a}
pr. *an inspector, overseer; a watcher, guardian,* 1
Peter 2:25; in N.T. *an ecclesiastical overseer,* Acts
20:28; Phil 1:1; 1 Tim 3:2; Titus 1:7*

ἐπισκοποῦντες   pres act ptcp nom pl masc
[2t; cv-1d(2a); 2174]   ἐπισκοπέω

ἐπισκόπους   acc pl masc
[Ac 20:28; n-2a; 2176]   ἐπίσκοπος
ἐπισπάσθω   pres mid imperative 3 sg
[1C 7:18; cv-1d(1b); 2177]   ἐπισπάομαι

ἐπισπάομαι   {2177, cv-1d(1b)}
[-, -, -, -, -] *to draw upon* or *after;* in N.T. mid. *to
obliterate circumcision* by artificial extension of
the foreskin, 1 Cor 7:18*

ἐπισπείρω   {2178, cv-2d(3)}
[-, ἐπέσπειρα, -, -, -] *to sow in* or *among,* Matt
13:25*

ἐπίσταμαι   {2179, cv-6b}
[(ἠπιστάμην), -, -, -, -, -] *to be versed in, to be
master of,* 1 Tim 6:4; *to be acquainted with,* Acts
18:25; 19:15; Jude 10: *to know,* Acts 10:28; *to
remember, comprehend, understand,* , Mark 14:68

ἐπίσταμαι   pres pass ind 1 sg
[2t; cv-6b; 2179]   ἐπίσταμαι
ἐπιστάμενος   pres pass ptcp nom sg masc
[4t; cv-6b; 2179]   "
ἐπίστανται   pres pass ind 3 pl   [2t; cv-6b; 2179]   "
ἐπιστάντες   aor act ptcp nom pl masc
[2t; cv-6a; 2392]   ἐφίστημι
ἐπιστάς   aor act ptcp nom sg masc
[4t; cv-6a; 2392]   "
ἐπιστᾶσα   aor act ptcp nom sg fem
[2t; cv-6a; 2392]   "
ἐπίστασθε   pres pass ind 2 pl
[5t; cv-6b; 2179]   ἐπίσταμαι
ἐπίστασιν   acc sg fem
[Ac 24:12; n-3e(5b); 2180]   ἐπίστασις

ἐπίστασις, εως, ἡ   {2180, n-3e(5b)}
pr. *care of, attention to,* 2 Cor 11:28

ἐπίστασις   nom sg fem   [2C 11:28; n-3e(5b); 2180]   "
ἐπιστάτα   voc sg masc   [7t; n-1f; 2181]   ἐπιστάτης
ἐπιστάται   pres pass ind 3 sg
[Ac 26:26; cv-6b; 2179]   ἐπίσταμαι

ἐπιστάτης, ου, ὁ   {2181, n-1f}
pr. *one who stands by; one who is set over;* in N.T.
in voc., equivalent to διδάσκαλε, or ῥαββί,
master, doctor, Luke 5:5; 8:24, 45; 9:33, 49; 17:13*

ἐπιστεῖλαι   aor act inf
[Ac 15:20; cv-2d(1); 2182]   ἐπιστέλλω

ἐπιστέλλω   {2182, cv-2d(1)}
[-, ἐπέστειλα, -, -, -] *to send word to, to send
injunctions,* Acts 15:20; 21:25; *to write to, write* a
letter, Heb 13:22*

ἐπίστευεν   imperf act ind 3 sg
[Jn 2:24; v-1a(6); 4409]   πιστεύω
ἐπιστεύετε   imperf act ind 2 pl
[2t; v-1a(6); 4409]   "
ἐπιστεύθη   aor pass ind 3 sg   [2t; v-1a(6); 4409]   "
ἐπιστεύθην   aor pass ind 1 sg
[2t; v-1a(6); 4409]   "
ἐπιστεύθησαν   aor pass ind 3 pl
[Rm 3:2; v-1a(6); 4409]   "
ἐπίστευον   imperf act ind 3 pl
[4t; v-1a(6); 4409]   "

ἐπίστευσα   aor act ind 1 sg
[2C 4:13; v-1a(6); 4409]   "
ἐπιστεύσαμεν   aor act ind 1 pl
[2t; v-1a(6); 4409]   "
ἐπίστευσαν   aor act ind 3 pl
[22t; v-1a(6); 4409]
ἐπίστευσας   aor act ind 2 sg   [2t; v-1a(6); 4409]   "
ἐπιστεύσατε   aor act ind 2 pl
[7t; v-1a(6); 4409]   "
ἐπίστευσεν   aor act ind 3 sg
[14t; v-1a(6); 4409]   "
ἐπιστῇ   aor act subj 3 sg
[Lk 21:34; cv-6a; 2392]   ἐφίστημι
ἐπίστηθι   aor act imperative 2 sg
[2Ti 4:2; cv-6a; 2392]   "

ἐπιστήμη, ης, ἡ   {2183, n-1b}
   understanding, knowledge, Phil 4:8 v.l.*

ἐπιστήμων, ον   {2184, a-4b(1)}
   knowing, discreet, understanding, James 3:13*

ἐπιστήμων   nom sg masc
[Jm 3:13; a-4b(1); 2184]   ἐπιστήμων
ἐπιστηρίζοντες   pres act ptcp nom pl masc
[Ac 14:22; cv-2a(2); 2185]   ἐπιστηρίζω

ἐπιστηρίζω   {2185, cv-2a(2)}
   [-, ἐπεστήριξα, -, -, -] pr. *to cause to rest* or *lean on,
   to settle upon*; met. *to conform, strengthen,
   establish*, Acts 11:2 v.l.; 14:22; 15:32, 41; 18:23 v.l.*

ἐπιστηρίζων   pres act ptcp nom sg masc
[2t; cv-2a(2); 2185]   "
ἐπιστολαί   nom pl fem
[2C 10:10; n-1b; 2186]   ἐπιστολή
ἐπιστολαῖς   dat pl fem   [2P 3:16; n-1b; 2186]   "
ἐπιστολάς   acc pl fem   [2t; n-1b; 2186]   "

ἐπιστολή, ῆς, ἡ   {2186, n-1b}
   word sent; an order, command; an epistle, letter,
   Acts 9:2; 15:30

ἐπιστολή   nom sg fem   [4t; n-1b; 2186]   "
ἐπιστολῇ   dat sg fem   [3t; n-1b; 2186]   "
ἐπιστολήν   acc sg fem   [6t; n-1b; 2186]   "
ἐπιστολῆς   gen sg fem   [3t; n-1b; 2186]   "
ἐπιστολῶν   gen pl fem   [4t; n-1b; 2186]   "
ἐπιστομίζειν   pres act inf
[Ti 1:11; cv-; 2187]   ἐπιστομίζω

ἐπιστομίζω   {2187, cv-2a(1)}
   [-, -, -, -, -] *to apply a curb* or *muzzle*; met. *to put
   to silence*, Titus 1:11*

ἐπιστραφείς   aor pass ptcp nom sg masc
[3t; cv-1b(1); 2188]   ἐπιστρέφω
ἐπιστραφήτω   aor pass imperative 3 sg
[Mt 10:13; cv-1b(1); 2188]   "
ἐπιστρέφειν   pres act inf   [2t; cv-1b(1); 2188]   "
ἐπιστρέφετε   pres act ind 2 pl
[Ga 4:9; cv-1b(1); 2188]   "
ἐπιστρέφουσιν   pres act ptcp dat pl masc
[Ac 15:19; cv-1b(1); 2188]   "

ἐπιστρέφω   {2188, cv-1b(1)}
   [ἐπιστρέψω, ἐπέστρεψα, -, -, ἐπεστράφην] trans.
   *to turn towards; to turn round; to bring back,
   convert*, Luke 1:16, 17; James 5:19, 20; intrans.

and mid. *to turn one's self upon* or *towards*, Acts
9:40; Rev 1:12; *to turn about*, Matt 9:22; *to turn
back, return*, Matt 12:44; met. *to be converted*,
Acts 28:27

ἐπιστρέψαι   aor act inf   [2t; cv-1b(1); 2188]   "
ἐπιστρέψαντες   aor act ptcp nom pl masc
[Ac 15:36; cv-1b(1); 2188]   "
ἐπιστρέψας   aor act ptcp nom sg masc
[6t; cv-1b(1); 2188]   "
ἐπιστρέψατε   aor act imperative 2 pl
[Ac 3:19; cv-1b(1); 2188]   "
ἐπιστρεψάτω   aor act imperative 3 sg
[3t; cv-1b(1); 2188]   "
ἐπιστρέψει   fut act ind 3 sg
[Lk 1:16; cv-1b(1); 2188]   "
ἐπιστρέψῃ   aor act subj 3 sg
[3t; cv-1b(1); 2188]   "
ἐπιστρέψω   fut act ind 1 sg
[Mt 12:44; cv-1b(1); 2188]   "
ἐπιστρέψωσιν   aor act subj 3 pl
[3t; cv-1b(1); 2188]   "

ἐπιστροφή, ῆς, ἡ   {2189, n-1b}
   a turning towards, a turning about; in N.T. met.
   conversion, Acts 15:3*

ἐπιστροφήν   acc sg fem
[Ac 15:3; n-1b; 2189]   ἐπιστροφή
ἐπιστώθης   aor pass ind 2 sg
[2Ti 3:14; v-1d(3); 4413]   πιστόω
ἐπισυναγαγεῖν   aor act inf
[Mt 23:37; cv-1b(2); 2190]   ἐπισυνάγω
ἐπισυνάγει   pres act ind 3 sg
[Mt 23:37; cv-1b(2); 2190]   "

ἐπισυνάγω   {2190, cv-1b(2)}
   [ἐπισυνάξω, ἐπισυνήγαγον or ἐπισυνῆξα, -,
   ἐπισύνηγμαι, ἐπισυνήχθην] *to gather to* a place;
   to gather together, assemble, convene, Matt 23:37;
   24:31; Luke 17:37

ἐπισυναγωγή, ῆς, ἡ   {2191, n-1b}
   the act of being gathered together or *assembled*, 2
   Thess 2:1; *an assembling together*, Heb 10:25*

ἐπισυναγωγήν   acc sg fem
[Hb 10:25; n-1b; 2191]   ἐπισυναγωγή
ἐπισυναγωγῆς   gen sg fem   [2Th 2:1; n-1b; 2191]   "
ἐπισυνάξαι   aor act inf
[Lk 13:34; cv-1b(2); 2190]   ἐπισυνάγω
ἐπισυνάξει   fut act ind 3 sg
[Mk 13:27; cv-1b(2); 2190]   "
ἐπισυνάξουσιν   fut act ind 3 pl
[Mt 24:31; cv-1b(2); 2190]   "
ἐπισυναχθεισῶν   aor pass ptcp gen pl fem
[Lk 12:1; cv-1b(2); 2190]   "
ἐπισυναχθήσονται   fut pass ind 3 pl
[Lk 17:37; cv-1b(2); 2190]   "
ἐπισυνηγμένη   perf pass ptcp nom sg fem
[Mk 1:33; cv-1b(2); 2190]   "
ἐπισυντρέχει   pres act ind 3 sg
[Mk 9:25; cv-1b(2); 2192]   ἐπισυντρέχω

ἐπισυντρέχω   {2192, cv-1b(2)}
   [-, -, -, -, -] *to run together* to a place, Mark 9:25*

ἐπισφαλοῦς gen sg masc
[Ac 27:9; a-4a; 2195]   ἐπισφαλής

ἐπισυρράπτω, v.l. for ἐπιράπτω at Mark 2:21* {2193}

ἐπισύστασις, εως, ἡ   {2194, n-3e(5b)}
a gathering, concourse, tumult, Acts 24:12 v.l.; *a
crowding* of calls upon the attention and
thoughts, 2 Cor 11:28 v.l.*

ἐπισφαλής, ές   {2195, a-4a}
on the verge of falling, unsteady; met. *insecure,
hazardous, dangerous*, Acts 27:9*

ἐπίσχυον imperf act ind 3 pl
[Lk 23:5; cv-1a(4); 2196]   ἐπισχύω

ἐπισχύω   {2196, cv-1a(4)}
[(ἐπίσχυον), -, -, -, -, -] *to strengthen*; intrans. *to
gather strength*; met. *to be urgent, to press on* a
point, *insist*, Luke 23:5*

ἐπισωρεύσουσιν fut act ind 3 pl
[2Ti 4:3; cv-1a(6); 2197]   ἐπισωρεύω

ἐπισωρεύω   {2197, cv-1a(6)}
[ἐπισωρεύσω, -, -, -, -] *to heap up, accumulate
largely*; met. *to procure in abundance*, 2 Tim 4:3*

ἐπιταγή, ῆς, ἡ   {2198, n-1b}
injunction, 1 Cor 7:6, 25; 2 Cor 8:8; *a decree*, Rom
16:26; 1 Tim 1:1; Titus 1:3; *authoritativeness,
strictness*, Titus 2:15*

ἐπιταγήν acc sg fem [6t; n-1b; 2198]   ἐπιταγή
ἐπιταγῆς gen sg fem [Ti 2:15; n-1b; 2198]   "
ἐπιτάξῃ aor act subj 3 sg
[Lk 8:31; cv-2b; 2199]   ἐπιτάσσω
ἐπιτάσσει pres act ind 3 sg [3t; cv-2b; 2199]   "
ἐπιτάσσειν pres act inf [Pm 8; cv-2b; 2199]   "

ἐπιτάσσω   {2199, cv-2b}
[-, ἐπέταξα, -, ἐπιτέταγμαι, -] with dat., *to set
over* or *upon; to enjoin, charge*, Mark 1:27; 6:39;
Luke 4:36

ἐπιτάσσω pres act ind 1 sg
[Mk 9:25; cv-2b; 2199]   "
ἐπιτελεῖν pres act inf
[Hb 8:5; cv-1d(2b); 2200]   ἐπιτελέω
ἐπιτελεῖσθαι pres pass inf
[1P 5:9; cv-1d(2b); 2200]   "
ἐπιτελεῖσθε pres mid ind 2 pl
[Ga 3:3; cv-1d(2b); 2200]   "
ἐπιτελέσαι aor act inf
[2C 8:11; cv-1d(2b); 2200]   "
ἐπιτελέσας aor act ptcp nom sg masc
[Rm 15:28; cv-1d(2b); 2200]   "
ἐπιτελέσατε aor act imperative 2 pl
[2C 8:11; cv-1d(2b); 2200]   "
ἐπιτελέσει fut act ind 3 sg
[Pp 1:6; cv-1d(2b); 2200]   "
ἐπιτελέσῃ aor act subj 3 sg
[2C 8:6; cv-1d(2b); 2200]   "

ἐπιτελέω   {2200, cv-1d(2b)}
[ἐπιτελέσω, ἐπετέλεσα, -, -, -] *to bring to an end;
to finish, complete, perfect*, Rom 15:28; 2 Cor 8:6,
11; *to perform*, Luke 13:32; *to carry into practice,
to realize*, 2 Cor 7:1; *to discharge*, Heb 9:6; *to
execute*, Heb 8:5; *to carry out to completion*, Phil

1:6; mid. *to end, make an end*, Gal 3:3; pass. *to be
fully undergone, endured*, 1 Peter 5:9

ἐπιτελοῦντες pres act ptcp nom pl masc
[2t; cv-1d(2b); 2200]   "
ἐπιτήδεια acc pl neut
[Jm 2:16; a-1a(1); 2201]   ἐπιτήδειος

ἐπιτήδειος, εία, ον   {2201, a-1a(1)}
fit, suitable, necessary, James 2:16; Acts 24:25 v.l.*

ἐπιτιθέασιν pres act ind 3 pl
[Mt 23:4; cv-6a; 2202]   ἐπιτίθημι
ἐπιτίθει pres act imperative 2 sg
[1Ti 5:22; cv-6a; 2202]   "
ἐπιτιθείς pres act ptcp nom sg masc
[Lk 4:40; cv-6a; 2202]   "
ἐπιτίθεσθαι pres mid inf
[Ac 15:28; cv-6a; 2202]   "

ἐπιτίθημι   {2202, cv-6a}
[(ἐπετίθην, ἐπιθήσω, ἐπέθηκα or ἐπέθην, -, -, -] *to
put, place*, or *lay upon*, Matt 9:18; Luke 4:40; *to
impose* a name, Mark 3:16, 17; *to inflict*, Acts
16:23; Luke 10:30; Rev 22:18; mid. *to impose*
with authority, Acts 15:28; 28:10; *to set* or *fall
upon, assail, assault, attack*, Acts 18:10

ἐπιτίθησιν pres act ind 3 sg
[Lk 15:5; cv-6a; 2202]   "
ἐπιτιμᾶν pres act inf
[2t; cv-1d(1a); 2203]   ἐπιτιμάω

ἐπιτιμάω   {2203, cv-1d(1a)}
[(ἐπετίμων), -, ἐπετίμησα, -, -, -] pr. *to set a value
upon; to assess a penalty; to allege as a crimination*;
hence, *to reprove, chide, censure, rebuke,
reprimand*, Matt 19:13; Luke 23:40; in N.T. *to
admonish strongly, enjoin strictly*, Matt 12:16;
Luke 17:3

ἐπιτιμῆσαι aor act opt 3 sg
[Jd 9; cv-1d(1a); 2203]   "
ἐπιτιμήσας aor act ptcp nom sg masc
[Lk 9:21; cv-1d(1a); 2203]   "
ἐπιτίμησον aor act imperative 2 sg
[3t; cv-1d(1a); 2203]   "

ἐπιτιμία, ας, ἡ   {2204, n-1a}
a punishment, penalty, 2 Cor 2:6*

ἐπιτιμία nom sg fem
[2C 2:6; n-1a; 2204]   ἐπιτιμία
ἐπιτιμῶν pres act ptcp nom sg masc
[2t; cv-1d(1a); 2203]   ἐπιτιμάω
ἐπιτρέπεται pres pass ind 3 sg
[2t; cv-1b(1); 2205]   ἐπιτρέπω
ἐπιτρέπῃ pres act subj 3 sg
[Hb 6:3; cv-1b(1); 2205]   "

ἐπιτρέπω   {2205, cv-1b(1)}
[-, ἐπέτρεψα, -, ἐπιτέτραμμαι, ἐπετράπην] *to give
over, to leave to the entire trust* or *management of*
any one; hence, *to permit, allow, suffer*, Matt 8:21;
Mark 5:13

ἐπιτρέπω pres act ind 1 sg
[1Ti 2:12; cv-1b(1); 2205]   "
ἐπιτρέψαντος aor act ptcp gen sg masc
[Ac 21:40; cv-1b(1); 2205]   "

ἐπιτρέψῃ   aor act subj 3 sg
[2t; cv-1b(1); 2205]   "
ἐπίτρεψον   aor act imperative 2 sg
[4t; cv-1b(1); 2205]   "

ἐπιτροπεύω   {2206, cv-1a(6)}
[-, -, -, -, -] *be procurator, governor,* Luke 3:1 v.l.*

ἐπιτροπή, ῆς, ἡ   {2207, n-1b}
a trust; a commission, permission, Acts 26:12*

ἐπιτροπῆς   gen sg fem
[Ac 26:12; n-1b; 2207]   ἐπιτροπή

ἐπίτροπος, ου, ὁ   {2208, n-2a}
one to whose charge or *control a thing is left; a
steward, bailiff, agent, manager,* Matt 20:8;
steward or *overseer of the revenue, treasurer,*
Luke 8:3; *a guardian* of children, Gal 4:2*

ἐπιτρόπου   gen sg masc [Lk 8:3; n-1b; 2207]   "
ἐπιτρόπους   acc pl masc [Ga 4:2; n-1b; 2207]   "
ἐπιτρόπῳ   dat sg masc [Mt 20:8; n-1b; 2207]   "

ἐπιτυγχάνω   {2209, cv-3a(2b)}
[-, ἐπέτυχον, -, -, -] *to light upon, find; to hit, reach;
to acquire, obtain, attain,* Rom 11:7; Heb 6:15;
11:33; James 4:2; Acts 13:29 v.l.*

ἐπιτυχεῖν   aor act inf
[Jm 4:2; cv-3a(2b); 2209]   ἐπιτυγχάνω
ἐπιφαινόντων   pres act ptcp gen pl neut
[Ac 27:20; cv-2d(4); 2210]   ἐπιφαίνω

ἐπιφαίνω   {2210, cv-2d(4)}
[-, ἐπέφανα -, -, ἐπεφάνην] *to make to appear, to
display;* pass. *to be manifested, revealed,* Titus
2:11; 3:4; intrans. *to give light, shine,* Luke 1:79;
Acts 27:20*

ἐπιφᾶναι   aor act inf   [Lk 1:79; cv-2d(4); 2210]   "

ἐπιφάνεια, ας, ἡ   {2211, n-1a}
appearance, manifestation, 1 Tim 6:14; 2 Tim 1:10;
glorious display, 2 Thess 2:8; 2 Tim 4:1, 8; Titus
2:13*

ἐπιφανείᾳ   dat sg fem
[2Th 2:8; n-1a; 2211]   ἐπιφάνεια
ἐπιφάνειαν   acc sg fem [3t; n-1a; 2211]   "
ἐπιφανείας   gen sg fem [2t; n-1a; 2211]   "
ἐπιφανῆ   acc sg fem
[Ac 2:20; a-4a; 2212]   ἐπιφανής

ἐπιφανής, ές   {2212, a-4a}
pr. *in full and clear view; splendid, glorious,
illustrious,* Acts 2:20*

ἐπιφαύσει   fut act ind 3 sg
[Ep 5:14; cv-5a; 2213]   ἐπιφαύσκω

ἐπιφαύσκω   {2213, cv-5a}
[ἐπιφαύσω, -, -, -, -] *to shine upon, give light to,
enlighten,* Eph 5:14*

ἐπιφέρω   {2214, cv-1c(1)}
[-, ἐπήνεγκον, -, -, -] *to bring upon* or *against,*
Acts 25:18 v.l.; Jude 9; *to inflict,* Rom 3:5; *to bring
to, apply to,* Acts 19:12 v.l.; *to bring in addition,
add,* Phil 1:16*

ἐπιφέρων   pres act ptcp nom sg masc
[Rm 3:5; cv-1c(1); 2214]   ἐπιφέρω

ἐπιφωνέω   {2215, cv-1d(2a)}
[(ἐπεφώνουν), -, -, -, -, -] *to cry aloud, raise a shout*
at a speaker, whether applaudingly, Acts 12:22;
or the contrary, *to clamor at,* Luke 23:21; Acts
21:34; 22:24*

ἐπιφωσκούσῃ   pres act ptcp dat sg fem
[Mt 28:1; cv-; 2216]   ἐπιφώσκω

ἐπιφώσκω   {2216, cv-5a}
[(ἐπέφωσκον), -, -, -, -, -] *to dawn,* Matt 28:1;
hence, used of the reckoned commencement of
the day, *to be near commencing, to dawn on,* Luke
23:54*

ἐπιχειρέω   {2217, cv-1d(2a)}
[(ἐπεχείρουν), -, ἐπεχείρησα, -, -, -] *to put hand to
a thing; to undertake, attempt,* Luke 1:1; Acts
9:29; 19:13*

ἐπιχείρησις, εως, ἡ   {2218, n-3e(5b)}
attempt, attack, Acts 12:3 v.l.*

ἐπιχέω   {2219, cv-1a(7)}
[-, -, -, -, -] *to pour upon,* Luke 10:34*

ἐπιχέων   pres act ptcp nom sg masc
[Lk 10:34; cv-1a(7); 2219]   ἐπιχέω

ἐπιχορηγέω   {2220, cv-1d(2a)}
[-, ἐπεχορήγησα, -, -, ἐπεχορηγήθην] *to supply
further; to superadd,* 2 Peter 1:5; *to supply, furnish,
give,* 2 Cor 9:10; Gal 3:5; 2 Peter 1:11; pass. *to
gather vigor,* Col 2:19*

ἐπιχορηγηθήσεται   fut pass ind 3 sg
[2P 1:11; cv-1d(2a); 2220]   ἐπιχορηγέω
ἐπιχορηγήσατε   aor act imperative 2 pl
[2P 1:5; cv-1d(2a); 2220]   "

ἐπιχορηγία, ας, ἡ   {2221, n-1a}
supply, aid, support, Eph 4:16; Phil 1:19*

ἐπιχορηγίας   gen sg fem
[2t; n-1a; 2221]   ἐπιχορηγία
ἐπιχορηγούμενον   pres pass ptcp nom sg neut
[Cl 2:19; cv-1d(2a); 2220]   ἐπιχορηγέω
ἐπιχορηγῶν   pres act ptcp nom sg masc
[2t; cv-1d(2a); 2220]   "

ἐπιχρίω   {2222, cv-1a(1)}
[-, ἐπέχρισα, -, -, -] *to smear upon, to anoint,* John
9:6, 11*

ἐπιψαύω   {2223, cv-1a(5)}
[-, -, -, -, -] with gen., *touch, grasp,* Eph 5:14 v.l.*

ἐπλανήθησαν   aor pass ind 3 pl
[2t; v-1d(1a); 4414]   πλανάω
ἐπλάνησεν   aor act ind 3 sg
[Rv 19:20; v-1d(1a); 4414]   "
ἐπλάσθη   aor pass ind 3 sg
[1Ti 2:13; v-2b; 4421]   πλάσσω
ἐπλέομεν   imperf act ind 1 pl
[Ac 21:3; v-1a(7); 4434]   πλέω
ἐπλεόνασεν   aor act ind 3 sg
[2t; v-2a(1); 4429]   πλεονάζω
ἐπλεονέκτησα   aor act ind 1 sg
[2C 12:17; v-1d(2a); 4430]   πλεονεκτέω
ἐπλεονεκτήσαμεν   aor act ind 1 pl
[2C 7:2; v-1d(2a); 4430]   "

ἐπλεονέκτησεν   aor act ind 3 sg
   [2C 12:18; v-1d(2a); 4430]   "
ἐπλήγη   aor pass ind 3 sg
   [Rv 8:12; v-2b; 4448]   πλήσσω
ἐπληθύνετο   imperf pass ind 3 sg
   [3t; v-1c(2); 4437]   πληθύνω
ἐπληθύνθη   aor pass ind 3 sg
   [Ac 7:17; v-1c(2); 4437]   "
ἐπλήρου   imperf act ind 3 sg
   [Ac 13:25; v-1d(3); 4444]   πληρόω
ἐπληροῦντο   imperf pass ind 3 pl
   [2t; v-1d(3); 4444]   "
ἐπληροῦτο   imperf pass ind 3 sg
   [Ac 7:23; v-1d(3); 4444]   "
ἐπληρώθη   aor pass ind 3 sg [6t; v-1d(3); 4444]   "
ἐπλήρωσαν   aor act ind 3 pl [2t; v-1d(3); 4444]   "
ἐπλήρωσεν   aor act ind 3 sg [4t; v-1d(3); 4444]   "
ἔπλησαν   aor act ind 3 pl
   [Lk 5:7; v-6a; 4398]   πίμπλημι
ἐπλήσθη   aor pass ind 3 sg [5t; v-6a; 4398]   "
ἐπλήσθησαν   aor pass ind 3 pl [12t; v-6a; 4398]   "
ἐπλούτησαν   aor act ind 3 pl
   [2t; v-1d(2a); 4456]   πλουτέω
ἐπλουτήσατε   aor act ind 2 pl
   [1C 4:8; v-1d(2a); 4456]   "
ἐπλουτίσθητε   aor pass ind 2 pl
   [1C 1:5; v-2a(1); 4457]   πλουτίζω
ἔπλυναν   aor act ind 3 pl
   [Rv 7:14; v-1c(2); 4459]   πλύνω
ἔπλυνον   imperf act ind 3 pl
   [Lk 5:2; v-1c(2); 4459]   "
ἔπνευσαν   aor act ind 3 pl
   [2t; v-1a(7); 4463]   πνέω
ἔπνιγεν   imperf act ind 3 sg
   [Mt 18:28; v-1b(2); 4464]   πνίγω
ἐπνίγοντο   imperf pass ind 3 pl
   [Mk 5:13; v-1b(2); 4464]   "
ἔπνιξαν   aor act ind 3 pl
   [Mt 13:7; v-1b(2); 4464]   "
ἐποίει   imperf act ind 3 sg
   [13t; v-1d(2a); 4472]   ποιέω
ἐποιεῖτε   imperf act ind 2 pl
   [Jn 8:39; v-1d(2a); 4472]   "
ἐποίησα   aor act ind 1 sg [10t; v-1d(2a); 4472]   "
ἐποιήσαμεν   aor act ind 1 pl
   [2t; v-1d(2a); 4472]   "
ἐποιησάμην   aor mid ind 1 sg
   [Ac 1:1; v-1d(2a); 4472]   "
ἐποίησαν   aor act ind 3 pl [15t; v-1d(2a); 4472]   "
ἐποίησας   aor act ind 2 sg [6t; v-1d(2a); 4472]   "
ἐποιήσατε   aor act ind 2 pl [8t; v-1d(2a); 4472]   "
ἐποίησεν   aor act ind 3 sg [75t; v-1d(2a); 4472]   "
ἐποικοδομεῖ   pres act ind 3 sg
   [3t; cv-1d(2a); 2224]   ἐποικοδομέω

ἐποικοδομέω   {2224, cv-1d(2a)}
   [-, ἐποικοδόμησα, -, -, ἐποικοδομήθην] to build
   upon, 1 Cor 3:10, 12, 14; pass. met. to be built
   upon as parts of a spiritual structure, Eph 2:20;
   to build up, carry up a building; met. to build up in
   spiritual advancement, Acts 20:32 v.l.; Col 2:7;
   Jude 20; 1 Peter 2:5 v.l.*

ἐποικοδομηθέντες   aor pass ptcp nom pl masc
   [Ep 2:20; cv-1d(2a); 2224]   "
ἐποικοδόμησεν   aor act ind 3 sg
   [1C 3:14; cv-1d(2a); 2224]   "
ἐποικοδομούμενοι   pres pass ptcp nom pl masc
   [Cl 2:7; cv-1d(2a); 2224]   "
ἐποικοδομοῦντες   pres act ptcp nom pl masc
   [Jd 20; cv-1d(2a); 2224]   "
ἐποίουν   imperf act ind 3 pl
   [3t; v-1d(2a); 4472]   ποιέω
ἐποιοῦντο   imperf mid ind 3 pl
   [Ac 27:18; v-1d(2a); 4472]   "

ἐποκέλλω   {2225, cv-2d(1)}
   [-, -, -, -, -] to run a ship aground, Acts 27:41*

ἐπολέμησεν   aor act ind 3 sg
   [Rv 12:7; v-1d(2a); 4482]   πολεμέω
ἐπονομάζῃ   pres pass ind 2 sg
   [Rm 2:17; cv-2a(1); 2226]   ἐπονομάζω

ἐπονομάζω   {2226, cv-2a(1)}
   [-, -, -, -, -] to attach a name to; pass. to be named,
   Rom 2:17*

ἐπόπται   nom pl masc
   [2P 1:16; n-1f; 2228]   ἐπόπτης
ἐποπτεύοντες   pres act ptcp nom pl masc
   [1P 2:12; cv-1a(6); 2227]   ἐποπτεύω
ἐποπτεύσαντες   aor act ptcp nom pl masc
   [1P 3:2; cv-1a(6); 2227]   "

ἐποπτεύω   {2227, cv-1a(6)}
   [-, ἐπώπτευσα -, -, -] to look upon, observe, watch;
   to witness, be an eye-witness of, 1 Peter 2:12; 3:2*

ἐπόπτης, ου, ὁ   {2228, n-1f}
   a looker-on, eye-witness, 2 Peter 1:16*

ἐπορεύετο   imperf mid ind 3 sg
   [6t; v-1a(6); 4513]   πορεύω
ἐπορεύθη   aor pass ind 3 sg [11t; v-1a(6); 4513]   "
ἐπορεύθησαν   aor pass ind 3 pl
   [5t; v-1a(6); 4513]   "
ἐπορευόμεθα   imperf mid ind 1 pl
   [Ac 21:5; v-1a(6); 4513]   "
ἐπορευόμην   imperf mid ind 1 sg
   [Ac 22:5; v-1a(6); 4513]   "
ἐπορεύοντο   imperf mid ind 3 pl
   [5t; v-1a(6); 4513]   "
ἐπόρθει   imperf act ind 3 sg
   [Ga 1:23; v-1d(2a); 4514]   πορθέω
ἐπόρθουν   imperf act ind 1 sg
   [Ga 1:13; v-1d(2a); 4514]   "
ἐπόρνευσαν   aor act ind 3 pl
   [3t; v-1a(6); 4519]   πορνεύω

ἔπος, ους, τό   {2229, n-3d(2b)}
   a word, that which is expressed by words; ὡς ἔπος
   εἰπεῖν, so to say, if the expression may be allowed,
   Heb 7:9*

ἔπος   acc sg neut [Hb 7:9; n-3d(2b); 2229]   ἔπος
ἐπότιζεν   imperf act ind 3 sg
   [2t; v-2a(1); 4540]   ποτίζω
ἐπότισα   aor act ind 1 sg
   [1C 3:2; v-2a(1); 4540]   "
ἐποτίσαμεν   aor act ind 1 pl
   [Mt 25:37; v-2a(1); 4540]   "

ἐποτίσατε aor act ind 2 pl [2t; v-2a(1); 4540]   "
ἐπότισεν aor act ind 3 sg
   [1C 3:6; v-2a(1); 4540]   "
ἐποτίσθημεν aor pass ind 1 pl
   [1C 12:13; v-2a(1); 4540]   "
ἐπουράνια nom pl neut
   [1C 15:40; a-3a; 2230]   ἐπουράνιος
ἐπουράνια acc pl neut [2t; a-3a; 2230]   "
ἐπουράνιοι nom pl masc [1C 15:48; a-3a; 2230]   "
ἐπουρανίοις dat pl neut [5t; a-3a; 2230]   "
ἐπουράνιον acc sg fem [2Ti 4:18; a-3a; 2230]   "

ἐπουράνιος, ον   {2230, a-3a}
   heavenly, in respect of locality, Eph 1:20; Phil
   2:10; τὰ ἐπουράνια, *the upper regions* of the air,
   Eph 6:12; *heavenly*, in respect of essence and
   character, *unearthly*, 1 Cor 15:48, 49; met. *divine*,
   spiritual, John 3:12

ἐπουράνιος nom sg masc [1C 15:48; a-3a; 2230]   "
ἐπουρανίου gen sg masc [1C 15:49; a-3a; 2230]   "
ἐπουρανίου gen sg fem [3t; a-3a; 2230]   "
ἐπουρανίῳ dat sg fem [Hb 12:22; a-3a; 2230]   "
ἐπουρανίων gen pl masc [Pp 2:10; a-3a; 2230]   "
ἐπουρανίων gen pl neut [2t; a-3a; 2230]   "
ἐπράθη aor pass ind 3 sg
   [Jn 12:5; v-5a; 4405]   πιπράσκω
ἔπραξα aor act ind 1 sg
   [Lk 19:23; v-2b; 4556]   πράσσω
ἐπράξαμεν aor act ind 1 pl
   [Lk 23:41; v-2b; 4556]   "
ἔπραξαν aor act ind 3 pl [2C 12:21; v-2b; 4556]   "
ἐπράξατε aor act ind 2 pl [Ac 3:17; v-2b; 4556]   "
ἔπραξεν aor act ind 3 sg [2t; v-2b; 4556]   "
ἔπρεπεν imperf act ind 3 sg
   [2t; v-1b(1); 4560]   πρέπω
ἐπρίσθησαν aor pass ind 3 pl
   [Hb 11:37; v-2a(1); 4569]   πρίζω
ἐπροφήτευον imperf act ind 3 pl
   [Ac 19:6; v-1a(6); 4736]   προφητεύω
ἐπροφητεύσαμεν aor act ind 1 pl
   [Mt 7:22; v-1a(6); 4736]   "
ἐπροφήτευσαν aor act ind 3 pl
   [Mt 11:13; v-1a(6); 4736]   "
ἐπροφήτευσεν aor act ind 3 sg
   [4t; v-1a(6); 4736]   "

ἑπτά   {2231, a-5b}
   seven, indecl. numeral, Matt 15:34, 37; by
   Jewish usage for a round number, Matt 12:45;
   Luke 11:26

ἑπτά indecl [88t; a-5b; 2231]   ἑπτά
ἔπταισαν aor act ind 3 pl
   [Rm 11:11; v-1a(2); 4760]   πταίω

ἑπτάκις   {2232, adverb}
   seven times, Matt 18:21, 22; Luke 17:4 (2t)*

ἑπτάκις adverb [4t; adverb; 2232]   ἑπτάκις

ἑπτακισχίλιοι, αι, α   {2233, a-1a(1)}
   seven thousand, Rom 11:4*

ἑπτακισχιλίους acc pl masc
   [Rm 11:4; a-1a(1); 2233]   ἑπτακισχίλιοι

ἑπταπλασίων, ον   {2234, a-3a}
   sevenfold, Luke 18:30 v.l.*

ἔπτυσεν aor act ind 3 sg
   [Jn 9:6; v-1a(4); 4772]   πτύω
ἐπτώχευσεν aor act ind 3 sg
   [2C 8:9; v-1a(6); 4776]   πτωχεύω
ἐπύθετο aor mid ind 3 sg
   [Jn 4:52; v-3a(2b); 4785]   πυνθάνομαι
ἐπυνθάνετο imperf mid ind 3 sg
   [5t; v-3a(2b); 4785]   "
ἐπυνθάνοντο imperf mid ind 3 pl
   [2t; v-3a(2b); 4785]   "
ἐπώλησεν aor act ind 3 sg
   [Ac 5:1; v-1d(2a); 4797]   πωλέω
ἐπώλουν imperf act ind 3 pl
   [Lk 17:28; v-1d(2a); 4797]   "
ἐπωρώθη aor pass ind 3 sg
   [2C 3:14; v-1d(3); 4800]   πωρόω
ἐπωρώθησαν aor pass ind 3 pl
   [Rm 11:7; v-1d(3); 4800]   "
ἐπώρωσεν aor act ind 3 sg
   [Jn 12:40; v-1d(3); 4800]   "
ἐράπισαν aor act ind 3 pl
   [Mt 26:67; v-2a(1); 4824]   ῥαπίζω
Ἔραστον acc sg masc
   [Ac 19:22; n-2a; 2235]   Ἔραστος

Ἔραστος, ου, ὁ   {2235, n-2a}
   Erastus, pr. name, Acts 19:22; Rom 16:23; 2 Tim
   4:20*

Ἔραστος nom sg masc [2t; n-2a; 2235]   "
ἐραυνᾷ pres act ind 3 sg
   [1C 2:10; v-1d(1a); 2236]   ἐραυνάω
ἐραυνᾶτε pres act ind 2 pl
   [Jn 5:39; v-1d(1a); 2236]   "

ἐραυνάω   {2236, v-1d(1a)}
   [-, ἠραύνησα, -, -, -] *to search*, *examine*,
   investigate, John 5:39; 7:52; Rom 8:27; 1 Cor 2:10;
   1 Peter 1:11; Rev 2:23*

ἐραύνησον aor act imperative 2 sg
   [Jn 7:52; v-1d(1a); 2236]   "
ἐραυνῶν pres act ptcp nom sg masc
   [2t; v-1d(1a); 2236]   "
ἐραυνῶντες pres act ptcp nom pl masc
   [1P 1:11; v-1d(1a); 2236]   "
ἔργα nom pl neut [15t; n-2c; 2240]   ἔργον
ἔργα acc pl neut [43t; n-2c; 2240]   "
ἐργάζεσθαι pres mid inf
   [6t; v-2a(1); 2237]   ἐργάζομαι
ἐργάζεσθε pres mid imperative 2 pl
   [2t; v-2a(1); 2237]   "
ἐργάζεσθε pres mid ind 2 pl
   [Jm 2:9; v-2a(1); 2237]   "
ἐργάζεται pres mid ind 3 sg [5t; v-2a(1); 2237] "
ἐργάζῃ pres mid ind 2 sg
   [Jn 6:30; v-2a(1); 2237]   "

ἐργάζομαι   {2237, v-2a(1)}
   [(ἠργαζόμην), -, ἠργασάμην or εἰργασάμην, -,
   εἴργασμαι, εἰργάσθην] intrans. *to work*, *labor*,
   Matt 21:28; Luke 13:14; *to trade*, *traffic*, *do*
   business, Matt 25:16; Rev 18:17; *to act*, *exert one's*
   power, *be active*, John 5:17; trans. *to do*, *perform*,

commit, Matt 26:10; John 6:28; *to be engaged in,
occupied upon,* 1 Cor 9:13; Rev 18:17; *to acquire,
gain by one's labor,* John 6:27

ἐργάζομαι   pres mid ind 1 sg [2t; v-2a(1); 2237]   "
ἐργαζόμενοι   pres mid ptcp nom pl masc
 [5t; v-2a(1); 2237]   "
ἐργαζόμενοι   pres mid ptcp voc pl masc
 [Mt 7:23; v-2a(1); 2237]   "
ἐργαζόμενος   pres mid ptcp nom sg masc
 [2t; v-2a(1); 2237]   "
ἐργαζομένους   pres mid ptcp acc pl masc
 [2Th 3:11; v-2a(1); 2237]   "
ἐργαζομένῳ   pres mid ptcp dat sg masc
 [3t; v-2a(1); 2237]   "
ἐργάζονται   pres mid ind 3 pl
 [Rv 18:17; v-2a(1); 2237]   "
ἐργάζου   pres mid imperative 2 sg
 [Mt 21:28; v-2a(1); 2237]   "
ἐργαζώμεθα   pres mid subj 1 pl
 [2t; v-2a(1); 2237]   "
ἐργάσῃ   aor mid subj 2 sg
 [3J 5; v-2a(1); 2237]   "

ἐργασία, ας, ἡ   {2238, n-1a}
 work, labor; in N.T. ἐργασίαν διδόναι, *to endeavor,
 strive,* Luke 12:58; *performance, practice,* Eph
 4:19; *a trade, business, craft,* Acts 19:25, *gain
 acquired by labor or trade, profit,* Acts 16:16, 19;
 19:24*

ἐργασίαν   acc sg fem [4t; n-1a; 2238]   ἐργασία
ἐργασίας   gen sg fem [2t; n-1a; 2238]   "
ἐργάται   nom pl masc [3t; n-1f; 2239]   ἐργάτης
ἐργάται   voc pl masc [Lk 13:27; n-1f; 2239]   "
ἐργάτας   acc pl masc [6t; n-1f; 2239]   "
ἐργάτην   acc sg masc [2Ti 2:15; n-1f; 2239]   "

ἐργάτης, ου, ὁ   {2239, n-1f}
 a workman, laborer, Matt 9:37, 38; 20:1, 2, 8; met.
 a spiritual workman or laborer, 2 Cor 11:13; *an
 artisan, artificer,* Acts 19:25; *a worker, practicer,*
 Luke 13:27

ἐργάτης   nom sg masc [3t; n-1f; 2239]   "
ἐργατῶν   gen pl masc [2t; n-1f; 2239]   "
ἔργοις   dat pl neut [13t; n-2c; 2240]   ἔργον

ἔργον, ου, τό   {2240, n-2c}
 anything done or *to be done; a deed, work, action,*
 John 3:21; Eph 2:10; 2 Cor 9:8, et al. freq.; *duty
 enjoined, office, charge, business,* Mark 13:34;
 John 4:34, et al. freq.; *a process, course of action,*
 James 1:4; *a work, product of an action* or *process,*
 Acts 7:41; Heb 1:10; *substance in effect,* Rom 2:15

ἔργον   nom sg neut [7t; n-2c; 2240]   "
ἔργον   acc sg neut [31t; n-2c; 2240]   "
ἔργου   gen sg neut [8t; n-2c; 2240]   "
ἔργῳ   dat sg neut [10t; n-2c; 2240]   "
ἔργων   gen pl neut [42t; n-2c; 2240]   "
ἐρεθίζετε   pres act imperative 2 pl
 [Cl 3:21; v-2a(1); 2241]   ἐρεθίζω

ἐρεθίζω   {2241, v-2a(1)}
 [-, ἠρέθισα, -, -, -] *to provoke, to irritate,
 exasperate,* Col 3:21; *to incite, stimulate,* 2 Cor
 9:2*

ἐρεῖ   fut act ind 3 sg [17t; v-1b(2); 3306]   λέγω

ἐρείδω   {2242, v-1b(3)}
 [-, ἤρεισα, -, ἤρεισμαι, -] *to make to lean upon; to
 fix firmly;* intrans. *to become firmly fixed, stick fast,*
 Acts 27:41*

ἔρεις   acc pl fem [Ti 3:9; n-3c(2); 2251]   ἔρις
ἐρεῖς   fut act ind 2 sg [4t; v-1b(2); 3306]   λέγω
ἐρείσασα   aor act ptcp nom sg fem
 [Ac 27:41; v-1b(3); 2242]   ἐρείδω
ἐρεῖτε   fut act ind 2 pl [5t; v-1b(2); 3306]   λέγω

ἐρεύγομαι   {2243, v-1b(2)}
 [ἐρεύξομαι, -, -, -, -] *to vomit;* met. *to utter, declare
 openly,* Matt 13:35*

ἐρευνάω, see ἐραυνάω

ἐρεύξομαι   fut mid ind 1 sg
 [Mt 13:35; v-1b(2); 2243]   ἐρεύγομαι

ἐρημία, ας, ἡ   {2244, n-1a}
 a solitude, uninhabited region, waste, desert, Matt
 15:33; Mark 8:4; 2 Cor 11:26; Heb 11:38*

ἐρημίᾳ   dat sg fem [2t; n-1a; 2244]   ἐρημία
ἐρημίαις   dat pl fem [Hb 11:38; n-1a; 2244]   "
ἐρημίας   gen sg fem [Mk 8:4; n-1a; 2244]   "
ἐρήμοις   dat pl masc [Mk 1:45; n-2b; 2245]   ἔρημος
ἐρήμοις   dat pl fem [2t; n-2b; 2245]   "
ἔρημον   acc sg masc [5t; n-2b; 2245]   "
ἔρημον   acc sg fem [8t; n-2b; 2245]   "

ἔρημος, ον   {2245, a-3a}
 lone, desert, waste, uninhabited, Matt 14:13, 15;
 Mark 6:31, 32, 35; *lone, abandoned* to ruin, Matt
 23:38; Luke 13:35; met. *lone, unmarried,* Gal
 4:27; as a subst. *a desert, uninhabited region,
 waste,* Matt 3:1; 24:26; Acts 7:36

ἔρημος   nom sg masc [3t; n-2b; 2245]   "
ἔρημος   nom sg fem [2t; n-2b; 2245]   "
ἐρήμου   gen sg fem [2t; n-2b; 2245]   "
ἐρήμους   acc pl fem [Lk 8:29; n-2b; 2245]   "
ἐρημοῦται   pres pass ind 3 sg
 [2t; v-1d(3); 2246]   ἐρημόω

ἐρημόω   {2246, v-1d(3)}
 [-, -, -, ἠρήμωμαι, ἠρημώθην] *to lay waste, make
 desolate, bring to ruin,* Matt 12:25; Luke 11:17;
 Rev 17:16; 18:17, 19*

ἐρήμῳ   dat sg masc [Lk 9:12; n-2b; 2245]   ἔρημος
ἐρήμῳ   dat sg fem [23t; n-2b; 2245]   "
ἐρημώσεως   gen sg fem
 [2t; n-3e(5b); 2247]   ἐρήμωσις

ἐρήμωσις, εως, ἡ   {2247, n-3e(5b)}
 desolation, devastation, Matt 24:15; Mark 13:14;
 Luke 21:20*

ἐρήμωσις   nom sg fem [Lk 21:20; n-3e(5b); 2247]   "
ἔριδες   nom pl fem [1C 1:11; n-3c(2); 2251]   ἔρις
ἔριδι   dat sg fem [Rm 13:13; n-3c(2); 2251]   "
ἔριδος   gen sg fem [Rm 1:29; n-3c(2); 2251]   "

ἐρίζω   {2248, v-2a(1)}
 [ἐρίσω, ἤρισα, -, -, -] *to quarrel; to wrangle; to use
 the harsh tone of a wrangler* or *brawler, to grate,*
 Matt 12:19*

ἐριθεία, ας, ἡ   {2249, n-1a}
the service of a party, party spirit; feud, faction, 2
Cor 12:20; *contentious disposition, selfish
ambition,* Gal 5:20; Phil 1:17; 2:3; James 3:14; by
impl. *untowardness, disobedience,* Rom 2:8;
James 3:16*

ἐριθεία   nom sg fem
   [Jm 3:16; n-1a; 2249]   ἐριθεία
ἐριθεῖαι   nom pl fem [2t; n-1a; 2249]   "
ἐριθείαν   acc sg fem [2t; n-1a; 2249]   "
ἐριθείας   gen sg fem [2t; n-1a; 2249]   "
ἔριν   acc sg fem [Pp 1:15; n-3c(2); 2251]   ἔρις

ἔριον, ου, τό   {2250, n-2c}
wool, Heb 9:19; Rev 1:14*

ἔριον   nom sg neut [Rv 1:14; n-2c; 2250]   ἔριον
ἐρίου   gen sg neut [Hb 9:19; n-2c; 2250]   "

ἔρις, ιδος, ἡ   {2251, n-3c(2)}
altercation, strife, Rom 13:13; *contentious
disposition,* Rom 1:29; Phil 1:15

ἔρις   nom sg fem [4t; n-3c(2); 2251]   ἔρις
ἐρίσει   fut act ind 3 sg
   [Mt 12:19; v-2a(1); 2248]   ἐρίζω
ἐρίφια   acc pl neut
   [Mt 25:33; n-2c; 2252]   ἐρίφιον

ἐρίφιον, ου, τό   {2252, n-2c}
the texts vary between ἐρίφιον and ἔριφος, *a
goat, kid,* Matt 25:33; Luke 15:29 v.l.*

ἔριφον   acc sg masc [Lk 15:29; n-2a; 2253]   ἔριφος

ἔριφος, ου, ὁ   {2253, n-2a}
the texts vary between ἔριφος and ἐρίφιον, *a
goat, kid,* Matt 25:32; Luke 15:29*

ἐρίφων   gen pl masc [Mt 25:32; n-2a; 2253]   "
Ἑρμᾶν   acc sg masc [Rm 16:14; n-1e; 2254]   Ἑρμᾶς

Ἑρμᾶς, ᾶ, ὁ   {2254, n-1e}
Hermas, pr. name, Rom 16:14*

Ἑρμῆν   acc sg masc [2t; n-1h; 2258]   Ἑρμῆς

ἑρμηνεία, ας, ἡ   {2255, n-1a}
interpretation, explanation, 1 Cor 14:26; meton.
the power or *faculty of interpreting,* 1 Cor 12:10*

ἑρμηνεία   nom sg fem
   [1C 12:10; n-1a; 2255]   ἑρμηνεία
ἑρμηνείαν   acc sg fem [1C 14:26; n-1a; 2255]   "
ἑρμηνεύεται   pres pass ind 3 sg
   [2t; v-1a(6); 2257]   ἑρμηνεύω
ἑρμηνευόμενος   pres pass ptcp nom sg masc
   [Hb 7:2; v-1a(6); 2257]   "

ἑρμηνευτής, οῦ, ὁ   {2256, n-1f}
translator, 1 Cor 14:28 v.l.*

ἑρμηνεύω   {2257, v-1a(6)}
[-, ἑρμήνευσα, -, -, -] *to explain, interpret,
translate,* Luke 24:27 v.l.; John 1:38 v.l., 42; 9:7;
Heb 7:2*

Ἑρμῆς, οῦ, ὁ   {2258, n-1h}
Hermes or *Mercury,* son of Jupiter and Maia, the
messenger and interpreter of the gods, and the
patron of eloquence, learning, etc., Acts 14:12;
Rom 16:14*

Ἑρμογένης, ους, ὁ   {2259, n-3d(2a)}
Hermogenes, pr. name, 2 Tim 1:15*

Ἑρμογένης   nom sg masc
   [2Ti 1:15; n-3d(2a); 2259]   Ἑρμογένης
ἐροῦμεν   fut act ind 1 pl
   [7t; v-1b(2); 3306]   λέγω
ἐροῦσιν   fut act ind 3 pl [5t; v-1b(2); 3306]   "
ἑρπετά   nom pl neut
   [Ac 10:12; n-2c; 2260]   ἑρπετόν
ἑρπετά   acc pl neut [Ac 11:6; n-2c; 2260]   "

ἑρπετόν, οῦ, τό   {2260, n-2c}
a creeping animal, a reptile, Acts 10:12; 11:6; Rom
1:23; James 3:7*

ἑρπετῶν   gen pl neut [2t; n-2c; 2260]   "
ἐρραβδίσθην   aor pass ind 1 sg
   [2C 11:25; v-2a(1); 4810]   ῥαβδίζω
ἐρράντισεν   aor act ind 3 sg
   [2t; v-2a(1); 4822]   ῥαντίζω
ἐρρέθη   aor pass ind 3 sg
   [10t; v-1b(2); 3306]   λέγω
ἐρρέθησαν   aor pass ind 3 pl
   [Ga 3:16; v-1b(2); 3306]   "
ἔρρηξεν   aor act ind 3 sg
   [Lk 9:42; v-3c(2); 4838]   ῥήγνυμι
ἐρριζωμένοι   perf pass ptcp nom pl masc
   [2t; v-1d(3); 4845]   ῥιζόω
ἐρριμμένοι   perf pass ptcp nom pl masc
   [Mt 9:36; v-4; 4849]   ῥίπτω
ἔρριπται   perf pass ind 3 sg [Lk 17:2; v-4; 4849]   "
ἔρριψαν   aor act ind 3 pl [2t; v-4; 4849]   "
ἐρρύσατο   aor mid ind 3 sg
   [4t; v-1a(4); 4861]   ῥύομαι
ἐρρύσθην   aor pass ind 1 sg
   [2Ti 4:17; v-1a(4); 4861]   "
ἔρρωσθε   perf pass imperative 2 pl
   [Ac 15:29; v-3c(1); 4874]   ῥώννυμι
ἐρυθρᾷ   dat sg fem
   [Ac 7:36; a-1a(1); 2261]   ἐρυθρός
ἐρυθράν   acc sg fem [Hb 11:29; a-1a(1); 2261]   "

ἐρυθρός, ά, όν   {2261, a-1a(1)}
red, Acts 7:36; Heb 11:29*

ἔρχεσθαι   pres mid inf
   [9t; v-1b(2); 2262]   ἔρχομαι
ἔρχεσθε   pres mid imperative 2 pl
   [2t; v-1b(2); 2262]   "
ἐρχέσθω   pres mid imperative 3 sg
   [2t; v-1b(2); 2262]   "
ἔρχεται   pres mid ind 3 sg [90t; v-1b(2); 2262]   "
ἔρχῃ   pres mid ind 2 sg [Mt 3:14; v-1b(2); 2262]   "
ἔρχηται   pres mid subj 3 sg [2t; v-1b(2); 2262]   "

ἔρχομαι   {2262, v-1b(2)}
[(ἠρχόμην), ἐλεύσομαι, ἦλθον or ἦλθα, ἐλήλυθα,
-, -] *to come, to go, to pass.* By the combination
of this verb with other terms, a variety of
meaning results, which, however, is due, not to
a change of meaning in the verb, but to the
adjuncts. Ὁ ἐρχόμενος, *He who is coming, the
expected Messiah,* Matt 11:3

ἔρχομαι   pres mid ind 1 sg [20t; v-1b(2); 2262]   "

ἐρχόμεθα   pres mid ind 1 pl
[Jn 21:3; v-1b(2); 2262]   "

ἐρχόμενα   pres mid ptcp acc pl neut
[2t; v-1b(2); 2262]   "

ἐρχομένη   pres mid ptcp nom sg fem
[2t; v-1b(2); 2262]   "

ἐρχομένης   pres mid ptcp gen sg fem
[1Th 1:10; v-1b(2); 2262]   "

ἐρχόμενοι   pres mid ptcp nom pl masc
[4t; v-1b(2); 2262]   "

ἐρχόμενον   pres mid ptcp acc sg masc
[16t; v-1b(2); 2262]   "

ἐρχόμενον   pres mid ptcp acc sg neut
[Mt 3:16; v-1b(2); 2262]   "

ἐρχόμενος   pres mid ptcp nom sg masc
[26t; v-1b(2); 2262]   "

ἐρχομένου   pres mid ptcp gen sg masc
[2t; v-1b(2); 2262]   "

ἐρχομένους   pres mid ptcp acc pl masc
[Mt 3:7; v-1b(2); 2262]   "

ἐρχομένῳ   pres mid ptcp dat sg masc
[3t; v-1b(2); 2262]   "

ἐρχομένῳ   pres mid ptcp dat sg neut
[Ac 13:44; v-1b(2); 2262]   "

ἐρχομένων   pres mid ptcp gen pl masc
[3J 3; v-1b(2); 2262]   "

ἔρχονται   pres mid ind 3 pl   [19t; v-1b(2); 2262]   "

ἔρχου   pres mid imperative 2 sg
[11t; v-1b(2); 2262]   "

ἐρῶ   fut act ind 1 sg   [8t; v-1b(2); 3306]   λέγω

ἐρωτᾷ   pres act ind 3 sg
[3t; v-1d(1a); 2263]   ἐρωτάω

ἐρωτᾷ   pres act subj 3 sg   [2t; v-1d(1a); 2263]   "

ἐρωτᾶν   pres act inf   [Jn 16:19; v-1d(1a); 2263]   "

ἐρωτᾷς   pres act ind 2 sg   [2t; v-1d(1a); 2263]   "

ἐρωτάω   {2263, v-1d(1a)}
[ἐρωτήσω, ἠρώτησα, -, -, ἠρωτήθην] *to ask,
interrogate, inquire of,* Matt 21:24; Luke 20:3; in
N.T. *to ask, request, beg, beseech,* Matt 15:23; Luke
4:38; John 14:16

ἐρωτῆσαι   aor act inf   [2t; v-1d(1a); 2263]   "

ἐρωτήσατε   aor act imperative 2 pl
[Jn 9:21; v-1d(1a); 2263]   "

ἐρωτήσετε   fut act ind 2 pl
[Jn 16:23; v-1d(1a); 2263]   "

ἐρωτήσῃ   aor act subj 3 sg
[1J 5:16; v-1d(1a); 2263]   "

ἐρώτησον   aor act imperative 2 sg
[Jn 18:21; v-1d(1a); 2263]   "

ἐρωτήσω   aor act subj 1 sg
[Lk 22:68; v-1d(1a); 2263]   "

ἐρωτήσω   fut act ind 1 sg   [4t; v-1d(1a); 2263]   "

ἐρωτήσωσιν   aor act subj 3 pl
[Jn 1:19; v-1d(1a); 2263]   "

ἐρωτῶ   pres act ind 1 sg   [9t; v-1d(1a); 2263]   "

ἐρωτῶμεν   pres act ind 1 pl   [3t; v-1d(1a); 2263]   "

ἐρωτῶν   pres act ptcp nom sg masc
[Lk 7:3; v-1d(1a); 2263]   "

ἐρωτῶντες   pres act ptcp nom pl masc
[Jn 8:7; v-1d(1a); 2263]   "

ἐρωτώντων   pres act ptcp gen pl masc
[Ac 18:20; v-1d(1a); 2263]   "

ἐσαλεύθη   aor pass ind 3 sg
[Ac 4:31; v-1a(6); 4888]   σαλεύω

ἐσάλευσεν   aor act ind 3 sg
[Hb 12:26; v-1a(6); 4888]   "

ἐσάλπισεν   aor act ind 3 sg
[7t; v-2a(1); 4895]   σαλπίζω

ἔσβεσαν   aor act ind 3 pl
[Hb 11:34; v-3c(1); 4931]   σβέννυμι

ἐσεβάσθησαν   aor pass ind 3 pl
[Rm 1:25; v-2a(1); 4933]   σεβάζομαι

ἐσείσθη   aor pass ind 3 sg
[2t; v-1a(3); 4940]   σείω

ἐσείσθησαν   aor pass ind 3 pl
[Mt 28:4; v-1a(3); 4940]   "

ἔσεσθαι   fut mid inf   [4t; v-6b; 1639]   εἰμί

ἔσεσθε   fut mid ind 2 pl   [12t; v-6b; 1639]   "

ἔσῃ   fut mid ind 2 sg   [8t; v-6b; 1639]   "

ἐσήμανεν   aor act ind 3 sg
[2t; v-2d(4); 4955]   σημαίνω

ἐσθής, ῆτος, ἡ   {2264, n-3c(1)}
also spelled ἔσθησις, *a robe, vestment, raiment,
garment,* Luke 23:11; 24:4; Acts 1:10 (v.l., the text
reads ἐσθήσεσι, from ἔσθησις); 10:30; 12:21;
James 2:2, 3*

ἐσθήσεσι   dat pl fem
[Ac 1:10; n-3c(1); 2264]   ἐσθής

ἔσθησις, see ἐσθής

ἐσθῆτα   acc sg fem   [3t; n-3c(1); 2264]   "

ἔσθητε   pres act subj 2 pl
[Lk 22:30; v-1b(3); 2266]   ἐσθίω

ἐσθῆτι   dat sg fem   [4t; n-3c(1); 2264]   ἐσθής

ἐσθίει   pres act ind 3 sg
[10t; v-1b(3); 2266]   ἐσθίω

ἐσθίειν   pres act inf   [6t; v-1b(3); 2266]   "

ἐσθίετε   pres act imperative 2 pl
[4t; v-1b(3); 2266]   "

ἐσθίετε   pres act ind 2 pl   [2t; v-1b(3); 2266]   "

ἐσθιέτω   pres act imperative 3 sg
[3t; v-1b(3); 2266]   "

ἐσθίῃ   pres act subj 3 sg   [2t; v-1b(3); 2266]   "

ἐσθίητε   pres act subj 2 pl
[1C 11:26; v-1b(3); 2266]   "

ἐσθίοντα   pres act ptcp acc sg masc
[2t; v-1b(3); 2266]   "

ἐσθίοντες   pres act ptcp nom pl masc
[4t; v-1b(3); 2266]   "

ἐσθίοντι   pres act ptcp dat sg masc
[Rm 14:20; v-1b(3); 2266]   "

ἐσθιόντων   pres act ptcp gen pl masc
[4t; v-1b(3); 2266]   "

ἐσθίουσιν   pres act ind 3 pl   [8t; v-1b(3); 2266]   "

ἐσθίω   {2266, v-1b(3)}
[φάγομαι, ἔφαγον, -, -, -] *to eat,* Matt 12:1; 15:27;
ἐσθίειν καὶ πίνειν, *to eat and drink, to eat and
drink* in the usual manner, *follow the common
mode of living,* Matt 11:18; also with the
associated notion of supposed security, Luke
17:27; *to feast, banquet,* Matt 24:49; met. *to
devour, consume,* Heb 10:27; James 5:3; from the
Hebrew, ἄρτον ἐσθίειν, *to eat bread, to take food,
take the usual meals,* Matt 15:2

ἐσθίων   pres act ptcp nom sg masc
   [11t; v-1b(3); 2266]   "
ἐσθίωσιν   pres act subj 3 pl [2t; v-1b(3); 2266]   "

ἔσθω, see ἐσθίω   {2267}

ἐσίγησαν   aor act ind 3 pl
   [2t; v-1d(1a); 4967]   σιγάω
ἐσίγησεν   aor act ind 3 sg
   [Ac 15:12; v-1d(1a); 4967]   "
ἐσιώπα   imperf act ind 3 sg
   [2t; v-1d(1a); 4995]   σιωπάω
ἐσιώπων   imperf act ind 3 pl
   [2t; v-1d(1a); 4995]   "
ἐσκανδαλίζοντο   imperf pass ind 3 pl
   [2t; v-2a(1); 4997]   σκανδαλίζω
ἐσκανδαλίσθησαν   aor pass ind 3 pl
   [Mt 15:12; v-2a(1); 4997]   "
ἔσκαψεν   aor act ind 3 sg
   [Lk 6:48; v-4; 4999]   σκάπτω
ἐσκήνωσεν   aor act ind 3 sg
   [Jn 1:14; v-1d(3); 5012]   σκηνόω
ἐσκίρτησεν   aor act ind 3 sg
   [2t; v-1d(1a); 5015]   σκιρτάω
ἐσκληρύνοντο   imperf pass ind 3 pl
   [Ac 19:9; v-1c(2); 5020]   σκληρύνω
ἐσκόρπισεν   aor act ind 3 sg
   [2C 9:9; v-2a(1); 5025]   σκορπίζω
ἐσκοτίσθη   aor pass ind 3 sg
   [Rm 1:21; v-2a(1); 5029]   σκοτίζω
ἐσκοτώθη   aor pass ind 3 sg
   [Rv 9:2; v-1d(3); 5031]   σκοτόω
ἐσκοτωμένη   perf pass ptcp nom sg fem
   [Rv 16:10; v-1d(3); 5031]   "
ἐσκοτωμένοι   perf pass ptcp nom pl masc
   [Ep 4:18; v-1d(3); 5031]   "
ἐσκυλμένοι   perf pass ptcp nom pl masc
   [Mt 9:36; v-2d(1); 5035]   σκύλλω

Ἐσλί, ὁ   {2268, n-3g(2)}
   Esli, pr. name, indecl., Luke 3:25*

Ἐσλί   indecl [Lk 3:25; n-3g(2); 2268]   Ἐσλί
ἐσμέν   pres act ind 1 pl [52t; v-6b; 1639]   εἰμί
ἐσμυρνισμένον   perf pass ptcp acc sg masc
   [Mk 15:23; v-2a(1); 5046]   σμυρνίζω
ἔσομαι   fut mid ind 1 sg [13t; v-6b; 1639]   εἰμί
ἐσόμεθα   fut mid ind 1 pl [4t; v-6b; 1639]   "
ἐσόμενον   fut mid ptcp acc sg neut
   [Lk 22:49; v-6b; 1639]   "
ἔσονται   fut mid ind 3 pl [31t; v-6b; 1639]   "

ἔσοπτρον, ου, τό   {2269, n-2c}
   mirror, James 1:23; 1 Cor 13:12*

ἐσόπτρου   gen sg neut
   [1C 13:12; n-2c; 2269]   ἔσοπτρον
ἐσόπτρῳ   dat sg neut [Jm 1:23; n-2c; 2269]   "
ἐσπαργανωμένον   perf pass ptcp acc sg neut
   [Lk 2:12; v-1d(3); 5058]   σπαργανόω
ἐσπαργάνωσεν   aor act ind 3 sg
   [Lk 2:7; v-1d(3); 5058]   "
ἐσπαρμένον   perf pass ptcp acc sg masc
   [Mk 4:15; v-2d(3); 5062]   σπείρω
ἐσπαρμένον   perf pass ptcp acc sg neut
   [Mt 13:19; v-2d(3); 5062]   "

ἐσπαταλήσατε   aor act ind 2 pl
   [Jm 5:5; v-1d(1a); 5059]   σπαταλάω
ἔσπειρα   aor act ind 1 sg
   [2t; v-2d(3); 5062]   σπείρω
ἐσπείραμεν   aor act ind 1 pl
   [1C 9:11; v-2d(3); 5062]   "
ἔσπειρας   aor act ind 2 sg [3t; v-2d(3); 5062]   "
ἔσπειρεν   aor act ind 3 sg
   [Mt 13:31; v-2d(3); 5062]   "

ἑσπέρα, ας, ἡ   {2270, n-1a}
   evening, Luke 24:29; Acts 4:3; 20:15 v.l.; 28:23*

ἑσπέρα   nom sg fem [Ac 4:3; n-1a; 2270]   ἑσπέρα
ἑσπέραν   acc sg fem [Lk 24:29; n-1a; 2270]   "
ἑσπέρας   gen sg fem [Ac 28:23; n-1a; 2270]   "

ἑσπερινός, ή, όν   {2271, a-1a(2a)}
   related to the evening (6-9 p.m.), Luke 12:38 v.l.*

ἔσπευδεν   imperf act ind 3 sg
   [Ac 20:16; v-1b(3); 5067]   σπεύδω
ἐσπιλωμένον   perf pass ptcp acc sg masc
   [Jd 23; v-1d(3); 5071]   σπιλόω
ἐσπλαγχνίσθη   aor pass ind 3 sg
   [6t; v-2a(1); 5072]   σπλαγχνίζομαι
ἐσπούδασα   aor act ind 1 sg
   [Ga 2:10; v-2a(1); 5079]   σπουδάζω
ἐσπουδάσαμεν   aor act ind 1 pl
   [1Th 2:17; v-2a(1); 5079]   "

Ἑσρώμ, ὁ   {2272, n-3g(2)}
   Hezron, pr. name, indecl., Matt 1:3; Luke 3:33*

Ἑσρώμ   indecl [3t; n-3g(2); 2272]   Ἑσρώμ

ἑσσόομαι   {2273, cv-1d(3)}
   [-, -, -, -, ἡσσώθην] *to be inferior to; to fare worse,
   to be in a less favored condition*, 2 Cor 12:13*

ἐστάθη   aor pass ind 3 sg [4t; v-6a; 2705]   ἵστημι
ἐστάθησαν   aor pass ind 3 pl
   [Lk 24:17; v-6a; 2705]   "
ἔσται   fut mid ind 3 sg [118t; v-6b; 1639]   εἰμί
ἑστάναι   perf act inf [3t; v-6a; 2705]   ἵστημι
ἐσταυρώθη   aor pass ind 3 sg
   [5t; v-1d(3); 5090]   σταυρόω
ἐσταυρωμένον   perf pass ptcp acc sg masc
   [4t; v-1d(3); 5090]   "
ἐσταυρωμένος   perf pass ptcp nom sg masc
   [Ga 3:1; v-1d(3); 5090]   "
ἐσταύρωσαν   aor act ind 3 pl [7t; v-1d(3); 5090]   "
ἐσταυρώσατε   aor act ind 2 pl
   [2t; v-1d(3); 5090]   "
ἐσταύρωται   perf pass ind 3 sg
   [Ga 6:14; v-1d(3); 5090]   "
ἐστε   pres act ind 2 pl [92t; v-6b; 1639]   εἰμί
ἐστέναξεν   aor act ind 3 sg
   [Mk 7:34; v-2a(2); 5100]   στενάζω
ἐστερεοῦντο   imperf pass ind 3 pl
   [Ac 16:5; v-1d(3); 5105]   στερεόω
ἐστερεώθησαν   aor pass ind 3 pl
   [Ac 3:7; v-1d(3); 5105]   "
ἐστερέωσεν   aor act ind 3 sg
   [Ac 3:16; v-1d(3); 5105]   "
ἐστεφανωμένον   perf pass ptcp acc sg masc
   [Hb 2:9; v-1d(3); 5110]   στεφανόω

ἐστεφάνωσας   aor act ind 2 sg
   [Hb 2:7; v-1d(3); 5110]   "
ἔστη   aor act ind 3 sg [9t; v-6a; 2705]   ἵστημι
ἔστηκα   perf act ind 1 sg [3t; v-6a; 2705]   "
ἑστήκαμεν   perf act ind 1 pl
   [Rm 5:2; v-6a; 2705]   "
ἕστηκας   perf act ind 2 sg [2t; v-6a; 2705]   "
ἑστήκασιν   perf act ind 3 pl [3t; v-6a; 2705]   "
ἑστήκατε   perf act ind 2 pl [4t; v-6a; 2705]   "
ἕστηκεν   imperf act ind 3 sg
   [Jn 8:44; v-1b(2); 5112]   στήκω
ἕστηκεν   perf act ind 3 sg [6t; v-6a; 2705]   ἵστημι
ἑστηκός   perf act ptcp acc sg neut
   [Rv 5:6; v-6a; 2705]   "
ἑστηκότα   perf act ptcp acc sg neut
   [Mk 13:14; v-6a; 2705]   "
ἑστηκότες   perf act ptcp nom pl masc
   [2t; v-6a; 2705]   "
ἑστηκότων   perf act ptcp gen pl masc
   [4t; v-6a; 2705]   "
ἑστηκώς   perf act ptcp nom sg masc
   [2t; v-6a; 2705]   "
ἐστηριγμένους   perf pass ptcp acc pl masc
   [2P 1:12; v-2a(2); 5114]   στηρίζω
ἐστήρικται   perf pass ind 3 sg
   [Lk 16:26; v-2a(2); 5114]   "
ἐστήρισεν   aor act ind 3 sg
   [Lk 9:51; v-2a(2); 5114]   "
ἔστησαν   aor act ind 3 pl [9t; v-6a; 2705]   ἵστημι
ἔστησεν   aor act ind 3 sg [7t; v-6a; 2705]   "
ἐστί   pres act ind 3 sg
   [Ac 18:10; v-6b; 1639]   εἰμί
ἐστιν   pres act ind 3 sg [896t; v-6b; 1639]   "
ἑστός   perf act ptcp nom sg neut
   [Rv 14:1; v-6a; 2705]   ἵστημι
ἑστός   perf act ptcp acc sg neut
   [Mt 24:15; v-6a; 2705]   "
ἐστράφη   aor pass ind 3 sg
   [Jn 20:14; v-1b(1); 5138]   στρέφω
ἐστράφησαν   aor pass ind 3 pl
   [Ac 7:39; v-1b(1); 5138]   "
ἔστρεψεν   aor act ind 3 sg [2t; v-1b(1); 5138]   "
ἐστρηνίασεν   aor act ind 3 sg
   [Rv 18:7; v-1d(1b); 5139]   στρηνιάω
ἐστρωμένον   perf pass ptcp acc sg neut
   [2t; v-3c(1); 5143]   στρωννύω
ἐστρώννυον   imperf act ind 3 pl
   [Mt 21:8; v-3c(1); 5143]   "
ἔστρωσαν   aor act ind 3 pl [2t; v-3c(1); 5143]   "
ἔστω   pres act imperative 3 sg
   [12t; v-6b; 1639]   εἰμί
ἑστώς   perf act ptcp nom sg masc
   [10t; v-6a; 2705]   ἵστημι
ἔστωσαν   pres act imperative 3 pl
   [2t; v-6b; 1639]   εἰμί
ἑστῶτα   perf act ptcp acc sg masc
   [7t; v-6a; 2705]   ἵστημι
ἑστῶτα   perf act ptcp acc pl neut
   [Lk 5:2; v-6a; 2705]   "
ἑστῶτας   perf act ptcp acc pl masc
   [6t; v-6a; 2705]   "
ἑστῶτες   perf act ptcp nom pl masc
   [5t; v-6a; 2705]   "

ἑστῶτος   perf act ptcp gen sg masc
   [Rv 10:8; v-6a; 2705]   "
ἑστώτων   perf act ptcp gen pl masc
   [Mt 16:28; v-6a; 2705]   "
ἐσυκοφάντησα   aor act ind 1 sg
   [Lk 19:8; v-1d(2a); 5193]   συκοφαντέω
ἐσύλησα   aor act ind 1 sg
   [2C 11:8; v-1d(1a); 5195]   συλάω
ἔσυρον   imperf act ind 3 pl
   [2t; v-1c(1); 5359]   σύρω
ἐσφάγης   aor pass ind 2 sg
   [Rv 5:9; v-2a(2); 5377]   σφάζω
ἐσφαγμένην   perf pass ptcp acc sg fem
   [Rv 13:3; v-2a(2); 5377]   "
ἐσφαγμένον   perf pass ptcp nom sg neut
   [Rv 5:12; v-2a(2); 5377]   "
ἐσφαγμένον   perf pass ptcp acc sg neut
   [Rv 5:6; v-2a(2); 5377]   "
ἐσφαγμένου   perf pass ptcp gen sg neut
   [Rv 13:8; v-2a(2); 5377]   "
ἐσφαγμένων   perf pass ptcp gen pl masc
   [2t; v-2a(2); 5377]   "
ἔσφαξεν   aor act ind 3 sg [2t; v-2a(2); 5377]   "
ἐσφράγισεν   aor act ind 3 sg
   [3t; v-2a(1); 5381]   σφραγίζω
ἐσφραγίσθητε   aor pass ind 2 pl
   [2t; v-2a(1); 5381]   "
ἐσφραγισμένοι   perf pass ptcp nom pl masc
   [3t; v-2a(1); 5381]   "
ἐσφραγισμένων   perf pass ptcp gen pl masc
   [Rv 7:4; v-2a(1); 5381]   "
ἔσχατα   nom pl neut [3t; a-1a(2a); 2274]   ἔσχατος
ἔσχατα   acc pl neut [Rv 2:19; a-1a(2a); 2274]   "
ἐσχάταις   dat pl fem [3t; a-1a(2a); 2274]   "
ἐσχάτας   acc pl fem [Rv 15:1; a-1a(2a); 2274]   "
ἐσχάτη   nom sg fem [3t; a-1a(2a); 2274]   "
ἐσχάτη   dat sg fem [8t; a-1a(2a); 2274]   "
ἔσχατοι   nom pl masc [9t; a-1a(2a); 2274]   "
ἔσχατον   acc sg masc [4t; a-1a(2a); 2274]   "
ἔσχατον   acc sg neut, can function
   adverbially [3t; a-1a(2a); 2274]   "
ἔσχατον   adverb [2t; a-1a(2a); 2274]   "

ἔσχατος, η, ον   {2274, a-1a(2a)}
   farthest; last, latest, Matt 12:45; Mark 12:6;
   lowest, Matt 19:30; 20:16; *in the lowest plight,* 1
   Cor 4:9

ἔσχατος   nom sg masc [6t; a-1a(2a); 2274]   "
ἐσχάτου   gen sg masc [2t; a-1a(2a); 2274]   "
ἐσχάτου   gen sg neut [3t; a-1a(2a); 2274]   "
ἐσχάτους   acc pl masc [1C 4:9; a-1a(2a); 2274]   "
ἐσχάτῳ   dat sg masc [2t; a-1a(2a); 2274]   "
ἐσχάτων   gen pl masc [Mt 20:8; a-1a(2a); 2274]   "
ἐσχάτων   gen pl fem [2t; a-1a(2a); 2274]   "

ἐσχάτως   {2275, adverb}
   to be in the last extremity, Mark 5:23*

ἐσχάτως   adverb [Mk 5:23; adverb; 2275]   ἐσχάτως
ἔσχεν   aor act ind 3 sg [5t; v-1b(2); 2400]   ἔχω
ἔσχες   aor act ind 2 sg [Jn 4:18; v-1b(2); 2400]   "
ἔσχηκα   perf act ind 1 sg
   [2C 2:13; v-1b(2); 2400]   "
ἐσχήκαμεν   perf act ind 1 pl [2t; v-1b(2); 2400]   "

ἔσχηκεν   perf act ind 3 sg
   [2C 7:5; v-1b(2); 2400]   "
ἐσχηκότα   perf act ptcp acc sg masc
   [Mk 5:15; v-1b(2); 2400]   "
ἐσχίσθη   aor pass ind 3 sg
   [6t; v-2a(1); 5387]   σχίζω
ἐσχίσθησαν   aor pass ind 3 pl
   [Mt 27:51; v-2a(1); 5387]   "
ἔσχομεν   aor act ind 1 pl
   [1Th 1:9; v-1b(2); 2400]   ἔχω
ἔσχον   aor act ind 1 sg [2t; v-1b(2); 2400]   "
ἔσχον   aor act ind 3 pl [3t; v-1b(2); 2400]   "

ἔσω   {2276, adverb}
   can function as an improper prep., *in, within, in
   the interior of,* Matt 26:58; John 20:26; ὁ, ἡ, τὸ
   ἔσω, *inner, interior, internal;* met. *within* the pale
   of community, 1 Cor 5:12; ὁ ἔσω ἄνθρωπος, *the
   inner man, the mind, soul,* Rom 7:22

ἔσω   adverb [9t; adverb; 2276]   ἔσω
ἐσῴζοντο   imperf pass ind 3 pl
   [Mk 6:56; v-2a(1); 5392]   σῴζω

ἔσωθεν   {2277, adverb}
   from within, from the interior, Mark 7:21, 23;
   within, in the internal parts, Matt 7:15; ὁ, ἡ, τὸ
   ἔσωθεν, *interior, internal,* Luke 11:39, 40; ὁ
   ἔσωθεν ἄνθρωπος, *the mind, soul,* 2 Cor 4:16

ἔσωθεν   adverb [12t; adverb; 2277]   ἔσωθεν
ἐσώθη   aor pass ind 3 sg
   [4t; v-2a(1); 5392]   σῴζω
ἐσώθημεν   aor pass ind 1 pl
   [Rm 8:24; v-2a(1); 5392]   "
ἔσωσεν   aor act ind 3 sg [4t; v-2a(1); 5392]   "
ἐσωτέραν   acc sg fem comparative
   [Ac 16:24; a-1a(1); 2278]   ἐσώτερος
ἐσώτερον   acc sg neut comparative, can
   function as an improper prep-gen
   [Hb 6:19; a-1a(1); 2278]   "

ἐσώτερος, α, ον   {2278, a-1a(1)}
   inner, interior, Acts 16:24; Heb 6:19*

ἑταῖρε   voc sg masc [3t; n-2a; 2279]   ἑταῖρος

ἑταῖρος, ου, ὁ   {2279, n-2a}
   a companion, associate, fellow-comrade, friend,
   Matt 11:16 v.l.; 20:13; 22:12; 26:50*

ἔταξαν   aor act ind 3 pl [2t; v-2b; 5435]   τάσσω
ἐτάξατο   aor mid ind 3 sg [Mt 28:16; v-2b; 5435]   "
ἐταπείνωσεν   aor act ind 3 sg
   [Pp 2:8; v-1d(3); 5427]   ταπεινόω
ἐτάραξαν   aor act ind 3 pl
   [2t; v-2b; 5429]   ταράσσω
ἐτάραξεν   aor act ind 3 sg
   [Jn 11:33; v-2b; 5429]   "
ἐταράχθη   aor pass ind 3 sg [3t; v-2b; 5429]   "
ἐταράχθησαν   aor pass ind 3 pl [2t; v-2b; 5429]   "
ἐτάφη   aor pass ind 3 sg [3t; v-4; 2507]   θάπτω
ἐτέθη   aor pass ind 3 sg
   [Lk 23:55; v-6a; 5502]   τίθημι
ἐτέθην   aor pass ind 1 sg [2t; v-6a; 5502]   "
ἐτέθησαν   aor pass ind 3 pl [2t; v-6a; 5502]   "
ἔτει   dat sg neut [Lk 3:1; n-3d(2b); 2291]   ἔτος
ἔτεκεν   aor act ind 3 sg [4t; v-1b(2); 5503]   τίκτω

ἐτεκνοτρόφησεν   aor act ind 3 sg
   [1Ti 5:10; v-1d(2a); 5452]   τεκνοτροφέω
ἐτελειώθη   aor pass ind 3 sg
   [Jm 2:22; v-1d(3); 5457]   τελειόω
ἐτελείωσεν   aor act ind 3 sg
   [Hb 7:19; v-1d(3); 5457]   "
ἐτέλεσαν   aor act ind 3 pl
   [2t; v-1d(2b); 5464]   τελέω
ἐτέλεσεν   aor act ind 3 sg [5t; v-1d(2b); 5464]   "
ἐτελέσθη   aor pass ind 3 sg [2t; v-1d(2b); 5464]   "
ἐτελεύτησεν   aor act ind 3 sg
   [4t; v-1d(1a); 5462]   τελευτάω
ἑτέρα   nom sg fem [6t; a-1a(1); 2283]   ἕτερος
ἑτέρᾳ   dat sg fem [4t; a-1a(1); 2283]   "
ἕτερα   acc pl neut [4t; a-1a(1); 2283]   "
ἕτεραι   nom pl fem [Lk 8:3; a-1a(1); 2283]   "
ἑτέραις   dat pl fem [3t; a-1a(1); 2283]   "
ἑτέραν   acc sg fem [3t; a-1a(1); 2283]   "
ἑτέρας   gen sg fem [2t; a-1a(1); 2283]   "
ἑτερογλώσσοις   dat pl masc
   [1C 14:21; a-3a; 2280]   ἑτερόγλωσσος

ἑτερόγλωσσος, ον   {2280, a-3a}
   one who speaks another or *foreign language,* 1 Cor
   14:21*

ἑτεροδιδασκαλεῖ   pres act ind 3 sg
   [1Ti 6:3; cv-1d(2b); 2281]   ἑτεροδιδασκαλέω
ἑτεροδιδασκαλεῖν   pres act inf
   [1Ti 1:3; cv-1d(2b); 2281]   "

ἑτεροδιδασκαλέω   {2281, cv-1d(2b)}
   [-, -, -, -, -] *to teach other* or *different doctrine,* and
   spc. *what is foreign to the Christian religion,* 1 Tim
   1:3; 6:3*

ἑτεροζυγέω   {2282, cv-1d(2a)}
   [-, -, -, -, -] *to be unequally yoked* or *matched,* 2 Cor
   6:14*

ἑτεροζυγοῦντες   pres act ptcp nom pl masc
   [2C 6:14; cv-1d(2a); 2282]   ἑτεροζυγέω
ἕτεροι   nom pl masc [6t; a-1a(1); 2283]   ἕτερος
ἑτέροις   dat pl masc [Ac 2:40; a-1a(1); 2283]   "
ἑτέροις   dat pl neut [Mt 11:16; a-1a(1); 2283]   "
ἕτερον   nom sg neut [7t; a-1a(1); 2283]   "
ἕτερον   acc sg masc [15t; a-1a(1); 2283]   "
ἕτερον   acc sg neut [4t; a-1a(1); 2283]   "

ἕτερος, α, ον   {2283, a-1a(1)}
   other, Matt 12:45; *another, some other,* Matt 8:21;
   besides, Luke 23:32; ὁ ἕτερος, *the other* of two,
   Matt 6:24; τῇ ἑτέρᾳ, *on the next* day, Acts 20:15;
   27:3; ὁ ἕτερος, *one's neighbor,* Rom 13:8; *different,*
   Luke 9:29; *foreign, strange,* Acts 2:4; 1 Cor 14:21;
   illicit, Jude 7

ἕτερος   nom sg masc [15t; a-1a(1); 2283]   "
ἑτέρου   gen sg masc [6t; a-1a(1); 2283]   "
ἑτέρους   acc pl masc [4t; a-1a(1); 2283]   "
ἑτέρῳ   dat sg masc [10t; a-1a(1); 2283]   "
ἑτέρῳ   dat sg neut [2t; a-1a(1); 2283]   "
ἑτέρων   gen pl masc [4t; a-1a(1); 2283]   "

ἑτέρως   {2284, adverb}
   otherwise, differently, Phil 3:15*

ἑτέρως   adverb [Pp 3:15; adverb; 2284]   ἑτέρως

ἔτεσιν   dat pl neut [2t; n-3d(2b); 2291]   ἔτος
ἐτέχθη   aor pass ind 3 sg
   [Lk 2:11; v-1b(2); 5503]   τίκτω
ἔτη   nom pl neut [7t; n-3d(2b); 2291]   ἔτος
ἔτη   acc pl neut [21t; n-3d(2b); 2291]   "
ἐτηρεῖτο   imperf pass ind 3 sg
   [Ac 12:5; v-1d(2a); 5498]   τηρέω
ἐτήρησα   aor act ind 1 sg
   [2C 11:9; v-1d(2a); 5498]   "
ἐτήρησαν   aor act ind 3 pl
   [Jn 15:20; v-1d(2a); 5498]   "
ἐτήρησας   aor act ind 2 sg [2t; v-1d(2a); 5498]   "
ἐτήρουν   imperf act ind 1 sg
   [Jn 17:12; v-1d(2a); 5498]   "
ἐτήρουν   imperf act ind 3 pl
   [2t; v-1d(2a); 5498]   "

ἔτι   {2285, adverb}
   yet, still, Matt 12:46; still, further, longer, Luke
   16:2; further, besides, in addition, Matt 18:16; with
   a compar. yet, still, Phil 1:9

ἔτι   adverb [93t; adverb; 2285]   ἔτι
ἐτίθει   imperf act ind 3 sg
   [2C 3:13; v-6a; 5502]   τίθημι
ἐτίθεσαν   imperf act ind 3 pl
   [Mk 6:56; v-6a; 5502]   "
ἐτίθουν   imperf act ind 3 pl [2t; v-6a; 5502]   "
ἔτιλλον   imperf act ind 3 pl
   [Lk 6:1; v-2d(1); 5504]   τίλλω
ἐτίμησαν   aor act ind 3 pl
   [Ac 28:10; v-1d(1a); 5506]   τιμάω
ἐτιμήσαντο   aor mid ind 3 pl
   [Mt 27:9; v-1d(1a); 5506]   "
ἕτοιμα   nom pl neut [2t; a-3b(2); 2289]   ἕτοιμος
ἕτοιμα   acc pl neut [2C 10:16; a-3b(2); 2289]   "
ἑτοίμαζε   pres act imperative 2 sg
   [Pm 22; v-2a(1); 2286]   ἑτοιμάζω

ἑτοιμάζω   {2286, v-2a(1)}
   [ἑτοιμάσω, ἡτοίμασα, ἡτοίμακα, ἡτοίμασμαι,
   ἡτοιμάσθην] to make ready, prepare, Matt 22:4;
   26:17

ἑτοιμάσαι   aor act inf [4t; v-2a(1); 2286]   "
ἑτοιμάσας   aor act ptcp nom sg masc
   [Lk 12:47; v-2a(1); 2286]   "
ἑτοιμάσατε   aor act imperative 2 pl
   [7t; v-2a(1); 2286]   "
ἑτοιμασθῇ   aor pass subj 3 sg
   [Rv 16:12; v-2a(1); 2286]   "

ἑτοιμασία, ας, ἡ   {2288, n-1a}
   preparation; preparedness, readiness, Eph 6:15*

ἑτοιμασίᾳ   dat sg fem
   [Ep 6:15; n-1a; 2288]   ἑτοιμασία
ἑτοίμασον   aor act imperative 2 sg
   [Lk 17:8; v-2a(1); 2286]   ἑτοιμάζω
ἑτοιμάσω   aor act subj 1 sg
   [Jn 14:3; v-2a(1); 2286]   "
ἑτοιμάσωμεν   aor act subj 1 pl
   [3t; v-2a(1); 2286]   "
ἑτοίμην   acc sg fem [2t; a-3b(2); 2289]   ἕτοιμος
ἕτοιμοι   nom pl masc [5t; a-3b(2); 2289]   "
ἕτοιμοι   nom pl fem [Mt 25:10; a-3b(2); 2289]   "

ἕτοιμον   acc sg neut [Mk 14:15; a-3b(2); 2289]   "

ἕτοιμος, η, ον   {2289, a-3b(2)}
   ready, prepared, Matt 22:4, 8; Mark 14:15

ἕτοιμος   nom sg masc [3t; a-3b(2); 2289]   "
ἑτοίμους   acc pl masc [Ti 3:1; a-3b(2); 2289]   "
ἑτοίμῳ   dat sg neut [2C 10:6; a-3b(2); 2289]   "

ἑτοίμως   {2290, adverb}
   in readiness, preparedly, Acts 21:13; 2 Cor 2:14;
   13:1 v.l.; 1 Pet 4:5*

ἑτοίμως   adverb [3t; adverb; 2290]   ἑτοίμως
ἐτόλμα   imperf act ind 3 sg
   [4t; v-1d(1a); 5528]   τολμάω
ἐτόλμησεν   aor act ind 3 sg [2t; v-1d(1a); 5528] "
ἐτόλμων   imperf act ind 3 pl
   [Lk 20:40; v-1d(1a); 5528]   "

ἔτος, ους, τό   {2291, n-3d(2b)}
   a year, Luke 2:41; 3:23

ἔτος   acc sg neut [2t; n-3d(2b); 2291]   ἔτος
ἐτρέχετε   imperf act ind 2 pl
   [Ga 5:7; v-1b(2); 5556]   τρέχω
ἔτρεχον   imperf act ind 3 pl
   [Jn 20:4; v-1b(2); 5556]   "
ἐτροποφόρησεν   aor act ind 3 sg
   [Ac 13:18; v-1d(2a); 5574]   τροποφορέω
ἐτρύγησεν   aor act ind 3 sg
   [Rv 14:19; v-1d(1a); 5582]   τρυγάω
ἐτρυφήσατε   aor act ind 2 pl
   [Jm 5:5; v-1d(1a); 5587]   τρυφάω
ἐτύθη   aor pass ind 3 sg
   [1C 5:7; v-1a(4); 2604]   θύω
ἐτυμπανίσθησαν   aor pass ind 3 pl
   [Hb 11:35; v-2a(1); 5594]   τυμπανίζω
ἔτυπτεν   imperf act ind 3 sg
   [Lk 18:13; v-4; 5597]   τύπτω
ἔτυπτον   imperf act ind 3 pl [3t; v-4; 5597]   "
ἐτύφλωσεν   aor act ind 3 sg
   [2t; v-1d(3); 5604]   τυφλόω
ἐτῶν   gen pl neut [15t; n-3d(2b); 2291]   ἔτος

εὖ   {2292, adverb}
   well, good, happily, rightly, Mark 14:7; Acts 15:29;
   Well! Well done! Matt 25:21, 23; Luke 19:17;
   Eph 6:3*

εὖ   adverb [5t; adverb; 2292]   εὖ

Εὕα, ας, ἡ   {2293, n-1a}
   Eve, pr. name, 2 Cor 11:3; 1 Tim 2:13*

Εὕα   nom sg fem [1Ti 2:13; n-1a; 2293]   Εὕα
εὐαγγελίζεσθαι   pres mid inf
   [2t; v-2a(1); 2294]   εὐαγγελίζω
εὐαγγελίζεται   pres mid ind 3 sg
   [2t; v-2a(1); 2294]   "
εὐαγγελίζεται   pres pass ind 3 sg
   [Lk 16:16; v-2a(1); 2294]   "
εὐαγγελίζηται   pres mid subj 3 sg
   [Ga 1:8; v-2a(1); 2294]   "
εὐαγγελίζομαι   pres mid ind 1 sg
   [Lk 2:10; v-2a(1); 2294]   "
εὐαγγελιζόμεθα   pres mid ind 1 pl
   [Ac 13:32; v-2a(1); 2294]   "

εὐαγγελιζόμενοι   pres mid ptcp nom pl masc
[7t; v-2a(1); 2294]   "

εὐαγγελιζόμενος   pres mid ptcp nom sg masc
[3t; v-2a(1); 2294]   "

εὐαγγελιζομένου   pres mid ptcp gen sg masc
[Lk 20:1; v-2a(1); 2294]   "

εὐαγγελιζομένῳ   pres mid ptcp dat sg masc
[Ac 8:12; v-2a(1); 2294]   "

εὐαγγελιζομένων   pres mid ptcp gen pl masc
[Rm 10:15; v-2a(1); 2294]   "

εὐαγγελίζονται   pres pass ind 3 pl
[2t; v-2a(1); 2294]   "

εὐαγγελίζω   {2294, v-2a(1)}
[(εὐηγγέλιζον), -, εὐηγγέλισα, -, εὐηγγέλισμαι,
εὐηγγελίσθην] *to address with good tidings*, Rev
10:7; 14:6; but elsewhere *to proclaim as good
tidings, to announce good tidings of*, Luke 1:19; *to
address with good tidings*, Acts 13:32; 14:15; *to
address with the Gospel teaching, evangelize*, Acts
16:10; Gal 1:9; absol. *to announce the good tidings
of the Gospel*, Luke 4:18; 9:6; pass. *to be
announced as good tidings*, Luke 16:16; *to be
addressed with good tidings*, Matt 11:5; Luke 7:22;
Heb 4:2

εὐαγγελίζωμαι   pres mid subj 1 sg
[2t; v-2a(1); 2294]   "

εὐαγγέλιον, ου, τό   {2295, n-2c}
glad tidings, good or *joyful news*, Matt 4:23; 9:35;
the Gospel; doctrines of the Gospel, Matt 26:13;
Mark 8:35; meton. *the preaching of*, or *instruction
in, the Gospel*, 1 Cor 4:15; 9:14

εὐαγγέλιον   nom sg neut
[5t; n-2c; 2295]   εὐαγγέλιον

εὐαγγέλιον   acc sg neut [36t; n-2c; 2295]   "

εὐαγγελίου   gen sg neut [23t; n-2c; 2295]   "

εὐαγγελίσαι   aor act inf
[Rv 14:6; v-2a(1); 2294]   εὐαγγελίζω

εὐαγγελισάμενοι   aor mid ptcp nom pl masc
[Ac 14:21; v-2a(1); 2294]   "

εὐαγγελισαμένου   aor mid ptcp gen sg masc
[1Th 3:6; v-2a(1); 2294]   "

εὐαγγελισαμένων   aor mid ptcp gen pl masc
[1P 1:12; v-2a(1); 2294]   "

εὐαγγελίσασθαι   aor mid inf [7t; v-2a(1); 2294] "

εὐαγγελισθέν   aor pass ptcp nom sg neut
[1P 1:25; v-2a(1); 2294]   "

εὐαγγελισθέν   aor pass ptcp acc sg neut
[Ga 1:11; v-2a(1); 2294]   "

εὐαγγελισθέντες   aor pass ptcp nom pl masc
[Hb 4:6; v-2a(1); 2294]   "

εὐαγγελιστάς   acc pl masc
[Ep 4:11; n-1f; 2296]   εὐαγγελιστής

εὐαγγελιστής, οῦ, ὁ   {2296, n-1f}
pr. *one who announces glad tidings; an evangelist,
preacher of the Gospel, teacher of the Christian
religion*, Acts 21:8; Eph 4:11; 2 Tim 4:5*

εὐαγγελιστοῦ   gen sg masc [2t; n-1f; 2296]   "

εὐαγγελίσωμαι   aor mid subj 1 sg
[1C 9:16; v-2a(1); 2294]   εὐαγγελίζω

εὐαγγελίῳ   dat sg neut
[12t; n-2c; 2295]   εὐαγγέλιον

Εὕαν   acc sg fem [2C 11:3; n-1a; 2293]   Εὕα

εὐαρεστεῖται   pres pass ind 3 sg
[Hb 13:16; cv-1d(2a); 2297]   εὐαρεστέω

εὐαρεστέω   {2297, cv-1d(2a)}
[-, εὐηρέστησα, εὐηρέστηκα, -, -] *to please*, Heb
11:5, 6; pass. *to take pleasure in, be well pleased
with*, Heb 13:16*

εὐαρεστηκέναι   perf act inf
[Hb 11:5; cv-1d(2a); 2297]   "

εὐαρεστῆσαι   aor act inf
[Hb 11:6; cv-1d(2a); 2297]   "

εὐάρεστοι   nom pl masc
[2C 5:9; a-3a; 2298]   εὐάρεστος

εὐάρεστον   nom sg neut [3t; a-3a; 2298]   "

εὐάρεστον   acc sg fem [2t; a-3a; 2298]   "

εὐάρεστον   acc sg neut [Hb 13:21; a-3a; 2298] "

εὐάρεστος, ον   {2298, a-3a}
well-pleasing, acceptable, grateful, Rom 12:1, 2

εὐάρεστος   nom sg masc [Rm 14:18; a-3a; 2298] "

εὐαρέστους   acc pl masc [Ti 2:9; a-3a; 2298]   "

εὐαρέστως   {2299, adverb}
acceptably, Heb 12:28

εὐαρέστως   adverb
[Hb 12:28; adverb; 2299]   εὐαρέστως

Εὔβουλος, ου, ὁ   {2300, n-2a}
Eubulus, pr. name, 2 Tim 4:21*

Εὔβουλος   nom sg masc
[2Ti 4:21; n-2a; 2300]   Εὔβουλος

εὖγε   {2301, adverb}
Well done! Luke 19:17*

εὖγε   adverb [Lk 19:17; adverb; 2301]   εὖγε

εὐγενεῖς   nom pl masc
[1C 1:26; a-4a; 2302]   εὐγενής

εὐγενέστεροι   nom pl masc comparative
[Ac 17:11; a-4a; 2302]   "

εὐγενής, ές   {2302, a-4a}
well-born, of high rank, honorable, Luke 19:12; 1
Cor 1:26; *generous, candid*, Acts 17:11*

εὐγενής   nom sg masc [Lk 19:12; a-4a; 2302]   "

εὐγλωττία, ας, ἡ   {2303, n-1a}
fluency of speech, Rom 16:18 v.l.*

εὐδία, ας, ἡ   {2304, n-1a}
serenity of the heavens, a cloudless sky, fair or *fine
weather*, Matt 16:2*

εὐδία   nom sg fem [Mt 16:2; n-1a; 2304]   εὐδία

εὐδοκεῖ   pres act ind 3 sg
[Hb 10:38; v-1d(2a); 2305]   εὐδοκέω

εὐδοκέω   {2305, v-1d(2a)}
[(ηὐδόκησα), -, εὐδόκησα or ηὐδόκησα, -, -, -] *to
think well, approve, consent, take delight* or
pleasure, Matt 3:17; 17:5; Mark 1:11; Luke 3:22;
12:32

εὐδόκησα   aor act ind 1 sg [5t; v-1d(2a); 2305] "

εὐδοκήσαμεν   aor act ind 1 pl
[1Th 3:1; v-1d(2a); 2305]   "

εὐδόκησαν   aor act ind 3 pl [2t; v-1d(2a); 2305] "

εὐδοκήσαντες   aor act ptcp nom pl masc
   [2Th 2:12; v-1d(2a); 2305]   "
εὐδόκησας   aor act ind 2 sg [2t; v-1d(2a); 2305]   "
εὐδόκησεν   aor act ind 3 sg [6t; v-1d(2a); 2305]   "

εὐδοκία, ας, ἡ   {2306, n-1a}
   good will, favor, Luke 2:14; *good pleasure, purpose,*
   intention, Matt 11:26; Luke 10:21; Eph 1:5, 9;
   Phil 2:13; *by impl. desire,* Rom 10:1; Phil 1:15; 2
   Thess 1:11*

εὐδοκία   nom sg fem [3t; n-1a; 2306]   εὐδοκία
εὐδοκίαν   acc sg fem [4t; n-1a; 2306]   "
εὐδοκίας   gen sg fem [2t; n-1a; 2306]   "
εὐδοκοῦμεν   imperf act ind 1 pl
   [1Th 2:8; v-1d(2a); 2305]   εὐδοκέω
εὐδοκοῦμεν   pres act ind 1 pl
   [2C 5:8; v-1d(2a); 2305]   "
εὐδοκῶ   pres act ind 1 sg
   [2C 12:10; v-1d(2a); 2305]   "

εὐεργεσία, ας, ἡ   {2307, n-1a}
   well-doing, a good deed, benefit conferred, Acts 4:9;
   duty, good offices, 1 Tim 6:2*

εὐεργεσίᾳ   dat sg fem
   [Ac 4:9; n-1a; 2307]   εὐεργεσία
εὐεργεσίας   gen sg fem [1Ti 6:2; n-1a; 2307]   "
εὐεργέται   nom pl masc
   [Lk 22:25; n-1f; 2309]   εὐεργέτης

εὐεργετέω   {2308, cv-1d(2}
   [-, -, -, -, -] *to do good, exercise beneficence,* Acts
   10:38*

εὐεργέτης, ου, ὁ   {2309, n-1f}
   a well-doer; a benefactor, Luke 22:25*

εὐεργετῶν   pres act ptcp nom sg masc
   [Ac 10:38; cv-1d(2; 2308]   εὐεργετέω
εὐηγγελίζετο   imperf mid ind 3 sg
   [3t; v-2a(1); 2294]   εὐαγγελίζω
εὐηγγελίζοντο   imperf mid ind 3 pl
   [Ac 8:25; v-2a(1); 2294]   "
εὐηγγελισάμεθα   aor mid ind 1 pl
   [Ga 1:8; v-2a(1); 2294]   "
εὐηγγελισάμην   aor mid ind 1 sg
   [4t; v-2a(1); 2294]   "
εὐηγγελίσατο   aor mid ind 3 sg
   [2t; v-2a(1); 2294]   "
εὐηγγέλισεν   aor act ind 3 sg
   [Rv 10:7; v-2a(1); 2294]   "
εὐηγγελίσθη   aor pass ind 3 sg
   [1P 4:6; v-2a(1); 2294]   "
εὐηγγελισμένοι   perf pass ptcp nom pl masc
   [Hb 4:2; v-2a(1); 2294]   "
εὐθεῖα   nom sg fem [Ac 8:21; adverb; 2318]   εὐθύς
εὐθεῖαν   acc sg fem [3t; adverb; 2318]   "
εὐθείας   acc pl fem [4t; adverb; 2318]   "
εὔθετον   nom sg neut
   [Lk 14:35; a-3a; 2310]   εὔθετος
εὔθετον   acc sg fem [Hb 6:7; a-3a; 2310]   "

εὔθετος, ον   {2310, a-3a}
   pr. *well arranged, rightly disposed; fit, proper,*
   adapted, Luke 9:62; 14:35; *useful,* Heb 6:7*

εὔθετος   nom sg masc [Lk 9:62; a-3a; 2310]   "

εὐθέως   {2311, adverb}
   immediately, instantly, at once, Matt 8:3; 13:5

εὐθέως   adverb [36t; adverb; 2311]   εὐθέως

εὐθυδρομέω   {2312, v-1d(2a)}
   [-, εὐθυδρόμησα, -, -, -] *to run on a straight course;*
   to sail on a direct course, Acts 16:11; 21:1*

εὐθυδρομήσαμεν   aor act ind 1 pl
   [Ac 16:11; v-1d(2a); 2312]   εὐθυδρομέω
εὐθυδρομήσαντες   aor act ptcp nom pl masc
   [Ac 21:1; v-1d(2a); 2312]   "
εὐθυμεῖ   pres act ind 3 sg
   [Jm 5:13; cv-1d(2a); 2313]   εὐθυμέω
εὐθυμεῖν   pres act inf
   [Ac 27:22; cv-1d(2a); 2313]   "
εὐθυμεῖτε   pres act imperative 2 pl
   [Ac 27:25; cv-1d(2a); 2313]   "

εὐθυμέω   {2313, cv-1d(2a)}
   [-, -, -, -, -] *to be cheerful, be in good spirits, take*
   courage, Acts 27:22, 25; James 5:13*

εὔθυμοι   nom pl masc
   [Ac 27:36; a-3a; 2314]   εὔθυμος

εὔθυμος, ον   {2314, a-3a}
   good cheer or *courage, cheerful,* Acts 27:36*

εὐθύμως   {2315, adverb}
   cheerfully, Acts 24:10*

εὐθύμως   adverb [Ac 24:10; adverb; 2315]   εὐθύμως
εὐθύνατε   aor act imperative 2 pl
   [Jn 1:23; v-1c(2); 2316]   εὐθύνω
εὐθύνοντος   pres act ptcp gen sg masc
   [Jm 3:4; v-1c(2); 2316]   "

εὐθύνω   {2316, v-1c(2)}
   [-, εὔθυνα, -, -, -] *to guide straight; to direct, guide,*
   steer a ship, James 3:4; *to make straight,* John
   1:23*

εὐθύς   {2317, adverb}
   straight forwards; directly, immediately, instantly,
   Matt 3:16; 13:20, 21

εὐθύς   adverb [51t; adverb; 2318]   εὐθύς

εὐθύς, εῖα, ύ   {2318, a-2b}
   straight, Matt 3:3; Mark 1:3; Luke 3:4f.; Acts
   9:11; 13:10; met. *right, upright, true,* Acts 8:21; 2
   Pet 2:15*

εὐθύτης, ητος, ἡ   {2319, n-3c(1)}
   righteousness, uprightness, equity, Heb 1:8*

εὐθύτητος   gen sg fem
   [Hb 1:8; n-3c(1); 2319]   εὐθύτης

εὐκαιρέω   {2320, v-1d(2a)}
   [(εὐκαίρουν or ηὐκαίρουν), -, εὐκαίρησα, -, -, -]
   to have convenient time or *opportunity, have*
   leisure, Mark 6:31; 1 Cor 16:12; *to be at leisure* for
   a thing, *to be disposed to attend, to give time,* Acts
   17:21*

εὐκαιρήσῃ   aor act subj 3 sg
   [1C 16:12; v-1d(2a); 2320]   εὐκαιρέω

εὐκαιρία, ας, ἡ   {2321, n-1a}
   convenient opportunity, favorable occasion, Matt
   26:16; Luke 22:6*

εὐκαιρίαν acc sg fem [2t; n-1a; 2321] εὐκαιρία
εὔκαιρον acc sg fem
    [Hb 4:16; a-3a; 2322] εὔκαιρος

εὔκαιρος, ον {2322, a-3a}
    timely, opportune, seasonable, convenient, Mark
    6:21; Heb 4:16*

εὐκαίρου gen sg fem [Mk 6:21; a-3a; 2322] "
εὐκαίρουν imperf act ind 3 pl
    [Mk 6:31; v-1d(2a); 2320] εὐκαιρέω

εὐκαίρως {2323, adverb}
    opportunely, seasonable, conveniently, Mark 6:31
    v.l.; 14:11; 2 Tim 4:2*

εὐκαίρως adverb [2t; adverb; 2323] εὐκαίρως

εὔκοπος, ον {2324, a-3a}
    easy, Matt 9:5; 19:24; Mark 2:9; 10:25; Luke 5:3;
    16:17; 18:25

εὐκοπώτερον nom sg neut comparative
    [7t; a-3a; 2324] εὔκοπος

εὐλάβεια, ας, ἡ {2325, n-1a}
    the disposition of one who is εὐλαβής, *caution,*
    circumspection; in N.T. *reverence* to God, *piety,*
    Heb 5:7; 12:28*

εὐλαβείας gen sg fem [2t; n-1a; 2325] εὐλάβεια
εὐλαβεῖς nom pl masc [2t; a-4a; 2327] εὐλαβής

εὐλαβέομαι {2326, v-1d(2a)}
    [-, -, -, -, ἠυλαβήθην] *to be cautious* or *afraid; to*
    fear, be afraid or *apprehensive,* Acts 23:10 v.l.; in
    N.T. absol. *to reverence* God, *to be influenced by*
    pious awe, Heb 11:7*

εὐλαβηθείς aor pass ptcp nom sg masc
    [Hb 11:7; v-1d(2a); 2326] εὐλαβέομαι

εὐλαβής, ές {2327, a-4a}
    pr. *taking hold of well,* i.e., *warily;* hence, *cautious,*
    circumspect; full of reverence towards God,
    devout, pious, religious, Luke 2:25; Acts 2:5; 8:2;
    22:12*

εὐλαβής nom sg masc [2t; a-4a; 2327] εὐλαβής
εὐλογεῖν pres act inf
    [Lk 24:51; v-1d(2a); 2328] εὐλογέω
εὐλογεῖται pres pass ind 3 sg
    [Hb 7:7; v-1d(2a); 2328] "
εὐλογεῖτε pres act imperative 2 pl
    [3t; v-1d(2a); 2328] "

εὐλογέω {2328, v-1d(2a)}
    [(εὐλόγουν and ἠυλόγουν), εὐλογήσω, εὐλόγησα,
    εὐλόγηκα, εὐλόγημαι, εὐλογήθην] pr. *to speak*
    well of, in N.T. *to bless, ascribe praise and*
    glorification, Luke 1:64; *to bless, invoke a blessing*
    upon, Matt 5:44; *to bless, confer a favor* or *blessing*
    upon, Eph 1:3; Heb 6:14; pass. *to be blessed, to be*
    an object of favor or *blessing,* Luke 1:28

εὐλόγηκεν perf act ind 3 sg
    [Hb 7:6; v-1d(2a); 2328] "
εὐλογημένη perf pass ptcp nom sg fem
    [v-1d(2a); 2328] "
εὐλογημένοι perf pass ptcp voc pl masc
    [Mt 25:34; v-1d(2a); 2328] "

εὐλογημένος perf pass ptcp nom sg masc
    [7t; v-1d(2a); 2328] "
εὐλογῇς pres act subj 2 sg
    [1C 14:16; v-1d(2a); 2328] "
εὐλογήσας aor act ptcp nom sg masc
    [5t; v-1d(2a); 2328] "
εὐλόγησεν aor act ind 3 sg [9t; v-1d(2a); 2328] "
εὐλογήσω fut act ind 1 sg
    [Hb 6:14; v-1d(2a); 2328] "

εὐλογητός, ή, όν {2329, a-1a(2a)}
    worthy of praise or *blessing, blessed,* Mark 14:61;
    Luke 1:68

εὐλογητός nom sg masc
    [7t; a-1a(2a); 2329] εὐλογητός
εὐλογητοῦ gen sg masc
    [Mk 14:61; a-1a(2a); 2329] "

εὐλογία, ας, ἡ {2330, n-1a}
    pr. *good speaking; fair speech, flattery,* Rom 16:18;
    in N.T. *blessing, praise, celebration,* 1 Cor 10:16;
    Rev 5:12, 13; *invocation of good, benediction,*
    James 3:10; *a divine blessing,* Rom 15:29; *a gift,*
    benevolence, 2 Cor 9:5; *a frank gift,* as opposed to
    πλεονεξία, 2 Cor 9:5; ἐπ᾽ εὐλογίαις, *liberally,* 2
    Cor 9:6

εὐλογία nom sg fem [4t; n-1a; 2330] εὐλογία
εὐλογίᾳ dat sg fem [Ep 1:3; n-1a; 2330] "
εὐλογίαις dat pl fem [2t; n-1a; 2330] "
εὐλογίαν acc sg fem [5t; n-1a; 2330] "
εὐλογίας gen sg fem [4t; n-1a; 2330] "
εὐλογοῦμεν pres act ind 1 pl
    [3t; v-1d(2a); 2328] εὐλογέω
εὐλογοῦντα pres act ptcp acc sg masc
    [Ac 3:26; v-1d(2a); 2328] "
εὐλογοῦνται pres pass ind 3 pl
    [Ga 3:9; v-1d(2a); 2328] "
εὐλογοῦντες pres act ptcp nom pl masc
    [2t; v-1d(2a); 2328] "
εὐλογῶν pres act ptcp nom sg masc
    [2t; v-1d(2a); 2328] "

εὐμετάδοτος, ον {2331, a-3a}
    liberal, bountiful, generous, 1 Tim 6:18*

εὐμεταδότους acc pl masc
    [1Ti 6:18; a-3a; 2331] εὐμετάδοτος

Εὐνίκη, ης, ἡ {2332, n-1b}
    Eunice, pr. name, 2 Tim 1:5*

Εὐνίκῃ dat sg fem [2Ti 1:5; n-1b; 2332] Εὐνίκη

εὐνοέω {2333, cv-1d(2a)}
    [-, -, -, -, -] *to have kind thoughts, be well affected*
    or *kindly disposed towards, make friends,* Matt
    5:25*

εὔνοια, ας, ἡ {2334, n-1a}
    good will, kindliness; heartiness, enthusiasm, Eph
    6:7*

εὐνοίας gen sg fem [Ep 6:7; n-1a; 2334] εὔνοια

εὐνουχίζω {2335, cv-2a(1)}
    [-, εὐνούχισα -, -, εὐνουχίσθην] *to emasculate,*
    make a eunuch; to impose chaste abstinence on, to
    bind to a practical emasculation, Matt 19:12*

εὐνούχισαν   aor act ind 3 pl
[Mt 19:12; cv-2a(1); 2335]   εὐνουχίζω
εὐνουχίσθησαν   aor pass ind 3 pl
[Mt 19:12; cv-2a(1); 2335]   "
εὐνοῦχοι   nom pl masc [3t; n-2a; 2336]   εὐνοῦχος

εὐνοῦχος, ου, ὁ   {2336, n-2a}
pr. *one who has charge of the bedchamber;* hence, *a eunuch, one emasculated,* Matt 19:12; as eunuchs in the East often rose to places of power and trust, hence, *a minister of a court,* Acts 8:27, 34, 36, 38f.*

εὐνοῦχος   nom sg masc [5t; n-2a; 2336]   "
εὐνοῶν   pres act ptcp nom sg masc
[Mt 5:25; cv-1d(2a); 2333]   εὐνοέω
εὐξαίμην   aor mid opt 1 sg
[Ac 26:29; v-1b(2); 2377]   εὔχομαι

Εὐοδία, ας, ἡ   {2337, n-1a}
Euodia, pr. name, Phil 4:2*

Εὐοδίαν   acc sg fem [Pp 4:2; n-1a; 2337]   Εὐοδία
εὐοδοῦσθαι   pres pass inf
[3J 2; cv-1d(3); 2338]   εὐοδόω
εὐοδοῦται   pres pass ind 3 sg
[3J 2; cv-1d(3); 2338]   "

εὐοδόω   {2338, cv-1d(3)}
[-, -, -, -, εὐοδώθην] *to give a prosperous journey; cause to prosper* or *be successful;* pass. *to have a prosperous journey, to succeed in a journey,* Rom 1:10; met. *to be furthered, to prosper,* temporally or spiritually, 1 Cor 16:2; 3 John 2 (2t)*

εὐοδωθήσομαι   fut pass ind 1 sg
[Rm 1:10; cv-1d(3); 2338]   "
εὐοδῶται   pres pass subj 3 sg
[1C 16:2; cv-1d(3); 2338]   "
εὐπάρεδρον   acc sg neut
[1C 7:35; a-3a; 2339]   εὐπάρεδρος

εὐπάρεδρος, ον   {2339, a-3a}
constantly attending; devoted to; τὸ εὐπάρεδρον, *devotedness,* 1 Cor 7:35*

εὐπειθής, ές   {2340, a-4a}
easily persuaded, compliant, James 3:17*

εὐπειθής   nom sg fem
[Jm 3:17; a-4a; 2340]   εὐπειθής
εὐπερίστατον   acc sg fem
[Hb 12:1; a-3a; 2342]   εὐπερίστατος

εὐπερισπαστος, ον   {2341, a-3a}
easily distracting, Heb 12:1 v.l.*

εὐπερίστατος, ον   {2342, a-3a}
easily or *constantly distracted,* Heb 12:1*

εὐποιΐα, ας, ἡ   {2343, n-1a}
doing good, beneficence, Heb 13:16*

εὐποιΐας   gen sg fem
[Hb 13:16; n-1a; 2343]   εὐποιΐα
εὐπορεῖτο   imperf mid ind 3 sg
[Ac 11:29; cv-1d(2); 2344]   εὐπορέω

εὐπορέω   {2344, cv-1d(2)}
[(εὐπόρουν), -, -, -, -, -] *to be in prosperous circumstances, enjoy plenty,* Acts 11:29*

εὐπορία, ας, ἡ   {2345, n-1a}
wealth, abundance, Acts 19:25*

εὐπορία   nom sg fem
[Ac 19:25; n-1a; 2345]   εὐπορία

εὐπρέπεια, ας, ἡ   {2346, n-1a}
grace, beauty, James 1:11*

εὐπρέπεια   nom sg fem
[Jm 1:11; n-1a; 2346]   εὐπρέπεια

εὐπρόσδεκτος, ον   {2347, a-3a}
acceptable, grateful, pleasing, Rom 15:16, 31; 2 Cor 6:2; 8:12; 1 Peter 2:5; in N.T. *gracious*

εὐπρόσδεκτος   nom sg masc
[2C 6:2; a-3a; 2347]   εὐπρόσδεκτος
εὐπρόσδεκτος   nom sg fem [3t; a-3a; 2347]   "
εὐπροσδέκτους   acc pl fem [1P 2:5; a-3a; 2347]   "

εὐπρόσεδρος, ον   {2348, a-3a}
constantly attending, assiduous, devoted to, 1 Cor 7:35 v.l.; equivalent to εὐπάρεδρος

εὐπροσωπέω   {2349, v-1d(2a)}
[-, εὐπροσώπησα, -, -, -] *to carry* or *make a fair appearance,* Gal 6:12*

εὐπροσωπῆσαι   aor act inf
[Ga 6:12; v-1d(2a); 2349]   εὐπροσωπέω

εὐρακύλων, ῶνος, ὁ   {2350, n-3f(1a)}
the north-east wind, from the Latin words Eurus and Aquilo, Acts 27:14*

εὐρακύλων, ωνος, ὁ   {2352, n-3f(1a)}
also spelled εὐρυκλύδων and εὐροκλύδων, which *BAGD* says was probably due to scribal error, *euraclyon,* the name of a tempestuous southeast wind, Acts 27:14*

εὐρακύλων   nom sg masc
[Ac 27:14; n-3f(1a); 2350]   εὐρακύλων
εὕραμεν   aor act ind 1 pl
[Lk 23:2; v-5b; 2351]   εὑρίσκω
εὑράμενος   aor mid ptcp nom sg masc
[Hb 9:12; v-5b; 2351]   "
εὑρεθείς   aor pass ptcp nom sg masc
[Pp 2:7; v-5b; 2351]   "
εὑρέθη   aor pass ind 3 sg [13t; v-5b; 2351]   "
εὑρεθῇ   aor pass subj 3 sg [4t; v-5b; 2351]   "
εὑρέθημεν   aor pass ind 1 pl
[Ga 2:17; v-5b; 2351]   "
εὑρέθην   aor pass ind 1 sg
[Rm 10:20; v-5b; 2351]   "
εὑρεθῆναι   aor pass inf [2P 3:14; v-5b; 2351]   "
εὑρέθησαν   aor pass ind 3 pl [2t; v-5b; 2351]   "
εὑρεθήσεται   fut pass ind 3 sg
[2P 3:10; v-5b; 2351]   "
εὑρεθησόμεθα   fut pass ind 1 pl
[2C 5:3; v-5b; 2351]   "
εὑρεθῆτε   aor pass subj 2 pl
[Ac 5:39; v-5b; 2351]   "
εὑρεθῶ   aor pass subj 1 sg [2t; v-5b; 2351]   "
εὑρεθῶσιν   aor pass subj 3 pl
[2C 11:12; v-5b; 2351]   "
εὑρεῖν   aor act inf [5t; v-5b; 2351]   "
εὗρεν   aor act ind 3 sg [16t; v-5b; 2351]   "
εὗρες   aor act ind 2 sg [2t; v-5b; 2351]   "

εὕρη   aor act subj 3 sg [5t; v-5b; 2351]   "
εὕρηκα   perf act ind 1 sg [2t; v-5b; 2351]   "
εὑρήκαμεν   perf act ind 1 pl [2t; v-5b; 2351]   "
εὑρηκέναι   perf act inf [Rm 4:1; v-5b; 2351]   "
εὑρήσει   fut act ind 3 sg [8t; v-5b; 2351]   "
εὑρήσεις   fut act ind 2 sg [Mt 17:27; v-5b; 2351]   "
εὑρήσετε   fut act ind 2 pl [10t; v-5b; 2351]   "
εὑρήσομεν   fut act ind 1 pl [Jn 7:35; v-5b; 2351]   "
εὑρήσουσιν   fut act ind 3 pl [2t; v-5b; 2351]   "
εὕρητε   aor act subj 2 pl [2t; v-5b; 2351]   "
εὑρίσκει   pres act ind 3 sg [12t; v-5b; 2351]   "
εὑρισκόμεθα   pres pass ind 1 pl [1C 15:15; v-5b; 2351]   "
εὑρίσκομεν   pres act ind 1 pl [Ac 23:9; v-5b; 2351]   "
εὕρισκον   imperf act ind 3 pl [Lk 19:48; v-5b; 2351]   "
εὑρίσκον   pres act ptcp nom sg neut [Lk 11:24; v-5b; 2351]   "
εὑρίσκοντες   pres act ptcp nom pl masc [2t; v-5b; 2351]   "

εὑρίσκω   {2351, v-5b}
[(εὕρισκον), εὑρήσω, εὗρον and εὗρα, εὕρηκα, -, εὑρέθην] *to find, to meet with;* Matt 18:28; 20:6; *to find out, to detect, discover,* Luke 23:2, 4, 14; *to acquire, obtain, win, gain,* Luke 1:30; 9:12; *to find* mentally, *to comprehend, recognize,* Acts 17:27; Rom 7:21; *to find* by experience, *observe, gather,* Rom 7:18; *to devise* as feasible, Luke 5:19; 19:48

εὑρίσκω   pres act ind 1 sg [6t; v-5b; 2351]   "
εὕροιεν   aor act opt 3 pl [Ac 17:27; v-5b; 2351]   "
εὕρομεν   aor act ind 1 pl [2t; v-5b; 2351]   "
εὗρον   aor act ind 1 sg [9t; v-5b; 2351]   "
εὗρον   aor act ind 3 pl [24t; v-5b; 2351]   "
εὑρόντες   aor act ptcp nom pl masc [8t; v-5b; 2351]   "
εὑροῦσα   aor act ptcp nom sg fem [Lk 15:9; v-5b; 2351]   "
εὑροῦσαι   aor act ptcp nom pl fem [Lk 24:23; v-5b; 2351]   "

εὐρύχωρος, ον   {2353, a-3a}
spacious; broad, wide, Matt 7:13*

εὐρύχωρος   nom sg fem [Mt 7:13; a-3a; 2353]   εὐρύχωρος
εὕρω   aor act subj 1 sg [2C 12:20; v-5b; 2351]   εὑρίσκω
εὕρωμεν   aor act subj 1 pl [Hb 4:16; v-5b; 2351]   "
εὑρών   aor act ptcp nom sg masc [10t; v-5b; 2351]   "
εὕρωσιν   aor act subj 3 pl [3t; v-5b; 2351]   "

εὐσέβεια, ας, ἡ   {2354, n-1a}
reverential feeling; piety, devotion, godliness, Acts 3:12; 1 Tim 2:2; 4:7, 8; *religion, the* Christian *religion,* 1 Tim 3:16

εὐσέβεια   nom sg fem [2t; n-1a; 2354]   εὐσέβεια
εὐσεβείᾳ   dat sg fem [3t; n-1a; 2354]   "
εὐσεβείαις   dat pl fem [2P 3:11; n-1a; 2354]   "
εὐσέβειαν   acc sg fem [7t; n-1a; 2354]   "

εὐσεβείας   gen sg fem [2t; n-1a; 2354]   "
εὐσεβεῖν   pres act inf [1Ti 5:4; cv-1d(2; 2355]   εὐσεβέω
εὐσεβεῖς   acc pl masc [2P 2:9; a-4a; 2356]   εὐσεβής
εὐσεβεῖτε   pres act ind 2 pl [Ac 17:23; cv-1d(2; 2355]   εὐσεβέω

εὐσεβέω   {2355, cv-1d(2}
[-, -, -, -, -] *to exercise piety;* towards a deity, *to worship,* Acts 17:23; towards relatives, *to be dutiful towards,* 1 Tim 5:4*

εὐσεβῆ   acc sg masc [Ac 10:7; a-4a; 2356]   εὐσεβής

εὐσεβής, ές   {2356, a-4a}
reverent; pious, devout, religious, Acts 10:2, 7; 2 Peter 2:9*

εὐσεβής   nom sg masc [Ac 10:2; a-4a; 2356]   "

εὐσεβῶς   {2357, adverb}
piously, religiously, 2 Tim 3:12; Titus 2:12*

εὐσεβῶς   adverb [2t; adverb; 2357]   εὐσεβῶς
εὔσημον   acc sg masc [1C 14:9; a-3a; 2358]   εὔσημος

εὔσημος, ον   {2358, a-3a}
pr. *well marked, strongly marked;* met. *significant, intelligible,* 1 Cor 14:9*

εὔσπλαγχνοι   nom pl masc [2t; a-3a; 2359]   εὔσπλαγχνος

εὔσπλαγχνος, ον   {2359, a-3a}
tender-hearted, compassionate, Eph 4:32; 1 Peter 3:8*

εὔσχημον   acc sg neut [1C 7:35; a-4b(1); 2363]   εὐσχήμων
εὐσχήμονα   nom pl neut [1C 12:24; a-4b(1); 2363]   "
εὐσχήμονας   acc pl fem [Ac 13:50; a-4b(1); 2363]   "

εὐσχημονέω   {2360, v-1d(2a)}
[-, -, -, -, -] *behave with dignity,* 1 Cor 13:5 v.l.*

εὐσχημόνων   gen pl fem [Ac 17:12; a-4b(1); 2363]   "

εὐσχημόνως   {2361, adverb}
in a becoming manner, with propriety, decently, gracefully, Rom 13:13; 1 Cor 14:40; 1 Thess 4:12*

εὐσχημόνως   adverb [3t; adverb; 2361]   εὐσχημόνως

εὐσχημοσύνη, ης, ἡ   {2362, n-1b}
comeliness, gracefulness; artificial *comeliness,* ornamental *array, embellishment,* 1 Cor 12:23*

εὐσχημοσύνην   acc sg fem [1C 12:23; n-1b; 2362]   εὐσχημοσύνη

εὐσχήμων, ον   {2363, a-4b(1)}
of good appearance, pleasing to look upon, comely, 1 Cor 12:24; met. *becoming, decent,* τὸ εὔσχημον, *decorum, propriety,* 1 Cor 7:35; *honorable, reputable, of high standing and influence,* Mark 15:43; Acts 13:50; 17:12, 34 v.l.*

εὐσχήμων   nom sg masc [Mk 15:43; a-4b(1); 2363]   εὐσχήμων

εὐτόνως   {2364, adverb}
intensely, vehemently, strenuously, Luke 23:10; Acts 18:28*

εὐτόνως   adverb [2t; adverb; 2364]   εὐτόνως

εὐτραπελία, ας, ἡ   {2365, n-1a}
   facetiousness, pleasantry; hence, *buffoonery,*
   coarse laughter, Eph 5:4*

εὐτραπελία   nom sg fem
   [Ep 5:4; n-1a; 2365]   εὐτραπελία

Εὔτυχος, ου, ὁ   {2366, n-2a}
   Eutychus, pr. name, Acts 20:9*

Εὔτυχος   nom sg masc [Ac 20:9; n-2a; 2366]
   Εὔτυχος

εὔφημα   nom pl neut [Pp 4:8; a-3a; 2368]   εὔφημος

εὐφημία, ας, ἡ   {2367, n-1a}
   pr. *use of words of good omen;* hence, *favorable*
   expression, praise, commendation, 2 Cor 6:8*

εὐφημίας   gen sg fem
   [2C 6:8; n-1a; 2367]   εὐφημία

εὔφημος, ον   {2368, a-3a}
   pr. *of good omen, auspicious;* hence, *of good report,*
   commendable, laudable, reputable, Phil 4:8*

εὐφορέω   {2369, v-1d(2a)}
   [-, εὐφόρησα, -, -, -] *to bear* or *bring forth well* or
   plentifully, yield abundantly, Luke 12:16*

εὐφόρησεν   aor act ind 3 sg
   [Lk 12:16; v-1d(2a); 2369]   εὐφορέω
εὐφραίνεσθαι   pres pass inf
   [Lk 15:24; v-2d(4); 2370]   εὐφραίνω
εὐφραίνεσθε   pres pass imperative 2 pl
   [Rv 12:12; v-2d(4); 2370]   "
εὐφραινόμενος   pres pass ptcp nom sg masc
   [Lk 16:19; v-2d(4); 2370]   "
εὐφραίνονται   pres pass ind 3 pl
   [Rv 11:10; v-2d(4); 2370]   "
εὐφραίνοντο   imperf pass ind 3 pl
   [Ac 7:41; v-2d(4); 2370]   "
εὐφραίνου   pres pass imperative 2 sg
   [2t; v-2d(4); 2370]   "

εὐφραίνω   {2370, v-2d(4)}
   [-, ηὔφρανα, -, -, ηὐφράνθην] *to gladden,* 2 Cor
   2:2; pass. *to be glad, exult, rejoice,* Luke 12:19;
   Acts 2:26; mid. *to feast in token of joy, keep a day*
   of rejoicing, Luke 15:23, 24, 29, 32

εὐφραίνων   pres act ptcp nom sg masc
   [2C 2:2; v-2d(4); 2370]   "
εὐφρανθῆναι   aor pass inf
   [Lk 15:32; v-2d(4); 2370]   "
εὐφράνθητε   aor pass imperative 2 pl
   [Rm 15:10; v-2d(4); 2370]   "
εὐφράνθητι   aor pass imperative 2 sg
   [Ga 4:27; v-2d(4); 2370]   "
εὐφρανθῶ   aor pass subj 1 sg
   [Lk 15:29; v-2d(4); 2370]   "
εὐφρανθῶμεν   aor pass subj 1 pl
   [Lk 15:23; v-2d(4); 2370]   "
Εὐφράτῃ   dat sg masc
   [Rv 9:14; n-1f; 2371]   Εὐφράτης
Εὐφράτην   acc sg masc [Rv 16:12; n-1f; 2371]   "

Εὐφράτης, ου, ὁ   {2371, n-1f}
   the river *Euphrates,* Rev 9:14; 16:12*

εὐφροσύνη, ης, ἡ   {2372, n-1b}
   joy, gladness, rejoicing, Acts 2:28; 14:17*

εὐφροσύνης   gen sg fem
   [2t; n-1b; 2372]   εὐφροσύνη
εὐχαριστεῖ   pres act ind 3 sg
   [2t; v-1d(2a); 2373]   εὐχαριστέω
εὐχαριστεῖν   pres act inf [2t; v-1d(2a); 2373]   "
εὐχαριστεῖς   pres act ind 2 sg
   [1C 14:17; v-1d(2a); 2373]   "
εὐχαριστεῖτε   pres act imperative 2 pl
   [1Th 5:18; v-1d(2a); 2373]   "

εὐχαριστέω   {2373, v-1d(2a)}
   [-, εὐχαρίστησα, -, -, εὐχαριστήθην] *to thank,*
   Luke 17:16; absol. *to give thanks,* Matt 15:36;
   26:27; pass. *to be made a matter of thankfulness,* 2
   Cor 1:11

εὐχαριστηθῇ   aor pass subj 3 sg
   [2C 1:11; v-1d(2a); 2373]   "
εὐχαριστήσαντος   aor act ptcp gen sg masc
   [Jn 6:23; v-1d(2a); 2373]   "
εὐχαριστήσας   aor act ptcp nom sg masc
   [9t; v-1d(2a); 2373]   "
εὐχαρίστησεν   aor act ind 3 sg
   [Ac 27:35; v-1d(2a); 2373]   "

εὐχαριστία, ας, ἡ   {2374, n-1a}
   gratitude, thankfulness, Acts 24:3; *thanks, the act*
   of giving thanks, thanksgiving, 1 Cor 14:16;
   conversation marked by the gentle cheerfulness of a
   grateful heart, as contrasted with the unseemly
   mirth of εὐτραπελία, Eph 5:4, of the Lord's
   Supper, 1 Cor 10:16 v.l.*

εὐχαριστία   nom sg fem
   [2t; n-1a; 2374]   εὐχαριστία
εὐχαριστίᾳ   dat sg fem [3t; n-1a; 2374]   "
εὐχαριστίαν   acc sg fem [4t; n-1a; 2374]   "
εὐχαριστίας   gen sg fem [4t; n-1a; 2374]   "
εὐχαριστίας   acc pl fem [1Ti 2:1; n-1a; 2374]   "
εὐχαριστιῶν   gen pl fem [2C 9:12; n-1a; 2374]   "
εὐχάριστοι   nom pl masc
   [Cl 3:15; a-3a; 2375]   εὐχάριστος

εὐχάριστος, ον   {2375, a-3a}
   grateful, pleasing; mindful of benefits, thankful,
   Col 3:15*

εὐχαριστοῦμεν   pres act ind 1 pl
   [4t; v-1d(2a); 2373]   εὐχαριστέω
εὐχαριστοῦντες   pres act ptcp nom pl masc
   [3t; v-1d(2a); 2373]   "
εὐχαριστῶ   pres act ind 1 sg
   [10t; v-1d(2a); 2373]   "
εὐχαριστῶν   pres act ptcp nom sg masc
   [2t; v-1d(2a); 2373]   "
εὔχεσθε   pres mid imperative 2 pl
   [Jm 5:16; v-1b(2); 2377]   εὔχομαι

εὐχή, ῆς, ἡ   {2376, n-1b}
   a wish, prayer, James 5:15; *a vow,* Acts 21:23; Acts
   18:18*

εὐχή   nom sg fem [Jm 5:15; n-1b; 2376]   εὐχή
εὐχήν   acc sg fem [2t; n-1b; 2376]   "

εὔχομαι   {2377, v-1b(2)}
[(εὐχόμην or ηὐχόμην), εὔξομαι, εὐξάμην, -, -, -]
to pray, offer prayer, Acts 26:29; 2 Cor 13:7, 9;
James 5:16 v.l.; *to wish, desire*, Acts 27:29; Rom
9:3; 3 John 2*

εὔχομαι   pres mid ind 1 sg
    [3J 2; v-1b(2); 2377]   εὔχομαι
εὐχόμεθα   pres mid ind 1 pl [2t; v-1b(2); 2377]   "
εὔχρηστον   nom sg neut
    [2Ti 2:21; a-3a; 2378]   εὔχρηστος
εὔχρηστον   acc sg masc [Pm 11; a-3a; 2378]   "

εὔχρηστος, ον   {2378, a-3a}
highly useful, very profitable, 2 Tim 2:21; 4:11; Phil
11*

εὔχρηστος   nom sg masc [2Ti 4:11; a-3a; 2378]   "

εὐψυχέω   {2379, cv-1d(2)}
[-, -, -, -, -] *to be animated, encouraged, in good
spirits*, Phil 2:19*

εὐψυχῶ   pres act subj 1 sg
    [Pp 2:19; cv-1d(2); 2379]   εὐψυχέω

εὐωδία, ας, ἡ   {2380, n-1a}
a sweet smell, grateful odor, fragrance, 2 Cor 2:15;
Eph 5:2; Phil 4:18*

εὐωδία   nom sg fem [2C 2:15; n-1a; 2380]   εὐωδία
εὐωδίας   gen sg fem [2t; n-1a; 2380]   "
εὐώνυμον   acc sg masc
    [Rv 10:2; a-3a; 2381]   εὐώνυμος
εὐώνυμον   acc sg fem [Ac 21:3; a-3a; 2381]   "

εὐώνυμος, ον   {2381, a-3a}
of good name or *omen*; used also as an
euphemism by the Greeks instead of ἀριστερός,
which was a word of bad import, as all omens
on the left denoted misfortune; *the left*, Matt
20:21, 23; 25:33, 41

εὐωνύμων   gen pl fem [2t; a-3a; 2381]   "
εὐωνύμων   gen pl neut [5t; a-3a; 2381]   "

εὐωχία, ας, ἡ   {2382, n-1a}
banquet, feasting, Jude 12 v.l.*

ἐφ'   prep-gen [7t; prep; 2093]   "
ἐφ'   prep-dat [15t; prep; 2093]   "
ἐφ'   prep-acc [60t; prep; 2093]   ἐπί
ἔφαγεν   aor act ind 3 sg
    [5t; v-1b(3); 2266]   ἐσθίω
ἐφάγετε   aor act ind 2 pl
    [Jn 6:26; v-1b(3); 2266]   "
ἐφάγομεν   aor act ind 1 pl [2t; v-1b(3); 2266]   "
ἔφαγον   aor act ind 1 sg [2t; v-1b(3); 2266]   "
ἔφαγον   aor act ind 3 pl [11t; v-1b(3); 2266]   "

ἐφάλλομαι   {2383, cv-2d(1)}
[-, ἐφαλόμην, -, -, -] *to leap* or *spring upon, assault*,
Acts 19:16*

ἐφαλόμενος   aor mid ptcp nom sg masc
    [Ac 19:16; cv-2d(1); 2383]   ἐφάλλομαι
ἐφανερώθη   aor pass ind 3 sg
    [11t; v-1d(3); 5746]   φανερόω
ἐφανερώθησαν   aor pass ind 3 pl
    [Rv 15:4; v-1d(3); 5746]   "

ἐφανέρωσα   aor act ind 1 sg
    [Jn 17:6; v-1d(3); 5746]   "
ἐφανέρωσεν   aor act ind 3 sg [5t; v-1d(3); 5746]   "
ἐφάνη   aor pass ind 3 sg
    [5t; v-2d(4); 5743]   φαίνω
ἐφάνησαν   aor pass ind 3 pl
    [Lk 24:11; v-2d(4); 5743]   "

ἐφάπαξ   {2384, adverb}
once for all, Rom 6:10; Heb 7:27; 9:12; 10:10; *at
once*, 1 Cor 15:6*

ἐφάπαξ   adverb [5t; adverb; 2384]   ἐφάπαξ
ἔφασκεν   imperf act ind 3 sg
    [Ac 25:19; v-5a; 5763]   φάσκω
ἐφείσατο   aor mid ind 3 sg
    [4t; v-1b(3); 5767]   φείδομαι
ἔφερεν   imperf act ind 3 sg
    [Mk 4:8; v-1c(1); 5770]   φέρω
ἐφερόμεθα   imperf pass ind 1 pl
    [Ac 27:15; v-1c(1); 5770]   "
ἔφερον   imperf act ind 3 pl [4t; v-1c(1); 5770]   "
ἐφέροντο   imperf pass ind 3 pl
    [Ac 27:17; v-1c(1); 5770]   "

Ἐφεσῖνος, α, ον   {2385, a-1a(1)}
see Ἐφέσιος, *Ephesian*, Rev 2:1 v.l.*

Ἐφέσιοι   voc pl masc
    [Ac 19:35; a-1a(1); 2386]   Ἐφέσιος
Ἐφέσιον   acc sg masc [Ac 21:29; a-1a(1); 2386]   "

Ἐφέσιος, α, ον   {2386, a-1a(1)}
Ephesian, belonging to Ephesus, Acts 19:28, 34,
35; 21:29*

Ἐφεσίων   gen pl masc [3t; a-1a(1); 2386]   "
Ἔφεσον   acc sg fem [8t; n-2b; 2387]   Ἔφεσος

Ἔφεσος, ου, ἡ   {2387, n-2b}
Ephesus, a celebrated city of Asia Minor, Acts
18:19, 21, 24; 1 Cor 15:32*

Ἐφέσου   gen sg fem [2t; n-2b; 2387]   "
ἐφέστηκεν   perf act ind 3 sg
    [2Ti 4:6; cv-6a; 2392]   ἐφίστημι
ἐφεστώς   perf act ptcp nom sg masc
    [Ac 22:20; cv-6a; 2392]   "
ἐφεστῶτα   perf act ptcp acc sg masc
    [Ac 28:2; cv-6a; 2392]   "
Ἐφέσῳ   dat sg fem [6t; n-2b; 2387]   Ἔφεσος
ἐφευρετάς   acc pl masc
    [Rm 1:30; n-1f; 2388]   ἐφευρετής

ἐφευρετής, οῦ, ὁ   {2388, n-1f}
an inventor, deviser, Rom 1:30*

ἔφη   imperf act ind 3 sg [43t; v-6b; 5774]   φημί

ἐφημερία, ας, ἡ   {2389, n-1a}
pr. *daily course; the daily service* of the temple; *a
class* of priests to which the daily service for a
week was allotted in rotation, Luke 1:5, 8*

ἐφημερίας   gen sg fem [2t; n-1a; 2389]   ἐφημερία

ἐφήμερος, ον   {2390, a-3a}
*lasting for a day; daily sufficient for a day,
necessary for every day*, James 2:15*

ἐφημέρου   gen sg fem
   [Jm 2:15; a-3a; 2390]   ἐφήμερος
ἐφθάσαμεν   aor act ind 1 pl
   [2t; v-3a(1); 5777]   φθάνω
ἔφθασεν   aor act ind 3 sg [4t; v-3a(1); 5777]   "
ἐφθείραμεν   imperf act ind 1 pl
   [2C 7:2; v-2d(3); 5780]   φθείρω
ἔφθειρεν   aor act ind 3 sg
   [Rv 19:2; v-2d(3); 5780]   "
ἐφικέσθαι   aor mid inf
   [2C 10:13; cv-3b; 2391]   ἐφικνέομαι

ἐφικνέομαι   {2391, cv-3b}
   [-, ἐφικόμην, -, -, -] to come or reach to, to reach a
   certain point or end; to reach, arrive at, 2 Cor
   10:13, 14*

ἐφικνούμενοι   pres mid ptcp nom pl masc
   [2C 10:14; cv-3b; 2391]   "
ἐφίλει   imperf act ind 3 sg
   [3t; v-1d(2a); 5797]   φιλέω
ἐφιμώθη   aor pass ind 3 sg
   [Mt 22:12; v-1d(3); 5821]   φιμόω
ἐφίμωσεν   aor act ind 3 sg
   [Mt 22:34; v-1d(3); 5821]   "
ἐφίσταται   pres mid ind 3 sg
   [1Th 5:3; cv-6a; 2392]   ἐφίστημι

ἐφίστημι   {2392, cv-6a}
   [-, ἐπέστην, ἐπέστην, -, ἐπεστάθην] trans. to place
   upon, over, close by; intrans. to stand by or near,
   Luke 2:38; 4:39; to come suddenly upon, Luke 2:9;
   24:4; to come upon, assault, Acts 6:12; 17:5; to
   come near, approach, Luke 10:40; to impend, be
   instant, to be at hand, 1 Thess 5:3; to be present,
   Acts 28:2; to be pressing, urgent, earnest, 2 Tim
   4:2

ἐφκάθετος, ον   {1588, a-3a}
   to incite someone to an evil act, lying in wait, as a
   noun spy, Luke 20:20*

ἐφκακέω   {1591, cv-1d(2a)}
   [-, ἐνεκάκησα, -, -, -] t.r. has ἐκκακέω, to be
   faint-hearted, be remiss, weary, tired, Luke 18:1; 2
   Cor 4:1, 16; Gal 6:9; Eph 3:13; 2 Thess 3:13*

ἐφοβεῖτο   imperf pass ind 3 sg
   [Mk 6:20; cv-1d(2a); 5828]   φοβέομαι
ἐφοβήθη   aor pass ind 3 sg [5t; cv-1d(2a); 5828]   "
ἐφοβήθησαν   aor pass ind 3 pl
   [14t; cv-1d(2a); 5828]   "
ἐφοβούμην   imperf pass ind 1 sg
   [Lk 19:21; cv-1d(2a); 5828]   "
ἐφοβοῦντο   imperf mid ind 3 pl
   [2t; cv-1d(2a); 5828]   "
ἐφοβοῦντο   imperf pass ind 3 pl
   [8t; cv-1d(2a); 5828]   "
ἐφονεύσατε   aor act ind 2 pl
   [2t; v-1a(6); 5839]   φονεύω

ἐφοράω   {2393, cv-1d(1a)}
   a proposed lexical form for the second aorist
   ἐπεῖδον

ἐφορέσαμεν   aor act ind 1 pl
   [1C 15:49; v-1d(2b); 5841]   φορέω

Ἐφραίμ, ὁ   {2394, n-3g(2)}
   Ephraim, pr. name, indecl. John 11:54*

Ἐφραίμ   indecl [Jn 11:54; n-3g(2); 2394]   Ἐφραίμ
ἔφραξαν   aor act ind 3 pl
   [Hb 11:33; v-2b; 5852]   φράσσω
ἐφρονεῖτε   imperf act ind 2 pl
   [Pp 4:10; v-1d(2a); 5858]   φρονέω
ἐφρόνουν   imperf act ind 1 sg
   [1C 13:11; v-1d(2a); 5858]   "
ἐφρούρει   imperf act ind 3 sg
   [2C 11:32; v-1d(2a); 5864]   φρουρέω
ἐφρουρούμεθα   imperf pass ind 1 pl
   [Ga 3:23; v-1d(2a); 5864]   "
ἐφρύαξαν   aor act ind 3 pl
   [Ac 4:25; v-2b; 5865]   φρυάσσω
ἔφυγεν   aor act ind 3 sg [5t; v-1b(2); 5771]   φεύγω
ἔφυγον   aor act ind 3 pl [7t; v-1b(2); 5771]   "
ἐφύλαξα   aor act ind 1 sg
   [3t; v-2b; 5875]   φυλάσσω
ἐφυλαξάμην   aor mid ind 1 sg
   [Mk 10:20; v-2b; 5875]   "
ἐφυλάξατε   aor act ind 2 pl
   [Ac 7:53; v-2b; 5875]   "
ἐφύλαξεν   aor act ind 3 sg [2P 2:5; v-2b; 5875]   "
ἐφυσιώθησαν   aor pass ind 3 pl
   [1C 4:18; v-1d(3); 5881]   φυσιόω
ἐφύτευον   imperf act ind 3 pl
   [Lk 17:28; v-1a(6); 5885]   φυτεύω
ἐφύτευσα   aor act ind 1 sg
   [1C 3:6; v-1a(6); 5885]   "
ἐφύτευσεν   aor act ind 3 sg [4t; v-1a(6); 5885]   "

ἐφφαθά   {2395, n-3g(2)}
   Aramaic, be thou opened, Mark 7:34*

ἐφφαθα   indecl
   [Mk 7:34; n-3g(2); 2395]   ἐφφαθά
ἐφώνει   imperf act ind 3 sg
   [Lk 8:8; v-1d(2a); 5888]   φωνέω
ἐφώνησαν   aor act ind 3 pl [2t; v-1d(2a); 5888]   "
ἐφώνησεν   aor act ind 3 sg [13t; v-1d(2a); 5888] "
ἐφώτισεν   aor act ind 3 sg
   [Rv 21:23; v-2a(1); 5894]   φωτίζω
ἐφωτίσθη   aor pass ind 3 sg
   [Rv 18:1; v-2a(1); 5894]   "
ἔχαιρεν   imperf act ind 3 sg
   [Lk 13:17; v-2d(2); 5897]   χαίρω
ἔχαιρον   imperf act ind 3 pl
   [Ac 13:48; v-2d(2); 5897]   "
ἐχαλάσθην   aor pass ind 1 sg
   [2C 11:33; v-1d(1b); 5899]   χαλάω
ἐχάρη   aor pass ind 3 sg
   [3t; v-2d(2); 5897]   χαίρω
ἐχάρημεν   aor pass ind 1 pl
   [2C 7:13; v-2d(2); 5897]   "
ἐχάρην   aor pass ind 1 sg [3t; v-2d(2); 5897]   "
ἐχάρησαν   aor pass ind 3 pl [5t; v-2d(2); 5897] "
ἐχάρητε   aor pass ind 2 pl
   [Jn 14:28; v-2d(2); 5897]   "
ἐχαρίσατο   aor mid ind 3 sg
   [6t; v-2a(1); 5919]   χαρίζομαι
ἐχαρίσθη   aor pass ind 3 sg
   [Pp 1:29; v-2a(1); 5919]   "

ἐχαρίτωσεν   aor act ind 3 sg
[Ep 1:6; v-1d(3); 5923]   χαριτόω
ἔχε   pres act imperative 2 sg
[4t; v-1b(2); 2400]   ἔχω
ἔχει   pres act ind 3 sg   [103t; v-1b(2); 2400]   "
ἔχειν   pres act inf   [30t; v-1b(2); 2400]   "
ἔχεις   pres act ind 2 sg   [28t; v-1b(2); 2400]   "
ἔχετε   pres act imperative 2 pl
[4t; v-1b(2); 2400]   "
ἔχετε   pres act ind 2 pl   [47t; v-1b(2); 2400]   "
ἐχέτω   pres act imperative 3 sg
[3t; v-1b(2); 2400]   "
ἔχῃ   pres act subj 3 sg   [11t; v-1b(2); 2400]   "
ἔχητε   pres act subj 2 pl   [11t; v-1b(2); 2400]   "

ἐχθές   {2396, adverb}
yesterday, John 4:52; Acts 7:28; 16:35 v.l.; Heb 13:8*

ἐχθές   adverb   [3t; adverb; 2396]   ἐχθές

ἔχθρα, ας, ἡ   {2397, n-1a}
enmity, discord, feud, Luke 23:12; Gal 5:20; *alienation,* Eph 2:14, 16; *a principle* or *state of enmity,* Rom 8:7; James 4:4*

ἔχθρα   nom sg fem   [2t; n-1a; 2397]   ἔχθρα
ἔχθρᾳ   dat sg fem   [Lk 23:12; n-1a; 2397]   "
ἔχθραι   nom pl fem   [Ga 5:20; n-1a; 2397]   "
ἔχθραν   acc sg fem   [2t; n-1a; 2397]   "
ἐχθρέ   voc sg masc
[Ac 13:10; a-1a(1); 2398]   ἐχθρός
ἐχθροί   nom pl masc   [6t; a-1a(1); 2398]   "
ἐχθρόν   acc sg masc   [2t; a-1a(1); 2398]   "

ἐχθρός, ά, όν   {2398, a-1a(1)}
hated, under disfavor, Rom 11:28; *inimical, hostile,* Matt 13:28; Col 1:21; as a subst., *an enemy, adversary,* Matt 5:43, 44; 10:36; Luke 27:35

ἐχθρός   nom sg masc   [7t; a-1a(1); 2398]   "
ἐχθροῦ   gen sg masc   [Lk 10:19; a-1a(1); 2398]   "
ἐχθρούς   acc pl masc   [13t; a-1a(1); 2398]   "
ἐχθρῶν   gen pl masc   [2t; a-1a(1); 2398]   "

ἔχιδνα, ης, ἡ   {2399, n-1c}
a viper, poisonous serpent, Acts 28:3; used also fig. of persons, Matt 3:7; 12:34; 23:33; Luke 3:7*

ἔχιδνα   nom sg fem   [Ac 28:3; n-1c; 2399]   ἔχιδνα
ἐχιδνῶν   gen pl fem   [4t; n-1c; 2399]   "
ἐχλεύαζον   imperf act ind 3 pl
[Ac 17:32; v-2a(1); 5949]   χλευάζω
ἔχοι   pres act opt 3 sg   [2t; v-1b(2); 2400]   ἔχω
ἔχοιεν   pres act opt 3 pl
[Ac 24:19; v-1b(2); 2400]   "
ἔχομεν   pres act ind 1 pl   [43t; v-1b(2); 2400]   "
ἐχόμενα   pres mid ptcp acc pl neut
[Hb 6:9; v-1b(2); 2400]   "
ἐχομένας   pres mid ptcp acc pl fem
[Mk 1:38; v-1b(2); 2400]   "
ἐχομένη   pres mid ptcp dat sg fem
[3t; v-1b(2); 2400]   "
ἔχον   pres act ptcp nom sg neut
[2t; v-1b(2); 2400]   "
ἔχον   pres act ptcp acc sg neut
[2t; v-1b(2); 2400]   "

ἔχοντα   pres act ptcp nom pl neut
[6t; v-1b(2); 2400]   "
ἔχοντα   pres act ptcp acc sg masc
[22t; v-1b(2); 2400]   "
ἔχοντας   pres act ptcp acc pl masc
[16t; v-1b(2); 2400]   "
ἔχοντες   pres act ptcp nom pl masc
[46t; v-1b(2); 2400]   "
ἔχοντι   pres act ptcp dat sg masc
[10t; v-1b(2); 2400]   "
ἔχοντος   pres act ptcp gen sg masc
[4t; v-1b(2); 2400]   "
ἔχοντος   pres act ptcp gen sg neut
[Rv 17:7; v-1b(2); 2400]   "
ἐχόντων   pres act ptcp gen pl masc
[9t; v-1b(2); 2400]   "
ἐχορτάσθησαν   aor pass ind 3 pl
[6t; v-2a(1); 5963]   χορτάζω
ἐχορτάσθητε   aor pass ind 2 pl
[Jn 6:26; v-2a(1); 5963]   "
ἔχουσα   pres act ptcp nom sg fem
[15t; v-1b(2); 2400]   ἔχω
ἔχουσαι   pres act ptcp nom pl fem
[3t; v-1b(2); 2400]   "
ἐχούσαις   pres act ptcp dat pl fem
[3t; v-1b(2); 2400]   "
ἔχουσαν   pres act ptcp acc sg fem
[6t; v-1b(2); 2400]   "
ἐχούσῃ   pres act ptcp dat sg fem
[1Th 5:3; v-1b(2); 2400]   "
ἐχούσης   pres act ptcp gen sg fem
[2t; v-1b(2); 2400]   "
ἔχουσι   pres act ind 3 pl   [3t; v-1b(2); 2400]   "
ἔχουσιν   pres act ind 3 pl   [33t; v-1b(2); 2400]   "
ἐχρηματίσθη   aor pass ind 3 sg
[Ac 10:22; v-2a(1); 5976]   χρηματίζω
ἐχρησάμεθα   aor mid ind 1 pl
[1C 9:12; v-1d(1a); 5968]   χράομαι
ἐχρησάμην   aor mid ind 1 sg
[2C 1:17; v-1d(1a); 5968]   "
ἔχρισας   aor act ind 2 sg
[Ac 4:27; v-1a(1); 5987]   χρίω
ἔχρισεν   aor act ind 3 sg   [3t; v-1a(1); 5987]   "
ἐχρῶντο   imperf mid ind 3 pl
[Ac 27:17; v-1d(1a); 5968]   χράομαι

ἔχω   {2400, v-1b(2)}
[(εἶχον), ἔξω, ἔσχον, ἔσχηκα, -, -] pluperfect., ἐσχήκειν, *to hold,* Rev 1:16; *to seize, possess* a person, Mark 16:8; *to have, possess,* Matt 7:29, et al. freq.; *to have, have ready, be furnished with,* Matt 5:23; John 5:36; 6:68; *to have* as a matter of crimination, Matt 5:23; Mark 11:25; *to have* at command, Matt 27:65; *to have* the power, *be able,* Matt 18:25; Luke 14:14; Acts 4:14; *to have* in marriage, Matt 14:4; *to have, be affected by, subjected to,* Matt 3:14; 12:10; Mark 3:10; John 12:48; 15:22, 24; 16:21, 22; Acts 23:29; 1 Tim 5:12; Heb 7:28; 1 John 1:8; 4:18; χάραν ἔχειν, *to feel gratitude, be thankful,* 1 Tim 1:12; 2 Tim 1:3; Phil 7; *to hold, esteem, regard,* Matt 14:5; Luke 14:18, 19; *to have* or *hold* as an object of knowledge, faith, or practice, John 5:38, 42; 14:21; 1 John 5:12; 2 John 9; *to hold on* in entire possession, *to*

retain, Rom 15:4; 2 Tim 1:13; Heb 12:28; intrans. with adverbs or adverbial expression, *to be, to fare*, Matt 9:12; Mark 2:17; 5:23; Luke 5:31; John 4:52; Acts 7:1; 12:15; 15:36; 21:13; 2 Cor 10:6; 12:14; 1 Tim 5:25; 1 Peter 4:5; τὸ νῦν ἔχον, *for the present*; in N.T. ἔχειν ἐν γαστρί, *to be pregnant*, Matt 1:18; as also ἔχειν κοίτην, Rom 9:10; ἔχειν δαιμόνιον, *to be possessed*, Matt 11:18; of time, *to have continued, to have lived*, John 5:5, 6; 8:57; of space, *to embrace, be distant*, Acts 1:12; mid. pr. *to hold by, cling to*; hence, *to border upon, be next*, Mark 1:38; Luke 13:33; Acts 20:15; 21:26; *to tend immediately to*, Heb 6:9

ἔχω   pres act ind 1 sg [43t; v-1b(2); 2400]   ἔχω
ἔχω   pres act subj 1 sg [5t; v-1b(2); 2400]   "
ἔχωμεν   pres act subj 1 pl [4t; v-1b(2); 2400]   "
ἔχων   pres act ptcp nom sg masc
    [86t; v-1b(2); 2400]   "
ἐχωρίσθη   aor pass ind 3 sg
    [Pm 15; v-2a(1); 6004]   χωρίζω
ἔχωσιν   pres act subj 3 pl [5t; v-1b(2); 2400]   ἔχω
ἐψευδομαρτύρουν   imperf act ind 3 pl
    [2t; cv-1d(2a); 6018]   ψευδομαρτυρέω
ἐψεύσω   aor mid ind 2 sg
    [Ac 5:4; v-1b(3); 6017]   ψεύδομαι
ἐψηλάφησαν   aor act ind 3 pl
    [1J 1:1; v-1d(1a); 6027]   ψηλαφάω
ἑώρακα   perf act ind 1 sg
    [3t; v-1d(1a); 3972]   ὁράω
ἑωράκαμεν   perf act ind 1 pl
    [5t; v-1d(1a); 3972]   "
ἑώρακαν   perf act ind 3 pl
    [Lk 9:36; v-1d(1a); 3972]   "
ἑώρακας   perf act ind 2 sg [4t; v-1d(1a); 3972]   "
ἑωράκασιν   perf act ind 3 pl
    [Jn 15:24; v-1d(1a); 3972]   "
ἑωράκατε   perf act ind 2 pl [3t; v-1d(1a); 3972]   "
ἑωράκει   pluperf act ind 3 sg
    [Ac 7:44; v-1d(1a); 3972]   "
ἑώρακεν   perf act ind 3 sg [10t; v-1d(1a); 3972]   "
ἑωρακέναι   perf act inf
    [Lk 24:23; v-1d(1a); 3972]   "
ἑωρακότες   perf act ptcp nom pl masc
    [Jn 4:45; v-1d(1a); 3972]   "
ἑωρακώς   perf act ptcp nom sg masc
    [2t; v-1d(1a); 3972]   "

ἕως   {2401, conj}
can function as an improper prep., *while, as long as*, John 9:4; *until*, Matt 2:9; Luke 15:4; as also in N.T. ἕως οὗ, ἕως ὅτου, Matt 5:18, 26; ἕως ἄρτι, *until now*, Matt 11:12; ἕως πότε, *until when, how long*, Matt 17:17; ἕως σήμερον, *until this day, to this time*, 2 Cor 3:15; as a prep. of time, *until*, Matt 24:21; of place, *unto, even to*, Matt 11:23; Luke 2:15; ἕως ἄνω, *to the brim*, John 2:7; ἕως εἰς, *even to, as far as*, Luke 24:50; ἕως κάτω, *to the bottom*; ἕως ὧδε, *to this place*, Luke 23:5; of state, *unto, even to*, Matt 26:38; of number, *even, so much as*, Rom 3:12, et al. freq.

ἕως   conj [146t; conj; 2401]   "

ζ

Ζαβουλών, ὁ   {2404, n-3g(2)}
Zebulun, pr. name, indecl., an Israelite tribe, Matt 4:13, 15; Rev 7:8; Luke 4:31 v.l.*

Ζαβουλών   indecl [3t; n-3g(2); 2404]   Ζαβουλών
Ζακχαῖε   voc sg masc
    [Lk 19:5; n-2a; 2405]   Ζακχαῖος
Ζακχαῖος, ου, ὁ   {2405, n-2a}
Zaccheus, pr. name, Luke 19:2, 5, 8*

Ζακχαῖος   nom sg masc [2t; n-2a; 2405]   "
Ζάρα, ὁ   {2406, n-3g(2)}
Zerah, pr. name, indecl., Matt 1:3*

Ζάρα   indecl [Mt 1:3; n-3g(2); 2406]   Ζάρα
Ζαχαρία   voc sg masc
    [Lk 1:13; n-1d; 2408]   Ζαχαρίας
Ζαχαρίαν   acc sg masc [2t; n-1d; 2408]   "
Ζαχαρίας, ου, ὁ   {2408, n-1d}
Zacharias, pr. name. (1) *Son of Barachias*, Matt 23:35; Luke 11:51. (2) *Father of John the Baptist*, Luke 1:5

Ζαχαρίας   nom sg masc [4t; n-1d; 2408]   "
Ζαχαρίου   gen sg masc [4t; n-1d; 2408]   "

ζάω   {2409, v-1d(1a)}
[ζήσω or ζήσομαι, ἔζησα, -, -, -] *to live, to be possessed of vitality, to exercise the functions of life*, Matt 27:63; Acts 17:28; τὸ ζῆν, *life*, Heb 2:15; *to have means of subsistence*, 1 Cor 9:14; *to live, to pass existence* in a specific manner, Luke 2:36; 15:13; *to be instinct with life and vigor*; hence, *living*, an epithet of God, in a sense peculiar to Himself; ἐλπὶς ζῶσα, *a living hope* in respect of vigor and constancy, 1 Peter 1:3; ὕδωρ ζῶν, *living water* in respect of a full and unfailing flow, John 4:10, 11; *to be alive* with cheered and hopeful feelings, 1 Thess 3:8; *to be alive* in a state of salvation from spiritual death, 1 John 4:9

Ζεβεδαῖον   acc sg masc
    [Mk 1:20; n-2a; 2411]   Ζεβεδαῖος
Ζεβεδαῖος, ου, ὁ   {2411, n-2a}
Zebedee, pr. name, the father of James and John, Matt 4:21; Mark 10:35; Luke 5:10; John 21:1*

Ζεβεδαίου   gen sg masc [11t; n-2a; 2411]   "
ζέοντες   pres act ptcp nom pl masc
    [Rm 12:11; v-1d(2a); 2417]   ζέω
ζεστός, ή, όν   {2412, a-1a(2a)}
pr. *boiled; boiling, boiling hot;* met. *glowing with zeal, fervent*, Rev 3:15, 16*

ζεστός   nom sg masc [3t; a-1a(2a); 2412]   ζεστός
ζεύγη   acc pl neut
    [Lk 14:19; n-3d(2b); 2414]   ζεῦγος
ζεύγνυμι   {2413, v-3c(2)}
[-, ἔζευξα, -, -, -] *connect, join*, Mark 10:9 v.l.*

ζεῦγος, ους, τό   {2414, n-3d(2b)}
a yoke of animals; *a pair, couple*, Luke 2:24; 14:19*

ζεῦγος   acc sg neut [Lk 2:24; n-3d(2b); 2414]   "

ζευκτηρία, ας, ἡ   {2415, n-1a}
   a fastening, band, Acts 27:40*

ζευκτηρίας   acc pl fem
   [Ac 27:40; n-1a; 2415]   ζευκτηρία

Ζεύς, Ζιός, ὁ   {2416, n-3g(1)}
   the supreme god of the Greeks answering to
   the *Jupiter* of the Romans, Acts 14:12, 13*

ζέω   {2417, v-1d(2a)}
   [-, -, -, -, -] *to boil, to be hot,* in N.T. met. *to be
   fervent, ardent, zealous,* Acts 18:25; Rom 12:11*

ζέων   pres act ptcp nom sg masc
   [Ac 18:25; v-1d(2a); 2417]   ζέω
ζῇ   pres act ind 3 sg [13t; v-1d(1a); 2409]   ζάω
ζήλευε   pres act imperative 2 sg
   [Rv 3:19; v-1a(6); 2418]   ζηλεύω

ζηλεύω   {2418, v-1a(6)}
   [-, -, -, -, -] *to be zealous, earnest, eager,* Rev 3:19*

ζηλοῖ   pres act ind 3 sg
   [1C 13:4; v-1d(3); 2420]   ζηλόω
ζῆλον   acc sg masc [4t; n-2a; 2419]   ζῆλος

ζῆλος, ους, τό   {2419, n-3d(2b)}
   also spelled ζῆλος, ου, τό (n-2a), *generous rivalry;
   noble aspiration;* in N.T. *zeal, ardor in behalf of,
   ardent affection,* John 2:17; Rom 10:2; in a bad
   sense, *jealousy, envy, malice,* Acts 13:45; Rom
   13:13; *indignation, wrath,* Acts 5:17

ζῆλος   nom sg masc [6t; n-2a; 2419]   "
ζῆλος   nom sg neut [2C 9:2; n-2a; 2419]   "
ζῆλος   acc sg neut [Pp 3:6; n-2a; 2419] "ζήλου   gen
   sg masc [2t; n-2a; 2419]   "
ζηλοῦσθαι   pres pass inf
   [Ga 4:18; v-1d(3); 2420]   ζηλόω
ζηλοῦσιν   pres act ind 3 pl
   [Ga 4:17; v-1d(3); 2420]   "
ζηλοῦτε   pres act imperative 2 pl
   [3t; v-1d(3); 2420]   "
ζηλοῦτε   pres act ind 2 pl
   [Jm 4:2; v-1d(3); 2420]   "
ζηλοῦτε   pres act subj 2 pl
   [Ga 4:17; v-1d(3); 2420]   "

ζηλόω   {2420, v-1d(3)}
   [ζηλώσω, ἐζήλωσα, -, -, -] *to have strong affection
   towards, be ardently devoted to,* 2 Cor 11:2; *to make
   a show of affection and devotion towards,* Gal 4:17;
   to desire earnestly, aspire eagerly after, 1 Cor 12:31;
   14:1, 39; absol. *to be fervent, to be zealous,* Rev
   3:19; *to be jealous, envious, spiteful,* Acts 7:9; 17:5;
   1 Cor 13:4; James 4:2; pass. *to be an object of
   warm regard and devotion,* Gal 4:18

ζήλῳ   dat sg masc [2t; n-2a; 2419]   ζῆλος
ζηλῶ   pres act ind 1 sg
   [2C 11:2; v-1d(3); 2420]   ζηλόω
ζηλώσαντες   aor act ptcp nom pl masc
   [2t; v-1d(3); 2420]   "
ζηλωταί   nom pl masc [3t; n-1f; 2421]   ζηλωτής
ζηλωτήν   acc sg masc [2t; n-1f; 2421]   "

ζηλωτής, οῦ, ὁ   {2421, n-1f}
   pr. *a generous rival, an imitator;* in N.T. *an
   aspirant,* 1 Cor 14:12; Titus 2:14; *a devoted
   adherent, a zealot,* Acts 21:20; 22:3; Gal 1:14

ζηλωτής   nom sg masc [3t; n-1f; 2421]   "

ζημία, ας, ἡ   {2422, n-1a}
   damage, loss, detriment, Acts 27:10, 21; Phil 3:7,
   8*

ζημίαν   acc sg fem [3t; n-1a; 2422]   ζημία
ζημίας   gen sg fem [Ac 27:10; n-1a; 2422]   "

ζημιόω   {2423, v-1d(3)}
   [-, -, -, -, ἐζημιώθην] *to visit with loss* or *harm;*
   pass. *to suffer loss* or *detriment,* 1 Cor 3:15; 2 Cor
   7:9; *to lose, to forfeit,* Matt 16:26; Mark 8:36; Luke
   9:25; Phil 3:8*

ζημιωθείς   aor pass ptcp nom sg masc
   [Lk 9:25; v-1d(3); 2423]   ζημιόω
ζημιωθῇ   aor pass subj 3 sg
   [Mt 16:26; v-1d(3); 2423]   "
ζημιωθῆναι   aor pass inf
   [Mk 8:36; v-1d(3); 2423]   "
ζημιωθήσεται   fut pass ind 3 sg
   [1C 3:15; v-1d(3); 2423]   "
ζημιωθῆτε   aor pass subj 2 pl
   [2C 7:9; v-1d(3); 2423]   "
ζῆν   pres act inf [12t; v-1d(1a); 2409]   ζάω
Ζηνᾶν   acc sg masc [Ti 3:13; n-3g(1); 2424]   Ζηνᾶς

Ζηνᾶς, ᾶν, ὁ   {2424, n-3g(1)}
   Zenas, pr. name, Titus 3:13*

ζῇς   pres act ind 2 sg [2t; v-1d(1a); 2409]   ζάω
ζήσασα   aor act ptcp nom sg fem
   [Lk 2:36; v-1d(1a); 2409]   "
ζήσει   fut act ind 3 sg [3t; v-1d(1a); 2409]   "
ζήσεσθε   fut mid ind 2 pl
   [Rm 8:13; v-1d(1a); 2409]   "
ζήσεται   fut mid ind 3 sg [9t; v-1d(1a); 2409]   "
ζήσετε   fut act ind 2 pl
   [Jn 14:19; v-1d(1a); 2409]   "
ζήσῃ   aor act subj 3 sg
   [Mk 5:23; v-1d(1a); 2409]   "
ζήσῃ   fut mid ind 2 sg
   [Lk 10:28; v-1d(1a); 2409]   "
ζήσομεν   fut act ind 1 pl [4t; v-1d(1a); 2409]   "
ζήσουσιν   fut act ind 3 pl
   [Jn 5:25; v-1d(1a); 2409]   "
ζήσω   aor act subj 1 sg [Ga 2:19; v-1d(1a); 2409]   "
ζήσωμεν   aor act subj 1 pl [4t; v-1d(1a); 2409]   "
ζῆτε   pres act ind 2 pl [Rm 8:13; v-1d(1a); 2409]   "
ζήτει   pres act imperative 2 sg
   [2t; v-1d(2a); 2426]   ζητέω
ζητεῖ   pres act ind 3 sg [9t; v-1d(2a); 2426]   "
ζητεῖν   pres act inf [2t; v-1d(2a); 2426]   "
ζητεῖς   pres act ind 2 sg [2t; v-1d(2a); 2426]   "
ζητεῖται   pres pass ind 3 sg
   [1C 4:2; v-1d(2a); 2426]   "
ζητεῖτε   pres act imperative 2 pl
   [7t; v-1d(2a); 2426]   "
ζητεῖτε   pres act ind 2 pl [15t; v-1d(2a); 2426]   "
ζητείτω   pres act imperative 3 sg
   [1C 10:24; v-1d(2a); 2426]   "

ζητέω   {2426, v-1d(2a)}
[(ἐζήτουν), ζητήσω, ἐζήτησα, -, -, ἐζητήθην] *to
seek, look for,* Matt 18:12; Luke 2:48, 49; *to search
after,* Matt 13:45; *to be on the watch for,* Matt
26:16; *to pursue, endeavor to obtain,* Rom 2:7; 1
Peter 3:11; *to desire, wish, want,* Matt 12:47; *to
seek, strive for,* Matt 6:33; *to endeavor,* Matt 21:46;
to require, demand, ask for, Mark 8:11; Luke 11:16;
12:48; *to inquire* or *ask questions, question,* John
16:19; *to deliberate,* Mark 11:18; Luke 12:29; in
N.T. from Hebrew, ζητεῖν τὴν ψυχήν, *to seek the
life* of any one, *to seek to kill,* Matt 2:20

ζητηθήσεται   fut pass ind 3 sg
    [Lk 12:48; v-1d(2a); 2426]   "

ζήτημα, ατος, τό   {2427, n-3c(4)}
a question; a subject of debate or *controversy,* Acts
15:2; 18:15; 23:29; 25:19; 26:3*

ζητήματα   nom pl neut
    [Ac 18:15; n-3c(4); 2427]   ζήτημα
ζητήματα   acc pl neut [Ac 25:19; n-3c(4); 2427]   "
ζητήματος   gen sg neut [Ac 15:2; n-3c(4); 2427]   "
ζητημάτων   gen pl neut [2t; n-3c(4); 2427]   "
ζητῆσαι   aor act inf
    [Lk 19:10; v-1d(2a); 2426]   ζητέω
ζητησάτω   aor act imperative 3 sg
    [1P 3:11; v-1d(2a); 2426]   "
ζητήσεις   acc pl fem [3t; n-3e(5b); 2428]   ζήτησις
ζητήσετε   fut act ind 2 pl
    [4t; v-1d(2a); 2426]   ζητέω
ζητήσεως   gen sg fem [2t; n-3e(5b); 2428]   ζήτησις
ζητήσῃ   aor act subj 3 sg
    [Lk 17:33; v-1d(2a); 2426]   ζητέω
ζήτησιν   acc sg fem
    [Ac 25:20; n-3e(5b); 2428]   ζήτησις

ζήτησις, εως, ἡ   {2428, n-3e(5b)}
*a seeking; an inquiry, a question; a dispute, debate,
discussion,* John 3:25; 1 Tim 6:4; *a subject of
dispute* or *controversy,* Acts 15:2, 7; 25:20; 2 Tim
2:23; Titus 3:9

ζήτησις   nom sg fem [Jn 3:25; n-3e(5b); 2428]   "
ζήτησον   aor act imperative 2 sg
    [Ac 9:11; v-1d(2a); 2426]   ζητέω
ζητήσουσιν   fut act ind 3 pl [2t; v-1d(2a); 2426]   "
ζητοῦν   pres act ptcp nom sg neut
    [2t; v-1d(2a); 2426]   "
ζητοῦντες   pres act ptcp nom pl masc
    [10t; v-1d(2a); 2426]   "
ζητοῦντι   pres act ptcp dat sg masc
    [Mt 13:45; v-1d(2a); 2426]   "
ζητούντων   pres act ptcp gen pl masc
    [2t; v-1d(2a); 2426]   "
ζητοῦσιν   pres act ind 3 pl [6t; v-1d(2a); 2426]   "
ζητοῦσιν   pres act ptcp dat pl masc
    [2t; v-1d(2a); 2426]   "
ζητῶ   pres act ind 1 sg [4t; v-1d(2a); 2426]   "
ζητῶν   pres act ptcp nom sg masc
    [9t; v-1d(2a); 2426]   "
ζιζάνια   nom pl neut [3t; n-2c; 2429]   ζιζάνιον
ζιζάνια   acc pl neut [4t; n-2c; 2429]   "

ζιζάνιον, ου, τό   {2429, n-2c}
zizanium, darnel, spurious wheat, a plant found

in Palestine, which resembles wheat both in its
stalk and grain, but is worthless, Matt 13:25, 26,
27, 29, 30, 36, 38, 40*

ζιζανίων   gen pl neut [Mt 13:36; n-2c; 2429]   "

Ζοροβαβέλ, ὁ   {2431, n-3g(2)}
Zorobabel, pr. name, indecl. (Ezra 2:2; 3:8), Matt
1:12, 13; Luke 3:27*

Ζοροβαβέλ   indecl [3t; n-3g(2); 2431]   Ζοροβαβέλ
ζόφον   acc sg masc [Jd 6; n-2a; 2432]   ζόφος

ζόφος, ου, ὁ   {2432, n-2a}
gloom, thick darkness, Heb 12:18; 2 Peter 2:4, 17;
Jude 6, 13*

ζόφος   nom sg masc [2t; n-2a; 2432]   "
ζόφου   gen sg masc [2P 2:4; n-2a; 2432]   "
ζόφῳ   dat sg masc [Hb 12:18; n-2a; 2432]   "
ζυγόν   acc sg masc [4t; n-1a; 2433]   ζυγός

ζυγός, οῦ, ὁ   {2433, n-2a}
also spelled ζυγόν, ου, τό (n-2c), pr. *a cross bar* or
band; a yoke; met. *a yoke* of servile condition, 1
Tim 6:1; *a yoke* of service or obligation, Matt
11:29, 30; Acts 15:10; Gal 5:1 ;*the beam* of a
balance; *a balance,* Rev 6:5*

ζυγός   nom sg masc [Mt 11:30; n-1a; 2433]   "
ζυγῷ   dat sg masc [Ga 5:1; n-1a; 2433]   "

ζύμη, ης, ἡ   {2434, n-1b}
leaven, yeast, Matt 16:12; 13:33; met. *leaven* of the
mind and conduct, by a system of doctrine or
morals, used in a bad sense, Matt 16:6, 11; 1 Cor
5:6

ζύμη   nom sg fem [2t; n-1b; 2434]   ζύμη
ζύμῃ   dat sg fem [4t; n-1b; 2434]   "
ζύμην   acc sg fem [1C 5:7; n-1b; 2434]   "
ζύμης   gen sg fem [6t; n-1b; 2434]   "
ζυμοῖ   pres act ind 3 sg [2t; v-1d(3); 2435]   ζυμόω

ζυμόω   {2435, v-1d(3)}
[-, -, -, -, ἐζυμώθην] *to leaven, cause to ferment,*
Matt 13:33; Luke 13:21; 1 Cor 5:6; Gal 5:9*

ζῶ   pres act ind 1 sg [6t; v-1d(1a); 2409]   ζάω
ζῷα   nom pl neut [8t; n-2c; 2442]   ζῷον

ζωγρέω   {2436, v-1d(2a)}
[-, -, -, ἐζώγρημαι, -] pr. *to take alive, take prisoner
in war* instead of killing; *to take captive, enthral,*
2 Tim 2:26; also, *to catch* animals, as fish; in
which sense it is used figuratively, Luke 5:10*

ζωγρῶν   pres act ptcp nom sg masc
    [Lk 5:10; v-1d(2a); 2436]   ζωγρέω

ζωή, ῆς, ἡ   {2437, n-1b}
life, living existence, Luke 16:25; Acts 17:25; in
N.T. spiritual *life* of deliverance from the
proper penalty of sin, which is expressed by
θάνατος, John 6:51; Rom 5:18; 6:4; the final *life* of
the redeemed, Matt 25:46; *life, source of* spiritual
life, John 5:39; 11:25; Col 3:4

ζωή   nom sg fem [24t; n-1b; 2437]   ζωή
ζωῇ   dat sg fem [4t; n-1b; 2437]   "
ζωήν   acc sg fem [60t; n-1b; 2437]   "
ζωῆς   gen sg fem [47t; n-1b; 2437]   "

ζῶμεν   pres act ind 1 pl [5t; v-1d(1a); 2409]   ζάω
ζῶμεν   pres act subj 1 pl [2t; v-1d(1a); 2409]   "
ζῶν   pres act ptcp nom sg masc
     [9t; v-1d(1a); 2409]   "
ζῶν   pres act ptcp acc sg neut
     [2t; v-1d(1a); 2409]   "
ζώνας   acc pl fem [2t; n-1b; 2438]   ζώνη

ζώνη, ῆς, ἡ   {2438, n-1b}
     a zone, belt, girdle, Matt 3:4; 10:9; Mark 1:6; 6:8;
     Acts 21:11; Rev 1:13; 15:6*

ζώνη   nom sg fem [Ac 21:11; n-1b; 2438]   "
ζώνην   acc sg fem [5t; n-1b; 2438]   "

ζώννυμι   {2439, v-3c(1)}
     [ζώσω, ἔζωσα, -, ἔζωσμαι, -] also spelled
     ζωννύω, *to gird, gird on, put on one's girdle*, John
     21:18 (2t), Acts 12:8*

ζωννύω, see ζώννυμι

ζῶντα   pres act ptcp acc sg masc
     [5t; v-1d(1a); 2409]   ζάω
ζῶντα   pres act ptcp acc pl neut
     [Ac 7:38; v-1d(1a); 2409]   "
ζῶντας   pres act ptcp acc pl masc
     [4t; v-1d(1a); 2409]   "
ζῶντες   pres act ptcp nom pl masc
     [7t; v-1d(1a); 2409]   "
ζῶντι   pres act ptcp dat sg masc
     [7t; v-1d(1a); 2409]   "
ζῶντος   pres act ptcp gen sg masc
     [13t; v-1d(1a); 2409]   "
ζῶντος   pres act ptcp gen sg neut
     [Jn 7:38; v-1d(1a); 2409]   "
ζώντων   pres act ptcp gen pl masc
     [5t; v-1d(1a); 2409]   "
ζωογονεῖσθαι   pres pass inf
     [Ac 7:19; v-1d(2a); 2441]   ζωογονέω

ζωογονέω   {2441, v-1d(2a)}
     [ζωογονήσω, -, -, -, -] pr. *to bring forth living
     creatures*; in N.T. *to preserve alive, save*, Luke
     17:33; Acts 7:19; 1 Tim 6:13*

ζωογονήσει   fut act ind 3 sg
     [Lk 17:33; v-1d(2a); 2441]   "
ζωογονοῦντος   pres act ptcp gen sg masc
     [1Ti 6:13; v-1d(2a); 2441]   "

ζῶον, ου, τό   {2442, n-2c}
     a living creature, animal, Heb 13:11; 2 Peter 2:12

ζῶον   nom sg neut [4t; n-2c; 2442]   ζῶον
ζωοποιεῖ   pres act ind 3 sg
     [3t; cv-1d(2a); 2443]   ζωοποιέω
ζωοποιεῖται   pres pass ind 3 sg
     [1C 15:36; cv-1d(2a); 2443]   "

ζωοποιέω   {2443, cv-1d(2a)}
     [ζωοποιήσω, ἐζωοποίησα, -, -, ἐζωοποιήθην] pr. *to
     engender living creatures; to quicken, make alive*,
     Rom 4:17; 8:11; 1 Cor 15:36; in N.T. met. *to
     quicken* with the life of salvation, John 6:63; 2
     Cor 3:6

ζωοποιηθείς   aor pass ptcp nom sg masc
     [1P 3:18; cv-1d(2a); 2443]   "

ζωοποιηθήσονται   fut pass ind 3 pl
     [1C 15:22; cv-1d(2a); 2443]   "
ζωοποιῆσαι   aor act inf
     [Ga 3:21; cv-1d(2a); 2443]   "
ζωοποιήσει   fut act ind 3 sg
     [Rm 8:11; cv-1d(2a); 2443]   "
ζωοποιοῦν   pres act ptcp nom sg neut
     [Jn 6:63; cv-1d(2a); 2443]   "
ζωοποιοῦν   pres act ptcp acc sg neut
     [1C 15:45; cv-1d(2a); 2443]   "
ζωοποιοῦντος   pres act ptcp gen sg masc
     [Rm 4:17; cv-1d(2a); 2443]   "
ζῴου   gen sg neut [3t; n-2c; 2442]   ζῶον
ζῶσα   pres act ptcp nom sg fem
     [1Ti 5:6; v-1d(1a); 2409]   ζάω
ζῶσαι   aor mid imperative 2 sg
     [Ac 12:8; v-3c(1); 2439]   ζώννυμι
ζῶσαν   pres act ptcp acc sg fem
     [5t; v-1d(1a); 2409]   ζάω
ζώσει   fut act ind 3 sg
     [Jn 21:18; v-3c(1); 2439]   ζώννυμι
ζῶσι   pres act subj 3 pl
     [1P 4:6; v-1d(1a); 2409]   ζάω
ζῶσιν   pres act ind 3 pl
     [Lk 20:38; v-1d(1a); 2409]   "
ζῶσιν   pres act subj 3 pl
     [2C 5:15; v-1d(1a); 2409]   "
ζῴων   gen pl neut [8t; n-2c; 2442]   ζῶον

η

ἤ   {2445, particle}
     can function as a conj (298t), *either, or*, Matt 6:24;
     after comparatives, and ἄλλος, ἕτερος,
     expressed or implied, *than*, Matt 10:15; 18:8;
     Acts 17:21; 24:21; intensive after ἀλλά and πρίν,
     Luke 12:51; Matt 1:18; it also serves to point an
     interrogation, Rom 3:29

ἤ   particle [343t; particle; 2445]   "

ἤ   {2446, adverb}
     truly, a particle occurring in the N.T. only in the
     combination ἦ μήν, introductory to the terms of
     an oath, Heb 6:14 v.l. *BAGD* list 1 Cor 9:10 and
     15, but our text has ἤ.

ἡ   nom sg fem [986t; a-1a(2b); 3836]   ὁ
ᾗ   dat sg fem [37t; a-1a(2b); 4005]   ὅς
ᾖ   pres act subj 3 sg [43t; v-6b; 1639]   εἰμί
ἤγαγεν   aor act ind 3 sg [8t; v-1b(2); 72]   ἄγω
ἠγάγετε   aor act ind 2 pl [2t; v-1b(2); 72]   "
ἤγαγον   aor act ind 3 pl [13t; v-1b(2); 72]   "
ἠγαλλιάσατο   aor mid ind 3 sg
     [4t; v-1d(1b); 22]   ἀγαλλιάω
ἠγαλλίασεν   aor act ind 3 sg
     [Lk 1:47; v-1d(1b); 22]   "
ἠγανάκτησαν   aor act ind 3 pl
     [3t; v-1d(2a); 24]   ἀγανακτέω
ἠγανάκτησεν   aor act ind 3 sg
     [Mk 10:14; v-1d(2a); 24]   "
ἠγάπα   imperf act ind 3 sg
     [5t; v-1d(1a); 26]   ἀγαπάω

ἠγαπᾶτε   imperf act ind 2 pl   [2t; v-1d(1a); 26]   "

ἠγαπήκαμεν   perf act ind 1 pl
   [1J 4:10; v-1d(1a); 26]   "

ἠγαπηκόσι   perf act ptcp dat pl masc
   [2Ti 4:8; v-1d(1a); 26]   "

ἠγαπημένην   perf pass ptcp acc sg fem
   [3t; v-1d(1a); 26]   "

ἠγαπημένοι   perf pass ptcp nom pl masc
   [Cl 3:12; v-1d(1a); 26]   "

ἠγαπημένοι   perf pass ptcp voc pl masc
   [2t; v-1d(1a); 26]   "

ἠγαπημένοις   perf pass ptcp dat pl masc
   [Jd 1; v-1d(1a); 26]   "

ἠγαπημένῳ   perf pass ptcp dat sg masc
   [Ep 1:6; v-1d(1a); 26]   "

ἠγάπησα   aor act ind 1 sg   [5t; v-1d(1a); 26]   "

ἠγάπησαν   aor act ind 3 pl   [3t; v-1d(1a); 26]   "

ἠγάπησας   aor act ind 2 sg   [5t; v-1d(1a); 26]   "

ἠγάπησεν   aor act ind 3 sg   [12t; v-1d(1a); 26]   "

ἠγγάρευσαν   aor act ind 3 pl
   [Mt 27:32; v-1a(6); 30]   ἀγγαρεύω

ἤγγιζεν   imperf act ind 3 sg
   [2t; v-2a(1); 1581]   ἐγγίζω

ἤγγικεν   perf act ind 3 sg   [14t; v-2a(1); 1581]   "

ἤγγισαν   aor act ind 3 pl   [2t; v-2a(1); 1581]   "

ἤγγισεν   aor act ind 3 sg   [7t; v-2a(1); 1581]   "

ἤγειραν   aor act ind 3 pl
   [Mt 8:25; v-2d(3); 1586]   ἐγείρω

ἤγειρεν   aor act ind 3 sg   [21t; v-2d(3); 1586]   "

ἡγεῖσθαι   pres mid inf
   [1Th 5:13; v-1d(2a); 2451]   ἡγέομαι

ἡγεῖσθε   pres mid imperative 2 pl
   [2t; v-1d(2a); 2451]   "

ἡγείσθωσαν   pres mid imperative 3 pl
   [1Ti 6:1; v-1d(2a); 2451]   "

ἡγεμόνα   acc sg masc [2t; n-3f(1b); 2450]   ἡγεμών

ἡγεμόνας   acc pl masc [2t; n-3f(1b); 2450]   "

ἡγεμονεύοντος   pres act ptcp gen sg masc
   [2t; v-1a(6); 2448]   ἡγεμονεύω

ἡγεμονεύω   {2448, v-1a(6)}
   [-, -, -, -, -] to be a guide, leader, chief; in N.T. to
   hold the office of a Roman provincial governor,
   Luke 2:2; 3:1*

ἡγεμόνι   dat sg masc [4t; n-3f(1b); 2450]   ἡγεμών

ἡγεμονία, ας, ἡ   {2449, n-1a}
   leadership, sovereignty; in N.T. a reign, Luke 3:1*

ἡγεμονίας   gen sg fem
   [Lk 3:1; n-1a; 2449]   ἡγεμονία

ἡγεμόνος   gen sg masc
   [5t; n-3f(1b); 2450]   ἡγεμών

ἡγεμόνων   gen pl masc [Mk 13:9; n-3f(1b); 2450]   "

ἡγεμόσιν   dat pl masc [2t; n-3f(1b); 2450]   "

ἡγεμών, όνος, ὁ   {2450, n-3f(1b)}
   a guide; a leader; a chieftain, prince, Matt 2:6; a
   Roman provincial governor, under whatever title,
   Matt 10:18; 27:2; Luke 20:20; Acts 23:24

ἡγεμών   nom sg masc [4t; n-3f(1b); 2450]   "

ἦγεν   imperf act ind 3 sg
   [Ac 5:26; v-1b(2); 72]   ἄγω

ἡγέομαι   {2451, v-1d(2a)}
   [ἡγήσομαι, ἡγησάμην, -, ἥγημαι, -] to lead the
   way; to take the lead, Acts 14:12; to be chief, to
   preside, govern, rule, Matt 2:6; Acts 7:10;
   ἡγούμενος, a chief officer in the church, Heb 13:7,
   17, 24; also, to think, consider, count, esteem,
   regard, Acts 26:2; 2 Cor 9:5

ἠγέρθη   aor pass ind 3 sg
   [18t; v-2d(3); 1586]   ἐγείρω

ἠγέρθησαν   aor pass ind 3 pl [2t; v-2d(3); 1586]   "

ἤγεσθε   imperf pass ind 2 pl
   [1C 12:2; v-1b(2); 72]   ἄγω

ἤγετο   imperf pass ind 3 sg [Lk 4:1; v-1b(2); 72]   "

ἥγημαι   perf mid ind 1 sg
   [Pp 3:7; v-1d(2a); 2451]   ἡγέομαι

ἥγημαι   perf pass ind 1 sg
   [Ac 26:2; v-1d(2a); 2451]   ἡγέομαι

ἡγησάμενος   aor mid ptcp nom sg masc
   [2t; v-1d(2a); 2451]   "

ἡγησάμην   aor mid ind 1 sg [2t; v-1d(2a); 2451]   "

ἡγήσασθε   aor mid imperative 2 pl
   [Jm 1:2; v-1d(2a); 2451]   "

ἡγήσατο   aor mid ind 3 sg [3t; v-1d(2a); 2451]   "

ἡγίασεν   aor act ind 3 sg
   [Jn 10:36; v-2a(1); 39]   ἁγιάζω

ἡγιάσθη   aor pass ind 3 sg
   [Hb 10:29; v-2a(1); 39]   "

ἡγιάσθητε   aor pass ind 2 pl
   [1C 6:11; v-2a(1); 39]   "

ἡγιασμένη   perf pass ptcp nom sg fem
   [Rm 15:16; v-2a(1); 39]   "

ἡγιασμένοι   perf pass ptcp nom pl masc
   [2t; v-2a(1); 39]   "

ἡγιασμένοις   perf pass ptcp dat pl masc
   [3t; v-2a(1); 39]   "

ἡγιασμένον   perf pass ptcp nom sg neut
   [2Ti 2:21; v-2a(1); 39]   "

ἡγίασται   perf pass ind 3 sg [2t; v-2a(1); 39]   "

ἡγνικότες   perf act ptcp nom pl masc
   [1P 1:22; v-2a(1); 49]   ἁγνίζω

ἡγνισμένον   perf pass ptcp acc sg masc
   [Ac 24:18; v-2a(1); 49]   "

ἠγνόουν   imperf act ind 3 pl
   [2t; v-1d(2a); 51]   ἀγνοέω

ἤγοντο   imperf pass ind 3 pl
   [Lk 23:32; v-1b(2); 72]   ἄγω

ἠγόραζον   imperf act ind 3 pl
   [Lk 17:28; v-2a(1); 60]   ἀγοράζω

ἠγόρασα   aor act ind 1 sg [2t; v-2a(1); 60]   "

ἠγόρασαν   aor act ind 3 pl [2t; v-2a(1); 60]   "

ἠγόρασας   aor act ind 2 sg [Rv 5:9; v-2a(1); 60]   "

ἠγόρασεν   aor act ind 3 sg
   [Mt 13:46; v-2a(1); 60]   "

ἠγοράσθησαν   aor pass ind 3 pl
   [Rv 14:4; v-2a(1); 60]   "

ἠγοράσθητε   aor pass ind 2 pl [2t; v-2a(1); 60]   "

ἠγορασμένοι   perf pass ptcp nom pl masc
   [Rv 14:3; v-2a(1); 60]   "

ἡγοῦμαι   pres mid ind 1 sg
   [3t; v-1d(2a); 2451]   ἡγέομαι

ἡγούμενοι   pres mid ptcp nom pl masc
   [2t; v-1d(2a); 2451]   "

ἡγουμένοις   pres mid ptcp dat pl masc
   [Hb 13:17; v-1d(2a); 2451]   "

ἡγούμενον   pres mid ptcp acc sg masc
   [Ac 7:10; v-1d(2a); 2451]   "

ἡγούμενος   pres mid ptcp nom sg masc
   [3t; v-1d(2a); 2451]   "

ἡγουμένους   pres mid ptcp acc pl masc
   [2t; v-1d(2a); 2451]   "

ἡγουμένων   pres mid ptcp gen pl masc
   [Hb 13:7; v-1d(2a); 2451]   "

ἡγοῦνται   pres mid ind 3 pl
   [2P 3:9; v-1d(2a); 2451]   "

ἡγωνίζοντο   imperf mid ind 3 pl
   [Jn 18:36; v-2a(1); 76]   ἀγωνίζομαι

ἡγώνισμαι   perf mid ind 1 sg
   [2Ti 4:7; v-2a(1); 76]   "

ᾔδει   pluperf act ind 3 sg
   [13t; v-1b(3); 3857]   οἶδα

ᾔδειν   pluperf act ind 1 sg [5t; v-1b(3); 3857]   "

ᾔδεις   pluperf act ind 2 sg [3t; v-1b(3); 3857]   "

ᾔδεισαν   pluperf act ind 3 pl
   [8t; v-1b(3); 3857]   "

ᾔδειτε   pluperf act ind 2 pl [3t; v-1b(3); 3857] "

ἡδέως   {2452, adverb}
   with pleasure, gladly, willingly, Mark 6:20; 12:37;
   2 Cor 11:19

ἡδέως   adverb [3t; adverb; 2452]   ἡδέως

ἤδη   {2453, adverb}
   before now, now, already, Matt 3:10; 5:28; ἤδη
   ποτέ, *at length*, Rom 1:10; Phil 4:10

ἤδη   adverb [61t; adverb; 2453]   ἤδη

ἠδίκησα   aor act ind 1 sg
   [Ac 25:10; v-1d(2a); 92]   ἀδικέω

ἠδικήσαμεν   aor act ind 1 pl
   [2C 7:2; v-1d(2a); 92]   "

ἠδικήσατε   aor act ind 2 pl
   [Ga 4:12; v-1d(2a); 92]   "

ἠδίκησεν   aor act ind 3 sg [2t; v-1d(2a); 92]   "

ἥδιστα   adverb-superlative
   [2t; adverb; 2452]   ἡδέως

ἡδοναῖς   dat pl fem [2t; n-1b; 2454]   ἡδονή

ἡδονή, ῆς, ἡ   {2454, n-1b}
   pleasure, gratification; esp. *sensual pleasure*, Luke
   8:14; Titus 3:3; James 4:3; 2 Peter 2:13; *a passion*,
   James 4:1*

ἡδονήν   acc sg fem [2P 2:13; n-1b; 2454]   "

ἡδονῶν   gen pl fem [2t; n-1b; 2454]   "

ἠδύναντο   imperf pass ind 3 pl
   [3t; v-6b; 1538]   δύναμαι

ἠδύνατο   imperf pass ind 3 sg [4t; v-6b; 1538]   "

ἠδυνήθη   aor pass ind 3 sg [Mk 7:24; v-6b; 1538] "

ἠδυνήθημεν   aor pass ind 1 pl [2t; v-6b; 1538]   "

ἠδυνήθην   aor pass ind 1 sg [1C 3:1; v-6b; 1538] "

ἠδυνήθησαν   aor pass ind 3 pl [3t; v-6b; 1538]   "

ἠδυνήθητε   aor pass ind 2 pl
   [Ac 13:38; v-6b; 1538]   "

ἡδύοσμον, ου, τό   {2455, n-2c}
   garden mint, Matt 23:23; Luke 11:42*

ἡδύοσμον   acc sg neut [2t; n-2c; 2455]   ἡδύοσμον

ἤθελεν   imperf act ind 3 sg
   [14t; v-1d(2c); 2527]   θέλω

ἤθελες   imperf act ind 2 sg
   [Jn 21:18; v-1d(2c); 2527]   "

ἠθέλησα   aor act ind 1 sg [3t; v-1d(2c); 2527]   "

ἠθελήσαμεν   aor act ind 1 pl
   [1Th 2:18; v-1d(2c); 2527]   "

ἠθέλησαν   aor act ind 3 pl [3t; v-1d(2c); 2527]   "

ἠθέλησας   aor act ind 2 sg [2t; v-1d(2c); 2527]   "

ἠθελήσατε   aor act ind 2 pl [3t; v-1d(2c); 2527] "

ἠθέλησεν   aor act ind 3 sg [8t; v-1d(2c); 2527]   "

ἤθελον   imperf act ind 1 sg
   [Ga 4:20; v-1d(2c); 2527]   "

ἤθελον   imperf act ind 3 pl [7t; v-1d(2c); 2527] "

ἠθέτησαν   aor act ind 3 pl
   [2t; v-1d(2a); 119]   ἀθετέω

ἤθη   acc pl neut [1C 15:33; n-3d(2b); 2456]   ἦθος

ἦθος, ους, τό   {2456, n-3d(2b)}
   pr. *a place of customary resort*; hence, *a settled
   habit of mind and manners*, 1 Cor 15:33*

ἠθροισμένους   perf pass ptcp acc pl masc
   [Lk 24:33; v-2a(1); 125]   ἀθροίζω

ᾔδει   pluperf act ind 3 sg
   [Jn 18:2; v-1b(3); 3857]   οἶδα

ἠκαιρεῖσθε   imperf mid ind 2 pl
   [Pp 4:10; v-1d(2b); 177]   ἀκαιρέομαι

ἥκασιν   pres act ind 3 pl
   [Mk 8:3; v-1b(2); 2457]   ἥκω

ἥκει   pres act ind 3 sg [4t; v-1b(2); 2457]   "

ἤκμασαν   aor act ind 3 pl
   [Rv 14:18; v-2a(1); 196]   ἀκμάζω

ἠκολούθει   imperf act ind 3 sg
   [14t; v-1d(2a); 199]   ἀκολουθέω

ἠκολουθήκαμεν   perf act ind 1 pl
   [Mk 10:28; v-1d(2a); 199]   "

ἠκολουθήσαμεν   aor act ind 1 pl
   [2t; v-1d(2a); 199]   "

ἠκολούθησαν   aor act ind 3 pl
   [18t; v-1d(2a); 199]   "

ἠκολούθησεν   aor act ind 3 sg
   [8t; v-1d(2a); 199]   "

ἠκολούθουν   imperf act ind 3 pl
   [2t; v-1d(2a); 199]   "

ἤκουεν   imperf act ind 3 sg
   [4t; v-1a(8); 201]   ἀκούω

ἤκουον   imperf act ind 3 pl [7t; v-1a(8); 201]   "

ἤκουσα   aor act ind 1 sg [35t; v-1a(8); 201]   "

ἠκούσαμεν   aor act ind 1 pl [10t; v-1a(8); 201] "

ἤκουσαν   aor act ind 3 pl [19t; v-1a(8); 201]   "

ἤκουσας   aor act ind 2 sg [5t; v-1a(8); 201]   "

ἠκούσατε   aor act ind 2 pl [26t; v-1a(8); 201] "

ἤκουσεν   aor act ind 3 sg [17t; v-1a(8); 201]   "

ἠκούσθη   aor pass ind 3 sg [4t; v-1a(8); 201]   "

ἠκρίβωσεν   aor act ind 3 sg
   [2t; v-1d(3); 208]   ἀκριβόω

ἠκυρώσατε   aor act ind 2 pl
   [Mt 15:6; v-1d(3); 218]   ἀκυρόω

ἥκω   {2457, v-1b(2)}
   [ἥξω, ἧξα, -, -, -] *to become, have arrived*, Matt
   8:11; Mark 8:3; Luke 15:27; Rev 15:4*

ἥκω   pres act ind 1 sg [3t; v-1b(2); 2457]   ἥκω

ἤλατο   aor mid ind 3 sg
   [Ac 14:10; v-2d(1); 256]   ἅλλομαι
ἠλαττόνησεν   aor act ind 3 sg
   [2C 8:15; v-1d(2a); 1782]   ἐλαττονέω
ἠλαττωμένον   perf pass ptcp acc sg masc
   [Hb 2:9; v-1d(3); 1783]   ἐλαττόω
ἠλάττωσας   aor act ind 2 sg
   [Hb 2:7; v-1d(3); 1783]   "
ἠλαύνετο   imperf pass ind 3 sg
   [Lk 8:29; v-3c(2); 1785]   ἐλαύνω
ἠλεήθημεν   aor pass ind 1 pl
   [2C 4:1; v-1d(2a); 1796]   ἐλεέω
ἠλεήθην   aor pass ind 1 sg [2t; v-1d(2a); 1796]   "
ἠλεήθητε   aor pass ind 2 pl
   [Rm 11:30; v-1d(2a); 1796]   "
ἠλεημένοι   perf pass ptcp nom pl masc
   [1P 2:10; v-1d(2a); 1796]   "
ἠλεημένος   perf pass ptcp nom sg masc
   [1C 7:25; v-1d(2a); 1796]   "
ἠλέησα   aor act ind 1 sg
   [Mt 18:33; v-1d(2a); 1796]   "
ἠλέησεν   aor act ind 3 sg [2t; v-1d(2a); 1796]   "
ἤλειφεν   imperf act ind 3 sg
   [Lk 7:38; v-1b(1); 230]   ἀλείφω
ἤλειφον   imperf act ind 3 pl
   [Mk 6:13; v-1b(1); 230]   "
ἤλειψας   aor act ind 2 sg [Lk 7:46; v-1b(1); 230]   "
ἤλειψεν   aor act ind 3 sg [2t; v-1b(1); 230]   "
ἠλευθέρωσεν   aor act ind 3 sg
   [2t; v-1d(3); 1802]   ἐλευθερόω
ἤλθαμεν   aor act ind 1 pl
   [Ac 28:14; v-1b(2); 2262]   ἔρχομαι
ἦλθαν   aor act ind 3 pl [5t; v-1b(2); 2262]   "
ἤλθατε   aor act ind 2 pl
   [Mt 25:36; v-1b(2); 2262]   "
ἦλθε   aor act ind 3 sg [Ac 19:6; v-1b(2); 2262]   "
ἦλθεν   aor act ind 3 sg [88t; v-1b(2); 2262]   "
ἦλθες   aor act ind 2 sg [3t; v-1b(2); 2262]   "
ἤλθομεν   aor act ind 1 pl [9t; v-1b(2); 2262]   "
ἦλθον   aor act ind 1 sg [20t; v-1b(2); 2262]   "
ἦλθον   aor act ind 3 pl [43t; v-1b(2); 2262]   "

ἠλί   {2458, n-3g(2)}
   My God!, Matt 27:46*

ἠλι   indecl [3t; n-3g(2); 2458]   ἠλί

Ἡλί   {2459, n-3g(2)}
   Eli, pr. name, indecl., Luke 3:23*

Ἡλί   indecl [Lk 3:23; n-3g(2); 2459]   Ἡλί
Ἡλίᾳ   dat sg masc [4t; n-1d; 2460]   Ἡλίας
Ἡλίαν   acc sg masc [7t; n-1d; 2460]   "

Ἡλίας, ου, ὁ   {2460, n-1d}
   Elijah, pr name, (1 Kgs 17-20), Matt 11:14; 17:3f.;
   Mark 15:35f.; Luke 1:7; John 1:21; James 5:17

Ἡλίας   nom sg masc [16t; n-1d; 2460]   "
ἡλίκην   acc sg fem
   [Jm 3:5; a-1a(2a); 2462]   ἡλίκος

ἡλικία, ας, ἡ   {2461, n-1a}
   a particular period of life; the period fitted for a
   particular function, prime, Heb 11:11; *full age,*
   years of discretion, John 9:21, 23; *perhaps, the*

whole duration of life, Matt 6:27; Luke 12:25;
   otherwise, *stature,* Luke 2:52; 19:3; Eph 4:13*

ἡλικίᾳ   dat sg fem [2t; n-1a; 2461]   ἡλικία
ἡλικίαν   acc sg fem [4t; n-1a; 2461]   "
ἡλικίας   gen sg fem [2t; n-1a; 2461]   "
ἡλίκον   nom sg neut
   [Jm 3:5; a-1a(2a); 2462]   ἡλίκος
ἡλίκον   acc sg masc [Cl 2:1; a-1a(2a); 2462]   "

ἡλίκος, η, ον   {2462, a-1a(2a)}
   as great as; how great, Col 2:1; James 3:5; Gal 6:11
   v.l.*

ἥλιον   acc sg masc [4t; n-2a; 2463]   ἥλιος

ἥλιος, ου, ὁ   {2463, n-2a}
   the sun, Matt 13:43; 17:2; Mark 1:32; meton. *light*
   of the sun, light, Acts 13:11

ἥλιος   nom sg masc [14t; n-2a; 2463]   "
ἡλίου   gen sg masc [14t; n-2a; 2463]   "
ἡλίῳ   dat sg masc [2t; n-2a; 2463]   "
ἤλλαξαν   aor act ind 3 pl
   [Rm 1:23; v-2b; 248]   ἀλλάσσω

ἧλος, ου, ὁ   {2464, n-2a}
   a nail, John 20:25 (2t)*

ἤλπιζεν   imperf act ind 3 sg
   [Lk 23:8; v-2a(1); 1827]   ἐλπίζω
ἠλπίζομεν   imperf act ind 1 pl
   [Lk 24:21; v-2a(1); 1827]   "
ἠλπίκαμεν   perf act ind 1 pl [2t; v-2a(1); 1827]   "
ἠλπίκατε   perf act ind 2 pl
   [Jn 5:45; v-2a(1); 1827]   "
ἤλπικεν   perf act ind 3 sg
   [1Ti 5:5; v-2a(1); 1827]   "
ἠλπικέναι   perf act inf
   [1Ti 6:17; v-2a(1); 1827]   "
ἠλπικότες   perf act ptcp nom pl masc
   [1C 15:19; v-2a(1); 1827]   "
ἠλπίσαμεν   aor act ind 1 pl
   [2C 8:5; v-2a(1); 1827]   "
ἥλων   gen pl masc [2t; n-2a; 2464]   ἧλος
ἥμαρτεν   aor act ind 3 sg
   [3t; v-3a(2a); 279]   ἁμαρτάνω
ἥμαρτες   aor act ind 2 sg
   [1C 7:28; v-3a(2a); 279]   "
ἡμαρτήκαμεν   perf act ind 1 pl
   [1J 1:10; v-3a(2a); 279]   "
ἥμαρτον   aor act ind 1 sg [4t; v-3a(2a); 279]   "
ἥμαρτον   aor act ind 3 pl [4t; v-3a(2a); 279]   "
ἡμᾶς   acc pl [166t; a-5a; 1609]   ἐγώ
ἥμεθα   imperf mid ind 1 pl [5t; v-6b; 1639]   εἰμί
ἡμεῖς   nom pl [127t; a-5a; 1609]   ἐγώ
ἠμέλησα   aor act ind 1 sg
   [Hb 8:9; v-1d(2a); 288]   ἀμελέω
ἤμελλεν   imperf act ind 3 sg
   [11t; v-1d(2c); 3516]   μέλλω
ἤμελλον   imperf act ind 1 sg
   [Rv 10:4; v-1d(2c); 3516]   "
ἦμεν   imperf act ind 1 pl [8t; v-6b; 1639]   εἰμί

ἡμέρα, ας, ἡ   {2465, n-1a}
   day, a day, the interval from sunrise to sunset, opp.
   to νύξ, Matt 4:2; 12:40; Luke 2:44; *the interval of*

twenty-four hours, comprehending day and night, Matt 6:34; 15:32; from the Hebrew, ἡμέρα καὶ ἡμέρα, day by day, every day, 2 Cor 4:16; ἡμέραν ἐξ ἡμέρας, from day to day, continually, 2 Peter 2:8; καθ᾽ ἡμέραν, every day, daily, Acts 17:17; Heb 3:13; a point or period of time, Luke 19:42; Acts 15:7; Eph 6:13; a judgement, trial, 1 Cor 4:3

ἡμέρα   nom sg fem [23t; n-1a; 2465]   ἡμέρα
ἡμέρᾳ   dat sg fem [84t; n-1a; 2465]   "
ἡμέραι   nom pl fem [26t; n-1a; 2465]   "
ἡμέραις   dat pl fem [49t; n-1a; 2465]   "
ἡμέραν   acc sg fem [58t; n-1a; 2465]   "
ἡμέρας   gen sg fem [59t; n-1a; 2465]   "
ἡμέρας   acc pl fem [68t; n-1a; 2465]   "
ἡμερῶν   gen pl fem [22t; n-1a; 2465]   "
ἡμετέρα   nom sg fem
       [1J 1:3; a-1a(1); 2466]   ἡμέτερος
ἡμετέραις   dat pl fem
       [Ac 2:11; a-1a(1); 2466]   "
ἡμετέραν   acc sg fem [Rm 15:4; a-1a(1); 2466]   "
ἡμετέρας   gen sg fem [Ac 26:5; a-1a(1); 2466]   "
ἡμέτεροι   nom pl masc
       [Ti 3:14; a-1a(1); 2466]   "
ἡμετέροις   dat pl masc
       [2Ti 4:15; a-1a(1); 2466]   "

ἡμέτερος, α, ον   {2466, a-1a(1)}
    our, Luke 16:12; Acts 2:11; 24:6; 26:5; Rom 15:4;
    2 Tim 4:15; Titus 3:14; 1 John 1:3; 2:2*

ἡμετέρων   gen pl fem [1J 2:2; a-1a(1); 2466]   "
ἤμην   imperf mid ind 1 sg [15t; v-6b; 1639]   εἰμί
ἡμιθανῆ   acc sg masc
       [Lk 10:30; a-4a; 2467]   ἡμιθανής

ἡμιθανής, ές   {2467, a-4a}
    half dead, Luke 10:30*

ἡμῖν   dat pl [169t; a-5a; 1609]   ἐγώ
ἡμίσια   acc pl neut [Lk 19:8; a-2b; 2468]   ἥμισυς
ἡμίσους   gen sg neut [Mk 6:23; a-2b; 2468]   "
ἥμισυ   acc sg neut [3t; a-2b; 2468]   "

ἥμισυς, εια, υ   {2468, a-2b}
    half, Mark 6:23; Luke 19:8; Rev 11:9, 11; 12:14*

ἡμιώριον, ου, τό   {2469, n-2c}
    also spelled ἡμίωρον, half an hour, Rev 8:1*

ἡμιώριον   acc sg neut
       [Rv 8:1; n-2c; 2469]   ἡμιώριον
ἠμύνατο   aor mid ind 3 sg
       [Ac 7:24; v-1c(2); 310]   ἀμύνομαι
ἠμφιεσμένον   perf pass ptcp acc sg masc
       [2t; cv-2a(1); 314]   ἀμφιάζω
ἡμῶν   gen pl [402t; a-5a; 1609]   ἐγώ
ἥν   acc sg fem [98t; a-1a(2b); 4005]   ὅς
ἦν   imperf act ind 3 sg [315t; v-6b; 1639]   εἰμί
ἠνάγκαζον   imperf act ind 1 sg
       [Ac 26:11; v-2a(1); 337]   ἀναγκάζω
ἠναγκάσατε   aor act ind 2 pl
       [2C 12:11; v-2a(1); 337]   "
ἠνάγκασεν   aor act ind 3 sg [2t; v-2a(1); 337]   "
ἠναγκάσθη   aor pass ind 3 sg
       [Ga 2:3; v-2a(1); 337]   "

ἠναγκάσθην   aor pass ind 1 sg
       [Ac 28:19; v-2a(1); 337]
ἤνεγκα   aor act ind 1 sg
       [Mk 9:17; v-1c(1); 5770]   φέρω
ἤνεγκαν   aor act ind 3 pl [3t; v-1c(1); 5770]
ἤνεγκεν   aor act ind 3 sg [5t; v-1c(1); 5770]
ἠνέχθη   aor pass ind 3 sg [2t; v-1c(1); 5770]
ἠνεῳγμένη   perf pass ptcp nom sg fem
       [Rv 4:1; cv-1b(2); 487]   ἀνοίγω
ἠνεῳγμένην   perf pass ptcp acc sg fem
       [Rv 3:8; cv-1b(2); 487]
ἠνεῳγμένον   perf pass ptcp acc sg masc
       [Rv 19:11; cv-1b(2); 487]
ἠνεῳγμένον   perf pass ptcp acc sg neut
       [2t; cv-1b(2); 487]
ἠνέῳξεν   aor act ind 3 sg [2t; cv-1b(2); 487]
ἠνεῴχθησαν   aor pass ind 3 pl
       [4t; cv-1b(2); 487]

ἡνίκα   {2471, particle
    when, 2 Cor 3:15, 16*

ἡνίκα   particle [2t; particle; 2471]   ἡνίκα
ἠνοίγη   aor pass ind 3 sg
       [3t; cv-1b(2); 487]   ἀνοίγω
ἠνοίγησαν   aor pass ind 3 pl
       [Mk 7:35; cv-1b(2); 487]
ἤνοιξεν   aor act ind 3 sg [16t; cv-1b(2); 487]
ἠνοίχθη   aor pass ind 3 sg
       [Rv 20:12; cv-1b(2); 487]
ἠνοίχθησαν   aor pass ind 3 pl
       [Rv 20:12; cv-1b(2); 487]
ἠντληκότες   perf act ptcp nom pl masc
       [Jn 2:9; v-1d(2a); 533]   ἀντλέω
ἥξει   fut act ind 3 sg [9t; v-1b(2); 2457]   ἥκω
ἠξίου   imperf act ind 3 sg
       [Ac 15:38; v-1d(3); 546]   ἀξιόω
ἠξίωσα   aor act ind 1 sg [Lk 7:7; v-1d(3); 546]
ἠξίωται   perf pass ind 3 sg
       [Hb 3:3; v-1d(3); 546]
ἥξουσιν   fut act ind 3 pl [6t; v-1b(2); 2457]   ἥκω
ἥξω   aor act subj 1 sg [Rv 2:25; v-1b(2); 2457]
ἥξω   fut act ind 1 sg [2t; v-1b(2); 2457]
ἠπατήθη   aor pass ind 3 sg
       [1Ti 2:14; v-1d(1a); 572]   ἀπατάω
ἠπείθησαν   aor act ind 3 pl
       [Rm 11:31; v-1d(2a); 578]   ἀπειθέω
ἠπειθήσατε   aor act ind 2 pl
       [Rm 11:30; v-1d(2a); 578]
ἠπείθουν   imperf act ind 3 pl
       [Ac 19:9; v-1d(2a); 578]
ἠπείλει   imperf act ind 3 sg
       [1P 2:23; cv-1d(2a); 580]   ἀπειλέω

ἤπερ   {2472, particle
    strengthened form of ἤ, than, John 12:43*

ἤπερ   particle [Jn 12:43; particle; 2472]   ἤπερ
ἤπιον   acc sg masc [2Ti 2:24; a-1a(1); 2473]   ἤπιο

ἤπιος, α, ον   {2473, a-1a(1)
    mild, gentle, kind, 2 Tim 2:24; 1 Thess 2:7 v.l.*

ἠπίστησαν   aor act ind 3 pl
       [2t; v-1d(2a); 601]   ἀπιστέω

ἠπίστουν imperf act ind 3 pl
 [2t; v-1d(2a); 601]   "
ἠπόρει imperf act ind 3 sg
 [Mk 6:20; v-1d(2a); 679] ἀπορέω

Ἥρ, ὁ   {2474, n-3g(2)}
 Er, pr. name, indecl., Luke 3:28*

Ἥρ indecl [Lk 3:28; n-3g(2); 2474] Ἥρ
ἦραν aor act ind 3 pl [12t; v-2d(2); 149] αἴρω
ἤρατε aor act ind 2 pl [3t; v-2d(2); 149] "
ἠργάζετο imperf mid ind 3 sg
 [Ac 18:3; v-2a(1); 2237] ἐργάζομαι
ἠργάσατο aor mid ind 3 sg [3t; v-2a(1); 2237] "
ἠρέθισεν aor act ind 3 sg
 [2C 9:2; v-2a(1); 2241] ἐρεθίζω
ἤρεμον acc sg masc [1Ti 2:2; a-3a; 2475] ἤρεμος

ἤρεμος, ον   {2475, a-3a}
 tranquil, quiet, 1 Tim 2:2*

ἦρεν aor act ind 3 sg [6t; v-2d(2); 149] αἴρω
ἤρεσεν aor act ind 3 sg [4t; v-5a; 743] ἀρέσκω
ἤρεσκον imperf act ind 1 sg [Ga 1:10; v-5a; 743] "
ἡρέτισα aor act ind 1 sg
 [Mt 12:18; v-2a(1); 147] αἱρετίζω
ἠρημώθη aor pass ind 3 sg
 [2t; v-1d(3); 2246] ἐρημόω
ἠρημωμένην perf pass ptcp acc sg fem
 [Rv 17:16; v-1d(3); 2246] "
ἤρθη aor pass ind 3 sg [3t; v-2d(2); 149] αἴρω
ἠριθμημέναι perf pass ptcp nom pl fem
 [Mt 10:30; v-1d(2a); 749] ἀριθμέω
ἠρίθμηνται perf pass ind 3 pl
 [Lk 12:7; v-1d(2a); 749] "
ἠρίστησαν aor act ind 3 pl
 [Jn 21:15; v-1d(1a); 753] ἀριστάω
ἦρκεν perf act ind 3 sg
 [Cl 2:14; v-2d(2); 149] αἴρω
ἠρμένον perf pass ptcp acc sg masc
 [Jn 20:1; v-2d(2); 149] "
ἡρμοσάμην aor mid ind 1 sg
 [2C 11:2; v-2a(1); 764] ἁρμόζω
ἠρνεῖτο imperf mid ind 3 sg
 [Mk 14:70; v-1d(2a); 766] ἀρνέομαι
ἠρνημένοι perf pass ptcp nom pl masc
 [2Ti 3:5; v-1d(2a); 766] "
ἠρνήσαντο aor mid ind 3 pl
 [Ac 7:35; v-1d(2a); 766] "
ἠρνήσασθε aor mid ind 2 pl [2t; v-1d(2a); 766] "
ἠρνήσατο aor mid ind 3 sg [8t; v-1d(2a); 766] "
ἠρνήσω aor mid ind 2 sg [2t; v-1d(2a); 766] "
ἤρνηται perf mid ind 3 sg
 [1Ti 5:8; v-1d(2a); 766] "
ἤρξαντο aor mid ind 3 pl [19t; v-1b(2); 806] ἄρχω
ἤρξατο aor mid ind 3 sg [41t; v-1b(2); 806] "
ἡρπάγη aor pass ind 3 sg
 [2C 12:4; v-2a(1); 773] ἁρπάζω
ἥρπασεν aor act ind 3 sg [Ac 8:39; v-2a(1); 773] "
ἡρπάσθη aor pass ind 3 sg
 [Rv 12:5; v-2a(1); 773] "
ἠρτυμένος perf pass ptcp nom sg masc
 [Cl 4:6; v-1a(4); 789] ἀρτύω
ἤρχετο imperf mid ind 3 sg
 [4t; v-1b(2); 2262] ἔρχομαι

ἤρχοντο imperf mid ind 3 pl [6t; v-1b(2); 2262] "
ἤρχου imperf mid ind 2 sg
 [Ac 9:17; v-1b(2); 2262] "
Ἡρῴδῃ dat sg masc [3t; n-1f; 2476] Ἡρῴδης
Ἡρῴδην acc sg masc [2t; n-1f; 2476] "

Ἡρῴδης, ου, ὁ   {2476, n-1f}
 Herod, pr. name. (1) *Herod the Great,* Matt 2:1. (2)
 Herod Antipas, tetrarch of Galilee and Peraea,
 Matt 14:1. (3) *Herod Agrippa,* Acts 12:1

Ἡρῴδης nom sg masc [25t; n-1f; 2476]
Ἡρῳδιάδα acc sg fem
 [2t; n-3c(2); 2478] Ἡρῳδιάς
Ἡρῳδιάδος gen sg fem [3t; n-3c(2); 2478] "

Ἡρῳδιανοί, ῶν, οἱ   {2477, n-2a}
 Herodians, partisans of Ἡρῴδης, *Herod Antipas,*
 Matt 22:16; Mark 3:6; 8:15 v.l.; 12:13*

Ἡρῳδιανῶν gen pl masc
 [3t; n-2a; 2477] Ἡρῳδιανοί

Ἡρῳδιάς, άδος, ἡ   {2478, n-3c(2)}
 Herodias, pr. name, the wife of Herod Antipas,
 Matt 14:3, 6; Mark 6:17, 19, 22; Luke 3:19*

Ἡρῳδιάς nom sg fem
 [Mk 6:19; n-3c(2); 2478] Ἡρῳδιάς

Ἡρῳδίων, ωνος, ὁ   {2479, n-3f(1a)}
 Herodian, pr. name, Rom 16:11*

Ἡρῳδίωνα acc sg masc
 [Rm 16:11; n-3f(1a); 2479] Ἡρῳδίων
Ἡρῴδου gen sg masc [13t; n-1f; 2476] Ἡρῴδης
ἠρώτα imperf act ind 3 sg
 [6t; v-1d(1a); 2263] ἐρωτάω
ἠρώτησαν aor act ind 3 pl [8t; v-1d(1a); 2263] "
ἠρώτησεν aor act ind 3 sg [6t; v-1d(1a); 2263] "
ἠρώτουν imperf act ind 3 pl
 [Mt 15:23; v-1d(1a); 2263] "
ἠρώτων imperf act ind 3 pl [7t; v-1d(1a); 2263] "
ἧς gen sg fem [49t; a-1a(2b); 4005] ὅς
ἦς imperf act ind 2 sg [6t; v-6b; 1639] εἰμί
ἧς pres act subj 2 sg [Rm 2:25; v-6b; 1639] "
Ἠσαΐᾳ dat sg masc [Mk 1:2; n-1d; 2480] Ἠσαΐας
Ἠσαΐαν acc sg masc [2t; n-1d; 2480] "

Ἠσαΐας, ου, ὁ   {2480, n-1d}
 Isaiah, pr. name, Matt 3:3; 13:14; Mark 1:2; Luke
 4:17; John 1:23; 12:38, 39, 41; Acts 8:28; Rom
 9:27, 29

Ἠσαΐας nom sg masc [10t; n-1d; 2480]
Ἠσαΐου gen sg masc [9t; n-1d; 2480]
ἦσαν imperf act ind 3 pl [95t; v-6b; 1639] εἰμί

Ἠσαῦ, ὁ   {2481, n-3g(2)}
 Esau, pr. name, indecl. (Gen 27-28), Rom 9:13;
 Heb 11:20; 12:16*

Ἠσαῦ indecl [3t; n-3g(2); 2481] Ἠσαῦ
ἠσέβησαν aor act ind 3 pl
 [Jd 15; v-1d(2a); 814] ἀσεβέω
ἦσθα imperf act ind 2 sg [2t; v-6b; 1639] εἰμί
ἠσθένει imperf act ind 3 sg
 [3t; v-1d(2a); 820] ἀσθενέω
ἠσθενήκαμεν perf act ind 1 pl
 [2C 11:21; v-1d(2a); 820] "

ἠσθένησα aor act ind 1 sg
[Mt 25:36; v-1d(2a); 820]   "

ἠσθένησεν aor act ind 3 sg [2t; v-1d(2a); 820]   "

ἤσθιον imperf act ind 3 pl
[4t; v-1b(3); 2266]   ἐσθίω

ἠσπάζοντο imperf mid ind 3 pl
[Mk 9:15; v-2a(1); 832]   ἀσπάζομαι

ἠσπάσατο aor mid ind 3 sg
[Lk 1:40; v-2a(1); 832]   "

ἧσσον acc sg neut comparative
can function adverbially
[2t; a-4b(1); 2482]   ἥσσων

ἡσσώθητε aor pass ind 2 pl
[2C 12:13; cv-1d(3); 2273]   ἐσσόομαι

ἥσσων, ον   {2482, a-4b(1)}
lesser, inferior, weaker, 1 Cor 11:17; 2 Cor 12:15;
Matt 20:28 v.l.*

ἠστόχησαν aor act ind 3 pl
[2t; v-1d(2a); 846]   ἀστοχέω

ἡσυχάζειν pres act inf
[1Th 4:11; v-2a(1); 2483]   ἡσυχάζω

ἡσυχάζω   {2483, v-2a(1)}
[-, ἡσύχασα, -, -, -] *to be still, at rest; to live
peaceably, be quiet,* 1 Thess 4:11; *to rest* from
labor, Luke 23:56; *to be silent* or *quiet, acquiesce,
to desist* from discussion, Luke 14:4; Acts 11:18;
21:14, 22:2 v.l.*

ἡσυχάσαμεν aor act ind 1 pl
[Ac 21:14; v-2a(1); 2483]   "

ἡσύχασαν aor act ind 3 pl [3t; v-2a(1); 2483]   "

ἡσυχία, ας, ἡ   {2484, n-1a}
rest, quiet, tranquillity; a quiet, tranquil life, 2
Thess 3:12; *silence, silent attention,* Acts 22:2; 1
Tim 2:11, 12; Acts 21:40 v.l.*

ἡσυχία dat sg fem [2t; n-1a; 2484]   ἡσυχία
ἡσυχίαν acc sg fem [Ac 22:2; n-1a; 2484]   "
ἡσυχίας gen sg fem [2Th 3:12; n-1a; 2484]   "
ἡσύχιον acc sg masc
[1Ti 2:2; a-3a; 2485]   ἡσύχιος

ἡσύχιος, ον   {2485, a-3a}
quiet, tranquil, peaceful, 1 Tim 2:2; 1 Peter 3:4*

ἡσυχίου gen sg neut [1P 3:4; a-3a; 2485]   "
ἠσφαλίσαντο aor mid ind 3 pl
[Mt 27:66; v-2a(1); 856]   ἀσφαλίζω
ἠσφαλίσατο aor mid ind 3 sg
[Ac 16:24; v-2a(1); 856]   "
ἠτακτήσαμεν aor act ind 1 pl
[2Th 3:7; v-1d(2a); 863]   ἀτακτέω
ἦτε imperf act ind 2 pl [10t; v-6b; 1639]   εἰμί
ἦτε pres act subj 2 pl [9t; v-6b; 1639]   "
ᾐτήκαμεν perf act ind 1 pl
[1J 5:15; v-1d(2a); 160]   αἰτέω
ᾐτήσαντο aor mid ind 3 pl [2t; v-1d(2a); 160]   "
ᾔτησας aor act ind 2 sg
[Jn 4:10; v-1d(2a); 160]   "
ᾐτήσασθε aor mid ind 2 pl
[Ac 3:14; v-1d(2a); 160]   "
ᾐτήσατε aor act ind 2 pl
[Jn 16:24; v-1d(2a); 160]   "
ᾐτήσατο aor mid ind 3 sg [6t; v-1d(2a); 160]   "

ἠτίμασαν aor act ind 3 pl
[Mk 12:4; v-2a(1); 869]   ἀτιμάζω
ἠτιμάσατε aor act ind 2 pl
[Jm 2:6; v-2a(1); 869]   "
ἥτις nom sg fem [38t; a-1a(2b); 4015]   ὅστις

ἤτοι   {2486, particle}
whether, with an elevated tone, Rom 6:16*

ἤτοι conj [Rm 6:16; particle; 2486]   ἤτοι
ἡτοίμακα perf act ind 1 sg
[Mt 22:4; v-2a(1); 2286]   ἑτοιμάζω
ἡτοίμασαν aor act ind 3 pl [6t; v-2a(1); 2286]   "
ἡτοίμασας aor act ind 2 sg [2t; v-2a(1); 2286]   "
ἡτοίμασεν aor act ind 3 sg [3t; v-2a(1); 2286]   "
ἡτοιμασμένην perf pass ptcp acc sg fem
[2t; v-2a(1); 2286]
ἡτοιμασμένοι perf pass ptcp nom pl masc
[Rv 9:15; v-2a(1); 2286]   "
ἡτοιμασμένοις perf pass ptcp dat pl masc
[Rv 9:7; v-2a(1); 2286]   "
ἡτοιμασμένον perf pass ptcp nom sg neut
[2Ti 2:21; v-2a(1); 2286]   "
ἡτοιμασμένον perf pass ptcp acc sg masc
[Rv 12:6; v-2a(1); 2286]   "
ἡτοιμασμένον perf pass ptcp acc sg neut
[Mt 25:41; v-2a(1); 2286]   "
ἡτοίμασται perf pass ind 3 sg
[2t; v-2a(1); 2286]   "
ᾐτοῦντο imperf mid ind 3 pl
[2t; v-1d(2a); 160]   αἰτέω

ἡττάομαι   {2487, v-1d(1a)}
[-, -, -, ἥττημαι, ἡττήθην] *to be less, inferior to; to
fare worse, to be in a less favored condition,* 2 Cor
12:13 v.l.; by impl. *to be overcome, vanquished,* 2
Peter 2:19, 20*

ἥττημα, ατος, τό   {2488, n-3c(4)}
an inferiority, to a particular standard; *default,
defeat, failure, shortcoming,* Rom 11:12; 1 Cor 6:7*

ἥττημα nom sg neut [2t; n-3c(4); 2488]   ἥττημα
ἥττηται perf pass ind 3 sg
[2P 2:19; v-1d(1a); 2487]   ἡττάομαι

ἥττων, see ἥσσων   {2489}

ἡττῶνται pres pass ind 3 pl
[2P 2:20; v-1d(1a); 2487]   "
ἤτω pres act imperative 3 sg
[2t; v-6b; 1639]   εἰμί
ηὐκαίρουν imperf act ind 3 pl
[Ac 17:21; v-1d(2a); 2320]   εὐκαιρέω
ηὐλήσαμεν aor act ind 1 pl
[2t; v-1d(2a); 884]   αὐλέω
ηὐλίζετο imperf mid ind 3 sg
[Lk 21:37; v-2a(1); 887]   αὐλίζομαι
ηὐλίσθη aor pass ind 3 sg
[Mt 21:17; v-2a(1); 887]   "
ηὔξανεν imperf act ind 3 sg
[6t; v-3a(1); 889]   αὐξάνω
ηὔξησεν aor act ind 3 sg [2t; v-3a(1); 889]   "
ηὑρίσκετο imperf pass ind 3 sg
[Hb 11:5; v-5b; 2351]   εὑρίσκω
ηὕρισκον imperf act ind 3 pl [2t; v-5b; 2351]   "

ἡὐφράνθη   aor pass ind 3 sg
   [Ac 2:26; v-2d(4); 2370]   εὐφραίνω
ἡὐχαρίστησαν   aor act ind 3 pl
   [Rm 1:21; v-1d(2a); 2373]   εὐχαριστέω
ἡὐχόμην   imperf mid ind 1 sg
   [Rm 9:3; v-1b(2); 2377]   εὔχομαι
ἡὔχοντο   imperf mid ind 3 pl
   [Ac 27:29; v-1b(2); 2377]   "
ἤφιεν   imperf act ind 3 sg
   [2t; cv-6a; 918]   ἀφίημι

ἠχέω   {2490, v-1d(2a)}
   [-, ἤχησα, -, ἤχημαι, ἠχήθην] to sound, ring, 1 Cor
   13:1; to roar, as the sea, Luke 21:25 v.l.*

ἤχθη   aor pass ind 3 sg [2t; v-1b(2); 72]   ἄγω
ἠχμαλώτευσεν   aor act ind 3 sg
   [Ep 4:8; v-1a(6); 169]   αἰχμαλωτεύω

ἦχος, ου, τό   {2491, n-2a}
   see spelling ἦχος, ους also, sound, noise, Acts 2:2;
   Heb 12:19; met. report, fame, rumor, Luke 4:37*

ἦχος, ους, τό   {2492, n-3d(2b)}
   see spelling ἦχος, ου also, roar, sound, noise,
   Luke 21:25, but see BAGD

ἦχος   nom sg masc [2t; n-2a; 2492]   ἦχος
ἤχους   gen sg neut [Lk 21:25; n-3d(2b); 2492]   "
ἠχρεώθησαν   aor pass ind 3 pl
   [Rm 3:12; v-1d(3); 946]   ἀχρειόω
ἤχῳ   dat sg masc [Hb 12:19; n-2a; 2491]   ἦχος
ἠχῶν   pres act ptcp nom sg masc
   [1C 13:1; v-1d(2a); 2490]   ἠχέω
ἤψαντο   aor mid ind 3 pl [2t; v-4; 721]   ἅπτω
ἤψατο   aor mid ind 3 sg [15t; v-4; 721]   "

θ

θάβιτα, v.l. for ῥαβιθα at Mark 5:41*   {2496}
Θαδδαῖον   acc sg masc
   [Mk 3:18; n-2a; 2497]   Θαδδαῖος

Θαδδαῖος, ου, ὁ   {2497, n-2a}
   Thaddaeus, pr. name, Matt 10:3; Mark 3:18*

Θαδδαῖος   nom sg masc [Mt 10:3; n-2a; 2497]   "

θάλασσα, ης, ἡ   {2498, n-1c}
   the sea, Matt 23:15, Mark 9:42; a sea, Acts 7:36; an
   inland sea, lake, Matt 8:24

θάλασσα   nom sg fem [6t; n-1c; 2498]   θάλασσα
θάλασσαν   acc sg fem [43t; n-1c; 2498]   "
θαλάσσῃ   dat sg fem [13t; n-1c; 2498]   "
θαλάσσης   gen sg fem [29t; n-1c; 2498]   "
θάλπει   pres act ind 3 sg
   [Ep 5:29; v-4; 2499]   θάλπω
θάλπῃ   pres act subj 3 sg [1Th 2:7; v-4; 2499]   "

θάλπω   {2499, v-4}
   [-, -, -, -, -] to impart warmth; met. to cherish,
   nurse, foster, comfort, Eph 5:29; 1 Thess 2:7*

Θαμάρ, ἡ   {2500, n-3g(2)}
   Tamar, (Gen 38), pr. name, indecl., Matt 1:3*

Θαμάρ   indecl [Mt 1:3; n-3g(2); 2500]   Θαμάρ

θαμβέω   {2501, v-1d(2a)}
   [(ἐθάμβουν), -, -, -, -, ἐθαμβήθην or ἐθαμβώθην] to
   be astonished, amazed, Acts 9:6; later, pass. to be
   astonished, amazed, awestruck, Matt 1:27; 10:24,
   32; Acts 3:11 v.l.; 9:6 v.l.;*

θάμβος, ους, τό   {2502, n-2a}
   astonishment, amazement, awe, Luke 4:36; 5:9;
   Acts 3:10*

θάμβος   nom sg neut [2t; n-2a; 2502]   θάμβος
θάμβους   gen sg neut [Ac 3:10; n-2a; 2502]   "
θανάσιμον   acc sg neut
   [Mk 16:18; a-3a; 2503]   θανάσιμος

θανάσιμος, ον   {2503, a-3a}
   deadly, mortal, fatal, Mark 16:18*

θάνατε   voc sg masc [2t; n-2a; 2505]   θάνατος

θανατηφόρος, ον   {2504, a-3a}
   bringing or causing death, deadly, fatal, James 3:8*

θανατηφόρου   gen sg masc
   [Jm 3:8; a-3a; 2504]   θανατηφόρος
θανάτοις   dat pl masc
   [2C 11:23; n-2a; 2505]   θάνατος
θάνατον   acc sg masc [25t; n-2a; 2505]   "

θάνατος, ου, ὁ   {2505, n-2a}
   death, the extinction of life, whether naturally,
   Luke 2:26; Mark 9:1; or violently, Matt 10:21;
   15:4; imminent danger of death, 2 Cor 4:11, 12;
   11:23; in N.T. spiritual death, as opposed to ζωή
   in its spiritual sense, in respect of a forfeiture of
   salvation, John 8:51; Rom 6:16

θάνατος   nom sg masc [24t; n-2a; 2505]   "
θανάτου   gen sg masc [53t; n-2a; 2505]   "
θανατούμεθα   pres pass ind 1 pl
   [Rm 8:36; v-1d(3); 2506]   θανατόω
θανατούμενοι   pres pass ptcp nom pl masc
   [2C 6:9; v-1d(3); 2506]   "
θανατοῦτε   pres act ind 2 pl
   [Rm 8:13; v-1d(3); 2506]   "

θανατόω   {2506, v-1d(3)}
   [θανατώσω, ἐθανάτωσα, -, -, ἐθανατώθην] to put
   to death, deliver to death, Matt 10:21; 26:59; Mark
   13:12; pass. to be exposed to imminent danger of
   death, Rom 8:36; in N.T. met. to subdue, Rom
   8:13; pass. to be dead to, to be rid, parted from, as
   if by the intervention of death, Rom 7:4

θανάτῳ   dat sg masc [15t; n-2a; 2505]   θάνατος
θανατωθείς   aor pass ptcp nom sg masc
   [1P 3:18; v-1d(3); 2506]   θανατόω
θανατῶσαι   aor act inf [2t; v-1d(3); 2506]   "
θανατώσουσιν   fut act ind 3 pl
   [3t; v-1d(3); 2506]   "
θανατώσωσιν   aor act subj 3 pl
   [Mt 26:59; v-1d(3); 2506]   "

θάπτω   {2507, v-4}
   [-, ἔθαψα, -, -, ἐτάφην] to bury, Matt 8:21, 22;
   14:12

Θάρα, ὁ   {2508, n-3g(2)}
Terah, Abraham's father, pr. name, indecl.,
Luke 3:34*

Θάρα   indecl [Lk 3:34; n-3g(2); 2508]   Θάρα

θαρρέω   {2509, v-1d(2a)}
[-, ἐθάρρησα, -, -, -] *to be confident, courageous*, 2
Cor 5:6, 8; 7:16; 10:1, 2; Heb 13:6*

θαρρῆσαι   aor act inf
   [2C 10:2; v-1d(2a); 2509]   θαρρέω
θαρροῦμεν   pres act ind 1 pl
   [2C 5:8; v-1d(2a); 2509]   "
θαρροῦντας   pres act ptcp acc pl masc
   [Hb 13:6; v-1d(2a); 2509]   "
θαρροῦντες   pres act ptcp nom pl masc
   [2C 5:6; v-1d(2a); 2509]   "
θαρρῶ   pres act ind 1 sg [2t; v-1d(2a); 2509]   "
θάρσει   pres act imperative 2 sg
   [4t; v-1d(2a); 2510]   θαρσέω
θαρσεῖτε   pres act imperative 2 pl
   [3t; v-1d(2a); 2510]   "

θαρσέω   {2510, v-1d(2a)}
[-, ἐθάρσησα, -, -, -] *to be of good courage, be of
good cheer*, Matt 9:2; *to be confident, hopeful; to be
bold, maintain a bold bearing*, Matt 9:22; 14:27;
Mark 6:50; 10:49; John 16:33; Acts 23:11*

θάρσος, ους, τό   {2511, n-3d(2b)}
courage, confidence, Acts 28:15*

θάρσος   acc sg neut
   [Ac 28:15; n-3d(2b); 2511]   θάρσος

θαῦμα, ατος, τό   {2512, n-3c(4)}
a wonder; wonder, admiration, astonishment, 2 Cor
11:14; Rev 17:6*

θαῦμα   nom sg neut
   [2C 11:14; n-3c(4); 2512]   θαῦμα
θαῦμα   acc sg neut [Rv 17:6; n-3c(4); 2512]   "
θαυμάζειν   pres act inf
   [2t; v-2a(1); 2513]   θαυμάζω
θαυμάζετε   pres act imperative 2 pl
   [2t; v-2a(1); 2513]   "
θαυμάζετε   pres act ind 2 pl [2t; v-2a(1); 2513] "
θαυμάζητε   pres act subj 2 pl
   [Jn 5:20; v-2a(1); 2513]   "
θαυμάζοντες   pres act ptcp nom pl masc
   [2t; v-2a(1); 2513]   "
θαυμαζόντων   pres act ptcp gen pl masc
   [2t; v-2a(1); 2513]   "

θαυμάζω   {2513, v-2a(1)}
[θαυμάσω ἐθαύμασα, -, -, ἐθαυμάσθην] *to admire,
regard with admiration, wonder at*, Luke 7:9; Acts
7:31; *to reverence, adore*, 2 Thess 1:10; absol. *to
wonder, be filled with wonder, admiration*, or
astonishment, Matt 8:10; Luke 4:22

θαυμάζω   pres act ind 1 sg
   [Ga 1:6; v-2a(1); 2513]   "
θαυμάζων   pres act ptcp nom sg masc
   [Lk 24:12; v-2a(1); 2513]   "
θαυμάσαι   aor act inf [Mt 15:31; v-2a(1); 2513] "
θαυμάσαντες   aor act ptcp nom pl masc
   [Lk 20:26; v-2a(1); 2513]   "

θαυμάσατε   aor act imperative 2 pl
   [Ac 13:41; v-2a(1); 2513]   "
θαυμάσῃς   aor act subj 2 sg
   [Jn 3:7; v-2a(1); 2513]   "
θαυμασθῆναι   aor pass inf
   [2Th 1:10; v-2a(1); 2513]   "
θαυμασθήσονται   fut pass ind 3 pl
   [Rv 17:8; v-2a(1); 2513]   "
θαυμάσια   acc pl neut
   [Mt 21:15; a-1a(1); 2514]   θαυμάσιος

θαυμάσιος, α, ον   {2514, a-1a(1)}
wonderful, admirable, marvellous; τὸ θαυμάσιον, *a
wonder, wonderful work*, Matt 21:15*

θαυμαστά   nom pl neut
   [Rv 15:3; a-1a(2a); 2515]   θαυμαστός
θαυμαστή   nom sg fem [2t; a-1a(2a); 2515]   "
θαυμαστόν   nom sg neut [Jn 9:30; a-1a(2a); 2515] "
θαυμαστόν   acc sg neut [2t; a-1a(2a); 2515]   "

θαυμαστός, ή, όν   {2515, a-1a(2a)}
wondrous, glorious, 1 Peter 2:9; Rev 15:1;
marvellous, strange, uncommon, Matt 21:42;
Mark 12:11; John 9:30; Rev 15:3*

θάψαι   aor act inf [4t; v-4; 2507]   θάπτω
θαψάντων   aor act ptcp gen pl masc
   [Ac 5:9; v-4; 2507]   "

θεά, ᾶς, ἡ   {2516, n-1a}
a goddess, Acts 19:27*

θεαθῆναι   aor pass inf
   [2t; v-1d(1b); 2517]   θεάομαι

θεάομαι   {2517, v-1d(1b)}
[-, ἐθεασάμην, -, τεθέαμαι, ἐθεάθην] *to gaze upon*,
Matt 6:1; 23:5; Luke 7:24; *to see, discern with the
eyes*, Mark 16:11, 14; Luke 5:27; John 1:14, 32,
38; *to see, visit*, Rom 15:24

θεᾶς   gen sg fem [Ac 19:27; n-1a; 2516]   θεά
θεασάμενοι   aor mid ptcp nom pl masc
   [2t; v-1d(1b); 2517]   θεάομαι
θεασαμένοις   aor mid ptcp dat pl masc
   [Mk 16:14; v-1d(1b); 2517]   "
θεασάμενος   aor mid ptcp nom sg masc
   [2t; v-1d(1b); 2517]   "
θεάσασθαι   aor mid inf [4t; v-1d(1b); 2517]   "
θεάσασθε   aor mid imperative 2 pl
   [Jn 4:35; v-1d(1b); 2517]   "
θεατριζόμενοι   pres pass ptcp nom pl masc
   [Hb 10:33; v-2a(1); 2518]   θεατρίζω

θεατρίζω   {2518, v-2a(1)}
[-, -, -, -, -] *to be exposed as in a theater, to be made
a gazing-stock, object of scorn*, Heb 10:33*

θέατρον, ου, τό   {2519, n-2c}
*a theater, a place where public games and spectacles
are exhibited*, Acts 19:29, 31; meton. *a show,
gazing-stock*, 1 Cor 4:9*

θέατρον   nom sg neut [1C 4:9; n-2c; 2519]   θέατρον
θέατρον   acc sg neut [2t; n-2c; 2519]   "
θεέ   voc sg masc [2t; n-2a; 2536]   θεός
θείας   gen sg fem [2t; a-1a(1); 2521]   θεῖος
θεῖναι   aor act inf [4t; v-6a; 5502]   τίθημι

θεῖον, ου, τό   {2520, n-2c}
brimstone, sulphur, Luke 17:29; Rev 9:17; 14:10;
19:20; 20:10; 21:8*

θεῖον   nom sg neut [Rv 9:17; n-2c; 2520]   θεῖον
θεῖον   acc sg neut [2t; a-1a(1); 2521]   θεῖος

θεῖος, α, ον   {2521, a-1a(1)}
divine, pertaining to God, 2 Peter 1:3, 4; τὸ θεῖον,
the divine nature, divinity, Acts 17:27 v.l., 29 Titus
1:9 v.l.*

θειότης, ητος, ἡ   {2522, n-3c(1)}
divinity, deity, godhead, divine majesty, Rom 1:20*

θειότης   nom sg fem
    [Rm 1:20; n-3c(1); 2522]   θειότης
θεῖου   gen sg neut [2t; n-2c; 2520]   θεῖον
θείς   aor act ptcp nom sg masc
    [4t; v-6a; 5502]   τίθημι
θείῳ   dat sg neut [3t; n-2c; 2520]   θεῖον
θειώδεις   acc pl masc
    [Rv 9:17; a-4a; 2523]   θειώδης

θειώδης, ες   {2523, a-4a}
of brimstone, sulphurous, Rev 9:17*

θέκλα, ῆς, ἡ   {2524, n-1c}
Thecla, 2 Tim 3:11 v.l.*

θέλει   pres act ind 3 sg
    [19t; v-1d(2c); 2527]   θέλω
θέλειν   pres act inf [4t; v-1d(2c); 2527]   "
θέλεις   pres act ind 2 sg [18t; v-1d(2c); 2527] "
θέλετε   pres act ind 2 pl [18t; v-1d(2c); 2527] "
θέλῃ   pres act subj 3 sg [8t; v-1d(2c); 2527]   "

θέλημα, ατος, τό   {2525, n-3c(4)}
will, bent, inclination, 1 Cor 16:12; Eph 2:3; 1
Peter 4:3; *resolve,* 1 Cor 7:37; *will, purpose,
design,* 2 Tim 2:26; 2 Peter 1:21; *will, sovereign
pleasure, behest,* Matt 18:14; Luke 12:47; Acts
13:22, et al. freq.; ἐν τῷ θελήματι θεοῦ, *Deo
permittente, if God please or permit,* Rom 1:10

θέλημα   nom sg neut [14t; n-3c(4); 2525]   θέλημα
θέλημα   acc sg neut [26t; n-3c(4); 2525]   "
θελήματα   acc pl neut [2t; n-3c(4); 2525]   "
θελήματι   dat sg neut [6t; n-3c(4); 2525]   "
θελήματος   gen sg neut [14t; n-3c(4); 2525]   "
θέλης   pres act subj 2 sg
    [4t; v-1d(2c); 2527]   θέλω
θελήσαντας   aor act ptcp acc pl masc
    [Lk 19:27; v-1d(2c); 2527]   "
θελήσῃ   aor act subj 3 sg [3t; v-1d(2c); 2527] "
θέλησιν   acc sg fem
    [Hb 2:4; n-3e(5b); 2526]   θέλησις

θέλησις, εως, ἡ   {2526, n-3e(5b)}
will, pleasure, Heb 2:4*

θελήσω   aor act subj 1 sg
    [2C 12:6; v-1d(2c); 2527]   θέλω
θελήσωσιν   aor act subj 3 pl
    [Rv 11:6; v-1d(2c); 2527]   "
θέλητε   pres act subj 2 pl [4t; v-1d(2c); 2527] "
θέλοι   pres act opt 3 sg [3t; v-1d(2c); 2527]   "
θέλομεν   pres act ind 1 pl [7t; v-1d(2c); 2527] "

θέλοντα   pres act ptcp acc sg masc
    [Mt 5:42; v-1d(2c); 2527]   "
θέλοντας   pres act ptcp acc pl masc
    [2P 3:5; v-1d(2c); 2527]   "
θέλοντες   pres act ptcp nom pl masc
    [ότ; v-1d(2c); 2527]   "
θέλοντες   pres act ptcp voc pl masc
    [Ga 4:21; v-1d(2c); 2527]   "
θέλοντι   pres act ptcp dat sg masc
    [2t; v-1d(2c); 2527]   "
θέλοντος   pres act ptcp gen sg masc
    [2t; v-1d(2c); 2527]   "
θελόντων   pres act ptcp gen pl masc
    [3t; v-1d(2c); 2527]   "
θέλουσιν   pres act ind 3 pl [6t; v-1d(2c); 2527] "

θέλω   {2527, v-1d(2c)}
[θελήσω, ἠθέλησα, -, -, ἐθελήθην] *to exercise the
will,* properly by an unimpassioned operation;
to be willing, Matt 17:4; *to be inclined, disposed,*
Rom 13:3; *to choose,* Luke 1:62; *to intend, design,*
Luke 14:28; *to will,* John 5:21; 21:22; ἤθελον, *I
could wish,* Gal 4:20

θέλω   pres act ind 1 sg [35t; v-1d(2c); 2527]   "
θέλω   pres act subj 1 sg [3t; v-1d(2c); 2527]   "
θέλων   pres act ptcp nom sg masc
    [13t; v-1d(2c); 2527]   "
θέλωσι   pres act subj 3 pl
    [Ac 26:5; v-1d(2c); 2527]   "
θεμέλια   acc pl neut
    [Ac 16:26; n-2c; 2528]   θεμέλιον
θεμέλιοι   nom pl masc
    [Rv 21:19; n-2a; 2529]   θεμέλιος

θεμέλιον, ου, τό   {2528, n-2c}
can also be θεμέλιος, ου, ο, *a foundation,* Luke
6:48, 49; Heb 11:10; met. *a foundation* laid in
elementary instruction, Heb 6:1; *a foundation* of
a superstructure of faith, doctrine, or hope, 1
Cor 3:10, 11, 12; Eph 2:20; 1 Tim 6:19; *a
foundation* laid in a commencement of
preaching the Gospel, Acts 16:26; Rom 15:20*

θεμέλιον   acc sg masc [8t; n-2a; 2529]   "

θεμέλιος, ου, ὁ, see θεμέλιον   {2529, n-2a}

θεμέλιος   nom sg masc [2t; n-2a; 2529]   "
θεμελίου   gen sg masc [Lk 6:49; n-2a; 2529]   "
θεμελίους   acc pl masc [2t; n-2a; 2529]   "

θεμελιόω   {2530, v-1d(3)}
[θεμελιώσω, ἐθεμελίωσα, -, τεθεμελίωμαι, -] *to
found, lay the foundation of,* Matt 7:25; Luke 6:48
v.l.; Heb 1:10; met. *to ground, establish, render
firm and unwavering,* Eph 3:17; Col 1:23; 1 Peter
5:10*

θεμελίῳ   dat sg masc [Ep 2:20; n-2a; 2529]   "
θεμελιώσει   fut act ind 3 sg
    [1P 5:10; v-1d(3); 2530]   θεμελιόω
θέμενος   aor mid ptcp nom sg masc
    [2t; v-6a; 5502]   τίθημι
θέντες   aor act ptcp nom pl masc
    [Ac 21:5; v-6a; 5502]   "
θέντος   aor act ptcp gen sg masc
    [Lk 14:29; v-6a; 5502]   "

θεοδίδακτοι nom pl masc
[1Th 4:9; a-3a; 2531]   θεοδίδακτος

θεοδίδακτος, ον   {2531, a-3a}
taught of God, divinely instructed, 1 Thess 4:9*

θεοί nom pl masc [5t; n-2a; 2536]   θεός
θεοῖς dat pl masc [Ga 4:8; n-2a; 2536]   "

θεολόγος, ου, ὁ   {2532, n-2a}
a person who speaks about God, in the inscription
to Rev*

θεομαχέω   {2533, cv-1d(2a)}
[-, -, -, -] *to fight* or *contend against God, to seek to
counteract the divine will,* Acts 23:9 v.l.*

θεομάχοι nom pl masc
[Ac 5:39; a-3a; 2534]   θεομάχος

θεομάχος, ον   {2534, a-3a}
fighting against God, in conflict with God, Acts
5:39*

θεόν acc sg masc [147t; n-2a; 2536]   θεός
θεόν acc sg fem [Ac 19:37; n-2a; 2536]   "

θεόπνευστος, ον   {2535, a-3a}
divinely inspired, 2 Tim 3:16*

θεόπνευστος nom sg fem
[2Ti 3:16; a-3a; 2535]   θεόπνευστος

θεός, οῦ, ὁ   {2536, n-2a}
a deity, Acts 7:43; 1 Cor 8:5; *an idol,* Acts 7:40;
God, the true God, Matt 3:9, et al. freq.; *God,
possessed of true godhead,* John 1:1; Rom 9:5; from
the Hebrew, applied to potentates, John 10:34,
35; τῷ θεῷ, an intensive term, from the Hebrew,
exceedingly, Acts 7:20, and, perhaps, 2 Cor 10:4

θεός nom sg masc [309t; n-2a; 2536]   θεός

θεοσέβεια, ας, ἡ   {2537, n-1a}
worshipping of God, reverence towards God, piety,
1 Tim 2:10*

θεοσέβειαν acc sg fem
[1Ti 2:10; n-1a; 2537]   θεοσέβεια

θεοσεβής, ές   {2538, a-4a}
*reverencing God, pious, godly, devout, a sincere
worshipper of God,* John 9:31*

θεοσεβής nom sg masc
[Jn 9:31; a-4a; 2538]   θεοσεβής
θεοστυγεῖς acc pl masc
[Rm 1:30; a-4a; 2539]   θεοστυγής

θεοστυγής, ές   {2539, a-4a}
God-hated; in N.T. *a hater and despiser of God,*
Rom 1:30*

θεότης, ητος, ἡ   {2540, n-3c(1)}
divinity, deity, godhead, Col 2:9*

θεότητος gen sg fem
[Cl 2:9; n-3c(1); 2540]   θεότης
θεοῦ gen sg masc [691t; n-2a; 2536]   θεός
θεούς acc pl masc [2t; n-2a; 2536]   "
Θεόφιλε voc sg masc [2t; n-2a; 2541]   Θεόφιλος

Θεόφιλος, ου, ὁ   {2541, n-2a}
Theophilus, pr. name, Luke 1:3; Acts 1:1*

θεραπεία, ας, ἡ   {2542, n-1a}
service, attendance; healing, cure, Luke 9:11; Rev
22:2; meton. *those who render service, servants,
domestics, family household,* Matt 24:45 v.l.; Luke
12:42*

θεραπείαν acc sg fem
[Rv 22:2; n-1a; 2542]   θεραπεία
θεραπείας gen sg fem [2t; n-1a; 2542]   "
θεραπεύει pres act ind 3 sg
[Lk 6:7; v-1a(6); 2543]   θεραπεύω
θεραπεύειν pres act inf [2t; v-1a(6); 2543]   "
θεραπεύεσθαι pres pass inf
[Lk 5:15; v-1a(6); 2543]   "
θεραπεύεσθε pres pass imperative 2 pl
[Lk 13:14; v-1a(6); 2543]   "
θεραπεύεται pres pass ind 3 sg
[Ac 17:25; v-1a(6); 2543]   "
θεραπεύετε pres act imperative 2 pl
[2t; v-1a(6); 2543]   "
θεραπευθῆναι aor pass inf
[Lk 8:43; v-1a(6); 2543]   "
θεραπεύοντες pres act ptcp nom pl masc
[Lk 9:6; v-1a(6); 2543]   "
θεραπεῦσαι aor act inf [3t; v-1a(6); 2543]   "
θεραπεύσει fut act ind 3 sg
[Mk 3:2; v-1a(6); 2543]   "
θεράπευσον aor act imperative 2 sg
[Lk 4:23; v-1a(6); 2543]   "
θεραπεύσω fut act ind 1 sg
[Mt 8:7; v-1a(6); 2543]   "

θεραπεύω   {2543, v-1a(6)}
[(ἐθεράπευον), θεραπεύσω, ἐθεράπευσα, -,
τεθεράπευμαι, ἐθεραπεύθην] *to heal, cure,* Matt
4:23, 24; 8:16; pass. *to receive service,* Acts 17:25;
*to serve, minister to, render service and attendance;
to render* divine *service, worship,* Acts 17:25

θεραπεύων pres act ptcp nom sg masc
[2t; v-1a(6); 2543]   "

θεράπων, οντος, ὁ   {2544, n-3c(5b)}
an attendant, a servant; a minister, Heb 3:5*

θεράπων nom sg masc
[Hb 3:5; n-3c(5b); 2544]   θεράπων
θερίζειν pres act inf
[Jn 4:38; v-2a(1); 2545]   θερίζω
θερίζεις pres act ind 2 sg
[Lk 19:21; v-2a(1); 2545]   "
θερίζουσιν pres act ind 3 pl [2t; v-2a(1); 2545]   "

θερίζω   {2545, v-2a(1)}
[θερίσω, ἐθέρισα, -, -, ἐθερίσθην] *to gather in
harvest, reap,* Matt 6:26; 25:24, 26; met. *to reap
the reward of labor,* 1 Cor 9:11; 2 Cor 9:6; *to reap
the harvest of vengeance,* Rev 14:15, 16

θερίζω pres act ind 1 sg
[Mt 25:26; v-2a(1); 2545]   "
θερίζων pres act ptcp nom sg masc
[5t; v-2a(1); 2545]   "
θερίσαι aor act inf [Rv 14:15; v-2a(1); 2545]   "
θερισάντων aor act ptcp gen pl masc
[Jm 5:4; v-2a(1); 2545]   "
θερίσει fut act ind 3 sg [5t; v-2a(1); 2545]   "

θερισμόν   acc sg masc [3t; n-2a; 2546]   θερισμός

θερισμός, οῦ, ὁ   {2546, n-2a}
a harvest, the act of gathering in the harvest,
reaping, John 4:35; met. *the harvest* of the
Gospel, Matt 9:37, 38; Luke 10:2; *a crop;* met. *the*
crop of vengeance, Rev 14:15

θερισμός   nom sg masc [6t; n-2a; 2546]   "
θερισμοῦ   gen sg masc [4t; n-2a; 2546]   "
θερίσομεν   fut act ind 1 pl
    [2t; v-2a(1); 2545]   θερίζω
θέρισον   aor act imperative 2 sg
    [Rv 14:15; v-2a(1); 2545]   "
θερισταί   nom pl masc
    [Mt 13:39; n-1f; 2547]   θεριστής
θερισταῖς   dat pl masc [Mt 13:30; n-1f; 2547]   "

θεριστής, οῦ, ὁ   {2547, n-1f}
one who gathers in the harvest, a reaper, Matt
13:30, 39*

θέρμα, ης, ἡ   {2549, n-1c}
also spelled θέρμη, *heat, warmth,* Acts 28:3*

θερμαίνεσθε   pres mid imperative 2 pl
    [Jm 2:16; v-2d(4); 2548]   θερμαίνω
θερμαινόμενον   pres mid ptcp acc sg masc
    [Mk 14:67; v-2d(4); 2548]   "
θερμαινόμενος   pres mid ptcp nom sg masc
    [3t; v-2d(4); 2548]   "

θερμαίνω   {2548, v-2d(4)}
[(ἐθέρμαινμον), -, -, -, -, -] *to warm;* mid. *to warm*
one's self, Matt 14:54, 67; John 18:18, 25; James
2:16*

θέρμη, see θέρμα

θέρμης   gen sg fem [Ac 28:3; n-1c; 2549]   θέρμα

θέρος, ους, τό   {2550, n-3d(2b)}
the warm season of the year, summer, Matt 24:32;
Mark 13:28; Luke 21:30*

θέρος   nom sg neut [3t; n-3d(2b); 2550]   θέρος
θέσθε   aor mid imperative 2 pl
    [Lk 9:44; v-6a; 5502]   τίθημι

Θεσσαλία, ας, ἡ   {2551, n-1a}
Thessaly, a region in Northeast Greece, Acts
17:15 v.l.*

Θεσσαλονικεύς, έως, ὁ   {2552, n-3e(3)}
Thessalonian, of Thessalonica, Acts 20:4; 27:2;
inscription to 1 and 2 Thess*

Θεσσαλονικέων   gen pl masc
    [3t; n-3e(3); 2552]   Θεσσαλονικεύς
Θεσσαλονικέως   gen sg masc
    [Ac 27:2; n-3e(3); 2552]   "

Θεσσαλονίκη, ης, ἡ   {2553, n-1b}
Thessalonica, a city of Macedonia, Acts 17:1, 11,
13; Phil 4:16; 2 Tim 4:10*

Θεσσαλονίκῃ   dat sg fem
    [2t; n-1b; 2553]   Θεσσαλονίκη
Θεσσαλονίκην   acc sg fem [2t; n-1b; 2553]   "
Θεσσαλονίκης   gen sg fem [Ac 17:13; n-1b; 2553] "
θέτε   aor act imperative 2 pl
    [Lk 21:14; v-6a; 5502]   τίθημι

Θευδᾶς, ᾶ, ὁ   {2554, n-1e}
Theudas, pr. name, Acts 5:36*

Θευδᾶς   nom sg masc [Ac 5:36; n-1e; 2554]   Θευδᾶς
θεῷ   dat sg masc [159t; n-2a; 2536]   θεός
θεωρεῖ   pres act ind 3 sg
    [9t; v-1d(2a); 2555]   θεωρέω
θεωρεῖν   pres act inf [2t; v-1d(2a); 2555]   "
θεωρεῖς   pres act ind 2 sg
    [Ac 21:20; v-1d(2a); 2555]   "
θεωρεῖτε   pres act imperative 2 pl
    [Hb 7:4; v-1d(2a); 2555]   "
θεωρεῖτε   pres act ind 2 pl [11t; v-1d(2a); 2555] "

θεωρέω   {2555, v-1d(2a)}
[(ἐθεώρουν), θεωρήσω, ἐθεώρησα, -, -, -] *to be a*
spectator, to gaze on, contemplate; to behold, view
with interest and attention, Matt 27:55; 28:1; *to*
contemplate mentally, *consider,* Heb 7:4; in N.T.
to see, perceive, Mark 3:11; *to come to a knowledge*
of, John 6:40; from the Hebrew, *to experience,*
undergo, John 8:51

θεωρῇ   pres act subj 3 sg
    [1J 3:17; v-1d(2a); 2555]   "
θεωρῆσαι   aor act inf [Mt 28:1; v-1d(2a); 2555] "
θεωρήσαντες   aor act ptcp nom pl masc
    [Lk 23:48; v-1d(2a); 2555]   "
θεωρήσῃ   aor act subj 3 sg
    [Jn 8:51; v-1d(2a); 2555]   "
θεωρήσουσιν   fut act ind 3 pl
    [Jn 7:3; v-1d(2a); 2555]   "
θεωρῆτε   pres act subj 2 pl
    [Jn 6:62; v-1d(2a); 2555]   "

θεωρία, ας, ἡ   {2556, n-1a}
a beholding; a sight, spectacle, Luke 23:48*

θεωρίαν   acc sg fem [Lk 23:48; n-1a; 2556]   θεωρία
θεωροῦντας   pres act ptcp acc pl masc
    [Rv 11:11; v-1d(2a); 2555]   θεωρέω
θεωροῦντες   pres act ptcp nom pl masc
    [5t; v-1d(2a); 2555]   "
θεωροῦντος   pres act ptcp gen sg masc
    [Ac 17:16; v-1d(2a); 2555]   "
θεωρούντων   pres act ptcp gen pl masc
    [Ac 28:6; v-1d(2a); 2555]   "
θεωροῦσαι   pres act ptcp nom pl fem
    [2t; v-1d(2a); 2555]   "
θεωροῦσιν   pres act ind 3 pl [3t; v-1d(2a); 2555] "
θεωρῶ   pres act ind 1 sg [4t; v-1d(2a); 2555]   "
θεωρῶν   pres act ptcp nom sg masc
    [4t; v-1d(2a); 2555]   "
θεωρῶσιν   pres act subj 3 pl
    [Jn 17:24; v-1d(2a); 2555]   "
θῇ   aor act subj 3 sg [2t; v-6a; 5502]   τίθημι

θήκη, ης, ἡ   {2557, n-1b}
a repository, receptacle; a case, sheath, scabbard,
John 18:11*

θήκην   acc sg fem [Jn 18:11; n-1b; 2557]   θήκη
θηλαζόντων   pres act ptcp gen pl masc
    [Mt 21:16; v-2a(1); 2558]   θηλάζω
θηλαζούσαις   pres act ptcp dat pl fem
    [3t; v-2a(1); 2558]   "

θηλάζω   {2558, v-2a(1)}
[-, ἐθήλασα, -, -, -] *to suckle, give suck,* Matt 24:19;
Mark 13:17; Luke 21:23; *to suck,* Matt 21:16;
Luke 11:27*

θήλειαι   nom pl fem [Rm 1:26; a-2b; 2559]   θῆλυς
θηλείας   gen sg fem [Rm 1:27; a-2b; 2559]   "
θῆλυ   nom sg neut [Ga 3:28; a-2b; 2559]   "
θῆλυ   acc sg neut [2t; a-2b; 2559]   "

θῆλυς, εια, υ   {2559, a-2b}
female; τὸ θῆλυ, sc. γένος, *a female,* Matt 19:4;
Mark 10:6; Gal 3:28; ἡ θήλεια, *woman,* Rom 1:26,
27*

θήρα, ας, ἡ   {2560, n-1a}
hunting, the chase; met. *means of capture, a cause
of destruction,* Rom 11:9*

θήραν   acc sg fem [Rm 11:9; n-1a; 2560]   θήρα
θηρεῦσαι   aor act inf
   [Lk 11:54; v-1a(6); 2561]   θηρεύω

θηρεύω   {2561, v-1a(6)}
[-, ἐθήρευσα, -, -, -] *to hunt, catch;* met. *to seize on,
lay hold of,* Luke 11:54*

θηρία   nom pl neut [Ti 1:12; n-2c; 2563]   θηρίον
θηρία   acc pl neut [Ac 11:6; n-2c; 2563]   "

θηριομαχέω   {2562, v-1d(2a)}
[-, ἐθηριομάχησα, -, -, -] *to fight with wild beasts;*
met. *to be exposed to furious hostility,* 1 Cor 15:32*

θηρίον, ου, τό   {2563, n-2c}
a beast, wild animal, Mark 1:13; Acts 10:12; met.
a brute, brutish man, Titus 1:12

θηρίον   nom sg neut [8t; n-2c; 2563]   "
θηρίον   acc sg neut [11t; n-2c; 2563]   "
θηρίου   gen sg neut [16t; n-2c; 2563]   "
θηρίῳ   dat sg neut [6t; n-2c; 2563]   "
θηρίων   gen pl neut [3t; n-2c; 2563]   "
θησαυρίζειν   pres act inf
   [2C 12:14; v-2a(1); 2564]   θησαυρίζω
θησαυρίζεις   pres act ind 2 sg
   [Rm 2:5; v-2a(1); 2564]   "
θησαυρίζετε   pres act imperative 2 pl
   [2t; v-2a(1); 2564]   "

θησαυρίζω   {2564, v-2a(1)}
[-, ἐθησαύρισα, -, τεθησαύρισμαι, -] *to collect and
lay up stores* or *wealth, treasure,* Matt 6:19, 20;
Luke 12:21; 2 Cor 12:14; James 5:3; *to heap up,
accumulate,* Rom 2:5; 1 Cor 16:2; *to reserve, keep
in store,* 2 Peter 3:7

θησαυρίζων   pres act ptcp nom sg masc
   [2t; v-2a(1); 2564]   "
θησαυροί   nom pl masc
   [Cl 2:3; n-2a; 2565]   θησαυρός
θησαυρόν   acc sg masc [5t; n-2a; 2565]   "

θησαυρός, οῦ, ὁ   {2565, n-2a}
a treasury, a store, treasure, precious deposit, Matt
6:19, 20, 21; *a receptacle in which precious articles
are kept, a casket,* Matt 2:11; *a storehouse,* Matt
12:35

θησαυρός   nom sg masc [2t; n-2a; 2565]   "
θησαυροῦ   gen sg masc [4t; n-2a; 2565]   "

θησαυρούς   acc pl masc [3t; n-2a; 2565]   "
θησαυρῷ   dat sg masc [Mt 13:44; n-2a; 2565]   "
θησαυρῶν   gen pl masc [Hb 11:26; n-2a; 2565]   "
θήσει   fut act ind 3 sg [2t; v-6a; 5502]   τίθημι
θήσεις   fut act ind 2 sg [Jn 13:38; v-6a; 5502]   "
θήσω   fut act ind 1 sg [3t; v-6a; 5502]   "
θήσω   aor act subj 1 sg [1C 9:18; v-6a; 5502]   "

θιγγάνω   {2566, v-3a(2b)}
[-, ἔθιγον, -, -, -] *to touch,* Col 2:21; Heb 12:20; *to
harm,* Heb 11:28*

θίγῃ   aor act subj 3 sg
   [2t; v-3a(2b); 2566]   θιγγάνω
θίγῃς   aor act subj 2 sg
   [Cl 2:21; v-3a(2b); 2566]   "
θλίβεσθαι   pres pass inf
   [1Th 3:4; v-1b(1); 2567]   θλίβω
θλιβόμεθα   pres pass ind 1 pl
   [2C 1:6; v-1b(1); 2567]   "
θλιβόμενοι   pres pass ptcp nom pl masc
   [3t; v-1b(1); 2567]   "
θλιβομένοις   pres pass ptcp dat pl masc
   [2t; v-1b(1); 2567]   "
θλίβουσιν   pres act ptcp dat pl masc
   [2Th 1:6; v-1b(1); 2567]   "

θλίβω   {2567, v-1b(1)}
[-, -, -, τέθλιμμαι, ἐθλίβην] *to squeeze, press; to
press upon, encumber, throng, crowd,* Mark 3:9;
met. *to distress, afflict,* 2 Cor 1:6; 4:8; pass. *to be
compressed, narrow,* Matt 7:14

θλίβωσιν   pres act subj 3 pl
   [Mk 3:9; v-1b(1); 2567]   "
θλίψει   dat sg fem [9t; n-3e(5b); 2568]   θλῖψις
θλίψεις   nom pl fem [Ac 20:23; n-3e(5b); 2568]   "
θλίψεσιν   dat pl fem [6t; n-3e(5b); 2568]   "
θλίψεων   gen pl fem [3t; n-3e(5b); 2568]   "
θλίψεως   gen sg fem [9t; n-3e(5b); 2568]   "
θλῖψιν   acc sg fem [10t; n-3e(5b); 2568]   "

θλῖψις, εως, ἡ   {2568, n-3e(5b)}
pr. *pressure, compression;* met. *affliction, distress
of mind,* 2 Cor 2:4; *distressing circumstances,
trial, affliction,* Matt 25:9

θλῖψις   nom sg fem [7t; n-3e(5b); 2568]   "

θνήσκω   {2569, v-5a; v-7}
[θανοῦμαι, ἔθανον, τέθνηκα, -, -] *to die;* in N.T. *to
be dead,* Matt 2:20; Mark 15:44

θνητά   acc pl neut
   [Rm 8:11; a-1a(2a); 2570]   θνητός
θνητῇ   dat sg fem [2C 4:11; a-1a(2a); 2570]   "
θνητόν   nom sg neut [2t; a-1a(2a); 2570]   "
θνητόν   acc sg neut [1C 15:53; a-1a(2a); 2570]   "

θνητός, ή, όν   {2570, a-1a(2a)}
mortal, subject to death, Rom 6:12; 8:11; 2 Cor
4:11; τὸ θνητόν, *mortality,* 1 Cor 15:53, 54; 2 Cor
5:4*

θνητῷ   dat sg neut [Rm 6:12; a-1a(2a); 2570]   "
θορυβάζῃ   pres pass ind 2 sg
   [Lk 10:41; v-2a(1); 2571]   θορυβάζω

θορυβάζω   {2571, v-2a(1)}
[-, -, -, -, -] *to be troubled, disturbed,* Luke 10:41*

θορυβεῖσθε pres pass imperative 2 pl
  [Ac 20:10; v-1d(2a); 2572]   θορυβέω
θορυβεῖσθε pres pass ind 2 pl
  [Mk 5:39; v-1d(2a); 2572]   "

θορυβέω   {2572, v-1d(2a)}
[(ἐθορύβουν), -, -, -, -, -] *to make a din, uproar;*
trans. *to disturb, throw into commotion,* Acts 17:5;
21:13 v.l.; in N.T. mid. *to manifest agitation of
mind, to raise a lament,* Matt 9:23; Mark 5:39;
Acts 20:10; Mark 13:7 v.l.*

θόρυβον acc sg masc [3t; n-2a; 2573]   θόρυβος

θόρυβος, ου, ὁ   {2573, n-2a}
*an uproar, din; an outward expression of mental
agitation, outcry,* Mark 5:38; *a tumult, commotion,*
Matt 26:5

θόρυβος nom sg masc [3t; n-2a; 2573]   "
θορύβου gen sg masc [Ac 24:18; n-2a; 2573]   "
θορυβούμενον pres pass ptcp acc sg masc
  [Mt 9:23; v-1d(2a); 2572]   θορυβέω

θραυματρίζω   {2574, v-2a(1)}
[-, -, -, -, -] *break,* Luke 4:18 v.l.*

θραύω   {2575, v-1a(5)}
[-, -, -, τέθραυσμαι, ἐθραύσθην] *to break, shiver;*
met., *shattered, crushed* by cruel oppression,
Luke 4:18*

θρέμμα, ατος, τό   {2576, n-3c(4)}
that which is reared (especially sheep and goats);
pl. *cattle,* John 4:12*

θρέμματα nom pl neut
  [Jn 4:12; n-3c(4); 2576]   θρέμμα

θρηνέω   {2577, v-1d(2a)}
[(ἐθρήνουν), θρηνήσω, ἐθρήνησα, -, -, -] *to lament,
bewail,* Matt 11:17; Luke 7:32; 23:27; John 16:20*

θρηνήσετε fut act ind 2 pl
  [Jn 16:20; v-1d(2a); 2577]   θρηνέω

θρῆνος, ου, ὁ   {2578, n-2a}
wailing, lamentation, dirge, Matt 2:18 v.l.*

θρησκεία, ας, ἡ   {2579, n-1a}
religious worship, Col 2:18; *religion, a religious
system,* Acts 26:5; *religion, piety,* James 1:26, 27*

θρησκεία nom sg fem [2t; n-1a; 2579]   θρησκεία
θρησκείᾳ dat sg fem [Cl 2:18; n-1a; 2579]   "
θρησκείας gen sg fem [Ac 26:5; n-1a; 2579]   "

θρησκός, όν   {2580, a-3a}
occupied with religious observances; in N.T.
religious, devout, pious, James 1:26*

θρησκός nom sg masc [Jm 1:26; a-3a; 2580] θρησκός
θριαμβεύοντι pres act ptcp dat sg masc
  [2C 2:14; v-1a(6); 2581]   θριαμβεύω
θριαμβεύσας aor act ptcp nom sg masc
  [Cl 2:15; v-1a(6); 2581]   "

θριαμβεύω   {2581, v-1a(6)}
[-, ἐθριάμβευσα, -, -, -] pr. *to celebrate a triumph;*
trans. *to lead in triumph, celebrate a triumph over,*

Col 2:15; in N.T. *to cause to triumph,* or, *to render
conspicuous,* 2 Cor 2:14*

θρίξ, τριχός, ἡ   {2582, n-3b(3)}
a hair; the hair of the head, Matt 5:36; 10:30; of an
animal, Matt 3:4; Mark 1:6

θρίξ nom sg fem [2t; n-3b(3); 2582]   θρίξ
θριξίν dat pl fem [4t; n-3b(3); 2582]   "
θροεῖσθαι pres pass inf
  [2Th 2:2; v-1d(2a); 2583]   θροέω
θροεῖσθε pres pass imperative 2 pl
  [2t; v-1d(2a); 2583]   "

θροέω   {2583, v-1d(2a)}
[-, -, -, -, ἐθροήθην] *to cry aloud;* in N.T. pass., *to
be disturbed, disquieted, alarmed, terrified,* Matt
24:6; Mark 13:7; 2 Thess 2:2; Luke 24:37 v.l.*

θρόμβοι nom pl masc
  [Lk 22:44; n-2a; 2584]   θρόμβος

θρόμβος, ου, ὁ   {2584, n-2a}
a lump; espec. *a clot* of blood, *drop,* Luke 22:44*

θρόνοι nom pl masc [Cl 1:16; n-2a; 2585]   θρόνος
θρόνον acc sg masc [7t; n-2a; 2585]   "

θρόνος, ου, ὁ   {2585, n-2a}
a seat, a throne, Matt 5:34; 19:28; Luke 1:52;
meton. *power, dominion,* Luke 1:32; Heb 1:8; *a
potentate,* Col 1:16

θρόνος nom sg masc [6t; n-2a; 2585]   "
θρόνου gen sg masc [32t; n-2a; 2585]   "
θρόνους acc pl masc [5t; n-2a; 2585]   "
θρόνῳ dat sg masc [9t; n-2a; 2585]   "
θρόνων gen pl masc [2t; n-2a; 2585]   "

θρύπτω   {2586, v-4}
[-, -, -, -, -] *break in pieces,* 1 Cor 11:24 v.l.*

Θυάτειρα, ων, τά   {2587, n-2c}
Thyatira, a city of Lydia, Acts 16:14; Rev 1:11;
2:18, 24*

Θυάτειρα acc pl neut
  [Rv 1:11; n-2c; 2587]   Θυάτειρα
Θυατείροις dat pl neut [2t; n-2c; 2587]   "
Θυατείρων gen pl neut [Ac 16:14; n-2c; 2587] "
θύγατερ voc sg fem
  [Mt 9:22; n-3f(2c); 2588]   θυγάτηρ
θυγατέρα acc sg fem [4t; n-3f(2c); 2588]   "
θυγατέρας acc pl fem [2C 6:18; n-3f(2c); 2588] "
θυγατέρες nom pl fem [2t; n-3f(2c); 2588]   "
θυγατέρες voc pl fem [Lk 23:28; n-3f(2c); 2588] "
θυγατέρων gen pl fem [Lk 1:5; n-3f(2c); 2588] "

θυγάτηρ, θυγατρός, ἡ   {2588, n-3f(2c)}
a daughter, Matt 9:18; 10:35, 37; in the vocative,
an expression of affection and kindness, Matt
9:22; from the Hebrew, *one of the female posterity*
of any one, Luke 1:5; met. *a city,* Matt 21:5; John
12:15; pl. *female inhabitants,* Luke 23:28

θυγάτηρ nom sg fem [13t; n-3f(2c); 2588]   "
θυγατρί dat sg fem [Mt 21:5; n-3f(2c); 2588] "

θυγάτριον, ου, τό   {2589, n-2c}
a little daughter, female child, Mark 5:23; 7:25*

θυγάτριον nom sg neut [2t; n-2c; 2589] θυγάτριον

θυγατρός   gen sg fem [4t; n-3f(2c); 2588]   θυγάτηρ
θύειν   pres act inf [2t; v-1a(4); 2604]   θύω

θύελλα, ης, ἡ   {2590, n-1c}
   a tempest, whirlwind, hurricane, Heb 12:18*

θυέλλῃ   dat sg fem [Hb 12:18; n-1c; 2590]   θύελλα
θύεσθαι   pres pass inf
   [Lk 22:7; v-1a(4); 2604]   θύω
θύϊνον   acc sg neut
   [Rv 18:12; a-1a(2a); 2591]

θύϊνος, η, ον   {2591, a-1a(2a)}
   thyme, of θυΐα, *thya,* an aromatic evergreen tree,
   arbor vitae, resembling the cedar, and found in
   Libya, Rev 18:12*

θυμίαμα, ατος, τό   {2592, n-3c(4)}
   *incense, any odoriferous substance burnt in
   religious worship,* Rev 5:8; 8:3, 4; 18:13; or, *the act
   of burning incense,* Luke 1:10, 11*

θυμιάματα   nom pl neut
   [Rv 8:3; n-3c(4); 2592]   θυμίαμα
θυμιάματα   acc pl neut [Rv 18:13; n-3c(4); 2592]   "
θυμιάματος   gen sg neut [2t; n-3c(4); 2592]   "
θυμιαμάτων   gen pl neut [2t; n-3c(4); 2592]   "
θυμιᾶσαι   aor act inf
   [Lk 1:9; v-1d(1b); 2594]   θυμιάω

θυμιατήριον   {2593, n-2c}
   an altar of burning incense, Heb 9:4*

θυμιατήριον   acc sg neut
   [Hb 9:4; n-2c; 2593]   θυμιατήριον

θυμιάω   {2594, v-1d(1b)}
   [-, ἐθυμίασα, -, -, -] *to burn incense,* Luke 1:9*

θυμοί   nom pl masc [2t; n-2a; 2596]   θυμός

θυμομαχέω   {2595, v-1d(2a)}
   [-, -, -, -, -] *to wage war fiercely; to be warmly
   hostile to, be enraged against,* Acts 12:20*

θυμομαχῶν   pres act ptcp nom sg masc
   [Ac 12:20; v-1d(2a); 2595]   θυμομαχέω
θυμόν   acc sg masc [3t; n-2a; 2596]   θυμός

θυμός, οῦ, ὁ   {2596, n-2a}
   pr. *the soul, mind;* hence, *a strong passion* or
   emotion of the mind; anger, wrath, Luke 4:28; Acts
   19:28; pl. *swellings of anger,* 2 Cor 12:20; Gal 5:20

θυμός   nom sg masc [3t; n-2a; 2596]   "
θυμοῦ   gen sg masc [10t; n-2a; 2596]   "

θυμόω   {2597, v-1d(3)}
   [-, -, -, -, ἐθυμώθην] *to provoke to anger;* pass. *to
   be angered, enraged,* Matt 2:16*

θύουσιν   pres act ind 3 pl [2t; v-1a(4); 2604]   θύω

θύρα, ας, ἡ   {2598, n-1a}
   a door, gate, Matt 6:6; Mark 1:33; *an entrance,*
   Matt 27:60; in N.T. met. *an opening, occasion,
   opportunity,* Acts 14:27; 1 Cor 16:9; meton. *a
   medium* or *means of entrance,* John 10:7, 9

θύρα   nom sg fem [6t; n-1a; 2598]   θύρα
θύρᾳ   dat sg fem [3t; n-1a; 2598]   "
θύραι   nom pl fem [2t; n-1a; 2598]   "
θύραις   dat pl fem [2t; n-1a; 2598]   "

θύραν   acc sg fem [14t; n-1a; 2598]   "
θύρας   gen sg fem [6t; n-1a; 2598]   "
θύρας   acc pl fem [2t; n-1a; 2598]   "
θυρεόν   acc sg masc [Ep 6:16; n-2a; 2599]   θυρεός

θυρεός, οῦ, ὁ   {2599, n-2a}
   a stone or *other material employed to close a
   doorway;* later, *a large oblong shield,* Eph 6:16*

θυρίδος   gen sg fem [2t; n-3c(2); 2600]   θυρίς

θυρίς, ίδος, ἡ   {2600, n-3c(2)}
   a small opening; a window, Acts 20:9; 2 Cor 11:33*

θυρῶν   gen pl fem [4t; n-1a; 2598]   θύρα

θυρωρός, οῦ, ὁ   {2601, n-2a}
   a door-keeper, porter, Mark 13:34; John 10:3;
   18:16, 17*

θυρωρός   nom sg masc [Jn 10:3; n-2a; 2601]   θυρωρός
θυρωρός   nom sg fem [Jn 18:17; n-2a; 2601]   "
θυρωρῷ   dat sg masc [Mk 13:34; n-2a; 2601]   "
θυρωρῷ   dat sg fem [Jn 18:16; n-2a; 2601]   "
θύσατε   aor act imperative 2 pl
   [Lk 15:23; v-1a(4); 2604]   θύω
θύσῃ   aor act subj 3 sg
   [Jn 10:10; v-1a(4); 2604]   "

θυσία, ας, ἡ   {2602, n-1a}
   sacrifice, the act of sacrificing, Heb 9:26; *the thing
   sacrificed, a victim,* Matt 9:13; 12:7; *the flesh of
   victims* eaten by the sacrificers, 1 Cor 10:18; in
   N.T. *an offering* or *service* to God, Phil 4:18

θυσία   nom sg fem [Hb 10:26; n-1a; 2602]   θυσία
θυσίᾳ   dat sg fem [Pp 2:17; n-1a; 2602]   "
θυσίαι   nom pl fem [Hb 9:9; n-1a; 2602]   "
θυσίαις   dat pl fem [3t; n-1a; 2602]   "
θυσίαν   acc sg fem [11t; n-1a; 2602]   "
θυσίας   gen sg fem [Hb 9:26; n-1a; 2602]   "
θυσίας   acc pl fem [8t; n-1a; 2602]   "
θυσιαστήρια   acc pl neut
   [Rm 11:3; n-2c; 2603]   θυσιαστήριον

θυσιαστήριον, ου, τό   {2603, n-2c}
   an altar, Matt 5:23, 24; Luke 1:11; spc. *the altar of
   burn-offering,* Matt 23:35; Luke 11:51; meton. *a
   class of sacrifices,* Heb 13:10

θυσιαστήριον   nom sg neut [Mt 23:19; n-2c; 2603]   "
θυσιαστήριον   acc sg neut [5t; n-2c; 2603]   "
θυσιαστηρίου   gen sg neut [11t; n-2c; 2603] "
θυσιαστηρίῳ   dat sg neut [5t; n-2c; 2603]   "
θυσιῶν   gen pl fem [2t; n-1a; 2602]   θυσία
θῦσον   aor act imperative 2 sg
   [2t; v-1a(4); 2604]   θύω

θύω   {2604, v-1a(4)}
   [(ἔθυον), -, ἔθυσα, -, τέθυμαι, ἐτύθην] *to offer; to
   kill in sacrifice, sacrifice, immolate,* Acts 14:13, 18;
   in N.T. *to slaughter* for food, Matt 22:4

θῶ   aor act subj 1 sg [5t; v-6a; 5502]   τίθημι
Θωμᾷ   dat sg masc [Jn 20:27; n-1e; 2605]   Θωμᾶς
Θωμᾶν   acc sg masc [2t; n-1e; 2605]   "

Θωμᾶς, ᾶ, ὁ   {2605, n-1e}
   Thomas, pr. name, Matt 10:3; Mark 3:18; Luke

6:15; John 11:16; 14:5; 20:24, 26, 27, 28; 21:2; Acts 1:13*

Θωμᾶς   nom sg masc [8t; n-1e; 2605]   "
θῶμεν   aor act subj 1 pl
    [Mk 4:30; v-6a; 5502]   τίθημι
θώρακα   acc sg masc [2t; n-3b(1); 2606]   θώραξ
θώραξ, ακός, ὁ   {2606, n-3b(1)}
    a breast-plate, armor for the body, consisting of
    two parts, one covering the breast and the
    other the back, Rev 9:9, 17; Eph 6:14; 1 Thess
    5:8*

θώρακας   acc pl masc [2t; n-3b(1); 2606]   "

ι

ἰαθείς   aor pass ptcp nom sg masc
    [Jn 5:13; v-1d(1b); 2615]   ἰάομαι
ἰάθη   aor pass ind 3 sg [4t; v-1d(1b); 2615]   "
ἰαθῇ   aor pass subj 3 sg
    [Hb 12:13; v-1d(1b); 2615]   "
ἰαθῆναι   aor pass inf [Lk 6:18; v-1d(1b); 2615]   "
ἰαθήσεται   fut pass ind 3 sg
    [Mt 8:8; v-1d(1b); 2615]   "
ἰάθητε   aor pass ind 2 pl
    [1P 2:24; v-1d(1b); 2615]   "
ἰαθῆτε   aor pass subj 2 pl
    [Jm 5:16; v-1d(1b); 2615]   "
ἰαθήτω   aor pass imperative 3 sg
    [Lk 7:7; v-1d(1b); 2615]   "

Ἰάϊρος, ου, ὁ   {2608, n-2a}
    also spelled Ἰάειρος, *Jairus,* pr. name, Mark
    5:22; Luke 8:41*

Ἰάϊρος   nom sg masc [2t; n-2a; 2608]   Ἰάϊρος

Ἰακώβ, ὁ   {2609, n-3g(2)}
    Jacob, pr. name, indecl. (1) *Son of Issac,* Matt 1:2.
    (2) *Father of Joseph, Mary's husband,* Matt 1:15, 16

Ἰακώβ   indecl [27t; n-3g(2); 2609]   Ἰακώβ
Ἰάκωβον   acc sg masc [16t; n-2a; 2610]   Ἰάκωβος

Ἰάκωβος, ου, ὁ   {2610, n-2a}
    James, pr. name (1) *Son of Zebedee,* Matt 4:21. (2)
    Son of Alphaeus and Mary, brother of Jude, Matt
    10:3. (3) *James the less, brother of Jesus,* Gal 1:19

Ἰάκωβος   nom sg masc [11t; n-2a; 2610]   "
Ἰακώβου   gen sg masc [13t; n-2a; 2610]   "
Ἰακώβῳ   dat sg masc [2t; n-2a; 2610]   "

ἴαμα, ατος, τό   {2611, n-3c(4)}
    healing, cure, 1 Cor 12:9, 28, 30*

ἰαμάτων   gen pl neut [3t; n-3c(4); 2611]   ἴαμα

Ἰαμβρῆς, ου, ὁ   {2612, n-1f}
    Jambres, pr. name, 2 Tim 3:8*

Ἰαμβρῆς   nom sg masc
    [2Ti 3:8; n-1f; 2612]   Ἰαμβρῆς

Ἰανναί, ὁ   {2613, n-3g(2)}
    Jannai, pr. name, indecl., Luke 3:24*

Ἰανναί   indecl [Lk 3:24; n-3g(2); 2613]   Ἰανναί

Ἰάννης, ου, ὁ   {2614, n-1f}
    Jannes, pr. name, 2 Tim 3:8*

Ἰάννης   nom sg masc [2Ti 3:8; n-1f; 2614]   Ἰάννης

ἰάομαι   {2615, v-1d(1b)}
    [(ἰώμην), ἰάσομαι, ἰασάμην, -, ἴαμαι, ἰάθην] *to*
    heal, cure, Matt 8:8; Luke 9:2; met. *to heal,*
    spiritually, *restore from a state of sin and*
    condemnation, Matt 13:15; Heb 12:13

Ἰάρετ, ὁ   {2616, n-3g(2)}
    Jared, pr. name, indecl., Luke 3:37*

Ἰάρετ   indecl [Lk 3:37; n-3g(2); 2616]   Ἰάρετ
ἰάσατο   aor mid ind 3 sg
    [4t; v-1d(1b); 2615]   ἰάομαι
ἰάσεις   acc pl fem
    [Lk 13:32; n-3e(5b); 2617]   ἴασις
ἰάσεως   gen sg fem [Ac 4:22; n-3e(5b); 2617]   "
ἰάσηται   aor mid subj 3 sg
    [Jn 4:47; v-1d(1b); 2615]   ἰάομαι
ἰᾶσθαι   pres mid inf [2t; v-1d(1b); 2615]   "
ἴασιν   acc sg fem [Ac 4:30; n-3e(5b); 2617]   ἴασις

ἴασις, εως, ἡ   {2617, n-3e(5b)}
    healing, cure, Luke 13:32; Acts 4:22, 30*

ἰάσομαι   fut mid ind 1 sg
    [3t; v-1d(1b); 2615]   ἰάομαι
Ἰάσονα   acc sg masc
    [Ac 17:6; n-3f(1b); 2619]   Ἰάσων
Ἰάσονος   gen sg masc [2t; n-3f(1b); 2619]   "
ἰάσπιδι   dat sg fem [2t; n-3c(2); 2618]   ἴασπις

ἴασπις, ιδος, ἡ   {2618, n-3c(2)}
    jasper, a precious stone of various colors, as
    purple, cerulian green, etc. Rev 4:3; 21:11, 18,
    19*

ἴασπις   nom sg fem [2t; n-3c(2); 2618]   "

Ἰάσων, ονος, ὁ   {2619, n-3f(1b)}
    Jason, pr. name, Acts 17:5-7, 9; 21:16 v.l.; Rom
    16:21*

Ἰάσων   nom sg masc [2t; n-3f(1b); 2619]   Ἰάσων
ἴαται   perf pass ind 3 sg
    [Mk 5:29; v-1d(1b); 2615]   ἰάομαι
ἰᾶται   pres mid ind 3 sg
    [Ac 9:34; v-1d(1b); 2615]   "
ἰᾶτο   imperf mid ind 3 sg [2t; v-1d(1b); 2615]   "
ἰατρέ   voc sg masc [Lk 4:23; n-2a; 2620]   ἰατρός
ἰατροῖς   dat pl masc [Lk 8:43; n-2a; 2620]   "

ἰατρός, οῦ, ὁ   {2620, n-2a}
    physician, Matt 9:12; Mark 2:17; 5:26; Luke 4:23;
    5:31; 8:43 v.l.; Col 4:14*

ἰατρός   nom sg masc [Cl 4:14; n-2a; 2620]   "
ἰατροῦ   gen sg masc [3t; n-2a; 2620]   "
ἰατρῶν   gen pl masc [Mk 5:26; n-2a; 2620]   "

Ἰαχίν, ὁ   {2621, n-3g(2)}
    Jachin, indecl., Luke 3:23ff. v.l.*

ιβ'   {2622}
    twelve, v.l. in Rev 7:5 (3t), 6 (3t), 7 (3t), 8 (3t).
    Our text has δώδεκα.

ἴδε   {2623, particle}
the imperative of εἶδον used as a particle, *Lo!*
Behold! John 16:29; 19:4, 5

ἴδε   particle [34t; part; 2623]   ἴδε

ἰδέα, ας, ἡ   {2624, n-1a}
form; look, aspect, Luke 9:29 v.l.*

ἰδεῖν   aor act inf [38t; v-1d(1a); 3972]   ὁράω
ἴδετε   aor act imperative 2 pl
[9t; v-1d(1a); 3972]   "
ἴδῃ   aor act subj 3 sg [5t; v-1d(1a); 3972]   "
ἴδῃς   aor act subj 2 sg
[Jn 1:33; v-1d(1a); 3972]   "
ἴδητε   aor act subj 2 pl [12t; v-1d(1a); 3972]   "
ἴδια   nom pl neut [Jn 10:12; a-1a(1); 2625]   ἴδιος
ἰδίᾳ   dat sg fem [12t; a-1a(1); 2625]   "
ἴδια   acc pl neut [8t; a-1a(1); 2625]   "
ἰδίαις dat pl fem [3t; a-1a(1); 2625]   "
ἰδίαν   acc sg fem [24t; a-1a(1); 2625]   "
ἰδίας   gen sg fem [4t; a-1a(1); 2625]   "
ἰδίας   acc pl fem [2t; a-1a(1); 2625]   "
ἴδιοι   nom pl masc [Jn 1:11; a-1a(1); 2625]   "
ἰδίοις dat pl masc [9t; a-1a(1); 2625]   "
ἰδίοις dat pl neut [1C 9:7; a-1a(1); 2625]   "
ἴδιον   acc sg masc [8t; a-1a(1); 2625]   "
ἴδιον   acc sg neut [10t; a-1a(1); 2625]   "

ἴδιος, ία, ιον   {2625, a-1a(1)}
one's own, Mark 15:20; John 7:18; *due, proper,*
specially assigned, Gal 6:9; 1 Tim 2:6; 6:15; Titus
1:3; also used in N.T. as a simple possessive,
Eph 5:22; τὰ ἴδια, *one's home, household, people,*
John 1:11; 16:32; 19:17, οἱ ἴδιοι, *members of one's*
own household, friends, John 1:11; Acts 24:23;
ἰδίᾳ, adverbially, *respectively,* 1 Cor 12:11; κατ'
ἰδίαν, adv., *privately, aside, by one's self, alone,*
Matt 14:13, 23

ἴδιος   nom sg masc [Ti 1:12; a-1a(1); 2625]   "
ἰδίου   gen sg masc [5t; a-1a(1); 2625]   "
ἰδίου   gen sg neut [6t; a-1a(1); 2625]   "
ἰδίους acc pl masc [5t; a-1a(1); 2625]   "
ἰδίῳ   dat sg masc [4t; a-1a(1); 2625]   "
ἰδίῳ   dat sg neut [3t; a-1a(1); 2625]   "
ἰδίων   gen pl masc [4t; a-1a(1); 2625]   "
ἰδίων   gen pl fem [Hb 7:27; a-1a(1); 2625]   "
ἰδίων   gen pl neut [2t; a-1a(1); 2625]   "
ἰδιῶται nom pl masc [2t; n-1f; 2626]   ἰδιώτης

ἰδιώτης, ου, ὁ   {2626, n-1f}
pr. *one in private life, one devoid of special learning*
or *gifts, a plain person,* Acts 4:13; 2 Cor 11:6;
ungifted, 1 Cor 14:16, 23, 24*

ἰδιώτης nom sg masc [2t; n-1f; 2626]   "
ἰδιώτου gen sg masc [1C 14:16; n-1f; 2626]   "
ἰδόντες aor act ptcp nom pl masc
[41t; v-1d(1a); 3972]   ὁράω

ἰδού   {2627}
aorist middle imperative of εἶδον used as an
intj, *Look! See! Lo!* Matt 1:23; Luke 1:38; Acts
8:36

ἰδού   interjection [200t; interj; 2627]   ἰδού

Ἰδουμαία, ας, ἡ   {2628, n-1a}
Idumaea, a country south of Judea, Mark 3:8;
Acts 2:9 v.l.*

Ἰδουμαίας gen sg fem
[Mk 3:8; n-1a; 2628]   Ἰδουμαία
ἰδοῦσα   aor act ptcp nom sg fem
[6t; v-1d(1a); 3972]   ὁράω

ἱδρώς, ῶτος, ὁ   {2629, n-3c(1)}
sweat, Luke 22:44*

ἱδρώς   nom sg masc
[Lk 22:44; n-3c(1); 2629]   ἱδρώς
ἴδω   aor act subj 1 sg [3t; v-1d(1a); 3972]   ὁράω
ἴδωμεν aor act subj 1 pl [5t; v-1d(1a); 3972]   "
ἰδών   aor act ptcp nom sg masc
[61t; v-1d(1a); 3972]   "
ἴδωσιν aor act subj 3 pl [9t; v-1d(1a); 3972]   "

Ἰεζάβελ, ἡ   {2630, n-3g(2)}
Jezebel, (1 Kgs 16:31), pr. name, indecl., Rev
2:20*

Ἰεζάβελ indecl [Rv 2:20; n-3g(2); 2630]   Ἰεζάβελ
ἱερά   acc pl neut [2t; a-1a(1); 2641]   ἱερός
Ἱεραπόλει dat sg fem
[Cl 4:13; n-3e(5b); 2631]   Ἱεράπολις

Ἱεράπολις, εως, ἡ   {2631, n-3e(5b)}
Hierapolis, a city of Phrygia, Col 4:13*

ἱερατεία, ας, ἡ   {2632, n-1a}
priesthood, sacerdotal office, Luke 1:9; Heb 7:5;
Rev 5:10 v.l.*

ἱερατείαν acc sg fem
[Hb 7:5; n-1a; 2632]   ἱερατεία
ἱερατείας gen sg fem [Lk 1:9; n-1a; 2632]   "
ἱερατεύειν pres act inf
[Lk 1:8; v-1a(6); 2634]   ἱερατεύω

ἱεράτευμα, ατος, τό   {2633, n-3c(4)}
a priesthood; meton. *a body of priests,* 1 Peter 2:5,
9*

ἱεράτευμα nom sg neut
[1P 2:9; n-3c(4); 2633]   ἱεράτευμα
ἱεράτευμα acc sg neut [1P 2:5; n-3c(4); 2633]   "

ἱερατεύω   {2634, v-1a(6)}
[-, -, -, -, -] *to officiate as a priest, perform sacred*
rites, Luke 1:8*

ἱερέα   acc sg masc [2t; n-3e(3); 2636]   ἱερεύς
ἱερεῖ   dat sg masc [3t; n-3e(3); 2636]   "
ἱερεῖς nom pl masc [6t; n-3e(3); 2636]   "
ἱερεῖς acc pl masc [5t; n-3e(3); 2636]   "
Ἱερεμίαν acc sg masc
[Mt 16:14; n-1d; 2635]   Ἱερεμίας

Ἱερεμίας, ου, ὁ   {2635, n-1d}
Jeremiah, pr. name, Matt 2:17; 16:14; 27:9*

Ἱερεμίου gen sg masc [2t; n-1d; 2635]   "

ἱερεύς, έως, ὁ   {2636, n-3e(3)}
a priest, one who performs sacrificial rites, Matt
8:4; Luke 1:5; John 1:19

ἱερεύς nom sg masc [11t; n-3e(3); 2636]   ἱερεύς
ἱερεῦσιν dat pl masc [2t; n-3e(3); 2636]   "

ἱερέων   gen pl masc   [2t; n-3e(3); 2636]   "

Ἰεριχώ, ἡ   {2637, n-3g(2)}
Jericho, a city of Palestine, Matt 20:29; Mark
10:46; Luke 10:30; 18:35; 19:1; Heb 11:30*

Ἰεριχώ   indecl   [7t; n-3g(2); 2637]   Ἰεριχώ
ἱερόθυτον   nom sg neut
  [1C 10:28; a-3a; 2638]   ἱερόθυτος

ἱερόθυτος, ον   {2638, a-3a}
offered in sacrifice, 1 Cor 10:28*

ἱερόν, οῦ, τό   {2639, n-2c}
temple, sanctuary, Matt 4:5; Luke 4:9; Acts 19:27

ἱερόν   acc sg neut   [21t; n-2c; 2639]   ἱερόν
ἱεροπρεπεῖς   acc pl fem
  [Ti 2:3; a-4a; 2640]   ἱεροπρεπής

ἱεροπρεπής, ές   {2640, a-4a}
*befitting what is sacred, holy; becoming holy
persons, worthy of honor,* Titus 2:3*

ἱερός, ά, όν   {2641, a-1a(1)}
holy, divine, set apart, 2 Tim 3:15; Col 4:13 v.l.; τὰ
ἱερά, *sacred rites,* 1 Cor 9:13 (2t), the shorter
ending of Mark (16:8)*

Ἰεροσόλυμα, ατος, τά and **ἡ**   {2642, n-1a}
Jerusalem, also spelled Ἰερουσαλήμ and
Ἰερουσαλήμ, Matt 2:3; Mark 3:8; Rev 21:2

Ἰεροσόλυμα   nom sg fem
  [Mt 2:3; n-1a; 2642]   Ἰεροσόλυμα
Ἰεροσόλυμα   nom pl neut [Mt 3:5; n-1a; 2642]   "
Ἰεροσόλυμα   acc pl neut [35t; n-1a; 2642]   "
Ἰεροσολυμῖται   nom pl masc
  [Mk 1:5; n-1f; 2643]   Ἰεροσολυμίτης

Ἰεροσολυμίτης, ου, ὁ   {2643, n-1f}
a native of Jerusalem, Mark 1:5; John 7:25*

Ἰεροσολυμιτῶν   gen pl masc [Jn 7:25; n-1f; 2643]   "
Ἰεροσολύμοις   dat pl neut
  [14t; n-1a; 2642]   Ἰεροσόλυμα
Ἰεροσολύμων   gen pl neut [11t; n-1a; 2642]   "
ἱεροσυλεῖς   pres act ind 2 sg
  [Rm 2:22; v-1d(2a); 2644]   ἱεροσυλέω

ἱεροσυλέω   {2644, v-1d(2a)}
[-, -, -, -, -] *to despoil temples, commit sacrilege,*
Rom 2:22*

ἱερόσυλος, ου, ὁ   {2645, n-2a}
one who despoils temples, commits sacrilege, Acts
19:37*

ἱεροσύλους   acc pl masc
  [Ac 19:37; n-2a; 2645]   ἱερόσυλος
ἱεροῦ   gen sg neut   [19t; n-2c; 2639]   ἱερόν

ἱερουργέω   {2646, cv-1d(2a)}
[-, -, -, -, -] *to officiate as priest, perform sacred rites;*
in N.T. *to minister* in a divine commission, Rom
15:16*

ἱερουργοῦντα   pres act ptcp acc sg masc
  [Rm 15:16; cv-1d(2a); 2646]   ἱερουργέω

Ἰερουσαλήμ   {2647, n-3g(2)}
Jerusalem, pr. name, indecl., see Ἰεροσόλυμα

Ἰερουσαλήμ   indecl [77t; n-3g(2); 2647] Ἰερουσαλήμ

ἱερῷ   dat sg neut   [32t; n-2c; 2639]   ἱερόν

ἱερωσύνη, ης, ἡ   {2648, n-1b}
a priesthood, sacerdotal office, Heb 7:11, 12, 24*

ἱερωσύνην   acc sg fem
  [Hb 7:24; n-1b; 2648]   ἱερωσύνη
ἱερωσύνης   gen sg fem   [2t; n-1b; 2648]   "

Ἰεσσαί, ὁ   {2649, n-3g(2)}
Jesse, father of David (1 Sam 16), pr. name,
indecl., Matt 1:5f.; Luke 3:32; Acts 13:22; Rom
15:12*

Ἰεσσαί   indecl [5t; n-3g(2); 2649]   Ἰεσσαί

Ἰεφθάε, ὁ   {2650, n-3g(2)}
Jephthah, (Judges 11f.), pr. name, indecl., Heb
11:32*

Ἰεφθάε   indecl [Hb 11:32; n-3g(2); 2650]   Ἰεφθάε
Ἰεχονίαν   acc sg masc
  [Mt 1:11; n-1d; 2651]   Ἰεχονίας

Ἰεχονίας, ου, ὁ   {2651, n-1d}
Jechoniah, pr. name, Matt 1:11, 12; Luke 3:23ff.*

Ἰεχονίας   nom sg masc [Mt 1:12; n-1d; 2651]   "
Ἰησοῦ   voc sg masc [10t; n-3g(1); 2652]   Ἰησοῦς
Ἰησοῦ   gen sg masc [225t; n-3g(1); 2652]   "
*Ἰησοῦ   dat sg masc [93t; n-3g(1); 2652]   "
Ἰησοῦν   acc sg masc [127t; n-3g(1); 2652]   "

Ἰησοῦς, οῦ, ὁ   {2652, n-3g(1)}
a Savior, Jesus, Matt 1:21, 25; 2:1, et al. freq.;
Joshua, Acts 7:45; Heb 4:8; *Jesus,* a Jewish
Christian, Col 4:11

Ἰησοῦς   nom sg masc [462t; n-3g(1); 2652]   "
ἱκανά   acc pl neut
  [Mt 28:12; a-1a(2a); 2653]   ἱκανός
ἱκαναί   nom pl fem [2t; a-1a(2a); 2653]   "
ἱκαναῖς   dat pl fem [Ac 27:7; a-1a(2a); 2653] "
ἱκανάς   acc pl fem [2t; a-1a(2a); 2653]   "
ἱκανοί   nom pl masc [5t; a-1a(2a); 2653]   "
ἱκανοῖς   dat pl masc [Lk 23:9; a-1a(2a); 2653] "
ἱκανόν   nom sg neut [2t; a-1a(2a); 2653]   "
ἱκανόν   acc sg masc [4t; a-1a(2a); 2653]   "
ἱκανόν   acc sg neut [3t; a-1a(2a); 2653]   "

ἱκανός, ή, όν   {2653, a-1a(2a)}
befitting; sufficient, enough, Luke 22:38; ἱκανὸν
ποιεῖν τινι, *to satisfy, gratify,* Mark 15:15; τὸ
ἱκανὸν λαμβάνειν, *to take security* or *bail* of any
one, Acts 17:9; or persons, *adequate, competent,
qualified,* 2 Cor 2:16; *fit, worthy,* Matt 3:11; 8:8; of
number or quantity, *considerable, large, great,
much,* and pl. *many,* Matt 28:12; Mark 10:46

ἱκανός   nom sg masc [10t; a-1a(2a); 2653]   "

ἱκανότης, ητος, ἡ   {2654, n-3c(1)}
sufficiency, ability, fitness, qualification, 2 Cor 3:5*

ἱκανότης   nom sg fem
  [2C 3:5; n-3c(1); 2654]   ἱκανότης
ἱκανοῦ   gen sg masc [2t; a-1a(2a); 2653]   ἱκανός
ἱκανούς   acc pl masc [2t; a-1a(2a); 2653]   "

ἱκανόω   {2655, v-1d(3)}
[-, ἱκάνωσα, -, -, -] *to make sufficient* or *competent,
qualify,* 2 Cor 3:6; Col 1:12*

ἱκανῷ   dat sg masc [2t; a-1a(2a); 2653]   "
ἱκανῶν   gen pl masc [2t; a-1a(2a); 2653]   "
ἱκανώσαντι   aor act ptcp dat sg masc
     [Cl 1:12; v-1d(3); 2655]   ἱκανόω
ἱκάνωσεν   aor act ind 3 sg
     [2C 3:6; v-1d(3); 2655]   "

ἱκετηρία, ας, ἡ   {2656, n-1a}
   pr. *an olive branch* borne by suppliants in their
   hands; *prayer, supplication*, Heb 5:7*

ἱκετηρίας   acc pl fem
     [Hb 5:7; n-1a; 2656]   ἱκετηρία
ἱκμάδα   acc sg fem [Lk 8:6; n-3c(2); 2657]   ἱκμάς

ἱκμάς, άδος, ἡ   {2657, n-3c(2)}
   moisture, Luke 8:6*

Ἰκόνιον, ου, τό   {2658, n-2c}
   Iconium, a city of Lycaonia, in Asia Minor, Acts
   13:51; 14:1, 19, 21; 16:2; 2 Tim 3:11*

Ἰκόνιον   acc sg neut [2t; n-2c; 2658]   Ἰκόνιον
Ἰκονίου   gen sg neut [Ac 14:19; n-2c; 2658]   "
Ἰκονίῳ   dat sg neut [3t; n-2c; 2658]   "
ἱλαρόν   acc sg masc
     [2C 9:7; a-1a(1); 2659]   ἱλαρός

ἱλαρός, ά, όν   {2659, a-1a(1)}
   cheerful, not grudging, 2 Cor 9:7*

ἱλαρότης, ητος, ἡ   {2660, n-3c(1)}
   cheerfulness, graciousness, Rom 12:8*

ἱλαρότητι   dat sg fem
     [Rm 12:8; n-3c(1); 2660]   ἱλαρότης
ἱλάσθητι   aor pass imperative 2 sg
     [Lk 18:13; v-5a; 2661]   ἱλάσκομαι
ἱλάσκεσθαι   pres mid inf [Hb 2:17; v-5a; 2661]   "

ἱλάσκομαι   {2661, v-5a}
   [ἱλάσομαι, ἱλασάμην -, -, ἱλάσθην] *to appease,*
   render propitious; in N.T. *to expiate, make an*
   atonement or *expiation for*, Heb 2:17; ἱλάσθητι, *be*
   gracious, show mercy, pardon, Luke 18:13*

ἱλασμόν   acc sg masc
     [1J 4:10; n-2a; 2662]   ἱλασμός

ἱλασμός, οῦ, ὁ   {2662, n-2a}
   atoning sacrifice, sin offering, propitiation,
   expiation; one who makes propitiation/expiation, 1
   John 2:2; 4:10*

ἱλασμός   nom sg masc [1J 2:2; n-2a; 2662]   "

ἱλαστήριον, ου, τό   {2663, n-2c}
   the cover of the ark of the covenant, the mercy-seat,
   the place of propitiation, Rom 3:25; Heb 9:5*

ἱλαστήριον   acc sg neut
     [2t; n-2c; 2663]   ἱλαστήριον

ἵλεως   {2664, a-5a}
   propitious, favorable, merciful, gracious, Heb 8:12;
   from the Hebrew, ἵλεως σοι (ὁ θεός) *God have*
   mercy on thee, God forbid, far be it from thee, Matt
   16:22*

ἵλεως   nom sg masc [2t; a-5a; 2664]   ἵλεως
Ἰλλυρικοῦ   gen sg neut
     [Rm 15:19; n-2c; 2665]   Ἰλλυρικόν

Ἰλλυρικόν, οῦ, τό   {2665, n-2c}
   Illyricum, a country between the Adriatic and
   the Danube, Rom 15:19*

ἱμάντα   acc sg masc [3t; n-3c(5a); 2666]   ἱμάς

ἱμάς, άντος, ὁ   {2666, n-3c(5a)}
   a strap or *thong of leather*, Acts 22:25; *a*
   shoe-latchet, Mark 1:7; Luke 3:16; John 1:27*

ἱμᾶσιν   dat pl masc [Ac 22:25; n-3c(5a); 2666]   "
ἱμάτια   nom pl neut [3t; n-2c; 2668]   ἱμάτιον
ἱμάτια   acc pl neut [26t; n-2c; 2668]   "

ἱματίζω   {2667, v-2a(1)}
   [-, -, -, ἱμάτισμαι, -] *to clothe*; pass. *to be clothed,*
   Mark 5:15; Luke 8:35*

ἱματίοις   dat pl neut [3t; n-2c; 2668]   "

ἱμάτιον, ου, τό   {2668, n-2c}
   a garment; the upper garment, mantle, Matt 5:40;
   9:16, 20, 21; pl. *the mantle and tunic together,*
   Matt 26:65; pl. genr. *garments, raiment*, Matt
   11:8; 24:18

ἱμάτιον   nom sg neut [2t; n-2c; 2668]   "
ἱμάτιον   acc sg neut [14t; n-2c; 2668]   "
ἱματίου   gen sg neut [8t; n-2c; 2668]   "
ἱματισμένον   perf pass ptcp acc sg masc
     [2t; v-2a(1); 2667]   ἱματίζω
ἱματισμόν   acc sg masc
     [Jn 19:24; n-2a; 2669]   ἱματισμός

ἱματισμός, οῦ, ὁ   {2669, n-2a}
   garment; raiment, apparel, clothing, Luke 7:25;
   9:29; John 19:24; Acts 20:33; 1 Tim 2:9*

ἱματισμός   nom sg masc [Lk 9:29; n-2a; 2669]   "
ἱματισμοῦ   gen sg masc [Ac 20:33; n-2a; 2669]   "
ἱματισμῷ   dat sg masc [2t; n-2a; 2669]   "
ἱματίῳ   dat sg neut
     [Mt 9:16; n-2c; 2668]   ἱμάτιον
ἱματίων   gen pl neut [3t; n-2c; 2668]   "

ἱμείρομαι   {2670, v-1c(1)}
   [-, -, -, -, -] see ὁμείρομαι, *to desire earnestly; long*
   for; by impl. *to have a strong affection for, love*
   fervently, 1 Thess 2:8 v.l.*

ἵνα   {2671, conj}
   that, in order that, Matt 19:13; Mark 1:38; John
   1:22; 3:15; 17:1; ἵνα μή, *that not, lest*, Matt 7:1; in
   N.T. equivalent to ὥστε, *so that, so as that*, John
   9:2; also, marking a simple circumstance, *the*
   circumstance that, Matt 10:25; John 4:34; 6:29; 1
   John 4:17; 5:3

ἵνα   conj [663t; conj; 2671]   ἵνα

ἱνατί   {2672, conj}
   Why is it that? For what reason? Why? Matt 9:4;
   27:46; Luke 13:7; Acts 4:25; 7:26; 1 Cor 10:29*

ἱνατί   conj [6t; conj; 2672]   ἱνατί

Ἰόππη, ης, ἡ   {2673, n-1b}
   Joppa, a city of Palestine, Acts 9:36, 38, 42f.; 10:5,
   8, 23, 32; 11:5, 13*

Ἰόππῃ   dat sg fem [4t; n-1b; 2673]   Ἰόππη
Ἰόππην   acc sg fem [4t; n-1b; 2673]   "
Ἰόππης   gen sg fem [2t; n-1b; 2673]   "

Ἰορδάνη   dat sg masc [2t; n-1f; 2674]   Ἰορδάνης
Ἰορδάνην   acc sg masc [2t; n-1f; 2674]   "

Ἰορδάνης, ου, ὁ   {2674, n-1f}
   the river Jordan, Matt 3:5; Mark 10:1; Luke 4:1;
   John 3:26

Ἰορδάνου   gen sg masc [11t; n-1f; 2674]   "

ἰός, οῦ, ὁ   {2675, n-2a}
   a missile weapon, arrow, dart; venom, poison, Rom
   3:13; James 3:8; *rust*, James 5:3*

ἰός   nom sg masc [2t; n-2a; 2675]   ἰός
ἰοῦ   gen sg masc [Jm 3:8; n-2a; 2675]   "
Ἰούδα   voc sg masc [Lk 22:48; n-1e; 2683]   Ἰούδας
Ἰούδα   gen sg masc [12t; n-1e; 2683]   "
Ἰούδᾳ   dat sg masc [Jn 13:26; n-1e; 2683]   "

Ἰουδαία, ας, ἡ   {2677, n-1a}
   Judea, the southern party of the country, below
   Samaria, Matt 2:1, 5, 22; 3:1; meton. *the
   inhabitants of Judea*

Ἰουδαία   nom sg fem [2t; n-1a; 2677]   Ἰουδαία
Ἰουδαίᾳ   dat sg fem [10t; n-1a; 2677]   "
Ἰουδαίαν   acc sg fem [8t; n-1a; 2677]   "
Ἰουδαίας   gen sg fem [27t; n-1a; 2677]   "
ἰουδαΐζειν   pres act inf
   [Ga 2:14; v-2a(1); 2678]   ἰουδαΐζω

Ἰουδαΐζω   {2678, v-2a(1)}
   [-, -, -, -, -] *to judaize, live like a Jew, follow the
   manners and customs of the Jews*, Gal 2:14*

Ἰουδαϊκοῖς   dat pl masc
   [Ti 1:14; a-1a(2a); 2679]   Ἰουδαϊκός

Ἰουδαϊκός, ή, όν   {2679, a-1a(2a)}
   Jewish, current among the Jews, Titus 1:14*

Ἰουδαϊκῶς   {2680, adverb}
   in the manner of Jews, according to Jewish custom,
   Gal 2:14*

Ἰουδαϊκῶς   adverb
   [Ga 2:14; adverb; 2680]   Ἰουδαϊκῶς
Ἰουδαῖοι   nom pl masc
   [55t; a-1a(1); 2681]   Ἰουδαῖος
Ἰουδαῖοι   voc pl masc [2t; a-1a(1); 2681]   "
Ἰουδαίοις   dat pl masc [26t; a-1a(1); 2681]   "
Ἰουδαῖον   acc sg masc [2t; a-1a(1); 2681]   "

Ἰουδαῖος, αία, αῖον   {2681, a-1a(1)}
   Jewish, Mark 1:5; John 3:22; Acts 16:1; 24:24; pr.
   one sprung from the tribe of Judah, or *a subject of
   the kingdom of Judah;* in N.T. *a descendant of Jacob,
   a Jew*, Matt 28:15; Mark 7:3; Acts 19:34; Rom
   2:28, 29

Ἰουδαῖος   nom sg masc [13t; a-1a(1); 2681]   "
Ἰουδαίου   gen sg masc [5t; a-1a(1); 2681]   "
Ἰουδαίους   acc pl masc [17t; a-1a(1); 2681]   "

Ἰουδαϊσμός, οῦ, ὁ   {2682, n-2a}
   *Judaism, the character and condition of a Jew;
   practice of the Jewish religion*, Gal 1:13, 14*

Ἰουδαϊσμῷ   dat sg masc
   [2t; n-2a; 2682]   Ἰουδαϊσμός
Ἰουδαίῳ   dat sg masc
   [3t; a-1a(1); 2681]   Ἰουδαῖος

Ἰουδαίων   gen pl masc [68t; a-1a(1); 2681]   "
Ἰούδαν   acc sg masc [8t; n-1e; 2683]   Ἰούδας

Ἰούδας, α, ὁ   {2683, n-1e}
   Judas, Jude, pr. name. (1) *Judah, son of Jacob; the
   tribe of Judah*, Matt 1:2; Luke 1:39. (2) *Juda, son of
   Joseph, of the ancestry of Jesus*, Luke 3:30. (3) *Juda,
   son of Joanna, of the ancestry of Jesus*, Luke 3:26.
   (4) *Judas, brother of James, Jude*, Luke 6:16; Jude
   1. (5) *Judas Iscariot, son of Simon*, Matt 10:4; John
   6:71. (6) *Judas, brother of Jesus*, Matt 13:55; Mark
   6:3. (7) *Judas of Galilee*, Acts 5:37 . (8) *Judas,
   surnamed Barsabas*, Acts 15:22. (9) *Judas of
   Damascus*, Acts 9:11

Ἰούδας   nom sg masc [21t; n-1e; 2683]   "
Ἰούδας   gen sg masc [Jn 13:2; n-1e; 2683]   "

Ἰουλία, ας, ἡ   {2684, n-1a}
   Julia, pr. name, Rom 16:15*

Ἰουλίαν   acc sg fem
   [Rm 16:15; n-1a; 2684]   Ἰουλία

Ἰούλιος, ου, ὁ   {2685, n-2a}
   Julius, pr. name, Acts 27:1, 3*

Ἰούλιος   nom sg masc
   [Ac 27:3; n-2a; 2685]   Ἰούλιος
Ἰουλίῳ   dat sg masc [Ac 27:1; n-2a; 2685]   "
Ἰουνιᾶν   acc sg masc
   [Rm 16:7; n-1e; 2687]   Ἰουνιᾶς

Ἰουνιᾶς, ᾶ, ὁ   {2687, n-1e}
   Junia, pr. name, Rom 16:7*

Ἰοῦστος, ου, ὁ   {2688, n-2a}
   Justus, pr. name (1) *Joseph Barsabas*, Acts 1:23
   (2) *Justus of Corinth*, Acts 18:7 (3) *Jesus, called
   Justus*, Col 4:11*

Ἰοῦστος   nom sg masc [2t; n-2a; 2688]   Ἰοῦστος
Ἰούστου   gen sg masc [Ac 18:7; n-2a; 2688]   "
ἱππεῖς   acc pl masc [2t; n-3e(3); 2689]   ἱππεύς

ἱππεύς, έως, ὁ   {2689, n-3e(3)}
   a horseman; pl. ἱππεῖς, *horsemen, cavalry*, Acts
   23:23, 32*

ἱππικός, ή, όν   {2690, a-1a(2a)}
   equestrian; τὸ ἱππικόν, *cavalry, horse*, Rev 9:16*

ἱππικοῦ   gen sg neut
   [Rv 9:16; a-1a(2a); 2690]   ἱππικός
ἵπποις   dat pl masc [2t; n-2a; 2691]   ἵππος

ἵππος, ου, ὁ   {2691, n-2a}
   a horse, James 3:3; Rev 6:2, 4, 5, 8; 9:7, 17; 18:13;
   19:11, 14

ἵππος   nom sg masc [5t; n-2a; 2691]   "
ἵππου   gen sg masc [2t; n-2a; 2691]   "
ἵππους   acc pl masc [Rv 9:17; n-2a; 2691]   "
ἵππων   gen pl masc [7t; n-2a; 2691]   "

ἶρις, ιδος, ἡ   {2692, n-3c(2)}
   a rainbow, iris, Rev 4:3; 10:1*

ἶρις   nom sg fem [2t; n-3c(2); 2692]   ἶρις
ἴσα   nom pl neut [Rv 21:16; a-1a(2a); 2698]   ἴσος
ἴσα   acc pl neut, can function
   adverbially [Pp 2:6] [2t; a-1a(2a); 2698]   "

Ἰσαάκ, ὁ {2693, n-3g(2)}
Isaac, pr. name, indecl., Matt 1:2; 8:11; 23:32;
Acts 3:13;. Rom 9:7f.; Gal 4:28; Heb 11:9ff.;
James 2:21

Ἰσαάκ   indecl [20t; n-3g(2); 2693]   Ἰσαάκ
ἰσάγγελοι   nom pl masc
  [Lk 20:36; a-3a; 2694]   ἰσάγγελος

ἰσάγγελος, ον {2694, a-3a}
equal or *similar to angels,* Luke 20:36*

ἴσαι   nom pl fem [Mk 14:56; a-1a(2a); 2698]   ἴσος
ἴσασι   perf act ind 3 pl
  [Ac 26:4; v-1b(3); 3857]   οἶδα

Ἰσαχάρ {2695, n-3g(2)}
Issachar, pr. name, indecl., Rev 7:7 v.l.*

ἴση   nom sg fem [Mk 14:59; a-1a(2a); 2698]   ἴσος
ἴσην   acc sg fem [Ac 11:17; a-1a(2a); 2698]   "
ἴσθι   pres act imperative 2 sg
  [5t; v-6b; 1639]   εἰμί

Ἰσκαριώθ, ὁ {2696, n-3g(2)}
also spelled Ἰσκαριώτης, *Iscariot,* indecl.
surname of Judas, Mark 3:19; 14:10; Luke 6:16

Ἰσκαριώθ   indecl [3t; n-3g(2); 2696]   Ἰσκαριώθ
Ἰσκαριώτην   acc sg masc
  [Lk 22:3; n-1f; 2697]   Ἰσκαριώτης

Ἰσκαριώτης, ου, ο {2697, n-1f}
also spelled Ἰσκαριώθ (2696), which is
indeclinable. The form in Luke 22:3
(Ἰσκαριώτην) is built on the declinable
Ἰσκαριώτης. *Iscariot,* surname of Judas*

Ἰσκαριώτης   nom sg masc [4t; n-1f; 2697]   "
Ἰσκαριώτου   gen sg masc [3t; n-1f; 2697]   "
ἴσον   acc sg masc [Jn 5:18; a-1a(2a); 2698]   ἴσος

ἴσος, η, ον {2698, a-1a(2a)}
equal, like, Matt 20:12; Luke 6:34; *on an equality,*
Phil 2:6; met. *correspondent, consistent,* Mark
14:56, 59

ἰσότης, ητος, ἡ {2699, n-3c(1)}
equality, equal proportion, 2 Cor 8:13, 14; *fairness,
equity, what is equitable,* Col 4:1*

ἰσότης   nom sg fem
  [2C 8:14; n-3c(1); 2699]   ἰσότης
ἰσότητα   acc sg fem [Cl 4:1; n-3c(1); 2699]   "
ἰσότητος   gen sg fem [2C 8:13; n-3c(1); 2699]   "
ἰσότιμον   acc sg fem
  [2P 1:1; a-3a; 2700]   ἰσότιμος

ἰσότιμος, ον {2700, a-3a}
of equal price, equally precious or *valuable,* 2 Peter
1:1*

ἴσους   acc pl masc [Mt 20:12; a-1a(2a); 2698]   ἴσος
ἰσόψυχον   acc sg masc
  [Pp 2:20; a-3a; 2701]   ἰσόψυχος

ἰσόψυχος, ον {2701, a-3a}
likeminded, of the same mind and spirit, Phil 2:20*

Ἰσραήλ, ὁ {2702, n-3g(2)}
Israel, pr. name, indecl.

Ἰσραήλ   indecl [68t; n-3g(2); 2702]   Ἰσραήλ

Ἰσραηλῖται   nom pl masc
  [2t; n-1f; 2703]   Ἰσραηλίτης
Ἰσραηλῖται   voc pl masc [5t; n-1f; 2703]   "

Ἰσραηλίτης, ου, ὁ {2703, n-1f}
an Israelite, a descendant of Ἰσραήλ, *Israel* or
Jacob, John 1:47; Acts 2:22

Ἰσραηλίτης   nom sg masc [2t; n-1f; 2703]   "

Ἰσσαχάρ, ὁ {2704, n-3g(2)}
Issachar, pr. name, indecl., Rev 7:7*

Ἰσσαχάρ   indecl [Rv 7:7; n-3g(2); 2704]   Ἰσσαχάρ
ἱστάνομεν   pres act ind 1 pl
  [Rm 3:31; v-6a; 2705]   ἵστημι
ἴστε   perf act imperative 2 pl
  [2t; v-1b(3); 3857]   οἶδα
ἴστε   perf act ind 2 pl [Hb 12:17; v-1b(3); 3857]   "

ἵστημι {2705, v-6a}
[στήσω, ἔστησα or ἔστην, ἕστηκα, -, ἐστάθην]
pluperfect, ἑστάμην, trans. *to make to stand, set,
place,* Matt 4:5; *to set forth, appoint,* Acts 1:23; *to
fix, appoint,* Acts 17:31; *to establish, confirm,* Rom
10:3; Heb 10:9; *to set down, impute,* Acts 7:60; *to
weigh out, pay,* Matt 26:15; intrans. *to stand,* Matt
12:46; *to stand fast, be firm, be permanent, endure,*
Matt 12:25; Eph 6:13; *to be confirmed, proved,*
Matt 18:16; 2 Cor 13:1; *to stop,* Luke 7:14; 8:44;
Acts 8:38

ἱστίον, ου, τό {2706}
sail, Acts 27:16 v.l.*

ἱστορέω {2707, v-1d(2a)}
[-, ἱστόρησα, -, -, -] *to ascertain by inquiry and
examination; to inquire of;* in N.T. *to visit* in order
to become acquainted with, Gal 1:18; Acts
17:23 v.l.*

ἱστορῆσαι   aor act inf
  [Ga 1:18; v-1d(2a); 2707]   ἱστορέω
ἰσχύει   pres act ind 3 sg
  [4t; v-1a(4); 2710]   ἰσχύω
ἰσχύειν   pres act inf [Mt 8:28; v-1a(4); 2710]   "
ἴσχυεν   imperf act ind 3 sg [2t; v-1a(4); 2710]   "
ἰσχύϊ   dat sg fem [2t; n-3e(1); 2709]   ἰσχύς
ἰσχύν   acc sg fem [Rv 5:12; n-3e(1); 2709]   "
ἴσχυον   imperf act ind 3 pl
  [3t; v-1a(4); 2710]   ἰσχύω
ἰσχύοντες   pres act ptcp nom pl masc
  [2t; v-1a(4); 2710]   "
ἰσχύοντος   pres act ptcp gen sg masc
  [Lk 14:29; v-1a(4); 2710]   "
ἰσχύος   gen sg fem [6t; n-3e(1); 2709]   ἰσχύς
ἰσχυρά   nom sg fem
  [Lk 15:14; a-1a(1); 2708]   ἰσχυρός
ἰσχυρά   voc sg fem [Rv 18:10; a-1a(1); 2708]   "
ἰσχυρᾷ   dat sg fem [Rv 18:2; a-1a(1); 2708]   "
ἰσχυρά   acc pl neut [1C 1:27; a-1a(1); 2708]   "
ἰσχυραί   nom pl fem [2C 10:10; a-1a(1); 2708]   "
ἰσχυράν   acc sg fem [Hb 6:18; a-1a(1); 2708]   "
ἰσχυρᾶς   gen sg fem [Hb 5:7; a-1a(1); 2708]   "
ἰσχυροί   nom pl masc [4t; a-1a(1); 2708]   "
ἰσχυρόν   acc sg masc [5t; a-1a(1); 2708]   "

ἰσχυρός, ά, όν {2708, a-1a(1)}
strong, mighty, robust, Matt 12:29; Luke 11:21;
powerful, mighty, 1 Cor 1:27; 4:10; 1 John 2:14;
strong, fortified, Rev 18:10; vehement, Matt 14:20;
energetic, 2 Cor 10:10; sure, firm, Heb 6:18

ἰσχυρός   nom sg masc [3t; a-1a(1); 2708]   "
ἰσχυρότεροι   nom pl masc comparative
[1C 10:22; a-1a(1); 2708]   "
ἰσχυρότερον   nom sg neut comparative
[1C 1:25; a-1a(1); 2708]   "
ἰσχυρότερος   nom sg masc comparative
[4t; a-1a(1); 2708]   "
ἰσχυροῦ   gen sg masc [2t; a-1a(1); 2708]   "
ἰσχυρῶν   gen pl masc [Rv 19:18; a-1a(1); 2708]   "
ἰσχυρῶν   gen pl fem [Rv 19:6; a-1a(1); 2708]   "

ἰσχύς, ύος, ἡ {2709, n-3e(1)}
strength, might, power, Rev 18:2; Eph 1:19;
faculty, ability, 1 Peter 4:11; Mark 12:30, 33; Luke
10:27

ἰσχύς   nom sg fem [Rv 7:12; n-3e(1); 2709]   ἰσχύς
ἰσχύσαμεν   aor act ind 1 pl
[2t; v-1a(4); 2710]   ἰσχύω
ἴσχυσαν   aor act ind 3 pl [3t; v-1a(4); 2710]   "
ἴσχυσας   aor act ind 2 sg
[Mk 14:37; v-1a(4); 2710]   "
ἰσχύσατε   aor act ind 2 pl
[Mt 26:40; v-1a(4); 2710]   "
ἴσχυσεν   aor act ind 3 sg [5t; v-1a(4); 2710]   "
ἰσχύσουσιν   fut act ind 3 pl
[Lk 13:24; v-1a(4); 2710]   "

ἰσχύω {2710, v-1a(4)}
[ἰσχύσω, ἴσχυσα, -, -, ἰσχύθην] to be strong, be
well, be in good health, Matt 9:12; to have power, be
able, Matt 8:28; 26:40; to have power or efficiency,
avail, be valid, Gal 5:6; Heb 9:17; to be of service,
be serviceable, Matt 5:13; meton. to prevail, Acts
19:16; Rev 12:8

ἰσχύω   pres act ind 1 sg [2t; v-1a(4); 2710]   "

ἴσως {2711, adverb}
equally; perhaps, it may be that, Luke 20:13*

ἴσως   adverb [Lk 20:13; adverb; 2711]   ἴσως

Ἰταλία, ας, ἡ {2712, n-1a}
Italy, Acts 18:2; 27:1, 6; subscription to Heb*

Ἰταλίαν   acc sg fem [2t; n-1a; 2712]   Ἰταλία
Ἰταλίας   gen sg fem [2t; n-1a; 2712]   "
Ἰταλικῆς   gen sg fem
[Ac 10:1; a-1a(2a); 2713]   Ἰταλικός

Ἰταλικός, ή, όν {2713, a-1a(2a)}
Italian, Acts 10:1*

Ἰτουραίας   gen sg fem
[Lk 3:1; a-1a(1); 2714]   Ἰτουραῖος

Ἰτουραῖος, α, ον {2714, a-1a(1)}
Ituraea, a district of Palestine beyond Jordan,
Luke 3:1*

ἰχθύας   acc pl masc [7t; n-3e(1); 2716]   ἰχθύς
ἰχθύδια   acc pl neut [2t; n-2c; 2715]   ἰχθύδιον

ἰχθύδιον, ου, τό {2715, n-2c}
a small fish, Matt 15:34; Mark 8:7*

ἰχθύες   nom pl masc
[Lk 9:13; n-3e(1); 2716]   ἰχθύς
ἰχθύν   acc sg masc [3t; n-3e(1); 2716]   "
ἰχθύος   gen sg masc [2t; n-3e(1); 2716]   "

ἰχθύς, ύος, ὁ {2716, n-3e(1)}
a fish, Matt 15:36; 17:27; Luke 5:6

ἰχθύων   gen pl masc [7t; n-3e(1); 2716]   "
ἴχνεσιν   dat pl neut [3t; n-3d(2b); 2717]   ἴχνος

ἴχνος, ους, τό {2717, n-3d(2b)}
a footstep, track; in N.T. pl. footsteps, line of
conduct, Rom 4:12; 2 Cor 12:18; 1 Peter 2:21*

Ἰωαθάμ, ὁ {2718, n-3g(2)}
Joatham, pr. name, indecl., Matt 1:9; Luke 3:23ff.
v.l.*

Ἰωαθάμ   indecl [2t; n-3g(2); 2718]   Ἰωαθάμ

Ἰωανάν, ὁ {2720, n-3g(2)}
Joanan, pr. name, indecl., Luke 3:27*

Ἰωανάν   indecl [Lk 3:27; n-3g(2); 2720]   Ἰωανάν

Ἰωάννα, ας, ἡ {2721, n-1a}
also spelled Ἰωάνα, Joanna, pr. name, Luke 8:3;
24:10*

Ἰωάννα   nom sg fem [2t; n-1a; 2721]   Ἰωάννα

Ἰωαννᾶς, see Ἰωάννης   {2723, n-3g(2)}

Ἰωάννῃ   dat sg masc [5t; n-1f; 2722]   Ἰωάννης
Ἰωάννην   acc sg masc [37t; n-1f; 2722]   "

Ἰωάννης, ου, ὁ {2722, n-1f}
also spelled Ἰωάνης, Joannes, John, pr. name (1)
John the Baptist, Matt 3:1, et al. (2) John, son of
Zebedee, the apostle, Matt 4:21, et al. (3) John,
surnamed Mark, Acts 12:12, et al. (4) John, the
high-priest, Acts 4:6

Ἰωάννης   nom sg masc [54t; n-1f; 2722]   "
Ἰωάννου   gen sg masc [39t; n-1f; 2722]   "

Ἰωάς, ὁ {2723, n-3g(2)}
Joash, a king of Judah, 2 Kgs 14:1, indecl., Matt
1:8 v.l.; Luke 3:23ff. v.l.*

Ἰώβ, ὁ {2724, n-3g(2)}
Job, pr. name, indecl., James 5:11*

Ἰώβ   indecl [Jm 5:11; n-3g(2); 2724]   Ἰώβ

Ἰωβήδ, ὁ {2725, n-3g(2)}
Obed, David's grandfather, pr. name, indecl.,
Matt 1:5; Luke 3:32*

Ἰωβήδ   indecl [3t; n-3g(2); 2725]   Ἰωβήδ

Ἰωδά, ὁ {2726, n-3g(2)}
Joda, pr. name, indecl., Luke 3:26*

Ἰωδά   indecl [Lk 3:26; n-3g(2); 2726]   Ἰωδά

Ἰωήλ, ὁ {2727, n-3g(2)}
Joel, an Old Testament prophet, pr. name,
indecl., Acts 2:16*

Ἰωήλ   indecl [Ac 2:16; n-3g(2); 2727]   Ἰωήλ
ἰώμενος   pres mid ptcp nom sg masc
[Ac 10:38; v-1d(1b); 2615]   ἰάομαι

Ἰωνᾶ   gen sg masc [7t; n-1e; 2731]   Ἰωνᾶς

Ἰωνάθας, ου, ὁ   {2728, n-1d}
Jonathas, Acts 4:6 v.l.*

Ἰωνάμ, ὁ   {2729, n-3g(2)}
Jonam, pr. name, indecl., Luke 3:30*

Ἰωνάμ   indecl [Lk 3:30; n-3g(2); 2729]   Ἰωνάμ

Ἰωνᾶς, ᾶ, ὁ   {2731, n-1e}
Jonas, pr. name (1) *Jonah, the prophet*, Matt
12:39; John 1:42 v.l.; 21:15-17 v.l. (2) *Jonas, father
of Simon Peter*, Matt 16:17 v.l.

Ἰωνᾶς   nom sg masc [2t; n-1e; 2731]   Ἰωνᾶς

Ἰωράμ, ὁ   {2732, n-3g(2)}
Joram, king of Judah (2 Kgs 8:16ff.), pr. name,
indecl., Matt 1:8; Luke 3:23ff. v.l.*

Ἰωράμ   indecl [2t; n-3g(2); 2732]   Ἰωράμ

Ἰωρίμ, ὁ   {2733, n-3g(2)}
Jorim, pr. name, indecl., Luke 3:29*

Ἰωρίμ   indecl [Lk 3:29; n-3g(2); 2733]   Ἰωρίμ·

Ἰωσαφάτ, ὁ   {2734, n-3g(2)}
Josaphat, king of Judah (1 Kgs 22:41), pr. name,
indecl., Matt 1:8; Luke 3:23f. v.l.*

Ἰωσαφάτ   indecl [2t; n-3g(2); 2734]   Ἰωσαφάτ

Ἰωσῆς, ῆτος, ὁ   {2736, n-3c(1)}
Joses, pr. name (1) *Joses, son of Eliezer*, Luke 3:29
v.l. (2) *Joses, son of Mary, brother of Jesus*, Matt
13:55 v.l. (3) *Joses, surnamed Barnabas*, Matt
27:56 v.l.; Acts 4:36 v.l.

Ἰωσῆτος   gen sg masc [3t; n-3c(1); 2736]   Ἰωσῆς

Ἰωσήφ, ὁ   {2737, n-3g(2)}
Joseph, pr. name, indecl. (1) *Joseph, son of Jacob*,
John 4:5. (2) *Joseph, son of Jonan*, Luke 3:30. (3)
Joseph, son of Judas, Luke 3:26. (4) *Joseph, son of
Mattathias*, Luke 3:24. (5) *Joseph, the husband of
Mary*, Matt 1:16. (6) *Joseph of Arimathea*, Matt
27:57. (7) *Joseph Barsabas*, Acts 1:23. (8) *Joseph
Barnabas*, Acts 4:36

Ἰωσήφ   indecl [34t; n-3g(2); 2737]   Ἰωσήφ

Ἰωσήχ, ὁ   {2738, n-3g(2)}
Josech, pr. name, indecl., Luke 3:26*

Ἰωσήχ   indecl [Lk 3:26; n-3g(2); 2738]   Ἰωσήχ
Ἰωσίαν   acc sg masc [Mt 1:10; n-1d; 2739]   Ἰωσίας

Ἰωσίας, ου, ὁ   {2739, n-1d}
Josiah, king of Judah (2 Kgs 22), Matt 1:10, 11;
Luke 3:23ff. v.l.*

Ἰωσίας   nom sg masc [Mt 1:11; n-1d; 2739]   "

ἰῶτα, τό   {2740, n-3g(2)}
iota; in N.T. used like the Hebrew, , the smallest
letter in the Hebrew alphabet, as an expression
for *the least* or *minutest part*; *a jot*, Matt 5:18*

ἰῶτα   indecl [Mt 5:18; n-3g(2); 2740]   ἰῶτα

Κ

κάβος, ου, ὁ   {2742, n-2a}
cab, a unit of dry measure, about one-half a
gallon, Luke 16:6 v.l.*

κἀγώ   {2743, a-5a}
and I, I also, but I, a crasis of καί and ἐγώ, dat.,
κἀμοί, acc., κἀμέ

κἀγώ   crasis [76t; a-5; 2743]   κἀγώ

κάδος, ου, ὁ   {2744, n-2a}
jar, container, Luke 16:6 v.l.*

καθ᾽   prep-acc [48t; prep; 2848]   κατά
καθ᾽   prep-gen [13t; prep; 2848]   "

καθά   {2745, conj}
can function as an adverb, *just as*, Matt 27:10;
6:12 v.l.; Luke 1:2 v.l.*

καθά   conj [Mt 27:10; conj; 2745]   καθά
καθαίρει   pres act ind 3 sg
     [Jn 15:2; v-2d(2); 2748]   καθαίρω
καθαιρεῖσθαι   pres pass inf
     [Ac 19:27; cv-1d(2a); 2747]   καθαιρέω
καθαίρεσιν   acc sg fem
     [3t; n-3e(5b); 2746]   καθαίρεσις

καθαίρεσις, εως, ἡ   {2746, n-3e(5b)}
tearing down, destruction, 2 Cor 10:4, 8; 13:10*

καθαιρέω   {2747, cv-1d(2a)}
[καθελῶ, καθεῖλον, -, -, -] *take* or *bring down*,
Mark 15:36, 46; Luke 1:52; 23:53; Acts 13:29; *tear
down, destroy*, Luke 12:18; Acts 13:19; 19:27; 2
Cor 10:4*

καθαιροῦντες   pres act ptcp nom pl masc
     [2C 10:4; cv-1d(2a); 2747]   καθαιρέω

καθαίρω   {2748, v-2d(2)}
[-, ἐκάθαρα, -, κεκάθαρμαι, -] *to cleanse* from
filth; *to clear* by pruning, *prune*, John 15:2; met.
to cleanse from sin, *make expiation*

καθάπερ   {2749, conj}
can function as an adverb, *even as, just as*, Rom
3:4; 4:6; 9:13; 10:15; 11:8; 12:4; 1 Cor 10:10; 12:12;
2 Cor 1:14; 3:13, 18; 8:11; 1 Thess 2:11; 3:6, 12;
4:5; Heb 4:2*

καθάπερ   conj [13t; conj; 2749]   καθάπερ

καθάπτω   {2750, cv-4}
[-, ἐκάθηψα, -, -, -] trans. *to fasten* or *fit to*; in N.T.
equivalent to καθάπτομαι, *to fix one's self upon,
fasten upon, take hold of, seize*, Acts 28:3*

καθαρά   nom sg fem
     [Jm 1:27; a-1a(1); 2754]   καθαρός
καθαρά   nom pl neut [3t; a-1a(1); 2754]   "
καθαρᾷ   dat sg fem [3t; a-1a(1); 2754]   "
καθαρᾶς   gen sg fem [3t; a-1a(1); 2754]   "
καθαριεῖ   fut act ind 3 sg
     [Hb 9:14; v-2a(1); 2751]   καθαρίζω
καθαρίζει   pres act ind 3 sg
     [1J 1:7; v-2a(1); 2751]   "

καθαρίζεσθαι   pres pass inf
   [Hb 9:23; v-2a(1); 2751]   "
καθαρίζεται   pres pass ind 3 sg
   [Hb 9:22; v-2a(1); 2751]   "
καθαρίζετε   pres act imperative 2 pl
   [Mt 10:8; v-2a(1); 2751]   "
καθαρίζετε   pres act ind 2 pl   [2t; v-2a(1); 2751]   "
καθαρίζονται   pres pass ind 3 pl
   [2t; v-2a(1); 2751]   "

καθαρίζω   {2751, v-2a(1)}
   [καθαριῶ, ἐκαθάρισα, -, κεκαθάρισμαι,
   ἐκαθαρίσθην] to cleanse, render pure, purify, Matt
   23:25; Luke 11:39; to cleanse from leprosy, Matt
   8:2, 3; 10:8; met. to cleanse from sin, purify by an
   expiatory offering, make expiation for, Heb 9:22,
   23; 1 John 1:7; to cleanse from sin, free from the
   influence of error and sin, Acts 15:9; 2 Cor 7:1; to
   pronounce ceremonially clean, Acts 10:15; 11:9

καθαρίζων   pres act ptcp nom sg masc
   [Mk 7:19; v-2a(1); 2751]   "
καθαρίσαι   aor act inf   [3t; v-2a(1); 2751]   "
καθαρίσας   aor act ptcp nom sg masc
   [2t; v-2a(1); 2751]   "
καθαρίσατε   aor act imperative 2 pl
   [Jm 4:8; v-2a(1); 2751]   "
καθαρίση   aor act subj 3 sg   [2t; v-2a(1); 2751]   "
καθαρίσθητι   aor pass imperative 2 sg
   [3t; v-2a(1); 2751]   "
καθαρισμόν   acc sg masc
   [2t; n-2a; 2752]   καθαρισμός

καθαρισμός, οῦ, ὁ   {2752, n-2a}
   ceremonial cleansing, purification, Luke 2:22;
   5:14; mode of purification, John 2:6; 3:35; cleansing
   of lepers, Mark 1:44; met. expiation, Heb 1:3; 2
   Peter 1:9*

καθαρισμοῦ   gen sg masc   [5t; n-2a; 2752]   "
καθάρισον   aor act imperative 2 sg
   [Mt 23:26; v-2a(1); 2751]   καθαρίζω
καθαρίσωμεν   aor act subj 1 pl
   [2C 7:1; v-2a(1); 2751]   "

κάθαρμα, ατος, τό   {2753, n-3c(4)}
   scapegoat, 1 Cor 4:13 v.l.*

καθαροί   nom pl masc   [4t; a-1a(1); 2754]   καθαρός
καθαροῖς   dat pl masc   [Ti 1:15; a-1a(1); 2754]   "
καθαρόν   nom sg neut   [4t; a-1a(1); 2754]   "
καθαρόν   acc sg neut   [3t; a-1a(1); 2754]   "

καθαρός, ά, όν   {2754, a-1a(1)}
   clean, pure, unsoiled, Matt 23:26; 27:59; met. clean
   from guilt, guiltless, innocent, Acts 18:6; 20:26;
   sincere, upright, virtuous, void of evil, Matt 5:8;
   John 15:3; clean ceremonially and morally,
   Luke 11:41

καθαρός   nom sg masc   [3t; a-1a(1); 2754]   "

καθαρότης, ητος, ἡ   {2755, n-3c(1)}
   cleanness; ceremonial purity, Heb 9:13*

καθαρότητα   acc sg fem
   [Hb 9:13; n-3c(1); 2755]   καθαρότης
καθαρῷ   dat sg masc
   [Rv 21:18; a-1a(1); 2754]   καθαρός

καθαρῷ   dat sg neut   [Hb 10:22; a-1a(1); 2754]   "

καθέδρα, ας, ἡ   {2756, n-1a}
   chair, seat, Matt 21:12; 23:2; Mark 11:15*

καθέδρας   gen sg fem   [Mt 23:2; n-1a; 2756]   καθέδρα
καθέδρας   acc pl fem   [2t; n-1a; 2756]   "

καθέζομαι   {2757, v-2a(1)}
   [(ἐκαθεζόμην), -, -, -, -, ἐκαθέσθην] to seat one's
   self, sit down, Matt 26:55; Luke 2:46; John 4:6; 6:3
   v.l.; 11:20; 20:12; Acts 6:15; 20:9*

καθεζόμενοι   pres mid ptcp nom pl masc
   [Ac 6:15; v-2a(1); 2757]   καθέζομαι
καθεζόμενον   pres mid ptcp acc sg masc
   [Lk 2:46; v-2a(1); 2757]   "
καθεζόμενος   pres mid ptcp nom sg masc
   [Ac 20:9; v-2a(1); 2757]   "
καθεζομένους   pres mid ptcp acc pl masc
   [Jn 20:12; v-2a(1); 2757]   "
καθεῖλεν   aor act ind 3 sg
   [Lk 1:52; cv-1d(2a); 2747]   καθαιρέω
καθελεῖν   aor act inf
   [Mk 15:36; cv-1d(2a); 2747]   "
καθελόντες   aor act ptcp nom pl masc
   [Ac 13:29; cv-1d(2a); 2747]   "
καθελῶ   fut act ind 1 sg
   [Lk 12:18; cv-1d(2a); 2747]   "
καθελών   aor act ptcp nom sg masc
   [3t; cv-1d(2a); 2747]   "

καθεξῆς   {2759, adverb}
   in a continual order or series, successively,
   consecutively, Luke 1:3; Acts 11:4; 18:23; ὁ, ἡ,
   καθεξῆς, succeeding, subsequent, Luke 8:1; Acts
   3:10 v.l., 24*

καθεξῆς   adverb   [5t; adverb; 2759]   καθεξῆς
καθεύδει   pres act ind 3 sg
   [3t; cv-1b(3); 2761]   καθεύδω
καθεύδειν   pres act inf
   [Mt 13:25; cv-1b(3); 2761]   "
καθεύδεις   pres act ind 2 sg
   [Mk 14:37; cv-1b(3); 2761]   "
καθεύδετε   pres act imperative 2 pl
   [Mt 26:45; cv-1b(3); 2761]   "
καθεύδετε   pres act ind 2 pl   [2t; cv-1b(3); 2761]   "
καθεύδη   pres act subj 3 sg
   Mk 4:27; cv-1b(3); 2761]   "
καθεύδοντας   pres act ptcp acc pl masc
   [5t; cv-1b(3); 2761]   "
καθεύδοντες   pres act ptcp nom pl masc
   [1Th 5:7; cv-1b(3); 2761]   "
καθεύδουσιν   pres act ind 3 pl
   [1Th 5:7; cv-1b(3); 2761]   "

καθεύδω   {2761, v-1b(3)}
   [(ἐκάθευδον), -, -, -, -, -] to sleep, be fast asleep,
   Matt 8:24; 9:24; met. to sleep in spiritual sloth,
   Eph 5:14; 1 Thess 5:6; to sleep the sleep of death,
   to die, 1 Thess 5:10

καθεύδωμεν   pres act subj 1 pl
   [2t; cv-1b(3); 2761]   "
καθεύδων   pres act ptcp nom sg masc
   [2t; cv-; 2761]   "

κάθη   pres mid ind 2 sg
  [Ac 23:3; v-6b; 2764]   κάθημαι
καθηγηταί   nom pl masc
  [Mt 23:10; n-1f; 2762]   καθηγητής

καθηγητής, ου, ὁ   {2762, n-1f}
  pr. *a guide, leader;* in N.T. *a teacher, instructor,*
  Matt 23:10*

καθηγητής   nom sg masc   [Mt 23:10; n-1f; 2762]   "
καθῆκαν   aor act ind 3 pl
  [2t; cv-6a; 2768]   καθίημι
καθῆκεν   imperf act ind 3 sg
  [Ac 22:22; cv-1b(2); 2763]   καθήκω
καθήκοντα   pres act ptcp acc pl neut
  [Rm 1:28; cv-1b(2); 2763]   "

καθήκω   {2763, cv-1b(2)}
  [-, -, -, -, -] *to reach, extend to;* καθήκει, impers. *it
  is fitting, meet,* Acts 22:22; τὸ καθῆκον, *what is fit,
  right, duty;* τὰ μὴ καθήκοντα, by litotes for *what
  is abominable* or *detestable,* Rom 1:28*

κάθημαι   {2764, v-6b}
  [καθήσομαι, -, -, -, -] *to sit, be sitting,* Matt 9:9;
  Luke 10:13; *to be seated,* 1 Cor 14:30; *to be
  enthroned,* Rev 18:7; *to dwell, reside,* Matt 4:16;
  Luke 1:79; 21:35

κάθημαι   pres mid ind 1 sg
  [Rv 18:7; v-6b; 2764]   καθημαι
καθήμεναι   pres mid ptcp nom pl fem
  [Mt 27:61; v-6b; 2764]   "
καθημένην   pres mid ptcp acc sg fem
  [Rv 17:3; v-6b; 2764]   "
καθημένης   pres mid ptcp gen sg fem
  [Rv 17:1; v-6b; 2764]   "
καθήμενοι   pres mid ptcp nom pl masc
  [7t; v-6b; 2764]   "
καθημένοις   pres mid ptcp dat pl masc
  [2t; v-6b; 2764]   "
καθημένοις   pres mid ptcp dat pl neut
  [2t; v-6b; 2764]   "
καθήμενον   pres mid ptcp acc sg masc
  [10t; v-6b; 2764]   "
καθήμενον   pres pass ptcp acc sg masc
  [Mk 5:15; v-6b; 2764]   "
καθήμενος   pres mid ptcp nom sg masc
  [16t; v-6b; 2764]   "
καθημένου   pres mid ptcp gen sg masc
  [9t; v-6b; 2764]   "
καθημένους   pres mid ptcp acc pl masc
  [6t; v-6b; 2764]   "
καθημένῳ   pres mid ptcp dat sg masc
  [8t; v-6b; 2764]   "
καθημένων   pres mid ptcp gen pl masc
  [Rv 19:18; v-6b; 2764]   "
καθημερινῇ   dat sg fem
  [Ac 6:1; a-1a(2a); 2766]   καθημερινός

καθημερινός, ή, όν   {2766, a-1a(2a)}
  daily, day by day, Acts 6:1*

καθήσεσθε   fut mid ind 2 pl
  [2t; v-6b; 2764]   καθημαι
καθῆσθαι   pres mid inf   [2t; v-6b; 2764]   "
κάθηται   pres mid ind 3 sg   [2t; v-6b; 2764]   "

καθῆψεν   aor act ind 3 sg
  [Ac 28:3; cv-4; 2750]   καθάπτω
καθιεμένην   pres pass ptcp acc sg fem
  [Ac 11:5; cv-6a; 2768]   καθίημι
καθιέμενον   pres pass ptcp acc sg neut
  [Ac 10:11; cv-6a; 2768]   "
καθίζετε   pres act ind 2 pl
  [1C 6:4; v-2a(1); 2767]   καθίζω

καθίζω   {2767, v-2a(1)}
  [καθίσω, ἐκάθισα, κεκάθικα, -, -] (1) trans. *to
  cause to sit, place;* καθίζομαι, *to be seated, sit,* Matt
  19:28; Luke 22:30; *to cause to sit* as judges, *place,
  appoint,* 1 Cor 6:4; (2) intrans. *to sit, sit down,*
  Matt 13:48; 26:36; *to remain, settle, stay, continue,
  live,* Luke 24:49

καθίημι   {2768, cv-6a}
  [-, καθῆκα, -, -, -] *to let down, lower,* Luke 5:19;
  Acts 9:25; 10:11; 11:5*

καθίσαι   aor act inf   [6t; v-2a(1); 2767]   "
καθίσαντες   aor act ptcp nom pl masc
  [2t; v-2a(1); 2767]   "
καθίσαντος   aor act ptcp gen sg masc
  [Mt 5:1; v-2a(1); 2767]   "
καθίσας   aor act ptcp nom sg masc
  [11t; v-2a(1); 2767]   "
καθίσατε   aor act imperative 2 pl
  [3t; v-2a(1); 2767]   "
καθίσει   fut act ind 3 sg
  [Mt 25:31; v-2a(1); 2767]   "
καθίσῃ   aor act subj 3 sg
  [Mt 19:28; v-2a(1); 2767]   "
καθιστάνοντες   pres act ptcp nom pl masc
  [Ac 17:15; cv-6a; 2770]   καθίστημι

καθιστάνω, see καθίστημι   {2769}

καθίσταται   pres pass ind 3 sg   [4t; cv-6a; 2770]   "

καθίστημι   {2770, cv-6a}
  [καταστήσω, κατέστησα, -, καθέσταμαι,
  κατεστάθην] and in N.T. καθιστάνω, *to place, set,*
  James 3:6; *to set, constitute, appoint,* Matt 24:45,
  47; Luke 12:14; *to set down* in a place, *conduct,*
  Acts 17:15; *to make, render,* or *cause to be,* 2 Peter
  1:8; pass. *to be rendered,* Rom 5:19

καθίστησιν   pres act ind 3 sg   [2t; cv-6a; 2770]   "
καθίσωμεν   aor act subj 1 pl
  [Mk 10:37; v-2a(1); 2767]   καθίζω
καθίσωσιν   aor act subj 3 pl
  [Mt 20:21; v-2a(1); 2767]   "

καθό   {2771, adverb}
  as, Rom 8:26; *according as, in proportion as, to the
  degree that,* 2 Cor 8:12; 1 Peter 4:13*

καθό   adverb [4t; adverb; 2771]   καθό

καθολικός, ή, όν   {2772, a-1a(2a)}
  general, universal, v.l., in the inscription to
  James

καθόλου   {2773, adverb}
  *on the whole, entirely, in general, altogether,
  completely;* with a negative, *not at all,* Acts 4:18*

καθόλου   adverb [Ac 4:18; adverb; 2773]   καθόλου

καθορᾶται   pres pass ind 3 sg
[Rm 1:20; cv-1d(1a); 2775]   καθοράω

καθοπλίζω   {2774, cv-2a(1)}
[-, ἐκαθόπλισα, -, καθώπλισμαι, -] middle, *to
arm oneself (completely)*, Luke 11:21*

καθοράω   {2775, cv-1d(1a)}
[-, -, -, -, -] pr. *to look down upon*, in the N.T. *to
mark, perceive, discern*, Rom 1:20*

καθότι   {2776, conj}
as, just as, according as, in proportion as, Acts
2:45; 4:35; *inasmuch as*, Luke 1:7; 19:9; Acts 2:24;
17:31*

καθότι   conj [6t; conj; 2776]   καθότι
κάθου   pres mid imperative 2 sg
[7t; v-6b; 2764]   κάθημαι
καθωπλισμένος   perf mid ptcp nom sg masc
[Lk 11:21; cv-; 2774]   καθοπλίζω

καθώς   {2777, adverb}
as, just as, in the manner that, Matt 21:6; 26:24;
how, in what manner, Acts 15:14; *according as*,
Mark 4:33; *inasmuch as*, John 17:2; *of time, when*,
Acts 7:17

καθώς   adverb [182t; adverb; 2777]   καθώς

καθώσπερ   {2778, adverb}
just as, exactly as, Heb 5:4; 2 Cor 3:18 v.l.*

καθώσπερ   adverb [Hb 5:4; adverb; 2778] καθώσπερ

καί   {2779, conj}
(1) *and*, Matt 2:2, 3, 11; 4:22; (2) καί ... καί, *both
... and;* (3) as a cumulative particle, *also, too*,
Matt 5:39; John 8:19; 1 Cor 11:6; (4) emphatic,
even, also, Matt 10:30; 1 Cor 2:10; in N.T.
adversative, *but*, Matt 11:19; also introductory
of the apodosis of a sentence, James 2:4; Gal,
3:28

καί   conj [9018t; conj; 2779]   καί
Καϊάφα   gen sg masc [4t; n-1e; 2780]   Καϊάφας
Καϊάφαν   acc sg masc [2t; n-1e; 2780]   "

Καϊάφας, ᾶ, ὁ   {2780, n-1e}
Caiaphas, pr. name, the high priest from A.D.
18-36, Matt 26:3, 57; Luke 3:2; John 11:49;
18:13f., 24, 28; Acts 4:6*

Καϊάφας   nom sg masc [3t; n-1e; 2780]   "

καίγε   {2781}
at least, were it only, Luke 19:42; *and even, yea too*,
Acts 2:18

καίεται   pres pass ind 3 sg
[Jn 15:6; v-2c; 2794]   καίω

Κάϊν, ὁ   {2782, n-3g(2)}
Cain, pr. name, indecl., Heb 11:4; 1 John 3:12;
Jude 11*

Κάϊν   indecl [3t; n-3g(2); 2782]   Κάϊν
καινά   nom pl neut
[2C 5:17; a-1a(2a); 2785]   καινός
καινά   acc pl neut [2t; a-1a(2a); 2785]   "
καιναῖς   dat pl fem [Mk 16:17; a-1a(2a); 2785]   "

Καϊνάμ, ὁ   {2783, n-3g(2)}
Cainan, pr. name, indecl., Luke 3:36, 37*

Καϊνάμ   indecl [2t; n-3g(2); 2783]   Καϊνάμ
καινή   nom sg fem [6t; a-1a(2a); 2785]   καινός
καινήν   acc sg fem [11t; a-1a(2a); 2785]   "
καινῆς   gen sg fem [3t; a-1a(2a); 2785]   "

Καϊνάν, ὁ   {2784, n-3g(2)}
Cainan, pr. name, indecl., (1) *Cainan, son of
Arphaxad*, Luke 3:36, 37, (2) *Cainan, son of Enos*,
Luke 3:37

καινόν   nom sg neut [2t; a-1a(2a); 2785]   "
καινόν   acc sg masc [3t; a-1a(2a); 2785]   "
καινόν   acc sg neut [5t; a-1a(2a); 2785]   "

καινός, ή, όν   {2785, a-1a(2a)}
new, recently made, Matt 9:17; Mark 2:22; *new* in
species, character, or mode, Matt 26:28, 29;
Mark 14:24, 25; Luke 22:20; John 13:34; 2 Cor
5:17; Gal 6:15; Eph 2:15; 4:24; 1 John 2:7; Rev
3:12; *novel, strange*, Mark 1:27; Acts 17:19; *new
to the possessor*, Mark 16:17; *unheard of,
unusual*, Mark 1:27; Acts 17:19; met. *renovated,
better, of higher excellence*, 2 Cor 5:17; Rev 5:9

καινότερον   acc sg neut comparative
[Ac 17:21; a-1a(2a); 2785]   "

καινότερος, α, ον   {a-1a(1)}
compar. of καινός, *newer, more recent;* but used
for the positive, *new, novel*, Acts 17:21

καινότης, ητος, ἡ   {2786, n-3c(1)}
newness, Rom 6:4; 7:6*

καινότητι   dat sg fem [2t; n-3c(1); 2786]   καινότης
καινοῦ   gen sg neut [2t; a-1a(2a); 2785]   καινός
καινούς   acc pl masc [4t; a-1a(2a); 2785]   "
καινῷ   dat sg neut [Mt 27:60; a-1a(2a); 2785]   "
καιόμεναι   pres pass ptcp nom pl fem
[Rv 4:5; v-2c; 2794]   καίω
καιομένη   pres pass ptcp nom sg fem
[Lk 24:32; v-2c; 2794]   "
καιομένη   pres pass ptcp dat sg fem
[Rv 21:8; v-2c; 2794]   "
καιομένης   pres pass ptcp gen sg fem
[Rv 19:20; v-2c; 2794]   "
καιόμενοι   pres pass ptcp nom pl masc
[Lk 12:35; v-2c; 2794]   "
καιόμενον   pres pass ptcp nom sg neut
[Rv 8:8; v-2c; 2794]   "
καιόμενος   pres pass ptcp nom sg masc
[2t; v-2c; 2794]   "
καίουσιν   pres act ind 3 pl [Mt 5:15; v-2c; 2794]   "

καίπερ   {2788, conj}
though, although; Phil 3:4; Heb 5:8; 7:5; 12:17; 2
Peter 1:12*

καίπερ   conj [5t; conj; 2788]   καίπερ
καιροί   nom pl masc [3t; n-2a; 2789]   καιρός
καιροῖς   dat pl masc [5t; n-2a; 2789]   "
καιρόν   acc sg masc [21t; n-2a; 2789]   "

καιρός, ου, ὁ   {2789, n-2a}
pr. *fitness, proportion, suitableness; a fitting
situation, suitable place*, 1 Peter 4:17; *a limited
period of time marked by a suitableness of
circumstances, a fitting season*, 1 Cor 4:5; 1 Tim
2:6; 6:15; Titus 1:3; *opportunity*, Acts 24:25; Gal

6:10; Heb 11:15; *a limited period of time marked by characteristic circumstances, a signal juncture, a marked season,* Matt 16:3; Luke 12:56; 21:8; 1 Peter 1:11; *a destined time,* Matt 8:29; 26:18; Mark 1:15; Luke 21:24; 1 Thess 5:1; *a season* in ordinary succession, equivalent to ὥρα, Matt 13:30; Acts 14:17; in N.T. *a limited time, a short season,* Luke 4:13; simply, *a point of time,* Matt 11:25; Luke 13:1

καιρός   nom sg masc   [17t; n-2a; 2789]   "
καιροῦ   gen sg masc   [7t; n-2a; 2789]   "
καιρούς   acc pl masc   [5t; n-2a; 2789]   "
καιρῷ   dat sg masc   [24t; n-2a; 2789]   "
καιρῶν   gen pl masc   [3t; n-2a; 2789]   "

Καῖσαρ, ρος, ὁ   {2790, n-3f(2a)}
   Caesar, pr. name

Καίσαρα   acc sg masc   [8t; n-3f(2a); 2790]   Καῖσαρ

Καισάρεια, ας, ἡ   {2791, n-1a}
   Caesarea (1) *Caesarea Philippi,* Matt 16:13; Mark 8:27; (2) *Caesarea Augusta,* Acts 8:40

Καισαρείᾳ   dat sg fem
    [Ac 10:1; n-1a; 2791]   Καισάρεια
Καισάρειαν   acc sg fem   [10t; n-1a; 2791]   "
Καισαρείας   gen sg fem   [6t; n-1a; 2791]   "
Καίσαρι   dat sg masc   [9t; n-3f(2a); 2790]   Καῖσαρ
Καίσαρος   gen sg masc   [12t; n-3f(2a); 2790]

καίτοι   {2792, particle}
   and yet, though, although, Acts 14:17; Heb 4:3*

καίτοι   part   [2t; particle; 2792]   καίτοι

καίτοιγε   {2793, particle}
   although indeed, and yet, John 4:2; Acts 14:17 v.l.*

καίτοιγε   conj   [Jn 4:2; particle; 2793]   καίτοιγε

καίω   {2794, v-2c}
   [καύσω, ἔκαυσα, ἐκέκαυκα, κεκαύμαι, ἐκαύθην] *to cause to burn, kindle, light,* Matt 5:15; pass. *to be kindled, burn, flame,* Luke 12:35; met. *to be kindled* into emotion, Luke 24:32; *to consume with fire,* John 15:6; 1 Cor 13:3

κακά   nom pl neut   [Ti 1:12; a-1a(2a); 2805]   κακός
κακά   acc pl neut   [5t; a-1a(2a); 2805]   "
κακαί   nom pl fem   [1C 15:33; a-1a(2a); 2805]   "

κἀκεῖ   {2795, adverb}
   crasis, *and there,* Matt 5:23; 10:11; *there also,* Mark 1:38 v.l.; *there also,* Acts 17:13

κἀκεῖ   crasis   [10t; adverb; 2795]   κἀκεῖ

κἀκεῖθεν   {2796, adverb}
   crasis, *and there,* Mark 10:1; Acts 7:4; 14:26; 20:15; 21:1; 27:4, 12; 28:15; *and then, afterwards,* Acts 13:21

κἀκεῖθεν   crasis   [10t; adverb; 2796]   κἀκεῖθεν
κἀκεῖνα   crasis   [4t; a-1a(2b); 2797]   κἀκεῖνος
κἀκεῖνοι   crasis   [7t; a-1a(2b); 2797]   "
κἀκεῖνον   crasis   [3t; a-1a(2b); 2797]   "

κἀκεῖνος, η, ο   {2797, a-1a(2b)}
   crasis, *and he, she, it; and this, and that,* Matt 15:18; 23:23; *he, she, it also; this also, that also,* Matt 20:4

κἀκεῖνος   crasis   [7t; a-1a(2b); 2797]   "
κἀκείνους   crasis   [Ac 18:19; a-1a(2b); 2797]   "
κακήν   acc sg fem   [Cl 3:5; a-1a(2a); 2805]   κακός

κακία, ας, ἡ   {2798, n-1a}
   malice, malignity, Rom 1:29; Eph 4:31; *wickedness, depravity,* Acts 8:22; 1 Cor 5:8; in N.T. *evil, trouble, calamity, misfortune,* Matt 6:34

κακία   nom sg fem   [Mt 6:34; n-1a; 2798]   κακία
κακίᾳ   dat sg fem   [4t; n-1a; 2798]   "
κακίαν   acc sg fem   [2t; n-1a; 2798]   "
κακίας   gen sg fem   [4t; n-1a; 2798]   "

κακοήθεια, ας, ἡ   {2799, n-1a}
   disposition for mischief, misfortune, malignity, Rom 1:29*

κακοηθείας   gen sg fem
    [Rm 1:29; n-1a; 2799]   κακοήθεια
κακοί   nom pl masc   [Mk 7:21; a-1a(2a); 2805] κακός

κακολογέω   {2800, cv-1d(2a)}
   [-, ἐκακολόγησα, -, -, -] *to speak evil of, revile, abuse, insult,* Mark 9:39; Acts 19:9; *to address with offensive language, to treat with disrespect,* Matt, 15:4; Mark 7:10*

κακολογῆσαι   aor act inf
    [Mk 9:39; cv-1d(2a); 2800]   κακολογέω
κακολογοῦντες   pres act ptcp nom pl masc
    [Ac 19:9; cv-1d(2a); 2800]   "
κακολογῶν   pres act ptcp nom sg masc
    [2t; cv-1d(2a); 2800]   "
κακόν   nom sg neut   [3t; a-1a(2a); 2805]   κακός
κακόν   acc sg neut   [21t; a-1a(2a); 2805]   "
κακοπαθεῖ   pres act ind 3 sg
    [Jm 5:13; cv-1d(2a) ; 2802]   κακοπαθέω

κακοπάθεια, ας, ἡ   {2801, n-1a}
   a state of suffering, affliction, trouble, in N.T. *endurance in affliction, perseverance,* James 5:10*

κακοπαθέω   {2802, cv-1d(2a) }
   [-, ἐκακοπάθησα, -, -, -] *to suffer evil* or *afflictions,* 2 Tim 2:9; *to be afflicted, troubled, dejected,* James 5:13; in N.T. *to show endurance in trials and afflictions,* 2 Tim 4:5*

κακοπάθησον   aor act imperative 2 sg
    [2Ti 4:5; cv-1d(2a) ; 2802]   "
κακοπαθίας   gen sg fem
    [Jm 5:10; n-1a; 2801]   κακοπάθεια
κακοπαθῶ   pres act ind 1 sg
    [2Ti 2:9; cv-1d(2a) ; 2802]   κακοπαθέω

κακοποιέω   {2803, cv-1d(2a)}
   [-, ἐκακοποίησα, -, -, -] *to cause evil, injure, do harm,* Mark 3:4; Luke 6:9; *to do evil, commit sin,* 1 Peter 3:17; 3 John 11*

κακοποιῆσαι   aor act inf
    [2t; cv-1d(2a); 2803]   κακοποιέω

κακοποιός, όν   {2804, a-3a}
   an evil-doer, 1 Peter 2:12, 14; 4:15; *a malefactor, criminal,* John 18:30 v.l.*

κακοποιός   nom sg masc
    [1P 4:15; a-3a; 2804]   κακοποιός

κακοποιοῦντας   pres act ptcp acc pl masc
   [1P 3:17; cv-1d(2a); 2803]   κακοποιέω
κακοποιῶν   gen pl masc [2t; a-3a; 2804]   κακοποιός
κακοποιῶν   pres act ptcp nom sg masc
   [3J 11; cv-1d(2a); 2803]   κακοποιέω

κακός, ή, όν   {2805, a-1a(2a)}
   bad, of a bad quality or *disposition, worthless,*
   corrupt, depraved, Matt 21:41; 24:48; Mark 7:21;
   wicked, criminal, morally bad; τὸ κακόν, *evil,*
   wickedness, crime, Matt 27:23; Acts 23:9;
   deceitful, 1 Peter 3:10; *mischievous, harmful,*
   destructive; τὸ κακόν, *evil mischief, harm, injury,*
   Titus 1:12; *afflictive;* τὸ κακόν, *evil, misery,*
   affliction, suffering, Luke 16;25

κακός   nom sg masc
   [Mt 24:48; a-1a(2a); 2805]   κακός
κακοῦ   gen sg neut [8t; a-1a(2a); 2805]   "
κακοῦργοι   nom pl masc
   [Lk 23:32; a-3a; 2806]   κακοῦργος

κακοῦργος, ον   {2806, a-3a}
   an evil-doer, malefactor, criminal, Luke 23:32, 33,
   39; 2 Tim 2:9*

κακοῦργος   nom sg masc [2Ti 2:9; a-3a; 2806]   "
κακούργους   acc pl masc [Lk 23:33; a-3a; 2806]   "
κακούργων   gen pl masc [Lk 23:39; a-3a; 2806]   "
κακούς   acc pl masc [3t; a-1a(2a); 2805]   κακός

κακουχέω   {2807, cv-1d(2a)}
   [-, -, -, -, -] *to torment, afflict, harass;* pass. *to be*
   afflicted, be oppressed with evils, Heb 11:37 13:3*

κακουχούμενοι   pres pass ptcp nom pl masc
   [Hb 11:37; cv-1d(2a); 2807]   κακουχέω
κακουχουμένων   pres pass ptcp gen pl masc
   [Hb 13:3; cv-1d(2a); 2807]   "

κακόω   {2808, v-1d(3)}
   [κακώσω, ἐκάκωσα, -, κεκάκωμαι, -] *to harm,*
   mistreat, cause evil to, oppress, Acts 7:6, 19; 12:1;
   18:10; 1 Peter 3:13; in N.T. *to make angry,*
   embitter, Acts 14:2*

κακῷ   dat sg neut [Rm 13:3; a-1a(2a); 2805]   κακός
κακῶν   gen pl neut [4t; a-1a(2a); 2805]   "

κακῶς   {2809, adverb}
   ill, badly; physically *ill, sick,* Matt 4:24; 8:16;
   grievously, vehemently, Matt 15:22; 17:5 v.l.;
   wretchedly, miserably, Matt 21:41; *wickedly,*
   reproachfully, Acts 23:5; *wrongly, criminally,* John
   18:23; *amiss,* James 4:3

κακῶς   adverb [16t; adverb; 2809]   κακῶς
κακῶσαι   aor act inf [2t; v-1d(3); 2808]   κακόω
κάκωσιν   acc sg fem
   [Ac 7:34; n-3e(5b); 2810]   κάκωσις

κάκωσις, εως, ή   {2810, n-3e(5b)}
   ill-treatment, affliction, oppression, misery, Acts
   7:34*

κακώσουσιν   fut act ind 3 pl
   [Ac 7:6; v-1d(3); 2808]   κακόω
κακώσων   fut act ptcp nom sg masc
   [1P 3:13; v-1d(3); 2808]   "

καλά   nom pl neut [2t; a-1a(2a); 2819]   καλός
καλά   acc pl neut [5t; a-1a(2a); 2819]   "

καλάμη, ῆς, ή   {2811, n-1b}
   the stalk of grain, *straw, stubble,* 1 Cor 3:12*

καλάμην   acc sg fem [1C 3:12; n-1b; 2811]   καλάμη
κάλαμον   acc sg masc [6t; n-2a; 2812]   κάλαμος

κάλαμος, ου, ό   {2812, n-2a}
   a reed, cane, Matt 11:7; 12:20; Luke 7:24; *a reed* in
   its various appliances, as, a wand, a staff, Matt
   27:29, 30, 48; Mark 15:19, 36; *a measuring-rod,*
   Rev 11:1; 21:15f.; a writer's *reed,* 3 John 13*

κάλαμος   nom sg masc [Rv 11:1; n-2a; 2812]   "
καλάμου   gen sg masc [3J 13; n-2a; 2812]   "
καλάμῳ   dat sg masc [4t; n-2a; 2812]   "
κάλει   pres act imperative 2 sg
   [Lk 14:13; v-1d(2b); 2813]   καλέω
καλεῖ   pres act ind 3 sg [4t; v-1d(2b); 2813]   "
καλεῖν   pres act inf [Hb 2:11; v-1d(2b); 2813]   "
καλεῖσθαι   pres pass inf [3t; v-1d(2b); 2813]   "
καλεῖται   pres pass ind 3 sg [5t; v-1d(2b); 2813] "
καλεῖτε   pres act ind 2 pl
   [Lk 6:46; v-1d(2b); 2813]   "
καλέσαι   aor act inf [4t; v-1d(2b); 2813]   "
καλέσαντα   aor act ptcp acc sg masc
   [1P 1:15; v-1d(2b); 2813]   "
καλέσαντες   aor act ptcp nom pl masc
   [Ac 4:18; v-1d(2b); 2813]   "
καλέσαντος   aor act ptcp gen sg masc
   [4t; v-1d(2b); 2813]   "
καλέσας   aor act ptcp nom sg masc
   [6t; v-1d(2b); 2813]   "
καλέσατε   aor act imperative 2 pl
   [Mt 22:9; v-1d(2b); 2813]   "
καλέσεις   fut act ind 2 sg [3t; v-1d(2b); 2813] "
καλέσητε   aor act subj 2 pl
   [Mt 23:9; v-1d(2b); 2813]   "
κάλεσον   aor act imperative 2 sg
   [Mt 20:8; v-1d(2b); 2813]   "
καλέσουσιν   fut act ind 3 pl
   [Mt 1:23; v-1d(2b); 2813]   "
καλέσω   fut act ind 1 sg
   [Rm 9:25; v-1d(2b); 2813]   "

καλέω   {2813, v-1d(2b)}
   [(ἐκάλουν), καλέσω, ἐκάλεσα, κέκληκα,
   κέκλημαι, ἐκλήθην] *to call, call to,* John 10:3; *to*
   call into one's presence, *send for* a person, Matt
   2:7; *to summon,* Matt 2:15; 25:14; *to invite,* Matt
   22:9; *to call* to the performance of a certain
   thing, Matt 9:13; Heb 11:8; *to call* to a
   participation in the privileges of the Gospel,
   Rom 8:30; 9:24; 1 Cor 1:9; 7:18; *to call* to an office
   or dignity, Heb 5:4; *to name, style,* Matt 1:21;
   pass. *to be styled, regarded,* Matt 5:9, 19

καλῇ   dat sg fem [2t; a-1a(2a); 2819]   καλός
καλήν   acc sg fem [11t; a-1a(2a); 2819]   "
καλῆς   gen sg fem [2t; a-1a(2a); 2819]   "
καλλιέλαιον   acc sg fem
   [Rm 11:24; n-2b; 2814]   καλλιέλαιος

καλλιέλαιος, οῦ, ή   {2814, n-2b}
   pr. adj. *productive of good oil;* as subst. *a*
   cultivated olive tree, Rom 11:24*

κάλλιον   adverb-comparative
[Ac 25:10; adverb; 2822]   καλῶς

καλοδιδάσκαλος, ον   {2815, a-3a}
teaching what is good; a teacher of good, Titus 2:3*

καλοδιδασκάλους   acc pl fem
[Ti 2:3; a-3a; 2815]   καλοδιδάσκαλος

Καλοὶ Λιμένες   {2816}
formed from καλός and λιμήν (n-3f[1b]), *Fair Havens,* a harbor of Crete, Acts 27:8*

καλοί   nom pl masc [1P 4:10; a-1a(2a); 2819]   καλός
καλοῖς   dat pl masc [Lk 21:5; a-1a(2a); 2819]   "
καλοῖς   dat pl neut [2t; a-1a(2a); 2819]   "

καλοκαγαθία, ας, ἡ   {2817, n-1a}
nobility of character, James 5:10 v.l.*

καλόν   nom sg neut [27t; a-1a(2a); 2819]   "
καλόν   acc sg masc [11t; a-1a(2a); 2819]   "
καλόν   acc sg neut [16t; a-1a(2a); 2819]   "

καλοποιέω   {2818, cv-1d(2a)}
[-, -, -, -, -] *to do well, do good, do what is right,* 2 Thess 3:13*

καλοποιοῦντες   pres act ptcp nom pl masc
[2Th 3:13; cv-1d(2a); 2818]   καλοποιέω

καλός, ή, όν   {2819, a-1a(2a)}
pr. *beautiful; good, of good quality* or *disposition; fertile, rich,* Matt 13:8, 23; *useful, profitable,* Luke 14:34; καλόν ἐστι(ν), *it is profitable, it is well,* Matt 18:8, 9; *excellent, choice, select, goodly,* Matt 7:17, 19; καλόν ἐστι(ν), *it is pleasant, delightful,* Matt 17:4; *just, full* measure, Luke 6:38; *honorable, distinguished,* James 2:7; *good, possessing moral excellence, worthy, upright, virtuous,* John 10:11, 14; 1 Tim 4:6; τὸ καλόν, and τὸ καλόν ἔργον, *what is good and right, a good deed, rectitude, virtue,* Matt 5:16; Rom 7:18, 21; *right, duty, propriety,* Matt 15:26; *benefit, favor,* John 10:32, 33

καλός   nom sg masc [7t; a-1a(2a); 2819]   καλός
καλοῦ   gen sg neut [3t; a-1a(2a); 2819]   "
καλουμένη   pres pass ptcp nom sg fem
[3t; v-1d(2b); 2813]   καλέω
καλουμένῃ   pres pass ptcp dat sg fem
[3t; v-1d(2b); 2813]   "
καλουμένην   pres pass ptcp acc sg fem
[3t; v-1d(2b); 2813]   "
καλουμένης   pres pass ptcp gen sg fem
[Ac 10:1; v-1d(2b); 2813]   "
καλούμενον   pres pass ptcp acc sg masc
[8t; v-1d(2b); 2813]   "
καλούμενον   pres pass ptcp acc sg neut
[3t; v-1d(2b); 2813]   "
καλούμενος   pres pass ptcp nom sg masc
[7t; v-1d(2b); 2813]   "
καλουμένου   pres pass ptcp gen sg masc
[Ac 7:58; v-1d(2b); 2813]   "
καλουμένου   pres pass ptcp gen sg neut
[Ac 1:12; v-1d(2b); 2813]   "
καλοῦνται   pres pass ind 3 pl
[Lk 22:25; v-1d(2b); 2813]   "
καλοῦντες   pres act ptcp nom pl masc
[Mk 3:31; v-1d(2b); 2813]   "

καλοῦντος   pres act ptcp gen sg masc
[4t; v-1d(2b); 2813]   "
καλούς   acc pl masc [4t; a-1a(2a); 2819]   καλός
καλοῦσα   pres act ptcp nom sg fem
[1P 3:6; v-1d(2b); 2813]   καλέω

κάλυμμα, ατος, τό   {2820, n-3c(4)}
a covering; a veil, 2 Cor 3:13; met. *a veil, a blind* to spiritual vision, 2 Cor 3:14, 15, 16*

κάλυμμα   nom sg neut [3t; n-3c(4); 2820]   κάλυμμα
κάλυμμα   acc sg neut [2C 3:13; n-3c(4); 2820]   "
καλύπτει   pres act ind 3 sg
[2t; v-4; 2821]   καλύπτω
καλύπτεσθαι   pres pass inf [Mt 8:24; v-4; 2821]   "

καλύπτω   {2821, v-4}
[καλύψω, ἐκάλυψα, -, κεκάλυμμαι, ἐκαλύφθην]
to cover, Matt 8:24; Luke 8:16; 23:30; *to hide, conceal,* Matt 10:26; 2 Cor 4:3; met. *to cover, throw a veil* of oblivion *over,* James 5:20; 1 Peter 4:8

καλύψατε   aor act imperative 2 pl
[Lk 23:30; v-4; 2821]   "
καλύψει   fut act ind 3 sg [Jm 5:20; v-4; 2821]   "
καλῷ   dat sg neut [Ga 4:18; a-1a(2a); 2819]   καλός
καλῶν   gen pl neut [6t; a-1a(2a); 2819]   "
καλῶν   pres act ptcp nom sg masc
[1Th 5:24; v-1d(2b); 2813]   καλέω

καλῶς   {2822, adverb}
well, rightly, suitable, with propriety, becomingly, 1 Cor 7:37; 14:17; Gal 4:17; 5:7; *truly, justly, correctly,* Mark 12:32; Luke 20:39; John 4:17; *appositely,* Matt 15:7; Mark 7:6; *becomingly, honorably,* James 2:3; *well, effectually,* Mark 7:9, 37; καλῶς εἰπεῖν, *to speak well, praise, applaud,* Luke 6:26; καλῶς ἔχειν, *to be convalescent,* Mark 16:18; καλῶς ποιεῖν, *to do good, confer benefits,* Matt 5:44; 12:12; *to do well, act virtuously,* Phil 4:14

καλῶς   adverb [36t; adverb; 2822]   καλῶς
κἀμέ   crasis [3t; a-5a; 2743]   κἀγώ
κάμηλον   acc sg masc
[Lk 18:25; n-2a; 2823]   κάμηλος
κάμηλον   acc sg fem [3t; n-2a; 2823]   "

κάμηλος, ου, ὁ or ἡ   {2823, n-2a/n-2b}
a camel, Matt 3:4; 23:24

καμήλου   gen sg fem [2t; n-2a; 2823]   "
κάμητε   aor act subj 2 pl
[Hb 12:3; v-3a(1); 2827]   κάμνω

κάμιλος, ου, ὁ   {2824, n-2a}
cable (on a ship), rope, v.l. in Matt 19:24, Mark 10:25, and Luke 18:25*

κάμινον   acc sg fem [2t; n-2b; 2825]   κάμινος

κάμινος, ου, ἡ   {2825, n-2b}
a furnace, oven, kiln, Matt 13:42, 50; Rev 1:15; 9:2*

καμίνου   gen sg fem [Rv 9:2; n-2b; 2825]   "
καμίνῳ   dat sg fem [Rv 1:15; n-2b; 2825]   "

καμμύω   {2826, v-1a(4)}
[-, ἐκάμμυσα, -, -, -] *to shut, close* the eyes, Matt
13:15; Acts 28:27*

κάμνοντα pres act ptcp acc sg masc
[Jm 5:15; v-3a(1); 2827]   κάμνω

κάμνω   {2827, v-3a(1)}
[-, ἔκαμον, κέκμηκα, -, -] *to tire with exertion,
labor to weariness; to be wearied, tired out,
exhausted, be discouraged,* Heb 12:3; *to labor
under disease, be sick,* James 5:15*

κἀμοί crasis [5t; a-5a; 2743]   κἀγώ

κάμπτω   {2828, v-4}
[κάμψω, ἔκαμψα, -, -, -] trans. *to bend, inflect* the
knee, Rom 11:4; Eph 3:14 intrans. *to bend, bow,*
Rom 14:11; Phil 2:10*

κάμπτω pres act ind 1 sg
[Ep 3:14; v-4; 2828]   κάμπτω
κάμψει fut act ind 3 sg [Rm 14:11; v-4; 2828]   "
κάμψῃ aor act subj 3 sg [Pp 2:10; v-4; 2828]   "

κἄν   {2829, particle}
crasis, *and if,* Mark 16:18; *also if,* Matt 21:21;
even if, if even, although, John 10:38; *if so much as,*
Heb 12:20; also in N.T. simply equivalent to
καί, as a particle of emphasis, by a pleonasm of
ἄν, *at least, at all events,* Mark 6:56; Acts 5:15; 2
Cor 11:16

κἄν crasis [17t; particle; 2829]   κἄν

Κανά, ἡ   {2830, n-3g(2)}
indecl. *Cana,* a town in Galilee, John 2:1, 11;
4:46; 21:2*

Κανά indecl [4t; n-3g(2); 2830]   Κανά
Καναναῖον acc sg masc
[Mk 3:18; n-2a; 2831]   Καναναῖος

Καναναῖος, ου, ὁ   {2831, n-2a}
a Canaanite, Matt 10:4; Mark 3:18*

Καναναῖος nom sg masc [Mt 10:4; n-2a; 2831]   "

Κανανίτης, ου, ὁ   {2832, n-1f}
Canaanite, Matt 10:4; Mark 3:18*

Κανδάκη, ης, ἡ   {2833, n-1b}
Candace, pr. name, Acts 8:27*

Κανδάκης gen sg fem [Ac 8:27; n-1b; 2833]
      Κανδάκη
κανόνα acc sg masc
[2C 10:15; n-3f(1b); 2834]   κανών
κανόνι dat sg masc [2t; n-3f(1b); 2834]   "
κανόνος gen sg masc [2C 10:13; n-3f(1b); 2834] "

κανών, όνος, ὁ   {2834, n-3f(1b)}
a measure, rule; in N.T. *prescribed range* of action
or duty, 2 Cor 10:13, 15, 16; met. *rule* of conduct
or doctrine, Gal 6:16; Phil 3:16 v.l.*

Καπερναούμ, ἡ, see Καφαρναούμ {2836, n-3g(2)}
Capernaum, indecl., a city of Galilee, v.l. only

καπηλεύοντες pres act ptcp nom pl masc
[2C 2:17; v-1a(6); 2836]   καπηλεύω

καπηλεύω   {2836, v-1a(6)}
[-, -, -, -, -] pr. *to be κάπηλος, a retailer; to peddle
with; to corrupt, adulterate,* 2 Cor 2:17*

καπνόν acc sg masc [2t; n-2a; 2837]   καπνός

καπνός, οῦ, ὁ   {2837, n-2a}
smoke, Acts 2:19; Rev 8:4

καπνός nom sg masc [6t; n-2a; 2837]   "
καπνοῦ gen sg masc [5t; n-2a; 2837]   "

Καππαδοκία, ας, ἡ   {2838, n-1a}
Cappadocia, a district of Asia Minor, Acts 2:9; 1
Peter 1:1*

Καππαδοκίαν acc sg fem
[Ac 2:9; n-1a; 2838]   Καππαδοκία
Καππαδοκίας gen sg fem [1P 1:1; n-1a; 2838]   "

καραδοκία, ας, ἡ   {2839, n-1a}
eager expectation, Phil 1:20 v.l.*

καρδία, ας, ἡ   {2840, n-1a}
the heart, regarded as the seat of feeling,
impulse, affection, desire, Matt 6:21; 22:37; Phil
1:7; *the heart,* as the seat of intellect, Matt 13:15;
Rom 1:21; *the heart,* as the inner and mental
frame, Matt 5:8; Luke 16:15; 1 Peter 3:4; *the
conscience,* 1 John 3:20, 21; *the heart, the inner
part, middle, center,* Matt 12:40

καρδία nom sg fem [19t; n-1a; 2840]   καρδία
καρδίᾳ dat sg fem [35t; n-1a; 2840]   "
καρδίαι nom pl fem [2t; n-1a; 2840]   "
καρδίαις dat pl fem [21t; n-1a; 2840]   "
καρδίαν acc sg fem [18t; n-1a; 2840]   "
καρδίας gen sg fem [32t; n-1a; 2840]   "
καρδίας acc pl fem [25t; n-1a; 2840]   "
καρδιογνῶστα voc sg masc
[Ac 1:24; n-1f; 2841]   καρδιογνώστης

καρδιογνώστης, ου, ὁ   {2841, n-1f}
heart-knower, searcher of hearts, Acts 1:24; 15:8*

καρδιογνώστης nom sg masc [Ac 15:8; n-1f; 2841] "
καρδιῶν gen pl fem [4t; n-1a; 2840]   καρδία
καρπόν acc sg masc [38t; n-2a; 2843]   καρπός

Κάρπος, ου, ὁ   {2842, n-2a}
Carpus, pr. name, 2 Tim 4:13*

καρπός, οῦ, ὁ   {2843, n-2a}
fruit, Matt 3:10; 21:19, 34; from the Hebrew,
καρπὸς κοιλίας, *fruit of the womb, offspring,* Luke
1:42; καρπὸς ὀσφύος, *fruit of the loins, offspring,
posterity,* Acts 2:30; καρπὸς χειλέων, *fruit of the
lips, praise,* Heb 13:15; met. *conduct, actions,*
Matt 3:8; 7:16; Rom 6:22; *benefit, profit,* Rom
1:13; 6:21; *reward,* Phil 4:17

καρπός nom sg masc [8t; n-2a; 2843]   "
καρποῦ gen sg masc [4t; n-2a; 2843]   "
καρπούς acc pl masc [10t; n-2a; 2843]   "
καρποφορεῖ pres act ind 3 sg
[2t; v-1d(2a); 2844]   καρποφορέω

καρποφορέω   {2844, v-1d(2a)}
[καρποφορήσω, ἐκαρποφόρησα, -, -, -] *to bear fruit,
yield,* Mark 4:28; met. *to bring forth the fruit* of
action or conduct, Matt 13:23; Rom 7:5; mid. *to*

expand by fruitfulness, to develop itself by success,
Col 1:6, 10

καρποφορῆσαι   aor act inf
    [Rm 7:5; v-1d(2a); 2844]   "
καρποφορήσωμεν   aor act subj 1 pl
    [Rm 7:4; v-1d(2a); 2844]   "

καρποφόρος, ον   {2845, a-3a}
fruitful, adapted to bring forth fruit, Acts 14:17;
John 15:2 v.l.*

καρποφορούμενον   pres mid ptcp nom sg neut
    [Cl 1:6; v-1d(2a); 2844]   "
καρποφοροῦντες   pres act ptcp nom pl masc
    [Cl 1:10; v-1d(2a); 2844]   "
καρποφόρους   acc pl masc
    [Ac 14:17; a-3a; 2845]   καρποφόρος
καρποφοροῦσιν   pres act ind 3 pl
    [2t; v-1d(2a); 2844]   καρποφορέω
Κάρπῳ   dat sg masc [2Ti 4:13; n-2a; 2842]   Κάρπος
καρπῶν   gen pl masc [6t; n-2a; 2843]   καρπός

καρτερέω   {2846, v-1d(2a)}
[-, ἐκαρτέρησα, -, -, -] *to be stout; to endure*
patiently, persevere, bear up with fortitude, Heb
11:27*

κάρφος, ους, τό   {2847, n-3d(2b)}
any small dry thing, as *chaff, stubble, splinter;*
Matt 7:3, 4, 5; Luke 6:41, 42*

κάρφος   acc sg neut [6t; n-3d(2b); 2847]   κάρφος
κατ᾽   prep-acc [67t; prep; 2848]   κατά
κατ᾽   prep-gen [18t; prep; 2848]   "

κατά   {2848, prep}
down from, Matt 8:32; *down upon, upon,* Mark
14:3; Acts 27:14; *down into;* κατὰ βάθους,
profound, deepest, 2 Cor 8:2; *down over,*
throughout a space, Luke 4:14; 23:5; *concerning,*
in cases of pointed allegation, 1 Cor 15:15;
against, Matt 12:30; *by,* in oaths, Matt 26:63;
with an acc. of place, *in the quarter of, about,*
near, at, Luke 10:32; Acts 2:10; *throughout,* Luke
8:39; *in,* Rom 16:5; *among,* Acts 21:21; *in the*
presence of, Luke 2:31; *in the direction of, towards,*
Acts 8:26; Phil 3:14; of time, *within the range of;*
during, in the course of, at, about, Acts 12:1; 27:27;
distributively, κατ᾽ οἶκον, *by houses, from house*
to house, Acts 2:46; κατὰ δύο, *two and two,* 1 Cor
14:27; καθ᾽ ἡμέραν, *daily,* Matt 26:55; trop.,
according to, conformable to, in proportion to, Matt
9:29; 25:15; *after the fashion* or *likeness of.* Heb
5:6; *in virtue of,* Matt 19:3; *as respects,* Rom 11:3;
Acts 25:14; Heb 9:9

κατά   prep-acc [284t; prep; 2848]   "
κατά   prep-gen [43t; prep; 2848]   "
καταβαίνει   pres act ind 3 sg
    [2t; cv-2d(6); 2849]   καταβαίνω
καταβαίνειν   pres act inf
    [Rv 13:13; cv-2d(6); 2849]   "
καταβαῖνον   pres act ptcp nom sg neut
    [Jm 1:17; cv-2d(6); 2849]   "
καταβαῖνον   pres act ptcp acc sg neut
    [6t; cv-2d(6); 2849]   "
καταβαίνοντα   pres act ptcp acc sg masc
    [3t; cv-2d(6); 2849]   "

καταβαίνοντας   pres act ptcp acc pl masc
    [Jn 1:51; cv-2d(6); 2849]   "
καταβαίνοντες   pres act ptcp gen sg neut
    [Lk 22:44; cv-2d(6); 2849]   "
καταβαίνοντος   pres act ptcp gen sg masc
    [Jn 4:51; cv-2d(6); 2849]   "
καταβαινόντων   pres act ptcp gen pl masc
    [2t; cv-2d(6); 2849]   "
καταβαίνουσα   pres act ptcp nom sg fem
    [Rv 3:12; cv-2d(6); 2849]   "
καταβαίνουσαν   pres act ptcp acc sg fem
    [3t; cv-2d(6); 2849]   "

καταβαίνω   {2849, cv-2d(6)}
[(κατέβαινον), καταβήσομαι, κατέβην,
καταβέβηκα, -, -] *to come* or *go down, descend,*
Matt 8:1; 17:9; *to lead down,* Acts 8:26; *to come*
down, fall, Matt 7:25, 27; *to be let down,* Acts
10:11; 11:5

καταβαίνων   pres act ptcp nom sg masc
    [2t; cv-2d(6); 2849]   "
καταβαλλόμενοι   pres mid ptcp nom pl masc
    [Hb 6:1; cv-2d(1); 2850]   καταβάλλω
καταβαλλόμενοι   pres pass ptcp nom pl masc
    [2C 4:9; cv-2d(1); 2850]   "

καταβάλλω   {2850, cv-2d(1)}
[-, -, -, -, -] *to cast down,* Rev 12:10 v.l.; *to*
prostrate, 2 Cor 4:9; mid. *to lay down, lay a*
foundation, Heb 6:1*

καταβάν   aor act ptcp acc sg neut
    [Ac 23:10; cv-2d(6); 2849]   καταβαίνω
καταβάντες   aor act ptcp nom pl masc
    [2t; cv-2d(6); 2849]   "
καταβάντος   aor act ptcp gen sg masc
    [Mt 8:1; cv-2d(6); 2849]   "

καταβαρέω   {2851, cv-1d(2a)}
[-, κατεβάρησα, -, -, -] pr. *to weigh down,* met. *to*
burden, be burdensome to, 2 Cor 12:16*

καταβαρυνόμενοι   pres mid ptcp nom pl masc
    [Mk 14:40; cv-1c(2); 2852]   καταβαρύνω

καταβαρύνω   {2852, cv-1c(2)}
[-, -, -, -, -] *to weigh down, depress,* pass., *be heavy,*
Mark 14:40*

καταβάς   aor act ptcp nom sg masc
    [12t; cv-2d(6); 2849]   καταβαίνω
καταβάσει   dat sg fem
    [Lk 19:37; n-3e(5b); 2853]   κατάβασις

κατάβασις, εως, ἡ   {2853, n-3e(5b)}
the act of descending; a way down, descent, Luke
19:37*

καταβάτω   aor act imperative 3 sg
    [5t; cv-2d(6); 2849]   καταβαίνω
καταβέβηκα   perf act ind 1 sg
    [2t; cv-2d(6); 2849]   "
καταβεβηκότες   perf act ptcp nom pl masc
    [Ac 25:7; cv-2d(6); 2849]   "
καταβῇ   aor act subj 3 sg [2t; cv-2d(6); 2849]   "
κατάβηθι   aor act imperative 2 sg
    [4t; cv-2d(6); 2849]   "
καταβῆναι   aor act inf [2t; cv-2d(6); 2849]   "

καταβήσεται   fut mid ind 3 sg
[2t; cv-2d(6); 2849]   "
καταβήση   fut mid ind 2 sg   [2t; cv-2d(6); 2849]   "

καταβιβάζω   {2854, cv-2a(1)}
[-, -, -, -, κατεβιβάσθην] *to cause to descend, bring*
or *thrust down,* Matt 11:23 v.l.; Luke 10:15 v.l.;
Acts 19:33 v.l.*

καταβοάω   {2855, cv-1d(3)}
[-, -, -, -, -] *cry out, complain,* Acts 18:13 v.l.*

καταβολή, ῆς, ἡ   {2856, n-1b}
pr. *a casting down; laying the foundation,*
foundation; beginning, commencement, Matt
13:35; 25:34; *conception* in the womb, Heb 11:11

καταβολήν   acc sg fem
[Hb 11:11; n-1b; 2856]   καταβολή
καταβολῆς   gen sg fem   [10t; n-1b; 2856]   "
καταβραβευέτω   pres act imperative 3 sg
[Cl 2:18; cv-2a(; 2857]   καταβραβεύω

καταβραβεύω   {2857, cv-1a(6)}
[-, -, -, -, -] pr. *to give an unfavorable decision as*
respects a prize; hence, *to decide against,* Col 2:18*

καταγαγεῖν   aor act inf
[Rm 10:6; cv-1b(2); 2864]   κατάγω
καταγάγη   aor act subj 3 sg
[Ac 23:15; cv-1b(2); 2864]   "
καταγάγης   aor act subj 2 sg
[Ac 23:20; cv-1b(2); 2864]   "
καταγαγόντες   aor act ptcp nom pl masc
[Lk 5:11; cv-1b(2); 2864]   "
καταγαγών   aor act ptcp nom sg masc
[Ac 22:30; cv-1b(2); 2864]   "

καταγγελεύς, έως, ὁ   {2858, n-3e(3)}
one who announces anything, *a proclaimer,*
publisher, Acts 17:18*

καταγγελεύς   nom sg masc
[Ac 17:18; n-3e(3); 2858]   καταγγελεύς
καταγγέλλειν   pres act inf
[2t; cv-2d(1); 2859]   καταγγέλλω
καταγγέλλεται   pres pass ind 3 sg
[3t; cv-2d(1); 2859]   "
καταγγέλλετε   pres act ind 2 pl
[1C 11:26; cv-2d(1); 2859]   "
καταγγέλλομεν   pres act ind 1 pl
[Cl 1:28; cv-2d(1); 2859]   "
καταγγέλλουσιν   pres act ind 3 pl
[3t; cv-2d(1); 2859]   "
καταγγέλλουσιν   pres act ptcp dat pl masc
[1C 9:14; cv-2d(1); 2859]   "

καταγγέλλω   {2859, cv-2d(1)}
[(κατήγγελλον), -, κατήγγειλα, κατήγγελκα, -,
κατηγγέλην] *to announce, proclaim,* Acts 13:38;
in N.T. *to laud, celebrate,* Rom 1:8

καταγγέλλω   pres act ind 1 sg
[2t; cv-2d(1); 2859]   "
καταγγέλλων   pres act ptcp nom sg masc
[1C 2:1; cv-2d(1); 2859]   "

καταγελάω   {2860, cv-1d(1b)}
[(κατεγέλων), -, κατεγέλασα, -, -, -] *to deride,*
laugh at, jeer, Matt 9:24; Mark 5:40; Luke 8:53*

καταγινώσκη   pres act subj 3 sg
[2t; cv-5a; 2861]   καταγινώσκω

καταγινώσκω   {2861, cv-5a}
[-, -, -, -, -] *to determine against, condemn, blame,*
reprehend, Gal 2:11; 1 John 3:20, 21; Mark 7:2 v.l.*

κατάγνυμι   {2862, cv-3c(2)}
[κατεάξω, κατέαξα, -, -, κατεάγην] *to break in*
pieces, crush, break in two, Matt 12:20; John 19:31,
32, 33*

καταγράφω   {2863, cv-1b(1)}
[(κατέγραφον), -, -, -, -, -] *to trace, draw in outline,*
write, John 8:6, 8 v.l.*

κατάγω   {2864, cv-1b(2)}
[-, κατήγαγον -, -, κατήχθην] *to lead, bring,* or
conduct down, Acts 9:30; 22:30; 23:15, 20, 28; *to*
bring a ship *to land;* pass. κατάγομαι, aor.
κατήχθην, *to come to land, land, touch,* Luke 5:11

καταγωνίζομαι   {2865, cv-2a(1)}
[-, κατηγωνισάμην, -, -, -] *to subdue, vanquish,*
overcome, conquer, Heb 11:33*

καταδέω   {2866, cv-1d(2b)}
[-, κατέδησα, -, -, -] *to bind up; to bandage* a
wound, Luke 10:34*

κατάδηλον   nom sg neut
[Hb 7:15; a-3a; 2867]   κατάδηλος

κατάδηλος, ον   {2867, a-3a}
quite clear or *evident,* Heb 7:15*

καταδικάζετε   pres act imperative 2 pl
[Lk 6:37; cv-2a(1); 2868]   καταδικάζω

καταδικάζω   {2868, cv-2a(1)}
[-, κατεδίκασα, -, -, κατεδικάσθην] *to give*
judgment against, condemn, Matt 12:7, 37; Luke
6:37; James 5:6*

καταδικασθήση   fut pass ind 2 sg
[Mt 12:37; cv-2a(1); 2868]   "
καταδικασθῆτε   aor pass subj 2 pl
[Lk 6:37; cv-2a(1); 2868]   "

καταδίκη, ῆς, ἡ   {2869, n-1b}
condemnation, sentence of condemnation, Acts
25:15*

καταδίκην   acc sg fem
[Ac 25:15; n-1b; 2869]   καταδίκη

καταδιώκω   {2870, cv-1b(2)}
[-, καταδίωξα, -, -, -] *to follow hard upon; to track,*
search for, follow perseveringly, Mark 1:36*

καταδουλοῖ   pres act ind 3 sg
[2C 11:20; cv-1d(3); 2871]   καταδουλόω

καταδουλόω   {2871, cv-1d(3)}
[καταδουλώσω, -, -, -, -] *to reduce to absolute*
servitude, make a slave of, 2 Cor 11:20; Gal 2:4*

καταδουλώσουσιν   fut act ind 3 pl
[Ga 2:4; cv-1d(3); 2871]   "
καταδυναστευομένους   pres pass ptcp acc pl masc
[Ac 10:38; cv-1a(6); 2872]   καταδυναστεύω
καταδυναστεύουσιν   pres act ind 3 pl
[Jm 2:6; cv-1a(6); 2872]   "

καταδυναστεύω {2872, cv-1a(6)}
[-, -, -, -, -] *to tyrannize over, oppress, exploit*, Acts 10:38; James 2:6*

κατάθεμα, ατος, τό {2873, n-3c(4)}
an execration, curse; by meton. *what is worthy of cursing* or *condemnation*, Rev 22:3*

κατάθεμα   nom sg neut
[Rv 22:3; n-3c(4); 2873]   κατάθεμα
καταθεματίζειν   pres act inf
[Mt 26:74; cv-2a(1); 2874]   καταθεματίζω

καταθεματίζω {2874, cv-2a(1)}
[-, -, -, -, -] *to curse*, Matt 26:74*

καταθέσθαι   aor mid inf
[2t; cv-6a; 2960]   κατατίθημι
καταισχύνει   pres act ind 3 sg
[3t; cv-1c(2); 2875]   καταισχύνω
καταισχύνετε   pres act ind 2 pl
[1C 11:22; cv-1c(2); 2875]   "
καταισχύνῃ   pres act subj 3 sg
[2t; cv-1c(2); 2875]   "
καταισχυνθῇ   aor pass subj 3 sg
[1P 2:6; cv-1c(2); 2875]   "
καταισχυνθήσεται   fut pass ind 3 sg
[2t; cv-1c(2); 2875]   "
καταισχυνθῶμεν   aor pass subj 1 pl
[2C 9:4; cv-1c(2); 2875]   "
καταισχυνθῶσιν   aor pass subj 3 pl
[1P 3:16; cv-1c(2); 2875]   "

καταισχύνω {2875, cv-1c(2)}
[(κατῄσχυνον), -, -, -, κατῄσχυμμαι, κατῃσχύνθην] *to humiliate, shame, put to shame*, 1 Cor 1:27; pass. *to be ashamed, be put to shame*, Luke 13:17; Matt 20:28 v.l.; *to dishonor, disgrace*, 1 Cor 11:4, 5; from the Hebrew, *to frustrate, disappoint*, Rom 5:5; 9:33; 1 Peter 2:6*

κατακαήσεται   fut pass ind 3 sg
[1C 3:15; cv-2c; 2876]   κατακαίω
κατακαίεται   pres pass ind 3 sg [2t; cv-2c; 2876]   "

κατακαίω {2876, cv-2c}
[(κατέκαιον), κατακαύσω, κατέκαυσα, -, -, κατεκάην or κατεκαύθην] *to burn up, consume with fire*, Matt 3:12; 13:30, 40

κατακαλύπτεσθαι   pres mid inf
[1C 11:7; cv-4; 2877]   κατακαλύπτω
κατακαλυπτέσθω   pres mid imperative 3 sg
[1C 11:6; cv-4; 2877]   "
κατακαλύπτεται   pres mid ind 3 sg
[1C 11:6; cv-4; 2877]   "

κατακαλύπτω {2877, cv-4}
[-, -, -, κατακεκάλυμμαι, -] *to veil*; mid. *to veil one's self, be veiled* or *covered*, 1 Cor 11:6, 7. In the pres act ind., 2nd sg, the personal ending σαι does not simplify as normal, κατακαυχᾶσαι*

κατακαυθήσεται   fut pass ind 3 sg
[Rv 18:8; cv-2c; 2876]   κατακαίω
κατακαῦσαι   aor act inf [Mt 13:30; cv-2c; 2876]   "
κατακαύσει   fut act ind 3 sg [2t; cv-2c; 2876]   "
κατακαύσουσιν   fut act ind 3 pl
[Rv 17:16; cv-2c; 2876]   "

κατακαυχάομαι {2878, cv-1d(1a)}
[-, -, -, -, -] *to boast, glory over, assume superiority over*, Rom 11:18; James 2:13; 3:14; 4:16 v.l.*

κατακαυχᾶσαι   pres mid ind 2 sg
[Rm 11:18; cv-1d(1a); 2878]   κατακαυχάομαι
κατακαυχᾶσθε   pres mid imperative 2 pl
[Jm 3:14; cv-1d(1a); 2878]   "
κατακαυχᾶται   pres mid ind 3 sg
[Jm 2:13; cv-1d(1a); 2878]   "
κατακαυχῶ   pres mid imperative 2 sg
[Rm 11:18; cv-1d(1a); 2878]   "

κατάκειμαι {2879, cv-6b}
[(κατεκείμην), -, -, -, -, -] *to lie, be in a recumbent position, be laid down*, Mark 1:30; 2:4; 5:40 v.l.; Luke 5:25; John 5:3, 6; Acts 9:33; 28:8; *to recline at table*, Mark 2:15; 14:3; Luke 5:29; 7:37; 1 Cor 8:10*

κατακείμενοι   pres mid ptcp nom pl masc
[Lk 5:29; cv-6b; 2879]   κατάκειμαι
κατακείμενον   pres mid ptcp acc sg masc
[3t; cv-6b; 2879]   "
κατακειμένου   pres mid ptcp gen sg masc
[Mk 14:3; cv-6b; 2879]   "
κατακεῖσθαι   pres mid inf [2t; cv-6b; 2879]   "
κατάκειται   pres mid ind 3 sg
[Lk 7:37; cv-6b; 2879]   "
κατακέκριται   perf pass ind 3 sg
[Rm 14:23; cv-1c(2); 2891]   κατακρίνω

κατακλάω {2880, cv-1d(1b)}
[-, κατέκλασα, -, -, -] *to break, break in pieces*, Mark 6:41; Luke 9:16*

κατακλείω {2881, cv-1a(3)}
[-, κατέκλεισα, -, -, -] *to close, shut fast; to shut up, confine*, Luke 3:20; Acts 26:10*

κατακληροδοτέω {2882, v-1d(2a)}
[-, κατεκληρονόμησα, -, -, -] *to divide out by lot, distribute by lot, give an inheritance*, Acts 13:19*

κατακληρονομέω {2883, cv-1d(2a)}
[-, κατεκληρονόμησα, -, -, -] same as κατακληροδοτέω, for which it is a v.l.

κατακλιθῆναι   aor pass inf
[Lk 24:30; cv-1c(2); 2884]   κατακλίνω
κατακλιθῇς   aor pass subj 2 sg
[Lk 14:8; cv-1c(2); 2884]   "
κατακλίνατε   aor act imperative 2 pl
[Lk 9:14; cv-1c(2); 2884]   "

κατακλίνω {2884, cv-1c(2)}
[-, κατέκλινα, -, -, κατεκλίθην] *to cause to lie down, cause to recline* at table, Luke 9:14, 15; mid. *to lie down, recline*, Luke 7:36; 14:8; 24:30*

κατακλύζω {2885, cv-2a(1)}
[-, -, -, -, κατεκλύσθην] *to inundate, flood, deluge*, 2 Peter 3:6*

κατακλυσθείς   aor pass ptcp nom sg masc
[2P 3:6; cv-2a(1); 2885]   κατακλύζω
κατακλυσμόν   acc sg masc
[2P 2:5; n-2a; 2886]   κατακλυσμός

κατακλυσμός, ου, ὁ {2886, n-2a}
flood, deluge, Matt 24:38, 39; Luke 17:27; 2 Peter 2:5*

κατακλυσμός nom sg masc [2t; n-2a; 2886] "
κατακλυσμοῦ gen sg masc [Mt 24:38; n-2a; 2886] "

κατακολουθέω {2887, cv-1d(2a)}
[-, κατηκολούθησα, -, -, -] *to follow closely or earnestly,* Luke 23:55; Acts 16:17*

κατακολουθήσασαι aor act ptcp nom pl fem
[Lk 23:55; cv-1d(2a); 2887] κατακολουθέω
κατακολουθοῦσα pres act ptcp nom sg fem
[Ac 16:17; cv-1d(2a); 2887] "

κατακόπτω {2888, cv-4}
[(κατέκοπτον), -, -, -, -, -] *to cut* or *dash in pieces; to mangle, wound,* Mark 5:5*

κατακόπτων pres act ptcp nom sg masc
[Mk 5:5; cv-4; 2888] κατακόπτω

κατακρημνίζω {2889, cv-2a(1)}
[-, κατεκρήμνισα, -, -, -] *to cast down headlong,* Luke 4:29*

κατακρημνίσαι aor act inf
[Lk 4:29; cv-2a(1); 2889] κατακρημνίζω
κατακριθήσεται fut pass ind 3 sg
[Mk 16:16; cv-1c(2); 2891] κατακρίνω
κατακριθῶμεν aor pass subj 1 pl
[1C 11:32; cv-1c(2); 2891] "

κατάκριμα, ατος, τό {2890, n-3c(4)}
punishment, condemnation, condemning sentence, Rom 5:16, 18; 8:1*

κατάκριμα nom sg neut
[Rm 8:1; n-3c(4); 2890] κατάκριμα
κατάκριμα acc sg neut [2t; n-3c(4); 2890] "
κατακρινεῖ fut act ind 3 sg
[2t; cv-1c(2); 2891] κατακρίνω
κατακρίνεις pres act ind 2 sg
[Rm 2:1; cv-1c(2); 2891] "
κατακρινοῦσιν fut act ind 3 pl
[4t; cv-1c(2); 2891] "

κατακρίνω {2891, cv-1c(2)}
[κατακρινῶ, κατέκρινα, -, κατακέκριμαι, κατεκρίθην] *to give judgment against, condemn,* Matt 27:3; John 8:10, 11; *to condemn, to place in a guilty light* by contrast, Matt 12:41, 42; Luke 11:31, 32; Heb 11:7

κατακρίνω pres act ind 1 sg
[Jn 8:11; cv-1c(2); 2891] "
κατακρινῶν pres act ptcp nom sg masc
[Rm 8:34; cv-1c(2); 2891] "
κατακρίσεως gen sg fem
[2C 3:9; n-3e(5b); 2892] κατάκρισις
κατάκρισιν acc sg fem [2C 7:3; n-3e(5b); 2892] "

κατάκρισις, εως, ἡ {2892, n-3e(5b)}
condemnation, 2 Cor 3:9; *censure,* 2 Cor 7:3*

κατακύπτω {2893, cv-4}
[-, κατέκυψα, -, -, -] *to bend down,* John 8:8*

κατακυριεύοντες pres act ptcp nom pl masc
[1P 5:3; cv-1a(6); 2894] κατακυριεύω

κατακυριεύουσιν pres act ind 3 pl
[2t; cv-1a(6); 2894] "
κατακυριεύσας aor act ptcp nom sg masc
[Ac 19:16; cv-1a(6); 2894] "

κατακυριεύω {2894, cv-1a(6)}
[κατακυριεύσω, κατεκυρίευσα, -, -, κατεκυριεύθην] *to get into one's power;* in N.T. *to bring under, master, overcome,* Acts 19:16; *to domineer over,* Matt 20:25; Mark 10:42; 1 Peter 5:3*

κατακύψας aor act ptcp nom sg masc
[Jn 8:8; cv-4; 2893] κατακύπτω
καταλαβέσθαι aor mid inf
[Ep 3:18; cv-3a(2b); 2898] καταλαμβάνω
καταλάβῃ aor act subj 3 sg
[3t; cv-3a(2b); 2898] "
καταλάβητε aor act subj 2 pl
[1C 9:24; cv-3a(2b); 2898] "
καταλαβόμενοι aor mid ptcp nom pl masc
[Ac 4:13; cv-3a(2b); 2898] "
καταλάβω aor act subj 1 sg
[Pp 3:12; cv-3a(2b); 2898] "
καταλαλεῖ pres act ind 3 sg
[Jm 4:11; cv-1d(2a); 2895] καταλαλέω
καταλαλεῖσθε pres pass ind 2 pl
[1P 3:16; cv-1d(2a); 2895] "
καταλαλεῖτε pres act imperative 2 pl
[Jm 4:11; cv-1d(2a); 2895] "

καταλαλέω {2895, cv-1d(2a)}
[-, -, -, -, -] *to blab out; to speak against, slander,* James 4:11; 1 Peter 2:12; 3:16*

καταλαλιά, ας, ἡ {2896, n-1a}
evil-speaking, detraction, backbiting, slandering, 2 Cor 12:20; 1 Peter 2:1*

καταλαλιαί nom pl fem
[2C 12:20; n-1a; 2896] καταλαλιά
καταλαλιάς acc pl fem [1P 2:1; n-1a; 2896] "

κατάλαλος, ον {2897, a-3a}
slanderous; a detractor, slanderer, Rom 1:30*

καταλάλους acc pl masc
[Rm 1:30; a-3a; 2897] κατάλαλος
καταλαλοῦσιν pres act ind 3 pl
[1P 2:12; cv-1d(2a); 2895] καταλαλέω
καταλαλῶν pres act ptcp nom sg masc
[Jm 4:11; cv-1d(2a); 2895] "
καταλαμβάνομαι pres mid ind 1 sg
[Ac 10:34; cv-3a(2b); 2898] καταλαμβάνω

καταλαμβάνω {2898, cv-3a(2b)}
[-, κατέλαβον, κατείληφα, κατείλημμαι, κατελήμφθην] *to lay hold of, grasp; to obtain, attain,* Rom 9:30; 1 Cor 9:24; Phil 3:12, 13; *to seize, to take possession of,* Mark 9:18; *to come suddenly upon; overtake, surprise,* John 12:35; 6:17 v.l.; 1 Thess 5:4; *to detect in the act, seize,* John 8:3, 4; met. *to comprehend, apprehend,* John 1:5; mid. *to understand, perceive,* Acts 4:13; 10:34; 25:25; Eph 3:18*

καταλεγέσθω pres pass imperative 3 sg
[1Ti 5:9; cv-1b(2); 2899] καταλέγω

καταλέγω   {2899, cv-1b(2)}
[-, -, -, -, -] *to select, enter in a list* or *catalog, enroll,*
1 Tim 5:9*

κατάλειμμα, ατος, τό   {2900, n-3c(4)}
a remnant, a small residue, Rom 9:27 v.l.*

καταλείπει   pres act ind 3 sg
[Lk 15:4; cv-1b(1); 2901]   καταλείπω
καταλειπομένης   pres pass ptcp gen sg fem
[Hb 4:1; cv-1b(1); 2901]   "
καταλείποντες   pres act ptcp nom pl masc
[2P 2:15; cv-1b(1); 2901]   "

καταλείπω   {2901, cv-1b(1)}
[(κατέλειπον), καταλείψω, κατέλειψα or
κατέλιπον, -, καταλέλειμμαι, κατελείφθην] *to
leave behind; to leave behind at death,* Mark 12:19;
to relinquish, let remain, Mark 14:52; *to quit,
depart from, forsake,* Matt 4:13; 16:4; *to neglect,*
Acts 6:2; *to leave alone,* or *without assistance,*
Luke 10:40; *to reserve,* Rom 11:4

καταλειφθῆναι   aor pass inf
[1Th 3:1; cv-1b(1); 2901]   "
καταλείψαντας   aor act ptcp acc pl masc
[Ac 6:2; cv-1b(1); 2901]   "
καταλείψει   fut act ind 3 sg [3t; cv-1b(1); 2901]   "
καταλελειμμένος   perf pass ptcp nom sg masc
[Ac 25:14; cv-1b(1); 2901]   "

καταλιθάζω   {2902, cv-2a(1)}
[καταλιθάσω, -, -, -, -] *to stone, kill by stoning,*
Luke 20:6*

καταλιθάσει   fut act ind 3 sg
[Lk 20:6; cv-2a(1); 2902]   καταλιθάζω
καταλίπῃ   aor act subj 3 sg
[Mk 12:19; cv-1b(1); 2901]   καταλείπω
καταλιπόντες   aor act ptcp nom pl masc
[Ac 21:3; cv-1b(1); 2901]   "
καταλιπών   aor act ptcp nom sg masc
[6t; cv-1b(1); 2901]   "
καταλλαγέντες   aor pass ptcp nom pl masc
[Rm 5:10; cv-2b; 2904]   καταλλάσσω

καταλλαγή, ῆς, ἡ   {2903, n-1b}
pr. *an exchange; reconciliation, restoration to favor,*
Rom 5:11; 11:15; 2 Cor 5:18, 19*

καταλλαγή   nom sg fem
[Rm 11:15; n-1b; 2903]   καταλλαγή
καταλλαγήν   acc sg fem [Rm 5:11; n-1b; 2903]   "
καταλλαγῆς   gen sg fem [2t; n-1b; 2903]   "
καταλλάγητε   aor pass imperative 2 pl
[2C 5:20; cv-2b; 2904]   καταλλάσσω
καταλλαγήτω   aor pass imperative 3 sg
[1C 7:11; cv-2b; 2904]   "
καταλλάξαντος   aor act ptcp gen sg masc
[2C 5:18; cv-2b; 2904]   "

καταλλάσσω   {2904, cv-2b}
[-, κατήλλαξα, -, -, κατηλλάγην] *to change,
exchange; to reconcile;* pass. *to be reconciled,* Rom
5:10; 1 Cor 7:11; 2 Cor 5:18, 19, 20; Acts 12:22
v.l.*

καταλλάσσων   pres act ptcp nom sg masc
[2C 5:19; cv-2b; 2904]   "

κατάλοιποι   nom pl masc
[Ac 15:17; a-3a; 2905]   κατάλοιπος

κατάλοιπος, ον   {2905, a-3a}
remaining; οἱ κατάλοιποι, *the rest,* Acts 15:17*

κατάλυε   pres act imperative 2 sg
[Rm 14:20; cv-1a(4); 2907]   καταλύω
καταλυθῇ   aor pass subj 3 sg
[2t; cv-1a(4); 2907]   "
καταλυθήσεται   fut pass ind 3 sg
[3t; cv-1a(4); 2907]   "

κατάλυμα, ατος, τό   {2906, n-3c(4)}
lodging, inn, Luke 2:7; *a guest-chamber,* Mark
14:14; Luke 22:11*

κατάλυμα   nom sg neut [2t; n-3c(4); 2906]
κατάλυμα
καταλύματι   dat sg neut [Lk 2:7; n-3c(4); 2906]   "
καταλῦσαι   aor act inf
[5t; cv-1a(4); 2907]   καταλύω
καταλύσει   fut act ind 3 sg
[Ac 6:14; cv-1a(4); 2907]   "
καταλύσω   fut act ind 1 sg
[Mk 14:58; cv-1a(4); 2907]   "
καταλύσωσιν   aor act subj 3 pl
[Lk 9:12; cv-1a(4); 2907]   "

καταλύω   {2907, cv-1a(4)}
[καταλύσω, κατέλυσα, -, -, κατελύθην] *to
dissolve; to destroy, demolish, overthrow, throw
down,* Matt 24:2; 26:61; met. *to nullify, abrogate,*
Matt 5:17; Acts 5:38, 39; absol. *to unloose
harness, etc., to halt, to stop for the night, lodge,*
Luke 9:12

καταλύων   pres act ptcp voc sg masc
[2t; cv-1a(4); 2907]   "
καταμάθετε   aor act imperative 2 pl
[Mt 6:28; cv-3a(2b); 2908]   καταμανθάνω
καταμαρτυροῦσιν   pres act ind 3 pl
[3t; cv-1d(2a); 2909]   καταμαρτυρέω

καταμανθάνω   {2908, cv-3a(2b)}
[-, κατέμαθον -, -, -] *to learn* or *observe
thoroughly; to consider accurately and diligently,
contemplate,* Matt 6:28*

καταμαρτυρέω   {2909, cv-1d(2a)}
[-, -, -, -, -] *to witness* or *testify against,* Matt
26:62; 27:13; Mark 14:60*

καταμένοντες   pres act ptcp nom pl masc
[Ac 1:13; cv-1c(2); 2910]   καταμένω

καταμένω   {2910, cv-1c(2)}
[καταμενῶ, -, -, -, -] *to remain; to abide, dwell,*
Acts 1:13; 1 Cor 16:6 v.l.*

καταμόνας   {2911}
can be written as two words, κατὰ μόνας, *alone,
apart, in private,* Mark 4:10; Luke 9:18

κατανάθεμα, ματος, τό   {2912, n-3c(4)}
see κατάθεμα, *a curse, execration;* meton. *one
accursed, execrable,* Rev 22:3 v.l.*

καταναθεματίζω   {2913, cv-2a(1)}
[-, -, -, -, -] *to curse,* Matt 26:74 v.l.*

καταναλίσκον   pres act ptcp nom sg neut
   [Hb 12:29; cv-5b; 2914]   καταναλίσκω

καταναλίσκω   {2914, cv-5b}
   [-, -, -, -, -] *to consume,* as fire, Heb 12:29*

καταναρκάω   {2915, cv-1d(1a)}
   [καταναρκήσω, κατενάρκησα, -, -, -] in N.T. *to be
   burdensome to the disadvantage of any one, to be a
   dead weight upon;* by impl. *to be troublesome,
   burdensome to,* in respect of maintenance, 2 Cor
   11:9; 12:13, 14*

καταναρκήσω   fut act ind 1 sg
   [2C 12:14; cv-1d(1a); 2915]   καταναρκάω

κατανεύω   {2916, cv-1a(6)}
   [-, κατένευσα, -, -, -] pr. *to nod, signify assent by
   a nod;* genr. *to make signs, beckon,* Luke 5:7*

κατανοεῖς   pres act ind 2 sg
   [2t; cv-1d(2a); 2917]   κατανοέω

κατανοέω   {2917, cv-1d(2a)}
   [(κατενόουν), -, κατενόησα, -, -, -] *to perceive,
   understand, apprehend,* Luke 20:23; *to observe,
   consider, contemplate,* Luke 12:24, 27; *to discern,
   detect,* Matt 7:3; *to have regard to, make account of,*
   Rom 4:19

κατανοῆσαι   aor act inf   [2t; cv-1d(2a); 2917]   "
κατανοήσας   aor act ptcp nom sg masc
   [Lk 20:23; cv-1d(2a); 2917]   "

καταντάω   {2918, cv-1d(1a)}
   [-, κατήντησα, κατήντηκα, -, -] *to come to, arrive
   at,* Acts 16:1; 20:15; of an epoch, *to come upon,* 1
   Cor 10:11; met. *to reach, attain to,* Acts 26:7

κατανοήσατε   aor act imperative 2 pl
   [3t; cv-1d(2a); 2917]   "
κατανοοῦντι   pres act ptcp dat sg masc
   [Jm 1:23; cv-1d(2a); 2917]   "
κατανοῶμεν   pres act subj 1 pl
   [Hb 10:24; cv-1d(2a); 2917]   "
καταντῆσαι   aor act inf
   [Ac 26:7; cv-1d(1a); 2918]   καταντάω
καταντήσαντες   aor act ptcp nom pl masc
   [Ac 27:12; cv-1d(1a); 2918]   "
καταντήσω   aor act subj 1 sg
   [Pp 3:11; cv-1d(1a); 2918]   "
καταντήσωμεν   aor act subj 1 pl
   [Ep 4:13; cv-1d(1a); 2918]   "
κατανύξεως   gen sg fem
   [Rm 11:8; n-3e(5b); 2919]   κατάνυξις

κατάνυξις, εως, ἡ   {2919, n-3e(5b)}
   in N.T. *deep sleep, stupor, dullness,* Rom 11:8*

κατανύσσομαι   {2920, cv-2b}
   [-, -, -, -, κατενύγην] *to pierce through; to pierce*
   with compunction and pain of heart, Acts 2:37*

καταξιόω   {2921, cv-1d(3)}
   [-, κατηξίωσα, -, -, κατηξιώθην] *to consider
   worthy of,* Luke 20:35; 21:36 v.l.; Acts 5:41; 2
   Thess 1:5*

καταξιωθέντες   aor pass ptcp nom pl masc
   [Lk 20:35; cv-1d(3); 2921]   καταξιόω

καταξιωθῆναι   aor pass inf
   [2Th 1:5; cv-1d(3); 2921]   "
καταπατεῖν   pres act inf
   [Lk 12:1; cv-1d(2a); 2922]   καταπατέω
καταπατεῖσθαι   pres pass inf
   [Mt 5:13; cv-1d(2a); 2922]   "

καταπατέω   {2922, cv-1d(2a)}
   [καταπατήσω, κατεπάτησα, -, -, κατεπατήθην] *to
   trample upon, tread down* or *under feet,* Matt 5:13;
   7:6; Luke 8:5; 12:1; met. *to trample on* by
   indignity, *spurn,* Heb 10:29*

καταπατήσας   aor act ptcp nom sg masc
   [Hb 10:29; cv-1d(2a); 2922]   "
καταπατήσουσιν   fut act ind 3 pl
   [Mt 7:6; cv-1d(2a); 2922]   "
καταπαύσεως   gen sg fem
   [Ac 7:49; n-3e(5b); 2923]   κατάπαυσις
κατάπαυσιν   acc sg fem   [8t; n-3e(5b); 2923]   "

κατάπαυσις, εως, ἡ   {2923, n-3e(5b)}
   pr. *the act of giving rest; a state of settled* or *final
   rest,* Heb 3:11, 18; 4:1, 3, 4, 5, 11; *a place of rest,
   place of abode, dwelling, habitation,* Acts 7:49*

καταπαύω   {2924, cv-1a(5)}
   [καταπαύσω, κατέπαυσα, -, -, -] *to cause to cease,
   restrain,* Acts 14:18; *to cause to rest, give final rest
   to, settle finally,* Heb 4:8; intrans. *to rest, desist
   from,* Heb 4:4, 10*

καταπεσόντων   aor act ptcp gen pl masc
   [Ac 26:14; cv-1b(3); 2928]   καταπίπτω

καταπέτασμα, ατος, τό   {2925, n-3c(4)}
   a veil, curtain, Matt 27:51; Mark 15:38; Luke
   23:45; Heb 6:19; 9:3; 10:20*

καταπέτασμα   nom sg neut
   [3t; n-3c(4); 2925]   καταπέτασμα
καταπέτασμα   acc sg neut   [Hb 9:3; n-3c(4); 2925]   "
καταπετάσματος   gen sg neut   [2t; n-3c(4); 2925]   "
καταπιεῖν   aor act inf
   [1P 5:8; cv-3a(1); 2927]   καταπίνω

καταπίμπρημι   {2926, cv-6a}
   [-, -, -, -, -] *to burn,* v.l. in 2 Peter 2:6 for
   κατέπ(ρ)ησεν*

καταπίνοντες   pres act ptcp voc pl masc
   [Mt 23:24; cv-3a(1); 2927]   "

καταπίνω   {2927, cv-3a(1)}
   [-, κατέπιον, -, -, κατεπόθην] *to drink, swallow,
   gulp down,* Matt 23:24; *to swallow up, absorb,* Rev
   12:16; 2 Cor 5:4; *to engulf, submerge, overwhelm,*
   Heb 11:29; *to swallow greedily, devour,* 1 Peter
   5:8; *to destroy, annihilate,* 1 Cor 15:54; 2 Cor 2:7*

καταπίπτειν   pres act inf
   [Ac 28:6; cv-1b(3); 2928]   καταπίπτω

καταπίπτω   {2928, cv-1b(3)}
   [-, κατέπεσον, -, -, -] *to fall down, fall prostrate,*
   Luke 8:6; Acts 26:14; 28:6*

καταπλέω   {2929, cv-1a(7)}
   [-, κατέπλευσα, -, -, -] *to sail towards land, to come
   to land,* Luke 8:26*

καταποθῇ   aor pass subj 3 sg
   [2t; cv-3a(1); 2927]   καταπίνω

καταπονέω   {2930, cv-1d(2a)}
   [-, -, -, -, -] *to exhaust by labor* or *suffering; to wear
   out,* 2 Peter 2:7; *to overpower, oppress,* Acts 7:24*

καταπονούμενον   pres pass ptcp acc sg masc
   [2P 2:7; cv-1d(2a); 2930]   καταπονέω
καταπονουμένῳ   pres pass ptcp dat sg masc
   [Ac 7:24; cv-1d(2a); 2930]   "
καταποντίζεσθαι   pres pass inf
   [Mt 14:30; cv-2a(1); 2931]   καταποντίζω

καταποντίζω   {2931, cv-2a(1)}
   [-, -, -, -, κατεποντίσθην] *to sink in the sea;* pass.
   to sink, Matt 14:30; *to be plunged, submerged,
   drowned,* Matt 18:6*

καταποντισθῇ   aor pass subj 3 sg
   [Mt 18:6; cv-2a(1); 2931]   "

κατάρα, ας, ἡ   {2932, n-1a}
   a cursing, execration, imprecation, James 3:10;
   from the Hebrew, *condemnation, doom,* Gal 3:10;
   Heb 6:8; 2 Peter 2:14; meton., *a doomed one, one
   on whom condemnation falls,* Gal 3:13*

κατάρα   nom sg fem [2t; n-1a; 2932]   κατάρα
κατάραν   acc sg fem [Ga 3:10; n-1a; 2932]   "

καταράομαι   {2933, cv-1d(1b)}
   [-, ἐκατηρασάμην, -, -, κατήραμαι] in N.T. perf.
   pass. part. κατηραμένος, *to curse, to wish evil to,
   imprecate evil upon,* Mark 11:21; Luke 6:28; Rom
   12:14; in N.T. pass. *to be doomed,* Matt 25:41;
   James 3:9*

κατάρας   gen sg fem [3t; n-1a; 2932]   "
καταρᾶσθε   pres mid imperative 2 pl
   [Rm 12:14; cv-1d(1b); 2933]   καταράομαι
καταργεῖ   pres act ind 3 sg
   [Lk 13:7; cv-1d(2a); 2934]   καταργέω
καταργεῖται   pres pass ind 3 sg
   [2t; cv-1d(2a); 2934]   "

καταργέω   {2934, cv-1d(2a)}
   [καταργήσω, κατήργησα, κατήργηκα,
   κατήργημαι, κατηργήθην] *to render useless* or
   unproductive, occupy unprofitable, Luke 13:7; *to
   render powerless,* Rom 6:6; *to make empty and
   unmeaning,* Rom 4:14; *to render null, to abrogate,
   cancel,* Rom 3:3, 31; Eph 2:15; *to bring to an end,*
   1 Cor 2:6; 13:8; 15:24, 26; 2 Cor 3:7; *to destroy,
   annihilate,* 2 Thess 2:8; Heb 2:14; *to free from,
   dissever from,* Rom 7:2, 6; Gal 5:4

καταργηθῇ   aor pass subj 3 sg
   [Rm 6:6; cv-1d(2a); 2934]   "
καταργηθήσεται   fut pass ind 3 sg
   [2t; cv-1d(2a); 2934]   "
καταργηθήσονται   fut pass ind 3 pl
   [1C 13:8; cv-1d(2a); 2934]   "
καταργῆσαι   aor act inf
   [Ga 3:17; cv-1d(2a); 2934]   "
καταργήσαντος   aor act ptcp gen sg masc
   [2Ti 1:10; cv-1d(2a); 2934]   "
καταργήσας   aor act ptcp nom sg masc
   [Ep 2:15; cv-1d(2a); 2934]   "

καταργήσει   fut act ind 3 sg
   [3t; cv-1d(2a); 2934]   "
καταργήσῃ   aor act subj 3 sg
   [3t; cv-1d(2a); 2934]   "
καταργοῦμεν   pres act ind 1 pl
   [Rm 3:31; cv-1d(2a); 2934]   "
καταργουμένην   pres pass ptcp acc sg fem
   [2C 3:7; cv-1d(2a); 2934]   "
καταργούμενον   pres pass ptcp nom sg neut
   [2C 3:11; cv-1d(2a); 2934]   "
καταργουμένου   pres pass ptcp gen sg neut
   [2C 3:13; cv-1d(2a); 2934]   "
καταργουμένων   pres pass ptcp gen pl masc
   [1C 2:6; cv-1d(2a); 2934]   "

καταριθμέω   {2935, cv-1d(2a)}
   [-, -, -, κατηρίθμημαι, -] *to enumerate, number
   with, count with,* Acts 1:17*

καταρτίζεσθε   pres pass imperative 2 pl
   [2C 13:11; cv-2a(1); 2936]   καταρτίζω
καταρτίζετε   pres act imperative 2 pl
   [Ga 6:1; cv-2a(1); 2936]   "
καταρτίζοντας   pres act ptcp acc pl masc
   [2t; cv-2a(1); 2936]   "

καταρτίζω   {2936, cv-2a(1)}
   [καταρτίσα, κατήρτισα, κατήρτισμαι,
   κατήρτισμαι, -] *to adjust thoroughly; to knit
   together, unite completely,* 1 Cor 1:10; *to frame,*
   Heb 11:3; *to prepare, provide,* Matt 21:16; Heb
   10:5; *to qualify fully, to complete* in character,
   Luke 6:40; Heb 13:21; 1 Peter 5:10; perf. pass.
   κατηρτισμένος, *fit, ripe,* Rom 9:22; *to repair, refit,*
   Matt 4:21; Mark 1:19; *to supply, make good,* 1
   Thess 3:10; *to restore* to a forfeited condition, *to
   reinstate,* Gal 6:1; 2 Cor 13:11*

καταρτίσαι   aor act inf
   [1Th 3:10; cv-2a(1); 2936]   "
καταρτίσαι   aor act opt 3 sg
   [Hb 13:21; cv-2a(1); 2936]   "
καταρτίσει   fut act ind 3 sg
   [1P 5:10; cv-2a(1); 2936]   "
κατάρτισιν   acc sg fem
   [2C 13:9; n-3e(5b); 2937]   κατάρτισις

κατάρτισις, εως, ἡ   {2937, n-3e(5b)}
   pr. *a complete adjustment; completeness* of
   character, *perfection,* 2 Cor 13:9*

καταρτισμόν   acc sg masc
   [Ep 4:12; n-2a; 2938]   καταρτισμός

καταρτισμός, ου, ὁ   {2938, n-2a}
   *a perfectly adjusted adaptation; complete
   qualification* for a specific purpose, Eph 4:12*

καταρώμεθα   pres mid ind 1 pl
   [Jm 3:9; cv-1d(1b); 2933]   καταράομαι
καταρωμένους   pres mid ptcp acc pl masc
   [Lk 6:28; cv-1d(1b); 2933]   "
κατασείσας   aor act ptcp nom sg masc
   [3t; cv-1a(3); 2939]   κατασείω

κατασείω   {2939, cv-1a(3)}
   [-, κατέσεισα, -, -, -] *to shake down* or *violently,*
   Acts 19:33; τὴν χεῖρα, or τῇ χειρί, *to wave the*

hand, beckon; to signal silence by waving the hand,
Acts 12:17; 13:16; 21:40*

κατασκάπτω {2940, cv-4}
[-, κατέσκαψα -, κατέσκαμμαι, -] pr. *to dig down
under, undermine;* by impl. *to overthrow;
demolish, raze,* Rom 11:3; τὰ κατεσκαμμένα,
ruins, Acts 15:16*

κατασκευάζεται pres pass ind 3 sg
[Hb 3:4; cv-2a(1); 2941]   κατασκευάζω
κατασκευαζομένης pres pass ptcp gen sg fem
[1P 3:20; cv-2a(1); 2941]   "

κατασκευάζω {2941, cv-2a(1)}
[κατασκευάσω, κατεσκεύασα, -, κατεσκεύασμαι,
κατεσκευάσθην] *to prepare, put in readiness,*
Matt 11:10; Mark 1:2; Luke 1:17; 7:27; *to
construct, form, build,* Heb 3:3, 4; 9:2, 6; 11:7; 1
Peter 3:20*

κατασκευάσας aor act ptcp nom sg masc
[2t; cv-2a(1); 2941]   "
κατασκευάσει fut act ind 3 sg
[3t; cv-2a(1); 2941]   "
κατασκηνοῦν pres act inf
[2t; cv-1d(3); 2942]   κατασκηνόω

κατασκηνόω {2942, cv-1d(3)}
[κατασκηνώσω, κατεσκήνωσα, -, -, -] *to pitch
one's tent;* in N.T. *to rest* in a place, *settle, abide,*
Acts 2:26; *to haunt, roost,* Matt 13:32; Mark 4:32;
Luke 13:19*

κατασκηνώσει fut act ind 3 sg
[Ac 2:26; cv-1d(3); 2942]   "
κατασκηνώσεις acc pl fem
[2t; n-3e(5b); 2943]   κατασκήνωσις

κατασκήνωσις, εως, ἡ {2943, n-3e(5b)}
pr. *the pitching a tent; a tent;* in N.T. *a
dwelling-place,* Matt 8:20; Luke 9:58*

κατασκιάζοντα pres act ptcp nom pl neut
[Hb 9:5; cv-2a(; 2944]   κατασκιάζω

κατασκιάζω {2944, cv-2a(1)}
[-, -, -, -, -] *to overshadow,* Heb 9:5*

κατασκοπέω {2945, cv-1d(2a)}
[-, κατεσκόπησα -, -, -] *to view closely and
accurately; to spy out,* Gal 2:4*

κατασκοπῆσαι aor act inf
[Ga 2:4; cv-1d(2a); 2945]   κατασκοπέω

κατάσκοπος, ου, ὁ {2946, n-2a}
a scout, spy, Heb 11:31; James 2:25 v.l.*

κατασκόπους acc pl masc
[Hb 11:31; n-2a; 2946]   κατάσκοπος

κατασοφίζομαι {2947, cv-2a(1)}
[-, κατεσοφισάμην -, -, -] *to exercise cleverness to
the detriment of* any one, *to outwit; to make a
victim of subtlety, to practice on the insidious
dealing,* Acts 7:19*

κατασοφισάμενος aor mid ptcp nom sg masc
[Ac 7:19; cv-2a(1); 2947]   κατασοφίζομαι
κατασταθήσονται fut pass ind 3 pl
[Rm 5:19; cv-6a; 2770]   καθίστημι

κατασταίλας aor act ptcp nom sg masc
[Ac 19:35; cv-2d(1); 2948]   καταστέλλω

καταστέλλω {2948, cv-2d(1)}
[-, κατέστειλα, -, κατέσταλμαι, -] *to arrange,
dispose in regular order; to appease, quiet, pacify,*
Acts 19:35, 36*

κατάστημα, ατος, τό {2949, n-3c(4)}
*determinate state, behavior, condition; personal
appearance,* Titus 2:3*

καταστήματι dat sg neut
[Ti 2:3; n-3c(4); 2949]   κατάστημα
καταστήσει fut act ind 3 sg
[3t; cv-6a; 2770]   καθίστημι
καταστήσῃς aor act subj 2 sg
[Ti 1:5; cv-6a; 2770]   "
καταστήσομεν fut act ind 1 pl
[Ac 6:3; cv-6a; 2770]   "
καταστήσω fut act ind 1 sg [2t; cv-6a; 2770]   "

καταστολή, ῆς, ἡ {2950, n-1b}
pr. *an arranging in order; adjustment of dress;* in
N.T. *apparel, dress,* 1 Tim 2:9*

καταστολῇ dat sg fem
[1Ti 2:9; n-1b; 2950]   καταστολή

καταστρέφω {2951, cv-1b(1)}
[-, κατέστρεψα, -, κατέστραμμαι, -] *to invert; to
overturn, upset, overthrow, throw down,* Matt
21:12; Mark 11:15; Acts 15:16 v.l.; James 2:15
v.l.*

καταστρηνιάσωσιν aor act subj 3 pl
[1Ti 5:11; cv-1d(1b); 2952]   καταστρηνιάω

καταστρηνιάω {2952, cv-1d(1b)}
[-, κατεστρηνίασα, -, -, -] *to be headstrong* or
wanton towards, 1 Tim 5:11*

καταστροφή, ῆς, ἡ {2953, n-1b}
an overthrow, destruction, 2 Peter 2:6; met.
overthrow of right principle or faith, *utter
detriment, perversion,* 2 Tim 2:14*

καταστροφῇ dat sg fem
[2t; n-1b; 2953]   καταστροφή

καταστρώννυμι {2954, cv-3c(1)}
[-, κατέστρωσα, -, -, κατεστρώθην] *to lay flat;*
pass. *to be laid prostrate* in death, 1 Cor 10:5*

κατασύρῃ pres act subj 3 sg
[Lk 12:58; cv-1c(1); 2955]   κατασύρω

κατασύρω {2955, cv-1c(1)}
[-, -, -, -, -] *to drag down, to drag away* by force,
Luke 12:58*

κατασφάζω {2956, cv-2a(2)}
[-, κατέσφαξα, -, -, -] also spelled κατασφάττω, *to
slaughter, slay,* Luke 19:27*

κατασφάξατε aor act imperative 2 pl
[Lk 19:27; cv-2a(2); 2956]   κατασφάζω

κατασφραγίζω {2958, cv-2a(1)}
[-, -, -, κατεσφράγισμαι, -] *to seal up,* Rev 5:1*

κατασχέσει dat sg fem
[Ac 7:45; n-3e(5b); 2959]   κατάσχεσις
κατάσχεσιν acc sg fem [Ac 7:5; n-3e(5b); 2959]   "

κατάσχεσις, εως, ἡ {2959, n-3e(5b)}
a possession, thing possessed, Acts 7:5, 45; 13:33
v.l.*

κατάσχωμεν aor act subj 1 pl
[2t; cv-1b(2); 2988] κατέχω

κατατίθημι {2960, cv-6a}
[-, κατέθηκα, -, -, -] *to lay down, deposit,* Mark
15:46 v.l.; mid. *to deposit* or *lay up for one's self;*
χάριν, or χάριτας, *to lay up a store of favor for one's
self, earn a title to favor* at the hands of a person,
to curry favor with, Acts 24:27; 25:9*

κατατομή, ῆς, ἡ {2961, n-1b}
mutilation, Phil 3:2*

κατατομήν acc sg fem
[Pp 3:2; n-1b; 2961] κατατομή

κατατοξεύω {2962, cv-1a(6)}
[-, -, -, -, -] *to shoot down* with arrows; *to transfix*
with an arrow or dart, Heb 12:20 v.l.*

κατατρέχω {2963, cv-1b(2)}
[-, κατέδραμον, -, -, -] *to run down,* Acts 21:32*

καταυγάζω {2964, cv-2a(1)}
[-, -, -, -, -] *illuminate,* 2 Cor 4:4 v.l.*

κατάφαγε aor act imperative 2 sg
[Rv 10:9; cv-1b(3); 2983] κατεσθίω
καταφάγεται fut mid ind 3 sg
[Jn 2:17; cv-1b(3); 2983] "
καταφάγῃ aor act subj 3 sg
[Rv 12:4; cv-1b(3); 2983] "
καταφαγών aor act ptcp nom sg masc
[Lk 15:30; cv-1b(3); 2983] "
καταφερόμενος pres pass ptcp nom sg masc
[Ac 20:9; cv-1c(1); 2965] καταφέρω
καταφέροντες pres act ptcp nom pl masc
[Ac 25:7; cv-1c(1); 2965] "

καταφέρω {2965, cv-1c(1)}
[-, κατήνεγκα, -, -, κατηνέχθην] *to bear down; to
overpower,* as sleep, Acts 20:9; καταφέρειν ψῆφον,
to give a vote or *verdict,* Acts 26:10; *to bring
charges,* Acts 25:7*

καταφεύγω {2966, cv-1b(2)}
[-, κατέφυγον, -, -, -] *to flee to* for refuge, Acts
14:6; Heb 6:18*

καταφθείρω {2967, cv-2d(3)}
[-, -, -, κατέφθαρμαι, κατεφθάρην] *to destroy,
cause to perish,* 2 Peter 2:12 v.l.; *to corrupt,
deprave,* 2 Tim 3:8*

καταφιλέω {2968, cv-1d(2a)}
[(κατεφίλουν), -, κατεφίλησα, -, -, -] *to kiss
affectionately* or *with a semblance of affection, to
kiss with earnest gesture,* Matt 26:49; Mark 14:45;
Luke 7:38, 45; 15:20; Acts 20:37*

καταφιλοῦσα pres act ptcp nom sg fem
[Lk 7:45; cv-1d(2a); 2968] καταφιλέω
καταφρονεῖς pres act ind 2 sg
[Rm 2:4; cv-1d(2a); 2969] καταφρονέω
καταφρονεῖτε pres act ind 2 pl
[1C 11:22; cv-1d(2a); 2969] "

καταφρονείτω pres act imperative 3 sg
[1Ti 4:12; cv-1d(2a); 2969] "
καταφρονείτωσαν pres act imperative 3 pl
[1Ti 6:2; cv-1d(2a); 2969] "

καταφρονέω {2969, cv-1d(2a)}
[καταφρονήσω, κατεφρόνησα, -, -, -] pr. *to look
down on; to scorn, despise,* Matt 18:10; Rom 2:4; *to
slight,* Matt 6:24; Luke 16:13; 1 Cor 11:22; 1 Tim
4:12; 6:2; 2 Peter 2:10; Titus 2:15 v.l.; *to disregard,*
Heb 12:2*

καταφρονήσας aor act ptcp nom sg masc
[Hb 12:2; cv-1d(2a); 2969] "
καταφρονήσει fut act ind 3 sg
[2t; cv-1d(2a); 2969] "
καταφρονήσητε aor act subj 2 pl
[Mt 18:10; cv-1d(2a); 2969] "
καταφρονηταί voc pl masc
[Ac 13:41; n-1f; 2970] καταφρονητής

καταφρονητής, ου, ὁ {2970, n-1f}
despiser, scorner, Acts 13:41*

καταφρονοῦντας pres act ptcp acc pl masc
[2P 2:10; cv-1d(2a); 2969] καταφρονέω
καταφυγόντες aor act ptcp nom pl masc
[Hb 6:18; cv-1b(2); 2966] καταφεύγω

καταφωνέω {2971, cv-1d(2a)}
[-, -, -, -, -] *cry out loudly,* Acts 22:24 v.l. for
ἐπιφωνέω*

καταχέω {2972, cv-1a(7)}
[-, κατέχεα, -, -, -] *to pour out* or *down upon,* Matt
26:7; Mark 14:3*

καταχθέντες aor pass ptcp nom pl masc
[Ac 28:12; cv-1b(2); 2864] κατάγω
καταχθονίων gen pl masc
[Pp 2:10; a-3a; 2973] καταχθόνιος

καταχθόνιος, ον {2973, a-3a}
under the earth, subterranean, infernal, Phil 2:10*

καταχράομαι {2974, cv-1d(1a)}
[-, κατεχρησάμην, -, -, -] *to use downright; to use
up, consume; to make an unrestrained use of, use
eagerly,* 1 Cor 7:31; *to use to the full, stretch to the
utmost, exploit,* 1 Cor 9:18*

καταχρήσασθαι aor mid inf
[1C 9:18; cv-1d(1a); 2974] καταχράομαι
καταχρώμενοι pres mid ptcp nom pl masc
[1C 7:31; cv-1d(1a); 2974] "

καταψηφίζομαι {2975, cv-2a(1)}
[-, -, -, -, -] *to be enrolled,* Acts 1:26 v.l.*

καταψύξῃ aor act subj 3 sg
[Lk 16:24; cv-1b(2); 2976] καταψύχω

καταψύχω {2976, cv-1b(2)}
[-, κατέψυξα, -, -, -] *to cool, refresh,* Luke 16:24*

κατεαγῶσιν aor pass subj 3 pl
[Jn 19:31; cv-3c(2); 2862] κατάγνυμι
κατέαξαν aor act ind 3 pl [2t; cv-3c(2); 2862] "
κατεάξει fut act ind 3 sg
[Mt 12:20; cv-3c(2); 2862] "
κατέβαινεν imperf act ind 3 sg
[2t; cv-2d(6); 2849] καταβαίνω

κατεβάρησα   aor act ind 1 sg
[2C 12:16; cv-1d(2a); 2851]   καταβαρέω
κατέβη   aor act ind 3 sg
[13t; cv-2d(6); 2849]   καταβαίνω
κατέβην   aor act ind 1 sg
[Ac 7:34; cv-2d(6); 2849]   "
κατέβησαν   aor act ind 3 pl [5t; cv-2d(6); 2849]   "
κατεγέλων   imperf act ind 3 pl
[3t; cv-1d(1b); 2860]   καταγελάω
κατεγνωσμένος   perf pass ptcp nom sg masc
[Ga 2:11; cv-5a; 2861]   καταγινώσκω
κατέγραφεν   imperf act ind 3 sg
[Jn 8:6; cv-1b(1); 2863]   καταγράφω
κατέδησεν   aor act ind 3 sg
[Lk 10:34; cv-1d(2b); 2866]   καταδέω
κατεδικάσατε   aor act ind 2 pl
[2t; cv-2a(1); 2868]   καταδικάζω
κατεδίωξεν   aor act ind 3 sg
[Mk 1:36; cv-1b(2); 2870]   καταδιώκω
κατέδραμεν   aor act ind 3 sg
[Ac 21:32; cv-1b(2); 2963]   κατατρέχω
κατείδωλον   acc sg fem
[Ac 17:16; a-3a; 2977]   κατείδωλος

κατείδωλος, ον   {2977, a-3a}
rife with idols, sunk in idolatry, grossly idolatrous,
Acts 17:16*

κατειλημμένην   perf pass ptcp acc sg fem
[Jn 8:3; cv-3a(2b); 2898]   καταλαμβάνω
κατείληπται   perf pass ind 3 sg
[Jn 8:4; cv-3a(2b); 2898]   "
κατειληφέναι   perf act inf
[Pp 3:13; cv-3a(2b); 2898]   "
κατειργάσατο   aor mid ind 3 sg
[3t; cv-2a(1); 2981]   κατεργάζομαι
κατειργάσθαι   perf mid inf
[1P 4:3; cv-2a(1); 2981]   "
κατειργάσθη   aor pass ind 3 sg
[2C 12:12; cv-2a(1); 2981]   "
κατειχόμεθα   imperf pass ind 1 pl
[Rm 7:6; cv-1b(2); 2988]   κατέχω
κατείχον   imperf act ind 3 pl
[2t; cv-1b(2); 2988]   "
κατεκάη   aor pass ind 3 sg
[3t; cv-2c; 2876]   κατακαίω
κατέκαιον   imperf act ind 3 pl
[Ac 19:19; cv-2c; 2876]   "
κατέκειτο   imperf mid ind 3 sg
[4t; cv-6b; 2879]   κατάκειμαι
κατέκλασεν   aor act ind 3 sg
[2t; cv-1d(1b); 2880]   κατακλάω
κατέκλεισα   aor act ind 1 sg
[Ac 26:10; cv-1a(3); 2881]   κατακλείω
κατέκλεισεν   aor act ind 3 sg
[Lk 3:20; cv-1a(3); 2881]   "
κατεκληρονόμησεν   aor act ind 3 sg
[Ac 13:19; cv-1d(2a); 2883]   κατακληρονομέω
κατεκλίθη   aor pass ind 3 sg
[Lk 7:36; cv-1c(2); 2884]   κατακλίνω
κατέκλιναν   aor act ind 3 pl
[Lk 9:15; cv-1c(2); 2884]   "
κατεκρίθη   aor pass ind 3 sg
[Mt 27:3; cv-1c(2); 2891]   κατακρίνω

κατέκριναν   aor act ind 3 pl
[Mk 14:64; cv-1c(2); 2891]   "
κατέκρινεν   aor act ind 3 sg [4t; cv-1c(2); 2891]   "
κατέλαβεν   aor act ind 3 sg
[2t; cv-3a(2b); 2898]   καταλαμβάνω
κατελαβόμην   aor mid ind 1 sg
[Ac 25:25; cv-3a(2b); 2898]   "
κατελείφθη   aor pass ind 3 sg
[Jn 8:9; cv-1b(1); 2901]   καταλείπω
κατελήμφθην   aor pass ind 1 sg
[Pp 3:12; cv-3a(2b); 2898]   καταλαμβάνω
κατελθεῖν   aor act inf
[2t; cv-1b(2); 2982]   κατέρχομαι
κατελθόντες   aor act ptcp nom pl masc
[Ac 15:1; cv-1b(2); 2982]   "
κατελθόντων   aor act ptcp gen pl masc
[Lk 9:37; cv-1b(2); 2982]   "
κατελθών   aor act ptcp nom sg masc
[3t; cv-1b(2); 2982]   "
κατέλιπε   aor act ind 3 sg
[Ac 24:27; cv-1b(1); 2901]   καταλείπω
κατέλιπεν   aor act ind 3 sg [3t; cv-1b(1); 2901]   "
κατέλιπον   aor act ind 1 sg
[Rm 11:4; cv-1b(1); 2901]   "
κατέλιπον   aor act ind 3 pl
[Lk 20:31; cv-1b(1); 2901]   "
κατέλυσα   aor act ind 1 sg
[Ga 2:18; cv-1a(4); 2907]   καταλύω

κατέναντι   {2978, adverb}
can function as an improper prep., *over against,*
opposite to, Mark 11:2; 12:41; 13:3; ὁ, ἡ, τό,
κατέναντι, *opposite,* Luke 19:30; *before, in the*
presence of, in the sight of, Rom 4:17; Matt 27:24
v.l.*

κατέναντι   adverb
[8t; adverb; 2978]   κατέναντι
κατενάρκησα   aor act ind 1 sg
[2t; cv-1d(1a); 2915]   καταναρκάω
κατένευσαν   aor act ind 3 pl
[Lk 5:7; cv-1a(6); 2916]   κατανεύω
κατενεχθείς   aor pass ptcp nom sg masc
[Ac 20:9; cv-1c(1); 2965]   καταφέρω
κατενόησεν   aor act ind 3 sg
[2t; cv-1d(2a); 2917]   κατανοέω
κατενόουν   imperf act ind 1 sg
[Ac 11:6; cv-1d(2a); 2917]   "
κατενόουν   imperf act ind 3 pl
[Ac 27:39; cv-1d(2a); 2917]   "
κατενύγησαν   aor pass ind 3 pl
[Ac 2:37; cv-2b; 2920]   κατανύσσομαι

κατενώπιον   {2979, adverb}
can function as an improper prep., *in the*
presence of, in the sight of, before; Eph 1:4; Col
1:22; Jude 24*

κατενώπιον   adverb [3t; adverb; 2979]   κατενώπιον
κατεξουσιάζουσιν   pres act ind 3 pl
[2t; cv-2a(; 2980]   κατεξουσιάζω

κατεξουσιάζω   {2980, cv-2a(1)}
[-, -, -, -, -] *to exercise lordship* or *authority over,*
domineer over, Matt 20:25; Mark 10:42*

κατεπατήθη   aor pass ind 3 sg
  [Lk 8:5; cv-1d(2a); 2922]   καταπατέω
κατέπαυσαν   aor act ind 3 pl
  [Ac 14:18; cv-1a(5); 2924]   καταπαύω
κατέπαυσεν   aor act ind 3 sg   [3t; cv-1a(5); 2924]   "
κατέπεσεν   aor act ind 3 sg
  [Lk 8:6; cv-1b(3); 2928]   καταπίπτω
κατεπέστησαν   aor act ind 3 pl
  [Ac 18:12; cv-6a; 2987]   κατεφίσταμαι
κατέπιεν   aor act ind 3 sg
  [Rv 12:16; cv-3a(1); 2927]   καταπίνω
κατέπλευσαν   aor act ind 3 pl
  [Lk 8:26; cv-1a(7); 2929]   καταπλέω
κατεπόθη   aor pass ind 3 sg
  [1C 15:54; cv-3a(1); 2927]   καταπίνω
κατεπόθησαν   aor pass ind 3 pl
  [Hb 11:29; cv-3a(1); 2927]   "
κατεργάζεσθαι   pres mid inf
  [Rm 7:18; cv-2a(1); 2981]   κατεργάζομαι
κατεργάζεσθε   pres mid imperative 2 pl
  [Pp 2:12; cv-2a(1); 2981]   "
κατεργάζεται   pres mid ind 3 sg
  [6t; cv-2a(1); 2981]   "

κατεργάζομαι   {2981, cv-2a(1)}
  [-, κατειργασάμην, -, κατείργασμαι,
  κατειργάσθην] *to work out; to effect, produce,
  bring out as a result,* Rom 4:15; 5:3; 7:13; 2 Cor
  4:17; 7:10; Phil 2:12; 1 Peter 4:3; James 1:3; *to
  work, practice, realize in practice,* Rom 1:27; 2:9; *to
  work* or *mould into fitness,* 2 Cor 5:5, *despatch,*
  Eph 6:13

κατεργάζομαι   pres mid ind 1 sg
  [3t; cv-2a(1); 2981]   "
κατεργαζομένη   pres mid ptcp nom sg fem
  [Rm 7:13; cv-2a(1); 2981]   "
κατεργαζόμενοι   pres mid ptcp nom pl masc
  [Rm 1:27; cv-2a(1); 2981]   "
κατεργαζομένου   pres mid ptcp gen sg masc
  [Rm 2:9; cv-2a(1); 2981]   "
κατεργασάμενοι   aor mid ptcp nom pl masc
  [Ep 6:13; cv-2a(1); 2981]   "
κατεργασάμενον   aor mid ptcp acc sg masc
  [1C 5:3; cv-2a(1); 2981]   "
κατεργασάμενος   aor mid ptcp nom sg masc
  [2C 5:5; cv-2a(1); 2981]   "

κατέρχομαι   {2982, cv-1b(2)}
  [-, κατῆλον, -, -, -] *to come* or *go down,* Luke 4:31;
  9:37; Acts 8:5; 9:32; *to land at, touch at,* Acts
  18:22; 27:5

κατερχομένη   pres mid ptcp nom sg fem
  [Jm 3:15; cv-1b(2); 2982]   κατέρχομαι
κατέσεισεν   aor act ind 3 sg
  [Ac 21:40; cv-1a(3); 2939]   κατασείω
κατεσθίει   pres act ind 3 sg
  [2t; cv-1b(3); 2983]   κατεσθίω
κατεσθίετε   pres act ind 2 pl
  [Ga 5:15; cv-1b(3); 2983]   "
κατεσθίοντες   pres act ptcp nom pl masc
  [Mk 12:40; cv-1b(3); 2983]   "
κατεσθίουσιν   pres act ind 3 pl
  [Lk 20:47; cv-1b(3); 2983]   "

κατεσθίω   {2983, cv-1b(3)}
  [καταφάγομαι, κατέφαγον, -, -, -] also spelled
  κατέσθω, *to eat up, devour,* Matt 13:4; *to consume,*
  Rev 11:5, *to expend, squander,* Luke 15:30; met. *to
  make a prey of, plunder,* Matt 23:13; Mark 12:40;
  Luke 20:47; 2 Cor 11:20; *to annoy, injure,* Gal
  5:15

κατέσθω, see κατέσθιω   {2984}

κατεσκαμμένα   perf pass ptcp acc pl neut
  [Ac 15:16; cv-4; 2940]   κατασκάπτω
κατέσκαψαν   aor act ind 3 pl
  [Rm 11:3; cv-4; 2940]   "
κατεσκεύασεν   aor act ind 3 sg
  [Hb 11:7; cv-2a(1); 2941]   κατασκευάζω
κατεσκευάσθη   aor pass ind 3 sg
  [Hb 9:2; cv-2a(1); 2941]   "
κατεσκευασμένον   perf pass ptcp acc sg masc
  [Lk 1:17; cv-2a(1); 2941]   "
κατεσκευασμένων   perf pass ptcp gen pl neut
  [Hb 9:6; cv-2a(1); 2941]   "
κατεσκήνωσεν   aor act ind 3 sg
  [Lk 13:19; cv-1d(3); 2942]   κατασκηνόω
κατεστάθησαν   aor pass ind 3 pl
  [Rm 5:19; cv-6a; 2770]   καθίστημι
κατεσταλμένους   perf pass ptcp acc pl masc
  [Ac 19:36; cv-2d(1); 2948]   καταστέλλω
κατέστησεν   aor act ind 3 sg
  [5t; cv-6a; 2770]   καθίστημι
κατέστρεψεν   aor act ind 3 sg
  [2t; cv-1b(1); 2951]   καταστρέφω
κατεστρώθησαν   aor pass ind 3 pl
  [1C 10:5; cv-3c(1); 2954]   καταστρώννυμι
κατεσφραγισμένον   perf pass ptcp acc sg neut
  [Rv 5:1; cv-2a(1); 2958]   κατασφραγίζω
κατευθῦναι   aor act inf
  [Lk 1:79; cv-1c(2); 2985]   κατευθύνω
κατευθῦναι   aor act opt 3 sg   [2t; cv-1c(2); 2985]   "

κατευθύνω   {2985, cv-1c(2)}
  [-, κατεύθυνα, -, -, -] optative, κατευθῦναι (3rd
  sg), *to make straight; to direct, guide aright,* Luke
  1:79; 1 Thess 3:11; 2 Thess 3:5*

κατευλόγει   imperf act ind 3 sg
  [Mk 10:16; cv-1d(2a); 2986]   κατευλογέω

κατευλογέω   {2986, cv-1d(2a)}
  [(κατευλόγουν), -, -, -, -, -] *to bless,* Mark 10:16*

κατέφαγεν   aor act ind 3 sg
  [4t; cv-1b(3); 2983]   κατεσθίω
κατέφαγον   aor act ind 1 sg
  [Rv 10:10; cv-1b(3); 2983]   "
κατεφθαρμένοι   perf pass ptcp nom pl masc
  [2Ti 3:8; cv-2d(3); 2967]   καταφθείρω
κατεφίλει   imperf act ind 3 sg
  [Lk 7:38; cv-1d(2a); 2968]   καταφιλέω
κατεφίλησεν   aor act ind 3 sg
  [3t; cv-1d(2a); 2968]   "
κατεφίλουν   imperf act ind 3 pl
  [Ac 20:37; cv-1d(2a); 2968]   "

κατεφίσταμαι   {2987, cv-6a}
  [-, κατεπέστην -, -, -] *to come upon suddenly, rush
  upon, assault,* Acts 18:12*

κατέφυγον   aor act ind 3 pl
    [Ac 14:6; cv-1b(2); 2966]   καταφεύγω

κατέχεεν   aor act ind 3 sg
    [2t; cv-1a(7); 2972]   καταχέω

κατέχειν   pres act inf
    [2t; cv-1b(2); 2988]   κατέχω

κατέχετε   pres act imperative 2 pl
    [1Th 5:21; cv-1b(2); 2988]   "

κατέχετε   pres act ind 2 pl [2t; cv-1b(2); 2988]   "

κατέχον   pres act ptcp acc sg neut
    [2Th 2:6; cv-1b(2); 2988]   "

κατέχοντες   pres act ptcp nom pl masc
    [2t; cv-1b(2); 2988]   "

κατεχόντων   pres act ptcp gen pl masc
    [Rm 1:18; cv-1b(2); 2988]   "

κατέχουσιν   pres act ind 3 pl
    [Lk 8:15; cv-1b(2); 2988]   "

κατέχω   {2988, cv-1b(2)}
  [(κατεῖχον), -, κατέσχον, -, -, -] (1) transitive, *to
hold down; to detain, retain*, Luke 4:42; Rom 1:18;
Phil 13; *to hinder, restrain*, 2 Thess 2:6, 7; *to hold
downright, hold in a firm grasp, to have in full and
secure possession*, 1 Cor 7:30; 2 Cor 6:10; *to come
into full possession of, seize upon; to keep, retain*, 1
Thess 5:21; *to occupy*, Luke 14:9; met. *to hold fast
mentally, retain*, Luke 8:15; 1 Cor 11:2; 15:2; *to
maintain*, Heb 3:6, 14; 10:23; (2) intransitive, a
nautical term, *to land, touch*, Acts 27:40; pass. *to
be in the grasp of, to be bound by*, Rom 7:6; *to be
afflicted with*, John 5:4 v.l.*

κατέχωμεν   pres act subj 1 pl
    [Hb 10:23; cv-1b(2); 2988]   "

κατέχων   pres act ptcp nom sg masc
    [2Th 2:7; cv-1b(2); 2988]   "

κατήγαγον   aor act ind 1 sg
    [Ac 23:28; cv-1b(2); 2864]   κατάγω

κατήγαγον   aor act ind 3 pl
    [Ac 9:30; cv-1b(2); 2864]   "

κατηγγείλαμεν   aor act ind 1 pl
    [Ac 15:36; cv-2d(1); 2859]   καταγγέλλω

κατήγγειλαν   aor act ind 3 pl
    [Ac 3:24; cv-2d(1); 2859]   "

κατηγγέλη   aor pass ind 3 sg
    [Ac 17:13; cv-2d(1); 2859]   "

κατήγγελλον   imperf act ind 3 pl
    [Ac 13:5; cv-2d(1); 2859]   "

κατηγορεῖν   pres act inf
    [6t; v-1d(2a); 2989]   κατηγορέω

κατηγορεῖσθαι   pres pass inf
    [Mt 27:12; v-1d(2a); 2989]   "

κατηγορεῖται   pres pass ind 3 sg
    [Ac 22:30; v-1d(2a); 2989]   "

κατηγορεῖτε   pres act ind 2 pl
    [Lk 23:14; v-1d(2a); 2989]   "

κατηγορείτωσαν   pres act imperative 3 pl
    [Ac 25:5; v-1d(2a); 2989]   "

κατηγορέω   {2989, v-1d(2a)}
  [(κατηγόρουν), κατηγορήσω, κατηγόρησα, -, -, -]
to speak against, accuse, Matt 12:10; 27:12; John
5:45

κατηγορήσω   fut act ind 1 sg
    [Jn 5:45; v-1d(2a); 2989]   "

κατηγορήσωσιν   aor act subj 3 pl
    [2t; v-1d(2a); 2989]   "

κατηγορία, ας, ἡ   {2990, n-1a}
  an accusation, crimination, John 18:29; 1 Tim
5:19; Titus 1:6; Luke 6:7 v.l.*

κατηγορίᾳ   dat sg fem
    [Ti 1:6; n-1a; 2990]   κατηγορία

κατηγορίαν   acc sg fem [2t; n-1a; 2990]   "

κατήγοροι   nom pl masc [2t; n-2a; 2991]   κατήγορος

κατηγόροις   dat pl masc   [Ac 23:30; n-2a; 2991]   "

κατήγορος, ου, ὁ   {2991, n-2a}
  an accuser, Acts 23:30, 35; 24:8 v.l.; Acts 25:16, 18;
Rev 12:10 v.l.*

κατηγοροῦμεν   pres act ind 1 pl
    [Ac 24:8; v-1d(2a); 2989]   κατηγορέω

κατηγορούμενος   pres pass ptcp nom sg masc
    [Ac 25:16; v-1d(2a); 2989]   "

κατηγόρουν   imperf act ind 3 pl
    [Mk 15:3; v-1d(2a); 2989]   "

κατηγοροῦντες   pres act ptcp nom pl masc
    [Lk 23:10; v-1d(2a); 2989]   "

κατηγορούντων   pres act ptcp gen pl masc
    [Rm 2:15; v-1d(2a); 2989]   "

κατηγόρους   acc pl masc
    [Ac 25:16; n-2a; 2991]   κατήγορος

κατηγοροῦσιν   pres act ind 3 pl
    [3t; v-1d(2a); 2989]   κατηγορέω

κατηγορῶν   pres act ptcp nom sg masc
    [2t; v-1d(2a); 2989]   "

κατηγωνίσαντο   aor mid ind 3 pl
    [Hb 11:33; cv-2a(1); 2865]   καταγωνίζομαι

κατήγωρ, ορος, ὁ   {2992, n-3f(2b)}
  an accuser, Rev 12:10, a barbarous form for
κατήγορος*

κατήγωρ   nom sg masc
    [Rv 12:10; n-3f(2b); 2992]   κατήγωρ

κατῆλθεν   aor act ind 3 sg
    [2t; cv-1b(2); 2982]   κατέρχομαι

κατήλθομεν   aor act ind 1 pl [2t; cv-1b(2); 2982]   "

κατῆλθον   aor act ind 3 pl [4t; cv-1b(2); 2982]   "

κατηλλάγημεν   aor pass ind 1 pl
    [Rm 5:10; cv-2b; 2904]   καταλλάσσω

κατήνεγκα   aor act ind 1 sg
    [Ac 26:10; cv-1c(1); 2965]   καταφέρω

κατήντηκεν   perf act ind 3 sg
    [1C 10:11; cv-1d(1a); 2918]   καταντάω

κατηντήσαμεν   aor act ind 1 pl
    [3t; cv-1d(1a); 2918]   "

κατήντησαν   aor act ind 3 pl
    [2t; cv-1d(1a); 2918]   "

κατήντησεν   aor act ind 3 sg
    [3t; cv-1d(1a); 2918]   "

κατηξιώθησαν   aor pass ind 3 pl
    [Ac 5:41; cv-1d(3); 2921]   καταξιόω

κατηραμένοι   perf pass ptcp voc pl masc
    [Mt 25:41; cv-1d(1b); 2933]   καταράομαι

κατηράσω   aor mid ind 2 sg
    [Mk 11:21; cv-1d(1b); 2933]   "

κατηργήθημεν   aor pass ind 1 pl
    [Rm 7:6; cv-1d(2a); 2934]   καταργέω

κατηργήθητε   aor pass ind 2 pl
  [Ga 5:4; cv-1d(2a); 2934]   "
κατήργηκα   perf act ind 1 sg
  [1C 13:11; cv-1d(2a); 2934]   "
κατήργηται   perf pass ind 3 sg
  [3t; cv-1d(2a); 2934]   "
κατηριθμημένος   perf pass ptcp nom sg masc
  [Ac 1:17; cv-1d(2a); 2935]   καταριθμέω
κατηρτίσθαι   perf pass inf
  [Hb 11:3; cv-2a(1); 2936]   καταρτίζω
κατηρτισμένα   perf pass ptcp acc pl neut
  [Rm 9:22; cv-2a(1); 2936]   "
κατηρτισμένοι   perf pass ptcp nom pl masc
  [1C 1:10; cv-2a(1); 2936]   "
κατηρτισμένος   perf pass ptcp nom sg masc
  [Lk 6:40; cv-2a(1); 2936]   "
κατηρτίσω   aor mid ind 2 sg   [2t; cv-2a(1); 2936]   "
κατῃσχύνθην   aor pass ind 1 sg
  [2C 7:14; cv-1c(2); 2875]   καταισχύνω
κατῃσχύνοντο   imperf pass ind 3 pl
  [Lk 13:17; cv-1c(2); 2875]   "

κατήφεια, ας, ἡ   {2993, n-1a}
  dejection, sorrow, James 4:9*

κατήφειαν   acc sg fem
  [Jm 4:9; n-1a; 2993]   κατήφεια

κατηχέω   {2994, cv-1d(2a)}
  [-, κατήχησα, -, κατήχημαι, κατηχήθην] pr. *to
  sound in the ears, make the ears ring; to instruct
  orally, to instruct, inform,* 1 Cor 14:19; pass. *to be
  taught, be instructed,* Luke 1:4; Rom 2:18; Gal
  6:6; *to be made acquainted,* Acts 18:25; *to receive
  information, hear report,* Acts 21:21, 24*

κατηχήθης   aor pass ind 2 sg
  [Lk 1:4; cv-1d(2a); 2994]   κατηχέω
κατηχήθησαν   aor pass ind 3 pl
  [Ac 21:21; cv-1d(2a); 2994]   "
κατηχημένος   perf pass ptcp nom sg masc
  [Ac 18:25; cv-1d(2a); 2994]   "
κατήχηνται   perf pass ind 3 pl
  [Ac 21:24; cv-1d(2a); 2994]   "
κατηχήσω   aor act subj 1 sg
  [1C 14:19; cv-1d(2a); 2994]   "
κατηχήθημεν   aor pass ind 1 pl
  [Ac 27:3; cv-1b(2); 2864]   κατάγω
κατηχούμενος   pres pass ptcp nom sg masc
  [2t; cv-1d(2a); 2994]   κατηχέω
κατηχοῦντι   pres act ptcp dat sg masc
  [Ga 6:6; cv-1d(2a); 2994]   "

κατιόω   {2995, v-1d(3)}
  [-, -, -, κατίωμαι, -] *to cover with rust;* pass. *to
  rust, become rusty* or *tarnished,* James 5:3*

κατίσχυον   imperf act ind 3 pl
  [Lk 23:23; cv-1a(4); 2996]   κατισχύω
κατισχύσητε   aor act subj 2 pl
  [Lk 21:36; cv-1a(4); 2996]   "
κατισχύσουσιν   fut act ind 3 pl
  [Mt 16:18; cv-1a(4); 2996]   "

κατισχύω   {2996, cv-1a(4)}
  [(κατίσχυον), κατισχύσω, κατίσχυσα, -, -, -] *to
  overpower,* Matt 16:18; absol. *to predominate, get
  the upper hand,* Luke 21:36; 23:23*

κατίωται   perf pass ind 3 sg
  [Jm 5:3; v-1d(3); 2995]   κατιόω
κατοικεῖ   pres act ind 3 sg
  [7t; cv-1d(2a); 2997]   κατοικέω
κατοικεῖν   pres act inf
  [Ac 17:26; cv-1d(2a); 2997]   "
κατοικεῖς   pres act ind 2 sg
  [Rv 2:13; cv-1d(2a); 2997]   "
κατοικεῖτε   pres act ind 2 pl
  [Ac 7:4; cv-1d(2a); 2997]   "

κατοικέω   {2997, cv-1d(2a)}
  [-, κατῴκησα, -, -, -] trans. *to inhabit,* Acts 1:19;
  absol. *to have an abode, dwell,* Luke 13:4; Acts
  11:29; *to take up* or *find an abode,* Acts 7:2; *to
  indwell,* Eph 3:17; James 4:5

κατοικῆσαι   aor act inf   [3t; cv-1d(2a); 2997]   "
κατοικήσας   aor act ptcp nom sg masc
  [Hb 11:9; cv-1d(2a); 2997]   "
κατοίκησιν   acc sg fem
  [Mk 5:3; n-3e(5b); 2998]   κατοίκησις

κατοίκησις, εως, ἡ   {2998, n-3e(5b)}
  an abode, dwelling, habitation, Mark 5:3*

κατοικητήριον, ου, τό   {2999, n-2c}
  an abode, dwelling, habitation, the same as
  κατοίκησις, Eph 2:22; Rev 18:2*

κατοικητήριον   nom sg neut
  [Rv 18:2; n-2c; 2999]   κατοικητήριον
κατοικητήριον   acc sg neut   [Ep 2:22; n-2c; 2999]   "

κατοικία, ας, ἡ   {3000, n-1a}
  habitation, i.q. κατοίκησις, Acts 17:26*

κατοικίας   gen sg fem
  [Ac 17:26; n-1a; 3000]   κατοικία

κατοικίζω   {3001, cv-2a(1)}
  [-, κατῴκισα, -, -, -] *to cause to dwell,* James 4:5*

κατοικοῦντας   pres act ptcp acc pl masc
  [9t; cv-1d(2a); 2997]   κατοικέω
κατοικοῦντες   pres act ptcp nom pl masc
  [8t; cv-1d(2a); 2997]   "
κατοικοῦντες   pres act ptcp voc pl masc
  [Ac 2:14; cv-1d(2a); 2997]   "
κατοικοῦντι   pres act ptcp dat sg masc
  [Mt 23:21; cv-1d(2a); 2997]   "
κατοικούντων   pres act ptcp gen pl masc
  [2t; cv-1d(2a); 2997]   "
κατοικοῦσιν   pres act ptcp dat pl masc
  [5t; cv-1d(2a); 2997]   "
κατοικῶν   pres act ptcp nom sg masc
  [Ac 1:20; cv-1d(2a); 2997]   "
κατοπτριζόμενοι   pres mid ptcp nom pl masc
  [2C 3:18; cv-; 3002]   κατοπτρίζω

κατοπτρίζω   {3002, cv-2a(1)}
  [-, -, -, -, -] *to show in a mirror; to present a clear
  and correct image* of a thing, mid. *to have
  presented in a mirror, to have a clear image
  presented,* or, *to reflect,* 2 Cor 3:18*

κατόρθωμα, ατος, τό   {3003, n-3c(4)}
  *anything happily and successfully accomplished; a
  beneficial and worthy deed,* Acts 24:2 v.l.*

κάτω {3004, adverb}
(1) *down, downwards,* Matt 4:6; Luke 4:9; John
8:6; Acts 20:9; (2) *beneath, below, under,* Matt
27:51; Mark 14:66; 15:38; Acts 2:19; Matt 2:16
v.l.; ὁ, ἡ, τό, κάτω, *what is below, earthly,* John
8:23*

κάτω adverb [9t; adverb; 3004] κάτω
κατῴκησεν aor act ind 3 sg
[3t; cv-1d(2a); 2997] κατοικέω
κατῴκισεν aor act ind 3 sg
[Jm 4:5; cv-2a(1); 3001] κατοικίζω
κατώτερα acc pl neut comparative
[Ep 4:9; a-1a(1); 3005] κατώτερος

κατώτερος, α, ον {3005, a-1a(1)}
lower, Eph 4:9*

κατωτέρω {3006, adverb}
lower, farther down; of time, *under,* Matt 2:16*

κατωτέρω adverb-comparative
[Mt 2:16; adverb; 3006] κατωτέρω

Καῦδα, ης, ἡ {3007, n-1c}
also spelled Κλαῦδα (3084) and Κλαῦδη (3085),
Cauda, indecl. prop. name of an island, Acts
27:16*

Καῦδα acc sg fem [Ac 27:16; n-1c; 3007] Καῦδα

καῦμα, ατος, τό {3008, n-3c(4)}
heat, scorching or *burning heat,* Rev 7:16; 16:9*

καῦμα nom sg neut [Rv 7:16; n-3c(4); 3008] καῦμα
καῦμα acc sg neut [Rv 16:9; n-3c(4); 3008] "

καυματίζω {3009, v-2a(1)}
[-, ἐκαυμάτισα, -, -, ἐκαυματίσθην] *to scorch,*
burn, Matt 13:6; Mark 4:6; Rev 16:8, 9*

καυματίσαι aor act inf
[Rv 16:8; v-2a(1); 3009] καυματίζω

καυματόω {3010, v-1d(3)}
[-, -, -, -, -] *be scorched* by heat, Matt 13:6 v.l.*

καῦσιν acc sg fem [Hb 6:8; n-3e(5b); 3011] καῦσις

καῦσις, εως, ἡ {3011, n-3e(5b)}
burning, being burned, Heb 6:8*

καυσούμενα pres pass ptcp nom pl neut
[2t; v-1d(3); 3012] καυσόω

καυσόω {3012, v-1d(3)}
[-, -, -, -, -] *to be on fire, burn intensely,* 2 Peter
3:10, 12*

καυστηριάζω {3013, v-2a(1)}
[-, -, -, κεκαυστηρίασμαι, -] also spelled
καυτηριάζω, *to cauterize, brand;* pass. met. *to be*
branded with marks of guilt, or, *to be seared* into
insensibility, 1 Tim 4:2*

καύσων, ῶνος, ὁ {3014, n-3f(1a)}
fervent scorching heat; the scorching of the sun,
Matt 20:12; *hot weather, a hot time,* Luke 12:55;
the scorching wind of the East, Eurus, James 1:11*

καύσων nom sg masc
[Lk 12:55; n-3f(1a); 3014] καύσων
καύσωνα acc sg masc [Mt 20:12; n-3f(1a); 3014] "
καύσωνι dat sg masc [Jm 1:11; n-3f(1a); 3014] "

καυτηριάζω, see καυστηριάζω {3015}

καυχάομαι {3016, v-1d(1a)}
[καυχήσομαι, ἐκαυχησάμην, -, κεκαύχημαι, -] *to*
glory, boast, Rom 2:17, 23; ὑπέρ τινος, *to boast of*
a person or thing, *to undertake a complimentary*
testimony to, 2 Cor 12:5; *to rejoice, exult,* Rom 5:2,
3, 11

καυχᾶσαι pres mid ind 2 sg
[3t; v-1d(1a); 3016] καυχάομαι
καυχᾶσθαι pres mid inf [3t; v-1d(1a); 3016] "
καυχᾶσθε pres mid ind 2 pl
[Jm 4:16; v-1d(1a); 3016] "
καυχάσθω pres mid imperative 3 sg
[4t; v-1d(1a); 3016] "

καύχημα, ατος, τό {3017, n-3c(4)}
a glorying, boasting, 1 Cor 5:6; *a ground* or *matter*
of glorying or *boasting,* Rom 4:2; *joy exultation,*
Phil 1:26; *complimentary testimony,* 1 Cor 9:15,
16; 2 Cor 9:3

καύχημα nom sg neut [5t; n-3c(4); 3017] καύχημα
καύχημα acc sg neut [5t; n-3c(4); 3017] "
καυχήματος gen sg neut [2C 5:12; n-3c(4); 3017] "
καυχήσασθαι aor mid inf
[2t; v-1d(1a); 3016] καυχάομαι
καυχήσεως gen sg fem
[3t; n-3e(5b); 3018] καύχησις
καυχήσηται aor mid subj 3 sg
[2t; v-1d(1a); 3016] καυχάομαι
καύχησιν acc sg fem [2t; n-3e(5b); 3018] καύχησις

καύχησις, εως, ἡ {3018, n-3e(5b)}
boasting, pride, a later equivalent to καύχημαι,
Rom 3:27; 2 Cor 7:4, 14; 11:10

καύχησις nom sg fem [6t; n-3e(5b); 3018] "
καυχήσομαι fut mid ind 1 sg
[5t; v-1d(1a); 3016] καυχάομαι
καυχησόμεθα fut mid ind 1 pl
[2C 10:13; v-1d(1a); 3016] "
καυχήσωμαι aor mid subj 1 sg
[3t; v-1d(1a); 3016] "
καυχήσωνται aor mid subj 3 pl
[Ga 6:13; v-1d(1a); 3016] "
καυχῶμαι pres mid ind 1 sg
[2C 9:2; v-1d(1a); 3016] "
καυχώμεθα pres mid ind 1 pl [2t; v-1d(1a); 3016] "
καυχώμενοι pres mid ptcp nom pl masc
[3t; v-1d(1a); 3016] "
καυχώμενος pres mid ptcp nom sg masc
[2t; v-1d(1a); 3016] "
καυχωμένους pres mid ptcp acc pl masc
[2C 5:12; v-1d(1a); 3016] "
καυχῶνται pres mid ind 3 pl [2t; v-1d(1a); 3016] "

Καφαρναούμ, ἡ {3019, n-3g(2)}
indecl. pr. name, *Capernaum*

Καφαρναούμ indecl
[16t; n-3g(2); 3019] Καφαρναούμ

Κεγχρεαί, ας, ἡ {3020, n-1a}
Cenchreae, the port of Corinth on the Saronic
Gulf; Acts 18:18; Rom 16:1*

Κεγχρεαῖς dat pl fem [2t; n-1a; 3020] Κεγχρεαί

κέδρος, ου, ἡ   {3021, n-2b}
a cedar, John 18:1 v.l., where Κέδρων is a false
reading for the proper name Κεδρών

Κεδρών, ὁ   {3022, n-3g(2)}
indecl. pr. name, *Kidron,* a valley near
Jerusalem, John 18:1*

Κεδρών   indecl [Jn 18:1; n-3g(2); 3022]   Κεδρών

κεῖμαι   {3023, v-6b}
[(ἔκειτο [3 sg]), -, -, -, -, -] *to lie, to be laid; to
recline, to be lying, to have been laid down,* Matt
28:6; Luke 2:12; *to have been laid, placed, set,* Matt
3:10; Luke 3:9; John 2:6; *to be situated,* as a city,
Matt 5:14; Rev 21:16; *to be in store,* Luke 12:19;
met. *to be constituted, established* as a law, 1 Tim
1:9; in N.T. of persons, *to be specially set,
solemnly appointed, destined,* Luke 2:34; Phil
1:17; 1 Thess 3:3; *to lie* under an influence, *to be
involved in,* 1 John 5:19

κεῖμαι   pres mid ind 1 sg
    [Pp 1:16; v-6b; 3023]   κεῖμαι
κείμεθα   pres mid ind 1 pl [1Th 3:3; v-6b; 3023]   "
κείμενα   pres mid ptcp acc pl neut
    [3t; v-6b; 3023]   "
κείμεναι   pres mid ptcp nom pl fem
    [Jn 2:6; v-6b; 3023]   "
κειμένη   pres mid ptcp nom sg fem
    [Mt 5:14; v-6b; 3023]   "
κειμένην   pres mid ptcp acc sg fem
    [Jn 21:9; v-6b; 3023]   "
κείμενον   pres mid ptcp acc sg masc
    [1C 3:11; v-6b; 3023]   "
κείμενον   pres mid ptcp acc sg neut
    [3t; v-6b; 3023]   "
κείμενος   pres mid ptcp nom sg masc
    [Lk 23:53; v-6b; 3023]   "
κειράμενος   aor mid ptcp nom sg masc
    [Ac 18:18; v-2d(3); 3025]   κείρω
κείραντος   aor act ptcp gen sg masc
    [Ac 8:32; v-2d(3); 3025]   "
κείρασθαι   aor mid inf [1C 11:6; v-2d(3); 3025]   "
κειράσθω   aor mid imperative 3 sg
    [1C 11:6; v-2d(3); 3025]   "

κειρία, ας, ἡ   {3024, n-1a}
a bandage, swath, in N.T. pl. *graveclothes,* John
11:44*

κειρίαις   dat pl fem [Jn 11:44; n-1a; 3024]   κειρία

κείρω   {3025, v-2d(3)}
[-, ἔκειρα, -, -, -] *to cut off* the hair, *shear, shave,*
Acts 8:32; 18:18; 1 Cor 11:6 (2t)*

κεῖται   pres mid ind 3 sg [7t; v-6b; 3023]   κεῖμαι
κεκαθαρισμένους   perf pass ptcp acc pl masc
    [Hb 10:2; v-2a(1); 2751]   καθαρίζω
κεκάθικεν   perf act ind 3 sg
    [Hb 12:2; v-2a(1); 2767]   καθίζω
κεκαλυμμένον   perf pass ptcp nom sg neut
    [3t; v-4; 2821]   καλύπτω
κεκαυμένῳ   perf pass ptcp dat sg neut
    [Hb 12:18; v-2c; 2794]   καίω
κεκαυστηριασμένων   perf pass ptcp gen pl masc
    [1Ti 4:2; v-2a(1); 3013]   καυστηριάζω

κεκαύχημαι   perf mid ind 1 sg
    [2C 7:14; v-1d(1a); 3016]   καυχάομαι
κεκένωται   perf pass ind 3 sg
    [Rm 4:14; v-1d(3); 3033]   κενόω
κεκερασμένου   perf pass ptcp gen sg masc
    [Rv 14:10; v-3c(1); 3042]   κεράννυμι
κεκλεισμένον   perf pass ptcp acc sg neut
    [Ac 5:23; v-1a(3); 3091]   κλείω
κεκλεισμένων   perf pass ptcp gen pl fem
    [2t; v-1a(3); 3091]   "
κέκλεισται   perf pass ind 3 sg
    [Lk 11:7; v-1a(3); 3091]   "
κέκληκεν   perf act ind 3 sg
    [2t; v-1d(2b); 2813]   καλέω
κεκληκότι   perf act ptcp dat sg masc
    [Lk 14:12; v-1d(2b); 2813]   "
κεκληκώς   perf act ptcp nom sg masc
    [Lk 14:10; v-1d(2b); 2813]   "
κεκλημένοι   perf pass ptcp nom pl masc
    [3t; v-1d(2b); 2813]   "
κεκλημένοις   perf pass ptcp dat pl masc
    [2t; v-1d(2b); 2813]   "
κεκλημένος   perf pass ptcp nom sg masc
    [Lk 14:8; v-1d(2b); 2813]   "
κεκλημένους   perf pass ptcp acc pl masc
    [2t; v-1d(2b); 2813]   "
κεκλημένων   perf pass ptcp gen pl masc
    [Lk 14:24; v-1d(2b); 2813]   "
κεκληρονόμηκεν   perf act ind 3 sg
    [Hb 1:4; v-1d(2a); 3099]   κληρονομέω
κέκληται   perf pass ind 3 sg
    [2t; v-1d(2b); 2813]   καλέω
κέκλικεν   perf act ind 3 sg
    [Lk 24:29; v-1c(2); 3111]   κλίνω
κεκοιμημένων   perf pass ptcp gen pl masc
    [2t; v-1d(1a); 3121]   κοιμάω
κεκοίμηται   perf pass ind 3 sg
    [2t; v-1d(1a); 3121]   "
κεκοίνωκεν   perf act ind 3 sg
    [Ac 21:28; v-1d(3); 3124]   κοινόω
κεκοινωμένους   perf pass ptcp acc pl masc
    [Hb 9:13; v-1d(3); 3124]   "
κεκοινώνηκεν   perf act ind 3 sg
    [Hb 2:14; v-1d(2a); 3125]   κοινωνέω
κεκονιαμένε   perf pass ptcp voc sg masc
    [Ac 23:3; v-1d(1b); 3154]   κονιάω
κεκονιαμένοις   perf pass ptcp dat pl masc
    [Mt 23:27; v-1d(1b); 3154]   "
κεκοπίακα   perf act ind 1 sg
    [Ga 4:11; v-1d(1b); 3159]   κοπιάω
κεκοπιάκασιν   perf act ind 3 pl
    [Jn 4:38; v-1d(1b); 3159]   "
κεκοπιάκατε   perf act ind 2 pl
    [Jn 4:38; v-1d(1b); 3159]   "
κεκοπίακες   perf act ind 2 sg
    [Rv 2:3; v-1d(1b); 3159]   "
κεκοπιακώς   perf act ptcp nom sg masc
    [Jn 4:6; v-1d(1b); 3159]   "
κεκορεσμένοι   perf pass ptcp nom pl masc
    [1C 4:8; v-3c(1); 3170]   κορέννυμι
κεκοσμημένην   perf pass ptcp acc sg fem
    [Rv 21:2; v-1d(2a); 3175]   κοσμέω

κεκοσμημένοι   perf pass ptcp nom pl masc
   [Rv 21:19; v-1d(2a); 3175]   "
κεκοσμημένον   perf pass ptcp acc sg masc
   [2t; v-1d(2a); 3175]   "
κεκόσμηται   perf pass ind 3 sg
   [Lk 21:5; v-1d(2a); 3175]   "
κέκραγεν   perf act ind 3 sg
   [Jn 1:15; v-2a(2); 3189]   κράζω
κεκρατηκέναι   perf act inf
   [Ac 27:13; v-1d(2a); 3195]   κρατέω
κεκράτηνται   perf pass ind 3 pl
   [Jn 20:23; v-1d(2a); 3195]
κέκρικα   perf act ind 1 sg
   [2t; v-1c(2); 3212]   κρίνω
κεκρίκατε   perf act ind 2 pl
   [Ac 16:15; v-1c(2); 3212]   "
κεκρίκει   pluperf act ind 3 sg
   [Ac 20:16; v-1c(2); 3212]   "
κέκρικεν   perf act ind 3 sg
   [1C 7:37; v-1c(2); 3212]   "
κεκριμένα   perf pass ptcp acc pl neut
   [Ac 16:4; v-1c(2); 3212]   "
κέκριται   perf pass ind 3 sg [2t; v-1c(2); 3212]   "
κεκρυμμένα   perf pass ptcp acc pl neut
   [Mt 13:35; v-4; 3221]   κρύπτω
κεκρυμμένον   perf pass ptcp nom sg neut
   [Lk 18:34; v-4; 3221]   "
κεκρυμμένος   perf pass ptcp nom sg masc
   [Jn 19:38; v-4; 3221]   "
κεκρυμμένου   perf pass ptcp gen sg neut
   [Rv 2:17; v-4; 3221]   "
κεκρυμμένῳ   perf pass ptcp dat sg masc
   [Mt 13:44; v-4; 3221]   "
κέκρυπται   perf pass ind 3 sg [Cl 3:3; v-4; 3221]   "
κεκυρωμένην   perf pass ptcp acc sg fem
   [Ga 3:15; v-1d(3); 3263]   κυρόω
κελεύεις   pres act ind 2 sg
   [Ac 23:3; v-1a(6); 3027]   κελεύω
κελεύσαντες   aor act ptcp nom pl masc
   [Ac 4:15; v-1a(6); 3027]   "
κελεύσαντος   aor act ptcp gen sg masc
   [Ac 25:23; v-1a(6); 3027]   "
κελεύσας   aor act ptcp nom sg masc
   [2t; v-1a(6); 3027]   "

κέλευσμα, ατος, τό   {3026, n-3c(4)}
   a word of command; a mutual cheer; hence, in N.T.
   a loud shout, an arousing outcry, 1 Thess 4:16*

κελεύσματι   dat sg neut
   [1Th 4:16; n-3c(4); 3026]   κέλευσμα
κέλευσον   aor act imperative 2 sg
   [2t; v-1a(6); 3027]   κελεύω

κελεύω   {3027, v-1a(6)}
   [(ἐκέλευον), -, ἐκέλευσα, -, -, -] *to order,*
   command, direct, bid, Matt 8:18; 14:19, 28

κενά   acc pl neut [Ac 4:25; a-1a(2a); 3031]   κενός
κενέ   voc sg masc [Jm 2:20; a-1a(2a); 3031]   "
κενή   nom sg fem [3t; a-1a(2a); 3031]   "
κενῆς   gen sg fem [Cl 2:8; a-1a(2a); 3031]   "

κενοδοξία, ας, ἡ   {3029, n-1a}
   empty conceit, Phil 2:3*

κενοδοξίαν   acc sg fem
   [Pp 2:3; n-1a; 3029]   κενοδοξία
κενόδοξοι   nom pl masc
   [Ga 5:26; a-3a; 3030]   κενόδοξος

κενόδοξος, ον   {3030, a-3a}
   boastful, Gal 5:26*

κενοῖς   dat pl masc [Ep 5:6; a-1a(2a); 3031]   κενός
κενόν   nom sg neut [1C 15:14; a-1a(2a); 3031]   "
κενόν   acc sg masc [3t; a-1a(2a); 3031]   "
κενόν   acc sg neut [5t; a-1a(2a); 3031]   "

κενός, ή, όν   {3031, a-1a(2a)}
   empty; having nothing, empty-handed, Mark 12:3;
   met. *vain, fruitless, void of effect,* Acts 4:25; 1 Cor
   15:10; εἰς κενόν, *in vain, to no purpose,* 2 Cor 6:1;
   hollow, fallacious, false, Eph 5:6; Col 2:8;
   inconsiderate, foolish, 1 Thess 3:5; James 2:20

κενός   nom sg masc [1C 15:58; a-1a(2a); 3031]   "
κενούς   acc pl masc [Lk 1:53; a-1a(2a); 3031]   "

κενοφωνία, ας, ἡ   {3032, n-1a}
   vain, empty babbling, vain disputation, fruitless
   discussion, 1 Tim 6:20; 2 Tim 2:16*

κενοφωνίας   acc pl fem [2t; n-1a; 3032]   κενοφωνία

κενόω   {3033, v-1d(3)}
   [κενώσω, ἐκένωσα, -, κεκένωμαι, ἐκενώθην] *to*
   empty, evacuate; ἑαυτόν, *to divest one's self of one's*
   prerogatives, abase one's self, Phil 2:7; *to deprive a*
   thing of its proper functions, Rom 4:14; 1 Cor
   1:17; *to show to be without foundation, falsify,* 1
   Cor 9:15; 2 Cor 9:3*

κέντρα   acc pl neut [2t; n-2c; 3034]   κέντρον

κέντρον, ου, τό   {3034, n-2c}
   a sharp point; a sting of an animal, Rev 9:10; *a*
   prick, stimulus, goad, Acts 9:5 v.l.; 26:14; met. of
   death, destructive power, deadly venom, 1 Cor
   15:55, 56*

κέντρον   nom sg neut [2t; n-2c; 3034]   "

κεντυρίων, ῶνος, ὁ   {3035, n-3f(1a)}
   in its original signification, *a commander of a*
   hundred foot-soldiers, *a centurion,* Mark 15:39,
   44, 45*

κεντυρίων   nom sg masc
   [Mk 15:39; n-3f(1a); 3035]   κεντυρίων
κεντυρίωνα   acc sg masc
   [Mk 15:44; n-3f(1a); 3035]   "
κεντυρίωνος   gen sg masc
   [Mk 15:45; n-3f(1a); 3035]   "
κενωθῇ   aor pass subj 3 sg
   [2t; v-1d(3); 3033]   κενόω

κενῶς   {3036, adverb}
   in vain, to no purpose, unmeaning, James 4:5*

κενῶς   adverb [Jm 4:5; adverb; 3036]   κενῶς
κενώσει   fut act ind 3 sg
   [1C 9:15; v-1d(3); 3033]   κενόω

κεραία, ας, ἡ   {3037, n-1a}
   pr. *a horn-like projection, a point, extremity;* in
   N.T. *an apex,* or *fine point;* as of letters, used for
   the minutest part, a tittle, Matt 5:18; Luke 16:17*

κεραία nom sg fem [Mt 5:18; n-1a; 3037] κεραία
κεραίαν acc sg fem [Lk 16:17; n-1a; 3037] "

κεραμεύς {3038, n-3e(3)}
a potter, Matt 27:7, 10; Rom 9:21*

κεραμεύς nom sg masc
[Rm 9:21; n-3e(3); 3038] κεραμεύς
κεραμέως gen sg masc [2t; n-3e(3); 3038] "
κεραμικά nom pl neut
[Rv 2:27; a-1a(2a); 3039] κεραμικός

κεραμικός, ή, όν {3039, a-1a(2a)}
made by a potter, earthen, Rev 2:27*

κεράμιον, ου, τό {3040, n-2c}
an earthenware vessel, a pitcher, jar, Mark 14:13;
Luke 22;10*

κεράμιον acc sg neut [2t; n-2c; 3040] κεράμιον

κέραμος, ου, ὁ {3041, n-2a}
potter's clay; earthenware; a roof, tile, tiling, Luke
5:19*

κεράμων gen pl masc [Lk 5:19; n-2a; 3041] κέραμος

κεράννυμι {3042, v-3c(1)}
[-, ἐκέρασα, -, κεκέρασμαι, ἐκράθην] *to mix,
mingle,* drink; *to prepare* for drinking, Rev 14:10;
18:6 (2t)*

κέρας, ατος, τό {3043, n-3c(6a)}
a horn, Rev 5:6; 12:3; *a horn-like projection* at the
corners of an altar, Rev 9:13; from the Hebrew,
a horn as a symbol of power, Luke 1:69

κέρας acc sg neut [Lk 1:69; n-3c(6a); 3043] κέρας
κεράσατε aor act imperative 2 pl
[Rv 18:6; v-3c(1); 3042] κεράννυμι
κέρατα nom pl neut [2t; n-3c(6a); 3043] κέρας
κέρατα acc pl neut [6t; n-3c(6a); 3043] "

κεράτιον, ου, τό {3044, n-2c}
pr. *a little horn;* in N.T. *a pod, the pod of the carob
tree,* or *Ceratonia siliqua* of Linnaeus, a common
tree in the East and the south of Europe,
growing to a considerable size, and producing
long slender pods, with a pulp of a sweetish
taste, and several brown shining seeds like
beans, sometimes eaten by the poorer people
in Syria and Palestine, and commonly used for
fattening swine, Luke 15:16*

κερατίων gen pl neut
[Lk 15:16; n-2c; 3044] κεράτιον
κεράτων gen pl neut [2t; n-3c(6a); 3043] κέρας

κερδαίνω {3045, v-2d(6)}
[κερδήσω, ἐκέρδησα or ἐκέρδανα, -, -, ἐκερδήθην]
to gain as a matter of profit, Matt 25:17; *to win,
acquire possession of,* Matt 16:26; *to profit in the
avoidance of, to avoid,* Acts 27:21; in N.T. Χριστόν,
to win Christ, *to become possessed of* the
privileges of the Gospel, Phil 3:8; *to win over*
from estrangement, Matt 18:15; *to win over* to
embrace the Gospel, 1 Cor 9:19, 20, 21, 22; 1
Peter 3:1; absol. *to make gain,* James 4:13

κερδάνω aor act subj 1 sg
[1C 9:21; v-2d(6); 3045] κερδαίνω
κέρδη nom pl neut [Pp 3:7; n-3d(2b); 3045] κέρδος

κερδηθήσονται fut pass ind 3 pl
[1P 3:1; v-2d(6); 3045] κερδαίνω
κερδῆσαι aor act inf [2t; v-2d(6); 3045] "
κερδήσας aor act ptcp nom sg masc
[Lk 9:25; v-2d(6); 3045] "
κερδήσῃ aor act subj 3 sg
[Mt 16:26; v-2d(6); 3045] "
κερδήσομεν fut act ind 1 pl
[Jm 4:13; v-2d(6); 3045] "
κερδήσω aor act subj 1 sg [5t; v-2d(6); 3045] "

κέρδος, ους, τό {3046, n-3d(2b)}
gain, profit, Phil 1:21; 3:7; Titus 1:11*

κέρδος nom sg neut
[Pp 1:21; n-3d(2b); 3046] κέρδος
κέρδους gen sg neut [Ti 1:11; n-3d(2b); 3046] "

κέρμα, ατος, τό {3047, n-3c(4)}
*something clipped small; small change, small pieces
of money, coin,* John 2:15*

κέρμα acc sg neut [Jn 2:15; n-3c(4); 3047] κέρμα
κερματιστάς acc pl masc
[Jn 2:14; n-1f; 3048] κερματιστής

κερματιστής, οῦ, ὁ {3048, n-1f}
a money changer, John 2:14*

κεφαλαί nom pl fem [3t; n-1b; 3051] κεφαλή

κεφάλαιον, ου, τό {3049, n-2c}
a sum total; a sum of money, capital, Acts 22:28; *the
crowning* or *ultimate point* to preliminary
matters, Heb 8:1*

κεφάλαιον nom sg neut
[Hb 8:1; n-2c; 3049] κεφάλαιον
κεφαλαίου gen sg neut [Ac 22:28; n-2c; 3049] "

κεφαλαιόω {3050, v-1d(3)}
[-, ἐκεφαλίωσα, -, -, -] *to sum up;* but in N.T.
equiv. to κεφαλίζω, *to wound on the head,* Mark
12:4

κεφαλάς acc pl fem [13t; n-1b; 3051] κεφαλή

κεφαλή, ῆς, ἡ {3051, n-1b}
the head, Matt 5:36; 6:17; *the head, top;* κεφαλὴ
γωνίας, *the head of the corner, the chief
corner-stone,* Matt 21:42; Luke 20:17; met. *the
head, superior, chief, principal, one to whom others
are subordinate,* 1 Cor 11:3; Eph 1:22

κεφαλή nom sg fem [11t; n-1b; 3051] "
κεφαλῇ dat sg fem [4t; n-1b; 3051] "
κεφαλήν acc sg fem [28t; n-1b; 3051] "
κεφαλῆς gen sg fem [15t; n-1b; 3051] "
κεφαλίδι dat sg fem
[Hb 10:7; n-3c(2); 3053] κεφαλίς

κεφαλιόω {3052, v-1d(3)}
[-, ἐκεφαλίωσα, -, -, -] *to hit the head,* Mark 12:4*

κεφαλίς, ίδος, ἡ {3053, n-3c(2)}
in N.T. *a roll, volume, division* of a book, Heb
10:7*

κεφαλῶν gen pl fem [Rv 13:3; n-1b; 3051] κεφαλή
κεχάρισμαι perf mid ind 1 sg
[2t; v-2a(1); 5919] χαρίζομαι
κεχάρισται perf mid ind 3 sg [2t; v-2a(1); 5919] "

κεχαριτωμένη   perf pass ptcp voc sg fem
[Lk 1:28; v-1d(3); 5923]   χαριτόω

κέχρημαι   perf mid ind 1 sg
[1C 9:15; v-1d(1a); 5968]   χράομαι

κεχρηματισμένον   perf pass ptcp nom sg neut
[Lk 2:26; v-2a(1); 5976]   χρηματίζω

κεχρημάτισται   perf pass ind 3 sg
[Hb 8:5; v-2a(1); 5976]   "

κεχρυσωμένη   perf pass ptcp nom sg fem
[2t; v-1d(3); 5998]   χρυσόω

κεχωρισμένος   perf pass ptcp nom sg masc
[Hb 7:26; v-2a(1); 6004]   χωρίζω

κηδεύω   {3054, v-1a(6)}
[-, κηδεῦσαι, -, -, -] *to take care of, bury* at corpse,
Mark 6:29 v.l.*

κημόω   {3055, v-1d(3)}
[κημώσω, -, -, -, -] *to muzzle,* 1 Cor 9:9*

κημώσεις   fut act ind 2 sg
[1C 9:9; v-1d(3); 3055]   κημόω

κῆνσον   acc sg masc [3t; n-2a; 3056]   κῆνσος

κῆνσος, ου, ὁ   {3056, n-2a}
*a census, assessment, enumeration of the people and
a valuation of their property;* in N.T. *tribute, tax,*
Matt 17:25; *poll-tax,* Matt 22:17, 19; Mark 12:14*

κήνσου   gen sg masc [Mt 22:19; n-2a; 3056] "

κῆπον   acc sg masc [Lk 13:19; n-2a; 3057]   κῆπος

κῆπος, ου, ὁ   {3057, n-2a}
a garden, any place planted with trees and herbs,
Luke 13:19; John 18:1, 26; 19:41*

κῆπος   nom sg masc [2t; n-2a; 3057]   "

κηπουρός, ου, ὁ   {3058, n-2a}
a garden-keeper, gardener, John 20:15*

κηπουρός   nom sg masc
[Jn 20:15; n-2a; 3058]   κηπουρός
κήπῳ   dat sg masc [2t; n-2a; 3057]   κῆπος

κηρίον, ου, τό   {3059, n-2c}
a honeycomb; a comb filled with honey, Luke 24:42
v.l.*

κήρυγμα, ατος, τό   {3060, n-3c(4)}
proclamation, proclaiming, public annunciation,
Matt 12:41; *public inculcation, preaching,* 1 Cor
2:4; 15:14; meton. *what is publicly inculcated,
doctrine,* Rom 16:25; Titus 1:3*

κήρυγμα   nom sg neut [3t; n-3c(4); 3060]   κήρυγμα
κήρυγμα   acc sg neut [4t; n-3c(4); 3060]   "
κηρύγματι   dat sg neut [Ti 1:3; n-3c(4); 3060] "
κηρύγματος   gen sg neut [1C 1:21; n-3c(4); 3060] "
κήρυκα   acc sg masc [2P 2:5; n-3b(1); 3061] κῆρυξ

κῆρυξ, ός, ὁ   {3061, n-3b(1)}
a herald, public messenger; in N.T. *a proclaimer,
publisher, preacher,* 1 Tim 2:7; 2 Tim 1:11; 2 Peter
2:5*

κῆρυξ   nom sg masc [2t; n-3b(1); 3061]   "
κηρύξαι   aor act inf [3t; v-2b; 3062]   κηρύσσω
κηρύξας   aor act ptcp nom sg masc
[1C 9:27; v-2b; 3062]   "

κηρύξατε   aor act imperative 2 pl
[2t; v-2b; 3062]   "
κήρυξον   aor act imperative 2 sg
[2Ti 4:2; v-2b; 3062]   "
κηρύξω   aor act subj 1 sg [Mk 1:38; v-2b; 3062] "
κηρύξωσιν   aor act subj 3 pl
[Rm 10:15; v-2b; 3062]   "
κηρύσσει   pres act ind 3 sg [2t; v-2b; 3062] "
κηρύσσειν   pres act inf [6t; v-2b; 3062]   "
κηρύσσεται   pres pass ind 3 sg
[1C 15:12; v-2b; 3062]   "
κηρύσσετε   pres act imperative 2 pl
[Mt 10:7; v-2b; 3062]   "
κηρύσσομεν   pres act ind 1 pl [4t; v-2b; 3062] "
κηρύσσοντα   pres act ptcp acc sg masc
[Rv 5:2; v-2b; 3062]   "
κηρύσσοντας   pres act ptcp acc pl masc
[Ac 15:21; v-2b; 3062]   "
κηρύσσοντος   pres act ptcp gen sg masc
[Rm 10:14; v-2b; 3062]   "
κηρύσσουσιν   pres act ind 3 pl
[Pp 1:15; v-2b; 3062]   "

κηρύσσω   {3062, v-2b}
[(ἐκήρυσσον), κηρύξω, ἐκήρυξα, -, κεκήρυγμαι,
ἐκηρύχθην] *to publish, proclaim,* as a herald, 1
Cor 9:27; *to announce openly and publicly,* Mark
1:4; Luke 4:18; *to noise abroad,* Mark 1:45; 7:36; *to
announce* as a matter of doctrine, *inculcate,
preach,* Matt 24:14; Mark 1:38; 13:10; Acts 15:21;
Rom 2:21

κηρύσσω   pres act ind 1 sg [2t; v-2b; 3062] "
κηρύσσων   pres act ptcp nom sg masc
[13t; v-2b; 3062]   "
κηρυχθείς   aor pass ptcp nom sg masc
[2C 1:19; v-2b; 3062]   "
κηρυχθέντος   aor pass ptcp gen sg neut
[Cl 1:23; v-2b; 3062]   "
κηρυχθῇ   aor pass subj 3 sg [2t; v-2b; 3062] "
κηρυχθῆναι   aor pass inf [2t; v-2b; 3062]   "
κηρυχθήσεται   fut pass ind 3 sg [2t; v-2b; 3062] "

κῆτος, ους, τό   {3063, n-3d(2b)}
a large fish, sea monster, whale, Matt 12:40*

κήτους   gen sg neut
[Mt 12:40; n-3d(2b); 3063]   κῆτος
Κηφᾶ   gen sg masc [1C 1:12; n-1e; 3064]   Κηφᾶς
Κηφᾷ   dat sg masc [2t; n-1e; 3064]   "
Κηφᾶν   acc sg masc [Ga 1:18; n-1e; 3064]   "

Κηφᾶς, ᾶ, ὁ   {3064, n-1e}
Cephas, Rock, rendered into Greek by Πέτρος,
John 1:42; 1 Cor 1:12; 3:22; 9:5; 15:5; Gal 1:18;
2:9, 11, 14*

Κηφᾶς   nom sg masc [5t; n-1e; 3064]   "

κιβώριον, ου, τό   {3065, n-2c}
ciborium, Acts 19:24 v.l.*

κιβωτόν   acc sg fem [4t; n-2b; 3066]   κιβωτός

κιβωτός, οῦ, ἡ   {3066, n-2b}
a chest, coffer; the ark of the covenant, Heb 9:4;
Rev 11:19; *the ark* of Noah, Matt 24:38; Luke
17:27; Heb 11:7; 1 Peter 3:20*

κιβωτός   nom sg fem [Rv 11:19; n-2b; 3066]   "
κιβωτοῦ   gen sg fem [1P 3:20; n-2b; 3066]   "

κιθάρα, ας, ἡ   {3067, n-1a}
a lyre, harp, 1 Cor 14:7; Rev 5:8; 14:2; 15:2*

κιθάρα   nom sg fem [1C 14:7; n-1a; 3067]   κιθάρα
κιθάραις   dat pl fem [Rv 14:2; n-1a; 3067]   "
κιθάραν   acc sg fem [Rv 5:8; n-1a; 3067]   "
κιθάρας   acc pl fem [Rv 15:2; n-1a; 3067]   "
κιθαριζόμενον   pres pass ptcp nom sg neut
   [1C 14:7; cv-; 3068]   κιθαρίζω
κιθαριζόντων   pres act ptcp gen pl masc
   [Rv 14:2; cv-; 3068]

κιθαρίζω   {3068, cv-2a(1)}
[-, -, -, -, -] *to play on a lyre* or *harp,* 1 Cor 14:7;
Rev 14:2*

κιθαρῳδός, ου, ὁ   {3069, n-2a}
*one who plays on the lyre and accompanies it with
his voice,* Rev 14:2; 18:22*

κιθαρῳδῶν   gen pl masc
   [2t; n-2a; 3069]   κιθαρῳδός

Κιλικία, ας, ἡ   {3070, n-1a}
Cilicia, a province of Asia Minor, Gal 1:21

Κιλικίαν   acc sg fem [3t; n-1a; 3070]   Κιλικία
Κιλικίας   gen sg fem [5t; n-1a; 3070]   "

Κίλιξ, ικος, ὁ   {3071, n-3b(1)}
a cilician, Acts 23:34 v.l.*

κινδυνεύει   pres act ind 3 sg
   [Ac 19:27; cv-1a(6); 3073]   κινδυνεύω
κινδυνεύομεν   pres act ind 1 pl
   [2t; cv-1a(6); 3073]   "

κινδυνεύω   {3073, cv-1a(6)}
[(ἐκινδύνευον), -, -, -, -, -] *to be in danger* or *peril,*
Luke 8:23; Acts 19:27, 40; 1 Cor 15:30*

κινδύνοις   dat pl masc [8t; n-2a; 3074]   κίνδυνος

κίνδυνος, ου, ὁ   {3074, n-2a}
danger, peril, Rom 8:35; 2 Cor 11:26*

κίνδυνος   nom sg masc [Rm 8:35; n-2a; 3074]   "

κινέω   {3075, v-1d(2a)}
[κινήσω, ἐκίνησα, -, -, ἐκινήθην] *to set a-going; to
move,* Matt 23:4; *to excite, agitate,* Acts 14:7 v.l.;
21:30; 24:5; *to remove,* Rev 2:5; 6:14; in N.T.
κεφαλήν, *to shake the head* in derision, Matt
27:39; Mark 15:29; mid., *to move, possess the
faculty of motion, exercise the functions of life,* Acts
17:28*

κινῆσαι   aor act inf
   [Mt 23:4; v-1d(2a); 3075]   κινέω

κίνησις, εως, ἡ   {3076, n-3e(5b)}
a moving, motion, John 5:3 v.l.*

κινήσω   fut act ind 1 sg [Rv 2:5; v-1d(2a); 3075]   "

κιννάμωμον, ου, τό   {3077, n-2c}
cinnamon, Rev 18:13*

κιννάμωμον   acc sg neut
   [Rv 18:13; n-2c; 3077]   κιννάμωμον

κινούμεθα   pres pass ind 1 pl
   [Ac 17:28; v-1d(2a); 3075]   κινέω
κινοῦντα   pres act ptcp acc sg masc
   [Ac 24:5; v-1d(2a); 3075]   "
κινοῦντες   pres act ptcp nom pl masc
   [2t; v-1d(2a); 3075]   "

Κίς, ὁ   {3078, n-3g(2)}
Kish, the father of Saul, pr. name, indecl., Acts
13:21*

Κίς   indecl [Ac 13:21; n-3g(2); 3078]   Κίς

κίχρημι   {3079, v-6a}
[-, ἔχρησα, -, -, -] *to lend,* Luke 11:5*

κλάδοι   nom pl masc [2t; n-2a; 3080]   κλάδος
κλάδοις   dat pl masc [2t; n-2a; 3080]   "

κλάδος, ου, ὁ   {3080, n-2a}
a bough, branch, shoot, Matt 13:32; 21:8; met. *a
branch* of a family stock, Rom 11:16, 21

κλάδος   nom sg masc [2t; n-2a; 3080]   "
κλάδους   acc pl masc [2t; n-2a; 3080]   "
κλάδων   gen pl masc [3t; n-2a; 3080]   "
κλαῖε   pres act imperative 2 sg
   [2t; v-2c; 3081]   κλαίω
κλαίειν   pres act inf [Rm 12:15; v-2c; 3081]   "
κλαίεις   pres act ind 2 sg [2t; v-2c; 3081]   "
κλαίετε   pres act imperative 2 pl
   [3t; v-2c; 3081]   "
κλαίετε   pres act ind 2 pl [Mk 5:39; v-2c; 3081]   "
κλαίοντας   pres act ptcp acc pl masc
   [2t; v-2c; 3081]   "
κλαίοντες   pres act ptcp nom pl masc
   [5t; v-2c; 3081]   "
κλαίοντες   pres act ptcp voc pl masc
   [Lk 6:21; v-2c; 3081]   "
κλαιόντων   pres act ptcp gen pl masc
   [Rm 12:15; v-2c; 3081]   "
κλαίουσα   pres act ptcp nom sg fem
   [3t; v-2c; 3081]   "
κλαίουσαι   pres act ptcp nom pl fem
   [Ac 9:39; v-2c; 3081]   "
κλαίουσαν   pres act ptcp acc sg fem
   [Jn 11:33; v-2c; 3081]   "
κλαίουσιν   pres act ind 3 pl
   [Rv 18:11; v-2c; 3081]   "
κλαίουσιν   pres act ptcp dat pl masc
   [Mk 16:10; v-2c; 3081]   "

κλαίω   {3081, v-2c}
[(ἔκλαιον), κλαύσω, ἔκλαυσα, -, -, -] intrans. *to
weep, shed tears,* Matt 26:75; Mark 5:38, 39; Luke
19:41; 23:28; trans. *to weep for, bewail,* Matt 2:18;
Rev 18:9 v.l.

κλαίων   pres act ptcp nom sg masc
   [Pp 3:18; v-2c; 3081]   "
κλάσαι   aor act inf
   [Ac 20:7; v-1d(1b); 3089]   κλάω
κλάσας   aor act ptcp nom sg masc
   [4t; v-1d(1b); 3089]   "
κλάσει   dat sg fem [2t; n-3e(5b); 3082]   κλάσις

κλάσις, εως, ἡ   {3082, n-3e(5b)}
a breaking, the act of breaking, Luke 24:35; Acts
2:42

κλάσμα, ατος, τό   {3083, n-3c(4)}
a piece broken off, fragment, Matt 14:20; 15:37;
Mark 6:43; 8:8, 19, 20; Luke 9:17; John 6:12f.*

κλάσματα   acc pl neut [2t; n-3c(4); 3083]   κλάσμα
κλασμάτων   gen pl neut [7t; n-3c(4); 3083]   "

Κλαύδη (3084) and Κλαῦδη (3085), see Καύδα

Κλαυδία, ας, ἡ   {3086, n-1a}
Claudia, pr. name, 2 Tim 4:21*

Κλαυδία   nom sg fem [2Ti 4:21; n-1a; 3086]
     Κλαυδία
Κλαύδιον   acc sg masc
     [Ac 18:2; n-2a; 3087]   Κλαύδιος

Κλαύδιος, ου, ὁ   {3087, n-2a}
Claudius, pr. name (1) *The fourth Roman
Emperor,* Acts 11:28; 18:2. (2) *Claudius Lysias, a
Roman captain,* Acts 23:26*

Κλαύδιος   nom sg masc [Ac 23:26; n-2a; 3087]   "
Κλαυδίου   gen sg masc [Ac 11:28; n-2a; 3087]   "

κλαυθμός, ου, ὁ   {3088, n-2a}
weeping, crying, Matt 2:18; 8:12

κλαυθμός   nom sg masc [9t; n-2a; 3088]   κλαυθμός
κλαύσατε   aor act imperative 2 pl
     [2t; v-2c; 3081]   κλαίω
κλαύσετε   fut act ind 2 pl [2t; v-2c; 3081]   "
κλαύσῃ   aor act subj 3 sg [Jn 11:31; v-2c; 3081] "
κλαύσουσιν   fut act ind 3 pl
     [Rv 18:9; v-2c; 3081]   "

κλάω   {3089, v-1d(1b)}
[κλάσω, ἔκλασα, -, -, ἐκλάσθην] *to break off;* in
N.T. *to break* bread, Matt 14:19; with figurative
reference to the violent death of Christ, 1 Cor
11:24

κλεῖδα   acc sg fem [Lk 11:52; n-3c(2); 3090]   κλείς
κλεῖδας   acc pl fem [Mt 16:19; n-3c(2); 3090]   "
κλείετε   pres act ind 2 pl
     [Mt 23:13; v-1a(3); 3091]   κλείω
κλεῖν   acc sg fem [2t; n-3c(2); 3090]   κλείς

κλείς, ιδός, ἡ   {3090, n-3c(2)}
a key, used in N.T. as the symbol of power,
authority, etc. Matt 16:19; Rev 1:18; 3:7; 9:1;
20:1; met. *the key* of entrance into knowledge,
Luke 11:52*

κλείς   nom sg fem [Rv 9:1; n-3c(2); 3090]   "
κλεῖς   acc pl fem [Rv 1:18; n-3c(2); 3090]   "
κλεῖσαι   aor act inf [2t; v-1a(3); 3091]   κλείω
κλείσας   aor act ptcp nom sg masc
     [Mt 6:6; v-1a(3); 3091]   "
κλείσει   fut act ind 3 sg [Rv 3:7; v-1a(3); 3091] "
κλείσῃ   aor act subj 3 sg
     [1J 3:17; v-1a(3); 3091]   "
κλεισθῶσιν   aor pass subj 3 pl
     [Rv 21:25; v-1a(3); 3091]   "

κλείω   {3091, v-1a(3)}
[κλείσω, ἔκλεισα, -, κέκλεισμαι, ἐκλείσθην] *to*

close, shut, Matt 6:6; 25:10; *to shut up* a person,
Rev 20:3; met. of the heavens, Luke 4:25; Rev
11:6; κλεῖσαι τὰ σπλάγχνα, *to shut one's bowels,
to be hard-hearted, void of compassion,* 1 John 3:17;
κλείειν τὴν βασιλεία τῶν οὐρανῶν, *to endeavor to
prevent entrance into the kingdom of heaven,* Matt
23:13

κλείων   pres act ptcp nom sg masc
     [Rv 3:7; v-1a(3); 3091]   "

κλέμμα, ατος, τό   {3092, n-3c(4)}
theft, Rev 9:21; Mark 7:22 v.l.*

κλεμμάτων   gen pl neut
     [Rv 9:21; n-3c(4); 3092]   κλέμμα
Κλεοπᾶς   nom sg masc
     [Lk 24:18; n-1e; 3093]   Κλεοπᾶς

Κλεοπᾶς, ᾶ, ὁ   {3093, n-1e}
Cleopas, pr. name, Luke 24:18*

κλέος, ους, τό   {3094, n-3d(2b)}
pr. *rumor, report; good report, praise, credit,* 1
Peter 2:20*

κλέος   nom sg neut [1P 2:20; n-3d(2b); 3094]   κλέος
κλέπται   nom pl masc [4t; n-1f; 3095]   κλέπτης
κλέπτειν   pres act inf
     [Rm 2:21; v-4; 3096]   κλέπτω
κλέπτεις   pres act ind 2 sg [Rm 2:21; v-4; 3096] "
κλεπτέτω   pres act imperative 3 sg
     [Ep 4:28; v-4; 3096]   "

κλέπτης, ου, ὁ   {3095, n-1f}
a thief, Matt 6:19, 20; 24:43; trop. *a thief* by
imposture, John 10:8

κλέπτης   nom sg masc [12t; n-1f; 3095]   κλέπτης
κλέπτουσιν   pres act ind 3 pl
     [2t; v-4; 3096]   κλέπτω

κλέπτω   {3096, v-4}
[κλέψω, ἔκλεψα, -, -, ἐκλάπην] *to steal,* Matt
6:19, 20; 19:18; *to take away stealthily, remove
secretly,* Matt 27:64; 28:13

κλέπτων   pres act ptcp nom sg masc
     [Ep 4:28; v-4; 3096]   "
κλέψεις   fut act ind 2 sg [2t; v-4; 3096]   "
κλέψῃ   aor act subj 3 sg [Jn 10:10; v-4; 3096] "
κλέψῃς   aor act subj 2 sg [2t; v-4; 3096]   "
κλέψωσιν   aor act subj 3 pl [Mt 27:64; v-4; 3096] "
κληθείς   aor pass ptcp nom sg masc
     [2t; v-1d(2b); 2813]   καλέω
κληθέν   aor pass ptcp nom sg neut
     [Lk 2:21; v-1d(2b); 2813]   "
κληθέντος   aor pass ptcp gen sg masc
     [Ac 24:2; v-1d(2b); 2813]   "
κληθῆναι   aor pass inf [3t; v-1d(2b); 2813]   "
κληθῇς   aor pass subj 2 sg [2t; v-1d(2b); 2813] "
κληθήσεται   fut pass ind 3 sg
     [11t; v-1d(2b); 2813]   "
κληθήσῃ   fut pass ind 2 sg [2t; v-1d(2b); 2813] "
κληθήσονται   fut pass ind 3 pl
     [2t; v-1d(2b); 2813]   "
κληθῆτε   aor pass subj 2 pl [2t; v-1d(2b); 2813] "
κληθῶμεν   aor pass subj 1 pl
     [1J 3:1; v-1d(2b); 2813]   "

κλῆμα, ατος, τό   {3097, n-3c(4)}
a branch, shoot, twig, esp. of the vine, John 15:2,
4-6*

κλῆμα   nom sg neut [2t; n-3c(4); 3097]   κλῆμα
κλῆμα   acc sg neut [Jn 15:2; n-3c(4); 3097]   "
κλήματα   nom pl neut [Jn 15:5; n-3c(4); 3097]   "
Κλήμεντος   gen sg masc
   [Pp 4:3; n-3c(5a); 3098]   Κλήμης

Κλήμης, μεντος, ὁ   {3098, n-3c(5a)}
Clemens, Clement, pr. name, Latin, Phil 4:3*

κλῆρον   acc sg masc [5t; n-2a; 3102]   κλῆρος
κληρονομεῖ   pres act ind 3 sg
   [1C 15:50; v-1d(2a); 3099]   κληρονομέω
κληρονομεῖν   pres act inf
   [Hb 1:14; v-1d(2a); 3099]

κληρονομέω   {3099, v-1d(2a)}
[κληρονομήσω, ἐκληρονόμησα, κεκληρονόμηκα,
-, -] pr. to acquire by lot; to inherit, obtain by
inheritance; in N.T. to obtain, acquire, receive
possession of, Matt 5:5; 19:29; absol. to be heir, Gal
4:30

κληρονομῆσαι   aor act inf [2t; v-1d(2a); 3099]   "
κληρονομήσατε   aor act imperative 2 pl
   [Mt 25:34; v-1d(2a); 3099]
κληρονομήσει   fut act ind 3 sg
   [3t; v-1d(2a); 3099]   "
κληρονομήσητε   aor act subj 2 pl
   [1P 3:9; v-1d(2a); 3099]
κληρονομήσουσιν   fut act ind 3 pl
   [4t; v-1d(2a); 3099]
κληρονομήσω   aor act subj 1 sg
   [Mk 10:17; v-1d(2a); 3099]
κληρονομήσω   fut act ind 1 sg
   [2t; v-1d(2a); 3099]

κληρονομία, ας, ἡ   {3100, n-1a}
an inheritance, patrimony, Matt 21:38; Mark 12:7;
a possession, portion, property, Acts 7:5; 13:33 v.l.;
20:32; in N.T. a share, participation in privileges,
Acts 20:32; Eph 1:14; 5:5

κληρονομία   nom sg fem [3t; n-1a; 3100] κληρονομία
κληρονομίαν   acc sg fem [7t; n-1a; 3100]   "
κληρονομίας   gen sg fem [4t; n-1a; 3100]   "
κληρονόμοι   nom pl masc
   [5t; n-2a; 3101]   κληρονόμος
κληρονόμοις   dat pl masc [Hb 6:17; n-2a; 3101]   "
κληρονόμον   nom sg neut [Rm 4:13; n-2a; 3101]   "
κληρονόμον   acc sg masc [Hb 1:2; n-2a; 3101]   "

κληρονόμος, ου, ὁ   {3101, n-2a}
an heir, Matt 21:38; Gal 4:1; a possessor, Rom
4:13; Heb 11:7; James 2:5

κληρονόμος   nom sg masc [6t; n-2a; 3101]   "
κληρονομούντων   pres act ptcp gen pl masc
   [Hb 6:12; v-1d(2a); 3099]   κληρονομέω
κληρονόμους   acc pl masc
   [Jm 2:5; n-2a; 3101]   κληρονόμος

κλῆρος, ου, ὁ   {3102, n-2a}
a lot, die, a thing used in determining chances,
Matt 27:35; Mark 15:24; Luke 23:34; John 19:24;
Acts 1:26; assignment, investiture, Acts 1:17, 25

v.l.; allotment, destination, Col 1:12; a part,
portion, share, Acts 8:21; 26:18; a constituent
portion of the Church, 1 Peter 5:3

κλῆρος   nom sg masc [2t; n-2a; 3102]   κλῆρος
κλήρου   gen sg masc [Cl 1:12; n-2a; 3102]   "
κλήρους   acc pl masc [2t; n-2a; 3102]   "

κληρόω   {3103, v-1d(3)}
[-, -, -, κεκλήρωμαι, ἐκληρώθην] to obtain by lot
or assignment; to obtain a portion, receive a share,
Eph 1:11*

κλήρων   gen pl masc [1P 5:3; n-2a; 3102]   "
κλήσει   dat sg fem [2t; n-3e(5b); 3104]   κλῆσις
κλήσεως   gen sg fem [6t; n-3e(5b); 3104]   "
κλῆσιν   acc sg fem [2t; n-3e(5b); 3104]   "

κλῆσις, εως, ἡ   {3104, n-3e(5b)}
a call, calling, invitation; in N.T. the call or
invitation to the privileges of the Gospel, Rom
11:29; Eph 1:18; Luke 11:42 v.l.; the favor and
privilege of the invitation, 2 Thess 1:11; 2 Peter
1:10; the temporal condition in which the call found
a person, 1 Cor 1:26; 7:20

κλῆσις   nom sg fem [Rm 11:29; n-3e(5b); 3104]   "
κλητοί   nom pl masc [3t; a-1a(2a); 3105]   κλητός
κλητοῖς   dat pl masc [5t; a-1a(2a); 3105]   "

κλητός, ή, όν   {3105, a-1a(2a)}
called, invited, in N.T. called to privileges or
function, Matt 20:16; 22:14; Rom 1:1, 6, 7; 8:28;
1 Cor 1:1, 2, 24; Jude 1; Rev 17:14

κλητός   nom sg masc [2t; a-1a(2a); 3105]   "
κλίβανον   acc sg masc [2t; n-2a; 3106]   κλίβανος

κλίβανος, ου, ὁ   {3106, n-2a}
an oven, Matt 6:30; Luke 12:28; Rev 2:22 v.l.*

κλίμα, ατος, τό   {3107, n-3c(4)}
pr. a slope; a portion of the ideal slope of the
earth's surface; a tract or region of country, Rom
15:23; 2 Cor 11:10; Gal 1:21*

κλίμασι   dat pl neut
   [Rm 15:23; n-3c(4); 3107]   κλίμα
κλίμασιν   dat pl neut [2C 11:10; n-3c(4); 3107]   "
κλίματα   acc pl neut [Ga 1:21; n-3c(4); 3107]   "

κλινάριον, ου, τό   {3108, n-2c}
a small bed or couch, Acts 5:15*

κλιναρίων   gen pl neut
   [Ac 5:15; n-2c; 3108]   κλινάριον
κλίνας   aor act ptcp nom sg masc
   [Jn 19:30; v-1c(2); 3111]   κλίνω
κλίνειν   pres act inf [Lk 9:12; v-1c(2); 3111]   "

κλίνη, ης, ἡ   {3109, n-1b}
a couch, bed, Matt 9:2, 6; Mark 4:21; 7:4 v.l.; Rev
2:22

κλίνη   pres act subj 3 sg [2t; v-1c(2); 3111]   "
κλίνην   acc sg fem [4t; n-1b; 3109]   κλίνη
κλίνης   gen sg fem [4t; n-1b; 3109]   "

κλινίδιον, ου, τό   {3110, n-2c}
a small couch or bed, Luke 5:19, 24*

κλινίδιον   acc sg neut
   [Lk 5:24; n-2c; 3110]   κλινίδιον

κλινιδίῳ   dat sg neut [Lk 5:19; n-2c; 3110]   "
κλινουσῶν   pres act ptcp gen pl fem
   [Lk 24:5; v-1c(2); 3111]   κλίνω

κλίνω   {3111, v-1c(2)}
   [κλινῶ, ἔκλινα, κέκλικα, -, ἐκλίθην] pr. trans. *to
   cause to slope* or *bend; to bow down*, Luke 24:5;
   John 19:30; *to lay down* to rest, Matt 8:20; Luke
   9:58; *to put to flight* troops, Heb 11:34; intrans. of
   the day, *to decline*, Luke 9:12; 24:29*

κλινῶν   gen pl fem [Mk 7:4; n-1b; 3109]   κλίνη

κλισία, ας, ἡ   {3112, n-1a}
   pr. *a place for reclining; a tent, seat, couch;* in N.T.
   a group of persons reclining at a meal. Luke 9:14*

κλισίας   acc pl fem [Lk 9:14; n-1a; 3112]   κλισία
κλοπαί   nom pl fem [2t; n-1b; 3113]   κλοπή

κλοπή, ῆς, ἡ   {3113, n-1b}
   theft, Matt 15:19; Mark 7:21*

κλύδων, ωνος, ὁ   {3114, n-3f(1a)}
   a wave, billow, surge, Luke 8:24; James 1:6*

κλύδωνι   dat sg masc [2t; n-3f(1a); 3114]   κλύδων

κλυδωνίζομαι   {3115, cv-2a(1)}
   [-, -, -, -, -] *to be tossed by waves;* met. *to fluctuate*
   in opinion, *be agitated, tossed to and fro*, Eph
   4:14*

κλυδωνιζόμενοι   pres pass ptcp nom pl masc
   [Ep 4:14; cv-; 3115]   κλυδωνίζομαι
κλῶμεν   pres act ind 1 pl
   [1C 10:16; v-1d(1b); 3089]   κλάω
κλῶντες   pres act ptcp nom pl masc
   [Ac 2:46; v-1d(1b); 3089]   "
Κλωπᾶ   gen sg masc [Jn 19:25; n-1e; 3116]   Κλωπᾶς

Κλωπᾶς, ᾶ, ὁ   {3116, n-1e}
   Cleopas, pr. name, John 19:25*

κνηθόμενοι   pres pass ptcp nom pl masc
   [2Ti 4:3; v-1b(3); 3117]   κνήθω

κνήθω   {3117, v-1b(3)}
   [-, -, -, -, -] *to scratch; to tickle, cause titillation;* in
   N.T. mid. met. *to procure pleasurable excitement
   for, to indulge an itching,* 2 Tim 4:3*

Κνίδον   acc sg fem [Ac 27:7; n-2b; 3118]   Κνίδος

Κνίδος, ου, ἡ   {3118, n-2b}
   Cnidus, a city of Caria, in Asia Minor, Acts 27:7*

κοδράντην   acc sg masc
   [Mt 5:26; n-1f; 3119]   κοδράντης

κοδράντης   {3119, n-1f}
   a Roman brass coin, equivalent to the *fourth part*
   of an *as,* or *ἀσσάριον,* or to the δύο λεπτά, Matt 5:26;
   Mark 12:42; Luke 12:59 v.l.*

κοδράντης   nom sg masc [Mk 12:42; n-1f; 3119]   "

κοιλία, ας, ἡ   {3120, n-1a}
   a cavity; the belly, Matt 15:17; Mark 7:19; Luke
   15:16 v.l.; *the stomach,* Matt 12:40; Luke 15:16;
   the womb, Matt 19:12; Luke 1:15; from the
   Hebrew, *the inner self,* John 7:38

κοιλία   nom sg fem [4t; n-1a; 3120]   κοιλία
κοιλία   dat sg fem [6t; n-1a; 3120]   "

κοιλίαι   nom pl fem [Lk 23:29; n-1a; 3120]   "
κοιλίαν   acc sg fem [4t; n-1a; 3120]   "
κοιλίας   gen sg fem [7t; n-1a; 3120]   "

κοιμάω   {3121, v-1d(1a)}
   [-, -, -, κεκοίμημαι, ἐκοιμήθην] *to lull to sleep;*
   pass. *to fall asleep, be asleep,* Matt 28:13; Luke
   22:45; met. *to sleep* in death, Acts 7:60; 13:36; 2
   Peter 3:4

κοιμηθέντας   aor pass ptcp acc pl masc
   [2t; v-1d(1a); 3121]   κοιμάω
κοιμηθέντες   aor pass ptcp nom pl masc
   [1C 15:18; v-1d(1a); 3121]   "
κοιμηθῇ   aor pass subj 3 sg
   [1C 7:39; v-1d(1a); 3121]   "
κοιμηθησόμεθα   fut pass ind 1 pl
   [1C 15:51; v-1d(1a); 3121]   "
κοιμήσεως   gen sg fem
   [Jn 11:13; n-3e(5b); 3122]   κοίμησις

κοίμησις, εως, ἡ   {3122, n-3e(5b)}
   sleep; meton. *rest, repose,* John 11:13*

κοιμώμενος   pres pass ptcp nom sg masc
   [Ac 12:6; v-1d(1a); 3121]   κοιμάω
κοιμωμένους   pres pass ptcp acc pl masc
   [Lk 22:45; v-1d(1a); 3121]   "
κοιμωμένων   pres pass ptcp gen pl masc
   [2t; v-1d(1a); 3121]   "
κοιμῶνται   pres pass ind 3 pl
   [1C 11:30; v-1d(1a); 3121]   "
κοινά   nom pl neut
   [Ac 4:32; a-1a(2a); 3123]   κοινός
κοινά   acc pl neut [Ac 2:44; a-1a(2a); 3123]   "
κοιναῖς   dat pl fem [2t; a-1a(2a); 3123]   "
κοινήν   acc sg fem [Ti 1:4; a-1a(2a); 3123]   "
κοινῆς   gen sg fem [Jd 3; a-1a(2a); 3123]   "
κοινοῖ   pres act ind 3 sg
   [6t; v-1d(3); 3124]   κοινόω
κοινόν   nom sg neut [5t; a-1a(2a); 3123]   κοινός
κοινόν   acc sg masc [Ac 10:28; a-1a(2a); 3123]   "
κοινόν   acc sg neut [2t; a-1a(2a); 3123]   "

κοινός, ή, όν   {3123, a-1a(2a)}
   common, belonging equally to several, Acts 2:44;
   4:32; in N.T. *common, profane,* Heb 10:29; Rev
   21:27; ceremonially *unclean,* Mark 7:2; Acts
   10:14

κοίνου   pres act imperative 2 sg
   [2t; a-1a(2a); 3123]   "
κοινοῦντα   pres act ptcp nom pl neut
   [2t; v-1d(3); 3124]   κοινόω

κοινόω   {3124, v-1d(3)}
   [-, ἐκοίνωσα, κεκοίνωκα, κεκοίνωμαι, -] *to make
   common,* in N.T. *to profane, desecrate,* Acts 21:28;
   to render ceremonially *unclean, defile, pollute,*
   Matt 15:11, 18, 20; 7:15, 18, 20, 23; Heb 9:13; *to
   pronounce unclean* ceremonially, Acts 10:15;
   11:9*

κοινώνει   pres act imperative 2 sg
   [1Ti 5:22; v-1d(2a); 3125]   κοινωνέω
κοινωνεῖ   pres act ind 3 sg
   [2J 11; v-1d(2a); 3125]   "

κοινωνεῖτε   pres act ind 2 pl
   [1P 4:13; v-1d(2a); 3125]   "
κοινωνείτω   pres act imperative 3 sg
   [Ga 6:6; v-1d(2a); 3125]   "

κοινωνέω   {3125, v-1d(2a)}
   [κοινωνήσω, ἐκοινώνησα, κεκοινώνηκα, -, -] *to
   have in common, share,* Heb 2:14; *to be associated
   in, to become a sharer in,* Rom 15:27; 1 Peter 4:13;
   to become implicated in, be a party to, 1 Tim 5:22;
   2 John 11; *to associate one's self with* by sympathy
   and assistance, *to communicate with* in the way
   of aid and relief, Rom 12:13; Gal 6:6; Phil 4:15*

κοινωνία, ας, ἡ   {3126, n-1a}
   fellowship, partnership, Acts 2:42; 2 Cor 6:14;
   13:13; Gal 2:9; Phil 3:10; 1 John 1:3; *participation,
   communion,* 1 Cor 10:16; *aid, relief,* Heb 13:16;
   contribution in aid, Rom 15:26

κοινωνία   nom sg fem [7t; n-1a; 3126]   κοινωνία
κοινωνίᾳ   dat sg fem [2t; n-1a; 3126]   "
κοινωνίαν acc sg fem [7t; n-1a; 3126]   "
κοινωνίας gen sg fem [3t; n-1a; 3126]   "

κοινωνικός, ή, όν   {3127, a-1a(2a)}
   social; in N.T. *generous, liberal, beneficent,* 1 Tim
   6:18*

κοινωνικούς   acc pl masc
   [1Ti 6:18; a-1a(2a); 3127]   κοινωνικός
κοινωνοί   nom pl masc [6t; n-2a; 3128]   κοινωνός
κοινωνόν   acc sg masc [Pm 17; n-2a; 3128]   "

κοινωνός, οῦ, ὁ ἡ   {3128, n-2a/n-2b}
   a fellow, partner, companion, Matt 23:30; Luke
   5:10; 1 Cor 10:18, 20; 2 Cor 8:23; Phil 17; Heb
   10:33; *a sharer, partaker,* 2 Cor 1:7; 1 Peter 5:1; 2
   Peter 1:4*

κοινωνός   nom sg masc [2t; n-2a; 3128]
κοινωνοῦντες   pres act ptcp nom pl masc
   [Rm 12:13; v-1d(2a); 3125]   κοινωνέω
κοινωνούς   acc pl masc
   [1C 10:20; n-2a; 3128]   κοινωνός
κοινῶσαι   aor act inf [2t; v-1d(3); 3124]   κοινόω
κοίταις   dat pl fem [Rm 13:13; n-1b; 3130]   κοίτη

κοίτη, ἧς, ἡ   {3130, n-1b}
   a bed, Luke 11:7; *the* conjugal *bed,* Heb 13:4;
   meton. *sexual intercourse, concubitus;* hence,
   lewdness, whoredom, chambering, Rom 13:13; in
   N.T. *conception,* Rom 9:10*

κοίτη   nom sg fem [Hb 13:4; n-1b; 3130]   "
κοίτην acc sg fem [2t; n-1b; 3130]   "

κοιτών, ῶνος, ὁ   {3131, n-3f(1a)}
   a bed-chamber, Acts 12:20*

κοιτῶνος   gen sg masc
   [Ac 12:20; n-3f(1a); 3131]   κοιτών
κοκκίνην   acc sg fem
   [Mt 27:28; a-1a(2a); 3132]   κόκκινος
κόκκινον   acc sg neut [3t; a-1a(2a); 3132]   "

κόκκινος, η, ον   {3132, a-1a(2a)}
   dyed with coccus, crimson, scarlet, Matt 27:28;
   Heb 9:19; Rev 17:3, 4; 18:12, 16*

κοκκίνου   gen sg neut [2t; a-1a(2a); 3132]   "

κόκκον   acc sg masc [3t; n-2a; 3133]   κόκκος

κόκκος, ου, ὁ   {3133, n-2a}
   a kernel, grain, seed, Matt 13:31; 17:20; Mark 4:31;
   Luke 13:19; 17:6; John 12:24; 1 Cor 15:37*

κόκκος   nom sg masc [Jn 12:24; n-2a; 3133]   "
κόκκῳ   dat sg masc [3t; n-2a; 3133]   "
κολαζομένους   pres pass ptcp acc pl masc
   [2P 2:9; v-2a(1); 3134]   κολάζω

κολάζω   {3134, v-2a(1)}
   [κολάσω, ἐκόλασα, -, -, ἐκολάσθην] pr. *to curtail,
   to coerce; to chastise, punish,* Acts 4:21; 1 Peter
   2:20 v.l.; 2 Peter 2:9*

κολακεία, ας, ἡ   {3135, n-1a}
   flattery, adulation, obsequiousness, 1 Thess 2:5*

κολακείας   gen sg fem
   [1Th 2:5; n-1a; 3135]   κολακεία
κόλασιν   acc sg fem [2t; n-3e(5b); 3136]   κόλασις

κόλασις, εως, ἡ   {3136, n-3e(5b)}
   chastisement, punishment, Matt 25:46; *painful
   disquietude, torment,* 1 John 4:18*

Κολασσαεύς   {3137}
   also spelled Κολοσσαεύς, Κολοσαεύς,
   Κολασαεύς, *Collosian, a Colossian,* as a v.l. in the
   title to the epistle to the Colossians

Κολασσαί see Κολοσσαί   {3138}
   Colossae, a city of Phrygia, Col 1:2 v.l.*

κολάσωνται   aor mid subj 3 pl
   [Ac 4:21; v-2a(1); 3134]   κολάζω
κολαφίζειν   pres act inf
   [Mk 14:65; v-2a(1); 3139]   κολαφίζω
κολαφίζῃ   pres act subj 3 sg
   [2C 12:7; v-2a(1); 3139]   "
κολαφιζόμεθα   pres pass ind 1 pl
   [1C 4:11; v-2a(1); 3139]   "
κολαφιζόμενοι   pres pass ptcp nom pl masc
   [1P 2:20; v-2a(1); 3139]   "

κολαφίζω   {3139, v-2a(1)}
   [-, ἐκολάφισα, -, -, -] *to beat with the fist, buffet,*
   Matt 26:67; Mark 14:65; met. *to maltreat, treat
   with excessive force,* 1 Cor 4:11; *to punish,* 1 Peter
   2:20; *to buffet, fret, afflict,* 2 Cor 12:7*

κολλᾶσθαι   pres pass inf
   [3t; v-1d(1a); 3140]   κολλάω

κολλάω   {3140, v-1d(1a)}
   [-, -, -, -, ἐκολλήθην] *to glue* or *weld together;* mid.
   to adhere to, Luke 10:11; met. *to attach one's self
   to, unite with, associate with,* Luke 15:15; Acts
   5:13; Rev 18:5

κολληθέντα   aor pass ptcp acc sg masc
   [Lk 10:11; v-1d(1a); 3140]   "
κολληθέντες   aor pass ptcp nom pl masc
   [Ac 17:34; v-1d(1a); 3140]   "
κολληθήσεται   fut pass ind 3 sg
   [Mt 19:5; v-1d(1a); 3140]   "
κολλήθητι   aor pass imperative 2 sg
   [Ac 8:29; v-1d(1a); 3140]   "

κολλούριον, ου, τό   {3141, n-2c}
also spelled κολλύριον, *collyrium, eye-salve*, Rev
3:18*

κολλούριον   acc sg neut
[Rv 3:18; n-2c; 3141]   κολλούριον

κολλυβιστής, ου, ὁ   {3142, n-1f}
a money-changer, Matt 21:12; Mark 11:15; Luke
19:45 v.l.; John 2:15*

κολλυβιστῶν   gen pl masc
[3t; n-1f; 3142]   κολλυβιστής

κολλύριον, see κολλούριον

κολλώμενοι   pres pass ptcp nom pl masc
[Rm 12:9; v-1d(1a); 3140]   κολλάω
κολλώμενος   pres pass ptcp nom sg masc
[2t; v-1d(1a); 3140]   "

κολοβόω   {3143, v-1d(3)}
[-, ἐκολόβωσα, -, κεκολόβωμαι, ἐκολοβώθην] in
N.T. of time, *to cut short, shorten*, Matt 24:22;
Mark 13:20*

κολοβωθήσονται   fut pass ind 3 pl
[Mt 24:22; v-1d(3); 3143]   κολοβόω

Κολοσσαεύς, έως, ὁ, see Κολασσαεύς   {3144}

Κολοσσαί, ῆς, ἡ   {3145, n-1b}
also spelled Κολασσαεύς, *Colossae*, a city of
Phrygia, Col 1:2; subscription to Phil*

Κολοσσαῖς   dat pl fem
[Cl 1:2; n-1b; 3145]   Κολοσσαί
κόλποις   dat pl masc [Lk 16:23; n-2a; 3146]   κόλπος
κόλπον   acc sg masc [4t; n-2a; 3146]   "

κόλπος, ου, ὁ   {3146, n-2a}
the bosom, Luke 16:22, 23; John 1:18; 13:23; *the
bosom of a garment*, Luke 6:38; *a bay, creek, inlet*,
Acts 27:39*

κόλπῳ   dat sg masc [Jn 13:23; n-2a; 3146]   "
κολυμβᾶν   pres act inf
[Ac 27:43; v-1d(1a); 3147]   κολυμβάω

κολυμβάω   {3147, v-1d(1a)}
[-, ἐκολύμβησα, -, -, -] *to dive*; in N.T. *to swim*,
Acts 27:43*

κολυμβήθρα, ας, ἡ   {3148, n-1a}
a place where any one may swim; a pond, pool, John
5:2, 4, 7; 9:7*

κολυμβήθρα   nom sg fem
[Jn 5:2; n-1a; 3148]   κολυμβήθρα
κολυμβήθραν   acc sg fem [2t; n-1a; 3148]   "

κολωνία, ας, ἡ   {3149, n-1a}
a Roman colony, Acts 16:12*

κολωνία   nom sg fem [Ac 16:12; n-1a; 3149]
κολωνία
κομᾷ   pres act subj 3 sg
[2t; v-1d(1a); 3150]   κομάω

κομάω   {3150, v-1d(1a)}
[-, -, -, -, -] *to have long hair, wear the hair long*, 1
Cor 11:14, 15*

κόμη, ῆς, ἡ   {3151, n-1b}
the hair; a head of long hair, 1 Cor 11:15*

κόμη   nom sg fem [1C 11:15; n-1b; 3151]   κόμη
κομιεῖσθε   fut mid ind 2 pl
[1P 5:4; v-2a(1); 3152]   κομίζω
κομιζόμενοι   pres mid ptcp nom pl masc
[1P 1:9; v-2a(1); 3152]   "

κομίζω   {3152, v-2a(1)}
[κομίσω or κομιῶ, ἐκόμισα, -, -, ἐκομίσθην] pr. *to
take into kindly keeping, to provide for; to convey,
bring*, Luke 7:37; mid. *to bring for one's self; to
receive, obtain*, 2 Cor 5:10; Eph 6:8; Heb 11:13
v.l.; 2 Peter 2:13 v.l.; *to receive again, recover*, Matt
25:27; Heb 11:19

κομίσασα   aor act ptcp nom sg fem
[Lk 7:37; v-2a(1); 3152]   "
κομίσεται   fut mid ind 3 sg [2t; v-2a(1); 3152]   "
κομίσησθε   aor mid subj 2 pl
[Hb 10:36; v-2a(1); 3152]   "
κομίσηται   aor mid subj 3 sg
[2C 5:10; v-2a(1); 3152]   "

κομψότερον   {3153, adverb}
in N.T. *in better health*, John 4:52*

κομψότερον   adverb-comparative
[Jn 4:52; adverb; 3153]   κομψότερον

κονιάω   {3154, v-1d(1b)}
[-, -, -, κεκονίαμαι, -] *to whitewash*, or, *plaster*,
Matt 23:27; Acts 23:3*

κονιορτόν   acc sg masc [5t; n-2a; 3155]   κονιορτός

κονιορτός, οῦ, ὁ   {3155, n-2a}
dust, Matt 10:14; Luke 9:5; 10:11; Acts 13:51;
22:23*

κοπάζω   {3156, v-2a(1)}
[-, ἐκόπασα, -, -, -] pr. *to grow weary, suffer
exhaustion; to abate, be stilled*, Matt 14:32; Mark
4:39; 6:51*

κοπετόν   acc sg masc [Ac 8:2; n-2a; 3157]   κοπετός

κοπετός, οῦ, ὁ   {3157, n-2a}
pr. *a beating* of the breast, etc., in token of grief;
a wailing, lamentation, Acts 8:2*

κοπή, ῆς, ἡ   {3158, n-1b}
a stroke, smiting; in N.T. *slaughter*, Heb 7:1*

κοπῆς   gen sg fem [Hb 7:1; n-1b; 3158]   κοπή
κοπιᾷ   pres act ind 3 sg
[Lk 12:27; v-1d(1b); 3159]   κοπιάω
κοπιάσαντες   aor act ptcp nom pl masc
[Lk 5:5; v-1d(1b); 3159]   "
κοπιάτω   pres act imperative 3 sg
[Ep 4:28; v-1d(1b); 3159]   "

κοπιάω   {3159, v-1d(1b)}
[-, ἐκοπίασα, κεκοπίακα, -, -] *to be wearied* or
spent with labor, faint from weariness, Matt 11:28;
John 4:6; in N.T. *to labor hard, to toil*, Luke 5:5;
John 4:38

κοπιῶ   pres act ind 1 sg
[Cl 1:29; v-1d(1b); 3159]   "
κοπιῶμεν   pres act ind 1 pl [2t; v-1d(1b); 3159]   "
κοπιῶντα   pres act ptcp acc sg masc
[2Ti 2:6; v-1d(1b); 3159]   "

κοπιῶντας   pres act ptcp acc pl masc
   [2t; v-1d(1b); 3159]   "
κοπιῶντες   pres act ptcp nom pl masc
   [1Ti 5:17; v-1d(1b); 3159]   "
κοπιῶντας   pres act ptcp voc pl masc
   [Mt 11:28; v-1d(1b); 3159]   "
κοπιῶντι   pres act ptcp dat sg masc
   [1C 16:16; v-1d(1b); 3159]   "
κοπιώσας   pres act ptcp acc pl fem
   [Rm 16:12; v-1d(1b); 3159]   "
κοπιῶσιν   pres act ind 3 pl
   [Mt 6:28; v-1d(1b); 3159]   "
κόποις   dat pl masc [3t; n-2a; 3160]   κόπος
κόπον   acc sg masc [5t; n-2a; 3160]   "

κόπος, ου, ὁ   {3160, n-2a}
   trouble, difficulty, uneasiness, Matt 26:10; Mark
   14:6; labor, wearisome labor, travail, toil, 1 Cor 3:8;
   15:58; meton. the fruit or consequence of labor,
   John 4:38; 2 Cor 10:15

κόπος   nom sg masc [2t; n-2a; 3160]   "
κόπου   gen sg masc [1Th 1:3; n-2a; 3160]   "
κόπους   acc pl masc [4t; n-2a; 3160]   "

κοπρία, ας, ἡ   {3161, n-1a}
   dung, manure, Luke 14:35*

κόπρια   acc pl neut [Lk 13:8; n-2c; 3162]   κόπριον
κοπρίαν   acc sg fem [Lk 14:35; n-1a; 3161]   κοπρία

κόπριον, ου, τό   {3162, n-2c}
   dung, manure, Luke 13:8*

κόπρος, ου, ἡ   {3163, n-2b}
   dung, manure, Luke 13:8 v.l.*

κόπτω   {3164, v-4}
   [(ἔκοπτον), κόψω, ἔκοψα, -, κέκομμαι, ἐκόπην] to
   smite, cut; to cut off or down, Matt 21:8; Mark
   11:8; mid. to beat one's self in mourning, lament,
   bewail, Matt 11:17; 24:30; Luke 8:52; 23:27; Rev
   1:7; 18:9*

κόπῳ   dat sg masc [2t; n-2a; 3160]   κόπος
κόπων   gen pl masc [Rv 14:13; n-2a; 3160]   "
κόρακας   acc pl masc
   [Lk 12:24; n-3b(1); 3165]   κόραξ

κόραξ, ός, ὁ   {3165, n-3b(1)}
   a raven, crow, Luke 12:24*

κοράσιον, ου, τό   {3166, n-2c}
   a girl, damsel, maiden, Matt 9:24, 25; 14:11; Mark
   5:41, 42; 6:22, 28*

κοράσιον   nom sg neut [4t; n-2c; 3166]   κοράσιον
κοράσιον   voc sg neut [Mk 5:41; n-2c; 3166]   "
κορασίῳ   dat sg neut [3t; n-2c; 3166]   "

κορβᾶν   {3167, n-3g(2)}
   corban, a gift, offering, oblation, anything
   consecrated to God, Mark 7:11*

κορβᾶν   indecl [Mk 7:11; n-3g(2); 3167]   κορβᾶν
κορβανᾶν   acc sg masc
   [Mt 27:6; n-1e; 3168]   κορβανᾶς

κορβανᾶς, ᾶ, ὁ   {3168, n-1e}
   temple treasury, the sacred treasury, Matt 27:6*

Κόρε, ὁ   {3169, n-3g(2)}
   Korah, Jude 11*

Κόρε   indecl [Jd 11; n-3g(2); 3169]   Κόρε

κορέννυμι   {3170, v-3c(1)}
   [-, -, -, κεκόρεσμαι, ἐκορέσθην] to satiate, satisfy,
   Acts 27:38; 1 Cor 4:8*

κορεσθέντες   aor pass ptcp nom pl masc
   [Ac 27:38; v-3c(1); 3170]   κορέννυμι
Κορίνθιοι   voc pl masc
   [2C 6:11; n-2a; 3171]   Κορίνθιος

Κορίνθιος, ου, ὁ   {3171, n-2a}
   Corinthian; an inhabitant of Κόρινθος, Corinth,
   Acts 18:8, 27 v.l.; 2 Cor 6:11, also in the titles to
   1 and 2 Cor, and the subscription to Rom*

Κορινθίων   gen pl masc [Ac 18:8; n-2a; 3171]   "
Κόρινθον   acc sg fem [2t; n-2b; 3172]   Κόρινθος

Κόρινθος, οῦ, ἡ or ὁ   {3172, n-2b/n-2a}
   Corinth, a celebrated city of Greece, Acts 18:1,
   27 v.l.; 19:1: 1 Cor 1:2; 2 Cor 1:1, 23; 2 Tim 4:20*

Κορίνθῳ   dat sg fem [4t; n-2b; 3172]   "
Κορνήλιε   voc sg masc [2t; n-2a; 3173]   Κορνήλιος

Κορνήλιος, ου, ὁ   {3173, n-2a}
   Cornelius, a Latin pr. name, Acts 10:1, 3, 17, 22,
   24f., 30f.*

Κορνήλιος   nom sg masc [5t; n-2a; 3173]   "
Κορνηλίου   gen sg masc [Ac 10:17; n-2a; 3173] "

κόρος, ου, ὁ   {3174, n-2a}
   a cor, the largest Jewish measure for things dry,
   equal to the homer, and about fifteen bushels
   English, according to Josephus, Luke 16:7*

κόρους   acc pl masc [Lk 16:7; n-2a; 3174]   κόρος
κοσμεῖν   pres act inf
   [1Ti 2:9; v-1d(2a); 3175]   κοσμέω
κοσμεῖτε   pres act ind 2 pl
   [Mt 23:29; v-1d(2a); 3175]   "

κοσμέω   {3175, v-1d(2a)}
   [(ἐκόσμουν), -, ἐκόσμησα, -, κεκόσμημαι, -]
   pluperfect, ἐκεκόσμητο (3 sg), to arrange, set in
   order; to adorn, decorate, embellish, Matt 12:44;
   23:29; to prepare, put in readiness, trim, Matt 25:7;
   met. to honor, dignify, Titus 2:10

κοσμικάς   acc pl fem
   [Ti 2:12; a-1a(2a); 3176]   κοσμικός
κοσμικόν   acc sg neut [Hb 9:1; a-1a(2a); 3176]   "

κοσμικός, ή, όν   {3176, a-1a(2a)}
   pr. belonging to the universe, in N.T.
   accommodated to the present state of things,
   adapted to this world, worldly, Titus 2:12; τὸ
   κοσμικόν, as a subst. the apparatus for the
   service of the tabernacle, Heb 9:1*

κόσμιον   acc sg masc
   [1Ti 3:2; a-3b(1); 3177]   κόσμιος

κόσμιος, (ία), ον   {3177, a-3b(1)}
   decorous, respectable, well-ordered, 1 Tim 2:9; 3:2*

κοσμίῳ   dat sg fem [1Ti 2:9; a-3b(1); 3177]   "
κοσμοκράτορας   acc pl masc
   [Ep 6:12; n-3f(2b); 3179]   κοσμοκράτωρ

κοσμοκράτωρ, ορος, ὁ {3179, n-3f(2b)}
pr. *monarch of the world;* in N.T. *a worldly prince,*
a power paramount in the world of the
unbelieving and ungodly, Eph 6:12*

κόσμον   acc sg masc [46t; n-2a; 3180]   κόσμος

κόσμος, ου, ὁ {3180, n-2a}
(1) pr. *order, regular disposition; ornament,*
decoration, embellishment, 1 Peter 3:3; (2) *the*
world, the material universe, Matt 13:35; *the*
world, the aggregate of sensitive existence, 1 Cor
4:9; *the lower world, the earth,* Mark 16:15; *the*
world, the aggregate of mankind, Matt 5:14; *the*
world, the public, John 7:4; in N.T. *the present*
order of things, the secular world, John 18:36; *the*
human race external to the Jewish nation, *the*
heathen *world,* Rom 11:12, 15; *the world* external
to the Christian body, 1 John 3:1, 13; *the world* or
material system of the Mosaic covenant, Gal 4:3;
Col 2:8, 20

κόσμος   nom sg masc [32t; n-2a; 3180]   "
κόσμου   gen sg masc [72t; n-2a; 3180]   "
κόσμῳ   dat sg masc [36t; n-2a; 3180]   "
κοσμῶσιν   pres act subj 3 pl
   [Ti 2:10; v-1d(2a); 3175]   κοσμέω

Κούαρτος, ου, ὁ {3181, n-2a}
Quartus, a Latin pr. name, Rom 16:23 and the
subscription to 1 Cor*

Κούαρτος   nom sg masc
   [Rm 16:23; n-2a; 3181]   Κούαρτος

κοῦμ {3182, n-3g(2)}
an Aramaic imperative, also spelled κοῦμι,
stand up, Mark 5:41*

κουμ   indecl [Mk 5:41; n-3g(2); 3182]   κοῦμ

κοῦμι, see κοῦμ {3183}

κουστωδία, ας, ἡ {3184, n-1a}
a watch, guard, Matt 27:65, 66; 28:11*

κουστωδίαν   acc sg fem
   [Mt 27:65; n-1a; 3184]   κουστωδία
κουστωδίας   gen sg fem [2t; n-1a; 3184]   "

κουφίζω {3185, v-2a(1)}
[(ἐκούφιζον), -, -, -, -, -] *to lighten, make light* or
less heavy, Acts 27:38*

κόφινοι   nom pl masc [Lk 9:17; n-2a; 3186]   κόφινος

κόφινος, ου, ὁ {3186, n-2a}
a large basket, Matt 14:20; 16:9; Mark 6:43; 8:19;
Luke 9:17; 13:8 v.l.; John 6:13*

κοφίνους   acc pl masc [4t; n-2a; 3186]   "
κοφίνων   gen pl masc [Mk 6:43; n-2a; 3186]   "
κόψαντες   aor act ptcp nom pl masc
   [Mk 11:8; v-4; 3164]   κόπτω
κόψονται   fut mid ind 3 pl [3t; v-4; 3164]   "
κραβάττοις   dat pl masc
   [Mk 6:55; n-2a; 3187]   κράβαττος
κράβαττον   acc sg masc [8t; n-2a; 3187]   "

κράβαττος, ου, ὁ {3187, n-2a}
also spelled κράββατος, *mattress, pallet, bed,*

Mark 2:4, 9, 11f.; 6:55; John 5:8-11; Acts 5:15;
9:33*

κραβάττου   gen sg masc [Ac 9:33; n-2a; 3187]   "
κραβάττων   gen pl masc [Ac 5:15; n-2a; 3187]   "

κράββατος, see κράβαττος {3188}

κράζει   pres act ind 3 sg
   [5t; v-2a(2); 3189]   κράζω
κράζειν   pres act inf [Mk 10:47; v-2a(2); 3189]   "
κράζομεν   pres act ind 1 pl
   [Rm 8:15; v-2a(2); 3189]   "
κρᾶζον   pres act ptcp acc sg neut
   [Ga 4:6; v-2a(2); 3189]   "
κράζοντας   pres act ptcp acc pl masc
   [Mt 21:15; v-2a(2); 3189]   "
κράζοντες   pres act ptcp nom pl masc
   [4t; v-2a(2); 3189]   "
κραζόντων   pres act ptcp gen pl masc
   [Ac 19:34; v-2a(2); 3189]   "
κράζουσιν   pres act ind 3 pl
   [Rv 7:10; v-2a(2); 3189]   "

κράζω {3189, v-2a(2)}
[(ἔκραζον), κράξω or κεκράξω, ἔκραξα or
ἐκέκραξα, κέκραγα, -, -] *to utter a cry,* Matt
14:26; *to exclaim, cry out,* Matt 9:27; John 1:15; *to*
cry for vengeance, James 5:4; *to cry* in
supplication, Rom 8:15; Gal 4:6

κράζων   pres act ptcp nom sg masc
   [2t; v-2a(2); 3189]   "

κραιπάλη, ης, ἡ {3190, n-1b}
also spelled κρεπάλη, *drunken dissipation,* Luke
21:34*

κραιπάλη   dat sg fem
   [Lk 21:34; n-1b; 3190]   κραιπάλη

κρανίον, ου, τό {3191, n-2c}
a skull, Matt 27:33; Mark 15:22; Luke 23:33; John
19:17*

κρανίον   acc sg neut
   [Lk 23:33; n-2c; 3191]   κρανίον
κρανίου   gen sg neut [3t; n-2c; 3191]   "
κράξαντες   aor act ptcp nom pl masc
   [Ac 7:57; v-2a(2); 3189]   κράζω
κράξας   aor act ptcp nom sg masc
   [4t; v-2a(2); 3189]   "
κράξουσιν   fut act ind 3 pl
   [Lk 19:40; v-2a(2); 3189]   "
κράσπεδα   acc pl neut
   [Mt 23:5; n-2c; 3192]   κράσπεδον

κράσπεδον, ου, τό {3192, n-2c}
a margin, border, edge, in N.T. *a fringe, tuft, tassel,*
Matt 9:20; 14:36; 23:5; Mark 6:56; Luke 8:44*

κρασπέδου   gen sg neut [4t; n-2c; 3192]   "
κραταιάν   acc sg fem
   [1P 5:6; a-1a(1); 3193]   κραταιός

κραταιός, ά, όν {3193, a-1a(1)}
strong, mighty, powerful, 1 Peter 5:6*

κραταιοῦσθε   pres pass imperative 2 pl
   [1C 16:13; v-1d(3); 3194]   κραταιόω

κραταιόω   {3194, v-1d(3)}
[(ἐκράταιουν), -, -, -, -, ἐκραταιώθην] *to
strengthen, render strong, corroborate, confirm;*
pass. *to grow strong, acquire strength,* Luke 1:80;
2:40; Eph 3:16; *to be firm, resolute,* 1 Cor 16:13*

κραταιωθῆναι   aor pass inf
   [Ep 3:16; v-1d(3); 3194]   "

κράτει   dat sg neut
   [Ep 6:10; n-3d(2b); 3197]   κράτος

κράτει   pres act imperative 2 sg
   [Rv 3:11; v-1d(2a); 3195]   κρατέω

κρατεῖν   pres act inf   [Mk 7:4; v-1d(2a); 3195]   "

κρατεῖς   pres act ind 2 sg
   [Rv 2:13; v-1d(2a); 3195]   "

κρατεῖσθαι   pres pass inf
   [Ac 2:24; v-1d(2a); 3195]   "

κρατεῖτε   pres act imperative 2 pl
   [2Th 2:15; v-1d(2a); 3195]   "

κρατεῖτε   pres act ind 2 pl
   [Mk 7:8; v-1d(2a); 3195]   "

κρατέω   {3195, v-1d(2a)}
[(ἐκράτουν), κρατήσω, ἐκράτησα, κεκράτηκα,
κεκράτημαι, ἐκρατήθην] pr. *to be strong; to be
superior* to any one, *subdue, vanquish,* Acts 2:24;
to get into one's power, lay hold of, seize, apprehend,
Matt 14:3; 18:28; 21:46; *to gain, compass, attain,*
Acts 27:13; in N.T. *to lay hold of, grasp, clasp,*
Matt 9:25; Mark 1:31; 5:41; *to retain, keep under
reserve,* Mark 9:10; met, *to hold fast, observe,*
Mark 7:3, 8; 2 Thess 2:15; *to hold to, adhere to,*
Acts 3:11; Col 2:19; *to restrain, hinder, repress,*
Luke 24:16; Rev 7:1; *to retain, not to remit,* sins,
John 20:23

κρατῆσαι   aor act inf   [4t; v-1d(2a); 3195]   "

κρατήσαντες   aor act ptcp nom pl masc
   [3t; v-1d(2a); 3195]   "

κρατήσας   aor act ptcp nom sg masc
   [6t; v-1d(2a); 3195]   "

κρατήσατε   aor act imperative 2 pl
   [3t; v-1d(2a); 3195]   "

κρατήσει   fut act ind 3 sg
   [Mt 12:11; v-1d(2a); 3195]   "

κρατήσωσιν   aor act subj 3 pl
   [Mt 26:4; v-1d(2a); 3195]   "

κρατῆτε   pres act subj 2 pl
   [Jn 20:23; v-1d(2a); 3195]   "

κράτιστε   voc sg masc superlative
   [3t; a-1a(2a); 3196]   κράτιστος

κράτιστος, η, ον   {3196, a-1a(2a)}
strongest; in N.T. κράτιστε, a term of respect,
most excellent, noble, or *illustrious,* Luke 1:3; Acts
23:26; 24:3; 26:25*

κρατίστῳ   dat sg masc superlative
   [Ac 23:26; a-1a(2a); 3196]   "

κράτος, ους, τό   {3197, n-3d(2b)}
strength, power, might, force, Acts 19:20; Eph
1:19; meton. *a display of might,* Luke 1:51; *power,
sway, dominion,* Heb 2:14; 1 Peter 4:11; 5:11

κράτος   nom sg neut   [6t; n-3d(2b); 3197]   κράτος
κράτος   acc sg neut   [4t; n-3d(2b); 3197]   "

κρατοῦντας   pres act ptcp acc pl masc
   [3t; v-1d(2a); 3195]   κρατέω

κρατοῦντες   pres act ptcp nom pl masc
   [Mk 7:3; v-1d(2a); 3195]   "

κρατοῦντος   pres act ptcp gen sg masc
   [Ac 3:11; v-1d(2a); 3195]   "

κράτους   gen sg neut
   [Ep 1:19; n-3d(2b); 3197]   κράτος

κρατοῦσιν   pres act ind 3 pl
   [Mk 14:51; v-1d(2a); 3195]   κρατέω

κρατῶμεν   pres act subj 1 pl
   [Hb 4:14; v-1d(2a); 3195]   "

κρατῶν   pres act ptcp nom sg masc
   [2t; v-1d(2a); 3195]   "

κραυγάζοντα   pres act ptcp nom pl neut
   [Lk 4:41; v-2a(1); 3198]   κραυγάζω

κραυγαζόντων   pres act ptcp gen pl masc
   [Ac 22:23; v-2a(1); 3198]   "

κραυγάζω   {3198, v-2a(1)}
[ἐκραύγαζον), κραυγάσω, ἐκραύγασα, -, -, -] *to
cry out, exclaim, shout,* Matt 12:19; Acts 22:23

κραυγάσει   fut act ind 3 sg
   [Mt 12:19; v-2a(1); 3198]   "

κραυγή, ῆς, ἡ   {3199, n-1b}
a cry, outcry, clamor, shouting, Matt 25:6; Luke
1:42; Acts 23:9; Eph 4:31; Rev 14:18 v.l.; *a cry* of
sorrow, *wailing, lamentation,* Rev 21:4; *a cry* for
help, *earnest supplication,* Heb 5:7*

κραυγή   nom sg fem   [4t; n-1b; 3199]   κραυγή
κραυγῇ   dat sg fem   [Lk 1:42; n-1b; 3199]   "
κραυγῆς   gen sg fem   [Hb 5:7; n-1b; 3199]   "
κρέα   acc pl neut   [2t; n-3c(6d); 3200]   κρέας

κρέας, έως, τό   {3200, n-3c(6d)}
flesh, meat, a later form of κρέατος, Rom 14:21; 1
Cor 8:13*

κρεῖσσον   nom sg neut comparative
   [Pp 1:23; a-4b(1); 3202]   κρείττων

κρεῖσσον   acc sg neut comparative
   [1C 11:17; a-4b(1); 3202]   "

κρεῖσσον   adverb-comparative
   [1C 7:38; a-4b(1); 3202]   "

κρείσσονα   acc pl neut comparative
   [Hb 6:9; a-4b(1); 3202]   "

κρείσσων, see κρείττων   {3201}

κρεῖττον   nom sg neut comparative
   [3t; a-4b(1); 3202]   "

κρεῖττον   acc sg neut comparative
   [2t; a-4b(1); 3202]   "

κρείττονα   acc sg fem comparative
   [Hb 10:34; a-4b(1); 3202]   "

κρείττονος   gen sg masc comparative
   [Hb 7:7; a-4b(1); 3202]   "

κρείττονος   gen sg fem comparative
   [5t; a-4b(1); 3202]   "

κρείττοσιν   dat pl fem comparative
   [2t; a-4b(1); 3202]   "

κρείττων, ον, gen., ονος   {3202, a-4b(1)}
also spelled κρείσσων, *better, more useful* or
profitable, more conducive to good, 1 Cor 7:8, 38;

superior, more excellent, of a higher nature, more valuable, Heb 1:4; 6:9; 7:7, 19, 22

κρείττων   nom sg masc comparative
[Hb 1:4; a-4b(1); 3202]   "

κρεμάμενον   pres mid ptcp acc sg neut
[Ac 28:4; v-3c(1); 3203]   κρεμάννυμι

κρεμάμενος   pres mid ptcp nom sg masc
[Ga 3:13; v-3c(1); 3203]   "

κρεμάννυμι   {3203, v-3c(1)}
[-, ἐκρέμασα, -, -, ἐκρεμάσθην] also spelled
κρέμαμαι and κρεμάζω, *to hang, suspend*, Acts
5:30; 10:39; pass. *to be hung, suspended*, Matt
18:6; Luke 23:39; mid. κρέμαμαι, *to hang, be
suspended*, Acts 28:4; Gal 3:13; met. κρέμαμαι ἐν,
to hang upon, to be referable to as an ultimate
principle, Matt 22:40

κρεμάσαντες   aor act ptcp nom pl masc
[2t; v-3c(1); 3203]   "

κρεμασθέντων   aor pass ptcp gen pl masc
[Lk 23:39; v-3c(1); 3203]   "

κρεμασθῇ   aor pass subj 3 sg
[Mt 18:6; v-3c(1); 3203]   "

κρέμαται   pres pass ind 3 sg
[Mt 22:40; v-3c(1); 3203]   "

κρεπάλη, see κραιπάλη

κρημνός, οῦ, ὁ   {3204, n-2a}
a hanging steep, precipice, a steep bank, Matt 8:32;
Mark 5:13; Luke 8:33*

κρημνοῦ   gen sg masc [3t; n-2a; 3204]   κρημνός

Κρής, ητός, ὁ   {3205, n-3c(1)}
a Cretan, an inhabitant of Κρήτη, Acts 2:11; Titus
1:12, subscription to Titus*

Κρήσκης, κεντος, τό   {3206, n-3c(5a)}
Crescens, a Latin pr. name, 2 Tim 4:10*

Κρήσκης   nom sg masc
[2Ti 4:10; n-3c(5a); 3206]   Κρήσκης

Κρῆτες   nom pl masc [2t; n-3c(1); 3205]   Κρής

Κρήτη, ης, ἡ   {3207, n-1b}
Crete, a large island in the eastern part of the
Mediterranean, Acts 27:7, 12f., 21, Titus 1:5*

Κρήτη   dat sg fem [Ti 1:5; n-1b; 3207]   Κρήτη

Κρήτην   acc sg fem [2t; n-1b; 3207]   "

Κρήτης   gen sg fem [2t; n-1b; 3207]   "

κριθή, ῆς, ἡ   {3208, n-1b}
barley, Rev 6:6*

κριθῆναι   aor pass inf [3t; v-1c(2); 3212] κρίνω

κριθήσεσθε   fut pass ind 2 pl
[Mt 7:2; v-1c(2); 3212]   "

κριθήσονται   fut pass ind 3 pl
[Rm 2:12; v-1c(2); 3212]   "

κριθῆτε   aor pass subj 2 pl [3t; v-1c(2); 3212]   "

κρίθινος, η, ον   {3209, a-1a(2a)}
made of barley, John 6:9, 13*

κριθίνους   acc pl masc
[Jn 6:9; a-1a(2a); 3209]   κρίθινος

κριθίνων   gen pl masc [Jn 6:13; a-1a(2a); 3209]   "

κριθῶν   gen pl fem [Rv 6:6; n-1b; 3208]   κριθή

κριθῶσι   aor pass subj 3 pl
[1P 4:6; v-1c(2); 3212]   κρίνω

κριθῶσιν   aor pass subj 3 pl
[2Th 2:12; v-1c(2); 3212]   "

κρίμα, ατος, τό   {3210, n-3c(4)}
judgment; a sentence, award, Matt 7:2; *a judicial
sentence*, Luke 23:40; 24:20; Rom 2:2; 5:16; *an
adverse sentence*, Matt 23:14; Rom 13:2; 1 Tim
5:12; James 3:1; *judgment, administration of
justice*, John 9:39; Acts 24:25; *execution of justice*,
1 Peter 4:17; *a lawsuit*; 1 Cor 6:7; in N.T. *judicial
visitation*, 1 Cor 11:29; 2 Peter 2:3; *an
administrative decree*, Rom 11:33

κρίμα   nom sg neut [5t; n-3c(4); 3210]   κρίμα

κρίμα   acc sg neut [16t; n-3c(4); 3210]   "

κρίματα   nom pl neut [Rm 11:33; n-3c(4); 3210]   "

κρίματα   acc pl neut [1C 6:7; n-3c(4); 3210]   "

κρίματι   dat sg neut [2t; n-3c(4); 3210]   "

κρίματος   gen sg neut [2t; n-3c(4); 3210]   "

κρίνα   acc pl neut [2t; n-2c; 3211]   κρίνον

κρῖναι   aor act inf [1P 4:5; v-1c(2); 3212] κρίνω

κρίναντας   aor act ptcp acc pl masc
[2C 5:14; v-1c(2); 3212]   "

κρίναντες   aor act ptcp nom pl masc
[2t; v-1c(2); 3212]   "

κρίναντος   aor act ptcp gen sg masc
[Ac 3:13; v-1c(2); 3212]   "

κρίνας   aor act ptcp nom sg masc
[Rv 18:8; v-1c(2); 3212]   "

κρίνατε   aor act imperative 2 pl
[5t; v-1c(2); 3212]   "

κρινεῖ   fut act ind 3 sg [6t; v-1c(2); 3212]   "

κρίνει   pres act ind 3 sg [7t; v-1c(2); 3212]   "

κρίνειν   pres act inf [4t; v-1c(2); 3212]   "

κρίνεις   pres act ind 2 sg [4t; v-1c(2); 3212]   "

κρίνεσθαι   pres mid inf [1C 6:1; v-1c(2); 3212]   "

κρίνεσθαι   pres pass inf [4t; v-1c(2); 3212]   "

κρίνεται   pres mid ind 3 sg
[1C 6:6; v-1c(2); 3212]   "

κρίνεται   pres pass ind 3 sg [4t; v-1c(2); 3212]   "

κρίνετε   pres act imperative 2 pl
[5t; v-1c(2); 3212]   "

κρίνετε   pres act ind 2 pl [5t; v-1c(2); 3212]   "

κρινέτω   pres act imperative 3 sg
[2t; v-1c(2); 3212]   "

κρίνῃ   aor act subj 3 sg
[Jn 3:17; v-1c(2); 3212]   "

κρίνομαι   pres pass ind 1 sg [3t; v-1c(2); 3212]   "

κρινόμενοι   pres pass ptcp nom pl masc
[1C 11:32; v-1c(2); 3212]   "

κρινόμενος   pres pass ptcp nom sg masc
[Ac 26:6; v-1c(2); 3212]   "

κρίνον, ου, τό   {3211, n-2c}
a lily, Matt 6:28; Luke 12:27*

κρίνοντα   pres act ptcp acc sg masc
[2t; v-1c(2); 3212]   "

κρίνοντες   pres act ptcp nom pl masc
[2t; v-1c(2); 3212]   "

κρίνοντι   pres act ptcp dat sg masc
[1P 2:23; v-1c(2); 3212]   "

κρινοῦμεν   fut act ind 1 pl
  [1C 6:3; v-1c(2); 3212]   "

κρινοῦσιν   fut act ind 3 pl
  [1C 6:2; v-1c(2); 3212]   "

κρίνω   {3212, v-1c(2)}
[(ἔκρινον), κρινῶ, ἔκρινα, κέκρικα, κέκριμαι,
ἐκρίθην] pluperfect, κεκρίκει (3 sg), pr. *to
separate; to make a distinction between; to exercise
judgment upon; to estimate*, Rom 14:5; *to judge, to
assume censorial power over, to call to account*,
Matt 7:1; Luke 6:37; Rom 2:1, 3; 14:3, 4, 10, 13;
Col 2:16; James 4:11, 12; *to bring under question*,
Rom 14:22; *to judge* judicially, *to try* as a judge,
John 18:31; *to bring to trial*, Acts 13:27; *to
sentence*, Luke 19:22; John 7:51; *to resolve on,
decree*, Acts 16:4; Rev 16:5; absol. *to decide,
determine, resolve*, Acts 3:13; 15:19; 27:1; *to deem*,
Acts 13:46; *to form a judgment, pass judgment*,
John 8:15; pass. *to be brought to trial*, Acts 25:10,
20; Rom 3:4; *to be brought to account, to incur
arraignment, be arraigned*, 1 Cor 10:29; mid. *to go
to law, litigate*, Matt 5:40; in N.T. *to judge, to visit
judicially*, Acts 7:7; 1 Cor 11:31, 32; 1 Peter 4:6; *to
judge, to right, to vindicate*, Heb 10:30; *to
administer government over, to govern*, Matt
19:28; Luke 22:30

κρινῶ   fut act ind 1 sg [2t; v-1c(2); 3212]   "
κρίνω   pres act ind 1 sg [5t; v-1c(2); 3212]   "
κρίνω   pres act subj 1 sg [Jn 8:16; v-1c(2); 3212]   "
κρίνωμεν   pres act subj 1 pl
  [Rm 14:13; v-1c(2); 3212]   "
κρίνων   pres act ptcp nom sg masc
  [6t; v-1c(2); 3212]   "
κρίνων   pres act ptcp voc sg masc
  [3t; v-1c(2); 3212]   "
κρίσει   dat sg fem [7t; n-3e(5b); 3213]   κρίσις
κρίσεις   nom pl fem [2t; n-3e(5b); 3213]   "
κρίσεως   gen sg fem [15t; n-3e(5b); 3213]   "
κρίσιν   acc sg fem [15t; n-3e(5b); 3213]   "

κρίσις, εως, ἡ   {3213, n-3e(5b)}
pr. *distinction; discrimination; judgment, decision,
award*, John 5:30; 7:24; 8:16; *a* judicial *sentence*,
John 3:19; James 2:13; *an* adverse *sentence*, Matt
23:33; Mark 3:29; *judgment, judicial process, trial*,
Matt 10:15; John 5:24; 12:31; 16:8; *judgment,
administration of justice*, John 5:22, 27; in N.T. *a
court of justice, tribunal*, Matt 5:21, 22; *an
impeachment*, 2 Peter 2:11; Jude 9; from the
Hebrew, *justice, equity*, Matt 12:18, 20; 23:23;
Luke 11:42

κρίσις   nom sg fem [8t; n-3e(5b); 3213]   "
Κρίσπον   acc sg masc [1C 1:14; n-2a; 3214]   Κρίσπος

Κρίσπος, ου, ὁ   {3214, n-2a}
Crispus, a Latin pr. name, Acts 18:8; 1 Cor 1:14;
2 Tim 4:10 v.l.*

Κρίσπος   nom sg masc [Ac 18:8; n-2a; 3214]   "
κριταί   nom pl masc [3t; n-1f; 3216]   κριτής
κριτάς   acc pl masc [Ac 13:20; n-1f; 3216]   "
κριτῇ   dat sg masc [2t; n-1f; 3216]   "
κριτήν   acc sg masc [3t; n-1f; 3216]   "
κριτήρια   acc pl neut [2t; n-2c; 3215]   κριτήριον

κριτήριον, ου, τό   {3215, n-2c}
pr. *a standard* or *means by which to judge,
criterion; a court of justice, tribunal*, James 2:6; *a
cause, controversy*, 1 Cor 6:2, 4*

κριτηρίων   gen pl neut [1C 6:2; n-2c; 3215]   "

κριτής, ου, ὁ   {3216, n-1f}
a judge, Matt 5:25; from the Hebrew, *a
magistrate, ruler*, Acts 13:20; 24:10

κριτής   nom sg masc [10t; n-1f; 3216]   κριτής

κριτικός, ή, όν   {3217, a-1a(2a)}
able or *quick to discern* or *judge*, Heb 4:12*

κριτικός   nom sg masc
  [Hb 4:12; a-1a(2a); 3217]   κριτικός
κρούειν   pres act inf
  [Lk 13:25; v-1a(8); 3218]   κρούω
κρούετε   pres act imperative 2 pl
  [2t; v-1a(8); 3218]   "
κρούοντι   pres act ptcp dat sg masc
  [2t; v-1a(8); 3218]   "
κρούσαντος   aor act ptcp gen sg masc
  [2t; v-1a(8); 3218]   "

κρούω   {3218, v-1a(8)}
[-, ἔκρουσα, -, -, -] *to knock* at a door, Matt 7:7, 8;
Luke 11:9, 10; 12:36; 13:25; Acts 12:13, 16; Rev
3:20*

κρούω   pres act ind 1 sg [Rv 3:20; v-1a(8); 3218]   "
κρούων   pres act ptcp nom sg masc
  [Ac 12:16; v-1a(8); 3218]   "
κρυβῆναι   aor pass inf [2t; v-4; 3221]   κρύπτω
κρυπτά   nom pl neut
  [1C 14:25; a-1a(2a); 3220]   κρυπτός
κρυπτά   acc pl neut [3t; a-1a(2a); 3220]   "

κρύπτη, ης, ἡ   {3219, n-1b}
a vault or *closet, a cell* for storage, *dark secret
place*, Luke 11:33*

κρύπτην   acc sg fem [Lk 11:33; n-1b; 3219]   κρύπτη
κρυπτόν   nom sg neut [4t; a-1a(2a); 3220]   κρυπτός

κρυπτός, ή, όν   {3220, a-1a(2a)}
hidden, concealed, secret, clandestine, Matt 6:4, 6,
18 v.l.; τὰ κρυπτά, *secrets*, Rom 2:16; 1 Cor 14:25

κρυπτός   nom sg masc [1P 3:4; a-1a(2a); 3220]   "

κρύπτω   {3221, v-4}
[κρύψω, ἔκρυψα, -, κέκρυμμαι, ἐκρύβην] *to hide,
conceal*, Matt 5:14; in N.T. *to lay up in store*, Col
3:3; Rev 2:17; κεκρυμμέμος, *concealed, secret*,
John 19:38

κρυπτῷ   dat sg neut [8t; a-1a(2a); 3220]   "
κρυσταλλίζοντι   pres act ptcp dat sg masc
  [Rv 21:11; cv-; 3222]   κρυσταλλίζω

κρυσταλλίζω   {3222, cv-2a(1)}
[-, -, -, -, -] *to be clear, brilliant like crystal*, Rev
21:11*

κρύσταλλον   acc sg masc
  [Rv 22:1; n-2a; 3223]   κρύσταλλος

κρύσταλλος, ου, ὁ   {3223, n-2a}
pr. *clear ice; crystal*, Rev 4:6; 22:1*

κρυστάλλῳ   dat sg masc [Rv 4:6; n-2a; 3223]   "

κρυφαῖος, α, ον   {3224, a-1a(1)}
   secret, hidden, Matt 6:18*

κρυφαίῳ   dat sg neut [2t; a-1a(1); 3224]   κρυφαῖος

κρυφῇ   {3225, adverb}
   in secret, secretly, not openly, Eph 5:12*

κρυφῇ   adverb [Ep 5:12; adverb; 3225]   κρυφῇ

κρύφιος, ία, ιον   {3226, a-1a(1)}
   hidden, secret, Matt 6:18 v.l.*

κρύψατε   aor act imperative 2 pl
   [Rv 6:16; v-4; 3221]   κρύπτω

κτάομαι   {3227, v-1d(1a)}
   [κτήσομαι, ἐκτησάμην, -, κέκτημαι, -] *to get,
procure, provide*, Matt 10:9; *to make gain, gain*,
Luke 18:12; *to purchase*, Acts 8:20; 22:28; *to be the
cause* or *occasion of purchasing*, Acts 1:18; *to
preserve, save*, Luke 21:19; *to get under control, to
be winning the mastery over*, 1 Thess 4:4; perf.
κέκτημαι, *to possess**

κτᾶσθαι   pres mid inf
   [2t; v-1d(1a); 3227]   κτάομαι

κτῆμα, ατος, τό   {3228, n-3c(4)}
   a possession, property, field, Matt 19:22; Mark
10:22; Acts 2:45; 5:1*

κτῆμα   acc sg neut [Ac 5:1; n-3c(4); 3228]   κτῆμα
κτήματα   acc pl neut [3t; n-3c(4); 3228]   "
κτήνη   acc pl neut [2t; n-3d(2b); 3229]   κτῆνος

κτῆνος, ους, τό   {3229, n-3d(2b)}
   pr. *property*, generally used in the plural, τὰ
κτήνη; *property* in animals; *a beast of burden,
domesticated animal*, Luke 10:34; Acts 23:24;
beasts, cattle, 1 Cor 15:39; Rev 18:13*

κτῆνος   acc sg neut [Lk 10:34; n-3d(2b); 3229]   "
κτηνῶν   gen pl neut [1C 15:39; n-3d(2b); 3229]   "
κτήσασθε   aor mid imperative 2 pl
   [Lk 21:19; v-1d(1a); 3227]   κτάομαι
κτήσησθε   aor mid subj 2 pl
   [Mt 10:9; v-1d(1a); 3227]   "
κτήτορες   nom pl masc
   [Ac 4:34; n-3f(2b); 3230]   κτήτωρ

κτήτωρ, ορος, ὁ   {3230, n-3f(2b)}
   a possessor, owner, Acts 4:34*

κτίζω   {3231, v-2a(1)}
   [-, ἔκτισα, -, ἔκτισμαι, ἐκτίσθην] pr. *to reduce
from a state of disorder and wildness*; in N.T. *to call
into being, to create*, Mark 13:19; *to call into
individual existence, to frame*, Eph 2:15; *to create
spiritually, to invest with a spiritual frame*, Eph
2:10; 4:24

κτίσαντα   aor act ptcp acc sg masc
   [Rm 1:25; v-2a(1); 3231]   κτίζω
κτίσαντι   aor act ptcp dat sg masc
   [Ep 3:9; v-2a(1); 3231]   "
κτίσαντος   aor act ptcp gen sg masc
   [Cl 3:10; v-2a(1); 3231]   "
κτίσας   aor act ptcp nom sg masc
   [Mt 19:4; v-2a(1); 3231]   "

κτίσει   dat sg fem [4t; n-3e(5b); 3232]   κτίσις
κτίσεως   gen sg fem [8t; n-3e(5b); 3232]   "
κτίσῃ   aor act subj 3 sg
   [Ep 2:15; v-2a(1); 3231]   κτίζω
κτισθέντα   aor pass ptcp acc sg masc
   [Ep 4:24; v-2a(1); 3231]   "
κτισθέντες   aor pass ptcp nom pl masc
   [Ep 2:10; v-2a(1); 3231]   "

κτίσις, εως, ἡ   {3232, n-3e(5b)}
   (1) pr. *a framing, founding*; (2) in N.T. *creation, the
act of creating*, Rom 1:20; *creation, the material
universe*, Mark 10:6; 13:19; Heb 9:11; 2 Peter 3:4;
a created thing, a creature, Rom 1:25; 8:39; Col
1:15; Heb 4:13; *the human creation*, Mark 16:15;
Rom 8:19, 20, 21, 22; Col 1:23; *a spiritual
creation*, 2 Cor 5:17; Gal 6:15; (3) *an institution,
ordinance*, 1 Peter 2:13

κτίσις   nom sg fem [7t; n-3e(5b); 3232]   κτίσις

κτίσμα, ατος, τό   {3233, n-3c(4)}
   pr. *a thing founded*; in N.T. *a created being,
creature*, 1 Tim 4:4; James 1:18; Rev 5:13; 8:9*

κτίσμα   nom sg neut
   [1Ti 4:4; n-3c(4); 3233]   κτίσμα
κτίσμα   acc sg neut [Rv 5:13; n-3c(4); 3233]   "
κτισμάτων   gen pl neut [2t; n-3c(4); 3233]   "
κτίστῃ   dat sg masc [1P 4:19; n-1f; 3234]   κτίστης

κτίστης, ου, ὁ   {3234, n-1f}
   a founder; in N.T. *a creator*, 1 Peter 4:19*

κτῶμαι   pres mid ind 1 sg
   [Lk 18:12; v-1d(1a); 3227]   κτάομαι

κυβεία, ας, ἡ   {3235, n-1a}
   also spelled κυβία, pr. *dice playing*; met.
craftiness, trickery, Eph 4:14*

κυβείᾳ   dat sg fem [Ep 4:14; n-1a; 3235]   κυβεία
κυβερνήσεις   acc pl fem
   [1C 12:28; n-3e(5b); 3236]   κυβέρνησις

κυβέρνησις, εως, ἡ   {3236, n-3e(5b)}
   government, office of a governor or *director*;
meton. *a director*, 1 Cor 12:28*

κυβερνήτῃ   dat sg masc
   [Ac 27:11; n-1f; 3237]   κυβερνήτης

κυβερνήτης, ου, ὁ   {3237, n-1f}
   a pilot, helmsman, Acts 27:11; Rev 18:17*

κυβερνήτης   nom sg masc [Rv 18:17; n-1f; 3237]   "

κυβία, see κυβεία

κυκλεύω   {3238, v-1a(6)}
   [-, ἐκύκλευσα, -, -, -] *to encircle, surround,
encompass*, Rev 20:9; John 10:24 v.l.*

κυκλόθεν   {3239, adverb}
   all around, round about, Rev 4:3, 4, 8*

κυκλόθεν   adverb [3t; adverb; 3239]   κυκλόθεν
κυκλουμένην   pres pass ptcp acc sg fem
   [Lk 21:20; v-1d(3); 3240]   κυκλόω

κυκλόω   {3240, v-1d(3)}
   [κυκλώσω, ἐκύκλωσα, -, -, ἐκυκλώθην] *to
encircle, surround, encompass, come around*. John

10:24; Acts 14:20; spc. *to lay siege to*, Luke 21:20; *to march round*, Heb 11:30*

κύκλω {3241, adverb}
from **κύκλος**, functions in the N.T. only as an improper prep., *a circle;* in N.T. κύκλω functions adverbially, *round, round about, around*, Mark 3:34; 6:6, 36

κύκλω adverb [8t; adverb; 3241] κύκλω
κυκλωθέντα aor pass ptcp nom pl neut
[Hb 11:30; v-1d(3); 3240] κυκλόω
κυκλωσάντων aor act ptcp gen pl masc
[Ac 14:20; v-1d(3); 3240] "

κύλισμα, ματος, τό {3242, n-3c(4)}
v.l. for κυλισμός, pr. *a rolling thing;* in N.T. *a place of rolling* or *wallowing, wallowing-place*, 2 Peter 2:22 v.l.*

κυλισμόν acc sg masc
[2P 2:22; n-2a; 3243] κυλισμός

κυλισμός, ου, ὁ {3243, n-2a}
also spelled κύλισμα, a rolling, wallowing, 2 Peter 2:22*

κυλίω {3244, v-1a(1)}
[(ἐκύλιον), κυλίσω, ἐκύλισα, -, κεκύλισμαι, ἐκυλίσθην] *to roll*, Luke 23:53 v.l.; mid. *to roll one's self, to wallow*, Mark 9:20

κυλλόν acc sg masc [2t; a-1a(2a); 3245] κυλλός

κυλλός, ή, όν {3245, a-1a(2a)}
pr. *crooked, bent, maimed, lame, crippled*, Matt 18:8; Mark 9:43, used as a noun meaning *cripple*, Matt 15:30ff.*

κυλλούς acc pl masc [2t; a-1a(2a); 3245] "

κῦμα, ατος, τό {3246, n-3c(4)}
a wave, surge, billow, Matt 8:24; 14:24; Mark 4:37; Acts 27:41 v.l.; Jude 13*

κύματα nom pl neut [2t; n-3c(4); 3246] κῦμα
κυμάτων gen pl neut [3t; n-3c(4); 3246] "

κύμβαλον, ου, τό {3247, n-2c}
a cymbal, 1 Cor 13:1*

κύμβαλον nom sg neut
[1C 13:1; n-2c; 3247] κύμβαλον

κύμινον, ου, τό {3248, n-2c}
cumin, cuminum salivum of Linnaeus, a plant, a native of Egypt and Syria, whose seeds are of an aromatic, warm, bitterish taste, with a strong but not disagreeable smell, and used by the ancients as a condiment, Matt 23:23*

κύμινον acc sg neut
[Mt 23:23; n-2c; 3248] κύμινον
κυνάρια nom pl neut [2t; n-2c; 3249] κυνάριον
κυναρίοις dat pl neut [2t; n-2c; 3249] "

κυνάριον, ου, τό {3249, n-2c}
a little or *worthless dog*, Matt 15:26, 27; Mark 7:27, 28*

κύνας acc pl masc [Pp 3:2; n-3f(1c); 3264] κύων
κύνες nom pl masc [2t; n-3f(1c); 3264] "
Κύπριοι nom pl masc
[Ac 11:20; n-2a; 3250] Κύπριος

Κύπριος, ου, ὁ {3250, n-2a}
a Cypriot, an inhabitant of Cyprus, Acts 4:36; 11:20; 21:16*

Κύπριος nom sg masc [Ac 4:36; n-2a; 3250] "
Κυπρίω dat sg masc [Ac 21:16; n-2a; 3250] "
Κύπρον acc sg fem [4t; n-2b; 3251] Κύπρος

Κύπρος, ου, ἡ {3251, n-2b}
Cyprus, an island in the eastern part of the Mediterranean, Acts 11:19; 13:4; 15:39; 21:3; 27:4*

Κύπρου gen sg fem [Ac 11:19; n-2b; 3251] "

κύπτω {3252, v-4}
[-, ἔκυψα, -, -, -] *to bend forwards, stoop down*, Mark 1:7; John 8:6, 8 v.l.*

Κυρηναῖοι nom pl masc
[Ac 11:20; n-2a; 3254] Κυρηναῖος
Κυρηναῖον acc sg masc [3t; n-2a; 3254] "

Κυρηναῖος, ου, ὁ {3254, n-2a}
a Cyrenian, an inhabitant of Cyrene, Matt 27:32; Mark 15:21; Luke 23:26; Acts 6:9; 11:20; 13:1*

Κυρηναῖος nom sg masc [Ac 13:1; n-2a; 3254] "
Κυρηναίων gen pl masc [Ac 6:9; n-2a; 3254] "

Κυρήνη, ης, ἡ {3255, n-1b}
Cyrene, a city founded by a colony of Greeks, in Northern Africa, Acts 2:10*

Κυρήνην acc sg fem [Ac 2:10; n-1b; 3255] Κυρήνη

Κυρήνιος, ου, ὁ {3256, n-2a}
Cyrenius (perhaps *Quirinus*) pr. name, the governor of Syria, Luke 2:2*

Κυρηνίου gen sg masc
[Lk 2:2; n-2a; 3256] Κυρήνιος

κυρία, ας, ἡ {3257, n-1a}
a lady, 2 John 1:1, 5*

κυρία voc sg fem [2J 5; n-1a; 3257] κυρία
κυρίᾳ dat sg fem [2J 1; n-1a; 3257] "
κυριακῇ dat sg fem
[Rv 1:10; a-1a(2a); 3258] κυριακός
κυριακόν acc sg neut [1C 11:20; a-1a(2a); 3258] "

κυριακός, ή, όν {3258, a-1a(2a)}
pertaining to the Lord Jesus Christ, the Lord's, 1 Cor 11:20; Rev 1:10*

κύριε voc sg masc [119t; n-2a; 3261] κύριος
κυριεύει pres act ind 3 sg
[2t; v-1a(6); 3259] κυριεύω
κυριεύομεν pres act ind 1 pl
[2C 1:24; v-1a(6); 3259] "
κυριευόντων pres act ptcp gen pl masc
[1Ti 6:15; v-1a(6); 3259] "
κυριεύουσιν pres act ind 3 pl
[Lk 22:25; v-1a(6); 3259] "
κυριεύσει fut act ind 3 sg
[Rm 6:14; v-1a(6); 3259] "
κυριεύσῃ aor act subj 3 sg
[Rm 14:9; v-1a(6); 3259] "

κυριεύω {3259, v-1a(6)}
[κυριεύσω, ἐκυρίευσα, -, -, ἐκυριεύθην] *to be lord over, to be possessed of, mastery over*, Rom 6:9, 14;

7:1; 14:9; 2 Cor 1:24; 1 Tim 6:15; *to exercise control over,* Luke 22:25; Acts 19:16 v.l.*

κύριοι nom pl masc [3t; n-2a; 3261]   κύριος
κύριοι voc pl masc [3t; n-2a; 3261]   "
κυρίοις dat pl masc [5t; n-2a; 3261]   "
κύριον acc sg masc [68t; n-2a; 3261]   "

κύριος, ου, ὁ {3261, n-2a}
a lord, master, Matt 12:8; *an owner, possessor,* Matt 20:8; *a potentate, sovereign,* Acts 25:26; *a power, deity,* 1 Cor 8:5; *the Lord, Jehovah,* Matt 1:22; *the Lord* Jesus Christ, Matt 24:42; Mark 16:19; Luke 10:1; John 4:1; 1 Cor 4:5; freq.; κύριε, a term of respect of various force, *Sir, Lord,* Matt 13:27; Acts 9:6, et al. freq.

κύριος nom sg masc [177t; n-2a; 3261]   "

κυριότης, ητος, ἡ {3262, n-3c(1)}
lordship; constituted authority, Eph 1:21; 2 Peter 2:10; Jude 8; pl. *authorities, potentates,* Col 1:16. The Ephesian and Colossian passage could also be speaking about angelic powers.*

κυριότητα acc sg fem
[Jd 8; n-3c(1); 3262]   κυριότης
κυριότητες nom pl fem [Cl 1:16; n-3c(1); 3262]   "
κυριότητος gen sg fem [2t; n-3c(1); 3262]   "
κυρίου gen sg masc [240t; n-2a; 3261]   κύριος

κυρόω {3263, v-1d(3)}
[-, ἐκύρωσα, -, κεκύρωμαι, -] *to confirm, ratify,* Gal 3:15; *to reaffirm, assure,* 2 Cor 2:8*

κυρίῳ dat sg masc [99t; n-2a; 3261]   "
κυρίων gen pl masc [3t; n-2a; 3261]   "
κυρῶσαι aor act inf
[2C 2:8; v-1d(3); 3263]   κυρόω
κυσίν dat pl masc [Mt 7:6; n-3f(1c); 3264]   κύων
κύψας aor act ptcp nom sg masc
[2t; v-4; 3252]   κύπτω

κύων, κυνός, ὁ {3264, n-3f(1c)}
a dog, Matt 7:6; Luke 16:21; 2 Peter 2:22; met. *a dog, a religious corrupter,* Phil 3:2; *miscreant,* Rev 22:15*

κύων nom sg masc [2P 2:22; n-3f(1c); 3264]   κύων
Κῶ acc sg fem [Ac 21:1; n-2e; 3271]   Κώς
κῶλα nom pl neut [Hb 3:17; n-2c; 3265]   κῶλον

κῶλον, ου, τό {3265, n-2c}
lit., *a member* or *limb of the body,* fig., *dead body, corpse,* Heb 3:17*

κωλύει pres act ind 3 sg
[2t; v-1a(4); 3266]   κωλύω
κωλύειν pres act inf [Ac 24:23; v-1a(4); 3266]   "
κωλύεσθαι pres pass inf
[Hb 7:23; v-1a(4); 3266]   "
κωλύετε pres act imperative 2 pl
[6t; v-1a(4); 3266]   "
κωλυθέντες aor pass ptcp nom pl masc
[Ac 16:6; v-1a(4); 3266]   "
κωλύοντα pres act ptcp acc sg masc
[Lk 23:2; v-1a(4); 3266]   "
κωλυόντων pres act ptcp gen pl masc
[2t; v-1a(4); 3266]   "
κωλῦσαι aor act inf [2t; v-1a(4); 3266]   "

κωλύσῃς aor act subj 2 sg
[Lk 6:29; v-1a(4); 3266]   "

κωλύω {3266, v-1a(4)}
[(ἐκώλυον), -, ἐκώλυσα, -, -, ἐκωλύθην] *to hinder, restrain, prevent,* Matt 19:14; Acts 8:36; Rom 1:13

κώμας acc pl fem [10t; n-1b; 3267]   κώμη

κώμη, ης, ἡ {3267, n-1b}
a village, a country town, Matt 9:35; 10:11; Luke 8:1

κώμην acc sg fem [13t; n-1b; 3267]   "
κώμης gen sg fem [4t; n-1b; 3267]   "
κῶμοι nom pl masc [Ga 5:21; n-2a; 3269]   κῶμος
κώμοις dat pl masc [2t; n-2a; 3269]   "
κωμοπόλεις acc pl fem
[Mk 1:38; n-3e(5b); 3268]   κωμόπολις

κωμόπολις, εως, ἡ {3268, n-3e(5b)}
a large village, market town, Mark 1:38*

κῶμος, ου, ὁ {3269, n-2a}
pr. *a festive procession, a merry-making;* in N.T. *a revel, lewd, immoral feasting,* Rom 13:13; Gal 5:21; 1 Peter 4:3*

κώνωπα acc sg masc
[Mt 23:24; n-3a(1); 3270]   κώνωψ

κώνωψ, ος, ὁ {3270, n-3a(1)}
a gnat, mosquito, which is found in wine when becoming sour, Matt 23:24*

Κῶς, ῶ, ἡ {3271, n-2e}
Cos, an island in the Aegean sea, Acts 21:1*

Κωσάμ, ὁ {3272, n-3g(2)}
Cosam, pr. name, indecl., Luke 3:28*

Κωσάμ indecl [Lk 3:28; n-3g(2); 3272]   Κωσάμ
κωφοί nom pl masc [2t; a-1a(2a); 3273]   κωφός
κωφόν nom sg neut [Lk 11:14; a-1a(2a); 3273]   "
κωφόν voc sg neut [Mk 9:25; a-1a(2a); 3273]   "
κωφόν acc sg masc [3t; a-1a(2a); 3273]   "

κωφός, ή, όν {3273, a-1a(2a)}
pr. *blunt, dull,* as a weapon; *dull* of hearing, *deaf,* Matt 11:5; Mark 7:32, 37; 9:25; Luke 7:22; *dumb, mute,* Matt 9:32, 33; 12:22; 15:30, 31; Luke 1:22; meton. *making dumb, causing dumbness,* Luke 11:14*

κωφός nom sg masc [4t; a-1a(2a); 3273]   "
κωφούς acc pl masc [3t; a-1a(2a); 3273]   "

λ

λάβε aor act imperative 2 sg
[2t; v-3a(2b); 3284]   λαμβάνω
λαβεῖν aor act inf [22t; v-3a(2b); 3284]   "
λάβετε aor act imperative 2 pl
[7t; v-3a(2b); 3284]   "
λαβέτω aor act imperative 3 sg
[2t; v-3a(2b); 3284]   "
λάβῃ aor act subj 3 sg [8t; v-3a(2b); 3284]   "
λάβητε aor act subj 2 pl
[Rv 18:4; v-3a(2b); 3284]   "

λάβοι   aor act opt 3 sg
  [Ac 25:16; v-3a(2b); 3284]   "

λαβόντα   aor act ptcp acc sg masc
  [Lk 19:15; v-3a(2b); 3284]

λαβόντας   aor act ptcp acc pl masc
  [Rv 19:20; v-3a(2b); 3284]   "

λαβόντες   aor act ptcp nom pl masc
  [15t; v-3a(2b); 3284]

λαβοῦσα   aor act ptcp nom sg fem
  [6t; v-3a(2b); 3284]

λαβοῦσαι   aor act ptcp nom pl fem
  [2t; v-3a(2b); 3284]   "

λάβω   aor act subj 1 sg
  [Jn 10:17; v-3a(2b); 3284]   "

λάβωμεν   aor act subj 1 pl [2t; v-3a(2b); 3284]   "

λαβών   aor act ptcp nom sg masc
  [40t; v-3a(2b); 3284]   "

λάβωσιν   aor act subj 3 pl [3t; v-3a(2b); 3284]   "

λαγχάνω   {3275, v-3a(2b)}
  [-, ἔλαχον, -, -, -] *to have assigned to one, to obtain,*
  receive, Acts 1:17; 2 Peter 1:1; *to have fall to one by*
  lot, Luke 1:9; absol. *to cast lots,* John 19:24*

Λάζαρε   voc sg masc [Jn 11:43; n-2a; 3276]   Λάζαρος
Λάζαρον   acc sg masc [6t; n-2a; 3276]   "

Λάζαρος, ου, ὁ   {3276, n-2a}
  Lazarus, pr. name

Λάζαρος   nom sg masc [8t; n-2a; 3276]   "
λαθεῖν   aor act inf
  [Mk 7:24; v-3a(2b); 3291]   λανθάνω

λάθρα   {3277, adverb}
  secretly, privately, Matt 1:19; 2:7; Mark 5:33 v.l.;
  John 11:28; Acts 16:37*

λάθρα   adverb [4t; adverb; 3277]   λάθρα
λαίλαπος   gen sg fem
  [2P 2:17; n-3a(1); 3278]   λαῖλαψ

λαῖλαψ, απος, ἡ   {3278, n-3a(1)}
  a squall of wind, a hurricane, Mark 4:37; Luke
  8:23; 2 Peter 2:17*

λαῖλαψ   nom sg fem [2t; n-3a(1); 3278]   "

λακάω   {3279, v-1d(1a)}
  [-, ἐλάκησα, -, -, -] *burst open,* Acts 1:18*

λακτίζειν   pres act inf
  [Ac 26:14; v-2a(1); 3280]   λακτίζω

λακτίζω   {3280, v-2a(1)}
  [-, ἐλάκτισα, -, -, -] *to kick,* Acts 26:14; 9:5 v.l.*

λάλει   pres act imperative 2 sg
  [3t; v-1d(2a); 3281]   λαλέω
λαλεῖ   pres act ind 3 sg [18t; v-1d(2a); 3281]   "
λαλεῖν   pres act inf [21t; v-1d(2a); 3281]   "
λαλεῖς   pres act ind 2 sg [4t; v-1d(2a); 3281] "
λαλεῖσθαι   pres pass inf
  [Hb 2:3; v-1d(2a); 3281]   "
λαλεῖτε   pres act imperative 2 pl
  [4t; v-1d(2a); 3281]   "
λαλείτω   pres act imperative 3 sg
  [1C 14:28; v-1d(2a); 3281]   "
λαλείτωσαν   pres act imperative 3 pl
  [1C 14:29; v-1d(2a); 3281]   "

λαλέω   {3281, v-1d(2a)}
  [(ἐλάλουν), λαλήσω, ἐλάλησα, λελάληκα,
  λελάλημαι, ἐλαλήθην] *to make vocal utterance; to*
  babble, to talk; in N.T. absol. *to exercise the faculty*
  of speech, Matt 9:33; *to speak,* Matt 10:20; *to hold*
  converse with, to talk with, Matt 12:46; Mark 6:50;
  Rev 1:12; *to discourse, to make an address,* Luke
  11:37; Acts 11:20; 21:39; *to make announcement, to*
  make a declaration, Luke 1:55; *to make mention,*
  John 12:41; Acts 2:31; Heb 4:8; 2 Peter 3:16;
  trans. *to speak, address, preach,* Matt 9:18; John
  3:11; Titus 2:1; *to give utterance to, utter,* Mark
  2:7; John 3:34; *to declare, announce, reveal,* Luke
  24:25 et al.; *to disclose,* 2 Cor 12:4

λαλῇ   pres act subj 3 sg
  [Jn 8:44; v-1d(2a); 3281]   "
λαληθείς   aor pass ptcp nom sg masc
  [Hb 2:2; v-1d(2a); 3281]   "
λαληθείσης   aor pass ptcp gen sg fem
  [Hb 9:19; v-1d(2a); 3281]   "
λαληθέντος   aor pass ptcp gen sg neut
  [Lk 2:17; v-1d(2a); 3281]   "
λαληθέντων   aor pass ptcp gen pl neut
  [Lk 2:18; v-1d(2a); 3281]   "
λαληθῆναι   aor pass inf [2t; v-1d(2a); 3281]   "
λαληθήσεται   fut pass ind 3 sg
  [4t; v-1d(2a); 3281]   "
λαληθησομένων   fut pass ptcp gen pl neut
  [Hb 3:5; v-1d(2a); 3281]   "
λαλῆσαι   aor act inf [22t; v-1d(2a); 3281]   "
λαλήσαντες   aor act ptcp nom pl masc
  [2t; v-1d(2a); 3281]   "
λαλήσας   aor act ptcp nom sg masc
  [2t; v-1d(2a); 3281]   "
λαλήσει   fut act ind 3 sg [4t; v-1d(2a); 3281] "
λαλήσῃ   aor act subj 3 sg [2t; v-1d(2a); 3281] "
λαλήσητε   aor act subj 2 pl [3t; v-1d(2a); 3281] "
λαλήσομεν   fut act ind 1 pl
  [3J 14; v-1d(2a); 3281]   "
λαλήσουσιν   fut act ind 3 pl [2t; v-1d(2a); 3281] "
λαλήσω   aor act subj 1 sg [2t; v-1d(2a); 3281] "
λαλήσω   fut act ind 1 sg [3t; v-1d(2a); 3281]   "

λαλιά, ας, ἡ   {3282, n-1a}
  talk, speech; in N.T. *matter of discourse,* John 4:42;
  8:43; *language, dialect,* Matt 26:73*

λαλιά   nom sg fem [Mt 26:73; n-1a; 3282]   λαλιά
λαλιάν   acc sg fem [2t; n-1a; 3282]   "
λαλοῦμεν   pres act ind 1 pl
  [10t; v-1d(2a); 3281]   λαλέω
λαλουμένη   pres pass ptcp nom sg fem
  [Ac 17:19; v-1d(2a); 3281]   "
λαλουμένοις   pres pass ptcp dat pl neut
  [3t; v-1d(2a); 3281]   "
λαλούμενον   pres pass ptcp nom sg neut
  [1C 14:9; v-1d(2a); 3281]   "
λαλούμενον   pres pass ptcp acc sg masc
  [Mk 5:36; v-1d(2a); 3281]   "
λαλοῦν   pres act ptcp nom sg neut
  [2t; v-1d(2a); 3281]   "
λαλοῦντα   pres act ptcp acc sg masc
  [Hb 12:25; v-1d(2a); 3281]   "

λαλοῦντας   pres act ptcp acc pl masc
   [Mt 15:31; v-1d(2a); 3281]   "

λαλοῦντες   pres act ptcp nom pl masc
   [7t; v-1d(2a); 3281]   "

λαλοῦντι   pres act ptcp dat sg masc
   [1C 14:11; v-1d(2a); 3281]   "

λαλοῦντι   pres act ptcp dat sg neut
   [Hb 12:24; v-1d(2a); 3281]   "

λαλοῦντος   pres act ptcp gen sg masc
   [17t; v-1d(2a); 3281]   "

λαλούντων   pres act ptcp gen pl masc
   [5t; v-1d(2a); 3281]   "

λαλοῦσαι   pres act ptcp nom pl fem
   [1Ti 5:13; v-1d(2a); 3281]   "

λαλοῦσαν   pres act ptcp acc sg fem
   [Rv 10:8; v-1d(2a); 3281]   "

λαλούσης   pres act ptcp gen sg fem
   [Rv 4:1; v-1d(2a); 3281]   "

λαλοῦσιν   pres act ind 3 pl   [2t; v-1d(2a); 3281]   "

λαλῶ   pres act ind 1 sg   [18t; v-1d(2a); 3281]   "

λαλῶ   pres act subj 1 sg
   [1C 13:1; v-1d(2a); 3281]   "

λαλῶν   pres act ptcp nom sg masc
   [16t; v-1d(2a); 3281]   "

λαλῶσιν   pres act subj 3 pl
   [1C 14:23; v-1d(2a); 3281]   "

λαμά   {3283}
   (Aramaic) *Why?* also spelled λαμμα, Matt 27:46
   v.l.; Mark 15:34 v.l.*

λαμβάνει   pres act ind 3 sg
   [18t; v-3a(2b); 3284]   λαμβάνω

λαμβάνειν   pres act inf   [4t; v-3a(2b); 3284]   "

λαμβάνεις   pres act ind 2 sg
   [Lk 20:21; v-3a(2b); 3284]   "

λαμβάνετε   pres act imperative 2 pl
   [2J 10; v-3a(2b); 3284]   "

λαμβάνετε   pres act ind 2 pl   [4t; v-3a(2b); 3284]   "

λαμβάνῃ   pres act subj 3 sg
   [Ac 8:19; v-3a(2b); 3284]   "

λαμβάνομεν   pres act ind 1 pl
   [2t; v-3a(2b); 3284]   "

λαμβανόμενον   pres pass ptcp nom sg neut
   [1Ti 4:4; v-3a(2b); 3284]   "

λαμβανόμενος   pres pass ptcp nom sg masc
   [Hb 5:1; v-3a(2b); 3284]   "

λαμβάνοντες   pres act ptcp nom pl masc
   [5t; v-3a(2b); 3284]   "

λαμβάνουσιν   pres act ind 3 pl
   [4t; v-3a(2b); 3284]   "

λαμβάνω   {3284, v-3a(2b)}
   [(ἐλάμβανον), λήμψομαι, ἔλαβον, εἴληφα,
   εἴλημμαι, ἐλήμφθην] *to take, take up, take in the
   hand,* Matt 10:38; 13:31, 33; *to take on one's self,
   sustain,* Matt 8:17; *to take, seize, seize upon,* Matt
   5:40; 21:34; Luke 5:26; 1 Cor 10:13; *to catch,*
   Luke 5:5; 2 Cor 12:16; *to assume, put on,* Phil 2:7;
   to make a rightful or *successful assumption of,*
   John 3:27; *to conceive,* Acts 28:15; *to take by way
   of provision,* Matt 16:5; *to get, get together,* Matt
   16:9; *to receive* as payment, Matt 17:24; Heb 7:8;
   to take to wife, Mark 12:19; *to admit, give
   reception to,* John 6:21; 2 John 10; met. *to give*

mental *reception to,* John 3:11; *to be* simply
recipient of, to receive, Matt 7:8; John 7:23, 39;
19:30; Acts 10:43; in N.T. λαμβάνειν πεῖραν, *to
make encounter of* a matter of difficulty or trial,
Heb 11:29, 36; λαμβάνειν ἀρχήν, *to begin,* Heb
2:3; λαμβάνειν συμβούλιον, *to take counsel,
consult,* Matt 12:14; λαμβάνειν λήθην, *to forget,* 2
Peter 1:9; λαμβάνειν ὑπόμνησιν, *to recollect, call
to mind,* 2 Tim 1:5; λαμβάειν περιτομήν, *to receive
circumcision, be circumcised,* John 7:23;
λαμβάνειν καταλλαγήν, *to be reconciled,* Rom
5:11; λαμβάνειν κρίμα, *to receive condemnation* or
punishment, be punished, Mark 12:40; from the
Hebrew, πρόσωπον λαμβάνειν, *to accept the
person* of any one, *show partiality towards,* Luke
20:21

λαμβάνω   pres act ind 1 sg   [2t; v-3a(2b); 3284]   "

λαμβάνων   pres act ptcp nom sg masc
   [6t; v-3a(2b); 3284]   "

Λάμεχ, ὁ   {3285, n-3g(2)}
   Lamech, pr. name, indecl., Luke 3:36*

Λάμεχ   indecl [Lk 3:36; n-3g(2); 3285]   Λάμεχ

λαμπάδας   acc pl fem   [3t; n-3c(2); 3286]   λαμπάς

λαμπάδες   nom pl fem   [3t; n-3c(2); 3286]   "

λαμπάδων   gen pl fem   [2t; n-3c(2); 3286]   "

λαμπάς, άδος, ἡ   {3286, n-3c(2)}
   a light, Acts 20:8; *a lamp,* Rev 4:5; 8:10, *a portable
   lamp, lantern, torch,* Matt 25:1, 3, 4, 7, 8; John
   18:3*

λαμπάς   nom sg fem   [Rv 8:10; n-3c(2); 3286]   "

λάμπει   pres act ind 3 sg
   [2t; v-1b(1); 3290]   λάμπω

λαμπρά   nom pl neut
   [Rv 18:14; a-1a(1); 3287]   λαμπρός

λαμπρᾷ   dat sg fem   [2t; a-1a(1); 3287]   "

λαμπράν   acc sg fem   [2t; a-1a(1); 3287]   "

λαμπρόν   acc sg masc   [Rv 22:1; a-1a(1); 3287]   "

λαμπρόν   acc sg neut   [2t; a-1a(1); 3287]   "

λαμπρός, ά, όν   {3287, a-1a(1)}
   bright, resplendent, shining, Rev 22:16; *clear,
   transparent,* Rev 22:1; *white, glistening,* Acts
   10:30; Rev 15:6; Rev 19:8; *of a bright color, gaudy,*
   Luke 23:11; by impl. *splendid, magnificent,
   sumptuous,* James 2:2, 3; Rev 18:14*

λαμπρός   nom sg masc   [Rv 22:16; a-1a(1); 3287]   "

λαμπρότης, ητος, ἡ   {3288, n-3c(1)}
   brightness, splendor, Acts 26:13*

λαμπρότητα   acc sg fem
   [Ac 26:13; n-3c(1); 3288]   λαμπρότης

λαμπρῶς   {3289, adverb}
   splendidly; magnificently, sumptuously, Luke
   16:19*

λαμπρῶς   adverb [Lk 16:19; adverb; 3289]   λαμπρῶς

λάμπω   {3290, v-1b(1)}
   [λάμψω, ἔλαμψα, -, -, -] *to shine, give light,* Matt
   5:15, 16; 17:2; *to flash, shine,* Luke 17:24; Acts
   12:7; 2 Cor 4:6*

λαμψάτω aor act imperative 3 sg
[Mt 5:16; v-1b(1); 3290] λάμπω
λάμψει fut act ind 3 sg [2C 4:6; v-1b(1); 3290] "
λανθάνει pres act ind 3 sg
[2P 3:5; v-3a(2b); 3291] λανθάνω
λανθάνειν pres act inf
[Ac 26:26; v-3a(2b); 3291] "
λανθανέτω pres act imperative 3 sg
[2P 3:8; v-3a(2b); 3291] "

λανθάνω {3291, v-3a(2b)}
[-, ἔλαθον, -, -, -] *to be unnoticed; to escape the knowledge* or *observation of* a person, Acts 26:26; 2 Peter 3:5, 8; absol. *to be concealed* or *hidden, escape detection,* Mark 7:24; Luke 8:47; with a participle of another verb, *to be unconscious* of an action while the subject or object of if, Heb 13:2*

λαξευτός, ή, όν {3292, a-1a(2a)}
cut in stone, hewn out of stone or *rock,* Luke 23:53*

λαξευτῷ dat sg neut
[Lk 23:53; a-1a(2a); 3292] λαξευτός

Λαοδίκεια, ας, ή {3293, n-1a}
Laodicea, a city of Phrygia in Asia Minor, Rev 3:14*

Λαοδικείᾳ dat sg fem [4t; n-1a; 3293] Λαοδίκεια
Λαοδίκειαν acc sg fem [Rv 1:11; n-1a; 3293] "
Λαοδικείας gen sg fem [Cl 4:16; n-1a; 3293] "

Λαοδικεύς, έως, ό {3294, n-3e(3)}
a Laodicean, an inhabitant of Laodicea, Col 4:16*

Λαοδικέων gen pl masc
[Cl 4:16; n-3e(3); 3294] Λαοδικεύς
λαοί nom pl masc [4t; n-2a; 3295] λαός
λαοῖς dat pl masc [2t; n-2a; 3295] "
λαόν acc sg masc [44t; n-2a; 3295] "

λαός, ου, ό {3295, n-2a}
a body of people; a concourse of people, a multitude, Matt 27:25; Luke 8:47; *the common people,* Matt 26:5; *a people, nation,* Matt 2:4; Luke 2:32; Titus 2:14; ὁ λαός, *the people* of Israel, Luke 2:10

λαός nom sg masc [25t; n-2a; 3295] "
λαοῦ gen sg masc [38t; n-2a; 3295] "

λάρυγξ, ός, ό {3296, n-3b(2)}
the throat, gullet, Rom 3:13*

λάρυγξ nom sg masc
[Rm 3:13; n-3b(2); 3296] λάρυγξ

Λασαία, ας, ή {3297, n-1a}
Lasaea, also spelled Λασέα, a maritime town in Crete, Acts 27:8

Λασαία nom sg fem [Ac 27:8; n-1a; 3297] Λασαία

Λασέα, ας, ή, see Λασσία {3298, n-1a}

λάσκω {3299}
BAGD say it is the incorrect lexical form of ἐλάκησεν in Acts 1:18, see λακάω, pr. *to emit a sound, ring;* hence, *to break with a sharp noise; to burst*

λατομέω {3300, v-1d(2a)}
[-, ἐλατόμησα, -, λελατόμημαι, -] *to hew stones; to*

cut out of stone, hew from stone, Matt 27:60; Mark 15:46; Luke 23:53*

λατρεία, ας, ή {3301, n-1a}
service, servitude; religious service, worship, John 16:2; Rom 9:4; 12:1; Heb 9:1, 6*

λατρεία nom sg fem [Rm 9:4; n-1a; 3301] λατρεία
λατρείαν acc sg fem [2t; n-1a; 3301] "
λατρείας gen sg fem [Hb 9:1; n-1a; 3301] "
λατρείας acc pl fem [Hb 9:6; n-1a; 3301] "
λατρεύειν pres act inf
[3t; v-1a(6); 3302] λατρεύω
λατρεῦον pres act ptcp nom sg neut
[Ac 26:7; v-1a(6); 3302]
λατρεύοντα pres act ptcp acc sg masc
[Hb 9:9; v-1a(6); 3302]
λατρεύοντας pres act ptcp acc pl masc
[Hb 10:2; v-1a(6); 3302]
λατρεύοντες pres act ptcp nom pl masc
[2t; v-1a(6); 3302]
λατρεύουσα pres act ptcp nom sg fem
[Lk 2:37; v-1a(6); 3302]
λατρεύουσιν pres act ind 3 pl
[2t; v-1a(6); 3302]
λατρεύσεις fut act ind 2 sg [2t; v-1a(6); 3302]
λατρεύσουσιν fut act ind 3 pl
[2t; v-1a(6); 3302]

λατρεύω {3302, v-1a(6)}
[λατρεύσω, ἐλάτρευσα, -, -, -] *to be a servant, to serve,* Acts 27:23; *to render religious service and homage, worship,* Matt 4:10; Luke 1:74; spc. *to offer sacrifices, present offerings,* Heb 8:5; 9:9

λατρεύω pres act ind 1 sg [4t; v-1a(6); 3302] "
λατρεύωμεν pres act subj 1 pl
[Hb 12:28; v-1a(6); 3302] "
λάχανα acc pl neut [Rm 14:2; n-2c; 3303] λάχανον

λάχανον, ου, τό {3303, n-2c}
a garden herb, vegetable, Matt 13:32; Mark 4:32; Luke 11:42; Rom 14:2*

λάχανον acc sg neut [Lk 11:42; n-2c; 3303] "
λαχάνων gen pl neut [2t; n-2c; 3303] "
λαχοῦσιν aor act ptcp dat pl masc
[2P 1:1; v-3a(2b); 3275] λαγχάνω
λάχωμεν aor act subj 1 pl
[Jn 19:24; v-3a(2b); 3275] "
λαῷ dat sg masc [26t; n-2a; 3295] λαός
λαῶν gen pl masc [3t; n-2a; 3295] "

Λεββαῖος, ου, ό {3304, n-2a}
Lebbaeus, pr. name, Matt 10:3 v.l.; Mark 3:18 v.l.*

λέγε pres act imperative 2 sg
[Ac 22:27; v-1b(2); 3306] λέγω
λέγει pres act ind 3 sg [338t; v-1b(2); 3306] "
λέγειν pres act inf [40t; v-1b(2); 3306] "
λέγεις pres act ind 2 sg [23t; v-1b(2); 3306] "
λέγεσθαι pres pass inf [4t; v-1b(2); 3306] "
λέγεται pres pass ind 3 sg [8t; v-1b(2); 3306] "
λέγετε pres act ind 2 pl [22t; v-1b(2); 3306] "
λέγετε pres act imperative 2 pl
[7t; v-1b(2); 3306] "

λεγέτω pres act imperative 3 sg
[Jm 1:13; v-1b(2); 3306] "

λεγεών see λεγιών

λέγῃ pres act subj 3 sg [3t; v-1b(2); 3306] "
λέγητε pres act subj 2 pl
[1C 1:10; v-1b(2); 3306] "

λεγιών, ῶνος, ἡ {3305, n-3f(1a)}
also spelled λεγεών, *a* Roman *legion*; in N.T.
used indefinitely for a great number, Matt
26:53; Mark 5:9, 15, Luke 8:30*

λεγιών nom sg fem [2t; n-3f(1a); 3305] λεγιών
λεγιῶνα acc sg masc [Mk 5:15; n-3f(1a); 3305] "
λεγιῶνας acc pl fem [Mt 26:53; n-3f(1a); 3305] "
λέγομεν pres act ind 1 pl
[4t; v-1b(2); 3306] λέγω
λεγόμενα pres pass ptcp acc pl neut
[Lk 18:34; v-1b(2); 3306] "
λεγομένη pres pass ptcp nom sg fem
[2t; v-1b(2); 3306] "
λεγομένην pres pass ptcp acc sg fem
[4t; v-1b(2); 3306] "
λεγομένης pres pass ptcp gen sg fem
[2t; v-1b(2); 3306] "
λεγόμενοι pres pass ptcp nom pl masc
[2t; v-1b(2); 3306] "
λεγομένοις pres pass ptcp dat pl neut
[4t; v-1b(2); 3306] "
λεγόμενον pres pass ptcp acc sg masc
[9t; v-1b(2); 3306] "
λεγόμενον pres pass ptcp acc sg neut
[Mt 26:36; v-1b(2); 3306] "
λεγόμενος pres pass ptcp nom sg masc
[12t; v-1b(2); 3306] "
λεγομένου pres pass ptcp gen sg masc
[Mt 26:3; v-1b(2); 3306] "
λέγον pres act ptcp nom sg neut
[Ac 20:23; v-1b(2); 3306] "
λέγοντα pres act ptcp nom pl neut
[Lk 4:41; v-1b(2); 3306] "
λέγοντα pres act ptcp acc sg masc
[4t; v-1b(2); 3306] "
λέγοντας pres act ptcp acc pl masc
[8t; v-1b(2); 3306] "
λέγοντες pres act ptcp nom pl masc
[149t; v-1b(2); 3306] "
λέγοντες pres act ptcp voc pl masc
[2t; v-1b(2); 3306] "
λέγοντι pres act ptcp dat sg masc
[Mt 12:48; v-1b(2); 3306] "
λέγοντος pres act ptcp gen sg masc
[18t; v-1b(2); 3306] "
λέγοντος pres act ptcp gen sg neut
[5t; v-1b(2); 3306] "
λεγόντων pres act ptcp gen pl masc
[6t; v-1b(2); 3306] "
λέγουσα pres act ptcp nom sg fem
[21t; v-1b(2); 3306] "
λέγουσαι pres act ptcp nom pl fem
[4t; v-1b(2); 3306] "
λέγουσαν pres act ptcp acc sg fem
[7t; v-1b(2); 3306] "

λεγούσης pres act ptcp gen sg fem
[7t; v-1b(2); 3306] "
λέγουσιν pres act ind 3 pl [60t; v-1b(2); 3306] "

λέγω {3306, v-1b(2)}
[(ἔλεγον), ἐρῶ, εἶπον or εἶπα, εἴρηκα, εἴρημαι,
ἐρρέθην or ἐρρήθην] *to lay, to arrange, to gather; to
say,* Matt 1:20; *to speak, make an address* or *speech,*
Acts 26:1; *to say* mentally, in thought, Matt 3:9;
Luke 3:8; *to say* in written language, Mark
15:28; Luke 1:63; John 19:37; *to say,* as
distinguished from acting, Matt 23:3; *to
mention, speak of,* Mark 14:71; Luke 9:31; John
8:27; *to tell, declare, narrate,* Matt 21:27; Mark
10:32; *to express,* Heb 5:11; *to put forth, propound,*
Luke 5:36; 13:6; John 16:29; *to mean, to intend to
signify,* 1 Cor 1:12; 10:29; *to say, declare, affirm,
maintain,* Matt 3:9; 5:18; Mark 12:18; Acts 17:7;
26:22; 1 Cor 1:10; *to enjoin,* Acts 15:24; 21:21;
Rom 2:22; *to term, designate, cull,* Matt 19:17;
Mark 12:37; Luke 20:37; 23:2; 1 Cor 8:5; *to call* by
a name, Matt 2:23; pass. *to be further named, to be
surnamed,* Matt 1:16; *to be explained, interpreted,*
John 4:25; 20:16, 24; in N.T. σὺ λέγεις, *you say,* a
form of affirmative answer to a question Matt
27:11; Mark 15:2; John 18:37

λέγω pres act ind 1 sg [209t; v-1b(2); 3306] "
λέγω pres act subj 1 sg [3t; v-1b(2); 3306] "
λέγων pres act ptcp nom sg masc
[178t; v-1b(2); 3306] "
λέγων pres act ptcp voc sg masc
[Rm 2:22; v-1b(2); 3306] "
λέγωσιν pres act subj 3 pl [3t; v-1b(2); 3306] "
λείας acc pl fem [Lk 3:5; a-1a(1); 3308] λεῖος

λεῖμμα, ατος, τό {3307, n-3c(4)}
pr. *a remnant;* in N.T. *a small residue,* Rom 11:5*

λεῖμμα nom sg neut
[Rm 11:5; n-3c(4); 3307] λεῖμμα

λεῖος, α, ον {3308, a-1a(1)}
smooth, level, plain, Luke 3:5*

λείπει pres act ind 3 sg
[Lk 18:22; v-1b(1); 3309] λείπω
λείπεται pres pass ind 3 sg
[Jm 1:5; v-1b(1); 3309] "
λείπῃ pres act subj 3 sg
[Ti 3:13; v-1b(1); 3309] "
λειπόμενοι pres pass ptcp nom pl masc
[2t; v-1b(1); 3309] "
λείποντα pres act ptcp acc pl neut
[Ti 1:5; v-1b(1); 3309] "

λείπω {3309, v-1b(1)}
[λείψω, ἔλιπον, λέλοιπα, λέλειμμαι, ἐλείφθην]
trans. *to leave, forsake;* pass. *to be left, deserted;* by
impl. *to be destitute of, deficient in,* James 1:4, 5;
2:15; intrans. *to fail, be wanting, be deficient,* Luke
18:22; Titus 1:5; 3:13*

λειτουργέω {3310, v-1d(2a)}
[(ἐλειτούργουν), -, ἐλειτούργησα, -, -, -] pr. *to
perform some public service at one's own expense;*
in N.T. *to officiate* as a priest, Heb 10:11; *to
minister* in the Christian Church, Acts 13:2;

Titus 1:9 v.l.; *to minister to, assist, succor,* Rom 15:27*

λειτουργῆσαι   aor act inf
[Rm 15:27; v-1d(2a); 3310]   λειτουργέω

λειτουργία, ας, ἡ   {3311, n-1a}
pr. *a public service discharged by a citizen at his own expense;* in N.T. *a* sacred *ministration,* Luke 1:23; Phil 2:17; Heb 8:6; 9:21; *a kind office, aid, relief,* 2 Cor 9:12; Phil 2:30*

λειτουργίᾳ   dat sg fem
[Pp 2:17; n-1a; 3311]   λειτουργία
λειτουργίας   gen sg fem [5t; n-1a; 3311]   "
λειτουργικά   nom pl neut
[Hb 1:14; a-1a(2a); 3312]   λειτουργικός

λειτουργικός, ή, όν   {3312, a-1a(2a)}
ministering; engaged in holy service, Heb 1:14*

λειτουργοί   nom pl masc
[Rm 13:6; n-2a; 3313]   λειτουργός
λειτουργόν   acc sg masc [2t; n-2a; 3313]   "

λειτουργός, οῦ, ὁ   {3313, n-2a}
pr. *a person of property who performed a public duty* or *service to the state at his own expense;* in N.T. *a minister* or *servant,* Rom 13:6; 15:16; Heb 1:7; 8:2; *one who ministers relief,* Phil 2:25*

λειτουργός   nom sg masc [Hb 8:2; n-2a; 3313]
λειτουργούντων   pres act ptcp gen pl masc
[Ac 13:2; v-1d(2a); 3310]   λειτουργέω
λειτουργούς   acc pl masc
[Hb 1:7; n-2a; 3313]   λειτουργός
λειτουργῶν   pres act ptcp nom sg masc
[Hb 10:11; v-1d(2a); 3310]   λειτουργέω

λείχω   {3314, v-1b(2)}
[-, -, -, -, -] *to lick,* Luke 16:21 v.l.*

Λέκτρα, ας, ἡ   {3315, n-1a}
Lectra, Aquilla's wife in 2 Tim 4:19 v.l.*

λελάληκα   perf act ind 1 sg
[11t; v-1d(2a); 3281]   λαλέω
λελάληκεν   perf act ind 3 sg [2t; v-1d(2a); 3281]   "
λελαλημένοις   perf pass ptcp dat pl neut
[Lk 1:45; v-1d(2a); 3281]   "
λελάληται   perf pass ind 3 sg
[Ac 27:25; v-1d(2a); 3281]   "
λελατομημένον   perf pass ptcp nom sg neut
[Mk 15:46; v-1d(2a); 3300]   λατομέω
λελουμένος   perf pass ptcp nom sg masc
[Jn 13:10; v-1a(8); 3374]   λούω
λελουσμένοι   perf pass ptcp nom pl masc
[Hb 10:22; v-1a(8); 3374]   "
λελυμένα   perf pass ptcp nom pl neut
[Mt 18:18; v-1a(4); 3395]   λύω
λελυμένον   perf pass ptcp nom sg neut
[Mt 16:19; v-1a(4); 3395]   "
λελύπηκεν   perf act ind 3 sg
[2t; v-1d(2a); 3382]   λυπέω
λέλυσαι   perf pass ind 2 sg
[1C 7:27; v-1a(4); 3395]   λύω

λεμά   {3316, n-3g(2)}
For what? Why? Wherefore? Matt 27:46; Mark 15:34*

λεμα   indecl [2t; n-3g(2); 3316]   λεμά

λέντιον, ου, τό   {3317, n-2c}
a coarse cloth, with which servants were girded, *a towel, napkin, apron,* John 13:4, 5*

λέντιον   acc sg neut [Jn 13:4; n-2c; 3317]   λέντιον
λεντίῳ   dat sg neut [Jn 13:5; n-2c; 3317]   "
λέοντι   dat sg masc [Rv 4:7; n-3c(5b); 3329]   λέων
λέοντος   gen sg masc [2t; n-3c(5b); 3329]   "
λεόντων   gen pl masc [3t; n-3c(5b); 3329]   "
λεπίδες   nom pl fem [Ac 9:18; n-3c(2); 3318]   λεπίς

λεπίς, ίδος, ἡ   {3318, n-3c(2)}
a scale, shell, rind, crust, incrustation, Acts 9:18*

λέπρα, ας, ἡ   {3319, n-1a}
the leprosy, Matt 8:3; Mark 1:42; Luke 5:12, 13*

λέπρα   nom sg fem [3t; n-1a; 3319]   λέπρα
λέπρας   gen sg fem [Lk 5:12; n-1a; 3319]   "
λεπροί   nom pl masc [4t; a-1a(1); 3320]   λεπρός

λεπρός, ά, όν   {3320, a-1a(1)}
leprous; a leper, Matt 8:2; 10:8

λεπρός   nom sg masc [2t; a-1a(1); 3320]
λεπροῦ   gen sg masc [2t; a-1a(1); 3320]
λεπρούς   acc pl masc [Mt 10:8; a-1a(1); 3320]
λεπτά   acc pl neut [2t; a-1a(2a); 3321]   λεπτός
λεπτόν   acc sg neut [Lk 12:59; a-1a(2a); 3321]   "

λεπτός, ή, όν   {3321, a-1a(2a)}
a mite, the smallest Jewish coin, equal to half a κοδράντης, Mark 12:42; Luke 12:59; 21:2*

Λευί, ὁ   {3322, n-3g(1)}
Levi, also spelled Λευίς (3323), pr. name. When the N.T. refers to the Λευί of the O.T., the word is indecl. (n-3g[2]); when it refers to a N.T. person, it is partially declined (n-3g[1]): Λευίς (nom); Λευίν (acc). (1) *Levi, son of Jacob,* Heb 7:5, 9; Rev 7:7. (2) *Levi, son of Symeon,* Luke 3:29 (3) *Levi, son of Melchi,* Luke 3:24

Λευί   indecl [4t; n-3g(1); 3322]   Λευί
Λευίν   acc sg masc [2t; n-3g(1); 3323]   "

Λευίς   {3323, n-3g(1)}
see Λευί, *Levi, son of Alphaeus, the publican,* Mark 2:14; Luke 5:27, 29*

Λευίς   nom sg masc [Lk 5:29; n-3g(1); 3323]   "
Λευίτας   acc pl masc [Jn 1:19; n-1f; 3324]   Λευίτης

Λευίτης, ου, ὁ   {3324, n-1f}
a Levite, one of the posterity of Levi, John 1:19; Luke 10:32; Acts 4:36*

Λευίτης   nom sg masc [2t; n-1f; 3324]
Λευιτικῆς   gen sg fem
[Hb 7:11; a-1a(2a); 3325]   Λευιτικός

Λευιτικός, ή, όν   {3325, a-1a(2a)}
Levitical, pertaining to the Levites, Heb 7:11*

λευκά   nom pl neut [2t; a-1a(2a); 3328]   λευκός
λευκά   acc pl neut [Rv 3:18; a-1a(2a); 3328]   "
λευκαί   nom pl fem [2t; a-1a(2a); 3328]   "

λευκαίνω   {3326, v-2d(4)}
[-, ἐλεύκανα, -, -, -] *to brighten, to make white,* Mark 9:3; Rev 7:14*

λευκαῖς   dat pl fem [Ac 1:10; a-1a(2a); 3328]   "
λευκᾶναι   aor act inf
    [Mk 9:3; v-2d(4); 3326]   λευκαίνω
λευκάς   acc pl fem [2t; a-1a(2a); 3328]   λευκός
λευκή   nom sg fem [2t; a-1a(2a); 3328]   "
λευκήν   acc sg fem [3t; a-1a(2a); 3328]   "

λευκοβύσσινος   {3327}
    white linen, v.l. for βύσσινον λευκόν in Rev
    19:14*

λευκοῖς   dat pl masc [Rv 19:14; a-1a(2a); 3328]   "
λευκοῖς   dat pl neut [4t; a-1a(2a); 3328]   "
λευκόν   nom sg neut [2t; a-1a(2a); 3328]   "
λευκόν   acc sg masc [Rv 20:11; a-1a(2a); 3328]   "
λευκόν   acc sg neut [Rv 19:14; a-1a(2a); 3328]   "

λευκός, ή, όν   {3328, a-1a(2a)}
    pr. *light, bright; white*, Matt 5:36; 17:2; *whitening,
    growing white*, John 4:35

λευκός   nom sg masc [3t; a-1a(2a); 3328]   "

λέων, οντος, ὁ   {3329, n-3c(5b)}
    a lion, Heb 11:33; 1 Peter 5:8; Rev 4:7; 9:8, 17;
    10:3; 13:2; met. *a lion, cruel adversary, tyrant*, 2
    Tim 4:17; *a lion, a hero, deliverer*, Rev 5:5*

λέων   nom sg masc [3t; n-3c(5b); 3329]   λέων

λήθη, ης, ἡ   {3330, n-1b}
    forgetfulness, oblivion, 2 Peter 1:9*

λήθην   acc sg fem [2P 1:9; n-1b; 3330]   λήθη
λήμψεσθε   fut mid ind 2 pl
    [5t; v-3a(2b); 3284]   λαμβάνω
λήμψεται   fut mid ind 3 sg [8t; v-3a(2b); 3284]   "
λήμψεως   gen sg fem
    [Pp 4:15; n-3e(5b); 3331]   λῆμψις

λῆμψις, εως, ἡ   {3331, n-3e(5b)}
    also spelled λῆψις, *taking, receiving*, Phil 4:15*

λημψόμεθα   fut mid ind 1 pl
    [Jm 3:1; v-3a(2b); 3284]   λαμβάνω
λήμψονται   fut mid ind 3 pl [4t; v-3a(2b); 3284]   "
ληνόν   acc sg fem [3t; n-2b; 3332]   ληνός

ληνός, οῦ, ἡ   {3332, n-2b}
    pr. *a tub. trough; a wine-press*, into which grapes
    were cast and trodden, Rev 14:19, 20; 19:15; *a
    wine-vat*, i.q. ὑπολήνιον, the lower vat into
    which the juice of the trodden grapes flowed,
    Matt 21:33*

ληνός   nom sg fem [Rv 14:20; n-2b; 3332]   "
ληνοῦ   gen sg fem [Rv 14:20; n-2b; 3332]   "

λῆρος, ου, ὁ   {3333, n-2a}
    idle talk; an empty tale, nonsense, Luke 24:11*

λῆρος   nom sg masc [Lk 24:11; n-2a; 3333]   λῆρος
λησταί   nom pl masc [3t; n-1f; 3334]   λῃστής
λῃσταῖς   dat pl masc [Lk 10:30; n-1f; 3334]   "
λῃστάς   acc pl masc [2t; n-1f; 3334]   "
λῃστήν   acc sg masc [3t; n-1f; 3334]   "

λῃστής, οῦ, ὁ   {3334, n-1f}
    a plunderer, robber, highwayman, Matt 21:13;
    26:55; Mark 11:17; Luke 10:30; 2 Cor 11:26; *a
    bandit, brigand*, Matt 27:38, 44; Mark 15:27; John

18:40; trop. *a robber, rapacious imposter*, John
    10:1, 8

λῃστής   nom sg masc [2t; n-1f; 3334]   "
λῃστῶν   gen pl masc [4t; n-1f; 3334]   "

λῆψις, see λῆμψις

λίαν   {3336, adverb}
    much, greatly, exceedingly, Matt 2:16; 4:8; 8:28

λίαν   adverb [12t; adverb; 3336]   λίαν
λίβα   acc sg masc [Ac 27:12; n-3a(2); 3355]   λίψ
λίβανον   acc sg masc [2t; n-2a; 3337]   λίβανος

λίβανος, ου, ὁ   {3337, n-2a}
    arbor thurifera, the tree producing frankincense,
    growing in Arabia and Mount Lebanon; in N.T.
    frankincense, the transparent gum that distils
    from incisions in the tree, Matt 2:11; Rev 18:13*

λιβανωτόν   acc sg masc [2t; n-2a; 3338]   λιβανωτός

λιβανωτός, οῦ, ὁ   {3338, n-2a}
    frankincense; in N.T. *a censer*, Rev 8:3, 5*

Λιβερτῖνος, ου, ὁ   {3339, n-2a}
    *a freedman, one who having been a slave has
    obtained his freedom*, or *whose father was a
    freed-man*; in N.T. the λιβερτῖνοι probably
    denote Jews who had been carried captive to
    Rome, and subsequently manumitted, Acts
    6:9*

Λιβερτίνων   gen pl masc
    [Ac 6:9; n-2a; 3339]   Λιβερτῖνος

Λιβύη, ης, ἡ   {3340, n-1b}
    Libya, a part of Africa, bordering on the west of
    Egypt, Acts 2:10*

Λιβύης   gen sg fem [Ac 2:10; n-1b; 3340]   Λιβύη

Λιβυστῖνος, ου, ὁ   {3341, n-2a}
    Libyan, v.l. for Λιβερτῖνος at Acts 6:9*

λιθάζειν   pres act inf
    [Jn 8:5; v-2a(1); 3342]   λιθάζω
λιθάζετε   pres act ind 2 pl
    [Jn 10:32; v-2a(1); 3342]   "
λιθάζομεν   pres act ind 1 pl
    [Jn 10:33; v-2a(1); 3342]   "

λιθάζω   {3342, v-2a(1)}
    [λιθάσω, ἐλίθασα, -, -, ἐλιθάσθην] *to stone, pelt* or
    kill with stones, John 8:5; 10:31, 32, 33; 11:8; Acts
    5:26; 14:19; 2 Cor 11:25; Heb 11:37*

λιθάσαι   aor act inf [Jn 11:8; v-2a(1); 3342]   "
λιθάσαντες   aor act ptcp nom pl masc
    [Ac 14:19; v-2a(1); 3342]   "
λιθασθῶσιν   aor pass subj 3 pl
    [Ac 5:26; v-2a(1); 3342]   "
λιθάσωσιν   aor act subj 3 pl
    [Jn 10:31; v-2a(1); 3342]   "
λίθινα   acc pl neut
    [Rv 9:20; a-1a(2a); 3343]   λίθινος
λίθιναι   nom pl fem [Jn 2:6; a-1a(2a); 3343]   "
λιθίναις   dat pl fem [2C 3:3; a-1a(2a); 3343]   "

λίθινος, η, ον   {3343, a-1a(2a)}
    made of stone, John 2:6; 2 Cor 3:3; Rev 9:20*

λιθοβολέω   {3344, v-1d(2a)}
[(ἐλιθοβόλουν), -, ἐλιθοβόλησα, -, -,
ἐλιθοβολήθην] *to stone, pelt with stones*, in order
to kill, Matt 21:35; 23:37

λιθοβοληθήσεται   fut pass ind 3 sg
[Hb 12:20; v-1d(2a); 3344]   λιθοβολέω
λιθοβολῆσαι   aor act inf
[Ac 14:5; v-1d(2a); 3344]   "
λιθοβολοῦσα   pres act ptcp voc sg fem
[2t; v-1d(2a); 3344]   "
λίθοι   nom pl masc   [4t; n-2a; 3345]   λίθος
λίθοις   dat pl masc   [3t; n-2a; 3345]   "
λίθον   acc sg masc   [26t; n-2a; 3345]   "

λίθος, ου, ὁ   {3345, n-2a}
a stone, Matt 3:9; 4:3, 6; used figuratively, of
Christ, Eph 2:20; 1 Peter 2:6; of believers, 1
Peter 2:5; meton. *a tablet of stone*, 2 Cor 3:7; *a
precious stone*, Rev 4:3

λίθος   nom sg masc   [9t; n-2a; 3345]   "
λιθόστρωτον   acc sg neut
[Jn 19:13; a-3a; 3346]   λιθόστρωτος

λιθόστρωτος, ον   {3346, a-3a}
a pavement made of blocks of stone, John 19:13*

λίθου   gen sg masc   [2t; n-2a; 3345]   λίθος
λίθους   acc pl masc   [3t; n-2a; 3345]   "
λίθῳ   dat sg masc   [10t; n-2a; 3345]   "
λίθων   gen pl masc   [2t; n-2a; 3345]   "

λικμάω   {3347, v-1d(1a)}
[λικμήσω, -, -, -, -] pr. *to winnow grain*; in N.T. *to
scatter like chaff, crush*, Matt 21:44; Luke 20:18*

λικμήσει   fut act ind 3 sg
[2t; v-1d(1a); 3347]   λικμάω
λιμένα   acc sg masc
[Ac 27:12; n-3f(1b); 3348]   λιμήν
λιμένας   acc pl masc   [Ac 27:8; n-3f(1b); 3348]   "
λιμένος   gen sg masc   [Ac 27:12; n-3f(1b); 3348]   "
λίμνη   nom sg fem   [Rv 20:14; n-1b; 3349]   λίμνη
λίμνῃ   dat sg fem   [Rv 21:8; n-1b; 3349]   "

λιμήν, ένος, ὁ   {3348, n-3f(1b)}
a port, haven, harbor, Καλὰ Λιμένες, Acts 27:8,
12*

λίμνη   {3349, n-1b}
a tract of standing water; a lake, Luke 5:1; Rev
20:14

λίμνην   acc sg fem   [8t; n-1b; 3349]   "
λίμνης   gen sg fem   [Lk 8:22; n-1b; 3349]   "
λιμοί   nom pl masc   [Lk 21:11; n-2a; 3350]   λιμός
λιμοί   nom pl fem   [2t; n-2a; 3350]   "
λιμόν   acc sg fem   [Ac 11:28; n-2a; 3350]   "

λιμός, οῦ, ὁ or **ἡ**   {3350, n-2a/n-2b}
famine, scarcity of food, want of grain, Matt 24:7;
famine, hunger, famishment, Luke 15:17; Rom
8:35

λιμοί   nom sg masc   [4t; n-2a; 3350]   "
λιμός   nom sg fem   [Lk 15:14; n-2a; 3350]   "
λιμῷ   dat sg masc   [2t; n-2a; 3350]   "
λιμῷ   dat sg fem   [Lk 15:17; n-2a; 3350]   "

λίνον, ου, τό   {3351, n-2c}
flax; by meton. *a flaxen wick*, Matt 12:20; *linen*,
Rev 15:6*

λίνον   acc sg neut   [2t; n-2c; 3351]   λίνον

Λίνος, ου, ὁ   {3352, n-2a}
some accent as Λῖνος, *Linus*, pr. name, 2 Tim
4:21*

Λίνος   nom sg masc   [2Ti 4:21; n-2a; 3352]   Λίνος
λιπαρά   nom pl neut
[Rv 18:14; a-1a(1); 3353]   λιπαρός

λιπαρός, ά, όν   {3353, a-1a(1)}
lit., *fat;* fig., *rich, sumptuous*, Rev 18:14*

λίτρα, ας, ἡ   {3354, n-1a}
a pound, libra, equivalent to about twelve
ounces (American), John 12:3; 19:39*

λίτραν   acc sg fem   [Jn 12:3; n-1a; 3354]   λίτρα
λίτρας   acc pl fem   [Jn 19:39; n-1a; 3354]   "

λίψ, ος, ὁ   {3355, n-3a(2)}
pr. *the south-west wind;* meton. *the south-west
quarter of the heavens*, Acts 27:12*

λογεία, ας, ἡ   {3356, n-1a}
collection of money, 1 Cor 16:1f.*

λογεῖαι   nom pl fem   [1C 16:2; n-1a; 3356]   λογεία
λογείας   gen sg fem   [1C 16:1; n-1a; 3356]   "
λόγια   nom pl neut   [1P 4:11; n-2c; 3359]   λόγιον
λόγια   acc pl neut   [2t; n-2c; 3359]   "
λογίζεσθαι   pres pass inf
[Rm 4:24; v-2a(1); 3357]   λογίζομαι
λογίζεσθε   pres mid imperative 2 pl
[2t; v-2a(1); 3357]   "
λογίζεσθε   pres mid ind 2 pl
[Jn 11:50; v-2a(1); 3357]   "
λογιζέσθω   pres mid imperative 3 sg
[3t; v-2a(1); 3357]   "
λογίζεται   pres mid ind 3 sg   [2t; v-2a(1); 3357]   "
λογίζεται   pres pass ind 3 sg   [3t; v-2a(1); 3357]   "
λογίζῃ   pres mid ind 2 sg
[Rm 2:3; v-2a(1); 3357]   "

λογίζομαι   {3357, v-2a(1)}
[(ἐλογιζόμην), -, ἐλογισάμην, -, -, ἐλογίσθην] (1)
pr. *to count, calculate; to count, enumerate*, Mark
15:28; Luke 22:37; *to set down* as a matter of
account, 1 Cor 13:5; 2 Cor 3:5; 12:6; *to impute*,
Rom 4:3; 2 Cor 5:19; 2 Tim 4:16; *to account*, Rom
2:26; 8:36; εἰς οὐδὲν λογισθῆναι, *to be set at
nought, despised*, Acts 19:27; *to regard, deem,
consider*, Rom 6:11; 14:14; 1 Cor 4:1; 2 Cor 10:2;
Phil 3:13; (2) *to infer, conclude, presume*, Rom 2:3;
3:28; 8:18; 2 Cor 10:2, 7, 11; Heb 11:19; 1 Peter
5:12; (3) *to think upon, ponder*, Phil 4:8; absol. *to
reason*, Mark 11:31; 1 Cor 13:11

λογίζομαι   pres mid ind 1 sg   [5t; v-2a(1); 3357]   "
λογιζόμεθα   pres mid ind 1 pl
[Rm 3:28; v-2a(1); 3357]   "
λογιζόμενος   pres mid ptcp nom sg masc
[2C 5:19; v-2a(1); 3357]   "
λογιζομένους   pres mid ptcp acc pl masc
[2C 10:2; v-2a(1); 3357]   "

λογιζομένῳ   pres mid ptcp dat sg masc
  [Rm 14:14; v-2a(1); 3357]   "
λογικήν   acc sg fem
  [Rm 12:1; a-1a(2a); 3358]   λογικός
λογικόν   acc sg neut [1P 2:2; a-1a(2a); 3358]   "

λογικός, ή, όν   {3358, a-1a(2a)}
  pertaining to speech; pertaining to reason; in N.T.
  rational, spiritual, pertaining to the mind and soul,
  Rom 12:1; 1 Peter 2:2*

λόγιον, ου, τό   {3359, n-2c}
  an oracle, a divine communication or *revelation,*
  Acts 7:38; Rom 3:2; Heb 5:12; 1 Peter 4:11*

λόγιος, α, ον   {3360, a-1a(1)}
  gifted with learning or *eloquence,* Acts 18:24*

λόγιος   nom sg masc
  [Ac 18:24; a-1a(1); 3360]   λόγιος
λογισάμενος   aor mid ptcp nom sg masc
  [Hb 11:19; v-2a(1); 3357]   λογίζομαι
λογίσασθαι   aor mid inf [2C 3:5; v-2a(1); 3357]   "
λογίσηται   aor mid subj 3 sg [2t; v-2a(1); 3357]   "
λογισθείη   aor pass opt 3 sg
  [2Ti 4:16; v-2a(1); 3357]   "
λογισθῆναι   aor pass inf [2t; v-2a(1); 3357]   "
λογισθήσεται   fut pass ind 3 sg
  [Rm 2:26; v-2a(1); 3357]   "

λογισμός, ου, ὁ   {3361, n-2a}
  pr. *a computation, act of computing; a thought,*
  cogitation, Rom 2:15; *a conception, device,* 2 Cor
  10:4*

λογισμούς   acc pl masc
  [2C 10:4; n-2a; 3361]   λογισμός
λογισμῶν   gen pl masc [Rm 2:15; n-2a; 3361]   "
λογίων   gen pl neut [Hb 5:12; n-2c; 3359]   λόγιον
λόγοι   nom pl masc [10t; n-2a; 3364]   λόγος
λόγοις   dat pl masc [17t; n-2a; 3364]   "
λογομαχεῖν   pres act inf
  [2Ti 2:14; v-1d(2a); 3362]   λογομαχέω

λογομαχέω   {3362, v-1d(2a)}
  [-, -, -, -, -] *to contend about words;* by impl. *to*
  dispute about trivial things, 2 Tim 2:14*

λογομαχία, ας, ἡ   {3363, n-1a}
  contention or *strife about words;* by impl. *a*
  dispute about trivial things, unprofitable
  controversy, 1 Tim 6:4; Titus 3:9 v.l.*

λογομαχίας   acc pl fem
  [1Ti 6:4; n-1a; 3363]   λογομαχία
λόγον   acc sg masc [130t; n-2a; 3364]   λόγος

λόγος, ου, ὁ   {3364, n-2a}
  a word, a thing uttered, Matt 12:32, 37; 1 Cor
  14:19; *speech, language, talk,* Matt 22:15; Luke
  20:20; 2 Cor 10:10; James 3:2; *converse,* Luke
  24:17; *mere talk, wordy show,* 1 Cor 4:19, 20; Col
  2:23; 1 John 3:18; *language, mode of discourse,*
  style of speaking, Matt 5:37; 1 Cor 1:17; 1 Thess
  2:5; *a saying, a speech,* Mark 7:29; Eph 4:29; *an*
  expression, form of words, formula, Matt 26:44;
  Rom 13:9; Gal 5:14; *a saying, a thing propounded*
  in discourse, Matt 7:24; 19:11; John 4:37; 6:60; 1
  Tim 1:15; *a message, announcement,* 2 Cor 5:19; *a*

prophetic announcement, John 12:38; *an account,*
statement, 1 Peter 3:15; *a story, report,* Matt 28:15;
John 4:39; 21:23; 2 Thess 2:2; *a written narrative,*
a treatise, Acts 1:1; *a set discourse,* Acts 20:7;
doctrine, John 8:31, 37; 2 Tim 2:17; *subject-matter,*
Acts 15:6; *reckoning, account,* Matt 12:36; 18:23;
25:19; Luke 16:2; Acts 19:40; 20:24; Rom 9:28;
Phil 4:15, 17; Heb 4:13; *a plea,* Matt 5:32; Acts
19:38; *a motive,* Acts 10:29; *reason,* Acts 18:14; ὁ
λόγος, *the word* of God, especially in the Gospel,
Matt 13:21, 22; Mark 16:20; Luke 1:2; Acts 6:4; ὁ
λόγος, *the* divine WORD, or *Logos,* John 1:1

λόγος   nom sg masc [68t; n-2a; 3364]   "
λόγου   gen sg masc [27t; n-2a; 3364]   "
λόγους   acc pl masc [23t; n-2a; 3364]   "

λόγχη, ῆς, ἡ   {3365, n-1b}
  pr. *the head of a javelin; a spear, lance,* John 19:34;
  Matt 27:49 v.l.*

λόγχῃ   dat sg fem [Jn 19:34; n-1b; 3365]   λόγχη
λόγῳ   dat sg masc [45t; n-2a; 3364]   λόγος
λόγων   gen pl masc [10t; n-2a; 3364]   "
λοιδορεῖς   pres act ind 2 sg
  [Ac 23:4; v-1d(2a); 3366]   λοιδορέω

λοιδορέω   {3366, v-1d(2a)}
  [-, ἐλοιδόρησα, -, -, -] *to revile, rail at, abuse,* John
  9:28; Acts 23:4; 1 Cor 4:12; 1 Peter 2:23*

λοιδορία, ας, ἡ   {3367, n-1a}
  reviling, railing, verbal abuse, 1 Tim 5:14; 1 Peter
  3:9*

λοιδορίαν   acc sg fem
  [1P 3:9; n-1a; 3367]   λοιδορία
λοιδορίας   gen sg fem [2t; n-1a; 3367]   "
λοίδοροι   nom pl masc
  [1C 6:10; n-2a; 3368]   λοίδορος

λοίδορος, ου, ὁ   {3368, n-2a}
  reviling, railing; as a subst. *a reviler, railer,* 1 Cor
  5:11; 6:10*

λοίδορος   nom sg masc [1C 5:11; n-2a; 3368]   "
λοιδορούμενοι   pres pass ptcp nom pl masc
  [1C 4:12; v-1d(2a); 3366]   λοιδορέω
λοιδορούμενος   pres pass ptcp nom sg masc
  [1P 2:23; v-1d(2a); 3366]   "
λοιμοί   nom pl masc [Lk 21:11; n-2a; 3369]   λοιμός
λοιμόν   acc sg masc [Ac 24:5; n-2a; 3369]   "

λοιμός, ου, ὁ   {3369, n-2a}
  a pestilence, plague, Matt 24:7 v.l.; Luke 21:11;
  met. *a pest, pestilent fellow,* Acts 24:5*

λοιπά   acc pl neut [3t; a-1a(2a); 3370]   λοιπός
λοιπαί   nom pl fem [2t; a-1a(2a); 3370]   "
λοιπάς   acc pl fem [2t; a-1a(2a); 3370]   "
λοιποί   nom pl masc [15t; a-1a(2a); 3370]   "
λοιποῖς   dat pl masc [7t; a-1a(2a); 3370]   "
λοιποῖς   dat pl neut [Rm 1:13; a-1a(2a); 3370]   "
λοιπόν   acc sg neut, can function adverbially
  [13t; a-1a(2a); 3370]

λοιπός, ή, όν   {3370, a-1a(2a)}
  remaining; the rest, remainder, Matt 22:6; as an
  adv., τοῦ λοιποῦ, *henceforth,* Gal 6:17; τὸ λοιπόν,
  or λοιπόν, *henceforward,* Matt 26:45; 2 Tim 4:8;

Acts 27:20; *as to the rest, besides,* 1 Cor 1:16; *finally,* Eph 6:10; ὃ δὲ λοιπόν, *but, now, furthermore,* 1 Cor 4:2

λοιποῦ   gen sg neut [2t; a-1a(2a); 3370]   "
λοιπούς   acc pl masc [3t; a-1a(2a); 3370]   "
λοιπῶν   gen pl masc [4t; a-1a(2a); 3370]   "
λοιπῶν   gen pl fem [Rv 8:13; a-1a(2a); 3370]   "
λοιπῶν   gen pl neut [2t; a-1a(2a); 3370]   "

Λουκᾶς, ᾶ, ὁ   {3371, n-1e}
Luke, pr. name

Λουκᾶς   nom sg masc [3t; n-1e; 3371]   Λουκᾶς

Λούκιος, ου, ὁ   {3372, n-2a}
Lucius, pr. name, (1) a person from Cyrene of Antioch, Acts 13:1. (2) a person who sends his greeting with Paul, Rom 16:21*

Λούκιος   nom sg masc [2t; n-2a; 3372]   Λούκιος
λουσαμένη   aor mid ptcp nom sg fem
       [2P 2:22; v-1a(8); 3374]   λούω
λούσαντες   aor act ptcp nom pl masc
       [Ac 9:37; v-1a(8); 3374]   "

λουτρόν, ου, τό   {3373, n-2c}
a bath, water for bathing; a bathing, washing, ablution, Eph 5:26; Titus 3:5*

λουτροῦ   gen sg neut [Ti 3:5; n-2c; 3373]   λουτρόν
λουτρῷ   dat sg neut [Ep 5:26; n-2c; 3373]   "

λούω   {3374, v-1a(8)}
[-, ἔλουσα, -, λέλουμαι or λέλουσμαι, -] pr. *to bathe the body,* as distinguished from washing only the extremities, John 13:10; *to bathe, wash,* Acts 9:37; 16:33; Heb 10:22; 2 Peter 2:22; met. *to cleanse* from sin, Rev 1:5 v.l.

Λύδδα, Λύδδας, ἡ   {3375, n-3g(1)}
Lydda, a town in Palestine, Acts 9:32, 35, 38*

Λύδδα   acc sg fem [2t; n-3g(1); 3375]   Λύδδα
Λύδδας   gen sg fem [Ac 9:38; n-3g(1); 3375]   "

Λυδία, ας, ἡ   {3376, n-1a}
Lydia, pr. name of a woman, Acts 16:14, 40*

Λυδία   nom sg fem [Ac 16:14; n-1a; 3376]   Λυδία
Λυδίαν   acc sg fem [Ac 16:40; n-1a; 3376]   "
λύει   pres act ind 3 sg
       [Lk 13:15; v-1a(4); 3395]   λύω
λύετε   pres act ind 2 pl [2t; v-1a(4); 3395]   "
λυθείσης   aor pass ptcp gen sg fem
       [Ac 13:43; v-1a(4); 3395]   "
λυθῇ   aor pass subj 3 sg
       [Jn 7:23; v-1a(4); 3395]   "
λυθῆναι   aor pass inf [3t; v-1a(4); 3395]   "
λυθήσεται   fut pass ind 3 sg [2t; v-1a(4); 3395]   "
λυθήσονται   fut pass ind 3 pl
       [2P 3:12; v-1a(4); 3395]   "

Λυκαονία, ας, ἡ   {3377, n-1a}
Lycaonia, a province of Asia Minor, Acts 14:6*

Λυκαονίας   gen sg fem
       [Ac 14:6; n-1a; 3377]   Λυκαονία

Λυκαονιστί   {3378, adverb}
in the dialect of Lycaonia, Acts 14:11*

Λυκαονιστί   adverb
       [Ac 14:11; adverb; 3378]   Λυκαονιστί

Λυκία, ας, ἡ   {3379, n-1a}
Lycia, a province of Asia Minor, Acts 27:5*

Λυκίας   gen sg fem [Ac 27:5; n-1a; 3379]   Λυκία
λύκοι   nom pl masc [2t; n-2a; 3380]   λύκος
λύκον   acc sg masc [Jn 10:12; n-2a; 3380]   "

λύκος, ου, ὁ   {3380, n-2a}
a wolf, Matt 10:16; Luke 10:3; John 10:12; met. *a person of wolf-like character,* Matt 7:15; Acts 20:29*

λύκος   nom sg masc [Jn 10:12; n-2a; 3380]   "
λύκων   gen pl masc [2t; n-2a; 3380]   "

λυμαίνω   {3381, v-2d(4)}
[(ἐλύμαινον), -, ἐλύμανα, -, -, -] some list as a deponent, λυμαίνομαι, *to outrage, harm, violently maltreat;* in N.T. *to make havoc of, ruin,* Acts 8:3*

λυομένων   pres pass ptcp gen pl neut
       [2P 3:11; v-1a(4); 3395]   λύω
λύοντες   pres act ptcp nom pl masc
       [Mk 11:5; v-1a(4); 3395]   "
λυόντων   pres act ptcp gen pl masc
       [Lk 19:33; v-1a(4); 3395]   "
λύουσιν   pres act ind 3 pl
       [Mk 11:4; v-1a(4); 3395]   "
λύπας   acc pl fem [1P 2:19; n-1b; 3383]   λύπη
λυπεῖσθαι   pres pass inf
       [2t; v-1d(2a); 3382]   λυπέω
λυπεῖται   pres pass ind 3 sg
       [Rm 14:15; v-1d(2a); 3382]   "
λυπεῖτε   pres act imperative 2 pl
       [Ep 4:30; v-1d(2a); 3382]   "

λυπέω   {3382, v-1d(2a)}
[-, ἐλύπησα, λελύπηκα, -, ἐλυπήθην] *to occasion grief* or *sorrow to, to distress,* 2 Cor 2:2, 5; 7:8; pass. *to be grieved, pained, distressed, sorrowful,* Matt 17:23; 19:22; *to aggrieve, cross, vex,* Eph 4:30; pass. *to feel pained,* Rom 14:15

λύπη, ης, ἡ   {3383, n-1b}
pain, distress, John 16:21; *grief, sorrow,* John 16:6, 20, 22; meton. *cause of grief, trouble, affliction,* 1 Peter 2:19

λύπη   nom sg fem [5t; n-1b; 3383]   λύπη
λύπῃ   dat sg fem [2t; n-1b; 3383]   "
λυπηθείς   aor pass ptcp nom sg masc
       [Mt 14:9; v-1d(2a); 3382]   λυπέω
λυπηθέντες   aor pass ptcp nom pl masc
       [1P 1:6; v-1d(2a); 3382]   "
λυπηθῆναι   aor pass inf
       [2C 7:11; v-1d(2a); 3382]   "
λυπηθήσεσθε   fut pass ind 2 pl
       [Jn 16:20; v-1d(2a); 3382]   "
λυπηθῆτε   aor pass subj 2 pl
       [2C 2:4; v-1d(2a); 3382]   "
λύπην   acc sg fem [5t; n-1b; 3383]   λύπη
λύπης   gen sg fem [3t; n-1b; 3383]   "
λυπῆσθε   pres pass subj 2 pl
       [1Th 4:13; v-1d(2a); 3382]   λυπέω

λυπούμενοι   pres pass ptcp nom pl masc
   [2t; v-1d(2a); 3382]   "

λυπούμενος   pres pass ptcp nom sg masc
   [3t; v-1d(2a); 3382]   "

λυπῶ   pres act ind 1 sg [2C 2:2; v-1d(2a); 3382]   "

λῦσαι   aor act inf [4t; v-1a(4); 3395]   λύω

Λυσανίας, ου, ὁ   {3384, n-1d}
   Lyssanias, pr. name, Luke 3:1*

Λυσανίου   gen sg masc
   [Lk 3:1; n-1d; 3384]   Λυσανίας

λύσαντες   aor act ptcp nom pl masc
   [2t; v-1a(4); 3395]   λύω

λύσαντι   aor act ptcp dat sg masc
   [Rv 1:5; v-1a(4); 3395]   "

λύσας   aor act ptcp nom sg masc
   [2t; v-1a(4); 3395]   "

λύσατε   aor act imperative 2 pl
   [3t; v-1a(4); 3395]   "

λύσῃ   aor act subj 3 sg [2t; v-1a(4); 3395]   "

λύσῃς   aor act subj 2 sg
   [Mt 16:19; v-1a(4); 3395]   "

λύσητε   aor act subj 2 pl
   [Mt 18:18; v-1a(4); 3395]   "

Λυσίας, ου, ὁ   {3385, n-1d}
   Lysias, pr. name, Acts 23:26; 24:7, 22*

Λυσίας   nom sg masc [2t; n-1d; 3385]   Λυσίας
λύσιν   acc sg fem [1C 7:27; n-3e(5b); 3386]   λύσις

λύσις, εως, ἡ   {3386, n-3e(5b)}
   a loosing; in N.T. *a release* from the marriage
   bond, *a divorce*, 1 Cor 7:27*

λυσιτελεῖ   pres act ind 3 sg
   [Lk 17:2; v-1d(2b); 3387]   λυσιτελέω

λυσιτελέω   {3387, v-1d(2b)}
   [-, -, -, -, -] pr. *to compensate for incurred expense*;
   by impl. *to be advantageous to, to profit,*
   advantage; impers. Luke 17:2*

λῦσον   aor act imperative 2 sg
   [2t; v-1a(4); 3395]   λύω

Λύστρα, ου, ἡ or **τό**   {3388, n-1a/n-2c}
   Lystra, a city of Lycaonia, in Asia Minor, Acts
   14:6, 8, 21; 16:1f.; 27:5 v.l.; 2 Tim 3:11*

Λύστραν   acc sg fem [3t; n-1a; 3388]   Λύστρα
Λύστροις   dat pl neut [3t; n-1a; 3388]   "
λύσω   aor act subj 1 sg
   [Jn 1:27; v-1a(4); 3395]   λύω

λύτρον, ου, τό   {3389, n-2c}
   pr. *price paid; a ransom*, Matt 20:28; Mark 10:45*

λύτρον   acc sg neut [2t; n-2c; 3389]   λύτρον
λυτροῦσθαι   pres mid inf
   [Lk 24:21; v-1d(3); 3390]   λυτρόω

λυτρόω   {3390, v-1d(3)}
   [-, ἐλύτρωσα, -, -, ἐλυτρώθην] *to release for a*
   ransom; mid, *to ransom, redeem, deliver, liberate*,
   Luke 24:21; Titus 2:14; 1 Peter 1:18; Acts 28:19
   v.l.*

λυτρώσηται   aor mid subj 3 sg
   [Ti 2:14; v-1d(3); 3390]   "

λύτρωσιν   acc sg fem [3t; n-3e(5b); 3391]   λύτρωσις

λύτρωσις, εως, ἡ   {3391, n-3e(5b)}
   redemption, Heb 9:12; *liberation, deliverance*,
   Luke 1:68; 2:38*

λυτρωτήν   acc sg masc
   [Ac 7:35; n-1f; 3392]   λυτρωτής

λυτρωτής, οῦ, ὁ   {3392, n-1f}
   a redeemer; a deliverer, Acts 7:35*

λυχνία, ας, ἡ   {3393, n-1a}
   a candlestick, lampstand, Matt 5:15; met. *a*
   candlestick, as a figure of a Christian church,
   Rev 1:12, 13, 20; of a teacher or prophet, Rev
   11:4

λυχνία   nom sg fem [Hb 9:2; n-1a; 3393]   λυχνία
λυχνίαι   nom pl fem [2t; n-1a; 3393]   "
λυχνίαν   acc sg fem [4t; n-1a; 3393]   "
λυχνίας   gen sg fem [Lk 8:16; n-1a; 3393]   "
λυχνίας   acc pl fem [2t; n-1a; 3393]   "
λυχνιῶν   gen pl fem [2t; n-1a; 3393]   "
λύχνοι   nom pl masc [Lk 12:35; n-2a; 3394]   λύχνος
λύχνον   acc sg masc [4t; n-2a; 3394]   "

λύχνος, ου, ὁ   {3394, n-2a}
   a light, lamp, candle, etc., Matt 5:15; Mark 4:21;
   met. *a lamp*, as a figure of a distinguished
   teacher, John 5:35

λύχνος   nom sg masc [6t; n-2a; 3394]   "
λύχνου   gen sg masc [2t; n-2a; 3394]   "
λύχνῳ   dat sg masc [2P 1:19; n-2a; 3394]   "

λύω   {3395, v-1a(4)}
   [(ἔλυον), λύσω, ἔλυσα, -, λέλυμαι, ἐλύθην] *to*
   loosen, unbind, unfasten, Mark 1:7; *to loose, untie*,
   Matt 21:2; John 11:44; *to disengage*, 1 Cor 7:27; *to*
   set free, set at liberty, deliver, Luke 13:16; *to break*,
   Acts 27:41; Rev 5:2, 5; *to break up, dismiss*, Acts
   13:43; *to destroy, demolish*, John 2:19; Eph 2:14;
   met *to infringe*, Matt 5:19; John 5:18; 7:23; *to*
   make void, nullify, John 10:35; in N.T. *to declare*
   free, of privileges, or, in respect of lawfulness,
   Matt 16:19

Λωΐδι   dat sg fem [2Ti 1:5; n-3c(2); 3396]   Λωΐς

Λωΐς, ΐδος, ἡ   {3396, n-3c(2)}
   Lois, pr. name of a woman, 2 Tim 1:5*

Λώτ, ὁ   {3397, n-3g(2)}
   Lot, pr. name, indecl., Luke 17:28, 29, 32; 2 Peter
   2:7*

Λώτ   indecl [3t; n-3g(2); 3397]   Λώτ

μ

Μάαθ, ὁ   {3399, n-3g(2)}
   Maath, pr. name, indecl., Luke 3:26*

Μάαθ   indecl [Lk 3:26; n-3g(2); 3399]   Μάαθ

Μαγαδάν, ἡ   {3400, n-3g(2)}
   also spelled Μαγδαλά, *Magadan*, pr. name,
   indecl., Matt 15:39; Mark 8:10 v.l.*

Μαγδαληνή   nom sg fem
   [11t; n-1b; 3402]   Μαγδαληνή
Μαγδαληνῇ   dat sg fem [Mk 16:9; n-1b; 3402]   "

Μαγδαλά, see Μαγαδάν   {3401}

Μαγδαληνή, ῆς, ἡ   {3402, n-1b}
   Magdalene, pr. name *(of Magdala),* John 20:18

Μαγδαληνῇ   dat sg fem
   [12t; n-1b; 3402]   Μαγδαληνή

Μαγε(δ)δών   {3403}
   see Ἁρμαγεδών, *Magadon,* indecl. pr. name, Rev
   16:16 v.l.*

μαγεία, ας, ἡ   {3404, n-1a}
   pr. *the system of the magians; magic,* Acts 8:11*

μαγείαις   dat pl fem [Ac 8:11; n-1a; 3404]   μαγεία

μαγεύω   {3405, v-1a(6)}
   [μαγεύσω, -, -, -, -] *to be a magician; to use magical
   arts, practise magic, sorcery,* Acts 8:9*

μαγεύων   pres act ptcp nom sg masc
   [Ac 8:9; v-1a(6); 3405]   μαγεύω
μάγοι   nom pl masc [Mt 2:1; n-2a; 3407]   μάγος
μάγον   acc sg masc [Ac 13:6; n-2a; 3407]   "

μάγος, ου, ὁ   {3407, n-2a}
   (1) *a magus, sage of the magician religion,
   magician, astrologer, wise man,* Matt 2:1, 7, 16; (2)
   a magician, sorcerer, Acts 13:6, 8*

μάγος   nom sg masc [Ac 13:8; n-2a; 3407]   "
μάγους   acc pl masc [Mt 2:7; n-2a; 3407]   "

Μαγώγ, ὁ   {3408, n-3g(2)}
   Magog, pr. name, indecl., Rev 20:8*

Μαγώγ   indecl [Rv 20:8; n-3g(2); 3408]   Μαγώγ
μάγων   gen pl masc [2t; n-2a; 3407]   μάγος

Μαδιάμ, ὁ   {3409, n-3g(2)}
   Madian, a district of Arabia Petra, Acts 7:29*

Μαδιάμ   gen sg masc
   [Ac 7:29; n-3g(2); 3409]   Μαδιάμ

μαζός, οῦ, ὁ   {3410, n-2a}
   breast, Rev 1:13 v.l.*

μαθεῖν   aor act inf [3t; v-3a(2b); 3443]   μανθάνω
μάθετε   aor act imperative 2 pl
   [4t; v-3a(2b); 3443]   "
μαθηταί   nom pl masc [109t; n-1f; 3412]   μαθητής
μαθηταῖς   dat pl masc [41t; n-1f; 3412]   "
μαθητάς   acc pl masc [39t; n-1f; 3412]   "
μάθητε   aor act subj 2 pl
   [1C 4:6; v-3a(2b); 3443]   μανθάνω
μαθητευθείς   aor pass ptcp nom sg masc
   [Mt 13:52; v-1a(6); 3411]   μαθητεύω
μαθητεύσαντες   aor act ptcp nom pl masc
   [Ac 14:21; v-1a(6); 3411]   "
μαθητεύσατε   aor act imperative 2 pl
   [Mt 28:19; v-1a(6); 3411]   "

μαθητεύω   {3411, v-1a(6)}
   [-, ἐμαθήτευσα, -, -, ἐμαθητεύθην] intrans. *to be a
   disciple, follow as a disciple,* Matt 27:57 v.l.; in
   N.T. trans. *to make a disciple of , to train in*

discipleship, Matt 28:19; Acts 14:21; pass. *to be
trained, disciplined, instructed,* Matt 13:52*

μαθητῇ   dat sg masc [3t; n-1f; 3412]   μαθητής
μαθητήν   acc sg masc [3t; n-1f; 3412]   "

μαθητής, ου, ὁ   {3412, n-1f}
   a disciple, Matt 10:24, 42, et al.

μαθητής   nom sg masc [20t; n-1f; 3412]   "
μαθητοῦ   gen sg masc [Mt 10:42; n-1f; 3412]   "

μαθήτρια, ας, ἡ   {3413, n-1a}
   a female disciple; a female Christian, Acts 9:36*

μαθήτρια   nom sg fem
   [Ac 9:36; n-1a; 3413]   μαθήτρια
μαθητῶν   gen pl masc [45t; n-1f; 3412]   μαθητής
Μαθθαῖον   acc sg masc [3t; n-3g(2); 3414]   Μαθθαῖος

Μαθθαῖος   {3414}
   Matthew, pr. name, Matt 10:3; Acts 1:13

Μαθθαῖος   nom sg masc [2t; n-3g(2); 3414]   "

Μαθθάν, see Ματθάτ

Μαθθάτ   {3415, n-3g(2)}
   also spelled Ματθάτ, *Mathat,* pr. name, indecl.,
   Luke 3:24, 29*

Μαθθάτ   gen sg masc [2t; n-3g(2); 3415]   Μαθθάτ
Μαθθίαν   acc sg masc [2t; n-3g(2); 3416]   Μαθθίας

Μαθθίας, ου, ὁ   {3416, n-1d}
   also spelled Ματθίας, *BAGD* suggest it is a
   shortened form of Ματταθίας, *Matthias,* pr.
   name, Acts 1:23, 26*

Μαθουσάλα, ὁ   {3417, n-3g(2)}
   Methuselah, pr. name, indecl., Luke 3:37*

Μαθουσαλά   gen sg masc
   [Lk 3:37; n-3g(2); 3417]   Μαθουσαλά
μαθών   aor act ptcp nom sg masc
   [2t; v-3a(2b); 3443]   μανθάνω

Μαϊνάν   {3418}
   see Μεννά, *Mainan,* pr. name, indecl., Luke 3:31
   v.l.*

μαίνεσθε   pres mid ind 2 pl
   [1C 14:23; v-2d(4); 3419]   μαίνομαι
μαίνεται   pres mid ind 3 sg
   [Jn 10:20; v-2d(4); 3419]   "
μαίνῃ   pres mid ind 2 sg [2t; v-2d(4); 3419]   "

μαίνομαι   {3419, v-2d(4)}
   [-, -, -, -, -] *to be disordered in mind, mad,* John
   10:20; Acts 12:15; 26:24, 25; 1 Cor 14:23*

μαίνομαι   pres mid ind 1 sg
   [Ac 26:25; v-2d(4); 3419]   "
μακαρία   nom sg fem [2t; a-1a(1); 3421]   μακάριος
μακάριαι   nom pl fem [Lk 23:29; a-1a(1); 3421]   "
μακαρίαν   acc sg fem [Ti 2:13; a-1a(1); 3421]   "
μακαρίζομεν   pres act ind 1 pl
   [Jm 5:11; v-2a(1); 3420]   μακαρίζω

μακαρίζω   {3420, v-2a(1)}
   [μακαριῶ, ἐμακάρισα, -, -, -] *to pronounce happy,
   fortunate,* Luke 1:48; James 5:11*

μακάριοι nom pl masc
[26t; a-1a(1); 3421] μακάριος
μακάριον nom sg neut [Ac 20:35; a-1a(1); 3421] "
μακάριον acc sg masc [Ac 26:2; a-1a(1); 3421] "

μακάριος, α, ον {3421, a-1a(1)}
happy, blessed, as a noun it can depict someone
who receives divine favor, Matt 5:3, 4, 5, 7;
Luke 1: 45

μακάριος nom sg masc [16t; a-1a(1); 3421] "
μακαρίου gen sg masc [1Ti 1:11; a-1a(1); 3421] "
μακαριοῦσιν fut act ind 3 pl
[Lk 1:48; v-2a(1); 3420] μακαρίζω
μακαρισμόν acc sg masc
[Rm 4:6; n-2a; 3422] μακαρισμός

μακαρισμός, ου, ὁ {3422, n-2a}
a happy calling, the act of pronouncing happy, Rom
4:6, 9; *self-congratulation,* Gal 4:15*

μακαρισμός nom sg masc [2t; n-2a; 3422] "
μακαριωτέρα nom sg fem comparative
[1C 7:40; a-1a(1); 3421] μακάριος
Μακεδόνας acc pl masc
[Ac 19:29; n-3f(1b); 3424] Μακεδών
Μακεδόνες nom pl masc [2C 9:4; n-3f(1b); 3424] "

Μακεδονία, ας, ἡ {3423, n-1a}
Macedonia, Acts 16:9; Rom 15:26; 1 Cor 16:5; 1
Thess 1:7; 1 Tim 1:3

Μακεδονία nom sg fem
[Rm 15:26; n-1a; 3423] Μακεδονία
Μακεδονίᾳ dat sg fem [3t; n-1a; 3423] "
Μακεδονίαν acc sg fem [11t; n-1a; 3423] "
Μακεδονίας gen sg fem [7t; n-1a; 3423] "
Μακεδόνος gen sg masc
[Ac 27:2; n-3f(1b); 3424] Μακεδών
Μακεδόσιν dat pl masc [2C 9:2; n-3f(1b); 3424] "

Μακεδών, όνος, ὁ {3424, n-3f(1b)}
a native of Macedonia, Acts 16:9; 19:29; 27:2; 2
Cor 9:2, 4*

Μακεδών nom sg masc [Ac 16:9; n-3f(1b); 3424] "

μάκελλον, ου, τό {3425, n-2c}
meat market, marketplace, slaughter house, 1 Cor
10:25*

μακέλλῳ dat sg neut
[1C 10:25; n-2c; 3425] μάκελλον
μακρά acc pl neut, can function adverbially
[2t; a-1a(1); 3431] μακρός

μακράν {3426, adverb}
far, far off, at a distance, far distant, Matt 8:30;
Mark 12:34; met. οἱ μακράν, *remote, alien,* Eph
2:13, 17; so οἱ εἰς μακράν, Acts 2:39

μακράν adverb [12t; adverb; 3426] μακράν

μακρόθεν {3427, adverb}
far off, at a distance, from afar, from a distance,
Mark 8:3; 11:13; preceded by ἀπό, in the same
sense, Matt 26:58

μακρόθεν adverb [14t; adverb; 3427] μακρόθεν
μακροθυμεῖ pres act ind 3 sg
[3t; v-1d(2a); 3428] μακροθυμέω

μακροθυμεῖτε pres act imperative 2 pl
[1Th 5:14; v-1d(2a); 3428] "

μακροθυμέω {3428, v-1d(2a)}
[-, ἐμακροθύμησα, -, -, -] *to be slow towards, be
long-enduring; to exercise patience, be
long-suffering, clement,* or *indulgent, to forbear,*
Matt 18:26, 29; 1 Cor 13:4; 1 Thess 5:14; 2 Peter
3:9; *to have patience, endure patiently, wait with
patient expectation,* Heb 6:15; James 5:7, 8; *to bear
long* with entreaties for deliverance and
avengement, Luke 18:7*

μακροθυμήσας aor act ptcp nom sg masc
[Hb 6:15; v-1d(2a); 3428] "
μακροθυμήσατε aor act imperative 2 pl
[2t; v-1d(2a); 3428] "
μακροθύμησον aor act imperative 2 sg
[2t; v-1d(2a); 3428] "

μακροθυμία, ας, ἡ {3429, n-1a}
patience; patient enduring of evil, fortitude, Col
1:11; Col 3:12; 1 Tim 1:16; 1 Peter 3:20; *slowness
of avenging injuries, long-suffering, forbearance,
clemency,* Rom 2:4; 9:22; 2 Cor 6:6; Gal 5:22; Eph
4:2; 2 Tim 4:2; James 5:10; *patient expectation,* 2
Tim 3:10; Heb 6:12; 2 Peter 3:15*

μακροθυμία nom sg fem [2t; n-1a; 3429]
μακροθυμία
μακροθυμίᾳ dat sg fem [4t; n-1a; 3429] "
μακροθυμίαν acc sg fem [4t; n-1a; 3429] "
μακροθυμίας gen sg fem [4t; n-1a; 3429] "
μακροθυμῶν pres act ptcp nom sg masc
[Jm 5:7; v-1d(2a); 3428] μακροθυμέω

μακροθύμως {3430, adverb}
patiently, Acts 26:3*

μακροθύμως adverb
[Ac 26:3; adverb; 3430] μακροθύμως

μακρός, ά, όν {3431, a-1a(1)}
long; of space, *far, distant, remote,* Luke 15:13;
19:12; of time, *of long duration,* Matt 23:14 v.l.;
Mark 12:40; Luke 20:47*

μακροχρόνιος, ον {3432, a-3a}
of long duration; long-lived, Eph 6:3*

μακροχρόνιος nom sg masc
[Ep 6:3; a-3a; 3432] μακροχρόνιος
μαλακά acc pl neut
[Mt 11:8; a-1a(2a); 3434] μαλακός

μαλακία, ας, ἡ {3433, n-1a}
*softness; listlessness, indisposition, weakness,
infirmity of body,* Matt 4:23; 9:35; 10:1*

μαλακίαν acc sg fem [3t; n-1a; 3433] μαλακία
μαλακοί nom pl masc
[1C 6:9; a-1a(2a); 3434] μαλακός
μαλακοῖς dat pl neut [2t; a-1a(2a); 3434] "

μαλακός, ή, όν {3434, a-1a(2a)}
soft; soft to the touch, delicate, Matt 11:8; Luke
7:25; met. *an instrument of unnatural lust,
effeminate,* 1 Cor 6:9*

Μαλελεήλ, ὁ {3435, n-3g(2)}
Maleleel, pr. name, indecl., Luke 3:37*

Μαλελεήλ   indecl
[Lk 3:37; n-3g(2); 3435]   Μαλελεήλ

μάλιστα   {3436, adverb}
most, most of all, chiefly, especially, Acts 20:38;
25:26

μάλιστα   adverb-superlative
[12t; adverb; 3436]   μάλιστα

μᾶλλον   {3437, adverb}
more, to a greater extent, in a higher degree, Matt
18:13; 27:24; John 5:18; 1 Cor 14:18; *rather, in
preference,* Matt 10:6; Eph 4:28; used in a
periphrasis for the comparative, Acts 20:35; as
an intensive with a comparative term, Matt
6:26; Mark 7:36; 2 Cor 7:13; Phil 1:23; μᾶλλον δέ,
yea rather, or, *more properly speaking,* Rom 8:34;
Gal 4:9; Eph 5:11

μᾶλλον   adverb-comparative
[81t; adverb; 3437]   μᾶλλον

Μάλχος, ου, ὁ   {3438, n-2a}
Malchus, pr. name, John 18:10*

Μάλχος   nom sg masc [Jn 18:10; n-2a; 3438]
Μάλχος

μάμμη, ης, ἡ   {3439, n-1b}
a mother; later, *a grandmother,* 2 Tim 1:5*

μάμμη   dat sg fem [2Ti 1:5; n-1b; 3439]   μάμμη
μαμωνᾶ   gen sg masc [Lk 16:9; n-1e; 3440] μαμωνᾶς
μαμωνᾷ   dat sg masc [3t; n-1e; 3440]   "

μαμωνᾶς, ᾶ, ὁ   {3440, n-1e}
wealth, riches, Luke 16:9, 11; personified, like
the Greek Πλοῦτος, *Mammon,* Matt 6:24; Luke
16:13*

Μαναήν, ὁ   {3441, n-3g(2)}
Manaen, pr. name, indecl., Acts 13:1*

Μαναήν   indecl [Ac 13:1; n-3g(2); 3441]   Μαναήν
Μανασσῆ   gen sg masc [Rv 7:6; n-1g; 3442]
Μανασσῆς
Μανασσῆ   acc sg masc [Mt 1:10; n-1g; 3442]   "

Μανασσῆς, ῆ, ὁ   {3442, n-1g}
Manasses, pr. name (1) *the tribe of Manasseh,* Rev
7:6 (2) *Manasseh, king of Judah,* Matt 1:10; Luke
3:23ff. v.l.*

Μανασσῆς   nom sg masc [Mt 1:10; n-1g; 3442]   "
μανθανέτω   pres act imperative 3 sg
[1Ti 2:11; v-3a(2b); 3443]   μανθάνω
μανθανέτωσαν   pres act imperative 3 pl
[2t; v-3a(2b); 3443]   "
μανθάνοντα   pres act ptcp acc pl neut
[2Ti 3:7; v-3a(2b); 3443]   "
μανθάνουσιν   pres act ind 3 pl
[1Ti 5:13; v-3a(2b); 3443]   "

μανθάνω   {3443, v-3a(2b)}
[-, ἔμαθον, μεμάθηκα, -, -] *to learn, be taught,*
Matt 9:13; 11:29; 24:32; *to learn* by practice or
experience, *acquire a custom* or *habit,* Phil 4:11; 1
Tim 5:4, 13; *to ascertain, be informed,* Acts 23:27;
to understand, comprehend, Rev 14:3

μανθάνωσιν   pres act subj 3 pl
[1C 14:31; v-3a(2b); 3443]   "

μανία, ας, ἡ   {3444, n-1a}
madness, insanity, Acts 26:24*

μανίαν   acc sg fem [Ac 26:24; n-1a; 3444]   μανία

μάννα, τό   {3445, n-3g(2)}
manna, the miraculous food of the Israelites
while in the desert, John 6:31, 49; Heb 9:4; Rev
2:17*

μάννα   indecl [4t; n-3g(2); 3445]   μάννα

μαντεύομαι   {3446, v-1a(6)}
[-, -, -, -, -] *to speak oracles, to divine,* Acts 16:16*

μαντευομένη   pres mid ptcp nom sg fem
[Ac 16:16; v-1a(6); 3446]   μαντεύομαι

μαραίνω   {3447, v-2d(4)}
[-, -, -, μεμάραμμαι, ἐμαράνθην] *to quench, cause
to decay, fade,* or *wither;* pass. *to wither, waste
away,* met. *to fade away, disappear, perish,* James
1:11*

μαράνα θά   {3448, interj}
(Aramaic), also spelled μαρὰν ἀθά, or κύριος
ἔρχεται, *the Lord comes* or *will come* to judgment,
1 Cor 16:22*

μαράνα θά   interjection
[1C 16:22; interj; 3448]   μαράνα θά
μαρανθήσεται   fut pass ind 3 sg
[Jm 1:11; v-2d(4); 3447]   μαραίνω
μαργαρῖται   nom pl masc
[Rv 21:21; n-1f; 3449]   μαργαρίτης
μαργαρίταις   dat pl masc [2t; n-1f; 3449]   "
μαργαρίτας   acc pl masc [2t; n-1f; 3449]   "
μαργαρίτῃ   dat sg masc [Rv 18:16; n-1f; 3449]   "
μαργαρίτην   acc sg masc [Mt 13:46; n-1f; 3449] "

μαργαρίτης, ου, ὁ   {3449, n-1f}
a pearl, Matt 7:6; 13:45, 46; 1 Tim 2:9; Rev 17:4;
18:12, 16; 21:21*

μαργαρίτου   gen sg masc [Rv 21:21; n-1f; 3449] "
μαργαριτῶν   gen pl masc [Rv 18:12; n-1f; 3449] "

Μάρθα, ας, ἡ   {3450, n-1a}
Martha, pr. name, John 12:2

Μάρθα   nom sg fem [8t; n-1a; 3450]   Μάρθα
Μάρθα   voc sg fem [2t; n-1a; 3450]   "
Μάρθαν   acc sg fem [2t; n-1a; 3450]   "
Μάρθας   gen sg fem [Jn 11:1; n-1a; 3450]   "

Μαρία, ας, ἡ   {3451, n-1a}
Mary, pr. name (1) The mother of Jesus, Matt
1:16; Acts 1:14. (2) *Mary,* wife of Clopas,
mother of James, Mark 15:40; Luke 24:10; John
19:25. (3) *Mary Magdalene,* Matt 27:56; Luke
20:18. (4) Sister of Martha and Lazarus, Luke
10:39; John 11:1; 12:3. (5) Mother of John
surnamed Mark, Acts 12:12 (6) A Christian at
Rome, Rom 16:6

Μαρία   nom sg fem [17t; n-1a; 3451]   Μαρία
Μαρίᾳ   dat sg fem [Mk 16:9; n-1a; 3451]   "

Μαριάμ, ἡ   {3452, n-3g(2)}
the indeclinable form of Μαρία

Μαριάμ   indecl [27t; n-3g(2); 3452]   Μαριάμ
Μαρίαν   acc sg fem [2t; n-1a; 3451]   Μαρία

Μαρίας   gen sg fem   [7t; n-1a; 3451]   "
Μᾶρκον   acc sg masc   [4t; n-2a; 3453]   Μᾶρκος

Μᾶρκος, ου, ὁ   {3453, n-2a}
    Mark, pr. name

Μᾶρκος   nom sg masc   [3t; n-2a; 3453]   "
Μάρκου   gen sg masc   [Ac 12:12; n-2a; 3453]   "

μάρμαρος, ου, ὁ   {3454, n-2a}
    a white glistening stone; marble, Rev 18:12*

μαρμάρου   gen sg masc
    [Rv 18:12; n-2a; 3454]   μάρμαρος
μάρτυρα   acc sg masc   [3t; n-3f(2a); 3459]   μάρτυς
μάρτυρας   acc pl masc   [Ac 6:13; n-3f(2a); 3459]   "
μαρτυρεῖ   pres act ind 3 sg
    [8t; v-1d(2a); 3455]   μαρτυρέω
μαρτυρεῖν   pres act inf
    [Ac 26:5; v-1d(2a); 3455]   "
μαρτυρεῖς   pres act ind 2 sg
    [Jn 8:13; v-1d(2a); 3455]   "
μαρτυρεῖται   pres pass ind 3 sg
    [Hb 7:17; v-1d(2a); 3455]   "
μαρτυρεῖτε   pres act ind 2 pl
    [3t; v-1d(2a); 3455]   "
μάρτυρες   nom pl masc   [10t; n-3f(2a); 3459]   μάρτυς

μαρτυρέω   {3455, v-1d(2a)}
    [(ἐμαρτύρουν), μαρτυρήσω, ἐμαρτύρησα,
    μεμαρτύρηκα, μεμαρτύρημαι, ἐμαρτυρήθην]
    trans. *to testify, depose*, John 3:11, 32; 1 John 1:2;
    Rev 1:2; 22:20; absol. *to give evidence*, John 18:23;
    to bear testimony, testify, Luke 4:22; John 1:7, 8; *to
    bear testimony* in confirmation, Acts 14:3; *to
    declare* distinctly and formally, John 4:44; pass.
    to be the subject of testimony, to obtain attestation
    to character, Acts 6:3; 10:22; 1 Tim 5:10; Heb
    11:2, 4; mid. equivalent to μαρτύρομαι, *to make a
    solemn appeal*, Acts 26:22; 1 Thess 2:12

μαρτυρηθέντες   aor pass ptcp nom pl masc
    [Hb 11:39; v-1d(2a); 3455]   μαρτυρέω
μαρτυρῆσαι   aor act inf   [2t; v-1d(2a); 3455]   "
μαρτυρήσαντος   aor act ptcp gen sg masc
    [1Ti 6:13; v-1d(2a); 3455]   "
μαρτυρήσας   aor act ptcp nom sg masc
    [Ac 13:22; v-1d(2a); 3455]   "
μαρτυρήσει   fut act ind 3 sg
    [Jn 15:26; v-1d(2a); 3455]   "
μαρτυρήσῃ   aor act subj 3 sg
    [3t; v-1d(2a); 3455]   "
μαρτύρησον   aor act imperative 2 sg
    [Jn 18:23; v-1d(2a); 3455]   "
μαρτυρήσω   aor act subj 1 sg
    [Jn 18:37; v-1d(2a); 3455]   "

μαρτυρία, ας, ἡ   {3456, n-1a}
    judicial *evidence*, Mark 14:55, 56, 59; Luke 22:71;
    testimony in general, Titus 1:13; 1 John 5:9
    testimony, declaration in a matter of fact or
    doctrine, John 1:19; 3:11; Acts 22:18; *attestation*
    to character, John 5:34, 36; *reputation*, 1 Tim 3:7

μαρτυρία   nom sg fem   [15t; n-1a; 3456]   μαρτυρία
μαρτυρίαι   nom pl fem   [Mk 14:56; n-1a; 3456]   "
μαρτυρίαν   acc sg fem   [19t; n-1a; 3456]   "
μαρτυρίας   gen sg fem   [2t; n-1a; 3456]   "

μαρτύριον, ου, τό   {3457, n-2c}
    testimony, evidence, 2 Cor 1:12; James 5:3; Acts
    4:33; in N.T. *testimony, mode of solemn
    declaration*, Matt 8:4; Luke 9:5; *testimony, matter
    of solemn declaration*, 1 Cor 1:6; 2:1; 1 Tim 2:6;
    σκηνὴ τοῦ μαρτυρίου, a title of the Mosaic
    tabernacle, Acts 7:44; Rev 15:5

μαρτύριον   nom sg neut   [4t; n-2c; 3457]   μαρτύριον
μαρτύριον   acc sg neut   [13t; n-2c; 3457]   "
μαρτυρίου   gen sg neut   [2t; n-2c; 3457]   "

μαρτύρομαι   {3458, v-1c(1)}
    [-, ἐμαρτυράμην, -, -, -] *to call to witness*; intrans.
    to make a solemn affirmation or *declaration*, Acts
    20:26; 26:22; Gal 5:3; *to make a solemn appeal*, Eph
    4:17; 1 Thess 2:12*

μαρτύρομαι   pres mid ind 1 sg
    [3t; v-1c(1); 3458]   μαρτύρομαι
μαρτυρόμενοι   pres mid ptcp nom pl masc
    [1Th 2:12; v-1d(2a); 3455]   μαρτυρέω
μαρτυρόμενος   pres mid ptcp nom sg masc
    [Ac 26:22; v-1d(2a); 3455]   "
μάρτυρος   gen sg masc
    [Ac 22:20; n-3f(2a); 3459]   μάρτυς
μαρτυροῦμεν   pres act ind 1 pl
    [4t; v-1d(2a); 3455]   μαρτυρέω
μαρτυρουμένη   pres pass ptcp nom sg fem
    [2t; v-1d(2a); 3455]   "
μαρτυρούμενος   pres pass ptcp nom sg masc
    [3t; v-1d(2a); 3455]   "
μαρτυρουμένους   pres pass ptcp acc pl masc
    [Ac 6:3; v-1d(2a); 3455]   "
μαρτυροῦν   pres act ptcp nom sg neut
    [1J 5:6; v-1d(2a); 3455]   "
μαρτυροῦντες   pres act ptcp nom pl masc
    [1J 5:7; v-1d(2a); 3455]   "
μαρτυροῦντι   pres act ptcp dat sg masc
    [Ac 14:3; v-1d(2a); 3455]   "
μαρτυροῦντος   pres act ptcp gen sg masc
    [Hb 11:4; v-1d(2a); 3455]   "
μαρτυρούντων   pres act ptcp gen pl masc
    [3J 3; v-1d(2a); 3455]   "
μαρτυροῦσαι   pres act ptcp nom pl fem
    [Jn 5:39; v-1d(2a); 3455]   "
μαρτυρούσης   pres act ptcp gen sg fem
    [Jn 4:39; v-1d(2a); 3455]   "
μαρτυροῦσιν   pres act ind 3 pl
    [Ac 10:43; v-1d(2a); 3455]   "
μαρτυρῶ   pres act ind 1 sg   [6t; v-1d(2a); 3455]   "
μαρτυρῶ   pres act subj 1 sg   [2t; v-1d(2a); 3455]   "
μαρτύρων   gen pl masc   [9t; n-3f(2a); 3459]   μάρτυς
μαρτυρῶν   pres act ptcp nom sg masc
    [4t; v-1d(2a); 3455]   μαρτυρέω

μάρτυς, ρος, ὁ   {3459, n-3f(2a)}
    (1) a judicial *witness, deponent*, Matt 18:16; Heb
    10:28; (2) generally, *a witness* to a circumstance,
    Luke 24:48; Acts 10:41; in N.T. *a witness, a
    testifier*, of a doctrine, Rev 1:5; 3:14; 11:3; (3) *a
    martyr*, Acts 22:20; Rev 2:13

μάρτυς   nom sg masc   [8t; n-3f(2a); 3459]   μάρτυς
μάρτυσιν   dat pl masc   [3t; n-3f(2a); 3459]   "

μασάομαι   {3460, v-1d(1a)}
[(ἐμασώμην), -, -, -, -, -] *to chew, masticate,* in N.T.
to gnaw, Rev 16:10*

μασθός, οῦ, ὁ   {3461}
v.l. for μαστός

μάστιγας   acc pl fem
    [Mk 3:10; n-3b(2); 3465]   μάστιξ
μαστιγοῖ   pres act ind 3 sg
    [Hb 12:6; v-1d(3); 3463]   μαστιγόω
μάστιγος   gen sg fem [2t; n-3b(2); 3465]   μάστιξ

μαστιγόω   {3463, v-1d(3)}
[μαστιγώσω, ἐμαστίγωσα, -, -, ἐμαστιγώθην] *to
scourge, whip,* Matt 10:17; 20:19; 23:34; Mark
10:34; Luke 18:33; John 19:1; met. *to chastise,*
Heb 12:6*

μαστίγων   gen pl fem [2t; n-3b(2); 3465]   "
μαστιγῶσαι   aor act inf
    [Mt 20:19; v-1d(3); 3463]   μαστιγόω
μαστιγώσαντες   aor act ptcp nom pl masc
    [Lk 18:33; v-1d(3); 3463]   "
μαστιγώσετε   fut act ind 2 pl
    [Mt 23:34; v-1d(3); 3463]   "
μαστιγώσουσιν   fut act ind 3 pl
    [2t; v-1d(3); 3463]   "
μαστίζειν   pres act inf
    [Ac 22:25; v-2a(1); 3464]   μαστίζω

μαστίζω   {3464, v-2a(1)}
[-, -, -, -, -] *to scourge,* Acts 22:25*

μάστιξιν   dat pl fem
    [Ac 22:24; n-3b(2); 3465]   μάστιξ

μάστιξ, ιγός, ἡ   {3465, n-3b(2)}
a scourge, whip, Acts 22:24; Heb 11:36; met. *a
scourge* of disease, Mark 3:10; 5:29, 34; Luke
7:21*

μαστοί   nom pl masc [2t; n-2a; 3466]   μαστός
μαστοῖς   dat pl masc [Rv 1:13; n-2a; 3466]   "

μαστός, οῦ, ὁ   {3466, n-2a}
the breast, pap, Luke 11:27; 23:29; Rev 1:13*

ματαία   nom sg fem
    [1C 15:17; a-1a(1); 3469]   μάταιος
ματαίας   gen sg fem [1P 1:18; a-1a(1); 3469]   "
μάταιοι   nom pl masc [1C 3:20; a-1a(1); 3469]   "
μάταιοι   nom pl fem [Ti 3:9; a-1a(1); 3469]   "

ματαιολογία, ας, ἡ   {3467, n-1a}
vain talking, idle disputation, 1 Tim 1:6*

ματαιολογίαν   acc sg fem
    [1Ti 1:6; n-1a; 3467]   ματαιολογία
ματαιολόγοι   nom pl masc
    [Ti 1:10; a-3a; 3468]   ματαιολόγος

ματαιολόγος, ον   {3468, a-3a}
a vain talker, given to vain talking or *trivial
disputation,* Titus 1:10*

μάταιος, αία, αιον   {3469, a-1a(1)}
idle, ineffective, worthless, 1 Cor 3:20; *groundless,
deceptive, fallacious,* 1 Cor 15:17; *useless, fruitless,
unprofitable,* Titus 3:9; James 1:26; from the
Hebrew, *erroneous* in principle, *corrupt,*

perverted, 1 Peter 1:18; τὰ μάταια, *superstition,
idolatry,* Acts 14:15*

μάταιος   nom sg fem
    [Jm 1:26; a-1a(1); 3469]   μάταιος

ματαιότης, ητος, ἡ   {3470, n-3c(1)}
vanity, folly, futility, from the Hebrew, *religious
error,* Eph 4:17; 2 Peter 2:18; *false religion,* Rom
8:20*

ματαιότητι   dat sg fem
    [2t; n-3c(1); 3470]   ματαιότης
ματαιότητος   gen sg fem [2P 2:18; n-3c(1); 3470]   "

ματαιόω   {3471, v-1d(3)}
[-, -, -, -, ἐματαιώθην] *to make vain;* from the
Hebrew, pass. *to fall into religious error, to be
perverted,* Rom 1:21*

ματαίων   gen pl neut
    [Ac 14:15; a-1a(1); 3469]   μάταιος

μάτην   {3472, adverb}
in vain, fruitlessly, without profit, Matt 15:9;
Mark 7:7*

μάτην   adverb [2t; adverb; 3472]   μάτην

Ματθαῖος, ου, ὁ   {3473, n-2a}
Matthew, pr. name, Matt 10:3; Acts 1:13

Ματθάν, ὁ   {3474, n-3g(2)}
Matthan, pr. name, indecl., Matt 1:15 (2t); Luke
3:24 v.l.*

Ματθάν   indecl [2t; n-3g(2); 3474]   Ματθάν

Ματθάτ, ὁ, see Μαθθάτ   {3475, n-3g(2)}

Ματθίας, ου, ὁ, see Μαθθίας   {3476, n-1d}

Ματταθά, ὁ   {3477, n-3g(2)}
Mattatha, pr. name, indecl.; Luke 3:31*

Ματταθά   indecl [Lk 3:31; n-3g(2); 3477]   Ματταθά

Ματταθίας, ου, ὁ   {3478, n-1d}
see also Μαθθίας, *Mattathias,* pr. name, Luke
3:25, 26*

Ματταθίου   gen sg masc [2t; n-1d; 3478]   Ματταθίας
μάχαι   nom pl fem [2t; n-1b; 3480]   μάχη

μάχαιρα, ης, ἡ   {3479, n-1c}
a large knife, dagger; a sword, Matt 26:47, 51; *the
sword* of the executioner, Acts 12:2; Rom 8:35;
Heb 11:37; hence, φορεῖν μάχαιραν, *to bear the
sword, to have the power of life and death,* Rom
13:4; meton. *war,* Matt 10:34

μάχαιρα   nom sg fem [2t; n-1c; 3479]   μάχαιρα
μάχαιραι   nom pl fem [Lk 22:38; n-1c; 3479]   "
μάχαιραν   acc sg fem [12t; n-1c; 3479]   "
μαχαίρῃ   dat sg fem [5t; n-1c; 3479]   "
μαχαίρης   gen sg fem [4t; n-1c; 3479]   "
μαχαιρῶν   gen pl fem [5t; n-1c; 3479]   "
μάχας   acc pl fem [2t; n-1b; 3480]   μάχη
μάχεσθαι   pres mid inf
    [2Ti 2:24; v-1b(2); 3481]   μάχομαι
μάχεσθε   pres mid ind 2 pl
    [Jm 4:2; v-1b(2); 3481]   "

μάχη, ης, ἡ   {3480, n-1b}
a fight, battle, conflict; in N.T. contention, dispute,
strife, controversy, 2 Cor 7:5; 2 Tim 2:23; Titus
3:9; James 4:1*

μάχομαι   {3481, v-1b(2)}
[(ἐμαχόμην), -, -, -, -, -] to fight; to quarrel, Acts
7:26; 2 Tim 2:24; to contend, dispute, John 6:52;
James 4:2*

μαχομένοις   pres mid ptcp dat pl masc
      [Ac 7:26; v-1b(2); 3481]   "
με   acc sg [291t; a-5a; 1609]   ἐγώ
μέγα   nom sg neut [8t; a-1a(2a); 3489]   μέγας
μέγα   acc sg neut [10t; a-1a(2a); 3489]   "
μεγάλα   nom pl neut [2t; a-1a(2a); 3489]   "
μεγάλα   acc pl neut [6t; a-1a(2a); 3489]   "
μεγάλαι   nom pl fem [Rv 11:15; a-1a(2a); 3489] "
μεγάλαις   dat pl fem [Lk 23:23; a-1a(2a); 3489] "
μεγάλας   acc pl fem [2t; a-1a(2a); 3489]   "

μεγαλαυχέω   {3482, v-1d(2a)}
[-, -, -, -, ἐμεγαλύνθην] to boast, vaunt; to cause a
great stir, James 3:5 v.l.*

μεγαλεῖα   acc pl neut
      [Ac 2:11; a-1a(1); 3483]   μεγαλεῖος

μεγαλεῖος, α, ον   {3483, a-1a(1)}
magnificent, splendid; τὰ μεγαλεῖα, great things,
wonderful works, Acts 2:11; Luke 1:49 v.l.*

μεγαλειότης, ητος, ἡ   {3484, n-3c(1)}
majesty, magnificence, glory, Luke 9:43; Acts
19:27; 2 Peter 1:16*

μεγαλειότητι   dat sg fem
      [Lk 9:43; n-3c(1); 3484]   μεγαλειότης
μεγαλειότητος · gen sg fem [2t; n-3c(1); 3484]   "
μεγάλη   nom sg fem [33t; a-1a(2a); 3489]   μέγας
μεγάλη   voc sg fem [2t; a-1a(2a); 3489]   "
μεγάλη   dat sg fem [34t; a-1a(2a); 3489]   "
μεγάλην   acc sg fem [19t; a-1a(2a); 3489]   "
μεγάλης   gen sg fem [16t; a-1a(2a); 3489]   "
μεγάλοι   nom pl masc [3t; a-1a(2a); 3489]   "
μεγάλοι   voc pl masc [Rv 19:5; a-1a(2a); 3489] "

μεγαλοπρεπής, ές   {3485, a-4a}
pr. becoming a great man; magnificent, glorious,
most splendid, 2 Peter 1:17*

μεγαλοπρεποῦς   gen sg fem
      [2P 1:17; a-4a; 3485]   μεγαλοπρεπής
μεγάλου   gen sg masc [7t; a-1a(2a); 3489]   μέγας
μεγάλους   acc pl masc [4t; a-1a(2a); 3489]   "
μεγαλύνει   pres act ind 3 sg
      [Lk 1:46; v-1c(2); 3486]   μεγαλύνω
μεγαλυνθῆναι   aor pass inf
      [2C 10:15; v-1c(2); 3486]   "
μεγαλυνθήσεται   fut pass ind 3 sg
      [Pp 1:20; v-1c(2); 3486]   "
μεγαλυνόντων   pres act ptcp gen pl masc
      [Ac 10:46; v-1c(2); 3486]   "
μεγαλύνουσιν   pres act ind 3 pl
      [Mt 23:5; v-1c(2); 3486]   "

μεγαλύνω   {3486, v-1c(2)}
[(ἐμεγάλυνον), μεγαλυνῶ, -, -, -, ἐμεγαλύνθην]
lit., to enlarge, amplify, Matt 23:5; 2 Cor 10:15; to

manifest in an extraordinary degree, Luke 1:58;
fig., to magnify, exalt, extol, Luke 1:46; Acts 5:13;
Acts 10:46; 19:17; Phil 1:20*

μεγάλῳ   dat sg masc [4t; a-1a(2a); 3489]   μέγας
μεγάλῳ   dat sg neut [Ac 26:29; a-1a(2a); 3489] "
μεγάλων   gen pl masc [2t; a-1a(2a); 3489]   "

μεγάλως   {3487, adverb}
greatly, very much, vehemently, Phil 4:10; Acts
15:4 v.l.*

μεγάλως   adverb [Pp 4:10; adverb; 3487]   μεγάλως

μεγαλωσύνη, ης, ἡ   {3488, n-1b}
greatness, majesty, Heb 1:3; 8:1; ascribed majesty,
Jude 25*

μεγαλωσύνη   nom sg fem
      [Jd 25; n-1b; 3488]   μεγαλωσύνη
μεγαλωσύνης   gen sg fem [2t; n-1b; 3488]   "
μέγαν   acc sg masc [13t; a-1a(2a); 3489]   μέγας

μέγας, μεγάλη, μέγα   {3489, a-1a(2a)}
great, large in size, Matt 27:60; Mark 4:32; great,
much, numerous, Mark 5:11; Heb 11:26; great,
grown up, adult, Heb 11:24; great, vehement,
intense, Matt 2:10; 28:8; great, sumptuous, Luke
5:29; great, important, weighty, of high importance,
1 Cor 9:11; 13:13; great, splendid, magnificent,
Rev 15:3; extraordinary, wonderful, 2 Cor 11:15;
great, solemn, John 7:37; 19:31; great in rank,
noble, Rev 11:18; 13:16; great in dignity,
distinguished, eminent, illustrious, powerful, Matt
5:19; 18:1, 4; great, arrogant, boastful, Rev 13:5

μέγας   nom sg masc [25t; a-1a(2a); 3489]   "

μέγεθος, ους, τό   {3490, n-3d(2b)}
greatness, vastness, Eph 1:19*

μέγεθος   nom sg neut
      [Ep 1:19; n-3d(2b); 3490]   μέγεθος
μέγιστα   acc pl neut superlative
      [2P 1:4; a-1a(2a); 3492]   μέγιστος

μεγιστάν, ᾶνος, ὁ   {3491, n-3f(1a)}
great men, lords, chiefs, nobles, princes, Mark 6:21;
Rev 6:15; 18:23*

μεγιστᾶνες   nom pl masc
      [2t; n-3f(1a); 3491]   μεγιστάν
μεγιστᾶσιν   dat pl masc [Mk 6:21; n-3f(1a); 3491] "

μέγιστος, η, ον   {3492, a-1a(2a)}
greatest; preeminent, 2 Peter 1:4*

μεθ'   prep-acc [2t; prep; 3552]   μετά
μεθ'   prep-gen [41t; prep; 3552]   "
μέθαι   nom pl fem [Ga 5:21; n-1b; 3494]   μέθη
μέθαις   dat pl fem [Rm 13:13; n-1b; 3494]   "
μεθερμηνεύεται   pres pass ind 3 sg
      [Ac 13:8; cv-1a(6); 3493]   μεθερμηνεύω
μεθερμηνευόμενον   pres pass ptcp nom sg neut
      [7t; cv-1a(6); 3493]   "

μεθερμηνεύω   {3493, cv-1a(6)}
[-, -, -, -, -] to translate, interpret, Matt 1:23; Mark
5:41; 15:22, 34; John 1:38, 41; Acts 4:36; 13:8*

μέθη, ῆς, ἡ   {3494, n-1b}
strong drink; drunkenness, Luke 21:34; *an indulgence in drinking*, Rom 13:13; Gal 5:21*

μέθη   dat sg fem   [Lk 21:34; n-1b; 3494]   μέθη

μεθιστάναι   pres act inf
[1C 13:2; cv-6a; 3496]   μεθίστημι

μεθίστημι   {3496, cv-6a}
[-, μετέστησα, -, -, μετεστάθην] *to cause a change of position; to remove, transport,* 1 Cor 13:2; *to transfer,* Col 1:13; met. *to cause to change sides;* by impl. *to pervert, mislead,* Acts 19:26; *to remove from office, dismiss, discard,* Luke 16:4; Acts 13:22*

μεθοδεία, ας, ἡ   {3497, n-1a}
wile, scheme, scheming, craftiness, Eph 4:14; 6:11, 12 v.l.*

μεθοδείαν   acc sg fem
[Ep 4:14; n-1a; 3497]   μεθοδεία
μεθοδείας   acc pl fem   [Ep 6:11; n-1a; 3497]   "

μεθόριον, ου, τό   {3498, n-2c}
confine, border, Mark 7:24 v.l.*

μεθύει   pres act ind 3 sg
[1C 11:21; v-1a(4); 3501]   μεθύω
μεθυόντων   pres act ptcp gen pl masc
[Mt 24:49; v-1a(4); 3501]   "
μεθύουσαν   pres act ptcp acc sg fem
[Rv 17:6; v-1a(4); 3501]   "
μεθύουσιν   pres act ind 3 pl   [2t; v-1a(4); 3501]   "
μεθυσθῶσιν   aor pass subj 3 pl
[Jn 2:10; v-5a; 3499]   μεθύσκω
μεθύσκεσθαι   pres pass inf
[Lk 12:45; v-5a; 3499]   "
μεθύσκεσθε   pres pass imperative 2 pl
[Ep 5:18; v-5a; 3499]   "
μεθυσκόμενοι   pres pass ptcp nom pl masc
[1Th 5:7; v-5a; 3499]   "

μεθύσκω   {3499, v-5a}
[-, -, -, -, ἐμεθύσθην] *to inebriate, make drunk;* pass. *to be intoxicated, to be drunk,* Luke 12:45; Eph 5:18; 1 Thess 5:7; Rev 17:2; *to drink freely,* John 2:10*

μέθυσοι   nom pl masc   [1C 6:10; n-2a; 3500] μέθυσος

μέθυσος, ου, ὁ   {3500, n-2a}
drunken; a drunkard, 1 Cor 5:11; 6:10*

μέθυσος   nom sg masc   [1C 5:11; n-2a; 3500]   "

μεθύω   {3501, v-1a(4)}
[-, -, -, -, -] *to be intoxicated, be drunk,* Matt 24:49; Acts 2:15; 1 Cor 11:21; 1 Thess 5:7; Rev 17:6*

μείγνυμι   {3502, v-3c(2)}
[-, ἔμειξα, -, μέμειγμαι, ἐμίγην] also spelled μειγνύω (3503) and μίγνυμι (3624), *to mix, mingle,* Matt 27:34; Luke 13:1; Rev 8:7; 15:2*

μεῖζον   nom sg neut comparative
[4t; a-1a(2a); 3489]   μέγας
μεῖζον   acc sg neut comparative
[Jm 3:1; a-1a(2a); 3489]   "
μεῖζον   adverb-comparative   [2t; a-1a(2a); 3489]   "

μείζονα   acc sg masc comparative
[Hb 11:26; a-1a(2a); 3489]   "
μείζονα   acc sg fem comparative
[3t; a-1a(2a); 3489]   "
μείζονα   acc pl neut comparative
[3t; a-1a(2a); 3489]   "
μείζονα   acc pl fem comparative
[Lk 12:18; a-1a(2a); 3489]   "
μείζονες   nom pl masc comparative
[2P 2:11; a-1a(2a); 3489]   "
μείζονος   gen sg masc comparative
[2t; a-1a(2a); 3489]   "
μείζονος   gen sg fem comparative
[Hb 9:11; a-1a(2a); 3489]   "
μειζοτέραν   acc sg fem comparative
[3J 4; a-1a(1); 3504]   μειζότερος

μειζότερος, α, ον   {3504, a-1a(1)}
greater, a superlative form of μέγας used as a comparative, 3 John 4*

μείζω   acc sg fem comparative
[Jn 5:36; a-1a(2a); 3489]   μέγας
μείζω   acc pl neut comparative
[Jn 1:50; a-1a(2a); 3489]   "

μείζων, ον   {3505, a-4b(1)}
greater, comparative of μέγας

μείζων   nom sg masc comparative
[23t; a-1a(2a); 3489]   "
μείζων   nom sg fem comparative
[3t; a-1a(2a); 3489]   "
μεῖναι   aor act inf   [6t; v-1c(2); 3531]   μένω
μείνατε   aor act imperative 2 pl
[5t; v-1c(2); 3531]   "
μείνῃ   aor act subj 3 sg   [6t; v-1c(2); 3531]   "
μείνητε   aor act subj 2 pl   [2t; v-1c(2); 3531]   "
μεῖνον   aor act imperative 2 sg
[Lk 24:29; v-1c(2); 3531]   "
μείνωσιν   aor act subj 3 pl   [3t; v-1c(2); 3531]   "
μέλαιναν   acc sg fem   [Mt 5:36; a-2a; 3506]   μέλας

μέλαν, see μέλας

μέλανι   dat sg neut   [2C 3:3; a-2a; 3506]   "
μέλανος   gen sg neut   [2t; a-2a; 3506]   "

μέλας, μέλαινα, μέλαν   {3506, a-2a}
black, Matt 5:36; Rev 6:5, 12, the form μέλαν means *ink,* 2 Cor 3:3; 2 John 12; 3 John 13

μέλας   nom sg masc   [2t; a-2a; 3506]   "

Μελεά, ὁ   {3507, n-3g(2)}
Melea, indecl. pr. name, Luke 3:31*

Μελεά   indecl   [Lk 3:31; n-3g(2); 3507]   Μελεά

μέλει   {3508, v-1d(2c)}
[(ἔμελεν), μελήσομαι, ἐμέλησα, -, -, ἐμελήθην] *there is a care, it concerns,* Matt 22:16; Acts 18:17; 1 Cor 7:21; 9:9

μέλει   pres act ind 3 sg
[7t; v-1d(2c); 3508]   μέλει
μέλεσιν   dat pl neut   [5t; n-3d(2b); 3517]   μέλος
μελέτα   pres act imperative 2 sg
[1Ti 4:15; v-1d(1a); 3509]   μελετάω

μελετάω   {3509, v-1d(1a)}
[-, ἐμελέτησα, -, -, -] *to care for; to bestow careful
thought upon, to give painful attention to, be
earnest in,* 1 Tim 4:15; *to devise,* Acts 4:25; absol.
to study beforehand, premeditate, Mark 13:11 v.l.*

μελέτω   pres act imperative 3 sg
   [1C 7:21; v-1d(2c); 3508]   μέλει
μέλη   nom pl neut [12t; n-3d(2b); 3517]   μέλος
μέλη   acc pl neut [10t; n-3d(2b); 3517]   "

μέλι, ιτος, τό   {3510, n-3c(6d)}
   honey, Matt 3:4; Mark 1:6; Rev 10:9, 10*

μέλι   nom sg neut [3t; n-3c(6d); 3510]   μέλι
μέλι   acc sg neut [Mk 1:6; n-3c(6d); 3510]   "

μελίσσιος, ον   {3513, a-3a}
   of bees, made by bees, BAGD say the v.l. form in
   Luke 24:42 goes rather with μελισσ(ε)ῖον (3511,
   3512)*

Μελίτη, ης, ἡ   {3514, n-1b}
   also spelled Μελιτήνη, *Malta,* an island in the
   Mediterranean, Acts 28:1*

Μελίτη   nom sg fem [Ac 28:1; n-1b; 3514]   Μελίτη
μέλλει   pres act ind 3 sg
   [16t; v-1d(2c); 3516]   μέλλω
μέλλειν   pres act inf [6t; v-1d(2c); 3516]   "
μέλλεις   pres act ind 2 sg [4t; v-1d(2c); 3516]   "
μέλλετε   pres act ind 2 pl [2t; v-1d(2c); 3516]   "
μέλλῃ   pres act subj 3 sg [3t; v-1d(2c); 3516]   "
μελλήσετε   fut act ind 2 pl
   [Mt 24:6; v-1d(2c); 3516]   "
μελλήσω   fut act ind 1 sg
   [2P 1:12; v-1d(2c); 3516]   "
μέλλομεν   pres act ind 1 pl
   [1Th 3:4; v-1d(2c); 3516]   "
μέλλον   pres act ptcp acc sg neut
   [3t; v-1d(2c); 3516]   "
μέλλοντα   pres act ptcp nom pl neut
   [2t; v-1d(2c); 3516]   "
μέλλοντα   pres act ptcp acc sg masc
   [2t; v-1d(2c); 3516]   "
μέλλοντα   pres act ptcp acc pl neut
   [2t; v-1d(2c); 3516]   "
μέλλοντας   pres act ptcp acc pl masc
   [3t; v-1d(2c); 3516]   "
μέλλοντες   pres act ptcp nom pl masc
   [4t; v-1d(2c); 3516]   "
μέλλοντι   pres act ptcp dat sg masc
   [3t; v-1d(2c); 3516]   "
μέλλοντι   pres act ptcp dat sg neut
   [Ac 27:2; v-1d(2c); 3516]   "
μέλλοντος   pres act ptcp gen sg masc
   [4t; v-1d(2c); 3516]   "
μέλλοντος   pres act ptcp gen sg neut
   [2t; v-1d(2c); 3516]   "
μελλόντων   pres act ptcp gen pl masc
   [3t; v-1d(2c); 3516]   "
μελλόντων   pres act ptcp gen pl neut
   [5t; v-1d(2c); 3516]   "
μέλλουσαν   pres act ptcp acc sg fem
   [4t; v-1d(2c); 3516]   "
μελλούσης   pres act ptcp gen sg fem
   [6t; v-1d(2c); 3516]   "

μέλλουσιν   pres act ind 3 pl   [2t; v-1d(2c); 3516]   "

μέλλω   {3516, v-1d(2c)}
   [(ἔμελλον and ἤμελλον), μελλήσω, -, -, -, -] *to be
   about to, be on the point of,* Matt 2:13; John 4:47;
   it serves to express in general a settled futurity,
   Matt 11:14; Luke 9:31; John 11:51; *to intend,*
   Luke 10:1; participle μέλλων, μέλλουσα, μέλλον,
   future as distinguished from past and present,
   Matt 12:32; Luke 13:9; *to be always, as it were,
   about to do, to delay, linger,* Acts 22:16

μέλλω   pres act ind 1 sg [2t; v-1d(2c); 3516]   "
μέλλων   pres act ptcp nom sg masc
   [9t; v-1d(2c); 3516]   "

μέλος, ους, τό   {3517, n-3d(2b)}
   a member, limb, any part of the body, Matt 5:29, 30;
   Rom 12:4; 1 Cor 6:15; 12:12

μέλος   nom sg neut [5t; n-3d(2b); 3517]   μέλος

Μελχί, ὁ   {3518, n-3g(2)}
   Melchi, pr. name, indecl., Luke 3:24, 28*

Μελχί   indecl [2t; n-3g(2); 3518]   Μελχί

Μελχισέδεκ, ὁ   {3519, n-3g(2)}
   Melchisedek, pr. name, indecl., Heb 5:6, 10; 6:20;
   7:1, 10f., 15, 17*

Μελχισέδεκ   indecl [8t; n-3g(2); 3519]   Μελχισέδεκ
μελῶν   gen pl neut [2t; n-3d(2b); 3517]   μέλος
μεμαθηκώς   perf act ptcp nom sg masc
   [Jn 7:15; v-3a(2b); 3443]   μανθάνω
μεμαρτύρηκα   perf act ind 1 sg
   [Jn 1:34; v-1d(2a); 3455]   μαρτυρέω
μεμαρτύρηκας   perf act ind 2 sg
   [Jn 3:26; v-1d(2a); 3455]   "
μεμαρτύρηκεν   perf act ind 3 sg
   [5t; v-1d(2a); 3455]   "
μεμαρτύρηται   perf pass ind 3 sg
   [2t; v-1d(2a); 3455]   "

μεμβράνα, ης, ἡ   {3521, n-1c}
   parchment, vellum, 2 Tim 4:13*

μεμβράνας   acc pl fem
   [2Ti 4:13; n-1c; 3521]   μεμβράνα
μεμενήκεισαν   pluperf act ind 3 pl
   [1J 2:19; v-1c(2); 3531]   μένω
μεμέρισται   perf pass ind 3 sg
   [2t; v-2a(1); 3532]   μερίζω
μεμεστωμένοι   perf pass ptcp nom pl masc
   [Ac 2:13; v-1d(3); 3551]   μεστόω
μεμιαμμένοις   perf pass ptcp dat pl masc
   [Ti 1:15; v-2d(4); 3620]   μιαίνω
μεμίανται   perf pass ind 3 sg
   [Ti 1:15; v-2d(4); 3620]   "
μεμιγμένα   perf pass ptcp nom pl neut
   [Rv 8:7; v-3c(2); 3624]   μίγνυμι
μεμιγμένην   perf pass ptcp acc sg fem
   [Rv 15:2; v-3c(2); 3624]   "
μεμιγμένον   perf pass ptcp acc sg masc
   [Mt 27:34; v-3c(2); 3624]   "
μεμισήκασιν   perf act ind 3 pl
   [Jn 15:24; v-1d(2a); 3631]   μισέω
μεμίσηκεν   perf act ind 3 sg
   [Jn 15:18; v-1d(2a); 3631]   "

μεμισημένου perf pass ptcp gen sg neut
[Rv 18:2; v-1d(2a); 3631] "

μεμνημένος perf pass ptcp nom sg masc
[2Ti 1:4; v-5a; 3630] μιμνήσκομαι

μέμνησθε perf mid ind 2 pl
[1C 11:2; v-5a; 3630] "

μεμονωμένη perf pass ptcp nom sg fem
[1Ti 5:5; v-1d(3); 3670] μονόω

μεμύημαι perf pass ind 1 sg
[Pp 4:12; v-1d(2a); 3679] μυέω

μέμφεται pres mid ind 3 sg
[Rm 9:19; v-1b(1); 3522] μέμφομαι

μέμφομαι {3522, v-1b(1)}
[-, ἐμεμψάμην, -, -, -] to find fault with, blame,
censure; to intimate dissatisfaction with, Heb 8:8;
absol. to find fault, Rom 9:19; Mark 7:2 v.l.*

μεμφόμενος pres mid ptcp nom sg masc
[Hb 8:8; v-1b(1); 3522] "

μεμψίμοιροι nom pl masc
[Jd 16; a-3a; 3523] μεμψίμοιρος

μεμψίμοιρος, ον {3523, a-3a}
finding fault or being discontented with one's lot,
querulous; a discontented, querulous person, a
complainer, Jude 16*

μέμψις, εως, ή {3524, n-3e(5b)}
reason for complaint, Col 3:13 v.l.*

μέν {3525, particle}
a particle serving to indicate that the term or
clause with which it is used stands
distin–guished from another, usually in the
sequel, and then mostly with δέ correspondent,
Matt 3:11; 9:39; Acts 1:1; ὁ μὲν ... ὁ δέ, this ... that,
the one ... the other, Phil 1:16, 17; one ... another,
οἱ μὲν ... οἱ δέ, some ... others, Matt 22:5; ὃς μὲν ...
ὃς δέ, one ... another, pl. some ... others, Matt 13:8;
21:35; ἄλλος μέν ... ἄλλος δέ, one ... another, 1 Cor
15:39; ὧδε μὲν ... ἐκεῖ δέ, here ... there, Heb 7:8;
τοῦτο μὲν ... τοῦτο δέ, partly ... partly, Heb 10:33

μέν particle [179t; particle; 3525] μέν
μένε pres act imperative 2 sg
[2Ti 3:14; v-1c(2); 3531] μένω
μενεῖ fut act ind 3 sg [1C 3:14; v-1c(2); 3531] "
μένει pres act ind 3 sg [28t; v-1c(2); 3531] "
μένειν pres act inf [5t; v-1c(2); 3531] "
μένεις pres act ind 2 sg
[Jn 1:38; v-1c(2); 3531] "
μενεῖτε fut act ind 2 pl [2t; v-1c(2); 3531] "
μένετε pres act imperative 2 pl
[5t; v-1c(2); 3531] "
μένετε pres act ind 2 pl
[1J 2:27; v-1c(2); 3531] "
μενέτω pres act imperative 3 sg
[5t; v-1c(2); 3531] "
μένῃ pres act subj 3 sg [4t; v-1c(2); 3531] "
μένητε pres act subj 2 pl
[Jn 15:4; v-1c(2); 3531] "

Μεννά, ό {3527, n-3g(2)}
Menna, pr. name, indecl., Luke 3:31*

Μεννά indecl [Lk 3:31; n-3g(2); 3527] Μεννά

μένομεν pres act ind 1 pl
[1J 4:13; v-1c(2); 3531] μένω
μένον pres act ptcp nom sg neut
[2t; v-1c(2); 3531] "
μένον pres act ptcp acc sg neut
[Jn 1:33; v-1c(2); 3531] "
μένοντα pres act ptcp acc sg masc
[Jn 5:38; v-1c(2); 3531] "
μένοντος pres act ptcp gen sg masc
[1P 1:23; v-1c(2); 3531] "

μενοῦν, see μενοῦνγε

μενοῦν particle [Lk 11:28; particle; 3528] μενοῦν

μενοῦνγε {3529, particle}
also spelled as two words, μενοῦν γε, a
combination of particles serving to take up
what has just preceded, with either emphasize
or to correct; indeed, really, truly, rather, Luke
11:28; Rom 9:20; 10:18; Phil 3:8*

μενοῦνγε particle [3t; particle; 3529] μενοῦνγε
μένουσαν pres act ptcp acc sg fem
[5t; v-1c(2); 3531] μένω
μένουσιν pres act ind 3 pl [2t; v-1c(2); 3531] "

μέντοι {3530, particle}
truly, certainly, sure, Jude 4:27; Jude 8

μέντοι particle [8t; particle; 3530] μέντοι

μένω {3531, v-1c(2)}
[ἔμενον), μενῶ, ἔμεινα, μεμένηκα, -, -]
pluperfect, μεμενήκειν, to stay, Matt 26:38; Acts
27:31; to continue; 1 Cor 7:11; 2 Tim 2:13; to dwell,
lodge, sojourn, John 1:39; Acts 9:43; to remain,
John 9:41; to rest, settle, John 1:32, 33; 3:36; to
last, endure, Matt 11:23; John 6:27; 1 Cor 3:14; to
survive, 1 Cor 15:6; to be existent, 1 Cor 13:13; to
continue unchanged, Rom 9:11; to be permanent,
John 15:16; 2 Cor 3:11; Heb 10:34; 13:14; 1 Peter
1:23; to persevere, be constant, be steadfast, 1 Tim
2:15; 2 Tim 3:14; to abide, to be in close and settled
union, John 6:56; 14:10; 15:4; to indwell, John
5:38; 1 John 2:14; trans. to wait for, Acts 20:5, 23

μενῶ fut act ind 1 sg
[Pp 1:25; v-1c(2); 3531] μένω
μένω pres act ind 1 sg [Jn 15:10; v-1c(2); 3531] "
μένων pres act ptcp nom sg masc
[7t; v-1c(2); 3531] "
μέρει dat sg neut [3t; n-3d(2b); 3538] μέρος
μέρη acc pl neut [11t; n-3d(2b); 3538] "
μερίδα acc sg fem [2t; n-3c(2); 3535] μερίς
μερίδος gen sg fem [Ac 16:12; n-3c(2); 3535] "

μερίζω {3532, v-2a(1)}
[μεριῶ, ἐμέρισα, μεμέρικα, μεμέρισμαι,
ἐμερίσθην] to divide; to divide out, distribute,
Mark 6:41; to assign, bestow, Rom 12:3; 1 Cor
7:17; 2 Cor 10:13; Heb 7:2; mid. to share, Luke
12:13; pass. to be subdivided, to admit distinctions,
Mark 3:24-26; 1 Cor 1:13; to be severed by
discord, be at variance, Matt 12:25, 26; to differ, 1
Cor 7:34*

μέριμνα, ης, ή {3533, n-1c}
care, Matt 13:22; Mark 4:19; Luke 8:14; 21:34;
anxiety, anxious interest, 2 Cor 11:28; 1 Peter 5:7*

μέριμνα　nom sg fem [2t; n-1c; 3533]　　μέριμνα
μεριμνᾷ　pres act ind 3 sg
　　[4t; v-1d(1a); 3534]　　　　　　μεριμνάω
μέριμναι　nom pl fem [Mk 4:19; n-1c; 3533]　μέριμνα
μερίμναις　dat pl fem [Lk 21:34; n-1c; 3533]　"
μέριμναν　acc sg fem [1P 5:7; n-1c; 3533]　"
μεριμνᾷς　pres act ind 2 sg
　　[Lk 10:41; v-1d(1a); 3534]　　　μεριμνάω
μεριμνᾶτε　pres act imperative 2 pl
　　[3t; v-1d(1a); 3534]　　　　　　"
μεριμνᾶτε　pres act ind 2 pl [2t; v-1d(1a); 3534]　"

μεριμνάω　　　　　　　　{3534, v-1d(1a)}
　[μεριμνήσω, ἐμερίμνησα, -, -, -] to be anxious, or
　solicitous, Phil 4:6; to expend careful thought, Matt
　6:27, 28, 31, 34a; 10:19; Luke 10:41; 12:11, 22, 25,
　26; to concern one's self, Matt 6:25, 34b v.l.; 1 Cor
　12:25; to have the thoughts occupied with, 1 Cor
　7:32, 33, 34; to feel an interest in, Phil 2:20*

μεριμνήσει　fut act ind 3 sg [2t; v-1d(1a); 3534]　"
μεριμνήσητε　aor act subj 2 pl
　　[4t; v-1d(1a); 3534]　　　　　　"
μεριμνῶν　gen pl fem [Lk 8:14; n-1c; 3533]　μέριμνα
μεριμνῶν　pres act ptcp nom sg masc
　　[2t; v-1d(1a); 3534]　　　　　　μεριμνάω
μεριμνῶσιν　pres act subj 3 pl
　　[1C 12:25; v-1d(1a); 3534]　　　"

μερίς, ίδος, ἡ　　　　　　　{3535, n-3c(2)}
　a part; a division of a country, district, region,
　tract, Acts 16:12; a portion, Luke 10:42; an
　allotted portion, Col 1:12; a portion in common,
　share, Acts 8:21; 2 Cor 6:15*

μερίς　nom sg fem [2t; n-3c(2); 3535]　　μερίς
μερίσασθαι　aor mid inf
　　[Lk 12:13; v-2a(1); 3532]　　　μερίζω
μερισθεῖσα　aor pass ptcp nom sg fem
　　[2t; v-2a(1); 3532]　　　　　　"
μερισθῇ　aor pass subj 3 sg [2t; v-2a(1); 3532]　"
μερισμοῖς　dat pl masc
　　[Hb 2:4; n-2a; 3536]　　　　　μερισμός

μερισμός, οῦ, ὁ　　　　　　{3536, n-2a}
　a dividing, act of dividing, Heb 4:12; distribution,
　gifts distributed, Heb 2:4*

μερισμοῦ　gen sg masc [Hb 4:12; n-2a; 3536]　"
μεριστήν　acc sg masc
　　[Lk 12:14; n-1f; 3537]　　　　μεριστής

μεριστής, οῦ, ὁ　　　　　　{3537, n-1f}
　a divider, arbitrator, Luke 12:14*

μέρος, ους, τό　　　　　　{3538, n-3d(2b)}
　a part, portion, division, of a whole, Luke 11:36;
　15:12; Acts 5:2; Eph 4:16; a piece, fragment, Luke
　24:42; John 19:23; a party, faction, Acts 23:9;
　allotted portion, lot, destiny, Matt 24:51; Luke
　12:46; a calling, craft, Acts 19:27; a partner's
　portion, partnership, fellowship, John 13:8; pl.
　μέρη, a local quarter, district, region, Matt 2:22;
　16:13; Acts 19:1; Eph 4:9; side of a ship, John
　21:6; ἐν μέρει, in respect, 2 Cor 3:10; 9:3; Col 2:16;
　1 Peter 4:16; μέρος τι, partly, in some part, 1 Cor
　11:18; ἀνὰ μέρος, alternately, one after another, 1
　Cor 14:27; ἀπὸ μέρους, partly, in some part or

measure, 2 Cor 1:14; ἐκ μέρους, individually, 1
Cor 12:27; partly, imperfectly, 1 Cor 13:9; κατὰ
μέρος, particularly, in detail, Heb 9:5

μέρος　nom sg neut [2t; n-3d(2b); 3538]　　μέρος
μέρος　acc sg neut [14t; n-3d(2b); 3538]　　"
μέρους　gen sg neut [12t; n-3d(2b); 3538]　"

μεσάζω　　　　　　　　{3539, v-2a(1)}
　[-, -, -, -, -] to be in the middle, John 7:14 v.l.*

μεσημβρία, ας, ἡ　　　　　{3540, n-1a}
　mid-day, noon, Acts 22:6; meton. the south, Acts
　8:26*

μεσημβρίαν　acc sg fem [2t; n-1a; 3540]　μεσημβρία
μέσης　gen sg fem [2t; a-1a(2a); 3545]　　μέσος

μεσιτεύω　　　　　　　　{3541, v-1a(6)}
　[-, ἐμεσίτευσα, -, -, -] to perform offices between
　two parties; to intervene, interpose, Heb 6:17*

μεσίτῃ　dat sg masc
　　[Hb 12:24; n-1f; 3542]　　　　μεσίτης

μεσίτης, ου, ὁ　　　　　　{3542, n-1f}
　one that acts between two parties; a mediator, one
　who interposes to reconcile two adverse parties, 1
　Tim 2:5; an arbitrator, one who is the medium of
　communication between two parties, a mid-party,
　Gal 3:19, 20; Heb 8:6; 9:15; 12:24*

μεσίτης　nom sg masc [4t; n-1f; 3542]　　"
μεσίτου　gen sg masc [Ga 3:19; n-1f; 3542]　"
μέσον　acc sg neut, can function as an adverb
　　and an improper prep
　　[16t; a-1a(2a); 3545]　　　　　μέσος

μεσονύκτιον, ου, τό　　　　{3543, n-2c}
　midnight, Luke 11:5, Mark 13:35; Luke 11:5;
　Acts 16:25; 20:7*

μεσονύκτιον　acc sg neut
　　[2t; n-2c; 3543]　　　　　　μεσονύκτιον
μεσονυκτίου　gen sg neut [2t; n-2c; 3543]　"

Μεσοποταμία, ας, ἡ　　　　{3544, n-1a}
　Mesopotamia, the country lying between the
　rivers Tigris and Euphrates, Acts 2:9; 7:2*

Μεσοποταμίᾳ　dat sg fem
　　[Ac 7:2; n-1a; 3544]　　　　　Μεσοποταμία
Μεσοποταμίαν　acc sg fem [Ac 2:9; n-1a; 3544]　"

μέσος, η, ον　　　　　　{3545, a-1a(2a)}
　mid, middle, Matt 25:6; Acts 26:13; τὸ μέσον, the
　middle, the midst, Matt 14:24 v.l.; ἀνὰ μέσον, in
　the midst; from the Hebrew, in, among, Matt
　13:25; between, 1 Cor 6:5; διὰ μέσου, through the
　midst of, Luke 4:30; εἰς τὸ μέσον, into, or in the
　midst, Mark 3:3; Luke 6:8; ἐκ μέσου, from the
　midst, out of the way, Col 2:14; 2 Thess 2:7; from
　the Hebrew, from, from among, Matt 13:49; ἐν τῷ
　μέσῳ, in the midst, Matt 10:16; in the midst, in
　public, publicly, Matt 14:6 ἐν μέσῳ, in the midst of;
　among, Matt 18:20; κατὰ μέσον τῆς νυκτός, about
　midnight, Acts 27:27

μέσος　nom sg masc [3t; a-1a(2a); 3545]　　μέσος

μεσότοιχον, ου, τό　　　　{3546, n-2c}
　a middle wall; a partition wall, a barrier, Eph 2:14*

μεσότοιχον   acc sg neut
   [Ep 2:14; n-2c; 3546]   μεσότοιχον
μέσου   gen sg neut [8t; a-1a(2a); 3545]   μέσος

μεσουράνημα, ατος, τό   {3547, n-3c(4)}
   the mid-heaven, mid-air, Rev 8:13; 14:6; 19:17*

μεσουρανήματι   dat sg neut
   [3t; n-3c(4); 3547]   μεσουράνημα
μεσούσης   pres act ptcp gen sg fem
   [Jn 7:14; v-1d(3); 3548]   μεσόω

μεσόω   {3548, v-1d(3)}
   [-, -, -, -, -] *to be in the middle* or *midst; to be
   advanced midway,* John 7:14*

Μεσσίαν   acc sg masc [Jn 1:41; n-1d; 3549] Μεσσίας

Μεσσίας, ου, ὁ   {3549, n-1d}
   the Messiah, the Anointed One, i.q. ὁ Χριστός,
   John 1:42, 4:25*

Μεσσίας   nom sg masc [Jn 4:25; n-1d; 3549]   "
μεστή   nom sg fem [2t; a-1a(2a); 3550]   μεστός
μεστοί   nom pl masc [2t; a-1a(2a); 3550]   "
μεστόν   nom sg neut [Jn 19:29; a-1a(2a); 3550]   "
μεστόν   acc sg masc [Jn 19:29; a-1a(2a); 3550]   "
μεστόν   acc sg neut [Jn 21:11; a-1a(2a); 3550]   "

μεστός, ή, όν   {3550, a-1a(2a)}
   full, full of, filled with, John 19:29; 21:11; *replete,*
   Matt 23:28; Rom 1:29; 15:14; James 3:8, 17; 2
   Peter 2:14*

μεστούς   acc pl masc [2t; a-1a(2a); 3550]

μεστόω   {3551, v-1d(3)}
   [-, -, -, μεμέστωμαι, -] *to fill;* pass. *to be filled, be
   full,* Acts 2:13*

μέσῳ   dat sg neut [29t; a-1a(2a); 3545]   μέσος
μετ᾽   prep-acc [5t; prep; 3552]   μετά
μετ᾽   prep-gen [126t; prep; 3552]   "

μετά   {3552, prep}
   (1) gen., *with, together with,* Matt 16:27; 12:41;
   26:55; *with, on the same side* or *party with, in aid
   of,* Matt 12:30; 20:20; *with, by means of,* Acts
   13:17; *with,* of conflict, Rev 11:7; *with, among,*
   Luke 24:5; *with, to, towards,* Luke 1:58, 72; (2)
   acc., *after,* of place, *behind,* Heb 9:3; of time, *after,*
   Matt 17:1; 24:29; followed by an infin. with the
   neut. article, *after, after that,* Matt 26:32; Luke
   22:20

μετά   prep-gen [198t; prep; 3552]   "
μετά   prep-acc [97t; prep; 3552]   "
μετάβα   aor act imperative 2 sg
   [Mt 17:20; cv-2d(6); 3553]   μεταβαίνω
μεταβαίνετε   pres act imperative 2 pl
   [Lk 10:7; cv-2d(6); 3553]   "

μεταβαίνω   {3553, cv-2d(6)}
   [μεταβήσομαι, μετέβην, μεταβέβηκα, -, -] *to go* or
   pass from one place to another, John 5:24; *to pass
   away, be removed,* Matt 17:20; *to go away, depart,*
   Matt 8:34

μεταβάλλω   {3554, cv-2d(1)}
   [-, μετέβαλον, -, -, -] *to change;* mid. *to change
   one's mind,* Acts 28:6*

μεταβαλόμενοι   aor mid ptcp nom pl masc
   [Ac 28:6; cv-2d(1); 3554]   μεταβάλλω
μεταβάς   aor act ptcp nom sg masc
   [3t; cv-2d(6); 3553]   μεταβαίνω
μεταβεβήκαμεν   perf act ind 1 pl
   [1J 3:14; cv-2d(6); 3553]   "
μεταβέβηκεν   perf act ind 3 sg
   [Jn 5:24; cv-2d(6); 3553]   "
μεταβῇ   aor act subj 3 sg [2t; cv-2d(6); 3553]   "
μετάβηθι   aor act imperative 2 sg
   [Jn 7:3; cv-2d(6); 3553]   "
μεταβήσεται   fut mid ind 3 sg
   [Mt 17:20; cv-2d(6); 3553]   "
μετάγεται   pres pass ind 3 sg
   [Jm 3:4; cv-1b(2); 3555]   μετάγω
μετάγομεν   pres act ind 1 pl
   [Jm 3:3; cv-1b(2); 3555]   "

μετάγω   {3555, cv-1b(2)}
   [-, μετήγαγον -, -, -] *to lead* or *move from one place
   to another; to change direction, turn about,* James
   3:3, 4; pass., *be brought back,* Acts 7:16 v.l.*

μεταδιδόναι   pres act inf
   [Ep 4:28; cv-6a; 3556]   μεταδίδωμι
μεταδιδούς   pres act ptcp nom sg masc
   [Rm 12:8; cv-6a; 3556]   "

μεταδίδωμι   {3556, cv-6a}
   [-, μετέδωκα, -, -, -] *to give a part, to share,* Luke
   3:11; *to impart, bestow,* Rom 1:11; 12:8; Eph 4:28;
   1 Thess 2:8*

μεταδότω   aor act imperative 3 sg
   [Lk 3:11; cv-6a; 3556]   "
μεταδοῦναι   aor act inf [1Th 2:8; cv-6a; 3556]   "
μεταδῶ   aor act subj 1 sg [Rm 1:11; cv-6a; 3556]   "
μεταθέσεως   gen sg fem
   [Hb 11:5; n-3e(5b); 3557]   μετάθεσις
μετάθεσιν   acc sg fem [Hb 12:27; n-3e(5b); 3557]   "

μετάθεσις, εως, ἡ   {3557, n-3e(5b)}
   a removal, translation, Heb 11:5; 12:27; *a
   transmutation, change by the abolition of one thing,
   and the substitution of another,* Heb 7:12*

μετάθεσις   nom sg fem [Hb 7:12; n-3e(5b); 3557]   "

μεταίρω   {3558, cv-3a(2b)}
   [-, μετῆρα, -, -, -] *to remove, transfer;* in N.T.
   intrans. *to go away, depart,* Matt 13:53; 19:1*

μετακάλεσαι   aor mid imperative 2 sg
   [Ac 10:32; cv-1d(2b); 3559]   μετακαλέω
μετακαλέσομαι   fut mid ind 1 sg
   [Ac 24:25; cv-1d(2b); 3559]   "

μετακαλέω   {3559, cv-1d(2b)}
   [μετακαλέσω, μετεκάλεσα, -, -, -] *to call from one
   place into another;* mid. *to call* or *send for, invite to
   come to oneself,* Acts 7:14; 10:32; 20:17; 24:25*

μετακινέω   {3560, cv-1d(2a)}
   [-, -, -, -, -] *to move away, remove;* pass. met. *to stir
   away from, to swerve,* Col 1:23*

μετακινούμενοι   pres pass ptcp nom pl masc
   [Cl 1:23; cv-1d(2a); 3560]   μετακινέω
μεταλαβεῖν   aor act inf
   [3t; cv-3a(2b); 3561]   μεταλαμβάνω

μεταλαβών   aor act ptcp nom sg masc
  [Ac 24:25; cv-3a(2b); 3561]   "
μεταλαμβάνει   pres act ind 3 sg
  [Hb 6:7; cv-3a(2b); 3561]   "
μεταλαμβάνειν   pres act inf
  [2Ti 2:6; cv-3a(2b); 3561]   "

μεταλαμβάνω   {3561, cv-3a(2b)}
  [(μετελάμβανον), -, μετέλαβον, μετείληφα, -, -] *to
  partake of , share in, Acts 2:46; 27:33f.; 2 Tim 2:6;
  Heb 6:7; 12:10; to get, obtain, find, Acts 24:25*

μετάλημψιν   acc sg fem
  [1Ti 4:3; n-3e(5b); 3562]   μετάλημψις

μετάλημψις, εως, ἡ   {3562, n-3e(5b)}
  a partaking of, a being partaken of, 1 Tim 4:3

μεταλλάσσω   {3563, cv-2b}
  [-, μετήλλαξα, -, -, -] *to exchange, change for* or
  into, transmute, Rom 1:25, 26

μεταμεληθείς   aor pass ptcp nom sg masc
  [2t; cv-1d(2c); 3564]   μεταμέλομαι
μεταμεληθήσεται   fut pass ind 3 sg
  [Hb 7:21; cv-1d(2c); 3564]   "

μεταμέλομαι   {3564, cv-1d(2c)}
  [(μετεμελόμην), -, -, -, -, μετεμελήθην] *to change
  one's judgment on past points of conduct; to change
  one's mind and purpose, Heb 7:21; to repent,
  regret, Matt 21:29, 32; 27:3; 2 Cor 7:8*

μεταμέλομαι   pres pass ind 1 sg
  [2C 7:8; cv-1d(2c); 3564]   "
μεταμορφούμεθα   pres pass ind 1 pl
  [2C 3:18; cv-1d(3); 3565]   μεταμορφόω
μεταμορφοῦσθε   pres pass imperative 2 pl
  [Rm 12:2; cv-1d(3); 3565]   "

μεταμορφόω   {3565, cv-1d(3)}
  [-, -, -, μεταμεμόρφωμαι, μετεμορφώθην] *to change
  the external form, transfigure; mid. to change one's
  form, be transfigured, Matt 17:2; Mark 9:2; to
  undergo a spiritual transformation Rom 12:2; 2
  Cor 3:18*

μετανοεῖν   pres act inf
  [2t; cv-1d(2a); 3566]   μετανοέω
μετανοεῖτε   pres act imperative 2 pl
  [3t; cv-1d(2a); 3566]   "

μετανοέω   {3566, cv-1d(2a)}
  [μετανοήσω, μετενόησα, -, -, -] *to undergo a
  change in frame of mind and feeling, to repent,
  Luke 17:3, 4; to make a change of principle and
  practice, to reform, Matt 3:2*

μετανοῆσαι   aor act inf
  [Rv 2:21; cv-1d(2a); 3566]   "
μετανοησάντων   aor act ptcp gen pl masc
  [2C 12:21; cv-1d(2a); 3566]   "
μετανοήσατε   aor act imperative 2 pl
  [2t; cv-1d(2a); 3566]   "
μετανοήσῃ   aor act subj 3 sg
  [2t; cv-1d(2a); 3566]   "
μετανοήσῃς   aor act subj 2 sg
  [Rv 2:5; cv-1d(2a); 3566]   "
μετανόησον   aor act imperative 2 sg
  [5t; cv-1d(2a); 3566]   "

μετανοήσουσιν   fut act ind 3 pl
  [Lk 16:30; cv-1d(2a); 3566]   "
μετανοήσωσιν   aor act subj 3 pl
  [Rv 2:22; cv-1d(2a); 3566]   "
μετανοῆτε   pres act subj 2 pl
  [2t; cv-1d(2a); 3566]   "

μετάνοια, ας, ἡ   {3567, n-1a}
  a change of mode of thought and feeling, repentance,
  Matt 3:8; Acts 20:21; 2 Tim 2:25; practical
  reformation, Luke 15:7; *reversal* of the past, Heb
  12:17

μετάνοιαν   acc sg fem [12t; n-1a; 3567]   μετάνοια
μετανοίας   gen sg fem [10t; n-1a; 3567]   "
μετανοοῦντι   pres act ptcp dat sg masc
  [2t; cv-1d(2a); 3566]   μετανοέω
μετανοῶ   pres act ind 1 sg
  [Lk 17:4; cv-1d(2a); 3566]   "
μετανοῶσιν   pres act subj 3 pl
  [Mk 6:12; cv-1d(2a); 3566]   "

μεταξύ   {3568, adverb}
  can function as an improper prep., *between,*
  Matt 23:35; Luke 11:51; 16:26; Acts 15:9; ἐν τῷ
  μεταξύ, sc. χρόνῳ, *in the meantime, meanwhile,*
  John 4:31; in N.T. ὁ μεταξύ, *following, succeeding,*
  Acts 13:42

μεταξύ   adverb [9t; adverb; 3568]   μεταξύ
μεταπεμπόμενος   pres mid ptcp nom sg masc
  [Ac 24:26; cv-1b(1); 3569]   μεταπέμπω

μεταπέμπω   {3569, cv-1b(1)}
  [-, μετέπεμψα, -, -, μετεπέμφθην] *to send after;*
  mid. *to send after* or *for* any one, *invite to come to
  one's self,* Acts 10:5, 22, 29; 11:13; 20:1; 24:24, 26;
  25:3*

μεταπεμφθείς   aor pass ptcp nom sg masc
  [Ac 10:29; cv-1b(1); 3569]   "
μετάπεμψαι   aor mid imperative 2 sg
  [2t; cv-1b(1); 3569]   "
μεταπεμψάμενος   aor mid ptcp nom sg masc
  [Ac 20:1; cv-1b(1); 3569]   "
μεταπέμψασθαι   aor mid inf
  [Ac 10:22; cv-1b(1); 3569]   "
μεταπέμψηται   aor mid subj 3 sg
  [Ac 25:3; cv-1b(1); 3569]   "
μετασταθῶ   aor pass subj 1 sg
  [Lk 16:4; cv-6a; 3496]   μεθίστημι
μεταστήσας   aor act ptcp nom sg masc
  [Ac 13:22; cv-6a; 3496]   "
μεταστραφήσεται   fut pass ind 3 sg
  [Ac 2:20; cv-1b(1); 3570]   μεταστρέφω

μεταστρέφω   {3570, cv-1b(1)}
  [-, μετέστρεψα, -, -, μετεστράφην] *to turn about;*
  convert into something else, *change,* Acts 2:20;
  James 4:9 v.l.; by impl. *to pervert,* Gal 1:7*

μεταστρέψαι   aor act inf
  [Ga 1:7; cv-1b(1); 3570]   "
μετασχηματίζεται   pres mid ind 3 sg
  [2C 11:14; cv-2a(1); 3571]   μετασχηματίζω
μετασχηματιζόμενοι   pres mid ptcp nom pl masc
  [2C 11:13; cv-2a(1); 3571]   "

μετασχηματίζονται   pres mid ind 3 pl
[2C 11:15; cv-2a(1); 3571]   "

μετασχηματίζω   {3571, cv-2a(1)}
[μετασχηματίσω, μετεσχημάτισα, -, -, -] *to remodel, transfigure,* Phil 3:21; mid. *to transform one's self,* 2 Cor 11:13, 14, 15; *to transfer* an imagination, 1 Cor 4:6*

μετασχηματίσει   fut act ind 3 sg
[Pp 3:21; cv-2a(1); 3571]   "

μετατιθεμένης   pres pass ptcp gen sg fem
[Hb 7:12; cv-6a; 3572]   μετατίθημι

μετατιθέντες   pres act ptcp nom pl masc
[Jd 4; cv-6a; 3572]   "

μετατίθεσθε   pres mid ind 2 pl
[Ga 1:6; cv-6a; 3572]

μετατίθημι   {3572, cv-6a}
[-, μετέθηκα, -, -, μετετέθην] *to transport,* Acts 7:16; *to transfer,* Heb 7:12; *to translate* out of the world, Heb 11:5; met. *to transfer* to other purposes, *to pervert,* Jude 4; mid. *to transfer one's self, to change over,* Gal 1:6*

μετατραπήτω   aor pass imperative 3 sg
[Jm 4:9; cv-1b(1); 3573]   μετατρέπω

μετατρέπω   {3573, cv-1b(1)}
[-, -, -, -, μετετράπην] *to turn around, change, alter,* James 4:9*

μεταφυτεύω   {3574, cv-1a(6)}
[-, -, -, -, μεταφυτεύθητι] *transplant,* Luke 17:6 v.l.*

μετέβη   aor act ind 3 sg
[Mt 11:1; cv-2d(6); 3553]   μεταβαίνω

μετέθηκεν   aor act ind 3 sg
[Hb 11:5; cv-6a; 3572]   μετατίθημι

μετεκαλέσατο   aor mid ind 3 sg
[2t; cv-1d(2b); 3559]   μετακαλέω

μετελάμβανον   imperf act ind 3 pl
[Ac 2:46; cv-3a(2b); 3561]   μεταλαμβάνω

μετεμελήθητε   aor pass ind 2 pl
[Mt 21:32; cv-1d(2c); 3564]   μεταμέλομαι

μετεμελόμην   imperf pass ind 1 sg
[2C 7:8; cv-1d(2c); 3564]   "

μετεμορφώθη   aor pass ind 3 sg
[2t; cv-1d(3); 3565]   μεταμορφόω

μετενόησαν   aor act ind 3 pl
[9t; cv-1d(2a); 3566]   μετανοέω

μετέπειτα   {3575, adverb}
afterwards, Heb 12:17*

μετέπειτα   adverb
[Hb 12:17; adverb; 3575]   μετέπειτα

μετεπέμψασθε   aor mid ind 2 pl
[Ac 10:29; cv-1b(1); 3569]   μεταπέμπω

μετεπέμψατο   aor mid ind 3 sg
[Ac 24:24; cv-1b(1); 3569]   "

μετέστησεν   aor act ind 3 sg
[2t; cv-6a; 3496]   μεθίστημι

μετέσχεν   aor act ind 3 sg
[Hb 2:14; cv-1b(2); 3576]   μετέχω

μετέσχηκεν   perf act ind 3 sg
[Hb 7:13; cv-1b(2); 3576]   "

μετεσχημάτισα   aor act ind 1 sg
[1C 4:6; cv-2a(1); 3571]   μετασχηματίζω

μετετέθη   aor pass ind 3 sg
[Hb 11:5; cv-6a; 3572]   μετατίθημι

μετετέθησαν   aor pass ind 3 pl
[Ac 7:16; cv-6a; 3572]   "

μετέχειν   pres act inf
[2t; cv-1b(2); 3576]   μετέχω

μετέχομεν   pres act ind 1 pl
[1C 10:17; cv-1b(2); 3576]   "

μετέχουσιν   pres act ind 3 pl
[1C 9:12; cv-1b(2); 3576]   "

μετέχω   {3576, cv-1b(2)}
[-, μετέσχον, μετέσχηκα, -, -] *to share in, partake,* 1 Cor 9:10, 12; 10:17, 21; 1 Cor 10:30; Heb 2:14; 5:13; *to be a member of,* Heb 7:13; Luke 1:34 v.l.*

μετέχω   pres act ind 1 sg
[1C 10:30; cv-1b(2); 3576]   "

μετέχων   pres act ptcp nom sg masc
[Hb 5:13; cv-1b(2); 3576]   "

μετεωρίζεσθε   pres pass imperative 2 pl
[Lk 12:29; cv-2a(1); 3577]   μετεωρίζομαι

μετεωρίζομαι   {3577, cv-2a(1)}
[-, -, -, -, -] *to raise aloft;* met. *to unsettle in mind;* pass. *to be excited with anxiety, be in anxious suspense,* Luke 12:29*

μετήλλαξαν   aor act ind 3 pl
[2t; cv-2b; 3563]   μεταλλάσσω

μετῆρεν   aor act ind 3 sg
[2t; cv-3a(2b); 3558]   μεταίρω

μετοικεσία, ας, ἡ   {3578, n-1a}
change of abode or *country, migration,* Matt 1:11, 12, 17*

μετοικεσίαν   acc sg fem
[Mt 1:12; n-1a; 3578]   μετοικεσία

μετοικεσίας   gen sg fem [3t; n-1a; 3578]   "

μετοικίζω   {3579, v-2a(1)}
[μετοικιῶ, μετῴκισα, -, -, -] *to cause to change abode, cause to emigrate,* Acts 7:4, 43 v.l.*

μετοικιῶ   fut act ind 1 sg
[Ac 7:43; v-2a(1); 3579]   μετοικίζω

μετοχή, ῆς, ἡ   {3580, n-1b}
a sharing, partaking; communion, fellowship, 2 Cor 6:14*

μετοχή   nom sg fem [2C 6:14; n-1b; 3580]   μετοχή
μέτοχοι   nom pl masc [2t; a-3a; 3581]   μέτοχος
μέτοχοι   voc pl masc [Hb 3:1; a-3a; 3581]   "
μετόχοις   dat pl masc [Lk 5:7; a-3a; 3581]   "

μέτοχος, ον   {3581, a-3a}
a partaker, Heb 3:1, 14; 6:4; 12:8; *an associate, partner, fellow,* Luke 5:7; Heb 1:9*

μετόχους   acc pl masc [2t; a-3a; 3581]
μετρεῖτε   pres act ind 2 pl
[3t; v-1d(2a); 3582]   μετρέω

μετρέω   {3582, v-1d(2a)}
[-, ἐμέτρησα, -, -, ἐμετρήθην] *to allot, measure,* Matt 7:2; Mark 4:24; Luke 6:38; Rev 11:1, 2; 21:15-17; met. *to estimate,* 2 Cor 10:12*

μετρηθήσεται   fut pass ind 3 sg
[2t; v-1d(2a); 3582]   "

μετρήσῃ   aor act subj 3 sg
[Rv 21:15; v-1d(2a); 3582]   "

μετρήσης   aor act subj 2 sg
[Rv 11:2; v-1d(2a); 3582]   "

μέτρησον   aor act imperative 2 sg
[Rv 11:1; v-1d(2a); 3582]   "

μετρητάς   acc pl masc
[Jn 2:6; n-1f; 3583]   μετρητής

μετρητής, οῦ, ὁ   {3583, n-1f}
pr. *a measurer*; also, *metretes*, Latin *metreta*,
equivalent to the Attic ἀμφορεύς, i.e.,
three-fourths of the Attic μέδιμνος, and
therefore equal to about nine gallons, John 2:6*

μετριοπαθεῖν   pres act inf
[Hb 5:2; cv-1d(2a); 3584]   μετριοπαθέω

μετριοπαθέω   {3584, cv-1d(2a)}
[-, -, -, -, -] *to moderate one's passions; to be gentle,
compassionate,* Heb 5:2*

μετρίως   {3585, adverb}
moderately; slightly; οὐ μετρίως *no little, not a
little, much, greatly,* Acts 20:12*

μετρίως   adverb [Ac 20:12; adverb; 3585]   μετρίως

μέτρον, ου, τό   {3586, n-2c}
measure, Matt 7:2; Mark 4:24; Luke 6:38; Rev
21:17; *measure, standard,* Eph 4:13; *extent,
compass,* 2 Cor 10:13; allotted *measure, specific
portion,* Rom 12:3; Eph 4:7, 16; ἐκ μέτρον, *by
measure, with definite limitation,* John 3:34

μέτρον   acc sg neut [8t; n-2c; 3586]   μέτρον
μέτρου   gen sg neut [2t; n-2c; 3586]   "
μετροῦντες   pres act ptcp nom pl masc
[2C 10:12; v-1d(2a); 3582]   μετρέω
μέτρῳ   dat sg neut [4t; n-2c; 3586]   μέτρον
μετῴκισεν   aor act ind 3 sg
[Ac 7:4; v-2a(1); 3579]   μετοικίζω

μέτωπον, ου, τό   {3587, n-2c}
forehead, front, Rev 7:3; 9:4; 14:1, 9; 22:4; Luke
23:48 v.l.*

μέτωπον   acc sg neut [3t; n-2c; 3587]   μέτωπον
μετώπου   gen sg neut [Rv 14:9; n-2c; 3587]   "
μετώπων   gen pl neut [4t; n-2c; 3587]   "

μέχρι   {3588, prep}
improper prep. and a conj (*until*), also spelled
μέχρις, *unto, even to,* Rom 15:19; Heb 3:6 v.l.; *of
time, until, till,* Matt 11:23; Mark 13:30

μέχρι   prep [14t; prep; 3588]   μέχρι

μέχρις see μέχρι   {3589, prep}

μέχρις   prep [3t; prep; 3588]   "

μή   {3590, particle}
a negative particle, can function as a conj, *not,*
for the particulars of its usage, especially as
distinguished from that of οὐ, consult a
grammar; as a conj., *lest, that not,* Matt 5:29, 30;
18:10; 24:6; Mark 13:36; μή, or μήτι, or μήποτε,
prefixed to an interrogative clause, is a mark of
tone, since it expresses an intimation either of

the reality of the matters respecting which the
question is asked, Matt 12:23; or the contrary,
John 4:12

μή   particle [1042t; particle; 3590]   μή

μήγε   {3591, particle}
a strengthened form for μή, Matt 6:1; 9:17

μηδ'   part [1P 5:3; particle; 3593]   μηδέ

μηδαμῶς   {3592, adverb}
by no means, Acts 10:14; 11:8*

μηδαμῶς   adverb [2t; adverb; 3592]   μηδαμῶς

μηδέ   {3593, particle}
negative disjunctive particle, can function as
an adverb and a conj, *neither,* and repeated,
neither-nor, Matt 6:25; 7:6; 10:9, 10; *not even, not
so much as,* Mark 2:2

μηδέ   particle [55t; particle; 3593]   μηδέ

μηδείς, μηδεμία, μηδέν   {3594, a-4b(2)}
not one, none, no one, Matt 8:4

μηδείς   nom sg masc [15t; a-4b(2); 3594]   μηδείς
μηδεμίαν   acc sg fem [7t; a-4b(2); 3594]   "
μηδέν   nom sg neut [4t; a-4b(2); 3594]   "
μηδέν   acc sg neut, can function as an
adverb [31t; a-4b(2); 3594]   "
μηδένα   acc sg masc [8t; a-4b(2); 3594]   "
μηδενί   dat sg masc [17t; a-4b(2); 3594]   "
μηδενί   dat sg neut [4t; a-4b(2); 3594]   "
μηδενός   gen sg neut [3t; a-4b(2); 3594]   "

μηδέποτε   {3595, adverb}
not at any time, never, 2 Tim 3:7*

μηδέποτε   adverb [2Ti 3:7; adverb; 3595]   μηδέποτε

μηδέπω   {3596, adverb}
not yet, not as yet, Heb 11:7*

μηδέπω   adverb [Hb 11:7; adverb; 3596]   μηδέπω
Μῆδοι   nom pl masc [Ac 2:9; n-2a; 3597]   Μῆδος

Μῆδος, ου, ὁ   {3597, n-2a}
a Mede, a native of Media in Asia, Acts 2:9*

μηθέν   acc sg neut
[Ac 27:33; a-4b(2); 3594]   μηδείς

μηκέτι   {3600, adverb}
no more, no longer, Mark 1:45; 2:2

μηκέτι   adverb [22t; adverb; 3600]   μηκέτι

μῆκος, ους, τό   {3601, n-3d(2b)}
length, Eph 3:18; Rev 21:16*

μῆκος   nom sg neut [3t; n-3d(2b); 3601]   μῆκος
μηκύνηται   pres pass subj 3 sg
[Mk 4:27; v-1c(2); 3602]   μηκύνω

μηκύνω   {3602, v-1c(2)}
[-, -, -, -, -] *to lengthen, prolong;* mid. *to grow up,*
as plants, Mark 4:27*

μηλωταῖς   dat pl fem [Hb 11:37; n-1b; 3603]   μηλωτή

μηλωτή, ῆς, ἡ   {3603, n-1b}
a sheepskin, Heb 11:37*

μήν, μηνός, ὁ   {3604, n-3f(1a)}
a month, Luke 1:24, 26, 36, 56; in N.T. *the new moon, the day of the new moon*, Gal 4:10

μήν   nom sg masc [2t; n-3f(1a); 3604]   μήν

μήν   {3605, particle}
used in conjunction with other particles. (1) εἰ μήν, used in oaths meaning *surely, certainly*, Heb 6:14. (2) καὶ μήν, *and yet, indeed*. (3) μήτε μήν, *not even*

μήν   part [Hb 6:14; particle; 3605]   μήν
μῆνα   acc sg masc [2t; n-3f(1a); 3604]   μήν
μῆνας   acc pl masc [14t; n-3f(1a); 3604]   "
μηνί   dat sg masc [Lk 1:26; n-3f(1a); 3604]   "
μηνυθείσης   aor pass ptcp gen sg fem
     [Ac 23:30; v-1a(4); 3606]   μηνύω
μηνύσαντα   aor act ptcp acc sg masc
     [1C 10:28; v-1a(4); 3606]   "
μηνύσῃ   aor act subj 3 sg
     [Jn 11:57; v-1a(4); 3606]   "

μηνύω   {3606, v-1a(4)}
[-, ἐμήνυσα, μεμήνυκα, -, ἐμηνύθην] *to disclose* what is secret, John 11:57; Acts 23:30; 1 Cor 10:28; *to declare, indicate*, Luke 20:37*

μήποτε   {3607, particle}
can function as an adverb, *BAGD* list it as a negative part., conj., and interrogative part., same signif. and usage as μή, Heb 9:17; Matt 4:6; 13:15; also, *whether*, Luke 3:15

μήποτε   particle [25t; particle; 3607]   μήποτε

μήπου   {3608, conj}
also written μή που, *that ... somewhere, that*, Acts 27:29*

μήπω   {3609, adverb}
not yet, not as yet, Rom 9:11; Heb 9:8*

μήπω   adverb [2t; adverb; 3609]   μήπω

μήπως   {3610, conj}
written in our texts as two words, μή πως, *lest in any way* or *means, that in no way*, Acts 27:29; Rom 11:21; 1 Cor 8:9; 9:27; *whether perhaps*, 1 Thess 3:5

μηρόν   acc sg masc [Rv 19:16; n-2a; 3611]   μηρός

μηρός, οῦ, ὁ   {3611, n-2a}
the thigh, Rev 19:16*

μήτε   {3612, conj}
neither; μήτε ... μήτε, or μή ... μήτε, or μηδὲ ... μήτε, *neither ... nor*, Matt 5:34, 35, 36; Acts 23:8; 2 Thess 2:2; in N.T. also equivalent to μηδέ, *not even, not so much as*, Mark 3:20

μήτε   conj [34t; conj; 3612]   μήτε
μητέρα   acc sg fem [26t; n-3f(2c); 3613]   μήτηρ
μητέρας   acc pl fem [2t; n-3f(2c); 3613]   "

μήτηρ, μητρός, ἡ   {3613, n-3f(2c)}
a mother, Matt 1:18; 12:49, 50, et al. freq.; *a parent city*, Gal 4:26; Rev 17:5

μήτηρ   nom sg fem [32t; n-3f(2c); 3613]   "

μήτι   {3614, particle}
interrogative particle, used in questions

expecting a negative answer; has the same use as μή in the form εἰ μήτε, Luke 9:3; also when prefixed to an interrogative clause, Matt 7:16; John 4:29

μήτι   particle [18t; particle; 3614]   μήτι

μήτιγε   {3615}
written in our texts as two words, μήτι γε, *surely then, much more then*, 1 Cor 6:3*

μήτρα, ας, ἡ   {3616, n-1a}
the womb, Luke 2:23; Rom 4:19*

μητραλῴας, ου, ὁ   {3617, n-1d}
also spelled μητρολῴας, *a strike* or *murderer of his mother, matricide*, 1 Tim 1:9*

μήτραν   acc sg fem [Lk 2:23; n-1a; 3616]   μήτρα
μήτρας   gen sg fem [Rm 4:19; n-1a; 3616]   "
μητρί   dat sg fem [11t; n-3f(2c); 3613]   μήτηρ
μητρολῴαις   dat pl masc
     [1Ti 1:9; n-1d; 3618]   μητρολῴας

μητρόπολις, εως, ἡ   {3619, n-3e(5b)}
a metropolis, chief city, in the subscription to 1 Tim*

μητρός   gen sg fem [12t; n-3f(2c); 3613]   μήτηρ
μία   nom sg fem [17t; a-4b(2); 1651]   εἷς
μιᾷ   dat sg fem [18t; a-4b(2); 1651]   "
μιαίνουσιν   pres act ind 3 pl
     [Jd 8; v-2d(4); 3620]   μιαίνω

μιαίνω   {3620, v-2d(4)}
[μιανῶ, ἐμίανα, -, μεμίαμμαι, ἐμιάνθην] pr. *to tinge, dye, stain; to pollute, defile*, ceremonially, John 18:28; *to corrupt, deprave*, Titus 1:15; Heb 12:15; Jude 8; Acts 5:38 v.l.*

μίαν   acc sg fem [36t; a-4b(2); 1651]   εἷς
μιανθῶσιν   aor pass subj 3 pl
     [2t; v-2d(4); 3620]   μιαίνω
μιᾶς   gen sg fem [8t; a-4b(2); 1651]   εἷς

μίασμα, ατος, τό   {3621, n-3c(4)}
pollution, moral *defilement, corruption*, 2 Peter 2:20*

μιάσματα   acc pl neut
     [2P 2:20; n-3c(4); 3621]   μίασμα

μιασμός, οῦ, ὁ   {3622, n-2a}
pollution, corruption, defiling, 2 Peter 2:10*

μιασμοῦ   gen sg masc [2P 2:10; n-2a; 3622]   μιασμός

μίγμα, ατος, τό   {3623, n-3c(4)}
a mixture, John 19:39*

μίγμα   acc sg neut [Jn 19:39; n-3c(4); 3623]   μίγμα

μίγνυμι   {3624, v-3c(2)}
[-, ἔμιξα, -, μέμιγμαι, -] also spelled μείγνυμι, *to mix, mingle*, Matt 27:34; Luke 13:1; Rev 8:7

μικρά   nom sg fem [2t; a-1a(1); 3625]   μικρός
μικράν   acc sg fem [Rv 3:8; a-1a(1); 3625]   "
μικροί   voc pl masc [Rv 19:5; a-1a(1); 3625]   "
μικρόν   nom sg neut [Jm 3:5; a-1a(1); 3625]   "
μικρόν   voc sg neut [Lk 12:32; a-1a(1); 3625]   "
μικρόν   acc sg masc [5t; a-1a(1); 3625]   "

μικρόν   acc sg neut, can function
   adverbially   [15t; a-1a(1); 3625]   "

μικρός, ά, όν   {3625, a-1a(1)}
   little, small in size quantity, etc. Matt 13:32;
   Luke 12:32; Rev 3:8; *small, little* in age, *young,
   not adult,* Mark 15:40; *little, short* in time, John
   7:33; μικρόν, sc. χρόνον, *a little while, a short time,*
   John 13:33; μετὰ μικρόν, *after a little while, a little
   while afterwards,* Matt 26:73; *little* in number,
   Luke 12:32; *small, little in dignity, low, humble,*
   Matt 10:42; 11:11; μικρόν, as an adv., *little, a
   little,* Matt 26:39

μικρός   nom sg masc [Lk 19:3; a-1a(1); 3625]   "
μικρότερον   nom sg neut comparative
   [2t; a-1a(1); 3625]   "
μικρότερος   nom sg masc comparative
   [3t; a-1a(1); 3625]   "
μικροῦ   gen sg masc [3t; a-1a(1); 3625]   "
μικρούς   acc pl masc [3t; a-1a(1); 3625]   "
μικρῷ   dat sg masc [Ac 26:22; a-1a(1); 3625]   "
μικρῶν   gen pl masc [6t; a-1a(1); 3625]   "
μικρῶν   gen pl neut [Mt 18:14; a-1a(1); 3625]   "
Μίλητον   acc sg fem [Ac 20:15; n-2b; 3626] Μίλητος

Μίλητος, οῦ, ἡ   {3626, n-2b}
   Miletus, a seaport city of Caria, on the west
   coast of Asia Minor, Acts 20:15, 17; 2 Tim 4:20*

Μιλήτου   gen sg fem [Ac 20:17; n-2b; 3626]   "
Μιλήτῳ   dat sg fem [2Ti 4:20; n-2b; 3626]   "

μίλιον, ου, τό   {3627, n-2c}
   a Roman mile, which contained *mille passuum,*
   1000 paces, or 8 stadia, 4, 854 feet, Matt 5:41*

μίλιον   acc sg neut [Mt 5:41; n-2c; 3627]   μίλιον
μιμεῖσθαι   pres mid inf
   [2t; v-1d(2a); 3628]   μιμέομαι
μιμεῖσθε   pres mid imperative 2 pl
   [Hb 13:7; v-1d(2a); 3628]   "

μιμέομαι   {3628, v-1d(2a)}
   [(ἐμιμούμην), μιμήσομαι, ἐμιμησάμην, -, -, -] *to
   imitate, follow* as an example, *strive to resemble,* 2
   Thess 3:7, 9; Heb 13:7; 3 John 11*

μιμηταί   nom pl masc [6t; n-1f; 3629]   μιμητής

μιμητής, οῦ, ὁ   {3629, n-1f}
   an imitator, follower, 1 Cor 4:16; 11:1; Eph 5:1; 1
   Thess 1:6; 2:14; Heb 6:12; 1 Peter 3:13 v.l.*

μιμνήσκεσθε   pres pass imperative 2 pl
   [Hb 13:3; v-5a; 3630]   μιμνήσκομαι
μιμνήσκῃ   pres pass ind 2 sg
   [Hb 2:6; v-5a; 3630]   "

μιμνήσκομαι   {3630, v-5a}
   [μνήσω, ἔμνησα, -, μέμνημαι, ἐμνήσθην] *to
   remember, recollect, call to mind,* Matt 26:75; Luke
   1:54, 72; 16:25; in N.T., in a passive sense, *to be
   called to mind, be borne in mind,* Acts 10:31; Rev
   16:19

μιμοῦ   pres mid imperative 2 sg
   [3J 11; v-1d(2a); 3628]   μιμέομαι
μισεῖ   pres act ind 3 sg
   [7t; v-1d(2a); 3631]   μισέω
μισεῖν   pres act inf [Jn 7:7; v-1d(2a); 3631]   "

μισεῖς   pres act ind 2 sg
   [Rv 2:6; v-1d(2a); 3631]   "

μισέω   {3631, v-1d(2a)}
   [(ἐμίσουν), μισήσω, ἐμίσησα, μεμίσηκα,
   μεμίσημαι, -] *to hate, regard with ill-will,* Matt
   5:43, 44; 10:22; *to detest, abhor,* John 3:20; Rom
   7:15; in N.T. *to regard with less affection, love less,
   esteem less,* Matt 6:24; Luke 14:26

μισῇ   pres act subj 3 sg
   [1J 4:20; v-1d(2a); 3631]   "
μισήσει   fut act ind 3 sg [2t; v-1d(2a); 3631]   "
μισήσεις   fut act ind 2 sg
   [Mt 5:43; v-1d(2a); 3631]   "
μισήσουσιν   fut act ind 3 pl [2t; v-1d(2a); 3631]   "
μισήσωσιν   aor act subj 3 pl
   [Lk 6:22; v-1d(2a); 3631]   "

μισθαποδοσία, ας, ἡ   {3632, n-1a}
   pr. *the discharge of wages; requital; reward,* Heb
   10:35; 11:26; *punishment,* Heb 2:2*

μισθαποδοσίαν   acc sg fem
   [3t; n-1a; 3632]   μισθαποδοσία

μισθαποδότης, ου, ὁ   {3633, n-1f}
   a bestower of remuneration; recompenser, rewarder,
   Heb 11:6*

μισθαποδότης   nom sg masc
   [Hb 11:6; n-1f; 3633]   μισθαποδότης
μίσθιοι   nom pl masc
   [Lk 15:17; n-2a; 3634]   μίσθιος

μίσθιος, ου, ὁ   {3634, n-2a}
   hired; as a subst., *a hired servant, hireling,* Luke
   15:17, 19, 21 v.l.*

μισθίων   gen pl masc [Lk 15:19; n-2a; 3634]   "
μισθόν   acc sg masc [18t; n-2a; 3635]   μισθός

μισθός, ου, ὁ   {3635, n-2a}
   hire, wages, Matt 20:8; James 5:4; *reward,* Matt
   5:12, 46; 6:1, 2, 5, 16; *punishment,* 2 Peter 2:13

μισθός   nom sg masc [7t; n-2a; 3635]   "
μισθοῦ   gen sg masc [4t; n-2a; 3635]   "

μισθόω   {3636, v-1d(3)}
   [-, ἐμίσθωσα, -, -, -] *to hire out, let out to hire;* mid.
   to hire, Matt 20:1, 7*

μίσθωμα, ατος, τό   {3637, n-3c(4)}
   hire, rent; in N.T. *a hired dwelling,* Acts 28:30*

μισθώματι   dat sg neut
   [Ac 28:30; n-3c(4); 3637]   μίσθωμα
μισθώσασθαι   aor mid inf
   [Mt 20:1; v-1d(3); 3636]   μισθόω

μισθωτός, οῦ, ὁ   {3638, n-2a}
   a hireling, Mark 1:20; John 10:12, 13*

μισθωτός   nom sg masc [2t; n-2a; 3638]   μισθωτός
μισθωτῶν   gen pl masc [Mk 1:20; n-2a; 3638]   "
μισούμενοι   pres pass ptcp nom pl masc
   [4t; v-1d(2a); 3631]   μισέω
μισοῦντες   pres act ptcp nom pl masc
   [2t; v-1d(2a); 3631]   "
μισούντων   pres act ptcp gen pl masc
   [Lk 1:71; v-1d(2a); 3631]   "

μισοῦσιν   pres act ptcp dat pl masc
[Lk 6:27; v-1d(2a); 3631]   "
μισῶ   pres act ind 1 sg   [2t; v-1d(2a); 3631]   "
μισῶν   pres act ptcp nom sg masc
[5t; v-1d(2a); 3631]   "

Μιτυλήνη, ης, ἡ   {3639, n-1b}
Mitylene, the capital city of Lesbos, in the
Aegean sea, Acts 20:14*

Μιτυλήνην   acc sg fem
[Ac 20:14; n-1b; 3639]   Μιτυλήνη

Μιχαήλ, ὁ   {3640, n-3g(2)}
Michael, the archangel, indecl., Jude 9; Rev 12:7*

Μιχαήλ   indecl [2t; n-3g(2); 3640]   Μιχαήλ

μνᾶ, ᾶς, ἡ   {3641, n-1h}
Latin *mina; a weight,* equivalent to 100
drachmae; also *a sum,* equivalent to 100
drachmas and the sixtieth part of a talent, Luke
19:13, 16, 18, 20, 24f.*

μνᾶ   nom sg fem   [3t; n-1h; 3641]   μνᾶ

μνάομαι   {3642, v-1d(1a)}
[-, -, -, μεμνησμένη, -] *to court for a bride,* the
participle can mean *engaged,* Luke 1:27 v.l.*

μνᾶν   acc sg fem [Lk 19:24; n-1h; 3641]   "
μνᾶς   acc pl fem [5t; n-1h; 3641]   "

Μνάσων, ωνος, ὁ   {3643, n-3f(1a)}
Mnason, pr. name, Acts 21:16*

Μνάσωνι   dat sg masc
[Ac 21:16; n-3f(1a); 3643]   Μνάσων

μνεία, ας, ἡ   {3644, n-1a}
remembrance, recollection, Phil 1:3; 1 Thess 3:6; 2
Tim 1:3; Rom 12:13 v.l.; *mention;* μνείαν
ποιεῖσθαι, *to make mention,* Rom 1:9; Eph 1:16; 1
Thess 1:2; Phil 4*

μνείᾳ   dat sg fem [Pp 1:3; n-1a; 3644]   μνεία
μνείαν   acc sg fem [6t; n-1a; 3644]   "

μνῆμα, ατος, τό   {3645, n-3c(4)}
pr. *a memorial, monument; a tomb, sepulchre,*
Mark 5:3, 5; Luke 8:27; 23:53; 24:1; Acts 2:29;
7:16; Rev 11:9; Mark 15:46 v.l.; Mark 16:2 v.l.*

μνῆμα   nom sg neut [Ac 2:29; n-3c(4); 3645]   μνῆμα
μνῆμα   acc sg neut [2t; n-3c(4); 3645]   "
μνήμασιν   dat pl neut [3t; n-3c(4); 3645]   "
μνήματι   dat sg neut [2t; n-3c(4); 3645]   "
μνημεῖα   nom pl neut [2t; n-2c; 3646]   μνημεῖον
μνημεῖα   acc pl neut [2t; n-2c; 3646]   "
μνημείοις   dat pl neut [Jn 5:28; n-2c; 3646]   "

μνημεῖον, ου, τό   {3646, n-2c}
monument, memorial, Luke 11:47; *grave, tomb,*
Matt 23:39; Mark 5:2; Luke 11:44; John 11:17, 31,
38; Acts 13:29

μνημεῖον   nom sg neut [2t; n-2c; 3646]   "
μνημεῖον   acc sg neut [15t; n-2c; 3646]   "
μνημείου   gen sg neut [10t; n-2c; 3646]   "
μνημείῳ   dat sg neut [5t; n-2c; 3646]   "
μνημείων   gen pl neut [3t; n-2c; 3646]   "

μνήμη, ης, ἡ   {3647, n-1b}
remembrance, recollection, memory; μνήμην
ποιεῖσθαι, *to make mention,* 2 Peter 1:15*

μνήμην   acc sg fem [2P 1:15; n-1b; 3647]   μνήμη
μνημόνευε   pres act imperative 2 sg
[3t; v-1a(6); 3648]   μνημονεύω
μνημονεύει   pres act ind 3 sg
[Jn 16:21; v-1a(6); 3648]   "
μνημονεύειν   pres act inf
[Ac 20:35; v-1a(6); 3648]   "
μνημονεύετε   pres act imperative 2 pl
[5t; v-1a(6); 3648]   "
μνημονεύετε   pres act ind 2 pl
[4t; v-1a(6); 3648]   "
μνημονεύητε   pres act subj 2 pl
[Jn 16:4; v-1a(6); 3648]   "
μνημονεύοντες   pres act ptcp nom pl masc
[2t; v-1a(6); 3648]   "

μνημονεύω   {3648, v-1a(6)}
[(ἐμνημόνευον), -, ἐμνημόνευσα, -, -, -] *to
remember, recollect, call to mind,* Matt 16:9; Luke
17:32; Acts 20:31; *to be mindful of, to fix the
thoughts upon,* Heb 11:15; *to make mention,
mention, speak of,* Heb 11:22

μνημονεύωμεν   pres act subj 1 pl
[Ga 2:10; v-1a(6); 3648]   "

μνημόσυνον, ου, τό   {3649, n-2c}
a record, memorial, Acts 10:4; *honorable
remembrance,* Matt 26:13; Mark 14:9*

μνημόσυνον   acc sg neut
[3t; n-2c; 3649]   μνημόσυνον
μνησθῆναι   aor pass inf
[3t; v-5a; 3630]   μιμνήσκομαι
μνησθῇς   aor pass subj 2 sg
[Mt 5:23; v-5a; 3630]   "
μνησθήσομαι   fut pass ind 1 sg
[Hb 10:17; v-5a; 3630]   "
μνήσθητε   aor pass imperative 2 pl
[2t; v-5a; 3630]   "
μνήσθητι   aor pass imperative 2 sg
[2t; v-5a; 3630]   "
μνησθῶ   aor pass subj 1 sg [Hb 8:12; v-5a; 3630]   "
μνηστευθείσης   aor pass ptcp gen sg fem
[Mt 1:18; v-1a(6); 3650]   μνηστεύω

μνηστεύω   {3650, v-1a(6)}
[-, -, -, ἐμνήστευμαι, ἐμνηστεύθην] *to ask in
marriage; to betroth;* pass. *to be betrothed, engaged,*
Matt 1:18; Luke 1:27; 2:5; Matt 1:16 v.l.*

μογγιλάλος, ον   {3651, a-3a}
to speak with a hoarse voice, Mark 7:32 v.l.*

μογιλάλον   acc sg masc
[Mk 7:32; a-3a; 3652]   μογιλάλος

μογιλάλος, ον   {3652, a-3a}
*having an impediment in one's speech, speaking
with difficulty, a stammerer,* Mark 7:32, 33 v.l.*

μόγις   {3653, adverb}
with difficulty, scarcely, hardly, Luke 9:39; 23:53
v.l.; Acts 14:18 v.l.; Rom 5:7 v.l.*

μόγις   adverb [Lk 9:39; adverb; 3653]   μόγις

μόδιον   acc sg masc [3t; n-2a; 3654]   μόδιος

μόδιος, ίου, ὁ   {3654, n-2a}
a modius, a Roman measure for things dry,
containing 16 sextarii, and equivalent to about
a peck (8.75 liters); in N.T. *a corn measure*, Matt
5:15; Mark 4:21; Luke 11:33*

μοι   dat sg [225t; a-5a; 1609]   ἐγώ
μοιχαλίδα   acc sg fem
   [Rm 7:3; n-3c(2); 3655]   μοιχαλίς
μοιχαλίδες   voc pl fem [Jm 4:4; n-3c(2); 3655]   "
μοιχαλίδι   dat sg fem [Mk 8:38; n-3c(2); 3655]   "
μοιχαλίδος   gen sg fem [2P 2:14; n-3c(2); 3655]   "

μοιχαλίς, ίδος, ἡ   {3655, n-3c(2)}
an adulteress, Rom 7:3; James 4:4; by meton., *an
adulterous appearance, lustful significance*, 2 Peter
2:14; from the Hebrew, spiritually *adulterous,
faithless, ungodly*, Matt 12:39; 16:4; Mark 8:38*

μοιχαλίς   nom sg fem [3t; n-3c(2); 3655]   "
μοιχᾶται   pres pass ind 3 sg
   [4t; v-1d(1a); 3656]   μοιχάω

μοιχάω   {3656, v-1d(1a)}
[-, -, -, -, -] act., *to cause to commit adultery*, pass.,
to commit or *be guilty of adultery*, Matt 5:32; 19:9;
Mark 10:11f.*

μοιχεία, ας, ἡ   {3657, n-1a}
adultery, Matt 15:19; Mark 7:22; John 8:3*

μοιχεία   dat sg fem [Jn 8:3; n-1a; 3657]   μοιχεία
μοιχεῖαι   nom pl fem [2t; n-1a; 3657]   "
μοιχεύει   pres act ind 3 sg
   [2t; v-1a(6); 3658]   μοιχεύω
μοιχεύειν   pres act inf [Rm 2:22; v-1a(6); 3658]   "
μοιχεύεις   pres act ind 2 sg [2t; v-1a(6); 3658]   "
μοιχευθῆναι   aor pass inf
   [Mt 5:32; v-1a(6); 3658]   "
μοιχευομένη   pres pass ptcp nom sg fem
   [Jn 8:4; v-1a(6); 3658]   "
μοιχεύοντας   pres act ptcp acc pl masc
   [Rv 2:22; v-1a(6); 3658]   "
μοιχεύσεις   fut act ind 2 sg [3t; v-1a(6); 3658]   "
μοιχεύσῃς   aor act subj 2 sg [3t; v-1a(6); 3658]   "

μοιχεύω   {3658, v-1a(6)}
[μοιχεύσω, ἐμοίχευσα, -, -, ἐμοιχεύθην] trans. *to
commit adultery with, debauch*, Matt 5:28; absol.
and mid. *to commit adultery*, Matt 5:27; John 8:4;
to commit spiritual *adultery, be guilty of idolatry*,
Rev 2:22

μοιχοί   nom pl masc [2t; n-2a; 3659]   μοιχός

μοιχός, ου, ὁ   {3659, n-2a}
an adulterer, Luke 18:11; 1 Cor 6:9; Heb 13:4;
James 4:4 v.l.*

μοιχούς   acc pl masc [Hb 13:4; n-2a; 3659]   "

μόλις   {3660, adverb}
with difficulty, scarcely, hardly, Acts 14:18; 27:7, 8,
16; Rom 5:7; 1 Peter 4:18; Luke 9:39 v.l.; Acts
23:29 v.l.*

μόλις   adverb [6t; adverb; 3660]   μόλις

Μολόχ, ὁ   {3661, n-3g(2)}
Moloch, pr. name, indecl., Acts 7:43*

Μολόχ   indecl [Ac 7:43; n-3g(2); 3661]   Μολόχ
μολύνεται   pres pass ind 3 sg
   [1C 8:7; v-1c(2); 3662]   μολύνω

μολύνω   {3662, v-1c(2)}
[-, ἐμόλυνα, -, -, ἐμολύνθην] pr. *to stain, sully; to
defile, contaminate* morally, 1 Cor 8:7; Rev 14:4;
to soil, Rev 3:4; Acts 5:38 v.l.*

μολυσμός, οῦ, ὁ   {3663, n-2a}
pollution, defilement, 2 Cor 7:1*

μολυσμοῦ   gen sg masc
   [2C 7:1; n-2a; 3663]   μολυσμός

μομφή, ῆς, ἡ   {3664, n-1b}
a complaint, cause or *ground of complaint*, Col
3:13*

μομφήν   acc sg fem [Cl 3:13; n-1b; 3664]   μομφή
μόνα   acc pl neut [Lk 24:12; a-1a(2a); 3668]   μόνος
μοναί   nom pl fem [Jn 14:2; n-1b; 3665]   μονή
μόνας   acc pl fem [2t; a-1a(2a); 3668]   μόνος

μονή, ῆς, ἡ   {3665, n-1b}
a stay in any place; an abode, dwelling, mansion,
John 14:2, 23*

μονήν   acc sg fem [2t; n-1b; 3665]   μονή
μονογενῆ   acc sg masc [3t; a-4a; 3666]   μονογενής

μονογενής, ές   {3666, a-4a}
only-begotten, only-born, Luke 7:12; 8:42; 9:38;
Heb 11:17; *only-begotten* in respect of peculiar
generation, *unique*, John 1:14, 18; 3:16, 18; 1
John 4:9*

μονογενής   nom sg masc [3t; a-4a; 3666]   "
μονογενής   nom sg fem [Lk 8:42; a-4a; 3666]   "
μονογενοῦς   gen sg masc [2t; a-4a; 3666]   "
μόνοι   nom pl masc [4t; a-1a(2a); 3668]   μόνος
μόνοις   dat pl masc [Mt 12:4; a-1a(2a); 3668]   "

μόνον   {3667, adverb}
only, Matt 5:47; 8:8; οὐ μόνον ... ἀλλὰ καί, *not
only ... but also*, Matt 21:21; John 5:18; μὴ μόνον
... ἀλλά, *not only ... but*, Phil 2:12. Is actually the
adjective μόνος used adverbially.

μόνον   nom sg masc, can function
   adverbially [Jn 17:3; a-1a(2a); 3668]   "
μόνον   acc sg masc [2t; a-1a(2a); 3668]   "
μόνον   adverb [70t; adverb; 3667]   μόνον

μόνος, η, ον   {3668, a-1a(2a)}
without accompaniment, alone, Mat. 14:23; 18:15;
Luke 10:40; *singly existent, sole, only*, John 17:3;
lone solitary, John 8:29; 16:32; *alone* in respect of
restriction, *only*, Matt 4:4; 12:4; *alone* in respect
of circumstances, *only*, Luke 24:18; *not
multiplied by reproduction, lone, barren*, John
12:24

μόνος   nom sg masc [20t; a-1a(2a); 3668]   μόνος
μόνου   gen sg masc [2t; a-1a(2a); 3668]   "
μόνους   acc pl masc [3t; a-1a(2a); 3668]   "
μονόφθαλμον   acc sg masc
   [2t; a-3a; 3669]   μονόφθαλμος

μονόφθαλμος, ον   {3669, a-3a}
one-eyed; deprived of an eye, Matt 18:9; Mark 9:47*

μονόω   {3670, v-1d(3)}
[-, -, -, μεμόνωμαι, -] *to leave alone;* pass. *to be left alone, be lone,* 1 Tim 5:5*

μόνῳ   dat sg masc [7t; a-1a(2a); 3668]   μόνος

μορφή, ῆς, ἡ   {3671, n-1b}
form, outward appearance, Mark 16:12; Phil 2:6, 7*

μορφῇ   dat sg fem [2t; n-1b; 3671]   μορφή
μορφήν   acc sg fem [Pp 2:7; n-1b; 3671]   "

μορφόω   {3672, v-1d(3)}
[-, -, -, μεμόρφωμαι, ἐμορφώθην] *to give shape to, mold, fashion,* Gal 4:19*

μορφωθῇ   aor pass subj 3 sg
    [Ga 4:19; v-1d(3); 3672]   μορφόω
μόρφωσιν   acc sg fem [2t; n-3e(5b); 3673]   μόρφωσις

μόρφωσις, εως, ἡ   {3673, n-3e(5b)}
pr. *a shaping, moulding;* in N.T. *external form, appearance,* 2 Tim 3:5; a settled *form.* prescribed *system,* Rom 2:20*

μόσχον   acc sg masc [3t; n-2a; 3675]   μόσχος

μοσχοποιέω   {3674, cv-1d(2a)}
[-, ἐμοσχοποίησα, -, -, -] *to form an image of a calf,* Acts 7:41*

μόσχος, ου, ὁ   {3675, n-2a}
pr. *a tender branch, shoot; a young animal; a calf, young bull,* Luke 15:23, 27, 30; Heb 12:19; Rev 4:7*

μόσχῳ   dat sg masc [Rv 4:7; n-2a; 3675]   "
μόσχων   gen pl masc [2t; n-2a; 3675]   "
μου   gen sg [564t; a-5a; 1609]   ἐγώ

μουσικός, ή, όν   {3676, a-1a(2a)}
pr. *devoted to the arts of the Muses; a musician;* in N.T., perhaps, *a singer,* Rev 18:22*

μουσικῶν   gen pl masc
    [Rv 18:22; a-1a(2a); 3676]   μουσικός
μόχθον   acc sg masc [1Th 2:9; n-2a; 3677]   μόχθος

μόχθος, ου, ὁ   {3677, n-2a}
wearisome labor, toil, travail, 2 Cor 11:27; 1 Thess 2:9; 2 Thess 3:8*

μόχθῳ   dat sg masc [2t; n-2a; 3677]   "

μυελός, ου, ὁ   {3678, n-2a}
marrow, Heb 4:12*

μυελῶν   gen pl masc [Hb 4:12; n-2a; 3678]   μυελός

μυέω   {3679, v-1d(2a)}
[-, -, -, μεμύημαι, -] *to initiate, instruct* in the sacred mysteries; in N.T. pass. *to be disciplined* in a practical lesson, *to learn* a lesson, Phil 4:12*

μύθοις   dat pl masc [3t; n-2a; 3680]   μῦθος

μῦθος, ου, ὁ   {3680, n-2a}
a word, speech, a tale; a fable, figment, 1 Tim 1:4; 4:7; 2 Tim 4:4; Titus 1:14; 2 Peter 1:16*

μύθους   acc pl masc [2t; n-2a; 3680]   "

μυκάομαι   {3681, v-1d(1a)}
[-, -, -, -, -] *to low, bellow,* as a bull; also, *to roar,* as a lion, Rev 10:3*

μυκᾶται   pres mid ind 3 sg
    [Rv 10:3; v-1d(1a); 3681]   μυκάομαι
μυκτηρίζεται   pres pass ind 3 sg
    [Ga 6:7; v-2a(1); 3682]   μυκτηρίζω

μυκτηρίζω   {3682, v-2a(1)}
[-, -, -, -, -] *to contract the nose in contempt and derision, toss up the nose; to mock, deride,* Gal 6:7*

μυλικός, ή, όν   {3683, a-1a(2a)}
of a mill, belonging to a mill, Luke 17:2; Mark 9:42 v.l.; Rev 18:21 v.l.*

μυλικός   nom sg masc
    [Lk 17:2; a-1a(2a); 3683]   μυλικός
μύλινον   acc sg masc
    [Rv 18:21; a-1a(2a); 3684]   μύλινος

μύλινος, η, ον   {3684, a-1a(2a)}
belonging to a mill, Rev 18:21*

μύλος, ου, ὁ   {3685, n-2a}
a millstone, Matt 18:6; 24:41; Mark 9:42; Rev 18:21 v.l., 22*

μύλος   nom sg masc [2t; n-2a; 3685]   μύλος
μύλου   gen sg masc [Rv 18:22; n-2a; 3685]   "
μύλῳ   dat sg masc [Mt 24:41; n-2a; 3685]   "

μυλών, ῶνος, ὁ   {3686, n-3f)1a)}
a mill-house, a place where the grinding of corn was performed, Matt 24:41 v.l.*

μυλωνικός, ή, όν   {3687, a-1a(2a)}
belonging to a mill house, Mark 9:42 v.l.*

Μύρα, ων τά   {3688, n-2c}
neuter plural, *Myra,* a city of Lycia, Acts 27:5; 21:1 v.l.*

μύρα   acc pl neut [2t; n-2c; 3693]   μύρον
μυριάδας   acc pl fem
    [Ac 19:19; n-3c(2); 3689]   μυριάς
μυριάδες   nom pl fem [2t; n-3c(2); 3689]   "
μυριάδων   gen pl fem [3t; n-3c(2); 3689]   "

μυριάς, άδος, ἡ   {3689, n-3c(2)}
a myriad, ten thousand, Acts 19:19; indefinitely, *a vast multitude,* Luke 12:1; Acts 21:20; Heb 12:22; Jude 14; Rev 5:11; 9:16*

μυριάσιν   dat pl fem [2t; n-3c(2); 3689]   "

μυρίζω   {3690, v-2a(1)}
[-, ἐμύρισα, -, -, -] *to anoint,* Mark 14:8*

μύριοι, αι, α   {3691, a-1a(1)}
indefinitely, *a great number;* specifically, μύριοι, *a myriad, ten thousand,* Matt 18:24*

μυρίος, α, ον   {3692, a-1a(1)}
innumerable, 1 Cor 4:15; 14:19*

μυρίους   acc pl masc [2t; a-1a(1); 3692]   μυρίος
μυρίσαι   aor act inf
    [Mk 14:8; v-2a(1); 3690]   μυρίζω
μυρίων   gen pl neut
    [Mt 18:24; a-1a(1); 3692]   μυρίος

μύρον, ου, τό   {3693, n-2c}
pr. *aromatic juice which distills from trees; ointment, unguent,* usually perfumed, Matt 26:7, 12; Mark 14:3, 4

μύρον   nom sg neut [2t; n-2c; 3693]   μύρον
μύρον   acc sg neut [2t; n-2c; 3693]   "
μύρου   gen sg neut [6t; n-2c; 3693]   "
μύρῳ   dat sg neut [3t; n-2c; 3693]   "

Μυσία, ας, ἡ   {3695, n-1a}
Mysia, a province of Asia Minor, Acts 16:7f.*

Μυσίαν   acc sg fem [2t; n-1a; 3695]   Μυσία
μυστήρια   acc pl neut [4t; n-2c; 3696]   μυστήριον

μυστήριον, ου, τό   {3696, n-2c}
a matter to the knowledge of which initiation is necessary; a secret which would remain such but for revelation, Matt 3:11; Rom 11:25; Col 1:26; *a concealed power* or *principle,* 2 Thess 2:7; *a hidden meaning* of a symbol, Rev 1:20: 17:7

μυστήριον   nom sg neut [8t; n-2c; 3696]   "
μυστήριον   acc sg neut [9t; n-2c; 3696]   "
μυστηρίου   gen sg neut [4t; n-2c; 3696]   "
μυστηρίῳ   dat sg neut [2t; n-2c; 3696]   "
μυστηρίων   gen pl neut [1C 4:1; n-2c; 3696]   "

μυωπάζω   {3697, v-2a(1)}
[-, -, -, -, -] pr. *to close the eyes, contract the eyelids, wink; to be nearsighted, partially blinded, slow to understand,* 2 Peter 1:9*

μυωπάζων   pres act ptcp nom sg masc
     [2P 1:9; v-2a(1); 3697]   μυωπάζω
μώλωπι   dat sg masc [1P 2:24; n-3a(1); 3698] μώλωψ

μώλωψ, ωπος, ὁ   {3698, n-3a(1)}
the mark of a blow; a stripe, a wound, 1 Peter 2:24*

μωμάομαι   {3699, v-1d(1a)}
[-, ἐμωμησάμην, -, -, ἐμωμήθην] *to find fault with, censure, blame,* 2 Cor 8:20; passively, 2 Cor 6:3*

μωμηθῇ   aor pass subj 3 sg
     [2C 6:3; v-1d(1a); 3699]   μωμάομαι
μωμήσηται   aor mid subj 3 sg
     [2C 8:20; v-1d(1a); 3699]   "
μῶμοι   nom pl masc [2P 2:13; n-2a; 3700]   μῶμος

μῶμος, ου, ὁ   {3700, n-2a}
blame, ridicule; a disgrace to society, *a stain,* 2 Peter 2:13*

μωρά   acc pl neut [1C 1:27; a-1a(1); 3704]   μωρός
μωραί   nom pl fem [3t; a-1a(1); 3704]   "

μωραίνω   {3701, v-2d(4)}
[-, ἐμώρανα, -, -, ἐμωράνθην] *to be foolish, to play the fool;* in N.T. trans. *to make foolish, convict of folly,* 1 Cor 1:20; pass. *to be convicted of folly, to incur the character of folly,* Rom 1:22; *to be rendered insipid,* Matt 5:13; Luke 14:34*

μωρανθῇ   aor pass subj 3 sg
     [2t; v-2d(4); 3701]   μωραίνω
μωράς   acc pl fem [2t; a-1a(1); 3704]   μωρός
μωρέ   voc sg masc [Mt 5:22; a-1a(1); 3704]   "

μωρία, ας, ἡ   {3702, n-1a}
foolishness, 1 Cor 1:18, 21, 23; 2:14; 3:19*

μωρία   nom sg fem [3t; n-1a; 3702]   μωρία
μωρίαν   acc sg fem [1C 1:23; n-1a; 3702]   "
μωρίας   gen sg fem [1C 1:21; n-1a; 3702]   "
μωροί   nom pl masc [1C 4:10; a-1a(1); 3704]   μωρός
μωροί   voc pl masc [Mt 23:17; a-1a(1); 3704]   "

μωρολογία, ας, ἡ   {3703, n-1a}
foolish talk, Eph 5:4*

μωρολογία   nom sg fem
     [Ep 5:4; n-1a; 3703]   μωρολογία
μωρόν   nom sg neut [1C 1:25; a-1a(1); 3704]   μωρός

μωρός, ά, όν   {3704, a-1a(1)}
pr. *dull; foolish,* Matt 7:26; 23:17; 25:2f., 8; 1 Cor 1:25, 27; 3:18; 4:10; 2 Tim 2:23; Titus 3:9; from the Hebrew, *a fool* in senseless wickedness, Matt 5:22*

μωρός   nom sg masc [1C 3:18; a-1a(1); 3704]   "
μωρῷ   dat sg masc [Mt 7:26; a-1a(1); 3704]   "

Μωσῆς, see Μωϋσῆς   {3706}
Moses, pr. name, v.l. in t.r. of Μωϋσέως

Μωϋσέα   acc sg masc
     [Lk 16:29; n-3g(1); 3707]   Μωϋσῆς
Μωϋσεῖ   dat sg masc [8t; n-3g(1); 3707]   "
Μωϋσέως   gen sg masc [23t; n-3g(1); 3707]   "
Μωϋσῇ   dat sg masc [Ac 7:44; n-3g(1); 3707]   "
Μωϋσῆν   acc sg masc [4t; n-3g(1); 3707]   "

Μωϋσῆς, Μωϋσέως, ὁ   {3707, n-3g(1)}
also spelled Μωσῆς and Μεσευς (3705), *Moses,* pr. name, Matt 8:4; John 1:17; Rom 5:14

ν

Ναασσών, ὁ   {3709, n-3g(2)}
Naasson, pr. name, indecl., Matt 1:4; Luke 3:32*

Ναασσών   indecl [3t; n-3g(2); 3709]   Ναασσών

Ναγγαί, ὁ   {3710, n-3g(2)}
Naggai, Nagge, pr. name, indecl., Luke 3:25*

Ναγγαί   indecl [Lk 3:25; n-3g(2); 3710]   Ναγγαί

Ναζαρά, ἡ, see Ναζαρέτ   {3711, n-3g(2)}

Ναζαρά   indecl [2t; n-3g(2); 3711]   Ναζαρά

Ναζαρέθ, ἡ, see Ναζαρέτ   {3714, n-3g(2)}

Ναζαρέθ   indecl [6t; n-3g(2); 3714]   Ναζαρέθ

Ναζαρέτ, ἡ   {3715, n-3g(2)}
also spelled Ναζαρά and Ναζαρέθ, *Nazareth,* a city of Galilee, indecl., Matt 4:13; Luke 4:16

Ναζαρέτ   indecl [4t; n-3g(2); 3715]   Ναζαρέτ
Ναζαρηνέ   voc sg masc
     [2t; a-1a(2a); 3716]   Ναζαρηνός
Ναζαρηνόν   acc sg masc [Mk 16:6; a-1a(2a); 3716]   "

Ναζαρηνός, ή, όν   {3716, a-1a(2a)}
an inhabitant of Nazareth, Mark 1:24; 10:47; 4:67; 16:6; Luke 4:34; 24:19; John 18:5 v.l.*

Ναζαρηνός   nom sg masc [Mk 10:47; a-1a(2a); 3716]   "

Ναζαρηνοῦ gen sg masc [2t; a-1a(2a); 3716]   "
Ναζωραῖον acc sg masc [3t; n-2a; 3717] Ναζωραῖος

Ναζωραῖος, ου, ὁ   {3717, n-2a}
   also spelled Ναζαρηνός, *a Nazarite; an inhabitant*
   of Nazareth, Matt 2:23; 26:69 v.l., 71; Luke 18:37;
   John 18:5, 7; 19:19; Acts 2:22; 3:6; 4:10; 6:14; 22:8;
   24:5; 26:9*

Ναζωραῖος nom sg masc [5t; n-2a; 3717]   "
Ναζωραίου gen sg masc [4t; n-2a; 3717]   "
Ναζωραίων gen pl masc [Ac 24:5; n-2a; 3717]   "

Ναθάμ, ὁ   {3718, n-3g(2)}
   also spelled Ναθάν, *Nathan,* pr. name, indecl.,
   Luke 3:31*

Ναθάμ indecl [Lk 3:31; n-3g(2); 3718]   Ναθάμ

Ναθαναήλ, ὁ   {3720, n-3g(2)}
   Nathanael, pr. name, indecl., John 1:45-49; 21:2

Ναθαναήλ indecl [6t; n-3g(2); 3720]   Ναθαναήλ

ναί   {3721, particle}
   a particle, used to strengthen an affirmation,
   certainly, Rev 22:20; to make an affirmation, or
   express an assent, *yea, yes,* Matt 5:37; Acts 5:8

ναί particle [33t; particle; 3721]   ναί

Ναιμάν, ὁ   {3722, n-3g(2)}
   also spelled Νεεμάν, *Naaman,* pr. name, indecl.,
   Luke 4:27*

Ναιμάν indecl [Lk 4:27; n-3g(2); 3722]   Ναιμάν

Ναΐν, ἡ   {3723, n-3g(2)}
   Nain, a town of Palestine, indecl., Luke 7:11*

Ναΐν indecl [Lk 7:11; n-3g(2); 3723]   Ναΐν
ναοῖς dat pl masc [Ac 17:24; n-2a; 3724]   ναός
ναόν acc sg masc [13t; n-2a; 3724]   "

ναός, οῦ, ὁ   {3724, n-2a}
   pr. *a dwelling; the dwelling* of a deity, *a temple,*
   Matt 26:61; Acts 7:48; used figuratively of
   individuals, John 2:19; 1 Cor 3:16; spc. *the cell of*
   a temple; hence, *the Holy Place* of the Temple of
   Jerusalem, Matt 23:35; Luke 1:9; *a model of a*
   temple, a shrine, Acts 19:24

ναός nom sg masc [10t; n-2a; 3724]   "
ναοῦ gen sg masc [12t; n-2a; 3724]   "

Ναούμ, ὁ   {3725, n-3g(2)}
   Naum, pr. name, indecl., Luke 3:25*

Ναούμ indecl [Lk 3:25; n-3g(2); 3725]   Ναούμ
ναούς acc pl masc [Ac 19:24; n-2a; 3724]   ναός

νάρδος, ου, ἡ   {3726, n-2b}
   spikenard, andropogon nardus of Linn., a species
   of aromatic plant with grassy leaves and a
   fibrous root, of which the best and strongest
   grows in India; in N.T. *oil of spikenard,* an oil
   extracted from the plant, which was highly
   prized and used as an ointment either pure or
   mixed with other substances, Mark 14:3; John
   12:3*

νάρδου gen sg fem [2t; n-2b; 3726]   νάρδος

Νάρκισσος, ου, ὁ   {3727, n-2a}
   Narcissus, pr. name, Rom 16:11*

Ναρκίσσου gen sg masc
   [Rm 16:11; n-2a; 3727]   Νάρκισσος

ναυαγέω   {3728, v-1d(2a)}
   [-, ἐναυάγησα, -, -, -] *to make shipwreck, be*
   shipwrecked, 2 Cor 11:25; 1 Tim 1:19*

ναύκληρος, ου, ὁ   {3729, n-2a}
   the master or *owner of a ship,* Acts 27:11*

ναυκλήρῳ dat sg masc
   [Ac 27:11; n-2a; 3729]   ναύκληρος
ναῦν acc sg fem [Ac 27:41; n-3e(2); 3730]   ναῦς

ναῦς, νεώς, ἡ   {3730, n-3e(2)}
   a ship, vessel, Acts 27:41*

ναύτης, ου, ὁ   {3731, n-1f}
   sailor, seaman, Acts 27:27, 30; Rev 18:17*

ναῦται nom pl masc [2t; n-1f; 3731]   ναύτης
ναυτῶν gen pl masc [Ac 27:30; n-1f; 3731]   "

Ναχώρ, ὁ   {3732, n-3g(2)}
   Nachor, pr. name, indecl., Luke 3:34*

Ναχώρ indecl [Lk 3:34; n-3g(2); 3732]   Ναχώρ
ναῷ dat sg masc [8t; n-2a; 3724]   ναός
Νέαν acc sg fem [Ac 16:11; a-1a(1); 3742]   νέος
νεανίαν acc sg masc
   [Ac 23:17; n-1d; 3733]   νεανίας

νεανίας, ου, ὁ   {3733, n-1d}
   a young man, youth, Acts 20:9; 23:17, 18, 22, all
   three being v.l.; used of *one who is in the prime*
   and vigor of life, Acts 7:58*

νεανίας nom sg masc [Ac 20:9; n-1d; 3733]   "
νεανίου gen sg masc [Ac 7:58; n-1d; 3733]   "
νεανίσκε voc sg masc
   [Lk 7:14; n-2a; 3734]   νεανίσκος
νεανίσκοι nom pl masc [2t; n-2a; 3734]   "
νεανίσκοι voc pl masc [2t; n-2a; 3734]   "
νεανίσκον acc sg masc [3t; n-2a; 3734]   "

νεανίσκος, ου, ὁ   {3734, n-2a}
   a young man, youth, Mark 14:51; 16:5; used of
   one in the prime of life, Mat. 19:20, 22; νεανίσκοι,
   soldiers, Mark 14:51

νεανίσκος nom sg masc [3t; n-2a; 3734]   "

Νεάπολις, εως, ἡ   {3736, n-3e(5b)}
   a compound noun that can be written as two
   words, Νεά πολις (3735), *Neapolis,* a city of
   Thrace on the Strymonic gulf, Acts 16:11

νέας gen sg fem [Hb 12:24; a-1a(1); 3742]   νέος
νέας acc pl fem [Ti 2:4; a-1a(1); 3742]   "

Νεεμάν, see Ναιμάν, ὁ   {3737, n-3g(2)}

νεκρά nom sg fem [3t; a-1a(1); 3738]   νεκρός
νεκράν acc sg fem [Ac 5:10; a-1a(1); 3738]   "
νεκροί nom pl masc [14t; a-1a(1); 3738]   "
νεκροῖς dat pl masc [2t; a-1a(1); 3738]   "
νεκρόν nom sg neut [2t; a-1a(1); 3738]   "
νεκρόν acc sg masc [Ac 28:6; a-1a(1); 3738]   "

νεκρός, ά, όν   {3738, a-1a(1)}
   dead, without life, Matt 11:5; 22:31; met. νεκρός
   τινι, *dead to a thing, no longer devoted to,* or *under*
   the influence of a thing, Rom 6:11; *dead* in respect

of fruitlessness, James 2:17, 20, 26; morally or
spiritually *dead*, Rom 6:13; Eph 5:14; *dead* in
alienation from God, Eph 2:1, 5; Col 2:13;
subject to death, mortal, Rom 8:10; *causing death
and misery, fatal, having a destructive power*, Heb
6:1; 9:14

νεκρός   nom sg masc   [9t; a-1a(1); 3738]   "
νεκροῦ   gen sg masc   [Rv 16:3; a-1a(1); 3738]   "
νεκρούς   acc pl masc   [19t; a-1a(1); 3738]   "

νεκρόω   {3739, v-1d(3)}
[-, ἐνέκρωσα, -, νενέκρωμαι, -] pr. *to put to death,
kill;* in N.T. met. *to deaden, mortify,* Col 3:5; pass.
to be rendered impotent, Rom 4:19; Heb 11:12*

νεκρῶν   gen pl masc   [74t; a-1a(1); 3738]   "
νεκρῶν   gen pl neut   [2t; a-1a(1); 3738]   "
νεκρώσατε   aor act imperative 2 pl
          [Cl 3:5; v-1d(3); 3739]   νεκρόω
νέκρωσιν   acc sg fem   [2t; n-3e(5b); 3740]   νέκρωσις

νέκρωσις, εως, ἡ   {3740, n-3e(5b)}
pr. *a putting to death; dying, abandonment to
death,* 2 Cor 4:10; *deadness, impotency,* Rom 4:19;
Mark 3:5 v.l.

νενεκρωμένον   perf pass ptcp acc sg neut
          [Rm 4:19; v-1d(3); 3739]   νεκρόω
νενεκρωμένου   perf pass ptcp gen sg masc
          [Hb 11:12; v-1d(3); 3739]   "
νενίκηκα   perf act ind 1 sg
          [Jn 16:33; v-1d(1a); 3771]   νικάω
νενικήκατε   perf act ind 2 pl
          [3t; v-1d(1a); 3771]   "
νενομοθέτηται   perf pass ind 3 sg
          [2t; v-1d(2a); 3793]   νομοθετέω

νεομηνία, ας, ἡ   {3741, n-1a}
new moon, first of the month, Col 2:16*

νεομηνίας   gen sg fem
          [Cl 2:16; n-1a; 3741]   νεομηνία
νέον   nom sg neut   [1C 5:7; a-1a(1); 3742]   νέος
νέον   acc sg masc   [8t; a-1a(1); 3742]   "

νέος, α, ον   {3742, a-1a(1)}
recent, new, fresh, Matt 9:17; 1 Cor 5:7; Col 3:10;
Heb 12:24; *young, youthful,* Titus 2:4. In Ac 16:11
is used in the name Νέαν πολις, which some
lexicons list as its own lexical form.

νέος   nom sg masc   [Lk 5:37; a-1a(1); 3742]   "

νεοσσός, see νοσσός

νεότης, ητος, ἡ   {3744, n-3c(1)}
youth, Matt 19:20

νεότητος   gen sg fem   [4t; n-3c(1); 3744]   νεότης
νεόφυτον   acc sg masc
          [1Ti 3:6; a-3a; 3745]   νεόφυτος

νεόφυτος, ον   {3745, a-3a}
newly or *recently planted* met. *a neophyte, one
newly implanted* into the Christian Church, *a
new convert,* 1 Tim 3:6*

Νέρων, ωνος, ὁ   {3746. n-3f(1a)}
Nero, pr. name v.l.

νεύει   pres act ind 3 sg
          [Jn 13:24; v-1a(6); 3748]   νεύω

Νεύης   {3747}
name of the rich man in Luke 16:19 v.l.*

νεύσαντος   aor act ptcp gen sg masc
          [Ac 24:10; v-1a(6); 3748]   "

νεύω   {3748, v-1a(6)}
[-, ἔνευσα, -, -, -] *to nod; to intimate by a nod* or
significant gesture, John 13:24; Acts 24:10*

νεφέλαι   nom pl fem   [Jd 12; n-1b; 3749]   νεφέλη
νεφέλαις   dat pl fem   [2t; n-1b; 3749]   "

νεφέλη, ης, ἡ   {3749, n-1b}
a cloud, Matt 17:5; 24:30; 26:64

νεφέλη   nom sg fem   [5t; n-1b; 3749]   "
νεφέλῃ   dat sg fem   [3t; n-1b; 3749]   "
νεφέλην   acc sg fem   [5t; n-1b; 3749]   "
νεφέλης   gen sg fem   [5t; n-1b; 3749]   "
νεφελῶν   gen pl fem   [4t; n-1b; 3749]   "

Νεφθαλίμ, ὁ   {3750, n-3g(2)}
also spelled Νεφθαλείμ, *Nephthalim,* pr. name,
indecl., Matt 4:13, 15; Rev 5:6; Luke 4:31 v.l.*

Νεφθαλίμ   indecl   [3t; n-3g(2); 3750]   Νεφθαλίμ

νέφος, ους, τό   {3751, n-3d(2b)}
a cloud; trop. *a cloud, a throng* of persons, Heb
12:1*

νέφος   acc sg neut   [Hb 12:1; n-3d(2b); 3751]   νέφος

νεφρός, οῦ, ὁ   {3752, n-2a}
a kidney; pl. νεφροί, *the kidneys, reins;* from the
Hebrew *the reins* regarded as a seat of desire
and affection, Rev 2:23*

νεφρούς   acc pl masc   [Rv 2:23; n-2a; 3752]   νεφρός
νεωκόρον   acc sg masc
          [Ac 19:35; n-2a; 3753]   νεωκόρος

νεωκόρος, ου, ὁ   {3753, n-2a}
pr. *one who sweeps* or *cleanses a temple;* generally,
one who has the charge of a temple; in N.T. *a
devotee* city, as having specially dedicated a
temple to some deity, Acts 19:35*

νεωτέρας   acc pl fem comparative
          [3t; a-1a(1); 3742]   νέος
νεωτερικάς   acc pl fem
          [2Ti 2:22; a-1a(2a); 3754]   νεωτερικός

νεωτερικός, ή, όν   {3754, a-1a(2a)}
juvenile, natural to youth, youthful, 2 Tim 2:22*

νεώτεροι   nom pl masc comparative
          [Ac 5:6; a-1a(1); 3742]   νέος
νεώτεροι   voc pl masc comparative
          [1P 5:5; a-1a(1); 3742]   "
νεώτερος   nom sg masc comparative
          [4t; a-1a(1); 3742]   "
νεωτέρους   acc pl masc comparative
          [2t; a-1a(1); 3742]   "

νή   {3755, particle}
by, BAGD calls it a "particle of strong
affirmation," and is followed by the person or

thing (in the acc) by which the person swears,
1 Cor 15:31*

νή   particle [1C 15:31; particle; 3755]   νή
νήθει   pres act ind 3 sg
    [Lk 12:27; v-1b(3); 3756]   νήθω
νήθουσιν   pres act ind 3 pl
    [Mt 6:28; v-1b(3); 3756]   "

νήθω   {3756, v-1b(3)}
    [-, -, -, -, -] *to spin,* Matt 6:28; Luke 12:27*

νηπιάζετε   pres act imperative 2 pl
    [1C 14:20; v-2a(1); 3757]   νηπιάζω

νηπιάζω   {3757, v-2a(1)}
    [-, -, -, -, -] *to be childlike,* 1 Cor 14:20*

νήπιοι   nom pl masc [3t; a-1a(1); 3758]   νήπιος
νηπίοις   dat pl masc [3t; a-1a(1); 3758]   "

νήπιος, α, ον   {3758, a-1a(1)}
    pr. *not speaking,* Latin *infans; an infant, babe,*
    child, Matt 21:16; 1 Cor 13:11; *one below the age of*
    manhood, a minor, Gal 4:1; 1 Thess 2:7 v.l.; met. *a*
    babe in knowledge, *unlearned, simple,* Matt
    11:25; Rom 2:20

νήπιος   nom sg masc [6t; a-1a(1); 3758]   "
νηπίου   gen sg masc [1C 13:11; a-1a(1); 3758]   "
νηπίων   gen pl masc [2t; a-1a(1); 3758]   "
Νηρέα   acc sg masc
    [Rm 16:15; n-3e(3); 3759]   Νηρεύς

Νηρεύς, έως, ὁ   {3759, n-3e(3)}
    Nereus, pr. name, Rom 16:15*

Νηρί, ὁ   {3760, n-3g(2)}
    Neri, pr. name, indecl., Luke 3:27*

Νηρί   indecl [Lk 3:27; n-3g(2); 3760]   Νηρί

νησίον, ου, τό   {3761, n-2c}
    a small island, Acts 27:16*

νησίον   acc sg neut [Ac 27:16; n-2c; 3761]   νησίον
νῆσον   acc sg fem [2t; n-2b; 3762]   νῆσος

νῆσος, ου, ἡ   {3762, n-2b}
    an island, Acts 13:6; 27:26

νῆσος   nom sg fem [3t; n-2b; 3762]   "
νήσου   gen sg fem [Ac 28:7; n-2b; 3762]   "

νηστεία, ας, ἡ   {3763, n-1a}
    fasting, want of food, 2 Cor 6:5; 11:27; *a fast,*
    religious *abstinence from food,* Matt 17:21; Luke
    2:37; spc. *the annual public fast of the Jews, the*
    great day of atonement, occurring in the month
    Tisri, corresponding to the new moon of
    October, Acts 27:9; Mark 9:29 v.l.; 1 Cor 7:5 v.l.

νηστείαις   dat pl fem [3t; n-1a; 3763]   νηστεία
νηστείαν   acc sg fem [Ac 27:9; n-1a; 3763]   "
νήστεις   acc pl masc [2t; n-3c(2); 3765]   νῆστις
νηστειῶν   gen pl fem
    [Ac 14:23; n-1a; 3763]   νηστεία
νηστεύειν   pres act inf
    [2t; v-1a(6); 3764]   νηστεύω
νηστεύητε   pres act subj 2 pl
    [Mt 6:16; v-1a(6); 3764]   "
νηστεύομεν   pres act ind 1 pl
    [Mt 9:14; v-1a(6); 3764]   "

νηστεύοντες   pres act ptcp nom pl masc
    [2t; v-1a(6); 3764]   "
νηστευόντων   pres act ptcp gen pl masc
    [Ac 13:2; v-1a(6); 3764]   "
νηστεύουσιν   pres act ind 3 pl
    [4t; v-1a(6); 3764]   "
νηστεῦσαι   aor act inf [Lk 5:34; v-1a(6); 3764]   "
νηστεύσαντες   aor act ptcp nom pl masc
    [Ac 13:3; v-1a(6); 3764]   "
νηστεύσας   aor act ptcp nom sg masc
    [Mt 4:2; v-1a(6); 3764]   "
νηστεύσουσιν   fut act ind 3 pl
    [3t; v-1a(6); 3764]   "

νηστεύω   {3764, v-1a(6)}
    [νηστεύσω, ἐνήστευσα, -, -, -] *to fast,* Matt 4:2;
    6:16, 17, 18; 9:15

νηστεύω   pres act ind 1 sg
    [Lk 18:12; v-1a(6); 3764]   "
νηστεύων   pres act ptcp nom sg masc
    [2t; v-1a(6); 3764]   "

νῆστις, ὁ or **ἡ**, gen. in **ιος**   {3765, n-3e(5a)}
    can also be masc. with a gen. in ιδος (n-3c[2]),
    fasting, hungry, Matt 15:32; Mark 8:3*

νήσῳ   dat sg fem [3t; n-2b; 3762]   νῆσος

νηφάλεος, α, ον   {3766, a-1a(1)}
    see νηφάλιος, *somber, temperate, abstinent in*
    respect to wine, etc.; in N.T. met., *vigilant,*
    circumspect, 1 Tim 3:2 v.l.; 3:11 v.l.*

νηφάλιον   acc sg masc
    [1Ti 3:2; a-1a(1); 3767]   νηφάλιος

νηφάλιος, ία, ιον   {3767, a-1a(1)}
    somber, temperate, abstinent in respect to wine,
    etc.; in N.T. met., *vigilant, circumspect,*
    self-controlled, 1 Tim 3:2, 11; Titus 2:2*

νηφαλίους   acc pl masc [Ti 2:2; a-1a(1); 3767]   "
νηφαλίους   acc pl fem [1Ti 3:11; a-1a(1); 3767]   "
νῆφε   pres act imperative 2 sg
    [2Ti 4:5; v-1b(1); 3768]   νήφω
νήφοντες   pres act ptcp nom pl masc
    [1P 1:13; v-1b(1); 3768]   "

νήφω   {3768, v-1b(1)}
    [-, ἔνηψα, -, -, -] *to be sober, not intoxicated;* in
    N.T. met., *to be vigilant, circumspect,* 1 Thess 5:6,
    8

νήφωμεν   pres act subj 1 pl [2t; v-1b(1); 3768]   "
νήψατε   aor act imperative 2 pl
    [2t; v-1b(1); 3768]   "

Νίγερ, ὁ   {3769, n-3g(2)}
    Niger, pr. name, probably not declined, Acts
    13:1*

Νίγερ   indecl [Ac 13:1; n-3g(2); 3769]   Νίγερ
νίκα   pres act imperative 2 sg
    [Rm 12:21; v-1d(1a); 3771]   νικάω
νικᾷ   pres act ind 3 sg [1J 5:4; v-1d(1a); 3771] "
Νικάνορα   acc sg masc
    [Ac 6:5; n-3f(2b); 3770]   Νικάνωρ

Νικάνωρ, ορος, ὁ   {3770, n-3f(2b)}
    Nicanor, pr. name, Acts 6:5*

νικάω   {3771, v-1d(1a)}
[νικήσω, ἐνίκησα, νενίκηκα, -, ἐνικήθην] *to*
conquer, overcome, vanquish, subdue, Luke 1:22;
John 16:33; absol. *to overcome, prevail,* Rev 5:5; *to*
come off superior in a judicial cause, Rom 3:4

νίκη, ῆς, ἡ   {3772, n-1b}
victory; meton. *a victorious principle,* 1 John 5:4*

νίκη   nom sg fem [1J 5:4; n-1b; 3772]   νίκη
νικῆσαι   aor act inf
        [Rv 13:7; v-1d(1a); 3771]   νικάω
νικήσασα   aor act ptcp nom sg fem
        [1J 5:4; v-1d(1a); 3771]   "
νικήσει   fut act ind 3 sg [2t; v-1d(1a); 3771]   "
νικήσεις   fut act ind 2 sg
        [Rm 3:4; v-1d(1a); 3771]   "
νικήσῃ   aor act subj 3 sg [2t; v-1d(1a); 3771]   "

Νικόδημος, ου, ὁ   {3773, n-2a}
Nicodemus, pr. name, John 3:1, 4, 9; 7:50; 19:39*

Νικόδημος   nom sg masc [5t; n-2a; 3773] Νικόδημος

Νικολαΐτης, ου, ὁ   {3774, n-1f}
a Nicolaitan, or follower of Nicolaus, a heresy of
the Apostolic age, Rev 2:6, 15*

Νικολαϊτῶν   gen pl masc
        [2t; n-1f; 3774]   Νικολαΐτης
Νικόλαον   acc sg masc
        [Ac 6:5; n-2a; 3775]   Νικόλαος

Νικόλαος, ου, ὁ   {3775, n-2a}
Nicolaus, pr. name, Acts 6:5*

Νικόπολιν   acc sg fem
        [Ti 3:12; n-3e(5b); 3776]   Νικόπολις

Νικόπολις, εως, ἡ   {3776, n-3e(5b)}
Nicopolis, a city of Macedonia, Titus 3:12*

νῖκος, ους, τό   {3777, n-3d(2b)}
victory, Matt 12:20; 1 Cor 15:54, 55, 57*

νῖκος   nom sg neut
        [1C 15:55; n-3d(2b); 3777]   νῖκος
νῖκος   acc sg neut [3t; n-3d(2b); 3777]   "
νικῶ   pres pass imperative 2 sg
        [Rm 12:21; v-1d(1a); 3771]   νικάω
νικῶν   pres act ptcp nom sg masc
        [8t; v-1d(1a); 3771]   "
νικῶντας   pres act ptcp acc pl masc
        [Rv 15:2; v-1d(1a); 3771]   "
νικῶντι   pres act ptcp dat sg masc
        [2t; v-1d(1a); 3771]   "

Νινευή, ἡ   {3778, n-3g(2)}
see Νινευΐται, *Nineveh,* indecl., Luke 11:32 v.l.*

Νινευΐ, ἡ   {3779, n-3g(2)}
see Νινευΐται, *Nineveh,* the capital of Assyria,
indecl., Luke 11:32 v.l.*

Νινευΐται   nom pl masc [2t; n-1f; 3780]   Νινευΐτης
Νινευΐταις   dat pl masc [Lk 11:30; n-1f; 3780]   "

Νινευΐτης, ου, ὁ   {3780, n-1f}
a Ninevite, an inhabitant of Nineveh, Matt 12:41;
Luke 11:30, 32*

νίπτειν   pres act inf [2t; v-4; 3782]   νίπτω
νίπτεις   pres act ind 2 sg [Jn 13:6; v-4; 3782]   "

νιπτήρ, ῆρος, ὁ   {3781, n-3f(2a)}
a basin for washing some part of the person,
John 13:5*

νιπτῆρα   acc sg masc
        [Jn 13:5; n-3f(2a); 3781]   νιπτήρ
νίπτονται   pres mid ind 3 pl
        [Mt 15:2; v-4; 3782]   νίπτω

νίπτω   {3782, v-4}
[-, ἔνιψα, -, -, -] *to wash;* spc. *to wash some part*
of the person, as distinguished from λούω,
Matt 6:17; John 13:8

νίψαι   aor mid imperative 2 sg
        [3t; v-4; 3782]   "
νιψάμενος   aor mid ptcp nom sg masc
        [Jn 9:11; v-4; 3782]   "
νίψασθαι   aor mid inf [Jn 13:10; v-4; 3782]   "
νίψῃς   aor act subj 2 sg [Jn 13:8; v-4; 3782]   "
νίψω   aor act subj 1 sg [Jn 13:8; v-4; 3782]   "
νίψωνται   aor mid subj 3 pl [Mk 7:3; v-4; 3782]   "
νόει   pres act imperative 2 sg
        [2Ti 2:7; v-1d(2a); 3783]   νοέω
νοεῖτε   pres act ind 2 pl [5t; v-1d(2a); 3783]   "
νοείτω   pres act imperative 3 sg
        [2t; v-1d(2a); 3783]   "

νοέω   {3783, v-1d(2a)}
[νοήσω, ἐνόησα, νενόηκα, -, -] *to perceive, observe;*
to mark attentively, Matt 24:15; Mark 13:14; 2
Tim 2:7; *to understand, comprehend,* Matt 15:17;
to conceive, Eph 3:20

νόημα, ατος, τό   {3784, n-3c(4)}
the mind, the understanding, intellect, 2 Cor 3:14;
4:4; Phil 4:7; *the heart, soul, affections, feelings,*
disposition, 2 Cor 11:3; *a conception of the mind,*
thought, purpose, device, 2 Cor 2:11; 10:5*

νόημα   acc sg neut [2C 10:5; n-3c(4); 3784]   νόημα
νοήματα   nom pl neut [2t; n-3c(4); 3784]   "
νοήματα   acc pl neut [3t; n-3c(4); 3784]   "
νοῆσαι   aor act inf [Ep 3:4; v-1d(2a); 3783]   νοέω
νοήσωσιν   aor act subj 3 pl
        [Jn 12:40; v-1d(2a); 3783]   "
νόθοι   nom pl masc [Hb 12:8; a-1a(2a); 3785] νόθος

νόθος, η, ον   {3785, a-1a(2a)}
spurious, bastard, Heb 12:8*

νοΐ   dat sg masc [6t; n-3e(4); 3808]   νοῦς

νομή, ῆς, ἡ   {3786, n-1b}
pasture, pasturage, John 10:9; ἔχειν νομήν, *to eat*
its way, spread corrosion, 2 Tim 2:17*

νομήν   acc sg fem [2t; n-1b; 3786]   νομή
νομίζει   pres act ind 3 sg
        [1C 7:36; v-2a(1); 3787]   νομίζω
νομίζειν   pres act inf [Ac 17:29; v-2a(1); 3787]   "
νομίζοντες   pres act ptcp nom pl masc
        [Ac 14:19; v-2a(1); 3787]   "
νομιζόντων   pres act ptcp gen pl masc
        [1Ti 6:5; v-2a(1); 3787]   "

νομίζω   {3787, v-2a(1)}
[(ἐνόμιζον), -, ἐνόμισα, -, -, -] *to own as settled and*
established; to deem, 1 Cor 7:26; 1 Tim 6:5; *to*

suppose, presume, Matt 5:17; 20:10; Luke 2:44; pass. to be usual, customary, Acts 16:13

νομίζω   pres act ind 1 sg
[1C 7:26; v-2a(1); 3787]   "
νομίζων   pres act ptcp nom sg masc
[Ac 16:27; v-2a(1); 3787]   "
νομικάς   acc pl fem
[Ti 3:9; a-1a(2a); 3788]   νομικός
νομικοί   nom pl masc [Lk 7:30; a-1a(2a); 3788]   "
νομικοῖς   dat pl masc [2t; a-1a(2a); 3788]   "
νομικόν   acc sg masc [Ti 3:13; a-1a(2a); 3788]   "

νομικός, ή, όν   {3788, a-1a(2a)}
pertaining to law; relating to the Mosaic law, Titus 3:9; as a subst., one skilled in law, a jurist, lawyer, Titus 3:13; spc. an interpreter and teacher of the Mosaic law, Matt 22:35

νομικός   nom sg masc [2t; a-1a(2a); 3788]   "
νομικούς   acc pl masc [Lk 14:3; a-1a(2a); 3788]   "
νομικῶν   gen pl masc [Lk 11:45; a-1a(2a); 3788]   "

νομίμως   {3789, adverb}
lawfully, agreeably to law or custom, rightfully, 1 Tim 1:8; 2 Tim 2:5*

νομίμως   adverb [2t; adverb; 3789]   νομίμως
νομίσαντες   aor act ptcp nom pl masc
[Lk 2:44; v-2a(1); 3787]   νομίζω
νομίσητε   aor act subj 2 pl [2t; v-2a(1); 3787]   "

νόμισμα, ατος, τό   {3790, n-3c(4)}
pr. a thing sanctioned by law or custom; lawful money, coin, Matt 22:19*

νόμισμα   acc sg neut
[Mt 22:19; n-3c(4); 3790]   νόμισμα
νομοδιδάσκαλοι   nom pl masc
[2t; n-2a; 3791]   νομοδιδάσκαλος

νομοδιδάσκαλος, ου, ὁ   {3791, n-2a}
a teacher and interpreter of the Mosaic law, Luke 5:17; Acts 5:34; 1 Tim 1:7

νομοδιδάσκαλος   nom sg masc [Ac 5:34; n-2a; 3791]
"

νομοθεσία, ας, ἡ   {3792, n-1a}
legislation; ἡ νομοθεσία, the gift of the Divine law, or the Mosaic law itself, Rom 9:4*

νομοθεσία   nom sg fem
[Rm 9:4; n-1a; 3792]   νομοθεσία

νομοθετέω   {3793, v-1d(2a)}
[-, ἐνομοθέτησα, -, νενομοθέτημαι, -] to impose a law, give laws; in N.T. pass., to have a law imposed on one's self, receive a law, Heb 7:11; to be enacted, constituted, Heb 8:6*

νομοθέτης, ου, ὁ   {3794, n-1f}
a legislator, lawgiver, James 4:12*

νομοθέτης   nom sg masc
[Jm 4:12; n-1f; 3794]   νομοθέτης
νόμον   acc sg masc [59t; n-2a; 3795]   νόμος

νόμος, ου, ὁ   {3795, n-2a}
a law, Rom 4:15; 1 Tim 1:9; the Mosaic law, Matt 5:17, et al. freq.; the Old Testament Scripture, John 10:34; a legal tie, Rom 7:2, 3; a law, a rule,

standard, Rom 3:27; a rule of life and conduct, Gal 6:2, James 1:25

νόμος   nom sg masc [34t; n-2a; 3795]   "
νόμου   gen sg masc [67t; n-2a; 3795]   "
νόμους   acc pl masc [2t; n-2a; 3795]   "
νόμῳ   dat sg masc [32t; n-2a; 3795]   "
νοός   gen sg masc [6t; n-3e(4); 3808]   νοῦς
νοοῦμεν   pres act ind 1 pl
[2t; v-1d(2a); 3783]   νοέω
νοούμενα   pres pass ptcp nom pl neut
[Rm 1:20; v-1d(2a); 3783]   "
νοοῦντες   pres act ptcp nom pl masc
[1Ti 1:7; v-1d(2a); 3783]   "

νοσέω   {3796, v-1d(2a)}
[-, -, -, -, -] to be sick; met. to have a diseased appetite or craving for a thing, have an excessive and vicious fondness for a thing, 1 Tim 6:4*

νόσημα, ατος, τό   {3797, n-3c(4)}
disease, sickness, John 5:4 v.l.*

νόσοις   dat pl fem [3t; n-2b; 3798]   νόσος
νόσον   acc sg fem [3t; n-2b; 3798]   "

νόσος, ου, ἡ   {3798, n-2b}
a disease, sickness, distemper, Matt 4:23, 24; 8:17; 9:35

νόσους   acc pl fem [3t; n-2b; 3798]   "

νοσσιά, ᾶς, ἡ   {3799, n-1a}
a brood of young birds, Luke 13:34*

νοσσία   acc pl neut [Mt 23:37; n-2c; 3800] νοσσίον
νοσσιάν   acc sg fem [Lk 13:34; n-1a; 3799] νοσσιά

νοσσίον, ου, τό   {3800, n-2c}
the young of birds, a chick; pl. a brood of young birds, Matt 23:37*

νοσσός, οῦ, ὁ   {3801, n-2a}
also spelled νεοσσός, the young of birds, a young bird, chick, Luke 2:24*

νοσσούς   acc pl masc [Lk 2:24; n-2a; 3801] νοσσός
νοσφιζομένους   pres mid ptcp acc pl masc
[Ti 2:10; v-2a(1); 3802]   νοσφίζω

νοσφίζω   {3802, v-2a(1)}
[-, ἐνόσφισα, -, -, -] to deprive, rob; mid. to misappropriate; to make secret reservation, Acts 5:2, 3; to purloin, Titus 2:10*

νοσφίσασθαι   aor mid inf [Ac 5:3; v-2a(1); 3802]   "
νόσων   gen pl fem [2t; n-2b; 3798]   νόσος
νοσῶν   pres act ptcp nom sg masc
[1Ti 6:4; v-1d(2a); 3796]   νοσέω
νότον   acc sg masc [Lk 12:55; n-2a; 3803]   νότος

νότος, ου, ὁ   {3803, n-2a}
the south wind, Luke 12:55; Acts 27:13; 28:13; meton. the south, the southern quarter of the heavens, Matt 12:42; Luke 11:31; 13:29; Rev 21:13*

νότου   gen sg masc [6t; n-2a; 3803]   νότος

νουθεσία, ας, ἡ   {3804, n-1a}
warning, admonition, 1 Cor 10:11; Eph 6:4; Titus 3:10*

νουθεσία   dat sg fem
[Ep 6:4; n-1a; 3804]   νουθεσία
νουθεσίαν   acc sg fem [2t; n-1a; 3804]   "
νουθετεῖν   pres act inf
[Rm 15:14; v-1d(2a); 3805]   νουθετέω
νουθετεῖτε   pres act imperative 2 pl
[2t; v-1d(2a); 3805]   "

νουθετέω   {3805, v-1d(2a)}
[νουθετήσω, ἐνουθέτησα, -, -, -] pr. *to put in mind;
to admonish, warn*, Acts 20:31; Rom 15:14; Titus
1:11 v.l.*

νουθετοῦντας   pres act ptcp acc pl masc
[1Th 5:12; v-1d(2a); 3805]   "
νουθετοῦντες   pres act ptcp nom pl masc
[2t; v-1d(2a); 3805]   "
νουθετῶν   pres act ptcp nom sg masc
[2t; v-1d(2a); 3805]   "

νουμηνία, see νεομηνία   {3806}

νοῦν   acc sg masc [9t; n-3e(4); 3808]   νοῦς

νουνεχῶς   {3807, adverb}
understandingly, sensibly, discreetly, Mark 12:34*

νουνεχῶς   adverb [Mk 12:34; adverb; 3807]
νουνεχῶς

νοῦς, νοός, νοΐ, νοῦν, ὁ   {3808, n-3e(4)}
the mind, intellect, 1 Cor 14:15, 19; *understanding,
intelligent faculty*, Luke 24:45; *intellect,
judgment*, Rom 7:23, 25; *opinion, sentiment*, Rom
14:5; 1 Cor 1:10; *mind, thought, conception*, Rom
11:34; 1 Cor 2:16; Phil 4:7; *settled state of mind*, 2
Thess 2:2; *frame of mind*, Rom 1:28; 12:2; Col
2:18; Eph 4:23; 1 Tim 6:5; 2 Tim 3:8; Titus 1:15

νοῦς   nom sg masc [3t; n-3e(4); 3808]   νοῦς
νύκτα   acc sg fem [4t; n-3c(1); 3816]   νύξ
νύκτας   acc pl fem [4t; n-3c(1); 3816]   "
νυκτί   dat sg fem [13t; n-3c(1); 3816]   "
νυκτός   gen sg fem [33t; n-3c(1); 3816]   "

Νύμφα, ας, ἡ   {3809, n-1a}
Nymphas, pr. name. Occurs in N.T. only at Col
4:15 as the acc. Νύμφαν, either from the fem.
Νύμφα (Attic, Νύμφη, ης), or from the masc.
Νυμφᾶς, ᾶς (3810). *BAGD* suggest is is a
shortened form of Νυμφόδωρος.*

Νύμφαν   acc sg fem [Cl 4:15; n-1a; 3809]   Νύμφαν

νύμφη, ης, ἡ   {3811, n-1b}
a bride, John 3:29; Rev 18:23; 21:2, 9; 22:17;
opposed to πενθερά, *a daughter-in-law*, Matt
10:35; Luke 12:53; Matt 25:1 v.l.*

νύμφη   nom sg fem [2t; n-1b; 3811]   νύμφη
νύμφην   acc sg fem [5t; n-1b; 3811]   "
νύμφης   gen sg fem [Rv 18:23; n-1b; 3811]   "
νυμφίον   acc sg masc [2t; n-2a; 3812]   νυμφίος

νυμφίος, ου, ὁ   {3812, n-2a}
a bridegroom, Matt 9:15; 25:1, 5, 6, 10

νυμφίος   nom sg masc [9t; n-2a; 3812]   "
νυμφίου   gen sg masc [5t; n-2a; 3812]   "

νυμφών, ῶνος, ὁ   {3813, n-3f(1a)}
a bridal-chamber; in N.T. υἱοὶ τοῦ νυμφῶνος, *sons*

*of the bridal-chamber, the bridegroom's attendant
friends, groomsmen*, perhaps the same as the
Greek παρανύμφιοι, Matt 9:15; Mark 2:19; Luke
5:34, Matt 22:10 v.l.*

νυμφῶνος   gen sg masc [3t; n-3f(1a); 3813]   νυμφών

νῦν   {3814, adverb}
now, at the present time, Mark 10:30; Luke 6:21,
et al. freq.; *just now*, John 11:8; *forthwith*, John
12:31; καὶ νῦν, *even now, as matters stand*, John
11:22; *now*, expressive of a marked tone of
address, Acts 7:34; 13:11; James 4:13; 5:1; τὸ νῦν,
the present time, Luke 1:48; τανῦν, or τὰ νῦν,
now, Acts 4:29

νῦν   adverb [147t; adverb; 3814]   νῦν

νυνί   {3815, adverb}
of time, *now, at this very moment*, an emphatic
form of νῦν although it now carries the same
meaning

νυνί   adverb [20t; adverb; 3815]   νυνί

νύξ, νυκτός, ἡ   {3816, n-3c(1)}
night, Matt 2:14; 28:13; John 3:2; met. spiritual
night, moral *darkness*, Rom 13:12; 1 Thess 5:5

νύξ   nom sg fem [7t; n-3c(1); 3816]   νύξ

νύσσω   {3817, v-2b}
[-, ἔνυξα, -, -, ἐνύγην] *to prick* or *pierce*, John
19:34; Matt 27:49 v.l.; Acts 12:7 v.l. *

νυστάζει   pres act ind 3 sg
[2P 2:3; v-2a(2); 3818]   νυστάζω

νυστάζω   {3818, v-2a(2)}
[-, ἐνύσταξα, -, -, -] *to nod; to nod in sleep; to sink
into a sleep*, Matt 25:5; *to slumber* in inactivity, 2
Peter 2:3*

νυχθήμερον, ου, τό   {3819, n-2c}
a day and night, twenty-four hours; 2 Cor 11:25*

νυχθήμερον   acc sg neut
[2C 11:25; n-2c; 3819]   νυχθήμερον

Νῶε, ὁ   {3820, n-3g(2)}
Noah, pr. name, indecl., Matt 24:37ff; Luke 3:36;
17:26f.; Heb 11:7; 1 Peter 3:20; 2 Peter 2:25*

Νῶε   indecl [8t; n-3g(2); 3820]   Νῶε

νωθροί   nom pl masc [2t; a-1a(1); 3821]   νωθρός

νωθρός, ά, όν   {3821, a-1a(1)}
slow, sluggish, lazy, Heb 5:11; 6:12*

νῶτος, ου, ὁ   {3822, n-2a}
the back of men or animals, Rom 11:10*

νῶτον   acc sg masc [Rm 11:10; n-2a; 3822]   νῶτος

ξ

ξαίνω   {3824}
comb, wool, Matt 6:28 v.l. See discussion in
BAGD

ξέναις   dat pl fem [Hb 13:9; a-1a(2a); 3828]   ξένος

ξενία, ας, ἡ {3825, n-1a}
pr. *state of being a guest;* then, *the reception of a guest* or *stranger, hospitality,* in N.T. *a lodging,* Acts 28:23; Phil 22*

ξενίαν acc sg fem [2t; n-1a; 3825] ξενία
ξενίζεσθε pres pass imperative 2 pl
[1P 4:12; v-2a(1); 3826] ξενίζω
ξενίζεται pres pass ind 3 sg [3t; v-2a(1); 3826] "
ξενίζοντα pres act ptcp acc pl neut
[Ac 17:20; v-2a(1); 3826] "
ξενίζονται pres pass ind 3 pl
[1P 4:4; v-2a(1); 3826] "

ξενίζω {3826, v-2a(1)}
[-, ἐξένισα, -, -, ἐξενίσθην] *to receive as a guest, entertain,* Acts 10:23; 28:7; Heb 13:2; pass. *to be entertained as a guest, to lodge* or *reside with,* Acts 10:6, 18, 32; 21:16; *to strike with a feeling of strangeness, to surprise;* pass. or mid. *to be struck with surprise, be staggered, be amazed,* 1 Peter 4:4, 12; intrans. *to be strange;* ξενίζοντα, *strange matters, novelties,* Acts 17:20; 1 Cor 16:19 v.l.*

ξενίσαντες aor act ptcp nom pl masc
[Hb 13:2; v-2a(1); 3826] "
ξενισθῶμεν aor pass subj 1 pl
[Ac 21:16; v-2a(1); 3826] "

ξενοδοχέω {3827, v-1d(2a)}
[-, ἐξενοδόχησα, -, -, -] *to receive and entertain strangers, exercise hospitality,* 1 Tim 5:10*

ξένοι nom pl masc [4t; a-1a(2a); 3828] ξένος
ξένοις dat pl masc [Mt 27:7; a-1a(2a); 3828] "
ξένον acc sg masc [2t; a-1a(2a); 3828] "

ξένος, η, ον {3828, a-1a(2a)}
strange, foreign, alien, Eph 2:12, 19; *strange, unexpected, surprising,* 1 Peter 4:12; *novel,* Heb 13:9; subst. *a stranger,* Matt 25:35, et al.; *a host,* Rom 16:23

ξένος nom sg masc [3t; a-1a(2a); 3828] "
ξένου gen sg neut [1P 4:12; a-1a(2a); 3828] "
ξένους acc pl masc [3J 5; a-1a(2a); 3828] "
ξένων gen pl neut [Ac 17:18; a-1a(2a); 3828] "

ξέστης, ου, ὁ {3829, n-1f}
a sextarius, a Roman measure, containing about one pint English; in N.T. used for *a small vessel, cup, pot,* Mark 7:4, 8 v.l.*

ξεστῶν gen pl masc [Mk 7:4; n-1f; 3829] ξέστης
ξηρά nom sg fem [Lk 6:6; a-1a(1); 3831] ξηρός
ξηραίνεται pres pass ind 3 sg
[Mk 9:18; v-2d(4); 3830] ξηραίνω

ξηραίνω {3830, v-2d(4)}
[-, ἐξήρανα, -, ἐξήραμμαι, ἐξηράνθην] *to dry up, parch,* James 1:11; pass. *to be parched,* Matt 13:6, et al.; *to be ripened* as corn, Rev 14:15; *to be withered, to wither,* Mark 11:20; of parts of the body, *to be withered,* Mark 3:1, 3; *to pine,* Mark 9:18

ξηράν acc sg fem [4t; a-1a(1); 3831] ξηρός
ξηρᾶς gen sg fem [Hb 11:29; a-1a(1); 3831] "

ξηρός, ά, όν {3831, a-1a(1)}
dry, withered, Luke 23:31; ἡ ξηρά, sc. γῆ, *the dry*

land, land, Matt 23:15; Heb 11:29; of parts of the body, *withered,* Matt 12:10

ξηρῷ dat sg neut [Lk 23:31; a-1a(1); 3831] "
ξηρῶν gen pl masc [Jn 5:3; a-1a(1); 3831] "
ξύλα acc pl neut [1C 3:12; n-2c; 3833] ξύλον
ξύλινα nom pl neut
[2Ti 2:20; a-1a(2a); 3832] ξύλινος
ξύλινα acc pl neut [Rv 9:20; a-1a(2a); 3832] "

ξύλινος, η, ον {3832, a-1a(2a)}
wooden, of wood, made of wood, 2 Tim 2:20; Rev 9:20*

ξύλον, ου, τό {3833, n-2c}
wood, timber, 1 Cor 3:12; Rev 18:12; *stocks,* Acts 16:24; *a club,* Matt 26:47, 55; *a post, cross, gibbet,* Acts 5:30; 10:29; 13:29; *a tree,* Luke 23:31; Rev 2:7

ξύλον nom sg neut [Rv 22:2; n-2c; 3833] ξύλον
ξύλον acc sg neut [4t; n-2c; 3833] "
ξύλου gen sg masc [Ac 10:39; n-2c; 3833] "
ξύλου gen sg neut [7t; n-2c; 3833] "
ξύλῳ dat sg neut [Lk 23:31; n-2c; 3833] "
ξύλων gen pl neut [5t; n-2c; 3833] "

ξυρᾶσθαι aor mid inf
[1C 11:6; v-1d(1a); 3834] ξυράω

ξυράω {3834, v-1d(1a)}
[ξυρήσω, -, -, ἐξύρημαι, -] *to cut off the hair, shear, shave,* Acts 21:24; 1 Cor 11:5, 6*

ξυρήσονται fut mid ind 3 pl
[Ac 21:24; v-1d(1a); 3834] ξυράω

Ο

ὁ, ἡ, τό {3836, a-1a(2b)}
the prepositive article, answering, to a considerable extent, to the English definite article; but, for the principle and facts of its usage, consult a grammar; ὁ μὲν ... ὁ δέ, *the one ... the other,* Phil 1:16, 17; Heb 7:5, 6, 20, 21, 23, 24; pl. *some ... others,* Matt 13:23; 22:5, 6; ὁ δέ, *but he,* Matt 4:4; 12:48; οἱ δέ, *but others,* Matt 28:17; used, in a poetic quotation, for a personal pronoun, Acts 17:28

ὁ nom sg masc [2934t; a-1a(2b); 3836] ὁ
ὅ nom sg neut [73t; a-1a(2b); 4005] ὅς
ὅ acc sg neut [177t; a-1a(2b); 4005] ὅς
ὀγδόῃ dat sg fem [2t; a-1a(2a); 3838] ὄγδοος

ὀγδοήκοντα {3837, a-5b}
indecl. numeral, *eighty,* Luke 2:37; 16:7*

ὀγδοήκοντα indecl [2t; a-5b; 3837] ὀγδοήκοντα
ὄγδοον acc sg masc
[2P 2:5; a-1a(2a); 3838] ὄγδοος

ὄγδοος, η, ον {3838, a-1a(2a)}
the eighth, Luke 1:59; Acts 7:8; 2 Pet 2:5; Rev 17:11; 21:20*

ὄγδοος nom sg masc [2t; a-1a(2a); 3838] "
ὄγκον acc sg masc [Hb 12:1; n-2a; 3839] ὄγκος

ὄγκος, ου, ὁ   {3839, n-2a}
pr. *bulk, weight; a burden, impediment,* Heb 12:1*

ὅδε, ἥδε, τόδε   {3840, a-1a(2b)}
this, that, he, she, it, Luke 10:39; 16:25; Acts 15:23

ὁδεύω   {3841, v-1a(6)}
[-, ὥδευσα, -, -, -] *to journey, travel,* Luke 10:33*

ὁδεύων   pres act ptcp nom sg masc
[Lk 10:33; v-1a(6); 3841]   ὁδεύω
ὁδηγεῖν   pres act inf
[Lk 6:39; v-1d(2a); 3842]   ὁδηγέω

ὁδηγέω   {3842, v-1d(2a)}
[ὁδηγήσω, -, -, -, -] *to lead, guide,* Matt 15:14;
Luke 6:39; Rev 7:17; met. *to instruct, teach,* John
16:13; Acts 8:31*

ὁδηγῇ   pres act subj 3 sg
[Mt 15:14; v-1d(2a); 3842]   "
ὁδηγήσει   fut act ind 3 sg [3t; v-1d(2a); 3842]   "
ὁδηγοί   nom pl masc
[Mt 15:14; n-2a; 3843]   ὁδηγός
ὁδηγοί   voc pl masc [2t; n-2a; 3843]   "
ὁδηγόν   acc sg masc [Rm 2:19; n-2a; 3843]   "

ὁδηγός, οῦ, ὁ   {3843, n-2a}
a guide, leader, Acts 1:16; met. *an instructor,
teacher,* Matt 15:14; 23:16, 24; Rom 2:19*

ὁδηγοῦ   gen sg masc [Ac 1:16; n-2a; 3843]   "
ὁδοί   nom pl fem [2t; n-2b; 3847]   ὁδός

ὁδοιπορέω   {3844, v-1d(2a)}
[-, ὡδοιπόρησα, -, -, -] *to journey, travel,* Acts
10:9*

ὁδοιπορία, ας, ἡ   {3845, n-1a}
to journey, journeying, travel, John 4:6; 2 Cor
11:26*

ὁδοιπορίαις   dat pl fem
[2C 11:26; n-1a; 3845]   ὁδοιπορία
ὁδοιπορίας   gen sg fem [Jn 4:6; n-1a; 3845]   "
ὁδοιπορούντων   pres act ptcp gen pl masc
[Ac 10:9; v-1d(2a); 3844]   ὁδοιπορέω
ὁδοῖς   dat pl fem [3t; n-2b; 3847]   ὁδός
ὁδόν   acc sg fem [51t; n-2b; 3847]   "
ὁδόντα   acc sg masc
[Mt 5:38; n-3c(5a); 3848]   ὁδούς
ὁδόντας   acc pl masc [2t; n-3c(5a); 3848]   "
ὁδόντες   nom pl masc [Rv 9:8; n-3c(5a); 3848]   "
ὁδόντος   gen sg masc [Mt 5:38; n-3c(5a); 3848]   "
ὁδόντων   gen pl masc [7t; n-3c(5a); 3848]   "

ὁδός, οῦ, ἡ   {3847, n-2b}
a way, road, Matt 2:12; 7:13, 14; 8:28; 22:9, 10;
means of access, approach, entrance, John 14:6;
Heb 9:8; *direction, quarter, region,* Matt 4:15; 10:5
the act of journeying, a journey, way, course, Matt
10:10; Mark 2:23; 1 Thess 3:11; *a journey,* as
regards extent, Acts 1:12; met. *a way,* systematic
course of pursuit, Luke 1:79; Acts 2:28; 16:17; *a
way,* systematic *course* of action or conduct,
Matt 21:32; Rom 11:33; 1 Cor 4:17; *a way, system
of doctrine,* Acts 18:26; ἡ ὁδός, *the way of the
Christian faith,* Acts 19:9, 23, 24:22

ὁδός   nom sg fem [5t; n-2b; 3847]   ὁδός

ὁδοῦ   gen sg fem [8t; n-2b; 3847]   "

ὁδούς, όντος, τό   {3848, n-3c(5a)}
a tooth, Matt 5:38; 8:12

ὁδούς   acc pl fem [8t; n-2b; 3847]   "
ὁδύναις   dat pl fem [1Ti 6:10; n-1b; 3850]   ὀδύνη
ὀδυνᾶσαι   pres pass ind 2 sg
[Lk 16:25; v-1d(1a); 3849]   ὀδυνάω

ὀδυνάω   {3849, v-1d(1a)}
[-, -, -, -, -] *to pain* either bodily or mentally;
pass. *to be in an agony, be tormented,* Luke 2:48;
16:24, 25; *to be distressed, grieved,* Acts 20:38*

ὀδύνη, ης, ἡ   {3850, n-1b}
pain of body of mind; *sorrow, grief,* Rom 9:2; 1
Tim 6:10; Matt 24:8 v.l.*

ὀδύνη   nom sg fem [Rm 9:2; n-1b; 3850]   ὀδύνη
ὀδυνῶμαι   pres pass ind 1 sg
[Lk 16:24; v-1d(1a); 3849]   ὀδυνάω
ὀδυνώμενοι   pres pass ptcp nom pl masc
[2t; v-1d(1a); 3849]   "
ὀδυρμόν   acc sg masc
[2C 7:7; n-2a; 3851]   ὀδυρμός

ὀδυρμός, οῦ, ὁ   {3851, n-2a}
bitter lamentation, wailing, Matt 2:18; meton.
sorrow, mourning, 2 Cor 7:7*

ὀδυρμός   nom sg masc [Mt 2:18; n-2a; 3851]   "
ὁδῷ   dat sg fem [23t; n-2b; 3847]   ὁδός
ὁδῶν   gen pl fem [Mt 22:9; n-2b; 3847]   "
ὄζει   pres act ind 3 sg
[Jn 11:39; v-2a(1); 3853]   ὄζω
Ὀζίαν   acc sg masc [Mt 1:8; n-1d; 3852]   Ὀζίας

Ὀζίας, ου, ὁ   {3852, n-1d}
Uzziah, pr. name, indeclinable, Luke 3:23ff.;
Matt 1:9 v.l.*

Ὀζίας   nom sg masc [Mt 1:9; n-1d; 3852]   "

ὄζω   {3853, v-2a(1)}
[-, -, -, -, -] *to smell, emit an odor; to have an
offensive smell, stink,* John 11:39*

ὅθεν   {3854, adverb}
whence, Matt 12:44; Acts 14:26; *from the place
where,* Matt 25:24, 26; *whence, from which
circumstance,* 1 John 2:18; *wherefore, whereupon,*
Matt 14:7

ὅθεν   adverb [15t; adverb; 3854]   ὅθεν

ὀθόνη, ης, ἡ   {3855, n-1b}
pr. *fine linen; a linen cloth; a sheet,* Acts 10:11;
11:5*

ὀθόνην   acc sg fem [2t; n-1b; 3855]   ὀθόνη
ὀθόνια   acc pl neut [3t; n-2c; 3856]   ὀθόνιον
ὀθονίοις   dat pl neut [Jn 19:40; n-2c; 3856]   "

ὀθόνιον, ου, τό   {3856, n-2c}
a linen cloth; in N.T. *a swath, bandage* for a
corpse, Luke 24:12

ὀθονίων   gen pl neut [Jn 20:7; n-2c; 3856]   "
οἱ   nom pl masc [1150t; a-1a(2b); 3836]   ὁ
οἷα   nom sg fem [2t; a-1a(1); 3888]   οἷος
οἷα   nom pl neut [2Ti 3:11; a-1a(1); 3888]   "

οἷα   acc pl neut [Mk 9:3; a-1a(1); 3888]   "

οἶδα   {3857, v-1b(3)}
[εἰδήσω or εἴσομαι, ᾔδειν, -, -, -] to know, Matt
6:8; to know how, Matt 7:11; from the Hebrew, to
regard with favor, 1 Thess 5:12. οἶδα is actually a
perfect form functioning as a present, and ᾔδειν
is actually a pluperfect form functioning as an
aorist.

οἶδα   perf act ind 1 sg [56t; v-1b(3); 3857]   οἶδα
οἴδαμεν   perf act ind 1 pl [43t; v-1b(3); 3857]   "
οἶδας   perf act ind 2 sg [17t; v-1b(3); 3857]   "
οἴδασιν   perf act ind 3 pl [7t; v-1b(3); 3857]   "
οἴδατε   perf act ind 2 pl [63t; v-1b(3); 3857]   "
οἶδεν   perf act ind 3 sg [22t; v-1b(3); 3857]   "
οἰέσθω   pres mid imperative 3 sg
[Jm 1:7; v-1d(2c); 3887]   οἴομαι
οἰκεῖ   pres act ind 3 sg
[4t; v-1d(2a); 3861]   οἰκέω
οἰκεῖν   pres act inf [2t; v-1d(2a); 3861]   "
οἰκεῖοι   nom pl masc
[Ep 2:19; a-3b(1); 3858]   οἰκεῖος

οἰκεῖος, (α), ον   {3858, a-3b(1)}
belonging to a house, domestic; pl. members of a
family, immediate kin, 1 Tim 5:8; members of a
spiritual family, Eph 2:19; members of a spiritual
brotherhood, Gal 6:10*

οἰκείους   acc pl masc [Ga 6:10; a-3b(1); 3858]   "
οἰκείων   gen pl masc [1Ti 5:8; a-3b(1); 3858]   "
οἰκέται   voc pl masc
[1P 2:18; n-1f; 3860]   οἰκέτης

οἰκετεία, ας, ἡ   {3859, n-1a}
the members, of a household, Matt 24:45*

οἰκετείας   gen sg fem
[Mt 24:45; n-1a; 3859]   οἰκετεία
οἰκέτην   acc sg masc
[Rm 14:4; n-1f; 3860]   οἰκέτης

οἰκέτης, ου, ὁ   {3860, n-1f}
pr. an inmate of a house; a domestic servant,
household slave, Luke 16:13; Acts 10:7; Rom 14:4;
1 Peter 2:18*

οἰκέτης   nom sg masc [Lk 16:13; n-1f; 3860]   "
οἰκετῶν   gen pl masc [Ac 10:7; n-1f; 3860]   "

οἰκέω   {3861, v-1d(2a)}
[οἰκήσω, ᾤκησα, -, -, -] to dwell in, inhabit, 1 Tim
6:16; intrans. to dwell, live; to cohabit, 1 Cor 7:12,
13; to be indwelling, indwell, Rom 7:17, 18, 20;
8:9, 11; 1 Cor 3:16*

οἴκημα, ατος, τό   {3862, n-3c(4)}
a dwelling; used in various conventional senses,
and among them, a prison, cell, Acts 12:7*

οἰκήματι   dat sg neut
[Ac 12:7; n-3c(4); 3862]   οἴκημα

οἰκητήριον, ου, τό   {3863, n-2c}
a habitation, dwelling, an abode, Jude 6; trop. the
personal abode of the soul, 2 Cor 5:2*

οἰκητήριον   acc sg neut
[2t; n-2c; 3863]   οἰκητήριον

οἰκία, ας, ἡ   {3864, n-1a}
a house, dwelling, an abode, Matt 2:11; 7:24, 27;
trop. the bodily abode of the soul, 2 Cor 5:1;
meton. a household, family, Matt 10:13; 12:25;
meton. goods, property, means, Matt 23:13

οἰκία   nom sg fem [9t; n-1a; 3864]   οἰκία
οἰκίᾳ   dat sg fem [26t; n-1a; 3864]   "
οἰκιακοί   nom pl masc
[Mt 10:36; n-2a; 3865]   οἰκιακός

οἰκιακός, οῦ, ὁ   {3865, n-2a}
belonging to a house; pl. the members of a
household or family, kindred, Matt 10:25, 36*

οἰκιακούς   acc pl masc [Mt 10:25; n-2a; 3865]   "
οἰκίαν   acc sg fem [40t; n-1a; 3864]   οἰκία
οἰκίας   gen sg fem [10t; n-1a; 3864]   "
οἰκίας   acc pl fem [7t; n-1a; 3864]   "
οἰκιῶν   gen pl fem [Ac 4:34; n-1a; 3864]   "
οἰκοδεσποτεῖν   pres act inf
[1Ti 5:14; cv-1d(2a); 3866]   οἰκοδεσποτέω

οἰκοδεσποτέω   {3866, cv-1d(2a)}
[-, -, -, -, -, -] pr. to be master of a household; to occupy
one's self in the management of a household, 1 Tim
5:14*

οἰκοδεσπότῃ   dat sg masc
[4t; n-1f; 3867]   οἰκοδεσπότης
οἰκοδεσπότην   acc sg masc [Mt 10:25; n-1f; 3867]   "

οἰκοδεσπότης, ου, ὁ   {3867, n-1f}
the master or head of a house or family, Matt 10:25;
13:27, 52

οἰκοδεσπότης   nom sg masc [5t; n-1f; 3867]   "
οἰκοδεσπότου   gen sg masc [2t; n-1f; 3867]   "
οἰκοδομαί   nom pl fem
[Mk 13:1; n-1b; 3869]   οἰκοδομή
οἰκοδομάς   acc pl fem [2t; n-1b; 3869]   "
οἰκοδομεῖ   pres act ind 3 sg
[4t; v-1d(2a); 3868]   οἰκοδομέω
οἰκοδομεῖν   pres act inf
[Lk 14:30; v-1d(2a); 3868]   "
οἰκοδομεῖσθε   pres pass ind 2 pl
[1P 2:5; v-1d(2a); 3868]   "
οἰκοδομεῖται   pres pass ind 3 sg
[1C 14:17; v-1d(2a); 3868]   "
οἰκοδομεῖτε   pres act imperative 2 pl
[1Th 5:11; v-1d(2a); 3868]   "
οἰκοδομεῖτε   pres act ind 2 pl
[3t; v-1d(2a); 3868]   "

οἰκοδομέω   {3868, v-1d(2a)}
[(ᾠκοδόμουν), οἰκοδομήσω, ᾠκοδόμησα, -,
οἰκοδόμημαι or ᾠκοδόμημαι, οἰκοδομήθην or
ᾠκοδομήθην] pluperfect, ᾠκοδόμητο (3 sg), to
build a house; to build, Matt 7:24; to repair,
embellish, and amplify a building, Matt 23:29; to
construct, establish, Matt 16:18; met. to contribute
to advancement in religious knowledge, to edify,
1 Cor 14:4, 17; to advance a person's spiritual
condition, to edify, 1 Cor 8:1; pass. to make
spiritual advancement, be edified, Acts 9:31; to
advance in presumption, 1 Cor 8:10

οἰκοδομή, ῆς, ἡ   {3869, n-1b}
pr. the act of building; a building, structure, Matt

24:1; in N.T. *a* spiritual *structure,* as instanced in the Christian body, 1 Cor 3:9; Eph 2:21; religious *advancement, edification,* Rom 14:19; 1 Cor 14:3

οἰκοδομή   nom sg fem   [2t; n-1b; 3869]   οἰκοδομή

οἰκοδομήθη   aor pass ind 3 sg
    [Jn 2:20; v-1d(2a); 3868]   οἰκοδομέω

οἰκοδομηθήσεται   fut pass ind 3 sg
    [1C 8:10; v-1d(2a); 3868]   "

οἰκοδομήν   acc sg fem   [11t; n-1b; 3869]   οἰκοδομή

οἰκοδομῆς   gen sg fem   [2t; n-1b; 3869]   "

οἰκοδομῆσαι   aor act inf
    [3t; v-1d(2a); 3868]   οἰκοδομέω

οἰκοδομήσαντι   aor act ptcp dat sg masc
    [Lk 6:49; v-1d(2a); 3868]   "

οἰκοδόμησεν   aor act ind 3 sg
    [Ac 7:47; v-1d(2a); 3868]   "

οἰκοδομήσετε   fut act ind 2 pl
    [Ac 7:49; v-1d(2a); 3868]   "

οἰκοδομῆσθαι   perf pass inf
    [Lk 6:48; v-1d(2a); 3868]   "

οἰκοδομήσω   fut act ind 1 sg
    [3t; v-1d(2a); 3868]   "

οἰκοδομία, ας, ἡ   {3870, n-1a}
    pr. *a building of a house;* met. spiritual *advancement, edification,* 1 Tim 1:4 v.l.*

οἰκοδόμος, ου, ὁ   {3871, n-2a}
    a builder, architect, Acts 4:11*

οἰκοδομουμένη   pres pass ptcp nom sg fem
    [Ac 9:31; v-1d(2a); 3868]   "

οἰκοδομοῦντες   pres act ptcp nom pl masc
    [4t; v-1d(2a); 3868]   "

οἰκοδομοῦντι   pres act ptcp dat sg masc
    [Lk 6:48; v-1d(2a); 3868]   "

οἰκοδομῶ   pres act ind 1 sg
    [Ga 2:18; v-1d(2a); 3868]   "

οἰκοδομῶ   pres act subj 1 sg
    [Rm 15:20; v-1d(2a); 3868]   "

οἰκοδόμων   gen pl masc
    [Ac 4:11; n-2a; 3871]   οἰκοδόμος

οἰκοδομῶν   pres act ptcp voc sg masc
    [2t; v-1d(2a); 3868]   οἰκοδομέω

οἴκοις   dat pl masc [Mt 11:8; n-2a; 3875]   οἶκος

οἶκον   acc sg masc [58t; n-2a; 3875]   "

οἰκονομεῖν   pres act inf
    [Lk 16:2; v-1d(2a); 3872]   οἰκονομέω

οἰκονομέω   {3872, v-1d(2a)}
    [-, -, οἰκονόμηκα, -, -] *to manage a household; to manage the affairs* of any one, *be steward,* Luke 16:2*

οἰκονομία, ας, ἡ   {3873, n-1a}
    pr. *the management of a household; a stewardship,* Luke 16:2, 3, 4; in N.T. *an* apostolic *stewardship, a* ministerial *commission* in the publication and furtherance of the Gospel, 1 Cor 9:17; 3:2; Col 1:25; or, *an arranged plan, a scheme,* Eph 1:10; *a due discharge of a commission,* 1 Tim 1:4, Eph 3:9*

οἰκονομία   nom sg fem
    [Ep 3:9; n-1a; 3873]   οἰκονομία

οἰκονομίαν   acc sg fem [6t; n-1a; 3873]   "

οἰκονομίας   gen sg fem   [2t; n-1a; 3873]   "

οἰκονόμοι   nom pl masc
    [1P 4:10; n-2a; 3874]   οἰκονόμος

οἰκονόμοις   dat pl masc [1C 4:2; n-2a; 3874]   "

οἰκονόμον   acc sg masc [3t; n-2a; 3874]   "

οἰκονόμος, ου, ὁ   {3874, n-2a}
    the manager of a household; a steward, Luke 12:42; 16:1, 3, 8; 1 Cor 4:2; *a manager, trustee,* Gal 4:2; *a* public *steward, treasurer,* Rom 16:23; *a* spiritual *steward, the holder of a commission* in the service of the Gospel, 1 Cor 4:1; Titus 1:7; 1 Peter 4:10*

οἰκονόμος   nom sg masc [3t; n-2a; 3874]   "

οἰκονόμους   acc pl masc [2t; n-2a; 3874]   "

οἶκος, ου, ὁ   {3875, n-2a}
    a house, dwelling, Matt 9:6, 7; Mark 2:1, 11; 3:20; *place of abode, seat, site,* Matt 23:38; Luke 13:35; met. *a* spiritual *house* or *structure,* 1 Peter 2:5; meton. *a household, family,* Luke 10:5; 11:17; *a* spiritual *household,* 1 Tim 3:15; Heb 3:6; *family, lineage,* Luke 1:27, 69; 2:4; from the Hebrew, *a people, nation,* Matt 10:6; 15:24

οἶκος   nom sg masc [17t; n-2a; 3875]   οἶκος

οἶκος   voc sg masc [Ac 7:42; n-2a; 3875]   "

οἴκου   gen sg masc [12t; n-2a; 3875]   "

οἰκουμένη, ῆς, ἡ   {3876, n-1b}
    some list as a participle, *the habitable earth, world,* Matt 24:14; Rom 10:18; Heb 1:6; used, however, with various restrictions of meaning, according to the context, Luke 2:1; Acts 17:6; meton. *the inhabitants of the earth, the whole human race, mankind,* Acts 17:31; 19:27; Rev 3:10. Some view this word as a participial form of οἰκέω.

οἰκουμένη   pres pass ptcp nom sg fem
    [Ac 19:27; n-1b; 3876]   οἰκουμένη

οἰκουμένη   dat sg fem   [2t; n-1b; 3876]   "

οἰκουμένην   pres pass ptcp acc sg fem
    [8t; n-1b; 3876]   "

οἰκουμένης   pres pass ptcp gen sg fem
    [4t; n-1b; 3876]   "

οἰκουργός, όν   {3877, a-3a}
    one who is occupied in domestic affairs, Titus 2:5*

οἰκουργούς   acc pl fem
    [Ti 2:5; a-3a; 3877]   οἰκουργός

οἰκουρός, ον   {3878, a-3a}
    pr. *a keeper* or *guard of a house; home-keeper, stay-at-home, domestic,* Titus 2:5

οἴκους   acc pl masc [4t; n-2a; 3875]   οἶκος

οἰκοῦσα   pres act ptcp nom sg fem
    [2t; v-1d(2a); 3861]   οἰκέω

οἰκτείρω, see οἰκτίρω   {3879, v-1c(1)}

οἰκτιρήσω   fut act ind 1 sg
    [Rm 9:15; v-1c(1); 3882]   οἰκτίρω

οἰκτιρμοί   nom pl masc
    [Pp 2:1; n-2a; 3880]   οἰκτιρμός

οἰκτίρμονες   nom pl masc
    [Lk 6:36; a-4b(1); 3881]   οἰκτίρμων

οἰκτιρμός, οῦ, ὁ   {3880, n-2a}
  compassion; kindness, in relieving sorrow and
  want, Phil 2:1; Col 3:12; Heb 10:28; *favor, grace,
  mercy*, Rom 12:1; 2 Cor 1:3*

οἰκτιρμοῦ   gen sg masc
  [Cl 3:12; n-2a; 3880]   οἰκτιρμός

οἰκτίρμων, ον   {3881, a-4b(1)}
  compassionate, merciful, Luke 6:36; James 5:11*

οἰκτίρμων   nom sg masc
  [2t; a-4b(1); 3881]   οἰκτίρμων
οἰκτιρμῶν   gen pl masc
  [3t; n-2a; 3880]   οἰκτιρμός

οἰκτίρω   {3882, v-1c(1)}
  [οἰκτιρήσω, -, -, -, -] also spelled οἰκτείρω, *to have
  compassion on, exercise grace* or *favor towards*,
  Rom 9:15*

οἰκτίρω   pres act subj 1 sg
  [Rm 9:15; v-1c(1); 3882]   οἰκτίρω
οἴκῳ   dat sg masc [20t; n-2a; 3875]   οἶκος
οἴκων   gen pl masc [1Ti 3:12; n-2a; 3875]   "
οἰκῶν   pres act ptcp nom sg masc
  [1Ti 6:16; v-1d(2a); 3861]   οἰκέω

οἶμαι, see οἴομα   {3883, v-1d(2c)}

οἶμαι   pres mid ind 1 sg
  [Jn 21:25; v-1d(2c); 3887]   οἴομαι
οἶνον   acc sg masc [19t; n-2a; 3885]   οἶνος

οἰνοπότης, ου, ὁ   {3884, n-1f}
  wine-drinking; in a bad sense, *a wine-bibber,
  tippler*, Matt 11:19; Luke 7:34*

οἰνοπότης   nom sg masc
  [2t; n-1f; 3884]   οἰνοπότης

οἶνος, ου, ὁ   {3885, n-2a}
  wine, Matt 9:17; Mark 2:22; meton. *the vine and
  its clusters*, Rev 6:6 met. οἶνος, *a potion*, οἶνος τοῦ
  θυμοῦ, *a furious potion*, Rev 14:8, 10; 16:19; 17:2,
  18:3

οἶνος   nom sg masc [4t; n-2a; 3885]   οἶνος
οἴνου   gen sg masc [7t; n-2a; 3885]   "

οἰνοφλυγία, ας, ἡ   {3886, n-1a}
  a debauch with wine, drunkenness, 1 Peter 4:3*

οἰνοφλυγίαις   dat pl fem
  [1P 4:3; n-1a; 3886]   οἰνοφλυγία
οἴνῳ   dat sg masc [4t; n-2a; 3885]   οἶνος
οἷοι   nom pl masc [2t; a-1a(1); 3888]   οἷος

οἴομαι   {3887, v-1d(2c)}
  [-, -, -, -, ᾠήθην] *to think, suppose, imagine,
  presume*, John 21:25; Phil 1:17; James 1:7*

οἰόμενοι   pres mid ptcp nom pl masc
  [Pp 1:17; v-1d(2c); 3887]   οἴομαι
οἶνον   acc sg masc [18t; n-2a; 3885]   οἶνος
οἶνον   acc sg neut [Jn 2:9; n-2a; 3885]   "
οἷον   acc sg masc [2t; a-1a(1); 3888]   "

οἷος, α, ον   {3888, a-1a(1)}
  what, of what kind or *sort, as*, Matt 24:21; Mark
  9:3; οὐχ, οἷον, *not so as, not as implying*, Rom 9:6;
  James 5:4 v.l.

οἷος   nom sg masc [3t; a-1a(1); 3888]   "
οἷους   acc pl masc [2t; a-1a(1); 3888]   "
οἷς   dat pl masc [27t; a-1a(2b); 4005]   ὅς
οἷς   dat pl neut [19t; a-1a(2b); 4005]   "
οἴσει   fut act ind 3 sg
  [Jn 21:18; v-1c(1); 5770]   φέρω
οἴσουσιν   fut act ind 3 pl
  [Rv 21:26; v-1c(1); 5770]   "
οἵτινες   nom pl masc [60t; a-1a(2b); 4015]   ὅστις

ὀκνέω   {3890, v-1d(2a)}
  [-, ὤκνησα, -, -, -] *to be slow; to delay, hesitate*,
  Acts 9:38*

ὀκνηρέ   voc sg masc
  [Mt 25:26; a-1a(1); 3891]   ὀκνηρός
ὀκνηροί   nom pl masc [Rm 12:11; a-1a(1); 3891]   "
ὀκνηρόν   nom sg neut [Pp 3:1; a-1a(1); 3891]   "

ὀκνηρός, ά, όν   {3891, a-1a(1)}
  slow; slothful, indolent, idle, Matt 25:26; Rom
  12:11; *tedious, troublesome*, Phil 3:1*

ὀκνήσῃς   aor act subj 2 sg
  [Ac 9:38; v-1d(2a); 3890]   ὀκνέω

ὀκταήμερος, ον   {3892, a-3a}
  on the eighth day, Phil 3:5*

ὀκταήμερος   nom sg masc
  [Pp 3:5; a-3a; 3892]   ὀκταήμερος

ὀκτώ   {3893, a-5b}
  eight, Luke 2:21; 9:28

ὀκτώ   indecl [8t; a-5b; 3893]   ὀκτώ

ὀλέθριος, ον   {3896, a-3a}
  deadly, destructive, 2 Thess 1:9 v.l.*

ὄλεθρον   acc sg masc [3t; n-2a; 3897]   ὄλεθρος

ὄλεθρος, ου, ὁ   {3897, n-2a}
  perdition, destruction, 1 Cor 5:5, 1 Thess 5:3; 2
  Thess 1:9; 1 Tim 6:9*

ὄλεθρος   nom sg masc [1Th 5:3; n-2a; 3897]   "
ὅλη   nom sg fem [8t; a-1a(2a); 3910]   ὅλος
ὅλῃ   dat sg fem [14t; a-1a(2a); 3910]   "
ὅλην   acc sg fem [20t; a-1a(2a); 3910]   "
ὅλης   gen sg fem [18t; a-1a(2a); 3910]   "
ὀλίγα   acc pl neut [6t; a-1a(2a); 3900]   ὀλίγος
ὀλίγαι   nom pl fem [Ac 17:4; a-1a(2a); 3900]   "
ὀλίγας   acc pl fem [2t; a-1a(2a); 3900]   "
ὀλίγην   acc sg fem [Ac 19:24; a-1a(2a); 3900]   "
ὀλίγης   gen sg fem [Ac 15:2; a-1a(2a); 3900]   "
ὀλίγοι   nom pl masc [7t; a-1a(2a); 3900]   "
ὀλίγοις   dat pl masc [Mk 6:5; a-1a(2a); 3900]   "
ὀλίγον   nom sg neut [Lk 7:47; a-1a(2a); 3900]   "
ὀλίγον   acc sg masc [2t; a-1a(2a); 3900]   "
ὀλίγον   acc sg neut, can function
  adverbially [10t; a-1a(2a); 3900]   "
ὀλιγόπιστε   voc sg masc
  [Mt 14:31; a-3a; 3899]   ὀλιγόπιστος

ὀλιγοπιστία, ας, ἡ   {3898, n-1a}
  littleness or *imperfectness of faith*, Matt 17:20*

ὀλιγοπιστίαν   acc sg fem
  [Mt 17:20; n-1a; 3898]   ὀλιγοπιστία

ὀλιγόπιστοι voc pl masc
[4t; a-3a; 3899]   ὀλιγόπιστος

ὀλιγόπιστος, ον   {3899, a-3a}
*scant of faith, of little faith, one whose faith is small
and weak*, Matt 6:30; 8:26; 14:31; 16:18; Luke
12:28*

ὀλίγος, η, ον   {3900, a-1a(2a)}
little, small, in number, etc.; pl. *few*, Matt 7:14;
9:37; 20:16; Luke 13:23; δι ὀλίγων, sc. λόγων, *in a
few words, briefly*, 1 Peter 5:12; *little* in time,
short, brief, Acts 14:28; Rev 12:12; πρὸς ὀλίγον,
sc. χρόνον, *for a short time, for a little while*, James
4:14; *little, small, light*, etc., in magnitude,
amount, etc., Luke 7:47; Acts 12:18; 15:2; ἐν
ὀλίγῳ, *concisely, briefly*, Eph 3:3; *almost*, Acts
26:28, 29

ὀλίγος nom sg masc [2t; a-1a(2a); 3900]   ὀλίγος
ὀλίγου gen sg masc [Ac 27:20; a-1a(2a); 3900]   "

ὀλιγόψυχος, ον   {3901, a-3a}
fainthearted, desponding, 1 Tim 5:14*

ὀλιγοψύχους acc pl masc
[1Th 5:14; a-3a; 3901]   ὀλιγόψυχος
ὀλίγῳ dat sg masc
[1Ti 5:23; a-1a(2a); 3900]   ὀλίγος
ὀλίγῳ dat sg neut [3t; a-1a(2a); 3900]   "
ὀλίγων gen pl neut [1P 5:12; a-1a(2a); 3900] "
ὀλιγώρει pres act imperative 2 sg
[Hb 12:5; cv-1d(2a); 3902]   ὀλιγωρέω

ὀλιγωρέω   {3902, cv-1d(2a)}
[-, -, -, -, -] *to neglect, regard slightly, make light of,
despise*, Heb 12:5*

ὀλίγως   {3903, adverb}
little, scarcely, 2 Peter 2:18*

ὀλίγως adverb [2P 2:18; adverb; 3903]   ὀλίγως

ὀλοθρευτής, οῦ, ὁ   {3904, n-1f}
a destroyer, 1 Cor 10:10*

ὀλοθρευτοῦ gen sg masc
[1C 10:10; n-1f; 3904]   ὀλοθρευτής

ὀλοθρεύω   {3905, v-1a(6)}
[-, ὠλέθρευσα, -, -, ὠλοθρεύθην] also spelled
ὀλεθρεύω, *to destroy, cause to perish*, Heb 11:28*

ὀλοθρεύων pres act ptcp nom sg masc
[Hb 11:28; v-1a(6); 3905]   ὀλοθρεύω

ὀλοκαύτωμα, ατος, τό   {3906, n-3c(4)}
a holocaust, whole burnt-offering, Mark 12:33;
Heb 10:6, 8*

ὀλοκαυτώματα acc pl neut
[2t; n-3c(4); 3906]   ὀλοκαύτωμα
ὀλοκαυτωμάτων gen pl neut
[Mk 12:33; n-3c(4); 3906]   "

ὀλοκληρία, ας, ἡ   {3907, n-1a}
perfect soundness, Acts 3:16*

ὀλοκληρίαν acc sg fem
[Ac 3:16; n-1a; 3907]   ὀλοκληρία
ὀλόκληροι nom pl masc
[Jm 1:4; a-3a; 3908]   ὀλόκληρος
ὀλόκληρον nom sg neut [1Th 5:23; a-3a; 3908] "

ὀλόκληρος, ον   {3908, a-3a}
*whole, having all its parts, sound, perfect, complete
in every part*; in N.T. *the whole*, 1 Thess 5:23;
morally, *perfect, faultless, blameless*, James 1:4*

ὀλολύζοντες pres act ptcp nom pl masc
[Jm 5:1; v-2a(1); 3909]   ὀλολύζω

ὀλολύζω   {3909, v-2a(1)}
[-, -, -, -, -] pr. *to cry aloud in invocation; to howl,
utter cries of distress, lament, bewail*, James 5:1*

ὅλον nom sg neut [17t; a-1a(2a); 3910]   ὅλος
ὅλον acc sg masc [13t; a-1a(2a); 3910]   "
ὅλον acc sg neut [5t; a-1a(2a); 3910]   "

ὅλος, η, ον   {3910, a-1a(2a)}
all, whole, entire, Matt 1:22; 4:23, 24

ὅλος nom sg masc [4t; a-1a(2a); 3910]   "
ὁλοτελεῖς acc pl masc
[1Th 5:23; a-4a; 3911]   ὁλοτελής

ὁλοτελής, ές   {3911, a-4a}
complete; all, the whole, 1 Thess 5:23*

ὅλου gen sg masc [2t; a-1a(2a); 3910]   ὅλος
ὅλου gen sg neut [Ac 10:22; a-1a(2a); 3910]   "
ὅλους acc pl masc [Ti 1:11; a-1a(2a); 3910]   "

Ὀλυμπᾶς, ᾶ, ὁ   {3912, n-1e}
Olympas, pr. name, Rom 16:15*

Ὀλυμπᾶν acc sg masc
[Rm 16:15; n-1e; 3912]   Ὀλυμπᾶς

ὄλυνθος, ου, ὁ   {3913, n-2a}
an unripe or *unseasonable fig*, such as, shaded by
the foliage, does not ripen at the usual season,
but hangs on the trees during winter, Rev 6:13*

ὀλύνθους acc pl masc
[Rv 6:13; n-2a; 3913]   ὄλυνθος
ὅλῳ dat sg masc [5t; a-1a(2a); 3910]   ὅλος
ὅλῳ dat sg neut [Pp 1:13; a-1a(2a); 3910]   "

ὅλως   {3914, adverb}
wholly, altogether; actually, really, 1 Cor 5:1; 6:7;
15:29; with a negative, *at all*, Matt 5:34*

ὅλως adverb [4t; adverb; 3914]   ὅλως

ὄμβρος, ου, ὁ   {3915, n-2a}
rain, a storm of rain, Luke 12:54*

ὄμβρος nom sg masc [Lk 12:54; n-2a; 3915]   ὄμβρος

ὀμείρομαι   {3916, v-1c(1)}
[-, -, -, -, -] also spelled ἱμείρομαι, *to desire
earnestly, have a strong affection for*, 1 Thess 2:8*

ὀμειρόμενοι pres mid ptcp nom pl masc
[1Th 2:8; v-1c(1); 3916]   ὀμείρομαι
ὁμιλεῖν pres act inf
[Lk 24:15; v-1d(2a); 3917]   ὁμιλέω

ὁμιλέω   {3917, v-1d(2a)}
[(ὡμίλουν), -, ὡμίλησα, -, -, -] *to be in company
with, associate with; to converse with, talk with*,
Luke 24:14, 15; Acts 20:11; 24:26*

ὁμιλήσας aor act ptcp nom sg masc
[Ac 20:11; v-1d(2a); 3917]   "

ὁμιλία, ας, ἡ   {3918, n-1a}
intercourse, communication, converse, 1 Cor
15:33*

ὁμιλίαι   nom pl fem
[1C 15:33; n-1a; 3918]   ὁμιλία

ὅμιλος, ου, ὁ   {3919, n-2a}
a multitude, company, crowd, Rev 18:17 v.l.*

ὁμίχλαι   nom pl fem [2P 2:17; n-1b; 3920]   ὁμίχλη

ὁμίχλη, ης, ἡ   {3920, n-1b}
a mist, fog, a cloud, 2 Pet 2:17*

ὄμμα, ατος, τό   {3921, n-3c(4)}
the eye, Matt 20:34; Mark 8:23*

ὄμματα   acc pl neut [Mk 8:23; n-3c(4); 3921]   ὄμμα
ὀμμάτων   gen pl neut [Mt 20:34; n-3c(4); 3921]   "
ὀμνύει   pres act ind 3 sg
[3t; v-3c(2); 3923]   ὀμνύω
ὀμνύειν   pres act inf [Mt 26:74; v-3c(2); 3923]   "
ὀμνύετε   pres act imperative 2 pl
[Jm 5:12; v-3c(2); 3923]   "
ὀμνύναι   pres act inf [Mk 14:71; v-3c(2); 3923]   "
ὀμνύουσιν   pres act ind 3 pl
[Hb 6:16; v-3c(2); 3923]   "

ὀμνύω   {3923, v-3c(2)}
[-, ὤμοσα, -, -, -] *to swear,* Matt 5:34; *to promise
with an oath,* Mark 6:23; Acts 2:30; 7:17

ὁμοθυμαδόν   {3924, adverb}
with one mind, with one accord, unanimously, Acts
1:14; Rom 15:6; *together, at once, at the same time,*
Acts 2:1, 46; 4:24

ὁμοθυμαδόν   adverb
[11t; adverb; 3924]   ὁμοθυμαδόν
ὅμοια   nom sg fem [13t; a-1a(1); 3927]   ὅμοιος
ὅμοια   nom pl neut [2t; a-1a(1); 3927]   "
ὅμοια   acc pl neut [Rv 13:11; a-1a(1); 3927]   "

ὁμοιάζω   {3925, v-2a(1)}
[-, -, -, -, -] *to be like, resemble,* Matt 23:27; 26:73;
Mark 14:70*

ὅμοιαι   nom pl fem [Rv 9:19; a-1a(1); 3927]   "
ὁμοίας   acc pl fem [Rv 9:10; a-1a(1); 3927]   "
ὅμοιοι   nom pl masc [7t; a-1a(1); 3927]   "
ὅμοιος   nom sg neut [5t; a-1a(1); 3927]   "
ὅμοιον   acc sg masc [3t; a-1a(1); 3927]   "
ὅμοιον   acc sg neut [Ac 17:29; a-1a(1); 3927]   "
ὁμοιοπαθεῖς   nom pl masc
[Ac 14:15; a-4a; 3926]   ὁμοιοπαθής

ὁμοιοπαθής, ές   {3926, a-4a}
being affected in the same way as another, *subject
to the same incidents, of like infirmities, subject to
the same frailties and evils,* Acts 14:15; James
5:17*

ὁμοιοπαθής   nom sg masc [Jm 5:17; a-4a; 3926]   "

ὅμοιος, οια, οιον   {3927, a-1a(1)}
like, similar, resembling, Matt 11:16; 13:31, 33, 44,
45, 47, 52; John 8:55, et al. freq.; *like, of similar
drift and force,* Matt 22:39; Mark 12:31 v.l.

ὅμοιος   nom sg masc [11t; a-1a(1); 3927]   ὅμοιος

ὁμοιότης, ητος, ἡ   {3928, n-3c(1)}
likeness, similitude, Heb 4:15; 7:15*

ὁμοιότητα   acc sg fem
[2t; n-3c(1); 3928]   ὁμοιότης

ὁμοιόω   {3929, v-1d(3)}
[ὁμοιώσω, ὡμοίωσα, -, ὡμοίωμαι, ὡμοιώθην] *to
make like, cause to be like* or *resemble, assimilate;*
pass. *to be made like, become like, resemble,* Matt
6:8; 13:24; 18:23; *to liken, compare,* Matt 7:24, 26;
11:16

ὁμοιωθέντες   aor pass ptcp nom pl masc
[Ac 14:11; v-1d(3); 3929]   ὁμοιόω
ὁμοιωθῆναι   aor pass inf
[Hb 2:17; v-1d(3); 3929]   "
ὁμοιωθήσεται   fut pass ind 3 sg
[3t; v-1d(3); 3929]   "
ὁμοιωθῆτε   aor pass subj 2 pl
[Mt 6:8; v-1d(3); 3929]   "

ὁμοίωμα, ατος, τό   {3930, n-3c(4)}
pr. *that which is conformed* or *assimilated; form,
shape, figure,* Rev 9:7; *likeness, resemblance,
similitude,* Rom 1:23; 5:14; 6:5; 8:3; Phil 2:7*

ὁμοιώματα   nom pl neut
[Rv 9:7; n-3c(4); 3930]   ὁμοίωμα
ὁμοιώματι   dat sg neut [5t; n-3c(4); 3930]   "

ὁμοίως   {3931, adverb}
likewise, in a similar manner, Matt 22:26; 27:41;
Mark 4:16 v.l.

ὁμοίως   adverb [30t; adverb; 3931]   ὁμοίως
ὁμοίωσιν   acc sg fem
[Jm 3:9; n-3e(5b); 3932]   ὁμοίωσις

ὁμοίωσις, εως, ἡ   {3932, n-3e(5b)}
pr. *assimilation; likeness, resemblance,* James 3:9*

ὁμοιώσω   fut act ind 1 sg
[Mt 11:16; v-1d(3); 3929]   ὁμοιόω
ὁμοιώσω   fut act ind 1 sg [3t; v-1d(3); 3929]   "
ὁμοιώσωμεν   aor act subj 1 pl
[Mk 4:30; v-1d(3); 3929]   "
ὁμολογεῖ   pres act ind 3 sg
[2t; v-1d(2a); 3933]   ὁμολογέω
ὁμολογεῖται   pres pass ind 3 sg
[Rm 10:10; v-1d(2a); 3933]   "

ὁμολογέω   {3933, v-1d(2a)}
[(ὡμολόγουν), ὁμολογήσω, ὡμολόγησα, -, -, -] *to
speak in accordance, adopt the same terms of
language; to engage, promise,* Matt 14:7; *to admit,
avow frankly,* John 1:20; Acts 24:14; *to confess,* 1
John 1:9; *to profess, confess,* John 9:22; 12:42; Acts
23:8; *to avouch, declare openly and solemnly,* Matt
7:23; in N.T. ὁμολογεῖν ἐν, *to accord belief,* Matt
10:32; Luke 12:8; *to accord approbation,* Luke
12:8; from the Hebrew, *to accord praise,* Heb
13:15

ὁμολογήσαντες   aor act ptcp nom pl masc
[Hb 11:13; v-1d(2a); 3933]   "
ὁμολογήσει   fut act ind 3 sg
[2t; v-1d(2a); 3933]   "
ὁμολογήσῃ   aor act subj 3 sg
[3t; v-1d(2a); 3933]   "

ὁμολογήσῃς   aor act subj 2 sg
[Rm 10:9; v-1d(2a); 3933]   "
ὁμολογήσω   fut act ind 1 sg   [3t; v-1d(2a); 3933]   "

ὁμολογία, ας, ἡ   {3934, n-1a}
assent, consent; profession, 2 Cor 9:13; 1 Tim 6:12,
13; Heb 3:1; 4:14; 10:23*

ὁμολογίαν   acc sg fem   [3t; n-1a; 3934]   ὁμολογία
ὁμολογίας   gen sg fem   [3t; n-1a; 3934]   "

ὁμολογουμένως   {3935, adverb}
confessedly, avowedly, without controversy, 1 Tim
3:16*

ὁμολογουμένως   adverb
[1Ti 3:16; adverb; 3935]   ὁμολογουμένως
ὁμολογοῦντες   pres act ptcp nom pl masc
[2J 7; v-1d(2a); 3933]   ὁμολογέω
ὁμολογούντων   pres act ptcp gen pl neut
[Hb 13:15; v-1d(2a); 3933]   "
ὁμολογοῦσιν   pres act ind 3 pl
[2t; v-1d(2a); 3933]   "
ὁμολογῶ   pres act ind 1 sg
[Ac 24:14; v-1d(2a); 3933]   "
ὁμολογῶμεν   pres act subj 1 pl
[1J 1:9; v-1d(2a); 3933]   "
ὁμολογῶν   pres act ptcp nom sg masc
[1J 2:23; v-1d(2a); 3933]   "
ὀμόσαι   aor act inf   [2t; v-3c(2); 3923]   ὀμνύω
ὀμόσας   aor act ptcp nom sg masc
[3t; v-3c(2); 3923]   "

ὁμόσε   {3936, adverb}
together, Acts 20:18 v.l.*

ὀμόσῃ   aor act subj 3 sg   [4t; v-3c(2); 3923]   "
ὀμόσῃς   aor act subj 2 sg
[Mt 5:36; v-3c(2); 3923]   "
ὁμότεχνον   acc sg masc
[Ac 18:3; a-3a; 3937]   ὁμότεχνος

ὁμότεχνος, ον   {3937, a-3a}
to the same trade or occupation, Acts 18:3*

ὁμοῦ   {3938, adverb}
together; in the same place, John 21:2; together at
the same time, John 4:36; 20:4; Acts 2:1*

ὁμοῦ   adverb   [4t; adverb; 3938]   ὁμοῦ
ὁμόφρονες   nom pl masc
[1P 3:8; a-4b(1); 3939]   ὁμόφρων

ὁμόφρων, ον   {3939, a-4b(1)}
of like mind, of the same mind, like-minded, 1 Peter
3:8*

ὅμως   {3940, adverb}
yet, nevertheless; with μέντοι, but nevertheless, but
for all that, John 12:42; even, though it be but, 1
Cor 14:7; Gal 3:15*

ὅμως   adverb   [3t; adverb; 3940]   ὅμως
ὅν   acc sg masc   [167t; a-1a(2b); 4005]   ὅς
ὅν   pres act ptcp nom sg neut
[Mk 4:31; v-6b; 1639]   εἰμί
ὀναίμην   aor mid opt 1 sg
[Pm 20; v-6a; 3949]   ὀνίνημι

ὄναρ, ατος, τό   {3941, n-3c(6b)}
a dream, Matt 1:20; 2:12, 13, 19, 22; 27:19*

ὄναρ   acc sg neut   [6t; n-3c(6b); 3941]   ὄναρ

ὀνάριον, ου, τό   {3942, n-2c}
a young ass, an ass's colt, John 12:14*

ὀνάριον   acc sg neut
[Jn 12:14; n-2c; 3942]   ὀνάριον
ὀνειδίζειν   pres act inf
[Mt 11:20; v-2a(1); 3943]   ὀνειδίζω
ὀνειδίζεσθε   pres pass ind 2 pl
[1P 4:14; v-2a(1); 3943]   "
ὀνειδίζοντος   pres act ptcp gen sg masc
[Jm 1:5; v-2a(1); 3943]   "
ὀνειδιζόντων   pres act ptcp gen pl masc
[Rm 15:3; v-2a(1); 3943]   "

ὀνειδίζω   {3943, v-2a(1)}
[(ὠνείδιζον), -, ὠνείδισα, -, -, -] to censure, inveigh
against, Matt 11:20; Mark 16:14; to reproach or
revile, James 1:5; to revile, insult with insulting
language, Matt 5:11

ὀνειδισμοί   nom pl masc
[Rm 15:3; n-2a; 3944]   ὀνειδισμός
ὀνειδισμοῖς   dat pl masc   [Hb 10:33; n-2a; 3944]   "
ὀνειδισμόν   acc sg masc   [3t; n-2a; 3944]   "

ὀνειδισμός, οῦ, ὁ   {3944, n-2a}
censure, 1 Tim 3:7; reproach, reviling, Rom 15:3

ὀνειδίσωσιν   aor act subj 3 pl
[2t; v-2a(1); 3943]   ὀνειδίζω

ὄνειδος, ους, τό   {3945, n-3d(2b)}
pr. fame, report, character; usually, reproach,
disgrace, Luke 1:25*

ὄνειδος   acc sg neut
[Lk 1:25; n-3d(2b); 3945]   ὄνειδος
Ὀνήσιμον   acc sg masc
[Pm 10; n-2a; 3946]   Ὀνήσιμος

Ὀνήσιμος, ου, ὁ   {3946, n-2a}
Onesimus, pr. name, Col 4:9; Phlm 10;
subscription of Col and Phlm*

Ὀνησίμῳ   dat sg masc   [Cl 4:9; n-2a; 3946]   "

Ὀνησίφορος, ου, ὁ   {3947, n-2a}
Onesiphorus, pr. name, 2 Tim 1:16; 4:19*

Ὀνησιφόρου   gen sg masc
[2t; n-2a; 3947]   Ὀνησίφορος

ὀνικός, ή, όν   {3948, a-1a(2a)}
pertaining to an ass; μύλος ὀνικός, a millstone
turned by an ass, a large or an upper millstone,
Matt 18:6; Mark 9:42; Luke 17:2 v.l.*

ὀνικός   nom sg masc   [2t; a-1a(2a); 3948]   ὀνικός

ὀνίνημι   {3949, v-6a}
[-, ὤνησα, -, -, -] optative, ὀναίμην, to receive
profit, pleasure, etc.; with a gen., to have joy of,
Phil 20*

ὄνομα, ατος, τό   {3950, n-3c(4)}
a name; the proper name of a person, etc., Matt
1:23, 25; 10:2; 27:32; a mere name or reputation,
Rev 3:1; in N.T. a name as the representative of
a person, Matt 6:9; Luke 6:22; 11:2; the name of
the author of a commission, delegated
authority, or religious profession, Matt 7:22;

10:22; 12:21; 18:5, 20; 19:29; 21:9; 28:19; Acts
3:16; 4:7, 12; εἰς ὄνομα, ἐν ὀνόματι, *on the score of
being* possessor of a certain character, Matt
10:41, 42; Mark 9:41

ὄνομα   nom sg neut [37t; n-3c(4); 3950]   ὄνομα
ὄνομα   acc sg neut [68t; n-3c(4); 3950]   "
ὀνομάζειν   pres act inf
   [Ac 19:13; v-2a(1); 3951]   ὀνομάζω
ὀνομαζέσθω   pres pass imperative 3 sg
   [Ep 5:3; v-2a(1); 3951]   "
ὀνομάζεται   pres pass ind 3 sg
   [Ep 3:15; v-2a(1); 3951]   "
ὀνομαζόμενος   pres pass ptcp nom sg masc
   [1C 5:11; v-2a(1); 3951]   "
ὀνομαζομένου   pres pass ptcp gen sg neut
   [Ep 1:21; v-2a(1); 3951]   "

ὀνομάζω   {3951, v-2a(1)}
   [-, ὠνόμασα, -, -, ὠνομάσθην] *to name,* Luke 6:14;
   to style, entitle, Luke 2:21 v.l.; 6:13; 1 Cor 5:11; *to
   make mention of,* 1 Cor 5:1 v.l.; Eph 5:3; *to make
   known,* Rom 15:20; *to pronounce* in exorcism,
   Acts 19:13; in N.T. *to profess,* 2 Tim 2:19

ὀνομάζων   pres act ptcp nom sg masc
   [2Ti 2:19; v-2a(1); 3951]   "
ὀνόματα   nom pl neut [6t; n-3c(4); 3950]   ὄνομα
ὀνόματα   acc pl neut [5t; n-3c(4); 3950]   "
ὀνόματι   dat sg neut [95t; n-3c(4); 3950]   "
ὀνόματος   gen sg neut [17t; n-3c(4); 3950]   "
ὀνομάτων   gen pl neut [2t; n-3c(4); 3950]   "
ὄνον   acc sg masc [2t; n-2a; 3952]   ὄνος
ὄνον   acc sg fem [2t; n-2a; 3952]   "

ὄνος, οὖ, ὁ (n-2a) or **ἡ** (n-2b)   {3952}
   donkey, ass,, male or female, Matt 21:2, 5, 7,
   Luke 14:5 v.l.

ὄνου   gen sg fem [Jn 12:15; n-2a; 3952]   "
ὄντα   pres act ptcp nom pl neut
   [2t; v-6b; 1639]   εἰμί
ὄντα   pres act ptcp acc sg masc
   [12t; v-6b; 1639]   "
ὄντα   pres act ptcp acc pl neut
   [5t; v-6b; 1639]   "
ὄντας   pres act ptcp acc pl masc
   [11t; v-6b; 1639]   "
ὄντες   pres act ptcp nom pl masc
   [26t; v-6b; 1639]   "
ὄντι   pres act ptcp dat sg masc
   [4t; v-6b; 1639]   "
ὄντος   pres act ptcp gen sg masc
   [14t; v-6b; 1639]   "
ὄντος   pres act ptcp gen sg neut
   [Ac 7:5; v-6b; 1639]   "
ὄντων   pres act ptcp gen pl masc
   [5t; v-6b; 1639]   "
ὄντων   pres act ptcp gen pl neut
   [Ac 19:36; v-6b; 1639]   "

ὄντως   {3953, adverb}
   really, in truth, truly, Mark 11:32; Luke 23:47.

ὄντως   adverb [10t; adverb; 3953]   ὄντως
ὀξεῖα   nom sg fem [2t; a-2b; 3955]   ὀξύς
ὀξεῖαν   acc sg fem [Rv 2:12; a-2b; 3955]   "

ὀξεῖς   nom pl masc [Rm 3:15; a-2b; 3955]   "

ὄξος, ους, τό   {3954, n-3d(2b)}
   vinegar; a wine of sharp flavor, posca, which was
   an ordinary beverage, and was often mixed
   with bitter herbs, etc., and this given to the
   condemned criminals in order to stupefy them,
   and lessen their sufferings, Matt 27:48; Mark
   15:36; Luke 23:36; John 19:29, 30

ὄξος   acc sg neut [2t; n-3d(2b); 3954]   ὄξος
ὄξους   gen sg neut [4t; n-3d(2b); 3954]   "
ὀξύ   acc sg neut [4t; a-2b; 3955]   ὀξύς

ὀξύς, εῖα, ύ   {3955, a-2b}
   sharp, keen, Rev 1:16; 2:12; 14:14, 17, 18; 19:15;
   swift, nimble, Rom 3:15*

ὀπαῖς   dat pl fem [Hb 11:38; n-1b; 3956]   ὀπή

ὀπή, ῆς, ἡ   {3956, n-1b}
   a hole; a hole, vent, opening, James 3:11; *a hole,
   cavern,* Heb 11:38*

ὀπῆς   gen sg fem [Jm 3:11; n-1b; 3956]   "

ὄπισθεν   {3957, adverb}
   can function as an improper prep., *from behind,
   behind, after, at the back of,* Matt 9:20; 15:23

ὄπισθεν   adverb [7t; adverb; 3957]   ὄπισθεν

ὀπίσω   {3958, adverb}
   can function as an improper prep., *behind, after,
   at one's back,* Matt 4:10; Luke 7:38; Rev 1:10; τὰ
   ὀπίσω, *the things which are behind,* Phil 3:14;
   ὀπίσω and εἰς τὰ ὀπίσω, *back, backwards,* Matt
   24:18; Mark 13:16; Luke 9:62, when an
   improper prep., takes the gen.

ὀπίσω   adverb [35t; adverb; 3958]   ὀπίσω
ὅπλα   nom pl neut [2C 10:4; n-2c; 3960]   ὅπλον
ὅπλα   acc pl neut [3t; n-2c; 3960]   "

ὁπλίζω   {3959, v-2a(1)}
   [-, ὥπλισα, -, -, -] *to arm, equip;* mid. *to arm one's
   self, equip one's self,* 1 Peter 4:1*

ὁπλίσασθε   aor mid imperative 2 pl
   [1P 4:1; v-2a(1); 3959]   ὁπλίζω

ὅπλον, ου, τό   {3960, n-2c}
   an implement, Rom 6:13; pl. τὰ ὅπλα, *arms,
   armor, weapons,* whether offensive or defensive,
   John 18:3; Rom 13:12; 2 Cor 6:7; 10:4*

ὅπλων   gen pl neut [2t; n-2c; 3960]   ὅπλον
ὁποίαν   acc sg fem
   [1Th 1:9; a-1a(1); 3961]   ὁποῖος
ὁποῖοι   nom pl masc [Ga 2:6; a-1a(1); 3961]   "
ὁποῖον   nom sg neut [1C 3:13; a-1a(1); 3961]   "

ὁποῖος, οία, οἶον   {3961, a-1a(1)}
   what, of what sort or *manner,* 1 Cor 3:13; Gal 2:6;
   1 Thess 1:9; James 1:24; after τοιοῦτος, *as,* Acts
   26:29*

ὁποῖος   nom sg masc [2t; a-1a(1); 3961]   "

ὁπότε   {3962, particle}
   when, Luke 6:3 v.l.*

ὅπου   {3963, particle}
   where, in which place, in what place, Matt 6:19, 20,

21; Rev 2:13; *whither, to what place,* John 8:21; 14:4; ὅπου ἄν, or ἐάν, *wherever, in whatever place,* Matt 24:28; *whithersoever,* Matt 8:19; James 3:4; met. *where, in which thing, state,* etc., Col 3:11; *whereas,* 1 Cor 3:3; 2 Peter 2:11

ὅπου   particle [82t; particle; 3963]   ὅπου

ὀπτάνομαι   {3964, v-3a(2a)}
[-, -, -, -, -] *to be seen, appear,* Acts 1:3*

ὀπτανόμενος   pres mid ptcp nom sg masc
  [Ac 1:3; v-3a(2a); 3964]   ὀπτάνομαι

ὀπτασία, ῆς, ἡ   {3965, n-1a}
  a vision, apparition, Luke 1:22; 24:23; Acts 26:19;
  2 Cor 12:1*

ὀπτασίᾳ   dat sg fem
  [Ac 26:19; n-1a; 3965]   ὀπτασία
ὀπτασίαν   acc sg fem [2t; n-1a; 3965]   "
ὀπτασίας   acc pl fem [2C 12:1; n-1a; 3965]   "

ὀπτός, ή, όν   {3966, a-1a(2a)}
  dressed by fire, roasted, broiled, etc., Luke 24:42*

ὀπτοῦ   gen sg masc
  [Lk 24:42; a-1a(2a); 3966]   ὀπτός

ὀπώρα, ας, ἡ   {3967, n-1a}
  autumn; the fruit season; meton. *fruits,* Rev
  18:14*

ὀπώρα   nom sg fem [Rv 18:14; n-1a; 3967]   ὀπώρα

ὅπως   {3968, adverb}
  can function as a conj., *how, in what way* or
  manner, by what means, Matt 22:5; Luke 24:20;
  conj. *that, in order that,* and ὅπως μή, *that not,*
  lest, Matt 6:2, 4, 5, 16, 18; Acts 9:2, et al. freq.

ὅπως   adverb [53t; adverb; 3968]   ὅπως
ὅρα   pres act imperative 2 sg
  [5t; v-1d(1a); 3972]   ὁράω
ὁρᾷ   pres act ind 3 sg
  [Lk 16:23; v-1d(1a); 3972]   "

ὅραμα, ατος, τό   {3969, n-3c(4)}
  a thing seen, sight, appearance, Acts 7:31; *a vision,*
  Matt 17:9; Acts 9:10, 12

ὅραμα   nom sg neut [2t; n-3c(4); 3969]   ὅραμα
ὅραμα   acc sg neut [5t; n-3c(4); 3969]   "
ὁράματι   dat sg neut [3t; n-3c(4); 3969]   "
ὁράματος   gen sg neut [2t; n-3c(4); 3969]   "
ὁράσει   dat sg fem [3t; n-3e(5b); 3970]   ὅρασις
ὁράσεις   acc pl fem [Ac 2:17; n-3e(5b); 3970]   "

ὅρασις, εως, ἡ   {3970, n-3e(5b)}
  seeing, sight; appearance, aspect, a vision, Acts
  2:17; Rev 9:17; 4:3*

ὁρατά   nom pl neut
  [Cl 1:16; a-1a(2a); 3971]   ὁρατός
ὁρᾶτε   pres act imperative 2 pl
  [7t; v-1d(1a); 3972]   ὁράω
ὁρᾶτε   pres act ind 2 pl
  [Jm 2:24; v-1d(1a); 3972]   "

ὁρατός, ή, όν   {3971, a-1a(2a)}
  visible, Col 1:16*

ὁράω   {3972, v-1d(1a)}
  [(ἑώρων), ὄψομαι, ὠψάμην, ἑώρακα or ἑόρακα, -,
  ὤφθην] pluperfect, ἑωράκειν, some list εἶδον as
  the second aorist of ὁράω, *to see, behold,* Matt 2:2,
  et al. freq.; *to look,* John 19:37; *to visit,* John
  16:22; Heb 13:23; *to mark, observe,* Acts 8:23;
  James 2:24; *to be admitted to witness,* Luke 17:22;
  John 3:36; Col 2:18; with Θεόν, *to be admitted*
  into the more immediate presence of God, Matt 5:8;
  Heb 12:14; *to attain to a true knowledge of God,* 3
  John 11; *to see to a thing,* Matt 27:4; Acts 18:15;
  ὅρα, *see, take care,* Matt 8:4; Heb 8:5; pass. *to*
  appear, Luke 1:11; Acts 2:3; *to reveal one's self,*
  Acts 26:16; *to present one's self,* Acts 7:26

ὀργή, ῆς, ἡ   {3973, n-1b}
  pr. *mental bent, impulse; anger, indignation,*
  wrath, Eph 4:31; Col 3:8; μετ' ὀργῆς, *indignantly,*
  Mark 3:5; *vengeance, punishment,* Matt 3:7; Luke
  3:7; 21:23; Rom 13:4, 5

ὀργή   nom sg fem [10t; n-1b; 3973]   ὀργή
ὀργῇ   dat sg fem [3t; n-1b; 3973]   "
ὀργήν   acc sg fem [9t; n-1b; 3973]   "
ὀργῆς   gen sg fem [14t; n-1b; 3973]   "
ὀργίζεσθε   pres pass imperative 2 pl
  [Ep 4:26; v-2a(1); 3974]   ὀργίζω
ὀργιζόμενος   pres pass ptcp nom sg masc
  [Mt 5:22; v-2a(1); 3974]   "

ὀργίζω   {3974, v-2a(1)}
  [ὀργιῶ, ὤργισα, -, -, ὠργίσθην] some list as
  deponent, ὀργίζομαι, *to provoke to anger, irritate;*
  pass. *to be angry, indignant, enraged,* Matt 5:22;
  18:34

ὀργίλον   acc sg masc
  [Ti 1:7; a-1a(2a); 3975]   ὀργίλος

ὀργίλος, η, ον   {3975, a-1a(2a)}
  prone to anger, irascible, passionate, Titus 1:7*

ὀργισθείς   aor pass ptcp nom sg masc
  [2t; v-2a(1); 3974]   ὀργίζω

ὀργυιά, ᾶς, ἡ   {3976, n-1a}
  the space measured by the arms outstretched; a
  fathom, Acts 27:28 (2t)*

ὀργυιάς   acc pl fem [2t; n-1a; 3976]   ὀργυιά
ὀρέγεται   pres mid ind 3 sg
  [1Ti 3:1; v-1b(2); 3977]   ὀρέγω
ὀρεγόμενοι   pres mid ptcp nom pl masc
  [1Ti 6:10; v-1b(2); 3977]   "
ὀρέγονται   pres mid ind 3 pl
  [Hb 11:16; v-1b(2); 3977]   "

ὀρέγω   {3977, v-1b(2)}
  [-, -, -, -, -] *to extend, stretch out;* mid. *to stretch*
  one's self out, to reach forward to, met. *to desire*
  earnestly, long after, 1 Tim 3:1; Heb 11:16; by
  impl. *to indulge in, be devoted to,* 1 Tim 6:10*

ὄρει   dat sg neut [11t; n-3d(2b); 4001]   ὄρος
ὀρεινῇ   dat sg fem
  [Lk 1:65; a-1a(2a); 3978]   ὀρεινός
ὀρεινήν   acc sg fem [Lk 1:39; a-1a(2a); 3978]   "

ὀρεινός, ή, όν   {3978, a-1a(2a)}
  mountainous, hilly, Luke 1:39, 65*

ὀρέξει   dat sg fem
[Rm 1:27; n-3e(5b); 3979]   ὄρεξις

ὄρεξις, εως, ἡ   {3979, n-3e(5b)}
desire, longing; lust, concupiscence, Rom 1:27*

ὄρεσιν   dat pl neut [4t; n-3d(2b); 4001]   ὄρος
ὀρέων   gen pl neut [Rv 6:15; n-3d(2b); 4001]   "
ὄρη   nom pl neut [2t; n-3d(2b); 4001]   "
ὄρη   acc pl neut [5t; n-3d(2b); 4001]   "
ὀρθάς   acc pl fem
[Hb 12:13; a-1a(2a); 3981]   ὀρθός

ὀρθοποδέω   {3980, cv-1d(2a)}
[-, -, -, -, -] *to walk in a straight course; to be
straightforward* in moral conduct, Gal 2:14*

ὀρθοποδοῦσιν   pres act ind 3 pl
[Ga 2:14; cv-1d(2a); 3980]   ὀρθοποδέω

ὀρθός, ή, όν   {3981, a-1a(2a)}
erect, upright, Acts 14:10; *plain, level, straight,*
Heb 12:13*

ὀρθός   nom sg masc
[Ac 14:10; a-1a(2a); 3981]   ὀρθός

ὀρθοτομέω   {3982, cv-1d(2a)}
[-, -, -, -, -] *to cut straight; to set forth truthfully,
without perversion* or *distortion,* 2 Tim 2:15*

ὀρθοτομοῦντα   pres act ptcp acc sg masc
[2Ti 2:15; cv-1d(2a); 3982]   ὀρθοτομέω

ὀρθρίζω   {3983, v-2a(1)}
[(ὤρθριζον), -, -, -, -, -] *to rise early in the morning;
to come with the dawn,* Luke 21:38*

ὀρθριναί   nom pl fem
[Lk 24:22; a-1a(2a); 3984]   ὀρθρινός

ὀρθρινός, ή, όν   {3984, a-1a(2a)}
a later form of ὄρθριος, *of* or *belonging to the
morning, morning,* Luke 24:22*

ὄρθριος, ία, ιον   {3985, a-1a(1)}
at daybreak, early, Luke 24:22*

ὄρθρον   acc sg masc [Ac 5:21; n-2a; 3986]   ὄρθρος

ὄρθρος, ου, ὁ   {3986, n-2a}
the dawn; the morning, John 8:2; Acts 5:21; ὄρθος
βαθύς, *the first streak of dawn, the early dawn,*
Luke 24:1*

ὄρθρου   gen sg masc [2t; n-2a; 3986]   "

ὀρθῶς   {3987, adverb}
straightly; rightly, correctly, Mark 7:35; Luke
7:43; 10:28; 20:21*

ὀρθῶς   adverb [4t; adverb; 3987]   ὀρθῶς
ὅρια   acc pl neut [4t; n-2c; 3990]   ὅριον
ὁρίζει   pres act ind 3 sg
[Hb 4:7; v-2a(1); 3988]   ὁρίζω

ὁρίζω   {3988, v-2a(1)}
[ὁριῶ or ὁρίσω, ὤρισα, -, ὤρισμαι, ὁρίσθην or
ὡρίσθην] *to set bounds to, to bound; to restrict,*
Heb 4:7; *to settle, appoint definitively,* Acts 17:26;
to fix determinately, Acts 2:23; *to decree, destine,*
Luke 22:22; *to constitute, appoint,* Acts 10:42;
17:31; *to characterize with precision, to set forth*

distinctively, Rom 1:4; absol. *to resolve,* Acts
11:29*

ὁρίοις   dat pl neut [2t; n-2c; 3990]   ὅριον

ὅριον, ου, τό   {3990, n-2c}
a limit, bound, border of a territory or *country;* pl.
τὰ ὅρια, *region, territory, district,* Matt 2:16; 4:13;
8:34

ὁρίσας   aor act ptcp nom sg masc
[Ac 17:26; v-2a(1); 3988]   ὁρίζω
ὁρισθέντος   aor pass ptcp gen sg masc
[Rm 1:4; v-2a(1); 3988]   "
ὁρίων   gen pl neut [6t; n-2c; 3990]   ὅριον

ὁρκίζω   {3991, v-2a(1)}
[-, -, -, -, -] *to put to an oath; to obtest, adjure,
conjure,* Mark 5:7; Acts 19:13; Matt 26:63 v.l.; 1
Thess 5:27 v.l.*

ὁρκίζω   pres act ind 1 sg
[2t; v-2a(1); 3991]   ὁρκίζω
ὅρκον   acc sg masc [2t; n-2a; 3992]   ὅρκος

ὅρκος, ου, ὁ   {3992, n-2a}
an oath, Matt 14:7, 9; 26:72; meton. *that which is
solemnly promised, a vow,* Matt 5:33

ὅρκος   nom sg masc [Hb 6:16; n-2a; 3992]   "
ὅρκου   gen sg masc [2t; n-2a; 3992]   "
ὅρκους   acc pl masc [3t; n-2a; 3992]   "
ὅρκῳ   dat sg masc [2t; n-2a; 3992]   "

ὁρκωμοσία, ας, ἡ   {3993, n-1a}
the act of taking an oath; an oath, Heb 7:20, 21, 28*

ὁρκωμοσίας   gen sg fem
[4t; n-1a; 3993]   ὁρκωμοσία

ὁρμάω   {3994, v-1d(1a)}
[-, ὥρμησα, -, -, -] pr. trans. *to put in motion,
incite;* intrans. *to rush,* Matt 8:32; Mark 5:13;
Luke 8:33

ὁρμή, ῆς, ἡ   {3995, n-1b}
impetus, impulse; assault, violent attempt, Acts
14:5; met. *impulse of mind, purpose, will,* James
3:4

ὁρμή   nom sg fem [2t; n-1b; 3995]   ὁρμή

ὅρμημα, ατος, τό   {3996, n-3c(4)}
violent or *impetuous motion; violence,* Rev 18:21*

ὁρμήματι   dat sg neut
[Rv 18:21; n-3c(4); 3996]   ὅρμημα
ὄρνεα   nom pl neut [Rv 19:21; n-2c; 3997]   ὄρνεον
ὀρνέοις   dat pl neut [Rv 19:17; n-2c; 3997]   "

ὄρνεον, ου, τό   {3997, n-2c}
a bird, fowl, Rev 18:2; 19:17, 21*

ὀρνέου   gen sg neut [Rv 18:2; n-2c; 3997]   "

ὄρνιξ, *bird,* Doric v.l. for ὄρνις (which is Attic) at Luke
13:34*   {n-3b(1)}

ὄρνις, ιθος, ἡ or **ὁ**   {3998, n-3c(3)}
bird, fowl; domestic *hen,* Matt 23:37; Luke 13:34*

ὄρνις   nom sg fem [2t; n-3c(3); 3998]   ὄρνις

ὁροθεσία, ας, ἡ   {3999, n-1a}
pr. *the act of fixing boundaries; a bound set, certain
bound, fixed limit,* Acts 17:26*

ὁροθεσίας   acc pl fem
[Ac 17:26; n-1a; 3999]   ὁροθεσία

ὄρος, ους, τό   {4001, n-3d(2b)}
a mountain, hill, Matt 5:1, 14; 8:1; 17:20

ὄρος   nom sg neut [4t; n-3d(2b); 4001]   ὄρος
ὄρος   acc sg neut [24t; n-3d(2b); 4001]   "
ὄρους   gen sg neut [12t; n-3d(2b); 4001]   "

ὀρύσσω   {4002, v-2b}
[-, ὤρυξα, -, -, ὠρύγην or ὠρύχθην] *to dig,
excavate,* Matt 21:33; 25:18; Mark 12:1*

ὀρφανός, ή, όν   {4003, a-1a(2a)}
bereaved of parents, *orphan,* James 1:27; Mark
12:40 v.l.; *bereaved, desolate,* John 14:18

ὀρφανούς   acc pl masc
[2t; a-1a(2a); 4003]   ὀρφανός

ὀρχέομαι   {4004, v-1d(2a)}
[(ὠρχούμην), -, ὠρχησάμην, -, -, -] *to dance,* Matt
11:6, 17; Mark 6:22; Luke 7:32*

ὀρχησαμένης   aor mid ptcp gen sg fem
[Mk 6:22; v-1d(2a); 4004]   ὀρχέομαι
ὁρῶ   pres act ind 1 sg [2t; v-1d(1a); 3972]   ὁράω
ὁρῶμεν   pres act ind 1 pl
[Hb 2:8; v-1d(1a); 3972]   "
ὁρῶν   pres act ptcp nom sg masc
[Hb 11:27; v-1d(1a); 3972]   "
ὁρῶντες   pres act ptcp nom pl masc
[1P 1:8; v-1d(1a); 3972]   "
ὁρῶσαι   pres act ptcp nom pl fem
[Lk 23:49; v-1d(1a); 3972]   "

ὅς, ἥ, ὅ   {4005, a-1a(2b)}
who, which, what, that, Matt 1:16, 23, 25; in N.T.
interrog. ἐφ᾽ ὅ, *wherefore, why,* Matt 26:50; in N.T.
ὅς μὲν ... ὅς δέ, for ὁ μὲν ... ὁ δέ, Matt 21:35; 2 Cor
2:16

ὅς   nom sg masc [217t; a-1a(2b); 4005]   ὅς
ὅσα   nom pl neut [7t; a-1a(2a); 4012]   ὅσος
ὅσα   acc pl neut [49t; a-1a(2a); 4012]   "
ὅσαι   nom pl fem [2C 1:20; a-1a(2a); 4012]   "

ὁσάκις   {4006, adverb}
as often as, 1 Cor 11:25, 26; Rev 11:6*

ὁσάκις   adverb [3t; adverb; 4006]   ὁσάκις
ὅσια   acc pl neut [Ac 13:34; a-1a(1); 4008]   ὅσιος
ὅσιον   acc sg masc [3t; a-1a(1); 4008]   "

ὅσιος, ία, ιον   {4008, a-1a(1)}
pr. *sanctioned by the supreme law of God, and
nature; pious, devout,* Titus 1:8; *pure,* 1 Tim 2:8;
supremely *holy,* Acts 2:27; 13:35; Heb 7:26; Rev
15:4; 16:5; τὰ ὅσια, *pledged bounties, mercies,* Acts
13:34*

ὅσιος   nom sg masc [3t; a-1a(1); 4008]   "

ὁσιότης, ητος, ἡ   {4009, n-3c(1)}
*piety, sacred observance of all duties towards God,
holiness,* Luke 1:75; Eph 4:24*

ὁσιότητι   dat sg fem [2t; n-3c(1); 4009]   ὁσιότης

ὁσίους   acc pl fem [1Ti 2:8; a-1a(1); 4008]   ὅσιος

ὁσίως   {4010, adverb}
piously, 1 Thess 2:10*

ὁσίως   adverb [1Th 2:10; adverb; 4010]   ὁσίως

ὀσμή, ῆς, ἡ   {4011, n-1b}
smell, odor; fragrant odor, John 12:3; Eph 5:2; Phil
4:18; met. 2 Cor 2:14, 16*

ὀσμή   nom sg fem [2t; n-1b; 4011]   ὀσμή
ὀσμήν   acc sg fem [3t; n-1b; 4011]   "
ὀσμῆς   gen sg fem [Jn 12:3; n-1b; 4011]   "
ὅσοι   nom pl masc [29t; a-1a(2a); 4012]   ὅσος
ὅσον   nom sg neut [Rv 21:16; a-1a(2a); 4012]   "
ὅσον   acc sg masc [8t; a-1a(2a); 4012]   "
ὅσον   acc sg neut [8t; a-1a(2a); 4012]   "

ὅσος, η, ον   {4012, a-1a(2a)}
as great, as much, Mark 7:36; John 6:11; Heb 1:4;
8:6; 10:25; ἐφ᾽ ὅσον χρόνον, *for how long a time,
while, as long as,* Rom 7:1; so, ἐφ᾽ ὅσον, sc. χρόνον,
Matt 9:15; ὅσον χρόνον, *how long,* Mark 2:19;
neut. ὅσον repeated, ὅσον ὅσον, used to give
intensity to other qualifying words, e.g.,
μικρόν, *the very least, a very little while,* Heb
10:37; ἐφ᾽ ὅσον, *in as much as,* Matt 25:40, 45;
καθ᾽ ὅσον, *by how much, so far as,* Heb 3:3; or, *in
as much as, as, so,* Heb 7:20; 9:27; pl. ὅσα, *so far
as, as much as,* Rev 1:2; 18:7; *how great, how much,
how many, what,* Mark 3:8; 5:19, 20; *how many, as
many as, all who,* 2 Cor 1:20; Phil 3:15; 1 Tim 6:1;
ὅσος ἄν, or ἐάν, *whoever, whatsoever,* Matt 7:12;
18:18

ὅσους   acc pl masc [3t; a-1a(2a); 4012]   "

ὅσπερ, ἥπερ, ὅπερ   {4013, a-1a(2b)}
an emphatic form of the relative pronoun ὅς,
Mark 15:6

ὀστέα   acc pl neut [Lk 24:39; n-2c; 4014]   ὀστέον

ὀστέον, ου, τό   {4014, n-2c}
contracted form, ὀστοῦν, οῦ, τό, *a bone,* Matt
23:27; Luke 24:39; John 19:36; Heb 11:22; Eph
5:30 v.l.*

ὀστέων   gen pl neut [2t; n-2c; 4014]   "

ὅστις, ἥτις, ὅ τι   {4015, a-1a(2b)}
whoever, whatever; whosoever, whatsoever, Matt
5:39, 41; 13:12; 18:4; its use in place of the
simple relative is also required in various
cases, which may be learned from the
grammars; ἕως ὅτου, sc. χρόνου, *until,* Luke
13:8; *while,* Matt 5:25

ὅστις   nom sg masc [26t; a-1a(2b); 4015]   ὅστις

ὀστοῦν, οῦ, τό, see ὀστέον   {4016, n-2d(2)}

ὀστοῦν   nom sg neut
[Jn 19:36; n-2c; 4014]   ὀστέον
ὀστράκινα   nom pl neut
[2Ti 2:20; a-1a(2a); 4017]   ὀστράκινος
ὀστρακίνοις   dat pl neut
[2C 4:7; a-1a(2a); 4017]   "

ὀστράκινος, η, ον   {4017, a-1a(2a)}
earthen, of earthenware, 2 Cor 4:7; 2 Tim 2:20*

ὄσφρησις, εως, ἡ   {4018, n-3e(5b)}
  smell, the sense of smelling, 1 Cor 12:17*

ὄσφρησις   nom sg fem
  [1C 12:17; n-3e(5b); 4018]   ὄσφρησις
ὀσφύας   acc pl fem
  [1P 1:13; n-3e(1); 4019]   ὀσφῦς
ὀσφύες   nom pl fem [Lk 12:35; n-3e(1); 4019]   "
ὀσφύϊ   dat sg fem [Hb 7:10; n-3e(1); 4019]   "
ὀσφύν   acc sg fem [3t; n-3e(1); 4019]   "
ὀσφύος   gen sg fem [2t; n-3e(1); 4019]   "

ὀσφῦς, ύος, ἡ   {4019, n-3e(1)}
  the loins, Matt 3:4; Mark 1:6

ὅσῳ   dat sg neut [3t; a-1a(2a); 4012]   ὅσος
ὅσων   gen pl neut [Lk 11:8; a-1a(2a); 4012]   "

ὅταν   {4020, particle}
  when, whenever, Matt 5:11; 6:2; Mark 3:11; Rev
  4:9, et al. freq.; in N.T. *in case of, on occasion of,*
  John 9:5; 1 Cor 15:27; Heb 1:6

ὅταν   particle [123t; particle; 4020]   ὅταν

ὅτε   {4021, particle}
  when, at the time that, at what time, Matt 7:28;
  9:25; Luke 13:35, et al. freq.

ὅτε   particle [103t; particle; 4021]   ὅτε

ὅτι   {4022, conj}
  originally was the neuter of ὅστις, *that,* Matt
  2:16, 22, 23; 6:5, 16; often used pleonastically in
  reciting another's words, Matt 9:18; Luke
  19:42; Acts 5:23; as a causal particle, *for that, for,
  because,* Matt 2:18; 5:3, 4, 5; 13:13; *because, seeing
  that, since,* Luke 23:40; Acts 1:17

ὅτι   conj [1296t; conj; 4022]   ὅτι
ὅτου   gen sg neut [5t; a-1a(2b); 4015]   ὅστις

οὗ   {4023, adverb}
  where, in what place, Matt 2:9; 18:20; *whither, to
  what place,* Luke 10:1; 22:10; 24:28; οὗ ἐάν,
  whithersoever, 1 Cor 16:6

οὗ   adverb [24t; adverb; 4023]   οὗ

οὐ   {4024, adverb}
  negative adverb, originally the gen. of ὅς,
  spelled οὐκ if followed by a word beginning
  with a vowel and a smooth breathing, οὐχ if
  followed by a vowel and rought breathing, *not,
  no,* Matt 5:37; 12:43; 23:37; for the peculiarities
  of its usage (especially as distinct from μή)
  consult a grammar

οὐ   adverb [693t; adverb; 4024]   οὐ
οὗ   gen sg masc [97t; a-1a(2b); 4005]   ὅς
οὗ   gen sg neut [18t; a-1a(2b); 4005]   "

οὐά   {4025, interj}
  expressive of insult and derision, *Ah! Ah!,*
  Mark 15:29; Matt 11:26 v.l.*

οὐά   interj [Mk 15:29; interj; 4025]   οὐά

οὐαί   {4026, interj}
  Wo! Alas! Matt 11:21; 18:7; 23:13, 14, 15, 16; ἡ
  οὐαί, subst., *a woe, calamity,* Rev 9:12; 11:14

οὐαί   interjection [46t; interjectio; 4026]   οὐαί

 οὐδ᾽   conj [9t; conj; 4028]   οὐδέ

οὐδαμῶς   {4027, adverb}
  by no means, Matt 2:6*

οὐδαμῶς   adverb [Mt 2:6; adverb; 4027]   οὐδαμῶς

οὐδέ   {4028, conj}
  negative conj., *neither, nor, and not, also not,*
  Matt 5:15; 6:15, 20, 26, 28; when single, *not even*
  Matt 6:29; 8:10

οὐδέ   conj [134t; conj; 4028]   οὐδέ

οὐδείς, οὐδεμία, οὐδέν   {4029, a-4b(2)}
  latter form, οὐθείς (4032), *not one, no one, none,
  nothing,* Matt 5:13; 6:24; 19:17; met. οὐδέν,
  nothing, of no account, naught, John 8:54; Acts
  21:24

οὐδείς   nom sg masc [98t; a-4b(2); 4029]   οὐδείς
οὐδεμία   nom sg fem [3t; a-4b(2); 4029]   "
οὐδεμίαν   acc sg fem [8t; a-4b(2); 4029]   "
οὐδέν   nom sg neut [21t; a-4b(2); 4029]   "
οὐδέν   acc sg neut [64t; a-4b(2); 4029]   "
οὐδένα   acc sg masc [16t; a-4b(2); 4029]   "
οὐδενί   dat sg masc [6t; a-4b(2); 4029]   "
οὐδενί   dat sg neut [3t; a-4b(2); 4029]   "
οὐδενός   gen sg masc [8t; a-4b(2); 4029]   "

οὐδέποτε   {4030, adverb}
  never, Matt 7:23; 21:16, 42, et al. freq.

οὐδέποτε   adverb [16t; adverb; 4030]   οὐδέποτε

οὐδέπω   {4031, adverb}
  not yet, never yet, never, Luke 23:53 v.l.; John
  7:39; 19:41; 20:9; Acts 8:16*

οὐδέπω   adverb [4t; adverb; 4031]   οὐδέπω

οὐθείς, see οὐδείς   {4032}

οὐθέν   nom sg neut
  [1C 13:2; a-4b(2); 4032]   οὐθείς
οὐθέν   acc sg neut [4t; a-4b(2); 4032]   "
οὐθενός   gen sg masc [2C 11:9; a-4b(2); 4032] "
οὐθενός   gen sg neut
  [Lk 22:35; a-4b(2); 4032]   "
οὐκ   adverb [825t; adverb; 4024]   οὐ

οὐκέτι   {4033, adverb}
  no longer, no more, Matt 22:46

οὐκέτι   adverb [47t; adverb; 4033]   οὐκέτι

οὐκοῦν   {4034, adverb}
  then, therefore; used interrogatively, John 18:37*

οὐκοῦν   adverb [Jn 18:37; adverb; 4034]   οὐκοῦν

οὖν   {4036, particle}
  then, now then, Matt 13:18; John 19:29; *then,
  thereupon,* Luke 15:28; John 6:14; *therefore,
  consequently,* Matt 5:48: Mark 10:9; it also serves
  to mark the resumption of discourse after an
  interruption by a parenthesis, 1 Cor 8:4.
  Sometimes it is not translated.

οὖν   particle [499t; particle; 4036]   οὖν

οὔπω   {4037, adverb}
  not yet, Matt 15:17; 16:9; 24:6 John 2:4; Phil 3:13
  v.l.

οὔπω   adverb [26t; adverb; 4037]   οὔπω

οὐρά, ᾶς, ἡ   {4038, n-1a}
a tail, Rev 9:10, 19; 12:4*

οὐρά   nom sg fem [Rv 12:4; n-1a; 4038]   οὐρά
οὐραί   nom pl fem [Rv 9:19; n-1a; 4038]   "
οὐραῖς   dat pl fem [2t; n-1a; 4038]   "
οὐρανέ   voc sg masc
   [Rv 18:20; n-2a; 4041]   οὐρανός

οὐράνιος, ον   {4039, a-3a}
heavenly, celestial, Matt 6:14, 26, 32; 15:13; 1 Cor
15:47 v.l.

οὐράνιος   nom sg masc [7t; a-3a; 4039]   οὐράνιος
οὐρανίου   gen sg fem [Lk 2:13; a-3a; 4039]   "
οὐρανίῳ   dat sg fem [Ac 26:19; a-3a; 4039]   "

οὐρανόθεν   {4040, adverb}
from heaven, Acts 14:17; 26:13*

οὐρανόθεν   adverb [2t; adverb; 4040]   οὐρανόθεν
οὐρανοί   nom pl masc [6t; n-2a; 4041]   οὐρανός
οὐρανοί   voc pl masc [Rv 12:12; n-2a; 4041]   "
οὐρανοῖς   dat pl masc [36t; n-2a; 4041]   "
οὐρανόν   acc sg masc [43t; n-2a; 4041]   "

οὐρανός, οῦ, ὁ   {4041, n-2a}
*heaven, the heavens, the visible heavens and all
their phenomena,* Matt 5:18; 16:1; 24:29, et al.
freq.; *the air, atmosphere,* in which the clouds
and tempests gather, the birds fly, etc., Matt
6:26; 16:2, 3; *heaven* as the peculiar seat and
abode of God, of angels, of glorified spirits,
etc., Matt 5:34, 45, 48; 6:1, 9, 10; 12:50; John 3:13,
31; 6:32, 38, 41, 42, 50, 51, 58; in N.T. *heaven* as a
term expressive of the Divine Being, His
administration, etc., Matt 19:14; 21:25; Luke
20:4, 5; John 3:27

οὐρανός   nom sg masc [12t; n-2a; 4041]   "
οὐρανοῦ   gen sg masc [92t; n-2a; 4041]   "
οὐρανούς   acc pl masc [5t; n-2a; 4041]   "
οὐρανῷ   dat sg masc [35t; n-2a; 4041]   "
οὐρανῶν   gen pl masc [42t; n-2a; 4041]   "
οὐράς   acc pl fem [Rv 9:10; n-1a; 4038]   οὐρά
Οὐρβανόν   acc sg masc
   [Rm 16:9; n-2a; 4042]   Οὐρβανός

Οὐρβανός, οῦ, ὁ   {4042, n-2a}
Urbanus, Urban, pr. name, Rom 16:9*

Οὐρίας, ου, ὁ   {4043, n-1d}
Urias, Uriah, pr. name (2 Sam 11; 12:24), Matt
1:6*

Οὐρίου   gen sg masc [Mt 1:6; n-1d; 4043]   Οὐρίας

οὖς, ὠτός, τό   {4044, n-3c(6c)}
the ear, Matt 10:27; Mark 7:33; Luke 22:50; Acts
7:57

οὖς   nom sg neut [2t; n-3c(6c); 4044]   οὖς
οὖς   acc sg neut [11t; n-3c(6c); 4044]   "
οὕς   acc pl masc [53t; a-1a(2b); 4005]   ὅς
οὖσα   pres act ptcp nom sg fem
   [6t; v-6b; 1639]   εἰμί
οὖσαι   pres act ptcp nom pl fem
   [Rm 13:1; v-6b; 1639]   "

οὖσαν   pres act ptcp acc sg fem
   [6t; v-6b; 1639]   "
οὔσῃ   pres act ptcp dat sg fem
   [4t; v-6b; 1639]   "
οὔσης   pres act ptcp gen sg fem
   [6t; v-6b; 1639]   "

οὐσία, ας, ἡ   {4045, n-1a}
substance, property, goods, fortune, Luke 15:12,
13*

οὐσίαν   acc sg fem [Lk 15:13; n-1a; 4045]   οὐσία
οὐσίας   gen sg fem [Lk 15:12; n-1a; 4045]   "
οὖσιν   pres act ptcp dat pl masc
   [9t; v-6b; 1639]   εἰμί
οὐσῶν   pres act ptcp gen pl fem
   [1Th 2:14; v-6b; 1639]   "

οὔτε   {4046, adverb}
neither, nor, Luke 20:36; οὔτε ... οὔτε, *or* οὔτε ...
οὔτε, *neither ... nor,* Luke 20:35; Gal 1:12; in N.T.
also used singly in the sense of οὐδέ, *not even,*
Mark 5:3; Luke 12:26; 1 Cor 3:2

οὔτε   adverb [87t; adverb; 4046]   οὔτε
οὗτοι   nom pl masc [74t; a-1a(2b); 4047]   οὗτος

οὗτος, αὕτη, τοῦτο   {4047, a-1a(2b)}
this, this person or thing, Matt 3:3, 9, 17; 8:9;
10:2; 24:34, et al. freq.; used by way of
contempt, *this fellow,* Matt 13:55; 27:47; αὐτὸ
τοῦτο, *this very thing, this same thing,* 2 Cor 2:3;
7:11; εἰς αὐτὸ τοῦτο, and elliptically, αὐτὸ τοῦτο,
for this same purpose, on this account, Eph 6:18,
22; 2 Peter 1:5; καὶ οὗτος, *and moreover,* Luke
7:12; 16:1; 20:30; καὶ τοῦτο, *and that too,* 1 Cor
6:6, 8; τοῦτο μὲν ... τοῦτο δέ, *partly ... partly,* Heb
10:33

οὗτος   nom sg masc [187t; a-1a(2b); 4047]   "
οὕτω   adverb [4t; adverb; 4048]   οὕτως

οὕτως   {4048, adverb}
thus, in this way, Matt 1:18; 2:5; 5:16; et al. freq.;
ὃς μὲν οὕτως, ὃς δὲ οὕτως, *one so, and another so,
one in one way, and another in another,* 1 Cor 7:7;
so, Matt 7:12; 12:40; 24:27, 37, et al. freq.; *thus,
under such circumstances,* Acts 20:11; *in such a
condition,* viz., one previously mentioned, Acts
27:17; 1 Cor 7:26, 40; and, perhaps, John 4:6; *in
an ordinary way, at ease,* like Latin *sic,* perhaps,
John 4:6

οὕτως   adverb [204t; adverb; 4048]   "
οὐχ   adverb [105t; adverb; 4024]   οὐ

οὐχί   {4049, adverb}
a strengthened form of οὐ, *not,* John 13:10, 11;
when followed by ἀλλά, *nay, not so, by no
means,* Luke 1:60; 12:51; used also in negative
interrogations, Matt 5:46, 47; 6:25

οὐχί   adverb [54t; adverb; 4049]   οὐχί
ὀφειλάς   acc pl fem [Rm 13:7; n-1b; 4051]   ὀφειλή
ὀφείλει   pres act ind 3 sg
   [11t; v-2d(1); 4053]   ὀφείλω
ὀφείλεις   pres act ind 2 sg [3t; v-2d(1); 4053]   "
ὀφειλέται   nom pl masc
   [3t; n-1f; 4050]   ὀφειλέτης
ὀφειλέταις   dat pl masc [Mt 6:12; n-1f; 4050]   "

ὀφείλετε   pres act imperative 2 pl
   [Rm 13:8; v-2d(1); 4053]   ὀφείλω
ὀφείλετε   pres act ind 2 pl
   [Jn 13:14; v-2d(1); 4053]   "

ὀφειλέτης, ου, ὁ   {4050, n-1f}
   a debtor, one who owes, Matt 18:24; met. one who
   is in any way bound, or under obligation to
   perform any duty, Rom 1:14; 8:12; 15:27; Gal
   5:3; in N.T. one who fails in duty, a delinquent,
   offender, Matt 6:12; a sinner, Luke 13:4, cf. v. 2*

ὀφειλέτης   nom sg masc
   [3t; n-1f; 4050]   ὀφειλέτης

ὀφειλή, ῆς, ἡ   {4051, n-1b}
   a debt, Matt 18:32; met. a duty, due, Rom 13:7; 1
   Cor 7:3*

ὀφείλημα, ατος, τό   {4052, n-3c(4)}
   a debt; a due, Rom 4:4, in N.T. a delinquency,
   offence, fault, sin, Matt 6:12, cf. v. 14*

ὀφείλημα   acc sg neut
   [Rm 4:4; n-3c(4); 4052]   ὀφείλημα
ὀφειλήματα   acc pl neut [Mt 6:12; n-3c(4); 4052]   "
ὀφειλήν   acc sg fem [2t; n-1b; 4051]   ὀφειλή
ὀφείλομεν   pres act ind 1 pl
   [7t; v-2d(1); 4053]   ὀφείλω
ὀφειλόμενον   pres pass ptcp acc sg neut
   [2t; v-2d(1); 4053]   "
ὀφείλοντες   pres act ptcp nom pl masc
   [Hb 5:12; v-2d(1); 4053]   "
ὀφείλοντι   pres act ptcp dat sg masc
   [Lk 11:4; v-2d(1); 4053]   "
ὀφείλουσιν   pres act ind 3 pl
   [2t; v-2d(1); 4053]   "

ὀφείλω   {4053, v-2d(1)}
   [(ὤφειλον), -, -, -, -, -] to owe, be indebted, Matt
   18:28, 30, 34; to incur a bond, to be bound to make
   discharge, Matt 23:16, 18; to be bound or obliged
   by what is due or fitting or consequently
   necessary, Luke 17:10; John 13:14; to incur
   desert, to deserve, John 19:7; to be due or fitting, 1
   Cor 7:3, 36; from the Aramaic, to be delinquent,
   Luke 11:4

ὄφεις   nom pl masc [Mt 10:16; n-3e(5b); 4058]   ὄφις
ὄφεις   voc pl masc [Mt 23:33; n-3e(5b); 4058]   "
ὄφεις   acc pl masc [Mk 16:18; n-3e(5b); 4058]   "

ὄφελον   {4054, particle}
   originally a ptcp (aor act ptcp nom sg neut)
   from ὀφείλω, used in N.T. as an interj. to
   introduce a wish that cannot be attained, O
   that! Would that! 1 Cor 4:8; 2 Cor 11:1; Gal 5:12;
   Rev 3:15*

ὄφελον   particle [4t; particle; 4054]   ὄφελον

ὄφελος, ους, τό   {4055, n-3d(2b)}
   profit, benefit, advantage, 1 Cor 15:32; James 2:14,
   16*

ὄφελος   nom sg neut [3t; n-3d(2b); 4055]   ὄφελος
ὄφεσιν   dat pl masc [Rv 9:19; n-3e(5b); 4058]   ὄφις
ὄφεων   gen pl masc [2t; n-3e(5b); 4058]   "
ὄφεως   gen sg masc [Rv 12:14; n-3e(5b); 4058]   "

ὀφθαλμοδουλεία, see ὀφθαλμοδουλία.

ὀφθαλμοδουλία, ας, ἡ   {4056, n-1a}
   also spelled ὀφθαλμοδουλεία, eye-service, service
   rendered only while under inspection, Eph 6:6; Col
   3:22*

ὀφθαλμοδουλία   dat sg fem
   [Cl 3:22; n-1a; 4056]   ὀφθαλμοδουλία
ὀφθαλμοδουλίαν   acc sg fem [Ep 6:6; n-1a; 4056]   "
ὀφθαλμοί   nom pl masc [15t; n-2a; 4057]   ὀφθαλμός
ὀφθαλμοῖς   dat pl masc [7t; n-2a; 4057]   "
ὀφθαλμόν   acc sg masc [Mt 5:38; n-2a; 4057]   "

ὀφθαλμός, οῦ, ὁ   {4057, n-2a}
   an eye, Matt 5:29, 38; 6:23; 7:3, 4, 5; ὀφθαλμὸς
   πονηρός, an evil eye, an envious eye, envy, Matt
   20:15; Mark 7:22; met. the intellectual eye, Matt
   13:15; Mark 8:18; John 12:40; Acts 26:18

ὀφθαλμός   nom sg masc [15t; n-2a; 4057]   "
ὀφθαλμοῦ   gen sg masc [6t; n-2a; 4057]   "
ὀφθαλμούς   acc pl masc [37t; n-2a; 4057]   "
ὀφθαλμῷ   dat sg masc [8t; n-2a; 4057]   "
ὀφθαλμῶν   gen pl masc [11t; n-2a; 4057]   "
ὀφθείς   aor pass ptcp nom sg masc
   [Ac 9:17; v-1d(1a); 3972]   ὁράω
ὀφθέντες   aor pass ptcp nom pl masc
   [Lk 9:31; v-1d(1a); 3972]   "
ὀφθέντος   aor pass ptcp gen sg masc
   [Ac 7:35; v-1d(1a); 3972]   "
ὀφθήσεται   fut pass ind 3 sg
   [Hb 9:28; v-1d(1a); 3972]   "
ὀφθήσομαι   fut pass ind 1 sg
   [Ac 26:16; v-1d(1a); 3972]   "
ὄφιν   acc sg masc [3t; n-3e(5b); 4058]   ὄφις

ὄφις, εως, ἡ   {4058, n-3e(5b)}
   a serpent, Matt 7:10; 10:16; an artificial serpent,
   John 3:14; used of the devil or Satan, Rev 12:9,
   14, 15; 20:2; met. a man of serpentine character,
   Matt 23:33

ὄφις   nom sg masc [4t; n-3e(5b); 4058]   "
ὀφρύος   gen sg fem
   [Lk 4:29; n-3e(1); 4059]   ὀφρῦς

ὀφρῦς, ύος, ἡ   {4059, n-3e(1)}
   a brow, eye-brow; the brow of a mountain, edge of
   a precipice, Luke 4:29*

ὀχετός, οῦ, ὁ   {4060, n-2a}
   drain, sewer, canal, Mark 7:19 v.l.*

ὀχλέω   {4061, v-1d(2a)}
   [-, -, -, -, -] pr. to mob; to disturb, trouble, Acts
   5:16; Luke 6:18 v.l.*

ὄχλοι   nom pl masc [28t; n-2a; 4063]   ὄχλος
ὄχλοις   dat pl masc [11t; n-2a; 4063]   "
ὄχλον   acc sg masc [35t; n-2a; 4063]   "

ὀχλοποιέω   {4062, cv-1d(2a)}
   [-, ὠχλοποίησα, -, -, -] to collect a mob, create a
   tumult, Acts 17:5*

ὀχλοποιήσαντες   aor act ptcp nom pl masc
   [Ac 17:5; cv-1d(2a); 4062]   ὀχλοποιέω

ὄχλος, ου, ὁ   {4063, n-2a}
   a crowd, a confused multitude of people, Matt 4:25;
   5:1; 7:28; spc. the common people, John 7:49; a

multitude, great number, Luke 5:29; 6:17; Acts
1:15; by impl. *tumult, uproar,* Luke 22:6; Acts
24:18

ὄχλος   nom sg masc [46t; n-2a; 4063]   ὄχλος
ὄχλου   gen sg masc [25t; n-2a; 4063]   "
ὀχλουμένους   pres pass ptcp acc pl masc
    [Ac 5:16; v-1d(2a); 4061]   ὀχλέω
ὄχλους   acc pl masc [17t; n-2a; 4063]   ὄχλος
ὄχλῳ   dat sg masc [12t; n-2a; 4063]   "
ὄχλων   gen pl masc [Lk 11:29; n-2a; 4063]   "

Ὀχοζίας, ου, ὁ   {4064, n-1f}
    Ahaziah (2 Kings 8:24), Matt 1:8 v.l.; Luke 3:23ff.
    v.l.*

ὀχύρωμα, ατος, τό   {4065, n-3c(4)}
    a stronghold; met. *an* opposing *bulwark* of error
    or vice, 2 Cor 10:4*

ὀχυρωμάτων   gen pl neut
    [2C 10:4; n-3c(4); 4065]   ὀχύρωμα
ὀψάρια   acc pl neut [Jn 6:9; n-2c; 4066]   ὀψάριον

ὀψάριον, ου, τό   {4066, n-2c}
    a little fish, John 6:9, 11; 21:9, 10, 13*

ὀψάριον   acc sg neut [2t; n-2c; 4066]   "
ὀψαρίων   gen pl neut [2t; n-2c; 4066]   "

ὀψέ   {4067, adverb}
    can function as an improper prep., *late;* put for
    the first watch, at evening, Mark 11:19; 13:35; ὀψὲ
    σαββάτων, *after the close of the Sabbath,* Matt 28:1

ὀψέ   adverb [3t; adverb; 4067]   ὀψέ
ὄψεσθε   fut mid ind 2 pl
    [13t; v-1d(1a); 3972]   ὁράω
ὄψεται   fut mid ind 3 sg [4t; v-1d(1a); 3972]   "
ὄψῃ   fut mid ind 2 sg [3t; v-1d(1a); 3972]   "
ὄψησθε   aor mid subj 2 pl
    [Lk 13:28; v-1d(1a); 3972]   "

ὀψία, see ὄψιος   {4068}

ὀψία   nom sg fem
    [Jn 6:16; see o[yio"; 4068]   ὀψία
ὀψίας   gen sg fem [14t; see o[yio"; 4068]   "
ὄψιμον   acc sg masc [Jm 5:7; a-3a; 4069]   ὄψιμος

ὄψιμος, ον   {4069, a-3a}
    late; latter, James 5:7; poetic and later prose for
    ὄψιος*

ὄψιν   acc sg fem [Jn 7:24; n-3e(5b); 4071]   ὄψις

ὄψιος, α, ον   {4070, a-1a(1)}
    late, Mark 11:11; ἡ ὀψία, sc. ὥρα, *evening,* two of
    which were reckoned by the Hebrews; one,
    from the ninth hour until sunset, Matt 8:16;
    14:15; and the other, from sunset until dark,
    Matt 14:23; 16:2

ὄψις, εως, ἡ   {4071, n-3e(5b)}
    a sight; the face, countenance, John 11:44; Rev
    1:16; *external appearance,* John 7:24*

ὄψις   nom sg fem [2t; n-3e(5b); 4071]   "
ὄψομαι   fut mid ind 1 sg
    [2t; v-1d(1a); 3972]   ὁράω
ὀψόμεθα   fut mid ind 1 pl
    [1J 3:2; v-1d(1a); 3972]   "

ὄψονται   fut mid ind 3 pl [8t; v-1d(1a); 3972]   "
ὀψώνια   nom pl neut
    [Rm 6:23; n-2c; 4072]   ὀψώνιον
ὀψωνίοις   dat pl neut [2t; n-2c; 4072]   "

ὀψώνιον, ου, τό   {4072, n-2c}
    provisions; a stipend or *pay* of soldiers, Luke
    3:14; 1 Cor 9:7; *wages* of any kind, 2 Cor 11:8;
    due *wages, a* stated *recompense,* Rom 6:23*

π

παγίδα   acc sg fem [3t; n-3c(2); 4075]   παγίς
παγιδεύσωσιν   aor act subj 3 pl
    [Mt 22:15; v-1a(6); 4074]   παγιδεύω

παγιδεύω   {4074, v-1a(6)}
    [-, ἐπαγίδευσα, -, -, -] *to ensnare, entrap, entangle,*
    Matt 22:15*

παγίδος   gen sg fem
    [2Ti 2:26; n-3c(2); 4075]   παγίς

παγίς, ίδος, ἡ   {4075, n-3c(2)}
    a snare, trap, Luke 21:35; met. *stratagem, device,
    wile,* 1 Tim 3:7; 6:9; 2 Tim 2:26; met. *a trap* of
    ruin, Rom 11:9*

παγίς   nom sg fem [Lk 21:35; n-3c(2); 4075]   "
πάγον   acc sg masc [Ac 17:19; n-2a; 4076]   πάγος

πάγος, ου, ὁ   {4076, n-2a}
    a hill, Ἄρειος πάγος, *Areopagus, the hill of Mars,*
    at Athens, Acts 17:19, 22

πάγου   gen sg masc [Ac 17:22; n-2a; 4076]   "
πάθει   dat sg neut [1Th 4:5; n-3d(2b); 4079] πάθος
παθεῖν   aor act inf [12t; v-5a; 4248]   πάσχω
πάθη   acc pl neut [Rm 1:26; n-3d(2b); 4079]   πάθος
πάθῃ   aor act subj 3 sg
    [Mk 9:12; v-5a; 4248]   πάσχω

πάθημα, ατος, τό   {4077, n-3c(4)}
    what is suffered; suffering, affliction, Rom 8:18; 2
    Cor 1:5, 6, 7; Phil 3:10; *emotion, passion,* Rom 7:5;
    Gal 5:24

πάθημα   acc sg neut [Hb 2:9; n-3c(4); 4077] πάθημα
παθήμασιν   dat pl neut [4t; n-3c(4); 4077]   "
παθήματα   nom pl neut [3t; n-3c(4); 4077]   "
παθήματα   acc pl neut [1P 1:11; n-3c(4); 4077] "
παθημάτων   gen pl neut [7t; n-3c(4); 4077]   "

παθητός, ή, όν   {4078, a-1a(2a)}
    passible, capable of suffering, liable to suffer; in
    N.T. *destined to suffer,* Acts 26:23*

παθητός   nom sg masc
    [Ac 26:23; a-1a(2a); 4078]   παθητός
παθόντας   aor act ptcp acc pl masc
    [1P 5:10; v-5a; 4248]   πάσχω
παθόντος   aor act ptcp gen sg masc
    [1P 4:1; v-5a; 4248]   "

πάθος, ους, τό   {4079, n-3d(2b)}
    suffering; an affection, passion, especially sexual,
    Rom 1:26

πάθος   acc sg neut [Cl 3:5; n-3d(2b); 4079]   πάθος
παθοῦσα   aor act ptcp nom sg fem
   [Mk 5:26; v-5a; 4248]   πάσχω
παθών   aor act ptcp nom sg masc
   [1P 4:1; v-5a; 4248]   "
παῖδα   acc sg masc [5t; n-3c(2); 4090]   παῖς
παιδαγωγόν   acc sg masc
   [Ga 3:25; n-2a; 4080]   παιδαγωγός

παιδαγωγός, οῦ, ὁ   {4080, n-2a}
   a pedagogue, childtender, a person, usually a
   slave or freedman, to whom the care of the
   boys of a family was committed, whose duty it
   was to attend them at their play, lead them to
   and from the public school, and exercise a
   constant superintendence over their conduct
   and safety; in N.T. an ordinary director or
   minister contrasted with an Apostle, as a
   pedagogue occupies an inferior position to a
   parent, 1 Cor 4:15; a term applied to the Mosaic
   law, as dealing with men as in a state of mere
   childhood and tutelage, Gal 3:24, 25*

παιδαγωγός   nom sg masc [Ga 3:24; n-2a; 4080]   "
παιδαγωγούς   acc pl masc [1C 4:15; n-2a; 4080]   "

παιδάριον, ου, τό   {4081, n-2c}
   a little boy, child; a boy, lad, John 6:9; Matt 11:16
   v.l.*

παιδάριον   nom sg neut
   [Jn 6:9; n-2c; 4081]   παιδάριον
παῖδας   acc pl masc [3t; n-3c(2); 4090]   παῖς

παιδεία, ας, ἡ   {4082, n-1a}
   education, training up, nurture of children, Eph
   6:4; instruction, discipline, 2 Tim 3:16; in N.T.
   correction, chastisement, Heb 12:5, 7, 8, 11*

παιδεία   nom sg fem [Hb 12:11; n-1a; 4082]   παιδεία
παιδείᾳ   dat sg fem [Ep 6:4; n-1a; 4082]   "
παιδείαν   acc sg fem [2t; n-1a; 4082]   "
παιδείας   gen sg fem [2t; n-1a; 4082]   "
παιδεύει   pres act ind 3 sg
   [2t; v-1a(6); 4084]   παιδεύω
παιδευθῶσιν   aor pass subj 3 pl
   [1Ti 1:20; v-1a(6); 4084]   "
παιδευόμεθα   pres pass ind 1 pl
   [1C 11:32; v-1a(6); 4084]   "
παιδευόμενοι   pres pass ptcp nom pl masc
   [2C 6:9; v-1a(6); 4084]   "
παιδεύοντα   pres act ptcp acc sg masc
   [2Ti 2:25; v-1a(6); 4084]   "
παιδεύουσα   pres act ptcp nom sg fem
   [Ti 2:12; v-1a(6); 4084]   "
παιδεύσας   aor act ptcp nom sg masc
   [2t; v-1a(6); 4084]   "
παιδευτάς   acc pl masc
   [Hb 12:9; n-1f; 4083]   παιδευτής
παιδευτήν   acc sg masc [Rm 2:20; n-1f; 4083]   "

παιδευτής, οῦ, ὁ   {4083, n-1f}
   a preceptor, instructor, teacher, pr. of boys; gener.
   Rom 2:20; in N.T. a chastiser, Heb 12:9*

παιδεύω   {4084, v-1a(6)}
   [(ἐπαίδευον), -, ἐπαίδευσα, -, πεπαίδευμαι,
   ἐπαιδεύθην] to educate, instruct children, Acts

7:22; 22:3; genr. παιδεύομαι, το be taught, learn, 1
   Tim 1:20; to admonish, instruct by admonition, 2
   Tim 2:25; Titus 2:12; in N.T. to chastise, chasten,
   1 Cor 11:32; 2 Cor 6:9; Heb 12:6, 7, 10; Rev 3:19;
   of criminals, to scourge, Luke 23:16, 22*

παιδεύω   pres act ind 1 sg
   [Rv 3:19; v-1a(6); 4084]   παιδεύω
παιδία   nom pl neut [6t; n-2c; 4086]   παιδίον
παιδία   voc pl neut [3t; n-2c; 4086]   "
παιδία   acc pl neut [4t; n-2c; 4086]   "

παιδιόθεν   {4085, adverb}
   from childhood, from a child, Mark 9:21*

παιδιόθεν   adverb
   [Mk 9:21; adverb; 4085]   παιδιόθεν
παιδίοις   dat pl neut [2t; n-2c; 4086]   παιδίον

παιδίον, ου, τό   {4086, n-2c}
   an infant, babe, Matt 2:8; but usually in N.T. as
   equiv. to παῖς, Matt 14:21; Mark 7:28, et al. freq.;
   pl. voc. used by way of endearment, my dear
   children, 1 John 2:18; also as a term of familiar
   address, children, my lads, John 21:5

παιδίον   nom sg neut [9t; n-2c; 4086]   "
παιδίον   voc sg neut [Lk 1:76; n-2c; 4086]   "
παιδίον   acc sg neut [17t; n-2c; 4086]   "
παιδίου   gen sg neut [6t; n-2c; 4086]   "
παιδίσκας   acc pl fem
   [Lk 12:45; n-1b; 4087]   παιδίσκη

παιδίσκη, ης, ἡ   {4087, n-1b}
   a girl, damsel, maiden; a female slave or servant,
   Matt 26:69; Mark 14:66, 69

παιδίσκη   nom sg fem [5t; n-1b; 4087]   "
παιδίσκην   acc sg fem [2t; n-1b; 4087]   "
παιδίσκης   gen sg fem [4t; n-1b; 4087]   "
παιδισκῶν   gen pl fem [Mk 14:66; n-1b; 4087]   "
παιδίων   gen pl neut [4t; n-2c; 4086]   παιδίον

παιδόθεν   {4088, adverb}
   from childhood, Mark 9:21 v.l.*

παιδός   gen sg masc [4t; n-3c(2); 4090]   παῖς
παιδός   gen sg fem [Lk 8:51; n-3c(2); 4090]   "
παίδων   gen pl masc [Lk 15:26; n-3c(2); 4090]   "
παίζειν   pres act inf
   [1C 10:7; v-2a(2); 4089]   -παίζω

παίζω   {4089, v-2a(2)}
   [παίξω, ἔπαιξα, -, -, ἐπαίχθην] to play in the
   manner of children; to sport, to practise the festive
   gestures of idolatrous worship, 1 Cor 10:7*

παῖς, ιδός, ἡ or ὁ   {4090, n-3c(2)}
   a child in relation to parents, of either sex, John
   4:51; a child in respect of age, either male or
   female, and of all ages from infancy up to
   manhood, a boy, youth, girl, maiden, Matt 2:16;
   17:18; Luke 2:43; 8:54; a servant, slave, Matt 8:6,
   8, 13, cf. v. 9; Luke 7:7, cf. v. 3, 10; an attendant,
   minister, Matt 14:2; Luke 1:69; Acts 4:25; also,
   Luke 1:54; or, perhaps, a child in respect of
   fatherly regard

παῖς   nom sg masc [8t; n-3c(2); 4090]   παῖς
παῖς   voc sg fem [Lk 8:54; n-3c(2); 4090]   "

παίσας   aor act ptcp nom sg masc
  [2t; v-1a(2); 4091]   παίω
παίσῃ   aor act subj 3 sg [Rv 9:5; v-1a(2); 4091]   "
παισίν   dat pl masc [Mt 14:2; n-3c(2); 4090]   παῖς

παίω   {4091, v-1a(2)}
  [-, ἔπαισα, -, -, -] *a strike, smite,* with the fist,
  Matt 26:68; Luke 22:64; with a sword, Mark
  14:47; John 18:10; *to strike* as a scorpion, *to sting,*
  Rev 9:5*

Πακατιανός, ή, όν   {4092, a-1a(2a)}
  Pacatiana, in the subscription to 1 Timothy,
  claiming Pacatiana as the original of the
  epistle.*

πάλαι   {4093, adverb}
  of old, long ago, Matt 11:21; Luke 10:13; Heb 1:1;
  Jude 4; οἱ πάλαι, *old, former,* 2 Peter 1:9; *some
  time since, already,* Mark 15:44

πάλαι   adverb [7t; adverb; 4093]   πάλαι
παλαιά   nom sg fem [1J 2:7; a-1a(1); 4094] παλαιός
παλαιᾷ   dat sg fem [1C 5:8; a-1a(1); 4094]   "
παλαιά   acc pl neut [Mt 13:52; a-1a(1); 4094]   "
παλαιάν   acc sg fem [2t; a-1a(1); 4094]   "
παλαιᾶς   gen sg fem [2C 3:14; a-1a(1); 4094]   "
παλαιόν   acc sg masc [3t; a-1a(1); 4094]   "
παλαιόν   acc sg neut [2t; a-1a(1); 4094]   "

παλαιός, ά, όν   {4094, a-1a(1)}
  old, not new or *recent,* Matt 9:16, 17; 13:52; Luke
  5:36

παλαιός   nom sg masc [2t; a-1a(1); 4094]   "

παλαιότης, ητος, ή   {4095, n-3c(1)}
  oldness, obsoleteness, Rom 7:6*

παλαιότητι   dat sg fem
  [Rm 7:6; n-3c(1); 4095]   παλαιότης
παλαιοῦ   gen sg neut
  [Mk 2:21; a-1a(1); 4094]   παλαιός
παλαιούμενα   pres pass ptcp acc pl neut
  [Lk 12:33; v-1d(3); 4096]   παλαιόω
παλαιούμενον   pres pass ptcp nom sg neut
  [Hb 8:13; v-1d(3); 4096]   "
παλαιούς   acc pl masc [3t; a-1a(1); 4094]   παλαιός

παλαιόω   {4096, v-1d(3)}
  [-, -, πεπαλαίωκα, -, ἐπαλαιώθην] *to make old;*
  pass. *to grow old, to become worn,* Luke 12:33;
  Heb 1:11; met. *to treat as antiquated, to abrogate,
  supersede,* Heb 8:13*

παλαιῷ   dat sg neut [2t; a-1a(1); 4094]   "
παλαιωθήσονται   fut pass ind 3 pl
  [Hb 1:11; v-1d(3); 4096]   παλαιόω

πάλη, ης, ή   {4097, n-1b}
  wrestling; struggle, contest, Eph 6:12*

πάλη   nom sg fem [Ep 6:12; n-1b; 4097]   πάλη

παλιγγενεσία, ας, ή   {4098, n-1a}
  a new birth; regeneration, renovation, Matt 19:28;
  Titus 3:5. See unpublished Ph.D. dissertation,
  William D. Mounce, *The Origin of the New
  Testament Metaphor of Rebirth,* University of
  Aberdeen, Scotland*

παλιγγενεσίᾳ   dat sg fem
  [Mt 19:28; n-1a; 4098]   παλιγγενεσία
παλιγγενεσίας   gen sg fem [Ti 3:5; n-1a; 4098]   "

πάλιν   {4099, adverb}
  pr. *back; again, back again,* John 10:17; Acts 10:16;
  11:10; *again* by repetition, Matt 26:43; *again* in
  continuation, *further,* Matt 5:33; 13:44, 45, 47,
  18:19; *again, on the other hand,* 1 John 2:8

πάλιν   adverb [141t; adverb; 4099]   πάλιν
παμπληθεί   adverb
  [Lk 23:18; adverb; 4101]   παμπληθεί

παμπληθεί   {4101, adverb}
  the whole multitude together, all at once, Luke
  23:18*

πάμπολυς, παμπόλλη, πάμπολυ   {4102, a-1a(2a)}
  very many, very great, vast, Mark 8:1 v.l.*

Παμφυλία, ας, ή   {4103, n-1a}
  Pamphylia, a country of Asia Minor, Acts 2:10;
  13:13; 14:24; 15:38; 16:6 v.l.; 27:5*

Παμφυλίαν   acc sg fem [3t; n-1a; 4103]   Παμφυλία
Παμφυλίας   gen sg fem [2t; n-1a; 4103]   "
πᾶν   nom sg neut [37t; a-2a; 4246]   πᾶς
πᾶν   acc sg neut [38t; a-2a; 4246]   "
πανδοχεῖ   dat sg masc
  [Lk 10:35; n-3e(3); 4107]   πανδοχεύς

πανδοχεῖον, ου, τό   {4106, n-2c}
  a public inn, place where travelers may lodge,
  called in the East by the name of *menzil, khan,
  caravanserai,* Luke 10:34*

πανδοχεῖον   acc sg neut
  [Lk 10:34; n-2c; 4106]   πανδοχεῖον

πανδοχεύς, έως, ὁ   {4107, n-3e(3)}
  the keeper of a public inn or *caravanserai, a host,*
  Luke 10:35*

πανηγύρει   dat sg fem
  [Hb 12:22; n-3e(5b); 4108]   πανήγυρις

πανήγυρις, εως, ή   {4108, n-3e(5b)}
  pr. *an assembly of an entire people; a solemn
  gathering at a festival; a festive convocation,* Heb
  12:22*

πανοικεί   {4109, adverb}
  also spelled πανοικί, *with one's whole household*
  or *family,* Acts 16:34*

πανοικεί   adverb [Ac 16:34; adverb; 4109] πανοικεί
πανοικί, see πανοικεί

πανοπλία, ας, ή   {4110, n-1a}
  panoply, complete armor, a complete suit of armor,
  both offensive and defensive, as the shield,
  sword, spear, helmet, breastplate, etc., Luke
  11:22; Eph 6:11, 13*

πανοπλίαν   acc sg fem [3t; n-1a; 4110]   πανοπλία

πανουργία, ας, ή   {4111, n-1a}
  knavery, craft, cunning, Luke 20:23; 1 Cor 3:19

πανουργίᾳ   dat sg fem [4t; n-1a; 4111]   πανουργία
πανουργίαν   acc sg fem [Lk 20:23; n-1a; 4111]   "

πανοῦργος, ον   {4112, a-3a}
pr. *ready to do anything;* hence, *crafty, cunning, artful, wily,* 2 Cor 12:16*

πανοῦργος nom sg masc
   [2C 12:16; a-3a; 4112]   πανοῦργος
πάντα nom pl neut [81t; a-2a; 4246]   πᾶς
πάντα voc pl neut [Rm 15:11; a-2a; 4246]   "
πάντα acc sg masc [20t; a-2a; 4246]   "
πάντα acc pl neut [161t; a-2a; 4246]   "
πάντας acc pl masc [90t; a-2a; 4246]   "

πανταχῇ   {4114, adverb}
everywhere, Acts 21:28*

πανταχῇ adverb [Ac 21:28; adverb; 4114] πανταχῇ

πανταχόθεν   {4115, adverb}
from all parts, from every direction, Mark 1:45 v.l.*

πανταχοῦ   {4116, adverb}
in all places, everywhere, Mark 16:20; Luke 9:6

πανταχοῦ adverb [7t; adverb; 4116]   πανταχοῦ
παντελές acc sg neut [2t; a-4a; 4117] παντελής

παντελής, ές   {4117, a-4a}
perfect, complete; εἰς τὸ παντελές, adverbially, *throughout, through all time, ever,* Heb 7:25; with a negative, *at all,* Luke 13:11*

πάντες nom pl masc [170t; a-2a; 4246] πᾶς
πάντες voc pl masc [7t; a-2a; 4246]   "

πάντη   {4118, adverb}
everywhere; in every way, in every instance, Acts 24:3*

πάντη adverb [Ac 24:3; adverb; 4118]   πάντη
παντί dat sg masc [34t; a-2a; 4246]   πᾶς
παντί dat sg neut [25t; a-2a; 4246]   "

πάντοθεν   {4119, adverb}
from every place, from all parts, on all sides, on every side, round about, Mark 1:45; Luke 19:43; Heb 9:4*

πάντοθεν adverb [3t; adverb; 4119] πάντοθεν
παντοκράτορος gen sg masc
   [2t; n-3f(2b); 4120]   παντοκράτωρ

παντοκράτωρ, ορος, ὁ   {4120, n-3f(2b)}
almighty, omnipotent, 2 Cor 6:18; Rev 1:8; 4:8

παντοκράτωρ nom sg masc [8t; n-3f(2b); 4120] "
παντός gen sg masc [19t; a-2a; 4246]   πᾶς
παντός gen sg neut [15t; a-2a; 4246]   "

πάντοτε   {4121, adverb}
always, at all times, ever, Matt 26:11; Mark 14:7; Luke 15:31; 18:1

πάντοτε adverb [41t; adverb; 4121]   πάντοτε
πάντων gen pl masc [86t; a-2a; 4246]   πᾶς
πάντων gen pl neut [48t; a-2a; 4246]   "

πάντως   {4122, adverb}
wholly, altogether; at any rate, by all means, 1 Cor 9:22; by impl. *surely, assuredly, certainly,* Luke 4:23; Acts 18:21 v.l.; 21:22; 28:4; 1 Cor 9:10; οὐ πάντως, *in nowise, not in the least,* Rom 3:9; 1 Cor 5:10; 16:12*

πάντως adverb [8t; adverb; 4122]   πάντως

παρ' prep-gen [28t; prep; 4123]   παρά
παρ' prep-dat [23t; prep; 4123]   "
παρ' prep-acc [9t; prep; 4123]   "

παρά   {4123, prep}
(1) gen., *from,* indicating source or origin, Matt 2:4, 7; Mark 8:11; Luke 2:1; οἱ παρ' αὐτοῦ, *his relatives* or *kinsmen,* Mark 3:21; τὰ παρ' αὐτῆς πάντα, *all her substance, property,* etc., Mark 5:26. (2) dat., *with, in, among,* etc., Matt 6:1; 19:26; 21:25; 22:25; παρ' ἑαυτῷ, *at home,* 1 Cor 16:2; *in the sight of, in the judgment* or *estimation of,* 1 Cor 3:19; 2 Peter 2:11; 3:8. (3) acc., motion, *by, near to, along,* Matt 4:18; motion, *towards, to, at,* Matt 15:30; Mark 2:13; motion terminating in rest, *at, by, near, by the side of,* Mark 4:1, 4; Luke 5:1; 8:5; *in deviation from, in violation of, inconsistently with,* Acts 18:13; Rom 1:26; 11:24; *above, more than,* Luke 13:2, 4; Rom 1:25. (4) After comparatives, Luke 3:13; 1 Cor 3:11; *except, save,* 2 Cor 11:24; *beyond, past,* Heb 11:11; *in respect of, on the score of,* 1 Cor 12:15, 16

παρά prep-gen [54t; prep; 4123]   "
παρά prep-dat [30t; prep; 4123]   "
παρά prep-acc [50t; prep; 4123]   "
παραβαίνετε pres act ind 2 pl
   [Mt 15:3; cv-2d(6); 4124]   παραβαίνω
παραβαίνουσιν pres act ind 3 pl
   [Mt 15:2; cv-2d(6); 4124]

παραβαίνω   {4124, cv-2d(6)}
[-, παρέβην, -, -, -] pr. *to step by the side of; to deviate;* met. *to transgress, violate,* Matt 15:2, 3, 2 John 9 v.l.; *to incur forfeiture,* Acts 1:25*

παραβάλλω   {4125, cv-2d(1)}
[παραβαλῶ, παρέβαλον, -, -, -] *to cast* or *throw by the side of;* met. *to compare,* Mark 4:30 v.l.; absol., a nautical term, *to bring-to, land,* Acts 20:15*

παραβάσει dat sg fem
   [1Ti 2:14; n-3e(5b); 4126]   παράβασις
παραβάσεων gen pl fem [2t; n-3e(5b); 4126] "
παραβάσεως gen sg fem [2t; n-3e(5b); 4126] "

παράβασις, εως, ἡ   {4126, n-3e(5b)}
a stepping by the side, deviation; a transgression, violation of law, Rom 2:23; 4:15

παράβασις nom sg fem [2t; n-3e(5b); 4126] "
παραβάται nom pl masc
   [Jm 2:9; n-1f; 4127]   παραβάτης
παραβάτην acc sg masc [2t; n-1f; 4127] "

παραβάτης, ου, ὁ   {4127, n-1f}
transgressor, violator of law, Rom 2:25, 27; Gal 2:18; James 2:9, 11*

παραβάτης nom sg masc [2t; n-1f; 4127] "

παραβιάζομαι   {4128, cv-2a(1)}
[-, παρεβιασάμην, -, -, -] *to force; to constrain press with urgent entreaties,* Luke 24:29; Acts 16:15*

παραβολαῖς dat pl fem [12t; n-1b; 4130] παραβολή
παραβολάς acc pl fem [4t; n-1b; 4130] "

παραβολεύομαι   {4129, cv-1a(6)}
[-, παρεβολευσάμην, -, -, -] also spelled

παραβουλεύομαι, *to stake* or *risk one's self*, Phil 2:30*

παραβολευσάμενος   aor mid ptcp nom sg masc
[Pp 2:30; cv-1a(6); 4129]   παραβολεύομαι

παραβολή, ῆς, ἡ   {4130, n-1b}
a placing one thing by the side of another; a comparing; a parallel case cited in illustration; a comparison, simile, similitude, Mark 4:30; Heb 11:19; *a parable,* a short relation under which something else is figured, or in which that which is fictitious is employed to represent that which is real, Matt 13:3, 10, 13, 18, 24, 31, 33, 34, 36, 53; 21:33, 45; 22:1; 24:32; in N.T. *a type, pattern, emblem,* Heb 9:9; *a sentiment, grave and significant precept, maxim,* Luke 14:7; *an obscure and enigmatical saying,* anything expressed in remote and ambiguous terms, Matt 13:35; Mark 7:17; *a proverb, adage,* Luke 4:23

παραβολή   nom sg fem [3t; n-1b; 4130]   παραβολή
παραβολῇ   dat sg fem [2t; n-1b; 4130]   "
παραβολήν   acc sg fem [26t; n-1b; 4130]   "
παραβολῆς   gen sg fem [3t; n-1b; 4130]   "

παραβουλεύομαι, see παραβολεύομαι   {4131}

παραγγείλαντες   aor act ptcp nom pl masc
[Ac 16:23; cv-2d(1); 4133]   παραγγέλλω
παραγγείλας   aor act ptcp nom sg masc
[4t; cv-2d(1); 4133]   "
παραγγείλῃς   aor act subj 2 sg
[1Ti 1:3; cv-2d(1); 4133]   "

παραγγελία, ας, ἡ   {4132, n-1a}
a command, order, charge, Acts 5:28; 16:24; *direction, precept,* 1 Thess 4:2; 1 Tim 1:5, 18*

παραγγελίᾳ   dat sg fem
[Ac 5:28; n-1a; 4132]   παραγγελία
παραγγελίαν   acc sg fem [2t; n-1a; 4132]   "
παραγγελίας   gen sg fem [1Ti 1:5; n-1a; 4132]   "
παραγγελίας   acc pl fem [1Th 4:2; n-1a; 4132]   "
παράγγελλε   pres act imperative 2 sg
[3t; cv-2d(1); 4133]   παραγγέλλω
παραγγέλλει   pres act ind 3 sg
[2t; cv-2d(1); 4133]   "
παραγγέλλειν   pres act inf
[Ac 15:5; cv-2d(1); 4133]   "
παραγγέλλομεν   pres act ind 1 pl
[3t; cv-2d(1); 4133]   "

παραγγέλλω   {4133, cv-2d(1)}
[(παρήγγελλον), -, παρήγγειλα, -, παρήγγελμαι, -] *to announce, notify; to command, direct, charge,* Matt 10:5; Mark 6:8, 8:6; Luke 9:21; *to charge, entreat solemnly,* 1 Tim 6:13

παραγγέλλω   pres act ind 1 sg
[3t; cv-2d(1); 4133]   "
παραγγέλλων   pres act ptcp nom sg masc
[1C 11:17; cv-2d(1); 4133]   "
παράγει   pres act ind 3 sg
[2t; cv-1b(2); 4135]   παράγω
παραγενόμενοι   aor mid ptcp nom pl masc
[6t; cv-1c(2); 4134]   παραγίνομαι
παραγενόμενον   aor mid ptcp acc sg masc
[Ac 9:39; cv-1c(2); 4134]   "

παραγενόμενος   aor mid ptcp nom sg masc
[11t; cv-1c(2); 4134]   "
παραγενομένου   aor mid ptcp gen sg masc
[Ac 25:7; cv-1c(2); 4134]   "
παραγενομένους   aor mid ptcp acc pl masc
[Lk 22:52; cv-1c(2); 4134]   "
παραγένωμαι   aor mid subj 1 sg
[1C 16:3; cv-1c(2); 4134]   "
παραγένωνται   aor mid subj 3 pl
[Ac 23:35; cv-1c(2); 4134]   "
παράγεται   pres pass ind 3 sg
[2t; cv-1b(2); 4135]   παράγω
παραγίνεται   pres mid ind 3 sg
[3t; cv-1c(2); 4134]   παραγίνομαι

παραγίνομαι   {4134, cv-1c(2)}
[(παρεγινόμην), -, παρεγενόμην, -, -, -] pluperfect, παραγεγόνει (3 sg), *to be by the side of; to come, approach, arrive,* Matt 2:1; 3:13; Mark 14:43; Luke 7:4; seq. ἐπί, *to come upon* in order to seize, Luke 22:52; *to come forth in public, make appearance,* Matt 3:1; Heb 9:11

παράγοντα   pres act ptcp acc sg masc
[Mk 15:21; cv-1b(2); 4135]   παράγω
παράγοντι   pres act ptcp dat sg masc
[Mt 9:27; cv-1b(2); 4135]   "

παράγω   {4135, cv-1b(2)}
[(παρῆγον), -, -, -, -, -] *to lead beside;* intrans. *to pass along* or *by,* Matt 20:30; John 9:1; *to pass on,* Matt 9:9, 27; intrans. and mid. *to pass away, be in a state of transition,* 1 Cor 7:31; 1 John 2:8, 17

παράγων   pres act ptcp nom sg masc
[4t; cv-1b(2); 4135]   "
παραδεδομένοι   perf pass ptcp nom pl masc
[Ac 14:26; cv-6a; 4140]   παραδίδωμι
παραδέδοται   perf pass ind 3 sg
[Lk 4:6; cv-6a; 4140]   "
παραδεδώκεισαν   pluperf act ind 3 pl
[Mk 15:10; cv-6a; 4140]   "
παραδεδωκόσι   perf act ptcp dat pl masc
[Ac 15:26; cv-6a; 4140]   "
παραδειγματίζοντας   pres act ptcp acc pl masc
[Hb 6:6; cv-2a(1); 4136]   παραδειγματίζω

παραδειγματίζω   {4136, cv-2a(1)}
[-, παρεδειγμάτισα, -, -, -] *to make an example of; to expose to ignominy and shame,* Heb 6:6; Matt 1:19 v.l.*

παράδεισον   acc sg masc
[2C 12:4; n-2a; 4137]   παράδεισος

παράδεισος, ου, ὁ   {4137, n-2a}
a park, a forest where wild beasts were kept for hunting; a pleasure-park, a garden of trees of various kinds; used in the LXX for *the Garden of Eden;* in N.T. the celestial *paradise,* Luke 23:43; 2 Cor 12:4; Rev 2:7*

παραδείσῳ   dat sg masc [2t; n-2a; 4137]   "
παραδέξονται   fut mid ind 3 pl
[Ac 22:18; cv-1b(2); 4138]   παραδέχομαι
παραδέχεσθαι   pres mid inf
[Ac 16:21; cv-1b(2); 4138]   "

παραδέχεται pres mid ind 3 sg
[Hb 12:6; cv-1b(2); 4138] "

παραδέχομαι {4138, cv-1b(2)}
[παραδέξομαι, παρεδεξάμην, -, -, παρεδέχθην] *to accept, receive*, met. *to receive, admit, yield assent to*, Mark 4:20; Acts 15:4; 16:21; 22:18; 1 Tim 5:19; in N.T. *to receive* or *embrace with favor, approve, love*, Heb 12:6*

παραδέχονται pres mid ind 3 pl
[Mk 4:20; cv-1b(2); 4138] "
παραδέχου pres mid imperative 2 sg
[1Ti 5:19; cv-1b(2); 4138] "

παραδιατριβή, ῆς, ἡ {4139, n-1b}
useless disputation, 1 Tim 6:5*

παραδιδόμεθα pres pass ind 1 pl
[2C 4:11; cv-6a; 4140] παραδίδωμι
παραδιδόναι pres act inf [2t; cv-6a; 4140] "
παραδιδόντα pres act ptcp acc sg masc
[Jn 13:11; cv-6a; 4140] "
παραδιδόντες pres act ptcp nom pl masc
[2t; cv-6a; 4140] "
παραδιδόντος pres act ptcp gen sg masc
[Lk 22:21; cv-6a; 4140] "
παραδίδοσθαι pres pass inf [2t; cv-6a; 4140] "
παραδίδοται pres pass ind 3 sg [7t; cv-6a; 4140] "
παραδιδούς pres act ptcp nom sg masc
[10t; cv-6a; 4140] "
παραδιδῷ pres act subj 3 sg
[1C 15:24; cv-6a; 4140] "

παραδίδωμι {4140, cv-6a}
[(παρεδίδων), παραδώσω, παρέδωκα, παραδέδωκα, παραδέδομαι, παρεδόθην]
pluperfect, παραδεδώκεισαν (3 pl), *to give over, hand over, deliver up*, Matt 4:12; 5:25; 10:4, 17; *to commit, intrust*, Matt 11:27; 25:14; *to commit, commend*, Acts 14:26; 15:40; *to yield up*, John 19:30; 1 Cor 15:24; *to abandon*, Acts 7:42; Eph 4:19; *to stake, hazard*, Acts 15:26; *to deliver* as a matter of injunction, instruction, etc., Mark 7:13; Luke 1:2; Acts 6:14; absol. *to render a yield, to be matured*, Mark 4:29

παραδίδως pres act ind 2 sg
[Lk 22:48; cv-6a; 4140] "
παραδοθείς aor pass ptcp nom sg masc
[Ac 15:40; cv-6a; 4140] "
παραδοθείσῃ aor pass ptcp dat sg fem
[Jd 3; cv-6a; 4140] "
παραδοθείσης aor pass ptcp gen sg fem
[2P 2:21; cv-6a; 4140] "
παραδοθῆναι aor pass inf [2t; cv-6a; 4140] "
παραδοθήσεσθε fut pass ind 2 pl
[Lk 21:16; cv-6a; 4140] "
παραδοθήσεται fut pass ind 3 sg
[3t; cv-6a; 4140] "
παραδοθῶ aor pass subj 1 sg
[Jn 18:36; cv-6a; 4140] "
παραδοῖ aor act subj 3 sg [4t; cv-6a; 4140] "
παραδόντος aor act ptcp gen sg masc
[Ga 2:20; cv-6a; 4140] "
παράδοξα acc pl neut
[Lk 5:26; a-3a; 4141] παράδοξος

παράδοξος, ον {4141, a-3a}
unexpected; strange, wonderful, astonishing, Luke 5:26*

παραδόσει dat sg fem
[Mk 7:13; n-3e(5b); 4142] παράδοσις
παραδόσεις acc pl fem [2t; n-3e(5b); 4142] "
παραδόσεων gen pl fem [Ga 1:14; n-3e(5b); 4142] "
παράδοσιν acc sg fem [9t; n-3e(5b); 4142] "

παράδοσις, εως, ἡ {4142, n-3e(5b)}
delivery, handing over, transmission; in N.T. *what is transmitted* in the way of teaching, *precept, doctrine*, 1 Cor 11:2; 2 Thess 2:15; 3:6; *tradition, traditionary law*, handed down from age to age, Matt 15:2, 3, 6

παραδοῦναι aor act inf
[3t; cv-6a; 4140] παραδίδωμι
παραδούς aor act ptcp nom sg masc
[4t; cv-6a; 4140] "
παραδῶ aor act subj 1 sg [1C 13:3; cv-6a; 4140] "
παραδῷ aor act subj 3 sg [3t; cv-6a; 4140] "
παραδώσει fut act ind 3 sg [7t; cv-6a; 4140] "
παραδῶσιν aor act subj 3 pl
[Mt 10:19; cv-6a; 4140] "
παραδώσουσιν fut act ind 3 pl [7t; cv-6a; 4140] "
παραδώσω fut act ind 1 sg
[Mt 26:15; cv-6a; 4140] "
παραδώσων fut act ptcp nom sg masc
[Jn 6:64; cv-6a; 4140] "
παραζηλοῦμεν pres act ind 1 pl
[1C 10:22; cv-1d(3); 4143] παραζηλόω

παραζηλόω {4143, cv-1d(3)}
[παραζηλώσω, παρεζήλωσα, -, -, -] *to provoke to jealousy*, Rom 10:19; *to excite to emulation*, Rom 11:11, 14; *to provoke to indignation*, 1 Cor 10:22*

παραζηλῶσαι aor act inf
[Rm 11:11; cv-1d(3); 4143] "
παραζηλώσω fut act ind 1 sg [2t; cv-1d(3); 4143] "
παραθαλασσίαν acc sg fem
[Mt 4:13; a-1a(1); 4144] παραθαλάσσιος

παραθαλάσσιος, ία, ιον {4144, a-1a(1)}
by the sea-side, situated on the sea-coast, maritime, Matt 4:13; Luke 4:31 v.l.*

παραθεῖναι aor act inf
[Lk 9:16; cv-6a; 4192] παρατίθημι

παραθεωρέω {4145, cv-1d(2a)}
[-, -, -, -, -] *to look at things placed side by side*, as in comparison, *to compare in thus looking, to regard less in comparison, overlook, neglect*, Acts 6:1*

παραθήκη, ῆς, ἡ {4146, n-1b}
a deposit, a thing committed to one's charge, a trust, 2 Tim 1:12; 1 Tim 6:20; 2 Tim 1:14*

παραθήκην acc sg fem [3t; n-1b; 4146] παραθήκη
παραθήσω fut act ind 1 sg
[Lk 11:6; cv-6a; 4192] παρατίθημι
παράθου aor mid imperative 2 sg
[2Ti 2:2; cv-6a; 4192] "

παραινέω   {4147, cv-1d(2b)}
[(παρήνουν), -, -, -, -, -] *to advise, exhort,* Acts
27:9, 22; Luke 3:18 v.l.*

παραινῶ   pres act ind 1 sg
   [Ac 27:22; cv-1d(2b); 4147]   παραινέω
παραιτεῖσθαι   pres mid inf
   [Lk 14:18; cv-1d(2a); 4148]   παραιτέομαι

παραιτέομαι   {4148, cv-1d(2a)}
[(παρητούμην), -, παρητησάμην, -, παρήτημαι, -]
to entreat; to beg off, excuse one's self, Luke 14:18,
19; *to deprecate, entreat against,* Acts 25:11; Heb
12:19; *to decline receiving, refuse, reject,* 1 Tim 4:7;
5:11; Titus 3:10; Heb 12:25; *to decline, avoid,
shun,* 2 Tim 2:23

παραιτησάμενοι   aor mid ptcp nom pl masc
   [Hb 12:25; cv-1d(2a); 4148]   "
παραιτήσησθε   aor mid subj 2 pl
   [Hb 12:25; cv-1d(2a); 4148]   "
παραιτοῦ   pres mid imperative 2 sg
   [4t; cv-1d(2a); 4148]   "
παραιτοῦμαι   pres mid ind 1 sg
   [Ac 25:11; cv-1d(2a); 4148]   "

παρακαθέζομαι   {4149, cv-2a(1)}
[-, -, -, -, παρεκαθέσθην] *to sit down by,* Luke
10:39*

παρακαθεσθεῖσα   aor pass ptcp nom sg fem
   [Lk 10:39; cv-2a(1); 4149]   παρακαθέζομαι

παρακαθίζω   {4150, cv-2a(1)}
[-, -, -, -, -] *to set beside;* intrans. *to sit by the side
of, sit near,* Luke 10:39 v.l.*

παρακάλει   pres act imperative 2 sg
   [4t; cv-1d(2b); 4151]   παρακαλέω
παρακαλεῖ   pres act ind 3 sg
   [Mk 5:23; cv-1d(2b); 4151]   "
παρακαλεῖν   pres act inf   [3t; cv-1d(2b); 4151]   "
παρακαλεῖσθε   pres pass imperative 2 pl
   [2C 13:11; cv-1d(2b); 4151]   "
παρακαλεῖται   pres pass ind 3 sg
   [Lk 16:25; cv-1d(2b); 4151]   "
παρακαλεῖτε   pres act imperative 2 pl
   [3t; cv-1d(2b); 4151]   "
παρακαλέσαι   aor act inf   [5t; cv-1d(2b); 4151]   "
παρακαλέσαι   aor act opt 3 sg
   [2Th 2:17; cv-1d(2b); 4151]   "
παρακαλέσας   aor act ptcp nom sg masc
   [2t; cv-1d(2b); 4151]   "
παρακαλέση   aor act subj 3 sg
   [2t; cv-1d(2b); 4151]   "
παρακάλεσον   aor act imperative 2 sg
   [2Ti 4:2; cv-1d(2b); 4151]   "

παρακαλέω   {4151, cv-1d(2b)}
[(παρεκάλουν), -, παρεκάλεσα, -, παρακέκλημαι,
παρεκλήθην] *to call for, invite to come, send for,*
Acts 28:20; *to call upon, exhort, admonish,
persuade,* Luke 3:18; Acts 2:40; 11:23; *to beg,
beseech, entreat, implore,* Matt 8:5, 31; 18:29;
Mark 1:40; *to animate, encourage, comfort,
console,* Matt 2:18; 5:4; 2 Cor 1:4, 6; pass. *to be
cheered, comforted,* Luke 16:25; Acts 20:12; 2 Cor
7:13

παρακαλούμεθα   pres pass ind 1 pl
   [2t; cv-1d(2b); 4151]   "
παρακαλοῦμεν   pres act ind 1 pl
   [6t; cv-1d(2b); 4151]   "
παρακαλοῦντες   pres act ptcp nom pl masc
   [4t; cv-1d(2b); 4151]   "
παρακαλοῦντος   pres act ptcp gen sg masc
   [2C 5:20; cv-1d(2b); 4151]   "
παρακαλοῦσιν   pres act ind 3 pl
   [2t; cv-1d(2b); 4151]   "

παρακαλύπτω   {4152, cv-4}
[-, -, -, παρακεκάλυμμαι, -] *to cover over, veil;*
met. pass. *to be veiled* from comprehension,
Luke 9:45*

παρακαλῶ   pres act ind 1 sg
   [20t; cv-1d(2b); 4151]   "
παρακαλῶν   pres act ptcp nom sg masc
   [9t; cv-1d(2b); 4151]   "
παρακαλῶνται   pres pass subj 3 pl
   [1C 14:31; cv-1d(2b); 4151]   "

παρακαταθήκη, ης, ἡ   {4153, n-1b}
a deposit, a thing committed to one's charge, a trust,
1 Tim 6:20 v.l.; 2 Tim 1:14 v.l.*

παράκειμαι   {4154, cv-6b}
[-, -, -, -, -] *to lie near, be adjacent;* met. *to be at
hand, be present,* Rom 7:18, 21*

παράκειται   pres mid ind 3 sg
   [2t; cv-6b; 4154]   παράκειμαι
παρακεκαλυμμένον   perf pass ptcp nom sg neut
   [Lk 9:45; cv-4; 4152]   παρακαλύπτω
παρακεκλήμεθα   perf pass ind 1 pl
   [2C 7:13; cv-1d(2b); 4151]   παρακαλέω
παρακεχειμακότι   perf act ptcp dat sg neut
   [Ac 28:11; cv-2a(1); 4199]   παραχειμάζω
παρακληθῆναι   aor pass inf
   [Mt 2:18; cv-1d(2b); 4151]   παρακαλέω
παρακληθήσονται   fut pass ind 3 pl
   [Mt 5:4; cv-1d(2b); 4151]   "
παρακληθῶσιν   aor pass subj 3 pl
   [Cl 2:2; cv-1d(2b); 4151]   "
παρακλήσει   dat sg fem
   [7t; n-3e(5b); 4155]   παράκλησις
παρακλήσεως   gen sg fem   [12t; n-3e(5b); 4155]   "
παράκλησιν   acc sg fem   [7t; n-3e(5b); 4155]   "

παράκλησις, εως, ἡ   {4155, n-3e(5b)}
a calling upon, exhortation, incitement, persuasion,
Rom 12:8; 1 Cor 14:3; *hortatory instruction,* Acts
13:15; 15:31; *entreaty, importunity, earnest
supplication,* 2 Cor 8:4; *solace, consolation,* Luke
2:25; Rom 15:4, 5; 2 Cor 1:3, 4, 5, 6, 7; *cheering
and supporting influence,* Acts 9:31; *joy, gladness,
rejoicing,* 2 Cor 7:13; *cheer, joy, enjoyment,* Luke
6:24

παράκλησις   nom sg fem   [3t; n-3e(5b); 4155]   "
παράκλητον   acc sg masc
   [2t; n-2a; 4156]   παράκλητος

παράκλητος, ου, ὁ   {4156, n-2a}
one called or *sent for to assist another; an advocate,
one who pleads the cause of another,* 1 John 2:1;
genr. *one present to render various beneficial*

service, and thus *the Paraclete*, whose influence and operation were to compensate for the departure of Christ himself, John 14:16, 26; 15:26; 16:7*

παράκλητος   nom sg masc [3t; n-2a; 4156]   "

παρακοή, ῆς, ἡ   {4157, n-1b}
an erroneous or *imperfect hearing; disobedience*, Rom 5:19; *a deviation from obedience*, 2 Cor 10:6; Heb 2:2*

παρακοή   nom sg fem [Hb 2:2; n-1b; 4157] παρακοή
παρακοήν   acc sg fem [2C 10:6; n-1b; 4157]   "
παρακοῆς   gen sg fem [Rm 5:19; n-1b; 4157]   "

παρακολουθέω   {4158, cv-1d(2a)}
[παρακολουθήσω, παρηκολούθησα, παρηκολούθηκα, -, -] *to follow* or *accompany closely; to accompany, attend, characterize*, Mark 16:17; *to follow* with the thoughts, *trace*, Luke 1:3; *to conform to*, 1 Tim 4:6; 2 Tim 3:10*

παρακολουθήσει   fut act ind 3 sg
[Mk 16:17; cv-1d(2a); 4158]   παρακολουθέω

παρακύπτω   {4160, cv-4}
[-, παρέκυψα, -, -, -] *to stoop beside; to stoop down* in order to take a view, Luke 24:12; John 20:5, 11; *to bestow a close and attentive look, to look intently, to penetrate*, James 1:25; 1 Peter 1:12*

παρακύσας   aor act ptcp nom sg masc
[Mk 5:36; cv-1a(8); 4159]   παρακούω
παρακούσῃ   aor act subj 3 sg
[2t; cv-1a(8); 4159]   "

παρακούω   {4159, cv-1a(8)}
[παρακούσω, παρήκουσα, -, -, -] *to overhear*, Mark 5:36; *to hear amiss, to fail to listen, neglect to obey, disregard*, Matt 18:17 (2t)*

παρακύψαι   aor act inf
[1P 1:12; cv-4; 4160]   παρακύπτω
παρακύψας   aor act ptcp nom sg masc
[3t; cv-4; 4160]   "
παράλαβε   aor act imperative 2 sg
[3t; cv-3a(2b); 4161]   παραλαμβάνω
παραλαβεῖν   aor act inf
[Mt 1:20; cv-3a(2b); 4161]   "
παραλαβόντα   aor act ptcp acc sg masc
[Ac 15:39; cv-3a(2b); 4161]   "
παραλαβόντες   aor act ptcp nom pl masc
[2t; cv-3a(2b); 4161]   "
παραλαβών   aor act ptcp nom sg masc
[10t; cv-3a(2b); 4161]   "
παραλαμβάνει   pres act ind 3 sg
[8t; cv-3a(2b); 4161]   "
παραλαμβάνεται   pres pass ind 3 sg
[2t; cv-3a(2b); 4161]   "
παραλαμβάνοντες   pres act ptcp nom pl masc
[Hb 12:28; cv-3a(2b); 4161]   "
παραλαμβάνουσιν   pres act ind 3 pl
[Mk 4:36; cv-3a(2b); 4161]   "

παραλαμβάνω   {4161, cv-3a(2b)}
[παραλήμψομαι, παρέλαβον, -, -, παρελήμφθην] pr. *to take to one's side; to take, receive to one's self*, Matt 1:20; John 14:3; *to take* with one's self, Matt 2:13, 14, 20, 21; 4:5, 8; Acts 16:35 v.l.; *to receive in*

charge or possession, Col 4:17; Heb 12:28; *to receive* as a matter of instruction, Mark 7:4; 1 Cor 11:23; 15:3; *to receive, admit, acknowledge*, John 1:11; 1 Cor 15:1; Col 2:6; pass. *to be carried off*, Matt 24:40, 41; Luke 17:34, 35, 36

παραλέγομαι   {4162, cv-1b(2)}
[(παρελεγόμην), -, -, -, -, -] *to gather a course along; to sail by, coast along*, Acts 27:8, 13*

παραλεγόμενοι   pres mid ptcp nom pl masc
[Ac 27:8; cv-1b(2); 4162]   παραλέγομαι
παραλελυμένα   perf pass ptcp acc pl neut
[Hb 12:12; cv-1a(4); 4168]   παραλύω
παραλελυμένοι   perf pass ptcp nom pl masc
[Ac 8:7; cv-1a(4); 4168]   "
παραλελυμένος   perf pass ptcp nom sg masc
[2t; cv-1a(4); 4168]   "
παραλελυμένῳ   perf pass ptcp dat sg masc
[Lk 5:24; cv-1a(4); 4168]   "
παραλημφθήσεται   fut pass ind 3 sg
[2t; cv-3a(2b); 4161]   παραλαμβάνω
παραλήμψομαι   fut mid ind 1 sg
[Jn 14:3; cv-3a(2b); 4161]   "

παράλιος, ον   {4163, a-3a}
adjacent to the sea, maritime; ἡ παράλιος, sc. χώρα, *the sea-coast*, Luke 6:17*

παραλίου   gen sg fem
[Lk 6:17; a-3a; 4163]   παράλιος

παραλλαγή, ῆς, ἡ   {4164, n-1b}
a shifting, mutation, change, James 1:17*

παραλλαγή   nom sg fem
[Jm 1:17; n-1b; 4164]   παραλλαγή
παραλογίζηται   pres mid subj 3 sg
[Cl 2:4; cv-2a(1); 4165]   παραλογίζομαι

παραλογίζομαι   {4165, cv-2a(1)}
[-, -, -, -, παρελογισάμην] *to misreckon, make a false reckoning; to impose upon, deceive, delude, circumvent*, Col 2:4; James 1:22*

παραλογιζόμενοι   pres mid ptcp nom pl masc
[Jm 1:22; cv-2a(1); 4165]   "
παραλυτικόν   acc sg masc
[2t; n-2a; 4166]   παραλυτικός

παραλυτικός, ή, όν   {4166, a-1a(2a)}
lame, palsied, used only as a noun in N.T., *paralytic*, Matt 4:24; 8:6; 9:2, 6; Luke 5:24 v.l.; John 5:3 v.l.

παραλυτικός   nom sg masc [2t; n-2a; 4166]   "
παραλυτικούς   acc pl masc [Mt 4:24; n-2a; 4166]   "
παραλυτικῷ   dat sg masc [5t; n-2a; 4166]   "

παραλύω   {4168, cv-1a(4)}
[-, -, -, παραλέλυμαι, -] *to unloose from proper fixity* or *consistency of substance; to enervate* or *paralyze* the body or limbs; pass. *to be enervated* or *enfeebled*, Heb 12:12; pass. perf. part. παραλελυμένος, *paralytic*, Luke 5:18, 24

παραμείνας   aor act ptcp nom sg masc
[Jm 1:25; cv-1c(2); 4169]   παραμένω
παραμένειν   pres act inf
[Hb 7:23; cv-1c(2); 4169]   "

παραμένω   {4169, cv-1c(2)}
[παραμενῶ, παρέμεινα, -, -, -] *to stay beside; to
continue, stay, abide*, 1 Cor 16:6; Heb 7:23; met. *to
remain constant in, persevere in*, Phil 1:25; James
1:25*

παραμενῶ   fut act ind 1 sg [2t; cv-1c(2); 4169]   "
παραμυθεῖσθε   pres mid imperative 2 pl
   [1Th 5:14; cv-1d(2a); 4170]   παραμυθέομαι

παραμυθέομαι   {4170, cv-1d(2a)}
[-, παρεμυθησάμην, -, -, -] *to exercise a gentle
influence by words; to soothe, comfort, console*,
John 11:19, 31; 1 Thess 5:14; *to cheer, exhort*, 1
Thess 2:12*

παραμυθήσωνται   aor mid subj 3 pl
   [Jn 11:19; cv-1d(2a); 4170]   "

παραμυθία, ας, ἡ   {4171, n-1a}
comfort, encouragement, 1 Cor 14:3*

παραμυθίαν   acc sg fem
   [1C 14:3; n-1a; 4171]   παραμυθία

παραμύθιον, ου, τό   {4172, n-2c}
gentle cheering, encouragement, Phil 2:1*

παραμύθιον   nom sg neut
   [Pp 2:1; n-2c; 4172]   παραμύθιον
παραμυθούμενοι   pres mid ptcp nom pl masc
   [2t; cv-1d(2a); 4170]   παραμυθέομαι

παρανομέω   {4174, cv-1d(2a)}
[-, -, -, -, -] *to violate* or *transgress the law*, Acts
23:3*

παρανομία, ας, ἡ   {4175, n-1a}
violation of the law, transgression, 2 Peter 2:16*

παρανομίας   gen sg fem
   [2P 2:16; n-1a; 4175]   παρανομία
παρανομῶν   pres act ptcp nom sg masc
   [Ac 23:3; cv-1d(2a); 4174]   παρανομέω
παραπεσόντας   aor act ptcp acc pl masc
   [Hb 6:6; cv-1b(3); 4178]   παραπίπτω

παραπικραίνω   {4176, cv-2d(4)}
[-, παρεπίκρανα, -, -, παρεπικράνθην] pr. *to incite
to bitter feelings; to provoke*; absol. *to act
provokingly, be rebellious*, Heb 3:16*

παραπικρασμός, οῦ, ὁ   {4177, n-2a}
exasperation, provocation; rebellion, Heb 3:8, 15*

παραπικρασμῷ   dat sg masc
   [2t; n-2a; 4177]   παραπικρασμός

παραπίπτω   {4178, cv-1b(3)}
[-, παρέπεσον, -, -, -] pr. *to fall by the side of*; met.
to fall off or *away from, make defection from*, Heb
6:6*

παραπλεῦσαι   aor act inf
   [Ac 20:16; cv-1a(7); 4179]   παραπλέω

παραπλέω   {4179, cv-1a(7)}
[-, παρέπλευσα, -, -, -] *to sail by* or *past a place*,
Acts 20:16*

παραπλήσιον   acc sg neut,
   can function adverbially
   [Pp 2:27; a-1a(1); 4180]   παραπλήσιος

παραπλήσιος, see παραπλήσιος

παραπλήσιος, ία, ιον   {4180, a-1a(1)}
pr. *near alongside*; met. *like, similar*; neut.
παραπλήσιον, adverbially, *near to, nearly, with a
near approach to*, Phil 2:27*

παραπλησίως   {4181, adverb}
like, in the same or *like manner*, Heb 2:14*

παραπλησίως   adverb
   [Hb 2:14; adverb; 4181]   παραπλησίως
παραπορεύεσθαι   pres mid inf
   [Mk 2:23; cv-1d(2a); 4182]   παραπορεύομαι

παραπορεύομαι   {4182, cv-1d(2a)}
[(παρεπορευόμην), -, -, -, -, -] *to pass by the side of;
to pass along*, Matt 27:39; Mark 2:23; 9:30; 11:20;
15:29*

παραπορευόμενοι   pres mid ptcp nom pl masc
   [3t; cv-1d(2a); 4182]   "

παράπτωμα, ατος, τό   {4183, n-3c(4)}
pr. *a stumbling aside, a false step*; in N.T. *a
trespass, fault, offence, transgression*, Matt 6:14,
15; Mark 11:25, 26; Rom 4:25; *a fall* in faith, Rom
11:11, 12

παράπτωμα   nom sg neut
   [3t; n-3c(4); 4183]   παράπτωμα
παραπτώμασιν   dat pl neut [3t; n-3c(4); 4183]   "
παραπτώματα   acc pl neut [6t; n-3c(4); 4183]   "
παραπτώματι   dat sg neut [4t; n-3c(4); 4183]   "
παραπτώματος   gen sg neut
   [Rm 5:18; n-3c(4); 4183]   "
παραπτωμάτων   gen pl neut [2t; n-3c(4); 4183]   "

παραρρέω   {4184, cv-1d(2a)}
[-, -, -, -, παρερύην] *to flow beside; to glide aside
from; to fall off* from profession, *decline* from
steadfastness, *make forfeit* of faith, Heb 2:1*

παραρυῶμεν   aor pass subj 1 pl
   [Hb 2:1; cv-1d(2a); 4184]   παραρρέω

παράσημος, ον   {4185, a-3a}
a distinguishing mark; an ensign of a ship, Acts
28:11*

παρασήμῳ   dat sg neut
   [Ac 28:11; a-3a; 4185]   παράσημος
παρασκευαζόντων   pres act ptcp gen pl masc
   [Ac 10:10; cv-2a(1); 4186]   παρασκευάζω

παρασκευάζω   {4186, cv-2a(1)}
[παρασκευάσω, -, -, παρεσκεύασμαι, -] *to
prepare, make ready*, 2 Cor 9:2, 3; 1 Pet 2:8 v.l.;
mid. *to prepare one's self, put one's self in
readiness*, Acts 10:10; 1 Cor 14:8*

παρασκευάσεται   fut mid ind 3 sg
   [1C 14:8; cv-2a(1); 4186]   "

παρασκευή, ῆς, ἡ   {4187, n-1b}
a getting ready, preparation, in N.T. *preparation
for a feast, day of preparation*, Matt 27:62; Mark
15:42

παρασκευή   nom sg fem [3t; n-1b; 4187] παρασκευή
παρασκευήν   acc sg fem [2t; n-1b; 4187]   "
παρασκευῆς   gen sg fem [Lk 23:54; n-1b; 4187] "

παραστάτις, ιδος, ἡ   {4188, n-3c(2)}
supporter, Rom 16:2 v.l.*

παραστῆναι   aor act inf
[Ac 27:24; cv-6a; 4225]   παρίστημι

παρατείνω   {4189, cv-2d(5)}
[-, παρέτεινα, -, -, -] *to extend, stretch out; to
prolong, continue*, Acts 20:7*

παρατηρέω   {4190, cv-1d(2a)}
[(παρετήρουν), -, παρετήρησα, -, -, -] *to watch
narrowly*, Acts 9:24; *to observe* or *watch
insidiously*, Mark 3:2; Luke 6:7; 14:1; 20:20; *to
observe scrupulously*, Gal 4:10*

παραστῆσαι   aor act inf [7t; cv-6a; 4225]   "
παραστήσατε   aor act imperative 2 pl
[2t; cv-6a; 4225]   "
παραστήσει   fut act ind 3 sg [3t; cv-6a; 4225]   "
παραστήσῃ   aor act subj 3 sg [Ep 5:27; cv-6a; 4225] "
παραστησόμεθα   fut mid ind 1 pl
[Rm 14:10; cv-6a; 4225]   "
παραστήσωμεν   aor act subj 1 pl
[Cl 1:28; cv-6a; 4225]   "
παραστῆτε   aor act subj 2 pl
[Rm 16:2; cv-6a; 4225]   "
παρασχών   aor act ptcp nom sg masc
[Ac 17:31; cv-1b(2); 4218]   παρέχω
παρατηρεῖσθε   pres mid ind 2 pl
[Ga 4:10; cv-1d(2a); 4190]   παρατηρέω
παρατηρήσαντες   aor act ptcp nom pl masc
[Lk 20:20; cv-1d(2a); 4190]   "
παρατηρήσεως   gen sg fem
[Lk 17:20; n-3e(5b); 4191]   παρατήρησις

παρατήρησις, εως, ἡ   {4191, n-3e(5b)}
careful watching, intent observation, Luke 17:20*

παρατηρούμενοι   pres mid ptcp nom pl masc
[Lk 14:1; cv-1d(2a); 4190]   παρατηρέω
παρατίθεμαι   pres mid ind 1 sg
[3t; cv-6a; 4192]   παρατίθημι
παρατιθέμενα   pres pass ptcp acc pl neut
[Lk 10:8; cv-6a; 4192]   "
παρατιθέμενον   pres pass ptcp acc sg neut
[1C 10:27; cv-6a; 4192]   "
παρατιθέμενος   pres mid ptcp nom sg masc
[Ac 17:3; cv-6a; 4192]   "
παρατιθέναι   pres act inf [Mk 8:7; cv-6a; 4192]   "
παρατιθέσθωσαν   pres mid imperative 3 pl
[1P 4:19; cv-6a; 4192]   "

παρατίθημι   {4192, cv-6a}
[παραθήσω, παρέθηκα, -, -, παρετέθην] *to place by
the side of*, or *near; to set before*, Mark 6:41; 8:6, 7;
Luke 9:16; met. *to set* or *lay before, propound*,
Matt 13:24, 31; Acts 28:23 v.l.; *to inculcate*, Acts
17:3; *to deposit, commit to the charge of, entrust*,
Luke 12:48; 23:46; *to commend*, Acts 14:23

παρατιθῶσιν   pres act subj 3 pl [2t; cv-6a; 4192]   "
παρατυγχάνοντας   pres act ptcp acc pl masc
[Ac 17:17; cv-3a(2b); 4193]   παρατυγχάνω

παρατυγχάνω   {4193, cv-3a(2b)}
[-, -, -, -, -] *to happen, to chance upon, chance to
meet*, Acts 17:17*

παραυτίκα   {4194, adverb}
instantly, immediately; ὁ, ἡ, τό, παραυτίκα,
momentary, transient, 2 Cor 4:17*

παραυτίκα   adverb
[2C 4:17; adverb; 4194]   παραυτίκα
παραφέρεσθε   pres pass imperative 2 pl
[Hb 13:9; cv-1c(1); 4195]   παραφέρω
παραφερόμεναι   pres pass ptcp nom pl fem
[Jd 12; cv-1c(1); 4195]   "

παραφέρω   {4195, cv-1c(1)}
[(παρέφερον), -, παρήνεγκον, -, παρενήνεγμαι,
παρηνέχθην] *to carry past; to cause to pass away*,
Mark 14:36; Luke 22:42; pass. *to be swept along*,
Jude 12; *to be led away, misled, seduced*, Heb 13:9*

παραφρονέω   {4196, cv-1d(2a)}
[-, -, -, -, -] *to be beside one's wits;* παραφρονῶν, *in
foolish style*, 2 Cor 11:23*

παραφρονία, ας, ἡ   {4197, n-1a}
madness, folly, 2 Peter 2:16*

παραφρονίαν   acc sg fem
[2P 2:16; n-1a; 4197]   παραφρονία
παραφρονῶν   pres act ptcp nom sg masc
[2C 11:23; cv-1d(2a); 4196]   παραφρονέω

παραφροσύνη, ης, ἡ   {4198, n-1b}
madness, insanity, 2 Pet 2:16 v.l.*

παραχειμάζω   {4199, cv-2a(1)}
[παραχειμάσω, παρεχείμασα, -, παρακεχείμακα,
-] *to winter, spend the winter*, Acts 27:12; 28:11; 1
Cor 16:6; Titus 3:12*

παραχειμάσαι   aor act inf
[2t; cv-2a(1); 4199]   παραχειμάζω

παραχειμασία, ας, ἡ   {4200, n-1a}
a wintering in a place, Acts 27:12*

παραχειμασίαν   acc sg fem
[Ac 27:12; n-1a; 4200]   παραχειμασία
παραχειμάσω   fut act ind 1 sg
[1C 16:6; cv-2a(1); 4199]   παραχειμάζω

παραχράομαι   {?4201, cv-1d(1a)}
[-, παρεχρησάμην, -, -, -] *misuse*, 1 Cor 7:31 v.l.*

παραχρῆμα   {4202, adverb}
at once, immediately, Matt 21:19, 20; Luke 1:64

παραχρῆμα   adverb [18t; adverb; 4202]   παραχρῆμα
παρδάλει   dat sg fem
[Rv 13:2; n-3e(5b); 4203]   πάρδαλις

πάρδαλις, εως, ἡ   {4203, n-3e(5b)}
a leopard or *panther*, Rev 13:2*

παρεβάλομεν   aor act ind 1 pl
[Ac 20:15; cv-2d(1); 4125]   παραβάλλω
παρέβη   aor act ind 3 sg
[Ac 1:25; cv-2d(6); 4124]   παραβαίνω
παρεβιάσαντο   aor mid ind 3 pl
[Lk 24:29; cv-2a(1); 4128]   παραβιάζομαι
παρεβιάσατο   aor mid ind 3 sg
[Ac 16:15; cv-2a(1); 4128]   "
παρεγένετο   aor mid ind 3 sg
[5t; cv-1c(2); 4134]   παραγίνομαι

παρεγενόμην   aor mid ind 1 sg
  [2t; cv-1c(2); 4134]   "
παρεγένοντο   aor mid ind 3 pl
  [4t; cv-1c(2); 4134]   "
παρεγίνοντο   imperf mid ind 3 pl
  [Jn 3:23; cv-1c(2); 4134]   "
παρεδέχθησαν   aor pass ind 3 pl
  [Ac 15:4; cv-1b(2); 4138]   παραδέχομαι
παρεδίδετο   imperf mid ind 3 sg
  [1C 11:23; cv-6a; 4140]   παραδίδωμι
παρεδίδοσαν   imperf act ind 3 pl
  [Ac 16:4; cv-6a; 4140]   "
παρεδίδου   imperf act ind 3 sg   [2t; cv-6a; 4140]   "
παρεδίδουν   imperf act ind 3 pl
  [Ac 27:1; cv-6a; 4140]   "
παρεδόθη   aor pass ind 3 sg   [4t; cv-6a; 4140]   "
παρεδόθην   aor pass ind 1 sg
  [Ac 28:17; cv-6a; 4140]   "
παρεδόθητε   aor pass ind 2 pl
  [Rm 6:17; cv-6a; 4140]   "
παρέδοσαν   aor act ind 3 pl   [Lk 1:2; cv-6a; 4140]   "
παρεδρεύοντες   pres act ptcp nom pl masc
  [1C 9:13; cv-1a(6); 4204]   παρεδρεύω

παρεδρεύω   {4204, cv-1a(6)}
  [-, -, -, -, -] to sit near; to attend, serve, 1 Cor 9:13*

παρέδωκα   aor act ind 1 sg
  [4t; cv-6a; 4140]   παραδίδωμι
παρεδώκαμεν   aor act ind 1 pl
  [Jn 18:30; cv-6a; 4140]   "
παρέδωκαν   aor act ind 3 pl   [6t; cv-6a; 4140]   "
παρέδωκας   aor act ind 2 sg   [2t; cv-6a; 4140]   "
παρεδώκατε   aor act ind 2 pl   [2t; cv-6a; 4140]   "
παρέδωκεν   aor act ind 3 sg   [17t; cv-6a; 4140]   "
παρέθεντο   aor mid ind 3 pl
  [2t; cv-6a; 4192]   παρατίθημι
παρεθεωροῦντο   imperf pass ind 3 pl
  [Ac 6:1; cv-1d(2a); 4145]   παραθεωρέω
παρέθηκαν   aor act ind 3 pl
  [Mk 8:6; cv-6a; 4192]   παρατίθημι
παρέθηκεν   aor act ind 3 sg   [3t; cv-6a; 4192]   "
πάρει   pres act ind 2 sg
  [Mt 26:50; cv-6b; 4205]   πάρειμι
παρειμένας   perf pass ptcp acc pl fem
  [Hb 12:12; cv-6a; 4223]   παρίημι

πάρειμι   {4205, cv-6b}
  [παρέσομαι, -, -, -, -] to be beside; to be present,
  Luke 13:1; to have come, Matt 26:50; John 7:6;
  11:28; Col 1:6; to be in possession, Heb 13:5; 2
  Peter 1:9, 12; part. παρών, οὖσα, όν, present, 1
  Cor 5:3; τὸ παρόν, the present time, the present,
  Heb 12:11

παρεῖναι   aor act inf   [Lk 11:42; cv-6a; 4223]   "
παρεῖναι   pres act inf   [3t; cv-6b; 4205]   πάρειμι

παρεισάγω   {4206, cv-1b(2)}
  [παρεισάξω, -, -, -, -] to introduce stealthily , 2
  Peter 2:1*

παρείσακτος, ον   {4207, a-3a}
  secretly introduced, brought in stealthily, Gal 2:4*

παρεισάκτους   acc pl masc
  [Ga 2:4; a-3a; 4207]   παρείσακτος

παρεισάξουσιν   fut act ind 3 pl
  [2P 2:1; cv-1b(2); 4206]   παρεισάγω

παρεισδύω   {4208, cv-3a(1)}
  [-, παρεισέδυσα, -, -, -] to enter secretly, creep in
  stealthily, Jude 4*

παρεισέδυσαν   aor act ind 3 pl
  [Jd 4; cv-3a(1); 4208]   παρεισδύω
παρεισενέγκαντες   aor act ptcp nom pl masc
  [2P 1:5; cv-1c(1); 4210]   παρεισφέρω

παρεισέρχομαι   {4209, cv-1b(2)}
  [-, παρεισῆλθον, -, -, -] to supervene, Rom 5:20; to
  steal in, Gal 2:4*

παρεισῆλθεν   aor act ind 3 sg
  [Rm 5:20; cv-1b(2); 4209]   παρεισέρχομαι
παρεισῆλθον   aor act ind 3 pl
  [Ga 2:4; cv-1b(2); 4209]   "
πάρεισιν   pres act ind 3 pl
  [Ac 17:6; cv-6b; 4205]   πάρειμι
παρειστήκεισαν   pluperf act ind 3 pl
  [Ac 1:10; cv-6a; 4225]   παρίστημι

παρεισφέρω   {4210, cv-1c(1)}
  [-, παρεισήνεγκα, -, -, -] to bring in beside; to bring
  into play, exhibit in addition, 2 Peter 1:5*

παρεῖχεν   imperf act ind 3 sg
  [Ac 16:16; cv-1b(2); 4218]   παρέχω
παρείχετο   imperf mid ind 3 sg
  [Ac 19:24; cv-1b(2); 4218]   "
παρεῖχον   imperf act ind 3 pl
  [Ac 28:2; cv-1b(2); 4218]   "
παρεκάλει   imperf act ind 3 sg
  [8t; cv-1d(2b); 4151]   παρακαλέω
παρεκάλεσα   aor act ind 1 sg
  [5t; cv-1d(2b); 4151]   "
παρεκάλεσαν   aor act ind 3 pl
  [6t; cv-1d(2b); 4151]   "
παρεκάλεσας   aor act ind 2 sg
  [Mt 18:32; cv-1d(2b); 4151]   "
παρεκάλεσεν   aor act ind 3 sg
  [3t; cv-1d(2b); 4151]   "
παρεκαλοῦμεν   imperf act ind 1 pl
  [Ac 21:12; cv-1d(2b); 4151]   "
παρεκάλουν   imperf act ind 3 pl
  [8t; cv-1d(2b); 4151]   "
παρεκλήθη   aor pass ind 3 sg
  [2C 7:7; cv-1d(2b); 4151]   "
παρεκλήθημεν   aor pass ind 1 pl
  [2t; cv-1d(2b); 4151]   "
παρεκλήθησαν   aor pass ind 3 pl
  [Ac 20:12; cv-1d(2b); 4151]   "

παρεκτός   {4211, adverb}
  can function as an improper prep., without, on
  the outside; except, Matt 5:32; 19:9 v.l.; Acts 26:29;
  τὰ παρεκτός, other matters, 2 Cor 11:28

παρεκτός   adverb   [3t; adverb; 4211]   παρεκτός
παρέκυψεν   aor act ind 3 sg
  [Jn 20:11; cv-4; 4160]   παρακύπτω
παρέλαβεν   aor act ind 3 sg
  [4t; cv-3a(2b); 4161]   παραλαμβάνω
παρέλαβες   aor act ind 2 sg
  [Cl 4:17; cv-3a(2b); 4161]   "

παρελάβετε   aor act ind 2 pl
[5t; cv-3a(2b); 4161]   "
παρέλαβον   aor act ind 1 sg [3t; cv-3a(2b); 4161]   "
παρέλαβον   aor act ind 3 pl [3t; cv-3a(2b); 4161]   "
παρελάβοσαν   aor act ind 3 pl
[2Th 3:6; cv-3a(2b); 4161]   "
παρελέγοντο   imperf mid ind 3 pl
[Ac 27:13; cv-1b(2); 4162]   παραλέγομαι
παρελεύσεται   fut mid ind 3 sg
[2t; cv-1b(2); 4216]   παρέρχομαι
παρελεύσονται   fut mid ind 3 pl
[5t; cv-1b(2); 4216]   "
παρεληλυθέναι   perf act inf
[Ac 27:9; cv-1b(2); 4216]   "
παρεληλυθώς   perf act ptcp nom sg masc
[1P 4:3; cv-1b(2); 4216]   "
παρελθάτω   aor act imperative 3 sg
[Mt 26:39; cv-1b(2); 4216]   "
παρελθεῖν   aor act inf [4t; cv-1b(2); 4216]   "
παρέλθη   aor act subj 3 sg [6t; cv-1b(2); 4216]   "
παρελθόντες   aor act ptcp nom pl masc
[Ac 16:8; cv-1b(2); 4216]   "
παρελθών   aor act ptcp nom sg masc
[2t; cv-1b(2); 4216]   "
παρέλθωσιν   aor act subj 3 pl
[Mt 24:35; cv-1b(2); 4216]   "

παρεμβάλλω   {4212, cv-2d(1)}
[παρεμβαλῶ, -, -, -, -] to cast up, set up, throw up
a palisade, Luke 19:43*

παρεμβαλοῦσιν   fut act ind 3 pl
[Lk 19:43; cv-2d(1); 4212]   παρεμβάλλω
παρεμβολάς   acc pl fem
[Hb 11:34; n-1b; 4213]   παρεμβολή

παρεμβολή, ῆς, ἡ   {4213, n-1b}
an insertion besides; later, a marshalling of an
army; an array of battle, army, Heb 11:34; a
camp, Heb 13:11, 12 v.l., 13; Rev 20:9; a standing
camp, fortress, citadel, castle, Acts 21:34, 37; 22:24;
23:10, 16, 32; 28:16 v.l.*

παρεμβολήν   acc sg fem [7t; n-1b; 4213]   "
παρεμβολῆς   gen sg fem [2t; n-1b; 4213]   "
παρένεγκε   aor act imperative 2 sg
[2t; cv-1c(1); 4195]   παραφέρω
παρενοχλεῖν   pres act inf
[Ac 15:19; cv-1d(2a); 4214]   παρενοχλέω

παρενοχλέω   {4214, cv-1d(2a)}
[-, -, -, -, -] to trouble, harass, Acts 15:19*

παρέξῃ   fut mid ind 2 sg
[Lk 7:4; cv-1b(2); 4218]   παρέχω
παρεπίδημοι   nom pl masc
[Hb 11:13; a-3a; 4215]   παρεπίδημος
παρεπιδήμοις   dat pl masc [1P 1:1; a-3a; 4215]   "

παρεπίδημος, ον   {4215, a-3a}
residing in a country not one's own, a sojourner,
stranger, Heb 11:13; 1 Peter 1:1; 2:11*

παρεπιδήμους   acc pl masc [1P 2:11; a-3a; 4215]   "
παρεπίκραναν   aor act ind 3 pl
[Hb 3:16; cv-2d(4); 4176]   παραπικραίνω
παρεπορεύοντο   imperf mid ind 3 pl
[Mk 9:30; cv-1d(2a); 4182]   παραπορεύομαι

παρέρχεσθε   pres mid ind 2 pl
[Lk 11:42; cv-1b(2); 4216]   παρέρχομαι
παρέρχεται   pres mid ind 3 sg
[Lk 18:37; cv-1b(2); 4216]   "

παρέρχομαι   {4216, cv-1b(2)}
[παρελεύσομαι, παρῆλθον, παρελήλυθα, -, -] to
pass beside, pass along, pass by, Matt 8:28; Mark
6:48; to pass, elapse, as time, Matt 14:15; Acts
27:19; to pass away, be removed, Matt 26:39, 42;
Mark 14:35; met. to pass away, disappear, vanish,
perish, Matt 5:18; 24:34, 35; to become vain, be
rendered void, Matt 5:18; Mark 13:31; trans. to
pass by, disregard, neglect, Luke 11:42; 15:29; Acts
17:15 v.l.; to come to the side of, come to, Luke
12:37; 17:7; Acts 24:7 v.l.

πάρεσιν   acc sg fem
[Rm 3:25; n-3e(5b); 4217]   πάρεσις

πάρεσις, εως, ἡ   {4217, n-3e(5b)}
a letting pass; a passing over, Rom 3:25*

παρεσκευασμένοι   perf mid ptcp nom pl masc
[2C 9:3; cv-2a(1); 4186]   παρασκευάζω
παρεσκεύασται   perf mid ind 3 sg
[2C 9:2; cv-2a(1); 4186]   "
πάρεσμεν   pres act ind 1 pl
[Ac 10:33; cv-6b; 4205]   πάρειμι
παρέσται   fut mid ind 3 sg [Rv 17:8; cv-6b; 4205]   "
πάρεστε   pres act ind 2 pl
[Ac 10:21; cv-6b; 4205]   "
παρέστη   aor act ind 3 sg [2t; cv-6a; 4225] παρίστημι
παρέστηκεν   perf act ind 3 sg [2t; cv-6a; 4225]   "
παρεστηκότων   perf act ptcp gen pl masc
[2t; cv-6a; 4225]   "
παρεστηκώς   perf act ptcp nom sg masc
[3t; cv-6a; 4225]   "
παρέστησαν   aor act ind 3 pl [3t; cv-6a; 4225]   "
παρεστήσατε   aor act ind 2 pl
[Rm 6:19; cv-6a; 4225]   "
παρέστησεν   aor act ind 3 sg [2t; cv-6a; 4225]   "
πάρεστιν   pres act ind 3 sg
[3t; cv-6b; 4205]   πάρειμι
παρεστῶσιν   perf act ptcp dat pl masc
[3t; cv-6a; 4225]   παρίστημι
παρεστῶτα   perf act ptcp acc sg masc
[Jn 19:26; cv-6a; 4225]   "
παρεστῶτες   perf act ptcp nom pl masc
[2t; cv-6a; 4225]   "
παρέσχον   aor act ind 3 pl
[Ac 22:2; cv-1b(2); 4218]   παρέχω
παρέτεινεν   imperf act ind 3 sg
[Ac 20:7; cv-2d(5); 4189]   παρατείνω
παρετήρουν   imperf act ind 3 pl
[Mk 3:2; cv-1d(2a); 4190]   παρατηρέω
παρετηροῦντο   imperf mid ind 3 pl
[2t; cv-1d(2a); 4190]   "
πάρεχε   pres act imperative 2 sg
[2t; cv-1b(2); 4218]   παρέχω
παρέχειν   pres act inf [Lk 18:5; cv-1b(2); 4218]   "
παρέχεσθε   pres mid imperative 2 pl
[Cl 4:1; cv-1b(2); 4218]   "
παρέχετε   pres act ind 2 pl [2t; cv-1b(2); 4218]   "
παρεχέτω   pres act imperative 3 sg
[Ga 6:17; cv-1b(2); 4218]   "

παρεχόμενος   pres mid ptcp nom sg masc
   [Ti 2:7; cv-1b(2); 4218]   "

παρέχοντι   pres act ptcp dat sg masc
   [1Ti 6:17; cv-1b(2); 4218]   "

παρέχουσιν   pres act ind 3 pl
   [1Ti 1:4; cv-1b(2); 4218]   "

παρέχω   {4218, cv-1b(2)}
   [(παρείχον), παρέξω, παρέσχον, παρέσχηκα, -, -]
   to hold beside; to hold out to, offer, present, Luke
   6:29; *to confer, render,* Luke 7:4; Acts 22:2; 28:2;
   Col 4:1; *to afford, furnish,* Acts 16:16; 17:31;
   19:24; 1 Tim 6:17; *to exhibit,* Titus 2:7; *to be the*
   cause of, occasion, Matt 26:10; Mark 14:6; Luke
   11:7

παρηγγείλαμεν   aor act ind 1 pl
   [2t; cv-2d(1); 4133]   παραγγέλλω

παρήγγειλαν   aor act ind 3 pl
   [2t; cv-2d(1); 4133]   "

παρήγγειλεν   aor act ind 3 sg
   [7t; cv-2d(1); 4133]   "

παρηγγέλλομεν   imperf act ind 1 pl
   [2Th 3:10; cv-2d(1); 4133]   "

παρηγγελμένα   perf pass ptcp acc pl neut
   [Mk 16:8; cv-2d(1); 4133]   "

παρηγορία, ας, ἡ   {4219, n-1a}
   exhortation; comfort, solace, consolation, Col 4:11*

παρηγορία   nom sg fem
   [Cl 4:11; n-1a; 4219]   παρηγορία

παρηκολούθηκας   perf act ind 2 sg
   [1Ti 4:6; cv-1d(2a); 4158]   παρακολουθέω

παρηκολουθηκότι   perf act ptcp dat sg masc
   [Lk 1:3; cv-1d(2a); 4158]   "

παρηκολούθησας   aor act ind 2 sg
   [2Ti 3:10; cv-1d(2a); 4158]   "

παρῆλθεν   aor act ind 3 sg
   [2t; cv-1b(2); 4216]   παρέρχομαι

παρῆλθον   aor act ind 1 sg
   [Lk 15:29; cv-1b(2); 4216]   "

παρῆνει   imperf act ind 3 sg
   [Ac 27:9; cv-1d(2b); 4147]   παραινέω

παρῆσαν   imperf act ind 3 pl
   [2t; cv-6b; 4205]   πάρειμι

παρητημένον   perf pass ptcp acc sg masc
   [2t; cv-1d(2a); 4148]   παραιτέομαι

παρητήσαντο   aor mid ind 3 pl
   [Hb 12:19; cv-1d(2a); 4148]   "

παρητοῦντο   imperf mid ind 3 pl
   [Mk 15:6; cv-1d(2a); 4148]   "

παρθενία, ας, ἡ   {4220, n-1a}
   virginity, Luke 2:36*

παρθενίας   gen sg fem
   [Lk 2:36; n-1a; 4220]   παρθενία

παρθένοι   nom pl masc
   [Rv 14:4; n-2a; 4221]   παρθένος

παρθένοι   nom pl fem   [3t; n-2a; 4221]   "

παρθένοις   dat pl fem   [Mt 25:1; n-2a; 4221]   "

παρθένον   acc sg fem   [5t; n-2a; 4221]   "

παρθένος, οῦ, ο (n-2a) **ἡ** (n-2b)   {4221}
   a virgin, maid, Matt 1:23; 25:1, 7, 11; Acts 21:9; in
   N.T. also masc., *chaste,* Rev 14:4

παρθένος   nom sg fem   [3t; n-2a; 4221]   "

παρθένου   gen sg fem   [Lk 1:27; n-2a; 4221]   "

παρθένων   gen pl fem   [1C 7:25; n-2a; 4221]   "

Πάρθοι, ου, ὁ   {4222, n-2a}
   a Parthian, a native of Parthia, in central Asia,
   Acts 2:9

Πάρθοι   nom pl masc   [Ac 2:9; n-2a; 4222]   Πάρθοι

παρίημι   {4223, cv-6a}
   [-, παρῆκα, -, παρεῖμαι, -] *to let pass beside, let fall*
   beside; to relax, Luke 11:42; perf. pass. part.
   παρειμένος, *hanging down helplessly, unstrung,*
   feeble, Heb 12:12*

παριστάνετε   pres act imperative 2 pl
   [Rm 6:13; cv-6a; 4225]   παρίστημι

παριστάνετε   pres act ind 2 pl
   [Rm 6:16; cv-6a; 4225]   "

παριστάνω, see παρίστημι   {4224, cv-6a}

παρίστημι   {4225, cv-6a}
   [παραστήσω, παρέστησα or παρέστην,
   παρέστηκα, -, παρεστάθην] pluperfect,
   παρειστήκειν, also spelled παριστάνω , trans. *to*
   place beside; to have in readiness, provide, Acts
   23:24; *to range beside, to place at the disposal of,*
   Matt 26:53; Acts 9:41; *to present* to God, *dedicate,*
   consecrate, devote, Luke 2:22; Rom 6:13, 19; *to*
   prove, demonstrate, show, Acts 1:3; 24:13; *to*
   commend, recommend, 1 Cor 8:8; intrans. perf.
   παρέστηκα, part. παρεστώς, pluperf.
   παρειστήκειν, 2 aor. παρέστην, and mid., *to stand*
   by or *before,* Acts 27:24; Rom 14:10; *to stand by, to*
   be present, Mark 14:47, 69, 70; *to stand in*
   attendance, attend, Luke 1:19; 1:24; of time, *to be*
   present, have come, Mark 4:29; *to stand by* in aid,
   assist, support, Rom 16:2

Παρμενᾶν   acc sg masc
   [Ac 6:5; n-1e; 4226]   Παρμενᾶς

Παρμενᾶς, ᾶ, ὁ   {4226, n-1e}
   Parmenas, pr. name, Acts 6:5*

πάροδος, ου, ἡ   {4227, n-2b}
   a way by; a passing by; ἐν παρόδῳ, *in passing, by*
   the way, 1 Cor 16:7*

παρόδῳ   dat sg fem   [1C 16:7; n-2b; 4227]   πάροδος

παροικεῖς   pres act ind 2 sg
   [Lk 24:18; cv-1d(2a); 4228]   παροικέω

παροικέω   {4228, cv-1d(2a)}
   [-, παρῴκησα, -, παρῴχημαι, -] *to dwell beside;*
   later, *to reside in a place as a stranger, sojourn, be a*
   stranger or *sojourner,* Luke 24:18; Heb 11:9*

παροικία, ας, ἡ   {4229, n-1a}
   a sojourning, temporary residence in a foreign land,
   Acts 13:17; 1 Peter 1:17*

παροικία   dat sg fem
   [Ac 13:17; n-1a; 4229]   παροικία

παροικίας   gen sg fem   [1P 1:17; n-1a; 4229]   "

πάροικοι   nom pl masc
   [Ep 2:19; a-3a; 4230]   πάροικος

πάροικον   nom sg neut   [Ac 7:6; a-3a; 4230]   "

πάροικος, ον	{4230, a-3a}
a neighbor; later, a sojourner, temporary resident,
stranger, Acts 7:6, 29; Eph 2:19; 1 Peter 2:11*

πάροικος nom sg masc [Ac 7:29; a-3a; 4230]	"
παροίκους acc pl masc [1P 2:11; a-3a; 4230]	"

παροιμία, ας, ή	{4231, n-1a}
a by-word, proverb, adage, 2 Peter 2:22; in N.T. an
obscure saying, enigma, John 16:25, 29; a parable,
similitude, figurative discourse, John 10:6*

παροιμίαις dat pl fem [2t; n-1a; 4231]	παροιμία
παροιμίαν acc sg fem [2t; n-1a; 4231]	"
παροιμίας gen sg fem [2P 2:22; n-1a; 4231]	"
πάροινον acc sg masc [2t; a-3a; 4232]	πάροινος

πάροινος, ον	{4232, a-3a}
pr. pertaining to wine, drunken; hence,
quarrelsome, insolent, overbearing, 1 Tim 3:3;
Titus 1:7*

παροίχομαι	{4233, cv-1d(2c)}
[-, -, -, παρῴχημαι, -] to have gone by; perf. part.
παρῳχημένος, by-gone, Acts 14:16*

παρόμοια   acc pl neut
   [Mk 7:13; a-3b(1); 4235]	παρόμοιος
παρομοιάζετε   pres act ind 2 pl
   [Mt 23:27; cv-2a(1); 4234]	παρομοιάζω

παρομοιάζω	{4234, cv-2a(1)}
[-, -, -, -, -] to be like, to resemble, Matt 23:27*

παρόμοιος, (α), ον	{4235, a-3b(1)}
nearly resembling, similar, like, Mark 7:13, 8 v.l.*

παρόν   pres act ptcp acc sg neut
   [Hb 12:11; cv-6b; 4205]	πάρειμι
παρόντες   pres act ptcp nom pl masc
   [2C 10:11; cv-6b; 4205]	"
παρόντος   pres act ptcp gen sg neut
   [Cl 1:6; cv-6b; 4205]	"
παροξύνεται   pres pass ind 3 sg
   [1C 13:5; cv-; 4236]	παροξύνω

παροξύνω	{4236, cv-3c(2)}
[(παρώξυνον), -, -, -, -, -] to sharpen; met. to incite,
stir up, Acts 17:16; to irritate, provoke, 1 Cor 13:5*

παροξυσμόν   acc sg masc
   [Hb 10:24; n-2a; 4237]	παροξυσμός

παροξυσμός, οῦ, ὁ	{4237, n-2a}
an inciting, incitement, Heb 10:24; a sharp fit of
anger, sharp contention, angry dispute, Acts
15:39*

παροξυσμός nom sg masc [Ac 15:39; n-2a; 4237]	"
παροργίζετε   pres act imperative 2 pl
   [Ep 6:4; cv-2a(1); 4239]	παροργίζω

παροργίζω	{4239, cv-2a(1)}
[παροργιῶ, παρώργισα, -, -, -] to provoke to anger,
irritate, exasperate, Rom 10:19; Eph 6:4; Col 3:21
v.l.*

παροργισμός, οῦ, ὁ	{4240, n-2a}
provocation to anger; anger excited, indignation,
wrath, Eph 4:26*

παροργισμῷ   dat sg masc
   [Ep 4:26; n-2a; 4240]	παροργισμός

παροργιῶ   fut act ind 1 sg
   [Rm 10:19; cv-2a(1); 4239]	παροργίζω

παροτρύνω	{4241, cv-1c(2)}
[-, παρώτρυνα, -, -, -] to stir up, incite, instigate,
Acts 13:50*

παρούσῃ   pres act ptcp dat sg fem
   [2P 1:12; cv-6b; 4205]	πάρειμι

παρουσία, ας, ή	{4242, n-1a}
presence, 2 Cor 10:10; Phil 2:12; a coming, arrival,
advent, Phil 1:26; Matt 24:3, 27, 37, 39; 1 Cor
15:23; 1:8 v.l.

παρουσία nom sg fem [6t; n-1a; 4242]	παρουσία
παρουσίᾳ dat sg fem [9t; n-1a; 4242]	"
παρουσίαν acc sg fem [3t; n-1a; 4242]	"
παρουσίας gen sg fem [6t; n-1a; 4242]	"
παροῦσιν   pres act ptcp dat pl neut
   [Hb 13:5; cv-6b; 4205]	πάρειμι
παροψίδος   gen sg fem
   [Mt 23:25; n-3c(2); 4243]	παροψίς

παροψίς, ίδος, ή	{4243, n-3c(2)}
pr. a dainty side-dish; meton. a plate, platter, Matt
23:25, 26 v.l.*

παρρησία, ας, ή	{4244, n-1a}
freedom in speaking, boldness of speech, Acts 4:13;
6:10 v.l.; 16:4 v.l.; παρρησίᾳ, as an adv., freely,
boldly, John 7:13, 26; so μετὰ παρρησίας, Acts
2:29; 4:29, 31; license, authority, Phil 8; confidence,
assurance, 2 Cor 7:4; Eph 3:12; Heb 3:6; 10:19;
openness, frankness, 2 Cor 3:12; παρρησίᾳ, and ἐν
παρρησίᾳ, adverbially, openly, plainly,
perspicuously, unambiguously, Mark 8:32; John
10:24; 16:29 v.l.; publicly, before all, John 7:4; Acts
14:19 v.l.

παρρησία nom sg fem [2t; n-1a; 4244]	παρρησία
παρρησίᾳ dat sg fem [14t; n-1a; 4244]	"
παρρησιάζεσθαι   pres mid inf
   [Ac 18:26; v-2a(1); 4245]	παρρησιάζομαι

παρρησιάζομαι	{4245, v-2a(1)}
[(ἐπαρρησιαζόμην), παρρησιάσομαι,
ἐπαρρησιασάμην, -, -, -] to speak plainly, freely,
boldly, and confidently, Acts 13:46; 14:3

παρρησιαζόμενοι   pres mid ptcp nom pl masc
   [Ac 14:3; v-2a(1); 4245]	"
παρρησιαζόμενος   pres mid ptcp nom sg masc
   [2t; v-2a(1); 4245]	"
παρρησίαν acc sg fem [10t; n-1a; 4244]	παρρησία
παρρησίας gen sg fem [5t; n-1a; 4244]	"
παρρησιασάμενοι   aor mid ptcp nom pl masc
   [Ac 13:46; v-2a(1); 4245]	παρρησιάζομαι
παρρησιάσωμαι   aor mid subj 1 sg
   [Ep 6:20; v-2a(1); 4245]	"
παρῴκησεν   aor act ind 3 sg
   [Hb 11:9; cv-1d(2a); 4228]	παροικέω
παρών   pres act ptcp nom sg masc
   [6t; cv-6b; 4205]	πάρειμι
παρωξύνετο   imperf pass ind 3 sg
   [Ac 17:16; cv-; 4236]	παροξύνω
παρώτρυναν   aor act ind 3 pl
   [Ac 13:50; cv-; 4241]	παροτρύνω

παρῳχημέναις   perf mid ptcp dat pl fem
   [Ac 14:16; cv-1d(2c); 4233]   παροίχομαι

πᾶς, πᾶσα, πᾶν   {4246, a-2a}
   all; in the sg. *the whole, entire,* usually when the
   substantive has the article, Matt 6:29; 8:32; Acts
   19:26; *every,* only with an anarthrous subst.,
   Matt 3:10; 4:4; pl. *all,* Matt 1:17, et al. freq.;
   πάντα, *in all respects,* Acts 20:35; 1 Cor 9:25;
   10:33; 11:2; by a Hebraism, a negative with πᾶς
   is sometimes equivalent to οὐδείς or μηδείς,
   Matt 24:22; Luke 1:37; Acts 10:14; Rom 3:20; 1
   Cor 1:29; Eph 4:29

πᾶς   nom sg masc [95t; a-2a; 4246]   πᾶς
πᾶς   voc sg masc [Rm 2:1; a-2a; 4246]   "
πᾶσα   nom sg fem [46t; a-2a; 4246]   "
πᾶσαι nom pl fem [16t; a-2a; 4246]   "
πᾶσαις dat pl fem [7t; a-2a; 4246]   "
πᾶσαν acc sg fem [57t; a-2a; 4246]   "
πάσας acc pl fem [9t; a-2a; 4246]   "
πάσῃ   dat sg fem [45t; a-2a; 4246]   "
πάσης gen sg fem [42t; a-2a; 4246]   "
πᾶσι   dat pl masc [3t; a-2a; 4246]   "
πᾶσι   dat pl neut [4t; a-2a; 4246]   "
πᾶσιν dat pl masc [48t; a-2a; 4246]   "
πᾶσιν dat pl neut [33t; a-2a; 4246]   "

πάσχα, τό   {4247, n-3g(2)}
   the passover, the paschal lamb, Matt 26:17; Mark
   14:12; met. used of Christ, the true *paschal lamb,*
   1 Cor 5:7; *the feast of the passover, the day on which
   the paschal lamb was slain and eaten,* the 14th of
   Nisan, Matt 26:18; Mark 14:1; Heb 11:28; more
   genr. *the whole paschal festival,* including the
   seven days of *the feast of unleavened bread,* Matt
   26:2; Luke 2:41; John 2:13

πάσχα   indecl [29t; n-3g(2); 4247]   πάσχα
πάσχει pres act ind 3 sg [2t; v-5a; 4248]   πάσχω
πάσχειν pres act inf [4t; v-5a; 4248]   "
πάσχετε pres act ind 2 pl [2Th 1:5; v-5a; 4248]   "
πασχέτω pres act imperative 3 sg
   [1P 4:15; v-5a; 4248]   "
πάσχοιτε pres act opt 2 pl [1P 3:14; v-5a; 4248] "
πάσχομεν pres act ind 1 pl [2C 1:6; v-5a; 4248] "
πάσχοντες pres act ptcp nom pl masc
   [2t; v-5a; 4248]   "

πάσχω   {4248, v-5a}
   [(ἔπασχον), πασχον, ἔπαθον, πέπονθα, -, -] *to be
   affected by* a thing, whether good or bad, *to
   suffer, endure* evil, Matt 16:21; 17:12, 15; 27:19;
   absol. *to suffer* death, Luke 22:15; 24:26

πάσχω   pres act ind 1 sg [2Ti 1:12; v-5a; 4248] "
πάσχων pres act ptcp nom sg masc
   [2t; v-5a; 4248]   "
πασῶν   gen pl fem [5t; a-2a; 4246]   πᾶς
πατάξαι aor act inf
   [Rv 11:6; v-2b; 4250]   πατάσσω
πατάξας aor act ptcp nom sg masc
   [3t; v-2b; 4250]   "
πατάξῃ   aor act subj 3 sg [Rv 19:15; v-2b; 4250] "
πατάξομεν fut act ind 1 pl
   [Lk 22:49; v-2b; 4250]   "

πατάξω   fut act ind 1 sg [2t; v-2b; 4250]   "

Πάταρα, ων, τά   {4249, n-2c}
   Patara, a city on the sea-coast of Lycia, in Asia
   Minor, Acts 21:1*

Πάταρα   acc pl neut [Ac 21:1; n-2c; 4249]   Πάταρα

πατάσσω   {4250, v-2b}
   [πατάξω, ἐπάταξα, -, -, -] *to strike, beat upon; to
   smite, wound,* Matt 26:51; Luke 22:49, 50; by
   impl. *to kill, slay,* Matt 26:31; Mark 14:27; Acts
   7:24; *to strike gently,* Acts 12:7; from the Hebrew,
   to smite with disease, plagues, etc., Acts 12:23;
   Rev 11:6; 19:15*

πατεῖ   pres act ind 3 sg
   [Rv 19:15; v-1d(2a); 4251]   πατέω
πατεῖν pres act inf [Lk 10:19; v-1d(2a); 4251]   "
πάτερ   voc sg masc [24t; n-3f(2c); 4252]   πατήρ
πατέρα acc sg masc [93t; n-3f(2c); 4252]   "
πατέρας acc pl masc [12t; n-3f(2c); 4252]   "
πατέρες nom pl masc [18t; n-3f(2c); 4252]   "
πατέρες voc pl masc [6t; n-3f(2c); 4252]   "
πατέρων gen pl masc [14t; n-3f(2c); 4252]   "

πατέω   {4251, v-1d(2a)}
   [πατήσω, ἐπάτησα, -, -, ἐπατήθην] intrans. *to
   tread,* Luke 10:19; trans. *to tread* the winepress,
   Rev 14:20; 19:15; *to trample,* Luke 21:24; Rev
   11:2*

πατήρ, πατρός, ὁ   {4252, n-3f(2c)}
   a father, Matt 2:22; 4:21, 22; spc. used of God, as
   the *Father* of man by creation, preservation,
   etc., Matt 5:16, 45, 48; and peculiarly as the
   Father of our Lord Jesus Christ, Matt 7:21; 2 Cor
   1:3; *the founder of a race, remote progenitor,
   forefather, ancestor,* Matt 3:9; 23:30, 32; *an elder,
   senior, father* in age, 1 John 2:13, 14; *a spiritual
   father,* 1 Cor 4:15; *father* by origination, John
   8:44; Heb 12:9; used as an appellation of honor,
   Matt 23:9; Acts 7:2

πατήρ   nom sg masc [110t; n-3f(2c); 4252]   "
πατήσουσιν fut act ind 3 pl
   [Rv 11:2; v-1d(2a); 4251]   πατέω

Πάτμος, ου, ὁ   {4253, n-2a}
   Patmos, an island in the Aegean sea, Rev 1:9*

Πάτμῳ   dat sg masc [Rv 1:9; n-2a; 4253]   Πάτμος
πατουμένη pres pass ptcp nom sg fem
   [Lk 21:24; v-1d(2a); 4251]   πατέω

πατραλῴας, see πατρολῴας   {4254}

πατράσιν dat pl masc [3t; n-3f(2c); 4252]   πατήρ
πατρί   dat sg masc [33t; n-3f(2c); 4252]   "

πατριά, ᾶς, ἡ   {4255, n-1a}
   descent, lineage; a family, tribe, race, Luke 2:4;
   Acts 3:25; Eph 3:15*

πατριά   nom sg fem [Ep 3:15; n-1a; 4255]   πατριά
πατριαί nom pl fem [Ac 3:25; n-1a; 4255]   "
πατριάρχαι nom pl masc
   [Ac 7:9; n-1f; 4256]   πατριάρχης
πατριάρχας acc pl masc [Ac 7:8; n-1f; 4256]   "

πατριάρχης, ου, ὁ {4256, n-1f}
a patriarch, head or founder of a family, Acts 2:29;
7:8, 9; Heb 7:4*

πατριάρχης   nom sg masc [Hb 7:4; n-1f; 4256]   "
πατριάρχου   gen sg masc [Ac 2:29; n-1f; 4256]   "
πατριᾶς   gen sg fem [Lk 2:4; n-1a; 4255]   πατριά
πατρίδα   acc sg fem [3t; n-3c(2); 4258]   πατρίς
πατρίδι   dat sg fem [5t; n-3c(2); 4258]   "

πατρικός, ή, όν {4257, a-1a(2a)}
from fathers or ancestors, ancestral, paternal, Gal
1:14*

πατρικῶν   gen pl fem
[Ga 1:14; a-1a(2a); 4257]   πατρικός

πατρίς, ίδος, ἡ {4258, n-3c(2)}
one's native place, country, or city, Matt 13:54, 57;
Mark 6:1, 4; Luke 2:3 v.l.; 4:23, 24; John 4:44;
Acts 18:25 v.l., 27 v.l.; a heavenly country, Heb
11:14

Πατροβᾶν   acc sg masc
[Rm 16:14; n-1e; 4259]   Πατροβᾶς

Πατροβᾶς, ᾶ, ὁ {4259, n-1e}
Patrobas, pr. name, Rom 16:14*

πατρολῴαις   dat pl masc
[1Ti 1:9; n-1d; 4260]   πατρολῴας

πατρολῴας, ου, ὁ {4260, n-1d}
also spelled πατραλῴας, one who kills one's
father, a patricide, 1 Tim 1:9*

πατροπαράδοτος, ον {4261, a-3a}
handed down or received by tradition from one's
fathers or ancestors, 1 Peter 1:18*

πατροπαραδότου   gen sg fem
[1P 1:18; a-3a; 4261]   πατροπαράδοτος
πατρός   gen sg masc [100t; n-3f(2c); 4252]   πατήρ
πατρῴοις   dat pl neut
[Ac 28:17; a-1a(1); 4262]   πατρῷος

πατρῷος, α, ον {4262, a-1a(1)}
received from one's ancestors, paternal, ancestral,
Acts 22:3; 24:14; 28:17*

πατρῴου   gen sg masc [Ac 22:3; a-1a(1); 4262]   "
πατρῴῳ   dat sg masc [Ac 24:14; a-1a(1); 4262]   "
παύεται   pres mid ind 3 sg
[Ac 6:13; v-1a(5); 4264]   παύω
Παῦλε   voc sg masc [2t; n-2a; 4263]   Παῦλος
Παῦλον   acc sg masc [30t; n-2a; 4263]   "

Παῦλος, ου, ὁ {4263, n-2a}
Paulus, Paul, pr. name. (1) Paul, the Apostle, Acts
13:9, et al. freq. (2) Sergius Paulus, the deputy or
proconsul of Cyprus, Acts 13:7

Παῦλος   nom sg masc [79t; n-2a; 4263]   "
Παύλου   gen sg masc [30t; n-2a; 4263]   "
Παύλῳ   dat sg masc [17t; n-2a; 4263]   "
παύομαι   pres mid ind 1 sg
[Ep 1:16; v-1a(5); 4264]   παύω
παυόμεθα   pres mid ind 1 pl
[Cl 1:9; v-1a(5); 4264]   "
παύσασθαι   aor mid inf [Ac 20:1; v-1a(5); 4264]   "

παυσάτω   aor act imperative 3 sg
[1P 3:10; v-1a(5); 4264]   "
παύσῃ   fut mid ind 2 sg
[Ac 13:10; v-1a(5); 4264]   "
παύσονται   fut mid ind 3 pl
[1C 13:8; v-1a(5); 4264]   "

παύω {4264, v-1a(5)}
[(ἔπαυον), παύσω, ἔπαυσα, -, πέπαυμαι, ἐπαύθην
or ἐπάην] to cause to pause or cease, restrain,
prohibit, 1 Peter 3:10; mid. perf. (pass. form)
πέπαυμαι, to cease, stop, leave off, desist, refrain,
Luke 5:4; 8:24

Πάφος, ου, ἡ {4265, n-2b}
Paphos, the chief city in the island of Cyprus

Πάφου   gen sg fem [2t; n-2b; 4265]   Πάφος

παχύνω {4266, v-1c(2)}
[-, -, -, -, ἐπαχύνθην] to fatten, make gross; met.
pass. to be rendered gross, dull, unfeeling, Matt
13:15; Acts 28:27*

πέδαις   dat pl fem [2t; n-1b; 4267]   πέδη
πέδας   acc pl fem [Mk 5:4; n-1b; 4267]   "

πέδη, ης, ἡ {4267, n-1b}
a fetter, shackle, Mark 5:4; Luke 8:29*

πεδινός, ή, όν {4268, a-1a(2a)}
level, flat, Luke 6:17*

πεδινοῦ   gen sg masc
[Lk 6:17; a-1a(2a); 4268]   πεδινός
πεζεύειν   pres act inf
[Ac 20:13; v-1a(6); 4269]   πεζεύω

πεζεύω {4269, v-1a(6)}
[-, -, -, -, -] pr. to travel on foot; to travel by land,
Acts 20:13*

πεζῇ {4270, adverb}
on foot, or, by land, Matt 14:13; Mark 6:33

πεζῇ   adverb [2t; adverb; 4270]   πεζῇ

πεζος, ή, όν {a-1a(2a)}
going by land, Matt 14:13 v.l.*

πειθαρχεῖν   pres act inf
[2t; v-1d(2a); 4272]   πειθαρχέω

πειθαρχέω {4272, v-1d(2a)}
[-, ἐπειθάρχησα, -, -, -] to obey one in authority,
Acts 5:29, 32; Titus 3:1; genr. to obey, follow, or
conform to advice, Acts 27:21*

πειθαρχήσαντας   aor act ptcp acc pl masc
[Ac 27:21; v-1d(2a); 4272]   "
πειθαρχοῦσιν   pres act ptcp dat pl masc
[Ac 5:32; v-1d(2a); 4272]   "
πείθεις   pres act ind 2 sg
[Ac 26:28; v-1b(3); 4275]   πείθω
πείθεσθαι   pres pass inf [2t; v-1b(3); 4275]   "
πείθεσθε   pres pass imperative 2 pl
[Hb 13:17; v-1b(3); 4275]   "
πειθοῖς   dat pl masc
[1C 2:4; a-1a(2a); 4273]   πειθός
πείθομαι   pres pass ind 1 sg
[Ac 26:26; v-1b(3); 4275]   πείθω

πειθόμεθα   pres pass ind 1 pl
   [Hb 13:18; v-1b(3); 4275]   "

πείθομεν   pres act ind 1 pl
   [2C 5:11; v-1b(3); 4275]   "

πειθομένοις   pres mid ptcp dat pl masc
   [Rm 2:8; v-1b(3); 4275]   "

πειθομένου   pres pass ptcp gen sg masc
   [Ac 21:14; v-1b(3); 4275]   "

πειθός, ή, όν   {4273, a-1a(2a)}
   also spelled πιθός, *persuasive, skillful,* 1 Cor 2:4*

πείθω   {4275, v-1b(3)}
   [(ἔπειθον), πείσω, ἔπεισα, πέποιθα, πέπεισμαι,
   ἐπείσθην] pluperfect, ἐπεποίθειν, *to persuade,
   seek to persuade, endeavor to convince,* Acts 18:4;
   19:8, 26; 28:23; *to persuade, influence by
   persuasion,* Matt 27:20; Acts 13:43; 26:28; *to
   incite, instigate,* Acts 14:19; *to appease, render
   tranquil, to quiet,* 1 John 3:19; *to strive to
   conciliate, aspire to the favor of,* Gal 1:10; *to pacify,
   conciliate, win over,* Matt 28:14; Acts 12:20; pass.
   and mid. *to be persuaded of, be confident of,* Luke
   20:6; Rom 8:38; Heb 6:9; *to suffer one's self to be
   persuaded, yield to persuasion, to be induced,* Acts
   21:14; *to be convinced, to believe, yield belief,* Luke
   16:31; Acts 17:4; *to assent, listen to, obey, follow,*
   Acts 5:36, 37, 40; 2 perf. πέποιθα, *to be assured, be
   confident,* 2 Cor 2:3; Phil 1:6; Heb 13:18; *to
   confide in , trust, rely on, place hope and confidence
   in,* Matt 27:43; Mark 10:24; Rom 2:19

πείθω   pres act ind 1 sg [Ga 1:10; v-1b(3); 4275]   "

πείθων   pres act ptcp nom sg masc
   [2t; v-1b(3); 4275]   "

πεῖν   aor act inf   [5t; v-3a(1); 4403]   πίνω

πεινᾷ   pres act ind 3 sg
   [2t; v-1d(1b); 4277]   πεινάω

πεινᾷ   pres act subj 3 sg
   [Rm 12:20; v-1d(1b); 4277]   "

πεινᾶν   pres act inf   [Pp 4:12; v-1d(1b); 4277]   "

πεινάσετε   fut act ind 2 pl
   [Lk 6:25; v-1d(1b); 4277]   "

πεινάσῃ   aor act subj 3 sg
   [Jn 6:35; v-1d(1b); 4277]   "

πεινάσουσιν   fut act ind 3 pl
   [Rv 7:16; v-1d(1b); 4277]   "

πεινάω   {4277, v-1d(1b)}
   [πεινάσω, ἐπείνασα, -, -, -] *to hunger, be hungry,*
   Matt 4:2; Mark 11:12; *to be exposed to hunger, be
   famished,* 1 Cor 4:11; Phil 4:12; met. *to hunger
   after, desire earnestly, long for,* Matt 5:6

πεινῶμεν   pres act ind 1 pl
   [1C 4:11; v-1d(1b); 4277]   "

πεινῶντα   pres act ptcp acc sg masc
   [2t; v-1d(1b); 4277]   "

πεινῶντας   pres act ptcp acc pl masc
   [Lk 1:53; v-1d(1b); 4277]   "

πεινῶντες   pres act ptcp nom pl masc
   [Mt 5:6; v-1d(1b); 4277]   "

πεινῶντες   pres act ptcp voc pl masc
   [Lk 6:21; v-1d(1b); 4277]   "

πεῖρα, ας, ἡ   {4278, n-1a}
   a trial, attempt, endeavor; λαμβάνειν πεῖραν, *to*

---

   attempt, Heb 11:29; also, *to experience,* Heb
   11:36*

πειράζει   pres act ind 3 sg
   [Jm 1:13; v-2a(1); 4279]   πειράζω

πειράζεται   pres pass ind 3 sg
   [Jm 1:14; v-2a(1); 4279]   "

πειράζετε   pres act imperative 2 pl
   [2C 13:5; v-2a(1); 4279]   "

πειράζετε   pres act ind 2 pl   [3t; v-2a(1); 4279]   "

πειράζῃ   pres act subj 3 sg
   [1C 7:5; v-2a(1); 4279]   "

πειράζομαι   pres pass ind 1 sg
   [Jm 1:13; v-2a(1); 4279]   "

πειραζομένοις   pres pass ptcp dat pl masc
   [Hb 2:18; v-2a(1); 4279]   "

πειραζόμενος   pres pass ptcp nom sg masc
   [4t; v-2a(1); 4279]   "

πειράζοντες   pres act ptcp nom pl masc
   [6t; v-2a(1); 4279]   "

πειράζω   {4279, v-2a(1)}
   [(ἐπείραζον), πειράσω, ἐπείρασα, -, πεπείρασμαι,
   ἐπειράσθην] *to make proof* or *trial of, put to the
   proof,* whether with good or mischievous
   intent, Matt 16:1; 22:35; absol. *to attempt,* Acts
   16:7; 24:6; in N.T. *to tempt,* Matt 4:1; *to try,
   subject to trial,* 1 Cor 10:13

πειράζων   pres act ptcp nom sg masc
   [4t; v-2a(1); 4279]   "

πεῖραν   acc sg fem   [2t; n-1a; 4278]   πεῖρα

πειράσαι   aor act inf   [2t; v-2a(1); 4279]   πειράζω

πειρασθείς   aor pass ptcp nom sg masc
   [Hb 2:18; v-2a(1); 4279]   "

πειρασθῆναι   aor pass inf   [2t; v-2a(1); 4279]   "

πειρασθῇς   aor pass subj 2 sg
   [Ga 6:1; v-2a(1); 4279]   "

πειρασθῆτε   aor pass subj 2 pl
   [Rv 2:10; v-2a(1); 4279]   "

πειρασμοῖς   dat pl masc   [3t; n-2a; 4280]   πειρασμός

πειρασμόν   acc sg masc   [11t; n-2a; 4280]   "

πειρασμός, οῦ, ὁ   {4280, n-2a}
   a putting to the proof, proof, trial, 1 Peter 4:12;
   Heb 3:8; direct *temptation* to sin, Luke 4:13; Acts
   15:26 v.l.; *trial, temptation,* Matt 6:13; 26:41; 1
   Cor 10:13; *trial, calamity, affliction,* Luke 22:28

πειρασμός   nom sg masc   [1C 10:13; n-2a; 4280]   "

πειρασμοῦ   gen sg masc   [4t; n-2a; 4280]   "

πειρασμῷ   dat sg masc   [1C 10:13; n-2a; 4280]   "

πειρασμῶν   gen pl masc   [Ac 20:19; n-2a; 4280]   "

πειράω   {4281, v-1d(1a)}
   [(ἐπείρων), -, -, -, πεπείραμαι, -] *to try, attempt,
   essay, endeavor,* Acts 9:26 v.l.; 26:21; Heb 4:15
   v.l.*

πείσαντες   aor act ptcp nom pl masc
   [2t; v-1b(3); 4275]   πείθω

πείσας   aor act ptcp nom sg masc
   [Ac 19:26; v-1b(3); 4275]   "

πεισθῇς   aor pass subj 2 sg
   [Ac 23:21; v-1b(3); 4275]   "

πεισθήσονται   fut pass ind 3 pl
   [Lk 16:31; v-1b(3); 4275]   "

πεισμονή, ῆς, ἡ   {4282, n-1b}
   a yielding to persuasion, assent, Gal 5:8*
πεισμονή   nom sg fem   [Ga 5:8; n-1b; 4282] πεισμονή
πείσομεν   fut act ind 1 pl
   [2t; v-1b(3); 4275]   πείθω
πελάγει   dat sg neut
   [Mt 18:6; n-3d(2b); 4283]   πέλαγος

πέλαγος, ους, τό   {4283, n-3d(2b)}
   the deep, the open sea, Matt 18:6; *a sea,*
   distinguished from the sea in general, and
   named from an adjacent country, Acts 27:5*
πέλαγος   acc sg neut   [Ac 27:5; n-3d(2b); 4283]   "

πελεκίζω   {4284, v-2a(1)}
   [-, -, -, πεπελέκισμαι, -] *to strike* or *cut with an*
   axe; to behead, Rev 20:4*
πέμπει   pres act ind 3 sg
   [2Th 2:11; v-1b(1); 4287]   πέμπω
πέμπειν   pres act inf   [Ac 25:25; v-1b(1); 4287]   "
πεμπομένοις   pres pass ptcp dat pl masc
   [1P 2:14; v-1b(1); 4287]   "
πέμποντα   pres act ptcp acc sg masc
   [Ac 25:27; v-1b(1); 4287]   "
πέμπτην   acc sg fem
   [Rv 6:9; a-1a(2a); 4286]   πέμπτος

πέμπτος, η, ον   {4286, a-1a(2a)}
   fifth, Rev 6:9; 9:1; 16:10; 21:20*
πέμπτος   nom sg masc   [3t; a-1a(2a); 4286]   "

πέμπω   {4287, v-1b(1)}
   [πέμψω, ἔπεμψα, πέπομφα, -, ἐπέμφθην] *to send,*
   to despatch on any message, embassy, business,
   etc., Matt 2:8; 11:2; 14:10; *to transmit,* Acts 11:29;
   Rev 1:11; *to dismiss, permit to go,* Mark 5:12; *to*
   send in or *among,* 2 Thess 2:11; *to thrust in,* or *put*
   forth, Rev 14:15, 18

πέμπω   pres act ind 1 sg
   [Jn 20:21; v-1b(1); 4287]   πέμπω
πεμφθέντες   aor pass ptcp nom pl masc
   [Lk 7:10; v-1b(1); 4287]   "
πέμψαι   aor act inf   [8t; v-1b(1); 4287]   "
πέμψαντα   aor act ptcp acc sg masc
   [7t; v-1b(1); 4287]   "
πέμψαντες   aor act ptcp nom pl masc
   [Ac 19:31; v-1b(1); 4287]   "
πέμψαντι   aor act ptcp dat sg masc
   [Jn 5:24; v-1b(1); 4287]   "
πέμψαντος   aor act ptcp gen sg masc
   [9t; v-1b(1); 4287]   "
πέμψας   aor act ptcp nom sg masc
   [15t; v-1b(1); 4287]   "
πέμψασιν   aor act ptcp dat pl masc
   [Jn 1:22; v-1b(1); 4287]   "
πέμψει   fut act ind 3 sg
   [Jn 14:26; v-1b(1); 4287]   "
πέμψῃς   aor act subj 2 sg
   [Lk 16:27; v-1b(1); 4287]   "
πέμψον   aor act imperative 2 sg
   [7t; v-1b(1); 4287]   "
πέμψουσιν   fut act ind 3 pl
   [Rv 11:10; v-1b(1); 4287]   "
πέμψω   fut act ind 1 sg   [4t; v-1b(1); 4287]   "

πέμψω   aor act subj 1 sg   [2t; v-1b(1); 4287]   "

πένης, ητος, ὁ   {4288, n-3c(1)}
   pr. *one who labors for his bread; poor, needy,* 2 Cor
   9:9*
πένησιν   dat pl masc   [2C 9:9; n-3c(1); 4288]   πένης
πενθεῖν   pres act inf
   [Mt 9:15; v-1d(2a); 4291]   πενθέω

πενθερά, ᾶς, ἡ   {4289, n-1a}
   a mother-in-law, Matt 8:14; 10:35; Mark 1:30;
   Luke 4:38; 12:53*
πενθερά   nom sg fem   [3t; n-1a; 4289]   πενθερά
πενθεράν   acc sg fem   [2t; n-1a; 4289]
πενθερᾶς   gen sg fem   [Mt 10:35; n-1a; 4289]   "

πενθερός, οῦ, ὁ   {4290, n-2a}
   a father-in-law, John 18:13*
πενθερός   nom sg masc
   [Jn 18:13; n-2a; 4290]   πενθερός

πενθέω   {4291, v-1d(2a)}
   [πενθήσω, ἐπένθησα, -, -, -] trans. *to lament over,*
   2 Cor 12:21; absol. *to lament, be sad, mourn,* Matt
   5:4; 9:15; Mark 16:10; mid. *to bewail one's self, to*
   feel guilt, 1 Cor 5:2
πενθήσατε   aor act imperative 2 pl
   [Jm 4:9; v-1d(2a); 4291]   πενθέω
πενθήσετε   fut act ind 2 pl
   [Lk 6:25; v-1d(2a); 4291]   "
πενθήσω   aor act subj 1 sg
   [2C 12:21; v-1d(2a); 4291]   "

πένθος, ους, τό   {4292, n-3d(2b)}
   mourning, sorrow, sadness, grief, James 4:9
πένθος   nom sg neut   [2t; n-3d(2b); 4292]   πένθος
πένθος   acc sg neut   [3t; n-3d(2b); 4292]   "
πενθοῦντες   pres act ptcp nom pl masc
   [3t; v-1d(2a); 4291]   πενθέω
πενθοῦσι   pres act ptcp dat pl masc
   [Mk 16:10; v-1d(2a); 4291]   "
πενθοῦσιν   pres act ind 3 pl
   [Rv 18:11; v-1d(2a); 4291]   "
πενιχράν   acc sg fem
   [Lk 21:2; a-1a(1); 4293]   πενιχρός

πενιχρός, ά, όν   {4293, a-1a(1)}
   poor, needy, Luke 21:2*

πεντάκις   {4294, adverb}
   five times, 2 Cor 11:24*
πεντάκις   adverb   [2C 11:24; adverb; 4294] πεντάκις

πεντακισχίλιοι, α, ον   {4295, a-1a(1)}
   five times one thousand, five thousand, Matt 14:21;
   16:9
πεντακισχίλιοι   nom pl masc
   [4t; a-1a(1); 4295]   πεντακισχίλιοι
πεντακισχιλίους   acc pl masc
   [Mk 8:19; a-1a(1); 4295]   "
πεντακισχιλίων   gen pl masc
   [Mt 16:9; a-1a(1); 4295]   "
πεντακόσια   acc pl neut
   [Lk 7:41; a-1a(1); 4296]   πεντακόσιοι

πεντακόσιοι, αι, α   {4296, a-1a(1)}
  five hundred, Luke 7:41; 1 Cor 15:6*

πεντακοσίοις   dat pl masc
  [1C 15:6; a-1a(1); 4296]   "

πέντε   {4297, a-5b}
  five, Matt 14:17, 19; 16:9

πέντε   indecl [38t; a-5b; 4297]   πέντε

πεντεκαιδέκατος, η, ον   {4298, a-1a(2a)}
  fifteenth, Luke 3:1*

πεντεκαιδεκάτω   dat sg neut
  [Lk 3:1; a-1a(2a); 4298]   πεντεκαιδέκατος

πεντήκοντα   {4299, a-5b}
  fifty, Mark 6:40; Luke 7:41

πεντήκοντα   indecl [7t; a-5b; 4299]   πεντήκοντα

πεντηκοστή, ῆς, ή   {4300, n-1b}
  Pentecost, or *the Feast of Weeks;* one of the three
  great Jewish festivals, so called because it was
  celebrated on the *fiftieth* day, reckoning from
  the second day of the feast of unleavened
  bread, i.e., from the 16th day of Nisan, Acts 2:1;
  20:16; 1 Cor 16:8*

πεντηκοστῆς   gen sg fem
  [3t; n-1b; 4300]   πεντηκοστή
πεπαιδευμένος   perf pass ptcp nom sg masc
  [Ac 22:3; v-1a(6); 4084]   παιδεύω
πεπαλαίωκεν   perf act ind 3 sg
  [Hb 8:13; v-1d(3); 4096]   παλαιόω
πέπαυται   perf mid ind 3 sg
  [1P 4:1; v-1a(5); 4264]   παύω
πεπειρασμένον   perf pass ptcp acc sg masc
  [Hb 4:15; v-2a(1); 4279]   πειράζω
πέπεισμαι   perf pass ind 1 sg
  [5t; v-1b(3); 4275]   πείθω
πεπείσμεθα   perf pass ind 1 pl
  [Hb 6:9; v-1b(3); 4275]   "
πεπεισμένος   perf pass ptcp nom sg masc
  [Lk 20:6; v-1b(3); 4275]   "
πεπελεκισμένων   perf pass ptcp gen pl masc
  [Rv 20:4; v-2a(1); 4284]   πελεκίζω
πεπιεσμένον   perf pass ptcp acc sg neut
  [Lk 6:38; v-2a(1); 4390]   πιέζω
πεπίστευκα   perf act ind 1 sg
  [2t; v-1a(6); 4409]   πιστεύω
πεπιστεύκαμεν   perf act ind 1 pl
  [2t; v-1a(6); 4409]   "
πεπίστευκας   perf act ind 2 sg
  [Jn 20:29; v-1a(6); 4409]   "
πεπιστεύκατε   perf act ind 2 pl
  [Jn 16:27; v-1a(6); 4409]   "
πεπιστεύκεισαν   pluperf act ind 3 pl
  [Ac 14:23; v-1a(6); 4409]   "
πεπίστευκεν   perf act ind 3 sg
  [2t; v-1a(6); 4409]   "
πεπιστευκόσιν   perf act ptcp dat pl masc
  [Ac 18:27; v-1a(6); 4409]   "
πεπιστευκότας   perf act ptcp acc pl masc
  [Jn 8:31; v-1a(6); 4409]   "
πεπιστευκότες   perf act ptcp nom pl masc
  [2t; v-1a(6); 4409]   "

πεπιστευκότων   perf act ptcp gen pl masc
  [2t; v-1a(6); 4409]   "
πεπιστευκότων   perf act ptcp gen pl neut
  [Ac 21:25; v-1a(6); 4409]   "
πεπιστευκώς   perf act ptcp nom sg masc
  [Ac 16:34; v-1a(6); 4409]   "
πεπίστευμαι   perf pass ind 1 sg
  [2t; v-1a(6); 4409]   "
πεπλανημένοις   perf pass ptcp dat pl neut
  [Mt 18:13; v-1d(1a); 4414]   πλανάω
πεπλάνησθε   perf pass ind 2 pl
  [Jn 7:47; v-1d(1a); 4414]   "
πεπλάτυνται   perf pass ind 3 sg
  [2C 6:11; v-1c(2); 4425]   πλατύνω
πεπληροφορημένοι   perf pass ptcp nom pl masc
  [Cl 4:12; v-1d(2a); 4442]   πληροφορέω
πεπληροφορημένων   perf pass ptcp gen pl neut
  [Lk 1:1; v-1d(2a); 4442]   "
πεπληρώκατε   perf act ind 2 pl
  [Ac 5:28; v-1d(3); 4444]   πληρόω
πεπλήρωκεν   perf act ind 3 sg [2t; v-1d(3); 4444]   "
πεπληρωκέναι   perf act inf
  [Rm 15:19; v-1d(3); 4444]   "
πεπλήρωμαι   perf pass ind 1 sg
  [2t; v-1d(3); 4444]   "
πεπληρωμένα   perf pass ptcp acc pl neut
  [Rv 3:2; v-1d(3); 4444]   "
πεπληρωμένη   perf pass ptcp nom sg fem
  [3t; v-1d(3); 4444]   "
πεπληρωμένην   perf pass ptcp acc sg fem
  [Jn 17:13; v-1d(3); 4444]   "
πεπληρωμένοι   perf pass ptcp nom pl masc
  [3t; v-1d(3); 4444]   "
πεπληρωμένους   perf pass ptcp acc pl masc
  [Rm 1:29; v-1d(3); 4444]   "
πεπλήρωται   perf pass ind 3 sg
  [5t; v-1d(3); 4444]   "
πεπλούτηκα   perf act ind 1 sg
  [Rv 3:17; v-1d(2a); 4456]   πλουτέω
πεποίηκα   perf act ind 1 sg
  [2t; v-1d(2a); 4472]   ποιέω
πεποιήκαμεν   perf act ind 1 pl
  [Lk 17:10; v-1d(2a); 4472]   "
πεποιήκατε   perf act ind 2 pl
  [Mk 11:17; v-1d(2a); 4472]   "
πεποιήκεισαν   pluperf act ind 3 pl
  [Mk 15:7; v-1d(2a); 4472]   "
πεποίηκεν   perf act ind 3 sg [5t; v-1d(2a); 4472]   "
πεποιηκέναι   perf act inf
  [Jn 12:18; v-1d(2a); 4472]   "
πεποιηκόσιν   perf act ptcp dat pl masc
  [Ac 3:12; v-1d(2a); 4472]   "
πεποιηκότες   perf act ptcp nom pl masc
  [Jn 18:18; v-1d(2a); 4472]   "
πεποιηκότος   perf act ptcp gen sg masc
  [Jn 12:37; v-1d(2a); 4472]   "
πεποιηκώς   perf act ptcp nom sg masc
  [2t; v-1d(2a); 4472]   "
πεποιημένων   perf pass ptcp gen pl neut
  [Hb 12:27; v-1d(2a); 4472]   "
πέποιθα   perf act ind 1 sg
  [2t; v-1b(3); 4275]   πείθω

πεποίθαμεν   perf act ind 1 pl
   [2Th 3:4; v-1b(3); 4275]   "
πέποιθας   perf act ind 2 sg
   [Rm 2:19; v-1b(3); 4275]   "
πέποιθεν   perf act ind 3 sg [2t; v-1b(3); 4275]   "
πεποιθέναι   perf act inf [Pp 3:4; v-1b(3); 4275]   "
πεποιθήσει   dat sg fem
   [4t; n-3e(5b); 4301]   πεποίθησις
πεποίθησιν   acc sg fem [2t; n-3e(5b); 4301]   "

πεποίθησις, εως, ἡ   {4301, n-3e(5b)}
   trust, confidence, reliance, 2 Cor 1:15

πεποιθότας   perf act ptcp acc pl masc
   [2t; v-1b(3); 4275]   πείθω
πεποιθότες   perf act ptcp nom pl masc
   [2t; v-1b(3); 4275]   "
πεποιθώς   perf act ptcp nom sg masc
   [5t; v-1b(3); 4275]   "
πεπολίτευμαι   perf mid ind 1 sg
   [Ac 23:1; v-1a(6); 4488]   πολιτεύομαι
πεπόνθασιν   perf act ind 3 pl
   [Lk 13:2; v-5a; 4248]   πάσχω
πέπονθεν   perf act ind 3 sg [Hb 2:18; v-5a; 4248]   "
πεπορευμένους   perf mid ptcp acc pl masc
   [1P 4:3; v-1a(6); 4513]   πορεύω
πεπότικεν   perf act ind 3 sg
   [Rv 14:8; v-2a(1); 4540]   ποτίζω
πεπραγμένον   perf pass ptcp nom sg neut
   [2t; v-2b; 4556]   πράσσω
πέπρακεν   perf act ind 3 sg
   [Mt 13:46; v-5a; 4405]   πιπράσκω
πεπραμένος   perf pass ptcp nom sg masc
   [Rm 7:14; v-5a; 4405]   "
πέπραχα   perf act ind 1 sg
   [Ac 25:11; v-2b; 4556]   πράσσω
πεπραχέναι   perf act inf [Ac 25:25; v-2b; 4556]   "
πέπτωκας   perf act ind 2 sg
   [Rv 2:5; v-1b(3); 4406]   πίπτω
πεπτωκότα   perf act ptcp acc sg masc
   [Rv 9:1; v-1b(3); 4406]   "
πεπτωκυῖαν   perf act ptcp acc sg fem
   [Ac 15:16; v-1b(3); 4406]   "
πεπυρωμένα   perf pass ptcp acc pl neut
   [Ep 6:16; v-1d(3); 4792]   πυρόω
πεπυρωμένης   perf pass ptcp gen sg fem
   [Rv 1:15; v-1d(3); 4792]   "
πεπυρωμένον   perf pass ptcp acc sg neut
   [Rv 3:18; v-1d(3); 4792]   "
πέπωκαν   perf act ind 3 pl
   [Rv 18:3; v-3a(1); 4403]   πίνω
πεπωρωμένη   perf pass ptcp nom sg fem
   [Mk 6:52; v-1d(3); 4800]   πωρόω
πεπωρωμένην   perf pass ptcp acc sg fem
   [Mk 8:17; v-1d(3); 4800]   "

περ   {4302, particle}
   enclitic particle, serving to add force to the
   word to which it is subjoined

Πέραια, ας, ἡ   {4303, n-1a}
   Pernaea, part of Palestine east of the Jordan,
   BAGD list as 2c under πέραν meaning *on the
   other side,* Luke 6:17 v.l.*

περαιτέρω   {4304, adverb}
   compar. adv. of πέραν, Acts 19:39*

περαιτέρω   adverb-comparative
   [Ac 19:39; adverb; 4304]   περαιτέρω

πέραν   {4305, adverb}
   can function as an improper prep., *across,
   beyond, over, on the other side,* Matt 4:15, 25; 19:1;
   John 6:1, 17; ὁ, ἡ, τό, πέραν, *farther, on the farther
   side,* and τὸ πέραν, *the farther side, the other side,*
   Matt 8:18, 28; 14:22

πέραν   adverb [23t; adverb; 4305]   πέραν

πέρας, ατος, τό   {4306, n-3c(6a)}
   an extremity, end, Matt 12:42; Luke 11:31; Acts
   13:33 v.l.; Rom 10:18; *an end, conclusion,
   termination,* Heb 6:16*

πέρας   nom sg neut [Hb 6:16; n-3c(6a); 4306] πέρας
πέρατα   acc pl neut [Rm 10:18; n-3c(6a); 4306]   "
περάτων   gen pl neut [2t; n-3c(6a); 4306]   "
Πέργαμον   acc sg fem
   [Rv 1:11; n-2c; 4307]   Πέργαμον

Πέργαμος, ου, ἡ   {4307, n-2b}
   Pergamus, a city of Mysia, in Asia Minor, Rev
   1:11; 2:12*

Περγάμῳ   dat sg fem [Rv 2:12; n-2c; 4307]   "

Πέργη, ης, ἡ   {4308, n-1b}
   Perga, the chief city of Pamphylia, in Asia
   Minor, Acts 13:13f.; 14:25

Πέργῃ   dat sg fem [Ac 14:25; n-1b; 4308]   Πέργη
Πέργην   acc sg fem [Ac 13:13; n-1b; 4308]   "
Πέργης   gen sg fem [Ac 13:14; n-1b; 4308]   "

περί   {4309, prep}
   pr. of place, (1) gen., *about, around; about,
   concerning, respecting,* Matt 2:8; 11:10; 22:31;
   John 8:18; Rom 8:3, et al. freq.; (2) acc., of place,
   about, around, round about, Matt 3:4; Mark 3:34;
   Luke 13:8; οἱ περί τινα, *the companions* of a
   person, Luke 22:49; *a person and his companions,*
   Acts 13:13; simply *a person,* John 11:19; τὰ περί
   τινα, *the condition, circumstances of* any one,
   Phil 2:23; of time, *about,* Matt 20:3, 5, 6, 9; *about,
   concerning, respecting, touching,* Luke 10:40; 1
   Tim 1:19; 6:21; Titus 2:7

περί   prep-gen [294t; prep; 4309]   περί
περί   prep-acc [39t; prep; 4309]   "
περιάγειν   pres act inf
   [1C 9:5; cv-1b(2); 4310]   περιάγω
περιάγετε   pres act ind 2 pl
   [Mt 23:15; cv-1b(2); 4310]   "

περιάγω   {4310, cv-1b(2)}
   [(περιῆγον), -, -, -, -, -] *to lead around, carry about*
   Acts 13:11 in one's company, 1 Cor 9:5; *to
   traverse,* Matt 4:23; 9:35; 23:15; Mark 6:6

περιάγων   pres act ptcp nom sg masc
   [Ac 13:11; cv-1b(2); 4310]   "
περιαιρεῖται   pres pass ind 3 sg
   [2C 3:16; cv-1d(2a); 4311]   περιαιρέω

περιαιρέω   {4311, cv-1d(2a)}
   [(περιεῖλον), -, περιελεῖν, -, -, -] *to take off, lift off,*

remove, 2 Cor 3:16; *to cast off,* Acts 27:40; met. *to cut off* hope, Acts 27:20; met. *to take away* sin, *remove the guilt* of sin, *make expiation for* sin, Heb 10:11

περιάπτω   {4312, cv-4}
[-, περιῆψα, -, -, -] *to light a fire, kindle,* Luke 22:55*

περιαστράπτω   {4313, cv-4}
[-, περιήστραψα, -, -, -] *to lighten around, shine like lightning around, shine like lightning around,* Acts 9:3; 22:6*

περιαστράψαι   aor act inf
    [Ac 22:6; cv-4; 4313]   περιαστράπτω
περιαψάντων   aor act ptcp gen pl masc
    [Lk 22:55; cv-4; 4312]   περιάπτω
περιβαλεῖται   fut mid ind 3 sg
    [Rv 3:5; cv-2d(1); 4314]   περιβάλλω
περιβάλῃ   aor mid subj 2 sg
    [Rv 3:18; cv-2d(1); 4314]   "
περιβάληται   aor mid subj 3 sg
    [Rv 19:8; cv-2d(1); 4314]   "

περιβάλλω   {4314, cv-2d(1)}
[περιβαλῶ, περιέβαλον, -, περιβέβλημαι, -] *to cast around; to clothe,* Matt 25:36, 38, 43; mid. *to clothe one's self, to be clothed,* Matt 6:29, 31; Luke 23:11; John 19:2; Acts 12:8; Rev 4:4; *to cast around* a city, *to draw* a line for a border, Luke 19:43 v.l.

περιβαλοῦ   aor mid imperative 2 sg
    [Ac 12:8; cv-2d(1); 4314]   "
περιβαλώμεθα   aor mid subj 1 pl
    [Mt 6:31; cv-2d(1); 4314]   "
περιβαλών   aor act ptcp nom sg masc
    [Lk 23:11; cv-2d(1); 4314]   "
περιβεβλημένη   perf pass ptcp nom sg fem
    [2t; cv-2d(1); 4314]   "
περιβεβλημένη   perf pass ptcp voc sg fem
    [Rv 18:16; cv-2d(1); 4314]   "
περιβεβλημένοι   perf pass ptcp nom pl masc
    [2t; cv-2d(1); 4314]   "
περιβεβλημένον   perf mid ptcp acc sg masc
    [Mk 16:5; cv-2d(1); 4314]   "
περιβεβλημένον   perf pass ptcp acc sg masc
    [Rv 10:1; cv-2d(1); 4314]   "
περιβεβλημένος   perf pass ptcp nom sg masc
    [2t; cv-2d(1); 4314]   "
περιβεβλημένους   perf pass ptcp acc pl masc
    [2t; cv-2d(1); 4314]   "

περιβλέπω   {4315, cv-1b(1)}
[(περιέβλεπον), -, περιέβλεψα, -, -, -] trans. *to look around upon,* Mark 3:5, 34; 11:11; Luke 6:10; absol. *to look around,* Mark 5:32; 9:8; 10:23*

περιβλεψάμενοι   aor mid ptcp nom pl masc
    [Mk 9:8; cv-1b(1); 4315]   περιβλέπω
περιβλεψάμενος   aor mid ptcp nom sg masc
    [5t; cv-1b(1); 4315]   "

περιβόλαιον, ου, τό   {4316, n-2c}
that which is thrown around any one, *clothing, covering; a cloak,* Heb 1:12; *a covering,* 1 Cor 11:15*

περιβόλαιον   acc sg neut
    [Hb 1:12; n-2c; 4316]   περιβόλαιον
περιβολαίου   gen sg neut   [1C 11:15; n-2c; 4316]   "

περιδέω   {4317, cv-1d(2b)}
[-, -, -, περιδέδεμαι, -] pluperfect, περιεδέδετο (pass., 3 sg), *to bind round about;* pass. *to be bound around, be bound up,* John 11:44*

περιεβάλετε   aor act ind 2 pl
    [2t; cv-2d(1); 4314]   περιβάλλω
περιεβάλετο   aor mid ind 3 sg
    [2t; cv-2d(1); 4314]   "
περιεβάλομεν   aor act ind 1 pl
    [Mt 25:38; cv-2d(1); 4314]   "
περιέβαλον   aor act ind 3 pl
    [Jn 19:2; cv-2d(1); 4314]   "
περιεβλέπετο   imperf mid ind 3 sg
    [Mk 5:32; cv-1b(1); 4315]   περιβλέπω
περιεδέδετο   pluperf pass ind 3 sg
    [Jn 11:44; cv-1d(2b); 4317]   περιδέω
περιέδραμον   aor act ind 3 pl
    [Mk 6:55; cv-1b(2); 4366]   περιτρέχω
περιεζωσμέναι   perf pass ptcp nom pl fem
    [Lk 12:35; cv-3c(1); 4322]   περιζώννυμι
περιεζωσμένοι   perf pass ptcp nom pl masc
    [Rv 15:6; cv-3c(1); 4322]   "
περιεζωσμένον   perf pass ptcp acc sg masc
    [Rv 1:13; cv-3c(1); 4322]   "
περιέθηκαν   aor act ind 3 pl
    [Mt 27:28; cv-6a; 4363]   περιτίθημι
περιέθηκεν   aor act ind 3 sg   [2t; cv-6a; 4363]   "
περιέκρυβεν   imperf act ind 3 sg
    [Lk 1:24; cv-; 4332]   περικρύβω
περιέλαμψεν   aor act ind 3 sg
    [Lk 2:9; cv-1b(1); 4334]   περιλάμπω
περιελεῖν   aor act inf
    [Hb 10:11; cv-1d(2a); 4311]   περιαιρέω
περιελόντες   aor act ptcp nom pl masc
    [2t; cv-1d(2a); 4311]   "
περιεπάτει   imperf act ind 3 sg
    [7t; cv-1d(2a); 4344]   περιπατέω
περιεπάτεις   imperf act ind 2 sg
    [Jn 21:18; cv-1d(2a); 4344]   "
περιεπατήσαμεν   aor act ind 1 pl
    [2C 12:18; cv-1d(2a); 4344]   "
περιεπατήσατε   aor act ind 2 pl
    [2t; cv-1d(2a); 4344]   "
περιεπάτησεν   aor act ind 3 sg
    [3t; cv-1d(2a); 4344]   "
περιεπάτουν   imperf act ind 3 pl
    [Jn 6:66; cv-1d(2a); 4344]   "
περιέπειραν   aor act ind 3 pl
    [1Ti 6:10; cv-2d(3); 4345]   περιπείρω
περιέπεσεν   aor act ind 3 sg
    [Lk 10:30; cv-1b(3); 4346]   περιπίπτω
περιεποιήσατο   aor mid ind 3 sg
    [Ac 20:28; cv-1d(2a); 4347]   περιποιέω
περίεργα   acc pl neut
    [Ac 19:19; a-3a; 4319]   περίεργος

περιεργάζομαι   {4318, cv-2a(1)}
[-, -, -, -, -] *to do a thing with excessive* or *superfluous care; to be a busy-body,* 2 Thess 3:11*

περιεργαζομένους   pres mid ptcp acc pl masc
  [2Th 3:11; cv-2a(1); 4318]   περιεργάζομαι
περίεργοι   nom pl fem
  [1Ti 5:13; a-3a; 4319]   περίεργος

περίεργος, ον   {4319, a-3a}
  over careful; officious, a busy-body, 1 Tim 5:13; in
  N.T. περίεργα, *magic arts, sorcery,* Acts 19:19*

περιέρχομαι   {4320, cv-1b(2)}
  [-, περιῆλθον, -, -, -] *to go about, wander about,
  rove,* Acts 13:6 v.l.; 19:13; Heb 11:37; *to go about,
  visit* from house to house, 1 Tim 5:13; *to take a
  circuitous course,* Acts 28:13*

περιερχόμεναι   pres mid ptcp nom pl fem
  [1Ti 5:13; cv-1b(2); 4320]   περιέρχομαι
περιερχομένων   pres mid ptcp gen pl masc
  [Ac 19:13; cv-1b(2); 4320]   "
περιεσπᾶτο   imperf pass ind 3 sg
  [Lk 10:40; cv-1d(1b); 4352]   περισπάω
περιέστησαν   aor act ind 3 pl
  [Ac 25:7; cv-6a; 4325]   περιΐστημι
περιεστῶτα   perf act ptcp acc sg masc
  [Jn 11:42; cv-6a; 4325]   "
περιέσχεν   aor act ind 3 sg
  [Lk 5:9; cv-1b(2); 4321]   περιέχω
περιέτεμεν   aor act ind 3 sg
  [2t; cv-3a(1); 4362]   περιτέμνω
περιετμήθητε   aor pass ind 2 pl
  [Cl 2:11; cv-3a(1); 4362]   "
περιέχει   pres act ind 3 sg
  [1P 2:6; cv-1b(2); 4321]   περιέχω

περιέχω   {4321, cv-1b(2)}
  [-, περιέσχον, -, -, -] *to encompass, enclose; to
  embrace, contain,* as a writing, Acts 15:23 v.l.;
  23:25 v.l.; met. *to encompass, seize on* the mind,
  Luke 5:9; περιέχει, impers. *it is contained, it is
  among the contents* of a writing, 1 Peter 2:6*

περιζώννυμι   {4322, cv-3c(1)}
  [περιζώσω, περιέζωσα, -, περιέζωσμαι, -] also
  spelled περιζωννύω, *to bind around with a girdle,
  gird;* in N.T. mid. *to gird one's self* in preparation
  for bodily motion and exertion, Luke 12:37;
  17:8; Acts 12:8 v.l.; *to wear a girdle,* Rev 1:13; 15:6

περιζωννύω, see περιζώννυμι   {4323}

περιζωσάμενοι   aor mid ptcp nom pl masc
  [Ep 6:14; cv-3c(1); 4322]   περιζώννυμι
περιζωσάμενος   aor mid ptcp nom sg masc
  [Lk 17:8; cv-3c(1); 4322]   "
περιζώσεται   fut mid ind 3 sg
  [Lk 12:37; cv-3c(1); 4322]   "
περιῆγεν   imperf act ind 3 sg
  [3t; cv-1b(2); 4310]   περιάγω
περιῆλθον   aor act ind 3 pl
  [Hb 11:37; cv-1b(2); 4320]   περιέρχομαι
περιῃρεῖτο   imperf pass ind 3 sg
  [Ac 27:20; cv-1d(2a); 4311]   περιαιρέω
περιήστραψεν   aor act ind 3 sg
  [Ac 9:3; cv-4; 4313]   περιαστράπτω
περιθείς   aor act ptcp nom sg masc
  [2t; cv-6a; 4363]   περιτίθημι
περιθέντες   aor act ptcp nom pl masc
  [Jn 19:29; cv-6a; 4363]   "

περιθέσεως   gen sg fem
  [1P 3:3; n-3e(5b); 4324]   περίθεσις

περίθεσις, εως, ἡ   {4324, n-3e(5b)}
  a putting on, wearing of dress, etc., 1 Peter 3:3*

περιΐστασο   pres mid imperative 2 sg
  [2t; cv-6a; 4325]   περιΐστημι

περιΐστημι   {4325, cv-6a}
  [-, περιέστην, περιέστηκα, -, -] *to place around;*
  intrans. 2 aor. περιέστην, perf. part. περιεστώς,
  to stand around, John 11:42; Acts 25:7; mid. *to
  keep aloof from, avoid, shun,* 2 Tim 2:16; Titus 3:9*

περικάθαρμα, ατος, τό   {4326, n-3c(4)}
  pr. *filth;* met. *refuse, outcast,* 1 Cor 4:13*

περικαθάρματα   nom pl neut
  [1C 4:13; n-3c(4); 4326]   περικάθαρμα

περικαθίζω   {4327, cv-2a(1)}
  [-, -, -, -, -] *to sit around,* Luke 22:55 v.l.*

περικαλύπτειν   pres act inf
  [Mk 14:65; cv-4; 4328]   περικαλύπτω

περικαλύπτω   {4328, cv-4}
  [-, περιεκάλυψα, -, περικεκάλυμμαι, -] *to cover
  round about, cover over; to cover* the face, Mark
  14:65; *to blindfold,* Luke 22:64; pass. *to be
  overlaid,* Heb 9:4*

περικαλύψαντες   aor act ptcp nom pl masc
  [Lk 22:64; cv-4; 4328]   περικαλύπτω

περίκειμαι   {4329, cv-6b}
  [-, -, -, -, -] *to lie around, be surround,* Heb 12:1; *to
  be hung around,* Mark 9:42; Luke 17:2; *to have
  around one's self, to wear,* Acts 28:20; *to be in
  submission to,* Heb 5:2*

περίκειμαι   pres mid ind 1 sg
  [Ac 28:20; cv-; 4329]   περίκειμαι
περικείμενον   pres mid ptcp acc sg neut
  [Hb 12:1; cv-; 4329]   "
περίκειται   pres mid ind 3 sg [3t; cv-; 4329]   "
περικεκαλυμμένην   perf pass ptcp acc sg fem
  [Hb 9:4; cv-4; 4328]   περικαλύπτω

περικεφαλαία, ας, ἡ   {4330, n-1a}
  a helmet, Eph 6:17; 1 Thess 5:8*

περικεφαλαίαν   acc sg fem
  [2t; n-1a; 4330]   περικεφαλαία
περικρατεῖς   nom pl masc
  [Ac 27:16; a-4a; 4331]   περικρατής

περικρατής, ές   {4331, a-4a}
  overpowering; περικρατὴς γενέσθαι, *to become
  master of, to secure,* Acts 27:16*

περικρύβω   {4332, cv-1b(1)}
  [(περιέκρυβον), -, -, -, -, -] also spelled
  περικρύπτω, *to hide* or *keep from sight, to conceal
  by envelopment; to conceal,* Luke 1:24*

περικρύπτω, see περικρύβω

περικυκλόω   {4333, cv-1d(3)}
  [περικυκλώσω, -, -, -, -] *to encircle, surround,*
  Luke 19:43*

περικυκλώσουσιν   fut act ind 3 pl
[Lk 19:43; cv-1d(3); 4333]   περικυκλόω

περιλάμπω   {4334, cv-1b(1)}
[-, περιέλαμψα, -, -, -] *to shine around*, Luke 2:9;
Acts 26:13*

περιλάμψαν   aor act ptcp acc sg neut
[Ac 26:13; cv-1b(1); 4334]   περιλάμπω

περιλείπομαι   {4335, cv-1b(1)}
[-, -, -, -, -] *to leave remaining*; pass. *to remain,
survive*, 1 Thess 4:15, 17*

περιλειπόμενοι   pres pass ptcp nom pl masc
[2t; cv-1b(1); 4335]   περιλείπομαι

περίλυπον   acc sg masc
[Lk 18:24; a-3a; 4337]   περίλυπος

περίλυπος, ον   {4337, a-3a}
greatly grieved, exceedingly sorrowful, Matt 26:38;
Mark 14:34

περίλυπος   nom sg masc [2t; a-3a; 4337]   "
περίλυπος   nom sg fem [2t; a-3a; 4337]   "
περιμένειν   pres act inf
[Ac 1:4; cv-1c(2); 4338]   περιμένω

περιμένω   {4338, cv-1c(2)}
[-, περιέμεινα, -, -, -] *to await, wait for*, Acts 1:4;
10:24 v.l.

πέριξ   {4339, adverb}
neighboring, Acts 5:16*

πέριξ   adverb [Ac 5:16; adverb; 4339]   πέριξ

περιοικέω   {4340, cv-1d(2a)}
[-, -, -, -, -] *to dwell around*, or *in the vicinity; to be
a neighbor*, Luke 1:65*

περίοικοι   nom pl masc
[Lk 1:58; a-3a; 4341]   περίοικος

περίοικος, ον   {4341, a-3a}
one who dwells in the vicinity, a neighbor, Luke
1:58*

περιοικοῦντας   pres act ptcp acc pl masc
[Lk 1:65; cv-1d(2a); 4340]   περιοικέω
περιούσιον   acc sg masc
[Ti 2:14; a-3a; 4342]   περιούσιος

περιούσιος, ον   {4342, a-3a}
chosen; peculiar, special, Titus 2:14*

περιοχή, ῆς, ἡ   {4343, n-1b}
lit., *a compass, circumference, contents*; fig., *a
section, a portion* of Scripture, Acts 8:32*

περιοχή   nom sg fem [Ac 8:32; n-1b; 4343] περιοχή
περιπάτει   pres act imperative 2 sg
[7t; cv-1d(2a); 4344]   περιπατέω
περιπατεῖ   pres act ind 3 sg
[3t; cv-1d(2a); 4344]   "
περιπατεῖν   pres act inf [10t; cv-1d(2a); 4344] "
περιπατεῖς   pres act ind 2 sg
[2t; cv-1d(2a); 4344]   "
περιπατεῖτε   pres act imperative 2 pl
[6t; cv-1d(2a); 4344]   "
περιπατεῖτε   pres act ind 2 pl
[3t; cv-1d(2a); 4344]   "

περιπατείτω   pres act imperative 3 sg
[1C 7:17; cv-1d(2a); 4344]   "

περιπατέω   {4344, cv-1d(2a)}
[(περιεπάτουν), περιπατήσω, περιεπάτησα, -, -, -]
pluperfect, περι(ε)πεπατήκει (3 sg), *to walk, walk
about*, Matt 9:5; 11:5; 14:25 , 26, 29; *to rove, roam*,
1 Peter 5:8; with μετά, *to accompany, follow, have
intercourse with*, John 6:66; Rev 3:4; *to walk,
frequent* a locality, John 7:1; 11:54; from the
Hebrew, *to maintain a* certain *walk* of life and
conduct, Rom 6:4; 8:1

περιπατῇ   pres act subj 3 sg
[3t; cv-1d(2a); 4344]   "
περιπατῆσαι   aor act inf [2t; cv-1d(2a); 4344] "
περιπατήσῃ   aor act subj 3 sg
[Jn 8:12; cv-1d(2a); 4344]   "
περιπατήσουσιν   fut act ind 3 pl
[2t; cv-1d(2a); 4344]   "
περιπατήσωμεν   aor act subj 1 pl
[3t; cv-1d(2a); 4344]   "
περιπατῆτε   pres act subj 2 pl
[2t; cv-1d(2a); 4344]   "
περιπατοῦμεν   pres act ind 1 pl
[2C 5:7; cv-1d(2a); 4344]   "
περιπατοῦντα   pres act ptcp acc sg masc
[4t; cv-1d(2a); 4344]   "
περιπατοῦντα   pres act ptcp acc pl neut
[3J 4; cv-1d(2a); 4344]   "
περιπατοῦντας   pres act ptcp acc pl masc
[6t; cv-1d(2a); 4344]   "
περιπατοῦντες   pres act ptcp nom pl masc
[5t; cv-1d(2a); 4344]   "
περιπατοῦντι   pres act ptcp dat sg masc
[Jn 1:36; cv-1d(2a); 4344]   "
περιπατοῦντος   pres act ptcp gen sg masc
[2t; cv-1d(2a); 4344]   "
περιπατοῦσιν   pres act ind 3 pl
[4t; cv-1d(2a); 4344]   "
περιπατοῦσιν   pres act ptcp dat pl masc
[2t; cv-1d(2a); 4344]   "
περιπατῶμεν   pres act subj 1 pl
[3t; cv-1d(2a); 4344]   "
περιπατῶν   pres act ptcp nom sg masc
[6t; cv-1d(2a); 4344]   "

περιπείρω   {4345, cv-2d(3)}
[-, περιέπειρα, -, -, -] *to put on a spit, transfix*; met.
to pierce, wound deeply, 1 Tim 6:10*

περιπέσητε   aor act subj 2 pl
[Jm 1:2; cv-1b(3); 4346]   περιπίπτω
περιπεσόντες   aor act ptcp nom pl masc
[Ac 27:41; cv-1b(3); 4346]   "

περιπίπτω   {4346, cv-1b(3)}
[-, περιέπεσον, -, -, -] *to fall around* or *upon, to fall
in with*, Luke 10:30; *to fall into, light upon*, Acts
27:41; *to be involved in*, James 1:2*

περιποιέω   {4347, cv-1d(2a)}
[περιποιήσω, περιεποίησα, -, -, -] *to cause to
remain over and above, to reserve, save*, Luke
17:33; mid. *to acquire, gain, earn*, 1 Tim 3:13; *to
purchase*, Acts 20:28*

περιποιήσασθαι   aor mid inf
   [Lk 17:33; cv-1d(2a); 4347]   περιποιέω

περιποιήσεως   gen sg fem
   [Ep 1:14; n-3e(5b); 4348]   περιποίησις

περιποίησιν   acc sg fem   [4t; n-3e(5b); 4348]   "

περιποίησις, εως, ἡ   {4348, n-3e(5b)}
   a laying up, keeping; an acquiring or *obtaining,
   acquisition,* 1 Thess 5:9; 2 Thess 2:14; *a saving,
   preservation,* Heb 10:39; *a peculiar possession,
   specialty,* Eph 1:14; 1 Pet 2:9*

περιποιοῦνται   pres mid ind 3 pl
   [1Ti 3:13; cv-1d(2a); 4347]   περιποιέω

περιρήγνυμι   {4351, cv-3c(2)}
   [-, περιέρηξα, -, -, -] also spelled περιρρήγνυμι, *to
   break* or *tear all around; to strip off,* Acts 16:22*

περιρήξαντες   aor act ptcp nom pl masc
   [Ac 16:22; cv-3c(2); 4351]   περιρήγνυμι

περισπάω   {4352, cv-1d(1b)}
   [(περιέσπων), -, -, -, -, -] *to draw off from around;
   to wheel about; to distract;* pass. *to be distracted,
   over-busied,* Luke 10:40*

περισσεία, ας, ἡ   {4353, n-1a}
   superabundance, Rom 5:17; 2 Cor 8:2; 10:15;
   James 1:21*

περισσεία   nom sg fem
   [2C 8:2; n-1a; 4353]   περισσεία

περισσείαν   acc sg fem   [3t; n-1a; 4353]   "

περισσεύει   pres act ind 3 sg
   [3t; v-1a(6); 4355]   περισσεύω

περισσεύειν   pres act inf   [5t; v-1a(6); 4355]   "

περισσεύετε   pres act ind 2 pl
   [2C 8:7; v-1a(6); 4355]   "

περισσεύῃ   pres act subj 3 sg
   [2t; v-1a(6); 4355]   "

περισσεύητε   pres act subj 2 pl
   [4t; v-1a(6); 4355]   "

περισσευθήσεται   fut pass ind 3 sg
   [2t; v-1a(6); 4355]   "

περίσσευμα, ατος, τό   {4354, n-3c(4)}
   more than enough, residue over and above, Mark
   8:8; *abundance, exuberance,* Matt 12:34; Luke
   6:45; *superabundance, affluence,* 2 Cor 8:14*

περίσσευμα   nom sg neut
   [2t; n-3c(4); 4354]   περίσσευμα

περισσεύματα   acc pl neut   [Mk 8:8; n-3c(4); 4354]   "

περισσεύματος   gen sg neut   [2t; n-3c(4); 4354]   "

περισσεύομεν   pres act ind 1 pl
   [1C 8:8; v-1a(6); 4355]   περισσεύω

περισσεῦον   pres act ptcp acc sg neut
   [2t; v-1a(6); 4355]   "

περισσεύονται   pres mid ind 3 pl
   [Lk 15:17; v-1a(6); 4355]   "

περισσεύοντες   pres act ptcp nom pl masc
   [2t; v-1a(6); 4355]   "

περισσεύοντος   pres act ptcp gen sg neut
   [2t; v-1a(6); 4355]   "

περισσεύουσα   pres act ptcp nom sg fem
   [2C 9:12; v-1a(6); 4355]   "

περισσεῦσαι   aor act inf   [2C 9:8; v-1a(6); 4355]   "

περισσεύσαι   aor act opt 3 sg
   [1Th 3:12; v-1a(6); 4355]   "

περισσεῦσαν   aor act ptcp nom sg neut
   [Lk 9:17; v-1a(6); 4355]   "

περισσεύσαντα   aor act ptcp acc pl neut
   [Jn 6:12; v-1a(6); 4355]   "

περισσεύσῃ   aor act subj 3 sg
   [2t; v-1a(6); 4355]   "

περισσεύω   {4355, v-1a(6)}
   [(ἐπερίσσευον), περισσεύσω, ἐπερίσσευσα, -, -,
   ἐπερισσεύθην] *to be over and above, to be
   superfluous,* Matt 14:20; Mark 12:44; Luke 21:4;
   to exist in full quantity, to abound, be abundant,
   Rom 5:15; 2 Cor 1:5; *to increase, be augmented,*
   Acts 16:5; *to be advanced, be rendered more
   prominent,* Rom 3:7; of persons, *to be abundantly
   gifted, richly furnished, abound,* Luke 15:17; Rom
   15:13; 1 Cor 14:12; 2 Cor 8:7; *to be possessed of a
   full sufficiency,* Phil 4:12, 18; *to abound in*
   performance, 1 Cor 15:58; *to be a gainer,* 1 Cor
   8:8; in N.T. trans., *to cause to be abundant,* 2 Cor
   4:15; 9:8; Eph 1:8; *to cause to be abundantly
   furnished, cause to abound,* 1 Thess 3:12; pass. *to
   be gifted with abundance,* Matt 13:12; 25:29

περισσεύω   pres act ind 1 sg
   [Pp 4:18; v-1a(6); 4355]   "

περισσόν   nom sg neut
   [3t; a-1a(2a); 4356]   περισσός

περισσόν   acc sg neut   [Mt 5:47; a-1a(2a); 4356]   "

περισσόν   acc sg neut, can function
   adverbially   [Jn 10:10; a-1a(2a); 4356]   "

περισσός, ή, όν   {4356, a-1a(2a)}
   over and above, Matt 5:37; *superfluous,* 2 Cor 9:1;
   extraordinary, Matt 5:47; compar. *more, greater,*
   Matt 11:9; 23:14; *excessive,* 2 Cor 2:7;
   adverbially, περισσόν, *in full abundance,* John
   10:10; περισσότερον, and ἐκ περισσοῦ,
   exceedingly, vehemently, Mark 6:51; 7:36; 1 Cor
   15:10; Eph 3:20; τὸ περισσόν, *pre-eminence,
   advantage,* Rom 3:1

περισσοτέρα   dat sg fem comparative
   [2C 2:7; a-1a(1); 4358]   περισσότερος

περισσοτέραν   acc sg fem comparative
   [3t; a-1a(1); 4358]   "

περισσότερον   nom sg neut comparative
   [Mk 12:33; a-1a(1); 4358]   "

περισσότερον   acc sg neut comparative
   [4t; a-1a(1); 4358]   "

περισσότερον   adverb-comparative
   [7t; a-1a(1); 4358]   "

περισσότερος, τέρα, τερον   {4358, a-1a(1)}
   comparative adj. from περισσός, *greater, more,*
   Mark 12:40; Luke 20:47; *even more,* Luke 12:48;
   1 Cor 15:10; *even more, so much more,* Mark 7:36

περισσοτέρως   {4359, adverb}
   *more, more abundantly, more earnestly, more
   vehemently,* Mark 15:14 v.l.; 2 Cor 7:13;
   exceedingly, Gal 1:14

περισσοτέρως   adverb-comparative
   [12t; adverb; 4359]   περισσοτέρως

περισσοῦ   gen sg neut
  [Mk 6:51; a-1a(2a); 4356]   περισσός

περισσῶς   {4360, adverb}
  much, abundantly, vehemently, Acts 26:11; *more,
  more abundantly*, Matt 27:23; Mark 10:26; 15:14*

περισσῶς   adverb [4t; adverb; 4360]   περισσῶς

περιστερά, ας, ἡ   {4361, n-1a}
  a dove, pigeon, Matt 3:16; 10:16

περιστεραί   nom pl fem
  [Mt 10:16; n-1a; 4361]   περιστερά
περιστεράν   acc sg fem [4t; n-1a; 4361]   "
περιστεράς   acc pl fem [4t; n-1a; 4361]   "
περιστερῶν   gen pl fem [Lk 2:24; n-1a; 4361]   "
περιτεμεῖν   aor act inf
  [2t; cv-3a(1); 4362]   περιτέμνω
περιτέμνειν   pres act inf [2t; cv-3a(1); 4362] "
περιτέμνεσθαι   pres pass inf
  [2t; cv-3a(1); 4362]   "
περιτεμνέσθω   pres pass imperative 3 sg
  [1C 7:18; cv-3a(1); 4362]   "
περιτέμνετε   pres act ind 2 pl
  [Jn 7:22; cv-3a(1); 4362]   "
περιτέμνησθε   pres pass subj 2 pl
  [Ga 5:2; cv-3a(1); 4362]   "
περιτεμνόμενοι   pres pass ptcp nom pl masc
  [Ga 6:13; cv-3a(1); 4362]   "
περιτεμνομένῳ   pres pass ptcp dat sg masc
  [Ga 5:3; cv-3a(1); 4362]   "

περιτέμνω   {4362, cv-3a(1)}
  [-, περιέτεμον, -, περιτέτμημαι, περιετμήθην] *to
  cut around; to circumcise, remove the prepuce*,
  Luke 1:59; 2:21; met. Col 2:11; mid. *to submit to
  circumcision*, Acts 15:1

περιτετμημένος   perf pass ptcp nom sg masc
  [1C 7:18; cv-3a(1); 4362]   "
περιτιθέασιν   pres act ind 3 pl
  [Mk 15:17; cv-6a; 4363]   περιτίθημι
περιτίθεμεν   pres act ind 1 pl
  [1C 12:23; cv-6a; 4363]   "

περιτίθημι   {4363, cv-6a}
  [(περιετίθην), -, περιέθηκα, -, -, περιετέθην] *to
  place around, put about* or *around*, Matt 21:33;
  27:28; met. *to attach, bestow*, 1 Cor 12:23

περιτιμηθῆναι   aor pass inf
  [Ga 2:3; cv-3a(1); 4362]   περιτέμνω
περιτμηθῆτε   aor pass subj 2 pl
  [Ac 15:1; cv-3a(1); 4362]   "

περιτομή, ῆς, ἡ   {4364, n-1b}
  circumcision, the act or *custom of circumcision*,
  John 7:22, 23; Acts 7:8; *the state of being
  circumcised, the being circumcised*, Rom 2:25, 26,
  27; 4:10; meton. *the circumcision, those who are
  circumcised*, Rom 3:30; 4:9 met. *spiritual
  circumcision* of the heart and affection, Rom
  2:29; Col 2:11; meton. *persons* spiritually
  circumcised, Phil 3:3

περιτομή   nom sg fem [9t; n-1b; 4364]   περιτομή
περιτομῇ   dat sg fem [5t; n-1b; 4364]   "
περιτομήν   acc sg fem [7t; n-1b; 4364]   "

περιτομῆς   gen sg fem [15t; n-1b; 4364]   "
περιτρέπει   pres act ind 3 sg
  [Ac 26:24; cv-1b(1); 4365]   περιτρέπω

περιτρέπω   {4365, cv-1b(1)}
  [-, -, -, -, -] *to turn about; to bring round* into any
  state, Acts 26:24*

περιτρέχω   {4366, cv-1b(2)}
  [(περιέτρεχον), -, περιέδραμον, -, -, -] *to run about,
  run up and down*, Mark 6:55*

περιφέρειν   pres act inf
  [Mk 6:55; cv-1c(1); 4367]   περιφέρω
περιφερόμενοι   pres pass ptcp nom pl masc
  [Ep 4:14; cv-1c(1); 4367]   "
περιφέροντες   pres act ptcp nom pl masc
  [2C 4:10; cv-1c(1); 4367]   "

περιφέρω   {4367, cv-1c(1)}
  [-, -, -, -, -] *to bear* or *carry about*, Mark 6:55; 2
  Cor 4:10; pass. *to be borne about hither and thither,
  to be whirled about, driven to and fro*, Eph 4:14;
  Heb 13:9 v.l.*

περιφρονείτω   pres act imperative 3 sg
  [Ti 2:15; cv-1d(2a); 4368]   περιφρονέω

περιφρονέω   {4368, cv-1d(2a)}
  [-, -, -, -, -] *to contemplate, reflect on; to despise,
  disregard*, Titus 2:15*

περίχωρον   acc sg fem [4t; a-3a; 4369]   περίχωρος

περίχωρος, ον   {4369, a-3a}
  neighboring; ἡ περίχωρος, sc. γῆ, *an adjacent
  region, country round about*, Matt 14:35; Mark
  1:28; meton. *inhabitants of the region round about*,
  Matt 3:5

περίχωρος   nom sg fem [Mt 3:5; a-3a; 4369]   "
περιχώρου   gen sg fem [3t; a-3a; 4369]   "
περιχώρῳ   dat sg fem [Lk 7:17; a-3a; 4369]   "

περίψημα, ατος, τό   {4370, n-3c(4)}
  filth which is wiped off; met. 1 Cor 4:13*

περίψημα   nom sg neut
  [1C 4:13; n-3c(4); 4370]   περίψημα
περπερεύεται   pres mid ind 3 sg
  [1C 13:4; v-1a(6); 4371]   περπερεύομαι

περπερεύομαι   {4371, v-1a(6)}
  [-, -, -, -, -] *to vaunt one's self*, 1 Cor 13:4*

Περσίδα   acc sg fem
  [Rm 16:12; n-3c(2); 4372]   Περσίς

Περσίς, ίδος, ἡ   {4372, n-3c(2)}
  Persis, pr. name, Rom 16:12*

πέρυσι   {4373, adverb}
  last year, a year ago, 2 Cor 8:10; 9:2*

πέρυσι   adverb [2t; adverb; 4373]   πέρυσι
πεσεῖν   aor act inf
  [Lk 16:17; v-1b(3); 4406]   πίπτω
πεσεῖται   fut mid ind 3 sg [2t; v-1b(3); 4406] "
πέσετε   aor act imperative 2 pl
  [2t; v-1b(3); 4406]   "
πέσῃ   aor act subj 3 sg [5t; v-1b(3); 4406]   "
πέσητε   aor act subj 2 pl
  [Jm 5:12; v-1b(3); 4406]   "

πεσόν   aor act ptcp nom sg neut
    [Lk 8:14; v-1b(3); 4406]   "

πεσόντα   aor act ptcp acc sg masc
    [Lk 10:18; v-1b(3); 4406]   "

πεσόντας   aor act ptcp acc pl masc
    [Rm 11:22; v-1b(3); 4406]   "

πεσόντες   aor act ptcp nom pl masc
    [Mt 2:11; v-1b(3); 4406]   "

πεσοῦνται   fut mid ind 3 pl [4t; v-1b(3); 4406]   "

πεσών   aor act ptcp nom sg masc
    [13t; v-1b(3); 4406]   "

πέσωσιν   aor act subj 3 pl
    [Rm 11:11; v-1b(3); 4406]   "

πετάομαι, see πέτομαι

πετεινά   nom pl neut [7t; n-2c; 4374]   πετεινόν
πετεινά   acc pl neut [4t; n-2c; 4374]   "

πετεινόν, οῦ, τό   {4374, n-2c}
    a bird, fowl, Matt 6:26; 8:20

πετεινῶν   gen pl neut [3t; n-2c; 4374]   "
πέτηται   pres mid subj 3 sg
    [Rv 12:14; v-1b(3); 4375]   πέτομαι

πέτομαι   {4375, v-1b(3)}
    [-, -, -, -, -] also spelled πετάομαι, *to fly*, Rev 4:7;
    8:13; 12:14; 14:6; 19:17*

πετομένοις   pres mid ptcp dat pl neut
    [Rv 19:17; v-1b(3); 4375]   "
πετόμενον   pres mid ptcp acc sg masc
    [Rv 14:6; v-1b(3); 4375]   "
πετομένου   pres mid ptcp gen sg masc
    [Rv 8:13; v-1b(3); 4375]   "
πετομένῳ   pres mid ptcp dat sg masc
    [Rv 4:7; v-1b(3); 4375]   "

πέτρα, ας, ἡ   {4376, n-1a}
    a rock, Matt 7:24, 25; met. Rom 9:33; 1 Peter 2:8;
    crags, clefts, Rev 6:15, 16; *stony ground*, Luke 8:6,
    13

πέτρα   nom sg fem [2t; n-1a; 4376]   πέτρα
πέτρᾳ   dat sg fem [2t; n-1a; 4376]   "
πέτραι   nom pl fem [Mt 27:51; n-1a; 4376]   "
πέτραις   dat pl fem [Rv 6:16; n-1a; 4376]   "
πέτραν   acc sg fem [5t; n-1a; 4376]   "
πέτρας   gen sg fem [3t; n-1a; 4376]   "
πέτρας   acc pl fem [Rv 6:15; n-1a; 4376]   "
Πέτρε   voc sg masc [3t; n-2a; 4377]   Πέτρος
Πέτρον   acc sg masc [26t; n-2a; 4377]   "

Πέτρος, ου, ὁ   {4377, n-2a}
    a stone; in N.T. the Greek rendering of the
    surname Cephas, given to the Apostle Simon,
    and having, therefore, the same sense as πέτρα,
    Peter, Matt 4:18; 8:14

Πέτρος   nom sg masc [100t; n-2a; 4377]   "
Πέτρου   gen sg masc [12t; n-2a; 4377]   "
Πέτρῳ   dat sg masc [15t; n-2a; 4377]   "
πετρῶδες   acc sg neut
    [Mk 4:5; a-4a; 4378]   πετρῶδης
πετρώδη   acc pl neut [3t; a-4a; 4378]   "

πετρώδης, ες   {4378, a-4a}
    like rock; stony, rocky, Matt 13:5, 20; Mark 4:5, 16*

πεφανερώμεθα   perf pass ind 1 pl
    [2C 5:11; v-1d(3); 5746]   φανερόω
πεφανερῶσθαι   perf pass inf [2t; v-1d(3); 5746]   "
πεφανέρωται   perf pass ind 3 sg
    [2t; v-1d(3); 5746]   "
πεφιλήκατε   perf act ind 2 pl
    [Jn 16:27; v-1d(2a); 5797]   φιλέω
πεφίμωσο   perf pass imperative 2 sg
    [Mk 4:39; v-1d(3); 5821]   φιμόω
πεφορτισμένοι   perf pass ptcp voc pl masc
    [Mt 11:28; v-2a(1); 5844]   φορτίζω
πεφυσιωμένοι   perf pass ptcp nom pl masc
    [1C 5:2; v-1d(3); 5881]   φυσιόω
πεφυσιωμένων   perf pass ptcp gen pl masc
    [1C 4:19; v-1d(3); 5881]   "
πεφυτευμένην   perf pass ptcp acc sg fem
    [Lk 13:6; v-1a(6); 5885]   φυτεύω
πεφωτισμένους   perf pass ptcp acc pl masc
    [Ep 1:18; v-2a(1); 5894]   φωτίζω
πηγαί   nom pl fem [2P 2:17; n-1b; 4380]   πηγή

πήγανον, ου, τό   {4379, n-2c}
    rue, a plant, *ruta graveolens* of Linnaeus, Luke
    11:42*

πήγανον   acc sg neut
    [Lk 11:42; n-2c; 4379]   πήγανον
πηγάς   acc pl fem [4t; n-1b; 4380]   πηγή

πηγή, ῆς, ἡ   {4380, n-1b}
    a source, spring, fountain, James 3:11, 12; *a well*,
    John 4:6; *an issue, flux, flow*, Mark 5:29; met.
    John 4:14

πηγή   nom sg fem [4t; n-1b; 4380]   "
πηγῇ   dat sg fem [Jn 4:6; n-1b; 4380]   "
πηγῆς   gen sg fem [Rv 21:6; n-1b; 4380]   "

πήγνυμι   {4381, v-3c(2)}
    [-, ἔπηξα, -, -, -] *to fasten; to pitch* a tent, Heb 8:2*

πηδάλιον, ου, τό   {4382, n-2c}
    a rudder, Acts 27:40; James 3:4*

πηδαλίου   gen sg neut
    [Jm 3:4; n-2c; 4382]   πηδάλιον
πηδαλίων   gen pl neut [Ac 27:40; n-2c; 4382]   "
πηλίκοις   dat pl neut
    [Ga 6:11; a-1a(2a); 4383]   πηλίκος

πηλίκος, η, ον   {4383, a-1a(2a)}
    how large, Gal 6:11; *how great* in dignity, Heb
    7:4*

πηλίκος   nom sg masc [Hb 7:4; a-1a(2a); 4383]   "
πηλόν   acc sg masc [5t; n-2a; 4384]   πηλός

πηλός, οῦ, ὁ   {4384, n-2a}
    moist earth, mud, slime, John 9:6, 11, 14, 15; *clay*,
    potter's *clay*, Rom 9:21*

πηλοῦ   gen sg masc [Rm 9:21; n-2a; 4384]   "

πήρα, ας, ἡ   {4385, n-1a}
    a leather bag or *sack* for provisions, *wallet*, Matt
    10:10; Mark 6:8

πήραν   acc sg fem [5t; n-1a; 4385]   πήρα
πήρας   gen sg fem [Lk 22:35; n-1a; 4385]   "

πηρόω   {4386, v-1d(3)}
[-, -, -, -, -] *to disable, maim,* occurs in N.T. only
as v.l. for πωρόω, Mark 8:17; John 12:20; Acts 5:3;
Rom 11:7*

πήρωσις, εως, ἡ   {4387, n-3e(5b)}
nearsightedness, blindness, used figuratively at
Mark 3:5 v.l.*

πῆχυν   acc sg masc [2t; n-3e(1); 4388]   πῆχυς

πῆχυς, εως, ὁ   {4388, n-3e(1)}
pr. *cubitus, the forearm;* hence, *a cubit,* a measure
of length, equal to the distance from the elbow
to the extremity of the little finger, usually
considered as equivalent to a foot and one half,
or 17 inches and one half, John 21:8; Rev 21:17;
met. of time, *a span,* Matt 6:27; Luke 12:25*

πηχῶν   gen pl masc [2t; n-3e(1); 4388]   "

πιάζω   {4389, v-2a(1)}
[-, ἐπίασα, -, -, ἐπιάσθην] *to press;* in N.T. *to take*
or *lay hold of,* Acts 3:7; *to take, catch* fish, etc.,
John 21:3, 10; Rev 19:20; *to take, seize, apprehend,
arrest,* John 7:30, 32, 44

πιάσαι   aor act inf [4t; v-2a(1); 4389]   πιάζω
πιάσας   aor act ptcp nom sg masc
  [2t; v-2a(1); 4389]   "
πιάσωσιν   aor act subj 3 pl [2t; v-2a(1); 4389]   "
πίε   aor act imperative 2 sg
  [Lk 12:19; v-3a(1); 4403]   πίνω

πιέζω   {4390, v-2a(1)}
[-, -, -, πεπίεσμαι, -] *to press, to press* or *squeeze
down, make compact by pressure,* Luke 6:38*

πιεῖν   aor act inf [8t; v-3a(1); 4403]   "
πίεσαι   fut mid ind 2 sg [Lk 17:8; v-3a(1); 4403] "
πίεσθε   fut mid ind 2 pl [2t; v-3a(1); 4403]   "
πίεται   fut mid ind 3 sg
  [Rv 14:10; v-3a(1); 4403]   "
πίετε   aor act imperative 2 pl
  [Mt 26:27; v-3a(1); 4403]   "
πίῃ   aor act subj 3 sg [2t; v-3a(1); 4403]   "
πίητε   aor act subj 2 pl [3t; v-3a(1); 4403]   "

πιθανολογία, ας, ἡ   {4391, n-1a}
persuasive speech, plausible discourse, Col 2:4*

πιθανολογίᾳ   dat sg fem
  [Cl 2:4; n-1a; 4391]   πιθανολογία

πιθός, see πειθός   {4392}

πικραίνεσθε   pres pass imperative 2 pl
  [Cl 3:19; v-2d(4); 4393]   πικραίνω

πικραίνω   {4393, v-2d(4)}
[πικρανῶ, ἐπίκρανα, -, -, ἐπικράνθην] *to embitter,
render bitter,* Rev 10:9; pass. *to be embittered, be
made bitter,* Rev 8:11; 10:10; met. pass. *to be
embittered, to grow angry, harsh,* Col 3:19*

πικρανεῖ   fut act ind 3 sg
  [Rv 10:9; v-2d(4); 4393]   "

πικρία, ας, ἡ   {4394, n-1a}
bitterness, Acts 8:23; Heb 12:15; met. *bitterness*
of spirit and language, *harshness,* Rom 3:14;
Eph 4:31*

πικρία   nom sg fem [Ep 4:31; n-1a; 4394]   πικρία
πικρίας   gen sg fem [3t; n-1a; 4394]   "
πικρόν   acc sg masc
  [Jm 3:14; a-1a(1); 4395]   πικρός
πικρόν   acc sg neut [Jm 3:11; a-1a(1); 4395]   "

πικρός, ά, όν   {4395, a-1a(1)}
bitter, James 3:11; met. *bitter, harsh,* James 3:14*

πικρῶς   {4396, adverb}
bitterly, Matt 26:75; Luke 22:62*

πικρῶς   adverb [2t; adverb; 4396]   πικρῶς
Πιλᾶτον   acc sg masc [7t; n-2a; 4397]   Πιλᾶτος

Πιλᾶτος, ου, ὁ   {4397, n-2a}
Pilate, pr. name

Πιλᾶτος   nom sg masc [39t; n-2a; 4397]   "
Πιλάτου   gen sg masc [3t; n-2a; 4397]   "
Πιλάτῳ   dat sg masc [6t; n-2a; 4397]   "

πίμπλημι   {4398, v-6a}
[-, ἔπλησα, -, πέπλησμαι, ἐπλήσθην] *to fill,* Matt
27:48; pass. *to be filled* mentally, *be under full
influence,* Luke 1:15; 4:28; *to be fulfilled,* Luke
21:22; of stated time, *to be brought to a close,
arrive at its close,* Luke 1:23, 57; 2:6, 21, 22

πίμπρασθαι   pres pass inf
  [Ac 28:6; v-6a; 4399]   πίμπρημι

πίμπρημι   {4399, v-6a}
[-, ἔπρησα, -, -, ἐπρήσθην] *to set on fire, burn,
inflame;* in N.T. pass., *to swell from inflamation,*
Acts 28:6*

πίνακι   dat sg masc [4t; n-3b(1); 4402]   πίναξ

πινακίδιον, ου, τό   {4400, n-2c}
a small tablet for writing, Luke 1:63*

πινακίδιον   acc sg neut
  [Lk 1:63; n-2c; 4400]   πινακίδιον

πινακίς, ίδος, ἡ   {4401, n-3c(2)}
small writing tablet made of wood, Luke 1:63
v.l.*

πίνακος   gen sg masc
  [Lk 11:39; n-3b(1); 4402]   πίναξ

πίναξ, ακός, ἡ   {4402, n-3b(1)}
pr. *a board* or *plank;* in N.T. *a plate, platter, dish* on
which food was served, Mark 14:8, 11

πίνει   pres act ind 3 sg
  [1C 11:29; v-3a(1); 4403]   πίνω
πίνειν   pres act inf [4t; v-3a(1); 4403]   "
πίνετε   pres act ind 2 pl [2t; v-3a(1); 4403]   "
πινέτω   pres act imperative 3 sg
  [2t; v-3a(1); 4403]   "
πίνῃ   pres act subj 3 sg [2t; v-3a(1); 4403]   "
πίνητε   pres act subj 2 pl [3t; v-3a(1); 4403]   "
πίνοντες   pres act ptcp nom pl masc
  [2t; v-3a(1); 4403]   "
πίνουσιν   pres act ind 3 pl
  [Lk 5:33; v-3a(1); 4403]   "

πίνω   {4403, v-3a(1)}
[(ἔπινον), πίομαι, ἔπιον, πέπωκα, -, ἐπόθην] *to
drink,* Matt 6:25, 31; 26:27, 29, et al. freq.; trop.
of the earth, *to drink in, imbibe,* Heb 6:7

πίνω   pres act ind 1 sg   [2t; v-3a(1); 4403]   "
πίνω   pres act subj 1 sg   [2t; v-3a(1); 4403]   "
πίνων   pres act ptcp nom sg masc
         [8t; v-3a(1); 4403]   "

πιότης, ητος, ἡ   {4404, n-3c(1)}
         fatness, richness, Rom 11:17*

πιότητος   gen sg fem
         [Rm 11:17; n-3c(1); 4404]   πιότης
πιοῦσα   aor act ptcp nom sg fem
         [Hb 6:7; v-3a(1); 4403]   πίνω
πιπρασκομένων   pres pass ptcp gen pl neut
         [Ac 4:34; v-5a; 4405]   πιπράσκω

πιπράσκω   {4405, v-5a}
         [(ἐπίπρασκον), -, -, πέπρακα, πέπραμαι, ἐπράθην]
         to sell, Matt 13:46; 18:25; met. with ὑπό, pass. *to
         be sold under, to be a slave to, be devoted to,* Rom
         7:14

πίπτει   pres act ind 3 sg
         [5t; v-1b(3); 4406]   πίπτω
πίπτοντες   pres act ptcp nom pl masc
         [Mk 13:25; v-1b(3); 4406]   "
πιπτόντων   pres act ptcp gen pl neut
         [2t; v-1b(3); 4406]   "

πίπτω   {4406, v-1b(3)}
         [(ἔπιπτον), πεσοῦμαι, ἔπεσον or ἔπεσα, πέπτωκα,
         -, -] *to fall,* Matt 15:27; Luke 10:18; *to fall, fall
         prostrate, fall down,* Matt 17:6; 18:29; Luke 17:16;
         to fall down dead, Luke 21:24; *to fall, fall in ruins,*
         Matt 7:25, 27; Luke 11:17; met. *to fall, come by
         chance,* as a lot, Acts 1:26; *to fall, to fail, become
         null and void, fall to the ground,* Luke 16:17; *to fall*
         into a worse state, Rev 2:5; *to come to ruin,* Rom
         11:11; Heb 4:11; *to fall* into sin, Rom 11:22; 1 Cor
         10:2; *to fall* in judgment, by condemnation, Rev
         14:8; *to fall* upon, *seize,* Rev 11:11; *to light* upon,
         Rev 7:16; *to fall under, incur,* James 5:12

Πισιδία, ας, ἡ   {4407, n-1a}
         Pisidia, a country of Asia Minor, Acts 14:24;
         13:14 v.l.*

Πισιδίαν   acc sg fem   [2t; n-1a; 4407]   Πισιδία

Πισίδιος, ία, ιον   {4408, a-1a(1)}
         Pisidian, Acts 13:14*

πιστά   acc pl neut   [2t; a-1a(2a); 4412]   πιστός
πιστάς   acc pl fem   [1Ti 3:11; a-1a(2a); 4412]   "
πιστέ   voc sg masc   [2t; a-1a(2a); 4412]   "
πίστει   dat sg fem   [58t; n-3e(5b); 4411]   πίστις
πίστευε   pres act imperative 2 sg
         [2t; v-1a(6); 4409]   πιστεύω
πιστεύει   pres act ind 3 sg   [3t; v-1a(6); 4409]   "
πιστεύειν   pres act inf   [5t; v-1a(6); 4409]   "
πιστεύεις   pres act ind 2 sg   [7t; v-1a(6); 4409]   "
πιστεύεται   pres pass ind 3 sg
         [Rm 10:10; v-1a(6); 4409]   "
πιστεύετε   pres act imperative 2 pl
         [10t; v-1a(6); 4409]   "
πιστεύετε   pres act ind 2 pl   [11t; v-1a(6); 4409]   "
πιστεύῃ   pres act subj 3 sg   [2t; v-1a(6); 4409]   "
πιστεύητε   pres act subj 2 pl   [2t; v-1a(6); 4409]   "
πιστευθῆναι   aor pass inf
         [1Th 2:4; v-1a(6); 4409]   "

πιστεύομεν   pres act ind 1 pl   [6t; v-1a(6); 4409]   "
πιστεύοντα   pres act ptcp acc sg masc
         [Ac 10:43; v-1a(6); 4409]
πιστεύοντας   pres act ptcp acc pl masc
         [4t; v-1a(6); 4409]   "
πιστεύοντες   pres act ptcp nom pl masc
         [7t; v-1a(6); 4409]   "
πιστεύοντι   pres act ptcp dat sg masc
         [4t; v-1a(6); 4409]   "
πιστευόντων   pres act ptcp gen pl masc
         [4t; v-1a(6); 4409]   "
πιστεύουσιν   pres act ind 3 pl
         [4t; v-1a(6); 4409]   "
πιστεύουσιν   pres act ptcp dat pl masc
         [10t; v-1a(6); 4409]   "
πιστεῦσαι   aor act inf   [6t; v-1a(6); 4409]   "
πιστεύσαντας   aor act ptcp acc pl masc
         [Jd 5; v-1a(6); 4409]   "
πιστεύσαντες   aor act ptcp nom pl masc
         [7t; v-1a(6); 4409]   "
πιστευσάντων   aor act ptcp gen pl masc
         [Ac 4:32; v-1a(6); 4409]   "
πιστεύσας   aor act ptcp nom sg masc
         [2t; v-1a(6); 4409]   "
πιστεύσασα   aor act ptcp nom sg fem
         [Lk 1:45; v-1a(6); 4409]   "
πιστεύσασιν   aor act ptcp dat pl masc
         [3t; v-1a(6); 4409]   "
πιστεύσει   fut act ind 3 sg
         [Lk 16:11; v-1a(6); 4409]   "
πιστεύσετε   fut act ind 2 pl   [2t; v-1a(6); 4409]   "
πιστεύσῃς   aor act subj 2 sg   [2t; v-1a(6); 4409]   "
πιστεύσητε   aor act subj 2 pl
         [11t; v-1a(6); 4409]   "
πιστεύσομεν   fut act ind 1 pl
         [Mt 27:42; v-1a(6); 4409]   "
πίστευσον   aor act imperative 2 sg
         [2t; v-1a(6); 4409]   "
πιστεύσουσιν   fut act ind 3 pl
         [Jn 11:48; v-1a(6); 4409]   "
πιστεύσω   aor act subj 1 sg   [2t; v-1a(6); 4409]   "
πιστεύσωμεν   aor act subj 1 pl
         [3t; v-1a(6); 4409]   "
πιστεύσωσιν   aor act subj 3 pl
         [4t; v-1a(6); 4409]   "

πιστεύω   {4409, v-1a(6)}
         [(ἐπίστευον), πιστεύσω, ἐπίστευσα, πεπίστευκα,
         πεπίστευμαι, ἐπιστεύθην] pluperfect,
         πεπιστεύκειν, *to believe, give credit to* , Mark 1:15;
         16:13; Luke 24:25; intrans. *to believe, have a
         mental persuasion,* Matt 8:13; 9:28; James 2:19; *to
         believe, be of opinion,* Rom 14:2; in N.T. πιστεύειν
         ἐν, εἰς, ἐπί, *to believe in* or *on,* Matt 18:6; 27:42;
         John 3:15, 16, 18; absol. *to believe, be a believer* in
         the religion of Christ, Acts 2:44; 4:4, 32; 13:48;
         trans. *to intrust, commit to the charge* or *power of,*
         Luke 16:11; John 2:24; pass. *to be intrusted with,*
         Rom 3:2; 1 Cor 9:17

πιστεύω   pres act ind 1 sg   [4t; v-1a(6); 4409]   "
πιστεύων   pres act ptcp nom sg masc
         [24t; v-1a(6); 4409]   "
πίστεως   gen sg fem   [94t; n-3e(5b); 4411]   πίστις

πιστή   nom sg fem
   [1Ti 5:16; a-1a(2a); 4412]   πιστός
πιστήν   acc sg fem [Ac 16:15; a-1a(2a); 4412]   "
πιστῆς   gen sg fem [Ac 16:1; a-1a(2a); 4412]   "
πιστικῆς   gen sg fem [2t; a-1a(2a); 4410]   πιστικός

πιστικός, ή, όν   {4410, a-1a(2a)}
   genuine, unadulterated, or (πίνω) *liquid,* Mark
   14:3; John 12:3*

πίστιν   acc sg fem [55t; n-3e(5b); 4411]   πίστις

πίστις, εως, ἡ   {4411, n-3e(5b)}
   faith, belief, firm persuasion, 2 Cor 5:7; Heb 11:1;
   assurance, firm conviction, Rom 14:23; *ground of*
   belief, guarantee, assurance, Acts 17:31; *good faith,*
   honesty, integrity, Matt 23:23; Gal 5:22; Titus
   2:10; *faithfulness, truthfulness,* Rom 3:3; in N.T.
   faith in God and Christ, Matt 8:10; Acts 3:16, et
   al. freq.; ἡ πίστις, *the* matter of Gospel *faith,* Acts
   6:7; Jude 3

πίστις   nom sg fem [36t; n-3e(5b); 4411]   "
πιστοί   nom pl masc [7t; a-1a(2a); 4412]   πιστός
πιστοῖς   dat pl masc [4t; a-1a(2a); 4412]   "
πιστόν   nom sg neut [1C 4:17; a-1a(2a); 4412]   "
πιστόν   acc sg masc [3t; a-1a(2a); 4412]   "
πιστόν   acc sg neut [3J 5; a-1a(2a); 4412]   "

πιστός, ή, όν   {4412, a-1a(2a)}
   faithful, true, trusty, Matt 24:45; 25:21, 23; Luke
   12:42; 2 Tim 2:2; *put in trust,* 1 Cor 7:25; *true,*
   veracious, Rev 1:5; 2:13; *credible, sure, certain,*
   indubitable, Acts 13:34; 1 Tim 1:15; *believing,*
   yielding belief and confidence, John 20:27; Gal 3:9;
   spc. *a* Christian *believer,* Acts 10:45; 16:1, 15; 2
   Cor 6:15; πιστόν, *in a true-hearted manner,*
   right-mindedly, 3 John 5

πιστός   nom sg masc [33t; a-1a(2a); 4412]   "
πιστοῦ   gen sg masc [2t; a-1a(2a); 4412]   "
πιστούς   acc pl masc [2t; a-1a(2a); 4412]   "

πιστόω   {4413, v-1d(3)}
   [-, -, -, -, ἐπιστώθην] *to make trustworthy;* pass. *to*
   be assured, feel sure belief, 2 Tim 3:14*

πιστῷ   dat sg masc [4t; a-1a(2a); 4412]   "
πιστῶν   gen pl masc [2t; a-1a(2a); 4412]   "
πίω   aor act subj 1 sg [6t; v-3a(1); 4403]   πίνω
πίωμεν   aor act subj 1 pl [2t; v-3a(1); 4403]   "
πιών   aor act ptcp nom sg masc
   [Lk 5:39; v-3a(1); 4403]   "
πίωσιν   aor act subj 3 pl
   [Mk 16:18; v-3a(1); 4403]   "
πλάκες   nom pl fem [Hb 9:4; n-3b(1); 4419]   πλάξ
πλανᾷ   pres act ind 3 sg
   [3t; v-1d(1a); 4414]   πλανάω
πλανᾶσθε   pres pass imperative 2 pl
   [4t; v-1d(1a); 4414]   "
πλανᾶσθε   pres pass ind 2 pl [3t; v-1d(1a); 4414]   "
πλανάτω   pres act imperative 3 sg
   [1J 3:7; v-1d(1a); 4414]   "

πλανάω   {4414, v-1d(1a)}
   [πλανήσω, ἐπλάνησα, -, πεπλάνημαι, ἐπλανήθην]
   to lead astray, cause to wander; pass. *to go astray,*
   wander about, stray, Matt 18:12, 13; 1 Peter 2:25;

met. *to mislead, deceive,* Matt 24:4, 5, 11, 24; pass.
to be deceived, err, mistake, Matt 22:29; *to seduce,*
delude, John 7:12; pass. *to be seduced* or *wander*
from the path of virtue, to sin, transgress, Titus
3:3; Heb 5:2; James 5:19

πλάνη, ης, ἡ   {4415, n-1b}
   a wandering; deceit, deception, delusion,
   imposture, fraud, Matt 27:64; 1 Thess 2:3;
   seduction, deceiving, Eph 4:14; 2 Thess 2:11; 1
   John 4:6; *error, false opinion,* 2 Peter 3:17;
   wandering from the path of truth and virtue,
   perverseness, wickedness, sin, Rom 1:27; James
   5:20; 2 Peter 2:18; Jude 11*

πλάνη   nom sg fem [Mt 27:64; n-1b; 4415]   πλάνη
πλάνη   dat sg fem [3t; n-1b; 4415]   "
πλανηθῇ   aor pass subj 3 sg
   [2t; v-1d(1a); 4414]   πλανάω
πλανηθῆτε   aor pass subj 2 pl
   [Lk 21:8; v-1d(1a); 4414]   "
πλάνης   gen sg fem [6t; n-1b; 4415]   πλάνη
πλανῆσαι   aor act inf [2t; v-1d(1a); 4414]   πλανάω
πλανήσῃ   aor act subj 3 sg [3t; v-1d(1a); 4414]   "
πλανήσουσιν   fut act ind 3 pl
   [3t; v-1d(1a); 4414]   "
πλανῆται   nom pl masc
   [Jd 13; n-1f; 4417]   πλανήτης

πλανήτης, ου, ὁ   {4417, n-1f}
   a rover, roving, a wanderer, wandering; ἀστὴρ
   πλανήτης, *a wandering star,* Jude 13*

πλάνοι   nom pl masc [2t; a-3a; 4418]   πλάνος
πλάνοις   dat pl neut [1Ti 4:1; a-3a; 4418]   "

πλάνος, ον   {4418, a-3a}
   a wanderer, vagabond; also act. *deceiving,*
   seducing; a deceiver, impostor, Matt 27:63; 2 Cor
   6:8; 1 Tim 4:1; 2 John 7*

πλάνος   nom sg masc [2t; a-3a; 4418]   "
πλανῶμεν   pres act ind 1 pl
   [1J 1:8; v-1d(1a); 4414]   πλανάω
πλανώμενοι   pres pass ptcp nom pl masc
   [4t; v-1d(1a); 4414]   "
πλανωμένοις   pres pass ptcp dat pl masc
   [Hb 5:2; v-1d(1a); 4414]   "
πλανώμενον   pres pass ptcp acc sg neut
   [Mt 18:12; v-1d(1a); 4414]   "
πλανῶν   pres act ptcp nom sg masc
   [2t; v-1d(1a); 4414]   "
πλανῶνται   pres pass ind 3 pl
   [Hb 3:10; v-1d(1a); 4414]   "
πλανῶντες   pres act ptcp nom pl masc
   [2Ti 3:13; v-1d(1a); 4414]   "
πλανώντων   pres act ptcp gen pl masc
   [1J 2:26; v-1d(1a); 4414]   "

πλάξ, πλακός, ἡ   {4419, n-3b(1)}
   a flat broad surface; a table, tablet, 2 Cor 3:3; Heb
   9:4*

πλαξίν   dat pl fem [2t; n-3b(1); 4419]   πλάξ
πλάσαντι   aor act ptcp dat sg masc
   [Rm 9:20; v-2b; 4421]   πλάσσω

πλάσμα, ατος, τό   {4420, n-3c(4)}
a thing formed or *fashioned*; spc. *a potter's vessel*,
Rom 9:20*

πλάσμα   nom sg neut
[Rm 9:20; n-3c(4); 4420]   πλάσμα

πλάσσω   {4421, v-2b}
[-, ἔπλασα, πέπλακα, -, ἐπλάσθην] *to form,
fashion, mould,* Rom 9:20; 1 Tim 2:13*

πλαστοῖς   dat pl masc
[2P 2:3; a-1a(2a); 4422]   πλαστός

πλαστός, ή, όν   {4422, a-1a(2a)}
formed, fashioned, moulded; met. *fabricated,
counterfeit, delusive,* 2 Peter 2:3*

πλατεῖα, ας, ἡ   {4423, n-1a}
a street, broad way, Matt 6:5; 12:19; Luke 10:10

πλατεῖα   nom sg fem [2t; a-2b; 4426]   πλατύς
πλατείαις   dat pl fem [2t; a-2b; 4426]   "
πλατείας   gen sg fem [2t; a-2b; 4426]   "
πλατείας   acc pl fem [3t; a-2b; 4426]   "
πλατειῶν   gen pl fem [Mt 6:5; a-2b; 4426]   "

πλάτος, ους, τό   {4424, n-3d(2b)}
breadth, Eph 3:18; Rev 20:9; 21:16*

πλάτος   nom sg neut [3t; n-3d(2b); 4424]   πλάτος
πλάτος   acc sg neut [Rv 20:9; n-3d(2b); 4424]   "
πλατύνθητε   aor pass imperative 2 pl
[2C 6:13; v-1c(2); 4425]   πλατύνω
πλατύνουσιν   pres act ind 3 pl
[Mt 23:5; v-1c(2); 4425]   "

πλατύνω   {4425, v-1c(2)}
[-, -, -, πεπλάτυμμαι, ἐπλατύνθην] *to make broad,
widen, enlarge,* Matt 23:5; pass. met. of the heart,
from the Hebrew, *to be expanded* with kindly
and genial feelings, 2 Cor 6:11, 13*

πλατύς, εῖα, ύ   {4426, a-2b}
broad, wide, Matt 7:13*

πλέγμα, ατος, τό   {4427, n-3c(4)}
anything plaited or *intertwined; a braid* of hair, 1
Tim 2:9*

πλέγμασιν   dat pl neut
[1Ti 2:9; n-3c(4); 4427]   πλέγμα
πλεῖν   pres act inf [Ac 27:2; v-1a(7); 4434]   πλέω
πλεῖον   nom sg neut comparative
[6t; a-1a(2a); 4498]   πολύς
πλεῖον   acc sg neut comparative
[4t; a-1a(2a); 4498]   "
πλεῖον   acc sg neut, can function as a
comparative adverb [8t; a-1a(2a); 4498]   "
πλείονα   acc sg masc comparative
[2t; a-1a(2a); 4498]   "
πλείονα   acc sg fem comparative
[2t; a-1a(2a); 4498]   "
πλείονα   acc pl neut comparative
[2t; a-1a(2a); 4498]   "
πλείονας   acc pl masc comparative
[5t; a-1a(2a); 4498]   "
πλείονας   acc pl fem comparative
[Ac 27:20; a-1a(2a); 4498]   "

πλείονες   nom pl masc comparative
[4t; a-1a(2a); 4498]   "
πλείονος   gen sg fem comparative
[Hb 3:3; a-1a(2a); 4498]   "
πλειόνων   gen pl masc comparative
[2t; a-1a(2a); 4498]   "
πλειόνων   gen pl neut comparative
[3t; a-1a(2a); 4498]   "
πλείοσιν   dat pl masc comparative
[2t; a-1a(2a); 4498]   "
πλείους   nom pl masc comparative
[4t; a-1a(2a); 4498]   "
πλείους   nom pl fem comparative
[Ac 24:11; a-1a(2a); 4498]   "
πλείους   acc pl fem comparative
[4t; a-1a(2a); 4498]   "
πλεῖσται   nom pl fem superlative
[Mt 11:20; a-1a(2a); 4498]   "
πλεῖστον   acc sg neut superlative
[1C 14:27; a-1a(2a); 4498]   "

πλεῖστος, η, ον   {a-1a(2a)}
most; very great, Matt 11:20; 21:8; τὸ πλεῖστον, as
an adv., *at most,* 1 Cor 14:27; superlative of
πολύς

πλεῖστος   nom sg masc superlative
[2t; a-1a(2a); 4498]   "
πλείω   adverb-comparative
[Mt 26:53; a-1a(2a); 4498]   "

πλείων, ον   {a-4b(1)}
more in number, Matt 21:36; 26:53; *more* in
quantity, Mark 12:43; Luke 21:3; οἱ πλείονες, or
πλείους, *the greater part, the majority,* Acts 19:32;
27:12; *the more,* 1 Cor 9:19; 2 Cor 4:15; neut.
πλεῖον, as an adv., *more,* Luke 7:42; ἐπὶ πλεῖον,
more, of time, *longer, further,* Acts 24:4; of space,
more widely, Acts 4:17; 2 Tim 2:16; 3:9; for the
positive, *much,* of time, *long,* Acts 20:9; *more,
higher, greater, more excellent, of higher value,*
Matt 5:20; 6:25

πλέκω   {4428, v-1b(2)}
[-, ἔπλεξα, -, πέπλεγμαι, ἐπλάκην] *to interweave,
weave, braid, plait,* Matt 27:29; Mark 15:17; John
19:2*

πλέξαντες   aor act ptcp nom pl masc
[3t; v-1b(2); 4428]   πλέκω
πλέον   acc sg neut comparative
[2t; a-1a(2a); 4498]   πολύς
πλέον   adverb-comparative
[Jn 21:15; a-1a(2a); 4498]   "
πλέον   pres act ptcp acc sg neut
[Ac 27:6; v-1a(7); 4434]   πλέω
πλεονάζει   pres act ind 3 sg
[2Th 1:3; v-2a(1); 4429]   πλεονάζω
πλεονάζοντα   pres act ptcp nom pl neut
[2P 1:8; v-2a(1); 4429]   "
πλεονάζοντα   pres act ptcp acc sg masc
[Pp 4:17; v-2a(1); 4429]   "

πλεονάζω   {4429, v-2a(1)}
[-, ἐπλεόνασα, -, -, -] *to be more than enough; to
have more than enough, to have in abundance,* 2
Cor 8:15; *to abound, be abundant,* 2 Thess 1:3; 2

Peter 1:8; *to increase, be augmented,* Rom 5:20; *to come into wider action, be more widely spread,* Rom 6:1; 2 Cor 4:15; in N.T. trans. *to cause to abound* or *increase, to augment,* 1 Thess 3:12

πλεονάσαι   aor act opt 3 sg
[1Th 3:12; v-2a(1); 4429]   "
πλεονάσασα   aor act ptcp nom sg fem
[2C 4:15; v-2a(1); 4429]   "
πλεονάσῃ   aor act subj 3 sg [2t; v-2a(1); 4429]   "
πλεονέκται   nom pl masc
[1C 6:10; n-1f; 4431]   πλεονέκτης
πλεονέκταις   dat pl masc [1C 5:10; n-1f; 4431]   "
πλεονεκτεῖν   pres act inf
[1Th 4:6; v-1d(2a); 4430]   πλεονεκτέω

πλεονεκτέω   {4430, v-1d(2a)}
[-, ἐπλεονέκτησα, -, -, ἐπλεονεκτήθην] *to have more* than another; *to take advantage of* ; *to overreach, make gain of* , 2 Cor 7:2; 12:17, 18; *to wrong,* 1 Thess 4:6; *to get the better,* or *an advantage of* , 2 Cor 2:11*

πλεονεκτηθῶμεν   aor pass subj 1 pl
[2C 2:11; v-1d(2a); 4430]   "

πλεονέκτης, ου, ὁ   {4431, n-1f}
one who has or *claims to have more than his share; a covetous, avaricious person, one who defrauds for the sake of gain,* 1 Cor 5:10, 11; 6:10; Eph 5:5*

πλεονέκτης   nom sg masc
[2t; n-1f; 4431]   πλεονέκτης

πλεονεξία, ας, ἡ   {4432, n-1a}
some advantage which one possesses over another; an inordinate desire of riches, covetousness, Luke 12:15; *grasping, overreaching, extortion,* Rom 1:29; 1 Thess 2:5; *a gift exacted by importunity and conferred with grudging, a hard-wrung gift,* 2 Cor 9:5; *a scheme of extortion,* Mark 7:22

πλεονεξία   nom sg fem
[Ep 5:3; n-1a; 4432]   πλεονεξία
πλεονεξίᾳ   dat sg fem [3t; n-1a; 4432]   "
πλεονεξίαι   nom pl fem [Mk 7:22; n-1a; 4432]   "
πλεονεξίαν   acc sg fem [2t; n-1a; 4432]   "
πλεονεξίας   gen sg fem [3t; n-1a; 4432]   "
πλέοντας   pres act ptcp acc pl masc
[Ac 27:24; v-1a(7); 4434]   πλέω
πλεόντων   pres act ptcp gen pl masc
[Lk 8:23; v-1a(7); 4434]   "

πλευρά, ᾶς, ἡ   {4433, n-1a}
pr. *a rib; the side* of the body, John 19:34; 20:20, 25, 27; Acts 12:7; Matt 27:49 v.l.*

πλευράν   acc sg fem [5t; n-1a; 4433]   πλευρά

πλέω   {4434, v-1a(7)}
[(ἐπλούν), -, ἔπλευσα, -, -, -] *to sail,* Luke 8:23; Acts 21:3; 27:2, 6, 24; Rev 18:17*

πλέων   pres act ptcp nom sg masc
[Rv 18:17; v-1a(7); 4434]   πλέω
πληγαί   nom pl fem [2t; n-1b; 4435]   πληγή
πληγαῖς   dat pl fem [3t; n-1b; 4435]   "
πληγάς   acc pl fem [6t; n-1b; 4435]   "

πληγή, ῆς, ἡ   {4435, n-1b}
a blow, stroke, stripe, Luke 10:30; 12:48; meton. *a*

wound, Acts 16:33; Rev 13:3, 12, 14; from the Hebrew, *a plague, affliction, calamity,* Rev 9:20; 11:6

πληγή   nom sg fem [3t; n-1b; 4435]   "
πληγῇ   dat sg fem [Rv 11:6; n-1b; 4435]   "
πληγήν   acc sg fem [Rv 13:14; n-1b; 4435]   "
πληγῆς   gen sg fem [Rv 16:21; n-1b; 4435]   "
πληγῶν   gen pl fem [5t; n-1b; 4435]   "
πλήθει   dat sg neut
[Hb 11:12; n-3d(2b); 4436]   πλῆθος
πλήθη   nom pl neut [Ac 5:14; n-3d(2b); 4436]   "

πλῆθος, ους, τό   {4436, n-3d(2b)}
fullness, amplitude, magnitude; a multitude, a great number, Luke 1:10; 2:13; 5:6; *a multitude, a crowd, throng,* Mark 3:7, 8; Luke 6:17

πλῆθος   nom sg neut [18t; n-3d(2b); 4436]   "
πλῆθος   acc sg neut [7t; n-3d(2b); 4436]   "
πλήθους   gen sg neut [4t; n-3d(2b); 4436]   "
πληθυνεῖ   fut act ind 3 sg
[2C 9:10; v-1c(2); 4437]   πληθύνω
πληθυνθείη   aor pass opt 3 sg [3t; v-1c(2); 4437]   "
πληθυνθῆναι   aor pass inf
[Mt 24:12; v-1c(2); 4437]   "
πληθυνόντων   pres act ptcp gen pl masc
[Ac 6:1; v-1c(2); 4437]   "

πληθύνω   {4437, v-1c(2)}
[(ἐπλήθυνον), πληθυνῶ, -, -, -, ἐπληθύνθην] optative, πληθύναι (3 sg), trans. *to multiply, cause to increase, augment,* 2 Cor 9:10; Heb 6:14; pass. *to be multiplied, increase, be accumulated,* Matt 24:12; Acts 6:7; 7:17; intrans. *to multiply, increase, be augmented,* Acts 6:1

πληθυνῶ   fut act ind 1 sg
[Hb 6:14; v-1c(2); 4437]   "
πληθύνων   pres act ptcp nom sg masc
[Hb 6:14; v-1c(2); 4437]   "
πλήκτην   acc sg masc [2t; n-1f; 4438]   πλήκτης

πλήκτης, ου, ὁ   {4438, n-1f}
a striker, one apt to strike; a quarrelsome, violent person, 1 Tim 3:3; Titus 1:7*

πλήμμυρα, ης, ἡ   {4439, n-1c}
the flood-tide; a flood, Luke 6:48*

πλημμύρης   gen sg fem
[Lk 6:48; n-1c; 4439]   πλήμμυρα

πλήν   {4440, adverb}
can function as an improper prep., *besides, except,* Mark 12:32; Acts 8:1; 20:23; as a conj. *but, however, nevertheless,* Matt 18:7; Luke 19:27; Eph 5:33; equivalent to ἀλλά, Luke 6:35; 12:31; Acts 27:22

πλήν   adverb [31t; adverb; 4440]   πλήν
πλήρεις   nom pl masc [Ac 19:28; a-4a; 4441] πλήρης
πλήρεις   acc pl masc [3t; a-4a; 4441]   "
πλήρεις   acc pl fem [Mt 15:37; a-4a; 4441]   "
πλήρη   acc sg masc [2J 8; a-4a; 4441]   "

πλήρης, ες   {4441, a-4a}
full, filled, Matt 14:20; 15:37; *full* of disease, Luke 5:12; met. *full of, abounding in, wholly occupied with, completely under the influence of,* or *affected*

by, Luke 4:1; John 1:14; Acts 9:36; *full, complete, perfect,* Mark 4:28

πλήρης   nom sg masc [5t; a-4a; 4441]   "
πλήρης   nom sg fem [Ac 9:36; a-4a; 4441]   "
πλήρης   voc sg masc [Ac 13:10; a-4a; 4441]   "
πλήρης   gen sg masc [Jn 1:14; a-4a; 4441]   "
πλήρης   acc sg masc [2t; a-4a; 4441]   "
πληροῖς   pres act subj 2 sg
          [Cl 4:17; v-1d(3); 4444]   πληρόω
πληρούμενον   pres pass ptcp nom sg neut
          [Lk 2:40; v-1d(3); 4444]   "
πληρουμένου   pres mid ptcp gen sg masc
          [Ep 1:23; v-1d(3); 4444]   "
πληροῦν   pres act inf [Lk 9:31; v-1d(3); 4444]   "
πληροῦσθε   pres pass imperative 2 pl
          [Ep 5:18; v-1d(3); 4444]   "
πληροφορείσθω   pres pass imperative 3 sg
          [Rm 14:5; v-1d(2a); 4442]   πληροφορέω

πληροφορέω   {4442, v-1d(2a)}
[-, ἐπληροφόρησα, -, πεπληροφόρημαι,
ἐπληροφορήθην] *to bring full measure, to give in
full; to carry out fully, to discharge completely,* 2
Tim 4:5, 17; pass. of things, *to be fully established*
as a matter of certainty, Luke 1:1; of persons, *to
be fully convinced, assured,* Rom 4:21; 14:15; Col
4:12*

πληροφορηθείς   aor pass ptcp nom sg masc
          [Rm 4:21; v-1d(2a); 4442]   "
πληροφορηθῇ   aor pass subj 3 sg
          [2Ti 4:17; v-1d(2a); 4442]   "
πληροφόρησον   aor act imperative 2 sg
          [2Ti 4:5; v-1d(2a); 4442]   "

πληροφορία, ας, ἡ   {4443, n-1a}
full conviction, firm persuasion, assurance, 1 Thess
1:5; Col 2:2; Rom 15:29 v.l.

πληροφορίᾳ   dat sg fem
          [2t; n-1a; 4443]   πληροφορία
πληροφορίαν   acc sg fem [Hb 6:11; n-1a; 4443]   "
πληροφορίας   gen sg fem [Cl 2:2; n-1a; 4443]   "

πληρόω   {4444, v-1d(3)}
[(ἐπλήρουν), πληρώσω, ἐπλήρωσα, πεπλήρωκα,
πεπλήρωμαι, ἐπληρώθην] pluperf., πεπληρώκει
(3 sg), *to fill, make full, fill up,* Matt 13:48; 23:32;
Luke 3:5; *to fill up* a deficiency, Phil 4:18, 19; *to
pervade,* John 12:3; Acts 2:2; *to pervade* with an
influence, *to influence fully, possess fully,* John
16:6; Acts 2:28; 5:3; Rom 1:29; Eph 5:18; *to
complete, perfect,* John 3:29; Eph 3:19; *to bring to
an end,* Luke 7:1; *to perform fully, discharge,* Matt
3:15; Acts 12:25; 13:25; 14:26; Rom 13:8; Col
4:17; *to consummate,* Matt 5:17; *to realize,
accomplish, fulfil,* Luke 1:20; 9:31; Acts 3:18;
13:27; from the Hebrew; *to set forth fully,* Rom
15:19; Col 1:25; pass. of time, *to be fulfilled, come
to an end, be fully arrived,* Mark 1:15; Luke 21:24;
John 7:8; of prophecy, *to receive fulfillment,* Matt
1:22, et al. freq.

πληρωθείσης   aor pass ptcp gen sg fem
          [Ac 24:27; v-1d(3); 4444]   πληρόω
πληρωθέντων   aor pass ptcp gen pl neut
          [Ac 7:30; v-1d(3); 4444]   "

πληρωθῇ   aor pass subj 3 sg [20t; v-1d(3); 4444] "
πληρωθῆναι   aor pass inf [2t; v-1d(3); 4444]   "
πληρωθήσεται   fut pass ind 3 sg
          [Lk 3:5; v-1d(3); 4444]   "
πληρωθήσονται   fut pass ind 3 pl
          [Lk 1:20; v-1d(3); 4444]   "
πληρωθῆτε   aor pass subj 2 pl [2t; v-1d(3); 4444] "
πληρωθῶ   aor pass subj 1 sg
          [2Ti 1:4; v-1d(3); 4444]   "
πληρωθῶσιν   aor pass subj 3 pl
          [5t; v-1d(3); 4444]   "

πλήρωμα, ατος, τό   {4445, n-3c(4)}
that which fills up; full measure, entire content,
Mark 8:20; 1 Cor 10:26, 28; *complement, full
extent, full number,* Gal 4:4; Eph 1:10; *that which
fills up a deficiency, a supplement, a patch,* Matt
9:16; *fulness, abundance,* John 1:16; *full measure,*
Rom 15:29; *a fulfilling, perfect performance,* Rom
13:10; *complete attainment* of entire belief, *full
acceptance,* Rom 11:12; *full development,
plenitude,* Eph 4:13; Col 1:19; 2:9

πλήρωμα   nom sg neut [7t; n-3c(4); 4445]   πλήρωμα
πλήρωμα   acc sg neut [4t; n-3c(4); 4445]   "
πληρώματα   acc pl neut [2t; n-3c(4); 4445]   "
πληρώματι   dat sg neut [Rm 15:29; n-3c(4); 4445] "
πληρώματος   gen sg neut [3t; n-3c(4); 4445]   "
πληρῶσαι   aor act inf [3t; v-1d(3); 4444]   πληρόω
πληρώσαι   aor act opt 3 sg
          [Rm 15:13; v-1d(3); 4444]   "
πληρώσαντες   aor act ptcp nom pl masc
          [Ac 12:25; v-1d(3); 4444]   "
πληρώσατε   aor act imperative 2 pl
          [2t; v-1d(3); 4444]   "
πληρώσει   fut act ind 3 sg
          [Pp 4:19; v-1d(3); 4444]   "
πληρώσεις   fut act ind 2 sg
          [Ac 2:28; v-1d(3); 4444]   "
πληρώσῃ   aor act subj 3 sg [2t; v-1d(3); 4444]   "
πλήσας   aor act ptcp nom sg masc
          [Mt 27:48; v-6a; 4398]   πίμπλημι
πλησθείς   aor pass ptcp nom sg masc
          [2t; v-6a; 4398]   "
πλησθῆναι   aor pass inf [Lk 21:22; v-6a; 4398]   "
πλησθῇς   aor pass subj 2 sg
          [Ac 9:17; v-6a; 4398]   "
πλησθήσεται   fut pass ind 3 sg
          [Lk 1:15; v-6a; 4398]   "

πλησίον   {4446, adverb}
can function as an improper prep., *near, near by,*
John 4:5; ὁ πλησίον, *a neighbor,* Matt 19:19; Rom
15:2; a friendly *neighbor,* Matt 5:43

πλησίον   adverb [17t; adverb; 4446]   πλησίον

πλησμονή, ῆς, ἡ   {4447, n-1b}
a filling up; met. *gratification, satisfaction,* Col
2:23*

πλησμονήν   acc sg fem
          [Cl 2:23; n-1b; 4447]   πλησμονή

πλήσσω   {4448, v-2b}
[(ἔπλησσον), -, ἔπληξα, -, πέπληγμαι, ἐπλήγην]

also spelled πλήττω, *to strike, smite;* from the Hebrew, *to smite, to plague, blast,* Rev 8:12

πλοῖα   nom pl neut [2t; n-2c; 4450]   πλοῖον
πλοῖα   acc pl neut [4t; n-2c; 4450]   "
πλοιάρια   nom pl neut
    [Jn 6:23; n-2c; 4449]   πλοιάριον
πλοιάρια   acc pl neut [Jn 6:24; n-2c; 4449]   "

πλοιάριον, ου, τό   {4449, n-2c}
a small vessel, boat, Mark 3:9; 4:36 v.l.; Luke 5:2 v.l.

πλοιάριον   nom sg neut [2t; n-2c; 4449]   "
πλοιαρίῳ   dat sg neut [Jn 21:8; n-2c; 4449]   "

πλοῖον, ου, τό   {4450, n-2c}
a vessel, ship, bark, whether large or small, Matt 4:21, 22; Acts 21:2, 3

πλοῖον   nom sg neut [4t; n-2c; 4450]   πλοῖον
πλοῖον   acc sg neut [29t; n-2c; 4450]   "
πλοίου   gen sg neut [12t; n-2c; 4450]   "
πλοίῳ   dat sg neut [14t; n-2c; 4450]   "
πλοίων   gen pl neut [2t; n-2c; 4450]   "

πλοκή, ῆς, ἡ   {n-1b}
braiding, braid, 1 Pet 3:3 v.l.*

πλοός   gen sg masc [Ac 27:9; n-3e(4); 4453]   πλοῦς
πλοῦν   acc sg masc [2t; n-3e(4); 4453]   "

πλοῦς, πλοός, ὁ   {4453, n-3e(4)}
contracted form of πλόος, *sailing, navigation, voyage,* Acts 21:7; 27:9, 10*

πλούσιοι   nom pl masc [3t; a-1a(1); 4454]   πλούσιος
πλούσιοι   voc pl masc [Jm 5:1; a-1a(1); 4454]   "
πλουσίοις   dat pl masc [2t; a-1a(1); 4454]   "
πλούσιον   acc sg masc [3t; a-1a(1); 4454]   "

πλούσιος, ια, ιον   {4454, a-1a(1)}
rich, opulent, wealthy; and pl. οἱ πλούσιοι, *the rich,* Matt 19:23, 24; 27:57; met. *rich, abounding in, distinguished for,* Eph 2:4; James 2:5; Rev 2:9; 3:17; *rich* in glory, dignity, bliss, etc., 2 Cor 8:9

πλούσιος   nom sg masc [13t; a-1a(1); 4454]   "
πλουσίου   gen sg masc [2t; a-1a(1); 4454]   "
πλουσίους   acc pl masc [4t; a-1a(1); 4454]   "

πλουσίως   {4455, adverb}
rich, largely, abundantly, Col 3:16

πλουσίως   adverb [4t; adverb; 4455]   πλουσίως
πλουτεῖν   pres act inf
    [2t; v-1d(2a); 4456]   πλουτέω

πλουτέω   {4456, v-1d(2a)}
[-, ἐπλούτησα, πεπλούτηκα, -, -] *to be* or *become rich,* Luke 1:25; 1 Tim 6:9; trop. Luke 12:21; met. *to abound in, be abundantly furnished with,* 1 Tim 6:18; *to be spiritually enriched,* 2 Cor 8:9

πλουτήσαντες   aor act ptcp nom pl masc
    [Rv 18:15; v-1d(2a); 4456]   "
πλουτήσῃς   aor act subj 2 sg
    [Rv 3:18; v-1d(2a); 4456]   "
πλουτήσητε   aor act subj 2 pl
    [2C 8:9; v-1d(2a); 4456]   "
πλουτιζόμενοι   pres pass ptcp nom pl masc
    [2C 9:11; v-2a(1); 4457]   πλουτίζω

πλουτίζοντες   pres act ptcp nom pl masc
    [2C 6:10; v-2a(1); 4457]   "

πλουτίζω   {4457, v-2a(1)}
[-, ἐπλούτισα, -, -, ἐπλουτίσθην] *to make rich, enrich;* met. *to enrich* spiritually, 1 Cor 1:5; 2 Cor 6:10; 9:11*

πλοῦτον   acc sg masc [3t; n-2a; 4458]   πλοῦτος

πλοῦτος, ου, ὁ   {4458, n-2a}
riches, wealth, opulence, Matt 13:22; Luke 8:14; in N.T., πλοῦτος τοῦ Θεοῦ, or Χριστοῦ, *those rich benefits, those abundant blessings which flow from God* or *Christ,* Eph 3:8; Phil 4:19; meton. *richness, abundance,* Rom 2:4; 11:33; 2 Cor 8:2; meton. *a* spiritual *enriching,* Rom 11:12

πλοῦτος   nom sg masc [5t; n-2a; 4458]   "
πλοῦτος   nom sg neut [Cl 1:27; n-2a; 4458]   "
πλοῦτος   acc sg neut [7t; n-2a; 4458]   "
πλούτου   gen sg masc [6t; n-2a; 4458]   "
πλουτοῦντας   pres act ptcp acc pl masc
    [Lk 1:53; v-1d(2a); 4456]   πλουτέω
πλουτῶν   pres act ptcp nom sg masc
    [2t; v-1d(2a); 4456]   "
πλύνοντες   pres act ptcp nom pl masc
    [Rv 22:14; v-1c(2); 4459]   πλύνω

πλύνω   {4459, v-1c(2)}
[(ἔπλυνον), πλυνῶ, ἔπλυνα, -, -, -] *to wash* garments, Luke 5:1; Rev 7:14; 22:14*

πνέῃ   pres act subj 3 sg
    [Rv 7:1; v-1a(7); 4463]   πνέω
πνεῖ   pres act ind 3 sg [Jn 3:8; v-1a(7); 4463]   "
πνέοντα   pres act ptcp acc sg masc
    [Lk 12:55; v-1a(7); 4463]   "
πνέοντος   pres act ptcp gen sg masc
    [Jn 6:18; v-1a(7); 4463]   "
πνεούσῃ   pres act ptcp dat sg fem
    [Ac 27:40; v-1a(7); 4463]   "

πνεῦμα, ατος, τό   {4460, n-3c(4)}
wind, air in motion, John 3:8; *breath,* 2 Thess 2:8; the substance *spirit,* John 3:6; *a spirit, spiritual being,* John 4:24; Acts 23:8, 9; Heb 1:14; *a bodiless spirit, specter,* Luke 24:37; *a foul spirit,* δαιμόνιον, Matt 8:16; Luke 10:20; *spirit,* as a vital principle, John 6:63; 1 Cor 15:45; *the* human *spirit, the soul,* Matt 26:41; 27:50; Acts 7:59; 1 Cor 7:34; James 2:26; *the spirit* as the seat of thought and feeling, *the mind,* Mark 8:12; Acts 19:21; *spirit, mental frame,* 1 Cor 4:21; 1 Peter 3:4; *a* characteristic *spirit, an influential principle,* Luke 9:55; 1 Cor 2:12; 2 Tim 1:7; *a pervading influence,* Rom 11:8; *spirit, frame of mind,* as distinguished from outward circumstances and action, Matt 5:3; *spirit* as distinguished from outward show and form. John 4:23; *spirit, a* divinely bestowed *spiritual frame,* characteristic of true believers, Rom 8:4; Jude 19; *spirit,* latent *spiritual import, spiritual significance,* as distinguished from the mere letter, Rom 2:29; 7:6; 2 Cor 3:6, 17; *spirit,* as a term for a process superior to a merely natural or carnal course of things, by the operation of the Divine Spirit, Rom 8:4; Gal 4:29; *a spiritual*

dispensation, or *a* sealing energy of the Holy Spirit, Heb 9:14; the Holy Spirit, Matt 3:16; 12:31; John 1:32, 33; *a gift of the Holy Spirit,* John 7:39; Acts 19:2; 1 Cor 14:12; *an operation* or *influence of the Holy Spirit,* 1 Cor 12:3; *a spiritual influence, an inspiration,* Matt 22:43; Luke 2:27; Eph 1:17; *a professedly divine communication,* or, *a professed possessor of a spiritual communication,* 1 Cor 12:10; 2 Thess 2:2; 1 John 4:1, 2, 3

πνεῦμα   nom sg neut [91t; n-3c(4); 4460]   πνεῦμα
πνεῦμα   voc sg neut [2t; n-3c(4); 4460]   "
πνεῦμα   acc sg neut [65t; n-3c(4); 4460]   "
πνεύμασι   dat pl neut [2t; n-3c(4); 4460]   "
πνεύμασιν   dat pl neut [3t; n-3c(4); 4460]   "
πνεύματα   nom pl neut [8t; n-3c(4); 4460]   "
πνεύματα   acc pl neut [10t; n-3c(4); 4460]   "
πνεύματι   dat sg neut [91t; n-3c(4); 4460]   "
πνευματικά   acc pl neut
    [4t; a-1a(2a); 4461]   πνευματικός
πνευματικαῖς   dat pl fem [2t; a-1a(2a); 4461]   "
πνευματικάς   acc pl fem [1P 2:5; a-1a(2a); 4461]   "
πνευματικῇ   dat sg fem [2t; a-1a(2a); 4461]   "
πνευματικῆς   gen sg fem [1C 10:4; a-1a(2a); 4461]   "
πνευματικοί   nom pl masc [Ga 6:1; a-1a(2a); 4461]   "
πνευματικοῖς   dat pl masc
    [1C 3:1; a-1a(2a); 4461]   "
πνευματικοῖς   dat pl neut [2t; a-1a(2a); 4461]   "
πνευματικόν   nom sg neut [4t; a-1a(2a); 4461]   "
πνευματικόν   acc sg neut [3t; a-1a(2a); 4461]   "

πνευματικός, ή, όν   {4461, a-1a(2a)}
spiritual, pertaining to the soul, as distinguished from what concerns the body, Rom 15:27; 1 Cor 9:11; *spiritual, pertaining to the nature of spirits,* 1 Cor 15:44; τὰ πνευματικὰ τῆς πονηρίας, i.q. τὰ πνεύματα τὰ πονηρά, *evil spirits,* Eph 6:12; *spiritual, pertaining* or *relating to the influences of the Holy Spirit,* of things, Rom 1:11; 7:14; τὰ πνευματικά, *spiritual gifts,* 1 Cor 12:1; 14:1; *superior in process to the natural course of things, miraculous,* 1 Cor 10:3; of persons, *gifted with a spiritual frame of mind, spiritually affected,* 1 Cor 2:13, 15; 15:47 v.l.; *endowed with spiritual gifts, inspired,* 1 Cor 14:37

πνευματικός   nom sg masc [4t; a-1a(2a); 4461]   "
πνευματικῶν   gen pl neut
    [1C 12:1; a-1a(2a); 4461]   "

πνευματικῶς   {4462, adverb}
spiritually, through spiritual views and affections, 1 Cor 2:13 v.l., 14; *spiritually, in a spiritual sense, allegorically,* Rev 11:8*

πνευματικῶς   adverb [2t; adverb; 4462]
    πνευματικῶς
πνεύματος   gen sg neut [96t; n-3c(4); 4460]   πνεῦμα
πνευμάτων   gen pl neut [11t; n-3c(4); 4460]   "

πνέω   {4463, v-1a(7)}
[-, ἔπνευσα, -, -, -] *to breathe; to blow,* as the wind, Matt 7:25, 27; Acts 27:15 v.l.

πνίγω   {4464, v-1b(2)}
[(ἔπνιγον), -, ἔπνιξα, -, -, ἐπνίγην] *to stifle,*

suffocate, choke, Mark 5:13; *to seize by the throat,* Mark 13:17; 18:28*

πνικτόν   acc sg neut
    [Ac 21:25; a-1a(2a); 4465]   πνικτός

πνικτός, ή, όν   {4465, a-1a(2a)}
strangled, suffocated; in N.T. τὸ πνικτόν, *the flesh of animals killed by strangulation* or *suffocation,* Acts 15:20, 29; 21:25*

πνικτοῦ   gen sg neut [Ac 15:20; a-1a(2a); 4465]   "
πνικτῶν   gen pl neut [Ac 15:29; a-1a(2a); 4465]   "

πνοή, ῆς, ἡ   {4466, n-1b}
breath, respiration, Acts 17:25; *a wind, a blast of wind, breeze,* Acts 2:2*

πνοήν   acc sg fem [Ac 17:25; n-1b; 4466]   πνοή
πνοῆς   gen sg fem [Ac 2:2; n-1b; 4466]   "
πόδα   acc sg masc [3t; n-3c(2); 4546]   πούς
πόδας   acc pl masc [55t; n-3c(2); 4546]   "
πόδες   nom pl masc [7t; n-3c(2); 4546]   "
ποδήρη   acc sg masc [Rv 1:13; a-4a; 4468]   ποδήρης

ποδήρης, ες   {4468, a-4a}
reaching to the feet; as subst. sc. ἐσθής, *a long, flowing robe reaching down to the feet,* Rev 1:13*

ποδινιπτήρ, ῆρος, ὁ   {4469, n-3f(2a)}
basin for washing feet, John 13:5 v.l.*

ποδός   gen sg masc [Ac 7:5; n-3c(2); 4546]   πούς
ποδῶν   gen pl masc [19t; n-3c(2); 4546]   "

πόθεν   {4470, adverb}
whence? from where, used of place, etc., Matt 15:33; met. of a state of dignity, Rev 2:5; used of origin, Matt 21:25; of cause, source, author, etc., Matt 13:27, 54, 56; Luke 1:43; *how? in what way?* Mark 8:4; 12:37

πόθεν   adverb [29t; adverb; 4470]   πόθεν

ποία, ας, ἡ   {4471, n-1a}
grass, herb, BAGD says it was at one time thought to be the word in James 4:14, but now thought to be the fem. of ποῖος.

ποία   nom sg fem [6t; a-1a(1); 4481]   ποῖος
ποία   dat sg fem [12t; a-1a(1); 4481]   "
ποῖα   acc pl neut [Lk 24:19; a-1a(1); 4481]   "
ποίαν   acc sg fem [Rv 3:3; a-1a(1); 4481]   "
ποίας   gen sg fem [2t; a-1a(1); 4481]   "
ποίας   acc pl fem [Mt 19:18; a-1a(1); 4481]   "
ποιεῖ   pres act imperative 2 sg
    [3t; v-1d(2a); 4472]   ποιέω
ποιεῖ   pres act ind 3 sg [28t; v-1d(2a); 4472]   "
ποιεῖν   pres act inf [25t; v-1d(2a); 4472]   "
ποιεῖς   pres act ind 2 sg [13t; v-1d(2a); 4472]   "
ποιεῖσθαι   pres mid inf [2t; v-1d(2a); 4472]   "
ποιεῖσθαι   pres pass inf
    [1Ti 2:1; v-1d(2a); 4472]   "
ποιεῖσθε   pres mid imperative 2 pl
    [Rm 13:14; v-1d(2a); 4472]   "
ποιεῖται   pres mid ind 3 sg
    [Ep 4:16; v-1d(2a); 4472]   "
ποιεῖτε   pres act imperative 2 pl
    [16t; v-1d(2a); 4472]   "
ποιεῖτε   pres act ind 2 pl [18t; v-1d(2a); 4472]   "

ποιείτω   pres act imperative 3 sg
　　[2t; v-1d(2a); 4472]   "

ποιέω   {4472, v-1d(2a)}
　　[(ἐποίουν), ποιήσω, ἐποίησα, πεποίηκα,
　　πεποίημαι, ἐποιήθην] pluperf., πεποιήκειν, *to
　　make, form, construct*, Matt 17:4; Mark 9:5; John
　　2:15; of God, *to create*, Matt 19:4; Acts 4:24; *to
　　make, prepare* a feast, etc., Matt 22:2; Mark 6:21;
　　met. *to make, establish, ratify,* a covenant, Heb
　　8:9; *to make, assume, consider, regard*, Matt 12:33;
　　*to make, effect, bring to pass, cause to take place, do,
　　accomplish*, Matt 7:22; 21:21; Mark 3:8; 6:5; 7:37;
　　met. *to perfect, accomplish, fulfil, put in execution*
　　a purpose, promise, etc., Luke 16:4; 19:48; *to
　　cause, make*, Matt 5:32; John 11:37; Acts 24:12; *to
　　make* gain, *gain, acquire*, Matt 25:16; Luke 19:18;
　　to get, procure, Luke 12:33; *to make, to cause to be
　　or become* a thing, Matt 21:13; 23:15; *to use, treat*,
　　Luke 15:19; *to make, constitute, appoint* to some
　　office, Matt 4:19; Mark 3:14; *to make, declare to
　　be*, 1 John 1:10; 5:10; *to do, to perform, execute,
　　practise, act*, Matt 5:46, 47, 6:2, 3; *to commit* evil,
　　Matt 13:41; 27:23; *to be devoted to, follow, practise*,
　　John 3:21; 5:29; Rom 3:12; *to do, execute, fulfil,
　　keep, observe, obey*, precepts, etc., Matt 1:24; 5:19;
　　7:21, 24, 26; *to bring* evil *upon, inflict*, Acts 9:13;
　　to keep, celebrate a festival, Matt 26:18; *to
　　institute the celebration of* a festival, Heb 11:28;
　　ποιεῖν τινα ἔξω, *to cause to leave* a place, i.q. ἔξω
　　ἄγειν, *to lead or conduct out*, Acts 5:34; *to pass,
　　spend* time, *continue for* a time, Matt 20:12; Acts
　　15:33; 18:23; James 4:13; *to bear*, as trees, *yield,
　　produce*, Matt 3:8, 10; 7:17, 18, 19; with a
　　substantive or adjective it forms a periphrasis
　　for the verb corresponding to the noun or
　　adjective, e.g. δῆλον ποιεῖν, i.q. δηλοῦν, *to make
　　manifest, betray*, Matt 26:73; ἐκδίκησιν ποιεῖν, i.q.
　　ἐδικεῖν, *to vindicate, avenge*, Luke 18:7, 8; ἔκθετον
　　ποιεῖν, i.q. ἐκτιθέναι, *to expose* infants, Acts 7:19;
　　ἐνέδραν ποιεῖν, i.q. ἐνεδρεύειν, *to lie in wait*, Acts
　　25:3; ἐξουσίαν ποιεῖν, i.q. ἐξουσιάζειν, *to exercise
　　power or authority*, Rev 13:12; κρίσιν ποιεῖν, i.q.
　　κρίνειν, *to judge, act as judge*, John 5:27;
　　λύτρωσιν ποιεῖν, i.q. λυτροῦν, *to deliver, set free*,
　　Luke 1:68; μονὴν ποιεῖν, i.q. μένειν, *to remain,
　　dwell*, John 14:23; πόλεμον ποιεῖν, i.q. πολεμεῖν,
　　to make or wage war, fight, Rev 11:7; συμβούλιον
　　ποιεῖν, i.q. συμβουλεύεσθαι, *to consult together,
　　deliberate*, Mark 3:6; συνωμοσίαν ποιεῖν, i.q.
　　συνομνύναι, and συστροφὴν ποιεῖν, i.q.
　　συστρέφεσθαι, *to conspire together, form a
　　conspiracy*, Acts 23:12, 13; φανερὸν ποιεῖν, i.q.
　　φανεροῦν, *to make known, betray*, Matt 12:16;
　　ἀναβολὴν ποιεῖσθαι, i.q. ἀναβάλλεσθαι, *to delay,
　　procrastinate*, Acts 25:17; βέβαιον ποιεῖσθαι, i.q.
　　βεβαιοῦν, *to confirm, render firm and sure*, 2 Peter
　　1:10; δεήσεις ποιεῖσθαι, i.q. δεῖσθαι, *to pray, offer
　　prayer*, Luke 5:33; ἐκβολὴν ποιεῖσθαι, i.q.
　　ἐκβάλλειν, *to cast out, throw overboard*, Acts
　　27:18; καθαρισμὸν ποιεῖσθαι, i.q. καθαρίζειν, *to
　　cleanse* from sin, Heb 1:3; κοινωνίαν ποιεῖσθαι,
　　i.q. κοινωνεῖν, *to communicate in liberality, bestow
　　alms*, Rom 15:26; κοπετὸν ποιεῖν, i.q. κόπτεσθαι,
　　to lament, bewail, Acts 8:2; λόγον ποιεῖσθαι, *to
　　regard, make account of*, Acts 20:24; μνείαν

　　ποιεῖσθαι, i.q. μνησθῆναι, *to call to mind*, Rom
　　1:9; μνήμην ποιεῖσθαι, *to remember, retain in
　　memory*, 2 Peter 1:15; πορείαν ποιεῖσθαι, i.q.
　　πορεύεσθαι, *to go, journey, travel*, Luke 13:22;
　　πρόνοιαν ποιεῖσθαι, i.q. προνοεῖσθαι, *to take care
　　of, provide for*, Rom 13:14; σπουδὴν ποιεῖσθαι, i.q.
　　σπουδάζειν, *to act with diligence and earnestness*,
　　Jude 3

ποιῇ   pres act subj 3 sg [3t; v-1d(2a); 4472]   "

ποίημα, ατος, τό   {4473, n-3c(4)}
　　*that which is made or done; a work, workmanship,
　　creation*, Rom 1:20; met. Eph 2:10*

ποίημα   nom sg neut
　　[Ep 2:10; n-3c(4); 4473]   ποίημα
ποιήμασιν   dat pl neut [Rm 1:20; n-3c(4); 4473]   "
ποιῇς   pres act subj 2 sg
　　[5t; v-1d(2a); 4472]   ποιέω
ποιῆσαι   aor act inf [47t; v-1d(2a); 4472]   "
ποιήσαιεν   aor act opt 3 pl
　　[Lk 6:11; v-1d(2a); 4472]   "
ποιησάμενοι   aor mid ptcp nom pl masc
　　[Ac 23:13; v-1d(2a); 4472]   "
ποιησάμενος   aor mid ptcp nom sg masc
　　[2t; v-1d(2a); 4472]   "
ποιήσαντες   aor act ptcp nom pl masc
　　[7t; v-1d(2a); 4472]   "
ποιήσαντι   aor act ptcp dat sg masc
　　[3t; v-1d(2a); 4472]   "
ποιήσας   aor act ptcp nom sg masc
　　[20t; v-1d(2a); 4472]   "
ποιήσασαν   aor act ptcp acc sg fem
　　[Mk 5:32; v-1d(2a); 4472]   "
ποιήσασθαι   aor mid inf
　　[Rm 15:26; v-1d(2a); 4472]   "
ποιήσατε   aor act imperative 2 pl
　　[11t; v-1d(2a); 4472]   "
ποιησάτω   aor act imperative 3 sg
　　[2t; v-1d(2a); 4472]   "
ποιήσει   dat sg fem
　　[Jm 1:25; n-3e(5b); 4474]   ποίησις
ποιήσει   fut act ind 3 sg
　　[17t; v-1d(2a); 4472]   ποιέω
ποιήσεις   fut act ind 2 sg [3t; v-1d(2a); 4472]   "
ποιήσετε   fut act ind 2 pl [2t; v-1d(2a); 4472]   "
ποιήση   aor act subj 3 sg [9t; v-1d(2a); 4472]   "
ποιήσῃς   aor act subj 2 sg
　　[Mk 10:35; v-1d(2a); 4472]   "
ποιήσητε   aor act subj 2 pl
　　[Lk 17:10; v-1d(2a); 4472]   "

ποίησις, εως, ἡ   {4474, n-3e(5b)}
　　*a making; an acting, doing, performance;
　　observance* of a law, James 1:25*

ποιησόμεθα   fut mid ind 1 pl
　　[Jn 14:23; v-1d(2a); 4472]   "
ποιήσομεν   fut act ind 1 pl [4t; v-1d(2a); 4472]   "
ποίησον   aor act imperative 2 sg
　　[9t; v-1d(2a); 4472]   "
ποιήσουσιν   fut act ind 3 pl [5t; v-1d(2a); 4472] "
ποιήσω   aor act subj 1 sg [16t; v-1d(2a); 4472]   "
ποιήσω   fut act ind 1 sg [9t; v-1d(2a); 4472]   "
ποιήσωμεν   aor act subj 1 pl [8t; v-1d(2a); 4472] "

ποιήσων   fut act ptcp nom sg masc
   [Ac 24:17; v-1d(2a); 4472]   "
ποιήσωσιν   aor act subj 3 pl   [4t; v-1d(2a); 4472]   "
ποιηταί   nom pl masc [2t; n-1f; 4475]   ποιητής
ποιῆτε   pres act subj 2 pl
   [7t; v-1d(2a); 4472]   ποιέω

ποιητής, οῦ, ὁ   {4475, n-1f}
   a maker; the maker or *author* of a song or poem, *a*
   poet, Acts 17:28; *a doer; a performer* of the
   enactments of a law, Rom 2:13

ποιητής   nom sg masc [3t; n-1f; 4475]   ποιητής
ποιητῶν   gen pl masc [Ac 17:28; n-1f; 4475]
ποικίλαις   dat pl fem
   [7t; a-1a(2a); 4476]   ποικίλος
ποικίλης   gen sg fem [1P 4:10; a-1a(2a); 4476]   "
ποικίλοις   dat pl masc [2t; a-1a(2a); 4476]   "

ποικίλος, η, ον   {4476, a-1a(2a)}
   of various colors, variegated, checkered; various,
   diverse, manifold, Matt 4:24

ποίμαινε   pres act imperative 2 sg
   [Jn 21:16; v-2d(4); 4477]   ποιμαίνω
ποιμαίνει   pres act ind 3 sg
   [1C 9:7; v-2d(4); 4477]   "
ποιμαίνειν   pres act inf   [2t; v-2d(4); 4477]   "
ποιμαίνοντα   pres act ptcp acc sg masc
   [Lk 17:7; v-2d(4); 4477]   "
ποιμαίνοντες   pres act ptcp nom pl masc
   [Jd 12; v-2d(4); 4477]   "

ποιμαίνω   {4477, v-2d(4)}
   [ποιμανῶ, ἐποίμανα, -, -, -] *to feed, pasture, tend a*
   flock, Luke 17:7; 1 Cor 9:7; trop. *to feed* with
   selfish indulgence, *to pamper,* Jude 12; met. *to*
   tend, direct, superintend, Matt 2:6; John 21:16; *to*
   rule, Rev 2:27

ποιμάνατε   aor act imperative 2 pl
   [1P 5:2; v-2d(4); 4477]   "
ποιμανεῖ   fut act ind 3 sg [4t; v-2d(4); 4477]   "
ποιμένα   acc sg masc [6t; n-3f(1b); 4478]   ποιμήν
ποιμένας   acc pl masc [Ep 4:11; n-3f(1b); 4478]   "
ποιμένες   nom pl masc [3t; n-3f(1b); 4478]   "
ποιμένων   gen pl masc [Lk 2:18; n-3f(1b); 4478]   "

ποιμήν, ένος, ὁ   {4478, n-3f(1b)}
   one who tends flocks or *herds, a shepherd,*
   herdsman, Matt 9:36; 25:32; met. *a pastor,*
   superintendent, guardian, John 10:11, 14, 16

ποιμήν   nom sg masc [7t; n-3f(1b); 4478]

ποίμνη, ῆς, ἡ   {4479, n-1b}
   a flock of sheep, Luke 2:8; 1 Cor 9:7; meton. *a*
   flock of disciples, Matt 26:31; John 10:16*

ποίμνη   nom sg fem [Jn 10:16; n-1b; 4479]   ποίμνη
ποίμνην   acc sg fem [2t; n-1b; 4479]   "
ποίμνης   gen sg fem [2t; n-1b; 4479]   "

ποίμνιον, ου, τό   {4480, n-2c}
   a flock; met. *a flock* of Christian disciples, Luke
   12:32; Acts 20:28, 29; 1 Peter 5:2, 3*

ποίμνιον   voc sg neut
   [Lk 12:32; n-2c; 4480]   ποίμνιον
ποίμνιον   acc sg neut [1P 5:2; n-2c; 4480]   "

ποιμνίου   gen sg neut [2t; n-2c; 4480]
ποιμνίῳ   dat sg neut [Ac 20:28; n-2c; 4480]   "
ποῖον   nom sg neut [1P 2:20; a-1a(1); 4481]   ποῖος
ποῖον   acc sg masc [2t; a-1a(1); 4481]   "
ποῖον   acc sg neut [Jn 10:32; a-1a(1); 4481]   "

ποῖος, α, ον   {4481, a-1a(1)}
   of what kind, sort or *species,* John 12:33; 21:19;
   what? which? Matt 19:18; 21:23, 24, 27

ποίου   gen sg masc [Rm 3:27; a-1a(1); 4481]   "
ποιοῦμαι   pres mid ind 1 sg
   [2t; v-1d(2a); 4472]   ποιέω
ποιοῦμεν   pres act ind 1 pl [4t; v-1d(2a); 4472]   "
ποιούμενοι   pres mid ptcp nom pl masc
   [1Th 1:2; v-1d(2a); 4472]   "
ποιούμενος   pres mid ptcp nom sg masc
   [5t; v-1d(2a); 4472]   "
ποιοῦν   pres act ptcp nom sg neut
   [6t; v-1d(2a); 4472]   "
ποιοῦντα   pres act ptcp nom pl neut
   [Rv 16:14; v-1d(2a); 4472]   "
ποιοῦντα   pres act ptcp acc sg masc
   [4t; v-1d(2a); 4472]   "
ποιοῦνται   pres mid ind 3 pl
   [Lk 5:33; v-1d(2a); 4472]   "
ποιοῦντας   pres act ptcp acc pl masc
   [3t; v-1d(2a); 4472]   "
ποιοῦντες   pres act ptcp nom pl masc
   [7t; v-1d(2a); 4472]   "
ποιοῦντι   pres act ptcp dat sg masc
   [Jm 4:17; v-1d(2a); 4472]   "
ποιοῦντι   pres act ptcp dat sg neut
   [Mt 21:43; v-1d(2a); 4472]   "
ποιοῦντος   pres act ptcp gen sg masc
   [Mt 6:3; v-1d(2a); 4472]   "
ποιοῦσιν   pres act ind 3 pl [11t; v-1d(2a); 4472]   "
ποιοῦσιν   pres act ptcp dat pl masc
   [Jm 3:18; v-1d(2a); 4472]   "
ποίῳ   dat sg masc [3t; a-1a(1); 4481]   ποῖος
ποίῳ   dat sg neut [2t; a-1a(1); 4481]   "
ποιῶ   pres act ind 1 sg
   [22t; v-1d(2a); 4472]   ποιέω
ποιῶ   pres act subj 1 sg
   [Jn 6:38; v-1d(2a); 4472]   "
ποιῶμεν   pres act subj 1 pl [2t; v-1d(2a); 4472]   "
ποιῶν   pres act ptcp nom sg masc
   [26t; v-1d(2a); 4472]   "
ποιῶν   pres act ptcp voc sg masc
   [Rm 2:3; v-1d(2a); 4472]   "
ποιῶσιν   pres act subj 3 pl [4t; v-1d(2a); 4472]   "
πόλει   dat sg fem [21t; n-3e(5b); 4484]   πόλις
πόλεις   nom pl fem [2t; n-3e(5b); 4484]   "
πόλεις   acc pl fem [10t; n-3e(5b); 4484]   "
πολεμεῖ   pres act ind 3 sg
   [Rv 19:11; v-1d(2a); 4482]   πολεμέω
πολεμεῖτε   pres act ind 2 pl
   [Jm 4:2; v-1d(2a); 4482]   "

πολεμέω   {4482, v-1d(2a)}
   [πολεμήσω, ἐπολέμησα, -, -, ἐπολεμήθην] *to make*
   or *wage war, fight,* Rev 2:16; 12:7; *to battle,*
   quarrel, James 4:2

πολεμῆσαι   aor act inf   [2t; v-1d(2a); 4482]   "

πολεμήσουσιν   fut act ind 3 pl
  [Rv 17:14; v-1d(2a); 4482]   "
πολεμήσω   fut act ind 1 sg
  [Rv 2:16; v-1d(2a); 4482]   "
πόλεμοι   nom pl masc [Jm 4:1; n-2a; 4483]   πόλεμος
πόλεμον   acc sg masc [10t; n-2a; 4483]   "

πόλεμος, ου, ὁ   {4483, n-2a}
  war, Matt 24:6; Mark 13:7; *battle, engagement,*
  combat, 1 Cor 14:8; Heb 11:34; *battling, strife,*
  James 4:1

πόλεμος   nom sg masc [Rv 12:7; n-2a; 4483]   "
πολέμους   acc pl masc [3t; n-2a; 4483]   "
πολέμῳ   dat sg masc [Hb 11:34; n-2a; 4483]   "
πολέμων   gen pl masc [2t; n-2a; 4483]   "
πόλεσιν   dat pl fem [2t; n-3e(5b); 4484]   πόλις
πόλεων   gen pl fem [6t; n-3e(5b); 4484]   "
πόλεως   gen sg fem [36t; n-3e(5b); 4484]   "
πόλιν   acc sg fem [64t; n-3e(5b); 4484]   "

πόλις, εως, ἡ   {4484, n-3e(5b)}
  a city, an enclosed and walled town, Matt 10:5, 11;
  11:1; meton. *the inhabitants of a city,* Matt 8:34;
  10:15; with a gen. of person, or a personal
  pronoun, *the city* of any one, *the city* of one's
  birth or residence, Matt 9:1; Luke 2:4, 11; ἡ
  πόλις, *the city,* κατ' ἐξοχήν, *Jerusalem,* Matt 21:18;
  28:11; met. *a place of permanent residence, abode,*
  home, Heb 11:10, 16; 13:14

πόλις   nom sg fem [22t; n-3e(5b); 4484]   "
πολῖται   nom pl masc
  [Lk 19:14; n-1f; 4489]   πολίτης
πολιτάρχας   acc pl masc
  [2t; n-1f; 4485]   πολιτάρχης

πολιτάρχης, ου, ὁ   {4485, n-1f}
  a ruler or *prefect of a city, city magistrate,* Acts
  17:6, 8*

πολιτεία, ας, ἡ   {4486, n-1a}
  the state of being a citizen; citizenship, the right or
  privilege of being a citizen, freedom of a city or
  state, Acts 22:28; *a commonwealth, community,*
  Eph 2:12*

πολιτείαν   acc sg fem
  [Ac 22:28; n-1a; 4486]   πολιτεία
πολιτείας   gen sg fem [Ep 2:12; n-1a; 4486]   "
πολιτεύεσθε   pres mid imperative 2 pl
  [Pp 1:27; v-1a(6); 4488]   πολιτεύομαι

πολίτευμα, ατος, τό   {4487, n-3c(4)}
  the administration of a commonwealth; in N.T.
  equivalent to πολιτεία, *a community,*
  commonwealth, Phil 3:20*

πολίτευμα   nom sg neut
  [Pp 3:20; n-3c(4); 4487]   πολίτευμα

πολιτεύομαι   {4488, v-1a(6)}
  [-, ἐπολιτευσάμην, -, πεπολίτευμαι, -] intrans. *to*
  be a citizen; trans. *to govern a city* or *state,*
  administer the affairs of a state; pass. *to be*
  governed; in N.T. *to order one's life and conduct,*
  converse, live, in a certain manner as to habits
  and principles, Acts 23:1; Phil 1:27*

πολίτην   acc sg masc [Hb 8:11; n-1f; 4489]   πολίτης

πολίτης, ου, ὁ   {4489, n-1f}
  a citizen, Luke 15:15; 19:14; Acts 21:39; Heb
  8:11*

πολίτης   nom sg masc [Ac 21:39; n-1f; 4489]   "
πολιτῶν   gen pl masc [Lk 15:15; n-1f; 4489]   "
πολλά   nom pl neut [14t; a-1a(2a); 4498]   πολύς
πολλά   acc pl neut [51t; a-1a(2a); 4498]   "
πολλαί   nom pl fem [6t; a-1a(2a); 4498]   "
πολλαῖς   dat pl fem [4t; a-1a(2a); 4498]   "

πολλάκις   {4490, adverb}
  many times, often, frequently, Matt 17:15; Mark
  5:4; 9:22

πολλάκις   adverb [18t; adverb; 4490]   πολλάκις
πολλαπλασίονα   acc pl neut
  [Lk 18:30; a-4b(1); 4491]   πολλαπλασίων

πολλαπλασίων, ον   {4491, a-4b(1)}
  manifold, many times more, Luke 18:30; Matt
  19:29 v.l.*

πολλάς   acc pl fem [11t; a-1a(2a); 4498]   πολύς
πολλή   nom sg fem [4t; a-1a(2a); 4498]   "
πολλῇ   dat sg fem [8t; a-1a(2a); 4498]   "
πολλήν   acc sg fem [9t; a-1a(2a); 4498]   "
πολλῆς   gen sg fem [13t; a-1a(2a); 4498]   "
πολλοί   nom pl masc [83t; a-1a(2a); 4498]   "
πολλοῖς   dat pl masc [5t; a-1a(2a); 4498]   "
πολλοῖς   dat pl neut [2t; a-1a(2a); 4498]   "
πολλοῦ   gen sg masc [5t; a-1a(2a); 4498]   "
πολλοῦ   gen sg neut [2t; a-1a(2a); 4498]   "
πολλούς   acc pl masc [23t; a-1a(2a); 4498]   "
πολλῷ   dat sg masc [5t; a-1a(2a); 4498]   "
πολλῷ   dat sg neut [15t; a-1a(2a); 4498]   "
πολλῶν   gen pl masc [20t; a-1a(2a); 4498]   "
πολλῶν   gen pl fem [3t; a-1a(2a); 4498]   "
πολλῶν   gen pl neut [16t; a-1a(2a); 4498]   "
πολύ   nom sg neut [8t; a-1a(2a); 4498]   "
πολύ   acc sg neut [5t; a-1a(2a); 4498]   "
πολύ   acc sg neut, can function
  adverbially [10t; a-1a(2a); 4498]   "

πολυεύσπλαγχνος, ον   {4492, a-3a}
  rich in comparison, James 5:11 v.l.*

πολύλαλος, ον   {4493, a-3a}
  talkative, BAGD says that πολύλαλοι could have
  been read for πολλοί in James 3:1*

πολυλογία, ας, ἡ   {4494, n-1a}
  wordiness, loquacity, Matt 6:7; Luke 11:2 v.l.*

πολυλογίᾳ   dat sg fem
  [Mt 6:7; n-1a; 4494]   πολυλογία

πολυμερῶς   {4495, adverb}
  in many parts or *ways,* Heb 1:1*

πολυμερῶς   adverb [Hb 1:1; adverb; 4495]
                                  πολυμερῶς
πολύν   acc sg masc [9t; a-1a(2a); 4498]   πολύς

πολυπλήθεια, ας, ἡ   {4496, n-1a}
  large crowd, Acts 14:17 v.l.*

πολυποίκιλος, ον   {4497, a-3a}
  exceedingly various, multiform, manifold; by impl.
  immense, infinite, Eph 3:10*

πολυποίκιλος nom sg fem
 [Ep 3:10; a-3a; 4497] πολυποίκιλος

πολύς, πολλή, πολύ {4498, a-1a(2a)}
 great in magnitude or quantity, *much, large,*
 Matt 13:5; John 3:23; 15:8; pl. *many,* Matt 3:7; in
 time, *long,* Matt 25:19; Mark 6:35; John 5:6; οἱ
 πολλοί, *the many, the mass,* Rom 5:15; 12:5; 1 Cor
 10:33; τὸ πολύ, *much,* 2 Cor 8:15; πολύ, as an
 adv., *much, greatly,* Mark 12:27; Luke 7:47; of
 time, ἐπὶ πολύ, *a long time,* Acts 28:6; μετ' οὐ
 πολύ, *not long after,* Acts 27:14; followed by a
 compar., *much,* 2 Cor 8:22; πολλῷ, *much, by*
 much, Matt 6:30; Mark 10:48; τὰ πολλά, as an
 adv., *most frequently, generally,* Rom 15:22;
 πολλά, as an adv., *much, greatly, vehemently,*
 Mark 1:45; 3:12; of time, *many times, frequently,*
 often, Matt 9:14

πολύς nom sg masc [26t; a-1a(2a); 4498] πολύς

πολύσπλαγχνος, ον {4499, a-3a}
 very merciful, very compassionate, James 5:11*

πολύσπλαγχνος nom sg masc
 [Jm 5:11; a-3a; 4499] πολύσπλαγχνος
πολυτελεῖ dat sg masc
 [1Ti 2:9; a-4a; 4500] πολυτελής
πολυτελές nom sg neut [1P 3:4; a-4a; 4500] "

πολυτελής, ές {4500, a-4a}
 expensive, costly, Mark 14:3; 1 Tim 2:9; *of great*
 value, very precious, 1 Peter 3:4*

πολυτελοῦς gen sg fem [Mk 14:3; a-4a; 4500] "
πολύτιμον acc sg masc
 [Mt 13:46; a-3a; 4501] πολύτιμος

πολύτιμος, ον {4501, a-3a}
 of great price, costly, precious, Matt 13:46; 26:7 v.l.;
 John 12:3; 1 Pet 1:7*

πολυτιμότερον nom sg neut comparative
 [1P 1:7; a-3a; 4501] "
πολυτίμου gen sg fem [Jn 12:3; a-3a; 4501] "

πολυτρόπως {4502, adverb}
 in many ways, in various modes, Heb 1:1*

πολυτρόπως adverb
 [Hb 1:1; adverb; 4502] πολυτρόπως

πόμα, ατος, τό {4503, n-3c(4)}
 drink, 1 Cor 10:4; 12:13 v.l.; Heb 9:10*

πόμα acc sg neut [1C 10:4; n-3c(4); 4503] πόμα
πόμασιν dat pl neut [Hb 9:10; n-3c(4); 4503] "
πονηρά nom sg fem [5t; a-1a(1); 4505] πονηρός
πονηρά nom pl neut [4t; a-1a(1); 4505] "
πονηρᾷ dat sg fem [2t; a-1a(1); 4505] "
πονηρά acc pl neut [4t; a-1a(1); 4505] "
πονηραί nom pl fem [2t; a-1a(1); 4505] "
πονηρᾶς gen sg fem [Hb 10:22; a-1a(1); 4505] "
πονηρέ voc sg masc [3t; a-1a(1); 4505] "

πονηρία, ας, ἡ {4504, n-1a}
 pr. *badness, bad condition;* in N.T. *evil disposition*
 of mind, *wickedness, mischief, malignity,* Matt
 22:18; pl. πονηρίαι, *wicked deeds, villanies,* Mark
 7:23; Acts 3:26

πονηρίᾳ dat sg fem [Rm 1:29; n-1a; 4504] πονηρία

πονηρίαι nom pl fem [Mk 7:22; n-1a; 4504] "
πονηρίαν acc sg fem [Mt 22:18; n-1a; 4504] "
πονηρίας gen sg fem [3t; n-1a; 4504] "
πονηριῶν gen pl fem [Ac 3:26; n-1a; 4504] "
πονηροί nom pl masc [5t; a-1a(1); 4505] πονηρός
πονηροῖς dat pl masc [3J 10; a-1a(1); 4505] "
πονηροῖς dat pl neut [2t; a-1a(1); 4505] "
πονηρόν nom sg neut [4t; a-1a(1); 4505] "
πονηρόν acc sg masc [3t; a-1a(1); 4505] "
πονηρόν acc sg neut [5t; a-1a(1); 4505] "

πονηρός, ά, όν {4505, a-1a(1)}
 bad, unsound, Matt 6:23; 7:17, 18; *evil, afflictive,*
 Eph 5:16; 6:13; Rev 16:2; *evil, wrongful,*
 malignant, malevolent, Matt 5:11, 39; Acts 28:21;
 evil, wicked, impious, and τὸ πονηρόν, *evil, wrong,*
 wickedness, Matt 5:37, 45; 9:4; *slothful, inactive,*
 Matt 25:26; Luke 19:22; ὁ πονηρός, *the evil one,*
 the devil, Matt 13:19, 38; John 17:15; *evil eye, i.q.*
 φθονερός *envious,* Matt 20:15; Mark 7:22; impl.
 covetous, Matt 7:11

πονηρός nom sg masc [8t; a-1a(1); 4505] "
πονηρότερα acc pl neut comparative
 [2t; a-1a(1); 4505] "
πονηροῦ gen sg masc [9t; a-1a(1); 4505] "
πονηροῦ gen sg neut [3t; a-1a(1); 4505] "
πονηρούς acc pl masc [7t; a-1a(1); 4505] "
πονηρῷ dat sg masc [1J 5:19; a-1a(1); 4505] "
πονηρῷ dat sg neut [Mt 5:39; a-1a(1); 4505] "
πονηρῶν gen pl masc [2t; a-1a(1); 4505] "
πονηρῶν gen pl neut [4t; a-1a(1); 4505] "
πόνον acc sg masc [Cl 4:13; n-2a; 4506] πόνος

πόνος, ου, ὁ {4506, n-2a}
 labor, travail; pain, misery, anguish, Col 4:13; Rev
 16:10, 11; 21:4*

πόνος nom sg masc [Rv 21:4; n-2a; 4506] "
πόνου gen sg masc [Rv 16:10; n-2a; 4506] "
Ποντικόν acc sg masc
 [Ac 18:2; a-1a(2a); 4507] Ποντικός

Ποντικός, ή, όν {4507, a-1a(2a)}
 belonging to or *an inhabitant of Pontus,* Acts 18:2*

Πόντιος, ου, ὁ {4508, n-2a}
 Pontius, pr. name, Acts 4:27

Πόντιος nom sg masc
 [Ac 4:27; n-2a; 4508] Πόντιος
Ποντίου gen sg masc [2t; n-2a; 4508] "
Πόντον acc sg masc [Ac 2:9; n-2a; 4509] Πόντος

Πόντος, ου, ὁ {4509, n-2a}
 Pontus, country of Asia Minor, Acts 2:9; 1 Peter
 1:1*

πόντος, ου, ὁ {4510; n-2a}
 the (high) sea, Rev 18:17 v.l.*

Πόντου gen sg masc [1P 1:1; n-2a; 4509] Πόντος
πόνων gen pl masc [Rv 16:11; n-2a; 4506] πόνος

Πόπλιος, ου, ὁ {4511, n-2a}
 Publius, pr. name, Acts 28:7, 8*

Ποπλίου gen sg masc [Ac 28:8; n-2a; 4511] Πόπλιος
Ποπλίῳ dat sg masc [Ac 28:7; n-2a; 4511] "

πορεία, ας, ἡ   {4512, n-1a}
  a going, progress; a journey, travel, Luke 13:22;
  from the Hebrew, *way* of life, *business,*
  occupation, James 1:11*

πορείαις   dat pl fem [Jm 1:11; n-1a; 4512]   πορεία
πορείαν   acc sg fem [Lk 13:22; n-1a; 4512]   "
πορεύεσθαι   pres mid inf
  [17t; v-1a(6); 4513]   πορεύω
πορεύεσθε   pres mid imperative 2 pl
  [7t; v-1a(6); 4513]   "
πορεύεται   pres mid ind 3 sg [7t; v-1a(6); 4513]   "
πορευθείς   aor pass ptcp nom sg masc
  [8t; v-1a(6); 4513]   "
πορευθεῖσα   aor pass ptcp nom sg fem
  [Mk 16:10; v-1a(6); 4513]   "
πορευθεῖσαι   aor pass ptcp nom pl fem
  [Mt 28:7; v-1a(6); 4513]   "
πορευθέντες   aor pass ptcp nom pl masc
  [15t; v-1a(6); 4513]   "
πορευθέντι   aor pass ptcp dat sg masc
  [Ac 27:3; v-1a(6); 4513]   "
πορευθῇ   aor pass subj 3 sg
  [Lk 16:30; v-1a(6); 4513]   "
πορευθῆναι   aor pass inf [2t; v-1a(6); 4513]   "
πορευθῆτε   aor pass subj 2 pl
  [Lk 21:8; v-1a(6); 4513]   "
πορευθητι   aor pass imperative 2 sg
  [4t; v-1a(6); 4513]   "
πορευθῶ   aor pass subj 1 sg [2t; v-1a(6); 4513]   "
πορευθῶσιν   aor pass subj 3 pl
  [Ac 23:23; v-1a(6); 4513]   "
πορεύομαι   pres mid ind 1 sg [8t; v-1a(6); 4513]   "
πορευομένη   pres pass ptcp nom sg fem
  [Ac 9:31; v-1a(6); 4513]   "
πορευόμενοι   pres mid ptcp nom pl masc
  [7t; v-1a(6); 4513]   "
πορευομένοις   pres mid ptcp dat pl masc
  [Mk 16:12; v-1a(6); 4513]   "
πορευόμενον   pres mid ptcp nom sg neut
  [Lk 9:53; v-1a(6); 4513]   "
πορευόμενον   pres mid ptcp acc sg masc
  [Ac 1:11; v-1a(6); 4513]   "
πορευόμενος   pres mid ptcp nom sg masc
  [3t; v-1a(6); 4513]   "
πορευομένου   pres mid ptcp gen sg masc
  [2t; v-1a(6); 4513]   "
πορευομένους   pres mid ptcp acc pl masc
  [2t; v-1a(6); 4513]   "
πορευομένῳ   pres mid ptcp dat sg masc
  [Ac 22:6; v-1a(6); 4513]   "
πορευομένων   pres mid ptcp gen pl masc
  [3t; v-1a(6); 4513]   "
πορευομένων   pres mid ptcp gen pl fem
  [Mt 28:11; v-1a(6); 4513]   "
πορεύου   pres mid imperative 2 sg
  [16t; v-1a(6); 4513]   "
πορεύσεται   fut mid ind 3 sg
  [Lk 11:5; v-1a(6); 4513]   "
πορεύσῃ   fut mid ind 2 sg
  [Ac 25:12; v-1a(6); 4513]   "
πορεύσομαι   fut mid ind 1 sg [2t; v-1a(6); 4513]   "

πορευσόμεθα   fut mid ind 1 pl
  [Jm 4:13; v-1a(6); 4513]   "
πορεύσονται   fut mid ind 3 pl
  [1C 16:4; v-1a(6); 4513]   "

πορεύω   {4513, v-1a(6)}
  [(ἐπορευόμην), πορεύσομαι, -, -, πεπόρευμαι,
  ἐπορεύθην] also listed as a deponent,
  πορεύομαι, *to go, pass from one place to another,*
  Matt 17:27; 18:12; *to go away, depart,* Matt 24:1;
  25:41; John 14:2, 3; trop. *to go away, depart,* from
  life, *to die,* Luke 22:22; *to go, pass on one's way,*
  journey, travel, Matt 2:8, 9; Luke 1:39; 2:41;
  πορεύομαι ὀπίσω, *to go after, to become a follower*
  or *partisan,* Luke 21:8; or, *to pursue after, be*
  devoted to, 2 Peter 2:10; from the Hebrew, *to go*
  or *proceed* in any way or course of life, *live* in
  any manner, Luke 1:6; 8:14; Acts 9:31

πορεύωμαι   pres mid subj 1 sg [2t; v-1a(6); 4513]   "

πορθέω   {4514, v-1d(2a)}
  [(ἐπόρθουν), -, ἐπόρθησα, -, -, -] *to lay waste,*
  destroy; impl. *to harass, ravage,* Acts 9:21; Gal
  1:13, 23*

πορθήσας   aor act ptcp nom sg masc
  [Ac 9:21; v-1d(2a); 4514]   πορθέω
πορισμόν   acc sg masc
  [1Ti 6:5; n-2a; 4516]   πορισμός

πορισμός, οῦ, ὁ   {4516, n-2a}
  a providing, procuring; meton. *source of gain,* 1
  Tim 6:5, 6*

πορισμός   nom sg masc [1Ti 6:6; n-2a; 4516]   "
Πόρκιον   acc sg masc
  [Ac 24:27; n-2a; 4517]   Πόρκιος

Πόρκιος, ου, ὁ   {4517, n-2a}
  Porcius, pr. name, Acts 24:27*

πόρναι   nom pl fem [2t; n-1b; 4520]   πόρνη

πορνεία, ας, ἡ   {4518, n-1a}
  fornication, whoredom, Matt 15:19; Mark 7:21;
  Acts 15:20, 29; *concubinage,* John 8:41; *adultery,*
  Matt 5:32; 19:9; *incest,* 1 Cor 5:1; *lewdness,*
  uncleanness, genr., Rom 1:29; from the Hebrew,
  put symbolically for *idolatry,* Rev 2:21; 14:8

πορνεία   nom sg fem [4t; n-1a; 4518]   πορνεία
πορνείᾳ   dat sg fem [4t; n-1a; 4518]   "
πορνεῖαι   nom pl fem [2t; n-1a; 4518]   "
πορνείαν   acc sg fem [3t; n-1a; 4518]   "
πορνείας   gen sg fem [11t; n-1a; 4518]   "
πορνείας   acc pl fem [1C 7:2; n-1a; 4518]   "
πορνεῦσαι   aor act inf
  [2t; v-1a(6); 4519]   πορνεύω
πορνεύσαντες   aor act ptcp nom pl masc
  [Rv 18:9; v-1a(6); 4519]   "

πορνεύω   {4519, v-1a(6)}
  [πορνεύσω, ἐπόρνευσα, -, -, -] *to commit*
  fornication, Mark 10:19 v.l.; 1 Cor 6:18; 10:8; Rev
  2:14, 20; from the Hebrew, *to commit* spiritual
  fornication, practise idolatry, Rev 17:2; 18:3, 9

πορνεύωμεν   pres act subj 1 pl
  [1C 10:8; v-1a(6); 4519]   "

πορνεύων   pres act ptcp nom sg masc
   [1C 6:18; v-1a(6); 4519]   "

πόρνη, ης, ἡ   {4520, n-1b}
   a prostitute, a whore, harlot, an unchaste female,
   Matt 21:31, 32; *from the Hebrew, an idolatress,*
   Rev 17:1, 5, 15

πόρνη   nom sg fem [3t; n-1b; 4520]   πόρνη
πόρνη   dat sg fem [1C 6:16; n-1b; 4520]   "
πόρνην   acc sg fem [2t; n-1b; 4520]   "
πόρνης   gen sg fem [2t; n-1b; 4520]   "
πόρνοι   nom pl masc [2t; n-2a; 4521]   πόρνος
πόρνοις   dat pl masc [4t; n-2a; 4521]   "

πόρνος, ου, ὁ   {4521, n-2a}
   a catamite; in N.T. *a fornicator, impure person,* 1
   Cor 5:9, 10, 11; 6:9

πόρνος   nom sg masc [3t; n-2a; 4521]   "
πόρνους   acc pl masc [Hb 13:4; n-2a; 4521]   "
πορνῶν   gen pl fem [2t; n-1b; 4520]   πόρνη

πόρρω   {4522, adverb}
   in advance, far advanced; far, far off, at a distance,
   Matt 15:8; Mark 7:6; Luke 14:32, can be an
   improper prep. with the gen. The comparative
   form of the adverb appears as πορρώτερον (v.l.
   πορρωτέρω) at Luke 24:28.*

πόρρω   adverb [3t; adverb; 4522]   πόρρω

πόρρωθεν   {4523, adverb}
   from a distance, from afar, Heb 11:13; *at a distance,*
   far, far off, Luke 17:12*

πόρρωθεν   adverb [2t; adverb; 4523]   πόρρωθεν
πορρώτερον   adverb-comparative
   [Lk 24:28; adverb; 4522]   πόρρω

πορρωτέρω, see πόρρω   {4524}
   farther, beyond, Luke 24:28 v.l.*

πορφύρα, ας, ἡ   {4525, n-1a}
   purpura, murex, a species of shell-fish that
   yielded the purple dye, highly esteemed by the
   ancients, its tint being a bright crimson; in N.T.
   a purple garment, robe of purple, Luke 16:19; Rev
   17:4 v.l.; 18:12

πορφύραν   acc sg fem [3t; n-1a; 4525]   πορφύρα
πορφύρας   gen sg fem [Rv 18:12; n-1a; 4525]   "

πορφύρεος, ον, see πορφυροῦς   {4526}

πορφυρόπωλις, ιδος, ἡ   {4527, n-3c(2)}
   a female seller of purple cloths, Acts 16:4*

πορφυρόπωλις   nom sg fem
   [Ac 16:14; n-3c(2); 4527]   πορφυρόπωλις
πορφυροῦν   acc sg neut [4t; a-1b; 4528]   πορφυροῦς

πορφυροῦς, ᾶ, οῦν   {4528, a-1b}
   uncontracted form, πορφύρεος, *purple,* John
   19:2, 5; *purple clothing* , Rev 17:4; 18:16*

πόσα   acc pl neut [2t; a-1a(2a); 4531]   πόσος
πόσαι   nom pl fem [Ac 21:20; a-1a(2a); 4531]   "

ποσάκις   {4529, adverb}
   How many times? How often? Matt 18:21; 23:37;
   Luke 13:34*

ποσάκις   adverb [3t; adverb; 4529]   ποσάκις

πόσας   acc pl fem [Mt 16:10; a-1a(2a); 4531]   πόσος
πόσει   dat sg fem [Cl 2:16; n-3e(5b); 4530]   πόσις
πόσην   acc sg fem [2C 7:11; a-1a(2a); 4531]   πόσος
ποσίν   dat pl masc [5t; n-3c(2); 4546]   πούς

πόσις, εως, ἡ   {4530, n-3e(5b)}
   drinking; drink, beverage, John 6:55; Rom 14:17;
   Col 2:16*

πόσις   nom sg fem [2t; n-3e(5b); 4530]   πόσις
πόσοι   nom pl masc
   [Lk 15:17; a-1a(2a); 4531]   πόσος
πόσον   nom sg neut [Mt 6:23; a-1a(2a); 4531]   "
πόσον   acc sg neut [2t; a-1a(2a); 4531]   "

πόσος, η, ον   {4531, a-1a(2a)}
   How great? How much? Matt 6:23; Luke 16:5, 7;
   2 Cor 7:11; πόσῳ, adverbially before a
   comparative, *How much? By how much?* Matt
   7:11; 10:25; Heb 10:29; of time, *How long?* Mark
   9:21; of number, pl. *How many?* Matt 15:34;
   16:9, 10

πόσος   nom sg masc [Mk 9:21; a-1a(2a); 4531]   "
πόσους   acc pl masc [5t; a-1a(2a); 4531]   "
πόσῳ   dat sg neut [11t; a-1a(2a); 4531]   "
πόσων   gen pl fem [Mk 8:20; a-1a(2a); 4531]   "
ποταμοί   nom pl masc [3t; n-2a; 4532]   ποταμός
ποταμόν   acc sg masc [5t; n-2a; 4532]   "

ποταμός, οῦ, ὁ   {4532, n-2a}
   a river, stream, Mark 1:5; Acts 16:13; met. and
   allegor. John 7:38; Rev 22:1, 2; *a flood, winter*
   torrent, for χείμαρρος ποταμός, Matt 7:25, 27

ποταμός   nom sg masc [2t; n-2a; 4532]   "
ποταμοῦ   gen sg masc [Rv 22:2; n-2a; 4532]   "
ποταμούς   acc pl masc [Rv 16:4; n-2a; 4532]   "
ποταμοφόρητον   acc sg fem
   [Rv 12:15; a-3a; 4533]   ποταμοφόρητος

ποταμοφόρητος, ον   {4533, a-3a}
   borne along or *carried away by a flood* or *torrent,*
   Rev 12:15*

ποταμῷ   dat sg masc [3t; n-2a; 4532]   ποταμός
ποταμῶν   gen pl masc [2t; n-2a; 4532]   "
ποταπαί   nom pl fem
   [Mk 13:1; a-1a(2a); 4534]   ποταπός
ποταπή   nom sg fem [Lk 7:39; a-1a(2a); 4534]   "
ποταπήν   acc sg fem [1J 3:1; a-1a(2a); 4534]   "
ποταποί   nom pl masc [Mk 13:1; a-1a(2a); 4534] "

ποταπός, ή, όν   {4534, a-1a(2a)}
   Of what country? in N.T. equivalent to ποῖος,
   What? Of what manner? Of what kind or sort?
   Luke 1:29; 7:37; denoting admiration, *What?*
   What kind of? How great? Matt 8:27; Mark 13:1

ποταπός   nom sg masc [2t; a-1a(2a); 4534]   "
ποταπούς   acc pl masc [2P 3:11; a-1a(2a); 4534] "

ποταπῶς   {4535; adverb}
   in what way, how, Acts 20:18 v.l.*

πότε   {4536, adverb}
   interrogative adverb, *When? At what time?*
   Matt 24:3; 25:37, 38, 39, 44; ἕως πότε, *until when?*
   how long? Matt 17:17

πότε   adverb [19t; adverb; 4536]   πότε

ποτέ   {4537, particle}
enclitic particle, *once, some time* or *other,* either
past or future; *formerly,* John 9:13; *at length,*
Luke 22:32; *at any time, ever,* Eph 5:29; Heb 2:1;
intensive after interrogatives, *ever,* 1 Cor 9:7;
Heb 1:5

πότε   part [29t; particle; 4537]   ποτέ

πότερον   {4538, particle}
interrogative of πότερος, α, ον, which never
occurs in N.T. other than in this form, *whether?,*
John 7:17*

πότερον   part [Jn 7:17; particle; 4538]   πότερον

ποτήριον, ου, τό   {4539, n-2c}
a vessel for drinking, cup, Matt 10:42; 23:25, 26;
meton. *the contents of a cup, liquor contained in a
cup,* Luke 22:20; 1 Cor 10:16; from the Hebrew,
the cup or *potion* of what God's administration
deals out, Matt 20:22, 23; 26:42 v.l.; Rev 14:10

ποτήριον   nom sg neut [4t; n-2c; 4539]   ποτήριον
ποτήριον   acc sg neut [20t; n-2c; 4539]   "
ποτηρίου   gen sg neut [4t; n-2c; 4539]   "
ποτηρίῳ   dat sg neut [2t; n-2c; 4539]   "
ποτηρίων   gen pl neut [Mk 7:4; n-2c; 4539]   "
πότιζε   pres act imperative 2 sg
          [Rm 12:20; v-2a(1); 4540]   ποτίζω
ποτίζει   pres act ind 3 sg
          [Lk 13:15; v-2a(1); 4540]   "

ποτίζω   {4540, v-2a(1)}
[(ἐπότιζον), -, ἐπότισα, πεπότικα, πεπότισμαι,
ἐποτίσθην] *to cause to drink, give drink to,* Matt
10:42; met. 1 Cor 3:2; Rev 14:8; *to water, irrigate,*
met. 1 Cor 3:6, 7, 8

ποτίζων   pres act ptcp nom sg masc
          [2t; v-2a(1); 4540]   "

Ποτίολοι, ων, οἱ   {4541, n-2a}
Puteoli, a town of Italy, Acts 28:13*

Ποτιόλους   acc pl masc
          [Ac 28:13; n-2a; 4541]   Ποτίολοι
ποτίσῃ   aor act subj 3 sg
          [2t; v-2a(1); 4540]   ποτίζω
πότοις   dat pl masc [1P 4:3; n-2a; 4542]   πότος

πότος, ου, ὁ   {4542, n-2a}
a drinking; a drinking together, drinking-bout, 1
Peter 4:3*

πού   {4543, adverb}
enclitic, *somewhere, in a certain place,* Heb 2:6;
4:4; with numerals, *thereabout,* Rom 4:19*

πού   adverb [4t; adverb; 4543]   πού

ποῦ   {4544, adverb}
interrogative, *where? In what place?* direct, Matt
2:2; Luke 8:25; John 1:39; indirect, Matt 2:4;
John 1:40; *whither,* John 3:8; 7:35; 13:36

ποῦ   adverb [48t; adverb; 4544]   ποῦ

Πούδης, δεντος, τό   {4545, n-3c(5a)}
Pudens, pr. name, Latin, 2 Tim 4:21*

Πούδης   nom sg masc
          [2Ti 4:21; n-3c(5a); 4545]   Πούδης

πούς, ποδός, ὁ   {4546, n-3c(2)}
the foot, Matt 4:6; 5:35; 7:6; 22:44; 28:9; Luke
1:79; Acts 5:9; Rom 3:15

πούς   nom sg masc [3t; n-3c(2); 4546]   πούς

πρᾶγμα, ατος, τό   {4547, n-3c(4)}
a thing done, fact, deed, work, transaction, Luke
1:1; James 3:16; *a matter, affair,* Matt 18:19; Rom
16:2; *a matter* of dispute, 1 Cor 6:1; *a thing,* genr.,
Heb 10:1; 11:1; τὸ πρᾶγμα, a euphemism for
unlawful sexual conduct, perhaps, 1 Thess 4:6

πρᾶγμα   nom sg neut
          [Jm 3:16; n-3c(4); 4547]   πρᾶγμα
πρᾶγμα   acc sg neut [2t; n-3c(4); 4547]   "

πραγματεία, ας, ἡ   {4548, n-1a}
an application to a matter of business; in N.T.
business, affair, transaction, 2 Tim 2:4*

πραγματείαις   dat pl fem
          [2Ti 2:4; n-1a; 4548]   πραγματεία

πραγματεύομαι   {4549, v-1a(6)}
[-, ἐπραγματευσάμην, -, -, -] *to be occupied with*
or *employed in any business, do business; to trade
traffic,* Luke 19:13*

πραγματεύσασθε   aor mid imperative 2 pl
          [Lk 19:13; v-1a(6); 4549]   πραγματεύομαι
πράγματι   dat sg neut [3t; n-3c(4); 4547]   πρᾶγμα
πράγματος   gen sg neut [Mt 18:19; n-3c(4); 4547] "
πραγμάτων   gen pl neut [4t; n-3c(4); 4547]   "
πραεῖς   nom pl masc [Mt 5:5; a-2b; 4558]   πραΰς
πραέως   gen sg neut [1P 3:4; a-2b; 4558]   "
πραθῇ   aor pass ptcp nom sg neut
          [Ac 5:4; v-5a; 4405]   πιπράσκω
πραθῆναι   aor pass inf [3t; v-5a; 4405]   "

πραιτώριον, ου, τό   {4550, n-2c}
when used in reference to a camp, *the tent of the
general* or *commander-in-chief;* hence, in
reference to a province, *the palace in which the
governor of the province resided,* Matt 27:27; Mark
15:16; Acts 23:35; *the camp occupied by the
praetorian cohorts at Rome, the praetorian camp,*
or, *the Roman emperor's palace,* Phil 1:13

πραιτώριον   nom sg neut
          [Mk 15:16; n-2c; 4550]   πραιτώριον
πραιτώριον   acc sg neut [5t; n-2c; 4550]   "
πραιτωρίῳ   dat sg neut [2t; n-2c; 4550]   "
πράκτορι   dat sg masc
          [Lk 12:58; n-3f(2b); 4551]   πράκτωρ

πράκτωρ, ορος, ὁ   {4551, n-3f(2b)}
an exactor of dues or *penalties; an officer* who
enforced payment of debts by imprisonment,
Luke 12:58*

πράκτωρ   nom sg masc [Lk 12:58; n-3f(2b); 4551]   "
πρᾶξαι   aor act inf [Ac 26:9; v-2b; 4556]   πράσσω
πράξαντες   aor act ptcp nom pl masc
          [Jn 5:29; v-2b; 4556]   "
πραξάντων   aor act ptcp gen pl masc
          [2t; v-2b; 4556]   "

πράξας   aor act ptcp nom sg masc
   [1C 5:2; v-2b; 4556]   "

πράξει   dat sg fem
   [Lk 23:51; n-3e(5b); 4552]   πρᾶξις

πράξεις   acc pl fem [2t; n-3e(5b); 4552]   "

πράξεσιν   dat pl fem [Cl 3:9; n-3e(5b); 4552]   "

πράξετε   fut act ind 2 pl
   [Ac 15:29; v-2b; 4556]   πράσσω

πράξῃς   aor act subj 2 sg [Ac 16:28; v-2b; 4556]   "

πράξιν   acc sg fem [2t; n-3e(5b); 4552]   πρᾶξις

πρᾶξις, εως, ἡ   {4552, n-3e(5b)}
   operation, business, office, Rom 12:4; πρᾶξις, and
   πράξεις, *actions, mode of acting, ways, deeds,*
   practice, behavior, Matt 16:27; Luke 23:51

πρᾶος, see πραΰς   {4553}
   mild; gentle, kind, Matt 11:29 v.l.*

πραότης, ητος, ἡ   {4554, n-3c(1)}
   see πραΰτης, *meekness, forbearance,* all v.l., 1 Cor
   4:21; Gal 5:23; *gentleness, kindness, benevolence,* 2
   Cor 10:1

πρασιά, ᾶς, ἡ   {4555, n-1a}
   a small area or *bed in a garden;* trop. *a company of*
   persons disposed in squares; from the Hebrew,
   πρασιαὶ πρασιαί, *by areas, by squares,* like beds
   in a garden, Mark 6:40*

πρασιαί   nom pl fem [2t; n-1a; 4555]   πρασιά

πράσσει   pres act ind 3 sg
   [Ac 26:31; v-2b; 4556]   πράσσω

πράσσειν   pres act inf [4t; v-2b; 4556]   "

πράσσεις   pres act ind 2 sg [Rm 2:1; v-2b; 4556]   "

πράσσετε   pres act imperative 2 pl
   [2t; v-2b; 4556]   "

πράσσῃς   pres act subj 2 sg
   [Rm 2:25; v-2b; 4556]   "

πράσσοντας   pres act ptcp acc pl masc
   [3t; v-2b; 4556]   "

πράσσοντες   pres act ptcp nom pl masc
   [2t; v-2b; 4556]   "

πράσσοντι   pres act ptcp dat sg masc
   [Rm 13:4; v-2b; 4556]   "

πράσσουσιν   pres act ind 3 pl
   [Ac 17:7; v-2b; 4556]   "

πράσσουσιν   pres act ptcp dat pl masc
   [Rm 1:32; v-2b; 4556]   "

πράσσω   {4556, v-2b}
   [(ἔπρασσον), πράξω, ἔπραξα, πέπραχα,
   πέπραγμαι, ἐπράχθην] *to do, execute, perform,*
   practise, act, transact, and of evil, *to commit,*
   Luke 22:23; 23:15; John 3:20; Acts 26:9, 20, 26,
   31; *to fulfil, obey, observe* a law, Rom 2:25; *to do to*
   any one, Acts 16:28; 5:35; *to occupy one's self*
   with, be engaged in, busy one's self about, Acts
   19:19; 1 Thess 4:11; absol. *to fare,* Acts 15:29; Eph
   6:21; *to exact, require, collect* tribute, money lent,
   etc., Luke 3:13; 19:23

πράσσω   pres act ind 1 sg [4t; v-2b; 4556]   "

πράσσων   pres act ptcp nom sg masc
   [Jn 3:20; v-2b; 4556]   "

πραϋπάθεια, ας, ἡ   {4557, n-1a}
   meekness, gentleness of mind, kindness, 1 Tim
   6:11*

πραϋπαθίαν   acc sg fem
   [1Ti 6:11; n-1a; 4557]   πραϋπάθεια

πραΰς, πραεῖα, πραΰ   {4558, a-2b}
   also spelled πρᾶος, *meek, gentle, kind, forgiving,*
   Matt 5:5; *mild, benevolent, humane,* Matt 11:29;
   21:5; 1 Peter 3:4*

πραΰς   nom sg masc [2t; a-2b; 4558]   πραΰς

πραΰτης, ητος, ἡ   {4559, n-3c(1)}
   also spelled πραότης, ητος, ἡ, *meekness, mildness,*
   forbearance, 1 Peter 3:15; *gentleness, kindness,*
   James 1:21; 3:13; Gal 5:23

πραΰτης   nom sg fem
   [Ga 5:23; n-3c(1); 4559]   πραΰτης

πραΰτητα   acc sg fem [2t; n-3c(1); 4559]   "

πραΰτητι   dat sg fem [3t; n-3c(1); 4559]   "

πραΰτητος   gen sg fem [5t; n-3c(1); 4559]   "

πρέπει   pres act ind 3 sg
   [3t; v-1b(1); 4560]   πρέπω

πρέπον   pres act ptcp nom sg neut
   [2t; v-1b(1); 4560]   "

πρέπω   {4560, v-1b(1)}
   [(ἔπρεπον), -, -, -, -, -] *it becomes, it is fitting, it is*
   proper, it is right, etc., and part. πρέπον,
   becoming, suitable, decorous, etc., Matt 3:15; 1
   Cor 11:13; Eph 5:3; 1 Tim 2:10

πρεσβεία, ας, ἡ   {4561, n-1a}
   eldership, seniority; an embassy, legation; a body of
   ambassadors, legates, Luke 14:32; 19:14*

πρεσβείαν   acc sg fem [2t; n-1a; 4561]   πρεσβεία

πρεσβεύομεν   pres act ind 1 pl
   [2C 5:20; v-1a(6); 4563]   πρεσβεύω

πρεσβεύω   {4563, v-1a(6)}
   [πρεσβεύσω, ἐπρέσβευσα, -, -, -] *to be elder; to be*
   an ambassador, perform the duties of an
   ambassador, 2 Cor 5:20; Eph 6:20*

πρεσβεύω   pres act ind 1 sg
   [Ep 6:20; v-1a(6); 4563]   "

πρεσβύτας   acc pl masc
   [Ti 2:2; n-1f; 4566]   πρεσβύτης

πρεσβυτέρας   acc pl fem comparative
   [1Ti 5:2; a-1a(1); 4565]   πρεσβύτερος

πρεσβυτέριον, ου, τό   {4564, n-2c}
   a body of old men, an assembly of elders; the Jewish
   Sanhedrin, Luke 22:66; Acts 22:5; *a body of elders*
   in the Christian church, *a presbytery,* 1 Tim 4:14*

πρεσβυτέριον   nom sg neut
   [2t; n-2c; 4564]   πρεσβυτέριον

πρεσβυτερίου   gen sg neut [1Ti 4:14; n-2c; 4564]   "

πρεσβύτεροι   nom pl masc
   [20t; a-1a(1); 4565]   πρεσβύτερος

πρεσβύτεροι   voc pl masc [Ac 4:8; a-1a(1); 4565]   "

πρεσβυτέροις   dat pl masc-comparative
   [5t; a-1a(1); 4565]   "

πρεσβύτερος, α, ον   {4565, a-1a(1)}
   elder, senior; older, more advanced in years, Luke

15:25; John 8:9; Acts 2:17; *an elder* in respect of age, *person advanced in years*, 1 Tim 5:1, 2; pl. spc. *ancients, ancestors, fathers*, Matt 15:2; Heb 11:2; as an appellation of dignity, *an elder*, local *dignitary*, Luke 7:3; *an elder, member of the Jewish Sanhedrin*, Matt 16:21; 21:23; 26:3, 47, 57, 59; *an elder* or *presbyter* of the Christian church, Acts 11:30; 14:23, et al. freq.

πρεσβύτερος   nom sg masc comparative
    [3t; a-1a(1); 4565]   "

πρεσβυτέρου   gen sg masc
    [1Ti 5:19; a-1a(1); 4565]   "

πρεσβυτέρους   acc pl masc [12t; a-1a(1); 4565]   "

πρεσβυτέρῳ   dat sg masc comparative
    [1Ti 5:1; a-1a(1); 4565]   "

πρεσβυτέρων   gen pl masc [22t; a-1a(1); 4565]   "

πρεσβύτης, ου, ὁ   {4566, n-1f}
    an old man, aged person, Luke 1:18; Titus 2:2; Phil 9*

πρεσβύτης   nom sg masc [2t; n-1f; 4566]   πρεσβύτης
πρεσβύτιδας   acc pl fem
    [Ti 2:3; n-3c(2); 4567]   πρεσβῦτις

πρεσβῦτις, ιδος, ἡ   {4567, n-3c(2)}
    an aged woman, Titus 2:3*

πρηνής, ές   {4568, a-4a}
    prone, head-foremost; πρηνὴς γενόμενος, *falling head-long*, Acts 1:18*

πρηνής   nom sg masc [Ac 1:18; a-4a; 4568]   πρηνής

πρίζω   {4569, v-2a(1)}
    [-, -, -, -, ἐπρίσθην] also spelled πρίω, *to saw, saw in two*, Heb 11:37*

πρίν   {4570, adverb}
    can function as a temporal conj. and an improper prep., *before*, of time, Matt 26:34, 75; Mark 14:72; πρὶν ἤ, *sooner than, before*, Matt 1:18; Luke 2:26

πρίν   adverb [13t; adverb; 4570]   πρίν

Πρίσκα, ης, ἡ   {4571, n-1c}
    see also Πρόσκιλλα, *Prisca*, pr. name, Rom 16:3; 1 Cor 16:19; 2 Tim 4:19*

Πρίσκα   nom sg fem [1C 16:19; n-1c; 4571]   Πρίσκα
Πρίσκαν   acc sg fem [2t; n-1c; 4571]   "

Πρίσκιλλα, ης, ἡ   {4572, n-1c}
    Priscilla, pr. name, the diminutive form of Πρίσκα, both words forms referring to the same person, the wife of Apollo, Acts 18:2, 18, 26; 1 Cor 16:19; Rom 16:3 v.l.*

Πρίσκιλλα   nom sg fem [2t; n-1c; 4572]   Πρίσκιλλα
Πρίσκιλλαν   acc sg fem [Ac 18:2; n-1c; 4572]   "

πρό   {4574, prep}
    before, of place, *in front of, in advance of*, Matt 11:10; Luke 1:76; Acts 5:23; *before*, of time, Matt 5:12; Luke 11:38; before an infin. with the gen. of the article, *before, before that*, Matt 6:8; Luke 2:21; *before, above, in preference*, James 5:12; 1 Peter 4:8

πρό   prep-gen [47t; prep; 4574]   πρό

προαγαγεῖν   aor act inf
    [2t; cv-1b(2); 4575]   προάγω

προαγαγών   aor act ptcp nom sg masc
    [Ac 16:30; cv-1b(2); 4575]   "

προάγει   pres act ind 3 sg [2t; cv-1b(2); 4575]   "
προάγειν   pres act inf [2t; cv-1b(2); 4575]   "
προάγοντες   pres act ptcp nom pl masc
    [3t; cv-1b(2); 4575]   "

προάγουσαι   pres act ptcp nom pl fem
    [1Ti 5:24; cv-1b(2); 4575]   "

προαγούσας   pres act ptcp acc pl fem
    [1Ti 1:18; cv-1b(2); 4575]   "

προαγούσης   pres act ptcp gen sg fem
    [Hb 7:18; cv-1b(2); 4575]   "

προάγουσιν   pres act ind 3 pl
    [Mt 21:31; cv-1b(2); 4575]   "

προάγω   {4575, cv-1b(2)}
    [(προῆγον), προάξω, προήγαγον, -, -, -] *to lead, bring*, or *conduct forth, produce*, Acts 12:6; 16:30; 25:26; intrans. *to go before, to go first*, Matt 2:9; 21:9; Mark 6:45; 1 Tim 5:24; part. προάγων, ουσα, ον, *preceding, previous, antecedent*, 1 Tim 1:18; Heb 7:18; hence, in N.T., trans. *to precede*, Matt 14:22; *to be in advance of*, Matt 21:31

προάγων   pres act ptcp nom sg masc
    [2t; cv-1b(2); 4575]   "

προαιρέω   {4576, cv-1d(2a)}
    [-, προεῖλον, προῄρημαι, -, -] *to prefer, choose*; met. *to purpose, intend considerately*, 2 Cor 9:7*

προαιτιάομαι   {4577, cv-1d(1b)}
    [-, προῃτιασάμην, -, -, -] pr. *to charge beforehand; to convince beforehand*, Rom 3:9, since the charges in the case in question were drawn from Scripture.*

προάξω   fut act ind 1 sg [2t; cv-1b(2); 4575]   "

προακούω   {4578, cv-1a(8)}
    [-, προήκουσα, -, -, -] *to hear beforehand* or *already*, Col 1:5*

προαμαρτάνω   {4579, cv-3a(2a)}
    [-, -, προημάρτηκα, -, -] *to sin before*; perf., *to have already sinned, have sinned heretofore*, 2 Cor 12:21; 13:2*

προαύλιον, ου, τό   {4580, n-2c}
    the exterior court before an edifice, Mark 14:68*

προαύλιον   acc sg neut
    [Mk 14:68; n-2c; 4580]   προαύλιον

προβαίνω   {4581, cv-2d(6)}
    [-, προέβην, προβέβηκα, -, -] *to go forward, advance*, Matt 4:21; Mark 1:19; *to advance* in life, Luke 1:7, 18; 2:36*

προβάλλω   {4582, cv-2d(1)}
    [(προέβαλλον), -, προέβαλον, -, -, -] *to cast before, project; to put* or *urge forward*, Acts 19:33; *to put forth*, as a tree its blossoms, etc., Luke 21:30*

προβαλόντων   aor act ptcp gen pl masc
    [Ac 19:33; cv-2d(1); 4582]   προβάλλω
προβάλωσιν   aor act subj 3 pl
    [Lk 21:30; cv-2d(1); 4582]   "

προβάς   aor act ptcp nom sg masc
    [2t; cv-2d(6); 4581]   προβαίνω
πρόβατα   nom pl neut [12t; n-2c; 4585]   πρόβατον
πρόβατα   acc pl neut [14t; n-2c; 4585]   "
προβατικῇ   dat sg fem
    [Jn 5:2; a-1a(2a); 4583]   προβατικός

προβατικός, ή, όν   {4583, a-1a(2a)}
    belonging or pertaining to sheep; ἡ προβατικὴ,
    (πύλη) the sheep-gate, John 5:2*

προβάτιον, ου, τό   {4584, n-2c}
    a little sheep, diminutive of πρόβατον, although
    it often has the same meaning, John 21:16, 17

πρόβατον, ου, τό   {4585, n-2c}
    a sheep, Matt 7:15; 9:36; 10:16; met. Matt 10:6;
    15:24

πρόβατον   nom sg neut
    [Ac 8:32; n-2c; 4585]   πρόβατον
πρόβατον   acc sg neut [2t; n-2c; 4585]   "
προβάτου   gen sg neut [Mt 12:12; n-2c; 4585]   "
προβάτων   gen pl neut [9t; n-2c; 4585]   "
προβεβηκότες   perf act ptcp nom pl masc
    [Lk 1:7; cv-2d(6); 4581]   προβαίνω
προβεβηκυῖα   perf act ptcp nom sg fem
    [2t; cv-2d(6); 4581]   "

προβιβάζω   {4586, cv-2a(1)}
    [-, προεβίβασα, -, -, προεβιβάσθην] to cause any
    one to advance, to lead forward; to advance, push
    forward, Acts 19:33 v.l.; met. to incite, instigate,
    Matt 14:8*

προβιβασθεῖσα   aor pass ptcp nom sg fem
    [Mt 14:8; cv-2a(1); 4586]   προβιβάζω

προβλέπω   {4587, cv-1b(1)}
    [(προέβλεπον), -, προέβλεψα, -, -, -] to foresee;
    mid. to provide beforehand, Heb 11:40*

προβλεψαμένου   aor mid ptcp gen sg masc
    [Hb 11:40; cv-1b(1); 4587]   προβλέπω
προγεγονότων   perf act ptcp gen pl neut
    [Rm 3:25; cv-1c(2); 4588]   προγίνομαι
προγεγραμμένοι   perf pass ptcp nom pl masc
    [Jd 4; cv-1b(1); 4592]   προγράφω

προγίνομαι   {4588, cv-1c(2)}
    [-, -, προγέγονα, -, -] to be or happen before, be
    previously done or committed; προγεγονώς,
    bygone, previous, Rom 3:25

προγινώσκοντες   pres act ptcp nom pl masc
    [2t; cv-5a; 4589]   προγινώσκω

προγινώσκω   {4589, cv-5a}
    [-, προέγνων, -, προέγνωσμαι, -] to know
    beforehand, to be previously acquainted with, Acts
    26:5; 2 Peter 3:17; to determine on beforehand, to
    fore-ordain, 1 Peter 1:20; in N.T., from the
    Hebrew, to foreknow, to appoint as the subject of
    future privileges, Rom 8:29; 11:2*

προγνώσει   dat sg fem
    [Ac 2:23; n-3e(5b); 4590]   πρόγνωσις
πρόγνωσιν   acc sg fem [1P 1:2; n-3e(5b); 4590]   "

πρόγνωσις, εως, ἡ   {4590, n-3e(5b)}
    foreknowledge; in N.T. previous determination,
    purpose, Acts 2:23; 1 Peter 1:2*

προγόνοις   dat pl masc
    [1Ti 5:4; a-3a; 4591]   πρόγονος

πρόγονος, ον   {4591, a-3a}
    born earlier, elder; a progenitor, pl. progenitors;
    parents, 1 Tim 5:4; forefathers, ancestors, 2 Tim
    1:3*

προγόνων   gen pl masc [2Ti 1:3; a-3a; 4591]   "

προγράφω   {4592, cv-1b(1)}
    [-, προέγραψα, -, προγέγραμμαι, προεγράφην] to
    write before, Rom 15:4; Eph 3:3; to make a subject
    of public notice; to set forth unreservedly and
    distinctly, Gal 3:1; to designate clearly, Jude 4*

πρόδηλα   nom pl neut
    [1Ti 5:25; a-3a; 4593]   πρόδηλος
πρόδηλοι   nom pl fem [1Ti 5:24; a-3a; 4593]   "
πρόδηλον   nom sg neut [Hb 7:14; a-3a; 4593]   "

πρόδηλος, ον   {4593, a-3a}
    previously manifest, before known; plainly
    manifest, very clear, prominently conspicuous, 1
    Tim 5:24, 25; Heb 7:14*

προδίδωμι   {4594, cv-6a}
    [-, προέδωκα, -, -, -] to give before, precede in
    giving; Rom 11:35; to give up, abandon, betray,
    Mark 14:10 v.l.*

προδόται   nom pl masc [2t; n-1f; 4595]   προδότης

προδότης, ου, ὁ   {4595, n-1f}
    a betrayer, traitor, Luke 6:16; Acts 7:52; 2 Tim 3:4*

προδότης   nom sg masc [Lk 6:16; n-1f; 4595]   "
προδραμών   aor act ptcp nom sg masc
    [Lk 19:4; cv-1b(2); 4731]   προτρέχω

πρόδρομος, ον   {4596, a-3a}
    a precursor, forerunner, one who advances to
    explore and prepare the way, Heb 6:20*

πρόδρομος   nom sg masc
    [Hb 6:20; a-3a; 4596]   πρόδρομος
προέγνω   aor act ind 3 sg
    [2t; cv-5a; 4589]   προγινώσκω
προεγνωσμένου   perf pass ptcp gen sg masc
    [1P 1:20; cv-5a; 4589]   "
προεγράφη   aor pass ind 3 sg
    [2t; cv-1b(1); 4592]   προγράφω
προέγραψα   aor act ind 1 sg
    [Ep 3:3; cv-1b(1); 4592]   "
προέδραμεν   aor act ind 3 sg
    [Jn 20:4; cv-1b(2); 4708]   προστρέχω
προέδωκεν   aor act ind 3 sg
    [Rm 11:35; cv-6a; 4594]   προδίδωμι
προεθέμην   aor mid ind 1 sg
    [Rm 1:13; cv-6a; 4729]   προτίθημι
προέθετο   aor mid ind 3 sg [2t; cv-6a; 4729]   "
προείπαμεν   aor act ind 1 pl
    [1Th 4:6; cv-1b(2); 4597]   προεῖπον
προεῖπεν   aor act ind 3 sg
    [Ac 1:16; cv-1b(2); 4597]   "

προεῖπον   {4597, cv-1b(2)}
[προερῶ, -, προείρηκα, προείρημαι, -] *to say, speak beforehand, foretell*, Matt 24:25; Acts 1:16; 1 Thess 4:6; Heb 10:15 v.l.

προεῖπον   aor act ind 1 sg
   [Ga 5:21; cv-1b(2); 4597]   "
προείρηκα   perf act ind 1 sg [4t; cv-1b(2); 4597]   "
προειρήκαμεν   perf act ind 1 pl
   [Ga 1:9; cv-1b(2); 4597]   "
προείρηκεν   perf act ind 3 sg
   [Rm 9:29; cv-1b(2); 4597]   "
προειρημένων   perf pass ptcp gen pl neut
   [2t; cv-1b(2); 4597]   "
προείρηται   perf pass ind 3 sg
   [Hb 4:7; cv-1b(2); 4597]   "
προέκοπτεν   imperf act ind 3 sg
   [Lk 2:52; cv-4; 4621]   προκόπτω
προέκοπτον   imperf act ind 1 sg
   [Ga 1:14; cv-4; 4621]   "
προέκοψεν   aor act ind 3 sg
   [Rm 13:12; cv-4; 4621]   "
προέλαβεν   aor act ind 3 sg
   [Mk 14:8; cv-3a(2b); 4624]   προλαμβάνω
προελέγομεν   imperf act ind 1 pl
   [1Th 3:4; cv-1b(2); 4625]   προλέγω
προελεύσεται   fut mid ind 3 sg
   [Lk 1:17; cv-1b(2); 4601]   προέρχομαι
προελθόντες   aor act ptcp nom pl masc
   [2t; cv-1b(2); 4601]   "
προελθών   aor act ptcp nom sg masc
   [2t; cv-1b(2); 4601]   "
προέλθωσιν   aor act subj 3 pl
   [2C 9:5; cv-1b(2); 4601]   "

προελπίζω   {4598, cv-2a(1)}
[-, -, προήλπικα, -, -] *to have hope and confidence* in a person or thing *beforehand*, Eph 1:12*

προενάρχομαι   {4599, cv-1b(2)}
[-, προενηρξάμην, -, -, -] *to begin before* a particular time, 2 Cor 8:6, 10*

προενήρξασθε   aor mid ind 2 pl
   [2C 8:10; cv-1b(2); 4599]   προενάρχομαι
προενήρξατο   aor mid ind 3 sg
   [2C 8:6; cv-1b(2); 4599]   "

προεπαγγέλλω   {4600, cv-2d(1)}
[-, προεπηγγειλάμην, -, προεπήγγελμαι, -] *to promise beforehand*, Rom 1:2; 2 Cor 9:5*

προέπεμπον   imperf act ind 3 pl
   [Ac 20:38; cv-1b(1); 4636]   προπέμπω
προεπηγγείλατο   aor mid ind 3 sg
   [Rm 1:2; cv-2d(1); 4600]   προεπαγγέλλω
προεπηγγελμένην   perf pass ptcp acc sg fem
   [2C 9:5; cv-2d(1); 4600]   "

προέρχομαι   {4601, cv-1b(2)}
[(προηρχόμην), προελεύσομαι, προῆλθον, -, -, -] *to go forwards, advance, proceed*, Matt 26:39; Mark 14:35; Acts 12:10; *to precede, go before* any one, Luke 22:47; *to precede* in time, *be a forerunner* or *precursor*, Luke 1:17; *to outgo, outstrip in going*, Mark 6:33; *to travel in advance of* any one, *precede*, Acts 12:13 v.l.; 20:5, 13; 2 Cor 9:5

προεστῶτες   perf act ptcp nom pl masc
   [1Ti 5:17; cv-6a; 4613]   προΐστημι
προέτειναν   aor act ind 3 pl
   [Ac 22:25; cv-2d(5); 4727]   προτείνω

προετοιμάζω   {4602, cv-2a(1)}
[-, προητοίμασα, -, -, -] *to prepare beforehand;* in N.T. *to appoint beforehand*, Rom 9:23; Eph 2:10*

προευαγγελίζομαι   {4603, cv-2a(1)}
[-, προευηγγελισάμην, -, -, -] *to announce joyful tidings beforehand*, Gal 3:8*

προευηγγελίσατο   aor mid ind 3 sg
   [Ga 3:8; cv-2a(1); 4603]   προευαγγελίζομαι
προεφήτευσεν   aor act ind 3 sg
   [Jd 14; v-1a(6); 4736]   προφητεύω
προέφθασεν   aor act ind 3 sg
   [Mt 17:25; cv-3a(1); 4740]   προφθάνω
προεχειρίσατο   aor mid ind 3 sg
   [Ac 22:14; cv-2a(1); 4741]   προχειρίζω
προεχόμεθα   pres mid ind 1 pl
   [Rm 3:9; cv-1b(2); 4604]   προέχω

προέχω   {4604, cv-1b(2)}
[-, -, -, -, -] *to have* or *hold before; intrans.* and *mid. to excel, surpass, have advantage* or *pre-eminence*, Rom 3:9*

προεωρακότες   perf act ptcp nom pl masc
   [Ac 21:29; cv-1d(1a); 4632]   προοράω
προήγαγον   aor act ind 1 sg
   [Ac 25:26; cv-1b(2); 4575]   προάγω
προῆγεν   imperf act ind 3 sg
   [Mt 2:9; cv-1b(2); 4575]   "

προηγέομαι   {4605, cv-1d(2a)}
[προηγήσομαι, -, -, -, -] *to go before, precede, lead onward;* met. *to endeavor to take the lead of, vie with,* or, *to give precedence to, to prefer,* Rom 12:10*

προηγούμενοι   pres mid ptcp nom pl masc
   [Rm 12:10; cv-1d(2a); 4605]   προηγέομαι
προηκούσατε   aor act ind 2 pl
   [Cl 1:5; cv-1a(8); 4578]   προακούω
προῆλθον   aor act ind 3 pl
   [2t; cv-1b(2); 4601]   προέρχομαι
προηλικότας   perf act ptcp acc pl masc
   [Ep 1:12; cv-2a(1); 4598]   προελπίζω
προημαρτηκόσιν   perf act ptcp dat pl masc
   [2C 13:2; cv-3a(2a); 4579]   προαμαρτάνω
προημαρτηκότων   perf act ptcp gen pl masc
   [2C 12:21; cv-3a(2a); 4579]   "
προῄρηται   perf mid ind 3 sg
   [2C 9:7; cv-1d(2a); 4576]   προαιρέω
προήρχετο   imperf mid ind 3 sg
   [Lk 22:47; cv-1b(2); 4601]   προέρχομαι
προῃτιασάμεθα   aor mid ind 1 pl
   [Rm 3:9; cv-1d(1b); 4577]   προαιτιάομαι
προητοίμασεν   aor act ind 3 sg
   [2t; cv-2a(1); 4602]   προετοιμάζω
προθέσει   dat sg fem [2t; n-3e(5b); 4606]   πρόθεσις
προθέσεως   gen sg fem [4t; n-3e(5b); 4606]   "
πρόθεσιν   acc sg fem [4t; n-3e(5b); 4606]   "

πρόθεσις, εως, ἡ   {4606, n-3e(5b)}
a setting forth or *before;* οἱ ἄρτοι τῆς προθέσεως,

and ἡ πρόθεσις τῶν ἄρτων, *the shewbread,* the twelve loaves of bread, corresponding to the twelve tribes, which were *set out* in two rows upon the golden table in the sanctuary, Matt 12:4; Mark 2:26; Luke 6:4; Heb 9:2; *predetermination, purpose,* Acts 11:23; 27:13; Rom 8:28; 2 Tim 3:10

πρόθεσις   nom sg fem   [2t; n-3e(5b); 4606]   "

προθεσμία, ας, ἡ   {4607, n-1a}
a time before appointed, set or *appointed time,* Gal 4:2*

προθεσμίας   gen sg fem
    [Ga 4:2; n-1a; 4607]   προθεσμία

προθυμία, ας, ἡ   {4608, n-1a}
promptness, readiness, eagerness of mind, willingness, Acts 17:11; 2 Cor 8:11, 12, 19; 9:2*

προθυμία   nom sg fem   [2t; n-1a; 4608]   προθυμία
προθυμίαν   acc sg fem   [2t; n-1a; 4608]   "
προθυμίας   gen sg fem   [Ac 17:11; n-1a; 4608]   "
πρόθυμον   nom sg neut   [3t; a-3a; 4609]   πρόθυμος

πρόθυμος, ον   {4609, a-3a}
ready in mind, prepared, prompt, willing, Matt 26:41; Mark 14:38; τὸ πρόθυμον, i.q. ἡ προθυμία, *readiness, eagerness of mind,* Rom 1:15*

προθύμως   {4610, adverb}
promptly, readily, willingly, heartily, cheerfully, 1 Peter 5:2*

προθύμως   adverb   [1P 5:2; adverb; 4610]   προθύμως
προιδοῦσα   aor act ptcp nom sg fem
    [Ga 3:8; cv-1d(1a); 4632]   προοράω
προιδών   aor act ptcp nom sg masc
    [Ac 2:31; cv-1d(1a); 4632]   "
πρόϊμον   acc sg masc
    [Jm 5:7; a-3a; 4611]   πρόϊμος

πρόϊμος, ον   {4611, a-3a}
also spelled πρώϊμος, *early,* James 5:7*

προϊστάμενοι   pres mid ptcp nom pl masc
    [1Ti 3:12; cv-6a; 4613]   προΐστημι
προϊστάμενον   pres mid ptcp acc sg masc
    [1Ti 3:4; cv-6a; 4613]   "
προϊστάμενος   pres mid ptcp nom sg masc
    [Rm 12:8; cv-6a; 4613]   "
προϊσταμένους   pres mid ptcp acc pl masc
    [1Th 5:12; cv-6a; 4613]   "
προΐστασθαι   pres mid inf   [2t; cv-6a; 4613]   "

προΐστημι   {4613, cv-6a}
[-, προέστησα, προέστηκα, -, -] *to set before;* met. *to set over, appoint with authority;* intrans. 2 aor. προῦστην, perf. προέστηκα, part. προεστώς, and mid. προΐσταμαι, *to preside, govern, superintend,* Rom 12:8; 1 Thess 5:12; 1 Tim 3:4, 5, 12; 5:17; mid. *to undertake resolutely, to practise diligently, to maintain the practice of,* Titus 3:8, 14*

προκαλέω   {4614, cv-1d(2b)}
[-, -, -, -, -] *to call out, challenge to fight; to provoke, irritate, with feelings of ungenerous rivalry,* Gal 5:26*

προκαλούμενοι   pres mid ptcp nom pl masc
    [Ga 5:26; cv-1d(2b); 4614]   προκαλέω
προκαταγγείλαντας   aor act ptcp acc pl masc
    [Ac 7:52; cv-2d(1); 4615]   προκαταγγέλλω

προκαταγγέλλω   {4615, cv-2d(1)}
[-, προκατήγγειλα, -, προκατήγγελμαι, -] *to declare* or *announce beforehand, foretell, predict,* Acts 3:18, 24 v.l.; 7:52; 2 Cor 9:5 v.l.*

προκαταρτίζω   {4616, cv-2a(1)}
[-, προκατήρτισα, -, -, -] *to make ready, prepare,* or *complete beforehand,* 2 Cor 9:5*

προκαταρτίσωσιν   aor act subj 3 pl
    [2C 9:5; cv-2a(1); 4616]   προκαταρτίζω
προκατήγγειλεν   aor act ind 3 sg
    [Ac 3:18; cv-2d(1); 4615]   προκαταγγέλλω

πρόκειμαι   {4618, cv-6b}
[-, -, -, -, -] *to lie* or *be placed before;* met. *to be proposed* or *set before,* as a duty, example, reward, etc., Heb 6:18; 12:1, 2; Jude 7; *to be at hand, be present,* 2 Cor 8:12*

προκειμένης   pres mid ptcp gen sg fem
    [2t; cv-6b; 4618]   πρόκειμαι
προκείμενον   pres mid ptcp acc sg masc
    [Hb 12:1; cv-6b; 4618]   "
πρόκεινται   pres mid ind 3 pl
    [Jd 7; cv-6b; 4618]   "
πρόκειται   pres mid ind 3 sg
    [2C 8:12; cv-6b; 4618]   "
προκεκυρωμένην   perf pass ptcp acc sg fem
    [Ga 3:17; cv-1d(3); 4623]   προκυρόω
προκεχειρισμένον   perf mid ptcp acc sg masc
    [Ac 3:20; cv-2a(1); 4741]   προχειρίζω
προκεχειροτονημένοις   perf pass ptcp dat pl masc
    [Ac 10:41; cv-1d(2a); 4742]   προχειροτονέω
προκηρύξαντος   aor act ptcp gen sg masc
    [Ac 13:24; cv-2b; 4619]   προκηρύσσω

προκηρύσσω   {4619, cv-2b}
[-, προεκήρυξα, -, προκεκήρυγμαι, -] *to announce publicly;* in N.T. *to announce before,* Acts 3:20 v.l.; 13:24*

προκοπή, ῆς, ἡ   {4620, n-1b}
advance upon a way; met. *progress, advancement, furtherance,* Phil 1:12, 25; 1 Tim 4:15*

προκοπή   nom sg fem   [1Ti 4:15; n-1b; 4620]   προκοπή
προκοπήν   acc sg fem   [2t; n-1b; 4620]   "

προκόπτω   {4621, cv-4}
[(προέκοπτον), προκόψω, προέκοψα, -, -, -] pr. *to cut* a passage *forward; to advance, make progress; to advance,* as time, *to be far spent,* Rom 13:12; met. *to advance* in wisdom, age, or stature, Luke 2:52; seq. ἐν, *to make progress* or *proficiency in,* Gal 1:14; προκόπτω ἐπὶ πλεῖον, *to proceed* or *advance further,* 2 Tim 2:16; 3:9; προκόπτω ἐπὶ τὸ χεῖρον, *to grow* worse and worse, 2 Tim 3:13*

προκόψουσιν   fut act ind 3 pl
    [3t; cv-4; 4621]   προκόπτω

πρόκριμα, ατος, τό   {4622, n-3c(4)}
previous judgment, prejudice, or, *preference, partiality,* 1 Tim 5:21*

προκρίματος   gen sg neut
[1Ti 5:21; n-3c(4); 4622]   πρόκριμα

προκυρόω   {4623, cv-1d(3)}
[-, -, -, προκεκύρωμαι, -] *to sanction and establish
previously, ratify and confirm before*, Gal 3:17*

προλαμβάνει   pres act ind 3 sg
[1C 11:21; cv-3a(2b); 4624]   προλαμβάνω

προλαμβάνω   {4624, cv-3a(2b)}
[-, προέλαβον, -, -, προελήμφθην] *to take before*
another, 1 Cor 11:21; trop. *to anticipate, do
beforehand*, Mark 14:8; *to take by surprise;* pass. *be
taken unexpectedly, be overtaken, be taken by
surprise*, Gal 6:1*

προλέγω   {4625, cv-1b(2)}
[-, προεῖπον or προεῖπα, -, προείρηκα or
προείρημαι, -] *to tell beforehand, to foretell*, Matt
24:25; Acts 1:16; Rom 9:29; 2 Cor 13:2; Gal 5:21;
1 Thess 3:4

προλέγω   pres act ind 1 sg
[2t; cv-1b(2); 4625]   προλέγω
προλη\μφθῇ   aor pass subj 3 sg
[Ga 6:1; cv-3a(2b); 4624]   προλαμβάνω

προμαρτύρομαι   {4626, cv-1c(1)}
[-, -, -, -, -] pr. *to witness* or *testify beforehand; to
declare beforehand, predict*, 1 Peter 1:11*

προμαρτυρόμενον   pres mid ptcp nom sg neut
[1P 1:11; cv-1c(1); 4626]   προμαρτύρομαι
προμελετᾶν   pres act inf
[Lk 21:14; cv-1d(1a); 4627]   προμελετάω

προμελετάω   {4627, cv-1d(1a)}
[-, -, -, -, -] *to practise beforehand; to premeditate*,
Luke 21:14*

προμεριμνᾶτε   pres act imperative 2 pl
[Mk 13:11; cv-1d(1a); 4628]   προμεριμνάω

προμεριμνάω   {4628, cv-1d(1a)}
[-, -, -, -, -] *to be anxious* or *solicitous beforehand,
to ponder beforehand*, Mark 13:11*

προνοεῖ   pres act ind 3 sg
[1Ti 5:8; cv-1d(2a); 4629]   προνοέω

προνοέω   {4629, cv-1d(2a)}
[-, -, -, -, -] *to perceive beforehand, foresee; to
provide for*, 1 Tim 5:8; mid. *to provide for one's self;*
by impl. *to apply one's self to* a thing, *practice,
strive to exhibit*, Rom 12:17; 2 Cor 8:21*

πρόνοια, ας, ἡ   {4630, n-1a}
forethought; providence, provident care, Acts 24:2;
provision, Rom 13:14*

πρόνοιαν   acc sg fem
[Rm 13:14; n-1a; 4630]   πρόνοια
προνοίας   gen sg fem   [Ac 24:2; n-1a; 4630]   "
προνοοῦμεν   pres act ind 1 pl
[2C 8:21; cv-1d(2a); 4629]   προνοέω
προνοούμενοι   pres mid ptcp nom pl masc
[Rm 12:17; cv-1d(2a); 4629]   "

προοράω   {4632, cv-1d(1a)}
[(προεώρων), -, προεῖδον, προεώρακα, -, -] *to
foresee*, Acts 2:31; Gal 3:8; *to see before*, Acts

21:29; in N.T. *to have vividly present to the mind,
to be mindful of*, Acts 2:25*

προορίζω   {4633, cv-2a(1)}
[-, προώρισα, -, -, προωρίσθην] *to limit* or *mark
out beforehand; to design definitely beforehand,
ordain beforehand, predestine*, Acts 4:28; Rom
8:29, 30

προορίσας   aor act ptcp nom sg masc
[Ep 1:5; cv-2a(1); 4633]   προορίζω
προορισθέντες   aor pass ptcp nom pl masc
[Ep 1:11; cv-2a(1); 4633]   "
προορώμην   imperf mid ind 1 sg
[Ac 2:25; cv-1d(1a); 4632]   προοράω
προπαθόντες   aor act ptcp nom pl masc
[1Th 2:2; cv-5a; 4634]   προπάσχω

προπάσχω   {4634, cv-5a}
[-, προέπαθον, -, -, -] *to experience previously*, of
ill treatment, 1 Thess 2:2*

προπάτορα   acc sg masc
[Rm 4:1; n-3f(2b); 4635]   προπάτωρ

προπάτωρ, ορος, ὁ   {4635, n-3f(2b)}
a grandfather; a progenitor, or *ancestor*, Rom 4:1*

προπεμπόντων   pres act ptcp gen pl masc
[Ac 21:5; cv-1b(1); 4636]   προπέμπω

προπέμπω   {4636, cv-1b(1)}
[(προέπεμπον), -, προέπεμψα, -, -, προεπέμφθην] *to
send on before; to accompany* or *attend out of
respect, escort, accompany for a certain distance on
setting out on a journey*, Acts 15:3; 20:38; 21:5; *to
furnish with things necessary for a journey*, Titus
3:13; 3 John 6

προπεμφθέντες   aor pass ptcp nom pl masc
[Ac 15:3; cv-1b(1); 4636]   "
προπεμφθῆναι   aor pass inf   [2t; cv-1b(1); 4636]   "
προπέμψας   aor act ptcp nom sg masc
[3J 6; cv-1b(1); 4636]   "
προπέμψατε   aor act imperative 2 pl
[1C 16:11; cv-1b(1); 4636]   "
προπέμψητε   aor act subj 2 pl
[1C 16:6; cv-1b(1); 4636]   "
πρόπεμψον   aor act imperative 2 sg
[Ti 3:13; cv-1b(1); 4636]   "
προπετεῖς   nom pl masc
[2Ti 3:4; a-4a; 4637]   προπετής
προπετές   acc sg neut   [Ac 19:36; a-4a; 4637]   "

προπετής, ές   {4637, a-4a}
falling forwards; meton. *precipitate, rash*, Acts
19:36; 2 Tim 3:4*

προπορεύομαι   {4638, cv-1a(6)}
[προπορεύσομαι, -, -, -, -] *to precede, go before*,
Acts 7:40; Luke 1:76*

προπορεύσῃ   fut mid ind 2 sg
[Lk 1:76; cv-1a(6); 4638]   προπορεύομαι
προπορεύσονται   fut mid ind 3 pl
[Ac 7:40; cv-1a(6); 4638]   "

πρός   {4639, prep}
from; met. *for the benefit of*, Acts 27:34; with a
dative, *near, by, at, by the side of, in the vicinity of*,
Mark 5:11; Luke 19:37; with an accusative, used

of the place to which anything tends, *to, unto, towards*, Matt 2:12; 3:5, 13; *at, close upon*, Matt 3:10; Mark 5:22; *near to, in the vicinity of*, Mark 6:45; after verbs of speaking, praying, answering to a charge, etc., *to*, Matt 3:15; 27:14; of place where, *with, in, among, by, at*, etc., Matt 26:55; Mark 11:4; Luke 1:80; of time, *for, during*, Luke 8:13; 1 Cor 7:5; *near, towards*, Luke 24:29; of the end, object, purpose for which an action is exerted, or to which any quality, etc., has reference, *to*, John 4:35; Acts 3:10; 27:12; before an infin. with τό, *in order to, that, in order that*, Matt 6:1; 13:30; 26:12; *so as to, so that*, Matt 5:28; of the relation which any action, state, quality, etc., bears to any person or thing, *in relation to, of, concerning, in respect to, with reference to*, Matt 19:8; Luke 12:41; 18:1; 20:19; *as it respects, as it concerns, with relation to*, Matt 27:4; John 21:22, 23; *according to, in conformity with*, Luke 12:47; 2 Cor 5:10; *in comparison with*, Rom 8:18; *in attention to*, Eph 3:4; of the actions, dispositions, etc., exhibited with respect to any one, whether friendly, *towards*, Gal 6:10; Eph 6:9; or unfriendly, *with, against*, Luke 23:12; Acts 23:30; after verbs signifying to converse, dispute, make a covenant, etc., *with*, Luke 24:14; Acts 2:7; 3:25

πρός   prep-gen   [3t; prep; 4639]   πρός
πρός   prep-dat   [7t; prep; 4639]   "
πρός   prep-acc   [690t; prep; 4639]   "

προσάββατον, ου, τό   {4640, n-2c}
the day before the sabbath, sabbath-eve, Mark 15:42*

προσάββατον   nom sg neut
     [Mk 15:42; n-2c; 4640]   προσάββατον
προσάγαγε   aor act imperative 2 sg
     [Lk 9:41; cv-1b(2); 4642]   προσάγω
προσαγάγῃ   aor act subj 3 sg
     [1P 3:18; cv-1b(2); 4642]   "
προσαγαγόντες   aor act ptcp nom pl masc
     [Ac 16:20; cv-1b(2); 4642]   "
προσάγειν   pres act inf
     [Ac 27:27; cv-1b(2); 4642]   "
προσαγορευθείς   aor pass ptcp nom sg masc
     [Hb 5:10; cv-1a(6); 4641]   προσαγορεύω

προσαγορεύω   {4641, cv-1a(6)}
[-, προσηγόρευσα -, -, προσηγορεύθην] *to speak to, accost, to name, declare*, Heb 5:10*

προσάγω   {4642, cv-1b(2)}
[(πρόσηγον), -, προσήγαγον, -, -, προσήχθην] *to lead* or *conduct to, bring*, Luke 9:41; Acts 12:6 v.l.; 16:20; *to conduct to the presence of, to procure access for*, Matt 18:24; 1 Peter 3:18; *to bring near; to near*, in a nautical sense, Acts 27:27*

προσαγωγή, ῆς, ἡ   {4643, n-1b}
approach; access, admission, to the presence of any one, Rom 5:2; Eph 2:18; 3:12*

προσαγωγήν   acc sg fem   [3t; n-1b; 4643]   προσαγωγή

προσαιτέω   {4644, cv-1d(2a)}
[-, -, -, -, -] *to ask for in addition; to ask earnestly,*

beg; to beg alms, John 9:8; Mark 10:46 v.l.; Luke 18:35 v.l.*

προσαίτης, ου, ὁ   {4645, n-1f}
a beggar, mendicant, Mark 10:46; John 9:8*

προσαίτης   nom sg masc   [2t; n-1f; 4645]   προσαίτης
προσαιτῶν   pres act ptcp nom sg masc
     [Jn 9:8; cv-1d(2a); 4644]   προσαιτέω

προσαναβαίνω   {4646, cv-2d(6)}
[-, προσανέβην, -, -, -] *to go up further*, Luke 14:10*

προσανάβηθι   aor act imperative 2 sg
     [Lk 14:10; cv-2d(6); 4646]   προσαναβαίνω

προσαναλίσκω   {4648, cv-5b}
[-, προσανέλωσα, -, -, -] also spelled προσαναλόω (4649), *to consume besides; to expend on a definite object*, Luke 8:43 v.l.*

προσαναλόω   {4649; cv-1d(3)}
[-, προσανάλωσα, -, -, -] alternate form for προσαναλίσκω; Lk 18:43 (προσαναλώσασα) shows this form

προσαναλώσασα   aor act ptcp nom sg fem
     [Lk 8:43; cv-1d(3); 4649]   προσαναλόω
προσαναπληροῦσα   pres act ptcp nom sg fem
     [2C 9:12; cv-1d(3); 4650]   προσαναπληρόω

προσαναπληρόω   {4650, cv-1d(3)}
[-, προσανεπλήρωσα -, -, -] *to fill up by addition; to supply* deficiencies, 2 Cor 9:12; 11:9*

προσανατίθημι   {4651, cv-6a}
[-, προσανέθηκα, -, -, -] occurs in the N.T. only as a middle, *to lay upon over and above*; mid. *to put one's self in free communication with, to confer with*, Gal 1:16; *to confer upon, to propound as a matter of consideration*, Gal 2:6*

προσανεθέμην   aor mid ind 1 sg
     [Ga 1:16; cv-6a; 4651]   προσανατίθημι
προσανέθεντο   aor mid ind 3 pl
     [Ga 2:6; cv-6a; 4651]   "
προσανεπλήρωσαν   aor act ind 3 pl
     [2C 11:9; cv-1d(3); 4650]   προσαναπληρόω

προσανέχω   {4652, cv-1b(2)}
[-, -, -, -, -] *to rise up toward*, followed by the dative, Acts 27:27 v.l.*

προσαπειλέω   {4653, cv-1d(2a)}
[-, προσαπείλησα, -, -, -] *to threaten in addition, utter additional threats*, Acts 4:21*

προσαπειλησάμενοι   aor mid ptcp nom pl masc
     [Ac 4:21; cv-1d(2a); 4653]   προσαπειλέω

προσαχέω   {4654, cv-1d(2a)}
[-, -, -, -, -] the Doric form of προσηχέω, *sound*, the sound made by the surf when close to shore, Acts 27:27 v.l.*

προσδαπανάω   {4655, cv-1d(1a)}
[-, προσεδαπάνησα, -, -, -] *to spend besides, expend over and above*, Luke 10:35*

προσδαπανήσῃς   aor act subj 2 sg
     [Lk 10:35; cv-1d(1a); 4655]   προσδαπανάω

προσδεξάμενοι   aor mid ptcp nom pl masc
   [Hb 11:35; cv-1b(2); 4657]   προσδέχομαι
προσδέξησθε   aor mid subj 2 pl
   [Rm 16:2; cv-1b(2); 4657]   "

προσδέομαι   {4656, cv-1d(2c)}
   [-, -, -, -, -] *to want besides* or *in addition, need,*
   Acts 17:25*

προσδεόμενος   pres mid ptcp nom sg masc
   [Ac 17:25; cv-1d(2c); 4656]   προσδέομαι
προσδέχεσθε   pres mid imperative 2 pl
   [Pp 2:29; cv-1b(2); 4657]   προσδέχομαι
προσδέχεται   pres mid ind 3 sg
   [Lk 15:2; cv-1b(2); 4657]   "

προσδέχομαι   {4657, cv-1b(2)}
   [(προσεδεχόμην), -, προσεδεξάμην, -, -, -] *to
   receive, accept; to receive, admit, grant access to.*
   Luke 15:2; *to receive, admit, accept,* and with οὐ,
   to reject, Heb 11:35; *to submit to,* Heb 10:34; *to
   receive kindly,* as a guest, *entertain,* Rom 16:2; *to
   receive, admit,* as a hope, Acts 24:15; *to look or
   wait for, expect, await,* Mark 15:43; Luke 1:21 v.l.;
   Luke 2:25; Acts 10:24 v.l.

προσδεχόμενοι   pres mid ptcp nom pl masc
   [3t; cv-1b(2); 4657]   "
προσδεχομένοις   pres mid ptcp dat pl masc
   [2t; cv-1b(2); 4657]   "
προσδεχόμενος   pres mid ptcp nom sg masc
   [2t; cv-1b(2); 4657]   "
προσδέχονται   pres mid ind 3 pl
   [Ac 24:15; cv-1b(2); 4657]   "

προσδίδωμι   {4658, cv-6a}
   [-, -, -, -, -] *to give (over),* Luke 24:30 v.l.*

προσδοκᾷ   pres act ind 3 sg
   [2t; cv-1d(1a); 4659]   προσδοκάω

προσδοκάω   {4659, cv-1d(1a)}
   [(προσεδόκων), -, προσεδόκησα, -, -, -] *to look for,
   be expectant of,* Matt 11:3; Luke 7:19, 20; Acts 3:5;
   2 Peter 3:12, 13, 14; *to expect,* Acts 28:6; *to wait
   for,* Luke 1:21; 8:40; Acts 10:24; 27:33; absol. *to
   think, anticipate,* Matt 24:50; Luke 12:46

προσδοκία, ας, ἡ   {4660, n-1a}
   a looking for, expectation, anticipation, Luke 21:26;
   meton. *expectation, what is expected* or
   anticipated, Acts 12:11*

προσδοκίας   gen sg fem   [2t; n-1a; 4660]   προσδοκία
προσδοκῶμεν   pres act ind 1 pl
   [4t; cv-1d(1a); 4659]   προσδοκάω
προσδοκῶν   pres act ptcp nom sg masc
   [3t; cv-1d(1a); 4659]   "
προσδοκῶντας   pres act ptcp acc pl masc
   [2P 3:12; cv-1d(1a); 4659]   "
προσδοκῶντες   pres act ptcp nom pl masc
   [3t; cv-1d(1a); 4659]   "
προσδοκῶντος   pres act ptcp gen sg masc
   [Lk 3:15; cv-1d(1a); 4659]   "
προσδοκώντων   pres act ptcp gen pl masc
   [Ac 28:6; cv-1d(1a); 4659]   "
προσδραμών   aor act ptcp nom sg masc
   [2t; cv-1b(2); 4708]   προστρέχω

προσεάω   {4661, cv-1d(1b)}
   [-, -, -, -, -] *to permit an approach,* Acts 27:7*

προσεγγίζω   {4662, cv-2a(1)}
   [-, -, -, -, -] *to approach, come near,* Mark 2:4; Acts
   10:25; 27:27*

προσεδέξασθε   aor mid ind 2 pl
   [Hb 10:34; cv-1b(2); 4657]   προσδέχομαι
προσεδέχετο   imperf mid ind 3 sg
   [Lk 23:51; cv-1b(2); 4657]   "
προσεδόκων   imperf act ind 3 pl
   [Ac 28:6; cv-1d(1a); 4659]   προσδοκάω

προσεδρεύω   {4663, cv-1a(6)}
   [-, -, -, -, -] *to sit near;* met. *to wait* or *attend upon,
   have charge of,* 1 Cor 9:13*

προσέθετο   aor mid ind 3 sg
   [3t; cv-6a; 4707]   προστίθημι
προσέθηκεν   aor act ind 3 sg
   [Lk 3:20; cv-6a; 4707]   "
προσεῖχον   imperf act ind 3 pl
   [3t; cv-1b(2); 4668]   προσέχω
προσεκαλέσατο   aor mid ind 3 sg
   [Lk 18:16; cv-1d(2a); 4673]   προσκαλέω
προσεκληρώθησαν   aor pass ind 3 pl
   [Ac 17:4; cv-1d(3); 4677]   προσκληρόω
προσεκλίθη   aor pass ind 3 sg
   [Ac 5:36; cv-1c(2); 4679]   προσκλίνω
προσέκοψαν   aor act ind 3 pl
   [2t; cv-4; 4684]   προσκόπτω
προσεκύλισεν   aor act ind 3 sg
   [Mk 15:46; cv-1a(1); 4685]   προσκυλίω
προσεκύνει   imperf act ind 3 sg
   [4t; cv-1d(2a); 4686]   προσκυνέω
προσεκύνησαν   aor act ind 3 pl
   [12t; cv-1d(2a); 4686]   "
προσεκύνησεν   aor act ind 3 sg
   [4t; cv-1d(2a); 4686]   "
προσεκύνουν   imperf act ind 3 pl
   [Mk 15:19; cv-1d(2a); 4686]   "
προσελάβετο   aor mid ind 3 sg
   [2t; cv-3a(2b); 4689]   προσλαμβάνω
προσελάβοντο   aor mid ind 3 pl
   [3t; cv-3a(2b); 4689]   "
προσεληλύθατε   perf act ind 2 pl
   [2t; cv-1b(2); 4665]   προσέρχομαι
πρόσελθε   aor act imperative 2 sg
   [Ac 8:29; cv-1b(2); 4665]   "
προσελθόντες   aor act ptcp nom pl masc
   [17t; cv-1b(2); 4665]   "
προσελθόντων   aor act ptcp gen pl masc
   [Mt 26:60; cv-1b(2); 4665]   "
προσελθοῦσα   aor act ptcp nom sg fem
   [2t; cv-1b(2); 4665]   "
προσελθοῦσαι   aor act ptcp nom pl fem
   [Mt 28:9; cv-1b(2); 4665]   "
προσελθών   aor act ptcp nom sg masc
   [23t; cv-1b(2); 4665]   "
προσενέγκαι   aor act inf
   [Mk 2:4; cv-1c(1); 4712]   προσφέρω
προσενέγκας   aor act ptcp nom sg masc
   [2t; cv-1c(1); 4712]   "
προσένεγκε   aor act imperative 2 sg
   [2t; cv-1c(1); 4712]   "

προσενέγκη   aor act subj 3 sg
   [Hb 8:3; cv-1c(1); 4712]   "
προσένεγκον   aor act imperative 2 sg
   [Mt 8:4; cv-1c(1); 4712]   "
προσενεχθείς   aor pass ptcp nom sg masc
   [Hb 9:28; cv-1c(1); 4712]   "
προσενήνοχεν   perf act ind 3 sg
   [Hb 11:17; cv-1c(1); 4712]   "
προσέπεσαν   aor act ind 3 pl
   [Mt 7:25; cv-1b(3); 4700]   προσπίπτω
προσέπεσεν   aor act ind 3 sg [5t; cv-1b(3); 4700]   "
προσέπιπτον   imperf act ind 3 pl
   [Mk 3:11; cv-1b(3); 4700]   "
προσεποιήσατο   aor mid ind 3 sg
   [Lk 24:28; cv-1d(2a); 4701]   προσποιέω

προσεργάζομαι   {4664, cv-2a(1)}
[-, προσηργασάμην or προσειργασάμην, -, -, -] pr.
to work in addition; to gain in addition in trade,
Luke 19:16*

προσέρηξεν   aor act ind 3 sg
   [2t; cv-3c(2); 4704]   προσρήσσω
προσέρχεσθαι   pres mid inf
   [Ac 10:28; cv-1b(2); 4665]   προσέρχομαι
προσέρχεται   pres mid ind 3 sg
   [1Ti 6:3; cv-1b(2); 4665]   "

προσέρχομαι   {4665, cv-1b(2)}
[(προσηρχόμην), προσελεύσομαι, προσῆλθον,
προσελήλυθα, -, -] *to come* or *go to* any one,
approach, Matt 4:3, 11; 5:1; 8:19, 25, et al. freq.;
trop. *to come* or *go to, approach, draw near,
spiritually*, Heb 7:25; 11:6; 4:16; 1 Peter 2:4; met.
to assent to, accede to, concur in, 1 Tim 6:3

προσερχόμενοι   pres mid ptcp nom pl masc
   [2t; cv-1b(2); 4665]   "
προσερχόμενον   pres mid ptcp acc sg masc
   [Hb 11:6; cv-1b(2); 4665]   "
προσερχομένου   pres mid ptcp gen sg masc
   [2t; cv-1b(2); 4665]   "
προσερχομένους   pres mid ptcp acc pl masc
   [2t; cv-1b(2); 4665]   "
προσέρχονται   pres mid ind 3 pl
   [2t; cv-1b(2); 4665]   "
προσερχώμεθα   pres mid subj 1 pl
   [2t; cv-1b(2); 4665]   "
προσέσχηκεν   perf act ind 3 sg
   [Hb 7:13; cv-1b(2); 4668]   προσέχω
προσέταξεν   aor act ind 3 sg
   [5t; cv-2b; 4705]   προστάσσω
προσετέθη   aor pass ind 3 sg
   [3t; cv-6a; 4707]   προστίθημι
προσετέθησαν   aor pass ind 3 pl
   [Ac 2:41; cv-6a; 4707]   "
προσετίθει   imperf act ind 3 sg
   [Ac 2:47; cv-6a; 4707]   "
προσετίθεντο   imperf pass ind 3 pl
   [Ac 5:14; cv-6a; 4707]   "
πρόσευξαι   aor mid imperative 2 sg
   [Mt 6:6; cv-1b(2); 4667]   προσεύχομαι
προσευξάμενοι   aor mid ptcp nom pl masc
   [5t; cv-1b(2); 4667]   "
προσευξάμενος   aor mid ptcp nom sg masc
   [Ac 28:8; cv-1b(2); 4667]   "

προσεύξασθαι   aor mid inf [6t; cv-1b(2); 4667]   "
προσευξάσθωσαν   aor mid imperative 3 pl
   [Jm 5:14; cv-1b(2); 4667]   "
προσεύξηται   aor mid subj 3 sg
   [Mt 19:13; cv-1b(2); 4667]   "
προσεύξομαι   fut mid ind 1 sg
   [2t; cv-1b(2); 4667]   "
προσεύξωμαι   aor mid subj 1 sg
   [2t; cv-1b(2); 4667]   "
προσευξώμεθα   aor mid subj 1 pl
   [Rm 8:26; cv-1b(2); 4667]   "
προσευχαί   nom pl fem [2t; n-1b; 4666]   προσευχή
προσευχαῖς   dat pl fem [6t; n-1b; 4666]   "
προσευχάς   acc pl fem [3t; n-1b; 4666]   "
προσεύχεσθαι   pres mid inf
   [6t; cv-1b(2); 4667]   προσεύχομαι
προσεύχεσθε   pres mid imperative 2 pl
   [13t; cv-1b(2); 4667]   "
προσεύχεσθε   pres mid ind 2 pl
   [Mk 11:24; cv-1b(2); 4667]   "
προσευχέσθω   pres mid imperative 3 sg
   [2t; cv-1b(2); 4667]   "
προσεύχεται   pres mid ind 3 sg
   [2t; cv-1b(2); 4667]   "

προσευχή, ῆς, ἡ   {4666, n-1b}
prayer, Matt 17:21; 21:13, 22; Luke 6:12; Acts
1:14; meton. *a place where prayer is offered, an
oratory*, perhaps, Acts 17:13, 16

προσευχή   nom sg fem [2t; n-1b; 4666]   προσευχή
προσευχῇ   dat sg fem [10t; n-1b; 4666]   "
προσεύχῃ   pres mid subj 2 sg
   [Mt 6:6; cv-1b(2); 4667]   προσεύχομαι
προσευχήν   acc sg fem [2t; n-1b; 4666]   προσευχή
προσευχῆς   gen sg fem [6t; n-1b; 4666]   "
προσεύχησθε   pres mid subj 2 pl
   [2t; cv-1b(2); 4667]   προσεύχομαι

προσεύχομαι   {4667, cv-1b(2)}
[(προσηυχόμην), προσεύξομαι, προσηυξάμην, -, -,
-] *to pray, offer prayer*, Matt 5:44; 6:5, 6

προσεύχομαι   pres mid ind 1 sg
   [Pp 1:9; cv-1b(2); 4667]   "
προσευχόμεθα   pres mid ind 1 pl
   [2Th 1:11; cv-1b(2); 4667]   "
προσευχομένη   pres mid ptcp nom sg fem
   [1C 11:5; cv-1b(2); 4667]   "
προσευχόμενοι   pres mid ptcp nom pl masc
   [10t; cv-1b(2); 4667]   "
προσευχόμενον   pres mid ptcp nom sg neut
   [Lk 1:10; cv-1b(2); 4667]   "
προσευχόμενον   pres mid ptcp acc sg masc
   [2t; cv-1b(2); 4667]   "
προσευχόμενος   pres mid ptcp nom sg masc
   [5t; cv-1b(2); 4667]   "
προσευχομένου   pres mid ptcp gen sg masc
   [2t; cv-1b(2); 4667]   "
προσεύχονται   pres mid ind 3 pl
   [Lk 20:47; cv-1b(2); 4667]   "
προσεύχωμαι   pres mid subj 1 sg
   [1C 14:14; cv-1b(2); 4667]   "
προσευχῶν   gen pl fem [5t; n-1b; 4666]   προσευχή

προσέφερεν imperf act ind 3 sg
   [Hb 11:17; cv-1c(1); 4712]   προσφέρω
προσέφερον imperf act ind 3 pl
   [3t; cv-1c(1); 4712]   "
προσεφώνει imperf act ind 3 sg
   [Ac 22:2; cv-1d(2a); 4715]   προσφωνέω
προσεφώνησεν aor act ind 3 sg
   [4t; cv-1d(2a); 4715]   "
πρόσεχε pres act imperative 2 sg
   [1Ti 4:13; cv-1b(2); 4668]   προσέχω
προσέχειν pres act inf [4t; cv-1b(2); 4668]   "
προσέχετε pres act imperative 2 pl
   [11t; cv-1b(2); 4668]   "
προσέχοντας pres act ptcp acc pl masc
   [1Ti 3:8; cv-1b(2); 4668]   "
προσέχοντες pres act ptcp nom pl masc
   [3t; cv-1b(2); 4668]   "

προσέχω   {4668, cv-1b(2)}
   [(προσεῖχον), -, προσέσχον, προσέσχηκα, -, -] *to*
   have in addition; to hold to, bring near; absol. to
   apply the mind to a thing, *to give heed to, attend*
   to, observe, consider, Acts 5:35; Heb 2:1; 2 Peter
   1:19; *to take care of, provide for,* Acts 20:28; when
   followed by ἀπό, μή, or μήποτε, *to beware of, take*
   heed of, guard against, Matt 6:1; 7:15; *to assent to,*
   yield credence to, follow, adhere or *be attached to,*
   Acts 8:6, 10, 11; 16:14; *to give one's self up to, be*
   addicted to, engage in, be occupied with, 1 Tim 1:4,
   3:8

προσεῶντος pres act ptcp gen sg masc
   [Ac 27:7; cv-1d(1b); 4661]   προσεάω
προσῆλθαν aor act ind 3 pl
   [2t; cv-1b(2); 4665]   προσέρχομαι
προσῆλθεν aor act ind 3 sg [8t; cv-1b(2); 4665] "
προσῆλθον aor act ind 3 pl [15t; cv-1b(2); 4665] "

προσηλόω   {4669, cv-1d(3)}
   [-, προσήλωσα -, -, -] *to nail to, affix with nails,*
   Col 2:14*

προσήλυτοι nom pl masc
   [Ac 2:11; n-2a; 4670]   προσήλυτος
προσήλυτον acc sg masc [2t; n-2a; 4670]   "

προσήλυτος, ου, ὁ   {4670, n-2a}
   pr. *a newcomer, a stranger;* in N.T. *a proselyte,*
   convert from paganism to Judaism, Matt 23:15;
   Acts 2:11; 6:5; 13:43*

προσηλύτων gen pl masc [Ac 13:43; n-2a; 4670] "
προσηλώσας aor act ptcp nom sg masc
   [Cl 2:14; cv-1d(3); 4669]   προσηλόω
προσήνεγκα aor act ind 1 sg
   [Mt 17:16; cv-1c(1); 4712]   προσφέρω
προσήνεγκαν aor act ind 3 pl
   [7t; cv-1c(1); 4712]   "
προσηνέγκατε aor act ind 2 pl
   [2t; cv-1c(1); 4712]   "
προσήνεγκεν aor act ind 3 sg
   [4t; cv-1c(1); 4712]   "
προσηνέχθη aor pass ind 3 sg
   [3t; cv-1c(1); 4712]   "
προσηνέχθησαν aor pass ind 3 pl
   [Mt 19:13; cv-1c(1); 4712]   "

προσηργάσατο aor mid ind 3 sg
   [Lk 19:16; cv-2a(1); 4664]   προσεργάζομαι
προσήρχοντο imperf mid ind 3 pl
   [Ac 28:9; cv-1b(2); 4665]   προσέρχομαι
προσηύξαντο aor mid ind 3 pl
   [Ac 8:15; cv-1b(2); 4667]   προσεύχομαι
προσηύξατο aor mid ind 3 sg [7t; cv-1b(2); 4667] "
προσηύχετο imperf mid ind 3 sg
   [5t; cv-1b(2); 4667]   "
προσθεῖναι aor act inf
   [2t; cv-6a; 4707]   προστίθημι
προσθείς aor act ptcp nom sg masc
   [Lk 19:11; cv-6a; 4707]   "
πρόσθες aor act imperative 2 sg
   [Lk 17:5; cv-6a; 4707]   "
πρόσκαιρα nom pl neut
   [2C 4:18; a-3a; 4672]   πρόσκαιρος
πρόσκαιροι nom pl masc [Mk 4:17; a-3a; 4672] "
πρόσκαιρον acc sg neut [Hb 11:25; a-3a; 4672] "

πρόσκαιρος, ον   {4672, a-3a}
   opportune, in N.T. *continuing for a limited time,*
   temporary, transient, Matt 13:21; Mark 4:17; 2
   Cor 4:18; Heb 11:25*

πρόσκαιρος nom sg masc [Mt 13:21; a-3a; 4672] "
προσκαλεῖται pres mid ind 3 sg
   [2t; cv-1d(2a); 4673]   προσκαλέω
προσκαλεσάμενοι aor mid ptcp nom pl masc
   [2t; cv-1d(2a); 4673]   "
προσκαλεσάμενος aor mid ptcp nom sg masc
   [20t; cv-1d(2a); 4673]   "
προσκαλεσάσθω aor mid imperative 3 sg
   [Jm 5:14; cv-1d(2a); 4673]   "
προσκαλέσηται aor mid subj 3 sg
   [Ac 2:39; cv-1d(2a); 4673]   "

προσκαλέω   {4673, cv-1d(2a)}
   [-, προσεκάλεσα, -, προσκέκλημαι, -] *to call to*
   one's self, summon, Matt 10:1; 15:10, 32; 18:2; *to*
   invite, Acts 2:39; *to call* to the performance of a
   thing, *appoint,* Acts 13:2; 16:10

προσκαρτερεῖτε pres act imperative 2 pl
   [Cl 4:2; cv-1d(2a); 4674]   προσκαρτερέω

προσκαρτερέω   {4674, cv-1d(2a)}
   [προσκαρτερήσω, -, -, -, -] *to persist in adherence*
   to a thing; *to be intently engaged in, attend*
   constantly to, Acts 1:14; 2:42; Rom 13:6; *to remain*
   constantly in a place, Acts 2:46; *to constantly*
   attend upon, continue near to, be at hand, Mark
   3:9; Acts 8:13; 10:7

προσκαρτερῇ pres act subj 3 sg
   [Mk 3:9; cv-1d(2a); 4674]   "
προσκαρτερήσει dat sg fem
   [Ep 6:18; n-3e(5b); 4675]   προσκαρτέρησις

προσκαρτέρησις, εως, ἡ   {4675, n-3e(5b)}
   perseverance, unremitting continuance in a thing,
   Eph 6:18*

προσκαρτερήσομεν fut act ind 1 pl
   [Ac 6:4; cv-1d(2a); 4674]   προσκαρτερέω
προσκαρτεροῦντες pres act ptcp nom pl masc
   [5t; cv-1d(2a); 4674]   "

προσκαρτερούντων pres act ptcp gen pl masc
[Ac 10:7; cv-1d(2a); 4674]   "

προσκαρτερῶν pres act ptcp nom sg masc
[Ac 8:13; cv-1d(2a); 4674]   "

προσκέκλημαι perf mid ind 1 sg
[Ac 13:2; cv-1d(2a); 4673]   προσκαλέω

προσκέκληται perf mid ind 3 sg
[Ac 16:10; cv-1d(2a); 4673]   "

προσκεφάλαιον, ου, τό   {4676, n-2c}
pr. *a cushion for the head, pillow;* also, *a boat-cushion,* Mark 4:38*

προσκεφάλαιον acc sg neut
[Mk 4:38; n-2c; 4676]   προσκεφάλαιον

προσκληρόω   {4677, cv-1d(3)}
[-, -, -, -, προσεκληρώθην] pr. *to assign by lot;* in N.T., *to adjoin one's self to, associate with, follow as a disciple,* Acts 17:4*

πρόσκλισιν acc sg fem
[1Ti 5:21; n-3e(5b); 4680]   πρόσκλισις

πρόσκλησις, εως, ἡ   {4678, n-3e(5b)}
advocacy, or, perhaps, *partiality,* 1 Tim 5:21*

προσκλίνω   {4679, cv-1c(2)}
[-, -, -, -, προσεκλίθην] pr. *to make to lean upon* or *against* a thing; met., *to join one's self to, follow as an adherent,* Acts 5:36*

πρόσκλισις, εως, ἡ   {4680, n-3e(5b)}
pr. *a leaning upon* or *towards* a thing; met. *a leaning towards* any one, *inclination* of mind *towards, partiality,* 1 Tim 5:21*

προσκολλάω   {4681, cv-1d(1a)}
[-, -, -, -, προσεκολλήθην] pr. *to glue to;* in N.T., *to join one's self to* any one, *follow as an adherent,* Acts 5:36 v.l.; *to cleave closely to,* Matt 19:5 v.l.; Mark 10:7; Eph 5:31*

προσκολληθήσεται fut pass ind 3 sg
[2t; cv-1d(1a); 4681]   προσκολλάω

πρόσκομμα, ατος, τό   {4682, n-3c(4)}
a stumbling, Rom 9:32, 33; 1 Peter 2:8; met. *a stumbling-block, an occasion of sinning, means of inducing to sin,* Rom 14:13; 1 Cor 8:9; met. *a moral stumbling, a shock* to the moral or religious sense, *a moral embarrassment,* Rom 14:20*

πρόσκομμα nom sg neut
[1C 8:9; n-3c(4); 4682]   πρόσκομμα
πρόσκομμα acc sg neut [Rm 14:13; n-3c(4); 4682] "
προσκόμματος gen sg neut [4t; n-3c(4); 4682]   "

προσκοπή, ῆς, ἡ   {4683, n-1b}
pr. *a stumbling; offence;* in N.T. *an offence, shock, ground of exception,* 2 Cor 6:3*

προσκοπήν acc sg fem
[2C 6:3; n-1b; 4683]   προσκοπή
προσκόπτει pres act ind 3 sg
[3t; cv-4; 4684]   προσκόπτω
προσκόπτουσιν pres act ind 3 pl
[1P 2:8; cv-4; 4684]   "

προσκόπτω   {4684, cv-4}
[-, προσέκοψα, -, -, -] *to dash against, to beat upon,*

Matt 7:27; *to strike* the foot *against,* Matt 4:6; Luke 4:11; *to stumble,* John 11:9, 10; met. *to stumble at, to take offence at,* Rom 9:32; 14:21; 1 Peter 2:8*

προσκόψῃς aor act subj 2 sg [2t; cv-4; 4684]   "
προσκυλίσας aor act ptcp nom sg masc
[Mt 27:60; cv-1a(1); 4685]   προσκυλίω

προσκυλίω   {4685, cv-1a(1)}
[-, προσεκύλισα, -, -, -] *to roll to* or *against,* Matt 27:60; Mark 15:46; Luke 23:53 v.l.*

προσκυνεῖ pres act ind 3 sg
[Rv 14:9; cv-1d(2a); 4686]   προσκυνέω
προσκυνεῖν pres act inf [3t; cv-1d(2a); 4686]   "
προσκυνεῖτε pres act ind 2 pl
[Jn 4:22; cv-1d(2a); 4686]   "

προσκυνέω   {4686, cv-1d(2a)}
[(προσεκύνουν), προσκυνήσω, προσεκύνησα, -, -, -] *to do reverence* or *homage by kissing the hand;* in N.T. *to do reverence* or *homage by prostration,* Matt 2:2, 8, 11; 20:20; Luke 4:7; 24:52; *to pay divine homage, worship, adore,* Matt 4:10; John 4:20, 21; Heb 1:6; *to bow one's self in adoration,* Heb 11:21

προσκυνῆσαι aor act inf [3t; cv-1d(2a); 4686]   "
προσκυνήσαντες aor act ptcp nom pl masc
[Lk 24:52; cv-1d(2a); 4686]   "
προσκυνήσατε aor act imperative 2 pl
[Rv 14:7; cv-1d(2a); 4686]   "
προσκυνήσάτωσαν aor act imperative 3 pl
[Hb 1:6; cv-1d(2a); 4686]   "
προσκυνήσει fut act ind 3 sg
[1C 14:25; cv-1d(2a); 4686]   "
προσκυνήσεις fut act ind 2 sg
[2t; cv-1d(2a); 4686]   "
προσκυνήσετε fut act ind 2 pl
[Jn 4:21; cv-1d(2a); 4686]   "
προσκυνήσῃς aor act subj 2 sg
[2t; cv-1d(2a); 4686]   "
προσκύνησον aor act imperative 2 sg
[2t; cv-1d(2a); 4686]   "
προσκυνήσουσιν fut act ind 3 pl
[7t; cv-1d(2a); 4686]   "
προσκυνήσω aor act subj 1 sg
[Mt 2:8; cv-1d(2a); 4686]   "
προσκυνήσων fut act ptcp nom sg masc
[2t; cv-1d(2a); 4686]   "
προσκυνήσωσιν aor act subj 3 pl
[2t; cv-1d(2a); 4686]   "
προσκυνηταί nom pl masc
[Jn 4:23; n-1f; 4687]   προσκυνητής

προσκυνητής, ου, ὁ   {4687, n-1f}
a worshipper, John 4:23*

προσκυνοῦμεν pres act ind 1 pl
[Jn 4:22; cv-1d(2a); 4686]   προσκυνέω
προσκυνοῦντας pres act ptcp acc pl masc
[5t; cv-1d(2a); 4686]
προσκυνοῦντες pres act ptcp nom pl masc
[Rv 14:11; cv-1d(2a); 4686]   "
προσκυνοῦσα pres act ptcp nom sg fem
[Mt 20:20; cv-1d(2a); 4686]   "

προσλαβόμενοι   aor mid ptcp nom pl masc
[2t; cv-3a(2b); 4689]   προσλαμβάνω
προσλαβόμενος   aor mid ptcp nom sg masc
[2t; cv-3a(2b); 4689]   "
προσλαβοῦ   aor mid imperative 2 sg
[Pm 17; cv-3a(2b); 4689]   "

προσλαλέω   {4688, cv-1d(2a)}
[-, προσελάλησα, -, -, -] *to speak to, converse with,*
Acts 13:43; 28:20*

προσλαλῆσαι   aor act inf
[Ac 28:20; cv-1d(2a); 4688]   προσλαλέω
προσλαλοῦντες   pres act ptcp nom pl masc
[Ac 13:43; cv-1d(2a); 4688]   "
προσλαμβάνεσθε   pres mid imperative 2 pl
[2t; cv-3a(2b); 4689]   προσλαμβάνω

προσλαμβάνω   {4689, cv-3a(2b)}
[-, προσέλαβον, προσείληφα, -, -] *to take to one's
self, assume, take as a companion* or *associate,* Acts
17:5; 18:26; *to take,* as food, Acts 27:33, 34 v.l., 36;
to receive kindly or *hospitably, admit to one's
society and friendship, treat with kindness,* Acts
28:2; Rom 14:1, 3; 15:7; Phil 12 v.l., 17; *to take* or
draw to one's self as a preliminary to an address
of admonition, Matt 16:22; Mark 8:32*

πρόσλημψις, εως, ἡ   {4691, n-3e(5b)}
also spelled πρόσληψις, *acceptance,* Rom 11:15*

πρόσλημψις   nom sg fem
[Rm 11:15; n-3e(5b); 4691]   πρόσλημψις

πρόσληψις, see πρόσλημψις   {4692}

προσμεῖναι   aor act inf
[1Ti 1:3; cv-1c(2); 4693]   προσμένω
προσμείνας   aor act ptcp nom sg masc
[Ac 18:18; cv-1c(2); 4693]   "
προσμένει   pres act ind 3 sg
[1Ti 5:5; cv-1c(2); 4693]   "
προσμένειν   pres act inf   [2t; cv-1c(2); 4693] "
προσμένουσιν   pres act ind 3 pl
[2t; cv-1c(2); 4693]   "

προσμένω   {4693, cv-1c(2)}
[-, προσέμεινα -, -, -] *to continue, remain, stay* in
a place, 1 Tim 1:3; *to remain* or *continue with* any
one, Matt 15:32; Mark 8:2; Acts 18:18; *to adhere
to,* Acts 11:23; met. *to remain constant in,
persevere in,* Acts 13:43; 1 Tim 5:5*

προσορμίζω   {4694, cv-2a(1)}
[-, -, -, -, προσωρμίσθην] *to bring a ship to its
station* or *to land;* mid. *to come to the land,* Mark
6:53*

προσοφείλεις   pres act ind 2 sg
[Pm 19; cv-2d(1); 4695]   προσοφείλω

προσοφείλω   {4695, cv-2d(1)}
[-, -, -, -, -] *to owe besides* or *in addition,* Phlm 19*

προσοχθίζω   {4696, cv-2a(1)}
[-, προσώχθισα, -, -, -] *to be vexed* or *angry at,* Heb
3:10, 17*

προσπαίω   {4697, cv-1a(2)}
[-, προσέπαισα, -, -, -] *beat against,* Matt 7:25*

πρόσπεινος, ον   {4698, a-3a}
very hungry, Acts 10:10*

πρόσπεινος   nom sg masc
[Ac 10:10; a-3a; 4698]   πρόσπεινος
προσπεσοῦσα   aor act ptcp nom sg fem
[Lk 8:47; cv-1b(3); 4700]   προσπίπτω

προσπήγνυμι   {4699, cv-3c(2)}
[-, προσέπηξα, -, -, -] *to fix to, affix to,* Acts 2:23*

προσπήξαντες   aor act ptcp nom pl masc
[Ac 2:23; cv-3c(2); 4699]   προσπήγνυμι

προσπίπτω   {4700, cv-1b(3)}
[(προσέπιπψον), -, προσέπεσον or προσέπεσα, -, -,
-] *to fall* or *impinge upon* or *against* a thing; *to fall
down to* any one, Mark 3:11; 7:25; *to rush
violently upon, beat against,* Matt 7:25

προσποιέω   {4701, cv-1d(2a)}
[-, προσεποίησα, -, -, -] *to add* or *attach;* mid. *to
attach to one's self; to claim* or *arrogate to one's self;
to assume the appearance of, make a show of,
pretend,* Luke 24:28, *to take notice,* John 8:6 v.l.*

προσπορεύομαι   {4702, cv-1a(6)}
[-, -, -, -, -] *to go* or *come to* any one, Mark 10:35*

προσπορεύονται   pres mid ind 3 pl
[Mk 10:35; cv-1a(6); 4702]   προσπορεύομαι

προσρήγνυμι, see προσρήσσω   {4703}

προσρήσσω   {4704, cv-3c(2)}
[-, προσέρηξα, -, -, -] also spelled προσρήγνυμι,
to break or *burst upon, dash against,* Luke 6:48, 49;
Matt 7:27 v.l.

προστάσσω   {4705, cv-2b}
[-, προσέταξα, -, προστέταγμαι, προσετάχθην or
προσετάγην] pr. *to place* or *station at* or *against;
to enjoin, command, direct,* Matt 1:24; 8:4; 21:6
v.l.; Mark 1:44; *to assign, constitute, appoint,* Acts
17:26

προστάτις, ιδος, ἡ   {4706, n-3c(2)}
a patroness, protectress, Rom 16:2*

προστάτις   nom sg fem
[Rm 16:2; n-3c(2); 4706]   προστάτις
προστεθῆναι   aor pass inf
[Hb 12:19; cv-6a; 4707]   προστίθημι
προστεθήσεται   fut pass ind 3 sg
[3t; cv-6a; 4707]   "
προστεταγμένα   perf pass ptcp acc pl neut
[Ac 10:33; cv-2b; 4705]   προστάσσω
προστεταγμένους   perf pass ptcp acc pl masc
[Ac 17:26; cv-2b; 4705]   "
προστῆναι   aor act inf
[1Ti 3:5; cv-6a; 4613]   προΐστημι

προστίθημι   {4707, cv-6a}
[(προσετίθην), προσθήσω, προσέθηκα, -, -,
προσετέθην] *to put to* or *near; to lay with* or *by the
side of,* Acts 13:36; *to add, super-add, adjoin,* Matt
6:27, 33; Luke 3:20; Acts 2:41, 47 v.l.; from the
Hebrew, denote *continuation,* or *repetition,*
Mark 14:25 v.l.; Luke 19:11; 20:11, 12; Acts 12:3

προστρέχοντες   pres act ptcp nom pl masc
[Mk 9:15; cv-1b(2); 4708]   προστρέχω

προστρέχω   {4708, cv-1b(2)}
[-, προσέδραμον, -, -, -] *to run to,* or *up,* Mark
9:15; 10:17; Acts 8:30; John 20:16 v.l.*

προσφάγιον, ου, τό   {4709, n-2c}
what is eaten besides; hence, genr. *victuals, food,*
John 21:5*

προσφάγιον   acc sg neut
[Jn 21:5; n-2c; 4709]   προσφάγιον
πρόσφατον   acc sg fem
[Hb 10:20; a-3a; 4710]   πρόσφατος

πρόσφατος, ον   {4710, a-3a}
pr. *recently killed;* hence, genr. *recent, new, newly*
or *lately made,* Heb 10:20*

προσφάτως   {4711, adverb}
newly, recently, lately, Acts 18:2*

προσφάτως   adverb
[Ac 18:2; adverb; 4711]   προσφάτως
πρόσφερε   pres act imperative 2 sg
[Mt 5:24; cv-1c(1); 4712]   προσφέρω
προσφέρει   pres act ind 3 sg
[Hb 9:7; cv-1c(1); 4712]   "
προσφέρειν   pres act inf   [3t; cv-1c(1); 4712]   "
προσφέρεται   pres pass ind 3 sg
[Hb 12:7; cv-1c(1); 4712]   "
προσφέρῃ   pres act subj 3 sg
[2t; cv-1c(1); 4712]   "
προσφέρῃς   pres act subj 2 sg
[Mt 5:23; cv-1c(1); 4712]   "
προσφερόμεναι   pres pass ptcp nom pl fem
[Hb 10:2; cv-1c(1); 4712]   "
προσφέρονται   pres pass ind 3 pl
[2t; cv-1c(1); 4712]   "
προσφέροντες   pres act ptcp nom pl masc
[Lk 23:36; cv-1c(1); 4712]   "
προσφερόντων   pres act ptcp gen pl masc
[Hb 8:4; cv-1c(1); 4712]   "
προσφέρουσιν   pres act ind 3 pl
[Hb 10:1; cv-1c(1); 4712]   "

προσφέρω   {4712, cv-1c(1)}
[(προσέφερον), -, προσήνεγκον or προσήνεγκα,
προσενήνοχα, -, προσηνέχθην] *to bear* or *bring to,*
Matt 4:24; 25:20; *to bring to* or *before* magistrates,
Luke 12:11; 23:14; *to bring near to, apply to,* John
19:29; *to offer, tender, proffer,* as money, Acts 8:18;
to offer, present, as gifts, oblations, etc., Matt
2:11; 5:23; Heb 5:7; *to offer* in sacrifice, Mark
1:44; Luke 5:14; *to offer up* any one as a sacrifice
to God, Heb 9:25, 28; 11:17; mid. *to bear one's self*
towards, behave or *conduct one's self towards, to*
deal with, treat any one, Heb 12:7

προσφέρων   pres act ptcp nom sg masc
[Hb 10:11; cv-1c(1); 4712]   "
προσφιλῆ   nom pl neut
[Pp 4:8; a-4a; 4713]   προσφιλής

προσφιλής, ές   {4713, a-4a}
friendly, grateful, acceptable, Phil 4:8*

προσφορά, ᾶς, ἡ   {4714, n-1a}
pr. *a bringing to;* in N.T. *an offering, an act of*
offering up or *sacrificing,* Heb 10:10, 14, 18; trop.
Rom 15:16; *an offering, oblation, a thing offered,*

Eph 5:2; Heb 10:5, 8; *a sacrifice, victim offered,*
Acts 21:26; 24:17*

προσφορά   nom sg fem [3t; n-1a; 4714]   προσφορά
προσφορᾷ   dat sg fem [Hb 10:14; n-1a; 4714]   "
προσφοράν   acc sg fem [2t; n-1a; 4714]   "
προσφορᾶς   gen sg fem [Hb 10:10; n-1a; 4714]   "
προσφοράς   acc pl fem [2t; n-1a; 4714]   "

προσφωνέω   {4715, cv-1d(2a)}
[(προσεφώνουν), -, προσεφώνησα, -, -, -] *to speak*
to, address, Matt 11:16; Luke 7:32; 13:12; *to*
address, harangue, Acts 22:2; *to call* to one's self,
Luke 6:13; Acts 11:2 v.l.

προσφωνοῦντα   pres act ptcp nom pl neut
[Mt 11:16; cv-1d(2a); 4715]   προσφωνέω
προσφωνοῦσιν   pres act ptcp dat pl neut
[Lk 7:32; cv-1d(2a); 4715]   "

προσχαίρω   {4716, cv-2d(2)}
[-, -, -, -, -] *be glad,* Mark 9:15 v.l.*

πρόσχυσιν   acc sg fem
[Hb 11:28; n-3e(5b); 4717]   πρόσχυσις

πρόσχυσις, εως, ἡ   {4717, n-3e(5b)}
an effusion, sprinkling, Heb 11:28*

προσψαύετε   pres act ind 2 pl
[Lk 11:46; cv-1a(5); 4718]   προσψαύω

προσψαύω   {4718, cv-1a(5)}
[-, -, -, -, -] *to touch upon, touch lightly,* with the
dative, Luke 11:46*

πρόσωπα   nom pl neut [2t; n-2c; 4725]   πρόσωπον
πρόσωπα   acc pl neut [5t; n-2c; 4725]   "
προσωπολημπτεῖτε   pres act ind 2 pl
[Jm 2:9; v-1d(2a); 4719]   προσωπολημπτέω

προσωπολημπτέω   {4719, v-1d(2a)}
[-, -, -, -, -] *show partiality,* James 2:9*

προσωπολήμπτης, ου, ὁ   {4720, n-1f}
one who shows partiality, Acts 10:34*

προσωπολήμπτης   nom sg masc
[Ac 10:34; n-1f; 4720]   προσωπολήμπτης

προσωπολημψία, ας, ἡ   {4721, n-1a}
respect of persons, partiality, Rom 2:11; Eph 6:9;
Col 3:25; James 2:1*

προσωπολημψία   nom sg fem
[3t; n-1a; 4721]   προσωπολημψία
προσωπολημψίαις   dat pl fem [Jm 2:1; n-1a; 4721]   "

προσωπολῃπτέω   {4722, cv-1d(2a)}
to accept or *respect the person* of any one, *to pay*
regard to external appearance, condition,
circumstances, etc., *to show partiality to,* James
2:9*

προσωπολήπτης, ου, ὁ   {4723, n-1f}
a respecter of persons, Acts 10:34*

προσωποληψία, ας, ἡ   {4724, n-1a}
respect of persons, partiality, Rom 2:11; Eph 6:9;
Col 3:25; James 2:1*

πρόσωπον, ου, τό   {4725, n-2c}
the face, countenance, visage, Matt 6:16, 17; 17:2,
6; according to late usage, *a person, individual,* 2

Cor 1:11; hence, *a personal presence*, 1 Thess 2:17; from the Hebrew, πρόσωπον πρὸς πρόσωπον, *face to face, clearly, perfectly*, 1 Cor 13:12; *face, surface, external form, figure, appearance*, Matt 16:3; Luke 12:56; *external circumstances*, or *condition* of any one, Matt 22:16; Mark 12:14; πρόσωπον λαμβάνειν, *to have respect to the external circumstances* of any one, Luke 20:21; Gal 2:6; ἐν προσώπῳ, *in presence of*, 2 Cor 2:10; ἀπὸ προσώπου, *from the presence of, from*, Acts 3:19; also, *from before*, Acts 7:45; εἰς πρόσωπον, *and* κατὰ πρόσωπον, *in the presence of, before*, Acts 3:13; 2 Cor 8:24; also, *openly*, Gal 2:11; κατὰ πρόσωπον, ἔχειν, *to have before one's face, to have* any one *present*, Acts 25:16; ἀπὸ προσώπου, *from*, Rev 12:14; πρὸ προσώπου, *before*, Acts 13:24

πρόσωπον   nom sg neut [4t; n-2c; 4725]   πρόσωπον
πρόσωπον   acc sg neut [39t; n-2c; 4725]   "
προσώπου   gen sg neut [18t; n-2c; 4725]   "
προσώπῳ   dat sg neut [7t; n-2c; 4725]   "
προσώπων   gen pl neut [2C 1:11; n-2c; 4725]   "
προσωρμίσθησαν   aor pass ind 3 pl
    [Mk 6:53; cv-2a(1); 4694]   προσορμίζω
προσώχθισα   aor act ind 1 sg
    [Hb 3:10; cv-2a(1); 4696]   προσοχθίζω
προσώχθισεν   aor act ind 3 sg
    [Hb 3:17; cv-2a(1); 4696]   "

προτάσσω   {4726, cv-2b}
    [-, -, -, -, -] *to place* or *arrange in front; to assign beforehand, foreordain*, Acts 17:26 v.l.*

προτείνω   {4727, cv-2d(5)}
    [-, προέτεινα, -, -, -] *to extend before; to stretch out*, Acts 22:25*

προτέραν   acc sg fem comparative
    [Ep 4:22; a-1a(1); 4728]   πρότερος
πρότερον   acc sg neut, can function as a
    comparative adverb [10t; a-1a(1); 4728]   "

πρότερος, α, ον   {4728, a-1a(1)}
    former, prior, Eph 4:22; *before, formerly*, John 6:62

προτίθημι   {4729, cv-6a}
    [προθήσω, προέθηκα, -, -, προετέθην] *to place before; to set forth, propose publicly*, Rom 3:25; mid. προτίθεμαι, *to purpose, determine, design beforehand*, Rom 1:13; Eph 1:9*

προτρέπω   {4730, cv-1b(1)}
    [-, προέτρεψα, -, -, -] *to turn forwards; to impel; to excite, urge, exhort*, Acts 18:27*

προτρεψάμενοι   aor mid ptcp nom pl masc
    [Ac 18:27; cv-1b(1); 4730]   προτρέπω

προτρέχω   {4731, cv-1b(2)}
    [-, προέδραμον, -, -, -] *to run before*, or *in advance*, Luke 19:4; John 20:4; Acts 10:25 v.l.*

προϋπάρχω   {4732, cv-1b(2)}
    [(προϋπῆρχον), -, -, -, -, -] *to be before*, or *formerly*, Luke 23:12; Acts 8:9*

προϋπῆρχεν   imperf act ind 3 sg
    [Ac 8:9; cv-1b(2); 4732]   προϋπάρχω
προϋπῆρχον   imperf act ind 3 pl
    [Lk 23:12; cv-1b(2); 4732]   "

προφάσει   dat sg fem [5t; n-3e(5b); 4733]   πρόφασις
πρόφασιν   acc sg fem [Jn 15:22; n-3e(5b); 4733]   "

πρόφασις, εως, ἡ   {4733, n-3e(5b)}
    pr. *that which appears in front, that which is put forward to hide the true state of things; a fair show* or *pretext*, Acts 27:30; *a specious cloak*, Matt 23:13; 1 Thess 2:5; *an excuse*, John 15:22; Matt 23:14 v.l.

προφέρει   pres act ind 3 sg
    [2t; cv-1c(1); 4734]   προφέρω

προφέρω   {4734, cv-1c(1)}
    [-, -, -, -, -] *to bring before, present; to bring forth* or *out, produce*, Luke 6:45 (2t)*

προφῆται   nom pl masc [20t; n-1f; 4737]   προφήτης
προφῆται   voc pl masc [Rv 18:20; n-1f; 4737]   "
προφήταις   dat pl masc [10t; n-1f; 4737]   "
προφήτας   acc pl masc [15t; n-1f; 4737]   "

προφητεία, ας, ἡ   {4735, n-1a}
    prophecy, a prediction of future events, Matt 13:14; 2 Peter 1:20, 21; *prophecy, a gifted faculty of setting forth and enforcing revealed truth*, 1 Cor 12:10; 13:2; *prophecy, matter of divine teaching set forth by special gift*, 1 Tim 1:18

προφητεία   nom sg fem [5t; n-1a; 4735]   προφητεία
προφητείᾳ   dat sg fem [1C 14:6; n-1a; 4735]   "
προφητεῖαι   nom pl fem [1C 13:8; n-1a; 4735]   "
προφητείαν   acc sg fem [2t; n-1a; 4735]   "
προφητείας   gen sg fem [8t; n-1a; 4735]   "
προφητείας   acc pl fem [2t; n-1a; 4735]   "
προφητεύειν   pres act inf
    [2t; v-1a(6); 4736]   προφητεύω
προφητεύητε   pres act subj 2 pl
    [2t; v-1a(6); 4736]   "
προφητεύομεν   pres act ind 1 pl
    [1C 13:9; v-1a(6); 4736]   "
προφητεύουσα   pres act ptcp nom sg fem
    [1C 11:5; v-1a(6); 4736]   "
προφητεύουσαι   pres act ptcp nom pl fem
    [Ac 21:9; v-1a(6); 4736]   "
προφητεῦσαι   aor act inf
    [Rv 10:11; v-1a(6); 4736]   "
προφητεύσαντες   aor act ptcp nom pl masc
    [1P 1:10; v-1a(6); 4736]   "
προφήτευσον   aor act imperative 2 sg
    [3t; v-1a(6); 4736]   "
προφητεύσουσιν   fut act ind 3 pl
    [3t; v-1a(6); 4736]   "

προφητεύω   {4736, v-1a(6)}
    [(ἐπροφήτευον), προφητεύσω, ἐπροφήτευσα, -, -, -] *to exercise the function of a* προφήτης; *to prophesy, to foretell the future*, Matt 11:13; *to divine*, Matt 26:68; Mark 14:65; Luke 22:64; *to prophesy, to set forth matter of divine teaching by special faculty*, 1 Cor 13:9; 14:1

προφητεύων   pres act ptcp nom sg masc
    [4t; v-1a(6); 4736]   "
προφητεύωσιν   pres act subj 3 pl
    [1C 14:24; v-1a(6); 4736]   "
προφήτῃ   dat sg masc
    [Mk 1:2; n-1f; 4737]   προφήτης

προφήτην   acc sg masc [12t; n-1f; 4737]   "

προφήτης, ου, ὁ   {4737, n-1f}
pr. *a spokesman for* another; spc. *a spokesman* or *interpreter* for a deity; *a prophet, seer,* Titus 1:12; in N.T. *a prophet, a divinely commissioned and inspired person,* Matt 14:5; Luke 7:16, 39; John 9:17; *a prophet* in the Christian church, *a person gifted for the exposition of divine truth,* 1 Cor 12:28, 29; *a prophet, a foreteller of the future,* Matt 1:22, et al. freq.; οἱ προφῆται, *the prophetic scriptures of the Old Testament,* Luke 16:29

προφήτης   nom sg masc [27t; n-1f; 4737]   "
προφητικόν   acc sg masc
   [2P 1:19; a-1a(2a); 4738]   προφητικός

προφητικός, ή, όν   {4738, a-1a(2a)}
prophetic, uttered by prophets, Rom 16:26; 2 Peter 1:19*

προφητικῶν   gen pl fem [Rm 16:26; a-1a(2a); 4738] "
προφῆτιν   acc sg fem
   [Rv 2:20; n-3c(2); 4739]   προφῆτις

προφῆτις, ιδος, ἡ   {4739, n-3c(2)}
a prophetess, a divinely gifted female teacher, Luke 2:36; Rev 2:20*

προφῆτις   nom sg fem [Lk 2:36; n-3c(2); 4739]   "
προφήτου   gen sg masc [26t; n-1f; 4737]   προφήτης
προφητῶν   gen pl masc [32t; n-1f; 4737]   "

προφθάνω   {4740, cv-3a(1)}
[-, προέφθασα, -, -, -] *to outstrip, anticipate; to anticipate* any one in doing or saying a thing, *be beforehand with,* Matt 17:25*

προχειρίζω   {4741, cv-2a(1)}
[-, προεχειρισάμην, -, προκεχείρισμαι, -] also listed as a deponent, προχειρίζομαι, *to take into the hand, to make ready for use* or *action; to constitute, destine,* Acts 3:20; 22:14; 26:16*

προχειρίσασθαι   aor mid inf
   [Ac 26:16; cv-2a(1); 4741]   προχειρίζω

προχειροτονέω   {4742, cv-1d(2a)}
[-, -, -, προκεχειροτόνημαι, -] pr. *to elect before* Acts 10:41*

Πρόχορον   acc sg masc
   [Ac 6:5; n-2a; 4743]   Πρόχορος

Πρόχορος, ου, ὁ   {4743, n-2a}
Prochorus, pr. name, Acts 6:5*

προώρισεν   aor act ind 3 sg
   [4t; cv-2a(1); 4633]   προορίζω

πρύμνα, ης, ἡ   {4744, n-1c}
the hinder part of a vessel, stern, Mark 4:38; Acts 27:29, 41*

πρύμνα   nom sg fem [Ac 27:41; n-1c; 4744]   πρύμνα
πρύμνη   dat sg fem [Mk 4:38; n-1c; 4744]   "
πρύμνης   gen sg fem [Ac 27:29; n-1c; 4744]   "

πρωΐ   {4745, adverb}
in the morning, early, Matt 16:3; 20:1; Mark 15:1; Acts 28:23; *the morning watch,* which ushers in the dawn, Mark 13:35

πρωΐ   adverb [12t; adverb; 4745]   πρωΐ

πρωΐα, ας, ἡ   {4746, n-1a}
morning, the morning hour, Matt 21:18 v.l.; 27:1; John 21:4; 18:28 v.l.*

πρωΐας   gen sg fem [2t; n-1a; 4746]   πρωΐα

πρώϊμος, ον   {4747, a-3a}
see πρόϊμος, *early,* James 5:7 v.l.

πρωϊνόν   acc sg masc
   [Rv 2:28; a-1a(2a); 4748]   πρωϊνός

πρωϊνός, ή, όν   {4748, a-1a(2a)}
belonging to the morning, morning, Rev 2:28; 22:16*

πρωϊνός   nom sg masc [Rv 22:16; a-1a(2a); 4748] "

πρῷρα, ης, ἡ   {4749, n-1c}
the forepart of a vessel, prow, Acts 27:30, 41*

πρῷρα   nom sg fem [Ac 27:41; n-1c; 4749]   πρῷρα
πρῴρης   gen sg fem [Ac 27:30; n-1c; 4749]   "
πρῶτα   nom pl neut
   [Rv 21:4; a-1a(2a); 4755]   πρῶτος
πρῶτα   acc pl neut [Rv 2:5; a-1a(2a); 4755]   "

πρωτεύω   {4750, cv-1a(6)}
[-, -, -, -, -] *to be first, to hold the first rank* or *highest dignity, have the pre-eminence, be chief,* Col 1:18*

πρωτεύων   pres act ptcp nom sg masc
   [Cl 1:18; cv-1a(6); 4750]   πρωτεύω
πρώτη   nom sg fem [12t; a-1a(2a); 4755]   πρῶτος
πρώτῃ   dat sg fem [6t; a-1a(2a); 4755]   "
πρώτην   acc sg fem [6t; a-1a(2a); 4755]   "
πρώτης   gen sg fem [5t; a-1a(2a); 4755]   "
πρῶτοι   nom pl masc [11t; a-1a(2a); 4755]   "
πρώτοις   dat pl masc [Mk 6:21; a-1a(2a); 4755] "
πρώτοις   dat pl neut [1C 15:3; a-1a(2a); 4755] "

πρωτοκαθεδρία, ας, ἡ   {4751, n-1a}
the first or *uppermost seat, the most honorable seat,* Matt 23:6; Mark 12:39; Luke 11:43; 20:46*

πρωτοκαθεδρίαν   acc sg fem
   [Lk 11:43; n-1a; 4751]   πρωτοκαθεδρία
πρωτοκαθεδρίας   acc pl fem [3t; n-1a; 4751]   "

πρωτοκλισία, ας, ἡ   {4752, n-1a}
the first place of reclining at table, *the most honorable place at table,* Matt 23:6; Mark 12:39; Luke 14:7, 8; 20:46

πρωτοκλισίαν   acc sg fem
   [2t; n-1a; 4752]   πρωτοκλισία
πρωτοκλισίας   acc pl fem [3t; n-1a; 4752]   "

πρωτόμαρτυς, υρος, ὁ   {n-3f(2a)}
first martyr, Acts 22:20 v.l.*

πρῶτον   {4754, adverb}
an acc sg neut form of πρῶτος that became solidified in function as an adverb, *first* in time, *in the first place,* Mark 4:28; 16:9; τὸ πρῶτον, *at the first, formerly,* John 12:16; 19:39; *first* in dignity, importance, etc., *before all things,* Matt 6:33

πρῶτον   nom sg neut
   [Rv 4:7; a-1a(2a); 4755]   πρῶτος
πρῶτον   acc sg masc [2t; a-1a(2a); 4755]   "
πρῶτον   acc sg neut [7t; a-1a(2a); 4755]   "

πρῶτον   adverb [55t; adverb; 4754]   πρῶτον

πρῶτος, η, ον   {4755, a-1a(2a)}
first in time, order, etc., Matt 10:2; 26:17; *first* in
dignity, importance, etc., *chief, principal, most
important*, Mark 6:21; Luke 19:47; Acts 13:50;
16:12; as an equivalent to the compar. πρότερος,
prior, John 1:5, 30; 15:18; Matt 27:64;
adverbially, *first*, John 1:42; 5:4; 8:7

πρῶτος   nom sg masc [30t; a-1a(2a); 4755]   πρῶτος
πρωτοστάτην   acc sg masc
   [Ac 24:5; n-1f; 4756]   πρωτοστάτης

πρωτοστάτης, ου, ὁ   {4756, n-1f}
pr. *one stationed in the first rank* of an army; *a
leader; a chief, ringleader*, Acts 24:5*

πρωτότοκα   acc pl neut
   [Hb 11:28; a-3a; 4758]   πρωτότοκος

πρωτοτόκια, ων, τά   {4757, n-2c}
the rights of primogeniture, birthright, Heb 12:16

πρωτοτόκια   acc pl neut
   [Hb 12:16; n-2c; 4757]   πρωτοτόκια
πρωτότοκον   acc sg masc
   [3t; a-3a; 4758]   πρωτότοκος

πρωτότοκος, ον   {4758, a-3a}
first-born, Matt 1:25 v.l.; Luke 2:7; Heb 11:28; in
N.T. *prior in generation*, Col 1:15; Heb 2:8 v.l.; *a
first-born* head of a spiritual family, Rom 8:29;
Heb 1:6; *first-born*, as possessed of the peculiar
privilege of spiritual generation, Heb 12:23

πρωτότοκος   nom sg masc [3t; a-3a; 4758]   "
πρωτοτόκων   gen pl masc [Hb 12:23; a-3a; 4758]   "
πρώτου   gen sg masc
   [Jn 19:32; a-1a(2a); 4755]   πρῶτος
πρώτου   gen sg neut [Rv 13:12; a-1a(2a); 4755]   "
πρώτους   acc pl masc [3t; a-1a(2a); 4755]   "
πρώτῳ   dat sg masc [3t; a-1a(2a); 4755]   "
πρώτῳ   dat sg neut [Mt 21:28; a-1a(2a); 4755]   "
πρώτων   gen pl masc [2t; a-1a(2a); 4755]   "
πρώτων   gen pl fem [Ac 17:4; a-1a(2a); 4755]   "
πρώτων   gen pl neut [4t; a-1a(2a); 4755]   "

πρώτως   {4759, adverb}
for the first time, Acts 11:26*

πρώτως   adverb [Ac 11:26; adverb; 4759]   πρώτως
πταίει   pres act ind 3 sg
   [Jm 3:2; v-1a(2); 4760]   πταίω
πταίομεν   pres act ind 1 pl
   [Jm 3:2; v-1a(2); 4760]   "
πταίσῃ   aor act subj 3 sg
   [Jm 2:10; v-1a(2); 4760]   "
πταίσητε   aor act subj 2 pl
   [2P 1:10; v-1a(2); 4760]   "

πταίω   {4760, v-1a(2)}
[-, ἔπταισα, -, -, -] *to cause to stumble*; intrans. *to
stumble, stagger, fall; to make a false step*; met. *to
err, transgress*, Rom 11:11; James 2:10; 3:2 (2t);
met. *to fail* of an object, 2 Peter 1:10*

πτέρνα, ης, ἡ   {4761, n-1c}
the heel, John 13:18*

πτέρναν   acc sg fem [Jn 13:18; n-1c; 4761]   πτέρνα

πτέρυγας   acc pl fem [3t; n-3b(2); 4763]   πτέρυξ
πτέρυγες   nom pl fem [Rv 12:14; n-3b(2); 4763]   "

πτερύγιον, ου, τό   {4762, n-2c}
a little wing; the extremity, the extreme point of a
thing; *a pinnacle*, or *apex* of a building, Matt 4:5;
Luke 4:9*

πτερύγιον   acc sg neut [2t; n-2c; 4762]   πτερύγιον
πτερύγων   gen pl fem
   [Rv 9:9; n-3b(2); 4763]   πτέρυξ

πτέρυξ, υγος, ἡ   {4763, n-3b(2)}
a wing, pinion, Matt 23:37; Luke 13:34

πτηνός, (ή), όν   {4764, a-3b(2)}
as adj., *winged, with feathers*; as noun, *a bird,
fowl*, 1 Cor 15:39*

πτηνῶν   gen pl neut
   [1C 15:39; a-3b(2); 4764]   πτηνός

πτοέω   {4765, v-1d(2a)}
[-, -, -, -, ἐπτοήθην] *to terrify, affright*; pass. *to be
terrified*, Luke 12:4 v.l.; 21:9; 24:37*

πτοηθέντες   aor pass ptcp nom pl masc
   [Lk 24:37; v-1d(2a); 4765]   πτοέω
πτοηθῆτε   aor pass subj 2 pl
   [Lk 21:9; v-1d(2a); 4765]   "
πτόησιν   acc sg fem
   [1P 3:6; n-3e(5b); 4766]   πτόησις

πτόησις, εως, ἡ   {4766, n-3e(5b)}
consternation, dismay, 1 Peter 3:6*

Πτολεμαΐδα   acc sg fem
   [Ac 21:7; n-3c(2); 4767]   Πτολεμαΐς

Πτολεμαΐς, ΐδος, ἡ   {4767, n-3c(2)}
Ptolemais, a city on the sea-coast of Galilee: the
modern *Acre*, Acts 21:7*

πτύξας   aor act ptcp nom sg masc
   [Lk 4:20; v-2b; 4771]   πτύσσω

πτύον, ου, τό   {4768, n-2c}
a fan, winnowing-shovel, Matt 3:12; Luke 3:17*

πτύον   nom sg neut [2t; n-2c; 4768]   πτύον
πτυρόμενοι   pres pass ptcp nom pl masc
   [Pp 1:28; v-1c(1); 4769]   πτύρω

πτύρω   {4769, v-1c(1)}
[-, -, -, -, -] *to scare, terrify*; pass. *to be terrified, be
in consternation*, Phil 1:28*

πτύσας   aor act ptcp nom sg masc
   [2t; v-1a(4); 4772]   πτύω

πτύσμα, ατος, τό   {4770, n-3c(4)}
spittle, saliva, John 9:6*

πτύσματος   gen sg neut
   [Jn 9:6; n-3c(4); 4770]   πτύσμα

πτύσσω   {4771, v-2b}
[-, ἔπτυξα, -, -, -] *to fold; to roll up* a scroll, Luke
4:20*

πτύω   {4772, v-1a(4)}
[πτύσω, ἔπτυσα, -, -, ἔπτυσθην] *to spit, spit out*,
Mark 7:33; 8:23; John 9:6

πτῶμα, ατος, τό   {4773, n-3c(4)}
a fall; a dead body, carcass, corpse, Matt 24:28; Mark 6:29

πτῶμα   nom sg neut [2t; n-3c(4); 4773]   πτῶμα
πτῶμα   acc sg neut [4t; n-3c(4); 4773]   "
πτῶματα   acc pl neut [Rv 11:9; n-3c(4); 4773]   "
πτῶσιν   acc sg fem
      [Lk 2:34; n-3e(5b); 4774]   πτῶσις

πτῶσις, εως, ἡ   {4774, n-3e(5b)}
a fall, crash, ruin, Matt 7:27; met. *downfall, ruin,* Luke 2:34*

πτῶσις   nom sg fem [Mt 7:27; n-3e(5b); 4774]   "
πτωχά   acc pl neut [Ga 4:9; a-1a(2a); 4777]   πτωχός

πτωχεία, ας, ἡ   {4775, n-1a}
begging; beggary; poverty, 2 Cor 8:2, 9; Rev 2:9*

πτωχεία   nom sg fem [2C 8:2; n-1a; 4775]   πτωχεία
πτωχείᾳ   dat sg fem [2C 8:9; n-1a; 4775]   "
πτωχείαν   acc sg fem [Rv 2:9; n-1a; 4775]   "

πτωχεύω   {4776, v-1a(6)}
[-, ἐπτώχευσα, -, -, -] *to be a beggar; to be* or *become poor, be in poverty,* 2 Cor 8:9*

πτωχή   nom sg fem [3t; a-1a(2a); 4777]   πτωχός
πτωχοί   nom pl masc [4t; a-1a(2a); 4777]   "
πτωχοί   voc pl masc [Lk 6:20; a-1a(2a); 4777]   "
πτωχοῖς   dat pl masc [9t; a-1a(2a); 4777]   "
πτωχόν   acc sg masc [2t; a-1a(2a); 4777]   "

πτωχός, ή, όν   {4777, a-1a(2a)}
reduced to beggary, mendicant; poor, indigent, Matt 19:21; 26:9, 11; met. spiritually *poor,* Rev 3:17; by impl. *a person of low condition,* Matt 11:4; Luke 4:18; 7:22; met. *beggarly, sorry,* Gal 4:9; 1 Cor 15:10 v.l.; met. *lowly,* Matt 5:3; Luke 6:20

πτωχός   nom sg masc [3t; a-1a(2a); 4777]   "
πτωχούς   acc pl masc [8t; a-1a(2a); 4777]   "
πτωχῷ   dat sg masc [Jm 2:3; a-1a(2a); 4777]   "
πτωχῶν   gen pl masc [2t; a-1a(2a); 4777]   "

πυγμή, ῆς, ἡ   {4778, n-1b}
together with the fore-arm, or, *with care, carefully,* Mark 7:3*

πυγμῇ   dat sg fem [Mk 7:3; n-1b; 4778]   πυγμή
πυθέσθαι   aor mid inf
      [Jn 13:24; v-3a(2b); 4785]   πυνθάνομαι
πυθόμενος   aor mid ptcp nom sg masc
      [Ac 23:34; v-3a(2b); 4785]

Πύθων, ωνος, ὁ   {4780, n-3f(1a)}
Python, the name of the mythological serpent slain by Apollo, thence named the Pythian; later, equivalent to ἐγγαστρίμαντις, *a soothsaying ventriloquist;* πνεῦμα πύθωνος, i.q. δαιμόνιον μαντικόν, *a soothsaying demon,* Acts 16:16*

πύθωνα   acc sg masc
      [Ac 16:16; n-3f(1a); 4780]   πύθων
πυκνά   acc pl neut, can function
      adverbially [Lk 5:33; a-1a(2a); 4781]   πυκνός
πυκνάς   acc pl fem [1Ti 5:23; a-1a(2a); 4781]   "

πυκνός, ή, όν   {4781, a-1a(2a)}
dense, thick; frequent, 1 Tim 5:23; πυκνά, as an adverb, *frequently, often,* Mark 7:3 v.l.; Luke 5:33; so the compar. πυκνότερον, *very frequently,* Acts 24:26*

πυκνότερον   acc sg neut, can function as a comparative adverb
      [Ac 24:26; a-1a(2a); 4781]   "

πυκτεύω   {4782, v-1a(6)}
[-, -, -, -, -] *to box, fight as a boxer,* 1 Cor 9:26*

πυκτεύω   pres act ind 1 sg
      [1C 9:26; v-1a(6); 4782]   πυκτεύω
πύλαι   nom pl fem [Mt 16:18; n-1b; 4783]   πύλη
πύλας   acc pl fem [Ac 9:24; n-1b; 4783]

πύλη, ης, ἡ   {4783, n-1b}
a gate, Matt 7:13, 14; Luke 7:12; 13:24 v.l.; Acts 12:10; πύλαι ᾅδου, *the gates of hades, the nether world and its powers, the powers of destruction, dissolution,* Matt 16:18

πύλη   nom sg fem [2t; n-1b; 4783]   "
πύλῃ   dat sg fem [2t; n-1b; 4783]   "
πύλην   acc sg fem [Ac 12:10; n-1b; 4783]   "
πύλης   gen sg fem [3t; n-1b; 4783]   "

πυλών, ῶνος, ὁ   {4784, n-3f(1a)}
a gateway, vestibule, Matt 26:71; Luke 16:20; *a gate,* Acts 14:13; Rev 21:12, 13, 15, 21, 25

πυλῶνα   acc sg masc [4t; n-3f(1a); 4784]   πυλών
πυλῶνας   acc pl masc [3t; n-3f(1a); 4784]   "
πυλῶνες   nom pl masc [6t; n-3f(1a); 4784]   "
πυλῶνος   gen sg masc [2t; n-3f(1a); 4784]   "
πυλώνων   gen pl masc [Rv 21:21; n-3f(1a); 4784]   "
πυλῶσιν   dat pl masc [2t; n-3f(1a); 4784]   "
πυνθάνεσθαι   pres mid inf
      [Ac 23:20; v-3a(2b); 4785]   πυνθάνομαι

πυνθάνομαι   {4785, v-3a(2b)}
[(ἐπυνθανόμην), -, ἐπυθόμην, -, -, -] *to ask, inquire,* Matt 2:4; Luke 15:26; *to investigate, examine judicially,* Acts 23:20; *to ascertain by inquiry, understand,* Acts 23:34

πυνθάνομαι   pres mid ind 1 sg
      [Ac 10:29; v-3a(2b); 4785]   "

πῦρ, ρός, τό   {4786, n-3f(2a)}
fire, Matt 3:10; 7:19; 13:40, et al. freq.; πυρός, used by Hebraism with the force of an adjective, *fiery, fierce,* Heb 10:27; *fire* used figuratively to express various circumstances of severe trial, Luke 12:49; 1 Cor 3:13; Jude 23

πῦρ   nom sg neut [10t; n-3f(2a); 4786]   πῦρ
πῦρ   acc sg neut [16t; n-3f(2a); 4786]   "

πυρά, ᾶς, ἡ   {4787, n-1a}
a fire, heap of combustibles, Acts 28:2, 3; Luke 22:55 v.l.*

πυράν   acc sg fem [2t; n-1a; 4787]   πυρά
πύργον   acc sg masc [3t; n-2a; 4788]   πύργος

πύργος, ου, ὁ   {4788, n-2a}
a tower, Matt 21:33; Mark 12:1; Luke 13:4; genr. *a castle, palace,* Luke 14:28*

πύργος   nom sg masc [Lk 13:4; n-2a; 4788]   "

πυρέσσουσα   pres act ptcp nom sg fem
    [Mk 1:30; v-2b; 4789]   πυρέσσω

πυρέσσουσαν   pres act ptcp acc sg fem
    [Mt 8:14; v-2b; 4789]   "

πυρέσσω   {4789, v-2b}
    [-, -, -, -, -] *to be feverish, be sick of a fever,* Matt
    8:14; Mark 1:30*

πυρετοῖς   dat pl masc
    [Ac 28:8; n-2a; 4790]   πυρετός

πυρετός, οῦ, ὁ   {4790, n-2a}
    scorching and noxious heat; a fever, Matt 8:15;
    Mark 1:31

πυρετός   nom sg masc [3t; n-2a; 4790]   "
πυρετῷ   dat sg masc [2t; n-2a; 4790]   "
πυρί   dat sg neut [17t; n-3f(2a); 4786]   πῦρ

πύρινος, η, ον   {4791, a-1a(2a)}
    pr. *of fire, fiery, burning; shining, glittering,* Rev
    9:17*

πυρίνους   acc pl masc
    [Rv 9:17; a-1a(2a); 4791]   πύρινος
πυρός   gen sg neut [28t; n-3f(2a); 4786]   πῦρ
πυροῦμαι   pres pass ind 1 sg
    [2C 11:29; v-1d(3); 4792]   πυρόω
πυρούμενοι   pres pass ptcp nom pl masc
    [2P 3:12; v-1d(3); 4792]   "
πυροῦσθαι   pres pass inf [1C 7:9; v-1d(3); 4792]   "

πυρόω   {4792, v-1d(3)}
    [-, -, -, πεπύρωμαι, ἐπυρώθην] *to set on fire, burn;*
    pass. *to be kindled, be on fire, burn, flame,* Eph
    6:16; 2 Peter 3:12; Rev 1:15; met. *to fire* with
    distressful feelings, 2 Cor 11:29; of lust, *to be
    inflamed, burn,* 1 Cor 7:9; *to be tried with fire,* as
    metals, Rev 3:18*

πυρράζει   pres act ind 3 sg
    [2t; v-2a(1); 4793]   πυρράζω

πυρράζω   {4793, v-2a(1)}
    [-, -, -, -, -] *to be fiery-red,* Matt 16:2, 3*

πυρρός, ά, όν   {4794, a-1a(1)}
    of the color of fire, fiery-red, Rev 6:4; 12:3*

πυρρός   nom sg masc [2t; a-1a(1); 4794]   πυρρός

Πύρρος, ου, ὁ   {4795, n-2a}
    Pyrrhus, pr. name, Acts 20:4*

Πύρρου   gen sg masc [Ac 20:4; n-2a; 4795]   Πύρρος
πυρώσει   dat sg fem
    [1P 4:12; n-3e(5b); 4796]   πύρωσις
πυρώσεως   gen sg fem [2t; n-3e(5b); 4796]   "

πύρωσις, εως, ἡ   {4796, n-3e(5b)}
    a burning, conflagration, Rev 18:9, 18; met. *a fiery
    test* of trying circumstances, 1 Peter 4:12*

πωλεῖ   pres act ind 3 sg
    [Mt 13:44; v-1d(2a); 4797]   πωλέω
πωλεῖται   pres pass ind 3 sg
    [Mt 10:29; v-1d(2a); 4797]   "

πωλέω   {4797, v-1d(2a)}
    [(ἐπώλουν), -, ἐπώλησα, -, -, -] *to sell,* Matt 10:29;
    13:44

πωλῆσαι   aor act inf [Rv 13:17; v-1d(2a); 4797]   "

πωλήσας   aor act ptcp nom sg masc
    [Ac 4:37; v-1d(2a); 4797]   "

πωλήσατε   aor act imperative 2 pl
    [Lk 12:33; v-1d(2a); 4797]   "

πωλησάτω   aor act imperative 3 sg
    [Lk 22:36; v-1d(2a); 4797]   "

πώλησον   aor act imperative 2 sg
    [3t; v-1d(2a); 4797]   "

πῶλον   acc sg masc [12t; n-2a; 4798]   πῶλος

πῶλος, ου, ὁ   {4798, n-2a}
    a youngling; a foal or *colt,* Matt 21:2, 5, 7; Mark
    11:2

πωλούμενον   pres pass ptcp acc sg neut
    [1C 10:25; v-1d(2a); 4797]   πωλέω

πωλοῦνται   pres pass ind 3 pl
    [Lk 12:6; v-1d(2a); 4797]   "

πωλοῦντας   pres act ptcp acc pl masc
    [5t; v-1d(2a); 4797]   "

πωλοῦντες   pres act ptcp nom pl masc
    [Ac 4:34; v-1d(2a); 4797]   "

πωλούντων   pres act ptcp gen pl masc
    [2t; v-1d(2a); 4797]   "

πωλοῦσιν   pres act ptcp dat pl masc
    [Jn 2:16; v-1d(2a); 4797]   "

πώποτε   {4799, adverb}
    ever yet, ever, at any time, Luke 19:30; John 1:18

πώποτε   adverb [6t; adverb; 4799]   πώποτε

πωρόω   {4800, v-1d(3)}
    [-, ἐπώρωσα, πεπώρωκα, πεπώρωμαι, ἐπωρώθην]
    to petrify; to harden; in N.T. *to harden* the
    feelings, John 12:40; pass. *to become callous,
    unimpressible,* Mark 6:52; 8:17; Rom 11:7; 2 Cor
    3:14*

πωρώσει   dat sg fem
    [Mk 3:5; n-3e(5b); 4801]   πώρωσις
πώρωσιν   acc sg fem [Ep 4:18; n-3e(5b); 4801]   "

πώρωσις, εως, ἡ   {4801, n-3e(5b)}
    a hardening; met. *hardness* of heart, *callousness,
    insensibility,* Mark 3:5; Rom 11:25; Eph 4:18*

πώρωσις   nom sg fem [Rm 11:25; n-3e(5b); 4801]   "

πῶς   {4802, particle}
    interrogative particle, *How? In what manner? By
    what means?* Matt 7:4; 22:12; John 6:52; used in
    interrogations which imply a negative, Matt
    12:26, 29, 34; 22:45; 23:33; Acts 8:31; put
    concisely for *How is it that? How does it come to
    pass that?* Matt 16:11; 22:43; Mark 4:40; John
    7:15; with an indirect interrogation, *how, in
    what manner,* Matt 6:28; 10:19; Mark 11:18; put
    for τί, *What?* Luke 10:26; put for ὡς, as a particle
    of exclamation, *how, how much, how greatly,*
    Mark 10:23, 24

πῶς   part [102t; particle; 4802]   πῶς

πώς   {4803, particle}
    enclitic particle, *in any way, by any means,* Acts
    27:12; Rom 1:10

πώς   part [14t; particle; 4803]   πώς

ρ

Ῥαάβ, ἡ   {4805, n-3g(2)}
Rahab, pr. name, indecl (Josh 2; 6:17, 25) Heb
11:31; James 2:25*

Ῥαάβ   indecl [2t; n-3g(2); 4805]   Ῥαάβ

ῥαββί   {4806, n-3g(2)}
also spelled ῥαββεί, *rabbi, my master, teacher,*
Matt 23:7, 8; 26:25, 49

ῥαββί   indecl [15t; n-3g(2); 4806]   ῥαββί

ῥαββονί   {4807, n-3g(2)}
also spelled ῥαββουνεί, ῥαββονί, ῥαββονεί,
rabboni, my master, the highest title of honor in
the Jewish schools, Mark 10:51; John 20:16

ῥαββουνί, see ῥαββονί   {4808, n-3g(2)}

ῥαββουνί   indecl [2t; n-3g(2); 4808]   ῥαββουνί
ῥαβδίζειν   pres act inf
    [Ac 16:22; v-2a(1); 4810]   ῥαβδίζω

ῥαβδίζω   {4810, v-2a(1)}
[-, -, -, -, ἐραβδίσθην] *to beat with rods,* Acts 16:22;
2 Cor 11:25*

ῥάβδον   acc sg fem [3t; n-2b; 4811]   ῥάβδος

ῥάβδος, ου, ἡ   {4811, n-2b}
a rod, wand, Heb 9:4; Rev 11:1; *a rod* of
correction, 1 Cor 4:21; *a staff,* Matt 10:10; Heb
11:21; *a scepter,* Heb 1:8; Rev 2:27

ῥάβδος   nom sg fem [3t; n-2b; 4811]   "
ῥάβδου   gen sg fem [Hb 11:21; n-2b; 4811]   "
ῥαβδοῦχοι   nom pl masc
    [Ac 16:38; n-2a; 4812]   ῥαβδοῦχος

ῥαβδοῦχος, ου, ὁ   {4812, n-2a}
the bearer of a wand of office; *a lictor, sergeant,* a
public servant who bore a bundle or rods
before the magistrates as insignia of their
office, and carried into execution the sentences
they pronounced, Acts 16:35, 38*

ῥαβδούχους   acc pl masc [Ac 16:35; n-2a; 4812]   "
ῥάβδῳ   dat sg fem [5t; n-2b; 4811]   ῥάβδος

Ῥαγαύ, ὁ   {4814, n-3g(2)}
Ragau, pr. name, indecl. Luke 3:35*

Ῥαγαύ   indecl [Lk 3:35; n-3g(2); 4814]   Ῥαγαύ

ῥᾳδιούργημα, ατος, τό   {4815, n-3c(4)}
pr. *anything done lightly, levity; reckless conduct,
crime,* Acts 18:14*

ῥᾳδιούργημα   nom sg neut
    [Ac 18:14; n-3c(4); 4815]   ῥᾳδιούργημα

ῥᾳδιουργία, ας, ἡ   {4816, n-1a}
facility of doing anything; *levity in doing;
recklessness, wickedness,* Acts 13:10*

ῥᾳδιουργίας   gen sg fem
    [Ac 13:10; n-1a; 4816]   ῥᾳδιουργία

ῥαίνω   {4817, v-2d(4)}
[-, ἔρρανα, -, -, -] *sprinkle,* Rev 19:13 v.l.*

Ῥαιφάν   {4818, n-3g(2)}
v.l.s include Ῥομφά, Ῥεμφάν, and Ῥεφά, pr.
name., *Rephan,* Acts 7:43*

Ῥαιφάν   gen sg masc
    [Ac 7:43; n-3g(2); 4818]   Ῥαιφάν

ῥακά   {4819, n-3g(2)}
raca, an Aramaic term of bitter contempt,
worthless fellow, fool, Matt 5:22*

ῥακά   indecl [Mt 5:22; n-3g(2); 4819]   ῥακά

ῥάκος, ους, τό   {4820, n-3d(2b)}
a piece torn off; a bit of cloth, cloth, Matt 9:16;
Mark 2:21*

ῥάκους   gen sg neut [2t; n-3d(2b); 4820]   ῥάκος

Ῥαμά, ἡ   {4821, n-3g(2)}
Rama, a city of Judea

Ῥαμά   indecl [Mt 2:18; n-3g(2); 4821]   Ῥαμά
ῥαντίζουσα   pres act ptcp nom sg fem
    [Hb 9:13; v-2a(1); 4822]   ῥαντίζω

ῥαντίζω   {4822, v-2a(1)}
[ῥαντιῶ, ἐράντισα, -, ῥεράντισμαι, -] *to sprinkle,*
Heb 9:13, 19, 21; Rev 19:13 v.l.; met. and by
impl. *to cleanse by sprinkling, purify, free from
pollution,* Heb 10:22; Mark 7:4 v.l.*

ῥαντισμόν   acc sg masc
    [1P 1:2; n-2a; 4823]   ῥαντισμός

ῥαντισμός, οῦ, ὁ   {4823, n-2a}
pr. *a sprinkling;* met. *a cleansing, purification,*
Heb 12:24; 1 Peter 1:2*

ῥαντισμοῦ   gen sg masc [Hb 12:24; n-2a; 4823]   "
ῥαπίζει   pres act ind 3 sg
    [Mt 5:39; v-2a(1); 4824]   ῥαπίζω

ῥαπίζω   {4824, v-2a(1)}
[ῥαπίσω, ἐράπισα, -, -, -] *to beat with rods; to strike
with the palm of the hand, cuff, clap,* Matt 5:39;
26:67*

ῥάπισμα, ατος, τό   {4825, n-3c(4)}
a blow with the palm of the hand, cuff, slap, Mark
14:65; John 18:22; 19:3*

ῥάπισμα   acc sg neut
    [Jn 18:22; n-3c(4); 4825]   ῥάπισμα
ῥαπίσμασιν   dat pl neut
    [Mk 14:65; n-3c(4); 4825]   "
ῥαπίσματα   acc pl neut [Jn 19:3; n-3c(4); 4825]   "
ῥαφίδος   gen sg fem [2t; n-3c(2); 4827]   ῥαφίς

ῥαφίς, ίδος, ἡ   {4827, n-3c(2)}
a needle, Matt 19:24; Mark 10:25; Luke 18:25 v.l.*

Ῥαχάβ, ἡ   {4829, n-3g(2)}
Rachab, pr. name, indecl., Matt 1:5*

Ῥαχάβ   indecl [Mt 1:5; n-3g(2); 4829]   Ῥαχάβ

Ῥαχήλ, ἡ   {4830, n-3g(2)}
Rachel, pr. name, indecl., Matt 2:18*

Ῥαχήλ   indecl [Mt 2:18; n-3g(2); 4830]   Ῥαχήλ

Ῥεβέκκα, ας, ἡ   {4831, n-1a}
Rebecca, pr. name, Rom 9:10*

Ῥεβέκκα   nom sg fem
    [Rm 9:10; n-1a; 4831]   Ῥεβέκκα

ῥέδη, ης, ἡ   {4832, n-1b}
    a carriage with four wheels for travelling, *a chariot*, Rev 18:13*

ῥεδῶν   gen pl fem [Rv 18:13; n-1b; 4832]   ῥέδη

Ῥεμφάν, see Ῥομφα   {4833, n-3g(2)}

ῥεραντισμένοι   perf pass ptcp nom pl masc
    [Hb 10:22; v-2a(1); 4822]   ῥαντίζω

ῥεύσουσιν   fut act ind 3 pl
    [Jn 7:38; v-1a(7); 4835]   ῥέω

ῥέω   {4835, v-1a(7)}
    [ῥεύσω, -, -, -, -] *flow, overflow with*, John 7:38*

Ῥήγιον, ου, τό   {4836, n-2c}
    Rhegium, a city at the southwestern extremity of Italy, Acts 28:13*

Ῥήγιον   acc sg neut
    [Ac 28:13; n-2c; 4836]   Ῥήγιον

ῥῆγμα, ατος, τό   {4837, n-3c(4)}
    a rent; a crash, ruin, Luke 6:49*

ῥῆγμα   nom sg neut
    [Lk 6:49; n-3c(4); 4837]   ῥῆγμα

ῥήγνυμι   {4838, v-3c(2)}
    [ῥήξω, ἔρ(ρ)ηξα, ἔρρηγα, -, ἐρ(ρ)άγη] also spelled ῥήσσω, *to rend, shatter; to break* or *burst in pieces* Matt 9:17; Mark 2:22; Luke 5:6 v.l., 37; *to rend, lacerate*, Matt 7:6; *to cast* or *dash* upon the ground, *convulse*, Mark 9:18; Luke 9:42; absol. *to break forth* into exclamation, Gal 4:27

ῥήγνυνται   pres pass ind 3 pl
    [Mt 9:17; v-3c(2); 4838]   ῥήγνυμι
ῥηθείς   aor pass ptcp nom sg masc
    [Mt 3:3; v-1b(2); 3306]   λέγω
ῥηθέν   aor pass ptcp nom sg neut
    [10t; v-1b(2); 3306]   "
ῥηθέν   aor pass ptcp acc sg neut
    [2t; v-1b(2); 3306]   "

ῥῆμα, ατος, τό   {4839, n-3c(4)}
    that which is spoken; declaration, saying, speech, word, Matt 12:36; 26:75; Mark 9:32; 14:72; *a command, mandate, direction*, Luke 3:2; 5:5; *a promise*, Luke 1:38; 2:29; *a prediction, prophecy*, 2 Peter 3:2; *a doctrine* of God or Christ, John 3:34; 5:47; 6:63, 68; Acts 5:20; *an accusation, charge, crimination*, Matt 5:11; 27:14; from the Hebrew, *a thing*, Matt 4:4; Luke 4:4; *a matter, affair, transaction, business*, Matt 18:16; Luke 1:65; 2 Cor 13:1

ῥῆμα   nom sg neut [10t; n-3c(4); 4839]   ῥῆμα
ῥῆμα   acc sg neut [12t; n-3c(4); 4839]   "
ῥήμασιν   dat pl neut [Jn 5:47; n-3c(4); 4839]   "
ῥήματα   nom pl neut [6t; n-3c(4); 4839]   "
ῥήματα   acc pl neut [21t; n-3c(4); 4839]   "
ῥήματι   dat sg neut [5t; n-3c(4); 4839]   "
ῥήματος   gen sg neut [7t; n-3c(4); 4839]   "
ῥημάτων   gen pl neut [6t; n-3c(4); 4839]   "
ῥήξει   fut act ind 3 sg
    [2t; v-3c(2); 4838]   ῥήγνυμι

ῥήξον   aor act imperative 2 sg
    [Ga 4:27; v-3c(2); 4838]   "
ῥήξωσιν   aor act subj 3 pl
    [Mt 7:6; v-3c(2); 4838]   "

Ῥησά, ὁ   {4840, n-3g(2)}
    Rhesa, pr. name, indecl., Luke 3:27*

Ῥησά   indecl [Lk 3:27; n-3g(2); 4840]   Ῥησά
ῥήσσει   pres act ind 3 sg
    [Mk 9:18; v-1b(2); 4841]   ῥήσσω
ῥήσσω, see ῥήγνυμι   {4841, v-1b(2)}
ῥήτορος   gen sg masc
    [Ac 24:1; n-3f(2b); 4842]   ῥήτωρ

ῥήτωρ, ορος, ὁ   {4842, n-3f(2b)}
    an orator, advocate, Acts 24:1*

ῥητῶς   {4843, adverb}
    in express words, expressly, 1 Tim 4:1*

ῥητῶς   adverb [1Ti 4:1; adverb; 4843]   ῥητῶς

ῥίζα, ης, ἡ   {4844, n-1c}
    a root of a tree, Matt 3:10; 13:6; met. ἔχειν ῥίζαν, or ἔχειν ῥίζαν ἐν ἑαυτῷ, *to be rooted* in faith, Matt 13:21; Mark 4:17; Luke 8:13; met. *cause, source, origin*, 1 Tim 6:10; Heb 12:15; by synec. *the trunk, stock* of a tree, met. Rom 11:16, 17, 18; met. *offspring, progeny, a descendant*, Rom 15:12; Rev 5:5; 22:16

ῥίζα   nom sg fem [7t; n-1c; 4844]   ῥίζα
ῥίζαν   acc sg fem [8t; n-1c; 4844]   "
ῥίζης   gen sg fem [Rm 11:17; n-1c; 4844]   "

ῥιζόω   {4845, v-1d(3)}
    [-, ἐρίζωσα, -, ἐρρίζωμαι, ἐριζώθην] *to root, cause to take root; firmly rooted, strengthened with roots*; met. *firm, constant, firmly fixed*, Eph 3:17; Col 2:7*

ῥιζῶν   gen pl fem [Mk 11:20; n-1c; 4844]   "

ῥιπή, ῆς, ἡ   {4846, n-1b}
    pr. *a rapid sweep, jerk; a wink, twinkling* of the eye, 1 Cor 15:52*

ῥιπῇ   dat sg fem [1C 15:52; n-1b; 4846]   ῥιπή
ῥιπιζομένῳ   pres pass ptcp dat sg masc
    [Jm 1:6; v-2a(1); 4847]   ῥιπίζω

ῥιπίζω   {4847, v-2a(1)}
    [-, -, -, -, -] *to fan, blow, ventilate; to toss, agitate*, e.g. the ocean by the wind, James 1:6*

ῥιπτέω   {4848}
    see ῥίπτω, frequent and repeated action, *to toss repeatedly, toss up* with violent gesture, Acts 22:23 (ῥιπτούντων)*

ῥιπτούντων   pres act ptcp gen pl masc
    [Ac 22:23; see rJivpt; 4848]   ῥιπτέω

ῥίπτω   {4849, v-4}
    [(ἐρ(ρ)ίπτουν), -, ἔρ(ρ)ιψα, -, ἔρ(ρ)ιμμαι, ἐρ(ρ)ίθην] also spelled ῥιπτέω, *to hurl, throw, cast; to throw* or *cast down*, Matt 27:5; Luke 4:35; 17:2; *to throw* or *cast out*, Acts 27:19, 29; *to lay down, set down*, Matt 15:30; pass. *to be dispersed, scattered*, Matt 9:36*

ῥίψαν   aor act ptcp nom sg neut
[Lk 4:35; v-4; 4849]   ῥίπτω
ῥίψαντες   aor act ptcp nom pl masc
[Ac 27:29; v-4; 4849]   "
ῥίψας   aor act ptcp nom sg masc
[Mt 27:5; v-4; 4849]   "

Ῥοβοάμ, ὁ   {4850, n-3g(2)}
Roboam, pr. name, indecl., Matt 1:7; Luke 3:23ff.
v.l.*

Ῥοβοάμ   indecl [2t; n-3g(2); 4850]   Ῥοβοάμ

Ῥόδη, ης, ἡ   {4851, n-1b}
Rhoda, pr. name, Acts 12:13*

Ῥόδη   nom sg fem [Ac 12:13; n-1b; 4851]   Ῥόδη
Ῥόδον   acc sg fem [Ac 21:1; n-2b; 4852]   Ῥόδος

Ῥόδος, ου, ἡ   {4852, n-2b}
Rhodes, an island in the Mediterranean, south
of Caria, Acts 21:1*

ῥοιζηδόν   {4853, adverb}
with a noise, with a crash, etc., 2 Peter 3:10*

ῥοιζηδόν   adverb
[2P 3:10; adverb; 4853]   ῥοιζηδόν

Ῥομφά, ὁ   {4854, n-3g(2)}
also spelled Ῥεμφάν and Ῥεφάν, pr. name,
Rompha, Acts 7:43 v.l.*

ῥομφαία, ας, ἡ   {4855, n-1a}
pr. a Thracian broad-sword; a sword, Luke 21:24
v.l.; Rev 1:16; 2:12; by meton. war, Rev 6:8; met.
a thrill of anguish, Luke 2:35

ῥομφαία   nom sg fem [3t; n-1a; 4855]   ῥομφαία
ῥομφαίᾳ   dat sg fem [3t; n-1a; 4855]   "
ῥομφαίαν   acc sg fem [Rv 2:12; n-1a; 4855]   "

ῥοπή, ῆς, ἡ   {4856, n-1b}
downward movement, 1 Cor 15:52 v.l.*

Ῥουβήν, ὁ   {4857, n-3g(2)}
Reuben, pr. name, indecl., Rev 7:5*

Ῥουβήν   indecl [Rv 7:5; n-3g(2); 4857]   Ῥουβήν

Ῥούθ, ἡ   {4858, n-3g(2)}
Ruth, pr. name, indecl., Matt 1:5*

Ῥούθ   indecl [Mt 1:5; n-3g(2); 4858]   Ῥούθ
Ῥοῦφον   acc sg masc
[Rm 16:13; n-2a; 4859]   Ῥοῦφος

Ῥοῦφος, ου, ὁ   {4859, n-2a}
Rufus, pr. name, Mark 15:21; Rom 16:13*

Ῥούφου   gen sg masc [Mk 15:21; n-2a; 4859]   "
ῥύεσθαι   pres mid inf
[2P 2:9; v-1a(4); 4861]   ῥύομαι
ῥύμαις   dat pl fem [Mt 6:2; n-1b; 4860]   ῥύμη
ῥύμας   acc pl fem [Lk 14:21; n-1b; 4860]   "

ῥύμη, ης, ἡ   {4860, n-1b}
pr. a rush or sweep of a body in motion; a street,
Acts 9:11; 12:10; a narrow street, lane, alley, as
distinguished from πλατεῖα, Matt 6:2; Luke
14:21*

ῥύμην   acc sg fem [2t; n-1b; 4860]   "

ῥύομαι   {4861, v-1a(4)}
[ῥύσομαι, ἐρ(ρ)υσάμην, -, -, ἐρ(ρ)ύσθην] to drag
out of danger, to rescue, save, Matt 6:13; 27:43;
Acts 5:15 v.l.; to be rescued, delivered, Luke 1:74;
11:4 v.l.; Rom 15:31; 2 Thess 3:2; 2 Tim 4:17

ῥυόμενον   pres mid ptcp acc sg masc
[1Th 1:10; v-1a(4); 4861]   ῥύομαι
ῥυόμενος   pres mid ptcp nom sg masc
[Rm 11:26; v-1a(4); 4861]   "

ῥυπαίνω   {4862, v-2d(4)}
[-, -, -, -, ἐρ(ρ)υπάνθην] to make filthy, defile, Rev
22:11*

ῥυπανθήτω   aor pass imperative 3 sg
[Rv 22:11; v-2d(4); 4862]   ῥυπαίνω
ῥυπαρᾷ   dat sg fem
[Jm 2:2; a-1a(1); 4865]   ῥυπαρός

ῥυπαρεύω   {4863, v-1a(6)}
[-, -, -, -, -] to be filthy, squalid, met. to be polluted,
Rev 22:11 v.l.*

ῥυπαρία, ας, ἡ   {4864, n-1a}
filth; met. moral filthiness, uncleanness, pollution,
James 1:21*

ῥυπαρίαν   acc sg fem
[Jm 1:21; n-1a; 4864]   ῥυπαρία

ῥυπαρός, ά, όν   {4865, a-1a(1)}
filthy, squalid, sordid, dirty, James 2:2; met.
defiled, polluted, Rev 22:11*

ῥυπαρός   nom sg masc
[Rv 22:11; a-1a(1); 4865]   ῥυπαρός

ῥύπος, ου, ὁ   {4866, n-2a}
filth, squalor, 1 Peter 3:21*

ῥύπου   gen sg masc [1P 3:21; n-2a; 4866]   ῥύπος

ῥυπόω   {4867, v-1d(3)}
[-, ῥυπωσάτω (imperative, 3 sg), -, -, -] to be
filthy; met. to be morally polluted, Rev 22:11 (2t)
v.l.*

ῥῦσαι   aor mid imperative 2 sg
[Mt 6:13; v-1a(4); 4861]   ῥύομαι
ῥυσάσθω   aor mid imperative 3 sg
[Mt 27:43; v-1a(4); 4861]   "
ῥύσει   dat sg fem [2t; n-3e(5b); 4868]   ῥύσις
ῥύσεται   fut mid ind 3 sg
[4t; v-1a(4); 4861]   ῥύομαι
ῥυσθέντας   aor pass ptcp acc pl masc
[Lk 1:74; v-1a(4); 4861]   "
ῥυσθῶ   aor pass subj 1 sg
[Rm 15:31; v-1a(4); 4861]   "
ῥυσθῶμεν   aor pass subj 1 pl
[2Th 3:2; v-1a(4); 4861]   "

ῥύσις, εως, ἡ   {4868, n-3e(5b)}
a flowing; a moɪ   Mark 5:25; Luke 8:43,
44*

ῥύσις   nom sg fem
[Lk 8:44; n-3e(5b)   ῥύσις
ῥυτίδα   acc sg fem
[Ep 5:27; n-3c(2),   ῥυτίς

ῥυτίς, ίδος, ἡ   {4869, n-3c(2)}
a wrinkle; met. a disfiguring wrinkle, flaw,
blemish, Eph 5:27*

Ῥωμαϊκός, η, ον   {4869, a-1a(2a)}
Roman, Latin, Luke 23:38*

Ῥωμαῖοι   nom pl masc [3t; a-1a(1); 4871]   Ῥωμαῖος
Ῥωμαίοις   dat pl masc [2t; a-1a(1); 4871]   "
Ῥωμαῖον   acc sg masc [Ac 22:25; a-1a(1); 4871]   "

Ῥωμαῖος, α, ον   {4871, a-1a(1)}
Roman; a Roman citizen, John 11:48; Acts 2:10;
16:21

Ῥωμαῖος   nom sg masc [4t; a-1a(1); 4871]   "
Ῥωμαίους acc pl masc [Ac 16:37; a-1a(1); 4871]   "

Ῥωμαϊστί   {4872, adverb}
in the Roman language, in Latin, John 19:20*

Ῥωμαϊστί   adverb
[Jn 19:20; adverb; 4872]   Ῥωμαϊστί
Ῥωμαίων   gen pl masc
[Ac 28:17; a-1a(1); 4871]   Ῥωμαῖος

Ῥώμη, ης, ἡ   {4873, n-1b}
Rome, Acts 18:2; 19:21; 23:11; 28:14, 16; Rom 1:7;
2 Tim 1:17; 1 Pet 5:13 v.l., the subscriptions to
Gal, Eph, Phil, Col, 2 Thess, 2 Tim, Phlm, and
Heb*

Ῥώμῃ   dat sg fem [3t; n-1b; 4873]   Ῥώμη

Ῥώμην acc sg fem [4t; n-1b; 4873]   "

Ῥώμης gen sg fem [Ac 18:2; n-1b; 4873]   "

ῥώννυμι   {4874, v-3c(1)}
[-, -, -, ἔρρωμαι, -] to strengthen, render firm; to be
well, enjoy firm health; at the end of letters, like
the Latin vale, farewell, Acts 15:29; 23:30 v.l.*

σ

σά   nom pl neut [3t; a-1a(2a); 5050]   σός
σά   acc pl neut [Lk 6:30; a-1a(2a); 5050]   "

σαβαχθάνι   {4876, n-3g(2)}
(Aramaic) sabacthani, you have forsaken me;
interrogatively, have you forsaken me? preceded
with λαμά, Why? Matt 27:46; Mark 15:34*

σαβαχθανι indecl [2t; n-3g(2); 4876]   σαβαχθάνι

Σαβαώθ   {4877, n-3g(2)}
(Hebrew) hosts, armies, indecl., Rom 9:29; James
5:4*

Σαβαώθ indecl [2t; n-3g(2); 4877]   Σαβαώθ
σάββασιν dat pl neut [13t; n-2c; 4879]   σάββατον
σάββατα   acc pl neut [Ac 17:2; n-2c; 4879]   "

σαββατισμός, οῦ, ὁ   {4878, n-2a}
pr. a keeping of a sabbath; a state of rest, a
sabbath-state, Heb 4:9*

σαββατισμός nom sg masc
[Hb 4:9; n-2a; 4878]   σαββατισμός

σάββατον, ου, τό   {4879, n-2c}
pr. cessation from labor, rest; the Jewish sabbath,
both in the sg. and pl., Matt 12:2, 5, 8; 28:1;
Luke 4:16; a week, sg. and pl., Matt 28:1; Mark
16:9; pl. sabbaths, or times of sacred rest, Col 2:16;
Mark 16:2 v.l.; 1 Cor 16:2 v.l.

σάββατον   nom sg neut [5t; n-2c; 4879]   σάββατον
σάββατον   acc sg neut [9t; n-2c; 4879]   "
σαββάτου   gen sg neut [13t; n-2c; 4879]   "
σαββάτῳ   dat sg neut [16t; n-2c; 4879]   "
σαββάτων   gen pl neut [11t; n-2c; 4879]   "

σαγήνη, ης, ἡ   {4880, n-1b}
a large net, Matt 13:47*

σαγήνῃ dat sg fem [Mt 13:47; n-1b; 4880]   σαγήνη
Σαδδουκαῖοι nom pl masc
[5t; n-2a; 4881]   Σαδδουκαῖος

Σαδδουκαῖος, ου, ὁ   {4881, n-2a}
a Sadducee, one belonging to the sect of the
Sadducees, which, according to the Talmudists,
was founded by one, Sadoc, about three
centuries before the Christian era: they were
directly opposed in sentiments to the
Pharisees, Matt 3:7; 16:1, 6, 11, 12; 22:23, 34;
Mark 12:18; Luke 20:27; Acts 4:1; 5:17; 23:6-8*

Σαδδουκαίους acc pl masc
[Mt 22:34; n-2a; 4881]   "
Σαδδουκαίων gen pl masc [8t; n-2a; 4881]   "

Σαδώκ, ὁ   {4882, n-3g(2)}
Zadok, pr. name, indecl., Matt 1:14; Luke 3:23ff.
v.l.*

Σαδώκ indecl [2t; n-3g(2); 4882]   Σαδώκ
σαίνεσθαι pres pass inf
[1Th 3:3; v-2d(4); 4883]   σαίνω

σαίνω   {4883, v-2d(4)}
[-, -, -, -, -] pr. to wag the tail; to fawn, flatter,
cajole; pass. to be cajoled; to be wrought upon, to be
perturbed, 1 Thess 3:3*

σάκκος, ου, ὁ   {4884, n-2a}
sackcloth, a species of very coarse black cloth
made of hair, Rev 6:12; a mourning garment of
sackcloth, Matt 11:21; Luke 10:13; Rev 11:3*

σάκκος   nom sg masc [Rv 6:12; n-2a; 4884]   σάκκος
σάκκους acc pl masc [Rv 11:3; n-2a; 4884]   "
σάκκῳ   dat sg masc [2t; n-2a; 4884]   "

Σαλά, ὁ   {4885, n-3g(2)}
Sala, pr. name, indecl., Luke 3:32, 35*

Σαλά indecl [2t; n-3g(2); 4885]   Σαλά

Σαλαθιήλ, ὁ   {4886, n-3g(2)}
Shealtiel, pr. name, indecl., Matt 1:12; Luke
3:27*

Σαλαθιήλ indecl [3t; n-3g(2); 4886]   Σαλαθιήλ
Σαλαμῖνι dat sg fem
[Ac 13:5; n-3f(1a); 4887]   Σαλαμίς

Σαλαμίς, ῖνος, ἡ   {4887, n-3f(1a)}
Salamis, a city in the island of Cyprus, Acts
13:5*

Σαλείμ indecl [Jn 3:23; n-3g(2); 4890]   Σαλίμ
σαλευθῆναι aor pass inf
[2t; v-1a(6); 4888]   σαλεύω

σαλευθήσονται   fut pass ind 3 pl
[3t; v-1a(6); 4888]   "

σαλευθῶ   aor pass subj 1 sg
[Ac 2:25; v-1a(6); 4888]   "

σαλευόμενα   pres pass ptcp nom pl neut
[Hb 12:27; v-1a(6); 4888]

σαλευόμενον   pres pass ptcp acc sg masc
[2t; v-1a(6); 4888]   "

σαλευομένων   pres pass ptcp gen pl neut
[Hb 12:27; v-1a(6); 4888]   "

σαλεῦσαι   aor act inf [Lk 6:48; v-1a(6); 4888]   "

σαλεύω   {4888, v-1a(6)}
[-, ἐσάλευσα, -, σεσάλευμαι, ἐσαλεύθην] *to make
to rock, to shake*, Matt 11:7; 24:29; Mark 13:25;
Luke 6:38, 48; 7:24; 21:26; Acts 4:31; 16:26; Heb
12:26; Rev 6:13 v.l.; met. *to stir up, excite* the
people, Acts 17:13; *to agitate, disturb* mentally,
Acts 2:25; 2 Thess 2:2; pass. impl. *to totter, be
ready to fall, be near to ruin*, met. Heb 12:27*

Σαλήμ, ἡ   {4889, n-3g(2)}
(Hebrew, meaning *peace*), *Salem*, pr. name,
indecl., Heb 7:1f.*

Σαλήμ   indecl [2t; n-3g(2); 4889]   Σαλήμ

Σαλίμ, τό   {4890, n-3g(2)}
Salim, indecl., a locality in Samaria; John 3:23*

Σαλμών, ὁ   {4891, n-3g(2)}
Salmon, pr. name, indecl., Matt 1:4f.; Luke 3:32
v.l.*

Σαλμών   indecl [2t; n-3g(2); 4891]   Σαλμών

Σαλμώνη, ης, ἡ   {4892, n-1b}
Salmone, a promontory, the eastern extremity
of Crete, Acts 27:7*

Σαλμώνην   acc sg fem [Ac 27:7; n-1b; 4892]
Σαλμώνη

σάλος, ου, ὁ   {4893, n-2a}
agitation, tossing, rolling, spc. of the sea, Luke
21:25*

σάλου   gen sg masc [Lk 21:25; n-2a; 4893]   σάλος
σάλπιγγα   acc sg fem
[Rv 9:14; n-3b(2); 4894]   σάλπιγξ
σάλπιγγας   acc pl fem [Rv 8:6; n-3b(2); 4894]   "
σάλπιγγες   nom pl fem [Rv 8:2; n-3b(2); 4894]   "
σάλπιγγι   dat sg fem [2t; n-3b(2); 4894]   "
σάλπιγγος   gen sg fem [5t; n-3b(2); 4894]   "

σάλπιγξ, ιγγός, ἡ   {4894, n-3b(2)}
trumpet, Matt 24:31 v.l.; 1 Cor 14:8; Heb 12:19;
Rev 1:10; 4:1; 8:2, 6; 13:9; 16:6 v.l.; 1 Thess 4:16;
sound of the trumpet, Matt 24:31; 1 Cor 15:52; 1
Thess 4:16*

σάλπιγξ   nom sg fem [1C 14:8; n-3b(2); 4894]   "
σαλπίζειν   pres act inf
[2t; v-2a(1); 4895]   σαλπίζω

σαλπίζω   {4895, v-2a(1)}
[σαλπίσω, ἐσάλπισα, -, -, -] *to sound a trumpet*,
Matt 6:2; 1 Cor 5:52; Rev 8:6, 7, 8, 10, 12, 13; 9:1,
13; 10:7; 11:15*

σαλπίσει   fut act ind 3 sg
[1C 15:52; v-2a(1); 4895]   "

σαλπίσῃς   aor act subj 2 sg
[Mt 6:2; v-2a(1); 4895]   "

σαλπιστής, οῦ, ὁ   {4896, n-1f}
a trumpeter, Rev 18:22*

σαλπιστῶν   gen pl masc
[Rv 18:22; n-1f; 4896]   σαλπιστής
σαλπίσωσιν   aor act subj 3 pl
[Rv 8:6; v-2a(1); 4895]   σαλπίζω

Σαλώμη, ης, ἡ   {4897, n-1b}
Salome, pr. name, a Galilean woman who
followed Jesus, Matt 27:56; Mark 15:40; 16:1*

Σαλώμη   nom sg fem [2t; n-1b; 4897]   Σαλώμη

Σαλωμών, see Σολομῶν, Acts 7:47 v.l.*   {4898}

Σαμάρεια, ας, ἡ   {4899, n-1a}
Samaria, the city and region so called, Acts 8:14

Σαμάρεια   nom sg fem
[Ac 8:14; n-1a; 4899]   Σαμάρεια
Σαμαρείᾳ   dat sg fem [Ac 1:8; n-1a; 4899]   "
Σαμάρειαν   acc sg fem [Ac 15:3; n-1a; 4899]   "
Σαμαρείας   gen sg fem [8t; n-1a; 4899]   "
Σαμαρῖται   nom pl masc
[Jn 4:40; n-1f; 4901]   Σαμαρίτης
Σαμαρίταις   dat pl masc [Jn 4:9; n-1f; 4901]

Σαμαρίτης, ου, ὁ   {4901, n-1f}
a Samaritan, an inhabitant of the city or *region of
Samaria*, applied by the Jews as a term of
reproach and contempt, Matt 10:5; John 4:9,
39f.; 8:48; Luke 9:52; 10:33; 17:16; Acts 8:25*

Σαμαρίτης   nom sg masc [3t; n-1f; 4901]   "
Σαμαρίτιδος   gen sg fem
[Jn 4:9; n-3c(2); 4902]   Σαμαρῖτις

Σαμαρῖτις, ιδος, ἡ   {4902, n-3c(2)}
a Samaritan woman, John 4:9*

Σαμαρῖτις   nom sg fem [Jn 4:9; n-3c(2); 4902]   "
Σαμαριτῶν   gen pl masc [4t; n-1f; 4901]   Σαμαρίτης

Σαμοθρᾴκη, ης, ἡ   {4903, n-1b}
Samothrace, an island in the northern part of the
Aegean sea, Acts 16:11*

Σαμοθρᾴκην   acc sg fem
[Ac 16:11; n-1b; 4903]   Σαμοθρᾴκη
Σάμον   acc sg fem [Ac 20:15; n-2b; 4904]   Σάμος

Σάμος, ου, ἡ   {4904, n-2b}
Samos, a celebrated island, in the Aegean sea,
Acts 20:15*

Σαμουήλ, ὁ   {4905, n-3g(2)}
(1 Sam 1:1-25:1), *Samuel*, pr. name, indecl. , Acts
3:24; 13:20; Heb 11:32*

Σαμουήλ   indecl [3t; n-3g(2); 4905]   Σαμουήλ

Σαμφουρειν   {4906, n-3g(2)}
Sepphoris, indecl., an area near Ephraim,
indecl., John 11:44 v.l.*

Σαμψών, ὁ   {4907, n-3g(2)}
(Judges 13-16), *Samson*, pr. name, indecl., Heb
11:32*

Σαμψών   indecl [Hb 11:32; n-3g(2); 4907]   Σαμψών

σανδάλια   acc pl neut [2t; n-2c; 4908]   σανδάλιον

σανδάλιον, ου, τό   {4908, n-2c}
   a sandal, a sole of wood or hide, covering the
   bottom of the foot, and bound on with leathern
   thongs, Mark 6:9, Acts 12:8*

σανίς, ίδος, ή   {4909, n-3c(2)}
   a board, plank, Acts 27:44*

σανίσιν   dat pl fem
   [Ac 27:44; n-3c(2); 4909]   σανίς

Σαούλ, ὁ   {4910, n-3g(2)}
   Saul, pr. name, indecl. I. *Saul, king of Israel,* Acts
   13:21; II. *The Apostle Paul,* Acts 9:4, 17; 22:7, 13;
   26:14*

Σαούλ   indecl [9t; n-3g(2); 4910]   Σαούλ

σαπρά   acc pl neut
   [Mt 13:48; a-1a(1); 4911]   σαπρός
σαπρόν   nom sg neut [3t; a-1a(1); 4911]   "
σαπρόν   acc sg masc [2t; a-1a(1); 4911]   "
σαπρόν   acc sg neut [Mt 12:33; a-1a(1); 4911]   "

σαπρός, ά, όν   {4911, a-1a(1)}
   pr. *rotten, putrid;* hence, *bad, of a bad quality,*
   Matt 7:17, 18; 12:33; Luke 6:43; *refuse,* Matt
   13:48; met. *corrupt, depraved, vicious, foul,*
   impure, Eph 4:29*

σαπρός   nom sg masc [Ep 4:29; a-1a(1); 4911]   "

Σάπφιρα, ης, ή   {4912, n-1c}
   Sapphira, wife of Ananias and a member of the
   Jerusalem church, Acts 5:1*

σαπφίρη   dat sg fem [Ac 5:1; n-1c; 4912]   Σάπφιρα

σάπφιρος, ου, ή   {4913, n-2b}
   a sapphire, a precious stone of a blue color in
   various shades, next in hardness and value to
   the diamond, Rev 21:19

σάπφιρος   nom sg fem
   [Rv 21:19; n-2b; 4913]   σάπφιρος

σαργάνη, ης, ή   {4914, n-1b}
   twisted or *plaited work; a netword of cords like a*
   basket, basket of ropes, etc. 2 Cor 11:33*

σαργάνη   dat sg fem
   [2C 11:33; n-1b; 4914]   σαργάνη

Σάρδεις, εων, αί   {4915, n-3e(5b)}
   Sardis, the capital city of Lydia, in Asia Minor
   Rev 1:11; 3:1, 4*

Σάρδεις   acc pl fem
   [Rv 1:11; n-3e(5b); 4915]   Σάρδεις
Σάρδεσιν   dat pl fem [2t; n-3e(5b); 4915]   "

σάρδινος, ου, ὁ, see σάρδιον   {4916, n-2a}

σάρδιον, ου, τό   {4917, n-2c}
   carnelian, a reddish precious stone, Rev 4:3
   (which has the later form σάρδινος as a v.l.);
   21:20*

σάρδιον   nom sg neut
   [Rv 21:20; n-2c; 4917]   σάρδιον
σαρδίῳ   dat sg neut [Rv 4:3; n-2c; 4917]   "

σαρδόνυξ, υχος, ή   {4918, n-3b(3)}
   sardonyx, a gem exhibiting the color of the

   carnelian and the white of the calcedony,
   intermingled in alternate layers, Rev 21:20*

σαρδόνυξ   nom sg fem
   [Rv 21:20; n-3b(3); 4918]   σαρδόνυξ

Σάρεπτα, ων, τά   {4919, n-2c}
   Sarepta, a city of Phoenicia, between Tyre and
   Sidon, Luke 4:26*

Σάρεπτα   acc pl neut [Lk 4:26; n-2c; 4919]   Σάρεπτα
σάρκα   acc sg fem [37t; n-3b(1); 4922]   σάρξ
σάρκας   acc pl fem [7t; n-3b(1); 4922]   "
σαρκί   dat sg fem [39t; n-3b(1); 4922]   "
σαρκικά   nom pl neut
   [2C 10:4; a-1a(2a); 4920]   σαρκικός
σαρκικά   acc pl neut [1C 9:11; a-1a(2a); 4920] "
σαρκικῇ   dat sg fem [2C 1:12; a-1a(2a); 4920] "
σαρκικοί   nom pl masc [2t; a-1a(2a); 4920]   "
σαρκικοῖς   dat pl neut [Rm 15:27; a-1a(2a); 4920] "

σαρκικός, ή, όν   {4920, a-1a(2a)}
   fleshly; pertaining to the body, corporeal, physical,
   Rom 15:27; 1 Cor 9:11; *carnal, pertaining to the*
   flesh, 1 Peter 2:11; *carnal, subject to the propensity*
   of the flesh, Rom 7:14 v.l.; *carnal, low in spiritual*
   knowledge and frame, 1 Cor 3:1 v.l., 3; *carnal,*
   human as opposed to divine, 2 Cor 1:12; 10:4;
   carnal, earthly, Heb 7:16 v.l.*

σαρκικῶν   gen pl fem [1P 2:11; a-1a(2a); 4920] "
σαρκίναις   dat pl fem
   [2C 3:3; a-1a(2a); 4921]   σάρκινος
σαρκίνης   gen sg fem [Hb 7:16; a-1a(2a); 4921] "
σαρκίνοις   dat pl masc [1C 3:1; a-1a(2a); 4921] "

σάρκινος, η, ον   {4921, a-1a(2a)}
   of flesh, fleshly, 2 Cor 3:3; Rom 7:14; 1 Cor 3:1;
   Heb 7:16; 2 Cor 1:12 v.l.*

σάρκινος   nom sg masc [Rm 7:14; a-1a(2a); 4921] "
σαρκός   gen sg fem [37t; n-3b(1); 4922]   σάρξ
σαρκῶν   gen pl fem [Rv 19:21; n-3b(1); 4922]   "

σάρξ, ός, ή   {4922, n-3b(1)}
   flesh, Luke 24:39; John 3:6; *the* human *body,* 2
   Cor 7:5; *flesh, human nature, human frame,* John
   1:13, 14; 1 Peter 4:1; 1 John 4:2; *kindred,* Rom
   11:14; *lineage,* Rom 1:3; 9:3; *flesh, humanity,*
   human beings, Matt 24:22; Luke 3:6; John 17:2;
   the circumstances of the body, material condition, 1
   Cor 5:5; 7:28; Phil 16; *flesh, mere humanity,*
   human fashion, 1 Cor 1:26; 2 Cor 1:17; *flesh* as the
   seat of passion and frailty, Rom 8:1, 3, 5;
   carnality, Gal 5:24; *materiality, material*
   circumstance, as opposed to the spiritual, Phil
   3:3, 4; Col 2:18; *a material system* or *mode,* Gal
   3:3; Heb 9:10

σάρξ   nom sg fem [26t; n-3b(1); 4922]   "
σαροῖ   pres act ind 3 sg
   [Lk 15:8; v-1d(3); 4924]   σαρόω

Σαρούχ, v.l. for Σερουχ at Luke 3:35*   {4923, n-3g(2)}

σαρόω   {4924, v-1d(3)}
   [-, ἐσάρωσα, -, σεσάρωμαι, ἐσαρώθην] *to sweep,*
   to clean with a broom, Matt 12:44; Luke 11:25;
   15:8*

Σάρρα, ας, ἡ   {4925, n-1a}
Sara, Sarah, pr. name, the wife of Abraham,
Rom 4:19; 9:9; Heb 11:11; 1 Peter 3:6*

Σάρρα   nom sg fem [2t; n-1a; 4925]   Σάρρα
Σάρρᾳ   dat sg fem [Rm 9:9; n-1a; 4925]   "
Σάρρας   gen sg fem [Rm 4:19; n-1a; 4925]   "

Σαρών, ῶνος, ὁ   {4926, n-3f(1a)}
Saron, a level tract of Palestine, between
Caesarea and Joppa, Acts 9:35*

Σαρῶνα   acc sg masc
    [Ac 9:35; n-3f(1a); 4926]   Σαρών
σάτα   acc pl neut [2t; n-2c; 4929]   σάτον

Σατάν, ὁ   {4927, n-3g(2)}
Satan, indecl., 2 Cor 12:7

σατανᾶ   voc sg masc [3t; n-1e; 4928]   Σατανᾶς
σατανᾶ   gen sg masc [10t; n-1e; 4928]   "
σατανᾷ   dat sg masc [2t; n-1e; 4928]   "
σατανᾶν acc sg masc [4t; n-1e; 4928]   "

Σατανᾶς, ᾶ, ὁ   {4928, n-1e}
an adversary, opponent, enemy, perhaps, Matt
16:23; Mark 8:33; Luke 4:8; elsewhere, Satan, the
devil, Matt 4:10; Mark 1:13

σατανᾶς   nom sg masc [17t; n-1e; 4928]   "

σάτον, ου, τό   {4929, n-2c}
a satum or seah, a Hebrew measure for things
dry, containing, as Josephus testifies, (Ant.
9.85) an Italian modius and one half, or 24
sextarii, and therefore equivalent to somewhat
less than three gallons English, Matt 13:33;
Luke 13:21*

Σαῦλον   acc sg masc [4t; n-2a; 4930]   Σαῦλος

Σαῦλος, ου, ὁ   {4930, n-2a}
Saul, the Hebrew name of the Apostle Paul,
Σαούλ with a Greek termination, Acts 7:58; 8:1,
3; 9:1; 22:7 v.l.; 26:14 v.l.

Σαῦλος   nom sg masc [8t; n-2a; 4930]   "
Σαύλου   gen sg masc [2t; n-2a; 4930]   "
Σαύλῳ   dat sg masc [Ac 9:24; n-2a; 4930]   "

σβέννυμι   {4931, v-3c(1)}
[σβέσω, ἔσβεσα, -, -, ἐσβέσθην] to extinguish,
quench, Matt 12:20; 25:8; Mark 9:44, 46, 48; Eph
6:16; Heb 11:34; met. to quench, damp, hinder,
thwart, 1 Thess 5:19*

σβέννυνται pres pass ind 3 pl
    [Mt 25:8; v-3c(1); 4931]   σβέννυμι
σβέννυται pres pass ind 3 sg
    [Mk 9:48; v-3c(1); 4931]   "
σβέννυτε pres act imperative 2 pl
    [1Th 5:19; v-3c(1); 4931]   "
σβέσαι   aor act inf [Ep 6:16; v-3c(1); 4931]   "
σβέσει   fut act ind 3 sg
    [Mt 12:20; v-3c(1); 4931]   "
σε   acc sg [197t; a-5a; 5148]   σύ
σεαυτόν   acc sg masc
    [33t; a-1a(2b); 4932]   σεαυτοῦ

σεαυτοῦ, ῆς   {4932, a-1a(2b)}
of yourself, to yourself, etc. Matt 4:6; 8:4; 19:19

σεαυτοῦ   gen sg masc [5t; a-1a(2b); 4932]   "
σεαυτῷ   dat sg masc [5t; a-1a(2b); 4932]   "

σεβάζομαι   {4933, v-2a(1)}
[-, -, -, -, ἐσεβάσθην] to feel dread of a thing; to
venerate, adore, worship, Rom 1:25*

σέβασμα, ατος, τό   {4934, n-3c(4)}
an object of religious veneration and worship, Acts
17:23; 2 Thess 2:4*

σέβασμα   acc sg neut
    [2Th 2:4; n-3c(4); 4934]   σέβασμα
σεβάσματα acc pl neut [Ac 17:23; n-3c(4); 4934]   "
Σεβαστῆς   gen sg fem
    [Ac 27:1; a-1a(2a); 4935]   σεβαστός
Σεβαστόν   acc sg masc [Ac 25:25; a-1a(2a); 4935]   "

σεβαστός, ή, όν   {4935, a-1a(2a)}
pr. venerable, august; ὁ Σεβαστός, i.q. Latin
Augustus, Acts 25:21, 25; Augustan, or, Sebastan,
named from the city Sebaste, Acts 27:1*

Σεβαστοῦ   gen sg masc [Ac 25:21; a-1a(2a); 4935]   "
σέβεσθαι   pres mid inf
    [Ac 18:13; v-1b(1); 4936]   σέβω
σέβεται   pres mid ind 3 sg
    [Ac 19:27; v-1b(1); 4936]   "
σεβομένας pres mid ptcp acc pl fem
    [Ac 13:50; v-1b(1); 4936]   "
σεβομένη   pres mid ptcp nom sg fem
    [Ac 16:14; v-1b(1); 4936]   "
σεβομένοις pres mid ptcp dat pl masc
    [Ac 17:17; v-1b(1); 4936]   "
σεβομένου pres mid ptcp gen sg masc
    [Ac 18:7; v-1b(1); 4936]   "
σεβομένων pres mid ptcp gen pl masc
    [2t; v-1b(1); 4936]   "
σέβονται   pres mid ind 3 pl [2t; v-1b(1); 4936]   "

σέβω   {4936, v-1b(1)}
[-, -, -, -, -] mid., to stand in awe; to venerate,
reverence, worship, adore, Matt 15:9; Mark 7:7;
Acts 18:13; 19:27; part. σεβόμενος, η, ον,
worshiping, devout, pious, a term applied to
proselytes to Judaism, Acts 13:43; 16:14; 18:7;
13:50; 17:4, 17*

σειομένη   pres pass ptcp nom sg fem
    [Rv 6:13; v-1a(3); 4940]   σείω

σειρά, ᾶς, ἡ   {4937, n-1a}
a cord, rope, band; in N.T. a chain, 2 Peter 2:4*

σειραῖς   dat pl fem [2P 2:4; n-1a; 4937]   σειρά

σειρός, see σιρός   {4938}

σεισμοί   nom pl masc [3t; n-2a; 4939]   σεισμός
σεισμόν   acc sg masc [Mt 27:54; n-2a; 4939]   "

σεισμός, οῦ, ὁ   {4939, n-2a}
pr. a shaking, agitation, concussion; an earthquake,
Matt 24:7; 27:54; a tempest, Matt 8:24

σεισμός   nom sg masc [9t; n-2a; 4939]   "
σεισμῷ   dat sg masc [Rv 11:13; n-2a; 4939]   "
σείσω   fut act ind 1 sg
    [Hb 12:26; v-1a(3); 4940]   σείω

σείω   {4940, v-1a(3)}
[σείσω, ἔσεισα, -, -, ἐσείσθην] *to shake, agitate,*
Heb 12:26; pass. *to quake,* Matt 27:51; 28:4; Rev
6:13; met. *to put in commotion, agitate,* Matt 21:10

Σεκοῦνδος, ου, ὁ   {4941, n-2a}
Secundus, pr. name, Acts 20:4*

Σεκοῦνδος   nom sg masc
   [Ac 20:4; n-2a; 4941]   Σεκοῦνδος

Σελεύκεια, ας, ἡ   {4942, n-1a}
Seleucia, a city of Syria, west of Antioch, on the
Orontes, Acts 13:4*

Σελεύκειαν   acc sg fem
   [Ac 13:4; n-1a; 4942]   Σελεύκεια

σελήνη, ης, ἡ   {4943, n-1b}
the moon, Matt 24:29; Mark 13:24

σελήνη   nom sg fem [5t; n-1b; 4943]   σελήνη
σελήνη   dat sg fem [Lk 21:25; n-1b; 4943]   "
σελήνης   gen sg fem [3t; n-1b; 4943]   "
σεληνιάζεται   pres pass ind 3 sg
   [Mt 17:15; v-2a(1); 4944]   σεληνιάζομαι

σεληνιάζομαι   {4944, v-2a(1)}
[-, -, -, -, -] *to be a lunatic,* Matt 4:24; 17:15*

σεληνιαζομένους   pres pass ptcp acc pl masc
   [Mt 4:24; v-2a(1); 4944]   "

Σεμεῖν, ὁ   {4946, n-3g(2)}
Semei, pr. name, indecl., Luke 3:26*

Σεμεΐν   indecl [Lk 3:26; n-3g(2); 4946]   Σεμεῖν
σεμίδαλιν   acc sg fem
   [Rv 18:13; n-3e(5b); 4947]   σεμίδαλις

σεμίδαλις, εως, ἡ   {4947, n-3e(5b)}
the finest flour, Rev 18:13*

σεμνά   nom pl neut [Pp 4:8; a-1a(2a); 4948]   σεμνός
σεμνάς   acc pl fem [1Ti 3:11; a-1a(2a); 4948]   "

σεμνός, ή, όν   {4948, a-1a(2a)}
august, venerable; honorable, reputable, Phil 4:8;
grave, serious, dignified, 1 Tim 3:8, 11; Titus 2:2*

σεμνότης, ητος, ἡ   {4949, n-3c(1)}
pr. *majesty; gravity, dignity, dignified seriousness,*
1 Tim 2:2; 3:4; Titus 2:7*

σεμνότητα   acc sg fem
   [Ti 2:7; n-3c(1); 4949]   σεμνότης
σεμνότητι   dat sg fem [1Ti 2:2; n-3c(1); 4949]   "
σεμνότητος   gen sg fem [1Ti 3:4; n-3c(1); 4949] "
σεμνούς   acc pl masc [2t; a-1a(2a); 4948]   σεμνός

Σέργιος, ου, ὁ   {4950, n-2a}
Sergius, pr. name, Acts 13:7*

Σεργίῳ   dat sg masc [Ac 13:7; n-2a; 4950]   Σέργιος

Σερούχ, ὁ   {4952, n-3g(2)}
Serug, proper name, Luke 3:35*

Σερούχ   indecl [Lk 3:35; n-3g(2); 4952]   Σερούχ
σεσαλευμένον   perf pass ptcp acc sg neut
   [Lk 6:38; v-1a(6); 4888]   σαλεύω
σεσαρωμένον   perf pass ptcp acc sg masc
   [2t; v-1d(3); 4924]   σαρόω

σέσηπεν   perf act ind 3 sg
   [Jm 5:2; v-1b(1); 4960]   σήπω
σεσιγημένου   perf pass ptcp gen sg neut
   [Rm 16:25; v-1d(1a); 4967]   σιγάω
σεσοφισμένοις   perf pass ptcp dat pl masc
   [2P 1:16; v-2a(1); 5054]   σοφίζω
σέσωκεν   perf act ind 3 sg
   [7t; v-2a(1); 5392]   σῴζω
σεσωρευμένα   perf pass ptcp acc pl neut
   [2Ti 3:6; v-1a(6); 5397]   σωρεύω
σεσωσμένοι   perf pass ptcp nom pl masc
   [2t; v-2a(1); 5392]   σῴζω
σέσωται   perf pass ind 3 sg
   [Ac 4:9; v-2a(1); 5392]   "
σῇ   dat sg fem [4t; a-1a(2a); 5050]   σός

Σήθ, ὁ   {4953, n-3g(2)}
Seth, (Gen. 4:25f.) pr. name, indecl., Luke 3:38*

Σήθ   indecl [Lk 3:38; n-3g(2); 4953]   Σήθ

Σήμ, ὁ   {4954, n-3g(2)}
Shem, (Gen. 5:32) pr. name, indecl., Luke 3:36*

Σήμ   indecl [Lk 3:36; n-3g(2); 4954]   Σήμ

σημαίνω   {4955, v-2d(4)}
[(ἐσήμαινον), -, ἐσήμανα, -, -, -] *to indicate by a
sign, to signal; to indicate, intimate,* John 12:33;
18:32; 21:19; *to make known, communicate,* Acts
11:28; Rev 1:1; *to specify,* Acts 25:27*

σημαίνων   pres act ptcp nom sg masc
   [3t; v-2d(4); 4955]   σημαίνω
σημᾶναι   aor act inf [Ac 25:27; v-2d(4); 4955]   "
σημεῖα   nom pl neut [6t; n-2c; 4956]   σημεῖον
σημεῖα   acc pl neut [26t; n-2c; 4956]   "
σημείοις   dat pl neut [4t; n-2c; 4956]   "

σημεῖον, ου, τό   {4956, n-2c}
a sign, a mark, token, by which anything is
known or distinguished, Matt 16:3; 24:3; 2
Thess 3:17; *a token, pledge, assurance,* Luke 2:12;
a proof, evidence, convincing token, Matt 12:38;
16:1; John 2:18; in N.T. *a sign, wonder, remarkable
event, wonderful appearance, extraordinary
phenomenon,* 1 Cor 14:22; Rev 12:1, 3; 15:1; *a
portent, prodigy,* Matt 24:30; Acts 2:19; *a
wonderful work, miraculous operation, miracle,*
Matt 24:24; Mark 16:17, 20; meton. *a sign, a
signal character,* Luke 2:34

σημεῖον   nom sg neut [18t; n-2c; 4956]   "
σημεῖον   acc sg neut [20t; n-2c; 4956]   "
σημειοῦσθε   pres mid imperative 2 pl
   [2Th 3:14; v-1d(3); 4957]   σημειόω

σημειόω   {4957, v-1d(3)}
[-, ἐσημείωσα, -, -, -] mid., *to mark, inscribe marks
upon;* mid. *to mark for one's self, note,* 2 Thess
3:14*

σημείων   gen pl neut [3t; n-2c; 4956]   σημεῖον

σήμερον   {4958, adverb}
to-day, this day, Matt 6:11, 30; 16:3; 21:28; *now, at
present,* Heb 13:8; 2 Cor 3:15; ἡ σήμερον, sc.
ἡμέρα, sometimes expressed, *this day, the
present day,* Acts 20:26; ἕως or ἄχρι τῆς σήμερον,
until this day, until our times, Matt 11:23; 27:8

σήμερον   adverb [41t; adverb; 4958]   σήμερον
σήν   acc sg fem [Jn 4:42; a-1a(2a); 5050]   σός

σήπω   {4960, v-1b(1)}
[-, -, σέσηπα, -, -] *to cause to putrify, rot, be
corrupted* or *rotten,* James 5:2*

σηρικός, see σιρικός   {4961}

σής, σητός, ὁ   {4962, n-3c(1)}
a moth, Luke 12:33; Matt 6:19f.*

σής   nom sg masc [3t; n-3c(1); 4962]   σής
σῆς   gen sg fem [3t; a-1a(2a); 5050]   σός
σητόβρωτα   nom pl neut
[Jm 5:2; a-3a; 4963]   σητόβρωτος

σητόβρωτος, ον   {4963, a-3a}
moth-eaten, James 5:2*

σθενόω   {4964, v-1d(3)}
[σθενώσω, -, -, -, -] *to strengthen, impart strength,*
1 Peter 5:10*

σθενώσει   fut act ind 3 sg
[1P 5:10; v-1d(3); 4964]   σθενόω
σιαγόνα   acc sg fem [2t; n-3f(1b); 4965]   σιαγών

σιαγών, όνος, ἡ   {4965, n-3f(1b)}
the jaw-bone; in N.T. *the cheek,* Matt 5:39; Luke
6:29*

σιαίνομαι   {4966}
[-, -, -, -, -] *to be disturbed, annoyed,* 1 Thess 3:13
v.l.*

σιγᾶν   pres act inf
[Ac 12:17; v-1d(1a); 4967]   σιγάω
σιγάτω   pres act imperative 3 sg
[2t; v-1d(1a); 4967]   "
σιγάτωσαν   pres act imperative 3 pl
[1C 14:34; v-1d(1a); 4967]   "

σιγάω   {4967, v-1d(1a)}
[-, ἐσίγησα, -, σεσίγημαι, -] *to be silent, keep
silence,* Luke 9:36; 20:26; Acts 15:12f.; 1 Cor
14:28, 30, 34; Luke 18:39; trans. *to keep in silence,
not to reveal, to conceal;* pass. *to be concealed, not
to be revealed,* Rom 16:25*

σιγή, ῆς, ἡ   {4968, n-1b}
silence, Acts 21:40; Rev 8:1*

σιγή   nom sg fem [Rv 8:1; n-1b; 4968]   σιγή
σιγῆς   gen sg fem [Ac 21:40; n-1b; 4968]   "
σιγῆσαι   aor act inf
[Ac 15:13; v-1d(1a); 4967]   σιγάω
σιγήσῃ   aor act subj 3 sg
[Lk 18:39; v-1d(1a); 4967]   "
σιδηρᾷ   dat sg fem [3t; a-1b; 4971]   σιδηροῦς
σιδηρᾶν   acc sg fem [Ac 12:10; a-1b; 4971]   "

σίδηρεος, uncontracted form of σιδηροῦς   {4969}

σίδηρος, ου, ὁ   {4970, n-2a}
iron, Rev 18:12*

σιδήρου   gen sg masc
[Rv 18:12; n-2a; 4970]   σίδηρος

σιδηροῦς, ᾶ, οῦν   {4971, a-1b}
Acts 12:10; Rev 2:27; 9:9; 12:5; 19:15*

σιδηροῦς   acc pl masc
[Rv 9:9; a-1b; 4971]   σιδηροῦς

Σιδών, ῶνος, ἡ   {4972, n-3f(1a)}
Sidon, a celebrated city of Phoenicia, Matt
11:21f.; Mark 3:8; 7:31; Luke 6:17; Acts 27:3

Σιδῶνα   acc sg fem [2t; n-3f(1a); 4972]   Σιδών
Σιδῶνι   dat sg fem [4t; n-3f(1a); 4972]   "
Σιδωνίας   gen sg fem
[Lk 4:26; a-1a(1); 4973]   Σιδώνιος
Σιδωνίοις   dat pl masc [Ac 12:20; a-1a(1); 4973]   "

Σιδώνιος, ία, ιον   {4973, a-1a(1)}
Sidonian; an inhabitant of Σιδών, *Sidon,* Acts
12:20; Luke 4:26*

Σιδῶνος   gen sg fem [3t; n-3f(1a); 4972]   Σιδών

σικάριος, ου, ὁ   {4974, n-2a}
an assassin, bandit, robber, Acts 21:38*

σικαρίων   gen pl masc
[Ac 21:38; n-2a; 4974]   σικάριος

σίκερα, τό   {4975, n-3g(2)}
strong or *inebriating drink,* Luke 1:15*

σίκερα   indecl [Lk 1:15; n-3g(2); 4975]   σίκερα
Σιλᾷ   dat sg masc [2t; n-1e; 4976]   Σίλας
Σίλαν   acc sg masc [6t; n-1e; 4976]   "

Σίλας, ᾶ, ὁ   {4976, n-1e}
Silas, pr. name, in Luke, Acts 15:22; see
Σιλουανός

Σιλᾶς   nom sg masc [4t; n-1e; 4976]   "

Σιλουανός, οῦ, ὁ   {4977, n-2a}
Silvanus, pr. name, 2 Cor 1:19; 1 Thess 1:1; 2
Thess 1:1; 1 Peter 5:12, see Σίλας*

Σιλουανός   nom sg masc [2t; n-2a; 4977] Σιλουανός
Σιλουανοῦ   gen sg masc [2t; n-2a; 4977]   "

Σιλωάμ, ὁ   {4978, n-3g(2)}
Siloam, a pool or fountain near Jerusalem, Luke
13:4; John 9:7, 11*

Σιλωάμ   indecl [3t; n-3g(2); 4978]   Σιλωάμ

Σιμαίας, ου, ὁ   {4979, n-1d}
Simaias, 2 Tim 4:19 v.l.*

Σιμεών, see Συμεών

σιμικίνθια   acc pl neut
[Ac 19:12; n-2c; 4980]   σιμικίνθιον

σιμικίνθιον, ου, τό   {4980, n-2c}
an apron, Acts 19:12*

Σίμων, ῶνος, ὁ   {4981, n-3f(1a)}
Simon, pr. name. (1) *Simon Peter,* Matt 4:18. (2)
Simon (the Canaanite) the Zealot, Matt 10:4; Acts
1:13 . (3) *Simon, brother of Jesus,* Matt 13:55;
Mark 6:3. (4) *Simon, the leper,* Matt 26:6; Mark
14:3. (5) *Simon, the Pharisee,* Luke 7:40. (6) *Simon
of Cyrene,* Matt 27:32. (7) *Simon, father of Judas
Iscariot,* John 6:71; 12:4 v.l. (8) *Simon, the sorcerer,*
Acts 8:9. (9) *Simon, the tanner, of Joppa,* Acts 9:43;
10:6

Σίμων   nom sg masc [27t; n-3f(1a); 4981]   Σίμων
Σίμων   voc sg masc [9t; n-3f(1a); 4981]   "

Σίμωνα   acc sg masc [16t; n-3f(1a); 4981]   "
Σίμωνι   dat sg masc [7t; n-3f(1a); 4981]   "
Σίμωνος gen sg masc [16t; n-3f(1a); 4981]   "

Σινά   {4982, n-3g(2)}
Mount Sinai, in Arabia, Acts 7:30, 38; Gal 4:24,
25*

Σινᾶ indecl [4t; n-3g(2); 4982]   Σινά
σινάπεως gen sg neut [5t; n-3e(5b); 4983] σίναπι

σίναπι, εως, ἡ   {4983, n-3e(5b)}
mustard; in N.T. probably the shrub, not the
herb, Khardal, Salvadora Persica L., the fruit of
which possesses the pungency of mustard,
Matt 13:31; 17:20; Mark 4:31; Luke 13:19; 17:6*

σινδόνα acc sg fem [3t; n-3f(1b); 4984]   σινδών
σινδόνι dat sg fem [3t; n-3f(1b); 4984]   "

σινδών, όνος, ἡ   {4984, n-3f(1b)}
sindon; pr. fine Indian cloth; fine linen; in N.T. a
linen garment, an upper garment or wrapper of fine
linen, worn in summer by night, and used to
envelope dead bodies, Matt 27:59; Mark 14:51,
52; 15:46; Luke 23:53*

σινιάζω   {4985, v-2a(1)}
[-, ἐσινίασα, -, -, -] to sift; met. to sift by trials
and temptations, Luke 22:31*

σινιάσαι aor act inf
   [Lk 22:31; v-2a(1); 4985]   σινιάζω

σιρικός, ή, όν   {4986, a-1a(2a)}
see also σηρικός, silk, of silk, silken; τὸ σηρικόν,
silken stuff, Rev 18:12*

σιρικοῦ gen sg neut
   [Rv 18:12; a-1a(2a); 4986]   σιρικός

σιρός, οῦ, ὁ   {4987, n-2a}
pit, cave, 2 Peter 2:4 v.l.*

σιτευτόν acc sg masc
   [3t; a-1a(2a); 4988]   σιτευτός

σιτευτός, ή, όν   {4988, a-1a(2a)}
fed, fatted, Luke 15:23, 27, 30*

σιτία acc pl neut [Ac 7:12; n-2c; 4989]   σιτίον

σιτίον, ου, τό   {4989, n-2c}
provision of corn, food, Acts 7:12*

σιτιστά nom pl neut
   [Mt 22:4; a-1a(2a); 4990]   σιτιστός

σιτιστός, ή, όν   {4990, a-1a(2a)}
fatted, a fatling, cattle, Matt 22:4*

σιτομέτριον, ου, τό   {4991, n-2c}
a certain measure of grain distributed for food at
set times to the slaves of a family, a ration, Luke
12:42*

σιτομέτριον acc sg neut
   [Lk 12:42; n-2c; 4991]   σιτομέτριον
σῖτον acc sg masc [9t; n-2a; 4992]   σῖτος

σῖτος, ου, ὁ   {4992, n-2a}
corn, grain, wheat, Matt 3:12; 13:25, 29, 30; Mark
4:28; pl. σῖτα, bread, food, Acts 7:12 v.l.

σίτου gen sg masc [5t; n-2a; 4992]   "

Σιχέμ , see Συχέμ   {4993}

Σιών, ἡ   {4994, n-3g(2)}
Zion, Mt. Zion, a hill within the city of Jerusalem,
indecl., Heb 12:22; Rev 14:1; poetic use, Matt
21:5; John 12:15; people of Israel, Rom 9:33; 11:26;
new Jerusalem of Christianity, 1 Peter 2:6*

Σιών indecl [7t; n-3g(2); 4994]   Σιών
σιώπα pres act imperative 2 sg
   [Mk 4:39; v-1d(1a); 4995]   σιωπάω

σιωπάω   {4995, v-1d(1a)}
[(ἐσιώπων), σιωπήσω, ἐσιώπησα, -, -, -] to be
silent, keep silence, hold one's peace, Matt 20:31;
26:63; Mark 3:4; 9:34; 10:48; 14:61; Luke 18:39
v.l.; 19:40; Acts 18:9; σιωπῶν, silent, dumb, Luke
1:20; met. to be silent, still, hushed, calm, as the
sea, Mark 4:39*

σιωπῇ   {4996, adverb}
an adverb formed from the dat. of σιωπή, ῆς, ἡ,
which does not occur in the N.T., quietly,
privately, John 11:28 v.l.*

σιωπήσῃ aor act subj 3 sg
   [Mk 10:48; v-1d(1a); 4995]   "
σιωπήσῃς aor act subj 2 sg
   [Ac 18:9; v-1d(1a); 4995]   "
σιωπήσουσιν fut act ind 3 pl
   [Lk 19:40; v-1d(1a); 4995]   "
σιωπήσωσιν aor act subj 3 pl
   [Mt 20:31; v-1d(1a); 4995]   "
σιωπῶν pres act ptcp nom sg masc
   [Lk 1:20; v-1d(1a); 4995]   "

σκάνδαλα acc pl neut [4t; n-2c; 4998]   σκάνδαλον
σκανδαλίζει pres act ind 3 sg
   [6t; v-2a(1); 4997]   σκανδαλίζω
σκανδαλίζεται pres pass ind 3 sg
   [2t; v-2a(1); 4997]   "
σκανδαλίζῃ pres act subj 3 sg
   [3t; v-2a(1); 4997]   "
σκανδαλίζονται pres pass ind 3 pl
   [Mk 4:17; v-2a(1); 4997]   "

σκανδαλίζω   {4997, v-2a(1)}
[-, ἐσκανδάλισα, -, ἐσκανδάλισμαι,
ἐσκανδαλίσθην] pr. to cause to stumble; met.
offend, Matt 17:27; to offend, shock, excite feeling of
repugnance, John 6:61; 1 Cor 8:13; pass. to be
offended, shocked, pained, Matt 15:12; Rom 14:21;
2 Cor 11:29; σκανδαλίζεσθαι ἔν τινι, to be affected
with scruples of repugnance towards any one as
respects his claims or pretensions, Matt 11:6;
13:57; met. to cause to stumble morally, to cause to
falter or err, Matt 5:29; 18:6; pass. to falter, fall
away, Matt 13:21

σκανδαλίσῃ aor act subj 3 sg
   [3t; v-2a(1); 4997]   "
σκανδαλισθῇ aor pass subj 3 sg
   [2t; v-2a(1); 4997]   "
σκανδαλισθήσεσθε fut pass ind 2 pl
   [2t; v-2a(1); 4997]   "
σκανδαλισθήσομαι fut pass ind 1 sg
   [Mt 26:33; v-2a(1); 4997]   "
σκανδαλισθήσονται fut pass ind 3 pl
   [3t; v-2a(1); 4997]   "

σκανδαλισθῆτε   aor pass subj 2 pl
[Jn 16:1; v-2a(1); 4997]   "

σκανδαλίσω   aor act subj 1 sg
[1C 8:13; v-2a(1); 4997]   "

σκανδαλίσωμεν   aor act subj 1 pl
[Mt 17:27; v-2a(1); 4997]   "

σκάνδαλον, ου, τό   {4998, n-2c}
pr. *a trap-spring;* also genr. *a stumbling-block,
anything against which one stumbles, an
impediment;* met. *a cause of ruin, destruction,
misery,* etc., Rom 9:33; 11:9; 1 Peter 2:8; *a cause* or
occasion of sinning, Matt 16:23; 18:7 (3t); Luke
17:1; Rom 14:13; 16:17; Rev 2:14; *scandal, offence,
cause of indignation,* Matt 13:41; 1 Cor 1:23; Gal
5:11; 1 John 2:10*

σκάνδαλον   nom sg neut [4t; n-2c; 4998] σκάνδαλον
σκάνδαλον   acc sg neut [4t; n-2c; 4998]   "
σκανδάλου   gen sg neut [2t; n-2c; 4998]   "
σκανδάλων   gen pl neut [Mt 18:7; n-2c; 4998]   "
σκάπτειν   pres act inf
[Lk 16:3; v-4; 4999]   σκάπτω

σκάπτω   {4999, v-4}
[σκάψω, ἔσκαψα, -, ἔσκαμμαι, ἐσκάφην] *to dig,
excavate,* Luke 6:48; 13:8; 16:3*

Σκαριώθ, v.l. for Ἰσκαριώθ in Mark 3:19 and John
6:71*   {5000}

σκάφη, ης, ἡ   {5002, n-1b}
pr. *anything excavated* or *hollowed; a boat, skiff,*
Acts 27:16, 30, 32*

σκάφην   acc sg fem [Ac 27:30; n-1b; 5002]   σκάφη
σκάφης   gen sg fem [2t; n-1b; 5002]   "
σκάψω   aor act subj 1 sg
[Lk 13:8; v-4; 4999]   σκάπτω
σκέλη   acc pl neut [3t; n-3d(2b); 5003]   σκέλος

σκέλος, ους, τό   {5003, n-3d(2b)}
the leg, John 19:31, 32, 33*

σκέπασμα, ατος, τό   {5004, n-3c(4)}
covering; clothing, raiment, 1 Tim 6:8*

σκεπάσματα   acc pl neut
[1Ti 6:8; n-3c(4); 5004]   σκέπασμα
Σκευᾶ   gen sg masc [Ac 19:14; n-1e; 5005]   Σκευᾶς

Σκευᾶς, ᾶ, ὁ   {5005, n-1e}
Sceva, pr. name, Acts 19:14*

σκεύει   dat sg neut [2t; n-3d(2b); 5007]   σκεῦος
σκεύεσιν   dat pl neut [2C 4:7; n-3d(2b); 5007]   "

σκευή, ῆς, ἡ   {5006, n-1b}
apparatus; tackle, Acts 27:19*

σκεύη   nom pl neut [3t; n-3d(2b); 5007]   "
σκεύη   acc pl neut [5t; n-3d(2b); 5007]   "
σκευήν   acc sg fem [Ac 27:19; n-1b; 5006]   σκευή

σκεῦος, ους, τό   {5007, n-3d(2b)}
a vessel, utensil for containing anything, Mark
11:16; Luke 8:16; Rom 9:21; *any utensil,
instrument;* σκεύη, *household stuff, furniture,
goods,* etc., Matt 12:29; Mark 3:27; *the mast of a
ship,* or, *the sail,* Acts 27:17; met. *an instrument,
means, organ, minister,* Acts 9:15; σκεύη ὀργῆς

and σκεύη ἐλέους, *vessels of wrath,* or, *of mercy,
persons visited by punishment,* or, *the divine favor,*
Rom 9:22, 23; *the vessel* or *frame* of the human
individual, 1 Thess 4:4; 1 Peter 3:7

σκεῦος   nom sg neut [4t; n-3d(2b); 5007]   σκεῦος
σκεῦος   acc sg neut [8t; n-3d(2b); 5007]   "
σκηναῖς   dat pl fem [Hb 11:9; n-1b; 5008]   σκηνή
σκηνάς   acc pl fem [4t; n-1b; 5008]   "
σκήνει   dat sg neut
[2C 5:4; n-3d(2b); 5011]   σκῆνος

σκηνή, ῆς, ἡ   {5008, n-1b}
a tent, tabernacle; genr. *any temporary dwelling; a
tent, booth,* Matt 17:4; Heb 11:9; *the tabernacle* of
the covenant, Heb 8:5; 9:1, 21; 13:10; allegor. *the*
celestial or true *tabernacle,* Heb 8:2; 9:11; *a
division* or *compartment of the tabernacle,* Heb 9:2,
3, 6; *a small portable tent* or *shrine,* Acts 7:43; *an
abode* or *seat* of a lineage, Acts 15:16; *a mansion,
habitation, abode, dwelling,* Luke 16:9; Rev 13:6

σκηνή   nom sg fem [4t; n-1b; 5008]   σκηνή
σκηνῇ   dat sg fem [Hb 13:10; n-1b; 5008]   "
σκηνήν   acc sg fem [6t; n-1b; 5008]   "
σκηνῆς   gen sg fem [4t; n-1b; 5008]   "

σκηνοπηγία, ας, ἡ   {5009, n-1a}
pr. *a pitching of tents* or *booths;* hence, *the feast of
tabernacles* or *booths,* instituted in memory of
the forty years' wandering of the Israelites in
the desert, and as a season of gratitude for the
ingathering of harvest, celebrated for eight
days, commencing on the 15th of Tisri, John 5:1
v.l.; 7:2*

σκηνοπηγία   nom sg fem
[Jn 7:2; n-1a; 5009]   σκηνοπηγία
σκηνοποιοί   nom pl masc
[Ac 18:3; n-2a; 5010]   σκηνοποιός

σκηνοποιός, οῦ, ὁ   {5010, n-2a}
a tent-maker, Acts 18:3*

σκῆνος, ους, τό   {5011, n-3d(2b)}
a tent, tabernacle, lodging; met. *the* corporeal
tabernacle, 2 Cor 5:1, 4*

σκηνοῦντας   pres act ptcp acc pl masc
[Rv 13:6; v-1d(3); 5012]   σκηνόω
σκηνοῦντες   pres act ptcp voc pl masc
[Rv 12:12; v-1d(3); 5012]   "
σκήνους   gen sg neut
[2C 5:1; n-3d(2b); 5011]   σκῆνος

σκηνόω   {5012, v-1d(3)}
[σκηνώσω, ἐσκήνωσα, -, -, -] *to pitch tent,
encamp; to tabernacle, dwell in a tent; to dwell, have
one's abode,* John 1:14; Rev 7:15; 12:12; 13:6; 21:3*

σκήνωμα, ατος, τό   {5013, n-3c(4)}
a habitation, abode, dwelling, Acts 7:46; *the*
corporeal *tabernacle* of the soul, 2 Peter 1:13, 14*

σκήνωμα   acc sg neut
[Ac 7:46; n-3c(4); 5013]   σκήνωμα
σκηνώματι   dat sg neut [2P 1:13; n-3c(4); 5013]   "
σκηνώματος   gen sg neut [2P 1:14; n-3c(4); 5013]   "
σκηνώσει   fut act ind 3 sg
[2t; v-1d(3); 5012]   σκηνόω

σκιά, ᾶς, ἡ   {5014, n-1a}
a shade, shadow, Mark 4:32; Acts 5:15; met. *a shadow, a foreshadowing, a vague outline*, in distinction from ἡ εἰκών, the perfect image or delineation, and τὸ σῶμα, the reality, Col 2:17; Heb 8:5; 10:1; *gloom*; σκιὰ θανάτου, *death-shade, the thickest darkness*, Matt 4:16; Luke 1:79; 1 John 2:8 v.l.*

σκιά   nom sg fem [2t; n-1a; 5014]   σκιά
σκιᾷ   dat sg fem [3t; n-1a; 5014]   "
σκιάν   acc sg fem [2t; n-1a; 5014]   "

σκιρτάω   {5015, v-1d(1a)}
[-, ἐσκίρτησα, -, -, -] *to leap*, Luke 1:41, 44; *to leap, skip, bound* for joy, Luke 6:23*

σκιρτήσατε   aor act imperative 2 pl
    [Lk 6:23; v-1d(1a); 5015]   σκιρτάω

σκληροκαρδία, ας, ἡ   {5016, n-1a}
hardness of heart, obstinacy, perverseness, Matt 19:8; Mark 10:5; 16:14*

σκληροκαρδίαν   acc sg fem
    [3t; n-1a; 5016]   σκληροκαρδία
σκληρόν   nom sg neut
    [Ac 26:14; a-1a(1); 5017]   σκληρός

σκληρός, ά, όν   {5017, a-1a(1)}
dry, hard to the touch; met. *harsh, severe, stern*, Matt 25:24; *vehement, violent, fierce*, James 3:4; *grievous, painful*, Acts 9:4 v.l.; 26:14; *grating* to the mind, *repulsive, offensive*, John 6:60; *stubborn, resistance to authority*, Jude 15*

σκληρός   nom sg masc [2t; a-1a(1); 5017]   "

σκληρότης, ητος, ἡ   {5018, n-3c(1)}
hardness; met. σκληρότης τῆς καρδίας, *hardness of heart, obstinacy, perverseness*, Rom 2:5*

σκληρότητα   acc sg fem
    [Rm 2:5; n-3c(1); 5018]   σκληρότης
σκληροτράχηλοι   voc pl masc
    [Ac 7:51; a-3a; 5019]   σκληροτράχηλος

σκληροτράχηλος, ον   {5019, a-3a}
stiff-necked, obstinate, Acts 7:51*

σκληρύνει   pres act ind 3 sg
    [Rm 9:18; v-1c(2); 5020]   σκληρύνω
σκληρύνητε   aor act subj 2 pl [3t; v-1c(2); 5020]   "
σκληρυνθῇ   aor pass subj 3 sg
    [Hb 3:13; v-1c(2); 5020]   "

σκληρύνω   {5020, v-1c(2)}
[(ἐσκλήρυνον), σκληρυνῶ, ἐσκλήρυνα, -, -, ἐσκληρύνθην] *to harden*; met. *to harden* morally, *to make stubborn*, Heb 3:8, 15; 4:7; as a negation of ἐλεεῖν, *to leave to stubbornness and contumacy*, Rom 9:18; mid. and pass. *to put on a stubborn frame*, Acts 19:9; Heb 3:13*

σκληρῶν   gen pl masc
    [Jm 3:4; a-1a(1); 5017]   σκληρός
σκληρῶν   gen pl neut [Jd 15; a-1a(1); 5017]   "
σκολιά   nom pl neut
    [Lk 3:5; a-1a(1); 5021]   σκολιός
σκολιᾶς   gen sg fem [2t; a-1a(1); 5021]   "
σκολιοῖς   dat pl masc [1P 2:18; a-1a(1); 5021]   "

σκολιός, ά, όν   {5021, a-1a(1)}
crooked, tortuous, Luke 3:5; met. *perverse, wicked*, Acts 2:40; Phil 2:15; *crooked, peevish, morose*, 1 Peter 2:18*

σκόλοψ, οπος, ὁ   {5022, n-3a(1)}
anything pointed; met. *a thorn, a plague*, 2 Cor 12:7*

σκόλοψ   nom sg masc
    [2C 12:7; n-3a(1); 5022]   σκόλοψ
σκόπει   pres act imperative 2 sg
    [Lk 11:35; v-1d(2a); 5023]   σκοπέω
σκοπεῖν   pres act inf [Rm 16:17; v-1d(2a); 5023]   "
σκοπεῖτε   pres act imperative 2 pl
    [Pp 3:17; v-1d(2a); 5023]   "

σκοπέω   {5023, v-1d(2a)}
[σκοπήσω, ἐσκόπησα, -, ἐσκόπημαι, -] *to view attentively, watch; to see, observe, take care, beware*, Luke 11:35; Gal 6:1; *to regard, have respect to*, 2 Cor 4:18; Phil 2:4; *to mark, note*, Rom 16:17; Phil 3:17*

σκοπόν   acc sg masc [Pp 3:14; n-2a; 5024]   σκοπός

σκοπός, οῦ, ὁ   {5024, n-2a}
also, *a watcher*; also, *a distant object on which the eye is kept fixed; a mark, goal*, Phil 3:14*

σκοποῦντες   pres act ptcp nom pl masc
    [Pp 2:4; v-1d(2a); 5023]   σκοπέω
σκοπούντων   pres act ptcp gen pl masc
    [2C 4:18; v-1d(2a); 5023]   "
σκοπῶν   pres act ptcp nom sg masc
    [Ga 6:1; v-1d(2a); 5023]   "
σκορπίζει   pres act ind 3 sg
    [3t; v-2a(1); 5025]   σκορπίζω

σκορπίζομαι   {5025, v-2a(1)}
[-, ἐσκόρπισα, -, -, ἐσκορπίσθην] some list as active σκορπίζω, *to disperse, scatter*, John 10:12; 16:32; *to dissipate, waste*, Matt 12:30; Luke 11:23; *to scatter abroad* one's gifts, *give liberally*, 2 Cor 9:9*

σκορπίοι   nom pl masc
    [Rv 9:3; n-2a; 5026]   σκορπίος
σκορπίοις   dat pl masc [Rv 9:10; n-2a; 5026]   "
σκορπίον   acc sg masc [Lk 11:12; n-2a; 5026]   "

σκορπίος, ου, ὁ   {5026, n-2a}
a scorpion, a large insect, sometimes several inches in length, shaped somewhat like a crab and furnished with a tail terminating in a stinger from which it emits a dangerous poison, Luke 10:19; 11:12; Rev 9:3, 5, 10*

σκορπίου   gen sg masc [Rv 9:5; n-2a; 5026]   "
σκορπισθῆτε   aor pass subj 2 pl
    [Jn 16:32; v-2a(1); 5025]   σκορπίζω
σκορπίων   gen pl masc
    [Lk 10:19; n-2a; 5026]   σκορπίος
σκότει   dat sg neut [5t; n-3d(2b); 5030]   σκότος
σκοτεινόν   nom sg neut
    [2t; a-1a(2a); 5027]   σκοτεινός
σκοτεινόν   acc sg neut [Lk 11:36; a-1a(2a); 5027]   "

σκοτεινός, ή, όν   {5027, a-1a(2a)}
dark, darkling, Matt 6:23; Luke 11:34, 36*

σκοτία, ας, ἡ   {5028, n-1a}
darkness, John 6:17; 20:1; *privacy,* Matt 10:27;
Luke 12:3; met. moral or spiritual *darkness,*
John 1:5 (2t); 8:12; 12:35, 46; Matt 4:16 v.l.; 1
John 1:5; 2:8, 9, 11*

σκοτία   nom sg fem [6t; n-1a; 5028]   σκοτία
σκοτίᾳ   dat sg fem [9t; n-1a; 5028]   "
σκοτίας gen sg fem [Jn 20:1; n-1a; 5028]   "

σκοτίζομαι   {5029, v-2a(1)}
[-, -, -, ἐσκότισμαι, ἐσκοτίσθην] some list as the
active σκοτίζω, *to darken, shroud in darkness;*
pass. *to be darkened, obscured,* Matt 24:29; Mark
13:24; Luke 23:45 v.l.; Rev 8:12; met. *to be
shrouded in* moral *darkness,* Rom 1:21; 11:10;
Eph 4:18 v.l.

σκοτισθῇ   aor pass subj 3 sg
   [Rv 8:12; v-2a(1); 5029]   σκοτίζω
σκοτισθήσεται   fut pass ind 3 sg
   [2t; v-2a(1); 5029]   "
σκοτισθήτωσαν   aor pass imperative 3 pl
   [Rm 11:10; v-2a(1); 5029]   "

σκότος, ους, τό   {5030, n-3d(2b)}
darkness, Matt 27:45; Acts 2:20; *gloom* of
punishment and misery, Matt 8:12; 2 Peter 2:17;
met. moral or spiritual *darkness,* Matt 4:16; John
3:19; Eph 5:11; *a realm of* moral *darkness,* Eph
5:8; 6:12; Heb 12:8 v.l.

σκότος nom sg neut [8t; n-3d(2b); 5030]   σκότος
σκότος acc sg neut [6t; n-3d(2b); 5030]   "
σκότους gen sg neut [12t; n-3d(2b); 5030]   "

σκοτόω   {5031, v-1d(3)}
[-, -, -, ἐσκότωμαι, ἐσκοτώθην] *to darken, shroud
in darkness,* Eph 4:18; Rev 9:2; 16:10

σκύβαλα   acc pl neut [Pp 3:8; n-2c; 5032] σκύβαλον

σκύβαλον, ου, τό   {5032, n-2c}
dung, sweepings, refuse, rubbish, Phil 3:8*

Σκύθης, ου, ὁ   {5033, n-1f}
A Scythian, a native of Scythia, the modern
Mongolia and Tartary, Col 3:11*

Σκύθης   nom sg masc [Cl 3:11; n-1f; 5033]   Σκύθης
σκυθρωποί   nom pl masc
   [2t; a-3b(2); 5034]   σκυθρωπός

σκυθρωπός, (ή), όν   {5034, a-3b(2)}
of a stern, morose, sour, gloomy, or *dejected
countenance,* Matt 6:16; Luke 24:17*

σκῦλα   acc pl neut [Lk 11:22; n-2c; 5036]   σκῦλον
σκύλλε   pres act imperative 2 sg
   [Lk 8:49; v-2d(1); 5035]   σκύλλω
σκύλλεις   pres act ind 2 sg
   [Mk 5:35; v-2d(1); 5035]   "
σκύλλου   pres pass imperative 2 sg
   [Lk 7:6; v-2d(1); 5035]   "

σκύλλω   {5035, v-2d(1)}
[-, -, -, ἔσκυλμαι, -] *to flay, lacerate;* met. *to vex,
trouble, annoy,* Mark 5:35; Luke 7:6; 8:49; pass.
met. ἐσκυλμένοι, *in sorry plight,* Matt 9:36*

σκῦλον, ου, τό   {5036, n-2c}
spoils stripped off an enemy; σκῦλα, *spoil, plunder,
booty,* Luke 11:22*

σκωληκόβρωτος, ον   {5037, a-3a}
eaten of worms, consumed by worms, Acts 12:23*

σκωληκόβρωτος   nom sg masc
   [Ac 12:23; a-3a; 5037]   σκωληκόβρωτος

σκώληξ, ηκος, ὁ   {5038, n-3b(1)}
a worm; met. *gnawing anguish,* Mark 9:44 v.l., 46
v.l., 48*

σκώληξ   nom sg masc
   [Mk 9:48; n-3b(1); 5038]   σκώληξ

σμαράγδινος, η, ον   {5039, a-1a(2a)}
of smaragdus or *emerald,* Rev 4:3*

σμαραγδίνῳ   dat sg masc
   [Rv 4:3; a-1a(2a); 5039]   σμαράγδινος

σμάραγδος, ου, ὁ   {5040, n-2a}
smaragdus, the emerald, a gem of a pure green
color; but under this name the ancients
probably comprised all stones of a fine green
color, Rev 21:19*

σμάραγδος   nom sg masc
   [Rv 21:19; n-2a; 5040]   σμάραγδος

σμύρνα, ης, ἡ   {5043, n-1c}
myrrh, an aromatic bitter resin, or gum, issuing
by incision, and sometimes spontaneously,
from the trunk and larger branches of a small
thorny tree growing in Egypt, Arabia, and
Abyssinia, much used by the ancients in
unguents, Matt 2:11; John 19:39*

Σμύρνα, ης, ἡ   {5044, n-1c}
Smyrna, a maritime city of Ionia, in Asia Minor,
Rev 1:11; 2:8*

Σμυρναῖος, α, ον   {5045, a-1a(1)}
Smyrnean; an inhabitant of Smyrna, Rev 2:8 v.l.*

σμύρναν acc sg fem [2t; n-1c; 5043]   σμύρνα
Σμύρνῃ   dat sg fem [Rv 2:8; n-1c; 5044]   Σμύρνα
σμύρνης gen sg fem [Jn 19:39; n-1c; 5043]   σμύρνα

σμυρνίζω   {5046, v-2a(1)}
[-, -, -, ἐσμύρνισμαι, -] *to mingle* or *flavor with
myrrh,* Mark 15:23*

Σόδομα, ων, τό   {5047, n-2c}
Sodom, (Gen. 19:24) one of the four cities of the
vale of Siddim, now covered by the Dead sea,
Matt 11:23f.; Luke 17:29; Rom 9:29; 2 Peter 2:6;
Rev 11:8

Σόδομα   nom pl neut [3t; n-2c; 5047]   Σόδομα
Σοδόμοις dat pl neut [2t; n-2c; 5047]   "
Σοδόμων   gen pl neut [4t; n-2c; 5047]   "
σοί   nom pl masc [2t; a-1a(2a); 5050]   σός
σοι   dat sg [215t; a-5a; 5148]   σύ

Σολομών, ῶνος, ὁ   {5048, n-3c(5b)}
Solomon, also spelled Σολομῶν, ῶντος, ο
(n-3f[1a]), pr. name, son and successor of
David, Matt 1:6f.; 6:29; Luke 11:31; John 10:23;
Acts 3:11; 7:47

Σολομών   nom sg masc [4t; n-3c(5b); 5048] Σολομών

Σολομῶνα   acc sg masc [Mt 1:6; n-3c(5b); 5048]   "
Σολομῶνος   gen sg masc [5t; n-3c(5b); 5048]   "
Σολομῶντος   gen sg masc [2t; n-3c(5b); 5048]   "
σόν   nom sg neut [2t; a-1a(2a); 5050]   σός
σόν   acc sg neut [2t; a-1a(2a); 5050]   "

σορός, οῦ, ἡ   {5049, n-2b}
a coffer; an urn for receiving the ashes of the dead; a coffin; in N.T. *a bier,* Luke 7:14*

σοροῦ   gen sg fem [Lk 7:14; n-2b; 5049]   σορός

σός, ἡ, όν   {5050, a-1a(2a)}
yours, Matt 7:3, 22; οἱ σοί, *your kindred, friends,* etc., Mark 5:19; τὸ σόν and τὰ σά, *what is yours, your property, goods,* etc., Matt 20:14; 25:25; Luke 6:30

σός   nom sg masc [Jn 17:17; a-1a(2a); 5050]   σός
σου   gen sg [481t; a-5a; 5148]   σύ
σουδάρια   acc pl neut
    [Ac 19:12; n-2c; 5051]   σουδάριον

σουδάριον, ου, τό   {5051, n-2c}
a handkerchief, napkin, etc., Luke 19:20; John 11:44; 20:7; Acts 19:12*

σουδάριον   acc sg neut [Jn 20:7; n-2c; 5051]   "
σουδαρίῳ   dat sg neut [2t; n-2c; 5051]   "
σούς   acc pl masc [Mk 5:19; a-1a(2a); 5050]   σός

Σουσάννα, ης, ἡ   {5052, n-1a}
Susanna, pr. name, Luke 8:3*

Σουσάννα   nom sg fem [Lk 8:3; n-1a; 5052]
    Σουσάννα

σοφία, ας, ἡ   {5053, n-1a}
wisdom in general, *knowledge,* Matt 12:42; Luke 2:40, 52; 11:31; Acts 7:10; *ability,* Luke 21:15; Acts 6:3, 10; practical *wisdom, prudence,* Col 4:5; *learning, science,* Matt 13:54; Mark 6:2; Acts 7:22; scientific *skill,* 1 Cor 1:17; 2:1; professed *wisdom,* human *philosophy,* 1 Cor 1:19, 20, 22; 2:4, 5, 6; superior *knowledge and enlightenment,* Col 2:23; in N.T. divine *wisdom,* Rom 11:33; Eph 3:10; Col 2:3; revealed *wisdom,* Matt 11:19; Luke 11:49; 1 Cor 1:24, 30; 2:7; Christian *enlightenment,* 1 Cor 12:8; Eph 1:8, 17; Col 1:9, 28, 3:16; James 1:5; 3:13

σοφία   nom sg fem [12t; n-1a; 5053]   σοφία
σοφίᾳ   dat sg fem [13t; n-1a; 5053]   "
σοφίαν   acc sg fem [14t; n-1a; 5053]   "
σοφίας   gen sg fem [12t; n-1a; 5053]   "

σοφίζω   {5054, v-2a(1)}
[(ἐσόφιζον), -, ἐσόφισα, -, σεσόφισμαι, -] *to make wise, enlighten,* 2 Tim 3:15; mid. *to invent skilfully, devise artfully,* pass. 2 Peter 1:16*

σοφίσαι   aor act inf
    [2Ti 3:15; v-2a(1); 5054]   σοφίζω
σοφοί   nom pl masc [3t; a-1a(2a); 5055]   σοφός
σοφοῖς   dat pl masc [Rm 1:14; a-1a(2a); 5055]   "

σοφός, ἡ, όν   {5055, a-1a(2a)}
wise generally, 1 Cor 1:25; *shrewd, clever,* Rom 16:19; 1 Cor 3:10; 6:5; *learned, intelligent,* Matt 11:25; Rom 1:14, 22; 1 Cor 1:19, 20, 26, 27; 3:18; in N.T. divinely *instructed,* Matt 23:34; *furnished*

with Christian *wisdom,* spiritually *enlightened,* James 3:13; *all-wise,* Rom 16:27; 1 Tim 1:17; Jude 25

σοφός   nom sg masc [6t; a-1a(2a); 5055]   "
σοφούς   acc pl masc [4t; a-1a(2a); 5055]   "
σοφῷ   dat sg masc [Rm 16:27; a-1a(2a); 5055]   "
σοφῶν   gen pl masc [4t; a-1a(2a); 5055]   "
σοφώτερον   nom sg neut comparative
    [1C 1:25; a-1a(2a); 5055]   "

Σπανία, ας, ἡ   {5056, n-1a}
Spain, Rom 15:24, 28*

Σπανίαν   acc sg fem [2t; n-1a; 5056]   Σπανία
σπαράξαν   aor act ptcp nom sg neut
    [Mk 1:26; v-2b; 5057]   σπαράσσω
σπαράξας   aor act ptcp nom sg masc
    [Mk 9:26; v-2b; 5057]   "
σπαράσσει   pres act ind 3 sg
    [Lk 9:39; v-2b; 5057]   "

σπαράσσω   {5057, v-2b}
[-, ἐσπάραξα, -, -, -] pr. *to tear, lacerate;* by impl. *to agitate greatly, convulse, distort by convulsion,* Mark 1:26; 9:20 v.l., 26; Luke 9:39*

σπαργανόω   {5058, v-1d(3)}
[-, ἐσπαργάνωσα, -, ἐσπαργάνωμαι, -] *to swathe, wrap in swaddling-cloths,* Luke 2:7, 12*

σπαρείς   aor pass ptcp nom sg masc
    [4t; v-2d(3); 5062]   σπείρω
σπαρέντες   aor pass ptcp nom pl masc
    [Mk 4:20; v-2d(3); 5062]   "
σπαρῇ   aor pass subj 3 sg [2t; v-2d(3); 5062]   "
σπασάμενος   aor mid ptcp nom sg masc
    [2t; v-1d(1b); 5060]   σπάω

σπαταλάω   {5059, v-1d(1a)}
[-, ἐσπατάλησα, -, -, -] *to live luxuriously, voluptuously, wantonly,* 1 Tim 5:6; James 5:5*

σπαταλῶσα   pres act ptcp nom sg fem
    [1Ti 5:6; v-1d(1a); 5059]   σπαταλάω

σπάω   {5060, v-1d(1b)}
[σπάσω, ἔπασα, -, -, ἐσπάσθην] *to draw, pull; to draw* a sword, Mark 14:47; Acts 16:27*

σπεῖρα, ης, ἡ   {5061, n-1c}
anything twisted or *wreathed, a cord, coil, band,* etc.; *a band of soldiers, company, troop;* used for a Roman *cohort,* about 600 soldiers, Matt 27:27; Acts 10:1; *the temple guard,* John 18:3, 12; Mark 15:16; Acts 21:31; 27:1*

σπεῖρα   nom sg fem [Jn 18:12; n-1c; 5061]   σπεῖρα
σπεῖραι   aor act inf [2t; v-2d(3); 5062]   σπείρω
σπεῖραν   acc sg fem [3t; n-1c; 5061]   σπεῖρα
σπείραντι   aor act ptcp dat sg masc
    [Mt 13:24; v-2d(3); 5062]   σπείρω
σπείραντος   aor act ptcp gen sg masc
    [Mt 13:18; v-2d(3); 5062]   "
σπείρας   aor act ptcp nom sg masc
    [Mt 13:39; v-2d(3); 5062]   "
σπείρει   pres act ind 3 sg
    [Mk 4:14; v-2d(3); 5062]   "
σπείρειν   pres act inf [4t; v-2d(3); 5062]   "
σπείρεις   pres act ind 2 sg [3t; v-2d(3); 5062]   "

σπείρεται   pres pass ind 3 sg   [6t; v-2d(3); 5062]   "

σπείρῃ   pres act subj 3 sg
[Ga 6:7; v-2d(3); 5062]   "

σπείρης   gen sg fem   [3t; n-1c; 5061]   σπεῖρα

σπειρόμενοι   pres pass ptcp nom pl masc
[2t; v-2d(3); 5062]   σπείρω

σπείροντι   pres act ptcp dat sg masc
[2C 9:10; v-2d(3); 5062]   "

σπείρουσιν   pres act ind 3 pl   [2t; v-2d(3); 5062]   "

σπείρω   {5062, v-2d(3)}
[-, ἔσπειρα, -, ἔσπαρμαι, ἐσπάρην] *to sow* seed,
Matt 6:26; 13:3, 4, 18, 24, 25, 27, 37, 39; in N.T.
used with variety of metaphors, Matt 13:19;
25:24; 1 Cor 9:11; 2 Cor 9:6; Gal 6:7

σπείρων   pres act ptcp nom sg masc
[11t; v-2d(3); 5062]   "

σπεκουλάτορα   acc sg masc
[Mk 6:27; n-3f(2b); 5063]   σπεκουλάτωρ

σπεκουλάτωρ, ορος, ὁ   {5063, n-3f(2b)}
a sentinel, life-guardsman, a kind of soldiers who
formed the body-guard of princes, etc., one of
whose duties was to put criminals to death,
Mark 6:27*

σπένδομαι   pres pass ind 1 sg
[2t; v-1b(3); 5064]   σπένδω

σπένδω   {5064, v-1b(3)}
[-, -, -, -, -] *to pour out a libation* or *drink-offering;*
in N.T. mid. *to make a libation of one's self* by
expending energy and life in the service of the
Gospel, Phil 2:17; pass. *to be in the act of being
sacrificed* in the cause of the Gospel, 2 Tim 4:6*

σπέρμα, ατος, τό   {5065, n-3c(4)}
seed, Matt 13:24, 27, 37, 38; *semen virile,* Heb
11:11; *offspring, posterity,* Matt 22:24, 25; John
7:42; *a seed* of future generations, Rom 9:29; in
N.T. met. *a seed* or *principle* of spiritual life, 1
John 3:9; 2 Cor 9:10 v.l.

σπέρμα   nom sg neut   [12t; n-3c(4); 5065]   σπέρμα
σπέρμα   acc sg neut   [12t; n-3c(4); 5065]   "
σπέρμασιν   dat pl neut   [Ga 3:16; n-3c(4); 5065]   "
σπέρματι   dat sg neut   [7t; n-3c(4); 5065]   "
σπέρματος   gen sg neut   [8t; n-3c(4); 5065]   "
σπερμάτων   gen pl neut   [3t; n-3c(4); 5065]   "

σπερμολόγος, ον   {5066, a-3a}
pr. *seed-picking; one who picks up and retails
scraps of information; a gossip; a babbler,* Acts
17:18*

σπερμολόγος   nom sg masc
[Ac 17:18; a-3a; 5066]   σπερμολόγος

σπεύδοντας   pres act ptcp acc pl masc
[2P 3:12; v-1b(3); 5067]   σπεύδω

σπεύδω   {5067, v-1b(3)}
[(ἔσπευδον), -, ἔσπευσα, -, -, -] trans. *to urge on,
impel, quicken; to quicken* in idea, *to be eager for
the arrival of,* 2 Peter 3:12; intrans. *to hasten,
make haste,* Acts 20:16; 22:18; the part. has the
force of an adverb, *quickly, hastily,* Luke 2:16;
19:5, 6*

σπεύσαντες   aor act ptcp nom pl masc
[Lk 2:16; v-1b(3); 5067]   "

σπεύσας   aor act ptcp nom sg masc
[2t; v-1b(3); 5067]   "

σπεῦσον   aor act imperative 2 sg
[Ac 22:18; v-1b(3); 5067]   "

σπήλαια   acc pl neut
[Rv 6:15; n-2c; 5068]   σπήλαιον

σπηλαίοις   dat pl neut   [Hb 11:38; n-2c; 5068]   "

σπήλαιον, ου, τό   {5068, n-2c}
a cave, cavern, den, hideout, Matt 21:13; Mark
11:17; Luke 19:46; John 11:38; Heb 11:38; Rev
6:5*

σπήλαιον   nom sg neut   [Jn 11:38; n-2c; 5068]   "
σπήλαιον   acc sg neut   [3t; n-2c; 5068]   "

σπιλάδες   nom pl fem
[Jd 12; n-3c(2); 5069]   σπιλάς

σπιλάς, άδος, ἡ   {5069, n-3c(2)}
a sharply-cleft portion of rock; in N.T. *a flaw,
stigma,* Jude 12*

σπίλοι   nom pl masc   [2P 2:13; n-2a; 5070]   σπίλος
σπίλον   acc sg masc   [Ep 5:27; n-2a; 5070]   "

σπίλος, ου, ὁ   {5070, n-2a}
a spot, stain, blot; a moral *blemish,* Eph 5:27; 2
Peter 2:13*

σπιλοῦσα   pres act ptcp nom sg fem
[Jm 3:6; v-1d(3); 5071]   σπιλόω

σπιλόω   {5071, v-1d(3)}
[-, -, -, ἐσπίλωμαι, -] *to spot, soil; to contaminate,
defile,* James 3:6; Jude 23*

σπλάγχνα   nom pl neut   [4t; n-2c; 5073]   σπλάγχνον
σπλάγχνα   acc pl neut   [5t; n-2c; 5073]   "

σπλαγχνίζομαι   {5072, v-2a(1)}
[-, -, -, -, ἐσπλαγχνίσθην] *to be moved with pity* or
compassion, Matt 9:36; 14:14; 20:34; Luke 7:13; *to
be compassionate,* Matt 18:27

σπλαγχνίζομαι   pres pass ind 1 sg
[2t; v-2a(1); 5072]   σπλαγχνίζομαι

σπλαγχνισθείς   aor pass ptcp nom sg masc
[4t; v-2a(1); 5072]   "

σπλάγχνοις   dat pl neut   [2t; n-2c; 5073]   σπλάγχνον

σπλάγχνον, ου, τό   {5073, n-2c}
the chief intestines, viscera; the entrails, bowels,
Acts 1:18; met. *the heart, the affections of the heart,
the tender affections,* Luke 1:78; 2 Cor 6:12; 7:15;
Phil 1:8, 2:1; Col 3:12; Phil 7, 20; 1 John 3:17;
meton. *a cherished one, dear as one's self,* Phil 12*

σπόγγον   acc sg masc   [3t; n-2a; 5074]   σπόγγος

σπόγγος, ου, ὁ   {5074, n-2a}
a sponge, Matt 27:48; Mark 15:36; John 19:29*

σποδός, οῦ, ἡ   {5075, n-2b}
ashes, Matt 11:21; Luke 10:13; Heb 9:13*

σποδός   nom sg fem   [Hb 9:13; n-2b; 5075]   σποδός
σποδῷ   dat sg fem   [2t; n-2b; 5075]   "

σπορά, ᾶς, ἡ   {5076, n-1a}
a sowing; seed sown; met. generative *seed,
generation,* 1 Peter 1:23*

σπορᾶς   gen sg fem [1P 1:23; n-1a; 5076]   σπορά

σπόριμος, ον   {5077, a-3a}
sown, fit to be sown; in N.T. τὰ σπόριμα, *fields which are sown, fields of grain, cornfields,* Matt 12:1; Mark 2:23; Luke 6:1*

σπορίμων   gen pl neut [3t; a-3a; 5077]   σπόριμος
σπόρον   acc sg masc [4t; n-2a; 5078]   σπόρος

σπόρος, ου, ὁ   {5078, n-2a}
a sowing; in N.T. *seed, that which is sown,* Mark 4:26, 27; Luke 8:5, 11; met. *the seed sown* in almsgiving, 2 Cor 9:10*

σπόρος   nom sg masc [2t; n-2a; 5078]   "
σπουδάζοντες   pres act ptcp nom pl masc
   [Ep 4:3; v-2a(1); 5079]   σπουδάζω

σπουδάζω   {5079, v-2a(1)}
[σπουδάσω, ἐσπούδασα, ἐσπούδακα, -, -] *to hurry; be bent upon,* Gal 2:10; *to endeavor earnestly, strive,* Eph 4:3

σπουδαῖον   acc sg masc
   [2C 8:22; a-1a(1); 5080]   σπουδαῖος

σπουδαῖος, α, ον   {5080, a-1a(1)}
earnest, eager, forward, zealous, 2 Cor 8:17, 22; as an adv., *earnestly,* 2 Tim 1:17 v.l.*

σπουδαιότερον   acc sg masc comparative
   [2C 8:22; a-1a(1); 5080]   "
σπουδαιότερος   nom sg masc comparative
   [2C 8:17; a-1a(1); 5080]   "
σπουδαιοτέρως   adverb-comparative
   [Pp 2:28; adverb; 5081]   σπουδαίως

σπουδαίως   {5081, adverb}
earnestly, eagerly, diligently, Luke 7:4; 2 Tim 1:17 v.l.; Titus 3:13; compar. σπουδαιοτέρως, *more earnestly, with special urgency,* Phil 2:28

σπουδαίως   adverb [3t; adverb; 5081]   "
σπουδάσατε   aor act imperative 2 pl
   [2t; v-2a(1); 5079]   σπουδάζω
σπούδασον   aor act imperative 2 sg
   [4t; v-2a(1); 5079]   "
σπουδάσω   fut act ind 1 sg
   [2P 1:15; v-2a(1); 5079]   "
σπουδάσωμεν   aor act subj 1 pl
   [Hb 4:11; v-2a(1); 5079]   "

σπουδή, ῆς, ἡ   {5082, n-1b}
haste; μετὰ σπουδῆς, *with haste, hastily, quickly,* Mark 6:25; Luke 1:39; *earnestness, earnest application, diligence, enthusiasm,* Rom 12:8, 11; 2 Cor 7:11, 12; 8:16; 8:7f.

σπουδῇ   dat sg fem [3t; n-1b; 5082]   σπουδή
σπουδήν   acc sg fem [6t; n-1b; 5082]   "
σπουδῆς   gen sg fem [3t; n-1b; 5082]   "
σπυρίδας   acc pl fem [3t; n-3c(2); 5083]   σπυρίς
σπυρίδι   dat sg fem [Ac 9:25; n-3c(2); 5083]   "
σπυρίδων   gen pl fem [Mk 8:20; n-3c(2); 5083]   "

σπυρίς, ίδος, ἡ   {5083, n-3c(2)}
also spelledσφυρίς, *a basket, hand-basket* for provision, Matt 15:37; 16:10; Mark 8:8, 20; Acts 9:25*

στάδιον, ου, τό   {5084, n-2c}
pr. *a fixed standard of measure; a stadium,* the eighth part of a Roman mile, and nearly equal to a furlong, containing 201.45 yards, *about 192 meters,* Luke 24:13; Matt 14:24; John 6:19; 11:18; Rev 14:20; 21:16; *a race-course, a race,* 1 Cor 9:24*

σταδίους   acc pl masc [3t; n-2c; 5084]   στάδιον
σταδίῳ   dat sg neut [1C 9:24; n-2c; 5084]   "
σταδίων   gen pl masc [2t; n-2c; 5084]   "
σταδίων   gen pl neut [Rv 21:16; n-2c; 5084]   "
σταθείς   aor pass ptcp nom sg masc
   [6t; v-6a; 2705]   ἵστημι
σταθέντα   aor pass ptcp acc sg masc
   [Ac 11:13; v-6a; 2705]   "
σταθέντες   aor pass ptcp nom pl masc
   [2t; v-6a; 2705]   "
σταθῇ   aor pass subj 3 sg [Mt 18:16; v-6a; 2705]   "
σταθῆναι   aor pass inf [4t; v-6a; 2705]   "
σταθήσεσθε   fut pass ind 2 pl
   [Mk 13:9; v-6a; 2705]   "
σταθήσεται   fut pass ind 3 sg [5t; v-6a; 2705]   "
σταθῆτε   aor pass subj 2 pl [Cl 4:12; v-6a; 2705]   "

στάμνος, ου, ὁ or **ἡ**   {5085, n-2a}
a wine-jar; a pot, jar, urn, vase, Heb 9:4*

στάμνος   nom sg fem [Hb 9:4; n-2a; 5085]   στάμνος
στάντος   aor act ptcp gen sg masc
   [Ac 24:20; v-6a; 2705]   ἵστημι
στάς   aor act ptcp nom sg masc
   [2t; v-6a; 2705]   "
στᾶσα   aor act ptcp nom sg fem
   [Lk 7:38; v-6a; 2705]   "
στάσει   dat sg fem
   [Mk 15:7; n-3e(5b); 5087]   στάσις
στάσεις   acc pl fem [Ac 24:5; n-3e(5b); 5087]   "
στάσεως   gen sg fem [3t; n-3e(5b); 5087]   "

στασιαστής, οῦ, ὁ   {5086, n-1f}
a partisan, rebel, revolutionary, Matt 15:7*

στασιαστῶν   gen pl masc
   [Mk 15:7; n-1f; 5086]   στασιαστής
στάσιν   acc sg fem [3t; n-3e(5b); 5087]   στάσις

στάσις, εως, ἡ   {5087, n-3e(5b)}
a setting; a standing; an effective *position, an* unimpaired *standing* or *dignity,* Heb 9:8; *a gathered party, a group;* hence, *a tumultuous assemblage, popular outbreak,* Mark 15:7; Acts 19:40; Luke 23:19, 25; *seditious movement,* Acts 24:5; *discord, dispute, dissension,* Acts 15:2; 23:7, 10*

στάσις   nom sg fem [Ac 23:7; n-3e(5b); 5087]   "

στατήρ, ῆρος, ὁ   {5088, n-3f(2a)}
pr. *a weight; a stater,* an Attic silver coin, equal in value to the Jewish shekel, or to four Attic or two Alexandrian drachmas, and equivalent to about eighty cents of American money, Matt 17:27; 26:15 v.l.*

στατῆρα   acc sg masc
   [Mt 17:27; n-3f(2a); 5088]   στατήρ
σταυρόν   acc sg masc [10t; n-2a; 5089]   σταυρός

σταυρός, οῦ, ὁ {5089, n-2a}
a stake; a cross, Matt 27:32, 40, 42; Phil 2:8; by impl. *the punishment of the cross, crucifixion,* Eph 2:16; Heb 12:2; meton. *the crucifixion* of Christ in respect of its import, *the doctrine of the cross,* 1 Cor 17:18; Gal 5:11; 6:12, 14; met. *to take up,* or *bear one's cross, to be ready to encounter any extremity,* Matt 10:38; 16:24; 10:21 v.l.

σταυρός   nom sg masc   [1C 1:17; n-2a; 5089]   "
σταυροῦ   gen sg masc   [12t; n-2a; 5089]   "
σταύρου   pres act imperative 2 sg
  [2t; v-1d(3); 5090]   σταυρόω
σταυροῦνται   pres pass ind 3 pl
  [Mt 27:38; v-1d(3); 5090]   "
σταυροῦσιν   pres act ind 3 pl   [2t; v-1d(3); 5090]   "

σταυρόω {5090, v-1d(3)}
[σταυρώσω, ἐσταύρωσα, -, ἐσταύρωμαι, ἐσταυρώθην] *to fix stakes;* later, *to crucify, affix to the cross,* Matt 20:19; 23:34; met. *to crucify, to mortify, to deaden, to make a sacrifice of,* Gal 5:24; pass. *to be cut off* from a thing, as by a violent death, *to be come dead to,* Gal 6:14

σταυρῷ   dat sg masc   [4t; n-2a; 5089]   σταυρός
σταυρωθῇ   aor pass subj 3 sg
  [3t; v-1d(3); 5090]   σταυρόω
σταυρωθῆναι   aor pass inf   [3t; v-1d(3); 5090]   "
σταυρωθήτω   aor pass imperative 3 sg
  [2t; v-1d(3); 5090]   "
σταυρῶσαι   aor act inf   [3t; v-1d(3); 5090]   "
σταυρώσαντες   aor act ptcp nom pl masc
  [Mt 27:35; v-1d(3); 5090]   "
σταυρώσατε   aor act imperative 2 pl
  [Jn 19:6; v-1d(3); 5090]   "
σταυρώσετε   fut act ind 2 pl
  [Mt 23:34; v-1d(3); 5090]   "
σταύρωσον   aor act imperative 2 sg
  [5t; v-1d(3); 5090]   "
σταυρώσω   aor act subj 1 sg
  [Jn 19:15; v-1d(3); 5090]   "
σταυρώσωσιν   aor act subj 3 pl
  [Mk 15:20; v-1d(3); 5090]   "
σταφυλαί   nom pl fem
  [Rv 14:18; n-1b; 5091]   σταφυλή
σταφυλάς   acc pl fem   [Mt 7:16; n-1b; 5091]   "

σταφυλή, ῆς, ἡ {5091, n-1b}
a cluster or *bunch of grapes,* Matt 7:16; Luke 6:44, Rev 14:18*

σταφυλήν   acc sg fem   [Lk 6:44; n-1b; 5091]
στάχυας   acc pl masc   [3t; n-1b; 5092]   στάχυς
στάχυϊ   dat sg masc   [Mk 4:28; n-1b; 5092]   "
Στάχυν   acc sg masc   [2t; n-3e(1); 5093]   Στάχυς

στάχυς, υος, ὁ {5092, n-1b}
an ear of corn, head of grain, Matt 12:1; Mark 2:23; 4:28; Luke 6:1*

Στάχυς, υος, ὁ {5093, n-3e(1)}
Stachys, pr. name, Rom 16:9*

στέγει   pres act ind 3 sg
  [1C 13:7; v-1b(2); 5095]   στέγω

στέγη, ης, ἡ {5094, n-1b}
a roof, flat roof of a house, Matt 8:8; Mark 2:4; Luke 7:6*

στέγην   acc sg fem   [3t; n-1b; 5094]   στέγη
στέγομεν   pres act ind 1 pl
  [1C 9:12; v-1b(2); 5095]   στέγω
στέγοντες   pres act ptcp nom pl masc
  [1Th 3:1; v-1b(2); 5095]   "

στέγω {5095, v-1b(2)}
[-, -, -, -, -] *to cover; to hold off, to hold in;* hence, *to hold out against, to endure patiently,* 1 Cor 9:12; 13:7; absol. *to contain one's self,* 1 Thess 3:1, 5*

στέγων   pres act ptcp nom sg masc
  [1Th 3:5; v-1b(2); 5095]   "

στεῖρα, ας, ἡ {5096, n-1a}
barren, incapable of bearing children, Luke 1:7, 36; 23:29; Gal 4:27; Heb 11:11*

στεῖρα   nom sg fem   [2t; n-1a; 5096]   στεῖρα
στεῖρα   voc sg fem   [Ga 4:27; n-1a; 5096]   "
στείρᾳ   dat sg fem   [Lk 1:36; n-1a; 5096]   "
στεῖραι   nom pl fem   [Lk 23:29; n-1a; 5096]   "
στέλλεσθαι   pres mid inf
  [2Th 3:6; v-2d(1); 5097]   στέλλω
στελλόμενοι   pres mid ptcp nom pl masc
  [2C 8:20; v-2d(1); 5097]   "

στέλλω {5097, v-2d(1)}
[στελῶ, ἔστειλα, ἔσταλκα, ἔσταλμαι, ἐστάλην] pr. *to place in set order, to arrange; to equip; to despatch; to stow;* mid. *to contract one's self, to shrink; to withdraw from, avoid, shun,* 2 Cor 8:20; 2 Thess 3:6*

στέμμα, ατος, τό {5098, n-3c(4)}
a crown, wreath, Acts 14:13*

στέμματα   acc pl neut
  [Ac 14:13; n-3c(4); 5098]   στέμμα
στεναγμοῖς   dat pl masc
  [Rm 8:26; n-2a; 5099]   στεναγμός

στεναγμός, οῦ, ὁ {5099, n-2a}
a sighing, groaning, groan, Acts 7:34; an inward *sighing,* Rom 8:26*

στεναγμοῦ   gen sg masc   [Ac 7:34; n-2a; 5099]   "
στενάζετε   pres act imperative 2 pl
  [Jm 5:9; v-2a(2); 5100]   στενάζω
στενάζομεν   pres act ind 1 pl   [3t; v-2a(2); 5100]   "
στενάζοντες   pres act ptcp nom pl masc
  [Hb 13:17; v-2a(2); 5100]   "

στενάζω {5100, v-2a(2)}
[στενάξω, ἐστέναξα, -, -, -] *to groan, sigh,* Rom 8:23; 2 Cor 5:2, 4; Heb 13:17; *to sigh* inwardly, Mark 7:34; *to give vent to querulous* or *censorious feelings,* James 5:9*

στενή   nom sg fem   [Mt 7:14; a-1a(2a); 5101]   στενός
στενῆς   gen sg fem   [2t; a-1a(2a); 5101]   "

στενός, ή, όν {5101, a-1a(2a)}
narrow, strait, Matt 7:13, 14; Luke 13:24*

στενοχωρεῖσθε   pres pass ind 2 pl
  [2t; cv-1d(2a); 5102]   στενοχωρέω

στενοχωρέω   {5102, cv-1d(2a)}
[-, -, -, -, -] *to crowd together into a narrow place,
straiten;* pass. met. *to be in straits, to be cooped up,
to be cramped* from action, 2 Cor 4:8; *to be
cramped* in feeling, 2 Cor 6:12*

στενοχωρία, ας, ἡ   {5103, n-1a}
pr. *narrowness of place, a narrow place;* met.
straits, distress, anguish, Rom 2:9; 8:35; 2 Cor 6:4;
12:10*

στενοχωρία   nom sg fem [2t; n-1a; 5103] στενοχωρία
στενοχωρίαις   dat pl fem [2t; n-1a; 5103]   "
στενοχωρούμενοι   pres pass ptcp nom pl masc
   [2C 4:8; cv-1d(2a); 5102]   στενοχωρέω
στερεά   nom sg fem
   [Hb 5:14; a-1a(1); 5104]   στερεός
στερεᾶς   gen sg fem [Hb 5:12; a-1a(1); 5104]   "
στερεοί   nom pl masc [1P 5:9; a-1a(1); 5104]   "

στερεός, ά, όν   {5104, a-1a(1)}
stiff, hard; of food, *solid,* as opposed to what is
liquid and light, Heb 5:12, 14; *firm, steadfast,* 2
Tim 2:19; 1 Peter 5:9*

στερεός   nom sg masc [2Ti 2:19; a-1a(1); 5104]   "

στερεόω   {5105, v-1d(3)}
[(ἐστέρεον), -, ἐστερέωσα, -, -, ἐστερεώθην] *to
make firm; to strengthen,* Acts 3:7, 16; *to settle,*
Acts 16:5*

στερέωμα, ατος, τό   {5106, n-3c(4)}
pr. *what is solid and firm;* met. *firmness,
steadfastness, constancy,* Col 2:5*

στερέωμα   acc sg neut
   [Cl 2:5; n-3c(4); 5106]   στερέωμα
Στεφανᾶ   gen sg masc [3t; n-1e; 5107]   Στεφανᾶς

Στεφανᾶς, ᾶ, ὁ   {5107, n-1e}
Stephanas, pr. name, 1 Cor 1:16; 16:15, 17*

στέφανοι   nom pl masc
   [Rv 9:7; n-2a; 5109]   στέφανος
στέφανον   acc sg masc [13t; n-2a; 5109]   "
Στέφανος   nom sg masc [5t; n-2a; 5108]   Στέφανος

Στέφανος, ου, ο)   {5108, n-2a}
Stephen, pr. name, Acts 6:5, 8f.; 7:1 v.l., 59; 8:2;
11:19; 22:20*

στέφανος, ου, ὁ   {5109, n-2a}
that which forms an encirclement; a crown, Matt
27:29; Rev 4:4, 10; *wreath,* conferred on a victor
in the public games, 1 Cor 9:25; met. *a crown,
reward, prize,* 2 Tim 4:8; James 1:12; *a crown,
ornament, honor, glory*

στέφανος   voc sg masc
   [Pp 4:1; n-2a; 5109]   στέφανος
Στεφάνου   gen sg masc
   [Ac 22:20; n-2a; 5108]   Στέφανος
στεφάνους   acc pl masc [2t; n-2a; 5109]   στέφανος
στεφανοῦται   pres pass ind 3 sg
   [2Ti 2:5; v-1d(3); 5110]   στεφανόω

στεφανόω   {5110, v-1d(3)}
[-, ἐστεφάνωσα, -, ἐστεφάνωμαι, ἐστεφανώθην] *to
crown; to crown* as victor in the games, 2 Tim 2:5;
met. *to crown, adorn, decorate,* Heb 2:7, 9*

Στεφάνῳ   dat sg masc [2t; n-2a; 5108]   Στέφανος
στήθη   acc pl neut [2t; n-3d(2b); 5111]   στῆθος
στῆθι   aor act imperative 2 sg
   [3t; v-6a; 2705]   ἵστημι

στῆθος, ους, τό   {5111, n-3d(2b)}
the breast, chest, Luke 18:13; 23:48; John 13:25;
21:20; Rev 15:6*

στῆθος   acc sg neut [3t; n-3d(2b); 5111]   στῆθος
στήκει   pres act ind 3 sg
   [Rm 14:4; v-1b(2); 5112]   στήκω
στήκετε   pres act imperative 2 pl
   [4t; v-1b(2); 5112]   "
στήκετε   pres act ind 2 pl [3t; v-1b(2); 5112]   "
στήκοντες   pres act ptcp nom pl masc
   [Mk 3:31; v-1b(2); 5112]   "

στήκω   {5112, v-1b(2)}
[-, ἔστηκα, -, -, -] *to stand,* Mark 11:25; 3:31; John
1:26; 8:44 (which could be from ἵστημι); met. *to
stand* when under judgment, *to be approved,*
Rom 14:4; *to stand firm, be constant, persevere,* 1
Cor 16:13; Gal 5:1; Phil 1:27; 4:1; 1 Thess 3:8; 2
Thess 2:15; Rev 12:4 v.l.*

στῆναι   aor act inf [4t; v-6a; 2705]   ἵστημι

στηριγμός, οῦ, ὁ   {5113, n-2a}
pr. *a fixing, settling; a state of firmness, fixedness;*
met. *firmness* of belief, *settle frame* of mind, 2
Peter 3:17*

στηριγμοῦ   gen sg masc
   [2P 3:17; n-2a; 5113]   στηριγμός

στηρίζω   {5114, v-2a(2)}
[στηρίξω or στηριῶ, ἐστήριξα or ἐστήρισα, -,
ἐστήριγμαι, ἐστηρίχθην] *to set fast; to set* in a
certain position or direction, Luke 9:51; met. *to
render* mentally *steadfast, to settle, confirm,* Luke
22:32; Acts 18:23 v.l.; Rom 1:11; *to stand
immovable,* Luke 16:26; met. *to be* mentally
settled, 2 Peter 1:12

στηρίξαι   aor act inf [3t; v-2a(2); 5114]   στηρίζω
στηρίξαι   aor act opt 3 sg
   [2Th 2:17; v-2a(2); 5114]   "
στηρίξατε   aor act imperative 2 pl
   [Jm 5:8; v-2a(2); 5114]   "
στηρίξει   fut act ind 3 sg [2t; v-2a(2); 5114]   "
στήρισον   aor act imperative 2 sg
   [2t; v-2a(2); 5114]   "
στηριχθῆναι   aor pass inf
   [Rm 1:11; v-2a(2); 5114]   "
στῆσαι   aor act inf [3t; v-6a; 2705]   ἵστημι
στήσαντες   aor act ptcp nom pl masc
   [2t; v-6a; 2705]   "
στήσει   fut act ind 3 sg [Mt 25:33; v-6a; 2705]   "
στήσῃ   aor act subj 3 sg [Hb 10:9; v-6a; 2705]   "
στήσῃς   aor act subj 2 sg [Ac 7:60; v-6a; 2705]   "
στήσητε   aor act subj 2 pl [Mk 7:9; v-6a; 2705]   "
στήσονται   fut mid ind 3 pl
   [Rv 18:15; v-6a; 2705]   "
στῆτε   aor act imperative 2 pl
   [2t; v-6a; 2705]   "
στιβάδας   acc pl fem
   [Mk 11:8; n-3c(2); 5115]   στιβάς

στιβάς, άδος, ή {5115, n-3c(2)}
a stuffing of leaves, boughs, etc., meton. *a bough,
branch*, Mark 11:8*

στίγμα, ατος, τό {5116, n-3c(4)}
a brand-mark, Gal 6:17*

στίγματα   acc pl neut
[Ga 6:17; n-3c(4); 5116]   στίγμα

στιγμή, ῆς, ή {5117, n-1b}
pr. *a point*; met. *a point* of time, *moment, instant,*
Luke 4:5*

στιγμῇ   dat sg fem [Lk 4:5; n-1b; 5117]   στιγμή
στίλβοντα   pres act ptcp nom pl neut
[Mk 9:3; v-1b(1); 5118]   στίλβω

στίλβω {5118, v-1b(1)}
[-, -, -, -, -] *to shine, glisten, be radiant*, Mark 9:3*

στοά, ᾶς, ή {5119, n-1a}
*a colonnade, cloister, covered walk supported by
columns*, John 5:2; 10:23; Acts 3:11; 5:12*

στοᾷ   dat sg fem [3t; n-1a; 5119]   στοά
στοάς   acc pl fem [Jn 5:2; n-1a; 5119]   "

στοιβάς, see στιβάς {5120}

Στοϊκός, ή, όν {5121, a-1a(2a)}
Stoic, Acts 17:18*

Στοϊκῶν   gen pl masc
[Ac 17:18; a-1a(2a); 5121]   Στοϊκός
στοιχεῖα   nom pl neut [2t; n-2c; 5122]   στοιχεῖον
στοιχεῖα   acc pl neut [4t; n-2c; 5122]   "
στοιχεῖν   pres act inf
[Pp 3:16; v-1d(2a); 5123]   στοιχέω

στοιχεῖον, ου, τό {5122, n-2c}
an element; an element of the natural universe, 2
Peter 3:10, 12; *an element* or *rudiment* of any
intellectual or religious system, Gal 4:3, 9; Col
2:8, 20; Heb 5:12*

στοιχεῖς   pres act ind 2 sg
[Ac 21:24; v-1d(2a); 5123]   "
στοιχείων   gen pl neut
[Cl 2:20; n-2c; 5122]   στοιχεῖον

στοιχέω {5123, v-1d(2a)}
[στοιχήσω, -, -, -, -] pr. *to advance in a line*; met.
to frame one's conduct by a certain rule, Acts
21:24; Rom 4:12; Gal 5:25; 6:16; Phil 3:16*

στοιχήσουσιν   fut act ind 3 pl
[Ga 6:16; v-1d(2a); 5123]   στοιχέω
στοιχοῦσιν   pres act ptcp dat pl masc
[Rm 4:12; v-1d(2a); 5123]   "
στοιχῶμεν   pres act subj 1 pl
[Ga 5:25; v-1d(2a); 5123]   "
στολαῖς   dat pl fem [2t; n-1b; 5124]   στολή
στολάς   acc pl fem [4t; n-1b; 5124]   "

στολή, ῆς, ή {5124, n-1b}
equipment; dress; a long garment, flowing robe,
worn by priests, kings, and persons of
distinction, Matt 12:38; 16:5; Luke 15:22; Rev
6:11

στολή   nom sg fem [Rv 6:11; n-1b; 5124]   "
στολήν   acc sg fem [2t; n-1b; 5124]   "

στόμα, ατος, τό {5125, n-3c(4)}
the mouth, Matt 12:34; 15:11, 17, 18; 21:16; *speech,
words*, Matt 18:16; 2 Cor 13:1; *command of speech,
facility of language*, Luke 21:15; from the
Hebrew, ἀνοίγειν τὸ στόμα, *to utter, to speak,*
Matt 5:2, 13:35; also, used of the earth, *to rend,
yawn*, Rev 12:16; στόμα πρὸς στόμα λαλεῖν, *to
speak mouth to mouth, face to face*, 2 John 12; 3
John 14; *the edge* or *point* of a weapon, Luke
21:24; Heb 11:34

στόμα   nom sg neut [10t; n-3c(4); 5125]   στόμα
στόμα   acc sg neut [18t; n-3c(4); 5125]   "
στόματα   acc pl neut [3t; n-3c(4); 5125]   "
στόματι   dat sg neut [11t; n-3c(4); 5125]   "
στόματος   gen sg neut [34t; n-3c(4); 5125]   "
στομάτων   gen pl neut [2t; n-3c(4); 5125]   "
στόμαχον   acc sg masc
[1Ti 5:23; n-2a; 5126]   στόμαχος

στόμαχος, ου, ό {5126, n-2a}
pr. *the gullet* leading to the stomach; hence,
later, *the stomach* itself, 1 Tim 5:23*

στρατεία, ας, ή {5127, n-1a}
a military expedition, campaign; and genr.
military service, warfare; met. *the* Christian
warfare, 2 Cor 10:4; *flight*, 1 Tim 1:18*

στρατείαν   acc sg fem
[1Ti 1:18; n-1a; 5127]   στρατεία
στρατείας   gen sg fem [2C 10:4; n-1a; 5127]   "
στρατεύεται   pres mid ind 3 sg
[1C 9:7; v-1a(6); 5129]   στρατεύομαι
στρατεύῃ   pres mid subj 2 sg
[1Ti 1:18; v-1a(6); 5129]   "

στράτευμα, ατος, τό {5128, n-3c(4)}
an army, Matt 22:7; Rev 19:14, 19; *an armed force,
corps*, Acts 23:10, 27; *troops, guards*, Luke 23:11;
Rev 9:16*

στράτευμα   acc sg neut
[Ac 23:10; n-3c(4); 5128]   στράτευμα

στρατεύομαι {5129, v-1a(6)}
[-, ἐστρατευσάμην, -, -, -] also spelled, στρατεύω,
to perform military duty, serve as a soldier, Luke
3:14; 1 Cor 9:7; 2 Tim 2:4; *to battle*, James 4:1; 1
Pet 2:11; *to be spiritually militant*, 2 Cor 10:3; 1
Tim 1:18*

στρατεύμασιν   dat pl neut
[Lk 23:11; n-3c(4); 5128]   "
στρατεύματα   nom pl neut
[Rv 19:14; n-3c(4); 5128]   "
στρατεύματα   acc pl neut [2t; n-3c(4); 5128]   "
στρατεύματι   dat sg neut
[Ac 23:27; n-3c(4); 5128]   "
στρατεύματος   gen sg neut
[Rv 19:19; n-3c(4); 5128]   "
στρατευμάτων   gen pl neut
[Rv 9:16; n-3c(4); 5128]   "
στρατευόμεθα   pres mid ind 1 pl
[2C 10:3; v-1a(6); 5129]   στρατεύομαι
στρατευόμενοι   pres mid ptcp nom pl masc
[Lk 3:14; v-1a(6); 5129]   "

στρατευόμενος   pres mid ptcp nom sg masc
[2Ti 2:4; v-1a(6); 5129]   "

στρατευομένων   pres mid ptcp gen pl fem
[Jm 4:1; v-1a(6); 5129]   "

στρατεύονται   pres mid ind 3 pl
[1P 2:11; v-1a(6); 5129]   "

στρατηγοί   nom pl masc [3t; n-2a; 5130]   στρατηγός
στρατηγοῖς   dat pl masc [3t; n-2a; 5130]   "

στρατηγός, οῦ, ὁ   {5130, n-2a}
  a leader or *commander of an army, general; a*
  Roman *praetor, provincial magistrate,* Acts 16:20,
  22, 35, 36, 38; στρατηγός τοῦ ἱεροῦ, *the captain* or
  prefect of the temple, the chief of the Levites who
  kept guard in and around the temple, Luke
  22:4, 52; Acts 4:1; 5:24, 26*

στρατηγός   nom sg masc [3t; n-2a; 5130]
στρατηγούς   acc pl masc [Lk 22:52; n-2a; 5130]   "

στρατιά, ᾶς, ἡ   {5131, n-1a}
  an army, host; from the Hebrew, στρατιὰ
  οὐράνιος, or τοῦ οὐρανοῦ, *the heavenly host, the
  host of heaven, the hosts of angels,* Luke 2:13; *the
  stars,* Acts 7:42; 2 Cor 10:4 v.l.*

στρατιᾷ   dat sg fem [Ac 7:42; n-1a; 5131]   στρατιά
στρατιᾶς   gen sg fem [Lk 2:13; n-1a; 5131]   "
στρατιῶται   nom pl masc
[9t; n-1f; 5132]   στρατιώτης
στρατιώταις   dat pl masc [3t; n-1f; 5132]   "
στρατιώτας   acc pl masc [5t; n-1f; 5132]   "
στρατιώτῃ   dat sg masc [2t; n-1f; 5132]   "
στρατιώτην   acc sg masc [Ac 10:7; n-1f; 5132]   "

στρατιώτης, ου, ὁ   {5132, n-1f}
  a soldier, Matt 8:9; 27:27; met. *a soldier* of Christ,
  2 Tim 2:3

στρατιώτης   nom sg masc [2Ti 2:3; n-1f; 5132]   "
στρατιωτῶν   gen pl masc [5t; n-1f; 5132]   "

στρατολογέω   {5133, v-1d(2a)}
  [-, ἐστρατολόγησα, -, -, -] *to collect* or *gather an
  army, enlist troops,* 2 Tim 2:4*

στρατολογήσαντι   aor act ptcp dat sg masc
[2Ti 2:4; v-1d(2a); 5133]   στρατολογέω

στρατοπεδάρχης   {5134}
  also spelled στρατοπέδαρχος, *a commandant of a
  camp; legionary tribune;* perhaps, *the prefect of the
  praetorian camp,* Acts 28:16 v.l.*

στρατοπέδαρχος, see στρατοπεδάρχης   {5135}

στρατόπεδον, ου, τό   {5136, n-2c}
  pr. *the site of an encampment; an encampment;*
  meton. *an army,* Luke 21:20*

στρατοπέδων   gen pl neut
[Lk 21:20; n-2c; 5136]   στρατόπεδον
στραφείς   aor pass ptcp nom sg masc
[10t; v-1b(1); 5138]   στρέφω
στραφεῖσα   aor pass ptcp nom sg fem
[Jn 20:16; v-1b(1); 5138]   "
στραφέντες   aor pass ptcp nom pl masc
[Mt 7:6; v-1b(1); 5138]   "
στραφῆτε   aor pass subj 2 pl
[Mt 18:3; v-1b(1); 5138]   "

στραφῶσιν   aor pass subj 3 pl
[Jn 12:40; v-1b(1); 5138]   "
στρεβλοῦσιν   pres act ind 3 pl
[2P 3:16; v-1d(3); 5137]   στρεβλόω

στρεβλόω   {5137, v-1d(3)}
  [-, -, -, -, -] pr. *to distort* the limbs *on a rack;* met.
  to wrench, distort, pervert, 2 Peter 3:16*

στρέφειν   pres act inf
[Rv 11:6; v-1b(1); 5138]   στρέφω
στρεφόμεθα   pres pass ind 1 pl
[Ac 13:46; v-1b(1); 5138]   "

στρέφω   {5138, v-1b(1)}
  [στρέψω, ἔστρεψα, -, ἔστραμμαι, ἐστράφην] *to
  twist;* to *turn,* Matt 5:39; *to make a change of*
  substance, *to change,* Rev 11:6; absol. *to change*
  or *turn* one's course of dealing, Acts 7:42; mid.
  to turn one's *self about,* Matt 16:23; Luke 7:9; *to
  turn back,* Acts 7:39; *to change one's direction, to
  turn* elsewhere, Acts 13:46; *to change one's course
  of principle and conduct, to be converted,* Matt 18:3

στρέψον   aor act imperative 2 sg
[Mt 5:39; v-1b(1); 5138]   "
στρηνιάσαντες   aor act ptcp nom pl masc
[Rv 18:9; v-1d(1b); 5139]   στρηνιάω

στρηνιάω   {5139, v-1d(1b)}
  [-, ἐστρηνίασα, -, -, -] *to be wanton, to revel, riot,*
  Rev 18:7, 9*

στρῆνος, ους, τό   {5140, n-3d(2b)}
  luxury, sensuality, Rev 18:3*

στρήνους   gen sg neut
[Rv 18:3; n-3d(2b); 5140]   στρῆνος
στρουθία   nom pl neut [2t; n-2c; 5141]   στρουθίον

στρουθίον, ου, τό   {5141, n-2c}
  any small bird, spc. *a sparrow,* Matt 10:29, 31;
  Luke 12:6, 7*

στρουθίων   gen pl neut [2t; n-2c; 5141]   "

στρώννυμι, see στρωννύω   {5142, v-6n}

στρωννύω   {5143, v-3c(1)}
  [(ἐστρώννυον), -, ἔστρωσα, -, ἔστρωμαι,
  ἐστρώθην] the thematic form of στρώννυμι, the
  μι form never being visible in the N.T., *to
  spread, to strew,* Matt 21:8; Mark 11:8; *to spread* a
  couch, *make your own bed,* Acts 9:34; used of a
  supper-chamber, pass. *to have the couches
  spread, to be prepared, furnished,* Mark 14:15;
  Luke 22:12*

στρῶσον   aor act imperative 2 sg
[Ac 9:34; v-3c(1); 5143]   στρώννυμι
στυγητοί   nom pl masc
[Ti 3:3; a-1a(2a); 5144]   στυγητός

στυγητός, ή, όν   {5144, a-1a(2a)}
  hateful, disgusting, detested, Titus 3:3*

στυγνάζω   {5145, v-2a(1)}
  [-, ἐστύγνασα, -, -, -] *to put on a gloomy and
  downcast look, to be shocked, appalled,* Mark 10:22;
  of the sky, *to lower,* Matt 16:3*

στυγνάζων   pres act ptcp nom sg masc
[Mt 16:3; v-2a(1); 5145]   στυγνάζω

στυγνάσας   aor act ptcp nom sg masc
   [Mk 10:22; v-2a(1); 5145]   "
στῦλοι   nom pl masc   [2t; n-2a; 5146]   στῦλος
στῦλον   acc sg masc   [Rv 3:12; n-2a; 5146]   "

στῦλος, ου, ὁ   {5146, n-2a}
   a pillar, column, Rev 10:1; used of persons of
   authority, influence, etc., a support or pillar of
   the Church, Gal 2:9; Rev 3:12; a support of true
   doctrine, 1 Tim 3:15*

στῦλος   nom sg masc   [1Ti 3:15; n-2a; 5146]   "

Στωϊκός, see Στοϊκος   {5147}

σύ   {5148, a-5}
   you, gen., σοῦ, dat., σοί, acc., σε, Matt 1:20; 2:6

σύ   nom sg   [174t; a-5a; 5148]   σύ

συγγένεια, ας, ἡ   {5149, n-1a}
   kindred; kinsfolk, kinsmen, relatives, Luke 1:61;
   Acts 7:3, 14*

συγγένειαν   acc sg fem
   [Ac 7:14; n-1a; 5149]   συγγένεια
συγγενείας   gen sg fem   [2t; n-1a; 5149]   "
συγγενεῖς   nom pl masc   [2t; a-4a; 5150]   συγγενής
συγγενεῖς   acc pl masc   [3t; a-4a; 5150]   "
συγγενεῦσιν   dat pl masc   [2t; a-4a; 5150]   "
συγγενῆ   acc sg masc   [Rm 16:11; a-4a; 5150]   "

συγγενής, ές   {5150, a-4a}
   kindred, akin; as a subst. a kinsman or
   kinswoman, relative; Mark 6:4; Luke 1:36 v.l., 58;
   2:44; 14:12; 21:16; John 18:26; Acts 10:24; one
   nationally akin, a fellow-countryman, Rom 9:3;
   16:7, 11, 21*

συγγενής   nom sg masc   [Jn 18:26; a-4a; 5150]   "

συγγενίς, ίδος, ἡ   {5151, n-3c(2)}
   a kinswoman, female relative, Luke 1:36*

συγγενίς   nom sg fem
   [Lk 1:36; n-3c(2); 5151]   συγγενίς
συγγενῶν   gen pl masc   [2t; a-4a; 5150]   συγγενής

συγγνώμη, ης, ἡ   {5152, n-1b}
   pardon; concession, leave, permission, 1 Cor 7:6*

συγγνώμην   acc sg fem
   [1C 7:6; n-1b; 5152]   συγγνώμη

συγκάθημαι   {5153, cv-6b}
   [-, -, -, -, -] to sit in company with, Mark 14:54;
   Acts 26:30*

συγκαθήμενοι   pres mid ptcp nom pl masc
   [Ac 26:30; cv-6b; 5153]   συγκάθημαι
συγκαθήμενος   pres mid ptcp nom sg masc
   [Mk 14:54; cv-6b; 5153]   "

συγκαθίζω   {5154, cv-2a(1)}
   [-, συνεκάθισα, -, -, -] trans. to cause to sit down
   with, seat in company with, Eph 2:6; intrans. to sit
   in company with; to sit down together, Luke 22:55*

συγκαθισάντων   aor act ptcp gen pl masc
   [Lk 22:55; cv-2a(1); 5154]   συγκαθίζω

συγκακοπαθέω   {5155, cv-1d(2a)}
   [-, συνεκακοπάθησα, -, -, -] to suffer evils along

with someone; to be enduringly adherent, 2 Tim
1:8; 2:3*

συγκακοπάθησον   aor act imperative 2 sg
   [2t; cv-1d(2a); 5155]   συγκακοπαθέω
συγκακουχεῖσθαι   pres mid inf
   [Hb 11:25; cv-1d(2a); 5156]   συγκακουχέομαι

συγκακουχέομαι   {5156, cv-1d(2a)}
   [-, -, -, -, -] to encounter adversity along with any
   one, Heb 11:25*

συγκαλεῖ   pres act ind 3 sg
   [2t; cv-1d(2b); 5157]   συγκαλέω
συγκαλεσάμενος   aor mid ptcp nom sg masc
   [3t; cv-1d(2b); 5157]   "
συγκαλέσασθαι   aor mid inf
   [Ac 28:17; cv-1d(2b); 5157]   "

συγκαλέω   {5157, cv-1d(2b)}
   [-, συνεκάλεσα, -, -, -] to call together, Mark
   15:16; Luke 15:6, 9; Acts 5:21; mid. to call around
   one's self, Luke 9:1; 15:6 v.l., 9 v.l.; 23:13; Acts
   5:21 v.l.; 10:24; 13:7 v.l.; 28:17*

συγκαλοῦσιν   pres act ind 3 pl
   [Mk 15:16; cv-1d(2b); 5157]   "

συγκαλύπτω   {5158, cv-4}
   [-, -, -, συγκεκάλυμμαι, -] to cover completely, to
   cover up; met. to conceal, Luke 12:2*

συγκάμπτω   {5159, cv-4}
   [-, συνέκαμψα, -, -, -] to bend or bow together; to
   bow down the back of any one afflictively, Rom
   11:10*

σύγκαμψον   aor act imperative 2 sg
   [Rm 11:10; cv-4; 5159]   συγκάμπτω

συγκαταβαίνω   {5160, cv-2d(6)}
   [-, συγκατέβην, -, -, -] to go down with anyone,
   Acts 25:5*

συγκαταβάντες   aor act ptcp nom pl masc
   [Ac 25:5; cv-2d(6); 5160]   συγκαταβαίνω

συγκατάθεσις, εως, ἡ   {5161, n-3e(5b)}
   assent; in N.T. accord, alliance, agreement, 2 Cor
   6:16*

συγκατάθεσις   nom sg fem
   [2C 6:16; n-3e(5b); 5161]   συγκατάθεσις

συγκατανεύω   {5162, cv-1a(6)}
   [-, -, -, -, -] agree, Acts 18:27 v.l.*

συγκατατεθειμένος   perf pass ptcp nom sg masc
   [Lk 23:51; cv-6a; 5163]   συγκατατίθημι

συγκατατίθημι   {5163, cv-6a}
   [-, -, -, -, -] to set down together with; mid. to agree,
   accord, Luke 23:51*

συγκαταψηφίζομαι   {5164, cv-2a(1)}
   [-, -, -, -, συγκατεψηφίσθην] to count, number
   with, be chosen together with, Acts 1:26*

συγκατεψηφίσθη   aor pass ind 3 sg
   [Ac 1:26; cv-2a(1); 5164]   συγκαταψηφίζομαι

σύγκειμαι   {5165, cv-6b}
   [-, -, -, -, -] recline together, Matt 9:10 v.l.*

συγκεκαλυμμένον   perf pass ptcp nom sg neut
[Lk 12:2; cv-4; 5158]   συγκαλύπτω
συγκεκερασμένους   perf pass ptcp acc pl masc
[Hb 4:2; cv-3c(1); 5166]   συγκεράννυμι

συγκεράννυμι   {5166, cv-3c(1)}
[-, συγκέρασα, -, συγκεκέρασμαι, -] pluperf.,
συνεκέκρατο (3 sg), to mix with, mingle together;
to blend, 1 Cor 12:24; pass. to be combined, united,
Heb 4:2*

συγκεχυμένη   perf pass ptcp nom sg fem
[Ac 19:32; cv-1a(7); 5177]   συγχέω

συγκινέω   {5167, cv-1d(2a)}
[(συνέκινουν), -, συνεκίνησα, -, -, -] to agitate,
put in turmoil; to excite, Acts 6:12*

συγκλειόμενοι   pres pass ptcp nom pl masc
[Ga 3:23; cv-1a(3); 5168]   συγκλείω

συγκλείω   {5168, cv-1a(3)}
[-, συνέκλεισα, -, -, -] to shut up together, to hem
in; to enclose, Luke 5:6; met. to band under a
sweeping sentence, Rom 11:32; Gal 3:22; pass.
to be banded under a bar of disability, Gal 3:23*

συγκληρονόμα   acc pl neut
[Ep 3:6; a-3a; 5169]   συγκληρονόμος
συγκληρονόμοι   nom pl masc [Rm 8:17; a-3a; 5169]"
συγκληρονόμοις   dat pl fem [1P 3:7; a-3a; 5169]   "

συγκληρονόμος, ον   {5169, a-3a}
pr. a coheir, Rom 8:17; a fellow-participant, Eph
3:6; Heb 11:9; 1 Peter 3:7*

συγκληρονόμων   gen pl masc [Hb 11:9; a-3a; 5169] "
συγκοινωνεῖτε   pres act imperative 2 pl
[Ep 5:11; cv-1d(2a); 5170]   συγκοινωνέω

συγκοινωνέω   {5170, cv-1d(2a)}
[-, συνεκοινώνησα, -, -, -] to be a joint partaker,
participate with a person; in N.T. to mix one's self
up in a thing, to involve one's self, be an accomplice
in, Eph 5:11; Rev 18:4; to sympathize actively in,
to relieve, Phil 4:14*

συγκοινωνήσαντες   aor act ptcp nom pl masc
[Pp 4:14; cv-1d(2a); 5170]   "
συγκοινωνήσητε   aor act subj 2 pl
[Rv 18:4; cv-1d(2a); 5170]   "

συγκοινωνός, οῦ, ὁ   {5171, n-2a}
one who partakes jointly; a coparticipant, Rom
11:17; a copartner in service, fellow, 1 Cor 9:23;
Phil 1:7; a sharer, 1 Cor 9:23; Rev 1:9*

συγκοινωνός   nom sg masc
[3t; n-2a; 5171]   συγκοινωνός
συγκοινωνούς   acc pl masc [Pp 1:7; n-2a; 5171]   "

συγκομίζω   {5172, cv-2a(1)}
[-, συνεκόμισα, -, -, συνεκομίσθην] to prepare for
burial, take charge of the funeral of any one, bury,
Acts 8:2*

συγκρῖναι   aor act inf
[2C 10:12; cv-1c(2); 5173]   συγκρίνω
συγκρίνοντες   pres act ptcp nom pl masc
[2t; cv-1c(2); 5173]   "

συγκρίνω   {5173, cv-1c(2)}
[-, συνέκρινα, -, -, -] to combine, compound; to

compare, to estimate by comparing with
something else, or, to match, 2 Cor 10:12 (2t); to
explain, to illustrate, or, to suit, 1 Cor 2:13*

συγκύπτουσα   pres act ptcp nom sg fem
[Lk 13:11; cv-4; 5174]   συγκύπτω

συγκύπτω   {5174, cv-4}
[-, -, -, -, -] to bend or bow together; to be bowed
together, bent over, Luke 13:11*

συγκυρία, ας, ἡ   {5175, n-1a}
concurrence, coincidence, chance, accident; κατὰ
συγκυρίαν, by chance, accidentally, Luke 10:31*

συγκυρίαν   acc sg fem
[Lk 10:31; n-1a; 5175]   συγκυρία
συγχαίρει   pres act ind 3 sg
[2t; cv-2d(2); 5176]   συγχαίρω
συγχαίρετε   pres act imperative 2 pl
[Pp 2:18; cv-2d(2); 5176]   "

συγχαίρω   {5176, cv-2d(2)}
[(συνέχαιρον), συγχαρήσω, -, -, -, συνεχάρην] to
rejoice with any one, sympathize in joy, Luke 1:58;
15:6, 9; Phil 2:17, 18; met. 1 Cor 12:26; to
sympathize in the advancement of, congratulate, 1
Cor 13:6*

συγχαίρω   pres act ind 1 sg
[Pp 2:17; cv-2d(2); 5176]   "
συγχάρητε   aor pass imperative 2 pl
[2t; cv-2d(2); 5176]   "

συγχέω   {5177, cv-1a(7)}
[(συνέχεον or συνέχυννεν), -, -, -, συγκέχυμαι,
συνεχύθην] to pour together, mingle by pouring
together; hence, to confound, perplex, amaze, Acts
2:6; to confound in dispute, Acts 9:22; 19:29 v.l.;
to throw into confusion, fill with uproar, Acts
19:32; 21:27, 31*

συγχράομαι   {5178, cv-1d(1a)}
[-, -, -, -, -] use in common; associate with, have
dealings with, John 4:9*

συγχρῶνται   pres mid ind 3 pl
[Jn 4:9; cv-1d(1a); 5178]   συγχράομαι
συγχύννεται   pres pass ind 3 sg
[Ac 21:31; cv-1a(7); 5177]   συγχέω

συγχύν(ν)ω, see συγχέω   {5179}

συγχύσεως   gen sg fem
[Ac 19:29; n-3e(5b); 5180]   σύγχυσις

σύγχυσις, εως, ἡ   {5180, n-3e(5b)}
pr. a pouring together; hence, confusion,
commotion, tumult, uproar, Acts 19:29*

συγχωρέω   {5181, cv-1d(2a)}
[-, -, -, -, -] permit, Acts 21:39 v.l.*

συζάω   {5182, cv-1d(1a)}
[συζήσω, -, -, -, -] to live with; to continue in life
with someone, 2 Cor 7:3; to coexist in life with
another, Rom 6:8; 2 Tim 2:11*

συζεύγνυμι   {5183, cv-3c(2)}
[-, συνέζευξα, -, -, -] to join together; trop. join
together, unite, Matt 19:6; Mark 10:9*

συζῆν   pres act inf
[2C 7:3; cv-1d(1a); 5182]   συζάω

συζήσομεν   fut act ind 1 pl [2t; cv-1d(1a); 5182]   "

συζητεῖν   pres act inf
[4t; cv-1d(2a); 5184]   συζητέω

συζητεῖτε   pres act ind 2 pl
[Mk 9:16; cv-1d(2a); 5184]   "

συζητέω   {5184, cv-1d(2a)}
[(συνεζήτουν), -, -, -, -, -] to seek, ask, or inquire
with another; to deliberate, debate, Mark 1:27;
9:10; Luke 24:15; to hold discourse with, argue,
reason, Mark 8:11; 12:28; Luke 22:23; Acts 6:9;
9:29; to question, dispute, quibble, Mark 9:14, 16*

συζήτησις, εως, ἡ   {5185, n-3e(5b)}
mutual discussion, debate, disputation, v.l. in Acts
15:2, 7, and 28:29*

συζητητής, οῦ, ὁ   {5186, n-1f}
a disputant, controversial reasoner, sophist, 1 Cor
1:20*

συζητητής   nom sg masc
[1C 1:20; n-1f; 5186]   συζητητής

συζητοῦντας   pres act ptcp acc pl masc
[Mk 9:14; cv-1d(2a); 5184]   συζητέω

συζητοῦντες   pres act ptcp nom pl masc
[2t; cv-1d(2a); 5184]   "

συζητούντων   pres act ptcp gen pl masc
[Mk 12:28; cv-1d(2a); 5184]   "

σύζυγε   voc sg masc [Pp 4:3; n-2a; 5187]   σύζυγος

σύζυγος, ου, ὁ   {5187, n-2a}
an associate, comrade, fellow-laborer, or it could be
the person's name, Phil 4:3*

συζωοποιέω   {5188, cv-1d(2a)}
[-, συνεζωοποίησα, -, -, -] to make alive together
with another; to make a sharer in the quickening of
another, Eph 2:5; Col 2:13*

σῦκα   acc pl neut [3t; n-2c; 5192]   σῦκον

συκάμινος, ου, ἡ   {5189, n-2b}
a sycamore-tree, mulberry tree, i.q. συκομοραία,
q.v., Luke 17:6*

συκαμίνῳ   dat sg fem
[Lk 17:6; n-2b; 5189]   συκάμινος

συκῆ, ῆς, ἡ   {5190, n-1h}
a fig tree, Matt 21:19

συκῆ   nom sg fem [5t; n-1h; 5190]   συκῆ
συκῇ   dat sg fem [Lk 13:7; n-1h; 5190]   "
συκῆν   acc sg fem [6t; n-1h; 5190]   "
συκῆς   gen sg fem [4t; n-1h; 5190]   "

συκομορέα, ας, ἡ   {5191, n-1a}
the fig-mulberry tree, sycamore fig, Luke 19:4*

συκομορέαν   acc sg fem
[Lk 19:4; n-1a; 5191]   συκομορέα

σῦκον, ου, τό   {5192, n-2c}
a fig, a ripe fig, Matt 7:16; Mark 11:13; Luke 6:44;
James 3:12*

συκοφαντέω   {5193, v-1d(2a)}
[-, ἐσυκοφάντησα, -, -, -] to inform against; to
accuse falsely; by impl. to wrong by false

accusations; to extort money by false informations,
Luke 3:14; 19:8*

συκοφαντήσητε   aor act subj 2 pl
[Lk 3:14; v-1d(2a); 5193]   συκοφαντέω

σύκων   gen pl neut [Mk 11:13; n-2c; 5192]   σῦκον

συλαγωγέω   {5194, cv-1d(2a)}
[-, -, -, -, -] to carry off as a prey or booty; met. to
make victims of fraud, Col 2:8*

συλαγωγῶν   pres act ptcp nom sg masc
[Cl 2:8; cv-1d(2a); 5194]   συλαγωγέω

συλάω   {5195, v-1d(1a)}
[-, ἐσύλησα, -, -, -] to strip; to rob, 2 Cor 11:8*

συλλαβεῖν   aor act inf
[3t; cv-3a(2b); 5197]   συλλαμβάνω

συλλαβέσθαι   aor mid inf
[Lk 5:7; cv-3a(2b); 5197]   "

συλλαβόμενοι   aor mid ptcp nom pl masc
[Ac 26:21; cv-3a(2b); 5197]   "

συλλαβόντες   aor act ptcp nom pl masc
[Lk 22:54; cv-3a(2b); 5197]   "

συλλαβοῦσα   aor act ptcp nom sg fem
[Jm 1:15; cv-3a(2b); 5197]   "

συλλαβοῦσιν   aor act ptcp dat pl masc
[Ac 1:16; cv-3a(2b); 5197]   "

συλλαλέω   {5196, cv-1d(2a)}
[(συνελάλουν), -, συνελάλησα, -, -, -] to talk,
converse, or discuss with, Matt 17:3; Mark 9:4;
Luke 4:36; 9:30; 22:4; Acts 18:12 v.l.; 25:12*

συλλαλήσας   aor act ptcp nom sg masc
[Ac 25:12; cv-1d(2a); 5196]   συλλαλέω

συλλαλοῦντες   pres act ptcp nom pl masc
[2t; cv-1d(2a); 5196]   "

συλλαμβάνου   pres mid imperative 2 sg
[Pp 4:3; cv-3a(2b); 5197]   συλλαμβάνω

συλλαμβάνω   {5197, cv-3a(2b)}
[συλλήμψομαι, συνέλαβον, συνείληφα, -,
συνελήμφθην] to catch; to seize, apprehend, Matt
26:55; Acts 1:16; to catch, as prey, Luke 5:9; to
conceive, become pregnant, Luke 1:24, 31, 36; 2:21;
met. James 1:15; mid. to help, aid, assist, Luke
5:7; Phil 4:3

συλλέγεται   pres pass ind 3 sg
[Mt 13:40; cv-1b(2); 5198]   συλλέγω

συλλέγοντες   pres act ptcp nom pl masc
[Mt 13:29; cv-1b(2); 5198]   "

συλλέγουσιν   pres act ind 3 pl
[2t; cv-1b(2); 5198]   "

συλλέγω   {5198, cv-1b(2)}
[συλλέξω, συνέλεξα, -, -, -] to collect, gather, Matt
7:16, 13:28-30, 40f., 48; Luke 6:44*

συλλέξατε   aor act imperative 2 pl
[Mt 13:30; cv-1b(2); 5198]   "

συλλέξουσιν   fut act ind 3 pl
[Mt 13:41; cv-1b(2); 5198]   "

συλλέξωμεν   aor act subj 1 pl
[Mt 13:28; cv-1b(2); 5198]   "

συλλημφθέντα   aor pass ptcp acc sg masc
[Ac 23:27; cv-3a(2b); 5197]   συλλαμβάνω

συλλημφθῆναι   aor pass inf
[Lk 2:21; cv-3a(2b); 5197]   "
συλλήμψῃ   fut mid ind 2 sg
[Lk 1:31; cv-3a(2b); 5197]   "

συλλογίζομαι   {5199, cv-2a(1)}
[-, συνελογισάμην, -, -, -] *to reason together; to
consider, deliberate, reason,* Luke 20:5*

συλλυπέω   {5200, cv-1d(2a)}
[-, -, -, -, -] *to be grieved together with; to be
grieved,* Mark 3:5*

συλλυπούμενος   pres pass ptcp nom sg masc
[Mk 3:5; cv-1d(2a); 5200]   συλλυπέω
συμβαίνειν   pres act inf
[Mk 10:32; cv-2d(6); 5201]   συμβαίνω
συμβαίνοντος   pres act ptcp gen sg neut
[1P 4:12; cv-2d(6); 5201]   "

συμβαίνω   {5201, cv-2d(6)}
[(συνέβαινον), -, συνέβην, συμβέβηκα, -,
συνέβην] *to step* or *come together; to happen, meet,
fall out,* Mark 10:32; Acts 20:19; 21:35; 1 Cor
10:11; 1 Peter 4:12; 2 Peter 2:22; Acts 3:10; Luke
24:14*

συμβαλεῖν   aor act inf
[Lk 14:31; cv-2d(1); 5202]   συμβάλλω
συμβάλλουσα   pres act ptcp nom sg fem
[Lk 2:19; cv-2d(1); 5202]   "

συμβάλλω   {5202, cv-2d(1)}
[(συνέβαλλον), -, συνέβαλον, συμβέβληκα, -, -]
pr. *to throw together; absol. to meet and join,* Acts
20:14; *to meet* in war, *to encounter, engage with,*
Luke 14:31; *to encounter* in discourse or dispute,
Acts 17:18; Luke 11:53 v.l.; *to consult together,*
Acts 4:15; mid. *to contribute, be of service to, to
aid,* Acts 18:27; συμβάλλειν ἐν τῇ καρδίᾳ, *to
revolve in mind, ponder upon,* Luke 2:19*

συμβάντων   aor act ptcp gen pl masc
[Ac 20:19; cv-2d(6); 5201]   συμβαίνω
συμβασιλεύσομεν   fut act ind 1 pl
[2Ti 2:12; cv-1a(6); 5203]   συμβασιλεύω
συμβασιλεύσωμεν   aor act subj 1 pl
[1C 4:8; cv-1a(6); 5203]   "

συμβασιλεύω   {5203, cv-1a(6)}
[συμβασιλεύσω, -, -, -, -] *to reign with;* met. *to
enjoy honor with,* 1 Cor 4:8; 2 Tim 2:12*

συμβέβηκεν   perf act ind 3 sg
[2P 2:22; cv-2d(6); 5201]   συμβαίνω
συμβεβηκότι   perf act ptcp dat sg neut
[Ac 3:10; cv-2d(6); 5201]   "
συμβεβηκότων   perf act ptcp gen pl neut
[Lk 24:14; cv-2d(6); 5201]   "
συμβιβαζόμενον   pres pass ptcp nom sg neut
[2t; cv-2a(1); 5204]   συμβιβάζω
συμβιβάζοντες   pres act ptcp nom pl masc
[Ac 16:10; cv-2a(1); 5204]   "

συμβιβάζω   {5204, cv-2a(1)}
[συμβιβάσω, συνεβίβασα, -, -, συνεβιβάσθην] pr.
to cause to come together; to unite, knit together,
Eph 4:16; Col 2:2, 19; *to infer, conclude,* Acts
16:10; by impl. *to prove, demonstrate,* Acts 9:22;
in N.T. *to teach, instruct,* 1 Cor 2:16; Acts 19:33*

συμβιβάζων   pres act ptcp nom sg masc
[Ac 9:22; cv-2a(1); 5204]   "
συμβιβάσει   fut act ind 3 sg
[1C 2:16; cv-2a(1); 5204]   "
συμβιβασθέντες   aor pass ptcp nom pl masc
[Cl 2:2; cv-2a(1); 5204]   "
συμβουλεύσας   aor act ptcp nom sg masc
[Jn 18:14; cv-1a(6); 5205]   συμβουλεύω

συμβουλεύω   {5205, cv-1a(6)}
[-, συνεβούλευσα, -, -, -] *to counsel, advise, exhort,*
John 18:14; Rev 3:18; mid. *to consult together,
plot,* Matt 26:4; John 11:53 v.l.; Acts 9:23*

συμβουλεύω   pres act ind 1 sg
[Rv 3:18; cv-1a(6); 5205]   "

συμβούλιον, ου, τό   {5206, n-2c}
counsel, consultation, mutual consultation, Matt
12:14; 22:15; 27:1, 7; 28:12; Mark 3:6; Acts 27:1,
7; 28:12; *a council of counsellors,* Acts 25:12*

συμβούλιον   acc sg neut
[7t; n-2c; 5206]   συμβούλιον
συμβουλίου   gen sg neut [Ac 25:12; n-2c; 5206]   "

σύμβουλος, ου, ὁ   {5207, n-2a}
a counsellor; advisor, one who shares one's counsel,
Rom 11:34*

σύμβουλος   nom sg masc
[Rm 11:34; n-2a; 5207]   σύμβουλος

Συμεών, ὁ   {5208, n-3g(2)}
Symeon, Simeon, pr. name. indecl. (1) *Simeon,*
son of Juda, Luke 3:30. (2) *Simeon,* son of Jacob,
Rev 7:7. (3) *Simeon,* a prophet of Jerusalem,
Luke 2:25, 34. (4) *Simeon,* or *Simon Peter,* Acts
15:14; 2 Peter 1:1. (5) *Simeon,* called Niger, Acts
13:1*

Συμεών   indecl [7t; n-3g(2); 5208]   Συμεών
συμμαθηταῖς   dat pl masc
[Jn 11:16; n-1f; 5209]   συμμαθητής

συμμαθητής, οῦ, ὁ   {5209, n-1f}
a fellow-disciple, John 11:16*

συμμαρτυρεῖ   pres act ind 3 sg
[Rm 8:16; cv-1d(2a); 5210]   συμμαρτυρέω

συμμαρτυρέω   {5210, cv-1d(2a)}
[-, -, -, -, -] *to testify* or *bear witness together with*
another, *confirm, add testimony,* Rom 2:15; 8:16;
9:1; Rev 22:18 v.l.*

συμμαρτυρούσης   pres act ptcp gen sg fem
[2t; cv-1d(2a); 5210]   "
συμμερίζονται   pres mid ind 3 pl
[1C 9:13; cv-2a(1); 5211]   συμμερίζω

συμμερίζω   {5211, cv-2a(1)}
[-, -, -, -, -] *to divide with* another so as to receive
a part to one's self, *share with, partake with,* 1
Cor 9:13*

συμμέτοχα   acc pl neut
[Ep 3:6; a-3a; 5212]   συμμέτοχος
συμμέτοχοι   nom pl masc [Ep 5:7; a-3a; 5212]   "

συμμέτοχος, ον   {5212, a-3a}
a partaker with any one, *a joint partaker,* Eph 3:6;
5:7*

συμμιμηταί   nom pl masc
[Pp 3:17; n-1f; 5213]   συμμιμητής

συμμιμητής, οῦ, ὁ   {5213, n-1f}
an imitator together with any one, *a joint-imitator,*
Phil 3:17*

συμμορφιζόμενος   pres pass ptcp nom sg masc
[Pp 3:10; cv-2a(1); 5214]   συμμορφίζω

συμμορφίζω   {5214, cv-2a(1)}
[-, -, -, -, -] *to conform to, take on the same form as,*
Phil 3:10*

σύμμορφον   acc sg neut
[Pp 3:21; a-3a; 5215]   σύμμορφος

σύμμορφος, ον   {5215, a-3a}
*of like form, assimilated, conformed, similar in
form,* Rom 8:29; Phil 3:21*

συμμόρφους   acc pl masc [Rm 8:29; a-3a; 5215]   "

συμμορφόω   {5216, cv-1d(3)}
[-, -, -, -, -] *to conform to, give the same form,* Phil
3:10 v.l.*

συμπαθεῖς   nom pl masc
[1P 3:8; a-4a; 5218]   συμπαθής

συμπαθέω   {5217, cv-1d(2a)}
[-, συνεπάθησα, -, -, -] *to sympathize with,* Heb
4:15; *to be compassionate,* Heb 10:34*

συμπαθής, ές   {5218, a-4a}
sympathizing, compassionate, 1 Peter 3:8*

συμπαθῆσαι   aor act inf
[Hb 4:15; cv-1d(2a); 5217]   συμπαθέω

συμπαραγενόμενοι   aor mid ptcp nom pl masc
[Lk 23:48; cv-1c(2); 5219]   συμπαραγίνομαι

συμπαραγίνομαι   {5219, cv-1c(2)}
[-, συμπαρεγενόμην, -, -, -] *to be present together
with; to come together, convene,* Luke 23:48; *to
stand by* or *support* one judicially, 2 Tim 4:16 v.l.*

συμπαρακαλέω   {5220, cv-1d(2b)}
[-, -, -, -, συμπαρεκλήθην] *to invite, exhort* along
with others; pass. *to share in mutual
encouragement,* Rom 1:12*

συμπαρακληθῆναι   aor pass inf
[Rm 1:12; cv-1d(2b); 5220]   συμπαρακαλέω

συμπαραλαβεῖν   aor act inf
[Ac 15:37; cv-3a(2b); 5221]   συμπαραλαμβάνω

συμπαραλαβόντες   aor act ptcp nom pl masc
[Ac 12:25; cv-3a(2b); 5221]   "

συμπαραλαβών   aor act ptcp nom sg masc
[Ga 2:1; cv-3a(2b); 5221]   "

συμπαραλαμβάνειν   pres act inf
[Ac 15:38; cv-3a(2b); 5221]   "

συμπαραλαμβάνω   {5221, cv-3a(2b)}
[-, συμπαρέλαβον, -, -, -] *to take along with, take as
a companion,* Acts 12:25; 15:37, 38; Gal 2:1*

συμπαραμένω   {5222, cv-1c(2)}
[συμπαραμενῶ, -, -, -, -] *to remain* or *continue
with* or *among* in order *to help,* Phil 1:25 v.l.*

συμπάρειμι   {5223, cv-6a}
[-, -, -, -, -] *to be present with* any one, Acts 25:24*

συμπαρόντες   pres act ptcp voc pl masc
[Ac 25:24; cv-6a; 5223]   συμπάρειμι

συμπάσχει   pres act ind 3 sg
[1C 12:26; cv-5a; 5224]   συμπάσχω

συμπάσχομεν   pres act ind 1 pl
[Rm 8:17; cv-5a; 5224]   "

συμπάσχω   {5224, cv-5a}
[-, συνέπαθον, -, -, -] *to suffer with, sympathize,* 1
Cor 12:26; *to suffer as* another, *endure
corresponding sufferings,* Rom 8:17*

συμπέμπω   {5225, cv-1b(1)}
[-, συνέπεμψα, -, -, -] *to send with* any one, 2 Cor
8:18, 22*

συμπεριέχω   {5226, cv-1b(2)}
[-, -, -, -, -] *surround, stand around,* Luke 12:1 v.l.*

συμπεριλαβών   aor act ptcp nom sg masc
[Ac 20:10; cv-3a(2b); 5227]   συμπεριλαμβάνω

συμπεριλαμβάνω   {5227, cv-3a(2b)}
[-, συμπεριέλαβον, -, -, -] *to embrace together; to
embrace,* Acts 20:10*

συμπίνω   {5228, cv-3a(1)}
[-, συνέπιον, -, -, -] *to drink with* any one, Acts
10:41*

συμπίπτω   {5229, cv-1b(3)}
[-, συνέπεσον, -, -, -] *fall together, collapse,* Luke
6: 49*

συμπληροῦσθαι   pres pass inf
[2t; cv-1d(3); 5230]   συμπληρόω

συμπληρόω   {5230, cv-1d(3)}
[(συνέπληρουν), -, -, -, -, -] *to fill, fill up,* Luke
8:23; pass., of time, *to be completed, have fully
come,* Luke 9:51; Acts 2:1*

συμπνίγει   pres act ind 3 sg
[Mt 13:22; cv-1b(2); 5231]   συμπνίγω

συμπνίγονται   pres pass ind 3 pl
[Lk 8:14; cv-1b(2); 5231]   "

συμπνίγουσιν   pres act ind 3 pl
[Mk 4:19; cv-1b(2); 5231]   "

συμπνίγω   {5231, cv-1b(2)}
[(συνέπνιγον), -, συνέπνιξα, -, -, -] *to throttle,
choke;* trop. *to choke* the growth or increase of
seed or plants, Matt 13:22; Mark 4:7, 19; Luke
8:14; *to press upon, crowd,* Luke 8:42; 12:1 v.l.*

συμπολῖται   nom pl masc
[Ep 2:19; n-1f; 5232]   συμπολίτης

συμπολίτης, ου, ὁ   {5232, n-1f}
a fellow-citizen, met. Eph 2:19*

συμπορεύομαι   {5233, cv-1a(6)}
[(συνεπορευόμην), -, -, -, -, -] *to go with,
accompany,* Luke 7:11; 14:25; 24:15; *to come
together, assemble,* Mark 10:1*

συμπορεύονται   pres mid ind 3 pl
[Mk 10:1; cv-1a(6); 5233]   συμπορεύομαι

συμποσία, ας, ἡ   {5234, n-1a}
common meal, Mark 6:39 v.l.*

συμπόσια   acc pl neut [2t; n-2c; 5235]   συμπόσιον

συμπόσιον, ου, τό {5235, n-2c}
a drinking together; a feast, banquet; a festive company; in N.T., pl. συμπόσια, *eating party,* Mark 6:39*

συμπρεσβύτερος, ου, ὁ {5236, n-2a}
a fellow-elder, fellow-presbyter, 1 Peter 5:1*

συμπρεσβύτερος   nom sg masc
[1P 5:1; n-2a; 5236]   συμπρεσβύτερος

συμφέρει   pres act ind 3 sg
[10t; cv-1c(1); 5237]   συμφέρω

συμφέρον   pres act ptcp nom sg neut
[2C 12:1; cv-1c(1); 5237]   "

συμφέρον   pres act ptcp acc sg neut
[2t; cv-1c(1); 5237]   "

συμφερόντων   pres act ptcp gen pl neut
[Ac 20:20; cv-1c(1); 5237]   "

συμφέρω {5237, cv-1c(1)}
[(συνέφερον), -, συνήνεγκα, -, -, -] *to bring together, collect,* Acts 19:19; absol. *be for the benefit* of any one, *be profitable, advantageous, expedient,* 1 Cor 6:12; *to suit best, be appropriate,* 2 Cor 8:10; *good, benefit, profit, advantage,* Acts 20:20; 1 Cor 7:35; 10:33 v.l.; *it is profitable, advantageous, expedient,* Matt 5:29, 30; 19:10

σύμφημι {5238, cv-6b}
[-, -, -, -, -, -] pr. *to agree with,* Rom 7:16*

σύμφημι   pres act ind 1 sg
[Rm 7:16; cv-6b; 5238]   σύμφημι

σύμφορον   acc sg neut   [2t; a-3a; 5239]   σύμφορος

σύμφορος, ον {5239, a-3a}
profitable, expedient, 1 Cor 7:35; 10:33*

συμφορτίζω {5240, cv-2a(1)}
[-, -, -, -, -] *to burden together,* Phil 3:10 v.l.*

συμφυεῖσαι   aor pass ptcp nom pl fem
[Lk 8:7; cv-1a(4); 5243]   συμφύω

συμφυλέτης, ου, ὁ {5241, n-1f}
pr. *one of the same tribe; a fellow-citizen, fellow-countryman,* 1 Thess 2:14*

συμφυλετῶν   gen pl masc
[1Th 2:14; n-1f; 5241]   συμφυλέτης

σύμφυτοι   nom pl masc
[Rm 6:5; a-3a; 5242]   σύμφυτος

σύμφυτος, ον {5242, a-3a}
pr. *planted together, grown together;* in N.T. met. *grown together, closely entwined* or *united with,* Rom 6:5*

συμφύω {5243, cv-1a(4)}
[-, -, -, -, συνεφύην] *to make to grow together;* pass. *to grow* or *spring up with,* Luke 8:7*

συμφωνέω {5244, cv-1d(2a)}
[συμφωνήσω, συνεφώνησα, -, -, συνεφωνήθην] *to sound together, to be in unison, be in accord;* trop. *to agree with, accord with* in purport, Acts 15:15; *to harmonize with, suit with,* Luke 5:36; *to agree with, make an agreement,* Matt 18:19; 20:2, 13; Acts 5:9*

συμφωνήσας   aor act ptcp nom sg masc
[Mt 20:2; cv-1d(2a); 5244]   συμφωνέω

συμφωνήσει   fut act ind 3 sg
[Lk 5:36; cv-1d(2a); 5244]   "

συμφώνησις, εως, ἡ {5245, n-3e(5b)}
unison, accord; agreement, 2 Cor 6:15*

συμφώνησις   nom sg fem
[2C 6:15; n-3e(5b); 5245]   συμφώνησις

συμφωνήσωσιν   aor act subj 3 pl
[Mt 18:19; cv-1d(2a); 5244]   συμφωνέω

συμφωνία, ας, ἡ {5246, n-1a}
symphony, harmony of sounds, concert of instruments, music, Luke 15:25*

συμφωνίας   gen sg fem
[Lk 15:25; n-1a; 5246]   συμφωνία

σύμφωνος, ον {5247, a-3a}
agreeing in sound; met. *harmonious, agreeing, accord, agreement,* 1 Cor 7:5*

συμφώνου   gen sg neut
[1C 7:5; a-3a; 5247]   σύμφωνος

συμφωνοῦσιν   pres act ind 3 pl
[Ac 15:15; cv-1d(2a); 5244]   συμφωνέω

συμψηφίζω {5248, cv-2a(1)}
[-, συνεψήφισα -, -, -] *to calculate together, compute, reckon up,* Acts 19:19; 1:26 v.l.*

σύμψυχοι   nom pl masc
[Pp 2:2; a-3a; 5249]   σύμψυχος

σύμψυχος, ον {5249, a-3a}
united in mind, at unity, Phil 2:2

σύν {5250, prep}
with, together with, Matt 25:27; 26:35; 27:38; *attendant on,* 1 Cor 15:10; *besides,* Luke 24:21; *with, with the assistance of,* 1 Cor 5:4; *with, in the same manner as,* Gal 3:9; εἶναι σύν τινι, *to be with any one, to be in company with, accompany,* Luke 2:13; 8:38; *to be on the side of, be a partisan of any one,* Acts 4:13; 14:4; οἱ σύν τινι, *those with any one, the companions of any one,* Mark 2:26; Acts 22:9; *the colleagues, associates of any one,* Acts 5:17, 21

σύν   prep-dat   [128t; prep; 5250]   σύν

συναγαγεῖν   aor act inf
[3t; cv-1b(2); 5251]   συνάγω

συναγάγετε   aor act imperative 2 pl
[2t; cv-1b(2); 5251]   "

συναγάγῃ   aor act subj 3 sg
[Jn 11:52; cv-1b(2); 5251]   "

συναγαγόντες   aor act ptcp nom pl masc
[2t; cv-1b(2); 5251]   "

συναγαγούσῃ   aor act ptcp dat sg fem
[Mt 13:47; cv-1b(2); 5251]   "

συναγαγών   aor act ptcp nom sg masc
[2t; cv-1b(2); 5251]   "

συνάγει   pres act ind 3 sg
[Jn 4:36; cv-1b(2); 5251]   "

συνάγεται   pres pass ind 3 sg
[Mk 4:1; cv-1b(2); 5251]   "

συνάγονται   pres pass ind 3 pl
[2t; cv-1b(2); 5251]   "

συνάγουσιν   pres act ind 3 pl
[2t; cv-1b(2); 5251]   "

συνάγω {5251, cv-1b(2)}
[συνάξω, συνήγαγον, -, συνῆγμαι, συνήχθην] *to bring together, collect, gather,* as grain, fruits, etc., Matt 3:12 6:26; 13:30, 47; *to collect* an assembly; pass. *to convene, come together, meet,* Matt 2:4; 13:2; 18:20; 22:10; in N.T. *to receive with kindness and hospitality, to entertain,* Matt 25:35, 38, 43; *advance, move,* Matt 20:28 v.l.

συνάγω pres act ind 1 sg
   [Mt 25:26; cv-1b(2); 5251]   "
συναγωγαῖς dat pl fem [15t; n-1b; 5252] συναγωγή
συναγωγάς acc pl fem [8t; n-1b; 5252]   "

συναγωγή, ῆς, ἡ {5252, n-1b}
a collecting, gathering; a Christian *assembly* or *congregation,* James 2:2; *the congregation* of a synagogue, Acts 9:2; hence, the place itself, *a synagogue,* Luke 7:5

συναγωγή nom sg fem [2t; n-1b; 5252]   "
συναγωγῇ dat sg fem [12t; n-1b; 5252]   "
συναγωγήν acc sg fem [12t; n-1b; 5252]   "
συναγωγῆς gen sg fem [6t; n-1b; 5252]   "
συναγωγῶν gen pl fem [Lk 13:10; n-1b; 5252] "
συνάγων pres act ptcp nom sg masc
   [3t; cv-1b(2); 5251]   συνάγω

συναγωνίζομαι {5253, cv-2a(1)}
[-, συνηγωνισάμην -, -, -] *to combat in company with* any one; *to exert one's strength with, to be earnest in aiding, help,* Rom 15:30*

συναγωνίσασθαι aor mid inf
   [Rm 15:30; cv-2a(1); 5253]   συναγωνίζομαι

συναθλέω {5254, cv-1d(2a)}
[-, συνήθλησα, -, -, -] pr. *to fight* or *work on the side of* any one; in N.T. *to cooperate vigorously with* a person, Phil 4:3; *to make effort in the cause of, in support of* a thing, Phil 1:27*

συναθλοῦντες pres act ptcp nom pl masc
   [Pp 1:27; cv-1d(2a); 5254]   συναθλέω

συναθροίζω {5255, cv-2a(1)}
[-, συνήθροισα, -, συνήθροισμαι, συνηθροίσθην] *to gather; to bring together,* Acts 19:25; pass. *to come together, convene,* Acts 12:12; Luke 24:33 v.l.*

συναθροίσας aor act ptcp nom sg masc
   [Ac 19:25; cv-2a(1); 5255]   συναθροίζω
συναίρει pres act ind 3 sg
   [Mt 25:19; cv-2d(2); 5256]   συναίρω
συναίρειν pres act inf
   [Mt 18:24; cv-2d(2); 5256]   "

συναίρω {5256, cv-2d(2)}
[-, συνῆρα, -, -, -] *to take up* a thing *with* any one; in N.T. συναίρειν λόγον, *to settle accounts, reckon* in order to payment, Matt 18:23, 24; 25:19*

συναιχμάλωτος, ου, ὁ {5257, n-2a}
a fellow-captive, Rom 16:7; Col 4:10; Phil 23*

συναιχμάλωτος nom sg masc
   [2t; n-2a; 5257]   συναιχμάλωτος
συναιχμαλώτους acc pl masc
   [Rm 16:7; n-2a; 5257]   "

συνακολουθέω {5258, cv-1d(2a)}
[(συνηκολούθουν), -, συνηκολούθησα, -, -, -] *to follow in company with, accompany,* Mark 5:37; 14:51; Luke 23:49; John 13:36 v.l.*

συνακολουθῆσαι aor act inf
   [Mk 5:37; cv-1d(2a); 5258]   συνακολουθέω
συνακολουθοῦσαι pres act ptcp nom pl fem
   [Lk 23:49; cv-1d(2a); 5258]   "
συναλιζόμενος pres mid ptcp nom sg masc
   [Ac 1:4; cv-2a(1); 5259]   συναλίζω

συναλίζω {5259, cv-2a(1)}
[-, -, -, -, -] *to cause to come together, collect, assemble, congregate;* mid. *to convene to one's self,* Acts 1:4*

συναλίσκομαι {5260, cv-5b}
[-, -, -, -, -] *be made captive,* Acts 1:4 v.l.*

συναλλάσσω {5261, cv-2b}
[(συνήλλασσον), -, -, -, -, -] *to negotiate* or *bargain with* someone; *to reconcile,* Acts 7:26*

συναναβαίνω {5262, cv-2d(6)}
[-, συνανέβην, -, -, -] *to go up, ascend with* someone, Mark 15:41; Acts 13:31*

συναναβᾶσαι aor act ptcp nom pl fem
   [Mk 15:41; cv-2d(6); 5262]   συναναβαίνω
συναναβᾶσιν aor act ptcp dat pl masc
   [Ac 13:31; cv-2d(6); 5262]   "

συνανάκειμαι {5263, cv-6b}
[(συνανεκείμην), -, -, -, -, -] *to recline with* someone at table, Matt 9:10; 14:9; Mark 2:15; 6:22; Luke 7:49; 14:10, 15*

συνανακείμενοι pres mid ptcp nom pl masc
   [Lk 7:49; cv-6b; 5263]   συνανάκειμαι
συνανακειμένοις pres mid ptcp dat pl masc
   [Mk 6:22; cv-6b; 5263]
συνανακειμένους pres mid ptcp acc pl masc
   [Mt 14:9; cv-6b; 5263]
συνανακειμένων pres mid ptcp gen pl masc
   [2t; cv-6b; 5263]   "

συναναμείγνυμι {5264, cv-3c(2)}
[-, -, -, -, -] *to mix together with;* mid. met. *to mingle one's self with, to associate with,* 1 Cor 5:9, 11; 2 Thess 3:14*

συναναμίγνυσθαι pres mid inf
   [3t; cv-3c(2); 5264]   συναναμείγνυμι

συναναπαύομαι {5265, cv-1a(5)}
[-, συνανεπαυσάμην, -, -, -] *to experience refreshment* or *rest in company with* someone, Rom 15:32*

συναναπαύσωμαι aor mid subj 1 sg
   [Rm 15:32; cv-1a(5); 5265]   συναναπαύομαι

συναναστρέφομαι {5266, cv-1b(1)}
[-, -, -, -, -] *associate with,* Acts 10:41 v.l.*

συνανέκειντο imperf mid ind 3 pl
   [2t; cv-6b; 5263]   συνανάκειμαι

συναντάω {5267, cv-1d(1a)}
[συναντήσω, συνήντησα, -, -, -] *to meet with, fall in with, encounter,* Luke 9:18 v.l., 37; 22:10; Acts

10:25; Heb 7:1, 10; *to occur, happen to, befall,* Acts 20:22*

συναντήσας   aor act ptcp nom sg masc
[2t; cv-1d(1a); 5267]   συναντάω

συναντήσει   fut act ind 3 sg
[Lk 22:10; cv-1d(1a); 5267]   "

συνάντησις, εως, ἡ   {5268, n-3e(5b)}
a meeting, Matt 8:34 v.l.; John 12:13 v.l.*

συναντήσοντα   fut act ptcp acc pl neut
[Ac 20:22; cv-1d(1a); 5267]   "

συναντιλάβηται   aor mid subj 3 sg
[Lk 10:40; cv-3a(2b); 5269]   συναντιλαμβάνομαι

συναντιλαμβάνεται   pres mid ind 3 sg
[Rm 8:26; cv-3a(2b); 5269]   "

συναντιλαμβάνομαι   {5269, cv-3a(2b)}
[-, συναντελαβόμην, -, -, -] pr. *to take hold of with*
someone; *to support, help, aid,* Luke 10:40; Rom 8:26*

συνάξει   fut act ind 3 sg
[Mt 3:12; cv-1b(2); 5251]   συνάγω

συνάξω   fut act ind 1 sg
[2t; cv-1b(2); 5251]   "

συναπαγόμενοι   pres pass ptcp nom pl masc
[Rm 12:16; cv-1b(2); 5270]   συναπάγω

συναπάγω   {5270, cv-1b(2)}
[-, -, -, -, συναπήχθην] *to lead* or *carry away with;
to seduce;* pass. *to be led away, carried astray,* Gal
2:13; 2 Peter 3:17; mid. *to conform one's self
willingly to* certain circumstances, Rom 12:16*

συναπαχθέντες   aor pass ptcp nom pl masc
[2P 3:17; cv-1b(2); 5270]   "

συναπεθάνομεν   aor act ind 1 pl
[2Ti 2:11; cv-5a; 5271]   συναποθνῄσκω

συναπέστειλα   aor act ind 1 sg
[2C 12:18; cv-2d(1); 5273]   συναποστέλλω

συναπήχθη   aor pass ind 3 sg
[Ga 2:13; cv-1b(2); 5270]   συναπάγω

συναποθανεῖν   aor act inf
[2t; cv-5a; 5271]   συναποθνῄσκω

συναποθνῄσκω   {5271, cv-5a}
[-, συναπέθανον, -, -, -] *to die together with* any
one, Mark 14:31; 2 Cor 7:3; met. *to die with,* in
respect of a spiritual likeness, 2 Tim 2:11*

συναπόλλυμι   {5272, cv-3c(2)}
[-, συναπώλεσα, -, -, -] *to destroy together with*
others; mid. *to perish* or *be destroyed with* others,
Heb 11:31*

συναποστέλλω   {5273, cv-2d(1)}
[-, συναπέστειλα, -, -, -] *to send forth together with*
someone, 2 Cor 12:18*

συναπώλετο   aor mid ind 3 sg
[Hb 11:31; cv-3c(2); 5272]   συναπόλλυμι

συνᾶραι   aor act inf
[Mt 18:23; cv-2d(2); 5256]   συναίρω

συναρμολογέω   {5274, cv-1d(2a)}
[-, -, -, -, -] *to join together fitly, fit* or *frame
together, compact,* Eph 2:21; 4:16*

συναρμολογουμένη   pres pass ptcp nom sg fem
[Ep 2:21; cv-1d(2a); 5274]   συναρμολογέω

συναρμολογούμενον   pres pass ptcp nom sg neut
[Ep 4:16; cv-1d(2a); 5274]   "

συναρπάζω   {5275, cv-2a(1)}
[-, συνήρπασα, συνήρπακα, -, συνηρπάσθην]
pluperf., συνηρπάκειν, *to snatch up, clutch; to
seize and carry off suddenly,* Acts 6:12; *to seize
with force and violence,* Luke 8:29; Acts 19:29;
pass. of a ship, *to be caught and swept on* by the
wind, Acts 27:15*

συναρπάσαντες   aor act ptcp nom pl masc
[Ac 19:29; cv-2a(1); 5275]   συναρπάζω

συναρπασθέντος   aor pass ptcp gen sg neut
[Ac 27:15; cv-2a(1); 5275]   "

συναυξάνεσθαι   pres pass inf
[Mt 13:30; cv-3a(1); 5277]   συναυξάνω

συναυξάνω   {5277, cv-3a(1)}
[-, -, -, -, -] pas., *to grow together* in company,
Matt 13:30*

συναχθέντες   aor pass ptcp nom pl masc
[Mt 28:12; cv-1b(2); 5251]   συνάγω

συναχθέντων   aor pass ptcp gen pl masc
[1C 5:4; cv-1b(2); 5251]   "

συναχθῆναι   aor pass inf   [2t; cv-1b(2); 5251]   "

συναχθήσονται   fut pass ind 3 pl
[2t; cv-1b(2); 5251]   "

συνάχθητε   aor pass imperative 2 pl
[Rv 19:17; cv-1b(2); 5251]   "

συνδεδεμένοι   perf pass ptcp nom pl masc
[Hb 13:3; cv-1d(2b); 5279]   συνδέω

σύνδεσμον   acc sg masc
[Ac 8:23; n-2a; 5278]   σύνδεσμος

σύνδεσμος, ου, ὁ   {5278, n-2a}
that which binds together, Col 2:19; *a band* of
union, Eph 4:3; Col 3:14; *a bundle,* or, *bond,* Acts
8:23*

σύνδεσμος   nom sg masc [Cl 3:14; n-2a; 5278]   "

συνδέσμῳ   dat sg masc [Ep 4:3; n-2a; 5278]   "

συνδέσμων   gen pl masc [Cl 2:19; n-2a; 5278]   "

συνδέω   {5279, cv-1d(2b)}
[-, -, -, συνδέδεμαι, -] *to bind together;* in N.T.
pass. *to be in bonds together,* Heb 13:3*

συνδοξάζω   {5280, cv-2a(1)}
[-, συνεδόξασα, -, -, συνεδοξάσθην] in N.T. *to
glorify together with, to exalt to a state of dignity
and happiness in company with,* to make to partake
in the glorification of another, Rom 8:17*

συνδοξασθῶμεν   aor pass subj 1 pl
[Rm 8:17; cv-2a(1); 5280]   συνδοξάζω

σύνδουλοι   nom pl masc [2t; n-2a; 5281] σύνδουλος

σύνδουλον   acc sg masc [Mt 18:33; n-2a; 5281] "

σύνδουλος, ου, ὁ   {5281, n-2a}
a fellow-slave, fellow-servant, Matt 24:49; 18:28f.,
31, 33; Col 4:7; Rev 6:11; 19:10; 22:9; *a
fellow-minister* of Christ, Col 1:7*

σύνδουλος   nom sg masc [4t; n-2a; 5281]   "

συνδούλου   gen sg masc [Cl 1:7; n-2a; 5281]   "

συνδούλους   acc pl masc [Mt 24:49; n-2a; 5281] "

συνδούλων   gen pl masc [Mt 18:28; n-2a; 5281]   "

συνδρομή, ῆς, ἡ   {5282, n-1b}
a running together, forming a mob, Acts 21:30*

συνδρομή   nom sg fem
   [Ac 21:30; n-1b; 5282]   συνδρομή
συνέβαινεν   imperf act ind 3 sg
   [1C 10:11; cv-2d(6); 5201]   συμβαίνω
συνεβάλετο   aor mid ind 3 sg
   [Ac 18:27; cv-2d(1); 5202]   συμβάλλω
συνέβαλλεν   imperf act ind 3 sg
   [Ac 20:14; cv-2d(1); 5202]   "
συνέβαλλον   imperf act ind 3 pl
   [2t; cv-2d(1); 5202]   "
συνέβη   aor act ind 3 sg
   [Ac 21:35; cv-2d(6); 5201]   συμβαίνω
συνεβίβασαν   aor act ind 3 pl
   [Ac 19:33; cv-2a(1); 5204]   συμβιβάζω
συνεβουλεύσαντο   aor mid ind 3 pl
   [2t; cv-1a(6); 5205]   συμβουλεύω

συνεγείρω   {5283, cv-2d(3)}
   [-, συνήγειρα, -, -, συνηγέρθην] *to raise up with*
   any one; *to raise up with* Christ by spiritual
   resemblance of His resurrection, Eph 2:6; Col
   2:12; 3:1*

συνέδραμεν   aor act ind 3 sg
   [Ac 3:11; cv-1b(2); 5340]   συντρέχω
συνέδραμον   aor act ind 3 pl
   [Mk 6:33; cv-1b(2); 5340]   "
συνέδρια   acc pl neut [2t; n-2c; 5284]   συνέδριον

συνέδριον, ου, τό   {5284, n-2c}
   pr. *a sitting together, assembly,* etc., in N.T. *the
   Sanhedrin,* the supreme council of the Jewish
   nation, Matt 5:22; 26:59; meton. *the Sanhedrin,*
   as including the members and place of
   meeting, Luke 22:66; Acts 4:15; genr. *a* judicial
   council, tribunal, Matt 10:17; Mark 13:9

συνέδριον   nom sg neut [3t; n-2c; 5284]   "
συνέδριον   acc sg neut [7t; n-2c; 5284]   "

συνέδριος, ου, ὁ   {5285, n-2a}
   BAGD say this is an erroneous form for
   σύνεδρος in Acts 5:35*

συνεδρίου   gen sg neut [3t; n-2c; 5284]   "
συνεδρίῳ   dat sg neut [7t; n-2c; 5284]   "
συνέζευξεν   aor act ind 3 sg
   [2t; cv-3c(2); 5183]   συζεύγνυμι
συνεζήτει   imperf act ind 3 sg
   [Ac 9:29; cv-1d(2a); 5184]   συζητέω
συνεζωοποίησεν   aor act ind 3 sg
   [2t; cv-1d(2a); 5188]   συζωοποιέω
συνέθεντο   aor mid ind 3 pl
   [2t; cv-6a; 5338]   συντίθημι
συνέθλιβον   imperf act ind 3 pl
   [Mk 5:24; cv-1b(1); 5315]   συνθλίβω
συνειδήσει   dat sg fem
   [3t; n-3e(5b); 5287]   συνείδησις
συνειδήσεσιν   dat pl fem
   [2C 5:11; n-3e(5b); 5287]   "
συνειδήσεως   gen sg fem [7t; n-3e(5b); 5287]   "
συνείδησιν   acc sg fem [16t; n-3e(5b); 5287]   "

συνείδησις, εως, ἡ   {5287, n-3e(5b)}
   consciousness, Heb 10:2; *a present idea, persisting
   notion, impression of reality,* 1 Cor 8:7 v.l.; 1 Peter
   2:19; *conscience,* as an inward moral impression
   of one's actions and principles, John 8:9 v.l.;
   Acts 23:1; 24:16; Rom 9:1; 2 Cor 1:12; *conscience,*
   as the inward faculty of moral judgment, Rom
   2:15; 13:5; 1 Cor 8:7b, 10, 12; 10:25, 27, 28, 29; 2
   Cor 4:2; 5:11; 1 Tim 1:5, 19; 3:9; 4:2; 2 Tim 1:3;
   conscience, as the inward moral and spiritual
   frame, Titus 1:15; Heb 9:9, 14; 10:22; 13:18; 1
   Peter 3:16, 21*

συνείδησις   nom sg fem [3t; n-3e(5b); 5287]   "
συνειδυίης   perf act ptcp gen sg fem
   [Ac 5:2; cv-1d(1a); 5328]   συνοράω
συνείληφεν   perf act ind 3 sg
   [Lk 1:36; cv-3a(2b); 5197]   συλλαμβάνω

σύνειμι   {5289, cv-6b}
   [(συνῆν [3 sg]), -, -, -, -, -] (1) from εἰμί, *to be with,
   be in company with,* Luke 9:18; Acts 22:11. (2)
   from συν + εἶμι (5290), *to come together,* Luke
   8:4*

συνείπετο   imperf mid ind 3 sg
   [Ac 20:4; cv-1d(3); 5299]   συνέπομαι

συνεισέρχομαι   {5291, cv-1b(2)}
   [-, συνεισῆλθον, -, -, -] *to enter with* someone,
   Mark 6:33 v.l.; John 18:15; *to embark with,* John
   6:22*

συνεισῆλθεν   aor act ind 3 sg
   [2t; cv-1b(2); 5291]   συνεισέρχομαι
συνείχετο   imperf pass ind 3 sg
   [Ac 18:5; cv-1b(2); 5309]   συνέχω
συνείχοντο   imperf pass ind 3 pl
   [Lk 8:37; cv-1b(2); 5309]   "
συνεκάθισεν   aor act ind 3 sg
   [Ep 2:6; cv-2a(1); 5154]   συγκαθίζω
συνεκάλεσαν   aor act ind 3 pl
   [Ac 5:21; cv-1d(2b); 5157]   συγκαλέω

συνέκδημος, ου, ὁ   {5292, n-2a}
   one who accompanies another *to foreign countries,
   fellow-traveller,* Acts 19:29; 2 Cor 8:19*

συνέκδημος   nom sg masc
   [2C 8:19; n-2a; 5292]   συνέκδημος
συνεκδήμους   acc pl masc [Ac 19:29; n-2a; 5292]   "
συνεκέρασεν   aor act ind 3 sg
   [1C 12:24; cv-3c(1); 5166]   συγκεράννυμι
συνεκίνησαν   aor act ind 3 pl
   [Ac 6:12; cv-1d(2a); 5167]   συγκινέω
συνέκλεισαν   aor act ind 3 pl
   [Lk 5:6; cv-1a(3); 5168]   συγκλείω
συνέκλεισεν   aor act ind 3 sg
   [2t; cv-1a(3); 5168]   "
συνεκλεκτή   nom sg fem
   [1P 5:13; a-1a(2a); 5293]   συνεκλεκτός

συνεκλεκτός, ή, όν   {5293, a-1a(2a)}
   chosen along with others; *elected* to Gospel
   privileges *along with,* 1 Peter 5:13*

συνεκόμισαν   aor act ind 3 pl
   [Ac 8:2; cv-2a(1); 5172]   συγκομίζω

συνεκπορεύομαι   {5294, cv-1a(6)}
[-, -, -, -, -] *to go out with*, Acts 3:11 v.l.*

συνέλαβεν   aor act ind 3 sg
[Lk 1:24; cv-3a(2b); 5197]   συλλαμβάνω

συνέλαβον   aor act ind 3 pl [2t; cv-3a(2b); 5197]   "

συνελάλησεν   aor act ind 3 sg
[Lk 22:4; cv-1d(2a); 5196]   συλλαλέω

συνελάλουν   imperf act ind 3 pl
[2t; cv-1d(2a); 5196]   "

συνελαύνω   {5295}
[-, συνήλασα, -, -, -] pr. *to drive together; to urge
to meet;* in N.T. *to urge* to union, Acts 7:26 v.l.*

συνέλεξαν   aor act ind 3 pl
[Mt 13:48; cv-1b(2); 5198]   συλλέγω

συνεληλύθεισαν   pluperf act ind 3 pl
[Ac 19:32; cv-1b(2); 5302]   συνέρχομαι

συνεληλυθότας   perf act ptcp acc pl masc
[Ac 10:27; cv-1b(2); 5302]   "

συνεληλυθυῖαι   perf act ptcp nom pl fem
[Lk 23:55; cv-1b(2); 5302]   "

συνελθεῖν   aor act inf   [3t; cv-1b(2); 5302]   "

συνέλθῃ   aor act subj 3 sg
[1C 14:23; cv-1b(2); 5302]   "

συνελθόντα   aor act ptcp acc sg masc
[Ac 15:38; cv-1b(2); 5302]   "

συνελθόντας   aor act ptcp acc pl masc
[Jn 11:33; cv-1b(2); 5302]   "

συνελθόντες   aor act ptcp nom pl masc
[Ac 1:6; cv-1b(2); 5302]   "

συνελθόντων   aor act ptcp gen pl masc
[3t; cv-1b(2); 5302]   "

συνελθούσαις   aor act ptcp dat pl fem
[Ac 16:13; cv-1b(2); 5302]   "

συνελογίσαντο   aor mid ind 3 pl
[Lk 20:5; cv-2a(1); 5199]   συλλογίζομαι

συνενέγκαντες   aor act ptcp nom pl masc
[Ac 19:19; cv-1c(1); 5237]   συμφέρω

συνέξουσιν   fut act ind 3 pl
[Lk 19:43; cv-1b(2); 5309]   συνέχω

συνεπαθήσατε   aor act ind 2 pl
[Hb 10:34; cv-1d(2a); 5217]   συμπαθέω

συνεπέθεντο   aor mid ind 3 pl
[Ac 24:9; cv-6a; 5298]   συνεπιτίθημι

συνεπέμψαμεν   aor act ind 1 pl
[2t; cv-1b(1); 5225]   συμπέμπω

συνέπεσεν   aor act ind 3 sg
[Lk 6:49; cv-1b(3); 5229]   συμπίπτω

συνεπέστη   aor act ind 3 sg
[Ac 16:22; cv-6a; 5308]   συνεφίστημι

συνεπιμαρτυρέω   {5296, cv-1d(2a)}
[-, -, -, -, -] *to join in according testimony; to
support by testimony, to confirm, sanction,* Heb
2:4*

συνεπιμαρτυροῦντος   pres act ptcp gen sg masc
[Hb 2:4; cv-1d(2a); 5296]   συνεπιμαρτυρέω

συνεπίομεν   aor act ind 1 pl
[Ac 10:41; cv-3a(1); 5228]   συμπίνω

συνεπίσκοπος, ου, ὁ   {5297, n-2a}
fellow overseer, Phil 1:1 v.l.*

συνεπιτίθημι   {5298, cv-6a}
[-, συνεπέθηκα, -, -, -] can also be spelled
συνεπιτίθεμαι, mid., *to set upon along with, join
with others* in an attack; *to unite in impeaching,*
Acts 24:9*

συνεπληροῦντο   imperf pass ind 3 pl
[Lk 8:23; cv-1d(3); 5230]   συμπληρόω

συνέπνιγον   imperf act ind 3 pl
[Lk 8:42; cv-1b(2); 5231]   συμπνίγω

συνέπνιξαν   aor act ind 3 pl
[Mk 4:7; cv-1b(2); 5231]   "

συνέπομαι   {5299, cv-1d(3)}
[(συνειπόμην), -, -, -, -, -] *to follow with, attend,
accompany,* Acts 20:4*

συνεπορεύετο   imperf mid ind 3 sg
[Lk 24:15; cv-1a(6); 5233]   συμπορεύομαι

συνεπορεύοντο   imperf mid ind 3 pl
[2t; cv-1a(6); 5233]   "

συνεργεῖ   pres act ind 3 sg
[Rm 8:28; cv-1d(2a); 5300]   συνεργέω

συνεργέω   {5300, cv-1d(2a)}
[(συνήργουν), -, συνήργησα, -, -, -] *to work
together with, to cooperate,* etc., 1 Cor 16:16; 2 Cor
6:1; *to assist, afford aid to,* Mark 16:20; James
2:22; absol. *to conspire actively* to a result, Rom
8:28*

συνεργοί   nom pl masc   [5t; n-2a; 5301]   συνεργός
συνεργόν   acc sg masc   [3t; n-2a; 5301]   "

συνεργός, οῦ, ὁ   {5301, n-2a}
a fellow-laborer, associate, helper, Rom 16:3, 9, 21;
2 Cor 1:24

συνεργός   nom sg masc   [2t; n-2a; 5301]   "
συνεργοῦντες   pres act ptcp nom pl masc
[2C 6:1; cv-1d(2a); 5300]   συνεργέω

συνεργοῦντι   pres act ptcp dat sg masc
[1C 16:16; cv-1d(2a); 5300]   "

συνεργοῦντος   pres act ptcp gen sg masc
[Mk 16:20; cv-1d(2a); 5300]   "

συνεργούς   acc pl masc
[Rm 16:3; n-2a; 5301]   συνεργός

συνεργῷ   dat sg masc   [Pm 1; n-2a; 5301]   "
συνεργῶν   gen pl masc   [Pp 4:3; n-2a; 5301]   "

συνέρχεσθε   pres mid ind 2 pl
[1C 11:17; cv-1b(2); 5302]   συνέρχομαι

συνέρχεται   pres mid ind 3 sg
[Mk 3:20; cv-1b(2); 5302]   "

συνέρχησθε   pres mid subj 2 pl
[2t; cv-1b(2); 5302]   "

συνέρχομαι   {5302, cv-1b(2)}
[(συνηρχόμην), συνελεύσομαι, συνῆλθον,
συνελήλυθα, -, -] pluperf., συνεληλύθεισαν (3
pl), *to come together; to assemble,* Mark 3:20; 6:33;
14:53; *to cohabit* matrimonially, Matt 1:18; 1 Cor
7:5; *to go* or *come with* any one, *to accompany,*
Luke 23:55; Acts 9:39; *to company with, associate
with,* Acts 1:21

συνερχόμενοι   pres mid ptcp nom pl masc
[1C 11:33; cv-1b(2); 5302]   "

συνερχομένων   pres mid ptcp gen pl masc
[2t; cv-1b(2); 5302]   "

συνέρχονται   pres mid ind 3 pl
  [2t; cv-1b(2); 5302]   "

συνέσει   dat sg fem [2t; n-3e(5b); 5304]   σύνεσις

συνέσεως   gen sg fem [2t; n-3e(5b); 5304]   "

συνεσθίει   pres act ind 3 sg
  [Lk 15:2; cv-1b(3); 5303]   συνεσθίω

συνεσθίειν   pres act inf
  [1C 5:11; cv-1b(3); 5303]   "

συνεσθίω   {5303, cv-1b(3)}
  [(συνήσθιον), -, συνέφαγον, -, -, -] to eat with,
  Acts 10:41; 11:3; 1 Cor 5:11; by impl. to associate
  with, live on familiar terms with, Luke 15:2; Gal
  2:12*

σύνεσιν   acc sg fem [3t; n-3e(5b); 5304]   σύνεσις

σύνεσις, εως, ἡ   {5304, n-3e(5b)}
  pr. a sending together, a junction, as of streams;
  met. understanding, intelligence, discernment,
  Luke 2:47; 1 Cor 1:19; meton. the understanding,
  intellect, mind, Mark 12:33; Eph 3:4; Col 1:9; 2:2;
  2 Tim 2:7*

συνεσπάραξεν   aor act ind 3 sg
  [2t; cv-2b; 5360]   συσπαράσσω

συνεσταλμένος   perf pass ptcp nom sg masc
  [1C 7:29; cv-2d(1); 5366]   συστέλλω

συνεσταυρώθη   aor pass ind 3 sg
  [Rm 6:6; cv-1d(3); 5365]   συσταυρόω

συνεσταύρωμαι   perf pass ind 1 sg
  [Ga 2:19; cv-1d(3); 5365]   "

συνεσταυρωμένοι   perf pass ptcp nom pl masc
  [Mk 15:32; cv-1d(3); 5365]   "

συνέστειλαν   aor act ind 3 pl
  [Ac 5:6; cv-2d(1); 5366]   συστέλλω

συνέστηκεν   perf act ind 3 sg
  [Cl 1:17; cv-6a; 5319]   συνίστημι

συνεστήσατε   aor act ind 2 pl
  [2C 7:11; cv-6a; 5319]   "

συνεστῶσα   perf act ptcp nom sg fem
  [2P 3:5; cv-6a; 5319]   "

συνεστῶτας   perf act ptcp acc pl masc
  [Lk 9:32; cv-6a; 5319]   "

συνέσχον   aor act ind 3 pl
  [Ac 7:57; cv-1b(2); 5309]   συνέχω

συνέταξεν   aor act ind 3 sg
  [3t; cv-2b; 5332]   συντάσσω

συνετάφημεν   aor pass ind 1 pl
  [Rm 6:4; cv-4; 5313]   συνθάπτω

σύνετε   aor act imperative 2 pl
  [Mk 7:14; cv-6a; 5317]   συνίημι

συνετέθειντο   pluperf mid ind 3 pl
  [Jn 9:22; cv-6a; 5338]   συντίθημι

συνετήρει   imperf act ind 3 sg
  [2t; cv-1d(2a); 5337]   συντηρέω

συνετός, ή, όν   {5305, a-1a(2a)}
  intelligent, discerning, wise, prudent, Matt 11:25;
  Luke 10:21; Acts 13:7; 1 Cor 1:19*

συνετῷ   dat sg masc
  [Ac 13:7; a-1a(2a); 5305]   συνετός

συνετῶν   gen pl masc [3t; a-1a(2a); 5305]   "

συνευδοκεῖ   pres act ind 3 sg
  [2t; cv-1d(2a); 5306]   συνευδοκέω

συνευδοκεῖτε   pres act ind 2 pl
  [Lk 11:48; cv-1d(2a); 5306]   "

συνευδοκέω   {5306, cv-1d(2a)}
  [-, συνηυδόκησα, -, -, -] to approve with another;
  to agree with in principle, Rom 1:32; to stamp
  approval, Luke 11:48; Acts 8:1; 22:20; to be
  willing, agreeable, 1 Cor 7:12, 13*

συνευδοκοῦσιν   pres act ind 3 pl
  [Rm 1:32; cv-1d(2a); 5306]   "

συνευδοκῶν   pres act ptcp nom sg masc
  [2t; cv-1d(2a); 5306]   "

συνευωχέομαι   {5307, cv-1d(2a)}
  [-, -, -, -, -] to feast together with, 2 Peter 2:13;
  Jude 12*

συνευωχούμενοι   pres pass ptcp nom pl masc
  [2t; cv-1d(2a); 5307]   συνευωχέομαι

συνέφαγες   aor act ind 2 sg
  [Ac 11:3; cv-1b(3); 5303]   συνεσθίω

συνεφάγομεν   aor act ind 1 pl
  [Ac 10:41; cv-1b(3); 5303]   "

συνεφίστημι   {5308, cv-6a}
  [-, συνεπέστην, -, -, -] to set together upon, join in
  an attack, Acts 16:22*

συνεφωνήθη   aor pass ind 3 sg
  [Ac 5:9; cv-1d(2a); 5244]   συμφωνέω

συνεφώνησας   aor act ind 2 sg
  [Mt 20:13; cv-1d(2a); 5244]   "

συνέχαιρον   imperf act ind 3 pl
  [Lk 1:58; cv-2d(2); 5176]   συγχαίρω

συνέχει   pres act ind 3 sg
  [2C 5:14; cv-1b(2); 5309]   συνέχω

συνέχεον   imperf act ind 3 pl
  [Ac 21:27; cv-1a(7); 5177]   συγχέω

συνέχομαι   pres pass ind 1 sg
  [2t; cv-1b(2); 5309]   συνέχω

συνεχομένη   pres pass ptcp nom sg fem
  [Lk 4:38; cv-1b(2); 5309]   "

συνεχόμενον   pres pass ptcp acc sg masc
  [Ac 28:8; cv-1b(2); 5309]   "

συνεχομένους   pres pass ptcp acc pl masc
  [Mt 4:24; cv-1b(2); 5309]   "

συνέχοντες   pres act ptcp nom pl masc
  [Lk 22:63; cv-1b(2); 5309]   "

συνέχουσιν   pres act ind 3 pl
  [Lk 8:45; cv-1b(2); 5309]   "

συνεχύθη   aor pass ind 3 sg
  [Ac 2:6; cv-1a(7); 5177]   συγχέω

συνέχυννεν   imperf act ind 3 sg
  [Ac 9:22; cv-1a(7); 5177]   "

συνέχω   {5309, cv-1b(2)}
  [(σύνειχον), συνέξω, συνέσχον, -, -, -] pr. to hold
  together; to confine, shut up, close; τὰ ὦτα, to stop
  the ears, Acts 7:57; to confine, as a besieged city,
  Luke 19:43; to hold, hold fast, have the custody of
  any one, Luke 22:63; to hem in, urge, press upon,
  Luke 8:45; to exercise a constraining influence on,
  2 Cor 5:14; pass. to be seized with, be affected with,
  as fear, disease, etc., Matt 4:24; Luke 4:38; 8:37;
  Acts 28:8; to be in a state of mental constriction, to
  be hard pressed by urgency of circumstances,
  Luke 12:50; Acts 18:5 v.l.; Phil 1:23*

συνεψήφισαν   aor act ind 3 pl
  [Ac 19:19; cv-2a(1); 5248]   συμψηφίζω

συνήδομαι   {5310, cv-1b(3)}
  [-, -, -, -, -] *to be pleased along with* others; *to
  congratulate; to delight in, approve cordially,* Rom
  7:22*

συνήγαγεν   aor act ind 3 sg
  [Rv 16:16; cv-1b(2); 5251]   συνάγω
συνηγάγετε   aor act ind 2 pl [2t; cv-1b(2); 5251]   "
συνηγάγομεν   aor act ind 1 pl
  [Mt 25:38; cv-1b(2); 5251]   "
συνήγαγον   aor act ind 3 pl [4t; cv-1b(2); 5251]   "
συνήγειρεν   aor act ind 3 sg
  [Ep 2:6; cv-2d(3); 5283]   συνεγείρω
συνηγέρθητε   aor pass ind 2 pl
  [2t; cv-2d(3); 5283]   "
συνηγμένα   perf pass ptcp acc pl neut
  [Rv 19:19; cv-1b(2); 5251]   συνάγω
συνηγμένοι   perf pass ptcp nom pl masc
  [3t; cv-1b(2); 5251]   "
συνηγμένων   perf pass ptcp gen pl masc
  [3t; cv-1b(2); 5251]   "
συνήδομαι   pres mid ind 1 sg
  [Rm 7:22; cv-; 5310]   συνήδομαι

συνήθεια, ας, ή   {5311, n-1a}
  use, custom; an established custom, practice, John
  18:39; 1 Cor 8:7; 11:16*

συνήθεια   nom sg fem
  [Jn 18:39; n-1a; 5311]   συνήθεια
συνηθείᾳ   dat sg fem [1C 8:7; n-1a; 5311]   "
συνήθειαν   acc sg fem [1C 11:16; n-1a; 5311]   "
συνήθλησαν   aor act ind 3 pl
  [Pp 4:3; cv-1d(2a); 5254]   συναθλέω
συνηθροισμένοι   perf pass ptcp nom pl masc
  [Ac 12:12; cv-2a(1); 5255]   συναθροίζω
συνήκαν   aor act ind 3 pl
  [6t; cv-6a; 5317]   συνίημι
συνήκατε   aor act ind 2 pl
  [Mt 13:51; cv-6a; 5317]   "
συνηκολούθει   imperf act ind 3 sg
  [Mk 14:51; cv-1d(2a); 5258]   συνακολουθέω
συνήλθαν   aor act ind 3 pl
  [Ac 10:45; cv-1b(2); 5302]   συνέρχομαι
συνῆλθεν   aor act ind 3 sg [2t; cv-1b(2); 5302]   "
συνῆλθον   aor act ind 3 pl [2t; cv-1b(2); 5302]   "
συνηλικιώτας   acc pl masc
  [Ga 1:14; n-1f; 5312]   συνηλικιώτης

συνηλικιώτης, ου, ό   {5312, n-1f}
  one of the same age, an equal in age, Gal 1:14*

συνήλλασσεν   imperf act ind 3 sg
  [Ac 7:26; cv-2b; 5261]   συναλλάσσω
συνήντησεν   aor act ind 3 sg
  [2t; cv-1d(1a); 5267]   συναντάω
συνήργει   imperf act ind 3 sg
  [Jm 2:22; cv-1d(2a); 5300]   συνεργέω
συνηρπάκει   pluperf act ind 3 sg
  [Lk 8:29; cv-2a(1); 5275]   συναρπάζω
συνήρπασαν   aor act ind 3 pl
  [Ac 6:12; cv-2a(1); 5275]   "
συνήρχετο   imperf mid ind 3 sg
  [Ac 5:16; cv-1b(2); 5302]   συνέρχομαι

συνήρχοντο   imperf mid ind 3 pl
  [Lk 5:15; cv-1b(2); 5302]   "
συνῆσαν   imperf act ind 3 pl
  [Lk 9:18; cv-6b; 5289]   σύνειμι
συνήσθιεν   imperf act ind 3 sg
  [Ga 2:12; cv-1b(3); 5303]   συνεσθίω
συνήσουσιν   fut act ind 3 pl
  [Rm 15:21; cv-6a; 5317]   συνίημι
συνῆτε   aor act subj 2 pl [2t; cv-6a; 5317]   "
συνήχθη   aor pass ind 3 sg
  [4t; cv-1b(2); 5251]   συνάγω
συνήχθησαν   aor pass ind 3 pl
  [9t; cv-1b(2); 5251]   "

συνθάπτω   {5313, cv-4}
  [-, -, -, -, συνετάφην] *to bury with;* pass. in N.T. *to
  be buried with* Christ symbolically, Rom 6:4; Col
  2:12*

συνθλασθήσεται   fut pass ind 3 sg
  [2t; cv-1d(1b); 5314]   συνθλάω

συνθλάω   {5314, cv-1d(1b)}
  [-, -, -, -, συνεθλάσθην] *to crush together; to break
  in pieces, shatter,* Matt 21:44; Luke 20:18*

συνθλίβοντα   pres act ptcp acc sg masc
  [Mk 5:31; cv-1b(1); 5315]   συνθλίβω

συνθλίβω   {5315, cv-1b(1)}
  [(συνέθλιβον), -, -, -, -, -] *to press together; to press
  upon, crowd,* Mark 5:24, 31*

συνθρύπτοντες   pres act ptcp nom pl masc
  [Ac 21:13; cv-4; 5316]   συνθρύπτω

συνθρύπτω   {5316, cv-4}
  [-, -, -, -, -] *to crush to pieces;* met. *to break* the
  heart of any one, *to make to recoil in fear,* Acts
  21:13*

συνιᾶσιν   pres act ind 3 pl
  [2C 10:12; cv-6a; 5317]   συνίημι
συνιδόντες   aor act ptcp nom pl masc
  [Ac 14:6; cv-1d(1a); 5328]   συνοράω
συνιδών   aor act ptcp nom sg masc
  [Ac 12:12; cv-1d(1a); 5328]   "
συνιείς   pres act ptcp nom sg masc
  [Mt 13:23; cv-6a; 5317]   συνίημι
συνιέναι   pres act inf [2t; cv-6a; 5317]   "
συνιέντος   pres act ptcp gen sg masc
  [Mt 13:19; cv-6a; 5317]   "
συνίετε   pres act imperative 2 pl
  [2t; cv-6a; 5317]   "
συνίετε   pres act ind 2 pl [2t; cv-6a; 5317]   "

συνίημι   {5317, cv-6a}
  [συνήσω, συνῆκα, -, -, -] also συνίω, see *BAGD*
  for a discussion, pr. *to send together;* met. *to
  understand, comprehend thoroughly,* Matt 13:51;
  Luke 2:50; 18:34; 24:45; *to perceive clearly,* Matt
  16:12; 17:13; Acts 7:25; Rom 15:21; Eph 5:17;
  absol. *to be well-judging, sensible,* 2 Cor 10:12; *to
  be* spiritually *intelligent,* Matt 13:13, 14, 15; Acts
  28:26, 27; *to be* religiously *wise,* Rom 3:11

συνιόντος   pres act ptcp gen sg masc
  [Lk 8:4; cv-6b; 5290]   σύνειμι
συνίουσιν   pres act ind 3 pl
  [Mt 13:13; cv-6a; 5317]   συνίημι

συνιστάνειν   pres act inf
[2C 3:1; cv-6a; 5319]   συνίστημι

συνιστάνομεν   pres act ind 1 pl
[2C 5:12; cv-6a; 5319]   "

συνιστάνοντες   pres act ptcp nom pl masc
[2C 4:2; cv-6a; 5319]   "

συνιστανόντων   pres act ptcp gen pl masc
[2C 10:12; cv-6a; 5319]   "

συνίσταντες   pres act ptcp nom pl masc
[2C 6:4; cv-6a; 5319]   "

συνιστάνω   pres act ind 1 sg
[Ga 2:18; cv-6a; 5319]   "

συνιστάνων   pres act ptcp nom sg masc
[2C 10:18; cv-6a; 5319]   "

συνίστασθαι   pres pass inf
[2C 12:11; cv-6a; 5319]   "

συνιστάω   {5318}
v.l. for συνίστημι at 2 Cor 4:2, 6:4, and 10:18*

συνίστημι   {5319, cv-6a}
[-, συνέστησα, συνέστηκα, -, συνετάθην] also
spelled συνιστάνω and συνιστάω, *to place
together; to recommend to favorable attention,* Rom
16:1; 2 Cor 3:1; 10:18; *to place in a striking point
of view,* Rom 3:5; 5:8; Gal 2:18; *to stand beside,*
Luke 9:32; *to have been permanently framed,* Col
1:17; *to possess consistence,* 2 Peter 3:5

συνίστημι   pres act ind 1 sg
[Rm 16:1; cv-6a; 5319]   "

συνίστησιν   pres act ind 3 sg   [3t; cv-6a; 5319]   "

συνίων   pres act ptcp nom sg masc
[Rm 3:11; cv-6a; 5317]   συνίημι

συνιῶσιν   pres act subj 3 pl   [2t; cv-6a; 5317]   "

συνοδεύοντες   pres act ptcp nom pl masc
[Ac 9:7; cv-1a(6); 5321]   συνοδεύω

συνοδεύω   {5321, cv-1a(6)}
[-, συνώδευσα, -, -, -] *to journey* or *travel with,
accompany on a journey,* Acts 9:7*

συνοδία, ας, ἡ   {5322, n-1a}
pr. *a journeying together;* meton. *a company of
fellow-travellers, caravan,* Luke 2:44*

συνοδίᾳ   dat sg fem   [Lk 2:44; n-1a; 5322]   συνοδία

σύνοιδα   {5323, cv-1b(3)}
[-, -, -, -, -] a defective verb that is actually
perfect in form but present in meaning, *to share
in the knowledge of* a thing; *to be privy to,* Acts 5:2;
to be conscious; οὐδὲν σύνοιδα, *to have a clear
conscience,* 1 Cor 4:4*

σύνοιδα   perf act ind 1 sg
[1C 4:4; cv-1d(1a); 5328]   συνοράω

συνοικέω   {5324, cv-1d(2a)}
[-, -, -, -, -] *to dwell with; to live* or *cohabit with,* 1
Peter 3:7*

συνοικοδομεῖσθε   pres pass ind 2 pl
[Ep 2:22; cv-1d(2a); 5325]   συνοικοδομέω

συνοικοδομέω   {5325, cv-1d(2a)}
[-, -, -, -, συνῳκοδομήθην] *to build in company
with* someone; pass. *to be built up, form a
constituent part of a structure,* Eph 2:22*

συνοικοῦντες   pres act ptcp nom pl masc
[1P 3:7; cv-1d(2a); 5324]   συνοικέω

συνομιλέω   {5326, cv-1d(2a)}
[-, -, -, -, -] pr. *to be in company with; to talk* or
converse with, Acts 10:27; *live with,* 1 Peter 3:7
v.l.*

συνομιλῶν   pres act ptcp nom sg masc
[Ac 10:27; cv-1d(2a); 5326]   συνομιλέω

συνομορέω   {5327, cv-1d(2a)}
[-, -, -, -, -] *to be next to, be next door,* Acts 18:7*

συνομοροῦσα   pres act ptcp nom sg fem
[Ac 18:7; cv-1d(2a); 5327]   συνομορέω

συνόντων   pres act ptcp gen pl masc
[Ac 22:11; cv-6b; 5289]   σύνειμι

συνοράω   {5328, cv-1d(1a)}
[-, συνεῖδον, -, -, -] *perceive, become aware of,
realize,* Acts 12:12; 14:6*

συνορία, ας, ἡ   {5329, n-1a}
neighboring country, Matt 4:24 v.l.*

συνοχή, ῆς, ἡ   {5330, n-1b}
pr. *a being held together; compression;* in N.T. met.
distress of mind, anxiety, Luke 21:25; 2 Cor 2:4

συνοχή   nom sg fem   [Lk 21:25; n-1b; 5330]   συνοχή
συνοχῆς   gen sg fem   [2C 2:4; n-1b; 5330]   "

συνταράσσω   {5331, cv-2a(2)}
[-, -, -, -, -] *throw into confusion,* Luke 9:42 v.l.*

συντάσσω   {5332, cv-2b}
[-, συνέταξα, -, -, -] pr. *to arrange* or *place in order
together;* in N.T. *to order, charge, direct,* Matt 21:6;
26:19; 27:10*

συνταφέντες   aor pass ptcp nom pl masc
[Cl 2:12; cv-4; 5313]   συνθάπτω

συντέλεια, ας, ἡ   {5333, n-1a}
*a complete combination, a completion,
consummation, end,* Matt 13:39, 40, 49; 24:3;
28:20; Heb 9:26*

συντέλεια   nom sg fem
[Mt 13:39; n-1a; 5333]   συντέλεια
συντελείᾳ   dat sg fem   [3t; n-1a; 5333]   "
συντελείας   gen sg fem   [2t; n-1a; 5333]   "
συντελεῖσθαι   pres pass inf
[2t; cv-1d(2a); 5334]   συντελέω
συντελέσας   aor act ptcp nom sg masc
[Lk 4:13; cv-1d(2a); 5334]   "
συντελεσθεισῶν   aor pass ptcp gen pl fem
[Lk 4:2; cv-1d(2a); 5334]   "
συντελέσω   fut act ind 1 sg
[Hb 8:8; cv-1d(2a); 5334]   "

συντελέω   {5334, cv-1d(2a)}
[συντελέσω, συνετέλεσα, -, -, συνετελέσθην] pr.
to bring to an end altogether; to finish, end, Matt
7:28 v.l.; Luke 4:13; *to consummate,* Rom 9:28; *to
ratify* a covenant, Heb 8:8; pass. *to be terminated,*
Luke 2:21 v.l.; 4:2; Acts 21:27; *to be fully realized,*
Mark 13:4; John 2:3 v.l.*

συντελῶν   pres act ptcp nom sg masc
[Rm 9:28; cv-1d(2a); 5334]   "

συντέμνω   {5335, cv-3a(1)}
[-, -, συντέτμηκα, συντέτμημαι, -] pr. *to cut short, contract by cutting off*; met. *to execute speedily*, or from the Hebrew, *to determine, decide, decree*, Rom 9:28 (2t)*

συντέμνων   pres act ptcp nom sg masc
     [Rm 9:28; cv-3a(1); 5335]   συντέμνω
συντετριμμένον   perf pass ptcp acc sg masc
     [Mt 12:20; cv-1b(1); 5341]   συντρίβω
συντετρίφθαι   perf pass inf
     [Mk 5:4; cv-1b(1); 5341]   "

συντεχνίτης, ου, ὁ   {5336, n-1f}
person who does the same trade, Acts 19:25 v.l.*

συντηρέω   {5337, cv-1d(2a)}
[(συνετήρουν), συντηρήσω, -, -, -, -] *to keep safe and sound*, Matt 9:17; Luke 5:38 v.l.; *to observe strictly*, or, *to secure from harm, protect*, Mark 6:20; *to preserve in memory, keep carefully in mind*, Luke 2:19*

συντηροῦνται   pres pass ind 3 pl
     [Mt 9:17; cv-1d(2a); 5337]   συντηρέω

συντίθημι   {5338, cv-6a}
[-, συνέθηκα, -, συντέθειμαι, -] pluperf., συνετεθείμην, *to agree together, come to a mutual understanding*, John 9:22; Acts 23:20; *to bargain, to pledge one's self*, Luke 22:5; *to second* a statement, Acts 24:9 v.l.*

συντόμως   {5339, adverb}
concisely, briefly, Acts 24:4; *short ending of Mark*

συντόμως   adverb [2t; adverb; 5339]   συντόμως
συντρεχόντων   pres act ptcp gen pl masc
     [1P 4:4; cv-1b(2); 5340]   συντρέχω

συντρέχω   {5340, cv-1b(2)}
[-, συνέδραμον, -, -, -] *to run together, flock together*, Mark 6:33; Acts 3:11; *to run in company with* others, met. 1 Peter 4:4*

συντρίβεται   pres pass ind 3 sg
     [Rv 2:27; cv-1b(1); 5341]   συντρίβω
συντριβήσεται   fut pass ind 3 sg
     [Jn 19:36; cv-1b(1); 5341]   "
συντρίβον   pres act ptcp nom sg neut
     [Lk 9:39; cv-1b(1); 5341]   "

συντρίβω   {5341, cv-1b(1)}
[συντρίψω, συνέτριψα, -, συντέτριμμαι, συνετρίβην] *to rub together; to shiver*, Mark 14:3; Rev 2:27; *to break, break in pieces*, Mark 5:4; John 19:36; *to break down, crush, bruise*, Matt 12:20; met. *to break the power of* any one, *deprive of strength, debilitate*, Luke 9:39; Rom 16:20; pass. *to be broken* in heart, *be contrite*, Luke 4:18 v.l.*

σύντριμμα, ατος, τό   {5342, n-3c(4)}
a breaking, bruising; in N.T. *destruction, ruin*, Rom 3:16*

σύντριμμα   nom sg neut
     [Rm 3:16; n-3c(4); 5342]   σύντριμμα
συντρίψασα   aor act ptcp nom sg fem
     [Mk 14:3; cv-1b(1); 5341]   συντρίβω
συντρίψει   fut act ind 3 sg
     [Rm 16:20; cv-1b(1); 5341]   "

σύντροφος, ον   {5343, a-3a}
nursed with another; *one brought up* (*NIV*) or *educated with* another, *intimate friend, friend of the court* (*RSV*) Acts 13:1*

σύντροφος   nom sg masc
     [Ac 13:1; a-3a; 5343]   σύντροφος

συντυγχάνω   {5344, cv-3a(2b)}
[-, συνέτυχον, -, -, -] *to meet* or *fall in with; join*, in N.T. *to get to, approach*, Luke 8:19; Acts 11:26 v.l.*

συντυχεῖν   aor act inf
     [Lk 8:19; cv-3a(2b); 5344]   συντυγχάνω

Συντύχη, ης, ἡ   {5345, n-1b}
Syntyche, pr. name, Phil 4:2*

Συντύχην   acc sg fem [Pp 4:2; n-1b; 5345]   Συντύχη

συντυχία, ας, ἡ   {5346, n-1a}
chance, Luke 10:31 v.l.*

συνυπεκρίθησαν   aor pass ind 3 pl
     [Ga 2:13; cv-1c(2); 5347]   συνυποκρίνομαι

συνυποκρίνομαι   {5347, cv-1c(2)}
[-, -, -, -, συνυπεκρίθην] *to dissemble, feign with*, or *in the same manner as* another, *join in the playing of the hypocrite*, Gal 2:13*

συνυπουργέω   {5348, cv-1d(2a)}
[-, -, -, -, -] *to aid along with* another, *help together*, 2 Cor 1:11*

συνυπουργούντων   pres act ptcp gen pl masc
     [2C 1:11; cv-1d(2a); 5348]   συνυπουργέω
συνωδίνει   pres act ind 3 sg
     [Rm 8:22; cv-1c(2); 5349]   συνωδίνω

συνωδίνω   {5349, cv-1c(2)}
[-, -, -, -, -] pr. *to travail at the same time with*; trop. *suffer together*, Rom 8:22*

συνωμοσία, ας, ἡ   {5350, n-1a}
a banding by oath; a combination, conspiracy, Acts 23:13*

συνωμοσίαν   acc sg fem
     [Ac 23:13; n-1a; 5350]   συνωμοσία
συνῶσιν   aor act subj 3 pl
     [2t; cv-6a; 5317]   συνίημι

Σύρα, ας, ἡ   {5351, n-1a}
Syrian woman, Mark 7:26 v.l.*

Συράκουσαι, ῶν, αἱ   {5352, n-1c}
Syracuse, a celebrated city of Sicily, Acts 28:12*

Συρακούσας   acc pl fem
     [Ac 28:12; n-1c; 5352]   Συράκουσαι
σύρει   pres act ind 3 sg
     [Rv 12:4; v-1c(1); 5359]   σύρω

Συρία, ας, ἡ   {5353, n-1a}
Syria, an extensive country of Asia, Matt 4:24; Luke 2:2; Acts 15:23

Συρίαν   acc sg fem [6t; n-1a; 5353]   Συρία
Συρίας   gen sg fem [2t; n-1a; 5353]   "
σύροντες   pres act ptcp nom pl masc
     [Jn 21:8; v-1c(1); 5359]   σύρω

Σύρος, ου, ὁ {5354, n-2a}
a Syrian, Luke 4:27*

Σύρος nom sg masc [Lk 4:27; n-2a; 5354] Σύρος

Συροφοινίκισσα, ης, ἡ {5355, n-1c}
a Syrophoenician woman, Phoenicia being
included in Syria, Mark 7:26*

Συροφοινίκισσα nom sg fem
[Mk 7:26; n-1c; 5355] Συροφοινίκισσα

συρρήγνυμι {5357, cv-3c(2)}
[-, -, -, -, -] dash together, Luke 6:49 v.l.*

Σύρτιν acc sg fem
[Ac 27:17; n-3e(5b); 5358] Σύρτις

Σύρτις, εως, ἡ {5358, n-3e(5b)}
a shoal, sand-bank, a place dangerous on account of
shoals, two of which were particularly famous
on the northern coast of Africa, one lying near
Carthage, and the other, the syrtis major, lying
between Cyrene and Leptis, which is probably
referred to in Acts 27:17*

σύρω {5359, v-1c(1)}
[(ἔσυρον), -, ἔσυρα, -, -, -] to draw, drag, John
21:8; Rev 12:4; to force away, hale before
magistrates, etc., Acts 8:3; 14:19; 17:6*

σύρων pres act ptcp nom sg masc
[Ac 8:3; v-1c(1); 5359] σύρω

συσπαράσσω {5360, cv-2b}
[-, συνεσπάραξα, -, -, -] to tear to pieces; to
convulse altogether, Mark 9:20; Luke 9:42*

σύσσημον, ου, τό {5361, n-2c}
a signal, Mark 14:44*

σύσσημον acc sg neut
[Mk 14:44; n-2c; 5361] σύσσημον
σύσσωμα acc pl neut [Ep 3:6; a-3a; 5362] σύσσωμος

σύσσωμος, ον {5362, a-3a}
united in the same body; met. pl. joint members in
a spiritual body, Eph 3:6*

συστασιαστής, οῦ, ὁ {5363, n-1f}
an accomplice in sedition, associate in insurrection,
Mark 15:7 v.l.*

συστατικῶν gen pl fem
[2C 3:1; a-1a(2a); 5364] συστατικός

συστατικός, ή, όν {5364, a-1a(2a)}
commendatory, recommendatory, 2 Cor 3:1 (2t)*

συσταυρόω {5365, cv-1d(3)}
[-, -, -, συνεσταύρωμαι, συνεσταυρώθην] to
crucify with another, Matt 27:44; Mark 15:32;
John 19:32; pass. met. to be crucified with
another in a spiritual resemblance, Rom 6:6;
Gal 2:20*

συσταυρωθέντες aor pass ptcp nom pl masc
[Mt 27:44; cv-1d(3); 5365] συσταυρόω
συσταυρωθέντος aor pass ptcp gen sg masc
[Jn 19:32; cv-1d(3); 5365] "

συστέλλω {5366, cv-2d(1)}
[-, ἐσυνέστειλα, -, συνέσταλμαι, -] to draw
together, contract, straiten; to enwrap; hence, i.q.

περιστέλλω, to lay out, prepare for burial, Acts 5:6,
10 v.l.; pass. to be shortened or to environed with
trials, 1 Cor 7:29*

συστενάζει pres act ind 3 sg
[Rm 8:22; cv-2a(2); 5367] συστενάζω

συστενάζω {5367, cv-2a(2)}
[-, -, -, -, -] to groan or lament together, Rom 8:22*

συστοιχεῖ pres act ind 3 sg
[Ga 4:25; cv-1d(2a); 5368] συστοιχέω

συστοιχέω {5368, cv-1d(2a)}
[-, -, -, -, -] pr. to be in the same row with; met. to
correspond to, Gal 4:25*

συστρατιώτῃ dat sg masc
[Pm 2; n-1f; 5369] συστρατιώτης
συστρατιώτην acc sg masc [Pp 2:25; n-1f; 5369] "

συστρατιώτης, ου, ὁ {5369, n-1f}
a fellow-soldier, co-militant, in the service of
Christ, Phil 2:25; Phil 2*

συστρεφομένων pres pass ptcp gen pl masc
[Mt 17:22; cv-1b(1); 5370] συστρέφω

συστρέφω {5370, cv-1b(1)}
[-, συνέστρεψα, -, -, -] to turn or roll together; to
collect, gather, Acts 28:3; 17:5 v.l.; Matt 17:22; v.l.
at Acts 10:41, 11:28, and 16:39*

συστρέψαντος aor act ptcp gen sg masc
[Ac 28:3; cv-1b(1); 5370] "

συστροφή, ῆς, ἡ {5371, n-1b}
a gathering, tumultuous assembly, Acts 19:40; a
combination, conspiracy, Acts 23:12*

συστροφήν acc sg fem
[Ac 23:12; n-1b; 5371] συστροφή
συστροφῆς gen sg fem [Ac 19:40; n-1b; 5371] "
συσχηματίζεσθε pres pass imperative 2 pl
[Rm 12:2; cv-2a(1); 5372] συσχηματίζω
συσχηματιζόμενοι pres pass ptcp nom pl masc
[1P 1:14; cv-2a(1); 5372] "

συσχηματίζω {5372, cv-2a(1)}
[-, -, -, -, -] to fashion in accordance with;
mid/pass. to conform or assimilate one's self to,
met. Rom 12:2; 1 Peter 1:14*

Συχάρ, ἡ {5373, n-3g(2)}
Sychar, indecl., a city of Samaria, John 4:5*

Συχάρ indecl [Jn 4:5; n-3g(2); 5373] Συχάρ

Συχέμ {5374, n-3g(2)}
Shechem, indecl., (1) fem., a city of Samaria,
Acts 7:16. (2) masc., proper name, son of
Hamor, Acts 7:16 v.l.*

Συχέμ indecl [2t; n-3g(2); 5374] Συχέμ

σφαγή, ῆς, ἡ {5375, n-1b}
slaughter, Acts 8:32; Rom 8:36; James 5:5*

σφαγήν acc sg fem [Ac 8:32; n-1b; 5375] σφαγή
σφαγῆς gen sg fem [2t; n-1b; 5375] "
σφάγια acc pl neut [Ac 7:42; n-2c; 5376] σφάγιον

σφάγιον, ου, τό {5376, n-2c}
a victim slaughtered in sacrifice, offering, Acts
7:42*

σφάζω   {5377, v-2a(2)}
[σφάξω, ἔσφαξα, -, ἔσφαγμαι, ἐσφάγην] also
spelled σφάττω, *to slaughter, kill, slay;* pr. used of
animals killed in sacrifice, etc., Rev 5:6, 9, 12;
13:8; of persons, etc., 1 John 3:12; Rev 6:4, 9;
18:24; *to wound mortally,* Rev 13:3*

σφάξουσιν fut act ind 3 pl
[Rv 6:4; v-2a(2); 5377]   σφάζω

σφόδρα   {5379, adverb}
much, greatly, exceedingly, Matt 2:10; 17:6; Mark
16:4; Luke 18:23; Acts 6:7

σφόδρα adverb [11t; adverb; 5379]   σφόδρα

σφοδρῶς   {5380, adverb}
exceedingly, vehemently, Acts 27:18*

σφοδρῶς adverb [Ac 27:18; adverb; 5380] σφοδρῶς
σφραγῖδα acc sg fem [10t; n-3c(2); 5382] σφραγίς
σφραγῖδας acc pl fem [3t; n-3c(2); 5382]   "
σφραγίδων gen pl fem [Rv 6:1; n-3c(2); 5382] "

σφραγίζω   {5381, v-2a(1)}
[-, ἐσφράγισα, -, ἐσφράγισμαι, ἐσφραγίσθην] *to
seal, stamp with a seal,* Matt 27:66; Rev 20:3; *to
seal up, to close up, conceal,* Rev 10:4; 22:10; *to set
a mark upon, distinguish by a mark,* Eph 1:13;
4:30; Rev 7:3, 4, 5, 8; *to seal, to mark distinctively*
as invested with a certain character, John 6:27;
mid. *to set one's own mark upon, seal as one's own,
to impress with a mark of acceptance,* 2 Cor 1:22; *to
deliver over safely to* someone, Rom 15:28; absol.
to set to one's seal, to make a solemn declaration,
John 3:33*

σφραγίς, ίδος, ἡ   {5382, n-3c(2)}
a seal, a signet ring, Rev 7:2; *an inscription on a
seal, motto,* 2 Tim 2:19; *a seal, the impression of a
seal,* Rev 5:1, 2, 5, 9, 6:1, 3, 5, 7, 9, 12; 8:1; *a seal,
a distinctive mark,* Rev 9:4; *a seal, a token, proof,* 1
Cor 9:2; *a token* of guarantee, Rom 4:11*

σφραγίς nom sg fem [1C 9:2; n-3c(2); 5382] "
σφραγισάμενος aor mid ptcp nom sg masc
[2t; v-2a(1); 5381]   σφραγίζω
σφραγίσαντες aor act ptcp nom pl masc
[Mt 27:66; v-2a(1); 5381]   "
σφραγίσῃς aor act subj 2 sg
[Rv 22:10; v-2a(1); 5381]   "
σφραγῖσιν dat pl fem
[Rv 5:1; n-3c(2); 5382]   σφραγίς
σφράγισον aor act imperative 2 sg
[Rv 10:4; v-2a(1); 5381]   σφραγίζω
σφραγίσωμεν aor act subj 1 pl
[Rv 7:3; v-2a(1); 5381]   "
σφυδρά nom pl neut [Ac 3:7; n-2c; 5383] σφυδρόν

σφυδρόν, οῦ, τό   {5383, n-2c}
ankle, Acts 3:7*

σφυρίς, ίδος, ἡ, see σπυρίς

σφυρόν, οῦ, τό   {5384, n-2c}
the ankle; pl. τὰ σφυρά, *the ankle bones* or *heel,*
Acts 3:7 v.l.*

σχεδόν   {5385, adverb}
pr. *near,* of place; hence, *nearly, almost,* Acts
13:44; 19:26; Heb 9:22*

σχεδόν adverb [3t; adverb; 5385]   σχεδόν

σχῆμα, ατος, τό   {5386, n-3c(4)}
fashion, form; fashion, external show, 1 Cor 7:31;
Phil 2:7*

σχῆμα nom sg neut [1C 7:31; n-3c(4); 5386] σχῆμα
σχήματι dat sg neut [Pp 2:7; n-3c(4); 5386] "
σχῆτε aor act subj 2 pl
[2C 1:15; v-1b(2); 2400]   ἔχω
σχιζομένους pres pass ptcp acc pl masc
[Mk 1:10; v-2a(1); 5387]   σχίζω

σχίζω   {5387, v-2a(1)}
[σχίσω, ἔσχισα, -, -, ἐσχίσθην] *to split,* Matt
27:51; Mark 15:38; *to rend, tear asunder,* Matt
27:51; Luke 5:36; 23:45; John 19:24; 21:11); mid.
to open or *unfold* with a chasm, Mark 1:10; pass.
met. *to be divided* into parties or factions, Acts
14:4; 23:7*

σχίσας aor act ptcp nom sg masc
[Lk 5:36; v-2a(1); 5387]   "
σχίσει fut act ind 3 sg [Lk 5:36; v-2a(1); 5387] "

σχίσμα, ατος, τό   {5388, n-3c(4)}
a split, Matt 9:16; Mark 2:21; met. *a division* into
parties, *schism,* John 7:43; 9:16; 10:19; 1 Cor 1:10;
11:18; 12:25*

σχίσμα nom sg neut [6t; n-3c(4); 5388]   σχίσμα
σχίσματα nom pl neut [1C 1:10; n-3c(4); 5388] "
σχίσματα acc pl neut [1C 11:18; n-3c(4); 5388] "
σχίσωμεν aor act subj 1 pl
[Jn 19:24; v-2a(1); 5387]   σχίζω
σχοινία acc pl neut
[Ac 27:32; n-2c; 5389]   σχοινίον

σχοινίον, ου, τό   {5389, n-2c}
pr. *a cord made of rushes;* genr. *a rope, cord,* John
2:15; Acts 27:32*

σχοινίων gen pl neut [Jn 2:15; n-2c; 5389] "
σχολάζοντα pres act ptcp acc sg masc
[Mt 12:44; v-2a(1); 5390]   σχολάζω

σχολάζω   {5390, v-2a(1)}
[-, ἐσχόλασα, -, -, -] *to be unemployed, to be at
leisure; to be at leisure* for a thing, *to devote one's
self entirely* to a thing, 1 Cor 7:5; *to be unoccupied,
empty,* Matt 12:44; Luke 11:25 v.l.*

σχολάσητε aor act subj 2 pl
[1C 7:5; v-2a(1); 5390]   "

σχολή, ῆς, ἡ   {5391, n-1b}
freedom from occupation; later, *ease, leisure; a
school,* Acts 19:9*

σχολῇ dat sg fem [Ac 19:9; n-1b; 5391]   σχολή
σχῶ aor act subj 1 sg [5t; v-1b(2); 2400]   ἔχω
σχῶμεν aor act subj 1 pl [2t; v-1b(2); 2400] "
σῷ dat sg masc [2t; a-1a(2a); 5050]   σός
σῷ dat sg neut [3t; a-1a(2a); 5050]   "
σῴζει pres act ind 3 sg
[1P 3:21; v-2a(1); 5392]   σῴζω
σῴζειν pres act inf [2t; v-2a(1); 5392]   "
σῴζεσθαι pres pass inf
[Ac 27:20; v-2a(1); 5392]   "

σῴζεσθε   pres pass ind 2 pl
   [1C 15:2; v-2a(1); 5392]   "

σῴζεται   pres pass ind 3 sg
   [1P 4:18; v-2a(1); 5392]   "

σῴζετε   pres act imperative 2 pl
   [Jd 23; v-2a(1); 5392]   "

σῳζόμενοι   pres pass ptcp nom pl masc
   [Lk 13:23; v-2a(1); 5392]   "

σῳζομένοις   pres pass ptcp dat pl masc
   [2t; v-2a(1); 5392]   "

σῳζομένους   pres pass ptcp acc pl masc
   [Ac 2:47; v-2a(1); 5392]   "

σῴζω   {5392, v-2a(1)}
   [(ἔσῳζον), σώσω, ἔσωσα, σέσωκα, σέσωσμαι or
   σέσωμαι, ἐσώθην] *to save, rescue; to preserve safe
   and unharmed*, Mark. 8:25; 10:22; 24:22; 27:40,
   42, 49; 1 Tim 2:15; σῴζειν εἰς, *to bring safely to*, 2
   Tim 4:18; *to cure, heal, restore to health*, Matt 9:21,
   22; Mark 5:23, 28, 34; 6:56; *to save, preserve* from
   being lost, Matt 16:25; Mark 3:4; 8:35; σῴζειν
   ἀπό, *to deliver from, set free from*, Matt 1:21; John
   12:27; Acts 2:40; in N.T. *to rescue* from unbelief,
   convert, Rom 11:14; 1 Cor 1:21; 7:16; *to bring
   within the pale of saving privilege*, Titus 3:5; 1
   Peter 3:21; *to save* from final ruin, 1 Tim 1:15;
   pass. *to be brought within the pale of saving
   privilege*, Acts 2:47; Eph 2:5, 8; *to be in the way of
   salvation*, 1 Cor 15:2; 2 Cor 2:15

σωθῇ   aor pass subj 3 sg [3t; v-2a(1); 5392]   "
σωθῆναι   aor pass inf [10t; v-2a(1); 5392]   "
σωθήσεται   fut pass ind 3 sg [13t; v-2a(1); 5392] "
σωθήσῃ   fut pass ind 2 sg [3t; v-2a(1); 5392]   "
σωθήσομαι   fut pass ind 1 sg [2t; v-2a(1); 5392]   "
σωθησόμεθα   fut pass ind 1 pl [2t; v-2a(1); 5392] "
σώθητε   aor pass imperative 2 pl
   [Ac 2:40; v-2a(1); 5392]   "
σωθῆτε   aor pass subj 2 pl
   [Jn 5:34; v-2a(1); 5392]   "
σωθῶ   aor pass subj 1 sg
   [Ac 16:30; v-2a(1); 5392]   "
σωθῶσιν   aor pass subj 3 pl [3t; v-2a(1); 5392]   "

σῶμα, ατος, τό   {5393, n-3c(4)}
   the body of an animal; *a living body*, Matt 5:29,
   30; 6:22, 23, 25; James 3:3; *a person, individual*, 1
   Cor 6:16; *a dead body; corpse, carcass*, Matt 14:12;
   27:52, 58; Heb 13:11; *the* human *body*
   considered as the seat and occasion of moral
   imperfection, as inducing to sin through its
   appetites and passions, Rom 7:24; 8:13; genr. *a
   body, a material substance*, 1 Cor 15:37, 38, 40; *the
   substance, reality*, as opposed to ἡ σκιά, Col 2:17;
   in N.T. met., *the aggregate body* of believers, *the
   body* of the Church, Rom 12:5; Col 1:18

σῶμα   nom sg neut [40t; n-3c(4); 5393]   σῶμα
σῶμα   acc sg neut [30t; n-3c(4); 5393]   "
σώματα   nom pl neut [6t; n-3c(4); 5393]   "
σώματα   acc pl neut [4t; n-3c(4); 5393]   "
σώματι   dat sg neut [25t; n-3c(4); 5393]   "
σωματική   nom sg fem
   [1Ti 4:8; a-1a(2a); 5394]   σωματικός

σωματικός, ή, όν   {5394, a-1a(2)}
   bodily, of or *belonging to the body*, 1 Tim 4:8;
   corporeal, material, Luke 3:22*

σωματικῷ   dat sg neut [Lk 3:22; a-1a(2a); 5394]   "

σωματικῶς   {5395, adverb}
   bodily, in a bodily frame, Col 2:9*

σωματικῶς   adverb [Cl 2:9; adverb; 5395]
   σωματικῶς

σώματος   gen sg neut [36t; n-3c(4); 5393]   σῶμα
σωμάτων   gen pl neut [Rv 18:13; n-3c(4); 5393]   "

Σώπατρος, ου, ὁ   {5396, n-2a}
   Sopater, pr. name, Acts 20:4*

Σώπατρος   nom sg masc
   [Ac 20:4; n-2a; 5396]   Σώπατρος
σωρεύσεις   fut act ind 2 sg
   [Rm 12:20; v-1a(6); 5397]   σωρεύω

σωρεύω   {5397, v-1a(6)}
   [σωρεύσω, -, -, σεσώρευμαι, -] *to heap* or *pile up*,
   Rom 12:20; met. pass. *to be filled* with sins, 2 Tim
   3:6*

σῶσαι   aor act inf [13t; v-2a(1); 5392]   σῴζω
σώσαντος   aor act ptcp gen sg masc
   [2Ti 1:9; v-2a(1); 5392]   "
σώσας   aor act ptcp nom sg masc
   [Jd 5; v-2a(1); 5392]   "
σωσάτω   aor act imperative 3 sg
   [Lk 23:35; v-2a(1); 5392]   "
σώσει   fut act ind 3 sg [6t; v-2a(1); 5392]   "
σώσεις   fut act ind 2 sg [3t; v-2a(1); 5392]   "
Σωσθένην   acc sg masc
   [Ac 18:17; n-3d(2a); 5398]   Σωσθένης

Σωσθένης, -ους, ὁ   {5398, n-3d(2a)}
   Sosthenes, pr. name, Acts 18:17; 1 Cor 1:1*

Σωσθένης   nom sg masc [1C 1:1; n-3d(2a); 5398]   "

Σωσίπατρος, ου, ὁ   {5399, n-2a}
   Sosipater, pr. name, Rom 16:21*

Σωσίπατρος   nom sg masc
   [Rm 16:21; n-2a; 5399]   Σωσίπατρος
σῶσον   aor act imperative 2 sg
   [7t; v-2a(1); 5392]   σῴζω
σώσω   aor act subj 1 sg [2t; v-2a(1); 5392]   "
σώσω   fut act ind 1 sg [Rm 11:14; v-2a(1); 5392]   "
σώσων   fut act ptcp nom sg masc
   [Mt 27:49; v-2a(1); 5392]   "

σωτήρ, ῆρος, ὁ   {5400, n-3f(2a)}
   a savior, preserver, deliverer, Luke 1:47; 2:11; Acts
   5:31

σωτήρ   nom sg masc [4t; n-3f(2a); 5400]   σωτήρ
σωτῆρα   acc sg masc [4t; n-3f(2a); 5400]   "
σωτῆρι   dat sg masc [2t; n-3f(2a); 5400]   "

σωτηρία, ας, ἡ   {5401, n-1a}
   a saving, preservation, Acts 27:34; Heb 11:7;
   deliverance, Luke 1:69, 71; Acts 7:25; *salvation*,
   spiritual and eternal, Luke 1:77; 19:9; Acts 4:12;
   Rev 7:10; *a being placed in a condition of salvation*
   by an embracing of the Gospel, Rom 10:1, 10; 2
   Tim 3:15; *means* or *opportunity of salvation*, Acts

13:26; Rom 11:11; Heb 2:3; ἡ σωτηρία, *the*
promised *deliverance* by the Messiah, John 4:22

σωτηρία   nom sg fem [8t; n-1a; 5401]   σωτηρία
σωτηρίαν   acc sg fem [18t; n-1a; 5401]   "
σωτηρίας   gen sg fem [20t; n-1a; 5401]   "
σωτήριον   nom sg neut
   [Ac 28:28; a-3a; 5403]   σωτήριος
σωτήριον   acc sg neut [2t; a-3a; 5403]   "

σωτήριος, ον   {5403, a-3a}
   imparting salvation, saving, Titus 2:11; Luke 2:30;
   3:6; Acts 28:28; Eph 6:17*

σωτήριος   nom sg fem [Ti 2:11; a-3a; 5402]   "
σωτηρίου   gen sg neut [Ep 6:17; a-3a; 5402]   "
σωτῆρος   gen sg masc [14t; n-3f(2a); 5400]   σωτήρ
σώφρονα   acc sg masc [2t; a-4b(1); 5409]   σώφρων
σώφρονας   acc pl masc [Ti 2:2; a-4b(1); 5409]   "
σώφρονας   acc pl fem [Ti 2:5; a-4b(1); 5409]   "
σωφρονεῖν   pres act inf
   [2t; v-1d(2a); 5404]   σωφρονέω

σωφρονέω   {5404, v-1d(2a)}
   [-, ἐσωφρόνησα, -, -, -] *to be of a sound mind, be in
   one's right mind, be sane*, Mark 5:15; Luke 8:35; *to
   be calm*, 2 Cor 5:13; *to be sober-minded, sedate*,
   Titus 2:6; 1 Peter 4:7; *to be of a modest, humble
   mind*, Rom 12:3*

σωφρονήσατε   aor act imperative 2 pl
   [1P 4:7; v-1d(2a); 5404]   "

σωφρονίζω   {5405, v-2a(1)}
   [-, -, -, -, -] *encourage, to restore to a right mind; to
   make sober-minded, to steady* by exhortation and
   guidance, Titus 2:4*

σωφρονίζωσιν   pres act subj 3 pl
   [Ti 2:4; v-2a(1); 5405]   σωφρονίζω

σωφρονισμός, οῦ, ὁ   {5406, n-2a}
   self discipline, prudence, 2 Tim 1:7*

σωφρονισμοῦ   gen sg masc
   [2Ti 1:7; n-2a; 5406]   σωφρονισμός
σωφρονοῦμεν   pres act ind 1 pl
   [2C 5:13; v-1d(2a); 5404]   σωφρονέω
σωφρονοῦντα   pres act ptcp acc sg masc
   [2t; v-1d(2a); 5404]   "

σωφρόνως   {5407, adverb}
   *in the manner of a person in his right mind; soberly,
   temperately*, Titus 2:12*

σωφρόνως   adverb [Ti 2:12; adverb; 5407] σωφρόνως

σωφροσύνη, ῆς, ἡ   {5408, n-1b}
   sanity, soundness of mind, a sane mind, Acts
   26:25; *female modesty*, 1 Tim 2:9, 15*

σωφροσύνης   gen sg fem
   [3t; n-1b] 5408]   σωφροσύνη

σώφρων, ον   {5409, a-4b(1)}
   of a sound mind, sane; temperate, discreet, 1 Tim
   3:2; Titus 1:8; 2:2; *modest, chaste*, Titus 2:5*

τ

τά   nom pl neut [217t; a-1a(2b); 3836]   ὁ
τά   voc pl neut [3t; a-1a(2b); 3836]   "
τά   acc pl neut [616t; a-1a(2b); 3836]   "

ταβέρναι, ῶν, αἱ   {5411, n-1b}
   a tavern, inn, Acts 28:15*

ταβερνῶν   gen pl fem
   [Ac 28:15; n-1b; 5411]   ταβέρναι

Ταβιθά, ἡ   {5412, n-3g(2)}
   antelope, Tabitha, pr. name, Acts 9:36, 40*

Ταβιθά   indecl [2t; n-3g(2); 5412]   Ταβιθά

τάγμα, ατος, τό   {5413, n-3c(4)}
   pr. *anything placed in order*; in N.T. *order of
   succession, class, group*, 1 Cor 15:23*

τάγματι   dat sg neut
   [1C 15:23; n-3c(4); 5413]   τάγμα
τάδε   acc pl neut [8t; a-1a(2b); 3840]   ὅδε
ταῖς   dat pl fem [203t; a-1a(2b); 3836]   ὁ
τακτῇ   dat sg fem
   [Ac 12:21; a-1a(2a); 5414]   τακτός

τακτός, ή, όν   {5414, a-1a(2a)}
   pr. *arranged; fixed, appointed, set*, Acts 12:21*

ταλαιπωρέω   {5415, v-1d(2a)}
   [(ἐταλαιπώρουν), -, ἐταλαιπώρησα, -, -, -] *to
   endure severe labor and hardship; to be harassed;
   complain*, James 4:9*

ταλαιπωρήσατε   aor act imperative 2 pl
   [Jm 4:9; v-1d(2a); 5415]   ταλαιπωρέω

ταλαιπωρία, ας, ἡ   {5416, n-1a}
   toil, difficulty, hardship; calamity, misery, distress,
   Rom 3:16; James 5:1*

ταλαιπωρία   nom sg fem
   [Rm 3:16; n-1a; 5416]   ταλαιπωρία
ταλαιπωρίαις   dat pl fem [Jm 5:1; n-1a; 5416]   "

ταλαίπωρος, ον   {5417, a-3a}
   pr. *enduring severe effort and hardship*; hence,
   wretched, miserable, afflicted, Rom 7:24; Rev 3:17*

ταλαίπωρος   nom sg masc
   [2t; a-3a; 5417]   ταλαίπωρος
τάλαντα   acc pl neut [10t; n-2c; 5419]   τάλαντον
ταλαντιαία   nom sg fem
   [Rv 16:21; a-1a(1); 5418]   ταλαντιαῖος

ταλαντιαῖος, α, ον   {5418, a-1a(1)}
   of a talent weight, weighing a talent, Rev 16:21*

τάλαντον, ου, τό   {5419, n-2c}
   the scale of a balance; a talent, which as a weight
   was among the Jews equivalent to 3000
   shekels, i.e., as usually estimated, 114 lbs. 15
   dwts. Troy; while the Attic talent, on the usual
   estimate, was only equal to 56 lbs. 11 oz. Troy,
   Matt 18:24; 25:15, 16, 20, 22, 24, 25, 28*

τάλαντον   acc sg neut [3t; n-2c; 5419]   τάλαντον
ταλάντων   gen pl neut [Mt 18:24; n-2c; 5419]   "

ταλιθά   {5420, n-3g(2)}
Aramaic, *(little) girl*, Mark 5:41*

ταλιθα indecl [Mk 5:41; n-3g(2); 5420]   ταλιθά
ταμείοις dat pl neut [2t; n-2c; 5421]   ταμεῖον

ταμεῖον, ου, τό   {5421, n-2c}
a storehouse, granary, barn, Luke 12:24; *a
chamber, closet, place of retirement and privacy*,
Matt 6:6; 24:26; Luke 12:3*

ταμεῖον nom sg neut [Lk 12:24; n-2c; 5421]   "
ταμεῖον acc sg neut [Mt 6:6; n-2c; 5421]   "

ταμιεῖον, ου, τό   {5422, n-2c}
hidden or *secret room*, Matt 24:26 v.l.*

τανῦν, see νῦν

ταξάμενοι aor mid ptcp nom pl masc
[Ac 28:23; v-2b; 5435]   τάσσω
τάξει dat sg fem [Lk 1:8; n-3e(5b); 5423]   τάξις
τάξιν acc sg fem [8t; n-3e(5b); 5423]   "

τάξις, εως, ἡ   {5423, n-3e(5b)}
*order, regular disposition, arrangement; order,
series, succession*, Luke 1:8; *an order, distinctive
class*, as of priests, Heb 5:6, 10; 6:20; 7:11, 17, 21
v.l.; *order, good order*, 1 Cor 14:40; *orderliness,
well-regulated conduct*, Col 2:5*

ταπεινοῖς dat pl masc
[3t; a-1a(2a); 5424]   ταπεινός

ταπεινός, ή, όν   {5424, a-1a(2a)}
low in situation; of condition, *humble, poor,
mean, depressed*, Luke 1:52; 2 Cor 7:6; James 1:9;
met. of the mind, *humble, lowly, modest*, Matt
11:29; Rom 12:16; 2 Cor 10:1; James 4:6; 1 Peter
5:5*

ταπεινός nom sg masc [3t; a-1a(2a); 5424]   "
ταπεινούς acc pl masc [2t; a-1a(2a); 5424]   "
ταπεινοῦσθαι pres pass inf
[Pp 4:12; v-1d(3); 5427]   ταπεινόω
ταπεινόφρονες nom pl masc
[1P 3:8; a-4b(1); 5426]   ταπεινόφρων

ταπεινοφροσύνη, ης, ἡ   {5425, n-1b}
lowliness or *humility of mind, modesty*, Acts
20:19; Eph 4:2; Phil 2:3; Col 2:18, 23; 3:12; 1
Peter 5:5*

ταπεινοφροσύνη dat sg fem
[3t; n-1b; 5425]   ταπεινοφροσύνη
ταπεινοφροσύνην acc sg fem [2t; n-1b; 5425]   "
ταπεινοφροσύνης gen sg fem [2t; n-1b; 5425]   "

ταπεινόφρων, ον   {5426, a-4b(1)}
humble-minded, 1 Peter 3:8*

ταπεινόω   {5427, v-1d(3)}
[ταπεινώσω, ἐταπείνωσα, -, τεταπείνωμαι,
ἐταπεινώθην] *to bring low, depress, level*, Luke
3:5; met. *to humble, abase*, Phil 2:8; mid. *to
descend to*, or *live in, a humble condition*, 2 Cor
11:7; Phil 4:12; *to humble, depress the pride of*, any
one, Matt 18:4; mid. *to humble one's self, exhibit
humility and contrition*, James 4:10; 1 Peter 5:6; *to
humble* with respect to hopes and expectations,
to depress with disappointment, Matt 23:12;
Luke 14:11; 18:14; 2 Cor 12:21*

ταπεινωθήσεται fut pass ind 3 sg
[4t; v-1d(3); 5427]   ταπεινόω
ταπεινώθητε aor pass imperative 2 pl
[2t; v-1d(3); 5427]   "
ταπεινῶν pres act ptcp nom sg masc
[3t; v-1d(3); 5427]   "
ταπεινώσει dat sg fem
[2t; n-3e(5b); 5428]   ταπείνωσις
ταπεινώσει fut act ind 3 sg
[2t; v-1d(3); 5427]   ταπεινόω
ταπεινώσεως gen sg fem
[Pp 3:21; n-3e(5b); 5428]   ταπείνωσις
ταπεινώσῃ aor act subj 3 sg
[2C 12:21; v-1d(3); 5427]   ταπεινόω
ταπείνωσιν acc sg fem
[Lk 1:48; n-3e(5b); 5428]   ταπείνωσις

ταπείνωσις, εως, ἡ   {5428, n-3e(5b)}
depression; low estate, abject condition, Luke 1:48;
Acts 8:33; Phil 3:21; James 1:10; Heb 11: 20 v.l.*

ταρασσέσθω pres pass imperative 3 sg
[2t; v-2b; 5429]   ταράσσω
ταράσσοντες pres act ptcp nom pl masc
[2t; v-2b; 5429]   "

ταράσσω   {5429, v-2b}
[(ἐτάρασσον), -, ἐτάραξα, -, τετάραγμαι,
ἐταράχθην] *to agitate, trouble*, as water, John 5:4
v.l., 7; met. *to agitate, trouble* the mind; with fear,
to terrify, put in consternation, Matt 2:3; 14:26;
with grief, etc., *affect with grief, anxiety*, etc.,
John 12:27; 13:21; with doubt, etc., *to unsettle,
perplex*, Acts 15:24; Gal 1:7

ταράσσων pres act ptcp nom sg masc
[Ga 5:10; v-2b; 5429]   "

ταραχή, ῆς, ἡ   {5430, n-1b}
agitation, troubling, of water, John 5:4 v.l.; met.
commotion, tumult, Matt 13:8 v.l.*

ταραχθῇ aor pass subj 3 sg [Jn 5:7; v-2b; 5429] "
ταραχθῆτε aor pass subj 2 pl
[1P 3:14; v-2b; 5429]   "

τάραχος, ου, ὁ   {5431, n-2a}
agitation, commotion; consternation, terror, Acts
12:18; *excitement, tumult, public contention*, Acts
19:23*

τάραχος nom sg masc [2t; n-2a; 5431]   τάραχος
Ταρσέα acc sg masc
[Ac 9:11; n-3e(3); 5432]   Ταρσεύς

Ταρσεύς, έως, ὁ   {5432, n-3e(3)}
of, or *a native of* Ταρσός, *Tarsus*, the metropolis
of Cilicia, Acts 9:11; 21:39*

Ταρσεύς nom sg masc [Ac 21:39; n-3e(3); 5432] "
Ταρσόν acc sg fem [2t; n-2b; 5433]   Ταρσός

Ταρσός, οῦ, ἡ   {5433, n-2b}
Tarsus, the chief city of Cilicia, and birth-place
of the Apostle Paul, Acts 9:30; 11:25; 21:39 v.l.,
22:3*

Ταρσῷ dat sg fem [Ac 22:3; n-2b; 5433]   "

ταρταρόω   {5434, v-1d(3)}
[-, ἐταρτάρωσα, -, -, -] *to cast* or *thrust down to*
Tartarus or *Gehenna*, 2 Peter 2:4*

ταρταρώσας   aor act ptcp nom sg masc
   [2P 2:4; v-1d(3); 5434]   ταρταρόω
τάς   acc pl fem [340t; a-1a(2b); 3836]   ὁ
τασσόμενος   pres pass ptcp nom sg masc
   [Lk 7:8; v-2b; 5435]   τάσσω

τάσσω   {5435, v-2b}
[τάξομαι, ἔταξα, τέταχα, τέταγμαι, ἐτάχθην] *to*
arrange; to set, appoint, in a certain station, Luke
7:8; Rom 13:1; Matt 8:9 v.l.; *to set, devote,* to a
pursuit, 1 Cor 16:15; *to dispose, frame,* for an
object, Acts 13:48; *to arrange, appoint,* place or
time, Matt 28:16; Acts 28:23; *to allot, assign,* Acts
22:10; *to settle, decide,* Acts 15:2; 18:2 v.l.*

ταῦροι   nom pl masc [Mt 22:4; n-2a; 5436]   ταῦρος

ταῦρος, ου, ὁ   {5436, n-2a}
a bull, ox, Matt 22:4; Acts 14:13; Heb 9:13; 10:4*

ταύρους   acc pl masc [Ac 14:13; n-2a; 5436]   "
ταύρων   gen pl masc [2t; n-2a; 5436]   "
ταῦτα   nom pl neut [44t; a-1a(2b); 4047]   οὗτος
ταῦτα   acc pl neut [195t; a-1a(2b); 4047]   "
ταύταις   dat pl fem [11t; a-1a(2b); 4047]   "
ταύτας   acc pl fem [9t; a-1a(2b); 4047]   "
ταύτῃ   dat sg fem [32t; a-1a(2b); 4047]   "
ταύτην   acc sg fem [53t; a-1a(2b); 4047]   "
ταύτης   gen sg fem [33t; a-1a(2b); 4047]   "

ταφή, ῆς, ἡ   {5438, n-1b}
burial, the act of burying, burial place, Matt 27:7*

ταφήν   acc sg fem [Mt 27:7; n-1b; 5438]   ταφή
τάφοις   dat pl masc [Mt 23:27; n-2a; 5439]   τάφος
τάφον   acc sg masc [3t; n-2a; 5439]   "

τάφος, ου, ὁ   {5439, n-2a}
a sepulchre, grave, tomb, Matt 23:27, 29; 27:61, 64,
66; 28:1; met. Rom 3:13*

τάφος   nom sg masc [Rm 3:13; n-2a; 5439]   "
τάφου   gen sg masc [Mt 27:61; n-2a; 5439]   "
τάφους   acc pl masc [Mt 23:29; n-2a; 5439]   "

τάχα   {5440, adverb}
pr. *quickly, soon; perhaps, possibly,* Rom 5:7; Phlm
15*

τάχα   adverb [2t; adverb; 5440]   τάχα
τάχει   dat sg neut [8t; n-3d(2b); 5443]   τάχος

ταχέως   {5441, adverb}
adverb of ταχύς, *quickly, speedily; soon, shortly,* 1
Cor 4:19; Gal 1:6; *hastily,* Luke 14:21; 16:6; *with*
inconsiderate haste, 1 Tim 5:22

ταχέως   adverb [10t; adverb; 5441]   ταχέως
ταχινή   nom sg fem
   [2P 1:14; a-1a(2a); 5442]   ταχινός
ταχινήν   acc sg fem [2P 2:1; a-1a(2a); 5442]   "

ταχινός, ή, όν   {5442, a-1a(2a)}
swift, speedy, 2 Peter 2:1; *near at hand, impending,*
2 Peter 1:14*

τάχιον   {adverb}
comparative adverb of ταχύς, *more swiftly, more*

quickly, more speedily, John 20:4; Heb 13:19;
quickly, speedily, John 13:27; 1 Tim 3:14 v.l.; Heb
13:23*

τάχιον   adverb-comparative
   [4t; adverb; 5441]   ταχέως

τάχιστα   {adverb}
superlative adverb of ταχύς, *most quickly, most*
speedily, very quickly; ὡς τάχιστα, *as soon as*
possible, Acts 17:15*

τάχιστα   adverb-superlative
   [Ac 17:15; adverb; 5441]   "

τάχος, ους, τό   {5443, n-3d(2b)}
swiftness, speed, quickness; ἐν τάχει, *with speed,*
quickly, speedily; soon, shortly, Luke 18:8; Acts
25:4; *hastily, immediately,* Acts 12:7; 22:18; Rom
16:20; 1 Tim 3:14; Rev 1:1; 22:6*

ταχύ   adverb [12t; a-2b; 5444]   ταχύς

ταχύς, εῖα, ύ   {5444, a-2b}
swift, fleet, quick; met. *ready, prompt,* James 1:19;
Matt 28:7f.; Mark 9:39; Luke 15:22; John 11:29

ταχύς   nom sg masc [Jm 1:19; a-2b; 5444]   "

τέ   {5445, particle}
enclitic, can function as a conj., serving either
as a lightly-appending link, Acts 1:15; *and,* Acts
2:3; or as an inclusive prefix, Luke 12:45; *both,*
Luke 24:20; Acts 26:16

τε   part [215t; particle; 5445]   τέ
τεθέαμαι   perf mid ind 1 sg
   [Jn 1:32; v-1d(1b); 2517]   θεάομαι
τεθεάμεθα   perf mid ind 1 pl
   [1J 4:14; v-1d(1b); 2517]   "
τεθέαται   perf mid ind 3 sg
   [1J 4:12; v-1d(1b); 2517]   "
τέθεικα   perf act ind 1 sg [2t; v-6a; 5502]   τίθημι
τεθείκατε   perf act ind 2 pl
   [Jn 11:34; v-6a; 5502]   "
τεθεικώς   perf act ptcp nom sg masc
   [2P 2:6; v-6a; 5502]   "
τεθειμένος   perf pass ptcp nom sg masc
   [Jn 19:41; v-6a; 5502]   "
τέθειται   perf pass ind 3 sg
   [Mk 15:47; v-6a; 5502]   "
τεθεμελιωμένοι   perf pass ptcp nom pl masc
   [2t; v-1d(3); 2530]   θεμελιόω
τεθεμελίωτο   pluperf pass ind 3 sg
   [Mt 7:25; v-1d(3); 2530]   "
τεθεραπευμέναι   perf pass ptcp nom pl fem
   [Lk 8:2; v-1a(6); 2543]   θεραπεύω
τεθεραπευμένον   perf pass ptcp acc sg masc
   [Ac 4:14; v-1a(6); 2543]   "
τεθεραπευμένῳ   perf pass ptcp dat sg masc
   [Jn 5:10; v-1a(6); 2543]   "
τεθῇ   aor pass subj 3 sg [2t; v-6a; 5502]   τίθημι
τεθῆναι   aor pass inf [Rv 11:9; v-6a; 5502]   "
τεθησαυρισμένοι   perf pass ptcp nom pl masc
   [2P 3:7; v-2a(1); 2564]   θησαυρίζω
τεθλιμμένη   perf pass ptcp nom sg fem
   [Mt 7:14; v-1b(1); 2567]   θλίβω
τεθνήκασιν   perf act ind 3 pl
   [Mt 2:20; v-5a; v-7; 2569]   θνήσκω

τέθνηκεν　perf act ind 3 sg　[3t; v-5a; v-7; 2569]　　"
τεθνηκέναι　perf act inf
　　[Ac 14:19; v-5a; v-7; 2569]　　"
τεθνηκότα　perf act ptcp acc sg masc
　　[Jn 19:33; v-5a; v-7; 2569]　　"
τεθνηκότος　perf act ptcp gen sg masc
　　[Ac 25:19; v-5a; v-7; 2569]　　"
τεθνηκώς　perf act ptcp nom sg masc
　　[2t; v-5a; v-7; 2569]　　"
τεθραμμένος　perf pass ptcp nom sg masc
　　[Lk 4:16; v-1b(1); 5555]　　τρέφω
τεθραυσμένους　perf pass ptcp acc pl masc
　　[Lk 4:18; v-1a(5); 2575]　　θραύω
τεθυμένα　perf pass ptcp nom pl neut
　　[Mt 22:4; v-1a(4); 2604]　　θύω
τεθῶσιν　aor pass subj 3 pl
　　[Hb 10:13; v-6a; 5502]　　τίθημι
τείχη　nom pl neut
　　[Hb 11:30; n-3d(2b); 5446]　　τεῖχος

τεῖχος, ους, τό　　　　　{5446, n-3d(2b)}
　a wall of a city, Acts 9:25; 2 Cor 11:33; Heb 11:30;
　Rev 21:12, 14f., 17-19*

τεῖχος　nom sg neut　[Rv 21:14; n-3d(2b); 5446]　　"
τεῖχος　acc sg neut　[3t; n-3d(2b); 5446]　　"
τείχους　gen sg neut　[4t; n-3d(2b); 5446]　　"
τεκεῖν　aor act inf　[4t; v-1b(2); 5503]　　τίκτω
τέκῃ　aor act subj 3 sg　[Rv 12:4; v-1b(2); 5503]　　"
τεκμηρίοις　dat pl neut
　　[Ac 1:3; n-2c; 5447]　　τεκμήριον

τεκμήριον, ου, τό　　　　{5447, n-2c}
　a sign, indubitable token, clear proof, Acts 1:3*

τέκνα　nom pl neut　[26t; n-2c; 5451]　　τέκνον
τέκνα　voc pl neut　[4t; n-2c; 5451]　　"
τέκνα　acc pl neut　[33t; n-2c; 5451]　　"
τεκνία　voc pl neut　[8t; n-2c; 5448]　　τεκνίον

τεκνίον, ου, τό　　　　{5448, n-2c}
　a little child; τεκνία, an endearing appellation,
　my dear children, John 13:33; Gal 4:19 v.l.; 1 John
　2:1, 12, 28; 3:7, 18; 4:4; 5:21*

τεκνογονεῖν　pres act inf
　　[1Ti 5:14; cv-1d(2a); 5449]　　τεκνογονέω

τεκνογονέω　　　　{5449, cv-1d(2a)}
　[-, -, -, -, -] to bear children, to rear a family, 1 Tim
　5:14*

τεκνογονία, ας, ή　　　　{5450, n-1a}
　the bearing of children, the rearing of a family, 1
　Tim 2:15*

τεκνογονίας　gen sg fem
　　[1Ti 2:15; n-1a; 5450]　　τεκνογονία
τέκνοις　dat pl neut　[8t; n-2c; 5451]　　τέκνον

τέκνον, ου, τό　　　　{5451, n-2c}
　a child, a son or daughter, Matt 2:18; Luke 1:7; pl.
　descendants, posterity, Matt 3:9; Acts 2:39; child,
　son, as a term of endearment, Matt 9:2; Mark
　2:5; 10:24; pl. children, inhabitants, people, of a
　city, Matt 23:37; Luke 19:44; from the Hebrew,
　met. a child or son in virtue of discipleship, 1
　Cor 4:17; 1 Tim 1:2; 2 Tim 1:2; Titus 1:4; Phlm
　10; 3 John 4; a child in virtue of gracious

acceptance, John 1:12; 11:52; Rom 8:16, 21; 1
John 3:1; a child in virtue of spiritual
conformity, John 8:39; Phil 2:15; 1 John 3:10; a
child of, one characterized by some condition or
quality, Matt 11:19; Eph 2:3; 5:8; 1 Peter 1:14; 2
Peter 2:14

τέκνον　nom sg neut　[4t; n-2c; 5451]　　"
τέκνον　voc sg neut　[8t; n-2c; 5451]　　"
τέκνον　acc sg neut　[4t; n-2c; 5451]　　"

τεκνοτροφέω　　　　{5452, v-1d(2a)}
　[-, ἐτεκνοτρόφησα, -, -, -] to rear a family, 1 Tim
　5:10*

τέκνου　gen sg neut　[2t; n-2c; 5451]　　"

τεκνόω　　　　{5453, v-1d(3)}
　[-, -, -, -, -] bear a child, Heb 11:11 v.l.*

τέκνῳ　dat sg neut　[3t; n-2c; 5451]　　"
τέκνων　gen pl neut　[7t; n-2c; 5451]　　"
τέκτονος　gen sg masc
　　[Mt 13:55; n-3f(1b); 5454]　　τέκτων

τέκτων, ονος, ὁ　　　　{5454, n-3f(1b)}
　an artisan; and spc. one who works with wood, a
　carpenter, Matt 13:55; Mark 6:3*

τέκτων　nom sg masc　[Mk 6:3; n-3f(1b); 5454]　　"
τελεῖ　pres act ind 3 sg
　　[Mt 17:24; v-1d(2b); 5464]　　τελέω
τελεία　nom sg fem
　　[1J 4:18; a-1a(1); 5455]　　τέλειος
τέλειοι　nom pl masc　[5t; a-1a(1); 5455]　　"
τελείοις　dat pl masc　[1C 2:6; a-1a(1); 5455]　　"
τέλειον　nom sg neut　[3t; a-1a(1); 5455]　　"
τέλειον　acc sg masc　[3t; a-1a(1); 5455]　　"
τέλειον　acc sg neut　[Jm 1:4; a-1a(1); 5455]　　"

τέλειος, α, ον　　　　{5455, a-1a(1)}
　brought to completion; fully accomplished, fully
　developed, James 1:4a; fully realized, thorough, 1
　John 4:18; complete, entire, as opposed to what is
　partial and limited, 1 Cor 13:10; full grown of
　ripe age, 1 Cor 14:20; Eph 4:13; Heb 5:14; fully
　accomplished in Christian enlightenment, 1 Cor
　2:6; Phil 3:15; Col 1:28; perfect in some point of
　character, without shortcoming in respect of a
　certain standard, Matt 5:48; 19:21; Col 4:12;
　James 1:4b; 3:2; perfect, consummate, Rom 12:2;
　James 1:17, 25; compar. of higher excellence and
　efficiency, Heb 9:11*

τέλειος　nom sg masc　[3t; a-1a(1); 5455]　　"
τελειοτέρας　gen sg fem comparative
　　[Hb 9:11; a-1a(1); 5455]　　"

τελειότης, ητος, ή　　　　{5456, n-3c(1)}
　completeness, perfectness, Col 3:14; ripeness of
　knowledge or practice, maturity, Heb 6:1*

τελειότητα　acc sg fem
　　[Hb 6:1; n-3c(1); 5456]　　τελειότης
τελειότητος　gen sg fem　[Cl 3:14; n-3c(1); 5456]　　"
τελειοῦμαι　pres pass ind 1 sg
　　[Lk 13:32; v-1d(3); 5457]　　τελειόω

τελειόω　　　　{5457, v-1d(3)}
　[-, ἐτελείωσα, τετελείωκα, τετελείωμαι,
　ἐτελειώθην] to execute fully, discharge, John 4:34;

5:36; 17:4; *to reach the end of, run through, finish,*
Luke 2:43; Acts 20:24; *to consummate, place in a*
condition of finality, Heb 7:19; *to perfect* a person,
advance a person *to final completeness of*
character, Heb 2:10; 5:9; 7:28; *to perfect* a person,
advance a person *to a completeness* of its kind,
which needs no further provision, Heb 9:9;
10:1, 14; pass. *to receive fulfillment,* John 19:28; *to*
be brought to the goal, to reach the end of one's
course, Luke 13:32; Phil 3:12; Heb 11:40; 12:23; *to*
be fully developed, 2 Cor 12:9; James 2:22; 1 John
2:5; 4:12, 17; *to be completely organized, to be*
closely embodied, John 17:23

τελεῖται   pres pass ind 3 sg
    [2C 12:9; v-1d(2b); 5464]   τελέω

τελεῖτε   pres act ind 2 pl [2t; v-1d(2b); 5464]   "

τελειωθείς   aor pass ptcp nom sg masc
    [Hb 5:9; v-1d(3); 5457]   τελειόω

τελειωθῇ   aor pass subj 3 sg
    [Jn 19:28; v-1d(3); 5457]   "

τελειωθῶσιν   aor pass subj 3 pl
    [Hb 11:40; v-1d(3); 5457]   "

τελείων   gen pl masc
    [Hb 5:14; a-1a(1); 5455]   τέλειος

τελείως   {5458, adverb}
    perfectly, completely, 1 Peter 1:13*

τελείως   adverb [1P 1:13; adverb; 5458]   τελείως

τελειῶσαι   aor act inf
    [4t; v-1d(3); 5457]   τελειόω

τελειωσάντων   aor act ptcp gen pl masc
    [Lk 2:43; v-1d(3); 5457]   "

τελειώσας   aor act ptcp nom sg masc
    [Jn 17:4; v-1d(3); 5457]   "

τελείωσις, εως, ἡ   {5459, n-3e(5b)}
    a completing; a fulfillment, an accomplishment of
    predictions, promised, etc., Luke 1:45; *finality*
    of function, *completeness* of operation and
    effect, Heb 7:11*

τελείωσις   nom sg fem
    [2t; n-3e(5b); 5459]   τελείωσις

τελειώσω   aor act subj 1 sg
    [2t; v-1d(3); 5457]   τελειόω

τελειωτήν   acc sg masc
    [Hb 12:2; n-1f; 5460]   τελειωτής

τελειωτής, οῦ, ὁ   {5460, n-1f}
    a finisher, one who completes and perfects a thing;
    one who brings through to final attainment,
    perfecter, Heb 12:2*

τελέσητε   aor act subj 2 pl
    [2t; v-1d(2b); 5464]   τελέω

τελεσθῇ   aor pass subj 3 sg [4t; v-1d(2b); 5464]   "

τελεσθῆναι   aor pass inf
    [Lk 22:37; v-1d(2b); 5464]   "

τελεσθήσεται   fut pass ind 3 sg
    [Lk 18:31; v-1d(2b); 5464]   "

τελεσθήσονται   fut pass ind 3 pl
    [Rv 17:17; v-1d(2b); 5464]   "

τελεσθῶσιν   aor pass subj 3 pl
    [Rv 15:8; v-1d(2b); 5464]

τελεσφορέω   {5461, cv-1d(2b)}
    [-, -, -, -, -] *to bring to maturity,* as fruits, etc.;
    met. Luke 8:14, 15 v.l.*

τελεσφοροῦσιν   pres act ind 3 pl
    [Lk 8:14; cv-1d(2b); 5461]   τελεσφορέω

τελέσωσιν   aor act subj 3 pl
    [Rv 11:7; v-1d(2b); 5464]   τελέω

τελευτᾷ   pres act ind 3 sg
    [Mk 9:48; v-1d(1a); 5462]   τελευτάω

τελευτᾶν   pres act inf [Lk 7:2; v-1d(1a); 5462]   "

τελευτάτω   pres act imperative 3 sg
    [2t; v-1d(1a); 5462]   "

τελευτάω   {5462, v-1d(1a)}
    [τελευτήσω, ἐτελεύτησα, τετελεύτηκα, -, -] *to end,*
    finish, complete; absol. *to end* one's life, *to die,*
    Matt 2:19; 15:4; 22:25; Mark 7:10; Luke 7:2; Acts
    7:15; Heb 11:22

τελευτή, ῆς, ἡ   {5463, n-1b}
    a finishing, end; hence, *end* of life, *death, decease,*
    Matt 2:15*

τελευτῆς   gen sg fem [Mt 2:15; n-1b; 5463]   τελευτή

τελευτήσαντος   aor act ptcp gen sg masc
    [Mt 2:19; v-1d(1a); 5462]   τελευτάω

τελευτῶν   pres act ptcp nom sg masc
    [Hb 11:22; v-1d(1a); 5462]   "

τελέω   {5464, v-1d(2b)}
    [τελέσω, ἐτέλεσα, τετέλεκα, τετέλεσμαι,
    ἐτελέσθην] *to finish, complete, conclude,* an
    operation, Matt 11:1; 13:53; 19:1; *to finish* a
    circuit, Matt 10:23; *to fulfil, to carry out into full*
    operation, Rom 2:27; Gal 5:16; James 2:8; *to pay*
    dues, Matt 17:24; pass. *to be fulfilled, realized,*
    Luke 12:50; 18:31; of time, *to be ended, elapse,*
    Rom 15:8; 20:3, 5, 7

τέλη   nom pl neut [1C 10:11; n-3d(2b); 5465]   τέλος

τέλη   acc pl neut [Mt 17:25; n-3d(2b); 5465]   "

τέλος, ους, τό   {5465, n-3d(2b)}
    an end attained, consummation; an end, closing act,
    Matt 24:6, 14; 1 Cor 15:24; *full performance,*
    perfect discharge, Rom 10:4; *fulfillment,*
    realization, Luke 22:37; *final dealing,* developed
    issue, James 5:11; *issue, final stage,* 1 Cor 10:11;
    issue, result, Matt 26:58; Rom 6:21, 22; 1 Peter
    1:9; antitypical *issue,* 2 Cor 3:13; practical *issue,*
    1 Tim 1:5; *ultimate destiny,* Phil 3:19; Heb 6:8; 1
    Peter 4:17; *a tax* or *dues,* Matt 17:25; Rom 13:7;
    εἰς τέλος, *to the full,* 1 Thess 2:16; εἰς τέλος,
    continually, Luke 18:5; εἰς τέλος, μέχρι, ἄχρι
    τέλους, *throughout,* Matt 10:22; Mark 13:13;
    John 13:1; Heb 3:6, 14; 6:11; Rev 2:26

τέλος   nom sg neut [16t; n-3d(2b); 5465]   "

τέλος   acc sg neut [17t; n-3d(2b); 5465]   "

τέλους   gen sg neut [5t; n-3d(2b); 5465]   "

τελοῦσα   pres act ptcp nom sg fem
    [Rm 2:27; v-1d(2b); 5464]   τελέω

τελῶναι   nom pl masc [8t; n-1f; 5467]   τελώνης

τελώνην   acc sg masc [Lk 5:27; n-1f; 5467]   "

τελώνης, ου, ὁ   {5467, n-1f}
    one who farms the public revenues; in N.T. *a*
    publican, collector of imposts, revenue officer, tax

gatherer, Matt 5:46; 9:10, 11; 10:3; Mark 2:15f.; Luke 3:12

τελώνης   nom sg masc   [5t; n-1f; 5467]   "

τελώνιον, ου, τό   {5468, n-2c}
a custom-house, toll-house; collector's office, Matt 9:9; Mark 2:14; Luke 5:27*

τελώνιον   acc sg neut   [3t; n-2c; 5468]   τελώνιον
τελωνῶν   gen pl masc   [7t; n-1f; 5467]   τελώνης
τέξεται   fut mid ind 3 sg
     [2t; v-1b(2); 5503]   τίκτω
τέξῃ   fut mid ind 2 sg   [Lk 1:31; v-1b(2); 5503]   "

τέρας, ατος, τό   {5469, n-3c(6a)}
a prodigy, portent, Acts 2:19; *a signal act, wonder, miracle*, Matt 13:22; John 4:48; Acts 2:43

τέρασι   dat pl neut
     [Ac 2:22; n-3c(6a); 5469]   τέρας
τέρασιν   dat pl neut   [3t; n-3c(6a); 5469]   "
τέρατα   nom pl neut   [2t; n-3c(6a); 5469]   "
τέρατα   acc pl neut   [9t; n-3c(6a); 5469]   "
τεράτων   gen pl neut   [Rm 15:19; n-3c(6a); 5469]   "

Τέρτιος, ου, ὁ   {5470, n-2a}
Tertius, pr. name, a helper of Paul, Rom 16:22*

Τέρτιος   nom sg masc
     [Rm 16:22; n-2a; 5470]   Τέρτιος

Τερτουλλος, ου, ὁ   {5471, n-2a}
Tertullus, pr. name, subscription to Phlm*

Τέρτυλλος, ου, ὁ   {5472, n-2a}
Tertullus, pr. name, an attorney, Acts 24:1f.*

Τέρτυλλος   nom sg masc
     [Ac 24:2; n-2a; 5472]   Τέρτυλλος
Τερτύλλου   gen sg masc   [Ac 24:1; n-2a; 5472]   "
τέσσαρα   nom pl neut   [5t; a-4b(2); 5475]   τέσσαρες
τέσσαρα   acc pl neut   [Jn 19:23; a-4b(2); 5475]   "

τεσσαράκοντα, v.l. for τεσσεράκοντα   {5473}

τεσσαρακονταετής, ές, v.l. for τεσσερακονταετής
     {5474}

τέσσαρας   acc pl masc   [4t; a-4b(2); 5475]   "
τέσσαρας   acc pl fem   [3t; a-4b(2); 5475]   "

τέσσαρες, τέσσαρα   {5475, a-4b(2)}
four, Matt 24:31; Mark 2:3

τέσσαρες   nom pl masc   [6t; a-4b(2); 5475]   "
τέσσαρες   nom pl fem   [4t; a-4b(2); 5475]   "
τέσσαρες   acc pl masc   [Rv 4:4; a-4b(2); 5475]   "
τεσσαρεσκαιδεκάτη   nom sg fem
     [Ac 27:27; a-1a(2a); 5476]   τεσσαρεσκαιδέκατος
τεσσαρεσκαιδεκάτην   acc sg fem
     [Ac 27:33; a-1a(2a); 5476]   "

τεσσαρεσκαιδέκατος, η, ον   {5476, a-1a(2a)}
the fourteenth, Acts 27:27, 33*

τέσσαρσιν   dat pl masc
     [Rv 7:2; a-4b(2); 5475]   τέσσαρες
τέσσαρσιν   dat pl fem   [3t; a-4b(2); 5475]   "
τέσσαρσιν   dat pl neut   [Ac 12:4; a-4b(2); 5475]   "
τεσσάρων   gen pl masc   [4t; a-4b(2); 5475]   "
τεσσάρων   gen pl neut   [8t; a-4b(2); 5475]   "

τεσσεράκοντα   {5477, a-5c}
forty, indecl., Matt 4:2; John 2:20; Acts 1:3; 23:13, 21; Heb 3:9; Rev 11:2; 21:17

τεσσεράκοντα   indecl
     [22t; a-5c; 5477]   τεσσεράκοντα
τεσσερακονταετῆ   acc sg masc
     [Ac 13:18; a-4a; 5478]   τεσσερακονταετής

τεσσερακονταετής, ές   {5478, a-4a}
forty years, Acts 7:23; 13:18*

τεσσερακονταετής   nom sg masc
     [Ac 7:23; a-4a; 5478]   "
τεταγμέναι   perf pass ptcp nom pl fem
     [Rm 13:1; v-2b; 5435]   τάσσω
τεταγμένοι   perf pass ptcp nom pl masc
     [Ac 13:48; v-2b; 5435]   "
τέτακται   perf pass ind 3 sg
     [Ac 22:10; v-2b; 5435]   "
τεταραγμένοι   perf pass ptcp nom pl masc
     [Lk 24:38; v-2b; 5429]   ταράσσω
τετάρακται   perf pass ind 3 sg
     [Jn 12:27; v-2b; 5429]   "

τεταρταῖος, α, ον   {5479, a-1a(1)}
on the fourth day, John 11:39*

τεταρταῖος   nom sg masc
     [Jn 11:39; a-1a(1); 5479]   τεταρταῖος
τετάρτῃ   dat sg fem
     [Mt 14:25; a-1a(2a); 5480]   τέταρτος
τετάρτην   acc sg fem   [2t; a-1a(2a); 5480]   "
τετάρτης   gen sg fem   [Ac 10:30; a-1a(2a); 5480]   "
τέταρτον   nom sg neut   [Rv 4:7; a-1a(2a); 5480]   "
τέταρτον   acc sg neut   [Rv 6:8; a-1a(2a); 5480]   "

τέταρτος, η, ον   {5480, a-1a(2a)}
fourth, Matt 14:25; *the fourth part, quarter*, Rev 6:8

τέταρτος   nom sg masc   [3t; a-1a(2a); 5480]   "
τετάρτου   gen sg neut   [Rv 6:7; a-1a(2a); 5480]   "
τετελείωκεν   perf act ind 3 sg
     [Hb 10:14; v-1d(3); 5457]   τελειόω
τετελείωμαι   perf pass ind 1 sg
     [Pp 3:12; v-1d(3); 5457]   "
τετελειωμένη   perf pass ptcp nom sg fem
     [1J 4:12; v-1d(3); 5457]   "
τετελειωμένοι   perf pass ptcp nom pl masc
     [Jn 17:23; v-1d(3); 5457]   "
τετελειωμένον   perf pass ptcp acc sg masc
     [Hb 7:28; v-1d(3); 5457]   "
τετελειωμένων   perf pass ptcp gen pl masc
     [Hb 12:23; v-1d(3); 5457]   "
τετελείωται   perf pass ind 3 sg
     [3t; v-1d(3); 5457]   "
τετέλεκα   perf act ind 1 sg
     [2Ti 4:7; v-1d(2b); 5464]   τελέω
τετέλεσται   perf pass ind 3 sg
     [2t; v-1d(2b); 5464]   "
τετελευτηκότος   perf act ptcp gen sg masc
     [Jn 11:39; v-1d(1a); 5462]   τελευτάω
τετήρηκα   perf act ind 1 sg
     [2t; v-1d(2a); 5498]   τηρέω
τετήρηκαν   perf act ind 3 pl
     [Jn 17:6; v-1d(2a); 5498]   "

τετήρηκας   perf act ind 2 sg
    [Jn 2:10; v-1d(2a); 5498]   "
τετήρηκεν   perf act ind 3 sg
    [Jd 6; v-1d(2a); 5498]   "
τετηρημένην   perf pass ptcp acc sg fem
    [1P 1:4; v-1d(2a); 5498]   "
τετηρημένοις   perf pass ptcp dat pl masc
    [Jd 1; v-1d(2a); 5498]   "
τετήρηται   perf pass ind 3 sg
    [2t; v-1d(2a); 5498]   "
τετιμημένου   perf pass ptcp gen sg masc
    [Mt 27:9; v-1d(1a); 5506]   τιμάω

τετρααρχέω   {5489, v-1d(2a)}
    [-, -, -, -, -] also spelled τετραρχέω, be tetrarch,
    Luke 3:1 (3t)*

τετραάρχης, ου, ὁ   {5490, n-1f}
    also spelled τετράρχης, a tetrarch, title of a
    prince, whose rank was lower than a king,
    Matt 14:1; Luke 3:19; 9:7; Acts 13:1*

τετραάρχης   nom sg masc
    [3t; n-1f; 5490]   τετραάρχης
τετραάρχου   gen sg masc [Ac 13:1; n-1f; 5490]   "
τετρααρχοῦντος   pres act ptcp gen sg masc
    [3t; v-1d(2a); 5489]   τετρααρχέω

τετράγωνος, ον   {5481, a-3a}
    four-angled, quadrangular, square, Rev 21:16*

τετράγωνος   nom sg fem
    [Rv 21:16; a-3a; 5481]   τετράγωνος
τετραδίοις   dat pl neut
    [Ac 12:4; n-2c; 5482]   τετράδιον

τετράδιον, ου, τό   {5482, n-2c}
    a set of four; a detachment of four men, Acts 12:4*

τετρακισχίλιοι, η, ον   {5483, a-1a(1)}
    four thousand, Matt 15:38; 16:10; Mark 8:9, 20;
    Acts 21:38*

τετρακισχίλιοι   nom pl masc
    [2t; a-1a(1); 5483]   τετρακισχίλιοι
τετρακισχιλίους   acc pl masc [2t; a-1a(1); 5483]   "
τετρακισχιλίων   gen pl masc
    [Mt 16:10; a-1a(1); 5483]
τετρακόσια   acc pl neut
    [2t; a-1a(1); 5484]   τετρακόσιοι

τετρακόσιοι, αι, α   {5484, a-1a(1)}
    four hundred, Acts 5:36; 7:6; 13:20; 21:38 v.l.; Gal
    3:17*

τετρακοσίοις   dat pl neut
    [Ac 13:20; a-1a(1); 5484]   "
τετρακοσίων   gen pl masc [Ac 5:36; a-1a(1); 5484] "

τετράμηνος, ον   {5485, a-3a}
    of four months, four months in duration, John
    4:35*

τετράμηνος   nom sg masc
    [Jn 4:35; a-3a; 5485]   τετράμηνος

τετραπλόος, όη, όον   {5486, a-1a(2a)}
    uncontracted form of τετραπλοῦς, quadruple,
    fourfold, Luke 19:8 v.l.*

τετραπλοῦν   acc sg neut, can function
    adverbially [Lk 19:8; a-1b; 5487]   τετραπλοῦς

τετραπλοῦς, ῆ, οῦν   {5487, a-1b}
    contracted form of τετραπλόος, four times (as
    much), fourfold, quadruple, Luke 19:8*

τετράποδα   nom pl neut
    [Ac 10:12; a-5; 5488]   τετράπους
τετράποδα   acc pl neut [Ac 11:6; a-5; 5488]   "
τετραπόδων   gen pl neut [Rm 1:23; a-5; 5488]   "

τετράπους   {5488, a-5}
    four-footed; quadrupeds, Acts 10:12; 11:6; Rom
    1:23*

τετραυματισμένους   perf pass ptcp acc pl masc
    [Ac 19:16; v-2a(1); 5547]   τραυματίζω
τετραχηλισμένα   perf pass ptcp nom pl neut
    [Hb 4:13; v-2a(1); 5548]   τραχηλίζω
τετύφλωκεν   perf act ind 3 sg
    [Jn 12:40; v-1d(3); 5604]   τυφλόω
τετυφωμένοι   perf pass ptcp nom pl masc
    [2Ti 3:4; v-1d(3); 5605]   τυφόομαι
τετύφωται   perf pass ind 3 sg
    [1Ti 6:4; v-1d(3); 5605]   "
τέτυχεν   perf act ind 3 sg
    [Hb 8:6; v-3a(2b); 5593]   τυγχάνω

τεφρόω   {5491, v-1d(3)}
    [-, ἐτέφρωσα, -, -, -] to reduce to ashes, to consume,
    destroy, 2 Peter 2:6*

τεφρώσας   aor act ptcp nom sg masc
    [2P 2:6; v-1d(3); 5491]   τεφρόω
τεχθείς   aor pass ptcp nom sg masc
    [Mt 2:2; v-1b(2); 5503]   τίκτω

τέχνη, ης, ἡ   {5492, n-1b}
    art, skill, Acts 17:29; an art, trade, craft, Acts 18:3;
    Rev 18:22*

τέχνη   dat sg fem [Ac 18:3; n-1b; 5492]   τέχνη
τέχνης   gen sg fem [2t; n-1b; 5492]   "
τεχνῖται   nom pl masc
    [Ac 19:38; n-1f; 5493]   τεχνίτης
τεχνίταις   dat pl masc [Ac 19:24; n-1f; 5493]   "

τεχνίτης, ου, ὁ   {5493, n-1f}
    an artisan; workman, mechanic, Acts 19:24, 25 v.l.,
    38; Rev 18:22; an architect, builder, Heb 11:10*

τεχνίτης   nom sg masc [2t; n-1f; 5493]   "
τῇ   dat sg fem [878t; a-1a(2b); 3836]   ὁ
τῇδε   dat sg fem [Lk 10:39; a-1a(2b); 3840]   ὅδε
τήκεται   pres pass ind 3 sg
    [2P 3:12; v-1b(2); 5494]   τήκω

τήκω   {5494, v-1b(2)}
    [-, -, -, -, ἐτάκην] to dissolve; pass. to be liquefied,
    melt, 2 Peter 3:12*

τηλαυγῶς   {5495, adverb}
    clearly, plainly, distinctly, Mark 8:25*

τηλαυγῶς   adverb [Mk 8:25; adverb; 5495]
    τηλαυγῶς
τηλικαῦτα   nom pl neut
    [Jm 3:4; a-1a(2b); 5496]   τηλικοῦτος
τηλικαύτης   gen sg fem [Hb 2:3; a-1a(2b); 5496]   "

τηλικοῦτος, αύτη, οῦτο   {5496, a-1a(2b)}
    so great, large, important, 2 Cor 1:10; Heb 2:3;
    James 3:4; Rev 16:18*

τηλικοῦτος   nom sg masc
   [Rv 16:18; a-1a(2b); 5496]   "
τηλικούτου   gen sg masc [2C 1:10; a-1a(2b); 5496]   "
τήν   acc sg fem [1528t; a-1a(2b); 3836]   ὁ
τήνδε   acc sg fem [Jm 4:13; a-1a(2b); 3840]   ὅδε

τηνικαῦτα   {5497, adverb}
   at that time, then, Phlm subscr.*

τήρει   pres act imperative 2 sg
   [2t; v-1d(2a); 5498]   τηρέω
τηρεῖ   pres act ind 3 sg [3t; v-1d(2a); 5498]   "
τηρεῖν   pres act inf [7t; v-1d(2a); 5498]   "
τηρεῖσθαι   pres pass inf [3t; v-1d(2a); 5498]   "
τηρεῖτε   pres act imperative 2 pl
   [Mt 23:3; v-1d(2a); 5498]   "

τηρέω   {5498, v-1d(2a)}
   [(ἐτήρουν), τηρήσω, ἐτήρησα, τετήρηκα,
   τετήρημαι, ἐτηρήθην] *to keep watch upon, guard,*
   Matt 27:36, 54; 28:4; Acts 12:6; *to watch over*
   protectively, guard, 1 John 5:18; Rev 16:15; *to*
   mark attentively, to heed, Rev 1:3; *to observe*
   practically, keep strictly, Matt 19:17; 23:3; 28:20;
   Mark 7:9; John 8:51; *to preserve, shield,* John
   17:15; *to store up, reserve,* John 2:10; 12:7; 1 Peter
   1:4; 2 Peter 2:4, 9, 17; *to keep in custody,* Acts 12:5;
   16:23; *to maintain,* Eph 4:3; 2 Tim 4:7; *to keep* in a
   condition, John 17:11, 12; 1 Cor 7:37; 2 Cor 11:9;
   1 Tim 5:22; James 1:27

τηρῇ   pres act subj 3 sg
   [1J 2:5; v-1d(2a); 5498]   "
τηρηθείη   aor pass opt 3 sg
   [1Th 5:23; v-1d(2a); 5498]   "
τηρηθῆναι   aor pass inf
   [Ac 25:21; v-1d(2a); 5498]   "
τηρῆσαι   aor act inf [1Ti 6:14; v-1d(2a); 5498]   "
τηρήσαντας   aor act ptcp acc pl masc
   [Jd 6; v-1d(2a); 5498]   "
τηρήσατε   aor act imperative 2 pl
   [Jd 21; v-1d(2a); 5498]   "
τηρήσει   dat sg fem
   [Ac 5:18; n-3e(5b); 5499]   τήρησις
τηρήσει   fut act ind 3 sg
   [Jn 14:23; v-1d(2a); 5498]   τηρέω
τηρήσετε   fut act ind 2 pl
   [Jn 14:15; v-1d(2a); 5498]   "
τηρήσῃ   aor act subj 3 sg [4t; v-1d(2a); 5498]   "
τηρήσῃς   aor act subj 2 sg
   [Jn 17:15; v-1d(2a); 5498]   "
τηρήσητε   aor act subj 2 pl
   [Jn 15:10; v-1d(2a); 5498]   "
τήρησιν   acc sg fem
   [Ac 4:3; n-3e(5b); 5499]   τήρησις

τήρησις, εως, ἡ   {5499, n-3e(5b)}
   a keeping, custody; meton. *a place of custody,*
   prison, ward, Acts 4:3; 5:18; met. *practical*
   observance, strict performance, 1 Cor 7:19*

τήρησις   nom sg fem [1C 7:19; n-3e(5b); 5499]   "
τήρησον   aor act imperative 2 sg
   [2t; v-1d(2a); 5498]   τηρέω
τηρήσουσιν   fut act ind 3 pl
   [Jn 15:20; v-1d(2a); 5498]   "
τηρήσω   fut act ind 1 sg [2t; v-1d(2a); 5498]   "

τηροῦμεν   pres act ind 1 pl
   [1J 3:22; v-1d(2a); 5498]   "
τηρούμενοι   pres pass ptcp nom pl masc
   [2P 3:7; v-1d(2a); 5498]   "
τηρουμένους   pres pass ptcp acc pl masc
   [2P 2:4; v-1d(2a); 5498]   "
τηροῦντες   pres act ptcp nom pl masc
   [4t; v-1d(2a); 5498]   "
τηρούντων   pres act ptcp gen pl masc
   [2t; v-1d(2a); 5498]   "
τηρῶ   pres act ind 1 sg [Jn 8:55; v-1d(2a); 5498] "
τηρῶμεν   pres act subj 1 pl [2t; v-1d(2a); 5498]   "
τηρῶν   pres act ptcp nom sg masc
   [6t; v-1d(2a); 5498]   "
τῆς   gen sg fem [1301t; a-1a(2b); 3836]   ὁ
τί   nom sg neut [88t; a-4b(2); 5515]   τίς
τί   acc sg neut [356t; a-4b(2); 5515]   "
Τιβεριάδος   gen sg fem
   [3t; n-3c(2); 5500]   Τιβεριάς

Τιβεριάς, άδος, ἡ   {5500, n-3c(2)}
   Tiberias, a city of Galilee, built by Herod
   Antipas, and named in honor of Tiberius, John
   6:1, 23; 21:1*

Τιβέριος, ου, ὁ   {5501, n-2a}
   Tiberius, the third Roman emperor, *14-37 A.D.,*
   Luke 3:1*

Τιβερίου   gen sg masc
   [Lk 3:1; n-2a; 5501]   Τιβέριος
τιθέασιν   pres act ind 3 pl
   [Mt 5:15; v-6a; 5502]   τίθημι
τιθείς   pres act ptcp nom sg masc
   [Mk 10:16; v-6a; 5502]   "
τιθέναι   pres act inf [2t; v-6a; 5502]   "
τιθέντες   pres act ptcp nom pl masc
   [Mk 15:19; v-6a; 5502]   "
τιθέτω   pres act imperative 3 sg
   [1C 16:2; v-6a; 5502]   "

τίθημι   {5502, v-6a}
   [(ἐτίθην), θήσω, ἔθηκα, τέθεικα, τέθειμαι, ἐτέθην]
   by-form of τιθέω, *to place, set, lay,* Matt 5:15;
   Mark 6:56; Luke 6:48; *to produce* at table, John
   2:10; *to deposit, lay,* Matt 27:60; Luke 23:53; Acts
   3:2; *to lay down,* Luke 19:21, 22; John 10:11, 15,
   17, 18; 1 John 3:16; *to lay aside, put off,* John 13:4;
   to allocate, assign, Matt 24:51; Luke 12:46; *to set,*
   appoint, John 15:16; Acts 13:47; Heb 1:2; *to*
   render, make, Matt 22:44; Rom 4:17; 1 Cor 9:18;
   mid. *to put* in custody, Matt 14:3; Acts 4:3; *to*
   reserve, Acts 1:7; *to commit* as a matter of charge,
   2 Cor 5:19; *to set,* with design, in a certain
   arrangement or position, Acts 20:28; 1 Cor
   12:18, 28; 1 Thess 5:9; 1 Tim 1:12; pass. 1 Tim
   2:7; 2 Tim 1:11; 1 Peter 2:8; τιθέναι τὰ γόνατα, *to*
   kneel down, Mark 15:19; Luke 22:41; Acts 7:60;
   9:40; 20:36; 21:5; τίθεσθαι ἐν τῇ καρδίᾳ, *to lay to*
   heart, ponder, Luke 1:66; also, εἰς τὰς καρδίας,
   Luke 21:14; *to design, resolve,* Acts 5:4; also, ἐν
   πνεύματι, Acts 19:21; also, βουλήν, Acts 17:12;
   τίθεσθαι εἰς τὰ ὦτα, *to give attentive audience to,*
   to listen to retentively, Luke 9:44

τίθημι   pres act ind 1 sg [5t; v-6a; 5502]   "
τίθησιν   pres act ind 3 sg [6t; v-6a; 5502]   "

τίκτει　pres act ind 3 sg
　　[Jm 1:15; v-1b(2); 5503]　　　　　　τίκτω
τίκτῃ　pres act subj 3 sg
　　[Jn 16:21; v-1b(2); 5503]　　　　　　"
τίκτουσα　pres act ptcp nom sg fem
　　[Hb 6:7; v-1b(2); 5503]　　　　　　"
τίκτουσα　pres act ptcp voc sg fem
　　[Ga 4:27; v-1b(2); 5503]　　　　　　"

τίκτω　　　　　　　　　　　　{5503, v-1b(2)}
　　[τέξομαι, ἔτεκον, -, -, ἐτέχθην] to bear, bring forth
　　children, Matt 1:21, 23; trop. to bear, produce, as
　　the earth, yield, Heb 6:7; met. to give birth to,
　　James 1:15

τίλλειν　pres act inf
　　[Mt 12:1; v-2d(1); 5504]　　　　　　τίλλω
τίλλοντες　pres act ptcp nom pl masc
　　[Mk 2:23; v-2d(1); 5504]　　　　　　"

τίλλω　　　　　　　　　　　　{5504, v-2d(1)}
　　[-, ἔτιλα, -, -, -] to pull, pluck off, Matt 12:1; Mark
　　2:23; Luke 6:1*

τίμα　pres act imperative 2 sg
　　[7t; v-1d(1a); 5506]　　　　　　τιμάω
τιμᾷ　pres act ind 3 sg　[3t; v-1d(1a); 5506]　　"

Τιμαῖος, ου, ὁ　　　　　　　　　{5505, n-2a}
　　Timaeus, pr. name, Mark 10:46*

Τιμαίου　gen sg masc
　　[Mk 10:46; n-2a; 5505]　　　　　　Τιμαῖος
τιμαῖς　dat pl fem　[Ac 28:10; n-1b; 5507]　　τιμή
τιμάς　acc pl fem　[2t; n-1b; 5507]　　　　"
τιμᾶτε　pres act imperative 2 pl
　　[1P 2:17; v-1d(1a); 5506]　　　　τιμάω

τιμάω　　　　　　　　　　　　{5506, v-1d(1a)}
　　[τιμήσω, ἐτίμησα, -, τετίμημαι, -] to estimate in
　　respect of worth; to hold in estimation, respect,
　　honor, reverence, Matt 15:4, 5, 8; 19:19; Mark
　　7:10; to honor with reverent service, John 5:23
　　(4t); 8:49; to treat with honor, manifest
　　consideration towards, Acts 28:10; to treat
　　graciously, visit with marks of favor, John 12:26;
　　mid. to price, Matt 27:9

τιμή, ῆς, ἡ　　　　　　　　　　{5507, n-1b}
　　a pricing, estimate of worth; price, value, Matt
　　27:9; price paid, Matt 27:6; meton. a thing of
　　price, and collectively, precious things, Rev
　　21:24, 26; preciousness, 1 Peter 2:7; substantial
　　value, real worth, Col 2:23; careful regard, honor,
　　state of honor, dignity, Rom 9:21; Heb 5:4; honor
　　conferred, observance, veneration, Rom 2:7, 10;
　　12:10; mark of favor and consideration, Acts 28:10;
　　honorarium, compensation, 1 Tim 5:7

τιμή　nom sg fem　[7t; n-1b; 5507]　　　τιμή
τιμῇ　dat sg fem　[5t; n-1b; 5507]　　　"
τιμήν　acc sg fem　[19t; n-1b; 5507]　　"
τιμῆς　gen sg fem　[7t; n-1b; 5507]　　　"
τιμήσατε　aor act imperative 2 pl
　　[1P 2:17; v-1d(1a); 5506]　　　　τιμάω
τιμήσει　fut act ind 3 sg　[2t; v-1d(1a); 5506]　"
τίμια　acc pl neut　[2P 1:4; a-1a(1); 5508]　τίμιος
τιμίαν　acc sg fem　[Ac 20:24; a-1a(1); 5508]　"
τίμιον　acc sg masc　[Jm 5:7; a-1a(1); 5508]　"

τίμιος, α, ον　　　　　　　　　{5508, a-1a(1)}
　　precious, costly, of great price, 1 Cor 3:12; Rev
　　18:12; precious, dear, valuable, Acts 20:24; 1 Peter
　　1:7, 19; honored, esteemed, respected, Acts 5:34;
　　Heb 13:4

τίμιος　nom sg masc　[2t; a-1a(1); 5508]　　"

τιμιότης, ητος, ἡ　　　　　　　{5509, n-1f}
　　preciousness, costliness; meton. precious things,
　　valuable merchandise, Rev 18:19*

τιμιότητος　gen sg fem
　　[Rv 18:19; n-1f; 5509]　　　　　　τιμιότης
τιμίου　gen sg masc
　　[Rv 18:12; a-1a(1); 5508]　　　　τίμιος
τιμίους　acc pl masc　[1C 3:12; a-1a(1); 5508]　"
τιμίῳ　dat sg masc　[3t; a-1a(1); 5508]　　　"
τιμίῳ　dat sg neut　[1P 1:19; a-1a(1); 5508]　"
τιμιωτάτου　gen sg neut superlative
　　[Rv 18:12; a-1a(1); 5508]　　　　"
τιμιωτάτῳ　dat sg masc superlative
　　[Rv 21:11; a-1a(1); 5508]　　　　"
Τιμόθεε　voc sg masc　[2t; n-2a; 5510]　Τιμόθεος
Τιμόθεον　acc sg masc　[6t; n-2a; 5510]　　"

Τιμόθεος, ου, ὁ　　　　　　　　{5510, n-2a}
　　Timotheus, Timothy, pr. name, son of Eunice,
　　traveling companion of Paul, Acts 16:1; Rom
　　16:21; 1 Cor 4:17; 2 Cor 1:1; Phil 1:1; Col 1:1; 1
　　Thess 1:1; 1 Tim 1:2, 18; 6:20; 2 Tim 1:2

Τιμόθεος　nom sg masc　[12t; n-2a; 5510]　　"
Τιμοθέου　gen sg masc　[2t; n-2a; 5510]　　"
Τιμοθέῳ　dat sg masc　[2t; n-2a; 5510]　　"
τιμῶ　pres act ind 1 sg
　　[Jn 8:49; v-1d(1a); 5506]　　　　τιμάω
τιμῶν　pres act ptcp nom sg masc
　　[Jn 5:23; v-1d(1a); 5506]　　　　"

Τίμων, ωνος, ὁ　　　　　　　　{5511, n-3f(1a)}
　　Timon, pr. name, Acts 6:5*

Τίμωνα　acc sg masc　[Ac 6:5; n-3f(1a); 5511]　Τίμων

τιμωρέω　　　　　　　　　　　{5512, v-1d(2a)}
　　[-, -, -, -, ἐτιμωρήθην] to avenge, someone; in N.T.
　　to punish, Acts 22:5; 26:11*

τιμωρηθῶσιν　aor pass subj 3 pl
　　[Ac 22:5; v-1d(2a); 5512]　　　　τιμωρέω

τιμωρία, ας, ἡ　　　　　　　　{5513, n-1a}
　　punishment, Heb 10:29*

τιμωρίας　gen sg fem
　　[Hb 10:29; n-1a; 5513]　　　　　τιμωρία
τιμωρῶν　pres act ptcp nom sg masc
　　[Ac 26:11; v-1d(2a); 5512]　　　τιμωρέω
τιμῶσι　pres act ind 3 pl
　　[Jn 5:23; v-1d(1a); 5506]　　　　τιμάω
τιμῶσι　pres act subj 3 pl
　　[Jn 5:23; v-1d(1a); 5506]　　　　"
τινα　nom pl neut　[2t; a-4b(2); 5516]　　τὶς
τινα　acc sg masc　[51t; a-4b(2); 5516]　　"
τινα　acc sg fem　[13t; a-4b(2); 5515]　　τίς
τινα　acc pl neut　[3t; a-4b(2); 5516]　　τὶς
τινας　acc pl masc　[20t; a-4b(2); 5516]　　"
τίνας　acc pl fem　[6t; a-4b(2); 5515]　　τίς

τίνες   nom pl masc [79t; a-4b(2); 5515]   "
τινες   nom pl fem [3t; a-4b(2); 5516]   τὶς
τίνι   dat sg masc [18t; a-4b(2); 5515]   τίς
τίνι   dat sg fem [3t; a-4b(2); 5515]   "
τίνι   dat sg neut [11t; a-4b(2); 5515]   "
τίνος   gen sg masc [28t; a-4b(2); 5516]   τὶς
τίνος   gen sg neut [6t; a-4b(2); 5515]   τίς

τίνω   {5514, v-3a(1)}
[τίσω or τείσω, -, -, -, -] *to pay; to pay* a penalty,
incur punishment, 2 Thess 1:9*

τινῶν   gen pl masc [10t; a-4b(2); 5516]   τὶς
τινῶν   gen pl fem [Ac 25:13; a-4b(2); 5516]   "
τίνων   gen pl neut [2t; a-4b(2); 5515]   τίς

τίς, τί   {5515, a-4b(2)}
Who? What? Matt 3:7; 5:13; 19:27; equivalent to
πότερος, *Whether? which* of two things? Matt
9:5; Mark 2:9; Phil 1:22; *Why?* Matt 8:26; 9:11,
14; τί ὅτι, *Why is it that?* Mark 2:16; John 14:22;
What? as an emphatic interrogative, Acts 26:8;
τί, *How very!* Matt 7:14; in indirect question,
Matt 10:11; 12:3 v.l.; Acts 13:25 v.l.; Matt 7:14

τίς   nom sg masc [349t; a-4b(2); 5515]   "

τὶς, τὶ   {5516, a-4b(2)}
a certain one, someone, Matt 12:47; pl. *some,
certain, several,* Luke 8:2; Acts 9:19; 2 Peter 3:16;
one, a person, Matt 12:29; Luke 14:8; John 6:50;
combined with the name of an individual, *one,*
Mark 15:21; *as it were in a manner, a kind of,* Heb
10:27; James 1:18; *any* whatever, Matt 8:28;
Luke 11:36; Rom 8:39; τις, *somebody* of
consequence, Acts 5:36; τι, *something* of
consequence, Gal 2:6; 6:3; τι, *anything* at all,
anything worth account, 1 Cor 3:7; 10:19; τι *at
all,* Phil 3:15; Phlm 18

τις   nom sg fem [34t; a-4b(2); 5516]   τὶς
τισιν dat pl masc [6t; a-4b(2); 5516]   "
τίσουσιν   fut act ind 3 pl
        [2Th 1:9; v-3a(1); 5514]   τίνω

Τίτιος, ου, ὁ   {5517, n-2a}
Titius, pr. name, Acts 18:7*

Τιτίου   gen sg masc [Ac 18:7; n-2a; 5517]   Τίτιος
τίτλον   acc sg masc [2t; n-2a; 5518]   τίτλος

τίτλος, ου, ὁ   {5518, n-2a}
an inscribed roll, superscription, John 19:19, 20*

Τίτον   acc sg masc [4t; n-2a; 5519]   Τίτος

Τίτος, ου, ὁ   {5519, n-2a}
Titus, pr. name, friend and helper of Paul, 2
Cor 2:13; 7:6; Gal 2:1; 2 Tim 4:10; Titus 1:4;
surnamed Justus, Acts 18:7 v.l.

Τίτος   nom sg masc [3t; n-2a; 5519]   "
Τίτου   gen sg masc [5t; n-2a; 5519]   "
Τίτῳ   dat sg masc [Ti 1:4; n-2a; 5519]   "
τό   nom sg neut [595t; a-1a(2b); 3836]   ὁ
τό   voc sg neut [5t; a-1a(2b); 3836]   "
τό   acc sg neut [1094t; a-1a(2b); 3836]   "
τοιᾶσδε   gen sg fem
        [2P 1:17; a-1a(2b); 5524]   τοιόσδε
τοιαῦτα   acc pl neut [9t; a-1a(2b); 5525]   τοιοῦτος

τοιαῦται   nom pl fem [Mk 6:2; a-1a(2b); 5525]   "
τοιαύταις dat pl fem [2t; a-1a(2b); 5525]   "
τοιαύτας   acc pl fem [Jn 8:5; a-1a(2b); 5525]   "
τοιαύτη   nom sg fem [3t; a-1a(2b); 5525]   "
τοιαύτην   acc sg fem [6t; a-1a(2b); 5525]   "

τοιγαροῦν   {5521, particle}
well then, so then, wherefore, for that reason, 1
Thess 4:8; Heb 12:1*

τοιγαροῦν   part [2t; particle; 5521]   τοιγαροῦν

τοίνυν   {5523, particle}
well then, therefore now, therefore, Luke 20:25; 1
Cor 9:26; Heb 13:13; James 2:24 v.l.*

τοίνυν   part [3t; particle; 5523]   τοίνυν

τοιόσδε, τοιάδε, τοιόνδε,   {5524, a-1a(2b)}
such as this; such as follows, 2 Peter 1:17*

τοιοῦτο   acc sg neut
        [Mt 18:5; a-1a(2b); 5525]   τοιοῦτος
τοιοῦτοι   nom pl masc [6t; a-1a(2b); 5525]   "
τοιούτοις   dat pl masc [2t; a-1a(2b); 5525]   "
τοιούτοις   dat pl neut [1C 7:15; a-1a(2b); 5525]   "
τοιοῦτον   acc sg masc [6t; a-1a(2b); 5525]   "

τοιοῦτος, τοιαύτη, τοιοῦτο   {5525, a-1a(2b)}
such, such like, of this kind or *sort,* Matt 18:5;
19:14; *such, so great,* Matt 9:8; Mark 6:2; ὁ
τοιοῦτος, *such a fellow,* Acts 22:22; also, *the one
alluded to,* 1 Cor 1:5; 2 Cor 2:6, 7; 12:2, 3, 5

τοιοῦτος   nom sg masc [5t; a-1a(2b); 5525]   "
τοιούτου   gen sg masc [2C 12:5; a-1a(2b); 5525]   "
τοιούτους   acc pl masc [5t; a-1a(2b); 5525]   "
τοιούτῳ   dat sg masc [2t; a-1a(2b); 5525]   "
τοιούτων   gen pl masc [Mt 19:14; a-1a(2b); 5525]   "
τοιούτων   gen pl neut [2t; a-1a(2b); 5525]   "
τοῖς   dat pl masc [458t; a-1a(2b); 3836]   ὁ
τοῖς   dat pl neut [166t; a-1a(2b); 3836]   "
τοῖχε   voc sg masc [Ac 23:3; n-2a; 5526]   τοῖχος

τοῖχος, ου, ὁ   {5526, n-2a}
a wall of a building, as distinct from a city wall
or fortification (τεῖχος) Acts 23:3*

τόκος, ου, ὁ   {5527, n-2a}
a bringing forth; offspring; met. *produce* of money
lent, *interest, usury,* Matt 25:27; Luke 19:23*

τόκῳ   dat sg masc [2t; n-2a; 5527]   τόκος
τολμᾷ   pres act ind 3 sg
        [2t; v-1d(1a); 5528]   τολμάω
τολμᾷ   pres act subj 3 sg
        [2C 11:21; v-1d(1a); 5528]   "
τολμᾶν   pres act inf [Pp 1:14; v-1d(1a); 5528]   "

τολμάω   {5528, v-1d(1a)}
[(ἐτόλμων), τολμήσω, ἐτόλμησα, -, -, -] *to assume
resolution* to do a thing, Mark 15:43; Rom 5:7;
Phil 1:14; *to make up the mind,* 2 Cor 10:12; *to
dare,* Acts 5:13; 7:32; *to presume,* Matt 22:46;
Mark 12:34; Luke 20:40; John 21:12; Rom 15:18;
Jude 9; *to have the face,* 1 Cor 6:1; absol. *to assume
a bold bearing, courageous,* 2 Cor 10:2; 11:21*

τολμηρότερον   {5530, adverb}
an adverb formed from τολμηρός, *more boldly,*
with more confidence, more freely, Rom 15:15*

τολμηρότερον   adverb-comparative
[Rm 15:15; adverb; 5530]   τολμηρός

τολμηροτέρως   {5531, adverb}
an adverb formed from τολμηρός, *more boldly,*
Rom 15:15 v.l.*

τολμῆσαι   aor act inf
[2C 10:2; v-1d(1a); 5528]   τολμάω

τολμήσας   aor act ptcp nom sg masc
[Mk 15:43; v-1d(1a); 5528]   "

τολμήσω   fut act ind 1 sg
[Rm 15:18; v-1d(1a); 5528]   "

τολμηταί   nom pl masc
[2P 2:10; n-1f; 5532]   τολμητής

τολμητής, οῦ, ὁ   {5532, n-1f}
one who is bold; in a bad sense, *a presumptuous,*
audacious person, 2 Peter 2:10*

τολμῶ   pres act ind 1 sg
[2C 11:21; v-1d(1a); 5528]   τολμάω

τολμῶμεν   pres act ind 1 pl
[2C 10:12; v-1d(1a); 5528]   "

τομός, ή, όν   {5533, a-1a(2a)}
cutting, sharp, sharper, Heb 4:12*

τομώτερος   nom sg masc comparative
[Hb 4:12; a-1a(2a); 5533]   τομός
τόν   acc sg masc [1581t; a-1a(2b); 3836]   ὁ

τόξον, ου, τό   {5534, n-2c}
a bow, Rev 6:2*

τόξον   acc sg neut [Rv 6:2; n-2c; 5534]   τόξον

τοπάζιον, ου, τό   {5535, n-2c}
a topaz, a gem of a yellowish color, different
from the modern topaz, Rev 21:20*

τοπάζιον   nom sg neut
[Rv 21:20; n-2c; 5535]   τοπάζιον
τόποις   dat pl masc [2t; n-2a; 5536]   τόπος
τόπον   acc sg masc [46t; n-2a; 5536]   "

τόπος, ου, ὁ   {5536, n-2a}
a place, locality, Matt 12:43; Luke 6:17; John
20:25 v.l.; *a* limited *spot* or *ground,* Matt 24:15;
27:33; John 4:20; Acts 6:13; *a precise spot* or
situation, Matt 28:6; Mark 16:6; Luke 14:9; *a*
dwelling place, abode, mansion, dwelling, seat,
John 14:2, 3; Acts 4:31; *a place* of ordinary
deposit, Matt 26:52; *a place, passage* in a book,
Luke 4:17; *place* occupied, *room, space,* Luke 2:7;
14:9, 22; *place, opportunity,* Acts 25:16; Heb
12:17; *place, condition, position,* 1 Cor 14:16

τόπος   nom sg masc [16t; n-2a; 5536]   "
τόπου   gen sg masc [7t; n-2a; 5536]   "
τόπους   acc pl masc [5t; n-2a; 5536]   "
τόπῳ   dat sg masc [15t; n-2a; 5536]   "
τόπων   gen pl masc [3t; n-2a; 5536]   "
τοσαῦτα   nom pl neut
[1C 14:10; a-1a(2b); 5537]   τοσοῦτος
τοσαῦτα   acc pl neut [3t; a-1a(2b); 5537]   "
τοσαύτην   acc sg fem [2t; a-1a(2b); 5537]   "

τοσοῦτο   acc sg neut [Hb 7:22; a-1a(2b); 5537]   "
τοσοῦτοι   nom pl masc [Mt 15:33; a-1a(2b); 5537]   "
τοσοῦτον   acc sg masc [3t; a-1a(2b); 5537]   "
τοσοῦτον   acc sg neut [Hb 12:1; a-1a(2b); 5537]   "

τοσοῦτος, τοσαύτη, τοσοῦτο   {5537, a-1a(2b)}
so great, so much, Matt 8:10; 15:33; *so long,* of
time, John 14:9; pl. *so many,* Matt 15:33

τοσοῦτος   nom sg masc [Rv 18:17; a-1a(2b); 5537]   "
τοσούτου   gen sg neut [2t; a-1a(2b); 5537]   "
τοσούτους   acc pl masc [Jn 6:9; a-1a(2b); 5537]   "
τοσούτῳ   dat sg masc [Jn 14:9; a-1a(2b); 5537]   "
τοσούτῳ   dat sg neut [2t; a-1a(2b); 5537]   "
τοσούτων   gen pl masc [Jn 21:11; a-1a(2b); 5537]   "

τότε   {5538, adverb}
then, at that time, Matt 2:17; 3:5; 11:20; *then,* Matt
12:29; 13:26; 25:31; ἀπὸ τότε, *from that time,* Matt
4:17; 16:21; ὁ τότε, *which then was,* 2 Peter 3:6

τότε   adverb [160t; adverb; 5538]   τότε
τοῦ   gen sg masc [1912t; a-1a(2b); 3836]   ὁ
τοῦ   gen sg neut [605t; a-1a(2b); 3836]   "

τοὐναντίον   {5539, adverb}
that which is opposite; as an adv., *on the contrary,*
on the other hand, 2 Cor 2:7; Gal 2:7; 1 Peter 3:9

τοὐναντίον   acc sg neut
[3t; adverb; 5539]   τοὐναντίον

τοὔνομα   {5540}
crasis of the article and ὄνομα, *the name;* in the
acc. *by name,* Matt 27:57

τοὔνομα   nom sg neut
[Mt 27:57; see o[noma; 5540]   τοὔνομα
τούς   acc pl masc [730t; a-1a(2b); 3836]   ὁ
τοῦτ'   nom sg neut [17t; a-1a(2b); 4047]   οὗτος

τουτέστι(ν)   {5542}
written in our texts as two words, τοῦτο ἔστιν,
that is, which signifies, which implies, Acts 19:4;
Acts 1:19

τοῦτο   nom sg neut [76t; a-1a(2b); 4047]   "
τοῦτο   acc sg neut [243t; a-1a(2b); 4047]   "
τούτοις   dat pl masc [5t; a-1a(2b); 4047]   "
τούτοις   dat pl neut [14t; a-1a(2b); 4047]   "
τοῦτον   acc sg masc [60t; a-1a(2b); 4047]   "
τούτου   gen sg masc [41t; a-1a(2b); 4047]   "
τούτου   gen sg neut [28t; a-1a(2b); 4047]   "
τούτους   acc pl masc [28t; a-1a(2b); 4047]   "
τούτῳ   dat sg masc [40t; a-1a(2b); 4047]   "
τούτῳ   dat sg neut [49t; a-1a(2b); 4047]   "
τούτων   gen pl masc [23t; a-1a(2b); 4047]   "
τούτων   gen pl fem [7t; a-1a(2b); 4047]   "
τούτων   gen pl neut [42t; a-1a(2b); 4047]   "

τράγος, ου, ὁ   {5543, n-2a}
a he-goat, Heb 9:12, 13, 19; 10:4*

τράγων   gen pl masc [4t; n-2a; 5543]   τράγος

τράπεζα, ης, ἡ   {5544, n-1c}
a table, an eating-table, Matt 15:27; Mark 7:28;
Heb 9:2; by impl. *a meal, feast,* Rom 11:9; 1 Cor
10:21; *a table* or *counter* of a money-changer,

Matt 21:12; *a bank,* Luke 19:23; by impl. pl. *money matters,* Acts 6:2

τράπεζα nom sg fem [2t; n-1c; 5544] τράπεζα
τραπέζαις dat pl fem [Ac 6:2; n-1c; 5544] "
τράπεζαν acc sg fem [2t; n-1c; 5544] "
τραπέζας acc pl fem [3t; n-1c; 5544] "
τραπέζης gen sg fem [7t; n-1c; 5544] "
τραπεζίταις dat pl masc
  [Mt 25:27; n-1f; 5545] τραπεζίτης

τραπεζίτης, ου, ὁ {5545, n-1f}
  a money-changer, broker, banker, who exchanges or loans money for a premium, Matt 25:27*

τραῦμα, ατος, τό {5546, n-3c(4)}
  a wound, Luke 10:34*

τραύματα acc pl neut
  [Lk 10:34; n-3c(4); 5546] τραῦμα

τραυματίζω {5547, v-2a(1)}
  [-, ἐτραυμάτισα, -, τετραυμάτισμαι, ἐτραυματίσθην] *to wound,* Luke 20:12; Acts 19:16*

τραυματίσαντες aor act ptcp nom pl masc
  [Lk 20:12; v-2a(1); 5547] τραυματίζω
τραχεῖαι nom pl fem [Lk 3:5; a-2b; 5550] τραχύς
τραχεῖς acc pl masc [Ac 27:29; a-2b; 5550] "

τραχηλίζω {5548, v-2a(1)}
  [-, -, -, τετραχήλισμαι, -] pr. *to grip the neck; to bend the neck back,* so as to make bare or expose the throat, as in slaughtering animals, etc.; met. *to lay bare in view,* Heb 4:13*

τράχηλον acc sg masc [7t; n-2a; 5549] τράχηλος

τράχηλος, ου, ὁ {5549, n-2a}
  the neck, Matt 18:6; Mark 9:42; Luke 15:20; 17:2; ἐπιθεῖναι ζυγὸν ἐπὶ τὸν τράχηλον, *to put a yoke upon the neck* of someone, met. *to bind to a burdensome observance,* Acts 15:10; 20:37; ὑποτιθέναι τὸν τράχηλον, *to lay down one's neck* under the axe of the executioner, *to imperil one's life,* Rom 16:4*

τραχύς, εῖα, ύ {5550, a-2b}
  rough, rugged, uneven, Luke 3:5; εἰς τραχεῖς τόπους, *on a rocky shore,* Acts 27:29*

Τραχωνίτιδος gen sg fem
  [Lk 3:1; n-3c(2); 5551] Τραχωνῖτις

Τραχωνῖτις, ιδος, ἡ {5551, n-3c(2)}
  Trachonitis, part of the tetrarchy of Herod Antipas, the north-easternmost habitable district east of the Jordan, Luke 3:1*

τρεῖς, τρία {5552, a-4a}
  three, Matt 12:40

τρεῖς nom pl masc [11t; a-4a; 5552] τρεῖς
τρεῖς nom pl fem [4t; a-4a; 5552] "
τρεῖς acc pl masc [9t; a-4a; 5552] "
τρεῖς acc pl fem [19t; a-4a; 5552] "
τρέμουσα pres act ptcp nom sg fem
  [2t; v-1c(2); 5554] τρέμω
τρέμουσιν pres act ind 3 pl
  [2P 2:10; v-1c(2); 5554] "

τρέμω {5554, v-1c(2)}
  [-, -, -, -, -] *to tremble, be agitated from fear,* Mark 5:33; Luke 8:47; Acts 9:6 v.l.; by impl. *to fear, be afraid,* 2 Peter 2:10*

τρέφει pres act ind 3 sg
  [2t; v-1b(1); 5555] τρέφω
τρέφεσθαι pres pass inf
  [Ac 12:20; v-1b(1); 5555] "
τρέφεται pres pass ind 3 sg
  [Rv 12:14; v-1b(1); 5555] "

τρέφω {5555, v-1b(1)}
  [-, ἔθρεψα, -, τέθραμμαι, -ετράφην] *to nourish; to feed, support, cherish, provide for,* Matt 6:26; 25:37; Luke 12:24; 23:29; Acts 12:20; Rev 12:6, 14; *to bring up, rear, educate,* Luke 4:16; *to gorge, pamper,* James 5:5*

τρέφωσιν pres act subj 3 pl
  [Rv 12:6; v-1b(1); 5555] "
τρέχει pres act ind 3 sg
  [Jn 20:2; v-1b(2); 5556] τρέχω
τρέχετε pres act imperative 2 pl
  [1C 9:24; v-1b(2); 5556] "
τρέχῃ pres act subj 3 sg
  [2Th 3:1; v-1b(2); 5556] "
τρέχοντες pres act ptcp nom pl masc
  [1C 9:24; v-1b(2); 5556] "
τρέχοντος pres act ptcp gen sg masc
  [Rm 9:16; v-1b(2); 5556] "
τρεχόντων pres act ptcp gen pl masc
  [Rv 9:9; v-1b(2); 5556] "
τρέχουσιν pres act ind 3 pl
  [1C 9:24; v-1b(2); 5556] "

τρέχω {5556, v-1b(2)}
  [(ἔτρεχον), -, ἔδραμον, -, -, -] *to run,* Matt 27:48; 28:8; *to run a race,* 1 Cor 9:24; met. 1 Cor 9:24, 26; Heb 12:1; in N.T. *to run a certain course of conduct,* Gal 5:7; *to run a course of exertion,* Rom 9:16; Gal 2:2; Phil 2:16; *to run, to progress freely, to advance rapidly,* 2 Thess 3:1

τρέχω pres act ind 1 sg [1C 9:26; v-1b(2); 5556] "
τρέχω pres act subj 1 sg [Ga 2:2; v-1b(2); 5556] "
τρέχωμεν pres act subj 1 pl
  [Hb 12:1; v-1b(2); 5556] "

τρῆμα, ατος, τό {5557, n-3c(4)}
  an aperture, hole, eye of a needle, Matt 19:24 v.l.; Luke 18:25*

τρήματος gen sg neut
  [Lk 18:25; n-3c(4); 5557] τρῆμα
τρία nom pl neut [1C 13:13; a-4a; 5552] τρεῖς
τρία acc pl neut [8t; a-4a; 5552] "

τριάκοντα {5558, a-5c}
  thirty, indecl., Matt 13:8, 23; Mark 4:8; Luke 3:23

τριάκοντα indecl [11t; a-5c; 5558] τριάκοντα

τριακόσιοι, αι, α {5559, a-1a(1)}
  three hundred, Mark 14:5; John 12:5*

τριακοσίων gen pl neut
  [2t; a-1a(1); 5559] τριακόσιοι

τρίβολος, ου, ὁ   {5560, n-2a}
    pr. *three-pronged; a thistle, thorn,* Matt 7:16; Heb 6:8*

τριβόλους   acc pl masc
    [Hb 6:8; n-2a; 5560]   τρίβολος
τριβόλων   gen pl masc [Mt 7:16; n-2a; 5560]   "

τρίβος, ου, ἡ   {5561, n-2b}
    a beaten track; a road, highway, Matt 3:3; Mark 1:3; Luke 3:4*

τρίβους   acc pl fem [3t; n-2b; 5561]   τρίβος

τριετία, ας, ἡ   {5562, n-1a}
    the space of three years, Acts 20:31, 18 v.l.*

τριετίαν   acc sg fem [Ac 20:31; n-1a; 5562]   τριετία
τρίζει   pres act ind 3 sg
    [Mk 9:18; v-2a(1); 5563]   τρίζω

τρίζω   {5563, v-2a(1)}
    [-, -, -, -, -] *to creak, grating sound; to gnash, grind the teeth,* Mark 9:18*

τρίμηνον   acc sg neut
    [Hb 11:23; a-3a; 5564]   τρίμηνος

τρίμηνος, ον   {5564, a-3a}
    the space of three months, Heb 11:23*

τρίς   {5565, adverb}
    three times, thrice, Matt 26:34, 75; ἐπὶ τρίς, *to the extent of thrice, as many as three times,* Acts 10:16; 11:10

τρίς   adverb [12t; adverb; 5565]   τρίς
τρισίν   dat pl masc [2t; a-4a; 5552]   τρεῖς
τρισίν   dat pl fem [4t; a-4a; 5552]   "

τρίστεγον, ου, τό   {5566, n-2c}
    the third floor, third story, Acts 20:9*

τριστέγου   gen sg neut
    [Ac 20:9; n-2c; 5566]   τρίστεγον
τρισχίλιαι   nom pl fem
    [Ac 2:41; a-1a(1); 5567]   τρισχίλιοι

τρισχίλιοι, α, ον   {5567, a-1a(1)}
    three thousand, Acts 2:41*

τρίτη   nom sg fem [3t; a-1a(2a); 5569]   τρίτος
τρίτῃ   dat sg fem [13t; a-1a(2a); 5569]   "
τρίτην   acc sg fem [3t; a-1a(2a); 5569]   "
τρίτης   gen sg fem [2t; a-1a(2a); 5569]   "
τρίτον   nom sg neut [12t; a-1a(2a); 5569]   "
τρίτον   acc sg neut, can function
    adverbially (8t) [13t; a-1a(2a); 5569]   "

τρίτος, η, ον   {5569, a-1a(2a)}
    third, Matt 20:3; 27:64; ἐκ τρίτου, *the third time, for the third time,* Matt 26:44; τὸ τρίτον, sc. μέρος, *the third part,* Rev 8:7, 12; τρίτον + τὸ τρίτον, *as an adv., the third time, for the third time,* Mark 14:21; Luke 23:22

τρίτος   nom sg masc [7t; a-1a(2a); 5569]   τρίτος
τρίτου   gen sg masc [2C 12:2; a-1a(2a); 5569]   "
τρίτου   gen sg neut [2t; a-1a(2a); 5569]   "
τρίχα   acc sg fem [Mt 5:36; n-3b(3); 2582]   θρίξ
τρίχας   acc pl fem [3t; n-3b(3); 2582]   "
τρίχες   nom pl fem [3t; n-3b(3); 2582]   "

τρίχινος, η, ον   {5570, a-1a(2a)}
    of hair, made of hair, Rev 6:12*

τρίχινος   nom sg masc
    [Rv 6:12; a-1a(2a); 5570]   τρίχινος
τριῶν   gen pl masc [6t; a-4a; 5552]   τρεῖς
τριῶν   gen pl fem [5t; a-4a; 5552]   "
τριῶν   gen pl fem [11t; a-4a; 5552]   τρεῖς

τρόμος, ου, ὁ   {5571, n-2a}
    pr. *a trembling, quaking; trembling from fear, fear, terror, agitation of mind,* Mark 16:8; *anxious, under solemn responsibility,* 1 Cor 2:3; *reverence, veneration, awe,* 2 Cor 7:15; Eph 6:5; Phil 2:12*

τρόμος   nom sg masc [Mk 16:8; n-2a; 5571]   τρόμος
τρόμου   gen sg masc [3t; n-2a; 5571]   "
τρόμῳ   dat sg masc [1C 2:3; n-2a; 5571]   "

τροπή, ῆς, ἡ   {5572, n-1b}
    a turning round; a turning back, change, mutation, James 1:17*

τροπῆς   gen sg fem [Jm 1:17; n-1b; 5572]   τροπή
τρόπον   acc sg masc [10t; n-2a; 5573]   τρόπος

τρόπος, ου, ὁ   {5573, n-2a}
    a turn; mode, manner, way, Jude 7; ὃν τρόπον, + καθ' ὃν τρόπον, *in which manner, as, even as,* Matt 23:37; Acts 15:11; κατὰ μηδένα τρόπον, *in no way, by no means,* 2 Thess 2:3; ἐν παντὶ τρόπῳ, and παντὶ τρόπῳ *in every way, by every means,* Phil 1:18; 2 Thess 3:16; *turn of mind or action, habit, disposition,* Heb 13:5

τρόπος   nom sg masc [Hb 13:5; n-2a; 5573]   "

τροποφορέω   {5574, v-1d(2a)}
    [-, ἐτροποφόρησα, -, -, -] *to bear with the disposition, manners, and conduct of any one, to put up with,* Acts 13:18*

τρόπῳ   dat sg masc [2t; n-2a; 5573]   τρόπος
τροφάς   acc pl fem [Jn 4:8; n-1b; 5575]   τροφή

τροφή, ῆς, ἡ   {5575, n-1b}
    nourishment, food, Matt 3:4; Luke 12:23; John 4:8; Acts 9:19; James 2:15; *provision,* Matt 24:45; *sustenance, maintenance,* Matt 10:10; met. *nourishment* of the mind, *of spiritual nourishment,* Heb 5:12, 14

τροφή   nom sg fem [2t; n-1b; 5575]   "
τροφήν   acc sg fem [2t; n-1b; 5575]   "
τροφῆς   gen sg fem [11t; n-1b; 5575]   "
Τρόφιμον   acc sg masc [2t; n-2a; 5576]   Τρόφιμος

Τρόφιμος, ου, ὁ   {5576, n-2a}
    Trophimus, pr. name, of Ephesus, a friend of Paul, Acts 20:4; 21:29; 2 Tim 4:20*

Τρόφιμος   nom sg masc [Ac 20:4; n-2a; 5576]   "

τροφός, οῦ, ἡ   {5577, n-2b}
    a nurse, 1 Thess 2:7*

τροφός   nom sg fem [1Th 2:7; n-2b; 5577]   τροφός

τροφοφορέω   {5578, v-1d(2a)}
    [-, ἐτροφοφόρησα -, -, -] *care for,* Acts 13:18 v.l.*

τροχιά, ᾶς, ἡ   {5579, n-1a}
a wheel-track; a track, way, path, met. Heb 12:13*

τροχιάς   acc pl fem [Hb 12:13; n-1a; 5579]   τροχιά
τροχόν   acc sg masc [Jm 3:6; n-2a; 5580]   τροχός

τροχός, οῦ, ὁ   {5580, n-2a}
pr. a runner; anything spherical, a wheel; drift,
course, with which signification the word is
usually written τρόχος, James 3:6*

τρύβλιον, ου, τό   {5581, n-2c}
a bowl, dish, Matt 26:23; Mark 14:20*

τρύβλιον   acc sg neut
[Mk 14:20; n-2c; 5581]   τρύβλιον
τρυβλίῳ   dat sg neut [Mt 26:23; n-2c; 5581]   "

τρυγάω   {5582, v-1d(1a)}
[τρυγήσω, ἐτρύγησα, -, -, -] to harvest, gather,
fruits, and spc. grapes, Luke 6:44; Rev 14:18,
19*

τρύγησον   aor act imperative 2 sg
[Rv 14:18; v-1d(1a); 5582]   τρυγάω
τρυγόνων   gen pl fem
[Lk 2:24; n-3f(1b); 5583]   τρυγών

τρυγών, όνος, ἡ   {5583, n-3f(1b)}
a turtle-dove, Luke 2:24*

τρυγῶσιν   pres act ind 3 pl
[Lk 6:44; v-1d(1a); 5582]   τρυγάω
τρυμαλιᾶς   gen sg fem
[Mk 10:25; n-1a; 5584]   τρυμαλιά

τρυμαλιά, ᾶς, ἡ   {5584, n-1a}
a hole, perforation; eye of a needle, Mark 10:25;
Matt 19:24 v.l.; Luke 18:25 v.l.*

τρύπημα, ατος, τό   {5585, n-3c(4)}
a hole; eye of a needle, Matt 19:24*

τρυπήματος   gen sg neut
[Mt 19:24; n-3c(4); 5585]   τρύπημα

Τρύφαινα, ης, ἡ   {5586, n-1c}
Tryphaena, pr. name, Rom 16:12*

Τρύφαιναν   acc sg fem
[Rm 16:12; n-1c; 5586]   Τρύφαινα

τρυφάω   {5587, v-1d(1a)}
[-, ἐτρύφησα, -, -, -] to live self-indulgently,
luxuriously, James 5:5*

τρυφή, ῆς, ἡ   {5588, n-1b}
indulgent living, luxury, Luke 7:25; 2 Pet 2:13*

τρυφῇ   dat sg fem [Lk 7:25; n-1b; 5588]   τρυφή
τρυφήν   acc sg fem [2P 2:13; n-1b; 5588]   "

Τρυφῶσα, ης, ἡ   {5589, n-1c}
Tryphosa, pr. name, Rom 16:12*

Τρυφῶσαν   acc sg fem
[Rm 16:12; n-1c; 5589]   Τρυφῶσα
Τρῳάδα   acc sg fem [3t; n-3c(2); 5590]   Τρῳάς
Τρῳάδι   dat sg fem [2t; n-3c(2); 5590]   "
Τρῳάδος   gen sg fem [Ac 16:11; n-3c(2); 5590]   "

Τρῳάς, άδος, ἡ   {5590, n-3c(2)}
Troas, a city on the coast of Phrygia, near the

site of ancient Troy, Acts 16:8, 11; 20:5f.; 2 Cor
2:12; 2 Tim 4:13*

τρώγοντες   pres act ptcp nom pl masc
[Mt 24:38; v-1b(2); 5592]   τρώγω

Τρωγύλλιον, ου, τό   {5591, n-2c}}
Trogyllium, a town and promontory on the
western coast of Ionia, opposite Samos, Acts
20:15 v.l.*

τρώγω   {5592, v-1b(2)}
[-, -, -, -, -] pr. to crunch; to eat, Matt 24:38; from
the Hebrew, ἄρτον τρώγειν, to take food, partake
of a meal, John 6:54, 56-58; 13:18*

τρώγων   pres act ptcp nom sg masc
[5t; v-1b(2); 5592]   "
τυγχάνοντες   pres act ptcp nom pl masc
[Ac 24:2; v-3a(2b); 5593]   τυγχάνω

τυγχάνω   {5593, v-3a(2b)}
[(ἐτύγχανον), τεύξω, ἔτυχον, τέτευχα, -, -] to hit
an object; to attain to, to obtain, acquire, enjoy,
Luke 20:35; Acts 24:2; 26:22; 27:3; 2 Tim 2:10;
Heb 8:6; 11:35; intrans. to happen, fall out, chance;
common, ordinary, Acts 19:11; 28:2; as an adv., it
may be, perchance, perhaps, 1 Cor 16:6; Luke
20:13 v.l., Acts 12:15 v.l.; εἰ τύχοι, as it so happens,
as the case may be, 1 Cor 14:10; 15:37; to be in a
certain condition, Luke 10:30 v.l.*

τυμπανίζω   {5594, v-2a(1)}
[-, -, -, -, ἐτυμπανίσθην] pr. to beat a drum; to
drum upon; in N.T. to torture, beat to death with
rods and clubs, Heb 11:35*

τυπικῶς   {5595, adverb}
figuratively, typically, 1 Cor 10:11*

τυπικῶς   adverb [1C 10:11; adverb; 5595]   τυπικῶς
τύποι   nom pl masc [2t; n-2a; 5596]   τύπος
τύπον   acc sg masc [10t; n-2a; 5596]   "

τύπος, ου, ὁ   {5596, n-2a}
pr. an impress; a print, mark, of a wound
inflicted, John 20:25; a delineation; an image,
statue, Acts 7:43; a formula, scheme, Rom 6:17;
form, Acts 23:25; a figure, counterpart, 1 Cor 10:6;
an anticipative figure, type, Rom 5:14; 1 Cor
10:11 v.l.; a model pattern, Acts 7:44; Heb 8:5; a
moral pattern, Phil 3:17; 1 Thess 1:7; 2 Thess 3:9;
1 Tim 4:12; Titus 2:7; 1 Peter 5:3*

τύπος   nom sg masc [2t; n-2a; 5596]   "
τύπους   acc pl masc [Ac 7:43; n-2a; 5596]   "
τύπτειν   pres act inf [4t; v-4; 5597]   τύπτω
τύπτεσθαι   pres pass inf [Ac 23:3; v-4; 5597]   "
τύπτοντες   pres act ptcp nom pl masc
[3t; v-4; 5597]   "
τύπτοντι   pres act ptcp dat sg masc
[Lk 6:29; v-4; 5597]   "

τύπτω   {5597, v-4}
[(ἔτυπτον), -, -, -, -, -] to beat, strike, smite, Matt
24:49; 27:30; to beat the breast, as expressive of
grief or strong emotion, Luke 18:13; 23:48; in
N.T. met. to wound or shock the conscience of
any one, 1 Cor 8:12; from the Hebrew, to smite
with evil, punish, Acts 23:3

τύραννος, ου, ὁ {5599, n-2a}
despotic ruler, tyrant, Acts 5:39 v.l.*

Τύραννος, ου, ὁ {5600, n-2a}
Tyrannus, an Ephesian, Acts 19:9*

Τυράννου gen sg masc
[Ac 19:9; n-2a; 5598] Τύραννος

τυρβάζω {v-2a(1)}
[-, -, -, -, -] *to stir up; to throw into a state of perturbation, disquiet;* mid. *to trouble one's self, be troubled, be disquieted,* Luke 10:41 v.l.*

Τυρίοις dat pl masc [Ac 12:20; n-2a; 5601] Τύριος

Τύριος, ου, ὁ {5601, n-2a}
a Tyrian, an inhabitant of Tyre, Acts 12:20, 22 v.l.*

Τύρον acc sg fem [2t; n-2b; 5602] Τύρος

Τύρος, ου, ἡ {5602, n-2b}
Tyre, a celebrated and wealthy commercial city of Phoenicia, Matt 11:21; 15:21; Mark 7:24; Acts 21:3, 7

Τύρου gen sg fem [5t; n-2b; 5602] "
Τύρῳ dat sg fem [4t; n-2b; 5602] "
τυφλέ voc sg masc
[Mt 23:26; a-1a(2a); 5603] τυφλός
τυφλοί nom pl masc [10t; a-1a(2a); 5603] "
τυφλοί voc pl masc [4t; a-1a(2a); 5603] "
τυφλοῖς dat pl masc [2t; a-1a(2a); 5603] "
τυφλόν acc sg masc [6t; a-1a(2a); 5603] "

τυφλός, ή, όν {5603, a-1a(2a)}
blind, Matt 9:27, 28; 11:5; 12:22; met. *mentally blind,* Matt 15:14; 23:16

τυφλός nom sg masc [14t; a-1a(2a); 5603] "
τυφλοῦ nom sg masc [Jn 9:32; a-1a(2a); 5603] "
τυφλοῦ gen sg masc [3t; a-1a(2a); 5603] "
τυφλούς acc pl masc [4t; a-1a(2a); 5603] "

τυφλόω {5604, v-1d(3)}
[-, ἐτύφλωσα, τετύφλωκα, -, -] *to blind, render blind;* met. John 12:40; 2 Cor 4:4; 1 John 2:11*

τυφλῷ dat sg masc [Jn 9:17; a-1a(2a); 5603] "
τυφλῶν gen pl masc [4t; a-1a(2a); 5603] "
τυφόμενον pres pass ptcp acc sg neut
[Mt 12:20; v-1b(1); 5606] τύφω

τυφόω {5605, v-1d(3)}
[-, -, -, τετύφωμαι, ἐτυφώθην] *to besmoke;* met. *to possess with the fumes* of conceit; pass. *to be demented with conceit, puffed up,* 1 Tim 3:6; 6:4; 2 Tim 3:4; 1 Tim 6:4*

τύφω {5606, v-1b(1)}
[-, -, -, -, -] *to raise a smoke;* pass. *to emit smoke, smoke, smoulder,* Matt 12:20*

τυφωθείς aor pass ptcp nom sg masc
[1Ti 3:6; v-1d(3); 5605] τυφόομαι

τυφωνικός, ή, όν {5607, a-1a(2a)}
stormy, tempestuous; with ἄνεμος it means *hurricane, typhoon, whirlwind,* Acts 27:14*

τυφωνικός nom sg masc
[Ac 27:14; a-1a(2a); 5607] τυφωνικός
τυχεῖν aor act inf [2t; v-3a(2b); 5593] τυγχάνω

Τύχικον acc sg masc [2t; n-2a; 5608] Τυχικός
Τύχικος nom sg masc [3t; n-2a; 5608] "

Τυχικός, οῦ, ὁ {5608, n-2a}
Tychicus, pr. name, a friend or companion of Paul, Acts 20:4; Eph 6:21; Col 4:7; 2 Tim 4:12; Titus 3:12; Eph subscr.; Col subscr.*

τύχοι aor act opt 3 sg
[2t; v-3a(2b); 5593] τυγχάνω
τυχόν aor act ptcp acc sg neut
[1C 16:6; v-3a(2b); 5593] "
τυχοῦσαν aor act ptcp acc sg fem
[Ac 28:2; v-3a(2b); 5593] "
τυχούσας aor act ptcp acc pl fem
[Ac 19:11; v-3a(2b); 5593] "
τυχών aor act ptcp nom sg masc
[Ac 26:22; v-3a(2b); 5593] "
τύχωσιν aor act subj 3 pl [2t; v-3a(2b); 5593] "
τῷ dat sg masc [827t; a-1a(2b); 3836] ὁ
τῷ dat sg neut [412t; a-1a(2b); 3836] "
τῶν gen pl masc [822t; a-1a(2b); 3836] "
τῶν gen pl fem [137t; a-1a(2b); 3836] "

υ

ὑακίνθινος, ίνη, ινον {5610, a-1a(2a)}
hyacinthine, resembling the hyacinth in color, dark blue, Rev 9:17*

ὑακινθίνους acc pl masc
[Rv 9:17; a-1a(2a); 5610] ὑακίνθινος

ὑάκινθος, ου, ὁ {5611, n-2a}
a hyacinth, a gem resembling the color of the *hyacinth flower, dark blue,* Rev 21:20*

ὑάκινθος nom sg masc
[Rv 21:20; n-2a; 5611] ὑάκινθος
ὑαλίνη nom sg fem
[Rv 4:6; a-1a(2a); 5612] ὑάλινος
ὑαλίνην acc sg fem [2t; a-1a(2a); 5612] "

ὑάλινος, η, ον {5612, a-1a(2a)}
made of glass; glassy, translucent, Rev 4:6; 15:2*

ὕαλος, ου, ἡ {5613, n-2b}
a transparent stone, crystal; also, *glass,* Rev 21:18, 21*

ὕαλος nom sg fem [Rv 21:21; n-2b; 5613] ὕαλος
ὑάλῳ dat sg masc [Rv 21:18; n-2b; 5613] "
ὕβρεσιν dat pl fem
[2C 12:10; n-3e(5b); 5615] ὕβρις
ὕβρεως gen sg fem [Ac 27:10; n-3e(5b); 5615] "
ὑβρίζεις pres act ind 2 sg
[Lk 11:45; v-2a(1); 5614] ὑβρίζω

ὑβρίζω {5614, v-2a(1)}
[-, ὕβρισα, -, -, ὑβρίσθην] *to run riot;* trans. *to outrage, to treat in an arrogant* or *spiteful manner,* Matt 22:6; Luke 11:45; 18:32; Acts 14:5; 1 Thess 2:2*

ὕβριν acc sg fem [Ac 27:21; n-3e(5b); 5615] ὕβρις

ὕβρις, εως, ἡ   {5615, n-3e(5b)}
insolence; shame, insult, outrage, 2 Cor 12:10;
damage by sea, Acts 27:10, 21*

ὑβρίσαι   aor act inf
   [Ac 14:5; v-2a(1); 5614]   ὑβρίζω
ὕβρισαν   aor act ind 3 pl
   [Mt 22:6; v-2a(1); 5614]   "
ὑβρισθέντες   aor pass ptcp nom pl masc
   [1Th 2:2; v-2a(1); 5614]   "
ὑβρισθήσεται   fut pass ind 3 sg
   [Lk 18:32; v-2a(1); 5614]   "
ὑβριστάς   acc pl masc
   [Rm 1:30; n-1f; 5616]   ὑβριστής
ὑβριστήν   acc sg masc [1Ti 1:13; n-1f; 5616]   "

ὑβριστής, οῦ, ὁ   {5616, n-1f}
an overbearing, violent person, Rom 1:30; 1 Tim
1:13*

ὑγιαίνειν   pres act inf
   [3J 2; v-2d(4); 5617]   ὑγιαίνω
ὑγιαίνοντα   pres act ptcp acc sg masc
   [2t; v-2d(4); 5617]   "
ὑγιαίνοντας   pres act ptcp acc pl masc
   [Ti 2:2; v-2d(4); 5617]   "
ὑγιαίνοντες   pres act ptcp nom pl masc
   [Lk 5:31; v-2d(4); 5617]   "
ὑγιαινόντων   pres act ptcp gen pl masc
   [2Ti 1:13; v-2d(4); 5617]   "
ὑγιαινούσῃ   pres act ptcp dat sg fem
   [3t; v-2d(4); 5617]   "
ὑγιαινούσης   pres act ptcp gen sg fem
   [2Ti 4:3; v-2d(4); 5617]   "
ὑγιαίνουσιν   pres act ptcp dat pl masc
   [1Ti 6:3; v-2d(4); 5617]   "

ὑγιαίνω   {5617, v-2d(4)}
[-, -, -, -, -] *to be sound, in health,* Matt 8:13 v.l.;
Luke 5:31; 7:10; *to be safe and sound,* Luke 15:27;
3 John 2; met. *to be healthful* or *sound* in faith,
doctrine, etc., Titus 1:9, 13; 2:1, 2; *sound, pure,*
uncorrupted, 1 Tim 1:10; 6:3; 2 Tim 1:13; 4:3

ὑγιαίνωσιν   pres act subj 3 pl
   [Ti 1:13; v-2d(4); 5617]   "
ὑγιεῖς   acc pl masc [Mt 15:31; a-4a; 5618]   ὑγιής
ὑγιῆ   acc sg masc [4t; a-4a; 5618]   "

ὑγιής, ές   {5618, a-4a}
sound, in health, Matt 12:13; 15:31; met. of
doctrine, *sound, pure, wholesome,* Titus 2:8

ὑγιής   nom sg masc [4t; a-4a; 5618]   "
ὑγιής   nom sg fem [2t; a-4a; 5618]   "

ὑγρός, ά, όν   {5619, a-1a(1)}
pr. *wet, moist, humid;* used of a tree, *full of sap,*
fresh, green, Luke 23:31*

ὑγρῷ   dat sg neut
   [Lk 23:31; a-1a(1); 5619]   ὑγρός
ὕδασιν   dat pl neut [Mt 8:32; n-3c(6b); 5623]   ὕδωρ
ὕδατα   nom pl neut [2t; n-3c(6b); 5623]   "
ὕδατα   acc pl neut [3t; n-3c(6b); 5623]   "
ὕδατι   dat sg neut [13t; n-3c(6b); 5623]   "
ὕδατος   gen sg neut [22t; n-3c(6b); 5623]   "
ὑδάτων   gen pl neut [12t; n-3c(6b); 5623]   "

ὑδρία, ας, ἡ   {5620, n-1a}
a water-pot, pitcher, John 2:6, 7; *a bucket, pail,*
John 4:28*

ὑδρίαι   nom pl fem [Jn 2:6; n-1a; 5620]   ὑδρία
ὑδρίαν   acc sg fem [Jn 4:28; n-1a; 5620]   "
ὑδρίας   acc pl fem [Jn 2:7; n-1a; 5620]   "
ὑδροπότει   pres act imperative 2 sg
   [1Ti 5:23; cv-1d(2a); 5621]   ὑδροποτέω

ὑδροποτέω   {5621, cv-1d(2a)}
[-, -, -, -, -] *to be only a water-drinker,* 1 Tim 5:23*

ὑδρωπικός, ή, όν   {5622, a-1a(2)}
dropsical, suffering from dropsey, Luke 14:2*

ὑδρωπικός   nom sg masc
   [Lk 14:2; a-1a(2a); 5622]   ὑδρωπικός

ὕδωρ, ὕδατος, τό   {5623, n-3c(6b)}
water, Matt 3:11, 16; 14:28, 29; 17:15; John 5:3, 4,
7; *watery fluid,* John 19:34; ὕδωρ ζῶν, *living water,*
fresh flowing water, John 4:11; met. of spiritual
refreshment, John 4:10; 7:38

ὕδωρ   nom sg neut [6t; n-3c(6b); 5623]   ὕδωρ
ὕδωρ   acc sg neut [17t; n-3c(6b); 5623]   "
ὑετόν   acc sg masc [3t; n-2a; 5624]   ὑετός

ὑετός, ου, ὁ   {5624, n-2a}
rain, Acts 14:17; 28:2; Heb 6:7; James 5:7 v.l., 18;
Rev 11:6*

ὑετός   nom sg masc [Rv 11:6; n-2a; 5624]   "
ὑετούς   acc pl masc [Ac 14:17; n-2a; 5624]   "
υἱέ   voc sg masc [9t; n-2a; 5626]   υἱός

υἱοθεσία, ας, ἡ   {5625, n-1a}
adoption, a placing in the condition of a son, Rom
8:15, 23; 9:4; Gal 4:5; Eph 1:5*

υἱοθεσία   nom sg fem
   [Rm 9:4; n-1a; 5625]   υἱοθεσία
υἱοθεσίαν   acc sg fem [3t; n-1a; 5625]   "
υἱοθεσίας   gen sg fem [Rm 8:15; n-1a; 5625]   "
υἱοί   nom pl masc [32t; n-2a; 5626]   υἱός
υἱοί   voc pl masc [Ac 13:26; n-2a; 5626]   "
υἱοῖς   dat pl masc [7t; n-2a; 5626]   "
υἱόν   acc sg masc [85t; n-2a; 5626]   "

υἱός, ου, ὁ   {5626, n-2a}
a son, Matt 1:21, 25; 7:9; 13:55 freq.; *a legitimate*
son, Heb 12:8; *a son* artificially constituted, Acts
7:21; Heb 11:24; *a descendant,* Matt 1:1, 20; Mark
12:35; in N.T. *the young* of an animal, Matt 21:5;
a spiritual son in respect of conversion or
discipleship, 1 Peter 5:13; from the Hebrew, *a*
disciple, perhaps, Matt 12:27; *a son* as implying
connection in respect of membership, service,
resemblance, manifestation, destiny, etc., Matt
8:12; 9:15; 13:38; 23:15; Mark 2:29; 3:17; Luke
5:34; 10:6; 16:8; 20:34, 36; John 17:12; Acts 2:25;
4:36; 13:10; Eph 2:2; 5:6; Col 3:6; 1 Thess 5:5; 2
Thess 2:3; υἱὸς θεοῦ, κ.τ.λ., *son of God* in respect
of divinity, Matt 4:3, 6; 14:33; Rom 1:4; also, in
respect of privilege and character, Matt 5:9, 45;
Luke 6:35; Rom 8:14, 19; 9:26; Gal 3:26; ὁ υἱὸς
τοῦ θεοῦ, κ.τ.λ., a title of the Messiah, Matt
26:63; Mark 3:11; 14:61; John 1:34, 50; 20:31; υἱὸς
ἀνθρώπου, *a son of man, a man,* Mark 3:28; Eph

3:5; Heb 2:6; ὁ υἱὸς τοῦ ἀνθρώπου, a title of the Messiah, Matt 8:20 freq.; as also, ὁ υἱὸς Δαβίδ, (Δαυίδ) Matt 12:23

υἱός   nom sg masc [161t; n-2a; 5626]   "
υἱοῦ   gen sg masc [36t; n-2a; 5626]   "
υἱούς   acc pl masc [14t; n-2a; 5626]   "
υἱῷ   dat sg masc [15t; n-2a; 5626]   "
υἱῶν   gen pl masc [17t; n-2a; 5626]   "

ὕλη, ης, ἡ   {5627, n-1b}
wood, a forest; in N.T. *firewood, a mass of fuel,* James 3:5*

ὕλην   acc sg fem [Jm 3:5; n-1b; 5627]   ὕλη
ὑμᾶς   acc pl [435t; a-5a; 5148]   σύ
ὑμεῖς   nom pl [236t; a-5a; 5148]   "

Ὑμέναιος, ου, ὁ   {5628, n-2a}
Hymenaeus, pr. name, 1 Tim 1:20; 2 Tim 2:17*

Ὑμέναιος   nom sg masc [2t; n-2a; 5628]   Ὑμέναιος
ὑμετέρα   nom sg fem
    [Lk 6:20; a-1a(1); 5629]   ὑμέτερος
ὑμετέρᾳ   dat sg fem [Ga 6:13; a-1a(1); 5629]   "
ὑμετέραν   acc sg fem [1C 15:31; a-1a(1); 5629]   "
ὑμετέρας   gen sg fem [2t; a-1a(1); 5629]   "
ὑμέτερον   acc sg masc
    [Jn 15:20; a-1a(1); 5629]   "
ὑμέτερον   acc sg neut [2t; a-1a(1); 5629]   "

ὑμέτερος, α, ον   {5629, a-1a(1)}
your, yours, Luke 6:20; John 7:6; 15:20

ὑμέτερος   nom sg masc [Jn 7:6; a-1a(1); 5629]   "
ὑμετέρῳ   dat sg masc
    [Jn 8:17; a-1a(1); 5629]   "
ὑμετέρῳ   dat sg neut
    [Rm 11:31; a-1a(1); 5629]   "
ὑμῖν   dat pl [608t; a-5a; 5148]   σύ

ὑμνέω   {5630, v-1d(2a)}
[(ὕμνουν), ὑμνήσω, ὕμνησα, -, -, -] *to hymn, praise, celebrate* or *worship with hymns,* Acts 16:25; Heb 2:12; absol. *to sing a hymn,* Matt 26:30; Mark 14:26*

ὑμνήσαντες   aor act ptcp nom pl masc
    [2t; v-1d(2a); 5630]   ὑμνέω
ὑμνήσω   fut act ind 1 sg
    [Hb 2:12; v-1d(2a); 5630]   "
ὕμνοις   dat pl masc [2t; n-2a; 5631]   ὕμνος

ὕμνος, ου, ὁ   {5631, n-2a}
a song; a hymn, song of praise to God, Eph 5:19; Col 3:16*

ὕμνουν   imperf act ind 3 pl
    [Ac 16:25; v-1d(2a); 5630]   ὑμνέω
ὑμῶν   gen pl [561t; a-5a; 5148]   σύ
ὑπ'   prep-gen [22t; prep; 5679]   ὑπό
ὑπ'   prep-acc [3t; prep; 5679]   "
ὕπαγε   pres act imperative 2 sg
    [24t; cv-1b(2); 5632]   ὑπάγω
ὑπάγει   pres act ind 3 sg [11t; cv-1b(2); 5632]   "
ὑπάγειν   pres act inf [5t; cv-1b(2); 5632]   "
ὑπάγεις   pres act ind 2 sg [5t; cv-1b(2); 5632]   "
ὑπάγετε   pres act imperative 2 pl
    [14t; cv-1b(2); 5632]   "

ὑπάγῃ   pres act subj 3 sg
    [Rv 14:4; cv-1b(2); 5632]   "
ὑπάγητε   pres act subj 2 pl
    [Jn 15:16; cv-1b(2); 5632]   "
ὑπάγοντας   pres act ptcp acc pl masc
    [Mk 6:33; cv-1b(2); 5632]   "
ὑπάγοντες   pres act ptcp nom pl masc
    [Mk 6:31; cv-1b(2); 5632]   "

ὑπάγω   {5632, cv-1b(2)}
[(ὑπῆγον), -, -, -, -, -] *to lead* or *bring under; to lead* or *bring from under; draw on* or *away;* in N.T. intrans. *to go away, depart,* Matt 8:4, 13; 9:6; ὕπαγε ὀπίσω μου, *Get behind me! Away! Begone!* Matt 4:10; 16:23; *to go,* Matt 5:41; Luke 12:58; *to depart* life, Matt 26:24

ὑπάγω   pres act ind 1 sg [14t; cv-1b(2); 5632]   "

ὑπακοή, ῆς, ἡ   {5633, n-1b}
a hearkening to; obedience, Rom 5:19; 6:16; 1 Peter 1:14; *submissiveness,* Rom 16:19; 2 Cor 7:15; *submission,* Rom 1:5; 15:18; 16:26; 2 Cor 10:5; Heb 5:8; 1 Peter 1:2, 22; *compliance,* Phlm 21

ὑπακοή   nom sg fem [2t; n-1b; 5633]   ὑπακοή
ὑπακοῇ   dat sg fem [2t; n-1b; 5633]   "
ὑπακοήν   acc sg fem [8t; n-1b; 5633]   "
ὑπακοῆς   gen sg fem [3t; n-1b; 5633]   "
ὑπακούει   pres act ind 3 sg
    [2t; cv-1a(8); 5634]   ὑπακούω
ὑπακούειν   pres act inf
    [Rm 6:12; cv-1a(8); 5634]   "
ὑπακούετε   pres act ind 2 pl
    [Rm 6:16; cv-1a(8); 5634]   "
ὑπακούετε   pres act imperative 2 pl
    [4t; cv-1a(8); 5634]   "
ὑπακούουσιν   pres act ind 3 pl
    [3t; cv-1a(8); 5634]   "
ὑπακούουσιν   pres act ptcp dat pl masc
    [2t; cv-1a(8); 5634]   "
ὑπακοῦσαι   aor act inf
    [Ac 12:13; cv-1a(8); 5634]   "

ὑπακούω   {5634, cv-1a(8)}
[(ὑπήκουον), ὑπακούσω, ὑπήκουσα, -, -, -] *to give ear; to listen,* Acts 12:13; *to obey,* Matt 8:27; Mark 1:27; in N.T. *to render submissive acceptance,* Acts 6:7; Rom 6:17; 2 Thess 1:8; Heb 5:9; absol. *to be submissive,* Phil 2:12

ὕπανδρος, ον   {5635, a-3a}
bound to a man, married, Rom 7:2*

ὕπανδρος   nom sg fem [Rm 7:2; a-3a; 5635]
    ὕπανδρος

ὑπαντάω   {5636, cv-1d(1a)}
[(ὑπήντων), -, ὑπήντησα, -, -, -] *to meet,* Matt 8:28; Luke 8:27; John 11:20, 30; 12:18

ὑπαντῆσαι   aor act inf
    [2t; cv-1d(1a); 5636]   ὑπαντάω
ὑπάντησιν   acc sg fem
    [3t; n-3e(5b); 5637]   ὑπάντησις

ὑπάντησις, εως, ἡ   {5637, n-3e(5b)}
a meeting, act of meeting, Matt 8:34; 25:1; John 12:13*

ὑπάρξεις   acc pl fem
  [Ac 2:45; n-3e(5b); 5638]   ὕπαρξις
ὕπαρξιν   acc sg fem [Hb 10:34; n-3e(5b); 5638]   "

ὕπαρξις, εως, ἡ   {5638, n-3e(5b)}
  goods possessed, substance, property, Acts 2:45;
  Heb 10:34*

ὑπάρχει   pres act ind 3 sg
  [3t; cv-1b(2); 5639]   ὑπάρχω
ὑπάρχειν   pres act inf   [6t; cv-1b(2); 5639]   "
ὑπάρχοντα   pres act ptcp nom pl neut
  [2t; cv-1b(2); 5639]   "
ὑπάρχοντα   pres act ptcp acc sg masc
  [Ac 17:27; cv-1b(2); 5639]   "
ὑπάρχοντα   pres act ptcp acc pl neut
  [5t; cv-1b(2); 5639]   "
ὑπάρχοντας   pres act ptcp acc pl masc
  [Ac 16:37; cv-1b(2); 5639]   "
ὑπάρχοντες   pres act ptcp nom pl masc
  [6t; cv-1b(2); 5639]   "
ὑπάρχοντος   pres act ptcp gen sg masc
  [2t; cv-1b(2); 5639]   "
ὑπάρχοντος   pres act ptcp gen sg neut
  [Ac 19:40; cv-1b(2); 5639]   "
ὑπαρχόντων   pres act ptcp gen pl neut
  [5t; cv-1b(2); 5639]   "
ὑπαρχούσης   pres act ptcp gen sg fem
  [Ac 27:21; cv-1b(2); 5639]   "
ὑπάρχουσιν   pres act ind 3 pl
  [Ac 21:20; cv-1b(2); 5639]   "
ὑπάρχουσιν   pres act ptcp dat pl neut
  [3t; cv-1b(2); 5639]   "

ὑπάρχω   {5639, cv-1b(2)}
  [(ὑπῆρχον), -, -, -, -, -] *to begin; to come into
  existence; to exist; to be, subsist,* Acts 19:40; 28:18;
  to be in possession, to belong, Acts 3:6; 4:37; *goods,
  possessions, property,* Matt 19:21; Luke 8:3; *to be,*
  Luke 7:25; 8:41

ὑπάρχων   pres act ptcp nom sg masc
  [15t; cv-1b(2); 5639]   "
ὑπάρχωσιν   pres act subj 3 pl
  [Jm 2:15; cv-1b(2); 5639]   "
ὑπέβαλον   aor act ind 3 pl
  [Ac 6:11; cv-2d(1); 5680]   ὑποβάλλω
ὑπέδειξα   aor act ind 1 sg
  [Ac 20:35; cv-3c(2); 5683]   ὑποδείκνυμι
ὑπέδειξεν   aor act ind 3 sg [2t; cv-3c(2); 5683]   "
ὑπεδέξατο   aor mid ind 3 sg
  [2t; cv-1b(2); 5685]   ὑποδέχομαι
ὑπέθηκαν   aor act ind 3 pl
  [Rm 16:4; cv-6a; 5719]   ὑποτίθημι
ὑπείκετε   pres act imperative 2 pl
  [Hb 13:17; cv-1b(2); 5640]   ὑπείκω

ὑπείκω   {5640, cv-1b(2)}
  [-, -, -, -, -] *to yield, give way;* absol. *to be
  submissive,* Heb 13:17*

ὑπέλαβεν   aor act ind 3 sg
  [Ac 1:9; cv-3a(2b); 5696]   ὑπολαμβάνω
ὑπελείφθην   aor pass ind 1 sg
  [Rm 11:3; cv-1b(1); 5699]   ὑπολείπω
ὑπέμειναν   aor act ind 3 pl
  [Ac 17:14; cv-1c(2); 5702]   ὑπομένω

ὑπεμείνατε   aor act ind 2 pl
  [Hb 10:32; cv-1c(2); 5702]   "
ὑπέμεινεν   aor act ind 3 sg [2t; cv-1c(2); 5702]   "
ὑπεμνήσθη   aor pass ind 3 sg
  [Lk 22:61; cv-5a; 5703]   ὑπομιμνῄσκω
ὑπεναντίον   nom sg neut
  [Cl 2:14; a-1a(1); 5641]   ὑπεναντίος

ὑπεναντίος, α, ον   {5641, a-1a(1)}
  over against; contrast, adverse, Col 2:14; ὁ
  ὑπεναντίος, *an opponent, adversary,* Heb 10:27*

ὑπεναντίους   acc pl masc
  [Hb 10:27; a-1a(1); 5641]   "
ὑπενεγκεῖν   aor act inf
  [1C 10:13; cv-1c(1); 5722]   ὑποφέρω
ὑπενόουν   imperf act ind 1 sg
  [Ac 25:18; cv-1d(2a); 5706]   ὑπονοέω
ὑπενόουν   imperf act ind 3 pl
  [Ac 27:27; cv-1d(2a); 5706]   "
ὑπεπλεύσαμεν   aor act ind 1 pl
  [2t; cv-1a(7); 5709]   ὑποπλέω

ὑπέρ   {5642, prep}
  (1) gen., *above, over;* met. *in behalf of,* Matt 5:44;
  Mark 9:40; John 17:19; *instead of* beneficially,
  Phlm 13; *in maintenance of,* Rom 15:8; *for the
  furtherance of,* John 11:4; 2 Cor 1:6, 8; *for the
  realization of,* Phil 2:13; equivalent to περί, *about,
  concerning,* with the further signification of
  interest or concern in the subject, Acts 5:41;
  Rom 9:27; 2 Cor 5:12; 8:23; 2 Thess 2:1. (2) acc.,
  over, beyond; met. *beyond, more than,* Matt 10:37;
  2 Cor 1:8; used after comparative terms, Luke
  16:8; 2 Cor 12:13; Heb 4:12. (3) in N.T. as an
  adv., *in a higher degree, in fuller measure,* 2 Cor
  11:23

ὑπέρ   prep-gen   [130t; prep; 5642]   "
ὑπέρ   prep-acc   [19t; prep; 5642]   "
ὑπέρ   adverbial usage   [2C 11:23; prep; 5642]   "
ὑπεραιρόμενος   pres mid ptcp nom sg masc
  [2Th 2:4; cv-2d(2); 5643]   ὑπεραίρω

ὑπεραίρω   {5643, cv-2d(2)}
  [-, -, -, -, -] *to raise* or *lift up above* or *over;* mid. *to
  lift up one's self;* met. *to be over-elated,* 2 Cor 12:7;
  to bear one's self arrogantly, to rear a haughty front,
  2 Thess 2:4*

ὑπεραίρωμαι   pres pass subj 1 sg
  [2t; cv-2d(2); 5643]   "

ὑπέρακμος, ον   {5644, a-3a}
  past the bloom of life, past one's prime, 1 Cor 7:36*

ὑπέρακμος   nom sg fem
  [1C 7:36; a-3a; 5644]   ὑπέρακμος

ὑπεράνω   {5645, adverb}
  can function as an improper prep., *above, over,
  far above;* of place, Eph 4:10; Heb 9:5; of rank,
  dignity, Eph 1:21*

ὑπεράνω   adverb   [3t; adverb; 5645]   ὑπεράνω

ὑπερασπίζω   {5646, cv-2a(1)}
  shield, protect, James 1:27 v.l.*

ὑπεραυξάνει   pres act ind 3 sg
  [2Th 1:3; cv-3a(1); 5647]   ὑπεραυξάνω

ὑπεραυξάνω {5647, cv-3a(1)}
[-, -, -, -, -] *to increase exceedingly,* 2 Thess 1:3*

ὑπερβαίνειν pres act inf
[1Th 4:6; cv-2d(6); 5648] ὑπερβαίνω

ὑπερβαίνω {5648, cv-2d(6)}
[-, -, -, -, -] *to overstep; to wrong, transgress,* 1 Thess 4:6*

ὑπερβάλλον pres act ptcp nom sg neut
[Ep 1:19; cv-2d(1); 5650] ὑπερβάλλω
ὑπερβάλλον pres act ptcp acc sg neut
[Ep 2:7; cv-2d(1); 5650] "

ὑπερβαλλόντως {5649, adverb}
exceedingly, above measure, 2 Cor 11:23*

ὑπερβαλλόντως adverb
[2C 11:23; adverb; 5649] ὑπερβαλλόντως
ὑπερβάλλουσαν pres act ptcp acc sg fem
[2t; cv-2d(1); 5650] ὑπερβάλλω
ὑπερβαλλούσης pres act ptcp gen sg fem
[2C 3:10; cv-2d(1); 5650] "

ὑπερβάλλω {5650, cv-2d(1)}
[-, -, -, -, -] pr. *to cast* or *throw over* or *beyond, to overshoot;* met. *to surpass, excel; surpassing,* 2 Cor 3:10; 9:14; Eph 1:19; 2:7; 3:19*

ὑπερβολή, ῆς, ἡ {5651, n-1b}
pr. *a throwing beyond, an overshooting; extraordinary amount* or *character, transcendency,* 2 Cor 12:7; 4:7; καθ᾽ ὑπερβολήν, adverbially, *exceedingly, extremely,* Rom 7:13; 2 Cor 1:8; Gal 1:13; *a far better way,* 1 Cor 12:31; *beyond all measure,* 2 Cor 4:17*

ὑπερβολή nom sg fem
[2C 4:7; n-1b; 5651] ὑπερβολή
ὑπερβολῇ dat sg fem [2C 12:7; n-1b; 5651] "
ὑπερβολήν acc sg fem [6t; n-1b; 5651] "

ὑπερέκεινα {5654, adverb}
BAGD list as an adverb used with the gen., others list as an improper prep., *beyond,* 2 Cor 10:16*

ὑπερέκεινα adverb
[2C 10:16; adverb; 5654] ὑπερέκεινα

ὑπερεκπερισσοῦ {5655, adverb}
in over abundance; beyond all measure, superabundantly, Eph 3:20; 1 Thess 3:10; 5:13*

ὑπερεκπερισσοῦ adverb
[3t; adverb; 5655] ὑπερεκπερισσοῦ

ὑπερεκπερισσῶς {5656, adverb}
beyond measure, 1 Thess 5:13; Mark 7:37 v.l.*

ὑπερεκτείνομεν pres act ind 1 pl
[2C 10:14; cv-2d(5); 5657] ὑπερεκτείνω

ὑπερεκτείνω {5657, cv-2d(5)}
[-, -, -, -, -] *to over-extend, over-stretch,* 2 Cor 10:14*

ὑπερεκχυννόμενον pres pass ptcp acc sg neut
[Lk 6:38; cv-3a(1); 5658] ὑπερεκχύννω

ὑπερεκχύννω {5658, cv-3a(1)}
[-, -, -, -, -] *to pour out above measure* or *in excess;* pass. *to run over, overflow,* Luke 6:38*

ὑπερεντυγχάνει pres act ind 3 sg
[Rm 8:26; cv-3a(2b); 5659] ὑπερεντυγχάνω

ὑπερεντυγχάνω {5659, cv-3a(2b)}
[-, -, -, -, -] *to intercede for,* Rom 8:26*

ὑπερεπερίσσευσεν aor act ind 3 sg
[Rm 5:20; cv-1a(6); 5668] ὑπερπερισσεύω
ὑπερεπλεόνασεν aor act ind 3 sg
[1Ti 1:14; cv-2a(1); 5670] ὑπερπλεονάζω
ὑπερέχον pres act ptcp acc sg neut
[Pp 3:8; cv-1b(2); 5660] ὑπερέχω
ὑπερέχοντας pres act ptcp acc pl masc
[Pp 2:3; cv-1b(2); 5660] "
ὑπερέχοντι pres act ptcp dat sg masc
[1P 2:13; cv-1b(2); 5660] "
ὑπερέχουσα pres act ptcp nom sg fem
[Pp 4:7; cv-1b(2); 5660] "
ὑπερεχούσαις pres act ptcp dat pl fem
[Rm 13:1; cv-1b(2); 5660] "

ὑπερέχω {5660, cv-1b(2)}
[ὑπερέξω, -, -, -, -] *to hold above;* intrans. *to stand out above, to overtop;* met. *to surpass, excel,* Phil 2:3; 4:7; τὸ ὑπερέχον, *excellence, pre-eminence,* Phil 3:8; *to be higher, superior,* Rom 13:1; 1 Peter 2:13*

ὑπερηφανία, ας, ἡ {5661, n-1a}
haughtiness, arrogance, Mark 7:22*

ὑπερηφανία nom sg fem
[Mk 7:22; n-1a; 5661] ὑπερηφανία
ὑπερήφανοι nom pl masc
[2Ti 3:2; a-3a; 5662] ὑπερήφανος
ὑπερηφάνοις dat pl masc [2t; a-3a; 5662] "

ὑπερήφανος, ον {5662, a-3a}
assuming, haughty, arrogant, Luke 1:51; Rom 1:30; 2 Tim 3:2; James 4:6; 1 Peter 5:5*

ὑπερηφάνους acc pl masc [2t; a-3a; 5662] "
ὑπεριδών aor act ptcp nom sg masc
[Ac 17:30; cv-1d(1a); 5666] ὑπεροράω

ὑπερλίαν {5663, adverb}
in the highest degree, pre-eminently, especially, superlatively, 2 Cor 11:5; 12:11*

ὑπερλίαν adverb [2t; adverb; 5663] ὑπερλίαν

ὑπερνικάω {5664, cv-1d(1a)}
[-, -, -, -, -] *to overpower in victory; to be abundantly victorious, prevail mightily,* Rom 8:37*

ὑπερνικῶμεν pres act ind 1 pl
[Rm 8:37; cv-1d(1a); 5664] ὑπερνικάω
ὑπέρογκα acc pl neut [2t; a-3a; 5665] ὑπέρογκος

ὑπέρογκος, ον {5665, a-3a}
pr. *swollen, overgrown;* of language, *swelling, pompous, boastful,* 2 Peter 2:18; Jude 16*

ὑπεροράω {5666, cv-1d(1a)}
[ὑπερόψομαι, ὑπερεῖδον, -, -, -] *overlook, disregard,* Acts 17:30*

ὑπεροχή, ῆς, ἡ {5667, n-1b}
prominence; met., *excellence, rare quality,* 1 Cor 2:1; *eminent station, authority,* 1 Tim 2:2*

ὑπεροχῇ   dat sg fem
  [1Ti 2:2; n-1b; 5667]   ὑπεροχή
ὑπεροχήν   acc sg fem [1C 2:1; n-1b; 5667]   "
ὑπερπερισσεύομαι   pres pass ind 1 sg
  [2C 7:4; cv-1a(6); 5668]   ὑπερπερισσεύω

ὑπερπερισσεύω   {5668, cv-1a(6)}
  [-, ὑπερεπερίσσευσα, -, -, -] *to superabound; to
  abound still more*, Rom 5:20; mid. *to be
  abundantly filled, overflow*, 2 Cor 7:4*

ὑπερπερισσῶς   {5669, adverb}
  *superabundantly, most vehemently, above all
  measure*, Mark 7:37*

ὑπερπερισσῶς   adverb
  [Mk 7:37; adverb; 5669]   ὑπερπερισσῶς

ὑπερπλεονάζω   {5670, cv-2a(1)}
  [-, ὑπερεπλεόνασα, -, -, -] *to superabound, be in
  exceeding abundance, over-exceed*, 1 Tim 1:14*

ὑπερυψόω   {5671, cv-1d(3)}
  [-, ὑπερύψωσα, -, -, -] *to exalt supremely*, Phil 2:9*

ὑπερύψωσεν   aor act ind 3 sg
  [Pp 2:9; cv-1d(3); 5671]   ὑπερυψόω
ὑπερφρονεῖν   pres act inf
  [Rm 12:3; cv-1d(2a); 5672]   ὑπερφρονέω

ὑπερφρονέω   {5672, cv-1d(2a)}
  [-, -, -, -, -] *to have lofty thoughts, be elated,
  haughty*, Rom 12:3*

ὑπερῷον, ου, τό   {5673, n-2c}
  the upper part of a house, upper room, or *chamber*,
  Acts 1:13; 9:37, 39; 20:8*

ὑπερῷον   acc sg neut [2t; n-2c; 5673]   ὑπερῷον
ὑπερῴῳ   dat sg neut [2t; n-2c; 5673]   "
ὑπεστειλάμην   aor mid ind 1 sg
  [2t; cv-2d(1); 5713]   ὑποστέλλω
ὑπέστελλεν   imperf act ind 3 sg
  [Ga 2:12; cv-2d(1); 5713]   "
ὑπέστρεφον   imperf act ind 3 pl
  [2t; cv-1b(1); 5715]   ὑποστρέφω
ὑπέστρεψα   aor act ind 1 sg
  [Ga 1:17; cv-1b(1); 5715]   "
ὑπέστρεψαν   aor act ind 3 pl
  [10t; cv-1b(1); 5715]   "
ὑπέστρεψεν   aor act ind 3 sg
  [6t; cv-1b(1); 5715]   "
ὑπεστρώννυον   imperf act ind 3 pl
  [Lk 19:36; cv-3c(1); 5716]   ὑποστρωννύω
ὑπετάγη   aor pass ind 3 sg
  [Rm 8:20; cv-2b; 5718]   ὑποτάσσω
ὑπετάγησαν   aor pass ind 3 pl
  [Rm 10:3; cv-2b; 5718]   "
ὑπέταξας   aor act ind 2 sg [Hb 2:8; cv-2b; 5718]   "
ὑπέταξεν   aor act ind 3 sg [3t; cv-2b; 5718]   "
ὑπέχουσαι   pres act ptcp nom pl fem
  [Jd 7; cv-1b(2); 5674]   ὑπέχω

ὑπέχω   {5674, cv-1b(2)}
  [-, ὑπέσχον, -, -, -] pr. *to hold under; to render,
  undergo, suffer*, Jude 7*

ὑπεχώρησεν   aor act ind 3 sg
  [Lk 9:10; cv-1d(2a); 5723]   ὑποχωρέω

ὑπῆγον   imperf act ind 3 pl
  [2t; cv-1b(2); 5632]   ὑπάγω
ὑπήκοοι   nom pl masc [2t; a-3a; 5675]   ὑπήκοος

ὑπήκοος, ον   {5675, a-3a}
  giving ear; obedient, submissive, Acts 7:39; 2 Cor
  2:9; Phil 2:8*

ὑπήκοος   nom sg masc [Pp 2:8; a-3a; 5675]   "
ὑπήκουον   imperf act ind 3 pl
  [Ac 6:7; cv-1a(8); 5634]   ὑπακούω
ὑπήκουσαν   aor act ind 3 pl
  [Rm 10:16; cv-1a(8); 5634]   "
ὑπηκούσατε   aor act ind 2 pl
  [2t; cv-1a(8); 5634]   "
ὑπήκουσεν   aor act ind 3 sg [3t; cv-1a(8); 5634]   "
ὑπήνεγκα   aor act ind 1 sg
  [2Ti 3:11; cv-1c(1); 5722]   ὑποφέρω
ὑπήντησαν   aor act ind 3 pl
  [2t; cv-1d(1a); 5636]   ὑπαντάω
ὑπήντησεν   aor act ind 3 sg
  [6t; cv-1d(1a); 5636]   "
ὑπηρέται   nom pl masc [9t; n-1f; 5677]   ὑπηρέτης
ὑπηρέταις   dat pl masc [Ac 5:26; n-1f; 5677]   "
ὑπηρέτας   acc pl masc [3t; n-1f; 5677]   "
ὑπηρετεῖν   pres act inf
  [Ac 24:23; v-1d(2a); 5676]   ὑπηρετέω

ὑπηρετέω   {5676, v-1d(2a)}
  [-, ὑπηρέτησα, -, -, -] *to subserve*, Acts 13:36; *to
  relieve, supply*, Acts 20:34; *to render kind offices*,
  Acts 24:23*

ὑπηρέτῃ   dat sg masc [2t; n-1f; 5677]   ὑπηρέτης
ὑπηρέτην   acc sg masc [2t; n-1f; 5677]   "

ὑπηρέτης, ου, ὁ   {5677, n-1f}
  pr. *an under-rower, a rower, one of a ship's crew; a
  minister, attendant, servant; an attendant* on a
  magistrate, *officer*, Matt 5:25; *an attendant* or
  officer of the Sanhedrin, Matt 26:58; *an
  attendant*, or *servant* of a synagogue, Luke 4:20;
  a minister, attendant, assistant in any work, Luke
  1:2; John 18:36

ὑπηρέτησαν   aor act ind 3 pl
  [Ac 20:34; v-1d(2a); 5676]   ὑπηρετέω
ὑπηρετήσας   aor act ptcp nom sg masc
  [Ac 13:36; v-1d(2a); 5676]   "
ὑπηρετῶν   gen pl masc [3t; n-1f; 5677]   ὑπηρέτης
ὑπῆρχεν   imperf act ind 3 sg
  [5t; cv-1b(2); 5639]   ὑπάρχω
ὑπῆρχον   imperf act ind 3 pl
  [2t; cv-1b(2); 5639]   "

ὕπνος, ου, ὁ   {5678, n-2a}
  sleep, Matt 1:24; Luke 9:32; John 11:13; Acts 20:9;
  met. spiritual *sleep*, religious *slumber*, Rom
  13:11*

ὕπνου   gen sg masc [4t; n-2a; 5678]   ὕπνος
ὕπνῳ   dat sg masc [2t; n-2a; 5678]   "

ὑπό   {5679, prep}
  (1) gen., *under*; hence, used to express
  influence, causation, agency; *by*, Matt 1:22
  freq.; *by the agency of, at the hands of*, 2 Cor 11:24;
  Heb 12:3. (2) acc., *under*, with the idea of
  motion associated, Matt 5:15; *under*, John 1:49;

1 Cor 10:1; *under* subjection to, Rom 6:14; 1 Tim 6:1; of time, *at, about,* Acts 5:21

ὑπό   prep-gen [139t; prep; 5679]   "
ὑπό   prep-acc [47t; prep; 5679]   ὑπό

ὑποβάλλω   {5680, cv-2d(1)}
[-, ὑπέβαλον, -, -, -] *to cast under;* met. *to suggest, instigate,* Acts 6:11*

ὑπογραμμόν   acc sg masc
[1P 2:21; n-2a; 5681]   ὑπογραμμός

ὑπογραμμός, οῦ, ὁ   {5681, n-2a}
pr. *a copy to write after;* met. *an example for imitation, pattern,* 1 Peter 2:21*

ὑποδέδεκται   perf mid ind 3 sg
[Ac 17:7; cv-1b(2); 5685]   ὑποδέχομαι
ὑποδεδεμένους   perf mid ptcp acc pl masc
[Mk 6:9; cv-1d(2b); 5686]   ὑποδέω

ὑπόδειγμα, ατος, τό   {5682, n-3c(4)}
a token, intimation; an example, model, proposed for imitation or admonition, John 13:15; Heb 4:11; James 5:10; 2 Peter 2:6; *a copy,* Heb 8:5; 9:23*

ὑπόδειγμα   acc sg neut
[3t; n-3c(4); 5682]   ὑπόδειγμα
ὑποδείγματα   acc pl neut
[Hb 9:23; n-3c(4); 5682]   "
ὑποδείγματι   dat sg neut [2t; n-3c(4); 5682]   "

ὑποδείκνυμι   {5683, cv-3c(2)}
[ὑποδείξω, ὑπέδειξα, -, -, -] also spelled ὑποδεικνύω, *to indicate,* Acts 20:35; *to intimate, suggest, show, prove,* Matt 3:7; Luke 3:7; 6:47; 12:5; Acts 9:16*

ὑποδεικνύω, see ὑποδείκνυμι   {5684}

ὑποδείξω   fut act ind 1 sg
[3t; cv-3c(2); 5683]   ὑποδείκνυμι
ὑποδεξαμένη   aor mid ptcp nom sg fem
[Jm 2:25; cv-1b(2); 5685]   ὑποδέχομαι

ὑποδέχομαι   {5685, cv-1b(2)}
[-, ὑπεδεξάμην, -, ὑποδέδεγμαι, -] *to give reception to; to receive as a guest, welcome, entertain,* Luke 10:38; 19:6; Acts 17:7; James 2:25*

ὑποδέω   {5686, cv-1d(2b)}
[-, ὑπέδησα, -, ὑποδέδεμαι, -] *to bind under,* mid. *to bind under one's self, put on one's own feet,* Acts 12:8; *to shoe,* Eph 6:15; pass. *to be shod,* Mark 6:9*

ὑπόδημα, ατος, τό   {5687, n-3c(4)}
anything bound under; a sandal, Matt 3:11; 10:10

ὑπόδημα   acc sg neut [2t; n-3c(4); 5687]   ὑπόδημα
ὑποδήματα   acc pl neut [4t; n-3c(4); 5687]   "
ὑποδήματος   gen sg neut [Jn 1:27; n-3c(4); 5687] "
ὑποδημάτων   gen pl neut [3t; n-3c(4); 5687]   "
ὑποδήσαι   aor mid imperative 2 sg
[Ac 12:8; cv-1d(2b); 5686]   ὑποδέω
ὑποδησάμενοι   aor mid ptcp nom pl masc
[Ep 6:15; cv-1d(2b); 5686]   "

ὑπόδικος, ον   {5688, a-3a}
under a legal process; also, *under a judicial*

sentence; *under verdict* to an opposed party in a suit, *liable to penalty,* Rom 3:19*

ὑπόδικος   nom sg masc
[Rm 3:19; a-3a; 5688]   ὑπόδικος
ὑποδραμόντες   aor act ptcp nom pl masc
[Ac 27:16; cv-1b(2); 5720]   ὑποτρέχω

ὑποζύγιον, ου, τό   {5689, n-2c}
an animal subject to the yoke, a beast of burden; in N.T. spc. *an ass, donkey,* Matt 21:5; 2 Peter 2:16*

ὑποζύγιον   nom sg neut
[2P 2:16; n-2c; 5689]   ὑποζύγιον
ὑποζυγίου   gen sg neut [Mt 21:5; n-2c; 5689]   "

ὑποζώννυμι   {5690, cv-3c(1)}
[-, -, -, -, -] *to gird under,* of persons; *to undergird* a ship with cables, chains, etc., Acts 27:17*

ὑποζωννύντες   pres act ptcp nom pl masc
[Ac 27:17; cv-3c(1); 5690]   ὑποζώννυμι

ὑποκάτω   {5691, adverb}
can function as an improper prep., *under, beneath, underneath,* Mark 6:11; 7:28; met. Heb 2:8

ὑποκάτω   adverb [11t; adverb; 5691]   ὑποκάτω

ὑπόκειμαι   {5692}
[-, -, -, -, -] *to be found,* Luke 6:42 v.l.*

ὑποκρίνομαι   {5693, cv-1c(2)}
[-, -, -, -, ὑπεκρίθην] *to answer, respond; to act a part* upon the stage; hence, *to assume a counterfeit character; to pretend, feign,* Luke 20:20*

ὑποκρινομένους   pres mid ptcp acc pl masc
[Lk 20:20; cv-1c(2); 5693]   ὑποκρίνομαι
ὑποκρίσει   dat sg fem
[2t; n-3e(5b); 5694]   ὑπόκρισις
ὑποκρίσεις   acc pl fem [1P 2:1; n-3e(5b); 5694]   "
ὑποκρίσεως   gen sg fem
[Mt 23:28; n-3e(5b); 5694]   "
ὑπόκρισιν   acc sg fem [Mk 12:15; n-3e(5b); 5694] "

ὑπόκρισις, εως, ἡ   {5694, n-3e(5b)}
a response, answer; an over-acting personification, acting; hypocrisy, simulation, Matt 23:28; Mark 12:15; Luke 12:1; Gal 2:13; 1 Tim 4:2; James 5:12 v.l.; 1 Peter 2:1*

ὑπόκρισις   nom sg fem [Lk 12:1; n-3e(5b); 5694]   "
ὑποκριτά   voc sg masc [2t; n-1f; 5695]   ὑποκριτής
ὑποκριταί   nom pl masc [3t; n-1f; 5695]   "
ὑποκριταί   voc pl masc [10t; n-1f; 5695]   "

ὑποκριτής, οῦ, ὁ   {5695, n-1f}
the giver of an answer or *response; a stageplayer, actor;* in N.T. *a* moral or religious *counterfeit, a hypocrite,* Matt 6:2, 5, 16; 7:5

ὑποκριτῶν   gen pl masc [2t; n-1f; 5695]   "
ὑπολαβών   aor act ptcp nom sg masc
[Lk 10:30; cv-3a(2b); 5696]   ὑπολαμβάνω
ὑπολαμβάνειν   pres act inf
[3J 8; cv-3a(2b); 5696]   "
ὑπολαμβάνετε   pres act ind 2 pl
[Ac 2:15; cv-3a(2b); 5696]   "

ὑπολαμβάνω   {5696, cv-3a(2b)}
[-, ὑπέλαβον, -, -, -] *to take up*, by placing one's
self underneath what is taken up; *to catch away,*
withdraw, Acts 1:9; *to take up* discourse by
continuation; hence, *to answer,* Luke 10:30; *to*
take up a notion, *to think, suppose,* Luke 7:43;
Acts 2:15; *receive as a guest,* 3 John 8*

ὑπολαμβάνω   pres act ind 1 sg
    [Lk 7:43; cv-3a(2b); 5696]   "

ὑπολαμπάς, άδος, ἡ   {5697, n-3c(2)}
window, Acts 20:8 v.l.*

ὑπόλειμμα, ατος, τό   {5698, n-3c(4)}
a remnant, Rom 9:27*

ὑπόλειμμα   nom sg neut
    [Rm 9:27; n-3c(4); 5698]   ὑπόλειμμα

ὑπολείπω   {5699, cv-1b(1)}
[-, -, -, -, ὑπελείφθην] *to leave remaining, leave*
behind; pass. *to be left surviving,* Rom 11:3*

ὑπολήνιον, ου, τό   {5700, n-2c}
a vat, placed under the press, ληνός, to receive
the juice, Mark 12:1*

ὑπολήνιον   acc sg neut
    [Mk 12:1; n-2c; 5700]   ὑπολήνιον

ὑπολιμπάνω   {5701}
[-, -, -, -, -] *to leave behind,* 1 Peter 2:21*

ὑπολιμπάνων   pres act ptcp nom sg masc
    [1P 2:21; cv-; 5701]   ὑπολιμπάνω
ὑπομείναντας   aor act ptcp acc pl masc
    [Jm 5:11; cv-1c(2); 5702]   ὑπομένω
ὑπομείνας   aor act ptcp nom sg masc
    [3t; cv-1c(2); 5702]   "
ὑπομεμενηκότα   perf act ptcp acc sg masc
    [Hb 12:3; cv-1c(2); 5702]   "
ὑπομένει   pres act ind 3 sg [2t; cv-1c(2); 5702]   "
ὑπομενεῖτε   fut act ind 2 pl
    [2t; cv-1c(2); 5702]   "
ὑπομένετε   pres act ind 2 pl
    [Hb 12:7; cv-1c(2); 5702]   "
ὑπομένομεν   pres act ind 1 pl
    [2Ti 2:12; cv-1c(2); 5702]   "
ὑπομένοντες   pres act ptcp nom pl masc
    [Rm 12:12; cv-1c(2); 5702]   "

ὑπομένω   {5702, cv-1c(2)}
[(ὑπέμενον), ὑπομενῶ, ὑπέμεινα, ὑπομεμένηκα, -,
-] intrans. *to remain* or *stay behind,* when others
have departed, Luke 2:43; trans. *to bear up*
under, endure, suffer patiently, 1 Cor 13:7; Heb
10:32; absol. *to continue firmly, hold out, remain*
constant, persevere, Matt 10:22; 24:13

ὑπομένω   pres act ind 1 sg
    [2Ti 2:10; cv-1c(2); 5702]   "
ὑπομίμνησκε   pres act imperative 2 sg
    [2t; cv-5a; 5703]   ὑπομιμνήσκω
ὑπομιμνήσκειν   pres act inf
    [2P 1:12; cv-5a; 5703]   "

ὑπομιμνήσκω   {5703, cv-5a}
[ὑπομνήσω, ὑπέμνησα, -, -, ὑπεμνήσθην]
remember, remind, John 14:26; Titus 3:1; 2 Peter
1:12; Jude 5; *to suggest recollection of, remind*

others *of,* 2 Tim 2:14; 3 John 10; *to call to mind,*
recollect, remember, Luke 22:61*

ὑπομνῆσαι   aor act inf   [Jd 5; cv-5a; 5703]   "
ὑπομνήσει   dat sg fem
    [2t; n-3e(5b); 5704]   ὑπόμνησις
ὑπομνήσει   fut act ind 3 sg
    [Jn 14:26; cv-5a; 5703]   ὑπομιμνήσκω
ὑπόμνησιν   acc sg fem
    [2Ti 1:5; n-3e(5b); 5704]   ὑπόμνησις

ὑπόμνησις, εως, ἡ   {5704, n-3e(5b)}
a putting in mind, act of reminding, 2 Peter 1:13;
3:1; *remembrance, recollection,* 2 Tim 1:5*

ὑπομνήσω   fut act ind 1 sg
    [3J 10; cv-5a; 5703]   ὑπομιμνήσκω

ὑπομονή, ῆς, ἡ   {5705, n-1b}
patient endurance, 2 Cor 12:12; Col 1:11; *patient*
awaiting, Luke 21:19; *a patient frame of mind,*
patience, Rom 5:3, 4; 15:4, 5; James 1:3;
perseverance, Rom 2:7; *endurance* in adherence
to an object, 1 Thess 1:3; 2 Thess 3:5; Rev 1:9; ἐν
ὑπομονῇ and δι᾿ ὑπομονῆς, *constantly,*
perseveringly, Luke 8:15; Rom 8:25; Heb 12:1; *an*
enduring of affliction, etc., *the act of suffering,*
undergoing, etc., 2 Cor 1:6; 6:4

ὑπομονή   nom sg fem [4t; n-1b; 5705]   ὑπομονή
ὑπομονῇ   dat sg fem [9t; n-1b; 5705]   "
ὑπομονήν   acc sg fem [11t; n-1b; 5705]   "
ὑπομονῆς   gen sg fem [8t; n-1b; 5705]   "
ὑπονοεῖτε   pres act ind 2 pl
    [Ac 13:25; cv-1d(2a); 5706]   ὑπονοέω

ὑπονοέω   {5706, cv-1d(2a)}
[(ὑπενόουν), -, ὑπενόησα, -, -, -] *to suspect; to*
suppose, deem, Acts 13:25; 25:18; 27:27*

ὑπόνοια, ας, ἡ   {5707, n-1a}
suspicion, surmise, 1 Tim 6:4*

ὑπόνοιαι   nom pl fem
    [1Ti 6:4; n-1a; 5707]   ὑπόνοια

ὑποπιάζω   {5708, cv-2a(1)}
v.l. spelling for ὑπωπιαχζω

ὑποπλέω   {5709, cv-1a(7)}
[-, ὑπέπλευσα, -, -, -] *to sail under; to sail under*
the lee, or, *to the south of,* an island, etc., Acts
27:4, 7*

ὑποπνέω   {5710, cv-1a(7)}
[-, ὑπέπνευσα, -, -, -] *to blow gently,* as the wind,
Acts 27:13*

ὑποπνεύσαντος   aor act ptcp gen sg masc
    [Ac 27:13; cv-1a(7); 5710]   ὑποπνέω

ὑποπόδιον, ου, τό   {5711, n-2c}
a footstool, James 2:3; Matt 22:44 v.l.

ὑποπόδιον   nom sg neut
    [2t; n-2c; 5711]   ὑποπόδιον
ὑποπόδιον   acc sg neut [5t; n-2c; 5711]   "
ὑποστάσει   dat sg fem
    [2t; n-3e(5b); 5712]   ὑπόστασις
ὑποστάσεως   gen sg fem [2t; n-3e(5b); 5712]   "

ὑπόστασις, εως, ἡ {5712, n-3e(5b)}
pr. *a standing under; a taking* of a thing *upon one's self; an assumed position, an assumption* of a specific character, 2 Cor 11:17; *an engagement undertaken* with regard to the conduct of others, *a vouching,* 2 Cor 9:4; or of one's self, *a pledged profession,* Heb 3:14; *an assured impression, a mental realizing,* Heb 11:1; *a substructure, basis; subsistence, essence,* Heb 1:3*

ὑπόστασις nom sg fem [Hb 11:1; n-3e(5b); 5712] "
ὑποστείληται aor mid subj 3 sg
[Hb 10:38; cv-2d(1); 5713] ὑποστέλλω

ὑποστέλλω {5713, cv-2d(1)}
[(ὑπέστελλον), -, ὑπέστειλα, -, -, -] pr. *to let down, to stow away; to draw back, withdraw,* Gal 2:12; mid. *to shrink back, recoil,* Heb 10:38; *to keep back, suppress, conceal,* Acts 20:20, 27*

ὑποστολή, ῆς, ἡ {5714, n-1b}
a shrinking back, Heb 10:39*

ὑποστολῆς gen sg fem
[Hb 10:39; n-1b; 5714] ὑποστολή
ὑπόστρεφε pres act imperative 2 sg
[Lk 8:39; cv-1b(1); 5715] ὑποστρέφω
ὑποστρέφειν pres act inf [4t; cv-1b(1); 5715] "
ὑποστρέφοντι pres act ptcp dat sg masc
[Hb 7:1; cv-1b(1); 5715] "

ὑποστρέφω {5715, cv-1b(1)}
[(ὑπέστρεφον), ὑποστρέψω, ὑπέστρεψα, -, -, -] *to turn back, return,* Mark 14:40; Luke 1:56; 2:39, 43, 45

ὑποστρέφων pres act ptcp nom sg masc
[Ac 8:28; cv-1b(1); 5715] "
ὑποστρέψαι aor act inf [2t; cv-1b(1); 5715] "
ὑποστρέψαντες aor act ptcp nom pl masc
[3t; cv-1b(1); 5715] "
ὑποστρέψαντι aor act ptcp dat sg masc
[Ac 22:17; cv-1b(1); 5715] "
ὑποστρέψασαι aor act ptcp nom pl fem
[2t; cv-1b(1); 5715] "
ὑποστρέψω fut act ind 1 sg
[Lk 11:24; cv-1b(1); 5715] "

ὑποστρωννύω {5716, cv-3c(1)}
[(ὑπεστρώννυον), -, ὑπέστρωσα, -, -, -] *to stow under, spread underneath,* Luke 19:36*

ὑποταγέντων aor pass ptcp gen pl masc
[1P 3:22; cv-2b; 5718] ὑποτάσσω

ὑποταγή, ῆς, ἡ {5717, n-1b}
subordination, 1 Tim 3:4; *submissiveness, obedience,* 2 Cor 9:13; Gal 2:5; 1 Tim 2:11*

ὑποταγῇ dat sg fem [4t; n-1b; 5717] ὑποταγή
ὑποταγῇ aor pass subj 3 sg
[1C 15:28; cv-2b; 5718] ὑποτάσσω
ὑποταγήσεται fut pass ind 3 sg
[1C 15:28; cv-2b; 5718] "
ὑποταγησόμεθα fut pass ind 1 pl
[Hb 12:9; cv-2b; 5718] "
ὑποτάγητε aor pass imperative 2 pl
[3t; cv-2b; 5718] "
ὑποτάξαι aor act inf [2t; cv-2b; 5718] "

ὑποτάξαντα aor act ptcp acc sg masc
[Rm 8:20; cv-2b; 5718] "
ὑποτάξαντι aor act ptcp dat sg masc
[1C 15:28; cv-2b; 5718] "
ὑποτάξαντος aor act ptcp gen sg masc
[1C 15:27; cv-2b; 5718] "
ὑποτάσσεσθαι pres pass inf [3t; cv-2b; 5718] "
ὑποτάσσεσθε pres pass imperative 2 pl
[Cl 3:18; cv-2b; 5718] "
ὑποτασσέσθω pres pass imperative 3 sg
[Rm 13:1; cv-2b; 5718] "
ὑποτασσέσθωσαν pres pass imperative 3 pl
[1C 14:34; cv-2b; 5718] "
ὑποτάσσεται pres pass ind 3 sg
[5t; cv-2b; 5718] "
ὑποτάσσησθε pres pass subj 2 pl
[1C 16:16; cv-2b; 5718] "
ὑποτασσόμεναι pres pass ptcp nom pl fem
[2t; cv-2b; 5718] "
ὑποτασσομένας pres pass ptcp acc pl fem
[Ti 2:5; cv-2b; 5718] "
ὑποτασσόμενοι pres pass ptcp nom pl masc
[2t; cv-2b; 5718] "
ὑποτασσόμενος pres pass ptcp nom sg masc
[Lk 2:51; cv-2b; 5718] "

ὑποτάσσω {5718, cv-2b}
[-, ὑπέταξα, -, ὑποτέταγμαι, ὑπετάγην] *to place* or *arrange under; to subordinate,* 1 Cor 15:27; *to bring under influence,* Rom 8:20; pass. *to be subordinated,* 1 Cor 14:32; *to be brought under a state* or *influence,* Rom 8:20; mid. *to submit one's self, render obedience, be submissive,* Luke 2:51; 10:17

ὑποτεταγμένα perf pass ptcp acc pl neut
[Hb 2:8; cv-2b; 5718] "
ὑποτέτακται perf pass ind 3 sg
[1C 15:27; cv-2b; 5718] "
ὑποτιθέμενος pres mid ptcp nom sg masc
[1Ti 4:6; cv-6a; 5719] ὑποτίθημι

ὑποτίθημι {5719, cv-6a}
[-, ὑπέθηκα, -, -, -] *to place under; to lay down* the neck beneath the sword of the executioner, *to set on imminent risk,* Rom 16:4; mid. *to suggest, recommend to attention,* 1 Tim 4:6*

ὑποτρέχω {5720, cv-1b(2)}
[-, ὑπέδραμον, -, -, -] *to run under;* as a nautical term, *to sail under* the lee of, Acts 27:16*

ὑποτύπωσιν acc sg fem
[2t; n-3e(5b); 5721] ὑποτύπωσις

ὑποτύπωσις, εως, ἡ {5721, n-3e(5b)}
a sketch, delineation; a form, formula, presentment, sample, 2 Tim 1:13; *a pattern, a model representation,* 1 Tim 1:16*

ὑποφέρει pres act ind 3 sg
[1P 2:19; cv-1c(1); 5722] ὑποφέρω

ὑποφέρω {5722, cv-1c(1)}
[-, ὑπήνεγκα, -, -, -] *to bear under; to bear up under, support, sustain,* 1 Cor 10:13; *to endure patiently,* 1 Peter 2:19; *to undergo,* 2 Tim 3:11*

ὑποχωρέω {5723, cv-1d(2a)}
[-, ὑπεχώρησα, -, -, -] *to withdraw, retire, retreat,*
Luke 5:16; 9:10; 20:20 v.l.*

ὑποχωρῶν pres act ptcp nom sg masc
[Lk 5:16; cv-1d(2a); 5723] ὑποχωρέω

ὑπωπιάζῃ pres act subj 3 sg
[Lk 18:5; v-2a(1); 5724] ὑπωπιάζω

ὑπωπιάζω {5724, v-2a(1)}
[-, -, -, -, -] pr. *to strike one upon the parts beneath
the eye; to beat black and blue;* hence, *to discipline
by hardship, coerce,* 1 Cor 9:27; met. *to weary* by
continual importunities, *pester,* Luke 18:5*

ὑπωπιάζω pres act ind 1 sg
[1C 9:27; v-2a(1); 5724] "

ὗς, ὑός, ἡ {5725, n-3e(1)}
a hog, swine, boar, sow, 2 Peter 2:22*

ὗς nom sg fem [2P 2:22; n-3e(1); 5725] ὗς

ὑσσός, οῦ, ὁ {5726, n-2a}
javelin, John 19:29 v.l.*

ὕσσωπος, οῦ, ἡ {5727, n-2b}
hyssop, in N.T., however, not the plant usually
so named, but probably the caper plant; *a
bunch of hyssop,* Heb 9:19; *a hyssop stalk,* John
19:29*

ὑσσώπου gen sg fem [Hb 9:19; n-2b; 5727] ὕσσωπος
ὑσσώπῳ dat sg fem [Jn 19:29; n-2b; 5727] "
ὑστερεῖ pres act ind 3 sg
[Mk 10:21; v-1d(2a); 5728] ὑστερέω
ὑστερεῖσθαι pres pass inf [3t; v-1d(2a); 5728] "

ὑστερέω {5728, v-1d(2a)}
[-, ὑστέρησα, ὑστέρηκα, ὑστέρημαι, ὑστερήθην]
to be behind in place or time, *to be in the rear; to
fall short of, be inferior to,* 2 Cor 11:5; 12:11; *to fail
of, fail to attain,* Heb 4:1; *to be in want of, lack,*
Luke 22:35; *to be wanting,* Mark 10:21; absol. *to
be defective, in default,* Matt 19:20; 1 Cor 12:24; *to
run short,* John 2:3; mid. *to come short of* a
privilege or standard, *to miss,* Rom 3:23; absol.
to come short, be below standard, 1 Cor 1:7; *to come
short* of sufficiency, *to be in need, want,* Luke
15:14; 2 Cor 11:9; Phil 4:12; Heb 11:37; *to be a
loser, suffer detriment,* 1 Cor 8:8; in N.T. ὑστερεῖν
ἀπό, *to be backwards with respect to, to slight,* Heb
12:15*

ὑστερηθείς aor pass ptcp nom sg masc
[2C 11:9; v-1d(2a); 5728] "
ὑστερηκέναι perf act inf [2t; v-1d(2a); 5728] "

ὑστέρημα, ατος, τό {5729, n-3c(4)}
a shortcoming, defect; personal *shortcoming,* 1
Cor 16:17; Phil 2:30; Col 1:24; 1 Thess 3:10; *want,
need, poverty, penury,* Luke 21:4; 2 Cor 8:14; 9:12;
11:9*

ὑστέρημα acc sg neut
[5t; n-3c(4); 5729] ὑστέρημα
ὑστερήματα acc pl neut [3t; n-3c(4); 5729] "
ὑστερήματος gen sg neut
[Lk 21:4; n-3c(4); 5729] "
ὑστέρησα aor act ind 1 sg
[2C 12:11; v-1d(2a); 5728] ὑστερέω

ὑστερήσαντος aor act ptcp gen sg masc
[Jn 2:3; v-1d(2a); 5728] "
ὑστερήσατε aor act ind 2 pl
[Lk 22:35; v-1d(2a); 5728] "
ὑστερήσεως gen sg fem
[Mk 12:44; n-3e(5b); 5730] ὑστέρησις
ὑστέρησιν acc sg fem [Pp 4:11; n-3e(5b); 5730] "

ὑστέρησις, εως, ἡ {5730, n-3e(5b)}
want, need, Mark 12:44; Phil 4:11*

ὑστέροις dat pl masc comparative
[1Ti 4:1; a-1a(1); 5731] ὕστερος
ὕστερον acc sg neut, can function
adverbially [11t; a-1a(1); 5731] "

ὕστερος, α, ον {5731, a-1a(1)}
posterior in place or time; *subsequent, later, last,
finally,* 1 Tim 4:1; Matt 21:31

ὑστερούμεθα pres pass ind 1 pl
[1C 8:8; v-1d(2a); 5728] ὑστερέω
ὑστερούμενοι pres pass ptcp nom pl masc
[Hb 11:37; v-1d(2a); 5728] "
ὑστερουμένῳ pres pass ptcp dat sg neut
[1C 12:24; v-1d(2a); 5728] "
ὑστεροῦνται pres mid ind 3 pl
[Rm 3:23; v-1d(2a); 5728] "
ὑστερῶ pres act ind 1 sg
[Mt 19:20; v-1d(2a); 5728] "
ὑστερῶν pres act ptcp nom sg masc
[Hb 12:15; v-1d(2a); 5728] "
ὑφ' prep-gen [8t; prep; 5679] "
ὑφ' prep-acc [Rm 3:9; prep; 5679] ὑπό

ὑφαίνω {5732, v-2d(4)}
[-, -, -, -, -] *to weave,* Luke 12:27 v.l.*

ὑφαντός, ή, όν {5733, a-1a(2a)}
woven, John 19:23*

ὑφαντός nom sg masc
[Jn 19:23; a-1a(2a); 5733] ὑφαντός
ὕψει dat sg neut [Jm 1:9; n-3d(2b); 5737] ὕψος
ὑψηλά acc pl neut [2t; a-1a(2a); 5734] ὑψηλός
ὑψηλοῖς dat pl masc [Hb 1:3; a-1a(2a); 5734] "
ὑψηλόν nom sg neut [Lk 16:15; a-1a(2a); 5734] "
ὑψηλόν acc sg neut [5t; a-1a(2a); 5734] "

ὑψηλός, ή, όν {5734, a-1a(2a)}
high, lofty, elevated, Matt 4:8; 17:1; τὰ ὑψηλά, *the
highest* heaven, Heb 1:3; *upraised,* Acts 13:17;
met. *highly esteemed,* Luke 16:15; φρονεῖν τὰ
ὑψηλά, *to have lofty thoughts, be proud, arrogant,*
Rom 12:16

ὑψηλότερος nom sg masc comparative
[Hb 7:26; a-1a(2a); 5734] "
ὑψηλοῦ gen sg masc [Ac 13:17; a-1a(2a); 5734] "
ὑψηλοφρονεῖν pres act inf
[1Ti 6:17; cv-1d(2a); 5735] ὑψηλοφρονέω

ὑψηλοφρονέω {5735, cv-1d(2a)}
[-, -, -, -, -] *to have lofty thoughts, be proud,
haughty,* Rom 11:20 v.l.; 1 Tim 6:17*

ὑψίστοις dat pl neut superlative
[4t; a-1a(2a); 5736] ὕψιστος

ὕψιστος, η, ον {5736, a-1a(2a)}
highest, loftiest, most elevated; τὰ ὕψιστα, from
the Hebrew, *the highest* heaven, Matt 21:9; Mark
11:10; met. ὁ ὕψιστος, *the Most High,* Mark 5:7

ὕψιστος nom sg masc superlative
 [Ac 7:48; a-1a(2a); 5736] "
ὑψίστου gen sg masc superlative
 [8t; a-1a(2a); 5736] "

ὕψος, ους, τό {5737, n-3d(2b)}
height, Eph 3:18; Rev 21:16; met. *exaltation,
dignity, eminence,* James 1:9; from the Hebrew,
the height of heaven, Luke 1:78; 24:49; Eph 4:8*

ὕψος nom sg neut [2t; n-3d(2b); 5737] ὕψος
ὕψος acc sg neut [Ep 4:8; n-3d(2b); 5737] "
ὕψους gen sg neut [2t; n-3d(2b); 5737] "

ὑψόω {5738, v-1d(3)}
[ὑψώσω, ὕψωσα, -, -, ὑψώθην] *to raise aloft, lift
up,* John 3:14; 8:28; met. *to elevate* in condition,
uplift, exalt, Matt 11:23; 23:12; Luke 1:52

ὑψωθείς aor pass ptcp nom sg masc
 [Ac 2:33; v-1d(3); 5738] ὑψόω
ὑψωθῆναι aor pass inf [2t; v-1d(3); 5738] "
ὑψωθήσεται fut pass ind 3 sg
 [3t; v-1d(3); 5738] "
ὑψωθήσῃ fut pass ind 2 sg [2t; v-1d(3); 5738] "
ὑψωθῆτε aor pass subj 2 pl
 [2C 11:7; v-1d(3); 5738] "
ὑψωθῶ aor pass subj 1 sg
 [Jn 12:32; v-1d(3); 5738] "

ὕψωμα, ατος, τό {5739, n-3c(4)}
height, Rom 8:39; *a towering* of self-conceit,
presumption, 2 Cor 10:5*

ὕψωμα nom sg neut
 [Rm 8:39; n-3c(4); 5739] ὕψωμα
ὕψωμα acc sg neut [2C 10:5; n-3c(4); 5739] "
ὑψῶν pres act ptcp nom sg masc
 [2t; v-1d(3); 5738] ὑψόω
ὑψώσει fut act ind 3 sg [2t; v-1d(3); 5738] "
ὕψωσεν aor act ind 3 sg [4t; v-1d(3); 5738] "
ὑψώσῃ aor act subj 3 sg
 [1P 5:6; v-1d(3); 5738] "
ὑψώσητε aor act subj 2 pl
 [Jn 8:28; v-1d(3); 5738] "

φ

φάγε aor act imperative 2 sg
 [4t; v-1b(3); 2266] ἐσθίω
φαγεῖν aor act inf [34t; v-1b(3); 2266] "
φάγεσαι fut mid ind 2 sg
 [Lk 17:8; v-1b(3); 2266] "
φάγεται fut mid ind 3 sg [2t; v-1b(3); 2266] "
φάγετε aor act imperative 2 pl
 [Mt 26:26; v-1b(3); 2266] "
φάγῃ aor act subj 3 sg [4t; v-1b(3); 2266] "
φάγῃς aor act subj 2 sg
 [Mk 14:12; v-1b(3); 2266] "
φάγητε aor act subj 2 pl [5t; v-1b(3); 2266] "

φάγοι aor act opt 3 sg [Mk 11:14; v-1b(3); 2266] "
φάγονται fut mid ind 3 pl
 [Rv 17:16; v-1b(3); 2266] "
φαγόντες aor act ptcp nom pl masc
 [2t; v-1b(3); 2266] "

φάγος, ου, ὁ {5741, n-2a}
a glutton, Matt 11:19; Luke 7:34*

φάγος nom sg masc [2t; n-2a; 5741] φάγος
φάγω aor act subj 1 sg [5t; v-1b(3); 2266] ἐσθίω
φάγωμεν aor act subj 1 pl [5t; v-1b(3); 2266] "
φάγωσιν aor act subj 3 pl [6t; v-1b(3); 2266] "
φαιλόνην acc sg masc
 [2Ti 4:13; n-1f; 5742] φαιλόνης

φαιλόνης, ου, ὁ {5742, n-1f}
a thick cloak for travelling, with a hood, 2 Tim
4:13*

φαίνει pres act ind 3 sg
 [3t; v-2d(4); 5743] φαίνω
φαίνεσθε pres mid ind 2 pl
 [Pp 2:15; v-2d(4); 5743] "
φαίνεσθε pres pass ind 2 pl
 [Mt 23:28; v-2d(4); 5743] "
φαίνεται pres mid ind 3 sg [2t; v-2d(4); 5743] "
φαίνεται pres pass ind 3 sg [2t; v-2d(4); 5743] "
φαινομένη pres pass ptcp nom sg fem
 [Jm 4:14; v-2d(4); 5743] "
φαινομένου pres mid ptcp gen sg masc
 [Mt 2:7; v-2d(4); 5743] "
φαινομένων pres mid ptcp gen pl neut
 [Hb 11:3; v-2d(4); 5743] "
φαίνονται pres pass ind 3 pl
 [Mt 23:27; v-2d(4); 5743] "
φαίνοντι pres act ptcp dat sg masc
 [2P 1:19; v-2d(4); 5743] "

φαίνω {5743, v-2d(4)}
[(ἐφαινόμην), φανοῦμαι, ἔφανα, -, -, ἐφάνην] *to
cause to appear, bring to light;* absol. *to shine,* John
1:5; 5:35; 2 Peter 1:19; 1 John 2:8; Rev 1:16; 8:12;
21:23; mid./pass. *to be seen, appear, be visible,*
Matt 1:20; 2:7, 13, 19; τὰ φαινόμενα, *things
visible, things obvious to the senses,* Heb 11:3;
φαίνομαι, *to appear, seen, be in appearance,* Matt
23:27; Luke 24:11; *to appear* in thought, *seen* in
idea, *be a notion,* Mark 14:64

φαίνων pres act ptcp nom sg masc
 [Jn 5:35; v-2d(4); 5743] "
φαίνωσιν pres act subj 3 pl
 [Rv 21:23; v-2d(4); 5743] "

Φάλεκ, ὁ {5744, n-3g(2)}
Peleg, also spelled Φάλεγ, pr. name, indecl.,
Luke 3:35*

Φάλεκ indecl [Lk 3:35; n-3g(2); 5744] Φάλεκ
φανεῖται fut mid ind 3 sg
 [1P 4:18; v-2d(4); 5743] φαίνω
φανερά nom sg fem
 [1Ti 4:15; a-1a(1); 5745] φανερός
φανερά nom pl neut [3t; a-1a(1); 5745] "
φανεροί nom pl masc [1C 11:19; a-1a(1); 5745] "
φανερόν nom sg neut [6t; a-1a(1); 5745] "
φανερόν acc sg masc [2t; a-1a(1); 5745] "

φανερόν   acc sg neut   [2t; a-1a(1); 5745]   "

φανερός, ά, όν   {5745, a-1a(1)}
apparent, manifest, clear, known, well-known,
Mark 4:22; 6:14; Gal 5:19; ἐν φανερῷ, *openly,*
Matt 6:4 v.l., 6 v.l.; also, *in outward guise,*
externally, Rom 2:28

φανερούμενοι   pres pass ptcp nom pl masc
  [2C 3:3; v-1d(3); 5746]   φανερόω
φανερούμενον   pres pass ptcp nom sg neut
  [Ep 5:14; v-1d(3); 5746]   "
φανεροῦντι   pres act ptcp dat sg masc
  [2C 2:14; v-1d(3); 5746]   "
φανερούς   acc pl masc
  [Pp 1:13; a-1a(1); 5745]   φανερός
φανεροῦται   pres pass ind 3 sg
  [Ep 5:13; v-1d(3); 5746]   φανερόω

φανερόω   {5746, v-1d(3)}
  [φανερώσω, ἐφανέρωσα, πεφανέρωκα,
  πεφανέρωμαι, ἐφανερώθην] *to bring to light, to set*
  in a clear light; to manifest, display, John 2:11; 7:4;
  9:3; *to show,* Rom 1:19; 2 Cor 7:12; *to declare,*
  make known, John 17:6; *to disclose,* Mark 4:22; 1
  Cor 4:5; Col 4:4; *to reveal,* Rom 3:21; 16:26; Col
  1:26; *to present to view,* John 21:1, 14; pass. *to*
  make an appearance, Mark 16:12, 14; spc. of
  Christ, *to be* personally *manifested,* John 1:31;
  Col 3:4; 1 Peter 1:20; 5:4; 1 John 3:5; *to be laid*
  bare, appear in true character, 2 Cor 5:10, 11

φανερῷ   dat sg neut   [2t; a-1a(1); 5745]   φανερός
φανερωθεῖσαν   aor pass ptcp acc sg fem
  [2Ti 1:10; v-1d(3); 5746]   φανερόω
φανερωθέντος   aor pass ptcp gen sg masc
  [2t; v-1d(3); 5746]   "
φανερωθέντος   aor pass ptcp gen sg neut
  [Rm 16:26; v-1d(3); 5746]   "
φανερωθῇ   aor pass subj 3 sg
  [10t; v-1d(3); 5746]   "
φανερωθῆναι   aor pass inf   [2t; v-1d(3); 5746]   "
φανερωθήσεσθε   fut pass ind 2 pl
  [Cl 3:4; v-1d(3); 5746]   "
φανερωθῶσιν   aor pass subj 3 pl
  [1J 2:19; v-1d(3); 5746]   "

φανερῶς   {5747, adverb}
  manifestly; clearly, plainly, distinctly, Acts 10:3;
  openly, publicly, Mark 1:45; John 7:10*

φανερῶς   adverb   [3t; adverb; 5747]   φανερῶς
φανερώσαντες   aor act ptcp nom pl masc
  [2C 11:6; v-1d(3); 5746]   φανερόω
φανερώσει   dat sg fem
  [2C 4:2; n-3e(5b); 5748]   φανέρωσις
φανερώσει   fut act ind 3 sg
  [1C 4:5; v-1d(3); 5746]   φανερόω
φανέρωσις, εως, ἡ   {5748, n-3e(5b)}
  a disclosure, clear display, 2 Cor 4:2; *an* outward
  evidencing of a latent principle, active *exhibition,*
  1 Cor 12:7*

φανέρωσις   nom sg fem
  [1C 12:7; n-3e(5b); 5748]   φανέρωσις
φανέρωσον   aor act imperative 2 sg
  [Jn 7:4; v-1d(3); 5746]   φανερόω

φανερώσω   aor act subj 1 sg
  [Cl 4:4; v-1d(3); 5746]   "
φάνῃ   aor act subj 3 sg   [2t; v-2d(4); 5743]   φαίνω
φανῇ   aor pass subj 3 sg
  [Rm 7:13; v-2d(4); 5743]   "
φανῇς   aor pass subj 2 sg
  [Mt 6:18; v-2d(4); 5743]   "
φανήσεται   fut pass ind 3 sg
  [Mt 24:30; v-2d(4); 5743]   "

φανός, οῦ, ὁ   {5749, n-2a}
  a torch, lantern, light, John 18:3*

Φανουήλ, ὁ   {5750, n-3g(2)}
  Phanuel, pr. name, indecl., Luke 2:36*

Φανουήλ   indecl   [Lk 2:36; n-3g(2); 5750]   Φανουήλ
φανταζόμενον   pres pass ptcp nom sg neut
  [Hb 12:21; v-2a(1); 5751]   φαντάζω
φαντάζω   {5751, v-2a(1)}
  [-, -, -, -, -] *to render visible, cause to appear;* pass.
  to appear, be seen; τὸ φανταζόμενον, *the sight,*
  spectacle, Heb 12:21*

φαντασία, ας, ἡ   {5752, n-1a}
  pr. *a rendering visible; a display; pomp, parade,*
  Acts 25:23*

φαντασίας   gen sg fem
  [Ac 25:23; n-1a; 5752]   φαντασία
φάντασμα, ατος, τό   {5753, n-3c(4)}
  a phantom, specter, Matt 14:26; Mark 6:49; Luke
  24:37 v.l.*

φάντασμα   nom sg neut   [2t; n-3c(4); 5753]   φάντασμα
φανῶμεν   aor pass subj 1 pl
  [2C 13:7; v-2d(4); 5743]   φαίνω
φανῶν   gen pl masc   [Jn 18:3; n-2a; 5749]   φανός
φανῶσιν   aor pass subj 3 pl
  [2t; v-2d(4); 5743]   φαίνω

φάραγξ, αγγος, ἡ   {5754, n-3b(2)}
  a cleft, ravine, valley, Luke 3:5*

φάραγξ   nom sg fem   [Lk 3:5; n-3b(2); 5754] φάραγξ
Φαραώ, ὁ   {5755, n-3g(2)}
  Pharaoh, pr. name, indecl., Acts 7:10, 13, 21;
  Rom 9:17; Heb 11:24*

Φαραώ   indecl   [5t; n-3g(2); 5755]   Φαραώ
Φαρές, ὁ   {5756, n-3g(2)}
  Perezs, pr. name, indecl., Matt 1:3; Luke 3:33*

Φαρές   indecl   [3t; n-3g(2); 5756]   Φαρές
Φαρισαῖε   voc sg masc
  [Mt 23:26; n-2a; 5757]   Φαρισαῖος
Φαρισαῖοι   nom pl masc   [44t; n-2a; 5757]   "
Φαρισαῖοι   voc pl masc   [6t; n-2a; 5757]   "
Φαρισαίοις   dat pl masc   [2t; n-2a; 5757]   "

Φαρισαῖος, ου, ὁ   {5757, n-2a}
  a Pharisee, a follower of the sect of the Pharisees, a
  numerous and powerful sect of the Jews,
  distinguished for their ceremonial
  observances, and apparent sanctity of life, and
  for being rigid interpreters of the Mosaic law;
  but who frequently violated its spirit by their
  traditional interpretations and precepts, to

which they ascribed nearly an equal authority with the Old Testament Scriptures, Matt 5:20; 12:2; 23:14

Φαρισαῖος   nom sg masc   [9t; n-2a; 5757]   "
Φαρισαίου   gen sg masc   [2t; n-2a; 5757]   "
Φαρισαίους   acc pl masc   [5t; n-2a; 5757]   "
Φαρισαίων   gen pl masc   [29t; n-2a; 5757]   "

φαρμακεία, ας, ἡ   {5758, n-1a}
employment of drugs for any purpose; *sorcery, magic, enchantment*, Rev 9:21 v.l.; 18:23; Gal 5:20*

φαρμακεία   nom sg fem
[Ga 5:20; n-1a; 5758]   φαρμακεία
φαρμακείᾳ   dat sg fem   [Rv 18:23; n-1a; 5758]   "

φαρμακεύς, έως, ὁ   {5759, n-3e(5b)}
pr. *one who deals in drugs; an enchanter, magician, sorcerer*, Acts 21:8 v.l.*

φάρμακοι   nom pl masc
[Rv 22:15; n-2a; 5761]   φάρμακος
φαρμάκοις   dat pl masc   [Rv 21:8; n-2a; 5761]   "

φάρμακον, ου, τό   {5760, n-2c}
a drug; an enchantment; magic potion, charm, Rev 9:21*

φάρμακος, ου, ὁ   {5761, n-2a}
a sorcerer, magician, Rev 21:8; 22:15*

φαρμάκων   gen pl neut
[Rv 9:21; n-2c; 5760]   φάρμακον
φασίν   pres act ind 3 pl   [Rm 3:8; v-6b; 5774]   φημί

φάσις, εως, ἡ   {5762, n-3e(5b)}
report, information, Acts 21:31*

φάσις   nom sg fem   [Ac 21:31; n-3e(5b); 5762]   φάσις
φάσκοντες   pres act ptcp nom pl masc
[2t; v-5a; 5763]   φάσκω

φάσκω   {5763, v-5a}
[(ἔφασκον), -, -, -, -, -] *to assert, affirm*, Acts 24:9; 25:19; Rom 1:22; Rev 2:2 v.l.*

φάτνη, ης, ἡ   {5764, n-1b}
a manger, stall, Luke 2:7, 12, 16; 13:15*

φάτνῃ   dat sg fem   [3t; n-1b; 5764]   φάτνη
φάτνης   gen sg fem   [Lk 13:15; n-1b; 5764]   "
φαῦλα   acc pl neut   [2t; a-1a(2a); 5765]   φαῦλος
φαῦλον   nom sg neut   [Jm 3:16; a-1a(2a); 5765]   "
φαῦλον   acc sg neut   [3t; a-1a(2a); 5765]   "

φαῦλος, η, ον   {5765, a-1a(2a)}
vile, refuse; evil, wicked; John 3:20; 5:29; Rom 9:11; 2 Cor 5:10; Titus 2:8; James 3:16*

φέγγος, ους, τό   {5766, n-3d(2b)}
light, splendor, radiance, Matt 24:29; Mark 13:24; Luke 11:33 v.l.*

φέγγος   acc sg neut   [2t; n-3d(2b); 5766]   φέγγος

φείδομαι   {5767, v-1b(3)}
[φείσομαι, ἐφεισάμην, -, -, -] *to spare; to be tender of*, Rom 8:32; *to spare*, in respect of hard dealing, Acts 20:29; Rom 11:21; 1 Cor 7:28; 2 Cor 1:23; 13:2; 2 Peter 2:4, 5; absol. *to forbear, abstain*, 2 Cor 12:6*

φείδομαι   pres mid ind 1 sg
[2t; v-1b(3); 5767]   φείδομαι
φειδόμενοι   pres mid ptcp nom pl masc
[Ac 20:29; v-1b(3); 5767]   "
φειδόμενος   pres mid ptcp nom sg masc
[2C 1:23; v-1b(3); 5767]   "

φειδομένως   {5768, adverb}
sparingly, 2 Cor 9:6 (2t)*

φειδομένως   adverb   [2t; adverb; 5768]   φειδομένως

φελόνης, ου, ὁ   {5769}
alternate spelling of φαιλόνης, *a thick cloak* for travelling, with a hood, 2 Tim 4:13 v.l.*

φείσεται   fut mid ind 3 sg
[Rm 11:21; v-1b(3); 5767]   φείδομαι
φείσομαι   fut mid ind 1 sg
[2C 13:2; v-1b(3); 5767]   "
φέρε   pres act imperative 2 sg
[3t; v-1c(1); 5770]   φέρω
φέρει   pres act ind 3 sg   [3t; v-1c(1); 5770]   "
φέρειν   pres act inf   [2t; v-1c(1); 5770]   "
φέρεσθαι   pres pass inf   [Hb 9:16; v-1c(1); 5770]   "
φέρετε   pres act imperative 2 pl
[7t; v-1c(1); 5770]   "
φέρετε   pres act ind 2 pl
[Jn 18:29; v-1c(1); 5770]   "
φέρῃ   pres act subj 3 sg
[Jn 15:2; v-1c(1); 5770]   "
φέρητε   pres act subj 2 pl   [2t; v-1c(1); 5770]   "
φερομένην   pres pass ptcp acc sg fem
[1P 1:13; v-1c(1); 5770]   "
φερομένης   pres pass ptcp gen sg fem
[Ac 2:2; v-1c(1); 5770]   "
φερόμενοι   pres pass ptcp nom pl masc
[2P 1:21; v-1c(1); 5770]   "
φέρον   pres act ptcp acc sg neut
[2t; v-1c(1); 5770]   "
φέροντες   pres act ptcp nom pl masc
[4t; v-1c(1); 5770]   "
φέρουσαι   pres act ptcp nom pl fem
[Lk 24:1; v-1c(1); 5770]   "
φέρουσαν   pres act ptcp acc sg fem
[Ac 12:10; v-1c(1); 5770]   "
φέρουσιν   pres act ind 3 pl   [6t; v-1c(1); 5770]   "

φέρω   {5770, v-1c(1)}
[(ἔφερον), οἴσω, ἤνεγκα, ἐνήνοχα, ἐνήνεκμαι, ἠνέχθην] *to bear, carry*, Mark 2:3; *to bring*, Matt 14:11, 18; *to conduct*, Matt 17:17; John 21:18; *to bear, endure*, Rom 9:22; Heb 12:20; 13:13; *to uphold, maintain, conserve*, Heb 1:3; *to bear, bring forth, produce*, Mark 4:8; John 12:24; 15:2; *to bring forward, advance, allege*, John 18:29; Acts 25:7; 2 Peter 2:11; *to offer, ascribe*, Rev 21:24, 26; absol. used of a gate, *to lead*, Acts 12:10; pass. *to be brought* within reach, *offered*, 1 Peter 1:13; *to be brought in, to enter*, Heb 9:16; *to be under a moving influence, to be moved*, 2 Peter 1:21; mid. *to rush, sweep*, Acts 2:2; *to proceed, come forth, have utterance*, 2 Peter 1:17, 18, 21; *to proceed, make progress*, Heb 6:1; used of a ship, *to drive* before the wind, Acts 27:15, 17

φερώμεθα   pres pass subj 1 pl
   [Hb 6:1; v-1c(1); 5770]						"

φέρων   pres act ptcp nom sg masc
   [2t; v-1c(1); 5770]						"

φεῦγε   pres act imperative 2 sg
   [3t; v-1b(2); 5771]					φεύγω

φεύγει pres act ind 3 sg [2t; v-1b(2); 5771]			"

φεύγετε   pres act imperative 2 pl
   [3t; v-1b(2); 5771]						"

φευγέτωσαν   pres act imperative 3 pl
   [3t; v-1b(2); 5771]						"

φεύγω						{5771, v-1b(2)}
   [φεύξομαι, ἔφυγον, πέφευγα, -, -] absol. *to flee,
   take to flight,* Matt 2:13; 8:33; *to shrink, stand
   fearfully aloof,* 1 Cor 10:14; *to make escape,* Matt
   23:33; trans. *to shun,* 1 Cor 6:18; 1 Tim 6:11; 2
   Tim 2:22; *to escape,* Heb 11:34; 12:25 v.l.

φεύξεται   fut mid ind 3 sg
   [Jm 4:7; v-1b(2); 5771]					"

φεύξονται   fut mid ind 3 pl
   [Jn 10:5; v-1b(2); 5771]					"

Φήλικα   acc sg masc
   [Ac 23:24; n-3b(1); 5772]				Φῆλιξ

Φήλικι dat sg masc [Ac 23:26; n-3b(1); 5772]		"

Φήλικος gen sg masc [Ac 25:14; n-3b(1); 5772]		"

Φῆλιξ, ός, ή					{5772, n-3b(1)}
   Felix, pr. name, Acts 23:24, 26; 24:3, 22, 24f., 27;
   25:14*

Φῆλιξ nom sg masc [5t; n-3b(1); 5772]			"
Φῆλιξ voc sg masc [Ac 24:3; n-3b(1); 5772]			"

φήμη, ης, ή					{5773, n-1b}
   pr. *a celestial* or *oracular utterance; an utterance;
   fame, rumor, report,* Matt 9:26; Luke 4:14*

φήμη nom sg fem [2t; n-1b; 5773]			φήμη

φημί						{5774, v-6b}
   [(ἔφη [3 sg]), -, -, -, -, -] *to utter; to say, speak,* Matt
   8:8; 14:8; 26:34, 61; *to say, allege, affirm,* Rom 3:8

φημι pres act ind 1 sg [4t; v-6b; 5774]			φημί

φημίζω						{5775, v-2a(1)}
   [-, -, -, -, -] *spread* a report *by word of mouth,* Matt
   28:15 v.l., Acts 13:43 v.l.*

φησίν pres act ind 3 sg [18t; v-6b; 5774]			"
Φῆστε voc sg masc [Ac 26:25; n-2a; 5776]		Φῆστος
Φῆστον acc sg masc [3t; n-2a; 5776]			"

Φῆστος, ου, ὁ					{5776, n-2a}
   Festus, pr. name, Acts 24:27; 25:1, 4, 12ff., 22ff.;
   26:24f., 32*

Φῆστος nom sg masc [7t; n-2a; 5776]			"
Φήστου gen sg masc [Ac 25:23; n-2a; 5776]		"
Φήστῳ dat sg masc [Ac 26:32; n-2a; 5776]		"

φθάνω						{5777, v-3a(1)}
   [-, ἔφθασα, ἔφθακα -, -] *come before, precede,* 1
   Thess 4:15; absol. *to advance, make progress,* 2
   Cor 10:14; Phil 3:16; *to come up* with, *come upon,
   be close at hand,* Matt 12:28; Luke 11:20; 1 Thess
   2:16; *to attain* an object of pursuit, Rom 9:31*

φθαρῇ   aor pass subj 3 sg
   [2C 11:3; v-2d(3); 5780]					φθείρω

φθαρήσονται   fut pass ind 3 pl
   [2P 2:12; v-2d(3); 5780]					"

φθαρτῆς   gen sg fem
   [1P 1:23; a-1a(2a); 5778]				φθαρτός

φθαρτοῖς dat pl neut [1P 1:18; a-1a(2a); 5778]		"

φθαρτόν nom sg neut [1C 15:54; a-1a(2a); 5778]		"

φθαρτόν acc sg masc [1C 9:25; a-1a(2a); 5778]		"

φθαρτόν acc sg neut [1C 15:53; a-1a(2a); 5778]		"

φθαρτός, ή, όν					{5778, a-1a(2a)}
   corruptible, perishable, Rom 1:23; 1 Cor 9:25;
   15:53f.; 1 Peter 1:18, 23*

φθαρτοῦ gen sg masc [Rm 1:23; a-1a(2a); 5778]		"

φθάσωμεν   aor act subj 1 pl
   [1Th 4:15; v-3a(1); 5777]					φθάνω

φθέγγεσθαι   pres mid inf
   [Ac 4:18; v-1b(2); 5779]				φθέγγομαι

φθέγγομαι					{5779, v-1b(2)}
   [-, -, ἐφθεγξάμην, -, -] *to emit a sound; to speak,*
   Acts 4:18; 2 Peter 2:16, 18*

φθεγγόμενοι   pres mid ptcp nom pl masc
   [2P 2:18; v-1b(2); 5779]					"

φθεγξάμενον   aor mid ptcp nom sg neut
   [2P 2:16; v-1b(2); 5779]					"

φθείρει   pres act ind 3 sg
   [1C 3:17; v-2d(3); 5780]					φθείρω

φθειρόμενον   pres pass ptcp acc sg masc
   [Ep 4:22; v-2d(3); 5780]					"

φθείρονται   pres pass ind 3 pl
   [Jd 10; v-2d(3); 5780]					"

φθείρουσιν   pres act ind 3 pl
   [1C 15:33; v-2d(3); 5780]					"

φθερεῖ fut act ind 3 sg [1C 3:17; v-2d(3); 5780]		"

φθείρω						{5780, v-2d(3)}
   [φθερῶ, ἔφθειρα, -, ἔφθαρμαι, ἐφθάρην] *to spoil,
   ruin,* 1 Cor 3:17; 2 Cor 7:2; *to corrupt,* morally
   deprave, 1 Cor 15:33; 2 Cor 11:3

φθινοπωρινά   nom pl neut
   [Jd 12; a-1a(2a); 5781]				φθινοπωρινός

φθινοπωρινός, ή, όν				{5781, a-1a(2a)}
   autumnal, bare, Jude 12*

φθόγγοις   dat pl masc
   [1C 14:7; n-2a; 5782]					φθόγγος

φθόγγος, ου, ὁ					{5782, n-2a}
   a vocal sound, Rom 10:18; 1 Cor 14:7*

φθόγγος nom sg masc [Rm 10:18; n-2a; 5782]		"

φθονέω						{5783, v-1d(2a)}
   [-, ἐφθόνησα, -, -, -] *to envy,* Gal 5:26; cf. James
   4:2 v.l.*

φθόνοι nom pl masc [Ga 5:21; n-2a; 5784]		φθόνος
φθόνον acc sg masc [4t; n-2a; 5784]			"

φθόνος, ου, ὁ					{5784, n-2a}
   envy, jealousy, spite, Matt 27:18; Mark 15:10;
   Rom 1:29; Gal 5:21; Phil 1:15; 1 Tim 6:4; Titus
   3:3; James 4:5; 1 Peter 2:1*

φθόνος nom sg masc [1Ti 6:4; n-2a; 5784]		"
φθόνου gen sg masc [Rm 1:29; n-2a; 5784]		"

φθονοῦντες   pres act ptcp nom pl masc
[Ga 5:26; v-1d(2a); 5783]   φθονέω
φθόνους   acc pl masc [1P 2:1; n-2a; 5784]   φθόνος
φθόνῳ   dat sg masc [Ti 3:3; n-2a; 5784]   "

φθορά, ᾶς, ἡ   {5785, n-1a}
corruption, decay, ruin, corruptibility, mortality,
Rom 8:21; 1 Cor 15:42; meton. *corruptible,*
perishable substance, 1 Cor 15:50; *killing,*
slaughter, 2 Peter 2:12; *spiritual ruin,* Gal 6:8;
Col 2:22; met. moral *corruption, depravity,* 2
Peter 1:4; 2:19*

φθορά   nom sg fem [1C 15:50; n-1a; 5785]   φθορά
φθορᾷ   dat sg fem [2t; n-1a; 5785]   "
φθοράν   acc sg fem [3t; n-1a; 5785]   "
φθορᾶς   gen sg fem [3t; n-1a; 5785]   "
φιάλας   acc pl fem [5t; n-1b; 5786]   φιάλη

φιάλη, ης, ἡ   {5786, n-1b}
a bowl, shallow cup, Rev 5:8; 15:7; 16:1, 2, 3, 4

φιάλην   acc sg fem [7t; n-1b; 5786]   "
φιλάγαθον   acc sg masc
[Ti 1:8; a-3a; 5787]   φιλάγαθος

φιλάγαθος, ον   {5787, a-3a}
a lover of goodness, or, *of the good, a fosterer of*
virtue, Titus 1:8*

Φιλαδέλφεια, ας, ἡ   {5788, n-1a}
Philadelphia, a city of Lydia, near Mount
Tmolus, Rev 1:11; 3:7*

φιλαδελφία   nom sg fem
[Hb 13:1; n-1a; 5789]   φιλαδελφία
φιλαδελφίᾳ   dat sg fem [2t; n-1a; 5789]   "
Φιλαδέλφειαν   acc sg fem [Rv 1:11; n-1a; 5788]   "

φιλαδελφία, ας, ἡ   {5789, n-1a}
brotherly love; in N.T. *love of the* Christian
brotherhood, Rom 12:10; 1 Thess 4:9; Heb 13:1; 1
Peter 1:22; 2 Peter 1:7*

φιλαδελφίᾳ   dat sg fem
[3t; n-1a; 5789]   φιλαδελφία
φιλαδελφίαν   acc sg fem [2t; n-1a; 5789]   "
φιλαδελφίας   gen sg fem [1Th 4:9; n-1a; 5789]   "
φιλάδελφοι   nom pl masc
[1P 3:8; a-3a; 5790]   φιλάδελφος

φιλάδελφος, ον   {5790, a-3a}
brother-loving; in N.T. *loving the members of the*
Christian *brotherhood,* 1 Peter 3:8*

φίλανδρος, ον   {5791, a-3a}
husband-loving; conjugal, Titus 2:4*

φιλάνδρους   acc pl fem
[Ti 2:4; a-3a; 5791]   φίλανδρος

φιλανθρωπία, ας, ἡ   {5792, n-1a}
philanthropy, love of mankind, Titus 3:4;
benevolence, humanity, Acts 28:2*

φιλανθρωπία   nom sg fem
[Ti 3:4; n-1a; 5792]   φιλανθρωπία
φιλανθρωπίαν   acc sg fem [Ac 28:2; n-1a; 5792]   "

φιλανθρώπως   {5793, adverb}
humanely, benevolently, kindly, Acts 27:3*

φιλανθρώπως   adverb
[Ac 27:3; adverb; 5793]   φιλανθρώπως

φιλαργυρία, ας, ἡ   {5794, n-1a}
love of money, covetousness, 1 Tim 6:10*

φιλαργυρία   nom sg fem
[1Ti 6:10; n-1a; 5794]   φιλαργυρία
φιλάργυροι   nom pl masc
[2t; a-3a; 5795]   φιλάργυρος

φιλάργυρος, ον   {5795, a-3a}
money-loving, covetous, Luke 16:14; 2 Tim 3:2*

φίλας   acc pl fem [Lk 15:9; a-1a(2a); 5813]   φίλος
φίλαυτοι   nom pl masc
[2Ti 3:2; a-3a; 5796]   φίλαυτος

φίλαυτος, ον   {5796, a-3a}
self-loving; selfish, 2 Tim 3:2*

φίλε   voc sg masc [2t; a-1a(2a); 5813]   φίλος
φιλεῖ   pres act ind 3 sg
[3t; v-1d(2a); 5797]   φιλέω
φιλεῖς   pres act ind 2 sg [3t; v-1d(2a); 5797]   "

φιλέω   {5797, v-1d(2a)}
[(ἐφίλουν), -, ἐφίλησα, πεφίληκα, -, -] pr. *to*
manifest some act or *token of kindness of affection;*
to kiss, Matt 26:48; Mark 14:44; Luke 22:47; *to*
love, regard with affection, have affection for, Matt
10:37; John 5:20; *to like, be fond of, delight in* a
thing, Matt 23:6; Rev 22:15; *to cherish*
inordinately, set store by, John 12:25; followed by
an infin. *to be wont,* Matt 6:5

φίλη, ης, ἡ   {5797}
substantive of the adjective φίλος, *a female*
friend, Luke 15:9

φιλήδονοι   nom pl masc
[2Ti 3:4; a-3a; 5798]   φιλήδονος

φιλήδονος, ον   {5798, a-3a}
pleasure-loving; a lover of pleasure, 2 Tim 3:4*

φίλημα, ατος, τό   {5799, n-3c(4)}
a kiss, Luke 7:45; 22:48; Rom 16:16; 1 Cor 16:20;
2 Cor 13:12; 1 Thess 5:26; 1 Peter 5:14*

φίλημα   acc sg neut
[Lk 7:45; n-3c(4); 5799]   φίλημα
φιλήματι   dat sg neut [6t; n-3c(4); 5799]   "
Φιλήμονι   dat sg masc
[Pm 1; n-3f(1b); 5800]   Φιλήμων

Φιλήμων, ονος, ὁ   {5800, n-3f(1b)}
Philemon, pr. name, Phlm 1; subscr. and title*

φιλῆσαι   aor act inf
[Lk 22:47; v-1d(2a); 5797]   φιλέω
φιλήσω   aor act subj 1 sg [2t; v-1d(2a); 5797]   "

Φίλητος, ου, ὁ   {5801, n-2a}
Philetus, pr. name, 2 Tim 2:17*

Φίλητος   nom sg masc
[2Ti 2:17; n-2a; 5801]   Φίλητος

φιλία, ας, ἡ   {5802, n-1a}
affection, fondness, love, James 4:4*

φιλία   nom sg fem [Jm 4:4; n-1a; 5802]   φιλία

Φίλιππε voc sg masc
[Jn 14:9; n-2a; 5805]   Φίλιππος

Φιλιππήσιοι voc pl masc
[Pp 4:15; n-2a; 5803]   Φιλιππήσιος

Φιλιππήσιος, ου, ὁ   {5803, n-2a}
a Philippian, a citizen of Φίλιπποι, Philippi, Phil
4:15; title*

Φίλιπποι, ων οἱ   {5804, n-2a}
Philippi, a considerable city of Macedonia, east
of Amphipolis, Acts 16:12; 20:6; Phil 1:1; 1
Thess 2:2; 1 & 2 Cor subscr.*

Φιλίπποις dat pl masc [2t; n-2a; 5804]   Φίλιπποι
Φίλιππον acc sg masc [9t; n-2a; 5805]   Φίλιππος

Φίλιππος, ου, ὁ   {5805, n-2a}
Philip, pr. name . (1) Philip, the Apostle, Matt
10:3. (2) Philip, the Evangelist, Acts 6:5. (3) Philip,
son of Herod the Great and Mariamne, Matt 14:3 .
(4) Philip, son of Herod the Great and Cleopatra,
Matt 16:13; Luke 3:1

Φίλιππος nom sg masc [14t; n-2a; 5805]   "
Φιλίππου gen sg masc [7t; n-2a; 5805]   "
Φιλίππους acc pl masc
[Ac 16:12; n-2a; 5804]   Φίλιπποι
Φιλίππῳ dat sg masc [5t; n-2a; 5805]   Φίλιππος
Φιλίππων gen pl masc
[Ac 20:6; n-2a; 5804]   Φίλιπποι
φιλόθεοι nom pl masc
[2Ti 3:4; a-3a; 5806]   φιλόθεος

φιλόθεος, ον   {5806, a-3a}
God-loving, pious; a lover of God, 2 Tim 3:4*

φίλοι nom pl masc [4t; a-1a(2a); 5813]   φίλος
φίλοις dat pl masc [Lk 12:4; a-1a(2a); 5813]   "
Φιλόλογον acc sg masc
[Rm 16:15; n-2a; 5807]   Φιλόλογος

Φιλόλογος, ου, ὁ   {5807, n-2a}
Philologus, pr. name, Rom 16:15*

φίλον acc sg masc [2t; a-1a(2a); 5813]   φίλος

φιλονεικία, ας, ἡ   {5808, n-1a}
a love of contention; rivalry, contention, Luke
22:24*

φιλονεικία nom sg fem
[Lk 22:24; n-1a; 5808]   φιλονεικία

φιλόνεικος, ον   {5809, a-3a}
fond of contention; contentious, disputations, 1
Cor 11:16*

φιλόνεικος nom sg masc
[1C 11:16; a-3a; 5809]   φιλόνεικος

φιλοξενία, ας, ἡ   {5810, n-1a}
kindness to strangers, hospitality, Rom 12:13; Heb
13:2*

φιλοξενίαν acc sg fem
[Rm 12:13; n-1a; 5810]   φιλοξενία
φιλοξενίας gen sg fem [Hb 13:2; n-1a; 5810]   "
φιλόξενοι nom pl masc
[1P 4:9; a-3a; 5811]   φιλόξενος
φιλόξενον acc sg masc [2t; a-3a; 5811]   "

φιλόξενος, ον   {5811, a-3a}
kind to strangers, hospitable, 1 Tim 3:2; Titus 1:8;
1 Peter 4:9*

φιλοπρωτεύω   {5812, v-1a(6)}
[-, -, -, -, -] to love or desire to be first or chief, affect
pre-eminence, 3 John 9*

φιλοπρωτεύων pres act ptcp nom sg masc
[3J 9; v-1a(6); 5812]   φιλοπρωτεύω

φίλος, η, ον   {5813, a-1a(2a)}
loved, dear; devoted; Acts 19:31; as a subst., a
friend, Luke 7:6; 11:5, 6, 8; a congenial associate,
Matt 11:19; Luke 7:34; James 4:4; used as a
word of courteous appellation, Luke 14:10

φίλος nom sg masc [8t; a-1a(2a); 5813]   φίλος

φιλοσοφία, ας, ἡ   {5814, n-1a}
a love of science; systematic philosophy; in N.T.
the philosophy of the Jewish gnosis, Col 2:8*

φιλοσοφίας gen sg fem
[Cl 2:8; n-1a; 5814]   φιλοσοφία

φιλόσοφος, ου, ὁ   {5815, n-2a}
pr. a lover of science, a systematic philosopher,
Acts 17:18*

φιλοσόφων gen pl masc
[Ac 17:18; n-2a; 5815]   φιλόσοφος
φιλόστοργοι nom pl masc
[Rm 12:10; a-3a; 5816]   φιλόστοργος

φιλόστοργος, ον   {5816, a-3a}
tenderly affectionate, Rom 12:10*

φιλότεκνος, ον   {5817, a-3a}
loving one's children, duly parental, Titus 2:4*

φιλοτέκνους acc pl fem
[Ti 2:4; a-3a; 5817]   φιλότεκνος
φιλοτιμεῖσθαι pres mid inf
[1Th 4:11; cv-1d(2a); 5818]   φιλοτιμέομαι

φιλοτιμέομαι   {5818, cv-1d(2a)}
[-, -, -, -, -] pr. to be ambitious of honor; by impl.
to exert one's self to accomplish a thing, use one's
utmost efforts, endeavor earnestly, Rom 15:20; 2
Cor 5:9; 1 Thess 4:11*

φιλοτιμούμεθα pres mid ind 1 pl
[2C 5:9; cv-1d(2a); 5818]   "
φιλοτιμούμενον pres mid ptcp acc sg masc
[Rm 15:20; cv-1d(2a); 5818]   "
φιλοῦντας pres act ptcp acc pl masc
[Ti 3:15; v-1d(2a); 5797]   φιλέω
φιλούντων pres act ptcp gen pl masc
[Lk 20:46; v-1d(2a); 5797]   "
φίλους acc pl masc [8t; a-1a(2a); 5813]   φίλος
φιλοῦσιν pres act ind 3 pl
[2t; v-1d(2a); 5797]   φιλέω

φιλοφρόνως   {5819, adverb}
with kindly feeling or manner, courteously, Acts
28:7*

φιλοφρόνως adverb
[Ac 28:7; adverb; 5819]   φιλοφρόνως

φιλόφρων, ον, gen., ονος   {5820, a-4b(1)}
kindly minded, courteous, friendly, 1 Peter 3:8 v.l.*

φιλῶ pres act ind 1 sg [3t; v-1d(2a); 5797]   φιλέω
φιλῶ pres act subj 1 sg
    [Rv 3:19; v-1d(2a); 5797]   "
φίλων gen pl masc [3t; a-1a(2a); 5813]   φίλος
φιλῶν pres act ptcp nom sg masc
    [4t; v-1d(2a); 5797]   φιλέω
φιμοῦν pres act inf
    [1P 2:15; v-1d(3); 5821]   φιμόω

φιμόω   {5821, v-1d(3)}
    [φιμώσω, ἐφίμωσα, -, πεφίμωμαι, ἐφιμώθην] *to*
    muzzle, 1 Cor 9:9 v.l.; 1 Tim 5:18; met. and by
    impl. *to silence, put to silence*; pass. *to be silent,*
    speechless, Matt 22:12, 34; 1 Peter 2:15; Mark
    1:25; trop. pass. *to be hushed*, as winds and
    waves, Mark 4:39; Luke 4:35*

φιμώθητι aor pass imperative 2 sg
    [2t; v-1d(3); 5821]   "
φιμώσεις fut act ind 2 sg
    [1Ti 5:18; v-1d(3); 5821]   "
Φλέγοντα acc sg masc
    [Rm 16:14; n-3c(5b); 5823]   Φλέγων

Φλέγων, οντος, ὁ   {5823, n-3c(5b)}
    Phlegon, pr. name, Rom 16:14*

φλόγα acc sg fem [2t; n-3b(2); 5825]   φλόξ
φλογί dat sg fem [2t; n-3b(2); 5825]   "
φλογιζομένη pres pass ptcp nom sg fem
    [Jm 3:6; v-2a(1); 5824]   φλογίζω
φλογίζουσα pres act ptcp nom sg fem
    [Jm 3:6; v-2a(1); 5824]   "

φλογίζω   {5824, v-2a(1)}
    [-, -, -, -, -] *to set in a flame, kindle, inflame*, James
    3:6 (2t)*

φλογός gen sg fem [2Th 1:8; n-3b(2); 5825]   φλόξ

φλόξ, φλογός, ἡ   {5825, n-3b(2)}
    a flame, Luke 16:24; Acts 7:30

φλόξ nom sg fem [2t; n-3b(2); 5825]   "

φλυαρέω   {5826, v-1d(2a)}
    [-, -, -, -, -] *to talk folly* or *nonsense*; in N.T. trans.,
    bring unjustified charges against, 3 John 10*

φλύαροι nom pl fem [1Ti 5:13; a-3a; 5827]   φλύαρος

φλύαρος, ον   {5827, a-3a}
    a gossip, tattler, 1 Tim 5:13*

φλυαρῶν pres act ptcp nom sg masc
    [3J 10; v-1d(2a); 5826]   φλυαρέω
φοβεῖσθαι pres pass inf
    [Rm 13:3; v-1d(2a); 5830]   φοβέομαι
φοβεῖσθε pres pass imperative 2 pl
    [12t; v-1d(2a); 5830   "
φοβερά nom sg fem
    [Hb 10:27; a-1a(1); 5829]   φοβερός
φοβερόν nom sg neut [2t; a-1a(1); 5829]   "

φοβερός, ά, όν   {5829, a-1a(1)}
    fearful; terrible, Heb 10:27, 31; 12:21*

φοβέομαι   {5830, v-1d(2a)}
    [ἐφοβούμην), -, -, -, -, ἐφοβήθην] has an active
    form, φοβέω (5828), but only occurs as a passive
    (deponent) in our literature, *to fear, dread*, Matt
    10:26; 14:5; *to fear reverentially, to reverence,*

Mark 6:20; Luke 1:50; Acts 10:2; Eph 5:33; Rev
11:18; *to be afraid* to do a thing, Matt 2:22; Mark
9:32; *to be reluctant, to scruple*, Matt 1:20; *to fear,*
be apprehensive, Acts 27:17; 2 Cor 11:3; 12:20; *to*
be fearfully anxious, Heb 4:1; absol. *to be fearful,*
afraid, alarmed, Matt 14:27; 17:6, 7; Mark 16:8; *to*
be fearfully impressed, Rom 11:20

φοβῇ pres pass ind 2 sg
    [Lk 23:40; v-1d(2a); 5830]   φοβέομαι
φοβηθείς aor pass ptcp nom sg masc
    [3t; v-1d(2a); 5830]   "
φοβηθεῖσα aor pass ptcp nom sg fem
    [Mk 5:33; v-1d(2a); 5830]   "
φοβηθέντες aor pass ptcp nom pl masc
    [Lk 8:25; v-1d(2a); 5830]   "
φοβηθῇ aor pass subj 3 sg
    [Rv 15:4; v-1d(2a); 5830]   "
φοβηθῇς aor pass subj 2 sg
    [Mt 1:20; v-1d(2a); 5830]   "
φοβηθήσομαι fut pass ind 1 sg
    [Hb 13:6; v-1d(2a); 5830]   "
φοβήθητε aor pass imperative 2 pl
    [3t; v-1d(2a); 5830]   "
φοβηθῆτε aor pass subj 2 pl [4t; v-1d(2a); 5830]   "
φοβηθῶμεν aor pass subj 1 pl
    [Hb 4:1; v-1d(2a); 5830]   "
φοβῆται pres pass subj 3 sg
    [Ep 5:33; v-1d(2a); 5830]   "
φόβητρα nom pl neut
    [Lk 21:11; n-2c; 5831]   φόβητρον

φόβητρον, ου, τό   {5831, n-2c}
    something which inspires terror; terrible sight or
    event, Luke 21:11*

φόβοι nom pl masc [2C 7:5; n-2a; 5832]   φόβος
φόβον acc sg masc [15t; n-2a; 5832]   "

φόβος, ου, ὁ   {5832, n-2a}
    fear, terror, affright, Matt 14:26; Luke 1:12;
    astonishment, amazement, Matt 28:8; Mark 4:41;
    trembling concern, 1 Cor 2:3; 2 Cor 7:15; meton.
    a terror, an object or *cause of terror*, Rom 13:5;
    reverential fear, awe, Acts 9:31; Rom 3:18; *respect,*
    deference, Rom 13:7; 1 Peter 2:18

φόβος nom sg masc [12t; n-2a; 5832]   "
φόβου gen sg masc [9t; n-2a; 5832]   "
φοβοῦ pres pass imperative 2 sg
    [13t; v-1d(2a); 5830]   φοβέομαι
φοβοῦμαι pres pass ind 1 sg [4t; v-1d(2a); 5830]   "
φοβούμεθα pres pass ind 1 pl
    [Mt 21:26; v-1d(2a); 5830]   "
φοβούμεναι pres pass ptcp nom pl fem
    [1P 3:6; v-1d(2a); 5830]   "
φοβούμενοι pres pass ptcp nom pl masc
    [3t; v-1d(2a); 5830]   "
φοβούμενοι pres pass ptcp voc pl masc
    [3t; v-1d(2a); 5830]   "
φοβουμένοις pres pass ptcp dat pl masc
    [2t; v-1d(2a); 5830]   "
φοβούμενος pres pass ptcp nom sg masc
    [6t; v-1d(2a); 5830]   "
φόβῳ dat sg masc [10t; n-2a; 5832]   φόβος

Φοίβη, ης, ἡ   {5833, n-1b}
Phoebe, pr. name, Rom 16:1*

Φοίβην   acc sg fem [Rm 16:1; n-1b; 5833]   Φοίβη
Φοίνικα   acc sg masc
[Ac 27:12; n-3b(1); 5837]   Φοῖνιξ
φοίνικες   nom pl masc
[Rv 7:9; n-3b(1); 5836]   φοῖνιξ

Φοινίκη, ης, ἡ   {5834, n-1b}
Phoenice, Phoenicia, a country on the east of the
Mediterranean, between Palestine and Syria,
anciently celebrated for commerce, Acts 11:19;
15:3; 21:2*

Φοινίκην   acc sg fem [2t; n-1b; 5834]   Φοινίκη
Φοινίκης   gen sg fem [Ac 11:19; n-1b; 5834]   "
φοινίκων   gen pl masc
[Jn 12:13; n-3b(1); 5836]   φοῖνιξ

φοῖνιξ, ικός, ὁ   {5836, n-3b(1)}
the palm-tree, the date-palm, John 12:13; Rev 7:9.
Identical in form to the word meaning phoenix,
the Egyptian bird.*

Φοῖνιξ, ικός, ἡ   {5837, n-3b(1)}
Phoenix, Phoenice, a city, with a harbor, on the
southeast coast of Crete, Acts 27:12*

φονέα   acc sg masc [Ac 3:14; n-3e(3); 5838]   φονεύς
φονεῖς   nom pl masc [2t; n-3e(3); 5838]   "
φονεῖς   acc pl masc [Mt 22:7; n-3e(3); 5838]   "
φονεύεις   pres act ind 2 sg
[Jm 2:11; v-1a(6); 5839]   φονεύω
φονεύετε   pres act ind 2 pl
[Jm 4:2; v-1a(6); 5839]   "

φονεύς, έως, ὁ   {5838, n-3e(3)}
a homicide, murderer, Matt 22:7; Acts 3:14; 7:52;
28:4; 1 Peter 4:15; Rev 21: 8; 22:15*

φονεύς   nom sg masc [2t; n-3e(3); 5838]   φονεύς
φονευσάντων   aor act ptcp gen pl masc
[Mt 23:31; v-1a(6); 5839]   φονεύω
φονεύσεις   fut act ind 2 sg [3t; v-1a(6); 5839]   "
φονεύσῃ   aor act subj 3 sg
[Mt 5:21; v-1a(6); 5839]   "
φονεύσῃς   aor act subj 2 sg [3t; v-1a(6); 5839]   "
φονεῦσιν   dat pl masc
[Rv 21:8; n-3e(3); 5838]   φονεύς

φονεύω   {5839, v-1a(6)}
[φονεύσω, ἐφόνευσα, -, -, ἐφονεύθην] to put out
death, kill, stay, Matt 23:31, 35; absol. to commit
murder, Matt 5:21

φόνοι   nom pl masc [2t; n-2a; 5840]   φόνος
φόνον   acc sg masc [3t; n-2a; 5840]   "

φόνος, ου, ὁ   {5840, n-2a}
a killing, slaughter, murder, Matt 15:19; Mark
7:21; 15:7

φόνου   gen sg masc [2t; n-2a; 5840]   "
φόνῳ   dat sg masc [Hb 11:37; n-2a; 5840]   "
φόνων   gen pl masc [Rv 9:21; n-2a; 5840]   "
φορεῖ   pres act ind 3 sg
[Rm 13:4; v-1d(2b); 5841]   φορέω
φορέσομεν   fut act ind 1 pl
[1C 15:49; v-1d(2b); 5841]   "

φορέω   {5841, v-1d(2b)}
[φορέσω, ἐφόρεσα, πεφόρηκα, -, -] to bear; to wear,
Matt 11:8; John 19:5; Rom 13:4; 1 Cor 15:49;
James 2:3

φόρον, ου, τό   {5842, n-2c}
a forum, marketplace; Φόρον Ἀππίου, Forum
Appii, the name of a small town on the Appian
way, according to Antoninus, forty-three
Roman miles from Rome, or about forty
English miles, Acts 28:15*

φόρον   acc sg masc [3t; n-2a; 5843]   φόρος

φόρος, ου, ὁ   {5843, n-2a}
tribute, tax, strictly such as is laid on dependent
and subject people, Luke 20:22; 23:2; Rom 13:6,
7*

φόρου   gen sg neut [Ac 28:15; n-2c; 5842]   φόρον
φοροῦντα   pres act ptcp acc sg masc
[Jm 2:3; v-1d(2b); 5841]   φορέω
φοροῦντες   pres act ptcp nom pl masc
[Mt 11:8; v-1d(2b); 5841]   "
φόρους   acc pl masc [2t; n-2a; 5843]   φόρος
φορτία   acc pl neut [2t; n-2c; 5845]   φορτίον
φορτίζετε   pres act ind 2 pl
[Lk 11:46; v-2a(1); 5844]   φορτίζω

φορτίζω   {5844, v-2a(1)}
[-, -, -, πεφόρτισμαι, -] to load, burden; met. Matt
11:28; Luke 11:46*

φορτίοις   dat pl neut
[Lk 11:46; n-2c; 5845]   φορτίον

φορτίον, ου, τό   {5845, n-2c}
a load, burden; of a ship, freight, cargo, Acts 27:10;
met. a burden of imposed precepts, etc., Matt
11:30; 23:4; Luke 11:46 (2t); of faults, sins, etc.,
Gal 6:5*

φορτίον   nom sg neut [Mt 11:30; n-2c; 5845]   "
φορτίον   acc sg neut [Ga 6:5; n-2c; 5845]   "
φορτίου   gen sg neut [Ac 27:10; n-2c; 5845]   "

φόρτος, ου, ὁ   {5846, n-2a}
a load, burden; freight, cargo, Acts 27:10 v.l.*

Φορτουνᾶτος, ου, ὁ   {5847, n-2a}
Fortunatus, pr. name, 1 Cor 16:15 v.l., 17;
subscr.*

Φορτουνάτου   gen sg masc
[1C 16:17; n-2a; 5847]   Φορτουνᾶτος
φορῶν   pres act ptcp nom sg masc
[Jn 19:5; v-1d(2b); 5841]   φορέω

φραγέλλιον, ου, τό   {5848, n-2c}
a whip, scourge, John 2:15*

φραγέλλιον   acc sg neut
[Jn 2:15; n-2c; 5848]   φραγέλλιον

φραγελλόω   {5849, v-1d(3)}
[-, ἐφραγέλλωσα, -, -, -] to scourge, Matt 27:26;
Mark 15:15*

φραγελλώσας   aor act ptcp nom sg masc
[2t; v-1d(3); 5849]   φραγελλόω
φραγῇ   aor pass subj 3 sg
[Rm 3:19; v-2b; 5852]   φράσσω

φραγήσεται   fut pass ind 3 sg
   [2C 11:10; v-2b; 5852]   "
φραγμόν   acc sg masc [2t; n-2a; 5850]   φραγμός

φραγμός, οῦ, ὁ   {5850, n-2a}
   a fence, hedge; a hedgeside path, Matt 21:33; Mark
   12:1; Luke 14:23; met. *a* parting *fence*, Eph 2:14*

φραγμοῦ   gen sg masc [Ep 2:14; n-2a; 5850]   "
φραγμούς   acc pl masc [Lk 14:23; n-2a; 5850]   "

φράζω   {5851, v-2a(1)}
   [-, ἔφρασα, -, -, -] pr. *to propound in distinct terms,
   to tell*; in N.T. *to explain, interpret, expound,* Matt
   13:36 v.l.; 15:15*

φράσον   aor act imperative 2 sg
   [Mt 15:15; v-2a(1); 5851]   φράζω

φράσσω   {5852, v-2b}
   [-, ἔφραξα, -, -, ἐφράγην] *to fence in*; by impl. *to
   obstruct, stop, close up*, Heb 11:33; met. *to silence,
   put to silence*, Rom 3:19; 2 Cor 11:10*

φρέαρ, φρέατος, τό   {5853, n-3c(6b)}
   a well, cistern, Luke 14:5; John 4:11, 12; *a pit,* Rev
   9:1, 2*

φρέαρ   nom sg neut [Jn 4:11; n-3c(6b); 5853]   φρέαρ
φρέαρ   acc sg neut [3t; n-3c(6b); 5853]   "
φρέατος   gen sg neut [3t; n-3c(6b); 5853]   "
φρεναπατᾷ   pres act ind 3 sg
   [Ga 6:3; cv-1d(1a); 5854]   φρεναπατάω
φρεναπάται   nom pl masc
   [Ti 1:10; n-1f; 5855]   φρεναπάτης

φρεναπατάω   {5854, cv-1d(1a)}
   [-, -, -, -, -] *to deceive the mind; to deceive, impose
   on*, Gal 6:3*

φρεναπάτης, ου, ὁ   {5855, n-1f}
   a deceiver, seducer, Titus 1:10*

φρεσίν   dat pl fem [2t; n-3f(1b); 5856]   φρήν

φρήν, ενός, ἡ   {5856, n-3f(1b)}
   pr. *the diaphragm, midriff; the mind, intellect,
   understanding*, 1 Cor 14:20 (2t)*

φρίσσουσιν   pres act ind 3 pl
   [Jm 2:19; v-2b; 5857]   φρίσσω

φρίσσω   {5857, v-2b}
   [-, ἔφριξα, πέφρικα, -, -] *to be ruffled, to bristle; to
   shiver, shudder* from fear, James 2:19*

φρόνει   pres act imperative 2 sg
   [Rm 11:20; v-1d(2a); 5858]   φρονέω
φρονεῖ   pres act ind 3 sg
   [Rm 14:6; v-1d(2a); 5858]   "
φρονεῖν   pres act inf [6t; v-1d(2a); 5858]   "
φρονεῖς   pres act ind 2 sg [3t; v-1d(2a); 5858] "
φρονεῖτε   pres act imperative 2 pl
   [3t; v-1d(2a); 5858]   "
φρονεῖτε   pres act ind 2 pl
   [Pp 3:15; v-1d(2a); 5858]   "

φρονέω   {5858, v-1d(2a)}
   [(ἐφρόνουν), φρονήσω, ἐφρόνησα, -, -, -] *to think,
   to mind; to be of opinion*, Acts 28:22; Phil 1:7; *to
   take thought, be considerate*, Phil 4:10; *to entertain
   sentiments* or *inclinations* of a specific kind, *to be*

minded, Rom 12:16; 15:5; 1 Cor 13:11; 2 Cor
13:11; Gal 5:10; Phil 2:2; 3:16; 4:2; *to be in a
certain frame of mind*, Rom 12:3; Phil 2:5; *to
imagine, entertain conceit*, 1 Cor 4:6; *to heed, pay
regard to*, Rom 14:6; *to incline to, be set upon,
mind*, Matt 16:23; Mark 8:33; Rom 8:5; Phil 3:15,
19; Col 3:2

φρόνημα, ατος, τό   {5859, n-3c(4)}
   frame of thought, will, aspirations, Rom 8:6, 7, 27*

φρόνημα   nom sg neut [4t; n-3c(4); 5859]   φρόνημα
φρονήσει   dat sg fem [2t; n-3e(5b); 5860]   φρόνησις
φρονήσετε   fut act ind 2 pl
   [Ga 5:10; v-1d(2a); 5858]   φρονέω

φρόνησις, εως, ἡ   {5860, n-3e(5b)}
   a thoughtful frame, sense, rightmindedness, Luke
   1:17; *intelligence*, Eph 1:8*

φρονῆτε   pres act subj 2 pl
   [Pp 2:2; v-1d(2a); 5858]   "
φρόνιμοι   nom pl masc [5t; a-3a; 5861]   φρόνιμος
φρόνιμοι   nom pl fem [3t; a-3a; 5861]   "
φρονίμοις   dat pl masc [1C 10:15; a-3a; 5861] "
φρονίμοις   dat pl fem [Mt 25:8; a-3a; 5861]   "

φρόνιμος, ον   {5861, a-3a}
   considerate, thoughtful, prudent, discreet, Matt
   7:24; 10:16; 24:45; 25:2, 4, 8, 9; Luke 12:42;
   sensible, wise, Rom 11:25; 12:16; 1 Cor 4:10;
   10:15; 2 Cor 11:19*

φρόνιμος   nom sg masc [2t; a-3a; 5861]   "
φρονίμῳ   dat sg masc [Mt 7:24; a-3a; 5861]   "

φρονίμως   {5862, adverb}
   considerately, providently, Luke 16:8*

φρονίμως   adverb [Lk 16:8; adverb; 5862]   φρονίμως
φρονιμώτεροι   nom pl masc comparative
   [Lk 16:8; a-3a; 5861]   φρόνιμος
φρονοῦντες   pres act ptcp nom pl masc
   [4t; v-1d(2a); 5858]   φρονέω
φρονοῦσιν   pres act ind 3 pl
   [Rm 8:5; v-1d(2a); 5858]   "

φροντίζω   {5863, v-2a(1)}
   [-, -, -, -, -] *to be considerate, be careful*, Titus 3:8*

φροντίζωσιν   pres act subj 3 pl
   [Ti 3:8; v-2a(1); 5863]   φροντίζω
φρονῶμεν   pres act subj 1 pl
   [Pp 3:15; v-1d(2a); 5858]   φρονέω
φρονῶν   pres act ptcp nom sg masc
   [Rm 14:6; v-1d(2a); 5858]   "

φρουρέω   {5864, v-1d(2a)}
   [(ἐφρούρουν), φρουρήσω, -, -, -, -] *to keep watch*;
   trans. *to guard, watch*, with a military guard, 2
   Cor 11:32; *to keep* in a condition of restraint, Gal
   3:23; *to keep* in a state of settlement or security,
   Phil 4:7; 1 Peter 1:5*

φρουρήσει   fut act ind 3 sg
   [Pp 4:7; v-1d(2a); 5864]   φρουρέω
φρουρουμένους   pres pass ptcp acc pl masc
   [1P 1:5; v-1d(2a); 5864]   "

φρυάσσω   {5865, v-2b}
   [-, ἐφρύαξα, -, -, -] pr. *to snort, neigh, stamp*, etc.;

as a high-spirited horse; hence, *to be noisy, fierce, insolent, and tumultuous, to rage, tumultuate,* Acts 4:25*

φρύγανον, ου, τό   {5866, n-2c}
a dry twig, branch, etc., Acts 28:3*

φρυγάνων gen pl neut
[Ac 28:3; n-2c; 5866]   φρύγανον

Φρυγία, ας, ἡ   {5867, n-1a}
Phrygia, an inland province of Asia Minor, Acts 2:10; 16:6; 18:23; 1 Tim subscr.*

Φρυγίαν acc sg fem [3t; n-1a; 5867]   Φρυγία

φυγαδεύω   {5868, v-1a(6)}
[-, -, -, -, ἐφυγαδεύθην] trans., *to banish as a fugitive,* Acts 7:29; intrans., *be a fugitive,* Acts 7:29 v.l.*

φυγεῖν aor act inf [3t; v-1b(2); 5771]   φεύγω

Φύγελος, ου, ὁ   {5869, n-2a}
Phygellus, pr. name, 2 Tim 1:15*

Φύγελος nom sg masc
[2Ti 1:15; n-2a; 5869]   Φύγελος

φυγή, ῆς, ἡ   {5870, n-1b}
a fleeing, flight, Matt 24:20; Mark 13:18 v.l.*

φυγή nom sg fem [Mt 24:20; n-1b; 5870]   φυγή
φύγητε aor act subj 2 pl
[Mt 23:33; v-1b(2); 5771]   φεύγω
φυέν aor pass ptcp nom sg neut
[2t; v-1a(4); 5886]   φύω
φυλαί nom pl fem [2t; n-1b; 5876]   φυλή
φυλαῖς dat pl fem [Jm 1:1; n-1b; 5876]   "
φυλακαῖς dat pl fem [3t; n-1b; 5871]   φυλακή
φύλακας acc pl masc [2t; n-3b(1); 5874]   φύλαξ
φυλακάς acc pl fem [3t; n-1b; 5871]   φυλακή
φύλακες nom pl masc
[Ac 12:6; n-3b(1); 5874]   φύλαξ

φυλακή, ῆς, ἡ   {5871, n-1b}
a keeping watch, ward, guard, Luke 2:8; *a place of watch,* Rev 18:2; *a watch, guard, body of guards,* Acts 12:10; *ward, custody, imprisonment,* 2 Cor 6:5; 11:23; Heb 11:36; *prison,* 1 Peter 3:19; *a place of custody, prison,* Matt 14:10; 25:39, 44; *a watch* or *division,* of the night, which in the time of our Savior was divided into watches of three hours each, called ὀψέ, μεσονύκτιον, ἀλεκτοροφωνία and πρωΐα, or πρωΐ, Matt 14:25; 24:43; Mark 6:48; Luke 12:38 (2t)

φυλακή nom sg fem [3t; n-1b; 5871]   φυλακή
φυλακῇ dat sg fem [17t; n-1b; 5871]   "
φυλακήν acc sg fem [15t; n-1b; 5871]   "
φυλακῆς gen sg fem [6t; n-1b; 5871]   "

φυλακίζω   {5872, v-2a(1)}
[-, -, -, -, -] *to deliver into custody, put in prison, imprison,* Acts 22:19*

φυλακίζων pres act ptcp nom sg masc
[Ac 22:19; v-2a(1); 5872]   φυλακίζω
φυλακτήρια acc pl neut
[Mt 23:5; n-2c; 5873]   φυλακτήριον

φυλακτήριον, ου, τό   {5873, n-2c}
the station of a guard or *watch; a preservative, safeguard;* hence, *a phylactery* or *amulet,* worn about the person; from which circumstance the word is used in the N.T. as a term for the Jewish *Tephillin* or *prayer-fillets,* which took their rise from the injunction in Deut 6:8; 11:18; Matt 23:5*

φύλαξ, ακός, ὁ   {5874, n-3b(1)}
a watchman, guard, sentinel, Matt 27:65 v.l.; Acts 5:23; 12:6, 19*

φυλάξαι aor act inf [2t; v-2b; 5875]   φυλάσσω
φυλάξατε aor act imperative 2 pl
[1J 5:21; v-2b; 5875]   "
φυλάξει fut act ind 3 sg [2t; v-2b; 5875]   "
φυλάξῃ aor act subj 3 sg [Jn 12:47; v-2b; 5875]   "
φυλάξῃς aor act subj 2 sg
[1Ti 5:21; v-2b; 5875]   "
φύλαξον aor act imperative 2 sg
[2t; v-2b; 5875]   "
φυλάς acc pl fem [2t; n-1b; 5876]   φυλή
φυλάσσειν pres act inf [2t; v-2b; 5875]   φυλάσσω
φυλάσσεσθαι pres mid inf
[Ac 21:25; v-2b; 5875]   "
φυλάσσεσθαι pres pass inf
[Ac 23:35; v-2b; 5875]   "
φυλάσσεσθε pres mid imperative 2 pl
[2t; v-2b; 5875]   "
φυλάσσῃ pres act subj 3 sg [2t; v-2b; 5875]   "
φυλασσόμενος pres pass ptcp nom sg masc
[Lk 8:29; v-2b; 5875]   "
φυλάσσοντες pres act ptcp nom pl masc
[2t; v-2b; 5875]   "
φυλάσσοντι pres act ptcp dat sg masc
[Ac 28:16; v-2b; 5875]   "
φυλάσσου pres mid imperative 2 sg
[2Ti 4:15; v-2b; 5875]   "
φυλάσσουσιν pres act ind 3 pl
[Ga 6:13; v-2b; 5875]   "

φυλάσσω   {5875, v-2b}
[φυλάξω, ἐφύλαξα, πεφύλαχα, -, ἐφυλάχθην] *to be on watch, keep* watch, Luke 2:8; *to have in keeping,* Acts 20:20; *to have in custody,* Acts 28:16; *to keep* under restraint, *confine,* Luke 8:29; Acts 12:4; 23:35; *to guard, defend,* Luke 11:21; *to keep safe, preserve,* John 12:25; 17:12; 2 Thess 3:3; 2 Peter 2:5; Jude 24; *to keep* in abstinence, Acts 21:25; 1 John 5:21; *to observe* a matter of injunction or duty, Matt 19:20 v.l.; Mark 10:20; Luke 11:28; 18:21 v.l.; Acts 7:53; 16:4; 21:24; mid. *to be on one's guard, beware,* Luke 12:15; 2 Tim 4:15; 2 Peter 3:17

φυλάσσων pres act ptcp nom sg masc
[2t; v-2b; 5875]   "

φυλή, ῆς, ἡ   {5876, n-1b}
a tribe, Matt 19:28; 24:30; Luke 2:36; *a people, nation,* Rev 1:7; 5:9

φυλήν acc sg fem [3t; n-1b; 5876]   φυλή
φυλῆς gen sg fem [20t; n-1b; 5876]   "
φύλλα nom pl neut [Rv 22:2; n-2c; 5877]   φύλλον
φύλλα acc pl neut [5t; n-2c; 5877]

φύλλον, ου, τό   {5877, n-2c}
   a leaf, Matt 21:19

φυλῶν   gen pl fem   [3t; n-1b; 5876]   φυλή
φύουσα   pres act ptcp nom sg fem
   [Hb 12:15; v-1a(4); 5886]   φύω

φύραμα, ατος, τό   {5878, n-3c(4)}
   *that which is mingled and reduced to a uniform
   consistence, by kneading, beating, treading,* etc.; *a
   mass* of potter's clay, Rom 9:21; of dough, 1 Cor
   5:6, 7; Gal 5:9; met. Rom 11:16*

φύραμα   nom sg neut   [2t; n-3c(4); 5878]   φύραμα
φύραμα   acc sg neut   [2t; n-3c(4); 5878]   "
φυράματος   gen sg neut   [Rm 9:21; n-3c(4); 5878]   "
φύσει   dat sg fem   [5t; n-3e(5b); 5882]   φύσις
φύσεως   gen sg fem   [2t; n-3e(5b); 5882]   "
φυσικά   nom pl neut
   [2P 2:12; a-1a(2a); 5879]   φυσικός
φυσικήν   acc sg fem   [2t; a-1a(2a); 5879]   "

φυσικός, ή, όν   {5879, a-1a(2a)}
   natural, agreeable to nature, Rom 1:26, 27;
   following the instinct of nature, as animals, 2
   Peter 2:12*

φυσικῶς   {5880, adverb}
   naturally, by natural instinct, Jude 10*

φυσικῶς   adverb   [Jd 10; adverb; 5880]   φυσικῶς
φύσιν   acc sg fem   [5t; n-3e(5b); 5882]   φύσις
φυσιοῖ   pres act ind 3 sg
   [1C 8:1; v-1d(3); 5881]   φυσιόω
φυσιούμενος   pres pass ptcp nom sg masc
   [Cl 2:18; v-1d(3); 5881]   "
φυσιοῦσθε   pres pass ind 2 pl
   [1C 4:6; v-1d(3); 5881]   "
φυσιοῦται   pres pass ind 3 sg
   [1C 13:4; v-1d(3); 5881]   "

φυσιόω   {5881, v-1d(3)}
   [-, -, -, πεφυσίωμαι, ἐφυσιώθην] *to inflate puff up;*
   met. *to inflate* with pride and vanity, 1 Cor 8:1;
   pass. *to be inflated* with pride, *to be proud, vain,
   arrogant,* 1 Cor 4:6, 18, 19; 5:2; 13:4; Col 2:18*

φύσις, εως, ἡ   {5882, n-3e(5b)}
   essence, Gal 4:8; *native condition, birth,* Rom 2:27;
   11:21, 24; Gal 2:15; Eph 2:3; *native species, kind,*
   James 3:7; *nature, natural frame,* 2 Peter 1:4;
   nature, native instinct, Rom 2:14; 1 Cor 11:14;
   nature, prescribed course of nature, Rom 1:26*

φύσις   nom sg fem   [2t; n-3e(5b); 5882]   φύσις
φυσιώσεις   nom pl fem
   [2C 12:20; n-3e(5b); 5883]   φυσίωσις

φυσίωσις, εως, ἡ   {5883, n-3e(5b)}
   pr. *inflation;* met. *inflation* of mind, *pride,* 2 Cor
   12:20*

φυτεία, ας, ἡ   {5884, n-1a}
   plantation, the act of planting; a plant, met. Matt
   15:13*

φυτεία   nom sg fem   [Mt 15:13; n-1a; 5884]   φυτεία
φυτεύει   pres act ind 3 sg
   [1C 9:7; v-1a(6); 5885]   φυτεύω

φυτεύθητι   aor pass imperative 2 sg
   [Lk 17:6; v-1a(6); 5885]   "

φυτεύω   {5885, v-1a(6)}
   [(ἐφύτευον), -, ἐφύτευσα, -, πεφύτευμαι,
   ἐφυτεύθην] *to plant, set,* Matt 21:33; Luke 13:6;
   17:6, 28; 20:9; met. Matt 15:13; Mark 12:1; *to
   plant* the Gospel, 1 Cor 3:6, 7, 8; 9:7*

φυτεύων   pres act ptcp nom sg masc
   [2t; v-1a(6); 5885]   "

φύω   {5886, v-1a(4)}
   [-, -, -, -, ἐφύην] *to generate, produce;* pass. *to be
   generated, produced;* of plants, *to germinate,
   sprout,* Luke 8:6, 8; intrans. *to germinate, spring*
   or *grow up,* Heb 12:15*

φωλεός, ου, ὁ   {5887, n-2a}
   a den, lair, burrow, Matt 8:20; Luke 9:58*

φωλεούς   acc pl masc   [2t; n-2a; 5887]   φωλεός
φωναί   nom pl fem   [6t; n-1b; 5889]   φωνή
φωναῖς   dat pl fem   [Lk 23:23; n-1b; 5889]   "
φωνάς   acc pl fem   [2t; n-1b; 5889]   "
φωνεῖ   pres act ind 3 sg   [6t; v-1d(2a); 5888]   φωνέω
φώνει   pres act imperative 2 sg
   [Lk 14:12; v-1d(2a); 5888]   "
φωνεῖτε   pres act ind 2 pl
   [Jn 13:13; v-1d(2a); 5888]   "

φωνέω   {5888, v-1d(2a)}
   [(ἐφώνουν), φωνήσω, ἐφώνησα, -, -, ἐφωνήθην] *to
   sound, utter a sound;* of the cock, *to crow,* Matt
   26:34, 74, 75; *to call,* or *cry out, exclaim,* Luke 8:8,
   54; 16:24; 23:46; *to call to,* Matt 27:47; Mark 3:31;
   to call, John 13:13; *to call, summon,* Matt 20:32; *to
   invite* to a feast, Luke 14:12

φωνή, ῆς, ἡ   {5889, n-1b}
   a sound, Matt 24:31; John 3:8; Rev 4:5; 8:5; *a cry,*
   Matt 2:18; *an* articulate *sound, voice,* Matt 3:3,
   17; 17:5; 27:46, 50; *voice, speech, discourse,* John
   10:16, 27; Acts 7:31; 12:22; 13:27; Heb 3:7, 15;
   tone of address, Gal 4:20; *language, tongue,
   dialect,* 1 Cor 14:10

φωνή   nom sg fem   [32t; n-1b; 5889]   φωνή
φωνῇ   dat sg fem   [33t; n-1b; 5889]   "
φωνηθῆναι   aor pass inf
   [Lk 19:15; v-1d(2a); 5888]   φωνέω
φωνήν   acc sg fem   [40t; n-1b; 5889]   φωνή
φωνῆς   gen sg fem   [23t; n-1b; 5889]   "
φωνῆσαι   aor act inf   [6t; v-1d(2a); 5888]   φωνέω
φωνῆσαν   aor act ptcp nom sg neut
   [Mk 1:26; v-1d(2a); 5888]   "
φωνήσαντες   aor act ptcp nom pl masc
   [Ac 10:18; v-1d(2a); 5888]   "
φωνήσας   aor act ptcp nom sg masc
   [5t; v-1d(2a); 5888]   "
φωνήσατε   aor act imperative 2 pl
   [Mk 10:49; v-1d(2a); 5888]   "
φωνήσει   fut act ind 3 sg
   [Lk 22:34; v-1d(2a); 5888]   "
φωνήσῃ   aor act subj 3 sg
   [Jn 13:38; v-1d(2a); 5888]   "
φώνησον   aor act imperative 2 sg
   [Jn 4:16; v-1d(2a); 5888]   "

φωνοῦσιν pres act ind 3 pl
[Mk 10:49; v-1d(2a); 5888]   "

φωνῶν gen pl fem [2t; n-1b; 5889]   φωνή

φῶς, φωτός, τό   {5890, n-3c(6c)}
light, Matt 17:2; 2 Cor 4:6; *daylight, broad day,*
Matt 10:27; Luke 12:3; *radiance, blaze of light,*
Matt 4:16; Acts 9:3; 12:7; *an instrument* or *means
of light, a light,* Matt 6:23; Acts 16:29; *a fire,* Mark
14:54; Luke 22:56; from the Hebrew, *the light* of
God's presence, 2 Cor 11:14; 1 Tim 6:16; met. *the
light* of Divine truth, spiritual *illumination,*
Luke 16:8; John 3:19; Rom 13:12; Eph 5:8; 1
Peter 2:9; 1 John 1:7; 2:8, 9, 10; *a source* or
dispenser of spiritual *light,* Matt 5:14; John 1:4, 5,
7, 8, 9; 8:12; 9:5; pure *radiance,* perfect *brightness,*
1 John 1:5

φῶς nom sg neut [24t; n-3c(6c); 5890]   φῶς
φῶς acc sg neut [24t; n-3c(6c); 5890]   "

φωστήρ, ρος, ὁ   {5891, n-3f(2a)}
a cause of light, illuminator; a light, luminary, star,
Phil 2:15; *radiance,* or, *luminary,* Rev 21:11*

φωστήρ nom sg masc
[Rv 21:11; n-3f(2a); 5891]   φωστήρ
φωστῆρες nom pl masc [Pp 2:15; n-3f(2a); 5891]   "

φωσφόρος, ον   {5892, a-3a}
light-bringing; sc. ἀστήρ, *Lucifer, the morning
star,* met. 2 Peter 1:19*

φωσφόρος nom sg masc
[2P 1:19; a-3a; 5892]   φωσφόρος
φῶτα acc pl neut [Ac 16:29; n-3c(6c); 5890]   φῶς
φωτεινή nom sg fem
[Mt 17:5; a-1a(2a); 5893]   φωτεινός
φωτεινόν nom sg neut [4t; a-1a(2a); 5893]   "

φωτεινός, ή, όν   {5893, a-1a(2a)}
radiant, lustrous, Matt 17:5; *enlightened,
illuminated,* Matt 6:22; Luke 11:34, 36 (2t)*

φωτί dat sg neut [9t; n-3c(6c); 5890]   φῶς
φωτίζει pres act ind 3 sg
[Jn 1:9; v-2a(1); 5894]   φωτίζω
φωτίζῃ pres act subj 3 sg
[Lk 11:36; v-2a(1); 5894]   "

φωτίζω   {5894, v-2a(1)}
[φωτίσω or φωτιῶ, ἐφώτισα, -, πεφώτισμαι,
ἐφωτίσθην] *to light, give light to, illuminate, shine
upon,* Luke 11:36; Rev 18:1; 21:23; 22:5 v.l.
(trans.); met. *to enlighten* spiritually, John 1:9;
Eph 1:18; 3:9; Heb 6:4; 10:32; *to reveal, to bring to
light, make known,* 1 Cor 4:5; Eph 3:9 v.l.; 2 Tim
1:10; intrans. *shine,* Rev 22:5*

φωτίσαι aor act inf [Ep 3:9; v-2a(1); 5894]
φωτίσαντος aor act ptcp gen sg masc
[2Ti 1:10; v-2a(1); 5894]   "
φωτίσει fut act ind 3 sg [2t; v-2a(1); 5894]   "
φωτισθέντας aor pass ptcp acc pl masc
[Hb 6:4; v-2a(1); 5894]   "
φωτισθέντες aor pass ptcp nom pl masc
[Hb 10:32; v-2a(1); 5894]   "
φωτισμόν acc sg masc [2t; n-2a; 5895]   φωτισμός

φωτισμός, οῦ, ὁ   {5895, n-2a}
*illumination; a shining forth, bringing to light,
enlightenment,* 2 Cor 4:4, 6*

φωτός gen sg neut [14t; n-3c(6c); 5890]   φῶς
φώτων gen pl neut [Jm 1:17; n-3c(6c); 5890]   "

χ

χαῖρε pres act imperative 2 sg
[5t; v-2d(2); 5897]   χαίρω
χαίρει pres act ind 3 sg [3t; v-2d(2); 5897]   "
χαίρειν pres act inf [7t; v-2d(2); 5897]   "
χαίρετε pres act imperative 2 pl
[11t; v-2d(2); 5897]   "
χαίρῃ pres act subj 3 sg
[Jn 4:36; v-2d(2); 5897]   "
χαίρομεν pres act ind 1 pl [2t; v-2d(2); 5897]   "
χαίροντες pres act ptcp nom pl masc
[6t; v-2d(2); 5897]   "
χαιρόντων pres act ptcp gen pl masc
[Rm 12:15; v-2d(2); 5897]   "
χαίρουσιν pres act ind 3 pl
[Rv 11:10; v-2d(2); 5897]   "

χαίρω   {5897, v-2d(2)}
[(ἔχαιρον), χαρήσομαι or χαροῦμαι, -, -, -,
ἐχάρην] *to rejoice, be glad, be joyful, be full of joy,*
Matt 2:10; 5:12; 18:13; Mark 14:11; Rom 12:12; 2
Cor 2:3; a term of salutation, *Hail!* Matt 26:49;
λέγω χαίρειν, *to greet,* 2 John 10:11; an epistolary
forth, *Health!* Acts 15:23

χαίρω pres act ind 1 sg [8t; v-2d(2); 5897]   "
χαίρωμεν pres act subj 1 pl
[Rv 19:7; v-2d(2); 5897]   "
χαίρων pres act ptcp nom sg masc
[4t; v-2d(2); 5897]   "

χάλαζα, ης, ἡ   {5898, n-1c}
hail, Rev 8:7; 11:19; 16:21 (2t)*

χάλαζα nom sg fem [3t; n-1c; 5898]   χάλαζα
χαλάζης gen sg fem [Rv 16:21; n-1c; 5898]   "
χαλάσαντες aor act ptcp nom pl masc
[2t; v-1d(1b); 5899]   χαλάω
χαλασάντων aor act ptcp gen pl masc
[Ac 27:30; v-1d(1b); 5899]   "
χαλάσατε aor act imperative 2 pl
[Lk 5:4; v-1d(1b); 5899]   "
χαλάσω fut act ind 1 sg [Lk 5:5; v-1d(1b); 5899]   "

χαλάω   {5899, v-1d(1b)}
[χαλάσω, ἐχάλασα, -, -, ἐχαλάσθην] *to slacken; to
let down, lower,* Mark 2:4; Luke 5:4, 5; Acts 9:25;
27:17, 30; 1 Cor 11:33*

Χαλδαῖος, ου, ὁ   {5900, n-2a}
a Chaldean, a native of Chaldea, a country of
central Asia, which seems to have included
Mesopotamia, Acts 7:4*

Χαλδαίων gen pl masc
[Ac 7:4; n-2a; 5900]   χαλδαῖος
χαλεποί nom pl masc [2t; a-1a(2a); 5901]   χαλεπός

χαλεπός, ή, όν   {5901, a-1a(2a)}
hard, rugged; furious, ferocious, Matt 8:28;
difficult, trying, 2 Tim 3:1*

χαλιναγωγῆσαι   aor act inf
[Jm 3:2; v-1d(2a); 5902]   χαλιναγωγέω

χαλιναγωγέω   {5902, v-1d(2a)}
[χαλιναγωγήσω, ἐχαλιναγώγησα, -, -, -] pr. *to
guide with a bridle;* met. *to bridle, control, sway,*
James 1:26; 3:2*

χαλιναγωγῶν   pres act ptcp nom sg masc
[Jm 1:26; v-1d(2a); 5902]   "

χαλινός, οῦ, ὁ   {5903, n-2a}
a bridle, bit, James 3:3; Rev 14:20*

χαλινούς   acc pl masc [Jm 3:3; n-2a; 5903]   χαλινός

χαλινόω   {5904, v-1d(3)}
[-, -, -, -, -] to *bridle, hold in check,* James 1:26 v.l.*

χαλινῶν   gen pl masc [Rv 14:20; n-2a; 5903]
χαλκᾶ   acc pl neut [Rv 9:20; a-1b; 5911]   χαλκοῦς

χάλκεος, uncontracted form of χαλκοῦς   {5905}

χαλκεύς, έως, ὁ   {5906, n-3e(3)}
pr. *a coppersmith;* hence, genr. *a worker in metals,
smith,* 2 Tim 4:14*

χαλκεύς   nom sg masc
[2Ti 4:14; n-3e(3); 5906]   χαλκεύς

χαλκηδών, όνος, ὁ   {5907, n-3f(1b)}
chalcedony, the name of a gem, generally of a
whitish, bluish, or gray color, susceptible of a
high and beautiful polish, and of which there
are several varieties, as the onyx, modern
carnelian, etc., Rev 21:19*

χαλκηδών   nom sg masc
[Rv 21:19; n-3f(1b); 5907]   χαλκηδών

χαλκίον, ου, τό   {5908, n-2c}
a vessel, copper, brazen utensil, Mark 7:4*

χαλκίων   gen pl neut [Mk 7:4; n-2c; 5908]   χαλκίον

χαλκολίβανον, ου, τό   {5909, n-2c}
orichalcum, fine bronze, a factitious metal of
which there were several varieties, the white
being of the highest repute, or, *deep-tinted
frankincense,* Rev 1:15; 2:18*

χαλκολιβάνῳ   dat sg neut
[2t; n-2c; 5909]   χαλκολίβανον
χαλκόν   acc sg masc [3t; n-2a; 5910]   χαλκός

χαλκός, οῦ, ὁ   {5910, n-2a}
copper, also, *bronze,* Rev 18:12; *a brazen musical
instrument,* 1 Cor 13:1; *copper money,* Matt 10:9;
money in general, Mark 6:8; 12:41*

χαλκός   nom sg masc [1C 13:1; n-2a; 5910]   "
χαλκοῦ   gen sg masc [Rv 18:12; n-2a; 5910]   "

χαλκοῦς, ῆ, οῦν   {5911, a-1b}
contracted form of χάλκεος, *made of copper,
brass,* or *bronze,* Rev 9:20*

χαλῶσι   pres act ind 3 pl
[Mk 2:4; v-1d(1b); 5899]   χαλάω

χαμαί   {5912, adverb}
on the ground, to the earth, John 9:6; 18:6*

χαμαί   adverb [2t; adverb; 5912]   χαμαί

Χανάαν, ἡ   {5913, n-3g(2)}
Canaan, the ancient name of Palestine, Acts
7:11; 13:19

Χανάαν   indecl [2t; n-3g(2); 5913]   χανάαν
Χαναναία   nom sg fem
[Mt 15:22; a-1a(1); 5914]   χαναναῖος

Χαναναῖος, α, ον   {5914, a-1a(1)}
Canaanitish, of Canaan, Matt 15:22*

χαρά, ᾶς, ἡ   {5915, n-1a}
joy, gladness, rejoicing, Matt 2:10; 13:20, 44; 28:8;
meton, *joy, cause of joy, occasion of rejoicing,* Luke
2:10; Phil 4:1; 1 Thess 2:19, 20; *bliss,* Matt 25:21,
23

χαρά   nom sg fem [16t; n-1a; 5915]   χαρά
χαρά   voc sg fem [Pp 4:1; n-1a; 5915]   "
χαρᾷ   dat sg fem [6t; n-1a; 5915]   "

χάραγμα, ατος, τό   {5916, n-3c(4)}
an imprinted mark, Rev 13:16, 17; 14:9, 11; 15:2
v.l.; 16:2; 19:20; 20:4; *sculpture,* Acts 17:29*

χάραγμα   acc sg neut [7t; n-3c(4); 5916]   χάραγμα
χαράγματι   dat sg neut [Ac 17:29; n-3c(4); 5916]   "
χάρακα   acc sg masc
[Lk 19:43; n-3b(1); 5918]   χάραξ

χαρακτήρ, ῆρος, ὁ   {5917, n-3f(2a)}
a graver, graving-tool; an engraven or *impressed
device; an impress, exact expression,* Heb 1:3*

χαρακτήρ   nom sg masc
[Hb 1:3; n-3f(2a); 5917]   χαρακτήρ
χαράν   acc sg fem [14t; n-1a; 5915]   χαρά

χάραξ, ακός, ὁ   {5918, n-3b(1)}
a stake; a military *palisade, rampart,* formed from
the earth thrown out of the ditch, and stuck
with sharp stakes or palisades, Luke 19:43*

χαρᾶς   gen sg fem [22t; n-1a; 5915]   "
χαρῆναι   aor pass inf [2t; v-2d(2); 5897]   χαίρω
χαρήσεται   fut pass ind 3 sg [2t; v-2d(2); 5897]   "
χαρήσομαι   fut pass ind 1 sg
[Pp 1:18; v-2d(2); 5897]   "
χαρήσονται   fut pass ind 3 pl
[Lk 1:14; v-2d(2); 5897]   "
χάρητε   aor pass imperative 2 pl
[Lk 6:23; v-2d(2); 5897]   "
χαρῆτε   aor pass subj 2 pl [2t; v-2d(2); 5897]   "
χαρίζεσθαι   pres mid inf
[Ac 25:16; v-2a(1); 5919]   χαρίζομαι
χαρίζεσθε   pres mid ind 2 pl
[2C 2:10; v-2a(1); 5919]   "

χαρίζομαι   {5919, v-2a(1)}
[χαρίσομαι, ἐχαρισάμην, -, κεχάρισμαι,
ἐχαρίσθην] *to gratify; to bestow* in kindness,
grant as a free favor, Luke 7:21; Rom 8:32; *to
grant the deliverance* of a person in favor to the
desire of others, Acts 3:14; 27:24; Phlm 22; *to
sacrifice* a person to the demand of enemies,

Acts 25:11; *to remit, forgive,* Luke 7:42; 2 Cor 2:7, 10

χαριζόμενοι   pres mid ptcp nom pl masc
[2t; v-2a(1); 5919]   "

χάριν   {5920, prep}
the acc. sg form of the noun χάριν which can be used as an im proper prep., *on account of,* Luke 7:47; Eph 3:1, 14; 1 John 3:12; *for the sake of, in order to,* Gal 3:19; Titus 1:5, 11; Jude 16; *on the score of,* 1 Tim 5:14*

χάριν   acc sg fem   [42t; n-3c(1); 5921]   χάρις
χάριν   prep   [9t; prep; 5920]   χάριν

χάρις, ιτος, ἡ   {5921, n-3c(1)}
pleasing show, charm; beauty, gracefulness; a pleasing circumstance, matter of approval, 1 Peter 2:19, 20; *kindly bearing, graciousness,* Luke 4:22; *a beneficial opportunity, benefit,* 2 Cor 1:15; Eph 4:29; *a charitable act, generous gift,* 1 Cor 16:3; 2 Cor 8:4, 6; *an act of favor,* Acts 25:3; *favor, acceptance,* Luke 1:30, 52; Acts 2:47; 7:10, 46; *free favor, free gift, grace,* John 1:14, 16, 17; Rom 4:4, 16; 11:5, 6; Eph 2:5, 8; 1 Peter 3:7; *free favor* specially manifested by God towards man in the Gospel scheme, *grace,* Acts 15:11; Rom 3:24; 5:15, 17, 20, 21; 6:1; 2 Cor 4:15; *a gracious provision, gracious scheme, grace,* Rom 6:14, 15; Heb 2:9; 12:28; 13:9; *gracious dealing* from God, *grace,* Acts 14:26; 15:40; Rom 1:7; 1 Cor 1:4; 15:10; Gal 1:15; *a commission graciously devolved* by God upon a human agent, Rom 1:5; 12:3; 15:15; 1 Cor 3:10; 2 Cor 1:12; Gal 2:9; Eph 3:8; *grace, graciously bestowed* divine *endowment* or *influence,* Luke 2:40; Acts 4:33; 11:23; Rom 12:6; 2 Cor 12:9; *grace,* Acts 11:43; Rom 5:2; Gal 5:4; 2 Peter 3:18; *an emotion correspondent to what is pleasing* or *kindly; sense of obligation,* Luke 17:9; *a grateful frame of mind,* 1 Cor 10:30; *thanks,* Luke 6:32, 33, 34; Rom 6:17; 1 Cor 15:57; χάριν or χάριτας καταθέσθαι, *to oblige, gratify,* Acts 24:27; 25:9

χάρις   nom sg fem   [60t; n-3c(1); 5921]   χάρις
χαρισάμενος   aor mid ptcp nom sg masc
[Cl 2:13; v-2a(1); 5919]   χαρίζομαι
χαρίσασθαι   aor mid inf   [2t; v-2a(1); 5919]   "
χαρίσασθε   aor mid imperative 2 pl
[2C 12:13; v-2a(1); 5919]   "
χαρίσεται   fut mid ind 3 sg
[Rm 8:32; v-2a(1); 5919]   "
χαρισθέντα   aor pass ptcp acc pl neut
[1C 2:12; v-2a(1); 5919]   "
χαρισθῆναι   aor pass inf
[Ac 3:14; v-2a(1); 5919]   "
χαρισθήσομαι   fut pass ind 1 sg
[Pm 22; v-2a(1); 5919]   "

χάρισμα, ατος, τό   {5922, n-3c(4)}
a free favor, free gift, Rom 5:15, 16; 6:23; 2 Cor 1:11; *benefit,* Rom 1:11; a divinely conferred *endowment,* 1 Cor 12:4, 9, 28, 30, 31

χάρισμα   nom sg neut   [4t; n-3c(4); 5922]   χάρισμα
χάρισμα   acc sg neut   [4t; n-3c(4); 5922]   "
χαρίσματα   nom pl neut   [2t; n-3c(4); 5922]   "

χαρίσματα   acc pl neut   [4t; n-3c(4); 5922]   "
χαρίσματι   dat sg neut   [1C 1:7; n-3c(4); 5922]   "
χαρίσματος   gen sg neut   [1Ti 4:14; n-3c(4); 5922]   "
χαρισμάτων   gen pl neut   [1C 12:4; n-3c(4); 5922]   "
χάριτα   acc sg fem   [2t; n-3c(1); 5921]   χάρις
χάριτι   dat sg fem   [24t; n-3c(1); 5921]   "
χάριτος   gen sg fem   [27t; n-3c(1); 5921]   "

χαριτόω   {5923, v-1d(3)}
[-, ἐχαρίτωσα, -, κεχαρίτωμαι, -] *to favor, visit with favor, to make an object of favor, to gift,* Eph 1:6; pass. *to be visited with free favor, be an object of gracious visitation,* Luke 1:28*

Χαρράν, ἡ   {5924, n-3g(2)}
Charran, a city in the northern part of Mesopotamia, Acts 7:2, 4*

Χαρράν   indecl   [2t; n-3g(2); 5924]   χαρράν

χάρτης, ου, ὁ   {5925, n-1f}
paper, 2 John 12*

χάρτου   gen sg masc   [2J 12; n-1f; 5925]   χάρτης

χάσμα, ατος, τό   {5926, n-3c(4)}
a chasm, gulf, Luke 16:26*

χάσμα   nom sg neut
[Lk 16:26; n-3c(4); 5926]   χάσμα
χείλεσιν   dat pl neut   [3t; n-3d(2b); 5927]   χεῖλος
χειλέων   gen pl neut   [Hb 13:15; n-3d(2b); 5927]   "
χείλη   acc pl neut   [2t; n-3d(2b); 5927]   "

χεῖλος, ους, τό   {5927, n-3d(2b)}
a lip, and pl. τὰ χείλη, *the lips,* Matt 15:8; Mark 7:6; Rom 3:13; Heb 13:15; 1 Peter 3:10; trop. χεῖλος τῆς θαλάσσης, *the seashore,* Heb 11:12; meton. *language, dialect,* 1 Cor 14:21*

χεῖλος   acc sg neut   [Hb 11:12; n-3d(2b); 5927]   "
χειμαζομένων   pres pass ptcp gen pl masc
[Ac 27:18; v-2a(1); 5928]   χειμάζω

χειμάζω   {5928, v-2a(1)}
[χειμάσω, ἐχείμασα, κεχείμακα, -, -] *to excite a tempest, toss with a tempest;* pass. *to be storm-tossed,* Acts 27:18*

χειμάρρου   gen sg masc
[Jn 18:1; n-2d(1); 5929]   χειμάρρους

χειμάρρους, ου, ὁ   {5929, n-2d(1)}
contracted form of χειμάρρος, *winter-flowing;* as a subst. *a stream which flows in winter,* but is dry in summer, *a brook,* John 18:1*

χειμών, ῶνος, ὁ   {5930, n-3f(1a)}
stormy weather, Matt 16:3; *a storm, tempest,* Acts 27:20; *winter,* Matt 24:20; Mark 13:18; John 10:22; 2 Tim 4:21*

χειμών   nom sg masc   [2t; n-3f(1a); 5930]   χειμών
χειμῶνος   gen sg masc   [4t; n-3f(1a); 5930]   "

χείρ, ρος, ἡ   {5931, n-3f(2a)}
a hand, Matt 3:12; 4:6; 8:15 freq.; from the Hebrew, χεὶρ Κυρίου, a special *operation of God,* Acts 11:21; 13:3; ἐν χειρί, *by agency,* Acts 7:35; Gal 3:19

χείρ   nom sg fem   [13t; n-3f(2a); 5931]   χείρ
χεῖρα   acc sg fem   [30t; n-3f(2a); 5931]   "

χειραγωγέω   {5932, v-1d(2a)}
[-, -, -, -, -] *to lead by the hand,* Acts 9:8; 22:11*

χειραγωγός, οῦ, ὁ   {5933, n-2a}
one who leads another by the hand, Acts 13:11*

χειραγωγούμενος   pres pass ptcp nom sg masc
   [Ac 22:11; v-1d(2a); 5932]   χειραγωγέω
χειραγωγοῦντες   pres act ptcp nom pl masc
   [Ac 9:8; v-1d(2a); 5932]   "
χειραγωγούς   acc pl masc
   [Ac 13:11; n-2a; 5933]   χειραγωγός
χεῖρας   acc pl fem [60t; n-3f(2a); 5931]   χείρ
χεῖρες   nom pl fem [2t; n-3f(2a); 5931]   "
χειρί   dat sg fem [20t; n-3f(2a); 5931]   "

χειρόγραφον, ου, τό   {5934, n-2c}
handwriting; a written form, literal instrument, as
distinguished from a spiritual dispensation,
Col 2:14*

χειρόγραφον   acc sg neut
   [Cl 2:14; n-2c; 5934]   χειρόγραφον
χεῖρον   nom sg neut comparative
   [3t; a-4b(1); 5937]   χείρων
χεῖρον   acc sg neut comparative
   [2t; a-4b(1); 5937]   "
χείρονα   nom pl neut comparative
   [3t; a-4b(1); 5937]   "
χείρονος   gen sg fem comparative
   [Hb 10:29; a-4b(1); 5937]   "
χειροποίητα   acc pl neut
   [Hb 9:24; a-3a; 5935]   χειροποίητος
χειροποίητοις   dat pl masc [2t; a-3a; 5935]   "
χειροποίητον   acc sg masc [Mk 14:58; a-3a; 5935] "

χειροποίητος, ον   {5935, a-3a}
made by hand, artificial, material, Mark 14:58;
Acts 7:48; 17:24; Eph 2:11; Heb 9:11, 24*

χειροποίητου   gen sg fem [2t; a-3a; 5935]   "
χειρός   gen sg fem [26t; n-3f(2a); 5931]   χείρ

χειροτονέω   {5936, v-1d(2a)}
[-, ἐχειροτόνησα, -, κεχειροτόνημαι,
ἐχειροτονήθην] *to stretch out the hand; to
constitute by voting; to appoint, constitute,* Acts
14:23; 2 Cor 8:19*

χειροτονηθείς   aor pass ptcp nom sg masc
   [2C 8:19; v-1d(2a); 5936]   χειροτονέω
χειροτονήσαντες   aor act ptcp nom pl masc
   [Ac 14:23; v-1d(2a); 5936]   "

χείρων, ον, gen., ονος   {5937, a-4b(1)}
worse, Matt 9:16; *more severe,* John 5:14; Heb
10:29

χείρων   nom sg masc comparative
   [1Ti 5:8; a-4b(1); 5937]   χείρων
χείρων   nom sg fem comparative
   [Mt 27:64; a-4b(1); 5937]   "
χειρῶν   gen pl fem [16t; n-3f(2a); 5931]   χείρ

Χερούβ, τό   {5938, n-3g(1)}
also spelled Χερουβείν and Χερουβίμ, indecl.
*cherub, a two-winged figure over the ark of the
covenant,* Heb 9:5*

Χερουβείν, see Χερούβ

Χερουβίμ, see Χερούβ

Χερουβίν   indecl [Hb 9:5; n-3g(1); 5938]   Χερούβ
χερσίν   dat pl fem [10t; n-3f(2a); 5931]   χείρ

χήρα, ας, ἡ   {5939, n-1a}
a widow, Matt 23:14; Luke 4:26

χήρα   nom sg fem [10t; n-1a; 5939]   χήρα
χῆραι   nom pl fem [3t; n-1a; 5939]   "
χήραις   dat pl fem [2t; n-1a; 5939]   "
χήραν   acc sg fem [3t; n-1a; 5939]   "
χήρας   acc pl fem [6t; n-1a; 5939]   "
χηρῶν   gen pl fem [2t; n-1a; 5939]   "

χθές   {5940, adverb}
v.l. for ἐχθές, *yesterday,* John 4:52; Acts 7:28; Heb
13:8*

χίλια   nom pl neut [5t; a-1a(1); 5943]   χίλιοι
χίλια   acc pl neut [3t; a-1a(1); 5943]   "
χιλιάδες   nom pl fem [19t; n-3c(2); 5942]   χιλιάς
χιλιάδων   gen pl fem [3t; n-3c(2); 5942]   "
χιλίαρχοι   nom pl masc
   [Rv 6:15; n-2a; 5941]   χιλίαρχος
χιλιάρχοις   dat pl masc [2t; n-2a; 5941]   "
χιλίαρχον   acc sg masc [3t; n-2a; 5941]   "

χιλίαρχος, ου, ὁ   {5941, n-2a}
commander of a thousand men; hence, genr. *a
commander, military chief,* Mark 6:21; Rev 6:15;
19:18; spc. *a legionary tribune,* Acts 21:31, 32,
33, 37; *the prefect* of the temple, John 18:12

χιλίαρχος   nom sg masc [10t; n-2a; 5941]   "
χιλιάρχῳ   dat sg masc [4t; n-2a; 5941]   "
χιλιάρχων   gen pl masc [Rv 19:18; n-2a; 5941]   "

χιλιάς, άδος, ἡ   {5942, n-3c(2)}
the number *one thousand, a thousand,* Luke
14:31; Acts 4:4

χιλίας   acc pl fem [2t; a-1a(1); 5943]   χίλιοι
χιλιάσιν   dat pl fem
   [Lk 14:31; n-3c(2); 5942]   χιλιάς

χίλιοι, αι, α   {5943, a-1a(1)}
a thousand, 2 Peter 3:8; Rev 11:3; 12:6; 14:20;
20:2-7*

χιλίων   gen pl masc
   [Rv 14:20; a-1a(1); 5943]   χίλιοι

χίος, ου, ἡ   {5944, n-2b}
Chios, an island near the coast of Asia Minor, in
the Aegean sea, between Samos and Lesbos,
Acts 20:15*

Χίου   gen sg fem [Ac 20:15; n-2b; 5944]   χίος

χιτών, ῶνος, ὁ   {5945, n-3f(1a)}
a tunic, vest, the inner garment which fitted
close to the body, having armholes, and
sometimes sleeves, and reaching below the
knees, worn by both sexes, Matt 5:40; 10:10; pl.
χιτῶνες, *clothes, garments* in general, Mark 14:63

χιτών   nom sg masc
   [Jn 19:23; n-3f(1a); 5945]   χιτών
χιτῶνα   acc sg masc [4t; n-3f(1a); 5945]   "
χιτῶνας   acc pl masc [6t; n-3f(1a); 5945]   "

χιών, όνος, ἡ   {5946, n-3f(1b)}
snow, Matt 28:3; Mark 9:3 v.l.; Rev 1:14*

χιών   nom sg fem [2t; n-3f(1b); 5946]   χιών
χλαμύδα   acc sg fem [2t; n-3c(2); 5948]   χλαμύς

χλαμύς, ύδος, ἡ   {5948, n-3c(2)}
chlamys, a type of *cloak*; a Roman military
commander's *cloak*, Matt 27:28, 31*

χλευάζω   {5949, v-2a(1)}
[(ἐχλεύαζον), -, -, -, -, -] *to jeer, scoff*, Acts 2:13 v.l.;
17:32*

χλιαρός, ά, όν   {5950, a-1a(1)}
warm, tepid; lukewarm, Rev 3:16*

χλιαρός   nom sg masc
[Rv 3:16; a-1a(1); 5950]   χλιαρός

χλόη, ης, ἡ   {5951, n-1b}
Chloe, pr. name, 1 Cor 1:11*

Χλόης   gen sg fem [1C 1:11; n-1b; 5951]   χλόη
χλωρόν   acc sg neut [Rv 9:4; a-1a(1); 5952]   χλωρός

χλωρός, ά, όν   {5952, a-1a(1)}
pale green; green, verdent, Mark 6:39; Rev 8:7; 9:4;
pale, sallow, Rev 6:8*

χλωρός   nom sg masc [2t; a-1a(1); 5952]   "
χλωρῷ   dat sg masc [Mk 6:39; a-1a(1); 5952]   "

χξς´   {5953; a-5b}
six hundred and sixty-six, the number denoted
by these letters; viz., χ´ = 600, ξ´ = 60, ς´ = 6, Rev
13:18 v.l. Our texts read ἑξακόσιοι ἑξήκοντα ἕξ.*

χοϊκοί   nom pl masc
[1C 15:48; a-1a(2a); 5954]   χοϊκός

χοϊκός, ή, όν   {5954, a-1a(2a)}
of earth, earthy, 1 Cor 15:47, 48, 49*

χοϊκός   nom sg masc [2t; a-1a(2a); 5954]   "
χοϊκοῦ   gen sg masc [1C 15:49; a-1a(2a); 5954]   "
χοίνικες   nom pl fem
[Rv 6:6; n-3b(1); 5955]   χοῖνιξ

χοῖνιξ, ικός, ἡ   {5955, n-3b(1)}
a choenix, an Attic measure for things dry, being
the 48th part of a medimnus, consequently
equal to the 8th part of the Roman modius, and
nearly equivalent to about one quart, being
considered a sufficient daily allowance for the
sustenance of one man, Rev 6:6 (2t)*

χοῖνιξ   nom sg fem [Rv 6:6; n-3b(1); 5955]   "
χοῖροι   nom pl masc [Lk 15:16; n-2a; 5956]   χοῖρος

χοῖρος, ου, ὁ   {5956, n-2a}
pr. *a young swine; a swine, hog*, or *sow*, Matt 8:30,
31, 32

χοίρους   acc pl masc [5t; n-2a; 5956]   "
χοίρων   gen pl masc [6t; n-2a; 5956]   "
χολᾶτε   pres act ind 2 pl
[Jn 7:23; v-1d(1a); 5957]   χολάω

χολάω   {5957, v-1d(1a)}
[-, -, -, -, -] pr. *to be melancholy;* used later as an
equivalent to χολοῦμαι, *to be angry, incensed*,
John 7:23*

χολή, ῆς, ἡ   {5958, n-1b}
the bile, gall; in N.T. *a bitter ingredient*, as
wormwood, Matt 27:34; χολὴ πικρίας, *intense
bitterness*, met. *thorough disaffection* to divine
truth, *utter estrangement*, Acts 8:23*

χολήν   acc sg fem [Ac 8:23; n-1b; 5958]   χολή
χολῆς   gen sg fem [Mt 27:34; n-1b; 5958]   "

χόος, uncontracted form of χοῦς   {5959}

Χοραζείν, see Χοραζίν

Χοραζίν, ἡ   {5960, n-3g(2)}
also spelled Χωραζίν and Χοραζείν, *Chorazin*, a
town of Galilee, probably near Bethsaida and
Capernaum, indecl., Matt 11:21; Luke 10:13*

Χοραζίν   indecl [2t; n-3g(2); 5960]   χοραζίν
χορηγεῖ   pres act ind 3 sg
[1P 4:11; v-1d(2a); 5961]   χορηγέω

χορηγέω   {5961, v-1d(2a)}
[χορηγήσω, ἐχορήγησα, -, -, ἐχορηγήθην] *to lead a
chorus;* at Athens, *to defray the cost of a chorus;*
hence, *to supply funds; to supply, furnish*, 2 Cor
9:10; 1 Peter 4:11*

χορηγήσει   fut act ind 3 sg
[2C 9:10; v-1d(2a); 5961]   "

χορός, οῦ, ὁ   {5962, n-2a}
dancing with music, Luke 15:25*

χορτάζεσθαι   pres pass inf
[Pp 4:12; v-2a(1); 5963]   χορτάζω
χορτάζεσθε   pres pass imperative 2 pl
[Jm 2:16; v-2a(1); 5963]   "

χορτάζω   {5963, v-2a(1)}
[-, ἐχόρτασα, -, -, ἐχορτάσθην] pr. *to feed* or *fill*
with grass, herbage, etc., *to fatten;* used of
animals of prey, *to satiate, gorge*, Rev 19:21; of
persons, *to satisfy with food*, Matt 14:20; 15:33,
37; met. *to satisfy* the desire of any one, Matt 5:6

χορτάσαι   aor act inf [2t; v-2a(1); 5963]   "
χορτασθῆναι   aor pass inf [3t; v-2a(1); 5963]   "
χορτασθήσεσθε   fut pass ind 2 pl
[Lk 6:21; v-2a(1); 5963]   "
χορτασθήσονται   fut pass ind 3 pl
[Mt 5:6; v-2a(1); 5963]   "

χόρτασμα, ατος, τό   {5964, n-3c(4)}
pasture, provender for cattle; *food, provision,
sustenance*, for men, Acts 7:11*

χορτάσματα   acc pl neut
[Ac 7:11; n-3c(4); 5964]   χόρτασμα
χόρτον   acc sg masc [6t; n-2a; 5965]   χόρτος

χόρτος, ου, ὁ   {5965, n-2a}
an enclosure; pasture-ground; fodder for beasts; in
N.T. *herbage, grass*, Mark 6:30; 14:19; *a plant* of
corn, Matt 13:26; Mark 4:28

χόρτος   nom sg masc [5t; n-2a; 5965]   "
χόρτου   gen sg masc [3t; n-2a; 5965]   "
χόρτῳ   dat sg masc [Mk 6:39; n-2a; 5965]   "
χορῶν   gen pl masc [Lk 15:25; n-2a; 5962]   χορός
Χουζᾶ   gen sg masc [Lk 8:3; n-1e; 5966]   χουζᾶς

χουζᾶς, ᾶ, ὁ   {5966, n-1e}
　　Chuzas, Chuza, pr. name, Luke 8:3*

χοῦν　acc sg masc [2t; n-3e(4); 5967]   χοῦς

χοῦς, χοός, ὁ   {5967, n-3e(4)}
　　uncontracted form χόος, *dust*, acc., χοῦν, Mark
　　6:11; Rev 18:19*

χράομαι   {5968, v-1d(1a)}
　　[(ἐχρώμην), -, ἐχρησάμην, -, κέχρημαι, -] *to use,*
　　make use of, employ, Acts 27:17; 1 Cor 7:31; *to take*
　　advantage of, 1 Cor 7:21; 9:12, 15; *to use, to treat,*
　　behave towards, Acts 27:3; 2 Cor 13:10

χρεία, ας, ἡ   {5970, n-1a}
　　use; need, necessity, requisiteness, Eph 4:29; Heb
　　7:11; personal *need, an* individual *want*, Acts
　　20:34; Rom 12:13; Phil 2:25; 4:16, 19; χρείαν ἔχω,
　　to need, require, want, Matt 6:8; 14:16; Mark 2:25;
　　John 2:25; ἐστὶ χρεία, *there is need*, Luke 10:42; τὰ
　　πρὸς τὴν χρείαν, *necessary things*, Acts 28:10; *a*
　　necessary business, affair, Acts 6:3

χρεία　nom sg fem [2t; n-1a; 5970]   χρεία
χρείαις　dat pl fem [2t; n-1a; 5970]   "
χρείαν　acc sg fem [40t; n-1a; 5970]   "
χρείας　gen sg fem [3t; n-1a; 5970]   "
χρείας　acc pl fem [2t; n-1a; 5970]   "
χρεοφειλέται　nom pl masc
　　[Lk 7:41; n-1f; 5971]   χρεοφειλέτης

χρεοφειλέτης, ου, ὁ   {5971, n-1f}
　　debtor, Luke 7:41; 16:5*

χρεωφειλέτης, ου, ὁ, see χρεοφειλέτης   {5972, n-1f}

χρεοφειλετῶν　gen pl masc [Lk 16:5; n-1f; 5971]   "

χρή   {5973, v-1d(2a)}
　　[-, -, -, -, -] impersonal verb, *there is need* or
　　occasion, it is necessary, it is requisite; it becomes,
　　it is proper, James 3:10*

χρή　pres act ind 3 sg
　　[Jm 3:10; v-1d(2a); 5973]   χρή
χρῄζει　pres act ind 3 sg
　　[Lk 11:8; v-2a(1); 5974]   χρῄζω
χρῄζετε　pres act ind 2 pl [2t; v-2a(1); 5974]   "
χρῄζῃ　pres act subj 3 sg
　　[Rm 16:2; v-2a(1); 5974]   "
χρῄζομεν　pres act ind 1 pl
　　[2C 3:1; v-2a(1); 5974]   "

χρῄζω   {5974, v-2a(1)}
　　[-, -, -, -, -] *to need, want, desire*, Matt 6:32; Luke
　　11:8; 12:30; Rom 16:2; 2 Cor 3:1*

χρῆμα, ατος, τό   {5975, n-3c(4)}
　　anything useful, or *needful*; pl. *wealth, riches*,
　　Mark 10:23, 24 v.l.; Luke 18:24; *money*, Acts 8:18,
　　20; 24:26; sg. *price*, Acts 4:37*

χρῆμα　acc sg neut [Ac 4:37; n-3c(4); 5975]   χρῆμα
χρήματα　nom pl neut [Ac 24:26; n-3c(4); 5975]   "
χρήματα　acc pl neut [3t; n-3c(4); 5975]   "
χρηματίζοντα　pres act ptcp acc sg masc
　　[Hb 12:25; v-2a(1); 5976]   χρηματίζω

χρηματίζω   {5976, v-2a(1)}
　　[χρηματίσω, ἐχρημάτισα, -, κεχρημάτισμαι,
　　ἐχρηματίσθην] *to have dealings, transact business;*

to negotiate; to give answer on deliberation; in N.T.
to utter a divine communication, Heb 12:25; pass.
to be divinely instructed, receive a revelation or
warning from God, Matt 2:12, 22; Luke 2:26 v.l.;
Acts 10:22; Heb 8:5; 11:7; intrans. *to receive an*
appellation, Acts 11:26; Rom 7:3*

χρηματίσαι　aor act inf
　　[Ac 11:26; v-2a(1); 5976]   "
χρηματίσει　fut act ind 3 sg
　　[Rm 7:3; v-2a(1); 5976]   "
χρηματισθείς　aor pass ptcp nom sg masc
　　[2t; v-2a(1); 5976]   "
χρηματισθέντες　aor pass ptcp nom pl masc
　　[Mt 2:12; v-2a(1); 5976]   "

χρηματισμός, οῦ, ὁ   {5977, n-2a}
　　in N.T. *a response from God, a divine*
　　communication, oracle, Rom 11:4*

χρηματισμός　nom sg masc
　　[Rm 11:4; n-2a; 5977]   χρηματισμός
χρημάτων　gen pl neut
　　[Ac 8:20; n-3c(4); 5975]   χρῆμα
χρῆσαι　aor mid imperative 2 sg
　　[1C 7:21; v-1d(1a); 5968]   χράομαι
χρησάμενος　aor mid ptcp nom sg masc
　　[Ac 27:3; v-1d(1a); 5968]   "
χρήσιμον　acc sg neut
　　[2Ti 2:14; a-1a(2a); 5978]   χρήσιμος

χρήσιμος, η, ον   {5978, a-1a(2a)}
　　useful, profitable, 2 Tim 2:14; Matt 20:28 v.l.*

χρῆσιν　acc sg fem [2t; n-3e(5b); 5979]   χρῆσις

χρῆσις, εως, ἡ   {5979, n-3e(5b)}
　　use, employment; manner of using, Rom 1:26, 27*

χρῆσον　aor act imperative 2 sg
　　[Lk 11:5; v-6a; 3079]   κίχρημι
χρηστά　acc pl neut
　　[1C 15:33; a-1a(2a); 5982]   χρηστός
χρηστεύεται　pres mid ind 3 sg
　　[1C 13:4; v-1a(6); 5980]   χρηστεύομαι

χρηστεύομαι   {5980, v-1a(6)}
　　[-, ἐχρηστευσάμην, -, -, ἐχρηστεύθην] *to be gentle,*
　　benign, kind, 1 Cor 13:4*

χρηστοί　nom pl masc
　　[Ep 4:32; a-1a(2a); 5982]   χρηστός

χρηστολογία, ας, ἡ   {5981, n-1a}
　　bland address, fair speaking, Rom 16:18*

χρηστολογίας　gen sg fem
　　[Rm 16:18; n-1a; 5981]   χρηστολογία
χρηστόν　nom sg neut
　　[Rm 2:4; a-1a(2a); 5982]   χρηστός

χρηστός, ή, όν   {5982, a-1a(2a)}
　　useful, profitable; good, agreeable, Luke 5:39; *easy,*
　　as a yoke, Matt 11:30; *gentle, benign, kind,*
　　obliging, gracious, Luke 6:35; Eph 4:32; Rom 2:4;
　　1 Peter 2:3; *good* in character, disposition, etc.,
　　virtuous, 1 Cor 15:33*

χρηστός　nom sg masc [4t; a-1a(2a); 5982]   "

χρηστότης, ητος, ἡ   {5983, n-3c(1)}
　　pr. *goodness, kindness, gentleness*, Rom 2:4; 9:23

v.l.; 11:22; 2 Cor 6:6; Gal 5:22; Col 3:12; Titus 3:4; *kindness* shown, *beneficence*, Eph 2:7; *goodness, virtue*, Rom 3:12*

χρηστότης   nom sg fem
    [3t; n-3c(1); 5983]   χρηστότης
χρηστότητα   acc sg fem [3t; n-3c(1); 5983]   "
χρηστότητι   dat sg fem [3t; n-3c(1); 5983]   "
χρηστότητος   gen sg fem [Rm 2:4; n-3c(1); 5983]   "
χρήσωμαι   aor mid subj 1 sg
    [2C 13:10; v-1d(1a); 5968]   χράομαι
χρῆται   pres mid subj 3 sg
    [1Ti 1:8; v-1d(1a); 5968]   "
χρίσας   aor act ptcp nom sg masc
    [2C 1:21; v-1a(1); 5987]   χρίω

χρῖσμα, ατος, τό   {5984, n-3c(4)}
    pr. *anything which is applied by smearing; ointment*; in N.T. *an anointing*, in the reception of spiritual privileges, 1 John 2:20, 27*

χρῖσμα   nom sg neut [2t; n-3c(4); 5984]   χρῖσμα
χρῖσμα   acc sg neut [1J 2:20; n-3c(4); 5984]   "
χριστέ   voc sg masc [Mt 26:68; n-2a; 5986]   χριστός
Χριστιανόν   acc sg masc
    [Ac 26:28; n-2a; 5985]   χριστιανός

Χριστιανός, οῦ, ὁ   {5985, n-2a}
    a Christian, follower of Christ, Acts 11:26; 26:28; 1 Peter 4:16*

Χριστιανός   nom sg masc [1P 4:16; n-2a; 5985]   "
Χριστιανούς   acc pl masc [Ac 11:26; n-2a; 5985]   "
Χριστόν   acc sg masc [65t; n-2a; 5986]   χριστός

Χριστός, οῦ, ὁ   {5986, n-2a}
    pr. *anointed*; ὁ Χριστός, *the Christ, the Anointed One*, i.q. Μεσσίας, *the Messiah*, Matt 1:16, 17; John 1:20, 25, 42; meton. *Christ, the word* or *doctrine of Christ*, 2 Cor 1:19; 21; Eph 4:20; *Christ, a* truly *Christian frame* of doctrine and affection, Rom 8:10; Gal 4:19; *Christ, the Church of Christ*, 1 Cor 12:12; *Christ the distinctive privileges of the Gospel of Christ*, Gal 3:27; Phil 3:8; Heb 3:14

Χριστός   nom sg masc [111t; n-2a; 5986]   "
Χριστοῦ   gen sg masc [249t; n-2a; 5986]   "
Χριστῷ   dat sg masc [103t; n-2a; 5986]   "

χρίω   {5987, v-1a(1)}
    [-, ἔχρισα, -, -, ἐχρίσθην] *to anoint*; in N.T. *to anoint*, by way of instituting to a dignity, function, or privilege, Luke 4:18; Acts 4:27; 10:38; 2 Cor 1:21; Heb 1:9*

χρονίζει   pres act ind 3 sg
    [2t; v-2a(1); 5988]   χρονίζω
χρονίζειν   pres act inf [Lk 1:21; v-2a(1); 5988]   "
χρονίζοντος   pres act ptcp gen sg masc
    [Mt 25:5; v-2a(1); 5988]   "

χρονίζω   {5988, v-2a(1)}
    [χρονίσω, -, -, -, -] *to spend time; to linger, delay, be long*, Matt 24:48; 25:5; Luke 1:21; 12:45; Heb 10:37*

χρονίσει   fut act ind 3 sg
    [Hb 10:37; v-2a(1); 5988]   "
χρόνοις   dat pl masc [2t; n-2a; 5989]   χρόνος

χρόνον   acc sg masc [27t; n-2a; 5989]   "

χρόνος, ου, ὁ   {5989, n-2a}
    time, whether in respect of duration or a definite point of its lapse, Matt 2:7; 25:19 freq.; *an epoch, era*, marked *duration*, Acts 1:7; 1 Thess 5:1

χρόνος   nom sg masc [7t; n-2a; 5989]   χρόνος

χρονοτριβέω   {5990, cv-1d(2a)}
    [-, ἐχρονοτρίβησα, -, -, -] *to spend time, waste time, linger, delay*, Acts 20:16*

χρονοτριβῆσαι   aor act inf
    [Ac 20:16; cv-1d(2a); 5990]   χρονοτριβέω
χρόνου   gen sg masc [4t; n-2a; 5989]   χρόνος
χρόνους   acc pl masc [3t; n-2a; 5989]   "
χρόνῳ   dat sg masc [5t; n-2a; 5989]   "
χρόνων   gen pl masc [6t; n-2a; 5989]   "
χρυσᾶ   nom pl neut [2Ti 2:20; a-1b; 5997]   χρυσοῦς
χρυσᾶ   acc pl neut [Rv 9:20; a-1b; 5997]   "
χρυσᾶν   acc sg fem [Rv 1:13; a-1b; 5997]   "
χρυσᾶς   acc pl fem [5t; a-1b; 5997]   "

χρύσεος, uncontracted form of χρυσοῦς   {5991}

χρυσῆ   nom sg fem [Hb 9:4; a-1b; 5997]   "

χρυσίον, ου, τό   {5992, n-2c}
    gold, 1 Cor 3:12 v.l.; Heb 9:4; 1 Peter 1:7; Rev 3:18; 21:18, 21; spc. *gold when coined* or *manufactured; golden ornaments*, 1 Tim 2:9; 1 Peter 3:3; Rev 17:4; 18:16; *gold coin, money*, Acts 3:6; 20:33; 1 Peter 1:18*

χρυσίον   nom sg neut [3t; n-2c; 5992]   χρυσίον
χρυσίον   acc sg neut [Rv 3:18; n-2c; 5992]   "
χρυσοῦ   gen sg masc [Rv 18:12; n-2a; 5996]   "
χρυσοῦ   gen sg neut [Rv 9:13; a-1b; 5997]   χρυσοῦς
χρυσίῳ   dat sg neut [5t; n-2c; 5992]   "
χρυσίων   gen pl neut [1P 3:3; n-2c; 5992]   "

χρυσοδακτύλιος, ον   {5993, a-3a}
    having rings of gold on the fingers, James 2:2*

χρυσοδακτύλιος   nom sg masc
    [Jm 2:2; a-3a; 5993]   χρυσοδακτύλιος

χρυσόλιθος, ου, ὁ   {5994, n-2a}
    chrysolite, a name applied by the ancients to all gems of a gold color; spc. the modern *topaz*, Rev 21:10*

χρυσόλιθος   nom sg masc
    [Rv 21:20; n-2a; 5994]   χρυσόλιθος
χρυσόν   acc sg masc [4t; n-2a; 5996]   χρυσός

χρυσόπρασος, ου, ὁ   {5995, n-2a}
    a chrsoprase, a species of gem of a golden green color like that of a leek, Rev 21:21*

χρυσόπρασος   nom sg masc
    [Rv 21:20; n-2a; 5995]   χρυσόπρασος

χρυσός, οῦ, ὁ   {5996, n-2a}
    gold, Matt 2:11; 23:16, 17; meton. *gold ornaments*, 1 Tim 2:9; *gold coin, money*, Matt 10:9

χρυσός   nom sg masc [2t; n-2a; 5996]   χρυσός
χρυσοῦ   gen sg neut [2t; a-1b; 5997]   χρυσοῦς
χρυσοῦν   acc sg masc [3t; a-1b; 5997]   "

χρυσοῦν   acc sg neut [3t; a-1b; 5997]   "

χρυσοῦς, ῆ, οῦν   {5997, a-1b}
golden, made of or *adorned with gold,* 2 Tim 2:20;
Heb 9:4; Rev 1:12, 13, 20; 9:13, 20, 21:15

χρυσοῦς   acc pl masc [Rv 4:4; a-1b; 5997]   "

χρυσόω   {5998, v-1d(3)}
[-, -, -, κεχρύσωμαι, -] *to gild, overlay with gold,*
adorn or *deck with gold,* Rev 17:4; 18:16*

χρυσῷ   dat sg masc [3t; n-2a; 5996]   χρυσός
χρυσῶν   gen pl fem [Rv 2:1; a-1b; 5997]   χρυσοῦς
χρῶ   pres mid imperative 2 sg
    [1Ti 5:23; v-1d(1a); 5968]   χράομαι
χρώμεθα   pres mid ind 1 pl
    [2C 3:12; v-1d(1a); 5968]   "
χρώμενοι   pres mid ptcp nom pl masc
    [1C 7:31; v-1d(1a); 5968]   "

χρώς, ωτός, ὁ   {5999, n-3c(1)}
the skin; the body surface; Acts 19:12*

χρωτός   gen sg masc [Ac 19:12; n-3c(1); 5999] χρώς
χωλοί   nom pl masc [4t; a-1a(2a); 6000]   χωλός
χωλόν   nom sg neut [Hb 12:13; a-1a(2a); 6000] "
χωλόν   acc sg masc [2t; a-1a(2a); 6000]   "

χωλός, ή, όν   {6000, a-1a(2a)}
crippled in the feet, limping, halting, lame, Matt
11:5; 15:30, 31; met. *limping, weak,* spiritually,
Heb 12:13; *maimed, deprived of a foot,* for
ἀναπηρός, Mark 9:45

χωλός   nom sg masc [2t; a-1a(2a); 6000]   "
χωλούς   acc pl masc [4t; a-1a(2a); 6000]   "
χωλῶν   gen pl masc [Jn 5:3; a-1a(2a); 6000]   "

χώρα, ας, ἡ   {6001, n-1a}
space, room; a country, region, tract, province,
Mark 5:10; Luke 2:8; *a district, territory, suburbs,*
Matt 8:28; meton. *the inhabitants of a country,*
region, etc., Mark 1:5; Acts 12:20; *the country,* as
opposed to the city or town, Luke 21:21; *a field,*
farm, Luke 12:16; John 4:35

χώρα   nom sg fem [2t; n-1a; 6001]   χώρα
χώρᾳ   dat sg fem [3t; n-1a; 6001]   "

Χωραζίν, see Χοραζίν   {6002}

χώραις   dat pl fem [Lk 21:21; n-1a; 6001]   "
χώραν   acc sg fem [14t; n-1a; 6001]   "
χώρας   gen sg fem [5t; n-1a; 6001]   "
χώρας   acc pl fem [3t; n-1a; 6001]   "
χωρεῖ   pres act ind 3 sg
    [2t; v-1d(2a); 6003]   χωρέω
χωρεῖν   pres act inf [2t; v-1d(2a); 6003]   "
χωρείτω   pres act imperative 3 sg
    [Mt 19:12; v-1d(2a); 6003]   "

χωρέω   {6003, v-1d(2a)}
[χωρήσω, ἐχώρησα, κεχώρηκα, -, -] *to make room,*
either by motion or capacity; *to move, pass,* Matt
15:17; 20:28 v.l.; *to proceed, go on,* 2 Pet 3:9; *to*
progress, make way, John 8:37; trans. *to hold* as
contents, *contain, afford room for,* Mark 2:2; John
2:6; 21:25; met. *to give* mental *admittance to, to*
yield accordance, Matt 19:11, 12; *to admit* to

approbation and esteem, *to regard cordially,* 2
Cor 7:2*

χωρῆσαι   aor act inf [2t; v-1d(2a); 6003]   "
χωρήσατε   aor act imperative 2 pl
    [2C 7:2; v-1d(2a); 6003]   "
χωρία   nom pl neut [Ac 28:7; n-2c; 6005]   χωρίον
χωρίζεσθαι   pres pass inf
    [2t; v-2a(1); 6004]   χωρίζω
χωριζέσθω   pres pass imperative 3 sg
    [1C 7:15; v-2a(1); 6004]   "
χωρίζεται   pres pass ind 3 sg
    [1C 7:15; v-2a(1); 6004]   "
χωριζέτω   pres act imperative 3 sg
    [2t; v-2a(1); 6004]   "

χωρίζω   {6004, v-2a(1)}
[χωρίσω, ἐχώρισα, -, κεχώρισμαι, ἐχωρίσθην] *to*
divide, separate, Matt 19:6; Mark 10:9; Rom 8:35,
39; *to dissociate one's self, to part,* 1 Cor 7:10, 11,
15; *to withdraw, depart,* Acts 1:4; 18:1, 2; Phlm 15;
to be aloof, Heb 7:26*

χωρίον, ου, τό   {6005, n-2c}
a place, spot; Matt 26:36; Mark 14:32; *a field, farm,*
estate, domain, John 4:5; Acts 1:18, 19; 4:34, 37
v.l.; 5:3, 8; 28:7*

χωρίον   acc sg neut [6t; n-2c; 6005]   χωρίον
χωρίου   gen sg neut [2t; n-2c; 6005]   "

χωρίς   {6006, adverb}
can function as an improper prep., *apart,* John
20:7; *apart from, parted from,* John 15:5; James
2:18, 20, 26; *alien from,* Eph 2:12; *apart from, on a*
distinct footing from, 1 Cor 11:11; *apart from,*
distinct from, without the intervention of, Rom
3:21, 28; 4:6; *apart from* the company of,
independently of, 1 Cor 4:8; Heb 11:40 *without* the
presence of, Heb 9:28; *without* the agency of,
John 1:3; Rom 10:14; *without* the employment
of, Matt 13:34; Mark 4:34; Heb 7:20, 21; 9:7, 18,
22; *without,* Luke 6:49; Phil 2:14; 1 Tim 2:8; 5:21;
Phlm 14; Heb 10:28; 11:6; 12:8, 14; *clear from,*
Heb 7:7; *irrespectively of,* Rom 7:8, 9; *without*
reckoning, besides, Matt 14:21; 15:38; 2 Cor 11:28;
with the exception of, Heb 4:15

χωρίς   adverb [41t; adverb; 6006]   χωρίς
χωρίσαι   aor act inf
    [Rm 8:39; v-2a(1); 6004]   χωρίζω
χωρίσει   fut act ind 3 sg
    [Rm 8:35; v-2a(1); 6004]   "
χωρισθείς   aor pass ptcp nom sg masc
    [Ac 18:1; v-2a(1); 6004]   "
χωρισθῇ   aor pass subj 3 sg
    [1C 7:11; v-2a(1); 6004]   "
χωρισθῆναι   aor pass inf
    [1C 7:10; v-2a(1); 6004]   "

χωρισμός, οῦ, ὁ   {6007, n-2a}
division, Acts 4:32 v.l.*

χωρίων   gen pl neut [Ac 4:34; n-2c; 6005]   χωρίον
χῶρον   acc sg masc [Ac 27:12; n-2a; 6008]   χῶρος

χῶρος, ου, ὁ   {6008, n-2a}
Corus, or *Caurus, the northwest wind;* meton. *the*
northwest quarter of the heavens, Acts 27:12*

χωροῦσαι   pres act ptcp nom pl fem
[Jn 2:6; v-1d(2a); 6003]   χωρέω
χωροῦσιν   pres act ind 3 pl
[Mt 19:11; v-1d(2a); 6003]   "

Ψ

ψαλλέτω   pres act imperative 3 sg
[Jm 5:13; v-2d(1); 6010]   ψάλλω
ψάλλοντες   pres act ptcp nom pl masc
[Ep 5:19; v-2d(1); 6010]   "

ψάλλω   {6010, v-2d(1)}
[ψαλῶ, -, -, -, -] *to move by a touch, to twitch; to
touch, strike* the strings or chords of an
instrument; absol. *to play on a stringed
instrument; to sing to music;* in N.T. *to sing
praises,* Rom 15:9; 1 Cor 14:15; Eph 5:19; James
5:13*

ψαλμοῖς   dat pl masc [3t; n-2a; 6011]   ψαλμός
ψαλμόν   acc sg masc [1C 14:26; n-2a; 6011]   "

ψαλμός, οῦ, ὁ   {6011, n-2a}
impulse, touch of the chords of stringed
instrument; in N.T. *a sacred song, psalm,* Luke
20:42; 24:44; Acts 1:20; 13:33; 1 Cor 14:26; Eph
5:19; Col 3:16*

ψαλμῷ   dat sg masc [Ac 13:33; n-2a; 6011]   "
ψαλμῶν   gen pl masc [2t; n-2a; 6011]   "
ψαλῶ   fut act ind 1 sg [3t; v-2d(1); 6010]   ψάλλω
ψευδαδέλφοις   dat pl masc
[2C 11:26; n-2a; 6012]   ψευδάδελφος

ψευδάδελφος, ου, ὁ   {6012, n-2a}
a false brother, a pretended Christian, 2 Cor 11:26;
Gal 2:4*

ψευδαδέλφους   acc pl masc [Ga 2:4; n-2a; 6012]   "
ψευδαπόστολοι   nom pl masc
[2C 11:13; n-2a; 6013]   ψευδαπόστολος

ψευδαπόστολος, ου, ὁ   {6013, n-2a}
a false apostle, pretended minister of Christ, 2 Cor
11:13*

ψεύδει   dat sg neut [2t; n-3d(2b); 6022]   ψεῦδος
ψευδεῖς   acc pl masc [2t; a-4a; 6014]   ψευδής
ψεύδεσθε   pres mid imperative 2 pl
[2t; v-1b(3); 6017]   ψεύδομαι
ψευδέσιν   dat pl masc [Rv 21:8; a-4a; 6014] ψευδής

ψευδής, ές   {6014, a-4a}
false, lying, Acts 6:13; Rev 2:2; in N.T. pl.
maintainers of religious *falsehood, corrupters of
the truth* of God, Rev 21:8*

ψευδοδιδάσκαλοι   nom pl masc
[2P 2:1; n-2a; 6015]   ψευδοδιδάσκαλος

ψευδοδιδάσκαλος, ου, ὁ   {6015, n-2a}
a false teacher, one who teaches false doctrines, 2
Peter 2:1*

ψευδολόγος, ον   {6016, a-3a}
false-speaking, 1 Tim 4:2*

ψευδολόγων   gen pl masc
[1Ti 4:2; a-3a; 6016]   ψευδολόγος

ψεύδομαι   {6017, v-1b(3)}
[ψεύσομαι, ἐψευσάμην, -, -, -] *lie,* Matt 5:11; Acts
5:4; 14:19 v.l.; Rom 9:1; 2 Cor 11:31; Gal 1:20;
deceive by lying, Acts 5:3

ψεύδομαι   pres mid ind 1 sg
[4t; v-1b(3); 6017]   ψεύδομαι
ψευδομάρτυρες   nom pl masc
[1C 15:15; n-3f(2a); 6020]   ψευδόμαρτυς

ψευδομαρτυρέω   {6018, cv-1d(2a)}
[(ἐψευδομαρτύρουν), ψευδομαρτυρήσω,
ἐψευδομαρτύρησα, -, -, -] *to bear false witness,
give false testimony,* Matt 19:18; Mark 10:19;
14:56, 57; Luke 18:20; Rom 13:9 v.l.*

ψευδομαρτυρήσεις   fut act ind 2 sg
[Mt 19:18; cv-1d(2a); 6018]   ψευδομαρτυρέω
ψευδομαρτυρήσῃς   aor act subj 2 sg
[2t; cv-1d(2a); 6018]   "

ψευδομαρτυρία, ας, ἡ   {6019, n-1a}
false witness, false testimony, Matt 15:19; 26:59*

ψευδομαρτυρίαι   nom pl fem
[Mt 15:19; n-1a; 6019]   ψευδομαρτυρία
ψευδομαρτυρίαν   acc sg fem [Mt 26:59; n-1a; 6019] "
ψευδομαρτύρων   gen pl masc
[Mt 26:60; n-3f(2a); 6020]   ψευδόμαρτυς

ψευδόμαρτυς, υρος, ὁ   {6020, n-3f(2a)}
a false witness, Matt 26:60 (2t); 1 Cor 15:15*

ψευδόμεθα   pres mid ind 1 pl
[1J 1:6; v-1b(3); 6017]   ψεύδομαι
ψευδόμενοι   pres mid ptcp nom pl masc
[Mt 5:11; v-1b(3); 6017]   "
ψεύδονται   pres mid ind 3 pl
[Rv 3:9; v-1b(3); 6017]   "
ψευδοπροφῆται   nom pl masc
[5t; n-1f; 6021]   ψευδοπροφήτης
ψευδοπροφήταις   dat pl masc [Lk 6:26; n-1f; 6021] "
ψευδοπροφήτην   acc sg masc [Ac 13:6; n-1f; 6021]   "

ψευδοπροφήτης, ου, ὁ   {6021, n-1f}
*a false prophet, one who falsely claims to speak by
divine inspiration,* whether as a foreteller of
future events, or as a teacher of doctrines, Matt
7:15; 24:24; Mark 13:22; Acts 13:6; 1 John 4:1;
Rev 16:13

ψευδοπροφήτης   nom sg masc [2t; n-1f; 6021]   "
ψευδοπροφήτου   gen sg masc [Rv 16:13; n-1f; 6021] "
ψευδοπροφητῶν   gen pl masc [Mt 7:15; n-1f; 6021] "

ψεῦδος, ους, τό   {6022, n-3d(2b)}
falsehood, John 8:44; Eph 4:25; 2 Thess 2:9, 11; 1
John 2:21, 27; in N.T. religious *falsehood,
perversion* of religious truth, *false religion,* Rom
1:25; *the practices of false religion,* Rev 14:15;
21:27; 22:15*

ψεῦδος   nom sg neut [3t; n-3d(2b); 6022]   ψεῦδος
ψεῦδος   acc sg neut [4t; n-3d(2b); 6022]   "
ψεύδους   gen sg neut [2Th 2:9; n-3d(2b); 6022] "
ψευδόχριστοι   nom pl masc
[2t; n-2a; 6023]   ψευδόχριστος

ψευδόχριστος, ου, ὁ   {6023, n-2a}
a false Christ, pretended Messiah, Matt 24:24;
Mark 13:22*

ψευδώνυμος, ον   {6024, a-3a}
falsely named, falsely called, 1 Tim 6:20*

ψευδωνύμου   gen sg fem
    [1Ti 6:20; a-3a; 6024]   ψευδώνυμος
ψεύσασθαι   aor mid inf
    [2t; v-1b(3); 6017]   ψεύδομαι

ψεῦσμα, ατος, τό   {6025, n-3c(4)}
a falsehood, lie; in N.T. *untruthfulness,* Rom 3:7*

ψεύσματι   dat sg neut
    [Rm 3:7; n-3c(4); 6025]   ψεῦσμα
ψεῦσται   nom pl masc [Ti 1:12; n-1f; 6026] ψεύστης
ψεύσταις   dat pl masc [1Ti 1:10; n-1f; 6026]   "
ψεύστην   acc sg masc [2t; n-1f; 6026]   "

ψεύστης, ου, ὁ   {6026, n-1f}
one who utters a falsehood, a liar, John 8:44, 55;
Rom 3:4; 1 Tim 1:10; Titus 1:9 v.l., 12; 1 John
1:10; 2:4, 22; 4:20; 5:10*

ψεύστης   nom sg masc [6t; n-1f; 6026]   "

ψηλαφάω   {6027, v-1d(1a)}
[-, ἐψηλάφησα, -, -, -] *to feel, handle,* Luke 24:39;
to feel or *grope for* or *after,* as persons in the dark,
Acts 17:27; Heb 12:18; 1 John 1:1*

ψηλαφήσατε   aor act imperative 2 pl
    [Lk 24:39; v-1d(1a); 6027]   ψηλαφάω
ψηλαφήσειαν   aor act opt 3 pl
    [Ac 17:27; v-1d(1a); 6027]   "
ψηλαφωμένῳ   pres pass ptcp dat sg neut
    [Hb 12:18; v-1d(1a); 6027]   "
ψηφίζει   pres act ind 3 sg
    [Lk 14:28; v-2a(1); 6028]   ψηφίζω

ψηφίζω   {6028, v-2a(1)}
[-, ἐψήφισα, -, -, ἐψηφίσθην] *to reckon by means of
pebbles, compute by counters;* hence genr. *to
compute, reckon, calculate,* Luke 14:28; Rev
13:18*

ψηφισάτω   aor act imperative 3 sg
    [Rv 13:18; v-2a(1); 6028]   "
ψῆφον   acc sg fem [3t; n-2b; 6029]   ψῆφος

ψῆφος, ου, ἡ   {6029, n-2b}
a small stone, pebble; a pebble variously
employed, especially in a ballot; hence, *a vote,
suffrage,* Acts 26:10; *a pebble* or *stone;* probably
given as a token, Rev 2:17 (2t)*

ψιθυρισμοί   nom pl masc
    [2C 12:20; n-2a; 6030]   ψιθυρισμός

ψιθυρισμός, οῦ, ὁ   {6030, n-2a}
a whispering; a calumnious *whispering, gossip,* 2
Cor 12:20*

ψιθυριστάς   acc pl masc
    [Rm 1:29; n-1f; 6031]   ψιθυριστής

ψιθυριστής, οῦ, ὁ   {6031, n-1f}
a whisperer; a whisperer, gossip, Rom 1:29*

ψίξ, χός, ἡ   {6032, n-3b(3)}
bit, crumb, Matt 15:27 v.l.; Luke 16:21 v.l.*

ψιχίον, ου, τό   {6033, n-2c}
a morsel, crumb, bit, Matt 15:27; Mark 7:28; Luke
16:21 v.l.*

ψιχίων   gen pl neut [2t; n-2c; 6033]   ψιχίον
ψυγήσεται   fut pass ind 3 sg
    [Mt 24:12; v-1b(2); 6038]   ψύχω
ψυχαί   nom pl fem [3t; n-1b; 6034]   ψυχή
ψυχαῖς   dat pl fem [3t; n-1b; 6034]   "
ψυχάς   acc pl fem [15t; n-1b; 6034]   "
ψύχει   dat sg neut
    [2C 11:27; n-3d(2b); 6036]   ψῦχος

ψυχή, ῆς, ἡ   {6034, n-1b}
breath; the principle of animal life; the life, Matt
2:20; 6:25; Mark 3:4; Luke 21:19; John 10:11; *an
inanimate being,* 1 Cor 15:45; *a* human *individual,
soul,* Acts 2:41; 3:23; 7:14; 27:37; Rom 13:1; 1
Peter 3:20; *the immaterial soul,* Matt 10:28; 1
Peter 1:9; 2:11, 25; 4:19; *the soul* as the seat of
religious and moral sentiment, Matt 11:29; Acts
14:2, 22; 15:24; Eph 6:6; *the soul,* as a seat of
feeling, Matt 12:18; 26:38; *the soul, the* inner *self,*
Luke 12:19

ψυχή   nom sg fem [15t; n-1b; 6034]   ψυχή
ψυχή   voc sg fem [Lk 12:19; n-1b; 6034]   "
ψυχῇ   dat sg fem [8t; n-1b; 6034]   "
ψυχήν   acc sg fem [41t; n-1b; 6034]   "
ψυχῆς   gen sg fem [12t; n-1b; 6034]   "
ψυχική   nom sg fem
    [Jm 3:15; a-1a(2a); 6035]   ψυχικός
ψυχικοί   nom pl masc [Jd 19; a-1a(2a); 6035]   "
ψυχικόν   nom sg neut [3t; a-1a(2a); 6035]   "

ψυχικός, ή, όν   {6035, a-1a(2a)}
pertaining to the life or *soul;* in N.T. *animal,* as
distinguished from spiritual subsistence, 1 Cor
15:44, 46; *occupied with mere animal things,
animal, sensual,* 1 Cor 2:14; James 3:15; Jude 19*

ψυχικός   nom sg masc [1C 2:14; a-1a(2a); 6035]   "

ψῦχος, ους, τό   {6036, n-3d(2b)}
cold, John 18:18; Acts 28:2; 2 Cor 11:27*

ψῦχος   nom sg neut
    [Jn 18:18; n-3d(2b); 6036]   ψῦχος
ψῦχος   acc sg neut [Ac 28:2; n-3d(2b); 6036]   "

ψυχρός, ά, όν   {6037, a-1a(1)}
cool, cold, Matt 10:42; met. Rev 3:15, 16*

ψυχρός   nom sg masc [3t; a-1a(1); 6037]   ψυχρός
ψυχροῦ   gen sg neut [Mt 10:42; a-1a(1); 6037]   "

ψύχω   {6038, v-1b(2)}
[-, ἔψυξα, -, -, ἐψύγην] *to breathe; to cool;* pass. *to
be cooled;* met. of affection, Matt 24:12*

ψυχῶν   gen pl fem [5t; n-1b; 6034]   ψυχή
ψώμιζε   pres act imperative 2 sg
    [Rm 12:20; v-2a(1); 6039]   ψωμίζω

ψωμίζω   {6039, v-2a(1)}
[-, ἐψώμισα, -, -, -] pr. *to feed by morsels;* hence,
genr. *to feed, supply with food,* Rom 12:20; *to
bestow in supplying food,* 1 Cor 13:3*

ψωμίον, ου, τό   {6040, n-2c}
a bit, morsel, mouthful, John 13:26, 27, 30*

ψωμίον   acc sg neut [4t; n-2c; 6040]   ψωμίον

ψωμίσω   aor act subj 1 sg
[1C 13:3; v-2a(1); 6039]   ψωμίζῶ

ψώχοντες   pres act ptcp nom pl masc
[Lk 6:1; v-1b(2); 6041]   ψώχω

ψώχω   {6041, v-1b(2)}
[-, -, -, -, -] *to rub in pieces,* as the ears of grain,
Luke 6:1*

ω

Ὦ   {6042, n-3g(2)}
Omega, the last letter of the Greek alphabet,
hence, met. τὸ Ω, *the last,* Rev 1:8, 11 v.l.; 21:6;
22:13*

Ὦ   indecl [3t; n-3g(2); 6042]   "

ὦ   {6043, interjection}
O!, Matt 15:28; Mark 9:19; Acts 1:1; Rom 2:1, 3;
11:33

ὦ   interj [17t; interj; 6043]   ὦ
ὦ   pres act subj 1 sg [2t; v-6b; 1639]   εἰμί
ᾧ   dat sg masc [79t; a-1a(2b); 4005]   ὅς
ᾧ   dat sg neut [40t; a-1a(2b); 4005]   "

Ὠβήδ   {6044}
Obed, pr. name indecl., v.l. for Ἰωβήδ in t.r. at
Matt 1:5; Luke 3:32

ᾠδαῖς   dat pl fem [2t; n-1b; 6046]   ᾠδή

ὧδε   {6045, adverb}
here, in this place, Matt 12:6, 41; ὧδε ἢ ὧδε, *here or
there,* Matt 24:23; τὰ ὧδε, *the state of things here,*
Col 4:9; met. *herein, in this thing,* Rev 13:10, 18;
to this place, Matt 8:29; 14:18

ὧδε   adverb [61t; adverb; 6045]   ὧδε

ᾠδή, ῆς, ἡ   {6046, n-1b}
an ode, song, hymn, Eph 5:19; Col 3:16; Rev 5:9;
14:3; 15:3*

ᾠδήν   acc sg fem [5t; n-1b; 6046]   ᾠδή

ὠδίν, ῖνος, ἡ   {6047, n-3f(1a)}
the spasms or *pains,* of a woman in travail, *a
birth-pang,* 1 Thess 5:3; pl. met. *birth-throes,
preliminary troubles* to the development of a
catastrophe, Matt 24:8; Mark 13:8; from the
Hebrew, *a stringent band, a snare, noose,* Acts
2:24*

ὠδίν   nom sg fem [1Th 5:3; n-3f(1a); 6047]   ὠδίν
ὠδίνας   acc pl fem [Ac 2:24; n-3f(1a); 6047]   "
ὠδίνουσα   pres act ptcp nom sg fem
[Rv 12:2; v-1c(2); 6048]   ὠδίνω
ὠδίνουσα   pres act ptcp voc sg fem
[Ga 4:27; v-1c(2); 6048]   "

ὠδίνω   {6048, v-1c(2)}
[-, -, -, -, -] *to be in travail,* Gal 4:27; Rev 12:2;
met. *to travail with, suffer birth pangs, to make
effort to bring to* spiritual birth, Gal 4:19*

ὠδίνω   pres act ind 1 sg
[Ga 4:19; v-1c(2); 6048]   "
ὠδίνων   gen pl fem [2t; n-3f(1a); 6047]   ὠδίν
ᾠκοδόμησεν   aor act ind 3 sg
[5t; v-1d(2a); 3868]   οἰκοδομέω
ᾠκοδόμητο   pluperf pass ind 3 sg
[Lk 4:29; v-1d(2a); 3868]   "
ᾠκοδόμουν   imperf act ind 3 pl
[Lk 17:28; v-1d(2a); 3868]   "
ὦμεν   pres act subj 1 pl [3t; v-6b; 1639]   εἰμί
ὡμίλει   imperf act ind 3 sg
[Ac 24:26; v-1d(2a); 3917]   ὁμιλέω
ὡμίλουν   imperf act ind 3 pl
[Lk 24:14; v-1d(2a); 3917]   "
ὡμοιώθη   aor pass ind 3 sg
[3t; v-1d(3); 3929]   ὁμοιόω
ὡμοιώθημεν   aor pass ind 1 pl
[Rm 9:29; v-1d(3); 3929]   "
ὡμολόγησας   aor act ind 2 sg
[1Ti 6:12; v-1d(2a); 3933]   ὁμολογέω
ὡμολόγησεν   aor act ind 3 sg
[4t; v-1d(2a); 3933]   "
ὡμολόγουν   imperf act ind 3 pl
[Jn 12:42; v-1d(2a); 3933]   "

ὦμος, ου, ὁ   {6049, n-2a}
the shoulder, Matt 23:4; Luke 15:5*

ὤμοσα   aor act ind 1 sg [2t; v-3c(2); 3923]   ὀμνύω
ὤμοσεν   aor act ind 3 sg [7t; v-3c(2); 3923]   "
ὤμους   acc pl masc [2t; n-2a; 6049]   ὦμος
ὦν   gen pl masc [31t; a-1a(2b); 4005]   ὅς
ὦν   gen pl fem [5t; a-1a(2b); 4005]   "
ὦν   gen pl neut [44t; a-1a(2b); 4005]   "
ὤν   pres act ptcp nom sg masc
[42t; v-6b; 1639]   εἰμί
ὤν   pres act ptcp voc sg masc
[2t; v-6b; 1639]   "
ὠνείδιζον   imperf act ind 3 pl
[2t; v-2a(1); 3943]   ὀνειδίζω
ὠνείδισεν   aor act ind 3 sg
[Mk 16:14; v-2a(1); 3943]   "

ὠνέομαι   {6050, v-1d(2a)}
[-, ὠνησάμην, -, -, -] *to buy, purchase,* Acts 7:16*

ὠνήσατο   aor mid ind 3 sg
[Ac 7:16; v-1d(2a); 6050]   ὠνέομαι
ὠνόμασεν   aor act ind 3 sg
[3t; v-2a(1); 3951]   ὀνομάζω
ὠνομάσθη   aor pass ind 3 sg
[Rm 15:20; v-2a(1); 3951]   "

ᾠόν, οῦ, τό   {6051, n-2c}
an egg, Luke 11:12*

ᾠόν   acc sg neut [Lk 11:12; n-2c; 6051]   ᾠόν

ὥρα, ας, ἡ   {6052, n-1a}
a limited portion of time, marked out by part of a
settled routine or train of circumstances; *a
season of the year; time of day,* Matt 14:15; Mark
6:35; 11:11; *an hour,* Matt 20:3; John 11:9; in N.T.
an eventful season, 1 John 2:18 (2t); Rev 3:10;
14:7; *due time,* John 16:21; Rom 13:11; *a destined
period, hour,* Matt 26:45; Mark 14:35; John 2:4;
7:30; *a short period,* Matt 26:40; John 5:35; 2 Cor

7:8; Gal 2:5; 1 Thess 2:17; Phlm 15; *a point of time, time,* Matt 8:13; 24:42; Luke 2:38

ὥρα   nom sg fem [33t; n-1a; 6052]   ὥρα
ὥρᾳ   dat sg fem [28t; n-1a; 6052]   "
ὧραι   nom pl fem [Jn 11:9; n-1a; 6052]   "
ὡραίᾳ   dat sg fem
          [Ac 3:10; a-1a(1); 6053]   ὡραῖος
ὡραίαν   acc sg fem [Ac 3:2; a-1a(1); 6053]   "
ὡραῖοι   nom pl masc [2t; a-1a(1); 6053]   "

ὡραῖος, α, ον   {6053, a-1a(1)}
    timely, seasonable; in prime, blooming; in N.T.
    beautiful, Matt 23:27; Acts 3:2, 10; Rom 10:15*

ὥραν   acc sg fem [22t; n-1a; 6052]   ὥρα
ὥρας   gen sg fem [20t; n-1a; 6052]   "
ὥρας   acc pl fem [Ac 19:34; n-1a; 6052]   "
ὠργίσθη   aor pass ind 3 sg
          [3t; v-2a(1); 3974]   ὀργίζω
ὠργίσθησαν   aor pass ind 3 pl
          [Rv 11:18; v-2a(1); 3974]   "
ὤρθριζεν   imperf act ind 3 sg
          [Lk 21:38; v-2a(1); 3983]   ὀρθρίζω
ὥρισαν   aor act ind 3 pl
          [Ac 11:29; v-2a(1); 3988]   ὁρίζω
ὥρισεν   aor act ind 3 sg
          [Ac 17:31; v-2a(1); 3988]   "
ὡρισμένη   perf pass ptcp dat sg fem
          [Ac 2:23; v-2a(1); 3988]   "
ὡρισμένον   perf pass ptcp acc sg neut
          [Lk 22:22; v-2a(1); 3988]   "
ὡρισμένος   perf pass ptcp nom sg masc
          [Ac 10:42; v-2a(1); 3988]   "
ὥρμησαν   aor act ind 3 pl
          [2t; v-1d(1a); 3994]   ὁρμάω
ὥρμησεν   aor act ind 3 sg [3t; v-1d(1a); 3994]   "
ὤρυξεν   aor act ind 3 sg [3t; v-2b; 4002]   ὀρύσσω

ὠρύομαι   {6054, v-1a(4)}
    [-, -, -, -, -] *to howl; to roar,* as a lion, 1 Peter 5:8*

ὠρυόμενος   pres mid ptcp nom sg masc
          [1P 5:8; v-1a(4); 6054]   ὠρύομαι
ὠρχήσασθε   aor mid ind 2 pl
          [2t; v-1d(2a); 4004]   ὀρχέομαι
ὠρχήσατο   aor mid ind 3 sg
          [Mt 14:6; v-1d(2a); 4004]   "
ὡρῶν   gen pl fem [Ac 5:7; n-1a; 6052]   ὥρα

ὡς   {6055, adverb}
    adverb formed from the relative pronoun ὅς,
    used as a comparative part. and conj., *as,*
    correlatively, Mark 4:26; John 7:46; Rom 5:15;
    as, like as, Matt 10:16; Eph 5:8; *according as,* Gal
    6:10; *as, as it were,* Rev 8:8; *as,* Luke 16:1; Acts
    3:12; before numerals, *about,* Mark 5:13; conj.
    that, Acts 10:28; *how,* Rom 11:2; *when,* Matt 28:9;
    Phil 2:23; as an exclamatory particle, *how,* Rom
    10:15; equivalent to ὥστε, *accordingly,* Heb 3:11;
    also, *on condition that, provided that,* Acts 20:24;
    ὡς εἰπεῖν, *so to speak,* Heb 7:9

ὡς   adverb [504t; adverb; 6055]   ὡς

ὡσάν   {6056, particle}
    as if, as it were, so to speak, 2 Cor 10:9

ὡσαννά   {6057, n-3g(2)}
    Hosanna! save now, help now, Matt 21:9, 15;
    Mark 11:9, 10; John 12:13*

ὡσαννά   indecl [6t; n-3g(2); 6057]   ὡσαννά

ὡσαύτως   {6058, adverb}
    just so, in just the same way or *manner, likewise,*
    Matt 20:5; 21:30

ὡσαύτως   adverb [17t; adverb; 6058]   ὡσαύτως

ὡσεί   {6059, particle}
    as if; as it were, as, like, Matt 3:16; 9:36; with
    terms of number or quantity, *about,* Matt 14:21;
    Luke 1:56; 22:41, 59

ὡσεί   particle [21t; particle; 6059]   ὡσεί

Ὡσηέ, ὁ   {6060, n-3g(2)}
    Hosea, pr. name, indecl., Rom 9:25*

Ὡσηέ   indecl [Rm 9:25; n-3g(2); 6060]   Ὡσηέ
ὠσίν   dat pl neut [6t; n-3c(6c); 4044]   οὖς
ὦσιν   pres act subj 3 pl [11t; v-6b; 1639]   εἰμί

ὥσπερ   {6061, particle}
    just as, as, Matt 6:2; 24:38; 1 Thess 5:3

ὥσπερ   particle [36t; particle; 6061]   ὥσπερ

ὡσπερεί   {6062, particle}
    just as if; as it were, 1 Cor 4:13 v.l.; 15:8*

ὡσπερεί   particle
          [1C 15:8; particle; 6062]   ὡσπερεί

ὥστε   {6063, conj}
    so that, so as that, so as to, Matt 8:24; Mark 2:12;
    Acts 14:1; Gal 2:13; as an illative particle,
    therefore, consequently, Matt 12:12; 23:31; in N.T.
    as a particle of design, *in order that, in order to,*
    Luke 9:52 v.l.

ὥστε   conj [83t; conj; 6063]   ὥστε
ὦτα   nom pl neut [2t; n-3c(6c); 4044]   οὖς
ὦτα   acc pl neut [15t; n-3c(6c); 4044]   "

ὠτάριον, ου, τό   {6064, n-2c}
    an ear, Matt 14:47; John 18:10*

ὠτάριον   acc sg neut [2t; n-2c; 6064]   ὠτάριον

ὠτίον, ου, τό   {6065, n-2c}
    in N.T. simply equivalent to οὖς, *an ear,* Matt
    26:51; Mark 14:47 v.l.; Luke 22:51; John 18:10
    v.l., 26*

ὠτίον   acc sg neut [2t; n-2c; 6065]   ὠτίον
ὠτίου   gen sg neut [Lk 22:51; n-2c; 6065]   "
ὤφειλεν   imperf act ind 3 sg
          [3t; v-2d(1); 4053]   ὀφείλω
ὠφείλετε   imperf act ind 2 pl
          [1C 5:10; v-2d(1); 4053]   "
ὠφείλομεν   imperf act ind 1 pl
          [Lk 17:10; v-2d(1); 4053]   "
ὤφειλον   imperf act ind 1 sg
          [2C 12:11; v-2d(1); 4053]   "
ὠφελεῖ   pres act ind 3 sg
          [4t; v-1d(2a); 6067]   ὠφελέω

ὠφέλεια, ας, ἡ   {6066, n-1a}
    help; profit, gain, advantage, benefit, Rom 3:1;
    Jude 16*

ὠφέλεια nom sg fem [Rm 3:1; n-1a; 6066] ὠφέλεια
ὠφελείας gen sg fem [Jd 16; n-1a; 6066] "
ὠφελεῖται pres pass ind 3 sg
   [Lk 9:25; v-1d(2a); 6067] ὠφελέω
ὠφελεῖτε pres act ind 2 pl
   [Jn 12:19; v-1d(2a); 6067] "

ὠφελέω {6067, v-1d(2a)}
[ὠφελήσω, ὠφέλησα, -, -, ὠφελήθην] *to help, profit,
benefit, accomplish,* Matt 27:24; Mark 7:11; Rom
2:25, *be of value,* John 6:63

ὠφεληθεῖσα aor pass ptcp nom sg fem
   [Mk 5:26; v-1d(2a); 6067] "
ὠφεληθῆς aor pass subj 2 sg
   [2t; v-1d(2a); 6067] "
ὠφελήθησαν aor pass ind 3 pl
   [Hb 13:9; v-1d(2a); 6067] "
ὠφεληθήσεται fut pass ind 3 sg
   [Mt 16:26; v-1d(2a); 6067] "
ὠφελήσει fut act ind 3 sg
   [Ga 5:2; v-1d(2a); 6067] "
ὠφέλησεν aor act ind 3 sg
   [Hb 4:2; v-1d(2a); 6067] "
ὠφελήσω fut act ind 1 sg
   [1C 14:6; v-1d(2a); 6067] "
ὠφέλιμα nom pl neut
   [Ti 3:8; a-3a; 6068] ὠφέλιμος

ὠφέλιμος, ον {6068, a-3a}
profitable, useful, beneficial; serviceable, 1 Tim 4:8
(2t); 2 Tim 3:16; Titus 3:8*

ὠφέλιμος nom sg fem [3t; a-3a; 6068] "
ὠφελοῦμαι pres pass ind 1 sg
   [1C 13:3; v-1d(2a); 6067] ὠφελέω
ὤφθη aor pass ind 3 sg
   [18t; v-1d(1a); 3972] ὁράω
ὤφθην aor pass ind 1 sg
   [Ac 26:16; v-1d(1a); 3972] "
ὤφθησαν aor pass ind 3 pl
   [Ac 2:3; v-1d(1a); 3972] "

Appendixes

Appendix

Quick reference chart

n-1 first declension stems

n-1a	ὥρα	ας	fem
n-1b	γραφή	ῆς	fem
n-1c	δόχη	ης	fem
n-1d	νεανίας	ου	masc
n-1e	σατανᾶς	ᾶ	masc
n-1f	προφήτης	ου	masc
n-1g	μανασσῆς	ῆ	masc
n-1h	μνᾶ	ᾶ	contract
	συκῆ	ῆς	contract

n-2 second declension stems

n-2a	λογος	ου	masc
n-2b	ὁδός	ου	fem
n-2c	ἔργον	ου	neut
n-2d(1)	χειμάρρους	ου	εο contract masc
n-2d(2)	ὀστοῦν	οῦ	οο contract neut
n-2e	κῶς	ῶ	εω stems

n-3 third declension stems

n-3a stems in a stop

n-3(1)	stems in labial		
n-3a(1)	λαῖλαψ	πος	π
n-3a(2)	ἄραψ	βος	β

n-3b stems in velar

n-3b(1)	σάρξ	κος	κ
n-3b(2)	σάλπιγξ	γος	γ
n-3b(3)	θρίξ	χος	χ

n-3c   dental

n-3c(1)	χάρις	ιτος	τ
n-3c(2)	ἐλπίς	ιδος	δ
n-3c(3)	ὄρνις	ιθος	θ
n-3c(4)	ὄνομα	ατος	ματ
n-3c(5a)	ὀδούς	όντος	ντ (σ in nom sg)
n-3c(5b)	ἄρχων	οντος	ντ (- in nom sg)
n-3c(6a)	τέρας	αρτος	ας
n-3c(6b)	ὕδωρ	ατος	ρ
n-3c(6c)	φῶς	ωτός	ς
n-3c(6d)	misc neuter stems		

n-3d   stems in ς

n-3d(1)	γήρας	ως	
n-3d(2a)	σωσθένης	ους	masc
n-3d(2b)	γένος	ους	neut
n-3d(3)	αἰδώς	οῦς	

n-3e stems in a sem i-vowel (Ϝ ι)

n-3e(1)	ἰχθύς	ύος	Ϝ
n-3e(2)	ναῦς	ώς	αϜ
n-3e(3)	βασιλεύς	έως	εϜ
n-3e(4)	νοῦς	ός	οϜ
n-3e(5a)	νῆστις	ιος/ιδος	ι (no ablaut)
n-3e(5b)	πόλις	εως	ι (ablaut)
n-3e(6)	πείθω	οῦς	ι

n-3f stems showing ablaut not listed below

n-3f(1a)	αἰών	ῶνος	ν (no ablaut)
n-3f(1b)	ἡγεμών	όνος	ν (strong/weak)
n-3f(1c)	κύων	ός	ν (strong/zero)
n-3f(2a)	σωτήρ	ῆρος	λ,ρ (no ablaut)
n-3f(2b)	ῥήτωρ	ορος	λ,ρ (strong/weak)
n-3f(2c)	ἀνήρ	ἀνδρός	λ,ρ (str, wk, zero)

n-3g(1) irregular and partially declined stems
n-3g(2   indeclinable stems

Adjectives

a-1a	adj using three endings (2-1-2)
a-1b	adj using three endings (contract stems)
a-2	adj using three endings (3-1-3)
a-3a	adj consistently using two endings (2-2)
a-3b	adj alternating between 2-2 and 2-1-2
a-4	adj using two endings (3-3)
a-5	irregular and indeclinable stems

Methodology

Following is a list of our basic guidelines as we constructed the data base, chose parsings and lexical forms, etc.

- Form was given preference over function. For example, if an adverb can also function as a preposition, we usually stated it as such but listed the form as an adverb. If a nominative is functioning as a vocative, we still list it as a nominative.

- Indeclinable words are listed as such. We did not specify the case in which they were functioning.

- We based the data base on the UBS 3rd edition revised. In choosing variants, we always agreed with the UBS text.

- The following verses are omitted from the UBS text and the analytical: Matt 17:21; 18:11; 23:14; Mark 7:16; 9:44, 46; 11:26; 15:28; Luke 17:36; 23:17; John 5:4; Acts 8:37; 15:34; 24:7; 28:29; Rom 16:24. 2 Cor 13:13-14 in the English is 2 Cor 13:13 in the Greek.

  We included both the shorter and longer ending to Mark as well as John 7:53-8:11.

- Forms listed in the text with square brackets were accepted. For example, [κατα]καίεται is recorded as κατακαίεται (see list below).

- In choosing lexical forms we tried to agree with the form of the word in *BAGD*. However, if their form disagreed with the form in the text, we sided with the text.

- Any alternate spelling for a word is listed in the lexical entry of the primary spelling and usually in the analytical listing. If the alternate form is evidenced in the text, it will have its own entry in the lexicon.

- Different texts categorize words such as adverbs, particles, conjunctions, and improper prepositions differently. Again, we agreed with *BAGD*.

- Crasis forms are listed as such.

- If a form could be either masculine or neuter and a decision could not be reached on the basis on the context, we list it as a (generic) masculine.

- Care was taken with those words that are spelled the same and are yet different because of a capital letter or a diacritical mark. See list below.

- If a verbal form could be middle or deponent, we tried to chose on the basis of function. If function were not clear, we tagged it as passive.

- Comparative and superlative forms are generally associated with the regular adjectival or adverbial form.

- εἶδον is listed as the aorist stem of ὁράω, and εἶπον is listed as the aorist stem of λέγω, both in the simple verb as well as compounds.

Bracketed forms

Whenever the UBS lists a form in brackets, we always used the full form of the word. For example, if the text listed κρ[αυγ]άζομτα, we list the word as κραυγάζομτα. Following is a list of all those words with the reference, form, a partial parsing of the word including the bracketed letters, and a parsing of the word not including the bracketed letters.

Mt 13:40	[κατα]καίεται	from κατακαίω	from καίω
Mt 14:12	αὐτό[ν]	acc sg masc	acc sg neut
Mk 3:17	ὀνόμα[τα]	acc neut pl	acc neut sg
Mk 4:28	πλήρη[ς]	nom sg masc	acc masc sg
Lk 4:41	κρ[αυγ]άζομτα	from κραυγάζω	from κράζω
Lk 11:10	ἀνοιγ[ήσ]εται	fut pas ind	pres pas ind
Lk 13:21	[ἐν]έκρυψεν	from ἐγκρύπτω	from κρύπτω
Lk 19:29	βηθανία[ν]	acc sg fem	acc sg fem
Lk 20:27	[ἀντι]λέγοντες	from ἀντιλέγω	from λέγω

Jn 6:23	πλοία[ρια]	from πλοιάριον	from πλοῖον
Jn 19:35	πιστεύ[σ]ητε	aor act subj	pres act subj
Jn 20:31	πιστεύ[σ]ητε	aor act subl	pres act subj
Acts 1:11	[ἐμ]βλέποντες	from ἐμβλέπω	from βλέπω
Acts 3:25	[ἐν]ευλογηθήσονται	from ἐνευλογεω	from εὐλογέω
Acts 13:14	[εἰσ]ελθόντες	from εἰσέρχομαι	from ἔρχομαι
Acts 16:12	πρώτη[ς]	gen sg fem	nom sg fem
Acts 19:1	[κατ]ελεῖν	from κατέρχομαι	from ἔρχομαι
1 Cor 4:14	νουθετῶ[ν]	pres act ptcp	pres act ind
2 Cor 12:15	ἀγαπῶ[ν]	pres act ptcp	pres act ind
Heb 3:6	ἐάν[περ]	from ἐάν	from ἐάνπερ
2 Pet 2:6	ἀσεβέ[σ]ιν	dat pl masc	pres act infinitive
Rev 13:1	ὀνόμα[τα]	acc pl neut	acc sg neut
Rev 16:6	[δ]έδωκας	perf act ind	aor act ind
Rev 17:3	γέμον[τα]	acc pl neut	acc sg masc/neut

Identical forms

The following lexical forms are identical in form if you ignore capital letters and diacritical marks.

G/K	Word	MBG tag	Definition
726	ἄρα	particle	then
727	ἀρα	particle	then
1003	βάτος, οὗ, ἡ and ὁ	n-2a(1)	bush
1004	βάτος, ου, ὁ	n-2a	bath
1124	Γάζα, ης, ἡ	n-1c	Gaza
1125	γάζα, ης, ἡ	n-1c	treasure
1528	δοῦλος, ου, ὁ	n-2a	slave
1529	δοῦλος, η, ον	a-1a(2a)	enslaved
1639	εἰμί	v-6b	I am
1640	εἶμι	v-6b	I will go
1650	εἰς	preposition	into
1651	εἷς, μία, ἕν	a-4b(2)	one
1760	ἐκτός	adverb	without
1761	ἕκτος, η, ον	a-1a(2a)	sixth
2317	εὐθύς	adverb	immediately
2318	εὐθύς, εῖα, ύ	a-2b	straight
2445	ἤ	particle	either
2446	ἦ	adverb	truly
2458	ἠλί	n-3g(2)	My God
2459	Ἡλί	n-3g(2)	Eli
2491	ἦχος, ου, ὁ	n-2a	sound, fame
2492	ἦχος, ους, τό	n-3d(2b)	sound, noise
2842	Κάρπος, ου, ὁ	n-2a	Carpus
2843	καρπός, ου, ὁ	n-2a	fruit

3604	μήν, μηνός, ὁ	n-3f(1a)	month
3605	μήν	particle	surely
3836	ὁ, ἡ, τό	a-1a(2b)	the
4005	ὅς, ἥ, ὅ	a-1a(2b)	what
4023	οὗ	adverb	where?
4024	οὐ	negative adverb	not
4509	πόντος, ου, ὁ	n-2a	sea
4510	Πόντος, ου, ὁ	n-2a	Pontus
4536	πότε	interrogative adverb	when?
4537	ποτέ	enclitic particle	once
4543	πού	enclitic adverb	somewhere
4544	ποῦ	interrogative adverb	where?
4794	πυρρός, ά, όν	a-1a(1)	fiery-red
4795	Πύρρος, ου, ὁ	n-2a	Pyrrhus
4802	πῶς	interrogative particle	how?
4803	πώς	enclitic particle	by any means
5043	σμύρνα, ης, ἡ	n-1c	myrrh
5044	Σμύρνα, ης, ἡ	n-1c	Smyrna
5092	στάχυς, υος, ὁ	n-1b	ear of corn
5093	Στάχυς, υος, ὁ	n-3e(1)	Stachys
5108	Στέφανος, ου, ὁ	n-2a	Stephen
5109	στέφανος, ου, ὁ	n-2a	crown
5289	σύνειμι	cv-6b	to be with
5290	σύνειμι	cv-6b	to come together
5515	τίς	interrogative adj (a-4b[2])	who?
5516	τὶς	indefinite adj (a-4b[2])	certain one
5599	τύραννος, ου, ὁ	n-2a	tyrant
5560	Τύραννος, ου, ὁ	n-2a	Tyrannus
5836	φοῖνιξ, ικός, ὁ	n-3b(1)	palm tree
5837	Φοῖνιξ, ικός, ἡ	n-3b(1)	Phoenix
6042	Ὠ	n-3g(2)	omega
6043	ὦ	interjection	O!

Crasis

All examples of crasis are listed with the combined form in the analytical. The breathing is optional.

κἀγώ (κἀμοι, κἀμέ)
κἄν
κἀκεῖ
κἀκεῖνος
κἀκεῖθεν
τοὔνομα
τοὐναντίον

Goodrick/Kohlenberger's numbers compared to Strong's numbers

This table lists the correspondence between the Goodrick/Kohlenberger numbers for the Greek New Testament (column 1) and Strong's numbering system (column 2).

When a G/K number corresponds to more than one Strong number, the ditto mark (") is used for each additional occurrence (94 times).

When more than one Strong number corresponds to one G/K number, the plus sign (+) is used to show the combination (30 times).

When no Strong number corresponds to the G/K number, the G/K number is followed by percent sign (%) (118 times).

G/K	Strong		G/K	Strong		G/K	Strong		G/K	Strong
1	1		45	44		88	87		133	127
2	2		46	45		89	88		134	128
3	3		47	46		90	89		135	129
4	4		48	47		91	90		136	130
5	5		49	48		92	91		137	131
6	6		50	49		93	92		138	132
7	7		51	50		94	93		139	133
8	8		52	51		95	94 + 2923		140	134
9	9		53	52		96	94		141	135
10	10		54	53		97	95		142	136
11	11		55	54		98	689		143	137
12	12		56	55		99	96		144	2056
13	13		57	56		100	97		145	138
14	14		58	57		101	98		146	139
15	18 + 2041		59	58		102	99		147	140
16	15		60	59		103	100		148	141
17	16		61	60		104	101		149	142
18	17		62	61		105	102		150	143
19	18		63	62		106	103		151	144
20	19		64	63		107	104		152	145
21	20		65	64		108	105		153	146
22	21		66	65		109	106		154	147
23	22		67	66		110	107		155	148
24	23		68	67		111	108		156	149
25	24		69	68		112	%		"	150
26	25		70	69		113	109		157	151
27	26		71	70		114	110		158	152
28	27		72	33		115	2288 + 1		159	153
29	28		"	71		116	111		160	154
30	29		73	72		117	112		161	155
31	30		74	73		118	113		162	156
32	31		75	74		119	114		163	157
33	518		76	75		120	115		164	4256
34	32		77	76		121	116		165	158
35	30		78	77		122	117		"	159
36	34		79	78		123	118		166	157
37	35		80	79		124	119		167	160
38	36		81	80		125	4867		168	161
39	37		82	81		126	120		169	162
40	38		83	82		127	121		170	163
41	39		84	83		128	122		171	164
"	40		85	84		129	123		172	165
42	41		86	85		130	124		173	166
43	42		87	86		131	125		174	167
44	43					132	126			

G/K	Strong		G/K	Strong		G/K	Strong		G/K	Strong
175	168		246	234		318	298		390	364
176	169		247	235		319	%		391	365
177	170		248	236		320	299		392	366
178	171		249	237		321	300		393	367
179	172		250	%		322	301		394	368
180	173		251	238		323	302		395	369
181	174		252	239		324	303		396	370
182	175		253	240		325	304		397	371
183	176		254	241		326	305		398	372
184	177		255	2087		327	306		399	373
185	178		256	242		328	307		400	374
186	179		257	243		329	308		401	376
187	180		258	244		330	309		402	375
188	180		259	245		331	310		403	450
189	181		260	246		332	311		404	377
190	182		261	247		333	508		405	378
191	183		262	248		334	312		406	379
192	184		263	249		335	313		407	4238
193	185		264	250		336	314		408	380
194	85		265	251		337	315		409	381
195	186		266	252		338	316		410	382
196	187		267	253		339	317		411	383
197	188		268	254		340	318		412	384
198	189		269	255		341	319		413	385
199	190		270	1		342	320		414	386
200	191		271	256		343	321		415	387
201	191		272	257		344	322		416	388
202	192		273	258		345	323		417	389
203	193		274	259		346	324		418	390
204	194		275	260		347	325		419	391
205	195		276	261		348	326		420	37
206	196		277	262		349	327		421	392
207	%		278	263		350	328		422	393
208	198		279	264		351	329		423	394
209	199		280	265		352	330		424	395
"	197		281	266		353	331		425	510
210	200		282	267		354	332		426	396
211	201		283	268		355	333		427	397
212	202		284	%		356	334		428	398
213	203		285	269		357	335		429	399
214	204		286	270		358	336		430	400
215	205		287	271		359	337		431	401
216	206		288	272		360	338		432	402
217	207		289	273		361	339		433	403
218	208		290	274		362	340		434	404
219	209		291	275		363	341		435	405
220	210		292	276		364	342		436	406
221	217		293	277		365	343		437	407
222	211		294	278		366	344		438	408
223	211		295	279		367	345		439	409
224	212		296	280		368	346		440	507 + 2821
225	213		297	281		369	347		441	410
226	214		298	282		370	348		442	411
227	215		299	283		371	349		443	412
228	216		300	284		372	%		444	413
229	217		301	%		373	350		445	414
230	218		302	285		374	351		446	415
231	219		303	286		375	617		447	448
232	220		304	287		376	352		448	416
233	221		305	880		377	353		449	417
234	222		306	288		378	354		450	418
235	223		307	289		379	355		451	419
236	224		308	290		380	242		452	420
237	225		309	291		381	356		453	421
238	226		310	292		382	357		454	422
239	227		311	906 + 293		383	358		455	423
240	228		312	293		384	355		456	424
241	229		313	294		385	359		457	425
242	230		314	294		386	360		458	426
243	231		315	295		387	361		459	427
244	232		316	296		388	362		460	428
245	233		317	297		389	363		461	429

462	430	533	501	602	570	674	634
463	431	534	502	603	571	675	635
464	432	535	503	604	573	676	636
465	433	536	504	605	572	677	637
466	434	537	505	606	573	678	638
467	435	538	506	607	574	679	639
468	436	539	507	608	575	680	640
469	437	540	509	609	576	681	641
470	438	541	510	610	577	682	642
471	439	542	511	611	578	683	643
472	440	543	512	612	579	684	644
473	441	544	513	613	580	685	645
474	442	545	514	614	581	686	646
475	443	546	515	615	582	687	647
476	444	547	516	616	583	688	3848
477	445	548	517	617	584	689	648
478	446	549	2456	618	585	690	649
479	447	550	518	619	586	691	650
480	448	551	519	620	586	692	651
481	449	552	520	621	587	693	652
482	450	553	521	622	588	694	653
483	451	554	522	623	589	695	654
484	452	555	523	624	590	696	655
485	453	556	524	625	591	697	656
486	454	557	525	626	592	698	657
487	455	558	526	627	593	699	658
488	456	559	527	628	594	700	659
489	457	560	528	629	595	701	660
490	458	561	529	630	596	702	661
491	459	562	530	631	597	703	662
492	460	563	531	632	598	704	663
493	453	564	532	633	599	705	664
494	461	565	533	634	600	706	665
495	462	566	575 + 737	635	600	707	666
496	463	567	534	636	601	708	667
497	464	568	535	637	602	709	668
498	465	569	536	638	603	710	669
499	466	570	537	639	604	711	670
500	467	571	782	640	605	712	671
501	468	572	538	641	606	713	672
502	469	573	539	642	607	714	673
503	470	574	540	643	608	715	674
504	472	575	541	644	609	716	675
505	473	576	1890	645	610	717	676
506	474	577	543	646	611	718	677
507	475	578	544	647	612	719	678
508	476	579	545	648	613	720	679
509	477	580	546	649	614	721	680
510	478	581	547	650	615	"	681
511	479	582	548	651	615	722	682
512	480	583	549	652	616	723	683
513	481	584	550	653	617	724	684
514	482	"	561	654	2980	725	685
515	471	585	551	655	618	726	686
"	483	586	552	656	619	727	687
516	484	587	553	657	620	728	688
517	485	588	554	658	621	729	%
518	486	589	555	659	5277	730	689
519	487	590	556	660	622	731	729
520	488	591	557	661	623	732	690
521	489	592	558	662	624	733	691
522	490	593	559	663	625	734	692
523	491	594	560	664	626	735	693
524	492	595	561	665	627	736	694
525	493	596	562	666	628	737	695
526	494	597	563	667	629	738	696
527	495	598	564	668	630	739	693
528	496	599	565	669	631	740	697
529	497	600	566	670	5278	741	698
530	498	"	567	671	632	742	699
531	499	"	568	672	633	743	700
532	500	601	569	673	575 + 3992	744	701

745	702	816	766	888	836	957	898
746	703	817	767	889	837	958	899
747	%	818	768	890	838	959	900
748	704	819	769	891	837	960	901
749	705	820	770	892	839	961	902
750	706	821	771	893	840	962	903
751	707	822	772	894	841	963	904
752	708	823	773	895	842	964	905
753	709	824	774	896	843	965	906
754	710	825	775	897	844	966	907
755	711	826	776	898	845	967	908
756	712	827	777	899	846	968	909
757	713	828	778	"	847	969	910
758	714	829	779	"	848	970	911
759	715	830	780	900	1888	971	920
760	715	831	781	901	849	972	912
761	716	832	782	902	3166	973	913
762	717	833	783	903	850	974	914
763	689	834	784	904	851	975	915
764	718	835	785	905	852	976	916
765	719	836	786	906	853	977	917
766	720	837	787	907	854	978	918
767	%	838	4565	908	855	979	919
768	721	839	788	909	856	980	920
769	722	840	789	910	857	981	920
770	723	841	790	911	858	982	921
771	724	842	791	912	859	983	922
772	725	843	792	913	860	984	923
773	726	844	793	914	861	985	924
774	727	845	794	915	862	986	925
775	728	846	795	916	90	987	926
776	730	847	796	917	90	988	927
777	731	848	797	918	863	989	928
778	732	849	798	919	864	990	929
779	732	850	799	920	865	991	930
780	733	851	800	921	866	992	931
781	730	852	801	922	867	993	932
782	734	853	802	923	868	994	933
783	735	854	803	924	869	"	934
784	736	855	804	925	870	995	935
785	737	856	805	926	871	996	936
786	738	857	806	927	542	997	937
787	739	858	807	"	872	998	937
788	740	859	808	928	873	999	938
789	741	860	809	929	874	1000	939
790	742	861	810	930	875	1001	940
791	743	862	811	931	876	1002	941
792	744	863	812	932	877	1003	942
793	745	864	813	933	878	1004	943
794	746	865	814	934	879	1005	944
795	747	866	815	935	650	1006	945
796	748	867	816	936	880	1007	946
797	749	868	817	937	881	1008	947
798	3027	869	818	938	882	1009	948
799	750	870	818	939	883	1010	949
800	751	871	819	940	884	1011	950
801	752	872	820	941	881	1012	951
802	753	873	821	942	886	1013	952
803	754	874	822	943	885	1014	953
804	755	875	823	944	887	1015	954
805	%	876	824	945	888	1016	955
806	756	877	825	946	889	1017	4476
"	757	878	826	947	890	1018	956
807	758	879	827	948	891	1019	957
808	759	880	828	949	892	1020	958
809	760	881	829	950	893	1021	958
810	761	882	830	951	894	1022	959
811	760	883	831	952	894	1023	960
812	762	884	832	953	895	1024	961
813	763	885	833	954	%	1025	%
814	764	886	834	955	896	1026	1007
815	765	887	835	956	897	1027	1007

1028	962	1100	1025	1172	1087	1244	1155
1029	963	1101	1026	1173	1088	1245	1156
1030	962	1102	1690	1174	1089	1246	1157
1031	964	1103	1027	1175	1090	1247	1155
1032	964	1104	1028	1176	1091	1248	1158
1033	965	1105	1029	1177	1092	1249	1156
1034	966	1106	1030	1178	1093	1250	1157
1035	966	1107	1031	1179	1094	1251	1159
1036	967	1108	1032	1180	1095	1252	1160
1037	968	1109	1033	1181	1096	1253	1138
1038	%	1110	1034	1182	1097	1254	1161
1039	969	1111	1035	1183	1098	1255	1162
1040	970	1112	1036	1184	1099	1256	1163
1041	971	1113	1037	1185	1100	1257	1164
1042	972	1114	1038	1186	1101	1258	1165
1043	973	1115	1039	1187	1102	1259	1166
1044	974	1116	1040	1188	1103	1260	1166
1045	974	1117	1041	1189	1104	1261	1167
1046	975	1118	%	1190	1105	1262	1168
1047	976	1119	1042	1191	1106	1263	%
1048	977	1120	1043	1192	1107	1264	1169
1049	978	1121	1044	1193	1110	1265	1170
1050	979	1122	1045	1194	1108	1266	%
1051	980	1123	1046	1195	1109	1267	1171
1052	981	1124	1048	1196	1110	1268	1172
1053	982	1125	1047	1197	1111	1269	%
1054	983	1126	1049	1198	1112	1270	1173
1055	984	1127	1050	1199	1113	1271	1173
1056	985	1128	1051	1200	1114	1272	1175
1057	985	1129	1052	1201	1115	1273	1174
1058	986	1130	1053	1202	1116	1274	1176
1059	987	1131	1054	1203	1117	1275	1177
1060	988	1132	1055	1204	1118	1276	1176 + 1803
1061	989	1133	1056	1205	1119	1277	1176 + 2532 +
1062	990	1134	1057	1206	1120		3638
1063	991	1135	1053	1207	1121	1278	1178
1064	992	1136	1058	1208	1122	1279	1179
1065	993	1137	1059	1209	1123	1280	1180
1066	994	1138	1060	1210	1124	1281	1181
1067	1003	1139	1061	1211	1125	"	1182
1068	995	1140	1061	1212	1126	1282	1183
1069	996	1141	1062	1213	1127	1283	1184
1070	997	1142	1063	1214	1128	1284	1185
1071	998	1143	1064	1215	1129	1285	1186
1072	999	1144	2802	1216	1130	1286	1187
1073	999	1145	1065	1217	1130	1287	1187
1074	1000	1146	1066	1218	1131	1288	1188
1075	1001	1147	1067	1219	1132	1289	1189
1076	1002	1148	1068	1220	1133	1290	127
1077	1003	1149	1068	1221	1134	1291	1190
1078	1003	1150	1069	1222	1135	1292	1191
1079	1004	1151	1070	1223	1136	1293	1192
1080	1005	1152	1071	1224	1137	1294	1193
1081	1006	1153	1072	1225	%	1295	2359
1082	1007	1154	1073	1226	1138	1296	1194
1083	1008	1155	1074	1227	1139	1297	1195
1084	1009	1156	1075	1228	1140	1298	1196
1085	1010	1157	1076	1229	1141	1299	1197
1086	1011	1158	1077	1230	1142	1300	1198
1087	1012	1159	1077	1231	1143	1301	1199
1088	1013	1160	1077	1232	1144	1302	1200
1089	1014	1161	1078	1233	1145	1303	1201
1090	1015	1162	1079	1234	1146	1304	1202
1091	1016	1163	1081	1235	1147	1305	1203
1092	1017	1164	1080	1236	1148	1306	1204
1093	1018	1165	1081	1237	1149	1307	1205
1094	1019	1166	1082	1238	1150	1308	1206
1095	1020	1167	1083	1239	1151	1309	1208
1096	1021	1168	1084	1240	1152	1310	1207
1097	1022	1169	1085	1241	1153	1311	1208
1098	1023	1170	1086	1242	1154	1312	1209
1099	1024	1171	1086	1243	%	1313	1210

G/K	Strong	G/K	Strong	G/K	Strong	G/K	Strong
1314	1211	1386	1277	1458	1337	1529	1401
1315	5081	1387	1278	1459	1338	1530	1402
1316	1212	1388	1279	1460	1339	1531	1403
1317	1213	1389	1280	1461	333	1532	1404
1318	1214	1390	1281	1462	1340	1533	1405
1319	1215	1391	1282	1463	2613	1534	1406
1320	1216	1392	1284	1464	1341	1535	1407
1321	1217	1393	1284	1465	1342	1536	1408
1322	1218	1394	%	1466	1343	1537	1409
1323	1219	1395	1283	1467	1344	1538	1410
1324	1220	1396	1284	1468	1345	1539	1411
1325	1221	1397	1285	1469	1346	1540	1412
1326	%	1398	1286	1470	1347	1541	1413
1327	1222	1399	1287	1471	1348	1542	1414
1328	1223	1400	1288	1472	1349	1543	1415
1329	1224	1401	1289	1473	1350	1544	1416
1330	1225	1402	1290	1474	1351	1545	1417
1331	1226	1403	1291	1475	1352	1546	1419
1332	1227	1404	1292	1476	1353	1547	1420
1333	1228	1405	1293	1477	1354	1548	1420
1334	1229	1406	1294	1478	1355	1549	1421
1335	1230	1407	1295	1479	1356	1550	%
1336	1231	1408	1296	1480	2735	1551	1422
1337	1232	1409	1297	1481	1357	1552	1423
1338	1233	1410	1298	1482	1358	1553	1424
1339	1234	1411	1299	1483	1359	1554	1425
1340	1235	1412	1300	1484	1360	1555	987
1341	1236	1413	1301	1485	1361	1556	1426
1342	1237	1414	1302	1486	1362	1557	1427
1343	1238	1415	1303	1487	1362	1558	1428
1344	1239	1416	1303	1488	1363	1559	1429
1345	1240	1417	1304	1489	1364	1560	1430
1346	1241	1418	1305	1490	1417 + 3461	1561	1431
1347	1242	1419	1306	1491	1365	1562	1432
1348	1243	1420	1307	1492	1366	1563	1433
1349	1244	1421	1307	1493	1367	1564	1434
1350	1245	1422	1308	1494	1368	1565	1435
1351	1245	1423	1309	1495	1369	1566	1248
1352	1246	1424	1310	1496	1370	1567	%
1353	1781	1425	1311	1497	1371	1568	1436
1354	1247	1426	1312	1498	1372	1569	1437
1355	1248	1427	1313	1499	1373	1570	1437 + 4007
1356	1249	1428	1314	1500	1374	1571	1438
1357	1250	1429	1315	1501	1375	1572	1439
1358	1251	1430	5512	1502	1376	1573	1440
1359	1252	1431	1316	1503	1377	1574	1441
1360	1253	1432	%	1504	1378	1575	1442
1361	1254	1433	%	1505	1379	1576	1443
1362	1255	1434	1317	1506	1380	1577	1444
1363	1256	1435	1318	1507	1381	1578	1445
1364	1257	1436	1319	1508	1381	1579	1446
1365	1258	1437	1320	1509	1382	1580	1447
1366	%	1438	1321	1510	1383	1581	1448
1367	1259	1439	1322	1511	1384	1582	1449
1368	1260	1440	1323	1512	1385	1583	1450
1369	1261	1441	1324	1513	1386	1584	1451
1370	1262	1442	1325	1514	1387	1585	1452
1371	1263	1443	1325	1515	1388	1586	1453
1372	1264	1444	1326	1516	1389	1587	1454
1373	1265	1445	1760	1517	1390	1588	1455
1374	1266	1446	1831	1518	1391	1589	1456
1375	1267	1447	1327	1519	1392	1590	1457
1376	1268	1448	2058	1520	1393	1591	1573
1377	1269	1449	1328	1521	1394	1592	1458
1378	1270	1450	1329	1522	1395	1593	1459
1379	1271	1451	1330	1523	1190	1594	1460
1380	1272	1452	1331	1524	1396	1595	2620
1381	1273	1453	1332	1525	1397	1596	1461
1382	1274	1454	1333	1526	1398	1597	2623
1383	1275	1455	1334	1527	1399	1598	1462
1384	3859	1456	1335	1528	1400	1599	1463
1385	1276	1457	1336	"	1401	1600	1464

1601	1465	1651	1520	1722	1587	1792	1649
1602	1466	"	3391	1723	1588	1793	1650
1603	1467	1652	1521	1724	1589	1794	1651
1604	1468	1653	1522	1725	1590	1795	1652
1605	1469	1654	1523	1726	1591	1796	1653
1606	1470	1655	1524	1727	1592	1797	1654
1607	1471	1656	1525	1728	1593	1798	1655
1608	1472	1657	1528	1729	1594	1799	1656
1609	1473	1658	1529	1730	1595	1800	1657
"	1691	1659	1530	1731	1596	1801	1658
"	1698	1660	1531	1732	1597	1802	1659
"	1700	1661	1532	1733	1598	1803	1660
"	2248	1662	1533	1734	1599	1804	1661
"	2249	1663	1534	1735	1537 + 4053	1805	1662
"	2254	1664	1535	1736	1600	1806	1662
"	2257	1665	1486	1737	1530	1807	3395
"	3165	1666	1537	1738	1601	1808	1663
"	3427	1667	1538	1739	1602	1809	1664
"	3450	1668	1539	1740	1603	1810	1665
1610	1474	1669	1540	1741	1604	1811	1666
1611	1475	1670	1541	1742	1605	1812	1666
1612	1476	1671	1542	1743	1606	1813	1507
1613	1477	1672	1543	1744	1607	"	1667
1614	1478	1673	1543	1745	1608	1814	1668
1615	1479	1674	1831	1746	1609	1815	1669
1616	1480	1675	1544	1747	%	1816	1670
1617	1481	1676	1545	1748	1610	1817	1671
1618	1482	1677	1816	1749	1611	1818	1672
1619	1483	1678	1546	1750	1612	1819	1673
1620	1484	1679	1547	1751	4982	1820	1674
1621	1485	1680	1548	1752	1613	1821	1675
1622	1486	1681	1549	1753	1614	1822	1676
1623	1487	1682	1550	1754	1615	1823	1677
1624	2397	1683	1551	1755	1616	1824	1677
1625	3708	1684	1552	1756	1618	1825	1678
1626	1491	1685	1553	1757	1617	1826	1678
1627	1493	1686	1554	"	1619	1827	1679
1628	1494	1687	1555	1758	1620	1828	1680
1629	1496	1688	1556	1759	1621	1829	1681
1630	1495	1689	1557	1760	1622	1830	1682
1631	1497	1690	1558	1761	1623	1831	1683
1632	1500	1691	1559	1762	1624	1832	1684
1633	1501	1692	1560	1763	1625	1833	1685
1634	1502	1693	1561	1764	1790	1834	1686
1635	1504	1694	1562	1765	1626	1835	1686
1636	1505	1695	1563	1766	1627	1836	1687
1637	1506	1696	1564	1767	1628	1837	1688
1638	2229 + 3375	1697	1565	1768	1629	1838	1689
1639	1488	1698	1566	1769	1630	1839	1690
"	1498	1699	1567	1770	1631	1840	1692
"	1510	1700	2214	1771	1537 + 5455	1841	1693
"	1511	1701	1568	1772	1632	1842	1694
"	1526	1702	1569	1773	1632	1843	1695
"	2070	1703	2296	1774	1633	1844	1696
"	2071	1704	1570	1775	1634	1845	1722 + 3319
"	2252	1705	1571	1776	1635	1846	1697
"	2258	1706	1572	1777	1636	1847	1699
"	2277	1707	1573	1778	1637	1848	%
"	2468	1708	1574	1779	1638	1849	1701
"	5600	1709	1575	1780	1639	1850	1702
"	5607	1710	1576	1781	1640	1851	1703
1640	%	1711	1577	1782	1641	1852	649
1641	1752	1712	1578	1783	1642	1853	1704
1642	1512	1713	1579	1784	1640	1854	1705
1643	1513	1714	1580	1785	1643	1855	1705
1644	1514	1715	1464	1786	1644	1856	1714
1645	1515	1716	1581	1787	1645	1857	1705
1646	1516	1717	1582	1788	1646	1858	1705
1647	1517	1718	1583	"	1647	1859	1714
1648	1518	1719	1584	1789	1648	1860	1706
1649	3004	1720	1585	1790	1653	1861	1707
1650	1519	1721	1586	1791	1650	1862	1708

1863	1709	1935	1770	2007	1834	2079	1966
1864	1710	1936	1771	2008	1835	2080	1897
1865	1711	1937	1772	2009	1836	2081	1898
1866	1712	1938	1722 + 3551	2010	1837	2082	1904
1867	1713	1939	1773	2011	1838	2083	1899
1868	1714	1940	1774	2012	1839	2084	1900
1869	1715	1941	3726	2013	1839	2085	1901
1870	1716	1942	1775	2014	1839	2086	1902
1871	1717	1943	1776	2015	1840	2087	1903
1872	1718	1944	1777	2016	1841	2088	1904
1873	1719	1945	1778	2017	1842	2089	1905
1874	1720	1946	1779	2018	1843	2090	1906
1875	1721	1947	1780	2019	1844	2091	1907
1876	5455	1948	1781	2020	1845	2092	1908
1877	1722	1949	1782	2021	1846	2093	1909
1878	1723	1950	1783	2022	1847	2094	1910
1879	1724	1951	%	2023	1847	2095	1911
1880	2177	1952	1784	2024	1848	2096	1912
1881	%	1953	1785	2025	1848	2097	1913
1882	1725	1954	1786	2026	1849	2098	1914
1883	1726	1955	1787	2027	1850	2099	1915
1884	%	1956	1788	2028	%	2100	1916
1885	1727	1957	1789	2029	1851	2101	1917
1886	1756	1958	1790	2030	1852	2102	1918
1887	1728	1959	1791	2031	1853	2103	1919
1888	1766	1960	1792	2032	1854	2104	1920
1889	863	1961	1793	2033	1855	2105	1921
1890	1729	1962	1794	2034	1856	2106	1922
1891	1730	1963	1795	2035	1857	2107	1923
1892	1731	1964	1796	2036	1503	2108	1924
1893	1732	1965	1797	2037	1858	2109	1925
1894	1733	1966	1798	2038	1859	2110	1926
1895	1734	1967	1799	2039	1860	2111	1927
1896	1735	1968	1800	2040	1861	2112	1928
1897	1736	1969	1801	2041	1862	2113	1929
1898	1737	1970	1802	2042	1863	2114	1930
1899	1738	1971	1803	2043	1864	2115	1931
1900	1739	1972	1804	2044	1865	2116	1932
1901	1740	1973	1805	2045	1866	2117	1933
1902	1741	1974	1806	2046	1867	2118	1934
1903	1742	1975	1807	2047	1868	2119	1935
1904	1743	1976	1808	2048	1869	2120	1936
1905	1744	1977	1809	2049	1870	2121	1937
1906	1745	1978	1810	2050	1871	2122	1938
1907	1746	1979	1811	2051	1872	2123	1939
1908	1739	1980	1812	2052	1873	2124	2380
1909	1747	1981	1813	2053	1874	2125	1940
1910	1748	1982	1814	2054	1875	2126	1941
1911	1749	1983	1815	2055	1876	2127	1942
1912	1750	1984	1816	2056	1877	2128	1943
1913	1751	1985	1817	2057	1878	2129	1944
1914	1752	1986	455	2058	1879	2130	1945
1915	1752	1987	1818	2059	1880	2131	2027
1916	1768	1988	1819	2060	1881	2132	2770
1917	1769	1989	1820	2061	1882	2133	2778
1918	1753	1990	1821	2062	1883	2134	1946
1919	1754	1991	%	2063	1944	2135	1947
1920	1755	1992	1822	2064	1884	2136	%
1921	1756	1993	1823	2065	1885	2137	1948
1922	1757	1994	1824	2066	1885	2138	1949
1923	1758	1995	1825	2067	%	2139	2989
1924	1759	1996	1826	2068	1886	2140	1950
1925	1782	1997	1832	2069	1887	2141	1951
1926	1760	1998	1827	2070	1888	2142	1952
1927	1761	1999	1828	2071	1889	2143	621
1928	1762	2000	1829	2072	1890	2144	1953
1929	1763	2001	1830	2073	1891	2145	1954
1930	4178	2002	1831	2074	1892	2146	1955
1931	1764	2003	1832	2075	1893	2147	1956
1932	1765	2004	1833	2076	1894	2148	1957
1933	1767	2005	1810	2077	1895	2149	1958
1934	1769	2006	%	2078	1896	2150	1959

2151	1960	2223	2017	2294	2097	2366	2161
2152	1961	2224	2026	2295	2098	2367	2162
2153	1962	2225	2027	2296	2099	2368	2163
2154	1963	2226	2028	2297	2100	2369	2164
2155	1964	2227	2029	2298	2101	2370	2165
2156	1965	2228	2030	2299	2102	2371	2166
2157	1967	2229	2031	2300	2103	2372	2167
2158	1968	2230	2032	2301	2095	2373	2168
2159	1969	2231	2033	2302	2104	2374	2169
2160	1971	2232	2034	2303	2129	2375	2170
2161	1972	2233	2035	2304	2105	2376	2171
2162	1973	2234	4179	2305	2106	2377	2172
2163	1974	2235	2037	2306	2107	2378	2173
2164	1975	2236	2045	2307	2108	2379	2174
2165	1976	2237	2038	2308	2109	2380	2175
2166	1977	2238	2039	2309	2110	2381	2176
2167	3982	2239	2040	2310	2111	2382	%
2168	1978	2240	2041	2311	2112	2383	2177
2169	1979	2241	2042	2312	2113	2384	2178
2170	1980	2242	2043	2313	2114	2385	2179
2171	643	2243	2044	2314	2115	2386	2180
2172	1981	2244	2047	2315	2115	2387	2181
2173	1982	2245	2048	2316	2116	2388	2182
2174	1983	2246	2049	2317	2117	2389	2183
2175	1984	2247	2050	2318	2117	2390	2184
2176	1985	2248	2051	2319	2118	2391	2185
2177	1986	2249	2052	2320	2119	2392	2186
2178	4687	2250	2053	2321	2120	2393	1896
2179	1987	2251	2054	2322	2121	2394	2187
2180	1999	2252	2055	2323	2122	2395	2188
2181	1988	2253	2056	2324	2123	2396	5504
2182	1989	2254	2057	2325	2124	2397	2189
2183	%	2255	2058	2326	2125	2398	2190
2184	1990	2256	1328	2327	2126	2399	2191
2185	1991	2257	2059	2328	2127	2400	2192
2186	1992	2258	2060	2329	2128	2401	2193
2187	1993	2259	2061	2330	2129	2402	%
2188	1994	2260	2062	2331	2130	2403	%
2189	1995	2261	2063	2332	2131	2404	2194
2190	1996	2262	2064	2333	2132	2405	2195
2191	1997	2263	2065	2334	2133	2406	2196
2192	1998	2264	2066	2335	2134	2407	4518
2193	1976	2265	2067	2336	2135	2408	2197
2194	1999	2266	2068	2337	2136	2409	2198
2195	2000	''	5315	2338	2137	2410	4570
2196	2001	2267	2068	2339	2145	2411	2199
2197	2002	2268	2069	2340	2138	2412	2200
2198	2003	2269	2072	2341	2139	2413	4801
2199	2004	2270	2073	2342	2139	2414	2201
2200	2005	2271	%	2343	2140	2415	2202
2201	2006	2272	2074	2344	2141	2416	2203
2202	2007	2273	2274	2345	2142	2417	2204
2203	2008	2274	2078	2346	2143	2418	2206
2204	2009	2275	2079	2347	2144	2419	2205
2205	2010	2276	2080	2348	2145	2420	2206
2206	2233	2277	2081	2349	2146	2421	2207
2207	2011	2278	2082	2350	2148	''	2208
2208	2012	2279	2083	2351	2147	2422	2209
2209	2013	2280	2084	2352	2148	2423	2210
2210	2014	2281	2085	2353	2149	2424	2211
2211	2015	2282	2086	2354	2150	2425	%
2212	2016	2283	2087	2355	2151	2426	2212
2213	2017	2284	2088	2356	2152	2427	2213
2214	2018	2285	2089	2357	2153	2428	2214
2215	2019	2286	2090	2358	2154	2429	2215
2216	2020	2287	1681	2359	2155	2430	4667
2217	2021	2288	2091	2360	807	2431	2216
2218	%	2289	2092	2361	2156	2432	2217
2219	2022	2290	2093	2362	2157	2433	2218
2220	2023	2291	2094	2363	2158	2434	2219
2221	2024	2292	2095	2364	2159	2435	2220
2222	2025	2293	2096	2365	2160	2436	2221

2437	2222	2508	2291	2580	2357	2652	2424
2438	2223	2509	2292	2581	2358	2653	2425
2439	2224	2510	2293	2582	2359	2654	2426
2440	2224	2511	2294	2583	2360	2655	2427
2441	2225	2512	2295	2584	2361	2656	2428
2442	2226	2513	2296	2585	2362	2657	2429
2443	2227	2514	2297	2586	%	2658	2430
2444	%	2515	2298	2587	2363	2659	2431
2445	2228	2516	2299	2588	2364	2660	2432
2446	2229	2517	2300	2589	2365	2661	2433
2447	2229 + 3375	2518	2301	2590	2366	2662	2434
2448	2230	2519	2302	2591	2367	2663	2435
2449	2231	2520	2303	2592	2368	2664	2436
2450	2232	2521	2304	2593	2369	2665	2437
2451	2233	2522	2305	2594	2370	2666	2438
2452	2234	2523	2306	2595	2371	2667	2439
"	2236	2524	%	2596	2372	2668	2440
2453	2235	2525	2307	2597	2373	2669	2441
2454	2237	2526	2308	2598	2374	2670	2442
2455	2238	2527	2309	2599	2375	2671	2443
2456	2239	2528	2310	2600	2376	2672	2444
2457	2240	2529	2310	2601	2377	2673	2445
2458	2241	2530	2311	2602	2378	2674	2446
2459	2242	2531	2312	2603	2379	2675	2447
2460	2243	2532	2312'	2604	2380	2676	2448
2461	2244	2533	2313	2605	2381	2677	2449
2462	2245	2534	2314	2606	2382	2678	2450
2463	2246	2535	2315	2607	%	2679	2451
2464	2247	2536	2316	2608	2383	2680	2452
2465	2250	2537	2317	2609	2384	2681	2453
2466	2251	2538	2318	2610	2385	2682	2454
2467	2253	2539	2319	2611	2386	2683	2455
2468	2255	2540	2320	2612	2387	2684	2456
2469	2256	2541	2321	2613	2388	2685	2457
2470	2256	2542	2322	2614	2389	2686	2456
2471	2259	2543	2323	2615	2390	2687	2458
2472	2260	2544	2324	2616	2391	2688	2459
2473	2261	2545	2325	2617	2392	2689	2460
2474	2262	2546	2326	2618	2393	2690	2461
2475	2263	2547	2327	2619	2394	2691	2462
2476	2264	2548	2328	2620	2395	2692	2463
2477	2265	2549	2329	2621	%	2693	2464
2478	2266	2550	2330	2622	%	2694	2465
2479	2267	2551	%	2623	2396	2695	2466
2480	2268	2552	2331	2624	2397	2696	2469
2481	2269	2553	2332	2625	2398	2697	2469
2482	2276	2554	2333	2626	2399	2698	2470
2483	2270	2555	2334	2627	2400	2699	2471
2484	2271	2556	2335	2628	2401	2700	2472
2485	2272	2557	2336	2629	2402	2701	2473
2486	2273	2558	2337	2630	2403	2702	2474
2487	2274	2559	2338	2631	2404	2703	2475
2488	2275	2560	2339	2632	2405	2704	2466
2489	2276	2561	2340	2633	2406	2705	2476
2490	2278	2562	2341	2634	2407	2706	%
2491	2279	2563	2342	2635	2408	2707	2477
2492	2279	2564	2343	2636	2409	2708	2478
2493	2279	2565	2344	2637	2410	2709	2479
2494	%	2566	2345	2638	1494	2710	2480
2495	3134	2567	2346	2639	2411	2711	2481
2496	5008	2568	2347	2640	2412	2712	2482
2497	2280	2569	2348	2641	2413	2713	2483
2498	2281	2570	2349	2642	2414	2714	2484
2499	2282	2571	5182	2643	2415	2715	2485
2500	2283	2572	2350	2644	2416	2716	2486
2501	2284	2573	2351	2645	2417	2717	2487
2502	2285	2574	2352	2646	2418	2718	2488
2503	2286	2575	2352	2647	2419	2719	%
2504	2287	2576	2353	2648	2420	2720	2489
2505	2288	2577	2354	2649	2421	2721	2489
2506	2289	2578	2355	2650	2422	"	2490
2507	2290	2579	2356	2651	2423	2722	2491

2723	%	2795	2546	2866	2611	2938	2677
2724	2492	2796	2547	2867	2612	2939	2678
2725	5601	2797	2548	2868	2613	2940	2679
2726	2455	2798	2549	2869	1349	2941	2680
2727	2493	2799	2550	2870	2614	2942	2681
2728	2491	2800	2551	2871	2615	2943	2682
2729	2494	2801	2552	2872	2616	2944	2683
2730	2494	2802	2553	2873	2652	2945	2684
2731	2495	2803	2554	2874	2653	2946	2685
2732	2496	2804	2555	2875	2617	2947	2686
2733	2497	2805	2556	2876	2618	2948	2687
2734	2498	2806	2557	2877	2619	2949	2688
2735	2499	2807	2558	2878	2620	2950	2689
2736	2500	2808	2559	2879	2621	2951	2690
2737	2501	2809	2560	2880	2622	2952	2691
2738	2501	2810	2561	2881	2623	2953	2692
2739	2502	2811	2562	2882	2624	2954	2693
2740	2503	2812	2563	2883	2624	2955	2694
2741	%	2813	2564	2884	2625	2956	2695
2742	943	2814	2565	2885	2626	2957	2695
2743	2504	2815	2567	2886	2627	2958	2696
2744	943	2816	2568	2887	2628	2959	2697
2745	2505	2817	2552	2888	2629	2960	2698
2746	2506	2818	2569	2889	2630	2961	2699
2747	2507	2819	2566	2890	2631	2962	2700
2748	2508	"	2570	2891	2632	2963	2701
2749	2509	2820	2571	2892	2633	2964	826
2750	2510	2821	2572	2893	2596 + 2955	2965	2702
2751	2511	2822	2573	2894	2634	2966	2703
2752	2512	2823	2574	2895	2635	2967	2704
2753	4027	2824	2574	2896	2636	2968	2705
2754	2513	2825	2575	2897	2637	2969	2706
2755	2514	2826	2576	2898	2638	2970	2707
2756	2515	2827	2577	2899	2639	2971	2019
2757	2516	2828	2578	2900	2640	2972	2708
2758	2596 + 1520	2829	2579	2901	2641	2973	2709
2759	2517	2830	2580	2902	2642	2974	2710
2760	2511	2831	2581	2903	2643	2975	4785
2761	2518	2832	2581	2904	2644	2976	2711
2762	2519	2833	2582	2905	2645	2977	2712
2763	2520	2834	2583	2906	2646	2978	2713
2764	2521	2835	2584	2907	2647	2979	2714
2765	2596 + 2250	2836	2585	2908	2648	2980	2715
2766	2522	2837	2586	2909	2649	2981	2716
2767	2523	2838	2587	2910	2650	2982	2718
2768	2524	2839	603	2911	2651	2983	2719
2769	2525	2840	2588	2912	2652	2984	2719
2770	2525	2841	2589	2913	2653	2985	2720
2771	2526	2842	2591	2914	2654	2986	2127
2772	2526'	2843	2590	2915	2655	2987	2721
2773	2527	2844	2592	2916	2656	2988	2722
2774	2528	2845	2593	2917	2657	2989	2723
2775	2529	2846	2594	2918	2658	2990	2724
2776	2530	2847	2595	2919	2659	2991	2725
2777	2531	2848	2596	2920	2660	2992	2725
2778	2509	2849	2597	2921	2661	2993	2726
2779	2532	2850	2598	2922	2662	2994	2727
2780	2533	2851	2599	2923	2663	2995	2728
2781	2534	2852	925	2924	2664	2996	2729
2782	2535	2853	2600	2925	2665	2997	2730
2783	2536	2854	2601	2926	%	2998	2731
2784	2536	2855	%	2927	2666	2999	2732
2785	2537	2856	2602	2928	2667	3000	2733
2786	2538	2857	2603	2929	2668	3001	2730
2787	2757	2858	2604	2930	2669	3002	2734
2788	2539	2859	2605	2931	2670	3003	2735
2789	2540	2860	2606	2932	2671	3004	2736
2790	2541	2861	2607	2933	2672	3005	2737
2791	2542	2862	2608	2934	2673	3006	2736
2792	2543	2863	1125	2935	2674	3007	2802
2793	2544	2864	2609	2936	2675	3008	2738
2794	2545	2865	2610	2937	2676	3009	2739

3010	2739	3082	2800	3154	2867	3225	2931
3011	2740	3083	2801	3155	2868	3226	2927
3012	2741	3084	2802	3156	2869	3227	2932
3013	2743	3085	2802	3157	2870	3228	2933
3014	2742	3086	2803	3158	2871	3229	2934
3015	2743	3087	2804	3159	2872	3230	2935
3016	2744	3088	2805	3160	2873	3231	2936
3017	2745	3089	2806	3161	2874	3232	2937
3018	2746	3090	2807	3162	2874	3233	2938
3019	2584	3091	2808	3163	2874	3234	2939
3020	2747	3092	2809	3164	2875	3235	2940
3021	2748	3093	2810	3165	2876	3236	2941
3022	2748	3094	2811	3166	2877	3237	2942
3023	2749	3095	2812	3167	2878	3238	2944
3024	2750	3096	2813	3168	2878	3239	2943
3025	2751	3097	2814	3169	2879	3240	2944
3026	2752	3098	2815	3170	2880	3241	2945
3027	2753	3099	2816	3171	2881	3242	2946
3028	%	3100	2817	3172	2882	3243	2946
3029	2754	3101	2818	3173	2883	3244	2947
3030	2755	3102	2819	3174	2884	3245	2948
3031	2756	3103	2820	3175	2885	3246	2949
3032	2757	3104	2821	3176	2886	3247	2950
3033	2758	3105	2822	3177	2887	3248	2951
3034	2759	3106	2823	3178	2887	3249	2952
3035	2760	3107	2824	3179	2888	3250	2953
3036	2761	3108	2825	3180	2889	3251	2954
3037	2762	3109	2825	3181	2890	3252	2955
3038	2763	3110	2826	3182	2891	3253	2956
3039	2764	3111	2827	3183	2891	3254	2956
3040	2765	3112	2828	3184	2892	3255	2957
3041	2766	3113	2829	3185	2893	3256	2958
3042	2767	3114	2830	3186	2894	3257	2959
3043	2768	3115	2831	3187	2895	3258	2960
3044	2769	3116	2832	3188	2895	3259	2961
3045	2770	3117	2833	3189	2896	3260	2958
3046	2771	3118	2834	3190	2897	3261	2962
3047	2772	3119	2835	3191	2898	3262	2963
3048	2773	3120	2836	3192	2899	3263	2964
3049	2774	3121	2837	3193	2900	3264	2965
3050	2775	3122	2838	3194	2901	3265	2966
3051	2776	3123	2839	3195	2902	3266	2967
3052	2775	3124	2840	3196	2903	3267	2968
3053	2777	3125	2841	3197	2904	3268	2969
3054	%	3126	2842	3198	2905	3269	2970
3055	5392	3127	2843	3199	2906	3270	2971
3056	2778	3128	2844	3200	2907	3271	2972
3057	2779	3129	%	3201	2908	3272	2973
3058	2780	3130	2845	3202	2908	3273	2974
3059	2781	3131	2846	"	2909	3274	%
3060	2782	3132	2847	3203	2910	3275	2975
3061	2783	3133	2848	3204	2911	3276	2976
3062	2784	3134	2849	3205	2912	3277	2977
3063	2785	3135	2850	3206	2913	3278	2978
3064	2786	3136	2851	3207	2914	3279	2997
3065	%	3137	2858	3208	2915	3280	2979
3066	2787	3138	2857	3209	2916	3281	2980
3067	2788	3139	2852	3210	2917	3282	2981
3068	2789	3140	2853	3211	2918	3283	2982
3069	2790	3141	2854	3212	2919	3284	2983
3070	2791	3142	2855	3213	2920	3285	2984
3071	2791	3143	2856	3214	2921	3286	2985
3072	2792	3144	2858	3215	2922	3287	2986
3073	2793	3145	2857	3216	2923	3288	2987
3074	2794	3146	2859	3217	2924	3289	2988
3075	2795	3147	2860	3218	2925	3290	2989
3076	2796	3148	2861	3219	2926	3291	2990
3077	2792	3149	2862	3220	2927	3292	2991
3078	2797	3150	2863	3221	2928	3293	2993
3079	5531	3151	2864	3222	2929	3294	2994
3080	2798	3152	2865	3223	2930	3295	2992
3081	2799	3153	2866	3224	2927	3296	2995

3297	2996	3366	3058	3436	3122	"	3189
3298	2996	3367	3059	3437	3123	3507	3190
3299	2997	3368	3060	3438	3124	3508	3199
3300	2998	3369	3061	3439	3125	3509	3191
3301	2999	3370	3062	3440	3126	3510	3192
3302	3000	"	3063	3441	3127	3511	3193
3303	3001	"	3064	3442	3128	3512	3193
3304	3002	3371	3065	3443	3129	3513	3193
3305	3003	3372	3066	3444	3130	3514	3194
3306	2036	3373	3067	3445	3131	3515	3194
"	2046	3374	3068	3446	3132	3516	3195
"	3004	3375	3069	3447	3133	3517	3196
"	4483	3376	3070	3448	3134	3518	3197
3307	3005	3377	3071	3449	3135	3519	3198
3308	3006	3378	3072	3450	3136	3520	3199
3309	3007	3379	3073	3451	3137	3521	3200
3310	3008	3380	3074	3452	3137	3522	3201
3311	3009	3381	3075	3453	3138	3523	3202
3312	3010	3382	3076	3454	3139	3524	3437
3313	3011	3383	3077	3455	3140	3525	3303
3314	621	3384	3078	3456	3141	3526	3104
3315	%	3385	3079	3457	3142	3527	%
3316	2982	3386	3080	3458	3143	3528	3304
3317	3012	3387	3081	3459	3144	3529	3304
3318	3013	3388	3082	3460	3145	3530	3305
3319	3014	3389	3083	3461	3149	3531	3306
3320	3015	3390	3084	3462	3145	3532	3307
3321	3016	3391	3085	3463	3146	3533	3308
3322	3017	3392	3086	3464	3147	3534	3309
3323	3018	3393	3087	3465	3148	3535	3310
3324	3019	3394	3088	3466	3149	3536	3311
3325	3020	3395	3089	3467	3150	3537	3312
3326	3021	3396	3090	3468	3151	3538	3313
3327	1039	3397	3091	3469	3152	3539	3322
3328	3022	3398	%	3470	3153	3540	3314
3329	3023	3399	3092	3471	3154	3541	3315
3330	3024	3400	3093	3472	3155	3542	3316
3331	3028	3401	3093	3473	3156	3543	3317
3332	3025	3402	3094	3474	3157	3544	3318
3333	3026	3403	717	3475	3158	3545	3319
3334	3027	3404	3095	3476	3159	3546	3320
3335	3028	3405	3096	3477	3160	3547	3321
3336	3029	3406	3095	3478	3161	3548	3322
3337	3030	3407	3097	3479	3162	3549	3323
3338	3031	3408	3098	3480	3163	3550	3324
3339	3032	3409	3099	3481	3164	3551	3325
3340	3033	3410	3149	3482	3166	3552	3326
3341	3032	3411	3100	3483	3167	3553	3327
3342	3034	3412	3101	3484	3168	3554	3328
3343	3035	3413	3102	3485	3169	3555	3329
3344	3036	3414	3156	3486	3170	3556	3330
3345	3037	3415	3158	3487	3171	3557	3331
3346	3038	3416	3159	3488	3172	3558	3332
3347	3039	3417	3103	3489	3173	3559	3333
3348	3040	3418	3104	3490	3174	3560	3334
3349	3041	3419	3105	3491	3175	3561	3335
3350	3042	3420	3106	3492	3176	3562	3336
3351	3043	3421	3107	3493	3177	3563	3337
3352	3044	3422	3108	3494	3178	3564	3338
3353	3045	3423	3109	3495	3179	3565	3339
3354	3046	3424	3110	3496	3179	3566	3340
3355	3047	3425	3111	3497	3180	3567	3341
3356	3048	3426	3112	3498	3181	3568	3342
3357	3049	3427	3113	3499	3182	3569	3343
3358	3050	3428	3114	3500	3183	3570	3344
3359	3051	3429	3115	3501	3184	3571	3345
3360	3052	3430	3116	3502	3396	3572	3346
3361	3053	3431	3117	3503	3396	3573	3344
3362	3054	3432	3118	3504	3186	3574	%
3363	3055	3433	3119	3505	3185	3575	3347
3364	3056	3434	3120	"	3187	3576	3348
3365	3057	3435	3121	3506	3188	3577	3349

3578	3350	3648	3421	3720	3482	3792	3548
3579	3351	3649	3422	3721	3483	3793	3549
3580	3352	3650	3423	3722	3497	3794	3550
3581	3353	3651	3424	3723	3484	3795	3551
3582	3354	3652	3424	3724	3485	3796	3552
3583	3355	3653	3425	3725	3486	3797	3553
3584	3356	3654	3426	3726	3487	3798	3554
3585	3357	3655	3428	3727	3488	3799	3555
3586	3358	3656	3429	3728	3489	3800	3556
3587	3359	3657	3430	3729	3490	3801	3502
3588	3360	3658	3431	3730	3491	3802	3557
3589	3360	3659	3432	3731	3492	3803	3558
3590	3361	3660	3433	3732	3493	3804	3559
3591	3361 + 1065	3661	3434	3733	3494	3805	3560
3592	3365	3662	3435	3734	3495	3806	3561
3593	3366	3663	3436	3735	3496	3807	3562
3594	3367	3664	3437	3736	3496	3808	3563
3595	3368	3665	3438	3737	3497	3809	3564
3596	3369	3666	3439	3738	3498	3810	3564
3597	3370	3667	3440	3739	3499	3811	3565
3598	3365	3668	3441	3740	3500	3812	3566
3599	3367	3669	3442	3741	3561	3813	3567
3600	3371	3670	3443	3742	3501	3814	3568
3601	3372	3671	3444	3743	3502	3815	3570
3602	3373	3672	3445	3744	3503	3816	3571
3603	3374	3673	3446	3745	3504	3817	3572
3604	3375	3674	3447	3746	3505	3818	3573
3605	3376	3675	3448	3747	%	3819	3574
3606	3377	3676	3451	3748	3506	3820	3575
3607	3379	3677	3449	3749	3507	3821	3576
3608	3361 + 4225	3678	3452	3750	3508	3822	3577
3609	3380	3679	3453	3751	3509	3823	%
3610	3381	3680	3454	3752	3510	3824	837
3611	3382	3681	3455	3753	3511	3825	3578
3612	3383	3682	3456	3754	3512	3826	3579
3613	3384	3683	3457	3755	3513	3827	3580
3614	3385	3684	3458	3756	3514	3828	3581
"	3387	3685	3458	3757	3515	3829	3582
3615	3386	3686	3459	3758	3516	3830	3583
3616	3388	3687	%	3759	3517	3831	3584
3617	3389	3688	3460	3760	3518	3832	3585
3618	3389	3689	3461	3761	3519	3833	3586
3619	3390	3690	3462	3762	3520	3834	3587
3620	3392	3691	3463	3763	3521	3835	%
3621	3393	3692	3463	3764	3522	3836	3588
3622	3394	3693	3464	3765	3523	"	5120
3623	3395	3694	3460	3766	3524	3837	3589
3624	3396	3695	3465	3767	3524	3838	3590
3625	3397	3696	3466	3768	3525	3839	3591
"	3398	3697	3467	3769	3526	3840	3592
3626	3399	3698	3468	3770	3527	3841	3593
3627	3400	3699	3469	3771	3528	3842	3594
3628	3401	3700	3470	3772	3529	3843	3595
3629	3402	3701	3471	3773	3530	3844	3596
3630	3403	3702	3472	3774	3531	3845	3597
3631	3404	3703	3473	3775	3532	3846	3598 + 4160
3632	3405	3704	3474	3776	3533	3847	3598
3633	3406	3705	3475	3777	3534	3848	3599
3634	3407	3706	3475	3778	3535	3849	3600
3635	3408	3707	3475	3779	3535	3850	3601
3636	3409	3708	%	3780	3536	3851	3602
3637	3410	3709	3476	3781	3537	3852	3604
3638	3411	3710	3477	3782	3538	3853	3605
3639	3412	3711	3478	3783	3539	3854	3606
3640	3413	3712	3478	3784	3540	3855	3607
3641	3414	3713	3478	3785	3541	3856	3608
3642	3415	3714	3478	3786	3542	3857	1492
3643	3416	3715	3478	3787	3543	3858	3609
3644	3417	3716	3479	3788	3544	3859	2322
3645	3418	3717	3480	3789	3545	3860	3610
3646	3419	3718	3481	3790	3546	3861	3611
3647	3420	3719	3481	3791	3547	3862	3612

G/K	Strong	G/K	Strong	G/K	Strong	G/K	Strong
3863	3613	3935	3672	4007	3739 + 1065	4067	3796
3864	3614	3936	%	4008	3741	4068	3798
3865	3615	3937	3673	4009	3742	4069	3797
3866	3616	3938	3674	4010	3743	4070	3798
3867	3617	3939	3675	4011	3744	4071	3799
3868	3618	3940	3676	4012	3745	4072	3800
3869	3619	3941	3677	4013	3746	4073	%
3870	3620	3942	3678	4014	3747	4074	3802
3871	3618	3943	3679	4015	3748	4075	3803
3872	3621	3944	3680	"	3755	4076	697
3873	3622	3945	3681	4016	3747	4077	3804
3874	3623	3946	3682	4017	3749	4078	3805
3875	3624	3947	3683	4018	3750	4079	3806
3876	3625	3948	3684	4019	3751	4080	3807
3877	3626	3949	3685	4020	3752	4081	3808
3878	3626	3950	3686	4021	3753	4082	3809
3879	3627	3951	3687	4022	3754	4083	3810
3880	3628	3952	3688	4023	3757	4084	3811
3881	3629	3953	3689	4024	3756	4085	3812
3882	3627	3954	3690	4025	3758	4086	3813
3883	3633	3955	3691	4026	3759	4087	3814
3884	3630	3956	3692	4027	3760	4088	3812
3885	3631	3957	3693	4028	3761	4089	3815
3886	3632	3958	3694	4029	3762	4090	3816
3887	3633	3959	3695	4030	3763	4091	3817
3888	3634	3960	3696	4031	3764	4092	3818
3889	%	3961	3697	4032	3762	4093	3819
3890	3635	3962	3698	4033	3765	4094	3820
3891	3636	3963	3699	4034	3766	4095	3821
3892	3637	3964	3700	4035	1695	4096	3822
3893	3638	3965	3701	4036	3767	4097	3823
3894	3644	3966	3702	4037	3768	4098	3824
3895	3645	3967	3703	4038	3769	4099	3825
3896	3639	3968	3704	4039	3770	4100	3824
3897	3639	3969	3705	4040	3771	4101	3826
3898	570	3970	3706	4041	3772	4102	3827
3899	3640	3971	3707	4042	3773	4103	3828
3900	3641	3972	3708	4043	3774	4104	3829
3901	3642	3973	3709	4044	3775	4105	3830
3902	3643	3974	3710	4045	3776	4106	3829
3903	3689	3975	3711	4046	3777	4107	3830
3904	3644	3976	3712	4047	3778	4108	3831
3905	3645	3977	3713	"	5023	4109	3832
3906	3646	3978	3714	"	5025	4110	3833
3907	3647	3979	3715	"	5026	4111	3834
3908	3648	3980	3716	"	5123	4112	3835
3909	3649	3981	3717	"	5124	4113	3826
3910	3650	3982	3718	"	5125	4114	3837
3911	3651	3983	3719	"	5126	4115	3836
3912	3652	3984	3720	"	5127	4116	3837
3913	3653	3985	3721	"	5128	4117	3838
3914	3654	3986	3722	"	5129	4118	3839
3915	3655	3987	3723	"	5130	4119	3840
3916	2442	3988	3724	4048	3779	4120	3841
3917	3656	3989	3733	4049	3780	4121	3842
3918	3657	3990	3725	4050	3781	4122	3843
3919	3658	3991	3726	4051	3782	4123	3844
3920	%	3992	3727	4052	3783	4124	3845
3921	3659	3993	3728	4053	3784	4125	3846
3922	3660	3994	3729	4054	3785	4126	3847
3923	3660	3995	3730	4055	3786	4127	3848
3924	3661	3996	3731	4056	3787	4128	3849
3925	3662	3997	3732	4057	3788	4129	3851
3926	3663	3998	3733	4058	3789	4130	3850
3927	3664	3999	3734	4059	3790	4131	3851
3928	3665	4000	%	4060	856	4132	3852
3929	3666	4001	3735	4061	3791	4133	3853
3930	3667	4002	3736	4062	3792	4134	3854
3931	3668	4003	3737	4063	3793	4135	3855
3932	3669	4004	3738	4064	%	4136	3856
3933	3670	4005	3739	4065	3794	4137	3857
3934	3671	4006	3740	4066	3795	4138	3858

4139	3859	4211	3924	4283	3989	4355	4052
4140	3860	4212	4016	4284	3990	4356	4053
4141	3861	4213	3925	4285	%	4357	4054
4142	3862	4214	3926	4286	3991	4358	4055
4143	3863	4215	3927	4287	3992	4359	4056
4144	3864	4216	3928	4288	3993	4360	4057
4145	3865	4217	3929	4289	3994	4361	4058
4146	3866	4218	3930	4290	3995	4362	4059
4147	3867	4219	3931	4291	3996	4363	4060
4148	3868	4220	3932	4292	3997	4364	4061
4149	3869	4221	3933	4293	3998	4365	4062
4150	3869	4222	3934	4294	3999	4366	4063
4151	3870	4223	3935	4295	4000	4367	4064
4152	3871	4224	3936	4296	4001	4368	4065
4153	3872	4225	3936	4297	4002	4369	4066
4154	3873	4226	3937	4298	4003	4370	4067
4155	3874	4227	3938	4299	4004	4371	4068
4156	3875	4228	3939	4300	4005	4372	4069
4157	3876	4229	3940	4301	4006	4373	4070
4158	3877	4230	3941	4302	4007	4374	4071
4159	3878	4231	3942	4303	%	4375	4072
4160	3879	4232	3943	4304	4012 + 2087	4376	4073
4161	3880	4233	3944	4305	4008	4377	4074
4162	3881	4234	3945	4306	4009	4378	4075
4163	3882	4235	3946	4307	4010	4379	4076
4164	3883	4236	3947	4308	4011	4380	4077
4165	3884	4237	3948	4309	4012	4381	4078
4166	3885	4238	5237	4310	4013	4382	4079
4167	3885	4239	3949	4311	4014	4383	4080
4168	3886	4240	3950	4312	681	4384	4081
4169	3887	4241	3951	4313	4015	4385	4082
4170	3888	4242	3952	4314	4016	4386	4456
4171	3889	4243	3953	4315	4017	4387	4457
4172	3890	4244	3954	4316	4018	4388	4083
4173	3913	4245	3955	4317	4019	4389	4084
4174	3891	4246	3956	4318	4020	4390	4085
4175	3892	4247	3957	4319	4021	4391	4086
4176	3893	4248	3958	4320	4022	4392	3981
4177	3894	4249	3959	4321	4023	4393	4087
4178	3895	4250	3960	4322	4024	4394	4088
4179	3896	4251	3961	4323	4024	4395	4089
4180	3897	4252	3962	4324	4025	4396	4090
4181	3898	4253	3963	4325	4026	4397	4091
4182	3899	4254	3964	4326	4027	4398	4130
4183	3900	4255	3965	4327	4776	4399	4092
4184	3901	4256	3966	4328	4028	4400	4093
4185	3902	4257	3967	4329	4029	4401	4093
4186	3903	4258	3968	4330	4030	4402	4094
4187	3904	4259	3969	4331	4031	4403	4095
4188	4368	4260	3964	4332	4032	4404	4096
4189	3905	4261	3970	4333	4033	4405	4097
4190	3906	4262	3971	4334	4034	4406	4098
4191	3907	4263	3972	4335	4035	4407	4099
4192	3908	4264	3973	4336	621	4408	4099
4193	3909	4265	3974	4337	4036	4409	4100
4194	3910	4266	3975	4338	4037	4410	4101
4195	3911	4267	3976	4339	4038	4411	4102
4196	3912	4268	3977	4340	4039	4412	4103
4197	3913	4269	3978	4341	4040	4413	4104
4198	3913	4270	3979	4342	4041	4414	4105
4199	3914	4271	3979	4343	4042	4415	4106
4200	3915	4272	3980	4344	4043	4416	4107
4201	2710	4273	3981	4345	4044	4417	4107
4202	3916	4274	3981	4346	4045	4418	4108
4203	3917	4275	3982	4347	4046	4419	4109
4204	4332	4276	4091	4348	4047	4420	4110
4205	3918	4277	3983	4349	%	4421	4111
4206	3919	4278	3984	4350	%	4422	4112
4207	3920	4279	3985	4351	4048	4423	4113
4208	3921	4280	3986	4352	4049	4424	4114
4209	3922	4281	3987	4353	4050	4425	4115
4210	3923	4282	3988	4354	4051	4426	4116

4427	4117	"	4119	4568	4248	4637	4312
4428	4120	"	4183	4569	4249	4638	4313
4429	4121	4499	4184	4570	4250	4639	4314
4430	4122	4500	4185	4571	4251	4640	4315
4431	4123	4501	4186	4572	4252	4641	4316
4432	4124	4502	4187	4573	4249	4642	4317
4433	4125	4503	4188	4574	4253	4643	4318
4434	4126	4504	4189	4575	4254	4644	4319
4435	4127	4505	4190	4576	4255	4645	4319
4436	4128	"	4191	4577	4256	4646	4320
4437	4129	4506	4192	4578	4257	4647	4355
4438	4131	4507	4193	4579	4258	4648	4321
4439	4132	4508	4194	4580	4259	4649	4321
4440	4133	4509	5117	4581	4260	4650	4322
4441	4134	4510	4195	4582	4261	4651	4323
4442	4135	4511	4196	4583	4262	4652	4317
4443	4136	4512	4197	4584	4263	4653	4324
4444	4137	4513	4198	4585	4263	4654	4317
4445	4138	4514	4199	4586	4264	4655	4325
4446	4139	4515	4197	4587	4265	4656	4326
4447	4140	4516	4200	4588	4266	4657	4327
4448	4141	4517	4201	4589	4267	4658	1929
4449	4142	4518	4202	4590	4268	4659	4328
4450	4143	4519	4203	4591	4269	4660	4329
4451	1708	4520	4204	4592	4270	4661	4330
4452	4144	4521	4205	4593	4271	4662	4331
4453	4144	4522	4206	4594	4272	4663	4332
4454	4145	4523	4207	4595	4273	4664	4333
4455	4146	4524	4208	4596	4274	4665	4334
4456	4147	4525	4209	4597	4302	4666	4335
4457	4148	4526	4210	4598	4276	4667	4336
4458	4149	4527	4211	4599	4278	4668	4337
4459	4150	4528	4210	4600	4279	4669	4338
4460	4151	4529	4212	4601	4281	4670	4339
4461	4152	4530	4213	4602	4282	4671	4286
4462	4153	4531	4214	4603	4283	4672	4340
4463	4154	4532	4215	4604	4284	4673	4341
4464	4155	4533	4216	4605	4285	4674	4342
4465	4156	4534	4217	4606	4286	4675	4343
4466	4157	4535	4458	4607	4287	4676	4344
4467	4217	4536	4219	4608	4288	4677	4345
4468	4158	4537	4218	4609	4289	4678	4346
4469	3537	4538	4220	4610	4290	4679	4347
4470	4159	4539	4221	4611	4406	4680	4346
4471	4169	4540	4222	4612	4407	4681	4347
4472	4160	4541	4223	4613	4291	4682	4348
4473	4161	4542	4224	4614	4292	4683	4349
4474	4162	4543	4225	4615	4293	4684	4350
4475	4163	4544	4226	4616	4294	4685	4351
4476	4164	4545	4227	4617	4284	4686	4352
4477	4165	4546	4228	4618	4295	4687	4353
4478	4166	4547	4229	4619	4296	4688	4354
4479	4167	4548	4230	4620	4297	4689	4355
4480	4168	4549	4231	4621	4298	4690	%
4481	4169	4550	4232	4622	4299	4691	4356
4482	4170	4551	4233	4623	4300	4692	4356
4483	4171	4552	4234	4624	4301	4693	4357
4484	4172	4553	4235	4625	4302	4694	4358
4485	4173	4554	4236	"	4277	4695	4359
4486	4174	4555	4237	"	4280	4696	4360
4487	4175	4556	4238	4626	4303	4697	%
4488	4176	4557	4236	4627	4304	4698	4361
4489	4177	4558	4239	4628	4305	4699	4362
4490	4178	4559	4240	4629	4306	4700	4363
4491	4179	4560	4241	4630	4307	4701	4364
4492	4184	4561	4242	4631	4308	4702	4365
4493	%	4562	4246	4632	4275	4703	4366
4494	4180	4563	4243	"	4308	4704	4366
4495	4181	4564	4244	4633	4309	4705	4367
4496	%	4565	4245	4634	4310	4706	4368
4497	4182	4566	4246	4635	3962	4707	4369
4498	4118	4567	4247	4636	4311	4708	4370

4709	4371	4780	4436	4851	4498	4923	4562
4710	4372	4781	4437	4852	4499	4924	4563
4711	4373	4782	4438	4853	4500	4925	4564
4712	4374	4783	4439	4854	4481	4926	4565
4713	4375	4784	4440	4855	4501	4927	4566
4714	4376	4785	4441	4856	4493	4928	4567
4715	4377	4786	4442	4857	4502	4929	4568
4716	4370	4787	4443	4858	4503	4930	4569
4717	4378	4788	4444	4859	4504	4931	4570
4718	4379	4789	4445	4860	4505	4932	4572
4719	4380	4790	4446	4861	4506	4933	4573
4720	4381	4791	4447	4862	4510	4934	4574
4721	4382	4792	4448	4863	4510	4935	4575
4722	4380	4793	4449	4864	4507	4936	4576
4723	4381	4794	4450	4865	4508	4937	4577
4724	4382	4795	%	4866	4509	4938	4577
4725	4383	4796	4451	4867	4510	4939	4578
4726	4384	4797	4453	4868	4511	4940	4579
4727	4385	4798	4454	4869	4512	4941	4580
4728	4386	4799	4455	4870	4513	4942	4581
"	4387	4800	4456	4871	4514	4943	4582
4729	4388	4801	4457	4872	4515	4944	4583
4730	4389	4802	4459	4873	4516	4945	4584
4731	4390	4803	4452	4874	4517	4946	4584
4732	4391	"	4458	4875	%	4947	4585
4733	4392	4804	%	4876	4518	4948	4586
4734	4393	4805	4460	4877	4519	4949	4587
4735	4394	4806	4461	4878	4520	4950	4588
4736	4395	4807	4462	4879	4521	4951	4562
4737	4396	4808	4462	4880	4522	4952	4562
4738	4397	4809	4462	4881	4523	4953	4589
4739	4398	4810	4463	4882	4524	4954	4590
4740	4399	4811	4464	4883	4525	4955	4591
4741	4400	4812	4465	4884	4526	4956	4592
4742	4401	4813	%	4885	4527	4957	4593
4743	4402	4814	4466	4886	4528	4958	4594
4744	4403	4815	4467	4887	4529	4959	4612
4745	4404	4816	4468	4888	4531	4960	4595
4746	4405	4817	911	4889	4532	4961	4596
4747	4406	4818	4481	4890	4530	4962	4597
4748	4407	4819	4469	4891	4533	4963	4598
4749	4408	4820	4470	4892	4534	4964	4599
4750	4409	4821	4471	4893	4535	4965	4600
4751	4410	4822	4472	4894	4536	4966	4525
4752	4411	4823	4473	4895	4537	4967	4601
4753	3144	4824	4474	4896	4538	4968	4602
4754	4412	4825	4475	4897	4539	4969	4603
4755	4413	4826	4486	4898	4672	4970	4604
4756	4414	4827	4476	4899	4540	4971	4603
4757	4415	4828	4469	4900	4540	4972	4605
4758	4416	4829	4477	4901	4541	4973	4606
4759	4412	4830	4478	4902	4542	4974	4607
4760	4417	4831	4479	4903	4543	4975	4608
4761	4418	4832	4480	4904	4544	4976	4609
4762	4419	4833	4481	4905	4545	4977	4610
4763	4420	4834	4481	4906	%	4978	4611
4764	4421	4835	4482	4907	4546	4979	%
4765	4422	4836	4484	4908	4547	4980	4612
4766	4423	4837	4485	4909	4548	4981	4613
4767	4424	4838	4486	4910	4549	4982	4614
4768	4425	4839	4487	4911	4550	4983	4615
4769	4426	4840	4488	4912	4551	4984	4616
4770	4427	4841	4486	4913	4552	4985	4617
4771	4428	4842	4489	4914	4553	4986	4596
4772	4429	4843	4490	4915	4554	4987	4577
4773	4430	4844	4491	4916	4555	4988	4618
4774	4431	4845	4492	4917	4556	4989	4621
4775	4432	4846	4493	4918	4557	4990	4619
4776	4433	4847	4494	4919	4558	4991	4620
4777	4434	4848	4495	4920	4559	4992	4621
4778	4435	4849	4496	4921	4560	4993	4965
4779	%	4850	4497	4922	4561	4994	4622

4995	4623	5067	4692	5136	4760	5201	4819
4996	2977	5068	4693	5137	4761	5202	4820
4997	4624	5069	4694	5138	4762	5203	4821
4998	4625	5070	4696	5139	4763	5204	4822
4999	4626	5071	4695	5140	4764	5205	4823
5000	2469	5072	4697	5141	4765	5206	4824
5001	2469	5073	4698	5142	4766	5207	4825
5002	4627	5074	4699	5143	4766	5208	4826
5003	4628	5075	4700	5144	4767	5209	4827
5004	4629	5076	4701	5145	4768	5210	4828
5005	4630	5077	4702	5146	4769	5211	4829
5006	4631	5078	4703	5147	4770	5212	4830
5007	4632	5079	4704	5148	4571	5213	4831
5008	4633	5080	4705	"	4671	5214	4833
5009	4634	"	4706	"	4675	5215	4832
5010	4635	"	4707	"	4771	5216	4833
5011	4636	5081	4708	"	5209	5217	4834
5012	4637	"	4709	"	5210	5218	4835
5013	4638	5082	4710	"	5213	5219	4836
5014	4639	5083	4711	"	5216	5220	4837
5015	4640	5084	4712	5149	4772	5221	4838
5016	4641	5085	4713	5150	4773	5222	4839
5017	4642	5086	4955	5151	4773	5223	4840
5018	4643	5087	4714	5152	4774	5224	4841
5019	4644	5088	4715	5153	4775	5225	4842
5020	4645	5089	4716	5154	4776	5226	%
5021	4646	5090	4717	5155	4777	5227	4843
5022	4647	5091	4718	5156	4778	5228	4844
5023	4648	5092	4719	5157	4779	5229	4098
5024	4649	5093	4720	5158	4780	5230	4845
5025	4650	5094	4721	5159	4781	5231	4846
5026	4651	5095	4722	5160	4782	5232	4847
5027	4652	5096	4723	5161	4783	5233	4848
5028	4653	5097	4724	5162	%	5234	4849
5029	4654	5098	4725	5163	4784	5235	4849
5030	4655	5099	4726	5164	4785	5236	4850
5031	4656	5100	4727	5165	4873	5237	4851
5032	4657	5101	4728	5166	4786	5238	4852
5033	4658	5102	4729	5167	4787	5239	4851
5034	4659	5103	4730	5168	4788	5240	4833
5035	4660	5104	4731	5169	4789	5241	4853
5036	4661	5105	4732	5170	4790	5242	4854
5037	4662	5106	4733	5171	4791	5243	4855
5038	4663	5107	4734	5172	4792	5244	4856
5039	4664	5108	4736	5173	4793	5245	4857
5040	4665	5109	4735	5174	4794	5246	4858
5041	3395	5110	4737	5175	4795	5247	4859
5042	3395	5111	4738	5176	4796	5248	4860
5043	4666	5112	4739	5177	4797	5249	4861
5044	4667	5113	4740	5178	4798	5250	4862
5045	4668	5114	4741	5179	4797	5251	4863
5046	4669	5115	4746	5180	4799	5252	4864
5047	4670	5116	4742	5181	2010	5253	4865
5048	4672	5117	4743	5182	4800	5254	4866
5049	4673	5118	4744	5183	4801	5255	4867
5050	4674	5119	4745	5184	4802	5256	4868
5051	4676	5120	4746	5185	4803	5257	4869
5052	4677	5121	4770	5186	4804	5258	4870
5053	4678	5122	4747	5187	4805	5259	4871
5054	4679	5123	4748	5188	4806	5260	4871
5055	4680	5124	4749	5189	4807	5261	4900
5056	4681	5125	4750	5190	4808	5262	4872
5057	4682	5126	4751	5191	4809	5263	4873
5058	4683	5127	4752	5192	4810	5264	4874
5059	4684	5128	4753	5193	4811	5265	4875
5060	4685	5129	4754	5194	4812	5266	%
5061	4686	5130	4755	5195	4813	5267	4876
5062	4687	5131	4756	5196	4814	5268	4877
5063	4688	5132	4757	5197	4815	5269	4878
5064	4689	5133	4758	5198	4816	5270	4879
5065	4690	5134	4759	5199	4817	5271	4880
5066	4691	5135	4759	5200	4818	5272	4881

5273	4882	5345	4941	5417	5005	5486	5073
5274	4883	5346	4795	5418	5006	5487	5073
5275	4884	5347	4942	5419	5007	5488	5074
5276	4871	5348	4943	5420	5008	5489	5075
5277	4885	5349	4944	5421	5009	5490	5076
5278	4886	5350	4945	5422	3569	5491	5077
5279	4887	5351	4949	5423	5010	5492	5078
5280	4888	5352	4946	5424	5011	5493	5079
5281	4889	5353	4947	5425	5012	5494	5080
5282	4890	5354	4948	5426	5391	5495	5081
5283	4891	5355	4949	5427	5013	5496	5082
5284	4892	5356	4949	5428	5014	5497	%
5285	%	5357	%	5429	5015	5498	5083
5286	%	5358	4950	5430	5016	5499	5084
5287	4893	5359	4951	5431	5017	5500	5085
5288	4894	5360	4952	5432	5018	5501	5086
5289	4895	5361	4953	5433	5019	5502	5087
5290	4896	5362	4954	5434	5020	5503	5088
5291	4897	5363	4955	5435	5021	5504	5089
5292	4898	5364	4956	5436	5022	5505	5090
5293	4899	5365	4957	5437	5024	5506	5091
5294	%	5366	4958	5438	5027	5507	5092
5295	4900	5367	4959	5439	5028	5508	5093
5296	4901	5368	4960	5440	5029	5509	5094
5297	4862 + 1985	5369	4961	5441	5030	5510	5095
5298	4934	5370	4962	"	5032	5511	5096
5299	4902	5371	4963	"	5033	5512	5097
5300	4903	5372	4964	5442	5031	5513	5098
5301	4904	5373	4965	5443	5034	5514	5099
5302	4905	5374	4966	5444	5035	5515	5101
5303	4906	5375	4967	"	5036	5516	5100
5304	4907	5376	4968	5445	5037	5517	2459
5305	4908	5377	4969	5446	5038	5518	5102
5306	4909	5378	%	5447	5039	5519	5103
5307	4910	5379	4970	5448	5040	5520	5104
5308	4911	5380	4971	5449	5041	5521	5105
5309	4912	5381	4972	5450	5042	5522	5105
5310	4913	5382	4973	5451	5043	5523	5106
5311	4914	5383	4974	5452	5044	5524	5107
5312	4915	5384	4974	5453	%	5525	5108
5313	4916	5385	4975	5454	5045	5526	5109
5314	4917	5386	4976	5455	5046	5527	5110
5315	4918	5387	4977	5456	5047	5528	5111
5316	4919	5388	4978	5457	5048	5529	5112
5317	4920	5389	4979	5458	5049	5530	5112
5318	4921	5390	4980	5459	5050	5531	5112
5319	4921	5391	4981	5460	5051	5532	5113
5320	4920	5392	4982	5461	5052	5533	5114
5321	4922	5393	4983	5462	5053	5534	5115
5322	4923	5394	4984	5463	5054	5535	5116
5323	4894	5395	4985	5464	5055	5536	5117
5324	4924	5396	4986	5465	5056	5537	5118
5325	4925	5397	4987	5466	5058	5538	5119
5326	4926	5398	4988	5467	5057	5539	5121
5327	4927	5399	4989	5468	5058	5540	5122
5328	4894	5400	4990	5469	5059	5541	3694
5329	%	5401	4991	5470	5060	5542	5123
5330	4928	5402	4992	5471	%	5543	5131
5331	4952	5403	4992	5472	5061	5544	5132
5332	4929	5404	4993	5473	5062	5545	5133
5333	4930	5405	4994	5474	5063	5546	5134
5334	4931	5406	4995	5475	5064	5547	5135
5335	4932	5407	4996	5476	5065	5548	5136
5336	%	5408	4997	5477	5062	5549	5137
5337	4933	5409	4998	5478	5063	5550	5138
5338	4934	5410	%	5479	5066	5551	5139
5339	4935	5411	4999	5480	5067	5552	5140
5340	4936	5412	5000	5481	5068	5553	5140 + 4999
5341	4937	5413	5001	5482	5069	5554	5141
5342	4938	5414	5002	5483	5070	5555	5142
5343	4939	5415	5003	5484	5071	5556	5143
5344	4940	5416	5004	5485	5072	5557	5169

5558	5144	5630	5214	5701	5277	5772	5344
5559	5145	5631	5215	5702	5278	5773	5345
5560	5146	5632	5217	5703	5279	5774	5346
5561	5147	5633	5218	5704	5280	5775	1310
5562	5148	5634	5219	5705	5281	5776	5347
5563	5149	5635	5220	5706	5282	5777	5348
5564	5150	5636	5221	5707	5283	5778	5349
5565	5151	5637	5222	5708	5299	5779	5350
5566	5152	5638	5223	5709	5284	5780	5351
5567	5153	5639	5224	5710	5285	5781	5352
5568	5154	"	5225	5711	5286	5782	5353
5569	5154	5640	5226	5712	5287	5783	5354
5570	5155	5641	5227	5713	5288	5784	5355
5571	5156	5642	5228	5714	5289	5785	5356
5572	5157	5643	5229	5715	5290	5786	5357
5573	5158	5644	5230	5716	5291	5787	5358
5574	5159	5645	5231	5717	5292	5788	5359
5575	5160	5646	784	5718	5293	5789	5360
5576	5161	5647	5232	5719	5294	5790	5361
5577	5162	5648	5233	5720	5295	5791	5362
5578	5159	5649	5234	5721	5296	5792	5363
5579	5163	5650	5235	5722	5297	5793	5364
5580	5164	5651	5236	5723	5298	5794	5365
5581	5165	5652	5228 + 1473	5724	5299	5795	5366
5582	5166	5653	5237	5725	5300	5796	5367
5583	5167	5654	5238	5726	%	5797	5368
5584	5168	5655	5240	5727	5301	5798	5369
5585	5169	5656	5240	5728	5302	5799	5370
5586	5170	5657	5239	5729	5303	5800	5371
5587	5171	5658	5240	5730	5304	5801	5372
5588	5172	5659	5241	5731	5305	5802	5373
5589	5173	5660	5242	"	5306	5803	5374
5590	5174	5661	5243	5732	%	5804	5375
5591	5175	5662	5244	5733	5307	5805	5376
5592	5176	5663	5244	5734	5308	5806	5377
5593	5177	5664	5245	5735	5309	5807	5378
5594	5178	5665	5246	5736	5310	5808	5379
5595	5179	5666	5237	5737	5311	5809	5380
5596	5179	5667	5247	5738	5312	5810	5381
5597	5180	5668	5248	5739	5313	5811	5382
5598	5181	5669	5249	5740	%	5812	5383
5599	%	5670	5250	5741	5314	5813	5384
5600	5182	5671	5251	5742	5341	5814	5385
5601	5183	5672	5252	5743	5316	5815	5386
5602	5184	5673	5253	5744	5317	5816	5387
5603	5185	5674	5254	5745	5318	5817	5388
5604	5186	5675	5255	5746	5319	5818	5389
5605	5187	5676	5256	5747	5320	5819	5390
5606	5188	5677	5257	5748	5321	5820	5391
5607	5189	5678	5258	5749	5322	5821	5392
5608	5190	5679	5259	5750	5323	5822	5417
5609	%	5680	5260	5751	5324	5823	5393
5610	5191	5681	5261	5752	5325	5824	5394
5611	5192	5682	5262	5753	5326	5825	5395
5612	5193	5683	5263	5754	5327	5826	5396
5613	5194	5684	5263	5755	5328	5827	5397
5614	5195	5685	5264	5756	5329	5828	5399
5615	5196	5686	5265	5757	5330	5829	5398
5616	5197	5687	5266	5758	5331	5830	5399
5617	5198	5688	5267	5759	5332	5831	5400
5618	5199	5689	5268	5760	5331	5832	5401
5619	5200	5690	5269	5761	5333	5833	5402
5620	5201	5691	5270	5762	5334	5834	5403
5621	5202	5692	%	5763	5335	5835	4949
5622	5203	5693	5271	5764	5336	5836	5404
5623	5204	5694	5272	5765	5337	5837	5405
5624	5205	5695	5273	5766	5338	5838	5406
5625	5206	5696	5274	5767	5339	5839	5407
5626	5207	5697	2985	5768	5340	5840	5408
5627	5208	5698	2640	5769	5341	5841	5409
5628	5211	5699	5275	5770	5342	5842	5410
5629	5212	5700	5276	5771	5343	5843	5411

5844	5412	5916	5480	5988	5549	6060	5617
5845	5413	5917	5481	5989	5550	6061	5618
5846	5414	5918	5482	5990	5551	6062	5619
5847	5415	5919	5483	5991	5552	6063	5620
5848	5416	5920	5484	5992	5553	6064	5621
5849	5417	5921	5485	5993	5554	6065	5621
5850	5418	5922	5486	5994	5555	6066	5622
5851	5419	5923	5487	5995	5556	6067	5623
5852	5420	5924	5488	5996	5557	6068	5624
5853	5421	5925	5489	5997	5552		
5854	5422	5926	5490	5998	5558		
5855	5423	5927	5491	5999	5559		
5856	5424	5928	5492	6000	5560		
5857	5425	5929	5493	6001	5561		
5858	5426	5930	5494	6002	5523		
5859	5427	5931	5495	6003	5562		
5860	5428	5932	5496	6004	5563		
5861	5429	5933	5497	6005	5564		
5862	5430	5934	5498	6006	5565		
5863	5431	5935	5499	6007	%		
5864	5432	5936	5500	6008	5566		
5865	5433	5937	5501	6009	%		
5866	5434	5938	5502	6010	5567		
5867	5435	5939	5503	6011	5568		
5868	%	5940	5504	6012	5569		
5869	5436	5941	5506	6013	5570		
5870	5437	5942	5505	6014	5571		
5871	5438	5943	5507	6015	5572		
5872	5439	5944	5508	6016	5573		
5873	5440	5945	5509	6017	5574		
5874	5441	5946	5510	6018	5576		
5875	5442	5947	5516	6019	5577		
5876	5443	5948	5511	6020	5575		
5877	5444	5949	5512	6021	5578		
5878	5445	5950	5513	6022	5579		
5879	5446	5951	5514	6023	5580		
5880	5447	5952	5515	6024	5581		
5881	5448	5953	5516	6025	5582		
5882	5449	5954	5517	6026	5583		
5883	5450	5955	5518	6027	5584		
5884	5451	5956	5519	6028	5585		
5885	5452	5957	5520	6029	5586		
5886	5453	5958	5521	6030	5587		
5887	5454	5959	5522	6031	5588		
5888	5455	5960	5523	6032	5589		
5889	5456	5961	5524	6033	5589		
5890	5457	5962	5525	6034	5590		
5891	5458	5963	5526	6035	5591		
5892	5459	5964	5527	6036	5592		
5893	5460	5965	5528	6037	5593		
5894	5461	5966	5529	6038	5594		
5895	5462	5967	5522	6039	5595		
5896	%	5968	5530	6040	5596		
5897	5463	5969	5531	6041	5597		
5898	5464	5970	5532	6042	5598		
5899	5465	5971	5533	6043	5599		
5900	5466	5972	5533	6044	5601		
5901	5467	5973	5534	6045	5602		
5902	5468	5974	5535	6046	5603		
5903	5469	5975	5536	6047	5604		
5904	5468	5976	5537	6048	5605		
5905	5470	5977	5538	6049	5606		
5906	5471	5978	5539	6050	5608		
5907	5472	5979	5540	6051	5609		
5908	5473	5980	5541	6052	5610		
5909	5474	5981	5542	6053	5611		
5910	5475	5982	5543	6054	5612		
5911	5470	5983	5544	6055	5613		
5912	5476	5984	5545	6056	5613 + 302		
5913	5477	5985	5546	6057	5614		
5914	5478	5986	5547	6058	5615		
5915	5479	5987	5548	6059	5616		

Strong's numbers compared to Goodrick/Kohlenberger's numbers

This table lists the correspondence between Strong's numbering system for the Greek New Testament (column 1) and the Goodrick/Kohlenberger numbers (column 2).

When a Strong number corresponds to more than one G/K number, the ditto mark (") is used for each additional occurrence.

When more than one G/K number corresponds to one Strong number, the plus sign (+) is used show the combination

When no G/K number corresponds to the Strong number, the Strong number is followed by a percent sign (%).

G/K 2717 and 3203 through 3302 were omitted by Strong.

1	1	43	44	86	87	128	134
"	270	44	45	87	88	129	135
2	2	45	46	88	89	130	136
3	3	46	47	89	90	131	137
4	4	47	48	90	91	132	138
5	5	48	49	"	916	133	139
6	6	49	50	"	917	134	140
7	7	50	51	91	92	135	141
8	8	51	52	92	93	136	142
9	9	52	53	93	94	137	143
10	10	53	54	94	96	138	145
11	11	54	55	95	97	139	146
12	12	55	56	96	99	140	147
13	13	56	57	97	100	141	148
14	14	57	58	98	101	142	149
15	16	58	59	99	102	143	150
16	17	59	60	100	103	144	151
17	18	60	61	101	104	145	152
18	19	61	62	102	105	146	153
19	20	62	63	103	106	147	154
20	21	63	64	104	107	148	155
21	22	64	65	105	108	149	156
22	23	65	66	106	109	150	156
23	24	66	67	107	110	151	157
24	25	67	68	108	111	152	158
25	26	68	69	109	113	153	159
26	27	69	70	110	114	154	160
27	28	70	71	111	116	155	161
28	29	71	72	112	117	156	162
29	30	72	73	113	118	157	163
30	31	73	74	114	119	"	166
"	35	74	75	115	120	158	165
31	32	75	76	116	121	159	165
32	34	76	77	117	122	160	167
33	72	77	78	118	123	161	168
34	36	78	79	119	124	162	169
35	37	79	80	120	126	163	170
36	38	80	81	121	127	164	171
37	39	81	82	122	128	165	172
"	420	82	83	123	129	166	173
38	40	83	84	124	130	167	174
39	41	84	85	125	131	168	175
40	41	85	194	126	132	169	176
41	42	"	86	127	133	170	177
42	43			"	1290		

171	178	239	252	309	330	379	406
172	179	240	253	310	331	380	408
173	180	241	254	311	332	381	409
174	181	242	256	312	334	382	410
175	182	"	380	313	335	383	411
176	183	243	257	314	336	384	412
177	184	244	258	315	337	385	413
178	185	245	259	316	338	386	414
179	186	246	260	317	339	387	415
180	187	247	261	318	340	388	416
"	188	248	262	319	341	389	417
181	189	249	263	320	342	390	418
182	190	250	264	321	343	391	419
183	191	251	265	322	344	392	421
184	192	252	266	323	345	393	422
185	193	253	267	324	346	394	423
186	195	254	268	325	347	395	424
187	196	255	269	326	348	396	426
188	197	256	271	327	349	397	427
189	198	257	272	328	350	398	428
190	199	258	273	329	351	399	429
191	200	259	274	330	352	400	430
"	201	260	275	331	353	401	431
192	202	261	276	332	354	402	432
193	203	262	277	333	355	403	433
194	204	263	278	"	1461	404	434
195	205	264	279	334	356	405	435
196	206	265	280	335	357	406	436
197	209	266	281	336	358	407	437
198	208	267	282	337	359	408	438
199	209	268	283	338	360	409	439
200	210	269	285	339	361	410	441
201	211	270	286	340	362	411	442
202	212	271	287	341	363	412	443
203	213	272	288	342	364	413	444
204	214	273	289	343	365	414	445
205	215	274	290	344	366	415	446
206	216	275	291	345	367	416	448
207	217	276	292	346	368	417	449
208	218	277	293	347	369	418	450
209	219	278	294	348	370	419	451
210	220	279	295	349	371	420	452
211	222	280	296	350	373	421	453
"	223	281	297	351	374	422	454
212	224	282	298	352	376	423	455
213	225	283	299	353	377	424	456
214	226	284	300	354	378	425	457
215	227	285	302	355	379	426	458
216	228	286	303	"	384	427	459
217	221	287	304	356	381	428	460
"	229	288	306	357	382	429	461
218	230	289	307	358	383	430	462
219	231	290	308	359	385	431	463
220	232	291	309	360	386	432	464
221	233	292	310	361	387	433	465
222	234	293	312	362	388	434	466
223	235	294	313	363	389	435	467
224	236	"	314	364	390	436	468
225	237	295	315	365	391	437	469
226	238	296	316	366	392	438	470
227	239	297	317	367	393	439	471
228	240	298	318	368	394	440	472
229	241	299	320	369	395	441	473
230	242	300	321	370	396	442	474
231	243	301	322	371	397	443	475
232	244	302	323	372	398	444	476
233	245	303	324	373	399	445	477
234	246	304	325	374	400	446	478
235	247	305	326	375	402	447	479
236	248	306	327	376	401	448	447
237	249	307	328	377	404	"	480
238	251	308	329	378	405	449	481

450	403	518	33	586	619	649	690
"	482	"	550	"	620	"	1852
451	483	519	551	587	621	650	691
452	484	520	552	588	622	"	935
453	485	521	553	589	623	651	692
"	493	522	554	590	624	652	693
454	486	523	555	591	625	653	694
455	487	524	556	592	626	654	695
"	1986	525	557	593	627	655	696
456	488	526	558	594	628	656	697
457	489	527	559	595	629	657	698
458	490	528	560	596	630	658	699
459	491	529	561	597	631	659	700
460	492	530	562	598	632	660	701
461	494	531	563	599	633	661	702
462	495	532	564	600	634	662	703
463	496	533	565	"	635	663	704
464	497	534	567	601	636	664	705
465	498	535	568	602	637	665	706
466	499	536	569	603	638	666	707
467	500	537	570	"	2839	667	708
468	501	538	572	604	639	668	709
469	502	539	573	605	640	669	710
470	503	540	574	606	641	670	711
471	515	541	575	607	642	671	712
472	504	542	927	608	643	672	713
473	505	543	577	609	644	673	714
474	506	544	578	610	645	674	715
475	507	545	579	611	646	675	716
476	508	546	580	612	647	676	717
477	509	547	581	613	648	677	718
478	510	548	582	614	649	678	719
479	511	549	583	615	650	679	720
480	512	550	584	"	651	680	721
481	513	551	585	616	652	681	721
482	514	552	586	617	375	"	4312
483	515	553	587	"	653	682	722
484	516	554	588	618	655	683	723
485	517	555	589	619	656	684	724
486	518	556	590	620	657	685	725
487	519	557	591	621	658	686	726
488	520	558	592	"	2143	687	727
489	521	559	593	"	3314	688	728
490	522	560	594	"	4336	689	98
491	523	561	584	622	660	"	730
492	524	"	595	623	661	"	763
493	525	562	596	624	662	690	732
494	526	563	597	625	663	691	733
495	527	564	598	626	664	692	734
496	528	565	599	627	665	693	735
497	529	566	600	628	666	"	739
498	530	567	600	629	667	694	736
499	531	568	600	630	668	695	737
500	532	569	601	631	669	696	738
501	533	570	602	632	671	697	740
502	534	"	3898	633	672	"	4076
503	535	571	603	634	674	698	741
504	536	572	605	635	675	699	742
505	537	573	604	636	676	700	743
506	538	"	606	637	677	701	744
507	539	574	607	638	678	702	745
508	333	575	608	639	679	703	746
509	540	576	609	640	680	704	748
510	425	577	610	641	681	705	749
"	541	578	611	642	682	706	750
511	542	579	612	643	683	707	751
512	543	580	613	"	2171	708	752
513	544	581	614	644	684	709	753
514	545	582	615	645	685	710	754
515	546	583	616	646	686	711	755
516	547	584	617	647	687	712	756
517	548	585	618	648	689	713	757

714	758	781	831	846	899	912	972
715	759	782	571	847	898	913	973
"	760	"	832	848	898	914	974
716	761	783	833	849	901	915	975
717	762	784	834	850	903	916	976
"	3403	"	5646	851	904	917	977
718	764	785	835	852	905	918	978
719	765	786	836	853	906	919	979
720	766	787	837	854	907	920	971
721	768	788	839	855	908	"	980
722	769	789	840	856	909	"	981
723	770	790	841	"	4060	921	982
724	771	791	842	857	910	922	983
725	772	792	843	858	911	923	984
726	773	793	844	859	912	924	985
727	774	794	845	860	913	925	986
728	775	795	846	861	914	"	2852
729	731	796	847	862	915	926	987
730	776	797	848	863	918	927	988
"	781	798	849	"	1889	928	989
731	777	799	850	864	919	929	990
732	778	800	851	865	920	930	991
"	779	801	852	866	921	931	992
733	780	802	853	867	922	932	993
734	782	803	854	868	923	933	994
735	783	804	855	869	924	934	994
736	784	805	856	870	925	935	995
737	785	806	857	871	926	936	996
738	786	807	858	872	927	937	997
739	787	"	2360	873	928	"	998
740	788	808	859	874	929	938	999
741	789	809	860	875	930	939	1000
742	790	810	861	876	931	940	1001
743	791	811	862	877	932	941	1002
744	792	812	863	878	933	942	1003
745	793	813	864	879	934	943	1004
746	794	814	865	880	936	"	2742
747	795	815	866	"	305	"	2744
748	796	816	867	881	937	944	1005
749	797	817	868	"	941	945	1006
750	799	818	869	882	938	946	1007
751	800	"	870	883	939	947	1008
752	801	819	871	884	940	948	1009
753	802	820	872	885	943	949	1010
754	803	821	873	886	942	950	1011
755	804	822	874	887	944	951	1012
756	806	823	875	888	945	952	1013
757	806	824	876	889	946	953	1014
758	807	825	877	890	947	954	1015
759	808	826	878	891	948	955	1016
760	809	"	2964	892	949	956	1018
"	811	827	879	893	950	957	1019
761	810	828	880	894	951	958	1020
762	812	829	881	"	952	"	1021
763	813	830	882	895	953	959	1022
764	814	831	883	896	955	960	1023
765	815	832	884	897	956	961	1024
766	816	833	885	898	957	962	1028
767	817	834	886	899	958	"	1030
768	818	835	887	900	959	963	1029
769	819	836	888	901	960	964	1031
770	820	837	889	902	961	"	1032
771	821	"	891	903	962	965	1033
772	822	"	3824	904	963	966	1034
773	823	838	890	905	964	"	1035
774	824	839	892	906	965	967	1036
775	825	840	893	907	966	968	1037
776	826	841	894	908	967	969	1039
777	827	842	895	909	968	970	1040
778	828	843	896	910	969	971	1041
779	829	844	897	911	970	972	1042
780	830	845	898	"	4817	973	1043

974	1044	1038	1114	1102	1187	"	1260
"	1045	1039	1115	1103	1188	1167	1261
975	1046	"	3327	1104	1189	1168	1262
976	1047	1040	1116	1105	1190	1169	1264
977	1048	1041	1117	1106	1191	1170	1265
978	1049	1042	1119	1107	1192	1171	1267
979	1050	1043	1120	1108	1194	1172	1268
980	1051	1044	1121	1109	1195	1173	1270
981	1052	1045	1122	1110	1193	"	1271
982	1053	1046	1123	"	1196	1174	1273
983	1054	1047	1125	1111	1197	1175	1272
984	1055	1048	1124	1112	1198	1176	1274
985	1056	1049	1126	1113	1199	1177	1275
"	1057	1050	1127	1114	1200	1178	1278
986	1058	1051	1128	1115	1201	1179	1279
987	1059	1052	1129	1116	1202	1180	1280
"	1555	1053	1130	1117	1203	1181	1281
988	1060	"	1135	1118	1204	1182	1281
989	1061	1054	1131	1119	1205	1183	1282
990	1062	1055	1132	1120	1206	1184	1283
991	1063	1056	1133	1121	1207	1185	1284
992	1064	1057	1134	1122	1208	1186	1285
993	1065	1058	1136	1123	1209	1187	1286
994	1066	1059	1137	1124	1210	"	1287
995	1068	1060	1138	1125	1211	1188	1288
996	1069	1061	1139	"	2863	1189	1289
997	1070	"	1140	1126	1212	1190	1291
998	1071	1062	1141	1127	1213	"	1523
999	1072	1063	1142	1128	1214	1191	1292
"	1073	1064	1143	1129	1215	1192	1293
1000	1074	1065	1145	1130	1216	1193	1294
1001	1075	1066	1146	"	1217	1194	1296
1002	1076	1067	1147	1131	1218	1195	1297
1003	1067	1068	1148	1132	1219	1196	1298
"	1077	"	1149	1133	1220	1197	1299
"	1078	1069	1150	1134	1221	1198	1300
1004	1079	1070	1151	1135	1222	1199	1301
1005	1080	1071	1152	1136	1223	1200	1302
1006	1081	1072	1153	1137	1224	1201	1303
1007	1026	1073	1154	1138	1226	1202	1304
"	1027	1074	1155	"	1253	1203	1305
"	1082	1075	1156	1139	1227	1204	1306
1008	1083	1076	1157	1140	1228	1205	1307
1009	1084	1077	1158	1141	1229	1206	1308
1010	1085	"	1159	1142	1230	1207	1310
1011	1086	"	1160	1143	1231	1208	1309
1012	1087	1078	1161	1144	1232	"	1311
1013	1088	1079	1162	1145	1233	1209	1312
1014	1089	1080	1164	1146	1234	1210	1313
1015	1090	1081	1163	1147	1235	1211	1314
1016	1091	"	1165	1148	1236	1212	1316
1017	1092	1082	1166	1149	1237	1213	1317
1018	1093	1083	1167	1150	1238	1214	1318
1019	1094	1084	1168	1151	1239	1215	1319
1020	1095	1085	1169	1152	1240	1216	1320
1021	1096	1086	1170	1153	1241	1217	1321
1022	1097	"	1171	1154	1242	1218	1322
1023	1098	1087	1172	1155	1244	1219	1323
1024	1099	1088	1173	"	1247	1220	1324
1025	1100	1089	1174	1156	1245	1221	1325
1026	1101	1090	1175	"	1249	1222	1327
1027	1103	1091	1176	1157	1246	1223	1328
1028	1104	1092	1177	"	1250	1224	1329
1029	1105	1093	1178	1158	1248	1225	1330
1030	1106	1094	1179	1159	1251	1226	1331
1031	1107	1095	1180	1160	1252	1227	1332
1032	1108	1096	1181	1161	1254	1228	1333
1033	1109	1097	1182	1162	1255	1229	1334
1034	1110	1098	1183	1163	1256	1230	1335
1035	1111	1099	1184	1164	1257	1231	1336
1036	1112	1100	1185	1165	1258	1232	1337
1037	1113	1101	1186	1166	1259	1233	1338

1234	1339	1302	1414	1367	1493	1436	1568
1235	1340	1303	1415	1368	1494	1437	1569
1236	1341	"	1416	1369	1495	1438	1571
1237	1342	1304	1417	1370	1496	1439	1572
1238	1343	1305	1418	1371	1497	1440	1573
1239	1344	1306	1419	1372	1498	1441	1574
1240	1345	1307	1420	1373	1499	1442	1575
1241	1346	"	1421	1374	1500	1443	1576
1242	1347	1308	1422	1375	1501	1444	1577
1243	1348	1309	1423	1376	1502	1445	1578
1244	1349	1310	1424	1377	1503	1446	1579
1245	1350	"	5775	1378	1504	1447	1580
"	1351	1311	1425	1379	1505	1448	1581
1246	1352	1312	1426	1380	1506	1449	1582
1247	1354	1313	1427	1381	1507	1450	1583
1248	1355	1314	1428	"	1508	1451	1584
"	1566	1315	1429	1382	1509	1452	1585
1249	1356	1316	1431	1383	1510	1453	1586
1250	1357	1317	1434	1384	1511	1454	1587
1251	1358	1318	1435	1385	1512	1455	1588
1252	1359	1319	1436	1386	1513	1456	1589
1253	1360	1320	1437	1387	1514	1457	1590
1254	1361	1321	1438	1388	1515	1458	1592
1255	1362	1322	1439	1389	1516	1459	1593
1256	1363	1323	1440	1390	1517	1460	1594
1257	1364	1324	1441	1391	1518	1461	1596
1258	1365	1325	1442	1392	1519	1462	1598
1259	1367	"	1443	1393	1520	1463	1599
1260	1368	1326	1444	1394	1521	1464	1600
1261	1369	1327	1447	1395	1522	"	1715
1262	1370	1328	1449	1396	1524	1465	1601
1263	1371	"	2256	1397	1525	1466	1602
1264	1372	1329	1450	1398	1526	1467	1603
1265	1373	1330	1451	1399	1527	1468	1604
1266	1374	1331	1452	1400	1528	1469	1605
1267	1375	1332	1453	1401	1528	1470	1606
1268	1376	1333	1454	"	1529	1471	1607
1269	1377	1334	1455	1402	1530	1472	1608
1270	1378	1335	1456	1403	1531	1473	1609
1271	1379	1336	1457	1404	1532	1474	1610
1272	1380	1337	1458	1405	1533	1475	1611
1273	1381	1338	1459	1406	1534	1476	1612
1274	1382	1339	1460	1407	1535	1477	1613
1275	1383	1340	1462	1408	1536	1478	1614
1276	1385	1341	1464	1409	1537	1479	1615
1277	1386	1342	1465	1410	1538	1480	1616
1278	1387	1343	1466	1411	1539	1481	1617
1279	1388	1344	1467	1412	1540	1482	1618
1280	1389	1345	1468	1413	1541	1483	1619
1281	1390	1346	1469	1414	1542	1484	1620
1282	1391	1347	1470	1415	1543	1485	1621
1283	1395	1348	1471	1416	1544	1486	1622
1284	1392	1349	1472	1417	1545	"	1665
"	1393	"	2869	1418	%	1487	1623
"	1396	1350	1473	1419	1546	1488	1639
1285	1397	1351	1474	1420	1547	1489	1623 + 1145
1286	1398	1352	1475	"	1548	1490	1623 + 1254 +
1287	1399	1353	1476	1421	1549		3590 + 1145
1288	1400	1354	1477	1422	1551	1491	1626
1289	1401	1355	1478	1423	1552	1492	3857
1290	1402	1356	1479	1424	1553	1493	1627
1291	1403	1357	1481	1425	1554	1494	1628
1292	1404	1358	1482	1426	1556	"	2638
1293	1405	1359	1483	1427	1557	1495	1630
1294	1406	1360	1484	1428	1558	1496	1629
1295	1407	1361	1485	1429	1559	1497	1631
1296	1408	1362	1486	1430	1560	1498	1639
1297	1409	"	1487	1431	1561	1499	1623 + 2779
1298	1410	1363	1488	1432	1562	1500	1632
1299	1411	1364	1489	1433	1563	1501	1633
1300	1412	1365	1491	1434	1564	1502	1634
1301	1413	1366	1492	1435	1565	1503	2036

Strong	G/K	Strong	G/K	Strong	G/K	Strong	G/K
1504	1635	1573	1591	1642	1783	1704	1853
1505	1636	"	1707	1643	1785	1705	1854
1506	1637	1574	1708	1644	1786	"	1855
1507	1813	1575	1709	1645	1787	"	1857
1508	1623 + 3590	1576	1710	1646	1788	"	1858
1509	1623 + 3590 + 5516	1577	1711	1647	1788	1706	1860
1510	1639	1578	1712	1648	1789	1707	1861
1511	1639	1579	1713	1649	1792	1708	1862
1512	1642	1580	1714	1650	1791	"	4451
1513	1643	1581	1716	"	1793	1709	1863
1514	1644	1582	1717	1651	1794	1710	1864
1515	1645	1583	1718	1652	1795	1711	1865
1516	1646	1584	1719	1653	1790	1712	1866
1517	1647	1585	1720	"	1796	1713	1867
1518	1648	1586	1721	1654	1797	1714	1856
1519	1650	1587	1722	1655	1798	"	1859
1520	1651	1588	1723	1656	1799	"	1868
1521	1652	1589	1724	1657	1800	1715	1869
1522	1653	1590	1725	1658	1801	1716	1870
1523	1654	1591	1726	1659	1802	1717	1871
1524	1655	1592	1727	1660	1803	1718	1872
1525	1656	1593	1728	1661	1804	1719	1873
1526	1639	1594	1729	1662	1805	1720	1874
1527	1651 + 2848	1595	1730	"	1806	1721	1875
1528	1657	1596	1731	1663	1808	1722	1877
1529	1658	1597	1732	1664	1809	1723	1878
1530	1659	1598	1733	1665	1810	1724	1879
"	1737	1599	1734	1666	1811	1725	1882
1531	1660	1600	1736	"	1812	1726	1883
1532	1661	1601	1738	1667	1813	1727	1885
1533	1662	1602	1739	1668	1814	1728	1887
1534	1663	1603	1740	1669	1815	1729	1890
1535	1664	1604	1741	1670	1816	1730	1891
1536	1623 + 5516	1605	1742	1671	1817	1731	1892
1537	1666	1606	1743	1672	1818	1732	1893
1538	1667	1607	1744	1673	1819	1733	1894
1539	1668	1608	1745	1674	1820	1734	1895
1540	1669	1609	1746	1675	1821	1735	1896
1541	1670	1610	1748	1676	1822	1736	1897
1542	1671	1611	1749	1677	1823	1737	1898
1543	1672	1612	1750	"	1824	1738	1899
"	1673	1613	1752	1678	1825	1739	1900
1544	1675	1614	1753	"	1826	"	1908
1545	1676	1615	1754	1679	1827	1740	1901
1546	1678	1616	1755	1680	1828	1741	1902
1547	1679	1617	1757	1681	1829	1742	1903
1548	1680	1618	1756	"	2287	1743	1904
1549	1681	1619	1757	1682	1830	1744	1905
1550	1682	1620	1758	1683	1831	1745	1906
1551	1683	1621	1759	1684	1832	1746	1907
1552	1684	1622	1760	1685	1833	1747	1909
1553	1685	1623	1761	1686	1834	1748	1910
1554	1686	1624	1762	"	1835	1749	1911
1555	1687	1625	1763	1687	1836	1750	1912
1556	1688	1626	1765	1688	1837	1751	1913
1557	1689	1627	1766	1689	1838	1752	1641
1558	1690	1628	1767	1690	1102	"	1914
1559	1691	1629	1768	"	1839	"	1915
1560	1692	1630	1769	1691	1609	1753	1918
1561	1693	1631	1770	1692	1840	1754	1919
1562	1694	1632	1772	1693	1841	1755	1920
1563	1695	"	1773	1694	1842	1756	1886
1564	1696	1633	1774	1695	1843	"	1921
1565	1697	1634	1775	"	4035	1757	1922
1566	1698	1635	1776	1696	1844	1758	1923
1567	1699	1636	1777	1697	1846	1759	1924
1568	1701	1637	1778	1698	1609	1760	1445
1569	1702	1638	1779	1699	1847	"	1926
1570	1704	1639	1780	1700	1609	1761	1927
1571	1705	1640	1781	1701	1849	1762	1928
1572	1706	"	1784	1702	1850	1763	1929
		1641	1782	1703	1851	1764	1931

1765	1932	1831	2002	1893	2075	1961	2152
1766	1888	"	1446	1894	2076	1962	2153
1767	1933	"	1674	1895	2077	1963	2154
1768	1916	1832	1997	1896	2078	1964	2155
1769	1917	"	2003	"	2393	1965	2156
"	1934	1833	2004	1897	2080	1966	2079
1770	1935	1834	2007	1898	2081	1967	2157
1771	1936	1835	2008	1899	2083	1968	2158
1772	1937	1836	2009	1900	2084	1969	2159
1773	1939	1837	2010	1901	2085	1970	%
1774	1940	1838	2011	1902	2086	1971	2160
1775	1942	1839	2012	1903	2087	1972	2161
1776	1943	"	2013	1904	2082	1973	2162
1777	1944	"	2014	"	2088	1974	2163
1778	1945	1840	2015	1905	2089	1975	2164
1779	1946	1841	2016	1906	2090	1976	2165
1780	1947	1842	2017	1907	2091	"	2193
1781	1353	1843	2018	1908	2092	1977	2166
"	1948	1844	2019	1909	2093	1978	2168
1782	1925	1845	2020	1910	2094	1979	2169
"	1949	1846	2021	1911	2095	1980	2170
1783	1950	1847	2022	1912	2096	1981	2172
1784	1952	"	2023	1913	2097	1982	2173
1785	1953	1848	2024	1914	2098	1983	2174
1786	1954	"	2025	1915	2099	1984	2175
1787	1955	1849	2026	1916	2100	1985	2176
1788	1956	1850	2027	1917	2101	1986	2177
1789	1957	1851	2029	1918	2102	1987	2179
1790	1764	1852	2030	1919	2103	1988	2181
"	1958	1853	2031	1920	2104	1989	2182
1791	1959	1854	2032	1921	2105	1990	2184
1792	1960	1855	2033	1922	2106	1991	2185
1793	1961	1856	2034	1923	2107	1992	2186
1794	1962	1857	2035	1924	2108	1993	2187
1795	1963	1858	2037	1925	2109	1994	2188
1796	1964	1859	2038	1926	2110	1995	2189
1797	1965	1860	2039	1927	2111	1996	2190
1798	1966	1861	2040	1928	2112	1997	2191
1799	1967	1862	2041	1929	2113	1998	2192
1800	1968	1863	2042	"	4658	1999	2180
1801	1969	1864	2043	1930	2114	"	2194
1802	1970	1865	2044	1931	2115	2000	2195
1803	1971	1866	2045	1932	2116	2001	2196
1804	1972	1867	2046	1933	2117	2002	2197
1805	1973	1868	2047	1934	2118	2003	2198
1806	1974	1869	2048	1935	2119	2004	2199
1807	1975	1870	2049	1936	2120	2005	2200
1808	1976	1871	2050	1937	2121	2006	2201
1809	1977	1872	2051	1938	2122	2007	2202
1810	1978	1873	2052	1939	2123	2008	2203
"	2005	1874	2053	1940	2125	2009	2204
1811	1979	1875	2054	1941	2126	2010	2205
1812	1980	1876	2055	1942	2127	"	5181
1813	1981	1877	2056	1943	2128	2011	2207
1814	1982	1878	2057	1944	2063	2012	2208
1815	1983	1879	2058	"	2129	2013	2209
1816	1677	1880	2059	1945	2130	2014	2210
"	1984	1881	2060	1946	2134	2015	2211
1817	1985	1882	2061	1947	2135	2016	2212
1818	1987	1883	2062	1948	2137	2017	2213
1819	1988	1884	2064	1949	2138	"	2223
1820	1989	1885	2065	1950	2140	2018	2214
1821	1990	"	2066	1951	2141	2019	2215
1822	1992	1886	2068	1952	2142	"	2971
1823	1993	1887	2069	1953	2144	2020	2216
1824	1994	1888	900	1954	2145	2021	2217
1825	1995	"	2070	1955	2146	2022	2219
1826	1996	1889	2071	1956	2147	2023	2220
1827	1998	1890	576	1957	2148	2024	2221
1828	1999	"	2072	1958	2149	2025	2222
1829	2000	1891	2073	1959	2150	2026	2224
1830	2001	1892	2074	1960	2151	2027	2131

"	2225	2095	2292	2159	2364	2227	2443
2028	2226	"	2301	2160	2365	2228	2445
2029	2227	2096	2293	2161	2366	2229	2446
2030	2228	2097	2294	2162	2367	2230	2448
2031	2229	2098	2295	2163	2368	2231	2449
2032	2230	2099	2296	2164	2369	2232	2450
2033	2231	2100	2297	2165	2370	2233	2206
2034	2232	2101	2298	2166	2371	"	2451
2035	2233	2102	2299	2167	2372	2234	2452
2036	3306	2103	2300	2168	2373	2235	2453
2037	2235	2104	2302	2169	2374	2236	2452
2038	2237	2105	2304	2170	2375	2237	2454
2039	2238	2106	2305	2171	2376	2238	2455
2040	2239	2107	2306	2172	2377	2239	2456
2041	2240	2108	2307	2173	2378	2240	2457
2042	2241	2109	2308	2174	2379	2241	2458
2043	2242	2110	2309	2175	2380	2242	2459
2044	2243	2111	2310	2176	2381	2243	2460
2045	2236	2112	2311	2177	1880	2244	2461
2046	3306	2113	2312	"	2383	2245	2462
2047	2244	2114	2313	2178	2384	2246	2463
2048	2245	2115	2314	2179	2385	2247	2464
2049	2246	"	2315	2180	2386	2248	1609
2050	2247	2116	2316	2181	2387	2249	1609
2051	2248	2117	2317	2182	2388	2250	2465
2052	2249	"	2318	2183	2389	2251	2466
2053	2250	2118	2319	2184	2390	2252	1639
2054	2251	2119	2320	2185	2391	2253	2467
2055	2252	2120	2321	2186	2392	2254	1609
2056	144	2121	2322	2187	2394	2255	2468
"	2253	2122	2323	2188	2395	2256	2469
2057	2254	2123	2324	2189	2397	"	2470
2058	1448	2124	2325	2190	2398	2257	1609
"	2255	2125	2326	2191	2399	2258	1639
2059	2257	2126	2327	2192	2400	2259	2471
2060	2258	2127	2328	2193	2401	2260	2472
2061	2259	"	2986	2194	2404	2261	2473
2062	2260	2128	2329	2195	2405	2262	2474
2063	2261	2129	2303	2196	2406	2263	2475
2064	2262	"	2330	2197	2408	2264	2476
2065	2263	2130	2331	2198	2409	2265	2477
2066	2264	2131	2332	2199	2411	2266	2478
2067	2265	2132	2333	2200	2412	2267	2479
2068	2266	2133	2334	2201	2414	2268	2480
"	2267	2134	2335	2202	2415	2269	2481
2069	2268	2135	2336	2203	2416	2270	2483
2070	1639	2136	2337	2204	2417	2271	2484
2071	1639	2137	2338	2205	2419	2272	2485
2072	2269	2138	2340	2206	2418	2273	2486
2073	2270	2139	2341	"	2420	2274	2273
2074	2272	"	2342	2207	2421	"	2487
2075	1639	2140	2343	2208	2421	2275	2488
2076	1639	2141	2344	2209	2422	2276	2482
2077	1639	2142	2345	2210	2423	"	2489
2078	2274	2143	2346	2211	2424	2277	1639
2079	2275	2144	2347	2212	2426	2278	2490
2080	2276	2145	2339	2213	2427	2279	2491
2081	2277	"	2348	2214	1700	"	2492
2082	2278	2146	2349	"	2428	"	2493
2083	2279	2147	2351	2215	2429	2280	2497
2084	2280	2148	2350	2216	2431	2281	2498
2085	2281	"	2352	2217	2432	2282	2499
2086	2282	2149	2353	2218	2433	2283	2500
2087	255	2150	2354	2219	2434	2284	2501
"	2283	2151	2355	2220	2435	2285	2502
2088	2284	2152	2356	2221	2436	2286	2503
2089	2285	2153	2357	2222	2437	2287	2504
2090	2286	2154	2358	2223	2438	2288	2505
2091	2288	2155	2359	2224	2439	2289	2506
2092	2289	2156	2361	"	2440	2290	2507
2093	2290	2157	2362	2225	2441	2291	2508
2094	2291	2158	2363	2226	2442	2292	2509

Strong	G/K	Strong	G/K	Strong	G/K	Strong	G/K
2293	2510	"	2582	2429	2657	2491	2722
2294	2511	2360	2583	2430	2658	"	2728
2295	2512	2361	2584	2431	2659	2492	2724
2296	1703	2362	2585	2432	2660	2493	2727
"	2513	2363	2587	2433	2661	2494	2729
2297	2514	2364	2588	2434	2662	"	2730
2298	2515	2365	2589	2435	2663	2495	2731
2299	2516	2366	2590	2436	2664	2496	2732
2300	2517	2367	2591	2437	2665	2497	2733
2301	2518	2368	2592	2438	2666	2498	2734
2302	2519	2369	2593	2439	2667	2499	2735
2303	2520	2370	2594	2440	2668	2500	2736
2304	2521	2371	2595	2441	2669	2501	2737
2305	2522	2372	2596	2442	2670	"	2738
2306	2523	2373	2597	"	3916	2502	2739
2307	2525	2374	2598	2443	2671	2503	2740
2308	2526	2375	2599	2444	2672	2504	2743
2309	2527	2376	2600	2445	2673	2505	2745
2310	2528	2377	2601	2446	2674	2506	2746
"	2529	2378	2602	2447	2675	2507	2747
2311	2530	2379	2603	2448	2676	2508	2748
2312	2531	2380	2124	2449	2677	2509	2749
2312'	2532	"	2604	2450	2678	"	2778
2313	2533	2381	2605	2451	2679	2510	2750
2314	2534	2382	2606	2452	2680	2511	2751
2315	2535	2383	2608	2453	2681	"	2760
2316	2536	2384	2609	2454	2682	2512	2752
2317	2537	2385	2610	2455	2683	2513	2754
2318	2538	2386	2611	"	2726	2514	2755
2319	2539	2387	2612	2456	549	2515	2756
2320	2540	2388	2613	"	2684	2516	2757
2321	2541	2389	2614	"	2686	2517	2759
2322	2542	2390	2615	2457	2685	2518	2761
"	3859	2391	2616	2458	2687	2519	2762
2323	2543	2392	2617	2459	2688	2520	2763
2324	2544	2393	2618	"	5517	2521	2764
2325	2545	2394	2619	2460	2689	2522	2766
2326	2546	2395	2620	2461	2690	2523	2767
2327	2547	2396	2623	2462	2691	2524	2768
2328	2548	2397	1624	2463	2692	2525	2769
2329	2549	"	2624	2464	2693	"	2770
2330	2550	2398	2625	2465	2694	2526	2771
2331	2552	2399	2626	2466	2695	2526'	2772
2332	2553	2400	2627	"	2704	2527	2773
2333	2554	2401	2628	2467	%	2528	2774
2334	2555	2402	2629	2468	1639	2529	2775
2335	2556	2403	2630	2469	2696	2530	2776
2336	2557	2404	2631	"	2697	2531	2777
2337	2558	2405	2632	"	5000	2532	2779
2338	2559	2406	2633	"	5001	2533	2780
2339	2560	2407	2634	2470	2698	2534	2781
2340	2561	2408	2635	2471	2699	2535	2782
2341	2562	2409	2636	2472	2700	2536	2783
2342	2563	2410	2637	2473	2701	"	2784
2343	2564	2411	2639	2474	2702	2537	2785
2344	2565	2412	2640	2475	2703	2538	2786
2345	2566	2413	2641	2476	2705	2539	2788
2346	2567	2414	2642	2477	2707	2540	2789
2347	2568	2415	2643	2478	2708	2541	2790
2348	2569	2416	2644	2479	2709	2542	2791
2349	2570	2417	2645	2480	2710	2543	2792
2350	2572	2418	2646	2481	2711	2544	2793
2351	2573	2419	2647	2482	2712	2545	2794
2352	2574	2420	2648	2483	2713	2546	2795
"	2575	2421	2649	2484	2714	2547	2796
2353	2576	2422	2650	2485	2715	2548	2797
2354	2577	2423	2651	2486	2716	2549	2798
2355	2578	2424	2652	2487	2717	2550	2799
2356	2579	2425	2653	2488	2718	2551	2800
2357	2580	2426	2654	2489	2720	2552	2801
2358	2581	2427	2655	"	2721	"	2817
2359	1295	2428	2656	2490	2722	2553	2802

Strong	G/K	Strong	G/K	Strong	G/K	Strong	G/K
2554	2803	2621	2879	2688	2949	2749	3023
2555	2804	2622	2880	2689	2950	2750	3024
2556	2805	2623	1597	2690	2951	2751	3025
2557	2806	"	2881	2691	2952	2752	3026
2558	2807	2624	2882	2692	2953	2753	3027
2559	2808	"	2883	2693	2954	2754	3029
2560	2809	2625	2884	2694	2955	2755	3030
2561	2810	2626	2885	2695	2956	2756	3031
2562	2811	2627	2886	"	2957	2757	2787
2563	2812	2628	2887	2696	2958	"	3032
2564	2813	2629	2888	2697	2959	2758	3033
2565	2814	2630	2889	2698	2960	2759	3034
2566	2819	2631	2890	2699	2961	2760	3035
2567	2815	2632	2891	2700	2962	2761	3036
2568	2816	2633	2892	2701	2963	2762	3037
2569	2818	2634	2894	2702	2965	2763	3038
2570	2819	2635	2895	2703	2966	2764	3039
2571	2820	2636	2896	2704	2967	2765	3040
2572	2821	2637	2897	2705	2968	2766	3041
2573	2822	2638	2898	2706	2969	2767	3042
2574	2823	2639	2899	2707	2970	2768	3043
"	2824	2640	2900	2708	2972	2769	3044
2575	2825	"	5698	2709	2973	2770	2132
2576	2826	2641	2901	2710	2974	"	3045
2577	2827	2642	2902	"	4201	2771	3046
2578	2828	2643	2903	2711	2976	2772	3047
2579	2829	2644	2904	2712	2977	2773	3048
2580	2830	2645	2905	2713	2978	2774	3049
2581	2831	2646	2906	2714	2979	2775	3050
"	2832	2647	2907	2715	2980	"	3052
2582	2833	2648	2908	2716	2981	2776	3051
2583	2834	2649	2909	2717	Omitted by	2777	3053
2584	2835	2650	2910		Strong	2778	2133
"	3019	2651	2911	2718	2982	"	3056
2585	2836	2652	2873	2719	2983	2779	3057
2586	2837	"	2912	"	2984	2780	3058
2587	2838	2653	2874	2720	2985	2781	3059
2588	2840	"	2913	2721	2987	2782	3060
2589	2841	2654	2914	2722	2988	2783	3061
2590	2843	2655	2915	2723	2989	2784	3062
2591	2842	2656	2916	2724	2990	2785	3063
2592	2844	2657	2917	2725	2991	2786	3064
2593	2845	2658	2918	"	2992	2787	3066
2594	2846	2659	2919	2726	2993	2788	3067
2595	2847	2660	2920	2727	2994	2789	3068
2596	2848	2661	2921	2728	2995	2790	3069
2597	2849	2662	2922	2729	2996	2791	3070
2598	2850	2663	2923	2730	2997	"	3071
2599	2851	2664	2924	"	3001	2792	3072
2600	2853	2665	2925	2731	2998	"	3077
2601	2854	2666	2927	2732	2999	2793	3073
2602	2856	2667	2928	2733	3000	2794	3074
2603	2857	2668	2929	2734	3002	2795	3075
2604	2858	2669	2930	2735	1480	2796	3076
2605	2859	2670	2931	"	3003	2797	3078
2606	2860	2671	2932	2736	3004	2798	3080
2607	2861	2672	2933	"	3006	2799	3081
2608	2862	2673	2934	2737	3005	2800	3082
2609	2864	2674	2935	2738	3008	2801	3083
2610	2865	2675	2936	2739	3009	2802	1144
2611	2866	2676	2937	"	3010	"	3007
2612	2867	2677	2938	2740	3011	"	3084
2613	1463	2678	2939	2741	3012	"	3085
"	2868	2679	2940	2742	3014	2803	3086
2614	2870	2680	2941	2743	3013	2804	3087
2615	2871	2681	2942	"	3015	2805	3088
2616	2872	2682	2943	2744	3016	2806	3089
2617	2875	2683	2944	2745	3017	2807	3090
2618	2876	2684	2945	2746	3018	2808	3091
2619	2877	2685	2946	2747	3020	2809	3092
2620	1595	2686	2947	2748	3021	2810	3093
"	2878	2687	2948	"	3022	2811	3094

Strong	G/K
2812	3095
2813	3096
2814	3097
2815	3098
2816	3099
2817	3100
2818	3101
2819	3102
2820	3103
2821	3104
2822	3105
2823	3106
2824	3107
2825	3108
"	3109
2826	3110
2827	3111
2828	3112
2829	3113
2830	3114
2831	3115
2832	3116
2833	3117
2834	3118
2835	3119
2836	3120
2837	3121
2838	3122
2839	3123
2840	3124
2841	3125
2842	3126
2843	3127
2844	3128
2845	3130
2846	3131
2847	3132
2848	3133
2849	3134
2850	3135
2851	3136
2852	3139
2853	3140
2854	3141
2855	3142
2856	3143
2857	3138
"	3145
2858	3137
"	3144
2859	3146
2860	3147
2861	3148
2862	3149
2863	3150
2864	3151
2865	3152
2866	3153
2867	3154
2868	3155
2869	3156
2870	3157
2871	3158
2872	3159
2873	3160
2874	3161
"	3162
"	3163
2875	3164
2876	3165
2877	3166
2878	3167
"	3168
2879	3169
2880	3170
2881	3171
2882	3172
2883	3173
2884	3174
2885	3175
2886	3176
2887	3177
"	3178
2888	3179
2889	3180
2890	3181
2891	3182
"	3183
2892	3184
2893	3185
2894	3186
2895	3187
"	3188
2896	3189
2897	3190
2898	3191
2899	3192
2900	3193
2901	3194
2902	3195
2903	3196
2904	3197
2905	3198
2906	3199
2907	3200
2908	3201
2909	3202
2910	3203
2911	3204
2912	3205
2913	3206
2914	3207
2915	3208
2916	3209
2917	3210
2918	3211
2919	3212
2920	3213
2921	3214
2922	3215
2923	3216
2924	3217
2925	3218
2926	3219
2927	3220
"	3224
"	3226
2928	3221
2929	3222
2930	3223
2931	3225
2932	3227
2933	3228
2934	3229
2935	3230
2936	3231
2937	3232
2938	3233
2939	3234
2940	3235
2941	3236
2942	3237
2943	3239
2944	3238
"	3240
2945	3241
2946	3242
"	3243
2947	3244
2948	3245
2949	3246
2950	3247
2951	3248
2952	3249
2953	3250
2954	3251
2955	3252
2956	3253
"	3254
2957	3255
2958	3256
"	3260
2959	3257
2960	3258
2961	3259
2962	3261
2963	3262
2964	3263
2965	3264
2966	3265
2967	3266
2968	3267
2969	3268
2970	3269
2971	3270
2972	3271
2973	3272
2974	3273
2975	3275
2976	3276
2977	3277
"	4996
2978	3278
2979	3280
2980	654
"	3281
2981	3282
2982	3283
"	3316
2983	3284
2984	3285
2985	3286
"	5697
2986	3287
2987	3288
2988	3289
2989	2139
"	3290
2990	3291
2991	3292
2992	3295
2993	3293
2994	3294
2995	3296
2996	3297
"	3298
2997	3279
"	3299
2998	3300
2999	3301
3000	3302
3001	3303
3002	3304
3003	3305
3004	1649
"	3306
3005	3307
3006	3308
3007	3309
3008	3310
3009	3311
3010	3312
3011	3313
3012	3317
3013	3318
3014	3319
3015	3320
3016	3321
3017	3322
3018	3323
3019	3324
3020	3325
3021	3326
3022	3328
3023	3329
3024	3330
3025	3332
3026	3333
3027	798
"	3334
3028	3331
"	3335
3029	3336
3030	3337
3031	3338
3032	3339
"	3341
3033	3340
3034	3342
3035	3343
3036	3344
3037	3345
3038	3346
3039	3347
3040	3348
3041	3349
3042	3350
3043	3351
3044	3352
3045	3353
3046	3354
3047	3355
3048	3356
3049	3357
3050	3358
3051	3359
3052	3360
3053	3361
3054	3362
3055	3363
3056	3364
3057	3365
3058	3366
3059	3367
3060	3368
3061	3369
3062	3370
3063	3370
3064	3370
3065	3371
3066	3372
3067	3373
3068	3374
3069	3375
3070	3376
3071	3377
3072	3378
3073	3379

Strong	G/K	Strong	G/K	Strong	G/K	Strong	G/K
3074	3380	3141	3456	3200	3521	3364	4024 + 3590
3075	3381	3142	3457	3201	3522	3365	3592
3076	3382	3143	3458	3202	3523	"	3598
3077	3383	3144	3459			3366	3593
3078	3384	"	4753	3203 to 3302		3367	3594
3079	3385	3145	3460	Omitted by Strong		"	3599
3080	3386	"	3462			3368	3595
3081	3387	3146	3463	3303	3525	3369	3596
3082	3388	3147	3464	3304	3528	3370	3597
3083	3389	3148	3465	"	3529	3371	3600
3084	3390	3149	3461	3305	3530	3372	3601
3085	3391	"	3461	3306	3531	3373	3602
3086	3392	"	3466	3307	3532	3374	3603
3087	3393	3150	3467	3308	3533	3375	3604
3088	3394	3151	3468	3309	3534	3376	3605
3089	3395	3152	3469	3310	3535	3377	3606
3090	3396	3153	3470	3311	3536	3378	3590 + 4024
3091	3397	3154	3471	3312	3537	3379	3607
3092	3399	3155	3472	3313	3538	3380	3609
3093	3400	3156	3414	3314	3540	3381	3610
"	3401	"	3473	3315	3541	3382	3611
3094	3402	3157	3474	3316	3542	3383	3612
3095	3404	3158	3415	3317	3543	3384	3613
"	3406	"	3475	3318	3544	3385	3614
3096	3405	3159	3416	3319	3545	3386	3615
3097	3407	"	3476	3320	3546	3387	3614
3098	3408	3160	3477	3321	3547	3388	3616
3099	3409	3161	3478	3322	3539	3389	3617
3100	3411	3162	3479	"	3548	"	3618
3101	3412	3163	3480	3323	3549	3390	3619
3102	3413	3164	3481	3324	3550	3391	1651
3103	3417	3165	1609	3325	3551	3392	3620
3104	3418	3166	902	3326	3552	3393	3621
"	3526	"	3482	3327	3553	3394	3622
3105	3419	3167	3483	3328	3554	3395	1807
3106	3420	3168	3484	3329	3555	"	3623
3107	3421	3169	3485	3330	3556	"	5041
3108	3422	3170	3486	3331	3557	"	5042
3109	3423	3171	3487	3332	3558	3396	3502
3110	3424	3172	3488	3333	3559	"	3503
3111	3425	3173	3489	3334	3560	"	3624
3112	3426	3174	3490	3335	3561	3397	3625
3113	3427	3175	3491	3336	3562	3398	3625
3114	3428	3176	3492	3337	3563	3399	3626
3115	3429	3177	3493	3338	3564	3400	3627
3116	3430	3178	3494	3339	3565	3401	3628
3117	3431	3179	3495	3340	3566	3402	3629
3118	3432	"	3496	3341	3567	3403	3630
3119	3433	3180	3497	3342	3568	3404	3631
3120	3434	3181	3498	3343	3569	3405	3632
3121	3435	3182	3499	3344	3570	3406	3633
3122	3436	3183	3500	"	3573	3407	3634
3123	3437	3184	3501	3345	3571	3408	3635
3124	3438	3185	3505	3346	3572	3409	3636
3125	3439	3186	3504	3347	3575	3410	3637
3126	3440	3187	3505	3348	3576	3411	3638
3127	3441	3188	3506	3349	3577	3412	3639
3128	3442	3189	3506	3350	3578	3413	3640
3129	3443	3190	3507	3351	3579	3414	3641
3130	3444	3191	3509	3352	3580	3415	3642
3131	3445	3192	3510	3353	3581	3416	3643
3132	3446	3193	3511	3354	3582	3417	3644
3133	3447	"	3512	3355	3583	3418	3645
3134	2495	"	3513	3356	3584	3419	3646
"	3448	3194	3514	3357	3585	3420	3647
3135	3449	"	3515	3358	3586	3421	3648
3136	3450	3195	3516	3359	3587	3422	3649
3137	3451	3196	3517	3360	3588	3423	3650
"	3452	3197	3518	"	3589	3424	3651
3138	3453	3198	3519	3361	3590	"	3652
3139	3454	3199	3508	3362	1569 + 3590	3425	3653
3140	3455	"	3520	3363	2671 + 3590	3426	3654

Strong	G/K	Strong	G/K	Strong	G/K	Strong	G/K
3427	1609	3488	3727	3554	3798	3623	3874
3428	3655	3489	3728	3555	3799	3624	3875
3429	3656	3490	3729	3556	3800	3625	3876
3430	3657	3491	3730	3557	3802	3626	3877
3431	3658	3492	3731	3558	3803	"	3878
3432	3659	3493	3732	3559	3804	3627	3879
3433	3660	3494	3733	3560	3805	"	3882
3434	3661	3495	3734	3561	3741	3628	3880
3435	3662	3496	3735	"	3806	3629	3881
3436	3663	"	3736	3562	3807	3630	3884
3437	3524	3497	3722	3563	3808	3631	3885
"	3664	"	3737	3564	3809	3632	3886
3438	3665	3498	3738	"	3810	3633	3883
3439	3666	3499	3739	3565	3811	"	3887
3440	3667	3500	3740	3566	3812	3634	3888
3441	3668	3501	3742	3567	3813	3635	3890
3442	3669	3502	3743	3568	3814	3636	3891
3443	3670	"	3801	3569	5422	3637	3892
3444	3671	3503	3744	3570	3815	3638	3893
3445	3672	3504	3745	3571	3816	3639	3896
3446	3673	3505	3746	3572	3817	"	3897
3447	3674	3506	3748	3573	3818	3640	3899
3448	3675	3507	3749	3574	3819	3641	3900
3449	3677	3508	3750	3575	3820	3642	3901
3450	1609	3509	3751	3576	3821	3643	3902
3451	3676	3510	3752	3577	3822	3644	3894
3452	3678	3511	3753	3578	3825	"	3904
3453	3679	3512	3754	3579	3826	3645	3895
3454	3680	3513	3755	3580	3827	"	3905
3455	3681	3514	3756	3581	3828	3646	3906
3456	3682	3515	3757	3582	3829	3647	3907
3457	3683	3516	3758	3583	3830	3648	3908
3458	3684	3517	3759	3584	3831	3649	3909
"	3685	3518	3760	3585	3832	3650	3910
3459	3686	3519	3761	3586	3833	3651	3911
3460	3688	3520	3762	3587	3834	3652	3912
"	3694	3521	3763	3588	3836	3653	3913
3461	3689	3522	3764	3589	3837	3654	3914
3462	3690	3523	3765	3590	3838	3655	3915
3463	3691	3524	3766	3591	3839	3656	3917
"	3692	"	3767	3592	3840	3657	3918
3464	3693	3525	3768	3593	3841	3658	3919
3465	3695	3526	3769	3594	3842	3659	3921
3466	3696	3527	3770	3595	3843	3660	3922
3467	3697	3528	3771	3596	3844	"	3923
3468	3698	3529	3772	3597	3845	3661	3924
3469	3699	3530	3773	3598	3847	3662	3925
3470	3700	3531	3774	3599	3848	3663	3926
3471	3701	3532	3775	3600	3849	3664	3927
3472	3702	3533	3776	3601	3850	3665	3928
3473	3703	3534	3777	3602	3851	3666	3929
3474	3704	3535	3778	3603	4005 + 1639	3667	3930
3475	3705	"	3779	3604	3852	3668	3931
"	3706	3536	3780	3605	3853	3669	3932
"	3707	3537	3781	3606	3854	3670	3933
3476	3709	"	4469	3607	3855	3671	3934
3477	3710	3538	3782	3608	3856	3672	3935
3478	3711	3539	3783	3609	3858	3673	3937
"	3712	3540	3784	3610	3860	3674	3938
"	3713	3541	3785	3611	3861	3675	3939
"	3714	3542	3786	3612	3862	3676	3940
"	3715	3543	3787	3613	3863	3677	3941
3479	3716	3544	3788	3614	3864	3678	3942
3480	3717	3545	3789	3615	3865	3679	3943
3481	3718	3546	3790	3616	3866	3680	3944
"	3719	3547	3791	3617	3867	3681	3945
3482	3720	3548	3792	3618	3868	3682	3946
3483	3721	3549	3793	"	3871	3683	3947
3484	3723	3550	3794	3619	3869	3684	3948
3485	3724	3551	3795	3620	3870	3685	3949
3486	3725	3552	3796	3621	3872	3686	3950
3487	3726	3553	3797	3622	3873	3687	3951

3688	3952	3754	4022	3822	4096	3885	4166
3689	3903	3755	4015	3823	4097	"	4167
"	3953	3756	4024	3824	4098	3886	4168
3690	3954	3757	4023	"	4100	3887	4169
3691	3955	3758	4025	3825	4099	3888	4170
3692	3956	3759	4026	3826	4101	3889	4171
3693	3957	3760	4027	"	4113	3890	4172
3694	3958	3761	4028	3827	4102	3891	4174
"	5541	3762	4029	3828	4103	3892	4175
3695	3959	"	4032	3829	4104	3893	4176
3696	3960	3763	4030	"	4106	3894	4177
3697	3961	3764	4031	3830	4105	3895	4178
3698	3962	3765	4033	"	4107	3896	4179
3699	3963	3766	4034	3831	4108	3897	4180
3700	3964	3767	4036	3832	4109	3898	4181
3701	3965	3768	4037	3833	4110	3899	4182
3702	3966	3769	4038	3834	4111	3900	4183
3703	3967	3770	4039	3835	4112	3901	4184
3704	3968	3771	4040	3836	4115	3902	4185
3705	3969	3772	4041	3837	4114	3903	4186
3706	3970	3773	4042	"	4116	3904	4187
3707	3971	3774	4043	3838	4117	3905	4189
3708	1625	3775	4044	3839	4118	3906	4190
"	3972	3776	4045	3840	4119	3907	4191
3709	3973	3777	4046	3841	4120	3908	4192
3710	3974	3778	4047	3842	4121	3909	4193
3711	3975	3779	4048	3843	4122	3910	4194
3712	3976	3780	4049	3844	4123	3911	4195
3713	3977	3781	4050	3845	4124	3912	4196
3714	3978	3782	4051	3846	4125	3913	4173
3715	3979	3783	4052	3847	4126	"	4197
3716	3980	3784	4053	3848	688	"	4198
3717	3981	3785	4054	"	4127	3914	4199
3718	3982	3786	4055	3849	4128	3915	4200
3719	3983	3787	4056	3850	4130	3916	4202
3720	3984	3788	4057	3851	4129	3917	4203
3721	3985	3789	4058	"	4131	3918	4205
3722	3986	3790	4059	3852	4132	3919	4206
3723	3987	3791	4061	3853	4133	3920	4207
3724	3988	3792	4062	3854	4134	3921	4208
3725	3990	3793	4063	3855	4135	3922	4209
3726	1941	3794	4065	3856	4136	3923	4210
"	3991	3795	4066	3857	4137	3924	4211
3727	3992	3796	4067	3858	4138	3925	4213
3728	3993	3797	4069	3859	1384	3926	4214
3729	3994	3798	4068	"	4139	3927	4215
3730	3995	"	4070	3860	4140	3928	4216
3731	3996	3799	4071	3861	4141	3929	4217
3732	3997	3800	4072	3862	4142	3930	4218
3733	3989	3801	3836 + 1639 +	3863	4143	3931	4219
"	3998		2779 + 2262	3864	4144	3932	4220
3734	3999	3802	4074	3865	4145	3933	4221
3735	4001	3803	4075	3866	4146	3934	4222
3736	4002	3804	4077	3867	4147	3935	4223
3737	4003	3805	4078	3868	4148	3936	4224
3738	4004	3806	4079	3869	4149	"	4225
3739	4005	3807	4080	"	4150	3937	4226
3740	4006	3808	4081	3870	4151	3938	4227
3741	4008	3809	4082	3871	4152	3939	4228
3742	4009	3810	4083	3872	4153	3940	4229
3743	4010	3811	4084	3873	4154	3941	4230
3744	4011	3812	4085	3874	4155	3942	4231
3745	4012	"	4088	3875	4156	3943	4232
3746	4013	3813	4086	3876	4157	3944	4233
3747	4014	3814	4087	3877	4158	3945	4234
"	4016	3815	4089	3878	4159	3946	4235
3748	4015	3816	4090	3879	4160	3947	4236
3749	4017	3817	4091	3880	4161	3948	4237
3750	4018	3818	4092	3881	4162	3949	4239
3751	4019	3819	4093	3882	4163	3950	4240
3752	4020	3820	4094	3883	4164	3951	4241
3753	4021	3821	4095	3884	4165	3952	4242

3953	4243	4018	4316	4088	4394	4154	4463
3954	4244	4019	4317	4089	4395	4155	4464
3955	4245	4020	4318	4090	4396	4156	4465
3956	4246	4021	4319	4091	4276	4157	4466
3957	4247	4022	4320	"	4397	4158	4468
3958	4248	4023	4321	4092	4399	4159	4470
3959	4249	4024	4322	4093	4400	4160	4472
3960	4250	"	4323	"	4401	4161	4473
3961	4251	4025	4324	4094	4402	4162	4474
3962	4635	4026	4325	4095	4403	4163	4475
"	4252	4027	2753	4096	4404	4164	4476
3963	4253	"	4326	4097	4405	4165	4477
3964	4254	4028	4328	4098	4406	4166	4478
"	4260	4029	4329	"	5229	4167	4479
3965	4255	4030	4330	4099	4407	4168	4480
3966	4256	4031	4331	"	4408	4169	4471
3967	4257	4032	4332	4100	4409	"	4481
3968	4258	4033	4333	4101	4410	4170	4482
3969	4259	4034	4334	4102	4411	4171	4483
3970	4261	4035	4335	4103	4412	4172	4484
3971	4262	4036	4337	4104	4413	4173	4485
3972	4263	4037	4338	4105	4414	4174	4486
3973	4264	4038	4339	4106	4415	4175	4487
3974	4265	4039	4340	4107	4416	4176	4488
3975	4266	4040	4341	"	4417	4177	4489
3976	4267	4041	4342	4108	4418	4178	4490
3977	4268	4042	4343	4109	4419	"	1930
3978	4269	4043	4344	4110	4420	4179	2234
3979	4270	4044	4345	4111	4421	"	4491
"	4271	4045	4346	4112	4422	4180	4494
3980	4272	4046	4347	4113	4423	4181	4495
3981	4273	4047	4348	4114	4424	4182	4497
"	4274	4048	4351	4115	4425	4183	4498
"	4392	4049	4352	4116	4426	4184	4492
3982	2167	4050	4353	4117	4427	"	4499
"	4275	4051	4354	4118	4498	4185	4500
3983	4277	4052	4355	4119	4498	4186	4501
3984	4278	4053	4356	4120	4428	4187	4502
3985	4279	4054	4357	4121	4429	4188	4503
3986	4280	4055	4358	4122	4430	4189	4504
3987	4281	4056	4359	4123	4431	4190	4505
3988	4282	4057	4360	4124	4432	4191	4505
3989	4283	4058	4361	4125	4433	4192	4506
3990	4284	4059	4362	4126	4434	4193	4507
3991	4286	4060	4363	4127	4435	4194	4508
3992	4287	4061	4364	4128	4436	4195	4510
3993	4288	4062	4365	4129	4437	4196	4511
3994	4289	4063	4366	4130	4398	4197	4512
3995	4290	4064	4367	4131	4438	"	4515
3996	4291	4065	4368	4132	4439	4198	4513
3997	4292	4066	4369	4133	4440	4199	4514
3998	4293	4067	4370	4134	4441	4200	4516
3999	4294	4068	4371	4135	4442	4201	4517
4000	4295	4069	4372	4136	4443	4202	4518
4001	4296	4070	4373	4137	4444	4203	4519
4002	4297	4071	4374	4138	4445	4204	4520
4003	4298	4072	4375	4139	4446	4205	4521
4004	4299	4073	4376	4140	4447	4206	4522
4005	4300	4074	4377	4141	4448	4207	4523
4006	4301	4075	4378	4142	4449	4208	4524
4007	4302	4076	4379	4143	4450	4209	4525
4008	4305	4077	4380	4144	4452	4210	4526
4009	4306	4078	4381	"	4453	"	4528
4010	4307	4079	4382	4145	4454	4211	4527
4011	4308	4080	4383	4146	4455	4212	4529
4012	4309	4081	4384	4147	4456	4213	4530
4013	4310	4082	4385	4148	4457	4214	4531
4014	4311	4083	4388	4149	4458	4215	4532
4015	4313	4084	4389	4150	4459	4216	4533
4016	4212	4085	4390	4151	4460	4217	4467
"	4314	4086	4391	4152	4461	"	4534
4017	4315	4087	4393	4153	4462	4218	4537

4219	4536	4283	4603	4346	4678	4407	4612
4220	4538	4284	4604	"	4680	"	4748
4221	4539	"	4617	4347	4681	4408	4749
4222	4540	4285	4605	"	4679	4409	4750
4223	4541	4286	4606	4348	4682	4410	4751
4224	4542	"	4671	4349	4683	4411	4752
4225	4543	4287	4607	4350	4684	4412	4754
4226	4544	4288	4608	4351	4685	"	4759
4227	4545	4289	4609	4352	4686	4413	4755
4228	4546	4290	4610	4353	4687	4414	4756
4229	4547	4291	4613	4354	4688	4415	4757
4230	4548	4292	4614	4355	4647	4416	4758
4231	4549	4293	4615	"	4689	4417	4760
4232	4550	4294	4616			4418	4761
4233	4551	4295	4618	4356	4691	4419	4762
4234	4552	4296	4619	"	4692	4420	4763
4235	4553	4297	4620	4357	4693	4421	4764
4236	4554	4298	4621	4358	4694	4422	4765
"	4557	4299	4622	4359	4695	4423	4766
4237	4555	4300	4623	4360	4696	4424	4767
4238	407	4301	4624	4361	4698	4425	4768
"	4556	4302	4625	4362	4699	4426	4769
4239	4558	"	4597	4363	4700	4427	4770
4240	4559	4303	4626	4364	4701	4428	4771
4241	4560	4304	4627	4365	4702	4429	4772
4242	4561	4305	4628	4366	4703	4430	4773
4243	4563	4306	4629	"	4704	4431	4774
4244	4564	4307	4630	4367	4705	4432	4775
4245	4565	4308	4631	4368	4188	4433	4776
4246	4562	"	4632	"	4706	4434	4777
"	4566	4309	4633	4369	4707	4435	4778
4247	4567	4310	4634	4370	4708	4436	4780
4248	4568	4311	4636	"	4716	4437	4781
4249	4569	4312	4637			4438	4782
"	4573	4313	4638	4371	4709	4439	4783
4250	4570	4314	4639	4372	4710	4440	4784
4251	4571	4315	4640	4373	4711	4441	4785
4252	4572	4316	4641	4374	4712	4442	4786
4253	4574	4317	4642	4375	4713	4443	4787
4254	4575	"	4652	4376	4714	4444	4788
4255	4576	"	4654	4377	4715	4445	4789
4256	164	4318	4643	4378	4717	4446	4790
"	4577	4319	4644	4379	4718	4447	4791
4257	4578	"	4645	4380	4719	4448	4792
4258	4579	4320	4646	"	4722	4449	4793
4259	4580	4321	4648	4381	4720	4450	4794
4260	4581	"	4649	"	4723	4451	4796
4261	4582	4322	4650	4382	4721	4452	4803
4262	4583	4323	4651	"	4724	4453	4797
4263	4584	4324	4653	4383	4725	4454	4798
"	4585	4325	4655	4384	4726	4455	4799
4264	4586	4326	4656	4385	4727	4456	4386
4265	4587	4327	4657	4386	4728	"	4800
4266	4588	4328	4659	4387	4728	4457	4387
4267	4590	4329	4660	4388	4729	"	4801
4268	4590	4330	4661	4389	4730	4458	4535
4269	4591	4331	4662	4390	4731	"	4803
4270	4592	4332	4204	4391	4732	4459	4802
4271	4593	"	4663	4392	4733	4460	4805
4272	4594	4333	4664	4393	4734	4461	4806
4273	4595	4334	4665	4394	4735	4462	4807
4274	4596	4335	4666	4395	4736	"	4808
4275	4632	4336	4667	4396	4737	"	4809
4276	4598	4337	4668	4397	4738	4463	4810
4277	4625	4338	4669	4398	4739	4464	4811
"	4597	4339	4670	4399	4740	4465	4812
4278	4599	4340	4672	4400	4741	4466	4814
4279	4600	4341	4673	4401	4742	4467	4815
4280	4625	4342	4674	4402	4743	4468	4816
"	4597	4343	4675	4403	4744	4469	4819
4281	4601	4344	4676	4404	4745	"	4828
4282	4602	4345	4677	4405	4746	4470	4820
				4406	4611		
				"	4747		

4471	4821	4532	4889	4596	4961	4664	5039
4472	4822	4533	4891	"	4986	4665	5040
4473	4823	4534	4892	4597	4962	4666	5043
4474	4824	4535	4893	4598	4963	4667	2430
4475	4825	4536	4894	4599	4964	"	5044
4476	1017	4537	4895	4600	4965	4668	5045
"	4827	4538	4896	4601	4967	4669	5046
4477	4829	4539	4897	4602	4968	4670	5047
4478	4830	4540	4899	4603	4969	4671	5148
4479	4831	"	4900	"	4971	4672	4898
4480	4832	4541	4901	4604	4970	"	5048
4481	4818	4542	4902	4605	4972	4673	5049
"	4833	4543	4903	4606	4973	4674	5050
"	4834	4544	4904	4607	4974	4675	5148
"	4854	4545	4905	4608	4975	4676	5051
4482	4835	4546	4907	4609	4976	4677	5052
4483	3306	4547	4908	4610	4977	4678	5053
4484	4836	4548	4909	4611	4978	4679	5054
4485	4837	4549	4910	4612	4959	4680	5055
4486	4826	4550	4911	"	4980	4681	5056
"	4838	4551	4912	4613	4981	4682	5057
"	4841	4552	4913	4614	4982	4683	5058
4487	4839	4553	4914	4615	4983	4684	5059
4488	4840	4554	4915	4616	4984	4685	5060
4489	4842	4555	4916	4617	4985	4686	5061
4490	4843	4556	4917	4618	4988	4687	2178
4491	4844	4557	4918	4619	4990	"	5062
4492	4845	4558	4919	4620	4991	4688	5063
4493	4846	4559	4920	4621	4989	4689	5064
"	4856	4560	4921	"	4992	4690	5065
4494	4847	4561	4922	4622	4994	4691	5066
4495	4848	4562	4923	4623	4995	4692	5067
4496	4849	"	4951	4624	4997	4693	5068
4497	4850	"	4952	4625	4998	4694	5069
4498	4851	4563	4924	4626	4999	4695	5071
4499	4852	4564	4925	4627	5002	4696	5070
4500	4853	4565	838	4628	5003	4697	5072
4501	4855	"	4926	4629	5004	4698	5073
4502	4857	4566	4927	4630	5005	4699	5074
4503	4858	4567	4928	4631	5006	4700	5075
4504	4859	4568	4929	4632	5007	4701	5076
4505	4860	4569	4930	4633	5008	4702	5077
4506	4861	4570	2410	4634	5009	4703	5078
4507	4864	"	4931	4635	5010	4704	5079
4508	4865	4571	5148	4636	5011	4705	5080
4509	4866	4572	4932	4637	5012	4706	5080
4510	4862	4573	4933	4638	5013	4707	5080
"	4863	4574	4934	4639	5014	4708	5081
"	4867	4575	4935	4640	5015	4709	5081
4511	4868	4576	4936	4641	5016	4710	5082
4512	4869	4577	4937	4642	5017	4711	5083
4513	4870	"	4938	4643	5018	4712	5084
4514	4871	"	4987	4644	5019	4713	5085
4515	4872	4578	4939	4645	5020	4714	5087
4516	4873	4579	4940	4646	5021	4715	5088
4517	4874	4580	4941	4647	5022	4716	5089
4518	2407	4581	4942	4648	5023	4717	5090
"	4876	4582	4943	4649	5024	4718	5091
4519	4877	4583	4944	4650	5025	4719	5092
4520	4878	4584	4945	4651	5026	4720	5093
4521	4879	"	4946	4652	5027	4721	5094
4522	4880	4585	4947	4653	5028	4722	5095
4523	4881	4586	4948	4654	5029	4723	5096
4524	4882	4587	4949	4655	5030	4724	5097
4525	4883	4588	4950	4656	5031	4725	5098
"	4966	4589	4953	4657	5032	4726	5099
4526	4884	4590	4954	4658	5033	4727	5100
4527	4885	4591	4955	4659	5034	4728	5101
4528	4886	4592	4956	4660	5035	4729	5102
4529	4887	4593	4957	4661	5036	4730	5103
4530	4890	4594	4958	4662	5037	4731	5104
4531	4888	4595	4960	4663	5038	4732	5105

4733	5106	4797	5177	4863	5251	4926	5326
4734	5107	"	5179	4864	5252	4927	5327
4735	5109	4798	5178	4865	5253	4928	5330
4736	5108	4799	5180	4866	5254	4929	5332
4737	5110	4800	5182	4867	125	4930	5333
4738	5111	4801	2413	"	5255	4931	5334
4739	5112	"	5183	4868	5256	4932	5335
4740	5113	4802	5184	4869	5257	4933	5337
4741	5114	4803	5185	4870	5258	4934	5298
4742	5116	4804	5186	4871	5259	"	5338
4743	5117	4805	5187	"	5260	4935	5339
4744	5118	4806	5188	"	5276	4936	5340
4745	5119	4807	5189	4872	5262	4937	5341
4746	5115	4808	5190	4873	5263	4938	5342
"	5120	4809	5191	"	5165	4939	5343
4747	5122	4810	5192	4874	5264	4940	5344
4748	5123	4811	5193	4875	5265	4941	5345
4749	5124	4812	5194	4876	5267	4942	5347
4750	5125	4813	5195	4877	5268	4943	5348
4751	5126	4814	5196	4878	5269	4944	5349
4752	5127	4815	5197	4879	5270	4945	5350
4753	5128	4816	5198	4880	5271	4946	5352
4754	5129	4817	5199	4881	5272	4947	5353
4755	5130	4818	5200	4882	5273	4948	5354
4756	5131	4819	5201	4883	5274	4949	5351
4757	5132	4820	5202	4884	5275	"	5355
4758	5133	4821	5203	4885	5277	"	5356
4759	5134	4822	5204	4886	5278	"	5835
"	5135	4823	5205	4887	5279	4950	5358
4760	5136	4824	5206	4888	5280	4951	5359
4761	5137	4825	5207	4889	5281	4952	5331
4762	5138	4826	5208	4890	5282	"	5360
4763	5139	4827	5209	4891	5283	4953	5361
4764	5140	4828	5210	4892	5284	4954	5362
4765	5141	4829	5211	4893	5287	4955	5086
4766	5142	4830	5212	4894	5288	"	5363
"	5143	4831	5213	"	5323	4956	5364
4767	5144	4832	5215	"	5328	4957	5365
4768	5145	4833	5214	4895	5289	4958	5366
4769	5146	"	5216	4896	5290	4959	5367
4770	5121	"	5240	4897	5291	4960	5368
"	5147	4834	5217	4898	5292	4961	5369
4771	5148	4835	5218	4899	5293	4962	5370
4772	5149	4836	5219	4900	5261	4963	5371
4773	5150	4837	5220	"	5295	4964	5372
"	5151	4838	5221	4901	5296	4965	4993
4774	5152	4839	5222	4902	5299	"	5373
4775	5153	4840	5223	4903	5300	4966	5374
4776	4327	4841	5224	4904	5301	4967	5375
"	5154	4842	5225	4905	5302	4968	5376
4777	5155	4843	5227	4906	5303	4969	5377
4778	5156	4844	5228	4907	5304	4970	5379
4779	5157	4845	5230	4908	5305	4971	5380
4780	5158	4846	5231	4909	5306	4972	5381
4781	5159	4847	5232	4910	5307	4973	5382
4782	5160	4848	5233	4911	5308	4974	5383
4783	5161	4849	5234	4912	5309	"	5384
4784	5163	"	5235	4913	5310	4975	5385
4785	2975	4850	5236	4914	5311	4976	5386
"	5164	4851	5237	4915	5312	4977	5387
4786	5166	"	5239	4916	5313	4978	5388
4787	5167	4852	5238	4917	5314	4979	5389
4788	5168	4853	5241	4918	5315	4980	5390
4789	5169	4854	5242	4919	5316	4981	5391
4790	5170	4855	5243	4920	5317	4982	1751
4791	5171	4856	5244	"	5320	"	5392
4792	5172	4857	5245	4921	5318	4983	5393
4793	5173	4858	5246	"	5319	4984	5394
4794	5174	4859	5247	4922	5321	4985	5395
4795	5175	4860	5248	4923	5322	4986	5396
"	5346	4861	5249	4924	5324	4987	5397
4796	5176	4862	5250	4925	5325	4988	5398

4989	5399	"	5468	5122	5540	5189	5607
4990	5400	5059	5469	5123	5542	5190	5608
4991	5401	5060	5470	5124	4047	5191	5610
4992	5402	5061	5472	5125	4047	5192	5611
"	5403	5062	5473	5126	4047	5193	5612
4993	5404	"	5477	5127	4047	5194	5613
4994	5405	5063	5474	5128	4047	5195	5614
4995	5406	"	5478	5129	4047	5196	5615
4996	5407	5064	5475	5130	4047	5197	5616
4997	5408	5065	5476	5131	5543	5198	5617
4998	5409	5066	5479	5132	5544	5199	5618
4999	5411	5067	5480	5133	5545	5200	5619
5000	5412	5068	5481	5134	5546	5201	5620
5001	5413	5069	5482	5135	5547	5202	5621
5002	5414	5070	5483	5136	5548	5203	5622
5003	5415	5071	5484	5137	5549	5204	5623
5004	5416	5072	5485	5138	5550	5205	5624
5005	5417	5073	5486	5139	5551	5206	5625
5006	5418	"	5487	5140	5552	5207	5626
5007	5419	5074	5488	5141	5554	5208	5627
5008	2496	5075	5489	5142	5555	5209	5148
"	5420	5076	5490	5143	5556	5210	5148
5009	5421	5077	5491	5144	5558	5211	5628
5010	5423	5078	5492	5145	5559	5212	5629
5011	5424	5079	5493	5146	5560	5213	5148
5012	5425	5080	5494	5147	5561	5214	5630
5013	5427	5081	1315	5148	5562	5215	5631
5014	5428	"	5495	5149	5563	5216	5148
5015	5429	5082	5496	5150	5564	5217	5632
5016	5430	5083	5498	5151	5565	5218	5633
5017	5431	5084	5499	5152	5566	5219	5634
5018	5432	5085	5500	5153	5567	5220	5635
5019	5433	5086	5501	5154	5568	5221	5636
5020	5434	5087	5502	"	5569	5222	5637
5021	5435	5088	5503	5155	5570	5223	5638
5022	5436	5089	5504	5156	5571	5224	5639
5023	4047	5090	5505	5157	5572	5225	5639
5024	5437	5091	5506	5158	5573	5226	5640
5025	4047	5092	5507	5159	5574	5227	5641
5026	4047	5093	5508	"	5578	5228	5642
5027	5438	5094	5509	5160	5575	5229	5643
5028	5439	5095	5510	5161	5576	5230	5644
5029	5440	5096	5511	5162	5577	5231	5645
5030	5441	5097	5512	5163	5579	5232	5647
5031	5442	5098	5513	5164	5580	5233	5648
5032	5441	5099	5514	5165	5581	5234	5649
5033	5441	5100	5516	5166	5582	5235	5650
5034	5443	5101	5515	5167	5583	5236	5651
5035	5444	5102	5518	5168	5584	5237	4238
5036	5444	5103	5519	5169	5557	"	5653
5037	5445	5104	5520	"	5585	"	5666
5038	5446	5105	5521	5170	5586	5238	5654
5039	5447	"	5522	5171	5587	5239	5657
5040	5448	5106	5523	5172	5588	5240	5655
5041	5449	5107	5524	5173	5589	"	5656
5042	5450	5108	5525	5174	5590	"	5658
5043	5451	5109	5526	5175	5591	5241	5659
5044	5452	5110	5527	5176	5592	5242	5660
5045	5454	5111	5528	5177	5593	5243	5661
5046	5455	5112	5529	5178	5594	5244	5662
5047	5456	"	5530	5179	5595	"	5663
5048	5457	"	5531	"	5596	5245	5664
5049	5458	5113	5532	5180	5597	5246	5665
5050	5459	5114	5533	5181	5598	5247	5667
5051	5460	5115	5534	5182	2571	5248	5668
5052	5461	5116	5535	"	5600	5249	5669
5053	5462	5117	5536	5183	5601	5250	5670
5054	5463	"	4509	5184	5602	5251	5671
5055	5464	5118	5537	5185	5603	5252	5672
5056	5465	5119	5538	5186	5604	5253	5673
5057	5467	5120	3836	5187	5605	5254	5674
5058	5466	5121	5539	5188	5606	5255	5675

5256	5676	5324	5751	"	5821	5461	5894
5257	5677	5325	5752	5393	5823	5462	5895
5258	5678	5326	5753	5394	5824	5463	5897
5259	5679	5327	5754	5395	5825	5464	5898
5260	5680	5328	5755	5396	5826	5465	5899
5261	5681	5329	5756	5397	5827	5466	5900
5262	5682	5330	5757	5398	5829	5467	5901
5263	5683	5331	5758	5399	5828	5468	5902
"	5684	"	5760	"	5830	"	5904
5264	5685	5332	5759	5400	5831	5469	5903
5265	5686	5333	5761	5401	5832	5470	5905
5266	5687	5334	5762	5402	5833	"	5911
5267	5688	5335	5763	5403	5834	5471	5906
5268	5689	5336	5764	5404	5836	5472	5907
5269	5690	5337	5765	5405	5837	5473	5908
5270	5691	5338	5766	5406	5838	5474	5909
5271	5693	5339	5767	5407	5839	5475	5910
5272	5694	5340	5768	5408	5840	5476	5912
5273	5695	5341	5742	5409	5841	5477	5913
5274	5696	"	5769	5410	5842	5478	5914
5275	5699	5342	5770	5411	5843	5479	5915
5276	5700	5343	5771	5412	5844	5480	5916
5277	659	5344	5772	5413	5845	5481	5917
"	5701	5345	5773	5414	5846	5482	5918
5278	670	5346	5774	5415	5847	5483	5919
"	5702	5347	5776	5416	5848	5484	5920
5279	5703	5348	5777	5417	5849	5485	5921
5280	5704	5349	5778	"	5822	5486	5922
5281	5705	5350	5779	5418	5850	5487	5923
5282	5706	5351	5780	5419	5851	5488	5924
5283	5707	5352	5781	5420	5852	5489	5925
5284	5709	5353	5782	5421	5853	5490	5926
5285	5710	5354	5783	5422	5854	5491	5927
5286	5711	5355	5784	5423	5855	5492	5928
5287	5712	5356	5785	5424	5856	5493	5929
5288	5713	5357	5786	5425	5857	5494	5930
5289	5714	5358	5787	5426	5858	5495	5931
5290	5715	5359	5788	5427	5859	5496	5932
5291	5716	5360	5789	5428	5860	5497	5933
5292	5717	5361	5790	5429	5861	5498	5934
5293	5718	5362	5791	5430	5862	5499	5935
5294	5719	5363	5792	5431	5863	5500	5936
5295	5720	5364	5793	5432	5864	5501	5937
5296	5721	5365	5794	5433	5865	5502	5938
5297	5722	5366	5795	5434	5866	5503	5939
5298	5723	5367	5796	5435	5867	5504	2396
5299	5708	5368	5797	5436	5869	"	5940
"	5724	5369	5798	5437	5870	5505	5942
5300	5725	5370	5799	5438	5871	5506	5941
5301	5727	5371	5800	5439	5872	5507	5943
5302	5728	5372	5801	5440	5873	5508	5944
5303	5729	5373	5802	5441	5874	5509	5945
5304	5730	5374	5803	5442	5875	5510	5946
5305	5731	5375	5804	5443	5876	5511	5948
5306	5731	5376	5805	5444	5877	5512	1430
5307	5733	5377	5806	5445	5878	"	5949
5308	5734	5378	5807	5446	5879	5513	5950
5309	5735	5379	5808	5447	5880	5514	5951
5310	5736	5380	5809	5448	5881	5515	5952
5311	5737	5381	5810	5449	5882	5516	5947
5312	5738	5382	5811	5450	5883	"	5953
5313	5739	5383	5812	5451	5884	5517	5954
5314	5741	5384	5813	5452	5885	5518	5955
5315	2266	5385	5814	5453	5886	5519	5956
5316	5743	5386	5815	5454	5887	5520	5957
5317	5744	5387	5816	5455	1876	5521	5958
5318	5745	5388	5817	"	5888	5522	5967
5319	5746	5389	5818	5456	5889	"	5959
5320	5747	5390	5819	5457	5890	5523	5960
5321	5426	5391	5426	5458	5891	"	6002
5322	5749	"	5820	5459	5892	5524	5961
5323	5750	5392	3055	5460	5893	5525	5962

5526	5963	5594	6038
5527	5964	5595	6039
5528	5965	5596	6040
5529	5966	5597	6041
5530	5968	5598	6042
5531	3079	5599	6043
"	5969	5600	1639
5532	5970	5601	2725
5533	5971	"	6044
"	5972	5602	6045
5534	5973	5603	6046
5535	5974	5604	6047
5536	5975	5605	6048
5537	5976	5606	6049
5538	5977	5607	1639
5539	5978	5608	6050
5540	5979	5609	6051
5541	5980	5610	6052
5542	5981	5611	6053
5543	5982	5612	6054
5544	5983	5613	6055
5545	5984	5614	6057
5546	5985	5615	6058
5547	5986	5616	6059
5548	5987	5617	6060
5549	5988	5618	6061
5550	5989	5619	6062
5551	5990	5620	6063
5552	5991	5621	6064
"	5997	"	6065
5553	5992	5622	6066
5554	5993	5623	6067
5555	5994	5624	6068
5556	5995		
5557	5996		
5558	5998		
5559	5999		
5560	6000		
5561	6001		
5562	6003		
5563	6004		
5564	6005		
5565	6006		
5566	6008		
5567	6010		
5568	6011		
5569	6012		
5570	6013		
5571	6014		
5572	6015		
5573	6016		
5574	6017		
5575	6020		
5576	6018		
5577	6019		
5578	6021		
5579	6022		
5580	6023		
5581	6024		
5582	6025		
5583	6026		
5584	6027		
5585	6028		
5586	6029		
5587	6030		
5588	6031		
5589	6032		
"	6033		
5590	6034		
5591	6035		
5592	6036		
5593	6037		

Principal Parts of Verbs Occurring
50 Times or More in the Greek Testament

The footnotes are drawn from the author's *The Basics of Biblical Greek,* and are fully explained in *The Morphology of Biblical Greek.* The principal parts that are not explained follow the basic rules of Greek morphology.

ἀγαπάω	ἀγαπήσω	ἠγάπησα	ἠγάπηκα	ἠγάπημαι	ἠγαπήθην
ἄγω	ἄξω	ἤγαγον[1]	-	ἦγμαι	ἤχθην
αἴρω	ἀρῶ	ἦρα	ἦρκα	ἦρμαι	ἤρθην
αἰτέω	αἰτήσω	ᾔτησα	ᾔτηκα	ᾔτημαι	-
ἀκολουθέω	ἀκολουθήσω	ἠκολούθησα	ἠκολούθηκα	-	-
ἀκούω	ἀκούσω	ἤκουσα	ἀκήκοα[2]	-	ἠκούσθην
ἀναβαίνω	ἀναβήσομαι	ἀνέβην	-	-	-
ἀνίστημι	ἀναστήσω	ἀνέστησα	ἀνέστηκα	ἀνέστημαι	ἀνεστάθην
ἀνοίγω	-	ἀνέῳξα[3]	-	-	ἀνεῴχθην[4]
ἀπέρχομαι	ἀπελεύσομαι	ἀπῆλθον	ἀπελήλυθα	-	-
ἀποθνήσκω	ἀποθανοῦμαι	ἀπέθανον	-	-	-
ἀποκρίνομαι	-	ἀπεκρινάμην	-	-	ἀπεκρίθην[5]
ἀποκτείνω	ἀποκτενῶ	ἀπέτεινα	-	-	ἀπεκτάνθην
ἀπόλλυμι[6]	ἀπολέσω	ἀπώλεσα	ἀπόλωλα[7]	-	-
ἀπολύω	ἀπολύσω	ἀπέλυσα	-	ἀπολέλυμαι	ἀπελύθην
ἀποστέλλω	ἀποστελῶ	ἀπέστειλα	ἀπέσταλκα	ἀπέσταλμαι	ἀπεστάλην
ἄρχω	ἄρξομαι	ἠρξάμην	-	-	-
ἀσπάζομαι	-	ἠσπασάμην	-	-	-
ἀφίημι	ἀφήσω	ἀφῆκα	-	ἀφέωμαι	ἀφέθην

---

1   *ἀγ. An unusual second aorist. There actually is a reduplication and an augment. The stem reduplicates (*ἀγ ‣ αγαγ) and then the reduplicated vowel lengthens (αγαγ ‣ ηγαγ ‣ ἤγαγον).
2   Because it is a second perfect, the tense formative is α, not κα.
3   Shows a double augment with the ι subscripting (ἀνοιγ + σα ‣ ανεοιξα ‣ ανεωιξα ‣ ἀνέῳξα). Can also be ἠνέῳξα, which adds a third augment by lengthening the first vowel.
4   Shows the same augmentation pattern as in the aorist active. Here the final stem gamma has changed to a χ because of the θ in the tense formative.
    Can also be ἠνεῴχθην .
5   Loses its stem ν before the θ. This is not normal.
6   *ἀπολε. This is a compound verb, as you can tell from the augment in the aorist active (ἀπώλεσα).
7   Second perfect.

βάλλω	βαλῶ	ἔβαλον[8]	βέβληκα[9]	βέβλημαι[10]	ἐβλήθην[11]
βαπτίζω	βαπτίσω	ἐβάπτισα	-	βεβάπτισμαι	ἐβαπτίσθην
βλέπω	βλέψω	ἔβλεψα	-	-	-
γεννάω	γεννήσω	ἐγέννησα	γεγέννηκα	γεγέννημαι	ἐγεννήθην
γίνομαι	γενήσομαι	ἐγενόμην	γέγονα[12]	γεγένημαι	ἐγενήθην
γινώσκω	γνώσομαι	ἔγνων	ἔγνωκα	ἔγνωσμαι	ἐγνώσθην
γράφω	γράψω	ἔγραψα	γέγραφα	γέγραμμαι	ἐγράφην
δεῖ	-	-	-	-	-
δέχομαι	δέξομαι	ἐδεξάμην	-	δέδεγμαι	ἐδέχθην
διδάσκω	διδάξω	ἐδίδαξα	-	-	ἐδιδάχθην
δίδωμι	δώσω	ἔδωκα	δέδωκα	δέδομαι	ἐδόθην
δοκέω	δόξω	ἔδοξα	-	-	-
δοξάζω	δοξάσω	ἐδόξασα	-	δεδόξασμαι	ἐδοξάσθην
δύναμαι	δυνήσομαι	-	-	-	ἠδυνήθην
ἐγείρω	ἐγερῶ	ἤγειρα	-	ἐγήγερμαι[13]	ἠγέρθην
		εἶδον[14]			
εἰμί	ἔσομαι	ἤμην[15]	-	-	-
εἰσέρχομαι	εἰσελεύσομαι	εἰσῆλθον	εἰσελήλυθα	-	-
ἐκβάλλω	ἐκβαλῶ	ἐξέβαλον	ἐκβέβληκα	ἐκβέβλημαι	ἐξεβλήθην
ἐξέρχομαι	ἐξελεύσομαι	ἐξῆλθον	ἐξελήλυθα	-	-
ἐπερωτάω	ἐπερωτήσω	ἐπηρώτησα	-	-	-
ἔρχομαι	ἐλεύσομαι[16]	ἦλθον[17]	ἐλήλυθα[18]	-	-
ἐρωτάω	ἐρωτήσω	ἠρώτησα	-	-	-
ἐσθίω	φάγομαι[19]	ἔφαγον[20]	-	-	-
εὐαγγελίζω	-	εὐηγγέλισα	-	εὐηγγέλισμαι	εὐηγγελίσθην

---

[8] Usually liquid aorists are first aorist and use the α as the tense formative. βάλλω follows the pattern of a normal second aorist.

[9] Due to ablaut, the stem vowel has dropped out and an η has been inserted before the tense formative. This form follows the normal rules.

[10] See the explanation for the perfect active tense form.

[11] See the explanation for the perfect active tense form.

[12] The stem vowel has shifted from ε to ο due to ablaut. It is a second perfect and therefore uses the tense formative α.

[13] Reduplicates and augments: εγερ ‣ εγεγερ ‣ εγηγερ ‣ ἐγήγερμαι.

[14] εἶδον is a second aorist of a verb that does not occur in any other tenses. Most associate it with ὁράω.

[15] Actually an imperfect, but we have included it here for clarity's sake.

[16] *ελευθ. Future middle deponent.

[17] *ελευθ, just like the future. The ευ has dropped out due to ablaut (*ελευθ ‣ ελθ ‣ ἦλθον). Second aorist.

[18] *ελευθ, just like the future. The form has both reduplicated and then augmented, and the ε has dropped out. It is a second perfect. *ελευθ ‣ ελελευθ ‣ εληλυθ ‣ ἐλήλυθα.

[19] *φαγ. Future middle deponent.

[20] *φαγ. Second aorist.

εὑρίσκω	εὑρήσω	εὗρον	εὕρηκα	-	εὑρέθην
ἔχω	ἕξω	ἔσχον	ἔσχηκα	-	-
ζητέω	ζητήσω	ἐζήτησα	-	-	ἐζητήθην
θέλω	θελήσω	ἠθέλησα	-	-	ἠθελήθην
θεωρέω	-	ἐθεώρησα	-	-	-
ἵστημι	στήσω	ἔστησα	ἕστηκα	ἕσταμαι	ἐστάθην
κάθημαι	καθήσομαι	-	-	-	-
καλέω	καλέσω	ἐκάλεσα	κέκληκα	κέκλημαι	ἐκλήθην
καταβαίνω	καταβήσομαι	κατέβην	-	-	-
κηρύσσω	κηρύξω	ἐκήρυξα	-	κεκήρυγμαι	ἐκηρύχθην
κράζω	κράξω	ἔκραξα	κέκραγα	-	-
κρατέω	κρατήσω	ἐκράτησα	κεκράτηκα	κεκράτημαι	-
κρίνω	κρινῶ	ἔκρινα	κέκρικα	κέκριμαι	ἐκρίθην
λαλέω	λαλήσω	ἐλάλησα	λελάληκα	λελάλημαι	ἐλαλήθην
λαμβάνω	λήμψομαι[21]	ἔλαβον[22]	εἴληφα[23]	εἴλημμαι[24]	ἐλήμφθην[25]
λέγω	ἐρῶ[26]	εἶπον[27]	εἴρηκα[28]	εἴρημαι[29]	ἐρρέθην[30]
μαρτυρέω	μαρτυρήσω	ἐμαρτύρησα	μεμαρτύρηκα	μεμαρτύρημαι	ἐμαρτυρήθην
μέλλω	μελλήσω	-	-	-	-
μένω	μενῶ	ἔμεινα	μεμένηκα	-	-
οἶδα	εἰδήσω	ᾔδειν			
ὁράω	ὄψομαι	ὠψάμην	ἑώρακα[31]	-	ὤφθην
ὀφείλω					
παραδίδωμι	παραδώσω	παρέδωκα	παραδέδωκα	παραδέδομαι	παρεδόθην
παρακαλέω	παρακαλέσω	παρεκάλεσα	παρακέκληκα	παρακέκλημαι	παρεκλήθην

---

[21] *λαβ. The α lengthens to η, a μ is inserted, and the β joins with the σ of the tense formative to form ψ. It is a future middle deponent.

*λαβ ‣ ληβ ‣ λημβ + σομαι ‣ λήμψομαι.

[22] *λαβ. Second aorist.

[23] *λαβ. The augment is ει instead of the usual ε (see *MBG* for an explanation), the stem vowel ε lengthens to η (ablaut), and the β is aspirated to a φ. It is a second perfect, so the tense formative is α and not κα.

*λαβ ‣ ειλαβ ‣ ειληβ ‣ ειληφ ‣ εἴληφα.

[24] The same changes present in the perfect active are active here as well. The β has changed to μ because of the following μ.

[25] The same changes present in the perfect active are active here as well, except that the augment is the simple ε. The β has changed to φ because of the following θ.

[26] *Ϝερ. Liquid future. The digamma (Ϝ) has dropped out.

[27] *Ϝιπ. Second aorist. It receives a syllabic augment, the digamma (Ϝ) drops out because it is between vowels, and they contract. ε + Ϝιπ + ο + ν ‣ εἶπον.

[28] *Ϝερ. It received the syllabic augment and the digamma (Ϝ) dropped out. It inserts an η before the tense stem. ε + Ϝερ + η + κα ‣ εερηκα ‣ εἴρηκα.

[29] Follows the same pattern of change as in the perfect active.

[30] *Ϝερ. When the digamma (Ϝ) was lost, evidently the ρ doubled. This is common in verbs beginning with ρ. An ε was inserted before the tense stem, much like an η can be inserted.

[31] There is both a lengthening and an augment: ορα ‣ ωρα ‣ εωρα ‣ ἑώρακα.

πείθω	πείσω	ἔπεισα	πέποιθα	πέπεισμαι	ἐπείσθην
περιπατέω	περιπατήσω	περιεπάτησα	-	-	περιεπατήθην
πίνω	πίομαι	ἔπιον	πέπωκα	-	ἐπόθην[32]
πίπτω	πεσοῦμαι[33]	ἔπεσον[34]	πέπτωκα[35]	-	-
πιστεύω	-	ἐπίστευσα	πεπίστευκα	πεπίστευμαι	ἐπιστεύθην
πληρόω	πληρώσω	ἐπλήρωσα	πεπλήρωκα	πεπλήρωμαι	ἐπληρώθην
ποιέω	ποιήσω	ἐποίησα	πεποίηκα	πεποίημαι	ἐποιήθην
πορεύομαι	πορεύσομαι	-	-	πεπόρευμαι	ἐπορεύθην
προσέρχομαι	προσελεύσομαι	προσῆλθον	προσελήλυθα	-	-
προσεύχομαι	προσεύξομαι	προσευξάμην	-	-	-
προσκυνέω	προσκυνήσω	προσεκύνησα	-	-	-
συνάγω	συνάξω	συνήγαγον	-	συνῆγμαι	συνήχθην
σῴζω	σώσω	ἔσωσα	σέσωκα	σέσωσμαι	ἐσώθην
τηρέω	τηρήσω	ἐτήρησα	τετήρηκα	τετήρημαι	ἐτηρήθην
τίθημι	θήσω	ἔθηκα	τέθεικα[36]	τέθειμαι[37]	ἐτέθην[38]
ὑπάγω	ὑπάξω	ὑπήγαγον	-	ὑπῆγμαι	ὑπήχθην
ὑπάρχω	ὑπάρξομαι	ὑπηρξάμην	-	-	-
φέρω	οἴσω	ἤνεγκα	ἐνήνοχα[39]	ἐνήνεγμαι	ἠνέχθην
φημί					
φοβέομαι	-	-	-	-	ἐφοβήθην
χαίρω	χαρήσομαι	-	-	-	ἐχάρην

---

[32] The stem vowel ι has shifted to ο due to ablaut.

[33] The τ has dropped out because of the σ tense formative, and for some reason there is a contraction.

*πετ + σ + ο + μαι › πεσομαι › πεσοῦμαι.

[34] Second aorist. The τ has dropped out because of the σ, which implies that πίπτω would have a first aorist. But actually it is a second aorist.

[35] The ε has dropped out and an ο has been inserted before the tense formative.

[36] The stem vowel has shifted to ει due to ablaut.

[37] The stem vowel has shifted to ει due to ablaut.

[38] Believe it or not, this form is regular. What is a little confusing is that the root *θε has shifted to τε ("transfer of aspiration"). When the θη is added for the aorist passive, there is the θεθ combination. The Greeks tried to avoid two aspirates (θ is an "aspirate") in successive vowels, so they "deaspirated" the first one, i.e., shifted it to a τ.

ε + *θε + θη + ν › εθεθην › ἐτέθην.

[39] Second perfect.